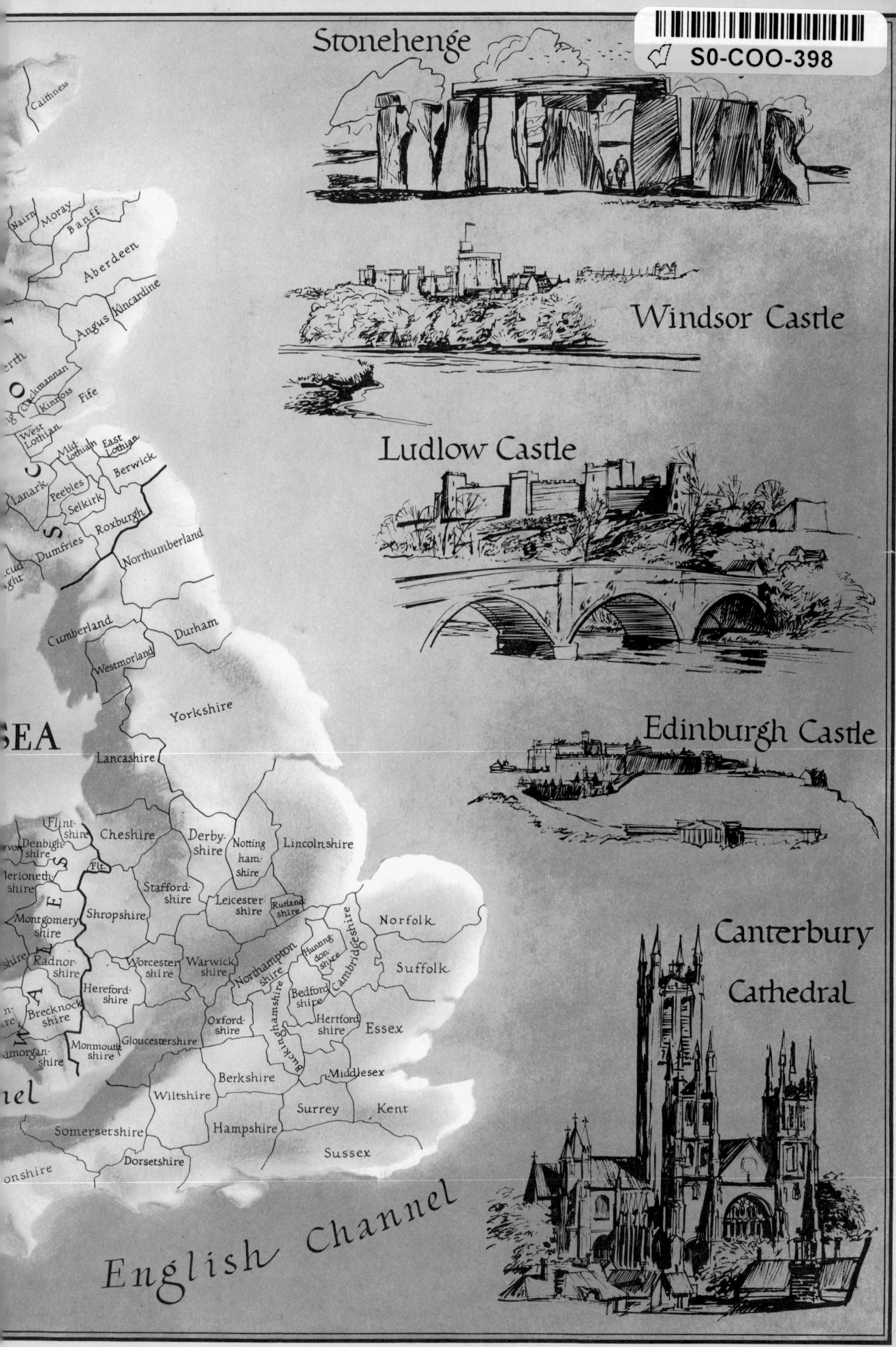

Stonehenge

Windsor Castle

Ludlow Castle

Edinburgh Castle

Canterbury
Cathedral

English Channel

BRITISH LITERATURE
from Beowulf *to* Sheridan

BRITISH LITERATURE

I. *From* Beowulf *to* Sheridan

EDITED BY *Hazelton Spencer*

II. *From* Blake *to the* Present Day

EDITED BY *Hazelton Spencer*

Walter E. Houghton

Herbert Barrows

British Literature

from
BEOWULF
to
SHERIDAN

Edited by
HAZELTON SPENCER

D. C. Heath and Company BOSTON

PUBLISHERS' PREFACE

THE EDITORS of this book have been mindful that literature has always been addressed to what is today called the "general reader" and his enjoyment. The student's intelligent enjoyment of the literature of the British people has been their first concern, both in selecting the texts and in providing explanatory comment. The introductions and notes are designed to supply the information which will most readily remove the barriers of space and time and allow the reader to confront without obstacle the permanence of the literature's thought and art. The explanatory material constitutes a large body of scholarship, historical and critical; no pain has been spared to make this a work of sound and accurate learning. But the scholarship has constantly been directed to the primary end of making the literature speak for itself.

The first volume, BRITISH LITERATURE FROM BEOWULF TO SHERIDAN, is entirely the work of Hazelton Spencer, late of The Johns Hopkins University. The second volume, BRITISH LITERATURE FROM BLAKE TO THE PRESENT DAY, is the work of Mr. Spencer, Walter E. Houghton of Wellesley College, and Herbert Barrows of the University of Michigan. Mr. Spencer edited and annotated the texts which appear in "The Romantic Period" and wrote the biographical introductions in that section. (For slight changes in this material and for the General Introduction the publishers' editors assume responsibility.) Mr. Houghton, with the valuable aid of his wife, Esther Rhoads Houghton, contributed "The Victorian Period"; Mr. Barrows, "The Modern Period." Mr. Karl Shapiro wrote the essay on prosody which stands at the end of each volume.

In the whole course of his work on the book, Mr. Spencer asked, and received generously, the opinions and advice of his colleagues at The Johns Hopkins University: Messrs. Don C. Allen, Charles R. Anderson, Raymond D. Havens, Kemp Malone, and Edward T. Norris. Mr. Spencer's appreciation and gratitude for their help, so frequently and heartily expressed to his publishers, he would wish to be recorded in the warmest terms. For their continued interest and helpfulness after his death, the publishers here record their own gratitude.

CONTENTS

viii

ix

THE EIGHTEENTH CENTURY

ILLUSTRATIONS AND MAPS

ILLUSTRATIONS AND MAPS

The end papers and other maps have been designed and drawn especially for this book by Mr. Aldren A. Watson.

Old English

OLD ENGLISH LITERATURE

THE CURTAIN goes up on Britain's history when the Romans first turn a calculating eye toward Gaul's northern neighbor. Though in 55 B. C. Julius Caesar threw a couple of legions across the English Channel, neither that brief landing nor the campaign of the following summer led to occupation. Julius, however, wielded pen as well as sword; his description helped maintain a lively interest in the island till the next invasion, under the emperor Claudius in 43 A. D. This time the success was complete, and the troops stayed. They made Britain, as far north as the Scottish Highlands, a Roman province; but neither the ancient Britons (a Celtic race) nor their Italian conquerors contributed to British literature, though both left their marks on the island in other ways. It remained part of the empire till the year 410, when a hard-pressed emperor recalled the garrison. Till that fateful event, the speech of Britannia, as the province was called, was Latin and Celtic.

THE ENGLISH CONQUEST

THOUGH the Picts of Caledonia (Scotland) and the Scots of Hibernia (Ireland) immediately renewed their pressure from the north and west, it was Angles, Saxons, and Jutes from the southern and southeastern shores of the North Sea who seized the helpless, beautiful country and gave it that magnificent thing, the English language. They were raiding tribesmen, bold sailors and savage fighters speaking dialects (highly inflected, in comparison with modern English) of the Germanic tongue's western branch, to which modern German as well as modern English belongs. For many decades they had found easy pickings along the fringes of the mighty but decaying empire. Combat and rapine came natural to these tough spearmen. The old civilization of the Mediterranean world that had brought Britain within its orbit inspired them, not with admiration for its refinement and order, but with contempt for its softness and greed for its riches. In 449, according to tradition, the Jutes established the first bridgehead on British soil, in Kent.

Widespread settlement followed the marauding forays, and by 600 the newcomers held about half the island. Such of the Britons as had not been killed,

enslaved, or assimilated either were living in the mountains of the west and north, rolled back from the areas of attack and infiltration, or had crossed salt water to Brittany. That is why varieties of the Celtic language survive to this day in the Scottish Highlands, Wales, and northwestern France.

Of the fight put up by the island's defenders history affords the scantiest of glimpses. Here and there local forces were rallied and a stand was made; but it was a lost cause they fought for. One attempt at resistance was perhaps headed by a leader named Artorius; in any event, later legend credited a leader so named with an heroic role in the British defense. Worked up long afterwards by poets and storytellers in the age of chivalry, this tradition flowered in the romances about King Arthur and his knights.

Out of the welter of hostile settlements, each with its own local king, there rose a number of states, small or large, with boundaries that shifted with the fortunes of war. Their number also varied; it was never stabilized until the royal house of Wessex made good its claim to the overlordship of all England. By that time Angles, Saxons, and Jutes alike were known as English. This was originally the name of the principal settlers in the north and northeast, where three kingdoms of Angles (or English) waxed and waned: Northumbria, which ran straight up the coast from the River Humber to the Firth of Forth beyond Edinburgh; Mercia, extending southward from the Humber to the Wash and thence nearly halfway to the English Channel; and, less important than the other two, East Anglia, which occupied the island's eastern hump. Britain's extreme southeastern tip, between the Thames estuary and the Strait of Dover, was settled by the Jutes, who also held the Isle of Wight and a strip of adjacent coast. The inhabitants of the main Jutish territory were called Kentishmen. The other principal kingdoms were Saxon. The East Saxons lived between the Thames and the lands of the East Angles. Along the southern coast between the two Jutish regions were the South Saxons. Most powerful and politically advanced of all, the West Saxons controlled a large area bounded on the west and north by Bristol Channel and the valley of the Severn, and on the south by the English Channel from the border of Cornwall to the Isle of Wight.

THE INVADERS, originally sea wolves, harriers, and plunderers, grew tamer, as settlers always do when they turn for subsistence from dependence on booty snatched with spear and sword to an economy based on agriculture. Yet the old rugged ideals lived on; and, in the ordinary course of events, there was still plenty of fighting: private feuds; struggles of the local chiefs and petty kings when a kingdom's throne, semihereditary yet elective, fell vacant; quarrels among the kingdoms; and, in the end, a desperate defense of Saxon England against the next wave of invasion, the terrible onslaught of the Danes. Christianity, which had been introduced during the Roman occupation, had been obliterated when the withdrawal of Rome's disciplined troops pulled the props from under the provincial government and left the island a prey to pagan attack. To the reign of Roman law and order there succeeded, while Britain was being conquered, shared, and reorganized by the English, a dreadful era of fire and sword.

The code of the Teutonic settlers was fierce and bloody; but it was better than no code at all, and it had its lofty side. Centuries earlier the Roman historian Tacitus had written of their German forebears—of their bravery, of their ideal of personal honor, of the devotion of the *comitatus* or warrior band whose duty was to die if need be to the last man in battle at their chieftain's side, of the lord's obligation to shield and reward his fighting men, of the special closeness (it appears, for example, in *Beowulf*) of the bond between uncle and nephew. The invaders who took Britain, their customs, their language, their religion of Woden and his fellow divinities of Germanic mythology, swept from the east and south nearly every trace of the Celto-Roman civilization.

The way of life which took its place rested on the warrior's loyalty to his kingly chief. The fighting men or "earls" formed a rude but proud military aristocracy. There were a few freedmen and even landholding yeomen who were not reckoned nobles; but the largest social class was the lowest, the bondmen. These serfs tilled the soil, tended the herds, caught the fish—menial tasks, beneath the dignity of the earls or "athelings." Justice was originally less a public concern than a matter of private revenge, on the principle of an eye for an eye or a tooth for a tooth. If someone killed a member of your family, you killed if you could the slayer or, as the next best thing, a member of his family. Yet, except when a man had committed the unpardonable offense of crime against an actual kinsman, the violent exaction of vengeance, even for murder, could be averted by

payment of blood money. That institution—it was a system of fines graduated according to the extent of the injury—was a long step toward civilization. It meant the triumph of law. To be an outlaw, exiled from home and beyond the pale of the code—that was a fearful fate.

CHRISTIANITY AND THE NORTHUMBRIAN REVIVAL

IF BY the end of the sixth century the Teutonic occupation was assured, it was not till late in the seventh that the first literary epoch arrived. For about a hundred years, till close to the year 800, education and the arts flourished; for a while English schools actually took the lead in European education. Since this cultural renascence occurred in the north, the home of the Angles, Britain's new language came to be known as English—Old English, we call it, because we speak its lineal descendant, enriched of course by subsequent large infusions from other tongues, especially Latin and French.

The Northumbrian revival was possible only because Christianity, at this stage of European history the western world's only hope of a better day, had meanwhile been brought back to England, with education in its train. Its return meant another sharp collision between two antagonistic cultures. But this time the result was not, as in the fifth century, the extermination of one; it was a compromise. Christianity absorbed some pagan things: Christmas customs, for instance, and the very name of Easter; while heathen ruthlessness and imperviousness to the beauty of the milder, gentler aspects of life began to melt in the light of the New Testament. In Old English poetry, allusions to Christian theology and ethics often stand cheek by jowl with ardent expression of the primitive heroic idealism and the old Teutonic tradition of violence.

Britain was reconverted from both the south and the north. In 597 a mission sent by Pope Gregory the Great and headed by an Italian priest named Augustine (not the famous theologian) landed in Kent, soon converted its king, and established in Canterbury a center of religious instruction from which the chief prelate of the Church of England still takes his title. Not long after, the marriage of a Kentish princess to a Northumbrian king gave the new religion a northern foothold, and York became England's second ecclesiastical capital. The heathen raged with considerable success when pagan Mercia overwhelmed Christian Northumbria, but this setback was temporary. In the west, Christianity had persevered among the Celts; about the time the Romans abandoned Britain, St. Patrick had converted Ireland. Thence missionaries carried their faith to western Scotland, and thence again it was brought southward into Northumbria. By 650 most of England was nominally Christian.

At first the Church in Britain was loosely organized; and, besides, there was dissension between adherents of the Celtic and advocates of the more directly Roman forms. At the Synod of Whitby in 664 both sides were heard by the Northumbrian king; he decided in favor of the southern or Roman practices. After that, organization proceeded rapidly, with the building of churches, the establishment of bishoprics under the archbishoprics of Canterbury and York, and the foundation of monasteries where, vowing themselves to poverty, chastity, and obedience, men or women, ruled by an abbot or an abbess, withdrew from the turmoil and anxieties of secular life. Long before the Wessex kings succeeded in replacing the separate and rival kingdoms with something like a national state, the Church had achieved a unity which fostered, at any rate on its own ever-increasing lands, an environment favorable to the arts of civilization and peace.

It was the Church that took the lead in education, literature, agriculture, and even industry. There were important schools at Canterbury and York; and, though Latin was long to remain the language of British scholarship, English as well as Latin was taught in the monasteries. Among the most valuable of the monkish contributions to enlightenment was the systematic reduplication of Latin and eventually of English manuscripts by the copyists who labored in the monastery's scriptorium. It was the incessant toil of these scribes that provided Anglo-Saxon Britain with its books, both the writings of the Church Fathers and some of the secular classics of Latin literature; and it preserved for us that fragment which has survived of what must once have been the considerable body of Old English literature.

The conversion of the English was an event of major importance to our literature. The marauders from over the North Sea undoubtedly had an oral literature—of ballads, songs, and snatches, of riddles (many of which got written down and have survived), of charms (against all and sundry of the aches and pains that flesh is heir to), of "gnomic verses"— these last embody pithy saws and general truths, half-truths, and maxims. There was also an important genre of more or less extemporized poetry, composed and sung by the scop or bard in early times. At the feast he raised his voice in praise of the deeds of heroes, thus honoring, either directly or by the subtler flattery of implied comparison, the chieftain

whom he served. He combined the functions of poet laureate, entertainer, and historian. Sometimes he was also the wandering minstrel, a welcome sojourner at many a court. Thus wide currency was given to an international body of Germanic history and legend. Few of the early English could write; though in the runes they had an alphabet, it was used chiefly for inscriptions. A literary epoch like the Northumbrian revival could not begin till Christianity had brought education.

BEDE

MANY of the historical facts already cited are recorded by the Venerable Bede (673–735) in his *Ecclesiastical History of the English People*. The honorary epithet which a succeeding generation tacked onto the name of the first English historian is a tribute to Bede's devotion to religion and scholarship; its continued employment acknowledges his permanent value as a major source for Anglo-Saxon history. Bede was a monk in the monastery at Jarrow on the Northumbrian coast; his writings are among the monuments of the cultural revival in that kingdom in the seventh and eighth centuries. Scholarship in the Middle Ages, and indeed as late as the Renaissance, was not specialized. Bede tackled many subjects; his most valuable contribution is the *Ecclesiastical History*.

Like all medieval scholars he wrote in Latin; hence a selection would be inappropriate here, even though an English translation was made early as King Alfred's time. Much of his book is intensely interesting to anyone who enjoys getting away from the necessarily arid condensations of textbook histories to firsthand, vividly detailed, and more nearly contemporary accounts. That is where the real flavor of history can be savored, though we ought to follow up our reading in the source books with the interpretive comment, synthesis, and considered judgment of the trained historian who has read everything that pertains to his specialty. There is a modern translation of the *Ecclesiastical History* in Everyman's Library. The standard Latin text (*Bedae Opera Historica*) was edited by C. Plummer in 1896. A good account is *Bede: His Life, Times, and Writings,* edited by A. H. Thompson, 1935.

CÆDMON, CYNEWULF, AND OTHER POETRY

IT IS in the pages of Bede's *Ecclesiastical History* that we first hear of an English poet. Cædmon, says the story, was a lay servant in the monastery at Whitby in Northumbria, well past the middle of the seventh century. When, according to custom, the harp passed from hand to hand of an evening and his turn came to contribute to the social glee, Cædmon felt his lack of poetry so keenly that he would leave the hall. One night, having crept away downheartedly, he was sleeping in the shed near the cattle he tended, when a vision bade him compose for the glory of God. This he did in his sleep; but when he awoke he recalled the poem, and he continued to versify, on themes from the Bible. Eventually he entered the Church.

The only bit of Cædmon's verse that has come down to us is a hymn which Bede quotes, with what accuracy no one knows. Several metrical paraphrases of portions of the Old Testament were once ascribed to Cædmon; their dates are unknown, but they are too late to be his. He remains obscure, a shadowy but appealing figure in the misty dawn of our literature. Some of the surviving "Cædmonian" poems rehearse, with a good deal of vitality, episodes from Genesis, Exodus, and Daniel; in them appears the compromise already mentioned between the two cultures, Christian and heathen: the Jewish battles are described in much the same terms and spirit as the heroic fights of Beowulf himself. For translations see *The Cædmonian Poems* (1916) by C. W. Kennedy.

The Christian strain continues in the "Cynewulfian" poems, also Northumbrian or possibly Mercian, about the end of the same century, the eighth. Of Cynewulf himself, nothing is known. That name is cryptically signed, in runes, to four religious poems —lives of Saints Juliana and Helena, *The Fates of the Apostles,* and one of three poems about Christ. *The Dream of the Rood* is not signed; but along with several others, most notably *Judith,* it seems to belong to the same school. It is included below, both in order to illustrate the Christian poetry of the Cynewulfian "cycle" and for the sake of its own beauty. For translations of the poems signed by Cynewulf and of others which have been attributed to him, see C. W. Kennedy's *The Poems of Cynewulf* (1910).

Still other poems, though none is a masterpiece, contain fine passages. There is charm in the Christian allegory of *The Phoenix,* adventure in *Apollonius of Tyre,* saintly martyrdom in *Andreas,* and the oddest of unnatural natural history in the pious *Bestiary.*

As for *Beowulf* and the lyrics which follow it in this book, they are all the work of nameless writers, and their dates are uncertain. *Beowulf* was probably composed in the eighth century. Its author was evidently a man of imagination and energy, whose genius helped make the Anglian revival a beginning worthy of the centuries of English song that have followed.

THE FIRST DANISH INVASION

BUT before that hopeful eighth century was over, history repeated itself; the promise of a long era of progress in the north was shattered by fresh onslaughts from overseas. The very name of the new invaders grew terrible to English ears, as the Christian culture of the Angles went down in the ninth century under the battle-axes of the Danes.

Meanwhile, in the seventh and early in the eighth centuries, first Northumbria and then Mercia had risen to a dominating position among the kingdoms; but in 830 Egbert, ruler of the West Saxons, having added Devonshire and Cornwall to his kingdom of Wessex and overcome Mercia and its dependencies, marched to Northumbria and received its king's submission. In the same year some of the Welsh chieftains acknowledged the West Saxon overlordship, though Wales was not permanently annexed till several centuries later. For the first time since Britain had ceased to be a Roman province, there was a semblance of political unity.

Winchester, the Wessex capital, was not, however, the seat of an effective insular government. Even before Egbert was accepted as a national monarch, the first raids of the Vikings had struck the coasts. In their shallow longboats, rowed by thirty or forty sailor-warriors, the Northmen could even run up the English rivers to ravage inland farms and pastures. Like everything else, literature suffered. How many of the monks' manuscripts vanished in the smoke of blazing towns and monasteries will never be known; but presumably only a fraction of the Old English literature remained unscathed in those libraries which escaped, first, the attentions of barbarians who cared as little for learning as for life, and, much later, the seizure of the Tudor monasteries by Henry VIII. Practically all the Old English poetry that is left, about 30,000 lines, has come down to us in four manuscripts: the *Beowulf* (British Museum, London), the Junius (Bodleian Library, Oxford), the Vercelli (at a monastery there, in Piedmont), and a fourth manuscript known as the Exeter Book (in the cathedral of the Devonshire city).

At first the Danes, who had no interest whatever in manuscripts, won their plunder in dashing piratical forays. Then the attacking fleets grew larger, the ravaging bands stronger, the duration of the raids longer. Better trained and fiercer than the English, in battle they seemed invincible. Eventually the independent units coalesced in "the army," as the natives called it. After a season of looting, the Danes would settle down for the winter in a fortified camp, to which they had brought the summer's booty. If local opposition mustered strongly enough to make it too hot for them, they could readily slip away, for they commanded the sea. But, as a rule, when it came to pitched battles the Danes won. Even important towns like Winchester, Canterbury, London, and York were sacked.

Permanent settlement was the third and final step; and by the time of King Alfred, Egbert's grandson (842?–c. 900), England was split in two. More or less under his control were all of the south, and the western half of the Midlands as far north as Chester; and he held London. But eastern Mercia, southern Northumbria, and all the east coast south of it clear down to the Thames comprised the "Danelaw." Danish, not English, law prevailed there. In 886 the heroic Alfred, who had led the English defense, formally accepted the division. Once more Britain received an infusion of new blood; the present inhabitants of the old Danelaw still average taller and blonder than their fellow countrymen.

Gradually the newcomers yielded to Christianity and their ways changed, till consciousness of national distinctions disappeared. Sea rovers always, the Danes were great traders; prosperous commercial towns sprang up in regions which they had once laid waste with sword and torch. It was Alfred who had stemmed the tide of their invasion, and bit by bit under his successors the English won back even the Danelaw.

ALFRED AND THE WEST SAXON REVIVAL

DURING Alfred's reign the Danes had been expelled from Wessex and the other territories controlled by the English crown; and at Winchester, in the comparatively peaceful era which ensued, there was a second flowering of Old English civilization. Alfred was seriously concerned over the cultural backwardness which had followed the submergence of the Northumbrian revival. Learning, he wrote,

> was so clean fallen off among the English that there were very few this side Humber who could understand their rituals in English or translate a letter from Latin into English, and I believe that there were not many beyond Humber. So few of them there were, that I can not think of even one south of Thames when I came to the throne. Thanks be to almighty God that we have some store of teachers now.

Alfred put the double weight of his authority and his example behind the renascence of letters. Monasteries and schools were founded, foreign scholars were attracted to Wessex by appointment to high places in the Church, and books were translated. Among these good works stand such of the Old English poems as have come down to us. Some, perhaps nearly all, were originally written in the Anglian dialect; we read them in West Saxon versions, the only ones that survived.

Alfred not only encouraged translation by others; he himself learned Latin in middle life in order to make translations of his own. His is a plain, honest style of no particular distinction; even when he inserts into a translation of Orosius's general *History* his own account of the Arctic and Baltic voyages of Ohthere and Wulfstan, two contemporary navigators, he misses what must have been a remarkable literary opportunity, for these narratives are of slight interest except to historians and geographers. Other works translated by Alfred and his co-workers are Bede's *Ecclesiastical History*, the *Pastoral Care* of Pope Gregory the Great, and the famous *Consolation of Philosophy* by the medieval Platonist, Boethius. Examples of Alfred's writing are available in *Select Translations from Old English Prose*, by A. S. Cook and C. B. Tinker (1908). For the life of this noble Englishman, see C. Plummer, *Life and Times of Alfred the Great* (1902) or Miss B. A. Lees, *Alfred the Great* (1915).

One further result of Alfred's belief in the national importance of literature is the *Anglo-Saxon Chronicle*, next to Bede's *Ecclesiastical History* the most important historical source for the Old English period. In several places, but first at Winchester under the King's direction, the monks began to systematize the annals already in their possession and to add yearly accounts of events of general importance. The national consciousness roused by the long struggle with the Danes is reflected in the grim story of the *Chronicle*. For two and a half centuries this unique national record was continued, even after the Norman Conquest. By 1154, the date of the last entry, the Old English period had long ended; the language had passed over, about a century before, into Middle English, a stage much closer to our present speech. There is a modern translation of the *Chronicle* in Everyman's Library. The best edition of the old text is that of C. Plummer, *Two of the Saxon Chronicles Parallel* (1892–99).

DANES AND NORMANS

WHILE the English under the West Saxon kings had been consolidating a national state, similar political developments had been proceeding in Scandinavia. Powerful kingdoms rose in Denmark, Norway, and Sweden; and the tenth century witnessed a new series of attacks on Britain. Early in the eleventh century the house of Wessex lost the throne to a wise and able Dane, King Cnut, who imposed his rule on the English and made them like it. After the death of Cnut's sons, the witan (literally, "the wise"), the council of the nation's leading men, elected Edward —the Confessor, as he was afterwards styled for his piety. This was in 1042; once more a prince of the Wessex line, a descendant of Alfred, wore the English crown.

But Edward had long been an exile in Normandy, and his reign was marked by a steadily increasing infiltration of Normans and of Norman culture. William, Duke of Normandy, claimed the right to succeed him. When Edward died the witan elected Harold, strongest of the English earls—by that time the word had come to mean, not as before a chief's fighting men, but the provincial viceroys whose power often eclipsed the monarch's. William's successful invasion and Harold's death at Hastings in 1066 opened the door still wider to Continental influences. French became the language of the nobility and the law courts. By 1100 the Old English period of history and literature was over.

TENTH-CENTURY LETTERS

LITERARY activity in Wessex had not ceased with Alfred's death. As in the earlier Northumbrian revival, much more was doubtless written than has survived. From the tenth century and the wars of the second Danish invasion come the two fine battle

poems of *Brunanburg* and *Maldon,* with which we end our glance at Old English literature. Like all the best things in it, they are the work of unknown writers.

Of less merit, yet the chief literary name in this later period, is Ælfric (c. 955–c. 1022), a Wessex priest and a voluminous author. He composed numerous homilies, edifying discourses for delivery by the clergy; he made translations; he wrote a variety of religious treatises, some in Latin. Cook and Tinker, cited below, give samples.

It is in the poetry, not the prose, of the Old English period that we find the highest expression of its literary genius; and we turn now to the noble epic which, like a trumpet blown from far away, still has power to stir the blood.

GENERAL REFERENCES

The selections which follow are necessarily scanty, though they constitute the best we have of what the Anglo-Saxons wrote. A wider range is available in *Select Translations from Old English Poetry* (1902) and *Select Translations from Old English Prose* (1908), both by A. S. Cook and C. B. Tinker. A good anthology culled from the original texts is W. J. Sedgefield's *An Anglo-Saxon Book of Verse and Prose* (1928); it contains notes and a glossary. An excellent literary history is A. R. Benham's *English Literature from Widsith to the Death of Chaucer* (1908). A recent survey of Old English poetry is C. W. Kennedy's *The Earliest English Poetry* (1943). For a sketch of the period in general see any good history of England, and for a full treatment R. H. Hodgkin's *A History of the Anglo-Saxons* (1935).

Beowulf

ENGLISH literature is not rich in epics; yet an English poem is the earliest of all the medieval works in that genre,[1] and the first great poem in any of the tongues of modern Europe. The unknown author of *Beowulf* was no Homer; but he knew how to write, and his mind had all the true poet's capability for taking fire at the thought of a noble or graceful action, a lofty sentiment, or a hero's serene fidelity to a code of honor.

He was a Christian, this gifted man; but he loved the heroic tradition. Probably he was a Northumbrian or Mercian; probably he lived in the eighth century. England is nowhere mentioned by this English author; his scene is laid in southeastern Denmark and southern Sweden. He is

dealing with old heroic times and battles long ago—long ago to him as well as to us. He draws admiringly on Scandinavian saga[2] and ballad, a vast stock of legend built up by generations of scops or bards on a slim foundation of historical fact. No doubt the oral literature the English brought with them to Britain included many related songs and stories. The *Beowulf* poet handles events which, if they occurred at all, happened at least two centuries before his day. The hero's uncle and lord, King Hygelac of Geatland, is known to history; he died in battle with the Franks near the mouths of the Rhine about the year 520. Possibly there really was a Beowulf, who fought so well on the fatal raid that in aftertimes legends clustered around his name—some dauntless warrior, famed for the abnormal strength of his

---

[1] *Genre,* as used in these introductions, means type, species, or branch of literature. The essay, lyric poetry, revenge tragedy are all genres.

[2] A saga is a medieval story, historical or legendary, usually in the form of an epiclike narrative, that is, on an heroic scale.

grip and for extraordinary feats of swimming. On the other hand the character may be sheer invention, without the slightest historical nucleus.

In either event, the main narrative material of the poem is older even than Hygelac's time. Either the author of *Beowulf* or the creator of some earlier version has brought together, with no remarkable display of structural skill, two separate stories from folklore, and has attached them to a single hero: he fights with trolls, and he slays a fiery dragon. Both these fables appear in one form or another in several Germanic sagas. In *Beowulf* they are elevated from the realm of popular lore and attached to an historical or pseudo-historical hero. But the English poet is not trying to paint an accurate picture of life on the Baltic in the sixth century, though some of his details may be precise. Just as Shake-speare depicts his Greeks and Romans by blending bits of local color, picked up from his reading, with a wealth of ideas, feelings, and customs ascribed by him to ancient times but actually the fruit of his own observation of human nature in Elizabethan London and Warwickshire, so we may presume the *Beowulf* poet wove into his tapestry of life in an earlier age and a distant land a great deal of what he saw in his own era and country, very likely as an ecclesiastic at some Anglian court. A profound conviction that honor is the root from which springs the good life is not weakened but sweetened by an infusion of Christian ethics; and in the beautiful closing lines we are reminded of the hero's benevolence as well as of his thirst for glory.

Yet the whole thing is haunted, in a quite unchristian manner, by one of humanity's most deeply rooted beliefs —"moods" is perhaps a more accurate word—a considera-tion that has always been a major stimulus of art. Every man is doomed. That is not a thought peculiar to the English or to their Germanic progenitors; nor is it fully accounted for by the long nights of the northern winter, when, locked in the icy grip of the hostile elements graph-ically introduced in some of the Old English lyrics, a book-less folk had ample time for brooding over the relative attractions of life and death. Nevertheless, a striking thing about this literature, alike in its pagan and in its Christian aspects, is the comparative absence of *joie de vivre* or zest for life. What little there is has to do chiefly with pleasures which dull the edge of life and therefore of pain by induc-ing a momentary oblivion—huge feeding and that variety of drinking which leads to stupefaction, not gaiety. Stormy times, a bad climate, a way of living the refinements of which were so recently acquired that civilization was still a veneer—such were the conditions of existence, and they encouraged the universal tendency of our kind to reflect that in the midst of life we are in death. Over all reflections, throughout the whole course of *Beowulf*, presides the grim conception, almost a deity, of *Wyrd* or Fate. To it, as in *Macbeth*, are largely due the poem's austerity and the harsh

yet exalted atmosphere of tragedy in which the action moves. From it stem the bitter lessons of fortitude, of cheer-fulness under fire, of doing one's possible; mindful of them, the eighth-century Englishman preferred, as his descendant prefers today, a grim understatement to a frantic claim. The famous strokes of ironical humor in the war speeches of Winston Churchill in 1940 and 1941 repeatedly touched the same iron string and produced the same grim tone. There is something in the fiber of the British that vibrates to that string, now as in Saxon times.

Despite this epic's northern origin, the unique manuscript which has preserved *Beowulf* for us was written in the West Saxon dialect; it was probably copied about the year 1000, at least two centuries after the poem was composed. Old English verse employs a line which contains regularly four stressed syllables, besides a varying number of unstressed syllables. The line is broken into two half-lines by a distinct pause in the middle. Rime is not used, but the repetitive effect of rime is secured by alliteration which ties the two half-lines together; the third stressed syllable in a line always alliterates with either the first or the second, and often with both. Note the alliteration and stresses in the following lines from the beginning and the end of *Beowulf*. (Any vowel alliterates with any other. The character þ represents the sound *th* in *thin*, ð the sound *th* in *then*.)

Hwæt, wē Gár-Déna   in géar-dágum,
þéod-cýninga   þrým gefrúnon,
hū ða æþelíngas   éllen frémedon.
Oft Scýld Scéfing   scéaþena þréatum
mónegum mǽgþum   méodo-setla oftéah,
égsode éorlas,   syððan ǽrest wéarð
féa-sceaft fúnden;   hē þæs frófre gebád,
wéox under wólcnum   wéorð-myndum þáh,
óð þæt him ǽghwylc   ýmbsíttendra
ofer hrónráde   hýran scólde,
gómban gýldan;   þæt wæs gód cýning!

* * * * * * *

Swā begnórnódon   Géata léode
hláfordes hrýre,   héorð-genéatas;
cwǽdon þæt hē wǽre   wýruld-cýninga
mánna míldust   ond món-ðwǽrust,
léodum líðost   ond lóf-geórnost.

There are other striking features of the poetic technique. A favorite device is reiteration by a lavish use of appositives —words, phrases, clauses, sentences—the poet exhibiting his skill and gaining his effect by playing an idea over with variations. Similes are rare, but the poet frequently uses "kennings" or descriptive circumlocutions: such are "whale-road" and "gannet's bath" for the sea, and "foamy-necked sea-goer" for a ship plunging along in blue water. How successfully the artistic level is sustained throughout the long narrative, you are about to discover, with the aid of Professor Kennedy's fine translation. That any translation must be used is a pity; to put the case with a pertinent example of Anglo-Saxon understatement, not everyone who has studied Old English sufficiently to be able to read *Beowulf* has thought his time wasted.

An excellent edition, with introduction, notes, and glossary, is F. Klaeber's (third and revised ed., 1936). Valuable and interesting treatises are those of W. W. Lawrence,

Beowulf and Epic Tradition (1928), and R. W. Chambers, *Beowulf: An Introduction to the Study of the Poem* (2nd ed., 1932). With permission of the Oxford University Press, the translation which follows is that of C. W. Kennedy. It has been reprinted in full, except for a few digressions in the poet's narrative and one passage of superfluous recapitulation. Summaries of these portions, as well as the division into sections and the descriptive section titles, are by the editor of the present volume.

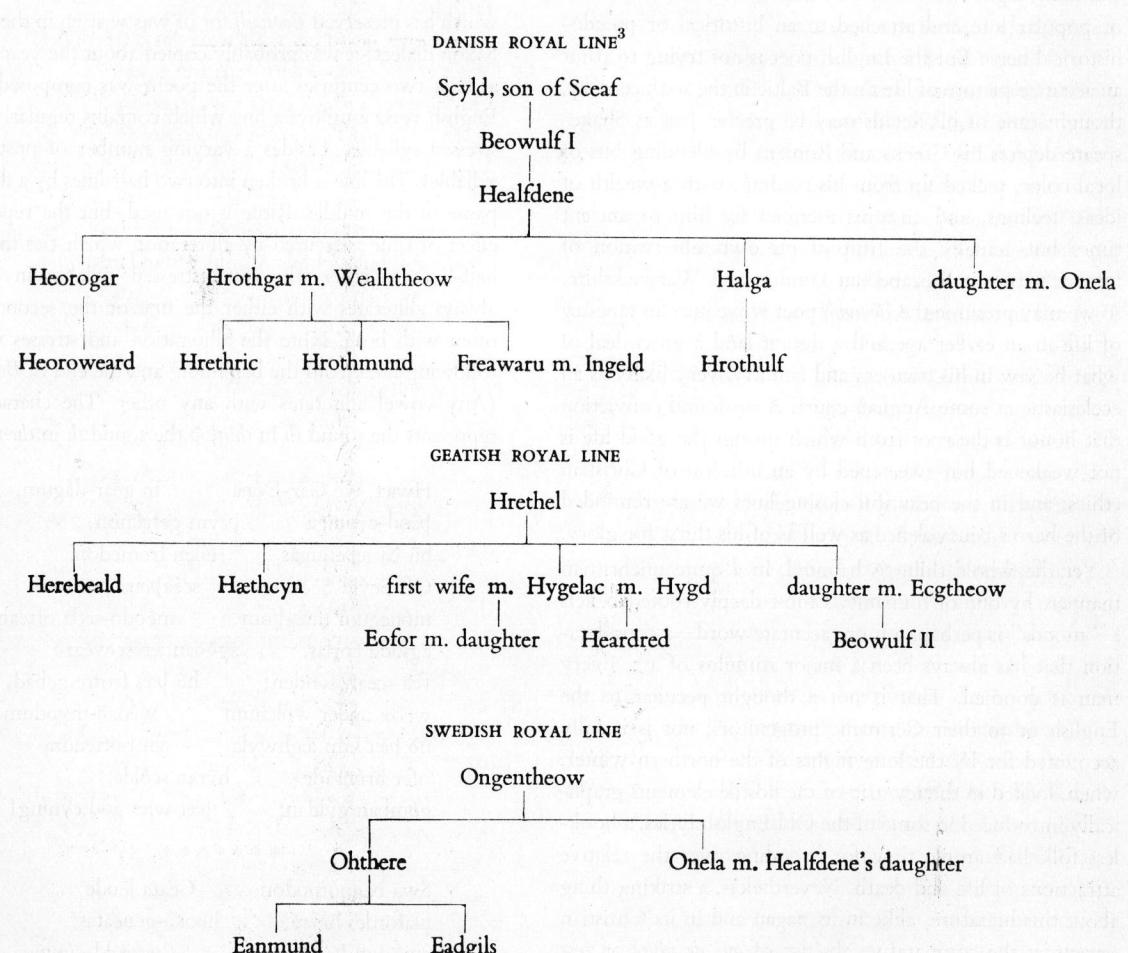

DANISH ROYAL LINE[3]

Scyld, son of Sceaf

Beowulf I

Healfdene

Heorogar   Hrothgar m. Wealhtheow   Halga   daughter m. Onela

Heoroweard   Hrethric   Hrothmund   Freawaru m. Ingeld   Hrothulf

GEATISH ROYAL LINE

Hrethel

Herebeald   Hæthcyn   first wife m. Hygelac m. Hygd   daughter m. Ecgtheow

Eofor m. daughter   Heardred   Beowulf II

SWEDISH ROYAL LINE

Ongentheow

Ohthere   Onela m. Healfdene's daughter

Eanmund   Eadgils

[3] These genealogies are adapted from Klaeber's edition, pp. xxi, xxxviii.

Beowulf

SCYLD OF THE SPEAR-DANES

*How he came as a foundling; how he ruled, conquered, and
established a dynasty; and how, when he died, his warriors gave
his body back to the sea.*

Lo! we have listened to many a lay
Of the Spear-Danes' fame, their splendor of old,
Their mighty princes, and martial deeds!
Many a mead-hall[1] Scyld, son of Sceaf,[2]
Snatched from the forces of savage foes.   5
From a friendless foundling, feeble and wretched,
He grew to a terror as time brought change.
He throve under heaven in power and pride
Till alien peoples beyond the ocean
Paid toll and tribute. A good king he!   10
To him thereafter an heir was born,
A son of his house, whom God had given
As stay to the people; God saw the distress
The leaderless nation had long endured.
The Giver of glory, the Lord of life,   15
Showered fame on the son of Scyld;
His name was honored, Beowulf[3] known,
To the farthest dwellings in Danish lands.
So must a young man strive for good
With gracious gifts from his father's store,   20
That in later seasons, if war shall scourge,
A willing people may serve him well:
'Tis by earning honor a man must rise
In every state. Then his hour struck,
And Scyld passed on to the peace of God.   25
As their leader had bidden, whose word was law
In the Scylding[4] realm which he long had ruled,
His loving comrades carried him down
To the shore of ocean; a ring-prowed[5] ship,
Straining at anchor and sheeted with ice,   30

Rode in the harbor, a prince's pride.
Therein they laid him, their well-loved lord,
Their ring-bestower,[6] in the ship's embrace,
The mighty prince at the foot of the mast
Amid much treasure and many a gem   35
From far-off lands. No lordlier ship
Have I ever heard of, with weapons heaped,
With battle-armor, with bills and byrnies.[7]
On the ruler's breast lay a royal treasure
As the ship put out on the unknown deep.   40
With no less adornment they dressed him round,
Or gift of treasure, than once they[8] gave
Who launched him first on the lonely sea
While still but a child. A golden standard
They raised above him, high over head,   45
Let the wave take him on trackless seas.
Mournful their mood and heavy their hearts;
Nor wise man nor warrior knows for a truth
Unto what haven that cargo came.

THE BUILDING OF HEOROT

*How Scyld's descendants ruled in Denmark, and how King
Hrothgar built a great mead-hall.*

Then Beowulf ruled o'er the Scylding realm,
Beloved and famous, for many a year—
The prince, his father, had passed away—
Till, firm in wisdom and fierce in war,
The mighty Healfdene held the reign,   5
Ruled, while he lived, the lordly Scyldings.
Four sons and daughters were seed of his line,
Heorogar and Hrothgar, leaders of hosts,
And Halga, the good. I have also heard
A daughter was Onela's consort and queen,   10
The fair bed-mate of the Battle-Scylfing.[9]
To Hrothgar was granted glory in war,
Success in battle; retainers bold
Obeyed him gladly; his band increased
To a mighty host. Then his mind was moved   15
To have men fashion a high-built hall,
A mightier mead-hall than man had known,
Wherein to portion to old and young

---

[1] Tribal headquarters and home of the warriors, where they slept, ate, and drank their mead.

[2] Shield, son of Sceaf. According to the myth, a mysterious ship brought the tribe a savior, apparently of divine origin. At the babe's head lay a sheaf, symbol of fertility and prosperity. (Scyld is pronounced *shilld*.)

[3] Not the hero of the poem, who is a Geat from the Swedish coast. Beowulf, the son of Scyld, was a Dane, an ancestor of the Danish king Hrothgar; it is in aid of Hrothgar that the hero of the poem, the later Beowulf, comes to Denmark. See the genealogical tables.

[4] Danish, belonging to the descendants of Scyld. To avoid excessive repetition, the poet uses various names for the Danes.

[5] Ornamented by the metal bands that strapped the timbers together.

[6] Liberality was expected of the ruler; he often bestowed rings and bracelets on his warriors. Cf. lines 19-22, above.

[7] Swords and coats of chain mail.

[8] His unknown parents or guardians.

[9] Swede. The Swedish royal family are "Scylfings," descendants of Scylf; the name is extended to the Swedes in general. Cf. *Scyldings* as a synonym for *Danes*.

All goodly treasure that God had given,
Save only the folk-land, and lives of men.[10]   20
His word was published to many a people
Far and wide o'er the ways of earth
To rear a folk-stead richly adorned;
The task was speeded, the time soon came
That the famous mead-hall was finished and done.   25
To distant nations its name was known,
The Hall of the Hart;[11] and the king kept well
His pledge and promise to deal out gifts,
Rings at the banquet. The great hall rose
High and horn-gabled, holding its place   30
Till the battle-surge of consuming flame
Should swallow it up; the hour was near
That the deadly hate of a daughter's husband
Should kindle to fury and savage feud.[12]

THE MURDERS OF GRENDEL

*How the warriors lived happily in the hall till the appearance of
Grendel, and how that wicked monster ravaged the Danes for
twelve long years.*

Then an evil spirit[13] who dwelt in the darkness
Endured it ill that he heard each day
The din of revelry ring through the hall,
The sound of the harp, and the scop's[14] sweet song.
A skillful bard sang the ancient story   5
Of man's creation; how the Maker wrought
The shining earth with its circling waters;
In splendor established the sun and moon
As lights to illumine the land of men;
Fairly adorning the fields of earth   10
With leaves and branches; creating life
In every creature that breathes and moves.
So the lordly warriors lived in gladness,
At ease and happy, till a fiend from hell
Began a series of savage crimes.   15
They called him Grendel, a demon grim
Haunting the fen-lands, holding the moors,
Ranging the wastes, where the wretched wight
Made his lair with the monster kin;
He bore the curse of the seed of Cain   20
Whereby God punished the grievous guilt
Of Abel's murder. Nor ever had Cain
Cause to boast of that deed of blood;

God banished him far from the fields of men;
Of his blood was begotten an evil brood,   25
Marauding monsters and menacing trolls,
Goblins and giants who battled with God
A long time. Grimly He gave them reward!
    Then at the nightfall the fiend drew near
Where the timbered mead-hall towered on high,   30
To spy how the Danes fared after the feast.
Within the wine-hall he found the warriors
Fast in slumber, forgetting grief,
Forgetting the woe of the world of men.
Grim and greedy the gruesome monster,   35
Fierce and furious, launched attack,
Slew thirty spearmen asleep in the hall,
Sped away gloating, gripping the spoil,
Dragging the dead men home to his den.
Then in the dawn with the coming of daybreak   40
The war-might of Grendel was widely known.
Mirth was stilled by the sound of weeping;
The wail of the mourner awoke with day.
And the peerless hero, the honored prince,
Weighed down with woe and heavy of heart,   45
Sat sorely grieving for slaughtered thanes,
As they traced the track of the cursed monster.
From that day onward the deadly feud
Was a long-enduring and loathsome strife.
    Not longer was it than one night later   50
The fiend returning renewed attack
With heart firm-fixed in the hateful war,
Feeling no rue for the grievous wrong.
'Twas easy thereafter to mark[15] the men
Who sought their slumber elsewhere afar,   55
Found beds in the bowers,[16] since Grendel's hate
Was so baldly blazoned in baleful signs.
He held himself at a safer distance
Who escaped the clutch of the demon's claw.
So Grendel raided and ravaged the realm,   60
One against all, in an evil war
Till the best of buildings was empty and still.
'Twas a weary while! Twelve winters' time
The lord of the Scyldings had suffered woe,
Sore affliction and deep distress.   65
And the malice of Grendel, in mournful lays,
Was widely sung by the sons of men,
The hateful feud that he fought with Hrothgar—
Year after year of struggle and strife,
And endless scourging, a scorning of peace   70
With any man of the Danish might.

---

[10] I.e., there were these limitations to the ruler's power.

[11] *Heorot* (hart) in Old English. The hart (stag) symbolized royalty,
and no doubt the hall was adorned with antlers. Hrothgar's court
was probably in Sjaelland, the largest of the Danish islands.

[12] An allusion to the destruction of Heorot in a subsequent war of
blood feud. Hrothgar tried to avert it by giving one of his
daughters in marriage to the enemy king.   [13] Grendel.

[14] Poet, singer, bard.

[15] One couldn't help noticing; i.e., everyone left the hall at night.
An example of the grim humor of the Old English poet; it
depends on understatement.

[16] Private sleeping quarters, near the hall.

No strength could move him to stay his hand,
Or pay for his murders; the wise knew well
They could hope for no halting of savage assault.
Like a dark death-shadow the ravaging demon, 75
Night-long prowling the misty moors,
Ensnared the warriors, wary or weak.
No man can say how these shades of hell
Come and go on their grisly rounds.

    With many an outrage, many a crime, 80
The fierce lone-goer, the foe of man,
Stained the seats of the high-built house,
Haunting the hall in the hateful dark.
But throne or treasure he might not touch,
Finding no favor or grace with God. 85
Great was the grief of the Scylding leader,
His spirit shaken, while many a lord
Gathered in council considering long
In what way brave men best could struggle
Against these terrors of sudden attack. 90
From time to time in their heathen temples
Paying homage they offered prayer
That the Slayer of souls[17] would send them succor
From all the torment that troubled the folk.
Such was the fashion and such the faith 95
Of their heathen hearts that they looked to hell,
Not knowing the Maker, the mighty Judge,
Nor how to worship the Wielder of glory,
The Lord of heaven, the God of hosts.
Woe unto him who in fierce affliction 100
Shall plunge his soul in the fiery pit
With no hope of mercy or healing change;
But well with the soul that at death seeks God,
And finds his peace in his Father's bosom.

    The son of Healfdene[18] was heavy-hearted, 105
Sorrowfully brooding in sore distress,
Finding no help in a hopeless strife;
Too bitter the struggle that stunned the people,
The long oppression, loathsome and grim.

THE COMING OF BEOWULF

*How news of Grendel's crimes reached the land of the Geats; how
Beowulf resolved to offer Hrothgar his services and, with fourteen
companions, set sail for Denmark; how the chief of the coast
guard marveled at their arrival but, accepting the hero's explanation, escorted the band to Heorot.*

Then tales of the terrible deeds of Grendel
Reached Hygelac's thane[19] in his home with the Geats;

---

[17] The Devil. Note the Christian touch; the poet assumes that in
pre-Christian times the tribes worshiped Satan. [18] Hrothgar.
[19] Beowulf, hero of the poem. *Thane* = warrior chief. Hygelac,
Beowulf's uncle, was the ruler of the Geats, another Germanic
tribe, who lived probably on the southern coast of Sweden.

Of living strong men he was the strongest,
Fearless and gallant and great of heart.
He gave command for a goodly vessel 5
Fitted and furnished; he fain would sail
Over the swan-road[20] to seek the king
Who suffered so sorely for need of men.
And his bold retainers found little to blame
In his daring venture, dear though he was; 10
They viewed the omens, and urged him on.
Brave was the band he had gathered about him,
Fourteen stalwarts seasoned and bold,
Seeking the shore where the ship lay waiting,
A sea-skilled mariner sighting the landmarks. 15
Came the hour of boarding; the boat was riding
The waves of the harbor under the hill.
The eager mariners mounted the prow;
Billows were breaking, sea against sand.
In the ship's hold snugly they stowed their trappings, 20
Gleaming armor and battle-gear;
Launched the vessel, the well-braced bark,
Seaward bound on a joyous journey.
Over breaking billows, with bellying sail
And foamy beak, like a flying bird 25
The ship sped on, till the next day's sun
Showed sea-cliffs shining, towering hills
And stretching headlands. The sea was crossed,
The voyage ended, the vessel moored.
And the Weder people[21] waded ashore 30
With clatter of trappings and coats of mail;
Gave thanks to God that His grace had granted
Sea-paths safe for their ocean-journey.

    Then the Scylding coast-guard watched from the
      sea-cliff
Warriors bearing their shining shields, 35
Their gleaming war-gear, ashore from the ship.
His mind was puzzled, he wondered much
What men they were. On his good horse mounted,
Hrothgar's thane made haste to the beach,
Boldly brandished his mighty spear 40
With manful challenge: "What men are you,
Carrying weapons and clad in steel,
Who thus come driving across the deep
On the ocean-lanes in your lofty ship?
Long have I served as the Scylding outpost, 45
Held watch and ward at the ocean's edge
Lest foreign foemen with hostile fleet
Should come to harry our Danish home,
And never more openly sailed to these shores
Men without password, or leave to land. 50
I have never laid eyes upon earl[22] on earth

---

[20] A kenning (see p. 9, above) for *sea*.
[21] Another name for the Geats, perhaps from a group of islands off
their coast. [22] Thane, noble warrior.

More stalwart and sturdy than one of your troop,
A hero in armor; no hall-thane he
Tricked out with weapons, unless looks belie him,
And noble bearing. But now I must know   55
Your birth and breeding, nor may you come
In cunning stealth upon Danish soil.
You distant-dwellers, you far sea-farers,
Hearken, and ponder words that are plain:
'Tis best you hasten to have me know   60
Who your kindred and whence you come."

    The lord of the seamen gave swift reply,
The prince of the Weders unlocked his word-hoard:
"We are sprung of a strain of the Geatish stock,
Hygelac's comrades and hearth-companions.   65
My father was famous in many a folk-land,
A leader noble, Ecgtheow his name!
Many a winter went over his head
Before death took him from home and tribe;
Well nigh every wise man remembers him well   70
Far and wide on the ways of earth.
With loyal purpose we seek your lord,
The prince of your people, great Healfdene's son.
Be kindly of counsel; weighty the cause
That leads us to visit the lord of the Danes;   75
Nor need it be secret, as far as I know!
You know if it's true, as we've heard it told,
That among the Scyldings some secret scather,
Some stealthy demon in dead of night,
With grisly horror and fiendish hate   80
Is spreading unheard-of havoc and death.
Mayhap I can counsel the good old king
What way he can master the merciless fiend,
If his coil of evil is ever to end
And feverish care grow cooler and fade—   85
Or else ever after his doom shall be
Distress and sorrow while still there stands
This best of halls on its lofty height."

    Then from the saddle the coast-guard spoke,
The fearless sentry: "A seasoned warrior   90
Must know the difference between words and deeds,
If his wits are with him. I take your word
That your band is loyal to the lord of the Scyldings.
Now go your way with your weapons and armor,
And I will guide you; I'll give command   95
That my good retainers may guard your ship,
Your fresh-tarred floater, from every foe,
And hold it safe in its sandy berth,
Till the curving prow once again shall carry
The loved man home to the land of the Geat.   100
To hero so gallant shall surely be granted
To come from the swordplay sound and safe."

    Then the Geats marched on; behind at her mooring,
Fastened at anchor, their broad-beamed boat

Safely rode on her swinging cable.   105
Boar-heads glittered on glistening helmets[23]
Above their cheek-guards, gleaming with gold;
Bright and fire-hardened the boar held watch
Over the column of marching men.
Onward they hurried in eager haste   110
Till their eyes caught sight of the high-built hall,
Splendid with gold, the seat of the king,
Most stately of structures under the sun;
Its light shone out over many a land.
The coast-guard showed them the shining hall,   115
The home of heroes; made plain the path;
Turned his horse; gave tongue to words:
"It is time to leave you! The mighty Lord
In His mercy shield you and hold you safe
In your bold adventure. I'll back to the sea   120
And hold my watch against hostile horde."

THE ARRIVAL AT HEOROT

*How the Geats were ceremoniously ushered into Heorot, where
Beowulf explained his purpose and his competence to execute it;
and how King Hrothgar welcomed the band, and they sat down
with the Danes and drank with them.*

The street had paving of colored stone;
The path was plain to the marching men.
Bright were their byrnies,[24] hard and hand-linked;
In their shining armor the chain mail sang
As the troop in their war-gear tramped to the hall.   5
The sea-weary sailors set down their shields,
Their wide, bright bucklers along the wall,
And sank to the bench. Their byrnies rang.
Their stout spears stood in a stack together
Shod with iron and shaped of ash.   10
'Twas a well-armed troop! Then a stately warrior
Questioned the strangers about their kin:
"Whence come you bearing your burnished shields,
Your steel-gray harness and visored helms,
Your heap of spears? I am Hrothgar's herald,[25]   15
His servant-thane. I have never seen strangers,
So great a number, of nobler mien.
Not exiles, I ween,[26] but high-minded heroes
In greatness of heart have you sought out Hrothgar."
Then bold under helmet the hero made answer,   20
The lord of the Weders, manful of mood,
Mighty of heart: "We are Hygelac's men,
His board-companions; Beowulf is my name.
I will state my mission to Healfdene's son,
The noble leader, your lordly prince,   25
If he will grant approach to his gracious presence."

---

[23] Their helmets bore metal figures of boars.
[24] Coats of chain mail.   [25] I.e., officer, court functionary.
[26] Suppose.

And Wulfgar answered, the Wendel[27] prince,
Renowned for merit in many a land,
For war-might and wisdom: "I will learn the wish
Of the Scylding leader, the lord of the Danes,   30
Our honored ruler and giver of rings,
Concerning your mission, and soon report
The answer our leader thinks good to give."

He swiftly strode to where Hrothgar sat
Old and gray with his earls about him;   35
Crossed the floor and stood face to face
With the Danish king; he knew courtly custom.
Wulfgar saluted his lord and friend:
"Men from afar have fared to our land
Over ocean's margin—men of the Geats,   40
Their leader called Beowulf—seeking a boon,
The holding of parley, my prince, with thee.
O gracious Hrothgar, refuse not the favor!
In their splendid war-gear they merit well
The esteem of earls; he's a stalwart leader   45
Who led this troop to the land of the Danes."

Hrothgar spoke, the lord of the Scyldings:
"Their leader I knew when he still was a lad.
His father was Ecgtheow; Hrethel the Geat[28]
Gave him in wedlock his only daughter.   50
Now is their son come, keen for adventure,
Finding his way to a faithful friend.
Sea-faring men who have voyaged to Geatland
With gifts of treasure as token of peace
Say that his hand-grip has thirty men's strength.   55
God, in His mercy, has sent him to save us—
So springs my hope—from Grendel's assaults.
For his gallant courage I'll load him with gifts!
Make haste now, marshal the men to the hall,
And give them welcome to Danish ground."   60

Then to the door went the well-known warrior,[29]
Spoke from the threshold welcoming words:
"The Danish leader, my lord, declares
That he knows your kinship; right welcome you come,
You stout sea-rovers, to Danish soil.   65
Enter now, in your shining armor
And vizored helmets, to Hrothgar's hall.
But leave your shields and the shafts of slaughter
To wait the issue and weighing of words."

Then the bold one rose with his band around him,   70
A splendid massing of mighty thanes;
A few stood guard, as the Geat gave bidding,
Over the weapons stacked by the wall.

They followed in haste on the heels of their leader
Under Heorot's roof. Full ready and bold   75
The helmeted warrior strode to the hearth;
Beowulf spoke; his byrny glittered,
His war-net woven by cunning of smith:
"Hail! King Hrothgar! I am Hygelac's thane,
Hygelac's kinsman. Many a deed   80
Of honor and daring I've done in my youth.
This business of Grendel was brought to my ears
On my native soil. The sea-farers say
This best of buildings, this boasted hall,
Stands dark and deserted when sun is set,   85
When darkening shadows gather with dusk.
The best of my people, prudent and brave,
Urged me, King Hrothgar, to seek you out;
They had in remembrance my courage and might.
Many had seen me come safe from the conflict,   90
Bloody from battle; five foes I bound
Of the giant kindred, and crushed their clan.
Hard-driven in danger and darkness of night
I slew the nicors[30] that swam the sea,
Avenged the woe they had caused the Weders,   95
And ended their evil—they needed the lesson!
And now with Grendel, the fearful fiend,
Single-handed I'll settle the strife!
Prince of the Danes, protector of Scyldings,
Lord of nations, and leader of men,   100
I beg one favor—refuse me not,
Since I come thus faring from far-off lands—
That I may alone with my loyal earls,
With this hardy company, cleanse Hart-Hall.
I have heard that the demon in proud disdain   105
Spurns all weapons; and I too scorn—
May Hygelac's heart have joy of the deed—
To bear my sword, or sheltering shield,
Or yellow buckler, to battle the fiend.
With hand-grip only I'll grapple with Grendel;   110
Foe against foe I'll fight to the death,
And the one who is taken must trust to God's grace!
The demon, I doubt not, is minded to feast
In the hall unaffrighted, as often before,
On the force of the Hrethmen, the folk of the Geats.   115
No need then to bury the body he mangles!
If death shall call me, he'll carry away
My gory flesh to his fen-retreat
To gorge at leisure and gulp me down,
Soiling the marshes with stains of blood.   120
There'll be little need longer to care for my body!
If the battle slays me, to Hygelac send
This best of corselets that covers my breast,

[27] Another Scandinavian tribe.
[28] Father of King Hygelac and of Beowulf's mother. Ecgtheow
   was probably a member of the Wylfing tribe. In his youth he
   had taken service with King Hrethel of Geatland. See also note
   32, below.   [29] Wulfgar.

[30] Nixes, water goblins or monsters.

Heirloom of Hrethel, and Wayland's[31] work,
Finest of byrnies. Fate goes as Fate must!"   125

Hrothgar spoke, the lord of the Scyldings:
"Deed of daring and dream of honor
Bring you, friend Beowulf, knowing our need!
Your father once fought the greatest of feuds,
Laid Heatholaf low, of the Wylfing line;[32]   130
And the folk of the Weders refused him shelter
For fear of revenge. Then he fled to the South-Danes,[33]
The Honor-Scyldings beyond the sea.
I was then first governing Danish ground,
As a young lad ruling the spacious realm,   135
The home-land of warriors. Heorogar was dead,
The son of Healfdene no longer living,
My older brother, and better than I!
Thereafter by payment composing the feud,
O'er the water's ridge I sent to the Wylfing   140
Ancient treasure; he swore me oaths!
It is sorrow sore to recite to another
The wrongs that Grendel has wrought in the hall,
His savage hatred and sudden assaults.
My war-troop is weakened, my hall-band is wasted;   145
Fate swept them away into Grendel's grip.
But God may easily bring to an end
The ruinous deeds of the ravaging foe.
Full often my warriors over their ale-cups
Boldly boasted, when drunk with beer,   150
They would bide in the beer-hall the coming of battle,
The fury of Grendel, with flashing swords.
Then in the dawn, when the daylight strengthened,
The hall stood reddened and reeking with gore,
Bench-boards wet with the blood of battle;   155
And I had the fewer of faithful fighters,
Beloved retainers, whom Death had taken.
Sit now at the banquet, unbend your mood,
Speak of great deeds as your heart may spur you!"

Then in the beer-hall were benches made ready   160
For the Geatish heroes. Noble of heart,
Proud and stalwart, they sat them down
And a beer-thane served them; bore in his hands
The patterned ale-cup, pouring the mead,

While the scop's sweet singing was heard in the hall.   165
There was joy of heroes, a host at ease,
A welcome meeting of Weder and Dane.

CAROUSAL IN HEOROT

*How a Danish thane, Unferth, taunted Beowulf, deriding his
conduct in his famous swim with Breca; how the hero met taunt
with taunt, relating the true story of that exploit, charging
Unferth with fratricide, and promising to show Grendel what a
Geat could do; and how Wealhtheow, Hrothgar's queen, honored Beowulf.*

Then out spoke Unferth,[34] Ecglaf's son,
Who sat at the feet of the Scylding lord,
Picking a quarrel—for Beowulf's quest,
His bold sea-voyaging, irked him sore;
He bore it ill that any man other   5
In all the earth should ever achieve
More fame under heaven than he himself:
"Are you the Beowulf that strove with Breca
In a swimming match in the open sea,
Both of you wantonly tempting the waves,   10
Risking your lives on the lonely deep
For a silly boast? No man could dissuade you,
Nor friend nor foe, from the foolhardy venture
Of ocean-swimming; with outstretched arms
You clasped the sea-stream, measured her streets,   15
With plowing shoulders parted the waves.
The sea-flood boiled with its wintry surges,
Seven nights you toiled in the tossing sea;
His strength was the greater, his swimming the stronger!
The waves upbore you at break of day   20
To the stretching beach of the Battle-Ræmas;[35]
And Breca departed, beloved of his people,
To the land of the Brondings,[36] the beauteous home,
The stronghold fair, where he governed the folk,
The city and treasure; Beanstan's son[37]   25
Made good his boast to the full against you!
Therefore, I ween, worse fate shall befall,
Stout as you are in the struggle of war,
In deeds of battle, if you dare to abide
Encounter with Grendel at coming of night."   30

Beowulf spoke, the son of Ecgtheow:
"My good friend Unferth, addled with beer
Much have you made of the deeds of Breca!
I count it true that I had more courage,
More strength in swimming than any other man.[38]   35

---

[31] The supernatural smith of Teutonic mythology. Cf. Vulcan.
[32] The passage is defective in the manuscript and subject to various
interpretations, among which the following agrees with the
translation given above. Ecgtheow, Beowulf's father, having
slain another Wylfing, named Heatholaf, was exiled by that
tribe. His wife's people, the Geats, refused him shelter; had they
taken him in, a feud would have ensued between them and the
Wylfings. The outcast found refuge with the Danes, whose
young king, Hrothgar, averted a feud by payment of blood
money to the Wylfings, in accordance with the code of the
blood feud. Ecgtheow lived to a ripe old age, but we are not
told where.
[33] Another name for the Danes or Scyldings.

[34] He is the *thyle*, court orator and official spokesman.
[35] In southern Norway.   [36] Another tribe, location unknown.
[37] Breca.
[38] Such boasting, frequent in heroic poetry, very likely reflects
actual procedure in early times.

A
Literary Map
OF THE
BRITISH
ISLES

Anglo-Saxon
Period

AW

SCOTS

PICTS

Firth of Forth

Lindisfarne

NORTHUMBRIA

Ruthwell ⊠

Jarrow ⊠
⊠ Wearmouth
Durham ⊠

⊠ Whitby

⊠ York

Humber River

BRITON

MERCIA

⊠ Chester

the Wash

EAST

⊠ Ely
ANGLIA

Maldon ⊠

ESSEX

Severn River

Thames River

London ⊠

Isle of
Thanet

⊠ Bath

KENT

Canterbury ⊠

Bristol Channel

Wedmore ⊠

⊠ Winchester

Hastings ⊠

Atlantic
Ocean

WESSEX

SUSSEX

Strait of Dover

Exeter ⊠

Isle of Wight

English Channel

ceꞇ eꞃ ᵹeꝥunꝺan· þᵹll ꝼꞃænᵹmꝺᵹt ꝥe þonꝺ ꞇimbꞃan· ac
hie ᵹnimlice· hæꝥum þhloꝺon hilꞇoꞃum ᵹeꝺalꝺeꞃ
þæꞃ oꝺþie· ᵹᵹhꝑile þonꝺᵹr· mæᵹ buꞃh ꝼꞃænꝺes ꞃᵹꝺꝺan
mic ꞇo þbꞃæꝺ· buꞃh hiꞃ mihꞇa ꝑ ꝑeꝺ· manna ꝑꝼꞃæce·

Surviving from about the year 1000 is this
volume of verse adaptations of Biblical
passages, now in the Bodleian Library at
Oxford. Its contents were once erroneously
attributed to Cædmon but are now known
to be of varying date and authorship. Scattered through the first section of the manuscript are 48 illustrations; those reproduced
here apparently deal with the story of
Nimrod (Genesis 10:8-10).

WANDERER IN THE EXETER BOOK

The Exeter Book is another specimen of
Anglo-Saxon bookmaking, of about the
same age as the Junius Manuscript; it was
presented to the library of Exeter Cathedral
about 1072. Its script has been described
as the "noblest of Anglo-Saxon hands."
The opening of *Wanderer* is shown here;
among the other poems in the manuscript
are *Deor*, *A Wife's Lament*, and *Seafarer*.

OFT him anhaᵹa aꞃe ᵹebiꝺeꝺ mᵹꞇuꝺiꝼ· milꞇ ꝼe þꞇihþe
he moꝺ cᵹꞇiꝡuᵹ ᵹᵹonꝺ laᵹu laꝺe lonᵹe ꝼcᵹlꝺe hꞃiþan
miꝺ honꝺum hꞃim cᵹlꝺe ꝥe ꝑaꝺan ꝼꞃaꞇ laᵹꞇaꞃ ꝑꝼꞃꝺ
biꝺ ꝼul aꞃeꝺ· Sꝑa cꝑᵹꝺ þꞃꝺ ꝼniꝺa· ꞇᵹꞃꝼᵹþa ᵹmꝑnꝺiᵹ
ꝑꞃaþꞃa ꝼᵹl ꞃᵹᵹulꞇᵹ ꝑine mᵹᵹa hꝑꞃꝑꝼ· Oꝼꞇ ic ꞃcᵹlꝺe
ana uhꞇna ᵹehꝑꞃlce mine cᵹꞃꝼ cꝑiþan niꞃ nu cꝑic
ꞃa nan þeic him moꝺ ꞃᵹꞇun minne ꝺuꞃꞃe ꝑꝑotule
aꞃiꞇᵹan ic ꞇo ꞃoþe ꝑaꞇ þ biþ inꞇꝑꝑle inꝺꞃꝑhꞇᵹh þᵹaꞃ
þaꞇ he hiꞃ ꝼᵹꞃꝺ locan ꝼᵹꞃꞇᵹ binꝺe· hᵹᵹloꝺe hiꞃ hoꞃꝺ
coꝼan hꞃᵹᵹe ꝑꝑahe ꝑille· Nᵹᵹmᵹᵹ ꝑꞃuᵹ moꝺ ꝑꝑꞃꝺe ꝑiꝺ
ꞃꞇoꞃꝺan nᵹþe hꞃᵹꝺ hᵹᵹe helꝼe ᵹꞃᵹnꞇinman· ꝼoꞃꝺon ꝺom
ᵹᵹꝑꞃne oꝼꞇꝼꞃⁱᵹne oꝼꞇ inhꝑꞃa bꞃᵹꝼꞇ coꝼan binꝺaꝺ
ꝼᵹꞃꞇᵹ· ꞃꞃa ic moꝺ ꞃꝼan minne ꝼcᵹlꝺe· oꝼꞇ ᵹᵹꞃⁱⁱm cᵹꞇiᵹ

In our youth we boasted—we were both of us boys—
We would risk our lives in the raging sea.
And we made it good! We gripped in our hands
Naked swords, as we swam in the waves,
Guarding us well from the whales' assault. 40
In the breaking seas he could not outstrip me,
Nor would I leave him. For five nights long
Side by side we strove in the waters
Till racing combers wrenched us apart,
Freezing squalls, and the falling night, 45
And a bitter north wind's icy blast.
Rough were the waves; the wrath of the sea-fish
Was fiercely roused; but my firm-linked byrny,
The gold-adorned corselet that covered my breast,
Gave firm defense from the clutching foe. 50
Down to the bottom a savage sea-beast
Fiercely dragged me and held me fast
In a deadly grip; none the less it was granted me
To pierce the monster with point of steel.
Death swept it away with the swing of my sword. 55
"The grisly sea-beasts again and again
Beset me sore; but I served them home
With my faithful blade as was well-befitting.
They failed of their pleasure to feast their fill
Crowding round my corpse on the ocean-bottom! 60
Bloody with wounds, at the break of day,
They lay on the sea-beach slain with the sword.
No more would they cumber the mariner's course
On the ocean deep. From the east came the sun,
Bright beacon of God, and the seas subsided; 65
I beheld the headlands, the windy walls.
Fate often delivers an undoomed earl
If his spirit be gallant! And so I was granted
To slay with the sword-edge nine of the nicors.
I have never heard tell of more terrible strife 70
Under dome of heaven in darkness of night,
Nor of man harder pressed on the paths of ocean.
But I freed my life from the grip of the foe
Though spent with the struggle. The billows bore me,
The swirling currents and surging seas, 75
To the land of the Finns.[39] And little I've heard
Of any such valiant adventures from you!
Neither Breca nor you in the press of battle
Ever showed such daring with dripping swords—
Though I boast not of it! But you stained your blade 80
With blood of your brothers, your closest of kin;
And for that you'll endure damnation in hell,
Sharp as you are! I say for a truth,
Son of Ecglaf, never had Grendel
Wrought such havoc and woe in the hall, 85
That horrid demon so harried your king,

If your heart were as brave as you'd have men think!
But Grendel has found that he never need fear
Revenge from your people, or valiant attack
From the Victor-Scyldings; he takes his toll, 90
Sparing none of the Danish stock.
He slays and slaughters and works his will
Fearing no hurt at the hands of the Danes!
But soon will I show him the stuff of the Geats,
Their courage in battle and strength in the strife; 95
Then let him who may go bold to the mead-hall
When the next day dawns on the dwellings of men,
And the sun in splendor shines warm from the south."
Glad of heart was the giver of treasure,
Hoary-headed and hardy in war; 100
The lordly leader had hope of help
As he listened to Beowulf's bold resolve.

There was revel of heroes and high carouse,
Their speech was happy; and Hrothgar's queen,
Of gentle manners, in jewelled splendor 105
Gave courtly greeting to all the guests.
The high-born lady first bore the beaker
To the Danish leader, lord of the land,
Bade him be blithe at the drinking of beer;
Beloved of his people, the peerless king 110
Joined in the feasting, had joy of the cup.
Then to all alike went the Helming[40] lady
Bearing the beaker to old and young,
Till the jewelled queen with courtly grace
Paused before Beowulf, proffered the mead. 115
She greeted the Geat and to God gave thanks,
Wise of word, that her wish was granted;
At last she could look to a hero for help,
Comfort in evil. He took the cup,
The hardy warrior, at Wealhtheow's hand 120
And, eager for battle, uttered his boast;
Beowulf spoke, the son of Ecgtheow:
"I had firm resolve when I set to sea
With my band of earls in my ocean-ship,
Fully to work the will of your people 125
Or fall in the struggle slain by the foe.
I shall either perform deeds fitting an earl
Or meet in this mead-hall the coming of death!"
Then the woman was pleased with the words he uttered,
The Geat-lord's boast; the gold-decked queen 130
Went in state to sit by her lord.

THE FIGHT WITH GRENDEL

How, without sword or armor, Beowulf watched that night in Heorot for Grendel; how that evil one came over the moors and murdered again; and how Beowulf and Grendel fought in the hall.

In the hall as of old were brave words spoken,
There was noise of revel; happy the host

---

[39] In northern Norway.

[40] I.e., she was a Wylfing by birth, Helm being ruler of that tribe.

Till the son of Healfdene would go to his rest.
He knew that the monster would meet in the hall
Relentless struggle when light of the sun   5
Was dusky with gloom of the gathering night,
And shadow-shapes crept in the covering dark,
Dim under heaven. The host arose.
Hrothgar graciously greeted his guest,
Gave rule of the wine-hall, and wished him well,   10
Praised the warrior in parting words:
"Never to any man, early or late,
Since first I could brandish buckler and sword,
Have I trusted this ale-hall save only to you!
Be mindful of glory, show forth your strength,   15
Keep watch against foe! No wish of your heart
Shall go unfulfilled if you live through the fight."
    Then Hrothgar withdrew with his host of retainers,
The prince of the Scyldings, seeking his queen,
The bed of his consort. The King of Glory   20
Had stablished a hall-watch, a guard against Grendel,
Dutifully serving the Danish lord,
The land defending from loathsome fiend.
The Geatish hero put all his hope
In his fearless might and the mercy of God!   25
He stripped from his shoulders the byrny of steel,
Doffed helmet from head; into hand of thane
Gave inlaid iron, the best of blades;
Bade him keep well the weapons of war.
Beowulf uttered a gallant boast,   30
The stalwart Geat, ere he sought his bed:
"I count myself nowise weaker in war
Or grapple of battle than Grendel himself.
Therefore I scorn to slay him with sword,
Deal deadly wound, as I well might do!   35
Nothing he knows of a noble fighting,
Of thrusting and hewing and hacking of shield,
Fierce as he is in the fury of war.
In the shades of darkness we'll spurn the sword
If he dares without weapon to do or to die.   40
And God in His wisdom shall glory assign,
The ruling Lord, as He deems it right."
Then the bold in battle bowed down to his rest,
Cheek pressed pillow; the peerless thanes
Were stretched in slumber around their lord.   45
Not one had hope of return to his home,
To the stronghold or land where he lived as a boy.
For they knew how death had befallen the Danes,
How many were slain as they slept in the wine-hall.
But the wise Lord wove them fortune in war,   50
Gave strong support to the Weder people;
They slew their foe by the single strength
Of a hero's courage. The truth is clear,
God rules forever the race of men.

    Then through the shades of enshrouding night   55
The fiend came stealing; the archers slept
Whose duty was holding the horn-decked hall—
Though one was watching—full well they knew
No evil demon could drag them down
To shades under ground if God were not willing.   60
But the hero watched, awaiting the foe,
Abiding in anger the issue of war.
    From the stretching moors, from the misty hollows,
Grendel came creeping, accursed of God,
A murderous ravager minded to snare   65
Spoil of heroes in high-built hall.
Under clouded heavens he held his way
Till there rose before him the high-roofed house,
Wine-hall of warriors gleaming with gold.
Nor was it the first of his fierce assaults   70
On the home of Hrothgar; but never before
Had he found worse fate or hardier hall-thanes!
Storming the building he burst the portal,
Though fastened of iron, with fiendish strength;
Forced open the entrance in savage fury   75
And rushed in rage o'er the shining floor.
A baleful glare from his eyes was gleaming
Most like to a flame. He found in the hall
Many a warrior sealed in slumber,
A host of kinsmen. His heart rejoiced;   80
The savage monster was minded to sever
Lives from bodies ere break of day,
To feast his fill of the flesh of men.
But he was not fated to glut his greed
With more of mankind when the night was ended!   85
    The hardy kinsman of Hygelac waited
To see how the monster would make his attack.
The demon delayed not, but quickly clutched
A sleeping thane in his swift assault,
Tore him in pieces, bit through the bones,   90
Gulped the blood, and gobbled the flesh,
Greedily gorged on the lifeless corpse,
The hands and the feet. Then the fiend stepped nearer,
Sprang on the Sea-Geat lying outstretched,
Clasping him close with his monstrous claw.   95
But Beowulf grappled and gripped him hard,
Struggled up on his elbow; the shepherd of sins
Soon found that never before had he felt
In any man other in all the earth
A mightier hand-grip; his mood was humbled,   100
His courage fled; but he found no escape!
He was fain to be gone; he would flee to the darkness,
The fellowship of devils. Far different his fate
From that which befell him in former days!
The hardy hero, Hygelac's kinsman,   105
Remembered the boast he had made at the banquet;

He sprang to his feet, clutched Grendel fast,
Though fingers were cracking, the fiend pulling free.
The earl pressed after; the monster was minded
To win his freedom and flee to the fens.   110
He knew that his fingers were fast in the grip
Of a savage foe. Sorry the venture,
The raid that the ravager made on the hall.

There was din in Heorot. For all the Danes,
The city-dwellers,[41] the stalwart Scyldings,   115
That was a bitter spilling of beer!
The walls resounded, the fight was fierce,
Savage the strife as the warriors struggled.
The wonder was that the lofty wine-hall
Withstood the struggle, nor crashed to earth,   120
The house so fair; it was firmly fastened
Within and without with iron bands
Cunningly smithied; though men have said
That many a mead-bench gleaming with gold
Sprang from its sill as the warriors strove.   125
The Scylding wise men had never weened
That any ravage could wreck the building,
Firmly fashioned and finished with bone,[42]
Or any cunning compass its fall,
Till the time when the swelter and surge of fire   130
Should swallow it up in a swirl of flame.[43]
Continuous tumult filled the hall;
A terror fell on the Danish folk
As they heard through the wall the horrible wailing,
The groans of Grendel, the foe of God   135
Howling his hideous hymn of pain,
The hell-thane shrieking in sore defeat.
He was fast in the grip of the man who was greatest
Of mortal men in the strength of his might,
Who would never rest while the wretch was living,   140
Counting his life-days a menace to man.

Many an earl of Beowulf brandished
His ancient iron to guard his lord,
To shelter safely the peerless prince.
They had no knowledge, those daring thanes,   145
When they drew their weapons to hack and hew,
To thrust to the heart, that the sharpest sword,
The choicest iron in all the world,
Could work no harm to the hideous foe.
On every sword he had laid a spell,   150
On every blade; but a bitter death
Was to be his fate; far was the journey
The monster made to the home of fiends.

Then he who had wrought such wrong to men,
With grim delight as he warred with God,   155
Soon found that his strength was feeble and failing
In the crushing hold of Hygelac's thane.
Each loathed the other while life should last!
There Grendel suffered a grievous hurt,
A wound in the shoulder, gaping and wide;   160
Sinews snapped and bone-joints broke,
And Beowulf gained the glory of battle.
Grendel, fated, fled to the fens,
To his joyless dwelling, sick unto death.
He knew in his heart that his hours were numbered,   165
His days at an end. For all the Danes
Their wish was fulfilled in the fall of Grendel.
The stranger from far, the stalwart and strong,
Had purged of evil the hall of Hrothgar,
And cleansed of crime; the heart of the hero   170
Joyed in the deed his daring had done.
The lord of the Geats made good to the East-Danes[44]
The boast he had uttered; he ended their ill,
And all the sorrow they suffered long
And needs must suffer—a foul offense.   175
The token was clear when the bold in battle
Laid down the shoulder and dripping claw—
Grendel's arm—in the gabled hall!

GRENDEL'S DEATH AND THE JOY OF THE DANES

*How the warriors tracked the monster to the fen where he died,
and how Hrothgar gave thanks to God and to Beowulf.*

When morning came, as they tell the tale,
Many a warrior hastened to hall,
Folk-leaders faring from far and near
Over wide-running ways, to gaze at the wonder,
The trail of the demon. Nor seemed his death   5
A matter of sorrow to any man
Who viewed the tracks of the vanquished monster
As he slunk weary-hearted away from the hall,
Doomed and defeated and marking his flight
With bloody prints to the nicors' pool.   10
The crimson currents bubbled and heaved
In eddying reaches reddened with gore;
The surges boiled with the fiery blood.
But the monster had sunk from the sight of men.
In that fenny covert the cursed fiend   15
Not long thereafter laid down his life,
His heathen spirit; and hell received him.

Then all the comrades, the old and young,
The brave of heart, in a blithesome band
Came riding their horses home from the mere.[45]   20
Beowulf's prowess was praised in song;

---

[41] I.e., the inhabitants of Heorot and its environs.
[42] I.e., adorned with horns.
[43] Another allusion to the later destruction of Heorot; see above,
    note 12.

[44] Another name for the Scyldings or Danes.   [45] Lake, pool.

And many men stated that south or north,
Over all the world, or between the seas,
Or under the heaven, no hero was greater,
More worthy of rule. But no whit they slighted   25
The gracious Hrothgar, their good old king.
Time and again they galloped their horses,
Racing their roans where the roads seemed fairest;
Time and again a gleeman chanted,
A minstrel mindful of saga and lay.   30
He wove his words in a winsome pattern,
Hymning the burden of Beowulf's feat,
Clothing the story in skillful verse.

[Forty-two lines, here omitted, are devoted to the bard's song.
He compliments Beowulf by praising an earlier slayer of monsters, Sigmund the Volsung,[46] and by citing the case of Heremod,
another hero, who unlike Beowulf failed to sustain his reputation.]

Time and again on their galloping steeds
Over yellow roads they measured the mile-paths;   35
Morning sun mounted the shining sky
And many a hero strode to the hall,
Stout of heart, to behold the wonder.
The worthy ruler, the warder of treasure,
Set out from the bowers with stately train;   40
The queen with her maidens paced over the mead-path.
    Then spoke Hrothgar; hasting to hall
He stood at the steps, stared up at the roof.
High and gold-gleaming; saw Grendel's hand:
"Thanks be to God for this glorious sight!   45
I have suffered much evil, much outrage from Grendel,
But the God of glory works wonder on wonder.
I had no hope of a haven from sorrow
While this best of houses stood badged with blood,
A woe far-reaching for all the wise   50
Who weened that they never could hold the hall
Against the assaults of devils and demons.
But now with God's help this hero has compassed
A deed our cunning could no way contrive.
Surely that woman may say with truth,   55
Who bore this son, if she still be living,
Our ancient God showed favor and grace
On her bringing-forth! O best of men,
I will keep you, Beowulf, close to my heart
In firm affection; as son to father   60
Hold fast henceforth to this foster-kinship.
You shall know not want of treasure or wealth
Or goodly gift that your wish may crave,
While I have power. For poorer deeds
I have granted guerdon, and graced with honor   65
Weaker warriors, feebler in fight.

---

[46] He appears in the Nibelungen cycle, whence Wagner adapts his
story in *Die Walküre*.

You have done such deeds that your fame shall flourish
Through all the ages! God grant you still
All goodly grace as He gave before."
    Beowulf spoke, the son of Ecgtheow: 70
"By the favor of God we won the fight,
Did the deed of valor, and boldly dared
The might of the monster. I would you could see
The fiend himself lying dead before you!
I thought to grip him in stubborn grasp   75
And bind him down on the bed of death,
There to lie straining in struggle for life,
While I gripped him fast lest he vanish away.
But I might not hold him or hinder his going,
For God did not grant it, my fingers failed.   80
Too savage the strain of his fiendish strength!
To save his life he left shoulder and claw,
The arm of the monster, to mark his track.
But he bought no comfort; no whit thereby
Shall the wretched ravager racked with sin,   85
The loathsome spoiler, prolong his life.
A deep wound holds him in deadly grip,
In baleful bondage; and black with crime
The demon shall wait for the day of doom
When the God of glory shall give decree."   90
    Then slower of speech was the son of Ecglaf,[47]
More wary of boasting of warlike deeds,
While the nobles gazed at the grisly claw,
The fiend's hand fastened by hero's might
On the lofty roof. Most like to steel   95
Were the hardened nails, the heathen's hand-spurs,
Horrible, monstrous; and many men said
No tempered sword, no excellent iron,
Could have harmed the monster or hacked away
The demon's battle-claw dripping with blood.   100

THE FEAST OF VICTORY

*How the Danes and Geats banqueted in Heorot; how Hrothgar
bestowed lordly gifts on Beowulf and his companions; and how
Queen Wealhtheow praised the hero and commended her sons to
his protection.*

In joyful haste was Heorot decked
And a willing host of women and men
Gaily dressed and adorned the guest-hall.
Splendid hangings with sheen of gold
Shone on the walls, a glorious sight   5
To eyes that delight to behold such wonders.
The shining building was wholly shattered
Though braced and fastened with iron bands;
Hinges were riven; the roof alone
Remained unharmed when the horrid monster,   10

---

[47] Unferth.

Foul with evil, slunk off in flight,
Hopeless of life. It is hard to flee
The touch of death, let him try who will;
Necessity urges the sons of men,
The dwellers on earth, to their destined place   15
Where the body, bound in its narrow bed,
After the feasting is fast in slumber.

    Soon was the time when the son of Healfdene
Went to the wine-hall; he fain would join
With happy heart in the joy of feasting.   20
I never have heard of a mightier muster
Of proud retainers around their prince.
All at ease they bent to the benches,
Had joy of the banquet; their kinsmen bold,
Hrothgar and Hrothulf,[48] happy of heart,   25
In the high-built hall drank many a mead-cup.
The hall of Hrothgar was filled with friends;
No treachery yet had troubled the Scyldings.[49]
Upon Beowulf, then, as a token of triumph,
Hrothgar bestowed a standard of gold,   30
A banner embroidered, a byrny and helm.
In sight of many, a costly sword
Before the hero was borne on high;
Beowulf drank of many a bowl.
No need for shame in the sight of heroes   35
For gifts so gracious! I never have heard
Of many men dealing in friendlier fashion,
To others on ale-bench, richer rewards,
Four such treasures fretted with gold!
On the crest of the helmet a crowning wreath,   40
Woven of wire-work, warded the head
Lest tempered swordblade, sharp from the file,
Deal deadly wound when the shielded warrior
Went forth to battle against the foe.
Eight horses also with plated headstalls   45
The lord of heroes bade lead into hall;
On one was a saddle skillfully fashioned
And set with jewels, the battle-seat
Of the king himself, when the son of Healfdene
Would fain take part in the play of swords;   50
Never in fray had his valor failed,
His kingly courage, when corpses were falling.
And the prince of the Ingwines[50] gave all these gifts
To the hand of Beowulf, horses and armor;
Bade him enjoy them! With generous heart   55
The noble leader, the lord of heroes,
Rewarded the struggle with steeds and with treasure,

So that none can belittle, and none can blame,
Who tells the tale as it truly happened.
    Then on the ale-bench to each of the earls   60
Who embarked with Beowulf, sailing the sea-paths,
The lord of princes dealt ancient heirlooms,
Gift of treasure, and guerdon of gold
To requite his slaughter whom Grendel slew,
As he would have slain others, but all-wise God   65
And the hero's courage had conquered Fate.
The Lord ruled over the lives of men
As He rules them still. Therefore understanding
And a prudent spirit are surely best!
He must suffer much of both weal and woe   70
Who dwells here long in these days of strife.
    Then song and revelry rose in the hall;
Before Healfdene's leader the harp was struck
And hall-joy wakened; the song was sung,
Hrothgar's gleeman rehearsed the lay   75
Of the sons of Finn when the terror befell them.

*[In ninety-two lines, here omitted, the bard sings of warfare
between the Danes and the Frisians.]*

So the song was sung, the lay recited,
The sound of revelry rose in the hall.
Stewards poured wine from wondrous vessels;
And Wealhtheow, wearing a golden crown,   80
Came forth in state where the two were sitting,
Courteous comrades, uncle and nephew,[51]
Each true to the other in ties of peace.
Unferth, the orator, sat at the feet
Of the lord of the Scyldings; and both showed trust   85
In his noble mind,[52] though he had no mercy
On kinsmen in swordplay; the Scylding queen spoke:
"My sovereign lord, dispenser of treasure,
Drink now of this flagon, have joy of the feast!
Speak to the Geats, O gold-friend of men,   90
In winning words as is well-befitting;
Be kind to the Geat-men and mindful of gifts
From the gold you have garnered from near and far.
You have taken as son, so many have told me,
This hardy hero. Heorot is cleansed,   95
The gleaming gift-hall. Rejoice while you may
In lavish bounty, and leave to your kin
People and kingdom when time shall come,
Your destined hour, to look on death.
I know the heart of my gracious Hrothulf,   100
That he'll safely shelter and shield our sons
When you leave this world, if he still is living.
I know he will favor with gracious gifts
These boys of ours, if he bears in mind

---

[48] Hrothgar's nephew, son of his younger brother Halga. After his
uncle's death Hrothulf killed his cousin Hrethric, Hrothgar's
heir, and seized the throne.

[49] The poet never forgets that the world is subject to change, and
life to death.

[50] Danes ("friends of Ing"—they worshiped this legendary ancestor
of many tribes).

[51] Hrothgar and Hrothulf.

[52] I.e., both Hrothgar and Hrothulf trusted Unferth.

The many honors and marks of love   105
We bestowed upon him while he still was a boy."[53]
  She turned to the bench where her boys were sitting,
Hrethric and Hrothmund, the sons of heroes,
The youth together; there the good man sat,
Beowulf of the Geats, beside the two brothers.   110
Then the cup was offered with gracious greeting,
And seemly presents of spiraled gold,
A corselet, and rings, and the goodliest collar
Of all that ever were known on earth.

[*At this point the poet digresses for eighteen lines,* here *omitted,
in order to compare the gift with the legendary necklace of Freya,
goddess of love and beauty, and to tell what eventually became
of it.*]

  The sound of revelry rose in the hall;   115
Wealhtheow spoke to the warrior host:
"Take, dear Beowulf, collar and corselet,
Wear these treasures with right good will!
Thrive and prosper and prove your might!
Befriend my boys with your kindly counsel;   120
I will remember and I will repay.
You have earned the undying honor of heroes
In regions reaching as far and wide
As the windy walls that the sea encircles.
May Fate show favor while life shall last!   125
I wish you wealth to your heart's content;
In your days of glory be good to my sons!
Here each hero is true to other,
Gentle of spirit, loyal to lord,
Friendly thanes and a folk united,   130
Wine-cheered warriors who do my will."
  Then she went to her seat. At the fairest of feasts
Men drank of the wine-cup, knowing not Fate,
Nor the fearful doom that befell the earls
When darkness gathered, and gracious Hrothgar   135
Sought his dwelling and sank to rest.

THE TROLL-WIFE'S VENGEANCE

*How Grendel's dam attacked Heorot and slew Æschere; how
Hrothgar lamented the loss of that good thane; and how he besought Beowulf to dare the dreadful pool where she harbored.*

A host of heroes guarded the hall
As they oft had done in the days of old.
They stripped the benches and spread the floor
With beds and bolsters. But one of the beer-thanes
Bowed to his hall-rest doomed to death.   5

---

[53] Wealhtheow fears Hrothulf as a potential candidate for the throne
after her husband's death. She urges Hrothgar to be generous,
partly because Beowulf merits reward, partly because she wishes
to cement his loyalty.

They set at their heads their shining shields,
Their battle-bucklers; and there on the bench
Above each hero his towering helmet,
His spear and corselet hung close at hand.
It was ever their wont to be ready for war   10
At home or in field, as it ever befell
That their lord had need. 'Twas a noble race!
  Then they sank to slumber. But one paid dear
For his evening rest, as had often happened
When Grendel haunted the lordly hall   15
And wrought such ruin, till his end was come,
Death for his sins; it was easily seen,
Though the monster was slain, an avenger survived
Prolonging the feud, though the fiend had perished.
The mother of Grendel, a monstrous hag,   20
Brooded over her misery, doomed to dwell
In evil waters and icy streams
From ancient ages when Cain had killed
His only brother, his father's son.
Banished and branded with marks of murder   25
Cain fled far from the joys of men,
Haunting the barrens, begetting a brood
Of grisly monsters; and Grendel was one,
The fiendish ogre who found in the hall
A hero on watch, and awaiting the fray.   30
The monster grappled; the Geat took thought
Of the strength of his might, that marvelous gift
Which the Lord had given; in God he trusted
For help and succor and strong support,
Whereby he humbled the fiend from hell,   35
Destroyed the demon; and Grendel fled,
Harrowed in heart and hateful to man,
Deprived of joy, to the place of death.
But rabid and raging his mother resolved
On a dreadful revenge for the death of her son!   40
  She stole to the hall where the Danes were sleeping,
And horror fell on the host of earls
When the dam of Grendel burst in the door.
But the terror was less as the war-craft is weaker,
A woman's strength, than the might of a man   45
When the hilted sword, well shaped by the hammer,
The blood-stained iron of tempered edge,
Hews the boar from the foeman's helmet.
Then in the hall was the hard-edged blade,
The stout steel, brandished above the benches;   50
Seizing their shields men stayed not for helmet
Or ample byrny, when fear befell.
As soon as discovered, the hag was in haste
To fly to the open, to flee for her life.
One of the warriors she swiftly seized,   55
Clutched him fast and made off to the fens.
He was of heroes the dearest to Hrothgar,
The best of comrades between two seas;

The warrior brave, the stout-hearted spearman,
She slew in his sleep. Nor was Beowulf there;   60
But after the banquet another abode
Had been assigned to the glorious Geat.
There was tumult in Heorot. She tore from its place
The blood-stained claw. Care was renewed!
It was no good bargain when both in turn _Litotes_   65
Must pay the price with the lives of friends!

    Then the white-haired warrior, the aged king,
Was numb with sorrow, knowing his thane
No longer was living, his dearest man dead.
Beowulf, the brave, was speedily summoned,   70
Brought to the bower; the noble prince
Came with his comrades at dawn of day
Where the wise king awaited if God would award
Some happier turn in these tidings of woe.
The hero came tramping into the hall   75
With his chosen band—the boards resounded—
Greeted the leader, the Ingwine lord,
And asked if the night had been peaceful and pleasant.

    Hrothgar spoke, the lord of the Scyldings:
"Ask not of pleasure; pain is renewed   80
For the Danish people. Æschere is dead!
Dead is Yrmenlaf's elder brother!
He was my comrade, closest of counsellors,
My shoulder-companion as side by side
We fought for our lives in the welter of war,   85
In the shock of battle when boar-helms crashed.
As an earl should be, a prince without peer,
Such was Æschere, slain in the hall
By the wandering demon! I know not whither
She fled to shelter, proud of her spoil,   90
Gorged to the full. She avenged the feud
Wherein yesternight you grappled with Grendel
And savagely slew him because so long
He had hunted and harried the men of my folk.
He fell in the battle and paid with his life.   95
But now another fierce ravager rises
Avenging her kinsman, and carries it far,
As it seems to many a saddened thane
Who grieves in his heart for his treasure-giver.
This woe weighs heavy! The hand lies still   100
That once was lavish of all delights.

    "Oft in the hall I have heard my people,
Comrades and counsellors, telling a tale
Of evil spirits their eyes have sighted,
Two mighty marauders who haunt the moors.   105
One shape, as clearly as men could see,
Seemed woman's likeness, and one seemed man,
An outcast wretch of another world,
And huger far than a human form.
Grendel my countrymen called him, not knowing   110
What monster-brood spawned him, what sire begot.

Wild and lonely the land they live in,
Wind-swept ridges and wolf-retreats,
Dread tracts of fen where the falling torrent
Downward dips into gloom and shadow   115
Under the dusk of the darkening cliff.
Not far in miles lies the lonely mere
Where trees firm-rooted and hung with frost
Overshroud the wave with shadowing gloom.
And there a portent appears each night,   120
A flame in the water; no man so wise
Who knows the bound of its bottomless depth.
The heather-stepper, the horned stag,
The antlered hart hard driven by hounds,
Invading that forest in flight from afar   125
Will turn at bay and die on the brink
Ere ever he'll plunge in that haunted pool.
'Tis an eerie spot! Its tossing spray
Mounts dark to heaven when high winds stir
The driving storm, and the sky is murky,   130
And with foul weather the heavens weep.
On your arm only rests all our hope!
Not yet have you tempted those terrible reaches,
The region that shelters that sinful wight.
Go if you dare! I will give requital   135
With ancient treasure and twisted gold,
As I formerly gave in guerdon of battle,
If out of that combat you come alive."

THE POOL

*How Beowulf pledged his life, and they rode to the dreadful
mere; how the hero shot a strange water-beast there; and how he
armed himself for battle.*

Beowulf spoke, the son of Ecgtheow:
"Sorrow not, brave one! Better for man
To avenge a friend than much to mourn.
All men must die; let him who may
Win glory ere death. That guerdon is best   5
For a noble man when his name survives him.
Then let us rise up, O ward of the realm,
And haste us forth to behold the track
Of Grendel's dam. And I give you pledge
She shall not in safety escape to cover,   10
To earthy cavern, or forest fastness,
Or gulf of ocean, go where she may.
This day with patience endure the burden
Of every woe, as I know you will."
Up sprang the ancient, gave thanks to God   15
For the heartening words the hero had spoken.

    Quickly a horse was bridled for Hrothgar,
A mettlesome charger with braided mane;
In royal splendor the king rode forth
Mid the trampling tread of a troop of shieldmen.   20

The tracks lay clear where the fiend had fared
Over plain and bottom and woodland path,
Through murky moorland making her way
With the lifeless body, the best of thanes
Who of old with Hrothgar had guarded the hall.   25
By a narrow path the king pressed on
Through rocky upland and rugged ravine,
A lonely journey, past looming headlands,
The lair of monster and lurking troll.
Tried retainers, a trusty few,   30
Advanced with Hrothgar to view the ground.
Sudden they came on a dismal covert
Of trees that hung over hoary stone,
Over churning water and blood-stained wave.
Then for the Danes was the woe the deeper,   35
The sorrow sharper for Scylding earls,
When they first caught sight, on the rocky sea-cliff,
Of slaughtered Æschere's severed head.
The water boiled in a bloody swirling
With seething gore as the spearmen gazed.   40
The trumpet sounded a martial strain;
The shield-troop halted. Their eyes beheld
The swimming forms of strange sea-dragons,
Dim serpent shapes in the watery depths,
Sea-beasts sunning on headland slopes;   45
Snakelike monsters that oft at sunrise
On evil errands scour the sea.
Startled by tumult and trumpet's blare,
Enraged and savage, they swam away;   50
But one the lord of the Geats brought low,
Stripped of his sea-strength, despoiled of life,
As the bitter bow-bolt pierced his heart.
His watery-speed grew slower, and ceased,
And he floated, caught in the clutch of death.   55
Then they hauled him in with sharp-hooked boar-spears,
By sheer strength grappled and dragged him ashore,
A wondrous wave-beast; and all the array
Gathered to gaze at the grisly guest.

    Beowulf donned his armor for battle,   60
Heeded not danger; the hand-braided byrny,[54]
Broad of shoulder and richly bedecked,
Must stand the ordeal of the watery depths.
Well could that corselet defend the frame
Lest hostile thrust should pierce to the heart   65
Or blows of battle beat down the life.
A gleaming helmet guarded his head
As he planned his plunge to the depths of the pool
Through the heaving waters—a helm adorned
With lavish inlay and lordly chains,   70
Ancient work of the weapon-smith
Skillfully fashioned, beset with the boar,[55]

---

[54] The coat of chain mail, made of hand-wrought interlinking rings.
[55] Engraved or embossed with the figure of a boar.

That no blade of battle might bite it through.
Not the least or the worst of his war-equipment
Was the sword the herald[56] of Hrothgar loaned   75
In his hour of need—Hrunting its name—
An ancient heirloom, trusty and tried;
Its blade was iron, with etched design,
Tempered in blood of many a battle.
Never in fight had it failed the hand   80
That drew it daring the perils of war,
The rush of the foe. Not the first time then
That its edge must venture on valiant deeds.
But Ecglaf's stalwart son[57] was unmindful
Of words he had spoken while heated with wine,   85
When he loaned the blade to a better swordsman.
He himself dared not hazard his life
In deeds of note in the watery depths;
And thereby he forfeited honor and fame.
Not so with that other undaunted spirit   90
After he donned his armor for battle.
Beowulf spoke, the son of Ecgtheow:
"O gracious ruler, gold-giver to men,
As I now set forth to attempt this feat,
Great son of Healfdene, hold well in mind   95
The solemn pledge we plighted of old,
That if doing your service I meet my death
You will mark my fall with a father's love.
Protect my kinsmen, my trusty comrades,
If battle take me. And all the treasure   100
You have heaped on me bestow upon Hygelac,
Hrothgar beloved! The lord of the Geats,
The son of Hrethel, shall see the proof,
Shall know as he gazes on jewels and gold,
That I found an unsparing dispenser of bounty,   105
And joyed, while I lived, in his generous gifts.
Give back to Unferth the ancient blade,
The sword-edge splendid with curving scrolls,
For either with Hrunting I'll reap rich harvest
Of glorious deeds, or death shall take me."   110

THE FIGHT WITH THE TROLL-WIFE

How Beowulf did battle in the hall under the pool; how his sword failed him and he fought on, relying on himself alone, "as a man must do"; and how the waiting Danes gave him up for lost and returned to Heorot, but the Geats stayed at the pool, staring hopelessly at the swirl of foam and blood.

After these words the prince of the Weders
Awaited no answer, but turned to the task,
Straightway plunged in the swirling pool.
Nigh unto a day he endured the depths
Ere he first had view of the vast sea-bottom.   5

---

[56] Unferth, the *thyle* or spokesman.   [57] Unferth.

Soon she found, who had haunted the flood,
A ravening hag, for a hundred half-years,
Greedy and grim, that a man was groping
In daring search through the sea-troll's home.
Swift she grappled and grasped the warrior   10
With horrid grip, but could work no harm,
No hurt to his body; the ring-locked byrny
Cloaked his life from her clutching claw;
Nor could she tear through the tempered mail
With her savage fingers. The she-wolf bore   15
The ring-prince down through the watery depths
To her den at the bottom; nor could Beowulf draw
His blade for battle, though brave his mood.
Many a sea-beast, strange sea-monsters,
Tasked him hard with their menacing tusks,   20
Broke his byrny and smote him sore.

    Then he found himself in a fearsome hall
Where water came not to work him hurt,
But the flood was stayed by the sheltering roof.[58]
There in the glow of firelight gleaming   25
The hero had view of the huge sea-troll.
He swung his war-sword with all his strength,
Withheld not the blow, and the savage blade
Sang on her head its hymn of hate.
But the bold one found that the battle-flasher   30
Would bite no longer, nor harm her life.
The sword-edge failed at his sorest need.
Often of old with ease it had suffered
The clash of battle, cleaving the helm,
The fated warrior's woven mail.   35
That time was first for the treasured blade
That its glory failed in the press of the fray.
But fixed of purpose and firm of mood
Hygelac's earl was mindful of honor;
In wrath, undaunted, he dashed to earth   40
The jewelled sword with its scrolled design,
The blade of steel; staked all on strength,
On the might of his hand, as a man must do
Who thinks to win in the welter of battle
Enduring glory; he fears not death.   45
The Geat-prince joyed in the straining struggle,
Stalwart-hearted and stirred to wrath,
Gripped the shoulder of Grendel's dam
And headlong hurled the hag to the ground.
But she quickly clutched him and drew him close,   50
Countered the onset with savage claw.
The warrior staggered, for all his strength,
Dismayed and shaken and borne to earth.
She knelt upon him and drew her dagger,

With broad bright blade, to avenge her son,   55
Her only issue. But the corselet's steel
Shielded his breast and sheltered his life
Withstanding entrance of point and edge.

    Then the prince of the Geats would have gone his
    journey,
The son of Ecgtheow, under the ground;   60
But his sturdy breast-net, his battle-corselet,
Gave him succor, and holy God,
The Lord all-wise, awarded the mastery;
Heaven's Ruler gave right decree.

    Swift the hero sprang to his feet;   65
Saw mid the war-gear a stately sword,
An ancient war-brand of biting edge,
Choicest of weapons worthy and strong,
The work of giants, a warrior's joy,
So heavy no hand but his own could hold it,   70
Bear to battle or wield in war.
Then the Scylding warrior, savage and grim,
Seized the ring-hilt and swung the sword,
Struck with fury, despairing of life,
Thrust at the throat, broke through the bone-rings; 75
The stout blade stabbed through her fated flesh.
She sank in death; the sword was bloody;
The hero joyed in the work of his hand.
The gleaming radiance shimmered and shone
As the candle of heaven shines clear from the sky.   80
Wrathful and resolute Hygelac's thane
Surveyed the span of the spacious hall;
Grimly gripping the hilted sword,
With upraised weapon he turned to the wall.
The blade had failed not the battle-prince;   85
A full requital he firmly planned
For all the injury Grendel had done
In numberless raids on the Danish race,
When he slew the hearth-companions of Hrothgar,
Devoured fifteen of the Danish folk   90
Clasped in slumber, and carried away
As many more spearmen, a hideous spoil.
All this the stout-heart had stern requited;
And there before him bereft of life
He saw the broken body of Grendel   95
Stilled in battle, and stretched in death,
As the struggle in Heorot smote him down.
The corpse sprang wide as he struck the blow,
The hard sword-stroke that severed the head.[59]

    Then the tried retainers, who there with Hrothgar 100
Watched the face of the foaming pool,
Saw that the churning reaches were reddened,
The eddying surges stained with blood.
And the gray, old spearmen spoke of the hero,

---

[58] In later versions of the saga the trolls live behind a waterfall, but
here the hall is a subterranean one and the water is kept out of it
by magic.

[59] Beowulf wants the head for a trophy; his action will also prevent
Grendel's ghost from haunting Heorot.

Having no hope he would ever return 105
Crowned with triumph and cheered with spoil.
Many were sure that the savage sea-wolf
Had slain their leader. At last came noon.
The stalwart Scyldings forsook the headland;
Their proud gold-giver departed home. 110
But the Geats sat grieving and sick in spirit,
Stared at the water with longing eyes,
Having no hope they would ever behold
Their gracious leader and lord again.

  Then the great sword, eaten with blood of battle, 115
Began to soften and waste away
In iron icicles, wonder of wonders,
Melting away most like to ice
When the Father looses the fetters of frost,
Slackens the bondage that binds the wave, 120
Strong in power of times and seasons;
He is true God! Of the goodly treasures
From the sea-cave Beowulf took but two,
The monster's head and the precious hilt
Blazing with gems; but the blade had melted, 125
The sword dissolved, in the deadly heat,
The venomous blood of the fallen fiend.

THE RETURN TO HEOROT

*How Beowulf came safe to shore, and the band marched back to
the hall; how the hero made his report to Hrothgar; how the old
King replied with praise and wise reflections on life's mystery;
and how, after feasting, they slept in peace at Heorot.*

Then he who had compassed the fall of his foes
Came swimming up through the swirling surge.
Cleansed were the currents, the boundless abyss,
Where the evil monster had died the death
And looked her last on this fleeting world. 5
With sturdy strokes the lord of the seamen
To land came swimming, rejoiced in his spoil,
Had joy of the burden he brought from the depths.
And his mighty thanes came forward to meet him,
Gave thanks to God they were granted to see 10
Their well-loved leader both sound and safe.
From the stalwart hero his helmet and byrny
Were quickly loosened; the lake lay still,
Its motionless reaches reddened with blood.
Fain[60] of heart men fared o'er the footpaths, 15
Measured the ways and the well-known roads.
From the sea-cliff's brim the warriors bore
The head of Grendel, with heavy toil;
Four of the stoutest, with all their strength,
Could hardly carry on swaying spear 20
Grendel's head to the gold-decked hall.

---

[60] Glad.

Swift they strode, the daring and dauntless,
Fourteen Geats, to the Hall of the Hart;
And proud in the midst of his marching men
Their leader measured the path to the mead-hall. 25
The hero entered, the hardy in battle,
The great in glory, to greet the king;
And Grendel's head by the hair was carried
Across the floor where the feasters drank—
A terrible sight for lord and for lady— 30
A gruesome vision whereon men gazed!

  Beowulf spoke, the son of Ecgtheow:
"O son of Healfdene, lord of the Scyldings!
This sea-spoil wondrous, whereon you stare,
We joyously bring you in token of triumph! 35
Barely with life surviving the battle,
The war under water, I wrought the deed
Weary and spent; and death had been swift
Had God not granted His sheltering strength.
My strong-edged Hrunting, stoutest of blades, 40
Availed me nothing. But God revealed—
Often His arm has aided the friendless—
The fairest of weapons hanging on wall,
An ancient broadsword; I seized the blade,
Slew in the struggle, as fortune availed, 45
The cavern-warders. But the war-brand old,
The battle-blade with its scrolled design,
Dissolved in the gush of the venomous gore;
The hilt alone I brought from the battle.
The record of ruin, and slaughter of Danes, 50
These wrongs I avenged, as was fitting and right.
Now I can promise you, prince of the Scyldings,
Henceforth in Heorot rest without rue
For you and your nobles; nor need you dread
Slaughter of follower, stalwart or stripling, 55
Or death of earl, as of old you did."
Into the hand of the aged leader,
The gray-haired hero, he gave the hilt,
The work of giants, the wonder of gold.
At the death of the demons the Danish lord 60
Took in his keeping the cunning craft,
The wondrous marvel, of mighty smiths;
When the world was freed of the ravaging fiend,
The foe of God, and his fearful dam
Marked with murder and badged with blood, 65
The bound hilt passed to the best of kings
Who ever held sceptre beside two seas,
And dealt out treasure in Danish land!

  Hrothgar spoke, beholding the hilt,
The ancient relic whereon was etched 70
An olden record of struggle and strife,
The flood that ravaged the giant race,
The rushing deluge of ruin and death.
That evil kindred were alien to God,

But the Ruler avenged with the wrath of the deep!   75
On the hilt-guards, likewise, of gleaming gold
Was rightly carven in cunning runes,
Set forth and blazoned, for whom that blade,
With spiral tooling and twisted hilt,
That fairest of swords, was fashioned and smithied.   80
Then out spoke Hrothgar, Healfdene's son,
And all the retainers were silent and still:
"Well may he say, whose judgment is just,
Recalling to memory men of the past,
That this earl was born of a better stock!   85
Your fame, friend Beowulf, is blazoned abroad
Over all wide ways, and to every people.
In manful fashion have you showed your strength,
Your might and wisdom. My word I will keep,
The plighted friendship we formerly pledged.   90
Long shall you stand as a stay to your people,
A help to heroes, as Heremod[61] was not
To the Honor-Scyldings, to Ecgwela's[62] sons!
Not joy to kindred, but carnage and death,
He wrought as he ruled o'er the race of the Danes.   95
In savage anger he slew his comrades,
His table-companions, till, lawless and lone,
An odious outcast, he fled from men.
Though God had graced him with gifts of strength,
Over all men exalting him, still in his breast   100
A bloodthirsty spirit was rooted and strong.
He dealt not rings to the Danes for glory;
His lot was eternal torment of woe,
And lasting affliction. Learn from his fate!
Strive for virtue! I speak for your good;   105
In the wisdom of age I have told the tale.
"'Tis a wondrous marvel how mighty God
In gracious spirit bestows on men
The gift of wisdom, and goodly lands,
And princely power! He rules over all!   110
He suffers a man of lordly line
To set his heart on his own desires,
Awards him fullness of worldly joy,
A fair home-land, and the sway of cities,
The wide dominion of many a realm,   115
An ample kingdom, till, cursed with folly,
The thoughts of his heart take no heed of his end.
He lives in luxury, knowing not want,
Knowing no shadow of sickness or age;
No haunting sorrow darkens his spirit,   120
No hatred or discord deepens to war;
The world is sweet, to his every desire,
And evil assails not—until in his heart
Pride overpowering gathers and grows!

---

[61] Already cited (p. 20, above) in contrast with the virtuous Beowulf.
[62] Apparently an earlier Danish king.

The warder slumbers, the guard of his spirit;   125
Too sound is that sleep, too sluggish the weight
Of worldly affairs, too pressing the Foe,
The Archer who looses the arrows of sin.
"Then is his heart pierced, under his helm,
His soul in his bosom, with bitter dart.   130
He has no defense for the fierce assaults
Of the loathsome Fiend. What he long has cherished
Seems all too little! In anger and greed
He gives no guerdon of plated rings.
Since God has granted him glory and wealth   135
He forgets the future, unmindful of Fate.
But it comes to pass in the day appointed
His feeble body withers and fails;
Death descends, and another seizes
His hoarded riches and rashly spends   140
The princely treasure, imprudent of heart.
Beloved Beowulf, best of warriors,
Avoid such evil and seek the good,
The heavenly wisdom. Beware of pride!
Now for a time you shall feel the fullness   145
And know the glory of strength, but soon
Sickness or sword shall strip you of might,
Or clutch of fire, or clasp of flood,
Or flight of arrow, or bite of blade,
Or relentless age; or the light of the eye   150
Shall darken and dim, and death on a sudden,
O lordly ruler, shall lay you low.
"A hundred half-years I've been head of the Ring-
   Danes,
Defending the folk against many a tribe
With spear-point and sword in the surges of battle   155
Till not one was hostile 'neath heaven's expanse.
But a loathsome change swept over the land,
Grief after gladness, when Grendel came,
That evil invader, that ancient foe!
Great sorrow of soul from his malice I suffered;   160
But thanks be to God, who has spared me to see
His bloody head at the battle's end!
Join now in the banquet; have joy of the feast,
O mighty in battle! And the morrow shall bring
Exchange of treasure in ample store."   165
Happy of heart the Geat leader hastened,
Took seat at the board as the good king bade.
Once more, as of old, brave heroes made merry
And tumult of revelry rose in the hall.
Then dark over men the night shadows deepened;   170
The host all arose, for Hrothgar was minded,
The gray, old Scylding, to go to his rest.
On Beowulf too, after labor of battle,
Came limitless longing and craving for sleep.
A hall-thane graciously guided the hero,   175
Weary and worn, to the place prepared,

Serving his wishes and every want
As befitted a mariner come from afar.
The stout-hearted warrior sank to his rest;
The lofty building, splendid and spacious,   180
Towered above him. His sleep was sound
Till the black-coated raven, blithesome of spirit,
Hailed the coming of Heaven's bliss.

THE PARTING

How Beowulf spoke his farewell; and how Hrothgar answered, weeping, for he loved him, and gave him twelve gifts.

Then over the shadows uprose the sun.
The Geats were in haste, and eager of heart
To depart to their people. Beowulf longed
To embark in his boat, to set sail for his home.
The hero tendered the good sword Hrunting   5
To the son of Ecglaf,[63] bidding him bear
The lovely blade; gave thanks for the loan,
Called it a faithful friend in the fray,
Bitter in battle. The greathearted hero
Spoke no word in blame of the blade!   10
Arrayed in war-gear, and ready for sea,
The warriors bestirred them; and, dear to the Danes,
Beowulf sought the high seat of the king.
The gallant in war gave greeting to Hrothgar;
Beowulf spoke, the son of Ecgtheow: 15
"It is time at last to tell of our longing!
Our homes are far, and our hearts are fain
To seek again Hygelac over the sea.
You have welcomed us royally, harbored us well
As a man could wish; if I ever can win   20
Your affection more fully, O leader of heroes,
Swift shall you find me to serve you again!
If ever I learn, o'er the levels of ocean,
That neighboring nations beset you sore,
As in former days when foemen oppressed,   25
With thanes by the thousand I will hasten to help.
For I know that Hygelac, lord of the Geats,
Prince of the people, though young in years,
Will favor and further by word and deed
That my arm may aid you, and do you honor,   30
With stout ash-spear and succor of strength
In the press of need. And if princely Hrethric[64]
Shall purpose to come to the court of the Geats,
He will find there a legion of loyal friends.
That man fares best to a foreign country   35
Who himself is stalwart and stout of heart."
    Hrothgar addressed him, uttered his answer:
"Truly, these words has the Lord of wisdom

Set in your heart, for I never have harkened
To speech so sage from a man so young.   40
You have strength, and prudence, and wisdom of word!
I count it true if it come to pass
That point of spear in the press of battle,
Or deadly sickness, or stroke of sword,
Shall slay your leader, the son of Hrethel,   45
The prince of your people, and you still live,
The Sea-Geats could have no happier choice
If you would be willing to rule the realm,
As king to hold guard o'er the hoard and the heroes.[65]
The longer I know you, the better I like you,   50
Beloved Beowulf! You have brought it to pass
That between our peoples a lasting peace
Shall bind the Geats to the Danish-born;
And strife shall vanish, and war shall cease,
And former feuds, while I rule this realm.   55
And many a man, in the sharing of treasure,
Shall greet another with goodly gifts
O'er the gannet's bath.[66] And the ring-stemmed ship
Shall bear over ocean bountiful riches
In pledge of friendship. Our peoples, I know,   60
Shall be firm united toward foe and friend,
Faultless in all things, in fashion of old."
    Then the son of Healfdene, shelter of earls,
Bestowed twelve gifts on the hero in hall,
Bade him in safety with bounty of treasure   65
Seek his dear people, and soon return.
The peerless leader, the Scylding lord,
Kissed the good thane and clasped to his bosom,
While tears welled fast from the old man's eyes.
Both chances he weighed in his wise, old heart,   70
But greatly doubted if ever again
They should meet at council or drinking of mead.
Nor could Hrothgar master—so dear was the man—
His swelling sorrow; a yearning love
For the dauntless hero, deep in his heart,   75
Burned through his blood. Beowulf, the brave,
Prizing his treasure and proud of the gold,
Turned away, treading the grassy plain.
The ring-stemmed sea-goer, riding at anchor,
Awaited her lord. There was loud acclaim   80
Of Hrothgar's gifts, as they went their way.
He was a king without failing or fault,
Till old age, master of all mankind,
Stripped him of power and pride of strength.

THE HOMECOMING OF BEOWULF

How the band took ship for Geatland; how King Hygelac and Queen Hygd welcomed and honored them, and heard the tale of

---

[63] Unferth.   [64] Hrothgar's elder son.

[65] Thrones were elective in Scandinavia, as in Shakespeare's *Hamlet*.
[66] Another kenning for *sea*.

*the hero's adventures; how he brought them noble presents; and
how Hygelac, in his turn, gave Beowulf land and hall.*

Then down to the sea came the band of the brave,
The host of young heroes in harness of war,
In their woven mail; and the coast-warden viewed
The heroes' return, as he heeded their coming!
No uncivil greeting he gave from the sea-cliff   5
As they strode to ship in their glistening steel;
But rode toward them and called their return
A welcome sight for their Weder kin.
There on the sand the ring-stemmed ship,
The broad-bosomed bark, was loaded with war-gear,   10
With horses and treasure; the mast towered high
Over the riches of Hrothgar's hoard.
A battle-sword Beowulf gave to the boatwarden
Hilted with gold; and thereafter in hall
He had the more honor because of the heirloom,   15
The shining treasure. The ship was launched.
Cleaving the combers of open sea
They dropped the shoreline of Denmark astern.
A stretching sea-cloth, a bellying sail,
Was bent on the mast; there was groaning of timbers;   20
A gale was blowing; the boat drove on.
The foamy-necked plunger plowed through the billows,
The ring-stemmed ship through the breaking seas,
Till at last they sighted the sea-cliffs of Geatland,
The well-known headlands; and, whipped by the wind,   25
The boat drove shoreward and beached on the sand.

    Straightway the harbor-watch strode to the seashore;
Long had he watched for the well-loved men,
Scanning the ocean with eager eyes!
The broad-bosomed boat he bound to the shingle   30
With anchor ropes, lest the rip of the tide
Should wrench from its mooring the comely craft.

    From the good ship Beowulf bade them bear
The precious jewels and plated gold,
The princely treasure. Not long was the path   35
That led to where Hygelac, son of Hrethel,
The giver of treasure, abode in his home
Hard by the sea-wall, hedged by his thanes.
Spacious the castle, splendid the king
On his high hall-seat; youthful was Hygd,   40
Wise and well-born—though winters but few
Hæreth's daughter had dwelt at court.
She was noble of spirit, not sparing in gifts
Of princely treasure to the people of the Geats.

*[The poet now digresses for thirty-two lines, omitted here, to
praise Hygd by telling the story of a queen of a different stamp,
the proud and wicked Thryth, notorious (before her marriage and
reform) for slaying her suitors.]*

Then the hero strode with his stalwart band   45
Across the stretches of sandy beach,
The wide sea-shingle. The world-candle shone,
The hot sun hasting on high from the south.
Marching together they made their way
To where in his stronghold the stout young king,   50
Ongentheow's[67] slayer, protector of earls,
Dispensed his treasure. Soon Hygelac heard
Of the landing of Beowulf, bulwark of men,
That his shoulder-companion had come to his court
Sound and safe from the strife of battle.   55

    The hall was prepared, as the prince gave bidding,
Places made ready for much travelled men.
And he who came safe from the surges of battle
Sat by the side of the king himself,
Kinsman by kinsman; in courtly speech   60
His liege lord greeted the loyal thane
With hearty welcome. And Hæreth's daughter[68]
Passed through the hall-building pouring the mead,
With courtesy greeting the gathered host,
Bearing the cup to the hands of the heroes.   65
In friendly fashion in high-built hall
Hygelac questioned his comrade and thane;
For an eager longing burned in his breast
To hear from the Sea-Geats the tale of their travels.
"How did you fare in your far sea-roving,   70
Beloved Beowulf, in your swift resolve
To sail to the conflict, the combat in Heorot,
Across the salt waves? Did you soften at all
The sorrows of Hrothgar, the weight of his woe?
Deeply I brooded with burden of care   75
For I had no faith in this far sea-venture
For one so beloved. Long I implored
That you go not against the murderous monster,
But let the South Danes settle the feud
Themselves with Grendel. To God be thanks   80
That my eyes behold you unharmed and unhurt."
    Beowulf spoke, the son of Ecgtheow:
"My dear lord Hygelac, many have heard
Of that famous grapple 'twixt Grendel and me,
The bitter struggle and strife in the hall   85
Where he formerly wrought such ruin and wrong,
Such lasting sorrow for Scylding men!
All that I avenged! Not any on earth
Who longest lives of that loathsome brood,
No kin of Grendel cloaked in his crime,   90
Has cause to boast of that battle by night!
First, in that country, I fared to the hall
With greeting for Hrothgar; Healfdene's kinsman
Learned all my purpose, assigned me a place

---

[67] A Swedish king. He fell in action against an army led by Hygelac,
    though not by Hygelac's hand.   [68] Queen Hygd.

Beside his own son. 'Twas a happy host!   95
I never have seen under span of heaven
More mirth of heroes sitting at mead!
The peerless queen, the peace-pledge of peoples,
Passed on her round through the princely hall;
There was spurring of revels, dispensing of rings,   100
Ere the noble woman went to her seat.

"At times in the host the daughter of Hrothgar
Offered the beaker to earls in turn;
Freawaru men called her, the feasters in hall,
As she held out to heroes the well-wrought cup.   105

[*In forty-six lines, here omitted, the hero predicts that Freawaru's
approaching marriage to Ingeld, a prince of a Germanic tribe
called the Heathobards, will not end the feud between them and
the Danes.*]

"I must now speak on, dispenser of treasure,
Further of Grendel, till fully you know
How we fared in that fierce and furious fight!
When the jewel of heaven[69] had journeyed o'er earth,
The wrathful demon, the deadly foe,   110
Stole through the darkness spying us out
Where still unharmed we guarded the gold-hall.
But doom in battle and bitter death
Were Hondscio's fate! He was first to perish
Though girded with weapon and famous in war,   115
Grendel murdered him, mangled his body,
Bolted the dear man's bloody corpse.
No sooner for that would the slaughterous spirit,
Bloody of tooth and brooding on evil,
Turn empty-handed away from the hall!   120
The mighty monster made trial of my strength
Clutching me close with his ready claw.
Wide and wondrous his huge pouch hung
Cunningly fastened, and fashioned with skill
From skin of dragon by devil's craft.   125
Therein the monster was minded to thrust me
Sinless and blameless, and many beside.
But it might not be, when I rose in wrath,
And fronted the hell-fiend face to face.
Too long is the tale how I took requital   130
On the cursed foe for his every crime,
But the deeds I did were a lasting honor,
Beloved prince, to your people's name.
He fled away, and a fleeting while
Possessed his life and the world's delights;   135
But he left in Heorot his severed hand,
A bloody reminder to mark his track.
Humbled in spirit and wretched in heart
Down he sank to the depths of the pool.
"When the morrow fell, and we feasted together,   140
The Scylding ruler rewarded me well
For the bloody strife, in guerdon bestowing

Goodly treasure of beaten gold.
There was song and revel. The aged Scylding
From well-stored mind spoke much of the past.   145
A warrior sang to the strains of the glee-wood,[70]
Sometimes melodies mirthful and joyous,
Sometimes lays that were tragic and true.
And the great-hearted ruler at times would tell
A tale of wonder in fitting words.   150
Heavy with years the white-haired warrior
Grieved for his youth and the strength that was gone;
And his heart was moved by the weight of his winters
And many a memory out of the past.
All the long day we made merry together   155
Till another night came to the children of men,
And quickly the mother of Grendel was minded
To wreak her vengeance; raging with grief
She came to the hall where the hate of the Weders
Had slain her son. But the hideous hag   160
Avenged his killing; with furious clutch
She seized a warrior—the soul of Æschere,
Wise and aged, went forth from the flesh!
Not at all could the Danes, when the morrow dawned,
Set brand to his body or burn on the bale[71]   165
Their well-loved comrade. With fiendish clasp
She carried his corpse through the fall of the force.[72]
That was to Hrothgar, prince of the people,
Sorest of sorrows that ever befell!
For your sake the sad-hearted hero implored me   170
To prove my valor and, venturing life,
To win renown in the watery depths.
He promised reward. Full well is it known
How I humbled the horrible guard of the gulf.
Hand to hand for a space we struggled   175
Till the swirling eddies were stained with blood;
With cleaving sword-edge I severed the head
Of Grendel's hag in that hall of strife.
Not easily thence did I issue alive,
But my death was not fated; not yet was I doomed!   180
"Then the son of Healfdene, the shelter of earls,
Gave many a treasure to mark the deed.
The good king governed with courtly custom;
In no least way did I lose reward,
The meed[73] of my might; but he gave me treasure,   185
Healfdene's son, to my heart's desire.
These riches I bring you, ruler of heroes,
And warmly tender with right good will.
Save for you, King Hygelac, few are my kinsmen,
Few are the favors but come from you."   190
Then he bade men bring the boar-crested headpiece,
The towering helmet, and steel-gray sark,[74]

---

69 The sun.   70 Harp.   71 Pyre.   72 Waterfall.
73 Recompense.   74 Shirt or coat of mail.

The splendid war-sword, and spoke this word:
"The good king Hrothgar gave me this gift,
This battle-armor, and first to you   195
Bade tell the tale of his friendly favor.
He said King Heorogar,[75] lord of the Scyldings,
Long had worn it, but had no wish
To leave the mail to his manful son,
The dauntless Heoroweard,[76] dear though he was!   200
Well may you wear it! Have joy of it all."
As I've heard the tale, he followed the trappings
With four bay horses, matched and swift,
Graciously granting possession of both,
The steeds and the wealth. 'Tis the way of a kinsman, 205
Not weaving in secret the wiles of malice
Nor plotting the fall of a faithful friend.
To his kinsman Hygelac, hardy in war,
The heart of the nephew was trusty and true;
Dear to each was the other's good!   210
To Hygd, as I've heard, he presented three horses
Gaily saddled, slender and sleek,
And the gleaming necklace Wealhtheow gave,
A peerless gift from a prince's daughter.
With the gracious guerdon, the goodly jewel,   215
Her breast thereafter was well bedecked.

So the son of Ecgtheow bore himself bravely,
Known for his courage and courteous deeds,
Strove after honor, slew not his comrades
In drunken brawling; nor brutal his mood.   220
But the bountiful gifts which the Lord God gave him
He held with a power supreme among men.
He had long been scorned, when the sons of the Geats
Accounted him worthless; the Weder lord
Held him not high among heroes in hall.   225
Laggard they deemed him, slothful and slack.
But time brought solace for all his ills![77]

Then the battle-bold king, the bulwark of heroes,
Bade bring a battle-sword banded with gold,
The heirloom of Hrethel;[78] no sharper steel,   230
No lovelier treasure, belonged to the Geats.
He laid the war-blade on Beowulf's lap,
Gave him a hall and a stately seat[79]
And hides seven thousand.[80] Inherited lands
Both held by birth-fee,[81] home and estate.   235

---

[75] Hrothgar's elder brother.
[76] He had not succeeded to his father's throne. After Heorogar and Hrothgar, Hrothulf became king of the Danes. Subsequently he was attacked by Heoroweard; in the battle Hrothulf was killed and Heoroweard took the throne, but he was soon murdered by a henchman of Hrothulf.
[77] The age-old motif of the Male Cinderella or Unpromising Hero.
[78] Hygelac's father, Beowulf's grandfather.
[79] I.e., high seat, post of authority.
[80] An enormous estate, that of a great earl, comparable to an English county in size. A hide equaled about 100 acres.
[81] I.e., the estates of both Hygelac and Beowulf were not mere life tenures but capable of transmission to their heirs.

But one[82] held rule o'er the spacious realm,
And higher therein his order and rank.

THE DRAGON'S HOARD

How Beowulf ruled the Geats for half a century; how a runaway thrall discovered a dragon-watched treasure in an ancient mound, and stole thence a gold cup; how in olden times that treasure was hidden there by the last survivor of a princely line; how the dragon had found it, and mounted guard for three hundred years, according to the nature of dragons; and how the fiery monster was enraged at the theft.

It later befell in the years that followed
After Hygelac sank in the surges of war,[83]
And the sword slew Heardred[84] under his shield
When the Battle-Scylfings, those bitter fighters,
Invaded the land of the victor-folk,   5
Overwhelming Hereric's nephew[85] in war,
That the kingdom came into Beowulf's hand.
For fifty winters he governed it well,
Aged and wise with the wisdom of years,
Till a fire-drake flying in darkness of night   10
Began to ravage and work his will.
On the upland heath he guarded a hoard,
A stone barrow[86] lofty. Under it lay
A path concealed from the sight of men.
There a thief broke in on the heathen treasure,   15
Laid hand on a flagon all fretted with gold,
As the dragon discovered, though cozened[87] in sleep
By the pilferer's cunning. The people soon found
That the mood of the dragon was roused to wrath!

Not at all with intent, of his own free will,   20
Did he ravish the hoard who committed the wrong;
But in dire distress the thrall[88] of a thane,
A guilty fugitive fleeing the lash,
Forced his way in. There a horror befell him!
Yet the wretched exile escaped from the dragon,   25
Swift in retreat when the terror arose.
A flagon he took. There, many such treasures
Lay heaped in that earth-hall where the owner of old
Had carefully hidden the precious hoard,
The countless wealth of a princely clan.   30
Death came upon them in days gone by
And he who lived longest, the last of his line,

---

[82] King Hygelac.
[83] The historical Hygelac was killed, about 520, on a raid which took him into the North Sea and up the Rhine. According to legend, Beowulf escaped by swimming.
[84] The widowed Queen Hygd had offered Beowulf the throne, which he loyally declined in the interest of Hygelac's young son, Heardred. The latter was killed during a Swedish (Scylfing) invasion of Geatland.
[85] Heardred. Hereric was his uncle, Queen Hygd's brother.
[86] Sepulchral mound.   [87] Beguiled, cheated.   [88] Slave.

Guarding the treasure and grieving for friend,
Deemed it his lot that a little while only
He too might hold that ancient hoard. 35
A barrow new-built near the ocean billows
Stood cunningly fashioned beneath the cliff;
Into the barrow the ring-warden[89] bore
The princely treasure, the precious trove
Of golden wealth, and these words he spoke: 40
"Keep thou, O Earth, what men could not keep—
This costly treasure—it came from thee!
Baleful slaughter has swept away,
Death in battle, the last of my blood;
They have lived their lives; they have left the mead-
     hall. 45
Now I have no one to wield the sword,
No one to polish the plated cup,
The precious flagon—the host[90] is fled.
The hard-forged helmet fretted with gold
Shall be stripped of its inlay; the burnishers sleep 50
Whose charge was to brighten the battle-masks.
Likewise the corselet that countered in war
Mid clashing of bucklers the bite of the sword—
Corselet and warrior decay into dust;
Mailed coat and hero are moveless and still. 55
No mirth of gleewood, no music of harp,
No good hawk swinging in flight through the hall;
No swift steed stamps in the castle yard;
Death has ravished an ancient race."
So sad of mood he bemoaned his sorrow, 60
Lonely and sole survivor of all,
Restless by day and wretched by night.
Till the clutch of death caught at his heart.
Then the goodly treasure was found unguarded
By the venomous dragon enveloped in flame, 65
The old naked night-foe flying in darkness,
Haunting the barrows; a bane that brings
A fearful dread to the dwellers of earth.
His wont is to hunt out a hoard under ground
And guard heathen gold, growing old with the years. 70
But no whit for that is his fortune more fair!

   For three hundred winters this waster of peoples
Held the huge treasure-hall under the earth
Till the robber aroused him to anger and rage,
Stole the rich beaker and bore to his master, 75
Imploring his lord for a compact of peace.
So the hoard was robbed and its riches plundered;
To the wretch was granted the boon that he begged;
And his liege-lord first had view of the treasure,
The ancient work of the men of old. 80
Then the worm[91] awakened and war was kindled,

The rush of the monster along the rock,
When the fierce one found the tracks of the foe;
He had stepped too close in his stealthy cunning
To the dragon's head. But a man undoomed 85
May endure with ease disaster and woe
If he has His favor who wields[92] the world.
Swiftly the fire-drake sought through the plain
The man who wrought him this wrong in his sleep.
Inflamed and savage he circled the mound, 90
But the waste was deserted—no man was in sight.
The worm's mood was kindled to battle and war;
Time and again he returned to the barrow
Seeking the treasure-cup. Soon he was sure
That a man had plundered the precious gold. 95
Enraged and restless the hoard-warden waited
The gloom of evening. The guard of the mound
Was swollen with anger; the fierce one resolved
To requite with fire the theft of the cup.
Then the day was sped, as the worm desired; 100
Lurking no longer within his wall
He sallied forth surrounded with fire,
Encircled with flame. For the folk of the land
The beginning was dread as the ending was grievous
That came so quickly upon their lord. 105

THE RAIDS OF THE DRAGON

*How Geatland was ravaged and Beowulf's own hall burned;
how the hero, to whom the thief's lord had sent the treasure-cup,
went with eleven companions to find the fiery foe, for he was
mindful of all the past occasions when he had fought and won;
and how he told his comrades of those valorous deeds, and announced that he would attack the dragon alone.*

Then the baleful stranger belched fire and flame,
Burned the bright dwellings—the glow of the blaze
Filled hearts with horror. The hostile flier
Was minded to leave there nothing alive.
From near and from far the war of the dragon, 5
The might of the monster, was widely revealed
So that all could see how the ravaging scather
Hated and humbled the Geatish folk.
Then he hastened back ere the break of dawn
To his secret den and the spoil of gold. 10
He had compassed the land with a flame of fire,
A blaze of burning; he trusted the wall,
The sheltering mound, and the strength of his might—
But his trust betrayed him! The terrible news
Was brought to Beowulf, told for a truth, 15
That his home was consumed in the surges of fire,
The goodly dwelling and throne of the Geats.
The heart of the hero was heavy with anguish,

---

89 Treasure-watchman.   90 Band of noble warriors.
91 Old English *wyrm*, dragon.

92 Governs.

The greatest of sorrows; in his wisdom he weened
He had grievously angered the Lord Everlasting,   20
Blamefully broken the ancient law.
Dark thoughts stirred in his surging bosom,
Welled in his breast, as was not his wont.
The flame of the dragon had levelled the fortress,
The people's stronghold washed by the wave.   25
But the king of warriors, prince of the Weders,
Exacted an ample revenge for it all.
The lord of warriors and leader of earls
Bade work him[93] of iron a wondrous shield,
Knowing full well that wood could not serve him   30
Nor linden defend him against the flame.
The stalwart hero was doomed to suffer
The destined end of his days on earth;
Likewise the worm, though for many a winter
He had held his watch o'er the wealth of the hoard.   35
The ring-prince scorned to assault the dragon
With a mighty army, or host of men.
He feared not the combat, nor counted of worth
The might of the worm, his courage and craft,
Since often aforetime, beset in the fray,   40
He had safely issued from many an onset,
Many a combat and, crowned with success,
Purged of evil the hall of Hrothgar
And crushed out Grendel's loathsome kin.

  Nor was that the least of his grim engagements   45
When Hygelac fell, great Hrethel's son;
When the lord of the people, the prince of the Geats,
Died of his wounds in the welter of battle,
Perished in Friesland,[94] smitten with swords.
Thence Beowulf came, by his strength in swimming;   50
Thirty sets of armor he bore on his back
As he hasted to ocean. The Hetware men[95]
Had no cause to boast of their prowess in battle
When they gathered against him with linden shields.
But few of them ever escaped his assault   55
Or came back alive to the homes they had left;
So the son of Ecgtheow swam the sea-stretches,
Lonely and sad, to the land of his kin.
Hygd then tendered him kingdom and treasure,
Wealth of riches and royal throne,   60
For she had no hope with Hygelac dead
That her son could defend the seat of his fathers
From foreign foemen. But even in need,
No whit the more could they move the hero
To be Heardred's[96] liege, or lord of the land.   65

But he fostered Heardred with friendly counsel,
With honor and favor among the folk,
Till he came of age and governed the Geats.
Then the sons of Ohthere fleeing in exile
Sought out Heardred over the sea.[97]   70
They had risen against the lord of the Scylfings,
Best of the sea-kings, bestower of rings,
An illustrious prince in the land of the Swedes.
So Heardred fell. For harboring exiles
The son of Hygelac died by the sword.   75
Ongentheow's son,[98] after Heardred was slain,
Returned to his home, and Beowulf held
The princely power and governed the Geats.
He was a good king, grimly requiting
In later days the death of his prince.   80
Crossing the sea with a swarming host
He befriended Eadgils, Ohthere's son,
In his woe and affliction, with weapons and men;
He took revenge in a savage assault,
And slew the king.[99] So Ecgtheow's son   85
Had come in safety through all his battles,
His bitter struggles and savage strife,
To the day when he fought with the deadly worm.
With eleven comrades, kindled to rage
The Geat lord went to gaze on the dragon.   90
Full well he knew how the feud arose,
The fearful affliction; for into his hold
From hand of finder the flagon had come.
The thirteenth man in the hurrying throng
Was the sorrowful captive[1] who caused the feud.   95
With woeful spirit and all unwilling
Needs must he guide them, for he only knew
Where the earth-hall stood near the breaking billows,
Filled with jewels and beaten gold.
The monstrous warden, waiting for battle,   100
Watched and guarded the hoarded wealth.
No easy bargain for any of men
To seize that treasure! The stalwart king,
Gold-friend of Geats, took seat on the headland,
Hailed his comrades and wished them well.   105
Sad was his spirit, restless and ready,
And the march of Fate immeasurably near;
Fate that would strike, seek his soul's treasure,
And deal asunder the spirit and flesh.
Not long was his life encased in the body!   110

[97] Eanmund and Eadgils, sons of Ohthere, having rebelled against
their uncle, King Onela of the Swedes (Scylfings), found refuge
at the court of King Heardred of Geatland. Onela therefore invaded Geatland, in 528; Heardred and Eanmund were killed.
Onela withdrew to his own country, and Beowulf became king
of the Geats. Eventually Beowulf avenged his cousin Heardred's
death (lines 79 ff.): a Geatish force aided Eadgils to seize the
Swedish throne and kill Onela.
[98] King Onela of the Swedes.   [99] Onela.
[1] I.e., the thrall.

[93] Ordered made for himself.
[94] The land of the Frisians, in the delta of the Rhine. See note 83,
above.
[95] A tribe of Franks living a little way up the Rhine.
[96] The young son of King Hygelac and Queen Hygd.

Beowulf spoke, the son of Ecgtheow:
"Many an ordeal I endured in youth,
And many a battle. I remember it all.
I was seven winters old when the prince of the people,
The lord of the treasure-hoard, Hrethel the king,   115
From the hand of my father[2] had me and held me,
Recalling our kinship with treasure and feast.
As long as he lived I was no less beloved,
As thane in his hall, than the sons of his house,
Herebeald and Hæthcyn and Hygelac, my lord.   120
For the eldest brother the bed of death
Was foully fashioned by brother's deed
When Hæthcyn let fly a bolt from his horn-bow,
Missed the mark,[3] and murdered his lord;
Brother slew brother with bloody shaft—   125
A tragic deed and beyond atonement,
A foul offense to sicken the heart!
Yet none the less was the lot of the prince
To lay down his soul and his life, unavenged.
    "Even so sad and sorrowful is it,   130
And bitter to bear, to an old man's heart,
Seeing his young son swing on the gallows.[4]
He wails his dirge and his wild lament
While his son hangs high, a spoil to the raven;
His aged heart can contrive no help.   135
Each dawn brings grief for the son that is gone
And his heart has no hope of another heir,
Seeing the one has gone to his grave.
In the house of his son he gazes in sorrow
On wine-hall deserted and swept by the wind,   140
Empty of joy. The horsemen and heroes
Sleep in the grave. No sound of the harp,
No welcoming revels as often of old!
He goes to his bed with his burden of grief;
To his spirit it seems that dwelling and land   145
Are empty and lonely, lacking his son.
    "So the helm of the Weders yearned after Herebeald
And welling sadness surged in his heart.
He could not avenge the feud on the slayer
Nor punish the prince for the loathsome deed,   150
Though he loved him no longer, nor held him dear.
Because of this sorrow that sore befell
He left life's joys for the heavenly light,
Granting his sons, as a good man will,
Cities and land, when he went from the world.   155
    "Then across the wide water was conflict and war,
A striving and struggle of Swedes and Geats,
A bitter hatred, when Hrethel died.

---

[2] Ecgtheow, King Hrethel's son-in-law.
[3] The killing was accidental.
[4] In lines 130–48 Hrethel's grief for his eldest son is compared to that which might be felt by a bereaved father whose only son has been hanged.

Ongentheow's sons[5] were dauntless and daring,
Cared not for keeping of peace overseas;   160
But often around Hreosnabeorh[6] slaughtered and slew.
My kinsmen avenged the feud and the evil,
As many have heard, though one of the Weders
Paid with his life—a bargain full bitter!
Hæthcyn's fate was to fall in the fight.   165
It is often recounted, a kinsman with sword-edge
Avenged in the morning the murderer's deed
When Ongentheow met Eofor.[7] Helm split asunder;
The aged Scylfing sank down to his death.
The hand that felled him remembered the feud   170
And drew not back from the deadly blow.
    "For all the rich gifts that Hygelac gave me
I repaid him in battle with shining sword,
As chance was given. He granted me land,
A gracious dwelling and goodly estate.   175
Nor needed he seek of the Gifths,[8] or the Spear-Danes,
Or in Swedish land, a lesser in war
To fight for pay; in the press of battle
I was always before him alone in the van.
So shall I bear me while life-days last,   180
While the sword holds out that has served me well
Early and late since I slew Dæghrefn,[9]
The Frankish hero, before the host.
He brought no spoil from the field of battle,
No corselet of mail to the Frisian king.   185
Not by the sword the warden of standards,
The stalwart warrior, fell in the fight.
My battle-grip shattered the bones of his body
And silenced the heart-beat. But now with the sword,
With hand and hard blade, I must fight for the
    treasure."   190

BEOWULF'S LAST FIGHT

How the hero ordered his band to stand aside, and challenged the dragon alone; how the old sword and the new shield availed not; and how young Wiglaf, untried in battle, dashed in to his lord's succor.

For the last time Beowulf uttered his boast:
"I came in safety through many a conflict
In the days of my youth; and now even yet,
Old as I am, I will fight this feud,
Do manful deeds, if the dire destroyer   5
Will come from his cavern to meet my sword."

---

[5] Ongentheow, King of the Swedes, had two sons, Ohthere (father of Eanmund and Eadgils) and Onela. See note 97, above.
[6] A hill in Geatland.
[7] After the fall of Hæthcyn, Hygelac routed the Swedes; Ongentheow was killed in a fight with the Geatish warrior Eofor and the latter's brother Wulf.
[8] An East Germanic tribe.
[9] During Hygelac's last and fatal expedition. See note 83, above.

The king for the last time greeted his comrades,
Bold helmet-bearers and faithful friends:
"I would bear no sword nor weapon to battle
With the evil worm, if I knew how else   10
I could close with the fiend, as I grappled with Grendel.
From the worm I look for a welling of fire,
A belching of venom, and therefore I bear
Shield and byrny. Not one foot's space
Will I flee from the monster, the ward of the mound.   15
It shall fare with us both in the fight at the wall
As Fate shall allot, the lord of mankind.
Though bold in spirit, I make no boast
As I go to fight with the flying serpent.
Clad in your corselets and trappings of war,   20
By the side of the barrow abide you to see
Which of us twain may best after battle
Survive his wounds. Not yours the adventure,
Nor the mission of any, save mine alone,
To measure his strength with the monstrous dragon   25
And play the part of a valiant earl.
By deeds of daring I'll gain the gold
Or death in battle shall break your lord."

　　　Then the stalwart rose with his shield upon him,
Bold under helmet, bearing his sark   30
Under the stone-cliff; he trusted the strength
Of his single might. Not so does a coward!
He who survived through many a struggle,
Many a combat and crashing of troops,
Saw where a stone-arch stood by the wall   35
And a gushing stream broke out from the barrow.
Hot with fire was the flow of its surge,
Nor could any abide near the hoard unburned,
Nor endure its depths, for the flame of the dragon.
Then the lord of the Geats in the grip of his fury   40
Gave shout of defiance; the strong-heart stormed.
His voice rang out with the rage of battle,
Resounding under the hoary stone.
Hate was aroused; the hoard-warden knew
'Twas the voice of a man. No more was there time   45
To sue for peace; the breath of the serpent,
A blast of venom, burst from the rock.
The ground resounded; the lord of the Geats
Under the barrow swung up his shield
To face the dragon; the coiling foe   50
Was gathered to strike in the deadly strife.
The stalwart hero had drawn his sword,
His ancient heirloom of tempered edge;
In the heart of each was fear of the other!
The shelter of kinsmen stood stout of heart   55
Under towering shield as the great worm coiled;
Clad in his war-gear he waited the rush.
In twisting folds the flame-breathing dragon
Sped to its fate. The shield of the prince

For a lesser while guarded his life and his body   60
Than heart had hoped. For the first time then
It was not his portion to prosper in war;
Fate did not grant him glory in battle!
Then lifted his arm the lord of the Geats
And smote the worm with his ancient sword;   65
But the brown edge failed as it fell on bone,
And cut less deep than the king had need
In his sore distress. Savage in mood
The ward of the barrow countered the blow
With a blast of fire; wide sprang the flame.   70
The ruler of Geats had no reason to boast;
His unsheathed iron, his excellent sword,
Had weakened as it should not, had failed in the fight.
It was no easy journey for Ecgtheow's son
To leave this world and against his will   75
Find elsewhere a dwelling! So every man shall
In the end give over this fleeting life.

　　　Not long was the lull. Swiftly the battlers
Renewed their grapple. The guard of the hoard
Grew fiercer in fury. His venomous breath   80
Beat in his breast. Enveloped in flame
The folk-leader suffered a sore distress.
No succoring band of shoulder-companions,
No sons of warriors aided him then
By valor in battle. They fled to the forest   85
To save their lives; but a sorrowful spirit
Welled in the breast of one of the band.
The call of kinship can never be stilled
In the heart of a man who is trusty and true.

　　　His name was Wiglaf, Weohstan's son,   90
A prince of the Scylfings,[10] a peerless thane,
Ælfhere's kinsman; he saw his king
Under his helmet smitten with heat.
He thought of the gifts which his lord had given,
The wealth and the land of the Wægmunding line   95
And all the folk-rights[11] his father had owned;
Nor could he hold back, but snatched up his buckler,
His linden shield and his ancient sword,
Heirloom of Eanmund, Ohthere's son,
Whom Weohstan slew with the sword in battle,[12]   100
Wretched and friendless and far from home.
The brown-hewed helmet he bore to his kinsmen,
The ancient blade and the byrny of rings.
These Onela gave him—his nephew's arms—

---

10 Presumably Wiglaf is a prince of the Swedish house through his
mother; she may have been the daughter or sister of Ælfhere,
mentioned in the next line, who was probably a member of the
Swedish royal family.

11 Share in the communal property of the tribe.

12 When King Onela invaded Geatland (see note 97, above). After
Onela's death and Eadgils's succession to the Swedish throne,
Weohstan, who was probably a Geat by birth, had to leave
Swedish territory and live in Geatland.

Nor called for vengeance, nor fought the feud,   105
Though Weohstan had slaughtered his brother's son.
He held the treasures for many half-years,
The byrny and sword, till his son was of age
For manful deeds, as his father before him.
Among the Geats he gave him of war-gear   110
Countless numbers of every kind;
Then, full of winters, he left the world,
Gave over this life. And Wiglaf, the lad,
Was to face with his lord the first of his battles,
The hazard of war. But his heart did not fail   115
Nor the blade of his kinsman weaken in war;
As the worm soon found when they met in the fight!

    Wiglaf spoke in sorrow of soul,
With bitter reproach rebuking his comrades:
"I remember the time, as we drank in the mead-hall,   120
When we swore to our lord who bestowed these rings
That we would repay for the war-gear and armor,
The hard swords and helmets, if need like this
Should ever befall him.[13] He chose us out
From all the host for this high adventure,   125
Deemed us worthy of glorious deeds,
Gave me these treasures, regarded us all
As high-hearted bearers of helmet and spear—
Though our lord himself, the shield of his people,
Thought single-handed to finish this feat,   130
Since of mortal men his measure was most
Of feats of daring and deeds of fame.
Now is the day that our lord has need
Of the strength and courage of stalwart men.
Let us haste to succor his sore distress   135
In the horrible heat and the merciless flame.
God knows I had rather the fire should enfold
My body and limbs with my gold-friend and lord.
Shameful it seems that we carry our shields
Back to our homes ere we harry the foe   140
And ward the life of the Weder king.
Full well I know it is not his due
That he alone, of the host of the Geats,
Should suffer affliction and fall in the fight.
One helmet and sword, one byrny and shield,   145
Shall serve for us both in the storm of strife."
Then Wiglaf dashed through the deadly reek
In his battle-helmet to help his lord.
Brief were his words: "Beloved Beowulf,
Summon your strength, remember the vow   150
You made of old in the years of youth
Not to allow your glory to lessen
As long as you lived. With resolute heart

---

[13] Like the hero's boast before battle, this superb exhortation is in
the best epic tradition. Of the *comitatus* or personal troop of the
chieftain, devotion to the death was expected.

And dauntless daring, defend your life
With all your force. I fight at your side!"   155

    Once again the worm, when the words were spoken,
The hideous foe in a horror of flame,
Rushed in rage at the hated men.
Wiglaf's buckler was burned to the boss
In the billows of fire; his byrny of mail   160
Gave the young hero no help or defense.
But he stoutly pressed on under shield of his kinsman
When his own was consumed in the scorching flame.
Then the king once more was mindful of glory,
Swung his great sword-blade with all his might   165
And drove it home on the dragon's head.
But Nægling broke, it failed in the battle,
The blade of Beowulf, ancient and gray.
It was not his lot that edges of iron
Could help him in battle; his hand was too strong,   170
Overtaxed, I am told, every blade with its blow.
Though he bore a wondrous hard weapon to war,
No whit the better was he thereby!

    A third time then the terrible scather,
The monstrous dragon inflamed with the feud,   175
Rushed on the king when the opening offered,
Fierce and flaming; fastened its fangs
In Beowulf's throat; he was bloodied with gore;
His life-blood streamed from the welling wound.

    As they tell the tale, in the king's sore need   180
His shoulder-companion showed forth his valor,
His craft and courage, and native strength.
To the head of the dragon he paid no heed,
Though his hand was burned as he helped his king.
A little lower the stalwart struck   185
At the evil beast, and his blade drove home
Plated and gleaming. The fire began
To lessen and wane. The king of the Weders
Summoned his wits; he drew the dagger
He wore on his corselet, cutting and keen,   190
And slit asunder the worm with the blow.
So they felled the foe and wrought their revenge;
The kinsmen together had killed the dragon.
So a man should be when the need is bitter!
That was the last fight Beowulf fought;   195
That was the end of his work in the world.

THE DEATH OF BEOWULF

*How the dying hero sent Wiglaf into the barrow to fetch out the
hoard; how he beheld it and was content; and how, for the last
time, he gave gold and war-gear.*

The wound which the dragon had dealt him began
To swell and burn; and soon he could feel
The baneful venom inflaming his breast.

The wise old warrior sank down by the wall
And stared at the work of the giants of old,   5
The arches of stone and the standing columns
Upholding the ancient earth-hall within.
His loyal thane, the kindest of comrades,
Saw Beowulf bloody and broken in war;
In his hands bore water and bathed his leader,   10
And loosened the helm from his dear lord's head.

    Beowulf spoke, though his hurt was sore,
The wounds of battle grievous and grim.
Full well he weened that his life was ended,
And all the joy of his years on earth;   15
That his days were done, and Death most near:
"My armor and sword I would leave to my son
Had Fate but granted, born of my body,
An heir to follow me after I'm gone.
For fifty winters I've ruled this realm,   20
And never a lord of a neighboring land
Dared strike with terror or seek with sword.
In my life I abode by the lot assigned,
Kept well what was mine, courted no quarrels,
Swore no false oaths. And now for all this   25
Though my hurt is grievous, my heart is glad.
When life leaves body, the Lord of mankind
Cannot lay to my charge the killing of kinsmen!
Go quickly, dear Wiglaf, to gaze on the gold
Beneath the hoar stone. The dragon lies still   30
In the slumber of death, despoiled of his hoard.
Make haste that my eyes may behold the treasure,
The gleaming jewels, the goodly store,
And, glad of the gold, more peacefully leave
The life and the realm I have ruled so long."   35

    Then Weohstan's son, as they tell the tale,
Clad in his corselet and trappings of war,
Hearkened at once to his wounded lord.
Under roof of the barrow he broke his way.
Proud in triumph he stood by the seat,   40
Saw glittering jewels and gold on the ground,
The den of the dragon, the old dawn-flier,
And all the wonders along the walls.
Great bowls and flagons of bygone men
Lay all unburnished and barren of gems,   45
Many a helmet ancient and rusted,
Many an arm-ring cunningly wrought.
Treasure and gold, though hid in the ground,
Override man's wishes, hide them who will!
High o'er the hoard he beheld a banner,   50
Greatest of wonders, woven with skill,
All wrought of gold; its radiance lighted
The vasty ground and the glittering gems.
But no sign of the worm! The sword-edge had slain him.
As I've heard the tale, the hero unaided   55
Rifled those riches of giants of old,

The hoard in the barrow, and heaped in his arms
Beakers and platters, picked what he would
And took the banner, the brightest of signs.
The ancient sword with its edge of iron   60
Had slain the worm who watched o'er the wealth,
In the midnight flaming, with menace of fire
Protecting the treasure for many a year
Till he died the death. Then Wiglaf departed
In haste returning enriched with spoil.   65
He feared, and wondered if still he would find
The lord of the Weders alive on the plain,
Broken and weary and smitten with wounds.
With his freight of treasure he found the prince,
His dear lord, bloody and nigh unto death.   70
With water he bathed him till words broke forth
From the hoard of his heart and, aged and sad,
Beowulf spoke, as he gazed on the gold:
"For this goodly treasure whereon I gaze
I give my thanks to the Lord of all,   75
To the Prince of glory, Eternal God,
Who granted me grace to gain for my people
Such dower of riches before my death.
I gave my life for this golden hoard.
Heed well the wants, the need of my people;   80
My hour is come, and my end is near.
Bid warriors build, when they burn my body,
A stately barrow on the headland's height.
It shall be for remembrance among my people
As it towers high on the Cape of the Whale,   85
And sailors shall know it as Beowulf's Barrow,
Sea-faring mariners driving their ships
Through fogs of ocean from far countries."
Then the great-hearted king unclasped from his throat
A collar of gold, and gave to his thane;   90
Gave the young hero his gold-decked helmet,
His ring and his byrny, and wished him well.
"You are the last of the Wægmunding line.
All my kinsmen, earls in their glory,
Fate has sent to their final doom,   95
And I must follow." These words were the last
The old king spoke ere the pyre received him,
The leaping flames of the funeral blaze,
And his breath went forth from his bosom, his soul
Went forth from the flesh, to the joys of the just.   100

    Then bitter it was for Beowulf's thane
To behold his loved one lying on earth
Suffering sore at the end of life.
The monster that slew him, the dreadful dragon,
Likewise lay broken and brought to his death.   105
The worm no longer could rule the hoard,
But the hard, sharp sword, the work of the hammer,
Had laid him low; and the winged dragon
Lay stretched near the barrow, broken and still.

No more in the midnight he soared in air, 110
Disclosing his presence, and proud of his gold;
For he sank to earth by the sword of the king.
But few of mankind, if the tales be true,
Has it prospered much, though mighty in war
And daring in deed, to encounter the breath 115
Of the venomous worm or plunder his wealth
When the ward of the barrow held watch o'er the mound.
Beowulf bartered his life for the treasure;
Both foes had finished this fleeting life.

THE TIDINGS OF EVIL

How Wiglaf reproached the craven thanes, and sent the dire
news to the Geatish host; how the messenger told it, predicting
evil days for the tribe; and how the warrior band arose and went
to the place where the hero had fallen.

Not long was it then till the laggards in battle
Came forth from the forest, ten craven in fight,
Who had dared not face the attack of the foe
In their lord's great need. The shirkers in shame
Came wearing their bucklers and trappings of war 5
Where the old man lay. They looked upon Wiglaf.
Weary he sat by the side of his leader
Attempting with water to waken his lord.
It availed him little; the wish was vain!
He could not stay his soul upon earth, 10
Nor one whit alter the will of God.
The Lord ruled over the lives of men
As He rules them still. With a stern rebuke
He reproached the cowards whose courage had failed.
Wiglaf addressed them, Weohstan's son; 15
Gazed sad of heart on the hateful men:
"Lo! he may say who would speak the truth
That the lord who gave you these goodly rings,
This warlike armor wherein you stand—
When oft on the ale-bench he dealt to his hall-men 20
Helmet and byrny, endowing his thanes
With the fairest he found from near or from far—
That he grievously wasted these trappings of war
When battle befell him. The king of the folk
Had no need to boast of his friends in the fight. 25
But the God of victory granted him strength
To avenge himself with the edge of the sword
When he needed valor. Of little avail
The help I brought in the bitter battle!
Yet still I strove, though beyond my strength, 30
To aid my kinsman. And ever the weaker
The savage foe when I struck with my sword;
Ever the weaker the welling flame!
Too few defenders surrounded our ruler
When the hour of evil and terror befell. 35
Now granting of treasure and giving of swords,

Inherited land-right and joy of the home,
Shall cease from your kindred. And each of your clan
Shall fail of his birthright when men from afar
Hear tell of your flight and your dastardly deed. 40
Death is better for every earl
Than life besmirched with the brand of shame!"
Then Wiglaf bade tell the tidings of battle
Up over the cliff in the camp of the host
Where the linden-bearers[14] all morning long 45
Sat wretched in spirit, and ready for both,
The return, or the death, of their dear-loved lord.
Not long did he hide, who rode up the headland,
The news of their sorrow, but spoke before all:
"Our leader lies low, the lord of the Weders, 50
The king of the Geats, on the couch of death.
He sleeps his last sleep by the deeds of the worm.
The dreadful dragon is stretched beside him
Slain with dagger-wounds. Not by the sword
Could he quell the monster or lay him low. 55
And Wiglaf is sitting, Weohstan's son,
Bent over Beowulf, living by dead.
Death watch he keeps in sorrow of spirit
Over the bodies of friend and foe.

[The messenger continues for ninety-eight lines, here omitted,
with an account of the Geats' old feuds, especially with the
Swedes, and a prediction that war will be renewed when the
enemy hears of Beowulf's death.]

"Let us go quickly to look on the king 60
Who brought us treasure, and bear his corpse
To the funeral pyre. The precious hoard
Shall burn with the hero. There lies the heap
Of untold treasure so grimly gained,
Jewels and gems he bought with his blood 65
At the end of life. All these at the last
The flames shall veil and the brands devour.
No man for remembrance shall take from the treasure,
Nor beauteous maiden adorn her breast
With gleaming jewel; bereft of gold 70
And tragic-hearted many shall tread
A foreign soil, now their lord has ceased
From laughter and revel and rapture of joy.
Many a spear in the cold of morning
Shall be borne in hand uplifted on high. 75
No sound of harp shall waken the warrior,
But the dusky raven despoiling the dead
Shall clamor and cry and call to the eagle
What fare he found at the carrion-feast
The while with the wolf he worried the corpses." 80

---

[14] Warriors. Linden was the favorite wood for shields.

So the stalwart hero had told his tidings,
His fateful message; nor spoke amiss
As to truth or telling. The host arose;
On their woeful way to the Eagles' Ness[15]
They went with tears to behold the wonder.   85
They found the friend, who had dealt them treasure
In former days, on the bed of death,
Stretched out lifeless upon the sand.
The last of the good king's days was gone;
Wondrous the death of the Weder prince!   90
They had sighted first, where it lay outstretched,
The monstrous wonder, the loathsome worm,
The horrible fire-drake, hideous-hued,
Scorched with the flame. The spread of its length
Was fifty foot-measures! Oft in the night   95
It sported in air, then sinking to earth
Returned to its den. Now moveless in death
It had seen the last of its earthly lair.
Beside the dragon were bowls and beakers,
Platters lying, and precious swords   100
Eaten with rust, where the hoard had rested
A thousand winters in the womb of earth.
That boundless treasure of bygone men,
The golden dower, was girt with a spell
So that never a man might ravage the ring-hall   105
Save as God himself, the Giver of victory—
He is the Shelter and Shield of men—
Might allow such man as seemed to Him meet,
Might grant whom He would, to gather the treasure.

[*In a passage of fifty-two lines, here omitted, the poet summarizes the fight for the treasure, and Wiglaf tells the host of Beowulf's dying wishes.*]

HEROIC FUNERAL

How the body of Beowulf was burned on a great pyre; how, as he had willed, they built a tall mound for his ashes and his treasure; and how the Geats mourned him who was of all rulers "mildest, most gentle, most eager for fame."

Then the son of Weohstan,[16] stalwart in war,
Bade send command to the heads of homes
To bring from afar the wood for the burning
Where the good king lay: "Now glede[17] shall devour,
As dark flame waxes, the warrior prince   5
Who has often withstood the shower of steel
When the storm of arrows, sped from the string,
Broke over shield, and shaft did service,

With feather-fittings guiding the barb."
Then the wise son of Weohstan chose from the
    host   10
Seven thanes of the king, the best of the band;
Eight heroes together they hied to the barrow
In under the roof of the fearful foe;
One of the warriors leading the way
Bore in his hand a burning brand.   15
They cast no lots who should loot the treasure
When they saw unguarded the gold in the hall
Lying there useless; little they scrupled
As quickly they plundered the precious store.
Over the sea-cliff into the ocean   20
They tumbled the dragon, the deadly worm,
Let the sea-tide swallow the guarder of gold.
Then a wagon was loaded with well-wrought treasure,
A countless number of every kind;
And the aged warrior, the white-haired king,   25
Was borne on high to the Cape of the Whale.
The Geat folk fashioned a peerless pyre
Hung round with helmets and battle-boards,[18]
With gleaming byrnies as Beowulf bade.
In sorrow of soul they laid on the pyre   30
Their mighty leader, their well-loved lord.
The warriors kindled the bale[19] on the barrow,
Wakened the greatest of funeral fires.
Dark o'er the blaze the wood-smoke mounted;
The winds were still, and the sound of weeping   35
Rose with the roar of the surging flame
Till the heat of the fire had broken the body.
With hearts that were heavy they chanted their sorrow,
Singing a dirge for the death of their lord;
And an aged woman with upbound[20] locks   40
Lamented for Beowulf, wailing in woe.
Over and over she uttered her dread
Of sorrow to come, of bloodshed and slaughter,
Terror of battle, and bondage, and shame.
The smoke of the bale-fire rose to the sky!   45
The men of the Weder folk fashioned a mound
Broad and high on the brow of the cliff,
Seen from afar by seafaring men.
Ten days they worked on the warrior's barrow
Inclosing the ash of the funeral flame   50
With a wall as worthy as wisdom could shape.
They bore to the barrow the rings and the gems,
The wealth of the hoard the heroes had plundered.
The olden treasure they gave to the earth,

---

[15] Cape.   [16] Wiglaf.   [17] Fire.

[18] Shields.   [19] Funeral fire.
[20] In contrast with the flowing hair of young women. Had Beowulf
left a widow, her lamentations would have been introduced
here; presumably the aged woman supplied that part of the
obsequies.

The gold to the ground, where it still remains 55
As useless to men as it was of yore.
Then round the mound rode the brave in battle,
The sons of warriors, twelve in a band,
Bemoaning their sorrow and mourning their king.
They sang their dirge and spoke of the hero, 60
Vaunting his valor and venturous deeds.

So is it proper a man should praise
His friendly lord with a loving heart,
When his soul must forth from the fleeting flesh.
So the folk of the Geats, the friends of his hearth, 65
Bemoaned the fall of their mighty lord;
Said he was kindest of worldly kings,
Mildest, most gentle, most eager for fame.

Shorter Old English Poems

DEOR

THERE is no way of telling whether in this lyric, as in the three that follow it, the writer is recording an event in his own life or whether he has invented an episode to express, even dramatize, a phase of human experience in general. If the latter is the case, the more skillful the poet, the more his poem will take on the appearance of specific auto-biography. In such matters the artist can deceive us—indeed, it is his business to deceive us.

The effectiveness of this sad but sturdy little poem, then, does not in the least depend on whether "Deor" is actually the name of the poet or, as seems more likely, of a fictitious character invented by him. Explicitly or implicitly, the artist generalizes about life from his own experience; and by the mysterious processes of art the individual experience is made available to everyone.

Nothing whatever is known about the author of this lyric; very likely, but not necessarily, he was a churchman. Guesses at his date have ranged from the fifth to the tenth century. His poem is preserved in the Exeter Book; since that manuscript belongs to the second half of the tenth century, *Deor* cannot have been written much later than 950. It may be a great deal earlier, but *c.* 900 is a fair possibility. In form *Deor* is far from typical of Old English poetry because of its refrain, the effect of which is to break it into irregular stanzas. On the other hand, its allusions to history and legend, except in their extreme meagerness, are characteristic; evidently the poet could assume his hearers' or readers' familiarity with heroic saga.

Like *Beowulf, Deor* was probably composed in an Anglian dialect, despite its survival only in West Saxon. The best edition, with full notes, glossary, and introduction, is by Kemp Malone (1933). All the following renderings from Old English are by Professor Malone, who reproduces meter and alliteration with remarkable fidelity but without the aesthetic sacrifices which disfigure most translations. These, with others, appear in his *Ten Old English Poems* (1941), from which they are reprinted with the permission of the Johns Hopkins Press.

Weland[1] from wounds underwent hardship,
the cunning kemp[2] bore cares full great,
he had for solace sorrow and longing,
winter-cold want; woe oft enough
he found, after Nithad laid fetters on him, 5
bonds of lithe sinew on the better man.
That now is gone; this[3] too will go.

Beadohild was less for her brothers' sake
than sake of herself so sore at heart:
full well was she aware of that, 10
that she was with child; choose she dared not
to think it through in her thoughts to the end.
That now is gone; this too will go.

We know that Mæthild's moans grew boundless,
grievous waxed the plaints of Geat's lady: 15
that ruthless love bereft her of all sleep.[4]
That now is gone; this too will go.

Theodric[5] held for thirty winters
Mæringaburg; to many that was known.
That now is gone; this too will go. 20

---

[1] The mythical smith of Germanic legend; cf. Vulcan. Once Weland was captured by King Nithad, who hamstrung him and made him work in the royal smithy. Weland revenged himself by killing the two princes, Nithad's sons, and fashioning bowls, gems, and brooches out of their skulls, eyeballs, and teeth; these he presented to the king, the queen, and their daughter Beadohild. Afterwards he ravished the princess, and then escaped by flying away. Beadohild bore a son, mentioned in line 11.
[2] Skillful champion.
[3] The poet's misfortune, described in the closing lines of the poem.
[4] This story is told in the widespread Scandinavian ballad of Gaute and Magnhild. The "ruthless love" is a water-demon's; Magnhild mourns because she expects him to seize her as she crosses a certain river. Fate has, in fact, so ordained; she falls in and drowns. Various versions have different endings. In one, Magnhild's husband, Gaute, raises her body and brings her back to life by the magic power of his harp.
[5] A famous king of the Franks; it was in battle with his army that King Hygelac of Geatland fell about 520 (see p. 31, note 83, above). According to legend, Theodric underwent exile; according to the poet, this was among the Mærings. Where they lived is unknown; probably they were Visigoths (West Goths).

We asked and learned Ermanaric's[6]
wolfishness of thought; wide shires he held
of the Gothic realm; he was grim, that lord.
Many a wight sat bewound in sorrows,
in ween[7] of woe; they wished much to see   25
that king in his realm overcome and fallen.
That now is gone; this too will go.

The man that is wretched sits bereft of gladness,
his soul darkens, it seems to him
the number of his hardships is never-ending;   30
he can bethink him, then, that through this world
God in his wisdom gives and withholds:
to many a man he metes out honor,
fame and fortune; their fill, to some, of woes.
That I will say, of myself to speak,   35
that the Heodenings[8] had me a while for scop,[9]
the king held me dear; Deor they called me.
For many winters my master was kind,
my hap was high, till Heorrenda[10] now,
a good man in song, was given the land   40
that my lord before had lent to me.
That now is gone; this too will go.

A WIFE'S LAMENT

OF THE artist who wrote this poignant lyric we do not
know the name, the century, or the place. His poem is
found in the Exeter Book. For the Old English text and
further discussion, see W. J. Sedgefield's *An Anglo-Saxon
Book of Verse and Prose* (1928) or Miss N. Kershaw's *Anglo-
Saxon and Norse Poems* (1922). The poem is also translated,
with a brief introduction, in C. W. Kennedy's *Old English
Elegies* (1936). The translation which follows is by Kemp
Malone.

I sing of myself, a sorrowful woman,
of my own unhap. All I have felt,
since I grew up, of ill let me say,
be it new or old—never more than now:
I have borne the cross of my cares, always.   5
First my friend[1] went far from home,
over the waves; I was awake at dawn,
I wondered where he was, day and night.

---

[6] King of the Ostrogoths (East Goths) in the second quarter of
the fourth century; he ruled from the Baltic to the Black Sea.
Deor considers him a tyrant, but elsewhere he is praised.
[7] Expectation.
[8] This tribe has not been identified; possibly their home was on
the coast of Pomerania.   [9] Bard, minstrel.
[10] The most famous minstrel of early Germanic legend. His mention here, as Deor's successful rival, indicates that Deor himself
is a romantic fiction.
[1] I.e., husband.

Then I went out, unhappy wife,
lonely and wretched, looking for fellowship.   10
The man's kindred, with minds of darkness,
began to plot to part us two,
that we might lead a life most hateful,
live most aloof, and I longed for him.
My lord bade me lodge in this hut.   15
Little I know of love-making here,
of sweet friendship. My soul is mournful
to find my man, my friend, my mate,
heavy-hearted, happy not at all,
hiding his mood, harboring ill   20
under a blithe bearing. We both made vow
that death alone should drive us asunder,
naught else in the world; that was, but is no more;
it is now as if it had never been,
that friendship of ours. Far and nigh now   25
I must bear the hate of my best beloved.
They drove me out to dwell in the woods
under an oak tree, in that old stone-heap.[2]
Fallen is this house, I am filled with yearning.
The dales are dim, the downs[3] are high,   30
the bitter yards with briars are grown,
the seats are sorrowful. I am sick at heart,
he is so far from me. There are friends on earth,
lovers living that lie together,
while I, early and all alone,   35
walk under the oak tree, wander through these halls.
There I must sit the summerlong day,
there I can rue my wretchedness,
bewail my many woes, my hardships,
for I cannot rest from my cares ever,   40
nor from all the longing that in this life befell me.
It is the way of a young man to be woeful in mood,
hard in his heart's thought; to have, besides,
a blithe bearing and a breast full of care,
a throng of woes alike when his worldly bliss   45
belongs all to him and when he lives an outcast
in a far country. My friend is sitting,
a cliff for shelter, cold in the storm,
a friend weary in mood, flooded with water
in his dismal dwelling, doomed to sorrow.   50
That man, my friend, is mindful too often
of a happier house. Hard is the lot
of one that longs for love in vain.

WANDERER

THE MISERY so powerfully expressed in this fine lyric
springs from the nature of early Teutonic society. The
speaker is a lordless thane or earl. His ruler's death has dis-

---

[2] A derogatory epithet for "house," equivalent to the modern
"hole in the ground."   [3] Hills.

persed the warrior band or *comitatus,* and thoughts of his lost security plunge the now aged exile into gloomy reflection on the insecurity of worldly joy. Once again we have no means of knowing whether this poem reflects a personal experience. Probably the unknown poet was not a wanderer, save in the sense that each of us is. Brooding over the instability of all things, he selects the figure of a lonely warrior as a striking example and uses his misfortune as an excuse for an elegy on the fate that awaits human hopes.

The Christian sentiments, especially in the closing lines, may have been added by some devout copyist; it is always possible that the monks tampered with the original texts of Old English poetry, injecting bits of pious moralizing at more or less appropriate points. But we have no evidence for that, except occasional incongruities of tone; and it seems more likely that the mixture of Christian and pagan ideals merely reflects their joint existence in the minds of the poets themselves. These men, being literate, were very likely ecclesiastics; it is also evident, from their writings, that their imaginations were fired by the traditions of the heroic age.

In those rough times every man's hand might be against an unattached warrior, for the core of the social structure was the relation of lord and thane. In *Wanderer,* Nature itself is also against him, not the beneficent Nature of Wordsworth, but an enemy, grim and harsh with blasts off the dark and wintry northern seas. As he ends, the poet recalls us to religion; yet he stoutly proclaims the stoic virtue that lives in a noble fortitude.

The author and date of *Wanderer* are unknown. Its very title, like those of the other Old English lyrics, is the invention of its modern editors. Its text is preserved in the Exeter Book, in West Saxon; but very likely the poem was originally composed in Northumbria or Mercia. For further discussion see the works of Kennedy, Kershaw, and Sedgefield mentioned above under *A Wife's Lament.* The following translation is by Kemp Malone.

Oft the lone man learns the favor,
the grace of God, though go he must
his ways on the deep, dreary and long,
arouse with hands the rime-cold[1] sea,
fare far from home; fate is unswerving.   5
So quoth the wanderer, of woes mindful,
of fell[2] slaughters, fall of dear ones:
"Oft at each daybreak I am doomed alone
to bewail my cares. Not one now is alive
that I to him openly dare   10
to say my mind. For sooth I know
that is a worthy wont[3] in a kemp[4]

that fast he bind his breast and keep
his thoughts to himself, think as he will.
No weary mood can ward a man,   15
no hot head can give help against fate;
therefore he that holds high his good name
oft binds in his bosom the bitter thought.
So I must fetter, lock fast my mood,
oft hounded with care, of home bereft,   20
far from fellows, friends and kinsmen,
since that day by-gone when the dark, the earth,
hid my gold-friend,[5] and I got me thence,
outcast, winter-sad, over ice-bound waves,
with heavy mood a hearth to seek   25
where I far or nigh might find a lord,
a man in mead-hall mindful of me,
one to befriend me, the friendless waif,
treat me kindly. They ken,[6] the wise,
how grim a mate grief is to him   30
who lives without a loved master.
The wanderer's path, not wound gold,[7] holds him,
a breast frozen, not bliss of earth.
He minds[8] the guests in hall, the gift-taking,
how at the board in years of youth his gold-friend   35
gave him tokens; gone is kindness, all.
For that he learns who long must fare without
his beloved leader's lore, wise sayings,
when sorrow and sleep at the same time together
press oft and bind the poor lone one: 40
to him it seems in mood that his sweet master
he clips[9] and kisses, and clasps at knee
with hands and head, as whilom[10] then
when in days of yore he yet held the throne.
The friendless wight[11] awakes at last,   45
the fallow[12] flood before him sees,
the birds bathing, broadening their feathers,
frost, snow and hail falling mingled.
Then are the heavier the heart's death-wounds,
sore for the loved one; sorrow is renewed.   50
Then the mood becomes mindful of kinsmen,
greets them with gladness, gazes fondly
at sight of his fellows; they swim oft away;[13]
the life of the fleeting ones brings little there
of the words he kens; care is renewed   55
for him who must send his soul wandering
over the ice-bound waves, his weary heart.
Therefore I cannot this world besee[14]
without thinking thoughts of darkness,
when I the life wholly behold of kemps,   60
how the hall they in haste gave up,

---

[1] Frosty.   [2] Cruel, deadly.   [3] Habit.   [4] Champion, warrior.

[5] Lord, dispenser of treasure.   [6] Know.
[7] Gold rings and bracelets.   [8] Remembers.   [9] Embraces.
[10] Formerly.   [11] Man.   [12] Brown, i.e., dark.
[13] I.e., the vision of kinsmen disappears in the sea.   [14] Behold.

the mood-bold thanes. So this middle-earth[15]
with every day down sinks and falls.
Not one can be wise at once, ere he own
winters in the world. The wise man is patient,   65
not too hot-headed nor too hasty-tongued,
nor too weak a fighter, nor too foolish-minded,
nor too fearful nor too fain nor too fee-greedy,
never too bold at boasting ere he know the better rede.[16]
The spearman, moved to speak a vow,   70
must wait, bide his time, till well he know
what turn his mood will take at last.
The tried kemp must grasp how ghastly it will be
when the weal of this world stands waste wholly,
as now in many a spot through this middle-earth   75
the wind-blown walls stand waste, befrosted,
the abodes of men lie buried in snow,
the wine-halls are dust in the wind, the rulers
dead, stripped of glee;—the dright[17] all fell,
by the wall the proud sought shield. War took off some,
brought some away; a bird took one[18]
over the high sea-flood; the hoar-grey wolf
dealt death to one; with dreary cheer
a kemp hid one in a cave of earth.
So the Maker of men made this borough waste   85
till all stood idle, the old work of giants,[19]
without the din of dwellers in hall."

He then, wise in soul, with weighty thought
thinks deeply upon this darksome life,
this fallen fastness,[20] far and oft minds   90
much spilling of blood, and speaks these words:
"Where came the horse, where the rider, where the
          ring-giver?[21]
Where came the house of feasting? Where is hall-gladness?
Alas, the bright mead-cup! Alas, the mailed fighter!
Alas, the prince's power! Past is that time,   95
grown dark in the night, as if it never were!
Where the tried warriors once trod stands now
a wall wondrous high, with worm-shapes dight.[22]
The might of spears, of maces death-greedy,
and fate, that famed one, they felled the kemps,   100
and the storm beats down upon these stone shelters,
the falling snow binds fast the ground,
the blaring winter. Then blackness comes,

[15] The world.   [16] Counsel.   [17] Warrior band.
[18] In the form of carrion from his corpse on the battlefield.
[19] Old ruins and old treasure or weapons or armor found in burial
     mounds were thought to be the work of giants. The speaker is
     viewing, or thinking of, some ancient ruin, probably a Roman
     one.   [20] The ruin.
[21] Lord, ruler.—This speech is written on the *ubi sunt* formula, a
     favorite device of the Roman elegiac writers. "Where are the
     snows of yesteryear?" No answer is expected to such questions;
     the answer is obvious—and unpleasant.
[22] Patterned with serpentine forms.

night-shades darken, the north sends out
fierce falls of hail to the fright of kemps.   105
Altogether hard is this earthly kingdom,
the word of the fates shifts the world under heaven.
Here kine[23] are fleeting, here kin are fleeting,
here men are fleeting, here mates are fleeting,
all this earthly frame[24] grows idle[25] at last."   110
So quoth the sage, sat apart in thought.
He is good who holds troth, his grief must he never
from his breast speak too soon, unless boot[26] first he know
to win boldly. He does well to seek help
of his Father above, where our bliss all stands.   115

SEAFARER

SOME think that this striking lyric came from the pen of
the same poet who wrote *Wanderer,* but there is no evidence
except their similarity. Much of what has been said in the
introductory note on pages 41–42 applies equally well to
Seafarer; the last paragraph applies precisely.

This time the poet chooses the figure of a sailor instead
of a lordless thane to make us see and feel a contrast between two ways of life. Despite the obvious resemblance
to *Wanderer, Seafarer* is essentially different: it winds up
with a little homily, a miniature sermon; the appeal to
stoicism is not repeated here. This Christian close—it begins with line 64—is disproportionately long; we must
admit the possibility that another hand added these less
admired but far from ineffective lines. More probably,
however, the conclusion embodies the generalizing
tendency we have already noticed as characteristic of
poetry. From his vivid picture of the hard life of seamen
the poet passes to its significance as a symbol of human
life in general.

The translation is by Kemp Malone.

I will tell a true tale of myself,
say my farings, how I far and oft
toil-days underwent and times of hardship.
Breast-cares I have borne, bitter enough,
care-seats many in keel I have known,   5
fearful roll of waves. There fell to me oft
hard night-watches at head or stern
when the ship lurches along the cliffs.
My feet were bound with frost, were bitten
with cold fetters; my cares moaned there   10
hot about the heart; hunger broke the mood
of the sea-weary soul from within.
The man that fares fairest on land
can never know how, numb with care,
I sailed the ice-cold sea all winter,   15
the road of the wretched, bereft of kinsmen,

[23] Cattle.   [24] The world.   [25] Empty, deserted.   [26] Remedy.

hung with icicles. Hail flew in showers.
There I heard only the ice-cold wave,
the sea, make song; the swan at times.
I took my glee in the gannet's voice,   20
had lay of whilp[1] for laughter of men,
and mew music for mead-drinking.
There tempests beat stone cliffs; there the tern gave
    answer,
the icy-feathered; full oft the eagle screamed there,
the wet-feathered. Not one of my kinsmen   25
could help my hapless heart in that faring.
The great of earth, the glad with wine,
who lead in towns a life of bliss,
little they mind how, many a time and oft,
I was doomed to bide on the deep, weary.   30
The night darkened, from the north came snow,
frost bound the fields, there was fall of hail,
coldest of seeds. They overcome me now,
the thoughts of my heart, till I think to try
high seas, the play of salt billows.   35
Deep goes the mood that drives my soul
to fare from home, that far away
I may find the stead[2] where strangers dwell.
Not a man on earth is so mood-lofty,
nor so good of his gifts, nor so glowing in youth, 40
nor in his deeds so daring, nor with so dear a lord
that he never has fear of his faring to sea,
what the Lord may list[3] to lay upon him.
He recks not of the harp, nor of ring-taking,
nor of lust for women, nor of worldly hopes,   45
he recks of naught but roll of waves;
but ever he feels longing who fares out to sea.
Blossoms take the woods, the towns grow fair,
the fields are in flower, fast goes the world:
all those move the man whose mood is bent,   50
whose thought is ready, who thinks even so
to fare afar, on the flood to ride.
And the cuckoo warns with woeful voice,
summer's ward sings, sorrow he heralds,
bitter, in breast-hoard. The blissful, the lucky   55
can never know what need some bear
who widest wander the way of outlaws.
    So, now, my soul soars from my bosom,
the mood of my mind moves with the sea-flood,
over the home of the whale, high flies and wide   60
to the ends of the earth; after, back to me
comes the lonely flier,[4] lustful and greedy,
whets me to the whale-way,[5] whelms with his bidding
over deep waters. Dearer, then, to me
the boons of the Lord than this life that is dead   65

---

[1] Song of sea bird; "whilp," like "gannet" and "mew," means a
   kind of gull.   [2] Place.   [3] Please.   [4] My soul.
[5] A kenning for *sea*.

in a land that passes; I believe no whit
that earthly weal is everlasting.
One woe of three ever awaits each man,
dooms him to doubt ere his day is come:
illness or eld or the edge of the sword   70
fails not to fell the fey[6] and the dying.
Therefore for every man after he is dead
that laud in the speech of the living is best
that he worked with a will, ere away he must,
to bring it about, braving his foes   75
in doughty deeds to the devil's hurt,
that the children of men should choose to praise him,
and his laud, after, should live with the angels
always, for aye, in everlasting bliss
with the heavenly host. Gone hence are the days,   80
all the high mood of earth's kingdom;
there is not a king nor a kaiser now,
nor a gold-giver[7] like the great of old,
when most they matched them in mighty deeds
and lived with fame in lordliest wise.   85
Gone is this glory, all; glee is departed.
The weaker walk this world and hold it,
spend it in hardship; splendor is stricken,
earthly honor ages and withers,
so now each of men through middle-earth:[8]   90
eld fares on him, his face turns pale,
the greybeard grieves; his good friends of yore,
begotten of athelings,[9] he knows given to earth.
When the soul flees it, then the flesh no whit
can swallow sweetness, nor soreness feel,   95
nor move a hand, nor with the mind take thought.
Though brother bury by his brothers dead
sundry hoardings, though he sow full wide
the grave with gold, it will not go with them.
The sinful soul can seek no help   100
in gold the wrath of God to face,
if he hides it away while here he lives.
Great is the fear of God: thereby goes the earth.
He fixed, made fast the firm bottoms,
the ends of the earth and the upper heavens.   105
Dull is he who dreads not his Lord; to him comes death
    unwarned.
Happy is he who humble lives; to him comes heaven's
    favor;
the Lord makes fast his mood, for he believes in its might.
The mood must steer a strong spirit, hold it steadfast and
    true
and worthy of man's trust, in its ways full clean.   110
Aright each man should rule evil,
to loved and loathed alike do no wrong,
though folded in fire he fain would have

---

[6] Doomed.   [7] Ruler, giver of treasure.   [8] The world.
[9] Noble warriors.

(or burnt on bale[10] to bone and ashes)
the friend he found! Fate is stronger, 115
God is greater than the grasp of a man.
Of the home we have, heedful let us be,
and care let us give how we come thither,
and try we must, too, to take our way
to the everlasting, endless bliss of heaven. 120
In the love of the Lord life, there, is set,
hope, in the heavens. To the Holy One be thanks
that he lifted us up, the Lord of hosts,
world without end, everlasting God. Amen.

THE DREAM OF THE ROOD

WE COME now to a fervent religious poem, probably inspired by the cult of the "True Cross," a piece of which
was presented to King Alfred. The date of the poem is,
however, uncertain; the cult was doubtless introduced into
Britain long before Alfred's time. *The Dream of the Rood*
survives in the Vercelli manuscript, which belongs to the
late tenth century. It gives a West Saxon version, but the
original poem was probably composed in an Anglian
dialect. That northern original was itself, in all likelihood,
an elaboration of an earlier and shorter Northumbrian
poem, quotations from which are carved in runes on an
eighteen-foot stone cross preserved at Ruthwell in southwestern Scotland. The Ruthwell cross appears to date from
the first half of the eighth century and the Northumbrian
revival. It has been suggested that the gift of the relic to
Alfred in 885 may have inspired the West Saxon poem;
but that is only a guess, and it ignores the probability of an
Anglian original. Nor is the author known, though it is
among the works ascribed by some to Cynewulf. There is
no evidence for that ascription; but the Anglian original
may have been written about the same time as Cynewulf's
signed poems, that is, about the end of the eighth century.
The surviving poem has some points of resemblance with
Cynewulf's work, but in poetic beauty it is superior to
anything that is certainly Cynewulf's.

This beauty appears chiefly in the first seventy-seven lines,
in which, with tender devotion and simple charm, the poet
relates from the point of view of the Cross itself the part
it played in the events on Calvary. The rest of the poem is
less touching, but it is characteristic of Old English religious verse in the way an earnest didacticism comes to
the front. If *The Dream of the Rood* was written when the
Christian civilization of Northumbria was menaced by
Danish fire and sword, there may be a special urgency in
the orthodox expression of longing for rest and peace in a
better world.

---

[10] Funeral pyre.

The best edition is by B. Dickins and A. S. C. Ross
(1934). For further discussion see C. W. Kennedy's *The
Poems of Cynewulf*. The following translation is by Kemp
Malone.

I am minded to tell a marvelous dream,
I will say what I dreamt in the deep of the night,
when the sons of men lay asleep and at rest.
I beheld, borne up on high, methought,
a wondrous rood,[1] bewound with light, 5
the brightest of beams. That beacon was all
overlaid with gold; lovely stood the gems
at the ends of the earth,[2] and up on the crossing
were five gems more. Fair from of old
the angel host looked on; no evil man's cross was that, 10
but hallowed souls beheld it there,
men upon earth, and every creature.
Lovely was the rood, and I laden with sins,
sunk in wickedness. I saw the tree,
garbed and decked and gladly shining, 15
adorned with gold; with dear-bought stones
the cross of Christ was clothed in splendor.
Yet through that gold I began to see
former work of men, the fall of blood
on the right-hand side. I was wretched with sorrow, 20
I was afraid at that sight. I saw that fair beacon
change garb and look: now with gore it was wet,
with blood it was drenched; now it was bright with
    treasure.
But I, lying a long time there,
ruefully gazed on the rood of my Savior, 25
till I was aware that it uttered words,
the cross of God began to speak:
    "It was many years ago—I remember it still—
that I was felled, afar, at the forest edge,
borne off from my roots. Evil men took me. 30
They were making a show, I was to be a mount for their
    felons.
Men bore me on their shoulders till they brought me to
    a hill;
there they set me. Then I saw that the Lord
was coming in haste to climb upon me.
When I saw the ends of the earth shaking[3] 35
I dared not bow or break, against
the Word of God. All at once I might
have struck his foes down, but I stood fast there.
Then the good youth stripped—that was God almighty—
his mind was set. He mounted to the gallows, 40
firm in the sight of many, to free mankind.

---

[1] Cross.
[2] It was customary to set a relic of the "True Cross" in a jeweled
crucifix. The poet has a vision of such a cross, so vast it fills the
sky. Its jeweled arms reach to the horizon.
[3] The earthquake mentioned in Matthew 27:51.

I quaked when he clasped me, but I could not bow to
    earth,
nor fall to the ground; it was my fate to stand.
As a rood I was raised; I bore my ruler up,
the king of the skies; I could not bow down.   45
They pierced me with dark nails; the places are on me still,
the wicked wounds are open. Not one of them dared I
    harm.
They railed at us both. I was all running with blood
as he gave up the ghost, with gore from his side.
A heavy burden I bore on that hill,   50
my lot was hard. I saw the Lord of hosts
most brutally racked. His body darkness
had clothed with clouds, the corpse of our Lord,
his shining splendor; a shadow went forth,
black over the earth. All fell to weeping,   55
every creature made moan; Christ was on the rood.
Yet willing ones from away came there,
from afar to the Lord. I looked upon it all.
I was burdened with sorrows but I bent for those men,
in meekness, low. Their Maker they took,   60
they lifted from that torment. They left me standing
bloody and wounded, all bruised and gashed.
They laid him down; by their Lord they stood;
they beheld God there; for a while he was resting,
tired after toil. A tomb they made for him   65
in the slayer's sight; they cut it in solid rock.
There they set their Redeemer. Over him they sang a
    dirge,
in the evening, sick at heart. Afterwards they went away,
they left their Lord; alone he rested there.
But we stood weeping woefully and long there,   70
we stood still there, when the steps of men
were heard no more. The house of the soul,
the body, grew cold. Then they brought us low,
that was a fearful fate, they felled us all to earth.
They buried us deep, in a dark pit there.   75
Yet holy men heard and hastened to free me;
they garbed me round with gold and silver.
    "Now thou wilt learn, my beloved child,
that I bore the deeds of baleful[4] souls,
troubles beset me. The time has now come   80
that far and wide they worship me,
the earth-dwellers and all things made,
they pray to this sign. On me he suffered a while,
the Child of God; for that I am glorious now,
high under heaven; I can heal one and all,   85
whoever is moved with awe before me.
Once I met the worst of fates,
I was loathly to all till I opened the way
to life everlasting for them that live on earth.

Lo, he lifted me, the Lord of glory,   90
the Helm[5] of heaven, highest among trees,
even as he made his mother, Mary herself,
almighty God, in all men's sight,
highest among the host of women.
    "Now I lay it upon thee, my beloved child,   95
that thou tell this sight to the sons of men,
the tale unfold of the tree of glory
that God almighty gave his life on,
to save mankind from the sin of old Adam,
and many works of wickedness.   100
Death he tasted, but from the dead he rose again
in all his might to give aid to mankind.
He went up to heaven. Hither afterwards,
to this middle-earth, to all men he shall come
on the day of doom, the dread Lord himself,   105
almighty God and his angels too.
Then will be meted out to every man
as he earlier here had earned for himself,
in former days, in this fleeting life.
Not anyone there can be unafraid   110
of that judgment that the Judge shall speak.
Among the many for that man he calls
who would lay down his life for his Lord, and taste
of such bitter death as he bore once on the rood.
But then they are afraid, and few can tell   115
what thing to say at the throne of Christ.
No need for him to know any fear
who has borne in his bosom the best of signs,
for through the rood he shall reach the kingdom,
every one from the ways of earth   120
that looks to life with his Lord in heaven."
    I prayed then to the cross, apart and happy,
with all my strength, where I stood alone,
far from the throng; my thought was fixed,
bent on the going hence; I bore them all,   125
the heavy days. Now it is the hope of my life
that I may fare to find the cross,
alone, more often than other men,
to worship it well; my will for that
is high in my heart, and my hope of grace   130
is lifted to the rood. No lords are stronger,
no friends of earth. But they went forth, went hence,
left worldly delights, sought the Lord of glory;
they live now in heaven, with the High Father,
they dwell in glory; and every day I hope   135
the time has come when the cross of my Lord,
which here on earth I beheld long ago,
shall fetch me away from this fleeting life
and bring me then there where bliss is great,
to the happiness of heaven, where the host of God   140

---

[4] Wicked.

[5] Guard.

is brought to the feast, where bliss is endless;
and shall put me then in the place where thenceforth
I may have my home, with the holy ones above,
where I may live in gladness. May the Lord be my friend,
he who here on earth of old suffered, 145
died on the cross for the evil deeds of man:
he redeemed us, for death he gave us life,
a heavenly home. Hope was made new
with blessing and with bliss, for those who burned in hell.
The Son was the winner in that warfaring, 150
mighty and matchless. Then with many he came,
with a host of souls, to his heavenly kingdom,
the Almighty went up to the angels, to bliss,
and to all the holy ones that in heaven already
were living in glory when their Lord came back, 155
almighty God, to his own again.

BRUNANBURG

THIS lyric is a paean of triumph for a decisive victory won
by an English army commanded by two grandsons of
Alfred the Great, King Athelstan and his brother Edmund,
who afterwards followed him on the throne. The enemy
forces consisted of Northumbrian Danes under King Anlaf,
other Viking bands he had picked up among the Northmen
who had seized part of Ireland, a contingent of Scots headed
by King Constantine II, and Celtic troops from Strath-
clyde under King Owen. Despite much speculation, the
location of the battlefield remains unknown; probably it
was somewhere in the northwest of England. Wherever it
was fought, the battle was an important one, for it greatly
strengthened the power of the Wessex royal line.

The poem constitutes the entry of the *Anglo-Saxon
Chronicle* for the year 937; it is one of several entries in
verse. Presumably its unknown author composed it soon
after the battle. Unlike the *Maldon* poet, he gives few details; it seems unlikely that he was an eyewitness.

On the *Chronicle,* see p. 7, above. Editions of *Brunanburg* may also be found in W. J. Sedgefield's *An Anglo-
Saxon Book of Verse and Prose* (1928) and Miss N. Kershaw's *Anglo-Saxon and Norse Poems* (1922). Tennyson's
translation, based on a prose version by his son, has often
been reprinted; it is not remarkable for fidelity to the
original. Professor Malone's, given below, is a great deal
closer to what the Old English poet actually wrote.

Athelstan the king, captain of earls,
bounteous lord of men, and his brother too,
Edmund the prince, won everlasting glory
in the onslaught of war, by the edge of the sword
at Bruna's borough; the board-wall[1] they clove, 5
they hewed shields low with hammers' leavings,[2]

---

[1] Line of shields.   [2] Hammer-wrought weapons.

the heirs of Edward;[3] it was inborn, handed down
from their forefathers, that in fight they oft
against each foe should defend their land,
their hoards and homes. Their haters perished, 10
the people of the Scots and the pirate host;
the fey[4] fell to earth. The field grew dark
with soldiers' blood after the sun rose up
in morningtide, the marvelous star,
glided across the sky, the bright candle of the Lord, 15
of God eternal, till the glorious creature
sank at eve, set. Many a soldier lay there,
many a man of the North, marred by the spear,
shot over the shield, many a shipman and Scot too,
weary, tired of war. The West-Saxons 20
pressed on in force all the day long,
pushed ahead after the hostile army,
hewed the fleeing down from behind fiercely,
with mill-sharp swords. The Mercians[5] withheld
the hard handplay no whit from a man 25
of those that with Anlaf came over the waves,
by ship invaded our shores from abroad,
warriors doomed to die in warplay.
On that field of battle lay five young kings,
put to sleep by the sword, and seven over that, 30
earls of Anlaf, endless numbers
of pirates and Scots. There was put to flight
the Northmen's prince, by need compelled
to seek his ship with a small band of men.
The keel pushed off, the king went out 35
on the fallow[6] flood, he was fated to live.
So there Constantinus came by flight too,
the cunning old king, to his kith in the north,
the grey-haired kemp;[7] he had no cause to be glad
of the crossing of swords; of his kin he was robbed, 40
of friends bereft on the field of battle,
he lost them in war, and he left his son
on the slaughter-ground, left him slain by wounds
in fight, the youth. The father had no cause
to boast about the battle-play of swords, 45
the evil old man, nor had Anlaf more;
with their loot they had no cause to laugh and say
they were better in strife, in battle-work
on the combat-ground, in the clash of banners,
the meeting of spears, men's encounter, 50
the weapon-crossing, the war game they played
with the sons of Edward on the slaughter-field.
Then the Northmen went with the nail-studded ships,
dreary darts' leavings, on Dingesmere,[8]
over deep water for Dublin bound, 55
back to Ireland, beaten, put to shame.

---

[3] King Edward the Elder, Alfred's son.   [4] Doomed.
[5] Mercia was now part of the English kingdom ruled by the royal
house of Wessex.   [6] Brown, i.e., dark.   [7] Warrior.
[8] Unidentified, but evidently water leading to the Irish Sea.

Likewise the brothers, both together,
the king and the prince, sought kith and home,
the land of Wessex, elate with the war.
The host of corpses behind them they left   60
to the black raven, the beak-faced one,
the dark-clothed one, and to the dun eagle,
the white-tailed erne,[9] hungry war-bird,
and to the greedy wolf, grey beast of the woods,
to devour and relish. So vast a slaughter   65
of men never yet was made before this
on this island of ours with the edge of the sword
(if we take for true what is told us in books
or by the old and wise), since from the east hither
the Angles and Saxons came up, to these shores,   70
over broad waters sought Britain out,
the keen war-smiths, overcame the Welshmen,
the worshipful kemps,[10] and won the land.

MALDON

WITH the heroic lines of *Maldon,* Old English poetry ends
—on a tragic note, for this battle of August 11, 991, cost
the English heavily in lives of brave men, and the victors
were Vikings from Norway. The time is the long, incapable reign of Ethelred the Unready, grandson of
Athelstan's brother, King Edmund, and father of Edward
the Confessor. The second wave of Scandinavian attack
was well on its way to the success that culminated in the
accession of King Cnut.

The engagement at Maldon was precipitated when
Byrhtnoth, the powerful earl or ealdorman of Essex,
threw his household troops and the *fyrd* or local levies of
the district across the path of a Viking raid. The enemy
fleet had ravaged the shores of Kent and then turned north
to sack Ipswich. Thence they ran up the estuary of the
Blackwater and camped on the island of Northey near
Maldon on the Essex coast. It was a strong defensive
position. But to march onto the mainland the Vikings had
to use a ford which was passable only at low tide; its ridge
is the "causeway" or "bridge" of the poem. This ford has
recently been identified; it is about eighty yards long.
Though it has been considerably built up since Saxon
times, it is still under water at high tide. Byrhtnoth, who
was sixty-five or thereabouts when he fought at Maldon,
was a hardy warrior—a giant of a man. But his generalship
is open to question. In his eagerness to bring the Norsemen
to battle he finally allowed them to cross the ford unmolested, with the result described in the poem.

Strangely enough, though its style and meter are not
fully up to former standards of Old English poetry, *Maldon*
incorporates more explicitly than any of the earlier pieces

the heroic code which the English had brought with them
to Britain five centuries before. There is a thorough appreciation of the warriors' conceptions of honor, and the
ignoble flight of the *fyrd* is contrasted with the exemplary
behavior of the *comitatus* or household troops. The poet is
less concerned with the battle as a military episode than
with the devoted conduct of a band of English heroes. He
therefore singles out the parts played by various individuals and compiles a roll of honor, instead of trying to
report the course of events as a whole. In the light of his
purpose, his success is complete; *Maldon* has been called the
best battle poem in our language.

It was among a number of works preserved in a West
Saxon manuscript which was known to Elizabethan
antiquarians. Early in the seventeenth century this document came into the possession of an important collector,
Sir Robert Cotton. Some time before the end of that
century several leaves were lost, perhaps two or three at
the beginning of the poem and one at the end. In 1731
the manuscript was almost completely destroyed in a fire
which damaged another and even more famous Cottonian
treasure, the manuscript which includes *Beowulf.* Fortunately a transcript, still extant, had been made of *Maldon,*
and the poem had been printed. Remaining bits of the
manuscript itself indicate that its date is late in the eleventh
century; no doubt the poem was composed shortly after
the battle, late in the tenth. It is unlikely that the writer
was present, but he has the facts. Doubtless he had talked
with survivors. Presumably he was an East Saxon.

The best edition of *Maldon,* with a full discussion of its
historical and aesthetic aspects, is by E. V. Gordon (1937).
The translation is by Kemp Malone.

       . . . were broken.
He[1] bade then each young man get off his horse,
drive it from him[2] and on foot go forward straight,
mindful that hands and heart be doughty.
As soon as it came to the kinsman of Offa[3]   5
that the earl[4] would never put up with slackness
he loosed from his hands his beloved hawk,
let it fly to the woods, and went to the fight.
By that one could tell that this young man
would not tire in strife when he took to weapons.   10
Eadric,[5] too, longed to aid his leader,
his lord, in the fight; forward he bore
spear in battle. His spirit was good
while in his hands he could hold a shield,
brandish a broadsword; he broke not his vow   15

[1] Byrhtnoth.
[2] As a rule the English did not fight mounted; driving the horses
away implies an intention of fighting it out to the death.
[3] Offa and at least two of his kinsmen are followers of Byrhtnoth.
[4] Byrhtnoth; he was Earl of Essex.
[5] Another of the Earl's followers.

EARLY MUSICIANS

From an illustration in an eighth-century psalter.

A MEDIEVAL BESTIARY

Bestiaries, or collections of fabulous and allegorical descriptions of animals, were popular in many countries in medieval times. The original Latin *Physiologus* was imitated in both Old and Middle English. These pages from a Latin manuscript of the twelfth or thirteenth century in the Cambridge University Library were decorated by an illustrator of great skill. One shows a fabulous tree which affords doves peculiar protection from dragons—a symbol of God's protection of the faithful. The other illustrates an account of the whale, said to be so easily mistaken for an island that mariners anchor their ship to it, to perish when it plunges beneath the surface. The whale symbolizes the wiles of the Devil.

MEDIEVAL AGRICULTURE

This scene, though drawn from the fourteenth-century Luttrell Psalter, depicts an activity common in the English countryside from a much earlier date. At the same time it points forward to *Piers Plowman* and to Chaucer's Plowman.

The Bayeux Tapestry, made probably soon after 1066, presents in a wonderfully living succession of embroidered scenes the events leading up to William I's conquest of England. Three small sections are shown here. (1) The Saxon earl Harold returns to England from an embassy which has arranged that William, Duke of Normandy, shall succeed Edward the Confessor on the English throne. (2) Harold, who has become king after Edward's death, is alarmed by news of a portent of disaster—Halley's Comet, which appeared on April 24-30, 1066. (3) Mounted Frenchmen and English foot soldiers fight savagely at Hastings, where Harold was killed and William established his claim to the throne.

to fight before his friend and master.

Then Byrhtnoth put the men[6] in battle array there:
he rode and taught, told the fighters
how they should stand and hold that stead,[7]
and bade them grip their boards[8] aright,   20
take them fast in hand and fear nothing.
When he had arrayed fairly the rank and file
he alighted then where he loved most to be,
with his hearth-fellows;[9] he knew they held him dearest.

On the shore[10] then stood, shouted sternly,   25
a speaker for the Vikings; he spoke with words,
he said the say of the seafarers,
stoutly threatened the earl where he stood on the bank:
"Seamen, bold men, have sent me to thee;
they bade me tell thee to bring quickly   30
thy best if ye would be spared, and it is better for you
to stop with tribute this storm of spears
than that we fight each other in fierce battle.
No lives need be lost if ye listen to this;
for gold we will gladly give you terms.   35
If thou be minded, who art master here,
willing to pay thy people's ransom,
give to the Vikings, as seems good in their sight,
a price for friendship, and take peace at our hands,
we will go with the tribute again on board,   40
and stand to sea and stay at peace with you."

Byrhtnoth spoke, brandished his slender spear,
lifted up his shield;[11] he uttered words,
angry and single-minded, he gave answer to him:
"Hearest thou, seafarer, what this folk sayeth?   45
On you they will spend spears for tribute,
the point that slays and swords from of old,
the heriot[12] that gives little help in strife.
Spokesman of the Vikings, speak once again,
tell to thy people a tale far worse,   50
that here stands unafraid an earl with his hearthmen
who is eager to fight for his own, this land,
the home of Ethelred, the earth and folk
of my dear master. They are doomed to fall,
the heathen, in battle. Too base it seems to me   55
to let you go with our gold to ship
unfought against, now that thus far hither
in ye have come, to our own country.
Look not so lightly to load treasure;
grim battle-play shall bring us together,   60
point and edge first, before we pay tribute."

Then he bade the men bear the shields forth,
go on till they stood at stream-side all.
Water parted the foes there, the one from the other:
there the tide came flowing, flood after ebb,   65
the sea-streams locked.[13] It seemed to them too long
until the time when the troops should join battle.

There they lined the Panta[14] in proud array,
the van of Essex and the Viking force;
the one could do no ill to the other of these,   70
unless someone should fall by flight of arrow.

The flood tide went out. The foe stood ready,
swarms of Vikings, set for the struggle.
Then the helm[15] of heroes bade a hard fighter
hold the crossing: that was Ceola's son,   75
as keen as his kin; he was called Wulfstan.[16]
At the causeway he slew with cast of spear
the first man (a bold one!) who set foot on it.
With Wulfstan watched there two warriors[17] great of
     heart,
Ælfere and Maccus, the unafraid.   80
The twain were not minded to take to flight,
but against the foes they stood fast at the bridge[18]
while they could hold in their hands a weapon.

When the seamen understood and saw clearly
what bitter keepers of the bridge they had found,   85
they turned to wiles, the wicked strangers,
they asked for leave to go up to land,
fare over the ford, lead their forces across.

The ealdorman then in his overboldness
yielded up to the enemy overmuch ground.   90
Then he called to them over cold water,
the son of Byrhtelm; the soldiers listened:
"Now space is given you: with speed come to us,
go, men, to battle. God only knows
who is fated to hold the field."   95

Then the wolves of slaughter waded west over Panta,
the host of the Vikings, heedless of the stream,
bore the linden[19] over bright water,
the shipmen carried their shields to land.
There before the fierce ones the fyrd stood ready,   100
Byrhtnoth and his men. He bade them make
the battle-hedge, that band, with their shields,
hold fast against the foe. The fight then was near,
honorable battle. The hour was come
when men there doomed to die should fall.   105

6 The *fyrd*, levied from the locality; not the Earl's personal troops.
7 Place.   8 Shields.
9 The *comitatus* or household troops.
10 Of the island, across the ford.
11 Both gestures are appeals for quiet during an announcement.
12 Feudal duty paid over to a lord in weapons.

13 The tidal channels around both sides of the island.
14 The River Blackwater, still called "Pant" (pronounced *Pont*)
   below Maldon.   15 Protector.
16 An extant will of a son of Wulfstan, probably this warrior, disposes of lands near Maldon.
17 Doubtless others were stationed at the ford, but the poet handles
   the battle in terms of individual feats.
18 The ford or "causeway."
19 Shields; linden was the favorite wood for them.

There a roar was raised. Ravens flew above,
the eagle, eager for meat. There was outcry below.
    They let fly then from hand the file-hard spear,
let go the dart, ground sharp and deadly.
Bows were busy, board took spear-point.   110
Bitter was the onslaught. Battle leaders fell
on either hand, young heirs lay slain.
Wulfmær was wounded, he went to his death,
Byrhtnoth's kinsman; with the bill[20] he was hewn,
his sister's son, sorely stricken.   115
Vengeance was taken on the Vikings there:
I heard that Edward[21] withheld not the stroke,
smote one of them with his sword so fiercely
that at his feet fell there the fey[22] warrior;
lord said thanks to thane for that,   120
to bower-henchman,[23] when he had a breathing-spell.
    Thus they stood their ground, the stouthearted,
the young, in the fight, they yearned to see
who first in that spot with flight of spear
could deal out death to a doomed warrior,   125
a seamen, with weapons. The slain fell to earth.
The band held firm, Byrhtnoth roused them,
whetted each thane to think on war
who sought for glory in battle against the Danes.
    Then a war-hard man came up, his weapon he
        raised,   130
his shield for defense, and went forward against
        Byrhtnoth.
Even so the unflinching earl went up against the yeoman:
each of them harbored harm for the other.
Then the seaman sent a southern spear,[24]
so that the lord of warriors was left wounded.   135
He shoved then with shield so that shaft broke off,
and the spear he shivered, so that it sprang out again.
The prince was angered: he pierced with his spear
the doughty Viking who dealt him that wound.
Wise was the fyrdman:[25] he made his weapon go   140
through the harding's[26] neck, the hand showed the way,
so that the shaft took the life of the ship-warrior.
    Then he speedily hurled his spear at another,
so that the sark[27] burst asunder; he suffered a breast-
        wound
through the net of rings. Nigh to his heart stood   145
the poisonous[28] point. The prince was the blither:
then the good man laughed, to God he said thanks
for the day's work done and to do that he gave him.

Then a man of the fleet let fly from his hand
a dart that went too deep, too straight,   150
through the noble thane of Ethelred.[29]
A beardless youth stood by him there,
a boy, in the battle; full boldly he drew
out of the warrior the wound-reddened spear.
That was Wulfstan's child, Wulfmær[30] the young;   155
he hurled the hard spear, made it hasten back.
It waded in, so that the warrior lay downed
who pierced his prince with that point before.
    A weaponed warrior then went to the earl;
he was minded to take the trappings of the man,   160
armor and rings and ornamented sword.
    Then Byrhtnoth drew his bill from its sheath,
broad and brown-edged, struck a blow at the sark.
Too swiftly one of the seamen stopped him,
when he crippled the earl in the arm that smote.   165
The fallow[31]-hilted sword fell then to earth:
he could not hold the hardened blade,
wield the weapon. Then yet words he spoke,
the hoary warrior, heartened the young men,
told his good followers to go forward.   170
He could then stand fast on his feet no longer;
he looked aloft, to his Lord above:
"I thank thee, O God, governor of peoples,
for all the blessings that on earth were mine.
Now, mild Master, I most have need   175
that thou grant to my ghost the grace of heaven,
that my soul have leave to seek thee out,
depart in peace, pass into thy keeping,
Prince of angels. I pray it of thee
that the fiends of hell afflict her not."[32]   180
    Then heathen fighters hewed him down,[33]
and both the stout ones that stood by him,
Ælfnoth and Wulmær; they went to their death,
beside their lord together they gave their lives.
    Then they who were loath to be there left the
        battle: 185
there the first to flee from the fight was Godric,
the son of Odda, and he forsook the earl,
who had bestowed many a steed upon him,
he leaped on the horse that his lord had there,
on the riding-gear he had no right to take;   190

[29] Byrhtnoth, King Ethelred's earl.
[30] Another youth, not the Earl's nephew.
[31] Yellow, i.e., golden.
[32] Byrhtnoth was noted for his piety and for protecting monas-
    teries.
[33] According to tradition recorded in a twelfth-century account,
    the "Danes" cut off his head. His body was buried in the Saxon
    church at Ely and reinterred when the Normans built the great
    cathedral. In 1769 the bones were moved to another spot there.
    No skull was found; the collarbone had been cut nearly in two;
    from the length of the bones Byrhtnoth's height was estimated
    at six feet nine.

[20] Sword.
[21] One of Byrhtnoth's followers, perhaps the same Edward ("the
    tall") mentioned in line 273.   [22] Doomed.
[23] Cf. hearth-fellows in line 24.
[24] Doubtless part of the loot from raids in England or France.
[25] Warrior, Byrhtnoth.
[26] A war-hard man, an experienced fighter.
[27] Coat of ringed mail.   [28] Baneful, ruinous.

and his brothers, too, both rode with him,
Godwin and Godwig; they forgot the battle
and went to the wood, away from the fight,
fled to the fastness[34] and found shelter,
with more men than it were meet[35] to be   195
if only they had thought of all the things
that he had done for a help to them.
Even so had Offa said on a day
at the meeting-place, when the moot[36] was held,
that many spoke there with much boldness   200
who would not bear up afterwards, at need.

  Then the people's prince was fallen,
Ethelred's earl. One and all they saw,
the hearth-fellows, that their head lay slain.
The proud thanes there then pushed forward,   205
men unafraid, they eagerly hastened:
they all meant to win then one of two things,
to die or avenge their dear leader.

  The child of Ælfric[37] thus cheered them on,
the young warrior; he used words then,   210
Ælfwin spoke and said with all his strength:
"Be mindful of the times when at mead we spoke,
when oft we voiced a vow on the bench,
we heroes in hall, about hard fighting:
it can straightway be proved who is stoutminded.   215
I will make known to all my noble descent;
from a mighty kindred of the Mercians I sprang,
my grandfather was rich in the goods of this world,
the wise ealdorman; Ealhelm[38] he was called.
The thanes of Mercia shall not think me a man   220
who was willing to leave, go away from this fyrd,
depart for home, now that my prince lies slain,
hewn down in battle. That is my deepest sorrow:
to me he was both, master and kinsman."
Then forward he went, of the fight he was mindful,   225
so that he pierced a man with the point of his spear,
a fighter of the fleet, so that he fell to earth,
killed by his weapon. He called on his friends,
comrades and fellows, to come forward.

  Then Offa spoke, shook his spear of ashwood: 230
"What! Thou, Ælfwin, hast whetted them all,
the thanes, in their need. Now that our leader,
the earl, is down, we all have need
that each of us hearten the other to fight,
to wield the weapons of war while he can,   235
as long as he can have and hold sharp blade,
spear and good sword. That spawn of Odda,

that wretched Godric, hath bewrayed[39] us all.
Many a man thought, when he mounted the steed,
rode the proud horse, that our prince was the rider.   240
So here on the field the folk hath been scattered,
the shield-wall broken. Shent[40] be his course,
who hath made so many men take to flight."

  Leofsunu[41] spoke and lifted his shield,
his board, in defense; that brave one he answered: 245
"I give my word not to go from hence,
not to flee a foot, but forward to go,
to avenge in fight my friend and lord.
The steadfast heroes in Sturmer need not
reproach me with words, now that my prince is
        fallen,   250
for faring home from the fight, lordless,
turning from warfare; but the weapon shall take me,
point and iron edge." He pushed on, full angry,
he fought firmly, held flight in scorn.

  Dunnere then spoke, a dart he shook,   255
the old yeoman[42] called out afar,
bade them all vow to avenge Byrhtnoth:
"He cannot flinch or fear for his life
who is minded to avenge his master in the field."

  Forward then they went, had no fear of death.   260
Then the household men fought hard and long,
the proud spearmen, and prayed to God
for might to avenge their master and friend
and bring down their foes to death in that fight.

  The hostage gladly gave them help;[43]   265
He belonged to a fighting line of Northumbrians,
the child of Ecglaf; Æscferth his name was.
He drew not back in the battle-play,
but let arrows speed forth often enough;
now shield, now bearer he would shoot into,   270
each moment he gave some man a wound
until he could wield weapons no longer.

  Then too in the forefront tall Edward stood,
ready and eager, spoke rousing words,
vowed not a foot to flee or yield,   275
disdained to fall back when his better lay dead.
He broke the boardwall and braved the foe
till he avenged his lord on the invader, the seamen,
before he fell on the field of slaughter.

  So did noble Ætheric, active comrade,   280
eager to go forward; he fought earnestly,
Sibyrht's brother, and the same did many,

---

[34] Place of safety, i.e., the wood.   [35] Proper.   [36] Council.
[37] Ælfric was once earl of Mercia; his subsequent banishment
    accounts for his son's being with their kinsman Byrhtnoth, who
    was probably of a Mercian family.
[38] Ælfwin's father, Ælfric, was the son-in-law of Ealhelm, a former
    earl of Mercia.

[39] Betrayed.   [40] Ruined.
[41] Another of Byrhtnoth's followers, evidently from Sturmer, a
    locality (now a village) on the River Stour in Essex.
[42] That is, he was a churl, not a noble.
[43] Why Byrhtnoth had a Northumbrian hostage is unknown. The
    latter's conduct was eminently correct, since a noble hostage got
    the same treatment from the lord as the members of the house-
    hold troop.

the keen ones held, they clove the shield;
rim of shield crashed and coat of mail sang
a fearsome song. Then in fight Offa 285
smote the seaman so that he sank to earth,
and Gad's kinsman[44] there got his death-wound,
full soon Offa was slain in battle.
He lived up to the vow that earlier he made
when he told his master that the two, lord and man, 290
should both ride back to borough untouched,
ride home all whole, or in the host lie dead,
fall, slain with wounds, on the field of slaughter.
He fell near his lord, as befitted a thane.
    Then there was shock of shields. The shipmen
      pushed on, 295
spurred by battle. The spear oft went through
the flesh of the fey. Forward then went Wistan,
the son of Thurstan[45] threw himself at these men.
The bane of three in the throng he was,
ere the son of Wigelm[46] sank on the field. 300
There was stubborn fighting. They stood fast there,
the warriors, in the fray. Warring men sank,
tired down by wounds. Dead men fell to earth.

    Oswold and Eadwold all the while,
both the brothers, made bold the men, 305
called on their kindly kinsmen with words
to take what came there in time of need,
without weakening wield their weapons still.
    Then Byrhtwold spoke, he brandished his spear,
raised up his shield; he was an old henchman; 310
full boldly he taught the band of men:
"Thought shall be the harder, heart the keener,
mood shall be the more, as our might lessens.
Here lies our earl, all hewn to earth,
the good one, on the ground. He will regret it always, 315
the one who thinks to turn from this war-play now.
My life has been long. Leave I will not,
but beside my lord I will sink to earth,
I am minded to die by the man so dear."
    Likewise the child of Æthelgar cheered them all, 320
spurred them to battle. Oft a spear he let fly,
the good Godric, against the Vikings;
so he led that army, went out in front,
cut down and felled till he was fallen in combat.
He was not the Godric that got away by flight.[47] 325

---

[44] Offa.   [45] Probably Wistan.   [46] Perhaps Offa.   [47] The rest of the manuscript is missing.

Middle English

MIDDLE ENGLISH LITERATURE

"To many of us," suggests G. G. Coulton in *Medieval Panorama,* "and perhaps especially to those whose daily task is most modern and monotonous, the medieval scene brings all the charm of foreign travel." The following selections, it is hoped, will give the reader of this book a taste of that kind of pleasure.

For a century and a half after the Norman Conquest, until, passing the year 1200, we get well into the thirteenth century, there is not much in the island's literary scene to reward the traveler. But then we come, with our first selections, and still more frequently in the fourteenth century, to English writings which need no apology. The masterpieces are not numerous, but they are splendid. Next follows another century of slower progress, the fifteenth, and that is the last desert stage. It leads, past several very fine oases, into the English Renaissance of the sixteenth century, a period second to none in all the world's literature. From the later decades of the 1500's, down to the present moment, though fashions have changed and genres and geniuses have come and gone, England has never been without great writers.

THE CONQUEST AND THE LANGUAGE

When, with the papal blessing, William I and his knights crossed the Channel in 1066 and at Hastings destroyed, along with King Harold, the military power of the English, they also doomed the islanders' language to a long eclipse. The invaders were racially a kindred stock. Early in the tenth century their Scandinavian forebears, the Northmen, had conquered Normandy much as the Danes had conquered part of England. But living among and beside the French had made them into Frenchmen, and Frenchmen they remained when they settled as conquerors on English soil. At one stroke the principal language of the governing class became French instead of English, even though the practical problems of administration obliged many members of the new aristocracy to learn and use the tongue of the vanquished as a second language. William and his successors called themselves kings of England; but it was long before any of them spoke English or thought of himself as an Englishman, and the same is true of

most of the great prelates who ruled the Church and of the barons whose services the Conqueror rewarded with immense grants of land. It was long, too, before the new line of monarchs came to realize that their future lay chiefly in their island kingdom and not in the possessions they retained as dukes of Normandy and counts of Anjou or acquired even farther south through marriage with French princesses. Even as late as the twelfth century, England was practically a province of an empire principally French. Norman French was the language of the law courts as well as of the aristocracy. Latin remained the language of the Church and of learning. And the noble English tongue fell almost to the status of illiteracy. It continued, of course, to be spoken by the bulk of the population; but until the thirteenth century any man who aspired to make his mark in literature was almost certain to choose French or Latin as his medium. Within a century of the Conquest even the *Anglo-Saxon Chronicle* petered out. It was after the two races had fused, after king and baron began thinking of themselves as Englishmen, after victorious campaigns against the French had made men proud of the English name, that a literature in English sprang up again.

Meanwhile, now that the English language was without the standardizing influence of a body of writings in national circulation, its various dialects continued to go their separate ways. Among them was East Midland, spoken in London and its vicinity, but destined to prevail as standard English for the obvious reason that it was the speech of the political and commercial capital. Luckily for the modern reader, the greatest of the medieval writers was a Londoner. Since the English we speak and write has developed straight from the dialect Chaucer wrote and spoke, it is far easier to read him now than it would be if his idiom had been the dialect of Yorkshire or of Somersetshire.

In the course of the period when the English language was mainly in oral use—and mainly in use by the common people for the affairs of daily life—the Old English system of declension and conjugation was much simplified. By Chaucer's time, in the fourteenth century, most of the old inflectional endings were well on the way toward disappearing. For the modern reader, this change is a decided gain. In sound and in appearance on the printed page, Middle English is a good deal closer to the language as we now speak and write it than Old English is. For a rough guide to the Middle English language see pp. 112–14, below.

During the time when it was primarily the tongue of the uneducated, who used only the words which stood for the simpler things of life, English lost a large part of its vocabulary. When intellectuals began writing it again, the words that had dropped out were replaced by importations from French and Latin. Since many of these originally foreign words have remained in constant use, the vocabulary of Middle English, like its grammar, is much less remote from our own than is that of Old English.

THE CONQUEST AND LITERATURE

IT IS a great mistake to suppose that the effect of the Norman Conquest on English culture was beneficent. The entire medieval cycle of a thousand years produced in France no poem equal in power and nobility to *Beowulf*. Had the Conquest never occurred or had it been postponed, Old English literature would doubtless have continued to flourish and to develop. The widespread notion that an uplifting French influence arrived in the train of William's army will not bear examination. There had been constant contact between the two sides of the Channel long before 1066; on the whole the Old English civilization was superior to that of contemporary Normandy; and what the Conquest did for English literature was to knock it out for over two centuries.

It is true that when, in the thirteenth and fourteenth centuries, we come once more on English writings of literary merit, they exhibit qualities both old and new. But in view of the lapse of two hundred and fifty years, there is no reason to suppose that the new things were a result of the Norman Conquest. They were the result of the steady ripening of medieval civilization as a whole and of English civilization along with it. Elegance, wit, the light touch, genial humor—these valued qualities of civilized manners and of literary art are practically nonexistent in the Old English writings. Not from one nor from all of these qualities could a *Beowulf* be made; but when they began to be reflected in English literature of the later Middle Ages, its range and its possibilities were vastly increased. Without them we should never have had a Chaucer. They go with an advanced culture such as that of the Late Middle Ages, and they appeared as soon as men began writing in English again. Presumably they would have appeared, anyway, at about that point in England's progress toward a modern civilization.

One important Continental influence, however, requires special mention, even though the Conquest was not its cause. It is generally reckoned that the two great subjects of art are death and love. There is death aplenty in Old English poetry, but little of love. In southeastern France, in Provence, a new school of poetry had arisen in the eleventh century, destined to affect the literature of all western Europe. Provençal poetry was lyric, and its subject was romantic love. The Church might insist that, in the shadow of death's imminence, anything but concentration on the saving of one's soul was a frivolous and dangerous waste of time; but it seems to be characteristic of lovers in every age to seek in their love the best defense against Time and Fate. The Provençal troubadours who composed this new poetry were, for the most part, men of gentle birth; they mirrored and to some extent formulated the aristocracy's view of these matters. They did not reject the love of God, but they sang about the love of man for woman.

Northward spread the cult of romantic love, in life and in literature. The Italians, too, even Dante and Petrarch, were powerfully influenced by the poetry of the troubadours. In actual life the cult was as pitifully at variance with the world as religion was. Marriage in the Middle Ages, for peasant no less than for noble, was founded on economic not romantic considerations. But when, either in lyric form or woven into the tale of high adventure, the poetry of love reached England and the new motif was accepted by native writers, English literature was not only enriched for the moment: it took, as a young man does when he comes to understand love on a spiritual plane, a long stride toward maturity. This ennobling conception of the love of man and woman was, as Professor Trevelyan says in *English Social History,* the medieval poets' great gift to the western world. "Here was a new and constant source of inspiration to the life of mankind, based on the facts of nature. It was an idea unknown to the Ancients, and unknown to the early Church."

THE SOCIAL STRUCTURE

TILL 1485, when Henry VII, first of the Tudor kings, won his crown in battle at Bosworth Field, feudalism prevailed in England. This system rested on the fighting man. Only one other man really counted, the man of prayer: war and the Church offered the only careers worth mentioning. Serfs, till the fourteenth century, continued to grow the crops and herd the cattle. They were not exactly slaves, but they were bound to the soil, which means they could not leave the estates they were born on. Even after they got their freedom and some of them rose to the status of yeomen or independent peasant landholders, farm laborers remained an exploited class. In time there were rich trading towns, but it was long before commerce and manufacturing developed to a point of economic or political rivalry with the interests of knight and prelate. The same is true of the lay professions. English medicine probably went backward in the Middle Ages, not forward. Till Chaucer's time the law was largely in the hands of the clergy. So were the universities. So were the administrative offices of government, high and low.

Theoretically the king of England owned all the land. William I had parceled it out to the great barons, and in return they and their successors owed him and his successors duties of obedience and support. It was a fighting aristocracy, obligated to provide the king with troops and money. In their turn the barons distributed lands to lesser nobles, and these smaller landholders were likewise bound as vassals to their immediate overlords, and so on down the scale.

As itself the holder of a large and ever increasing share of the land, the Church had to contribute to the king's support, despite its foreign allegiance to the Pope. In their relation to the Crown the lords of the Church, the bishops, stood much as the barons did, though when the king needed soldiers they gave money in lieu of raising troops. Throughout the Middle Ages there was an incessant tug of war between the kings and the Popes for supremacy over the English Church. On the whole the kings had the upper hand, though not till the sixteenth century, when Henry VIII severed the national Church from Rome, was the issue finally settled.

The Church's own organization was a good deal like the feudal system. From parish priest up through bishop and archbishop to cardinal and Pope it ran. The parish priests and their superiors were known as the "secular" clergy, for they were bound by vows less rigorous than those of the monks and friars. The two latter groups—the monks withdrawn from the world to a cloistered existence in the monasteries, the friars sallying forth bent on charitable works or on conversion—were known as the "regular" clergy, because of their submission to a special *regula* or rule. No love was lost between the monks and friars on the one hand and the parish priests and bishops on the other. It was easy for either side to accuse the other, for by the fourteenth century, as we shall see when we come to *Piers Plowman* and to Chaucer, both were in need of reform. To make that statement is not to take sides on the question of whether the Reformation itself, the Protestant schism that occurred about the time of the Renaissance, was the best remedy. That remedial measures were needed was widely recognized as early as the fourteenth century, not only by heretics but also by loyal reformers within the Catholic Church. We must not suppose that the satirical strokes of a writer like Chaucer are evidence of irreligion or anti-Catholicism. Chaucer wrote a good deal of religious literature himself; and his own recognition of the beauty of holiness in, for example, his Parson makes him all the more critical of rascally individuals like his Friar and his Summoner.

In the hands of the Church lay scholarship and science; too often they reposed there. Looking backward for its inspiration and for its right to command obedience, the Church, as an institution, a way of life, and a means of instruction, required the acceptance of authority. Since it was incomparably the principal institution of the Middle Ages, the most powerful and, however imperfect, the most valuable to humanity, its influence dominated secular thinking, as far as there was any. Medieval medicine, for instance, rested on authority, the authority of the medical writings of ancient Greece. When a scientific experimentalist, like the great Oxford friar Roger Bacon (d. 1292), advocated new theories derived from observation, he got into trouble. Content with her own understanding of the divine purpose, and confident of the worthlessness of earthly existence, the Church inevitably tended to throw her weight against change, either in theory or in practice. Set against an eternity to be passed amid either the indescribable joys of heaven or the unspeakable torments of hell, the longest human life was obviously of inconsiderable duration, and of no real importance except as a preparation for the life to come.

For the two consequential classes of medieval society which have been described, books were written —on the one hand for the noble, the knight, the gentleman, the lady; on the other for the priest, the scholar, the "clerk." Not that the gentry were great readers. Most of them could neither read nor write; and much of the literature addressed to them was, till toward the end of the Middle Ages, sung or chanted or recited by the troubadour. In this literature pride of place belongs to the romances which constituted his stock in trade. Love and adventure were their themes.

Written by and for the clerk, that is, the man of some learning, almost always in orders[1] though not necessarily a priest, and chiefly distinguished from the rest of the population by his ability to read and write, were theological studies, historical works in the form of chronicles, and a few "philosophical" treatises bearing on other subjects, such as science.

For the rest of the population, the great mass of the people, the provision was very different. Two kinds of works were composed in great numbers by the clergy especially for the laity, both the aristocracy and the commons. The first type comprised sermons and devotional works—prayers, for instance, and other aids to piety. Of all the literary categories of the period the sermon probably was the largest; it was primarily for reading aloud to the people. Not often, however, in this or any other period, does the sermon take high rank as literature. Second, the most striking, as we shall see, of the later medieval writings addressed to the laity consisted of the working up in dramatic form, not for readers but for audiences, of the principal episodes of the Bible story, from both the Old and the New Testament. These plays were originally staged by the clergy, but afterwards by the townsfolk themselves. There was also, of and for the people, an oral literature of story and ballad, for the most part never committed to writing till long after the Middle Ages were past.

Under one or another of these three headings come all the English writings of the later Middle Ages: literature for the aristocracy (especially the romances); literature for the clerk (especially theological works); literature for the people (especially the religious drama, ballads, and sermons).

THE ELEVENTH AND TWELFTH CENTURIES

OF THE barren century and a half (1066–c.1200) which followed the Norman Conquest little more need be said. William I was not merely a bold general; he was also an able executive who speedily brought the country to heel and kept it there. Strong castles, with their massive central towers or keeps, dotted the land and insured submission. Under the Conqueror's successors, though with notable exceptions, the centralization of authority continued. As we have seen, it was an imperial rather than a national authority; but

---

[1] The orders of the Christian ministry. Major or holy orders: priest, deacon, subdeacon; minor orders: acolyte, exorcist, lector, doorkeeper.

however internationally minded their masters, in the people there remained, dimly perceived perhaps but essentially unbroken, that sense of continuity with the past which is still one of the strongest characteristics of the English. The people had not forgotten Alfred; dumbly in most cases but doggedly they resisted the Frenchifying tendencies of the Norman aristocracy. England remained English.

The tenacity of the people preserved but did not express, and nothing of permanent value in English literature came out of this period. Yet there were important events not unrelated to the future of literature. A university was in existence at Oxford by the end of the twelfth century, and another was founded at Cambridge early in the thirteenth. Indirectly the Crusades of the eleventh, twelfth, and thirteenth centuries may have stimulated literature; at any rate, they greatly expanded the horizon of western Europe.

THE THIRTEENTH CENTURY

WITH the thirteenth century we arrive at better days. A good deal of excellent lyric verse, both religious and secular, was written; and a religious drama of charm and strength showed signs of developing out of the rudimentary playlets which had originated as embellishments of the liturgy.

Meanwhile, in France, in the twelfth as well as the thirteenth century, the romance had come to be the chief artistic expression of the feudal element in medieval society. This, the most important of all the literary genres of the Middle Ages, is a fairly long adventure story, usually in verse but in later times often in prose, addressed to the aristocratic audience. Some of its themes it found in ancient myth and history, especially in narratives about Thebes, Troy, and Alexander the Great. Others it took from tales of Charlemagne and his heroic knight Roland. Others were based on old Celtic legends; among these are the romances of King Arthur and his Table Round. In the thirteenth century many romances were reworked for English hearers and eventually English readers, too, though the earlier examples have little in them but plain fighting. We have to wait till the next century for the best example, *Sir Gawain and the Green Knight,* and till the next, the fifteenth, for Malory's retelling of the Arthurian cycle.

The genre received its name of "romance" from the family of modern languages it was first written in. These were originally dialects of Latin, the language of Rome—the Romance (i.e., Romanish) languages, as we call them now. Though addressed to the aristocracy, the romances were composed in the vernacular tongues, especially in Provençal and French, and later, not only by troubadours but also by writers for readers, in all the languages of western Europe, including English.

In general, the romances glorify, in the persons of their heroes, the chivalric ideals of physical strength, skill in the use of weapons, courage, honor, and devotion to the Christian faith and to the protection and reverent admiration of womanhood. The addition of the last of these articles to the knightly code was very likely suggested by an increased fervor in the veneration of the Blessed Virgin. It has even been asserted that an improvement in the status of women in real life can be traced to the cult of Mary, but this is incapable of proof. Theoretically and in law, man was master, with the right to administer even corporal punishment to a wife in need of correction. But in practice, though the range of her activities was much more limited, the medieval wife and mother was probably little less mistress of her household than is her modern sister. To be sure, fanatics, amply fortified with quotations from the Church Fathers, poured out a steady stream of invective against the sex; and just as the mother-in-law joke still survives in vaudeville and on the radio today, satirical literary hits at women's foibles were always good for a laugh. The tone of the romances is quite different. To the troubadours the gentlewoman, at least, seemed nobler and more important in the scheme of things, partly because for all save the abnormal the furious diatribes of the ascetics were losing their force and credibility, and partly because the merit of Our Lady, the Mother of God, raised all ladies in dignity.

This attitude toward women was, like love itself, considered possible only for the aristocrat. The knights of the romances are not concerned for the honor of peasant girls or servingmaids, nor was the churl thought capable of the sentiment of love. "Courtly love" this part of the aristocratic code is called. In the introductory note to our selection from Malory's *Morte d'Arthur* we shall return to this subject, for the romances are full of it. In this respect their heroes differ radically from the heroes of the older epics. It would be difficult to imagine Beowulf as a courtly lover, but Lancelot is one.

It is often said that the hero of fiction now becomes an eminently Christian hero, that he fights in a higher cause than the blood feuds of his petty chieftain—for a great king like Charlemagne; for Holy Cross against the Saracens of Spain, Barbary, and the Levant; for truth and right against infidels, wizards, sorcerers, and evildoers in general. There is some truth in this; but, apart from his love affairs, the hero

of the romances does not really differ essentially from Beowulf. On the whole his Christianity is still of less importance as the mainspring of his conduct than his desire to live up to the chivalric code. Unquestionably the romances reflect the feudal character of medieval society, but the picture they paint is an idealized one. Yet however hopes were disappointed, the nobly born were expected to be worthy of their birth, to exemplify the virtues of the aristocratic code, some of which coincided with the Christian virtues. Others, most notably courtly love, were contrary to the Church's teaching. The strongest motivation of the good knight of romance was certainly not the imitation of Christ; it was the great principle of *noblesse oblige*.

Nor was there anything new in the romances' fondness for impossible wonders. There is nothing peculiar to the Middle Ages in a love for the marvelous, nor in the meek acceptance of authority which, rather than a free and bold inquiry after truth, was a general tendency. Thus saith the text or the book or the ancient writer revered by manifold generations of scholars. Thus saith the traveler, too, even as in the days of Herodotus; and many were the tall tales travelers told in the Middle Ages—of dog-headed men, for instance, and a single-footed human species that inconveniently had to hop its course through life, but by way of compensation could shade itself in hot weather by lying down and sticking up its huge foot umbrellalike against the sun. We always, even today, have to suspend our skepticism when we abandon ourselves to the enjoyment of any writer of fiction. Audiences in the Middle Ages, who had heard on the best authority of a myriad of actual wonders on sea and land, were not automatically inclined to incredulity when a romance brought in enchanted castles, giants, and magicians. The supernatural world and the constant possibility of its intervention in human affairs were a closer and a more vivid reality than now. We are not to suppose that our forefathers believed all they were told. But they were less predisposed to disbelief than most of us like to think we are.

It is possible that the romance came to England in the train of Eleanor of Aquitaine. In 1152 this brilliant French princess was married to Henry II (d. 1189), the Conqueror's great-grandson. In addition to England, Henry held as his birthright Normandy, Maine, Anjou, and Touraine; and he was overlord of Brittany. Eleanor brought him all the rest of western France from the Loire to the Pyrenees. Henry ruled half the country. He was really a Frenchman; his right to the English crown came through his mother, not his father. Eleanor, his wife, was a patroness of chivalry and of the troubadours. Whether or not the romance crossed the Channel because the rulers of England were in the twelfth century the masters of an Anglo-French empire, the genre flourished there all through the next two centuries.

THE FOURTEENTH CENTURY

FOR fifty years of the fourteenth century (1327–1377) England was ruled by the able Edward III, grandson of Edward I, who was the great-grandson of Henry II and Eleanor. Twice, about the middle of the century, the English army with its archers, recruited and in fact usually drafted into service from the ranks of the common people, faced the vastly larger array of the French chivalry and the horde of peasants that supported it, and at Crécy (1346) and at Poitiers (1356) emerged triumphant. The French knights toppling from their mounts under the arrows of the English longbowmen symbolized a great deal more than merely the defeat of a nation by its neighbor. Feudalism itself was falling; no longer was the knightly horseman on whom it rested supreme in battle.

In England the end of serfdom was accelerated by the Black Death, a fearful epidemic of the bubonic plague. In two years it reduced the population by about forty or fifty percent. Farm laborers were at a premium; and those who survived were eventually enabled to better their lot, though not without struggle and such violence as accompanied the Peasants' Revolt of 1381. The increasing importance of that part of the population, by far the largest part, which spoke neither French nor Latin hastened the day when the native tongue regained its supremacy. And after the campaigns in France a victorious English nationalism could hardly tolerate the continued exaltation of the language of the soundly beaten foe. Between the dates of Crécy and the still more shattering victory at Poitiers, Ralph Higden in his *Polychronicon* called for educating English children in English, not French. Before the century was over this significant reform had been effected.

From every point of view, intellectual as well as material, the fourteenth century was one of change and accomplishment. The serf was lifting himself to freedom. Parliament, in which the industrial middle class was now represented, was claiming political power. The rising merchant class was pushing England's trade with foreign countries. Towns were increasing in importance. The arts, especially architecture, flourished. A liberal party was proposing

drastic reforms of ecclesiastical abuses; and its guiding spirit, the Oxford priest and theologian John Wyclif (d. 1384), was overseeing an English translation of the Latin Bible, and questioning the truth of certain orthodox beliefs and practices.

It was in this fourteenth century, with its intellectual ferment, that medieval literature in England touched its highest point—in the works of Geoffrey Chaucer, who died in its closing year. Yet if Chaucer had never lived, the epoch would have been a distinguished one in our literary history—"ours," for at least till we are well into the seventeenth century, English literature belongs almost as much to the background of the civilization which sprang up three centuries later on the western shores of the North Atlantic as to the English background. Lyric poetry, religious and secular, continued to blossom in the fourteenth century. The drama, exclusively religious, showed amazing vitality. The dour author of *Piers Plowman* bent his rough energy to a mystical yet realistic depiction and denunciation of sin in high and low places. And the unknown artist now called the Pearl Poet gave us, among other things, a masterpiece of storytelling and chivalric idealism in *Sir Gawain and the Green Knight*.

A number of Chaucer's poems illustrate the vogue of allegory in the Middle Ages, and the framework of *Piers Plowman* is allegorical. An allegory is an extended metaphor or symbol, a story in which most of the important characters are not individuals but personified abstractions. In *Piers Plowman,* for instance, we are introduced to the Seven Deadly Sins, not as abstract concepts but as persons, acting and speaking, under the names of Pride, Avarice, Gluttony, and the rest. Though Bunyan's *Pilgrim's Progress* (1678) has long held an audience, the rise of nineteenth-century realism has made allegory less palatable to the modern reader. The Middle Ages loved it. It was a way of bringing the immaterial close and making it real and understandable.

Piers Plowman, Sir Gawain and the Green Knight in the main part of its stanza, and many other fourteenth-century poems were written in unrimed alliterative verse of much the same general character as the meter of *Beowulf*. This alliterative revival, accompanying as it did the reappearance in England of first-rate literary genius, is a remarkable example of the continuity of English literature.

THE FIFTEENTH CENTURY

AFTER the death of Chaucer, in 1400, we enter another relatively barren stretch of English literary history, though its infertility has been exaggerated by most historians. In high achievement the fifteenth century falls far below the fourteenth; but productivity did not slacken, and there are important exceptions to the generally low level of quality. The drama and the popular ballad kept on flowering, many short lyric poems were composed, and as the Middle Ages drew to their end Sir Thomas Malory recast the Arthurian romances in his *Morte d'Arthur*. During the course of the century there was a substantial advance in education. Many schools were founded; and the number of "literate laymen," a significant phrase, greatly increased. Otherwise there is not much to be said for the 1400's. No really great writer appears, unless Malory be accounted such. Chaucer had his imitators, especially in Scotland, but they produced nothing worthy of him. England was occupied with the last stages of the wicked Hundred Years War (1337–1453) in France and, after St. Joan (d.1431) and the defeat which cost the English their French possessions, with the even wickeder Wars of the Roses (1455–85).

A century and more of foreign and civil wars, of death in battle and pestilence and on the scaffold, sufficed to exterminate the old feudal nobility. In 1399 the throne had been seized by Henry IV, first of the Lancastrian kings and grandson of Edward III. Civil war was England's portion under Henry IV (d.1413), and foreign war under his son and successor, Henry V, who beat the French again at Agincourt in 1415, once more against overwhelming odds. Again the freeborn archers of England shot down the French nobles and their men-at-arms. By now the people's weapon, the longbow, trivial in cost compared with the weapons and armor of the knight, was the mainstay of the English army. As early as the reign of Edward III the government attempted, of course in vain, to abolish all other sports even in time of peace and restrict the English peasant, whether serf or freeman, to practicing with the bow. The longbow was distinctly English, and vastly superior to the crossbow of the Continental armies. The English yeoman did not "draw" the bow with his right hand, like the French; he "bent" it with his left arm, and put the whole weight of his body into

that arm. As late as 1477 the Commons declared that "the defence of this land standeth much by archers"; and in Shakespeare's time, a century later, army conservatives were still arguing for reliance on the bow and against the equipment of the British infantry with the musket. After the death of Henry V (1422) came the long and ineffectual reign of his son Henry VI (d.1471). It was stained by the bloody contest between the rival houses of York and Lancaster, both descended from Edward III. The reigns of the Yorkist kings, Edward IV (d.1483), Edward V (d.1483?), and Richard III (d.1485), were brief. Richard was dethroned in 1485 by the great Elizabeth's grandfather, Henry Tudor, heir of the Lancastrian party. By marrying the daughter of Edward IV he united the rival claims, and with his accession as Henry VII we are on the threshold of the Renaissance.

Already, since 1474, the press of William Caxton (d.1491), England's first printer, had been turning out printed books in English; and the great voyages of discovery were soon to enlarge men's minds as well as extend the range of their activities. To the world the world now turned; and while the other world, on which the Church had always insisted, was still very present to men's thinking, it no longer absorbed the best of men's thinking.

GENERAL REFERENCES

An authoritative and interesting introduction to life in the Middle Ages is G. G. Coulton's *Medieval Panorama: the English Scene from Conquest to Reformation* (1938). There is a briefer sketch in G. M. Trevelyan's *English Social History* (1942), chapters 1–3. Further selections from the literature may be found in A. S. Cook's *A Literary Middle English Reader* (1915), in Jessie L. Weston's *Chief Middle English Poets* (1914), and in W. A. Neilson and K. G. T. Webster's *Chief British Poets of the Fourteenth and Fifteenth Centuries* (1916). The standard bibliography for the period is J. E. Wells's *A Manual of the Writings in Middle English, 1050–1400* (1916, with supplements from time to time). For historical accounts, see A. R. Benham's *English Literature from Widsith to the Death of Chaucer* (1908) and W. P. Ker's *English Literature, Medieval* (1912).

Middle English Lyrics

It was in lyric poetry that English literary genius first re-asserted itself, after the long silence which followed the Norman Conquest. The thirteenth and fourteenth centuries were rich in song; in the fifteenth there is a falling off, not in quantity but in quality; with the sixteenth a new out-pouring was to begin, that of the Renaissance, when England had its finest lyric hour. To the great songs and sonnets of the sixteenth and early seventeenth centuries these medieval lyrics bear somewhat the same relation that the Italian primitives bear to the great paintings by the masters of the Italian Renaissance. They are farther away from modern styles, not so deep in coloring nor so realistic in drawing; but the best of them are exquisite in their delicacy and simple charm.

They fall into two main classes, secular and religious. Love is the chief subject of the former; with it is frequently allied the theme of spring, time of Nature's renewal and of a special joy in the earth's beauty. The religious lyrics are more numerous. Among the common types are reminders of death's tyranny, hymns, prayers, praise of the Blessed Virgin, songs of the Nativity, poems about the Crucifixion, and injunctions to righteous living.

Few of the authors are known. Their lyrics survive in commonplace-books copied by other hands, mostly those of monks and friars. Latin and French verses as well as English appear in these miscellanies, along with memorabilia of various sorts. Some of these manuscripts were compiled by individuals; others were communal enterprises of religious establishments. They are principally but not exclusively in the dialects of the south and the southwest (hence the frequency of "ich" for "I"); yet no doubt some of the poems which have come down to us in those dialectal forms were originally composed in other regions. The musical notation for many of the thirteenth-century songs has also been preserved. The lyric of the fourteenth century was more independently literary, but the rise of the carol in the fifteenth once again brought the lyric closer to music.

For the texts of over four hundred of these poems see Carleton Brown's *English Lyrics of the XIIIth Century* (1932), *Religious Lyrics of the XIVth Century* (1924), and *Religious Lyrics of the XVth Century* (1939). Other useful collections are R. L. Greene's *The Early English Carols* (1935) and E. K. Chambers and F. Sidgwick's *Early English Lyrics: Amorous, Divine, Moral & Trivial* (1921).

Attempts to render the Middle English lyric into modern English have failed; either the translator sacrifices fidelity, or in sticking to the letter he loses the spirit. There is nothing for it but to present these selections in the original, with an assurance that they are worth the effort required to read them. The first step is to use the footnotes and associate the right meaning with each of the words, many of which, once pronounced, will not seem so strange as they look. The second step is to look on pages 112–14 at the rules for pronouncing Middle English and then to read the poem aloud, slowly, marking if necessary those of the final e's which have syllabic value. Third and last, read aloud at a normal pace for the lyrical effect, that is, for sound as well as sense. If you will take this trouble, you may be surprised to find how much loveliness is still fresh in these little poems, apparently so fragile, of six and seven hundred years ago.

SUMER IS ICUMEN IN

This merry song, still a favorite for round singing, is preserved, words and music, in a commonplace-book (now in the British Museum) into which monks of Reading Abbey copied various things. The song was probably composed rather early in the thirteenth century. The poet is unknown.

> Sumer is icumen[1] in;
>   Lhude[2] sing cuccu!
> Groweth sed and bloweth[3] med[4]
>   And springth the wude nu.[5]
>   Sing cuccu!
>
> Awe[6] bleteth after lomb,
>   Lhouth[7] after calve cu,
> Bulluc sterteth,[8] bucke verteth;[9]
>   Murie[10] sing cuccu!
>   Cuccu! cuccu!
>   Wel singes thu, cuccu.
>   Ne swik thu naver nu![11]

LENTEN YS COME WITH LOVE

This lyric, too, is a spring song; but for this poet the coming of spring is inseparable from the coming of love. What to me is the rapture of all Nature, if the one I love will not have me? The poem is preserved in another commonplace-book in the British Museum, one of the most important collections of Middle English lyrics, which may have been compiled at Leominster Priory in Herefordshire. This manuscript also includes "Alysoun," "With longying y am lad," and "Wynter wakeneth al my care." The authors'

---

[1] Come.   [2] Loudly.   [3] Blooms.
[4] Mead, meadow.   [5] Springs up the wood now.
[6] Ewe.   [7] Lows.   [8] Leaps.   [9] Breaks wind.
[10] Merrily.   [11] Cease not thou, never, now.

names are not given. They were probably thirteenth-century poets, though at least part of the manuscript was written in the early fourteenth century.

Lenten[1] ys come with love to toune,
With blosmen and with briddes roune,[2]
   That al this blisse bryngeth;
Dayes-eyes[3] in this[4] dales,
Notes suete[5] of nyhtegales—   5
   Uch foul[6] song singeth.
The threstelcoc him threteth oo;[7]
Away is huere wynter woo,
   When woderove[8] springeth.
This foules singeth ferly fele[9]   10
And wrytleth on huere wunne wele,[10]
   That al the wode ryngeth.

The rose rayleth hire rode;[11]
The leves on the lyhte[12] wode
   Waxen al with wille.[13]   15
The mone mandeth hire bleo;
The lilie is lossom to seo,
   The fenyl and the fille;
Wowes[14] this wilde drakes,
Miles murgeth huere makes,[15]   20
   Ase strem that striketh stille;
Mody meneth, so doh mo:
Ichot ycham on of tho,
   For love that likes ille.

The mone mandeth[16] hire lyht,   25
So doth the semly[17] sonne bryht,
   When briddes singeth breme;[18]
Deawes donketh the dounes;[19]
Deores with huere derne rounes,
   Domes forte deme;   30
Wormes woweth under cloude;[20]
Wymmen waxeth wounder proude,
   So wel hit[21] wol them seme.[22]

Yef me shal wonte wille of on,[23]
This wunne weole y wole forgon   35
   And wyht in wode be fleme.

ALYSOUN

Alice's admirer also begins on the thrilling note of spring. He devotes his poem, however, to the depiction of a lover's joy, praise, fear, and woe, the four themes on which countless Elizabethan as well as medieval lyrics are built.

Bytuene Mersh and Averil,
   When spray beginneth to springe,
The lutel foul[1] hath hire wyl
   On hyre lud[2] to synge.
Ich libbe[3] in lovelonginge   5
For semlokest[4] of alle thynge;
He[5] may me blisse bringe:
Icham[6] in hire baundoun.[7]
   An hendy hap ichabbe yhent—[8]
   Ichot[9] from hevene it is me sent: 10
   From alle wymmen mi love is lent[10]
And lyht[11] on Alysoun.

On heu hire her is fayr ynoh,[12]
   Hire browe broune, hire eye blake;
With lossum chere he on me loh;[13]   15
   With middel smal and wel ymake.[14]
Bote he me wolle[15] to hire take
Forte buen hire owen make,[16]
Longe to lyven ichulle[17] forsake
And feye[18] fallen adoun.   20
   An hendy hap &c.

Nihtes when y wende[19] and wake[20]—
   For-thi myn wonges waxeth won[21]—
Levedi,[22] al for thine sake,
   Longinge is ylent[23] me on.   25
In world nis non so wyter mon[24]
That al hire bounte[25] telle con;
Hire swyre[26] is whittore then the swon,

---

[1] Spring.   [2] With blossoms and with birds' song.
[3] Daisies.   [4] These.   [5] Sweet.   [6] Each bird.
[7] Lines 7–8: The male thrush scolds away constantly; /gone is their winter woe.   [8] Woodruff (an herb).
[9] Wondrous much.
[10] And warble of their delightful state of well-being.
[11] Arrays (dons) her complexion.   [12] Light, bright.
[13] Lines 15–18: All grow with a will./The moon shows her face;/The lily is lovesome to see,/The fennel and (probably) the chervil (another herb).   [14] Woo.
[15] Lines 20–24: Animals make merry their mates,/Like (a) stream that flows ever;/(The) proud (man) complains, as do others:/I know I am one of those,/On account of love that pleases ill.
[16] Sends forth.   [17] Goodly.   [18] Clearly.
[19] Lines 28–30: Dews moisten the hills;/Deer (are engaged) in their private talk,/Opinions to give.
[20] Clod.   [21] It, i. e., pride.   [22] Beseem, become.

---

[23] Lines 34–36: If to me shall be lacking (the) good will of a certain one,/ This delightful weal (i. e., the joys of the world in spring) I will forgo/And be a banished wight in the wood.

[1] Little bird.   [2] In her language.   [3] I live.
[4] Seemliest, fairest.   [5] She.   [6] I am.   [7] Power.
[8] A goodly fortune I have got.   [9] I wot, I know.
[10] Gone.   [11] Alighted.
[12] In hue her hair is fair enough.
[13] With lovesome face she on me laughed, i.e., smiled.
[14] Made, shaped.   [15] Unless she me will.
[16] For to be her own mate.   [17] I shall.   [18] Fated to die.
[19] (Twist and) turn.   [20] Stay awake.
[21] Therefore my cheeks grow pale.   [22] Lady.   [23] Come.
[24] Is none so wise (a) man.   [25] Goodness.   [26] Neck.

And feyrest may[27] in toune.
  An hendi &c.   30

Icham for wowyng al forwake,[28]
  Wery so water in wore;
Lest eny reve me my make
  Ychabbe y-yyrned yore.
Betere is tholien whyle sore   35
  Then mournen evermore.
Geynest under gore,[29]
  Herkne to my roun.[30]
    An hendi &c.

WITH LONGYNG Y AM LAD

An almost blunt expression of physical longing distinguishes this poem; here is nothing of love's joy or tenderness or playfulness, and little even of praise. The lyric's effectiveness springs from the directness and intensity with which the poet concentrates on a single idea, that of the final passionate line, to which everything builds up.

With longyng y am lad,[1]
On molde[2] y waxe mad,
  A maide marreth me;
Y grede,[3] y grone unglad,
For selden y am sad[4]   5
  That semly forte se.
    Levedi, thou rewe me!
To routhe thou havest me rad;
Be bote of that y bad!
  My lyf is long[5] on the.   10

Levedy of alle londe,
Les[6] me out of bonde!
  Broht icham[7] in wo.
Have resting on honde,[8]
And sent[9] thou me thi sonde[10]   15

Sone,[11] er thou me slo![12]
My reste is with the ro.[13]
Thah men to me han onde,[14]
To love nuly noht wonde
  Ne lete for non of tho.   20

Levedi, with al my miht
My love is on the liht,[15]
  To menske[16] when y may.
Thou rew and red[17] me ryht!
To dethe thou havest me diht;[18]   25
  Y deye longe er my day.
    Thou leve upon mi lay![19]
Treuthe ichave the plyht,
To don that ich have hyht
  Whil mi lif leste[20] may.   30

Lylie-whyt hue[21] is,
Hire rode so rose on rys,[22]
  That reveth[23] me mi rest.
Wymmon war[24] and wys,
Of prude hue bereth the pris,[25]   35
  Burde[26] on[27] of the best.
    This wommon woneth[28] by west,
Brihtest under bys.[29]
Hevene y tolde[30] al his
  That o[31] nyht were hire gest.   40

WYNTER WAKENETH AL MY CARE

This poet loves the green of wood and field—so much that when the world's beauty withers and dies he is deeply moved. In winter's coming he sees a symbol of our common doom; it shocks him, and he ends his poem with an anguished cry for divine help.

Wynter wakeneth al my care,
  Nou this[1] leves waxeth bare;
Ofte y sike[2] and mourne sare[3]
  When hit cometh in my thoht
  Of this worldes joie hou hit geth[4] al to noht.   5

---

27 Maid.
28 Lines 31–36: I am, on account of wooing, all worn out by lying awake,/Weary as water (which incessantly beats) on (the) strand;/Lest anyone take away from me my sweetheart/(Whom) I have desired for long./Better it is to suffer (this love-sickness) awhile sorely/Than to mourn (her loss, through having given up the suit) evermore.
29 (Thou who art) comeliest under clothes, i. e., prettiest of those who wear them.   30 Words.

1 Led.   2 Earth.   3 Cry.
4 Lines 5–9: For seldom am I satisfied/That lovely (one) for to see./Lady, pity thou me!/To sorrow thou hast subjected me;/Be (the) remedy of what I proclaimed (i. e., my love-sickness)!
5 Dependent.   6 Loose.   7 Brought I am.
8 Hand; i. e., take measures for my rest.   9 Send.
10 Sending, message.

11 Soon.   12 Slay.
13 The (hunted) deer; i. e., I have no rest.
14 Lines 18–20: Though men to me have enmity,/From loving will I not refrain/Nor cease for any of those.
15 On thee lighted.   16 Honor.   17 Pity and counsel.
18 Sentenced.
19 Lines 27–29: Believe thou in my faith!/Troth I have thee plighted,/To do what I have promised.   20 Last.
21 She.   22 Her complexion as rose on spray.   23 Robs.
24 (A) woman prudent.   25 For pride she takes the prize.
26 Lady.   27 One.   28 Dwells.
29 Byssus (a fine fabric); cf. note 29 on the preceding poem.
30 Would count, would consider.   31 One.

1 Now these.   2 I sigh.   3 Sore, grievously.
4 Goes.

Nou hit is, and nou hit nys[5]—
  Also hit ner nere ywys;[6]
That moni mon seith soth hit ys:
  Al goth bote godes wille;
  Alle we shule deye thah us like ylle.   10

Al that gren me graueth grene;[7]
  Nou hit faleweth al by-dene.
Jhesu, help that hit be sene,[8]
  Ant shild us from helle!
  For y not whider y shal ne hou longe her duelle.[9]   15

I SYNG OF A MYDEN

Though both are examples of the religious lyric, the pain
of the preceding poem is entirely absent from this one,
perhaps the most exquisite of all the efforts of the medieval
writers to sing the Virgin's praise. A fifteenth-century
manuscript in the British Museum contains seventy-four
songs and carols, probably composed in the fourteenth and
fifteenth centuries. Among them are *I syng of a myden* and
Adam lay i-bowndyn.

I syng of a myden[1]
  That is makeles;[2]
Kyng of alle kynges
  To[3] here sone che ches.[4]

He cam also[5] stylle   5
  There[6] his moder was
As dew in Aprylle,
  That fallyt[7] on the gras.

He cam also stylle
  To his moderes bowr   10
As dew in Aprille,
  That fallyt on the flour.

He cam also stylle
  There his moder lay
As dew in Aprille,   15
  That fallyt on the spray.

Moder and mayden
  Was never non but che;
Wel may swych[8] a lady
  Godes moder be.   20

ADAM LAY I-BOWNDYN

Humor mingles with devotion in this charming tribute to
the Virgin. The Paradox of the Fortunate Fall first appeared
in Christian writings many centuries earlier. Theologians
held that, while Adam's sin was deplorable and involved
all his descendants, it was nevertheless a cause for rejoicing,
since it led to the Incarnation and Redemption. Had it not
been for guilty old Adam, a Saviour would not have been
needed, nor, adds the poet, would Our Lady have been
exalted.

Adam lay i-bowndyn,[1] bowndyn in a bond;
Fowre thowsand wynter[2] thowt he not to long;[3]
And al was for an appil, an appil that he tok,
As clerkis fyndyn wretyn in here book.[4]

Ne hadde[5] the appil take ben, the appil taken ben,   5
Ne hadde never Our Lady a ben[6] hevene qwen.
Blyssid be the tyme that appil take was!
Ther-fore we mown syngyn,[7] "Deo gracias!"[8]

TIMOR MORTIS

Death is inescapable; on that dread fact medieval Christianity was insistent, in order to ask, "What will *your* lot be
after death?" Everything reminds the poet of it, from bird
on bough to Christ on the Cross. This lyric is preserved in
the commonplace-book of one Richard Hill, who was employed by Alderman (afterwards Mayor) John Wyngar, a
London grocer; Hill compiled it throughout the first third
of the sixteenth century. "Timor Mortis" was probably
composed in the fifteenth; the author is unknown. Hill's
manuscript is in the library of Balliol College, Oxford.

In what state that ever I be,
  Timor mortis conturbat me.[1]

As I me walked in on[2] mornyng,
  I hard a birde both wepe and synge;
  This was the tenor of her talkynge: 5
  Timor mortis conturbat me.

---

[5] Is not.
[6] Lines 7–10: As if it had never existed, indeed;/So that many (a) man says it is true (as follows):/All goes except God's will;/We shall all die though it please us ill.
[7] Lines 11–12: All that green grows green for me;/Now it turns brown all at once.
[8] I. e., that the truth of the foregoing observations may be gen-erally recognized.   [9] I know not whither I shall (go) nor how long (I shall) dwell there.

[1] Maiden.   [2] Matchless.   [3] I.e., for.   [4] She chose.
[5] All so, as.   [6] Where.   [7] Falls.

[8] Such.

[1] Bound.
[2] The time from Adam's fall to his delivery from hell by Jesus after the Crucifixion. See the Apocryphal gospel of Nicodemus.
[3] Thought he not too long; i.e., since at the end of this term he went to heaven.   [4] As scholars find written in their book.
[5] Had not.   [6] Have been.   [7] May sing.
[8] *Deo gratias,* thanks to God.

[1] The fear of death perturbs me.   [2] One.

I asked this birde what he ment;
He said, "I am a musket[3] gent;[4]
For dred of deth I am nygh shent;[5]
Timor mortis conturbat me.   10

Jhesu Cryst, whan he shuld dye,
To his fader lowd gan he crye:

"Fader," he said, "in trynyte,
Timor mortis conturbat me."

Whan I shall dye know I no day;   15
Therfore this songe synge I may,
In what place or contrey can I not say:
Timor mortis conturbat me.

Piers Plowman

EVEN the briefest survey of medieval British literature would be unthinkable without some representation of the huge, sprawling, inartistic, savage diatribe somewhat inaccurately known as *The Vision of William concerning Piers the Plowman.* Who "William" was is quite uncertain. Early but not contemporary notes in some of the manuscripts give his surname as Langland; and it was long supposed that he came to London from the west of England, where his poem opens on the Malvern Hills. He certainly lived in the second half of the fourteenth century, but some scholars have rejected the name Langland and even doubted whether the poem was written by a single author.

On that last point there is sharp divergence of opinion. The question is complicated by the existence of three versions, now called the A, B, and C texts. Possible references to contemporary events have been used in attempts to establish their approximate dates. Some think A was composed about 1362; it consists of a prologue and twelve "passus" or cantos. Perhaps the date of B falls about halfway between A and C, though the process of rewriting and enlargement may have gone on for many years. In B, in addition to much revision, there are ten new passus; this version runs to over 7000 lines, nearly three times the length of A. The C text, which some date about 1395, is a thoroughgoing revision of B; its length is approximately the same. That the revisions were not made by the original author is the opinion of numerous scholars; others believe that all three versions came from a single pen. In the light of present knowledge a positive conclusion is impossible.

In view of this uncertainty, the word portraits of the author by certain critics are, to say the least, superfluous. Perhaps the author was, as alleged, a somewhat uncouth but nobly austere zealot whose heart bled for erring humanity. But the great clown is sometimes a dreadfully sober person off stage, and the most rampant of reformers may be a charming fellow in private life. We must therefore address ourselves to the work, not the workman.

It is not a work of poetic genius. It has hardly any poetry

at all; the music of the prologue's opening lines is not characteristic, and there is far more of blunt statement than of imaginative exploration or reconstruction of life. Its chief merit is its force, but that is a matter more of vigor than of power. In style, as in point of view, the contrast with Chaucer is inevitable and striking. Will, as he calls himself, has little grace and no urbanity; you would not choose Will—that is, the personage set forth in the poem— to go fishing with. He is intolerant and perennially scandalized. He regards the world as a pretty vile place.

To be sure, we can easily understand the horror with which he contemplates worldly churchmen and the spiritual shepherd who has betrayed his flock. The priesthood was in a bad way in his time. Comparatively few of its members were university graduates; many were completely ignorant of Latin, though the ritual was in that language. There are cases on record of pastors who knew so little of the Scriptures that they were unable to locate the Lord's Prayer or name its author. A substantial number of churches were served by men who were not priests at all. Some had taken neither major orders (priest, deacon, subdeacon) nor minor (acolyte, exorcist, reader, doorkeeper), and thus had no title to the status even of "clerk." Ten percent of the parishioners' produce or income, including crops and animals, was supposed to go to the Church as tithes; but the rectors who received them were too often absentees and sometimes not even individuals but monastic establishments. In such cases pastoral duties were performed by a vicar (that is, a substitute), who, though he was given life tenure, received but a fraction of what the parish paid in, or by a curate, a hireling who subsisted on a miserable salary from the recipient of the tithes. By the sixteenth century about one third of the English rectories had become vicarages, which meant that the bulk of the ecclesiastical tax was being spent outside the parish. Another vice was "pluralism." Since the benefice or ecclesiastical "living" was at the disposal, not of the parishioners, but of monasteries, bishops, or lay patrons, several livings were often assigned to a single favored individual. Against such conditions the author of *Piers*

---

[3] Sparrow hawk.   [4] Noble.   [5] Ruined, lost.

Plowman bitterly, and justly, complains. But when all is said and done, the impression William creates is certainly that of an haranguing fanatic.

Why, then, read him? For one thing, the fanatical, obsessed, or haunted are often more interesting than the normal. The sheer intensity of Will's fulminations keeps them from dullness. In the second place, if he owns few or none of the more attractive gifts of a poet, he does have a gift for rough but striking portraiture. For example, the lines which introduce the figure of Avarice are etched with acid; they bite, and they do what their author meant them to: they make you *see*. Third, the poem is worth reading as a medieval panorama, a mural of the fourteenth-century scene, splashed on in a big way, not by an amused and civilized and very wise master like Chaucer, but by a deeply moved religious enthusiast. Yet with all his crudeness and violence in depicting it, the writer does not hate humanity, any more than Chaucer does. He writes in an agony of apprehension for sinful men; and the second of our selections closes with a fervent proclamation of mercy and hope, which, if completely lacking in charm, is not wholly without tenderness. Nor (fourth)—and here he differs from many reformers—is the author of *Piers Plowman* entirely without humor. He can be tickled by the foibles of our kind; and to their correction, as in Envy's account of his service in the nunnery, he sometimes brings the flickering lash of ridicule instead of the heavy knout of denunciation. Fifth, to read a poem as close as this is to the dirt and sweat of everyday existence is to widen our appreciation of certain unchanging aspects of human nature, some agreeable, others less so. In the fourteenth century, too, as Avarice explains in his confession, they put the poorer berries below the top of the box and sold at two prices out of the same barrel. It is not a pleasant but it is an interesting reflection that one touch of that side of human nature is still able to make us doubly kin with our forefathers of six hundred years ago. Finally, the note of social protest gives the poem a special interest for us.

Piers Plowman was written as the peasant began raising himself out of serfdom. About the middle of the fourteenth century the bubonic plague or "Black Death" came close to cutting the population of England in half. Despite efforts by the governing classes to freeze labor's status by regulatory legislation, the consequent widespread shortage of workers encouraged owners of large estates to lease parcels to tenant farmers. Serfdom gradually died out, as free property-holders became much more numerous. This fundamental change in the structure of society was not accomplished without violence. One of the great causes of unrest was heavy taxation, and in 1381 attempts to enforce a recently invented form of class legislation, the poll tax, precipitated the Peasants' Revolt. This was the first great uprising of the exploited classes. Throughout the south-

eastern half of England—that is, the more thickly settled, prosperous, and progressive half—the nobility, landed gentry, and monastic proprietors were attacked. There were spontaneous protest marches on the capital; and eventually a people's champion, Wat Tyler, assumed leadership of the rioters. For several days a mob held London; but the rebellion soon collapsed, partly through the adroitness and courage of the boy king, Richard II, who in 1377 had succeeded to the throne occupied for half a century by his grandfather, Edward III.

On its social side *Piers Plowman,* at least in its earliest version, is among the rumblings of discontent which preceded the storm of 1381. Among the causes of that rebellion was one which has several points of contact with the poem, the contemporary religious revival under the great Oxford priest and scholar John Wyclif. The poem's attacks on ecclesiastical abuses are directly in line with, if not actually a consequence of, Wyclif's advocacy of reform. Since many churchmen were neglecting their spiritual duties, an unauthorized itinerant clergy had sprung up in competition with the parish priests and the friars. These Lollards, as they were called, were sympathizers with Wyclif; and in spite of brutal persecution they assumed the task of carrying his ideas to the masses. They preached in English, and they circulated English versions of the Scriptures. It was likewise for the common people that *Piers Plowman* was written, in their own idiom, possibly by a Lollard, certainly by someone who approved of Wyclif's views. In its lack of finesse, its coarseness, and its employment of homely illustration, the poem is evidently addressed to plain folk by a moralist who is one of them or wishes them to think he is one of them.

Piers Plowman belongs to the alliterative revival of the fourteenth century, when the versification of the Old English poets once more came into vogue. As in *Beowulf,* the unit is the four-stressed line, with a pause near the middle of each line, and alliteration of several stressed syllables. But the pattern is much less rigidly observed. Numerous unstressed syllables often make a line indistinguishable from prose; and while it is normally the first two and the third of the stressed syllables that agree, many lines omit the alliteration of one of these, others alliterate the fourth stress instead of the third, some entirely lack alliteration, and others alliterate all four of the stressed syllables. There are even some lines in which a different alliteration is used for each of the half lines. The following line-for-line rendering, though intended to be more faithful to the original than previous verse translations, does not attempt to follow it in every syllabic or alliterative detail. But the line's "feminine" ending, that is, the regular appearance of an unstressed syllable at the close, has been strictly held to, since it is among the most marked features of the original verse.

Except in punctuation and capitalization, the opening lines of the prologue run as follows in the Middle English. Pronounce þ as *th* and ʒ like *ch* in German *ich* or *ach*. For the vowels, see the headnote to Chaucer (pp. 112 f., below). Note that prefixes are often ignored in the alliteration: *love* and *belongeth* agree perfectly. *H* often appears to alliterate with a vowel; but in virtually all such cases the *h* is actually silent, and the alliteration results from the principle that any vowel alliterates with any other. *F* and *v* alliterate.

> In a somer seson   whan soft was the sonne,
> I shope me in shroudes   as I a shepe were;
> In habite as an heremite   unholy of workes,
> Went wyde in þis world   wondres to here.
> Ac on a May mornynge   on Malverne hulles,
> Me byfel a ferly,   of fairy me thouʒte.
> I was wery forwandred   and went me to reste
> Under a brode banke   bi a bornes side;
> And as I lay and lened   and loked in þe wateres,
> I slombred in a slepyng,   it sweyed so merye.

The poem belongs to the genre of vision literature; Will has a series of dreams, in the course of which various subjects are presented to his mind. The theme is frankly ethical and the treatment allegorical. The necessity of moral conduct as a preparation for salvation is insisted on, both in exhortations by characters who personify various virtues and aids to right living, and also in racy scenes from the life of the people, illustrative of the gulf that separates precept from practice, the ideal from the real.

Piers Plowman has survived in many manuscripts; it must have been very popular. The standard text was edited by W. W. Skeat (Oxford, 1886); partial translations have been made by H. W. Wells (1935) and Nevill Coghill (1949). For a more extensive, more confident, and more eulogistic analysis than the one above, see "Piers Plowman: A Comparative Study" in R. W. Chambers's *Man's Unconquerable Mind* (1939). The following selections, translated by the present editor, give the Prologue from the A text (with some additional lines from Passus I of B), and the description of the seven deadly sins from Passus VII and VIII of the C text.

THE VISION OF WILLIAM CONCERNING PIERS THE PLOWMAN

[PROLOGUE. THE FIELD FULL OF FOLK]

In a summer season, when soft was the sunshine,
In shrouds[1] did I shape me,[2] like as a poor shepherd;
In habit[3] as an hermit, unholy[4] of living,
Went wide in this world, wonders to hear of.
But on a May morning, on a Malvern hillside,[5]   5
A marvel I met with, of magical semblance.
I was weary with wandering, and went for to rest me
Under a broad bankside, by a brooklet's margin;
And as I lay and leaned there, and looked into the waters,
I slumbered in a sleeping, it sounded so merry.   10

Thereon fell I to dreaming a dream full of marvels:
That I was in a wilderness—where, never wist[6] I.
Then as I held my eyes eastward, on high where the
     sun was,
I saw a keep[7] on a crest, cunningly builded.
A deep dale was below, a dungeon[8] within it,   15
With deep ditches and dark and dreadful of appearance.

A fair field full of folk[9] I found there between them,
Of every manner of men, the mean[10] and the wealthy,
Working and wandering, as the way of the world is.

Some were putting themselves to plow—played they
     full seldom: 20
In setting[11] and in sowing sweat they full harshly,
And won what the wasteful with gluttony squander.

And some applied themselves to pride, appareling
     themselves congruently;
In the cut of their clothing came they decked strangely.[12]

To prayers and to penitence put themselves many;   25
All for love of our Lord they lived very strictly,
In hope of their having heaven's kingdom's gladness—
Like hermits and anchorites in their cells fast harbored,
Unwishful of wandering their way round the country
For a sumptuous sustenance, their senses to coddle.   30

And others' bent was for business: their success was the
     better,
As it seemeth to our sight that such men do prosper.

And others mirths for to make as minstrels are gifted

---

[1] Garments.   [2] Clothe myself.
[3] Garb. Evidently fourteenth-century hermits dressed much like shepherds.
[4] A hermit was supposed to occupy himself with his devotions and not go gadding.
[5] The Malvern Hills, in Worcestershire, on the border of Herefordshire.   [6] Knew.
[7] Tower, castle. Later in the poem it is identified as the Abode of Truth.   [8] Subsequently identified as the Castle of Care.

[9] I.e., the world, set between heaven and hell.   [10] Lowly.
[11] Planting.   [12] I.e., extravagantly clad.

And gather gold with their glee; guiltless I hold them.[13]
But jesters and jabberers, Judas's children,   35
Feign for themselves fantasies and make themselves
    foolish,
Yet have their wits at their will,[14] and could work if
    they cared to.
What Paul preacheth of them[15] I will not herewith
    publish—
Qui turpiloquium loquitur[16] is Lucifer's servant.

Bidders[17] and beggars fast about hastened   40
With their bellies and their budgets[18] of bread full to
    bursting,
Falsified for their food there, fought at the alehouse;
In gluttony, God knoweth, go they to bedward,
And rise up with ribaldry, those rascally robbers.
Sleep and sorest sloth pursue them for ever.   45

Pilgrims and palmers[19] pledged themselves together
To seek out Saint James[20] and in Rome, too, the saints
    there.
They went forth on their way, with many wise
    inventions,
And had leave for to lie all their life after.
I saw some who said that saints they had sought for: 50
To every tale that they told was their tongue well
    tempered for lying
More than to say sooth,[21] as it seemed by their speeches.

Hermits in an heap, with staves all hook-shaped,
Went off to Walsingham,[22] and their wenches with them.
Big lubbers and lengthy, that loath were to labor,   55
Clothed themselves in copes,[23] for to be clearly
    distinguished,
In garments like hermits', so they'd have things most easy.

I found there the friars, all the four orders,[24]
Preaching to the people themselves for to profit,

Straining true Scripture as their aims suited,   60
For personal profit explaining it as they wished to.
Many of these master-friars may wear what they fancy,
For their money and merchandise march on together;[25]
For since Charity hath been chapman[26] and chief to
    shrive great ones,[27]
Frequent marvels we've marked within years far from
    many!   65
Unless Holy Church and they hold better together,
The worst evil on earth will be amplified greatly.

There was preaching a pardoner as though he a priest
    were.
He brought forth a bull,[28] with the seals of a bishop,
And said he himself could absolve all and sundry   70
Of falsehood in fasting, of vows that were broken.
Laymen believed him and liked what he told them,
And came up there kneeling and kissing his parchments.
He banged away with his brevet;[29] their eyes he made
    bleary,
And bagged with his bull both rings and fine brooches. 75
Thus their gold did they give, for the maintenance of
    gluttons,
Believing such lubbers as cling to their lechery.
If the bishop were blessed, of both his ears worthy,[30]
His seal he'd not send to deceive thus the people.
But 't is naught against the bishop that the knave
    preacheth,[31]   80
For the parish priest and the pardoner part[32] all the silver,
Which the poor of the parish but for them might be
    granted.

Parsons and parish priests complained to the bishop
That their parishes were poor since the time of the
    pestilence,[33]
Asking license and leave to dwell up at London   85
And sing there for simony,[34] for sweet is the silver.

---

[13] An unexpected concession to honest artists.
[14] Under their control.
[15] 2 Thessalonians 3:10: "We commanded you that if any would
not work, neither should he eat."
[16] He who says something base.   [17] Mendicants.
[18] Bags, sacks.
[19] A palm branch was the sign of a pilgrim who had visited the
Holy Land. Many who called themselves palmers were impostors.
[20] At the famous shrine of Santiago de Compostela in northwestern Spain.   [21] Truth.
[22] The famous shrine of the Virgin, in Norfolk. The reformers
were opposed to the commercialization, hypocrisy, and licen-
tiousness of pilgrimages. In the fourteenth century a hermit did
not necessarily live in retirement; but see note 4, above.
[23] Ecclesiastical capes.
[24] Dominicans (black or preaching friars), Franciscans (Minorites
or gray friars), Carmelites (white friars), and Augustinians. The
friars were a thorn in the flesh of the parish clergy.

[25] I.e., they multiply.   [26] Merchant.
[27] Great folk now have as confessor some friar (whose proper concern is works of charity, but who is likely to be on the make)
instead of an honest parish priest.
[28] His license for selling indulgences.   [29] License.
[30] I.e., fit to keep his ears, instead of having them cropped as a
punishment.
[31] I.e., though he was licensed *as a pardoner* by the bishop, the latter
is not to blame because the pardoner *preaches,* nor does the
bishop get a share in the proceeds. In fact, the large collections
taken up by the pardoner reduce the amount of tithes paid in
by the parish, part of which goes to the bishop.   [32] Divide.
[33] One of the three fourteenth-century epidemics of the Black
Death. The parishes were "poor" because half the parishioners
had died and the tithes were correspondingly reduced.
[34] I.e., money. Simony is the buying or selling of ecclesiastical
office. There was much complaint against the absentee priest,
who found it profitable to secure a place singing masses for the
repose of the soul of someone who had left money for that purpose. His income from his parish continued; he either neglected
his duties there completely or hired a low-paid substitute.

Bishops and bachelors,[35] both masters and doctors,[36]
That have cure[37] under Christ, and crowning[38] in token
And sign that they should be shriving their parishioners,
Preaching and praying for them, the poor folk feeding, 90
Are living in London, in Lent[39] and all seasons.
Some are serving the King and his silver counting,
In Checker[40] and in Chancery,[41] challenging his income,[42]
His waifs and his strays[43] from the wards and the
    ward-moots.[44]
And some are serving as servants of lords and of ladies 95
And instead of stewards sit and give judgment.[45]
Their masses and matins[46] and many of their hours
Are void of devotion. I fear at the Judgment
Lest Christ in his council accurse them, full many.
I was positive that the power that Peter had in
    keeping,   100
To bind and to unbind,[47] as the Book doth tell us,
He left with love, as our Lord commanded,
In charge of four virtues, the best of all virtues,[48]
That "cardinal" are called and "closing of portals"[49]
Where Christ's in his kingdom, to close and to shut it,
And also to open it, and to heaven's bliss give access. 106
As for the cardinals at the court,[50] who have caught up
    that title,
And power postulate as theirs a pope to make choice of
To have that power that was Peter's, impugn it I will not;
For in love and learning also the election belongs
    there—   110
Wherefore I can, and cannot, of court things speak
    further.[51]

Also hovered there an hundred, in silk finely hooded,
Sergeants[52] as it seemed, who served at the bar there.
For pennies[53] and pounds they were pleading their cases,
For love of our Lord their lips never unloosing.   115

Thou mightst easier measure the mist on Malvern hilltops
Than get one mumble from their mouths unless money
    were shown them.

Barons there and burgesses[54] and bondmen, too,
I saw in this assembly, as ye shall hear later.
Bakers and brewers and butchers a many,   120
Woolen websters[55] and weavers of linen,
Tailors and tinkers and tollers[56] in markets,
Masons and miners and many other craftsmen,
Of every living kind of laborers leaped forth some there,
As ditchers and delvers, that do their work badly   125
And drive forth[57] the long day with *Dieu vous save*,[58]
    Dame Emma!
Cooks and their kitchen help cried, "Hot pies, hot ones!
Good pigs and geese! Go dine! go now!"
Taverners there to them told the same story:
"White wine of Osey[59] and red wine of Gascony,[60]   130
Of the Rhine and of Rochelle[61] for the roast's digestion!"
All this saw I sleeping and seven times more, too.

[*The Prologue concluded, a lovely lady named Holy Church tells
the poet that the two castles are heaven and hell, and exhorts him
to virtue. The dream continues with the proposed marriage of
False to the gorgeously appareled maiden Meed. Her name is
ambiguous, meaning Reward or Bribery; she symbolizes the
power of money in human affairs, including government. Theology objects, and they all go to London to consult the lawyers.
The king breaks off the match and commands the knight Conscience to wed Lady Meed. He refuses, and opposing views of
life are expounded by him and Meed. The king summons Reason
to his council. Peace complains against wrong, and there is a general debate on government. The poet awakes, but he soon goes
back to sleep and has another vision of the field full of folk.
Reason preaches so effectively that the next episode (Passus VII,
in the C text) is the confession of*]

THE SEVEN DEADLY SINS.

With that, ran Repentance and repeated his[1] teaching,
And made Will[2] to weep with his eyes full of water.

Confessio Superbiae

Parnel Proud-heart[3] then plumped down and groveled;
Long 't was ere she looked up and "Lord, mercy!"
    clamored,

---

35 I.e., novices, ecclesiastical beginners.
36 Of theology.   37 Cure of souls, spiritual charge of a parish.
38 Tonsure, shaven heads.
39 Even in Lent, when they ought to be performing extra services
   in their parishes.
40 The Court of Exchequer, which had jurisdiction in revenue
   matters. It was one of the three principal courts of law, the
   others being King's Bench and Common Pleas.
41 Formerly the highest court in England, next to Parliament itself.
42 I.e., claiming the king's dues and perquisites.
43 Unclaimed property and strayed cattle.
44 City wards and their courts.
45 I.e., they administer great estates and hold the manorial courts.
46 The earliest of the day's appointed "hours" for prayers and
   devotions.   47 I.e., of admitting or denying entrance to heaven.
48 Prudence, temperance, fortitude, and justice.
49 A pun, *cardo* being Latin for "hinge." St. Peter, according to the
   poet, lovingly committed his control of heaven's gates to the
   four *cardinal* virtues.   50 The Papal court.
51 I.e., there is plenty I would like to say about affairs at Rome;
   but I must not, since the Papacy is too holy a subject.
52 King's barristers, leading lawyers.   53 Coins.

54 Substantial citizens.   55 Weavers.   56 Tax collectors.
57 Pass.
58 God save you. Perhaps the refrain of some popular song. Elsewhere the poet mentions a Dame Emma of Shoreditch, a disreputable London suburb.   59 A corruption of "Alsace."
60 Formerly the great southwestern province of France.
61 La Rochelle, on the west coast of France.   1 Reason's.
2 The poet.
3 Of the seven deadly sins, a common medieval conception, pride
   was considered the chief.—Parnel (Latin *Petronilla*) is a proper
   name but was proverbial for a bold or flashily dressed woman.

And vowed unto Him that all of us fashioned 5
She would unsew her smock and an hair-shirt would set
  there
For to vanquish her flesh, that fierce was for sinning:
"Shall never high be my heart, but I'll hold myself lowly
And suffer even slander—and so did I never.
But now meek I'll make myself; mercy I'll ask for 10
Of all that I have in my heart ever hated."

"Repent thee!" quoth Repentance, "as Reason hath
  preached to thee,
And shrive[4] thyself sharply, and shake off all pride now!"

"I, Pride, patiently penance I ask for.[5]
For I foremost and first to father and to mother 15
Disobedient have been—I beg God for mercy—
Disobedient been, not abashed in offending
God and all good men, my heart swelled so greatly—
Disobedient to Holy Church, to her and her servants.
Some I censured for their evil vices, and excited others 20
Through my words and my wit their evil works to
  exhibit,
And scorned them and others if I could find an opening,
Laughing all aloud so the ignorant who listened
Might ween[6] I was witty and wiser than another;
A scorner and unreasonable to them that spoke
  reasonably, 25
By all manner of means I sought notoriety,
Setting up for superior when so it befell me
To tell any tale—I trowed I was wiser
To discuss or to counsel than the learned or the laity.
I was proud of appearing appareled among the people 30
Otherwise than I owned,[7] both inside and outside,
Hoping men would think that I, in my having,
Was rich and reasonable and rightful of living;[8]
Boasting and bragging with many bold blasphemies,
Vaunting in my vanity in defiance of reprimand; 35
And yet so singular by myself[9] that in the sight of the
  people
Was none such as myself; nor none so pope-holy,[10]
Sometimes in one sect and sometimes in another.
In all kinds of covetousness I schemed how I could be
Held to be holy, an hundred times, with that motive. 40
I wished men should ween that my works ever the best
  were,

And me cleverest of my calling, clerkly or otherwise,
And strongest on earth, and stoutest under girdle,[11]
And loveliest to look on, and in bed the most likable.
And liking of such a life as no law praiseth, 45
I was vain of my fair features and faculty of loud singing.
And what I gave for God's love I told to my gossips,[12]
So they'd ween that I was unworldly and charitable.
And none so bold a beggar as I, to bid for and covet.
Tales I would tell, in the streets and in the taverns— 50
Such thing as was never thought, and yet I swore that
  I saw it,
And lied on my own body[13] and on my life also.
Works that I well did I call folk to witness,
And say thus to such as are sitting beside me:
'Lo, if ye believe me not or ween that I'm lying, 55
Ask of him, or of her; and they can inform you
What I suffered and saw and had in possession,
And was clever at, and knew, and what kin I came of.'
I was eager that all should know aught I was proud of,
So the people might praise me, though poor my
  appearance.[14] 60
(Si hominibus placerem, Christi servus non essem.[15]
Nemo potest duobus dominis servire.)"[16]

"Now God in his goodness give thee grace for
  amendment,"
Quoth Repentance plainly. And promptly rose Envy.

Confessio Invidiae

Envy with heavy heart then asked to be shriven 65
And cried, "Mea culpa!"[17] cursing all his enemies.
He was clothed all in curses and in cutting phrases.
He shook his fist in his wrath; had his wishes been
  realized,
No one's life would have lasted that on his land ventured.
Chiding and slandering, such was his chief livelihood, 70
And blaming men behind their back, and wishing they'd
  fare badly.
All that he wist[18] about Will[19] to Watkin he told it,
And what he knew about Watkin told it to Will
  thereafter,
And made foes of friends through his tongue false and
  fickle.

---

[4] Confess.
[5] This speech, apparently by another spokesman, is somewhat in-
consistently transferred to this point in the C text from a later
place in the B text, where the poet had indulged in a second
account of the seven deadly sins.   [6] Suppose.
[7] I.e., in costlier raiment than my income warranted, but also (as
the next phrase indicates) with reference to spiritual pretensions.
[8] I.e., not living beyond my means nor less piously than I pretended.   [9] I.e., unique.   [10] Hypocritical.

[11] I.e., a tough one, a regular ironsides.   [12] Cronies.
[13] I.e., swore falsely by it.   [14] I.e., in the sight of God.
[15] For if I yet pleased men, I should not be the servant of Christ.
(Galatians 1:10.)
[16] No man can serve two masters. (Matthew 6:24.)
[17] My sin, my fault. (A portion of the formula of confession.)
[18] Knew.
[19] Not the poet; like "Watkin" (Little Walter) a typical name: all
he knew about Smith he told Jones.

"Either through strength of speech or through many
    deceptions   75
I've avenged myself often or else fretted inwardly
Like a clothier's shears[20] and have cursed my fellow
    Christian,
Against the counsel of Christ, as the clergy find in
    Scripture:
Cuius maledictione os plenum est et amaritudine et dolo; sub
    lingua eius labor et dolor.[21]
Filii hominum, dentes eorum arma et sagittae, et lingua eorum
    gladius acutus.[22]   80
When I miss having the mastery, such melancholy I suffer
That I catch the cramp or a cardiac ailment
Or else an ague, in such an anger, and sometimes a fever
That attacketh me all a twelvemonth until I abandon
Leechcraft[23] from our Lord and believe in witchcraft, 85
And say that no cleric has power, nor Christ himself
    either,
To[24] the shoemaker[25] of Southwark,[26] such is his
    salvation.[27]
For God or God's word gave me grace or help never,
But through a charm I had good chance and my chief
    healing.
I could not eat for many a year as a man ought to,   90
For envy and ill will are evil for the digestion.
Can no sugar nor sweet thing assuage these my
    swellings,[28]
Nor some precious potion from my heart expel it,
Nor can shame or shrift, unless someone scrapes my
    stomach?"
"Yes, presently," quoth Repentance, "if thou profess
    thou art sorry,   95
For thy sovereign sin beseeching God for mercy."

"I am ever sorry!" said Envy. "I am seldom otherwise!
That maketh me so meager—because I miss my
    vengeance.
Yet am I backbiting's broker: men's wares I call
    blemished
Among merchants many times, especially in London. 100
When they sold and I didn't, I soon was quite ready
To lie and to lower and belittle my neighbors,
Their works and their words, where I would be sitting.

Now I am contrite in conscience because of that
    conduct.—
Lord, ere I leave life, for love of Thyself now   105
Grant to me, good Lord, grace for amendment."

Confessio Irae

With two white eyes[29] then Wrath awakened.
With a snuffling nose,[30] gnawing his lips, too.
"I am Wrath," quoth that fellow, "most ready at smiting
Both with stone and with staff, and stealing upon mine
    enemy;   110
For to slay him slyly I think up stratagems.
Though I sat here this seven year, I could not tell suitably
The harm that I have done with hand and tongue also.
Impatient in all penances, I complained, as you might say,
'Gainst God, when aught grieved me, and grumbled at
    his mandates: 115
As, sometimes in summer and so, too, in harvest,
Unless the weather pleased my wish, I was wont to
    blame God for it—
For all forms of misfortune that I felt or was touched by.
'Mongst all manner of men my dwelling is sometimes,
Whether learned or laity, that like for to hear   120
Harm of any man, in the past or the future.
Friars follow my fashion often and frequently,
And prove that the prelates of Holy Church are
    imperfect.[31]
And prelates complain of them, since their people they
    are shriving
Without license and leave, and wrath therein liveth.[32] 125
Thus they speak and dispute, till each despiseth the other.
Thus beggars and barons[33] at debate are often;
Till I, Wrath, rise up high and run with both factions.—
Either till both be beggars, and live by their calling,[34]
Or till all ride like rich men,[35] I, Wrath, shall rest not: 130
That I must follow these folk, my fortune is none other.

"I have as aunts a nun and also an abbess.
They would rather swoon away or die than suffer any
    penance.
I have been cook in their kitchen,[36] and have served the
    convent
Many months, both with them and with monks also. 135

---

[20] The blades of which, at their inner edges, are constantly chafing.
[21] Cf. Psalms 10:7: "His mouth is full of cursing and deceit and
    fraud: under his tongue is mischief and vanity."
[22] Cf. Psalms 57:4 ". . . the sons of men, whose teeth are spears
    and arrows, and their tongue a sharp sword."
[23] I.e., innocent medical art.
[24] In comparison with.
[25] Evidently a practicer of black magic.
[26] A suburb of London, at the south end of London Bridge.
[27] Power to save.   [28] I.e., indigestion.

[29] For in his anger he rolled them.   [30] Another sign of anger.
[31] The friars were not under the jurisdiction of the bishops.
[32] I.e., in the friars' encroachments there is ample occasion for
    anger on the part of the parish priests and their bishops. Cf.
    Prologue, lines 58–67, and Prologue, note 27, above.
[33] I.e., the lords of the church, the bishops.
[34] The fact of their being ecclesiastics. I.e., till the prelates renounce
    their riches and beg like the friars for subsistence.
[35] I.e., or till the friars get as rich as the prelates. There will never
    be peace as long as the inequality exists.
[36] Cooks were supposed to be especially prone to anger.

I was the prioress's potager[37] and other poor ladies',
And made their broths out of scandals:[38] 'Dame Johanna
 was a bastard;
And Dame Clarice, a knight's daughter, her sire was a
 cuckold;[39]
Dame Parnel[40] a priest's miss[41]—she will never be
 prioress,
For she had a child in the chicken house—she was
 challenged at the election.'   140
Thus they sit, these sisters, sometimes disputing
Till 'Thou liest!' and 'Thou liest!' over them all be lady;
And then I, Wrath, am roused and ready for vengeance.
Then I[42] cry and cratch[43] with my keen fingernails,
Both bite and beat and display such a bearing   145
That all ladies do loathe me who love proper dignity.

" 'Mongst wives and 'mongst widows I am wont to be
 sitting,
Parked up[44] in the pews. The parson has knowledge
How little's my love for Lettice at the Stile;[45]
For she had her holy bread[46] ere I—my heart then
 began to alter.[47]   150
Afterward, after meat, did she and I[48] quarrel;
And I, Wrath, was ready and wroth with the pair of
 them,
Till each called the other whore, and off went their
 clothing[49]
Till both their heads were laid bare and bloody their
 cheeks were.

"Among monks, too, might I be; but many times I
 avoid them,   155
For there are many fierce fellows my affairs to spy into,
That is, the prior and the superior[50] and our pater abbas.[51]
And if I tell any tales they betake themselves unto counsel
And make me fast Fridays on bread and on water.
Yet am I charged with it like a child before the whole
 chapter   160
And beaten on the bare buttocks, no breeches intervening!
I've no delight, believe me, 'mongst monks for to linger.
For they eat more fish than flesh, and feeble[52] ale their
 drink is.

---

[37] Soup and stew maker.
[38] I.e., I cooked up scandals about them.   [39] Deceived husband.
[40] See p. 70, note 3, above.   [41] I.e., concubine.
[42] I.e., not as Wrath itself, but in the persons of the angry nuns.
[43] Scratch.   [44] Enclosed.
[45] Apparently a proper name. Cf. line 211, below.
[46] Either the Eucharist or ordinary bread blessed by the priest and
 distributed in small pieces.   [47] Toward her.
[48] This angry wife or widow.
[49] I.e., they tore off each other's outer garments, hoods, and perhaps hair.
[50] A prior was the second in authority at an abbey; in less important establishments either he or a "superior" might be in
 charge.   [51] Father abbot, the head of the monastery.   [52] Weak.

But other times, when wine cometh and when I drink all
 evening,
I have a flux from a foul mouth[53] well five days after.   165
All that I wist of wickedness about any of our convent[54]
I coughed it up in our cloister, so all the convent knew
 it."

"Now repent thee!" quoth Repentance, "and never
 publish
What secrets thou possessest, by speech or by visage!
And drink not overdelicately nor too deep neither,   170
That thy will or thy reason may not turn unto anger!
Esto sobrius!"[55] he said, and absolved him thereafter,
And bade him pray unto God, by his bounty to live better.

Confessio Luxuriae

Then said Lechery, "Alas!" and cried to our Lady:
"Lady, to thy loved Son bend for me low now,   175
That He pity me, a fornicator, of his pure grace and
 mercy.
And then I shall," quoth that scoundrel, "for love of
 thee, Saturdays
Drink but with the duck[56] and keep but one mealtime.
I, guilty in spirit, to God I'm confessing
My liking of lechery, my culpable lewdness,   180
In words and in weeds[57] and in wantonly eying.
To every maid that I met I made her a signal,
A symbol of sinning; and some of them I tasted
Around the sweet mouth; and beneath I began
 reaching,   184
Till our two wills were one. To work then we hurried,
No less on fasting days than on Fridays and eves of high
 feast days,[58]
As lief in Lent as out of Lent, alike on all occasions:
Such actions were with us never at all out of season—
Till we could manage no more. Then had we merry
 stories
Of prurience and of paramours, and experimented—
 with speeches,   190
Handling and hugging, and also with kissing—
Exciting ourselves each the other, to our old iniquity.
I made songs most subtle, and old bawds I sent out
For to win unto my will women, with guilefulness,
By sorcery sometimes, and sometimes overpowering
 them.   195
I lay with the loveliest, and loved them never after.
When I was old and hoar, and had no more vigor,
I had liking for to laugh at lecherous stories.
Now, Lord, for thy promise, on lechers have mercy!"

---

[53] I.e., a bad taste in my mouth.
[54] Formerly applied to monasteries as well as nunneries.
[55] Be sober.   [56] I.e., stick to water.   [57] Clothes.
[58] Important church festivals. Abstinence was prescribed on the
 "eve" of a feast, that is, on the day before the holy day.

Confessio Avaritiae

Then came Covetousness; I cannot describe him,   200
So hungry and so hollow Harvey[59] himself looked then.
He was beetle-browed and blubber-lipped, his two eyes
      were bleary,
And like a leathern purse his cheeks sagged lopping
Well under his chin, with age all a-tremble—
Like bondmen's bacon[60] his beard was close shaven—   205
With his hood on his head and his hat on likewise,
In a tattered tabard[61] of twelve winters' wearing.
Unless a louse could leap—on my faith I believe it—
He would not wander on that Welsh,[62] it was so
      threadbare.[63]

"I have been covetous," quoth this caitiff,[64] "I do here
      proclaim it.   210
With Sim of the Stile for some time I took service
And was his prentice pledged,[65] his profit to see to.
First I learned how to lie, one lie or a couple.
Wickedly to weigh out was my first lesson.
I went to the fair at Weyhill and at Winchester[66]   215
With many kinds of merchandise, as my master bade me.
Had not the grace of guile[67] 'mongst my goods been
      present,
They had been unsold this seven year, so may God help
      me!
I dwelt next among drapers,[68] my primer to drudge at:[69]
To stretch out the selvage so 't would seem longer.   220
'Mongst the costly striped cloths I conned a new lesson:
To pierce them with a pack-needle and bind them
      together.
I put them in presses and pinned them down in them,
Till ten yards or twelve to thirteen were extended.

"My wife was a weaver, and woolen cloth made she.   225
She spoke to the spinsters to spin the thread thinly.
The weight she paid wages by weighed well a quarter
More than my steelyard[70] when I weighed honestly.
I bought her barley; she brewed it to sell it.

Penny-ale and pudding-ale, she poured them
      together;[71]   230
For laborers and low folk, apart lay those brewings.
The best lay in my bower[72] and in my bedchamber;
And who tasted thereof he bought it thereafter,
A gallon for a groat[73]—yet got not full measure,
Since it came in by cupfuls—my wife was thus
      crafty.   235
Rose the Retailer was her name rightly.
She hath been a huckster this eleven winter."

"Repent didst thou never?" quoth Repentance, "nor pay
      restitution?"

"Yes, once," quoth he,[74] "at a hostelry with a heap of
      merchants.
I arose and rifled their bags when at rest they lay
      sleeping."   240

"That was a powerful repayment, forsooth!" quoth
      Repentance.
"Here or in hell thou'lt be hanging high for it.
Didst thou ever practice usury[75] in all thy lifetime?"

"Not so, truly," he asserted, "save when I was younger.
I learned among Lombards[76] and from Jews a lesson: 245
To weigh pence with a weight and pare down the
      heaviest;[77]
And I lent for love of the pledge, which I believed better
And worth more than the money or the men I had
      lent to.[78]
I lent folk willing to lose a little from every noble;[79]
And with letters from Lombards I lent gold at Rome,
      too.   250
Thus the person who borrowed from me the time paid
      for."[80]

"Didst thou lend ever to a lord for love of his behavior?"

"I have lent to lords and to ladies—that never loved me
      after.

---

[71] I.e., thin and thick alike came out of the same cask. The latter
was worth four times the former.   [72] Private quarters.
[73] A silver coin worth fourpence. The far greater purchasing
power of money in earlier times must be taken into account.
[74] Pretending to take "restitution" to mean robbery.
[75] The Church held charging interest a sin.
[76] Milan, the capital of Lombardy, was famous for its bankers and
brokers, some of whom were established in London.
[77] The edges of medieval coins were not milled and could sometimes be clipped.
[78] The pledge, pawned by the borrower, was worth more than
the loan—more, indeed, than the borrower himself.
[79] A gold coin worth six shillings eightpence. The borrowers carelessly accepted clipped coin.
[80] Had to pay interest for the term of the loan.

---

[59] Possibly this name had some previous association with covetousness.   [60] A bondman would get but a thin slice.
[61] Jacket.   [62] A kind of cloth, probably flannel.
[63] I.e., without a nap there was no foothold for crawling and it
would take a good jumper to get across.   [64] Scoundrel.
[65] An apprentice was "bound" for seven years of service while he
learned the business.
[66] Both these towns, in Hampshire and Wiltshire, were noted for
annual fairs.   [67] I.e., not God's favor, but guile's.
[68] Cloth merchants.   [69] I.e., to study more lessons in cheating.
[70] A kind of scales, with a movable weight on the longer of the
two arms.

I have made many a knight both mercer[81] and draper,
Without payment for their apprenticeships—not one
    pair of gloves, even. 255
Who did business with my assistance seldom succeeded."

"Now clearly," quoth Repentance, "and by the Cross, I
    am confident
Shall never executor well bestow the silver that thou
    leavest him,
Nor thine heirs, as I guess, have the joy of what thou
    gainedst.
For the Pope has no power, nor all his priestly
    confessors, 260
To absolve thee of thy sinfulness, *sine restitutione:*[82]
Nunquam dimittitur peccatum, nisi restituatur ablatum."[83]

"With false words and with wiles I have won my
    possessions,
And with guile and gulling what is mine I have gathered.
I mixed up my merchandise and made a good
    showing: 265
The worst lay unseen—very smart I considered it.
And if my neighbor had a servant or some kind of
    animal
More profitable than mine, I made many devices:
To how I might get it, all my wits I devoted.
Unless I got it some other way, in the end I stole it, 270
Or privily shook out his purse and unpicked his locks,
    too.
And if I went to the plow, I pinched off from his
    half-acre;
So a foot of land or a furrow I was able to fetch myself—
Of my nearest neighbor's some earth to nip away.
And if I reaped, I'd reach over, or order the reapers 275
To seize for me with their sickles what I sowed never.[84]

"On holy days at holy church, when I heard masses,
I never had will, I warrant, to pray for mercy
For my misdeeds; so that I mourned more often
For loss of goods, believe me, than for bodily
    guiltiness. 280
Though deadly the sin I did, I dreaded it not so sorely
As when I lent and believed it lost or too long without
    payment.
And if I sent oversea my servant to Bruges
Or into Prussia my prentice my profit to see to,

To do business with money and make their exchanges, 285
Never could I in the mean time be comforted by anyone—
Neither matins nor mass, nor no manner of pageant;
Never penance I practiced nor paternoster recited:
So my mind ever was more on my possessions
Than on God's own grace and his great almightiness. 290
Ubi thesaurus tuus, ibi et cor tuum."[85]

"Now, certainly," quoth Repentance, "I am sorry about
    thy conduct.
Were I a friar, in good faith, not for all earth's treasure
Would I apparel myself with thy goods or repair our
    church buildings[86]
Or take meat of yours for one meal; if my heart were
    certain 295
That thou art such as thou sayest—I would rather die
    starving:
Melius est mori quam male vivere.[87]
I counsel no faithful friar to feast at thy table.
I would liefer, by our Lord, live on water cresses
Than have my food and my finding[88] from false men's
    winnings. 300
Servus es alterius cum fercula pinguia queris;
Pane tuo potius vescere, liber eris.[89]
Thou art an unnatural creature; I cannot absolve thee
Till thou hast made, as thou canst, to all men restitution.
For all that shared in thy goods, as God is my
    witness, 305
Will be held at the great Judgment to help thee make
    restitution.
The priest that taketh thy tithe—him, I trow, and no
    other—
Shall have a part with thee in purgatory and help pay
    thy debts there,
If he knew thou wert such when he accepted thine
    offering.
Who believes that I lie, let him look in the Psalter
    notes: 310
At *Ecce enim veritatem dilexisti.*[90]
There shall he learn manifestly the meaning of usury
And what penance the priest shall have that is proud of
    thy tithing.
For an whore from her tail-earnings may give tithes
    with more hardihood
Than an arrant[91] usurer, as God doth hear me, 315
And sooner shall come to heaven, by Christ that did
    make me!"

---

[81] Textiles seller. This may mean that the knights sold to Avarice goods which they obtained abroad either as gifts or as booty.
[82] Without restitution.
[83] Never shall a sin be forgiven unless restitution is made of what was taken.
[84] A medieval field was often cultivated in extremely narrow strips, by several farmers.
[85] Where your treasure is, there will your heart be also. (Matthew 6:21.)
[86] I.e., I would not accept a gift, since your money is tainted.
[87] Better it is to die than evilly to live.   [88] Keep.
[89] Thou art the slave of another when thou seekest after dainty dishes; if thou eatest rather thine own bread, thou shalt be free.
[90] For, lo, you have loved truth. (Cf. Psalms 51:6.)
[91] Manifest, downright.

Then was there a Welshman who was wondrous repentant;

He was called Evan Give-it-back—"if I have it left over—
All that I guilefully got since I grew up from childhood;
And though I lack for a living, delay I will never   320
Till each man has what is his, ere hence I must pass away.
For I had rather in this life go in rags begging
Than to live in delight and lose life and soul, too."

Robert[92] the Robber on *reddite*[93] considered.
Since the wherewithal was not, he wept very sorely.   325
And yet that sinful scoundrel said unto heaven:
"Christ, that on Calvary on the Cross didst perish,
When Dismas,[94] my brother, begged for thy mercy,
And thou hadst mercy on that man, for *memento*'s[95] sake,
Have rue on me, Robert, that *reddere*[96] have not   330
Nor am able to earn with such skill as I'm owner of.
Out of thy mighty mercy, mitigation I ask for.
Damn me not at Doomsday because I did such evil!"

What became of this criminal I cannot clearly show you.
Well I know he wept copiously, with his eyes watering;   335
And to Christ yet again he acknowledged his guiltiness:
His pikestaff[97] called Penance he would polish up freshly,
For he had lain with *Latro*,[98] aunt of Lucifer.

"By the Cross!" said Repentance, "thy pilgrimage is toward heaven,
If thou hast in thine heart what thy tongue is rehearsing.   340
Trust in His mighty mercy, and thou mayest yet be rescued.
For all the woefulness of this world and deeds of wickedness
Fare but as a spark of fire that in Thames' midst hath fallen
And died there, by one drop of water; so do all transgressions
Of all manner of men that with good intention   345
Confess contritely and cry for mercy: they shall come to hell never.
Omnis iniquitas quoad misericordiam Dei est quasi scintilla in medio maris.[99]

Repent thee promptly," quoth Repentance plainly to the usurer,
"And have His mercy in thy mind. Forget matters of business,
For thou ownest nothing, by my faith, not enough to buy a loaf with.   350
The goods that thou hast got, their beginning was in falsehood;
As long as thou livest on them, thou'rt not restoring but borrowing.
And if thou hast no idea to whom nor where is due restitution,
Bear it to the bishop and of his grace bid him
To dispose of it himself as is best for thy soul's health.   355
For he must answer for thee at the high seat of Judgment;
For thee and for many more that man shall be accountable
For what he taught you to live by and to take you from thievery."

Confessio Gulae

Now beginneth Gluttony for to go to confession
And to get himself churchward, his guilt to lay open.   360
Fasting on a Friday, forward he started
By Betty the brewer's house, who bade him good morrow;
And whither was he bound, the brew-wife did ask him.

"To holy church," quoth he, "for to hear the mass there,
And then to sit and be shriven and nevermore be sinful."   365

"I have good ale, gossip.[1] Glutton, wilt thou taste?"

"What hast thou?" quoth he; "any hot spices?"

"I have pepper and peony seed and a pound of garlic
And a farthingworth[2] of fennel seed for days of fasting."

Then goeth Glutton in, and his great vows with him.[3]   370
Cissy the seamstress on the bench was sitting;
Wat the warrener[4] and his wife were drinking—
Tommy the tinker and two of his workmen,
Hick the hackneyman[5] and Hugh the needle seller,
Clarice of Cock's Lane,[6] the clerk of the church, too,   375

---

[92] Similarity in sound had earlier and inevitably associated this name with the word *robbery*.   [93] Make restitution.

[94] According to the Apocryphal gospel of Nicodemus, the name of the penitent thief.

[95] "Domine, *memento* mei, cum veneris in regnum tuum": Lord, remember me when thou comest into thy kingdom. (Luke 23:42.)   [96] Means of restitution.

[97] Spiked walking stick, a necessity to a pilgrim.   [98] Robber.

[99] All sin, in comparison with the mercy of God, is like a spark in the midst of the sea.

[1] Crony, friend.

[2] A farthing was a small silver coin worth half a cent (one quarter of an English penny).

[3] I.e., his vow to confess was broken.   [4] Gamekeeper.

[5] Livery stable owner or employee.

[6] Prostitution flourished in this well-known London street.

Sir Piers of Prydie[7] and Parnel of Flanders,[8]
An hayward[9] and an hermit and the hangman of
    Tyburn,[10]
Davy the ditcher, with a dozen rascals—
Some porters and some pickpurses and bald tooth-pullers,
A rebec[11] player and a rat catcher, a raker[12] and his
    helper,   380
A ropemaker and a reding-king[13] and Rosie the dish-
    seller,
Godfrey the garlic-monger and Griffin the Welshman,
And a lot of second-hand merchants. Early in that
    morning
Gave they Glutton with glad cheer good ale for a starter.

Clement the cobbler cast off his mantle   385
And at this odd kind of fair put it up to exchange it.
Hick the hackneyman heaved down his hood likewise,
And asked Bat the butcher for to be in his interest.
The goods to appraise, there were appointed price-fixers,
So he that had the hood should not have the cloak,
    too: 390
Less boot by the arbiters should be added to the better
    thing.[14]
Two rose then rapidly and reasoned together,
Appraising the pennyworths apart from the rest of them;
And there were oaths a plenty, since each tried to best
    the other.
They could not, "in their conscience,"[15] accord, to speak
    truly.   395
Till Robin the ropemaker to rise they requested
And bade him be an umpire, and debate was abolished.
Hick the hackneyman had thus the mantle,
On covenant that Clement the cup should replenish
And have the hackneyman's hood and hold himself
    satisfied;[16]   400
And the first who dissented should stand up directly
And with a gallon of ale give greeting to Sir Glutton.

There was laughing and lowering and "Let's have the
    tankard!"
Trading and tippling in turn kept them busy.

And so till evensong rang they sat there, singing
    sometimes,   405
Till Glutton had gulped down a gallon and a gill,
    too. . . .[17]
He could neither step nor stand till a staff he had taken;
Then gan he to go[18] like the bitch of a gleeman,[19]
Sometimes aside and sometimes quite backward,
Like him who setteth strings to snare the birds with.   410
And when he drew to the door, then his eyes got dimmer;
He faltered at the threshold and fell on the floor there.
Then Clement the cobbler caught him by the middle;
For to lift him aloft, on his knees he laid him.
But Glutton was a great churl, and groaned in the
    lifting   415
And coughed up a caudle in the lap of Clement.
There's no hound so hungry in the whole of
    Hertfordshire
That he'd lap up those leavings, so unlovely their flavor.

With all the woe in the world, his wife and his
    maidservant
Bore him to his bed and brought him inside it;   420
And after all this excess he had a fit of indolence:
He slept Saturday and Sunday till sunset was over.
Then awaked he most wan, and wishful for drinking.
The first word that he spoke was, "Who's holding the
    bowl up?"[20]
His spouse and his inward sense blamed him for his
    sinning;   425
He was struck ashamed, that scoundrel, and confessed
    himself swiftly
To Repentance plainly: "Have for me," he said, "pity,
Thou Lord that aloft art and made all things living!
To thee, God, I, Glutton, my guilt I acknowledge
In my trespass with tongue—I cannot tell how often   430
I swore 'Thy soul and thy sides!' and 'So help me, God
    almighty!'
When need there was none, many times, falsely.
I oversupped at my supper, and sometimes at noonday—
More than man's able to manage digestively;
And like an hound that eats grass began I to vomit,   435
And spilled what I could have saved—I cannot speak for
    shame of
The villainy of my foul mouth and of my foul stomach.
On fasting days before noon with ale I fed myself,
Out of reason, 'mongst the ribald, to their ribaldry to
    listen.
Thereof, good God, grant to me forgiveness   440

[7] Unidentified. "Sir" was a courtesy title of priests, equivalent to
    Dominus.
[8] A number of London's prostitutes were Flemish women.
[9] His duty was to keep up hedges and fences.
[10] London's famous place of public execution.
[11] An early form of the viol.   [12] Scavenger.
[13] The meaning of this expression is now unknown.
[14] I.e., the idea was to exchange them. The question was whether
    the articles were of equal value and, if not, what should be
    added on each side till an equal balance should be struck.
[15] Thus they swore.
[16] I.e., Hick's hood was judged worth more than Clement's cloak;
    so Clement had to give boot, that is, make up the difference by
    setting up the drinks.

[17] Here the poet goes into physiological details of the aftereffects
    of Glutton's potations. Five lines are omitted.   [18] Walk.
[19] A blind minstrel, led by a dog.
[20] I.e., keeping longer than is fair the cup that should pass freely
    from hand to hand.

For all my evil living in all my lifetime.
For I vow to very God not for thirst nor for hunger
Shall ever fish on Friday digest in my belly
Till from Abstinence, mine aunt, I have due permission—
And yet have I hated her all my lifetime."[21]   445

Confessio Accidiae

Then came Sloth, all beslobbered, with two eyes all
          slimy.
"I must sit to be shriven," quoth he, "or else shall I nap
          off.
I cannot stand nor stoop nor without a stool do my
          kneeling.
Were I tucked into bed, unless my tail-end required it,
No ringing should make me rise till I were ready for
          dining.   5
"*Benedicite!*"[22] he began with a belch, and his breast
          knocked at,
Stretched himself, roared, and snored away finally.

"What! wake up, man!" quoth Repentance, "prepare for
          confession!"

"If I did," quoth he, "this day, I doubt very seriously
If I know perfectly my paternoster, as the priest recites
          it.   10
I know rimes of Robin Hood[23] and of Randolph, Earl
          of Chester;[24]
But of our Lord or of our Lady, the least that there ever
          was.
I have vowed forty vows, and they vanished next
          morning.
I practiced never the penance that the priest directed;
I saw never the time I was sorry for my sinfulness.   15
If I offer any prayers, unless it be in anger,[25]
What I tell with my tongue from my heart's ten mile
          distant.
I am occupied each day, holy days and others,
With idle tales at an alehouse and even in churches.
God's[26] pain and his passion[27] appear seldom in my
          memory.   20
I never visited a feeble[28] man nor a fettered man in
          prison.
I am fonder of hearing vile tales or of laughing at
          falsehoods,

Or reproaching men, with comparisons unpleasantly
          uttered,
Than of all that Mark made, or John, Luke, or Matthew.
Vigils[29] and fasting days, I can forget them all freely.   25
I lie abed in Lent, with my arms round my leman,[30]
Till matins and mass are done; then I get the friars to
          remember me.[31]
I seldom seek shriving, unless sickness impels it—
Not twice in ten year. Yet I've not told the half of it:
I have been priest and parson passing thirty winter;   30
Yet can I neither sol-fa nor sing, nor read in a saint's life.
But I can find in a field and in a furlong a rabbit,
And hold court for a knight[32] and check accounts with
          an overseer;
But I cannot construe Cato[33] nor read like a clergyman.[34]
If I buy or borrow aught, unless it be recorded   35
I easily forget it; and if any man asks for it,
Six times or even seven, with oaths I forswear it.
Thus honest men have I harmed on ten hundred
          occasions.
And sometimes the salary of my servants is behindhand:
'T is pity to hear the process when accounts are
          computed,   40
With so wicked a will I pay off my workmen.
If any man does me a benefit or helps me when I need it,
I am hostile toward helpfulness—I cannot comprehend it.
For I have and have had somewhat hawklike manners:
I am not lured by love unless under thumb lies
          something.[35]   45
The kindness my fellow Christian accorded me formerly,
Sixty times, I, Sloth, have forgotten it subsequently.
In speech or in sparing of speech, I spoiled very often
Both flesh[36] and also fish; and victuals I have hoarded
Till any living man loathed for to look at or smell
          them,   50
Both bread and ale, and milk, cheese, and butter.
I was slothful in my services and set fire to houses,[37]
In youth roamed all around and disrelished thriftiness,
And a beggar have been since, for my foul slothfulness:
Heu mihi, quod sterilem duxi vitam iuvenilem!"[38]   55

"Repent thee!" quoth Repentance; and presently he[39]
          fainted,

---

21 The last line of Passus VII in the C text; the next are the opening
     lines of Passus VIII.   22 Bless ye.
23 Apparently the earliest mention of him. Some of the "rimes"
     will be found below, among the medieval ballads.
24 There were two famous earls of this name and title; the earlier
     died in 1153, his grandson and namesake in 1232.
25 I.e., "ejaculatory" prayers asking God to damn someone.
26 Christ's.   27 Suffering.   28 Sick.

29 Eves of holy days, when fasting was prescribed.
30 Mistress.
31 I.e., for a small fee I get the friars to mention me in their prayers.
32 I.e., hold the manorial court as his steward.
33 Dionysius Cato, the reputed author of the popular *Distichs,* a
     collection of moralizing Latin verses of the third or fourth
     century A.D.   34 I.e., read Latin.
35 I.e., unless, as in training a falcon, he who wants me to come
     has a reward in his hand.   36 Meat.
37 I.e., through my negligence.
38 Alas for me, that I lived as a youth a life so barren!   39 Sloth.

Till *Vigilate* the watchman from his eyes fetched some
water
And flung it on his face, and firmly cried to him
And said, "Beware of despair, for it will betray thee!
'I am sorry for my sinning,' say to thyself now!   60
And beat thyself on the breast, and God's blessing be
asking!
For there is no guilt so great that his goodness is not
greater."

Then Sloth did sit up and signed[40] himself often
And made a vow before God for his foul slothfulness:
"Shall be no Sunday this seven year, unless sickness
cause it,   65
That I'll not get me ere day to the church I love dearly
And hear matins and mass as if I a monk were.
After eating, no alehouse shall ever detain me
Till I have heard evensong—by the Cross I do swear it!"

[*At this point a passage of fifty-five lines, here omitted, is inserted from the B text; in it the poet expounds the various
causes of sloth.*]

Then was Repentance prepared, and did prompt them to
fall kneeling: 70
"I shall beseech our Saviour for grace for the sinful
To amend us of doing amiss and to deal us all mercy.—
God, in thy goodness thou began the world's creation,
And from nothing madest something, and man in thine
image.
Thou hast suffered him to sin, a sickness to all of us,   75
And yet for the best, I'll be bound, whatever the Book
telleth:
O felix culpa! O necessarium peccatum Adae![41]
For through that sin thy Son was sent down to earth here,
And became man by a maid, for mankind's amendment.
Thou madest thyself with thy Son to our soul and body
physician: 80
'*Ego in patre, et pater in me est; et qui videt me, patrem
meum videt.*'[42]
Then like one of ourselves, as it seemed, didst thou
perish;
On a Friday, in man's form, thou didst feel our sorrow:
Captivam duxit captivitatem.[43]
The sun for sorrow thereat lost light for an interval,   85
About midday, when there's most light and the saints
have their mealtime.[44]

Then feddest thou with thy fresh blood in hell our
forefathers:[45]
Populus qui ambulabat in tenebris lucem magnam vidit.[46]
The light that shone out of thee, Lucifer it blinded,
And brought thy blessed ones thence into the bliss of
heaven.   90
The third day thereafter thou went in man's image;
A sinful Mary[47] saw thee ere Saint Mary thy mother.
And all to solace the sinful thou sufferedst it should
happen:
Non veni vocare iustos sed peccatores ad penitentiam.[48]
And all that Mark hath mentioned, Luke and John and
Matthew,   95
Of thy doughtiest deeds was done in man's image:
Verbum caro factum est.[49]
And by that token it seemeth that we may with all
sureness
Pray and beseech thee, if such be thy will now,
That art first our Father, and in flesh our brother,   100
And finally our Saviour, and with thy tongue asserted
That whenever we sinful men are minded to be sorry
For deeds that we have done evilly, damned shall we
never be
If we own them and cry unto Christ for his mercy:
*Quandocumque ingemuerit peccator, omnes iniquitates eius non
recordabor amplius.*[50]   105
And for that great mercy and the love of Mary thy
mother,
Have pity on all these paltry folk that repent very sorely
That ever they sinned against thee, God, in deed or in
spirit!"

Then seized Hope an horn, of *Deus, tu conversus
vivificabis nos,*[51]
And blew it with *Beati quorum remissae sunt iniquitates, et
cetera,*[52]   110
Till all the saints with sinful men sang out with David:
"*Homines et iumenta salvabis, Domine, quemadmodum
multiplicasti misericordiam tuam, Deus!*"[53]

---

40 Crossed.
41 O happy guilt! O necessary sin of Adam! (For the theology involved in this conception see the headnote to "Adam lay
i-bowndyn," p. 65, above.)
42 I am in the Father, and the Father is in me; and he that sees me
sees my Father. (Cf. John 14:9–11.)
43 He led captivity captive. (Ephesians 4:8.)
44 The Christian being spiritually refreshed by the blood shed on
the Cross at that hour.
45 This was at "the harrowing of hell." According to the Apocryphal gospel of Nicodemus, Christ visited that region in order
to free Adam and the other patriarchs.
46 The people that walked in darkness have seen a great light.
(Isaiah 9:2.)   47 Mary Magdalene. See Mark 16:9.
48 I am not come to call the righteous, but sinners to repentance.
(Matthew 9:13.)   49 The Word was made flesh. (John 1:14.)
50 Whenever a sinner laments, all his iniquities I shall remember
no more. (Cf. Jeremiah 31:34.)
51 God, thou shalt quicken us again. (Cf. Psalms 71:20.)
52 Blessed are they whose transgressions are forgiven, and so forth.
(Cf. Psalms 32:1.)
53 Men and beasts thou shalt preserve, Lord, according as thou
hast multiplied thy lovingkindness, God. (Psalms 35:7, in the
Latin Vulgate; cf., in the English Bible, Psalms 36:7, 8.)

Sir Gawain and the Green Knight

NEXT to Chaucer's poetry and possibly a few anonymous lyrics, the romance of *Sir Gawain and the Green Knight* is by common consent the finest thing written in England between the Norman Conquest and the end of the Middle Ages. In it appears, along with a keen relish of the pleasures of social intercourse and (most unusual in medieval art) a sensitive appreciation of the earth's beauty even in its wilder aspects, the most exquisite feeling for the aristocratic codes of honor and of manners. In addition to these marks of a poetic nature perfectly attuned to the best that worldly life affords both in nature and in society, the poem reflects a simple devotion to the Christian faith which seems all the more profound because the author and his hero take it for granted.

The name of this accomplished man, after Chaucer the best storyteller of his age, is not known. His poem is preserved in a manuscript, evidently from Lancashire, in the Cottonian collection of the British Museum. Three other poems are also contained in it. From the first, *The Pearl*, comes the name by which the author of *Sir Gawain* is known today: "the Pearl poet." *The Pearl* is an elaborate and in certain parts a very beautiful elegy. The poet has lost a spotless pearl—it has slipped away out of his hand into the grass. But we soon discover that the pearl is really a little girl, perhaps his daughter, not two years old when she died and left him heartbroken. On her grave he falls asleep and has a vision: beyond a river he sees her, robed in white, in a land of gemlike radiance, the New Jerusalem. He tries to cross over to her, but in vain; she is the bride of Christ, to whom he resigns her. The poem is uneven, at any rate from the modern reader's point of view. Much of it is abandoned to tedious exposition of theology; but some passages are extremely moving, and it is clearly from the pen of a writer of extraordinary powers.

Patience is a homily or moral preachment, with the story of Jonah as its *exemplum* or illustrative narrative. *Cleanness* is also a homily, chiefly on purity. Like *Sir Gawain and the Green Knight*, the manuscript's fourth poem, all these works are composed in the alliterative verse already described in the headnote to *Piers Plowman*. In dialect (West Midland), in vocabulary, and in style, all four (*The Pearl, Patience, Cleanness,* and *Sir Gawain*) are sufficiently alike to encourage the belief that they were written by the same man;

but about that we cannot be certain. One other poem, *St. Erkenwald*, preserved in another manuscript, may be the work of the Pearl poet.

Sir Gawain is the best of the metrical romances, which constitute one of the most important branches of medieval European literature. Though the moral note is struck more clearly than is typical of its genre, the poem is not primarily didactic. First of all, it is a masterly piece of artistic narrative. Medieval romances are usually pretty rambling; but this author is as studious of his effects, as careful in his management of detail, and as much concerned for the tightness and balance of the whole as any modern short-story writer. Two old motifs—the Beheading Game, with its tests of courage and fidelity, and the Temptation, with its tests of truth and chastity—each of which had repeatedly done duty in earlier romance, are here woven together in such a way as to make the outcome of one depend upon the outcome of the other. The materials are probably of Celtic origin. No immediate source is known; but it seems likely (though the point has been disputed) that the poet was working from some French romance which, like all the old Arthurian tales, was spun from Celtic legend. The poet, however, is not an antiquarian; like the author of *Beowulf,* he tells his story against a background composed out of the ideals and sometimes the actual facts of his own times. Various details—for instance, the descriptions of the hero's armor and the Green Knight's castle—are so precise as to fix the date late in the fourteenth century.

But the poem is not merely a skillfully told story. The great thing about *Sir Gawain* is its nobility. Like Hamlet, Gawain is a conception of universal appeal; he is what every man would like to be—in his courage and fortitude, his poise, his exquisite manners, the fineness of his moral nature. Any writer, if he offers a character who thoroughly deserves, as this hero does, the title of "the Good," runs the risk of turning him into a prig. Gawain is nothing of the sort. One reason is the sincerity of his modesty; others are his two lapses from perfection, minor though they be. Whatever his own anguish over these failures, in our eyes Gawain loses no stature by them; they help to make him human. The ethical issue raised by these events is clear, but the poet does not seize the opportunity for a sermon. The obligation of loyalty to one's pledged word, the duty of resistance not so much to this or that temptation of the flesh as to the thing which a man knows in his heart is the wrong thing for him, the conflict between the dictates of self-interest and of honor—in literature, considerations such as these can be the greatest bore in the world; here they buttress the thrust of the poem's soaring artistic effect and make the reading of *Sir Gawain* not merely interesting but exhilarating.

The poem is divided into four "fits" or cantos. The stanza, an odd one, varies in length. Down to its last five lines, its meter is that of the alliterative revival, normally with four stresses to the line; but the stanza is finished off with a "bob" and a "wheel." The bob is a very short, one-stress line, the fifth from the end; it rimes with lines two and four of the wheel. The wheel consists of four lines, riming alternately. In the wheel there is usually alliteration of two of the stressed syllables of the normally three-stress line; and the line is regularly iambic, that is, each stressed syllable is preceded by a single unstressed syllable. The difficulty of the dialect necessitates a translation for readers unversed in Middle English. The following stanza, the first, illustrates the original text. The character þ has the sound of *th*. The character ʒ has three values: before *t*, it is pronounced like *ch* in German *ich* or *ach*; before a vowel, somewhat like *y* in *you*; at the end of a word, usually somewhat like *z*.

Siþen þe sege & þe assaut watʒ sesed at Troye,
Þe borʒ brittened & brent to brondeʒ & askeʒ,
Þe tulk þat þe trammes of tresoun þer wroʒt
Watʒ tried for his tricherie, þe trewest on erthe
Hit watʒ Ennias þe athel & his highe kynde
Þat siþen depreced prouinces, & patrounes bicome

Welneʒe of al þe wele in þe west iles.
Fro riche Romulus to Rome ricchis hym swyþe;
With gret bobbaunce þat burʒe he biges vpon fyrst,
& neuenes hit his aune nome, as hit now hat;
Ticius to Tuskan, & teldes bigynnes;
Langaberde in Lumbardie lyftes vp homes;
& fer ouer þe French flod Felix Brutus
On mony bonkkes ful brode Bretayn he setteʒ,
    With wynne;
    Where werre & wrake & wonder
    Bi syþeʒ hatʒ wont þerinne,
    & oft boþe blysse and blunder
    Ful skete hatʒ skyfted synne.

By permission of Appleton-Century-Crofts, Inc., the following translation is that of Professor Theodore H. Banks, Jr., who notes that he has modified the original meter to the extent of reducing to not more than two an excessive number of unstressed syllables occurring between two stresses. For the pattern of fourteenth-century alliterative verse, see p. 67, above. In *Sir Gawain* it is followed more precisely and conservatively than in *Piers Plowman*.

A good edition of the original text, with introduction, notes, and glossary, is that of I. Gollancz (revised ed. by Mabel Day and Mary Serjeantson, 1940). The earlier, and for beginners the preferable, edition of J. R. R. Tolkien and E. V. Gordon (revised impression, 1936) reproduces one of the manuscript's illustrations in color, showing the lady of the castle, not without charm, at Gawain's bedside. For an elaborate account of the literary history of the poem's narrative elements, see G. L. Kittredge, *A Study of Gawain and the Green Knight* (1916).

SIR GAWAIN AND THE GREEN KNIGHT

I

When the siege and assault ceased at Troy, and the city
Was broken, and burned all to brands and to ashes,
The warrior who wove there the web of his treachery
Tried was for treason, the truest on earth.[1]
'T was Aeneas, who later with lords of his lineage   5
Provinces quelled, and became the possessors
Of well-nigh the whole of the wealth of the West Isles.[2]
Then swiftly to Rome rich Romulus journeyed,
And soon with great splendor builded that city,
Named with his own name, as now we still know it.   10

Ticius[3] to Tuscany turns for his dwellings;
In Lombardy Langobard[4] lifts up his homes;
And far o'er the French flood fortunate Brutus[5]
With happiness Britain on hillsides full broad
                             Doth found.   15
        War, waste, and wonder there
        Have dwelt within its bound;
        And bliss has changed to care
        In quick and shifting round.

And after this famous knight founded his Britain,   20
Bold lords were bred there, delighting in battle,
Who many times dealt in destruction. More marvels

---

[1] I.e., the clearest case there ever was. According not to the *Aeneid* but to medieval tradition, Aeneas was tried by the Greeks and exiled from Troy because his concealment of the maiden Polyxena, whom Achilles loved, had lured that Greek champion to his death.

[2] Probably a vague term for the western part of the then known world.

[3] Unidentified. Evidently to be taken as another descendant of Aeneas.

[4] Legendary descendant of Japhet (Noah's son) and nephew of Brutus (see note 5).

[5] Legendary grandson of Aeneas and founder of Britain.

Befell in those fields since the days of their finding
Than anywhere else upon earth that I know of.
Yet of all kings who came there was Arthur[6] most
    comely;[7]   25
My intention is, therefore, to tell an adventure
Strange and surprising, as some men consider,
A strange thing among all the marvels of Arthur.
And if you will list to the lay[8] for a little,
Forthwith I shall tell it, as I in the town   30
                        Heard it told
         As it doth fast endure
         In story brave and bold,
         Whose words are fixed and sure,
         Known in the land of old.[9]   35

In Camelot[10] Arthur the King lay at Christmas,
With many a peerless lord princely companioned,
The whole noble number of knights of the Round Table;[11]
Here right royally held his high revels,
Care-free and mirthful. Now much of the company,   40
Knightly born gentlemen, joyously jousted,
Now came to the court to make caroles;[12] so kept they
For full fifteen days this fashion of feasting,
All meat and all mirth that a man might devise.
Glorious to hear was the glad-hearted gaiety,   45
Dancing at night, merry din in the daytime;
So found in the courts and the chambers the fortunate
Ladies and lords the delights they best loved.
In greatest well-being abode they together:
The knights whose renown was next to the Savior's,   50
The loveliest ladies who ever were living,
And he who held court, the most comely of kings.
For these fine folk were yet in their first flush of youth
                     Seated there,
         The happiest of their kind,   55
         With a king beyond compare.
         It would be hard to find
         A company so fair.

And now while the New Year was young were the
    nobles
Doubly served[13] as they sat on the dais,   60
When Arthur had come to the hall with his court,
In the chapel had ceased the singing of mass;
Loud shouts were there uttered by priests and by others,

Anew praising Noel, naming it often.
Then hastened the lords to give handsel,[14] cried loudly 65
These gifts of the New Year, and gave them in person;
Debated about them busily, briskly.
Even though they were losers,[15] the ladies laughed loudly,
Nor wroth was the winner, as well ye may know.
All this manner of mirth they made till meat-time;   70
Then, when they had washed, they went to be seated,
Were placed in the way that appeared most proper,
The best men above. And Guinevere,[16] beautiful,
Was in the midst of the merriment seated
Upon the rich dais, adorned all about: 75
Fine silks on all sides, and spread as a canopy
Tapestries treasured of Tars[17] and Toulouse,
Embroidered and set with stones most splendid—
They'd prove of great price if ye pence gave to buy them
                     Some day.   80
         The comeliest was the Queen,
         With dancing eyes of grey.
         That a fairer he had seen
         No man might truly say.

But Arthur would eat not till all were attended;   85
Youthfully mirthful and merry in manner,
He loved well his life, and little it pleased him
Or[18] long to be seated, or long to lie down,
His young blood and wild brain were so busy and brisk.
Moreover, the King was moved by a custom   90
He once had assumed in a spirit of splendor:
Never to fall to his feast on a festival
Till a strange story of something eventful
Was told him, some marvel that merited credence
Of kings, or of arms, or all kinds of adventures;   95
Or some one besought him to send a true knight
To join him in proving the perils of jousting,
Life against life, each leaving the other
To have, as fortune would help him, the fairer lot.
This, when the King held his court, was his custom   100
At every fine feast 'mid his followers, freemen,
                     In hall.
         And so with countenance clear
         He stands there strong and tall,
         Alert on that New Year,   105
         And makes much mirth with all.

At his place the strong King stands in person, full
    courtly
Talking of trifles before the high table.

---

6 See p. 177, below, on this legendary ruler.
7 Pleasing, gracious.   8 Song, poem.
9 Either a reference to the poet's source in an earlier romance, or
  merely his way of encouraging his audience to believe his story.
10 The legendary capital of Arthur.
11 The legendary table at which Arthur's knights sat, and hence
  the corps of knights.
12 Originally dances in a ring accompanied by singing. The translator spells with an *e* to distinguish them from the later "carols."
13 They got two helpings on the holiday.

14 Gift at the beginning of a period or enterprise.
15 Presumably those whose gifts or arguments in praise of their
  gifts were considered inferior. Possibly gifts were offered in a
  game of handy-dandy or which-hand-is-it-in, so that some
  were literally losers.   16 Arthur's queen.
17 Turkestan.   18 Either.

There sat the good Gawain[19] by Guinevere's side,
And Sir Agravain, he of the Hard Hand, also,   110
True knights, and sons of the sister of Arthur.
At the top, Bishop Baldwin the table begins,
And Ywain beside him ate, Urien's son.
On the dais these sat, and were served with distinction;
Then many a staunch, trusty man at the side tables.   115
The first course was served to the sharp sound of trumpets,
With numerous banners beneath hanging brightly.
Then newly the kettledrums sounded and noble pipes;
Wild and loud warbles awakened such echoes
That many a heart leaped on high at their melody.   120
Came then the choice meats, cates rare and costly,
Of fair and fresh food such profusion of dishes
'T was hard to find place to put by the people
The silver that carried the various stews
                              On the cloth.   125
              Each to his best loved fare
              Himself helps, nothing loth;
              Each two,[20] twelve dishes share,
              Good beer and bright wine both.

And now I will say nothing more of their service,   130
For well one may know that naught there was wanted.
Now another new noise drew nigh of a sudden,
To let all the folk take their fill of the feast.
And scarcely the music had ceased for a moment,
The first course been suitably served in the court,   135
When a being most dreadful burst through the hall-door,
Among the most mighty of men in his measure.
From his throat to his thighs so thick were his sinews,
His loins and his limbs so large and so long,
That I hold him half-giant, the hugest of men,   140
And the handsomest, too, in his height, upon horseback.
Though stalwart in breast and in back was his body,
His waist and his belly were worthily small;
Fashioned fairly he was in his form, and in features
                              Cut clean.   145
              Men wondered at the hue
              That in his face was seen.
              A splendid man to view
              He came, entirely green.[21]

All green was the man, and green were his garments:

---

[19] In the older Arthurian romances the greatest of the knights.
    Later on he was belittled in character and in prowess, to exalt
    new heroes. In *Idylls of the King* Tennyson unhappily follows
    the later conception. His mother being Arthur's half sister,
    Gawain is the King's nephew, a relationship of special signifi-
    cance in medieval story, as we have seen in *Beowulf*. Agravain
    is Gawain's brother. Their father was King Lot of Orkney.
    Ywain is another of the most famous knights and also Arthur's
    nephew; his mother, Queen Brimesent, was another half sister
    of Arthur.
[20] Either two or four persons constituted a mess and ate out of the
    same dish.   [21] A fairy color.

A coat, straight and close, that clung to his sides,   151
A bright mantle on top of this, trimmed on the inside
With closely-cut fur, right fair, that showed clearly,
The lining with white fur most lovely, and hood too,
Caught back from his locks, and laid on his shoulders,   155
Neat stockings that clung to his calves, tightly stretched,
Of the same green, and under them spurs of gold shining
Brightly on bands of fine silk, richly barred;
And under his legs, where he rides, guards of leather.
His vesture was verily color of verdure: 160
Both bars of his belt and other stones, beautiful,
Richly arranged in his splendid array
On himself and his saddle, on silken designs.
'T would be truly too hard to tell half the trifles
Embroidered about it with birds and with flies   165
In gay, verdant green with gold in the middle;
The bit-studs, the crupper, the breast-trappings' pendants,
And everything metal enamelled in emerald.
The stirrups he stood on the same way were colored,
His saddle-bows too, and the studded nails splendid,   170
That all with green gems ever glimmered and glinted.
The horse he bestrode was in hue still the same,
                              Indeed;
              Green, thick, and of great height,
              And hard to curb, a steed   175
              In broidered bridle bright
              That such a man would need.

This hero in green was habited gaily,
And likewise the hair on the head of his good horse;
Fair, flowing tresses enfolded his shoulders,   180
And big as a bush a beard hung on his breast.
This, and the hair from his head hanging splendid,
Was clipped off evenly over his elbows,
In cut like a king's hood, covering the neck,
So that half of his arms were held underneath it.   185
The mane of the mighty horse much this resembled,
Well curled and combed, and with many knots covered,
Braided with gold threads about the fair green,
Now a strand made of hair, now a second of gold.
The forelock and tail were twined in this fashion,   190
And both of them bound with a band of bright green.
For the dock's length the tail was decked with stones
              dearly,
And then was tied with a thong in a tight knot,
Where many bright bells of burnished gold rang.
In the hall not one single man's seen before this   195
Such a horse here on earth, such a hero as on him
                              Goes.
              That his look was lightning bright
              Right certain were all those
              Who saw. It seemed none might   200
              Endure beneath his blows.

Yet the hero carried nor helmet nor hauberk,[22]
But bare was of armor, breastplate or gorget,[23]
Spear-shaft or shield, to thrust or to smite.
But in one hand he bore a bough of bright holly,   205
That grows most greenly when bare are the groves,
In the other an axe, gigantic, awful,
A terrible weapon, wondrous to tell of.
Large was the head, in length a whole ell-yard,
The blade of green steel and beaten gold both;   210
The bit had a broad edge, and brightly was burnished,
As suitably shaped as sharp razors for shearing.
This steel by its strong shaft the stern hero gripped:
With iron it was wound to the end of the wood,
And in work green and graceful was everywhere
          graven.   215
About it a fair thong was folded, made fast
At the head, and oft looped down the length of the
          handle.
To this were attached many splendid tassels,
On buttons of bright green richly embroidered.
Thus into the hall came the hero, and hastened   220
Direct to the dais, fearing no danger.
He gave no one greeting, but haughtily gazed,
And his first words were, "Where can I find him who
          governs
This goodly assemblage? for gladly that man
I would see and have speech with." So saying, from
          toe   225

> To crown
> On the knights his look he threw,
> And rolled it up and down;
> He stopped to take note who
> Had there the most renown.   230

There sat all the lords, looking long at the stranger,
Each man of them marvelling what it might mean
For a horse and a hero to have such a hue.
It seemed to them green as the grown grass, or greener,
Gleaming more bright than on gold green enamel.   235
The nobles who stood there, astonished, drew nearer,
And deeply they wondered what deed he would do.
Since never a marvel they'd met with like this one,
The folk all felt it was magic or phantasy.
Many great lords then were loth to give answer,   240
And sat stone-still, at his speaking astounded,
In swooning silence that spread through the hall.
As their speech on a sudden was stilled, fast asleep

> They did seem.
> They felt not only fright   245
> But courtesy, I deem.
> Let him address the knight,
> Him whom they all esteem.

---

[22] Coat of mail.   [23] Throat armor.

This happening the King, ever keen and courageous,
Saw from on high, and saluted the stranger   250
Suitably, saying, "Sir, you are welcome.
I, the head of this household, am Arthur;
In courtesy light, and linger, I pray you,
And later, my lord, we shall learn your desire."
"Nay, so help me He seated on high," quoth the hero,   255
"My mission was not to remain here a moment;
But, sir, since thy name is so nobly renowned,
Since thy city the best is considered, thy barons
The stoutest in steel gear that ride upon steeds,
Of all men in the world the most worthy and brave,   260
Right valiant to play with in other pure pastimes,
Since here, I have heard, is the highest of courtesy—
Truly, all these things have brought me at this time.
Sure ye may be by this branch that I bear
That I pass as in peace, proposing no fight.   265
If I'd come with comrades, equipped for a quarrel,
I have at my home both hauberk and helmet,
Shield and sharp spear, brightly shining, and other
Weapons to wield, full well I know also.
Yet softer my weeds[24] are, since warfare I wished not;   270
But art thou as bold as is bruited[25] by all,
Thou wilt graciously grant me the game that I ask for

> By right."
> Arthur good answer gave,
> And said, "Sir courteous knight,   275
> If battle here you crave,
> You shall not lack a fight."

"Nay, I ask for no fight; in faith, now I tell thee
But beardless babes are about on this bench.
Were I hasped in my armor, and high on a horse,   280
Here is no man to match me, your might is so feeble.
So I crave but a Christmas game in this court;
Yule and New Year are come, and here men have
          courage;
If one in this house himself holds so hardy,
So bold in his blood, in his brain so unbalanced   285
To dare stiffly strike one stroke for another,
I give this gisarme, this rich axe, as a gift to him,
Heavy enough, to handle as pleases him;
Bare as I sit, I shall bide the first blow.
If a knight be so tough as to try what I tell,   290
Let him leap to me lightly; I leave him this weapon,
Quitclaim it forever, to keep as his own;
And his stroke here, firm on this floor, I shall suffer,
This boon if thou grant'st me, the blow with another

> To pay;   295
> Yet let his respite be
> A twelvemonth and a day.

---

[24] Garments.   [25] Reported.

Come, let us quickly see
If one here aught dare say."

If at first he had startled them, stiller then sat there   300
The whole of the court, low and high, in the hall.
The knight on his steed turned himself in his saddle,
And fiercely his red eyes he rolled all around,
Bent his bristling brows, with green gleaming brightly,
And waved his beard, waiting for one there to rise.   305
And when none of the knights spoke, he coughed right
    noisily,
Straightened up proudly, and started to speak:
"What!" quoth the hero, "Is this Arthur's household,
The fame of whose fellowship fills many kingdoms?
Now where is your vainglory? Where are your
    victories?   310
Where is your grimness, your great words, your anger?
For now the Round Table's renown and its revel
Is worsted by one word of one person's speech,
For all shiver with fear before a stroke 's shown."
Then so loudly he laughed that the lord was grieved
    greatly,   315
And into his fair face his blood shot up fiercely
              For shame.
    As wroth as wind he grew,
    And all there did the same.
    The King that no fear knew   320
    Then to that stout man came.

And said, "Sir, by heaven, strange thy request is;
As folly thou soughtest, so shouldest thou find it.
I know that not one of the knights is aghast
Of thy great words. Give me thy weapon, for God's
    sake,   325
And gladly the boon thou hast begged I shall grant thee."
He leaped to him quickly, caught at his hand,
And fiercely the other lord lights on his feet.
Now Arthur lays hold of the axe by the handle,
As if he would strike with it, swings it round sternly.   330
Before him the strong man stood, in stature
A head and more higher than all in the house.
Stroking his beard, he stood with stern bearing,
And with a calm countenance drew down his coat,
No more frightened or stunned by the axe Arthur
    flourished   335
Than if on the bench some one brought him a flagon
              Of wine.
    Gawain by Guinevere
    Did to the King incline:
    "I pray in accents clear   340
    To let this fray be mine."

"If you now, honored lord," said this knight to King
    Arthur,
"Would bid me to step from this bench, and to stand
    there
Beside you—so could I with courtesy quit then
The table, unless my liege lady disliked it—   345
I'd come to your aid before all your great court.
For truly I think it a thing most unseemly
So boldly to beg such a boon in your hall here,
Though you in person are pleased to fulfil it,
While here on the benches such brave ones are seated,   350
Than whom under heaven, I think, none are higher
In spirit, none better in body for battle.
I am weakest and feeblest in wit, I know well,
And my life, to say truth, would be least loss of any.
I only since you are my uncle have honor;   355
Your blood the sole virtue I bear in my body.
Unfit is this foolish affair for you. Give it
To me who soonest have sought it, and let
All this court if my speech is not seemly, decide
              Without blame."   360
    The nobles gather round,
    And all advise the same:
    To free the King that's crowned,
    And Gawain give the game.

The King then commanded his kinsman to rise,   365
And quickly he rose up and came to him courteously,
Kneeled by the King, and caught the weapon;
He left it graciously, lifted his hand,
And gave him God's blessing, and gladly bade him
Be sure that his heart and his hand both were hardy.   370
"Take care," quoth the King, "how you start, coz,[26]
    your cutting,
And truly, I think, if rightly you treat him,
That blow you'll endure that he deals you after."
Weapon in hand, Gawain goes to the hero,
Who boldly remains there, dismayed none the more.   375
Then the knight in the green thus greeted Sir Gawain,
"Let us state our agreement again ere proceeding.
And now first, sir knight, what your name is I beg
That you truly will tell, so in that I may trust."
"In truth," said the good knight, "I'm called Sir
    Gawain,   380
Who fetch you this blow, whatsoever befalls,
And another will take in return, this time twelve-month,
From you, with what weapon you will; with no other
              I'll go."
    The other made reply: 385
    "By my life here below,
    Gawain, right glad am I
    To have you strike this blow.

---

[26] Cousin, kinsman; here, nephew.

"By God," said the Green Knight, "Sir Gawain, it pleases me—
Here, at thy hand, I shall have what I sought. 390
Thou hast rightly rehearsed to me, truly and readily,
All of the covenant asked of King Arthur;
Except that thou shalt, by thy troth, sir, assure me
Thyself and none other shalt seek me, wherever
Thou thinkest to find me, and fetch thee what wages 395
Are due for the stroke that today thou dost deal me
Before all this splendid assembly." "Where should I,"
Said Gawain, "go look for the land where thou livest?
The realm where thy home is, by Him who hath wrought me,
I know not, nor thee, sir, thy court nor thy name. 400
Truly tell me thy title, and teach me the road,
And I'll use all my wit to win my way thither.
And so by my sure word truly I swear."
" 'T is enough. No more now at New Year is needed,"
The knight in the green said to Gawain the courteous: 405
"If truly I tell when I've taken your tap
And softly you've struck me, if swiftly I tell you
My name and my house and my home, you may then
Of my conduct make trial, and your covenant keep;
And if no speech I speak, you speed all the better: 410
No longer need look, but may stay in your land.
But ho!
Take your grim tool with speed,
And let us see your blow."
Stroking his axe, "Indeed," 415
Said Gawain, "gladly so."

With speed then the Green Knight took up his stand,
Inclined his head forward, uncovering the flesh,
And laid o'er his crown his locks long and lovely,
And bare left the nape of his neck for the business. 420
His axe Gawain seized, and swung it on high;
On the floor his left foot he planted before him,
And swiftly the naked flesh smote with his weapon.
The sharp edge severed the bones of the stranger,
Cut through the clear flesh and cleft it in twain, 425
So the blade of the brown steel bit the ground deeply.
The fair head fell from the neck to the floor,
So that where it rolled forth with their feet many spurned it.
The blood on the green glistened, burst from the body;
And yet neither fell nor faltered the hero, 430
But stoutly he started forth, strong in his stride;
Fiercely he rushed 'mid the ranks of the Round Table,
Seized and uplifted his lovely head straightway;
Then back to his horse went, laid hold of the bridle,
Stepped into the stirrup and strode up aloft, 435
His head holding fast in his hand by the hair.
And the man as soberly sat in his saddle

As if he unharmed were, although now headless,
Instead.
His trunk around he spun, 440
That ugly body that bled.
Frightened was many a one
When he his words had said.

For upright he holds the head in his hand,
And confronts with the face the fine folk on the dais. 445
It lifted its lids, and looked forth directly,
Speaking this much with its mouth, as ye hear:
"Gawain, look that to go as agreed you are ready,
And seek for me faithfully, sir, till you find me,
As, heard by these heroes, you vowed in this hall. 450
To the Green Chapel go you, I charge you, to get
Such a stroke as you struck. You are surely deserving,
Sir knight, to be promptly repaid at the New Year.
As Knight of the Green Chapel many men know me;
If therefore to find me you try, you will fail not; 455
Then come, or be recreant called as befits thee."
With furious wrench of the reins he turned round,
And rushed from the hall-door, his head in his hands,
So the fire of the flint flew out from the foal's hoofs.
Not one of the lords knew the land where he went to, 460
No more than the realm whence he rushed in among them.
What then?
The King and Gawain there
At the Green Knight laughed again;
Yet this the name did bear 465
Of wonder among men.

Though much in his mind did the courtly King marvel,
He let not a semblance be seen, but said loudly
With courteous speech to the Queen, most comely:
"To-day, my dear lady, be never alarmed; 470
Such affairs are for Christmas well fitted to sing of
And gaily to laugh at when giving an interlude,[27]
'Mid all the company's caroles, most courtly.
None the less I may go now to get my meat;
For I needs must admit I have met with a marvel." 475
He glanced at Sir Gawain, and gladsomely said:
"Now sir, hang up thine axe; enough it has hewn."
O'er the dais 't was placed, to hang on the dosser,[28]
That men might remark it there as a marvel,
And truly describing, might tell of the wonder. 480
Together these two then turned to the table,
The sovereign and good knight, and swiftly men served them
With dainties twofold, as indeed was most fitting,

---

[27] Play.   [28] Tapestry.

All manner of meat and of minstrelsy both.
So the whole day in pleasure they passed till night fell   485
                    O'er the land.
              Now take heed, Gawain, lest,
              Fearing the Green Knight's brand,[29]
              Thou shrinkest from the quest
              That thou hast ta'en in hand.   490

                              II

    This sample had Arthur of strange things right early,
When young was the year, for he yearned to hear boasts.[30]
Though such words when they went to be seated were
                    wanting,
Yet stocked are they now with handfuls of stern work.
In the hall glad was Gawain those games to begin,   5
But not strange it would seem if sad were the ending;
For though men having drunk much are merry in mind,
Full swift flies a year, never yielding the same,
The start and the close very seldom according.
So past went this Yule, and the year followed after,   10
Each season in turn succeeding the other.
There came after Christmas the crabbed Lenten,
With fish and with plainer food trying the flesh;
But then the world's weather with winter contends;
Down to earth shrinks the cold, the clouds are uplifted; 15
In showers full warm descends the bright rain,
And falls on the fair fields. Flowers unfold;
The ground and the groves are green in their garments;
Birds hasten to build, blithesomely singing
For soft summer's solace ensuing on slopes   20
                    Everywhere.
              The blossoms swell and blow,
              In hedge-rows rich and rare,
              And notes most lovely flow
              From out the forest fair.   25

    After this comes the season of soft winds of summer,
When Zephyrus[31] sighs on the seeds and the green plants.
The herb that then grows in the ground is right happy,
When down from the leaves drops the dampening dew
To abide the bright sun that is blissfully shining.   30
But autumn comes speeding, soon grows severe,
And warns it to wax full ripe for the winter.
With drought then the dust is driven to rise,
From the face of the fields to fly to the heaven.
With the sun the wild wind of the welkin[32] is
                    struggling;   35

The leaves from the limbs drop, and light on the ground;
And withers the grass that grew once so greenly.
Then all ripens that formerly flourished, and rots;
And thus passes the year in yesterdays many,
And winter, in truth, as the way of the world is,   40
                    Draws near,
              Till comes the Michaelmas[33] moon
              With pledge of winter sere.
              Then thinks Sir Gawain soon
              Of his dread voyage drear.   45

    Till the tide of Allhallows[34] with Arthur he tarried;
The King made ado on that day for his sake
With rich and rare revel of all of the Round Table,
Knights most courteous, comely ladies,
All of them heavy at heart for the hero.   50
Yet nothing but mirth was uttered, though many
Joyless made jests for that gentleman's sake.
After meat, with sorrow he speaks to his uncle,
And openly talks of his travel, saying:
"Liege lord of my life, now I ask of you leave.   55
You know my case and condition, nor care I
To tell of its troubles even a trifle.
I must, for the blow I am bound to, to-morrow
Go seek as God guides me the man in the green."
Then came there together the best in the castle: 60
Ywain, Eric, and others full many,
Sir Dodinel de Sauvage, the Duke of Clarence,
Lancelot,[35] Lyonel, Lucan the good,
Sir Bors and Sir Bedevere,[36] both of them big men,
Mador de la Port, and many more nobles.   65
All these knights of the court came near to the King
With care in their hearts to counsel the hero;
Heavy and deep was the dole in the hall
That one worthy as Gawain should go on that errand,
To suffer an onerous stroke, and his own sword   70
                    To stay.
              The knight was of good cheer:
              "Why should I shrink away
              From a fate stern and drear?
              A man can but essay."   75

    He remained there that day; in the morning made
                    ready.
Early he asked for his arms; all were brought him.
And first a fine carpet was laid on the floor,
And much was the gilt gear that glittered upon it.

[33] September 29.
[34] Time of All Saints' Day, November 1.
[35] The most famous of the knights in this list. In later romance he
    displaces Gawain as the best of Arthur's knights. Lyonel is his
    cousin.
[36] According to the version worked up by Malory (and followed
    by Tennyson), the sole survivor of Arthur's knights in the last
    battle.

---

[29] Sword.
[30] On heroic boasting see p. 16, note 38, above. Here the poet
    means especially the knights' vows to undertake quests.
[31] The west wind.   [32] Sky, air.

Thereon stepped the strong man, and handled the steel, 80
Dressed in a doublet[37] of Tars that cost dearly,
A hood made craftily,[38] closed at the top,
And about on the lining bound with a bright fur.
Then they set on his feet shoes fashioned of steel,
And with fine greaves of steel encircled his legs. 85
Knee-pieces to these were connected, well polished,
Secured round his knees with knots of gold.
Then came goodly cuisses, with cunning enclosing
His thick, brawny thighs; with thongs they attached
   them.
Then the man was encased in a coat of fine mail, 90
With rings of bright steel on a rich stuff woven,
Braces well burnished on both of his arms,
Elbow-pieces gay, good, and gloves of plate,
All the goodliest gear that would give him most succor
               That tide: 95
      Coat armor[39] richly made,
      His gold spurs fixed with pride,
      Girt his unfailing blade
      By a silk sash to his side.[40]

When in arms he was clasped, his costume was
   costly; 100
The least of the lacings or loops gleamed with gold.
And armed in this manner, the man heard mass,
At the altar adored and made offering, and afterward
Came to the King and all of his courtiers,
Gently took leave of the ladies and lords; 105
Him they kissed and escorted,[41] to Christ him
   commending.
Then was Gringolet ready, girt with a saddle
That gaily with many a gold fringe was gleaming,
With nails studded newly, prepared for the nonce.[42]
The bridle was bound about, barred with bright gold; 110
With the bow of the saddle, the breastplate, the splendid
   skirts,
Crupper, and cloth in adornment accorded,
With gold nails arrayed on a groundwork of red,
That glittered and glinted like gleams of the sun.
Then he caught up his helm, and hastily kissed it; 115
It stoutly was stapled and stuffed well within,
High on his head, and hasped well behind,
With a light linen veil laid over the visor,
Embroidered and bound with the brightest of gems
On a silken border; with birds on the seams 120
Like painted parroquets preening; true love-knots
As thickly with turtledoves tangled as though

Many women had been at the work seven winters
         In town.
      Great was the circle's price 125
      Encompassing his crown;
      Of diamonds its device,
      That were both bright and brown.

Then they showed him his shield, sheer gules,[43]
   whereon shone
The pentangle[44] painted in pure golden hue. 130
On his baldric[45] he caught, and about his neck cast it;
And fairly the hero's form it befitted.
And why that great prince the pentangle suited
Intend I to tell, in my tale though I tarry.
'T is a sign that Solomon formerly set 135
As a token, for so it doth symbol, of truth.
A figure it is that with five points is furnished;
Each line overlaps and locks in another,
Nor comes to an end; and Englishmen call it
Everywhere, hear I, the endless knot.[46] 140
It became then the knight and his noble arms also,
In five ways, and five times each way still faithful.[47]
Sir Gawain was known as the good, refined gold,
Graced with virtues of castle,[48] of villainy void,
              Made clean. 145
      So the pentangle new
      On shield and coat was seen,
      As man of speech most true,
      And gentlest knight of mien.

First, in his five wits he faultless was found; 150
In his five fingers too the man never failed;
And on earth all his faith was fixed on the five wounds
That Christ, as the creed tells, endured on the cross.
Wheresoever this man was midmost in battle,
His thought above everything else was in this, 155
To draw all his fire from the fivefold joys[49]
That the fair Queen of Heaven felt in her child.
And because of this fitly he carried her image
Displayed on his shield, on its larger part,
That whenever he saw it his spirit should sink not.[50] 160
The fifth five the hero made use of, I find,
More than all were his liberalness, love of his fellows,
His courtesy, chasteness, unchangeable ever,

---

[43] Red.
[44] Or pentacle, a five-pointed star, an ancient geometric symbol of
  perfection; in the Middle Ages it was supposed to have magic
  power against demons.   [45] Shoulder belt.
[46] Because drawn in one continuous yet interlacing line.
[47] Each of the five points symbolized a virtue of Gawain, and each
  of those virtues had reference to five things.
[48] I.e., such virtues as grace the best society.
[49] These were usually reckoned as the Annunciation, Nativity,
  Resurrection, Ascension, and Assumption.
[50] It was evidently painted on the inner side of the shield.

---

[37] Jacket.   [38] Skillfully.
[39] A vest or tunic worn over the armor and displaying the knight's
  heraldic bearings.
[40] The poet puts his hero into fourteenth-century armor.
[41] To the mounting block.   [42] Present occasion.

And pity, all further traits passing. These five
In this hero more surely were set than in any.   165
In truth now, fivefold they were fixed in the knight,
Linked each to the other without any end,
And all of them fastened on five points unfailing;
Each side they neither united nor sundered,
Evermore endless at every angle,   170
Where equally either they ended or started.
And so his fair shield was adorned with this symbol,
Thus richly with red gold wrought on red gules,
So by people the pentangle perfect 't was called,
       As it ought.   175
    Gawain in arms is gay;
    Right there his lance he caught,
    And gave them all good-day
    For ever, as he thought.

He set spurs to his steed, and sprang on his way   180
So swiftly that sparks from the stone flew behind him.
All who saw him, so seemly, sighed, sad at heart;
The same thing, in sooth, each said to the other,
Concerned for that comely man: "Christ, 't is a shame
Thou, sir knight, must be lost whose life is so noble!   185
To find, faith! his equal on earth is not easy.
'T would wiser have been to have acted more warily,
Dubbed yonder dear one a duke. He seems clearly
To be in the land here a brilliant leader:
So better had been than brought thus to naught,   190
By an elf-man beheaded for haughty boasting.
Who e'er knew any king such counsel to take,
As foolish as one in a Christmas frolic?"
Much was the warm water welling from eyes
When the seemly hero set out from the city   195
       That day.
    Nowhere he abode,
    But swiftly went his way;
    By devious paths he rode,
    As I the book heard say.   200

Through the realm of Logres[51] now rides this lord,
Sir Gawain, for God's sake, no game though he thought
 it.
Oft alone, uncompanioned he lodges at night
Where he finds not the fare that he likes set before him.
Save his foal, he 'd no fellow by forests and hills;   205
On the way, no soul but the Savior to speak to.
At length he drew nigh unto North Wales, and leaving
To left of him all of the islands of Anglesey,

Fared by the forelands and over the fords
Near the Holy Head; hastening hence to the mainland,   210
In Wyral he went through the wilderness. There,
Lived but few who loved God or their fellows with good
 heart.
And always he asked of any he met,
As he journeyed, if nearby a giant they knew of,
A green knight, known as the Knight of the Green
 Chapel.   215
All denied it with nay, in their lives they had never
Once seen any hero who had such a hue
       Of green.
    The knight takes roadways strange
    In many a wild terrene;[52]   220
    Often his feelings change
    Before that chapel's seen.

Over many cliffs climbed he in foreign countries;[53]
From friends far sundered, he fared as a stranger;
And wondrous it were, at each water or shore   225
That he passed, if he found not before him a foe,
So foul too and fell[54] that to fight he could fail not.
The marvels he met with amount to so many
Too tedious were it to tell of the tenth part.
For sometimes with serpents he struggled and wolves
 too,   230
With wood-trolls sometimes in stony steeps dwelling,
And sometimes with bulls and with bears and with boars;
And giants from high fells hunted and harassed him.
If he'd been not enduring and doughty, and served God,
These doubtless would often have done him to death.   235
Though warfare was grievous, worse was the winter,
When cold, clear water was shed from the clouds
That froze ere it fell to the earth, all faded.
With sleet nearly slain, he slept in his armor
More nights than enough on the naked rocks,   240
Where splashing the cold stream sprang from the summit,
And hung in hard icicles high o'er his head.
Thus in peril and pain and desperate plights,
Till Christmas Eve wanders this wight through the
 country
       Alone.   245
    Truly the knight that tide
    To Mary made his moan,
    That she direct his ride
    To where some hearth-fire shone.

By a mount on the morn he merrily rides   250
To a wood dense and deep that was wondrously wild;
High hills on each hand, with forests of hoar oaks
Beneath them most huge, a hundred together.

---

[51] An old name for England south of the Humber. The geographical details which follow fail, perhaps intentionally, to
indicate Gawain's route clearly. The district of Wirral is near
Chester; it had a bad reputation in the fourteenth century as
the lair of bandits. Thence some think Gawain goes north, into
Cumberland.

[52] Terrain. The Middle English word is *bonk*, hill.
[53] I.e., strange regions.   [54] Fierce.

Thickly the hazel and hawthorn were tangled,
Everywhere mantled with moss rough and ragged,   255
With many a bird on the bare twigs, mournful,
That piteously piped for pain of the cold.
Sir Gawain on Gringolet goes underneath them
Through many a marsh and many a mire,
Unfriended, fearing to fail in devotion,   260
And see not His service, that Sire's, on that very night
Born of a Virgin to vanquish our pain.
And so sighing he said: "Lord, I beseech Thee,
And Mary, the mildest mother so dear,
For some lodging wherein to hear mass full lowly,   265
And matins, meekly I ask it, to-morrow;
So promptly I pray my pater and ave[55]

> And creed."
>> Thus rode he as he prayed,
>> Lamenting each misdeed;   270
>> Often the sign he made,
>> And said, "Christ's cross me speed."

He scarcely had signed himself thrice, ere he saw
In the wood on a mound a moated mansion,
Above a fair field, enfolded in branches   275
Of many a huge tree hard by the ditches:
The comeliest castle that knight ever kept.
In a meadow 't was placed, with a park all about,
And a palisade, spiked and pointed, set stoutly
Round many a tree for more than two miles.   280
The lord on that one side looked at the stronghold
That shimmered and shone through the shapely oak trees;
Then duly his helm doffed, and gave his thanks humbly
To Jesus and Julian,[56] both of them gentle,
For showing him courtesy, hearing his cry.   285
"Now good lodging," quoth Gawain, "I beg you to
> grant me."
Then with spurs in his gilt heels he Gringolet strikes,
Who chooses the chief path by chance that conducted
The man to the bridge-end ere many a minute
> Had passed.   290
>> The bridge secure was made,
>> Upraised; the gates shut fast;
>> The walls were well arrayed.
>> It feared no tempest's blast.

The hero abode on his horse by the bank   295
Of the deep, double ditch that surrounded the dwelling.
The wall stood wonderfully deep in the water,
And again to a huge height sprang overhead;
Of hard, hewn rock that reached to the cornices,
Built up with outworks under the battlements   300

Finely; at intervals, turrets fair fashioned,
With many good loopholes that shut tight; this lord
Had ne'er looked at a barbican[57] better than this one.
Further in he beheld the high hall; here and there
Towers were stationed set thickly with spires,   305
With finials[58] wondrously long and fair fitting,
Whose points were cunningly carven, and craftily.
There numerous chalk-white chimneys he noticed
That bright from the tops of the towers were gleaming.
Such pinnacles painted, so placed about everywhere,   310
Clustering so thick 'mid the crenels,[59] the castle
Surely appeared to be shaped to cut paper.
The knight on his foal it fair enough fancies
If into the court he may manage to come,
In that lodging to live while the holiday lasts   315
> With delight.
>> A porter came at call,
>> His mission learned, and right
>> Civilly from the wall
>> Greeted the errant knight.   320

Quoth Gawain: "Good sir, will you go on my errand,
Harbor to crave of this house's high lord?"
"Yea, by Peter. I know well, sir knight," said the porter,
"You're welcome as long as you list here to tarry."
Then went the man quickly, and with him, to
> welcome   325
The knight to the castle, a courteous company.
Down the great drawbridge they dropped, and went
> eagerly
Forth; on the frozen earth fell on their knees
To welcome this knight in the way they thought worthy;
Threw wide the great gate for Gawain to enter.   330
He bid them rise promptly, and rode o'er the bridge.
His saddle several seized as he lighted,
And stout men in plenty stabled his steed.
And next there descended knights and esquires
To lead to the hall with delight this hero.   335
When he raised his helmet, many made haste
From his hand to catch it, to care for the courtly man.
Some of them took then his sword and his shield both.
Then Gawain graciously greeted each knight;
Many proud men pressing to honor that prince,   340
To the hall they led him, all hasped in his harness,
Where fiercely a fair fire flamed on the hearth.
Then came the lord of this land from his chamber
To fittingly meet the man on the floor,
And said: "You are welcome to do what your will is; 345
To hold as your own, you have all that is here

---

[55] Paternoster (the Lord's Prayer, beginning "Our Father") and
Ave Maria (a prayer to the Virgin, beginning "Hail, Mary").
[56] The patron saint of travelers.

[57] Outer defense work.
[58] Ornamental tips of pinnacles or gables.
[59] Embrasures in battlements.

In this place."
"Thank you," said Gawain then,
"May Christ reward this grace."
The two like joyful men   350
Each other then embrace.

Gawain gazed at the man who so graciously greeted
   him;
Doughty he looked, the lord of that dwelling,
A hero indeed huge, hale, in his prime;
His beard broad and bright, its hue all of beaver;[60] 355
Stern, and on stalwart shanks steadily standing;
Fell faced as the fire, in speech fair and free.
In sooth, well suited he seemed, thought Gawain,
To govern as prince of a goodly people.
To his steward the lord turned, and strictly
   commanded   360
To send men to Gawain to give him good service;
And prompt at his bidding were people in plenty.
To a bright room they brought him, the bed nobly
   decked
With hangings of pure silk with clear golden hems,
And curious coverings with comely panels,   365
Embroidered with bright fur above at the edges;
On cords curtains running with rings of red gold;
From Tars and Toulouse were the tapestries covering
The walls; under foot on the floor more to match.
There he soon, with mirthful speeches, was stripped 370
Of his coat of linked mail and his armor; and quickly
Men ran, and brought him rich robes, that the best
He might pick out and choose as his change of apparel.
When lapped was the lord in the one he selected,
That fitted him fairly with flowing skirts,   375
The fur by his face, in faith it seemed made,
To the company there, entirely of colors,
Glowing and lovely; beneath all his limbs were.
That never made Christ a comelier knight
           They thought.   380
On earth, or far or near,
It seemed as if he ought
To be a prince sans peer
In fields where fierce men fought.

A chair by the chimney where charcoal was burning 385
For Gawain was fitted most finely with cloths,
Both cushions and coverlets, cunningly made.
Then a comely mantle was cast on the man,
Of a brown, silken fabric bravely embroidered,
Within fairly furred with the finest of skins,   390
Made lovely with ermine, his hood fashioned likewise.
He sat on that settle in clothes rich and seemly;
His mood, when well he was warmed, quickly mended.

[60] Reddish brown.

Soon was set up a table on trestles most fair;
With a clean cloth that showed a clear white it was
   covered,   395
With top-cloth and salt-cellar, spoons too of silver.
When he would the man washed, and went to his meat,
And seemly enough men served him with several
Excellent stews in the best manner seasoned,
Twofold[61] as was fitting, and various fishes;   400
In bread some were baked, some broiled on the coals,
Some seethed,[62] some in stews that were savored with
   spices;
And ever such subtly made sauces as pleased him.
He freely and frequently called it a feast,
Most courtly; the company there all acclaimed him 405
           Well-bred.
"But now this penance[63] take,
And soon 't will mend," they said.
That man much mirth did make,
As wine went to his head.   410

They enquired then and queried in guarded questions
Tactfully put to the prince himself,
Till he courteously owned he came of the court
The lord Arthur, gracious and goodly, alone holds,
Who rich is and royal, the Round Table's King;   415
And that Gawain himself in that dwelling was seated,
For Christmas come, as the case had befallen.
When he learned that he had that hero, the lord
Laughed loudly thereat so delightful he thought it.
Much merriment made all the men in that castle   420
By promptly appearing then in his presence;
For all prowess and worth and pure polished manners
Pertain to his person. He ever is praised;
Of all heroes on earth his fame is the highest.
Each knight full softly said to his neighbor,   425
"We now shall see, happily, knightly behavior,
And faultless terms of talking most noble;
What profit's in speech we may learn without seeking,
For nurture's fine father[64] has found here a welcome;
In truth God has graciously given His grace   430
Who grants us to have such a guest as Gawain
When men for His birth's sake sit merry and sing.
           To each
Of us this hero now
Will noble manners teach;   435
Who hear him will learn how
To utter loving speech."

When at length the dinner was done, and the lords
Had risen, the nighttime nearly was come.

[61] Double helpings.   [62] Boiled.
[63] Days before holy days were days of abstinence; hence the fish
   dinner, jokingly called a penance by the people of the castle.
[64] Exemplar of good breeding. Gawain was famed as the most
   courteous of Arthur's knights.

The chaplains went their way to the chapels   440
And rang right joyfully, just as they should do,
For evensong solemn this festival season.
To this goes the lord, and the lady likewise;
She comes in with grace to the pew closed and comely,
And straightway Gawain goes thither right gaily;   445
The lord by his robe took him, led to a seat,
Acknowledged him kindly and called him by name,
Saying none in the world was as welcome as he was.
He heartily thanked him; the heroes embraced,
And together they soberly sat through the service.   450
Then longed the lady to look on the knight,
And emerged from her pew with many fair maidens;
In face she was fairest of all, and in figure,
In skin and in color, all bodily qualities;
Lovelier, Gawain thought, even than Guinevere.   455
He goes through the chancel to greet her, so gracious.
By the left hand another was leading her, older
Than she, a lady who looked as if aged,
By heroes around her reverenced highly.
The ladies, however, unlike were to look on: 460
If fresh was the younger, the other was yellow;
Rich red on the one was rioting everywhere,
Rough wrinkled cheeks hung in rolls on the other;
One's kerchiefs, with clear pearls covered and many,
Displayed both her breast and her bright throat all
          bare,   465
Shining fairer than snow on the hillsides falling;
The second her neck in a neck-cloth enswathed,
That enveloped in chalk-white veils her black[65] chin;
Her forehead in silk was wrapped and enfolded
Adorned and tricked with trifles about it   470
Till nothing was bare but the lady's black brows,
Her two eyes, her nose, and her lips, all naked,
And those were bleared strangely, and ugly to see.
A goodly lady, so men before God
          Might decide!   475
          Her body thick and short,
          Her hips were round and wide;
          One of more pleasant sort
          She led there by her side.

When Gawain had gazed on that gay one so
          gracious   480
In look, he took leave of the lord and went toward them,
Saluted the elder, bowing full lowly,
The lovelier lapped in his two arms a little,
And knightly and comely greeted and kissed her.[66]
They craved his acquaintance, and quickly he asked   485
To be truly their servant if so they desired it.

They took him between them, and led him with talk
To the sitting room's hearth; then straightway for spices
They called, which men sped to unsparingly bring,
And with them as well pleasant wine at each coming.   490
Up leaped right often the courteous lord,
Urged many a time that the men should make merry,
Snatched off his hood, on a spear gaily hung it,
And waved it, that one for a prize might win it
Who caused the most mirth on that Christmas season.   495
"I shall try, by my faith, to contend with the finest
Ere hoodless I find myself, helped by my friends."
Thus with laughing speeches the lord makes merry
That night, to gladden Sir Gawain with games.
          So they spent   500
          The evening in the hall.
          The king[67] for lights then sent,
          And taking leave of all
          To bed Sir Gawain went.

On the morn when the Lord, as men all remember,   505
Was born, who would die for our doom, in each dwelling
On earth grows happiness greater for His sake;
So it did on that day there with many a dainty:
With dishes cunningly cooked at meal-times,
With doughty men dressed in their best on the dais.   510
The old lady was seated the highest; beside her
Politely the lord took his place, I believe;
The gay lady and Gawain together sat, midmost,
Where fitly the food came, and afterward fairly
Was served through the hall as beseemed them the
          best,   515
Of the company each in accord with his station.
There was meat and mirth, there was much joy, too
          troublous
To tell, though I tried in detail to describe it;
Yet I know both the lovely lady and Gawain
So sweet found each other's society (pleasant   520
And polished their converse, courtly and private;
Unfailing their courtesy, free from offence)
That surpassing, in truth, any play of a prince was
          Their game.
          There trumpets, drums, and airs   525
          Of piping loudly came.
          Each minded his affairs,
          And those two did the same.

Much mirth was that day and the day after made,
And the third followed fast, as full of delight.   530
Sweet was the joy of St. John's Day[68] to hear of,
The last, as the folk there believed, of the festival.

[65] Swarthy.
[66] The conventional thing for a gentleman to do; nothing more
     than courtesy was implied by it.

[67] The reading of the manuscript, probably in error for *lord.*
[68] December 27.

Guests were to go in the grey dawn, and therefore
They wondrously late were awake with their wine,
And danced delightful, long-lasting caroles.   535
At length when 't was late they took their leave,
Each strong man among them to start on his way.
Gawain gave him good-day; then the good man laid hold
          of him,
Led to the hearth in his own room the hero;
There took him aside, and gave suitable thanks   540
For the gracious distinction that Gawain had given
In honoring his house that holiday season,
And gracing his castle with courteous company.
"I'll truly as long as I live be the better
That Gawain at God's own feast was my guest."   545
"Gramercy," said Gawain, "by God, sir, not mine
Is the worth, but your own; may the high King reward
          you.
I am here at your will to work your behest,
As in high and low it behooves me to do
                    By right."   550
          The lord intently tries
          Longer to hold the knight;
          Gawain to him replies
          That he in no way might.

     Then the man with courteous question enquired   555
What dark deed that feast time had driven him forth,
From the King's court to journey alone with such
          courage,
Ere fully in homes was the festival finished.
"In sooth," said the knight, "sir, ye say but the truth;
From these hearths a high and a hasty task took me.   560
Myself, I am summoned to seek such a place
As to find it I know not whither to fare.
I'd not fail to have reached it the first of the New Year,
So help me our Lord, for the whole land of Logres;
And therefore, I beg this boon of you here, sir;   565
Tell me, in truth, if you ever heard tale
Of the Chapel of Green, of the ground where it stands,
And the knight, green colored, who keeps it. By solemn
Agreement a tryst was established between us,
That man at that landmark to meet if I lived.   570
And now there lacks of New Year but little;
I'd look at that lord, if God would but let me,
More gladly than own any good thing, by God's Son.
And hence, by your leave, it behooves me to go;
I now have but barely three days to be busy.   575
As fain would I fall dead as fail of my mission."
Then laughing the lord said: "You longer must stay,
For I'll point out the way to that place ere the time's end,
The ground of the Green Chapel. Grieve no further;
For, sir, you shall be in your bed at your ease   580
Until late, and fare forth the first of the year,
To your meeting place come by mid-morning; to do
          there
                    Your pleasure.
          Tarry till New Year's day,
          Then rise and go at leisure.   585
          I'll set you on your way;
          Not two miles is the measure."

     Then was Gawain right glad, and gleefully laughed.
"Now for this more than anything else, sir, I thank you.
I have come to the end of my quest; at your will   590
I shall bide, and in all things act as you bid me."
The lord then seized him, and set him beside him,
And sent for the ladies to better delight him.
Seemly the pleasure them among in private.
So gay were the speeches he spoke, and so friendly,   595
The host seemed a man well-nigh mad in behavior.
He called to the knight there, crying aloud:
"Ye have bound you to do the deed that I bid you.
Here, and at once, will you hold to your word, sir?"
"Yes, certainly, sir," the true hero said;   600
"While I bide in your house I obey your behest."
"You have toiled," said the lord; "from afar have
          travelled,
And here have caroused, nor are wholly recovered
In sleep or in nourishment, know I for certain.
In your room you shall linger, and lie at your ease   605
To-morrow till mass-time, and go to your meat
When you will, and with you my wife to amuse you
With company, till to the court I return.
                    You stay
          And I shall early rise,   610
          And hunting go my way."
          Bowing in courteous wise,
          Gawain grants all this play.

     "And more," said the man, "let us make an agreement:
Whatever I win in the wood shall be yours;   615
And what chance you shall meet shall be mine in
          exchange.
Sir, let's so strike our bargain and swear to tell truly
Whate'er fortune brings, whether bad, sir, or better."
Quoth Gawain the good: "By God, I do grant it.
What pastime you please appears to me pleasant."   620
"On the beverage brought us the bargain is made,"
So the lord of the land said. All of them laughed,
And drank, and light-heartedly revelled and dallied,
Those ladies and lords, as long as they liked.
Then they rose with elaborate politeness, and
          lingered,   625
With many fair speeches spoke softly together,
Right lovingly kissed, and took leave of each other.
Gay troops of attendants with glimmering torches

In comfort escorted each man to his couch

To rest.   630

Yet ere they left the board

Their promise they professed

Often. That people's lord

Could well maintain a jest.

III

Betimes[1] rose the folk ere the first of the day;
The guests that were going then summoned their grooms,
Who hastily sprang up to saddle their horses,
Packed their bags and prepared all their gear.
The nobles made ready, to ride all arrayed;   5
And quickly they leaped and caught up their bridles,
And started, each wight on the way that well pleased him.
The land's beloved lord not last was equipped
For riding, with many a man too. A morsel
He hurriedly ate when mass he had heard,   10
And promptly with horn to the hunting field hastened.
And ere any daylight had dawned upon earth,
Both he and his knights were high on their horses.
The dog-grooms, accomplished, the hounds then coupled,
The door of the kennel unclosed, called them out,   15
On the bugle mightily blew three single notes;[2]
Whereupon bayed with a wild noise the brachets,[3]
And some they turned back that went straying, and
     punished.
The hunters, I heard, were a hundred. To station

They go,   20

The keepers of the hounds,

And off the leashes throw.

With noise the wood resounds

From the good blasts they blow.

At the first sound of questing, the wild creatures
     quaked;   25
The deer fled, foolish from fright, in the dale,
To the high ground hastened, but quickly were halted
By beaters, loud shouting, stationed about
In a circle. The harts[4] were let pass with their high heads,
And also the bucks, broad-antlered and bold;   30
For the generous lord by law had forbidden
All men with the male deer to meddle in close season.
The hinds were hemmed in with hey! and ware!
The does to the deep valleys driven with great din.
You might see as they loosed them the shafts swiftly
     soar—   35
At each turn of the forest their feathers went flying—

[1] Early.
[2] Three "moots" or long blasts. The hunting horn of the fourteenth century had but one note; variety was secured by using
combinations of long and short blasts.   [3] Hounds.
[4] The male of the red deer; the hinds were the female.

That deep into brown hides bit with their broad heads;
Lo! they brayed on the hill-sides, bled there, and died,
And hounds, fleet-footed, followed them headlong.
And hunters after them hastened with horns   40
So loud in their sharp burst of sound as to sunder
The cliffs. What creatures escaped from the shooters,
Hunted and harried from heights to the waters,
Were pulled down and rent at the places there ready;
Such skill the men showed at these low-lying stations,   45
So great were the greyhounds that quickly they got them
And dragged them down, fast as the folk there might look

At the sight.

Carried with bliss away,

The lord did oft alight,   50

Oft gallop; so that day

He passed till the dark night.

Thus frolicked the lord on the fringe of the forest,
And Gawain the good in his gay bed reposed,
Lying snugly, till sunlight shone on the walls,   55
'Neath a coverlet bright with curtains about it.
As softly he slumbered, a slight sound he heard
At his door, made with caution, and quickly it opened.
The hero heaved up his head from the clothes;
By a corner he caught up the curtain a little,   60
And glanced out with heed to behold what had happened.
The lady it was, most lovely to look at,
Who shut the door after her stealthily, slyly,
And turned toward the bed. Then the brave man,
     embarrassed,
Lay down again subtly to seem as if sleeping;   65
And stilly she stepped, and stole to his bed,
There cast up the curtain, and creeping within it,
Seated herself on the bedside right softly,
And waited a long while to watch when he woke.
And the lord too, lurking, lay there a long while,   70
Wondering at heart what might come of this happening,
Or what it might mean—a marvel he thought it.
Yet he said to himself, " 'T would be surely more seemly
By speaking at once to see what she wishes."
Then roused he from sleep, and stretching turned toward
     her,   75
His eyelids unlocked, made believe that he wondered,
And signed himself so by his prayers to be safer

From fall.

Right sweet in chin and cheek,

Both white and red withal,   80

Full fairly she did speak

With laughing lips and small.

"Good morrow, Sir Gawain," that gay lady said,
"You're a sleeper unwary, since so one may steal in.
In a trice you are ta'en! If we make not a truce,   85

In your bed, be you certain of this, I shall bind you."
All laughing, the lady delivered those jests.
"Good morrow, fair lady," said Gawain the merry,
"You may do what you will, and well it doth please me,
For quickly I yield me, crying for mercy;   90
This method to me seems the best—for I must!"
So the lord in turn jested with laughter right joyous.
"But if, lovely lady, you would, give me leave,
Your prisoner release and pray him to rise,
And I'd come from this bed and clothe myself better; 95
So could I converse with you then with more comfort."
"Indeed no, fair sir," that sweet lady said,
"You'll not move from your bed; I shall manage you
        better;
For here—and on that side too—I shall hold you,
And next I shall talk with the knight I have taken.   100
For well do I know that your name is Sir Gawain,
By everyone honored wherever you ride;
Most highly acclaimed is your courtly behavior
With lords and ladies and all who are living.
And now you're here, truly, and none but we two;   105
My lord and his followers far off have fared;
Other men remain in their beds, and my maidens;
The door is closed, and secured with a strong hasp;
Since him who delights all I have in my house,
My time, as long as it lasts, I with talking   110
                                Shall fill.
        My body's gladly yours;
        Upon me work your will.
        Your servant I, perforce,
        Am now, and shall be still."   115

"In faith," quoth Sir Gawain, "a favor I think it,
Although I am now not the knight you speak of;
To reach to such fame as here you set forth,
I am one, as I well know myself, most unworthy.
By God, should you think it were good, I'd be glad   120
If I could or in word or action accomplish
Your ladyship's pleasure—a pure joy 't would prove."
"In good faith, Sir Gawain," the gay lady said,
"Ill-bred I should be if I blamed or belittled
The worth and prowess that please all others.   125
There are ladies enough who'd be now more delighted
To have you in thraldom, as here, sir, I have you,
To trifle gaily in talk most engaging,
To give themselves comfort and quiet their cares,
Than have much of the gold and the goods they
        command.   130
But to Him I give praise that ruleth the heavens,
That wholly I have in my hand what all wish."
                                So she
        Gave him good cheer that day,
        She who was fair to see.   135

To what she chanced to say
With pure speech answered he.

Quoth the merry man, "Madam, Mary reward you,
For noble, in faith, I've found you, and generous.
People by others pattern their actions,   140
But more than I merit to me they give praise;
'T is your courteous self who can show naught but
        kindness."
"By Mary," said she, "to me it seems other!
Were I worth all the host of women now living,
And had I the wealth of the world in my hands,   145
Should I chaffer and choose to get me a champion,
Sir, from the signs I've seen in you here
Of courtesy, merry demeanor, and beauty,
From what I have heard, and hold to be true,
Before you no lord now alive would be chosen."   150
"A better choice, madam, you truly have made;
Yet I'm proud of the value you put now upon me.
Your servant as seemly,[5] I hold you my sovereign,
Become your knight, and Christ give you quittance."[6]
Thus of much they talked till mid-morning was past.   155
The lady behaved as if greatly she loved him,
But Gawain, on guard, right gracefully acted.
"Though I were the most lovely of ladies," she thought,
"The less would he take with him love." He was seeking,
                                With speed,   160
        Grief that must be: the stroke
        That him should stun indeed.
        She then of leaving spoke,
        And promptly he agreed.

Then she gave him good-day, and glanced at him,
        laughing,   165
And startled him, speaking sharp words as she stood:
"He who blesses all words reward this reception!
I doubt if indeed I may dub you[7] Gawain."
"Wherefore?" he queried, quickly enquiring,
Afraid that he'd failed in his fashion of speech.   170
But the fair lady blessed him, speaking as follows:
"One as good as is Gawain the gracious considered
(And courtly behavior 's found wholly in him),
Not lightly so long could remain with a lady
Without, in courtesy, craving a kiss   175
At some slight subtle hint at the end of a story."
"Let it be as you like, lovely lady," said Gawain;
"As a knight is so bound, I'll kiss at your bidding,
And lest he displease you, so plead no longer."
Then closer she comes, and catches the knight   180
In her arms, and salutes him, leaning down affably.

---

[5] In due propriety.   [6] Reward.
[7] If I may call you; i.e., if you really are.

Kindly each other to Christ they commend.
She goes forth at the door without further ado,
And he quickly makes ready to rise, and hastens,
Calls to his chamberlain, chooses his clothes,   185
And merrily marches, when ready, to mass.
Then he fared to his meat, and fitly he feasted,
Made merry all day with amusements till moonrise.

None knew

A knight to better fare   190
With dames so worthy, two:
One old, one younger. There
Much mirth did then ensue.

Still was absent the lord of that land on his pleasure,
To hunt barren hinds in wood and in heath.   195
By the set of the sun he had slain such a number
Of does and different deer that 't was wondrous.
Eagerly flocked in the folk at the finish,
And quickly made of the killed deer a quarry;[8]
To this went the nobles with numerous men;   200
The game whose flesh was the fattest they gathered;
With care, as the case required, cut them open.
And some the deer searched at the spot of assay,[9]
And two fingers of fat they found in the poorest.
They slit at the base of the throat, seized the stomach, 205
Scraped it away with a sharp knife and sewed it;[10]
Next slit the four limbs and stripped off the hide;
Then opened the belly and took out the bowels
And flesh of the knot, quickly flinging them out.
They laid hold of the throat, made haste to divide,
then,   210
The windpipe and gullet, and tossed out the guts;
With their sharp knives carved out the shoulders and
carried them
Held through a small hole to have the sides perfect.[11]
The breast they sliced, and split it in two;
And then they began once again at the throat,   215
And quickly as far as its fork they cut it;
Pulled out the pluck,[12] and promptly thereafter

---

[8] Collection of carcasses.

[9] Test. It was formally made by the ranking member of a hunting party, while the carcass was held for him by the chief
huntsman. The assay was made by slitting the brisket, the lower
part of the breast. Throughout his hunting scenes the poet's
terminology follows the established codes of procedure.

[10] The usual thing was to stuff the stomach with blood and fat.

[11] A gentleman was supposed to know how to cut up a deer. This
line is explained by a passage on that subject in the authoritative
treatise The Noble Art of Venery or Hunting (1576), ascribed to
George Turberville; procedure had not changed much since the
fourteenth century. In cutting off the shoulder the operator
sticks in his knife above the "elbow joint" and then "raiseth out
the sinew or muscle with his knife, and putteth his forefinger of
his left hand through under the said muscle to hold the leg by."

[12] The fore part of the numbles or viscera.

Beside the ribs swiftly severed the fillets,
Cleared them off readily right by the backbone,
Straight down to the haunch, all hanging together.   220
They heaved it up whole, and hewed it off there,
And the rest by the name of the numbles—and rightly—

They knew.

Then where divide the thighs,
The folds behind they hew,   225
Hasten to cut the prize
Along the spine in two.

And next both the head and the neck off they hewed;
The sides from the backbone swiftly they sundered;
The fee of the ravens they flung in the branches.   230
They ran through each thick side a hole by the ribs,
And hung up both by the hocks of the haunches,
Each fellow to have the fee[13] that was fitting.
On the fair beast's hide, they fed their hounds
With the liver and lights[14] and the paunch's lining,   235
Among which bread steeped in blood was mingled.
They blew boldly the blast for the prize;[15] the hounds
barked.
Then the venison took they and turned toward home,
And stoutly many a shrill note they sounded.
Ere close of the daylight, the company came   240
To the comely castle where Gawain in comfort

Sojourned.

And when he met the knight
As thither he returned,
Joy had they and delight,   245
Where the fire brightly burned.

In the hall the lord bade all his household to gather,
And both of the dames to come down with their damsels.
In the room there before all the folk he ordered
His followers, truly, to fetch him his venison.   250
Gawain he called with courteous gaiety,
Asked him to notice the number of nimble beasts,
Showed him the fairness of flesh on the ribs.
"Are you pleased with this play? Have I won your praise?
Have I thoroughly earned your thanks through my
cunning?"   255
"In faith," said Sir Gawain, "this game is the fairest
I've seen in the season of winter these seven years."
"The whole of it, Gawain, I give you," the host said;
"Because of our compact, as yours you may claim it."
"That is true," the knight said, "and I tell you the
same: 260
That this I have worthily won within doors,
And surely to you with as good will I yield it."
With both of his arms his fair neck he embraced,

---

[13] I.e., portion of the deer.   [14] Lungs.

[15] The special call that meant the deer was taken.

And the hero as courteously kissed as he could.
"I give you my gains. I got nothing further;   265
I freely would grant it, although it were greater."
"It is good," said the good man; "I give you my thanks.
Yet things so may be that you'd think it better
To tell where you won this same wealth by your wit."
" 'T was no part of our pact," said he; "press me no
        more;   270
For trust entirely in this, that you've taken
                        Your due."
                With laughing merriment
                And knightly speech and true,
                To supper soon they went   275
                With store of dainties new.

In a chamber they sat, by the side of the chimney,
Where men right frequently fetched them mulled[16] wine.
In their jesting, again they agreed on the morrow
To keep the same compact they came to before: 280
That whatever should chance, they'd exchange at evening,
When greeting again, the new things they had gotten.
Before all the court they agreed to the covenant;
Then was the beverage brought forth in jest.
At last they politely took leave of each other,   285
And quickly each hero made haste to his couch.
When the cock but three times had crowed and cackled,
The lord and his men had leaped from their beds.
So that duly their meal was dealt with, and mass,
And ere daylight they'd fared toward the forest, on
        hunting   290
                        Intent.
                The huntsmen with loud horns
                Through level fields soon went,
                Uncoupling 'mid the thorns
                The hounds swift on the scent.   295

Soon they cry for a search by the side of a swamp.
The huntsmen encourage the hounds that first catch there
The scent, and sharp words they shout at them loudly;
And thither the hounds that heard them hastened,
And fast to the trail fell, forty at once.   300
Then such clamor and din from the dogs that had come
        there
Arose that the rocks all around them rang.
With horn and with mouth the hunters heartened them;
They gathered together then, all in a group,
'Twixt a pool in that copse and a crag most
        forbidding.   305
At a stone-heap, beside the swamp, by a cliff,
Where the rough rock had fallen in rugged confusion,

---

16 Heated, sweetened, and spiced. (The translator's rendering, for alliteration's sake, of *walle,* choice.)

They fared to the finding, the folk coming after.
Around both the crag and the rubble-heap searched
The hunters, sure that within them was hidden   310
The beast whose presence was bayed by the blood-hounds.
Then they beat on the bushes, and bade him rise up,
And wildly he made for the men in his way,
Rushing suddenly forth, of swine the most splendid.
Apart from the herd he'd grown hoary with age,   315
For fierce was the beast, the biggest of boars.
Then many men grieved, full grim when he grunted,
For three at his first thrust he threw to the earth,
And then hurtled forth swiftly, no harm doing further.
They shrilly cried hi! and shouted hey! hey!   320
Put bugles to mouth, loudly blew the recall.
The men and dogs merry in voice were and many;
With outcry they all hurry after this boar
                        To slay.
                He maims the pack when, fell,   325
                He oftens stands at bay.
                Loudly they howl and yell,
                Sore wounded in the fray.

Then to shoot at him came up the company quickly.
Arrows that hit him right often they aimed,   330
But their sharp points failed that fell on his shoulders'
Tough skin, and the barbs would not bite in his flesh;
But the smooth-shaven shafts were shivered in pieces,
The heads wherever they hit him rebounding.
But when hurt by the strength of the strokes they
        struck,   335
Then mad for the fray he falls on the men,
And deeply he wounds them as forward he dashes.
Then many were frightened, and drew back in fear;
But the lord galloped off on a light horse after him,
Blew like a huntsman right bold the recall   340
On his bugle, and rode through the thick of the bushes,
Pursuing this swine till the sun shone clearly.
Thus the day they passed in doing these deeds,
While bides our gracious knight Gawain in bed,
With bedclothes in color right rich, at the castle   345
                        Behind.
                The dame did not forget
                To give him greetings kind.
                She soon upon him set,
                To make him change his mind.   350

Approaching the curtain, she peeps at the prince,
And at once Sir Gawain welcomes her worthily.
Promptly the lady makes her reply.
By his side she seats herself softly, heartily
Laughs, and with lovely look these words delivers: 355
"If you, sir, are Gawain, greatly I wonder
That one so given at all times to goodness

Should be not well versed in social conventions,
Or, made once to know, should dismiss them from mind.
You have promptly forgotten what I in the plainest   360
Of talk that I knew of yesterday taught you."
"What is that?" said the knight. "For truly I know not;
If it be as you say, I am surely to blame."
"Yet I taught you," quoth the fair lady, "of kissing;
When clearly he's favored, quickly to claim one   365
Becomes each knight who practices courtesy."
"Cease, dear lady, such speech," said the strong man;
"I dare not for fear of refusal do that.
'T would be wrong to proffer and then be repulsed."
"In faith, you may not be refused," said the fair one;   370
"Sir, if you please, you have strength to compel it,
Should one be so rude as to wish to deny you."
"By God, yes," said Gawain, "good is your speech;
But unlucky is force in the land I live in,
And every gift that with good will's not given.   375
Your word I await to embrace when you wish;
You may start when you please, and stop at your
    pleasure."

               With grace
    The lady, bending low,
    Most sweetly kissed his face.   380
    Of joy in love and woe
    They talked for a long space.

    "I should like," said the lady, "from you, sir, to learn,
If I roused not your anger by asking, the reason
Why you, who are now so young and valiant,   385
So known far and wide as knightly and courteous
(And principally, picked from all knighthood, is praised
The sport of true love and the science of arms;
For to tell of these true knights' toil, it is surely
The title inscribed and the text of their deeds,   390
How men their lives for their leal[17] love adventured,
Endured for their passion doleful days,
Then themselves with valor avenged, and their sorrow
Cast off, and brought bliss into bowers by their virtues),
Why you, thought the noblest knight of your time,   395
Whose renown and honor are everywhere noted,
Have so let me sit on two separate occasions
Beside you, and hear proceed from your head
Not one word relating to love, less or more.
You so goodly in vowing your service and gracious   400
Ought gladly to give to a young thing your guidance,
And show me some sign of the sleights[18] of true love.
What! know you nothing, and have all renown?
Or else do you deem me too dull, for your talking
               Unfit?   405
    For shame! Alone I come;

---

[17] Loyal, true.   [18] Skill, finesse.

    To learn some sport I sit;
    My lord is far from home;
    Now, teach me by your wit."

    "In good faith," said Gawain, "God you reward;   410
For great is the happiness, huge the gladness
That one so worthy should want to come hither,
And pains for so poor a man take, as in play
With your knight with looks of regard; it delights me.
But to take up the task of telling of true love,   415
To touch on those themes, and on tales of arms
To you who've more skill in that art, I am certain,
By half than a hundred men have such as I,
Or ever shall have while here upon earth,
By my faith, 't would be, madam, a manifold folly.   420
Your bidding I'll do, as in duty bound,
To the height of my power, and will hold myself ever
Your ladyship's servant, so save me the Lord."
Thus the fair lady tempted and tested him often
To make the man sin—whate'er more she'd in mind;   425
But so fair his defence was, no fault was apparent,
Nor evil on either side; each knew but joy
               On that day.
    At last she kissed him lightly,
    After long mirth and play,   430
    And took her leave politely,
    And went upon her way.

    The man bestirs himself, springs up for mass.
Then made ready and splendidly served was their dinner;
In sport with the ladies he spent all the day.   435
But the lord through fields oft dashed as he followed
The savage swine, that sped o'er the slopes,
And in two bit the backs of the best of his hounds
Where he stood at bay; till 't was broken by bowmen,
Who made him, despite himself, move to the open,   440
The shafts flew so thick when the throng had assembled.
Yet sometimes he forced the stoutest to flinch,
Till at last too weary he was to run longer,
But came with such haste as he could to a hole
In a mound, by a rock whence the rivulet runs out.   445
He started to scrape the soil, backed by the slope,
While froth from his mouth's ugly corners came foaming.
White were the tushes he whetted. The bold men
Who stood round grew tired of trying from far
To annoy him, but dared not for danger draw nearer.   450
               Before,
    So many he did pierce
    That all were loth a boar
    So frenzied and so fierce
    Should tear with tusks once more,   455

    Till the hero himself came, spurring his horse,
Saw him standing at bay, the hunters beside him.

He leaped down right lordly, leaving his courser,
Unsheathed a bright sword and strode forth stoutly,
Made haste through the ford where that fierce one was
    waiting.   460
Aware of the hero with weapon in hand,
So savagely, bristling his back up, he snorted
All feared for the wight lest the worst befall him.
Then rushed out the boar directly upon him,
And man was mingled with beast in the midst   465
Of the wildest water. The boar had the worse,
For the man aimed a blow at the beast as he met him,
And surely with sharp blade struck o'er his breast bone,
That smote to the hilt, and his heart cleft asunder.
He squealing gave way, and swift through the water   470
                   Went back.
          By a hundred hounds he's caught,
          Who fiercely him attack;
          To open ground he's brought,
          And killed there by the pack.   475

The blast for the beast's death was blown on sharp
    horns,
And the lords there loudly and clearly hallooed.
At the beast bayed the brachets, as bid by their masters,
The chief, in that hard, long chase, of the hunters.
Then one who was wise in woodcraft began   480
To slice up this swine in the seemliest manner.
First he hews off his head, and sets it on high;
Then along the back roughly rends him apart.
He hales out the bowels, and broils them on hot coals,
With these mixed with bread, rewarding his brachets.   485
Then slices the flesh in fine, broad slabs,
And pulls out the edible entrails properly.
Whole, though, he gathers the halves together,
And proudly upon a stout pole he places them.
Homeward they now with this very swine hasten,   490
Bearing in front of the hero the boar's head,
Since him at the ford by the force of his strong hand
                   He slew.
          It seemed long till he met
          In hall Sir Gawain, who   495
          Hastened, when called, to get
          The payment that was due.

The lord called out loudly, merrily laughed
When Gawain he saw, and gladsomely spoke.
The good ladies were sent for, the household
    assembled;   500
He shows them the slices of flesh, and the story
He tells of his largeness and length, and how fierce
Was the war in the woods where the wild swine had fled.
Sir Gawain commended his deeds right graciously,
Praised them as giving a proof of great prowess.   505

Such brawn on a beast, the bold man declared,
And such sides on a swine he had ne'er before seen.
Then they handled the huge head; the courteous hero
Praised it, horror-struck, honoring his host.
Quoth the good man, "Now, Gawain, yours is this game
By our covenant, fast and firm, you know truly."   511
"It is so," said the knight; "and as certain and sure
All I get I'll give you again as I pledged you."
He about the neck caught, with courtesy kissed him,
And soon a second time served him the same way.   515
Said Gawain, "We've fairly fulfilled the agreement
This evening we entered on, each to the other
                   Most true."
          "I, by Saint Giles,[19] have met
          None," said the lord, "like you.   520
          Riches you soon will get,
          If you such business do."

And then the tables they raised upon trestles,
And laid on them cloths; the light leaped up clearly
Along by the walls, where the waxen torches   525
Were set by the henchmen who served in the hall.
A great sound of sport and merriment sprang up
Close by the fire, and on frequent occasions
At supper and afterward, many a splendid song,
Conduits[20] of Christmas, new carols,[21] all kinds   530
Of mannerly mirth that a man may tell of.
Our seemly knight ever sat at the side
Of the lady, who made so agreeable her manner,
With sly, secret glances to glad him, so stalwart,
That greatly astonished was Gawain, and wroth   535
With himself; he in courtesy could not refuse her,
But acted becomingly, courtly, whatever
The end, good or bad, of his action might be.
                  When quite
          Done was their play at last,   540
          The host called to the knight,
          And to his room they passed
          To where the fire burned bright.

The men there make merry and drink, and once more
The same pact for New Year's Eve is proposed;   545
But the knight craved permission to mount on the
    morrow:
The appointment approached where he had to appear.
But the lord him persuaded to stay and linger,
And said, "On my word as a knight I assure you
You'll get to the Green Chapel, Gawain, on New
    Year's,   550

[19] Noted for his humility and imperviousness to temptation. He
even refused a king who tried with honors to draw him from
his life of solitude.
[20] Originally a kind of motet; here, merely songs.
[21] See p. 82, note 12, above.

And far before prime,[22] to finish your business.
Remain in your room then, and take your rest.
I shall hunt in the wood and exchange with you winnings,
As bound by our bargain, when back I return,
For twice I've found you were faithful when tried: 555
In the morning 'best be the third time,' remember.
Let's be mindful of mirth while we may, and make
      merry,
For care when one wants it is quickly encountered."
At once this was granted, and Gawain is stayed;
Drink blithely was brought him; to bed they were
      lighted.   560

                    The guest
            In quiet and comfort spent
            The night, and took his rest.
            On his affairs intent,
            The host was early dressed.   565

After mass a morsel he took with his men.
The morning was merry; his mount he demanded.
The knights who'd ride in his train were in readiness,
Dressed and horsed at the door of the hall.
Wondrous fair were the fields, for the frost was
      clinging;   570
Bright red in the cloud-rack rises the sun,
And full clear sails close past the clouds in the sky.
The hunters unleashed all the hounds by a woodside:
The rocks with the blast of their bugles were ringing.
Some dogs there fall on the scent where the fox is,   575
And trail oft a traitoress[23] using her tricks.
A hound gives tongue at it; huntsmen call to him;
Hastens the pack to the hound sniffing hard,
And right on his track run off in a rabble,
He scampering before them. They started the fox
      soon;   580
When finally they saw him, they followed fast,
Denouncing him clearly with clamorous anger.
Through many a dense grove he dodges and twists,
Doubling back and harkening at hedges right often;
At last by a little ditch leaps o'er a thorn-hedge,   585
Steals out stealthily, skirting a thicket
In thought from the wood to escape by his wiles
From the hounds; then, unknowing, drew near to a
      hunting-stand.
There hurled themselves, three at once, on him strong
      hounds,
                        All grey.   590
            With quick swerve he doth start

---

[22] About nine in the morning.
[23] There is a vixen as well as a dog-fox in the wood. Her scent is
less strong than his; but since she keeps doubling back to the
covert, the hounds are confused when her scent crosses his.
Eventually a hound gives tongue, and the dog-fox leaves the
covert.

Afresh without dismay.
            With great grief in his heart
            To the wood he goes away.

Huge was the joy then to hark to the hounds.   595
When the pack all met him, mingled together,
Such curses they heaped on his head at the sight
That the clustering cliffs seemed to clatter down round
      them
In heaps. The men, when they met him, hailed him,
And loudly with chiding speeches hallooed him;   600
Threats were oft thrown at him, thief he was called;
At his tail were the greyhounds, that tarry he might not.
They rushed at him oft when he raced for the open,
And ran to the wood again, reynard the wily.
Thus he led them, all muddied, the lord and his men,   605
In this manner along through the hills until mid-day.
At home, the noble knight wholesomely slept
In the cold of the morn within comely curtains.
But the lady, for love, did not let herself sleep,
Or fail in the purpose fixed in her heart;   610
But quickly she roused herself, came there quickly,
Arrayed in a gay robe that reached to the ground,
The skins of the splendid fur skillfully trimmed close.
On her head no colors save jewels, well-cut,
That were twined in her hair-fret[24] in clusters of
      twenty.   615
Her fair face was completely exposed, and her throat;
In front her breast too was bare, and her back.
She comes through the chamber-door, closes it after her,
Swings wide a window, speaks to the wight,
And rallies him soon in speech full of sport   620
                        And good cheer.
            "Ah! man, how can you sleep?
            The morning is so clear."
            He was in sorrow deep,
            Yet her he then did hear.   625

In a dream muttered Gawain, deep in its gloom,
Like a man by a throng of sad thoughts sorely moved
Of how fate was to deal out his destiny to him
That morn, when he met the man at the Green
      Chapel,
Bound to abide his blow, unresisting.   630
But as soon as that comely one came to his senses,
Started from slumber and speedily answered,
The lovely lady came near, sweetly laughing,
Bent down o'er his fair face and daintily kissed him.
And well, in a worthy manner, he welcomed her.   635
Seeing her glorious, gaily attired,
Without fault in her features, most fine in her color,
Deep joy came welling up, warming his heart.

---

[24] The ornamental net that confined her hair.

With sweet, gentle smiling they straightway grew
    merry;
So passed naught between them but pleasure, joy,   640
            And delight.
        Goodly was their debate,
        Nor was their gladness slight.
        Their peril had been great
        Had Mary quit her knight.   645

For that noble princess pressed him so closely,
Brought him so near the last bound, that her love
He was forced to accept, or, offending, refuse her:
Concerned for his courtesy not to prove caitiff,[25]
And more for his ruin if wrong he committed,   650
Betraying the hero, the head of that house.
"God forbid," said the knight; "that never shall be";
And lovingly laughing a little, he parried
The words of fondness that fell from her mouth.
She said to him, "Sir, you are surely to blame   655
If you love not the lady beside whom you're lying,
Of all the world's women most wounded in heart,
Unless you've one dearer, a lover you like more,
Your faith to her plighted, so firmly made fast
You desire not to loosen it—so I believe.   660
Now tell me truly I pray you; the truth,
By all of the loves that in life are,[26] conceal not
            Through guile."
        The knight said, "By Saint John,"
        And pleasantly to smile   665
        Began, "In faith I've none,
        Nor will have for a while."

"Such words," said the lady, "the worst are of all;
But in sooth I am answered, and sad it seems to me.
Kiss me now kindly, and quickly I'll go;   670
I on earth may but mourn, as a much loving mortal."
Sighing she stoops down, and kisses him seemly;
Then starting away from him, says as she stands,
"Now, my dear, at parting, do me this pleasure:
Give me some gift, thy glove if it might be,   675
To bring you to mind, sir, my mourning to lessen."
"On my word," quoth the hero, "I would that I had
    here,
For thy sake, the thing that I think the dearest
I own, for in sooth you've deserved very often
A greater reward than one I could give.   680
But a pledge of love would profit but little;
'T would help not your honor to have at this time
For a keepsake a glove, as a gift of Gawain.
I've come on a mission to countries most strange;

I've no servants with splendid things filling their
    sacks: 685
That displeases me, lady, for love's sake, at present;
Yet each man without murmur must do what he may
            Nor repine."
        "Nay, lord of honors high,
        Though I have naught of thine,"   690
        Quoth the lovely lady, "I
        Shall give you gift of mine."

She offered a rich ring, wrought in red gold,
With a blazing stone that stood out above it,
And shot forth brilliant rays bright as the sun;   695
Wit you well that wealth right huge it was worth.
But promptly the hero replied, refusing it,
"Madam, I care not for gifts now to keep;
I have none to tender and naught will I take."
Thus he ever declined her offer right earnest,   700
And swore on his word that he would not accept it;
And, sad he declined, she thereupon said,
"If my ring you refuse, since it seems too rich,
If you would not so highly to me be beholden,
My girdle, that profits you less, I'll give you."   705
She swiftly removed the belt circling her sides,
Round her tunic knotted, beneath her bright mantle;
'T was fashioned of green silk, and fair made with gold,
With gold, too, the borders embellished and beautiful.
To Gawain she gave it, and gaily besought him   710
To take it, although he thought it but trifling.
He swore by no manner of means he'd accept
Either gold or treasure ere God gave him grace
To attain the adventure he'd there undertaken.
"And, therefore, I pray, let it prove not displeasing,   715
But give up your suit, for to grant it I'll never
            Agree.
        I'm deeply in your debt
        For your kind ways to me.
        In hot and cold I yet   720
        Will your true servant be."

"Refuse ye this silk," the lady then said,
"As slight in itself? Truly it seems so.
Lo! it is little, and less is its worth;
But one knowing the nature knit up within it,   725
Would give it a value more great, peradventure;
For no man girt with this girdle of green,
And bearing it fairly made fast about him,
Might ever be cut down by any on earth,
For his life in no way in the world could be taken."   730
Then mused the man, and it came to his mind
In the peril appointed him precious 't would prove,
When he'd found the chapel, to face there his fortune.
The device, might he slaying evade, would be splendid.

---

[25] I.e., ungentlemanly.
[26] For the love of everyone by whom men swear according to the
    formula "for the love of. . . ."

Her suit then he suffered, and let her speak; 735
And the belt she offered him, earnestly urging it
(And Gawain consented), and gave it with good will,
And prayed him for her sake ne'er to display it,
But, true, from her husband to hide it. The hero
Agreed that no one should know of it ever. 740
                    Then he
          Thanked her with all his might
          Of heart and thought; and she
          By then to this stout knight
          Had given kisses three. 745

Then the lady departs, there leaving the lord,
For more pleasure she could not procure from that prince.
When she's gone, then quickly Sir Gawain clothes
          himself,
Rises and dresses in noble array,
Lays by the love-lace[27] the lady had left him, 750
Faithfully hides it where later he'd find it.
At once then went on his way to the chapel,
Approached in private a priest, and prayed him
To make his life purer, more plainly him teach
How his soul, when he had to go hence, should be
          saved. 755
He declared his faults, confessing them fully,
The more and the less, and mercy besought,
And then of the priest implored absolution.
He surely absolved him, and made him as spotless,
Indeed, as if doomsday were due on the morrow. 760
Then among the fair ladies he made more merry
With lovely caroles, all kinds of delights,
That day than before, until darkness fell.
                    All there
          Were treated courteously, 765
          "And never," they declare,
          "Has Gawain shown such glee
          Since hither he did fare."

In that nook where his lot may be love let him linger!
The lord's in the meadow still, leading his men. 770
He has slain this fox that he followed so long;
As he vaulted a hedge to get view of the villain,
Hearing the hounds that hastened hard after him,
Reynard from out a rough thicket came running,
And right at his heels in a rush all the rabble. 775
He, seeing that wild thing, wary, awaits him,
Unsheathes his bright brand and strikes at the beast.
And he swerved from its sharpness and back would have
          started;
A hound, ere he could, came hurrying up to him;
All of them fell on him fast by the horse's feet, 780
Worried that sly one with wrathful sound.

And quickly the lord alights, and catches him,
Takes him in haste from the teeth of the hounds,
And over his head holds him high, loudly shouting,
Where brachets, many and fierce, at him barked. 785
Thither huntsmen made haste with many a horn,
The recall, till they saw him, sounding right clearly.
As soon as his splendid troop had assembled,
All bearing a bugle blew them together,
The others having no horns all hallooed. 790
'T was the merriest baying that man ever heard
That was raised for the soul of reynard with sounding
                    Din.
          They fondle each dog's head
          Who his reward did win. 795
          Then take they reynard dead
          And strip him of his skin.

And now, since near was the night, they turned
          homeward,
Strongly and sturdily sounding their horns.
At last at his loved home the lord alighted, 800
A fire on the hearth found, the hero beside it,
Sir Gawain the good, who glad was withal,
For he had 'mong the ladies in love much delight.
A blue robe that fell to the floor he was wearing;
His surcoat, that softly was furred, well beseemed
          him; 805
A hood of the same hue hung on his shoulders,
And both were bordered with white all about.
He, mid-most, met the good man in the hall,
And greeted him gladly, graciously saying:
"Now shall I first fulfil our agreement 810
We struck to good purpose, when drink was not spared."
Then Gawain embraced him, gave him three kisses,
The sweetest and soundest a man could bestow.
"By Christ, you'd great happiness," quoth then the host,
"In getting these wares, if good were your bargains." 815
"Take no care for the cost," the other said quickly,
"Since plainly the debt that is due I have paid."
Said the other, "By Mary, mine's of less worth.
The whole of the day I have hunted, and gotten
The skin of this fox—the fiend take its foulness!— 820
Right poor to pay for things of such price
As you've pressed on me here so heartily, kisses
                    So good."
          "Say no more," Gawain saith;
          "I thank you, by the rood!"[28] 825
          How the fox met his death
          He told him as they stood.

With mirth and minstrelsy, meat at their pleasure,
They made as merry as any men might

27 Love-belt, i.e., token.

28 Cross.

(With ladies' laughter, and launching of jests   830
Right glad were they both, the good man and Gawain)
Unless they had doted or else had been drunken.
Both the man and the company make many jokes,
Till the time is come when the two must be parted,
When finally the knights are forced to go bedward.   835
And first of the lord his respectful leave
This goodly man took, and graciously thanked him:
"May God you reward for the welcome you gave me
This high feast, the splendid sojourn I've had here.
I give you myself, if you'd like it, to serve you.   840
I must, as you know, on the morrow move on;
Give me some one to show me the path, as you said,
To the Green Chapel, there, as God will allow me,
On New Year the fate that is fixed to perform."
"With a good will, indeed," said the good man;
          "whatever   845
I promised to do I deem myself ready."
He a servant assigns on his way to set him,
To take him by hills that no trouble he'd have,
And through grove and wood by the way most direct
                              Might repair.   850
          The lord he thanked again
          For the honor done him there.
          The knight his farewell then
          Took of those ladies fair.

     To them with sorrow and kissing he spoke,   855
And besought them his thanks most sincere to accept;
And they, replying, promptly returned them,
With sighings full sore to the Savior commended him.
Then he with courtesy quitted the company,
Giving each man that he met his thanks   860
For kindness, for trouble he'd taken, for care
Whereby each had sought to serve him right eagerly.
Pained was each person to part with him then,
As if long they in honor had lived with that noble.
With people and lights he was led to his chamber,   865
To bed gaily brought there to be at his rest;
Yet I dare not say whether soundly he slept,
For much, if he would, on the morn to remember
                              Had he.
          Let him lie stilly there   870
          Near what he sought to see.
          What happened I'll declare,
          If you will silent be.

IV

The New Year draws near, and the nighttime now
          passes;
The day, as the Lord bids, drives on to darkness.
Outside, there sprang up wild storms in the world;

The clouds cast keenly the cold to the earth
With enough of the north sting to trouble the naked;   5
Down shivered the snow, nipping sharply the wild beasts;
The wind from the heights, shrilly howling, came
          rushing,
And heaped up each dale full of drifts right huge.
Full well the man listened who lay in his bed.
Though he shut tight his lids, he slept but a little;   10
He knew by each cock that crowed 't was the tryst time,
And swiftly ere dawn of the day he arose,
For there shone then the light of a lamp in his room;
To his chamberlain called, who answered him quickly,
And bade him his saddle to bring and his mail-shirt.   15
The other man roused up and fetched him his raiment,
Arrayed then that knight in a fashion right noble.
First he clad him in clothes to ward off the cold,
Then his other equipment, carefully kept:
His pieces of plate armor, polished right cleanly,   20
The rings of his rich mail burnished from rust.
All was fresh as at first; he was fain to give thanks
                              To the men.
          He had on every piece
          Full brightly burnished then.   25
          He, gayest from here to Greece,
          Ordered his steed again.

     He garbed himself there in the loveliest garments
(His coat had its blazon of beautiful needlework
Stitched upon velvet for show, its rich stones   30
Set about it and studded, its seams all embroidered,
Its lovely fur in the fairest of linings),
Yet he left not the lace, the gift of the lady:
That, Gawain did not, for his own sake, forget.
When the brand[29] on his rounded thighs he had
          belted,   35
He twisted his love-token two times about him.
That lord round his waist with delight quickly wound
The girdle of green silk, that seemed very gay
Upon royal red cloth that was rich to behold.
But Gawain the girdle wore not for its great price,   40
Or pride in its pendants although they were polished,
Though glittering gold there gleamed on the ends,
But himself to save when he needs must suffer
The death, nor could stroke then of sword or of knife
                              Him defend.   45
          Then was the bold man dressed;
          Quickly his way did wend;
          To all the court expressed
          His great thanks without end.

     Then was Gringolet ready that great was and huge, 50
Who had safely, as seemed to him pleasant, been stabled;

_____
[29] Sword.

That proud horse pranced, in the pink of condition.
The lord then comes to him, looks at his coat,
And soberly says, and swears on his word,
"In this castle's a company mindful of courtesy, 55
Led by this hero. Delight may they have;
And may love the dear lady betide all her lifetime.
If they for charity cherish a guest,
And give so great welcome, may God reward them,
Who rules the heaven on high, and the rest of you. 60
Might I for long live my life on the earth,
Some repayment with pleasure I'd make, if 't were
    possible."
He steps in the stirrup, strides into the saddle,
Receives on his shoulder the shield his man brings him,
And spurs into Gringolet strikes with his gilt heels; 65
Who leaps on the stones and lingers no longer
              To prance.
        The knight on his horse sits,
        Who bears his spear and lance,
        The house to Christ commits, 70
        And wishes it good chance.

Then down the drawbridge they dropped, the broad
    gates
Unbarred, and on both sides bore them wide open.
He blessed them quickly, and crossed o'er the planks
    there
(He praises the porter, who knelt by the prince 75
Begging God to save Gawain, and gave him good-day),
And went on his way with but one man attended
To show him the turns to that sorrowful spot
Where he must to that onerous onset submit.
By hillsides where branches were bare they both
    journeyed; 80
They climbed over cliffs where the cold was clinging.
The clouds hung aloft, but 't was lowering beneath them.
On the moor dripped the mist, on the mountains melted;
Each hill had a hat, a mist-cloak right huge.
The brooks foamed and bubbled on hillsides about
    them, 85
And brightly broke on their banks as they rushed down.
Full wandering the way was they went through the
    wood,
Until soon it was time for the sun to be springing.
             Then they
        Were on a hill full high; 90
        White snow beside them lay.
        The servant who rode nigh
        Then bade his master stay.

"I have led you hither, my lord, at this time,
And not far are you now from that famous place 95
You have sought for, and asked so especially after.

Yet, sir, to you surely I'll say, since I know you,
A man in this world whom I love right well,
If you'd follow my judgment, the better you'd fare.
You make haste to a place that is held full of peril; 100
One dwells, the worst in the world, in that waste,
For he's strong and stern, and takes pleasure in striking.
No man on the earth can equal his might;
He is bigger in body than four of the best men
In Arthur's own household, Hestor[30] or others. 105
And thus he brings it about at the chapel:
That place no one passes so proud in his arms
That he smites him not dead with a stroke of his hand.
He's a man most immoderate, showing no mercy;
Be it chaplain or churl[31] that rides by the chapel, 110
Monk or priest, any manner of man,
Him to slay seems as sweet as to still live himself.
So I say, as sure as you sit in your saddle
You're killed, should the knight so choose, if you come
    here;
That take as the truth, though you twenty lives had 115
             To spend.
        He's lived in this place long
        In battles without end.
        Against his strokes right strong
        You cannot you defend. 120

    "So let him alone, good Sir Gawain, and leave
By a different road, for God's sake, and ride
To some other country where Christ may reward you.
And homeward again I will hie me, and promise
To swear by the Lord and all his good saints 125
(So help me the oaths on God's halidom[32] sworn)
That I'll guard well your secret, and give out no story
You hastened to flee any hero I've heard of."
"Thank you," said Gawain, and grudgingly added,
"Good fortune go with you for wishing me well. 130
And truly I think you'd not tell; yet though never
So surely you hid it, if hence I should hasten,
Fearful, to fly in the fashion you tell of,
A coward I'd prove, and could not be pardoned.
The chapel I'll find whatsoever befalls, 135
And talk with that wight the way that I want to,
Let weal or woe follow as fate may wish.
             Though the knave,
        Hard to subdue and fell,
        Should stand there with a stave,[33] 140
        Yet still the Lord knows well
        His servants how to save."

---

[30] Apparently a variant of *Hector,* the Trojan hero. This form also
    occurs in several French romances.   [31] Common fellow.
[32] Holy thing, relic, anything sacred.
[33] Stick—doubtless a long and heavy one.

Quoth the man, "By Mary, you've said now this
   much:
That you wish to bring down your own doom on your
   head.
Since you'd lose your life, I will stay you no longer. 145
Put your helm on your head, take your spear in your
   hand,
And ride down this road by the side of that rock
Till it brings you down to the dale's rugged bottom;
Then look at the glade on the left hand a little:
You'll see in the valley that selfsame chapel, 150
And near it the great-limbed knight who is guarding it.
Gawain the noble, farewell now, in God's name!
I would not go with thee for all the world's wealth,
Nor in fellowship ride one more foot through the forest."
The man in the trees there then turns his bridle, 155
As hard as he can hits his horse with his heels,
And across the fields gallops, there leaving Sir Gawain
                              Alone.
         "By God," the knight said, "now
         I'll neither weep nor groan. 160
         Unto God's will I bow,
         And make myself his own."

He strikes spurs into Gringolet, starts on the path;
By a bank at the side of a small wood he pushes in,
Rides down the rugged slope right to the dale. 165
Then about him he looks, and the land seems wild,
And nowhere he sees any sign of a shelter,
But slopes on each side of him, high and steep,
And rocks, gnarled and rough, and stones right rugged.
The clouds there seemed to him scraped by the crags. 170
Then he halted and held back his horse at that time,
And spied on all sides in search of the chapel;
Such nowhere he saw, but soon, what seemed strange,
In the midst of a glade a mound, as it might be,
A smooth, swelling knoll by the side of the water, 175
The falls of a rivulet running close by;
In its banks the brook bubbled as though it were boiling.
The knight urged on Gringolet, came to the glade,
There leaped down lightly and tied to the limb
Of a tree, right rugged, the reins of his noble steed, 180
Went to the mound, and walked all about it,
Debating what manner of thing it might be:
On the end and on each side an opening; everywhere
Over it grass was growing in patches,
All hollow inside, it seemed an old cave 185
Or a crag's old cleft: which, he could not decide.
                    Said the knight,
         "Is this the chapel here?
         Alas, dear Lord! here might
         The fiend, when midnight's near, 190
         His matin prayers recite.

"Of a truth," said Gawain, "the glade here is gloomy;
The Green Chapel's ugly, with herbs overgrown.
It greatly becomes here that hero, green-clad,
To perform in the devil's own fashion his worship. 195
I feel in my five senses this is the fiend[34]
Who has made me come to this meeting to kill me.
Destruction fall on this church of ill-fortune!
The cursedest chapel that ever I came to!"
With helm on his head and lance in his hand 200
He went right to the rock of that rugged abode.
From that high hill he heard, from a hard rock over
The stream, on the hillside, a sound wondrous loud.
Lo! it clattered on cliffs fit to cleave them, as though
A scythe on a grindstone some one were grinding. 205
It whirred, lo! and whizzed like a water-mill's wheel;
Lo! it ground and it grated, grievous to hear.
"By God, this thing, as I think," then said Gawain,
"Is done now for me, since my due turn to meet it
                         Is near. 210
         God's will be done! 'Ah woe!'
         No whit doth aid me here.
         Though I my life forego
         No sound shall make me fear."

And then the man there[35] commenced to call loudly,
"Who here is the master, with me to hold tryst? 216
For Gawain the good now is going right near.
He who craves aught of me let him come hither quickly;
'T is now or never; he needs to make haste."
Said somebody, "Stop," from the slope up above him, 220
"And promptly you'll get what I promised to give you."
Yet he kept up the whirring noise quickly a while,
Turned to finish his sharpening before he'd descend.
Then he came by a crag, from a cavern emerging,
Whirled out of a den with a dreadful weapon, 225
A new Danish axe to answer the blow with:
Its blade right heavy, curved back to the handle,
Sharp filed with the filing tool, four feet in length,
'T was no less, by the reach of that lace[36] gleaming
                          brightly.
The fellow in green was garbed as at first, 230
Both his face and his legs, his locks and his beard,
Save that fast o'er the earth on his feet he went fairly,
The shaft on the stone set, and stalked on beside it.
On reaching the water, he would not wade it;
On his axe he hopped over, and hastily strode, 235
Very fierce, through the broad field filled all about him
                    With snow.
         Sir Gawain met the man,
         And bowed by no means low,
         Who said, "Good sir, men can 240
         Trust you to tryst to go."

---

[34] The Devil.   [35] Gawain.   [36] Measured by its thong.

Said the green man, "Gawain, may God you guard!
You are welcome indeed, sir knight, at my dwelling.
Your travel you've timed as a true man should,
And you know the compact we came to between us; 245
A twelvemonth ago you took what chance gave,
And I promptly at New Year was pledged to repay you.
In truth, we are down in this dale all alone;
Though we fight as we please, here there's no one to
      part us.
Put your helm from your head, and have here your
      payment;   250
Debate no further than I did before,
When you slashed off my head with a single stroke."
"Nay," quoth Gawain, "by God who gave me my spirit,
I'll harbor no grudge whatever harm happens.
Exceed not one stroke and still I shall stand;   255
You may do as you please, I'll in no way oppose
                                    The blow."
            He left the flesh all bare,
            Bending his neck down low
            As if he feared naught there,   260
            For fear he would not show.

Then the man in green raiment quickly made ready,
Uplifted his grim tool Sir Gawain to smite;
With the whole of his strength he heaved it on high,
As threateningly swung it as though he would slay
      him.   265
Had it fallen again with the force he intended
That lord, ever brave, from the blow had been lifeless.
But Gawain a side glance gave at the weapon
As down it came gliding to do him to death;
With his shoulders shrank from the sharp iron a little. 270
The other with sudden jerk stayed the bright axe,
And reproved then that prince with proud words in
      plenty:
"Not Gawain thou art who so good is considered,
Ne'er daunted by host in hill or in dale;
Now in fear, ere thou feelest a hurt, thou art
      flinching;   275
Such cowardice never I knew of that knight.
When you swung at me, sir, I fled not nor started;
No cavil I offered in King Arthur's castle.
My head at my feet fell, yet never I flinched,
And thy heart is afraid ere a hurt thou feelest,   280
And therefore thy better I'm bound to be thought
                              On that score."
            "I shrank once," Gawain said,
            "And I will shrink no more;
            Yet cannot I my head,   285
            If it fall down, restore.

"But make ready, sir, quickly, and come to the point;
My destiny deal me, and do it forthwith;

For a stroke I will suffer, and start no further
Till hit with thy weapon; have here my pledged
      word."   290
Quoth the other, heaving it high, "Have at thee!"
As fierce in his manner as if he were mad,
He mightily swung but struck not the man,
Withheld on a sudden his hand ere it hurt him.
And firmly he waited and flinched in no member,   295
But stood there as still as a stone or a stump
In rocky ground held by a hundred roots.
Then the Green Knight again began to speak gaily:
"It behooves me to hit, now that whole is thy heart.
Thy high hood that Arthur once gave you now hold
      back,   300
Take care that your neck at this cut may recover."
And Gawain full fiercely said in a fury,
"Come! lay on, thou dread man; too long thou art
      threatening.
I think that afraid of your own self you feel."
"In sooth," said the other, "thy speech is so savage   305
No more will I hinder thy mission nor have it
                              Delayed."
            With puckered lips and brow
            He stands with ready blade.
            Not strange 't is hateful now   310
            To him past hope of aid.

He lifts his axe lightly, and lets it down deftly,
The blade's edge next to the naked neck.
Though he mightily hammered he hurt him no more
Than to give him a slight nick that severed the skin
      there.   315
Through fair skin the keen axe so cut to the flesh
That shining blood shot to the earth o'er his shoulders.
As soon as he saw his blood gleam on the snow
He sprang forth in one leap, for more than a spear length;
His helm fiercely caught up and clapped on his head;   320
With his shoulders his fair shield shot round in front of
      him,[37]
Pulled out his bright sword, and said in a passion
(And since he was mortal man born of his mother
The hero was never so happy by half),
"Cease thy violence, man; no more to me offer,   325
For here I've received, unresisting, a stroke.
If a second thou strikest I soon will requite thee,
And swiftly and fiercely, be certain of that,
                              Will repay.
            One stroke on me might fall   330
            By bargain struck that way,
            Arranged in Arthur's hall;
            Therefore, sir knight, now stay!"

---

[37] Evidently it has been hanging on his back or shoulder, held by
   a strap; with a jerk of his shoulders he now slings it around in
   front of him.

The man turned away, on his weapon rested,
The shaft on the ground set, leaned on the sharp
    edge,   335
And gazed at Sir Gawain there in the glade;
Saw that bold man, unblenching, standing right bravely,
Full-harnessed and gallant; at heart he was glad.
Then gaily the Green Knight spoke in a great voice,
And said to the man in speech that resounded,   340
"Now be not so savage, bold sir, for towards you
None here has acted unhandsomely, save
In accord with the compact arranged in the King's court.
I promised the stroke you've received, so hold you
Well paid. I free you from all duties further.   345
If brisk I had been, peradventure a buffet
I'd harshly have dealt that harm would have done you.
In mirth, with a feint I menaced you first,
With no direful wound rent you; right was my deed,
By the bargain that bound us both on the first night,   350
When, faithful and true, you fulfilled our agreement,
And gave me your gain as a good man ought to.
The second I struck at you, sir, for the morning
You kissed my fair wife and the kisses accorded me.
Two mere feints for both times I made at you, man,   355
                Without woe.
        True men restore by right,
        One fears no danger so;
        You failed the third time, knight,
        And therefore took that blow.   360

" 'T is my garment you're wearing, that woven girdle,
Bestowed by my wife, as in truth I know well.
I know also your kisses and all of your acts
And my wife's advances; myself, I devised them.
I sent her to try you, and truly you seem   365
The most faultless of men that e'er fared on his feet.
As a pearl compared to white peas is more precious,
So next to the other gay knights is Sir Gawain.
But a little you lacked, and loyalty wanted,
Yet truly 't was not for intrigue or for wooing,   370
But love of your life; the less do I blame you."
Sir Gawain stood in a study a great while,
So sunk in disgrace that in spirit he groaned;
To his face all the blood in his body was flowing;
For shame, as the other was talking, he shrank.   375
And these were the first words that fell from his lips:
"Be cowardice cursed, and coveting! In you
Are vice and villainy, virtue destroying."
The lace he then seized, and loosened the strands,
And fiercely the girdle flung at the Green Knight.   380
"Lo! there is faith-breaking! evil befall it.
To coveting came I, for cowardice caused me
From fear of your stroke to forsake in myself
What belongs to a knight: munificence, loyalty.

I'm faulty and false, who've been ever afraid   385
Of untruth and treachery; sorrow betide both
                And care!
        Here I confess my sin;
        All faulty did I fare.
        Your good will let me win,   390
        And then I will beware."

Then the Green Knight laughed, and right graciously
    said,
"I am sure that the harm is healed that I suffered.
So clean you're confessed, so cleared of your faults,
Having had the point of my weapon's plain penance,   395
I hold you now purged of offence, and as perfectly
Spotless as though you'd ne'er sinned in your life.
And I give to you, sir, the golden-hemmed girdle,
As green as my gown. Sir Gawain, when going
Forth on your way among famous princes,   400
Think still of our strife and this token right splendid,
'Mid chivalrous knights, of the chapel's adventure.
This New Year you'll come to my castle again,
And the rest of this feast in revel most pleasant
                Will go."   405
        Then pressed him hard the lord:
        "My wife and you, I know
        We surely will accord,
        Who was your bitter foe."

"No indeed," quoth the hero, his helm seized and
    doffed it   410
Graciously, thanking the Green Knight; "I've stayed
Long enough. May good fortune befall you; may He
Who all fame doth confer give it fully to you, sir.
To your lady, gracious and lovely, commend me,
To her and that other, my honored ladies,   415
That so with their sleights deceived their knight subtly.
But no marvel it is for a fool to act madly,
Through woman's wiles to be brought to woe.
So for certain was Adam deceived by some woman;
By several Solomon; Samson besides,   420
Delilah dealt him his doom;[38] and David
Was duped by Bath-sheba, enduring much sorrow.[39]
Since these were grieved by their guile, 't would be great
    gain
To love them yet never believe them, if knights could.
For formerly these[40] were most noble and fortunate,   425
More than all others who lived on the earth;
                And these few
        By women's wiles were caught
        With whom they had to do.
        Though I'm beguiled, I ought   430
        To be excused now too.

---

[38] Judges 16.   [39] 2 Samuel 11.   [40] Adam and the others.

"But your girdle," said Gawain, "may God you
    reward!
With a good will I'll use it, yet not for the gold,
The sash or the silk, or the sweeping pendants,
Or fame, or its workmanship wondrous, or cost,   435
But in sign of my sin I shall see it oft.
When in glory I move, with remorse I'll remember
The frailty and fault of the stubborn flesh,
How soon 't is infected with stains of defilement;
And thus when I'm proud of my prowess in arms,   440
The sight of this sash shall humble my spirit.
But one thing I pray, if it prove not displeasing;
Because you are lord of the land where I stayed
In your house with great worship (may He now reward
    you
Who sitteth on high and upholdeth the heavens),   445
What name do you bear? No more would I know."
And then "That truly I'll tell," said the other;
"Bercilak de Hautdesert[41] here am I called.
Through her might who lives with me, Morgan le Fay,[42]
Well-versed in the crafts and cunning of magic   450
(Many of Merlin's[43] arts she has mastered,
For long since she dealt in the dalliance of love
With him whom your heroes at home know, that sage
                 Without blame.
      'Morgan the goddess,'[44] so   455
      She's rightly known by name.
      No one so proud doth go
      That him she cannot tame),

"I was sent in this way to your splendid hall
To make trial of your pride, and to see if the people's   460
Tales were true of the Table's great glory.
This wonder she sent to unsettle your wits,
And to daunt so the Queen[45] as to cause her to die
From fear at the sight of that phantom speaker
Holding his head in his hand at the high table.   465
Lives she at home there, that ancient lady;
She's even thine aunt, King Arthur's half-sister,
Tyntagel's duchess's[46] daughter, whom Uther

Made later the mother of mighty Lord Arthur.
I beg thee, sir, therefore, come back to thine aunt;   470
In my castle make merry. My company love thee,
And I, sir, wish thee as well, on my word,
As any on earth for thy high sense of honor."
He said to him, nay, this he'd never consent to.
The men kiss, embrace, and each other commend   475
To the Prince of Paradise; there they part
                 In the cold.
      Gawain on his fair horse
      To Arthur hastens bold;
      The bright Green Knight his course   480
      Doth at his pleasure hold.

Through the wood now goes Sir Gawain by wild ways
On Gringolet, given by God's grace his life.
Oft in houses, and oft in the open he lodged,
Met many adventures, won many a victory: 485
These I intend not to tell in this tale.
Now whole was the hurt he had in his neck,
And about it the glimmering belt he was bearing,
Bound to his side like a baldric obliquely,
Tied under his left arm, that lace, with a knot   490
As a sign that with stain of sin he'd been found.
And thus to the court he comes all securely.
Delight in that dwelling arose when its lord knew
That Gawain had come; a good thing he thought it.
The King kissed the lord, and the Queen did likewise,   495
And next many knights drew near him to greet him
And ask how he'd fared; and he wondrously answered,
Confessed all the hardships that him had befallen,
The happenings at chapel, the hero's behavior,
The lady's love, and lastly the lace.   500
He showed them the nick in his neck all naked,
The blow that the Green Knight gave for deceit,
                 Him to blame.
      In torment this he owned;
      Blood in his face did flame;   505
      With wrath and grief he groaned,
      When showing it with shame.

Laying hold of the lace, quoth the hero, "Lo! lord!
The band of this fault I bear on my neck;
And this is the scathe and damage I've suffered,   510
For cowardice caught there, and coveting also,
The badge of untruth in which I was taken.
And this for as long as I live I must wear,
For his fault none may hide without meeting misfortune,
For once it is fixed, it can ne'er be unfastened."   515
To the knight then the King gave comfort; the court too
Laughed greatly, and made this gracious agreement:
That ladies and lords to the Table belonging,

41 High hermitage, mountain cell.—The given name is actually
    Bertilak, though the manuscript spells it with a *c*.
42 Already introduced as the hag at Bertilak's castle; she is King
    Arthur's half sister.
43 The famous wizard at Arthur's court. Infatuated with Morgan,
    he instructed her in magic. That accounts for the Green Knight's
    appearance and powers. It was after Morgan went in for magic
    that she lost her beauty and appeared aged.
44 She is called goddess in some of the chronicles and romances.
45 The sorceress hates the Queen because Guinevere's discovery of
    her intrigue with a knight, a cousin of the Queen, was respon-
    sible for Morgan's having to leave the court.
46 Igraine, Duchess of Tintagel, mother of Arthur and Morgan.
    She was first the wife and then the widow of Gorlois. She be-
    came the mother of Arthur after King Uther Pendragon was
    enabled by Merlin's art to visit her in the likeness of Gorlois.

All of the brotherhood, baldrics should bear
Obliquely about them, bands of bright green,   520
Thus following suit for the sake of the hero.
For the Round Table's glory was granted that lace,
And he held himself honored who had it thereafter,
As told in the book, the best of romances.
In the days of King Arthur this deed was done   525
Whereof witness is borne by Brutus's book.[47]

Since Brutus, that bold man, first came here to Britain,
When ceased, indeed, had the siege and assault
              At Troy's wall,
Full many feats ere now   530
Like this one did befall.
May He with thorn-crowned brow
To His bliss bring us all. Amen.

Hony soyt qui mal pence.[48]

Geoffrey Chaucer

c. 1343–1400

CHAUCER was born probably not much before 1345; he died in 1400, the final year of that brilliant century whose most impressive English monument is his works. He came of upper-middle-class stock, a family of wealthy wine merchants. Perhaps after attending one of London's grammar schools, he became, undoubtedly through family influence, a page in the service of Elizabeth, wife of Edward III's second son, Prince Lionel. In this household Chaucer was presumably instructed in the various accomplishments, military, athletic, and cultural, which every gentleman was expected to acquire. Evidently he had, among other bents, a natural inclination to books; eventually he became one of the best-read Englishmen of his time, especially in Latin, Italian, and French literature. How long he remained with Lionel and Elizabeth is uncertain; the bulk of his career was directly in the service of the Crown, first of Edward III, who reigned from 1327 to 1377, and then of his grandson and successor, Richard II, who reigned from 1377 to 1399. Chaucer found a patron in John of Gaunt, Duke of Lancaster, the most famous of Edward's sons and at times the most powerful man in England. It was Lancaster's son, Henry Bolingbroke, who in 1399 dethroned his cousin, Richard II, and seized the crown as Henry IV.

A courtier and a public official, Chaucer had a busy and varied career, full of worldly experience, the fruits of which appear in what he wrote. He was still in his teens when he served in the campaign of 1359–60 and was captured by the French, near Reims. He was speedily ransomed, King Edward himself contributing £16 (perhaps the equivalent of about $2400 now) to the required sum. A few months later Chaucer was carrying letters from France to England for Prince Lionel; this was the first of numerous errands as courier or diplomat. Next come seven years without a

surviving record of Chaucer. Some of them he very likely spent at the Inner Temple, one of the "inns of court" which provided training in law and business administration. That Chaucer had more than a grammar school education seems certain. When documentary evidence again becomes available, he is receiving a small stipend as a servant of King Edward.

Shortly before, probably about 1366, he had married Philippa, daughter of Sir Payne Roet and sister of Katherine Swynford. Katherine was for years the mistress and afterwards the third wife of John of Gaunt. Philippa was also attached to the court, in the queen's service and later in that of Constance of Castile, John of Gaunt's second wife. As early as 1368 we find Chaucer enrolled among the esquires of the royal household, and for the next few years he was often sent abroad on the king's affairs. There was a second military interlude in 1369—John of Gaunt's raid in Picardy. For English literature, however, the most significant event of these years was the Italian journey of 1372–73. Chaucer's business was to negotiate a trade agreement with Genoa; the important thing is that he also went to Florence, the center of the Italian Renaissance. England was still in the Middle Ages; culturally it was far behind Italy. Personal contact with the capital of European literature and art must have been a tremendous stimulus to the Englishman's creative genius. Whether he met any of the great Italian writers, Petrarch and Boccaccio for example, is unknown.

[48] Shamed be he who thinks evil [of it]; the famous motto of the Order of the Garter. Its appearance here and the adoption of Gawain's "lace" by the court seem to point to some connection between the poem and the Order; but none of the orders has had green baldrics or collars as insignia. Possibly the poem was composed to offer, by way of indirect compliment to the wearers of the Garter, a parallel case in which an article of attire became a symbol of honor. The Order, the highest of British knighthood, was established about the middle of the fourteenth century.

[47] Unidentified; probably a reference to British chronicles in general.

Back in his own country, he was appointed in 1374 controller of the customs on wools, skins, and hides, an important post since the export duty on wool was the Crown's principal source of revenue. The appointment stipulated that Chaucer must keep his records in his own hand; they consisted of check lists in verification of the collectors' accounts. For the next twelve years his home was evidently in London, where he received rent free the lease of a house in the tower of Aldgate, at the east end of the city, not a great way from the wharves. Further marks of royal favor also brought substantial sums of money. These included profitable wardships of landed minors and the grant of a fine incurred by a violator of the customs regulations. There were also diplomatic missions in France and the Low Countries during the remainder of Edward's reign; they covered a wide variety of public affairs. In 1377 Chaucer was again abroad, on a commission relating to the marriage of the young king, Richard; and the following year saw him once more in Italy. Thereafter the records are almost exclusively of activities in England. In 1382 he became controller of the customs on wine and other goods, with the right to hire a deputy.

The lucrative customs work ended in 1386. Chaucer probably went to live not far from London, in the county of Kent, where in the same year he was elected to the House of Commons as knight of the shire. He was already a justice of the peace there. He was not re-elected to Parliament. How seriously he was personally involved in politics is unknown; no doubt he belonged to the faction of John of Gaunt. The rise to power, during the great Duke's absence from the country (1386–89), of an opposition party, hostile both to the King's intimates and to the Lancastrians, was probably the cause of Chaucer's retirement from the customs. Richard had to submit to the control of a parliamentary commission, one of the first acts of which was to throw out Lancastrian officeholders.

In May, 1389, King Richard seized the reins of government, and in October the Duke of Lancaster came back to England. Chaucer's fortunes took an immediate turn for the better. He soon became clerk of the king's works, which meant that he was in charge of building and repairs on such Crown properties as the Tower of London, the palace at Westminster, and several other royal residences. He was also on the commission for walls, bridges, sewers, and ditches along the Thames below London. Why he relinquished the clerkship two years later is unrecorded. About the same time he was made a deputy forester in Somersetshire; this appointment was renewed in 1398. To what extent its duties required absence from London is uncertain. Evidently he maintained a home near the capital, in Kent. Throughout the nineties numerous gifts and payments are on record; they leave no doubt of his standing at court. When, in 1399, Henry IV, son of Chaucer's old

patron, ascended the throne, he promptly confirmed the poet in certain grants (they included an annual hogshead of wine), and added a fresh annuity. At the end of that year Chaucer took a long lease on a house in the garden of Westminster Abbey. Perhaps he expected to settle down there and finish *The Canterbury Tales,* secure in the sunshine of the new sovereign's favor; but he died in less than a year. He was buried in the Abbey.

The significant thing about all these appointments and rewards is not their proof of Chaucer's versatility and his success as courtier and public servant but their revelation of the scope of an artist's experience. He doubtless knew most of the leading Englishmen of his day. On his Continental travels he must have met many European notables. Yet his observations ranged from top to bottom of the social structure. For example, as clerk of the king's works he bossed large gangs of craftsmen and laborers. He had opportunities for seeing everything, and to those opportunities he brought an uncommonly observant eye and a deep understanding of human nature. Since he also made himself a master of the art of literary expression, he was equipped, as few men have been before or since, to compose a record both accurate and entrancing of the whole human comedy.

CHAUCER'S WORKS

CHAUCER lived before the invention of printing; his works circulated in manuscripts copied by scribes, to one of whom he addresses a playful remonstrance invoking, unless the copyist's accuracy improves, the curse of a scabby disease known as the scall.

CHAUCERS WORDES UNTO ADAM, HIS OWNE SCRIVEYN

Adam scriveyn, if ever it thee bifalle
Boece or *Troylus* for to wryten newe,
Under thy long lokkes thou most[1] have the scalle,
But[2] after my makyng thou wryte more trewe—
So ofte a-daye I mot[3] thy werk renewe,
It to correcte and eek to rubbe and scrape;
And al is thorugh thy negligence and rape.[4]

The multiplication of the manuscripts by scribes who lacked Chaucer's supervision was doubtless still more negligent, and those which have survived often disagree. Not yet have scholars been able to establish with complete certainty Chaucer's lines as he actually wrote them, though recent textual studies have made a good deal of progress.

Nor has the problem of chronology been solved; there is still uncertainty about the dates of Chaucer's various writings. It is, however, possible to group them roughly under four categories: early, transitional, middle, and late.

---

[1] Mayest thou.   [2] Unless.   [3] Must.   [4] Haste.

Some prefer to name each group according to the paramount literary influence under which Chaucer was working at the time: the early period is the French; the transitional is Franco-Italian; the third is Italian; and the fourth and last is English, the poet having outgrown foreign tutelage.

The early (or French) group consists of poems written before 1372, prior, that is, to the first Italian journey. The most important of these is *The Book of the Duchess.* Chaucer wrote it in memory of the first wife of John of Gaunt, the Duchess Blanche, who died in 1369. Falling asleep over a book, the poet dreams of an encounter with a knight dressed in black, who is mourning the loss of his lady. Love is discussed, the Duchess is praised, and the poet offers the bereaved husband his sympathy. This performance is largely lacking in the realism characteristic of Chaucer's best work, but anticipations of it are mingled with the conventions drawn from medieval French poetry, especially French allegorical love-visions. The most influential of these poems, the *Roman de la Rose,* Chaucer had probably already translated, in whole or in part.

The second group is called transitional because, while it still shows French influence, the Italian is beginning. It also bears the marks of Chaucer's widening acquaintance with Latin authors. The principal work of this period, which extends from 1372 to 1380, two years after the second trip to Italy, is *The House of Fame.* Like *The Book of the Duchess,* it uses the conventional framework of the vision. The poet dreams that he is caught up into the air by an eagle and borne to the palace of Fame, where he is an interested observer of Fame's dealings with the ambitions of humankind. He next visits the House of Rumor, where he is on the verge of hearing a sensational announcement when the poem breaks off unfinished. While inferior to Chaucer's greatest work, this long poem contains a number of effective passages; and the eagle, whose erudition is equaled by his condescension in instructing the woefully ignorant Chaucer, is portrayed with much charm and humor. To this period also belong, among a variety of pieces, a life of Saint Cecilia and a collection of stanzas called "tragedies," both afterwards used in *The Canterbury Tales,* where they are assigned respectively to the Second Nun and the Monk.

In the third or middle period (1380–86) the Italian influence is thoroughly assimilated. Several important poems belong to this group. There is another love-vision, the fresh and charming *Parliament of Fowls.* Professing ignorance of love, the poet seeks knowledge in books but as usual falls asleep. He dreams that an ancient Roman guides him to a temple of Venus and thence to a rendezvous of all the birds, who, obedient to Nature's law, have assembled on St. Valentine's Day to choose their mates. Three eagles are rival suitors for the favor of a beautiful female eagle. They debate their claims in the language of courtly love, and the less aristocratic birds add their comments, idealistic or cynical, on the nature of love. The romance of *Palamon and Arcite,* an adaptation from Boccaccio, also falls in the third group; Chaucer later incorporated it in *The Canterbury Tales,* assigning it to the Knight. In the same period, too, comes Chaucer's somewhat heavy translation of the popular treatise *De Consolatione Philosophiae* by the Roman philosopher Boethius (died 524 A. D.), which is the source of most of the extended passages of philosophizing in Chaucer's poems.

But the major work of this third period is *Troilus and Criseyde,* a long narrative poem which is still the best thing of its kind in English. That is not to put it above *The Canterbury Tales,* which offers more variety and belongs to a different genre; but the *Troilus* is fully its equal in the art of narrative, in metrical virtuosity, and in characterization. The current premium on originality in fiction was nonexistent in the Middle Ages. If an author told the story better than his predecessors had, he was justified. Chaucer found the plot of *Troilus and Criseyde* in the *Filostrato* of Boccaccio, who in turn was much indebted to a long line of medieval embellishments of the Homeric account of the Trojan War. In Chaucer's hands the grand passion of Prince Troilus and his subsequent betrayal by the all-too-human Criseyde are related with a wisdom and tolerance that spring from largeness of experience, a genius's power of penetrating below the surface of life, and a profound understanding of the human heart. To the richly painted and humane portraits of the two lovers Chaucer adds a third, the figure of Pandarus, the heroine's uncle, a humorous but sympathetic onlooker, eager to further the amour of his niece and his best friend and vicariously thrilled by it. His character is one of Chaucer's sagest and most comic inventions. All three of the principals are in Boccaccio, but simply conceived and executed without complexity or subtlety. Troilus is little changed by Chaucer, but as studies in human nature Criseyde and Pandarus are his own.

With *The Legend of Good Women* the third period closes. This poem begins with an ecstatic tribute to the joys of spring and especially to the English daisy, which alone can draw the poet away from his books.

> And as for me, though that I konne but lyte,[1]
> On bokes for to rede I me delyte;
> And to hem yive I feyth and ful credence,
> And in myn herte have hem in reverence
> So hertely, that ther is game noon
> That fro my bokes maketh me to goon,
> But yt be seldom on the holyday,[2]

---

[1] Know but little. Chaucer delights, in both his early and his late work, in representing himself as ignorant of life and naive in his observation of it.

[2] Unless it be occasionally on a holy day.

Save, certeynly, whan that the month of May
Is comen, and that I here the foules synge,
And that the floures gynnen for to sprynge,
Farwel my bok and my devocioun!
   Now have I thanne eek[3] this condicioun,
That, of al the floures in the mede,
Thanne love I most thise floures white and rede,
Swiche as men callen daysyes in our toun.
To hem have I so gret affeccioun,
As I seyde erst,[4] whanne comen is the May,
That in my bed ther daweth[5] me no day
That I nam[6] up, and walkyng in the mede
To seen this flour agein[7] the sonne sprede,
Whan it upryseth erly by the morwe.[8]
That blisful sighte softneth al my sorwe,
So glad am I, whan that I have presence
Of it, to doon it alle reverence,
As she that is of alle floures flour,
Fulfilled of al vertu and honour,
And ever ilyke faire, and fressh of hewe;
And I love it, and ever ylike newe,
And evere shal, til that myn herte dye.
Al[9] swere I nat, of this I wol nat lye:
Ther loved no wight hotter in his lyve.
And whan that hit[10] ys eve, I renne blyve,[11]
As sone as evere the sonne gynneth weste,[12]
To seen this flour, how it wol go to reste,
For fere of nyght, so hateth she derknesse.
Hir chere[13] is pleynly[14] sprad in the brightnesse
Of the sonne, for ther yt wol unclose.
Allas! that I ne had Englyssh, ryme or prose,
Suffisant this flour to preyse aryght!

After a day spent in such devoted observation of the daisy, the poet falls asleep and dreams that he is back in the meadow, where he encounters the God of Love and the beautiful queen Alceste. The God of Love censures him harshly as a heretic: in the *Troilus* and in the translation of the *Roman de la Rose* Chaucer has been guilty of defaming women by describing them as fickle in love. Alceste comes to his defense: in some of his works he has praised women; besides, to one so ignorant and so lowly it befits the mighty God of Love to be merciful. Chaucer is ordered to do penance by composing a "legendary" or collection of saints' lives—only they are to be lives of Cupid's saints, the "good" women of the title, good, that is, as devotees of Cupid. Waking, Chaucer begins with an account of Cleopatra and follows it with narratives of other ladies unlike Criseyde because, whatever their shortcomings in other respects, they were all faithful lovers. The series breaks off in the middle of the legend of the tenth "saint."

---

3 Also.
4 Before.   5 Dawns.   6 Am not.   7 Toward.
8 In the morning.   9 Although.   10 It.
11 Run quickly.   12 Begins westering.   13 Countenance.
14 Fully.

Toward the beginning of the fourth, the late (or English), period (1387–1400), Chaucer wrote a few stories for *The Canterbury Tales* and also the superb general prologue to that collection. Here, too, belongs the translation and adaptation *A Treatise on the Astrolabe,* a scientific prose work describing the instrument, a predecessor of the sextant, and its use in the solution of forty astronomical problems. During the remaining years of this period the rest of *The Canterbury Tales* and several more short poems were written.

HOW TO READ CHAUCER

CHAUCER'S language is not so distant from our own as it looks at first sight. Chaucer wrote in East Midland, that one of the Middle English dialects which, because it was spoken in London, eventually became standard English speech; hence his language offers fewer difficulties than that of his contemporaries who spoke other dialects—for example, the Pearl Poet and the author of *Piers Plowman.* The following directions apply in particular to Chaucer and, less precisely, to Middle English writings in general.

Pronunciation

1. CONSONANTS. These are pronounced as in modern English except *gh* (= the German or Scottish *ch* in *ich, ach,* or *licht, loch*) and *r* (regularly trilled). There are no silent consonants; pronounce the *k* in *knyght,* the *g* in *gnawe,* the *l* in *folk,* both *n*'s in *sonne. Ch* is pronounced as in *church, ng* as in *finger.*

2. VOWELS AND DIPHTHONGS. Here the special catch is a final unstressed *e,* usually pronounced lightly *uh* (like *a* in *China*), but regularly elided (that is, not pronounced) before a vowel or an *h* at the beginning of the following word. (This final unstressed *e* is not to be confused with the final long *e* of such words as *be, charite.*) In general the vowels have the so-called "continental" values with which you are familiar if you know almost any foreign language. Note that long vowels are often doubled in spelling without having their sound changed thereby; for example, *rote* and *roote* are pronounced alike; so are *swete* and *sweete.* For the beginner the table on the following page, while not complete, is sufficiently accurate.

Note especially that the spelling *ou (ow)* sometimes represents long *u,* sometimes a diphthong. In general, modern pronunciation provides a guide to the distinction; Chaucer's long *u* becomes modern *ou* as in *house,* his diphthong becomes an *o* sound. Test this generalization by the examples given in the table.

Inflections

THE following notes are not intended as an abstract of Chaucer's grammar but as practical hints to the beginner.

SPELLING		PRONUNCIATION	EXAMPLES
Long a	a, aa	like *a* in *father*	bathed, maad
Short a	a	like the preceding sound shortened	that
Long e	e, ee	like *a* in *ale, care*[1]	feet, heeth, swete
Short e	e	like *e* in *tender*	tendre
Neutral e	e (final)	like *a* in *China*	roote
Long i	i, y	like *i* in *machine*	rise, lyke
Short i	i, y	like *i* in *ill*	in, kyng
Long o	o, oo	like *o* in *no, nor*[2]	foot, old
Short o	o	like *o* in *odd*	Engelond, ofte
Long u	ou, ow	like *oo* in *food*	flour, fowles
Short u	u, o	like *u* in *full*	but, yong[3]
iu	u, ew	like *u* in *unite*	vertu, salewe
au	au, aw	like *ou* in *out*	cause, drawe
ei	ai, ay, ei, ey	like *ay* in *day*[4]	day, veyne
eu	eu, ew	like long *e* + long *u*[5]	reule, lewed
oi	oi, oy	like *oi* in *boil*	roial, coy
ou	ou, ow, o (before gh)	like long *o* + long *u*[5]	soule, knowe, fo(u)ghte

(For a clear and systematic yet brief account see F. N. Robinson's edition, pp. xxviii–xxxi.)

1. The final -*e* of many nouns was a surviving trace of the word's original vowel ending, and it was regularly pronounced. Thus in Old English the nominative case of the noun we know as *son* was *sunu*; but by Chaucer's time the final *u* had dwindled into the indeterminate, lightly pronounced final -*e* of *sone*. Moreover, many words which now have the inflectional ending -*s* ended in Chaucer's day in -*es*—*dayes, nihtes*. In other words, many words were pronounced in Chaucer's day with one more syllable than they have today.

2. NOUNS. A few nouns have no ending in the possessive singular (e. g., *his lady grace*, his lady's grace). The plural ending -*en* (still seen in *oxen*) is more frequent in Chaucer (*eyen* or *yën*, eyes; *pesen*, peas).

3. PRONOUNS. *I* is sometimes *ich*; *its* is *his*; *their* and *them* are *hire* (*here, hir, her*) and *hem*. (The beginner should be on his guard against translating the word for *their* as *her*.)

4. ADVERBS. In addition to the suffix -*ly* (*gladly*) Chaucer has -*e* and -*liche* (*smerte*, smartly; *royalliche*, royally).

5. VERBS. The ending of the plural, the infinitive, and frequently the past participle is -*en* or -*e*. The imperative often ends in -*eth*. The past participle frequently has the prefix *y*- (*yronne*).

Versification

CHAUCER's usual line in the *Canterbury Tales* is regularly iambic pentameter; that is, it consists of five stressed syllables each preceded by an unstressed syllable. But the normal iambic foot (x /) is sometimes replaced by a trochee (/ x), that is, a foot in which the unstressed syllable follows the stressed one. Because of the frequency of a final unaccented syllable, many lines have eleven syllables instead of ten. Occasionally the opening unstressed syllable of a line is omitted. Final unstressed -*e* is regularly elided before a vowel or an *h* at the beginning of the following word, and elsewhere it is regularly pronounced; but sometimes the rhythm of the line demands that it be retained before a vowel or an *h*, and elided or sounded very rapidly and

[1] Actually, as these examples indicate, long *e* has two values, according as it is "close" or "open," but the beginner cannot be expected to distinguish between them. In the examples given, *feet* has long close *e*, pronounced like *a* in *ale*; *heeth* has long open *e*, pronounced like *a* in *care*; *swete* has long close *e* when it means *sweet* and long open *e* when it means *sweat*.

[2] Long *o*, like long *e*, has two values, close and open; of the examples given, *foot* has the close sound (as in *no*), *old* the open sound (as in *nor*).

[3] The spelling *o* designates a short *u* generally in words having a short *u* in modern pronunciation, such as *sone* (son), *sonne* (sun), *yong* (young), etc.

[4] Chaucer's pronunciation of this diphthong is a matter of dispute; this approximation is as satisfactory as any for beginners.

[5] Chaucer distinguishes here between two pronunciations, one beginning with a close sound, the other with an open sound.

lightly before a consonant. Two readers will frequently disagree as to the precise rhythm of a line.

GENERAL REFERENCES

THE best edition of Chaucer is the one-volume Cambridge
edition by F. N. Robinson (1933). The text of the follow-
ing selections is based partly on it and partly on J. M.
Manly's useful but incomplete edition of *The Canterbury
Tales* (1928). Both these volumes contain helpful glossaries,
notes, and introductions. The *Chaucer Handbook* of R. D.
French (1927) is valuable. For literary criticism see G. L.
Kittredge, *Chaucer and His Poetry* (1915); J. L. Lowes,
Geoffrey Chaucer and the Development of his Genius (1934);
and R. K. Root, *The Poetry of Chaucer* (revised ed., 1922).

Geoffrey Chaucer

THE CANTERBURY TALES

COLLECTIONS of short stories held together by some unifying thread are common enough in literature; the *Arabian
Nights* and Longfellow's *Tales of a Wayside Inn* are well-
known examples from widely separated periods. As an
excuse to bring together originally separate narratives, the
author constructs a framework: an occasion is invented, a
group of people is assembled, and for one reason or another
they are set to telling stories. In most such frame stories the
unifying device has little more than structural value. For
example, Boccaccio's *Decameron* brings together three ladies
and seven gentlemen, all of the same social class, who have
been driven by the pestilence from Florence to a villa in
the country, and who while away the time by telling
stories—a hundred of them in all. The interest lies almost
entirely in the stories, not in the frame nor in the relation
of the stories to it. Chaucer's handling of the frame is far
superior to Boccaccio's. His pilgrimage brings into temporary association representatives of many ranks and callings; and since he differentiates his characters sharply and
in general adjusts the tales carefully to their tellers, the
stories have a rich variety and a dramatic propriety lacking
in Boccaccio. Some of Chaucer's best strokes are in the
links between the stories; there he develops much incidental
drama in the relations of the pilgrims, out of which some
of the stories spring directly. For that reason several of the
links have been included in the following selections.

That the book was not completed has been a cause for
lamentation by five and a half centuries of readers. According to the plan announced in the General Prologue, each
pilgrim was to tell two tales on the outward journey and
two more on the way back. Only twenty were finished;
two were interrupted dramatically in the telling; two were
left unfinished by Chaucer. They run the gamut of human
experience, from hilarious farce to religious ecstasy. There
is not much in the way of human nature that has escaped
this keen but kindly glance, this serenely comic pen.

Here bygynneth the Book of the Tales of Caunterbury.

Whan that Aprill with his shoures soote[1]
The droghte of March hath perced to the roote,
And bathed every veyne in swich licour[2]
Of which vertu[3] engendred is the flour;
Whan Zephirus eek[4] with his swete breeth   5
Inspired hath in every holt and heeth[5]
The tendre croppes,[6] and the yonge sonne
Hath in the Ram his halfe cours yronne;[7]
And smale foweles maken melodye,
That slepen al the nyght with open yë—   10
So priketh hem nature in hir corages;[8]
Thanne longen folk to goon on pilgrimages,
And palmeres for to seken straunge strondes[9]
To ferne halwes, kowthe[10] in sondry londes;
And specially from every shires ende   15
Of Engelond to Caunterbury they wende,
The hooly, blisful martir[11] for to seke,
That hem hath holpen whan that they were seeke.[12]

---

[1] Sweet.—Note that this line lacks the usual opening unaccented
syllable.   [2] Such moisture; i.e., sap.   [3] Power.
[4] Also.   [5] Wood and open land; i.e., everywhere.
[6] Shoots, sprouts.
[7] It is mid-April. Since the calendar year formerly began on
March 25, the sun is still "young." The Ram is Aries, one of
the twelve constellations of the zodiac. The sun is nearly through
the second half of its course in Aries, the first of the constellations along its annual track.—The *y* in *yronne* is a sign of the
past participle.
[8] So nature spurs them on in their inclinations or feelings.
[9] Strands, shores.   [10] Distant shrines, known (i.e., famous).
[11] St. Thomas à Becket, Archbishop of Canterbury, where he was
assassinated in the cathedral in 1170. He was canonized in 1173,
and his tomb became the most popular shrine in England.
[12] Sick.

Bifil that in that seson on a day,
In Southwerk[13] at the Tabard[14] as I lay, 20
Redy to wenden on my pilgrymage
To Caunterbury with ful devout corage,
At nyght were come into that hostelrye
Wel nyne and twenty in a compaignye
Of sondry folk, by aventure yfalle[15] 25
In felaweshipe; and pilgrimes were they alle,
That toward Caunterbury wolden ryde.
The chambres and the stables weren wyde,
And wel we weren esed atte beste.[16]
And, shortly,[17] whan the sonne was to reste, 30
So hadde I spoken with hem everychon,[18]
That I was of hir felaweshipe anon,[19]
And made forward[20] erly for to ryse,
To take oure wey ther-as I yow devyse.[21]

But nathelees,[22] whil I have tyme and space, 35
Er that I ferther in this tale pace,[23]
Me thynketh it acordaunt to resoun[24]
To telle yow al the condicioun[25]
Of ech of hem, so as it semed me,
And whiche they weren, and of what degree 40
And eek in what array that they were inne;
And at a knyght than wol I first bigynne.

A KNYGHT ther was, and that a worthy man,
That, fro the tyme that he first bigan
To riden out, he loved chivalrie, 45
Trouthe and honour, fredom[26] and curteisie.
Ful worthy was he in his lordes[27] werre,[28]
And therto hadde he riden, no man ferre,[29]
As wel in cristendom as in hethenesse,[30]
And evere honoured for his worthynesse. 50
At Alisaundre[31] he was whan it was wonne.
Ful ofte tyme he hadde the bord bigonne[32]

Aboven alle nacions in Pruce;[33]
In Lettow[34] hadde he reysed[35] and in Ruce—[36]
No Cristen man so ofte of his degree. 55
In Gernade at the seege eek hadde he be
Of Algezir,[37] and riden in Belmarye.[38]
At Lyeys was he and at Satalye,[39]
Whan they were wonne; and in the Grete See[40]
At many a noble armee[41] hadde he be. 60
At mortal batailles hadde he been fiftene,
And foughten for oure feith at Tramyssene[42]
In lystes thries, and ay slayn his foo.
This ilke[43] worthy knyght hadde been also
Somtyme with the lord of Palatye[44] 65
Agayn[45] another hethen in Turkye.
And everemoore he hadde a sovereyn prys;[46]
And though that he were worthy, he was wys,[47]
And of his port[48] as meeke as is a mayde.
He nevere yet no vileynye[49] ne sayde 70
In al his lyf unto no maner wight.
He was a verray,[50] parfit, gentil[51] knyght.
But for to tellen yow of his array,
His hors[52] weren goode, but he was nat gay;
Of fustian[53] he wered a gypon[54] 75
Al bismotered[55] with his habergeon;[56]
For he was late ycome from his viage,[57]
And wente for to doon his pilgrymage.

With hym ther was his sone, a yong SQUIER,
A lovyere and a lusty bacheler,[58] 80
With lokkes crulle as they were[59] leyd in presse.
Of twenty yeer of age he was, I gesse.
Of his stature he was of evene lengthe,[60]
And wonderly delyvere,[61] and of greet strengthe.
And he hadde been somtyme in chyvachie[62] 85
In Flaundres, in Artoys, and Pycardie,
And born hym weel, as of so litel space,[63]
In hope to stonden in his lady[64] grace.

---

[13] Southwark, a London suburb, where the Canterbury road came in at the south end of London Bridge.
[14] Inns were identified by painted signs; a tabard was a short, sleeveless jacket. There actually was an inn of this name in Southwark in Chaucer's time. [15] By chance fallen.
[16] Accommodated in the best manner.
[17] I.e., to make a long story short.
[18] With them, everyone.
[19] Was of their fellowship immediately.
[20] (We) made an agreement.
[21] Where I am (now) relating to you.
[22] No[ne] the less, nevertheless. [23] Pass, proceed.
[24] I.e., proper.
[25] State; i.e., rank, character, appearance, etc. [26] Generosity.
[27] His feudal lord's. [28] War; i.e., campaigns. [29] Farther.
[30] The Knight's military exploits, listed in the following lines, fall into three general campaigns: (1) against the pagans in Prussia, Lithuania, and Russia; (2) against the Mohammedans in Asia Minor and Egypt; (3) against the Moors in North Africa.
[31] Alexandria was captured by Pierre de Lusignan, king of Cyprus, in 1365. [32] Been seated at the head of the table.

[33] Prussia, i.e., East Prussia. He had evidently campaigned with the Teutonic Knights. [34] Lithuania. [35] Campaigned.
[36] Russia.
[37] Algeciras, besieged in 1342. Granada was a Moorish kingdom in Spain. [38] The territory of the Beni-Marin in Morocco.
[39] The cities of Ayas and Adalia, in Asia Minor; both figured in the campaigns of Pierre de Lusignan. [40] Mediterranean.
[41] Armada, expedition. [42] Tlemçen, in Algeria.
[43] Same. [44] Probably Balat, in Asia Minor. [45] Against.
[46] Noble reputation.
[47] Though he was a man of importance, he was level headed (i.e., not conceited). [48] Demeanor.
[49] Rudeness, boorishness. [50] True. [51] Well-bred.
[52] Horses. [53] Coarse cotton cloth. [54] Tunic.
[55] Smutted, stained. [56] Hauberk, coat of mail.
[57] Voyage, journey. [58] Aspirant to knighthood.
[59] As curly as if they had been. [60] Medium height.
[61] Agile. [62] On a cavalry raid.
[63] Considering the shortness of the time.
[64] Lady's, sweetheart's.

Embrouded[65] was he as it were a meede,
Al ful of fresshe floures, whyte and reede.   90
Syngynge he was, or floytynge,[66] al the day;
He was as fressh as is the monthe of May.
Short was his gowne, with sleves longe and wyde.
Wel koude he sitte on hors and faire ryde;
He koude songes make, and wel endite,[67]   95
Juste,[68] and eek daunce, and weel purtreye[69] and write.
So hoote he lovede that by nyghtertale[70]
He slepte namoore than dooth a nyghtyngale.
Curteis he was, lowely, and servysable,
And carf[71] biforn his fader at the table.   100

A YEMAN[72] hadde he,[73] and servantz namo[74]
At that tyme, for hym liste[75] ride soo.
And he was clad in cote and hood of grene;
A sheef of pecok arwes, bright and kene,
Under his belt he bar ful thriftily—   105
Wel koude he dresse his takel[76] yemanly:
His arwes drouped noght with fetheres lowe—
And in his hand he baar a myghty bowe.
A not heed[77] hadde he, with a broun visage.
Of woodecraft wel koude[78] he al the usage.   110
Upon his arm he baar a gay bracer,[79]
And by his syde a swerd and a bokeler,[80]
And on that oother syde a gay daggere,
Harneised[81] wel and sharpe as point of spere,
A Cristophere[82] on his brest, of silver sheene.[83]   115
An horn he bar, the bawdryk[84] was of grene.
A forster[85] was he soothly,[86] as I gesse.

Ther was also a nonne, a PRIORESSE,
That of hir smylyng was ful symple and coy;[87]
Hire gretteste ooth was but by Seinte Loy.[88]   120
And she was cleped[89] Madame Eglentyne.
Ful weel she soong the service dyvyne,
Entuned in hir nose ful semely;[90]

And Frenssh she spak ful faire and fetisly—[91]
After the scole of Stratford-atte-Bowe,[92]   125
For Frenssh of Parys was to hire unknowe.
    At mete wel ytaught was she withalle:
She leet no morsel from hir lippes falle,
Ne wette hir fyngres in hir sauce depe;
Wel koude she carie a morsel, and wel kepe   130
That no drope ne fille upon hire brest—
In curteisie was set ful muchel hir lest.[93]
Hire over-lippe wyped she so clene
That in hir coppe ther was no ferthyng[94] sene
Of grece, whan she dronken hadde hir draughte.   135
Ful semely after hir mete she raughte.[95]
And, sikerly,[96] she was of greet desport,[97]
And full plesaunt, and amyable of port,
And peyned hire to countrefete cheere[98]
Of court, and been estatlich[99] of manere,   140
And to ben holden digne[1] of reverence.
    But for to speken of hire conscience,[2]
She was so charitable and so pitous
She wolde wepe if that she saugh a mous
Kaught in a trappe, if it were deed or bledde.   145
Of smale houndes hadde she, that she fedde
With rosted flessh, or milk and wastel-breed;[3]
But soore wepte she if oon of hem were deed,
Or if men[4] smoot it with a yerde smerte.[5]
And al was conscience and tendre herte.   150
    Ful semyly hir wympul pynched was,[6]
Hire nose tretys,[7] hir eyen greye as glas,[8]
Hir mouth ful smal and therto[9] softe and reed;
But sikerly she hadde a fair forheed.
It was almoost a spanne brood, I trowe;   155
For, hardily,[10] she was nat undergrowe.
Ful fetys[11] was hir cloke, as I was war.
Of smal coral aboute hire arm she bar
A peire of bedes,[12] gauded al with grene;[13]
And theron heng a brooch of gold ful sheene,   160

---

65 Embroidered, i.e., adorned. As a meadow is embroidered by
    flowers of red and white, so his complexion was beautified.
    Possibly the reference is to his costume.
66 Playing the flute (or, possibly, whistling).
67 Write down words to them.   68 Joust, fight in tournaments.
69 Draw.   70 At night.
71 A squire's duty, and an accomplishment every gentleman was
    supposed to acquire.   72 Yeoman.   73 The Knight.
74 No more.   75 It pleased him to.
76 Keep his equipment (tackle) in order.
77 Nut-head; i.e., his hair was clipped short.   78 Knew.
79 Guard (for the left forearm).   80 Buckler, shield.
81 Equipped (with a sheath).
82 St. Christopher was patron saint of foresters; the Yeoman wore
    his image to avert injury.   83 Bright.
84 Shoulder belt or sash.   85 Forester.   86 Truly.
87 Quiet, modest.
88 St. Eligius, a seventh-century saint famous for his craftsmanship
    as a goldsmith.   89 Called.
90 As was and is the custom of ecclesiastics.

91 Gracefully.
92 At Bromley, Middlesex, adjoining Stratford le Bow, two miles
    east of London, there was a Benedictine convent, St. Leonard's.
    After the scole means according to the (inferior) manner or style.
93 Desire.   94 Farthing, bit.   95 Reached.
96 Certainly.   97 Merriment.
98 Took pains to imitate the deportment.   99 Stately.

1 Worthy.   2 Sensibility.   3 Fine white bread.
4 I.e., anyone.   5 With a stick sharply (smartly).
6 Very becomingly her head-covering was pleated. This, like
    several other strokes in the portrait, suggests a touch of world-
    liness. Nunneries in Chaucer's time were not so much for the
    poor or the devout as for the well-to-do spinster; she had to
    bring a dowry with her.   7 Well formed.   8 Blue.
9 In addition.   10 Certainly.   11 Elegant.
12 A string of beads, i.e., a rosary.
13 Furnished at intervals with green beads. The small **coral** beads
    stood for Ave Marias, the green beads for Paternosters.

On which ther was first write a crowned A,[14]
And after *Amor vincit omnia.*[15]

Another NONNE with hire hadde she,
That was hire chapeleyne,[16] and PREESTES thre.[17]

A MONK ther was, a fair for the maistrie,[18]   165
An outridere,[19] that lovede venerie,[20]
A manly man, to been an abbot able.
Ful many a deyntee[21] hors hadde he in stable;
And whan he rood, men myghte his brydel heere
Gynglen in a whistlynge wynd als cleere   170
And eek as loude as dooth the chapel belle.
    Ther-as[22] this lord was kepere of the celle,[23]
The reule[24] of Seint Maure, or of Seint Beneit,[25]
By cause that it was old, and somdel streit,[26]
This ilke Monk leet olde thynges pace,   175
And heeld after the newe world the space.[27]
He yaf nat of[28] that text a pulled[29] hen
That seith that hunters ben nat hooly men,[30]
Ne that a monk whan he is recchelees[31]
Is likned til a fissh that is waterlees,   180
This is to seyn, a monk out of his cloystre;
But thilke[32] text heeld he nat worth an oystre.
And I seyde his opinion was good.
What[33] sholde he studie and make hymselven wood,[34]
Upon a book in cloystre alwey to poure,   185
Or swynken[35] with his handes and laboure,
As Austyn bit?[36] How shal the world be served?
Lat Austyn have his swynk to him reserved.
Therfore he was a prikasour[37] aright.
Grehoundes he hadde as swift as fowel in flight.   190

Of prikyng[38] and of huntyng for the hare
Was al his lust; for no cost wolde he spare.
I seigh[39] his sleves purfiled[40] at the hond
With grys,[41] and that the fyneste of a lond;
And, for to festne his hood under his chyn,   195
He hadde of gold ywroght a ful curious pyn—
A love knotte in the gretter ende ther was.
His heed was balled, that shoon as any glas—
And eek his face, as he hadde been enoynt;
He was a lord ful fat and in good poynt.[42]   200
His eyen stepe[43] and rollynge in his heed,
That stemed as a forneys of a leed;[44]
His bootes souple, his hors in greet estaat.[45]
Now certeinly he was a fair prelaat;
He was nat pale, as a forpyned[46] goost.   205
A fat swan loved he best of any roost.
His palfrey was as broun as is a berye.

    A FRERE ther was, a wantowne[47] and a merye;
A lymytour,[48] a ful solempne[49] man.
In alle the ordres foure[50] is noon that kan[51]   210
So muchel of daliaunce[52] and fair langage.
He hadde maad ful many a mariage
Of yonge wommen at his owene cost.[53]
Unto his ordre he was a noble post.[54]
Ful wel biloved and famulier was he   215
With frankeleyns[55] over-al[56] in his contree,
And eek with worthy wommen of the toun;
For he hadde power of confessioun,
As seyde hymself, moore than a curat,
For of his ordre he was licenciat.[57]   220
Ful swetely herde he confession,
And plesaunt was his absolucion.
He was an esy man to yeve[58] penaunce
Ther-as he wiste to have a good pitaunce.[59]

---

[14] A capital A with a crown over it.   [15] Love conquers all.

[16] Private secretary or assistant.

[17] Three would bring the number of pilgrims to thirty-one, instead of twenty-nine (see line 24, above). Nor is it likely that
the Prioress would be attended by more than one priest. There
may be a scribal error or simply an inconsistency left by Chaucer
in this uncompleted work.

[18] A good candidate for pre-eminence, i.e., a very fine one.

[19] Rider out (to inspect the monastery's farms).

[20] Hunting. By Chaucer's time the monastic orders had, in practice,
considerably relaxed the rules prescribing poverty, meager diet,
manual labor, and claustration or restriction to the cloister.

[21] Fine.   [22] Where.

[23] Cells were monastic establishments, such as priories, subject to
others, such as abbeys.   [24] Monastic regulations.

[25] St. Benedict founded monasticism in western Europe in 529.
St. Maurus was believed to have introduced the Benedictine
order into France.   [26] Somewhat strict.

[27] I.e., meanwhile.   [28] Cared (gave) not for.

[29] Plucked.

[30] St. Jerome, not Holy Writ, seems to be responsible for this
widely current idea.

[31] Reckless, i.e., careless in observing the monastic discipline.—The
comparison, in the next line, to a fish out of water was a commonplace in religious writings.   [32] That same.

[33] What for, why.   [34] Mad.   [35] Toil.

[36] As Augustine bids.   [37] Mounted hunter.

[38] Following the hare by its tracks.   [39] Saw.

[40] Trimmed.   [41] A costly gray fur.

[42] In good physical condition, plump.   [43] Large, prominent.

[44] Glowed like a furnace under a cauldron.   [45] Fine condition.

[46] Wasted away by torture or suffering.   [47] Sportive.

[48] A friar licensed to beg within a limited area.

[49] Gay, festive.

[50] The Carmelites or White Friars, the Franciscans or Gray Friars,
the Dominicans or Black Friars, and the Augustinians.

[51] Knows.   [52] Pleasures of society.

[53] By putting up the cash for their dowries he arranged marriages
for the girls he seduced.—Chaucer is more contemptuous, in
the portrait of the Friar, than is usual with him. The friars'
orders, established in a spirit of reform inspired by the growing
laxity of the monastic orders, had themselves fallen away from
the ideals of their founders.   [54] I.e., pillar.

[55] Large landowners, not nobles, but ranking just below the
baronage.   [56] Everywhere.

[57] He had from his order a license to hear confessions. The parish
clergy complained of the friars' venality and their laxity in
imposing penance.   [58] Give.

[59] Where he knew he would have a good allowance (of gifts).

For unto a poure ordre for to yive[60] 225
Is signe that a man is wel yshryve;
For if he yaf,[61] he dorste make avaunt,[62]
He wiste[63] that a man was repentaunt,
For many a man so harde is of his herte
He may nat wepe althogh hym soore smerte. 230
Therfore, instede of wepynge and preyeres,
Men moote[64] yeve silver to the poure freres.
His typet[65] was ay farsed[66] ful of knyves
And pynnes, for to yeven yonge wyves.
And certeinly he hadde a murye note; 235
Wel koude he synge, and pleyen on a rote;[67]
Of yeddynges he baar outrely the pris.[68]
His nekke whit was as the flour-de-lys;
Therto he strong was as a champion.
He knew the tavernes wel in every toun, 240
And everich hostiler[69] and tappestere,[70]
Bet than a lazar or a beggestere;[71]
For unto swich a worthy man as he
Acorded nat, as by his facultee,[72]
To have with sike lazars aqueyntaunce. 245
It is nat honeste—it may nat avaunce[73]—
For to deelen with no swich poraille,[74]
But al with riche and selleres of vitaille.[75]
And over-al, ther-as profit sholde arise,
Curteis he was and lowely of servyse. 250
Ther nas[76] no man, nowher, so vertuous:
He was the beste beggere in his hous;[77]
For thogh a wydwe hadde noght a sho,[78]
So plesaunt was his *In principio*[79]
Yet wolde he have a ferthyng er he wente. 255
His purchas was wel bettre than his rente.[80]
And rage[81] he koude, as it were right a whelpe.[82]
In love-dayes[83] ther koude he muchel helpe;
For there he was nat lyk a cloysterer[84]

With a thredbare cope,[85] as is a poure scoler, 260
But he was lyk a maister[86] or a pope.
Of double worstede was his semycope,[87]
That rounded as a belle out of the presse.[88]
Somwhat he lipsed,[89] for his wantownesse,
To make his Englissh sweete upon his tonge; 265
And in his harpyng, whan that he hadde songe,
His eyen twynkled in his heed aryght
As doon the sterres in the frosty nyght.
This worthy lymytour was cleped Huberd.

A MARCHANT was ther, with a forked berd, 270
In mottelee,[90] and hye on horse[91] he sat;
Upon his heed a Flaundryssh bevere hat;
His bootes clasped faire and fetisly.
His resons[92] he spak ful solempnely,
Sownynge[93] alway th' encrees of his wynnyng. 275
He wolde the see were kept for anything
Bitwixe Middelburgh and Orewelle.[94]
Wel koude he in eschaunge sheeldes[95] selle.
This worthy man ful wel his wit bisette:[96]
Ther wiste no wight that he was in dette, 280
So estatly was he of his governaunce
With his bargaynes and with his chevyssaunce.[97]
For sothe[98] he was a worthy man withalle;[99]
But sooth to seyn, I noot[1] how men hym calle.

A CLERK ther was of Oxenford also, 285
That unto logyk hadde longe ygo.[2]
As leene was his hors as is a rake;
And he nas nat right fat, I undertake,
But looked holwe, and therto sobrely.
Ful thredbare was his overeste courtepy;[3] 290
For he hadde geten hym yet no benefice,[4]
Ne was so worldly for to have office.[5]

---

60 Give. 61 Gave. 62 Boast. 63 Knew.
64 One may, must, ought to.
65 Hanging part of a garment; here probably some kind of scarf in
which these objects were tied up. 66 Stuffed.
67 An ancestor of the violin.
68 For songs he utterly bore off the prize. 69 Innkeeper.
70 Tapster, barmaid.
71 Better than (he did) a leper or a beggar woman.
72 Position. 73 Advance, be profitable. 74 Poor folk.
75 Victuals, provisions. 76 Was not.
77 The best of his convent at begging supplies for them. (*Vertuous*
in line 251 means capable, efficient.) Unlike the monastic houses,
those of the friars were not supposed to hold property but to
live from hand to mouth on donations. 78 Shoe.
79 *In principio erat verbum* (in the beginning was the Word), John
1:1. The first fourteen verses of this gospel were thought to
have a special efficacy, and the friars were fond of reciting them
as they went from house to house in quest of donations.
80 What he picked up on the side (*purchase*) came to more than
his regular income (*rent*). *Purchase* carried a suggestion of goods
obtained by shady methods.
81 Play, i.e., he was playful as a puppy. 82 Dog, pup.
83 Arbitration days for settling minor disputes. 84 Recluse.

85 Cape.
86 Master of Arts, i.e., college graduate. Few university students
took even the B.A., which was hardly a degree; it was the M.A.
that marked the graduate. 87 Short cape. 88 Mold.
89 Lisped. 90 Motley, figured cloth of more than one color.
91 In an especially high saddle. 92 Remarks.
93 Talking about, proclaiming.
94 He wished the sea to be held (against pirates), at all costs, between Middleburg (the wool market on the Dutch coast) and
Orwell (an old port near Harwich and Ipswich).
95 The French *écus*, worth about $.87 each. If the Merchant made
a profit in foreign exchange he was breaking the law.
96 Bestowed, applied.
97 Dealing. Both *bargaynes* and *chevyssaunce* often imply dis-
honesty. *Chevyssaunce* was also used as a euphemism for *usury*.
98 Forsooth, in truth. 99 Besides, for all that.

1 Know not.
2 Gone. Since logic belonged to the curriculum of candidates for
the B. A., the Clerk may be studying for the M. A.
3 Outside jacket.
4 Ecclesiastical "living," e.g., appointment as rector or vicar.
5 Secular office. See *Piers Plowman*, Prologue, lines 87 ff., for a
complaint against ecclesiastics in secular employment.

For hym was levere[6] have at his beddes heed
Twenty bookes, clad in blak or reed,
Of Aristotle and his philosophie   295
Than robes riche, or fithele,[7] or gay sautrie.
But al be that he was a philosophre,[8]
Yet hadde he but litel gold in cofre;
But al that he myghte of his freendes hente[9]
On bookes and on lernynge he it spente;   300
And bisily gan for the soules preye
Of hem that yaf hym wherwith to scoleye.[10]
Of studie took he moost cure[11] and moost heede.
Noght o[12] word spak he moore than was neede;
And that was seyd in forme and reverence,[13]   305
And short, and quyk, and ful of hy sentence.[14]
Sownynge in[15] moral vertu was his speche;
And gladly wolde he lerne, and gladly teche.

A SERGEANT OF THE LAWE,[16] war and wys,[17]
That often hadde been at the Parvys,[18]   310
Ther was also, ful riche of excellence.
Discreet he was, and of greet reverence—
He semed swich, his wordes weren so wise.
Justice he was ful often in assise,
By patente and by pleyn commissioun.[19]   315
For his science and for his heigh renoun,
Of fees and robes[20] hadde he many oon.
So greet a purchasour[21] was nowher noon:
Al was fee symple to hym in effect;[22]
His purchasyng myghte nat been infect.[23]   320
Nowher so bisy a man as he ther nas;
And yet he semed bisier than he was.

6 He would rather.
7 Fiddle. The psaltery (*sautrie*) was somewhat like a zither.
8 Philosophy included science, even alchemy, which sought for
the "philosopher's stone," a chemical preparation that the
alchemists believed would turn other metals into gold. The
Clerk is not a philosopher in that sense; Chaucer is joking.—As
for his twenty books, they constituted a substantial private
library; there were no printed books, and manuscripts were
not plentiful.   9 Get.   10 Pursue scholarship.
11 Care.   12 One.   13 In due form and with respect.
14 Lofty maxims.   15 Tending to.
16 One of the king's legal servants, chosen from the most eminent
barristers of at least sixteen years' experience. From the ranks of
the sergeants the judges of the royal courts were appointed.
There were about twenty sergeants in Chaucer's time.
17 Wary and wise, cautious and prudent.
18 Porch, perhaps the porch of St. Paul's, where lawyers consulted
their clients. Whether this was the practice as early as the
fourteenth century is uncertain, however. Possibly the reference
is to a courtroom or to a meeting place of law students.
19 The assizes were the regular county courts. A patent was a
royal letter of appointment as justice; a plain commission
authorized justices to try cases.
20 Suits of clothes, as fees.   21 Buyer of land for himself.
22 However unsatisfactory the seller's evidence of tenure, the
Sergeant's legal knowledge was such that he always got as good
a title as tenure in fee simple, that is, unrestricted ownership.
23 Could not be invalidated.

In termes[24] hadde he caas and doomes[25] alle
That from the tyme of Kyng William[26] were falle.
Therto he koude endite and make a thyng,   325
Ther koude no wight pynche at[27] his writyng.
And every statut koude he pleyn by rote.
He rood but hoomly, in a medlee[28] cote,
Girt with a ceint[29] of silk, with barres[30] smale;
Of his array telle I no lenger tale.   330

A FRANKELEYN[31] was in his compaignye.
Whit was his berd as is a dayesye;
Of his complexion he was sangwyn.[32]
Wel loved he by the morwe[33] a sop in wyn.[34]
To lyven in delit was evere his wone;[35]   335
For he was Epicurus owene sone,
That heeld opinion that pleyn delit
Was verraily felicitee parfit.[36]
An housholdere, and that a greet, was he;
Seint Julian[37] was he in his contree.   340
His breed, his ale, was alweys after oon;[38]
A bettre envyned[39] man was nowher noon.
Withoute bake mete was nevere his hous,
Of fissh and flessh, and that so plentevous
It snewed in his hous of mete and drynke,   345
Of alle deyntees that men koude thynke.
After the sondry sesons of the yeer,
So chaunged he his mete and his soper.
Ful many a fat partrich hadde he in muwe,[40]
And many a breem and many a luce[41] in stuwe.[42]   350
Wo was his cook but if[43] his sauce were
Poynaunt and sharpe, and redy al his geere.
His table dormant[44] in his halle alway
Stood redy covered al the longe day.

24 Precisely.
25 Cases and judgments. This mastery of the common law was in
addition to his memorized knowledge of the statutes, mentioned
in line 327.   26 The Conqueror.
27 Find fault with.   28 Cloth of mixed weave.   29 Girdle.
30 Metal strips across the girdle, presumably for ornament.
31 Franklins were landed proprietors, and apparently ranked as
gentlemen, however limited their opportunities of acquiring
polish. They are comparable to the country squire of the
eighteenth century.
32 Medieval and Renaissance literature is full of allusions to the
old physiology based on the four "humors" or moistures: blood,
phlegm, yellow bile or choler, and black bile or melancholy.
The individual's temperament or "complexion" was due to the
mixture of the four in him, harmonious or unbalanced. Hence
the predomination of one humor made a man sanguine, phlegmatic, bilious or choleric, or melancholy.
33 I.e., as a morning dish.   34 Bread soaked in wine.
35 Wont, custom.
36 An inadequate summary of Epicurus's views!
37 Patron saint of hospitality.
38 Invariable; i.e., uniformly good.   39 Stocked with wine.
40 Mew, coop.   41 Bream and pike.   42 Stew, fishpond.
43 Unless.
44 I.e., fixed; it was not, like most, a removable board laid on
trestles.

At sessions[45] ther was he lord and sire;   355
Ful ofte tyme he was knyght of the shire.[46]
An anlaas,[47] and a gipser al of silk,
Heeng at his girdel, whit as morne milk.
A shirreve[48] hadde he been, and a countour.[49]
Was nowher swich a worthy vavasour.[50]   360

AN HABERDASSHERE,[51] and a CARPENTER,
A WEBBE,[52] a DYERE, and a TAPYCER[53]—
And they were clothed alle in o lyveree,
Of a solempne and a greet fraternitee.[54]
Ful fressh and newe hir geere apiked[55] was.   365
Hir knyves were chaped,[56] noght with bras,
But al with silver; wroght ful clene and weel
Hire girdles and hir pouches everydeel.
Wel semed ech of hem a fair burgeys[57]
To sitten in a yeldehalle[58] on a deys.[59]   370
Everich, for the wisdom that he kan,
Was shaply[60] for to been an alderman;
For catel[61] hadde they ynogh, and rente,
And eek hir wyves wolde it wel assente;
And elles certeyn were they to blame—   375
It is ful fair to been ycleped "Madame,"
And goon to vigiliies al bifore,[62]
And have a mantel roialliche ybore.

A COOK they hadde with hem, for the nones,[63]
To boille the chiknes, with the marybones   380
And poudre-marchant tart[64] and galyngale.[65]
Wel koude he knowe a draughte of London ale.
He koude rooste, and sethe,[66] and broille, and frye,
Maken mortreux,[67] and wel bake a pye.
But greet harm was it, as it thoughte me,   385
That on his shyne a mormal[68] hadde he.
For blankmanger,[69] that made he with the beste.

A SHIPMAN was ther, wonynge fer by[70] weste;
For aught I woot he was of Dertemouthe.
He rood upon a rouncy,[71] as he kouthe,[72]   390
In a gowne of faldyng[73] to the knee.
A daggere hangynge on a laas[74] hadde he
Aboute his nekke under his arm adoun.
The hoote somer hadde maad his hewe al broun;
And certeinly he was a good felawe:[75]   395
Ful many a draughte of wyn had he ydrawe
Fro Burdeux-ward,[76] whil that the chapman sleepe.
Of nyce conscience[77] took he no keepe:[78]
If that he faught and hadde the hyer hond,
By water he sente hem hoom to every lond.[79]   400
But of his craft,[80] to rekene wel his tydes,
His stremes,[81] and his daungers hym bisides,
His herberwe,[82] and his moone, his lodemenage,[83]
Ther nas noon swich from Hulle to Cartage.[84]
Hardy he was and wys, to undertake.[85]   405
With many a tempest hadde his berd been shake.
He knew alle the havenes, as they were,
Fro Gootlond[86] to the Cape of Fynystere,[87]
And every cryke in Britaigne and in Spayne.
His barge ycleped was the Maudelayne.   410

With us ther was a DOCTOUR OF PHISIK.
In al this world ne was ther noon hym lik,
To speke of[1] phisik and of surgerye,
For he was grounded in astronomye.[2]
He kepte[3] his pacient a ful greet deel   415
In houres[4] by his magyk natureel.[5]
Wel koude he fortunen the ascendent
Of his ymages for his pacient;[6]
He knew the cause of everich maladye,

[45] Of justices of the peace; they held the local courts.
[46] Member of Parliament for his county.
[47] A dagger tapering to its point. Gipser = bag, pouch, purse.
[48] Sheriff, a royal official of the county, ranking next to the Lord Lieutenant.   [49] Probably, accountant or auditor of the shire.
[50] Substantial landholder, ranking below the baron.
[51] Seller of miscellaneous small wares.   [52] Weaver.
[53] Tapestry maker.
[54] Probably a religious guild (they all belonged to different trade guilds).   [55] Trimmed.   [56] Mounted.
[57] Citizen.   [58] Guildhall.
[59] Dais, raised platform where the municipal dignitaries sat.
[60] Fitted.   [61] Chattels, property.
[62] Have precedence at religious services on the eves of feast days.
[63] For the nonce, for the once, for the occasion. Often, however, the phrase is a virtually meaningless tag.
[64] Pungent flavoring powder.
[65] Flavoring made from a variety of cyperus or sedge.
[66] Boil.   [67] Stews. The x was probably pronounced s.
[68] Ulcerous sore.
[69] Not our blancmange, but an elaborate dish of creamed chicken cooked with eggs, rice, sugar, and almonds.

[70] Dwelling far in the.
[71] Exactly what kind of horse is uncertain; probably a big and heavy one, rather than a fine riding horse.
[72] As well as he knew how; i.e., he rode like a sailor.
[73] Frieze, heavy woolen cloth.   [74] Lace, cord.
[75] Slang for rascal.
[76] I.e., he stole the wine on the voyage home from Bordeaux.
[77] Sensibility, tender feelings.   [78] Heed.
[79] I.e., he made his prisoners walk the plank.
[80] Skill at his profession.   [81] Currents.   [82] Harborage.
[83] Pilotage.   [84] Probably the Spanish port of Cartagena.
[85] He was daring and shrewd in carrying out any project.
[86] The island of Gottland in the Baltic, off the coast of Sweden.
[87] In northwestern Spain.

[1] I.e., if you are talking (or thinking) of; with respect to.
[2] Which included astrology.   [3] Watched.
[4] I.e., he chose the most favorable astrological hours.
[5] Legitimate science, as distinguished from black magic or necromancy.
[6] He made his images (either representations of the patient or symbols) at the moment when favorable planets were rising (and when the malefic planets were in positions where they could do no harm).

Were it of hoot or cold or moyste or drye,[7]   420
And where they engendred, and of what humour;[8]
He was a verray,[9] parfit praktisour.
The cause yknowe and of his harm the roote,
Anon he yaf the sike man his boote.[10]
Ful redy hadde he his apothecaries   425
To sende him drogges and his letuaries;[11]
For ech of hem made oother for to wynne—[12]
Hir[13] frendshipe nas nat newe to bigynne.
Wel knew he the oldë Esculapius,[14]
And Deÿscorides, and eek Rufus,   430
Olde Ypocras, Haly, and Galyen,
Serapion, Razis, and Avycen,
Averrois, Damascien, and Constantyn,
Bernard, and Gatesden, and Gilbertyn.
Of his diete mesurable[15] was he,   435
For it was of no superfluitee.
But of greet norissyng and digestible.
His studie was but litel on the Bible.[16]
In sangwyn[17] and in pers[18] he clad was al,
Lyned with taffata and with sendal;[19]   440
And yet he was but esy of dispence,[20]
He kepte that he wan in pestilence.[21]
For gold in phisik is a cordial;[22]
Therfore he lovede gold in special.

A good WIF[23] was ther, OF biside BATHE;   445
But she was somdel[24] deef, and that was scathe.[25]
Of clooth-makyng she hadde swich an haunt[26]
She passed hem of Ypres and of Gaunt.[27]
In al the parisshe, wif ne was ther noon
That to the offrynge bifore hire sholde goon;[28]   450
And if ther dide, certeyn so wrooth was she
That she was out of alle charitee.
Hir coverchiefs[29] ful fyne weren of ground;[30]

I dorste swere they weyeden ten pound
That on a Sonday weren upon hir heed.   455
Hir hosen weren of fyn scarlet reed,
Ful streite yteyd,[31] and shoes ful moyste[32] and newe.
Boold was hir face, and fair, and reed of hewe.
She was a worthy womman al hir lyve;
Housbondes at chirche dore[33] she hadde fyve,   460
Withouten[34] oother compaignye in youthe—
But therof nedeth nat to speke as nowthe.[35]
And thries hadde she been at Jerusalem;
She hadde passed many a straunge strem.
At Rome she hadde been, and at Boloigne,[36]   465
In Galice[37] at Seint Jame, and at Coloigne.[38]
She koude muchel of wandrynge by the weye.
Gat-tothed[39] was she, soothly for to seye.
Upon an amblere[40] esily she sat,
Ywympled wel, and on hir heed an hat   470
As brood as is a bokeler or a targe;[41]
A foot-mantel[42] aboute hir hipes large,
And on hire feet a paire of spores sharpe.
In felaweshipe wel koude she laughe and carpe.[43]
Of remedies of love she knew per chaunce,   475
For she koude of that art the olde daunce.[44]

A good man was ther of religioun,
And was a poure PERSON[45] of a toun;
But riche he was of hooly thoght and werk.
He was also a lerned man, a clerk,   480
That Cristes gospel trewely wolde preche.
His parisshens[46] devoutly wolde he teche.
Benygne he was, and wonder diligent,
And in adversitee ful pacient,
And swich he was ypreved ofte sithes.[47]   485
Ful looth were hym to cursen for his tithes,[48]
But rather wolde he yeven, out of doute,

---

[7] The four elementary "qualities." Combined they produced the four "elements": earth (cold and dry), air (hot and moist), water (cold and moist), and fire (hot and dry).

[8] For the humors, see note 32, on line 333, above. Blood was hot and moist; phlegm, cold and moist; yellow bile or choler, hot and dry; black bile or melancholy, cold and dry.   [9] True.

[10] Remedy.   [11] Electuaries, remedies.   [12] Profit.

[13] Their.

[14] The father of medicine, according to Greek legend. The following lines list the medical authorities, Greek, Arabian, and medieval, esteemed in Chaucer's day.   [15] Moderate.

[16] Cf. the proverb *Ubi tres medici, duo athei:* where (there are) three doctors (there are) two atheists.   [17] Blood-red.

[18] Persian blue, blue-gray.   [19] Thin silk.

[20] Slow to spend.   [21] What he gained during an epidemic.

[22] *Aurum potabile,* gold in solution, was used medicinally.

[23] Woman.   [24] Somewhat.   [25] A pity.   [26] Skill.

[27] Ghent. Both these cities of Flanders were famous for woolen goods.

[28] Precedence in going to the offering at church was a bone of contention among women. Cf. line 377.   [29] Kerchiefs.

[30] Texture.

[31] Tied.   [32] Fresh, new, not worn before.

[33] The marriage ceremony was performed on the church porch, and the wedding party then heard Mass before the altar.

[34] Not counting.   [35] As now, at present.

[36] There was a famous shrine of the Virgin at Boulogne, on the French side of the Strait of Dover.

[37] Galicia in northwestern Spain, where, at Compostela, was the famous shrine of St. James.

[38] A shrine of the Three Kings was at Cologne, on the Rhine.

[39] Gap-toothed or gate-toothed; i.e., with teeth spaced widely, a sign (in popular belief) of a bold and amorous nature.

[40] A "pacer," which moves the fore and hind legs of the same side at the same time. Hence, loosely, an easy-gaited horse.

[41] Buckler, target, shield.

[42] An outer riding-skirt; women rode astride.   [43] Talk.

[44] All the rules of the game.

[45] Parish priest, in this case a rector, since he has the tithes, such as they were in his poor parish.   [46] Parishioners.

[47] So he was proved oftentimes.

[48] Parishioners who failed to pay their tithes might be excommunicated ("cursed"). The parish priest could only exclude from the sacraments; excommunication was pronounced by the bishop.

Unto his poure parisshens aboute
Of his offryng[49] and eek of his substaunce;[50]
He koude in litel thyng have suffisaunce.[51]   490
Wyd was his parisshe, and houses fer asonder,
But he ne lefte[52] nat, for reyn ne[53] thonder,
In siknesse nor in meschief[54] to visite
The ferreste[55] in his parisshe, muche and lite,[56]
Upon his feet, and in his hand a staf.   495
This noble ensample to his sheepe he yaf,
That firste he wroghte and afterward he taughte.[57]
Out of the gospel he tho[58] wordes caughte,
And this figure he added eek therto:
That if gold ruste, what shal iren doo?   500
For if a preest be foul, on whom we truste,
No wonder is a lewed man[59] to ruste;
And shame it is—if a prest take keep—
A shiten[60] shepherde and a clene sheep.
Wel oghte a preest ensample for to yive,   505
By his clennesse, how that his sheep sholde lyve.
    He sette nat his benefice to hyre[61]
And leet[62] his sheepe encombred in the myre,
And ran to London, unto Seint Poules,
To seken hym a chaunterie for soules,[63]   510
Or with a bretherhed to been withholde,[64]
But dwelte at hoom and kepte wel his folde,
So that the wolf ne made it nat myscarie:
He was a shepherde and noght a mercenarie.
And though he hooly were and vertuous,   515
He was to synful men nat despitous,[65]
Ne of his speche daungerous ne digne,[66]
But in his techyng discreet and benygne.
To drawen folk to hevene by fairnesse,
By good ensample, this was his bisynesse.   520
But it were[67] any persone obstinat,
What-so he were, of heigh or lough estat,
Hym wolde he snybben[68] sharply for the nonys.[69]
A bettre preest I trowe that nowher noon ys.
He waiteth after[70] no pompe and reverence,   525

Ne maked him a spiced[71] conscience;
But Cristes loore and his apostles twelve
He taughte, but first he folwed it hymselve.

With hym ther was a PLOWMAN,[72] was his brother,
That hadde ylad of dong ful many a fother;[73]   530
A trewe swynkere[74] and a good was he,
Lyvynge in pees and parfit charitee.
God loved he best, with al his hoole herte,
At alle tymes, thogh him gamed or smerte,[75]
And thanne his neighebore right as hymselve: 535
He wolde thresshe, and therto dyke[76] and delve,
For Cristes sake, for every poure wight,
Withouten hire, if it lay in his myght.
His tithes payde he ful faire and wel
Bothe of his propre swynk and his catel.[77]   540
In a tabard[78] he rood upon a mere.[79]

Ther was also a reve, and a millere;
A somnour, and a pardoner also;
A maunciple, and myself—ther were namo.

The MILLERE was a stout carl for the nones;[80]   545
Ful byg he was of brawn,[81] and eek of bones.
That proved wel,[82] for over-al ther[83] he cam,
At wrastlynge he wolde have alwey the ram.[84]
He was short-sholdred, brood, a thikke knarre;[85]
Ther was no dore that he nolde heve of harre,[86]   550
Or breke it, at a rennyng with his heed.[87]
His berd as any sowe or fox was reed,
And therto brood as though it were a spade.
Upon the cop right[88] of his nose he hade
A werte; and theron stood a toft of herys,   555
Reed as the brustles of a sowes erys;[89]
His nosethirles[90] blake were and wyde.
A swerd and a bokeler bar he by his syde.
His mouth as greet was as a greet forneys.[91]

[49] In addition to his tithes the priest received voluntary offerings.
[50] His own goods.   [51] Enough, sufficiency.
[52] Neglected.   [53] Nor.   [54] Misfortune.
[55] Farthest.   [56] I.e., high and low.
[57] This idea is derived from Matthew 5:19.   [58] Those.
[59] Layman.   [60] Dung-covered, i.e., befouled.
[61] I.e., he did not hire a curate to perform the duties of his rectory.
[62] Left.
[63] Absentee priests found it profitable to chant masses for the soul of someone who had established a foundation for that purpose. See the complaint in Piers Plowman, Prologue, lines 83 ff. and note 34.
[64] Or to be retained (as a chaplain) by a guild (brotherhood).
[65] Spiteful.   [66] Arrogant nor haughty.
[67] Were it, if it were.   [68] Snub, rebuke.
[69] On the occasion, to be sure, indeed.   [70] Demanded.

[71] Overnice, too scrupulous. I.e., he was not unreasonable with his parishioners; he did not exaggerate the importance of minor matters.
[72] Probably a small tenant farmer, and neither a serf nor a free laborer working for wages.
[73] Had drawn (i.e., carted onto his fields) very many a load of dung.   [74] Worker.   [75] I.e., in pleasure or pain.
[76] Make dikes or ditches.
[77] Both of his own services and his goods.   [78] Sleeveless jacket.
[79] Mare; regarded as a mount for a poor man.
[80] Indeed. Here this overworked phrase is merely intensive.
[81] Flesh, muscle.   [82] That was clearly demonstrated.
[83] Everywhere where.
[84] Often a prize in wrestling matches at fairs.
[85] Knot (in wood); hence, a tough fellow.
[86] Heave off hinge.
[87] Running with his head for a battering-ram.
[88] Right on the tip.   [89] Ears.   [90] Nostrils.
[91] Furnace.

He was a janglere[92] and a goliardeys,[93]   560
And that[94] was moost of synne and harlotries.[95]
Wel koude he stelen corn[96] and tollen thries;[97]
And yet he hadde a thombe of gold,[98] pardee.[99]
A whit cote and a blew hood wered he.
A baggepipe wel koude he blowe and sowne,[1]   565
And therwithal[2] he broghte us out of towne.

A gentil[3] MAUNCIPLE[4] was ther of a Temple,[5]
Of which achatours[6] myghte take exemple
For to be wise in byynge of vitaille;
For wheither that he payde or took by taille,[7]   570
Algate[8] he wayted so in his achaat[9]
That he was ay biforn[10] and in good staat.[11]
Now is nat that of God a ful fair grace
That swich a lewed[12] mannes wit shal pace
The wisdom of an heepe of lerned men?   575
Of maistres hadde he mo[13] than thries ten,
That weren of lawe expert and curious,[14]
Of whiche ther weren a duszeyne in that hous
Worthy to been stywardes of rente and lond
Of any lord that is in Engelond,   580
To maken hym lyve by his propre good,[15]
In honour dettelees, but-if he were wood,[16]
Or lyve as scarsly as hym list desire;
And able for to helpen al a shire
In any caas that myghte falle or happe;   585
And yet this Manciple sette hir aller cappe.[17]

The REVE[18] was a sclendre, colerik[19] man.
His berd was shave as ny as ever he kan;
His heer was by his erys round yshorn;
His top was dokked lyk a preest biforn.[20]   590
Ful longe were his legges and ful lene,
Ylyk a staf; ther was no calf ysene.
Wel koude he kepe a gerner[21] and a bynne;
Ther was noon auditour koude on him wynne.[22]
Wel wiste he by the droghte and by the reyn   595
The yeldynge of his seed and of his greyn.
His lordes sheep, his neet,[23] his dayerye,
His swyn, his hors, his stoor,[24] and his pultrye
Was hoolly in this Reves governyng;
And by his covenant yaf the rekenyng   600
Syn[25] that his lord was twenty yeer of age.
Ther koude no man brynge hym in arrerage.[26]
Ther nas baillif, ne hierde,[27] nor oother hyne,[28]
That he ne knew his sleighte[29] and his covyne;[30]
They were adrad of hym as of the deeth.   605
    His wonyng[31] was ful faire upon an heeth;
With grene trees yshadwed was his place.
He koude bettre than his lord purchace;
Ful riche he was astored pryvely.[32]
His lord wel koude he plesen subtilly,   610
To yeve and lene hym of his owene good[33]
And have a thank and yet a gowne and hood.[34]
In youthe he hadde lerned a good myster;[35]
He was a wel good wrighte, a carpenter.
This Reve sat upon a ful good stot,[36]   615
That was al pomely[37] grey and highte[38] Scot.
A long surcote of pers[39] upon he hade,
And by his syde he baar a rusty blade.
Of Northfolk was this Reve of which I telle,
Biside a toun men clepen Baldeswelle.[40]   620
Tukked[41] he was, as is a frere, aboute;
And evere he rood the hyndreste of oure route.

---

[92] Babbler, chatterer.
[93] Coarse buffoon. Originally a goliard was a scholar or would-be scholar who went in for literary buffoonery.
[94] The substance of his talk.   [95] Wickedness, ribaldry.
[96] Grain.
[97] Take three times his rightful toll (of what he ground).
[98] I.e., cheater though he is, this Miller is relatively honest—as millers go. The reference is to the proverb "An honest miller has a golden thumb," i.e., all millers are dishonest.
[99] Indeed, to be sure. (Literally, *by God.*)

[1] Sound, play.
[2] With it, to the sound of it.   [3] Worthy.
[4] Manciple, servant who purchased supplies for a college or an inn of court.
[5] Either the Inner or Middle Temple off the Strand in London. The buildings originally belonged to the Knights Templars but were now occupied by societies of lawyers. These inns of court provided an education not only in law but also in business administration.   [6] Purchasing agents, caterers.
[7] Whether he paid cash or charged his purchases. *Taille* = tally, a notched stick indicating the amount of a debt.
[8] In every way, at all events.
[9] He looked out so carefully in his purchasing.
[10] In a favorable position.   [11] Estate, financial condition.
[12] Unlearned.   [13] More.   [14] Careful, skillful.
[15] Within his own income.   [16] Unless he were crazy.
[17] Set the caps of them all, made fools of them all.

[18] Overseer. The status of reeves varied in different times and localities. They were usually subordinate to the steward and the bailiff, but this one seems to have been directly responsible to the lord of the manor.
[19] Choleric, hot-tempered. On choler and the humors, see note 32, on line 333, above.
[20] A sign of his menial status. Reeves were originally serfs.
[21] Garner, granary.   [22] Get the better of him.   [23] Cattle.
[24] Stock.   [25] Since.   [26] Catch him in arrears.
[27] Herdsman, shepherd.   [28] Hind, farm laborer.
[29] Trickery.   [30] Agreement with intent to defraud.
[31] Dwelling.   [32] Provided for secretly.
[33] He could please his lord very craftily by lending to him out of his own (the lord's) goods.   [34] As a present.   [35] Trade.
[36] Horse.   [37] Apple-spotted, dappled.   [38] Called.
[39] Outer coat of blue-gray cloth.
[40] Bawdswell, in northern Norfolk.
[41] With his coat hitched up by a belt.

A Somonour[42] was ther with us in that place,
That hadde a fyr-reed cherubynnes[43] face,
For sawcefleem[44] he was, with eyen narwe.[45]   625
As hoot he was and lecherous as a sparwe,
With scalled[46] browes blake and piled[47] berd.
Of his visage children were aferd.
Ther nas quyksilver, lytarge,[48] ne brymstoon,
Boras,[49] ceruce,[50] ne oille of tartre noon,   630
Ne oynement that wolde clense and byte,
That hym myghte helpen of the whelkes white[51]
Nor of the knobbes[52] sittynge on his chekes.
Wel loved he garleek, oynons, and eek lekes,
And for to drynken strong wyn, reed as blood.   635
Thanne wolde he speke and crie as he were wood.[53]
And whan that he wel dronken hadde the wyn,
Than wolde he speke no word but Latyn.
A fewe termes hadde he, two or thre,
That he had lerned out of som decree.   640
No wonder is—he herde it al the day;
And eek ye knowen wel how that a jay
Kan clepen "Watte"[54] as wel as kan the pope.
But whoso koude in oother thyng hym grope,[55]
Thanne hadde he spent al his philosophie.[56]   645
Ay[57] Questio quid iuris![58] wolde he crie.
He was a gentil harlot[59] and a kynde.
A bettre felawe[60] sholde men noght fynde.
He wolde suffre[61] for a quart of wyn
A good felawe to have his concubyn   650
A twelf monthe, and excuse hym atte fulle;[62]
And prively[63] a fynch eek koude he pulle.[64]
And if he foond owher[65] a good felawe,
He wolde techen him to have noon awe,
In swich caas, of the ercedekenes curs[66]—   655
But-if[67] a mannes soule were in his purs,
For in his purs he sholde ypunysshed be.

"Purs is the ercedekenes helle," seyde he.
But wel I woot he lyed right in dede;
Of cursyng oghte ech gilty man him drede,   660
For curs wol slee, right as assoillyng[68] savith—
And also war him of a Significavit.[69]
In daunger[70] hadde he at his owene gise[71]
The yonge girles[72] of the diocise;
And knew hir conseil,[73] and was al hir reed.[74]   665
A gerland hadde he set upon his heed,
As greet as it were for an ale-stake.[75]
A bokeleer hadde he maad him of a cake.

With hym ther rood a gentil Pardoner[76]
Of Rouncivale,[77] his freend and his compeer,[78]   670
That streight was comen fro the court of Rome.[79]
Ful loude he soong "Com hider, love, to me!"
This Somonour bar to hym a stif burdoun;[80]
Was nevere trompe of half so greet a soun.
This Pardoner hadde heer as yelow as wex,   675
But smothe it heeng as dooth a strike[81] of flex;
By ounces[82] henge his lokkes that he hadde,
And therwith he his shuldres overspradde;
But thynne it lay, by colpons,[83] oon and oon.
But hood, for jolitee, wered he noon,   680
For it was trussed up in his walet;
Hym thoughte he rood al of the newe jet:[84]
Dischevelee, save his cappe, he rood al bare.
Swiche glarynge eyen hadde he as an hare.
A vernycle[85] hadde he sowed upon his cappe.   685
His walet lay biforn hym in his lappe,
Bret-ful[86] of pardon, comen from Rome al hoot.

---

42 Apparitor, summoner of persons required to appear before an
ecclesiastical court. Numerous classes of offenders came under
the jurisdiction of such courts, presided over by archdeacons,
rather than of the civil courts.
43 Cherubs appeared in paintings with fire-red faces.
44 Pimply.
45 I.e., his eyelids were swollen. The symptoms and suggested
treatment indicate a form of leprosy.
46 Scabby.   47 Peeled; with hair falling out.
48 Litharge, protoxide of lead.   49 Borax.
50 White lead.   51 From the white blotches.
52 I.e., pimples.   53 Crazy.
54 Can say "Wat" (Walt, Walter).   55 Question searchingly.
56 Then had the Summoner used up all his learning.   57 Ever.
58 The question (is) what part of the law (is applicable).
59 Fine rascal.   60 Rascal.   61 Allow.
62 At the full, fully.   63 Secretly, privately.
64 Pluck a finch; a slang phrase for illicit sexual intercourse;
"finch" = girl.   65 Anywhere.
66 In such a case, of the archdeacon's curse. The archdeacon headed
the ecclesiastical court and thus had much to do with the sentence
of excommunication.   67 Unless.

68 Exactly as absolution.
69 After the bishop had excommunicated an offender, he might
require his arrest by the civil authorities, whose writ began
Significavit nobis venerabilis pater (The reverend father has signified to us).   70 Control, influence.
71 Guise, way, discretion.   72 Young people (of both sexes).
73 Counsel, secrets.   74 Counsel, adviser.
75 The usual sign of a tavern was a horizontal pole over the door;
from it hung an ivy bush or a hoop wreathed with leaves and
flowers.
76 Salesman of papal indulgences, documents granting remission
of punishment in purgatory for sins already forgiven in confession. This Pardoner, like many, was a fraud. Very likely he
was in minor orders, that is, neither a priest or deacon on the
one hand, nor a layman on the other.
77 Hospital of the Blessed Mary of Rouncivalle, near Charing
Cross, between London and Westminster. In the 1380's unauthorized sales of pardons were made by persons who represented themselves as agents of the hospital.   78 Pal, crony.
79 This was the time of the Great Schism, with rival popes established at Rome and at Avignon in Provence. The English church
acknowledged the former.   80 Bass.   81 Hank, bunch.
82 I.e., small portions.   83 Shreds.   84 Fashion.
85 Little Veronica; i.e., a small copy of the handkerchief St.
Veronica was supposed to have lent Christ on the way to
Calvary. According to the legend he wiped his face, and it was
miraculously imprinted on the handkerchief.   86 Brimful.

A voys he hadde as smal as hath a goot.
No berd hadde he, ne nevere sholde have;
As smothe it was as it were late shave. 690
I trowe he were a geldyng or a mare.[87]

But of his craft,[88] fro Berwyk into Ware,[89]
Ne was ther swich another pardoner.
For in his male[90] he hadde a pilwebeer[91]
Which that he seyde was oure Lady veyl; 695
He seyde he hadde a gobet[92] of the seyl
That Seint Peter hadde whan that he wente
Upon the see, til Jesu Crist hym hente.[93]
He hadde a croys[94] of laton[95] ful of stones,
And in a glas he hadde pigges bones. 700
But with thise relikes whan that he fond
A poure person[96] dwellynge upon lond,
Upon a day he gat hym moore moneye
Than that the person gat in monthes tweye.
And thus with feyned flaterye and japes[97] 705
He made the person and the peple his apes.[98]
But trewely to tellen atte laste,
He was in chirche a noble ecclesiaste.
Wel koude he rede a lesson or a storie,[99]
But alderbest[1] he song an offertorie; 710
For wel he wiste, whan that song was songe,
He moste preche and wel affile[2] his tonge
To wynne silver, as he ful wel koude;
Therefore he song the murierly and loude.

Now have I toold you shortly, in a clause, 715
The staat, tharray, the nombre, and eek the cause
Why that assembled was this compaignye
In Southwerk, at this gentil hostelrye
That highte the Tabard, faste by the Belle.[3]
But now is tyme to yow for to telle 720
How that we baren us that ilke nyght,
Whan we were in that hostelrie alyght.
And after wol I telle of our viage,
And al the remenaunt of oure pilgrimage.

But first I pray yow, of youre curteisye, 725
That ye n'arette it nat my vileynye,[4]
Thogh that I pleynly speke in this mateere,
To telle yow hir wordes and hir cheere,[5]
Ne thogh I speke hir wordes proprely.

For this ye knowen al so wel as I: 730
Whoso shal telle a tale after a man,
He moote reherce as ny as evere he kan
Everich a word, if it be in his charge,
Al[6] speke he never so rudeliche or large;[7]
Or ellis he moot telle his tale untrewe, 735
Or feyne thyng, or fynde wordes newe.
He may nat spare, althogh he were his brother;
He moot as wel seye o word as another.
Crist spak hymself ful brode in hooly writ,
And wel ye woot no vileynye is it. 740
Eek Plato seith[8]—whoso that kan hym rede—
The wordes moote be cosyn to the dede.
Also I prey yow to foryeve it me,
Al have I nat set folk in hir degree[9]
Heere in this tale, as that they sholde stonde; 745
My wit is short, ye may wel understonde.

Greet chiere[10] made oure Hoost us everichon,
And to the soper sette he us anon.
He served us with vitaille at the beste;
Strong was the wyn, and wel to drynke us leste.[11] 750
A semely man oure HOOSTE[12] was withalle
For to been a marchal in an halle.
A large man he was, with eyen stepe—[13]
A fairer burgeys is ther noon in Chepe—[14]
Boold of his speche, and wys, and well ytaught; 755
And of manhod hym lakkede right naught.
Eek therto he was right a myrie man;
And after soper pleyen he bigan,
And spak of myrthe amonges othere thynges,
Whan that we hadde maad our rekenynges,[15] 760
And seyde thus: "Now, lordynges, trewely,
Ye been to me right welcome, hertely;
For by my trouthe, if that I shal nat lye,
I saugh nat this yeer so myrie a compaignye
Atones[16] in this herberwe[17] as is now. 765
Fayn wolde I doon yow myrthe, wiste I how.
And of a myrthe I am right now bythoght
To doon yow ese, and it shal coste noght.

"Ye goon to Caunterbury—God yow speede!
The blisful martir quite yow youre meede!—[18] 770

---

[6] Although.   [7] Broadly.
[8] In the "Timaeus"; but Chaucer gained his knowledge of the Dialogues not from the Greek but through Latin intermediaries. In this case he seems to be indebted to Boethius.
[9] According to their rank.   [10] Ample entertainment.
[11] It pleased us.
[12] Harry Bailly is his name, as we learn later on. An innkeeper of that name was taxed in Southwark in 1380–81 and is very likely the same person who was member of Parliament for Southwark (1376–79) and held various local offices (1377–94).
[13] Large and protruding.
[14] Across the Thames in Cheapside, the heart of London itself.
[15] Paid our bills.   [16] At once.   [17] Harbor, inn.
[18] Pay you your reward.

[87] I.e., he was not a normal man but effeminate.   [88] Trade.
[89] From Berwick on Tweed (at the Scottish border) to Ware (in Hertfordshire, just north of London).
[90] Mail, traveling bag.   [91] Pillowcase.   [92] Piece, bit.
[93] Caught.   [94] Cross.
[95] Lattin, a compound of copper and zinc.   [96] Parson, priest.
[97] Tricks.   [98] I.e., fools.
[99] A liturgical series of lessons dealing with Bible stories and saints' lives.   [1] Best of all.   [2] File, smooth.
[3] A Southwark inn, not certainly identified.
[4] Do not attribute it to my being ill-mannered.
[5] Behavior.

And wel I woot, as ye goon by the weye,
Ye shapen yow to talen[19] and to pleye;
For trewely confort ne myrthe is noon
To ride by the weye doumb as a stoon.
And therfore wol I maken yow disport, 775
As I seyde erst,[20] and doon yow som confort.
And if yow liketh alle, by oon assent,
For to stonden at my juggement,
And for to werken as I shal yow seye,
Tomorwe, whan ye riden by the weye, 780
Now by my fader soule that is deed,
But-if ye be myrie, I wol yeve yow myn heed!
Hoold up youre hondes, withouten moore speche!"
Oure conseil was nat longe for to seche.[21]
Us thoughte it was noght worth to make it wys,[22] 785
And graunted hym withouten moore avys,[23]
And bad him seye his voirdit[24] as hym leste.
    "Lordynges,"[25] quod[26] he, "now herkneth,[27] for the
        beste;
But taak it nought, I prey yow, in desdeyn.
This is the poynt, to speken short and pleyn, 790
That ech of yow, to shorte with oure weye,
In this viage shal telle tales tweye—[28]
To Caunterbury-ward, I mene it so;
And homward he shal tellen othere two—
Of aventures that whilom[29] han bifalle. 795
And which of yow that bereth hym best of alle,
That is to seyn, that telleth in this caas
Tales of best sentence[30] and moost solaas,[31]
Shal have a soper at oure aller cost,[32]
Heere in this place, sittynge by this post, 800
Whan that we come agayn fro Caunterbury.
And for to make yow the moore mury,
I wol myselven goodly with yow ryde,
Right at myn owene cost, and be youre gyde.
And whoso wole my juggement withseye[33] 805
Shal paye al that we spenden by the weye.
And if ye vouchesauf that it be so,
Tel me anon withouten wordes mo,
And I wol erly shape me therfore."
    This thyng was graunted, and oure othes swore 810
With ful glad herte, and preyden hym also
That he wolde vouchesauf for to do so,
And that he wolde been oure governour,

And of our tales juge and reportour,[34]
And sette a soper at a certeyn pris, 815
And we wol reuled been at his devys[35]
In heigh and lough.[36] And thus by oon assent
We been acorded to his juggement.
And therupon the wyn was fet[37] anon;
We dronken, and to reste wente echon 820
Withouten any lenger taryynge.
    Amorwe,[38] whan that day gan for to sprynge,
Up roos oure Hoost, and was oure aller cok[39]
And gadrede us togidre, alle in a flok;
And forth we riden a litel moore than paas[40] 825
Unto the wateryng of Seint Thomas.[41]
And there oure Hoost bigan his hors areste,
And seyde, "Lordynges, herkneth, if yow leste!
Ye woot youre foreward[42] and I it yow recorde.[43]
If even-song and morwe-song accorde,[44] 830
Lat se now who shal telle the firste tale.
As evere mote I drynke wyn or ale,
Whoso be rebel to my juggement
Shal paye for al that by the wey is spent.
Now draweth cut,[45] er that we ferrer twynne;[46] 835
He which that hath the shorteste shal bigynne.
Sire Knyght," quod he, "my mayster and my lord,
Now draweth cut, for that is myn accord.
Cometh neer,"[47] quod he, "my lady Prioresse.
And ye, sire Clerk, lat be your shamefastnesse,[48] 840
Ne studieth noght. Ley hond to, every man!"
    Anon to drawen every wight bigan;
And shortly for to tellen as it was,
Were it by aventure or sort or cas,[49]
The sothe is this, the cut fil to the Knyght, 845
Of which ful blithe and glad was every wyght;
And telle he moste his tale, as was reson,
By foreward and by composicion,[50]
As ye han herd. What nedeth wordes mo?
And whan this goode man saugh that it was so, 850
As he that wys was and obedient
To kepe his foreward by his free assent,
He seyde, "Syn I shal bigynne the game,
What, welcome be the cut, a Goddes name!
Now lat us ryde and herkneth what I seye." 855
And with that word we ryden forth oure weye;
And he bigan, with right a myrie cheere,
His tale anon, and seyde in this manere.

---

[19] You plan to tell stories.   [20] At first, before.
[21] It did not take us long to arrive at an opinion.
[22] It did not seem to us profitable to go through the forms of
deliberation.   [23] Advice, consideration.
[24] Verdict, decision.   [25] Sirs.   [26] Quoth, said.
[27] Listen. The imperative in -eth is common in Chaucer; it is the
full form, used in polite or careful speech.
[28] Shall tell two stories on this journey, with which to shorten our
way.   [29] Formerly.   [30] Content, instruction.
[31] Solace, entertainment.   [32] At the cost of us all.
[33] Gainsay.

[34] Commentator, referee.
[35] Device, direction.   [36] I.e., in all.   [37] Fetched.
[38] On the morrow.   [39] The cock for us all; he woke us.
[40] At a walk a bit faster than a footpace.
[41] A brook at the second milestone on the Kent road.
[42] Agreement.   [43] Recall it to you.
[44] I.e., if you are going to stick this morning to what you agreed
on last evening.   [45] Lot.   [46] Depart (from London).
[47] Nearer.   [48] Bashfulness.
[49] All three nouns mean luck or chance.   [50] Compact.

[*There follows* THE KNIGHT'S TALE, *a fine specimen of the chivalric romance, which relates the rivalry of Palamon and Arcite for the love of Emily.*]

Heere folwen the words bitwene the Hoost and the Millere.

Whan that the Knyght had thus his tale ytoold,
In al the route nas ther yong ne oold
That he ne seyde it was a noble storie,
And worthy for to drawen to memorie;
And namely the gentils everichon.[1]   5
Oure Hooste lough[2] and swoor, "So moot I gon,[3]
This gooth aright; unbokeled is the male.[4]
Lat se now who shal telle another tale;
For trewely the game is wel bigonne.
Now telleth on, sire Monk, if that ye konne,   10
Somwhat to quite with[5] the Knyghtes tale."

   The Millere, that for dronken[6] was al pale,
So that unnethe[7] upon his hors he sat,
He nolde avalen[8] neither hood ne hat,
Ne abyde[9] no man for his curteisie;   15
But in Pilates voys[10] he gan to crie,
And swoor, "By armes, and by blood and bones,[11]
I kan[12] a noble tale for the nones,
With which I wol now quite the Knyghtes tale."

   Oure Hooste saugh that he was dronke of ale,   20
And seyde, "Abyd, Robyn, my leeve[13] brother;
Som bettre man shal telle us first another.
Abyde, and lat us werken thriftily."

   "By Goddes soule," quod he, "that wol nat I;
For I wol speke, or elles go my wey."   25

   Oure Hoost answerde, "Tel on, a devele wey!
Thou art a fool; thy wit is overcome."

   "Now herkneth," quod the Millere, "alle and some!
But first I make a protestacioun
That I am dronke—I knowe it by my soun—   30
And therfore if that I mysspeke or seye,[14]
Wyte it[15] the ale of Southwerk, I you preye;
For I wol telle a legende and a lyf
Bothe of a carpenter and of his wyf,
How that a clerk hath set the wrightes cappe."[16]   35

   The Reve answerde and seyde, "Stynt thy clappe![17]
Lat be thy lewed, dronken harlotrye!
It is a synne and eek a greet folye

To apeyren[18] any man or hym defame,
And eek to bryngen wyves in swich fame.   40
Thou mayst ynogh of othere thynges seyn."

   This dronke Millere spak ful soone ageyn
And seyde, "Leve brother Osewold,
Who hath no wyf, he is no cokewold.[19]
But I say nat therfore that thou art oon;   45
Ther been ful goode wyves many oon,
And evere a thousand goode ayeyns oon badde.
That knowestow wel thyself, but-if thou madde.[20]
Why artow angry with my tale now?
I have a wyf, pardee, as wel as thow;   50
Yet nolde[21] I, for the oxen in my plogh,
Take upon me moore than ynogh,
As demen[22] of myself that I were oon.
I wol bileve wel that I am noon.
An housbonde shal nat been inquisityf   55
Of Goddes pryvetee[23] nor of his wyf.
So he may fynde Goddes foyson[24] there,
Of the remenant[25] nedeth nat enquere."

   What sholde I moore seyn, but this Millere
He nolde his wordes for no man forbere,   60
But tolde his cherles tale in his manere.
M'athynketh[26] that I shal reherce it heere.
And therfore every gentil wight I preye,
For Goddes love, demeth nat that I seye
Of yvel entente, but that I moot[27] reherce   65
Hir[28] tales alle, be they bettre or werse,
Or elles falsen som of my mateere.
And therfore, whoso list it nat yheere,
Turne over the leef and chese[29] another tale;
For he shal fynde ynowe, grete and smale,   70
Of storial thyng that toucheth gentillesse,[30]
And eek moralitee and hoolynesse.
Blameth nat me if that ye chese amys.
The Millere is a cherl, ye knowe wel this;
So was the Reve, and othere manye mo;   75
And harlotrie[31] they tolden bothe two.
Avyseth yow,[32] and put me out of blame;
And eek[33] men shal nat maken ernest of game.

[*The Miller and the Reeve continue their feud in their stories. Each of the tales is a fabliau, that is, it belongs to a special genre of medieval narrative verse, short and realistic, usually comic, often extremely coarse. The butt of* THE MILLER'S TALE *is a carpenter (as the Reeve was), and* THE REEVE'S TALE *is a retaliatory account of how two Cambridge students beguiled a*

---

1 Especially the gentlefolk, every one.   2 Laughed.
3 So may I (continue to be able to) walk. A kind of oath: by my
   desire to (be able to) walk!
4 I.e., we're off; the bag of stories is opened.   5 Match.
6 On account of being drunk.
7 Uneasily, i.e., scarcely, with difficulty.   8 Would not doff.
9 I.e., yield to, give way to.
10 Like Herod, Pilate was a violent character in the medieval plays
   on the life of Christ.   11 By Christ's arms, blood, and bones.
12 Know.   13 Lief, dear.   14 Missay.
15 Blame it on.   16 Made a fool of the workman.
17 Cease thy babble. (The Reeve, remember, was a carpenter.)

18 Impair, injure.   19 Cuckold, husband of an unfaithful wife.
20 Unless you're crazy.   21 Would not.
22 As to conclude or suppose.   23 Private matters.
24 Plenty; i.e., provided his wife satisfies his desires.
25 I.e., what is left over, the rest.   26 I regret.
27 Must.   28 Their.   29 Choose.   30 Gentility.
31 Ribaldry.   32 Consider.   33 Moreover.

miller. Both stories are told with great narrative skill, and both
are replete with vulgarity. Yet their humor is so rich and so
constantly in the foreground that, while they are certainly improper, they are scarcely obscene. At any rate, their coarseness is
honest and hearty, not sly and unhealthy. Hodge of Ware, the
Cook, is so pleased with the Reeve's offering that he volunteers
another; but Chaucer left THE COOK'S TALE unfinished. We have
only the opening lines; evidently it was to be another fabliau.
And so ends the First Fragment of The Canterbury Tales.

The Second Fragment begins at ten o'clock on the morning of
April 18, when the Host calls on the MAN OF LAW and he obliges
with the adventures of Constance, a Roman emperor's daughter,
whose Christian endurance of sufferings comparable to those of
the saints and martyrs makes her story a monument to fortitude.
Then the Host, with an oath, requires a tale of the Parson, who
promptly rebukes him for swearing. At this display of the good
man's gift for snibbing, the Host retorts that he can "smell a
Lollard in the wind," an allusion to the reforming sect engaged
in popularizing the opinions of Wyclif (see pp. 60, 67, above).
Many reformers—and both in England and on the Continent
their stand was considered heretical—held it unchristian to swear,
even when testifying in court. The suggestion of lurking heresy
scandalizes, of all people, the Shipman (or the Summoner—the
manuscripts name various pilgrims as the objector), who seeks to
forestall a long-winded religious discourse by telling another story.
He promises a merry one to wake up the company (the implication is that the Man of Law's story has put everybody to sleep).
Apparently Chaucer never wrote it, for the Second Fragment
ends here.

The Third opens with a racy exposition by the Wife of Bath
of her theories and experience of marriage and her subversive
opinion that in it the woman should have the upper hand. This
introduction, one of Chaucer's most remarkable performances,
is wonderfully sustained for 828 lines; but before she begins her
tale, the Friar and the Summoner have a quarrel. As we have
seen in Piers Plowman, there was no love lost between the
"regular" clergy (monks and friars) and the "secular" clergy
(parish priests and their superiors, the bishops). The Summoner
is an employee of the court of a bishop and his archdeacon, and is
therefore prejudiced on the subject of friars.]

Biholde the wordes bitwene the Somonour and the Frere.

The Frere lough, whan he hadde herd al this.
"Now, dame," quod he, "so have I joye or blis,
This is a long preamble of a tale."
And whan the Somonour herde the Frere gale,[1]
"Lo," quod the Somonour, "Goddes armes two!   5
A frere wol entremette him[2] everemo.

Lo, goode men, a flye and eek a frere
Wol falle in every dyssh and eek mateere.
What spekestow of preambulacioun?
What! amble, or trotte, or pees, or go sit doun!   10
Thou lettest[3] oure disport in this manere."
    "Ye, woltow so, sire Somonour?" quod the Frere.
"Now, by my feith, I shal, er that I go,
Telle of a somonour swich a tale or two
That alle the folk shal laughen in this place."   15
    "Now elles,[4] Frere, I bishrewe[5] thy face,"
Quod this Somonour; "and I bishrewe me
But-if I telle tales two or thre
Of freres, er I come to Sidyngborne,[6]
That I shal make thyn herte for to morne,   20
For wel I woot thy pacience is gon."
    Oure Hooste cride, "Pees! and that anon!"
And seyde, "Lat the womman telle hire tale.
Ye fare as folk that dronken ben of ale.
Do, dame, telle forth youre tale, and that is best."   25
    "Al redy, sire," quod she, "right as yow lest,
If I have licence of this worthy Frere."
    "Yis,[7] dame," quod he; "tel forth, and I wol heere."

[THE WIFE OF BATH'S TALE *rounds out her argument; for its hero,
a knight whose embrace frees a Loathly Lady from enchantment
(cf. the ballad of "Kemp Owyne," below), is offered his choice
of having her ugly and faithful, or fair and quite free to bestow
her favors wherever she pleases. The knight puts himself completely in her hands by leaving the decision to her. Since the lady
rewards him by proving both fair and faithful, the contention of
the Wife of Bath is aptly exemplified. Later on we return to the
question of supremacy in marriage. Meanwhile, the Friar and the
Summoner resume their dispute. The former leads off with
another fabliau, witty, graphic, and this time relatively free from
coarseness. It is one of Chaucer's best comic efforts.]*

The Prologe of the Freres Tale.

This worthy lymytour, this noble Frere,
He made alwey a maner louryng chiere[1]
Upon the Somonour, but for honestee[2]
No vileyns word as yet to hym spak he.
But atte laste he seyde unto the Wyf,   5
"Dame," quod he, "God yeve yow right good lyf!
Ye han heer touched, al so moot I thee,[3]
In scole-matere[4] greet difficultee.
Ye han seyd muche thyng right wel, I seye;
But, dame, heere as we ryde by the weye,   10
Us nedeth nat to speken but of game,

---

[3] You hinder.
[4] (If you do) otherwise; i.e., go right ahead.   [5] Curse.
[6] Sittingbourne, about forty miles from London.   [7] Yes indeed!

[1] A kind of lowering look.   [2] As a matter of decorum.
[3] So may I thrive.   [4] I.e., scholastic subjects.

---

[1] Exclaim.   [2] Interfere, butt in.

A Literary Map OF THE BRITISH ISLES Middle English Period A W

North Sea

Atlantic Ocean

English Channel

Dunfermline
Aberdour
Edinburgh
Glasgow
Berwick on Tweed
Flodden Field ✗

Carlisle
Durham

York

Wakefield

Dublin

Anglesey

Chester
Lincoln

Sherwood Forest
Wells next the Sea

Nottingham
Walsingham
Bawdswell
Norwich

Bosworth Field ✗
Peterborough

Malvern Hills
Coventry
Warwick
Ely
Cambridge
Bury St. Edmunds

Oxford
Ware

Malmesbury
LONDON
Deptford
Bath
Reading
Greenwich
Rochester
Glastonbury
Amesbury
Sittingbourne
Canterbury
Salisbury
Winchester
Dover

Hastings

Tintagel
Exeter

Dartmouth

THE ELLESMERE MANUSCRIPT

Many copies of Chaucer's works survive in manuscript—good evidence of his popularity with his contemporaries and immediate successors. The most authoritative copy of *The Canterbury Tales* is the Ellesmere Manuscript, made soon after Chaucer's death. Its decorations include figures of the pilgrims. Here is a representation of Chaucer himself, placed at the beginning of his Tale of Melibee. (Henry E. Huntington Library, San Marino, California)

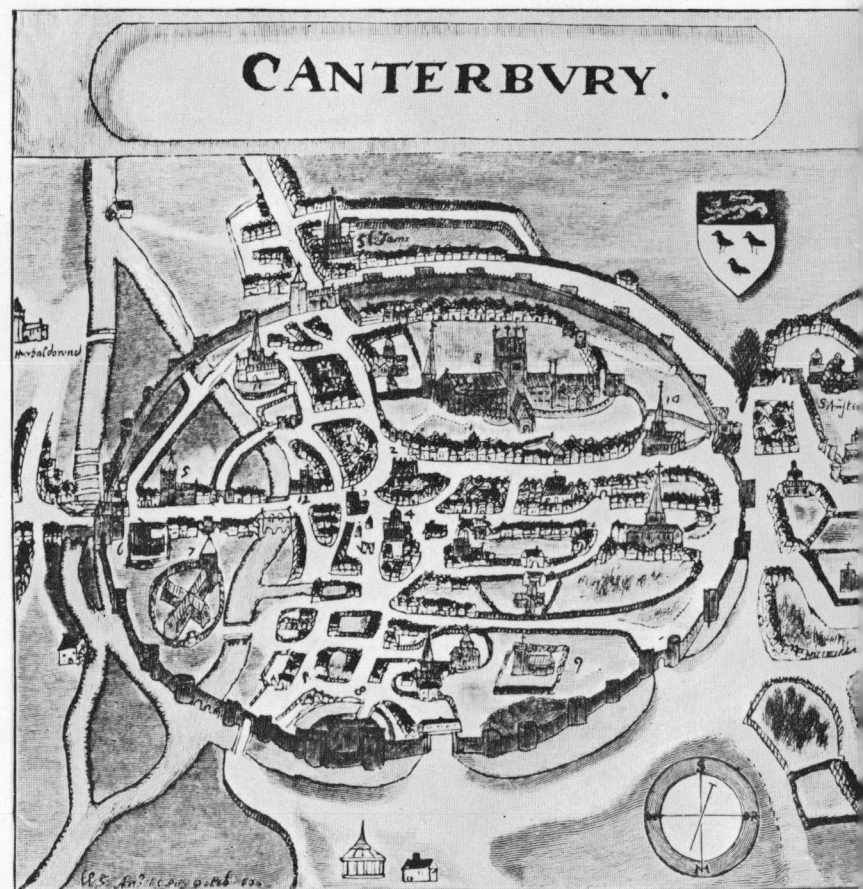

CANTERBURY

This plan of Canterbury, though from a later source, shows the walled town essentially as it was known to the Middle Ages and gives a sense of its compactness and the dominance of its ecclesiastical establishments. The cathedral, which contained the shrine of St. Thomas à Becket, is slightly above and to the right of the center.

GEOFFREY CHAUCER

The so-called Seddon portrait is perhaps no earlier than the sixteenth century, but it follows the tradition of such manuscript miniatures as we see illustrated in the Ellesmere miniature on the opposite page, which were much more nearly contemporary with Chaucer. (Harvard College Library)

MANDEVILLE'S
TRAVELS

Many besides the Wife of Bath made pilgrimages to Jerusalem. One of the most popular medieval books, *The Travels of Sir John Mandeville,* begins as a guide book for pilgrims to Jerusalem, though it is better known for its accounts of marvels in more remote places. Originally written in French in the fourteenth century, it was soon widely translated. This late fifteenth-century German manuscript contains what purports to be a portrait of the author (whose name was not actually Mandeville). (Spencer Collection, New York Public Library)

Here are scenes from two famous romances. (Left) An illustration from the manuscript copy of *Sir Gawain and the Green Knight*. The Green Knight holds up his severed head to deliver instructions to Sir Gawain for the return encounter at the Green Chapel (see p. 86, lines 432 ff.). (Above) A wood cut from an early printed edition of Malory's *Morte d'Arthur*, issued by Wynkyn de Worde in 1529.

A MEDIEVAL JOUST

In this depiction of a scene common in romance both combatants have been unhorsed and are fighting on foot with swords. The miniature is from a fifteenth-century French manuscript copy of *Petit Artus de Bretaigne*, a romance later translated into English as *Arthur of Little Britain* by John Bourchier, Lord Berners, who is more famous as the translator of Froissart. (Spencer Collection, New York Public Library)

And lete auctoritees,[5] on Goddes name,
To prechyng and to scole eek of clergye.
And if it lyke to this compaignye,
I wol yow of a somonour telle a game.   15
Pardee, ye may wel knowe by the name
That of a somonour may no good be sayd;
I praye that noon of you be yvele apayd.[6]
A somonour is a rennere[7] up and doun
With mandementz[8] for fornicacioun,[9]   20
And is ybet[10] at every townes ende."

Oure Hoost tho spak: "A, sire, ye sholde be hende[11]
And curteys, as a man of youre estaat.
In compaignye we wol have no debaat.
Telleth youre tale, and lat the Somonour be."   25

"Nay," quod the Somonour, "lat hym seye to me
What-so hym list. Whan it comth to my lot,
By God, I shal hym quiten every grot.[12]
I shal hym tellen which a greet honour
It is to be a flaterynge lymytour;   30
And of many another manere cryme,
Which nedeth nat rehercen at this tyme;
And his office I shal hym telle, ywis."[13]

Oure Hoost answerde, "Pees, namoore of this!"
And after this he seyde unto the Frere,   35
"Tel forth youre tale, leeve maister deere."

[THE FRIAR'S TALE]

Heere bigynneth the Freres Tale.

Whilom[14] ther was dwellynge in my contree
An erchedekene, a man of heigh degree,
That boldely dide execucioun
In punysshynge of fornicacioun,
Of wicchecraft, and eek of bawderye,[15]   5
Of diffamacioun,[16] and avowtrye,[17]
Of chirche reves,[18] and of testamentz,[19]
Of contractes, and of lakke of sacramentz,
Of usure,[20] and of symonye[21] also.
But, certes, lecchours dide he grettest wo;   10
They sholde syngen, if that they were hent;[22]
And smale tytheres weren foule yshent,[23]
If any persone[24] wolde upon hem pleyne.[25]

Ther myghte asterte hym no pecunyal peyne.[26]
For smale tithes and for smal offrynge   15
He made the peple pitously to synge.
For er the bisshope caughte hem with his hook,[27]
They weren in the erchedeknes book;
And thanne hadde he thurgh his jurisdiccion
Power to doon on hem correccion.   20

He hadde a somonour redy to his hond.
A slyer boye was noon in Engelond;
For subtilly he hadde his espiaille,[28]
That taughtë hym wel wher hym myghte availle.
He koude spare of lecchours oon or two,   25
To techen hym to foure and twenty mo.[29]
For thogh this Somonour wood were as an hare,[30]
To telle his harlotrye[31] I wol nat spare;
For we been out of his correccion.
They han of us no jurisdiccion,[32]   30
Ne nevere shullen, terme of al hir lyves.

"Peter! so been wommen of the styves,"[33]
Quod the Somonour, "yput out of oure cure."[34]

"Pees, with myschance, and with mysaventure!"[35]
Thus seyde oure Hoost; "and lat hym telle his tale.   35
Now telleth forth, thogh that the Somonour gale,[36]
Ne spareth nat, myn owene maister deere!"

This false theef, this somonour—quod the Frere—
Hadde alwey bawdes redy to his hond
As any hauk to lure[37] in Engelond,   40
That tolde hym al the secree that they knewe.
For hire[38] acqueyntance was nat come of newe;
They weren his approwours[39] prively.
He took hymself a greet profit therby;
His maister knew nat alwey what he wan.[40]   45
Withouten mandement[41] a lewed[42] man
He koude somne, on peyne of Cristes curs.[43]
And they were glade for to fille his purs,
And make hym grete feestes atte nale.[44]
And right as Judas hadde purses smale   50
And was a theef, right swich a theef was he;

---

[26] No monetary penalty could escape him; i.e., he always imposed a fine.
[27] Crosier; the bishop's staff of office, resembling a shepherd's crook.
[28] Espial, corps of spies.
[29] I.e., he would let some off, provided they would serve him as informers.   [30] Cf. "mad as a March hare."
[31] Rascality.
[32] The mendicant orders (friars), like the monastic orders (monks), were responsible directly to the Pope; the bishops had no control over them.
[33] Stews, brothels. They were not subject to ecclesiastical control but were licensed by civil authority.   [34] Care, supervision.
[35] I.e., mischance and mishap be yours if you aren't quiet.
[36] Exclaim.
[37] The lure was made of leather and feathers, resembling a bird. It was used to recall the falcon to her master.   [38] Their.
[39] Informers.   [40] Won, gained.   [41] Writ of summons.
[42] Ignorant, i.e., humble, ordinary.   [43] Excommunication.
[44] At an alehouse.

---

[5] Leave texts or citation of authorities.   [6] Be dissatisfied.
[7] Runner.   [8] Summonses (to the archdeacon's court).
[9] Sexual irregularities came under the jurisdiction of the ecclesiastical courts.   [10] Beaten.   [11] Pleasant.
[12] Pay him back every particle. A groat was a very small coin.
[13] Certainly.   [14] Formerly.
[15] Bawdry, illicit intercourse.   [16] Slander.
[17] Adultery.   [18] Of robberies of churches.
[19] Wills.
[20] Usury, taking interest. It was forbidden by canon law.
[21] Simony, buying and selling of ecclesiastical appointments.
[22] Caught.   [23] Injured, ruined.   [24] Parson.
[25] Complain.

His maister hadde but half his duëtee.[45]
He was, if I shal yeven hym his laude,
A theef, and eek a somnour, and a baude.
He hadde eek wenches at his retenue,
That wheither that Sir Robert, or Sir Huwe,[46]   55
Or Jakke, or Rauf,[47] or whoso that it were
That lay by hem, they tolde it in his ere.
Thus was the wenche and he of oon assent;
And he wolde fecche a feyned mandement,
And somne hem to the chapitre,[48] bothe two,   60
And pile[49] the man and lete the wenche go.
Thanne wolde he seye, "Freend, I shal for thy sake
Do striken hire out[50] of oure lettres blake.
Thee thar namoore, as in this cas, travaille;[51]   65
I am thy freend ther[52] I thee may availle."
Certeyn, he knew of briberyes[53] mo
Than possible is to telle in yeres two;
For in this world nys[54] dogge for the bowe[55]
That kan an hurt deer from an hool yknowe   70
Bet than this somnour knew a sly lecchour,
Or an avowtier,[56] or a paramour.
And for that was the fruyt of al his rente,[57]
Therfore on it he sette al his entente.

    And so bifel that ones on a day   75
This somnour, evere waityng on his pray,
Rood for to somne an old wydwe, a ribibe,[58]
Feynynge a cause, for he wolde brybe.
And happed that he saugh bifore hym ryde
A gay yeman, under a forest syde.   80
A bowe he bar and arwes brighte and kene;
He hadde upon a courtepy[59] of grene,
An hat upon his heed with frenges blake.
"Sire," quod this somnour, "hayl, and wel atake!"[60]

    "Welcome," quod he, "and every good felawe!   85
Wher rydestow, under this grene-wode shawe?"[61]
Seyde this yeman; "wiltow fer today?"

    This somnour hym answerde, and seyde, "Nay.
Heere faste by," quod he,"is myn entente
To ryden, for to reysen up a rente   90
That longeth[62] to my lordes duëtee."

    "Artow thanne a bailly?"[63] "Ye,"[64] quod he.
He dorste nat, for verray filthe and shame,

Seye that he was a somonour, for the name.[65]
"Depardieux,"[66] quod this yeman, "deere broother,   95
Thou art a bailly, and I am another.
I am unknowen as in this contree;
Of thyn aqueyntance I wolde praye thee,
And eek of bretherhede, if that yow leste.
I have gold and silver in my cheste;   100
If that thee happe to comen in oure shire,
Al shal be thyn, right as thou wolt desire."

    "Grantmercy,"[67] quod this somonour, "by my feith!"
Everych in ootheres hand his trouthe[68] leith,
For to be sworne bretheren til they deye.   105
In daliance they ryden forth hir weye.
This somonour, that was as ful of jangles[69]
As ful of venym[70] been thise waryangles,[71]
And evere enqueryng upon everythyng,
"Brother," quod he, "where is now youre dwellyng,   110
Another day if that I sholde yow seche?"

    This yeman hym answerde in softe speche,
"Brother," quod he, "fer in the north contree,[72]
Where-as I hope somtyme I shal thee see.
Er we departe,[73] I shal thee so wel wisse[74]   115
That of myn hous ne shaltow nevere mysse."

    "Now, brother," quod this somonour, "I yow preye,
Teche me, whil that we ryden by the weye,
Syn that ye been a baillif as am I,
Som subtiltee, and tel me feithfully   120
In myn office how that I may moost wynne;
And spareth nat for conscience ne synne,
But as my brother tel me how do ye."

    "Now by my trouthe, brother deere," seyde he,
"As I shal tellen thee a feithful tale.   125
My wages been ful streitë[75] and ful smale.
My lord is hard to me, and daungerous,[76]
And myn officë is ful laborous;
And therfore by extorcions I lyve.
Forsothe, I take all that men wol me yive.   130
Algate,[77] by sleyghtë or by violence,
Fro yeer to yeer I wynne al my dispence.[78]
I kan no bettre telle, feithfully."

    "Now certes," quod this somonour, "so fare I.
I spare nat to taken, God it woot,   135
But-if it be to hevy or to hoot.
What I may gete in conseil prively,
No maner conscience of that have I.
Nere[79] myn extorcioun, I myghte nat lyven.

---

45 Duty, fees.
46 Probably priests, since "sir" was their regular title.
47 Ralph.   48 Chapter, assembly of officials of the diocese.
49 Pillage, rob.   50 Have her struck out.
51 To thee it is necessary in this case no more to labor; i.e., trouble
    yourself no more.   52 Where.   53 Ways of robbing.
54 Is not.
55 Dog accompanying a bowman in order to follow the deer.
56 Adulterer.
57 Because that was the substance of all his income.
58 Slang for old woman; literally, fiddle.   59 Jacket.
60 Overtaken.   61 Wood.   62 Belongs.
63 Bailiff, administrator of a lord's estate.   64 Yea, yes.

65 On account of (the shamefulness of) the name.   66 By God!
67 Gramercy, much thanks.   68 Troth, promise.
69 Jabber.   70 Venom, i.e., malice.
71 Shrikes, butcherbirds; they impale their prey (insects) on thorns.
72 Apparently an innocent admission; but the north was associated
    with the infernal regions.   73 Separate.   74 Inform.
75 Strait, scanty.   76 Hard to please.   77 In every way.
78 All I spend.   79 Were it not for.

Nor of swiche japes wol I nat be shryven; 140
Stomak[80] ne conscience ne knowe I noon;
I shrewe thise shrifte-fadres everychoon.[81]
Wel be we met, by God and by Seint Jame!
But, leeve brother, tel me thanne thy name,"
Quod this somonour. In this meene while, 145
This yeman gan a litel for to smyle.

"Brother," quod he, "wiltow that I thee telle?
I am a feend; my dwellyng is in helle.
And heere I ryde aboute my purchasyng,[82]
To wite[83] wher men wol yeve me anythyng. 150
My purchas is th' effect of al my rente.[84]
Looke how thou rydest for the same entente,
To wynne good, thou rekkest nevere how;
Right so fare I, for ryde wolde I now
Unto the worldes ende for a preye." 155

"A!" quod this somonour, "benedicite![85] what say ye?
I wende[86] ye were a yeman trewely;
Ye han a mannes shape as wel as I.
Han ye a figure thanne determinat[87]
In helle, ther ye been in youre estat?" 160

"Nay, certeinly," quod he; "ther have we noon;
But whan us liketh we kan take us oon,
Or elles make yow seme[88] we been shape
Somtyme lyk a man or lyk an ape,
Or lyk an angel kan I ryde or go.[89] 165
It is no wonder thyng thogh it be so;
A lowsy jogelour[90] kan deceyve thee,
And pardee, yet kan I moore craft than he."

"Why," quod this somonour, "ryde ye thanne or goon
In sondry shape, and nat alwey in oon?" 170

"For we," quod he, "wol us swiche formes make
As moost able is oure preyes for to take."

"What maketh yow to han al this labour?"

"Ful many a cause, leeve sire somonour,"
Seyde this feend. "But alle thyng hath tyme; 175
The day is short, and it is passed pryme,[91]
And yet ne wan I nothyng in this day.
I wol entende to wynnen if I may,
And nat entende oure wittes to declare.
For, brother myn, thy wit is al to bare 180
To understonde, althogh I tolde hem thee.
But, for thou axest why labouren we—
For somtyme we been Goddes instrumentz,
And meenes to doon his comandementz,
Whan that hym list, upon his creatures, 185
In divers art and in diverse figures.

Withouten hym we have no myght, certayn,
If that hym list to stonden ther-agayn.[92]
And somtyme, at oure prayere, han we leve
Oonly the body and nat the soule greve; 190
Witnesse on Job, whom that we diden wo.
And somtyme han we myght of bothe two,
This is to seyn, of soule and body eke.
And somtyme be we suffred for to seke[93]
Upon a man and doon his soule unreste 195
And nat his body. And al is for the beste.
Whan he withstandeth oure temptacioun,
It is a cause of his savacioun;
Al be it that it was nat oure entente
He sholde be sauf,[94] but that we wolde hym hente.[95] 200
And somtyme be we servant unto man;
As to the ercebisshope, Seint Dunstan;
And to the apostles servant eek was I."[96]

"Yet tel me," quod the somonour, "feithfully,
Make ye yow newe bodies thus alway 205
Of elementz?" The feend answerde, "Nay.
Somtyme we feyne; and somtyme we aryse
With dede bodyes, in ful sondry wyse,
And speke as renably[97] and faire and wel
As to the Phitonissa[98] dide Samuel. 210
And yet wol som men seye it was nat he—[99]
I do no fors of youre dyvynytee.[1]
But o thyng warne I thee, I wol nat jape:[2]
Thou wolt algates wite how we been shape.
Thou shalt herafterwardes, my brother deere, 215
Come there thee nedeth nat of me to leere;[3]
For thou shalt, by thyn owene experience,
Konne in a chayer rede of this sentence[3]
Bet than Virgile while he was on lyve,
Or Dant[4] also. Now lat us ryde blyve,[5] 220
For I wole holde compaignye with thee
Til it be so that thou forsake me."

"Nay," quod this somonour, "that shal nat bityde.
I am a yeman, knowen is ful wyde;
My trouthe wol I holde, as in this cas. 225
For though thou were the devel Sathanas,
My trouthe wol I holde to my brother,
As I am sworn—and ech of us til oother—

---

[80] Compassion.
[81] I curse every one of these father confessors.
[82] Procuring, obtaining.   [83] Learn.
[84] What I pick up is the sum total of my income.   [85] Bless ye!
[86] Weened, supposed.   [87] Fixed.   [88] Make it seem to you.
[89] Walk.   [90] Juggler, sleight-of-hand performer.
[91] 9 a.m.

[92] Thereagainst.   [93] Harass.
[94] Safe, secure from damnation.   [95] Seize.
[96] There were stories of the apostles' control of devils, but not of
St. Dunstan's (d.988).   [97] Readily, fluently.
[98] Pythoness, Witch of Endor; see 1 Samuel 28:7–20.
[99] One theory was that the witch did not raise Samuel but a demon
impersonating him.

[1] Make no force of, take no stock in, your theology.
[2] Jest.
[3] Be able in a (professorial) chair to read (a lecture) on this subject.
[4] Vergil and Dante were specialists, both having made trips to hell.
[5] In a lively way, quickly.

For to be trewe brother in this cas.
And bothe we goon abouten oure purchas.   230
Taak thou thy part, what that men wol thee yive,
And I shal myn; thus may we bothe lyve.
And if that any of us have moore than oother,
Lat hym be trewe and parte it with his brother."

"I graunte," quod the devel, "by my fey!"[6]   235
And with that word, they ryden forth hir wey.
And right at the entryng of the townes ende,
To which this somonour shoope hym for to wende,[7]
They saugh a cart that charged[8] was with hey,
Which that a cartere droof forth in his wey.   240
Deepe was the wey, for which the carte stood.[9]

The cartere smoot, and cryde as he were wood,
"Hayt,[10] Brok![11] hayt, Scot! what spare ye for the stones?
The feend," quod he, "yow fecche, body and bones,
As ferforthly as[12] evere were ye foled,   245
So muche wo as I have with yow tholed![13]
The devel have al, bothe hors and cart and hey!"

This somonour seyde, "Heere shal we have a pley."
And neer the feend he drough, as noght ne were,[14]
Ful prively, and rowned[15] in his ere: 250
"Herkne, my brother! herkne, by thy feith!
Herestow nat how that the cartere seith?
Hent it anon, for he hath yeve it thee—
Bothe hey and cart, and eek his caples[16] thre."

"Nay," quod the devel, "God woot, never a deel.[17] 255
It is nat his entente, trust me weel.
Axe hym thyself, if thou nat trowest[18] me;
Or elles stynt a while, and thou shalt see."

This cartere thakketh his hors upon the croupe,
And they bigonne to drawen and to stoupe.   260
"Heyt now!" quod he, "ther Jesu Crist yow blesse,
And al his handwerk, bothe moore and lesse!
That was wel twight,[19] myn owene lyard[20] boy.
I pray God save thee, and Seinte Loy![21]
Now is my cart out of the slow,[22] pardee."   265

"Lo, brother," quod the feend, "what tolde I thee?
Heere may ye se, myn owene deere brother,
The carl[23] spak oon thing, but he thoghte another.
Lat us go forth abouten oure viage;
Heere wynne I nothyng upon cariage."[24]   270

Whan that they coomen somwhat out of towne,
This somonour to his brother gan to rowne:
"Brother," quod he, "heere woneth[25] an old rebekke,[26]
That hadde almoost as lief to lese[27] hire nekke
As for to yeve a peny of hir good.   275
I wole han twelf pens,[28] though that she be wood,
Or I wol sompne hire unto oure office;
And yet, God woot, of hire knowe I no vice.
But, for[29] thou kanst nat as in this contree
Wynne thy cost, taak heer ensample of me."   280

This somonour clappeth[30] at the wydwes gate.
"Com out," quod he, "thou olde virytrate![31]
I trowe thou hast som frere or preest with thee."

"Who clappeth there?" seyde this wyf, "benedicite!
God save you, sire. What is youre sweete wille?"   285

"I have," quod he, "of somonce here a bille.
Up peyne[32] of cursyng, looke that thou be
Tomorn bifore the erchedeknes knee,
T'answere to the court of certeyn thynges."

"Now, Lord," quod she, "Crist Jesu, kyng of kynges,
So wisly[33] helpe me, as I ne may.[34]   291
I have been syk, and that ful many a day.
I may nat go so fer," quod she, "ne ryde,
But I be deed,[35] so priketh it in my syde.
May I nat axe a libel,[36] sire somonour,   295
And answere there by my procuratour[37]
To swich thyng as men wole opposen me?"

"Yis," quod this somonour; "pay anon—lat se—
Twelf pens to me, and I wol thee acquite.
I shal no profit han therby but lite;   300
My maister hath the profit and nat I.
Com of,[38] and lat me ryden hastily;
Yif me twelf pens; I may no lenger tarye."

"Twelf pens!" quod she, "now, lady Seinte Marie
So wisly help me out of care and synne,   305
This wyde world thogh that I sholde wynne,
Ne have I nat twelf pens withinne myn hoold.[39]
Ye knowen wel that I am poure and oold;
Kithe youre almesse[40] on me, poure wrecche."

"Nay thanne," quod he, "the foule feend me fecche 310
If I th'excuse, though thou shul be spilt!"[41]

"Allas!" quod she; "God woot, I have no gilt."

---

6 Faith.   7 Planned to go.   8 Loaded.
9 The road was deep (in mud), on account of which the wagon
was stuck.   10 Get up.
11 Badger; a common name for a gray horse.
12 Precisely to the extent that.   13 Endured.
14 Just as if nothing were up.   15 Whispered.
16 Cart horses.   17 God knows, never a bit.   18 Believe.
19 Twitched, pulled.   20 Gray.
21 Patron saint of teamsters.   22 Slough, mudhole.
23 Churl, fellow.
24 As a payment by the carter on consideration of my giving up
my claim to his cart and team.

25 Dwells.
26 Old woman; literally, fiddle. Cf. *ribibe*, line 77, above.
27 Lose.
28 Equivalent to at least six dollars in our money.   29 Since.
30 Knocks.
31 Evidently a contemptuous term for an old woman; this is the
only known case of its survival.   32 On pain.
33 Surely.   34 As I cannot.
35 Without its being the death of me.
36 Ask for a copy of the indictment.
37 Attorney, representative.
38 Come off, i.e., quit holding back.   39 Possession.
40 Show your alms.   41 Destroyed.

"Pay me," quod he, "or by the sweete Seinte Anne,
As I wol bere awey thy newe panne
For dette which thou owest me of old.   315
Whan that thou madest thyn housbonde cokewold,
I payde at hoom for thy correccioun."

"Thou lixt!"[42] quod she; "by my savacioun,
Ne was I nevere er now, wydwe ne wyf,
Somoned unto youre court in al my lyf;   320
Ne nevere I nas but of my body trewe.[43]
Unto the devel, blak and rough of hewe,
Yeve I thy body and my panne also!"

And whan the devel herde hire cursen so
Upon hir knees, he seyde in this manere: 325
"Now, Mabely, myn owene moder deere,
Is this youre wyl in ernest that ye seye?"

"The devel," quod she, "so fecche hym er he deye,
And panne and al, but[44] he wol hym repente!"

"Nay, olde stot,[45] that is nat myn entente,"   330
Quod this somonour, "for to repente me
For anythyng that I have had of thee.
I wolde I hadde thy smok and every clooth."

"Now, brother," quod the devel, "be nat wrooth;
Thy body and this panne been myne by right;   335
Thou shalt with me to helle yet tonyght,
Where thou shalt knowen of oure privetee
Moore than a maister of dyvynytee."

And with that word this foule feend hym hente;
Body and soule he with the devel wente   340
Where-as that[46] somonours han[47] hir heritage.
And God, that makede after his ymage
Mankynde, save and gyde us, alle and some,
And leve[48] thise somonours goode men bicome!

"Lordynges, I koude han toold yow," quod this Frere,
"Hadde I had leyser, for this Somnour heere,   346
After the text of Crist, Poul,[49] and John,
And of oure othere doctours many oon,
Swiche peynes that youre hertes myghte agryse;[50]
Al be it so[51] no tonge may it devyse,   350
Thogh that I myghte a thousand wynter telle
The peynes of thilke cursed hous of helle.
But, for to kepe us fro that cursed place,
Waketh, and preyeth Jesu for his grace
So kepe us fro the temptour, Sathanas.   355
Herketh this word! beth war,[52] as in this cas:
The leoun sit in his awayt[53] alway
To sle the innocent, if that he may.

---

[42] Liest.
[43] Nor never was I with respect to my body (anything) but chaste.
[44] Unless.   [45] Usually, horse; here, evidently a term of abuse.
[46] Went where.   [47] Have.   [48] Let.
[49] Probably a dissyllable.   [50] Shudder.
[51] Although it be such as.   [52] Be wary.   [53] Ambush.

Disposeth ay youre hertes to withstonde
The feend, that yow wolde make thral and bonde.   360
He may[54] nat tempte yow over youre myght,[55]
For Crist wol be youre champion and knyght.
And prayeth that thise somonours hem repente
Of hir mysdedes, er that the feend hem hente!"

Heere endeth the Freres Tale.

[*The Summoner retorts, by way of prologue, with a scandalous account of how the friars are domiciled in hell, and then tells his story. Like his enemy's, it is a fabliau. The subject is a trick of monumental vulgarity played by Goodman Thomas on a rapacious friar. With* THE SUMMONER'S TALE *the Third Fragment closes.*

The Fourth Fragment resumes the theme introduced by the Wife of Bath. (The tales of Fragments Three, Four, and Five are sometimes called the Marriage Group, though obviously the quarrel of the Friar and the Summoner breaks the continuity.) In effect, THE CLERK'S TALE, *with which the Fourth Fragment begins, is a reply to the feministic thesis of the Wife of Bath. He tells the old story of Patient Griselda, subjected by her misguided husband to a series of cruel tests which she meekly accepts and endures with more than human resignation, till at long last he is satisfied and her troubles are over. The next is a tale of another sort of wife, an impudent deceiver of her foolish old husband. It is told by the* MERCHANT, *in keeping with the bitterness his own unhappy marriage has brought him.*

The Fifth Fragment opens with THE SQUIRE'S TALE, *a highly romantic story of adventure and magic. It was left incomplete, as Milton complains in "Il Penseroso." Then comes* THE FRANKLIN'S TALE, *one of Chaucer's best, thoroughly romantic, yet full of wisdom about life in general and the relations of man and woman in particular. Here romantic love, which the troubadours (see p. 56, above) held impossible to the wedded, is the cherished support of a beautiful marriage. It is, of course, this view of marriage which has gradually come, in the centuries since Chaucer, to prevail in the English-speaking world.*]

Heere folwen the wordes of the Frankelyn to the Squier, and the wordes of the Hoost to the Frankelyn.

"In feith, Squier, thow hast thee wel yquit[1]
And gentilly; I preise wel thy wit,"
Quod the Frankeleyn, "consideringe thy yowthe.
So feelyngly thou spekest, sire, I allowe the.[2]
As to my doom,[3] ther is noon that is heere,   5
Of eloquence that shal be thy peere,

---

[54] Can.   [55] Above your power (to resist).
[1] Acquitted.   [2] Commend thee.
[3] As for my judgment, i.e., in my opinion.

If that thou lyve. God yeve thee good chaunce,
And in vertu sende thee continuaunce!
For of thy speche I have greet deyntee.[4]
I have a sone, and by the Trinitee,   10
I hadde levere than twenty pound worth lond,[5]
Though it right now were fallen in myn hond,
He were a man of swich discrecion
As that ye been. Fy on possession,
But-if a man be vertuous[6] withal!   15
I have my sone snybbed[7] and yet shal,
For he to vertu listeth nat entende;
But for to pleye at dees,[8] and to despende
And lese al that he hath, is his usage;
And he hath levere talken with a page   20
Than to comune with any gentil wight
There he myghte lerne gentillesse[9] aright."

  "Straw for youre gentillesse!" quod our Hoost;
"What, Frankeleyn! pardee, sire, wel thou woost[10]
That ech of yow moot tellen atte leste   25
A tale or two, or breken his biheste."[11]

  "That knowe I wel, sire," quod the Frankeleyn;
"I prey yow haveth me nat in desdeyn,
Though to this man I speke a word or two."

  "Telle on thy tale, withouten wordes mo!"   30
"Gladly, sire Hoost," quod he, "I wole obeye
Unto your wyl; now herkneth what I seye.
I wol yow nat contrarien in no wyse
As fer as that my wittes wol suffyse.
I prey to God that it may plesen yow;   35
Thanne woot I wel that it is good ynow."[12]

The Prologe of the Frankeleyns Tale.

Thise olde gentil[13] Britons[14] in hir dayes
Of diverse aventures maden layes,[15]
Rymeyed[16] in hir firste Briton tonge;
Whiche layes with hir instrumentz they songe,   40
Or elles redden hem, for hir plesance;
And oon of hem have I in remembrance,
Which I shal seyn with good wyl as I kan.

  But, sires, bycause I am a burel[17] man,
At my bigynnyng first I yow biseche,   45
Have me excused of my rude speche.
I lerned nevere rethorik, certeyn;
Thyng that I speke, it moot be[18] bare and pleyn.

I sleep nevere on the Mount of Pernaso,[19]
Ne lerned Marcus Tullius Scithero.[20]   50
Colours[21] ne knowe I none, withouten drede,[22]
But swiche colours as growen in the mede,
Or elles swichë as men dye or peynte.
Colours of rethoryke been to queynte;[23]
My spirit feeleth noght of swich mateere.   55
But if yow list, my tale shul ye heere.

[THE FRANKLIN'S TALE]

Heere bigynneth the Frankeleyns Tale.

In Armorik,[24] that called is Britayne,
Ther was a knyght that loved and dide his payne
To serve[25] a lady in his beste wise;
And many a labour, many a greet emprise,[26]
He for his lady wroghte, er she were wonne.   5
For she was oon the faireste[27] under sonne,
And eek therto comen of so heigh kynrede
That wel unnethes[28] dorste this knyght, for drede,
Telle hire his wo, his peyne, and his distresse.
But atte laste she, for his worthynesse,   10
And namely[29] for his meke obeÿsance,
Hath swich a pitee caught of his penance
That pryvely she fil of his accord[30]
To take hym for hir housbonde and hir lord—
Of swich lordshipe as men han over hir wyves.   15
And for to lede the moore in blisse hir lyves,
Of his free wyl he swoor hire as a knyght
That nevere in al his lyf he, day ne nyght,
Ne sholde upon hym take no maistrie
Agayn hir wyl, ne kithe hire[31] jalousie,   20
But hire obeye and folwe hir wyl in al,
As any lovere to his lady shal,
Save that the name of soveraynetee,
That wolde he have, for shame of his degree.[32]

  She thanked hym, and with ful greet humblesse   25
She seyde, "Sire, sith of youre gentillesse
Ye profre me to have so large a reyne,[33]
Ne wolde nevere God bitwixe us tweyne
As in my gilt were outher werre or stryf.[34]

---

[4] Delight.   [5] Land renting for twenty pounds a year.
[6] Accomplished, able.   [7] Snubbed, checked.   [8] Dice.
[9] Good breeding.   [10] Knowest.   [11] Promise.
[12] Enough.   [13] Worthy.
[14] Bretons, inhabitants of Brittany in northwestern France.
[15] Lays. Usually, lyrics; here, short poems of romantic narrative.
[16] Rimed.
[17] Plain; from borel, a kind of coarse woolen cloth.
[18] Must be, is bound to be.

[19] Parnassus, home of the Muses.
[20] Cicero.   [21] Rhetorical ornaments.
[22] Without doubt, certainly.   [23] Too elaborate or artful.
[24] Armorica, Brittany.
[25] According to the rules of courtly love. They are described in
    the introductory note to Malory (pp. 177 f., below). An ex-
    ception should be noted here: as usually in Chaucer, marriage is
    considered the proper goal of lovers.   [26] Enterprise.
[27] One of the fairest.   [28] Hardly.   [29] Especially.
[30] Fell to agreement with him.   [31] Display to her.
[32] I.e., so that his position (as husband) would not be humiliating.
[33] Reign, rule.
[34] It would never be God's will that between us twain there should
    be either war or strife through my fault.

Sire, I wol be youre humble, trewe wyf. 30
Have heer my trouthe, til that myn herte breste."[35]
Thus been they bothe in quiete and in reste.

For o[36] thyng, sires, saufly dar I seye,
That freendes everych oother moot obeye
If they wol longe holden compaignye. 35
Love wol nat been constreyned by maistrye;
Whan maistrie comth, the God of Love anon
Beteth hise wynges, and, farewel, he is gon!
Love is a thyng as any spirit free.
Wommen, of kynde,[37] desiren libertee, 40
And nat to been constreyned as a thral;
And so doon men, if I sooth seyen shal.
Looke who that is moost pacient in love,
He is at his avantage al above.
Pacience is an heigh vertu, certeyn, 45
For it venquysseth, as thise clerkes seyn,
Thynges that rigour sholde nevere[38] atteyne.
For every word men may nat chide or pleyne.
Lerneth to suffre, or elles, so moot I goon,[39]
Ye shul it lerne, wher-so ye wole or noon;[40] 50
For in this world, certein, ther no wight is
That he ne dooth or seith somtyme amys.
Ire, siknesse, or constellacion,[41]
Wyn, wo, or chaungynge of complexion,[42]
Causeth ful ofte to doon amys or speken. 55
On every wrong a man may nat be wreken;[43]
After the tyme moste be temperance
To every wight that kan on governance.[44]
And therfore hath this wise, worthy knyght,
To lyve in ese, suffrance[45] hire bihight;[46] 60
And she to hym ful wisly gan to swere
That nevere sholde ther be defaute in here.[47]

Heere may men seen an humble, wys accord;
Thus hath she take hir servant and hir lord—
Servant in love and lord in mariage. 65
Thanne was he bothe in lordshipe and servage.
Servage? nay; but in lordshipe above,
Sith he hath bothe his lady and his love—
His lady, certes, and his wyf also,
The which that lawe of love acordeth to. 70
And whan he was in this prosperitee,
Hoom with his wyf he gooth to his contree,

Nat fer fro Pedmark,[48] ther his dwellyng was,
Whereas he lyveth in blisse and in solas.

Who koude telle, but he hadde wedded be, 75
The joye, the ese, and the prosperitee
That is bitwixe an housbonde and his wyf?
A yeer and moore lasted this blisful lyf,
Til that the knyght, of which I speke of thus,
That of Kayrrud was cleped Arveragus,[49] 80
Shoope hym[50] to goon and dwelle a yeer or tweyne
In Engelond, that cleped was eek Briteyne,
To seke in armes worshipe and honour;
For al his lust he sette in swich labour;
And dwelled there two yeer—the book seith thus. 85

Now wol I stynten of[51] this Arveragus,
And speken I wole of Dorigen his wyf,
That loveth hire housbonde as hire hertes lyf.
For his absence wepeth she and siketh,[52]
As doon thise noble wyves whan hem liketh.[53] 90
She moorneth, waketh, wayleth, fasteth, pleyneth;
Desir of his presence hire so distreyneth[54]
That al this wyde world she sette at noght.
Hire freendes, whiche that knewe hir hevy thoght,
Conforten hire in al that ever they may. 95
They prechen hire;[55] they telle hire nyght and day
That causelees she sleeth hirself, allas!
And every confort possible in this cas
They doon to hire, with all hire bisynesse,
Al for to make hire leve hire hevynesse. 100

By proces,[56] as ye knowen everichoon,
Men may so longe graven in a stoon
Til som figure therinne emprented be.
So longe han they conforted hire, til she
Receyved hath, by hope and by reson, 105
The emprentyng of hire consolacion;
Thurgh which hir grete sorwe gan aswage;
She may nat alwey duren in swich rage.[57]
And eek Arveragus, in al this care,
Hath sent hire lettres hoom of his welfare, 110
And that he wol come hastily agayn;
Or elles hadde this sorwe hir herte slayn.

Hire freendes sawe hir sorwe gan to slake,
And preyde hire on knees, for Goddes sake,
To come and romen hire[58] in compaignye, 115
Awey to dryve hire derke fantasye.[59]
And finally she graunted that requeste,
For wel she saugh that it was for the beste.

---

[35] Break; i.e., stop.   [36] One.   [37] By their nature.
[38] Never would (be able to).   [39] May I be able to walk.
[40] None, i.e., no.
[41] Planetary influence.
[42] Temperament. See, on the humors, p. 119, note 32, above.
[43] Wreaked, avenged.
[44] Has skill in governing.
[45] Patience, submission.   [46] Promised her.
[47] Fault or defect in her.

[48] The modern Penmarc'h, a cape and commune in northwest Brittany near Quimper.
[49] Who was called Arveragus of Kayrrud.   [50] Planned.
[51] Cease concerning.   [52] Sighs.   [53] It pleases them.
[54] Constrains.   [55] To her.   [56] In course of time.
[57] Violent emotion.   [58] I.e., go for a walk.
[59] Imagination.

Now stood hire castel faste by the see;
And often with hire freendes walketh shee,   120
Hire to disporte, upon the bank an heigh,[60]
Where-as she many a shipe and barge seigh[61]
Seillynge hir cours, where-as hem liste go.
But thanne was that a parcel[62] of hire wo,
For to hirself ful ofte, "Allas!" seith she,   125
"Is ther no shipe, of so manye as I se,
Wol bryngen hom my lord? Thanne were myn herte
Al warisshed[63] of his[64] bittre peynes smerte."
    Another tyme ther wolde she sitte and thynke,
And caste hir eyen dounward fro the brynke.   130
But whan she saugh the grisly rokkes blake,
For verray feere so wolde hir herte quake
That on hire feet she myghte hire noght sustene.
Thanne wolde she sitte adoun upon the grene,
And pitously into the see biholde,   135
And seyn right thus, with sorweful sikes[65] colde:
    "Eterne God, that thurgh thy purveiaunce[66]
Ledest the world by certein governaunce,
In ydel,[67] as men seyn, ye nothyng make.
But, Lord, thise grisly, feendly rokkes blake,   140
That semen rather a foul confusion
Of werk than any fair creacion
Of swich a parfit wys God and a stable—
Why han ye wroght this werk unresonable?
For by this werk, south, north, ne west, ne eest,   145
Ther nys yfostred man, ne bryd,[68] ne beest.
It dooth no good, to my wit,[69] but anoyeth.[70]
Se ye nat, Lord, how mankynde it destroyeth?
An hundred thousand bodyes of mankynde
Han rokkes slayn, al be they nat in mynde,[71]   150
Which mankynde is so fair part of thy werk
That thou it madest lyk to thyn owene merk.[72]
    "Thanne semed it ye hadde a greet chiertee[73]
Toward mankynde; but how thanne may it bee
That ye swiche meenes make it to destroyen,   155
Whiche meenes do no good but evere anoyen?
I woot wel clerkes wol seyn as hem leste,
By argumentz, that al is for the beste,
Though I ne kan the causes nat yknowe.
But thilke[74] God that made wynd to blowe   160
As[75] kepe my lord! This my conclusion.
To clerkes lete I[76] al this disputison.[77]

But wolde God that alle thise rokkes blake
Were sonken into helle for his sake!
Thise rokkes sleen myn herte, for the feere."[78]   165
Thus wolde she seyn, with many a pitous teere.
    Hire freendes sawe that it was no disport
To romen by the see, but disconfort,
And shopen for to pleyen somwher elles.
They leden hire by ryveres and by welles,[79]   170
And eek in othere places delitables.[80]
They dauncen, and they pleyen at ches and tables.[81]
    So on a day, right in the morwe-tyde,[82]
Unto a gardyn that was ther bisyde,
In which that they hadde maad hir ordinance   175
Of vitaille and of oother purveiance,[83]
They goon and pleye hem al the longe day.
And this was in the sixte morwe of May,
Which May hadde peynted with his softe shoures
This gardyn ful of leves and of floures.   180
And craft of mannes hand so curiously
Arrayed hadde this gardyn, trewely,
That nevere was ther gardyn of swich prys,[84]
But if it were the verray paradys.
The odour of floures and the fresshe sighte   185
Wolde han maked any herte lighte
That evere was born, but-if to greet[85] siknesse
Or to greet sorwe helde it in distresse,
So ful it was of beautee with plesaunce.[86]
    At after-dyner gonne they to daunce   190
And synge also, save Dorigen allone;
Which made alwey hir compleint and hir moone,
For she ne saugh hym on the daunce go
That was hir housbonde and hir love also.
But nathelees she moste[87] a tyme abyde,   195
And with good hope lete hir sorwe slyde.
    Upon this daunce, amonges othere men,
Daunced a squier biforn Dorigen,
That fressher was and jolyer of array,
As to my doom,[88] than is the monthe of May.   200
He syngeth, daunceth, passynge any man
That is, or was, sith that the world bigan.
Therwith he was, if men sholde hym discryve,[89]
Oon of the beste faryngе[90] man on lyve,
Yong, strong, right vertuous, and riche, and wys,   205
And wel biloved, and holden in greet prys.
And shortly, if the sothe I tellen shal,
Unwityng of[91] this Dorigen at al,
This lusty squier, servant to Venus,
Which that ycleped was Aurelius,   210

---

60 On high.   61 Saw.   62 Part.
63 Cured.   64 Its.   65 Sighs.   66 Providence.
67 Vain.   68 Man is not fostered, nor bird.
69 Understanding.   70 Harms.
71 I.e., even though we may forget their existence.   72 Image.
73 Affection.   74 That same.
75 A particle often introducing the imperative or the subjunctive,
    as here.   76 To the learned I leave.
77 Disputation, argument.

78 For fear.   79 Springs.   80 Delightful places.
81 Backgammon.   82 Morning time.   83 Provision.
84 Price, worth.   85 Unless too great.   86 Delight.
87 Must   88 In my judgment.   89 Describe.
90 Handsomest.   91 Unknown to.

Hadde loved hire best of any creature
Two yeer and moore, as was his aventure,[92]
But nevere dorste he tellen hire his grevance.
Withouten coppe[93] he drank al his penance.
He was despeyred; nothyng dorste he seye,   215
Save in his songes somwhat wolde he wreye[94]
His wo, as in a general compleynyng;
He seyde he lovede, and was biloved nothyng.
Of swich matere made he manye layes,[95]
Songes, compleintes,[96] roundels,[97] virelayes,[98]   220
How that he dorste nat his sorwe telle,
But langwissheth as a furye dooth in helle.
And dye he moste, he seyde, as dide Ekko
For Narcisus, that dorste nat telle hir wo.
In oother manere than ye heere me seye   225
Ne dorste he nat to hire his wo biwreye,[99]
Save that, paraventure,[1] somtyme at daunces,
Ther[2] yonge folk kepen hir observaunces,[3]
It may wel be he looked on hir face
In swich a wise as man that asketh grace.   230
But nothyng wiste she of his entente.
Nathelees it happed, er they thennes wente,
Bycause that he was hire neighebour,
And was a man of worship[4] and honour,
And hadde[5] yknowen hym of tyme yoore,   235
They fille[6] in spechë; and forth, moore and moore,
Unto this purpos drough[7] Aurelius.
And whan he saugh his tyme, he seyde thus:
"Madame," quod he, "by God, that this world made,
So that I wiste[8] it myghte youre herte glade,   240
I wolde that day that youre Arveragus
Wente over the see that I, Aurelius,
Hadde went ther[9] nevere I sholde have come agayn.
For wel I woot my servyce[10] is in vayn;
My gerdon is but brestyng[11] of myn herte.   245
Madame, reweth[12] upon my peynes smerte,
For with a word ye may me sleen or save.
Heere at youre feet God wolde that I were grave![13]
I ne have as now no leyser[14] moore to seye;
Have mercy, sweete, or ye wol do[15] me deye."   250
  She gan to looke upon Aurelius.
"Is this youre wyl?" quod she, "and sey ye thus?
Nevere erst,"[16] quod she, "ne wiste I what ye mente.

But now, Aurelie, I knowe youre entente,
By thilke God that yaf me soule and lyf,   255
Ne shal I nevere been untrewe wyf,
In word ne werk, as fer as I have wit;
I wol been his to whom that I am knyt.
Taak this for fynal answere, as of me."
But after that, in pley, thus seyde she: 260
"Aurelie," quod she, "by heighe God above,
Yet wolde I graunte yow to been youre love,
Syn I yow se so pitously complayne,
Looke what day that endelong Britayne[17]
Ye remoeve alle the rokkes, stoon by stoon,   265
That they ne lette[18] ship ne boot to goon.
I seye, whan ye han maad the coost so clene
Of rokkes that ther nys no stoon ysene,
Thanne wol I love yow best of any man.
Have heer my trouthe, in al that evere I kan.   270
For wel I woot that it shal never bityde.
Lat swiche folies out of youre herte slyde!
What deyntee[19] sholde a man han in his lyf
For to go love another mannes wyf,
That hath hir body whan-so that hym liketh?"   275
  Aurelius ful ofte soore siketh.
"Is ther noon oother grace[20] in yow?" quod he.
  "No, by that Lord," quod she, "that maked me!"
  Wo was Aurelie whan that he this herde,
And with a sorweful herte he thus answerde: 280
"Madame," quod he, "this were an inpossible!
Thanne moot[21] I dye of sodeyn deth horrible."
And with that word he turned hym anon.
  Tho coome[22] hir othere freendes many oon,
And in the aleyes[23] romeden up and doun;   285
And nothyng wiste of this conclusioun.
But sodeynly bigonne revel newe,
Til that the brighte sonne loste his hewe,
For th'orisonte hath reft the sonne his lyght—
This is as muche to seye as it was nyght![24]—   290
And hoom they goon, in joye and in solas,
Save oonly wrecche[25] Aurelius, allas!
He to his hous is goon with sorweful herte.
He seeth he may nat fro his deeth asterte;[26]
Hym semed that he felte his herte colde.[27]   295
Up to the hevene his handes he gan holde,
And on his knowes[28] bare he sette hym doun,
And in his ravyng seyde his orisoun.[29]
For verray wo out of his wit he breyde.[30]
He nyste[31] what he spak, but thus he seyde   300

---

92 Lot.   93 I.e., not in small draughts.
94 Betray, disclose.   95 Lyrics.   96 Love songs.
97 Rondels, roundelays, lyric poems with fixed refrains.
98 Ballads in which a rime is carried over from one stanza to the
    next.   99 Reveal.
1 Perhaps.   2 Where.
3 Pay their respects.   4 Repute.   5 She had.   6 Fell.
7 Drew.   8 If I knew.   9 Where, whence.
10 As a lover, according to the code of courtly love.
11 My reward is but the breaking.   12 Have pity.
13 Buried.   14 Opportunity.   15 Make.   16 Before.

17 Along the length of Brittany.
18 So that they do not hinder.   19 Pleasure.
20 Favor, mercy.   21 Must.   22 Then came.   23 Paths.
24 Chaucer is making fun of poets' fondness for circumlocutions.
25 Wretched.   26 Escape.   27 Grow cold.   28 Knees.
29 Prayer.   30 He started out of his senses.
31 He knew not.

With pitous herte; his pleynt hath he bigonne
Unto the goddes, and first unto the sonne.

He seyde: "Appollo, god, and governour
Of every plaunte, herbe, tree, and flour,
That yevest, after thy declinacion,[32]   305
To ech of hem his tyme and his seson
As thyn herberwe[33] chaungeth lowe or heighe,
Lord Phebus, cast thy merciable eighe
On wrecche Aurelie, which that am but lorn![34]
Lo, lord, my lady hath my deeth ysworn   310
Withoute gilt, but[35] thy benignytee
Upon my dedly[36] herte have som pitee.
For wel I woot, lord Phebus, if yow lest,[37]
Ye may me helpen—save my lady—best.
Now voucheth sauf that I may yow devyse[38]   315
How that I may been holpen, and in what wyse.

"Youre blisful suster, Lucina the sheene,[39]
That of the see is chief goddesse and queene—
Though Neptunus have deitee in the see,
Yet emperisse aboven hym is she—   320
Ye knowen wel, lord, that right as hir desir
Is to be quyked and lightned of[40] youre fir,
For which she folweth yow ful bisily,
Right so the see desireth naturelly
To folwen hire, as she that is goddesse   325
Bothe in the see and ryveres moore and lesse.[41]
Wherfore, lord Phebus, this is my requeste:
Do this miracle or do myn herte breste[42]—
That now next at this opposicion,[43]
Which in the signe shal be of the Leon,[44]   330
As prieeth hire[45] so greet a flood to brynge
That fyve fadme[46] at the leeste it oversprynge
The hyeste rokke in Armorik Briteyne;
And lat this flood endure yeres tweyne.
Thanne, certes, to my lady may I seye,   335
'Holdeth youre heste,[47] the rokkes been aweye.'

"Lord Phebus, dooth this miracle for me.
Preye hire she go no faster cours than ye;[48]
I seye, preyeth your suster that she go
No faster cours than ye thise yeres two.   340
Thanne shal she been evene atte fulle alway,
And spryng flood laste bothe nyght and day.
And but she vouche sauf in swich manere
To graunte me my sovereyn lady deere,

Prey hire to synken every rok adoun   345
Into hir owene dirke regioun,[49]
Under the ground ther Pluto dwelleth inne,
Or nevere mo shal I my lady wynne.
Thy temple in Delphos[50] wol I barefoot seke.
Lord Phebus, se the teeris on my cheke,   350
And of my peyne have som compassioun!"
And with that word, in swowne he fil adoun,
And longe tyme he lay forth in a traunce.

His brother, which that knew of his penaunce,
Up caughte hym, and to bedde he hath hym broght.   355
Dispeyred in this torment and this thoght,[51]
Lete I this woful creature lye;
Chese he, for me,[52] wheither he wol lyve or dye.

Arveragus, with heele[53] and greet honour,
As he that was of chivalrie the flour,   360
Is comen hoom, and othere worthy men.
O, blisful artow now, thou Dorigen!
That hast thy lusty housbonde in thyne armes,
The fresshe knyght, the worthy man of armes,
That loveth thee as his owene hertes lyf.   365
Nothyng list hym to been ymaginatyf
If[54] any wight had spoke, whil he was oute,[55]
To hire of love. He hadde of it no doute;[56]
He noght entendeth to no swich mateere,
But daunceth, justeth, maketh hire good cheere.   370
And thus in joye and blisse I lete hem dwelle,
And of the sike Aurelius wol I telle.

In langour, and in torment furyus,
Two yeer and moore lay wrecche Aurelyus
Er any foot he myghte on erthe gon;   375
Ne confort in this tyme hadde he noon,
Save of his brother, which that was a clerk.
He knew of al this wo and al this werk;
For to noon oother creature, certeyn,
Of this matere he dorste no word seyn.   380
Under his brest he baar it moore secree
Than evere dide Pamphilus for Galathee.[57]
His brest was hool, withoute for to sene,
But in his herte ay was the arwe kene.
And wel ye knowe that of a sursanure[58]   385
In surgerye is perilous the cure,
But men myghte[59] touche the arwe or come therby.
His brother weep and wayled pryvely,
Til atte laste hym fil in remembrance

---

[32] Distance from the celestial equator, i.e., height in the sky.
[33] Lodging.   [34] Lost.   [35] Unless.   [36] Dying.
[37] If it pleases you.   [38] Explain.   [39] Diana the bright.
[40] Quickened and made light by.   [41] Large and small.
[42] Make my heart break.
[43] Since the highest tides come when the sun and moon are either
in conjunction or 180° apart (in "opposition").
[44] I.e., when the sun is in Leo, its own "mansion" (station), and
the moon in opposition.   [45] Ask her.   [46] Fathom.
[47] Keep your promise.
[48] I.e., that she remain in "opposition."

[49] Proserpina, goddess of the underworld, was identified with
Diana.   [50] Delphi.   [51] Anxiety.
[52] Let him choose, for all of me.—*Wheither* is to be pronounced,
as it was often spelled, *wher*.   [53] Health.
[54] It does not please him to be suspicious whether.   [55] Abroad.
[56] Fear, suspicion.
[57] Galatea, in the medieval Latin poem "Pamphilus de Amore."
[58] A wound healed on the surface but not within.
[59] Unless one can.

That whiles he was at Orliens[60] in France— 390
As yonge clerkes, that been lykerous[61]
To reden artes that been curious,[62]
Seken in every halke and every herne[63]
Particuler sciences for to lerne—
He hym remembred that upon a day 395
At Orliens in studie a book he say[64]
Of magyk natureel,[65] which his felawe,
That was that tyme a bacheler of lawe,
Al were he[66] ther to lerne another craft,
Hadde prively upon his desk ylaft; 400
Which book spak muchel of the operacions
Touchynge the eighte and twenty mansions[67]
That longen[68] to the moone, and swich folye
As in oure dayes is nat worth a flye—
For Hooly Chirches feith in oure bileve 405
Ne suffreth noon illusion us to greve.
And whan this book was in his remembraunce,
Anon for joye his herte gan to daunce;
And to hymself he seyde pryvely:
"My brother shal be warisshed[69] hastily; 410
For I am siker[70] that ther be sciences
By whiche men make diverse apparences,[71]
Swiche as thise subtile tregetoures[72] pleye.
For ofte at feestes have I wel herd seye
That tregetours withinne an halle large 415
Have maad come in a water and a barge,
And in the halle rowen up and doun.
Somtyme hath semed come a grym leoun;
And somtyme floures sprynge as in a mede;
Somtyme a vyne, and grapes white and rede; 420
Somtyme a castel, al of lym and stoon;
And whan hym lyked, voyded[73] it anoon—
Thus semed it to every mannes sighte.
    "Now thanne conclude I thus: that if I myghte
At Orliens som oold felawe yfynde 425
That hadde this moones mansions in mynde,
Or oother magyk natureel above,
He sholde wel make my brother han his love.
For with an apparence a clerk may make,
To mannes sighte, that alle the rokkes blake 430
Of Britaigne weren yvoyded everichon,
And shippes by the brynke comen and gon,
And in swich forme enduren a wowke[74] or two.
Thanne were my brother warisshed of his wo;

Thanne moste she nedes holden hire biheste, 435
Or elles he shal shame hire atte leeste."
    What sholde I make a lenger tale of this?
Unto his brotheres bed he comen is,
And swich confort he yaf hym for to gon
To Orliens that he up stirte anon,[75] 440
And on his wey forthward thanne is he fare
In hope for to been lissed[76] of his care.
    Whan they were come almoost to that citee,
But-if it were a two furlong or thre,
A yong clerk romynge by hymself they mette, 445
Which that in Latyn thriftily hem grette,[77]
And after that he seyde a wonder thyng.
"I knowe," quod he, "the cause of youre comyng."
And er they ferther any foote wente,
He tolde hem al that was in hire entente. 450
    This Briton[78] clerk hym asked of felawes
The whiche that he had knowe in olde dawes.[79]
And he answerde hym that they dede were,
For which he weep ful ofte many a teere.
    Doun of his hors Aurelius lighte anon, 455
And with this mágicien forth is he gon
Hoom to his hous; and made[80] hem wel at ese.
Hem lakked no vitaille that myghte hem plese.
So wel arrayed hous as ther was oon
Aurelius in his lyf saugh nevere noon. 460
    He shewed hym er he wente to soper
Forestes, parkes ful of wilde deer;
Ther saugh he hertes with hir hornes hye,
The gretteste that evere were seyn with yë.
He saugh of hem an hondred slayn with houndes, 465
And somme with arwes blede of bittre woundes.
He saugh, whan voyded were thise wilde deer,
This[81] fauconers upon a fair ryver,[82]
That with hir haukes han the heron slayn.
Tho saugh he knyghtes justyng in a playn. 470
And after this he dide hym swich plesaunce
That he hym shewed his lady on a daunce,
On which hymself he daunced, as hym thoughte.
    And whan this maister that this magyk wroughte
Saugh it was tyme, he clapte his handes two, 475
And farewel! al oure revel was ago.[83]
And yet remoeved they nevere out of the hous
Whil they saugh al this sighte merveillous,
But in his studie, ther-as his bookes be,
They seten stille, and no wight but they thre. 480
    To hym this maister called his squier,
And seyde hym thus: "Is redy oure soper?

60 The University of Orleans.
61 Greedy.   62 To study out-of-the-way subjects.
63 Every nook and every corner.   64 Saw.
65 Natural; i.e., legitimate, not "black."
66 Though he was.
67 Stations, one for each day of the lunar cycle.   68 Belong.
69 Cured.   70 Sure.   71 Apparitions, false shows.
72 Jugglers.   73 Removed.   74 Week.

75 Up he started at once.   76 Relieved.
77 Greeted them worthily.   78 The Breton, Aurelius's brother.
79 Days.   80 He (the magician) made.   81 I.e., some.
82 River bank.   83 The whole entertainment was gone.

Almoost an houre it is, I undertake,[84]
Sith[85] I yow bad oure soper for to make,
Whan that thise worthy men wenten with me   485
Into my studie, ther-as my bookes be."

"Sire," quod this squier, "whan it liketh yow,
It is al redy, though ye wol right now."

"Go we thanne soupe," quod he, "as for the beste;
This amorous folk somtyme moote han hir reste."   490

At after-soper fille they in tretee[1]
What somme sholde this maistres gerdon be
To remooven alle the rokkes of Britayne
And eek from Gerounde to the mouth of Sayne.[2]

He made it straunge,[3] and swoor, so God hym save,   495
Lasse than a thousand pound he wolde nat have;
Ne gladly for that somme he wolde nat goon.

Aurelius, with blisful herte anoon,
Answerde thus: "Fy on a thousand pound!
This wyde world, which that men seye is round,[4]   500
I wolde it yeve, if I were lord of it.
This bargayn is ful dryve, for we been knyt.[5]
Ye shal be payed trewely, by my trouthe;
But looketh now for no necligence or slouthe
Ye tarie us heere no lenger than tomorwe."   505

"Nay," quod this clerk, "have heer my feith to
     borwe."[6]

To bedde is goon Aurelius whan hym leste,
And wel ny al that nyght he hadde his reste.
What for his labour and his hope of blisse,
His woful herte of penaunce hadde a lisse.[7]   510

Upon the morwe, whan that it was day,
To Britaigne tooke they the righte[8] way,
Aurelius and this mágicien bisyde,
And been descended ther they wolde abyde.
And this was, as thise bookes me remembre,   515
The colde, frosty seson of Decembre.
Phebus wex old and hewed lyk laton,[9]
That in his hoote declynacion[10]
Shoon as the burned[11] gold with stremes[12] brighte;
But now in Capricorn adoun he lighte,   520
Where-as he shoon ful pale, I dar wel seyn.
The bittre frostes, with the sleet and reyn,
Destroyed hath the grene in every yerd.
Janus sit by the fyr, with double berd,[13]
And drynketh of his bugle horn the wyn;   525

Biforn hym stant brawn of the tusked swyn,
And "Nowel!"[14] crieth every lusty[15] man.

Aurelius in al that evere he kan
Dooth to his maister chiere and reverence,
And preyeth hym to doon his diligence   530
To bryngen hym out of his peynes smerte,
Or with a swerd that he wolde slitte his herte.

This subtil clerk swich routhe[16] had of this man
That nyght and day he spedde hym that he kan[17]
To wayten[18] a tyme of his conclusion;[19]   535
This is to seye, to maken illusion
By swich an apparence, or jogelrye—
I ne kan no termes of astrologye[20]—
That she and every wight sholde wene[21] and seye
That of Britaigne the rokkes were aweye,   540
Or ellis they were sonken under grounde.
So, atte laste, he hath his tyme yfounde
To maken his japes[22] and his wrecchednesse
Of swich a supersticious cursednesse.
His tables Tolletanes[23] forth he brought,   545
Ful wel corrected; ne ther lakked nought,
Neither his collect ne his expans yeeris,
Ne his rootes, ne his othere geeris,
As been his centris, and his argumentz,
And his proporcioneles convenientz   550
For his equacions in every thyng.
And by his eighte speere in his wirkyng
He knew ful wel how fer Alnath was shove
Fro the heed of thilke fixe Aries above
That in the nynte speere considered is;   555
Ful subtilly he hadde kalkuled al this.

Whan he hadde founde his firste mansion,
He knew the remenant by proporcion;
And knew the arisyng of his moone weel,
And in whos face, and terme, and everydeel;   560
And knew ful weel the moones mansion
Acordaunt to his operacion;
And knew also his othere observances
For swiche illusions and swiche meschances
As hethen folk useden in thilke dayes.   565
For which no lenger maked he delayes;
But thurgh his magik for a wyke[24] or tweye
It semed that alle the rokkes were aweye.

[14] Latin *natalem*, birthday; especially Christ's; i.e., Merry Christmas. Medieval Christmas festivities lasted from December 25 to January 6 (Twelfth Day).
[15] Joyous.   [16] Pity.
[17] As best he knew how.   [18] To watch for.
[19] Astrological exercise.
[20] The Franklin is speaking. His disclaimer is belied by what follows.
[21] Suppose.   [22] Tricks.
[23] Astronomical tables. There follows a parade of astrological terminology, the purpose of which is of course to make the clerk's feat seem more plausible.
[24] Week.

[84] Warrant, declare.   [85] Since.   [1] Treaty, negotiation.
[2] The Gironde . . . the Seine.   [3] Held off.
[4] This was regular scientific doctrine in the Middle Ages.
[5] Is all driven, for we are agreed.   [6] As pledge.
[7] Had a release from suffering.   [8] Straight.
[9] Copper-colored.
[10] When he was in the sign Cancer, in midsummer.
[11] Burnished.   [12] Beams.
[13] For Janus had two faces. It is January.

Aurelius, which that yet despeired is
Wher[25] he shal han his love or fare amys,   570
Awaiteth nyght and day on this myracle;
And whan he knew that ther was noon obstacle,
That voyded were thise rokkes everychon,
Doun to hise maistres feet he fil anon,
And seyde, "I, woful wrecche Aurelius,   575
Thanke yow, lord, and lady myn Venus,
That me han holpen fro my cares colde."[26]
And to the temple his wey forth hath he holde,
Where-as he knew he sholde his lady see.
And whan he saugh his tyme, anon-right hee,   580
With dredful[27] herte and with ful humble cheere,
Salewed[28] hath his sovereyn lady deere.

"My righte lady," quod this woful man,
"Whom I moost drede, and love as I best kan,
And lothest were of al this world displese;   585
Nere it[29] that I for yow have swich disese[30]
That I moste dyen heere at youre foot anon,
Noght wolde I telle how me is wo bigon;
But certes, outher[31] moste I dye or pleyne.[32]
Ye sle me, giltelees, for verray peyne.   590
But of my deeth thogh that ye have no routhe,
Avyseth yow[33] er that ye breke youre trouthe.
Repenteth yow, for thilke God above,
Er ye me sleen bycause that I yow love;
For, madame, wel ye woot what ye han hight.[34]   595
Nat that I chalange[35] anythyng of right
Of yow, my sovereyn lady, but youre grace;[36]
But in a gardyn yond, at swich a place,
Ye woot right wel what ye bihighten me;
And in myn hand youre trouthe plighten ye   600
To love me best. God woot, ye seyde so,
Al be that I unworthy be therto.
Madame, I speke it for the honour of yow,
Moore than to save myn hertes lyf right now.
I have do so as ye comanded me;   605
And if ye vouche sauf, ye may go see.
Dooth as yow list; have youre biheste in mynde;
For, quyk or deed, right there[37] ye shal me fynde.
In yow lith[38] al to do[39] me lyve or deye.
But wel I woot the rokkes been aweye."   610

He taketh his leve; and she astonied stood;
In al hir face nas a drope of blood.
She wende nevere han come[40] in swich a trappe.
"Allas," quod she, "that evere this sholde happe!

For wende I nevere by possibilitee   615
That swich a monstre[41] or merveille myghte be;
It is agayns the proces of nature."
And hoom she goth a sorweful creature;
For verray feere unnethe may she go.[42]
She wepeth, wailleth, al a day or two,   620
And swowneth, that it routhe was to see.
But why it was to no wight tolde shee,
For out of towne was goon Arveragus.
But to hirself she spak, and seyde thus,
With face pale and with ful sorweful cheere,   625
In hire compleynt, as ye shal after heere:

"Allas!" quod she; "on thee, Fortune, I pleyne,[43]
That unwar[44] wrapped hast me in thy cheyne;
For which t'escape woot I no socour
Save oonly deeth or elles dishonour.   630
Oon of thise two bihoveth me to chese;
But nathelees, yet have I levere to lese[45]
My lif than of my body have a shame,
Or knowe myselven fals, or lese my name.
And with my deth I may be quyt,[46] ywis.[47]   635
Hath ther nat many a noble wyf er this,
And many a mayde, yslayn hirself, allas!
Rather than with hir body doon trespas?
"Yis, certes; lo, thise stories[48] beren witnesse.
Whan thritty tirauntz[49] ful of cursednesse   640
Hadde slayn Phidon in Atthenes atte feste,
They comanded his doghtres for t'areste
And bryngen hem biforn hem in despit,[50]
Al naked, to fulfille hir foul delit;
And in hir fadres blood they made hem daunce   645
Upon the pavement, God yeve hem myschaunce!
For which thise woful maydens, ful of drede,
Rather than they wolde lese hir maydenhede,[51]
They prively been stirt[52] into a welle,
And dreynte[53] hemselven, as the bookes telle.   650
"They of Mecene[54] leete enquere and seke[55]
Of Lacedomye[56] fifty maydens eke,
On whiche they wolden doon hir lecherye.
But was ther noon of al that compaignye
That she nas[57] slayn, and with a good entente   655

---

[25] Whether.   [26] Chilling, fatal.
[27] Full of fear, timid.   [28] Saluted.   [29] Were it not.
[30] Discomfort, misery.   [31] Either.
[32] I.e., make a formal love "complaint."
[33] Advise yourself, reflect.   [34] Promised.   [35] Claim.
[36] But of your favor (contrasted with "of right").
[37] I.e., waiting for the fulfillment of your promise.   [38] Lies.
[39] Make.   [40] She never expected to have come.

[41] Monstrosity, unnatural state.   [42] Hardly can she walk.
[43] Complain. Her speech exemplifies the formal "complaint," common in medieval poetry.   [44] Unawares.
[45] I had rather lose.   [46] Set free.   [47] Certainly.
[48] The stories which follow are from St. Jerome's treatise *Against Jovinian*. Citation of a long string of *exempla*, that is, of illustrative cases from history and myth, is a favorite device of medieval writers.
[49] The Thirty Tyrants of Athens fell in 403 B.C.
[50] Spite, malice.   [51] Maidenhood, virginity.
[52] Secretly jumped.   [53] Drenched, drowned.
[54] Messene, in the Peloponnesus.
[55] Caused to be inquired and sought for.   [56] Lacedaemonia.
[57] Was not.

Chees rather for to dye than assente
To been oppressed[58] of hir maydenhede.
Why sholde I, thanne, to dye been in drede?

"Lo eek the tiraunt Aristoclides,[59]
That loved a mayden heet Stymphalides,[60]   660
Whan that hir fader slayn was on a nyght,
Unto Dianes temple goth she right,
And hente[61] the ymage in hir handes two;
Fro which ymage wolde she nevere go—
No wight ne myghte hir handes of it arace—[62]   665
Til she was slayn right in the selve[63] place.

"Now sith that maydens hadden swich despit[64]
To been defouled with mannes foul delit,
Wel oghte a wyf rather hirselven slee
Than be defouled, as it thynketh me.   670

"What shal I seyn of Hasdrubales wyf,
That at Cartage birafte hirself hir lyf?[65]
For whan she saugh that Romayns wan the toun,
She took hir children alle and skipte adoun
Into the fyr, and chees rather to dye   675
Than any Romayn dide hire vileynye.

"Hath nat Lucresse[66] yslayn hirself—allas!—
At Rome, whan that she oppressed was
Of Tarquyn,[67] for hire thoughte it was a shame
To lyven whan she hadde lost hir name?   680

"The sevene maydens of Melesie[68] also
Han slayn hemself for verray drede and wo
Rather than folk of Gawle hem sholde oppresse.
Mo than a thousand stories, as I gesse,
Koude I now telle as touchynge this mateere.   685

"Whan Habradate[69] was slayn, his wyf so deere
Hirselven slow, and leet hir blood to glyde
In Habradates woundes depe and wyde,
And seyde, 'My body, at the leeste way,
Ther shal no wight defoulen if I may.'[70]   690

"What sholde I mo ensamples heerof sayn?
Sith that so manye han hemselven slayn
Wel rather than they wolde defouled be,
I wol conclude that it is bet for me
To sleen myself than been defouled thus.   695
I wol be trewe unto Arveragus
Or rather sleen myself in som manere,

As dide Demociones[71] doghter deere
Bycause that she wolde nat defouled be.

"O Cedasus,[72] it is ful greet pitee   700
To reden how thy doghtren deyde, allas!
That slowe hemself for swich a manere cas.[73]

"As greet a pitee was it, or wel moore,
The Theban mayden that for Nichanore[74]
Hirselven slow, right for swich manere wo.   705

"Another Theban mayden dide right so,
For oon of Macidonye[75] hadde hire oppressed;
She with hire deeth hir maydenhede redressed.

"What shal I seye of Nicerates[76] wyf,
That for swich cas birafte hirself hir lyf?   710

"How trewe eek was to Alcebiades
His love,[77] that rather for to dyen chees
Than for to suffre his body unburyed be.

"Lo, which a wyf was Alceste![78] quod she.

"What seith Omer of goode Penalopee?[79]   715
Al Grece knoweth of hire chastitee.

"Pardee, of Laodomya[80] is writen thus,
That whan at Troie was slayn Protheselaus,
No lenger wolde she lyve after his day.

"The same of noble Porcia[81] telle I may;   720
Withoute Brutus koude she nat lyve,
To whom she hadde al hool hir herte yive.

"The parfit wyfhod of Arthemesie[82]
Honured is thurgh al the Barbarie.[83]

"O Teuta, queene,[84] thy wyfly chastitee   725
To alle wyves may a mirour bee.

"The same thyng I seye of Bilyea,[85]

---

[71] Demotion, an Athenian of the fourth century B.C. On learning of her fiancé's death his virgin daughter, regarding herself as spiritually his bride, killed herself to avoid marrying someone else.   [72] Scedasus of Boeotia.
[73] On account of such a kind of case (i.e., misfortune). According to Plutarch, they killed each other after being violated.
[74] On account of Nicanor. At the capture of Thebes (336 B.C.) he was one of the officers of Alexander the Great.
[75] Macedonia.
[76] Nicerates was executed by the Thirty Tyrants (see note 49 of this series).
[77] His concubine, Timandra. Alcibiades, the Athenian politician and general, died in 404 B.C. See Plutarch's *Lives*.
[78] Alcestis, wife of Admetus, king of Pherae in Thessaly. Hers was a famous myth. She died as a substitute for her husband, in order to prolong his life; but Hercules invaded Hades and brought her back to him.
[79] Penelope, wife of Odysseus, in Homer's *Odyssey*.
[80] Laodamia, wife of Protesilaus. Ovid tells her story (*Heroides*, xiii).
[81] Portia, wife of Marcus Junius Brutus, one of the assassins of Julius Caesar. See Plutarch's *Lives*.
[82] Artemisia, queen of Caria, builder of the Mausoleum for her husband, King Mausolus, who died in 365 B.C.
[83] Barbarian territory (from the Greek point of view).
[84] Widow of Agron, king of the Illyrians. She was famous for her chastity and her force as a ruler.
[85] Bilia, wife of Dullius, victor of a naval battle with the Carthaginians in 260 B.C.

---

[58] Violated.
[59] Tyrant of Orchomenos in Arcadia.   [60] Stymphalis.
[61] Seized.   [62] From it erase, i.e., tear away.
[63] Exactly in the very.   [64] Scorn.
[65] In the Third Punic War, 146 B.C. Hasdrubal was king of Carthage.
[66] Lucrece, Lucretia, wife of Lucius Tarquinius Collatinus. Shakespeare tells her story in his poem *Lucrece* (1594).
[67] Tarquinius Sextus, son of the last of the Roman kings.
[68] Miletus, sacked in 276 B.C., according to St. Jerome by the Gauls.
[69] Abradatas, king of Susa. This story is told by Xenophon.
[70] If I can (prevent it).

Of Rodogone,[86] and eek Valeria."[87]

Thus pleyned Dorigene a day or tweye,
Purposynge evere that she wolde deye.   730
But nathelees, upon the thridde[88] nyght,
Hoom cam Arveragus, this worthy knyght,
And asked hire why that she weep so soore.
And she gan wepen ever lenger the moore.

"Allas," quod she, "that evere I was born!   735
Thus have I seyd," quod she; "thus have I sworn."
And toold hym al, as ye han herd bifore;
It nedeth nat reherce it yow namoore.

This housbonde, with glad chiere, in freendly wyse,
Answerde and seyde, as I shal yow devyse: 740
"Is ther oght elles, Dorigen, but this?"

"Nay, nay," quod she, "God helpe me so as wys![89]
This is to muche, and[90] it were Goddes wille!"

"Ye,[91] wyf," quod he; "lat slepen that[92] is stille.
It may be wel, paraventure,[93] yet today.   745
Ye shul youre trouthe[94] holden, by my fay;
For God so wisly[95] have mercy upon me,
I hadde wel levere ystiked[96] for to be,
For verray love which that I to yow have,
But-if ye sholde youre trouthe kepe and save.   750
Trouthe is the hyeste thyng that man may kepe."[97]
But with that word he brast[98] anon to wepe,
And seyde, "I yow forbede, up[99] peyne of deeth,
That nevere, whil thee lasteth lyf ne breeth,
To no wight telle thou of this aventure—   755
As I may best, I wol my wo endure—
Ne make no contenance of hevynesse,[1]
That folk of yow may demen[2] harm or gesse."

And forth he cleped[3] a squier and a mayde.
"Gooth forth anon with Dorigen," he sayde,   760
"And bryngeth hire to swich a place anon."
They take hir leve and on hir wey they gon,
But they ne wiste why she thider wente;
He nolde no wight tellen his entente.

Paraventure an heepe of yow, ywis,   765
Wol holden hym a lewed[4] man in this,
That he wol putte his wyf in jupartie.[5]
Herkneth the tale er ye upon hire crie.

---

[86] Rhodogune, daughter of Darius. She killed her nurse for urging her to marry again.
[87] Wife of Servius. She, too, refused to consent to a second marriage.   [88] Third.   [89] As (it is) certain.
[90] (Even) if.   [91] Yea.
[92] What. Cf. "Let sleeping dogs lie."   [93] Perhaps.
[94] Troth, promise.   [95] Surely.
[96] I had much rather be stabbed.
[97] The first moral of the story.   [98] Burst out.   [99] Upon.

[1] Show no appearance of sadness.   [2] Deem, suppose.
[3] Called.   [4] Ignorant, unwise.   [5] Jeopardy.

She may have bettre fortune than yow semeth;[6]
And whan that ye han herd the tale, demeth.[7]   770

This squier, which that highte Aurelius,
On Dorigen that was so amorus,
Of aventure happed hire to meete
Amydde the toun, right in the quykkest[8] strete,
As she was bown[9] to goon the wey forth right   775
Toward the gardyn ther-as she had hight.
And he was to the gardyn-ward also;
For wel he spyed whan she wolde go
Out of hir hous to any maner place.
But thus they mette, of aventure or grace,[10]   780
And he saleweth hire with glad entente,
And asked of hire whiderward she wente.

And she answerde, half as she were mad,
"Unto the gardyn, as myn housbonde bad,
My trouthe for to holde, allas! allas!"   785

Aurelius gan wondren on this cas,
And in his herte hadde greet compassion
Of hire, and of hire lamentacion,
And of Arveragus the worthy knyght,
That bad hire holden al that she had hight,   790
So looth hym was his wyf sholde breke hir trouthe;
And in his herte he caughte, of this, greet routhe,[11]
Considerynge the beste on every syde,
That fro his lust yet were hym levere abyde[12]
Than doon so heigh[13] a cherlyssh wrecchednesse   795
Agayns franchise[14] and alle gentillesse;[15]
For which, in fewe wordes seyde he thus:

"Madame, seyth to youre lord Arveragus
That sith I se[16] his grete gentillesse
To yow—and eek I se wel youre distresse—   800
That him were levere han[17] shame—and that were routhe—
Than ye to me sholde breke thus youre trouthe,
I have wel levere evere to suffre wo
Than I departe[18] the love bitwix yow two.
I yow relesse, madame, into youre hond,   805
Quyt,[19] every surement[20] and every bond
That ye han maad to me as heerbiforn
Sith thilke tyme which that ye were born.
My trouthe I plighte I shal yow never repreve
Of no biheste.[21] And heere I take my leve   810
As of the treweste and the beste wyf
That evere yet I knew in al my lyf.

---

[6] It seems to you.   [7] Judge.   [8] Liveliest, busiest.
[9] Ready, bound.   [10] By chance or God's grace.
[11] Pity.
[12] That it would be preferable to him to live without his desire.
[13] High, i.e., extreme.   [14] Nobleness.
[15] Courtesy, nobility.   [16] Since I see.   [17] Have.
[18] Than (that) I should part.   [19] Paid, satisfied.
[20] Assurance.   [21] Reproach you for a (broken) promise.

"But every wyf be war of hire biheeste;
On Dorigene remembreth atte leeste!
Thus kan a squier doon a gentil dede   815
As wel as kan a knyght, withouten drede."[22]

She thonketh hym upon hir knees al bare,
And hoom unto hir housbonde is she fare;
And tolde hym al, as ye han herd me sayd.
And be ye siker he was so weel apayd[23]   820
That it were inpossible me to wryte.

What sholde I lenger of this cas endyte?
Arveragus and Dorigene his wyf
In sovereyn blisse leden forth hir lyf.
Nevere eft[24] ne was ther angre[25] hem bitwene.   825
He cherisseth hire as though she were a queene,
And she was to hym trewe for everemoore—
Of thise folk ye gete of me namoore.

Aurelius, that his cost hath al forlorn,[26]
Curseth the tyme that evere he was born.   830
"Allas," quod he, "allas, that I bihighte
Of pured gold a thousand pound of wighte[27]
Unto this philosophre! How shal I do?
I se namoore but that I am fordo.[28]
Myn heritage moot I nedes selle   835
And been a beggere. Heere may I nat dwelle,
And shamen al my kynrede in this place,
But[29] I of hym[30] may gete bettre grace.
But nathelees I wole of hym assaye
At certeyn dayes yeer by yeer to paye,   840
And thanke hym of his grete curteisye;
My trouthe wol I kepe—I wol nat lye."

With herte soor he gooth unto his cofre,
And broghte gold unto this philosophre,
The value of fyve hundred pound, I gesse,   845
And hym bisecheth, of his gentilesse,
To graunte hym dayes of[31] the remenaunt;
And seyde, "Maister, I dar wel make avaunt,[32]
I failled nevere of my trouthe as yit.
For sikerly my dette shal be quyt   850
Towardes yow, howevere that I fare—
To goon a-begged[33] in my kirtle bare.[34]
But wolde ye vouchesauf, upon seuretee,[35]
Two yeer or thre for to respiten me,
Thanne were I wel; for elles moot I selle   855
Myn heritage; ther is namoore to telle."

This philosophre sobrely answerde
And seyde thus, whan he thise wordes herde:

"Have I nat holden covenant unto thee?"
"Yes, certes; wel and trewely," quod he.   860
"Hastow nat had thy lady as thee liketh?"
"No, no!" quod he; and sorwefully he siketh.
"What was the cause? tel me if thou kan."
Aurelius his tale anon bigan,
And tolde hym al, as ye han herd bifoore.   865
It nedeth nat to yow reherce it moore.
He seide Arveragus, of gentillesse,
Hadde levere dye in sorwe and in distresse
Than that his wyf were of hir trouthe fals.
The sorwe of Dorigen he tolde hym als,   870
How looth hire was to been a wikked wyf,
And that she levere had lost that day hir lyf,
And that hir trouthe she swoor thurgh innocence—
She nevere erst hadde herd speke of apparence.
"That made me han of hire so greet pitee,   875
And right as frely as he sente hire me
As frely sente I hire to hym ageyn.
This al and som;[36] ther is namoore to seyn."

This philosophre answerde: "Leeve brother,
Everich of yow dide gentilly[37] til oother.   880
Thou art a squier, and he is a knyght;
But God forbede, for his blisful myght,
But-if a clerk koude doon a gentil dede
As wel as any of yow, it is no drede.

"Sire, I releesse thee thy thousand pound,   885
As thou right now were cropen[38] out of the ground
Ne nevere er now ne haddest knowen me.
For, sire, I wol nat taken a peny of thee
For al my craft, ne noght for my travaille.
Thou hast ypayed wel for my vitaille.   890
It is ynogh; and farewel, have good day!"
And took his hors and forth he goth his way.

Lordynges, this question thanne wolde I aske now:
Which was the mooste fre,[39] as thynketh yow?
Now telleth me, er that ye ferther wende.   895
I kan namoore; my tale is at an ende.

Heere is ended the Frankeleyns Tale.

[THE FRANKLIN'S TALE *is the last of Fragment V. The Sixth
Fragment begins abruptly with* THE PHYSICIAN'S TALE, *a retelling of the classical account of how the Roman knight Virginius
killed his daughter Virginia to save her from the wicked judge*

---

22 Undoubtedly.   23 Be ye sure he was so well satisfied.
24 Again.   25 Anguish, vexation.   26 Completely lost.
27 Weight.   28 Fordone, ruined.   29 Unless.
30 The magician.   31 Days of grace for.   32 Boast.
33 I.e., even if I should have to go begging.
34 I.e., clad only in my tunic.   35 On (my giving) security.

36 This is the whole and every part, i.e., the long and short of it.
37 Honorably, nobly.
38 Crept; i.e., as if you had just made your original appearance on earth.
39 Magnanimous, generous. Such questions are a favorite device of medieval storytellers. In this one is implied the second moral of the tale: the beauty of "gentilesse" or noble behavior, and the possibility of its appearance in any man or woman.

Appius. The Host is much moved by it, and to counteract the sadness into which it has plunged him calls on the Pardoner for something more sprightly. That impudent fraud responds with a frank description of how, as an itinerant preacher, he prevails on his hearers to buy his fake relics, and then, in THE PARDONER'S TALE, *launches into an* exemplum, *as if he were actually delivering one of his sermons. The* exemplum *was a regular feature of the medieval sermon; it consisted of a story illustrating the text. The Pardoner tells his well—so well that . . . but we are getting ahead of Chaucer's narrative. To return to the Host's reaction to the Physician's tale:*]

The wordes of the Hoost to the Phisicien and the Pardoner.

Oure Hooste gan to swere as he were wood;[1]
"Harrow!"[2] quod[3] he, "by nayles and by blood![4]
This was a fals cherl and a fals justise!
As shameful deeth as herte may devyse
Come to thise juges and hire advocatz!   5
Algate[5] this sely[6] mayde is slayn, allas!
Allas, to deere boughte she beautee!
Wherfore I seye al day that men may see
That yiftes of Fortune and of Nature
Been cause of deeth to many a creature.   10
Hire beautee was hire deth, I dar wel sayn.
Allas, so pitously as she was slayn!
Of bothe yiftes that I speke of now
Men han ful ofte moore for harm than prow.[7]
    "But trewely, myn owene maister deere,   15
This is a pitous tale for to heere.
But natheles, passe over! is no fors.[8]
I pray to God, so save thy gentil cors,[9]
And eek thyne urynals[10] and thy jurdones,[11]
Thyn ypocras and eek thy galiones,[12]   20
And every boyste[13] ful of thy letuarie;[14]
God blesse hem, and oure Lady Seinte Marie!
So moot I theen,[15] thou art a propre[16] man,
And lyk a prelat, by Seint Ronyan![17]

Seyde I nat wel? I kan nat speke in terme,[18]   25
But wel I woot thou doost myn herte to erme,[19]
That I almoost have caught a cardynacle.[20]
By corpus bones![21] but I have triacle,[22]
Or elles a draughte of moyste[23] and corny[24] ale,
Or but I heere anon a myrie tale,   30
Myn herte is lost for pitee of this mayde.
    "Thou beel amy,[25] thou Pardoner," he sayde,
"Telle us som myrthe or japes[26] right anon."[27]
    "It shal be doon," quod he, "by Seint Ronyon!
But first," quod he, "heere at this ale-stake[28]   35
I wol bothe drynke, and eten of a cake."
    But right anon the gentils gonne[29] to crye,
"Nay! lat hym telle us of no ribaudye.[30]
Telle us som moral thyng that we may leere[31]
Some wit,[32] and thanne wol we gladly heere."   40
    "I graunte, ywis,[33]" quod he, "but I moot thynke
Upon som honeste thyng while that I drynke."

Heere folweth the Prologe of the Pardoners Tale.

RADIX MALORUM EST CUPIDITAS. AD THIMOTHEUM, 6°.[34]

Lordynges,[35]—quod he,—in chirches whan I preche,
I peyne me to han an hauteyn speche,[36]
And rynge it out as round as gooth a belle,   45
For I kan al by rote[37] that I telle.
My theme[38] is alwey oon and evere was:
Radix malorum est Cupiditas.
First I pronounce whennes that I come,
And thanne my bulles[39] shewe I, alle and some.   50
Oure lige lordes[40] seel on my patente,[41]
That shewe I first, my body to warente,[42]
That no man be so boold, ne preest ne clerk,
Me to destourbe of Cristes hooly werk.
And after that thanne telle I forth my tales;   55
Bulles of popes and of cardynales,
Of patriarkes and bisshoppes I shewe;
And in Latyn I speke a wordes fewe,

---

1 Crazy.
2 Help! The old Norman cry rallying the community in pursuit of a criminal. The Host feels like raising the hue and cry against the unjust judge and the false churl who aided and abetted him.
3 Quoth.
4 By the nails of the Cross and the blood shed by Christ.
5 Anyhow.   6 Innocent, poor.   7 Profit, advantage.
8 It is no matter.   9 Body, self.
10 Vessels for holding urine (for use in diagnosis).
11 Jordans, chamber pots.
12 Hippocras was a beverage made of wine, sugar, and spices, used as a cordial; it was named after Hippocrates, the great Greek physician.—No other occurrence of the word *galiones* is known. Very likely the Host invents it on the spur of the moment as a parallel (unintentionally jocose) to *ypocras,* as if there were another cordial named after the other great Greek physician, Galen.   13 Box.   14 Electuary, remedy.
15 As I may (i.e., hope to) thrive.   16 Handsome, fine.
17 A trisyllable; in line 34 it is dissyllabic. Apparently a saint of the Host's invention.

18 Technical phraseology.
19 Well I know you make my heart grieve.
20 Cardiacle, pain in the heart.
21 A vulgar and blundering oath: by the bones of (Christ's) body.
22 Unless I have (a) remedy.   23 New.   24 Strong.
25 *Bel ami,* fair friend.   26 Jokes.   27 Right now.
28 A horizontal pole above the door, with a wreath or bush hanging from it, denoted an alehouse.   29 Began.
30 Ribaldry.   31 Learn.   32 Knowledge.
33 Certainly.
34 The love of money [cupidity] is the root of [all] evil. [The First Epistle . . .] to Timothy 6 [:10].   35 Sirs.
36 Take pains to have a loud way of speaking.
37 Know by heart all.   38 Text.   39 Papal letters.
40 I.e., bishop's.
41 License. Cf. *Piers Plowman,* Prologue, lines 68–82, where the bishop, as well as the pardoner who preaches as if he were a priest, is condemned.   42 Myself to warrant.

To saffron with[43] my predicacion,[44]
And for to stire hem to devocion.   60
Thanne shewe I forth my longe cristal stones,[45]
Ycrammed ful of cloutes[46] and of bones—
Relikes been they, as wenen they echoon.[47]
Thanne have I in laton[48] a sholder boon
Which that was of an hooly Jewes[49] sheep.   65
   "Goode men," I seye, "taak of my wordes keep:[50]
If that this boon be wasshe in any welle,
If cow or calf or sheepe or oxe swelle
That any worm[51] hath ete, or worm[52] ystonge,
Taak water of that welle and wassh his tonge,   70
And it is hool anon; and forthermoor,
Of pokkes and of scabbe and every soor
Shal every sheepe be hool that of this welle
Drynketh a draughte. Taak kepe eek what I telle:
If that the goode man that the beestes oweth[53]   75
Wol every wyke, er that the cok hym croweth,
Fastynge, drinken of this welle a draughte,
As thilke hooly Jew oure eldres taughte,
His beestes and his stoor[54] shal multiplie.
And, sires, also it heeleth jalousie;   80
For though a man be falle in jalous rage,
Lat maken with this water his potage,[55]
And nevere shal he moore his wyf mystriste,[56]
Though he the soothe of hir defaute wiste—[57]
Al[58] had she taken preestes[59] two or thre.   85
   "Heere is a miteyn eek that ye may se.
He that his hand wol putte in this mitayn,
He shal have multipliyng of his grayn,
Whan he hath sowen, be it whete or otes,
So[60] that he offre pens, or elles grotes.   90
   "Goode men and wommen, o thyng warne I yow!
If any wight be in this chirche now
That hath doon synnë horrible, that he
Dar nat, for shame, of it yshryven be,
Or any womman, be she yong or old,   95
That hath ymaked hir housbonde cokewold,[61]
Swich folk shal have no power ne no grace
To offren to my relikes in this place.
And whoso fyndeth hym out of swich blame,
He wol come up and offre, in Goddes name,   100

And I assoille[62] hem by the auctoritee
Which that by bulle ygraunted was to me."
   By this gaude[63] have I wonne, yeer by yeer,
An hundred mark,[64] sith I was pardoner.
I stonde lyk a clerk[65] in my pulpet,   105
And whan the lewed[66] peple is doun yset,
I preche so as ye han herd bifoore,
And telle an hundred false japes[67] moore.
Thanne peyne I me[68] to strecche forth the nekke,
And est and west upon the peple I bekke,[69]   110
As dooth a dowve sittynge on a berne.[70]
Myne handes and my tonge goon so yerne[71]
That it is joye to se my bisynesse.
Of avarice and of swich cursednesse
Is al my prechyng, for to make hem free   115
To yeven hir pens, and namely[72] unto me.
For myn entente is nat but for to wynne,
And nothyng for correccion of synne;
I rekke nevere, whan that they been beryed,
Though that hir soules goon a-blakeberyed.[73]   120
   For certes, many a predicacion
Comth ofte tyme of yvel entencion:
Som for plesance of folk and flaterye,
To been avaunced by ypocrisye;
And som for veyne glorie; and som for hate—   125
For whan I dar noon oother weyes debate,[74]
Thanne wol I stynge hym[75] with my tonge smerte
In prechyng, so that he shal nat asterte[76]
To been defamed falsly, if that he
Hath trespased to my bretheren or to me.   130
For though I telle noght his propre name,
Men shal wel knowe that it is the same,
By signes and by othere circumstances.
Thus quyte[77] I folk that doon us displesances;
Thus spitte I out my venym under hewe   135
Of hoolynesse, to semen hooly and trewe.
   But, shortly, myn entente I wol devyse:[78]
I preche of nothyng but for coveityse.
Therfore my theme is yet, and evere was:
Radix malorum est Cupiditas.   140
Thus kan I preche agayn that same vice
Which that I use, and that is avarice.

---

[43] To give color and flavor to. Saffron was used for these purposes. In color it was a rich yellow.   [44] Preaching, sermon.
[45] Glass cases.   [46] Pieces of cloth.
[47] As they suppose, each one.
[48] I.e., set in latten, a composition of copper and zinc.
[49] I.e., belonging to one of the patriarchs of the Old Testament.
[50] Heed.
[51] Certain diseases of livestock were supposed to be the result of eating worms.   [52] Snake.   [53] Owns.
[54] Possessions.   [55] Soup.   [56] Mistrust.
[57] Though he knew the truth of her fault.
[58] Although, even if.   [59] As lovers.
[60] Provided.   [61] Cuckold; i.e., that has committed adultery.

[62] Absolve.   [63] Trick.
[64] A sum equivalent, in purchasing power, to about $10,000 of our money. A mark was worth two-thirds of a pound.
[65] Ecclesiastic.   [66] Simple.   [67] Tricks.
[68] I take pains.   [69] Beckon, nod.   [70] Barn.
[71] Eagerly, quickly.   [72] Especially.
[73] Go blackberrying; i.e., go wandering, instead of home to heaven.—The extraordinary cynicism and shamelessness of the Pardoner are entirely consistent with his character as drawn in the Prologue, but it should be remembered that on the present occasion his tongue is loosened with drink.   [74] Quarrel.
[75] The person I hate.   [76] Escape.   [77] Pay back.
[78] Explain.

But though myself be gilty in that synne,
Yet kan I maken oother folk to twynne[79]
From avarice and soore to repente.   145
But that is nat my principal entente;
I preche nothyng but for coveitise.
Of this mateere it oghte ynogh suffise.

Thanne telle I hem ensamples[80] many oon
Of olde stories longe tyme agoon;   150
For lewed peple loven tales olde—
Swiche thynges kan they wel reporte and holde.
What! trowe[81] ye that whiles I may preche,
And wynne gold and silver for[82] I teche,
That I wol lyve in poverte wilfully?   155
Nay, nay! I thoghte it nevere, trewely!
For I wol preche and begge in sondry landes;
I wol nat do no labour with myne handes,
Ne make baskettes[83] and lyve therby,
Bycause I wol nat beggen ydelly.   160
I wol noon of the apostles countrefete;[84]
I wol have moneie, wolle, chese, and whete,
Al were it yeven of the pouereste page,
Or of the pouereste wydwe in a village,
Al sholde hir children sterve for famyne.   165
Nay, I wol drynke licour of the vyne,
And have a joly wenche in every toun.

But herkneth, lordynges, in conclusioun:
Youre likyng is that I shal telle a tale;
Now have I dronke a draughte of corny ale,   170
By God, I hope I shal yow telle a thyng
That shal by reson been at youre likyng;
For though myself be a ful vicious man,
A moral tale yet I yow telle kan,
Which I am wont to preche, for to wynne.   175
Now hoold youre pees! my tale I wol bigynne.

[THE PARDONER'S TALE]

Heere bigynneth the Pardoners Tale.

In Flaundres whilom[1] was a compaignye
Of yonge folk that haunteden folye,
As riot,[2] hasard,[3] stywes,[4] and tavernes,
Where-as with harpes, lutes, and gyternes[5]   180

---

[79] Depart.
[80] Examples, *exempla*. A regular part of the medieval sermon was
the *exemplum*, example, illustrative story. See lines 174 f.,
below. The main narrative of the Pardoner's tale is an *exemplum;*
his whole performance is a mock sermon.
[81] Think, suppose.   [82] Because.
[83] As did Paul the Hermit, according to St. Jerome.
[84] Imitate.

[1] Formerly, once upon a time.
[2] Riotous living, debauchery.
[3] The dice game now known as craps.   [4] Stews, brothels.
[5] Citterns, guitars.

They daunce and pleyen at dees[6] bothe day and nyght,
And eten also and drynken over hir myght;
Thurgh which they doon the devel sacrifise
Withinne that develes temple,[7] in cursed wise,
By superfluytee abhomynable.   185
Hir othes been so grete and so dampnable
That it is grisly for to heere hem swere.
Oure blissed Lordes body they to-tere—[8]
Hem thoughte that Jewes rente hym noght ynough—
And ech of hem at otheres synne lough.   190
And right anon thanne comen tombesteres[9]
Fetys[10] and smale, and yonge frutesteres,[11]
Syngeres with harpes, baudes, wafereres—[12]
Whiche been the verray develes officeres
To kyndle and blowe the fyr of lecherye,   195
That is annexed unto glotonye.
The hooly writ take I to my witnesse
That luxurie[13] is in wyn and dronkenesse.

Lo, how that dronken Looth,[14] unkyndely,[15]
Lay by his doghtres two, unwityngly;   200
So dronke he was he nyste[16] what he wroghte.
Herodes[17]—whoso wel the stories soghte—[18]
Whan he of wyn was repleet at his feeste,
Right at his owene table he yaf his heeste[19]
To sleen the Baptist John, ful giltelees.[20]   205
Senec[21] seith a good word doutelees.
He seith he kan no difference fynde
Bitwix a man that is out of his mynde
And a man which that is dronkelewe,[22]
But that woodnesse, fallen in a shrewe,[23]   210
Persevereth lenger than dooth dronkenesse.

O glotonye, ful of cursednesse!
O cause first of oure confusion![24]
O original of oure dampnacion,
Til Crist hadde boght us with his blood agayn!   215
Lo, how deere, shortly for to sayn,
Aboght was thilke cursed vileynye!
Corrupt was al this world for glotonye.
Adam oure fader and his wyf also
Fro Paradys to labour and to wo   220
Were dryven for that vice, it is no drede;[25]
For whil that Adam fasted, as I rede,

---

[6] Dice.   [7] I.e., the tavern.
[8] Tore to pieces (by swearing by the parts of Christ's body).
[9] Dancing girls.   [10] Shapely.   [11] Female fruit-sellers.
[12] Sellers of wafers, cakes, and confections; they had a bad reputation.   [13] Lechery. See Ephesians 5:18.
[14] Lot. See Genesis 19:33-35.   [15] Unnaturally.
[16] Ne wiste, knew not.   [17] Herod.
[18] Whoever should examine (seek) well the stories (would find).
[19] Gave his order (hest).   [20] See Matthew 14:1-12.
[21] Seneca, Roman Stoic philosopher and tragic dramatist of the
first century A.D. See his *Epistles,* especially lxxxiii.
[22] Drunken.   [23] Having occurred in a wretch.
[24] Ruin. See lines 222 ff., below.   [25] Doubt.

He was in Paradys; and whan that he
Eet of the fruyt deffended[26] on the tree,
Anon he was out cast to wo and peyne. 225
O glotonye, on thee wel oghte us pleyne![27]
O, wiste a man how manye maladyes
Folwen of excesse and of glotonyes,
He wolde been the moore mesurable
Of his diete, sittynge at his table. 230
Allas! the shorte throte,[28] the tendre mouth,
Maketh that est and west and north and south,
In erthe, in eir, in water, men to swynke[29]
To gete a gloton deyntee mete and drynke.
Of this matiere, O Paul, wel kanstow trete: 235
"Mete unto wombe,[30] and wombe eek unto mete,
Shal God destroyen bothe," as Paulus seith.[31]
Allas! a foul thyng is it, by my feith,
To seye this word, and fouler is the dede,
Whan man so drynketh of the white and rede 240
That of his throte he maketh his pryvee,[32]
Thurgh thilke cursed superfluitee.

The apostel wepyng seith ful pitously:
"Ther walken manye, of whiche yow toold have I—
I seye it now wepyng, with pitous voys— 245
That they been enemys of Cristes croys,
Of which the ende is deeth; wombe is hir god."[33]
O wombe! O bely! O stynkyng cod,[34]
Fulfilled[35] of dong and of corrupcioun!
At either ende of thee foul is the soun.[36] 250
How greet labour and cost is thee to fynde![37]
This cookes, how they stampe, and streyne, and grynde,
And turnen substaunce[38] into accident,[39]
To fulfillen[40] al thy likerous talent![41]
Out of the harde bones knokke they 255
The mary,[42] for they caste noght awey
That may go thurgh the golet softe and swoote.
Of spicerie of leef, and bark, and roote
Shal been his sauce ymaked, by delit
To make hym yet a newer appetit. 260
But certes, he that haunteth swiche delices
Is deed, whil that he lyveth in tho vices.[43]

A lecherous thyng is wyn, and dronkenesse
Is ful of stryvyng and of wrecchednesse.

O dronke man, disfigured is thy face, 265
Sour is thy breeth, foul artow to embrace,
And thurgh thy dronke nose semeth the soun
As though thou seydest ay, "Sampsoun, Sampsoun!"
And yet, God woot, Sampsoun drank nevere no wyn.
Thou fallest as it were a styked swyn;[44] 270
Thy tonge is lost, and al thyn honeste cure;[45]
For dronkenesse is verray sepulture
Of mannes wit and his discrecion.
In whom that drynke hath dominacion,
He kan no conseil kepe, it is no drede. 275
Now kepe yow fro the white and fro the rede,
And namely fro the white wyn of Lepe,[46]
That is to selle in Fysshstrete[47] or in Chepe.[48]
This wyn of Spaigne crepeth subtilly
In othere wynes growynge faste by,[49] 280
Of which ther ryseth swich fumositee[50]
That whan a man hath dronken draughtes thre,
And weneth that he be at hoom in Chepe,
He is in Spaigne, right at the toune of Lepe—
Nat at the Rochele,[51] ne at Burdeux toun;[52] 285
And thanne wol he seye, "Sampsoun, Sampsoun!"

But herkneth, lordynges, o word, I yow preye:
That alle the sovereyn actes, dar I seye,
Of victories in the Olde Testament,
Thurgh verray God, that is omnipotent, 290
Were doon in abstinence and in preyere;
Looketh the Bible and ther ye may it leere.[53]

Looke, Attilla,[54] the grete conquerour,
Deyde in his sleepe, with shame and dishonour,
Bledynge ay at his nose in dronkenesse. 295
A capitayn sholde lyve in sobrenesse.
And over al[55] this, avyseth yow[56] right wel
What was comaunded unto Lamuel—
Nat Samuel, but Lamuel,[57] seye I;
Redeth the Bible and fynde it expresly— 300
Of wyn-yevyng to[58] hem that han justise.[59]
Namoore of this, for it may wel suffise.

---

26 Forbidden.   27 Complain, lament.
28 I.e., how brief the pleasure of tasting.   29 Labor.
30 Belly.   31 1 Corinthians 6:13.   32 Privy, toilet.
33 Philippians 3:18–19.   34 Bag, stomach.   35 Filled full.
36 Sound.   37 Keep, provide for.
38 Actuality, the real essence. Like *accident,* a term in contemporary
   philosophy. Both figured in the Wyclifite controversy over the
   real presence of Christ's body in the Eucharist, according to
   the doctrine of transubstantiation.
39 The outward qualities by which a thing is apprehended: color,
   weight, texture, shape, etc.   40 Satisfy.
41 Greedy taste.   42 Marrow.   43 Cf. 1 Timothy 5:6.

44 Stuck pig.   45 Care for decency.
46 A town in Spain near Cadiz.
47 Fish Street, near London Bridge; it was in a district of wine
   merchants.
48 Cheapside, in the center of London; there were numerous taverns in the vicinity.
49 Spanish wines were both heavier and cheaper than those of
   southwestern France; evidently the latter were adulterated with
   the former.
50 Vapor rising from the stomach and affecting the brain.
51 La Rochelle, on the west coast of France.
52 Bordeaux, center of the southwestern French wine trade.
53 Learn.
54 Leader of the Huns, d. 453 A.D. According to several accounts
   he died, as described, on his wedding night.   55 Besides.
56 Consider.   57 Lemuel; see Proverbs 31:4–5.
58 Of giving wine to.
59 Them that have judicial functions.

And now that I have spoken of glotonye,
Now wol I yow deffenden hasardrye.[60]
Hasard is verray mooder of lesynges,[61]   305
And of deceite, and cursed forswerynges,[62]
Blasphemyng of Crist, manslaughtre, and wast also
Of catel[63] and of tyme; and forthermo,
It is repreeve[64] and contrarie of honour
For to ben holde a commune hasardour.   310
And ever the hyer he is of estaat,
The moorë is he holden desolaat.[65]
If that a pryncë useth hasardrye,
In alle governance and policye
He is, as by commune opinion,   315
Yholde the lasse in reputacion.

Stilbon,[66] that was a wys embassadour,
Was sent to Corynthe in ful greet honour
Fro Lacidomye,[67] to maken hire alliaunce.
And whan he cam, hym happede par chaunce   320
That alle the gretteste that were of that lond
Pleyynge atte hasard he hem fond;
For which, as soonë as it myghte be,
He stal hym hoom agayn to his contree,
And seyde: "Ther wol I nat lese[68] my name,   325
Ne I wol nat take on me so greet defame
Yow for to allie unto none hasardours.
Sendeth othere wise embassadours;
For, by my trouthe, me were levere dye
Than I yow sholde to hasardours allye.   330
For ye that been so glorious in honours
Shul nat allyen yow with hasardours,
As by my wyl, ne as by my tretee."
This wise philosophre, thus seyde hee.

Looke eek[69] that to the kyng Demetrius[70]   335
The kyng of Parthes,[71] as the book seith us,
Sente him a paire of dees of gold in scorn,
For he hadde used hasard ther-biforn;
For which he heeld his glorie or his renoun
At no value or reputacioun.   340
Lordes may fynden oother maner pley
Honeste ynough to dryve the day awey.

Now wol I speke of othes false and grete
A word or two, as olde bookes trete.
Gret sweryng is a thyng abhominable,   345
And fals sweryng is yet moore reprevable.
The heighe God forbad sweryng at al—

Witnesse on Mathew;[72] but in special
Of sweryng seith the hooly Jeremye,[73]
"Thou shalt seye sooth thyne othes, and nat lye,   350
And swere in doom,[74] and eek in rightwisnesse";
But ydel sweryng is a cursednesse.
Bihoold and se that in the firste table[75]
Of heighe Goddes heestes honurable
Hou that the seconde heeste[76] of hym is this: 355
"Take nat my name in ydel or amys."
Lo, rather[77] he forbedeth swich sweryng
Than homycide or many a cursed thyng.
I seye that as by ordre thus it stondeth;
This knowen, that his heestes understondeth,   360
How that the seconde heeste of God is that.
And forther-over, I wol thee telle al plat[78]
That vengeance shal nat parten[79] from his hous
That of his othes is to outrageous.
"By Goddes precious herte," and "By his nayles,"   365
And "By the blood of Crist that is in Hayles,[80]
Sevene is my chaunce and thyn is cynk and treye!"[81]
"By Goddes armes, if thou falsly pleye,
This daggere shal thurghout thyn herte go!"—
This fruyt cometh of the bicched[82] bones two: 370
Forsweryng, ire, falsnesse, homycide.
Now for the love of Crist, that for us dyde,
Lete[83] youre othes, bothe grete and smale!
But, sires, now wol I telle forth my tale.[84]

Thise riotoures thre of whiche I telle,   375
Longe erst er[85] prime[86] rong of any belle,
Were set hem in a taverne for to drynke.
And as they sat, they herde a belle clynke
Biforn a cors, was[87] caried to his grave.
That oon[88] of hem gan callen to his knave:[89]   380
"Go bet,"[90] quod he, "and axe redily
What cors is this that passeth heer forby;
And looke that thou reporte his name weel."

"Sire," quod this boy, "it nedeth never-a-deel;
It was me toold er ye cam heer two houres.   385
He was, pardee, an old felawe of youres;

---

[72] Matthew 5:34.   [73] Cf. Jeremiah 4:2.   [74] Judgment.
[75] The first four commandments, teaching man's duty to God.
   (The rest deal with his duty to society.)
[76] The second commandment according to the Catholic number-
   ing, which combines the Protestants' first two and divides into
   two the Protestants' tenth.
[77] Earlier, sooner.
[78] And furthermore, I will tell you quite flatly.   [79] Depart.
[80] The Abbey of Hales, in Gloucestershire, treasured a vial said to
   contain some of Christ's blood.
[81] Five and three. Then as now seven and eleven were the best
   throws.   [82] Bitched, execrable.   [83] Leave, forsake.
[84] And now he launches into his *exemplum.*   [85] Long before.
[86] The earliest of the day's canonical hours, 6 to 9 a.m. I.e., it was
   not yet nine.   [87] Which was.   [88] The one, one.
[89] Servant, boy.
[90] Go better, faster (a hunting call to the dogs); i.e., hurry.

---

[60] Forbid gambling.
[61] Mother of lies.   [62] Swearing falsely.   [63] Chattels.
[64] (A) reproach, shame.   [65] Lost (to shame).
[66] This name occurs in one of Seneca's *Dialogues;* but the story is
   told of one Chilon in John of Salisbury's *Polycraticus.*
[67] Lacedaemon, i.e., Sparta.   [68] Lose.   [69] Also.
[70] Unidentified, though Chaucer got the story from the *Polycraticus* (see note 66, above).   [71] Parthians.

And sodeynly he was yslayn tonyght,[91]
Fordronke,[92] as he sat on his bench upright.
Ther cam a privee[93] theef men clepeth Deeth,
That in this contree al the peple sleeth,
And with his spere he smoot his herte atwo,   390
And wente his wey withouten wordes mo.
He hath a thousand slayn this pestilence.[94]
And, maister, er ye come in his presence,
Me thynketh that it were necessarie   395
For to be war of swich an adversarie.
Beth redy for to meete hym everemoore!
Thus taughte me my dame; I sey namoore."
     "By Seinte Marie," seyde this taverner,[95]
"The child seith sooth; for he hath slayn this yeer, 400
Henne[96] over a mile, withinne a greet village,
Bothe man and womman, child, and hyne,[97] and page;
I trowe his habitacion be there.
To been avysed greet wysdom it were,
Er that he dide a man a dishonour."   405
     "Ye, Goddes armes!"[98] quod this riotour.
"Is it swich peril with hym for to meete?
I shal hym seke by wey and eek by strete,
I make avow to Goddes digne[99] bones!
Herkneth, felawes! we thre been al ones.[1]   410
Lat ech of us holde up his hand til[2] oother,
And ech of us bicomen otheres brother;[3]
And we wol sleen this false traytour Deeth.
He shal be slayn which that so manye sleeth,
By Goddes dignitee, er it be nyght!"   415
     Togidres han thise thre hir trouthes plight
To lyve and dyen, ech of hem for oother,
As though he were his owene yboren brother.
And up they stirte, al dronken in this rage;
And forth they goon towardes that village   420
Of which the taverner hadde spoke biforn.
And many a grisly ooth thanne han they sworn,
And Cristes blessed body they to-rente—
Deeth shal be deed, if that they may hym hente![4]
     Whan they han goon nat fully half a mile,   425
Right as they wolde han troden over a stile,
An oold man and a poure with hem mette.
This olde man ful mekely hem grette,[5]
And seyde thus: "Now, lordes, God yow see!"[6]
     The proudeste of thise riotoures three   430
Answerde agayn: "What, carl,[7] with sory grace![8]

Why artow al forwrapped[9] save thy face?
Why lyvestow so longe in so greet age?"
     This olde man gan looke in his visage,
And seyde thus: "For I ne kan nat fynde   435
A man, though that I walked into Ynde,[10]
Neither in citee nor in no village,
That wolde chaunge his youthe for myn age;
And therfore moot I han myn age stille
As longe tyme as it is Goddes wille.   440
Ne Deeth, allas, ne wol nat han my lyf!
Thus walke I, lyk a restelees kaityf,[11]
And on the ground, which is my moodres gate,
I knokke with my staf, bothe erly and late,
And seye, 'Leeve[12] mooder, leet me in!   445
Lo, how I vanysshe, flessh and blood and skyn!
Allas! whan shul my bones been at reste?
Mooder, with yow wolde I chaunge my cheste,[13]
That in my chambre longe tyme hath be,
Ye, for an heyre clowt[14] to wrappe me.'   450
But yet to me she wol nat do that grace,
For which ful pale and welked[15] is my face.
     "But, sires, to yow it is no curteisye
To speken to an old man vileynye,
But[16] he trespasse in word or elles in dede.   455
In hooly writ[17] ye may yourself wel rede:
'Agayns[18] an oold man, hoor upon his heed,
Ye sholde arise'; wherfore I yeve yow reed,[19]
Ne dooth unto an oold man noon harm now,
Namoore than that ye wolde men did to yow   460
In agë, if that ye so longe abyde.
And God be with yow, where ye go[20] or ryde!
I moote[21] go thider as I have to go."
     "Nay, olde cherl, by God thou shalt nat so,"
Seyde this oother hasardour anon;   465
"Thou partest nat so lightly, by Seint John!
Thou spak right now of thilke traytour Deeth,
That in this contree alle oure freendes sleeth.
Have heer my trouthe, as thou art his espye;[22]
Telle where he is, or thou shalt it abye,[23]   470
By God and by the hooly sacrement!
For, soothly, thou art oon of his assent
To sleen us yonge folk, thou false theef!"
     "Now, sires," quod he, "if that ye be so leef[24]
To fynde Deeth, turne up this croked wey;   475
For in that grove I lafte hym, by my fey,[25]
Under a tree; and there he wole abyde;

---

[91] Last night.   [92] Very drunk.   [93] Secret.
[94] During this epidemic (of the bubonic plague).
[95] Tavernkeeper.   [96] Hence.   [97] Servant.
[98] Yea, by the arms of Christ!   [99] Worthy.

[1] All of one mind.   [2] To.   [3] I.e., sworn brother.
[4] Catch.   [5] Greeted.   [6] I.e., protect.
[7] Churl, fellow.   [8] I.e., the Devil take you!

[9] Why art thou all wrapped up?   [10] India.
[11] Caitiff, wretch.   [12] Dear.
[13] Exchange my clothes-chest.
[14] Haircloth, hair shirt, the garment of penance; here, a shroud.
[15] Withered.   [16] Unless.   [17] Cf. Leviticus 19:32.
[18] In the presence of.   [19] Counsel.   [20] Walk.
[21] Must.   [22] Spy.   [23] Pay for it, suffer.
[24] Lief, eager.   [25] Faith.

Noght for youre boost he wole him no thyng hyde.
Se ye that ook? Right there ye shal hym fynde.
God save yow, that boghte agayn mankynde,   480
And yow amende!" thus seyde this olde man.

    And everich of thise riotoures ran
Til he cam to that tree, and ther they founde
Of floryns[26] fyne of gold ycoyned rounde
Wel ny an eighte busshels, as hem thoughte.[27]   485
No lenger thannë after Deeth they soughte;
But ech of hem so glad was of that sighte,
For that the floryns been so faire and brighte,
That doun they sette hem by this precious hoord.
The worste of hem, he spak the firste word.   490
    "Bretheren," quod he, "taak keep[28] what I seye;
My wit is greet, though that I bourde[29] and pleye.
This tresor hath Fortune unto us yiven,
In myrthe and joliftee oure lyf to lyven;
And lightly as it comth so wol we spende.   495
Ey, Goddes precious dignitee! who wende[30]
Today that we sholde han so fair a grace?
But myghte this gold be caried fro this place
Hoom to myn hous, or elles unto youres—
For wel ye woot that al this gold is oures—   500
Thanne were we in heigh felicitee.
But trewely, by daye it may nat bee;
Men wolde seyn that we were theves stronge,[31]
And for oure owene tresor doon us honge.[32]
This tresor moste ycaried be by nyghte   505
As wisely and as slyly as it myghte.
Wherfore I rede that cut among us alle
Be drawe, and lat se wher the cut wol falle;
And he that hath the cut with herte blithe
Shal renne to the towne, and that ful swithe,[33]   510
And brynge us breed and wyn ful prively;
And two of us shul kepen subtilly
This tresor wel; and if he wol nat tarie,
Whan it is nyght we wol this tresor carie,
By oon assent, where-as us thynketh best."   515
    That oon of hem the cut broghte in his fest,[34]
And bad hem drawe, and looke where it wol falle.
And it fil[35] on the yongeste of hem alle,
And forth toward the toun he wente anon.
    And al so soonë as that he was gon,   520
That oon of hem spak thus unto that oother:
"Thow knowest wel thou art my sworen brother;
Thy profit wol I telle thee anon.
Thou woost wel that oure felawe is agon;

And heere is gold, and that ful greet plentee,   525
That shal departed[36] been among us thre;
But nathelees, if I kan shape it so
That it departed were among us two,
Hadde I nat doon a freendes torn[37] to thee?"
    That oother answerde: "I noot[38] hou that may be;   530
He woot how that the gold is with us tweye.
What shal we doon? What shal we to hym seye?"
    "Shal it be conseil?"[39] seyde the firste shrewe,[40]
"And I shal tellen in a wordes fewe
What we shal doon, and bryngen it wel aboute."   535
    "I graunte," quod that oother, "out of doute,
That, by my trouthe, I shal thee nat biwreye."[41]
    "Now," quod the firste, "thou woost wel we be tweye;
And two of us shul strenger be than oon.
Look whan that he is set, that right anoon[42]   540
Arys as though thou woldest with hym pleye,
And I shal ryve hym thurgh the sydes tweye
Whil that thou strogelest with hym as in game;
And with thy daggere looke thou do the same.
And thanne shal al this gold departed be,   545
My deere freend, bitwixen me and thee.
Thanne may we bothe oure lustes all fulfille,
And pleye at dees right at oure owene wille."
And thus acorded been thise shrewes tweye
To sleen the thridde, as ye han herd me seye.   550
    This yongeste, which that wente unto the toun,
Ful ofte in herte he rolleth up and doun
The beautee of thise floryns newe and brighte.
"O Lord," quod he, "if so were that I myghte
Have al this tresor to myself allone,   555
Ther is no man that lyveth under the trone
Of God that sholde lyve so murye as I!"
And atte laste the feend, oure enemy,
Putte in his thought that he sholde poyson beye,[43]
With which he myghte sleen his felawes tweye;   560
For-why[44] the feend foond hym in swich lyvynge
That he hadde leve[45] hym to sorwe brynge.
For this was outrely his fulle entente,
To sleen hem bothe and nevere to repente.
And forth he gooth—no lenger wolde he tarie—   565
Into the toun unto a pothecarie,
And preydë hym that he hym wolde selle
Som poyson, that he myghte his rattes quelle;[46]
And eek ther was a polcat in his hawe,[47]
That, as he seyde, his capons hadde yslawe;[48]   570
And fayn he wolde wreke[49] hym, if he myghte,
On vermyn that destroyed[50] hym by nyghte.

[26] The English florin was worth about $1.65; in purchasing power it was the equivalent of twenty-five or thirty times that in our currency.   [27] It seemed to them.   [28] Heed.
[29] Jest.   [30] Would have supposed.
[31] Violent; i.e., highwaymen.   [32] Cause us to be hanged.
[33] Quickly.   [34] Fist.   [35] Fell.

[36] Divided.
[37] Turn, act.   [38] Ne wot, know not.   [39] Secret.
[40] Rogue.   [41] Betray.   [42] At once.   [43] Buy.
[44] Because.   [45] Permission (from God).   [46] Kill.
[47] Within his hedge; i.e., in his yard.   [48] Slain.
[49] Wreak, avenge.   [50] Harassed.

The pothecarie answerde: "And thou shalt have
A thyng that, al so God my soule save,
In al this world ther is no creature   575
That eten or dronken hath of this confiture[51]
Noght but the montance of a corn[52] of whete
That he ne shal his lif anon forlete;[53]
Ye, sterve[54] he shal, and that in lasse while
Than thou wolt goon a-paas[55] nat but a mile,   580
This poyson is so strong and violent."

   This cursed man hath in his hond yhent
This poyson in a box, and sith he ran
Into the nexte strete unto a man
And borwed of hym large botels thre.   585
And in the two his poyson poured he;
The thridde he kepte clene for his owene drynke,
For al the nyght he shoope hym for to swynke[56]
In cariynge of the gold out of that place.
And whan this riotour—with sory grace!—   590
Hadde filled with wyn his grete botels thre,
To his felawes agayn repaireth he.

   What nedeth it to sermone of it moore?
For right as they hadde cast[57] his deeth bifoore,
Right so they han hym slayn, and that anon.   595
   And whan that this was doon, thus spak that oon:
"Now lat us sitte and drynke, and make us merie,
And afterward we wol his body berie."
And with that word it happed hym par cas[58]
To take the botel ther the poyson was,   600
And drank, and yaf his felawe drynke also;
For which anon they storven[59] bothe two.

   But certes, I suppose that Avycen[60]
Wroot nevere in no canon[61] ne in no fen[62]
Mo wonder signes[63] of empoisonyng   605
Than hadde thise wrecches two er hir endyng.
Thus ended been thise homycides two,
And eek the false empoysonere also.

   O cursed synne, of alle cursednesse!
O traytours homycide! O wikkednesse!   610
O glotonye, luxurie, and hasardrye!
Thou blasphemour of Crist with vileynye
And othes grete, of usage and of pride!
Allas, mankynde! how may it bitide
That to thy Creatour, which that the wroghte,   615
And with his precious herte-blood thee boghte,
Thou art so fals and so unkynde,[64] allas?

   Now, goode men, God foryeve yow youre trespas,
And ware yow fro the synne of avarice!

Myn hooly pardon may yow alle warice,[65]   620
So that ye offre nobles,[66] or sterlynges,[67]
Or elles silver broches, spoones, rynges.
Boweth youre heed under this hooly bulle!
Com up, ye wyves; offreth of youre wolle![68]
Youre names I entre heer in my rolle anon;   625
In-to the blisse of hevene shul ye gon.
I yow assoille[69] by myn heigh power,
Yow that wol offre, as clene and eek as cleer
As ye were born.—
                                 "And lo, sires, thus I preche.
And Jesu Crist, that is oure soules leche,[70]   630
So graunte yow his pardon to receyve,
For that is best; I wol yow nat deceyve.[71]

   "But, sires, o[72] word forgat I in my tale:
I have relikes and pardon in my male,[73]
As faire as any man in Engelond,   635
Whiche were me yeven by the popes hond.
If any of yow wole, of devocion,
Offren, and han myn absolucion,
Com forth anon, and kneleth heere adoun,
And mekely receyveth my pardoun;   640
Or elles taketh pardon as ye wende,
Al newe and fressh at every miles ende,
So that ye offren, alwey newe and newe,
Nobles or pens whiche that be goode and trewe.

   "It is an honour to everich[74] that is heer   645
That ye mowe have a suffisant[75] pardoneer
T'assoille yow, in contree as ye ryde,
For aventures whiche that may bityde.
Paraventure[76] ther may fallen oon or two
Doun of his hors and breke his nekke atwo.   650
Looke which a seuretee is it to yow alle
That I am in youre felaweshipe yfalle,
That may assoille yow, bothe moore and lasse,[77]
Whan that the soule shal fro the body passe.
I rede that oure Hoost heere shal bigynne,   655
For he is moost envoluped[78] in synne.

   "Com forth, sire Hoost, and offre first anon,
And thou shalt kisse my relikes everychon—
Ye, for a grote![79] Unbokele anon thy purs!"

   "Nay, nay," quod he, "thanne have I Cristes curs!   660
Lat be," quod he; "it shal nat be, so theech![80]

[51] Mixture.   [52] The amount of a grain.   [53] Leave, give up.
[54] Die.   [55] Walk at a footpace.   [56] Planned to labor.
[57] Plotted.   [58] By chance.   [59] Died.
[60] Avicenna, the great Arabian medical authority of the eleventh
century.   [61] Rule of procedure.
[62] Section (of his book).   [63] Symptoms.   [64] Unnatural.

[65] Cure.
[66] Their value was the same as the florin's. See note 26, above.
[67] Silver pennies.   [68] Wool.   [69] Absolve.
[70] Leech, physician.
[71] The Pardoner's tongue has been loosened by drink, but the
intoxication with which he boasts of his rascality is due to his
pride in it. Now, for a moment, his better nature asserts itself;
but in the next line he reverts to his shameless mendacity.
[72] One.   [73] Bag.   [74] Everyone.
[75] Sufficient, adequate.   [76] Perhaps.   [77] High and low.
[78] Enveloped.   [79] Groat, a trivial coin.
[80] So may I thrive!

Thou woldest make me kisse thyn olde breech
And swere it were a relyk of a seint,
Though it were with thy fundement depeint![81]
But, by the croys[82] which that Seint Eleyne fond, 665
I wolde I hadde thy coillons[83] in myn hond
In stide of relikes or of seintuarie.[84]
Lat kutte hem of:[85] I wol thee helpe hem carie;
They shul be shryned in an hogges toord!"[86]

This Pardoner answerde nat a word; 670
So wrooth he was, no word ne wolde he seye.

"Now," quod oure Hoost, "I wol no lenger pleye
With thee, ne with noon oother angry man."

But right anon the worthy Knyght bigan,
Whan that he saugh that al the peple lough:[87] 675
"Namoore of this, for it is right ynough!
Sire Pardoner, be glad and myrie of cheere!
And ye, sire Hoost, that been to me so deere,
I prey yow that ye kisse the Pardoner.
And, Pardoner, I prey thee drawe thee neer;[88] 680
And as we diden, lat us laughe and pleye."
Anon they kiste, and ryden forth hir weye.

Heere is ended the Pardoners Tale.

[*Here ends, also, Fragment VI.* THE SHIPMAN'S TALE *opens the Seventh Fragment. It recounts the beguiling of a merchant by his wife, who is enamored of a monk. She fools her husband with complete success, but the monk fools her. This fabliau is followed by* THE PRIORESS'S TALE, *which in subject and tone is at the opposite pole. It relates one of the numerous medieval legends of Christian children murdered by Jews. It is an expression of un-reasoning credulity and prejudice, but it is exquisitely told. This story belongs to the genre of Miracles of Our Lady, for the Virgin interposes and restores her little devotee temporarily to life while he sings her praise. The following excerpt illustrates Chaucer's use of the seven-line stanza called rime royal (riming ababbcc), which he chose for four of the Canterbury tales and also for* The Parliament of Fowls *and* Troilus and Criseyde.]

[from THE PRIORESS'S TALE]

. . . This litel child his litel book lernynge,
As he sat in the scole at his prymer,[1]
He *Alma Redemptoris*[2] herde synge,
As children lerned hire antiphoner;[3]
And as he dorste, he drough hym ner[4] and ner, 5

And herkned ay the wordes and the noote,
Til he the firste vers koude al by rote.[5]

Noght wiste he what this Latyn was to seye,
For he so yong and tendre was of age;
But on a day his felawe gan he preye 10
T'expounden hym this song in his langage
Or telle hym why this song was in usage.
This preyde he hym to construe and declare
Ful often tyme upon his knowes[6] bare.

His felawe, which that elder was than he, 15
Answerde hym thus: "This song, I have herd seye,
Was maked of oure blisful Lady free,[7]
Hire to salue,[8] and eek hire for to preye
To been oure help and socour whan we deye.
I kan namoore expounde in this mateere; 20
I lerne song, I kan but smal grammeere."

"And is this song maked in reverence
Of Cristes mooder?" seyde this innocent.
"Now certes I wol do my diligence
To konne it al er Cristemasse is went; 25
Though that I for my prymer shal be shent,[9]
And shal be beten thries in an houre,
I wol it konne oure Lady for to honoure."

His felawe taughte hym homward prively,
Fro day to day, til he koude it by rote; 30
And thanne he song it wel and boldely
Fro word to word, acordynge with the note.
Twies a day it passed thurgh his throte,
To scoleward and homward whan he wente;
On Cristes mooder set was his entente. 35

As I have seyd, thurghout the Juërie[10]
This litel child, as he cam to and fro,
Ful murily than wolde he synge and crie
O *Alma Redemptoris* everemo.
The swetnesse hath his herte perced so 40
Of Cristes mooder that, to hire to preye,
He kan nat stynte[11] of syngyng by the weye.

* * * * * * * *

Bihoold the murye wordes of the Hoost to Chaucer.

Whan seyd was al this miracle, every man
As sobre was that wonder was to se,
Til that oure Hooste japen[12] tho[13] bigan;
And thanne at erst[14] he looked upon me,

---

[81] Daubed with thy excrement.
[82] Cross; i.e., the True Cross, said to have been found by St. Helen, the mother of the emperor Constantine.
[83] Cullions, testicles. [84] Sacred objects.
[85] Let them be cut off! [86] Enshrined in a hog's excrement.
[87] Laughed. [88] Nearer. [1] Prayer book.
[2] The anthem beginning *Alma Redemptoris mater*, gracious mother of the Redeemer. [3] Anthem book. [4] Nearer.

[5] Knew by heart. [6] Knees. [7] Noble. [8] Salute.
[9] Disgraced, scolded. [10] Jews' quarter, ghetto.
[11] Cease. [12] To joke. [13] Then. [14] First.

And seyde thus: "What man artow?" quod he.   5
"Thou lookest as thou woldest fynde an hare,[15]
For evere upon the ground I se thee stare.

"Approche neer, and looke up murily.—
Now war yow,[16] sires, and lat this man have place!
He in the waast is shape as wel as I;[17]   10
This were a popet[18] in an arm t'enbrace
For any womman smal and fair of face.
He semeth elvyssh[19] by his contenaunce,
For unto no wight dooth he daliance.[20]

"Sey now somwhat, syn[21] oother folk han sayd.   15
Telle us a tale of myrthe, and that anon!"[22]
    "Hooste," quod I, "ne beth nat yvele apayd,[23]
For oother tale certes kan I noon
But of a rym I lerned longe agoon."
    "Ye, that is good," quod he. "Now shul we heere   20
Som deyntee[24] thyng, me thynketh by his cheere."

[CHAUCER'S TALE OF SIR THOPAS *is a burlesque of the metrical romance, with a ludicrous knight for a hero. He does not get very far with it before he is vigorously called to a halt.*]

Heere the Hoost stynteth Chaucer of his Tale of Thopas.

"Namoore of this, for Goddes dignitee!"
Quod oure Hooste, "for thou makest me
So wery of thy verray lewednesse[25]
That, also wisly[26] God my soule blesse,
Min eres aken of thy drasty[27] speche.   5
Now swich a rym the devel I biteche![28]
This may wel be rym dogerel," quod he.
    "Why so?" quod I; "why wiltow lette[29] me
Moore of my tale than another man,
Syn that it is the beste tale I kan?"   10
    "By God," quod he, "for pleynly, at a word,
Thy drasty ryming is nat worth a toord![30]
Thou doost noght elles but despendest tyme.
Sire, at o word, thou shalt no lenger ryme.
Lat se wher thou kanst tellen aught in geeste,[31]   15
Or telle in prose somwhat, at the leeste,
In which ther be som murthe or som doctryne."[32]

"Gladly," quod I, "by Goddes sweete pyne![33]
I wol yow telle a litel thyng in prose. . . ."

[CHAUCER'S TALE OF MELIBEE *turns out to be no "litel thyng" but it does prove prosy in the worst sense of the word. Its moralizing may have pleased more in the fourteenth century than in the twentieth; at any rate, it draws a vigorous response from the Host.*]

Whan ended was my tale of Melibee
And of Prudence and hire benignytee,
Oure Hooste seyde, "As I am feithful man,
And by that precious corpus Madrian,[34]
I hadde levere than a barel ale   5
That Goodelief, my wyf, hadde herd this tale.
For she nys no thyng of swich pacience
As was this Melibeus wyf Prudence.
By Goddes bones, whan I bete my knaves,
She bryngeth me forth the grete clobbed staves,   10
And crieth, 'Slee the dogges everichoon,
And brek hem, bothe bak and every boon!'
And if that any neighebore of myne
Wol nat in chirche to my wyf enclyne,
Or be so hardy to hire to trespace,   15
Whan she comth home, she rampeth in my face,
And crieth, 'False coward, wrek[35] thy wyf!
By corpus bones,[36] I wol have thy knyf,
And thou shalt have my distaf and go spynne!'
Fro day to nyght right thus she wol bigynne.   20
'Allas,' she seith, 'that evere I was shape[37]
To wedden a milksope or a coward ape,
That wol been overlad with[38] every wight!
Thou darst nat stonden by thy wyves right!'
    "This is my lif but-if[39] that I wol fighte.   25
And out at dore anon I moot me dighte,[40]
Or elles I am but lost, but-if that I
Be lik a wilde leon, fool-hardy.
I woot wel, she wol do me slee[41] som day
Som neighebore and thanne go my way;[42]   30
For I am perilous with knyf in honde,
Al be it that I dar hire nat withstonde;
For she is byg in armes, by my feith!
That shal he fynde that hire mysdooth or seith."

[*The Host then demands a story from the Monk, on whose unmonkish appearance he expends much jocularity. If he expects a*

[15] By following its tracks.   [16] Observe.
[17] From these lines and another in his "Lenvoy a Scogan," it appears that Chaucer was a bit fat.   [18] Puppet, dainty one.
[19] Elfish, as if of another world.
[20] He chats with no one. This reticence is hardly consistent with Chaucer's account of his easy mingling with the pilgrims at the Tabard, but the Host seeks to stir up mirth after the sober tale of the Prioress.   [21] Since.   [22] At once.
[23] Ill satisfied.   [24] Rare, excellent.   [25] Ignorance.
[26] As surely (as I would have).   [27] Worthless.
[28] I commit to the Devil.   [29] Stop.
[30] Turd, piece of dung.
[31] I.e., in the proper style of a gest or tale of adventure.
[32] Some entertainment or some instruction.

[33] I.e., Christ's suffering on the Cross.
[34] The body of Madrian, apparently a saint invented by the Host.
    —*Feithful* (line 3) = of the Christian faith.
[35] Avenge.   [36] Another blundering oath.   [37] Made.
[38] Overled by, browbeaten by.   [39] Unless.
[40] I must betake myself.   [41] Make me slay.
[42] Into exile or outlawry, or to the gallows.

worldly tale from him, however, he is disappointed, for THE
MONK'S TALE *is a series of bald and dismal recitals of what the
Middle Ages called "tragedies"—stories of celebrated falls from
high estate. At last the Knight protests; and the Monk gives way
to the* NUN'S PRIEST, *whose story ends the Seventh Fragment
with one of Chaucer's best tales. This example of the beast epic
is a masterpiece of the mock-heroic style.*]

The prologe of the Nonnes Preestes Tale.

"Hoo!" quod the Knyght, "good sire, namoore of this!
That[1] ye han seyd is right ynough, ywis,[2]
And muchel moore; for litel hevynesse[3]
Is right ynough to muche folk, I gesse.
I seye for me, it is a greet disese,[4]   5
Where-as men han been in greet welthe and ese,
To heeren of hire sodeyn fal, allas!
And the contrarie is joye and greet solas,
As whan a man hath ben in poure estaat,
And clymbeth up, and wexeth fortunat,   10
And there abideth in prosperitee—
Swich thyng is gladsom, as it thynketh me,
And of swich thyng were goodly for to telle."
    "Ye," quod oure Hooste, "by Seint Poules[5] belle,
Ye seye right sooth. This Monk he clappeth[6] lowde.   15
He spak how Fortune covered with a clowde
I noot[7] nevere what; and also of a tragedie
Right now ye herde; and, pardee,[8] no remedie
It is for to biwaille ne compleyne
That that is doon; and als[9] it is a peyne,   20
As ye han seyd, to heere of hevynesse.
    "Sire Monk, namoore of this, so God yow blesse!
Youre tale anoyeth all this compaignye.
Swich talkyng is nat worth a boterflye,
For therinne is ther no desport ne game.   25
Wherfore, sire Monk, or Daun[10] Piers,[11] by youre name,
I pray yow hertely telle us somwhat elles;
For sikerly,[12] nere[13] clynkyng of youre belles,
That on youre bridel hange on every syde,
By hevene Kyng, that for us alle dyde,   30
I sholde er this han fallen doun for sleepe,
Althogh the slough had never been so deepe.
Thanne hadde your talë al be toold in veyn;
For certeinly, as that thise clerkes seyn,
Where-as[14] a man may have noon audience,   35
Noght helpeth it to tellen his sentence.[15]

---

[1] What.
[2] Certainly.   [3] Sadness.   [4] Discomfort, unpleasantness.
[5] St. Paul's, the cathedral in London.   [6] Chatters.
[7] Know not.
[8] Literally, by God; actually, a mild asseveration: truly, verily.
[9] Also.   [10] Don, sir; from the Latin *dominus*.
[11] Peter.   [12] Surely.   [13] Were it not for.
[14] Where, i.e., when.   [15] Meaning.

And wel I woot the substance is in me,
If any thyng shal wel reported be.
Sir, sey somwhat of huntyng, I yow preye."
    "Nay," quod this Monk, "I have no lust to pleye.   40
Now lat another telle, as I have toold."
    Thanne spak oure Hoost with rude speche and boold,
And seyde unto the Nonnes Preest anon:
"Com neer, thou preest; com hyder, thou Sir John![16]
Telle us swich thyng as may oure hertes glade.   45
Be blithe, though thou ryde upon a jade.[17]
What thogh thyn hors be bothe foule and lene?
If he wol serve thee, rekke nat a bene.[18]
Looke that thyn herte be murie everemo."
    "Yis,[19] sir," quod he; "yis, Hoost, so moot I go;   50
But[20] I be myrie, ywis I wol be blamed."
And right anon his tale he hath attamed;[21]
And thus he seyde unto us everichon,
This sweete preest, this goodly man, Sir John.

[THE NUN'S PRIEST'S TALE]

*Heere bigynneth the Nonnes Preestes Tale of the Cok and Hen,
Chauntecleer and Pertelote.*

A poure wydwe somdel stape[22] in age
Was whilom dwellyng in a narwe cotage
Beside a grove, stondynge in a dale.
This wydwe of which I telle yow my tale,
Syn thilke[23] day that she was last a wyf,   5
In pacience ladde a ful symple lyf,
For litel was hir catel and hir rente.[24]
By housbondrie of swich as God hire sente
She foond[25] hirself and eek hire doghtren two.
Thre large sowes hadde she and namo,   10
Three keen,[26] and eek a sheep that highte Malle.[27]
Ful sooty was hir bour and eek hire halle,[28]
In which she eet ful many a sklendre meel.
Of poynaunt sauce hir neded never a deel;
No deyntee morsel passed thurgh hir throte,   15
Hir diete was accordant to hir cote.
Repleccioun[29] ne made hire nevere sik;
Attempree[30] diete was al hir phisik,
And exercise, and hertes suffisaunce.[31]

---

[16] A common nickname for a priest, but here apparently the
actual name also (see line 54).   [17] Poor horse.
[18] Care not a bean.   [19] Yes indeed.   [20] Unless.
[21] Broached, begun.   [22] Somewhat advanced (stepped).
[23] That same.   [24] Her property (chattels) and her income.
[25] Kept, provided for.   [26] Kine, cows.
[27] Was called Moll.
[28] The main dining-living room and the private apartments of a
great house. The use of *hall* and *bower* for the widow's humble
dwelling is humorous and ironical.   [29] Repletion, surfeit.
[30] Temperate, moderate.   [31] Sufficiency, contentment.

The goute lette hire nothyng for to daunce,[32]   20
N'apoplexie shente[33] nat hir heed.
No wyn ne drank she, neither whit ne reed;
Hir bord was served moost with whit and blak—
Milk and broun breed, in which she foond no lak,
Seynd[34] bacon, and somtyme an ey or tweye;[35]   25
For she was, as it were, a maner deye.[36]

A yeerd she hadde, enclosed al aboute
With stikkes, and a drye dych withoute,
In which she hadde a cok, hight Chauntecleer.
In al the land of crowyng nas his peer: 30
His voys was murier than the murie orgon
On messedayes that in the chirche gon;[37]
Wel sikerer[38] was his crowyng in his logge[39]
Than is a clokke or an abbey orlogge.[40]
By nature he knew eche ascencioun   35
Of the equynoxial[41] in thilke toun;
For whan degrees fiftene weren ascended,
Thanne crew he, that it myghte nat been amended.[42]
His coomb was redder than the fyn coral,
And batailled as it were a castel wal;   40
His byle was blak, and as the jeet it shoon;
Lyk asure were his legges and his toon;[43]
His nayles whiter than the lylye flour;
And lyk the burned gold was his colour.

   This gentil cok hadde in his governaunce   45
Sevene hennes for to doon al his plesaunce,
Whiche were his sustres and his paramours,
And wonder lyk to hym as of colours;
Of whiche the faireste-hewed on hir throte
Was cleped faire damoysele Pertelote.   50
Curteys she was, discreet, and debonaire,[44]
And compaignable, and bar hyrself so faire,
Syn thilke day that she was seven nyght oold,
That trewely she hath the herte in hoold[45]
Of Chauntecleer, loken in every lith.[46]   55
He loved hire so that wel was hym therwith.[47]
But swiche a joye was it to here hem synge,
Whan that the brighte sonne bigan to sprynge,

In sweete accord, "My lief is faren in londe!"[48]
For thilke tyme, as I have understonde,   60
Beestes and briddes koude speke and synge.
   And so bifel that in the dawenynge,
As Chauntecleer among hise wyves alle
Sat on his perche, that was in the halle,
And next hym sat this faire Pertelote,   65
This Chauntecleer gan gronen in his throte
As man that in his dreem is drecched[49] soore.
And whan that Pertelote thus herde hym roore,
She was agast, and seyde, "O herte deere,
What eyleth yow, to grone in this manere?   70
Ye been a verray sleper! fy! for shame!"
   And he answerde and seyde thus, "Madame,
I pray yow that ye take it nat agrief.[50]
By God, me thoughte I was in swich meschief,[51]
Right now, that yet myn herte is soore afright.   75
Now God," quod he, "my swevene recche aright,[52]
And kepe my body out of foul prisoun!
Me mette[53] how that I romed up and doun
Withinne our yeerd, wheer-as I saugh a beest,
Was lyk an hound, and wolde han maad areest   80
Upon my body, and han had me deed.
His colour was bitwixe yelow and reed,
And tipped was his tayl and bothe hise eeris
With blak, unlyk the remenant of his heeris;
His snowte smal, with glowynge eyen tweye.   85
Yet of his look, for feere, almoost I deye.
This caused me my gronyng, doutelees."
   "Avoy!"[54] quod she, "fy on yow, hertelees![55]
Allas!" quod she, "for, by that God above,
Now han ye lost myn herte and al my love!   90
I kan nat love a coward, by my feith;
For certes, what-so any womman seith,
We alle desiren, if it myghte bee,
To han housbondes hardy, wise, and free,[56]
And secree,[57] and no nygard, ne no fool,   95
Ne hym that is agast of every tool,[58]
Ne noon avauntour,[59] by that God above!
How dorste ye seyn, for shame, unto youre love
That anythyng myghte make yow aferd?
Have ye no mannes herte, and han a berd?   100
Allas! and konne ye been agast of swevenys?
Nothyng, God woot, but vanitee[60] in swevene is.
Swevenes engendren of[61] repleccions,[62]

---

32 The gout in no way kept her from dancing.   33 Injured.
34 Singed, broiled.   35 An egg or two.
36 A sort of dairywoman.
37 Go, agreeing with *orgon*, regularly plural in Middle English, probably because of the number of pipes.
38 Much more certain.   39 Lodge.
40 Horologe, timepiece. Some elaborate ones showed the movement of the planets, as well as the time of day.
41 The equinoctial circle of the heavens, made by extending the plane of the earth's equator. According to the old, geocentric astronomy, it made a complete revolution every twenty-four hours. Thus fifteen degrees "ascended" every hour, and the cock crowed every hour on the hour.
42 It could not be bettered.   43 Toes.   44 Gentle.
45 In (her) keeping.   46 Locked in every limb.
47 It was well with him on that account.

48 My dear has gone to the country. This is the first line of a song (it has survived) of lament for the beloved's absence.
49 Vexed.   50 Amiss.   51 Misfortune.
52 My dream interpret favorably.   53 I dreamed.   54 Fie!
55 Faintheart!   56 Liberal.   57 Trusty.   58 Weapon.
59 Boaster (of favors granted by women).
60 Emptiness, nothingness.   61 Engender from, result from.
62 Repletions, eating or drinking too much.

And ofte of fume[63] and of compleccions,[64]
Whan humours been to habundant in a wight.   105
Certes, this dreem which ye han met tonyght[65]
Cometh of the greete superfluytee
Of youre rede colera,[66] pardee,
Which causeth folk to dreden in hir dremes
Of arwes,[67] and of fyr with rede lemes,[68]   110
Of rede beestes that they wol hem byte,
Of contekes,[69] and of whelpes[70] grete and lyte—
Right as the humour of malencolie
Causeth ful many a man in sleepe to crie
For feere of blake beres, or boles[71] blake,   115
Or elles blake develes wole hem take.
Of othere humours koude I telle also
That werken many a man in sleepe ful wo,
But I wol passe as lightly as I kan.
    "Lo, Caton,[72] which that was so wys a man,   120
Seyde he nat thus—'Ne do no fors of[73] dremes'?
    "Now, sire," quod she, "whan ye flee fro the bemes,[74]
For Goddes love, as[75] taak som laxatyf!
Up[76] peril of my soule and of my lyf,
I conseille yow the beste, I wol nat lye,   125
That bothe of colere and of malencolye[77]
Ye purge yow; and, for ye shal nat[78] tarie,
Though in this toun is noon apothecarie,
I shal myself to herbes techen yow
That shul been for youre hele[79] and for youre prow.[80]   130
And in oure yeerd tho[81] herbes shal I fynde
The whiche han of hire propretee by kynde[82]
To purge yow bynethe and eek above.
Foryet nat this, for Goddes owene love!
Ye been ful coleryk of compleccion.   135
Ware the sonne in his ascencion
Ne fynde yow nat repleet of humours hoote.
And if it do, I dar wel leye a grote[83]
That ye shul have a fevere terciane,[84]
Or an agu that may be youre bane.   140
A day or two ye shul have digestyves
Of wormes, er ye take youre laxatyves

---

[63] Vapor. It supposedly rose from the stomach into the brain.
[64] Temperaments, the mixtures of humors in men's systems. On
    the four humors, see p. 119, note 32, above.
[65] Last night, this past night.
[66] Choler, yellow bile.
[67] Arrows.   [68] Flames.   [69] Conflicts.   [70] Dogs.
[71] Bulls.
[72] Dionysius Cato, supposed author of the popular collection of
    maxims, Disticha.   [73] Attach no importance to.
[74] I.e., fly down from your roost.
[75] A meaningless particle, used with the imperative.   [76] On.
[77] Of yellow and of black bile.
[78] In order that you may not.
[79] Health.   [80] Profit.   [81] Those.   [82] By nature.
[83] Bet a groat (a trivial coin).
[84] Tertian fever recurred every third day. It was thought to be due
    to an excess of both kinds of bile.

Of lawriol, centaure, and fumetere,[85]
Or elles of ellebor[86] that groweth there,
Of katapucë,[87] or of gaitrys beryis,[88]   145
Of herbe yve[89] growyng in oure yeerd, ther mery is.[90]
Pekke hem up right as they growe, and ete hem yn!
Be myrie, housbonde, for youre fader kyn!
Dredeth no dreem! I kan sey yow namoore."
    "Madame," quod he, "graunt mercy[91] of youre
        loore!   150
But nathelees, as touchyng Daun Catoun,
That hath of wysdom swich a greet renoun,
Though that he bad no dremes for to drede,
By God, men may in olde bookes rede
Of many a man moore of auctorite   155
Than evere Caton was, so moot I thee,[92]
That al the revers seyn of this sentence,[93]
And han wel founden by experience
That dremes been significacions
As wel of joye as of tribulacions   160
That folk enduren in this lif present.
Ther nedeth make of this noon argument;
The verray preeve[94] sheweth it in dede.
    "Oon of the gretteste auctours that men rede[95]
Seith thus: that whilom two felawes wente   165
On pilgrimage, in a ful good entente,[96]
And happed so they coomen in a toun
Wher-as ther was swich congregacioun
Of peple and eek so streit[97] of herbergage[98]
That they ne founde as muche as o cotage   170
In which they bothe myghte logged bee.
Wherfore they mosten of necessitee,
As for that nyght, departen compaignye.
And ech of hem gooth to his hostelrye,
And took his loggyng as it wolde falle.[99]   175
That oon[1] of hem was logged in a stalle,
Fer[2] in a yeerd, with oxen of the plough;
That oother man was logged wel ynough,
As was his aventure or his fortune,
That us governeth alle as in commune.   180
    "And so bifel that, longe er it were day,
This man mette[3] in his bed, ther-as he lay,
How that his felawe gan upon hym calle
And seyde, 'Allas! for in an oxes stalle
This nyght I shal be mordred ther I lye.   185

---

[85] Spurge-laurel, centaury, and fumitory.   [86] Hellebore.
[87] Caper-spurge.   [88] Dogwood berries.   [89] Ground ivy.
[90] Where it is pleasant—referring to the herb garden, not to the
    nauseous "herbe yve."   [91] Gramercy, thanks.
[92] So may I thrive.   [93] Opinion.
[94] The true test (proof), i.e., experience.
[95] Both Cicero and Valerius Maximus tell this story.
[96] With very good intentions.   [97] I.e., crowded.
[98] Harborage, lodgings.   [99] Chance.   [1] The one, one.
[2] Far.   [3] Dreamed.

Now helpe me, deere brother, or I dye!
In alle haste com to me!' he sayde.
    "This man out of his sleepe for feere abrayde;[4]
But whan that he was wakened of his sleep,
He turned hym and took of it no keep.[5]   190
Hym thoughte his dreem nas but[6] a vanitee.
Thus twies in his slepyng dremed hee;
And atte thridde tyme yet his felawe
Cam, as hym thoughte, and seide, 'I am now slawe.[7]
Bihoold my bloody woundes depe and wyde!   195
Arys up erly in the morwe tyde,
And at the west gate of the toun,' quod he,
'A carte ful of donge ther shaltow se,
In which my body is hid ful prively.
Do thilke carte arresten boldely.   200
My gold caused my mordre, sooth to sayn.'
And tolde hym every point how he was slayn,
With a ful pitous[8] face, pale of hewe.
    "And truste wel, his dreem he foond ful trewe;
For on the morwe, as soone as it was day,   205
To his felawes in he took the way;
And whan that he cam to this oxes stalle,
After his felawe he bigan to calle.
    "The hostiler answerede hym anon,
And seyde, 'Sire, your felawe is agon;   210
As soone as day he wente out of the toun.'
    "This man gan fallen in suspecioun,
Remembrynge on hise dremes that he mette,
And forth he gooth—no lenger wolde he lette—[9]
Unto the west gate of the toun, and fond   215
A dong-carte, wente as it were to donge lond,
That was arrayed in that same wise
As ye han herd the dede man devyse.[10]
And with an hardy herte he gan to crye
Vengeance and justice of this felonye.   220
'My felawe mordred is this same nyght,
And in this carte heere he lith gapyng upright![11]
I crye out on the ministres,'[12] quod he,
'That sholden kepe and reulen this citee.
Harrow![13] allas! heere lith my felawe slayn!'   225
    "What sholde I moore unto this tale sayn?
The peple out-sterte, and caste the cart to grounde,
And in the myddel of the dong they founde
The dede man, that mordred was al newe.
    "O blisful God, that art so just and trewe,   230
Lo, how that thou biwreyest[14] mordre alway!
Mordre wol out, that se we day by day.

Mordre is so wlatsom[15] and abhomynable
To God, that is so just and resonable,
That he ne wol nat suffre it heled[16] be,   235
Though it abyde a yeer or two or thre.
Mordre wol out, this[17] my conclusioun!
    "And right anon[18] ministres of that toun
Han hent[19] the carter and so soore hym pyned,[20]
And eek the hostiler so soore engyned,[21]   240
That they biknewe[22] hire wikkednesse anon,
And were anhanged by the nekke-bon.
    "Heere may men seen that dremes been to drede.
And certes in the same book I rede,
Right in the nexte chapitre after this—   245
I gabbe[23] nat, so have I joye or blis!—
Two men that wolde han passed over see
For certeyn cause into a fer contree,
If that the wynd ne hadde been contrarie,
That made hem in a citee for to tarie,   250
That stood ful myrie upon an haven syde—
But on a day, agayn the even tyde,[24]
The wynd gan chaunge, and blew right as hem leste.[25]
Jolif and glad, they wente unto hir reste,
And casten hem[26] ful erly for to saille.   255
    "But to that o man fil[27] a greet mervaille.
That oon of hem, in slepyng as he lay,
Hym mette a wonder dreem agayn the day.
Him thoughte a man stood by his beddes syde
And hym comanded that he sholde abyde,   260
And seyde hym thus, 'If thou tomorwe wende,
Thow shalt be dreynt;[28] my tale is at an ende.'
    "He wook and tolde his felawe what he mette,
And preyde hym his viage for to lette;[29]
As for that day he preyde hym to byde.   265
    "His felawe, that lay by his beddes syde,
Gan for to laughe, and scorned him ful faste.
'No dreem,' quod he, 'may so myn herte agaste
That I wol lette for to do my thynges.
I sette nat a straw by thy dremynges;   270
For swevenes been but vanytees and japes.[30]
Men dreme al day of owles or of apes,
And eek of many a maze[31] therwithal;
Men dreme of thyng that nevere was ne shal.
But sith[32] I see that thou wolt heere abyde,   275

[15] Heinous.   [16] Concealed.   [17] This is.
[18] Immediately.   [19] Seized.   [20] Pained, tortured.
[21] Tortured, racked.   [22] Acknowledged.
[23] Speak idly. But Chaucer certainly intends us to recognize that
    as a husband the pompous Chauntecleer is full of gab.
[24] Toward evening.
[25] Exactly as it pleased them.
[26] Planned.   [27] Fell, happened.   [28] Drowned.
[29] To give up his voyage.   [30] Jokes, nonsense.
[31] Bewildering thing.—*Owls and apes* (line 272) = absurdities.
[32] Since.

[4] Started up.   [5] Heed.
[6] Was not save, was merely.   [7] Slain.   [8] Pitiable.
[9] Stop.   [10] Describe.   [11] Stretched out.
[12] Officers.
[13] The old Norman cry of alarm, calling on the community to
    join in apprehending a criminal.   [14] Revealest.

And thus forslewthen[33] wilfully thy tyde,[34]
God woot, it reweth me;[35] and have good day!'
  "And thus he took his leve, and wente his way.
But er that he hadde half his cours yseyled—
Noot I nat why, ne what myschaunce it eyled—   280
But, casuelly,[36] the shippes botme rente,
And shipe and man under the water wente,
In sighte of othere shippes it bisyde,
That with hem seyled at the same tyde.
And therfore, faire Pertelote so deere,   285
By swiche ensamples olde yet maistow leere[37]
That no man sholde been to recchelees[38]
Of dremes; for I seye thee, doutelees,
That many a dreem ful soore is for to drede.
  "Lo, in the lyf of Seint Kenelm[39] I rede,   290
That was Kenulphus sone, the noble kyng
Of Mercenrike, how Kenelm mette a thyng.
A lite er he was mordred, on a day,
His mordre in his avysion he say.[40]
His norice hym expowned every deel[41]   295
His swevene, and bad hym for to kepe hym weel
For traison;[42] but he nas but seven yeer oold,
And therfore litel tale hath he toold
Of any dreem, so hooly was his herte.
By God! I hadde levere[43] than my sherte   300
That ye hadde rad his legende as have I.
  "Dame Pertelote, I sey yow trewely,
Macrobeus, that writ the avision
In Affrike of the worthy Cipion,[44]
Affermeth dremes, and seith that they been   305
Warnynge of thynges that men after seen.
And forthermoore, I pray yow, looketh wel
In the Olde Testament, of Daniel,[45]
If he heeld dremes any vanitee.
Reed eek of Joseph,[46] and ther shul ye see   310
Wher dremes be somtyme—I sey nat alle—
Warnynge of thynges that shul after falle.
Looke of Egipte the kyng, Daun Pharao,
His baker and his butiller also—
Wher they ne felte noon effect in dremes.   315
Whoso wol seken actes of sondry remes[47]
May rede of dremes many a wonder thyng.

Lo, Cresus, which that was of Lyde[48] kyng,
Mette he nat that he sat upon a tree—
Which signified he sholde anhanged bee?   320
Lo, heere Andromacha, Ectores wyf—
That day that Ector sholde lese[49] his lyf,
She dremed on the same nyght biforn
How that the lyf of Ector sholde be lorn[50]
If thilke day he wente into bataille.   325
She warned hym, but it myghte nat availle;
He wente for to fighte natheles.
But he was slayn anon of Achilles.
But thilke tale is al to longe to telle,
And eek it is ny day; I may nat dwelle.   330
Shortly I seye, as for conclusion,
That I shal han of this avision
Adversitee. And I seye, forthermoor,
That I ne telle[51] of laxatyves no stoor,[52]
For they been venymous, I woot it weel.   335
I hem diffye;[53] I love hem never a deel!
  "Now let us speke of myrthe, and stynte[54] al this.
Madame Pertelote, so have I blis,
Of o thyng God hath sent me large grace!
For whan I se the beautee of youre face,   340
Ye been so scarlet reed aboute youre yën,
It maketh al my drede for to dyen;
For, al so siker as In principio,[55]
Mulier est hominis confusio.—[56]
Madame, the sentence[57] of this Latyn is,   345
'Womman is mannes joye and al his blis.'
For whan I feele a-nyght your softe syde
(Al be it that I may nat on yow ryde,
For that oure perche is maad so narwe, allas!)
I am so ful of joye and of solas   350
That I diffye bothe swevene and dreem."
  And with that word, he fley doun fro the beem—
For it was day—and eke his hennes alle;
And with a chuk he gan hem for to calle,
For he hadde founde a corn, lay in the yerd.   355
Real[58] he was; he was namoore aferd.
He fethered Pertelote twenty tyme,
And trad[59] her eke as ofte, er it was pryme.[60]
He looketh as it were a grym leoun,
And on hise toos he rometh up and doun;   360

---

[33] Slothfully waste.   [34] Time.
[35] I am sorry for it.   [36] Accidentally.
[37] Mayest thou learn.   [38] Reckless, heedless.
[39] In 821, at the age of seven, Kenelm (Cenhelm) succeeded his father Kenulphus (Cenwulf) on the throne of Mercia. He was murdered at the instigation of his aunt and guardian.
[40] In his vision he saw.
[41] His nurse expounded to him every bit.
[42] For fear of treason.   [43] Liefer, rather.
[44] The Dream of Scipio may be found in Book VI of Cicero's De Republica. About 400 A.D. Macrobius wrote an elaborate commentary on it.   [45] See Daniel 2, 4, 7, 8, 10.
[46] See Genesis 37, 40, 41.   [47] Realms.

[48] Croesus, king of Lydia, was killed by Cyrus the Great in 546 B.C.
[49] Lose. This story is not in Homer; it was added to the Troy legend by medieval writers.   [50] Lost.   [51] Reckon.
[52] I.e., I set no store by laxatives.   [53] Renounce.
[54] Cease.
[55] I.e., as sure as gospel. In principio is the opening phrase of John's gospel.
[56] Woman is man's ruin. A common medieval sentiment.
[57] Meaning.   [58] Regal.
[59] Trod, copulated with. Feathered, i.e., covered with his feathers, means the same thing.   [60] 9 a.m.

Hym deigned nat to sette his foote to grounde.
He chukketh whan he hath a corn yfounde,
And to hym rennen thanne hise wyves alle.
Thus roial, as a prince is in an halle,
Leve I this Chauntecleer in his pasture,   365
And after wol I telle his aventure.

Whan that the monthe in which the world bigan,
That highte March, whan God first maked man,[61]
Was compleet, and ypassed were also,
Syn March bigan, thritty dayes and two,   370
Bifel that Chauntecleer in al his pryde,
His sevene wyves walkynge by his syde,
Caste up his eyen to the brighte sonne,
That in the signe of Taurus[62] hadde yronne
Twenty degrees and oon and somwhat moore,   375
And knew by kynde[63] and by noon oother loore[64]
That it was pryme, and crew with blisful stevene.[65]
"The sonne," he seyde, "is clomben up on hevene
Fourty degrees and oon and moore, ywis.[66]
Madame Pertelote, my worldes blis,   380
Herkneth thise blisful briddes how they synge,
And se the fresshe floures how they sprynge!
Ful is myn herte of revel and solas."

But sodeynly hym fil a sorweful cas;[67]
For evere the latter ende of joye is wo.   385
God woot that worldly joye is soone ago;
And if a rethor[68] koude faire endite,
He in a cronycle saufly myghte it write
As for a sovereyn notabilitee.
Now every wys man lat him herkne me: 390
This storie is al so trewe, I undertake,
As is the book of Launcelot de Lake,[69]
That wommen holde in ful greet reverence.
Now wol I come agayn to my sentence.

A colfox,[70] ful of sly iniquitee,   395
That in the grove hadde wonned[71] yeres three,
By heigh ymaginacion forn-cast,[72]
The same nyght thurghout the hegges brast[73]
Into the yerd, ther Chauntecleer the faire
Was wont, and eek his wyves, to repaire;   400
And in a bed of wortes[74] stille he lay
Til it was passed undren[75] of the day,
Waitynge his tyme on Chauntecleer to falle,

As gladly doon thise homycides alle
That in await liggen[76] to mordre men.   405
O false mordrour lurkynge in thy den!
O newe Scariot![77] newe Genylon![78]
False dissymulour, O Greek Synon,[79]
That broghtest Troye al outrely to sorwe!
O Chauntecleer, acursed be that morwe   410
That thou into that yerd flaugh fro the bemes!
Thou were ful wel ywarned by thy dremes
That thilke day was perilous to thee.
But what that God forwoot moot nedes bee,[80]
After the opinion of certein clerkis.   415
Witnesse on hym that any parfit clerk is
That in scole is greet altercacion
In this mateere and greet disputison,[81]
And hath been of an hundred thousand men.
But I ne kan nat bulte it to the bren,[82]   420
As kan the hooly doctour Augustyn,[83]
Or Boece,[84] or the Bisshope Bradwardyn;[85]
Wheither that Goddes worthy forwityng[86]
Streyneth[87] me nedely[88] to doon a thyng—
"Nedely" clepe I[89] symple necessitee;   425
Or elles, if free choys be graunted me
To do that same thyng or do it noght,
Though God forwoot it er that it was wroght;
Or if his wityng[90] streyneth never a deel
But by necessitee condicioneel.[91]   430
I wil nat han to do of swich mateere;
My tale if of a cok, as ye may heere,
That took his conseil of his wyf—with sorwe![92]
To walken in the yerd upon that morwe
That he hadde met that dreem that I yow tolde.   435

---

76 Lie.   77 Judas Iscariot.
78 Ganelon, the traitor of *The Song of Roland,* the great French epic of the exploits of Charlemagne's knights against the Saracens.
79 Sinon, the treacherous Greek who persuaded the Trojans to take in the wooden horse by means of which the Greeks got into Troy.   80 What God foreknows must needs be.
81 Disputation.
82 Sift (bolt) it to the bran, thoroughly analyze it.
83 St. Augustine (d.430) was the orthodox authority on the questions of predestination and "necessity," and whether they restricted free will, that is, man's power to choose.
84 Boethius (d. 524 A.D.), the Roman philosopher. A passage in his *De Consolatione Philosophiae* discusses foreordination, and distinguishes between "simple necessity" and "conditional necessity" (lines 425-30, below).
85 Lecturer at Oxford on predestination and, at his death in 1349, Archbishop of Canterbury.   86 Foreknowledge.
87 Constrains, forces.   88 Necessarily.   89 I call.
90 Knowledge.
91 Necessity conditioned by God's foreknowledge. By "simple necessity" God's foreknowledge would compel a man to act in a certain way, and the human will would not be free. By "conditional necessity" God has foreknowledge and a man's choice is certain to conform to it, but his will is nevertheless free to choose.   92 I.e., blast her!

---

61 The time of the Creation was supposed to have been the vernal equinox.
62 The Bull, the second of the twelve signs of the zodiac. It is 9 a.m., May 3.   63 Nature.   64 Lore, learning.
65 Sound.   66 Certainly.   67 Sad occasion.
68 Rhetorician.   69 I.e., it is not true.
70 Coal-fox, a fox tipped with black.   71 Lived.
72 By divine foresight foreordained.
73 Through the hedges burst.   74 Herbs.
75 Mid-morning.

Wommennes conseils been ful ofte colde;[93]
Wommannes conseil broghte us first to wo,
And made Adam fro Paradys to go,
Ther-as[94] he was ful myrie and wel at ese.
But for I noot[95] to whom it myght displese[96]   440
If I conseil of wommen wolde blame,
Passe over, for I seyde it in my game.[97]
Rede auctours,[98] where they trete of swich mateere,
And what they seyn of wommen ye may heere.
Thise been the cokkes wordes, and nat myne;   445
I kan noon harm of no womman divyne.[99]

    Faire in the soond,[1] to bathe hire myrily,
Lith Pertelote, and alle hire sustres by,
Agayn the sonne; and Chauntecleer so free[2]
Soong murier than the mermayde[3] in the see—   450
For Phisiologus[4] seith sikerly[5]
How that they syngen wel and myrily.
    And so bifel that as he cast his yë
Among the wortes on a boterflye,
He was war of this fox, that lay ful lowe.   455
Nothyng ne liste hym[6] thanne for to crowe,
But cride anon, "Cok-cok!"[7] and up he sterte,
As man that was affrayed in his herte.
For natureelly a beest desireth flee
Fro his contrarie,[8] if he may it see,   460
Though he never erst[9] hadde seyn it with his yë.
    This Chauntecleer, whan he gan hym espye,
He wolde han fled, but that the fox anon
Seyde, "Gentil sire, allas! wher wol ye gon?
Be ye affrayed of me, that am youre freend?   465
Now, certes, I were worse than a feend,
If I to yow wolde harm or vileynye.
I am nat come your conseil for t'espye;
But trewely the cause of my comynge
Was oonly for to herkne how that ye synge.   470
For trewely ye have as myrie a stevene[10]
As any aungel hath that is in hevene,
Therwith ye han in musyk moore feelynge
Than hadde Boece,[11] or any that kan synge.
My lord youre fader—God his soule blesse!—   475
And eek youre mooder, of hire gentillesse,[12]
Han in myn hous ybeen, to my greet ese.
And certes, sire, ful fayn wolde I yow plese.

But for men speke of syngyng, I wol seye,
So moote I brouke[13] wel myne eyen tweye,   480
Save yow, I herde nevere man so synge
As dide youre fader in the morwenynge.
Certes, it was of herte, al that he song.
And for to make his voys the moore strong,
He wolde so peyne[14] hym that with bothe his yën   485
He moste wynke,[15] so loude he wolde cryen,
And stonden on his tiptoon therwithal,
And strecche forth his nekke long and smal.
And eek he was of swich discrecion
That ther nas no man in no region   490
That hym in song or wisedom myghte passe.
I have wel rad in Daun Burnel the Asse,[16]
Among hise vers, how that ther was a cok,
For that a preestes sone yaf hym a knok
Upon his leg, whil he was yong and nyce,[17]   495
He made hym for to lese his benefice.[18]
But certeyn, ther nys no comparison
Bitwixe the wisedom and discrecion
Of youre fader and of his subtiltee.
Now syngeth, sire; for seinte charitee,   500
Lat se konne ye[19] youre fader countrefete!"[20]
    This Chauntecleer his wynges gan to bete,
As man that koude his trayson nat espie,
So was he ravysshed with his flaterie.
    Allas! ye lordes, many a fals flatour[21]   505
Is in youre courtes, and many a losengeour,[22]
That plesen yow wel moore, by my feith,
Than he that soothfastnesse[23] unto yow seith.
Redeth Ecclesiaste[24] of flaterye;
Beth war, ye lordes, of hir trecherye.   510
    This Chauntecleer stood hye upon his toos,
Strecchynge his nekke, and heeld his eyen cloos,
And gan to crowe loude for the nones.[25]
And Daun Russell the foxe stirte up atones,[26]
And by the gargat hente[27] Chauntecleer,   515

---

93 Disastrous.
94 Where.   95 But since I know not.   96 Be displeasing.
97 Joke.   98 Authors, authorities.   99 Guess, declare.
1 Sand.   2 Noble.
3 Mermaids were often confused with the sirens of classical myth.
4 The Latin Bestiary, a collection of fanciful moral and theological
  interpretations of animals.   5 Surely, indeed.
6 It pleased him not at all, he had no desire.
7 The cock's rapid cry of alarm.
8 Every creature was supposed to have an opposite, toward which
  it felt a natural antipathy.   9 Before.   10 Voice.
11 Who wrote a treatise on music.   12 Politeness.

13 So may I enjoy.   14 Exert.
15 I.e., he shut both his eyes.
16 Burnellus is the hero of this twelfth-century Latin poem by
  Nigel Wireker, the subtitle of which is Speculum Stultorum (The
  Mirror of Fools). It satirizes the worldly ambitions of the regular
  clergy by relating the ass's adventures in search of means of
  increasing the length of his tail.   17 Foolish.
18 Ecclesiastical post. This cock avenged himself on Gundulfus, his
  tormentor, five years later. The priest's son was now ready for
  consecration and succession to his father's benefice; but the cock
  refused to crow that morning, Gundulfus overslept, and the
  living was lost to him.
19 I.e., demonstrate whether you can.   20 Imitate, match.
21 Flatterer.   22 Flatterer.   23 Truth.
24 The Apocryphal book of Ecclesiasticus (chap. 12).
25 On the occasion; indeed.
26 At once.—Russell is the name of a young fox in a Dutch version
  of the medieval European beast epic Reynard the Fox.
27 By the throat seized.

And on his bak toward the wode hym beer,
For yet ne was ther no man that hym sewed.[28]

O Destinee, that mayst nat been eschewed![29]
Allas, that Chauntecleer fleigh fro the bemes!
Allas, his wyf ne roghte[30] nat of dremes!   520
And on a Friday fil al this meschaunce.

O Venus, that art goddesse of plesaunce,
Syn that thy servant was this Chauntecleer,
And in thy servyce dide al his poweer,
Moore for delit than world to multiplye,[31]   525
Why woldestow suffre hym on thy day to dye?

O Gaufred,[32] deere maister soverayn,
That whan thy worthy kyng Richard was slayn
With shot, compleynedest his deeth so soore,
Why ne hadde I now thy sentence[33] and thy loore,   530
The Friday for to chide as diden ye?
For on a Friday, soothly, slayn was he.
Thanne wolde I shewe yow how that I koude pleyne[34]
For Chauntecleres drede and for his peyne.

Certes, swich cry ne lamentacion   535
Was nevere of ladyes maad whan Ylion[35]
Was wonne, and Pirrus[36] with his streite[37] swerd,
Whan he hadde hent Kyng Priam by the berd
And slayn hym—as seith us Eneÿdos[38]—
As maden alle the hennes in the clos,[39]   540
Whan they had seyn of Chauntecleer the sighte.
But sodeynly dame Pertelote shrighte[40]
Ful louder than dide Hasdrubales[41] wyf
Whan that hir housbonde hadde lost his lyf
And that the Romayns hadde brend Cartage.   545
She was so ful of torment and of rage[42]
That wilfully into the fyr she sterte,
And brende hirselven with a stedefast herte.

O woful hennes, right so criden ye
As, whan that Nero brende the citee   550
Of Rome, cryden senatoures wyves
For that hir husbondes losten alle hir lyves—
Withouten gilt this Nero hath hem slayn.
Now wole I turne to my tale agayn.

This sely[43] wydwe and eek hir doghtres two   555
Herden thise hennes crie and maken wo;
And out at dores stirten they anon,
And syen the fox toward the grove gon,

And bar upon his bak the cok away,
And cryden "Out! harrow!" and "Weylaway!"   560
"Ha, ha, the fox!" and after hym they ran,
And eek with staves many another man.
Ran Colle oure dogge, and Talbot, and Gerland,
And Malkyn,[44] with a dystaf in hir hand;
Ran cow and calf and eek the verray hogges,   565
So fered for[45] the berkyng of the dogges
And shoutyng of the men and wommen eke,
They ronne so hem thoughte hir herte breke.[46]
They yolleden as feendes doon in helle;
The dokes cryden as men wolde hem quelle;[47]   570
The gees for feere flowen over the trees;
Out of the hyve cam the swarm of bees.
So hydous was the noyse, a! benedicitee![48]
Certes, he[49] Jakke Straw[50] and his meynee[51]
Ne made nevere shoutes half so shrille,   575
Whan that they wolden any Flemyng[52] kille,
As thilke day was maad upon the fox.
Of bras they broghten bemes,[53] and of box,[54]
Of horn, of boon, in whiche they blewe and powped;[55]
And therwithal they skriked and they howped:[56]   580
It semed as that hevene sholde falle.

Now, goode men, I pray yow herkneth alle.
Lo, how Fortune turneth sodeynly
The hope, and pryde eek, of hir enemy!
This cok, that lay upon the foxes bak,   585
In al his drede unto the fox he spak,
And seyde, "Sire, if that I were as ye,
Yet wolde I seyn, as wys[57] God helpe me,
'Turneth agayn, ye proude cherles alle!
A verray pestilence upon yow falle!   590
Now am I come unto the wodes syde,
Maugree youre heed,[58] the cok shal heere abyde;
I wol hym ete, in feith, and that anon.'"
The fox answerde, "In feith, it shal be don."
And as he spak that word, al sodeynly   595
This cok brak from his mouth delyverly,[59]
And heighe upon a tree he fleigh anon.

And whan the fox saugh that the cok was gon,
"Allas," quod he, "O Chauntecleer, allas!
I have to yow," quod he, "ydoon trespas,   600

---

[28] Pursued.   [29] Escaped.
[30] Recked, heeded.
[31] More for pleasure than for procreation.
[32] Geoffrey de Vinsauf, whose treatise on the art of poetry appeared soon after the death of Richard I (1199). As an example of a lamentation he includes some lines of his own on Richard's death; they allude to Friday, the day Richard was wounded.
[33] Insight.   [34] Complain, lament.   [35] Ilion, Troy.
[36] Pyrrhus, son of Achilles.   [37] Drawn.
[38] The Aeneid (II, 550 ff.).   [39] Close, yard.   [40] Shrieked.
[41] Hasdrubal, king of Carthage. The city was burned in 146 B.C.
[42] Violent grief.   [43] Innocent, good.

[44] Molly, a conventional name for a country maid. Talbot and Gerland may be dogs or men.   [45] Scared by.
[46] So it seemed to them their heart would break.   [47] Kill.
[48] Bless ye! Here, as often, contracted to a trisyllable: pronounce béndistaý or bénsitaý.   [49] I.e., the famous.
[50] One of the leaders of the Peasants' Revolt, in 1381.
[51] Retinue, gang.
[52] Flemings resident in London were attacked by the rebels for their part in the woolen industry, which encouraged English landowners, contrary to the peasants' interest, to turn their land into sheep pasturage.   [53] Trumpets.   [54] Boxwood.
[55] Blew.   [56] Whooped.   [57] Surely.
[58] Despite your head, in spite of you.   [59] Nimbly.

Inasmuche as I maked yow aferd
Whan I yow hente and broght out of the yerd.
But, sire, I dide it of no wikke[60] entente.
Com doun, and I shal telle yow what I mente.
I shal seye sooth to yow, God help me so!"   605
    "Nay, thanne," quod he, "I shrewe[61] us bothe two.
And first I shrewe myself, bothe blood and bones,
If thou bigyle me ofter than ones.
Thou shalt namoore thurgh thy flaterye
Do[62] me to synge and wynke with myn yë;   610
For he that wynketh whan he sholde see,
Al wilfully, God lat him nevere thee!"[63]
    "Nay," quod the fox, "but God yeve hym meschaunce
That is so undiscreet of governaunce
That jangleth[64] whan he sholde holde his pees."   615
    Lo, swich it is for to be recchelees
And necligent, and truste on flaterye.
    But ye that holden this tale a folye,
As of a fox, or of a cok and hen,
Taketh the moralite, goode men.   620
For Seint Paul seith that al that writen is,
To oure doctrine[65] it is ywrite, ywis.
Taketh the fruyt and lat the chaf be stille.[66]
    Now, goode God, if that it be thy wille,
As seith my lord,[67] so make us alle goode men,   625
And brynge us to his heighe blisse! Amen!

                              Heere is ended the Nonnes Preestes Tale.

[*The Eighth Fragment begins with* THE SECOND NUN'S TALE.
*Like her superior, the Prioress, she tells a Christian legend, the
life of St. Cecilia. Then the pilgrims are overtaken by another
ecclesiastic, a Canon, who comes galloping after them in such
eagerness to join the party that both he and his horse are wringing
wet*—"*it was,*" *says Chaucer,* "*joye for to seen hym swete!*" *To
the discomfiture of this Canon, who soon withdraws, his Yeoman confides that the reverend father is an alchemist; and he
volunteers, in* THE CANON'S YEOMAN'S TALE, *further details of
his practices as well as a story about another canon-alchemist and
the swindling of a priest.*

The Ninth Fragment consists of a prologue and THE MAN-
CIPLE'S TALE, *of how a talking crow's disclosure of the adultery
of his master's wife was punished instead of rewarded by the
ungrateful husband.*

THE PARSON'S TALE *with its prologue constitutes the concluding Tenth Fragment. The good man promises the pilgrims "a
myrie tale in prose," but it turns out to be a dreadfully dull discourse on the seven deadly sins.*

*Finally, come the notorious "Retractations." If Chaucer really
wrote these lines, he did so in a mood of revulsion that we can
only hope was temporary. For in them he repudiates, on moral
grounds, all his best work, deploring that he ever composed
Troilus and Criseyde, most of The Canterbury Tales, "and
many another book . . . and many a song and many a leccherous
lay," and excepting only his saints' legends, homilies, moral and
devotional pieces, and translation of Boethius on philosophy.
Needless to say, the world has not agreed with this estimate of a
great life's work. It has been, for more than five centuries, with
the keenest regret that the eyes of readers have come to rest on the
final lines of the manuscripts or of the books which reproduce
them:*]

*Heere is ended the book of the tales of Caunterbury, compiled
by Geffrey Chaucer, of whos soule Jhesu Crist have mercy.
Amen.*

Medieval Drama

THE great and all-inclusive art of drama, carried by the
Greeks to a height which has been equaled only once, declined under the Romans and at last vanished from Europe.
Its reappearance in the Middle Ages broadly parallels the
course of medieval painting. Both arts were revived by
the Church. The subjects of the early dramatists, like those
of the monkish painters, were exclusively religious; and
they were drawn chiefly from Biblical narrative. Secularization gradually invaded both fields. With the coming
of the Renaissance, painter and playwright were no longer
required to work within the Church, though many were
content to continue under her patronage; and in subject
matter the scope of both, while still often scriptural, included contemporary life.

Drama was reborn within the consecrated edifice, from
a germ in the liturgy itself. One of the Easter services
contained a special bit of dialogue, in the form of question
and answer by the choir:

ANGELS. Whom seek ye in the sepulchre?
THE THREE MARYS. Jesus of Nazareth, who was crucified.
ANGELS. He is not here; he is risen, as he said.
    Go quickly, and tell his disciples!

In successive steps, the dialogue was expanded; impersona-
tion, pantomime, action, and properties were introduced;

---

[60] Wicked.   [61] Curse.   [62] Make.   [63] Prosper.
[64] Prates.   [65] Instruction.   [66] I.e., let the chaff alone.
[67] What or who is meant is uncertain.

the language of the people replaced the original Latin; episodes unwarranted in Holy Writ were invented; dramatic effects, horrific or comic, were built up for their own sake. Eventually a whole series of scenes on the events of the Passion and another on the Christmas story were acted out on platforms set up at various points inside a church, with a different stage for each episode.

The next phase was the removal of this drama, already in process of secularization, to the churchyard and finally into the hands of the guilds, the medieval associations of craftsmen. This transfer did not take place everywhere; in some monastic establishments the clergy went on performing plays down to the seventeenth century. But in many places the drama became wholly the possession of the guilds and was acted by the local tanners, armorers, bakers, shipwrights, goldsmiths, painters, and carpenters, to mention but a few of the crafts. In some localities these amateurs, whose duties as dramatic producers were laid out by the strictest municipal regulation, took special pride and pains in an annual performance of all the local plays. It was the big event of the year, to which people poured in from the rural districts for miles around; and the players, who were also businessmen, were well aware that their show brought money into town. One of the great festivals of the Church, Corpus Christi Day, which comes two months after Easter, was a favorite time for staging these cycles. In some cases they had grown to such proportions that a single performance occupied the entire day and handled selected episodes all the way from the Creation to the Judgment. Besides these "mystery" or "miracle" plays, as they were also often called, there was the non-scriptural play depicting the miraculous in the life of a local saint or the patron saint of the church or monastery. Some scholars use "mystery" for the Biblical plays and "miracle" for the plays about saints, but this distinction of terminology was not made by the English playwriters themselves. "Mystery" seems to come from the French *mystère*, a play acted by a craft guild.

The number of cities and towns that became centers of this kind of dramatic activity is unknown, but surviving manuscripts have preserved at least a part of four of the most remarkable cycles. York, the ecclesiastical capital of the north, had an elaborate cycle. So, apparently, did Wakefield, in the same county. Another of the existing cycles was performed at Chester; and there is yet another, the location of which, though it is sometimes called the Coventry cycle, remains uncertain. Undoubtedly, however, there was much playing at Coventry, only a few miles from Stratford-on-Avon, where Shakespeare grew up. In all probability he saw at Coventry, in his boyhood, performances of types of drama that were already becoming archaic. Fragments of the Coventry cycle, as well as of the cycles of Norwich and Newcastle, survive.

Long after the heyday of the religious drama, its characters remained firmly fixed in the popular imagination. Among them was the furious slaughterer of innocents, whose frantic behavior on the medieval stage we still allude to when we speak of out-Heroding Herod. The Devil and his satellites, rushing off stage with the persons of their sinful victims into a luridly painted version of Hell Mouth, were indelibly impressed on the minds of all who had seen them in childhood. Another celebrated character was Noah's wife, always a cantankerous creature with a mind of her own and a fixed contempt in it for her husband's prognostications. She regards the Ark's projected voyage as a harebrained enterprise and refuses to go aboard till persuaded in a farcical scene of scolding and wife beating.

There is no evidence that there were any of these plays in England, even in their earliest forms, till after the Norman Conquest. The religious drama seems to have been a slow growth, though it sprang up all over western Europe. How early the mysteries took root in England is not known. Unquestionably they were flourishing by the fourteenth century, and presumably it was the second half of that century and the first half of the next that saw their greatest popularity and development. At their height, they were usually presented processionally. There was a separate stage for each episode, that is, for each of the separate plays; it was a good deal like a float, providing a platform for the acting, with a space below curtained off for a dressing room. In turn each "pageant" or stage-wagon would be hauled to the successive stations throughout the town. Pageant 1, having played Station A, rolled off to Station B, at another square or corner, as Pageant 2 replaced it at Station A. There was not much attempt at scenery, but sometimes a movable curtain was used for discovery scenes.

In merit the performances doubtless varied greatly from year to year and from place to place. So did the plays themselves. They were not the work of well-known authors. From time to time a cycle would be overhauled and modernized; then there would be additions, excisions, and revisions, according to the taste and talent of the new writer. At its best the result was excellent; and the more one reads certain cycles, especially the Wakefield, the more respect one has for the men who wrote, acted, and assumed the really prodigious task of producing them. There are forty-eight plays in the York cycle; and even if the guilds were reduced by sheer lack of daylight to playing half of them in alternate years, the management obviously had to face many problems. We have contemporary evidence that, at least in some towns and on some occasions, these were admirably solved and that performances of exemplary smoothness ensued. Such productions probably remain the highwater mark of amateur theatricals in the English-speaking world.

During the second half of the fifteenth century another type of drama came to the front, the morality play. While it never equaled the mysteries in either literary or dramatic power, yet by cutting loose from the Bible story it gave playwrights wider scope for invention. In its final form, early in the sixteenth century, when a good many of the "moral interludes" were not religious at all, it provided a transitional step away from the medieval types toward a modern and secular drama. But in the fifteenth century, and in some cases even later, the morality was still mostly religious in subject. Its usual theme was the conflict of good and evil for the soul of Man; and its characters were not historical and Biblical individuals, like those of the mystery plays, but personified abstractions. Thus in *The Castle of Perseverance* the World, the Flesh, and the Devil appear, attended by all seven of the Deadly Sins, as well as Back-biter and other rascals, against whom are arrayed the Seven Virtues, aided and abetted by Confession, Penance, and the

Four Daughters of God, namely Mercy, Peace, Truth, and Righteousness. God and Death are also characters. Both parties are out to win Mankind's soul, which after his death appears as yet another character. In short, the morality play is a dramatic allegory.

Most of these pieces are pretty dull. The most famous of them is *Everyman*, still occasionally revived. This morality, which has some fine moments, is probably a translation of a Dutch play.

The standard treatise on the English drama in the Middle Ages is *The Medieval Stage,* by E. K. Chambers (2 vols., 1903). The four great cycles have been separately edited for the Early English Text Society. Lucy T. Smith also edited the York cycle (1885). Well-edited selections, with copious glossarial notes, are available in J. Q. Adams's *Chief Pre-Shakespearean Dramas* (1924). The best short history of English drama in general is Allardyce Nicoll's *British Drama* (1925).

The Second Shepherds' Play

THE *Secunda Pastorum,* as it is entitled in its manuscript, is the second of two plays on the same subject in a cycle almost certainly acted at Wakefield, in the West Riding of Yorkshire. Its relation to Shakespeare's *Twelfth Night* or Jonson's *The Alchemist* is that of the primitives of the monkish painters to the full glory of the great works of Rubens, Rembrandt, and El Greco. Yet the best of the mystery plays, and this one is by all odds the best on the comic side, are a culmination as well as a beginning. Centuries earlier, the good tidings of the angelic chorus and the shepherds' coming to Bethlehem had been cast in simple dramatic form as a special feature of the Christmas liturgy. Pantomime, the singing of the choirboys from a gallery high up near the roof of the church, and a brief Latin dialogue of the adoration at the manger combined to form the germ of a play. Successive generations expanded it. The Magi were added, and eventually the Slaughter of the Innocents and the Flight into Egypt. Latin was discarded, and realistic strokes of character and incident brought the story more closely home to delighted audiences. The scene is still Judea, but the dramatist models his characters on English types he has observed directly. The outburst of the First Shepherd reflects the desire of the English peasant to shake off the tyranny of the feudal system.

When it occurred to some reviser of the text to differentiate the shepherds, the door was opened to a comic amplification, which by the early fifteenth century, if not sooner, had resulted in the extraordinary disproportion of

the play before us. No doubt its abrupt transition from the long and racy scenes of the sheep stealing to the brief treatment of the Biblical episode itself seemed less grotesque to the medieval audience than it does to us. The Church embraced nearly all of life's interests, and it was able to absorb a farcical play as easily as the Gothic design of its architecture took an occasional gargoyle. Nor must we neglect, after the fun of the huge gag to which the greater part of the piece builds up, the charm of the closing scene, so touching in its tenderness and simplicity.

When the revision of the shepherds' play reached this final form is uncertain; perhaps it was in the second quarter of the fifteenth century. The manuscript which preserves its cycle was probably copied about the middle of that century. Though there is small doubt that these plays were given at Wakefield, the cycle is often called the Towneley, from the name of the family in whose possession the manuscript was discovered.

For the cycle, of which thirty-two plays have survived, see *The Towneley Plays,* edited for the Early English Text Society by G. England and A. W. Pollard (1897). Annotated editions, also in Middle English, of the *Second Shepherds' Play* and other plays apparently from the pen of the Wakefield Master, as he has been called, are included in Dr. Adams's anthology. The unknown dramatist was not highly gifted as a poet, but he certainly had a flair for the dramatic and above all was endowed with a rich sense of humor.

The opening stanza will serve to illustrate the metrical form:

> Lord, what these weders ar cold! and I am ill happyd;
> I am nere hande dold, so long have I nappyd;
> My legys they fold; my fyngers ar chappyd;
> It is not as I wold, for I am al lappyd
>   In sorow.
> In storms and tempest,
> Now in the eest, now in the west,
> Wo is hym has neuer rest,
>   Myd day nor morrow!

It will be observed that in terms of the rime scheme the first four lines, each with four stresses, are equivalent to eight two-stress lines riming alternately. The fifth line, single-stressed, rimes with the ninth, a two-stress line. Lines six to eight, with two stresses each, all rime. Four rimes thus appear in the nine-line stanza, in the scheme *abababdcdddc*. The complexity of the stanza drives the dramatist to the occasional use, in order to wring out a rime, of conventional tags, sometimes virtually meaningless, and also of a good many farfetched expressions and forms. All this makes the modernizer's task difficult. The following rendering, by the present editor, is an attempt to put the play into a readable idiom while maintaining a reasonable degree of fidelity to the original. Some liberties have been taken with the rime; it should be noted, however, that the occasional replacement of rime by assonance (that is, identity of vowel sound but not of consonant sound: e. g., *done, some*) has a precedent in the original. The original stage directions are indicated in the footnotes; others have been added by the editor.

THE SECOND SHEPHERDS' PLAY

A plain, in Judea, but remarkably similar to a Yorkshire moor

Enter COLL, *the* FIRST SHEPHERD

1ST SHEP. Lord, this weather is cold! And I am ill wrapped.
I am almost dulled, so long have I napped.
My legs they do fold. My fingers are chapped.
It is not as I would, for I am all lapped
  In sorrow.   5
In storms and tempest,[1]
Now in the east, now in the west,
Woe is his who lacks rest
  Midday or morrow.

But the wretched sheephand, that walks on the moer,   10
The time's near at hand he'll be out of the door.[2]
No wonder, as things stand, if we be poor!
For the tilth of our land lies fallow as the floor,[3]
  As ye ken.[4]
We are so hammed,[5]   15
O'ertaxed and rammed,
That as tame things we're ranked
  By these "gentry" men.

Thus they rob us of our rest—accurse them Saint Mary!
These men so lord-fast,[6] they make the plow tarry. 20
What men say is for the best, we find it contrary.
Thus are husbandmen[7] oppressed, so they're bound to
    miscarry
  In life.
Thus hold they us under,
Thus they bring us in blunder;[8]   25
It would be great wonder
  If ever we should thrive.

Let a man get a sleeve or a brooch[9] nowadays,
And woe to who grieves or against him aught says!
Snubs from none he receives, however lordly his ways. 30
And yet no one believes one word that he says,
  No letter.
He has power to commandeer;[10]
Boast and brag we must hear;
For he has the ear   35
  Of men that are greater.

There shall come a swain,[11] as proud as a po.[12]
He must borrow my wain,[13] my plow also.
Then I am full fain to grant ere he go.
Thus live we in pain, anger, and woe,   40

---

[1] Here and often (as also in the original) the rime scheme necessitates "wrenching" the word accent from its normal position.
[2] Done out of house and home.
[3] I.e., our arable land is not under cultivation because we lack the money required to farm it.
[4] As you know. Note the occasional frank recognition of the presence of the audience; it is characteristic of English drama through the Elizabethan period.
[5] Possibly: hamstrung, crippled. More likely: kept in harness; from *hames*, the curved wooden or metal pieces attached to the collar of a workhorse, or the collar itself.—*Rammed* (line 16) = battered, pushed about.
[6] Attached in service to a lord and engaged as his agent in squeezing his tenants. [7] Farmers. [8] Trouble.
[9] I.e., an embroidered sleeve or a badge as livery, showing he is in a lord's service.
[10] I.e., to requisition supplies and services at prices fixed by himself. [11] Attendant, follower. [12] Peacock.
[13] He says he must borrow my cart.

By night and day.
What he fancies takes he,
Though 't is needed by me.
Better hanged might I be
    Than once say him nay.   45

It does me good as I walk, thus all alone,
Of this world for to talk and its ways to bemoan.
To my sheep will I stalk, and hearken anon,
And abide on a balk[14] or sit on a stone
    Full soon.   50
For I trow, pardie,[15]
Of true[16] men, if such they be,
We'll get more company
    Ere it be noon.

    The FIRST SHEPHERD *steps aside and sits down. Enter* GIB,
    the SECOND SHEPHERD

2ND SHEP. (*to himself*). Benste and Dominus![17] what may
    all this mean?   55
Why fares the world thus? Such we seldom have seen.
Lord! this storm's hard on us, and the winds are full keen,
And the frosts hideous, so they water mine een,[18]
    No lie!
Now in dry, now in wet,   60
Now in snow, now in sleet!
When my shoes freeze to my feet,
    All's not easy, say I.

But, as far as I ken, or yet as I go,
We wretched wed men suffer much woe.   65
We have sorrow then and then[19]—it happens oft so.
Poor Caple, our hen, both to and fro
    She cackles,
But when starts she to croak,
To groan, or to cluck,   70
Then woe to our cock:
    He is in the shackles.

These men that are wed have not all their will;
When they're hard bestead,[20] they sigh their fill;
God knows they are led full hard and full ill;   75
In bower or in bed, their answer is nil.[21]
    This tide[22]
My part I have found;
What I've learned I'll expound:
Woe to him that is bound,   80
    For he must abide.

But now, late in our lives—such a marvel to me,
That I think my heart rives such wonders to see!
What destiny ordains, it has so to be—
Some men have two wives, and some men three,   85
    In store.[23]
Some men have woe that have any;
But in this am I canny:[24]
Woe is his that has many,
    For he suffers sore.   90

Young wooers, to this cling, by God that you bought:[25]
Be wary of wedding, and think in your thought,
"Had I known" is a thing that's exactly worth nought.
Much silent mourning has wedding home brought,
    And griefs,   95
With many a sharp shower.
For thou may catch in an hour
What will savor full sour
    As long as thou lives.

Sure as I read epistle,[26] I have one for my dear   100
As sharp as a thistle or briar—she's their peer!
She has eyebrows that bristle with a sour-looking cheer.[27]
If she once wet her whistle, she could sing full clear
    Her paternoster.[28]
She's as great as a whale;   105
She has a gallon of gall;
By Him that died for us all,
    I wish I'd run till I'd lost her.

1ST SHEP. (*rising*). What's over the row?[29]—Full deafly
    ye stand.

2ND SHEP. The Devil trip thy toe, for a tarrying
    hand![30]   110
Saw thou where Daw did go?

1ST SHEP.   Yea, on a lea land
I heard him blow.[31] He comes here at hand,
    Not far.
Stand still.

2ND SHEP. Why?

1ST SHEP. For he's coming, hope I.   115

2ND SHEP. He will tell us both a lie
    Unless we beware.

---

14 Unplowed strip between two plowed strips.
15 I believe, verily.   16 Honest.
17 Common ejaculations. *Benste* = *benedicite*, bless us! *Dominus* =
    Lord.   18 Eyes.   19 Continually.
20 In a difficult situation.   21 I.e., they don't dare answer back.
22 Time.

23 As a sum total. (Not, at the same time.)
24 Knowing.
25 Christ who redeemed you.
26 I.e., Scripture.
27 Expression.
28 Lord's Prayer. I.e., give her a drink and she'll talk her head off.
    From *paternoster* in this sense is derived our *patter.*
29 Either hedgerow or row of the plowed field.
30 A loitering sheephand.   31 His shepherd's horn or pipe.

They step aside. Enter DAW, *the* THIRD SHEPHERD[32]

3RD SHEP. Christ's Cross me speed and Saint Nicholas!
Thereof had I need; it is worse than it was.
No matter who heed, and let the world pass,[33]   120
It is aye full of dread and brittle as glass
        And sliding.[34]
This world fared never so,
With marvels mo[35] and mo,
Now in weal, now in woe;   125
        And all is writhing.[36]

Ne'er since Noah's flood were such floods seen,
Winds and rains so rude, and storms so keen.
Some staggered, some stood—in fear, as I ween.
Now God turn all to good! I say as I mean,   130
        To ponder.
These floods so they drown
Both in fields and in town,
And bear all down!
        And that is a wonder.   135

We that walk in the nights our cattle to keep,
We see sudden sights when other men sleep.—
Yet methinks my heart lights:[37] I see shrews peep!—
Ye are two bad wights! I will give my sheep
        A turn.—   140
But full ill have I meant:[38]
As I walk on this bent,[39]
I might easily repent
        If my toes I should spurn.[40]

                [He sees the other SHEPHERDS

Ah, sir, God you save, and master mine!   145
A drink would I have, and also I'd dine.
1ST SHEP. Christ's curse, my knave! Thou'rt a lazy hind.[41]
2ND SHEP. Lo, the boy likes to rave.—Thou canst wait for
        thine
        Till we've made it.[42]
Ill thrift on thy pate!—   150
Though the rascal came late,
Yet he's in a state
        To dine—if he had it.

3RD SHEP. Such servants as I, that sweats and swinks,[43]
Eat our bread full dry; and that's wrong, methinks.   155
Wet and weary we hie, while master still winks;[44]
Yet late's the supply of our dinners and drinks.
        But greatly
Both our dame and our sire,
When we've run in the mire,   160
Can nip at our hire[45]
        And pay us full lately.

But hear my pledge, sir! for the fare that you make,[46]
Henceforth I'll bestir myself just as I take.[47]
I'll do little, I aver, and sport often make.   165
For from my supper I ne'er got stomach-ache
        In the field.
But why my wrongs cite
When my staff[48] has such might?
And men say bargains light[49]   170
        A bad profit yield.

1ST SHEP. Thou'dst be an ill lad to go for a ride
With one whose purse had but little inside.[50]
2ND SHEP. Peace, boy, I bade! shut up! subside!
Or I'll make thee afraid, so heaven's King me guide!   175
        With thy gauds![51]
Where's the sheep, boy? We scorn![52]
3RD SHEP. Sir, this same day at morn
Them I left in the corn,[53]
        When they rang Lauds.[54]   180

They have pasture good; they cannot go wrong.
1ST SHEP. That is right.[55]—By the Rood,[56] these nights
        they are long!
Ere we go, much I would one might give us a song.
2ND SHEP. So I thought, as I stood—mirth to make us
        among.
3RD SHEP. I grant.[57]   185
1ST SHEP. The tenor let me try.
2ND SHEP. And I the treble so high.
3RD SHEP. Then the mean[58] take will I.
        Let's see how ye chant.   [*They sing*

---

[32] Though he probably speaks standing still, his soliloquy is understood by the audience to be uttered en route; when he sees the others, he has arrived.
[33] I. e., even though some see the condition of affairs but don't give it their attention.   [34] Unstable.   [35] More.
[36] Awry.
[37] Grows light because he sees shrewmice, whose appearance is an old sign of a change from bad to fair weather. Then he recalls that they sometimes injured animals; hence his decision to give the sheep a turn.
[38] I.e., he changes his mind about going out on the moor to the sheep.   [39] Moor.   [40] I.e., strike against something.
[41] Farmhand.   [42] Had our meal.

[43] Toils.
[44] Sleeps.   [45] Hold back part of our wages.
[46] Because of the fuss you make (about giving me food).
[47] Receive. I'll work in proportion to what I get.
[48] Shepherd's crook, the symbol of my calling. I.e., I can get another job.   [49] Easy. This statement is a proverb.
[50] I. e., you would be an expensive companion on account of your appetite.   [51] Tricks, pretences.   [52] We jeer (at you).
[53] Field of grain.   [54] A religious service at dawn.
[55] Said, of course, ironically. Evidently the Third Shepherd is not serious; they do not believe he has left the sheep in the grain.
[56] Cross.   [57] Agree.
[58] Alto. The manuscript fails to include the song.

Then MAC *enters, in a cloak thrown over his smock*[59]

MAC (*to himself*). Now, Lord, by thy names seven,[60] who
made both moon and stars,   190
Well more than I can mention, thy will my conduct
bars:[61]
I am very wicked—my brain that often jars.
Now would God I were in heaven—babies' weeping
never mars
    Those haunts.
1ST SHEP. Who is that pipes so poor?   195
MAC. Would ye knew why I'm sore!
Lo, a man that walks on the moor,
    And has not all his wants!

2ND SHEP. Mac, whence hast thou come? What tidings
dost bring?
3RD SHEP. Is it he? Then each one should take heed to his
thing![62]   200
              [*And he pulls off* MAC's *cloak*
MAC. Lo, ich[63] be, I vum, a yeoman! of the king!
The selfsame! I come from a lord I'm serving,
    And sich!
Fie on you! Go ye hence,
Out of my presence!   205
I must have reverence!
    Why, "Who be ich!"

1ST SHEP. Why make ye it so quaint?[64] Mac, ye do wrong.
2ND SHEP. But, Mac, ye'd play the saint? I trow that ye
long.[65]
3RD SHEP. I trow the rogue can paint,[66] may the Devil
him hang!   210
MAC. I shall make complaint, and a taste of the thong
    You'll endure,
And I'll tell on you—both!
1ST SHEP. But Mac, is that sooth?[67]
Now take that southern tooth[68]   215
    And stick it in the manure!

---

[59] This stage direction appears in the manuscript, in Latin.
[60] In rabbinical writings.
[61] I.e., I don't do thy will. Mac, in prayer, admits his true character
—in order to inform the audience.
[62] Watch his property. Mac is a northerner, evidently one of the
thievish Scots.—The following stage direction is from the Latin
of the manuscript.
[63] Mac affects a southern dialect, hoping the shepherds will be
sufficiently impressed not to detain him. *Ich* = I, *vum* = declare,
sich = such.
[64] Why do you put on such airs?
[65] To do so.
[66] Counterfeit, deceive.   [67] True.
[68] I.e., drop your southern accent. See note 63, above. The author
is drawing the shepherds of Palestine in terms of those he knows
in Yorkshire.

2ND SHEP. Mac, the Devil in your ee! I've a good mind
to sock you!
3RD SHEP. Mac, know ye not me? By God, I could knock
you!
MAC (*pretending to recognize them for the first time*). God
keep you all three! Methought that I saw you.
You're a fair company.
1ST SHEP.   To your senses you've brought you!   220
2ND SHEP. Fine feat!
Thus late as thou goes,
What will men suppose,
Since your repute grows
    For stealing of sheep?   225

MAC. I am true[69] as steel—so all men say.
But a sickness I feel, that hot makes me stay.
My belly fares not weel—it's upset today.
3RD SHEP. Seldom lies the Deil dead by the way.[70]
MAC. Therefore   230
Full sore am I and ill
If I stand stone-still.
I ate not a needle's fill
    This month and more.

1ST SHEP. How's thy wife? By my hood, how does she
do?   235
MAC. At the fire, by the Rood, sprawls the long day
through!
And the house full of her brood! She drinks well, too.
Ill fares any other good that she will do,
    'T is true.
Eats as fast as a hound,   240
And, each year that comes round,
Has a brat, I'll be bound,
    And some years two!

If I hadn't a heart and weren't richer than some,
I'd be eaten, from the start, out of house and of home.   245
And she's a foul tart, if nigh her ye come!
Who a worse can report, I can tell you, there's none
    Than I kens.
Now will ye see what I proffer?—
To give all in my coffer   250
Tomorrow morning to offer
    Her head-mass pence.[71]

---

[69] Honest.
[70] Road. A proverb; i.e., the Devil is usually going about his
business. Mac, in spite of the innocent reasons he has given for
being so early on the moor, is compared to the Devil, who is
a notorious walker to and fro.
[71] Fee for her funeral service.

2ND SHEP. One so tired you'd behold nowhere else in
    this shire.
I would sleep, if less gold I received for my hire.
3RD SHEP. I am naked and cold, and would have a fire. 255
1ST SHEP. I have weariness untold, from running in the
    mire.—
    Watch, you!   [He lies down
2ND SHEP. Nay, I'll lie down hard by.
I need sleep, that is why.   [He lies down
3RD SHEP. As good a man's son was I   260
    As either of you two.[72]

But, come here, Mac! Between do thou lie here![73]
MAC. Then I'd keep you, I ween, from whispering
    there.—
    Indeed!—[74]
From my top to my toe,   265
Manus tuas commendo,[75]
Poncio Pilato.—
    Christ's Cross me speed!
            [*They lie down; the* SHEPHERDS *go to sleep*

Then he gets up, the SHEPHERDS *being asleep, and says*[76]

Now 't is time for a guy that lacks what he would
In secret to hie unto a fold   270
And his trade there to ply, yet be not too bold—
One might pay too high, if the truth were told,
    At the ending.[77]
Now I'll put on some speed.
He must cleverly deal   275
Who would like a good meal
    But has little for spending.—

A circle round you,[78] as round as a moon,
I'll draw till I'm through, until it be noon.
Stone-still lie this crew, until I have done!   280
And to fix it, a few of good words I'll say soon
    In the height:—[79]
Over your heads my hand I lift:
Out go your een! Sight, vanish swift!—
But yet I must make better shift,   285
    If it's to be right.   [*The* SHEPHERDS *snore*

---

[72] I.e., I also object to taking the watch.
[73] Possibly two lost lines originally preceded this one.
[74] Unquestionably. Apparently the preceding line is a flimsy excuse offered by Mac to avoid lying where the shepherds will
wake if he gets up. But they insist, with gestures, and he consents.
[75] (Into) thy hands I commend (my spirit). (Luke 23:46.) The
graceless Mac gets mixed up and commends his soul to the
keeping of Pontius Pilate.   [76] From the manuscript.
[77] I. e., in the long run.
[78] A charmed circle. He is casting a spell.
[79] Aloud, plainly, openly. Cf. line 299.

Lord! they're all fast asleep—(*to the audience*) that may ye
    all hear.
Never tended I sheep. I must learn how, that's clear.
To the flock I must creep, even though they may fear.—
Lo, here come the sheep! Now mends our cheer   290
    From sorrow!
A fat sheep, I dare say!
A good fleece, dare I lay![80]
I'll pay back when I may,
    But this will I borrow.   295

    MAC *takes the sheep and crosses to the other side of the
    stage. At the same time,* JILL *enters and lies at her ease*

Hey! Jill! art thou in? Get us some light!
JILL.[81] Who makes such a din this time of the night?
I'm all set for to spin. I wouldn't arise
Even a penny to win. Them I curse in the height
    That so roars.   300
A housewife like I've been,
Torn betwixt and between![82]
Here no work can be seen
    To, for such small chores.[83]

MAC. Good wife, open the heck![84] Seest thou not what I
    bring?   305
JILL (*rising*). I can let thee draw the sneck![85]—Ah, come
    in, my sweeting!
MAC. Yea, thou dost not reck[86] of my long standing.
JILL. By the naked neck thou art likely to swing.
MAC. Go 'way!
I am worthy my meat.   310
In a fix I can get
More than they that swink and sweat
    All the long day.

Thus it fell to my lot, Jill; I had such grace.
JILL. It were a foul blot to be hanged for the case.   315
MAC. I've oft 'scaped, Jillotte, from as tight a place.
JILL. But if long goes the pot to the water, men says,
    At last
Comes it home broken.
MAC. Well know I the token,   320
But let it never be spoken.—
    But come and help fast!

I would he were slain; I want to eat.
This twelvemonth was I not so fain[87] of a sheep's meat.

---

[80] Bet.
[81] Manuscript *Uxor eius,* his wife. The speech tags and stage
directions of the manuscript are in Latin; e. g., the First Shepherd's speeches are tagged *Primus Pastor.*
[82] I.e., interrupted in the midst of my duties.
[83] I.e., I can't accomplish anything if I have to stop my work and
open the door.   [84] Hatch, door.   [85] Latch.
[86] Care for, heed.   [87] Desirous.

JILL. Come they ere he be slain, and hear the sheep
  bleat—   325
MAC. Then might I be ta'en: it gives me a cold sweat.
  Go bar
The front door.
JILL.   Yes, Mac.
For if they come at thy back—
MAC. Then might I suffer, what with all the pack,   330
  The devil and even more.

JILL. A good trick have I spied, since thou knowest none:
Him here let us hide, until they be gone;
In my cradle he'll abide—let me alone—[88]
And I'll lie beside in childbed and groan.   335
MAC. Thou hast said!
And I'll say thou wast light[89]
Of a knave[90] child this night.
JILL. Now that day was full bright
  Whereon I was bred.   340

'T is a good disguise and a farsighted cast.[91]
Ever woman's advice helps out at the last.
I know not where are spies: again go thou fast!
MAC. Unless I'm there when they rise, they will blow a
  cold blast.
  I will go sleep.—   [He returns to the SHEPHERDS 345
So in sleep they still lie!
I'll step quietly by
As if 't was never I
  That carried their sheep.
                  [He lies down and pretends to sleep

IST SHEP. (suddenly waking and jumping up). Resurex a
  mortruis![92] Catch hold of my hand!   350
Judas carnas dominus![93] I cannot well stand.
My foot sleeps, by Jesus! From hunger I'll collapse.
I thought[94] we'd laid us near the English land.
2ND SHEP. (stretching). Ah—ee—ee!
Lord, lo! I have slept weel;   355
As fresh as an eel,
As light do I feel
  As leaf on a tree.

3RD SHEP. (waking in a fright). Blessing be herein! So my
  body doth quake
My heart's out of my skin, such a noise it doth make! 360
Who makes all this din, so my forehead doth ache?
To the door will I win.[95]—Hark, fellows! awake!

Four were we.
Do you see Mac here now?
1ST SHEP. We were up before thou.   365
2ND SHEP. Man, to God I avow
  Nowhere yet has gone he.

3RD SHEP. Methought he was lapped in a wolf's own skin.
1ST SHEP. Now are many so wrapped, especially within.
3RD SHEP. When we long had napped, methought with a
  gin[96]   370
A fat sheep he trapped; but he made no din.
2ND SHEP. Be still!
Thy dream makes thee wood;[97]
'T is but phantom, by the Rood!   [He points to MAC
1ST SHEP. Now God turn all to good,   375
  If it be his will!

2ND SHEP. Rise, Mac! for shame! thou liest right long!
MAC. Now Christ's holy name be us among!
What is this, by Saint Jame? I can't walk along.
I think I'm the same.—Ah, my neck has lain wrong   380
  Enough—
Much obliged[98]—since yestereven.
Now, by Saint Stephen,
I was tortured by dreaming
  That treated me rough.   385

I thought Jill gan croak and travail full sad,
Well nigh the first cock, with a young lad
To add to our flock. So I'll never be glad.
I have tow on my rock more[99] than ever I had.
  Ah, my head.   390
Of young bellies a full house!
Their brains the Devil knock out!
Woe when brats are about
  And for them little bread!

I must go home, by your leave, to Jill—as I thought! 395
I pray, search my sleeve, to see I steal nought!
I'd be loath you to grieve or from you take aught.
3RD SHEP. Go! ill may thou achieve!—Now would I we
  sought   [MAC leaves the SHEPHERDS
  This morn
Whether we've all our store.[1]   400
1ST SHEP. Then I'll go before.
Let us meet.

[96] Trap, contrivance.   [97] Crazy.
[98] Either a shepherd now straightens Mac's head, which he has
  been holding at some absurd angle, or else Mac is making an
  airy and ironical acknowledgment to the unseen powers that
  create trouble for mortals.
[99] More tow to spin on my distaff, i.e., a bigger job on my hands.

[1] I.e., to see whether we have all our sheep.

[88] Leave it to me.   [89] Lightened, delivered.   [90] Boy.
[91] Plan.
[92] Dog Latin, like the next italicized phrase. Here the sense is clear:
  resurrection from the dead.
[93] Perhaps: Judas, lord of the flesh.   [94] I.e., dreamed.
[95] Reach, get, go.

2ND SHEP.   Where?

3RD SHEP. At the crooked thorn.   [Exeunt SHEPHERDS[2]

MAC (arriving at his house). Undo this door! Who's there?
    How long shall I stand?

JILL. Who is roaring out there? Walk where moonlight
    has wanned![3]   405

MAC. Ah, Jill, what cheer? 'T is I, Mac, your husband!

JILL. Then may we see here the Devil in a band,[4]
    Sir Guile!
Lo, he comes with a croak,
As if the rope were round his throat.   410
Myself to work I can't devote
    For any while!

MAC (to the audience). Hear the rumpus she makes,
    proclaiming her woes!
Yet does nought, her ease takes, and tickles her toes!

JILL. Why, who wanders, who wakes, who comes, who
    goes,   415
Who brews, who bakes, who makes me thus hoarse?[5]
    Besides,
It is sad to behold,
Now in hot, now in cold:
Unhappy the household   420
    Where no woman resides!

But what end hast thou made with the herdsmen, Mac?

MAC. The last word they said when I turned my back
Was they'd look that they had of their sheep the whole
    pack.
They'll be sore, I'm afraid, when they their sheep lack,   425
    Pardie!
But, however the game goes,
It's me, they will suppose,
And make a foul noise,
    And cry out upon me.   430

To our plan thou must stick.

JILL.   I agree to it still.
I shall swaddle him slick; my cradle he'll fill.
                          [She puts the carcass in it
If 't were a greater trick, I could help with my skill.
I will lie down quick. Tuck me in!

MAC.   I will.

JILL. Behind!   435
Come Coll and his pal by,

---

[2] Or, possibly, they remain at the other side of the stage from
Mac and Jill.
[3] In the waning of the moon, an unlucky time.
[4] In bonds, fetters; perhaps with an allusion to the hangman's
noose.
[5] She is wheezing—from overwork, she implies. Very likely the
actor hiccups before hoarse.

They will nip us full nigh.

MAC. But "Help!" I must cry,
    The sheep if they find.

JILL. Hearken for when they call; they will come
    anon.   440
Come, make ready all, and sing on thine own:
Sing lullay thou shalt, for I must groan
And cry by the wall on Mary and John,
    For sore.[6]
Sing lullay fast,   445
When thou hearest them at last.
If I don't play a false cast,[7]
    Trust me no more.

Re-enter the SHEPHERDS, meeting at the other side of the
stage

3RD SHEP. Ah, Coll, good morn! Why sleepest thou not?

1ST SHEP. Alas that ever I was born! We have a foul
    blot.   450
A fat wether[8] must we mourn.

3RD SHEP.   God forbid such a lot!

2ND SHEP. Who would do us that scorn? 'T would be a
    foul spot.

1ST SHEP. Some shrew.[9]
I have sought with my dogs
All Horbury[10] Shrogs,   455
And of fifteen hogs[11]
    Found all but one ewe.

3RD SHEP. Now believe me, if ye will: by Saint Thomas
    of Kent,[12]
Either Mac or Jill has not been absent.

1ST SHEP. Peace, man! be still! I saw when he went.   460
Thou slanders him ill; thou ought to repent
    With speed.

2ND SHEP. Now, thrive as may I,
If I should here die,
That 't was he I'd reply,   465
    That did that same deed.

3RD SHEP. Straight thither let's tread, and run on our feet!
I shall never eat bread till the truth is complete.

1ST SHEP. Nor drink in my head till with him I meet.

2ND SHEP. I will rest in no bed until him I greet,   470
    My brother.

---

[6] In pain.   [7] Trick.
[8] Castrated ram. In line 457, for the sake of rime, it is called a ewe.
[9] Rogue.
[10] A village three miles southwest of Wakefield, where the play
    was given. Shrogs = brush land.   [11] Yearling sheep.
[12] Thomas à Becket, martyred at Canterbury.

One pledge will I plight:
Till I have him in sight
I'll ne'er sleep one night
    Where I do another.   475

They cross to the other side. MAC *sings a raucous lullaby;*
    JILL *groans*

3RD SHEP. How their voices do break! Hear the proud
    father boom!
1ST SHEP. Heard I never voice crack so far out of tune.
Call on him!
2ND SHEP.   Hey, Mac! undo your door soon!
MAC. Who is it that spake, as if it were noon
    Aloft?   480
Who is that? I say.
3RD SHEP. Good fellows, were it day.[13]
MAC. As far as ye may,
    Good sirs, speak soft,

Over a sick woman's head, that discomfort knows.   485
I had liefer be dead than to worry her expose.
JILL. Go elsewhere instead; I can't breathe with repose.
Each foot that ye tread goes right through my nose,
    Ye see.
1ST SHEP. Tell us, Mac, if ye may,   490
How fare ye, I say.
MAC. Why! are ye in this town today?
    Now how fare ye?

Ye have run in the mire and still are wet.
I shall make you a fire, if ye will sit.—   495
A nurse would I hire.—Just think! One more yet!
Well earned is my hire. My dream this is it,
    In due season.
I have bairns,[14] if ye knew,
Well more than a few;   500
But we must drink as we brew,
    And that is but reason.

I would ye dined ere ye went; methinks that ye sweat.
2ND SHEP. Nay, we'll not change our bent, for drink or
    for meat.
MAC. Is aught but good to you sent?
3RD SHEP.   Yea, our sheep that we get   505
Are stolen—as they went; our loss it is great.
MAC. Sirs, drink! [*He hands them a tankard of ale, from*
If I had been there,   *which they drink in turn*
Some had paid very dear.
1ST SHEP. Marry, some say ye were!   510
    Which it pains us to think.

---

13 If there were light by which you could recognize us.
14 Children.

2ND SHEP. Mac, some men trows that it might be ye.
3RD SHEP. Either ye or your spouse, so say we.
MAC. Now if ye suppose it was Jill or me,
Come rip our house, and then ye can see   515
    Who had her.
If any sheep I got,
Or a cow or a stot,[15]
(And Jill, my wife, rose not
    Since down she laid her),   520

As I am true and leal,[16] to God here I pray
That this be the first meal I shall eat this day.
                          [*He points to the supposed child*
1ST SHEP. So God bliss to me deal! consider, Mac, I say:
Any thief that could steal could also say nay.[17]
JILL. I swelt![18]   [*They search the house*   525
Out, thieves, from my home!
Ye come to steal all we own!
MAC. Hear ye not how she doth groan?
    Your hearts ought to melt.

JILL. Out, thieves, from my bairn! To him come not
    nigh!   530
MAC. If ye knew how she'd fared, you would sorrow and
    sigh.
Ye do wrong, I declare, that thus you come by
To a woman that has fared—but no more say I.
JILL. Ah! my middle!—
I pray to God so mild   535
If ever you I beguiled
That I may eat this child
    That lies in this cradle.

MAC. Peace, woman, for God's pain, and cry not so!
Thou hurtest thy brain and makest me full woe.   540
2ND SHEP. I guess our sheep's slain. Find ye nought also?
3RD SHEP. We're working in vain; we may as well go.
    But hatters![19]
I can find no flesh,
Hard or nesh,[20]   545
Salt or fresh,
    But two bare platters.

Of live cattle, save this (*pointing at the cradle*), tame or
    wild,
None, so may I have bliss, quite so strong as he[21]
    smelled.
JILL. No! so grant me bliss and give me joy of my
    child!   550
1ST SHEP. We have aimed all amiss; I think we're beguiled.

---

15 Horse.   16 Loyal, i.e., honest.
17 I.e., deny it. The line is a proverb.   18 Faint.
19 By (Christ's) clothes.   20 Tender.   21 The lost sheep.

2ND SHEP. Sir, 'don!²²
Sir, our Lady him save!
Is your child a knave?²³
MAC. Any lord might well have   555
  This child for his son.

When he wakens he grips;²⁴ a joy 't is to see.
3RD SHEP. Good luck to his hips, and happy be he!
But who was his gossips,²⁵ so quickly ready?
MAC. All good to their lips!
1ST SHEP. (aside).   A lie I foresee.   560
MAC. May God them thank!
Perkin and Gibbon Waller, I vow,
And gentle John Horne, believe me thou—
He kicked up all the row—
  With the big shank.²⁶   565

2ND SHEP. Mac, friends will we be, for we are all one.
MAC. We! Nothing doing! not me! for amends get I
  none.
Farewell all three! I'd be glad were ye gone.
          [*The* SHEPHERDS *leave, but pause outside the house*
3RD SHEP. Fair words there may be, but love is there none,
  Not this year.   570
1ST SHEP. Gave ye the child anything?
2ND SHEP. Not a single farthing.
3RD SHEP. Fast again in I'll fling;
  Abide ye me here!   [*He goes back into the house*

Mac, harm don't conceive; from thy bairn don't me
  bar!   575
MAC. Nay, thou dost me aggrieve, and my peace thou
  dost mar.
3RD SHEP. The child 't will not grieve, that little daystar!
Mac, with your leave, let me give him from far
  But six pence.
MAC. Nay! get out! He sleeps.   580
3RD SHEP. Methinks he peeps.
MAC. When he wakens, he weeps.
  I pray you, go hence!   [*The other* SHEPHERDS *come inside*

---

22 Pardon.   23 Boy.
24 I.e., seizes with his hand, as babies do.
25 Godparents, sponsors at baptism. The point is the speed of the
  alleged christening.
26 This line describes long-legged John Horne (he is a shepherd in
  the other, the first, shepherds' play of this cycle), and not how
  he kicked up the row. If there had been a child, there might
  (ignoring the element of time) have been a christening, at
  which there might have been a row, which might have been
  caused by John, a godparent. There was, however, no child.
  Mac's allegations are "merely corroborative detail, intended,"
  in the words of Pooh-Bah, "to give artistic verisimilitude to an
  otherwise bald and unconvincing narrative."

3RD SHEP. Give me leave him to kiss and lift up the
  clout.²⁷—   [*He pulls down the blanket*
What the devil is this? He has a long snout!   585
          [*He steps back*
1ST SHEP. (glancing at the cradle). He is marked all amiss.²⁸
  Let's not wait hereabout!   [*He starts toward the door*
2ND SHEP. Weft ill spun, iwis, always comes foul
  out.—²⁹
  Ay, so!   [*He looks into the cradle*
He is like to our sheep!
3RD SHEP. How! Gib! may I peep?   590
1ST SHEP. I see Nature will creep
  Where it cannot go.³⁰

2ND SHEP. We were thoroughly sold. A farsighted cast!
'T was a fraud very bold.
3RD SHEP.   Yea, sirs, was't.
We should burn her, I hold; come, bind this bawd
  fast!—   595
Ah, false scold, hang at the last
  Shalt thou!—
Will ye see how thy swaddle
His four feet in the middle?
Saw I never in the cradle   600
  A horned lad till now!

MAC. Peace bid I! Lo, your speeches spare!
It was I him begat, and yon woman did bear.
1ST SHEP. What the Deil name the brat? "Mac"? Lo,
  God! Mac's heir!
2ND SHEP. Let be all that! Now God give him care,   605
  I say!
JILL. A pretty child is he
As sits on a woman's knee;
A dillydown,³¹ pardie,
  To make a man gay!   610

3RD SHEP. His ear shows the mark, and that's a good token.
MAC. I tell you, sirs, hark! his nose was broken!
I was told by a clerk³² that some spell had been spoken.
1ST SHEP. This is a false work; my vengeance is awoken!
  Get a weapon!   615
JILL. He was taken by an elf!³³
I saw it myself!
When the clock struck twelve
  Was he misshapen!

---

27 Cloth.   28 I.e., disfigured.
29 A proverb. I.e., what could one expect of the child of such
  parents? *Iwis* = certainly.
30 Walk. A proverb. I.e., every man is bound to act according to
  his nature.   31 Darling.   32 Learned man.
33 An old popular superstition attributed a child's deformity to
  the elves' having spirited away the real child, a misshapen
  "changeling" being left by them as a substitute.

2ND SHEP. Gifts ye two do display—here in one place,
    indeed![34]   620
3RD SHEP. Since their theft they maintain, let's see them
    both dead!
MAC (*falling on his knees*). If I trespass again, strike off my
    head!
In your hands I remain.
1ST SHEP.   Sirs, do this instead:
  For this loss
We will neither curse nor smite,   625
Scold nor fight,
But to end soon and right
  Him in canvas we'll toss.

They take MAC *outside the house and toss him*

1ST SHEP. Lord, lo, I am sore, about ready to bust.
In faith, I can no more; therefore will I rest.   630
                      [*Exeunt* MAC *and* JILL
2ND SHEP. As a sheep of seven score he weighed in my fist.
For to sleep some more methinks now I list.[35]
3RD SHEP. Now, I pray,
On this green won't you lie?
1ST SHEP. On those thieves still think I.   635
3RD SHEP. Why let that thought come nigh?
  Do as I say!   [*They lie down and sleep*

An ANGEL *sings "Gloria in Excelsis";*[36] *after that let him
say*

ANG. Rise, herdsmen hind![37] for now is He born
That shall take from the Fiend what Adam lost long.[38]
That warlock[39] to rend, this night is He born.   640
God is made your friend now at this morn.
  He doth mean
Ye at Bedlem[40] to see
Where lies He so free[41]
In a crib full poorly   645
  Two beasts between.
             [*Exit the* ANGEL. *The* SHEPHERDS *rise*

1ST SHEP. As quaint a strain even as ever yet I heard!
A marvel's to us given, thus to be scared.
2ND SHEP. Of God's Son from heaven he aloft declared.
All the wood in a levin[42] methought it flared.   650
  When he came near.

3RD SHEP. Of a bairn he did say
In Bedlem today.
1ST SHEP. That star shows the way;
  Let us seek him there.   655

2ND SHEP. Say, what was his song? Heard ye how he
    sang with skill,
Three breves to a long?[43]
3RD SHEP.   Yea, marry, he could trill!
Not a crotchet[44] was wrong, there was nothing of ill.
1ST SHEP. How to sing us among, with his very same trill,
    I know.   660
2ND SHEP. Let's see how ye croon!
Can ye bark at the moon?
3RD SHEP. Hold your tongues! Have done!
1ST SHEP. Then here we go.   [*They sing*

2ND SHEP. To Bedlem he bade that we should gang;[45] 665
I am afraid that we tarry too long.
3RD SHEP. Be merry, not sad! Of mirth is our song!
Everlastingly glad, to our meed[46] go along
    Noiselessly!
1ST SHEP. Then thither hie we,   670
Though wet and weary we be,
To that Child and that Lady!
  Lose it never shall we!

2ND SHEP. We find prophets certify—let be your din!—
Both David and Isay,[47] and more than I ken,   675
By clergy[48] prophesy that a virgin within
Should He alight and lie, to lessen our sin
    And slake[49] it—
Our kind from woe;
For Isay said so: 680
Ecce virgo
  Concipiet[50] a child that is naked.

3RD SHEP. Full glad may we be and abide that day,
That Lovely to see that all things obey.
Lord, 't were well for me, for once and for aye,   685
Could I kneel on my knee some word for to say
    To that Child.
But the angel said
In a crib was he laid
And poorly arrayed,   690
  Both lowly and mild.

---

[34] I.e., it is going some to find two like you in the same place.
[35] Desire.
[36] Glory (to God) in the highest. This stage direction is in the
manuscript.   [37] Peasant.
[38] Shall redeem from the Devil mankind, lost in sin because of
Adam's fall.   [39] Wizard, i.e., the Devil.
[40] Bethlehem.   [41] Noble.   [42] Flash of lightning.

[43] In old musical notation a breve (equal to two of our whole
notes) was equivalent to one-third or one-half a long, according
to the "mode" of the composition.
[44] Our quarter note, in value one-quarter of a semibreve (our
whole note).   [45] Go.   [46] Reward.   [47] Isaiah.
[48] Knowledge, learning.   [49] Abate.
[50] Behold, a virgin shall conceive (Isaiah 7:14).

IST SHEP. Patriarchs that have been, and prophets before,
They desired to have seen this Child that is born.
They are gone full clean;[51] that they've lost evermore.
We shall see him, I ween, ere it be morn,   695
  For a token.
When I see him and feel,
Then I'll know full weel
It is true as steel
  What prophets have spoken: 700

To poor men, as we are, that he would appear,
First find, and declare by his messenger.
2ND SHEP. Go we now! Let us fare! The place is quite
   near.
3RD SHEP. I am ready, I swear. Let's together seek there
  That bright One.—   [They kneel 705
Lord, if thy will it be,
We are plain folk all three:
Grant us something for glee
  To comfort thy Son.

As they are kneeling, MARY *enters with the* CHILD.[52] *The*
SHEPHERDS *rise, cross the stage, and kneel in adoration*

IST SHEP. Hail, comely and clean![53] Hail, young
   Child!   710
Hail, Maker, as I mean,[54] from a maiden so mild.
Thou hast cursed, I ween, the warlock so wild,
The false guiler of teen;[55] now goes he beguiled.—[56]
  Lo, He merry is!
Lo, He laughs!—My sweeting!—   715
A happy meeting!
I've kept promise of greeting!
  Have a bob[57] of cherries!

2ND SHEP. Hail, Saviour of power, for thou hast us sought!
Hail, noble shoot and flower, that all things hast
   wrought!   720
Hail, gracious in bower, that made all from nought!
Hail! I kneel and cower. A bird have I brought
  To my bairn from far.

Hail, little tiny mop![58]
Of our creed thou art crop.[59]   725
I would drink of thy cup,[60]
  Little daystar.

3RD SHEP. Hail, darling dear, full of Godhead![61]
I pray thee be near when that I have need!
Hail! Sweet is thy cheer.[62] My heart would bleed   730
To see thee sit here in so poor a weed[63]
  With no pennies.
Put forth thy hand so small!
I bring thee but a ball.
Have it, and play withal,[64]   735
  And go to the tennis!

MARY. The Father of heaven, God omnipotent,
That made all in seven, his Son has he sent.
He[65] named my name given, and lighted ere he went;
I conceived him[66] then even,[67] through his might, as he
   meant;   740
  And now is he born.
May he keep you from woe!
I shall pray him even so.
Tell this forth, as ye go!
  And remember this morn!   745

IST SHEP. Farewell, Lady free, so fair to behold,
With thy Child on thy knee!
2ND SHEP.   But he's lying full cold.
                 [He tucks the CHILD in
Lord, well is me! Now we go. Do thou behold![68]
3RD SHEP. Forsooth, ready are we. This seems to be told
  Full oft.[69]   750
IST SHEP. What grace doth abound!   [They leave the stable
2ND SHEP. Come! Salvation we've found!
3RD SHEP. To sing are we bound![70]
  Let it ring aloft!   [Exeunt, the SHEPHERDS singing

Thus endeth the pageant of the SHEPHERDS[71]

---

51 Utterly.
52 Or, possibly, a curtain was drawn revealing the tableau at the
   manger.—In response to the shepherds' prayer, we must suppose, the objects they are to present to Jesus are miraculously
   conveyed into the long sleeves which serve them as pockets.
53 Lovely and pure.   54 Creator, I mean to say.
55 Beguiler who works iniquity.   56 I.e., defeated, foiled.
57 Bunch.

58 Baby.
59 Head; i.e., you are the leader of all Christians.
60 The Communion cup.   61 Divinity.   62 Face.
63 Garb.   64 With it.   65 God the Father.
66 God the Son.   67 Without sin.
68 Watch over me (a prayer).
69 I.e., we are not the first to tell this story. The actor steps out of
   character for a moment.   70 Ready.
71 Original stage direction.

Sir Thomas Malory

d. 1471

THE MOST remarkable effort by any of the medieval English prose writers comes at the end of the period, on the threshold of the Renaissance. Chiefly from French sources Sir Thomas Malory drew the collection of stories which goes under the not very accurate title of *Le Morte d'Arthur,* that is, *The Death of Arthur.* Malory was not, however, merely a translator. His book not only selects and condenses earlier romances; it presents a fifteenth-century English gentleman's conception of the chivalric ideals.

Structurally, it is a rambling and ill-unified performance. It begins with Arthur's birth and ends with his death and the dispersal of the corps of knights known as the Round Table, but for long stretches neither the King nor his principal knights appear. A number of its "books" are given over to unrelated adventures; a substantial portion deals with the knights' quest for the Holy Grail, the cup used by Jesus at the Last Supper. Gawain is still of first-rate importance; but his fame is eclipsed by that of Lancelot, in the later of the French romances the foremost of the knights. Much of the narrative is, by present-day standards, pretty flat. We accompany knight after knight in adventure after adventure, too many of them meaningless, narrated baldly, and tiresomely repetitive in their catalogues of wicked warriors unhorsed, sinister dwarfs circumvented, giants beheaded, sorceresses foiled, and damsels rescued from worse than death. There is far too much that neither illuminates life nor exhibits any remarkable degree of competence in the art of narration. Suspense, racy detail, those touches of nature that make a reader share a character's experience, these are too often absent; and a great deal of Malory's story is a procession of doll figures against backgrounds sketched in the palest of water colors.

Nevertheless, the book's success was immediate, and it continued throughout the sixteenth century. Naturally, it waned after the appearance of the full-bodied masterpieces of the Renaissance. The seventeenth and eighteenth centuries had no great love for Malory. The revival of his popularity in the nineteenth was a consequence of the Romantic movement and its interest in things medieval. Our own century has seen another decline. Drastically expurgated, stories from Malory's book have a perennial appeal for children. Toned up by Tennyson with a complete set of Victorian morals, they are still mildly palatable even to adults. Whatever the faults of *The Idylls of the King,* the credit is mainly Tennyson's for keeping popular interest in Arthurian story alive. He succeeds in giving some of the figures a depth, a third dimension, which, if largely false

to Malory's age, at least makes them interesting human beings.

It is with his style, not his gifts for storytelling, that Malory wins his place. That style is an irregular one, blandly defiant of all the rules of sentence structure; but its cadences are graceful and delicately rhythmical, and they lure a reader on. With all his shortcomings in the manipulation of narrative and the delineation of character, Malory was a great artist in the important matter of arranging words beautifully.

From these reservations, with which you are not obliged to agree if you think them too severe, certain portions of Malory's work must be excepted, especially the selection which follows, Book XXI. Here, at the end of the whole performance, and most sharply for the reader to whom, since he has persevered throughout all that precedes, the names of the principal actors have come to suggest a long past of glory and of suffering, there is a fine cumulative effect and the level reaches the dignity of tragedy. And, indeed, it may be said of Malory in general that, however he muddles along through a series of routine adventures, he can rise to a great occasion, as he also does in the best scenes of the stories about the Grail.

The subject itself is, of course, sheer legend. We have already noticed (p. 3) that around the name of a certain Artorius there appear in later centuries to have clustered tales of an heroic leader's defense of Britain in the fifth and sixth. But the historian Gildas, who lived about the time when King Arthur is supposed to have flourished, fails to mention his allegedly celebrated contemporary, though he describes the wars of the Britons and Saxons and the great British victory at Mount Badon. Not till the ninth century and the *Historia Britonum* of Nennius do we find a written account, not yet of a king, but of an Arthur who commanded against the invaders. By the eleventh century a large body of legend had become attached to his name; and in the twelfth Geoffrey of Monmouth, in his *Historia Regum Britanniae,* really let himself go. Geoffrey's book became the cornerstone of the splendid palace of myth to which his successors, both chroniclers and poets, long continued to add striking features. Among these writers was the gifted twelfth-century romancer, Chrestien de Troyes, in whose poetry the stories of the quest for the Grail, not originally part of the Arthurian cycle, were joined with it.

By the French romancers, too, "courtly love" was introduced into the Arthurian tales. According to this cult, only the gentry were capable of love, and of the lover was required the strictest conformity to an elaborate code of conduct. It included undeviating courtesy, especially toward noble ladies. To the lady whom he served, the lover or "servant" was required to render unquestioning obedience, however capricious her will. All this had nothing to do with marriage, which was dictated by economic "convenience" rather than by love. Though constancy was expected of the lover even when he saw no prospect of attaining his desire, courtly love sanctioned adultery and therefore the secrecy which such a relationship ordinarily involves. "Romantic" love was thus illicit; between husband and wife it was, according to the code, an impossibility. This convention is reflected in Malory's pages, most notably in the adultery of Queen Guinevere. She and Lancelot are guilty; yet their love ennobles them.

But it was not only from his reading of French romances that Malory acquired his feeling for chivalry; he drew it also from the circumstances of his own life. If the orthodox identification of Malory is correct (and there is small doubt that it is, though few details have come to light), he was a Warwickshire man, a gentleman of ancient lineage, reasonably well educated, a veteran of the latter part of the Hundred Years' War with France, a member of Parliament, and a figure of some prominence on the Lancastrian side in the Wars of the Roses. He was a follower of Richard de Beauchamp, Earl of Warwick, one of the greatest lords of his time. Beauchamp's life was like a hero's of romance, and he was famous throughout western Europe as "the father of courtesy." It is the ideals of his own youth, when the fifteenth century was also young, that Malory depicts. There is nothing of the antiquarian about him. Arthur and the Round Table are not British chieftains of the fifth and sixth centuries but idealizations of the knights who charged at Agincourt or lightly gave their lives for the honor of the white rose or the red. In a way his book is a swan song of chivalry. The year of its publication, 1485, also saw Bosworth Field, last of the feudal battles for the throne. There the power of the English baronage was finally broken, and the first of the Tudor monarchs seized the crown and proceeded to make its authority supreme.

Malory died in 1471, shortly after completing his book and fourteen years before its publication. Most of his last twenty years were spent in prison. He was arrested in 1451 for a variety of crimes, the charges arising from his violent entry into the abbey at Coombe, which he was accused of robbing. The political setting of this episode is unknown; it is quite possible that Malory was within his rights from his own point of view. However that may have been, he was in trouble for the rest of his life and was in prison when he died, having been excluded by name from a general pardon issued by Edward IV, the Yorkist king. Presumably Malory wrote his book, his only one as far as is known, to occupy himself during his imprisonment.

Le Morte d'Arthur was published in 1485 by William Caxton (d. 1491), the first English printer and hence the possessor of a venerated name in the annals of the English-speaking world. (See below, p. 218.) The recent discovery of a manuscript version closer to Malory's own text, in the Fellows' Library, Winchester College, shows that Caxton made considerable revision of the original. The Winchester manuscript has been edited by E. Vinaver (*The Works of Sir Thomas Malory*, 3 vols., 1947). Of Caxton's text there is no good modern annotated edition. The standard one is that of H. O. Sommer (3 vols., 1889–91). The complete text, modernized, is available in Everyman's Library (2 vols.). There is a good short introduction in W. E. Mead's *Selections from Sir Thomas Malory's Morte Darthur* (1897). For a fuller and more recent treatment, see E. Vinaver, *Malory* (1929). The following reprint of Book XXI follows Caxton's text except for alterations in spelling, punctuation, capitalization, and paragraphing.

The love of Lancelot and the Queen is indirectly responsible for the fall of Arthur and of the chivalry of the Round Table. Sir Gawain's brother, Sir Agravaine, and his half brother, Sir Mordred, have taken the lead in exposing Guinevere's adultery. They succeed in trapping her lover in her chamber, but Lancelot fights his way out and makes his escape. In doing so he kills, among others, Agravaine and two sons of Gawain. For this Gawain bears no grudge; he and his other brothers, Sir Gaheris and Sir Gareth, have expressed in advance their disapproval of the plot against Lancelot and the Queen. The latter is condemned to be burnt, but Lancelot appears at the stake and carries her off to his northern castle of Joyous Gard. In rescuing Guinevere, however, he unfortunately kills Gaheris and Gareth, Gawain's brothers and his own friends, who are present on orders from the King against their wishes and are entirely unarmed. Lancelot fails to recognize them in the thick of the fighting. Gawain is unable to forgive him and insists on Arthur's making war. The royal army besieges Joyous Gard without advantage; but in obedience to the Pope's commands Lancelot surrenders the Queen to her husband, who makes peace with her and would do the same with Lancelot but for Gawain. Lancelot then goes overseas to his own lands in the southwest of France; Arthur and Gawain follow with their army. During the ensuing campaign Gawain is twice wounded by Lancelot in single combat. Meanwhile, Sir Mordred seizes Arthur's throne. It is at this point that the final book opens.

Sir Thomas Malory

LE MORTE D'ARTHUR

BOOK XXI

CHAPTER I

How Sir Mordred presumed and took on him to be king of England, and would have married the Queen, his father's wife.[1]

As Sir Mordred was ruler of all England, he did do make[2] letters as though that they came from beyond the sea; and the letters specified that King Arthur was slain in battle with Sir Lancelot. Wherefore Sir Mordred made a parliament and called the lords together, and there he made them to choose him king. And so was he crowned at Canterbury, and held a feast there fifteen days; and afterward he drew him unto Winchester. And there he took the Queen Guinevere, and said plainly that he would wed her which was his uncle's wife and his father's wife. And so he made ready for the feast, and a day prefixed[3] that they should be wedded; wherefore Queen Guinevere was passing heavy.[4] But she durst not discover her heart, but spake fair, and agreed to Sir Mordred's will.

Then she desired of Sir Mordred for to go to London, to buy all manner of things that longed[5] unto the wedding. And because of her fair speech Sir Mordred trusted her well enough, and gave her leave to go. And so, when she came to London, she took the Tower of London; and suddenly in all haste possible she stuffed it with all manner of victual, and well garnished it with men, and so kept it. Then when Sir Mordred wist[6] and understood how he was beguiled, he was passing wroth, out of measure.

And, a short tale for to make, he went and laid a mighty siege about the Tower of London, and made many great assaults thereat, and threw many great engines unto them, and shot great guns. But all might not prevail Sir Mordred, for Queen Guinevere would never, for fair speech nor for foul, would never trust to come in his hands again.

Then came the Bishop of Canterbury, the which was a noble clerk[7] and an holy man, and thus he said to Sir Mordred: "Sir, what will ye do? Will ye first displease God and sithen[8] shame yourself and all knighthood? Is not King Arthur your uncle, no farther but your mother's brother, and on her himself King Arthur begat you upon his own sister? Therefore how may you wed your father's wife? Sir," said the noble clerk, "leave this opinion, or I shall curse you with book and bell and candle."[9]

"Do thou thy worst!" said Sir Mordred. "Wit[10] thou well I shall defy thee!"

"Sir," said the Bishop, "and wit you well I shall not fear me to do that[11] me ought to do. Also, where ye noise where my lord Arthur is slain, and that is not so, and therefore ye will make a foul work in this land."

"Peace, thou false priest!" said Sir Mordred, "for and[12] thou chafe me any more, I shall make strike off thy head."

So the Bishop departed and did the cursing in the most orgulous[13] wise that might be done. And then Sir Mordred sought the Bishop of Canterbury, for to have slain him. Then the Bishop fled, and took part of his goods with him, and went nigh unto Glastonbury;[14] and there he was a priest hermit in a chapel, and lived in poverty and in holy prayers. For well he understood that mischievous war was at hand. Then Sir Mordred sought on Queen Guinevere by letters and sonds,[15] and by fair means and foul means, for to have her to come out of the Tower of London; but all this availed not, for she answered him shortly, openly and privily, that she had liefer slay herself than to be married with him.

---

[1] This and the following chapter headings are from Caxton's table of contents.—Arthur's mother was Igraine, Duchess of Tintagel. She was first the wife and then the widow of Gorlois. She gave birth to Arthur after King Uther Pendragon had been enabled by Merlin's magic art to visit her in the likeness of Gorlois. Arthur was conceived shortly after the death of Gorlois, of which Igraine was then unaware. King Uther afterwards married her, but Arthur was brought up from infancy by one of Uther's knights, in ignorance of his real origin. Soon after he came to the throne and before he learned who his true parents were, Arthur had a brief love affair with the Queen of Orkney, one of Igraine's three daughters (another was Morgan le Fay, whom we have already met in *Sir Gawain and the Green Knight*), and therefore Arthur's elder half sister, though neither was aware of the relationship. Sir Mordred was the fruit of this amour. When Arthur goes overseas in pursuit of Lancelot, he leaves Mordred in England as regent. [2] Caused to be written.
[3] Set in advance. [4] Very sad.
[5] Belonged, were appropriate. [6] Knew.

[7] Ecclesiastic. [8] Then.
[9] I.e., excommunicate you. The ceremony ended by closing the book, ringing the bell, and putting out the candle.
[10] Know. [11] What. [12] If. [13] Haughtiest.
[14] In Somersetshire. It is still famous for the ruins of its ancient abbey. [15] Messages.

Then came word to Sir Mordred that King Arthur had araised the siege for Sir Lancelot, and he was coming homeward with a great host, to be avenged upon Sir Mordred; wherefore Sir Mordred made write writs to all the barony of this land, and much people drew to him. For then was the common voice among them that with Arthur was none other life but war and strife, and with Sir Mordred was great joy and bliss. Thus was Sir Arthur depraved[16] and evil said of. And many there were that King Arthur had made up of nought, and given them lands, might not then say him a good word.

Lo, ye all Englishmen, see ye not what a mischief here was? For he that was the most king and knight of the world, and most loved the fellowship of noble knights, and by him they were all upholden, now might not these Englishmen hold them content with him. Lo, thus was the old custom and usage of this land; and also men say that we of this land have not yet lost nor forgotten that custom and usage.[17] Alas, this is a great default of us Englishmen, for there may no thing please us no term.

And so fared the people at that time: they were better pleased with Sir Mordred than they were with King Arthur; and much people drew unto Sir Mordred, and said they would abide with him for better and for worse. And so Sir Mordred drew with a great host to Dover, for there he heard say that Sir Arthur would arrive, and so he thought to beat his own father from his lands; and the most party of all England held with Sir Mordred, the people were so newfangle.

CHAPTER 2

How after that King Arthur had tidings he returned and came to Dover, where Sir Mordred met him to let[18] his landing; and of the death of Sir Gawain.

And so, as Sir Mordred wa[s] at Dover with his host, there came King Arthur with a great navy of ships and galleys[19] and carracks.[20] And there was Sir Mordred ready awaiting upon his landage,[21] to let his own father to land up the land that he was king over. Then there was launching of great boats and small, and full of noble men of arms; and there was much slaughter of gentle[22] knights, and many a full[23] bold baron was laid full low, on both parties.

But King Arthur was so courageous that there might no manner of knights let him to land, and his knights fiercely followed him; and so they landed maugre[24] Sir Mordred's and all his power,[25] and put Sir Mordred aback, that he fled and all his people. So when this battle was done, King Arthur let bury his people that were dead. And then was noble Sir Gawain found in a great boat, lying more than half dead.

When Sir Arthur wist that Sir Gawain was laid so low, he went unto him; and there the King made sorrow out of measure, and took Sir Gawain in his arms, and thrice he there swooned. And then when he awaked, he said: "Alas, Sir Gawain, my sister's son,[26] here now thou liest, the man in the world that I loved most; and now is my joy gone, for now, my nephew, Sir Gawain, I will discover me unto your person: in Sir Lancelot and you I most had my joy and mine affiance,[27] and now have I lost my joy of you both; wherefore all mine earthly joy is gone from me."

"Mine uncle, King Arthur," said Sir Gawain, "wit you well my death day is come, and all is through mine own hastiness and willfulness; for I am smitten upon the old wound the which Sir Lancelot gave me, on the which I feel well I must die; and had Sir Lancelot been with you as he was, this unhappy war had never begun; and of all this am I causer, for Sir Lancelot and his blood, through their prowess, held all your cankered enemies in subjection and danger.[28] And now," said Sir Gawain, "ye shall miss Sir Lancelot. But, alas, I would not accord with him; and therefore," said Sir Gawain, "I pray you, fair uncle, that I may have paper, pen, and ink, that I may write to Sir Lancelot a schedule[29] with mine own hands."

And then, when paper and ink was brought, then Gawain was set up weakly by King Arthur, for he was shriven a little tofore;[30] and then he wrote thus, as the French book maketh mention: "Unto Sir Lancelot, flower of all noble knights that ever I heard of or saw by my days,[31] I, Sir Gawain, King Lot's son of Orkney, sister['s] son unto the noble King Arthur, send thee greeting, and let thee have knowledge that the tenth day of May I was smitten upon the old wound that thou gavest me afore the city of Benwick;[32] and through the same wound that thou

---

[16] Defamed.
[17] An allusion to the Wars of the Roses, the current struggle between the factions of Lancaster and York.   [18] Prevent.
[19] Bargelike vessels, using oars as well as sail.
[20] Big sailing ships.   [21] Landing.   [22] Honorable.
[23] Very.

[24] In spite of.   [25] Army.
[26] Gawain was one of the sons of King Lot of Orkney by his queen, Arthur's half sister. It was he that had urged Arthur to prosecute the war with Lancelot, against whom Gawain sought revenge.   [27] Trust.   [28] Power.   [29] Scroll, note.
[30] Absolved a little while before.   [31] In my time.
[32] Identified by Malory as Bayonne, in southwestern France.

gavest me, I am come to my death day. And I will that all the world wit, that I, Sir Gawain, knight of the Table Round, sought my death, and not through thy deserving, but it was mine own seeking. Wherefore I beseech thee, Sir Lancelot, to return again unto this realm and see my tomb and pray some prayer, more or less, for my soul. And this same day that I wrote this schedule, I was hurt to the death in the same wound the which I had of thy hand, Sir Lancelot. For of a more nobler man might I not be slain. Also, Sir Lancelot, for all the love that ever was betwixt us, make no tarrying, but come over the sea in all haste, that thou mayst with thy noble knights rescue that noble king that made thee knight, that is my lord Arthur. For he is full straightly bestead with[33] a false traitor, that is my half brother, Sir Mordred; and he hath let crown him king, and would have wedded my lady Queen Guinevere, and so had he done had she not put herself in the Tower of London. And so the tenth day of May last past, my lord Arthur and we all landed upon them at Dover; and there we put that false traitor, Sir Mordred, to flight, and there it misfortuned me to be stricken upon thy stroke. And at the date of this letter was written, but two hours and a half afore my death, written with mine own hand, and so subscribed with part of my heart's blood. And I require thee, most famous knight of the world, that thou wilt see my tomb."

And then Sir Gawain wept, and King Arthur wept; and then they swooned both. And when they awaked both, the King made Sir Gawain to receive his Saviour.[34] And then Sir Gawain prayed the King for to send for Sir Lancelot, and to cherish him above all other knights. And so at the hour of noon Sir Gawain yielded up the spirit; and then the King let inter him in a chapel within Dover Castle. And there yet all men may see the skull of him, and the same wound is seen that Sir Lancelot gave him in battle.

Then was it told the King that Sir Mordred had pight[35] a new field upon Barham Down.[36] And upon the morn the King rode thither to him, and there was a great battle betwixt them, and much people was slain on both parties; but at the last Sir Arthur's party stood best, and Sir Mordred and his party fled unto Canterbury.

How, after, Sir Gawain's ghost appeared to King Arthur and warned him that he should not fight that day.

And then the King let search all the towns for his knights that were slain, and interred them; and salved them with soft salves that so sore were wounded. Then much people drew unto King Arthur. And then they said that Sir Mordred warred upon King Arthur with wrong. And then King Arthur drew him with his host down by the seaside westward toward Salisbury; and there was a day assigned betwixt King Arthur and Sir Mordred, that they should meet upon a down[37] beside Salisbury, and not far from the seaside; and this day was assigned on a Monday after Trinity Sunday, whereof King Arthur was passing glad, that he might be avenged upon Sir Mordred. Then Sir Mordred araised much people about London; for they of Kent, Southsex, and Surrey, Estsex, and of Southfolk, and of Northfolk, held the most party with Sir Mordred. And many a full noble knight drew unto Sir Mordred and to the King. But they loved Sir Lancelot drew unto Sir Mordred.

So, upon Trinity Sunday at night, King Arthur dreamed a wonderful dream, and that was this: that him seemed he sat upon a chaflet[38] in a chair, and the chair was fast to a wheel, and thereupon sat King Arthur in the richest cloth of gold that might be made. And the King thought there was under him, far from him, an hideous deep black water, and therein were all manner of serpents and worms and wild beasts, foul and horrible. And suddenly the King thought the wheel turned up so down, and he fell among the serpents and every beast took him by a limb; and then the King cried as he lay in his bed and slept, "Help!" And then knights, squires, and yeomen awaked the King; and then he was so amazed that he wist not where he was; and then he fell on slumbering again, not sleeping nor thoroughly waking. So the King seemed[39] verily that there came Sir Gawain unto him, with a number of fair ladies with him. And when King Arthur saw him, then he said: "Welcome, my sister's son; I weened[40] thou hadst been dead, and, now I see thee alive, much am I beholding unto Almighty Jesu. O fair nephew and my sister's son, what be these ladies that hither be come with you?"

"Sir," said Sir Gawain, "all these be ladies for whom I have foughten when I was man living, and

---

[33] He is very hard beset by.
[34] The sacrament of Communion.
[35] Pitched, picked, encamped on.
[36] Near Canterbury.

[37] Hill.
[38] Platform, stage.
[39] It seemed to the King.   [40] Thought, supposed.

all these are those that I did battle for in righteous quarrel; and God hath given them that grace at their great prayer, because I did battle for them, that they should bring me hither unto you. Thus much hath God given me leave, for to warn you of your death; for, and ye fight as tomorn with Sir Mordred, as ye both have assigned, doubt ye not ye must be slain, and the most party of your people on both parties. And for the great grace and goodness that Almighty Jesu hath unto you, and for pity of you and many more other good men there shall be slain, God hath sent me to you of his special grace, to give you warning that in no wise ye do battle as tomorn, but that ye take a treatise[41] for a month day;[42] and proffer you largely,[43] so as tomorn to be put in a delay. For within a month shall come Sir Lancelot with all his noble knights, and rescue you worshipfully,[44] and slay Sir Mordred and all that ever will hold with him."

Then Sir Gawain and all the ladies vanished. And anon the King called upon his knights, squires, and yeomen, and charged them wightly[45] to fetch his noble lords and wise bishops unto him. And when they were come, the King told them his avision, what Sir Gawain had told him and warned him, that if he fought on the morn he should be slain. Then the King commanded Sir Lucan de Butler, and his brother, Sir Bedivere, with two bishops with them, and charged them in any wise, and they might: "Take a treatise for a month day with Sir Mordred, and spare not! Proffer him lands and goods as much as ye think best!"

So then they departed, and came to Sir Mordred, where he had a grim host of an hundred thousand men. And there they entreated Sir Mordred long time; and at the last Sir Mordred was agreed for to have Cornwall and Kent, by Arthur's days: after, all England, after the days of King Arthur.

CHAPTER 4

How by misadventure of an adder the battle began, where Mordred was slain, and Arthur hurt to the death.

Then were they condescended that King Arthur and Sir Mordred should meet betwixt both their hosts, and every each of them should bring fourteen persons; and they came with this word unto Arthur. Then said he, "I am glad that this is done." And so he went into the field. And when Arthur should depart, he warned all his host that, and they see any sword drawn, "Look ye come on fiercely, and slay that traitor, Sir Mordred, for I in no wise trust him."

In like wise Sir Mordred warned his host that, "And ye see any sword drawn, look that ye come on fiercely, and so slay all that ever before you standeth; for in no wise I will not trust for this treatise, for I know well my father will be avenged on me."

And so they met as their pointment was, and so they were agreed and accorded thoroughly; and wine was fetched, and they drank. Right so came an adder out of a little heath bush, and it stung a knight on the foot. And when the knight felt him stung, he looked down and saw the adder; and then he drew his sword to slay the adder, and thought of none other harm. And when the host on both parties saw that sword drawn, then they blew bemes,[46] trumpets, and horns, and shouted grimly. And so both hosts dressed them together. And King Arthur took his horse, and said, "Alas, this unhappy day!" and so rode to his party. And Sir Mordred in like wise.

And never was there seen a more dolefuller battle in no Christian land; for there was but rushing and riding, foining[47] and striking, and many a grim word was there spoken either to other, and many a deadly stroke. But ever King Arthur rode throughout the battle[48] of Sir Mordred many times, and did full nobly as a noble king should; and at all times he fainted never. And Sir Mordred that day put him in devoir[49] and in great peril. And thus they fought all the long day, and never stinted till the noble knights were laid to the cold earth; and ever they fought still till it was near night, and by that time was there an hundred thousand laid dead upon the down. Then was Arthur wood[50] wroth out of measure, when he saw his people so slain from him.

Then the King looked about him, and then was he ware, of all his host and of all his good knights, were left no more alive but two knights: that one was Sir Lucan de Butler, and his brother Sir Bedivere; and they were full sore wounded. "Jesu mercy!" said the King, "where are all my noble knights become? Alas that ever I should see this doleful day! For now," said Arthur, "I am come to mine end. But would to God that I wist where were that traitor Sir Mordred, that hath caused all this mischief." Then was King Arthur ware where Sir Mordred leaned upon his sword among a great heap of dead men. "Now give me my spear," said Arthur unto Sir Lucan, "for

---

[41] Treaty. [42] A month's time.
[43] Offer generous concessions. [44] Honorably.
[45] Quickly.

[46] Trumpets. [47] Thrusting.
[48] Army. [49] Did his duty. [50] Violently.

yonder I have espied the traitor that all this woe hath wrought."

"Sir, let him be," said Sir Lucan, "for he is unhappy;[51] and if ye pass this unhappy day ye shall be right well revenged upon him. Good lord, remember ye of your night's dream, and what the spirit of Sir Gawain told you this night; yet God of his great goodness hath preserved you hitherto. Therefore, for God's sake, my lord, leave off by this. For blessed b[e] God ye have won the field, for here we be three alive, and with Sir Mordred is none alive; and if ye leave off now, this wicked day of destiny is past."

"Tide me death, betide me life," saith the King, "now I see him yonder alone he shall never escape mine hands, for at a better avail shall I never have him."

"God speed you well," said Sir Bedivere.

Then the King gat his spear in both his hands, and ran toward Sir Mordred, crying, "Traitor, now is thy death day come!" And when Sir Mordred heard Sir Arthur, he ran until him with his sword drawn in his hand. And there King Arthur smote Sir Mordred under the shield, with a foin of his spear, throughout the body, more than a fathom. And when Sir Mordred felt that he had his death's wound, he thrust himself with the might that he had up to the burr[52] of King Arthur's spear. And right so he smote his father, Arthur, with his sword holden in both his hands, on the side of the head, that[53] the sword pierced the helmet and the brainpan, and therewithal Sir Mordred fell stark dead to the earth; and the noble Arthur fell in a swoon to the earth, and there he swooned ofttimes. And Sir Lucan de Butler and Sir Bedivere ofttimes heave[d] him up. And so weakly they led him betwixt them both, to a little chapel not far from the seaside. And when the King was there, he thought him well eased.

Then heard they people cry in the field. "Now go thou, Sir Lucan," said the King, "and do me to wit[54] what betokens that noise in the field." So Sir Lucan departed, for he was grievously wounded in many places. And so as he yede,[55] he saw and hearkened by the moonlight how that pillers[56] and robbers were come into the field, to pill and rob many a full noble knight of brooches and beads, of many a good ring, and of many a rich jewel; and who that were not dead all out, there they slew them for their harness[57] and their riches.

When Sir Lucan understood this work, he came to the King as soon as he might,[58] and told him all what he had heard and seen. "Therefore by my rede,"[59] said Sir Lucan, "it is best that we bring you to some town."

"I would it were so," said the King.

CHAPTER 5

How King Arthur commanded to cast his sword Excalibur into the water, and how he was delivered to ladies in a barge.

"But I may[60] not stand, mine head works so. Ah, Sir Lancelot," said King Arthur, "this day have I sore missed thee. Alas, that ever I was against thee! for now have I my death, whereof Sir Gawain me warned in my dream." Then Sir Lucan took up the King the one part, and Sir Bedivere the other part, and in the lifting the King swooned; and Sir Lucan fell in a swoon with the lift, that the part of his guts fell out of his body, and therewith the noble knight's heart brast.[61] And when the King awoke, he beheld Sir Lucan, how he lay foaming at the mouth, and part of his guts lay at his feet. "Alas," said the King, "this is to me a full heavy sight, to see this noble duke so die for my sake; for he would have holpen me, that had more need of help than I. Alas, he would not complain him, his heart was so set to help me! Now Jesu have mercy upon his soul!"

Then Sir Bedivere wept for the death of his brother. "Leave this mourning and weeping," said the King, "for all this will not avail me. For wit thou well: and I might live myself, the death of Sir Lucan would grieve me evermore; but my time hieth fast," said the King. "Therefore," said Arthur unto Sir Bedivere, "take thou Excalibur, my good sword, and go with it to yonder waterside; and when thou comest there I charge thee throw my sword in that water, and come again and tell me what thou there seest."

"My lord," said Bedivere, "your commandment shall be done, and lightly[62] bring you word again." So Sir Bedivere departed, and by the way he beheld that noble sword, that the pommel and the haft was all of precious stones; and then he said to himself, "If I throw this rich sword in the water, thereof shall never come good, but harm and loss." And then Sir Bedivere hid Excalibur under a tree. And so, as soon as he might, he came again unto the King, and said he had been at the water and had thrown the sword into the water.

[51] Unlucky (for you).
[52] A broad ring just behind the part of the spear gripped by the hand.   [53] So that.   [54] Cause me to know.
[55] Went.   [56] Pillagers, looters.   [57] Armor.

[58] Could.   [59] Counsel.   [60] Can.   [61] Burst.
[62] Swiftly.

"What saw thou there?" said the King.

"Sir," he said, "I saw nothing but waves and winds."

"That is untruly said of thee," said the King; "therefore go thou lightly again, and do my commandment. As thou art to me lief[63] and dear, spare not, but throw it in!"

Then Sir Bedivere returned again, and took the sword in his hand; and then him thought[64] sin and shame to throw away that noble sword, and so eft[65] he hid the sword, and returned again, and told to the King that he had been at the water and done his commandment.

"What saw thou there?" said the King.

"Sir," he said, "I saw nothing but the waters wap[66] and waves wan."[67]

"Ah, traitor untrue," said King Arthur, "now hast thou betrayed me twice. Who would have weened that thou, that hast been to me so lief and dear, and thou art named a noble knight, and would betray me for the riches of the sword? But now go again lightly, for thy long tarrying putteth me in great jeopardy of my life, for I have taken cold. And but if[68] thou do now as I bid thee, if ever I may see thee I shall slay thee mine own hands; for thou wouldst for my rich sword see me dead."

Then Sir Bedivere departed, and went to the sword, and lightly took it up, and went to the waterside; and there he bound the girdle about the hilts, and then he threw the sword as far into the water as he might. And there came an arm and an hand above the water and met it, and caught it, and so shook it thrice and brandished; and then vanished away the hand with the sword in the water. So Sir Bedivere came again to the King, and told him what he saw.

"Alas," said the King, "help me hence, for I dread me I have tarried overlong." Then Sir Bedivere took the King upon his back, and so went with him to that waterside. And when they were at the waterside, even fast by the bank hoved[69] a little barge, with many fair ladies in it, and among them all was a queen; and all they had black hoods, and all they wept and shrieked when they saw King Arthur. "Now put me into the barge," said the King; and so he did softly. And there received him three queens with great mourning, and so they set him down, and in one of their laps King Arthur laid his head.

And then that queen said, "Ah, dear brother, why have ye tarried so long from me? Alas, this wound on your head hath caught overmuch cold." And so then they rowed from the land, and Sir Bedivere beheld all those ladies go from him.

Then Sir Bedivere cried, "Ah, my lord Arthur, what shall become of me, now ye go from me and leave me here alone among mine enemies?"

"Comfort thyself," said the King, "and do as well as thou mayst, for in me is no trust for to trust in; for I will into the vale of Avilion,[70] to heal me of my grievous wound. And if thou hear nevermore of me, pray for my soul!" But ever the queens and ladies wept and shrieked, that it was pity to hear. And as soon as Sir Bedivere had lost the sight of the barge, he wept and wailed, and so took the forest; and so he went all that night, and in the morning he was ware, betwixt two holts hoar,[71] of a chapel and an hermitage.

CHAPTER 6

How Sir Bedivere found him on the morn dead in an hermitage, and how he abode there with the hermit.

Then was Sir Bedivere glad, and thither he went; and when he came into the chapel, he saw where lay an hermit groveling on all four, there fast by a tomb was[72] new graven.[73] When the hermit saw Sir Bedivere, he knew him well, for he was, but little tofore, Bishop of Canterbury, that Sir Mordred flemed.[74] "Sir," said Sir Bedivere, "what man is there interred that ye pray so fast for?"

"Fair son," said the hermit, "I wot[75] not verily, but by my deeming.[76] But this night, at midnight, here came a number of ladies, and brought hither a dead corse, and prayed me to bury him; and here they offered an hundred tapers, and they gave me an hundred bezants."[77]

"Alas," said Sir Bedivere, "that was my lord King Arthur, that here lieth buried in this chapel." Then Sir Bedivere swooned; and when he awoke he prayed the hermit he might abide with him still there, to live with fasting and prayers. "For from hence will I never go," said Sir Bedivere, "by my will, but all the days of my life here to pray for my lord Arthur."

"Ye are welcome to me," said the hermit, "for I know you better than ye ween that I do. Ye are the bold Bedivere, and the full noble duke, Sir Lucan de Butler, was your brother."

---

[70] Avalon; in Celtic romance, an island paradise in fairyland. Malory confuses it with Glastonbury.

[71] Ancient wooded hills.   [72] Which was.   [73] Dug.

[74] Put to flight.   [75] Know.   [76] Supposition, inference.

[77] A coin, gold or silver, originally struck at Byzantium (Constantinople, Istanbul); in England the gold bezant fluctuated in value up to about five dollars.

---

[63] Dear.   [64] It seemed to him.

[65] Again.   [66] Lap.   [67] Darken.   [68] Unless.

[69] Waited.

Then Sir Bedivere told the hermit all as ye have heard tofore. So there bode Sir Bedivere with the hermit that was tofore Bishop of Canterbury; and there Sir Bedivere put upon him poor clothes, and served the hermit full lowly in fasting and in prayers.

Thus of Arthur I find never more written in books that be authorized, nor more of the very certainty of his death heard I never read, but thus was he led away in a ship wherein were three queens: that one was King Arthur's sister, Queen Morgan le Fay; the other was the Queen of North Wales; the third was the Queen of the Waste Lands. Also there was Nimue, the chief Lady of the Lake, that had wedded Pelleas the good knight;[78] and this lady had done much for King Arthur. For she would never suffer Sir Pelleas to be in no place where he should be in danger of his life; and so he lived to the uttermost of his days with her in great rest. More of the death of King Arthur could I never find, but that ladies brought him to his burials; and such one was buried there, that the hermit bore witness that sometime was Bishop of Canterbury; but yet the hermit knew not in certain that he was verily the body of King Arthur: for this tale Sir Bedivere, knight of the Table Round, made it to be written.

CHAPTER 7

Of the opinion of some men of the death of King Arthur, and how Queen Guinevere made her a nun in Amesbury.

Yet some men say in many parts of England that King Arthur is not dead, but had by the will of our Lord Jesu into another place; and men say that he shall come again, and he shall win the Holy Cross. I will not say that it shall be so, but rather I will say: here in this world he changed his life. But many men say that there is written upon his tomb this verse: *Hic jacet Arthurus, rex quondam rexque futurus.*[79] Thus leave I here Sir Bedivere with the hermit, that dwelled that time in a chapel beside Glastonbury, and there was his hermitage. And they lived in their prayers and fastings and great abstinence.

And when Queen Guinevere understood that King Arthur was slain, and all the noble knights, Sir Mordred, and all the remnant, then the Queen stole away, and five ladies with her, and so she went to Amesbury;[80] and there she let make herself a nun, and wore white clothes and black, and great penance

she took, as ever did sinful lady in this land. And never creature could make her merry, but lived in fasting, prayers, and alms deeds, that all manner of people marveled how virtuously she was changed. Now leave we Queen Guinevere in Amesbury, a nun in white clothes and black, and there she was abbess and ruler, as reason would; and turn we from her, and speak we of Sir Lancelot du Lake.

CHAPTER 8

How when Sir Lancelot heard of the death of King Arthur, and of Sir Gawain, and other matters, he came into England.

And when he heard in his country that Sir Mordred was crowned king in England and made war against King Arthur, his own father, and would let him to land in his own land; also it was told Sir Lancelot how that Sir Mordred had laid siege about the Tower of London, because the Queen would not wed him: then was Sir Lancelot wroth out of measure, and said to his kinsmen: "Alas, that double traitor, Sir Mordred, now me repenteth that ever he escaped my hands, for much shame hath he done unto my lord Arthur; for all I feel by the doleful letter that my lord Sir Gawain sent me, on whose soul Jesu have mercy, that my lord Arthur is full hard bestead. Alas," said Sir Lancelot, "that ever I should live to hear that most noble king that made me knight thus to be overset with his subject in his own realm. And this doleful letter that my lord, Sir Gawain, hath sent me afore his death, praying me to see his tomb, wit you well his doleful words shall never go from mine heart. For he was a full noble knight as ever was born; and in an unhappy hour was I born that ever I should have that unhap to slay, first Sir Gawain, Sir Gaheris the good knight, and mine own friend Sir Gareth, that full noble knight.[81] Alas, I may say I am unhappy," said Sir Lancelot, "that ever I should do thus unhappily, and, alas, yet might I never have hap to slay that traitor, Sir Mordred."

"Leave your complaints," said Sir Bors,[82] "and first revenge you of the death of Sir Gawain; and it will be well done that ye see Sir Gawain's tomb, and secondly that ye revenge my lord Arthur and my lady Queen Guinevere."

"I thank you," said Sir Lancelot, "for ever ye will my worship."[83]

Then they made them ready in all the haste that might be, with ships and galleys, with Sir Lancelot

---

[78] This story is told in Book IV. It was from the Lady of the Lake that Arthur had received Excalibur in his youth; hence his instructions to Sir Bedivere.
[79] Here lies Arthur, king formerly and future king.
[80] In Wiltshire, near Salisbury.

[81] See the summary of the earlier action, p. 178, above.
[82] Sir Bors de Ganis, Lancelot's cousin and a leading figure in the quest for the Grail.   [83] Desire my honor.

and his host to pass into England. And so he passed over the sea till he came to Dover, and there he landed with seven kings, and the number was hideous to behold. Then Sir Lancelot speered[84] of men of Dover where was King Arthur become. Then the people told him how that he was slain, and Sir Mordred and an hundred thousand died on a day; and how Sir Mordred gave King Arthur there the first battle at his landing, and there was good Sir Gawain slain; and on the morn Sir Mordred fought with the King upon Barham Down, and there the King put Sir Mordred to the worse.

"Alas," said Sir Lancelot, "this is the heaviest tidings that ever came to me. Now, fair sirs," said Sir Lancelot, "show me the tomb of Sir Gawain." And then certain people of the town brought him into the Castle of Dover, and showed him the tomb. Then Sir Lancelot kneeled down and wept, and prayed heartily for his soul. And that night he made a dole; and all they that would come had as much flesh, fish, wine, and ale, and every man and woman had twelve pence, come who would. Thus with his own hand dealt he this money, in a mourning gown; and ever he wept, and prayed them to pray for the soul of Sir Gawain. And on the morn all the priests and clerks that might be gotten in the country were there, and sang mass of requiem. And there offered first Sir Lancelot, and he offered an hundred pound; and then the seven kings offered forty pound apiece; and also there was a thousand knights, and each of them offered a pound. And the offering dured from morn till night, and Sir Lancelot lay two nights on his tomb in prayers and weeping.

Then on the third day Sir Lancelot called the kings, dukes, earls, barons, and knights, and said thus: "My fair lords, I thank you all of your coming into this country with me, but we came too late; and that shall repent me while I live, but against death may no man rebel. But sithen[85] it is so," said Sir Lancelot, "I will myself ride and seek my lady Queen Guinevere; for, as I hear say, she hath had great pain and much disease,[86] and I heard say that she is fled into the west. Therefore ye all shall abide me here; and but if[87] I come again within fifteen days, then take your ships and your fellowship, and depart into your country: for I will do as I say to you."

How Sir Lancelot departed to seek the Queen Guinevere, and how he found her at Amesbury.

Then came Sir Bors de Ganis and said: "My lord Sir Lancelot, what think ye for to do? Now to ride in this realm, wit you well ye shall find few friends."

"Be as be may," said Sir Lancelot, "keep you still here; for I will forth on my journey, and no man nor child shall go with me." So it was no boot[88] to strive, but he departed and rode westerly, and there he sought a seven or eight days; and at the last he came to a nunnery, and then was Queen Guinevere ware of Sir Lancelot as he walked in the cloister. And when she saw him there she swooned thrice, that all the ladies and gentlewomen had work enough to hold the Queen up.

So, when she might speak, she called ladies and gentlewomen to her and said, "Ye marvel, fair ladies, why I make this fare. Truly," she said, "it is for the sight of yonder knight that yonder standeth; wherefore, I pray you all, call him to me." When Sir Lancelot was brought to her, then she said to all the ladies: "Through this man and me hath all this war been wrought, and the death of the most noblest knights of the world; for through our love that we have loved together is my most noble lord slain. Therefore, Sir Lancelot, wit thou well I am set in such a plight[89] to get my soul health; and yet I trust, through God's grace, that after my death to have a sight of the blessed face of Christ, and at doomsday to sit on his right side,[90] for as sinful as ever I was are saints in heaven. Therefore, Sir Lancelot, I require thee and beseech thee heartily, for all the love that ever was betwixt us, that thou never see me more in the visage; and I command thee, on God's behalf, that thou forsake my company, and to thy kingdom thou turn again, and keep well thy realm from war and wrack. For as well as I have loved thee, mine heart will not serve me to see thee; for through thee and me is the flower of kings and knights destroyed. Therefore, Sir Lancelot, go to thy realm, and there take thee a wife, and live with her with joy and bliss; and I pray thee heartily, pray for me to our Lord, that I may amend my misliving."

"Now, sweet madam," said Sir Lancelot, "would ye that I should turn again unto my country, and there to wed a lady? Nay, madam, wit you well that shall I never do; for I shall never be so false to you of that I have promised; but the same destiny that ye

---

84 Inquired.
85 Since.   86 Lack of ease, trouble.   87 Unless.

88 Profit, use.   89 State, condition.
90 I.e., to be among the saved, when they are separated from the damned.

have taken you to, I will take me unto, for to please Jesu, and ever for you I cast me[91] specially to pray."

"If thou wilt do so," said the Queen, "hold thy promise; but I may never believe but that thou wilt turn to the world again."

"Well, madam," said he, "ye say as pleaseth you; yet wist you me never false of my promise, and God defend[92] but I should forsake the world as ye have done. For in the quest of the Sangreal[93] I had forsaken the vanities of the world, had not your lord been. And if I had done so at that time, with my heart, will, and thought, I had passed all the knights that were in the Sangreal, except Sir Galahad my son. And therefore, lady, sithen ye have taken you to perfection, I must needs take me to perfection, of right. For I take record of God, in you I have had mine earthly joy. And if I had found you now so disposed, I had cast me to have had you into mine own realm.

CHAPTER 10

How Sir Lancelot came to the hermitage where the Archbishop of Canterbury was, and how he took the habit[94] on him.

"But sithen I find you thus disposed, I ensure you faithfully I will ever take me to penance, and pray while my life lasteth, if that I may find any hermit, either gray or white,[95] that will receive me. Wherefore, madam, I pray you kiss me, and never no more."

"Nay," said the Queen, "that shall I never do; but abstain you from such works." And they departed.[96] But there was never so hard an hearted man but he would have wept to see the dolor that they made; for there was lamentation as they had been stung with spears, and many times they swooned; and the ladies bore the Queen to her chamber. And Sir Lancelot awoke and went and took his horse, and rode all that day and all night in a forest, weeping.

And at the last he was ware of an hermitage and a chapel stood betwixt two cliffs; and then he heard a little bell ring to mass, and thither he rode and alit, and tied his horse to the gate, and heard mass. And he that sang mass was the Bishop of Canterbury. Both the Bishop and Sir Bedivere knew Sir Lancelot, and they spake together after mass. But when Sir Bedivere had told his tale all whole, Sir Lancelot's heart almost brast for sorrow; and Sir Lancelot

threw his arms abroad and said: "Alas, who may trust this world?"

And then he kneeled down on his knee, and prayed the Bishop to shrive him and assoil[97] him. And then he besought the Bishop that he might be his brother. Then the Bishop said, "I will gladly." And there he put an habit upon Sir Lancelot, and there he served God day and night with prayers and fastings.

Thus the great host abode at Dover. And then Sir Lionel[98] took fifteen lords with him, and rode to London to seek Sir Lancelot; and there Sir Lionel was slain and many of his lords. Then Sir Bors de Ganis made the great host for to go home again; and Sir Bors, Sir Ector de Maris,[99] Sir Blamore, Sir Bleoberis, with more other of Sir Lancelot's kin, took on them to ride all England overthwart and endlong, to seek Sir Lancelot. So Sir Bors by fortune rode so long till he came to the same chapel where Sir Lancelot was; and so Sir Bors heard a little bell knell, that rang to mass; and there he alit and heard mass. And when mass was done, the Bishop, Sir Lancelot, and Sir Bedivere came to Sir Bors. And when Sir Bors saw Sir Lancelot in that manner clothing, then he prayed the Bishop that he might be in the same suit. And so there was an habit put upon him, and there he lived in prayers and fasting. And within half a year, there was come Sir Galihud, Sir Galihodin, Sir Blamore, Sir Bleoberis, Sir Villiars, Sir Clarras, and Sir Gahalantine. So all these seven noble knights there abode still. And when they saw Sir Lancelot had taken him to such perfection, they had no l[u]st to depart, but took such an habit as he had.

Thus they endured in great penance six year; and then Sir Lancelot took the habit of priesthood of the Bishop, and a twelvemonth he sang mass. And there was none of these other knights but they read in books, and holp for to sing mass, and rang bells, and did bodily all manner of service. And so their horses went where they would, for they took no regard of no worldly riches. For when they saw Sir Lancelot endure such penance, in prayers and fastings, they took no force[1] what pain they endured, for to see the noblest knight of the world take such abstinence that he waxed full lean.

And thus, upon a night, there came a vision to Sir Lancelot, and charged him, in remission of his sins, to haste him unto Amesbury: "And by then th[ou] come there, thou shall find Queen Guinevere dead.

---

[91] Plan, intend.   [92] Forbid.
[93] Holy Grail, the cup which was the object of the quest.
[94] Garb (of a monk).   [95] Franciscan or Carmelite.
[96] Parted, separated.

[97] Absolve.   [98] Like Sir Bors, Lancelot's cousin.
[99] Lancelot's younger brother.

[1] Account.

And therefore take thy fellows with thee, and purvey them of an horse bier, and fetch thou the corse of her, and bury her by her husband, the noble King Arthur." So this avision came to Sir Lancelot thrice in one night.

CHAPTER II

How Sir Lancelot went with his eight fellows to Amesbury, and found there Queen Guinevere dead, whom they brought to Glastonbury.

Then Sir Lancelot rose up ere day, and told the hermit. "It were well done," said the hermit, "that ye made you ready, and that ye disobey not the avision." Then Sir Lancelot took his eight fellows with him, and on fo[ot] they yede[2] from Glaston-bury to Amesbury, the which is little more than thirty mile. And thither they came within two days, for they were weak and feeble to go.

And when Sir Lancelot was come to Amesbury, within the nunnery, Queen Guinevere died but half an hour afore. And the ladies told Sir Lancelot that Queen Guinevere told them all ere she passed: that Sir Lancelot had been priest near a twelvemonth. "And hither he cometh as fast as he may to fetch my corse; and beside my lord, King Arthur, he shall bury me." Wherefore the Queen said, in hearing of them all, "I beseech Almighty God that I may never have power to see Sir Lancelot with my worldly eyne." And thus, said all the ladies, was ever her prayer these two days, till she was dead. Then Sir Lancelot saw her visage; but he wept not greatly, but sighed. And so he did all the observance of the service himself, both the dirge, and on the morn he sang mass. And there was ordained an horse bier; and so with an hundred torches ever burning about the corse of the Queen, and ever Sir Lancelot with his eight fellows went about the horse bier, singing and reading many an holy orison, and frankincense upon the corpse incensed.

Thus Sir Lancelot and his eight fellows went on foot from Amesbury unto Glastonbury; and when they were come to the chapel and the hermitage, there she had a dirge, with great devotion. And on the morn the hermit, that sometime was Bishop of Canterbury, sang the mass of requiem with great devotion. And Sir Lancelot was the first that offered, and then also his eight fellows. And then she was wrapped in cered[3] cloth of Rennes,[4] from the top to the toe, in thirtyfold; and, after, she was put in a web of lead, and then in a coffin of marble. And when she was put in the earth Sir Lancelot swooned, and lay long still, while the hermit came and awaked him, and said, "Ye be to blame, for ye displease God with such manner of sorrow making."

"Truly," said Sir Lancelot, "I trust I do not displease God, for he knoweth mine intent; for my sorrow was not, nor is not, for any rejoicing of sin; but my sorrow may never have end. For when I remember of her beauty, and of her noblesse, that was both with her king and with her, so when I saw his corpse and her corpse so lie together, truly mine heart would not serve to sustain my careful[5] body. Also, when I remember me how by my default and mine orgueil[6] and my pride, that they were both laid full low, that were peerless that ever was living of Christian people, wit you well," said Sir Lancelot, "this remembered, of their kindness and mine unkindness, sank so to mine heart, that I might not sustain myself." So the French book maketh mention.

CHAPTER 12

How Sir Lancelot began to sicken, and after died, whose body was borne to Joyous Gard for to be buried.

Then Sir Lancelot never after ate but little meat, nor drank, till he was dead. For then he sickened more and more, and dried, and dwined[7] away; for the Bishop nor none of his fellows might not make him to eat, and little he drank, that he was waxen by a cubit shorter than he was, that the people could not know him. For evermore day and night he prayed, but sometime he slumbered a broken sleep; ever he was lying groveling on the tomb of King Arthur and Queen Guinevere. And there was no comfort that the Bishop, nor Sir Bors, nor none of his fellows, could make him; it availed not.

So, within six week after, Sir Lancelot fell sick and lay in his bed; and then he sent for the Bishop that there was hermit, and all his true fellows. Then Sir Lancelot said with dreary steven,[8] "Sir Bishop, I pray you give to me all my rights that longeth to a Christian man."

"It shall not need you," said the hermit and all his fellows; "it is but heaviness of your blood; ye shall be well mended, by the grace of God, tomorn."

"My fair lords," said Sir Lancelot, "wit you well my careful body will into the earth. I have warning more than now I will say; therefore give me my rights." So, when he was houseled and aneled,[9] and had all that a Christian man ought to have, he

---

[2] Went.   [3] Waxed.   [4] In Brittany.

[5] Sorrowful.
[6] Haughtiness.   [7] Dwindled.   [8] Voice.
[9] Had received the Eucharist and extreme unction.

prayed the Bishop that his fellows might bear his body to Joyous Gard.[10] Some men say it was Alnwick, and some may say it was Hamborow. "Howbeit," said Sir Lancelot, "me repenteth sore, but I made mine avow sometime, that in Joyous Gard I would be buried. And because of breaking of mine avow, I pray you all, lead me thither." Then there was weeping and wringing of hands among his fellows. So at a season of the night they all went to their beds, for they all lay in one chamber.

And so, after midnight, against[11] day, the Bishop th[at] was hermit, as he lay in his bed asleep, he fell upon a great laughter. And therewith all the fellowship awoke, and came to the Bishop, and asked him what he ailed. "Ah, Jesu mercy!" said the Bishop, "why did ye awake me? I was never in all my life so merry and so well at ease."

"Wherefore?" said Sir Bors.

"Truly," said the Bishop," here was Sir Lancelot with me with more angels than ever I saw men in one day. And I saw the angels heave up Sir Lancelot unto heaven, and the gates of heaven opened against him."

"It is but dretching of swevens,"[12] said Sir Bors, "for I doubt not Sir Lancelot aileth nothing but good."

"It may well be," said the Bishop; "go ye to his bed, and then shall ye prove the sooth." So when Sir Bors and his fellows came to his bed they found him stark dead, and he lay as he had smiled, and the sweetest savor about him that ever they felt.[13] Then was there weeping and wringing of hands, and the greatest dole[14] they made that ever made men. And on the morn the Bishop did his mass of requiem; and, after, the Bishop and all the nine knights put Sir Lancelot in the same horse bier that Queen Guinevere was laid in tofore that she was buried. And so the Bishop and they all together went with the body of Sir Lancelot daily, till they came to Joyous Gard; and ever they had an hundred torches burning about him.

And so within fifteen days they came to Joyous Gard. And there they laid his corpse in the body of the choir,[15] and sang and read many psalters and prayers over him and about him. And ever his visage was laid open and naked, that all folks might behold him. For such was the custom in those days, that all men of worship should so lie with open visage till that they were buried. And right thus as they were at their service, there came Sir Ector de Maris, that had seven year sought all England, Scotland, and Wales, seeking his brother, Sir Lancelot.

CHAPTER 13

How Sir Ector found Sir Lancelot his brother dead, and how Constantine reigned next after Arthur; and of the end of this book.

And when Sir Ector heard such noise and light in the choir of Joyous Gard, he alit and put his horse from him, and came into the choir; and there he saw men sing and weep. And all they knew Sir Ector, but he knew not them. Then went Sir Bors unto Sir Ector, and told him how there lay his brother, Sir Lancelot, dead; and then Sir Ector threw his shield, sword, and helm from him. And when he beheld Sir Lancelot's visage, he fell down in a swoon. And when he waked it were hard any tongue to tell the doleful complaints that he made for his brother. "Ah, Lancelot," he said, "thou were head of all Christian knights, and now I dare say," said Sir Ector, "thou, Sir Lancelot, there thou liest, that thou were never matched of earthly knight's hand. And thou were the courteousest knight that ever bore shield. And thou were the truest friend to thy lover that ever bestrode horse. And thou were the truest lover, of a sinful man, that ever loved woman. And thou were the kindest man that ever struck with sword. And thou were the goodliest person that ever came among press of knights. And thou was the meekest man and the gentlest that ever ate in hall among ladies. And thou were the sternest knight to thy mortal foe that ever put spear in the breast." Then there was weeping and dolor out of measure.

Thus they kept Sir Lancelot's corpse aloft fifteen days, and then they buried it with great devotion. And then at leisure they went all with the Bishop of Canterbury to his hermitage, and there they were together more than a month. Then Sir Constantine, that was Sir Cador's son of Cornwall, was chosen king of England. And he was a full noble knight, and worshipfully he ruled this realm. And then this King Constantine sent for the Bishop of Canterbury, for he heard say where he was; and so he was restored unto his bishopric, and left that hermitage. And Sir Bedivere was there ever still hermit, to his life's end. Then Sir Bors de Ganis, Sir Ector de Maris, Sir Gahalantine, Sir Galihud, Sir Galihodin, Sir Blamore, Sir Bleoberis, Sir Villiars le Valiant, Sir

---

[10] Lancelot's English castle, in the north. Alnwick is in Northumberland. So is Bamborough, for which *Hamborow* may be a mistake.
[11] Toward.   [12] Troubling of dreams.
[13] A wicked person's body was supposed to exude an evil odor at death; in this case the sweet savor, like the Bishop's dream, indicates Lancelot's salvation.   [14] Sorrow.
[15] I.e., the choir of the castle's chapel.

Clarras of Cleremont,—all these knights drew them to their countries. Howbeit King Constantine would have had them with him, but they would not abide in this realm; and there they all lived in their countries as holy men.

And some English books make mention that they went never out of England after the death of Sir Lancelot, but that was but favor of makers.[16] For the French book maketh mention, and is authorized, that Sir Bors, Sir Ector, Sir Blamore, and Sir Bleoberis went into the Holy Land, thereas Jesu Christ was quick and dead, and anon as they had stablished their lands.[17] For the book saith so Sir Lancelot commanded them for to do, or ever[18] he passed out of this world. And these four knights did many battles upon the miscreants[19] or Turks. And there they died upon a Good Friday, for God's sake.

Here is the end of the book of King Arthur, and of his noble knights of the Round Table, that when they were whole together there was ever an hundred and forty. And here is the end of *The Death of Arthur*. I pray you all, gentlemen and gentlewomen that read this book of Arthur and his knights from the beginning to the ending, pray for me while I am alive, that God send me good deliverance;[20] and when I am dead, I pray you all pray for my soul. For this book was ended the ninth year of the reign of King Edward the Fourth,[21] by Sir Thomas Maleore, knight, as Jesu help him for his great might, as he is the servant of Jesu both day and night.

Thus endeth this noble and joyous book, entitled *Le Morte d'Arthur* notwithstanding it treateth of the birth, life, and acts of the said King Arthur, of his noble knights of the Round Table, their marvellous inquests and adventures, the achieving of the Sangreal, and in the end the dolorous death and departing out of this world of them all; which book was reduced into English by Sir Thomas Malory, knight, as afore is said, and by me divided into twenty-one books, chaptered, and imprinted, and finished in the Abbey, Westminster, the last day of July, the year of Our Lord MCCCCLXXXV.

CAXTON ME FIERI FECIT[22]

The Popular Ballads

THE BEST of the poems known as ballads are called popular because they once belonged almost exclusively to the common people. As a rule they were composed for the people, often by men of the people, though rarely about them; and once made and sung and liked, a ballad circulated from place to place by word of mouth and was handed on from generation to generation of the people. Any ballad singer felt free to introduce any changes that occurred to him; and that freedom helped take the ballad farther away from the original and soon quite forgotten composer and to make it, like the proverb, the possession of the common people as a whole. It is impossible to give the authentic text of a true ballad; an editor can only choose among such versions as have chanced to survive. Many of the ballads have come down to us in an astonishing variety of versions.

The ballad form arose in the Middle Ages. But though the original versions of some of the surviving poems were medieval compositions, chiefly of the fourteenth and fifteenth centuries, many ballads were made in the sixteenth century and a few must be dated as late as the seventeenth. Not till the seventeenth and eighteenth centuries were any but a very few written down. That is why their spelling varies so oddly, and it also accounts for the mutilated form in which some have been preserved. Their life was not, till toward the nineteenth century, in books. They lived on the lips that sang them. Sir Walter Scott was a great collector of them, and was scolded to his face by the old mother of James Hogg (1770–1835), "the Ettrick Shepherd." She objected to their being put into print: "They were made for singin' an' no' for readin'; but ye hae broken the charm noo, an' they'll never be sung mair."

The origin of the popular ballad has been much discussed. A widely credited theory, now generally discarded, held that such pieces were not composed by individuals but by assembled communities or groups. Such "communal composition" is not unknown among primitive races, but there is small likelihood that it accounts for the origin of any of the English and Scottish ballads. Nor does

---

[16] Partiality of poets.
[17] I.e., as soon as they had regained possession of their lands.
[18] Before.

[19] Misbelievers, infidels.
[20] From prison. See introduction to Malory, above.
[21] March 4, 1469—March 3, 1470.   [22] Caxton had me made.

it seem likely that these poems were to any great extent composed, as a variant of the same theory suggests, by individuals improvising in the presence of a crowd which shared in the process of creation by chanting back refrains in response to the verses of the leader. Like the folksong, to which a similar mysterious origin used to be attributed, the ballad is a work of art, though sometimes a humble and even illiterate branch of art; and works of art are composed by artists. It was an artist who made "Edward," though it is quite possible that he could neither read nor write and that he was not a professional poet.

A second class of ballad was composed by the minstrels, and these poems were often picked up by one minstrel from another. Being a professional entertainer, a minstrel was likely to decorate his poem with more description, details, and literary flourishes than ordinarily appear in the folk ballad. Meanwhile something stark and elemental vanished. Occasionally, however, a minstrel ballad was taken over by the common people, and then it went the way of the folk ballad.[1]

The major forms of oral entertainment, song and story, are united in the ballad, which is a narrative song. As a rule it tells its story with little or no attention to characterization, and usually without comment or moralizing. Mood is often suggested, but casually, as if artlessly. Narrative is almost all. Often the folk ballad is stripped to the bare essentials of it; hence the abrupt transitions, the omission of "he said," the speed with which we proceed from one crucial point to the next. Repetition and refrain are common, and contribute to the lyrical effect. Often the repetition is "incremental": each time a line is repeated, the alteration of a word or phrase puts us in possession of another fact or carries the story one step further.

The subjects of the ballads are extremely varied. Folklore, legend, romance, but also historical events and indeed any happening that seemed likely to interest people, might inspire someone to compose a ballad. The metrical form also varies. The most common ballad stanza has four iambic lines; lines 1 and 3 regularly have four stresses, and lines 2 and 4, which rime, have three. "The Douglas Tragedy" is a good example.

Since most true ballads were never put on paper by their anonymous composers but owed their circulation and survival exclusively to oral transmission, they were long neglected by literary men; and when, in the eighteenth century, the Antiquarian Movement and the allied Romantic Movement at last directed the attention of readers to this delightful branch of literature, the ballads had first to be "collected." The texts then published were derived partly from such manuscripts as had come into existence and partly from the laborious but fascinating process of persuading old country people to sing over the ballads they had heard in their youth and memorized more or less accurately, while the collector took down the words. Among the most diligent rescuers of ballads were Bishop Thomas Percy and Sir Walter Scott. Percy's *Reliques of Ancient English Poetry,* the first great collection of ballad texts, appeared in 1765; Scott's three volumes of *Minstrelsy of the Scottish Border* were published in 1802–3.

Ballad collecting continues today, for many of the old ballads live on independently of printed texts, in America as well as in Great Britain. Especially in the southern Appalachians, mountain folk of English and Scottish stock still sing versions of the medieval ballads their forefathers brought with them across the Atlantic in the seventeenth century, not in books or manuscripts, but as oral tradition.

The standard edition is F. J. Child's *English and Scottish Popular Ballads* (5 vols., 1882–98). He gives 305 ballads, in many versions. From this monumental work a single volume of selections was edited under the same title by Helen S. Sargent and G. L. Kittredge (1904); it includes all the ballads, but not all the versions. For an account of ballad origins, see G. H. Gerould's *The Ballad of Tradition* (1932).

THE DOUGLAS TRAGEDY

This version of a very old story is a typical ballad in the speed of its narrative and in its abrupt opening, like an epic's, with a leap *in medias res.*[1] We are given only the essential details; suspense is aroused for and interest concentrated on the flight and fortunes of the lovers. Lady Douglas's injunctions in the first two stanzas are subsequent to her daughter's elopement with Lord William, which is described in the third. Evidently Lord Douglas recovers and lives to pursue the objects of his wrath beyond the grave.

"Rise up, rise up, now, Lord Douglas," she says,
  "And put on your armour so bright;
Let it never be said that a daughter of thine
  Was married to a lord under night.

"Rise up, rise up, my seven bold sons,   5
  And put on your armour so bright,
And take better care of your youngest sister,
  For your eldest's awa the last night."

---

[1] In the sixteenth century and later, so-called "ballads," most of them the work of hack writers, were printed on broadsides (that is, on single sheets like handbills) and peddled, somewhat as tabloid newspapers are now, to simple folk who yearned for the latest news, especially about murders. These broadside ballads, not being composed for oral circulation, are not true ballads, even though they could be sung by purchaser or vendor, for they were always written with a particular tune in mind.

[1] Into the midst of things (instead of at the beginning).

He's mounted her on a milk-white steed,
    And himself on a dapple grey,   10
With a bugelet horn hung down by his side,
    And lightly they rode away.

Lord William lookit oer his left shoulder,
    To see what he could see,
And there he spy'd her seven brethren bold,   15
    Come riding over the lee.[2]

"Light down, light down, Lady Margret," he said,
    "And hold my steed in your hand,
Until that against your seven brethren bold
    And your father I mak a stand."   20

She held his steed in her milk-white hand,
    And never shed one tear,
Until that she saw her seven brethren fa,[3]
    And her father hard fighting, who lovd her so dear.

"O hold your hand, Lord William!" she said,   25
    "For your strokes they are wondrous sair:[4]
True lovers I can get many a ane,
    But a father I can never get mair."

O she's taen out her handkerchief,
    It was o the holland sae fine,   30
And aye she dighted[5] her father's bloody wounds,
    That were redder than the wine.

"O chuse, O chuse, Lady Margret," he said,
    "O whether will ye gang or bide?"[6]
"I'll gang, I'll gang, Lord William," she said,   35
    "For ye have left me no other guide."

He's lifted her on a milk-white steed,
    And himself on a dapple grey,
With a bugelet horn hung down by his side,
    And slowly they baith rade away.   40

O they rade on, and on they rade,
    And a' by the light of the moon,
Until they came to yon wan water,
    And there they lighted down.

They lighted down to tak a drink   45
    Of the spring that ran sae clear,
And down the stream ran his gude heart's blood,
    And sair she gan to fear.

"Hold up, hold up, Lord William" she says,
    "For I fear that you are slain."   50
" 'Tis naething but the shadow of my scarlet cloak,
    That shines in the water sae plain."

O they rade on, and on they rade,
    And a' by the light of the moon,
Until they cam to his mother's ha[7] door,   55
    And there they lighted down.

"Get up, get up, lady mother," he says,
    "Get up, and let me in!
Get up, get up, lady mother," he says,
    "For this night my fair lady I've win.   60

"O mak my bed, lady mother," he says,
    "O mak it braid and deep,
And lay Lady Margret close at my back,
    And the sounder I will sleep."

Lord William was dead lang ere midnight,   65
    Lady Margaret lang ere day,
And all true lovers that go thegither,
    May they have mair luck than they!

Lord William was buried in St. Mary's kirk,
    Lady Margret in Mary's quire;   70
Out o' the lady's grave grew a bonny red rose,
    And out o' the knight's a briar.

And they twa met, and they twa plat,[8]
    And fain they wad be near;
And a' the warld might ken[9] right weel   75
    They were twa lovers dear.

But bye[10] and rade the Black Douglas,
    And wow but he was rough!
For he pulled up the bonny brier,
    And flang 't in St. Mary's Loch.   80

EDWARD

For stark, swift tragedy "Edward" has no superior among
the ballads. This is, in its way, a perfect poem: despite its
extreme compression, a bold but logical structure supports
a passion of terrible intensity. The refrains "Edward,
Edward" and "Mither, mither" exemplify a characteristic
device of ballads. Another is the incremental repetition in
the questions and answers; by it suspense is heightened, and
the truth dawns, as it usually does in life, by degrees.

---

[2] Lea, plain, ground.   [3] Fall, die.   [4] Sore, grievous.
[5] Dressed.   [6] Go or stay.

[7] Hall, mansion.
[8] Plaited, intertwined.   [9] Know.   [10] Past, near.

"Why dois your brand[1] sae[2] drap wi bluid,
  Edward, Edward?
Why dois your brand sae drap wi bluid,
  And why sae sad gang yee O?"
"O I hae killed my hauke sae guid,   5
  Mither, mither,
O I hae killed my hauke sae guid,
  And I had nae mair bot[3] hee O."

"Your haukis bluid was nevir sae reid,[4]
  Edward, Edward, 10
Your haukis bluid was never sae reid,
  My deir son I tell thee O."
"O I hae killed my reid-roan steid,
  Mither, mither,
O I hae killed my reid-roan steid,   15
  That erst[5] was sae fair and frie[6] O."

"Your steid was auld, and ye hae gat mair,
  Edward, Edward,
Your steid was auld, and ye hae gat mair;
  Sum other dule ye drie[7] O."
"O I hae killed my fadir deir,   20
  Mither, mither,
O I hae killed my fadir deir,
  Alas, and wae is mee O!"

"And whatten penance wul ye drie for that,   25
  Edward, Edward?
And whatten penance wul ye drie for that?
  My deir son, now tell me O."
"Ile set my feit in yonder boat,
  Mither, mither,   30
Ile set my feit in yonder boat,
  And Ile fare ovir the sea O."

"And what wul ye doe wi your towirs and your ha,
  Edward, Edward?
And what wul ye doe wi your towirs and your ha,   35
  That were sae fair to see O?"
"Ile let thame stand tul they doun fa,
  Mither, mither,
Ile let thame stand tul they doun fa,
  For here nevir mair maun[8] I bee O."   40

"And what wul ye leive to your bairns[9] and your wife,
  Edward, Edward?
And what wul ye leive to your bairns and your wife,
  Whan ye gang ovir the sea O?"
"The warldis room; late them beg thrae[10] life,   45
  Mither, mither;
The warldis room, late them beg thrae life,
  For thame nevir mair wul I see O."

"And what wul ye leive to your ain mither deir,
  Edward, Edward?   50
And what wul ye leive to your ain mither deir?
  My deir son, now tell me O."
"The curse of hell frae[11] me sall[12] ye beir,
  Mither, mither,
The curse of hell frae me sall ye beir,   55
  Sic[13] counseils ye gave to me O."

BABYLON, OR
THE BONNIE BANKS O' FORDIE

Charm, rather than force, marks this favorite ballad; and its charm resides less in the extraordinary coincidence which forms its story than in its general simplicity, the unexpected beauty of the line "For to bear the red rose company," and the curious effectiveness of "my wee penknife." Though not repeated in the version which follows, the refrains (lines 2 and 4) reappeared in every stanza when the piece was sung. Such was, and still is, a regular feature of many ballads, including others here reprinted.

There were three ladies lived in a bower,
  Eh vow bonnie,
And they went out to pull a flower,
  On the bonnie banks o Fordie.

They hadna pu'ed a flower but ane,   5
When up started to them a banisht man.

He's taen the first sister by her hand,
And he's turned her round and made her stand.

"It's whether will ye be a rank robber's wife,
  Or will ye die by my wee penknife?"   10

"It's I'll not be a rank robber's wife,
  But I'll rather die by your wee penknife."

He's killed this may,[1] and he's laid her by,
  For to bear the red rose company.

---

[1] Sword.   [2] So, thus.   [3] No more but.   [4] Red.
[5] Formerly.   [6] Free, noble.
[7] Dole you dree, grief you undergo.   [8] Shall.

[9] Children.   [10] Through.   [11] From.   [12] Shall.
[13] Such.   [1] Maid.

He's taken the second ane by the hand,   15
And he's turned her round and made her stand.

"It's whether will ye be a rank robber's wife,
Or will ye die by me wee penknife?"

"I'll not be a rank robber's wife,
But I'll rather die by your wee penknife."   20

He's killed this may, and he's laid her by,
For to bear the red rose company.

He's taken the youngest ane by the hand,
And he's turned her round and made her stand.

Says, "Will ye be a rank robber's wife,   25
Or will ye die by my wee penknife?"

"I'll not be a rank robber's wife,
Nor will I die by your wee penknife.

"For I hae a brother in this wood;
And gin ye kill me, it's he'll kill thee."   30

"What's thy brother's name? come tell to me."
"My brother's name is Baby Lon."

"O sister, sister, what have I done!
O have I done this ill to thee!

"O since I've done this evil deed,   35
Good sall never be seen o me."

He's taken out his wee penknife,
And he's twyned[2] himsel o his ain sweet life.

HIND HORN

Among the medieval romances is *King Horn,* an important
feature of which is the hero's return disguised as a palmer.
Some minstrel evidently lifted that episode and from it
made the unpretentious piece which follows. He was a
popularizer of materials composed for the aristocratic
audience; thus his work illustrates a type less original than
the true folk ballad but like it in being addressed to the
common people. There is nothing particularly remarkable
about "Hind Horn" till line 41. Up to that point it jogs
along conventionally; but the disclosure of identity is
treated with passionate intensity, and its whirlwind finish
makes this ballad one of the best.

In Scotland there was a babie born,
    Lill lal, etc.,
And his name it was called young Hind[1] Horn,
    With a fal lal, etc.

He sent a letter to our king   5
That he was in love with his daughter Jean.

He's gien to her a silver wand,
With seven living lavrocks[2] sitting thereon.

She's gien to him a diamond ring,
With seven bright diamonds set therein.   10

"When this ring grows pale and wan,
You may know by it my love is gane."

One day as he looked his ring upon,
He saw the diamonds pale and wan.

He left the sea and came to land,   15
And the first that he met was an old beggar man.

"What news, what news?" said young Hind Horn.
"No news, no news," said the old beggar man.

"No news," said the beggar, "no news at a',
But there is a wedding in the king's ha.   20

"But there is a wedding in the king's ha,
That has halden these forty days and twa."

"Will ye lend me your begging coat?
And I'll lend you my scarlet cloak.

"Will you lend me your beggar's rung?[3]   25
And I'll gie you my steed to ride upon.

"Will you lend me your wig o hair,
To cover mine, because it is fair?"

The auld beggar man was bound for the mill,
But young Hind Horn for the king's hall.   30

The auld beggar man was bound for to ride,
But young Hind Horn was bound for the bride.

When he came to the king's gate,
He sought a drink for Hind Horn's sake.

---

[2] Twined, parted, sundered.

[1] Boy, lad.   [2] Larks.   [3] Staff.

The bride came down with a glass of wine,   35
When he drank out the glass and dropt in the ring.

"O got ye this by sea or land?
Or got ye it off a dead man's hand?"

"I got not it by sea, I got it by land,
And I got it, madam, out of your own hand."   40

"O I'll cast off my gowns of brown,
And beg wi you frae town to town.

"O I'll cast off my gowns of red,
And I'll beg wi you to win my bread."

"Ye needna cast off your gowns of brown,   45
For I'll make you lady o many a town.

"Ye needna cast off your gowns of red;
It's only a sham, the begging o my bread."

The bridegroom he had wedded the bride,
But young Hind Horn he took her to bed.   50

THE THREE RAVENS

There were many versions of "The Three Ravens"; in
some the dead knight is deserted by all. Not story but
mood, the mood of wonder, distinguishes this ballad. It
is removed from the ordinary course of events by the disappointed ravens and the enchanted lady, but the last
stanza voices the desire of all men.

There were three ravens sat on a tree,
    Downe a downe, hay down, hay downe,
There were three ravens sat on a tree,
    With a downe,
There were three ravens sat on a tree,   5
They were as blacke as they might be,
    With a downe derrie, derrie, derrie, downe, downe.

The one of them said to his mate,
"Where shall we our breakefast take?"

"Downe in yonder greene field,   10
There lies a knight slain under his shield.

"His hounds they lie downe at his feete,
So well they can their master keepe.

"His haukes they flie so eagerly,
There's no fowle dare him come nie."   15

Downe there comes a fallow[1] doe,
As great with yong as she might goe.

She lift up his bloudy hed,
And kist his wounds that were so red.

She got him up upon her backe,   20
And carried him to earthen lake.[2]

She buried him before the prime,[3]
She was dead herselfe ere evensong time.

God send every gentleman
Such haukes, such hounds, and such a leman.[4] 25

KEMP OWYNE

Here we have a variant of the Loathly Lady theme. Redemption, as often, depends on a hero's kiss; and that depends on his nerve, since the wicked stepmother is a witch
and has changed the maid into a sea monster. These narrative elements are common in folklore. What makes this
ballad remarkable is its air of wildness and strangeness.

Her mother died when she was young,
    Which gave her cause to make great moan;
Her father married the warst woman
    That ever lived in Christendom.

She served her with foot and hand,   5
    In every thing that she could dee,[1]
Till once, in an unlucky time,
    She threw her in ower Craigy's sea.

Says, "Lie you there, dove Isabel,
    And all my sorrows lie with thee;   10
Till Kemp[2] Owyne come ower the sea,
    And borrow[3] you with kisses three;
Let all the warld do what they will,
    Oh, borrowed shall you never be!"

Her breath grew strang, her hair grew lang,   15
    And twisted thrice about the tree;
And all the people, far and near,
    Thought that a savage beast was she.

---

[1] Brown; hence the name of a European deer, smaller than the
red deer.   [2] Pit, grave.
[3] One of the canonical "hours" of the Church; about 9 a.m.
[4] Sweetheart.

[1] Do.
[2] Warrior, champion. Perhaps Owyne is the knight Ywain (see
Sir Gawain and the Green Knight, I, 113, and note 19, p. 83,
above); if so, the ballad maker is adapting Arthurian romance.
[3] Redeem.

These news did come to Kemp Owyne,
　　Where he lived, far beyond the sea;　　20
He hasted him to Craigy's sea,
　　And on the savage beast lookd he.

Her breath was strang, her hair was lang,
　　And twisted was about the tree;
And with a swing she came about:　　25
　　"Come to Craigy's sea, and kiss with me.

"Here is a royal belt," she cried,
　　"That I have found in the green sea;
And while your body it is on,
　　Drawn shall your blood never be;　　30
But if you touch me, tail or fin,
　　I vow my belt your death shall be."

He stepped in, gave her a kiss;
　　The royal belt he brought him wi;
Her breath was strang, her hair was lang,　　35
　　And twisted twice about the tree;
And with a swing she came about:
　　"Come to Craigy's sea, and kiss with me.

"Here is a royal ring," she said,
　　"That I have found in the green sea;　　40
And while your finger it is on,
　　Drawn shall your blood never be;
But if you touch me, tail or fin,
　　I swear my ring your death shall be."

He stepped in, gave her a kiss;　　45
　　The royal ring he brought him wi;
Her breath was strang, her hair was lang,
　　And twisted ance about the tree;
And with a swing she came about:
　　"Come to Craigy's sea, and kiss with me.　　50

"Here is a royal brand," she said,
　　"That I have found in the green sea;
And while your body it is on,
　　Drawn shall your blood never be;
But if you touch me, tail or fin,　　55
　　I swear my brand your death shall be."

He stepped in, gave her a kiss;
　　The royal brand he brought him wi;
Her breath was sweet, her hair grew short,
　　And twisted nane about the tree;　　60
And smilingly she came about,
　　As fair a woman as fair could be.

SIR PATRICK SPENCE

This favorite ballad may be historical, though no such person as Sir Patrick is known to have been connected with the disastrous voyages on royal missions between Norway and Scotland which are mentioned in other versions. Such missions and disasters did occur in the thirteenth century. Though others add striking details, the version which follows is the most effective, in its terseness and grim humor.

The king sits in Dumferling[1] toune,
　　Drinking the blude-reid wine:
"O whar will I get a guid sailor,
　　To sail this schip of mine?"

Up and spak an eldern knicht,　　5
　　Sat at the kings richt kne:
"Sir Patrick Spence is the best sailor
　　That sails upon the se."

The king has written a braid[2] letter,
　　And signd it wi his hand,　　10
And sent it to Sir Patrick Spence,
　　Was walking on the sand.

The first line that Sir Patrick red,
　　A loud lauch[3] lauched he;
The next line that Sir Patrick red,　　15
　　The teir blinded his ee.

"O wha[4] is this has don this deid,
　　This ill deid don to me,
To send me out this time o' the yeir,
　　To sail upon the se?　　20

"Mak hast, mak haste, my mirry men all,
　　Our guid schip sails the morne."
"O say na sae,[5] my master deir,
　　For I feir a deadlie storme.

"Late late yestreen I saw the new moone,　　25
　　Wi the auld moone in her arme,
And I feir, I feir, my deir master,
　　That we will cum to harme."

O our Scots nobles wer richt laith[6]
　　To weet[7] their cork-heild schoone;[8]　　30
Bot lang owre[9] a' the play wer playd,
　　Thair hats they swam aboone.[10]

---

[1] Dunfermline, near Edinburgh.
[2] Broad, i.e., plainspoken.　　[3] Laugh.　　[4] Who.
[5] So.　　[6] Loath.　　[7] Wet.　　[8] Shoes.　　[9] Ere.
[10] Above; i.e., the water was over their heads.

O lang, lang may their ladies sit,
  Wi thair fans into their hand,
Or eir[11] they se Sir Patrick Spence
  Cum sailing to the land.

O lang, lang may the ladies stand,
  Wi thair gold kems[12] in their hair,
Waiting for thair ain deir lords,
  For they'll se thame na mair.

Haf owre, half owre[13] to Aberdour,
  It's fiftie fadom deip;
And thair lies guid Sir Patrick Spence,
  Wi the Scots lords at his feit.

CHILD WATERS

The Patient Wife, in this case a patient sweetheart, is a favorite theme of medieval fiction. She is always outrageously tested by the man she loves, and then, having passed the test, suitably rewarded—at least according to her view of the matter. The humility of its heroine may not recommend this piece to contemporary taste, but her devotion does; and she wins our sympathy, even before the test begins, by the intensity (lines 21 ff.) of her declaration of love and by her contempt for worldly prudence. This is a romantic story, not a moral lesson; yet it should not go unnoted that Our Lady herself comes to Ellen's aid.

Childe[1] Watters in his stable stoode,
  And stroaket his milke-white steede;
To him came a ffaire young ladye
  As ere[2] did weare womans weede.[3]

Saies, "Christ you save, good Chyld Waters!"
  Sayes, "Christ you save and see!
My girdle of gold, which was too longe,
  Is now to short ffor mee.

"And all is with one chyld of yours,
  I ffeele sturre att my side;
My gowne of greene, it is to strayght;[4]
  Before it was to wide."

"If the child be mine, Faire Ellen," he sayd,
  "Be mine, as you tell mee,
Take you Cheshire and Lancashire both,
  Take them your owne to bee.

"If the child be mine, Ffaire Ellen," he said,
  "Be mine, as you doe sweare,
Take you Cheshire and Lancashire both,
  And make that child your heyre."

Shee saies, "I had rather have one kisse,
  Child Waters, of thy mouth,
Then[5] I wold have Cheshire and Lancashire both,
  That lyes by north and south.

"And I had rather have a twinkling,
  Child Waters, of your eye,
Then I wold have Cheshire and Lancashire both,
  To take them mine oune to bee!"

"Tomorrow, Ellen, I must forth ryde
  Soe ffarr into the north countrye;
The ffairest lady that I can ffind,
  Ellen, must goe with mee."
"And ever I pray you, Child Watters,
  Your ffootpage let me bee!"

"If you will my ffootpage be, Ellen,
  As you doe tell itt mee,
Then you must cutt your gowne of greene
  An inche above your knee.

"Soe must you doe your yellow lockes,
  Another inch above your eye;
You must tell noe man what is my name;
  My ffootpage then you shall bee."

All this long day Child Waters rode,
  Shee ran bareffoote by his side;
Yett was he never soe curteous a knight
  To say, "Ellen, will you ryde?"

But all this day Child Waters rode,
  Shee ran barffoote thorow the broome;
Yett he was never soe curteous a knight
  As to say, "Put on your shoone."

"Ryde softlye,"[6] shee said, "Child Watters;
  Why doe you ryde soe ffast?
The child which is no mans but yours
  My bodye itt will burst."

He sayes, "Sees thou yonder water, Ellen,
  That fflowes from banke to brim?"
"I trust to God, Child Waters," shee said,
  "You will never see mee swime."

---

[11] Ere ever, i.e., before. [12] Combs.
[13] Half over, i.e., halfway back on the return voyage to Aberdour, on the Firth of Forth.
[1] Young. [2] Ever. [3] Clothes. [4] Tight.
[5] Than. [6] Slowly.

But when shee came to the waters side,
    Shee sayled[7] to the chinne:
"Except the Lord of heaven be my speed,[8]
    Now must I learne to swime."   60

The salt waters bare up Ellens clothes,
    Our Ladye bare upp her chinne,
And Child Waters was a woe man, good Lord,   65
    To ssee Faire Ellen swime.

And when shee over the water was,
    Shee then came to his knee:
He said, "Come hither, Ffaire Ellen;
    Loe yonder what I see!   70

"Seest thou not yonder hall, Ellen?
    Of redd gold shine the yates.[9]
There's four and twenty ffayre ladyes;
    The ffairest is my worldlye make.[10]

"Seest thou not yonder hall, Ellen?   75
    Of redd gold shineth the tower;
There is four and twenty ffaire ladyes;
    The fairest is my paramoure."

"I doe see the hall now, Child Waters,
    That of redd gold shineth the yates;   80
God give good then of your selfe
    And of your worldlye make!

"I doe see the hall now, Child Waters,
    That of redd gold shineth the tower;
God give good then of your selfe   85
    And of your paramoure!"

There were foure and twenty ladyes,
    Were playing att the ball;
And Ellen, was the ffairest ladye,
    Must bring his steed to the stall.   90

There were four and twenty faire ladyes
    Was playing att the chesse;
And Ellen, shee was the ffairest ladye,
    Must bring his horsse to grasse.

And then bespake Child Waters sister,   95
    And these were the words said shee:
"You have the prettyest ffootpage, brother,
    That ever I saw with mine eye;

"But that his belly it is soe bigg,
    His girdle goes wonderous hye;   100
And ever I pray you, Child Waters,
    Let him goe into the chamber with mee."

"It is more meete for a little ffootpage,
    That has run through mosse and mire,
To take his supper upon his knee   105
    And sitt downe by the kitchin fyer,
Then to goe into the chamber with any ladye
    That weares soe [rich] attyre."

But when they had supped every one,
    To bedd they took the way;   110
He sayd, "Come hither, my little footpage;
    Harken what I doe say.

"And goe thee downe into yonder towne,
    And low into the street;
The ffairest ladye that thou can find,   115
    Hyer her in mine armes to sleepe,
And take her up in thine armes two,
    For filinge of[11] her ffeete."

Ellen is gone into the towne,
    And low into the street;   120
The fairest ladye that shee cold[12] find
    Shee hyred in his armes to sleepe,
And tooke her in her armes two,
    For filing of her ffeete.

"I pray you now, good Child Waters,   125
    That I may creepe in att your bedds feete;
For there is noe place about this house
    Where I may say[13] a sleepe."

This [night] and itt drove on affterward
    Till itt was neere the day: 130
He sayd, "Rise up, my litle ffootepage,
    And give my steed corne[14] and hay;
And soe doe thou the good blacke oates,
    That he may carry me the better away."

And up then rose Ffaire Ellen,   135
    And gave his steed corne and hay;
And soe shee did, and the good blacke oates,
    That he might carry him the better away.

Shee layned her backe to the manger side,
    And greivouslye did groane;   140

---

[7] Assailed, attempted.   [8] Help.   [9] Gates.
[10] Match, mate.

[11] On account of defiling, i.e., so that she will not soil.
[12] Could.   [13] Attempt.   [14] Grain, not maize.

And that beheard his mother deere,
And heard her make her moane.

Shee said, "Rise up, thou Child Waters;
I thinke thou art a cursed man;
For yonder is a ghost in thy stable,   145
That greivouslye doth groane,
Or else some woman laboures of child,
Shee is soe woe begone."

But up then rose Child Waters,
And did on his shirt of silke;   150
Then he put on his other clothes
On his body as white as milke.

And when he came to the stable-dore,
Full still that hee did stand,
That hee might heare now Faire Ellen,   155
How shee made her monand.[15]

Shee said, "Lullabye, my owne deere child!
Lullabye, deere child, deere!
I wold thy father were a king,
Thy mother layd on a beere!"   160

"Peace now," he said, "good Faire Ellen,
And be of good cheere, I thee pray;
And the bridall and the churching[16] both,
They shall bee upon one day."

SWEET WILLIAM'S GHOST

Love that does not die with the beloved's death is a favorite
theme, and there are many versions and variations of the
dead lover's return. In its humble way this sad little ballad
effectively expresses a universal experience, one of the
bitterest life brings.

There came a ghost to Margret's door,
With many a grievous groan,
And ay he tirled[1] at the pin,
But answer made she none.

"Is that my father Philip,   5
Or is't my brother John?
Or is't my true-love, Willy,
From Scotland new come home?"

---

[15] Moaning.   [16] Blessing after childbirth.

[1] Rasped. The "pin" or "risp" was a small bar of iron which
came straight out from the door and then turned down a few
inches. One edge was notched, and with a ring attached to it a
grating or rasping sound could be made by a visitor who wished
to announce his presence.

" 'Tis not thy father Philip,   10
Nor yet thy brother John;
But 'tis thy true-love, Willy,
From Scotland new come home.

"O sweet Margret, O dear Margret,
I pray thee speak to me;
Give me my faith and troth, Margret,   15
As I gave it to thee."

"Thy faith and troth thou's[2] never get,
Nor yet will I thee lend,
Till that thou come within my bower,
And kiss my cheek and chin."   20

"If I should come within thy bower,
I am no earthly man;
And should I kiss thy rosy lips,
Thy days will not be lang.

"O sweet Margret, O dear Margret,   25
I pray thee speak to me;
Give me my faith and troth, Margret,
As I gave it to thee."

"Thy faith and troth thou's never get,
Nor yet will I thee lend,   30
Till you take me to yon kirk,
And wed me with a ring."

"My bones are buried in yon kirk-yard,
Afar beyond the sea,
And it is but my spirit, Margret,   35
That's now speaking to thee."

She stretchd out her lilly-white hand,
And, for to do her best,
"Hae,[3] there's your faith and troth, Willy,
God send your soul good rest."   40

Now she has kilted her robes of green
A piece below her knee,
And a' the live-lang winter night
The dead corp followed she.

"Is there any room at your head, Willy?   45
Or any room at your feet?
Or any room at your side, Willy,
Wherein that I may creep?"

---

[2] Thou shalt.
[3] Have, i.e., take.

"There's no room at my head, Margret,
　　There's no room at my feet;
There's no room at my side, Margret,
　　My coffin's made so meet."[4]　　　　　50

Then up and crew the red, red cock,
　　And up then crew the gray:
" 'Tis time, 'tis time, my dear Margret,　　55
　　That you were going away."

No more the ghost to Margret said,
　　But, with a grievous groan,
Evanished in a cloud of mist,
　　And left her all alone.　　　　　　60

"O stay, my only true-love, stay!"
　　The constant Margret cry'd;
Wan grew her cheeks, she closed her een,
　　Stretched her soft limbs, and dy'd.

LITTLE MUSGRAVE AND
LADY BARNARD

This is among the most dramatic of the ballads. The narrative is handled with unerring instinct for the critical
situations; and, while Musgrave is merely the mainspring
of the plot, Barnard, his wife, and the page are drawn
with a warm humanity which makes them, as characters,
more vivid than those usually to be found in ballads.

As it fell one holy-day,
　　Hay downe,
　　As many be in the yeare,
When young men and maids together did goe,
　　Their mattins[1] and masse to heare,　　5

Little Musgrave came to the church dore;
　　The preist was at private masse;
But he had more minde of the faire women
　　Then he had of our Lady grace.

The one of them was clad in green,　　10
　　Another was clad in pall,[2]
And then came in my lord Bernard's wife,
　　The fairest amonst them all.

She cast an eye on Little Musgrave,
　　As bright as the summer sun;　　15
And then bethought this Little Musgrave,
　　This lady's heart have I woonn.

Quoth she, "I have loved thee, Little Musgrave,
　　Full long and many a day."
"So have I loved you, fair lady,　　20
　　Yet never word durst I say."

"I have a bower at Buckelsfordbery,[3]
　　Full daintyly it is deight;[4]
If thou wilt wend thither, thou Little Musgrave,
　　Thou's lig[5] in mine armes all night."　　25

Quoth he, "I thank yee, faire lady,
　　This kindnes thou showest to me;
But whether it be to my weal or woe,
　　This night I will lig with thee."

With that he heard, a little tynë page,　　30
　　By his ladye's coach as he ran:
"All though I am my ladye's foot-page,
　　Yet I am Lord Barnard's man.

"My lord Barnard shall knowe of this,
　　Whether I sink or swim."　　35
And ever where the bridges were broake
　　He laid him downe to swimme.

"Asleepe or wake, thou Lord Barnard,
　　As thou art a man of life,
For Little Musgrave is at Bucklesfordbery,　　40
　　Abed with thy own wedded wife."

"If this be true, thou little tinny page,
　　This thing thou tellest to me,
Then all the land in Bucklesfordbery
　　I freely will give to thee.　　45

"But if it be a ly, thou little tinny page,
　　This thing thou tellest to me,
On the hyest tree in Bucklesfordbery
　　Then hanged shalt thou be."

He called up his merry men all:　　50
　　"Come saddle me my steed;
This night must I to Buckellsfordbery,
　　For I never had greater need."

And some of them whistld, and some of them sung,
　　And some these words did say,　　55
And ever when my lord Barnard's horn blew,
　　"Away, Musgrave, away!"

"Methinks I hear the thresel-cock,[6]
    Methinks I hear the jaye;
Methinks I hear my lord Barnard,   60
    And I would I were away."

"Lye still, lye still, thou Little Musgrave,
    And huggell me from the cold;
'Tis nothing but a shephard's boy,
    A driving his sheep to the fold.   65

"Is not thy hawke upon a perch?
    Thy steed eats oats and hay;
And thou a fair lady in thine armes,
    And wouldst thou bee away?"

With that my lord Barnard came to the dore, 70
    And lit[7] a stone upon;
He plucked out three silver keys,
    And he opend the dores each one.

He lifted up the coverlett,
    He lifted up the sheet: 75
"How now, how now, thou Littell Musgrave,
    Doest thou find my lady sweet?"

"I find her sweet," quoth Little Musgrave,
    "The more 'tis to my paine;
I would gladly give three hundred pounds 80
    That I were on yonder plaine."

"Arise, arise, thou Littell Musgrave,
    And put thy clothës on;
It shall nere be said in my country
    I have killed a naked[8] man.   85

"I have two swords in one scabberd,
    Full deere they cost my purse;
And thou shalt have the best of them,
    And I will have the worse."

The first stroke that Little Musgrave stroke, 90
    He hurt Lord Barnard sore;
The next stroke that Lord Barnard stroke,
    Little Musgrave nere struck more.

With that bespake this faire lady,
    In bed whereas she lay: 95
"Although thou'rt dead, thou Little Musgrave,
    Yet I for thee will pray.

"And wish well to thy soule will I,
    So long as I have life;
So will I not for thee, Barnard,   100
    Although I am thy wedded wife."

He cut her paps from off her brest;
    Great pitty it was to see
That some drops of this ladie's heart's blood
    Ran trickling downe her knee.   105

"Woe worth you, woe worth, my mery men all,
    You were nere borne for my good;
Why did you not offer[9] to stay my hand,
    When you see me wax so wood?[10]

"For I have slaine the bravest sir knight 110
    That ever rode on steed;
So have I done the fairest lady
    That ever did woman's deed.

"A grave, a grave," Lord Barnard cryd,
    "To put these lovers in;   115
But lay my lady on the upper hand,
    For she came of the better kin."

BONNY BARBARA ALLAN

British settlers brought this plaintive little piece to America,
where in one version or another it has had wide currency
among rural and especially mountain folk.

It was in and about the Martinmas time,[1]
    When the green leaves were a falling,
That Sir John Graeme, in the West Country,
    Fell in love with Barbara Allan.

He sent his man down through the town,   5
    To the place where she was dwelling:
"O haste and come to my master dear,
    Gin[2] ye be Barbara Allan."

O hooly,[3] hooly rose she up,
    To the place where he was lying,   10
And when she drew the curtain by,
    "Young man, I think you're dying."

"O it's I'm sick, and very, very sick,
    And 'tis a' for Barbara Allan."
"O the better for me ye's never be,   15
    Tho your heart's blood were a spilling.

<hr>

[6] Throstle, thrush.   [7] Alighted, dismounted.
[8] Unarmed.

[9] Attempt.   [10] Madly enraged.
[1] November 11.   [2] If.   [3] Slowly.

"O dinna ye mind,[4] young man," said she,
  "When ye was in the tavern a drinking,
That ye made the healths gae round and round,
    And slighted Barbara Allan?"   20

He turnd his face unto the wall,
  And death was with him dealing:
"Adieu, adieu, my dear friends all,
    And be kind to Barbara Allan."

And slowly, slowly raise she up,   25
  And slowly, slowly left him,
And sighing said she could not stay,
    Since death of life had reft him.

She had not gane a mile but twa,
  When she heard the dead-bell ringing;   30
And every jow[5] that the dead-bell geid,[6]
    It cry'd "Woe to Barbara Allan!"

"O mother, mother, make my bed!
  O make it soft and narrow!
Since my love died for me today,   35
    I'll die for him tomorrow."

ROBIN HOOD AND ALLEN A DALE

In the metrical romances the medieval gentry were provided with heroes who exemplified the code of knightly chivalry. Robin Hood is even less historical than King Arthur. There is no reason to suppose there ever was any such person; but the balladmakers who invented him provided the common people with a yeoman hero after their own hearts. His legend grew. It is fully narrated in *A Gest of Robyn Hode,* a ballad so long that it comes near being an epic. No doubt it was composed by a minstrel who knew the earlier and less ambitious popular ballads.

In later ballads Robin Hood is often less interesting and admirable than members of his band; but in "Allen a Dale" the great outlaw is still at his best as righter of wrongs, friend of the poor and friendless, and enemy of all oppressors. The opening line, with its direct bid for the attention of an audience, shows that this is not a folk ballad but the composition of a professional entertainer, that is, a minstrel.

Come listen to me, you gallants so free,
  All you that loves mirth for to hear,
And I will you tell of a bold outlaw,
    That lived in Nottinghamshire.

As Robin Hood in the forrest stood,   5
  All under the greenwood tree,
There was he ware of a brave[1] young man,
    As fine as fine might be.

The youngster was clothed in scarlet red,
  In scarlet fine and gay;   10
And he did frisk it over the plain,
    And chanted a roundelay.

As Robin Hood next morning stood,
  Amongst the leaves so gay,
There did he espy the same young man   15
    Come drooping along the way.

The scarlet he wore the day before,
  It was clean cast away;
And every step he fetcht a sigh,
    "Alack and a well a day!"   20

Then stepped forth brave Little John,
  And Nick the miller's son,
Which made the young man bend his bow,
    Whenas he see them come.

"Stand off, stand off!" the young man said.   25
  "What is your will with me?"
"You must come before our master straight,
    Under yon greenwood tree."

And when he came bold Robin before,
  Robin askt him courteously,   30
"O hast thou any money to spare
    For my merry men and me?"

"I have no money," the young man said,
  "But five shillings and a ring;
And that I have kept this seven long years,   35
    To have it at my wedding.

"Yesterday I should have married a maid,
  But she is now from me tane,
And chosen to be an old knight's delight,
    Whereby my poor heart is slain."   40

"What is thy name?" then said Robin Hood.
  "Come tell me, without any fail!"
"By the faith of my body," then said the young man,
    "My name it is Allen a Dale."[2]

---

[4] Don't you remember.   [5] Stroke.   [6] Gave.

[1] Fine.   [2] Allen of the dale.

"What wilt thou give me," said Robin Hood,   45
  "In ready gold or fee,
To help thee to thy true-love again,
  And deliver her unto thee?"

"I have no money," then quoth the young man,
  "No ready gold nor fee;   50
But I will swear upon a book
  Thy true servant for to be."

"How many miles is it to thy true-love?
  Come tell me without any guile!"
"By the faith of my body," then said the young man,   55
  "It is but five little mile."

Then Robin he hasted over the plain,
  He did neither stint nor lin,[3]
Until he came unto the church
  Where Allin should keep his wedding.   60

"What dost thou do here?" the bishop he said,
  "I prethee now tell to me."
"I am a bold harper," quoth Robin Hood,
  "And the best in the north countrey."

"O welcome, O welcome!" the bishop he said,   65
  "That musick best pleaseth me."
"You shall have no musick," quoth Robin Hood,
  "Till the bride and the bridegroom I see."

With that came in a wealthy knight,
  Which was both grave and old,   70
And after him a finikin[4] lass,
  Did shine like glistering gold.

"This is no fit match," quoth bold Robin Hood,
  "That you do seem to make here;
For since we are come into the church,   75
  The bride she shall chuse her own dear."

Then Robin Hood put his horn to his mouth,
  And blew blasts two or three;
When four and twenty bowmen bold
  Came leaping over the lee.[5]   80

And when they came into the churchyard,
  Marching all on a row,
The first man was Allin a Dale,
  To give bold Robin his bow.

"This is thy true-love," Robin he said,   85
  "Young Allin, as I hear say;
And you shall be married at this same time,
  Before we depart away."

"That shall not be," the bishop he said,
  "For thy word shall not stand;   90
They shall be three times askt[6] in the church,
  As the law is of our land."

Robin Hood pulled off the bishop's coat,
  And put it upon Little John;
"By the faith of my body," then Robin said,   95
  "This cloath doth make thee a man."

When Little John went into the quire,
  The people began for to laugh;
He askt them seven times in the church,
  Lest three times should not be enough.   100

"Who gives me this maid?" then said Little John;
  Quoth Robin, "That do I,
And he that doth take her from Allin a Dale
  Full dearly he shall her buy."

And thus having ended this merry wedding,   105
  The bride lookt as fresh as a queen;
And so they returnd to the merry greenwood,
  Amongst the leaves so green.

ROBIN HOOD'S DEATH

In an earlier version of this ballad an old woman, perhaps a witch, curses Robin on his way to the priory where he is to be let blood. In the *Gest* his kinswoman is the prioress; she conspires with a knight she loves, and Robin Hood is slain, but why we are not told. The *Gest* ends with stanza 456:

> *Christ have mercy on his soule,*
>   *That dyed on the rode!*
> *For he was a good outlawe,*
>   *And dyde pore men moch god.*

When Robin Hood and Little John,
  Down a down a down a down,
Went oer yon bank of broom,
Said Robin Hood bold to Little John,
  "We have shot for many a pound."   5
Hey down a down a down.

---

[3] Both words mean *stop*.
[4] Handsomely dressed.   [5] Ground.

[6] A reference to the prescribed banns. Marriage intentions had to be announced at church on three consecutive Sundays, in order to facilitate disclosure of any impediment.

"But I am not able to shoot one shot more;
 My broad arrows[1] will not flee.
But I have a cousin lives down below;
 Please God, she will bleed me."   10

Now Robin he is to fair Kirkly[2] gone,
 As fast as he can win;[3]
But before he came there, as we do hear,
 He was taken very ill.

And when he came to fair Kirkly-hall,   15
 He knockd all at the ring;[4]
But none was so ready as his cousin herself
 For to let bold Robin in.

"Will you please to sit down, cousin Robin," she said,
 "And drink some beer with me?"   20
"No, I will neither eat nor drink,
 Till I am blooded by thee."

"Well, I have a room, cousin Robin," she said,
 "Which you did never see,
And if you please to walk therein,   25
 You blooded by me shall be."

She took him by the lily-white hand,
 And led him to a private room;
And there she blooded bold Robin Hood,
 While one drop of blood would run down. 30

She blooded him in a vein of the arm,
 And locked him up in the room;
There did he bleed all the livelong day,
 Until the next day at noon.

He then bethought him of a casement there, 35
 Thinking for to get down,
But was so weak he could not leap;
 He could not get him down.

He then bethought him of his bugle-horn,
 Which hung low down to his knee,   40
He set his horn unto his mouth,
 And blew out weak blasts three.

Then Little John, when hearing him,
 As he sat under a tree:
"I fear my master is now near dead,   45
 He blows so wearily."

Then Little John to fair Kirkly is gone,
 As fast as he can dree;[5]
But when he came to Kirkly-hall,
 He broke locks two or three: 50

Until he came bold Robin to see;
 Then he fell on his knee.
"A boon, a boon," cries Little John,
 "Master, I beg of thee."

"What is that boon," said Robin Hood,   55
 "Little John, [thou] begs of me?"
"It is to burn fair Kirkly-hall,
 And all their nunnery."

"Now nay, now nay," quoth Robin Hood,
 "That boon I'll not grant thee;   60
I never hurt woman in all my life,
 Nor men in woman's company.

"I never hurt fair maid in all my time,
 Nor at mine end shall it be;
But give me my bent bow in my hand,   65
 And a broad arrow I'll let flee,
And where this arrow is taken up,
 There shall my grave digged be.

"Lay me a green sod under my head,
 And another at my feet;   70
And lay my bent bow by my side,
 Which was my music sweet;
And make my grave of gravel and green,
 Which is most right and meet.

"Let me have length and breadth enough,   75
 With a green sod under my head;
That they may say, when I am dead
 Here lies bold Robin Hood."

These words they readily granted him,
 Which did bold Robin please;   80
And there they buried bold Robin Hood,
 Within the fair Kirkleys.

CHEVY CHASE

"I never," wrote Sir Philip Sidney in 1583 in his *Defense of Poesy,* "heard the old song of Percy and Douglas that I found not my heart moved more than with a trumpet." Its popularity, as a song, continued throughout the seventeenth century; and in 1711 Joseph Addison (see *Spectator,* nos. 70

---

[1] A kind of arrow with a broad head.
[2] Unidentified. There is a village of Kirk Lees in Yorkshire.
[3] Make his way.   [4] A circular knocker.

[5] Endure; i.e., manage.

and 74) called it still "the favorite ballad of the common people of England." Both "Chevy Chase," or "The Hunting of the Cheviot," as an older version entitles it, and another ballad on "The Battle of Otterburn" were inspired by a fight between the English and Scots on August 19, 1388. For a contemporary and doubtless more accurate account of it, see Froissart's *Chronicles*.

God prosper long our noble king,
    our liffes and saftyes all!
A woefull hunting once there did
    in Chevy Chase befall.

To drive the deere with hound and horne   5
    Erle Pearcy took the way.
The child may rue that is unborne
    the hunting of that day.

The stout Erle of Northumberland
    a vow to God did make   10
His pleasure in the Scottish woods
    three sommers days to take,

The cheefest harts[1] in Chevy C[h]ase
    to kill and beare away;
These tydings to Erle Douglas came   15
    in Scotland, where he lay,

Who sent Erle Pearcy present word
    he wold prevent his sport.
The English erle, not fearing that,
    did to the woods resort,   20

With fifteen hundred bowmen bold,
    all chosen men of might,
Who knew ffull well in time of neede
    to ayme their shafts arright.

The gallant greyhound[s] swiftly ran   25
    to chase the fallow[2] deere;
On Munday they began to hunt,
    ere daylight did appeare.

And long before high noone the[3] had
    a hundred fat buckes slaine;   30
Then, having dined, the drovyers went
    to rouze the deare againe.

The bowmen mustered on the hills,
    well able to endure;
Theire backsids all with speciall care   35
    that day were guarded sure.

The hounds ran swiftly through the woods
    the nimble deere to take,
That with their cryes the hills and dales
    an eccho shrill did make.   40

Lord Pearcy to the querry[4] went
    to view the tender deere.
Quoth he, "Erle Douglas promised once
    this day to meete me heere;

"But if I thought he wold not come,   45
    noe longer wold I stay."
With that a brave younge gentlman
    thus to the erle did say:

"Loe, yonder doth Erle Douglas come,
    hys men in armour bright;   50
Full twenty hundred Scottish speres
    all marching in our sight.

"All men of pleasant Tivydale,[5]
    fast by the river Tweede."
"O ceaze your sportts!" Erle Pearcy said,   55
    "and take your bowes with speede.

"And now with me, my countrymen,
    your courage forth advance!
For there was never champion yett,
    in Scottland nor in Ffrance,   60

"That ever did on horsbacke come,
    [but], and if my hap it were,
I durst encounter man for man,
    with him to break a spere."

Erle Douglas on his milke-white steede,   65
    most like a baron bold,
Rode formost of his company,
    whose armor shone like gold.

"Shew me," sayd hee, "whose men you bee
    that hunt soe boldly heere,   70
That without my consent doe chase
    and kill my fallow deere."

The first man that did answer make
    was noble Pearcy hee,
Who sayd, "Wee list[6] not to declare   75
    nor shew whose men wee bee.

[1] Stags.   [2] Yellow.   [3] They.

[4] Quarry, heap of carcasses.
[5] Teviotdale, the county of Roxburgh, Scotland.   [6] Desire.

"Yett wee will spend our deerest blood
  thy cheefest harts to slay."
Then Douglas swore a solempne oathe,
  and thus in rage did say: 80

"Ere thus I will outbraved bee,
  one of us tow shall dye;
I know thee well: an erle thou art;
  Lord Pearcy, soe am I.

"But trust me, Pearcye, pittye it were,   85
  and great offence, to kill
Then any of these our guiltlesse men,
  for they have done none ill.

"Let thou and I the battell trye,
  and set our men aside."   90
"Accurst bee [he!]" Erle Pearcye sayd,
  "by whome it is denyed."

Then stept a gallant squire forth—
  Witherington was his name—
Who said, "I wold not have it told   95
  To Henery our king, for shame,

"That ere my captaine fought on foote,
  and I stand looking on.
You bee two Erles," quoth Witherington,
  "and I a squier alone.   100

"I'le doe the best that doe I may,
  while I have power to stand;
While I have power to weeld my sword,
  I'le fight with hart and hand."

Our English archers bent their bowes;   105
  their harts were good and trew;
Att the first flight of arrowes sent,
  full foure score Scotts the slew.

To drive the deere with hound and horne,
  Douglas bade on the bent.[7]   110
Two captaines moved with mickle[8] might;
  their speres to shivers went.

They closed full fast on everye side;
  noe slacknes there was found;
But many a gallant gentleman   115
  lay gasping on the ground.

O Christ! it was great greeve to see
  how eche man chose his spere,
And how the blood out of their brests
  did gush like water cleare.   120

At last these two stout erles did meet,
  like captaines of great might;
Like lyons woode[9] they layd on lode;[10]
  the made a cruell fight.

The fought untill they both did sweat,   125
  with swords of tempered steele,
Till blood downe their cheekes like raine
  the trickling downe did feele.

"O yeeld thee, Pearcye!" Douglas sayd,
  "And in faith I will thee bringe   130
Where thou shall high advanced bee
  by James our Scottish king.

"Thy ransome I will freely give,
  and this report of thee:
Thou art the most couragious knight   135
  [that ever I did see.]"

"Noe, Douglas!" quoth Erle Percy then,
  "thy profer I doe scorne;
I will not yeelde to any Scott
  that ever yett was borne!"   140

With that there came an arrow keene,
  out of an English bow,
Which stroke Erle Douglas on the brest
  a deepe and deadlye blow.

Who never sayd more words than these: 145
  "Fight on, my merry men all!
For why, my life is att [an] end;
  Lord Pearcy sees my fall."

Then leaving liffe, Erle Pearcy tooke
  the dead man by the hand;   150
Who said, "Erle Dowglas, for thy life,
  wold I had lost my land!

"O Christ! my verry hart doth bleed
  for sorrow for thy sake,
For, sure, a more redoubted knight   155
  mischance cold never take."

---

[7] Grassy field.   [8] Much.

[9] Madly.   [10] Struck heavily.

A knight amongst the Scotts there was
    which saw Erle Douglas dye,
Who streight in hart did vow revenge
    upon the Lord Pearcye.   160

Sir Hugh Mountgomerye was he called,
    who, with a spere full bright,
Well mounted on a gallant steed,
    ran feircly through the fight,

And past the English archers all,   165
    without all dread or feare,
And through Erle Percyes body then
    he thrust his hatfull spere.

With such a vehement force and might
    his body he did gore,   170
The staff ran through the other side
    a large cloth-yard and more.

Thus did both those nobles dye,
    whose courage none cold staine.
An English archer then perceived   175
    the noble erle was slaine.

He had [a] good bow in his hand,
    made of a trusty tree;
An arrow of a cloth-yard long
    to the hard head haled hee.   180

Against Sir Hugh Mountgomerye
    his shaft full right he sett;
The grey-goose-winge that was thereon
    in his harts bloode was wett.

This fight from breake of day did last   185
    till setting of the sun,
For when the rung the evening bell
    the battele scarse was done.

With stout Erle Percy there was slaine
    Sir John of Egerton,   190
Sir Robert Harcliffe and Sir William,
    Sir James, that bold barron.

And with Sir George and Sir James,
    both knights of good account,
Good Sir Raphe Rebbye there was slaine, 195
    whose prowesse did surmount.

For Witherington needs must I wayle
    as one in dolefull dumpes,
For when his leggs were smitten of,
    he fought upon his stumpes.   200

And with Erle Dowglas there was slaine
    Sir Hugh Mountgomerye
And Sir Charles Morrell, that from feelde
    one foote wold never flee;

Sir Roger Hever of Harcliffe, tow,   205
    his sisters sonne was hee;
Sir David Lambwell, well esteemed,
    but saved he cold not bee.

And the Lord Maxwell, in like case,
    with Douglas he did dye;   210
Of twenty hundred Scottish speeres,
    scarce fifty-five did flye.

Of fifteen hundred Englishmen
    went home but fifty-three;
The rest in Chevy Chase were slaine,   215
    under the greenwoode tree.

Next day did many widdowes come
    their husbands to bewayle;
They washt their wounds in brinish teares,
    but all wold not prevayle.   220

Theyr bodyes, bathed in purple blood,
    the bore with them away;
They kist them dead a thousand times
    ere the were cladd in clay.

The newes was brought to Eddenborrow,   225
    were Scottlands king did rayne,
That brave Erle Douglas soddainlye
    was with an arrow slaine.

"O heavy newes!" King James can say;
    "Scottland may wittenesse bee   230
I have not any captaine more
    of such account as hee."

Like tydings to King Henery came,
    within as short a space,
That Pearcy of Northumberland   235
    was slaine in Chevy Chase.

"Now God be with him!" said our king,
    "sith[11] it will noe better bee;
I trust I have within my realme
    five hundred as good as hee.   240

---

[11] Since.

"Yett shall not Scotts nor Scottland say
    but I will vengeance take,
And be revenged on them all
    for brave Erle Percyes sake."

This vow the king did well performe   245
    after on Humble-downe;
In one day fifty knights were slayne,
    with lords of great renowne.

And of the rest, of small account,
    did many hundreds dye: 250
Thus endeth the hunting in Chevy Chase,
    made by the Erle Pearcye.

God save our king and blesse this land
    with plentye, joy, and peace,
And grant hencforth that foule debate   255
    twixt noble men may ceaze!

MARY HAMILTON

Among the attendants of Mary Stuart, Queen of Scots,
were four well-born ladies, all named Mary. None met the
fate ascribed to Mary Hamilton in the ballad, which was
probably inspired by a scandalous incident at Queen Mary's
court in 1563. This piece is therefore too late to be one
of the medieval ballads, but it belongs with them in form
and spirit.

Word's gane to the kitchen,
    And word's gane to the ha,
That Marie Hamilton gangs wi' bairn[1]
    To the hichest[2] Stewart of a'.

He's courted her in the kitchen;   5
    He's courted her in the ha';
He's courted her in the laigh[3] cellar,
    And that was warst of a'.

She's tyed it in her apron,
    And she's thrown it in the sea;   10
Says, "Sink ye, swim ye, bonny wee babe,
    You'll neer get mair o me!"

Down then came the auld queen,
    Goud tassels tying her hair:
"O Marie, where's the bonny wee babe   15
    That I heard greet[4] sae sair?"

"There was never a babe intill my room,
    As little designs to be;
It was but a touch o my sair side,
    Come oer my fair bodie."   20

"O Marie, put on your robes o black,
    Or else your robes o brown,
For ye maun gang wi me the night,[5]
    To see fair Edinbro town."

"I winna put on my robes o black,   25
    Nor yet my robes o brown;
But I'll put on my robes o white,
    To shine through Edinbro town."

When she gaed up the Cannogate,[6]
    She laughd loud laughters three;   30
But whan she cam down the Cannogate,
    The tear blinded her ee.

When she gaed up the Parliament stair,
    The heel cam aff her shee;
And lang or she cam down again,   35
    She was condemnd to dee.

When she cam down the Cannogate,
    The Cannogate sae free,[7]
Many a ladie lookd oer her window,
    Weeping for this ladie.   40

"Ye need nae weep for me," she says,
    "Ye need nae weep for me;
For had I not slain mine own sweet babe,
    This death I wadna dee.

"Bring me a bottle of wine," she says,   45
    "The best that eer ye hae,
That I may drink to my weil-wishers,
    And they may drink to me.

"Here's a health to the jolly sailors,
    That sail upon the main;   50
Let them never let on to my father and mother
    But what I'm coming hame.

"Here's a health to the jolly sailors,
    That sail upon the sea;
Let them never let on to my father and mother   55
    That I cam here to dee.

---

[1] Goes with child.
[2] Highest; i.e., the king, Henry Stuart, Lord Darnley, Queen
Mary's husband.   [3] Low.   [4] Cry.

[5] Tonight.
[6] Canongate, an avenue leading from Holyrood Palace to the
city of Edinburgh.   [7] Noble, fine.

"Oh little did my mother think,
   The day she cradled me,
What lands I was to travel through,
   What death I was to dee.   60

"Oh little did my father think,
   The day he held up me,
What lands I was to travel through,
   What death I was to dee.

"Last night I washd the queen's feet,   65
   And gently laid her down;
And a' the thanks I've gotten the nicht
   To be hangd in Edinbro town!

"Last nicht there was four Maries;
   The nicht there'l be but three: 70
There was Marie Seton and Marie Beton
   And Marie Carmichael and me."

GET UP AND BAR THE DOOR

Our final ballad represents that very rare type, the humorous ballad.

It fell about the Martinmas[1] time,
   And a gay time it was then,
When our good wife got puddings[2] to make,
   And she's boild them in the pan.

The wind sae cauld blew south and north,   5
   And blew into the floor;
Quoth our goodman to our goodwife,
   "Gae out and bar the door."

"My hand is in my hussyfskap,[3]
   Goodman, as ye may see;   10
An it shoud nae be barrd this hundred year,
   It's[4] no be barrd for me."

They made a paction[5] tween them twa,
   They made it firm and sure,
That the first word whaeer[6] shoud speak,   15
   Shoud rise and bar the door.

Then by there came two gentlemen,
   At twelve oclock at night,
And they could neither see house nor hall,
   Nor coal nor candle-light.   20

"Now whether is this a rich man's house,
   Or whether is it a poor?"
But neer a word wad ane o them speak,
   For barring of the door.

And first they ate the white puddings,   25
   And then they ate the black;
Tho muckle[7] thought the goodwife to hersel,
   Yet neer a word she spake.

Then said the one unto the other,
   "Here, man, tak ye my knife;   30
Do ye tak aff the auld man's beard,
   And I'll kiss the goodwife."

"But there's nae water in the house,
   And what shall we do than?"
"What ails ye at[8] the pudding-broo,[9]   35
   That boils into the pan?"

O up then started our goodman,
   An angry man was he:
"Will ye kiss my wife before my een,
   And scad[10] me wi pudding-bree?"   40

Then up and started our goodwife,
   Gied three skips on the floor:
"Goodman, you've spoken the foremost word;
   Get up and bar the door."

---

[1] November 11.   [2] Sausages.   [3] Housewifery.
[4] It shall.

[5] Agreement.   [6] Whoever.   [7] Then much.
[8] What's the matter with; i.e., why not use. . . ?
[9] Broth. (So also *bree* in line 40.)   [10] Scald.

The Renaissance

THE RENAISSANCE

THE TERM *Renaissance* is merely a catchword for a changing state of the European mind. We shall not begin with a definition, since a short one is impracticable. The Renaissance had several aspects, and has meant different things to different men. Yet by the time a faithful reader arrives at the last page of this introduction he ought to have a fairly comprehensive grip on the term's significance. The effort is worth making. The importance of the Renaissance for a number of things Americans care deeply about can hardly be overstated. Foremost among these is our belief in the value of freedom for the human spirit.

During the Renaissance the rigid class organization of society began breaking down in England. The class rules and regulations of the Middle Ages make even the most bureaucratic of modern democracies look as free as air. By and large, the medieval tendency was to crush individualism. People were people, then as now; but the medieval *ideal* subordinated the spiritual side of life to the Church and the material side to the social class. You lived according to your class, not yourself. The very cut and quality of your clothes were prescribed according to the class you belonged to.

If the Renaissance did not break these molds, it cracked them. It gave the individual a scope which the feudal system and the medieval Church had withheld. It was one of the great liberating epochs of history, and on the whole its great books were liberating books. That is true not only for ideological works, such as the *Essays* of Montaigne (d. 1592), in which there is a clear purpose of helping strike the shackles from men's minds, but also for many of the greatest works of the imagination. Shakespeare wrote his plays as popular entertainments, and if he had any formulated political views he was probably a conservative; yet the *effect* of his plays on the mind is a liberating effect. One comes from the reading of them fortified in optimistic convictions about the durability and soundness of human nature, and buoyed up with renewed belief in mankind's possibilities. Without that faith no thinking man can be an advocate of freedom.

Liberation requires time. A man cannot be free by taking thought and saying, "I am free." All he can do is to work toward freedom. No one can give freedom to another; it has to be won privately, in the mind. The most effective helps are books. The centuries since the Renaissance have discernibly, though stumblingly, followed the lead it gave. The twentieth century, in its second quarter, has witnessed the most serious threat the Renaissance ideal has yet had to face. If by the year 2000 the human spirit still retains the degree of freedom it has hitherto enjoyed in the western democracies, it will be because thinking men understand, are jealous of, and are willing to work and, if necessary, to fight for the ideas with which we are concerned in this introduction.

Literally, *renaissance* or *renascence* means *rebirth;* like most new things, the Renaissance was partly a revival of old ones. But as the name of an epoch in European history it stands for a period of transition which ended the Middle Ages and ushered in the modern world. In this book we shall group under "The Renaissance" the English authors who flourished between 1485 and 1603. Obviously, this does not mean that in 1485, when Henry Tudor seized the throne, everyone in England stopped being medieval. Many, perhaps most, of the changes which were taking place during the Renaissance were well under way before the end of the Middle Ages, in some cases centuries before; and much that we think of as characteristically medieval survived into and long after the Renaissance. Nor does our choosing 1603 for the end of the epoch in England mean that when Queen Elizabeth died the prologue ended and the curtain rose abruptly on the seventeenth century, Act I of modern times. Those are simply convenient dates.

Since, however, many literary careers begun in the sixteenth century carried on far into the seventeenth, we shall have to be a little arbitrary in assigning certain writers to this or the next section of this book. The force, the drive, of Renaissance enthusiasm and spontaneity were still potent in the earlier part of the seventeenth century; but a new tone was becoming dominant. In poetry, for example, the key changed from a bold major to a less confident minor. Disillusion was in the air, even though occasional strains of the old Elizabethan rapture could still be heard. Shakespeare lived till 1616; but he is clearly an Elizabethan, a sixteenth-century man, a poet of the Renaissance. John Donne, on the other hand, though he was born in 1572, only eight years after Shakespeare, and though his first poems were written before the end of the century, is even in those poems rebellious against certain Elizabethan standards and ideas. We shall therefore hold him in reserve, along with Jonson and Bacon, who also began writing before 1600, for our section on the seventeenth century.

THE ITALIAN REVIVAL

THE RENAISSANCE was the product of Mediterranean culture. The fairest art and the noblest philosophy had flourished in ancient Greece. By ancient Rome the largest section of the western world ever successfully unified was politically organized. Long before the barbarian invaders from the North wrecked the Roman Empire, literature and the other arts had declined; but throughout the Dark Ages which followed, the major force for internationalism was still Italian, the Papacy. In the Mediterranean basin western civilization was preserved, and there it had a new birth in fourteenth-century Italy.

It is easy for us of the twentieth century, living in the midst of educational systems, libraries, and other storage agencies of culture, to assume that once a thing has been known it will always be known. History does not bear out this assumption. During the Dark (that is, the earlier Middle) Ages, Europe lost sight of much that the Greeks and Romans had accomplished in ancient times. Political and legal principles, scientific formulas, the fruits of philosophical inquiry, glorious works of art and literature, were ignored, lost, or actually destroyed. Some of the manuscripts in which man's past achievements and hopes for the future were recorded went up, as we have seen, in flames kindled by illiterate conquerors from lands outside the Mediterranean circle. Others, despised by the Christian clergy, dropped out of circulation or were misinterpreted. The only organized intellectual and spiritual force was the Church, and the Church concentrated on the soul's preparation for life eternal. "Vanity of vanities, all is vanity," an extreme and oversimplified statement of one aspect of the truth, was the official view of man's life on earth; and although few men successfully followed this principle in actual daily living, its pressure

on the mold of culture was constant. In sharp contrast to the busy Romans and the beauty-loving Athenians, the medieval Church insisted that the material be rigorously subordinated to the service of the spiritual.

But in the Middle East, among the Arabs, and in what was left of the Byzantine or eastern half of the Roman Empire, a great deal had survived from the wreckage of Greek and Greco-Roman civilization; and from the East this knowledge of the past finally began to seep back into western Europe. It came by way of Italy. Italy's geographical position had always kept her, at least to a greater extent than her western and northern neighbors, in touch with eastern culture. Most of Europe's eastern trading was done by Italian merchants; and as their commerce prospered, their cities rose to wealth and power. Especially to Venice the ships returned with the superior wares of the East. Not only Florence but also Milan and several other cities of northern Italy, because they lay not far from the Alpine passes which led to the markets of the North, became famous for their own manufactures and for their financial institutions. It was a solid basis of commercial activity that supported the culture which flowered in fourteenth- and fifteenth-century Italy. The revival, moreover, was partly nourished by the fact that the dwellers in the great towns, busy in the world of trade and practical affairs, had become increasingly indifferent to the Church's modes of idealism.

Long before the Turks took Constantinople in 1453, eastern scholars began emigrating to Italy. Often they brought precious manuscripts from monastic libraries, which gave glimpses of a conception of man and nature very different from the orthodox medieval view. It began to dawn slowly on western men that the relics of ancient culture failed to support the contempt for man's secular state set forth by the Church's extremists. A tremendous upsurge of interest in the intellectual, scientific, literary, and artistic achievements of classical times began. Rulers, nobles, bankers, wealthy merchants, bishops, cardinals, and popes were swept by enthusiasm for scholarship and art, and became their patrons. Later on the Church was to condemn the whole movement; but for the present the tide carried everything before it.

THE ARTISTIC OUTBURST

THE GREEKS' curiosity about the world, their intense admiration of its beauties, and their urge to represent them in art lived again in the Italian Renaissance. Under the new stimulus the Renaissance artist, scholar, and scientist (often one man was all three) turned his back on the medieval contemplation of another world and plunged into an ardent scrutiny of this. Such an artist was the painter and sculptor Michelangelo (1475–1564). Under his hand, and with the enthusiastic approval of the Pope who hired him, the decoration of the Sistine Chapel and of St. Peter's came to express, not discontent with mundane things, but man's pride and magnificence, and the beauty of the world's colors and forms—even of the forms of man's mortal body. Leonardo da Vinci (1452–1519) was painter, sculptor, architect, scientist, and engineer. In love with the world and burning with a genius's imperative desire to communicate the glory of his own experience, his passionate cry to all mankind was "Open your eyes!" The greatest art of the Middle Ages was Gothic architecture. Its cathedral towers and spires sprang heavenward and spoke a different message from Leonardo's. Their injunction was not to open the eyes but to lift them up.

In general, the domed and pillared architecture of the Renaissance reverted to classical forms. Its keynote was regularity; in its balance, symmetry, and solidity it kept down to earth where the Gothic had soared away from it.

Rome had long been the capital of western civilization; now Florence became the world capital of art. This fundamental shift in orientation is illustrated by the course which painting took. The "primitive" or pre-Renaissance Italian paintings were the work of monks. Almost exclusively religious in subject, they are often exquisite in color and in composition. Yet there is rarely a suggestion that under the robes of those awkward, appealing figures there are bodies. These paintings are not attempts to show us the world; they are relatively abstract. Here is a Madonna with the Holy Child in her lap, and kneeling saints ringed round her. The artist is giving us not so much men and women as a symbol of religious adoration. But when Raphael (1483–1520) paints a Madonna, it is a real woman he is trying to get onto his canvas, the sweet fleshly grace of the pretty model, perhaps his own mistress.

The Middle Ages had put a premium, at any rate theoretically, on selflessness. Most medieval art is anonymous, and one man copied another's work without anyone's reproaching him with plagiarism. To the Renaissance, personality seemed immensely worth while; it was cultivated in art and in conduct with a renewed energy and pride. People as people fascinate the great Renaissance artists, whether like many of the portrait painters they remain on the surface of the flesh, or like El Greco (1548?–1625) they try also for the soul within.

This is not to maintain—it would be folly to do so in our times, which have seen a healthy reaction against literal fidelity to nature as the grand object of art—that the preoccupation with the appearance of things which we call realism or naturalism is art's best sphere. The point is that the greatest creations of Renaissance art came in the main out of rebellion against the medieval ideal of otherworldliness, and often out of an artist's intoxication with the world in which, because we can see, hear, feel, touch, and taste it, we live and move and at all save our greatest moments have our being. Hence the intensity of the colors from the palette of Titian (1477–1576), and his glowing Venetian women, with their rich robes and jewels and their flaming auburn hair. Hence the energy of the tremendous nudes in which Rubens (1577–1640) glorified the flesh; for by his time the Renaissance, though it had collided with the Reformation, had stirred the North, and Flanders as well as the Holland of Rembrandt (1606–69) had been set ablaze with color. The human body had long been held a shameful thing. Now it was unveiled with an exultation in its beauty which extended to every object in nature.

THE REVIVAL OF LETTERS

PAGAN literature had not been completely forgotten in the Middle Ages, though much of it had been lost to sight. Plautus, the best of Rome's dramatists, for example, was in postclassical times almost ignored, till the sensational discovery, in 1429, of manuscripts which gave twelve of his plays. With some of the great pagan authors the medieval intellectuals had remained well acquainted, but often they were valued for reasons that would have seemed very strange to them. Practically all the intellectuals were churchmen, the clerics or "clerks"; and they sought in the classics their own values. The *Aeneid* was read as an allegory of man's journey through life. Terence was esteemed not for his comic genius but for the pithy moralistic observations with which he larded his plays.

In the Renaissance men gradually learned to approach the classics on their own ground—to look in them for what their authors had intended, not for what a biased reader hoped to find. Latin was studied with renewed interest, and now a wider range of pagan authors was included. Knowledge of Greek, key to a richer literature than the Romans', had declined. Now its study was revived, first in Italy and then throughout western Europe. In England the backbone of the curriculum in both school and university became the language, literature, and history of Rome, and to some extent of Greece. Such it remained till late in the nineteenth century.

But in creative writing, familiarity with the classics led to translation, imitation, and emulation, in that order. Though as late as the seventeenth century there were still a few Englishmen who doubted the suitability of their native language for serious works, the vernacular, the tongue of the people, eventually won out everywhere. As we have seen, this trend had begun in the Middle Ages. Dante (1265–1321), the last of Italy's medieval great men, chose the vernacular for the *Divine Comedy*. Francis Petrarch (1304–74), her pioneer Renaissance man, and his disciple Giovanni Boccaccio (1313–75) made a major contribution to the molding of the standard literary language of modern Italy. Their precedent was followed in other countries. Before the sixteenth century was over, Latin had been relegated to second place everywhere, except in the educational system and in the Catholic Church.

The revival of the classics worked in two opposite directions. In some writers it stimulated a creative independence which resulted, as in the plays of the Elizabethan dramatists, in works markedly different from the classical models. On the whole that was the case in England, at any rate till toward the end of the seventeenth century. Even as staunch an advocate of neoclassicism as Ben Jonson held that the ancients should be our guides, not our commanders. But the Renaissance also encouraged that general human weakness which is apt to turn veneration for a great mind of the past into worship of the books or other works it gave us. By some the spirit was forgotten in a blind adherence to the letter; and Renaissance pedants, first Italian scholars and afterwards French critics, wove an intricate fabric of rules out of certain wise observations of Aristotle and others, less wise, of Horace. In Italy and France the neoclassical rules triumphed, and many of the best Renaissance writings conformed to them. In England a freer and more romantic spirit prevailed till late in the seventeenth century.

THE QUESTIONING OF AUTHORITY

One of the most important aspects of the new spirit set free in the world by the Renaissance was unwillingness to accept the unsupported say-so of ancient authorities, and awakening faith in the ability of the human reason to attain fresh truth. The weight of the medieval Church had naturally been exerted largely in the direction of the acceptance of authority:

the Bible as God's inspired Word; the Church Fathers as guides to the Christian life; the Church itself as custodian and interpreter of what God had revealed, and therefore as the sole means to salvation. In science and philosophy, emphasis was laid on the experience of the distant past, embalmed in books. For example, Galen (d. 200?) and Hippocrates (d. 359?) were still the greatest names in medicine; and Aristotle was revered above all the rest, not as a model in the spirit of inquiry but as a source of truth.

The Renaissance spirit was one of intense curiosity about the world, though it took a long time for experimental methods to supplant the appeal to authority. Some of the sciences that we now take for granted made slow progress or none during this period. But in general men pressed the pursuit of scientific truth no less ardently than the voyagers plowed unknown seas and found continents.

Probably the most influential of the new hypotheses was that of the Polish astronomer Copernicus (1473–1543). He rejected the ancient Ptolemaic theory of planetary spheres revolving around the earth, and substituted an earth turning daily on its own axis and, along with neighboring planets, periodically circling the sun. To his contemporaries the most startling feature of the Copernican astronomy was the denial that the earth is the center of the universe. This conception clashed sharply with orthodox religious teachings; its gradual acceptance shook the foundations of belief and encouraged free scientific inquiry. In sixteenth-century England, astronomy and mathematics made strides which led to a general scientific and philosophical advance in the next century.

In the year which saw the publication of the Copernican astronomy, 1543, appeared the first landmark in modern medicine, a treatise on anatomy by the Flemish physician Vesalius (1514–1564). Dissection was still considered impious by many ecclesiastics, since it desecrated bodies made in the image of God. Vesalius argued (and acted on his convictions) that the road to a knowledge of anatomy and physiology necessarily lay through the dissecting room rather than in the writings of the ancients.

HUMANISM

Just as in his own way the scientist turned to a direct examination of the phenomena of nature, and the artist in his to the same world—the landscape, the human face, the gorgeous costume, the flesh under the costume, and the anatomical structure under the flesh—so many a Renaissance scholar turned his back on the scholastic speculations of the Middle Ages concerning the dogmas of theology and applied himself to the study of man viewed not as a candidate for immortality but as a citizen of the present world. This humanistic approach to man was stimulated by the new reading of classical literature. Petrarch has been called the first modern man chiefly because he wanted to see Latin used, not for the hairsplitting disputations of the medieval schoolmen, who propounded fantastic refinements of theological problems in order to solve them by ingenious applications of Aristotelian logic, but as a key to a better and more enlightened understanding of human life. It was to that end that he prosecuted his textual labors on the ancient manuscripts, encouraged others to go in for classical scholarship, and called for the foundation of libraries.

This Renaissance humanism did not greatly affect England till the sixteenth century. The study of Greek, however, had been revived at Oxford before the end of the fifteenth. In 1496 John Colet (1466–1519) began an epoch-making series of lectures there on the epistles of St. Paul, handling them with a strictly historical and critical technique, like any other ancient texts. The English humanists, at Oxford and afterwards at Cambridge, were devout Catholics; in no sense was their interest in the New Learning a rebellion against religion. Against a number of orthodox beliefs and practices, however, they vigorously remonstrated. Their movement had a strong ethical bias. Remaining within the Church's fold, they hoped to reconcile the tenets of Christianity with the wisdom of the Greeks and Romans, and to use the resultant synthesis as a means to the good life. They were fervent idealists, and their ideal philosopher was Plato. Like many Renaissance Catholics, Colet was sceptical about the value of relics and pilgrimages, favored making the Bible available to all in English, rejected the tissue of subtleties and allegories which medieval students had read into it, and called for a spiritual reform of the Church.

Among the leaders of the English humanists was Thomas Linacre (d. 1524). He had gone on from Oxford to Italy, where he studied medicine and also the philosophy of Plato. On his return he had a distinguished career as a physician and a teacher of Greek. Colet and Sir Thomas More, who was also in the van of humanism, were among Linacre's pupils. Another leader was John Fisher (d. 1535), Bishop of Rochester. While chancellor of Cambridge University he brought the great Dutch scholar, Desiderius Erasmus (1467–1537), the leading humanist of all Europe, to teach Greek there. Fisher was completely free from Protestant leanings and refused to follow Henry VIII in separating the English Church from Rome. Like More he sealed his Catholic faith with martyrdom.

Despite the unwillingness of its leaders to divorce humanism from religion, the ultimate tendency of the movement in England was toward the secularization of life and especially of education.

NATIONALISM

THE OUTBURST of artistic expression, the revival of letters, and the progress of science were important results of a general awakening of the western mind. About the same time a number of inventions began revolutionizing the organization of European affairs. There was some use of cannon in the fourteenth century; and once firearms established themselves as supreme in war, the feudal warrior was doomed. His castle was now vulnerable despite its encircling moat. The heavy cavalry of the armored knights, already more than matched by the fire power of the English longbowmen, was in the fifteenth century rendered even more hopelessly obsolete by the application of gunpowder to small arms. Now it was the day of the monarch, backed by a national treasury, able to support a standing corps of disciplined household troops, a train of artillery, and a fleet. The way lay open to the centralization of authority, and to eventual imperialism and the exploitation of the badly armed non-European races.

Italy and Germany were exceptions and did not achieve national unity till the nineteenth century. England had long enjoyed it, though in the fifteenth century it was submerged for a time in the Wars of the Roses. With the accession of the Tudor family under Henry VII in 1485, the royal power was once more consolidated. Henry VIII had artillery and a navy; under Elizabeth a national militia was organized. In France and Spain strong monarchies were established during the Renaissance. For a time the latter moved in the orbit of the so-called Holy Roman Empire, a German combination but not a nation, long in the grasp of the Austrian house of Hapsburg. France, Spain, and the Empire were at various times more or less dominant in Italy, which was often their battleground.

But the most important cause of the decline of feudalism was the growing importance of cities and towns. The feudal system was based on ownership of the soil by a military aristocracy; the medieval economy was essentially agrarian. During the later Middle Ages towns rapidly increased in number and in size, and they were only indirectly dependent on agriculture. The tradesmen of the town steadily resisted the local baron's efforts to control them. The rise of the towns contributed to the Renaissance because the close association of city dwellers provides in itself an intellectual stimulus. In the city the artist and the writer find the principal market for their wares, which for the Renaissance painter, sculptor, or poet meant not so much the general public as the existence of the wealthy patron. In Elizabethan England the drama, with its direct appeal to the public, was a remarkable exception; but it too depended, even more than the other arts, on urban life.

Whether the new nationalism and the immense emotional force (patriotism) which it has acquired have proved a blessing or a curse is among the most highly debatable questions of our time. One conclusion is obvious: nationalism was a strong card in a Renaissance king's hand. In England it enabled the monarch to seize control of the Church and of education. And it unquestionably had a good deal to do with the amazing outburst of literary masterpieces in the last decade of the sixteenth century.

PRINTING

EDUCATION was revitalized in sixteenth-century England; literacy, already much increased during the fifteenth century, went on increasing; scholarship even became fashionable. Behind these developments stood the invention of printing, and behind that the invention of paper to replace parchment made of skins. Like gunpowder, printing and papermaking were an old story in China. The first two were re-invented in Europe; the art of papermaking was learned from the Chinese through the Arabs. Printing was a German contribution. Priority is disputed, but the first book printed from movable types on linen paper seems to have been the Bible which in 1454 came from the press of Johannes Gutenberg of Mainz. The fifteenth century is called the cradle-time of printing, which is why books printed before 1500 are known as incunabula (Latin *cunae*=cradle). The Gutenberg Bible is a Latin text; but soon, in every country, the presses were pouring off a larger stream of vernacular works than of Latin. Caxton, the first English printer, probably learned the art in Cologne. In 1474 the first printed book in English came from his shop in Bruges, and two years later he set up the first printing press in England.

Printing was more an effect than a cause of the revival of learning. But it was a powerful agent in spreading the Renaissance, not only geographically but also from top to bottom of the literate population. Books were far cheaper to manufacture than manuscripts, and there were more of them. Slowly the door opened to a larger participation by the middle class in intellectual and political affairs, formerly monopolized by the clergy and the aristocracy.

THE GEOGRAPHICAL DISCOVERIES

MEDIEVAL Europeans lived in a small world. That it could not be flat had long been generally known; such was the conclusion of the Greek astronomer Ptolemy in the second century after Christ. But the existence of the American continents was unknown, despite the temporary settlement of Norsemen from Greenland on the New England coast in the tenth century.

The Crusades of the eleventh, twelfth, and thirteenth centuries helped push the horizon back and put the West in closer touch with the Middle East. With a certain naive wonder, western Europeans became aware of old cultures in Asia Minor and North Africa. They learned of luxuries and refinements of living beyond anything Europe could offer. They found that in some fields of learning, for example medicine, the torch of enlightenment was in the hands of the Arabs. Another point of contact was Spain, where the final conquest of another Mohammedan people, the Moors, was not accomplished till 1492, under Ferdinand and Isabella.

Long before that event, the Venetian traveler Marco Polo (1254–1323) had made his way to China, whence he returned with news of civilizations in central and eastern Asia more ancient and in some ways more advanced than Europe had ever known. A number of Italian cities, especially Venice, began opening up trade routes to Asia Minor, Persia, India, and China—by sea to Syria, and thence overland by caravan. Increasing commercial penetration intensified the stimulus to Europe's imagination. Mixed with the truths brought back by the traders were the most fantastic exaggerations and myths. A voyager who had pushed far to the south or east actually witnessed so many scarcely credible things that when he heard of fresh wonders a few miles farther on he believed the tale and told it at home as sober fact.

Indeed, the Renaissance mind was so suddenly confronted with so much new truth, difficult to believe but requiring acceptance, that in the midst of all the scientific ferment there was an urge to credulity. The age believed in wonders and had an insatiable appetite for more—not merely for accounts of

> the Cannibals that each other eat,
> The Anthropophagi, and men whose heads
> Do grow beneath their shoulders,

but for astrology, alchemy, fortune telling, and get-rich-quick schemes of every description. On the whole, however, the effect of the deluge of marvels was probably salutary. It quickened the most important of all the mind's qualities, the imagination; and this stimulus, which so powerfully affected all the arts and especially creative literature, was for the moment hardly less beneficent to science as well.

The lure of what lay beyond the horizon, however mixed up it might be with greed or commercialism, was much like the impulse that gave no rest to the poet, the artist, the scientist, and the scholar. The revival of learning had placed the astronomy and geography of the Greeks at the disposal of the Renaissance explorer. The compass, which came into general use in the fifteenth century, relieved seamen of the necessity of hugging the coast. Nation after nation took up the challenge. For a time Portugal held the lead. Down the West African coast and out among its islands pushed the ships, till in 1486 the Cape of Good Hope was doubled and in 1498 Vasco Da Gama at last showed the way to India. The great prize was Spain's, the great date 1492, and the greatest name Columbus. The Genoese seaman struck boldly westward for the Far East, and went to his grave believing he had found the best way to it. From the vast American empire to which his voyages led, gold poured into the coffers of the Spanish kings and made them the terror of Europe, till England broke their sea power in 1588.

England and France were late entrants in the race; but before the sixteenth century was over, the voyages that Raleigh organized had paved the way for the English-speaking nations of North America, while the sun of Spain had begun to set. The discovery of the New World put England, hitherto located at a margin of the civilized world, in a strategic position on what was to become one of the world's main thoroughfares, the North Atlantic. Commerce and manufacturing increased by leaps and bounds. Evidence of the new wealth is still visible in the surviving Tudor manorhouses and in the architecture of many public buildings. One of the most important aspects of the age is the rise of capitalism. Already under way in fourteenth-century England, it was fostered by the premium the Renaissance put on individualism. With the founding of merchant trading companies and banks, money itself became a dominating political as well as commercial power. Capitalism replaced the old guilds, both as the economic system and as the ruling influence in local and eventually in national government.

As THE Middle Ages neared their end, the Church seemed firmly established. It had the allegiance of all western Europe. It was a temporal power in Italy, where the Pope ruled a sizable state. Rebellions against its spiritual authority, such as the Wyclifite or Lollard heresy in fourteenth-century England, had been easily crushed. The Church was rich. Its enormous estates were untaxed. It levied its own tax, the tithes, theoretically (though not actually) one tenth of all the land's produce. It controlled education. The laity were subject not only to the civil law of the various states but also to the canon law of the Church, the jurisdiction of whose courts extended to everything that pertained to marriage, divorce, and the probate of wills.

Yet, despite its unique foundation, the Church was an organization; it was operated by human beings; and into it, as sooner or later into every institution, abuses had crept. Reform was inevitable. This was recognized not only by the Protestants, who finally separated themselves from Rome, but by many Catholics, including some of the saintliest figures in the Church's history.

Among the practices which roused the ire of the reformers were certain methods by which the Popes increased their revenues. Licenses for the sale of indulgences or pardons had reached scandalous proportions. Another point of attack was the Popes' encouragement of the sin of simony (traffic in ecclesiastical appointments) by accepting presents from candidates for high office in the Church. Another was the exaction of First Fruits, by which a new bishop paid the Pope half his first year's income. In an era of growing nationalism, these practices came to be regarded by many as a form of foreign taxation. In Germany this resentment was strengthened by the progress of humanism in the universities, where the revival of learning took a narrower and more religious turn than in Italy. Scholars like Erasmus labored to establish a more accurate text of the Bible, and insisted on the primary authority of that book over and above the interpretations of the Church. In his *Praise of Folly* the great Dutchman attacked with telling satire a number of ecclesiastical abuses and popular superstitions. No name stands higher in the humanist movement anywhere, but Erasmus worked steadily for the main cause of intellectual enlightenment and held aloof from the party which eventually broke with Rome.

The leader of that party was Martin Luther (1483–1546), an Augustinian friar and professor of theology at the University of Wittenberg in Saxony. Having come to doubt the Catholic program of salvation by faith and good works, he declared that through faith and faith alone lay the way to heaven. In the fall of 1517 he nailed his ninety-five points or "theses" to a church door in Wittenberg, thus indicating his readiness to argue the case against the practice of granting indulgences.

The fight was on. The Pope proclaimed Luther a heretic, and the young emperor Charles V took the Pope's side. But the reform movement had attracted so much support that neither could halt it. Under the protection of German princes who had turned Protestant, the Lutheran Church was organized; monasteries were confiscated; indulgences, pilgrimages, and other practices were condemned. The colorful and dramatic ritual of the Catholic Church was simplified; German replaced Latin in the Lutheran service of prayer, psalm, and sermon; and Luther, having renounced his monastic vows and married a former nun, began a German translation of the Bible. Soon after his death in 1546 came the first of the religious wars which long ravaged Germany; but the Peace of Augsburg in 1555 gave the Lutherans legal standing, and the unity of the Christian Church in western Europe was a thing of the past.

Protestantism spread rapidly north and west. In Italy and Spain it was suppressed. In France ensued a period of civil war and massacre. The leader of the Protestants was Henry of Navarre, and he had to fight for his rightful succession to the throne as Henry IV, greatest of modern French kings. In the end he turned Catholic; but while he was still campaigning he was aided with men and money by Queen Elizabeth. Under his rule the Huguenots or French Protestants won toleration. In northern Germany and Scandinavia the reformers made a clean sweep.

Switzerland gave the Protestants one of their hardest fights, but by the middle of the sixteenth century Geneva was one of the strongholds of the new faith. There John Calvin (1509-1564), an exiled French lawyer, had settled after the publication in 1536 of his *Institutes of the Christian Religion*. In this book, a masterpiece of logical argument (provided you accept the premises), Calvin formulated a theory for a church and a state strictly in accordance with the Bible's teachings. Untouched by the more genial aspects of the Renaissance, he agreed with the medieval theologians that man's sole task in this world is to prepare for life eternal in the next. His view of human nature was low. He held that most of humanity is, without any injustice on God's part, foreordained to damnation.

In his conception of the state, Calvin broke with the German leaders of the Reformation. In Germany the Protestant church was controlled by the princes; but Geneva was a republic, and Calvin held that the primitive Christian churches were democracies. In Scotland his doctrines soon triumphed under the preaching of John Knox (1502-72); and in England the Puritan movement was nourished on his teachings, though by the time it grew to be a serious threat to the established order the Church of England had long been separated from Rome. That separation was more political than doctrinal, but the Puritans attacked the Church of England at those points where they thought it still smacked of Rome. They particularly disliked the ritual and the rule of the bishops. They followed Calvin in his conception of God as the sternest of autocrats and of man as a worm, in his doctrine of predestination, and in his insistence on a rigid austerity of conduct and a harsh interference with private lives by church officials. In the next century Calvin's teaching was exported to the New World by the founders of the Massachusetts Bay Colony.

The Reformation was both a part of the Renaissance and a reaction against it. The impetus it gave to individualism is obvious. Private judgment, not the pronouncement of the Church, was to be the authority for belief and conduct. A man must seek by his own efforts to learn God's will and to find salvation. The mediation of the clergy was rejected in favor of the individual's direct application to the throne of God. But in its exaltation of the Bible as the only and sufficient guide and in the Calvinistic insistence on the depravity of man, the Reformation broke sharply with the humanistic impulse of the Renaissance, to the liberating forces of which it had partly owed its origin. In the end the Reformation became the deadly enemy of much for which most enlightened men account themselves the thankful debtors of the Renaissance. All that has been said in these pages about Renaissance optimism, buoyancy, and aspiration is perfectly true. But, as so often in the course of human affairs, while certain fine notions were uppermost in many minds, exactly the opposite conceptions were also present. In some minds they were dominant. Plenty of pessimists were certain that this brave modern world was taking the shortest route to hell. And no man could avoid thinking sometimes of the most certain of all the facts of life—death. Any picture of the Elizabethan epoch which bathed the scene of "Merry England" in uninterrupted sunlight would be a false picture. It was in fact full of shadows. To the more thoroughgoing of the Puritans it was mostly shadows, for their faith laid on every soul the awful responsibility of finding its own way to God. This was a never-ending source of worry, often of dreadful agony.

The effect of the Reformation on the Catholic Church went far beyond the alienation of large areas from its authority. The Church was itself stimulated to a self-administered Counter Reformation. Reforms were instituted in the parish priesthood and the monastic orders, and new orders were founded. The most important of these was the Society of Jesus, which speedily assumed leadership in the educational and missionary enterprises of Catholicism. The Jesuit fathers were particularly aggressive in the effort the Church now made to win the heretic back to the fold. About the middle of the sixteenth century the lead in the Counter Reformation was taken by the Papacy itself.

If there was ever any chance of uniting the two movements of reform (the one within, the other outside the Catholic Church), it was never grasped. Eventually both parties resorted to arms. As we have seen, Protestantism turned its back on the Renaissance. Under the Popes who renounced the luxury of some of their predecessors, Catholicism did likewise.

HENRY VIII AND THE CHURCH OF ENGLAND

THE PURITAN wing of the Protestant movement was deeply exercised over theological, organizational, and ritualistic issues; but most Englishmen were probably little interested. To them the important feature of the Reformation in England was the transfer of authority over the Church from the Pope to the King.

Henry VII had defeated and killed Richard III, last of the Yorkist monarchs, in 1485. Through his mother, Henry had a Lancastrian strain in his blood; his marriage to the Yorkist princess, daughter of Edward IV, ended the rivalry of the two houses. Many of the feudal nobility had fallen in France or during the Wars of the Roses, and Henry succeeded in making his throne supreme. The barons were forbidden to maintain private armies and were subjected to a new court known as Star Chamber, which did the King's will. Parliament was preserved, but under the Tudors it played a secondary role. The new monarch ruled personally. He amassed a huge fortune, and hoarded it. When he died, in 1509, his son was crowned Henry VIII, and proceeded to spend it.

Meanwhile the New Learning had won many followers in England. Henry VIII himself had been educated in the light of humanism, and the progressives were joyful over his accession. They thought their royal pupil would be a great power for good. In six visits to England between 1499 and 1517, Erasmus helped bring first Oxford and then Cambridge into line with the Renaissance. John Colet (see p. 217, above) became dean of St. Paul's, London's cathedral church, and founded St. Paul's School for boys, with a curriculum based on the New Learning.

Sir Thomas More (1478–1535)—or St. Thomas More, for he has recently been canonized—was a warm friend of Erasmus and Colet. As lord chancellor and therefore head of the administration under Henry VIII, he was to give his life for his Catholic faith; but he was an ardent advocate of humanism. His *Utopia* (1516) was written in Latin and therefore lies outside English literature. Its importance was in its criticism of contemporary politics, society, and religious life. It was in fact a humanist manifesto. More makes his points partly by direct attack, partly by describing Utopia, a mythical land of Nowhere, in which men live communistically in peace and happiness.

The high hopes of the reformers were blighted as Henry VIII matured. Tyrannical by nature and ambitious for personal glory, the King visualized himself in a leading role on the stage of European politics. England was weaker than either France or Spain, but in their rivalry Henry saw his chance to wield the balance of power. The dawn of permanent international peace, which the humanists believed they might live to see, never came. Henry warred repeatedly, with Scotland and with France.

He had married a Spanish princess, Catherine of Aragon, daughter of Ferdinand and Isabella. She was the widow of his older brother Arthur, who had died young. For her second marriage, to her brother-in-law, a papal dispensation was secured. Sons were born, but they soon died; only a daughter, Mary Tudor, lived beyond infancy. Henry wanted a male successor. In 1527 he made up his mind to marry Anne Boleyn, a pretty maid of honor with whom he had fallen wildly in love. Throughout long years of debate, Henry's request for a divorce was denied by the Pope, who could not risk giving mortal offense to Queen Catherine's nephew, the German Emperor Charles V, king of Spain. The question became the major issue of English politics. When the King concluded that his chancellor, Cardinal Wolsey, had not pushed the divorce negotiations vigorously, he dismissed Wolsey and appointed More in his place.

Henry's principal adviser, however, was now the able but sinister Thomas Cromwell, who at once proceeded to wrest from the Pope control of the Church in England. In 1531 its Convocation acknowledged Henry as its head. First Fruits were abolished, and appeals to Rome from the ecclesiastical courts were prohibited. In 1533 Thomas Cranmer, Archbishop of Canterbury, granted the divorce from Catherine. Anne was crowned queen. The Pope retaliated by excommunicating the King; but in 1534 Parliament passed an Act of Supremacy, confirming Henry's authority over the Church of England and completely severing the tie with Rome. More was among those who refused to take an oath accepting the Act of Supremacy, and he was executed for "treason" in 1535.

Henry was not by nature much subject to the influence of spiritual considerations, and the Protestantism of Cromwell was more political than religious. Cromwell's idea was to make the King supreme by breaking the only other power in England, and so he led an all-out attack on the Church's wealth. In 1536 Parliament agreed to the confiscation of the monasteries. The plunder was enormous. Most of the lands were sold off to the country squires at bargain prices for the benefit of the royal treasury—it had been emptied by the pleasure-loving and war-making King. A few of the monastic properties were distributed as gifts to members of the new aristocracy the Tudors were building up. With some of the proceeds of the Dissolution, schools and churches were endowed, but not enough to compensate for the large number wiped out.

THE PROTESTANT AND CATHOLIC EXTREMISTS

ON THE whole there was little change in the articles of faith while Henry lived; his own opinions were conservative. His last years were a reign of terror. The handsome and hopeful prince of the humanists had degenerated into the bloated and brutish king. Heads rolled with appalling frequency. Cromwell went to the block in 1540, charged with treason. Two of Henry's six wives, Anne Boleyn and Catherine Howard, died by the headsman's ax. But it was under his successor, Edward VI, his son by his third wife, that the Protestants really took control.

This king—he reigned from 1547 to 1553—was a boy; and the Lord Protector, his uncle, the Duke of Somerset, put through with the help of Archbishop Cranmer a series of parliamentary acts introducing radical changes. The requirement of celibacy for the priesthood was abolished. So was the use of holy water. Images, which the Protestant extremists con-

sidered an invitation to superstition, were ripped down in the churches. English replaced Latin in the ritual, which was standardized in 1549 by the first Book of Common Prayer. The practice of family worship became widespread.

Somerset's career ended in 1552 with his execution. A genuine reformer, he had taken the side of the people in one of the periodic clashes between the small farmers and the great landlords who were fencing off for sheep pasturage not only the plowed lands they owned but also tracts long used in common by the whole population. Somerset's fall did not halt the radical trend in religion. Under his successor, the Duke of Northumberland, Catholics were persecuted. Mobs were allowed to smash the stained glass of the churches or anything else that to the fanatics savored of popery. A new formulation of doctrine was adopted.

On Edward's death, Mary, the elder of his two sisters, ascended the throne. She reigned from 1553 to 1558. Now there was a violent swing to Catholicism, for the Queen was the daughter of Catherine of Aragon. She might have realized her ambition of leading England back to the Catholic faith; a majority of the population probably favored the old religion. But they would not follow her in her effort to re-establish papal supremacy. Nor could she restore the confiscated estates of the monasteries—too many people of importance had shared in the loot. Most of the other measures of the reforming parliaments were repealed. Mary's marriage in 1554 to Philip II, son and successor to Charles V on the throne of Spain, strengthened her determination to convert her subjects at any cost. Again the fires of martyrdom were lighted. Archbishop Cranmer was but one of many who perished at the stake.

ELIZABETH

WITH Mary's death began the long reign (1558–1603) of Elizabeth. As Anne Boleyn's daughter, the new Queen was bound to be a Protestant, that is, politically, for the Catholics denied her legitimacy and hence her right to the throne. Hers was not a temperament predisposed to strong religious feeling. She had been educated in the humanist tradition; and though it was during her reign that Protestantism permanently won the ascendancy in England, she was more the child of the Renaissance than of the Reformation. Catholics were persecuted; there were torments and burnings; a Jesuit caught anywhere in the realm was doomed. But the Catholic laity were not greatly molested, and England escaped the horrors which afflicted a number of other countries.

Acts were soon passed renewing the sovereign's supremacy over the Church and prescribing conformity to the Book of Common Prayer and to the Thirty-nine Articles, a revision of the doctrinal formulation that had been adopted during the reign of Edward VI. Elizabeth's comparative moderation suited the English character. Shakespeare was like his queen in this respect; if he was strongly inclined toward either Protestantism or Catholicism, he fails to reveal it in his plays. Nevertheless, in addition to a Catholic minority, two groups of Protestants remained dissatisfied with the Queen's policy. Of these the more moderate were the Puritans. They were a party inside the Church of England desirous of pushing its reform still further. The Separatists or Brownists (so called after a leader) considered the Anglican establishment little less tainted than the Roman Church itself, and by leaving the Church of England made themselves liable to persecution. Thus the Puritans proper constituted a liberal left wing within the Church, while the Separatists were the out-and-out radicals. The name of Puritan, however, came to be applied loosely to anyone who advocated a more thoroughgoing Protestant reform.

In her tastes and scholarship Elizabeth was one of the most cultivated persons who have ever occupied England's throne. She had a tough mind, an excellent education, and a hard-driving personality. She was willful, inordinately vain and therefore susceptible to the grossest flattery, mean about money, devious in her political methods, violent in temper, rude in manner, and coarse in speech. She may not have been a great woman, or even a great lady; she was certainly a great queen—keenly intelligent, a superb executive, gifted with a special knack for selecting capable ministers, and utterly devoted to her job of guarding England's greatness. She was overfond of diplomatic finesse, her adroitness at which she loved to display; but her statesmanship steered her country safely through a sea of difficulties, domestic and foreign. Parliament remained of minor importance. Elizabeth governed mainly through her Privy Council, to which she appointed the best talent she could discover. Its leader was the able and cautious Lord Treasurer, William Cecil, first baron Burghley.

From the very beginning Spain, strongest of the Catholic powers, was a constant menace. Its king had been the consort of Elizabeth's sister and predecessor. From his father, the Emperor Charles V, Philip II had inherited the Netherlands as well as Spain and the Spanish possessions in Italy and in the New World, while the title of emperor had passed

to his uncle, founder of the younger, Austrian branch of the Hapsburgs. Ownership of the Low Countries by a Spanish king was a dagger pointed at England's heart.

The war started unofficially when the great English admirals, among them Sir John Hawkins (1532–95) and Sir Francis Drake (1540?–96), began preying on Spanish commerce in the Atlantic, especially the treasure fleets from America. Elizabeth naturally withheld official approval of such acts; but when in 1580 Drake returned to Plymouth from his voyage around the world, in the course of which he had plundered the Spanish towns on the west coast of the Americas, Elizabeth knighted him on the quarter-deck of his flagship, the *Golden Hind,* and took her cut of the immense treasure he brought home.

King Philip was a religious fanatic. His attempts to suppress the Protestantism of the Dutch had goaded them into rebellion in 1568, under William the Silent, Prince of Orange. This noble leader was assassinated in 1584, but the heroic struggle went on. It lasted for eighty years. Elizabeth's motives were chiefly political; but many of her subjects felt profoundly for their persecuted coreligionists both in France and in the Low Countries, and went overseas as volunteers to fight for Protestantism. The Queen sent help to Henry of Navarre, while he was still a Protestant hero, and by 1585 she was openly aiding the Dutch. In 1587, alarmed by a plot against her life, she ordered the execution of her Catholic kinswoman, Mary Stuart, the exiled Queen of Scots, to whom the Pope had awarded the English throne when he excommunicated Elizabeth.

In the summer of the following year, Philip struck. The huge fleet called the Invincible Armada sailed for the Netherlands to cover the projected invasion of England. The Spanish conception of naval tactics was still the ancient one of grappling ship to ship and boarding with an overwhelming force of soldiers. The English, who exalted seamanship, were beginning to understand that a warship was essentially a maneuverable platform for the broadside batteries. The Armada was badly mauled by the lighter but handier English ships in an eight-day running engagement as it went through the Channel, and a subsequent attack by fireships took the fight out of it. The Spaniards decided to make for home by a circuit north of the British Isles, but ran into a series of storms which wrecked nearly all their ships.

Not even during her wars against Louis XIV, nor in Napoleonic times, in fact not till the summer of 1940, was England to face again so serious a threat to her island home. With Spain's immense effort shattered, the English now took the offensive, in war and in commerce. In 1596 an English fleet was victorious at Cadiz on the Spanish mainland. In the years just before the great Armada, Raleigh had financed several voyages to Virginia and the first attempt at colonization there. English seamen also sailed the eastern Mediterranean, and before long in the Far East a brisk commerce sprang up with India and the spice islands. For trading in these quarters merchants banded together to form the Levant Company and the East India Company. With Russia and parts of the Middle East commercial relations were established by the Muscovy Company.

The relief and exultant pride of 1588 intensified English nationalism and undoubtedly was a factor in the intensity of the literary outburst which began immediately and continued throughout the remainder of the Queen's reign. She was herself keenly interested in literature. We have seen how Oxford was the original English stronghold of humanism. Toward the end of the reign of Henry VIII, Sir Thomas Cheke, a pupil of Erasmus, became professor of Greek there. Cheke's favorite pupil was Roger Ascham, and Elizabeth's girlhood tutors were Ascham and one of his own pupils, William Grindal. Thus the influence of the New Learning reached the Queen in a kind of apostolic succession from the master humanist himself. She acquired a good knowledge of both Latin and Greek literature, and she could speak Latin, French, and Italian.

Elizabeth's court provided an audience for England's new literature; it was also one of its sources, since among her courtier poets were some of the best writers. The court was the center of English life, and the Queen was the center of the court. Her position was enhanced by a sentimental attitude toward her virginity. Political considerations, as well as a personal aversion which was probably pathological, dissuaded her from marrying. For many years she played France against Spain by keeping several matrimonial candidates dangling. Meanwhile, and indeed to the last of her old age, she expected from her courtiers professions of love as well as loyalty. These must be ardent but respectful. Though she formed emotional attachments with the Earl of Leicester, Sir Walter Raleigh, the Earl of Essex, and others, it is probable that no one actually became her lover; and she did not allow affection to cloud her judgment of a man's capacity for public affairs. However grim and realistic the machinery of government behind the scenes, the court was a kind of stage, and court life almost a drama. Grace in expression was a requirement for success there.

ONE obvious effect of the Renaissance on England was linguistic. Enthusiasm for the classics encouraged the importation into English of many words of Latin origin. Some of them failed to stick; others are now so familiar that we are quite unconscious of how their use began early in the modern English period. For a while there was a lively controversy, and conservatives fumed against these "inkhorn terms." Some of the borrowing was on a fantastic scale, but the language was certainly enriched. A multiplicity of synonyms always increases its ability to make nice discriminations: *happiness* does not mean precisely the same thing as *felicity*. When the dying Hamlet implores his loyal friend to live and tell his story, the beautiful line "Absént thee from felicity awhile" is no less beautiful and no less English because both *absent* and *felicity* came into the language, not with the basic stock of Germanic words, but from Latin.

The language was also considerably though temporarily affected by Latin syntax and rhetoric, which tended to make the English sentence less direct and less clear. Phonological changes also took place; that is, many words were pronounced differently, chiefly because vowel sounds were shifting. The change from Chaucer's pronunciation to our own (see pp. 112 f., above) had begun in the fifteenth century. A hundred years after Chaucer's death it had gone so far that no one knew how to pronounce his lines. By Renaissance readers he was thought a clumsy versifier. Since the final *e*, which gives many of Chaucer's words one more syllable than their present forms, was rarely sounded in the sixteenth century, his lines were considered barbarously rough and jerky.

The necessity of disfiguring the following pages with a profusion of glossarial notes shows that the language was still to pass through a long period of change, especially in semantics or the meanings of words, before it reached the phase which we speak and write today. In the sixteenth century it was, however, definitely no longer Middle English but, as the linguists term it, Early Modern English.

PROSE

CLOSELY associated with the Reformation was the work of putting the Bible into the various modern languages. For England William Tyndale, a zealous reformer, translated the New Testament and parts of the Old, not from the Vulgate (the Latin text), but from the original tongues. His work was scholarly, though it had a Protestant bias. Its literary excellence was such that later translations, down through the King James Version of 1611, are hardly more than revisions. Tyndale aimed at a simplicity which should make the Bible an open book to any "boy that driveth the plow." Though many an Elizabethan writer, like John Lyly in his *Euphues* (1578), adopted an ornate style, only too characteristic of the Renaissance love of display and quite the reverse of what we now consider good writing, there remained from that day to this the example of the plain, forceful, idiomatic prose of Tyndale.

The Book of Common Prayer, chiefly from the pen of Archbishop Cranmer, was also in its simplicity and rhythm a good influence on prose. So were some of the sermons, for example those of Cranmer's fellow martyr Hugh Latimer (d.1555). As in medieval times, the sermon was still an important branch of literature; there was a steady demand for it in print. To this list of religious works should be added another, not for its style, but because practically all Elizabethans read it and its popularity continued for two centuries. This was John Foxe's *Acts and Monuments of These Latter and Perilous Times,* commonly called *The Book of Martyrs,* a collection of lurid accounts of Christian martyrs, particularly the Protestants who suffered under Queen Mary.

Some of the best prose of the period was written by the dramatists. An audience cannot turn back the leaf for a second reading; it must be made to understand, through the ear, immediately. This ever-present requirement encouraged a straightforward style in works designed for the theater. Outside it, the overdecorated style found favor with many. The age loved ornament for its own sake. Hence, even in the drama, the lavish use of extravagant figures of speech, and the intrusion of puns even when the mood is entirely serious. Eventually, from 1588 on, poetry and drama came to overshadow the prose books. Yet throughout the period prose, especially the prose of the Bible and sermons, reached more people.

Historians, or rather chroniclers, were active. A long series of chronicles, each to some extent appropriating and then continuing its predecessor, culminates in two books which are still interesting for the vivid detail with which they often describe great moments in English history. These are Edward Halle's *The Union of the Two Noble Families of Lancaster and York* (1542) and the *Chronicles of England, Scotland, and Ireland* (1578) by Raphael Holinshed and others. Shakespeare drew repeatedly on them for his historical plays. Another important chronicler was John Stowe (d.1605), a London tailor so in love with historical studies that in middle life he left "his own peculiar gains" and gave himself to

scholarship. His *Chronicles of England* first appeared in 1580, and *A Survey of London* in 1598. The latter, in the enlarged edition of 1603, is our chief authority for the metropolis in Elizabethan times.

Another source of plots for the dramatists, and a favorite with the reading public, was anthologies of tales, mostly translated from Italian and French collections. William Painter's *Palace of Pleasure* (1566–69) and Geoffrey Fenton's *Tragical Discourses* (1567), to mention only two of them, are full of stories (usually in an Italian setting) of violent death and no less violent love. In these volumes something of the fiercer side of the Italian Renaissance was brought to England, and sober Englishmen came to regard Italy as a place where anything could happen. To this sinister aspect of the Renaissance and the depiction of Italy as the scene of ceaseless political and private intrigue, assassination by steel and poison, and unbridled lust, a misunderstanding of the ideas of Niccolò Machiavelli (1469-1527) made a powerful contribution. Depressed by the chaotic state of Italian politics, Machiavelli concluded that only the benevolent despot promised any hope of order and peace. Accordingly, in *The Prince,* he laid down a program of realistic method which, misrepresented by hostile writers, came to stand in the eyes of the sixteenth-century Englishman (to whom it was not available in English) as a symbol of everything unscrupulous and ruthless in political theory and practice. To English conservatives, therefore, a young Englishman rounding out his education with a grand tour of the Continent ran the risk of losing all his native virtues if he ventured into Italy; and the Italianate Englishman, back from Italy with a new suit of clothes and a set of foreign manners and morals, was an object sometimes of ridicule, sometimes of alarm.

An important agency in bringing England within the orbit of the Renaissance was a series of translations from the classics. Sir Thomas North's rendering (1579) of a French version of Plutarch's *Lives of the Noble Greeks and Romans* made available a Greek book which, throughout this period and long after, was an important formative influence on the modern mind. From North's translation Shakespeare took, not only the plots of his Roman plays, but also chunks of phraseology. Other Greek writings, both prose and poetry, were also translated; but none, not even the Homer of George Chapman, which moved Keats to a great sonnet, assumed a comparable place in English literature. Nor did any of the numerous translations of the Roman poets, dramatists, historians, and philosophers, Christian or pagan, win much of a place, even though some of England's greatest writers were indebted to them, as Shakespeare was to Arthur Golding's verse translation of the *Metamorphoses* of Ovid. There were also many translations and adaptations of modern Continental works. The most important of these was John Florio's spirited prose translation (1603) of the *Essays* of Montaigne (1533–92). From Florio's Montaigne English writers, Shakespeare among them, picked up many a modern idea.

Another kind of Elizabethan letters was the prose romance, a long and usually rambling narrative of heroic adventures in an idyllic pastoral setting, with idealized shepherds and their sweethearts. Sir Philip Sidney and Robert Greene, of whom more hereafter, were leaders in this prolific but not very important genre, the former with his *Arcadia* (published in 1590), the latter with a whole string of romances. Another influential romance was Thomas Lodge's *Rosalind* (1590), whence Shakespeare took the plot of *As You Like It*. The realistic novel was yet to be invented; but in Thomas Nashe's *Jack Wilton* (1591) the adventurous hero is a rogue, and his fantastic doings are described with realistic touches.

Of slender literary merit, but much read, were the "courtesy books," manuals of manners and conduct. The most famous were Italian. Of one of these, *Il Cortegiano* by Baldassare Castiglione (d.1529), Sir Thomas Hoby made a popular English version, *The Courtier* (1561). It describes the finished gentleman who was the ideal of the humanists, a figure of all-round accomplishment. The courtier must be trained for war, proficient in sports and horsemanship, graceful in speech and manners, and adroit in diplomacy; as a Renaissance man he must, moreover, be well read, something of a poet, a good dancer, and enough of a musician to read and carry his part in a song. Even more popular than *The Courtier* was George Pettie and Bartholomew Young's *Civil Conversation* (1581–86), a translation of a treatise by another Italian, Stefano Guazzo (1530–93), whose book, a product of the Counter Reformation, was addressed to the plain man rather than the courtier. Other famous treatises were Sir Thomas Elyot's *The Book of the Governor*, a political manual, and two by Roger Ascham: *The Schoolmaster*, in which he sets forth his views on education, and *Toxophilus*, still a standard work on archery.

A very popular kind of sixteenth-century writing was the pamphlet. The day of the newspaper was yet to come; but with the spread of literacy, pamphlets furnished a medium for disseminating news and for debating public questions, religious, political, and social. They cost little and sold well. In this form

appeared interesting descriptions of London life, especially on its seamier side. The follies of the day, the devious ways of the underworld, calamities such as visitations of the plague—these were the main subjects. Robert Greene and Thomas Dekker, to whom we shall return later on, were the most gifted authors of this type of pamphlet. Controversial pamphlets were also numerous. Rarely do they rise to literary importance, but there are a few exceptions. Among the most celebrated pamphlet wars was the Marprelate controversy of 1587–89. Under the pseudonym of Martin Marprelate, a furious attack was launched by the Puritans against the episcopacy; and the harassed bishops hired professional writers, among them Tom Nashe, to take up the cudgels.

One remarkable book on controversial questions rises serenely above the level of the squabbling pamphleteers, Richard Hooker's *The Laws of Ecclesiastical Polity*, a monument of eloquent yet unaffected English prose. Hooker (1554?–1600), whose surviving sermons are also notable for their style, wished to replace the vituperation of the controversialists by coolness and reason. His treatise is a temperately argued defense of the Church of England.

Of literary criticism Elizabethan England produced little of importance. The best is Sidney's ringing *Defense of Poesy*, part of which is reprinted below.

POETRY

THE TUDOR poetry which still gives pleasure begins under Henry VIII with the courtier poets Wyatt and Surrey, both of whom helped transmit the Renaissance to England. Wyatt introduced the sonnet and the influence of Petrarch. Surrey brought in blank verse, the unrimed iambic pentameter line. A great deal of the best poetry in English was destined to be composed in these two forms. Then, as far as merit goes, there is a gap till well into the reign of Elizabeth, though *A Mirror for Magistrates* (1559), a collection of moralizing narratives from history and legend versified by various writers, went through a series of progressively enlarged editions.

Once more it was the courtier poet who led off. His verses were handed round the court circle. He sought the praise of that circle and its sovereign; for popular acclaim he felt, or at least affected, complete disdain. Gentlemen of taste kept commonplace-books into which they copied things they liked. In these a good deal of the court poetry was preserved, but much was lost.

In addition to the epochmaking *Songs and Sonnets* published by the printer Richard Tottel in 1557 and usually referred to as *Tottel's Miscellany,* a series of similar anthologies made some of the new poetry available to the public. These volumes came out with fancy titles, such as *The Paradise of Dainty Devices* and *The Gorgeous Gallery of Gallant Inventions.* But for most of the great works we have to wait till toward the end of the century, when a brilliant group of professional men of letters began offering their books directly to the public. The subsequent course of Elizabethan verse is traced in the introductions to the various poets represented in this section.

A special word should, however, be said about the sonnet and its immense vogue for about eight years after the posthumous publication of Sir Philip Sidney's *Astrophel and Stella* in 1591. This cycle was followed by twenty-four others brought out before 1599. The vogue was brief, but it inspired some of the most moving poems in our language. In all about two thousand sonnets found their way into print. During the twenty years from 1599 to 1619, when Michael Drayton's *Idea* received its final revision, only five new cycles appeared; but one of them was Shakespeare's. The others were by friends of Drayton, and more or less under his influence. The peculiar form of the sonnet is described below (p. 247), in the introduction to Wyatt and Surrey.

THE DRAMA

DRAWN as it was to the world of men and nature, the Renaissance, for all its deep idealistic and intellectual currents, took also an intensely sensuous direction. Contact with that world through the wide-opened avenues of the five senses, and freedom from the moral considerations emphasized by medieval thought, seemed to some the essence of the new order and led to a gross materialism and to sensualities gross or subtly refined. In England practically everyone except the Puritan loved show. It was an age of ostentation. The gentleman's dress, as well as the lady's, was extravagant beyond anything we see today—in cut, in color, in costliness. No wonder the sixteenth and early seventeenth centuries produced England's greatest drama.

The early morality plays (p. 165, above) were severely religious. In the Renaissance their scope was expanded to embrace many kinds of subject matter. Under Henry VIII there was a fairly close connection between humanism and drama; the reformers sometimes used interludes, as the later moralities were called, for propaganda. It chanced, however, that the best of the interlude writers was a Catholic, John Heywood (1497–c.1580), a connection by marriage of Henry's martyred chancellor, Sir Thomas

More. Heywood, a disciple of Chaucer, is full of rich and racy humor. Though his one-act farces are little more than short dialogues, scarcely dramatic in form, they are excellent comic literature. Heywood was to die in an exile imposed by his Catholic convictions; yet for much of his material he went in good humanistic style to ecclesiastical abuses—the rascally pardoner, the lying pilgrim, the mercenary friar, the greedy priest. What his playlets lack is development of plot, and form in general. Eventually English drama was supplied with these essentials from the classical Latin dramatists. They were studied in the schools, and sometimes acted there. Then Englishmen began writing imitative plays in Latin, and at last adaptations and imitations in English. Plautus and Terence were the models in comedy, Seneca in tragedy.

By 1590 John Lyly had composed several polished and sophisticated prose comedies, Thomas Kyd with his well-plotted *The Spanish Tragedy* (c.1586) had formed the mold which was long to serve the genre of revenge tragedy, and Marlowe and probably Shakespeare had begun providing the London stage with poetic dramas in which a literary excellence superior to Kyd's was united with a robust appeal lacking in Lyly's work. Marlowe's *Doctor Faustus* is reprinted below. At the universities an academic drama, tied too closely to the ancient models, persisted throughout the period; but when Kyd, Shakespeare, and Marlowe threw in their lot with the public theater (the first one was built in 1576) they laid the foundations of a great popular art, out of which came the finest contributions England has made to the world's literature.

Their lead was followed by the poets George Peele and Robert Greene. All the important members of this pioneer group had died or left the stage by 1594, except Shakespeare, whose pre-eminence was not seriously challenged for several years. Toward the end of the nineties new men began coming on the stage: Thomas Dekker (represented below by *The Shoemakers' Holiday*), George Chapman (translator of Homer and author of many tragedies and comedies, among the former his powerful *Bussy d'Ambois*), John Marston (who first attracted attention during a brief vogue of satirical poetry at the turn of the century, and then had a short but brilliant career in the theater—his best play is *The Malcontent*), Thomas Heywood (author of the domestic tragedy *A Woman Killed with Kindness*), John Webster (whose work is illustrated in our seventeenth-century section by *The Duchess of Malfi*), and Ben Jonson, one of the major writers of English comedy.

On the whole, the plays of the years from 1586 to 1615, loosely styled the Elizabethan drama, remain the finest body of dramatic art the world has seen, with the possible exceptions of the ancient Greek tragedies and of Moli`re's comedies.

THE ELIZABETHAN STAGE

The principal feature of the stage which produced the plays of Marlowe, Shakespeare, and Jonson was a large platform, sometimes about forty feet wide and more than half as deep. This platform projected into the central "yard" of the theater. Around the unroofed yard, where the "groundlings" stood, ran a circular or polygonal tier of galleries, usually three. For an additional fee you could sit or stand in a gallery, among the more genteel spectators, with a roof over your head. If you were eager to display your fine clothes, you could even hire a stool and sit on the stage, puffing away at the latest fashionable vice, your pipe of Virginia tobacco.

Performances in a "public" theater (it had room for about a thousand persons) were in the afternoon, by the plain light of day. There were also a few "private" theaters, no less open to the public, where prices were higher. These houses were smaller and wholly roofed; artificial light was required there. Shakespeare's company eventually had two playhouses: from spring to fall they used the Globe, a fine public theater in a suburb on the south bank of the Thames; in the winter they played at the Blackfriars, a private theater inside the city.

The section of the public theater behind the stage was known as the tiring house; its inner façade served as a permanent setting for the stage. It contained lounging, dressing, and storage rooms and the company's library of playscripts. Part of its lower floor was taken up by an inner stage (the "study"), separated from the outer platform by sliding curtains. Rushes strewed the floor of this rear stage, as in Elizabethan houses. There was no scenery. Properties were, however, elaborate; and costumes, though usually Elizabethan whatever the time and scene of the play, were gorgeous.

Most of the acting was close to the audience, well down on the outer platform; but courtroom, bedroom, and other scenes requiring substantial properties could be played partly on the inner stage. Having been placed there while the preceding scene was being acted on the platform, they could be "discovered," as on our own stage, by pulling aside the curtains. Once an interior scene was under way, the platform and study were usually assumed to be one room. If, however, the dramatist wished to show an interior and exterior simultaneously, that too was possible. Or, with the study curtains closed, the platform might itself be an interior; in that case the curtains could be the tapestry or painted cloth with which contemporary rooms were hung. They gave a fine opportunity to a character without whom many a dramatic plot would falter, the eavesdropper. In exterior scenes the curtains were ignored.

Above the study, on the second of the galleries, was another curtained stage, handy for any scene which needed an upper level. Serenaded ladies or besieged citizens on their battlements could appear on this balcony stage, though for the former it seems likely that windows were available in the tiring house façade, above the doors which opened directly from the tiring house onto the platform. That, by the way, was the normal mode of entrance; as a regular thing the actor walked directly onto the platform by one of the downstage doors, though entrance to the platform through the inner stage was also possible.

The platform was partly sheltered from the weather, exactly how is uncertain. Apparently the top of the tiring house overhung the platform to some extent. We know that two stout posts stood on the platform, or ran up through it; but whether they helped support this overhang is unknown. We hear of a "shadow" or "cover"; but the few surviving pictures fail to solve its relation to the "heavens," as the upper region was called. There, in a "hut" or garret, were housed the devices for some of the stage's elaborate mechanical effects. In many a play on mythological themes, divinities and heroes were lowered to the platform or hoisted aloft; for example: "Jupiter first ascends on the eagle, and after him Ganymede," and "From the heavens descends a hand in a cloud, that, from the place where Hercules was burnt, brings up a star and fixeth it in the firmament." And there were several trapdoors, some with elevators on which the ghosts rose majestically from lower regions. Music, too, was plentiful in the Elizabethan theater. Many of the plays are studded with exquisite songs; and there was a room, somewhere aloft, for a little band of players on the lute, viol, recorder, and oboe. Ravishing were their strains, for this was the great age of English music, when it was the finest in all Europe.

Yet, however ingenious the machinery, realistic the properties, and charming the music, the absence of scenery and historical costumes left a great deal to the imagination of Elizabethan audiences. The spoken word ruled this theater. Today the electrician turns on the dawn. In *Hamlet*, Shakespeare and the actors bring it on:

But look, the morn, in russet mantle clad,
Walks o'er the dew of yon high eastward hill.

By these well-arranged words a scenic mirage is artfully created, and it adds to our pleasure to hear them spoken well. Read the opening scene of *The Tempest* to see how effectively a medley of shouted orders, fragments of excited conversation, and at last the wild cry, "We split!" stage a whole shipwreck *in words*. The great Elizabethan dramatists, Shakespeare above all, became masters of suggestion; the whole technique of their theater was impressionistic. Thus, since there was no way of darkening the stage, characters in a night scene came on carrying torches or candles; and without conscious effort the audience accepted these as indications of surrounding darkness. But words were even more important, and it is Shakespeare who lowers the lights in *Macbeth* with

Light thickens, and the crow
Makes wing to th' rooky wood.
Good things of day begin to droop and drowse,
Whiles night's black agents to their preys do rouse.

Sometimes, however, a scene is entirely unlocated in time or space. Two characters must have a talk, if the plot is to move forward. So they meet; and often we are not told whether they are in a private room, a garden, or a public square. Everything the dramatist wants us to know he weaves into his dialogue; if it is not there, it is of no importance—indeed it does not exist. Many of the scene headings and stage directions in modern editions of these playwrights have no warrant in the text.

That in an Elizabethan stage direction a character points to a tree or even climbs a tree does not mean they brought a tree on stage. The actor waves vaguely in this direction or that, or (like Orlando in *As You Like It*) hangs his verses on one of the two great posts, or (if he must spy out the country round) shinnies a few feet up the post, or (if he must talk at length from a treetop) goes up onto the gallery stage. It was not a realistic theater, but that does not mean it was an unconvincing one. The convincing, that is, the enforcing of the audience's willing suspension of disbelief, as Coleridge calls it, was achieved mainly by words. Asked once how he wrote his poetry, Carl Sandburg replied, "I just take words and lay down a barrage, hoping to create a mirage." The most realistic scenery cannot equal this method of making an audience forget it is in the theater. For that, two things are necessary: great dramatic writing and great acting. And that is what the Elizabethan theater, which is to say the corps of dramatists and actors who staffed it, supplied in abundance.

The leading actors, like Richard Burbage of Shakespeare's company and Edward Alleyn of the Lord Admiral's (which produced most of Marlowe's plays), were accomplished men, courted by the nobility and gentry as well as admired by the theater-going public. The principal parts were played by the "members" (shareholders) of the company. A secondary class of actors consisted of "hirelings" or salaried actors. The third class, the apprentices, was of great importance, for to the best of the boys were entrusted the roles of the youthful heroines. Older heroines, like a Lady Macbeth, who required stronger playing than an Ophelia or a Rosalind, were probably acted by youths in their late teens or early twenties. Older men, as a rule, would take eccentric and "character" roles, such as Juliet's Nurse. Occasionally the regular troupes had stiff competition from companies composed entirely of boys; how seriously the art of even a thirteen-year-older could be taken is evident from Jonson's epitaph on a talented boy whose specialty was old men; this charming poem is reprinted below, in our seventeenth-century section.

GENERAL REFERENCES

The foregoing introduction is longer than others in this book because with the Renaissance we come to the modern world. For a well-classified bibliography see V. de Sola Pinto's *The English Renaissance* (1938); this is volume II of *Introductions to English Literature* (edited by B. Dobrée).

A useful treatise on the general intellectual background is H. Craig's *The Enchanted Glass: the Elizabethan Mind in Literature* (1936). *Shakespeare's England: an Account of the Life & Manners of His Age* (2 vols., 1916) is a valuable series of monographs on special topics.

A good introduction to the first part of the period is J. M. Berdan's *Early Tudor Poetry, 1485–1547* (1920). The best general survey is still F. E. Schelling's *English Literature in the Lifetime of Shakespeare* (revised ed., 1927).

On the English humanists an interesting book is F. Seebohm's *The Oxford Reformers of 1489* (1867; also available in Everyman's Library). For More, see R. W. Chambers's *Sir Thomas More* (1935).

Tottel's Miscellany and the other sixteenth-century anthologies have been edited by H. E. Rollins. The importance of Holinshed is brought out in A. and J. Nicoll's *Holinshed's Chronicle as Used in Shakespeare's Historical Plays* (Everyman's Library). Stowe's *Survey of London* was edited by C. L. Kingsford (1908). Richard Hakluyt's voyage literature is available in Everyman's Library (9 vols.).

For an account of Elizabethan prose fiction, see A. E. Baker's *The History of the English Novel*, vol. II (1929). G. G. Smith's *Elizabethan Critical Essays* (2 vols., 1904),

J. E. Spingarn's *A History of Literary Criticism in the Renaissance* (2nd ed., 1908), H. O. Taylor's *Thought and Expression in the Sixteenth Century* (2 vols., 1920), and G. M. Trevelyan's *English Social History* (1942), chaps. 3–7, are all valuable.

On practically every aspect of the Elizabethan drama in general the standard reference work is E. K. Chambers's *The Elizabethan Stage* (4 vols., 1923). An excellent introduction is T. Brooke's *The Tudor Drama*. H. Spencer's *Elizabethan Plays* gives twenty-eight texts. Inexpensive reprints, several plays to a volume, are available in Everyman's Library, the Mermaid series, and the Belles Lettres series. For a brief summary of present knowledge of the Elizabethan stage, see H. Spencer's *The Art and Life of William Shakespeare* (1940), chap. 2.

Numerous other special references will be found in the introductions to the various authors treated below.

Except as otherwise noted, all the selections in this and the remaining sections of this volume have been modernized in spelling and punctuation. Occasionally, however, an old spelling has been retained when it appears to indicate an old pronunciation.

The English Bible

IF, AS seems certain, the King James Version of the Bible, published in 1611, has had a greater effect on English and American literature than any other book, William Tyndale (see pp. 224 f.) must be recognized as the most influential writer of English prose. The committee of scholars whose labors ended in 1611 were wise enough to see that on the whole his work was beyond their power to improve. About nine-tenths of the King James Version of the New Testament and a great deal of the Old are essentially Tyndale's. Accordingly, despite its publication in the reign of James I, the King James Version is really a sixteenth-century book.

Tyndale had translated the New Testament and parts of the Old Testament. Miles Coverdale (d.1568) brought out a complete translation in his Great Bible (1535). A composite version—it probably included, along with what Tyndale had printed, the unpublished remainder of his manuscript, and filled in the rest of the Old Testament from Coverdale's translation—appeared on the Continent and became the basic text for a series of revisions down through the King James Version.

With the accuracy of the King James Version as a transla-

tion neither Catholics nor Protestants have been content. The official Catholic text was an English rendering of the standard Latin Bible, the Vulgate. This translation was prepared by exiled English Catholics in France; the New Testament was published at Rheims in 1582 and the Old at Douai in 1609–10. Since then there have been other versions by Catholics, and a new one has just been completed. Many Protestants have come to prefer, not the King James Version, but the "Revised Version" of 1881–85. With further changes, this was brought out again in 1901 as the "American Standard Version." A new revision of the text of 1901, the "Revised Standard Version," is now nearing completion.

Our concern is of course with the Bible as a non-English work which has become a part of English literature, and hence with the King James Version. Of the English texts between Coverdale's and the King James, the most important for literary influence was the Geneva Bible, translated by English Calvinists in Geneva and published in 1560. This popular version was the Bible Shakespeare knew; but it is the King James Version of 1611 that in countless phrases has become a part of living English speech.

THE SECOND BOOK OF SAMUEL

This book—it is part of a history—begins with the anointing of David, warrior and poet, as king of Judah, one of the Israelite "tribes." The following episode is among the best examples of Old Testament narrative, both for the story itself and for the vivid characterization of the three principal actors in it.

CHAPTER II

And it came to pass, after the year was expired, at the time when kings go forth to battle, that David sent Joab,[1] and his servants with him, and all Israel;[2]

and they destroyed the children of Ammon,[3] and besieged Rabbah. But David tarried still at Jerusalem.

2 ¶ And it came to pass in an evening-tide, that David arose from off his bed, and walked upon the roof of the king's house: and from the roof he saw a woman washing herself; and the woman was very beautiful to look upon.

3 And David sent and enquired after the woman. And one said, Is not this Bath-sheba, the daughter of Eliam, the wife of Uriah the Hittite?[4]

---

[1] His general.   [2] The Jews as a whole.

[3] The people of Ammon, northeast of the Dead Sea. Rabbah was its capital. Judah lay between the Dead Sea and the Mediterranean.

[4] An ancient people whose capital was near Ankara, Turkey.

4 And David sent messengers, and took her: and she came in unto him, and he lay with her; for she was purified from her uncleanness: and she returned unto her house.

5 And the woman conceived, and sent and told David, and said, I am with child.

6 And David sent to Joab, saying, Send me Uriah the Hittite. And Joab sent Uriah to David.

7 And when Uriah was come unto him, David demanded of him how Joab did, and how the people did, and how the war prospered.

8 And David said to Uriah, Go down to thy house, and wash thy feet. And Uriah departed out of the king's house, and there followed him a mess of meat from the king.

9 But Uriah slept at the door of the king's house with all the servants of his lord, and went not down to his house.

10 And when they had told David, saying, Uriah went not down unto his house, David said unto Uriah, Camest thou not from thy journey? why then didst thou not go down unto thine house?

11 And Uriah said unto David, The ark,[5] and Israel, and Judah,[6] abide in tents; and my lord Joab, and the servants of my lord, are encamped in the open fields; shall I then go into mine house, to eat and to drink, and to lie with my wife? As thou livest, and as thy soul liveth, I will not do this thing.

12 And David said to Uriah, Tarry here to-day also, and to-morrow I will let thee depart. So Uriah abode in Jerusalem that day and the morrow.

13 And when David had called him, he did eat and drink before him; and he made him drunk: and at even he went out to lie on his bed with the servants of his lord, but went not down to his house.

14 ¶ And it came to pass in the morning, that David wrote a letter to Joab, and sent it by the hand of Uriah.

15 And he wrote in the letter, saying, Set ye Uriah in the fore front of the hottest battle, and retire ye from him, that he may be smitten, and die.

16 And it came to pass, when Joab observed the city, that he assigned Uriah unto a place where he knew that valiant men were.

17 And the men of the city went out and fought with Joab: and there fell some of the people of the servants of David; and Uriah the Hittite died also.

18 ¶ Then Joab sent and told David all the things concerning the war;

19 And charged the messenger, saying, When thou hast made an end of telling the matters of the war unto the king,

20 And if so be that the king's wrath arise, and he say unto thee, Wherefore approached ye so nigh unto the city when ye did fight? knew ye not that they would shoot from the wall?

21 Who smote Abimelech the son of Jerubbesheth? did not a woman cast a piece of a millstone upon him from the wall, that he died in Thebez?[7] why went ye nigh the wall? then say thou, Thy servant Uriah the Hittite is dead also.

22 ¶ So the messenger went, and came and showed David all that Joab had sent him for.

23 And the messenger said unto David, Surely the men prevailed against us, and came out unto us into the field, and we were upon them even unto the entering of the gate.

24 And the shooters shot from off the wall upon thy servants; and some of the king's servants be dead, and thy servant Uriah the Hittite is dead also.

25 Then David said unto the messenger, Thus shalt thou say unto Joab, Let not this thing displease thee, for the sword devoureth one as well as another: make thy battle more strong against the city, and overthrow it: and encourage thou him.

26 ¶ And when the wife of Uriah heard that Uriah her husband was dead, she mourned for her husband.

27 And when the mourning was past, David sent and fetched her to his house, and she became his wife, and bare him a son. But the thing that David had done displeased the Lord.

CHAPTER 12

And the Lord sent Nathan[8] unto David. And he came unto him, and said unto him, There were two men in one city; the one rich, and the other poor.

2 The rich man had exceeding many flocks and herds:

3 But the poor man had nothing, save one little ewe lamb, which he had bought and nourished up: and it grew up together with him, and with his children; it did eat of his own meat, and drank of his own cup, and lay in his bosom, and was unto him as a daughter.

4 And there came a traveller unto the rich man, and he spared to take of his own flock and of his own herd, to dress for the wayfaring man that was come unto him; but took the poor man's lamb, and dressed it for the man that was come to him.

---

[5] A sacred chest in which some of the holiest relics were kept.
[6] The tribe of Judah.

[7] A hill town in north central Palestine. It had figured in a previous campaign (see Judges 9:50).
[8] A prophet. His "Thou art the man!" is dramatically the high point of the narrative.

5 And David's anger was greatly kindled against the man; and he said to Nathan, As the Lord liveth, the man that hath done this thing shall surely die:

6 And he shall restore the lamb fourfold, because he did this thing, and because he had no pity.

7 ¶ And Nathan said to David, Thou art the man. Thus saith the Lord God of Israel, I anointed thee king over Israel, and I delivered thee out of the hand of Saul;[9]

8 And I gave thee thy master's house, and thy master's wives into thy bosom, and gave thee the house of Israel and of Judah: and if that had been too little, I would moreover have given unto thee such and such things.

9 Wherefore hast thou despised the commandment of the Lord, to do evil in his sight? thou hast killed Uriah the Hittite with the sword, and hast taken his wife to be thy wife, and hast slain him with the sword of the children of Ammon.

10 Now therefore the sword shall never depart from thine house; because thou hast despised me, and hast taken the wife of Uriah the Hittite to be thy wife.

11 Thus saith the Lord, Behold, I will raise up evil against thee out of thine own house, and I will take thy wives before thine eyes, and give them unto thy neighbour, and he shall lie with thy wives in the sight of this sun.

12 For thou didst it secretly; but I will do this thing before all Israel, and before the sun.

13 And David said unto Nathan, I have sinned against the Lord. And Nathan said unto David, The Lord also hath put away thy sin; thou shalt not die.

14 Howbeit, because by this deed thou hast given great occasion to the enemies of the Lord to blaspheme, the child also that is born unto thee shall surely die.

15 ¶ And Nathan departed unto his house. And the Lord struck the child that Uriah's wife bare unto David, and it was very sick.

16 David therefore besought God for the child; and David fasted, and went in, and lay all night upon the earth.

17 And the elders of his house arose, and went to him, to raise him up from the earth: but he would not, neither did he eat bread with them.

18 And it came to pass on the seventh day, that the child died. And the servants of David feared to tell him that the child was dead: for they said, Behold, while the child was yet alive, we spake unto him, and he would not hearken unto our voice: how will he then vex himself, if we tell him that the child is dead?

19 But when David saw that his servants whispered, David perceived that the child was dead: therefore David said unto his servants, Is the child dead? And they said, He is dead.

20 Then David arose from the earth, and washed, and anointed himself, and changed his apparel, and came into the house of the Lord, and worshipped: then he came to his own house; and when he required, they set bread before him, and he did eat.

21 Then said his servants unto him, What thing is this that thou hast done? thou didst fast and weep for the child, while it was alive; but when the child was dead, thou didst rise and eat bread.

22 And he said, While the child was yet alive, I fasted and wept: for I said, Who can tell whether God will be gracious to me, that the child may live?

23 But now he is dead, wherefore should I fast? can I bring him back again? I shall go to him, but he shall not return to me.

24 ¶ And David comforted Bath-sheba his wife, and went in unto her, and lay with her: and she bare a son, and he called his name Solomon: and the Lord loved him.

25 And he sent by the hand of Nathan the prophet; and he called his name Jedidiah, because of the Lord.

26 ¶ And Joab fought against Rabbah of the children of Ammon, and took the royal city.

27 And Joab sent messengers to David, and said, I have fought against Rabbah and have taken the city of waters.

28 Now therefore gather the rest of the people together, and encamp against the city, and take it: lest I take the city, and it be called after my name.

29 And David gathered all the people together, and went to Rabbah, and fought against it, and took it.

30 And he took their king's crown from off his head, the weight whereof was a talent of gold[10] with the precious stones: and it was set on David's head. And he brought forth the spoil of the city in great abundance.

31 And he brought forth the people that were therein, and put them under saws, and under harrows of iron, and under axes of iron, and made them pass through the brickkiln: and thus did he unto all the cities of the children of Ammon. So David and all the people returned unto Jerusalem.

---

[9] His predecessor on the throne, who had tried to kill him.

[10] About equal in weight to bullion worth $3000.

The story of Job is cast in dramatic form. Both the moral significance and the dramatic intensity are expressed less by the chain of events than by the impact of character on character, and above all by the speeches themselves. The bulk of the book is dialogue, sometimes passionately lyrical. This great poem is one of the most moving portions of the Bible. Unshakable trust in God is displayed by many of the Old Testament personages (see, for example, the story of Abraham, Genesis 22:1–19), but none is treated with greater subtlety and verbal beauty than Job. As the notes below occasionally indicate, the Hebrew text bristles with problems; some of it is unintelligible, though recent archeological discoveries are clearing up a number of difficulties.

CHAPTER I

There was a man in the land of Uz,[11] whose name was Job: and that man was perfect and upright, and one that feared God, and eschewed evil.

2 And there were born unto him seven sons and three daughters.

3 His substance also was seven thousand sheep, and three thousand camels, and five hundred yoke of oxen, and five hundred she asses, and a very great household; so that this man was the greatest of all the men of the east.

4 And his sons went and feasted in their houses, every one his day; and sent and called for their three sisters to eat and to drink with them.

5 And it was so, when the days of their feasting were gone about, that Job sent and sanctified them, and rose up early in the morning, and offered burnt offerings according to the number of them all: for Job said, It may be that my sons have sinned, and cursed God in their hearts. Thus did Job continually.

6 ¶ Now there was a day when the sons of God[12] came to present themselves before the Lord, and Satan came also among them.

7 And the Lord said unto Satan, Whence comest thou? Then Satan answered the Lord, and said, From going to and fro in the earth, and from walking up and down in it.

8 And the Lord said unto Satan, Hast thou considered my servant Job, that there is none like him in the earth, a perfect and an upright man, one that feareth God, and escheweth evil?

9 Then Satan answered the Lord, and said, Doth Job fear God for nought?

10 Hast not thou made an hedge about him, and about his house, and about all that he hath on every side? Thou hast blessed the work of his hands, and his substance is increased in the land:

11 But put forth thine hand now, and touch all that he hath, and he will curse thee to thy face.

12 And the Lord said unto Satan, Behold, all that he hath is in thy power; only upon himself put not forth thine hand. So Satan went forth from the presence of the Lord.

13 ¶ And there was a day when his sons and his daughters were eating and drinking wine in their eldest brother's house:

14 And there came a messenger unto Job, and said, The oxen were plowing, and the asses feeding beside them;

15 And the Sabeans[13] fell upon them, and took them away; yea, they have slain the servants with the edge of the sword; and I only am escaped alone to tell thee.

16 While he was yet speaking, there came also another, and said, The fire of God is fallen from heaven, and hath burnt up the sheep, and the servants, and consumed them; and I only am escaped alone to tell thee.

17 While he was yet speaking, there came also another, and said, The Chaldeans[14] made out three bands, and fell upon the camels, and have carried them away, yea, and slain the servants with the edge of the sword; and I only am escaped alone to tell thee.

18 While he was yet speaking, there came also another, and said, Thy sons and thy daughters were eating and drinking wine in their eldest brother's house:

19 And, behold, there came a great wind from the wilderness, and smote the four corners of the house, and it fell upon the young men, and they are dead; and I only am escaped alone to tell thee.

20 Then Job arose, and rent his mantle, and shaved his head, and fell down upon the ground, and worshipped,

21 And said, Naked came I out of my mother's womb, and naked shall I return thither; the Lord gave, and the Lord hath taken away; blessed be the name of the Lord.

22 In all this Job sinned not, nor charged God foolishly.

---

[11] Somewhere in northern Arabia. [12] Angels.

[13] From Sheba, an Arab tribe. [14] From southern Iraq.

Again there was a day when the sons of God came to present themselves before the Lord, and Satan came also among them, to present himself before the Lord.

2 And the Lord said unto Satan, From whence comest thou? And Satan answered the Lord, and said, From going to and fro in the earth, and from walking up and down in it.

3 And the Lord said unto Satan, Hast thou considered my servant Job, that there is none like him in the earth, a perfect and an upright man, one that feareth God, and escheweth evil? and still he holdeth fast his integrity, although thou movedst me against him, to destroy him without cause.

4 And Satan answered the Lord, and said, Skin for skin, yea, all that a man hath will he give for his life:

5 But put forth thine hand now, and touch his bone and his flesh, and he will curse thee to thy face.

6 And the Lord said unto Satan, Behold, he is in thine hand; but save his life.

7 ¶ So went Satan forth from the presence of the Lord, and smote Job with sore boils from the sole of his foot unto his crown.

8 And he took him a potsherd to scrape himself withal;[15] and he sat down among the ashes.

9 ¶ Then said his wife unto him, Dost thou still retain thine integrity? curse God, and die.

10 But he said unto her, Thou speakest as one of the foolish women speaketh. What! shall we receive good at the hand of God, and shall we not receive evil? In all this did not Job sin with his lips.

11 ¶ Now when Job's three friends heard of all this evil that was come upon him, they came every one from his own place; Eliphaz the Temanite,[16] and Bildad the Shuhite,[17] and Zophar the Naamathite:[18] for they had made an appointment together to come to mourn with him and to comfort him.

12 And when they lifted up their eyes afar off, and knew him not, they lifted up their voice, and wept; and they rent every one his mantle, and sprinkled dust upon their heads toward heaven.

13 So they sat down with him upon the ground seven days and seven nights, and none spake a word unto him: for they saw that his grief was very great.

---

15 With.   16 From northern Arabia.
17 From Iraq, along the Euphrates.   18 Location unknown.

CHAPTER 3

After this opened Job his mouth, and cursed his day.

2 And Job spake, and said,

3 Let the day perish wherein I was born, and the night in which it was said, There is a man-child conceived.

4 Let that day be darkness; let not God regard it from above, neither let the light shine upon it.

5 Let darkness and the shadow of death stain it; let a cloud dwell upon it; let the blackness of the day terrify it.

6 As for that night, let darkness seize upon it; let it not be joined unto the days of the year; let it not come into the number of the months.

7 Lo, let that night be solitary; let no joyful voice come therein.

8 Let them curse it that curse the day, who are ready to raise up their mourning.

9 Let the stars of the twilight thereof be dark; let it look for light, but have none; neither let it see the dawning of the day:

10 Because it shut not up the doors of my mother's womb, nor hid sorrow from mine eyes.

11 Why died I not from the womb? why did I not give up the ghost when I came out of the belly?

12 Why did the knees prevent me? or why the breasts that I should suck?

13 For now should I have lain still and been quiet, I should have slept: then had I been at rest

14 With kings and counsellors of the earth, which built desolate places for themselves;

15 Or with princes that had gold, who filled their houses with silver:

16 Or as an hidden untimely birth I had not been; as infants which never saw light.

17 There the wicked cease from troubling; and there the weary be at rest.

18 There the prisoners rest together; they hear not the voice of the oppressor.

19 The small and great are there; and the servant is free from his master.

20 Wherefore is light given to him that is in misery, and life unto the bitter in soul;

21 Which long for death, but it cometh not; and dig for it more than for hid treasures;

22 Which rejoice exceedingly, and are glad, when they can find the grave?

23 Why is light given to a man whose way is hid, and whom God hath hedged in?

24 For my sighing cometh before I eat, and my roarings are poured out like the waters.

25 For the thing which I greatly feared is come upon me, and that which I was afraid of is come unto me.

26 I was not in safety, neither had I rest, neither was I quiet; yet trouble came.

[*The prologue, as it might be termed, having ended with chapter 2, the dialogue between Job and his friends begins with the lyric outburst of chapter 3. The friends, in chapters 4–11, open the inquiry into the book's main subject, the reason why the wicked flourish and why a good and omnipotent God permits human suffering, a mystery called by philosophers the Problem of Evil. The theory of the friends, that suffering is a punishment for sin, is rejected by Job as inadequate.*]

CHAPTER 12

And Job answered and said,

2 No doubt but ye are the people, and wisdom shall die with you.

3 But I have understanding as well as you; I am not inferior to you: yea, who knoweth not such things as these?

4 I am as one mocked of his neighbour, who calleth upon God, and he answereth him: the just upright man is laughed to scorn.

5 He that is ready to slip with his feet is as a lamp despised in the thought of him that is at ease.

6 The tabernacles[19] of robbers prosper, and they that provoke God are secure; into whose hand God bringeth abundantly.

7 But ask now the beasts, and they shall teach thee; and the fowls of the air, and they shall tell thee:

8 Or speak to the earth, and it shall teach thee: and the fishes of the sea shall declare unto thee.

9 Who knoweth not in all these that the hand of the Lord hath wrought this?

10 In whose hand is the soul of every living thing, and the breath of all mankind.

11 Doth not the ear try words? and the mouth taste his meat?

12 With the ancient is wisdom; and in length of days understanding.

13 With him is wisdom and strength, he hath counsel and understanding.

14 Behold, he breaketh down, and it cannot be built again: he shutteth up a man, and there can be no opening.

15 Behold, he withholdeth the waters, and they dry up: also he sendeth them out, and they overturn the earth.

16 With him is strength and wisdom: the deceived and the deceiver are his.

17 He leadeth counsellors away spoiled, and maketh the judges fools.

18 He looseth the bond of kings, and girdeth their loins with a girdle.

19 He leadeth princes away spoiled, and overthroweth the mighty.

20 He removeth away the speech of the trusty, and taketh away the understanding of the aged.

21 He poureth contempt upon princes, and weakeneth the strength of the mighty.

22 He discovereth[20] deep things out of darkness, and bringeth out to light the shadow of death.

23 He increaseth the nations, and destroyeth them: he enlargeth the nations, and straiteneth[21] them again.

24 He taketh away the heart of the chief of the people of the earth, and causeth them to wander in a wilderness where there is no way.

25 They grope in the dark without light, and he maketh them to stagger like a drunken man.

CHAPTER 13

Lo, mine eye hath seen all this, mine ear hath heard and understood it.

2 What ye know, the same do I know also: I am not inferior unto you.

3 Surely I would speak to the Almighty, and I desire to reason with God.

4 But ye are forgers of lies, ye are all physicians of no value.

5 O that ye would altogether hold your peace! and it should be your wisdom.

6 Hear now my reasoning, and hearken to the pleadings of my lips.

7 Will ye speak wickedly for God? and talk deceitfully for him?

8 Will ye accept[22] his person? will ye contend for God?

9 Is it good that he should search you out? or as one man mocketh another, do ye so mock him?

10 He will surely reprove you, if ye do secretly accept persons.

11 Shall not his excellency make you afraid? and his dread fall upon you?

12 Your remembrances are like unto ashes, your bodies to bodies of clay.

13 Hold your peace, let me alone, that I may speak, and let come on me what will.

---

[19] Tents.

[20] Reveals. [21] Reduces. [22] Show partiality to.

14 Wherefore do I take my flesh in my teeth, and put my life in mine hand?

15 Though he slay me, yet will I trust in him: but I will maintain mine own ways before him.

16 He also shall be my salvation: for an hypocrite shall not come before him.

17 Hear diligently my speech, and my declaration with your ears.

18 Behold now, I have ordered my cause; I know that I shall be justified.

19 Who is he that will plead with me? for now, if I hold my tongue, I shall give up the ghost.

20 Only do not two things unto me; then will I not hide myself from thee.

21 Withdraw thine hand far from me; and let not thy dread make me afraid:

22 Then call thou, and I will answer; or let me speak, and answer thou me.

23 How many are mine iniquities and sins? make me to know my transgression and my sin.

24 Wherefore hidest thou thy face, and holdest me for thine enemy?

25 Wilt thou break a leaf driven to and fro? and wilt thou pursue the dry stubble?

26 For thou writest bitter things against me, and makest me to possess the iniquities of my youth.

27 Thou puttest my feet also in the stocks, and lookest narrowly unto all my paths; thou settest a print upon the heels of my feet.

28 And he, as a rotten thing, consumeth, as a garment that is moth-eaten.

CHAPTER 14

Man that is born of a woman is of few days, and full of trouble.

2 He cometh forth like a flower, and is cut down: he fleeth also as a shadow, and continueth not.

3 And dost thou open thine eyes upon such an one, and bringest me into judgment with thee?

4 Who can bring a clean thing out of an unclean? not one.

5 Seeing his days are determined, the number of his months are with thee, thou hast appointed his bounds that he cannot pass;

6 Turn from him, that he may rest, till he shall accomplish, as an hireling, his day.

7 For there is hope of a tree, if it be cut down, that it will sprout again, and that the tender branch thereof will not cease.

8 Though the root thereof wax old in the earth, and the stock thereof die in the ground;

9 Yet through the scent of water it will bud, and bring forth boughs like a plant.

10 But man dieth, and wasteth away; yea, man giveth up the ghost, and where is he?

11 As the waters fail from the sea, and the flood decayeth and drieth up;

12 So man lieth down, and riseth not: till the heavens be no more, they shall not awake, nor be raised out of their sleep.

13 O that thou wouldest hide me in the grave, that thou wouldest keep me secret, until thy wrath be past, that thou wouldest appoint me a set time, and remember me!

14 If a man die, shall he live again? All the days of my appointed time will I wait, till my change come.

15 Thou shalt call, and I will answer thee: thou wilt have a desire to the work of thine hands.

16 For now thou numberest my steps: dost thou not watch over my sin?

17 My transgression is sealed up in a bag, and thou sewest up mine iniquity.

18 And surely the mountain falling cometh to nought, and the rock is removed out of his place.

19 The waters wear the stones: thou washest away the things which grow out of the dust of the earth; and thou destroyest the hope of man.

20 Thou prevailest for ever against him, and he passeth: thou changest his countenance, and sendest him away.

21 His sons come to honour, and he knoweth it not; and they are brought low, but he perceiveth it not of them.

22 But his flesh upon him shall have pain, and his soul within him shall mourn.

[*The debate goes on throughout chapters 15–37. It is joined by Elihu, a younger man, who has heard with impatience both Job's self-justification and the conventional arguments of the friends. Elihu offers another solution of the problem: through suffering God calls men to repentance. But Job and the friends, too, disdain to reply. As a sudden storm comes up, Elihu launches into an apostrophe to the majesty and power of God. This theme is continued by the voice of the Lord himself; and the book closes with an endorsement of Job, who, though a questioner, has held fast in his faith.*]

CHAPTER 38

Then the Lord answered Job out of the whirlwind, and said,

2 Who is this that darkeneth counsel by words without knowledge?

3 Gird up now thy loins like a man; for I will demand[23] of thee, and answer thou me.

---

[23] Ask.

4 Where wast thou when I laid the foundations of the earth? declare, if thou hast understanding.

5 Who hath laid the measures thereof, if thou knowest? or who hath stretched the line upon it?

6 Whereupon are the foundations thereof fastened? or who laid the corner stone thereof;

7 When the morning stars sang together, and all the sons of God shouted for joy?

8 Or who shut up the sea with doors, when it brake forth, as if it had issued out of the womb?

9 When I made the cloud the garment thereof, and thick darkness a swaddlingband[24] for it.

10 And brake up for it my decreed place, and set bars and doors,

11 And said, Hitherto shalt thou come, but no further: and here shall thy proud waves be stayed?

12 Hast thou commanded the morning since thy days; and caused the dayspring[25] to know his[26] place;

13 That it might take hold of the ends of the earth, that the wicked might be shaken out of it?

14 It is turned as clay to the seal; and they stand as a garment.

15 And from the wicked their light is withholden, and the high arm shall be broken.

16 Hast thou entered into the springs of the sea? or hast thou walked in the search of the depth?

17 Have the gates of death been opened unto thee? or hast thou seen the doors of the shadow of death?

18 Hast thou perceived the breadth of the earth? declare if thou knowest it all.

19 Where is the way where light dwelleth? and as for darkness, where is the place thereof,

20 That thou shouldest take it to the bound thereof, and that thou shouldest know the paths to the house thereof?

21 Knowest thou it, because thou wast then born? or because the number of thy days is great?

22 Hast thou entered into the treasures of the snow? or hast thou seen the treasures of the hail,

23 Which I have reserved against the time of trouble, against the day of battle and war?

24 By what way is the light parted, which scattereth the east wind upon the earth?

25 Who hath divided a watercourse for the overflowing of waters, or a way for the lightning of thunder;

26 To cause it to rain on the earth, where no man is; on the wilderness, wherein there is no man;

27 To satisfy the desolate and waste ground; and to cause the bud of the tender herb to spring forth?

28 Hath the rain a father? or who hath begotten the drops of dew?

29 Out of whose womb came the ice? and the hoary frost of heaven, who hath gendered it?

30 The waters are hid as with a stone, and the face of the deep is frozen.

31 Canst thou bind the sweet influences of Pleiades, or loose the bands of Orion?

32 Canst thou bring forth Mazzaroth[27] in his season? or canst thou guide Arcturus with his sons?

33 Knowest thou the ordinances of heaven? canst thou set the dominion thereof in the earth?

34 Canst thou lift up thy voice to the clouds, that abundance of waters may cover thee?

35 Canst thou send lightnings, that they may go, and say unto thee, Here we are?

36 Who hath put wisdom in the inward parts? or who hath given understanding to the heart?

37 Who can number the clouds in wisdom? or who can stay the bottles of heaven,

38 When the dust groweth into hardness, and the clods cleave fast together?

39 Wilt thou hunt the prey for the lion, or fill the appetite of the young lions,

40 When they couch in their dens, and abide in the covert to lie in wait?

41 Who provideth for the raven his food? when his young ones cry unto God, they wander for lack of meat.

CHAPTER 39

Knowest thou the time when the wild goats of the rock bring forth? or canst thou mark when the hinds[28] do calve?

2 Canst thou number the months that they fulfil? or knowest thou the time when they bring forth?

3 They bow themselves, they bring forth their young ones, they cast out their sorrows.

4 Their young ones are in good liking,[29] they grow up with corn; they go forth, and return not unto them.

5 Who hath sent out the wild ass free? or who hath loosed the bands of the wild ass?

6 Whose house I have made the wilderness, and the barren land his dwellings.

7 He scorneth the multitude of the city, neither regardeth he the crying of the driver.

8 The range of the mountains is his pasture, and he searcheth after every green thing.

---

24 Cloth wrapped around a newborn child.　　25 Dawn.
26 Its.

27 The signs of the zodiac.
28 Female deer.　　29 Plump.

9 Will the unicorn be willing to serve thee, or abide by thy crib?

10 Canst thou bind the unicorn with his band in the furrow? or will he harrow the valleys after thee?

11 Wilt thou trust him, because his strength is great? or wilt thou leave thy labour to him?

12 Wilt thou believe him, that he will bring home thy seed, and gather it into thy barn?

13 Gavest thou the goodly wings unto the peacocks? or wings and feathers unto the ostrich?

14 Which leaveth her eggs in the earth, and warmeth them in dust,

15 And forgetteth that the foot may crush them, or that the wild beast may break them.

16 She is hardened against her young ones, as though they were not hers: her labour is in vain without fear;

17 Because God hath deprived her of wisdom, neither hath he imparted to her understanding.

18 What time she lifteth up herself on high, she scorneth the horse and his rider.

19 Hast thou given the horse strength? hast thou clothed his neck with thunder?

20 Canst thou make him afraid as a grasshopper? the glory of his nostrils is terrible.

21 He paweth in the valley, and rejoiceth in his strength: he goeth on to meet the armed men.

22 He mocketh at fear, and is not affrighted; neither turneth he back from the sword.

23 The quiver rattleth against him, the glittering spear and the shield.

24 He swalloweth the ground with fierceness and rage; neither believeth he that it is the sound of the trumpet.

25 He saith among the trumpets, Ha, ha! and he smelleth the battle afar off, the thunder of the captains, and the shouting.

26 Doth the hawk fly by thy wisdom, and stretch her wings toward the south?

27 Doth the eagle mount up at thy command, and make her nest on high?

28 She dwelleth and abideth on the rock, upon the crag of the rock, and the strong place.

29 From thence she seeketh the prey, and her eyes behold afar off.

30 Her young ones also suck up blood: and where the slain are, there is she.

CHAPTER 40

Moreover the Lord answered Job, and said,

2 Shall he that contendeth with the Almighty instruct him? he that reproveth God, let him answer it.

3 ¶ Then Job answered the Lord, and said,

4 Behold, I am vile; what shall I answer thee? I will lay mine hand upon my mouth.

5 Once have I spoken; but I will not answer: yea, twice; but I will proceed no further.

6 ¶ Then answered the Lord unto Job out of the whirlwind, and said,

7 Gird up thy loins now like a man: I will demand of thee, and declare thou unto me.

8 Wilt thou also disannul my judgment? wilt thou condemn me, that thou mayest be righteous?

9 Hast thou an arm like God? or canst thou thunder with a voice like him?

10 Deck thyself now with majesty and excellency, and array thyself with glory and beauty.

11 Cast abroad the rage of thy wrath: and behold every one that is proud, and abase him.

12 Look on every one that is proud, and bring him low; and tread down the wicked in their place.

13 Hide them in the dust together; and bind their faces in secret.

14 Then will I also confess unto thee that thine own right hand can save thee.

15 ¶ Behold now behemoth,[30] which I made with thee; he eateth grass as an ox.

16 Lo now, his strength is in his loins, and his force is in the navel of his belly.

17 He moveth his tail like a cedar: the sinews of his stones[31] are wrapped together.

18 His bones are as strong pieces of brass; his bones are like bars of iron.

19 He is the chief of the ways of God: he that made him can make his sword to approach unto him.

20 Surely the mountains bring him forth food, where all the beasts of the field play.

21 He lieth under the shady trees, in the covert of the reed, and fens.

22 The shady trees cover him with their shadow; the willows of the brook compass him about.

23 Behold, he drinketh up a river, and hasteth not: he trusteth that he can draw up Jordan into his mouth.

24 He taketh it with his eyes; his nose pierceth through snares.

CHAPTER 41

Canst thou draw out leviathan[32] with an hook? or his tongue with a cord which thou lettest down?

2 Canst thou put an hook into his nose? or bore his jaw through with a thorn?

3 Will he make many supplications unto thee? will he speak soft words unto thee?

---

[30] A legendary land-monster. [31] Testicles.
[32] An aquatic monster; here, the crocodile.

4 Will he make a covenant with thee? wilt thou take him for a servant for ever?

5 Wilt thou play with him as with a bird? or wilt thou bind him for thy maidens?

6 Shall thy companions make a banquet of him? shall they part him among the merchants?

7 Canst thou fill his skin with barbed irons? or his head with fish spears?

8 Lay thine hand upon him, remember the battle, do no more.

9 Behold, the hope of him is in vain: shall not one be cast down even at the sight of him?

10 None is so fierce that dare stir him up: who then is able to stand before me?

11 Who hath prevented me, that I should repay him? whatsoever is under the whole heaven is mine.

12 I will not conceal his parts, nor his power, nor his comely proportion.

13 Who can discover the face of his garment? or who can come to him with his double bridle?

14 Who can open the doors of his face? his teeth are terrible round about.

15 His scales are his pride, shut up together as with a close seal.

16 One is so near to another, that no air can come between them.

17 They are joined one to another, they stick together, that they cannot be sundered.

18 By his neesings[33] a light doth shine, and his eyes are like the eyelids of the morning.

19 Out of his mouth go burning lamps, and sparks of fire leap out.

20 Out of his nostrils goeth smoke, as out of a seething pot or caldron.

21 His breath kindleth coals, and a flame goeth out of his mouth.

22 In his neck remaineth strength, and sorrow is turned into joy before him.

23 The flakes of his flesh are joined together: they are firm in themselves; they cannot be moved.

24 His heart is as firm as a stone; yea, as hard as a piece of the nether[34] millstone.

25 When he raiseth up himself, the mighty are afraid: by reason of breakings they purify themselves.[35]

26 The sword of him that layeth at him cannot hold: the spear, the dart, nor the habergeon.[36]

27 He esteemeth iron as straw, and brass as rotten wood.

28 The arrow cannot make him flee: slingstones are turned with him into stubble.

29 Darts are counted as stubble: he laugheth at the shaking of a spear.

30 Sharp stones are under him: he spreadeth sharp pointed things[37] upon the mire.

31 He maketh the deep to boil like a pot: he maketh the sea like a pot of ointment.

32 He maketh a path to shine after him; one would think the deep to be hoary.

33 Upon earth there is not his like, who is made without fear.

34 He beholdeth all high things: he is a king over all the children of pride.

CHAPTER 42

Then Job answered the Lord, and said,

2 I know that thou canst do every thing, and that no thought can be withholden from thee.

3 Who is he that hideth counsel without knowledge? therefore have I uttered that I understood not; things too wonderful for me, which I knew not.

4 Hear, I beseech thee, and I will speak: I will demand of thee, and declare thou unto me.

5 I have heard of thee by the hearing of the ear: but now mine eye seeth thee.

6 Wherefore I abhor myself, and repent in dust and ashes.

7 ¶ And it was so, that after the Lord had spoken these words unto Job, the Lord said to Eliphaz the Temanite, My wrath is kindled against thee, and against thy two friends: for ye have not spoken of me the thing that is right, as my servant Job hath.

8 Therefore take unto you now seven bullocks and seven rams, and go to my servant Job, and offer up for yourselves a burnt offering; and my servant Job shall pray for you: for him will I accept: lest I deal with you after your folly, in that ye have not spoken of me the thing which is right, like my servant Job.

9 So Eliphaz the Temanite and Bildad the Shuhite and Zophar the Naamathite went, and did according as the Lord commanded them: the Lord also accepted Job.

10 And the Lord turned the captivity of Job, when he prayed for his friends: also the Lord gave Job twice as much as he had before.

11 Then came there unto him all his brethren, and all his sisters, and all they that had been of his acquaintance before, and did eat bread with him in his house: and they bemoaned him, and comforted him

---

33 Sneezings.   34 The lower of the two stones used for grinding.
35 Translated literally from the Hebrew, which at this point is unintelligible.   36 Coat of mail.

37 The Hebrew is obscure.

over all the evil that the Lord had brought upon him: every man also gave him a piece of money, and every one an earring of gold.

12 So the Lord blessed the latter end of Job more than his beginning: for he had fourteen thousand sheep, and six thousand camels, and a thousand yoke of oxen, and a thousand she asses.

13 He had also seven sons and three daughters.

14 And he called the name of the first, Jemima; and the name of the second, Kezia; and the name of the third, Keren-happuch.

15 And in all the land were no women found so fair as the daughters of Job: and their father gave them inheritance among their brethren.

16 After this lived Job an hundred and forty years, and saw his sons, and his sons' sons, even four generations.

17 So Job died, being old and full of days.

THE BOOK OF PSALMS

Even as translated into English prose, anyone can see that the psalms are lyric poems. Adequate translations of poetry are rare. Like their originals, these vary in mood and in literary merit; the best are among the noblest poems in our language.

PSALM 8

To the chief Musician upon Gittith,[38] *A Psalm of David*

O Lord our Lord, how excellent is thy name in all the earth! who hast set thy glory above the heavens.

2 Out of the mouth of babes and sucklings hast thou ordained strength because of thine enemies, that thou mightest still the enemy and the avenger.

3 When I consider thy heavens, the work of thy fingers, the moon and the stars, which thou hast ordained;

4 What is man, that thou art mindful of him? and the son of man, that thou visitest him?

5 For thou hast made him a little lower than the angels, and hast crowned him with glory and honour.

6 Thou madest him to have dominion over the works of thy hands; thou hast put all things under his feet:

7 All sheep and oxen, yea, and the beasts of the field;

8 The fowl of the air, and the fish of the sea, and whatsoever passeth through the paths of the seas.

9 O Lord our Lord, how excellent is thy name in all the earth!

PSALM 19

To the chief Musician, A Psalm of David

The heavens declare the glory of God; and the firmament showeth his handywork.

2 Day unto day uttereth speech, and night unto night showeth knowledge.

3 There is no speech nor language where their voice is not heard.

4 Their line is gone out through all the earth, and their words to the end of the world. In them hath he set a tabernacle for the sun;

5 Which is as a bridegroom coming out of his chamber, and rejoiceth as a strong man to run a race.

6 His going forth is from the end of the heaven, and his circuit unto the ends of it: and there is nothing hid from the heat thereof.

7 The law of the Lord is perfect, converting the soul: the testimony of the Lord is sure, making wise the simple:

8 The statutes of the Lord are right, rejoicing the heart: the commandment of the Lord is pure, enlightening the eyes:

9 The fear of the Lord is clean, enduring for ever: the judgments of the Lord are true and righteous altogether.

10 More to be desired are they than gold, yea, than much fine gold; sweeter also than honey, and the honeycomb.

11 Moreover by them is thy servant warned: and in keeping of them there is great reward.

12 Who can understand his errors? cleanse thou me from secret faults.

13 Keep back thy servant also from presumptuous sins; let them not have dominion over me: then shall I be upright, and I shall be innocent from the great transgression.

14 Let the words of my mouth, and the meditation of my heart, be acceptable in thy sight, O Lord, my strength, and my redeemer.

PSALM 24

A Psalm of David

The earth is the Lord's, and the fullness thereof; the world, and they that dwell therein:

2 For he hath founded it upon the seas, and established it upon the floods.

---

[38] Some kind of air.

3 Who shall ascend into the hill of the Lord? or who shall stand in his holy place?

4 He that hath clean hands, and a pure heart; who hath not lifted up his soul unto vanity, nor sworn deceitfully.

5 He shall receive the blessing from the Lord, and righteousness from the God of his salvation.

6 This is the generation of them that seek him, that seek thy face, O Jacob.[39] Selah.[40]

7 Lift up your heads, O ye gates; and be ye lift up, ye everlasting doors; and the King of glory shall come in.

8 Who is this King of glory? The Lord strong and mighty, the Lord mighty in battle.

9 Lift up your heads, O ye gates; even lift them up, ye everlasting doors; and the King of glory shall come in.

10 Who is this King of glory? The Lord of hosts, he is the King of glory. Selah.

PSALM 90

A Prayer of Moses the man of God

Lord, thou hast been our dwelling place in all generations.

2 Before the mountains were brought forth, or ever thou hadst formed the earth and the world, even from everlasting to everlasting, thou art God.

3 Thou turnest man to destruction; and sayest, Return, ye children of men.

4 For a thousand years in thy sight are but as yesterday when it is past, and as a watch in the night.

5 Thou carriest them away as with a flood; they are as a sleep: in the morning they are like grass which groweth up.

6 In the morning it flourisheth, and groweth up; in the evening it is cut down, and withereth.

7 For we are consumed by thine anger, and by thy wrath are we troubled.

8 Thou hast set our iniquities before thee, our secret sins in the light of thy countenance.

9 For all our days are passed away in thy wrath; we spend our years as a tale that is told.

10 The days of our years are threescore years and ten; and if by reason of strength they be fourscore years, yet is their strength labour and sorrow; for it is soon cut off, and we fly away.

11 Who knoweth the power of thine anger? even according to thy fear,[41] so is thy wrath.

12 So teach us to number our days, that we may apply our hearts unto wisdom.

13 Return, O Lord, how long? and let it repent thee concerning thy servants.

14 O satisfy us early with thy mercy; that we may rejoice and be glad all our days.

15 Make us glad according to the days wherein thou hast afflicted us, and the years wherein we have seen evil.

16 Let thy work appear unto thy servants, and thy glory unto their children.

17 And let the beauty of the Lord our God be upon us: and establish thou the work of our hands upon us; yea, the work of our hands establish thou it.

ECCLESIASTES; OR, THE PREACHER

The following chapters close this short book, which ends as it began, with a wearied philosopher's conclusion that all is vanity—in the original Latin sense of that word: emptiness. He believes in God, but questions the utility of belief.

CHAPTER II

Cast thy bread upon the waters: for thou shalt find it after many days.

2 Give a portion to seven, and also to eight; for thou knowest not what evil shall be upon the earth.

3 If the clouds be full of rain, they empty themselves upon the earth: and if the tree fall toward the south, or toward the north, in the place where the tree falleth, there it shall be.

4 He that observeth the wind shall not sow; and he that regardeth the clouds shall not reap.

5 As thou knowest not what is the way of the spirit, nor how the bones do grow in the womb of her that is with child; even so thou knowest not the works of God who maketh all.

6 In the morning sow thy seed, and in the evening withhold not thine hand; for thou knowest not whether shall prosper, either this or that, or whether they both shall be alike good.

7 ¶ Truly the light is sweet, and a pleasant thing it is for the eyes to behold the sun:

8 But if a man live many years, and rejoice in

---

[39] I.e., God of Jacob. The word *God* appears in the Greek text but has dropped out of the surviving Hebrew texts.
[40] A solemn pause.

[41] Our fear of thee.

them all, yet let him remember the days of darkness; for they shall be many. All that cometh is vanity.

9 ¶ Rejoice, O young man, in thy youth, and let thy heart cheer thee in the days of thy youth, and walk in the ways of thine heart, and in the sight of thine eyes: but know thou, that for all these things God will bring thee into judgment.

10 Therefore remove sorrow from thy heart, and put away evil from thy flesh: for childhood and youth are vanity.

CHAPTER 12

Remember now thy Creator in the days of thy youth, while the evil days come not, nor the years draw nigh, when thou shalt say, I have no pleasure in them;

2 While the sun, or the light, or the moon, or the stars, be not darkened, nor the clouds return after the rain:

3 In the day when the keepers of the house shall tremble,[42] and the strong men shall bow themselves, and the grinders cease, because they are few, and those that look out of the windows be darkened,

4 And the doors shall be shut in the streets, when the sound of the grinding is low, and he shall rise up at the voice of the bird, and all the daughters of music shall be brought low;[43]

5 Also when they shall be afraid of that which is high, and fears shall be in the way, and the almond tree shall flourish, and the grasshopper shall be a burden,[44] and desire shall fail; because man goeth to his long home; and the mourners go about the streets:

6 Or ever the silver cord be loosed, or the golden bowl be broken, or the pitcher be broken at the fountain, or the wheel broken at the cistern:

7 Then shall the dust return to the earth as it was; and the spirit shall return unto God who gave it.

8 ¶ Vanity of vanities, saith the Preacher; all is vanity.

9 And moreover, because the Preacher was wise, he still taught the people knowledge; yea, he gave good heed, and sought out, and set in order many proverbs.

10 The Preacher sought to find out acceptable words; and that which was written was upright, even words of truth.

11 The words of the wise are as goads, and as nails fastened by the masters of assemblies, which are given from one shepherd.[45]

12 And further, by these, my son, be admonished: of making many books there is no end; and much study is a weariness of the flesh.

13 ¶ Let us hear the conclusion of the whole matter: Fear God, and keep his commandments: for this is the whole duty of man.

14 For God shall bring every work into judgment, with every secret thing, whether it be good, or whether it be evil.

THE SONG OF SOLOMON

This book of eight short chapters is a collection of love poems, unsurpassed for lyrical expression of the physical side of love. Sometimes the bride seems to be a country girl and the bridegroom a prince. From the second verse of Chapter 1 through the seventh of Chapter 2, the theme is apparently their wedding, and both speak. Then, through 3:5, the bride recites details of the courtship. The third lyric—it continues through 5:1—appears to describe the betrothal.

CHAPTER 1

The song of songs, which is Solomon's.

2 Let him kiss me with the kisses of his mouth: for thy love is better than wine.

3 Because of the savour of thy good ointments thy name is as ointment poured forth, therefore do the virgins love thee.

4 Draw me, we will run after thee: the king hath brought me into his chambers: we will be glad and rejoice in thee, we will remember thy love more than wine: the upright love thee.

5 I am black,[46] but comely, O ye daughters of Jerusalem, as the tents of Kedar,[47] as the curtains of Solomon.

6 Look not upon me, because I am black, because the sun hath looked upon me: my mother's children were angry with me; they made me the keeper of the vineyards; but mine own vineyard have I not kept.

7 Tell me, O thou whom my soul loveth, where thou feedest, where thou makest thy flock to rest at

---

[42] With palsy. Age also brings the stooped figure, loss of teeth, and dimmed sight.

[43] In their deafness the aged can barely hear the perpetual sound of the grinding of the household's meal. They take little pleasure in sleep, and so rise with the lark. In music, likewise, they have no delight.

[44] The meaning is obscure.   [45] The meaning is obscure.
[46] Swarthy.   [47] A tribe in northern Arabia.

noon: for why should I be as one that turneth aside by the flocks of thy companions?

8 ¶ If thou know not, O thou fairest among women, go thy way forth by the footsteps of the flock, and feed thy kids beside the shepherds' tents.

9 I have compared thee, O my love, to a company of horses in Pharaoh's[48] chariots.

10 Thy cheeks are comely with rows of jewels, thy neck with chains of gold.

11 We will make thee borders of gold with studs of silver.

12 ¶ While the king sitteth at his table, my spikenard[49] sendeth forth the smell thereof.

13 A bundle of myrrh is my well-beloved unto me; he shall lie all night betwixt my breasts.

14 My beloved is unto me as a cluster of camphire in the vineyards of En-gedi.[50]

15 Behold, thou art fair, my love; behold, thou art fair; thou hast doves' eyes.

16 Behold, thou art fair, my beloved, yea, pleasant: also our bed is green.

17 The beams of our house are cedar, and our rafters of fir.

CHAPTER 2

I am the rose of Sharon, and the lily of the valleys.

2 As the lily among thorns, so is my love among the daughters.

3 As the apple tree among the trees of the wood, so is my beloved among the sons. I sat down under his shadow with great delight, and his fruit was sweet to my taste.

4 He brought me to the banqueting house, and his banner over me was love.

5 Stay me with flagons, comfort me with apples: for I am sick of love.

6 His left hand is under my head, and his right hand doth embrace me.

7 I charge you, O ye daughters of Jerusalem, by the roes,[51] and by the hinds of the field, that ye stir not up, nor awake my love, till he please.

8 ¶ The voice of my beloved! behold, he cometh leaping upon the mountains, skipping upon the hills.

9 My beloved is like a roe or a young hart:[52] behold, he standeth behind our wall, he looketh forth at the windows, shewing[53] himself through the lattice.

10 My beloved spake, and said unto me, Rise up, my love, my fair one, and come away.

11 For, lo, the winter is past, the rain is over and gone;

12 The flowers appear on the earth; the time of the singing of birds is come, and the voice of the turtle[54] is heard in our land;

13 The fig tree putteth forth her green figs, and the vines with the tender grape give a good smell. Arise, my love, my fair one, and come away.

14 O my dove, that art in the clefts of the rock, in the secret places of the stairs, let me see thy countenance, let me hear thy voice; for sweet is thy voice, and thy countenance is comely.

15 Take us the foxes, the little foxes, that spoil the vines: for our vines have tender grapes.

16 ¶ My beloved is mine, and I am his: he feedeth among the lilies.

17 Until the day break, and the shadows flee away, turn, my beloved, and be thou like a roe or a young hart upon the mountains of Bether.[55]

CHAPTER 3

By night on my bed I sought him whom my soul loveth: I sought him, but I found him not.

2 I will rise now, and go about the city in the streets, and in the broad ways I will seek him whom my soul loveth: I sought him, but I found him not.

3 The watchmen that go about the city found me: to whom I said, Saw ye him whom my soul loveth?

4 It was but a little that I passed from them, but I found him whom my soul loveth: I held him, and would not let him go, until I had brought him into my mother's house, and into the chamber of her that conceived me.

5 I charge you, O ye daughters of Jerusalem, by the roes, and by the hinds of the field, that ye stir not up, nor awake my love, till he please.

6 ¶ Who is this that cometh out of the wilderness like pillars of smoke, perfumed with myrrh and frankincense, with all powders of the merchant?

7 Behold his bed, which is Solomon's; threescore valiant men are about it, of the valiant of Israel.

8 They all hold swords, being expert in war: every man hath his sword upon his thigh, because of fear in the night.

9 King Solomon made himself a chariot of the wood of Lebanon.[56]

10 He made the pillars thereof of silver, the bottom thereof of gold, the covering of it of purple, the

---

[48] The king of Egypt's.   [49] Like myrrh, a perfume.
[50] An oasis on the western shore of the Dead Sea.—*Camphire* (camphor) means the blossoms of the plant.
[51] Roe deer.   [52] Stag.   [53] Showing.

[54] Turtledoves.   [55] Location unknown.   [56] Probably fir.

midst thereof being paved with love, for the daughters of Jerusalem.

11 Go forth, O ye daughters of Zion, and behold king Solomon with the crown wherewith his mother crowned him in the day of his espousals, and in the day of the gladness of his heart.

CHAPTER 4

Behold, thou art fair, my love; behold, thou art fair; thou hast doves' eyes within thy locks: thy hair is as a flock of goats, that appear from mount Gilead.[57]

2 Thy teeth are like a flock of sheep that are even shorn, which came up from the washing; whereof every one bear twins, and none is barren among them.

3 Thy lips are like a thread of scarlet, and thy speech is comely: thy temples are like a piece of a pomegranate within thy locks.

4 Thy neck is like the tower of David builded for an armoury, whereon there hang a thousand bucklers, all shields of mighty men.

5 Thy two breasts are like two young roes that are twins, which feed among the lilies.

6 Until the day break, and the shadows flee away, I will get me to the mountain of myrrh, and to the hill of frankincense.

7 Thou art all fair, my love; there is no spot in thee.

8 ¶ Come with me from Lebanon, my spouse, with me from Lebanon: look from the top of Amana,[58] from the top of Shenir and Hermon,[59] from the lions' dens, from the mountains of the leopards.

9 Thou hast ravished my heart, my sister, my spouse; thou hast ravished my heart with one of thine eyes, with one chain of thy neck.

10 How fair is thy love, my sister, my spouse! how much better is thy love than wine! and the smell of thine ointments than all spices!

11 Thy lips, O my spouse, drop as the honeycomb: honey and milk are under thy tongue; and the smell of thy garments is like the smell of Lebanon.

12 A garden enclosed is my sister, my spouse; a spring shut up, a fountain sealed.

13 Thy plants are an orchard of pomegranates, with pleasant fruits; camphire, with spikenard,

14 Spikenard and saffron; calamus and cinnamon, with all trees of frankincense; myrrh and aloes, with all the chief spices:

15 A fountain of gardens, a well of living waters, and streams from Lebanon.

16 ¶ Awake, O north wind; and come, thou south; blow upon my garden, that the spices thereof may flow out. Let my beloved come into his garden, and eat his pleasant fruits.

THE GOSPEL ACCORDING TO ST. MATTHEW

The following New Testament selection is from Jesus's "Sermon on the Mount."

CHAPTER 5

And seeing the multitudes, he went up into a mountain: and when he was set, his disciples came unto him:

2 And he opened his mouth, and taught them, saying,

3 Blessed are the poor in spirit: for theirs is the kingdom of heaven.

4 Blessed are they that mourn: for they shall be comforted.

5 Blessed are the meek: for they shall inherit the earth.

6 Blessed are they which do hunger and thirst after righteousness: for they shall be filled.

7 Blessed are the merciful: for they shall obtain mercy.

8 Blessed are the pure in heart: for they shall see God.

9 Blessed are the peacemakers: for they shall be called the children of God.

10 Blessed are they which are persecuted for righteousness' sake: for theirs is the kingdom of heaven.

11 Blessed are ye when men shall revile you, and persecute you, and shall say all manner of evil against you falsely, for my sake.

12 Rejoice, and be exceeding glad; for great is your reward in heaven: for so persecuted they the prophets which were before you. . . .

---

[57] Northwest of the Dead Sea, in Transjordania.

[58] The Anti-Lebanon Mountains, north of Damascus.
[59] A peak at the southern end of the Anti-Lebanon range. *Shenir* is another name for it.

Take heed that ye do not your alms before men, to be seen of them; otherwise ye have no reward of your Father which is in heaven.

2 Therefore, when thou doest thine alms, do not sound a trumpet before thee, as the hypocrites do in the synagogues and in the streets, that they may have glory of men. Verily I say unto you, They have their reward.

3 But when thou doest alms, let not thy left hand know what thy right hand doeth;

4 That thine alms may be in secret: and thy Father which seeth in secret himself shall reward thee openly.

5 ¶ And when thou prayest, thou shalt not be as the hypocrites are: for they love to pray standing in the synagogues and in the corners of the streets, that they may be seen of men. Verily I say unto you, They have their reward.

6 But thou, when thou prayest, enter into thy closet, and when thou hast shut thy door, pray to thy Father which is in secret; and thy Father which seeth in secret shall reward thee openly.

7 But when ye pray, use not vain repetitions, as the heathen do: for they think that they shall be heard for their much speaking.

8 Be not ye therefore like unto them: for your Father knoweth what things ye have need of before ye ask him.

9 After this manner therefore pray ye; Our Father which art in heaven, Hallowed be thy name.

10 Thy kingdom come. Thy will be done in earth, as it is in heaven.

11 Give us this day our daily bread.

12 And forgive us our debts, as we forgive our debtors.

13 And lead us not into temptation, but deliver us from evil: For thine is the kingdom, and the power, and the glory, for ever. Amen.

14 For if ye forgive men their trespasses, your heavenly Father will also forgive you:

15 But if ye forgive not men their trespasses, neither will your Father forgive your trespasses.

16 ¶ Moreover, when ye fast, be not, as the hypocrites, of a sad countenance: for they disfigure their faces, that they may appear unto men to fast. Verily I say unto you, They have their reward.

17 But thou, when thou fastest, anoint thine head, and wash thy face;

18 That thou appear not unto men to fast, but unto thy Father which is in secret: and thy Father, which seeth in secret, shall reward thee openly.

19 ¶ Lay not up for yourselves treasures upon earth, where moth and rust doth corrupt, and where thieves break through and steal:

20 But lay up for yourselves treasures in heaven, where neither moth nor rust doth corrupt, and where thieves do not break through nor steal:

21 For where your treasure is, there will your heart be also.

22 The light of the body is the eye: if therefore thine eye be single,[60] thy whole body shall be full of light.

23 But if thine eye be evil, thy whole body shall be full of darkness. If therefore the light that is in thee be darkness, how great is that darkness!

24 No man can serve two masters: for either he will hate the one, and love the other; or else he will hold to the one, and despise the other. Ye cannot serve God and mammon.[61]

25 Therefore I say unto you, Take no thought for your life, what ye shall eat, or what ye shall drink; nor yet for your body, what ye shall put on. Is not the life more than meat, and the body than raiment?

26 Behold the fowls of the air: for they sow not, neither do they reap, nor gather into barns; yet your heavenly Father feedeth them. Are ye not much better than they?

27 Which of you, by taking thought, can add one cubit[62] unto his stature?

28 And why take ye thought for raiment? Consider the lilies of the field, how they grow: they toil not, neither do they spin:

29 And yet I say unto you, That even Solomon in all his glory was not arrayed like one of these.

30 Wherefore, if God so clothe the grass of the field, which to-day is, and to-morrow is cast into the oven, shall he not much more clothe you, O ye of little faith?

31 Therefore take no thought, saying, What shall we eat? or, What shall we drink? or, Wherewithal shall we be clothed?

32 (For after all these things do the Gentiles seek;) for your heavenly Father knoweth that ye have need of all these things.

33 But seek ye first the kingdom of God, and his righteousness; and all these things shall be added unto you.

34 Take therefore no thought for the morrow: for the morrow shall take thought for the things of itself. Sufficient unto the day is the evil thereof.

---

[60] Honest.   [61] Riches.
[62] Eighteen inches.

Active as a missionary in the first century of the Christian era, St. Paul (d. *c.* 62) was not only an organizer of genius but a gifted writer. His epistles are pastoral letters in admonition and supervision of various Christian communities, in this case the church at Corinth. The word *charity*, as Paul uses it, means love for humanity and in some recent translations of the New Testament is replaced by *love*.

CHAPTER 13

Though I speak with the tongues of men and of angels, and have not charity, I am become as sounding brass, or a tinkling[63] cymbal.

2 And though I have the gift of prophecy, and understand all mysteries, and all knowledge; and though I have all faith, so that I could remove mountains, and have not charity, I am nothing.

3 And though I bestow all my goods to feed the poor, and though I give my body to be burned, and have not charity, it profiteth me nothing.

4 Charity suffereth long, and is kind; charity envieth not; charity vaunteth not itself, is not puffed up,

5 Doth not behave itself unseemly, seeketh not her own, is not easily provoked, thinketh no evil;

6 Rejoiceth not in iniquity, but rejoiceth in the truth;

7 Beareth all things, believeth all things, hopeth all things, endureth all things.

8 Charity never faileth: but whether there be prophecies, they shall fail; whether there be tongues, they shall cease; whether there be knowledge, it shall vanish away.

9 For we know in part, and we prophesy in part.

10 But when that which is perfect is come, then that which is in part shall be done away.

11 When I was a child, I spake as a child, I understood as a child, I thought as a child; but when I became a man, I put away childish things.

12 For now we see through a glass, darkly;[64] but then face to face: now I know in part; but then shall I know even as also I am known.

13 And now abideth faith, hope, charity, these three; but the greatest of these is charity.

Wyatt and Surrey

1503–1542   1517?–1547

SIR THOMAS WYATT and Henry Howard, Earl of Surrey, were not collaborators. It is likely they knew each other; but even that is uncertain, for they belonged to opposite factions: Wyatt, at any rate politically, was a strong Protestant, while Surrey inclined to the old religion. Yet their names are forever linked. They were the first good poets after Chaucer, the earliest good poets of Tudor England. Above all, they helped bring in the Renaissance there. Both were "courtly makers," that is, poets of aristocratic birth and station.

WYATT was the older. His life was lived at a faster pace than is normal in our times. He had his Cambridge B.A. at fifteen and his M.A. at seventeen. By the latter date he was married, and within the year he had a son. The poet's father had been one of Henry VIII's guardians, and young Wyatt's place at court was waiting for him. By his twenty-fourth year he was noted for "feats of arms" in the tournaments which, with elaborate safeguards, were still held at

the Tudor court. Diplomatic missions to France and Italy enriched his culture, and for several years he lived in France as marshal of Calais.

Wyatt's marriage was unhappy; his wife and he soon separated. In 1536 he was thrown into the Tower of London under suspicion of having been Anne Boleyn's lover. Henry VIII had divorced and executed that gay and imprudent lady, his second wife, the year before. Wyatt may have had an affair with her prior to her marriage; the point has never been cleared up. He was soon released, knighted, and sent abroad as ambassador to Spain. The year 1541 found him in the Tower again, maliciously charged with disloyalty. Such were a Tudor courtier's ups and downs. Wyatt easily cleared himself. In the last year of his life he was elected to Parliament, and he was on another royal errand when he died of a fever.

It was Wyatt's trip to Italy, in 1527, that put him directly in touch with the Renaissance. Petrarch had died in 1374; but the young Englishman read his love sonnets, as well as

---

[63] Ringing.

[64] Early glass was imperfectly transparent.

the works of the more recent Italian masters. With contemporary French verse he also had an intimate acquaintance. In the last decade of the sixteenth century England saw an amazing outburst of sonneteering. Something like two thousand sonnets got into print, to say nothing of those which circulated only in manuscript. Wyatt laid the foundations of the vogue when he composed the first group of sonnets in English. Some he adapted from Petrarch, often improving on his source. On the whole, however, his best pieces are his songs.

Many of Wyatt's poems were first printed in 1557, fifteen years after his death, in *Tottel's Miscellany* (see above, pp. 226 f.). During his lifetime their circulation was doubtless chiefly among the courtiers. Others remained in manuscript till the nineteenth century. Tottel's texts often vary from those of surviving manuscripts; since some of the latter are more authoritative, they have been followed here. Tottel's smoothed-up versions are inferior to the rougher, more pungent originals. The standard edition is Miss A. K. Foxwell's *The Poems of Sir Thomas Wiat* (2 vols., 1913). (Apropos of the variants in the spelling of the poet's surname, it should be noted that the sixteenth century had not accepted the notion that for most words there is but one correct form. Sometimes a man's own signature varied in spelling.) There is a good selection, with comment, in E. M. W. Tillyard's *The Poetry of Sir Thomas Wyatt* (1929). E. K. Chambers has an essay in *Sir Thomas Wyatt and Some Collected Studies* (1933).

THE EARL OF SURREY was an earl by virtue of the custom of giving a peer's eldest son the second of his father's titles —a courtesy title it is called. Henry Howard came of proud stock. His father, the leading English general of the day, was Thomas Howard, Duke of Norfolk. As heir to England's premier dukedom, Surrey did not grow up in an atmosphere to foster humility. According to a contemporary he proved, at twenty-two, "the most foolish proud boy that is in England"; but his rank brought such advantages as his visit, in 1532, to the French court. Already— and when he went to France he was only fifteen—he was married. He began living with his bride when he was eighteen.

Like Wyatt's, the life of Surrey was full of adventure; and it was even shorter. He was a fiery youth, and never quite outgrew his youth. When he was twenty he struck a fellow courtier at the royal palace of Hampton Court. It was a serious offense—the penalty was loss of the right hand; and such was Surrey's sentence, though it was commuted. Twice, in his middle twenties, his violent temper landed him in Fleet prison. He took part in the political maneuvering which ended the career of Thomas Cromwell, the upstart statesman who headed the Protestant party. The Howards followed the King, but they were a

Catholic family. Surrey fought in campaigns against the Scots and the French; in two of these he held important commands. At court he cut a dazzling figure. But it all ended in a charge of high treason, growing out of the question of the succession to the throne. A week before Henry died, Surrey lost his head on Tower Hill.

Surrey followed Wyatt's example in exploiting the new modes of Italian and French verse. A number of his poems first appeared in *Tottel's Miscellany,* where his name stands alone on the title page. Tottel also printed his translation of Books II and IV of the *Aeneid;* for this Surrey adopted blank verse. He found the meter in his Italian reading, and to him we owe its introduction into England, a step of first-rate importance, since this ten-syllable, unrimed line was afterwards used by the greatest English poets and above all by the major Elizabethan dramatists.

Surrey also imitated the Italian sonnet. Two of his sonnets and two of Wyatt's are given below. Wyatt's stick reasonably close to the Italian form, with octave and sestet (i.e., two parts of eight and six lines respectively), the former riming *abbaabba,* the latter in various ways, though to close the sestet with a rimed couplet was a departure from the strict Italian pattern. Surrey experimented with sonnet structure, and the second of our selections from his sonnets is in the precise form later practiced by Shakespeare and called by his name, i.e., three quatrains and a rimed couplet (*abab, cdcd, efef, gg*). Surrey was not the first to compose in the quatrain pattern, but his use of it helped make it the normal Elizabethan type. As a poet, Surrey lacks Wyatt's imagination and passion. He handles his meters more smoothly.

The standard edition is by F. M. Padelford (revised ed., 1928). A handy volume of selections from Wyatt as well as from Surrey is Padelford's *Early Sixteenth Century Lyrics* (1907). For a biography, see E. Casady's *Henry Howard, Earl of Surrey* (1938).

Sir Thomas Wyatt

FORGET NOT YET

This is a song; its music has survived in manuscript. The note struck here, a lover's complaint against a lady's hard heart, continues to reverberate throughout the lyric poetry of the sixteenth century.

> Forget not yet the tried intent
> Of such a truth as I have meant,
> My great travail so gladly spent—
> Forget not yet!

Forget not yet when first began 5
The weary life ye know, since whan
The suit, the service, none tell can—
　　Forget not yet!

Forget not yet the great assays,
The cruel wrong, the scornful ways, 10
The painful patience in denays[1]—
　　Forget not yet!

Forget not yet, forget not this:
How long ago hath been, and is,
The mind that never meant amiss— 15
　　Forget not yet!

Forget not then thine own approved,[2]
The which so long hath thee so loved,
Whose steadfast faith yet never moved—
　　Forget not this!

THE LOVER COMPARETH HIS STATE TO A SHIP IN PERILOUS STORM TOSSED ON THE SEA

Like many another, this sonnet (a translation of Petrarch's 189th) embodies an extended metaphor. The poet's beloved disdains him; accordingly, Love is his foe and steers his vessel, that is, his life. The poem's effectiveness does not come from clearness—in fact, it is a little obscure—but from the vividness and strangeness of the scene pictured in the metaphor. The title is from Tottel's version.

My galley, chargèd with forgetfulness,[3]
Thorough sharp seas, in winter nights doth pass
'Tween rock and rock; and eke mine enemy, alas,
That is my lord, steereth with cruelness;
And every oar a thought in readiness 5
As though that[4] death were light in such a case.
An endless wind doth tear the sail apace
Of forcèd sighs, and trusty fearfulness.
A rain of tears, a cloud of dark disdain,
Hath done the wearied cords great hinderance, 10
Wreathèd[5] with error, and eke with ignorance.
The stars be hid that led me to this pain;
Drownèd is reason, that should me comfórt;
And I remain despairing of the port.

---

1 Denials.
2 Tested one, i.e., lover.
3 I.e., so weighted with love that I am oblivious to everything else.
4 As though. I.e., my constant thought is how, in such a plight as mine, death would be a small matter.
5 I.e., the ropes are tangled.

A RENOUNCING OF LOVE

Farewell, Love, and all thy laws for ever!
Thy baited hooks shall tangle me no more.
Senec[6] and Plato call me from thy lore
To perfect wealth my wit for to endeavor.
In blind error when I did persever, 5
Thy sharp repulse, that pricketh aye so sore,
Hath taught me to set in trifles no store,
And 'scape forth, since liberty is lever.[7]
Therefore, farewell! go trouble younger hearts,
And in me claim no more authority. 10
With idle youth go use thy property,[8]
And thereon spend thy many brittle darts.
For hitherto though I have lost all my time,
Me lusteth no lenger[9] rotten boughs to climb.

THE LOVER COMPLAINETH THE UNKINDNESS OF HIS LOVE

My lute, awake! Perform the last
Labor that thou and I shall waste,
　And end that[10] I have now begun!
For when this song is sung and past,
　My lute, be still, for I have done! 5

As to be heard where ear is none,
As lead to grave[11] in marble stone,
　My song may pierce her heart as soon.
Should we then sigh, or sing, or moan?
　No, no, my lute, for I have done. 10

The rocks do not so cruelly
Repulse the waves continually
　As she my suit and affectiön;
So that I am past remedy,
　Whereby my lute and I have done. 15

Proud of the spoil that thou hast got
Of simple hearts thorough Love's shot,
　By whom, unkind, thou hast them won,
Think not he hath his bow forgot,
　Although my lute and I have done. 20

Vengeance shall fall on thy disdain,
That makest but game on[12] earnest pain;
　Think not alone under the sun
Unquit[13] to cause thy lovers plain,[14]
　Although my lute and I have done. 25

---

6 Seneca, the Roman Stoic philosopher of the first century A.D.
7 Dearer.　　8 Act according to thy nature.
9 It pleases me no longer.　　10 What.
11 As (a tool made of) lead (is able) to engrave.　12 Of.
13 Unrequited; i.e., with impunity.　　14 To complain, to sorrow.

Per chance thee lie[15] withered and old
In winter nights, that are so cold,
Plaining in vain unto the moon.
Thy wishes then dare not be told:
Care then who list,[16] for I have done.   30

And then may chance thee to repent
The time that thou hast lost and spent,
To cause thy lovers sigh and swoon.
Then shalt thou know beauty but lent,
And wish and want, as I have done.   35

Now cease, my lute! This is the last
Labor that thou and I shall waste,
And ended is that we begun.
Now is this song both sung and past.
My lute, be still, for I have done!   40

THE LOVER SHOWETH HOW HE IS FORSAKEN OF SUCH AS HE SOMETIME ENJOYED

They flee from me that sometime[17] did me seek,
With naked foot stalking in my chamber.
I have seen them gentle, tame, and meek,
That now are wild, and do not remember
That sometime they put themselves in danger   5
    To take bread at my hand; and now they range,
    Busily seeking with a continual change.

Thanked be Fortune, it hath been otherwise,
Twenty times better; but once, in special,
In thin array, after a pleasant guise,[18]   10
    When her loose gown did from her shoulders fall,
    And she me caught in her arms long and small,
        Therewith all sweetly did me kiss
        And softly said, "Dear heart, how like you this?"

It was no dream; I lay broad waking.   15
But all is turnèd thorough my gentleness
Into a strange fashion of forsaking;
    And I have leave to go, of her goodness,[19]
    And she also to use newfangleness.[20]
        But since that I so kindly[21] am servèd,   20
        I fain would know what she hath deservèd?

Henry Howard, Earl of Surrey

DESCRIPTION OF SPRING, WHEREIN EACH THING RENEWS, SAVE ONLY THE LOVER

An adaptation from Petrarch, and a decided improvement. Aside from its charming freshness, there is nothing remarkable about this sonnet's catalogue of signs of spring; but the reserving of the sharp contrast till the last four words has a sudden and poignant effect.

The soote[22] season that bud and bloom forth brings,
With green hath clad the hill and eke the vale;
The nightingale with feathers new she sings;
The turtle[23] to her make[24] hath told her tale.
Summer is come, for every spray now springs;   5
The hart hath hung his old head on the pale;[25]
The buck in brake[26] his winter coat he flings;
The fishes float with new repairèd scale;
The adder all her slough away she slings;
The swift swallow pursueth the flies small;   10
The busy bee her honey now she mings.[27]
Winter is worn, that was the flowers' bale.
And thus I see among these pleasant things
Each care decays, and yet my sorrow springs.

VOW TO LOVE FAITHFULLY HOWSOEVER HE BE REWARDED

This sonnet is also from Petrarch.

Set me whereas the sun doth parch the green,
Or where his beams may not dissolve the ice;
In temperate heat, where he is felt and seen;
In presence prest of people, mad or wise;
Set me in high or yet in low degree;   5
In longest night, or in the shortest day;
In clearest sky, or where clouds thickest be;
In lusty youth, or when my hairs are gray:
Set me in heaven, in earth, or else in hell;
In hill, or dale, or in the foaming flood;   10
Thrall, or at large, alive whereso I dwell;
Sick or in health, in evil fame or good:
Hers will I be, and only with this thought
Content myself, although my chance be nought.

---

[15] It may befall thee to lie.
[16] Wishes to.   [17] Formerly.   [18] In a delightful way.
[19] This is ironical, of course.   [20] To practice fickleness.
[21] Also ironic. Pronounced as a trisyllable, *kindely.*

[22] Sweet.   [23] Turtledove.   [24] Mate.
[25] I.e., has rubbed off his old set of horns against the fence of the enclosure he is kept in.   [26] Thicket.   [27] Mixes.

HOW NO AGE IS CONTENT WITH HIS OWN ESTATE,[28] AND HOW THE AGE OF CHILDREN IS THE HAPPIEST, IF THEY HAD SKILL[29] TO UNDERSTAND IT

This poem alternates iambic hexameters (six-foot lines) and heptameters (seven-foot lines). The hexameter has never been a favorite meter in England; in the so-called "four-teener," however, a great deal of sixteenth-century verse was composed. The combination of the two, as in this poem, is called "poulter's measure."

Laid in my quiet bed, in study as I were,
I saw within my troubled head a heap of thoughts appear;
And every thought did show so lively in mine eyes,
That now I sighed and then I smiled, as cause of thought
    doth rise.
I saw the little boy in thought, how oft that he   5
Did wish of God, to scape the rod, a tall young man to
    be;
The young man eke that feels his bones with pains[30]
    opprest,
How he would be a rich old man, to live and lie at rest;
The rich old man, that sees his end draw on so sore,
How he would be a boy again, to live so much the more.
Whereat full oft I smiled, to see how all these three,   11

From boy to man, from man to boy, would chop[31] and
    change degree.
And, musing thus, I think the case is very strange,
That man from wealth, to live in woe, doth ever seek to
    change.
Thus thoughtful as I lay, I saw my withered skin,   15
How it doth show my dented chews,[32] the flesh was
    worn so thin.
And eke my toothless chaps,[33] the gates of my right way,
That opes and shuts as I do speak, do thus unto me say:
"Thy white and hoarish hairs, the messengers of age,
That show, like lines of true belief, that this life doth
    assuage,[34]   20
Bids thee lay hand and feel them hanging on thy chin,
The which do write[35] two ages past, the third now
    coming in.
Hang up therefore the bit of thy young wanton[36] time,
And thou that therein beaten art, the happiest life
    define."
Whereat I sighed, and said: "Farewell, my wonted joy!
Truss up thy pack,[37] and trudge from me to every little
    boy;   26
And tell them thus from me: their time most happy is,
If, to their time, they reason had, to know the truth of
    this."

John Lyly

1554?–1606

There is a great puzzle about Lyly. How did the man who could perpetrate the absurd and pretentious prose of *Euphues, the Anatomy of Wit* rise to the crystal-clear, chaste beauty of the lyrics which adorn his comedies? To that question a simple answer has been proposed: that someone else wrote the lyrics. They first appear, not in the earliest editions of the plays, but long after Lyly's death, in a collected volume of 1632 entitled *Six Court Comedies*. Most scholars, however, think the chances favor Lyly's authorship, and recently discovered evidence also points that way. There is no dodging the fact that John Lyly, however he misused it, had an uncommon knack with a pen. He was no genius, but he was a very clever fellow indeed.

Nothing is known of Lyly's early life. He was educated principally at Oxford, where he took his B.A. in 1573 and his M.A. in 1575. For some reason Elizabeth's great minister, Lord Burghley, was interested in him; eventually

Lyly became a courtier. Being a courtier was practically a profession; you made yourself useful to a greater courtier than yourself, and if possible to the sovereign, hoping to be rewarded by gifts, grants, and offices. All of Lyly's work, dramatic and nondramatic, was addressed more to the courtly audience than to the general public. His great ambition was to be Master of the Revels, that is, head of the bureau which censored plays and supervised entertainments at court. He was admirably suited for the post; but though he obtained some recognition and a modest status at court, nothing really good ever came his way.

His literary successes were all relatively early. He was twenty-four when *Euphues* made him famous. It is really only a piece of cleverness, and some considered him the merest smart aleck. The academic world always had its doubts about him; in *Euphues* he fires some hot shot at his own university. Two years later he brought out a sequel,

---

[28] Its own state, condition.   [29] Reason; i.e., sense enough.
[30] Toil.

[31] Swap, exchange.   [32] Sunken jaws.   [33] Jaws.
[34] Pass away.   [35] Which signify.   [36] Sportive.
[37] I.e., tie up, like a peddler, your pack of youthful pleasures.

Euphues and His England. For a while he found a patron in the Earl of Oxford, himself a minor poet; and soon Lyly was writing and producing comedies. They were acted by companies composed exclusively of boys, especially by one which had grown out of the choir of St. Paul's. The best of Lyly's plays are graceful; but they are overliterary, prettified, and tame. Though some of them are daring in their allusions to current topics, they all shy away from strong emotion—Lyly is incapable of the note of genuine passion. After Shakespeare, Marlowe, and Kyd had given the stage their robust dramas of action and passion, Lyly's plays seemed thin and his vogue declined. He had enjoyed from 1578 through the eighties a spectacular success; but he was still in his thirties when his creative fires, such as they were, flickered out. They had sparkled, but they had never given off much heat. Yet he was a refining influence on the formative period of Elizabethan drama. That even Shakespeare learned from Lyly how to apply the light, smart touch to witty comedy seems clear enough in *Love's Labour's Lost.*

As for *Euphues,* of which a sample is given below, in form it is prose fiction. Actually, the story is simply an excuse for essaylike commentaries on a variety of things, particularly on how a bright young man should conduct himself; and even these observations are of less concern to the author than his style. Lyly is chiefly interested in his attempt to establish an artistic English prose, and he adopts a particularly gaudy one. It had been worked up earlier from a variety of sources by a minor writer named George Pettie, whose taste may be measured by the title he gave his book, *A Petite Palace of Pettie His Pleasure* (1576). It was the hit *Euphues* made that gave the style its name and its immense popularity. Not everyone succumbed to it— Sidney scorned it and in his *Arcadia* invented a far from ideal substitute of his own—but the vogue of euphuism continued throughout the century. The publisher of *Six Court Comedies* declares that

our nation are in his debt for a new English which he taught them. . . . All our ladies were then his scholars, and that beauty in court which could not parley euphuism was as little regarded as she which now there speaks not French.

Euphuism is an extremely mannered and self-conscious style, the reverse of what we consider good English prose today. It does not aim at simplicity and directness; instead, it bristles with overelaborate figures of speech, which are introduced not to insure clearness or force, but purely for their decorative effect. Short sentences it avoids, preferring to build up a fantastic architecture of either parallel or antithetic constructions on formulas like these: *As A is like X, and B like Y, so C is like Z;* or *Though M acts on the principle a+b, yet N on the contrary behaves in accordance with the formula x−y.* The reader may amuse himself by working

out typical patterns in the sample below. He will discover also that the words which are balanced or contrasted in the structure are often made to sound alike as well: frequently they alliterate, sometimes in elaborate patterns; often there is assonance, and occasionally even rime. Plays on words are numerous. Another species of decoration consists of allusions to alleged happenings in the lives of famous Greeks and Romans, to classical mythology, and to the "unnatural natural history" which the Elizabethans picked up chiefly from the writings of Pliny the Elder (d. 79 A.D.). These allusions are mostly in the form of comparisons or analogies; numerous examples will be found in the passage below. For a cultivated Elizabethan they increased the pleasures of reading by adding the pleasure of recognition, since study of the Latin language and literature was the cornerstone of education.

Most readers find that a little of *Euphues* goes a long way. Still, however far removed it is from what we consider good prose today, the latter owes it a debt for its emphasis on firmly controlled structure and artistic finish.

The standard edition is *The Complete Works of John Lyly* by R. W. Bond (3 vols., 1902); a life is included. Annotated editions of the best plays, *Campaspe* and *Endymion,* may be found in, respectively, J. Q. Adams's *Chief Pre-Shakespearean Dramas* (1924) and H. Spencer's *Elizabethan Plays* (1933). On the historical significance of euphuism, see G. P. Krapp's *The Rise of English Literary Prose* (1915).

CUPID AND MY CAMPASPE

This lyric and the following one are from Lyly's play *Campaspe.* The first, which Tennyson called one of the most elegant things in English, is sung to Campaspe, a maiden captive of Alexander the Great, by the conqueror's court painter, Apelles, who loves her. Grace, however, not passion, is the effect Lyly seeks.

> Cupid and my Campaspe played
> At cards for kisses; Cupid paid.
> He stakes his quiver, bow, and arrows,
> His mother's[1] doves and team of sparrows;
> Loses them, too. Then down he throws   5
> The coral of his lip, the rose
> Growing on's cheek (but none knows how);
> With these, the crystal of his brow,
> And then the dimple of his chin:
> All these did my Campaspe win.   10
> At last he set[2] her both his eyes;
> She won, and Cupid blind did rise.
> O Love, has she done this to thee?
> What shall, alas! become of me?

---

[1] Venus.   [2] Staked, bet.

WHAT BIRD SO SINGS?

What bird so sings, yet so does wail?
Oh, 'tis the ravished nightingale.[3]
"Jug, jug, jug, jug, tereu," she cries;
And still her woes at midnight rise.
Brave[4] prick song![5] who is't now we hear?   5
None but the lark so shrill and clear;
Now at heaven's gates she claps her wings,
The morn not waking till she sings.
Hark, hark, with what a pretty throat
Poor robin redbreast tunes his note!   10
Hark how the jolly cuckoos sing,
"Cuckoo," to welcome in the spring,
"Cuckoo," to welcome in the spring!

from EUPHUES, THE ANATOMY[6] OF WIT

Euphues, a well-to-do young Athenian, travels to Naples, "a place of more pleasure than profit," where he applies himself to the former. Deploring his frivolity, an old gentleman gives him a friendly lecture, but Euphues flatly rejects his advice.

EUPHUES,[7] having thus ended his talk, departed, leaving this old gentleman in a great quandary; who, perceiving that he was more inclined to wantonness than to wisdom, with a deep sigh, the tears trickling down his cheeks, said: "Seeing thou wilt not buy counsel at the first hand good cheap,[8] thou shalt buy repentance at the second hand, at such an unreasonable rate that thou wilt curse thy hard pennyworth, and ban[9] thy hard heart." And immediately he went to his own house, heavily bewailing the young man's unhappiness.

Here ye may behold, gentlemen,[10] how lewdly wit[11] standeth in his own light, how he deemeth no penny good silver but his own, preferring the blossom before the fruit, the bud before the flower, the green blade before the ripe ear of corn,[12] his own wit before all men's wisdoms. Neither is that geason,[13] seeing for the most part it is proper to[14] all

those of sharp capacity to esteem of themselves as most proper; if one be hard in conceiving they pronounce him a dolt, if given to study they proclaim him a dunce, if merry a jester, if sad a saint, if full of words a sot, if without speech a cipher; if one argue with them boldly, then is he impudent; if coldly, an innocent;[15] if there be reasoning of divinity,[16] they cry, "Quae supra nos nihil ad nos";[17] if of humanity, "Sententias loquitur carnifex."[18] Hereof cometh such great familiarity between the ripest wits, when they shall see the disposition the one of the other, the *sympathia* of affections and as it were but a pair of shears to go between their natures,[19] one flattereth another in his own folly, and layeth cushions under the elbow of his fellow[20] when he seeth him take a nap with fancy; and as their wit wresteth them to vice, so it forgeth them some feat[21] excuse to cloak their vanity.

Too much study doth intoxicate their brains, for (say they), although iron the more it is used the brighter it is, yet silver with much wearing doth waste to nothing; though the cammock[22] the more it is bowed the better it serveth, yet the bow the more it is bent and occupied[23] the weaker it waxeth; though the camomile[24] the more it is trodden and pressed down the more it spreadeth, yet the violet the oftener it is handled and touched the sooner it withereth and decayeth. Besides this, a fine wit, a sharp sense, a quick understanding, is able to attain to more in a moment or a very little space than a dull and blockish head in a month; the scythe cutteth far better and smoother than the saw; the wax yieldeth better and sooner to the seal than the steel to the stamp or hammer; the smooth and plain beech is easier to be carved and occupied than the knotty box. For neither is there any thing but that hath his contraries. Such is the nature of these novices that think to have learning without labor, and treasure without travail, either not understanding or else not remembering that the finest edge is made with the blunt whetstone, and the fairest jewel fashioned with the hard hammer. I go not about, gentlemen, to inveigh against wit, for then I were witless; but, frankly to confess mine own little wit, I have ever

---

[3] In classical mythology, the daughter of a king of Attica (in some versions of the story her name is Philomela) was changed by the gods into a nightingale after she had been ravished. Hence the plaintiveness of the bird's song.   [4] Fine.
[5] Melody. (Originally a song "pricked," i.e., written down in musical notation.)
[6] Structure, science (literally, dissection).
[7] Literally, well-natured.   [8] At a bargain.
[9] Condemn.
[10] I.e., readers. Note that for the next two paragraphs Lyly characteristically abandons his narrative in favor of a brief essay.
[11] Cleverness.   [12] Grain.   [13] Rare.   [14] Characteristic of.

[15] Simpleton.
[16] Discussion of theology.
[17] What is above us is nothing to us.
[18] The hangman pronounces sentence; i.e., an unqualified base rascal offers his opinions.
[19] I.e., they are alike; they are cut from the same cloth.
[20] I.e., flatters him.   [21] Neat.   [22] Crooked staff, crook.
[23] Used.
[24] A genus of daisylike plants. Lyly was not the first to use this alleged phenomenon for purposes of comparison. Shakespeare later on has a laugh at the figure, in *1 Henry IV*, II, iv, 441 ff.

thought so superstitiously of wit that I fear I have committed idolatry against wisdom; and if Nature had dealt so beneficially with me to have given me any wit, I should have been readier in the defence of it to have made an apology than any way to turn to apostasy. But this I note, that for the most part they stand so on their pantofles[25] that they be secure[26] of perils, obstinate in their own opinions, impatient of labor, apt to conceive wrong, credulous to believe the worst, ready to shake off their old acquaintance without cause, and to condemn them without color. All which humors[27] are by so much the more easier to be purged by how much the less they have festered the sinews. But return we again to Euphues.

Euphues having sojourned by the space of two months in Naples, whether he were moved by the courtesy of a young gentleman named Philautus, or enforced by destiny; whether his pregnant wit or his pleasant conceits[28] wrought the greater liking in the mind of Euphues, I know not for certainty. But Euphues showed such entire love towards him that he seemed to make small accompt of any others, determining to enter into such an inviolable league of friendship with him as neither time by piecemeal should impair, neither fancy utterly dissolve, nor any suspicion infringe. "I have read," saith he, "and well I believe it, that a friend is in prosperity a pleasure, a solace in adversity, in grief a comfort, in joy a merry companion, at all times an other I,[29] in all places the express image of mine own person; insomuch that I cannot tell whether the immortal gods have bestowed any gift upon mortal men either more noble or more necessary than friendship. Is there anything in the world to be reputed (I will not say compared) to friendship? Can any treasure in this transitory pilgrimage be of more value than a friend? In whose bosom thou mayst sleep secure without fear, whom thou mayst make partner of all thy secrets without suspicion of fraud and partaker of all thy misfortune without mistrust of fleeting, who will accompt thy bale his bane,[30] thy mishap his misery, the pricking of thy finger the piercing of his heart. But whither am I carried? Have I not also learned that one should eat a bushel of salt with him[31] whom he meaneth to make his friend? that trial maketh trust? that there is falsehood in fellowship? And what

then? Doth not the sympathy of manners make the conjunction of minds? Is it not a byword, 'like will to like'? Not so common as commendable it is, to see young gentlemen choose them such friends with whom they may seem being absent to be present, being asunder to be conversant, being dead to be alive. I will therefore have Philautus for my fere;[32] and by so much the more I make myself to have Philautus, by how much the more I view in him the lively image of Euphues."

Although there be none so ignorant that doth not know, neither any so impudent that will not confess, friendship to be the jewel of human joy; yet whosoever shall see this amity grounded upon a little affection will soon conjecture that it shall be dissolved upon a light occasion: as in the sequel of Euphues and Philautus you shall see, whose hot love waxed soon cold. For as the best wine doth make the sharpest vinegar, so the deepest love turneth to the deadliest hate. Who deserved the most blame, in mine opinion it is doubtful, and so difficult that I dare not presume to give verdict. For love being the cause for which so many mischiefs have been attempted, I am not yet persuaded whether[33] of them was most to be blamed, but certainly neither of them was blameless. I appeal to your judgment, gentlemen, not that I think any of you of the like disposition able to decide the question, but being of deeper discretion than I am, are more fit to debate the quarrel. Though the discourse of their friendship and falling out be somewhat long, yet being somewhat strange, I hope the delightfulness of the one will attenuate the tediousness of the other.

Euphues had continual access to the place of Philautus, and no little familiarity with him, and finding him at convenient leisure, in these short terms unfolded his mind unto him: "Gentleman and friend, the trial I have had of thy manners cutteth off divers terms which to another I would have used in the like matter. And sithens[34] a long discourse argueth folly, and delicate words incur the suspicion of flattery, I am determined to use neither of them, knowing either of them to breed offence. Weighing with myself the force of friendship by the effects, I studied ever since my first coming to Naples to enter league with such a one as might direct my steps being a stranger, and resemble my manners being a scholar, the which two qualities as I find in you able to satisfy my desire, so I hope I shall find a heart in you willing to accomplish my request. Which if I may

---

25 High-heeled shoes.   26 Careless.
27 Whims. On the physiological humors, see p. 119, note 32, above.
28 Notions.
29 For a number of the ideas in this passage, see Cicero, *De Amicitia*, xx–xxii, and George Pettie's *Palace of Pleasure* (1576).
30 Thy sorrow his woe.
31 I.e., see a good deal of him before swearing eternal friendship.

32 Companion.   33 Which.   34 Since.

obtain, assure yourself that Damon to his Pythias,[35] Pylades[36] to his Orestes, Titus to his Gysippus,[37] Theseus to his Pyrothus,[38] Scipio to his Laelius,[39] was never found more faithful than Euphues will be to his Philautus."

Philautus, by how much the less he looked for this discourse, by so much the more he liked it, for he saw all qualities both of body and mind in Euphues, unto whom he replied as followeth: "Friend Euphues (for so your talk warranteth me to term you), I dare neither use a long process, neither loving speech, lest unwittingly I should cause you to convince[40] me of those things which you have already condemned. And verily I am bold to presume upon your courtesy, since you yourself have used so little curiosity,[41] persuading myself that my short answer will work as great an effect in you as your few words did in me. And seeing we resemble (as you say) each other in qualities, it cannot be that the one should differ from the other in courtesy; seeing the sincere affection of the mind cannot be expressed by the mouth, and that no art can unfold the entire love of the heart, I am earnestly to beseech you not to measure the firmness of my faith by the fewness of my words, but rather think that the overflowing waves of good will leave no passage for many words. Trial shall prove trust; here is my hand, my heart, my lands, and my life at thy commandment. Thou mayst well perceive that I did believe thee, that so soon I did love thee; and I hope thou wilt the rather love me, in that I did believe thee."

After many embracings and protestations one to another, they walked to dinner, where they wanted neither meat, neither music, neither any other pastime; and, having banqueted, to digest their sweet confections they danced all that afternoon; they used not only one board but one bed, one book (if so be it they thought not one too many). Their friendship augmented every day, insomuch that the one could not refrain the company of the other one minute;

all things went in common between them, which all men accompted commendable. Philautus being a town-born child, both for his own continuance[42] and the great countenance which his father had while he lived, crept into credit[43] with Don Ferardo, one of the chief governors of the city, who, although he had a courtly crew of gentlewomen sojourning in his palace, yet his daughter, heir to his whole revenues, stained the beauty of them all, whose modest bashfulness caused the other to look wan for envy, whose lily cheeks dyed with a vermilion red made the rest to blush at her beauty. For as the finest ruby staineth the color of the rest that be in place, or as the sun dimmeth the moon that[44] she cannot be discerned, so this gallant girl, more fair than fortunate, and yet more fortunate than faithful, eclipsed the beauty of them all and changed their colors. Unto her had Philautus access, who won her by right of love and should[45] have worn her by right of law, had not Euphues by strange destiny broken the bonds of marriage and forbidden the bans of matrimony.[46]

It happened that Don Ferardo had occasion to go to Venice about certain his own affairs, leaving his daughter the only steward of his household, who spared not to feast Philautus, her friend, with all kinds of delights and delicates,[47] reserving only her honesty[48] as the chief stay of her honor. Her father being gone, she sent for her friend[49] to supper, who came not as he was accustomed, solitarily alone, but accompanied with[50] his friend Euphues. The gentlewoman, whether it were for niceness[51] or for niggardness of courtesy, gave him such a cold welcome that he repented that he was come.

Euphues, though he knew himself worthy every way to have a good countenance,[52] yet could he not perceive her willing any way to lend him a friendly look. Yet lest he should seem to want gestures,[53] or to be dashed out of conceit[54] with her coy countenance, he addressed him to a gentlewoman called Livia, unto whom he uttered this speech: "Fair lady, if it be the guise[55] of Italy to welcome strangers[56] with strangeness,[57] I must needs say the custom is strange and the country barbarous; if the manner of ladies to salute gentlemen with coyness, then I am enforced to think the women without courtesy to

35 Under sentence of death by the tyrant Dionysius of Syracuse (d. 367 B.C.), Pythias, according to the story, was permitted to absent himself for a time on condition that his friend Damon pledge his own life.
36 The trusty comrade of Orestes, the Hamlet-like avenger of Greek tragedy.
37 Characters in a contemporary English play which has not survived. Its source was evidently the eighth story of the tenth day of Boccaccio's Decameron. Titus and Gisippus are rivals, first in love, but later in generosity and friendship.
38 Pirithoüs, a legendary king of Thessaly. He invaded Attica; but such was his admiration for his opponent, Theseus, that the two became fast friends.
39 Gaius Laelius fought under Scipio Africanus the Elder throughout most of the latter's campaigns.   40 Convict.
41 Ceremony, ceremonious phraseology.

42 On account of his own continuing—i.e., in the favor his father had enjoyed.   43 Favor.   44 So that.
43 Would certainly.
46 Successive formal announcements of matrimonial intentions.
47 Delicacies.   48 Chastity.   49 Lover, suitor.
50 By.   51 Prudery.
52 Reception, favor.
53 Lack poise.   54 Out of his wits.   55 Fashion.
56 Foreigners.   57 Offishness.

use such welcome, and the men past shame that will come. But hereafter I will either bring a stool on mine arm, for[58] an unbidden guest, or a vizard[59] on my face, for a shameless gossip."

Livia replied: "Sir, our country is civil, and our gentlewomen are courteous; but in Naples it is compted a jest, at every word to say, 'In faith you are welcome.'"

As she was yet talking, supper was set on the board; then Philautus spake thus unto Lucilla: "Yet, gentlewoman, I was the bolder to bring my shadow with me," meaning Euphues, "knowing that he should be the better welcome for my sake."

Unto whom the gentlewoman replied: "Sir, as I never when I saw you thought that you came without your shadow, so now I cannot a little marvel to see you so overshot in bringing a new shadow with you."

Euphues, though he perceived her coy nip, seemed not to care for it,[60] but taking her by the hand said: "Fair lady, seeing the shade doth often shield your beauty from the parching sun, I hope you will the better esteem of the shadow; and by so much the less it ought to be offensive, by how much the less it is able to offend you; and by so much the more you ought to like it, by how much the more you use to lie in it."

"Well, gentleman," answered Lucilla, "in arguing of the shadow, we forgo the substance. Pleaseth it you[61] therefore to sit down to supper."

And so they all sat down. But Euphues fed of one dish, which ever stood before him: the beauty of Lucilla.

Sir Philip Sidney

1554–1586

SIDNEY wrote his name high as a poet and a scholar; but that is not his chief claim to fame, even now. It is a strange fact that his name still rouses, in an age of profoundly altered ideals, echoes of the hero worship lavishly accorded in his own day, when he was the idol of Elizabeth's court. His existence and afterwards his memory seemed to many the best justification of that often satirized type, the courtier; and he also exemplified, as was recognized not only in England but on the Continent, the Renaissance ideal of the complete gentleman.

Sidney was born an aristocrat. His paternal grandfather had commanded the right wing against the Scots at Flodden. His father, Sir Henry Sidney (d. 1586), was a wealthy knight who served three English sovereigns as soldier and administrator and became Queen Elizabeth's Lord Deputy in Ireland. His mother was the daughter of the Duke of Northumberland and the sister of Robert Dudley, Earl of Leicester (d. 1588), long the Queen's favorite courtier. By birth Sidney was destined to command, and he acquired the personal skills in arms and horsemanship expected of a young man of his position. His were the manners, too, of the ideal chevalier, both in grace and in a knightly enthusiasm for the heroic action and the heroic gesture. He had a high conception of public service. And in him there flowered, along with all these tokens of loyalty to the

great principle of *noblesse oblige,* the new humanism of the Renaissance. Sidney was a student of literature; had he been a poor boy, unmarked at Oxford except by his intellectual brilliance, he would perhaps have devoted to scholarship a life that might have lasted longer. As it was, he wrote some of the best sonnets in English and an exposition of the importance of poetry, parts of which are no less valuable today than when he penned it. Like Surrey, he was a "courtly maker," the finest of the many who adorned the Tudor courts. But above all he was a pure and noble spirit.

In his eighteenth year Sidney left Oxford without a degree and went to the Continent, where he stayed three years. Paris came first, and he was living at the English embassy when the Massacre of St. Bartholomew shocked all Protestant Europe. Sidney was speedily dispatched to Germany; doubtless his experience in Paris fortified him in his Protestantism. His travels—they also included Austria, Hungary, Italy, Poland, and the Low Countries—brought him more closely in touch with both the Renaissance and the Reformation. In those days such journeying by a serious-minded youth involved a good deal more than satisfying a tourist's curiosity; it was the rounding out of his education. For a young courtier, special objects were the acquirement of foreign languages and a knowledge of European politics. Sidney made long sojourns in

---

[58] As.   [59] Mask.

[60] Not to mind it.   [61] May it please you.

the company of celebrated scholars, and he gained the acquaintance of numerous men of affairs.

Then he came back to England and began the courtier's life. He was only twenty-three when he was sent abroad again as special emissary to the German emperor. His was not a diplomatic career of great importance, but he had a remarkable gift for winning the confidence of statesmen and rulers. William the Silent, the heroic leader of the Dutch, was devoted to him. Sidney was now an enthusiast for the general cause of European Protestantism and hoped to aid in forming a coalition of Protestant states. His uncle Leicester was a leader of the party hostile to the Queen's proposed marriage to the Duke of Anjou and Alençon, younger brother of the French king. In 1580, after his return to England, Sidney in a letter to Elizabeth took so strong a stand against it that for a while it seemed best for him to keep away from court.

He spent most of this year of retirement in Wiltshire, at the country seat of his sister Mary, Countess of Pembroke, a patroness of poets and scholars. At Wilton, Sidney wrote at least part of his *Arcadia,* a long pastoral romance, in a way a forerunner of the modern novel but marred by too ornate a style and by the artificial conventions of prose fiction which had developed on the Continent, especially in Spain. The *Arcadia* is prose, with a number of poems scattered through it. Sidney afterwards revised and enlarged it; but it was not published till 1590, several years after his death. All of Sidney's major works were published posthumously; during his lifetime they circulated among his friends in manuscript, in accordance with the courtly convention that regarded the printing and sale of a gentleman's writings as a species of vulgarity. After its publication *Arcadia* was an immensely popular book in England for nearly a century.

Meanwhile, in 1579, a fanatical Puritan named Stephen Gosson had brought out an attack on plays and poetry under the apt title of *The School of Abuse.* Most inappropriately he had ventured to dedicate it to Sidney. Just when the latter wrote his magnificent reply, *The Defense of Poesy,* is uncertain; probably it was in the early eighties. This essay, of which a substantial portion is given below, is a remarkable blend of learning, eloquence, and charm. It is still one of the best attempts to explain the claims of poetry on the attention of all serious men. The *Defense* was not printed till 1595, when it appeared in two editions, one of which bears a variant title, *An Apology for Poetry.*

Besides the *Arcadia* and *The Defense of Poesy,* Sidney left a third work, his greatest. This is the sonnet cycle *Astrophel and Stella* (star-lover and star), probably begun about 1580, but not published till 1591 and then without authorization from the family. Since the time of Wyatt and Surrey, the Petrarchan sonnet had enjoyed a great vogue in France. There, and later on when he went to Italy, the youthful

Sidney had rediscovered its availability for English poetry. It was the posthumous publication of *Astrophel and Stella* that made Sidney one of the chief influences on Elizabethan letters, for it set off the outburst of sonnet cycles in the 1590's.

Sidney had met, probably in his twenty-first year, Penelope Devereux, the young daughter of the first Earl of Essex; to her he was eventually betrothed, but the engagement was afterwards broken and Penelope married the wealthy Lord Rich. There is no means now of telling whether Sidney was hurt or whether, like most marriages among great folk in those times, this one had been projected by the two families solely for reasons of property, not love. Sidney may have fallen in love with Penelope after her marriage. She is almost certainly the Stella of the sonnets (if not, the persistence with which he plays on the word "rich" in sonnets 24 and 37 is hard to account for), and one of their recurring themes is the bitterness of love recognized too late. Unfortunately, one can rarely be certain whether an Elizabethan sonnet is a poetical exercise in the fashionable genre or whether it comes from the heart. Many of Sidney's sonnets have every appearance of coming straight from the heart, but it is the business of a poet who writes sonnets to give that impression. We shall discuss this problem again when we come to Shakespeare's sonnets. All one can say of Sidney's is that the best are very beautiful poems, which speak of love, probably that of the poet for Penelope Rich, but possibly only making of that episode an excuse for writing idealistically of love. If the last of these possibilities should chance to be the right one, we should be wrong if we called the sonnets insincere. We may be confident that many of them reflect some of the moods, of pain or of joy, which were a part of the experience of Sidney—and of every sensitive being who has known what it is to love.

To return from Sidney's three major works, *Arcadia,* *The Defense of Poesy,* and *Astrophel and Stella,* to his life. In 1583 he married and was knighted. His wife, at least a dozen years younger than he, was the daughter of one of Elizabeth's principal ministers, Sir Francis Walsingham. She bore a daughter in 1585.

Admired as Sidney was, he had never roused the Queen's personal interest sufficiently to gain any great employment or office. Though he sat in Parliament, and as joint Master of the Ordnance had a good deal to do with preparations for the threatened Spanish invasion, he chafed at his relative inactivity and at the Queen's indecisive foreign policy. He was projecting an expedition with Sir Francis Drake to attack the Spaniards in the New World when, toward the end of 1585, he was appointed governor of Flushing, a key town to the river system of the Scheldt. It was held by Elizabeth as security for her expenses in aid of the Dutch war of liberation. In the fall of the next year,

HENRY VIII

Hans Holbein the younger (1497-1543), the German painter of this portrait of Henry, came to England in 1528 with a letter of introduction from Erasmus to Sir Thomas More. By the 30's he had become the great portrait painter of English royalty and aristocracy. His paintings communicate the physical splendor of the Renaissance and, beyond this, from his skill at seizing character, the personalities of some of its leading figures.

ANNO · ÆTATIS · · SVÆ · XLIX ·

HAMPTON COURT

Hampton Court Palace was built about 1520 by Cardinal Wolsey, then chief minister of Henry VIII. The richness of the building and its furnishings made it a general object of wonder and envy. After Wolsey's fall in 1529 and Henry's break with Rome, it became the King's favorite palace. The architecture is in a modified style of the medieval castle, but the medallions with heads of Roman emperors, visible here, and other decorations were by Italian craftsmen, forerunners of changing styles in English building.

A
Literary Map
OF THE
BRITISH ISLES
1500-1800

A W

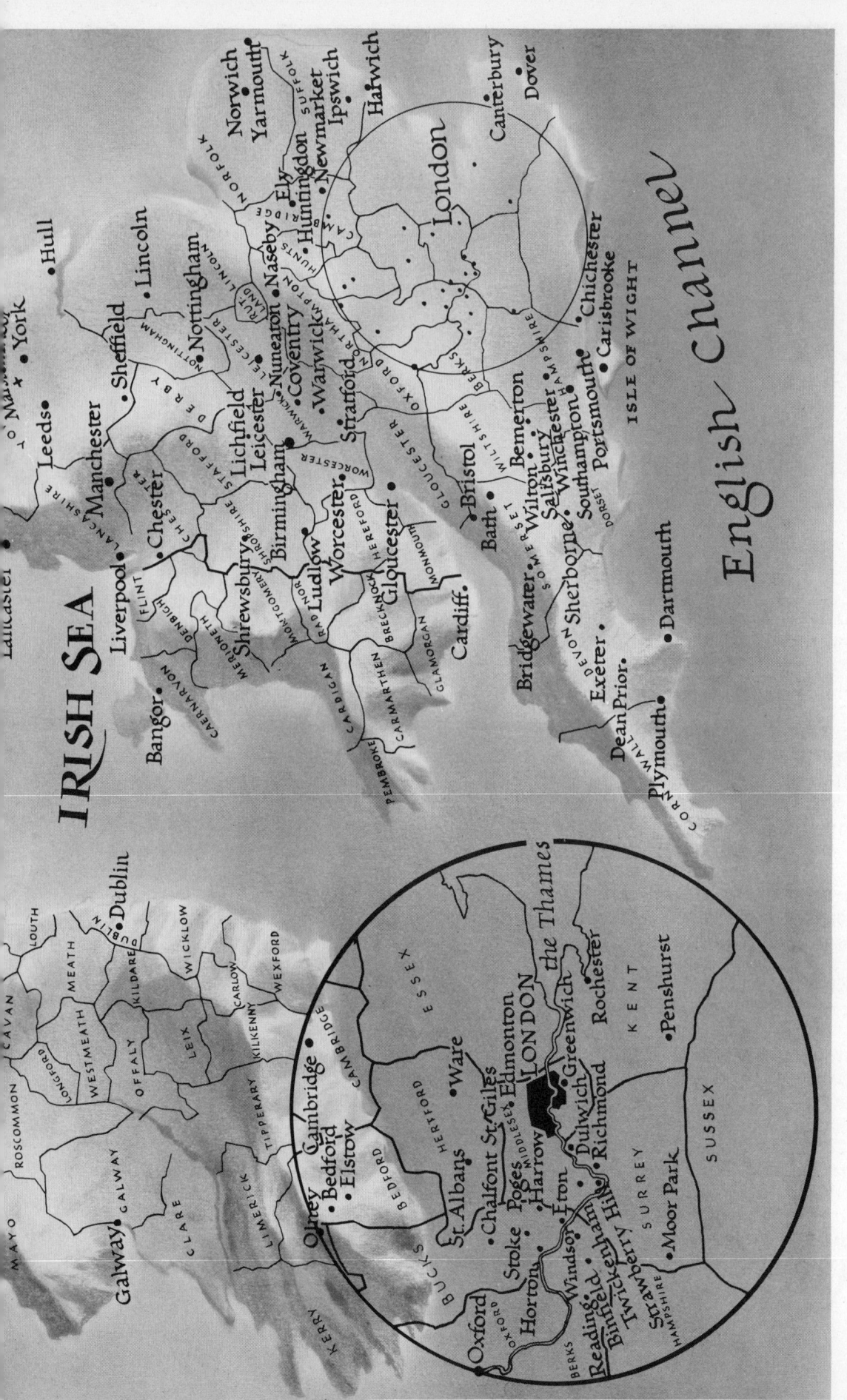

IRISH SEA

ENGLISH CHANNEL

London

English Channel

the Thames

LONDON

ISLE OF WIGHT

Norwich
Yarmouth
Newmarket
Ipswich
Harwich
Dover
Canterbury
Ely
Huntingdon
Naseby
Nuneaton
Coventry
Warwick
Stafford
Lichfield
Leicester
Nottingham
Lincoln
Hull
York
Leeds
Manchester
Sheffield
Liverpool
Chester
Shrewsbury
Birmingham
Ludlow
Worcester
Gloucester
Cardiff
Bristol
Bath
Bridgewater
Sherborne
Exeter
Dean Prior
Plymouth
Dartmouth
Wilton
Bemerton
Salisbury
Winchester
Southampton
Portsmouth
Chichester
Carisbrooke
Lancaster
Bangor
Dublin
Galway

Oundle
Cambridge
Bedford
Elstow
St. Albans
Ware
Chalfont St. Giles
Edmonton
Stoke Poges
Harrow
Eton
Windsor
Dulwich
Greenwich
Rochester
Penshurst
Richmond
Twickenham
Strawberry Hill
Binfield
Reading
Horton
Oxford
Moor Park

MAYO
ROSCOMMON
GALWAY
CLARE
KERRY
LIMERICK
TIPPERARY
LEIX
OFFALY
KILKENNY
CARLOW
WEXFORD
WICKLOW
KILDARE
DUBLIN
MEATH
WESTMEATH
LONGFORD
CAVAN
LOUTH

ESSEX
HERTFORD
BEDFORD
BUCKS
OXFORD
BERKS
HAMPSHIRE
MIDDLESEX
SURREY
KENT
SUSSEX

LANCASHIRE
FLINT
DENBIGH
CARNARVON
MERIONETH
MONTGOMERY
CARDIGAN
RADNOR
PEMBROKE
CARMARTHEN
BRECKNOCK
GLAMORGAN
MONMOUTH
HEREFORD
SHROPSHIRE
STAFFORD
CHESTER
DERBY
NOTTINGHAM
LEICESTER
RUTLAND
LINCOLN
NORFOLK
SUFFOLK
CAMBRIDGE
HUNTS
NORTHAMPTON
WARWICK
WORCESTER
GLOUCESTER
WILTSHIRE
SOMERSET
DEVON
DORSET
HAMPSHIRE
BERKS
CORNWALL

THE COVERDALE BIBLE

This first complete printed English Bible, translated in large part by Miles Coverdale, was produced on the Continent. It appeared in 1535 with a dedication to Henry VIII, who a year earlier had secured from Parliament the act separating the English Church from Rome. The title page (from a copy in the New York Public Library) is shown here.

The psalter.

al.108. d

att.27.c

ß

ßal.70.a

fue.7.a
Re.14.b

and were helped:they put their trust in the, and were not côfounded. But as for me, I am a worme and no man:a very scorne of mê and the outcast of the people. All thoy ý se me,laugh me to scorne:they shute out their lippes,and shake their heades. He trusted in God,let him delyuer him:let him helpe hî, yf he wil haue him. But thou art he that toke me out of my mothers wôbe:thou wast my hope, when I hanged yet vpon my mo thers brestes. I haue bene left vnto the euer sence I was borne,thou art my God, euê fro my mothers wombe. O go not fro me thê, for trouble is harde at honde, and here is no ne to helpe me. Greate bulles are come a boute me, fatt oxen close me in on euery syde. They gape vpon me with their mouthes,as it were a rampinge and roaringe lyon.

I am poured out like water, all my bones are out of ioynt: my hert in the myddest off my body is euen lyke melting waxe. My strength is dryed vp like a potsherde, my tunge cleueth to my goomes, and thou hast brought me into the dust of death. For dogges are come aboute me,the coũcell of ý wicked hath layed sege agaynst me. They pearsed my hondes and my fete, I might haue tolde all my bones:as for them,they stode staring and lokinge vpon me. They haue par-

The xxiiij. psalme.

Psal.101.c

A
Ioh.10.a
1.Pe.2.c

Pro.10.b

A
Deu.10.c
Iere.27.a
1.Cor.10.c
Iob.38.a

the dust,and lyue so hardly, shall fall downe before him. The sede shall serue him, and preach of the LORDE for euer. They shal come, z declare his rightuousines:vnto a peo ple that shal be borne, whô the LORDE hath made.

The XXII. A psalme of Dauid.

THe LORDE is my shepherde, I can wante nothinge. He fedeth me in a grene pasture,ãd ledeth me to a fresh water. He quickeneth my soule, z bringeth me forth in the waye of rightuousnes for his names sake. Though I shulde walke now in the valley of the shadowe of death, yet I feare no euell,for thou art with me:thy staffe z thy shepehoke côforte me. Thou prepa rest a table before me agaynst mine enemies: thou anoyntest my heade with oyle, z fyllest my cuppe full. Oh let thy louynge kyndnes z mercy felowe me all the dayes off my life, that I maye dwell in the house off the LOR DE for euer.

The XXIII. A psalme of Dauid.

THe earth is the LORDES, z all that therin is:the côpase of the worlde, ãd all ý dwell therin. For he hath foû ded it vpô the sees, z buylded it vpon the flou des. Who shal go vp in to the hill off the LORDE:Or,who shal remayne in his holy

Above is a portion of the page containing the Twenty-third Psalm (here numbered XXII because Psalms 9 and 10 are printed together as 9, in accordance with a practice of long standing). The book is printed in black-letter type, which was used for all English books until well into the sixteenth century, for Bibles until well into the seventeenth century, and for law books and Acts of Parliament until late in the eighteenth century.

1586, in a minor operation at Zutphen, Sidney was mortally wounded. He lingered on for nearly a month, setting a superb example of calmness and fortitude. Then he died, and all Europe mourned. "It was accounted a sin," says a contemporary account, "for any gentleman of quality, for many months after, to appear at court or City in any light or gaudy apparel."

The standard edition of Sidney's works was edited by A. Feuillerat (4 vols., 1912–26). There is a separate edition of *The Defense of Poesy,* with annotations, by A. S. Cook

(1890). Fulke Greville's life of Sidney is available in a modern reprint (1907); it is generally reckoned the earliest piece of good biography in English. There is a life and general study by Mona Wilson (*Sir Philip Sidney,* 1931), and another, more formidable but better documented, by M. W. Wallace (*The Life of Sir Philip Sidney,* 1915). For the background of Sidney's views as a critic, see J. E. Spingarn's *A History of Literary Criticism in the Renaissance* (revised ed., 1912) and K. O. Myrick's *Sir Philip Sidney as a Literary Craftsman* (1935).

Sir Philip Sidney

from ASTROPHEL AND STELLA

1

Loving in truth, and fain in verse my love to show,
That she, dear she, might take some pleasure of my pain
(Pleasure might cause her read, reading might make her
    know,
Knowledge might pity win, and pity grace obtain),
I sought fit words to paint the blackest face of woe,   5
Studying inventions fine, her wits to entertain,
Oft turning others' leaves, to see if thence would flow
Some fresh and fruitful shower upon my sunburnt brain.
But words came halting[1] forth, wanting Invention's stay;[2]
Invention, Nature's child, fled stepdame Study's blows;   10
And others' feet[3] still[4] seemed but strangers in my way.
Thus, great with child to speak, and helpless in my throes,
Biting my truant pen, beating myself for spite,
"Fool," said my Muse to me, "look in thy heart, and
    write!"

3

Let dainty wits cry on the Sisters nine,[5]
That, bravely masked, their fancies may be told;
Or Pindar's apes[6] flaunt in their phrases fine,
Enameling with flowers[7] their thoughts of gold;
Or else let them in stately glory shine,   5
Ennobling new-found tropes[8] with problems[9] old;
Or with strange similes[10] enrich each line,
Of herbs or beasts which Inde or Afric hold.
For me, in sooth,[11] no Muse but one I know;
Phrases and problems from my reach do grow,   10
And strange things cost too dear for my poor sprites:[12]
How then? even thus. In Stella's face I read

---

[1] Limping.   [2] Support.   [3] I.e., metrical works, poems.
[4] Ever.   [5] Appeal to the Muses.
[6] Imitators of Pindar, the Greek poet of the fifth century B.C.
[7] Flowers of rhetoric, figures of speech.   [8] Figures of speech.
[9] Subjects.   [10] Like those of Lyly and other euphuistic writers.
[11] Truth.   [12] Spirits.

What Love and Beauty be. Then all my deed
But copying is, what in her Nature writes.

14

Alas, have I not pain enough, my friend,
Upon whose breast a fiercer gripe doth tire[13]
Than did on him who first stole down the fire,[14]
While Love on me doth all his quiver spend—
But with your rhubarb words you must contend,   5
To grieve me worse, in saying that Desire
Doth plunge my well-formed soul even in the mire
Of sinful thoughts, which do in ruin end?
If that be sin which doth the manners frame,
Well stayed with truth in word, and faith of deed,   10
Ready of wit, and fearing nought but shame—
If that be sin which in fixed hearts doth breed
A loathing of all loose unchastity,
Then love is sin, and let me sinful be.

15

You that do search for every purling spring
Which from the ribs of old Parnassus[15] flows,
And every flower, not sweet perhaps, which grows
Near thereabout, into your poems wring;
You that do dictionary method bring   5
Into your rimes, running in rattling rows;
You that poor Petrarch's long-deceasèd woes
With newborn sighs and denizened[16] wit do sing:
You take wrong ways; those far-fet[17] helps be such
As do bewray a want of inward touch,[18]   10
And, sure, at length stolen goods do come to light;
But if, both for your love and skill, your name
You seek to nurse at fullest breasts of Fame,
Stella behold, and then begin to indite!

---

[13] Vulture doth tear.
[14] Prometheus, the Titan who gave man fire, wh___he stole from heaven. [15] The Greek mountain sacred to Ap___the Muses.
[16] Naturalized; i.e., imported, borrowed from ___
[17] Farfetched.   [18] Emotion.

31

With how sad steps, O Moon, thou climb'st the skies!
How silently, and with how wan a face!
What, may it be that even in heavenly place
That busy archer his sharp arrows tries?
Sure, if that long-with-love-acquainted eyes   5
Can judge of love, thou feel'st a lover's case;
I read it in thy looks; thy languished grace,
To me, that feel the like, thy state descries.
Then, even of fellowship, O Moon, tell me,
Is constant love deemed there but want of wit?[19]   10
Are beauties there as proud as here they be?
Do they above love to be loved, and yet
Those lovers scorn whom that love doth possess?
Do they call virtue there ungratefulness?[20]

41

Having this day my horse, my hand, my lance
Guided so well that I obtained the prize,
Both by the judgment of the English eyes
And of some sent from that sweet enemy, France,
Horsemen my skill in horsemanship advance,[21]   5
Townfolks my strength; a daintier judge applies
His praise to sleight,[22] which from good use[23] doth rise;
Some lucky wits impute it but to chance;
Others, because of[24] both sides I do take
My blood from them who did excel in this,   10
Think Nature me a man-at-arms did make.
How far they shot awry! The true cause is,
Stella looked on, and from her heavenly face
Sent forth the beams which made so fair my race.

74

I never drank of Aganippe[25] well,
Nor never did in shade of Tempe[26] sit;
And Muses scorn with vulgar brains to dwell—
Poor layman I, for sacred rites unfit.
Some do I hear of poets' fury[27] tell,   5
But, God wot,[28] wot not what they mean by it;
And this I swear by blackest brook of hell,
I am no pickpurse of another's wit.
How falls it then, that with so smooth an ease
My thoughts I speak; and what I speak doth flow   10

In verse; and that my verse best wits doth please?
Guess we the cause! What, is it this? Fie, no!
Or so?[29] Much less.[30] How then? Sure thus it is:
My lips are sweet, inspired with Stella's kiss.

90

Stella, think not that I by verse seek fame,
Who seek, who hope, who love, who live but thee:
Thine eyes my pride, thy lips my history—
If thou praise not, all other praise is shame.
Nor so ambitious am I as to frame   5
A nest for my young praise in laurel[31] tree;
In truth, I swear I wish not there should be
Graved in my epitaph a poet's name.
Nor, if I would, could I just title make,
That any laud thereof to me should grow,   10
Without my plumes from others' wings I take—[32]
For nothing from my wit or will doth flow,
Since all my words thy beauty doth endite,
And Love doth hold my hand, and makes me write.

LEAVE ME, O LOVE

The following sonnet, a noble one, is not from *Astrophel
and Stella,* with which it is in sharp conflict. What was
Sidney's final opinion? That is a natural but an unanswerable question. Nor would the answer, if we knew it, be of
much importance, however it might gratify our curiosity.
Every great poem reflects a mood of the poet or a facet of
life; and each is true, or has its moment of truth.

Leave me, O Love, which reachest but to dust,
And thou, my mind, aspire to higher things!
Grow rich in that which never taketh rust:
Whatever fades, but fading pleasure brings.
Draw in thy beams, and humble all thy might   5
To that sweet yoke where lasting freedoms be,
Which breaks the clouds and opens forth the light
That doth both shine and give us sight to see.
Oh, take fast hold! Let that light be thy guide
In this small course which birth draws out to death; 10
And think how evil[33] becometh him to slide
Who seeketh heaven, and comes of heavenly breath.
Then farewell, world! thy uttermost I see.
Eternal Love, maintain thy life in me!

---

[19] Intelligence, good sense.
[20] Do they consider ingratitude a virtue?   [21] Praise.
[22] Dexterity.   [23] Practice.   [24] On.
[25] Aganippe's. She was a nymph and thus one of the minor divinities of nature; her spring at the foot of Mt. Helicon in central
Greece was sacred to the Muses.
[26] A beautiful valley in Thessaly, supposed to be a favorite spot of
Apollo's.
[27] The inspired frenzy anciently ascribed to poets.   [28] Knows.

[29] Such and such.
[30] I.e., still further from the truth.
[31] Sacred to Apollo, the god of poetry.
[32] I.e., unless I borrow from other poets.
[33] Then pronounced as a monosyllable: *eel,* almost *ill.*

Sidney begins with an account of the antiquity of poetry, "which, in the noblest nations and languages that are known, hath been the first light-giver to ignorance," and of the esteem in which poetry was held by the ancient Greeks and Romans as indicated by the names they bestowed upon the poet (ποιητής = maker, *vates* = prophet). His explanation of the appropriateness of the Greek term, with which our excerpt begins, makes clear that in this essay he is using the words *poetry* and *poesy* to designate imaginative literature in general.

THE GREEKS called him[1] ποιητήν,[2] which name hath, as the most excellent, gone through other languages. It cometh of this word ποιεῖν,[3] which is "to make"; wherein I know not whether by luck or wisdom we Englishmen have met with the Greeks in calling him a "maker."[4] Which name how high and incomparable a title it is, I had rather were known by marking the scope of other sciences than by any partial allegation.

There is no art delivered unto mankind that hath not the works of nature for his principal object, without which they could not consist, and on which they so depend as they become actors and players, as it were, of what nature will have set forth. So doth the astronomer look upon the stars and, by that he seeth, set down what order nature hath taken therein. So doth the geometrician and arithmetician in their divers sorts of quantities. So doth the musician in times tell you which by nature agree, which not. The natural philosopher thereon hath his name; and the moral philosopher standeth upon the natural virtues, vices, and passions of man, and "Follow nature," saith he therein, "and thou shalt not err." The lawyer saith what men have determined, the historian what men have done. The grammarian speaketh only of the rules of speech; and the rhetorician and logician, considering what in nature will soonest prove and persuade, thereon give artificial[5] rules, which still are compassed within the circle of a question, according to the proposed matter. The physician weigheth the nature of man's body, and the nature of things helpful or hurtful unto it. And the metaphysic,[6] though it be in the second and abstract notions, and therefore be counted supernatural, yet doth he, indeed, build upon the depth of nature.

Only the poet, disdaining to be tied to any such subjection, lifted up with the vigor of his own invention, doth grow, in effect, into another nature, in making things either better than nature bringeth forth, or, quite anew, forms such as never were in nature, as the heroes, demigods, cyclops, chimeras, furies, and such like; so as[7] he goeth hand in hand with nature, not enclosed within the narrow warrant of her gifts, but freely ranging within the zodiac of his own wit. Nature never set forth the earth in so rich tapestry as divers poets have done—neither with so pleasant rivers, fruitful trees, sweet-smelling flowers, nor whatsoever else may make the too-much-loved earth more lovely. Her world is brazen; the poets only deliver[8] a golden.

But let those things alone, and go to man—for whom as the other things are, so it seemeth in him her uttermost cunning is employed—and know whether she have brought forth so true a lover as Theagenes,[9] so constant a friend as Pylades;[10] so valiant a man as Orlando;[11] so right a prince as Xenophon's Cyrus;[12] so excellent a man every way as Vergil's Aeneas? Neither let this be jestingly conceived, because the works of the one be essential, the other in imitation or fiction; for any understanding knoweth the skill of each artificer standeth in that *idea,* or fore-conceit of the work, and not in the work itself. And that the poet hath that *idea* is manifest, by delivering them forth in such excellency as he hath imagined them. Which delivering forth, also, is not wholly imaginative, as we are wont to say by[13] them that build castles in the air; but so far substantially it worketh, not only to make a Cyrus, which had been but a particular excellency, as Nature might have done, but to bestow a Cyrus upon the world to make many Cyruses, if they will learn aright why and how that maker made him. Neither let it be deemed too saucy a comparison to balance the highest point of man's wit with the efficacy of nature; but rather give right honor to the heavenly Maker of that maker, who, having made man to his own likeness, set him beyond and over all the works of that second nature. Which in nothing he showeth

---

[7] That.   [8] Tell of.
[9] A character in a Greek romance by Heliodorus (the "Ethiopic History"), probably of the third century A.D.
[10] The faithful friend of Orestes in Greek tragedies dealing with vengeance for the murder of Agamemnon.
[11] Or Roland, the knight of Charlemagne, in epic story. He is the hero of Ariosto's *Orlando Furioso.*
[12] The hero of Xenophon's *Cyropaedia* (fifth century B.C.).
[13] Concerning.

---

[1] The poet.   [2] Pronounced *poi-ai-taín* (*ai* as in *rain*).
[3] Pronounced *poi-aín.*
[4] The word was a favorite with the Scottish Chaucerians of the fifteenth century.   [5] Artful.
[6] Metaphysician, philosopher.

so much as in poetry; when, with the force of a divine breath, he bringeth things forth surpassing her doings, with no small arguments to the incredulous of that first accursed fall of Adam; since our erected wit maketh us know what perfection is, and yet our infected will keepeth us from reaching unto it. But these arguments will by few be understood, and by fewer granted; thus much I hope will be given me, that the Greeks, with some probability of reason, gave him the name above all names of learning.

Now let us go to a more ordinary opening[14] of him, that the truth may be the more palpable; and so, I hope, though we get not so unmatched a praise as the etymology of his names will grant, yet his very description, which no man will deny, shall not justly be barred from a principal commendation.

Poesy, therefore, is an art of imitation; for so Aristotle termeth it in the word μίμησις;[15] that is to say, a representing, counterfeiting, or figuring forth: to speak metaphorically, a speaking picture, with this end, to teach and delight.[16]

Of this have been three general kinds: the chief, both in antiquity and excellency, were they that did imitate the inconceivable excellencies of God. Such were David in his Psalms; Solomon in his Song of Songs, in his Ecclesiastes, and Proverbs; Moses[17] and Deborah[18] in their hymns; and the writer of Job; which, beside other, the learned Emanuel Tremellius and Franciscus Junius[19] do entitle the poetical part of the Scripture; against these none will speak that hath the Holy Ghost in due holy reverence. In this kind, though in a full wrong divinity,[20] were Orpheus, Amphion,[21] Homer in his hymns, and many other, both Greeks and Romans. And this poesy must be used by whosoever will follow St. James his counsel in singing psalms when they are merry,[22] and I know is used with the fruit of comfort by some when, in sorrowful pangs of their death-bringing sins, they find the consolation of the never-leaving goodness.

The second kind is of them that deal with matters philosophical: either moral, as Tyrtaeus, Phocylides,

Cato;[23] or natural, as Lucretius,[24] and Vergil's Georgics;[25] or astronomical, as Manilius[26] and Pontanus;[27] or historical, as Lucan;[28] which who mislike, the fault is in their judgment, quite out of taste, and not in the sweet food of sweetly uttered knowledge.

But because this second sort is wrapped within the fold of the proposed subject, and takes not the free course of his own invention, whether they properly be poets or no let grammarians dispute; and go to the third, indeed right poets, of whom chiefly this question ariseth; betwixt whom and these second is such a kind of difference as betwixt the meaner sort of painters, who counterfeit only such faces as are set before them, and the more excellent, who having no law but wit, bestow that in colors upon you which is fittest for the eye to see: as the constant though lamenting look of Lucretia,[29] when she punished in herself another's fault; wherein he painteth not Lucretia, whom he never saw, but painteth the outward beauty of such a virtue. For these third be they which most properly do imitate to teach and delight; and to imitate, borrow nothing of what is, hath been, or shall be; but range, only reined with learned discretion, into the divine consideration of what may be, and should be. These be they that, as the first and most noble sort, may justly be termed *vates;* so these are waited on in the excellentest languages and best understandings, with the foredescribed name of poets. For these, indeed, do merely make to imitate, and imitate both to delight and teach, and delight to move men to take that goodness in hand which, without delight, they would fly as from a stranger, and teach to make them know that goodness whereunto they are moved; which being the noblest scope to which ever any learning was directed, yet want there not idle tongues to bark at them.

These be subdivided into sundry more special denominations. The most notable be the heroic, lyric, tragic, comic, satiric, iambic, elegiac, pastoral, and certain others, some of these being termed according

---

14 Exposition.
15 Pronounced *mí-mai-sis* (*i* as in *it*).
16 In this statement of the poet's aims, as well as in the categories of poetry, Sidney follows the neoclassical critics of the Italian Renaissance, especially Scaliger (1540–1609).
17 See Exodus 15:1–9 and Deuteronomy 32:1–43.
18 See Judges 5.
19 Biblical scholars, contemporaries of Sidney.
20 An erroneous theology.
21 A legendary Greek poet and musician.
22 James 5:13.

23 Dionysius Cato, reputed author of an ancient collection of maxims much read in the Middle Ages and Renaissance. Tyrtaeus and Phocylides were Greek poets of the seventh and sixth centuries B.C.
24 A Roman philosophical poet of the first century A.D. who wrote *On the Nature of Things.*
25 Poems describing and praising country life.
26 A Roman poet of the first century A.D.
27 A fifteenth-century Italian poet and scholar.
28 Author (first century A.D.) of the epic *Pharsalia,* on the civil war between Pompey and Julius Caesar.
29 Lucrece, the Roman matron who killed herself after rape by Tarquinius Sextus.

to the matter they deal with, some by the sort of verse they liked best to write in; for indeed the greatest part of poets have appareled their poetical inventions in that numberous kind of writing which is called verse. Indeed but appareled, verse being but an ornament and no cause to poetry, since there have been many most excellent poets that never versified, and now swarm many versifiers that need never answer to the name of poets. For Xenophon, who did imitate so excellently as to give us *effigiem justi imperii*—the portraiture of a just empire under the name of Cyrus[30] (as Cicero saith of him)—made therein an absolute heroical poem; so did Heliodorus in his sugared[31] invention of that picture of love in Theagenes and Chariclea;[32] and yet both these wrote in prose. Which I speak to show that it is not riming and versing that maketh a poet—no more than a long gown maketh an advocate, who, though he pleaded in armor, should be an advocate and no soldier—but it is that feigning notable images of virtues, vices, or what else, with that delightful teaching, which must be the right describing note to know a poet by. Although indeed the senate of poets hath chosen verse as their fittest raiment, meaning, as in matter they passed all in all, so in manner to go beyond them—not speaking, table-talk fashion, or like men in a dream, words as they chanceably fall from the mouth, but peising[33] each syllable of each word by just proportion, according to the dignity of the subject.

Now therefore it shall not be amiss, first to weigh this latter sort of poetry by his works, and then by his parts; and if in neither of these anatomies[34] he be condemnable, I hope we shall obtain a more favorable sentence. This purifying of wit, this enriching of memory, enabling of judgment, and enlarging of conceit,[35] which commonly we call learning, under what name soever it come forth or to what immediate end soever it be directed, the final end is to lead and draw us to as high a perfection as our degenerate souls, made worse by their clay lodgings, can be capable of. This, according to the inclination of man, bred many-formed impressions. For some that thought this felicity principally to be gotten by knowledge, and no knowledge to be so high or heavenly as acquaintance with the stars, gave themselves to astronomy; others, persuading themselves to be demigods if they knew the causes of things, be-

came natural and supernatural philosophers. Some an admirable delight drew to music, and some the certainty of demonstration to the mathematics; but all, one and other, having this scope:—to know; and by knowledge to lift up the mind from the dungeon of the body to the enjoying his own divine essence. But when by the balance[36] of experience it was found that the astronomer, looking to the stars, might fall into a ditch, that the inquiring philosopher might be blind in himself, and the mathematician might draw forth a straight line with a crooked heart; then lo! did proof, the overruler of opinions, make manifest that all these are but serving sciences, which, as they have each a private end in themselves, so yet are they all directed to the highest end of the mistress-knowledge, by the Greeks called ἀρχιτεκτονική,[37] which stands, as I think, in the knowledge of a man's self, in the ethic and politic consideration, with the end of well-doing, and not of well-knowing only—even as the saddler's next[38] end is to make a good saddle, but his further end to serve a nobler faculty, which is horsemanship; so the horseman's to soldiery; and the soldier not only to have the skill, but to perform the practice of a soldier. So that the ending end of all earthly learning being virtuous action, those skills that most serve to bring forth that have a most just title to be princes over all the rest; wherein, if we can show, the poet is worthy to have it before any other competitors.

Among whom as principal challengers step the moral philosophers, whom, methinks, I see coming towards me with a sullen gravity, as though they could not abide vice by daylight, rudely clothed for to witness outwardly their contempt of outward things; with books in their hands against glory, whereto they set their names; sophistically speaking against subtlety, and angry with any man in whom they see the foul fault of anger. These men, casting largess as they go of definitions, divisions, and distinctions, with a scornful interrogative do soberly ask whether it be possible to find any path so ready to lead a man to virtue as that which teacheth what virtue is, and teacheth it not only by delivering forth his[39] very being, his causes and effects, but also by making known his enemy, vice, which must be destroyed, and his cumbersome servant, passion, which must be mastered; by showing the generalities that contain it, and the specialities that are derived from it; lastly, by plain setting down how it extends itself, out of the limits of a man's own little world, to the

---

30 See note 12, above.
31 Charming.   32 See note 9, above.
33 Poising, giving weight to.   34 Dissections.
35 Imagination.

36 Scales.
37 Architectonics. Sidney proceeds to define his meaning.
38 Nearest, immediate.   39 Explaining its.

government of families and maintaining of public societies.

The historian scarcely gives leisure to the moralist to say so much, but that he (loaden with old mouse-eaten records, authorizing himself, for the most part, upon other histories, whose greatest authorities are built upon the notable foundation hearsay, having much ado to accord differing writers, and to pick truth out of partiality; better acquainted with a thousand years ago than with the present age, and yet better knowing how this world goes than how his own wit runs; curious for antiquities, and inquisitive of novelties, a wonder to young folks, and a tyrant in table-talk) denieth, in a great chafe, that any man for teaching of virtue and virtuous actions is comparable to him. "I am *Testis temporum, lux veritatis, vita memoriae, magistra vitae, nuntia vetustatis*.[40] The philosopher," saith he, "teacheth a disputative virtue, but I do an active. His virtue is excellent in the dangerless academy of Plato; but mine showeth forth her honorable face in the battles of Marathon, Pharsalia, Poitiers,[41] and Agincourt. He teacheth virtue by certain abstract considerations; but I only bid you follow the footing of them that have gone before you. Old-aged experience goeth beyond the fine-witted philosopher; but I give the experience of many ages. Lastly, if he make the songbook, I put the learner's hand to the lute; and if he be the guide, I am the light." Then would he allege you innumerable examples, confirming story by stories, how much the wisest senators and princes have been directed by the credit of history, as Brutus,[42] Alphonsus of Aragon[43]—and who not, if need be? At length, the long line of their disputation makes a point in this: that the one giveth the precept, and the other the example.

Now whom shall we find, since the question standeth for the highest form[44] in the school of learning, to be moderator? Truly, as me seemeth, the poet; and if not a moderator, even the man that ought to carry the title from them both, and much more from all other serving sciences. Therefore compare we the poet with the historian, and with the moral philosopher; and if he go beyond them both,

no other human skill can match him. For as for the divine, with all reverence, he is ever to be excepted; not only for having his scope as far beyond any of these as eternity exceedeth a moment, but even for passing each of these in themselves. And for[45] the lawyer, though *Jus*[46] be the daughter of Justice, the chief of virtues, yet because he seeks to make men good rather *formidine poenae* than *virtutis amore*[47] (or, to say righter, doth not endeavor to make men good, but that their evil hurt not others, having no care, so[48] he be a good citizen, how bad a man he be), therefore, as our wickedness maketh him necessary, and necessity maketh him honorable, so is he not in the deepest truth to stand in rank with these, who all endeavor to take naughtiness[49] away and plant goodness even in the secretest cabinet of our souls. And these four are all that any way deal in the consideration of men's manners,[50] which being the supreme knowledge, they that best breed it deserve the best commendation.

The philosopher, therefore, and the historian are they which would win the goal, the one by precept, the other by example; but both, not having both, do both halt. For the philosopher, setting down with thorny arguments the bare rule, is so hard of utterance and so misty to be conceived that one that hath no other guide but him shall wade in him till he be old, before he shall find sufficient cause to be honest. For his knowledge standeth so upon the abstract and general that happy is that man who may understand him, and more happy that can apply what he doth understand. On the other side, the historian, wanting the precept, is so tied, not to what should be but to what is, to the particular truth of things and not to the general reason of things, that his example draweth no necessary consequence, and therefore a less fruitful doctrine.

Now doth the peerless poet perform both; for whatsoever the philosopher saith should be done, he gives a perfect picture of it in someone by whom he presupposeth it was done, so as he coupleth the general notion with the particular example. A perfect picture, I say; for he yieldeth to the powers of the mind an image of that whereof the philosopher bestoweth but a wordish description, which doth neither strike, pierce, nor possess the sight of the soul so much as that other doth. For as, in outward things, to a man that had never seen an elephant or a rhinoceros, who should tell him most exquisitely all their

---

[40] Witness of the times, light of truth, life of memory, mistress of life, messenger of antiquity. (Cicero, *On Oratory*.)

[41] Victories of the Athenians against the Persians, of Julius Caesar against Pompey the Great, and of the English against the French in 1356 and 1415.

[42] Marcus Junius Brutus (d. 42 B.C.). The reference is probably not to his part in the assassination of Caesar but to his reading habits when campaigning.

[43] Alphonsus V (d. 1454). This Renaissance monarch was a friend of learning.   [44] Grade.

[45] As for.   [46] Law.

[47] Rather from fear of punishment than from love of virtue. (Cf. Horace, *Epistles*, I, xvi.)   [48] Provided that.

[49] Wickedness.   [50] Conduct.

shape, color, bigness, and particular marks; or of a gorgeous palace, an architector,[51] who, declaring the full beauties, might well make the hearer able to repeat, as it were by rote, all he had heard: yet should never satisfy his inward conceit with being witness to itself of a true, lively knowledge; but the same man, as soon as he might see those beasts well painted, or that house well in model, should straightways grow, without need of any description, to a judicial comprehending of them: so no doubt the philosopher, with his learned definitions, be it of virtues or vices, matters of public policy or private government, replenisheth the memory with many infallible grounds of wisdom, which notwithstanding lie dark before the imaginative and judging power, if they be not illuminated or figured forth by the speaking picture of poesy.

Tully[52] taketh much pains, and many times not without poetical helps, to make us know the force love of our country hath in us. Let us but hear old Anchises[53] speaking in the midst of Troy's flames, or see Ulysses, in the fullness of all Calypso's[54] delights, bewail his absence from barren and beggarly Ithaca. Anger, the Stoics said, was a short madness. Let but Sophocles[55] bring you Ajax on a stage, killing and whipping sheep and oxen, thinking them the army of Greeks, with their chieftains Agamemnon and Menelaus, and tell me if you have not a more familiar insight into anger, than finding in the schoolmen his genus and difference.[56] See whether wisdom and temperance in Ulysses and Diomedes, valor in Achilles,[57] friendship in Nisus and Euryalus,[58] even to an ignorant man carry not an apparent shining. And, contrarily, the remorse of conscience in Oedipus;[59] the soon-repenting pride of Agamemnon;[60] the self-devouring cruelty in his father Atreus;[61] the violence of ambition in the two

Theban brothers;[62] the sour sweetness of revenge in Medea;[63] and, to fall lower, the Terentian Gnatho[64] and our Chaucer's Pandar[65] so expressed that we now use their names to signify their trades. And finally, all virtues, vices, and passions so, in their own natural states, laid to the view, that we seem not to hear of them but clearly to see through them.

But even in the most excellent determination of goodness, what philosopher's counsel can so readily direct a prince, as the feigned Cyrus in Xenophon? or a virtuous man in all fortunes, as Aeneas in Vergil? or a whole commonwealth, as the way of Sir Thomas More's *Utopia*?[66] I say the way, because where Sir Thomas More erred it was the fault of the man and not of the poet; for that way of patterning a commonwealth was most absolute,[67] though he perchance hath not so absolutely performed it.[68] For the question is, whether the feigned image of poesy or the regular instruction of philosophy hath the more force in teaching. Wherein if the philosophers have more rightly showed themselves philosophers than the poets have attained to the high top of their profession—as, in truth,

Mediocribus esse poetis
Non dei, non homines, non concessere columnae—[69]

it is, I say again, not the fault of the art, but that by few men that art can be accomplished. Certainly, even our Saviour Christ could as well have given the moral commonplaces of uncharitableness and humbleness as the divine narration of Dives and Lazarus,[70] or of disobedience and mercy as that heavenly discourse of the lost child and the gracious father,[71] but that his through-searching wisdom knew the estate[72] of Dives burning in hell, and of Lazarus in Abraham's bosom, would more constantly, as it were, inhabit both the memory and judgment. Truly, for myself, meseems, I see before mine eyes the lost child's disdainful prodigality turned to envy a swine's dinner; which by the learned divines are thought not historical acts, but instructing parables.

---

[51] Architect.

[52] Marcus Tullius Cicero (d. 43 B.C.), the Roman statesman and author.

[53] Father of Aeneas, who carried him from burning Troy. See *Aeneid*, II, 634–50.

[54] The sea nymph who detained Ulysses on his way home to the island of Ithaca after the fall of Troy. See *Odyssey*, V, 149–58.

[55] In his *Ajax*.   [56] Distinguishing mark.

[57] Three of the most famous of the Greek heroes in the *Iliad*.

[58] Two friends who die together in the *Aeneid* (IX, 176–82, 433–45).

[59] In Sophocles's *Oedipus the King*, one of the greatest of all plays. The hero finally learns that certain acts of his in the past, which he supposed guiltless, were actually horrible crimes.

[60] In Aeschylus's *Agamemnon*. His pride is partly responsible for his murder.

[61] Mentioned in the *Agamemnon* and in other Greek and Roman tragedies. Thyestes having seduced the wife of his brother Atreus, the latter takes vengeance by killing his nephews and serving their father with their flesh at a banquet.

[62] Eteocles and Polynices, in Aeschylus's *Seven against Thebes*. Unwilling to share the throne, these brothers finally kill each other.

[63] In the great tragedy of Euripides, so entitled.

[64] A parasite in Terence's *Eunuch*. Hence *gnathonic*, flattering.

[65] Pandarus in *Troilus and Criseyde*.   [66] See p. 221, above.

[67] Perfect.

[68] A reference to More's break with Henry VIII, Elizabeth's father, when he was chancellor. It cost him his head.

[69] Mediocrity in poets is condemned by gods, men, and booksellers. (Horace, *Art of Poetry*.)   [70] Luke 16:19–31.

[71] The parable of the prodigal son (Luke 15:11–32).

[72] State, condition.

For conclusion, I say the philosopher teacheth, but he teacheth obscurely, so as the learned only can understand him; that is to say, he teacheth them that are already taught. But the poet is the food for the tenderest stomachs; the poet is, indeed, the right[73] popular philosopher. Whereof Aesop's tales give good proof; whose pretty allegories, stealing under the formal tales of beasts, makes many, more beastly than beasts, begin to hear the sound of virtue from those dumb speakers.

But now may it be alleged that, if this imagining of matters be so fit for the imagination, then must the historian needs surpass, who brings you images of true matters, such as indeed were done, and not such as fantastically[74] or falsely may be suggested to have been done. Truly, Aristotle himself, in his Discourse of Poesy,[75] plainly determineth this question, saying that poetry is φιλοσοφώτερον and σπουδαιότε-ρον,[76] that is to say, it is more philosophical and more studiously serious than history. His reason is, because poesy dealeth with καθόλου,[77] that is to say, with the universal consideration, and the history καθ' ἕκαστον,[78] the particular. "Now," saith he, "the universal weighs what is fit to be said or done, either in likelihood or necessity—which the poesy considereth in his imposed names;[79] and the particular only marketh whether Alcibiades[80] did or suffered this or that."

Thus far Aristotle. Which reason of his, as all his, is most full of reason. For, indeed, if the question were whether it were better to have a particular act truly or falsely set down, there is no doubt which is to be chosen, no more than whether you had rather have Vespasian's[81] picture right[82] as he was, or, at the painter's pleasure, nothing resembling. But if the question be, for your own use and learning, whether it be better to have it set down as it should be, or as it was, then certainly is more doctrinable[83] the feigned Cyrus in Xenophon than the true Cyrus in Justin,[84] and the feigned Aeneas in Vergil than the

right Aeneas in Dares Phrygius;[85] as, to a lady that desired to fashion her countenance to the best grace, a painter should more benefit her to portrait a most sweet face, writing Canidia upon it, than to paint Canidia as she was, who, Horace[86] sweareth, was full ill-favored. If the poet do his part aright, he will show you in Tantalus,[87] Atreus, and such like, nothing that is not to be shunned; in Cyrus, Aeneas, Ulysses, each thing to be followed; where[88] the historian, bound to tell things as things were, cannot be liberal—without[89] he will be poetical—of a perfect pattern; but, as in Alexander or Scipio[90] himself, show doings, some to be liked, some to be misliked; and then how will you discern what to follow, but by your own discretion, which you had without reading Q. Curtius?[91] And whereas a man may say, though in universal consideration of doctrine the poet prevaileth, yet that the history, in his saying such a thing was done, doth warrant a man more in that[92] he shall follow; the answer is manifest: that if he stand upon that *was,* as if he should argue because it rained yesterday therefore it should rain today, then indeed[93] hath it some advantage to a gross conceit. But if he know an example only informs[94] a conjectured likelihood, and so go by reason, the poet doth so far exceed him, as he is to frame his example to that which is most reasonable, be it in warlike, politic,[95] or private matters; where the historian in his bare *was* hath many times that which we call fortune to overrule the best wisdom. Many times he must tell events whereof he can yield no cause; and if he do, it must be poetically. . . .[96]

I conclude, therefore, that [the poet] excelleth history, not only in furnishing the mind with knowledge, but in setting it forward to that which deserves to be called and accounted good; which setting forward, and moving to well-doing, indeed setteth the laurel crown upon the poet as victorious, not only of the historian, but over the philosopher, howsoever in teaching it may be questionable. For suppose it be granted—that which I suppose with great reason may be denied—that the philosopher,

---

73 Truly.   74 Fancifully.

75 *Poetics,* chapter 9. This distinction is of the utmost importance to anyone who wishes to understand the importance of art.

76 Pronounce *filosofóteron* and *spūdióteron* (unmarked vowels short).

77 Pronounce *kathólū.*   78 Pronounce *kath hékaston.*

79 Which poetry considers under the names it gives. I.e., poetry ostensibly deals with the particular, since it gives particular names to, for example, the characters in a play; actually, however, it deals through them with the universal.

80 The Athenian politician and general (d. 404 B.C.).

81 Roman emperor (d. 79 A.D.).   82 Exactly.

83 Instructive.

84 A Roman historian of the second century A.D.

85 Reputed author of an account of the Trojan War much read and accepted as true in the Middle Ages.

86 *Satires,* I, viii; *Epodes,* v.

87 In Greek mythology. His punishment in hell is variously described as being placed close to inaccessible food and drink or near a rock which threatened to topple onto him.

88 Whereas.   89 Unless.

90 Scipio Africanus Major (d. 183 B.C.), victor over Hannibal.

91 Quintus Curtius, a Roman historian who wrote on Alexander.

92 What.   93 Imagination; i.e., to a dull or limited mind.

94 Gives form to.   95 Political.

96 A short passage has been omitted, in which Sidney gives further illustrations of his point.

in respect of his methodical proceeding, teach more perfectly than the poet, yet do I think that no man is so much φιλοφιλόσοφος[97] as to compare the philosopher in moving with the poet. And that moving is of a higher degree than teaching, it may by this appear: that it is well nigh both the cause and the effect of teaching. For who will be taught, if he be not moved with desire to be taught? And what so much good doth that teaching bring forth—I speak still of moral doctrine—as that it moveth one to do that which it doth teach? For, as Aristotle saith, it is not γνῶσις but πρᾶξις[98] must be the fruit; and how πρᾶξις cannot be, without being moved to practice, it is no hard matter to consider. The philosopher showeth you the way; he informeth you of the particularities, as well of the tediousness of the way as of the pleasant lodging you shall have when your journey is ended, as of the many by-turnings that may divert you from your way. But this is to no man but to him that will read him, and read him with attentive, studious painfulness; which constant desire, whosoever hath in him hath already passed half the hardness of the way, and therefore is beholding[99] to the philosopher but for the other half. Nay, truly, learned men have learnedly thought that where once reason hath so much overmastered passion as that the mind hath a free desire to do well, the inward light each mind hath in itself is as good as a philosopher's book, since in nature we know it is well to do well, and what is well and what is evil, although not in the words of art which philosophers bestow upon us; for out of natural conceit[1] the philosophers drew it. But to be moved to do that which we know, or to be moved with desire to know, *hoc opus, hic labor est*.[2]

Now therein of all sciences—I speak still of human[3] and according to the human conceit—is our poet the monarch. For he doth not only show the way, but giveth so sweet a prospect into the way as will entice any man to enter into it. Nay, he doth, as if your journey should lie through a fair vineyard, at the very first give you a cluster of grapes, that full of that taste you may long to pass further. He beginneth not with obscure definitions, which must blur the margent[4] with interpretations and load the memory with doubtfulness. But he cometh to you with words set in delightful proportion, either accompanied with, or prepared for, the well-enchanting skill of music; and with a tale, forsooth,[5] he cometh unto you, with a tale which holdeth children from play and old men from the chimney-corner; and, pretending no more, doth intend the winning of the mind from wickedness to virtue, even as the child is often brought to take most wholesome things, by hiding them in such other as have a pleasant taste—which, if one should begin to tell them the nature of the aloes or rhubarb[6] they should receive, would sooner take their physic at their ears than at their mouth. So is it in men, most of which are childish in the best things, till they be cradled in their graves,—glad they will be to hear the tales of Hercules, Achilles, Cyrus, Aeneas; and, hearing them, must needs hear the right description of wisdom, valor, and justice; which, if they had been barely, that is to say philosophically, set out, they would swear they be brought to school again.

That imitation whereof poetry is, hath the most conveniency to nature of all other; insomuch that, as Aristotle saith,[7] those things which in themselves are horrible, as cruel battles, unnatural monsters, are made in poetical imitation delightful. Truly, I have known men that, even with reading *Amadis de Gaule*,[8] which, God knoweth, wanteth much of a perfect poesy, have found their hearts moved to the exercise of courtesy, liberality, and especially courage. Who readeth Aeneas carrying old Anchises on his back, that wisheth not it were his fortune to perform so excellent an act?[9] Whom do not those words of Turnus move, the tale of Turnus having planted his image in the imagination,

Fugientem haec terra videbit?
Usque adeone mori miserum est?[10]

Where the philosophers, as they think scorn to delight, so must they be content little to move—saving wrangling whether *virtus*[11] be the chief or the only good, whether the contemplative or the active life do excel—which Plato and Boethius[12] well knew, and therefore made Mistress Philosophy very often borrow the masking raiment of Poesy. For even those hard-hearted, evil men who think virtue a

---

[97] A philosopher-lover. (Pronounce *filofilósofos*.)
[98] Not knowledge but practice. (Pronounce *gnôsis* and *prahxis*.) See Aristotle, *Ethics*, I, 3.   [99] Beholden, indebted.
[1] Out of their conception of nature.
[2] This is the work, this is the end. (*Aeneid*, VI, 129.)
[3] I.e., excluding theology.
[4] Margin. Such a note as this you are reading would normally appear, in an Elizabethan book, not at the foot of the page but in the margin.

[5] Indeed.   [6] Used as purgatives.   [7] *Poetics*, chap. 4.
[8] A famous Spanish or Portuguese chivalric romance of uncertain date and origin.   [9] *Aeneid*, II, 705 ff.
[10] Shall this land see [my] flight? Is it so very wretched a thing to die? (*Aeneid*, XII, 645–46.)   [11] Virtue.
[12] Roman philosopher (d. 524 A.D.).

school-name, and know no other good but *indulgere genio,*[13] and therefore despise the austere admonitions of the philosopher and feel not the inward reason they stand upon, yet will be content to be delighted, which is all the good-fellow poet seems to promise; and so steal to see the form of goodness, which seen, they cannot but love, ere themselves be aware, as if they took a medicine of cherries.

Infinite proofs of the strange effects of this poetical invention might be alleged. Only two shall serve, which are so often remembered as I think all men know them. The one of Menenius Agrippa, who, when the whole people of Rome had resolutely divided themselves from the senate, with apparent show of utter ruin, though he were, for that time, an excellent orator, came not among them upon trust either of figurative speeches or cunning insinuations, and much less with far-fet maxims of philosophy, which, especially if they were Platonic, they must have learned geometry before they could well have conceived; but, forsooth, he behaveth himself like a homely and familiar poet. He telleth them a tale, that there was a time when all the parts of the body made a mutinous conspiracy against the belly, which they thought devoured the fruits of each other's labor. They concluded they would let so unprofitable a spender starve. In the end, to be short (for the tale is notorious,[14] and as notorious that it was a tale), with punishing the belly they plagued themselves. This, applied by him, wrought such effect in the people as I never read that only words brought forth but then so sudden and so good an alteration, for upon reasonable conditions a perfect reconcilement ensued.

The other is of Nathan the prophet,[15] who, when the holy David had so far forsaken God as to confirm adultery with murther, when he was to do the tenderest office of a friend, in laying his own shame before his eyes, sent by God to call again so chosen a servant, how doth he it? But by telling of a man whose beloved lamb was ungratefully taken from his bosom. The application most divinely true, but the discourse itself feigned; which made David (I speak of the second and instrumental cause) as in a glass see his own filthiness, as that heavenly Psalm of Mercy well testifieth.

By these, therefore, examples and reasons, I think it may be manifest that the poet, with that same hand of delight, doth draw the mind more effectually than any other art doth. And so a conclusion not unfitly ensueth: that, as virtue is the most excellent resting-place for all worldly learning to make his end of, so poetry, being the most familiar to teach it, and most princely to move towards it, in the most excellent work is the most excellent workman. . . .[16]

Since, then, poetry is of all human learnings the most ancient, and of most fatherly antiquity, as from whence other learnings have taken their beginnings; since it is so universal that no learned nation doth despise it, nor barbarous nation is without it; since both Roman and Greek gave such divine names unto it, the one of prophesying, the other of making, and that indeed that name of making is fit for him, considering that where all other arts retain themselves within their subject, and receive, as it were, their being from it, the poet only, only bringeth his own stuff, and doth not learn a conceit out of a matter, but maketh matter for a conceit; since neither his description nor end containeth any evil, the thing described cannot be evil; since his effects be so good as to teach goodness, and delight the learners of it; since therein (namely in moral doctrine, the chief of all knowledges) he doth not only far pass the historian, but, for instructing, is well nigh comparable to the philosopher, for moving leaveth him behind him; since the Holy Scripture (wherein there is no uncleanness) hath whole parts in it poetical, and that even our Saviour Christ vouchsafed to use the flowers of it; since all his kinds are not only in their united forms but in their severed dissections fully commendable; I think, and think I think rightly, the laurel crown appointed for triumphant captains doth worthily, of all other learnings, honor the poet's triumph.

[*In the remainder of the essay Sidney answers specific objections raised by "poet-haters" and then surveys English poetry, of which he finds little good to say. Chaucer and Surrey are among the few who are praised: "Chaucer undoubtedly did excellently in his Troilus and Criseyde; of whom, truly, I know not whether to marvel more, either that he in that misty time could see so clearly, or that we in this clear age go so stumblingly after him. Yet had he great wants, fit to be forgiven in so reverend an antiquity. . . . And in the Earl of Surrey's lyrics, [are] many things tasting of a noble birth, and worthy of a noble mind." From his general condemnation of English drama only the impossible tragedy of Gorboduc is excepted; Sidney had too great a respect for the neoclassical rules, but on the other hand it must be remembered that he wrote before the great flowering of Elizabethan drama. His criticism of the artificiality and over-elaboration of much contemporary love-poetry and prose shows*]

---

13 To indulge one's nature.
14 Famous. See, e.g., Shakespeare's *Coriolanus*, I, i, 99 ff. Of Oriental origin, the tale became attached to legends of early Rome and was assigned to Menenius. 15 See 2 Samuel 12.

16 Sidney next examines, in a passage here omitted, the various genres of poetry and certain criticisms of them.

firmer taste. All through the Defense *there are shrewd critical strokes; and for any lover of Elizabethan literature it is fascinating to see what this highly gifted and sensitive spirit made of it. With characteristic humor he concludes, after enjoining upon the reader a proper esteem for poetry:*]

Thus doing, your name shall flourish in the printers' shops. Thus doing, you shall be most fair, most rich, most wise, most all; you shall dwell upon superlatives.[17] Thus doing, though you be *libertino patre natus,*[18] you shall suddenly grow *Herculea proles,*[19]

> Si quid mea carmina possunt.[20]

Thus doing, your soul shall be placed with Dante's Beatrix, or Vergil's Anchises.

But if (fie of such a but!) you be born so near the dull-making cataract of Nilus that you cannot hear the planetlike music of poetry; if you have so earth-creeping a mind that it cannot lift itself up to look to the sky of poetry, or rather, by a certain rustical disdain, will become such a mome[21] as to be a Momus[22] of poetry; then, though I will not wish unto you the ass's ears of Midas,[23] nor to be driven by a poet's verses, as Bubonax[24] was, to hang himself, nor to be rimed to death, as is said to be done in Ireland; yet thus much curse I must send you in the behalf of all poets: that while you live, you live in love, and never get favor for lacking skill of a sonnet; and when you die, your memory die from the earth for want of an epitaph.

An Elizabethan Garland

GOOD *anthologies are N. Ault's* ELIZABETHAN LYRICS *(3rd ed., 1949), M. W. Black's* ELIZABETHAN AND SEVENTEENTH-CENTURY LYRICS *(1938), E. K. Chambers's* THE OXFORD BOOK OF SIXTEENTH CENTURY VERSE *(1932), J. W. Hebel and H. H. Hudson's* POETRY OF THE ENGLISH RENAISSANCE, 1509-1660 *(1929), and A. H. Bullen's* LYRICS FROM THE SONG-BOOKS OF THE ELIZABETHAN AGE *(revised ed., 1889).*

Anonymous

WESTERN WIND, WHEN WILL THOU BLOW?

In the stark simplicity of its emotion this poem is reminiscent of the ballads, and in some earlier form it may have been composed considerably before the sixteenth century. It certainly antedates the reign of Elizabeth.

> Western wind, when will thou blow,
>   The small rain down can rain?
> Christ, if my love were in my arms,
>   And I in my bed again!

BACK AND SIDE GO BARE

This fine drinking song must have been written before 1575, since an inferior version appears as an entr'acte lyric in *Gammer Gurton's Needle,* a comedy printed in that year. The song may be a good deal older.

> But if that[1] I may have truly
>   Good ale my belly full,
> I shall look like one, by sweet Saint John,
>   Were shorn against the wool.[2]
> Though I go bare, take you no care—   5
>   I am nothing cold,

[17] I.e., you will be praised in such terms in the dedicatory epistles to books by poets whom you have subsidized as patron.
[18] Born of a father who was a freed slave.
[19] The offspring of Hercules.
[20] If my songs are of any avail. (*Aeneid*, IX, 446.)

[21] Buffoon; foolish person.
[22] A god personifying mocking criticism and ridicule; a carping critic.
[23] A king of Phrygia who was given ass's ears by Apollo because he preferred Pan's playing to Apollo's.
[24] The Greek sculptor Bupalus was driven by the satire of the poet Hipponax to hang himself. Sidney's memory seems to have betrayed him into combining these two names.
[1] Unless.   [2] I.e., who has been rubbed the wrong way.

I stuff my skin so full within
Of jolly good ale and old.
Back and side go bare, go bare,
Both hand and foot go cold;
But belly, God send thee good ale enough,   10
Whether it be new or old!

I cannot eat but little meat—
My stomach is not good;
But sure I think that I could drink   15
With him that weareth an hood.[3]
Drink is my life; although my wife
Sometime do chide and scold,
Yet spare I not to ply the pot
Of jolly good ale and old.   20
Back and side, etc.

I love no roast but a brown toast,
Or a crab[4] in the fire;
A little bread shall do me stead,[5]
Much bread I never desire.   25
Nor frost nor snow nor wind, I trow,[6]
Can hurt me if it wold,[7]
I am so wrapped within and lapped
With jolly good ale and old.
Back and side, etc.   30

I care right nought, I take no thought
For clothes to keep me warm;
Have I good drink, I surely think
Nothing can do me harm.
For truly than[8] I fear no man,   35
Be he never so bold,
When I am armed and throughly warmed
With jolly good ale and old.
Back and side, etc.

But now and than I curse and ban,   40
They make their ale so small.
God give them care and evil to fare!
They stry[9] the malt and all.
Such peevish pew,[10] I tell you true,
Not for a crown of gold   45
There cometh one sip within my lip,
Whether it be new or old.
Back and side, etc.

Good ale and strong maketh me among[11]
Full jocund and full light,   50
That oft I sleep and take no keep[12]
From morning until night.
Then start I up and flee to the cup—
The right[13] way on I hold;
My thirst to staunch, I fill my paunch   55
With jolly good ale and old.
Back and side, etc.

And Kit my wife, that as her life
Loveth well good ale to seek,
Full oft drinketh she, that ye may see   60
The tears run down her cheek.
Then doth she troll[14] to me the bowl,
As a good maltworm[15] shold,
And say, "Sweetheart, I have take my part
Of jolly good ale and old."   65
Back and side, etc.

They that do drink till they nod and wink,[16]
Even as good fellows should do,
They shall not miss to have the bliss
That good ale hath brought them to.   70
And all poor souls that scour black[17] bowls
And them hath lustily trolled,
God save the lives of them and their wives,
Whether they be young or old!
Back and side, etc.   75

MY LOVE IN HER ATTIRE

This exquisite poem was printed anonymously in one of
the numerous miscellanies of the period, Francis Davison's
Poetical Rhapsody (1602).

My love in her attire doth show her wit,[18]
It doth so well become her.
For every season she hath dressings fit,
For winter, spring, and summer.
No beauty she doth miss   5
When all her robes are on;
But Beauty's self she is
When all her robes are gone.

---

[3] I.e., a monk or friar.   [4] Crab apple.
[5] Service; i.e., be sufficient.   [6] Believe, am certain.
[7] Would, should wish.   [8] Then.
[9] Destroy, i.e., waste.
[10] Phew, i.e., nauseous stuff.—*Peevish* = senseless.

[11] Now and then.   [12] Heed.   [13] Direct.
[14] Circulate, pass.   [15] Toper.
[16] Shut their eyes, i.e., doze off.
[17] Dirty, i.e., used—there being no more left to drink.
[18] Mental powers.

WEEP YOU NO MORE, SAD FOUNTAINS

This lovely lyric, a masterpiece of versification, was set by the great lutenist and songwriter John Dowland (d. 1626?) and appeared in his *Third and Last Book of Songs or Airs of Four Parts with Tablature for the Lute* (1603). An arrangement for solo voice and piano is available in Frederick Keel's *Elizabethan Love-Songs, Second Set* (1913).

> Weep you no more, sad fountains!
>   What need you flow so fast?
> Look, how the snowy mountains
>   Heaven's sun doth gently waste.
> But my sun's heavenly eyes   5
>   View not your weeping,
>   That now lies sleeping
> Softly, now softly lies
>   Sleeping.
>
> Sleep is a reconciling,   10
>   A rest that peace begets.
> Doth not the sun rise smiling
>   When fair at even he sets?
> Rest you then, rest, sad eyes,
>   Melt not in weeping,   15
>   While she lies sleeping
> Softly, now softly lies
>   Sleeping.

SWEET CUPID, RIPEN HER DESIRE

William Corkine wrote the fine setting of this lyric, which made its appearance in his *Airs to Sing and Play to the Lute and Bass Viol* (1610). With all its elegance, a graver note is struck in this little poem. There is a modern arrangement of Corkine's music for it in Frederick Keel's *Elizabethan Love-Songs, First Set* (1909).

> Sweet Cupid, ripen her desire!
>   Thy joyful harvest may begin.
> If age approach a little nigher,
>   'Twill be too late to get it in.
>
> Cold winter storms lay standing corn,   5
>   Which once too ripe will never rise;
> And lovers wish themselves unborn,
>   When all their joys lie in their eyes.
>
> Then, sweet, let us embrace and kiss!
>   Shall beauty shale[19] upon the ground?   10
> If age bereave us of this bliss,
>   Then will no more such sport be found.

---

[19] Fall like a seed that drops from the pod; i.e., be lost because unreaped.

THERE IS A LADY SWEET AND KIND

Though this charming song was first published in *Music of Sundry Kinds* (1607) by Thomas Ford (d. 1648), it is now best known in the graceful setting of Edward Purcell (d. 1740), son of the greatest of English composers, Henry Purcell (d. 1695).

> There is a lady sweet and kind,
>   Was never face so pleased my mind;
> I did but see her passing by,
>   And yet I love her till I die.
>
> Her gesture, motion, and her smiles,   5
>   Her wit, her voice, my heart beguiles,
> Beguiles my heart, I know not why,
>   And yet I love her till I die.
>
> Her free behavior, winning looks,
>   Will make a lawyer burn his books;   10
> I touched her not, alas! not I,
>   And yet I love her till I die.
>
> Had I her fast betwixt mine arms,
>   Judge you that think such sports were harms,
> Were't any harm? no, no! fie, fie!   15
>   For I will love her till I die.
>
> Should I remain confinèd there
>   So long as Phoebus in his sphere,[20]
> I to request, she to deny,
>   Yet would I love her till I die.   20
>
> Cupid is wingèd and doth range,
>   Her country so my love doth change;
> But change she earth, or change she sky,
>   Yet will I love her till I die.

---

[20] According to the Ptolemaic astronomy, the heavenly bodies, including the sun (Phoebus), were fixed in several spheres which revolved around the earth.

Sir Edward Dyer

1543–1607

ALL THE famous Renaissance poets thus far represented in this book were courtiers or men who hoped to make their way at court. Like his bosom friend Sidney, Dyer too was a courtier poet. Not much of his work has survived, nor is much known about his early life. It was probably after some years at Oxford that he was introduced by the Earl of Leicester at court, where he became a prominent figure. The Queen frequently employed him on diplomatic missions; he was active in Parliament; his services were rewarded, but not with any great post. His poetic career, if it can be called that, presumably began in the 1560's and flourished in the seventies and eighties. For the text of his poems and a biography which contains an interesting account of the sort of life led by the courtiers, see R. M. Sargent's *At the Court of Queen Elizabeth: The Life and Lyrics of Sir Edward Dyer* (1935).

THE LOWEST TREES HAVE TOPS

A version of this poem was printed in Francis Davison's *Poetical Rhapsody* (1602), and with a musical setting by John Dowland in his *Third and Last Book of Songs* (1603). Its appearance in a manuscript commonplace-book of about a dozen years before points to the likelihood of its dating at least as early as the eighties. It is only a minor lyric, but the last line has been much admired.

The lowest trees have tops, the ant her gall,
   The fly her spleen, the little sparks their heat;
The slender hairs cast shadows, though but small,
   And bees have stings, although they be not great;
Seas have their source, and so have shallow springs;   5
And love is love, in beggars as in kings.

Where rivers smoothest run, deep are the fords;
   The dial stirs, yet none perceives it move;
The firmest faith is in the fewest words;
   The turtles[21] cannot sing, and yet they love: 10
True hearts have eyes and ears, no tongues to speak;
They hear and see, and sigh, and then they break.

MY MIND TO ME A KINGDOM IS

The earliest printed version of this poem appeared in 1588, in the *Psalms, Sonnets, and Songs* of William Byrd (d. 1623), greatest of Elizabethan composers. It remained for at least a quarter of a century one of the most popular songs of the time. The idea around which it is written is obviously not original with Dyer—to whom has this thought not occurred? But Dyer voices it with a remarkable blend of sturdy bluntness and appealing simplicity.

My mind to me a kingdom is,
   Such perfect joy therein I find,
That it excels all other bliss
   That earth affords or grows by kind:[22]
Though much I want which most would have,   5
Yet still my mind forbids to crave.

No princely pomp, no wealthy store,
   No force to win the victory,
No wily wit to salve a sore,
   No shape to feed a loving eye—   10
To none of these I yield as thrall.
For why? My mind doth serve for all.

I see how plenty suffers oft,
   And hasty climbers soon do fall;
I see that those which are aloft   15
   Mishap doth threaten most of all;
They get with toil, they keep with fear.
Such cares my mind could never bear.

Content to live, this is my stay;
   I seek no more than may suffice;   20
I press to bear no haughty sway;
   Look, what I lack my mind supplies:
Lo, thus I triumph like a king,
Content with that my mind doth bring.

Some have too much, yet still do crave;   25
   I little have, and seek no more;
They are but poor, though much they have,
   And I am rich with little store:
They poor, I rich; they beg, I give;
They lack, I leave: they pine, I live.   30

I laugh not at another's loss;
   I grudge not at another's gain;
No worldly waves my mind can toss;
   My state at one doth still remain.
I fear no foe, I fawn no friend;   35
I loathe not life, nor dread no end.

---

[21] Turtledoves.

[22] Nature.

Some weigh their pleasure by their lust,
　　Their wisdom by their rage of will;
Their treasure is their only trust;
　　A cloakèd craft their store of skill.　　　40
But all the pleasure that I find
Is to maintain a quiet mind.

My wealth is health and perfect ease;
　　My conscience clear my chief defense;
I neither seek by bribes to please,　　　45
　　Nor by desert to breed offense:
Thus do I live, thus will I die;
Would all did so as well as I!

Robert Greene

1558–1592

GREENE was not a courtier poet but one of the group of professional writers called "university wits." The members of this group lived by their pens, tossing off, with a great deal of gaiety and scant respect for what sober citizens might think, plays, romantic and realistic fiction, lyric poetry, and satirical pamphlets on the manners and controversies of the day. Next to Marlowe, Greene was the most promising of the group. Born at Norwich, he received most of his education at Cambridge, went to London, threw himself into the world of Bohemia, burned his candle at both ends, and flickered out in his early thirties.

Before he died, in squalor and despair, he had given posterity ample cause for regretting his unwritten masterpieces. Two of his plays, *Friar Bacon and Friar Bungay* and *James the Fourth,* are among the best non-Shakespearean pieces of their time; Greene's heroines are the most appealing women in English drama before Shakespeare's. He wrote several prose romances, adorned with beautiful songs. His pamphlets describing the contemporary underworld of crooks, swindlers, and whores contain some of the raciest of Elizabethan prose. Others are more or less autobiographical; for with all his genius the man was a poseur, and in the course of repenting in public enjoyed telling the world how wicked he had been.

The standard edition of Greene's *Plays and Poems* is by J. C. Collins (2 vols., 1905). H. Spencer's *Elizabethan Plays* (1933) reprints *Friar Bacon and Friar Bungay.* Greene's other writings may be found in A. B. Grosart's edition of his *Complete Works* (15 vols., 1881–86). The semi-autobiographical and the "cony-catching"[23] pamphlets have been reprinted by G. B. Harrison in the Bodley Head Quartos (1923–24).

---

[23] Rabbit-catching. *Cony* (rabbit) was slang for *dupe.* A cony-catcher was a swindler of suckers.

The following poems are typically Elizabethan in the conventionality of their themes. Their merit lies in simple beauty of phrase and line, and in the poet's great gift for suddenly possessing our imagination with something profoundly stirring, still simply but intensely expressed, and suggestive of thoughts that lie almost too deep for words.

FAIR IS MY LOVE

This lyric is full of the conventional comparisons which constitute the "conceits" of Elizabethan verse; many of them are Petrarchan in origin. But the first line, which John Masefield has echoed in *Enslaved,* is one of the finest in English love poetry. "Fair is my love" first appeared in Greene's prose tale *Perimedes the Blacksmith* (1588).

Fair is my love for April in her face,
　　Her lovely breasts September claims his part,
And lordly Júly in her eyes takes place;
　　But cold December dwelleth in her heart.
Blest be the months that sets my thoughts on fire,　　　5
Accurst that month that hind'reth my desire!

Like Phoebus' fire, so sparkles both her eyes;
　　As air perfumed with amber is her breath;
Like swelling waves her lovely teats do rise;
　　As earth her heart, cold, dateth me to death.　　　10
Ay me, poor man, that on the earth do live,
When unkind earth death and despair doth give!

In pomp sits mercy seated in her face;
　　Love 'twixt her breasts his trophies doth imprint;
Her eyes shines favor, courtesy, and grace;　　　15
　　But touch her heart—ah, that is framed of flint;
That, 'fore my harvest in the grass bears grain,
The rock will wear, washed with a winter's rain.

AH, WERE SHE PITIFUL

Greene's authorship of this full-throated song of love is probable but not certain; his *Pandosto* appeared in 1588, but not till an edition of 1677 was "Ah, were she pitiful" included. In this story, on which Shakespeare drew for *The Winter's Tale,* "Dorastus, in love-passion, writes these lines in praise of his loving and best-beloved Fawnia." The poem is remarkable for its unbroken outpouring of ecstasy and for the magnificent hyperbole of its closing lines.

Ah, were she pitiful as she is fair,
  Or but as mild as she is seeming so,
Then were my hopes greater than my despair,
  Then all the world were heaven, nothing woe.
Ah, were her heart relenting as her hand,   5
  That seems to melt e'en with the mildest touch,
Then knew I where to seat me in a land
  Under the wide heavens, but yet not such.
Just as she shows, so seems the budding rose,
  Yet sweeter far than is an earthly flower;   10
Sovereign of beauty! like the spray she grows,
  Compassed she is with thorns and cankered bower.[24]
Yet were she willing to be plucked and worn,
She would be gathered, though she grew on thorn.

Ah, when she sings, all music else be still!   15
  For none must be comparèd to her note;
Ne'er breathed such glee[25] from Philomela's[26] bill,
  Nor from the morning singer's[27] swelling throat.
Ah, when she riseth from her blissful bed,
  She comforts all the world, as doth the sun,   20
And at her sight the night's foul vapor's fled;
  When she is set, the gladsome day is done.
O glorious sun! imagine me the west,
Shine in my arms, and set thou in my breast!

SEPHESTIA'S SONG TO HER CHILD

Here we have a little picture, a family group, charming in its simplicity. This is from another of Greene's euphuistic prose romances, *Menaphon* (1589). It is sung by a wife whom misfortune has temporarily separated from her husband.

Weep not, my wanton,[28] smile upon my knee;
When thou art old there's grief enough for thee.

  Mother's wag, pretty boy,
  Father's sorrow, father's joy;
  When thy father first did see   5
  Such a boy by him and me,

He was glad, I was woe;
Fortune changed made him so,
When he left his pretty boy,
Last his sorrow, first his joy.   10
Weep not, my wanton, smile upon my knee;
When thou art old there's grief enough for thee.

  Streaming tears that never stint,
  Like pearl drops from a flint,
  Fell by course[29] from his eyes,   15
  That one another's[30] place supplies;
  Thus he grieved in every part,
  Tears of blood fell from his heart,
  When he left his pretty boy,
  Father's sorrow, father's joy.   20
Weep not, my wanton, smile upon my knee;
When thou art old there's grief enough for thee.

  The wanton smiled, father wept,
  Mother cried, baby leapt;
  More he crowed, more we cried;   25
  Nature could not sorrow hide.
  He must go, he must kiss
  Child and mother, baby bliss,[31]
  For he left his pretty boy,
  Father's sorrow, father's joy.   30
Weep not, my wanton, smile upon my knee;
When thou art old there's grief enough for thee.

THE SHEPHERD'S WIFE'S SONG

In this example of the pastoral tradition Greene treats with his characteristic homely charm a favorite theme of the Elizabethan poets. This lyric is from *Greene's Mourning Garment* (1590).

  Ah, what is love? It is a pretty thing,
  As sweet unto a shepherd as a king,
    And sweeter too;
  For kings have cares that wait upon a crown,
  And cares can make the sweetest love to frown.   5
    Ah then, ah then,
  If country loves such sweet desires do gain,
  What lady would not love a shepherd swain?[32]

  His flocks once folded, he comes home at night
  As merry as a king in his delight,   10
    And merrier too;
  For kings bethink them what the state[33] require,
  Where shepherds careless carol by the fire.

---

[24] The original reading is *flower*. The meaning may be a bower infested with cankerworms, a corrupt bower, or a bower of inferior roses (dog roses).   [25] Melody.
[26] Nightingale's.   [27] The lark's.   [28] Little rascal.

[29] By turns.   [30] So that each takes its predecessor's place.
[31] Give his blessing to.   [32] Gallant, lover.
[33] Governmental affairs.

Ah then, ah then,
If country loves such sweet desires gain,   15
What lady would not love a shepherd swain?

He kisseth first, then sits as blithe to eat
His cream and curds as doth the king his meat,
    And blither too;
For kings have often fears when they do sup,   20
Where shepherds dread no poison in their cup.
    Ah then, ah then,
If country loves such sweet desires gain,
What lady would not love a shepherd swain?

To bed he goes, as wanton then, I ween,   25
As is a king in dalliance with a queen,
    More wanton too;
For kings have many griefs, affects[34] to move,
Where shepherds have no greater grief than love.
    Ah then, ah then,   30
If country loves such sweet desires gain,
What lady would not love a shepherd swain?

Upon his couch of straw he sleeps as sound
As doth the king upon his beds of down,
    More sounder too;   35
For cares cause kings full oft their sleep to spill,[35]
Where weary shepherds lie and snort[36] their fill.
    Ah then, ah then,
If country loves such sweet desires gain,
What lady would not love a shepherd swain?   40

Thus with his wife he spends the year, as blithe
As doth the king, at every tide or sithe,[37]
    And blither too;
For kings have wars and broils to take in hand,
Where shepherds laugh and love upon the land.   45
    Ah then, ah then,
If country loves such sweet desires gain,
What lady would not love a shepherd swain?

SWEET ARE THE THOUGHTS

These stanzas from *Greene's Farewell to Folly* (1591), like
those of "The Shepherd's Wife's Song," express a common thought, so full of consolation for the weary or
wounded spirit that the poets return to it again and again.

Sweet are the thoughts that savor of content;
    The quiet mind is richer than a crown;
Sweet are the nights in careless slumber spent;
    The poor estate scorns fortune's angry frown:

---

34 Feelings.   35 Lose.   36 Snore.
37 *Tide* and *sithe* both mean *time,* as in "time and tide."

Such sweet content, such minds, such sleep, such bliss,   5
Beggars enjoy, when princes oft do miss.

The homely house that harbors quiet rest,
    The cottage that affords no pride nor care,
The mean that 'grees with country music best,
    The sweet consort of mirth and music's fare.   10
Obscurèd life sets down a type of bliss:
A mind content both crown and kingdom is.

PHILOMELA'S ODE

This beautiful tribute to the peace that love can bring is
"Philomela's ode that she sung in her arbor" in Greene's
Philomela (1592).

Sitting by a river's side,
Where a silent stream did glide,
Muse I did of many things
That the mind in quiet brings.
I 'gan think how some men deem   5
Gold their god, and some esteem
Honor is the chief content
That to man in life is lent,
And some others do contend
Quiet none like to a friend;   10
Others hold there is no wealth
Cómpared to a perfect health;
Some man's mind in quiet stands
When he is lord of many lands.
But I did sigh, and said all this   15
Was but a shade[38] of perfect bliss;
And in my thoughts I did approve
Nought so sweet as is true love.
Love 'twixt lovers passeth these,
When mouth kisseth and heart 'grees,   20
With folded arms and lips meeting,
Each soul another sweetly greeting;
For by the breath the soul fleeteth,
And soul with soul in kissing meeteth.
If love be so sweet a thing,   25
That such happy bliss doth bring,
Happy is love's sugared thrall;
But unhappy maidens all,
Who esteem your virgin blisses
Sweeter than a wife's sweet kisses.   30
No such quiet to the mind
As true love with kisses kind!
But if a kiss prove unchaste,
Then is true love quite disgraced.
Though love be sweet, learn this of me: 35
No love sweet but honesty.[39]

---

38 Shadow.   39 Chastity, i.e., chaste love.

George Peele
1558?–1597?

HAVING graduated from Oxford, Peele joined the group of "university wits" in London. He had an intense vision of beauty and was lyrically gifted for expressing it, but his lack of solidity and staying power weakens most of his work. Of his plays, *The Old Wife's Tale*, *The Arraignment of Paris*, and *David and Bethsabe* all have gorgeous things in them; none is first-rate drama either in construction or in characterization. The following lyric, almost certainly Peele's, is from his *Polyhymnia* (1590). This work describes one of the tournaments in which Elizabeth's courtiers played at medieval chivalry. Sir Henry Lee (1530–1610), a nephew of Sir Thomas Wyatt, was the Queen's personal champion; every year on her birthday he challenged all comers in her honor. In 1590, when he decided to retire from tilting, the tournament ended with this song. Peele's works were edited by A. H. Bullen (2 vols., 1888).

HIS GOLDEN LOCKS TIME HATH TO SILVER TURNED

His[40] golden locks time hath to silver turned;
  O time too swift, O swiftness never ceasing!
His youth 'gainst time and age hath ever spurned,
  But spurned in vain; youth waneth by increasing:
Beauty, strength, youth are flowers but fading seen;   5
Duty, faith, love are roots, and ever green.

His helmet now shall make a hive for bees,
  And, lovers' sonnets turned to holy psalms,
A man-at-arms must now serve on his knees,
  And feed on prayers, which are age his[41] alms: 10
But though from court to cottage he depart,
His saint[42] is sure of his unspotted heart.

And when he saddest sits in homely cell,
  He'll teach his swains[43] this carol for a song:
"Blest be the hearts that wish my sovereign well,   15
  Curst be the souls that think her any wrong."
Goddess, allow this agèd man his right,
To be your beadsman[44] now that was your knight.

Thomas Nashe
1567–1601

A GRADUATE of Cambridge, Nashe was another of London's "university wits," one of the most reckless, caustic, and realistic of the lot. He had talents, and for invective almost a genius; but he failed to touch the heights in any of the genres he tried. His best single effort is the spring song here reprinted; the old grannies in the sun are a fine realistic stroke, in the midst of all the ecstasy. *The Unfortunate Traveler, or The Life of Jack Wilton* (1594) is the first picaresque novel of any merit in England; it is racy stuff— a fantastic adventure story with realistic trimmings and a wandering rogue for a hero. Both the lyrics which follow, in such sharp contrast with each other, are from one of Nashe's plays, *Summer's Last Will and Testament* (1592). His complete works were edited by R. B. McKerrow (5 vols., 1904–10).

SPRING, THE SWEET SPRING

Spring, the sweet spring, is the year's pleasant king;
Then blooms each thing, then maids dance in a ring,
Cold doth not sting, the pretty birds do sing,
  "Cuckoo, jug-jug, pu-we, to-witta-woo!"

The palm[45] and may[46] make country houses gay,   5
Lambs frisk and play, the shepherds pipe all day,
And we hear aye birds tune this merry lay,
  "Cuckoo, jug-jug, pu-we, to-witta-woo."

The fields breathe sweet, the daisies kiss our feet,
Young lovers meet, old wives a-sunning sit,   10
In every street these tunes our ears do greet,
  "Cuckoo, jug-jug, pu-we, to-witta-woo!"
    Spring, the sweet spring!

ADIEU, FAREWELL EARTH'S BLISS

    Adieu, farewell earth's bliss!
    This world uncertain is;
    Fond[47] are life's lustful joys:
    Death proves them all but toys.[48]
    None from his darts can fly;   5
    I am sick, I must die.
      Lord, have mercy on us!

---

40 Lee's.   41 Age's.   42 I.e., the Queen.
43 Attendants.
44 I.e., to serve you by devoting myself to prayer for you.

45 Pussywillow; in northern countries, branches of various kinds of willow were sometimes substituted on Palm Sunday for palm branches.   46 Hawthorn.   47 Foolish.
48 Trifles.

Rich men, trust not in wealth;
Gold cannot buy you health;
Physic himself must fade.   10
All things to end are made;
The plague full swift goes by;
I am sick, I must die.
   Lord, have mercy on us!

Beauty is but a flow'r,   15
Which wrinkles will devour;
Brightness falls from the [h]air;
Queens have died young and fair;
Dust hath closed Helen's eye.
I am sick, I must die.   20
   Lord, have mercy on us!

Strength stoops unto the grave;
Worms feed on Hector brave;
Swords may not fight with fate;
Earth still holds ope her gate;   25

"Come, come!" the bells do cry.
I am sick, I must die.
   Lord, have mercy on us!

Wit with his wantonness
Tasteth death's bitterness;   30
Hell's executioner
Hath no ears for to hear
What vain art can reply.
I am sick, I must die.
   Lord, have mercy on us!   35

Haste, therefore, each degree,
To welcome destiny!
Heaven is our heritage,
Earth but a player's stage;
Mount we unto the sky.   40
I am sick, I must die.
   Lord, have mercy on us!

Sir Walter Raleigh

1552?–1618

LIKE other men, Walter Raleigh was an imperfect mortal creature. There is a good deal on his record that does not make pretty reading; yet no Elizabethan Englishman except Shakespeare has appealed more warmly to subsequent generations. No Englishman was more typical of his times; no man's life ever afforded stranger contrasts in worldly success and failure; no Elizabethan comes more alive as a human being out of the pages of history. This vividness reflects the impression he made on his contemporaries. He dazzled them with the gorgeous clothes in which he shone at court—there was, for example, a pair of jeweled shoes allegedly worth "six thousand six hundred gold pieces." He was famous, even in that age of versatility, for the ease with which he turned to one after another of most of the great concerns of the human mind and adorned everything he touched. Poet, historian, general, admiral, naval architect, explorer, colonizer, politician, courtier, dabbler in music and chemistry, patron of learning and letters and science—all these he was; but in them all he was first and foremost the man: curious, adventuring, restless, like the age he stands for. But a man like a character in a play, one of Marlowe's aspiring heroes, a planner of designs beyond even his own immense scope, a stormer of heights impossibly remote.

Like several other of the greatest Elizabethan captains, Raleigh was a Devonshire man, son of a country gentleman there and brought up a staunch Protestant. Of his education nothing is known save that he went to Oxford but like Sidney took no degree. He was only sixteen or seventeen when he underwent his baptism of fire, fighting for the Huguenots in the civil wars of France. Like his half brother, Sir Humphrey Gilbert, Raleigh may have served in the Low Countries. With him he sailed in 1578 on a stormy and unsuccessful voyage from which they turned back after a defeat at the Spaniards' hands off Cape Verde. In 1580 Raleigh was in Ireland, sharing in the bloody work of battle and (only too prominently) of massacre, and speedily acquiring a reputation for daring and resourcefulness. As for the atrocities he committed, they were in line with the government's policy; and Raleigh, whose Guiana voyages were to be marked by a noble humanity toward the Indians, never abandoned advocacy of the sternest repression in Ireland.

It was his return with dispatches in 1581 that first brought him to Elizabeth's notice; and though the famous story of how he threw his cloak over a muddy spot in her path may or may not be true, he was soon in personal attendance, partly on the Earl of Leicester's recommendation, partly because he got the ear of the Privy Council by finding fault with Grey's handling of Irish affairs, and not least by reason of his charm. Elizabeth liked to have personable young men about her, making themselves useful in administrative matters and assuring her of their passionate but respectful and hopeless devotion. Raleigh proved particularly useful; and, as his writings testify, he had an exquisite talent for turning the graceful phrase.

Appointment after appointment was showered on him. He was soon Captain of the Yeomen of the Guard and thus constantly near the Queen; he was Vice-admiral of Devon and Cornwall; he was Warden of the Stannaries, that is, administrator of the tin mines of Cornwall and Devonshire. These were but three of his many posts, some of which brought him a great deal of money. Like Spenser, he obtained an estate in Ireland; it was an enormous tract of confiscated lands. And the Queen gave him several manors in England, so that he was a landowner in at least six counties. One of these estates, Sherborne in Dorsetshire, became his home. A lucrative appointment was the wine-selling monopoly; every vintner had to obtain his license from Raleigh, for a fee. In 1584 he was elected to Parliament, of which he was long a leading member; he was not identified with any party or faction, but played a lone hand. He was unquestionably greedy for riches, though no miser. What he got he spent, by no means always on himself; in the Virginia voyages alone he sank a fortune.

For all his courtiership, Raleigh was essentially a Renaissance artist—in his versatility and in his flamboyance. His greatest quality was imagination. To it was due his own literary achievement, as well as his patronage of scientific research and philosophical speculation, the boldness of which was such that he and his associates got the name of atheists, a term of condemnation hurled about pretty freely in those times at anyone who deviated from orthodoxy in either religion or science. Thomas Harriot (d. 1621), a brilliant mathematician and astronomer, and of the poets the wild genius Christopher Marlowe as well as the "sage and serious" Spenser, were among his friends.

Raleigh's imaginative powers were obviously, too, behind the grand schemes for colonization, and also for getting rich quick, that make him so interesting to us now but finally brought him to ruin. His mind was one of the few, and perhaps the first, that grasped some notion of what might result from planting English settlements in the New World. Only the Queen's express veto kept him from the Newfoundland voyage of 1583 from which Gilbert never returned. The next year Raleigh sent out two ships at his own expense to explore Virginia, as the Elizabethans called the whole Middle Atlantic coast; in 1585 he equipped a little fleet under his cousin Sir Richard Grenville.

This was the origin of the settlement on Roanoke Island, in North Carolina. It was not Raleigh's fault that the col-

onists Grenville left there grew discouraged and sailed for England on a ship of Drake's when he came by the following summer on his way home from a marauding voyage to the West Indies. Raleigh had not forgotten them; but the relief ships under Grenville arrived after Drake's fleet had left. The next year, 1587, saw yet another Virginia voyage, the fourth of Raleigh's efforts; a hundred persons were left established on Roanoke. But in 1588 came the long-threatened attempt against the homeland; with the Spaniards' Armada in the offing, the relief fleet for Virginia was countermanded. Two boats of twenty-five and thirty tons were actually dispatched but returned without completing their mission. Raleigh turned his interests over to a company; it was not till 1590 that the next expedition anchored off Roanoke, and by that time the Lost Colony had disappeared. Its fate is still unknown. Raleigh's endeavors had ended in failure; yet they paved the way for the successful plantation at Jamestown in 1607. The originality of his colonial views and his persistence in them have linked his name more closely with the early voyages to Virginia than those of the colonists and seamen themselves. He did not introduce potatoes into Europe, but their introduction is popularly associated with him. As for tobacco, its importation was a direct result of the expeditions he sponsored; and his own adoption of the habit stimulated the spread of smoking.

Apparently Raleigh was not aboard the fleet that fought the Armada; his service was by land. He was a member of the committee which prepared an elaborate report on England's defenses, and as Lord Lieutenant of Cornwall he was in charge of preparations there. About 1592 he forfeited the royal favor. The disclosure of his secret marriage to Elizabeth Throgmorton, one of her maids of honor, threw the Queen into a fury. She did not rain influence and wealth on a gallant member of her entourage in order to see him give his heart to another. Of late her special pet had been the handsome and dashing young Robert Devereux, second earl of Essex. She put Raleigh into the Tower, whence he had to buy his way out by turning over the spoil of a captured ship. His income was largely derived from his sea ventures; like Drake's, his privateers preyed on Spanish shipping.

Raleigh was not long in prison, but for several years he was in disgrace. In 1595, his presence at court no longer demanded by the Queen, he crossed the Atlantic to "Guiana," that is, Venezuela, and then went on up the Orinoco. He published his *Discoveries of Guiana* the following year. The territory about the headwaters of the Orinoco and Amazon is still a somewhat mysterious region; to the Elizabethans it was a land of wonders, and Raleigh believed they were golden wonders. He failed to find them; but he was convinced, to his ultimate undoing, that he had come very close to them.

After this voyage his thoughts were more than ever of England's future empire. Spain, he saw, was the chief obstacle to English expansion overseas; and he was certain she meant to strike first. To forestall an invasion of England, he urged a descent on Cadiz. The expedition sailed in 1596, under Essex as general. The admiral was Lord Charles Howard of Effingham, soon to be Earl of Nottingham; he had commanded against the Armada of 1588. It was Raleigh, however, who devised the tactical plan which resulted in a huge naval victory and the destruction of the Spanish port; and it was his own squadron that led the attack.

For a while thereafter, though it was about a year before the Queen restored Raleigh to favor, he worked politically in harmony with Essex and Sir Robert Cecil (d. 1612), son and successor of Lord Burghley (d. 1598). In 1597 he was joined with Essex and another of Elizabeth's seadogs, Lord Thomas Howard, in command of the "Island Voyage" to the Azores, where in the absence of his colleagues Raleigh attacked and beat the Spaniards. The consequence was ineradicable jealousy on the part of the brilliant but petulant Earl, who was about fourteen years Raleigh's junior. From then on these two were bitter rivals, till the rebellion and execution of Essex in 1601.

With the fall of Essex, Raleigh was at his height. He was appointed Governor of Jersey and resumed his leadership in the affairs of Parliament. But though his fitness was obvious for membership in the Privy Council, the real governing body, he was never appointed though often consulted. He had powerful and treacherous enemies. One of them was Robert Cecil, who pretended the firmest friendship but meant to play the leading role in the next administration. As the end of Elizabeth's life approached, it was Cecil who nursed the King of Scotland's claim and presided over his peaceful succession to the throne in 1603. Cecil had already poisoned the King's mind against Raleigh. No greater contrast could be imagined than the bold Elizabethan captain and the mean and supercautious Stuart. Toward the close of his career Essex had been in close touch with James, who now regarded the Earl as almost a martyr and hated his rival.

Many of Raleigh's appointments, including several major sources of his income, were immediately canceled; and before long he was on trial for his life, charged with plotting against James in the interests of Spain. Considering his lifelong hostility to that nation and to Catholicism, it is impossible to believe there was anything substantial in the accusation; but Raleigh knew the pack was in full cry. In a frenzy of despair he may have tried to kill himself, thereby to prevent his son's disinheritance as the offspring of a condemned traitor; but the wound was in his right breast, and it is possible that his object was only to inspire sympathy. When his trial came on he fought for his life with skill and dignity. The great legal light Sir Edward Coke (d. 1634), eventually to be a famous patriot and opponent of the King's policies, prosecuted as attorney general. But in 1603 Coke was a willing tool, and his conduct of the trial was grossly unfair and abusive. Raleigh was adjudged guilty of high treason and sentenced to be drawn, hanged, and quartered.

He was not executed—not yet. James seized practically all he owned and threw him into the Tower; it was his home for the next twelve years. He was allowed many privileges, including the companionship of his devoted wife. He turned at once to an elaborate program of reading, writing, and scientific experiment, the last in a hen house he was allowed to convert into a chemistry laboratory. His most ambitious project was his *History of the World*—the very title is characteristic, both of Raleigh and of an age which saw in boundaries and limits only a challenge. The *History*, though he never completed it, was published in 1614. Perhaps Raleigh was discouraged by the death in 1612 of his admiring patron, Prince Henry, the heir to the throne. The malevolent James termed the book "too saucy" in its comments on kings, but for a hundred years it was a standard work in England and the American colonies. In common with most of Raleigh's efforts it fell far short of his design; he begins with the Creation and gets down only to the second century B.C. and the Roman conquest of Greece.

The restless spirit was not tamed by imprisonment nor by the labors of scholarship. Ever since his Guiana voyage Raleigh had clung to the belief that he could find gold there. His chief enemies at court were now dead, and he persuaded the King to set him free for one last venture. He was allowed to sail on his promise not to break the peace with Spain, though it was to territory claimed by Spain that he was bound. Into this voyage Raleigh put the little that was left from the wreck of his estate and all that he could persuade his friends to invest. He left England in the early summer of 1617. Everything went wrong. Even before the fleet weighed anchor a copy of Raleigh's plans had been handed to Count Gondomar, the Spanish ambassador. James's policy was now pro-Spanish; to that policy Raleigh's hopes of recouping his fortunes, and eventually his life, were to be sacrificed.

It was November when they reached the Orinoco. Ill with fever, Raleigh lay off one of its mouths while his son Wat went ashore with a party which pushed inland to find the mine that was the expedition's goal. This detachment was ambushed by the Spaniards; Wat fell at the head of his men. To his father, who idolized him, the blow was a terrible one. He sent Lady Raleigh the sad news: "I was loath to write, because I know not how to comfort you; and, God knows, I never knew what sorrow meant till now." Lawrence Kemys, one of his tried followers, had taken charge of the survivors. They captured the Spanish settlement; but when they marched on they ran into opposition sufficiently formidable to discourage their leader, who fell back on the ships for reinforcements. Raleigh reproached him bitterly, and Kemys killed himself. Meanwhile a second shore party, under a nephew of Raleigh, made another push but failed to find the mine.

By this time Raleigh knew he was done for. He was still at sea on the long voyage home when, though the Spaniards had taken the initiative in the Guiana skirmish, Gondomar charged him with piracy and King James readily concurred. He was arrested on his arrival, accused of treason, and after a futile attempt to flee the country sentenced to death. On October 29, 1618, with a superb exhibition of fortitude, he calmly laid his white head on the block on Tower Hill. The final paragraph of his own *History* is a kind of epitaph; it is severe but not inapplicable to its author:

For the rest, if we seek a reason of the succession and continuance of this boundless ambition in mortal men, we may add to that which hath been already said that the kings and princes of the world have always laid before them the actions, but not the ends, of those great ones which preceded them. They are always transported with the glory of the one; but they never mind[1] the misery of the other, till they find the experience in themselves. They neglect the advice of God while they enjoy life or hope it, but they follow the counsel of Death upon his first approach. It is he that puts into man all the wisdom of the world, without speaking a word, which God, with all the words of his law, promises, or threats, doth not infuse. Death, which hateth and destroyeth man, is believed; God, which hath made him and loves him, is always deferred. "I have considered," saith Solomon, "all the works that are under the sun; and, behold, all is vanity and vexation of spirit."[2] But who believes it, till Death tells it us? It was Death which, opening the conscience of Charles the Fifth,[3] made him enjoin his son Philip to restore Navarre; and King Francis the First of France, to command that justice should be done upon the murderers of the Protestants in Mérindol and Cabrières,[4] which till then he neglected. It is therefore Death alone that can suddenly make man to know himself. He tells the proud and insolent that they are but abjects, and humbles them at the instant, makes them cry, complain, and repent, yea, even to hate their forepast happiness. He takes the account of the rich and proves him a beggar, a naked beggar, which hath interest in nothing but in the gravel that fills his mouth. He holds a glass before the eyes of the most beautiful, and makes them see therein their deformity and rottenness, and they acknowledge it.

O eloquent, just, and mighty Death! whom none could advise, thou hast persuaded; what none hath dared, thou hast done; and whom all the world hath flattered, thou only hast cast out of the world and despised. Thou hast drawn together all the farstretched greatness, all the pride, cruelty, and ambition of man, and covered it all over with these two narrow words, *Hic jacet!*[5]

The standard edition of Raleigh's works is still that of 1829 (8 vols.). G. E. Hadow edited a volume of selections from the *History of the World* and the letters (1926). A court poet, Raleigh preferred private circulation in manuscript, subscribing to the foolish convention of his time against a gentleman's coming publicly forward as an artist. The bulk of his poetry has doubtless vanished. What we have, surviving here and there in printed miscellanies and in manuscript commonplace-books, stamps him as a transitional poet. He was an Elizabethan rather than a seventeenth-century man; but in none of his multifarious activities was he one to rest content with the day's popular modes. There is a good deal in his verse that looks forward to the work of Donne and the new Jacobean poets. His poems' appeal for us lies much in their intensely personal character. "Lofty, insolent, and passionate," his contemporary George Puttenham called them in *The Art of English Poesy* (1589). They are often tart, sometimes bitter.[6] The standard edition of the poems is by Agnes M. C. Latham (1929). F. C. Hersey gives a selection of both poetry and prose in *Sir Walter Ralegh: "The Shepherd of the Ocean"* (1916)—the subtitle repeats Spenser's phrase for Raleigh in *Colin Clout's Come Home Again*.

There are numerous biographies, among them W. Stebbing's (1891), M. Waldman's (1928), and E. Thompson's (1936). Although, like Shakespeare, Raleigh seems to have preferred another spelling of his name (*Ralegh*) to the one long in common use, the standard American form is *Raleigh*.

---

[1] Notice.   [2] Ecclesiastes 1:14.
[3] Holy Roman Emperor and King of Spain (d. 1558).
[4] In Vaucluse, in southeastern France. There was a massacre of the Vaudois at these places in 1545.

[5] Here lies. . . .
[6] Raleigh's well-known reply to Marlowe's "Come live with me and be my love" will be found below, in our seventeenth-century selection, under Izaak Walton, who quotes it in *The Complete Angler*.

Sir Walter Raleigh

OUR PASSIONS ARE MOST LIKE

This poem is a gracefully turned compliment, the sort of thing that might have been composed during an evening of parlor games at court. It was not printed in Raleigh's lifetime; and though the manuscript from which the following text is derived entitles it "Sir Walter Raleigh to the Queen," it is only probable, not certain, that she was the recipient and he the author.

Our passions are most like to floods and streams:
  The shallow murmur, but the deep are dumb.
So when affections yield discourse, it seems
  The bottom is but shallow whence they come.
They that are rich in words must needs discover[1]   5
That they are poor in that which makes a lover.

Wrong not, dear empress of my heart,
  The merit of true passion
With thinking that he feels no smart
  That sues for no compassion: 10
Since, if my plaints serve not to prove
  The conquest of your beauty,
It comes not from defect of love
  But from excess of duty.

For, knowing that I sue to serve   15
  A saint of such perfection
As all desire (but none deserve)
  A place in her affection,
I rather choose to want relief
  Than venture the revealing.   20
When glory recommends the grief,
  Despair distrusts the healing.

Thus those desires that aim too high
  For any mortal lover,
When reason cannot make them die,   25
  Discretion will them cover.
Yet when discretion doth bereave
  The plaints that they should utter,
Then your discretion may perceive
  That silence is a suitor.   30

Silence in love bewrays[2] more woe
  Than words, though ne'er so witty;
A beggar that is dumb, ye know,
  Deserveth double pity.
Then misconceive not, dearest heart,   35
  My true though secret passion!
He smarteth most that hides his smart
  And sues for no compassion.

---

[1] Cannot avoid revealing.   [2] Betrays, indicates.

GO, SOUL, THE BODY'S GUEST

That Raleigh wrote this poem in bitterness of heart during one of the periods when he was out of the Queen's favor seems likely enough; but though it appears in a manuscript of 1595, its precise date is unknown.

Go, soul, the body's guest,
  Upon a thankless arrant;[3]
Fear not to touch the best—
  The truth shall be thy warrant;
Go, since I needs must die,   5
  And give the world the lie!

Say to the court it glows
  And shines like rotten wood;
Say to the Church it shows
  What's good, yet doth no good!   10
If court and Church reply,
  Give court and Church the lie!

Tell potentates they live
  Acting by others' actions,
Not loved unless they give,   15
  Not strong but by affections!
If potentates reply,
  Give potentates the lie!

Tell men of high condition,
  That tend affairs of state,   20
Their purpose is ambition,
  Their practice is but hate;
And if they once reply,
  Then give them all the lie!

Tell those that brave it most[4]   25
  They beg for more by spending,
Who in their greatest cost
  Have nothing but commending;[5]
And if they do reply,
  Give each of them the lie!   30

Tell zeal[6] it wants devotion,
  Tell love it is but lust,
Tell time it meets but motion,
  Tell flesh it is but dust;
And wish them not reply,   35
  For thou must give the lie!

---

[3] Errand.   [4] Are most ostentatious.
[5] I.e., courtiers who try to ingratiate themselves by spending lavishly in hope of being rewarded with profitable appointments but receive instead only fair words.   [6] Religious fervor.

Tell age it daily wasteth,
  Tell honor how it alters,
Tell beauty how she blasteth,[7]
  Tell favor[8] how it falters;   40
And if they shall reply,
  Give every one the lie!

Tell wit how much it wrangles
  In tickle points of niceness,
Tell wisdom she entangles   45
  Herself in overwiseness;
And when they do reply,
  Straight give them both the lie!

Tell physic[9] of her boldness,
  Tell skill[10] it is prevention,[11]   50
Tell charity of coldness,
  Tell law it is contention;
And as they do reply,
  So give them still the lie!

Tell fortune of her blindness,   55
  Tell nature of decay,
Tell friendship of unkindness,
  Tell justice of delay;
And if they will reply,
  Then give them all the lie!   60

Tell arts they have no soundness
  But vary by contriving,
Tell schools they lack profoundness
  And stand too much on striving;
If arts and schools reply,   65
  Give arts and schools the lie!

Tell faith it's fled the city,
  Tell how the country erreth,
Say manhood shakes off pity,
  Say virtue none preferreth;[12]   70
And if they do reply,
  Spare not to give the lie!

So when thou hast, as I
  Commanded thee, done blabbing,
Although to give the lie   75
  Deserves no less than stabbing,[13]
Stab at thee he that will,
  No stab the soul can kill.

---

[7] Withers.   [8] Attractiveness, "looks."   [9] Medicine.
[10] Expert knowledge.
[11] The securing of an advantage by forestalling someone else.
[12] I.e., promotes no one's career.
[13] The code of honor prescribed the sword as the proper reply to being called a liar.

GIVE ME MY SCALLOP-SHELL OF QUIET

This poem was probably written while Raleigh lay under sentence of death late in 1603. Like our other selections from his verses, it seems to have been left by its author without a title. Several manuscripts and the earliest edition (1651) call it "Sr Walter Raleighes Pilgrimage." It has every appearance of being a very personal lyric.

Give me my scallop-shell[14] of quiet,
  My staff of faith to walk upon,
My scrip[15] of joy, immortal diet,
  My bottle of salvation,
My gown of glory, hope's true gauge;   5
And thus I'll take my pilgrimage.

Blood[16] must be my body's balmer—
  No other balm will there be given;
Whilst my soul, like a white palmer,[17]
  Travels to the land of heaven,   10
Over the silver mountains,
Where spring the nectar fountains.
    And there I'll kiss
    The bowl of bliss,
Drinking my eternal fill   15
Upon every milken hill.
My soul will be a-dry before,
But after it, will ne'er thirst more.

And by the happy, blissful way,
  More peaceful pilgrims I shall see,   20
That have shook off their gowns of clay
  And walk appareled fresh like me.
    I'll bring them first
    To slake their thirst
And then taste those nectar suckets[18] 25
    At the clear wells
    Where sweetness dwells,
Drawn up by saints in crystal buckets.

And when our bottles and all we
Are filled with immortality,   30
Then the holy paths we'll travel,
Strewed with rubies thick as gravel—
Ceilings of diamonds, sapphire floors,
High walls of coral, and pearly bowers.

---

[14] Worn by returning pilgrims.
[15] Knapsack; pilgrims carried provisions in them.
[16] Of the crucified Christ.
[17] Pilgrim back from the Holy Land, wearing a bit of palm leaf as a sign. Here, since the "palmer" is a resurrected spirit, he will be clad in white.   [18] Candies.

From thence to heaven's bribeless hall, 35
Where no corrupted voices brawl,
No conscience molten into gold,
Nor forged accusers bought and sold,
No cause deferred, nor vain-spent journey,
For there Christ is the King's attorney, 40
Who pleads for all, without degrees,[19]
And He hath angels,[20] but no fees.

And when the grand twelve-million jury
Of our sins, with direful fury,
'Gainst our souls black verdicts give, 45
Christ pleads His death, and then we live.
Be thou my speaker, taintless pleader,
Unblotted lawyer, true proceeder!
Thou movest salvation, even for alms,
Not with a bribèd lawyer's palms. 50

And this is my eternal plea
To Him that made heaven, earth, and sea:
Seeing my flesh must die so soon,
And want a head to dine next noon,

Just at the stroke, when my veins start and spread, 55
Set on my soul an everlasting head!
Then am I ready, like a palmer fit,
To tread those blest paths which before I writ.[21]

EVEN SUCH IS TIME

An earlier version of these poignant lines, but without the
final couplet, constitutes the last stanza of one of Raleigh's
love poems. According to statements in circulation not
long after his execution, the verses were found in their revised form in his Bible, where he had copied them the
night before he died.

Even such is time, which takes in trust
Our youth, our joys, and all we have,
And pays us but with earth and dust:
Who, in the dark and silent grave,
When we have wandered all our ways, 5
Shuts up the story of our days.
But from this earth, this grave, this dust,
My God shall raise me up, I trust.

THE LAST FIGHT OF THE *REVENGE* AT SEA

SUCH is the running head of the pamphlet Raleigh wrote
and had published in the fall of 1591 about the heroic death
of his cousin, Sir Richard Grenville, in action against the
national enemy, Spain. The title which immediately precedes the text below is from the title page of 1591. Richard
Hakluyt (d. 1616) had already issued, in a single volume,
his *Principal Navigations, Voyages, Traffics, and Discoveries
of the English Nation* (1589); when he expanded this work
to three volumes (1598–1600), he included Raleigh's narrative. The present text, modernized but uncut, is from the
pamphlet of 1591, with a few corrections from Hakluyt's
reprint.

Hakluyt's "prose epic of the modern English nation" is
available in twentieth-century editions (Hakluyt Society,
12 volumes; Everyman, 9 volumes); it is fascinating reading. Hakluyt was an enthusiast, resolved that the maritime
exploits of his countrymen should not run the risk of being
forgotten. And so, whenever a weather-beaten captain
turned up from voyaging in far waters or singeing the
king of Spain's beard or tugging under the lash at an oar
in a Turkish galley, Hakluyt added the pamphlet the
wanderer wrote about his adventures to the collection on
which the *Principal Navigations* was based.

None of the Elizabethan commanders was a tougher
specimen of dash and hardihood than Grenville. Both
Raleigh and Tennyson, whose poem on the *Revenge* was
inspired by Raleigh's narrative, put his conduct in the
most favorable light and exaggerate the odds against him.
The fact is, Grenville's judgment was poor, and he was a
violent man whom his subordinates disliked; but of his
great courage there can be no question. The odds were not
fifty-three but fifteen to one; the sober truth is sufficiently
amazing.

Under Admiral Lord Thomas Howard, Sir Richard
Grenville (1542–1591), already distinguished in the Virginia voyages sent out by Raleigh, was ordered to the
Azores in the summer of 1591 as vice-admiral of a small
English fleet, whose task was to intercept the great flotilla
of Spanish treasure ships on their annual voyage home from
the West Indies. He sailed in the *Revenge*, of 500 tons and
250 men; she had been Drake's flagship against the Invincible Armada. The English plan fell through when
Philip II dispatched a powerful force to meet and convoy
the eastbound ships; it was the largest fleet Spain had sent
to sea since the immense effort of 1588.

---

[19] Irrespective of rank.   [20] A pun on *angel,* a gold coin.

[21] One of the manuscripts adds:
"Of death and judgment, heaven and hell,
    Who oft doth think, must needs die well."

It caught Howard and Grenville unprepared for action. They were anchored off the north shore of the island of Flores, waiting for promised supply ships from England which never came. Disease had played havoc with their crews. Such of the seamen as were fit for duty were cleaning out the vessels' holds and shipping new ballast when a scouting craft brought the news that the Spaniards were near. The day they arrived the wind was from the east. As the enemy squadrons, screened by the island, came up from the south, the English had barely time to put themselves in sailing trim. Most of the Spanish craft were transports and cargo ships; but even so, the enemy was vastly superior in numbers, firepower, and readiness for engagement. It was a near thing; there was just time for the English to get away, close-hauled, on a northeast course. Howard very properly retired at top speed, and saved his ships.

Why Grenville was delayed is far from clear, despite Raleigh's statement. Possibly his station as vice-admiral was to bring up the rear and by the time his turn came to get under way it was too late to cut across the bow of the leading Spaniard. When he was advised by his navigating officer to take the only sensible course and run westward before the wind, staking his safety on outstripping the enemy in a stern chase, Grenville evidently lost his temper and, mistakenly supposing that the speed and handiness of the *Revenge* would see him through, insisted on attempting to pass between the Spanish squadrons by setting his course northeast after Howard and running the gauntlet of their fire. This meant opposing one ship with 150 effectives to fifteen men-of-war and a fleet that had about 5000 combatants aboard. When, as Raleigh's account explains, Grenville lost the wind, he doubtless concluded that, having got his ship into an inextricable predicament, the only honorable thing was to go down fighting and take as many of the enemy with him as he could. He must have known he was a dead man when at long last he consented to go aboard the Spanish flagship.

Raleigh's account of this stirring episode, one of the most famous in naval history, is a splendid example of straightforward narrative prose. There is an excellent biography of Grenville by A. L. Rowse, *Sir Richard Grenville of the Revenge: An Elizabethan Hero* (1937).

A REPORT OF THE TRUTH OF THE FIGHT ABOUT THE ISLES OF AZORES THIS LAST SUMMER BETWIXT THE *Revenge,* ONE OF HER MAJESTY'S SHIPS, AND AN ARMADA OF THE KING OF SPAIN

BECAUSE the rumors are diversely spread, as well in England as in the Low Countries and elsewhere, of this late encounter between her Majesty's ships and

the armada of Spain, and that[1] the Spaniards according to their usual manner fill the world with their vainglorious vaunts, making great appearance of victories, when on the contrary themselves are most commonly and shamefully beaten and dishonored, thereby hoping to possess the ignorant multitude by anticipating and forerunning false reports, it is agreeable with all good reason, for manifestation of the truth, to overcome falsehood and untruth, that the beginning, continuance, and success[2] of this late honorable encounter of Sir Richard Grenville and other her Majesty's captains with the armada of Spain should be truly set down and published without partiality or false imaginations. And it is no marvel that the Spaniard should seek by false and slanderous pamphlets, advisoes,[3] and letters, to cover their own loss and to derogate from others their due honors, especially in this fight, being performed far off; seeing they were not ashamed in the year 1588, when they purposed the invasion of this land, to publish in sundry languages, in print, great victories in words, which they pleaded to have obtained against this realm; and spread the same in a most false sort over all parts of France, Italy, and elsewhere. When, shortly after, it was happily manifested in very deed to all nations how their navy, which they termed invincible, consisting of 240 sail of ships, not only of their own kingdom, but strengthened with the greatest argosies,[4] Portugal carracks,[5] Florentines,[6] and huge hulks of other countries, were by thirty of her Majesty's own ships of war and a few of our own merchants,[7] by the wise, valiant, and most advantageous conduction of the Lord Charles Howard, High Admiral of England, beaten and shuffled together; even from the Lizard[8] in Cornwall, first to Portland, where they shamefully left Don Pedro de Valdes with his mighty ship; from Portland to Calais, where they lost Hugo de Moncado, with the galleass[9] of which he was captain; and from Calais driven with squibs[10] from their anchors, were chased out of the sight of England, round about Scotland and Ireland. Where, for the sympathy of their barbarous religion hoping to find succor and assistance, a great part of them were crushed against the rocks, and those other that landed, being very many in number, were notwithstanding broken, slain, and taken, and so sent from village to village, coupled in

---

[1] Because.   [2] Outcome.   [3] Dispatches.
[4] Especially large ships.
[5] Galleons, ships of three or four decks.   [6] Ships of Florence.
[7] Merchantmen.
[8] A headland, England's extreme southern point.
[9] A large galley carrying heavy guns.   [10] Fire bombs.

halters, to be shipped into England. Where her Majesty, of her princely and invincible disposition, disdaining to put them to death and scorning either to retain or entertain them, they were all sent back again to their countries, to witness and recount the worthy achievements of their invincible and dreadful navy. Of which the number of soldiers, the fearful burthen of their ships, the commanders' names of every squadron, with all other their magazines of provisions, were put in print, as an army and navy unresistible and disdaining prevention. With all which so great and terrible an ostentation, they did not in all their sailing round about England so much as sink or take one ship, bark, pinnace, or cockboat of ours, or ever burnt so much as one sheepcote of this land. Whenas on the contrary Sir Francis Drake, with only 800 soldiers, not long before landed in their Indies and forced Santiago, Santo Domingo, Cartagena, and the forts of Florida. And after that Sir John Norris marched from Peniche[11] in Portugal, with a handful of soldiers, to the gates of Lisbon, being above 40 English miles. Where the Earl of Essex himself and other valiant gentlemen braved the city of Lisbon, encamped at the very gates; from whence after many days' abode, finding neither promised party nor provision to batter,[12] they made retreat by land in despite of all their garrisons, both of horse and foot.

In this sort I have a little digressed from my first purpose, only by the necessary comparison of theirs and our actions: the one covetous of honor without vaunt or ostentation; the other so greedy to purchase the opinion of their own affairs and by false rumors to resist the blasts of their own dishonors as[13] they will not only not blush to spread all manner of untruths, but even for the least advantage, be it but for the taking of one poor adventurer of the English, will celebrate the victory with bonfires in every town, always spending more in faggots than the purchase[14] was worth they obtained. Whenas we never yet thought it worth the consumption of two billets[15] when we have taken eight or ten of their Indian ships at one time and twenty of the Brazil fleet. Such is the difference between true valor and ostentation, and between honorable actions and frivolous vainglorious vaunts. But now to return to my first purpose.

The Lord Thomas Howard, with six of her Majesty's ships, six victualers of London, the bark Raleigh, and two or three pinnaces, riding at anchor near unto Flores, one of the westerly islands of the Azores, the last of August in the afternoon, had intelligence by one Captain Middleton of the approach of the Spanish armada. Which Middleton, being in a very good sailer, had kept them company three days before, of good purpose both to discover their forces the more as also to give advice to my Lord Thomas of their approach. He had no sooner delivered the news but the fleet was in sight. Many of our ships' companies were on shore in the island, some providing ballast for their ships, others filling of water and refreshing themselves from the land with such things as they could either for money or by force recover.[16] By reason whereof our ships being all pestered[17] and rummaging,[18] every thing out of order, very light for want of ballast; and that which was most to our disadvantage, the one-half part of the men of every ship sick and utterly unserviceable. For in the Revenge there were ninety diseased; in the Bonaventure not so many in health as could handle her mainsail. For had not twenty men been taken out of a bark of Sir George Cary's, his being commanded to be sunk, and those appointed to her, she had hardly ever recovered England. The rest for the most part were in little better state. The names of her Majesty's ships were these as followeth: the Defiance, which was admiral;[19] the Revenge, vice-admiral; the Bonaventure, commanded by Captain Cross; the Lion, by George Fenner; the Foresight, by M.[20] Thomas Vavasour; and the Crane, by Duffeild. The Foresight and the Crane being but small ships; only the other were of the middle size; the rest, besides the bark Raleigh commanded by Captain Thin, were victualers and of small force or none.

The Spanish fleet, having shrouded their approach by reason of the island, were now so soon at hand as our ships had scarce time to weigh their anchors, but some of them were driven to let slip their cables and set sail. Sir Richard Grenville was the last weighed, to recover the men that were upon the island, which otherwise had been lost. The Lord Thomas with the rest very hardly recovered the wind, which Sir Richard Grenville not being able to do was persuaded[21] by the master and others to cut his mainsail

---

[11] On Cape Carvoeiro, north of Lisbon. This was Drake's great expedition (Raleigh accompanied it) in 1589, the unsuccessful attempt of the English at reprisals for the attack of the Armada the year before.   [12] Means of bombardment.
[13] That.   [14] Booty.   [15] Small sticks of wood.

[16] Obtain.   [17] Encumbered.
[18] Cleaning out holds, dumping old ballast, and shipping new.
[19] Flagship.   [20] Master, mister.
[21] Urged. I.e., part of the Spanish fleet being already to the east and on his windward side ("the weather bow"), the only hope of avoiding action was to run to the westward before the wind.

and cast about, and to trust to the sailing of his ship; for the squadron of Seville were on his weather bow. But Sir Richard utterly refused to turn from the enemy, alleging that he would rather choose to die than to dishonor himself, his country, and her Majesty's ship, persuading his company that he would pass through the two squadrons[22] in despite of them, and enforce those of Seville to give him way. Which he performed upon divers of the foremost, who, as the mariners term it, sprang their luff,[23] and fell under the lee of the Revenge. But the other course had been the better, and might right well have been answered in so great an impossibility of prevailing.[24] Notwithstanding, out of the greatness of his mind he could not be persuaded.

In the meanwhile, as he attended[25] those which were nearest him, the great San Philip, being in the wind[26] of him and coming towards him, becalmed his sails in such sort as the ship could neither way[27] nor feel the helm, so huge and high carged[28] was the Spanish ship, being of a thousand and five hundred tons. Who after laid the Revenge aboard.[29] When he was thus bereft of his sails, the ships that were under his lee, luffing up, also laid him aboard; of which the next[30] was the admiral of the Biscayans,[31] a very mighty and puissant ship commanded by Bertendona.[32] The said Philip carried three tier of ordnance on a side, and eleven pieces in every tier. She shot eight forthright out of her chase,[33] besides those of her stern ports.

After the Revenge was entangled with this Philip, four other boarded her, two on her larboard and two on her starboard. The fight thus beginning at three of the clock in the afternoon continued very terrible all that evening. But the great San Philip having received the lower tier of the Revenge, discharged with crossbar shot, shifted herself with all diligence from her sides, utterly misliking her first entertainment. Some say that the ship foundered, but we cannot report it for truth unless we were assured. The Spanish ships were filled with companies of soldiers, in some two hundred besides the mariners,

in some five, in others eight hundred. In ours there were none at all beside the mariners, but the servants of the commanders and some few voluntary gentlemen only.[34] After many interchanged volleys of great ordnance and small shot, the Spaniards deliberated to enter the Revenge, and made divers attempts, hoping to force her by the multitudes of their armed soldiers and musketeers, but were still repulsed again and again, and at all times beaten back into their own ships or into the seas.

In the beginning of the fight the George Noble of London, having received some shot through her by the armadas, fell under the lee of the Revenge and asked Sir Richard what he would command him, being but one of the victualers and of small force. Sir Richard bid him save himself and leave him to his fortune.

After the fight had thus without intermission continued while the day lasted and some hours of the night, many of our men were slain and hurt, and one of the great galleons of the armada and the admiral of the hulks[35] both sunk, and in many other of the Spanish ships great slaughter was made. Some write that Sir Richard was very dangerously hurt almost in the beginning of the fight and lay speechless for a time ere he recovered. But two of the Revenge's own company, brought home in a ship of Lyme[36] from the Islands, examined by some of the lords and others, affirmed that he was never so wounded as that he forsook the upper deck, till an hour before midnight; and then, being shot into the body with a musket, as he was a-dressing was again shot into the head, and withal[37] his chirurgeon[38] wounded to death. This agreeth also with an examination taken by Sir Francis Godolphin of 4 other mariners of the same ship being returned, which examination the said Sir Francis sent unto Master William Killigrew of her Majesty's Privy Chamber.[39]

But to return to the fight, the Spanish ships which attempted to board the Revenge, as they were wounded and beaten off, so always others came in their places, she having never less than two mighty galleons by her sides and aboard her. So that ere the morning, from three of the clock the day before, there had fifteen several armadas[40] assailed her; and

---

[22] There were two Spanish squadrons, from Viscaya and from Seville.

[23] Brought their ships' heads nearer to the wind, probably altering course from north to northeast. Grenville now had Spanish ships to both port and starboard.

[24] I.e., might have been justified in view of the odds against him.

[25] Gave his attention to.

[26] To the windward, the advantageous side.   [27] Keep moving.

[28] Tall in the hull.   [29] Afterwards came alongside the Revenge.

[30] Nearest.   [31] The ships from Viscaya.

[32] General Martin de Bertendona, commanding the Viscayan squadron.   [33] Bow battery, which could fire straight ahead.

[34] Gentlemen volunteers.

[35] Flagship of the Spanish transports.

[36] Lyme Regis, a port in Dorset.   [37] Besides, in addition.

[38] Surgeon.

[39] Killigrew, afterwards Sir William, was a Groom of the Chamber and a lifelong servant of the Queen.

[40] Usually this word means fleets; occasionally, as here, it refers to single (large) ships.

all so ill approved their entertainment as they were by the break of day far more willing to hearken to a composition[41] than hastily to make any more assaults or entries. But as the day increased, so our men decreased; and as the light grew more and more, by so much more grew our discomforts. For none appeared in sight but enemies, saving one small ship called the *Pilgrim,* commanded by Jacob Whiddon, who hovered all night to see the success, but in the morning, bearing with the *Revenge,* was hunted like a hare amongst many ravenous hounds, but escaped.

All the powder of the *Revenge* to the last barrel was now spent, all her pikes broken, forty of her best men slain, and the most part of the rest hurt. In the beginning of the fight she had but one hundred free from sickness, and fourscore and ten sick, laid in hold upon the ballast. A small troop to man such a ship, and a weak garrison to resist so mighty an army! By those hundred all was sustained, the volleys, boardings, and enterings of fifteen ships of war, besides those which beat her at large. On the contrary, the Spanish were always supplied with soldiers brought from every squadron, all manner of arms and powder at will. Unto ours there remained no comfort at all, no hope, no supply either of ships, men, or weapons; the masts all beaten overboard, all her tackle cut asunder, her upper work altogether razed, and in effect evened she was with the water, but the very foundation or bottom of a ship, nothing being left overhead either for flight or defense.

Sir Richard, finding himself in this distress and unable any longer to make resistance, having endured in this fifteen hours' fight the assault of fifteen several armadas all by turns aboard him, and by estimation eight hundred shot of great artillery, besides many assaults and entries; and that himself and the ship must needs be possessed by the enemy, who were now all cast in a ring round about him, the *Revenge* not able to move one way or other but as she was moved with the waves and billow of the sea; commanded the master gunner, whom he knew to be a most resolute man, to split and sink the ship; that thereby nothing might remain of glory or victory to the Spaniards, seeing in so many hours' fight and with so great a navy they were not able to take her, having had fifteen hours' time, fifteen thousand men, and fifty and three sail of men-of-war to perform it withal;[42] and persuaded the company, or as many as he could induce, to yield themselves unto God and to the mercy of none else, but as they had

like valiant, resolute men repulsed so many enemies they should not now shorten the honor of their nation by prolonging their own lives for a few hours or a few days.

The master gunner readily condescended,[43] and divers others; but the captain and the master[44] were of another opinion and besought Sir Richard to have care of them, alleging that the Spaniard would be as ready to entertain a composition as they were willing to offer the same; and that there being divers sufficient[45] and valiant men yet living, and whose wounds were not mortal, they might do their country and prince[46] acceptable service hereafter. And that where[47] Sir Richard had alleged that the Spaniards should never glory to have taken one ship of her Majesty's, seeing that they had so long and so notably defended themselves, they answered that the ship had six foot water in hold, three shot under water which were so weakly stopped as with the first working of the sea she must needs sink, and was besides so crushed and bruised as she could never be removed out of the place.

And as the matter was thus in dispute, and Sir Richard refusing to hearken to any of those reasons, the master of the *Revenge* (while the captain won unto him the greater party) was convoyed aboard the general,[48] Don Alfonso Bazan. Who, finding none overhasty to enter the *Revenge* again, doubting lest Sir Richard would have blown them up and himself, and perceiving by the report of the master of the *Revenge* his dangerous disposition, yielded that all their lives should be saved, the company sent for England, and the better sort to pay such reasonable ransom as their estate would bear, and in the mean season to be free from galley[49] or imprisonment. To this he so much the rather condescended as well, as I have said, for fear of further loss and mischief to themselves, as also for the desire he had to recover Sir Richard Grenville, whom for his notable valor he seemed greatly to honor and admire.

When this answer was returned, and that[50] safety of life was promised, the common sort being now at the end of their peril, the most drew back from Sir Richard and the master gunner, being no hard matter to dissuade men from death to life. The master gunner, finding himself and Sir Richard thus prevented and mastered by the greater number, would have slain himself with a sword, had he not been by force withheld and locked into his cabin.

<hr>

[41] Agreement, terms of conditional surrender.   [42] With.

[43] Assented.   [44] Navigating officer.   [45] Competent.
[46] Monarch, the Queen.   [47] Whereas.
[48] I.e., the ship of the commander-in-chief.
[49] From forced service in the Spanish galleys.   [50] When.

Then the general sent many boats aboard the *Revenge,* and divers of our men, fearing Sir Richard's disposition, stole away aboard the general and other ships. Sir Richard, thus overmatched, was sent unto by Alfonso Bazan to remove out of the *Revenge,* the ship being marvelous unsavory, filled with blood and bodies of dead and wounded men like a slaughterhouse. Sir Richard answered that he might do with his body what he list, for he esteemed it not; and as he was carried out of the ship he swounded,[51] and reviving again desired the company to pray for him. The general used Sir Richard with all humanity, and left nothing unattempted that tended to his recovery, highly commending his valor and worthiness, and greatly bewailing the danger wherein he was, being unto them a rare spectacle and a resolution seldom approved,[52] to see one ship turn toward so many enemies, to endure the charge and boarding of so many huge armadas, and to resist and repel the assaults and entries of so many soldiers. All which and more is confirmed by a Spanish captain of the same armada, and a present actor in the fight, who being severed from the rest in a storm was by the *Lion* of London (a small ship) taken, and is now prisoner in London.

The general commander of the armada was Don Alfonso Bazan, brother to the Marquess of Santa Cruz. The admiral of the Biscayan squadron was Bertendona. Of the squadron of Seville, Marquess of Arumburu. The hulks and flyboats[53] were commanded by Luis Couitiño. There were slain and drowned in this fight well near two thousand[54] of the enemy's, and two especial commanders, Don Luis de Sant John, and Don George de Prunaria de Malaga, as the Spanish captain confesseth, besides divers others of special account whereof as yet report is not made.

The admiral of the hulks and the *Ascension* of Seville were both sunk by the side of the *Revenge;* one other recovered the road of St. Michael's[55] and sunk also there; a fourth ran herself with the shore to save her men. Sir Richard died, as it is said, the second or third day aboard the general, and was by them greatly bewailed. What became of his body, whether it were buried in the sea or on the land, we know not; the comfort that remaineth to his friends is that he hath ended his life honorably in respect of the reputation won to his nation and country, and of the same

to his posterity, and that being dead he hath not outlived his own honor.

For the rest of her Majesty's ships that entered not so far into the fight as the *Revenge,* the reasons and causes were these. There were of them but six in all, whereof two but small ships; the *Revenge* engaged past recovery; the island of Flores was on the one side, 53 sail of the Spanish, divided into squadrons, on the other, all as full filled with soldiers as they could contain; almost the one-half of our men sick and not able to serve; the ships grown foul, unrummaged, and scarcely able to bear any sail for want of ballast, having been six months at the sea before. If all the rest had entered, all had been lost. For the very hugeness of the Spanish fleet, if no other violence had been offered, would have crushed them between them into shivers. Of which the dishonor and loss to the Queen had been far greater than the spoil or harm that the enemy could any way have received. Notwithstanding, it is very true that the Lord Thomas would have entered between the squadrons, but the rest would not condescend; and the master of his own ship offered to leap into the sea rather than to conduct that her Majesty's ship and the rest to be a prey to the enemy, where there was no hope nor possibility either of defense or victory. Which also in my opinion had ill sorted or answered the discretion and trust of a general, to commit himself and his charge to an assured destruction, without hope or any likelihood of prevailing, thereby to diminish the strength of her Majesty's navy, and to enrich the pride and glory of the enemy. The *Foresight* of the Queen's, commanded by Master Thomas Vavasour, performed a very great fight and stayed two hours as near the *Revenge* as the weather would permit him, not forsaking the fight till he was like to be encompassed by the squadrons, and with great difficulty cleared himself. The rest gave divers volleys of shot, and entered as far as the place permitted and their own necessities to keep the weather gauge of the enemy, until they were parted by night.

A few days after the fight was ended and the English prisoners dispersed into the Spanish and Indy ships, there arose so great a storm from the west and northwest that all the fleet was dispersed, as well the Indian fleet which were then come unto them as the rest of the armada which attended their arrival, of which 14 sail, together with the *Revenge* and in her 200 Spaniards, were cast away upon the isle of St. Michael's. So it pleased them to honor the burial of that renowned ship the *Revenge,* not suffering her to perish alone, for the great honor she

---

51 Swooned.   52 Demonstrated.
53 Fast sailing-vessels, used for scouting and dispatches.
54 Hakluyt reduces this figure to 1000.
55 The largest of the Azores.

achieved in her lifetime. On the rest of the islands there were cast away in this storm, 15 or 16 more of the ships of war; and of a hundred and odd sail of the Indian fleet, expected this year in Spain, what in this tempest and what before in the bay of Mexico and about the Bermudas, there were 70 and odd consumed and lost, with those taken by our ships of London, besides one very rich Indian ship, which set herself on fire, being boarded by the *Pilgrim,* and five other taken by Master Watts his ships of London, between the Havana and Cape S. Antonio.[56] The fourth of this month of November we received letters from the Terceira,[57] affirming that there are 3000 bodies of men remaining in that island saved out of the perished ships, and that by the Spaniards' own confession there are 10,000 cast away in this storm, besides those that are perished between the islands and the main.[58] Thus it hath pleased God to fight for us and to defend the justice of our cause against the ambitious and bloody pretences of the Spaniard, who, seeking to devour all nations, are themselves devoured. A manifest testimony how injust and displeasing their attempts are in the sight of God, who hath pleased to witness by the success of their affairs his mislike of their bloody and injurious designs purposed and practiced against all Christian princes, over whom they seek unlawful and ungodly rule and empery.[59]

One day or two before this wrack happened to the Spanish fleet, whenas some of our prisoners desired to be set on shore upon the islands, hoping to be from thence transported into England, which liberty was formerly by the general promised, one Maurice Fitzjohn, son of old John of Desmond, a notable traitor, cousin-german[60] to the late Earl of Desmond, was sent to the English from ship to ship, to persuade them to serve the King of Spain. The arguments he used to induce them were these: the increase of pay, which he promised to be trebled; advancement to the better sort; and the exercise of the true Catholic religion, and safety of their souls to all. For the first, even the beggarly and unnatural behavior of those English and Irish rebels that served the King in that present action, was sufficient to answer that first argument of rich pay. For so poor and beggarly they were as for want of apparel they

stripped their poor countrymen prisoners out of their ragged garments, worn to nothing by six months' service, and spared not to despoil them even of their bloody shirts from their wounded bodies and the very shoes from their feet—a notable testimony of their rich entertainment and great wages! The second reason was hope of advancement if they served well and would continue faithful to the King. But what man can be so blockishly ignorant ever to expect place or honor from a foreign king, having no other argument or persuasion than his own disloyalty: to be unnatural to his own country that bred him; to his parents that begat him; and rebellious to his true prince, to whose obedience he is bound by oath, by nature, and by religion? No, they are only assured to be employed in all desperate enterprises, to be held in scorn and disdain ever among those whom they serve. And that ever traitor was either trusted or advanced I could never yet read, neither can I at this time remember any example. And no man could have less beccommed the place of an orator for such a purpose than this Maurice of Desmond. For the Earl his cousin, being one of the greatest subjects in that kingdom of Ireland (having almost whole countries in his possession, so many goodly manors, castles, and lordships, the Count Palatine of Kerry, five hundred gentlemen of his own name and family to follow him, besides others, all which he possessed in peace for three or four hundred years), was in less than three years after his adhering to the Spaniards and rebellion beaten from all his holds, not so many as ten gentlemen of his name left living, himself taken and beheaded by a soldier of his own nation, and his land given by a parliament to her Majesty and possessed by the English; his other cousin, Sir John of Desmond, taken by Master John Zouch and his body hanged over the gates of his native city to be devoured by ravens; the third brother, Sir James, hanged, drawn, and quartered in the same place. If he had withal vaunted of this success of his own house, no doubt the argument would have moved much and wrought great effect; which because he for that present forgot, I thought it good to remember in his behalf. For matter of religion, it would require a particular volume if I should set down how irreligiously they cover their greedy and ambitious pretences with that veil of piety. But sure I am that there is no kingdom or commonwealth in all Europe but, if they be reformed,[61] they then invade it for religion sake; if it be, as they term, Catholic, they pretend title, as if

---

[56] The western tip of Cuba.
[57] In the Azores.   [58] Mainland (of Europe).
[59] Imperial sway.
[60] First cousin.—The Earl was the rebel Gerald Fitzgerald, fifteenth Earl of Desmond, who was killed in 1583. The Desmond lands were declared forfeit in 1586. The Irish estates of both Raleigh and Edmund Spenser were granted from these lands.

[61] Protestant.

the kings of Castile were the natural heirs of all the world; and so, between both, no kingdom is unsought. Where they dare not with their own forces to invade, they basely entertain the traitors and vagabonds of all nations, seeking by those and by their runagate[62] Jesuits to win parts, and have by that mean ruined many noble houses and others in this land, and have extinguished both their lives and families. What good, honor, or fortune ever man yet by them achieved is yet unheard of or unwritten. And if our English papists do but look into Portugal, against whom they have no pretence of religion,[63] how the nobility are put to death, imprisoned, their rich men made a prey, and all sorts of people captived, they shall find that the obedience even of the Turk is easy and a liberty in respect of the slavery and tyranny of Spain. What they have done in Sicil, in Naples, Milan, and in the Low Countries; who hath there been spared for religion at all? And it cometh to my remembrance of a certain burgher of Antwerp, whose house being entered by a company of Spanish soldiers when they first sacked the city, he besought them to spare him and his goods, being a good Catholic and one of their own party and faction. The Spaniards answered that they knew him to be of a good conscience for himself; but his money, plate, jewels, and goods were all heretical and therefore good prize. So they abused and tormented the foolish Fleming, who hoped that an Agnus Dei[64] had been a sufficient target[65] against all force of that holy and charitable nation. Neither have they at any time, as they protest, invaded the kingdoms of the Indies and Peru and elsewhere, but only led thereunto rather to reduce the people to Christianity than for either gold or empery. Whenas in one only island, called Hispaniola,[66] they have wasted thirty hundred thousand of the natural[67] people, besides many millions else in other places of the Indies, a poor and harmless people, created of God, and might have been won to His knowledge, as many of them were, and almost as many as ever were persuaded thereunto. The story whereof is at large written by a bishop of their own nation called Bartholomew de las Casas,[68] and translated into English and many other languages, entitled *The Spanish Cruelties.* Who would therefore repose trust in such a nation of ravenous strangers, and especially in those Spaniards which more greedily thirst after English blood than after the lives of any other people of Europe, for the many overthrows and dishonors they have received at our hands, whose weakness we have discovered to the world, and whose forces at home, abroad, in Europe, in India,[69] by sea and land, we have even with handfuls of men and ships overthrown and dishonored. Let not therefore any Englishman, of what religion soever, have other opinion of the Spaniards but that those whom he seeketh to win of our nation he esteemeth base and traitorous, unworthy persons, or unconstant fools; and that he useth his pretence of religion for no other purpose but to bewitch us from the obedience of our natural Prince, thereby hoping in time to bring us to slavery and subjection, and then none shall be unto them so odious and disdained as the traitors themselves, who have sold their country to a stranger,[70] and forsaken their faith and obedience contrary to nature or religion and contrary to that human and general honor, not only of Christians, but of heathen and irreligious nations, who have always sustained what labor soever, and embraced even death itself, for their country, prince, or commonwealth.

To conclude, it hath ever to this day pleased God to prosper and defend her Majesty, to break the purposes of malicious enemies, of forsworn traitors, and of unjust practices[71] and invasions. She hath ever been honored of the worthiest kings, served by faithful subjects, and shall by the favor of God resist, repel, and confound all whatsoever attempts against her sacred person or kingdom. In the meantime, let the Spaniard and traitor vaunt of their success; and we, her true and obedient vassals, guided by the shining light of her virtues, shall always love her, serve her, and obey her to the end of our lives.

---

[62] Fugitive. Raleigh is thinking of the expulsion of the Jesuits from England. Many of these priests ran the risk of discovery and execution by returning in disguise to promote the interests of their church and minister to its adherents.

[63] Against whom the Spaniards lack the excuse of (a hostile) religion.

[64] Lamb of God; a disk stamped with the image of a lamb as a symbol of Christ, much used by Catholics.   [65] Shield.

[66] The island of Haiti.   [67] Native.

[68] "Apostle to the Indies" and crusader against slavery in the Spanish possessions (d. 1566). The title which follows was supplied by the English adapter.   [69] West Indies.

[70] Foreigner.   [71] Conspiracies.

Edmund Spenser

1552?-1599

SPENSER was the next major poet after Chaucer. In his time modern English poetry was in the making; and he put important elements into the crucible. To our taste, he was soon surpassed in sheer poetic excellence; but till Milton no one came forward with so large, so dignified, so impressive a contribution. Spenser was not the best singer in the Elizabethan choir, yet he was immediately accepted as its principal musician. English verse, when he began writing it, still lagged behind the poetry of Italy and France. Spenser learned his art not only from Chaucer and from the Latin authors he read at school and college, but also from the new poets of the Italian and the French Renaissance. His contemporaries were well aware that it was Spenser who had made English poetry contemporary.

A Londoner born, Spenser prepared at the Merchant Tailors School. Its headmaster, Richard Mulcaster, was an enlightened teacher; without neglecting his pupils' Latin studies, he was an advocate of such unorthodox subjects as English composition, music, dramatic art, and physical education. Spenser's college at Cambridge was Pembroke Hall, where the Puritans were strongly entrenched. Doubtless he was confirmed in his Protestantism by listening to constant attacks both on the old religion itself and on what the Puritans regarded as Romanizing tendencies within the Established Church. Spenser took his B.A. and M.A., the latter in 1576 after seven years at the university. He had struck up a friendship there with a learned Fellow of his college, Gabriel Harvey, a pedant and a boor, but a progressive and a reformer, alive to the new intellectual currents. Perhaps it was Harvey who encouraged him to try for a career at court. At any rate, Spenser was soon making himself useful to men of affairs as secretary or courier: to an influential bishop, formerly the head of his college; probably to Sir Henry Sidney, Elizabeth's Lord Deputy in Ireland; very likely to the Earl of Leicester, who was politically if not religiously aligned with the Puritans. In a letter to Harvey, Spenser boasts of intimacy with the Earl's nephew, Sir Henry's son, Philip Sidney, and adds that he has had an interview with Elizabeth herself. It began to look as though a career was opening.

This was in the late seventies, and already Spenser was showing what he could do with a pen. It was in 1579, just after Lyly's *Euphues* (1578) and just before Philip Sidney's temporary retirement from court (1580), that *The Shepherd's Calendar,* a series of pastoral poems, one for each month, was anonymously published with a dedication to Sidney. In it Spenser himself appears as Colin Clout, and

there seem to be allusions to a long and tempestuous love affair. "Rosalind," the woman in the case, has not been identified. There are references to her and to another lady in Spenser's correspondence with Harvey; and there is evidence, but it is not conclusive, that the poet may have married in 1579.

In *The Shepherd's Calendar* Elizabethan poetry comes of age. For all its indebtedness to classical models and to the modern pastorals of Italy and France, this work reveals Spenser consciously attempting to base his art on Chaucer. "He hath labored," says "E. K.," an unknown contemporary whose explanatory comments were printed with the poem, "to restore, as to their rightful heritage, such good and natural English words as have been long time out of use and almost clean disinherited." Nothing is more characteristic of Spenser's style than this effort to rehabilitate archaic words. At its best it is charming, but it occasionally invests his lines with a kind of moldy quaintness.

Besides *The Shepherd's Calendar* Spenser wrote, at this stage of his career, a number of poems which have not survived and several others not immediately published. Among the latter were "hymns" to love and beauty, and the original version of his satirical *Mother Hubberd's Tale.* And already he had begun *The Faery Queen.* Some, perhaps all, of these early works were circulating in manuscript; and their author's talent was recognized in important circles.

Political employment followed, but not in England; the sharpness of *Mother Hubberd's Tale* had evidently offended powerful personages. To Ireland Spenser went in 1580, as secretary to its governor, the new Deputy, Lord Grey de Wilton. For about eight years the poet's residence was in or near Dublin. Though, like other Elizabethan men of letters who held appointments there, he regarded his lot as exile, Ireland was to be his home for the rest of his life. He served in various secretaryships, and toward the close of his career was sheriff of Cork. From 1588 to 1598 he lived in the province of Munster in the southwest of the island, for his rewards as a minor official included the tumble-down castle of Kilcolman and three thousand acres about halfway between Cork and Limerick. This estate was a grant from the vast forfeited possessions of the rebel Earl of Desmond. The native population in this part of Ireland had dwindled to almost nothing, such were the ravages of war, disease, and famine. The "undertakers," as the new landlords were called, were supposed to colonize their estates by settling English farmers on them. Spenser eventually had half a dozen tenants, all English. Though he endorsed Grey's cruel policy of repression with its attendant horrors of massacre and starvation, it would be unfair to judge Spenser's attitude toward Ireland and its people by current democratic standards. But he never saw more than the surface of the problems the English faced in their efforts to reduce the island to order. Inevitably, his tenure of Kilcolman was marked by litigation and ended by violence.

Soon after he went there, in the summer of 1589, he received a visit from Sir Walter Raleigh, who had left England to look over his own Irish holdings. Spenser showed his guest the first three books of *The Faery Queen*, and in the fall accompanied him back to London. Raleigh was to be his patron; presumably both men hoped to improve their standing with the Queen by presenting her with the new poem. It was published early in 1590, and Spenser's fame was assured. He was rewarded more tangibly with a pension equal in purchasing power to upwards of $2,000 a year in our currency; but if he had expected that this literary demonstration of his genius and loyalty would win him an important post, he returned to Ireland a disappointed man. In *Colin Clout's Come Home Again*, a draft of which he dispatched to Raleigh soon afterwards, Spenser has his say on life at court. He probably realized that the way was barred. William Cecil, Lord Burghley, able and cold, dominated the administration; he had no confidence in Raleigh, and he was not won over by his own appearance among the recipients of the seventeen dedicatory sonnets in the volume of 1590. Perhaps he knew that, years before, some of the satire of *Mother Hubberd's Tale* had been aimed at him. In this middle period of Spenser's literary career some shorter poems also fall; along with others composed earlier, they were collected in the volume entitled *Complaints* (1591). *Daphnaïda* (also 1591) is an elegy frankly imitative of Chaucer's *Book of the Duchess*.

At Kilcolman Spenser now settled down, and there in 1594 he brought his bride, Elizabeth Boyle, an English lady who had come to live in Ireland; she was a connection of the family which afterwards held the earldom of Cork. Among her wedding gifts was one the like of which few women, however loved, have ever received. It was her husband's *Epithalamion*, his song of their marriage, and his finest poem. Many of his sonnets, too, were inspired by his love for her.

The year after his marriage Spenser went over to London again with three more books of *The Faery Queen*. They were published in 1596. Meanwhile, in 1595, *Colin Clout's Come Home Again* was printed, and also "Astrophel," Spenser's elegy for Sidney, probably written considerably earlier. Other works now given the press include his *Four Hymns* in praise first of earthly love and beauty and then of heavenly, and his *Prothalamion*. This last is another wedding poem, inferior to its predecessor but memorable for its exquisite refrain, "Sweet Thames, run softly till I end my song." Presumably about this time, though it was not published till long after his death, Spenser wrote, in prose, *A View of the State of Ireland*.

He probably went home to Kilcolman with every intention of completing the large design of his most ambitious work; but of the twelve projected books of *The Faery Queen* only six and a fragment of the seventh were ever composed. He had, in fact, but three more years to live. In the summer of 1598 the Irish of Munster rose under the Earl of Tyrone and furiously assailed their English oppressors. They came to Kilcolman with sword and torch; Spenser, his wife, and their four children fled to the walled town of Cork. He was soon sent off to London to report on the rebellion. Hardship and perhaps heartbreak were too much for him; on January 16, 1599, not long after his arrival, he died. He was buried near Chaucer in Westminster Abbey.

Of the poetical works there are good one-volume editions by R. E. N. Dodge (1908) and by J. C. Smith and E. de Sélincourt (1921). The standard edition of *The Faery Queen* was edited by E. Greenlaw and others (6 vols., 1932–38). A useful guide is H. S. V. Jones's *A Spenser Handbook* (1930). There has been much critical and interpretive commentary. As good a book as any is B. E. C. Davis's *Edmund Spenser* (1933).

The original spelling is preserved in the following selections; the punctuation has been modernized. Note that the ending -*ed* is always pronounced as a separate syllable. E.g., *seemed* has two syllables; if Spenser wants the modern pronunciation he spells *seemd*.

from THE FAERY QUEEN

SPENSER's plan for *The Faery Queen*, only partially executed and even then not consistently, is set forth in his prefatory epistle to Raleigh, in which you will discern his agreement with Sidney on the function and nature of poetry. As he tells Raleigh, the poem is "a continued Allegory." A vast deal of scholarship has gone to the untangling of its meaning, but many points are still disputed; for the action moves on shifting planes of reality and unreality, amid reflections (often indecipherably blurred) of Elizabethan England, the world of Platonic idealism, and Spenser's own land of [10] utter faery. The notes indicate the main thread of the allegory in the excerpt below.

One of the most pleasing things about *The Faery Queen* is its stanza, an adaptation of Chaucer's rime royal. Chaucer's stanza has seven lines, riming *ababbcc*. Spenser splits [15] Chaucer's *c* rimes with another *b,* and then adds a ninth and closing line riming *c,* so that his final scheme is *ababbcbcc*. Unlike the rest, the ninth line is not an iambic pentameter, the five-stress line common in English narrative verse, but an Alexandrine or six-stress line. The effect is to apply a brake to the stanza's speed: it rolls gently to a stop—or, to put it more aesthetically, there is a pleasing [20] retard at the music's close. It is therefore not a stanza for rapid narrative; but story for its own sake is the least of Spenser's concerns. His main purpose is beautifully served by the pictorial and musical potentialities of the Spenserian stanza; and he exploits them with unflagging energy [25] through many thousands of lines.

A LETTER OF THE AUTHOR'S EXPOUNDING HIS WHOLE INTENTION IN THE COURSE OF THIS WORKE: WHICH, FOR THAT IT GIVETH GREAT LIGHT TO THE [30] READER, FOR THE BETTER UNDERSTANDING IS HEREUNTO ANNEXED.

To the Right noble and Valorous SIR WALTER RALEIGH, *knight, Lo. Wardein of the Stanneryes,*[1] [35] *and her Majestie's liefetenaunt of the County of Cornewayll.*

SIR, knowing how doubtfully all Allegories may be construed, and this booke of mine, which I have en- [40] tituled the Faery Queene, being a continued Allegory, or darke conceit,[2] I haue thought good, as well for avoyding of gealous opinions and misconstructions, as also for your better light in reading thereof, (being so by you commanded,) to discover unto [45] you the general intention and meaning, which in the whole course thereof I have fashioned, without ex-

pressing of any particular purposes or by-accidents[3] therein occasioned. The generall end therefore of all the booke is to fashion a gentleman or noble person in vertuous and gentle discipline: Which, for that I [5] conceived shoulde be most plausible[4] and pleasing, being coloured with an historicall fiction, the which the most part of men delight to read, rather for variety of matter then[5] for profite of the ensample,[6] I chose the historye of king Arthure, as most fitte for the excellency of his person, being made famous by many men's former workes, and also furthest from the daunger of envy, and suspition of present time. In which I have followed all the antique Poets historicall: first Homere, who in the Persons of Aga- [15] memnon and Ulysses hath ensampled a good governour and a vertuous man, the one in his Ilias, the other in his Odysseis;[7] then Virgil, whose like intention was to doe in the person of Aeneas; after him, Ariosto comprised them both in his Orlando; and lately Tasso[8] disseuered them againe and formed both parts in two persons—namely that part which they in Philosophy call Ethice or vertues of a private man, coloured in his Rinaldo, the other named Politice in his Godfredo. By ensample of which ex- [25] cellente Poets, I labour to pourtraict in Arthure, before he was king, the image of a brave knight, perfected in the twelve private morall vertues, as Aristotle hath devised;[9] the which is the purpose of these first twelve bookes:[10] which if I finde to be [30] well accepted, I may be perhaps encoraged to frame the other part of polliticke vertues in his person, after that hee came to be king.

To some, I know, this Methode will seeme displeasaunt, which had rather have good discipline[11] delivered plainly in way of precepts, or sermoned at large, as they use, then thus clowdily enwrapped in Allegoricall devises. But such, me seeme, should be satisfide with the use of these dayes, seeing all things accounted by their showes,[12] and nothing esteemed of, that is not delightfull and pleasing to commune sence. For this cause is Xenophon preferred before Plato, for that the one, in the exquisite depth of his judgement, formed a Commune welth, such as it should be; but the other in the person of Cyrus, and

---

[3] Incidental matters.   [4] Pleasing.   [5] Than.
[6] Example.   [7] *Iliad . . . Odyssey.*
[8] Ludovico Ariosto (d. 1533) and Torquato Tasso (d. 1595) were Italian epic poets.   [9] Divided.
[10] Spenser did not complete his project. He finished six books and left part of a seventh.   [11] Teaching.
[12] Valued by their appearance.

---

[1] Lord Warden of the Stannaries; i.e., head of the tin mines of Devonshire and Cornwall—there was a separate judicial administration for them.   [2] Obscure conception.

the Persians, fashioned a governement, such as might best be:[13] So much more profitable and gratious is doctrine by ensample, then by rule. So have I laboured to doe in the person of Arthure: whome I conceive, after his long education by Timon, to whom he was by Merlin delivered to be brought up, so soone as he was borne of the Lady Igrayne, to have seene in a dream or vision the Faery Queen, with whose excellent beauty ravished, he awaking resolved to seeke her out; and so being by Merlin armed, and by Timon throughly instructed, he went to seeke her forth in Faerye land. In that Faery Queene I meane glory in my generall intention, but in my particular I conceive the most excellent and glorious person of our soveraine, the Queene, and her kingdome in Faery land. And yet, in some places els, I doe otherwise shadow[14] her. For, considering she beareth two persons, the one of a most royall Queene or Empresse, the other of a most vertuous and beautifull Lady, this latter part in some places I doe expresse in Belphoebe, fashioning her name according to your owne excellent conceipt of Cynthia, (Phoebe and Cynthia being both names of Diana.) So in the person of Prince Arthure I sette forth magnificence in particular; which vertue, for that (according to Aristotle and the rest) it is the perfection of all the rest, and conteineth in it them all, therefore in the whole course I mention the deedes of Arthure applyable to that vertue, which I write of in that booke. But of the xii. other vertues, I make xii. other knights the patrones, for the more variety of the history—of which these three bookes[15] contayn three: The first, of the knight of the Redcrosse, in whome I expresse Holynes; the seconde, of Sir Guyon, in whome I sette forth Temperaunce; the third, of Britomartis, a Lady knight, in whome I picture Chastity.

But, because the beginning of the whole worke seemeth abrupte and as depending[16] upon other antecedents, it needs that ye know the occasion of these three knights' severall adventures. For the Methode of a Poet historical is not such as of an Historiographer. For an Historiographer discourseth of affayres orderly as they were donne, accounting as well the times as the actions; but a Poet thrusteth into the middest,[17] even where it most concerneth him, and there recoursing to the thinges forepaste,

and divining of thinges to come, maketh a pleasing Analysis of all.

The beginning therefore of my history,[18] if it were to be told by an Historiographer, should be the twelfth booke, which is the last; where I devise[19] that the Faery Queene kept her Annuall feaste xii. dayes; uppon which xii. severall[20] dayes, the occasions of the xii. severall adventures hapned, which, being undertaken by xii. severall knights, are in these xii. books severally handled and discoursed. The first was this. In the beginning of the feast, there presented him selfe a tall clownishe younge man, who falling before the Queene of Faries desired a boone (as the manner then was), which during that feast she might not refuse; which was that hee might have the atchievement of any adventure which during that feaste should happen; that being graunted, he rested him on the floore, unfitte through his rusticity for a better place. Soone after entred a faire Ladye in mourning weedes, riding on a white Asse, with a dwarfe behind her leading a warlike steed, that bore the Armes of a knight, and his speare in the dwarfe's hand. Shee, falling before the Queene of Faeries, complayned that her father and mother, an ancient King and Queene, had bene by an huge dragon many years shut up in a brasen Castle, who thence suffred them not to yssew; and therefore besought the Faery Queene to assygne her some one of her knights to take on him that exployt. Presently[21] that clownish person, upstarting, desired that adventure; whereat the Queene much wondering, and the Lady much gainesaying, yet he earnestly importuned his desire. In the end the Lady told him that unlesse that armour which she broughte would serve him (that is, the armour of a Christian man specified by Saint Paul, v Ephes.[22]), that he could not succeed in that enterprise; which being forthwith put upon him with dewe furnitures thereunto, he seemed the goodliest man in al that company, and was well liked of the Lady. And eftesoones[23] taking on him knighthood, and mounting on that straunge Courser, he went forth with her on that adventure: where beginneth the first book, vz.,

A gentle knight was pricking on the playne, &c.

The second day there came in a Palmer,[24] bearing an Infant with bloody hands, whose Parents he com-

---

13 The comparison is between the philosophical *Republic* of Plato and the romantic *Cyropaedia* of Xenophon.
14 Faintly represent.
15 First published in 1590, with the letter to Raleigh. Books IV-VI did not appear till 1596.   16 As if it depended.
17 Begins in the middle of the story, as Horace prescribes in his *Art of Poetry: in medias res,* into the middle of things.

18 Story.   19 Explain.   20 Separate.
21 Immediately.
22 Spenser's reference is wrong; the passage occurs in Ephesians 6:11 ff.   23 Soon afterwards.
24 A pilgrim who had visited the Holy Land. A palm leaf was his token.

plained to have bene slayn by an Enchaunteresse called Acrasia, and therefore craved of the Faery Queene to appoint him some knight to performe that adventure; which being assigned to Sir Guyon, he presently went forth with that same Palmer: which is the beginning of the second booke and the whole subject thereof. The third day there came in a Groome, who complained before the Faery Queene that a vile Enchaunter, called Busirane, had in hand a most faire Lady, called Amoretta, whom he kept in most grievous torment, because she would not yield him the pleasure of her body. Whereupon Sir Scudamour, the lover of that Lady, presently tooke on him that adventure. But being unable to performe it by reason of the hard Enchauntments, after long sorrow, in the end met with Britomartis, who succoured him and reskewed his love.

But by occasion hereof many other adventures are intermedled,[25] but rather as Accidents then intendments, as: the love of Britomart, the overthrow of Marinell, the misery of Florimell, the vertuousnes of Belphoebe, the lasciviousnes of Hellenora, and many the like.

Thus much, Sir, I have briefly overronne[26] to direct your understanding to the wel-head of the History; that from thence gathering the whole intention of the conceit, ye may as in a handfull gripe al the discourse, which otherwise may happily[27] seeme tedious and confused. So, humbly craving the continuance of your honorable favour towards me, and th' eternall establishment of your happines, I humbly take leave.

23. JANUARY. 1589.
Yours most humbly affectionate.
ED. SPENSER.

THE FIRST BOOKE OF THE FAERIE QUEENE

Contayning the Legende of the Knight of the Red Crosse, or of Holinesse

1

Lo, I, the man whose Muse whilome[1] did maske,
As time her taught, in lowly Shepheard's weeds,[2]
Am now enforst, a farre unfitter taske,
For trumpets sterne to chaunge mine Oaten reeds,[3]
And sing of Knights' and Ladies' gentle deeds;   5
Whose prayses having slept in silence long,

Me, all too meane, the sacred Muse[4] areeds[5]
To blazon broad emongst her learned throng:
Fierce warres and faithfull loves shall moralize my song.

2

Helpe then, O holy Virgin, chief of nyne,[6]   10
Thy weaker Novice to performe thy will;
Lay forth out of thine everlasting scryne[7]
The antique rolles, which there lye hidden still,
Of Faerie knights, and fayrest Tanaquill,[8]
Whom that most noble Briton Prince[9] so long   15
Sought through the world, and suffered so much ill,
That I must rue his undeserved wrong:
O, helpe thou my weake wit, and sharpen my dull tong!

3

And thou, most dreaded impe[10] of highest Jove,
Faire Venus' sonne, that with thy cruell dart   20
At that good knight so cunningly didst rove[11]
That glorious fire it kindled in his hart,
Lay now thy deadly Heben[12] bowe apart,
And with thy mother milde come to mine ayde!
Come, both! and with you bring triumphant Mart,[13]   25
In loves and gentle jollities arrayd,
After his murdrous spoiles and bloudy rage allayd!

4

And with them eke,[14] O Goddesse[15] heavenly bright,
Mirrour of grace and Majestie divine,
Great Lady of the greatest Isle, whose light   30
Like Phœbus' lampe[16] throughout the world doth shine,
Shed thy faire beames into my feeble eyne,
And raise my thoughts, too humble and too vile,
To thinke of that true glorious type[17] of thine,
The argument[18] of mine afflicted stile:[19]   35
The which to heare, vouchsafe, O dearest dred,[20] a-while!

[4] Clio, the Muse of history; to Spenser his subject, since it related to King Arthur, seemed historical.
[5] Decrees; i.e., commissions.
[6] See note 4, above. There were nine Muses.
[7] Chest, box of records (rolls).
[8] Or Gloriana, daughter of Oberon, the fairy king; here, Queen Elizabeth.   [9] Arthur.
[10] Scion, shoot; i.e., Cupid. His mother was Venus; and, according to one version of the myth, his father was Jove.
[11] Shoot an arrow. To rove was to shoot at an unpremeditated object, instead of at a fixed target on a measured range. The intention of such shooting in archery practice was to gain proficiency in estimating ranges.   [12] Ebony.
[13] Mars, god of war; he was Venus's lover.   [14] Also.
[15] Queen Elizabeth.   [16] Apollo's light, the sun.
[17] Representative; i.e., the faery queen, symbol of Elizabeth.
[18] Theme.
[19] I.e., lowly pen, the poet being abashed by the greatness of his theme.   [20] Supreme in inspiring awe; i.e., Elizabeth.

---

[25] Intermingled.   [26] Run over.   [27] Perhaps.   [1] Formerly.
[2] Garments. A reference to Spenser's *Shepherd's Calendar*.
[3] The primitive pipes of the shepherd; here, a symbol of pastoral poetry, as trumpets were of epic.

CANTO I

The Patron of true Holinesse
Foule Errour doth defeate;
Hypocrisie, him to entrape,
Doth to his home entreate.

1

A gentle Knight was pricking[1] on the plaine,
Ycladd in mightie armes and silver shielde,
Wherein old dints of deepe wounds did remaine,
The cruell markes of many a bloudy fielde;
Yet armes till that time did he never wield.   5
His angry steede did chide his foming bitt,
As[2] much disdayning to the curbe to yield.
Full jolly[3] knight he seemd, and faire did sitt,
As one for knightly giusts[4] and fierce encounters fitt.

2

But on his brest a bloudie Crosse he bore,   10
The deare remembrance of his dying Lord,
For whose sweete sake that glorious badge he wore,
And dead, as living, ever him ador'd.
Upon his shield the like was also scor'd,
For soveraine hope[5] which in his helpe he had.   15
Right faithfull true he was in deede and word,
But of his cheere[6] did seeme too solemne sad;
Yet nothing did he dread, but ever was ydrad.[7]

3

Upon a great adventure he was bond,
That greatest Gloriana[8] to him gave—   20
That greatest Glorious Queene of Faery lond—
To winne him worshippe, and her grace to have,
Which of all earthly things he most did crave.
And ever as he rode, his hart did earne[9]
To prove his puissance[10] in battell brave   25
Upon his foe, and his new force to learne—
Upon his foe, a Dragon[11] horrible and stearne.

4

A lovely Ladie[12] rode him faire beside,
Upon a lowly Asse[13] more white then snow,

Yet she much whiter; but the same did hide   30
Under a vele, that wimpled[14] was full low;
And over all a blacke stole[15] shee did throw,
As one that inly mournd—so was she sad,
And heavie sate upon her palfrey slow.
Seemed in heart some hidden care she had;   35
And by her, in[16] a line, a milke white lambe[17] she lad.[18]

5

So pure an innocent as that same lambe
She was in life and every vertuous lore,
And by descent from Royall lynage came
Of ancient Kings and Queenes, that had of yore   40
Their scepters stretcht from East to Westerne shore,
And all the world in their subjection held
Till that infernall feend with foule uprore
Forwasted[19] all their land, and them expeld;
Whom to avenge, she had this Knight from far
        compeld.   45

6

Behind her farre away a Dwarfe[20] did lag,
That lasie seemd, in being ever last,
Or wearied with bearing of her bag
Of needments at his backe. Thus as they past,
The day with cloudes was suddeine overcast,   50
And angry Jove[21] an hideous storme of raine
Did poure into his Leman's[22] lap so fast
That everie wight to shrowd[23] it did constrain;
And this faire couple eke to shroud themselves were fain.

7

Enforst to seeke some covert nigh at hand,   55
A shadie grove not far away they spide,
That promist ayde the tempest to withstand;
Whose loftie trees, yclad with sommer's pride,
Did spred so broad, that heaven's light did hide,
Not perceable with power of any starr.   60
And all within were pathes and alleies wide,
With footing worne, and leading inward farre.
Faire harbour that them seems;[24] so in they entred arre.

---

[1] Spurring, i.e., riding.   [2] As if.   [3] A very gallant.
[4] Jousts, tilts.   [5] On account of the great hope.
[6] Face, demeanor.   [7] Dreaded.
[8] See note 8 of the preceding series.   [9] Yearn.
[10] Strength.   [11] In the allegory it represents Sin.
[12] Named, as we learn later on, Una. She stands for Truth, that is,
    true religion as exemplified (in Spenser's opinion) by English
    Protestantism.   [13] Symbol of Humility.

[14] Pleated.
[15] A long, loose robe.   [16] On.   [17] Symbol of Innocence.
[18] Led.   [19] Completely laid waste.
[20] Symbol of Prudence.   [21] I.e., the heavens.
[22] Sweetheart's, mistress's; i.e., the earth's.
[23] Get under cover.   [24] That seems to them.

8

And foorth they passe, with pleasure forward led,
Joying to heare the birdes' sweete harmony,   65
Which, therein shrouded from the tempest dred,
Seemd in their song to scorne the cruell sky.
Much can they prayse the trees so straight and hy:
The sayling[25] Pine; the Cedar proud and tall;
The vine-prop Elme; the Poplar never dry;[26]   70
The builder Oake, sole king of forrests all;
The Aspine, good for staves; the Cypresse funerall;[27]

9

The Laurell, meed[28] of mightie Conquerours
And Poets sage; the Firre that weepeth still;[29]
The Willow, worne of[30] forlorne Paramours;   75
The Eugh,[31] obedient to the bender's will;
The Birch for shaftes;[32] the Sallow[33] for the mill;
The Mirrhe, sweete-bleeding in the bitter wound;[34]
The warlike[35] Beech; the Ash, for nothing ill;
The fruitfull Olive; and the Platane[36] round;   80
The carver Holme;[37] the Maple seeldom inward sound.

10

Led with delight, they thus beguile[38] the way,
Untill the blustring storme is overblowne;
When, weening[39] to returne whence they did stray,
They cannot finde that path which first was showne,   85
But wander too and fro in wayes unknowne,
Furthest from end then, when they neerest weene—
That makes them doubt[40] their wits be not their owne:
So many pathes, so many turnings seene,
That which of them to take, in diverse doubt they been. 90

11

At last, resolving forward still to fare,
Till that some end they finde, or[41] in or out,
That path they take that beaten seemd most bare,
And like to lead the labyrinth about;

Which when by tract they hunted had throughout,   95
At length it brought them to a hollow cave,
Amid the thickest woods. The champion stout
Eftsoones dismounted from his courser brave,
And to the dwarfe a while his needlesse[42] spere he gave.

12

"Be well aware," quoth then that ladie milde,   100
"Least suddaine mischiefe ye too rash provoke.
The danger hid, the place unknowne and wilde,
Breedes dreadfull doubts; oft fire is without smoke,
And perill without show. Therefore your stroke,
Sir knight, with-hold, till further triall made."   105
"Ah, ladie," said he, "shame were to revoke
The forward footing for an hidden shade.[43]
Vertue gives her selfe light, through darkenesse for to
         wade."

13

"Yea, but," quoth she, "the perill of this place
I better wot[44] then you; though nowe too late   110
To wish you backe returne with foule disgrace,
Yet wisedome warnes, whilest foot is in the gate,
To, stay the steppe, ere forced to retrate.
This is the wandring wood, this Errour's den,
A monster vile, whom God and man does hate.   115
Therefore I read[45] beware." "Fly, fly!" quoth then
The fearefull dwarfe. "This is no place for living men."

14

But full of fire and greedy hardiment,[46]
The youthfull knight could not for ought be staide;
But forth unto the darksome hole he went,   120
And looked in. His glistring armor made
A little glooming light, much like a shade,
By which he saw the ugly monster plaine,
Halfe like a serpent horribly displaide;
But th' other halfe did woman's shape retaine,   125
Most lothsome, filthie, foule, and full of vile disdaine.

15

And, as she lay upon the durtie ground,
Her huge long taile her den all overspred,
Yet was in knots and many boughtes[47] upwound,
Pointed with mortall sting. Of her there bred   130

---

[25] Since pine was used for the masts of sailing ships.
[26] Withered.—The catalog of trees is a commonplace in Latin poetry.   [27] Since it symbolizes death.   [28] Reward.
[29] Ever. It weeps by reason of its exuding pitch.
[30] By. The willow was a symbol of forsaken love.
[31] Yew, from which the longbow was made.   [32] Arrows.
[33] Broad-leaved willow.
[34] I.e., exuding an aromatic gum when its bark is pierced.
[35] According to Theophrastus (a Greek philosopher of the third century B.C.), beech was used in ancient times for war chariots.
[36] Plane tree.   [37] Holm oak, good material for woodcarvers.
[38] While away.   [39] Supposing, thinking.
[40] Suspect, fear.   [41] Either.

[42] Since it was practically useless to a dismounted knight.
[43] I.e., it would be shameful to turn back on account of the possibility of danger.
[44] Know. For Truth instinctively senses the presence of Error.
[45] Counsel.   [46] Insatiable boldness.   [47] Coils.

A thousand yong ones, which she dayly fed,
Sucking upon her poisnous dugs; each one
Of sundry shapes, yet all ill-favored.[48]
Soone as that uncouth[49] light upon them shone,
Into her mouth they crept, and suddain all were gone. 135

16

Their dam upstart[50] out of her den effraide,[51]
And rushed forth, hurling her hideous taile
About her cursed head, whose folds displaid[52]
Were stretcht now forth at length without entraile.[53]
She lookt about, and seeing one in mayle,   140
Armed to point,[54] sought backe to turne againe;
For light she hated as the deadly bale,[55]
Ay wont[56] in desert darknesse to remaine,
Where plaine none might see her, nor she see any plaine.

17

Which when the valiant Elfe[57] perceiv'd, he lept   145
As Lyon fierce upon the flying pray,
And with his trenchand[58] blade her boldly kept
From turning backe, and forced her to stay.
Therewith enrag'd she loudly gan to bray,
And turning fierce her speckled taile advaunst,   150
Threatning her angry sting, him to dismay;
Who, nought aghast, his mightie hand enhaunst:[59]
The stroke down from her head unto her shoulder
    glaunst.[60]

18

Much daunted with that dint, her sence was dazd;
Yet kindling rage her selfe she gathered round,   155
And all attonce her beastly body raizd
With doubled forces high above the ground.
Tho,[61] wrapping up her wrethed sterne arownd,
Lept fierce upon his shield, and her huge traine
All suddenly about his body wound,   160
That[62] hand or foot to stirre he strove in vaine.
God helpe the man so wrapt in Errour's endlesse traine!

19

His Lady, sad to see his sore constraint,
Cride out, "Now, now, Sir knight, shew what ye bee!
Add faith unto your force, and be not faint!   165

Strangle her! els she sure will strangle thee!"
That when he heard, in great perplexitie,
His gall did grate[63] for griefe[64] and high disdaine;
And, knitting all his force, got one hand free,
Wherewith he grypt her gorge[65] with so great paine 170
That soone to loose her wicked bands did her constraine.

20

Therewith she spewd out of her filthy maw[66]
A floud of poyson horrible and blacke,
Full of great lumpes of flesh and gobbets[67] raw,
Which stunck so vildly[68] that it forst him slacke   175
His grasping hold, and from her turne him backe.
Her vomit full of bookes and papers[69] was,
With loathly frogs and toades, which eyes did lacke,
And creeping sought way in the weedy gras:
Her filthy parbreake[70] all the place defiled has.   180

21

As when old father Nilus gins to swell
With timely pride above the Aegyptian vale,
His fattie waves do fertile slime outwell,
And overflow each plaine and lowly dale;
But when his later spring gins to avale,[71]   185
Huge heapes of mudd he leaves, wherein there breed
Ten thousand kindes of creatures, partly male
And partly female of his fruitfull seed:
Such ugly monstrous shapes elswhere may no man reed.[72]

22

The same so sore annoyed has the knight   190
That, welnigh choked with the deadly stinke,
His forces faile, ne[73] can no longer fight;
Whose corage when the feend perceiv'd to shrinke,
She poured forth out of her hellish sinke
Her fruitfull cursed spawne of serpents small,   195
Deformed monsters, fowle and blacke as inke,
Which swarming all about his legs did crall,
And him encombred sore, but could not hurt at all.

23

As gentle Shepheard in sweete even-tide,
When ruddy Phoebus gins to welke[74] in west,   200
High on an hill, his flocke to vewen wide,

---

48 Ugly.   49 Unfamiliar.   50 Started up.   51 Frightened.
52 Spread out.   53 Coiling.   54 Completely.   55 Destruction.
56 Ever accustomed.
57 The Redcross knight was of fairy birth.
58 Trenchant, sharp.   59 Enhanced, raised.
60 Glanced, struck obliquely.   61 Then.   62 So that.

63 Stir. The gall was supposed to be the seat of resentment.
64 Pain.   65 Throat.   66 Stomach.   67 Bits of flesh.
68 Vilely.
69 Pamphlets attacking the Church of England and the Queen's
government.   70 Vomit.
71 Flood begins to subside.   72 Perceive.   73 Nor.
74 Wane, decline.

Markes which do byte their hasty supper best;
A cloud of combrous gnattes do him molest,
All striving to infixe their feeble stings,
That from his noyance he no where can rest,   205
But with his clownish hands their tender wings
He brusheth oft, and oft doth mar their murmurings:

24

Thus ill bestedd,[75] and fearefull more of shame
Then of the certaine perill he stood in,
Halfe furious unto his foe he came,   210
Resolv'd in minde all suddenly to win
Or soone to lose, before he once would lin,[76]
And strooke at her with more then manly[77] force,
That from her body full of filthie sin
He raft[78] her hatefull head without remorse.   215
A streame of cole black bloud forth gushed from her
    corse.

25

Her scattred brood, soone as their Parent deare
They saw so rudely falling to the ground,
Groning full deadly, all with troublous feare,
Gathred themselves about her body round,   220
Weening their wonted entrance to have found
At her wide mouth; but being there withstood
They flocked all about her bleeding wound,
And sucked up their dying mother's blood,
Making her death their life, and eke her hurt their
    good.   225

26

That détestable sight him much amazde,
To see th'unkindly Impes,[79] of heaven accurst,
Devoure their dam; on whom, while so he gazd,
Having all satisfide their bloudy thurst,
Their bellies swolne he saw with fulnesse burst,   230
And bowels gushing forth. Well worthy end
Of such as drunke her life, the which them nurst!
Now needeth him no lenger labour spend;
His foes have slaine themselves, with whom he should
    contend.

27

His Ladie, seeing all that chaunst from farre,   235
Approcht in hast to greet his victorie,
And said, "Faire knight, borne under happy starre,

Who see your vanquisht foes before you lye,
Well worthy be you of that Armorie[80]
Wherein ye have great glory wonne this day,   240
And proov'd your strength on a strong enimie,
Your first adventure. Many such I pray,
And henceforth ever wish, that like succeed it may."

28

Then mounted he upon his Steede againe,
And with the Lady backward sought to wend.   245
That path he kept which beaten was most plaine,
Ne ever would to any by-way bend,
But still did follow one unto the end,
The which at last out of the wood them brought.
So forward on his way (with God to frend[81])   250
He passed forth, and new adventure sought.
Long way he travelled before he heard of ought.

29

At length they chaunst to meet upon the way
An aged Sire, in long blacke weedes yclad,
His feete all bare, his beard all hoarie gray,   255
And by his belt his booke[82] he hanging had.
Sober he seemde, and very sagely sad,[83]
And to the ground his eyes were lowly bent,
Simple in shew, and voide of malice bad;
And all the way he prayed as he went,   260
And often knockt his brest, as one that did repent.

30

He faire the knight saluted, louting[84] low,
Who faire him quited,[85] as that[86] courteous was;
And after asked him if he did know
Of straunge adventures, which abroad did pas.   265
"Ah, my dear Sonne," quoth he, "how should, alas,
Silly[87] old man, that lives in hidden cell,
Bidding[88] his beades[89] all day for his trespas,
Tydings of warre and worldly trouble tell?
With holy father sits not[90] with such thinges to
    mell.[91]   270

31

"But if of daunger which hereby doth dwell
And homebred evil ye desire to heare,
Of a straunge man I can you tidings tell,
That wasteth all this countrey, farre and neare."

[75] Beset.　[76] Cease.　[77] Human.
[78] Bereft.　[79] Unnatural offspring.

[80] Armor (of Christianity).　[81] For his friend.
[82] Prayer book.　[83] Solemn.　[84] Bowing.
[85] Repaid (with a return bow).　[86] As.　[87] Simple.
[88] Telling, counting.　[89] I.e., praying.　[90] It is not fitting.
[91] Mix, meddle.

"Of such," saide he, "I chiefly doe inquere,   275
And shall you well reward to shew the place
In which that wicked wight[92] his dayes doth weare;
For to all knighthood it is foule disgrace,
That such a cursed creature lives so long a space."

32

"Far hence," quoth he, "in wastfull wildernesse   280
His dwelling is, by which no living wight
May ever passe, but[93] thorough great distresse."
"Now," saide the Ladie, "draweth toward night,
And well I wote that of your later fight
Ye all forwearied[94] be; for what so strong,   285
But, wanting rest, will also want of might?
The Sunne, that measures heaven all day long,
At night doth baite[95] his steedes[96] the Ocean waves
  emong.

33

"Then with the Sunne take, Sir, your timely rest,
And with new day new worke at once begin.   290
Untroubled night, they say, gives counsell best."
"Right well, Sir knight, ye have advised bin,"
Quoth then that aged man; "the way to win
Is wisely to advise. Now day is spent;
Therefore with me ye may take up your In   295
For this same night." The knight was well content;
So with that godly father to his home they went.

34

A litle lowly Hermitage it was,
Downe in a dale, hard by a forest's side,
Far from resort of people that did pas   300
In travell to and froe. A litle wyde[97]
There was an holy Chappell edifyde,[98]
Wherein the Hermite dewly wont to say
His holy things each morne and eventyde.
Thereby a Christall streame did gently play,   305
Which from a sacred fountaine welled forth alway.

35

Arrived there, the little house they fill,
Ne looke for entertainement[99] where none was.
Rest is their feast, and all things at their will;
The noblest mind the best contentment has.   310

With faire discourse the evening so they pas;
For that old man of pleasing wordes had store,
And well could file[1] his tongue as smooth as glas.
He told of Saintes and Popes,[2] and evermore
He strowd an Ave-Mary after and before.   315

36

The drouping Night thus creepeth on them fast,
And the sad humour[3] loading their eye liddes,
As messenger of Morpheus[4] on them cast
Sweet slombring deaw, the which to sleepe them biddes.
Unto their lodgings then his guestes he riddes;[5]   320
Where when all drownd in deadly sleepe he findes,
He to his study goes, and there amiddes
His Magick bookes and artes of sundry kindes,
He seekes out mighty charmes, to trouble sleepy mindes.

37

Then choosing out few wordes most horrible   325
(Let none them read), thereof did verses frame,
With which and other spelles like terrible,
He bad awake blacke Plutoe's griesly Dame,[6]
And cursed heaven, and spake reprochfull shame
Of highest God, the Lord of life and light—   330
A bold, bad man, that dar'd to call by name
Great Gorgon,[7] Prince of darknesse and dead night,
At which Cocytus quakes, and Styx[8] is put to flight.

38

And forth he cald out of deepe darknesse dred
Legions of Sprights, the which like little flyes   335
Fluttring about his ever damned hed,
A-waite whereto their service he applyes,
To aide his friends, or fray[9] his enimies.
Of those he chose out two, the falsest twoo,
And fittest for to forge true-seeming lyes: 340
The one of them he gave a message too;
The other by him selfe staide, other worke to doo.

39

He,[10] making speedy way through spersed[11] ayre,
And through the world of waters wide and deepe,
To Morpheus' house doth hastily repaire.   345

[1] Polish.
[2] The old hermit, Archimago by name, symbolizes Hypocrisy.
  As a Roman Catholic he is an object of suspicion to adherents
  of the state religion.   [3] Heavy moisture.
[4] God of sleep.   [5] Dismisses.
[6] Proserpina, wife of Pluto and hence queen of Hades.
[7] The demon Demogorgon.   [8] Rivers of Hades.
[9] Affright.   [10] The sprite sent by Archimago.
[11] Dispersed, thin.

[92] Person.   [93] Except.
[94] Completely wearied.   [95] Feed, i.e., put up.
[96] The horses of the sun god's chariot.   [97] Apart.
[98] Built.   [99] Accommodation.

Amid the bowels of the earth full steepe[12]
And low, where dawning day doth never peepe,
His dwelling is; there Tethys[13] his wet bed
Doth ever wash, and Cynthia[14] still[15] doth steepe
In silver deaw his ever-drouping hed,   350
Whiles sad Night over him her mantle black doth spred.

40

Whose double gates he findeth locked fast,
The one faire fram'd of burnisht Yvory,
The other all with silver overcast;
And wakefull dogges before them farre do lye,   355
Watching to banish Care, their enimy,
Who oft is wont to trouble gentle Sleepe.
By them the Sprite doth passe in quietly,
And unto Morpheus comes, whom drowned deepe
In drowsie fit he findes: of nothing he takes keepe.[16] 360

41

And more, to lulle him in his slumber soft,
A trickling streame from high rocke tumbling downe
And ever-drizling raine upon the loft,[17]
Mixt with a murmuring winde, much like the sowne
Of swarming Bees, did cast him in a swowne.   365
No other noyse, nor people's troublous cryes,
As still are wont t'annoy the walled[18] towne,
Might there be heard; but carelesse Quiet lyes,
Wrapt in eternall silence farre from enemyes.

42

The messenger approching to him spake,   370
But his wast wordes returnd to him in vaine;
So sound he slept that nought mought[19] him awake.
Then rudely he him thrust, and pusht with paine,
Whereat he gan to stretch; but he againe
Shooke him so hard that forced him to speake.   375
As one then in a dreame, whose dryer braine[20]
Is tost with troubled sights and fancies weake,
He mumbled soft, but would not all his silence breake.

43

The Sprite then gan more boldly him to wake,
And threatned unto him the dreaded name   380
Of Hecatë;[21] whereat he gan to quake,

And, lifting up his lumpish head, with blame
Halfe angry asked him for what he came.
"Hether," quoth he, "me Archimago sent,
He that the stubborne Sprites can wisely tame;   385
He bids thee to him send for his intent
A fit false dreame, that can delude the sleeper's sent.[22]"

44

The God obayde and, calling forth straight way
A diverse[23] dreame out of his prison darke,
Delivered it to him, and downe did lay   390
His heavie head, devoide of careful carke,[24]
Whose sences all were straight benumbd and starke.
He, backe returning by the Yvorie dore,[25]
Remounted up as light as chearefull Larke;
And on his litle winges the dreame he bore   395
In hast unto his Lord, where he him left afore.

45

Who all this while, with charmes and hidden artes,
Had made a Lady of that other Spright,
And fram'd of liquid ayre her tender partes,
So lively and so like in all men's sight   400
That weaker sence it could have ravisht quight;
The maker selfe, for all his wondrous witt,
Was nigh beguiled with so goodly sight.
Her all in white he clad, and over it
Cast a black stole, most like to seeme for Una fit.   405

46

Now, when that ydle[26] dreame was to him brought,
Unto that Elfin knight he bad him fly,
Where he slept soundly void of evill thought,
And with false shewes abuse his fantasy,[27]
In sort as[28] he him schooled privily;   410
And that new creature, borne without her dew,[29]
Full of the maker's guyle, with usage sly
He taught to imitate that Lady trew
Whose semblance she did carrie under feigned hew.

47

Thus well instructed, to their worke they hast,   415
And comming where the knight in slomber lay,
The one upon his hardy head him plast,
And made him dreame of loves and lustfull play,

---

[12] Precipitous.
[13] Wife of Oceanus, god of the sea.   [14] The moon goddess.
[15] Ever.   [16] Heed.   [17] Top of the house.
[18] And hence good-sized.   [19] Could.
[20] Moisture was supposed to induce a sound and dreamless sleep.
See line 317, above.
[21] A nocturnal goddess of the moon, magic, and Hades.

[22] Sensation, senses.   [23] Distracting, misleading.
[24] Worry.
[25] The exit for false dreams; true ones went out by the gate of horn.
[26] Empty, false.
[27] With false shows (apparitions) deceive his imagination.
[28] In the way that.   [29] Due; i.e., unnaturally.

That nigh his manly hart did melt away,
Bathed in wanton blis and wicked joy.
Then seemed him his Lady by him lay,   420
And to him playnd[30] how that false winged boy
Her chast hart had subdewd, to learne Dame Pleasure's
    toy.[31]

48

And she her selfe, of beautie soveraigne Queene,
Faire Venus, seemde unto his bed to bring   425
Her whom he waking evermore did weene
To be the chastest flowre that ay did spring
On earthly braunch, the daughter of a king,
Now a loose Leman[32] to vile service bound.
And eke the Graces seemed all to sing   430
Hymen iō Hymen,[33] dauncing all around,
Whilst freshest Flora[34] her with Yuie girlond crownd.

49

In this great passion of unwonted lust,
Or wonted feare of doing ought amis,
He started up, as seeming to mistrust   435
Some secret ill or hidden foe of his.
Lo, there before his face his Lady is,
Under blake stole hyding her bayted hooke,[35]
And as halfe blushing offred him to kis,
With gentle blandishment and lovely looke,   440
Most like that virgin true, which for her knight him took.

50

All cleane dismayd to see so uncouth[36] sight,
And halfe enraged at her shameless guise,
He thought have slaine her in his fierce despight;[37]
But hasty heat tempring with sufferance[38] wise,   445
He stayde his hand and gan himselfe advise
To prove his sense, and tempt her faigned truth.
Wringing her hands, in wemen's pitteous wise,[39]
Tho can[40] she weepe, to stirre up gentle ruth,[41]
Both for her noble bloud and for her tender youth.   450

51

And said, "Ah, Sir, my liege Lord and my love,
Shall I accuse the hidden cruell fate

And mightie causes wrought in heaven above
Or the blind God,[42] that doth me thus amate,[43]
For hoped love to winne me certaine hate?   455
Yet thus perforce he bids me do, or die.
Die is my dew. Yet rew my wretched state
You, whom my hard avenging destinie
Hath made judge of my life or death indifferently!

52

"Your owne deare sake forst me at first to leave   460
My Father's kingdome—" there she stopt with teares:
Her swollen hart her speach seemd to bereave;
And then againe begun, "My weaker yeares
Captiv'd to fortune and frayle worldly feares,
Fly to your faith for succour and sure ayde.   465
Let me not dye in languor and long teares!"
"Why, Dame," quoth he, "what hath ye thus dismayd?"
What frayes[44] ye, that were wont to comfort me affrayd?"

53

"Love of your selfe," she said, "and deare[45] constraint
Lets me not sleepe, but wast the wearie night   470
In secret anguish and unpittied plaint,
Whiles you in carelesse sleepe are drowned quight."
Her doubtfull words made that redoubted knight
Suspect her truth; yet, since no'untruth he knew,
Her fawning love with foule, disdainefull spight   475
He would not shend,[46] but said, "Deare dame, I rew,
That for my sake unknowne such griefe unto you grew.

54

"Assure your selfe, it fell not all to ground;
For all so deare as life is to my hart
I deeme your love, and hold me to you bound.   480
Ne let vaine feares procure your needlesse smart,
Where cause is none; but to your rest depart!"
Not all content, yet seemd she to appease
Her mournefull plaintes, beguiled of her art
And fed with words that could not chuse but please.   485
So, slyding softly forth, she turnd as to her ease.

55

Long after lay he musing at her mood,
Much griev'd to thinke that gentle Dame so light,
For whose defence he was to shed his blood.
At last dull wearinesse of former fight   490
Having yrockt asleepe his irkesome spright,[47]

---

30 Complained, lamented.   31 Trifle, trifling.
32 Mistress.
33 Hymen, ho, Hymen! I.e., a marriage song, Hymen being god
   of marriage.   34 Goddess of flowers.
35 I.e., her body's beauty.   36 Strange.   37 Anger.
38 Patience.   39 Way.
40 Then did. For can in the sense of began, did, see also line 68,
   above.   41 Pity.

42 Cupid, god of love.
43 Daunt, overcome.   44 Frightens.   45 Urgent.
46 Blame, revile.   47 His own spirit or consciousness.

That troublous dreame gan freshly tosse his braine,
With bowres, and beds, and Ladies' deare delight;
But when he[48] saw his labour all was vaine,
With that misformed spright he backe returnd againe. 495

CANTO II

The guilefull great Enchaunter parts
The Redcrosse Knight from Truth:
Into whose stead faire falshood steps,
And workes him wofull ruth.

1

By this the Northerne wagoner had set
His sevenfold teme[1] behind the stedfast starre[2]
That was in Ocean waves yet never wet,
But firme is fixt and sendeth light from farre
To all that in the wide deepe wandring arre;   5
And chearefull Chaunticlere with his note shrill
Had warned once that Phoebus' fiery carre
In hast was climbing up the Easterne hill,
Full envious that night so long his roome did fill.

2

When those accursed messengers of hell,   10
That feigning dreame and that faire-forged Spright,
Came to their wicked maister and gan tell
Their bootelesse paines and ill succeeding night;
Who all in rage to see his skilfull might
Deluded so, gan threaten hellish paine   15
And sad Proserpine's wrath, them to affright.
But when he saw his threatning was but vaine,
He cast about and searcht his balefull bookes againe.

3

Eftsoones he tooke that miscreated faire
And that false other Spright, on whom he spred   20
A seeming body of the subtile aire,
Like a young Squire, in loves and lusty-hed
His wanton dayes that ever loosely led,
Without regard of armes and dreaded fight;
Those two he tooke, and in a secret bed,   25
Covered with darknesse and misdeeming[3] night,
Them both together laid, to joy in vaine delight.

4

Forthwith he runnes with feigned faithfull hast
Unto his guest, who after troublous sights
And dreames gan now to take more sound repast,[4]   30
Whom suddenly he wakes with fearefull frights,
As one aghast with feends or damned sprights,
And to him cals, "Rise, rise, unhappy Swaine,
That here wex old in sleepe, whiles wicked wights
Have knit themselves in Venus' shamefull chaine;   35
Come, see where your false Lady doth her honour staine."

5

All in amaze he suddenly up start
With sword in hand, and with the old man went;
Who soone him brought into a secret part,
Where that false couple were full closely ment[5]   40
In wanton lust and lewd embracement;
Which when he saw, he burnt with gealous fire;
The eye of reason was with rage yblent,[6]
And would have slaine them in his furious ire,
But hardly was restreined of that aged sire.   45

6

Returning to his bed in torment great
And bitter anguish of his guiltie sight,
He could not rest, but did his stout heart eat,
And wast his inward gall with deepe despight,
Yrkesome[7] of life and too long lingring night.   50
At last faire Hesperus in highest skie
Had spent his lampe and brought forth dawning light.
Then up he rose, and clad him hastily.
The Dwarfe him brought his steed; so both away do fly.

7

Now when the rosy-fingred Morning faire,   55
Weary of aged Tithone's[8] saffron bed,
Had spred her purple robe through deawy aire,
And the high hils Titan[9] discovered,
The royall virgin shooke off drowsy-hed,
And rising forth out of her baser bowre,   60
Lookt for her knight, who far away was fled,
And for her Dwarfe, that wont to wait each houre;
Then gan she waile and weepe, to see that woefull
        stowre.[10]

---

[48] The dream spirit, which now returns to Archimago in company
with the other spirit made in the image of Una.

[1] The seven stars of the Dipper, sometimes called Charles's Wain
(Wagon).   [2] The North Star.
[3] Misleading, creating misunderstanding.

[4] I.e., sleep.
[5] Mingled.   [6] Blinded.   [7] Wearied.
[8] Tithonus's. He was beloved of Aurora, goddess of the dawn,
who persuaded Jove to grant him immortality but neglected to
ask for eternal youth.   [9] The sun.   [10] Calamity.

8

And after him she rode with so much speede
As her slow beast could make; but all in vaine: 65
For him so far had borne his light-foot steede,
Pricked with wrath and fiery fierce disdaine,
That him to follow was but fruitlesse paine;
Yet she her weary limbes would never rest,
But every hill and dale, each wood and plaine   70
Did search, sore grieved in her gentle brest,
He so ungently left her, whom she loved best.

* * * * *

from AMORETTI

That it is usually impossible to be sure whether an Elizabethan sonnet is autobiographical or merely conventional
has already been remarked in the introductory note on
Sidney. The case is clearer with Spenser's. He may have
had some sonnets on hand and worked them into his cycle;
but there is small doubt that most of these poems were
inspired by Elizabeth Boyle. Certainly the whole cycle
achieves a unity of tone. In all there are eighty-nine of these
"little love" poems. In structure Spenser follows the
English rather than the Italian form (see p. 247, above):
his sonnet consists of three quatrains and a closing couplet.
The quatrains are, however, more closely linked than is
customary, by the extension of one of the rimes of each
quatrain into the next: *abab bcbc cdcd ee*, an arrangement
reminiscent of the Spenserian stanza itself.

I

Happy, ye leaves,[1] when as[2] those lilly hands
Which hold my life in their dead doing[3] might
Shall handle you and hold in love's soft bands,
Lyke captives trembling at the victor's sight!
And happy lines, on which with starry light   5
Those lamping[4] eyes will deigne sometimes to look
And reade the sorrowes of my dying spright,[5]
Written with teares in hart's close bleeding book!
And happy rymes, bath'd in the sacred brooke
Of Helicon,[6] whence she derived is,   10
When ye behold that Angel's blessed looke,
My soule's long lacked foode, my heaven's blis!
Leaves, lines, and rymes, seeke her to please alone!
Whom if ye please, I care for other none.

70

Fresh spring, the herald of love's mighty king,[7]
In whose cote armour[8] richly are displayd
All sorts of flowers the which on earth do spring
In goodly colours gloriously arrayd,
Goe to my love, where she is carelesse layd,   5
Yet in her winter's bowre not well awake:
Tell her the joyous time wil not be staid
Unlesse she doe him by the forelock take!
Bid her therefore her selfe soone ready make,
To wayt on love amongst his lovely crew,   10
Where every one that misseth then her make[9]
Shall be by him amearst[10] with penance dew!
Make hast therefore, sweet love, whilest it is prime![11]
For none can call againe the passed time.

75

One day I wrote her name upon the strand,
But came the waves and washed it away;
Agayne I wrote it with a second hand,
But came the tyde and made my paynes his pray.
"Vayne man," sayd she, "that doest in vaine assay   5
A mortall thing so to immortalize!
For I my selfe shall lyke to this decay,
And eek my name bee wyped out lykewize."
"Not so," quod I; "let baser things devize[12]
To dy in dust, but you shall live by fame.   10
My verse your vertues rare shall eternize,
And in the hevens wryte your glorious name.
Where, whenas death shall all the world subdew,
Our love shall live and later life renew."

82

Joy of my life, full oft for loving you
I blesse my lot, that was so lucky placed.
But then the more your owne mishap I rew,[13]
That are so much by so meane love embased.[14]
For, had the equall hevens so much you graced   5
In this as in the rest, ye mote invent[15]
Som hevenly wit, whose verse could have enchased[16]
Your glorious name in golden moniment.
But since ye deignd so goodly to relent
To me, your thrall, in whom is little worth,   10
That little that I am shall all be spent
In setting your immortall prayses forth:
Whose lofty argument,[17] uplifting me,
Shall lift you up unto an high degree.

---

1 Sheets of paper on which the sonnets are written.
2 Whenas, when.   3 Death dealing.   4 Shining.
5 Spirit.
6 The Greek mountain, in Boeotia, sacred to Apollo and the
Muses.

7 Cupid.
8 The herald's tabard, an outer garment bright with armorial
   bearings.   9 Mate.   10 Amerced, fined, punished.
11 Spring.   12 Plan.   13 Pity.   14 Degraded.
15 Might find.   16 Engraved.   17 Theme.

EPITHALAMION *also to Elizabeth Boyle*

In this magnificent tone-poem of happy love Spenser overcomes his tendency to diffuseness; and his music, so often
melodious but thin, is fully orchestrated. It is not always
true that a man's best poem must spring from direct experience, but it is clear that this one did. The word *epithalamion* is Greek in origin and means *nuptial song*.

Ye learned sisters which have oftentimes
Beene to me ayding, others to adorne[18]
Whom ye thought worthy of your gracefull rymes,
That[19] even the greatest did not greatly scorne
To heare theyr names sung in your simple layes,   5
But joyed in theyr prayse
(And when ye list your owne mishaps to mourne,[20]
Which death or love or fortune's wreck did rayse,
Your string could soone to sadder tenor turne,
And teach the woods and waters to lament   10
Your dolefull dreriment),
Now lay those sorrowfull complaints aside,
And, having all your heads with girland crownd,
Helpe me mine owne love's prayses to resound,
Ne let the same of any be envide![21]   15
So Orpheus did for his owne bride;[22]
So I unto my selfe alone will sing:
The woods shall to me answer and my Eccho ring.

Early before the world's light-giving lampe
His golden beame upon the hils doth spred,   20
Having disperst the night's unchearefull dampe,
Doe ye awake, and with fresh lusty-hed[23]
Go to the bowre[24] of my beloved love,
My truest turtledove!
Bid her awake; for Hymen[25] is awake   25
And long since ready forth his maske[26] to move,
With his bright Tead[27] that flames with many a flake,[28]
And many a bachelor to waite on him,
In theyr fresh garments trim!
Bid her awake therefore and soone her dight,[29]   30
For lo! the wished day is come at last,
That shall for al the paynes and sorrowes past
Pay to her usury of long delight!
And whylest she doth her dight,
Do ye to her of joy and solace sing,   35
That all the woods may answer and your eccho ring!

Bring with you all the Nymphes that you can heare,
Both of the rivers and the forrests greene
And of the sea that neighbours to her neare,[30]
Al with gay girlands goodly wel beseene.[31]   40
And let them also with them bring in hand
Another gay girlánd
For my fayre love of lillyes and of roses,
Bound truelove-wize with a blew silke ribánd.
And let them make great store of bridale poses,[32]   45
And let them eeke[33] bring store of other flowers
To deck the bridale bowers.
And let the ground whereas[34] her foot shall tread,
For feare the stones her tender foot should wrong,
Be strewed with fragrant flowers all along   50
And diapred[35] lyke the discolored mead.[36]
Which done, doe at her chamber dore awayt,
For she will waken strayt,[37]
The whiles doe ye this song unto her sing:
The woods shall to you answer and your Eccho ring.   55

Ye Nymphes of Mulla,[38] which with carefull heed
The silver scaly trouts doe tend full well
And greedy pikes which use therein to feed
(Those trouts and pikes all others doo excell),
And ye likewise which keepe the rushy lake   60
Where none doo fishes take,
Bynd up the locks the which hang scatterd light,
And in his waters which your mirror make
Behold your faces as the christall bright,
That when you come whereas my love doth lie   65
No blemish she may spie.
And eke ye lightfoot mayds[39] which keepe the dere
That on the hoary mountayne use to towre,[40]
And the wylde wolves which seeke them to devoure
With your steele darts doo chace from comming neer,   70
Be also present heere
To helpe to decke her and to help to sing,
That all the woods may answer and your eccho ring.

Wake now, my love, awake, for it is time;
The Rosy Morne long since left Tithone's[41] bed,   75
All ready to her silver coche to clyme,
And Phoebus gins to shew his glorious hed.

---

[30] Elizabeth Boyle, whom Spenser married, lived at Kilcoran, County Cork, on the Bay of Youghal.
[31] Appareled, adorned.   [32] Posies, nosegays.   [33] Also.
[34] Where.   [35] Patterned (with flowers).
[36] Variegated meadow.   [37] Directly, soon.
[38] Spenser's name for the River Awbeg, near his home at Kilcol-man. His castle stood close to the "rushy lake" of line 60, and the mountain of line 68 was also near.
[39] I.e., more nymphs, in classical mythology minor divinities of nature.   [40] Climb to high altitudes.
[41] Tithonus's. He was the mortal youth who loved Aurora, the dawn goddess.

[18] I.e., ye nine Muses, who have often helped me write verses to others.   [19] So that.
[20] An allusion to Spenser's poem *The Tears of the Muses*.
[21] Nor let my beloved be hated by anyone (because I show her this attention).   [22] Eurydice.   [23] Lustihood, vigor.
[24] Bedchamber.   [25] God of marriage.
[26] Processional rite, celebration.   [27] Torch, Hymen's symbol.
[28] Spark.   [29] Quickly dress herself.

Hark how the cheerefull birds do chaunt theyr laies
And carroll of love's praise.
The merry Larke hir mattins[42] sings aloft,   80
The thrush replyes, the Mavis[43] descant playes,[44]
The Ouzell[45] shrills, the Ruddock[46] warbles soft,
So goodly all agree with sweet consent[47]
To this daye's merriment.
Ah! my deere love, why doe ye sleepe thus long,   85
When meeter were that ye should now awake,
T'awayt the comming of your joyous make,[48]
And hearken to the birds' love-learned song,
The deawy leaves among?
For they of joy and pleasance to you sing,   90
That all the woods them answer and theyr eccho ring.

My love is now awake out of her dreames,
And her fayre eyes, like stars that dimmed were
With darksome cloud, now shew theyr goodly beams
More bright then[49] Hesperus[50] his head doth rere.   95
Come now, ye damzels,[51] daughters of delight,
Helpe quickly her to dight!
But first come ye, fayre Houres,[52] which were begot
In Jove's sweet paradice, of Day and Night,
Which doe the seasons of the yeare allot,   100
And al that ever in this world is fayre
Do make and still repayre.
And ye three handmayds[53] of the Cyprian Queene,[54]
The which doe still adorne her beautie's pride,
Helpe to addorne my beautifullest bride!   105
And as ye her array, still throw betweene
Some graces to be seene;
And, as ye use to Venus, to her sing,
The whiles the woods shal answer and your eccho ring.

Now is my love all ready forth to come.   110
Let all the virgins therefore well awayt;
And ye fresh boyes, that tend upon her groome,
Prepare your selves, for he is comming strayt.
Set all your things in seemely good aray,
Fit for so joyfull day,   115
The joyfulst day that ever sunne did see!
Faire Sun, shew forth thy favourable ray,
And let thy lifull[55] heat not fervent be,
For feare of burning her sunshyny face,

Her beauty to disgrace.   120
O fayrest Phoebus,[56] father of the Muse,
If ever I did honour thee aright,
Or sing the thing that mote[57] thy mind delight,
Doe not thy servant's simple boone refuse,
But let this day, let this one day be myne—   125
Let all the rest be thine!
Then I thy soverayne prayses loud wil sing,
That all the woods shal answer and theyr eccho ring.

Harke how the Minstrels gin to shrill aloud
Their merry Musick that resounds from far,   130
The pipe, the tabor,[58] and the trembling Croud,[59]
That well agree withouten breach or jar.
But most of all the Damzels doe delite,
When they their tymbrels[60] smyte,
And thereunto doe daunce and carrol sweet,   135
That all the sences they doe ravish quite,
The whyles the boyes run up and downe the street,
Crying aloud with strong confused noyce,
As if it were one voyce.
"Hymen, iö Hymen, Hymen!"[61] they do shout,   140
That even to the heavens theyr shouting shrill
Doth reach and all the firmament doth fill;
To which the people, standing all about,
As in approvance doe thereto applaud,
And loud advaunce her laud,   145
And evermore they "Hymen, Hymen" sing,
That al the woods them answer and theyr eccho ring.

Loe, where she comes along with portly pace,[62]
Lyke Phoebe,[63] from her chamber of the East,
Arysing forth to run her mighty race,   150
Clad all in white, that seemes[64] a virgin best.
So well it her beseemes that ye would weene
Some angell she had beene.
Her long loose yellow locks lyke golden wyre,
Sprinckled with perle, and perling flowers atweene,   155
Doe lyke a golden mantle her attyre,
And being crowned with a girland greene,
Seeme lyke some mayden Queene.
Her modest eyes, abashed to behold
So many gazers as on her do stare,   160
Upon the lowly ground affixed are;
Ne dare lift up her countenance too bold,
But blush to heare her prayses sung so loud,
So farre from being proud.

---

42 Morning songs.   43 Song thrush.
44 I.e., sings a "part," which harmonizes.
45 Blackbird; the European variety is a songbird.   46 Robin.
47 Accord, harmony.   48 Mate.   49 Than.
50 The evening star, Venus.   51 The bridesmaids.
52 The Horae of classical mythology, goddesses of the seasons and
   of orderliness. They were the daughters of Jove.
53 The Graces, sister goddesses.
54 I.e., goddess. Aphrodite or Venus, supposed to have been born
   at Cyprus.   55 Lifeful, life-giving.

56 Apollo, in classical mythology the god of poetry and music,
   but not the Muses' father.   57 Might.   58 Small drum.
59 Crowd, an ancestor of the fiddle.   60 Tambourines.
61 The Romans' joyous cry in honor of Hymen.
62 Stately step.
63 Diana, goddess of the moon. Cf. Psalms 19:4–5.   64 Becomes.

Nathlesse doe ye still loud her prayses sing,   165
That all the woods may answer and your eccho ring.

Tell me, ye merchants' daughters, did ye see
So fayre a creature in your towne before,
So sweet, so lovely, and so mild as she,
Adornd with beautye's grace and vertue's store?   170
Her goodly eyes lyke Saphyres shining bright,
Her forehead yvory white,
Her cheekes lyke apples which the sun hath rudded,
Her lips lyke cherryes charming men to byte,
Her brest like to a bowle of creame uncrudded,[65]   175
Her paps lyke lyllies budded,
Her snowie necke lyke to a marble towre,
And all her body like a pallace fayre,
Ascending uppe with many a stately stayre,
To honour's seat and chastitie's sweet bowre.[66]   180
Why stand ye still, ye virgins, in amaze
Upon her so to gaze,
Whiles ye forget your former lay to sing,
To which the woods did answer and your eccho ring?

But if ye saw that which no eyes can see,   185
The inward beauty of her lively spright,[67]
Garnisht with heavenly guifts of high degree,
Much more then would ye wonder at that sight
And stand astonisht lyke to those which red[68]
Medusae's mazeful[69] hed.   190
There dwels sweet love and constant chastity,
Unspotted fayth and comely womanhood,
Regard of honour and mild modesty;
There vertue raynes as Queene in royal throne,
And giveth lawes alone,   195
The which the base affections[70] doe obay
And yeeld theyr services unto her will;
Ne thought of thing uncomely ever may
Thereto approch to tempt her mind to ill.
Had ye once seene these her celestial threasures   200
And unrevealed pleasures,
Then would ye wonder and her prayses sing,
That al the woods should answer and your eccho ring.

Open the temple gates[71] unto my love,
Open them wide that she may enter in,   205
And all the postes adorne as doth behove,
And all the pillours deck with girlands trim,

For to recyve this Saynt with honour dew,
That commeth in to you!
With trembling steps and humble reverence   210
She commeth in, before th'almightie's vew.
Of her, ye virgins, learne obedience:
When so ye come into those holy places,
To humble your proud faces!
Bring her up to th'high altar, that she may   215
The sacred ceremonies there partake,
The which do endlesse matrimony make;
And let the roring Organs loudly play
The praises of the Lord in lively notes,
The whiles with hollow throates   220
The Choristers the joyous Antheme sing,
That al the woods may answere and their eccho ring!

Behold, whiles she before the altar stands
Hearing the holy priest that to her speakes
And blesseth her with his two happy hands,   225
How the red roses flush up in her cheekes,
And the pure snow with goodly vermill stayne,
Like crimsin dyde in grayne,[72]
That even th'Angels which continually
About the sacred Altare doe remaine   230
Forget their service and about her fly,
Ofte peeping in her face that seemes more fayre,
The more they on it stare.
But her sad[73] eyes still fastened on the ground
Are governed with goodly modesty,   235
That suffers not one looke to glaunce awry
Which may let in a little thought unsownd.
Why blush ye, love, to give to me your hand,
The pledge of all our band?[74]
Sing ye, sweet Angels, Alleluya sing,   240
That all the woods may answer and your eccho ring!

Now al is done; bring home the bride againe,
Bring home the triumph of our victory,
Bring home with you the glory of her gaine,[75]
With joyance bring her and with jollity!   245
Never had man more joyfull day then this,
Whom heaven would heape with blis.
Make feast therefore now all this livelong day—
This day for ever to me holy is—
Poure out the wine without restraint or stay,   250
Poure not by cups, but by the bellyfull,
Poure out to all that wull,[76]
And sprinkle all the postes and wals with wine,[77]
That they may sweat and drunken be withall!

[65] Uncurdled.
[66] The head, seat of the mind.   [67] Spirit, soul.
[68] Looked upon.
[69] Confounding. According to the myth, whoever looked at the
    head of the Gorgon Medusa, with her hair of snakes, was
    turned to stone.   [70] Inclinations, passions.
[71] I.e., the church doors.

[72] Fast.   [73] Serious.
[74] Bond (of marriage).   [75] Of having won her.
[76] Will, wish.   [77] A Roman custom.

Crowne ye God Bacchus with a coronall, 255
And Hymen also crowne with wreathes of vine,
And let the Graces daunce unto the rest,
For they can doo it best!
The whiles the maydens doe theyr carroll sing, 259
To which the woods shall answer and theyr eccho ring.

Ring ye the bels, ye yong men of the towne,
And leave your wonted labours for this day!
This day is holy: doe ye write it downe,
That ye for ever it remember may!
This day the sunne is in his chiefest hight, 265
With Barnaby[78] the bright,
From whence declining daily by degrees
He somewhat loseth of his heat and light,
When once the Crab[79] behind his back he sees.
But for this time it ill ordained was 270
To chose the longest day in all the yeare
And shortest night, when longest fitter weare;
Yet never day so long, but late would passe.
Ring ye the bels, to make it weare away,
And bonefiers make all day 275
And daunce about them and about them sing,
That all the woods may answer and your eccho ring.

Ah, when will this long, weary day have end
And lende me leave to come unto my love?
How slowly do the houres theyr numbers spend! 280
How slowly does sad Time his feathers move!
Hast thee, O fayrest Planet,[80] to thy home
Within the Westerne fome!
Thy tyred steedes long since have need of rest.
Long though it be, at last I see it gloome, 285
And the bright evening star with golden creast
Appeare out of the East.
Fayre childe of beauty, glorious lampe of love,
That all the host of heaven in rankes doost lead,
And guydest lovers through the nightès dread, 290
How chearefully thou lookest from above
And seemst to laugh atweene thy twinkling light,
As joying in the sight
Of these glad many which for joy doe sing,
That all the woods them answer and theyr eccho ring. 295

Now ceasse, ye damsels, your delights forepast;
Enough is it that all the day was youres;
Now day is doen, and night is nighing fast:
Now bring the Bryde into the brydall boures!
Now night is come, now soone her disaray, 300

Behold, how goodly my faire love does ly 305
In proud humility,
Like unto Maia,[82] when-as Jove her tooke,
In Tempe,[83] lying on the flowry gras,
Twixt sleepe and wake, after she weary was,
With bathing in the Acidalian brooke![84] 310
Now it is night; ye damsels may be gon,
And leave my love alone,
And leave likewise your former lay to sing;
The woods no more shal answer nor your eccho ring.

Now welcome, night, thou night so long expected, 315
That long daie's labour doest at last defray,
And all my cares, which cruell love collected,
Hast sumd in one and cancelled for aye!
Spread thy broad wing over my love and me,
That no man may us see, 320
And in thy sable mantle us enwrap,
From feare of perrill and foule horror free.
Let no false treason seeke us to entrap,
Nor any dread disquiet once annoy
The safety of our joy; 325
But let the night be calme and quietsome,
Without tempestuous storms or sad afray,
Lyke as when Jove with fayre Alcmena lay,
When he begot the great Tirynthian groome;[85]
Or lyke as when he with thy selfe did lie, 330
And begot Majesty![86]
And let the mayds and yongmen cease to sing,
Ne let the woods them answer nor theyr eccho ring!

Let no lamenting cryes nor dolefull teares
Be heard all night within nor yet without; 335
Ne let false whispers, breeding hidden feares,
Breake gentle sleepe with misconceived dout!
Let no deluding dreames nor dreadful sights
Make sudden sad affrights;
Ne let housefyres nor lightning's helpelesse[87] harmes, 340
Ne let the Pouke[88] nor other evill sprights,
Ne let mischívous witches with theyr charmes,

---

[81] Famous for its textiles, especially tapestry.
[82] Mother of Hermes or Mercury.
[83] A vale in Thessaly, famous in mythology, but not for this episode. [84] I.e., the fountain Acidalius, in Boeotia.
[85] Hercules. It was in the service of King Eurystheus of Tiryns (in Argos) that he performed his twelve labors.
[86] Apparently this episode is Spenser's invention; his references to mythology are often inaccurate. [87] Irreparable.
[88] In Celtic folklore a malicious goblin. Shakespeare arbitrarily makes Robin Goodfellow (Puck in *A Midsummer Night's Dream*) merely mischievous.

---

[78] St. Barnabas. His day, June 11, coincided in the old calendar (which by Spenser's time had lagged behind the sun) with the summer solstice, the longest day of the year.
[79] Cancer, a sign of the zodiac. The sun leaves it in June.
[80] The sun.

And in her bed her lay;
Lay her in lillies and in violets,
And silken courteins over her display,
And odourd sheetes, and Arras[81] coverlets.

Ne let hob Goblins, names whose sence we see not,
Fray[89] us with things that be not.
Let not the shriech[90] Oule nor the Storke be heard;   345
Nor the night Raven that still deadly yels,
Nor damned ghosts cald up with mighty spels,
Nor griesly vultures make us once affeard;
Ne let th'unpleasant Quyre of Frogs still croking
Make us to wish theyr choking;   350
Let none of these theyr drery accents sing,
Ne let the woods them answer, nor theyr eccho ring!

But let stil Silence trew night watches keepe,
That sacred peace may in assurance rayne,
And tymely sleep, when it is tyme to sleepe,   355
May poure his limbs forth on your pleasant playne,
The whiles an hundred little winged loves,
Like divers fethered doves,
Shall fly and flutter round about your bed,
And in the secret darke, that none reproves,   360
Their prety stealthes shal worke and snares shal spread
To filch away sweet snatches of delight,
Conceald through covert night.
Ye sonnes of Venus, play your sports at will,
For greedy pleasure, carelesse of your toyes,   365
Thinks more upon her paradise of joyes,
Then what ye do, albe it[91] good or ill.
All night therefore attend your merry play,
For it will soone be day!
Now none doth hinder you, that say or sing,   370
Ne will the woods now answer nor your Eccho ring.

Who is the same which at my window peepes?
Or whose is that faire face that shines so bright?
Is it not Cinthia,[92] she that never sleepes,
But walkes about high heaven al the night?   375
O fayrest goddesse, do thou not envý
My love with me to spy!
For thou likewise didst love, though now unthought,
And for a fleece of woll, which privily
The Latmian shephard[93] once unto thee brought,   380
His pleasures with thee wrought.
Therefore to us be favorable now;
And sith of wemen's labours thou hast charge[94]
And generation goodly dost enlarge,
Encline thy will t' effect our wishfull vow,   385
And the chast wombe informe with timely seed,

That may our comfort breed!
Till which we cease our hopefull hap[95] to sing,
Ne let the woods us answere nor our Eccho ring.

And thou, great Juno, which with awful might   390
The lawes of wedlock still dost patronize,
And the religion of the faith first plight
With sacred rites hast taught to solemnize,
And eeke for comfort often called art
Of women in their smart,   395
Eternally bind thou this lovely band,
And all thy blessings unto us impart!
And thou, glad Genius,[96] in whose gentle hand
The bridale bowre and geniall[97] bed remaine,
Without blemish or staine,   400
And the sweet pleasures of theyr love's delight
With secret ayde dost succour and supply
Till they bring forth the fruitfull progeny,
Send us the timely fruit of this same night!
And thou, fayre Hebe,[98] and thou Hymen free,   405
Grant that it may so be!
Til which we cease your further prayse to sing,
Ne any woods shal answer nor your Eccho ring.

And ye high heavens, the temple of the gods,
In which a thousand torches flaming bright   410
Doe burne, that to us wretched earthly clods
In dreadfull darknesse lend desired light,
And all ye powers which in the same remayne,
More then we men can fayne,[99]
Poure out your blessings on us plentiously   415
And happy influence upon us raine,
That we may raise a large posterity,
Which from the earth, which they may long possesse
With lasting happinesse,
Up to your haughty pallaces may mount,   420
And for the guerdon[1] of theyr glorious merit
May heavenly tabernacles there inherit,
Of blessed Saints for to increase the count!
So let us rest, sweet love, in hope of this,
And cease till then our tymely joyes to sing,   425
The woods no more us answer nor our eccho ring.

Song made in lieu of many ornaments
With which my love should duly have bene dect,
Which cutting off through hasty accidents
Ye would not stay your dew time to expect[2]   430
But promist both to recompens,
Be unto her a goodly ornament
And for short time an endlesse moniment!

---

[89] Frighten.
[90] Screech. Why the stork should appear among the birds of ill omen Spenser does not explain.   [91] Whether it be.
[92] The moon, Diana.
[93] Endymion, the shepherd boy of Mt. Latmos. The moon saw him and loved him, as he lay sleeping. Spenser alters the myth.
[94] In this "aspect" Diana was known as Lucina. Juno, also, was often invoked in childbirth; hence lines 394-95.

[95] Good fortune.   [96] Guardian spirit.   [97] Nuptial, procreative.
[98] Goddess of youth.   [99] Feign, imagine.   [1] Reward.
[2] Await. Apparently "accidents of haste" had advanced the date of the marriage, and the ornaments the poet had intended to offer his bride could not be procured in time.

Christopher Marlowe

1564–1593

MARLOWE has been called the first *sublime* English poet. In any art, elevation is not obtained by the exercise of caution. Marlowe threw in everything he had, into life and into his writing, with a headlong recklessness which, joined with an intense adoration of beauty and an unbounded curiosity about man's role in the universe, was to make him for future generations the very pattern of a Renaissance artist.

He was born in Canterbury in 1564, about two months before the probable date of Shakespeare's birth. His father was a successful shoemaker. Scholarships at King's School in Canterbury and at Corpus Christi College, Cambridge, took the poet to his B.A. in 1584 and his M.A. three years later. He was absent from Cambridge for lengthy periods presumably spent as an agent in one of the secret services maintained by the great ministers of state, and when the university authorities hesitated to bestow the M.A. they received a direct order from the Privy Council.

Marlowe had begun to write at Cambridge. When he left for London, where he seems to have spent the six years that remained to him, it was to put his pen to work as a "university wit" and professional man of letters. Except for the fragmentary *Hero and Leander,* his nondramatic poems are of slight importance.[1] He had no natural aptitude for the stage, as Shakespeare had; his first play, *Tamburlaine* (in two parts, *c.* 1587), is more epic than dramatic. It made, however, a tremendous impression in the theater; and the thundering lines of its all-conquering hero established blank verse as the principal medium of Elizabethan dramatic poetry. The next play, *Doctor Faustus,* is considerably more suited to the stage; and after *The Jew of Malta* (which influenced *The Merchant of Venice* and the Elizabethan stage villain in general), Marlowe's career as playwright closed with *Edward II,* dramatically though not poetically the best of his plays. These five pieces (he wrote two other plays of little merit) display such a rapid development in dramatic art that many have wondered whether, had he lived, he might have rivaled Shakespeare. For he possessed, from the first, the most important of a poet's attributes: imaginative power in the highest degree, and the most sensitive and even sensuous feeling for words. What he lacked at first, but was gaining as he worked on *Edward II,* was a dramatist's feeling for human nature, an eye for its manifestations in human actions, and a sense of humor; in these vital departments of a playwright's equip-

ment he never came abreast of Shakespeare, from whom (as his last play shows) he was learning fast.

All Marlowe's plays except the last are marked by immense and original force. Their heroes are embodiments of insatiable and implacable desire, the eternal thrusting of man's spirit against all that says, "Thus far and no farther." Tamburlaine seeks the ultimate by force of arms, Faustus through knowledge, Barabas, the hero-villain of *The Jew of Malta,* through the power of money. These men are all less credible as human beings than the characters of *Edward II,* but each is a flaming symbol of human aspiration and a typical expression of one side of the Renaissance. Marlowe is dead in earnest about them; his vein is exclusively high seriousness, and in none of his plays is there any comic scene certainly of his own writing.

This brilliant career ended on May 30, 1593, in Marlowe's thirtieth year. The inquest concluded that he had been stabbed by a drinking companion in a quarrel over a tavern bill; but the affair remains obscure, and there may have been a political angle to it. As a government spy the poet had dealings with some extremely shady characters. His own reputation with sober, conventional folk was bad— for his quarrelsomeness, for several acts of violence, and for atheism. On the last count only was he maligned; the charge of atheism arose from his connection with Raleigh's circle and from the picturesque vigor of some of Marlowe's objections to Trinitarian orthodoxy. In Elizabethan times atheistic views were regarded as bordering on treason.

Moralizing over the excesses of a turbulent genius is both priggish and useless. At any rate, Marlowe's genius was neither petulant nor complacent; and, cut short though it was, his was a durable achievement.

> What is beauty, saith my sufferings, then?
> If all the pens that ever poets held
> Had fed the feeling of their masters' thoughts,
> And every sweetness that inspired their hearts,
> Their minds, and muses on admirèd themes;
> If all the heavenly quintessence they still[2]
> From their immortal flowers of poesy,
> Wherein, as in a mirror, we perceive
> The highest reaches of a human wit;[3]
> If these had made one poem's period,[4]
> And all combined in beauty's worthiness,
> Yet should there hover in their restless heads
> One thought, one grace, one wonder, at the least,
> Which into words no virtue[5] can digest.[6]

---

[1] His best-known lyric will be found below, in our seventeenth-century section, under Izaak Walton, who quotes it in *The Complete Angler.*

[2] Distill.   [3] Intelligence.   [4] End, goal.   [5] Power.
[6] *1 Tamburlaine,* V, ii, 97–110.

That is the right attitude for an artist toward his art and the subject of his art. That is honor and integrity and purity, however the spirit was troubled or even muddied on other and nonprofessional occasions. All of which is not to deny the wish that in Marlowe's case the bright steel of genius might have been grasped by a steadier hand.

The standard edition of Marlowe's works was edited by R. H. Case and others (6 vols., 1930–33). For the life, see the first of these volumes (edited by T. Brooke) and F. S. Boas's *Christopher Marlowe* (1940). Inexpensive collections of the plays are available in Everyman's Library and The World's Classics.

from HERO AND LEANDER

Hero and Leander is a masterpiece of literary painting; in opulence of form and richness of color it resembles many a glowing canvas, likewise mythological in subject, of such another sixteenth-century master as Titian. Here is that sheer delight in the glory of the flesh that marks a great deal of Renaissance art, and the poem belongs to the same category of erotic narrative verse as Shakespeare's *Venus and Adonis*.

The story of the famous lovers is an old one; Ovid's is the most notable version before Marlowe's. When the latter's was composed is uncertain. Marlowe left it unfinished. George Chapman (d. 1634), dramatist and translator of Homer, completed it; the entire text was published in 1598. Presumably it was Chapman who divided the poem into six "sestiads"—*sestiad* from Sestos, the town, on the analogy of the *Iliad*, which deals with Ilium or Troy. The first two sestiads are Marlowe's; Chapman's four are decidedly inferior. The passage which follows includes nearly all of the First Sestiad. Its remaining lines (385–484) deal only indirectly with Hero and Leander.

On Hellespont,[1] guilty of true love's blood,
In view and opposite two cities stood,
Sea-borderers, disjoined by Neptune's might:
The one Abydos, the other Sestos hight.[2]
At Sestos Hero dwelt: Hero the fair,   5
Whom young Apollo courted for her hair,[3]
And offered as a dower his burning throne,
Where she should sit for men to gaze upon.
The outside of her garments were of lawn,
The lining purple silk with gilt stars drawn,   10
Her wide sleeves green and bordered[4] with a grove
Where Venus in her naked glory strove
To please the careless and disdainful eyes
Of proud Adonis that before her lies;
Her kirtle blue, whereon was many a stain,   15
Made with the blood of wretched lovers slain.
Upon her head she ware a myrtle wreath,
From whence her veil reached to the ground beneath;
Her veil was artificial flowers and leaves,
Whose workmanship both man and beast deceives.   20
Many would praise the sweet smell as she passed,
When 'twas the odor which her breath forth cast;
And there for honey bees have sought in vain,
And beat from thence have lighted there again.
About her neck hung chains of pebble-stone,   25
Which, lightened by her neck, like diamonds shone.
She ware no gloves, for neither sun nor wind
Would burn or parch her hands, but to her mind[5]
Or warm or cool them, for they took delight
To play upon those hands, they were so white.   30
Buskins[6] of shells all silvered usèd she,
And branched with blushing coral to the knee;
Where sparrows perched, of hollow pearl and gold,
Such as the world would wonder to behold.
Those with sweet water oft her handmaid fills,   35
Which as she went would cherup through the bills.[7]
Some say, for her the fairest Cupid pined,
And looking in her face was strooken blind.
But this is true, so like was one the other,
As he imagined Hero was his mother;[8]   40
And oftentimes into her bosom flew,
About her naked neck his bare arms threw,
And laid his childish head upon her breast,
And with still panting rocked, there took his rest.
So lovely-fair was Hero, Venus' nun,[9]   45
As nature wept, thinking she was undone,[10]
Because she took more from her than she left
And of such wondrous beauty her bereft.
Therefore, in sign her treasure suffered wrack,
Since Hero's time hath half the world[11] been black.   50

Amorous Leander, beautiful and young,
Whose tragedy divine Musaeus[12] sung,

---

[1] The Dardanelles.   [2] Named.
[3] As often in this poem, Marlowe invents this bit of mythology.
[4] Embroidered.

[5] According to her inclination.
[6] High boots.
[7] Such devices for imitating the songs of birds were common.
[8] Venus.   [9] I.e., priestess.   [10] Ruined.
[11] I.e., half the world's population.
[12] This Greek poem of the fifth century after Christ was mistakenly attributed to the semilegendary Musaeus of the sixth century B.C.

Dwelt at Abydos; since him dwelt there none
For whom succeeding times make greater moan.
His dangling tresses that were never shorn,   55
Had they been cut and unto Colchos[13] borne,
Would have allured the vent'rous youth of Greece
To hazard more than for the Golden Fleece.
Fair Cynthia[14] wished his arms might be her sphere;[15]
Grief makes her pale, because she moves not there.   60
His body was as straight as Circe's[16] wand;
Jove might have sipped out nectar from his hand.
Even as delicious meat[17] is to the taste,
So was his neck in touching, and surpassed
The white of Pelops' shoulder.[18] I could tell ye   65
How smooth his breast was, and how white his belly,
And whose immortal fingers did imprint
That heavenly path, with many a curious[19] dint,
That runs along his back; but my rude pen
Can hardly blazon forth the loves of men,   70
Much less of powerful gods: let it suffice
That my slack muse sings of Leander's eyes,
Those orient[20] cheeks and lips, exceeding his[21]
That leapt into the water for a kiss
Of his own shadow and, despising many,   75
Died ere he could enjoy the love of any.
Had wild Hippolytus[22] Leander seen,
Enamored of his beauty had he been:
His presence made the rudest peasant melt
That in the vast uplandish country dwelt;   80
The barbarous Thracian soldier, moved with nought,
Was moved with[23] him, and for his favor sought.
Some swore he was a maid in man's attire,
For in his looks were all that men desire:
A pleasant smiling cheek, a speaking eye,   85
A brow for love to banquet royally;
And such as knew he was a man would say,
"Leander, thou art made for amorous play.
Why art thou not in love, and loved of all?
Though thou be fair, yet be not thine own thrall."   90

The men of wealthy Sestos every year,
For his sake whom their goddess held so dear,
Rose-cheeked Adonis,[24] kept a solemn feast.
Thither resorted many a wand'ring guest
To meet their loves; such as had none at all,   95
Came lovers home from this great festival.

For every street, like to a firmament,
Glistered with breathing stars, who, where they went,
Frighted the melancholy earth, which deemed
Eternal heaven to burn, for so it seemed   100
As if another Phaëthon[25] had got
The guidance of the sun's rich chariot.
But far above the loveliest Hero shined,
And stole away th' enchanted gazer's mind;
For like sea-nymphs' inveigling harmony,   105
So was her beauty to the standers by,
Nor that night-wandering, pale, and watery star[26]
(When yawning dragons draw her thirling[27] car
From Latmus'[28] mount up to the gloomy sky,
Where, crowned with blazing light and majesty,   110
She proudly sits) more over-rules[29] the flood,
Than she the hearts of those that near her stood.
Even as when gaudy nymphs pursue the chase,
Wretched Ixion's shaggy-footed race,[30]
Incensed[31] with savage heat, gallop amain   115
From steep pine-bearing mountains to the plain,
So ran the people forth to gaze upon her,
And all that viewed her were enamored on her.
And as, in fury of a dreadful fight,
Their fellows being slain or put to flight,   120
Poor soldiers stand with fear of death dead-strooken,
So at her presence all, surprised and tooken,
Await the sentence of her scornful eyes:
He whom she favors lives; the other dies.
There might you see one sigh, another rage,   125
And some (their violent passions to assuage)
Compile sharp satires, but alas too late,
For faithful love will never turn to hate.
And many, seeing great princes were denied,
Pined as they went, and thinking on her died.   130

On this feast day—O cursèd day and hour!—
Went Hero thorough Sestos, from her tower
To Venus' temple, where, unhappily
As after chanced, they did each other spy.
So fair a church as this had Venus none;   135
The walls were of discolored[32] jasper stone,
Wherein was Proteus[33] carved, and overhead
A lively[34] vine of green-sea agate spread,

---

13 Colchis, now Georgia, in the Caucasus.
14 Diana, the moon.   15 Orbit.
16 The sorceress encountered by Ulysses.   17 Food.
18 His lost shoulder was replaced, according to the myth, with an
   ivory one.   19 Exquisite.   20 Radiant.
21 Narcissus.
22 Who scorned love and devoted himself to hunting. See the great
   tragedy by Euripides.   23 By.
24 The mortal youth loved by Venus. See Shakespeare's poem.

25 Who drove the sun god's chariot so recklessly that Zeus killed
   him with a thunderbolt to avert a general conflagration.
26 The moon.   27 Flying like a missile.
28 Latmos, on the southwestern coast of Asia Minor, a mountain
   associated with Cynthia or Diana.   29 Rules over.
30 The centaurs (half man, half horse), progeny of Ixion; his
   wretchedness was due to his punishment in hell, where he was
   chained to a ceaselessly revolving wheel.   31 Inflamed.
32 Variegated.
33 A sea god; he had power to assume different forms.
34 Lifelike.

Where by one hand light-headed Bacchus hung,
And with the other wine from grapes out-wrung. 140
Of crystal shining fair the pavement was;
The town of Sestos called it Venus' glass.
There might you see the gods in sundry shapes
Committing heady riots, incest, rapes:
For know that underneath this radiant floor 145
Was Danaë's[35] statue in a brazen tower,
Jove slily stealing from his sister's bed
To dally with Idalian Ganymede,[36]
And for his love Europa bellowing loud,[37]
And tumbling with the rainbow in a cloud;[38] 150
Blood-quaffing Mars, heaving the iron net
Which limping Vulcan and his Cyclops[39] set;
Love kindling fire, to burn such towns as Troy;[40]
Sylvanus[41] weeping for the lovely boy
That now is turned into a cypress tree, 155
Under whose shade the wood gods love to be.
And in the midst a silver altar stood;
There Hero sacrificing turtles'[42] blood,
Vailed[43] to the ground, vailing[44] her eyelids close,
And modestly they opened as she rose. 160
Thence flew Love's[45] arrow with the golden head,
And thus Leander was enamorèd.
Stone still he stood, and evermore he gazed,
Till with the fire that from his count'nance blazed
Relenting Hero's gentle heart was strook: 165
Such force and virtue[46] hath an amorous look.

It lies not in our power to love, or hate,
For will in us is over-ruled by fate.
When two are stripped, long ere the course[47] begin
We wish that one should lose, the other win; 170
And one especially do we affect[48]
Of two gold ingots like in each respect.
The reason no man knows; let it suffice,
What we behold is censured[49] by our eyes.
Where both deliberate, the love is slight: 175
Who ever loved, that loved not at first sight?

---

[35] In the form of a golden shower Zeus or Jove visited her in her
prison. The god's sister and wife was Hera or Juno.
[36] A beautiful boy who served as the gods' cupbearer. According
to some versions of the myth his home was on Mt. Ida, near
Troy.
[37] Since, when he carried her off, he took the form of a bull.
[38] As Jupiter Pluvius he was a rainmaker.—The rainbow was Iris.
[39] I.e., the Cyclopes, the giants who labored in the workshops of
Vulcan, god of fire and metal working. He trapped his wife
Venus with her lover Mars in a net of his own manufacture.
[40] Since Helen was the cause of the Trojan War.
[41] A wood god, enamored of the youth Cyparissus.
[42] Turtledoves'.   [43] Bowed down.   [44] Lowering.
[45] Cupid's.   [46] Power.   [47] Race.   [48] Prefer.
[49] Judged.

He kneeled, but unto her devoutly prayed.
Chaste Hero to herself thus softly said,
"Were I the saint he worships, I would hear him";
And, as she spake those words, came somewhat near
        him. 180
He started up, she blushed as one ashamed;
Wherewith Leander much more was inflamed.
He touched her hand; in touching it she trembled:
Love deeply grounded, hardly is dissembled.
These lovers parlèd[50] by the touch of hands: 185
True love is mute, and oft amazèd[51] stands.
Thus, while dumb signs their yielding hearts entangled,
The air with sparks of living fire was spangled;
And Night, deep drenched in mystic Acheron,[52]
Heaved up her head, and half the world upon 190
Breathed darkness forth (dark night is Cupid's day).
And now begins Leander to display
Love's holy fire, with words, with sighs and tears,
Which like sweet music entered Hero's ears;
And yet at every word she turned aside, 195
And always cut him off as he replied.
At last, like to a bold sharp sophister,[53]
With cheerful hope thus he accosted her.
        "Fair creature, let me speak without offence:
I would my rude words had the influence 200
To lead thy thoughts as thy fair looks do mine;
Then shouldst thou be his prisoner who is thine.
Be not unkind and fair; misshapen stuff[54]
Are of behavior boisterous and rough.
Oh, shun me not, but hear me ere you go; 205
God knows I cannot force love, as you do.
My words shall be as spotless as my youth,
Full of simplicity and naked truth.
This sacrifice, whose sweet perfúme descending
From Venus' altar to your footsteps bending, 210
Doth testify that you exceed her far
To whom you offer, and whose nun you are.
Why should you worship her? Her you surpass
As much as sparkling diamonds flaring[55] glass.
A diamond set in lead his[56] worth retains; 215
A heavenly nymph, beloved of human swains,
Receives no blemish, but ofttimes more grace:
Which makes me hope, although I am but base—
Base in respect of thee, divine and pure—
Dutiful service may thy love procure; 220
And I in duty will excel all other,
As thou in beauty dost exceed Love's mother.
Nor heaven nor thou were made to gaze upon;
As heaven preserves all things, so save thou one.[57]

[50] Parleyed, spoke.   [51] Stunned.
[52] The river of woe in Hades.   [53] Sophist, smart arguer.
[54] I.e., only ugly persons.   [55] Gaudy.   [56] Its.
[57] I.e., my life.

A stately builded ship, well rigged and tall,   225
The ocean maketh more majestical:
Why vowest thou then to live in Sestos here,
Who on love's seas more glorious wouldst appear?
Like untuned golden strings all women are,
Which long time lie[58] untouched, will harshly jar.   230
Vessels of brass, oft handled, brightly shine;
What difference betwixt the richest mine
And basest mold, but use? For both, not used,
Are of like worth. Then treasure is abused
When misers keep it; being put to loan,   235
In time it will return us two for one.
Rich robes themselves and others do adorn;
Neither themselves nor others, if not worn.
Who builds a palace and rams up the gate
Shall see it ruinous and desolate.   240
Ah, simple Hero, learn thyself to cherish!
Lone women, like to empty houses, perish.
Less sins the poor rich man that starves himself
In heaping up a mass of drossy pelf,
Than such as you: his golden earth remains,   245
Which after his decease some other gains;
But this fair gem, sweet in the loss alone,
When you fleet hence can be bequeathed to none.
Or if it could, down from th' enamelled sky
All heaven would come to claim this legacy,   250
And with intestine broils the world destroy,
And quite confound nature's sweet harmony.
Well therefore by the gods decreed it is
We human creatures should enjoy that bliss.
One is no number;[59] maids are nothing, then,   255
Without the sweet society of men.
Wilt thou live single still?—one shalt thou be,[60]
Though never-singling[61] Hymen[62] couple thee.
Wild savages, that drink of running springs,
Think water far excels all earthly things;   260
But they that daily taste neat wine despise it:
Virginity, albeit some highly prize it,
Compared with marriage, had you tried them both,
Differs as much as wine and water doth.
Base bullion for the stamp's sake we allow;   265
Even so for men's impression do we you,
By which alone, our reverend fathers say,
Women receive perfection every way.
This idol which you term virginity
Is neither essence subject to the eye,   270
No, nor to any one exterior sense,
Nor hath it any place of residence,

Nor is 't of earth or mold celestiäl,
Or capable of any form at all.
Of that which hath no being, do not boast;   275
Things that are not at all are never lost.
Men foolishly do call it virtuous—
What virtue is it, that is born with us?
Much less can honor be ascribed thereto:
Honor is purchased by the deeds we do.   280
Believe me, Hero, honor is not won
Until some honorable deed be done.
Seek you, for chastity, immortal fame,
And know that some have wronged Diana's name?
Whose name is it, if she be false or not,   285
So[63] she be fair, but some vile tongues will blot?
But you are fair, ay me, so wondrous fair,
So young, so gentle, and so debonair,
As Greece will think, if thus you live alone,
Someone or other keeps you as his own.   290
Then, Hero, hate me not, nor from me fly,
To follow swiftly blasting infamy.
Perhaps thy sacred priesthood makes thee loath:
Tell me, to whom mad'st thou that heedless oath?"
   "To Venus," answered she; and as she spake,   295
Forth from those two tralucent[64] cisterns brake
A stream of liquid pearl, which down her face
Made milk-white paths, whereon the gods might trace[65]
To Jove's high court. He thus replied: "The rites
In which love's beauteous empress most delights   300
Are banquets, Doric music, midnight revel,
Plays, masques, and all that stern age counteth evil.
Thee as a holy idiot doth she scorn;
For thou in vowing chastity hast sworn
To rob her name[66] and honor, and thereby   305
Commit'st a sin far worse than perjury,
Even sacrilege against her deity,
Through regular and formal purity.
To expiate which sin, kiss and shake hands;
Such sacrifice as this Venus demands."   310
   Thereat she smiled, and did deny him so
As, put[67] thereby, yet might he hope for mo;[68]
Which makes him quickly reinforce his speech,
And her in humble manner thus beseech:
"Though neither gods nor men may thee deserve,   315
Yet, for her sake whom you have vowed to serve,
Abandon fruitless cold virginity,
The gentle queen of love's sole enemy.
Then shall you most resemble Venus' nun,
When Venus' sweet rites are performed and done.   320
Flint-breasted Pallas[69] joys in single life,
But Pallas and your mistress are at strife.

---

[58] Lie they, if they lie.
[59] Aristotle, *Metaphysics*, XIV, I.
[60] I.e., if you marry you will discover another kind of unity.
[61] Ever uniting.   [62] God of marriage.

[63] Provided that.   [64] Translucent.   [65] Walk.
[66] Injure her reputation.   [67] Repelled.   [68] More.
[69] Pallas Athena or Minerva, goddess of wisdom.

Love, Hero, then, and be not tyrannous,
But heal the heart that thou hast wounded thus,
Nor stain thy youthful years with avarice:[70]   325
Fair fools delight to be accounted nice.[71]
The richest corn[72] dies, if it be not reaped;
Beauty alone is lost, too warily kept."
These arguments he used, and many more,
Wherewith she yielded, that was won before.   330
Hero's looks yielded, but her words made war;
Women are won when they begin to jar.[73]
Thus having swallowed Cupid's golden hook,
The more she strived, the deeper was she strook.

    Yet, evilly feigning anger, strove she still,   335
And would be thought to grant against her will.
So, having paused awhile, at last she said:
"Who taught thee rhetoric to deceive a maid?
Ay me! such words as these should I abhor,
And yet I like them for the orator."   340

    With that Leander stooped, to have embraced her,
But from his spreading arms away she cast her,
And thus bespake him: "Gentle youth, forbear
To touch the sacred garments which I wear.
Upon a rock, and underneath a hill,   345
Far from the town (where all is whist and still,
Save that the sea, playing on yellow sand,
Sends forth a rattling murmur to the land,
Whose sound allures the golden Morpheus[74]
In silence of the night to visit us)   350
My turret stands; and there, God knows, I play
With Venus' swans and sparrows all the day.
A dwarfish beldame bears me company,

That hops about the chamber where I lie,
And spends the night, that might be better spent, 355
In vain discourse and apish merriment.
Come thither." As she spake this, her tongue tripped,
For unawares "Come thither" from her slipped;
And suddenly her former color changed,
And here and there her eyes through anger ranged. 360
And like a planet moving several ways
At one self instant, she, poor soul, assays,
Loving, not to love at all; and every part
Strove to resist the motions of her heart.
And hands so pure, so innocent, nay such   365
As might have made heaven stoop to have a touch,
Did she uphold to Venus, and again
Vowed spotless chastity, but all in vain:
Cupid beats down her prayers with his wings;
Her vows above the empty air he flings;   370
All deep enraged, his sinewy bow he bent,
And shot a shaft that burning from him went;
Wherewith she, strooken, looked so dolefully,
As made Love sigh to see his tyranny.
And as she wept, her tears to pearl he turned,   375
And wound them on his arm, and for her mourned.
Then towards the palace of the Destinies,
Laden with languishment and grief, he flies,
And to those stern nymphs humbly made request
Both might enjoy each other, and be blest.   380
But with a ghastly, dreadful countenance,
Threat'ning a thousand deaths at every glance,
They answered Love, nor would vouchsafe so much
As one poor word, their hate to him was such.

DOCTOR FAUSTUS

As Tamburlaine aspires to mastery of the world by force of arms, Faustus seeks it through knowledge; thus Marlowe exhibits in this play another aspect of the Renaissance will to power and freedom. Unfortunately, though the play was probably produced about 1589, the first edition appeared only in 1604. By that time, eleven years after its author's death, it had been mutilated by alterations made in the theater. A later edition, in 1616, gives us a text widely at variance with that of 1604. No doubt there was constant tampering, and as late as 1663 a version appeared with grotesque additions in part adapted from *The Jew of Malta*. The tendency of the early stage was to treat the Devil as a comic character; and as new material was successively introduced for the low comedians, the original text was repeatedly pared down to make room for it.

Doctor Faustus, then, is to be approached like a temple of the antique world: we are the losers if we allow partial collapse, inartistic restoration, and unauthentic and impudent addition to obscure the surviving traces of its beauty. Aside from the interpolation of new lines and the discarding of old, the most serious changes are the mangling of meter and the substitution of prose paraphrases for some of the original verse.

The bulk of the new passages consists of slapstick farce, mostly quite witless. The humorous effects must have come largely from the funny faces and antics of the comedians. Let the reader, when he comes to one of these scenes of tedious foolery, try to imagine it cast with his favorites among the leading comedians of today's stage and screen. As a rule, the laughter they inspire in us is far more the result of their own genius for clowning than of their script writers' efforts. Whether any of the sad stuff provided for their forerunners in *Faustus* was the work of Marlowe we

[70] I.e., hoarding your beauty.   [71] Coy.   [72] Grain.
[73] Dispute, argue.   [74] God of sleep.

cannot tell, since in no play do we have for purposes of comparison any farcical passage that is certainly his. It seems likely that the comic scenes in prose were added by Thomas Nashe (see p. 274, above), not as a collaborator but soon after Marlowe's death, when the play was about five years old. In turn they were probably altered and further debased before the appearance of the first edition.

Marlowe's source was an English adaptation of the German *Historia von D. Johann Fausten* (1587). Since the first extant edition of this English *Faust Book* was published in 1592, some scholars have placed *Doctor Faustus* among the last of Marlowe's writings; but new evidence points to the probability that there was an earlier edition of the *Faust Book* and that 1589 is about right for the date of the play.

The moral application of the story is a prominent feature of the *Faust Book,* and in the contention between the good and evil angels for the hero's soul we have a link with the old morality plays. But it is the impetuous imagination of Marlowe that gives *Doctor Faustus* its vitality and its representative character as a document of Renaissance reluctance to accept the limitations which circumscribe the desires and hopes of man. Its hero, however wicked his courses, is a Renaissance man in his desire to see and experience everything.

The historical Faustus took his baccalaureate in divinity at Heidelberg in 1509. Legends arose concerning his prowess as a magician, and to them the credulous attached

the ancient motif of the scholar who sells himself to the Devil. Sermons held him up as a horrible example. The core of the Faustus legend in its literary treatments is the bargain with the Devil; any drama on this subject must begin with the making of the compact and end with the exaction of its terms. The playwright's structural problem is to determine what elements of the story to fill the intervening acts with. Gounod's opera employs the Gretchen or Marguerite intrigue. In the *Faust Book* the interval is replete with a wide variety of episodes, including those with the Pope, the horse-courser, and the clowns. Whether or not Marlowe did anything with this material, he was clearly more interested in the boundless aspiration of Faustus. With that fact in mind the reader must attempt as best he may to hold in his mind's eye the noble outlines of the original structure. "How greatly," said Goethe, "is it all planned!"

The play held the stage, in versions progressively degraded, till well into the eighteenth century. A New York revival in 1937, with Orson Welles in the title role, was successful beyond all expectations. With the kind permission of the publishers, D. C. Heath and Company, the text which follows is reprinted (somewhat altered, especially in the notes) from H. Spencer's *Elizabethan Plays* (1933). It should be noted that division of the dramas of this period into acts and scenes is seldom made in the earliest texts; it is largely the work of modern editors. There has also been some expansion of the original stage directions.

THE TRAGICAL HISTORY OF DOCTOR FAUSTUS

DRAMATIS PERSONAE

THE POPE	SCHOLARS, FRIARS, and ATTENDANTS
CARDINAL OF LORRAINE	
CHARLES V, EMPEROR OF GERMANY	
DUKE OF VANHOLT[1]	DUCHESS OF VANHOLT
FAUSTUS	
VALDES	
CORNELIUS } friends to FAUSTUS	LUCIFER
	BELZEBUB
WAGNER, servant to FAUSTUS	MEPHISTOPHILIS
CLOWN	GOOD ANGEL
ROBIN	EVIL ANGEL
RALPH	THE SEVEN DEADLY SINS
VINTNER	DEVILS
HORSE-COURSER[2]	SPIRITS in the shapes of ALEXANDER THE GREAT,
KNIGHT	of his PARAMOUR, and of HELEN OF TROY
OLD MAN	CHORUS

THE SCENE—*Wittenberg, Rome, and palaces of the German Emperor and of the Duke of Vanholt*

---

[1] Anhalt, in central Germany.   [2] Horse trader.

Enter CHORUS[3]

CHORUS. Not marching now in fields of Thrasimene,[4]
Where Mars did mate[5] the Carthaginians,
Nor sporting in the dalliance of love
In courts of kings where state is overturned,
Nor in the pomp of proud, audacious deeds,   5
Intends our Muse to vaunt[6] his heavenly verse;
Only this, gentlemen: we must perform
The form of[7] Faustus' fortunes, good or bad.
To patient judgments we appeal our plaud,[8]
And speak for Faustus in his infancy.   10
Now is he born, his parents base of stock,
In Germany, within a town called Rhodes;[9]
Of riper years to Wittenberg[10] he went,
Whereas[11] his kinsmen chiefly brought him up.
So soon he profits in divinity,[12]   15
The fruitful plot of scholarism graced,[13]
That shortly he was graced[14] with doctor's name,
Excelling all whose sweet delight disputes[15]
In heavenly matters of theology;
Till, swoln with cunning,[16] of a self-conceit,   20
His waxen[17] wings did mount above his reach,
And melting heavens conspired his overthrow;
For, falling to a devilish exercise,
And glutted more with learning's golden gifts,
He surfeits upon cursèd necromancy.   25
Nothing so sweet as magic is to him,
Which he prefers before his chiefest bliss.
And this the man that in his study sits.   [*Exit*

SCENE I[18]

Enter FAUSTUS *in his study*

FAUST. Settle thy studies, Faustus, and begin
To sound the depth of that thou wilt profess.[19]

Having commenced,[20] be a divine in show;
Yet level[21] at the end of every art,
And live and die in Aristotle's works.   5
Sweet Analytics,[22] 't is thou hast ravished me:
Bene disserere est finis logices.[23]
Is to dispute well logic's chiefest end?
Affords this art no greater miracle?
Then read no more; thou hast attained the end—   10
A greater subject fitteth Faustus' wit.
Bid ὂν καὶ μὴ ὄν[24] farewell, Galen[25] come:
Seeing *Ubi desinit philosophus ibi incipit medicus,*[26]
Be a physician, Faustus, heap up gold,
And be eternized for some wondrous cure.   15
Summum bonum medicinae sanitas:
The end of physic is our body's health.
Why, Faustus, hast thou not attained that end?
Is not thy common talk sound Aphorisms?[27]
Are not thy bills[28] hung up as monuments,   20
Whereby whole cities have escaped the plague,
And thousand desp'rate maladies been eased?
Yet art thou still but Faustus and a man.
Wouldst thou make man to live eternally,
Or, being dead, raise them to life again?   25
Then this profession were to be esteemed.
Physic, farewell. Where is Justinian?   [*Reads*
*Si una eademque res legatur duobus,
Alter rem, alter valorem rei, &c.*[29]
A petty case of paltry legacies!   [*Reads*   30
Exhaereditare filium non potest pater nisi. . . .[30]
Such is the subject of the *Institute*
And universal body of the law.
His study fits a mercenary drudge,
Who aims at nothing but external trash;   35
Too servile and illiberal for me.
When all is done, divinity is best;

---

[3] A single actor. This is a faint survival of the actual chorus of classical drama, with its comment on the action.
[4] Lake Trasimenus, in central Italy, near Perugia.
[5] Defeat. But Hannibal won this battle against the Romans (217 B.C.). The author may be confused; the whole speech may be non-Marlovian.   [6] Proudly display.   [7] We must enact.
[8] For our applause.   [9] Roda, in Saxe-Altenburg, near Jena.
[10] The famous university in Saxon Prussia.   [11] Where.
[12] Theology.   [13] Full of grace.
[14] Punning on the official "grace" at Cambridge, by virtue of which a candidate received his degree.
[15] Who take pleasure in disputations.
[16] Puffed up with knowledge.
[17] I.e., insecure, like the wings of Icarus. According to the myth, they melted when he flew too near the sun.
[18] Wittenberg. Faustus is "discovered" on the inner stage, a curtained room behind the main platform or outer stage.
[19] Be a professor of.

[20] Taken a degree.   [21] Aim.   [22] Aristotelian logic.
[23] For the meaning see the next line, as often in this play.
[24] Aristotle's "being and not being."
[25] The great Greek medical authority of the second century.
[26] Where the philosopher leaves off, there the physician begins. Adapted, as is line 16, from Aristotle (d. 322 B.C.), the great Greek philosopher.
[27] Medical memoranda, so called from the *Aphorisms* of Hippocrates, the famous Greek physician of the fifth and fourth centuries B.C.   [28] Prescriptions.
[29] If one and the same thing is bequeathed to two persons, one shall take the thing and the other its value. An incorrect version of a rule in the *Institutes* of the Emperor Justinian (d. 565), codifier of the Roman law.
[30] A father cannot disinherit his son, except . . . . (Adapted from the *Institutes.*)

Jerome's Bible,[31] Faustus, view it well.   [*Reads*
Stipendium peccati mors est.[32] Ha! *Stipendium, &c.:*
The reward of sin is death.—That's hard.   [*Reads* 40
Si peccasse negamus, fallimur, et nulla est in nobis veritas:[33]
If we say that we have no sin we deceive ourselves, and
there's no truth in us.—Why then, belike we must sin and
so consequently die.
Ay, we must die an everlasting death.   45
What doctrine call you this, *Che sera, sera:*
"What will be shall be"?—Divinity, adieu!
These metaphysics of magicians
And necromantic books are heavenly;
Lines, circles, schemes, letters, and characters,   50
Ay, these are those that Faustus most desires.
O what a world of profit and delight,
Of power, of honor, of omnipotence
Is promised to the studious artisan!
All things that move between the quiet poles   55
Shall be at my command. Emperors and kings
Are but obeyed in their several provinces,
Nor can they raise the wind or rend the clouds;
But his dominion that exceeds[34] in this
Stretcheth as far as doth the mind of man.   60
A sound magician is a mighty god:
Here, Faustus, try thy brains to gain a deity.
Wagner!

Enter WAGNER

Commend me to my dearest friends,
The German Valdes and Cornelius;
Request them earnestly to visit me.   65
WAG. I will, sir.   [*Exit*
FAUST. Their conference[35] will be a greater help to me
Than all my labors, plod I ne'er so fast.

Enter the GOOD ANGEL *and the* EVIL ANGEL

G. ANG. O Faustus, lay that damnèd book aside
And gaze not on it, lest it tempt thy soul   70
And heap God's heavy wrath upon thy head.
Read, read the Scriptures; that is blasphemy.
E. ANG. Go forward, Faustus, in that famous art,
Wherein all Nature's treasury is contained;
Be thou on earth as Jove is in the sky,   75
Lord and commander of these elements.   [*Exeunt* ANGELS
FAUST. How am I glutted with conceit of this![36]
Shall I make spirits fetch me what I please,
Resolve me of all ambiguities,[37]

Perform what desperate enterprise I will?   80
I'll have them fly to India for gold,
Ransack the oceän for orient[38] pearl,
And search all corners of the new-found world
For pleasant fruits and princely delicates.
I'll have them read me strange philosophy,   85
And tell the secrets of all foreign kings.
I'll have them wall all Germany with brass,
And make swift Rhine circle fair Wittenberg.
I'll have them fill the public schools[39] with silk,[40]
Wherewith the students shall be bravely clad.   90
I'll levy soldiers with the coin they bring,
And chase the Prince of Parma[41] from our land,
And reign sole king of all our provinces;
Yea, stranger engines for the brunt of war
Than was the fiery keel[42] at Antwerp's bridge,   95
I'll make my servile spirits to invent.
Come, German Valdes and Cornelius,
And make me blest with your sage conference.

Enter VALDES *and* CORNELIUS

Valdes, sweet Valdes, and Cornelius,
Know that your words have won me at the last   100
To practice magic and concealèd arts;
Yet not your words only, but mine own fantasy,
That will receive no object;[43] for my head
But ruminates on necromantic skill.
Philosophy is odious and obscure;   105
Both law and physic are for petty wits;
Divinity is basest of the three,
Unpleasant, harsh, contemptible, and vild:[44]
'T is magic, magic, that hath ravished me.
Then, gentle friends, aid me in this attempt;   110
And I, that have with concise syllogisms
Graveled the pastors of the German church,
And made the flow'ring pride of Wittenberg
Swarm to my problems,[45] as the infernal spirits
On sweet Musaeus[46] when he came to hell,   115
Will be as cunning as Agrippa[47] was,
Whose shadows[48] made all Europe honor him.
VALD. Faustus, these books, thy wit, and our experience
Shall make all nations to canónize us.

---

[38] Lustrous.   [39] University lecture-rooms.
[40] Which Cambridge regulations forbade the students to wear.
[41] Spanish governor-general (1579–92) of the Netherlands.
[42] A Dutch fireship damaged a bridge at the siege of Antwerp.
[43] I.e., my own fancy, which will entertain no regular academic
subject, nor anything else except necromancy, the black art.
[44] Vile.   [45] Lectures on mathematics and logic.
[46] A legendary Greek poet. See *Aeneid*, VI, 667.
[47] Henry Cornelius Agrippa von Nettesheim, a friend of the historical Faustus.   [48] Shades raised from the dead.

---

[31] The Vulgate, the Latin text chiefly by St. Jerome (d. 420).
[32] Romans 6:23.   [33] 1 John 1:8.   [34] Excels.
[35] A conference with them.
[36] How am I filled with this idea.
[37] I.e., free me from all uncertainties by answering my questions.

As Indian Moors[49] obey their Spanish lords,   120
So shall the subjects of every element
Be always serviceable to us three.
Like lions shall they guard us when we please,
Like Almain rutters[50] with their horsemen's staves
Or Lapland giants trotting by our sides;   125
Sometimes like women or unwedded maids,
Shadowing[51] more beauty in their airy[52] brows
Than in the white breasts of the Queen of Love.[53]
From Venice shall they drag huge argosies,[54]
And from America the golden fleece   130
That yearly stuffs[55] old Philip's treasury,
If learned Faustus will be resolute.
   FAUST. Valdes, as resolute am I in this
As thou to live; therefore object it not.
   CORN. The miracles that magic will perform   135
Will make thee vow to study nothing else.
He that is grounded in astrology,
Enriched with tongues, well seen[56] in minerals,
Hath all the principles magic doth require.
Then doubt not, Faustus, but to be renowmed,[57]   140
And more frequented for this mystery[58]
Than heretofore the Delphian oracle.
The spirits tell me they can dry the sea
And fetch the treasure of all foreign wracks,
Ay, all the wealth that our forefathers hid   145
Within the massy entrails of the earth.
Then tell me, Faustus, what shall we three want?
   FAUST. Nothing, Cornelius. O, this cheers my soul!
Come, show me some demonstrations magical,
That I may conjure in some lusty[59] grove,   150
And have these joys in full possessiön.
   VALD. Then haste thee to some solitary grove,
And bear wise Bacon's[60] and Albanus'[61] works,
The Hebrew Psalter, and New Testament;
And whatsoever else is requisite   155
We will inform thee ere our conference cease.
   CORN. Valdes, first let him know the words of art;
And then, all other ceremonies learned,
Faustus may try his cunning by himself.
   VALD. First I'll instruct thee in the rudiments,   160
And then wilt thou be perfecter than I.

---

49 American Indians.   50 German troopers.
51 Exhibiting.   52 Because insubstantial.   53 Venus.
54 Large merchant ships.
55 Ed. 1616 reads *stuff'd*, an alteration made after the death of
Philip II (1527–98), King of Spain. His predecessor, the Emperor Charles V (1500–58), nevertheless appears later on in this
play.   56 Versed.   57 Renowned.
58 More sought after because of this profession.   59 Pleasant.
60 Roger Bacon, the great thirteenth-century English scientist,
long reputed a magician.
61 Either Pietro d'Albano, a thirteenth-century alchemist, or (mis-
printed) Albertus Magnus, a German Dominican of the same
century, supposed to be a magician.

FAUST. Then come and dine with me, and after meat
We'll canvass every quiddity[62] thereof;
For ere I sleep I'll try what I can do:
This night I'll conjure though I die therefore. [*Exeunt*   165

SCENE II[1]

Enter two SCHOLARS

   1ST SCHOL. I wonder what's become of Faustus, that was
wont to make our schools ring with *sic probo?*[2]
   2ND SCHOL. That shall we know, for see here comes his
boy.

Enter WAGNER

   1ST SCHOL. How now, sirrah![3] Where's thy master?   5
   WAG. God in heaven knows.
   2ND SCHOL. Why, dost not thou know?
   WAG. Yes, I know; but that follows not.
   1ST SCHOL. Go to, sirrah; leave your jesting, and tell us
where he is.   10
   WAG. That follows not necessary by force of argument,
that you, being licentiate,[4] should stand upon 't; therefore acknowledge your error and be attentive.
   2ND SCHOL. Why, didst thou not say thou knew'st?
   WAG. Have you any witness on 't?   15
   1ST SCHOL. Yes, sirrah, I heard you.
   WAG. Ask my fellow if I be a thief.[5]
   2ND SCHOL. Well, you will not tell us?
   WAG. Yes, sir, I will tell you; yet if you were not dunces,
you would never ask me such a question; for is not   [20
he *corpus naturale?*[6] and is not that *mobile?* Then wherefore
should you ask me such a question? But that I am by nature
phlegmatic, slow to wrath, and prone to lechery—to love,
I would say—it were not for you to come within forty
foot of the place of execution,[7] although I do not   [25
doubt to see you both hanged the next sessions. Thus having triumphed over you, I will set my countenance like a
precisian,[8] and begin to speak thus:—Truly, my dear
brethren, my master is within at dinner, with Valdes and
Cornelius, as this wine, if it could speak, it would   [30
inform your worships; and so the Lord bless you, preserve you, and keep you, my dear brethren, my dear
brethren.   [*Exit*

---

62 Minute point.

1 Before Faustus's house.   2 Thus I prove.
3 A contemptuous vocative, used either in anger or (as here) to
an inferior. Wagner is Faustus's *famulus*, a poor scholar earning
his way as a servant.
4 Licensed to ascend to a higher degree.
5 A proverbial expression.
6 A physical body. Like *mobile* (*movable*, with a pun on the
meaning *capable of anger*), a current term in physics.
7 I.e., where I wreak my wrath.   8 Puritan.

1ST SCHOL. Nay, then, I fear he has fall'n into that damned art, for which they two are infamous through the world. 36

2ND SCHOL. Were he a stranger, and not allied to me, yet should I grieve for him. But come, let us go and inform the Rector,[9] and see if he by his grave counsel can reclaim him. 40

1ST SCHOL. O, but I fear me nothing can reclaim him.

2ND SCHOL. Yet let us try what we can do. [*Exeunt*

SCENE III[10]

Enter FAUSTUS *to conjure*

FAUST. Now that the gloomy shadow of the earth,
Longing to view Orion's drizzling look,
Leaps from th' antarctic world unto the sky
And dims the welkin with her pitchy breath,
Faustus, begin thine incantatïons, 5
And try if devils will obey thy hest,
Seeing thou hast prayed and sacrificed to them.
Within this circle is Jehovah's name
Forward and backward anagrammatized,
The breviated names of holy saints, 10
Figures of every adjunct to[11] the heavens,
And characters of signs and erring stars,[12]
By which the spirits are enforced to rise.
Then fear not, Faustus, but be resolute
And try the uttermost magic can perform. 15

Sint mihi Dei Acherontis propitii! Valeat numen triplex Iehovae! Ignei, aerii, aquatici spiritus, salvete! Orientis Princeps Belzebub, inferni ardentis monarcha, et Demogorgon, propitiamus vos, ut appareat et surgat Mephistophilis. Quid tu moraris? Per Iehovam, Gehennam, et consecratam aquam [20 *quam nunc spargo, signumque crucis quod nunc facio, et per vota nostra, ipse nunc surgat nobis dicatus Mephistophilis!*[13]

Enter a DEVIL

I charge thee to return and change thy shape;
Thou art too ugly to attend on me.
Go, and return an old Franciscan friar; 25
That holy shape becomes a devil best. [*Exit* DEVIL

---

[9] The head of the university.   [10] A grove.
[11] Astrological diagrams of every possible planetary combination in.   [12] Comets.—*Signs* = signs of planets.
[13] Unto me be the gods of Acheron propitious. May the triple name of Jehovah prevail. Spirits of fire, air, and water, hail! Belzebub, prince of the East, sovereign of burning hell, and Demogorgon, we propitiate you, that Mephistophilis may appear and rise. Why delayest thou? By Jehovah, Gehenna, and the holy water which now I sprinkle, and the sign of the cross which now I make, and by our prayer, may Mephistophilis, by us summoned, now arise.—From a stage direction in the quarto of 1616 it seems likely that the actor playing Mephistophilis did not enter till line 34, and that at line 22 a dragon entered, perhaps on a trap.

I see there's virtue in my heavenly words;
Who would not be proficient in this art?
How pliant is this Mephistophilis,
Full of obedience and humility, 30
Such is the force of magic and my spells!
Now, Faustus, thou art conjuror laureate;
Thou canst command great Mephistophilis:
Quin regis Mephistophilis fratris imagine.[14]

Re-enter MEPHISTOPHILIS, *like a Franciscan friar*

MEPH. Now, Faustus, what wouldst thou have me do?
FAUST. I charge thee wait upon me whilst I live, 36
To do whatever Faustus shall command,
Be it to make the moon drop from her sphere
Or the oceän to overwhelm the world.
MEPH. I am a servant to great Lucifer, 40
And may not follow thee without his leave;
No more than he commands must we perform.
FAUST. Did he not charge thee to appear to me?
MEPH. No, I came now hither of mine own accord.
FAUST. Did not my conjuring speeches raise thee? Speak!
MEPH. That was the cause, but yet per accident; 46
For when we hear one rack[15] the name of God,
Abjure the Scriptures and his Saviour Christ,
We fly, in hope to get his glorious soul;
Nor will we come, unless he use such means 50
Whereby he is in danger to be damned.
Therefore the shortest cut for conjuring
Is stoutly to abjure the Trinity,
And pray devoutly to the Prince of Hell.
FAUST. So Faustus hath 55
Already done, and holds this principle:
There is no chief but only Belzebub,
To whom Faustus doth dedicate himself.
This word "damnation" terrifies not him,
For he confounds hell in[16] Elysium; 60
His ghost be with the old philosophers!
But, leaving these vain trifles of men's souls,
Tell me what is that Lucifer, thy lord?
MEPH. Archregent and commander of all spirits.
FAUST. Was not that Lucifer an angel once? 65
MEPH. Yes, Faustus, and most dearly loved of God.
FAUST. How comes it then that he is prince of devils?
MEPH. Oh, by aspiring pride and insolence,
For which God threw him from the face of heaven.
FAUST. And what are you that live with Lucifer? 70
MEPH. Unhappy spirits that fell with Lucifer,
Conspired against our God with Lucifer,
And are for ever damned with Lucifer.

---

[14] Indeed thou rulest Mephistophilis in his likeness of a friar.
[15] Torture into anagrams, i.e., rearrange the letters. Cf. line 9.
[16] Makes no distinction between hell and.

FAUST. Where are you damned?

MEPH. In hell.   75

FAUST. How comes it then that thou art out of hell?

MEPH. Why, this is hell, nor am I out of it!
Think'st thou that I, who saw the face of God,
And tasted the eternal joys of heaven,
Am not tormented with ten thousand hells   80
In being deprived of everlasting bliss?
O Faustus, leave these frivolous demands,
Which strike a terror to my fainting soul.

FAUST. What, is great Mephistophilis so passionate[17]
For being deprivèd of the joys of heaven?   85
Learn thou of Faustus manly fortitude,
And scorn those joys thou never shalt possess.
Go bear these tidings to great Lucifer:
Seeing Faustus hath incurred eternal death
By desp'rate thoughts against Jove's[18] deity,   90
Say he surrenders up to him his soul,
So[19] he will spare him four-and-twenty years,
Letting him live in all voluptuousness,
Having thee ever to attend on me,
To give me whatsoever I shall ask,   95
To tell me whatsoever I demand,
To slay mine enemies and aid my friends
And always be obedient to my will.
Go, and return to mighty Lucifer,
And meet me in my study at midnight,   100
And then resolve[20] me of thy master's mind.

MEPH. I will, Faustus.   [Exit

FAUST. Had I as many souls as there be stars,
I'd give them all for Mephistophilis.
By him I'll be great emp'ror of the world,   105
And make a bridge through[21] the moving air,
To pass the ocean with a band of men;
I'll join the hills that bind the Afric shore,
And make that country continent to[22] Spain,
And both contributory to my crown.   110
The Emperor shall not live but by my leave,
Nor any potentate of Germany.
Now that I have obtained what I desire,
I'll live in speculation[23] of this art
Till Mephistophilis return again.   [Exit   115

---

17 Emotionally disturbed, grieved.
18 Common in Elizabethan literature for the Christian God.
19 Provided that.
20 Inform.
21 Dissyllabic.
22 Adjoining.
23 Contemplative study.

Enter WAGNER *and the* CLOWN

WAG. Sirrah boy, come hither.

CLOWN. How, "boy"! Swowns,[25] "boy"! I hope you
have seen many boys with such pickadevaunts[26] as I have.
"Boy," quotha![27]

WAG. Tell me, sirrah, hast thou any comings in?   5

CLOWN. Ay, and goings out too. You may see else.

WAG. Alas, poor slave! See how poverty jesteth in his
nakedness! The villain is bare and out of service, and so
hungry that I know he would give his soul to the Devil for
a shoulder of mutton, though it were blood-raw.   10

CLOWN. How? My soul to the Devil for a shoulder of
mutton, though 't were blood-raw! Not so, good friend.
By'r Lady, I had need have it well roasted and good sauce
to it, if I pay so dear.   14

WAG. Well, wilt thou serve me, and I'll make thee go
like *Qui mihi discipulus?*[28]

CLOWN. How, in verse?

WAG. No, sirrah; in beaten silk[29] and stavesacre.[30]

CLOWN. How, how, Knave's acre![31] Ay, I thought that
was all the land his father left him. Do ye hear? I would
be sorry to rob you of your living.   21

WAG. Sirrah, I say in stavesacre.

CLOWN. Oho! Oho! Stavesacre! Why, then, belike, if I
were your man I should be full of vermin.

WAG. So thou shalt, whether thou beest with me   [25
or no. But, sirrah, leave your jesting, and bind yourself
presently unto me for seven years, or I'll turn all the lice
about thee into familiars,[32] and they shall tear thee in
pieces.   29

CLOWN. Do you hear, sir? You may save that labor; they
are too familiar with me already. Swowns! they are as
bold with my flesh as if they had paid for my meat and
drink.

WAG. Well, do you hear, sirrah? Hold, take these guilders.

CLOWN. Gridirons! what be they?   35

WAG. Why, French crowns.

CLOWN. Mass, but for the name of French crowns, a
man were as good have as many English counters.[33] And
what should I do with these?

---

24 Unlocated.   25 Zounds, God's wounds.
26 Pointed beards.
27 Said he.—*Comings in* (next line) means *income; goings out* refers
   to the holes in his clothes.
28 The first words of W. Lily's *Ad discipulos carmen de moribus;* i.e.,
   you shall be my pupil.
29 Silk with metal embroidery hammered into it.
30 A kind of larkspur, used to kill lice.
31 Poultney Street, Soho, where junk dealers were established.
32 Familiar spirits.
33 Worthless tokens used in computing. Most of the French
   crowns circulating in England were spurious.

WAG. Why, now, sirrah, thou art at an hour's [40
warning, whensoever or wheresoever the Devil shall
fetch thee.

CLOWN. No, no. Here, take your gridirons again.

WAG. Truly, I'll none of them.

CLOWN. Truly, but you shall. 45

WAG. (to the audience). Bear witness I gave them him.

CLOWN. Bear witness I give them you again.

WAG. Well, I will cause two devils presently to fetch thee
away—Baliol[34] and Belcher.

CLOWN. Let your Baliol and your Belcher come [50
here, and I'll knock them, they were never so knocked
since they were devils. Say I should kill one of them, what
would folks say? "Do ye see yonder tall[35] fellow in the
round slop?[36]—he has killed the Devil." So I should be
called Kill-devil all the parish over. 55

WAG. Baliol and Belcher!

Enter two DEVILS, *and the* CLOWN *runs up and down
crying*

Spirits, away! [*Exeunt* DEVILS

CLOWN. What, are they gone? A vengeance on them;
they have vild long nails! There was a he-devil, and a she-
devil; I'll tell you how you shall know them: all he- [60
devils has horns, and all she-devils has clifts and cloven feet.

WAG. Well, sirrah, follow me.

CLOWN. But, do you hear—if I should serve you, would
you teach me to raise up Banios and Belcheos? 64

WAG. I will teach thee to turn thyself to anything; to a
dog, or a cat, or a mouse, or a rat, or anything.

CLOWN. How? a Christian fellow to a dog or a cat, a
mouse or a rat? No, no, sir; if you turn me into anything,
let it be in the likeness of a little pretty frisking flea, that I
may be here and there and everywhere. O, I'll tickle [70
the pretty wenches' plackets;[37] I'll be amongst them, i' faith.

WAG. Well, sirrah, come.

CLOWN. But, do you hear, Wagner?

WAG. How!—Baliol and Belcher!

CLOWN. O Lord! I pray, sir, let Banio and Belcher go
sleep. 76

WAG. Villain, call me Master Wagner, and let thy left
eye be diametarily fixed upon my right heel, with *quasi
vestigias nostras insistere*.[38] [*Exit*

CLOWN. God forgive me, he speaks Dutch fustian![39]
Well, I'll follow him; I'll serve him; that's flat. [*Exit* 81

ACT II

SCENE I

Enter FAUSTUS *in his study*

FAUST. Now, Faustus, must
Thou needs be damned, and canst thou not be saved!
What boots it then to think of God or heaven?
Away with such vain fancies, and despair!
Despair in God, and trust in Belzebub!— 5
Now, go not backward; no, Faustus, be resolute!
Why waverest thou? O, something soundeth in mine ears,
"Abjure this magic; turn to God again."
Ay, and Faustus will turn to God again.—
To God? He loves thee not; 10
The God thou servest is thine own appetite,
Wherein is fixed the love of Belzebub;
To him I'll build an altar and a church,
And offer lukewarm blood of newborn babes.

Enter GOOD ANGEL *and* EVIL ANGEL

G. ANG. Sweet Faustus, leave that execrable art. 15

E. ANG. Go forward, Faustus, in that famous art.

FAUST. Contrition, prayer, repentance! What of them?

G. ANG. O, they are means to bring thee unto heaven.

E. ANG. Rather illusions, fruits of lunacy,
That makes men foolish that do trust them most. 20

G. ANG. Sweet Faustus, think of heaven, and heavenly
things.

E. ANG. No, Faustus, think of honor and wealth.
[*Exeunt* ANGELS

FAUST. Of wealth!
Why, the signiory of Emden[1] shall be mine.
When Mephistophilis shall stand by me,
What God can hurt thee, Faustus? Thou art safe; 25
Cast[2] no more doubts. Come, Mephistophilis,
And bring glad tidings from great Lucifer!—
Is 't not midnight?—Come, Mephistophilis:
Veni, veni, Mephistophile!

---

[34] Belial; with a pun on *belly-all*. Cf. *Belcher*.   [35] Valiant.
[36] Loose breeches.

[37] Slits in skirts and petticoats.
[38] As if to tread in my tracks.   [39] Highfalutin.
[1] Then a great port.   [2] Reckon up.

Enter MEPHISTOPHILIS

Now tell me, what says Lucifer, thy lord?   30
MEPH. That I shall wait on Faustus while he lives,
So he will buy my service with his soul.
  FAUST. Already Faustus hath hazarded that for thee.
  MEPH. But, Faustus, thou must bequeath[3] it solemnly
And write a deed of gift with thine own blood,   35
For that security craves great Lucifer.
If thou deny it, I will back to hell.
  FAUST. Stay, Mephistophilis! and tell me what good
Will my soul do thy lord.
  MEPH.   Enlarge his kingdom.
  FAUST. Is that the reason why he tempts us thus?   40
  MEPH. *Solamen miseris socios habuisse doloris.*[4]
  FAUST. Why, have you any pain, that[5] tortures others?
  MEPH. As great as have the human souls of men.
But tell me, Faustus, shall I have thy soul?
And I will be thy slave, and wait on thee,   45
And give thee more than thou hast wit to ask.
  FAUST. Ay, Mephistophilis, I give it thee.
  MEPH. Then, Faustus, stab thine arm courageously,
And bind thy soul that at some certain day
Great Lucifer may claim it as his own;   50
And then be thou as great as Lucifer.
  FAUST. Lo, Mephistophilis, for love of thee
I cut mine arm, and with my proper[6] blood
Assure my soul to be great Lucifer's,
Chief lord and regent of perpetual night.   55
View here the blood that trickles from mine arm,
And let it be propitious for my wish.
  MEPH. But, Faustus, thou must
Write it in manner of a deed of gift.
  FAUST. Ay, so I will. (*Writes.*) But, Mephistophilis,   60
My blood congeals, and I can write no more.
  MEPH. I'll fetch thee fire to dissolve it straight.   [*Exit*
  FAUST. What might the staying of my blood portend?
Is it unwilling I should write this bill?
Why streams it not that I may write afresh?   65
"Faustus gives to thee his soul." Ah, there it stayed.
Why shouldst thou not? Is not thy soul thine own?
Then write again, "Faustus gives to thee his soul."

Re-enter MEPHISTOPHILIS *with a chafer[7] of coals*

  MEPH. Here's fire. Come, Faustus, set it[8] on.
  FAUST. So; now the blood begins to clear again;   70
Now will I make an end immediately.   [*Writes*
  MEPH. (*aside*). O, what will not I do to obtain his soul?

_____
[3] Give.
[4] I.e., misery loves company.   [5] You who.   [6] Own.
[7] Pan.   [8] The dish of blood.

FAUST. *Consummatum est:* this bill is ended,
And Faustus hath bequeathed his soul to Lucifer.
But what is this inscription on mine arm?   75
Homo, fuge![9] Whither should I fly?
If unto God, he'll throw thee down to hell.
My senses are deceived; here's nothing writ!—
I see it plain; here in this place is writ
Homo, fuge! Yet shall not Faustus fly.   80
  MEPH. (*aside*). I'll fetch him somewhat to delight his
    mind.   [*Exit*

Re-enter MEPHISTOPHILIS *with* DEVILS, *giving crowns
and rich apparel to* FAUSTUS, *and dance, and then depart*

  FAUST. Speak, Mephistophilis. What means this show?
  MEPH. Nothing, Faustus, but to delight thy mind withal,
And to show thee what magic can perform.
  FAUST. But may I raise up spirits when I please?   85
  MEPH. Ay, Faustus, and do greater things than these.
  FAUST. Then there's enough for a thousand souls.
Here, Mephistophilis, receive this scroll,
A deed of gift of body and of soul,
But yet conditionally that thou perform   90
All articles prescribed between us both.
  MEPH. Faustus, I swear by hell and Lucifer
To effect all promises between us made.
  FAUST. Then hear me read them: "On these conditions
following. First, that Faustus may be a spirit in form   [95
and substance. Secondly, that Mephistophilis shall be his
servant, and at his command. Thirdly, that Mephistophilis
shall do for him and bring him whatsoever. Fourthly, that
he shall be in his chamber or house invisible. Lastly, that
he shall appear to the said John Faustus, at all times,   [100
in what form or shape soever he please. I, John Faustus, of
Wittenberg, Doctor, by these presents do give both body
and soul to Lucifer, prince of the East, and his minister,
Mephistophilis; and furthermore grant unto them, that
four-and-twenty years being expired, the articles   [105
above written inviolate, full power to fetch or carry the
said John Faustus, body and soul, flesh, blood, or goods,
into their habitation wheresoever. By me, John Faustus."
  MEPH. Speak, Faustus; do you deliver this as your deed?
  FAUST. Ay, take it, and the Devil give thee good on 't.
  MEPH. Now, Faustus, ask what thou wilt.   111
  FAUST. First will I question with thee about hell.
Tell me, where is the place that men call hell?
  MEPH. Under the heavens.
  FAUST. Ay, so are all things else; but whereabout?   115
  MEPH. Within the bowels of these elements,
Where we are tortured and remain for ever.
Hell has no limits, nor is circumscribed

_____
[9] Man, fly!

In one self place; for where we are is hell,
And where hell is there must we ever be;   120
And, to conclude, when all the world dissolves,
And every creature shall be purified,
All places shall be hell that is not heaven.

FAUST. Come, I think hell's a fable.

MEPH. Ay, think so still, till experience change thy mind.

FAUST. Why, think'st thou then that Faustus shall be
    damned?   126

MEPH. Ay, of necessity; for here's the scroll
Wherein thou hast given thy soul to Lucifer.

FAUST. Ay, and body too; but what of that?
Think'st thou that Faustus is so fond[10] to imagine   130
That after this life there is any pain?
Tush! these are trifles, and mere old wives' tales!

MEPH. But, Faustus, I am an instance to prove the
    contrary,
For I am damned, and am now in hell.

FAUST. How? now in hell!   135
Nay, an this be hell, I'll willingly be damned here;
What, walking, disputing, etc.?
But, leaving off this, let me have a wife,
The fairest maid in Germany;
For I am wanton and lascivious,   140
And cannot live without a wife.

MEPH. How? a wife?
I prithee, Faustus, talk not of a wife.

FAUST. Nay, sweet Mephistophilis, fetch me one, for I
    will have one.

MEPH. Well, thou wilt have one. Sit there till I come.
I'll fetch thee a wife in the Devil's name.   [Exit   146

Re-enter MEPHISTOPHILIS *with a* DEVIL *dressed like a
woman, with fireworks*

MEPH. Tell, Faustus, how dost thou like thy wife?

FAUST. A plague on her for a hot whore!

MEPH. Tut, Faustus,
Marriage is but a ceremonial toy;   150
If thou lovest me, think no more of it.
I'll cull thee out the fairest courtesans
And bring them ev'ry morning to thy bed;
She whom thine eye shall like thy heart shall have,
Be she as chaste as was Penelope,[11]   155
As wise as Saba, or as beautiful
As was bright Lucifer before his fall.
Hold, take this book; peruse it thoroughly.
The iterating of these lines brings gold.
The framing of this circle on the ground   160
Brings whirlwinds, tempests, thunder and lightning.

Pronounce this thrice devoutly to thyself,
And men in armor shall appear to thee,
Ready to execute what thou desirest.

FAUST. Thanks, Mephistophilis; yet fain would I have a
book wherein I might behold all spells and incanta-   [166
tions, that I might raise up spirits when I please.

MEPH. Here they are, in this book.   [*There turn to them*

FAUST. Now would I have a book where I might see all
characters and planets of the heavens, that I might know
their motions and dispositions.   171

MEPH. Here they are too.   [*Turn to them*

FAUST. Nay, let me have one book more—and then I
have done—wherein I might see all plants, herbs, and trees
that grow upon the earth.   175

MEPH. Here they be.

FAUST. O, thou art deceived.

MEPH. Tut, I warrant thee.   [*Turn to them. Exeunt*

SCENE II[12]

Enter FAUSTUS *in his study, and* MEPHISTOPHILIS

FAUST. When I behold the heavens, then I repent;
And curse thee, wicked Mephistophilis,
Because thou hast deprived me of those joys.

MEPH. Why, Faustus,
Think'st thou heaven is such a glorious thing?   5
I tell thee 't is not half so fair as thou,
Or any man that breathes on earth.

FAUST. How provest thou that?

MEPH. It was made for man; therefore is man more
    excellent.

FAUST. If it were made for man, 't was made for me! 10
I will renounce this magic and repent.

Enter GOOD ANGEL *and* EVIL ANGEL

G. ANG. Faustus, repent; yet God will pity thee.

E. ANG. Thou art a spirit; God cannot pity thee.

FAUST. Who buzzeth in mine ears I am a spirit?
Be I a devil, yet God may pity me;   15
Ay, God will pity me if I repent.

E. ANG. Ay, but Faustus never shall repent.
                  [*Exeunt* ANGELS

FAUST. My heart's so hard'ned I cannot repent.
Scarce can I name salvation, faith, or heaven,
But fearful echoes thunder in mine ears,   20
"Faustus, thou art damned!" Then swords and knives,
Poison, guns, halters, and envenomed steel
Are laid before me to despatch myself;

---

[10] Foolish.

[11] The faithful wife of Ulysses.—*Saba* = the Queen of Sheba.

---

[12] The same. Very likely another scene, perhaps a comic one,
originally stood between the present scenes i and ii.

And long ere this I should have slain myself,
Had not sweet pleasure conquered deep despair.   25
Have I not made blind Homer sing to me
Of Alexander's[13] love and Oenon's death?
And hath not he that built the walls of Thebes
With ravishing sound of his melodious harp
Made music with my Mephistophilis?   30
Why should I die then, or basely despair?
I am resolved; Faustus shall ne'er repent.
Come, Mephistophilis, let us dispute again,
And argue of divine astrology.
Tell me, are there many heavens above the moon?   35
Are all celestial bodies but one globe,
As is the substance of this centric earth?

MEPH. As are the elements, such are the spheres
Mutually folded in each other's orb;
And, Faustus,   40
All jointly move upon one axletree,
Whose terminine[14] is termed the world's wide pole;
Nor are the names of Saturn, Mars, or Jupiter
Feigned, but are erring stars.

FAUST. But tell me, have they all one motion, both   [45
situe et tempore?[15]

MEPH. All jointly move from east to west in four-and-
twenty hours upon the poles of the world, but differ in
their motion upon the poles of the zodiac.

FAUST. Tush! These slender trifles Wagner can decide. [50
Hath Mephistophilis no greater skill?
Who knows not the double motion of the planets?
The first is finished in a natural day;
The second thus: as Saturn in thirty years; Jupiter in
twelve; Mars in four; the sun, Venus, and Mercury   [55
in a year; the moon in twenty-eight days. Tush, these are
freshmen's suppositions. But tell me, hath every sphere a
dominion or intelligentia?

MEPH. Ay.

FAUST. How many heavens, or spheres, are there?   [60

MEPH. Nine: the seven planets, the firmament, and the
empyreal heaven.

FAUST. Well, resolve me in this question: Why have we
not conjunctions, oppositions, aspects, eclipses, all at one
time, but in some years we have more, in some less?   [65

MEPH. Per inaequalem motum respectu totius.[16]

FAUST. Well, I am answered. Tell me who made the
world.

MEPH. I will not.

FAUST. Sweet Mephistophilis, tell me.

---

[13] Paris's. Oenone was the wife he deserted for Helen.—The
allusion in the next two lines is to Amphion.
[14] Termine, term, end.
[15] In both the direction and the duration (of their revolutions).
[16] On account of their unequal motion in relation to the whole.

MEPH. Move me not, for I will not tell thee.   70

FAUST. Villain, have I not bound thee to tell me anything?

MEPH. Ay, that is not against our kingdom; but this is.
Think thou on hell, Faustus, for thou art damned.

FAUST. Think, Faustus, upon God that made the world.

MEPH. Remember this.   [Exit   75

FAUST. Ay, go, accursèd spirit, to ugly hell;
'T is thou hast damned distressèd Faustus' soul.
Is 't not too late?

Re-enter GOOD ANGEL *and* EVIL ANGEL

E. ANG.   Too late.

G. ANG. Never too late, if Faustus can repent.

E. ANG. If thou repent, devils shall tear thee in pieces. 80

G. ANG. Repent, and they shall never raze thy skin.
                                          [*Exeunt* ANGELS

FAUST. Ah, Christ, my Saviour,
Seek to save distressèd Faustus' soul.

Enter LUCIFER, BELZEBUB, *and* MEPHISTOPHILIS

LUC. Christ cannot save thy soul, for he is just;
There's none but I have int'rest in the same.   85

FAUST. O, who art thou that look'st so terrible?

LUC. I am Lucifer,
And this is my companion prince in hell.

FAUST. O Faustus, they are come to fetch away thy soul!

LUC. We come to tell thee thou dost injure us;   90
Thou talk'st of Christ, contráry to thy promise;
Thou shouldst not think of God: think of the Devil,
And of his dam, too.

FAUST. Nor will I henceforth. Pardon me in this,
And Faustus vows never to look to heaven,   95
Never to name God, or to pray to him,
To burn his Scriptures, slay his ministers,
And make my spirits pull his churches down.

LUC. Do so, and we will highly gratify thee. Faustus, we
are come from hell to show thee some pastime. Sit down,
and thou shalt see all the Seven Deadly Sins appear   [101
in their proper shapes.

FAUST. That sight will be pleasing unto me
As Paradise was to Adam the first day
Of his creation.   105

LUC. Talk not of Paradise nor creation, but mark this
show; talk of the Devil, and nothing else.—Come away!

Enter the SEVEN DEADLY SINS

Now, Faustus, examine them of their several names and
dispositions.

FAUST. What art thou—the first?

PRIDE. I am Pride. I disdain to have any parents.   [111
I am like to Ovid's flea:[17] I can creep into every corner of

---

[17] The *Carmen de Pulice,* probably of medieval origin, was attributed to Ovid.

a wench; sometimes, like a periwig, I sit upon her brow; or like a fan of feathers, I kiss her lips; indeed I do—what do I not? But, fie, what a scent is here! I'll not speak another word, except the ground were perfumed, and covered with cloth of arras.   117

FAUST. What art thou—the second?

COVET. I am Covetousness, begotten of an old churl in an old leathern bag; and might I have my wish, I would desire that this house and all the people in it were   [121 turned to gold, that I might lock you up in my good chest. O, my sweet gold!

FAUST. What art thou—the third?

WRATH. I am Wrath. I had neither father nor mother: I leaped out of a lion's mouth when I was scarce half   [126 an hour old; and ever since I have run up and down the world with this case[18] of rapiers, wounding myself when I had nobody to fight withal. I was born in hell; and look to it, for some of you shall be[19] my father.   130

FAUST. What art thou—the fourth?

ENVY. I am Envy, begotten of a chimney sweeper and an oyster-wife. I cannot read, and therefore wish all books were burnt. I am lean with seeing others eat. O, that there would come a famine through all the world, that all might die, and I live alone! Then thou shouldst see how   [136 fat I would be. But must thou sit and I stand? Come down with a vengeance!

FAUST. Away, envious rascal!—What art thou—the fifth?

GLUT. Who, I, sir? I am Gluttony. My parents are all dead, and the devil a penny they have left me, but a   [141 bare pension, and that is thirty meals a day and ten bevers[20]—a small trifle to suffice nature. O, I come of a royal parentage! My grandfather was a gammon of bacon, my grandmother a hogshead of claret wine; my godfathers were these: Peter Pickleherring and Martin Martle-   [146 mas-beef.[21] O, but my godmother, she was a jolly gentle-woman, and well beloved in every good town and city; her name was Mistress Margery March-beer. Now, Faustus, thou hast heard all my progeny,[22] wilt thou bid me to supper?   151

FAUST. No, I'll see thee hanged; thou wilt eat up all my victuals.

GLUT. Then the Devil choke thee!

FAUST. Choke thyself, glutton!—Who art thou—the sixth?   156

SLOTH. I am Sloth. I was begotten on a sunny bank, where I have lain ever since; and you have done me great injury to bring me from thence. Let me be carried thither

again by Gluttony and Lechery. I'll not speak another word for a king's ransom.   161

FAUST. What are you, Mistress Minx—the seventh and last?

LECH. Who, I, sir? I am one that loves an inch of raw mutton[23] better than an ell of fried stockfish;[24] and the first letter of my name begins with Lechery. (lust)   166

LUC. Away! to hell, to hell!   [Exeunt the SINS—Now, Faustus, how dost thou like this?

FAUST. O, this feeds my soul!

LUC. Tut, Faustus, in hell is all manner of delight.   170

FAUST. O, might I see hell, and return again, How happy were I then!

LUC. Thou shalt; I will send for thee at midnight. In meantime take this book; peruse it throughly, And thou shalt turn thyself into what shape thou wilt.

FAUST. Great thanks, mighty Lucifer!   176
This will I keep as chary as my life.

LUC. Farewell, Faustus, and think on the Devil.

FAUST. Farewell, great Lucifer!—Come, Mephistophilis.

[Exeunt omnes

SCENE III[25]

Enter ROBIN *the ostler with a book in his hand*

ROBIN. O, this is admirable! Here I ha' stol'n one of Dr. Faustus' conjuring books, and i' faith I mean to search some circles[26] for my own use! Now will I make all the maidens in our parish dance at my pleasure, stark naked before me; and so by that means I shall see more than   [5 e'er I felt or saw yet.

Enter RALPH[27] *calling* ROBIN

RALPH. Robin, prithee come away; there's a gentleman tarries to have his horse, and he would have his things rubbed and made clean. He keeps such a chafing with my mistress about it, and she has sent me to look thee   [10 out. Prithee come away!

ROBIN. Keep out, keep out, or else you are blown up, you are dismembered, Ralph; keep out, for I am about a roaring piece of work.

RALPH. Come, what doest thou with that same   [15 book? Thou canst not read.

ROBIN. Yes, my master and mistress shall find that I can read, he for his forehead,[28] she for her private study; she's born to bear with me, or else my art fails.

---

[18] Pair.
[19] One of you devils is doubtless.
[20] Between-meals refreshments.
[21] I.e., beef salted about Martinmas time (Nov. 11).
[22] Lineage.

[23] Punning on *mutton* = wench, harlot.
[24] Salted or dried fish.   [25] An innyard.
[26] Drawn by magicians conjuring up spirits.
[27] The original edition has *Rafe* throughout.
[28] Innumerable jokes in Elizabethan plays allude to the horns which were supposed to grow in the forehead of the cuckold or deceived husband.

RALPH. Why, Robin, what book is that? 20

ROBIN. What book! Why, the most intolerable book for conjuring that e'er was invented by any brimstone devil.

RALPH. Canst thou conjure with it?

ROBIN. I can do all these things easily with it; first, I can make thee drunk with ippocras[29] at any tavern in [25 Europe for nothing; that's one of my conjuring works.

RALPH. Our Master Parson says that's nothing.

ROBIN. True, Ralph; and more, Ralph, if thou hast any mind to Nan Spit, our kitchenmaid, then turn her and wind her to thy own use, as often as thou wilt, and at midnight. 31

RALPH. O brave, Robin, shall I have Nan Spit, and to mine own use? On that condition I'll feed thy devil with horsebread[30] as long as he lives, of free cost.

ROBIN. No more, sweet Ralph; let's go and make [35 clean our boots, which lie foul upon our hands, and then to our conjuring in the Devil's name. [Exeunt

ACT III

Enter WAGNER, *solus*[1]

WAG. Learnèd Faustus, to know the secrets of astronomy
Graven in the book of Jove's high firmament,
Did mount himself to scale Olympus' top,
Being seated in a chariot burning bright,
Drawn by the strength of yoky dragons'[2] necks. 5
He views the clouds, the planets, and the stars,
The tropic zones, and quarters of the sky,
From the bright circle of the hornèd moon
Even to the height of *Primum Mobile;*[3]
And, whirling round with this circumference, 10
Within the concave compass of the pole,
From east to west his dragons swiftly glide
And in eight days did bring him home again.
Not long he stayed within his quiet house,
To rest his bones after his weary toil; 15
But new exploits do hale him out again,
And, mounted then upon a dragon's back,
That with his wings did part the subtle air,
He now is gone to prove cosmography,[4]
That measures coasts and kingdoms of the earth: 20
And, as I guess, will first arrive at Rome,
To see the Pope and manner of his court,
And take some part of holy Peter's feast,
That to this day is highly solemnized. [Exit

SCENE I[5]

Enter FAUSTUS *and* MEPHISTOPHILIS

FAUST. Having now, my good Mephistophilis,
Passed with delight the stately town of Trier,[6]
Environed round with airy mountain tops,[7]
With walls of flint, and deep entrenchèd lakes,
Not to be won by any conquering prince; 5
From Paris next, coasting the realm of France,
We saw the river Main fall into Rhine,
Whose banks are set with groves of fruitful vines.
Then up to Naples, rich Campania,[8]
Whose buildings fair and gorgeous to the eye, 10
The streets straight forth, and paved with finest brick,
Quarters the town in four equivalents.
There saw we learnèd Maro's[9] golden tomb,
The way he cut, an English mile in length,
Thorough a rock of stone in one night's space. 15
From thence to Venice, Padua, and the rest,
In midst of which a sumptuous temple[10] stands,
That threats the stars with her aspiring top,
Whose frame is paved with sundry-colored stones
And roofed aloft with curious work in gold. 20
Thus hitherto hath Faustus spent his time.
But tell me, now, what resting place is this?
Hast thou, as erst I did command,
Conducted me within the walls of Rome?

MEPH. I have, my Faustus; and, for proof thereof, 25
This is the goodly palace of the Pope;
And 'cause we are no common guests,
I choose his privy-chamber for our use.

FAUST. I hope his Holiness will bid us welcome.

MEPH. All's one,[11] for we'll be bold with his ven'son. 30
And now, my Faustus, that thou mayst perceive
What Rome containeth to delight thee with,
Know that this city stands upon seven hills
That underprops the groundwork of the same.
Just through the midst runs flowing Tiber's stream, 35
With winding banks that cut it in two parts,

---

[29] Hippocras, sugared and spiced wine.

[1] Alone. Here he acts as chorus, to inform the audience.

[2] Among properties for this play in a contemporary list is a dragon. Perhaps Faustus alights from it at the opening of III, i.

[3] "The axle of the heavens, that moveth the whole firmament" (English *Faust Book*)

[4] I.e., to test (the accuracy of) geographers.

[5] Rome. The Pope's privy-chamber or private room.

[6] In the Rhineland.

[7] Evidently Marlowe misread the *Faust Book's* "monuments."

[30] A coarse bread, fed to horses.

[8] The *Faust Book* reads "to Campania [i.e., the province] in the Kingdom of Naples." Marlowe evidently took "Campania" as another name for the *city* of Naples.

[9] Vergil's. A tunnel near it was supposed to be the work of his magic.

[10] St. Mark's, at Venice. Padua is here taken as a Venetian possession; "the rest" are the other territories of Venice.

[11] It makes no difference.

Over the which four stately bridges lean,
That makes safe passage to each part of Rome.
Upon the bridge called Ponto Angelo
Erected is a castle passing strong, 40
Within whose walls such store of ordnance are,
And double cannons, framed of carvèd brass,
As match the days within one complete year;
Besides the gates and high pyrámidès,[12]
Which Julius Caesar brought from Africa. 45
  FAUST. Now by the kingdoms of infernal rule,
Of Styx, Acheron,[13] and the fiery lake
Of ever-burning Phlegethon, I swear
That I do long to see the monuments
And situation of bright-splendent Rome: 50
Come, therefore; let's away.
  MEPH. Nay, Faustus, stay; I know you'd fain see the
    Pope,
And take some part of holy Peter's feast,
Where thou shalt see a troop of bald-pate friars,
Whose *summum bonum* is in belly-cheer. 55
  FAUST. Well, I am content to compass, then, some
    sport,
And by their folly make us merriment.
Then charm me, that I may be invisible, to do what I
    please,
Unseen of any whilst I stay in Rome.
                    [MEPHISTOPHILIS *charms him*
  MEPH. So, Faustus; now 60
Do what thou wilt, thou shalt not be discerned.

Sound a sennet.[14] *Enter the* POPE *and the* CARDINAL *of*
LORRAINE *to the banquet, with* FRIARS *attending*

  POPE. My Lord of Lorraine, wilt please you draw near?
  FAUST. Fall to, and the Devil choke you an you spare!
  POPE. How now! Who's that which spake?—Friars,
    look about.
  1ST FRIAR. Here's nobody, if it like[15] your Holiness. 65
  POPE. My Lord, here is a dainty dish was sent me from
the Bishop of Milan.
  FAUST. I thank you, sir.   [*Snatch it*
  POPE. How now! Who's that which snatched the meat
from me? Will no man look?—My Lord, this dish [70
was sent me from the Cardinal of Florence.
  FAUST. You say true; I'll ha 't.   [*Snatch it*
  POPE. What, again?—My Lord, I'll drink to your Grace.
  FAUST. I'll pledge your Grace.   [*Snatch the cup*
  C. OF LOR. My Lord, it may be some ghost newly [75
crept out of purgatory, come to beg a pardon of your
Holiness.

  POPE. It may be so.—Friars, prepare a dirge to lay the
fury of this ghost.—Once again, my Lord, fall to.
                    [*The* POPE *crosseth himself*
  FAUST. What, are you crossing of yourself? Well, [80
use that trick no more, I would advise you.—(*Cross again.*)
Well, there's the second time. Aware the third, I give you
fair warning. [*Cross again, and* FAUSTUS *hits him a box of
                the ear; and they all run away*
Come on, Mephistophilis, what shall we do?
  MEPH. Nay, I know not. We shall be cursed with [85
bell, book, and candle.
  FAUST. How! bell, book, and candle,—candle, book, and
    bell,
Forward and backward to curse Faustus to hell!
Anon you shall hear a hog grunt, a calf bleat, and an ass
    bray,
Because it is Saint Peter's holiday. 90

Re-enter all the FRIARS, *to sing the dirge*

  1ST FRIAR. Come, brethren, let's about our business with
good devotion.

Sing this

  Cursed be he that stole away his Holiness' meat from
the table! *Maledicat Dominus!*[16]
  Cursed be he that struck his Holiness a blow on [95
the face! *Maledicat Dominus!*
  Cursed be he that took Friar Sandelo a blow on the pate!
Maledicat Dominus!
  Cursed be he that disturbeth our holy dirge! *Maledicat
Dominus!* 100
  Cursed be he that took away his Holiness' wine! *Maledicat
Dominus! Et omnes sancti!*[17] *Amen!*

            [MEPHISTOPHILIS *and* FAUSTUS *beat the* FRIARS,
              and fling fireworks among them, and so exeunt

SCENE II[18]

Enter ROBIN *and* RALPH *with a silver goblet*

  ROBIN. Come, Ralph, did not I tell thee we were for
ever made by this Doctor Faustus book? *Ecce signum,*[19]
here's a simple purchase[20] for horsekeepers; our horses shall
eat no hay as long as this lasts.

Enter the VINTNER

  RALPH. But, Robin, here comes the vintner. 5

[12] Obelisks.
[13] Rivers of Hades. Phlegethon was another.
[14] Fanfare of trumpets.   [15] Please.
[16] May the Lord curse him.   [17] And all the saints.
[18] The inn.   [19] Behold the evidence.
[20] Piece of loot.—Since it is theirs, they will provide their horses
     with better fodder than hay.

ROBIN. Hush! I'll gull him supernaturally.—Drawer, I hope all is paid; God be with you.—Come, Ralph.

VINT. Soft, sir; a word with you. I must yet have a goblet paid from you, ere you go.

ROBIN. I, a goblet, Ralph; I, a goblet! I scorn you, [10 and you are but a &c.[21] I, a goblet! Search me.

VINT. I mean so, sir, with your favor. [Searches him
ROBIN. How say you now?

VINT. I must say somewhat to your fellow. You, sir!

RALPH. Me, sir! me, sir! Search your fill. 15
(VINTNER searches him.) Now, sir, you may be ashamed to burden honest men with a matter of truth.

VINT. Well, t' one of you hath this goblet about you.

ROBIN (aside). You lie, drawer; 't is afore me.—Sirrah you, I'll teach ye to impeach honest men; stand by; [20 I'll scour you for a goblet! Stand aside you had best, I charge you in the name of Belzebub.—(Aside to RALPH) Look to the goblet, Ralph.

VINT. What mean you, sirrah?

ROBIN. I'll tell you what I mean. (He reads [from the [25 book.]) Sanctobulorum, Periphrasticon—Nay, I'll tickle you, vintner.—(Aside) Look to the goblet, Ralph.—(Reads.) Polypragmos Belseborams framanto pacostiphos tostu, Mephistophilis, etc.

Enter MEPHISTOPHILIS, sets squibs at their backs, and then exit. They run about

VINT. O nomine Domine![22] what mean'st thou, [30 Robin? Thou hast no goblet.

RALPH. Peccatum peccatorum![23] Here's thy goblet, good vintner.

ROBIN. Misericordia pro nobis![24] What shall I do? Good Devil, forgive me now, and I'll never rob thy library more. 36

Re-enter to them MEPHISTOPHILIS

MEPH. Vanish, villains!
Th' one like an ape, another like a bear, the third an ass, for doing this enterprise.—[25] [Exit VINTNER
Monarch of hell, under whose black survey 40
Great potentates do kneel with awful fear,
Upon whose altars thousand souls do lie,
How am I vexèd with these villains' charms!
From Constantinople am I hither come
Only for pleasure of these damnèd slaves. 45

ROBIN. How? from Constantinople? You have had a great journey. Will you take sixpence in your purse to pay for your supper, and be gone?

MEPH. Well, villains, for your presumption, I transform thee into an ape, and thee into a dog; and so, begone! [50
[Exit

ROBIN. How, into an ape? That's brave![26] I'll have fine sport with the boys. I'll get nuts and apples enow.

RALPH. And I must be a dog.

ROBIN. I' faith, thy head will never be out of the pottage pot. [Exeunt 55

ACT IV

Enter CHORUS

CHORUS. When Faustus had with pleasure ta'en the
      view
Of rarest things and royal courts of kings,
He stayed his course and so returnèd home;
Where such as bear his absence but with grief,
I mean his friends and near'st companiöns, 5
Did gratulate his safety with kind words.
And in their conference of what befell,
Touching his journey through the world and air,
They put forth questions of astrology,
Which Faustus answered with such learnèd skill 10
As they admired and wond'red at his wit.
Now is his fame spread forth in every land;
Amongst the rest the Emperor is one:
Carolus the Fifth, at whose palace now
Faustus is feasted 'mongst his noblemen. 15
What there he did in trial of his art,
I leave untold—your eyes shall see performed. [Exit

SCENE I[1]

*Enter EMPEROR, FAUSTUS, MEPHISTOPHILIS, and a
KNIGHT, with Attendants*

EMP. Master Doctor Faustus, I have heard strange report of thy knowledge in the black art, how that none in my empire nor in the whole world can compare with thee for the rare effects of magic; they say thou hast a familiar

---

21 The comedian was expected to supply a string of racy invectives. Cf., after the nonsensical verbiage in lines 26–29, the *etc.*
22 The Vintner's imperfect Latin for "in the name of the Lord."

23 Sin of sins.   24 Mercy on us.
25 Most modern editions omit this speech; it may be an alternative ending for the scene. The double transformation indicates corruption. So do the squibs.   26 Fine.

1 A room in a palace of Charles V (1500–58), Holy Roman Emperor.

spirit, by whom thou canst accomplish what thou   [5
list. This, therefore, is my request, that thou let me see
some proof of thy skill, that mine eyes may be witnesses
to confirm what mine ears have heard reported; and here
I swear to thee, by the honor of mine imperial crown, that
whatever thou doest thou shalt be no ways prejudiced or
endamaged.   11

KNIGHT (*aside*). I' faith he looks much like a conjuror.

FAUST. My gracious Sovereign, though I must confess
myself far inferior to the report men have published, and
nothing answerable[2] to the honor of your imperial   [15
Majesty, yet for that[3] love and duty binds me thereunto I
am content to do whatsoever your Majesty shall command
me.

EMP. Then, Doctor Faustus, mark what I shall say.
As I was sometime solitary set   20
Within my closet, sundry thoughts arose
About the honor of mine ancestors,
How they had won by prowess such exploits,
Got such riches, subdued so many kingdoms,
As we that do succeed, or they that shall   25
Hereafter possess our throne, shall
(I fear me) ne'er attain to that degree
Of high renown and great authority.
Amongst which kings is Alexander the Great,
Chief spectacle of the world's pre-eminence,   30
The bright shining of whose glorious acts
Lightens the world with his[4] reflecting beams,
As,[5] when I heard but motion[6] made of him,
It grieves my soul I never saw the man.
If, therefore, thou by cunning of thine art   35
Canst raise this man from hollow vaults below,
Where lies entombed this famous conqueror,
And bring with him his beauteous paramour,
Both in their right shapes, gesture, and attire
They used to wear during their time of life,   40
Thou shalt both satisfy my just desire
And give me cause to praise thee whilst I live.

FAUST. My gracious Lord, I am ready to accomplish your
request so far forth as by art, and power of my spirit, I am
able to perform.   45

KNIGHT (*aside*). I' faith, that's just nothing at all.

FAUST. But, if it like your Grace, it is not in my ability
to present before your eyes the true substantial bodies of
those two deceased princes, which long since are consumed
to dust.   50

KNIGHT (*aside*). Ay, marry, Master Doctor, now there's
a sign of grace in you, when you will confess the truth.

FAUST. But such spirits as can lively resemble Alexander
and his paramour shall appear before your Grace in that

manner that they best lived in, in their most flourish-   [55
ing estate;[7] which I doubt not shall sufficiently content
your imperial Majesty.

EMP. Go to, Master Doctor; let me see them presently.[8]

KNIGHT. Do you hear, Master Doctor? You bring Alexander and his paramour before the Emperor!   60

FAUST. How then, sir?

KNIGHT. I' faith, that's as true as Diana turned me to a
stag![9]

FAUST. No, sir, but when Actaeon died, he left the horns
for you.[10] Mephistophilis, begone!   65

[*Exit* MEPHISTOPHILIS

KNIGHT. Nay, an you go to conjuring, I'll be gone.

[*Exit* KNIGHT

FAUST. I'll meet with you anon for interrupting me so.—
Here they are, my gracious Lord.

Re-enter MEPHISTOPHILIS *with spirits in the shapes of*
ALEXANDER *and his* PARAMOUR

EMP. Master Doctor, I heard this lady while she lived had
a wart or mole in her neck. How shall I know whether it
be so or no?   71

FAUST. Your Highness may boldly go and see.

[*Exeunt* SPIRITS

EMP. Sure these are no spirits, but the true substantial
bodies of those two deceased princes.

FAUST. Will't please your Highness now to send   [75
for the knight that was so pleasant with me here of late?

EMP. One of you call him forth.   [*Exit* Attendant

Re-enter the KNIGHT *with a pair of horns on his head*

How now, Sir Knight! Why, I had thought thou hadst
been a bachelor; but now I see thou hast a wife, that not
only gives thee horns, but makes thee wear them. Feel on
thy head.   81

KNIGHT. Thou damnèd wretch and execrable dog,
Bred in the concave of some monstrous rock,
How dar'st thou thus abuse a gentleman?
Villain, I say, undo what thou hast done!   85

FAUST. O, not so fast, sir; there's no haste. But, good,[11]
are you remb'red how you crossed me in my conference with the Emperor? I think I have met with you
for it.

EMP. Good Master Doctor, at my entreaty release   [90
him; he hath done penance sufficient.

FAUST. My gracious Lord, not so much for the injury
he off'red me here in your presence, as to delight you with
some mirth, hath Faustus worthily requited this injurious

---

[2] In no respect adequate.   [3] Since.
[4] Its.   [5] To the extent that.   [6] Mention.

[7] State, condition.   [8] At once.
[9] According to the myth Actaeon was thus punished and then
    hunted by his own hounds for having seen the goddess bathing.
[10] See II, iii, note 28, above.   [11] My dear sir.

knight; which being all I desire, I am content to re- [95
lease him of his horns. And, Sir Knight, hereafter speak
well of scholars.—Mephistophilis, transform him straight!
(MEPHISTOPHILIS *removes the horns.*) Now, my good Lord,
having done my duty, I humbly take my leave.

EMP. Farewell, Master Doctor; yet, ere you go,   100
Expect from me a bounteous reward.   [*Exeunt*

SCENE II[12]

Enter FAUSTUS *and* MEPHISTOPHILIS

FAUST. Now, Mephistophilis, the restless course
That Time doth run with calm and silent foot,
Short'ning my days and thread of vital life,
Calls for the payment of my latest years.
Therefore, sweet Mephistophilis, let us   5
Make haste to Wittenberg.

MEPH. What, will you go on horseback or on foot?

FAUST. Nay, till I am past this fair and pleasant green,
I'll walk on foot.

Enter a HORSE-COURSER

HORSE-C. I have been all this day seeking one   [10
Master Fustian; mass, see where he is!—God save you,
Master Doctor!

FAUST. What, horse-courser! You are well met.

HORSE-C. Do you hear, sir? I have brought you forty
dollars for your horse.   15

FAUST. I cannot sell him so; if thou lik'st him for fifty,
take him.

HORSE-C. Alas, sir, I have no more.—I pray you speak
for me.   19

MEPH. I pray you let him have him; he is an honest
fellow, and he has a great charge, neither wife nor child.

FAUST. Well, come, give me your money. (HORSE-
COURSER *gives* FAUSTUS *the money.*) My boy will deliver
him to you. But I must tell you one thing before you have
him: ride him not into the water[13] at any hand.   25

HORSE-C. Why, sir, will he not drink of all waters?

FAUST. O yes, he will drink of all waters, but ride him
not into the water; ride him over hedge or ditch, or where
thou wilt, but not into the water.

HORSE-C. Well, sir.—(*Aside*) Now am I made man   [30
for ever. I'll not leave my horse for forty.[14] If he had but
the quality of hey ding ding, hey ding ding, I'd make a
brave living on him; he has a buttock as slick as an eel.—

Well, God buy,[15] sir; your boy will deliver him me. But
hark ye, sir; if my horse be sick or ill at ease, if I bring   [35
his water to you, you'll tell me what it is?

FAUST. Away, you villain; what, dost think I am a horse-
doctor?—   [*Exit* HORSE-COURSER
What art thou, Faustus, but a man condemned to die?
Thy fatal time doth draw to final end.   40
Despair doth drive distrust unto my thoughts;
Confound these passions with a quiet sleep.
Tush, Christ did call the thief upon the cross;
Then rest thee, Faustus, quiet in conceit.[16]

[*Sleep in his chair*

Re-enter HORSE-COURSER, *all wet, crying*

HORSE-C. Alas, alas! Doctor Fustian, quotha?   [45
Mass, Doctor Lopus[17] was never such a doctor. Has given
me a purgation has purged me of forty dollars; I shall
never see them more. But yet, like an ass as I was, I would
not be ruled by him, for he bade me I should ride him
into no water. Now I, thinking my horse had had   [50
some rare quality that he would not have had me known
of, I, like a vent'rous youth, rid him into the deep pond at
the town's end. I was no sooner in the middle of the pond,
but my horse vanished away, and I sat upon a bottle[18] of
hay, never so near drowning in my life. But I'll seek   [55
out my Doctor, and have my forty dollars again, or I'll
make it the dearest horse—O, yonder is his snipper-
snapper.[19]—Do you hear? You hey-pass,[20] where's your
master?

MEPH. Why, sir, what would you? You cannot speak
with him.   61

HORSE-C. But I will speak with him.

MEPH. Why, he's fast asleep. Come some other time.

HORSE-C. I'll speak with him now, or I'll break his glass
windows[21] about his ears.   65

MEPH. I tell thee he has not slept this eight nights.

HORSE-C. An he have not slept this eight weeks, I'll
speak with him.

MEPH. See where he is, fast asleep.

HORSE-C. Ay, this is he.—God save ye, Master   [70
Doctor! Master Doctor, Master Doctor Fustian!—Forty
dollars, forty dollars for a bottle of hay!

MEPH. Why, thou seest he hears thee not.

HORSE-C. So ho, ho!—so ho, ho! (*Holla in his ear.*) No,
will you not wake? I'll make you wake ere I go.   [75
(*Pull him by the leg, and pull it away.*) Alas, I am undone![22]
What shall I do?

---

[12] A green; afterwards Faustus's house. The wreckage of several
scenes probably confronts us here.
[13] Demons could not cross water.
[14] I.e., any number of others.—The next lines allude to the horse's
possibilities for breeding.

[15] Goodbye.
[16] With quiet thoughts.
[17] Queen Elizabeth's physician, Roderigo Lopez, a Spanish Jew.
He was charged with conspiracy to poison her and was executed
in 1594, nearly a year after Marlowe's death!   [18] Truss.
[19] Whippersnapper.   [20] Juggler, since this was his cry.
[21] Spectacles.   [22] Ruined.

FAUST. O, my leg, my leg! Help, Mephistophilis! Call the officers! My leg, my leg!

MEPH. Come, villain, to the constable. 80

HORSE-C. O Lord, sir, let me go, and I'll give you forty dollars more.

MEPH. Where be they?

HORSE-C. I have none about me. Come to my ostry[23] and I'll give them you. 85

MEPH. Begone quickly! [HORSE-COURSER *runs away*

FAUST. What, is he gone? Farewell he! Faustus has his leg again, and the horse-courser, I take it, a bottle of hay for his labor. Well, this trick shall cost him forty dollars more. 90

Enter WAGNER

How now, Wagner, what's the news with thee?

WAG. Sir, the Duke of Vanholt doth earnestly entreat your company.

FAUST. The Duke of Vanholt! an honorable gentleman, to whom I must be no niggard of my cunning. [95 Come, Mephistophilis, let's away to him. [*Exeunt*

SCENE III[24]

Enter the DUKE *of* VANHOLT, *the* DUCHESS, FAUSTUS, *and* MEPHISTOPHILIS

DUKE. Believe me, Master Doctor, this merriment hath much pleased me.

FAUST. My gracious Lord, I am glad it contents you so well.—But it may be, madam, you take no delight in this. I have heard that great-bellied[25] women do long for [5 some dainties or other. What is it, madam? Tell me, and you shall have it.

ACT V

SCENE I[1]

Enter WAGNER, *solus*

WAG. I think my master means to die shortly,
For he hath given to me all his goods;
And yet, methinks if that death were near,
He would not banquet and carouse and swill
Amongst the students, as even now he doth, 5
Who are at supper with such belly-cheer
As Wagner ne'er beheld in all his life.
See where they come! Belike the feast is ended. [*Exit*

---

[23] Hostelry, inn.

[24] A residence of the Duke of "Vanholt." Another scene doubtless intervened in the original. [25] Pregnant.

[1] Wittenberg. A room in Faustus's house.

DUCHESS. Thanks, good Master Doctor; and for I see your courteous intent to pleasure me, I will not hide from you the thing my heart desires; and were it now [10 summer, as it is January and the dead time of the winter, I would desire no better meat than a dish of ripe grapes.

FAUST. Alas, madam, that's nothing.—Mephistophilis, begone! (*Exit* MEPHISTOPHILIS.)—Were it a greater thing than this, so it would content you, you should have it. [15

Re-enter MEPHISTOPHILIS *with the grapes*

Here they be, madam; wilt please you taste on them?

DUKE. Believe me, Master Doctor, this makes me wonder above the rest, that being in the dead time of winter and in the month of January, how you should come by these grapes. 20

FAUST. If it like your Grace, the year is divided into two circles over the whole world, that[26] when it is here winter with us, in the contrary circle it is summer with them, as in India, Saba,[27] and farther countries in the East; and by means of a swift spirit that I have, I had them brought [25 hither, as ye see.—How do you like them, madam; be they good?

DUCHESS. Believe me, Master Doctor, they be the best grapes that e'er I tasted in my life before.

FAUST. I am glad they content you so, madam. 30

DUKE. Come, madam, let us in, where you must well reward this learned man for the great kindness he hath showed to you.

DUCHESS. And so I will, my Lord; and whilst I live, rest beholding for this courtesy. 35

FAUST. I humbly thank your Grace.

DUKE. Come, Master Doctor, follow us and receive your reward. [*Exeunt*

Enter FAUSTUS, *with two or three* SCHOLARS, *and* MEPHISTOPHILIS

1ST SCHOL. Master Doctor Faustus, since our conference about fair ladies, which was the beautiful'st in all the [10 world, we have determined with ourselves that Helen of Greece was the admirablest lady that ever lived. Therefore, Master Doctor, if you will do us that favor as to let us see that peerless dame of Greece, whom all the world admires for majesty, we should think ourselves much beholding unto you. 16

FAUST. Gentlemen,
For that I know your friendship is unfeigned,
And Faustus' custom is not to deny

---

[26] So that. [27] Sheba, an ancient Arabian kingdom.

The just requests of those that wish him well,   20
You shall behold that peerless dame of Greece,
No otherways for pomp and majesty
Than when Sir Paris crossed the seas with her
And brought the spoils to rich Dardania.[2]
Be silent, then; for danger is in words.   25

Music sounds, and HELEN *passeth over the stage*

2ND SCHOL. Too simple is my wit to tell her praise,
Whom all the world admires for majesty.

3RD SCHOL. No marvel though the angry Greeks
      pursued
With ten years' war the rape[3] of such a queen,
Whose heavenly beauty passeth all compare.   30

1ST SCHOL. Since we have seen the pride of Nature's
      works
And only paragon of excellence,
Let us depart; and for this glorious deed
Happy and blest be Faustus evermore.

FAUST. Gentlemen, farewell; the same I wish to
      you.   [*Exeunt* SCHOLARS   35

Enter an OLD MAN

OLD MAN. Ah, Doctor Faustus, that I might prevail
To guide thy steps unto the way of life,
By which sweet path thou mayst attain the goal
That shall conduct thee to celestial rest!
Break heart, drop blood, and mingle it with tears,   40
Tears falling from repentant heaviness[4]
Of thy most vild and loathsome filthiness,
The stench whereof corrupts the inward soul
With such flagitious crimes of heinous sins
As no commiseration may expel,   45
But mercy, Faustus, of thy Saviour sweet,
Whose blood alone must wash away thy guilt.

FAUST. Where art thou, Faustus? Wretch, what hast
      thou done?
Damned art thou, Faustus, damned. Despair and die!
Hell calls for right, and with a roaring voice   50
Says, "Faustus, come; thine hour is almost come!"
And Faustus now will come to do thee right.
            [MEPHISTOPHILIS *gives him a dagger*

OLD MAN. Ah, stay, good Faustus, stay thy desperate
      steps!
I see an angel hovers o'er thy head,
And with a vial full of precious grace   55
Offers to pour the same into thy soul.
Then call for mercy, and avoid despair!

FAUST. Ah, my sweet friend, I feel
Thy words do comfort my distressèd soul.
Leave me awhile to ponder on my sins.   60

OLD MAN. I go, sweet Faustus, but with heavy cheer,
Fearing the ruin of thy hopeless soul.   [*Exit*

FAUST. Accursèd Faustus, where is mercy now?
I do repent, and yet I do despair;
Hell strives with grace for conquest in my breast.   65
What shall I do to shun the snares of death?

MEPH. Thou traitor, Faustus, I arrest thy soul
For disobedience to my sovereign lord.
Revolt, or I'll in piecemeal tear thy flesh.

FAUST. I do repent I e'er offended him;   70
Sweet Mephistophilis, entreat thy lord
To pardon my unjust presumptiön,
And with my blood again I will confirm
My former vow I made to Lucifer.

MEPH. Do it now then quickly, with unfeignèd heart, 75
Lest danger do attend thy drift.

FAUST. Torment, sweet friend, that base and crooked
      age,[5]
That durst dissuade me from my Lucifer,
With greatest torments that our hell affords.

MEPH. His faith is great; I cannot touch his soul.   80
But what I may afflict his body with
I will attempt, which is but little worth.

FAUST. One thing, good servant, let me crave of thee,
To glut the longing of my heart's desire,
That I might have unto my paramour   85
That heavenly Helen, which I saw of late,
Whose sweet embracings may extinguish clean
These thoughts that do dissuade me from my vow,
And keep mine oath I made to Lucifer.

MEPH. Faustus, this or what else thou shalt desire   90
Shall be performed in twinkling of an eye.

Re-enter HELEN

FAUST. Was this the face that launched a thousand ships,
And burnt the topless[6] towers of Ilium?[7]
Sweet Helen, make me immortal with a kiss.—
Her lips sucks forth my soul; see where it flies!—   95
Come, Helen, come, give me my soul again.
Here will I dwell, for heaven be in these lips,
And all is dross that is not Helena.
I will be Paris, and for love of thee,
Instead of Troy shall Wittenberg be sacked;   100

---

[5] Old man.   [6] Incomparably lofty.
[7] Troy. It fell, according to the legend, after a long siege by the
      Greeks; their object was to restore Helen, whom Paris had
      seduced, to her husband Menelaus (line 101). Achilles (line 103)
      was the Greeks' best fighter; he was invulnerable except in the
      heel.

---

[2]Troy.   [3] Seizure.   [4] Sorrow.

And I will combat with weak Menelaus,
And wear thy colors on my plumèd crest;
Yea, I will wound Achilles in the heel,
And then return to Helen for a kiss.
O, thou art fairer than the evening air 105
Clad in the beauty of a thousand stars;
Brighter art thou than flaming Jupiter
When he appeared to hapless Semele;[8]
More lovely than the monarch of the sky[9]
In wanton Arethusa's azured arms; 110
And none but thou shalt be my paramour.

Re-enter OLD MAN. *Exeunt the others*

OLD MAN. Accursèd Faustus, miserable man,
That from thy soul exclud'st the grace of heaven,[10]
And fliest the throne of his tribunal seat!

Enter the DEVILS

Satan begins to sift[11] me with his pride.[12] 115
As in this furnace God shall try my faith,
My faith, vile hell, shall triumph over thee.
Ambitious fiends, see how the heavens smiles
At your repulse, and laughs your state to scorn!
Hence, hell! for hence I fly unto my God. [*Exeunt* 120

SCENE II[13]

Enter FAUSTUS *with the* SCHOLARS

FAUST. Ah, gentlemen!

1ST SCHOL. What ails Faustus?

FAUST. Ah, my sweet chamber-fellow, had I lived with
thee, then had I lived still! But now I die eternally. Look,
comes he not? comes he not? 5

2ND SCHOL. What means Faustus?

3RD SCHOL. Belike he is grown into some sickness by
being oversolitary.

1ST SCHOL. If it be so, we'll have physicians to cure him.
—'T is but a surfeit; never fear, man. 10

FAUST. A surfeit of deadly sin that hath damned both
body and soul.

2ND SCHOL. Yet, Faustus, look up to heaven; remember
God's mercies are infinite.

FAUST. But Faustus' offence can ne'er be pardoned; [15
the serpent that tempted Eve may be saved, but not
Faustus. Ah, gentlemen, hear me with patience, and

---

[8] At her request he allowed her to see him in his splendor, and
his lightnings destroyed her.
[9] Presumably Apollo, but this alleged amour is unknown in
mythology.　[10] God.　[11] Cf. Luke 22:31.
[12] Display (of power).　[13] The same.

tremble not at my speeches. Though my heart pants and
quivers to remember that I have been a student here these
thirty years, oh, would I had never seen Wittenberg, [20
never read book! And what wonders I have done, all
Germany can witness, yea, all the world; for which Faustus
hath lost both Germany and the world, yea, heaven itself,
heaven, the seat of God, the throne of the blessed, the
kingdom of joy, and must remain in hell for ever, [25
hell, ah, hell, for ever! Sweet friends, what shall become of
Faustus, being in hell for ever?

3RD SCHOL. Yet, Faustus, call on God.

FAUST. On God, whom Faustus hath abjured! On God,
whom Faustus hath blasphemed! Ah, my God, I [30
would weep, but the Devil draws in my tears. Gush forth
blood instead of tears! Yea, life and soul—oh, he stays my
tongue! I would lift up my hands, but see, they hold them,
they hold them!

ALL. Who, Faustus? 35

FAUST. Lucifer and Mephistophilis. Ah, gentlemen! I
gave them my soul for my cunning.

ALL. God forbid!

FAUST. God forbade it indeed; but Faustus hath done it.
For vain pleasure of four-and-twenty years hath [40
Faustus lost eternal joy and felicity. I writ them a bill with
mine own blood; the date is expired, the time will come,
and he will fetch me.

1ST SCHOL. Why did not Faustus tell us of this before,
that divines might have prayed for thee? 45

FAUST. Oft have I thought to have done so; but the
Devil threat'ned to tear me in pieces if I named God, to
fetch both body and soul if I once gave ear to divinity;
and now 't is too late. Gentlemen, away! lest you perish
with me. 50

2ND SCHOL. Oh, what shall we do to save Faustus?

FAUST. Talk not of me, but save yourselves, and depart.

3RD SCHOL. God will strengthen me. I will stay with
Faustus. 54

1ST SCHOL. Tempt not God, sweet friend; but let us into
the next room, and there pray for him.

FAUST. Ay, pray for me, pray for me! And what noise
soever ye hear come not unto me, for nothing can rescue
me. 59

2ND SCHOL. Pray thou, and we will pray that God may
have mercy upon thee.

FAUST. Gentlemen, farewell. If I live till morning I'll
visit you; if not, Faustus is gone to hell.

ALL. Faustus, farewell!

[*Exeunt* SCHOLARS. *The clock strikes eleven*

FAUST. Ah, Faustus, 65
Now hast thou but one bare hour to live,
And then thou must be damned perpetually!
Stand still, you ever-moving spheres of heaven,
That time may cease and midnight never come!

Fair Nature's eye, rise, rise again and make 70
Perpetual day; or let this hour be but
A year, a month, a week, a natural day,
That Faustus may repent and save his soul!
O lente, lente, currite noctis equi![14]
The stars move still,[15] time runs, the clock will strike, [75
The Devil will come, and Faustus must be damned.
O, I'll leap up to my God! Who pulls me down?
See, see where Christ's blood streams in the firmament!
One drop would save my soul—half a drop! ah, my
    Christ!—
Ah, rend not my heart for naming of my Christ!— 80
Yet will I call on him!—O, spare me, Lucifer!—
Where is it now? 'T is gone; and see where God
Stretcheth out his arm, and bends his ireful brows!—
Mountains and hills, come, come and fall on me,
And hide me from the heavy wrath of God! 85
No! no!—
Then will I headlong run into the earth!—
Earth, gape!—O no, it will not harbor me!—
You stars that reigned at my nativity,
Whose influence hath allotted death and hell, 90
Now draw up Faustus like a foggy mist
Into the entrails of yon lab'ring cloud,
That when you vomit forth into the air,
My limbs may issue from their smoky mouths,
So that my soul may but ascend to heaven. 95
        [*The watch strikes*
Ah, half the hour is past! 'T will all be past anon!—
O God,
If thou wilt not have mercy on my soul,
Yet for Christ's sake, whose blood hath ransomed me,
Impose some end to my incessant pain: 100
Let Faustus live in hell a thousand years,
A hundred thousand, and at last be saved!—
O, no end is limited to damnèd souls!
Why wert thou not a creature wanting soul?
Or why is this immortal that thou hast? 105

Ah, Pythagoras' metempsychosis![16] were that true,
This soul should fly from me, and I be changed
Unto some brutish beast! All beasts are happy,
For when they die
Their souls are soon dissolved in elements; 110
But mine must live, still to be plagued in hell.
Cursed be the parents that engend'red me!
No, Faustus, curse thyself, curse Lucifer,
That hath deprived thee of the joys of heaven.
        [*The clock striketh twelve*
O, it strikes, it strikes! Now, body, turn to air, 115
Or Lucifer will bear thee quick to hell!
        [*Thunder and lightning*
O soul, be changed into little water-drops,
And fall into the ocean—ne'er be found!—
My God, my God, look not so fierce on me!

Enter DEVILS

Adders and serpents, let me breathe awhile!— 120
Ugly hell, gape not!—Come not, Lucifer!—
I'll burn my books!—Ah, Mephistophilis!
        [*Exeunt with him*

Enter CHORUS

CHORUS. Cut is the branch that might have grown full
    straight,
And burnèd is Apollo's laurel bough,
That sometime[17] grew within this learnèd man. 125
Faustus is gone; regard his hellish fall,
Whose fiendful fortune may exhort the wise
Only to wonder at unlawful things,
Whose deepness doth entice such forward wits
To practice more than heavenly power permits. 130
        [*Exit*

Terminat hora diem; terminat author opus.[18]

---

[16] Pythagoras, a Greek philosopher of the sixth century B.C., was
identified with the theory that souls transmigrate into successive
bodily forms, both human and animal.   [17] Formerly.
[18] The hour ends the day; the author ends his work.

---

[14] Run slowly, slowly, steeds of the night (Ovid, *Amores*, I, xiii,
40).   [15] Unceasingly.

Samuel Daniel

1563?–1619

DANIEL is not a comet, like Marlowe and Raleigh. Thomas Fuller, the antiquarian (1608-61), declares in his *Worthies of England* that "as the Tortoise burieth himself all the Winter in the ground, so Mr. Daniel would lie hid at his garden house . . . nigh London for some months together (the more retiredly to enjoy the company of the Muses), and then would appear in public to converse with his friends." He was a careful craftsman, and even after his poems were printed went on revising them for later editions. There is nothing spectacular about Daniel or his poetry, but in the course of a quiet life which led him into neither the hurly-burly of the political world nor the tumultuous world of the public theaters he wrote some excellent poetry. His was no idle boast:

> I know I shall be read, among the rest,
> So long as men read English.

A native of Somerset and a former student at Oxford, he found some means of traveling to Italy, possibly as someone's secretary. Sidney's sister Mary, Countess of Pembroke, became his patroness. She presided over a literary circle; and at Wilton, the Herberts' country seat in Wiltshire (p. 256, above), Daniel was encouraged in his literary ambitions. Another acquaintance and perhaps patron was Fulke Greville, Sidney's friend and first biographer. It was he, says Daniel,

> By whose mild grace and gentle hand at first
> My infant Muse was brought in open sight
> And made to be partaker of the light.

These three lines, by the way, are a fair sample of much of Daniel's verse—smooth, dignified, and tame. So, evidently, was he. But not always. As the following selections show, he was capable of the note of passion; and on those rare occasions when he strikes it hard, the result is unforgettable.

Sidney's *Astrophel and Stella* was posthumously published in 1591. The family had not authorized this volume; nor had Daniel, a number of whose sonnets the printer included. The appearance of this book led Daniel to bring out a corrected version in 1592: *Delia: Containing Certain Sonnets, with the Complaint of Rosamond*. The poem on the unfortunate mistress of Henry II is of slight importance; but a number of the sonnets (nine are reprinted below) are very fine.

On this early work of Daniel's rests his reputation to-day. To his contemporaries others among his writings may have seemed more significant, though none of them was a popular success. For a time he earned his livelihood by tutoring. Unlike Shakespeare and Marlowe, Daniel did not throw in his lot with the popular drama, nor could he have done so successfully, for his style lacks humor, raciness, and gusto. His *Cleopatra* (1594) is a rimed neo-classical tragedy, an academic affair, written on the Senecan model. In a long poem on *The Civil Wars between the Two Houses of Lancaster and York* (1595-1609) he injudiciously chose a subject already treated much more successfully by Shakespeare in *2* and *3 Henry VI*. In 1603 Daniel published a volume of poetic *Epistles* to various aristocratic contemporaries; they are not exciting, but they contain passages of noble sentiment. In the same year appeared *A Defense of Rime,* Daniel's able reply, in prose, to a pamphlet by Thomas Campion (see below), who in his *Observations on English Poesy* had attacked riming and the "artlessness" of English versification compared with the classical. Daniel's defense is admirable. He appeals to nature and freedom, and with ease and good temper completely disposes of Campion's argument.

On the succession of James, Daniel was introduced to Anne, the new queen, by another patroness, the Countess of Bedford. He was commissioned to write a masque for the court; and he received a small appointment, soon terminated, as licenser of a theatrical company known as the Children of the Queen's Revels—they had to fee him for permission to act. But in the fall of 1604 his second tragedy, *Philotas,* was thought to touch dangerously on the rebellion of the Earl of Essex in 1601. Such may in fact have been his intention, though he denied it; and, whether or not on account of this episode, he seems to have abandoned hope of a career as courtier. Apparently he divided his time between farming and writing. Whether he married is not clear. Though his farm was in Somersetshire, he still enjoyed the patronage of Queen Anne and was occasionally at court. Two pastoral plays and a masque of his were performed there. His prose *History of England,* left unfinished, proved to be the most popular of his books; the first instalment appeared in 1612.

Four years after his death in 1619, his *Whole Works* were published. The standard edition is by A. B. Grosart (1883). A. C. Sprague has edited a volume of selections, with a critical estimate: *Poems and a Defence of Rhyme* (1930).

Daniel must have been acquainted with manuscripts of Sidney's sonnets when he lived at Wilton; but his own, however influenced by them, are not essentially imitative. Who Delia was is one of those questions of no importance to which everyone would like to know the answer. The usual possibilities are open to us (cf.: on Sidney, p. 256, above; on Shakespeare, pp. 339 f., below). The least probable hypothesis is that Daniel addressed a cycle to some girl he had fallen in love with. Possibly they were intended as a graceful tribute to the Countess of Pembroke: not an amorous plea, but a compliment in the prevalent amorous idiom. The likeliest theory is that they are of various origin and inspiration, personal or literary, often drawn from Daniel's reading in the Italian and French sonneteers, and on the whole inspired more by a poet's moods and his desire to compose than by an overwhelming experience. Though *Delia* was first printed in 1592, some of the sonnets had doubtless been written years before. Daniel continued to polish them in successive editions; the texts which follow incorporate his final revisions.

6

Fair is my love, and cruel as sh' is fair;
Her brow shades frowns, although her eyes are sunny;
Her smiles are lightning, though her pride despair;
And her disdains are gall, her favors honey.
A modest maid, decked with a blush of honor,　　5
Whose feet do tread green paths of youth and love!
The wonder of all eyes that look upon her,
Sacred on earth, designed a saint above!
Chastity and beauty, which were deadly foes,
Live reconcilèd friends within her brow;　　10
And had she pity, to conjoin with those,
Then who had heard the plaints I utter now?
For had she not been fair and thus unkind,
My muse had slept, and none had known my mind.

39

Look, Delia, how w' esteem the half-blown rose,
The image of thy blush and summer's honor,
Whilst yet her tender bud doth undisclose
That full of beauty Time bestows upon her!
No sooner spreads her glory in the air　　5
But straight her wide-blown pomp comes to decline;
She then is scorned that late adorned the fair:
So fade the roses of those cheeks of thine.
No April can revive thy with'red flowers
Whose springing grace adorns thy glory now;　　10
Swift, speedy Time, feath'red with flying hours,
Dissolves the beauty of the fairest brow.
Then do not thou such treasure waste in vain;
But love now, whilst thou mayst be loved again!

But love whilst that thou mayst be loved again,
Now whilst thy May hath filled thy lap with flowers,
Now whilst thy beauty bears without a stain;
Now use the summer smiles ere winter lours.
And whilst thou spread'st unto the rising sun　　5
The fairest flow'r that ever saw the light,
Now joy thy time before thy sweet be done;
And, Delia, think thy morning must have night!—
And that thy brightness sets at length to west,
When thou wilt close up that which now thou show'st;[10
And think the same becomes thy fading best,
Which then shall most inveil and shadow most!
Men do not weigh the stalk for that it was,
When once they find her flow'r, her glory, pass.

41

When men shall find thy flow'r, thy glory, pass,
And thou with careful[1] brow sitting alone
Receivèd hast this message from thy glass,
That tells the truth and says that all is gone:
Fresh shalt thou see in me the wounds thou madest;　　5
Though spent thy flame, in me the heat remaining;
I that have loved thee thus before thou fadest,
My faith shall wax when thou art in thy waning.
The world shall find this miracle in me,
That fire can burn when all the matter's spent.　　10
Then what my faith hath been thyself shalt see,
And that thou wast unkind thou mayst repent.
Thou mayst repent that thou hast scorned my tears,
When winter snows upon thy sable hairs.

42

When winter snows upon thy sable hairs,
And frost of age hath nipped thy beauties near,
When dark shall seem thy day that never clears,
And all lies with'red that was held so dear:
Then take this picture which I here present thee,　　5
Limned with a pencil not all unworthy;
Here see the gifts that God and nature lent thee;
Here read thyself and what I suff'red for thee!
This may remain thy lasting monument,
Which happily[2] posterity may cherish—　　10
These colors with thy fading are not spent;
These may remain when thou and I shall perish.
If they remain, then thou shalt live thereby;
They will remain, and so thou canst not die.

---

[1] Full of cares.　　　　　[2] Perhaps.

Thou canst not die whilst any zeal abound
In feeling hearts that can conceive these lines;
Though thou, a Laura, hast no Petrarch[3] found,
In base attire yet clearly beauty shines.
And I, though born within a colder clime,   5
Do feel mine inward heat as great (I know it):
He never had more faith, although more rime;
I love as well, though he could better show it.
But I may add one feather to thy fame,
To help her flight throughout the fairest isle;   10
And if my pen could more enlarge thy name,
Then shouldst thou live in an immortal style.
For though that Laura better limnèd be,
Suffice, thou shalt be loved as well as she.

50

Beauty, sweet love, is like the morning dew,
Whose short refresh upon the tender green
Cheers for a time, but till the sun doth shew,
And straight 'tis gone as it had never been.
Soon doth it fade that makes the fairest flourish;   5
Short is the glory of the blushing rose,
The hue which thou so carefully dost nourish,
Yet which at length thou must be forced to lose.
When thou, surcharged with burthen of thy years,
Shalt bend thy wrinkles homeward to the earth;   10
And that,[4] in beauty's lease expired, appears
The date of age, the calends[5] of our death—
But ah, no more! this must not be foretold,
For women grieve to think they must be old.

54

Care-charmer Sleep, son of the sable Night,
Brother to Death, in silent darkness born,
Relieve my languish, and restore the light;
With dark forgetting of my cares return.
And let the day be time enough to mourn   5
The shipwrack of my ill-advent'red youth;
Let waking eyes suffice to wail their scorn,
Without the torment of the night's untruth.
Cease, dreams, the images of day desires,
To model forth the passions of the morrow;   10
Never let rising sun approve[6] you liars,
To add more grief to aggravate my sorrow.
Still let me sleep, embracing clouds in vain,
And never wake to feel the day's disdain.

55

Let others sing of knights and paladins
In agèd accents and untimely words,[7]
Paint shadows in imaginary lines,
Which well the reach of their high wits records;
But I must sing of thee, and those fair eyes   5
Authentic shall my verse in time to come,
When yet th' unborn shall say, "Lo where she lies
Whose beauty made him speak that else was dumb!"
These are the arcs,[8] the trophies, I erect,
That fortify thy name against old age;   10
And these thy sacred virtues must protect
Against the dark and Time's consuming rage.
Though th' error of my youth in them appear,
Suffice, they show I lived and loved thee dear.

from MUSOPHILUS

In 1599 Daniel published a dialogue in verse entitled
Musophilus: Containing a General Defense of Learning. It is a
didactic piece, infrequently poetic; Musophilus, the Muse-
lover, lectures his friend Philocosmus, World-lover. The
poem consists of nearly a thousand lines. Occasionally, as
in the following passage near the close, it rises to an imaginative level. Here Daniel voices a poet's love for words
and belief in their power, an appeal to his countrymen
against allowing their literature to remain inferior to the
Italian and the French, a vision of an English-speaking
empire across the Atlantic, and a tribute to the supremacy
of poetry among the arts of expression.

Pow'r above pow'rs, O heavenly Eloquence,
    That with the strong rein of commanding words
Dost manage, guide, and master th' eminence
    Of men's affections[9] more than all their swords,
Shall we not offer to thy excellence   5
    The richest treasure that our wit affords?

Thou that canst do much more with one poor pen
    Than all the pow'rs of princes can effect,
And draw, divert, dispose, and fashion men
    Better than force or rigor can direct,   10
Should we this ornament of glory then,
    As th' unmaterial fruits of shades, neglect?

Or should we careless come behind the rest
    In pow'r of words, that go before in worth,
Whenas our accents, equal to the best,   15
    Is able greater wonders to bring forth,
When all that ever hotter spirits expressed
    Comes bettered by the patience of the north?

---

[3] See pp. 216, 246 f., above. It was to Laura that Petrarch addressed his sonnets.   [4] When.
[5] Prelude; age is the beginning of death.   [6] Prove.

[7] I.e., in archaic meter and vocabulary; this is probably an allusion
to Spenser and *The Faery Queen.*
[8] Arches; i.e., commemorative monuments.   [9] Feelings.

QUEEN ELIZABETH

This engraving of about 1595-1600 by William Rogers was probably based upon a painting or drawing now lost. The dress is said to be the one in which the Queen received her victorious forces after the defeat of the Spanish Armada in 1588.

THE SPANISH ARMADA

Soon after 1588 Admiral Lord Thomas Howard, who had commanded the English forces against the Armada, commissioned a series of tapestries depicting incidents of the attempted invasion. This eighteenth-century engraving copies one of the tapestries. The English ships (on the left) are attacking the larger and more unwieldy Spanish vessels, which are drawn up in crescent formation.

THE BANKSIDE

Though the first public theaters were built to the north of London, others were soon erected on the south bank of the Thames. In this section of a view of London by Merian, 1638, the Globe, the Bear Garden, and the Swan are numbered 37, 38, and 39, respectively. (Folger Shakespeare Library, Washington, D.C. Photograph by Horydczak.)

The Swan theater deeply impressed a Dutch visitor to London in 1596, Johannes de Witt, who wrote a description of it after his return home. The accompanying sketch shows that his memory of the stage was somewhat faulty, but it suggests clearly the arrangement of the spectators.

A far more reliable idea of the Elizabethan stage may be gained from this reconstruction of the stage of Shakespeare's theater, the Globe, by a modern scholar, Professor John C. Adams. (Folger Shakespeare Library

And who, in time, knows whither we may vent
  The treasure of our tongue, to what strange shores   20
This gain of our best glory shall be sent
  T' enrich unknowing nations with our stores?
What worlds in th' yet unformèd occident
  May come refined with th' accents that are ours?

Or who can tell for what great work in hand   25
  The greatness of our style is now ordained?
What pow'rs it shall bring in, what spirits command,
  What thoughts let out, what humors[10] keep restrained,
What mischief it may pow'rfully withstand,
  And what fair ends may thereby be attained?   30

And as for Poesy, mother of this force,
  That breeds, brings forth, and nourishes this might,
Teaching it in a loose yet measured course
  With comely motions how to go[11] upright,
And, fost'ring it with bountiful discourse,   35
  Adorns it thus in fashions of delight,

What should I say? since it is well approved
  The speech of heaven, with whom they have commérce
That only seem out of themselves removed[12]
  And do with more than human skills converse: 40
Those numbers wherewith heaven and earth are moved
  Show weakness speaks in prose, but pow'r in verse.

ARE THEY SHADOWS?

This grave and thoughtful poem is from Daniel's court masque, *Tethys' Festival* (1610). This type of entertainment, which combined drama, poetry, music, dance, and scenic effects, was more than ever in vogue at the court of James I, who spent huge sums on masques. The fleeting character of the world's beauty is a favorite theme of the poets. Daniel's song is remarkable because the elaboration of his idea (see note 13) does not spoil the poem's lyricism.

Are they shadows that we see?
And can shadows pleasure give?
Pleasures only shadows be,
Cast by bodies we conceive,[13]
And are made the things we deem   5
In those figures which they seem.

But these pleasures vanish fast
Which by shadows are expressed.
Pleasures are not, if they last;
In their passing is their best.   10
Glory is most bright and gay
In a flash, and so away.

Feed apace then, greedy eyes,
On the wonder you behold.
Take it sudden as it flies,   15
Though you take it not to hold.
When your eyes have done their part,
Thought must length it in the heart.

William Shakespeare

1564-1616

SHAKESPEARE, who has as good a claim as anyone to first place among the world's geniuses, came of undistinguished yeoman stock. Both his grandfathers were farmers. His father's principal occupation was the making and selling of gloves. The poet was born in Warwickshire, at the town of Stratford-on-Avon, probably about April 23, 1564. Presumably he attended the local "grammar" school. It was a good one; a student could prepare there for Oxford. Shakespeare's father was a prosperous businessman; he took a leading part in the town's affairs and held in succession most of the municipal offices, including that of bailiff or mayor. But when William was about thirteen, financial difficulties began plaguing John Shakespeare; according to a tradition that circulated in Stratford later, his

son had to leave school. The next we hear of him, at the age of eighteen, he is marrying Anne Hathaway, a near-by farmer's daughter seven or eight years his senior. Susanna, the first child, was born six months later, and in two years more the twins, Hamnet and Judith. The boy died in his twelfth year, but both daughters survived their father.

After the birth of the twins comes a gap of seven years without documentary evidence of Shakespeare's whereabouts. It is fairly likely that he taught school for a while; probably he soon made his way to London and went on the stage. He became a good actor, though not a great one. By 1592—from then on references are numerous— he was a successful playwright. During the next two years,

---

[10] Notions.   [11] Walk.
[12] I.e., divinely inspired; this is the doctrine of poetic inspiration.

[13] This is a statement of the Platonic philosopher's view that concrete objects are only shadows of ideas, and that the material is thus less real than the ideal. If such is the case, pleasures derived from concrete objects are only the shadows of shadows.

while an outbreak of the bubonic plague kept the theaters closed, he published two narrative poems, *Venus and Adonis* and *Lucrece*. These somewhat artificial but graceful poetic exercises immediately won Shakespeare a high reputation in the world of letters. It was clear now that he was the coming poet; his popularity with, for example, the undergraduates at the universities was immense. In the young Earl of Southampton he found what all Renaissance artists longed for, a generous patron.

When the earliest of his plays were written and staged is uncertain; it was probably about 1589. Most of his first works were either comedies or "histories," as the Elizabethans called a type of play, very popular in the 1590's, which attempted to depict, sometimes in far too scattered a series of scenes, the most striking events of the reign of one or another of the English kings.

By 1594 the other poets who had helped lay the foundations of Elizabethan drama were dead or had ceased writing for the stage. Till the appearance, about the turn of the century, of Ben Jonson and several other new men, Shakespeare had no important rival. His plays were popular with the public, and his company often gave command performances at court. By 1596 he had written *Romeo and Juliet, A Midsummer Night's Dream,* and *The Merchant of Venice,* three plays still often acted; his experimental period was over. He followed up *The Merchant* with a string of masterpieces, the romantic comedies *Much Ado about Nothing, As You Like It,* and *Twelfth Night.* About the same time, in the closing years of the sixteenth century, he was also composing the best of his histories, based on the English chronicles of Edward Halle and of Raphael Holinshed. In *Henry IV* the gaiety of nations was permanently increased by the invention of Sir John Falstaff, perhaps the richest of all the comic characters in the world's literature.

In *Julius Caesar* (1599) Shakespeare was working out of chronicle-history into tragedy; and then his supreme

A LIST OF THE PLAYS, WITH APPROXIMATE DATES OF COMPOSITION

		TRAGEDIES	COMEDIES	HISTORIES (chronicles)
I	1589	Titus Andronicus	The Comedy of Errors	
	1590		?The Taming of the Shrew	1 Henry VI
	1591			2 Henry VI
	1592			3 Henry VI
	1593		The Two Gentlemen of Verona	Richard III
	1594		Love's Labour's Lost	King John
II	1595	Romeo and Juliet	A Midsummer Night's Dream	Richard II
	1596		The Merchant of Venice	
	1597			1 Henry IV
	1598		Much Ado about Nothing	2 Henry IV
	1599	Julius Caesar	As You Like It	Henry V
	1600	Hamlet	Twelfth Night	
	1601		The Merry Wives of Windsor	
III	1602		Troilus and Cressida	
	1603		All's Well That Ends Well	
	1604	Othello	Measure for Measure	
	1605	King Lear		
	1606	Macbeth		
	1607	Antony and Cleopatra		
	1608	Coriolanus	Pericles	
IV	1609	?Timon of Athens	Cymbeline	
	1610		The Winter's Tale	
	1611		The Tempest	
	1612			
	1613		The Two Noble Kinsmen	Henry VIII (both with Fletcher)

achievements began: *Hamlet, Othello, King Lear,* and *Macbeth,* four tragedies which constitute one of the mightiest efforts of the human mind. At the same time he went on in comedy, turning from the happy narratives of romantic love to a series of less successful and more realistic comedies. Before he retired, about 1611, he wrote several more tragedies, among them another masterpiece, *Antony and Cleopatra.* His career closed with a group of new comedies, his dramatic romances; in these, after the storms and agonies of the tragedies, he strikes a note of quiet serenity. The best of this group are *The Winter's Tale* and *The Tempest.*

Meanwhile Shakespeare seems to have led a normal sort of existence, working hard and laying up treasure in Warwickshire as well as fame in London. He invested his money chiefly in Stratford real estate; on his retirement he went to live there at New Place, the second largest of its dwellings. He had already induced the heralds to grant his father a coat of arms and had thus raised himself, as many Elizabethans did, from yeoman to gentleman in the caste system of the time. He derived his capital principally from the earnings of his company, which was London's leading troupe (he was one of a dozen sharcholding members), and from the proceeds of his share in the syndicate which owned the Globe and Blackfriars theaters. His was a dignified and prominent position in London life, and afterwards in Stratford. Both Queen Elizabeth and King James delighted in his plays, and he held minor but honorable appointments at their courts. Under James his company received official status as the "King's Men."

After his retirement Shakespeare collaborated on two more plays with John Fletcher, who succeeded him as the King's Men's principal dramatist. He made sojourns in London, and in Stratford renewed his friendships among the Stratford townsfolk and enjoyed the society of the local gentry. He died on April 23, 1616, and was buried in Stratford church.

Quite aside from his primacy as a dramatist, Shakespeare was, if anyone deserves that title, the greatest of poets. His incomparable imagination, his matchless power over words, and his uncanny insight into human nature with its attendant power to go out of himself when he drew his characters, are more important sources of his greatness than his mastery, important though that was, of the special arts and artifices of the stage. The supreme manifestations of his poetic power are to be found, however, in his plays. Nevertheless, since no one is likely to read this volume who is not already familiar with several of the dramas, and since these are all readily available, Shakespeare's dramatic art is not represented here. The following selections are from his sonnets and from the songs he scattered through his plays.

The best one-volume edition of Shakespeare's complete works is by G. L. Kittredge (1936). H. Spencer's *The Art and Life of William Shakespeare* (1940) contains (besides a biography) a description of the Elizabethan stage, an explanation of Shakespeare's versification, an introduction to each of the plays (including criticism and a résumé of stage history), and a classified bibliography. E. K. Chambers's *William Shakespeare: A Study of Facts and Problems* (2 vols., 1930) is an invaluable encyclopedia of Shakespeare scholarship.

William Shakespeare

SONNETS

SHAKESPEARE'S *Sonnets* appeared in 1609 in an unauthorized edition; how the publisher got hold of them is unknown. He dedicated the little book to "the only begetter of these ensuing sonnets, Mr. W. H." This gentleman's identity remains a secret; that he was the person who procured the manuscript is as good a guess as any.

Whether the 154 sonnets form a coherent sequence addressed to actual persons, or whether they are poetic exercises inspired, not by love, but by the fashionable vogue of the early and middle 1590's, is a much debated question, on which extreme views are held by some. The truth probably lies between. A number of the poems are addressed to a handsome young man averse to matrimony. The poet compliments him, declares his undying affection for him, and urges him to perpetuate his good looks by marrying and begetting children. Attempts to identify this youth with the Earl of Southampton or (perhaps a likelier possibility) the Earl of Pembroke remain conjectural, and many of the sonnets which critics have included in this group may have been written to a woman.

Nor can the sonnets be dated. Even their arrangement in the volume of 1609 may not follow Shakespeare's intention, if he had any. Besides these obstacles, a third and fourth stand in the way of the search for clues to the poet's private life. Some of the poems are clearly to a man, and others clearly to a woman, the "dark lady"; but others may be to either, and some may not have been addressed to any individual. Finally, a love sonnet is no good unless it looks autobiographical; it ought to *appear* to come from the heart. In his plays Shakespeare was constantly composing speeches that appear to come from a character's heart, but certainly are not from his own. In any one of his sonnets he may be practicing an artistic deception on us: read what he says on that score himself in Sonnet 110 (see below), where he seems to be speaking in person, with the mask off.

Every year or two some amateur or crank comes forward with a new proposal about Shakespeare's sonnets; but we shall never know more about them, unless and until some new document comes to light. Who would not welcome new facts illuminating the great heart and mind that made these poems? But the important thing is their existence. What they tell us is, not whether Shakespeare was faithful to his lawful wedded wife or had a love affair with a brunette charmer, but how from time to time he felt about the great experiences and mysteries of life and death. And so, whatever their inspiration, these poems are true; for they express the moods of a very great genius, who (like ordinary people, but perhaps more intensely) knew joy and longing and wonder and pain and love.

The best edition is by H. E. Rollins (2 vols., 1944). There is a good account of the sonnet's early history in Lisle C. John's *The Elizabethan Sonnet Sequences* (1938); see also Lu E. Pearson's *Elizabethan Love Conventions* (1933).

15

When I consider everything that grows
Holds in perfection but a little moment,
That this huge stage presenteth nought but shows
Whereon the stars in secret influence comment;
When I perceive that men as[1] plants increase,   5
Cheerèd and checked even by the self-same sky,
Vaunt in their youthful sap, at height decrease,
And wear their brave state out of memory—
Then the conceit[2] of this inconstant stay
Sets you most rich in youth before my sight,   10
Where wasteful Time debateth with Decay,
To change your day of youth to sullied night;
    And all in war with Time for love of you,
    As he takes from you, I engraft you new.

18

Shall I compare thee to a summer's day?
Thou art more lovely and more temperate:
Rough winds do shake the darling buds of May,
And summer's lease hath all too short a date;
Sometime too hot the eye of heaven shines,   5
And often is his gold complexion dimmed,
And every fair from fair[3] sometime declines,
By chance or nature's changing course untrimmed;
But thy eternal summer shall not fade
Nor lose possession of that fair thou ow'st,[4]   10
Nor shall Death brag thou wand'rest in his shade
When in eternal lines to time thou grow'st.[5]
    So long as men can breathe or eyes can see,
    So long lives this, and this gives life to thee.

23

As an unperfect actor[6] on the stage
Who with his fear is put besides his part,
Or some fierce thing replete with too much rage,
Whose strength's abundance weakens his own heart,
So I, for fear of trust,[7] forget to say   5
The perfect ceremony of love's rite,
And in mine own love's strength seem to decay,
O'ercharged with burthen of mine own love's might.
O, let my looks be then the eloquence
And dumb presagers of my speaking breast,   10
Who plead for love, and look for recompense,
More than that tongue that more hath more expressed.
    O, learn to read what silent love hath writ!
    To hear with eyes belongs to love's fine wit.

25

Let those who are in favor with their stars
Of public honor and proud titles boast,
Whilst I, whom fortune of such triumph bars,
Unlooked for joy in that I honor[8] most.
Great princes' favorites their fair leaves spread   5
But as the marigold at the sun's eye;
And in themselves their pride lies burièd,
For at a frown they in their glory die.
The painful[9] warrior famousèd for fight,
After a thousand victories, once foiled,   10
Is from the book of honor razèd quite,
And all the rest forgot for which he toiled.
    Then happy I, that love and am beloved
    Where I may not remove nor be removed.

[1] Like.   [2] Conception, idea.
[3] The first *fair* = beautiful object; the second (as also in line 10) = beauty. Note the emphatic Elizabethan *from* = away from.
[4] Own, possess.   [5] You become a part of time.

[6] An actor who has failed to memorize his part perfectly.
[7] Fearful of trusting myself.
[8] Contrary to expectation, take delight in what I honor (not, like other people, in what I receive honor from).
[9] Industrious, laboring devotedly at his profession (cf. *toiled* in line 12).

29

When, in disgrace with Fortune and men's eyes,
I all alone beweep my outcast state
And trouble deaf heaven with my bootless cries
And look upon myself and curse my fate,
Wishing me like to one more rich in hope,   5
Featured like him, like him with friends possessed,
Desiring this man's art and that man's scope,
With what I most enjoy contented least:
Yet in these thoughts myself almost despising,
Haply I think on thee, and then my state,   10
Like to the lark at break of day arising
From sullen earth, sings hymns at heaven's gate.
   For thy sweet love rememb'red such wealth brings
   That then I scorn to change my state with kings.

30

When to the sessions of sweet silent thought
I summon up remembrance of things past,
I sigh the lack of many a thing I sought
And with old woes new wail my dear time's waste.
Then can I drown an eye, unused to flow,   5
For precious friends hid in death's dateless night,
And weep afresh love's long-since-canceled woe,
And moan th' expense of many a vanished sight.
Then can I grieve at grievances foregone,
And heavily from woe to woe tell o'er   10
The sad account of fore-bemoanèd moan,
Which I new pay as if not paid before.
   But if the while I think on thee, dear friend,
   All losses are restored and sorrows end.

32

If thou survive my well-contented day
When that churl Death my bones with dust shall cover,
And shalt by fortune once more resurvey
These poor rude lines of thy deceasèd lover,
Compare them with the bett'ring of the time,   5
And, though they be outstripped by every pen,
Reserve them for my love, not for their rime,
Exceeded by the height of happier[10] men.
O, then vouchsafe me but this loving thought:
"Had my friend's muse grown with this growing age,   10
A dearer birth than this his love had brought,[11]
To march in ranks of better equipage.
   But since he died, and poets better prove,
   Theirs for their style I'll read, his for his love."

[10] More fortunate, i.e., more gifted.
[11] His love for me would have brought forth poems more precious
    than these.

33

Full many a glorious morning have I seen
Flatter the mountain-tops with sovereign eye,
Kissing with golden face the meadows green,
Gilding pale streams with heavenly alchemy;
Anon permit the basest clouds to ride   5
With ugly rack[12] on his celestial face,
And from the forlorn world his visage hide,
Stealing unseen to west with this disgrace.
Even so my sun one early morn did shine
With all-triumphant splendor on my brow;   10
But, out, alack! he was but one hour mine;
The region cloud[13] hath masked him from me now.
   Yet him for this my love no whit disdaineth;
   Suns of the world may stain[14] when heaven's sun
      staineth.

Not marble, nor the gilded monuments
Of princes, shall outlive this pow'rful rime;
But you shall shine more bright in these contents
Than unswept stone, besmeared with sluttish time.
When wasteful war shall statues overturn,   5
And broils root out the work of masonry,
Nor Mars his sword nor war's quick fire shall burn
The living record of your memory.
'Gainst death and all-oblivious enmity
Shall you pace forth; your praise shall still find room   10
Even in the eyes of all posterity
That wear this world out to the ending doom.[15]
   So, till the judgment that[16] yourself arise,
   You live in this, and dwell in lovers' eyes.

Like as the waves make towards the pebbled shore,
So do our minutes hasten to their end;
Each changing place with that which goes before,
In sequent toil all forwards do contend.
Nativity, once in the main of light,   5
Crawls to maturity, wherewith being crowned,
Crooked eclipses 'gainst his glory fight,
And Time that gave doth now his gift confound.
Time doth transfix the flourish set on youth
And delves the parallels[17] in beauty's brow,   10
Feeds on the rarities of nature's truth,
And nothing stands but for his scythe to mow:
   And yet to times in hope my verse shall stand,
   Praising thy worth, despite his cruel hand.

[12] Cloudy vapor.   [13] Cloud of the upper air.
[14] Become dim or dull.   [15] Judgment Day.
[16] The Judgment Day, when.   [17] Digs the trenches, i.e., wrinkles.

WILLIAM SHAKESPEARE

When I have seen by Time's fell hand defaced
The rich proud cost of outworn buried age;
When sometime lofty towers I see down-razed,
And brass eternal slave to mortal rage;
When I have seen the hungry ocean gain   5
Advantage on the kingdom of the shore,
And the firm soil win of the wat'ry main,
Increasing store with loss and loss with store;
When I have seen such interchange of state,
Or state itself confounded to decay;   10
Ruin hath taught me thus to ruminate,
That Time will come and take my love away.
  This thought is as a death, which cannot choose
  But weep to have that which it fears to lose.

Since brass, nor stone, nor earth, nor boundless sea,
But sad mortality o'ersways their power,
How with this rage shall beauty hold a plea,
Whose action is no stronger than a flower?
O, how shall summer's honey breath hold out   5
Against the wrackful[18] siege of batt'ring days,
When rocks impregnable are not so stout,
Nor gates of steel so strong, but Time decays?
O fearful meditation! Where, alack,
Shall Time's best jewel[19] from Time's chest lie hid?   10
Or what strong hand can hold his swift foot back?
Or who his spoil of beauty can forbid?
  O, none!—unless this miracle have might,
  That in black ink my love may still shine bright.

Tired with all these, for restful death I cry:
As, to behold desert a beggar born,
And needy nothing trimmed in jollity,
And purest faith unhappily forsworn,
And gilded honor shamefully misplaced,   5
And maiden virtue rudely strumpeted,
And right perfection wrongfully disgraced,
And strength by limping sway disablèd,
And art made tongue-tied by authority,
And folly (doctor-like) controlling skill,   10
And simple truth miscalled simplicity,
And captive good attending captain ill.
  Tired with all these, from these would I be gone,
  Save that, to die, I leave my love alone.

---

[18] Wrecking.   [19] I.e., beauty.

No longer mourn for me when I am dead
Than you shall hear the surly sullen bell
Give warning to the world that I am fled
From this vile world, with vilest worms to dwell.
Nay, if you read this line, remember not   5
The hand that writ it; for I love you so
That I in your sweet thoughts would be forgot
If thinking on me then should make you woe.
O, if, I say, you look upon this verse
When I, perhaps, compounded am with clay,   10
Do not so much as my poor name rehearse,
But let your love even with my life decay:
  Lest the wise world should look into your moan
  And mock you with me after I am gone.

That time of year thou mayst in me behold
When yellow leaves, or none, or few, do hang
Upon those boughs which shake against the cold,
Bare ruined choirs, where late the sweet birds sang.
In me thou seest the twilight of such day   5
As after sunset fadeth in the west,
Which by and by black night doth take away,
Death's second self, that seals up all in rest.
In me thou seest the glowing of such fire
That[20] on the ashes of his[21] youth doth lie,   10
As the deathbed whereon it must expire,
Consumed with that which it was nourished by.
  This thou perceivest, which makes thy love more
    strong,
  To love that well which thou must leave ere long.

Why is my verse so barren of new pride,[22]
So far from variation or quick change?
Why, with the time, do I not glance aside
To new-found methods and to compounds strange?
Why write I still all one, ever the same,   5
And keep invention in a noted weed,[23]
That[24] every word doth almost tell my name,
Showing their birth, and where[25] they did proceed?
O, know, sweet love, I always write of you,
And you and love are still my argument:[26]   10
So all my best is dressing old words new,
Spending again what is already spent.
  For as the sun is daily new and old,
  So is my love still telling what is told.

[20] As.   [21] Its.
[22] Ornamentation. Some think this alludes to Drayton's sonnet
"To the Reader" (see p. 349, below).   [23] Familiar dress.
[24] So that.   [25] Whence.   [26] Theme.

Then hate me when thou wilt! if ever, now!
Now, while the world is bent my deeds to cross,
Join with the spite of fortune, make me bow,
And do not drop in for an after-loss:[27]
Ah, do not, when my heart hath scaped this sorrow,   5
Come in the rearward of a conquered woe;
Give not a windy night a rainy morrow,
To linger out a purposed overthrow.
If thou wilt leave me, do not leave me last,
When other, petty griefs have done their spite,   10
But in the onset come. So shall I taste
At first the very worst of fortune's might;
    And other strains[28] of woe, which now seem woe,
    Compared with loss of thee will not seem so.

97

How like a winter hath my absence been
From thee, the pleasure of the fleeting year!
What freezings have I felt, what dark days seen!
What old December's bareness everywhere!
And yet this time removed[29] was summer's time,   5
The teeming autumn, big with rich increase,
Bearing the wanton burthen of the prime,[30]
Like widowed wombs after their lords' decease.
Yet this abundant issue seemed to me
But hope of orphans and unfathered fruit;   10
For summer and his pleasures wait on thee,
And, thou away, the very birds are mute;
    Or, if they sing, 'tis with so dull a cheer
    That leaves look pale, dreading the winter's near.

98

From you have I been absent in the spring,
When proud-pied[31] April, dressed in all his trim,
Hath put a spirit of youth in everything,
That heavy Saturn laughed and leapt with him.
Yet nor the lays of birds nor the sweet smell   5
Of different flowers in odor and in hue
Could make me any summer's story tell,
Or from their proud lap pluck them where they grew;
Nor did I wonder at the lily's white,
Nor praise the deep vermilion in the rose: 10
They were but sweet, but figures of delight,
Drawn after you, you pattern of all those.
    Yet seemed it winter still, and, you away,
    As with your shadow I with these did play.

When in the chronicle of wasted time
I see descriptions of the fairest wights,[32]
And beauty making beautiful old rime
In praise of ladies dead and lovely knights,
Then, in the blazon[33] of sweet beauty's best,   5
Of hand, of foot, of lip, of eye, of brow,
I see their antique pen would have expressed
Even such a beauty as you master now.
So all their praises are but prophecies
Of this our time, all you prefiguring;   10
And, for they looked but with divining eyes,
They had not skill enough your worth to sing:
    For we, which now behold these present days,
    Have eyes to wonder, but lack tongues to praise.

109

O, never say that I was false of heart,
Though absence seemed my flame to qualify.[34]
As easy might I from myself depart
As from my soul, which in thy breast doth lie.
That is my home of love. If I have ranged,   5
Like him that travels I return again,
Just to the time, not with the time exchanged,
So that myself bring water for my stain.
Never believe, though in my nature reigned
All frailties that besiege all kinds of blood,[35]   10
That it could so preposterously be stained
To[36] leave for nothing all thy sum of good:
    For nothing this wide universe I call,
    Save thou, my rose; in it thou art my all.

110

Alas, 'tis true I have gone here and there
And made myself a motley to the view,
Gored mine own thoughts, sold cheap what is most dear,
Made old offences of affections new.
Most true it is that I have looked on truth   5
Askance and strangely; but, by all above,
These blenches[37] gave my heart another youth,
And worse essays proved thee my best of love.
Now all is done, have what shall have no end!
Mine appetite I nevermore will grind   10
On newer proof, to try an older friend,
A god in love, to whom I am confined.
    Then give me welcome, next my heaven the best,
    Even to thy pure and most most loving breast.

---

[27] As is often the case, the meaning of this line is explained by
what follows.   [28] Kinds.
[29] When we were separated.   [30] Spring.
[31] Gorgeously variegated.

[32] Men and women.   [33] Description.   [34] Weaken.
[35] Emotions.   [36] As to.   [37] Inconstancies.

WILLIAM SHAKESPEARE

Let me not to the marriage of true minds
Admit impediments. Love is not love
Which alters when it alteration finds
Or bends with the remover to remove.
O, no! it is an ever-fixèd mark,   5
That looks on tempests and is never shaken;
It is the star to every wand'ring bark,
Whose worth's unknown, although his height be taken.
Love's not Time's fool, though rosy lips and cheeks
Within his bending sickle's compass come;   10
Love alters not with his brief hours and weeks,
But bears it out even to the edge of doom.
    If this be error and upon me proved,
    I never writ, nor no man ever loved.

130

My mistress' eyes are nothing like the sun;
Coral is far more red than her lips' red;
If snow be white, why then her breasts are dun;
If hairs be wires, black wires grow on her head.
I have seen roses damasked,[38] red and white,   5
But no such roses see I in her cheeks;
And in some perfumes is there more delight
Than in the breath that from my mistress reeks.
I love to hear her speak, yet well I know
That music hath a far more pleasing sound;   10
I grant I never saw a goddess go;[39]
My mistress, when she walks, treads on the ground.
    And yet, by heaven, I think my love as rare
    As any she[40] belied with false compare.

146

Poor soul, the center of my sinful earth,
Thrall to[41] these rebel powers that thee array,
Why dost thou pine within and suffer dearth,
Painting thy outward walls so costly gay?
Why so large cost, having so short a lease,   5
Dost thou upon thy fading mansion spend?
Shall worms, inheritors of this excess,
Eat up thy charge?[42] Is this thy body's end?
Then, soul, live thou upon thy servant's loss,
And let that pine to aggravate thy store;   10
Buy terms divine[43] in selling hours of dross;
Within be fed, without be rich no more:
    So shalt thou feed on Death, that feeds on men,
    And Death once dead, there's no more dying then.

---

[38] Variegated.   [39] Walk.   [40] Woman.
[41] This line is defective in the earliest text; the reading here printed
is one of many proposed corrections.   [42] Expenditure.
[43] I.e., eternity.

That Shakespeare's lyric gift was of the highest order is
attested by the eagerness with which three centuries of
composers have flocked to the task of setting his songs.
Few examples of the original music have survived. Most
of the more familiar settings were composed in the eighteenth century, though Franz Schubert (1797–1828) contributed several exquisite ones. Even without the music
these poems, whether grave or gay, are little masterpieces
of the rapid and expert evocation of mood. A good book
is E. W. Naylor's *Shakespeare and Music* (new ed., 1931).

from THE TWO GENTLEMEN OF VERONA

Who is Silvia?[1] What is she,
    That all our swains commend her?
Holy, fair, and wise is she:
    The heaven such grace did lend her,
That she might admirèd be.   5

Is she kind as she is fair?
    For beauty lives with kindness.
Love doth to her eyes repair
    To help him of his blindness,
And, being helped, inhabits there.   10

Then to Silvia let us sing,
    That Silvia is excelling;
She excels each mortal thing
    Upon the dull earth dwelling.
To her let us garlands bring.   15

from LOVE'S LABOUR'S LOST

1

When daisies pied and violets blue
    And lady smocks[2] all silver-white
And cuckoo-buds of yellow hue
    Do paint the meadows with delight,
The cuckoo then, on every tree,   5
Mocks married men; for thus sings he:
    "Cuckoo!
Cuckoo, cuckoo!"—O word of fear,
Unpleasing to a married ear![3]

---

[1] Sung by serenaders under her window in IV, ii. The setting by
Schubert is one of his most famous songs. The play is one of
Shakespeare's earlier comedies (c. 1593).
[2] Or cuckooflowers.—This and the following song are sung, respectively, by Spring and Winter, garbed as cuckoo and owl,
to close the entertainment presented for the royalties and their
courtiers in the last scene of the play, one of Shakespeare's earlier
comedies (c. 1594).
[3] Since the word *cuckold* is derived from the name of the bird,
which is notorious for laying eggs in other birds' nests.

When shepherds pipe on oaten straws,   10
  And merry larks are plowmen's clocks,
When turtles tread,[4] and rooks and daws,
  And maidens bleach their summer smocks,
The cuckoo then, on every tree,
Mocks married men; for thus sings he: 15
      "Cuckoo!
Cuckoo, cuckoo!"—O word of fear,
Unpleasing to a married ear!

II

When icicles hang by the wall,
  And Dick the shepherd blows his nail,[5]
And Tom bears logs into the hall,
  And milk comes frozen home in pail,
When blood is nipped, and ways[6] be foul,   5
Then nightly sings the staring owl:
     ["To-who!]
Tu-whit, tu-who!" a merry note,
While greasy Joan doth keel[7] the pot.

When all aloud the wind doth blow,   10
  And coughing drowns the parson's saw,[8]
And birds sit brooding in the snow,
  And Marian's nose looks red and raw,
When roasted crabs[9] hiss in the bowl,
Then nightly sings the staring owl: 15
     ["To-who!]
Tu-whit, tu-who!" a merry note,
While greasy Joan doth keel the pot.

from MUCH ADO ABOUT NOTHING

Sigh no more, ladies, sigh no more!
  Men were deceivers ever,
One foot in sea and one on shore,
  To one thing constant never:
Then sigh not so, but let them go,   5
  And be you blithe and bonny,
Converting all your sounds of woe
  Into Hey nonny, nonny!

Sing no more ditties, sing no moe,[10]
  Of dumps[11] so dull and heavy!   10
The fraud of men was ever so,
  Since summer first was leavy.

Then sigh not so, but let them go,
  And be you blithe and bonny,
Converting all your sounds of woe   15
  Into Hey nonny, nonny!

from AS YOU LIKE IT

I

Under the greenwood tree[12]
  Who loves to lie with me,
  And turn his merry note
  Unto the sweet bird's throat,
Come hither, come hither, come hither!   5
    Here shall he see
    No enemy
But winter and rough weather.

Who doth ambition shun,
  And loves to live i' th' sun,   10
  Seeking the food he eats
  And pleased with what he gets,
Come hither, come hither, come hither!
    Here shall he see
    No enemy   15
But winter and rough weather.

II

Blow, blow, thou winter wind![13]
Thou art not so unkind
  As man's ingratitude.
Thy tooth is not so keen,
Because thou art not seen,   5
  Although thy breath be rude.

Heigh-ho, sing heigh-ho, unto the green holly!
Most friendship is feigning, most loving mere folly:
  Then, heigh-ho, the holly!
  This life is most jolly.   10

Freeze, freeze, thou bitter sky!
That dost not bite so nigh
  As benefits forgot.
Though thou the waters warp,
Thy sting is not so sharp   15
  As friend rememb'red not.

Heigh-ho, sing heigh ho! &c.

---

[4] Turtledoves copulate.   [5] To warm the ends of his fingers.
[6] Roads.
[7] Cool (as by skimming it, to keep it from boiling over).
[8] Saying.
[9] Crab apples; they were sometimes added to drinks, especially ale.
[10] More.—Balthasar entertains the Prince and his courtiers with this gay song in II, iii. *Much Ado* was written *c*. 1598.
[11] Doleful tunes.—*Leavy* (line 12) = leafy.

[12] This song and the next are familiar in fine settings by Dr. Thomas Arne, composed for the Drury Lane revival of 1740. *As You Like It* was first produced *c.*1599. Amiens sings "Under the greenwood tree" (II, v) and "Blow, blow" (II, vii) in the forest where he lives with the outlawed duke.
[13] Pronounce here with a long *i*.

III

It was a lover and his lass[14]
  (With a hey, and a ho, and a hey nonino)
That o'er the green cornfield did pass
  In springtime, the only pretty ring-time,
When birds do sing, hey ding a ding, ding—   5
Sweet lovers love the spring.

Between the acres of the rye
  (With a hey, and a ho, and a hey nonino)
These pretty country folks would lie
  In springtime, the only pretty ring-time,   10
When birds do sing, hey ding a ding, ding—
Sweet lovers love the spring.

This carol they began that hour
  (With a hey, and a ho, and a hey nonino),
How that a life was but a flower   15
  In springtime, the only pretty ring-time,
When birds do sing, hey ding a ding, ding—
Sweet lovers love the spring.

And therefore take the present time
  (With a hey, and a ho, and a hey nonino),   20
For love is crownèd with the prime[15]
  In springtime, the only pretty ring-time,
When birds do sing, hey ding a ding, ding—
Sweet lovers love the spring.

from TWELFTH NIGHT

I

O mistress mine, where are you roaming?[16]
O, stay and hear! your true-love's coming,
  That can sing both high and low.
Trip no further, pretty sweeting;
Journeys end in lovers meeting,   5
  Every wise man's son doth know.

What is love? 'Tis not hereafter;
Present mirth hath present laughter;
  What's to come is still unsure:
In delay there lies no plenty;   10
Then come kiss me, sweet and twenty!
  Youth's a stuff will not endure.

II

When that I was and a little tiny boy,
  With hey, ho, the wind and the rain,
A foolish thing was but a toy,[17]
  For the rain it raineth every day.

But when I came to man's estate,   5
  With hey, ho, the wind and the rain,
'Gainst knaves and thieves men shut their gate,[18]
  For the rain it raineth every day.

But when I came, alas! to wive,
  With hey, ho, the wind and the rain,   10
By swaggering could I never thrive,[19]
  For the rain it raineth every day.

But when I came unto my beds,[20]
  With hey, ho, the wind and the rain,
With tosspots still had drunken heads,[21]   15
  For the rain it raineth every day.

A great while ago the world begun,[22]
  With hey, ho, the wind and the rain;
But that's all one,[23] our play is done,
  And we'll strive to please you every day.   20

from CYMBELINE

I

Hark, hark! the lark at heaven's gate sings,
  And Phoebus[24] gins arise,
His steeds to water at those springs
  On chaliced flowers that lies;
And winking Mary-buds[25] begin   5
  To ope their golden eyes,
With every thing that pretty is,
  My lady sweet, arise!
    Arise, arise!

[17] Trifle; i.e., I was so young that no one minded my little follies. —This charming song, sung by Feste, comes at the end of the play, after all the rest have left the stage.
[18] I.e., now I had grown up I found the world a harder place to get along in.   [19] I.e., I couldn't bluff my wife.
[20] I.e., got really old.
[21] I.e., when I consorted with topers I inevitably got drunk.
[22] (And it is not going to change its ways for the likes of you and me.)   [23] Never mind, that makes no difference.
[24] Apollo; the sun was his chariot. Shakespeare has him watering his horses with the dew in the flowers' cups.—This *aubade* or morning serenade (Schubert's perfect setting is famous) is sung in II, iii for the heroine, Imogen, by musicians brought by her suitor, the villainous Cloten. *Cymbeline* was probably produced c.1609.
[25] Marigold buds with their eyes shut (in sleep).

[14] Sung (in V, iii) by two pages to the court jester Touchstone and Audrey, his rustic sweetheart. The setting by one of Shakespeare's great contemporaries, Thomas Morley, has survived in his *First Book of Airs or Little Short Songs* (1600).   [15] Spring.
[16] Sung by the Fool, Feste, in II, iii, to the reveling knights, Sir Toby and Sir Andrew. *Twelfth Night* was written c.1600.

II

Fear no more the heat o' th' sun,[26]
　　Nor the furious winter's rages;
Thou thy worldly task hast done,
　　Home art gone, and ta'en thy wages.
Golden lads and girls all must,　　　　　　5
　　As[27] chimney-sweepers, come to dust.

Fear no more the frown o' th' great;
　　Thou art past the tyrant's stroke.
Care no more to clothe and eat;
　　To thee the reed is as the oak.　　　　10
The scepter, learning, physic,[28] must
　　All follow this, and come to dust.

Fear no more the lightning flash,
　　Nor th' all-dreaded thunder-stone;
Fear not slander, censure rash;　　　　　15
　　Thou hast finished joy and moan.
All lovers young, all lovers must
　　Consign to thee, and come to dust.

No exorciser harm thee!
　　Nor no witchcraft charm thee!　　　　20
Ghost unlaid forbear thee!
　　Nothing ill come near thee!
Quiet consummation have,
　　And renownèd be thy grave!

from THE WINTER'S TALE

When daffodils begin to peer
　　(With hey! the doxy[29] over the dale)
Why, then comes in the sweet o' the year,
　　For the red blood reigns in the winter's pale.

The white sheet bleaching on the hedge　　5
　　(With hey! the sweet birds, O, how they sing!)
Doth set my pugging[30] tooth on edge,
　　For a quart of ale is a dish for a king.

The lark, that tirra-lirra chants
　　(With hey! with hey! the thrush and the jay!)　10
Are summer songs for me and my aunts,[31]
　　While we lie tumbling in the hay.

from THE TEMPEST

I

Come unto these yellow sands,
　　And then take hands.
Curtsied when you have and kissed,[32]
　　The wild waves whist,[33]
Foot it featly[34] here and there;　　　　　5
And, sweet sprites, the burthen[35] bear.
　　Hark, hark!
　　　(Burthen, dispersedly.) Bow-wow!
The watchdogs bark!
　　　(Burthen, dispersedly.) Bow-wow!　　10
Hark, hark! I hear
The strain of strutting chanticleer
　　Cry cock-a-diddle-dow!

II

Full fadom five[36] thy father lies:
　　Of his bones are coral made;
Those are pearls that were his eyes;
　　Nothing of him that doth fade
But doth suffer a sea-change　　　　　　5
Into something rich and strange.
Sea nymphs hourly ring his knell:
　　　(Burthen.) Ding-dong!
Hark! now I hear them—Ding-dong, bell!

III

Where the bee sucks, there suck I;[37]
　　In a cowslip's bell I lie;
There I couch when owls do cry.
　　On the bat's back I do fly
After summer merrily.　　　　　　　5
Merrily, merrily shall I live now
Under the blossom that hangs on the bough.

---

[26] Sung in IV, ii as a funeral dirge for the supposedly dead Imogen by King Cymbeline's two young sons, near the mountain cave where they live in ignorance of their rank.　　[27] Like.

[28] I.e., even the practitioner of medical art.

[29] Wench, sweetheart, mistress.—This lilting lyric is sung by the merry rogue and small-time thief Autolycus, as he enters in IV, iii—to himself, out of his sheer exuberance and delight in his way of life. *The Winter's Tale* was probably produced c.1610.

[30] Thievish. The idea is to steal and sell the sheet, and drink up the proceeds.　　[31] Whores, mistresses.

[32] Certain old dances began with a formal kiss.—Ariel, Prospero's airy spirit, invisibly lures on the shipwrecked Prince Ferdinand with music, singing both this song and the next in I, ii. *The Tempest* (c.1611) is very likely the last play Shakespeare wrote, except for two later pieces on which he collaborated.

[33] Quiet.　　　　[34] Dance nimbly.

[35] The drone, a monotone in the bass; here, "bow-wow."

[36] Five fathoms deep.

[37] Sung by Ariel as he waits on Prospero in V, i.

Michael Drayton

1563–1631

LIKE Shakespeare, Drayton was a poor boy from Warwickshire and came of yeoman stock. Their upbringing,
however, was quite different. Drayton was reared as a
page in the household of Henry Goodere of Polesworth
(1534–95), a friend of Sir Philip Sidney. This was Drayton's
education, a childhood in a cultivated family, with of course
some formal schooling. Apparently he attended neither of
the universities.

From the first, he wanted to be a poet. In his "Epistle to
Henry Reynolds" he tells how

> To my mild tutor merrily I came
> (For I was then a proper, goodly page,
> Much like a pigmy, scarce ten years of age),
> Clasping my slender arms about his thigh:
> "O my dear master! cannot you," quoth I,
> "Make me a poet? Do it, if you can!
> And you shall see I'll quickly be a man."

But it proved to be his own hard and persistent toil, not
the release of a natural facility, that made a poet of Michael
Drayton.

Goodere and his family remained steadfast friends. With
Anne, the younger daughter of the house, Drayton fell in
love. He could scarcely have cherished serious hopes; but
his devotion endured throughout his life, even after Anne
married. Drayton never married. Evidently he sublimated
his passion, became her firm friend and her husband's, and
found a kind of refuge in the homely philosophy of resignation which is reflected in his sonnets to "Idea," as he
calls her. We must not let their frequent sallies of humor
blind us to the deep and steady emotion which underlies
them. When Anne died is unknown, but it was after the
poet who adored her; on his deathbed he was still writing
verses in her praise. As Goodere's life drew near its close,
he "bequeathed" his protégé to Lucy Harington (d. 1627),
who in 1594 at fourteen (not then an unusual age for
matrimony) married Edward Russell, Earl of Bedford. She
lives in history as a great patroness of the poets. Perhaps
Drayton was her tutor. How well and how long she served
his career is uncertain.

Drayton's earliest volumes are of little merit. His first
good poems appeared in 1594, in *Idea's Mirror*, the first
version of the sonnets inspired by Anne Goodere. This
cycle was very popular with the reading public; there
were eleven editions in Drayton's lifetime. Not that such a
success solved the problem of livelihood. Royalties for
authors are a relatively recent invention; an outright and
arbitrary sum was paid down by the publisher, who might

then reprint as often as he pleased. An Elizabethan, unless
he wrote for the theater, was more or less dependent on
the patronage of the great. Among Drayton's other works
of the middle nineties were his *Mortimeriados* (1596), an
account in Chaucer's rime royal of the contest between
Edward II and his barons, and *England's Heroical Epistles*
(1597), modeled on Ovid's *Heroides*. Neither volume rises
above mediocrity. In the latter his love of England's past
finds further scope, as he versifies imaginary letters by
amorous heroes and heroines from the pages of history.
About the same time began his career as a playwright, an
undistinguished one. Fortunately he found another patron
in Sir Walter Aston (1583–1639) and thus escaped actual
want.

Drayton tried everything; none of the poetic genres of
the day was to lack at least one contribution from his pen.
In 1604 he published a satire, *The Owl*. A collected volume
of his verse was issued in 1605, and in 1606 a new *Poems*.
In the last of these volumes are some of his finest achievements, the "Odes," of which the two best are reprinted
below. In 1612 appeared the first part of *Poly-Olbion*. In
this extraordinary performance—it ran eventually to
15,000 lines—Drayton undertakes to describe *all* his country's natural features: every river, every mountain, every
forest, as well as the fauna and flora of each region. The
poet's sheer ambition crowns this labor of love with an
odd dignity of its own, despite the hopelessly unpoetic
character of most of the verse. The remainder of the poem
was brought out in 1622, still unfinished. In the meantime,
1619 saw the publication, in that kind of tall, thick format
known as a folio, of *Poems by Michael Drayton, Esquire,
Collected into One Volume*. And in 1627, as if to show yet
another facet of his versatility, came, in a new book of
poems, the humorous but dainty mock-heroic, *Nymphidia*.
Fairyland being the subject, *A Midsummer Night's Dream* is
much in the poet's mind; but, as always, Drayton's own
quality gives the work its savor, a puckish one. He continued writing to the last. *The Moon-Calf* (1627) is notable
for its rough satire. In *The Muses' Elysium* (1630) he carries
on the pastoral tradition of Spenser.

Drayton died in 1631 and was buried in Westminster
Abbey. His popularity continued for several generations
and then faded out, largely because his work is uneven.
At his best he is very good, but too much of his excursion-
ing in English history is rambling and prosy. Yet except
in *Poly-Olbion* he is rarely, in the works of his maturity,
uninteresting; one likes Drayton for his versatility, his

manliness, the way he goes all out for what he believes in. None of his contemporaries had a nobler concept of poetry as the highest wisdom; none gave himself more devotedly to its composition as a sacred responsibility. And, with all this high seriousness, there is no priggishness about him; he is like Shakespeare in his ample possession of the saving grace of humor.

Jealous he may have been of other men's successes, but he does not seem to have allowed that emotion to cloud his judgment. He is certainly critical; but when he puts himself on record about his contemporaries (as in sonnet 3 from *Idea*, below) he is modest enough, though sturdily insistent on the independent character of his own contribution. The most notable of his critical judgments are in the epistle "of poets and poesy" addressed "To Henry Reynolds"; on the whole they agree with prevailing estimates today.

The standard edition of his works is by J. W. Hebel and others (5 vols., 1931–41). For his life and a criticism of his poetry, see the companion volume, valuable though often conjectural, by B. H. Newdigate, *Michael Drayton and His Circle* (1941). The poems on which his reputation rests are collected, with an introduction, in C. Brett's *Minor Poems of Michael Drayton* (1907).

from IDEA

Drayton stuck to what he believed in; his doggedness is one of his most attractive qualities. The text of the following sonnets agrees with his final revisions. From *Idea's Mirror* of 1594, through several intervening editions, to *Idea: In Sixty-three Sonnets* (in the *Poems* of 1619), he rejected some sonnets, added others, and reworked many. He did not abandon sonneteering because most of his colleagues were tired of it; and unlike most of them, though his first sonnets appeared in 1594 at the height of the vogue, he did not translate from his Italian and French predecessors. To be sure, many of his conceits were already current in English poetry; but Drayton has his own flavor, and it is a tart one. Had he not loved Anne Goodere, these poems might have been different; but the fact that they are personally inspired does not alter their general applicability, which is emphasized by his title. In the last of our selections, "Since there's no help," he achieved one of the great English sonnets, a poem of universal significance, at any rate for all who have loved.

To the Reader of These Sonnets

Into these loves[1] who but for passion looks,
At this first sight here let him lay them by
And seek elsewhere, in turning other books
Which better may his labor satisfy.
No far-fetched sigh shall ever wound my breast,   5
Love from mine eye a tear shall never wring,
Nor in "Ah me's!" my whining sonnets drest:
A libertine,[2] fantastic'ly I sing.
My verse is the true image of my mind,
Ever in motion, still desiring change;   10
And as thus, to variety inclined,
So in all humors[3] sportively I range!
My Muse is rightly of the English strain,
That cannot long one fashion entertain.

3

Many there be excelling in this kind,[4]
Whose well-tricked[5] rimes with all invention swell.
Let each commend as best shall like his mind,
Some Sidney, Constable, some Daniel.[6]
That thus their names familiarly I sing   5
Let none think them disparagèd to be;
Poor men with reverence may speak of a king,
And so may these be spoken of by me.
My wanton verse ne'er keeps one certain stay:
But now at hand, then seeks invention far,   10
And with each little motion runs astray,
Wild, madding, jocund, and irregular.
Like me that lust,[7] my honest, merry rimes
Nor care for critic nor regard the times.

4

Bright star of Beauty, on whose eyelids sit
A thousand nymph-like and enamored Graces,
The goddesses of memory and wit,[8]
Which there in order take their several places;
In whose dear bosom, sweet delicious Love   5
Lays down his quiver, which he once did bear,
Since he that blessèd paradise did prove,[9]
And leaves his mother's[10] lap, to sport him there,—
Let others strive to entertain with words;
My soul is of a braver[11] mettle made: 10
I hold that vile which vulgar wit affords;
In me's that faith which time cannot invade.
Let what I praise be still[12] made good by you:
Be you most worthy, whilst I am most true.

[1] Love poems; the subtitle of the first edition is *Amours in Quatorzains,* i.e., in fourteen lines.
[2] A free spirit. But the sonnets which follow belie this airy introduction.   [3] Whims, notions.

[4] Sonnets.
[5] Artfully adorned.
[6] For Sidney's and Daniel's sonnets, see pp. 257 f., 335 f., above. Henry Constable (1562–1613) wrote a famous sonnet cycle, *Diana* (1592).   [7] Lists, chooses, wishes.
[8] Reason.   [9] Try.
[10] Cupid was the son of Venus.   [11] Finer.
[12] Always.

9

As other men, so I myself do muse
Why in this sort I wrest invention[13] so,
And why these giddy metaphors I use,
Leaving the path the greater part do go.
I will resolve you:[14] I am lunatic!   5
And ever this in madmen you shall find:
What they last thought of when the brain grew sick,
In most distraction they keep that in mind.
Thus talking idly, in this Bedlam[15] fit,
Reason and I, you must conceive, are twain;   10
'Tis nine years now since first I lost my wit.
Bear with me, then, though troubled be my brain.
With diet and correction[16] men distraught,
Not too far past, may to their wits be brought.

20

An evil spirit, your beauty, haunts me still,
Wherewith, alas, I have been long possest;
Which ceaseth not to tempt me to each ill,
Nor give me once but one poor minute's rest.
In me it speaks, whether I sleep or wake;   5
And when by means to drive it out I try,
With greater torments then it me doth take,
And tortures me in most extremity.
Before my face it lays down my despairs,
And hastes me on unto a sudden death,[17]   10
Now tempting me to drown myself in tears,
And then in sighing to give up my breath.
Thus am I still provoked to every evil,
By this good-wicked spirit, sweet angel-devil.

24

I hear some say, "This man is not in love."
"Who? can he love? a likely thing!" they say.
"Read but his verse, and it will eas'ly prove."
O, judge not rashly, gentle sir, I pray!
Because I loosely trifle in this sort,   5
As one that fain his sorrows would beguile,
You now suppose me all this time in sport,
And please yourself with this conceit[18] the while.
Ye shallow censures! sometime, see ye not,
In greatest perils some men pleasant be—   10
Where fame by death is only to be got,
They resolute? So stands the case with me:
Where other men in depth of passion cry,
I laugh at Fortune, as in jest to die.

25[19]

The glorious sun went blushing to his bed
When my soul's sun, from her fair cabinet,[20]
Her golden beams had now discoverèd,[21]
Light'ning the world, eclipsèd by his set.
Some mused[22] to see the earth envý the air   5
Which from her lips exhaled refinèd sweet,
A world to see, yet how he[23] joyed to hear
The dainty grass make music with her feet.
But my most marvel was when, from the skies,
So comet-like each star advanced her light,   10
As though the heaven had now awaked her eyes
And summoned angels to this blessèd sight.
No cloud was seen, but crystalline the air,
Laughing for joy upon my lovely fair.

37

Dear, why should you command me to my rest,
When now the night doth summon all to sleep?
Methinks this time becometh lovers best;
Night was ordained together friends to keep.
How happy are all other living things,   5
Which, though the day disjoin by sev'ral flight,
The quiet evening yet together brings,
And each returns unto his love at night![24]
O thou that art so courteous else to all,
Why shouldst thou, Night, abuse me only thus,   10
That ev'ry creature to his kind dost call,
And yet 'tis thou dost only sever us?
Well could I wish it would be ever day,
If when night comes you bid me go away.

42

Some men there be which like my method well,
And much commend the strangeness of my vein;
Some say I have a passing[25] pleasing strain,
Some say that in my humor I excel;
Some, who not kindly relish my conceit,   5
They say, as poets do I use to feign,
And in bare words paint out my passion's pain;
Thus sundry men their sundry minds repeat.
I pass not,[26] I, how men affected be,
Nor who commends or discommends my verse;   10
It pleaseth me if I may woes rehearse,
And in my lines if she my love may see.
Only, my comfort still consists in this:
Writing her praise, I cannot write amiss.

---

[13] I.e., rack my brain.   [14] Explain to you.
[15] Mad. *Bedlam* (for *Bethlehem*) was London's insane asylum.
[16] Starvation and whipping, then in use for the cure of the insane.
[17] There was always danger that a spirit might be the Devil, one
of whose methods of obtaining souls was to persuade to suicide.
[18] Notion.

[19] So numbered in *Idea's Mirror* (1594); but Drayton never reprinted this lovely and joyous sonnet.   [20] Boudoir.
[21] Revealed.   [22] Marveled.   [23] The earth.
[24] This thought has occurred to many poets, since the time of
Sappho (*c.* 600 B.C.).   [25] Surpassingly, very.   [26] Care.

Whilst thus my pen strives to eternize thee,
Age rules my lines with wrinkles in my face,
Where, in the map[27] of all my misery,
Is modeled out the world of my disgrace.
Whilst, in despite of tyrannizing times,5
Medea-like[28] I make thee young again,
Proudly thou scorn'st my world-outwearing rimes,
And murther'st virtue with thy coy disdain.
And though in youth my youth untimely perish
To keep thee from oblivion and the grave,10
Ensuing ages yet my rimes shall cherish,
Where I, entombed, my better part shall save;
And though this earthly body fade and die,
My name shall mount upon eternity.[29]

Thou leaden brain, which censur'st what I write
And sayst my lines be dull and do not move,
I marvel not thou feel'st not my delight,
Which[30] never felt'st my fiery touch of love.
But thou whose pen hath like a pack horse served,5
Whose stomach unto gall hath turned thy food,
Whose senses like poor pris'ners hunger-starved,
Whose grief hath parched thy body, dried thy blood;
Thou which hast scornèd life and hated death,
And in a moment mad, sober, glad, and sorry,10
Thou which hath banned[31] thy thoughts and cursed thy
birth
With thousand plagues, more than in purgatory:
Thou, thus whose spirit Love in his fire refines,
Come thou and read, admire, applaud my lines!

You, best discerned of my mind's inward eyes,
And yet your graces outwardly divine,
Whose dear remembrance in my bosom lies,
Too rich a relic for so poor a shrine;
You, in whom Nature chose herself to view5
When she her own perfection would admire,
Bestowing all her excellence on you,
At whose pure eyes Love lights his hallowed fire:
Ev'n as a man that in some trance hath seen
More than his wond'ring utt'rance can unfold,10
That, rapt in spirit, in better worlds hath been,
So must your praise distractedly be told—
Most of all short, when I should show you most,
In your perfections so much am I lost.

---

[27] Which is full of crinkly lines.
[28] After helping Jason obtain the Golden Fleece, she magically
restored his father to youth.
[29] Note the variation on the conventional statement that the poet's
lines will immortalize the lady.[30] Who.[31] Cursed.

60

Define my weal, and tell the joys of heaven;
Express my woes, and show the pains of hell;
Declare what fate unlucky stars have given,
And ask a world upon my life to dwell;
Make known the faith that Fortune could not move;5
Compare my worth with others' base desert;
Let virtue be the touchstone of my love,
So may the heavens read wonders in my heart;
Behold the clouds which have eclipsed my sun,
And view the crosses which my course do let;[32]10
Tell me if ever since the world begun
So fair a rising had so foul a set:
And see if Time, if he would strive to prove,
Can show a second to so pure a love.

61

Since there's no help, come let us kiss and part—
Nay, I have done: you get no more of me;
And I am glad, yea, glad with all my heart,
That thus so cleanly I myself can free.
Shake hands[33] for ever, cancel all our vows;5
And when we meet at any time again,
Be it not seen in either of our brows
That we one jot of former love retain.
Now, at the last gasp of Love's latest breath,
When, his pulse failing, Passion speechless lies,10
When Faith is kneeling by his bed of death,
And Innocence is closing up his eyes,—
Now, if thou wouldst, when all have given him over,
From death to life thou mightst him yet recover.

ODE TO THE VIRGINIAN VOYAGE

Drayton's inspiration, when he introduced this new kind
of lyric into English verse, was the odes of Horace; but
his tone is actually more reminiscent of English balladry.
Both the following poems appeared in 1606. Drayton had
read Hakluyt (see p. 281, above), his imagination was
fired, he had invested in the Virginia Voyage. Though
Raleigh's ventures had failed, they had paved the way; and
in December of 1606 the expedition sailed which was to
establish, at Jamestown, the first permanent English settlement. A number of the details and claims about Virginia
are straight from Hakluyt's pages. For Americans, especially, this is a stirring poem.

You brave heroic minds,
Worthy your country's name,
That honor still pursue,
Go and subdue,
Whilst loit'ring hinds[34]5
Lurk here at home with shame!

---

[32] Obstruct. The term survives in tennis.
[33] Say goodbye, part.[34] Peasants.

Britons, you stay too long!
Quickly aboard bestow you,
   And with a merry gale
   Swell your stretched sail,   10
With vows as strong
As the winds that blow you!

Your course securely steer,
West-and-by-south forth keep!
   Rocks, lee shores, nor shoals,   15
   When Aeolus[35] scowls,
You need not fear,
So absolute the deep.

And, cheerfully at sea,
Success you still entice,   20
   To get the pearl and gold,
   And ours to hold,
Virginia,
Earth's only paradise;

Where Nature hath in store   25
Fowl, venison, and fish,
   And the fruitful'st soil—
   Without your toil,
Three harvests more,
All greater than your wish;   30

And the ambitious vine
Crowns with his purple mass
   The cedar reaching high
   To kiss the sky,
The cypress, pine,   35
And useful sassafras;

To whose,[36] the Golden Age
Still Nature's laws doth give,
   Nor other cares attend
   But them to defend   40
From winter's rage,
That long there doth not live.

When-as the luscious smell
Of that delicious land,
   Above the seas that flows,   45
   The clear wind throws,
Your hearts to swell,
Approaching the dear strand,

In kenning[37] of the shore
(Thanks to God first given)   50
   O you, the happi'st men,
   Be frolic then!
Let cannons roar,
Frighting the wide heaven!

And in regions far,   55
Such heroes bring ye forth
   As those from whom we came,
   And plant our name
Under that star
Not known unto our North!   60

And as there plenty grows
The laurel everywhere,
   Apollo's sacred tree,
   You it may see
A poet's brows   65
To crown, that may sing there.

Thy Voyages attend,
Industrious Hakluyt!
   Whose reading shall inflame
   Men to seek fame,   70
And much commend
To after times thy wit.

BALLAD OF AGINCOURT

On October 25, 1415, an English army raiding northern
France attacked and defeated, near the village of Azincourt
in the vicinity of St. Pol, an intercepting French army at
least four times its size, chiefly because the fire of the
English archers proved disastrous to the French nobility,
who on this occasion fought dismounted in the vanguard.
About four thousand of them were killed. Drayton's
source for his "ballad," the best battle poem in English
since the tenth-century *Maldon* (see p. 48, above), was a
book to which Shakespeare had repeatedly resorted for
his historical plays, the *Chronicles* of Raphael Holinshed
(d. 1580?). In the poem's full title Drayton dedicates it to
the Welsh: "Ode to the Cambro-Britons and Their Harp,
His Ballad of Agincourt."

Fair stood the wind for France,
When we our sails advance,
Nor now to prove our chance
   Longer will tarry;
But putting to the main,   5
At Caux, the mouth of Seine,
With all his martial train
   Landed King Harry;[38]

---

[35] God of the winds.
[36] The inhabitants. The idea behind these lines is the prehistoric
   "Golden Age," when man was supposed to have been closer to
   nature and uncorrupted by civilization.

[37] Recognition.   [38] Henry V.

And taking many a fort,
Furnished in warlike sort,
Marcheth towards Agincourt   10
    In happy hour,
Skirmishing day by day
With those that stopped his way,
Where the French gen'ral lay   15
    With all his power;[39]

Which, in his height of pride,
King Henry to deride,
His ransom to provide
    To the King sending;   20
Which he neglects the while,
As from a nation vile,
Yet with an angry smile,
    Their fall portending.

And, turning to his men,   25
Quoth our brave Henry then,
"Though they to one be ten,
    Be not amazèd!
Yet have we well begun;
Battles so bravely won   30
Have ever to the sun
    By Fame been raisèd!

"And for myself," quoth he,
"This my full rest[40] shall be:
England ne'er mourn for me,   35
    Nor more esteem me!
Victor I will remain,
Or on this earth lie slain;
Never shall she sustain
    Loss to redeem me.   40

"Poitiers and Cressy[41] tell,
When most their pride did swell,
Under our swords they fell.
    No less our skill is,
Than when our grandsire great,[42]   45
Claiming the regal seat,[43]
By many a warlike feat
    Lopped the French lilies."

The Duke of York[44] so dread
The eager vaward[45] led;   50

With the main, Henry sped
    Amongst his henchmen;
Excester[46] had the rear,
A braver man not there;
O Lord, how hot they were   55
    On the false Frenchmen!

They now to fight are gone;
Armor on armor shone,
Drum now to drum did groan,
    To hear was wonder;   60
That with cries they make
The very earth did shake,
Trumpet to trumpet spake,
    Thunder to thunder.

Well it thine age became,   65
O noble Erpingham,[47]
Which didst the signal aim
    To our hid forces;
When from a meadow by,
Like a storm suddenly,   70
The English archery
    Stuck the French horses,

With Spanish yew[48] so strong,
Arrows a cloth-yard long,
That like to serpents stung,   75
    Piercing the weather;
None from his fellow starts,
But playing manly parts,
And like true English hearts,
    Stuck close together.   80

When down their bows they threw,
And forth their bilboes[49] drew,
And on the French they flew,
    Not one was tardy;
Arms were from shoulders sent,   85
Scalps to the teeth were rent,
Down the French peasants[50] went;
    Our men were hardy.

46 Exeter, i.e., the duke of that title; he was the King's uncle.
47 Sir Thomas Erpingham; he was sixty-eight. When the King decided to attack, Erpingham was sent forward to deploy the archers.
48 The favorite wood for the English longbow, which was 5½ to 6 feet long.
49 Swords. Bilbao in northern Spain manufactured them. The charge by the archers was to exploit gaps in the French line made by wounded horses galloping back from two ineffective cavalry charges delivered from the flanks of the French army; its center fought on foot.
50 Here a contemptuous term for the French in general. As a matter of fact, it was the French aristocracy that suffered most heavily in this battle. The field was a sea of mud, and they were literally stuck in it.

39 Army.   40 Resolve.   41 Crécy. See p. 60, above.
42 Great-grandfather; Edward III.   43 The throne of France.
44 This grandson of Edward III and second cousin of the King was killed in the battle.
45 Vanguard. In this battle it formed the right wing, since on account of their numerical inferiority the English had troops enough for only one line.

This while our noble King,
His broadsword brandishing,
Down the French host did ding,   90
    As to o'erwhelm it;
And many a deep wound lent,
His arms with blood besprent,[51]
And many a cruel dent   95
    Bruisèd his helmet.

Gloster, that Duke so good,
Next of the royal blood,
For famous England stood
    With his brave brother;[52]   100
Clarence in steel so bright,
Though but a maiden[53] knight,
Yet in that furious fight
    Scarce such another.

Warwick[54] in blood did wade,   105
Oxford[55] the foe invade,
And cruel slaughter made,
    Still as they ran up;
Suffolk[56] his ax did ply,
Beaumont and Willoughby   110
Bare them right doughtily,
    Ferrers[57] and Fanhope.

Upon Saint Crispin's day
Fought was this noble fray,
Which fame did not delay   115
    To England to carry.
O when shall Englishmen
With such acts fill a pen,
Or England breed again
    Such a King Harry?   120

Thomas Dekker

1572?–1632?

DEKKER was born in London and, like Charles Lamb and Charles Dickens, became almost a professional Londoner. City ways and byways, the color and bustle and clatter of the metropolis, fascinated him and furnished him with inexhaustible materials for plays and pamphlets. He was probably not a university man. There may have been an interlude of wandering on the Continent, possibly of soldiering in the Low Countries, before he turns up in his native place as a playwright.

Presumably his career began in the mid-nineties; in all, he had a hand in more than forty plays. With *The Shoemakers' Holiday* (1599) and still more with *The Honest Whore* (1604), both written before Ben Jonson's first masterpiece, Dekker must have looked for a while like the most promising dramatist next to the already well-established Shakespeare. In the course of a literary squabble known as the War of the Theaters, Jonson took him seriously enough to attack him along with John Marston in a play, *Poetaster* (1601). In the same year Dekker retaliated in a satirical drama of his own, *Satiromastix*.

But he never fulfilled the promise of 1599–1604. He was a prolific writer, but a great deal of his output is hack work. He collaborated with many playwrights, he wrote some exquisite lyric verse, he turned out a string of prose pamphlets which made him the most distinguished successor of Greene and Nashe. Something, however, he lacked, some element of toughness. Few of his works are sustained. There are flashes of great power and beauty, and they are frequent enough to place him among the most remarkable writers of Renaissance England; but not in his career as a whole, nor throughout any but a very few of his separate works, was he able to hold himself steadily to the high level he nevertheless always seems capable of.

James came to the throne in an evil year. The bubonic plague was reigning in the summer of 1603, and the royal Scot had to wait till it abdicated before he could proceed with the ceremonies of his English coronation. His son Charles I succeeded in another virulent plague-time, 1625. Both these dreadful scourges are described by Dekker in pamphlets (*The Wonderful Year*, 1603; *A Rod for Runaways*, 1625) which are uncompromisingly realistic in the detail of their reporting, and yet full of sorrow for the city's anguish: "O London, thou mother of my life, nurse of my being, a hard-hearted son might I be counted if here I should not dissolve all into tears."

---

[51] Sprinkled.

[52] Humphrey, Duke of Gloucester, the King's brother (d. 1447), was afterwards famous as a patron of literature. He figures prominently in Shakespeare's *2 Henry VI*. Gloucester was actually younger than his brothers, the King and the Duke of Clarence.

[53] Inexperienced. Actually, he had already seen much service.

[54] Richard de Beauchamp, Earl of Warwick.

[55] Richard de Vere, eleventh Earl of Oxford.

[56] Michael de la Pole, third Earl of Suffolk. He was killed at Agincourt; his father had been killed earlier in the campaign.

[57] Holinshed says Henry had knighted him during the march up the River Somme which preceded the battle, and gives the three other names as those of lords who were with the Duke of York in charge of the archers.

As a Londoner and a close observer of London, Dekker is socially minded, and no less an artist for his intense interest in the moral problems of urban life. Nothing separates our own time more strikingly from his than the callousness, as it seems to us, of the Elizabethans. Dekker, long before the eighteenth-century age of humanitarianism, repeatedly exhibits a sympathy rare among the artists of his time for the little man, the plain citizen, the honest bourgeois. Unlike most of the dramatists, he does not view the people with condescending amusement from the eminence of his own superiority, either of position or of intellect. And for the poor and wronged, for the decent unfortunate caught in the web of the law, for suffering animals, even, he has a fund of pity and sadness far from characteristic of his period. "Oh, what a deal of wretchedness," he writes of the miserable tenants of London's thirteen prisons, "can make shift to lie in a little room." And again, of a favorite Elizabethan sport:

Methought this whipping of the blind bear moved as much pity in my breast towards him as the leading of poor starved wretches to the whipping posts in London, when they had more need to be relieved with food, ought to move the breasts of citizens, though it be the fashion now to laugh at the punishment.

It is the underdog (or man or bear) that wrings his heart, not the spectacle of fallen greatness. Toward rogues and fools he can be stern enough, as in *The Gull's Hornbook* (1609), which is to say the fool's A B C, a caustic guide to the follies of the day, including those of playhouse and tavern. And among his other pamphlets there are *The Seven Deadly Sins of London* (1606) and *The Bellman of London* (1608), in which, fascinated still by every aspect of metropolitan manners and customs, he exposes the ways of crooks and sharpers. He had seen the underworld, intimately, from some of its chief points of rendezvous, the jails. Poverty was a constant menace; it may have crushed him. For years he lay in debtors' prison, forgotten by nearly all his friends. Family he apparently had none.

Lamb said rightly that Dekker had "poetry enough for anything." His best poetry is not in his songs but in certain impassioned speeches of *The Honest Whore;* to quote them detached from their context would be unjust to them. The play which follows is a new reader's best introduction to Dekker, but there is more of poetry, imagination, and high seriousness in the main plot of *The Honest Whore*.

Both parts of that masterpiece are reprinted in H. Spencer's *Elizabethan Plays* (1933). There is no good collected edition. The surviving plays are available in the faulty Pearson reprint of 1873 (4 vols.), and the non-dramatic works in A. B. Grosart's edition (5 vols., 1884–6). F. P. Wilson edited *The Plague Pamphlets of Thomas Dekker* (1925). For *The Gull's Hornbook* see R. B. McKerrow's reprint (1907).

ART THOU POOR?

This lyric and the next are from an inferior play, *Patient Grissill* (1603), of which Dekker was co-author, along with Henry Chettle and William Haughton. They are sung by a poor basket-weaver; the second is a lullaby to his grandchildren. Dekker's authorship of these songs has been questioned, but nothing in the known work of the poetasters who collaborated with him suggests that they were capable of them.

Art thou poor, yet hast thou golden slumbers?
    O sweet content!
Art thou rich, yet is thy mind perplexèd?
    O punishment!
Dost thou laugh to see how fools are vexèd   5
To add to golden numbers golden numbers?
O sweet content! O sweet, O sweet content!
    Work apace, apace, apace, apace;
    Honest labor bears a lovely face;
Then hey nonny nonny, hey nonny nonny!   10

Canst drink the waters of the crispèd[1] spring?
    O sweet content!

---
[1] Rippled.

Swimm'st thou in wealth, yet sink'st in thine own tears?
    O punishment!
Then he that patiently want's burden bears   15
No burden bears, but is a king, a king!
O sweet content! O sweet, O sweet content!
    Work apace, apace, apace, apace;
    Honest labor bears a lovely face;
Then hey nonny nonny, hey nonny nonny!   20

GOLDEN SLUMBERS

Golden slumbers kiss your eyes;
Smiles awake you when you rise.
Sleep, pretty wantons, do not cry,
And I will sing a lullaby:
Rock them, rock them, lullaby.   5

Care is heavy, therefore sleep you;
You are care, and care must keep you.
Sleep, pretty wantons, do not cry,
And I will sing a lullaby:
Rock them, rock them, lullaby.   10

Thomas Dekker

THE SHOEMAKERS' HOLIDAY

ORIGINALLY produced in 1599 by the principal rival of Shakespeare's company, the Lord Admiral's Men, this favorite comedy is based on several tales about shoemakers in Thomas Deloney's prose tract, *The Gentle Craft* (1598). Here may be found, with unhistorical embellishments, the story of that early-fifteenth-century worthy Sir Simon Eyre, from the hiring of the new foreign workman to the feasting of the apprentices. Here also are the return of the wife supposed dead and the legend of St. Crispin, who, in his adoption of the gentle craft and his clandestine marriage, is emulated by Lacy.

These materials are deftly interwoven by Dekker, and highly colored from his own intimate acquaintance with London life. True, the rise of Eyre is pretty rapid, even for

a romantic comedy. Nor is the dramatist critical, like Jonson, as he surveys the contemporary scene. This is a play of romantic plot curiously allied with realistic manners, the first so charming, and the second depicted with a gusto so nearly Chaucerian, that the combination is irresistible. Simon Eyre wins every reader's heart as easily as he wins the King's. And it is the heart, not the mind, that Dekker, on the threshold of his career, addresses in this play.

There was a successful New York revival in 1938 by Orson Welles and his Mercury Theater. The present text (reprinted, with revisions, by kind permission of D. C. Heath and Company, from H. Spencer's *Elizabethan Plays*) is based on the quarto of 1600.

THE SHOEMAKERS' HOLIDAY
A PLEASANT COMEDY OF THE GENTLE CRAFT

DRAMATIS PERSONAE

KING HENRY V

THE EARL OF CORNWALL

SIR HUGH LACY, EARL OF LINCOLN

ROWLAND LACY,
  for a time disguised as } his nephews
  HANS
ASKEW

SIR ROGER OATELEY, LORD MAYOR OF LONDON

HAMMON }
WARNER } citizens of London
SCOTT }

SIMON EYRE, a shoemaker

ROGER }
FIRK } EYRE's journeymen
RALPH }

LOVELL

DODGER, a servant to the EARL OF LINCOLN

A DUTCH SKIPPER

ROSE, daughter to SIR ROGER

SYBIL, her maid

MARGERY, wife to SIMON EYRE

JANE, wife to RALPH

Courtiers, Attendants, Officers, Soldiers, Hunters, Shoemakers, Apprentices, Boys, and Servants

THE SCENE—*London and Old Ford*

THE PROLOGUE

As it was pronounced before the Queen's Majesty

As wretches in a storm, expecting day,
With trembling hands and eyes cast up to heaven,
Make prayers the anchor of their conquered hopes,
So we, dear Goddess, wonder of all eyes,
Your meanest vassals, through mistrust and fear   5
To sink into the bottom of disgrace
By our imperfect pastimes, prostrate thus
On bended knees, our sails of hope do strike,
Dreading the bitter storms of your dislike.

Since then, unhappy men, our hap is such   10
That to ourselves ourselves no help can bring,
But needs must perish, if your saintlike ears,
Locking the temple where all mercy sits,
Refuse the tribute of our begging tongues,
Oh, grant, bright mirror of true chastity,   15
From those life-breathing stars, your sunlike eyes,
One gracious smile: for your celestial breath
Must send us life or sentence us to death.

ACT I[1]

Enter the LORD MAYOR *and the* EARL OF LINCOLN

LINC. My Lord Mayor, you have sundry times
Feasted myself and many courtiers more.
Seldom or never can we be so kind
To make requital of your courtesy.
But leaving this, I hear my cousin[2] Lacy   5
Is much affected to[3] your daughter Rose.

L. MAYOR. True, my good Lord, and she loves him so
    well
That I mislike her boldness in the chase.

LINC. Why, my Lord Mayor, think you it then a shame,
To join a Lacy with an Oateley's name?   10

L. MAYOR. Too mean is my poor girl for his high birth;
Poor citizens must not with courtiers wed,
Who will in silks and gay apparel spend
More in one year than I am worth, by far.
Therefore your Honor need not doubt[4] my girl.   15

LINC. Take heed, my Lord, advise you what you do!
A verier unthrift lives not in the world
Than is my cousin; for I'll tell you what:
'T is now almost a year since he requested
To travel countries for experience.   20
I furnished him with coin, bills of exchange,
Letters of credit, men to wait on him,
Solicited my friends in Italy
Well to respect[5] him. But, to see the end,
Scant had he journeyed through half Germany,   25
But all his coin was spent, his men cast off,
His bills embezzled,[6] and my jolly coz,[7]
Ashamed to show his bankrupt presence here,
Became a shoemaker in Wittenberg—
A goodly science for a gentleman   30
Of such descent! Now judge the rest by this:
Suppose your daughter have a thousand pound,
He did consume me more in one half-year;
And, make him heir to all the wealth you have,
One twelvemonth's rioting will waste it all.   35
Then seek, my Lord, some honest citizen
To wed your daughter to.

L. MAYOR.   I thank your Lordship.—
(*Aside*) Well, fox, I understand your subtlety.—
As for your nephew, let your Lordship's eye
But watch his actions, and you need not fear,   40
For I have sent my daughter far enough.
And yet your cousin Rowland might do well,
Now he hath learned an occupation.—
(*Aside*) And yet I scorn to call him son-in-law.

LINC. Ay, but I have a better trade for him.   45
I thank his Grace,[8] he hath appointed him
Chief colonel of all those companies
Must'red in London and the shires about,
To serve his Highness in those wars of France.
See where he comes!

Enter LOVELL, LACY, *and* ASKEW

                Lovell, what news with you?   50

LOVELL. My Lord of Lincoln, 't is his Highness' will
That presently[9] your cousin ship for France
With all his powers;[10] he would not for a million
But they should land at Dieppe within four days.

LINC. Go certify his Grace it shall be done.   55

[*Exit* LOVELL

Now, Cousin Lacy, in what forwardness
Are all your companies?

LACY.   All well prepared.
The men of Hertfordshire lie at Mile End;
Suffolk and Essex train in Tothill Fields;
The Londoners and those of Middlesex,   60
All gallantly prepared in Finsbury,
With frolic spirits long for their parting hour.

L. MAYOR. They have their imprest,[11] coats, and
    furniture;[12]
And, if it please your cousin Lacy come
To the Guildhall, he shall receive his pay;   65
And twenty pounds besides my brethren[13]
Will freely give him, to approve[14] our loves
We bear unto my Lord, your uncle here.

LACY. I thank your Honor.

LINC.   Thanks, my good Lord Mayor.

L. MAYOR. At the Guildhall we will expect[15] your
    coming.   [*Exit*   70

LINC. To approve your loves to me? No, subtlety!
Nephew, that twenty pound he doth bestow
For joy to rid you from his daughter Rose.
But, cousins both, now here are none but friends,
I would not have you cast an amorous eye   75
Upon so mean a project as the love
Of a gay, wanton, painted citizen.
I know this churl even in the height of scorn
Doth hate the mixture of his blood with thine.
I pray thee, do thou so! Remember, coz,   80
What honorable fortunes wait on thee.

---

[1] A street in London.
[2] Nephew. Used of anyone collaterally related, except a brother
or sister.   [3] Fond of.   [4] Be apprehensive concerning.
[5] Regard.   [6] Squandered.   [7] Cousin, nephew.

[8] The King.   [9] At once.   [10] Troops.
[11] Advance pay.   [12] Equipment.   [13] Trisyllabic.
[14] Attest.   [15] Await.

Increase the King's love, which so brightly shines,
And gilds thy hopes. I have no heir but thee—
And yet not thee, if with a wayward spirit
Thou start from the true bias[16] of my love.   85

LACY. My Lord, I will for honor, not desire
Of land or livings, or to be your heir,
So guide my actions in pursuit of France
As shall add glory to the Lacys' name.

LINC. Coz, for those words here's thirty Portuguese,[17]
And, nephew Askew, there's a few for you.   91
Fair Honor, in her loftiest eminence,
Stays in France for you, till you fetch her thence.
Then, nephews, clap swift wings on your designs.
Begone, begone! make haste to the Guildhall;   95
There presently I'll meet you. Do not stay!
Where honor beckons shame attends delay.   [Exit

ASKEW. How gladly would your uncle have you gone!

LACY. True, coz, but I'll o'erreach his policies.
I have some serious business for three days,   100
Which nothing but my presence can dispatch.
You, therefore, cousin, with the companies,
Shall haste to Dover; there I'll meet with you.
Or, if I stay past my prefixèd time,
Away for France; we'll meet in Normandy.   105
The twenty pounds my Lord Mayor gives to me
You shall receive, and these ten Portuguese,
Part of mine uncle's thirty. Gentle coz,
Have care to our great charge; I know your wisdom
Hath tried itself in higher consequence.   110

ASKEW. Coz, all myself am yours; yet have this care,
To lodge in London with all secrecy.
Our uncle Lincoln hath, besides his own,
Many a jealous eye, that in your face
Stares only to watch means for your disgrace.   115

LACY. Stay, cousin, who be these?

Enter SIMON EYRE, *his wife* MARGERY, HODGE, FIRK,
JANE, *and* RALPH[18] *with a piece*[19]

EYRE. Leave whining, leave whining! Away with this
whimp'ring, this puling, these blubb'ring tears, and these
wet eyes! I'll get thy husband discharged, I warrant thee,
sweet Jane; go to!   120

HODGE. Master, here be the captains.

EYRE. Peace, Hodge; husht, ye knave, husht!

FIRK. Here be the cavaliers and the colonels, master.

EYRE. Peace, Firk; peace, my fine Firk! Stand by with
your pishery-pashery,[20] away! I am a man of the   [125
best presence; I'll speak to them, an they were popes.—
Gentlemen, captains, colonels, commanders! Brave men,

brave leaders, may it please you to give me audience. I am
Simon Eyre, the mad shoemaker of Tower Street; this
wench with the mealy mouth[21] that will never tire   [130
is my wife, I can tell you; here's Hodge, my man and my
foreman; here's Firk, my fine firking[22] journeyman, and
this is blubbered Jane. All we come to be suitors for this
honest Ralph. Keep him at home, and as I am a true shoemaker and a gentleman of the gentle craft, buy   [135
spurs yourself, and I'll find ye boots these seven years.

MARG. Seven years, husband?

EYRE. Peace, midriff,[23] peace! I know what I do. Peace!

FIRK. Truly, master cormorant,[24] you shall do God
good service to let Ralph and his wife stay together.   [140
She's a young new-married woman; if you take her husband away from her a-night, you undo[25] her; she may
beg in the daytime; for he's as good a workman at a prick
and an awl as any is in our trade.

JANE. Oh, let him stay, else I shall be undone.   145

FIRK. Ay, truly, she shall be laid at one side like a pair
of old shoes else, and be occupied[26] for no use.

LACY. Truly, my friends, it lies not in my power;
The Londoners are pressed,[27] paid, and set forth
By the Lord Mayor; I cannot change a man.   150

HODGE. Why, then you were as good be a corporal as a
colonel, if you cannot discharge one good fellow; and I
tell you true, I think you do more than you can answer, to
press a man within a year and a day of his marriage.[28]

EYRE. Well said, melancholy Hodge! gramercy,[29]   [155
my fine foreman!

MARG. Truly, gentlemen, it were ill done for such as
you, to stand so stiffly against a poor young wife, considering her case, she is new married; but let that pass. I pray,
deal not roughly with her; her husband is a young   [160
man, and but newly ent'red;[30] but let that pass.

EYRE. Away with your pishery-pashery, your pols and
your edipols![31] Peace, midriff; silence, Cicely Bum-
trinket![32] Let your head[33] speak.

FIRK. Yea, and the horns[34] too, master.   165

EYRE. Too soon, my fine Firk, too soon! Peace, scoundrels!—See you this man? Captains, you will not release
him? Well, let him go; he's a proper shot; let him vanish!

---

21 I.e., Margery is soft-spoken, given to mincing matters.
22 Frisking.
23 Diaphragm; probably a slighting allusion to Margery's cor-
pulence.   24 For colonel, often spelled *coronel*.
25 Ruin.   26 With a play on an indecent meaning.
27 Into the army.   28 See Deuteronomy 24:5.
29 Thanks.
30 Recently entered upon his profession. The chief comic effect of
Margery's speech resides in her unintentional double-entendres.
31 Both words = asseverations, from Latin *pol*, a contraction of
Pollux, and *edepol* = by Pollux.
32 Probably only an epithet for Margery; cf. II, iii, 38, where it
is applied to one of her maids.   33 Eyre.
34 The familiar jocose allusion to the constant imminence of
cuckoldom.

---

16 Propensity.   17 Gold coins worth about $20 each.
18 Old eds. *Rafe* or *Raph*, throughout.   19 Musket.
20 Trifling talk.

Peace, Jane, dry up thy tears; they'll make his powder
dankish. Take him, brave men; Hector of Troy   [170
was an hackney to him, Hercules and Termagant[35] scoundrels, Prince Arthur's Round Table—by the Lord of Ludgate—ne'er fed such a tall,[36] such a dapper swordman; by
the life of Pharaoh, a brave resolute swordman! Peace,
Jane! I say, no more, mad knaves!   175

FIRK. See, see, Hodge, how my master raves in commendation of Ralph!

HODGE. Ralph, th'art a gull,[37] by this hand, an[38] thou
goest.

ASKEW. I am glad, good Master Eyre, it is my hap   180
To meet so resolute a soldier.
Trust me, for your report and love to him,
A common slight regard shall not respect[39] him.

LACY. Is thy name Ralph?

RALPH.   Yes, sir.

LACY.   Give me thy hand;
Thou shalt not want, as I am a gentleman.   185
Woman, be patient; God, no doubt, will send
Thy husband safe again; but he must go:
His country's quarrel says it shall be so.

HODGE. Th'art a gull, by my stirrup,[40] if thou dost not
go. I will not have thee strike thy gimlet into these   [190
weak vessels; prick thine enemies, Ralph.

Enter DODGER

DODGER. My Lord, your uncle on the Tower Hill
Stays with the Lord Mayor and the aldermen,
And doth request you, with all speed you may,
To hasten thither.

ASKEW.   Cousin, let's go.   195

LACY. Dodger, run you before; tell them we come.—
                                    [*Exit* DODGER
(*Aside to* ASKEW) This Dodger is mine uncle's parasite,
The arrant'st varlet that e'er breathed on earth.
He sets more discord in a noble house
By one day's broaching of his pickthank tales,[41]   200
Than can be salved[42] again in twenty years.
And he, I fear, shall go with us to France,
To pry into our actions.

ASKEW.   Therefore, coz,
It shall behove you to be circumspect.

LACY. Fear not, good cousin.—Ralph, hie to your
    colors.   [*Exeunt* LACY *and* ASKEW   205

RALPH. I must, because there's no remedy.—
But, gentle master and my loving dame,

As you have always been a friend to me,
So in mine absence think upon my wife.

JANE. Alas, my Ralph.

MARG.   She cannot speak for weeping.   210

EYRE. Peace, you cracked groats,[43] you mustard tokens![44]
disquiet not the brave soldier!—Go thy ways, Ralph!

JANE. Ay, ay, you bid him go; what shall I do
When he is gone?

FIRK. Why, be doing with me or my fellow   [215
Hodge; be not idle.

EYRE. Let me see thy hand, Jane. This fine hand, this
white hand, these pretty fingers must spin, must card, must
work; work, you bombast cotton-candle[45] quean;[46] work
for your living, with a pox to you!—Hold thee,   [220
Ralph, here's five sixpences for thee. Fight for the honor
of the gentle craft, for the gentlemen shoemakers, the
courageous cordwainers, the flower of St. Martin's,[47] the
mad knaves of Bedlam, Fleet Street, Tower Street, and
Whitechapel! Crack me the crowns of the French   [225
knaves, a pox on them, crack them! Fight, by the Lord of
Ludgate; fight, my fine boy!

FIRK. Here, Ralph, here's three twopences: two carry
into France; the third shall wash our souls at parting, for
sorrow is dry. For my sake, firk[48] the *Basa-mon-*   [230
cues.[49]

HODGE. Ralph, I am heavy[50] at parting; but here's a
shilling for thee. God send[51] thee to cram thy slops[52] with
French crowns, and thy enemies' bellies with bullets.

RALPH. I thank you, master, and I thank you all.—   [235
Now, gentle wife, my loving lovely Jane,
Rich men, at parting, give their wives rich gifts,
Jewels and rings, to grace their lily hands.
Thou know'st our trade makes rings for women's heels:
Here take this pair of shoes, cut out by Hodge,   240
Stitched by my fellow Firk, seamed by myself,
Made up and pinked[53] with letters for thy name.
Wear them, my dear Jane, for thy husband's sake,
And every morning when thou pull'st them on,
Remember me, and pray for my return.   245
Make much of them; for I have made them so
That I can know them from a thousand mo.

Sound drum. Enter LORD MAYOR, EARL OF LINCOLN,
LACY, ASKEW, DODGER, *and* Soldiers. *They pass over
the stage;* RALPH *falls in amongst them;* FIRK *and the
rest cry "Farewell," etc., and so exeunt*

[43] I.e., worthless ones. A sound groat was worth only about
    fourpence.
[44] I.e., worthless ones; originally, a token given to a purchaser of
    mustard, entitling him to a small repayment when a certain
    number had been accumulated.
[45] Candle with a cotton wick; *bombast* = (1) cotton; (2) padded,
    perhaps with an allusion to Jane's plumpness.   [46] Hussy.
[47] The parish of St. Martin's Le Grand, a center of the craft.
[48] Trounce.   [49] The kiss-my-tails.   [50] Sad.   [51] Grant.
[52] Breeches.   [53] Decorated (by piercing them with small holes).

---

[35] A blustering character in the morality plays and interludes; he
    was supposed to be a Mohammedan deity.   [36] Valiant.
[37] Fool, ass.   [38] If.
[39] He shall not be held in slight regard.
[40] The shoemaker's strap, by which he keeps his last on his knee.
[41] Sycophantic tattling.   [42] Cured.

ACT II

SCENE I[1]

Enter ROSE, alone, making a garland

ROSE. Here sit thou down upon this flow'ry bank
And make a garland for thy Lacy's head.
These pinks, these roses, and these violets,
These blushing gilliflowers, these marigolds,
The fair embroidery of his coronet,   5
Carry not half such beauty in their cheeks
As the sweet count'nance of my Lacy doth.
O my most únkind father! O my stars,
Why low'red you so at my nativity,
To make me love, yet live robbed of my love?   10
Here as a thief am I imprisonèd
For my dear Lacy's sake within those walls,
Which by my father's cost were builded up
For better purposes. Here must I languish
For him that doth as much lament, I know,   15
Mine absence, as for him I pine in woe.

Enter SYBIL

SYBIL. Good morrow, young mistress. I am sure you
make that garland for me, against I shall be Lady of the
Harvest.
ROSE. Sybil, what news at London?   20
SYBIL. None but good; my Lord Mayor, your father, and
Master Philpot, your uncle, and Master Scott, your cousin,
and Mistress Frigbottom by Doctors' Commons,[2] do all,
by my troth, send you most hearty commendations.[3]
ROSE. Did Lacy send kind greetings to his love?   25
SYBIL. Oh, yes, out of cry,[4] by my troth! I scant knew
him; here 'a wore a scarf, and here a scarf, here a bunch of
feathers, and here precious stones and jewels, and a pair of
garters—oh, monstrous! like one of our yellow silk curtains
at home here in Old Ford House here, in Master   [30
Bellymount's chamber. I stood at our door in Cornhill,
looked at him, he at me indeed, spake to him, but he not
to me, not a word; marry, gup,[5] thought I, with a wanion![6]
He passed by me as proud—Marry, foh! are you grown
humorous?[7] thought I; and so shut the door, and in   [35
I came.
ROSE. Oh, Sybil, how dost thou my Lacy wrong!
My Rowland is as gentle as a lamb;
No dove was ever half so mild as he.

SYBIL. Mild? yea, as a bushel of stamped crabs.[8]   [40
He looked upon me as sour as verjuice.[9] Go thy ways,
thought I; thou mayst be much in my gaskins,[10] but
nothing in my netherstocks.[11] This is your fault, mistress,
to love him that loves not you. He thinks scorn to do as
he's done to; but if I were as you, I'd cry, "Go by,   [45
Jeronimo, go by!"[12]
I'd set mine old debts against my new driblets,[13]
And the hare's foot against the goose giblets;
For if ever I sigh, when sleep I should take,
Pray God I may lose my maidenhead when I wake.   50
ROSE. Will my love leave me then, and go to France?
SYBIL. I know not that, but I am sure I see him stalk
before the soldiers. By my troth, he is a proper[14] man;
but he is proper that proper doth. Let him go snick up,[15]
young mistress.   55
ROSE. Get thee to London, and learn perfectly
Whether my Lacy go to France, or no.
Do this, and I will give thee for thy pains
My cambric apron and my Romish gloves,
My purple stockings, and a stomacher.   60
Say, wilt thou do this, Sybil, for my sake?
SYBIL. Will I, quoth 'a? At whose suit? By my troth,
yes, I'll go. A cambric apron, gloves, a pair of purple
stockings, and a stomacher! I'll sweat in purple, mistress,
for you; I'll take anything that comes, a' God's   [65
name. Oh, rich! a cambric apron! Faith, then have at[16]
up-tails-all.[17] I'll go jiggy-joggy to London, and be here
in a trice, young mistress.   [*Exit*
ROSE. Do so, good Sybil.—Meantime wretched I
Will sit and sigh for his lost company.   [*Exit* 70

SCENE II[18]

Enter ROWLAND LACY, like a Dutch shoemaker

LACY. How many shapes have gods and kings devised,
Thereby to compass their desirèd loves!
It is no shame for Rowland Lacy, then,
To clothe his cunning with the gentle craft,

---

8 Crushed crab apples.
9 The sour juice of green fruits.   10 Breeches.
11 Stockings. I.e., we are acquainted, but we are not intimate
friends.
12 From Thomas Kyd's *The Spanish Tragedy*, IV, v, 30. This play
of *c.* 1586 was now a byword, though it was still popular with
the unsophisticated.
13 Petty debts.—The next line is a proverbial saying; Sybil's application is "Off with the old love, on with the new."
14 Handsome.   15 Go hang.   16 Now for.
17 A card game; also a tune.   18 London. Tower Street.

---

1 The garden of Oateley's house at Old Ford (northeast of the City).
2 The buildings of the College of Doctors of Civil Law, south of
St. Paul's.   3 Regards.   4 Beyond measure.
5 Go up. Cf. "come up."   6 With a vengeance.
7 Capricious.

That, thus disguised, I may unknown possess 5
The only happy presence of my Rose.
For her have I forsook my charge in France,
Incurred the King's displeasure, and stirred up
Rough hatred in mine uncle Lincoln's breast.
O love, how powerful art thou, that canst change 10
High birth to baseness, and a noble mind
To the mean semblance of a shoemaker!
But thus it must be; for her cruel father,
Hating the single union of our souls,
Has secretly conveyed my Rose from London, 15
To bar me of her presence; but I trust
Fortune and this disguise will furder[19] me
Once more to view her beauty, gain her sight.
Here in Tower Street with Eyre the shoemaker
Mean I awhile to work; I know the trade: 20
I learnt it when I was in Wittenberg.
Then cheer thy hoping spirits, be not dismayed;
Thou canst not want: do Fortune what she can,
The gentle craft is living for a man. *[Exit*

SCENE III[20]

Enter EYRE, *making himself ready*

EYRE. Where be these boys, these girls, these drabs, these
scoundrels? They wallow in the fat brewis[21] of my bounty,
and lick up the crumbs of my table, yet will not rise to
see my walks cleansed.—Come out, you powder-beef[22]
queans! What, Nan! what, Madge Mumble-crust! [5
Come out, you fat-midriff, swag-belly whores, and sweep
me these kennels, that the noisome stench offend not the
nose of my neighbors.—What, Firk, I say! what, Hodge!
Open my shop windows! What, Firk, I say!

Enter FIRK

FIRK. Oh, master, is't you that speak bandog[23] and [10
Bedlam this morning? I was in a dream, and mused what
madman was got into the street so early. Have you drunk
this morning that your throat is so clear?

EYRE. Ah, well said, Firk; well said, Firk. To work, my
fine knave, to work! Wash thy face, and thou't be [15
more blest.

FIRK. Let them wash my face that will eat it. Good
master, send for a souse-wife,[24] if you'll have my face
cleaner.

---

[19] Further.   [20] The same. Before Eyre's house.
[21] Broth.   [22] Corned beef.
[23] A chained dog; i.e., speak so ferociously.
[24] Pickled-pork woman.

Enter HODGE

EYRE. Away, sloven! avaunt, scoundrel!—Good [20
morrow, Hodge; good morrow, my fine foreman.

HODGE. Oh, master, good morrow; y' are an early stirrer.
Here's a fair morning.—Good morrow, Firk. I could have
slept this hour. Here's a brave day towards.[25]

EYRE. Oh, haste to work, my fine foreman, haste [25
to work!

FIRK. Master, I am dry as dust to hear my fellow Roger
talk of fair weather; let us pray for good leather, and let
clowns[26] and plowboys and those that work in the fields
pray for brave days. We work in a dry shop; what [30
care I if it rain?

Enter EYRE's *wife* MARGERY

EYRE. How now, Dame Margery, can you see to rise?
Trip and go; call up the drabs, your maids.

MARG. See to rise? I hope 't is time enough; 't is early
enough for any woman to be seen abroad. I marvel [35
how many wives in Tower Street are up so soon. Gods
me, 't is not noon—here 's a yawling![27]

EYRE. Peace, Margery, peace! Where's Cicely Bum-
trinket, your maid? She has a privy fault: she farts in her
sleep. Call the quean up; if my men want shoe- [40
thread, I'll swinge[28] her in a stirrup.

FIRK. Yet, that's but a dry beating; here's still a sign of
drought.

Enter LACY *disguised, singing*

LACY. *Der was een bore van Gelderland,*
Frolick sie byen; 45
He was als dronck he cold nyet stand,
Upsolce sie byen.
Tap eens de canneken,
Drincke, schone mannekin.[29]

FIRK. Master, for my life, yonder's a brother of [50
the gentle craft; if he bear not St. Hugh's bones,[30] I'll
forfeit my bones; he's some uplandish[31] workman. Hire
him, good master, that I may learn some gibble-gabble; 't
will make us work the faster.

---

[25] A fine day impending.   [26] Rustics.   [27] Bawling.   [28] Beat.
[29] There was a boor from Gelderland
    (Merry they be)
He was so drunk he could not stand
    (Dead drunk they be).
Draw once the cannikin;
Drink, pretty mannikin.
[30] According to Deloney, St. Hugh was befriended by journeymen shoemakers, "in requital of which kindness he called them
Gentlemen of the Gentle Craft" and bequeathed them his bones.
After his martyrdom they secretly secured his skeleton, which
they made into the tools of their trade, "which ever since have
been called S. Hugh's bones."   [31] Outlandish.

EYRE. Peace, Firk! a hard world! Let him pass, [55 let him vanish; we have journeymen enow. Peace, my fine Firk!

MARG. Nay, nay, y' are best follow your man's counsel; you shall see what will come on 't. We have not men enow, but we must entertain every butter-box;[32] [60 but let that pass.

HODGE. Dame, 'fore God, if my master follow your counsel, he'll consume little beef. He shall be glad of men an he can catch them.

FIRK. Ay, that he shall. 65

HODGE. 'Fore God, a proper man, and I warrant, a fine workman.—Master, farewell; dame, adieu; if such a man as he cannot find work, Hodge is not for you. [Offer to go

EYRE. Stay, my fine Hodge.

FIRK. Faith, an your foreman go, dame, you must [70 take a journey to seek a new journeyman; if Roger remove, Firk follows. If St. Hugh's bones shall not be set a-work, I may prick mine awl in the walls, and go play. Fare ye well, master; God buy, dame.

EYRE. Tarry, my fine Hodge, my brisk foreman! [75 Stay, Firk!—(To MARGERY) Peace, pudding-broth!—By the Lord of Ludgate, I love my men as my life. Peace, you gallimaufry![33] Hodge, if he want work, I'll hire him. One of you to him; stay—he comes to us.

LACY. Goeden dach, meester, ende u vro oak.[34] 80

FIRK. Nails,[35] if I should speak after him without drinking, I should choke.—And you, friend Oak, are you of the gentle craft?

LACY. Yaw, yaw, ik bin den skomawker.

FIRK. Den skomaker, quoth 'a! And hark you, [85 skomaker, have you all your tools, a good rubbing-pin, a good stopper, a good dresser, your four sorts of awls, and your two balls of wax, your paring knife, your hand and thumb leathers, and good St. Hugh's bones to smooth up your work? 90

LACY. Yaw, yaw; be niet vorveard.[36] Ik hab all de dingen voour mack skoes groot and cleane.[37]

FIRK. Ha, ha! Good master, hire him; he'll make me laugh so that I shall work more in mirth than I can in earnest. 95

EYRE. Hear ye, friend, have ye any skill in the mystery[38] of cordwainers?

LACY. Ik weet niet wat yow seg; ich verstaw you niet.[39]

FIRK. Why, thus, man! (imitating by gesture a shoemaker at work)—Ich verste u niet, quoth 'a. 100

LACY. Yaw, yaw, yaw; ick can dat wel doen.

FIRK. Yaw, yaw! He speaks yawing like a jackdaw that gapes to be fed with cheesecurds. Oh, he'll give a villainous pull at a can of double-beer; but Hodge and I have the vantage: we must drink first, because we are the [105 eldest journeymen.

EYRE. What is thy name?

LACY. Hans—Hans Meulter.

EYRE. Give me thy hand; th'art welcome.—Hodge, entertain him; Firk, bid him welcome; come, Hans. [110 Run, wife, bid your maids, your trullibubs,[40] make ready my fine men's breakfasts. To him, Hodge!

HODGE. Hans, th'art welcome; use thyself friendly, for we are good fellows; if not, thou shalt be fought with, wert thou bigger than a giant. 115

FIRK. Yea, and drunk with, wert thou Gargantua.[41] My master keeps no cowards, I tell thee.—Ho, boy, bring him an heel-block;[42] here's a new journeyman.

Enter a Boy

LACY. O, ich wersto you; ich moet een halve dossen cans betaelen. Here, boy, nempt dis skilling; tap eens freelicke.[43] [120
[Exit Boy

EYRE. Quick, snipper-snapper, away! Firk, scour thy throat; thou shalt wash it with Castilian liquor.

Re-enter Boy

Come, my last of the fives,[44] give me a can. Have to thee, Hans; here, Hodge; here, Firk; drink, you mad Greeks, and work like true Trojans, and pray for Simon [125 Eyre, the shoemaker.—Here, Hans, and th'art welcome.

FIRK. Lo, dame, you would have lost a good fellow that will teach us to laugh. This beer came hopping in well.

MARG. Simon, it is almost seven.

EYRE. Is't so, Dame Clapper-dudgeon?[45] is't seven [130 a'clock, and my men's breakfast not ready? Trip and go, you soused conger,[46] away! Come, you mad Hyperboreans;[47] follow me, Hodge; follow me, Hans; come after, my fine Firk; to work, to work awhile, and then to breakfast! [Exit 135

FIRK. Soft! Yaw, yaw, good Hans, though my master have no more wit but to call you afore me, I am not so foolish to go behind you, I being the elder journeyman.
[Exeunt

---

[40] Trillibubs, the (edible) entrails of animals; i.e., trifles.
[41] Rabelais's gigantic hero.
[42] Used in fastening a lift to a shoe.
[43] Oh, I understand you; I must pay for half a dozen cans. Here, boy, take this shilling; draw once freely.
[44] Alluding to the diminutive stature of the boy, since number five is a small last.
[45] Because her tongue is as noisy as the wooden cover of a beggar's clap-dish.   [46] Pickled conger-eel.
[47] A fabulous people, in Greek mythology, who lived far to the north in a state of perpetual happiness.

---

[32] Dutchman.   [33] Hash, hodge-podge.
[34] Good-day, master, and you, goodwife, also.
[35] By God's nails.   [36] Don't be afraid.
[37] All the things for making shoes large and small.   [38] Craft.
[39] I don't know what you say; I don't understand you.

SCENE IV[48]

Hollowing[49] within. Enter WARNER *and* HAMMON, *like hunters*

HAM. Cousin, beat every brake; the game's not far;
This way with wingèd feet he fled from death,
Whilst the pursuing hounds, scenting his steps,
Find out his highway to destructiön.
Besides, the miller's boy told me even now   5
He saw him take soil,[50] and he halloaed him,
Affirming him [to have been] so embossed[51]
That long he could not hold.

WARN.   If it be so,
'T is best we trace these meadows by Old Ford.

A noise of hunters within. Enter a Boy

HAM. How now, boy? Where's the deer? speak!
    saw'st thou him?   10

BOY. Oh, yea; I saw him leap through a hedge, and then
over a ditch, then at my Lord Mayor's pale; over he skipped
me,[52] and in he went me; and "holla" the hunters cried,
and "There, boy! there, boy!" But there he is, a' mine
honesty.   15

HAM. Boy, God-a-mercy.[53] Cousin, let's away;
I hope we shall find better sport today.   [*Exeunt*

SCENE V[54]

Hunting within. Enter ROSE *and* SYBIL

ROSE. Why, Sybil, wilt thou prove a forester?

SYBIL. Upon some,[55] no. Forester? Go by! no, faith,
mistress. The deer came running into the barn through the
orchard and over the pale; I wot well I looked as pale as a
new cheese to see him. But whip, says Goodman   [5
Pinclose, up with his flail, and our Nick with a prong,
and down he fell, and they upon him, and I upon them.
By my troth, we had such sport; and in the end, we ended
him; his throat we cut, flayed him, unhorned him, and my
Lord Mayor shall eat of him anon, when he comes.   10
          [*Horns sound within*

ROSE. Hark, hark, the hunters come; y' are best take heed:
They'll have a saying to you for this deed.

---

[48] A field near Old Ford.
[49] Hallooing.—*Like* = costumed as.
[50] Take refuge in a stretch of water.   [51] Exhausted.
[52] The "ethical" dative, now virtually meaningless.
[53] Thanks.
[54] Not precisely located; perhaps the garden at Old Ford.
[55] Cf. "upon my honor."

Enter HAMMON, WARNER, Huntsmen, *and* Boy

HAM. God save you, fair ladies.

SYBIL.   Ladies! Oh, gross![56]

WARN. Came not a buck this way?

ROSE.   No, but[57] two does.

HAM. And which way went they? Faith, we'll hunt at
    those.   15

SYBIL. At those? Upon some, no! When, can you tell?

WARN. Upon some, ay.

SYBIL.   Good Lord!

WARN.   Wounds![58] then farewell!

HAM. Boy, which way went he?

BOY.   This way, sir, he ran.

HAM. This way he ran indeed, fair Mistress Rose;
Our game was lately in your orchard seen.   20

WARN. Can you advise which way he took his flight?

SYBIL. Follow your nose; his horns will guide you right.

WARN. Th'art a mad wench.

SYBIL.   Oh, rich!

ROSE.   Trust me, not I.
It is not like that the wild forest deer
Would come so near to places of resort.   25
You are deceived; he fled some other way.

WARN. Which way, my sugar-candy, can you show?

SYBIL. Come up, good honeysops! upon some, no!

ROSE. Why do you stay, and not pursue your game?

SYBIL. I'll hold my life, their hunting nags be lame.   30

HAM. A deer more dear is found within this place.

ROSE. But not the deer, sir, which you had in chase.

HAM. I chased the deer, but this dear chaseth me.

ROSE. The strangest hunting that ever I see.
But where's your park?   [*She offers[59] to go away*

HAM.   'T is here. Oh, stay!   35

ROSE. Impale[60] me, and then I will not stray.

WARN. They wrangle, wench; we are more kind than
    they.

SYBIL. What kind of hart is that dear heart you seek?

WARN. A hart,[61] dear heart.

SYBIL.   Who ever saw the like?

ROSE. To lose your heart, is't possible you can?   40

HAM. My heart is lost.

ROSE.   Alack, good gentleman!

HAM. This poor lost heart would I wish you might find.

ROSE. You, by such luck, might prove your hart a
    hind.[62]

HAM. Why Luck had horns, so have I heard some say.

ROSE. Now, God, an't be his will, send Luck into your
    way.   45

---

[56] How stupid.   [57] Merely.   [58] By God's wounds.
[59] Tries, starts.   [60] Fence in.
[61] Stag.   [62] Doe.

Enter LORD MAYOR *and* Servants

L. MAYOR. What, Master Hammon? Welcome to Old
    Ford!

SYBIL. Gods pittikins!⁶³ hands off, sir! Here's my Lord.

L. MAYOR. I hear you had ill luck, and lost your game.

HAM. 'T is true, my Lord.

L. MAYOR.   I am sorry for the same.
What gentleman is this?

HAM.   My brother-in-law.   50

L. MAYOR. Y' are welcome both; sith⁶⁴ Fortune offers
    you
Into my hands, you shall not part from hence,

Until you have refreshed your wearied limbs.
Go, Sybil, cover the board! You shall be guest
To no good cheer, but even a hunter's feast.   55

HAM. I thank your Lordship.—Cousin, on my life,
For our lost venison I shall find a wife.

L. MAYOR. In, gentlemen; I'll not be absent long.

                         [Exeunt all but MAYOR

This Hammon is a proper gentleman,
A citizen by birth, fairly allied.⁶⁵   60
How fit an husband were he for my girl!
Well, I will in, and do the best I can
To match my daughter to this gentleman.   *[Exit*

ACT III

SCENE I¹

Enter LACY *as* HANS, SKIPPER, HODGE, *and* FIRK

SKIP. *Ick sal yow wat seggen,² Hans; dis skip dat comen from
Candy³ is all wol,⁴ by Got's sacrament, van sugar, civet,
almonds, cambrick, end alle dingen, towsand towsand ding.
Nempt⁵ it, Hans, nempt it vor u meester. Daer be de bils van
laden. Your meester Simon Eyre sal hae good copen.⁶   [5
Wat seggen yow, Hans?*

FIRK. *Wat seggen de reggen de copen-slopen*—laugh, Hodge,
laugh!

HANS. *Mine liever⁷ broder Firk, bringt Meester Eyre to den
signe un Swannekin;⁸ daer sal yow finde dis skipper end*   [10
*me. Wat seggen yow, broder Firk? Doot⁹ it, Hodge.—Come,
skipper.*   *[Exeunt* HANS *and* SKIPPER

FIRK. Bring him, quod you? Here's no knavery, to bring
my master to buy a ship worth the lading of two or three
hundred thousand pounds. Alas, that's nothing; a   [15
trifle, a bauble, Hodge.

HODGE. The truth is, Firk, that the merchant owner of
the ship dares not show his head, and therefore this skipper
that deals for him, for the love he bears to Hans, offers my
master Eyre a bargain in the commodities. He shall   [20
have a reasonable day of payment; he may sell the wares
by that time, and be an huge gainer himself.

FIRK. Yea, but can my fellow Hans lend my master
twenty porpentines¹⁰ as an earnest penny?

HODGE. Portuguese, thou wouldst say; here they   [25
be, Firk; hark, they jingle in my pocket like St. Mary
Overy's¹¹ bells.

Enter EYRE *and his wife* MARGERY

FIRK. Mum! here comes my dame and my master. She'll
scold, on my life, for loitering this Monday; but all's one:¹²
let them all say what they can, Monday's our holiday.   [30

MARG. You sing, Sir Sauce, but I beshrew¹³ your heart:
I fear for this your singing we shall smart.

FIRK. Smart for me, dame; why, dame, why?

HODGE. Master, I hope you'll not suffer my dame to
take down your journeymen.   35

FIRK. If she take me down, I'll take her up; yea, and
take her down too, a buttonhole lower.

EYRE. Peace, Firk!—Not I, Hodge; by the life of Pharaoh,
by the Lord of Ludgate, by this beard, every hair whereof
I value at a king's ransom, she shall not meddle   [40
with you.—Peace, you bombast cotton-candle quean!
Away, queen of clubs!¹⁴ Quarrel not with me and my
men, with me and my fine Firk; I'll firk¹⁵ you, if you do.

MARG. Yea, yea, man, you may use me as you please;
but let that pass.   45

EYRE. Let it pass, let it vanish away! Peace! Am I not
Simon Eyre? Are not these my brave men, brave shoemakers, all gentlemen of the gentle craft? Prince am I none,
yet am I nobly born, as being the sole son of a shoemaker.¹⁶

---

⁶³ By God's pity.   ⁶⁴ Since.

¹ A room in Eyre's house.

² I'll tell you what.   ³ Candia, Crete.   ⁴ Full.

⁵ Take.   ⁶ A good bargain.   ⁷ Dear.

⁸ I.e., to the sign of the Swan, to the Swan Inn.   ⁹ Do.

¹⁰ Porcupines.

⁶⁵ Well connected.

¹¹ This church, also called St. Saviour's, later became the cathedral of the diocese of Southwark.

¹² It makes no difference.   ¹³ Curse. (A mild oath.)

¹⁴ I.e., of the prentices, clubs being their weapons.   ¹⁵ Beat.

¹⁶ An allusion to the vaunt of Crispianus that "a shoemaker's son
is a prince born"; his brother Crispin's son by the Princess
Ursula made good the boast.

Away, rubbish! vanish, melt! melt, like kitchen-stuff.[17] [50

MARG. Yea, yea, 't is well; I must be called rubbish, kitchen-stuff, for a sort[18] of knaves.

FIRK. Nay, dame, you shall not weep and wail in woe for me.—Master, I'll stay no longer; here's an inventory of my shop tools. Adieu, master; Hodge, farewell.   55

HODGE. Nay, stay, Firk; thou shalt not go alone.

MARG. I pray, let them go; there be mo maids than Mawkin, more men than Hodge, and more fools than Firk.

FIRK. Fools? Nails! if I tarry now, I would my guts might be turned to shoe-thread.   60

HODGE. And if I stay, I pray God I may be turned to a Turk, and set in Finsbury[19] for boys to shoot at.—Come, Firk.

EYRE. Stay, my fine knaves, you arms of my trade, you pillars of my profession. What, shall a tittle-tattle's [65 words make you forsake Simon Eyre?—Avaunt, kitchen-stuff! Rip,[20] you brown-bread[21] Tannikin;[22] out of my sight! Move me not! Have not I ta'en you from selling tripes in Eastcheap, and set you in my shop, and made you hail-fellow with Simon Eyre, the shoemaker? [70 And now do you deal thus with my journeymen? Look, you powder-beef quean, on the face of Hodge: here's a face for a lord.

FIRK. And here's a face for any lady in Christendom.

EYRE. Rip, you chitterling,[23] avaunt![24] Boy!   75

Enter Boy

Bid the tapster of the Boar's Head fill me a dozen cans of beer for my journeymen.

FIRK. A dozen cans? O, brave! Hodge, now I'll stay.

EYRE (*aside to the* Boy). An the knave fills any more than two, he pays for them.   [*Exit* Boy   80
—A dozen cans of beer for my journeymen.

Re-enter Boy

Here, you mad Mesopotamians,[25] wash your livers with this liquor. Where be the odd ten?—No more, Madge, no more.—Well said.[26] Drink and to work!—What work dost thou, Hodge? What work?   [*Exit* Boy   85

HODGE. I am a making a pair of shoes for my Lord Mayor's daughter, Mistress Rose.

FIRK. And I a pair of shoes for Sybil, my Lord's maid. I deal with her.

EYRE. Sybil? Fie, defile not thy fine workmanly [90 fingers with the feet of kitchen-stuff and basting-ladles. Ladies of the court, fine ladies, my lads, commit their feet to our appareling: put gross work to Hans. Yark[27] and seam, yark and seam!

FIRK. For yarking and seaming let me alone,[28] an [95 I come to 't.

HODGE. Well, master, all this is from the bias.[29] Do you remember the ship my fellow Hans told you of? The skipper and he are both drinking at the Swan. Here be the Portuguese to give earnest. If you go through [100 with it, you cannot choose but be a lord at least.

FIRK. Nay, dame, if my master prove not a lord, and you a lady, hang me.

MARG. Yea, like enough, if you may loiter and tipple thus.   105

FIRK. Tipple, dame? No, we have been bargaining with Skellum Skanderbag[30] Can-you-Dutch-spreaken for a ship of silk cypress, laden with sugar-candy.

EYRE. Peace, Firk! Silence, Tittle-tattle! Hodge, I'll go through with it. Here's a seal-ring, and I have sent [110 for a guarded[31] gown and a damask cassock.

Re-enter the Boy *with a velvet coat and an alderman's gown.* EYRE *puts them on*

See where it comes; look here, Maggy; help me, Firk; apparel me, Hodge; silk and satin, you mad Philistines,[32] silk and satin.

FIRK. Ha, ha, my master will be as proud as a dog [115 in a doublet, all in beaten[33] damask and velvet.

EYRE. Softly, Firk, for rearing of[34] the nap, and wearing threadbare my garments. How dost thou like me, Firk? How do I look, my fine Hodge?

HODGE. Why, now you look like yourself, mas- [120 ter. I warrant you, there's few in the city but will give you the wall,[35] and come upon you with[36] the Right Worshipful.

FIRK. Nails, my master looks like a threadbare cloak new turned and dressed. Lord, Lord, to see what good [125 raiment doth! Dame, dame, are you not enamored?

EYRE. How say'st thou, Maggy, am I not brisk? Am I not fine?

---

17 I.e., the greasy refuse of the kitchen.   18 Set.
19 A field to the north of the City, where archery was practiced.
20 Move on.   21 Homely, unrefined.   22 Dutchwoman.
23 Frill.   24 Begone.
25 Eyre employs this and other Middle East names because he likes their sound and exotic flavor.
26 Well done, good for you.

27 Twitch (the stitch tight).
28 Leave it to me.   29 Beside the point.
30 John Castriota, the Albanian patriot, called by the Turks Iskanderbey = Prince Alexander.—*Skellum* = rogue.
31 Ornamented.   32 Cf. note 25, above.
33 Wrought with metal trimmings.
34 Be careful . . . so as not to ruffle up.
35 I.e., show you deference.
36 Approach you with the title of.—Eyre is disguising himself as a magnate in order to induce the skipper to sell him the cargo. In Deloney much more is made of this trick.

MARG. Fine? By my troth, sweetheart, very fine! By my troth, I never liked thee so well in my life, sweet-   [130 heart; but let that pass. I warrant there be many women in the city have not such handsome husbands, but only for their apparel; but let that pass, too.

Re-enter LACY *as* HANS, *and* SKIPPER

HANS. *Godden day, mester. Dis be de skipper dat heb de skip van marchandice; de commodity ben good; nempt it,*   [135 *master, nempt it.*

EYRE. God-a-mercy, Hans. Welcome, skipper. Where lies this ship of merchandise?

SKIP. *De skip ben in rovere;*[37] *dor be van sugar, civet, almonds, cambricke, and a towsand, towsand tings. Gotz sacra-*   [140 *ment; nempt it, mester: yo sal heb good copen.*

FIRK. To him, master! O sweet master! O sweet wares! Prunes, almonds, sugar-candy, carrot-roots, turnips! O brave fatting meat! Let not a man buy a nutmeg but yourself.   145

EYRE. Peace, Firk! Come, skipper, I'll go aboard with you.—Hans, have you made him drink?

SKIP. *Yaw, yaw, ic heb veale gedrunck.*[38]

EYRE. Come, Hans, follow me.—Skipper, thou shalt have my countenance[39] in the city.   150

[*Exeunt* EYRE, HANS, *and* SKIPPER

FIRK. *Yaw heb veale gedrunck,* quoth 'a. They may well be called butter-boxes, when they drink fat veal and thick beer too. But come, dame, I hope you'll chide us no more.

MARG. No, faith, Firk; no, perdy,[40] Hodge. I do feel honor creep upon me, and, which is more, a certain   [155 rising in my flesh; but let that pass.

FIRK. Rising in your flesh do you feel, say you? Ay, you may be with child; but why should not my master feel a rising in his flesh, having a gown and a gold ring on? But you are such a shrew, you'll soon pull him down.   [160

MARG. Ha, ha! prithee, peace! Thou mak'st my Worship laugh; but let that pass. Come, I'll go in; Hodge, prithee, go before me; Firk, follow me.

FIRK. Firk doth follow: Hodge, pass out in state.

[*Exeunt*

SCENE II[41]

Enter EARL OF LINCOLN *and* DODGER

LINC. How now, good Dodger; what's the news in France?

DODGER. My Lord, upon the eighteen day of May
The French and English were prepared to fight;
Each side with eager fury gave the sign
Of a most hot encounter. Five long hours   5
Both armies fought together; at the length
The lot of victory fell on our sides.
Twelve thousand of the Frenchmen that day died,
Four thousand English, and no man of name[42]
But Captain Hyam and young Ardington,   10
Two gallant gentlemen; I knew them well.
LINC. But Dodger, prithee, tell me, in this fight
How did my cousin Lacy bear himself?
DODGER. My Lord, your cousin Lacy was not there.
LINC. Not there?
DODGER.   No, my good Lord.
LINC.   Sure, thou mistakest.   15
I saw him shipped, and a thousand eyes beside
Were witnesses of the farewells which he gave,
When I with weeping eyes bid him adieu.
Dodger, take heed.
DODGER.   My Lord, I am advised
That what I spake is true; to prove it so,   20
His cousin Askew, that supplied his place,
Sent me for him from France, that secretly
He might convey himself hither.[43]
LINC.   Is't even so?
Dares he so carelessly venture his life
Upon the indignation of a king?   25
Hath he despised my love, and spurned those favors
Which I with prodigal hand poured on his head?
He shall repent his rashness with his soul!
Since of my love he makes no estimate,
I'll make him wish he had not known my hate.   30
Thou hast no other news?
DODGER.   None else, my Lord.
LINC. None worse I know thou hast.—Procure the King
To crown his giddy brows with ample honors,
Send him chief colonel,[44] and all my hope
Thus to be dashed! But 't is in vain to grieve;   35
One evil cannot a worse relieve.
Upon my life, I have found out his plot:
That old dog, Love, that fawned upon him so,
Love to that puling girl, his fair-cheeked Rose,
The Lord Mayor's daughter, hath distracted him;   40
And in the fire of that love's lunacy
Hath he burnt up himself, consumed his credit,[45]
Lost the King's love, yea, and I fear, his life,
Only to get a wanton to his wife.
Dodger, it is so.
DODGER.   I fear so, my good Lord.   45

---

[37] River.
[38] Drunk much.   [39] Favor, support.
[40] *Par Dieu* (a mild oath).
[41] Unlocated; perhaps a room in the Earl's house.

[42] Reputation.   [43] I.e., thither.   [44] Trisyllabic.
[45] Reputation.

LINC. It is so—nay, sure it cannot be!
I am at my wits' end, Dodger!

DODGER.   Yea, my Lord.

LINC. Thou art acquainted with my nephew's haunts;
Spend this gold for thy pains: go seek him out.
Watch at my Lord Mayor's—there if he live,   50
Dodger, thou shalt be sure to meet with him.
Prithee, be diligent.—Lacy, thy name
Lived once in honor; now 't is dead in shame.—
Be circumspect.   [Exit

DODGER.   I warrant you, my Lord.   [Exit

SCENE III[46]

Enter LORD MAYOR *and* MASTER SCOTT

L. MAYOR. Good Master Scott, I have been bold with
        you
To be a witness to a wedding knot
Betwixt young Master Hammon and my daughter.
Oh, stand aside; see where the lovers come.

Enter HAMMON *and* ROSE

ROSE. Can it be possible you love me so?   5
No, no; within those eyeballs I espy
Apparent likelihoods of flattery.
Pray now, let go my hand.

HAM.   Sweet Mistress Rose,
Misconstrue not my words, nor misconceive
Of my affection, whose devoted soul   10
Swears that I love thee dearer than my heart.

ROSE. As dear as your own heart? I judge it right,
Men love their hearts best when th'are out of sight.

HAM. I love you, by this hand.

ROSE.   Yet hands off now!
If flesh be frail, how weak and frail's your vow!   15

HAM. Then by my life I swear.

ROSE.   Then do not brawl;
One quarrel loseth wife and life and all.
Is not your meaning thus?

HAM.   In faith, you jest.

ROSE. Love loves to sport; therefore leave love, y'are
        best.

L. MAYOR (*aside to* SCOTT). What? square[47] they, Master
        Scott?

SCOTT (*aside to* MAYOR).   Sir, never doubt,   20
Lovers are quickly in, and quickly out.

HAM. Sweet Rose, be not so strange[48] in fancying me.
Nay, never turn aside, shun not my sight;

---

[46] A room in the Lord Mayor's house in London.
[47] Quarrel.   [48] Offish.

I am not grown so fond,[49] to fond[50] my love
On any that shall quit[51] it with disdain;   25
If you will love me, so.[52] If not, farewell.

L. MAYOR (*advancing*). Why, how now, lovers, are you
        both agreed?

HAM. Yes, faith, my Lord.

L. MAYOR.   'T is well; give me your hand;
Give me yours, daughter.—How now, both pull back!
What means this, girl?

ROSE.   I mean to live a maid.   30

HAM (*aside*). But not to die one; pause, ere that be said.

L. MAYOR. Will you still cross me, still be obstinate?

HAM. Nay, chide her not, my Lord, for doing well;
If she can live an happy virgin's life,
'T is far more blessèd than to be a wife.   35

ROSE. Say, sir, I cannot; I have made a vow,
Whoever be my husband, 't is not you.

L. MAYOR. Your tongue is quick; but Master Hammon,
        know
I bade you welcome to another end.

HAM. What, would you have me pule and pine and
        pray,   40
With "lovely lady," "mistress of my heart,"
"Pardon your servant"? and the rimer play,
Railing on Cupid and his tyrant's-dart?
Or shall I undertake some martial spoil,[53]
Wearing your glove at tourney and at tilt,   45
And tell how many gallants I unhorsed?
Sweet, will this pleasure you?

ROSE.   Yea; when wilt begin?
What, love rimes, man? Fie on that deadly sin!

L. MAYOR. If you will have her, I'll make her agree.

HAM. Enforcèd love is worse than hate to me.—   50
(*Aside*) There is a wench keeps shop in the Old Change;[54]
To her will I (it is not wealth I seek—
I have enough) and will prefer her love
Before the world.—My good Lord Mayor, adieu;
Old love for me: I have no luck with new.   [Exit   55

L. MAYOR. Now, mammet,[55] you have well behaved
        yourself;
But you shall curse your coyness if I live.—
Who's within there? See you convey your mistress
Straight to th' Old Ford!—I'll keep you straight[56]
        enough.—
'Fore God, I would have sworn the puling girl   60
Would willingly accepted Hammon's love;
But banish him, my thoughts!—Go, minion,[57] in!—
                                                    [Exit ROSE

---

[49] Foolish.   [50] As to found, punning on *fond*.   [51] Requite.
[52] Well and good.   [53] Expedition.
[54] Old Exchange. The Royal Exchange, at Threadneedle Street
and Cornhill, was built in 1564–71 by Sir Thomas Gresham as
a meeting place for merchants.   [55] Maumet, puppet.
[56] Strictly confined.   [57] Mistress.

Now tell me, Master Scott, would you have thought
That Master Simon Eyre, the shoemaker,
Had been of wealth to buy such merchandise?   65
SCOTT. 'T was well, my Lord, your Honor and myself
Grew partners with him; for your bills of lading
Show that Eyre's gains in one commodity
Rise at the least to full three thousand pound,
Besides like gain in other merchandise.   70
L. MAYOR. Well, he shall spend some of his thousands now,
For I have sent for him to the Guildhall.[58]

Enter EYRE

See, where he comes.—Good morrow, Master Eyre.
EYRE. Poor Simon Eyre, my Lord, your shoemaker.
L. MAYOR. Well, well, it likes[59] yourself to term you
so.—   75

Enter DODGER

Now Master Dodger, what's the news with you?
DODGER. I'd gladly speak in private to your Honor.
L. MAYOR. You shall, you shall.—Master Eyre and
Master Scott,
I have some business with this gentleman;
I pray, let me entreat you to walk before   80
To the Guildhall; I'll follow presently.
Master Eyre, I hope ere noon to call you sheriff.
EYRE. I would not care, my Lord, if you might call me
King of Spain.—Come, Master Scott.

                    [*Exeunt* EYRE *and* SCOTT

L. MAYOR. Now, Master Dodger, what's the news you
bring?   85
DODGER. The Earl of Lincoln by me greets your
Lordship,
And earnestly requests you if you can
Inform him where his nephew Lacy keeps.
L. MAYOR. Is not his nephew Lacy now in France?
DODGER. No, I assure your Lordship, but disguised   90
Lurks here in London.
L. MAYOR.   London? Is't even so?
It may be; but upon my faith and soul,
I know not where he lives, or whether he lives.
So tell my Lord of Lincoln. Lurk in London?
Well, Master Dodger, you perhaps may start[60] him.   95
Be but the means to rid him into France,
I'll give you a dozen angels[61] for your pains;
So much I love his Honor, hate his nephew.
And, prithee, so inform thy lord from me.

---

[58] The seat of the municipal government.   [59] Is pleasing to.
[60] Rouse (as in hunting).
[61] Gold coins worth about $2.50 each.

DODGER. I take my leave.   [*Exit*
L. MAYOR.   Farewell, good Master
Dodger.—   100
Lacy in London? I dare pawn my life
My daughter knows thereof, and for that cause
Denied young Master Hammon in his love.
Well, I am glad I sent her to Old Ford.
God's Lord, 't is late! to Guildhall I must hie;   105
I know my brethren stay[62] my company.   [*Exit*

SCENE IV[63]

Enter FIRK, *Eyre's wife* MARGERY, LACY *as* HANS, *and*
ROGER

MARG. Thou goest too fast for me, Roger.—Oh, Firk.
FIRK. Ay, forsooth.
MARG. I pray thee, run—do you hear?—run to Guildhall,
and learn if my husband, Master Eyre, will take that worshipful vocation of Master Sheriff upon him. Hie   [5
thee, good Firk.
FIRK. Take it? Well, I go; an he should not take it, Firk
swears to forswear him. Yes, forsooth, I go to Guildhall.
MARG. Nay, when![64] Thou art too compendious and
tedious.   10
FIRK. O rare! your excellence is full of eloquence; how
like a new cartwheel my dame speaks, and she looks like
an old musty ale-bottle[65] going to scalding.
MARG. Nay, when! Thou wilt make me melancholy.
FIRK. God forbid your Worship should fall into   [15
that humor[66]—I run.   [*Exit*
MARG. Let me see now, Roger and Hans.
HODGE. Ay, forsooth, dame—mistress, I should say, but
the old term so sticks to the roof of my mouth, I can
hardly lick it off.   20
MARG. Even what thou wilt, good Roger; "dame" is a
fair name for any honest Christian; but let that pass. How
dost thou, Hans?
HANS. *Mee tanck you, vro.*[67]
MARG. Well, Hans and Roger, you see God hath   [25
blessed your master; and, perdy, if ever he comes to be
Master Sheriff of London—as we are all mortal—you shall
see, I will have some odd thing or other in a corner for
you: I will not be your backfriend;[68] but let that pass.—
Hans, pray thee, tie my shoe.   30
HANS. *Yaw, ic sal, vro.* (*aside to* SCOTT). What
MARG. Roger, thou know'st the length of my foot: as it
is none of the biggest, so I thank God, it is handsome
enough. Prithee, let me have a pair of shoes made—cork,[69]
good Roger, wooden heel too.   35

---

[62] Await.
[63] Before Eyre's house.   [64] An exclamation of impatience.
[65] I.e., a leathern one.   [66] State of mind (and body).
[67] Mistress.   [68] False friend.
[69] I.e., with a raised sole, to add height.

WILLIAM CECIL, LORD BURGHLEY

William Cecil, Lord Burghley (1520-98), was Elizabeth's cautious guide for forty years from the day of her accession in 1558, when he drew up her first proclamation within an hour of Queen Mary's death. "This judgment I have of you," said the Queen, "that you will not be corrupted by any manner of gifts, and that you will be faithful to the state." This engraving was made in the eighteenth century by Jacobus Houbraken. (Boston Public Library)

BURGHLEY HOUSE

Elizabeth's reign saw the establishment of a new landed gentry, of which Lord Burghley was a conspicuous member. He lavished all the arts of the new architecture of the Renaissance on Burghley House, typical of many great houses rising in England in the latter part of the sixteenth century and the early part of the seventeenth. Fortification had disappeared. These new palaces of the nobility came near being, as was said of one of them, "all window and no wall." (Harvard College Library)

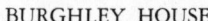

To the Reader.

This Figure, that thou here feeſt put,
    It was for gentle Shakeſpeare cut;
Wherein the Grauer had a ſtrife
    with Nature, to out-doo the life :
O, could he but haue drawne his wit
    As well in braſſe, as he hath hit
His face ; the Print would then ſurpaſſe
    All, that vvas euer vvrit in braſſe.
But, ſince he cannot, Reader, looke
    Not on his Picture, but his Booke.

B. I.

THE SHAKESPEARE FIRST FOLIO

When Shakespeare died in 1616, less than half of his plays had been printed. Seven years later appeared the first collected edition—an imposing volume of 908 double-column pages, the page size about 8 x 13 inches ("folio" size). The engraved portrait by Martin Droeshout is perhaps a more faithful likeness than any other surviving portrait of Shakespeare. The lines above face the title page; B. I. may possibly have been Ben Jonson. (Harvard College Library)

Mr. WILLIAM
SHAKESPEARES
COMEDIES,
HISTORIES, &
TRAGEDIES.
Publiſhed according to the True Originall Copies.

LONDON
Printed by Iſaac Iaggard, and Ed. Blount. 1623.

GEORGE CHAPMAN

This portrait of Chapman, the translator of the *Ili[ad]* and the *Odyssey*, appeared in the 1616 edition of *T[he] Whole Works of Homer*. It was this edition that Kea[ts] and his friend Charles Cowden Clarke spent most of [a] night reading together two hundred years later, just b[e]fore Keats wrote his great sonnet "On First Looking in[to] Chapman's Homer."

HODGE. You shall.

MARG. Art thou acquainted with never a farthingale-maker, nor a French-hood-maker? I must enlarge my bum,[70] ha, ha! How shall I look in a hood, I wonder! Perdy, oddly, I think.   40

HODGE (aside). As a cat out of[71] a pillory.—Very well, I warrant you, mistress.

MARG. Indeed, all flesh is grass; and, Roger, canst thou tell where I may buy a good hair?

HODGE. Yes, forsooth, at the poulterer's in Gracious   [45 Street.

MARG. Thou art an ungracious wag; perdy, I mean a false hair for my periwig.

HODGE. Why, mistress, the next time I cut my beard, you shall have the shavings of it; but they are all   [50 true hairs.

MARG. It is very hot; I must get me a fan or else a mask.

HODGE (aside). So you had need, to hide your wicked face.

MARG. Fie upon it, how costly this world's calling is; perdy, but that it is one of the wonderful works of   [55 God, I would not deal with it.—Is not Firk come yet?— Hans, be not so sad; let it pass and vanish, as my husband's Worship says.

HANS. Ick bin vrolicke; lot see yow soo.[72]

HODGE. Mistress, will you drink[73] a pipe of   [60 tobacco?

MARG. Oh, fie upon it, Roger, perdy! These filthy to-bacco pipes are the most idle slavering baubles that ever I felt. Out upon it! God bless us, men look not like men that use them.   65

Enter RALPH *with a crutch, being lame*

HODGE. What, fellow Ralph?—Mistress, look here, Jane's husband!—Why, how now, lame?—Hans, make much of him; he's a brother of our trade, a good workman, and a tall[74] soldier.

HANS. You be welcome, broder.   70

MARG. Perdy, I knew him not.—How dost thou, good Ralph? I am glad to see thee well.

RALPH. I would God you saw me, dame, as well As when I went from London into France.

MARG. Trust me, I am sorry, Ralph, to see thee   [75 impotent. Lord, how the wars have made him sunburnt! The left leg is not well; 't was a fair gift of God the in-firmity took not hold a little higher, considering thou camest from France;[75] but let that pass.

RALPH. I am glad to see you well, and I rejoice   80 To hear that God hath blessed my master so Since my departure.

---

[70] Backside (with the hoops of the farthingale).
[71] I.e., looking out of; for the French hood framed the wearer's face with a large fold.   [72] I'm merry; let's see you so.
[73] The usual verb then.   [74] Brave.
[75] Alluding to syphilis, "the French disease."

MARG. Yea, truly, Ralph, I thank my Maker; but let that pass.

HODGE. And, sirrah Ralph, what news, what news   [85 in France?

RALPH. Tell me, good Roger, first, what news in England? How does my Jane? When didst thou see my wife? Where lives my poor heart? She'll be poor indeed, Now I want limbs to get whereon to feed.   90

HODGE. Limbs? Hast thou not hands, man? Thou shalt never see a shoemaker want bread, though he have but three fingers on a hand.

RALPH. Yet all this while I hear not of my Jane.

MARG. Oh, Ralph, your wife—perdy, we know   [95 not what's become of her. She was here awhile and, be-cause she was married, grew more stately than became her; I checked her, and so forth; away she flung, never re-turned, nor said bye nor bah; and, Ralph, you know, "ka me, ka thee."[76] And, so as I tell ye—Roger, is not   [100 Firk come yet?

HODGE. No, forsooth.

MARG. And so, indeed, we heard not of her; but I hear she lives in London; but let that pass. If she had wanted, she might have opened her case to me or my hus-   [105 band, or to any of my men; I am sure, there's not any of them, perdy, but would have done her good to his power. —Hans, look if Firk be come.

HANS. Yaw, ik sal, vro.   [Exit

MARG. And so, as I said—but Ralph, why dost   [110 thou weep? Thou knowest that naked we came out of our mother's womb, and naked we must return; and, there-fore, thank God for all things.

HODGE. No, faith, Jane is a stranger here; but, Ralph, pull up a good heart; I know thou hast one. Thy   [115 wife, man, is in London; one told me, he saw her awhile ago very brave[77] and neat; we'll ferret her out, an London hold her.

MARG. Alas, poor soul, he's overcome with sorrow; he does but as I do, weep for the loss of any good   [120 thing.—But, Ralph, get thee in, call for some meat and drink; thou shalt find me worshipful towards thee.

RALPH. I thank you, dame; since I want limbs and lands, I'll trust to God, my good friends, and to these my hands.
                                                                    [Exit

Enter LACY *as* HANS, *and* FIRK, *running*

FIRK. Run, good Hans! O Hodge! O mistress!   [125 Hodge, heave up thine ears; mistress, smug up[78] your looks; on with your best apparel: my master is chosen, my master is called, nay, condemned by the cry of the country, to be

---

[76] If you "ka" me, I'll "ka" thee; i.e., scratch my back and I'll scratch yours. *Ka* occurs only in this expression.
[77] Well dressed.   [78] Spruce up.

sheriff of the city for this famous year now to come. And, time now being, a great many men in black gowns [130 were asked for their voices[79] and their hands, and my master had all their fists about his ears presently, and they cried "Ay, ay, ay, ay"—and so I came away—

Wherefore without all other grieve
I do salute you, Mistress Shrieve.[80]   135

HANS. *Yaw, my mester is de groot man, de shrieve.*

HODGE. Did not I tell you, mistress? Now I may boldly say, "Good morrow to your Worship."

MARG. Good morrow, good Roger.—I thank you, my good people all.—Firk, hold up thy hand: here's a [140 threepenny piece for thy tidings.

FIRK. 'T is but three halfpence, I think. Yes, 't is three-pence, I smell the rose.[81]

HODGE. But, mistress, be ruled by me, and do not speak so pulingly.   145

FIRK. 'T is her Worship speaks so, and not she. No, faith, mistress, speak me in the old key: "To it, Firk!" "there, good Firk!" "ply your business, Hodge!" "Hodge, with a full mouth!" "I'll fill your bellies with good cheer, till they cry twang!"   150

Enter SIMON EYRE *wearing a gold chain*

HANS. *See, myn liever broder, heer compt my meester.*

MARG. Welcome home, Master Shrieve; I pray God continue you in health and wealth.

EYRE. See here, my Maggy, a chain, a gold chain for Simon Eyre. I shall make thee a lady; here's a French [155 hood for thee; on with it, on with it! dress thy brows with this flap of a shoulder of mutton, to make thee look lovely.—Where be my fine men?—Roger, I'll make over my shop and tools to thee; Firk, thou shalt be the foreman; Hans, thou shalt have an hundred for twenty.[82] [160 Be as mad knaves as your master Sim Eyre hath been, and you shall live to be sheriffs of London.—How dost thou like me, Margery?—Prince am I none, yet am I princely born.—Firk, Hodge, and Hans!

ALL THREE. Ay, forsooth, what says your Wor- [165 ship, Master Sheriff?

EYRE. Worship and honor, you Babylonian knaves, for the gentle craft. But I forgot myself; I am bidden by my Lord Mayor to dinner to Old Ford: he's gone before; I must after.—Come, Madge, on with your trinkets! [170 —Now, my true Trojans, my fine Firk, my dapper Hodge, my honest Hans, some device, some odd crotchets, some morris,[83] or suchlike, for the honor of the gentle shoe-

makers. Meet me at Old Ford; you know my mind.— Come, Madge, away.—Shut up the shop, knaves, [175 and make holiday.

[Exeunt EYRE *and* MARGERY

FIRK. O rare! O brave! Come, Hodge; follow me, Hans; We'll be with them for a morris dance.   *[Exeunt*

SCENE V [84]

Enter LORD MAYOR, ROSE, EYRE, *his wife* MARGERY *in a French hood,* SYBIL, *and other* Servants.

L. MAYOR. Trust me, you are as welcome to Old Ford
As I myself.

MARG.   Truly, I thank your Lordship.

L. MAYOR. Would our bad cheer were worth the thanks
you give.

EYRE. Good cheer, my Lord Mayor, fine cheer! A fine
house, fine walls, all fine and neat.   5

L. MAYOR. Now, by my troth, I'll tell thee, Master Eyre,
It does me good, and all my brethren,[85]
That such a madcap fellow as thyself
Is ent'red into our society.

MARG. Ay, but, my Lord, he must learn now to [10
put on gravity.

EYRE. Peace, Maggy; a fig for gravity! When I go to
Guildhall in my scarlet gown, I'll look as demurely as a
saint, and speak as gravely as a justice of peace; but now I
am here at Old Ford, at my good Lord Mayor's [15
house, let it go by, vanish, Maggy; I'll be merry; away
with flip-flap, these fooleries, these gulleries. What, honey?
Prince am I none, yet am I princely born. What says my
Lord Mayor?

L. MAYOR. Ha, ha, ha! I had rather than a thousand [20
pound, I had an heart but half so light as yours.

EYRE. Why, what should I do, my Lord? A pound of
care pays not a dram of debt. Hum, let's be merry, whiles
we are young; old age, sack, and sugar will steal upon us,
ere we be aware.   25

THE FIRST THREE-MAN'S SONG [86]

Oh, the month of May, the merry month of May,
    So frolic, so gay, and so green, so green, so green!
Oh, and then did I unto my true-love say,
    "Sweet Peg, thou shalt be my summer's queen.

"Now the nightingale, the pretty nightingale,   30
    The sweetest singer in all the forest's choir,
Entreats thee, sweet Peggy, to hear thy true-love's tale;
    Lo, yonder she sitteth, her breast against a brier.

---

[79] Votes.   [80] Sheriff.
[81] The silver threepence of Elizabeth had the Queen's head and a rose on the obverse side. It was not in general circulation, but was used for maundy money. Margery is acting the role of a sovereign dispensing alms.
[82] In return for his loan of the "Portuguese."
[83] Mumming dance.

[84] A room in the Lord Mayor's house at Old Ford.
[85] Trisyllabic.
[86] Both songs are printed before the play in the old editions, which fail to indicate when they were sung.

"But oh, I spy the cuckoo, the cuckoo, the cuckoo;
    See where she sitteth—come away, my joy;   35
Come away, I prithee! I do not like the cuckoo
    Should sing where my Peggy and I kiss and toy."

Oh, the month of May, the merry month of May,
    So frolic, so gay, and so green, so green, so green!
And then did I unto my true-love say,   40
    "Sweet Peg, thou shalt be my summer's queen."

L. MAYOR. It's well done.—Mistress Eyre, pray, give good
counsel to my daughter.

MARG. I hope Mistress Rose will have the grace to take
nothing that's bad.   45

L. MAYOR. Pray God she do; for i' faith, Mistress Eyre,
I would bestow upon that peevish[87] girl
A thousand marks more than I mean to give her,
Upon condition she'd be ruled by me.
The ape still crosseth me. There came of late   50
A proper[88] gentleman of fair revenues,
Whom gladly I would call son-in-law:
But my fine cockney would have none of him.—
You'll prove a coxcomb[89] for it, ere you die;
A courtier, or no man, must please your eye.   55

EYRE. Be ruled, sweet Rose; th'art ripe for a man. Marry
not with a boy that has no more hair on his face than thou
hast on thy cheeks. A courtier, wash![90] go by! stand not
upon pishery-pashery: those silken fellows are but painted
images, outsides, outsides, Rose; their inner linings   [60
are torn. No, my fine mouse, marry me with a gentleman
grocer like my Lord Mayor, your father; a grocer is a
sweet trade—plums, plums! Had I a son or daughter should
marry out of the generation and blood of the shoemakers,
he should pack. What! the gentle trade is a living   [65
for a man through Europe, through the world!

[A noise within of a tabor[91] and a pipe

L. MAYOR. What noise is this?

EYRE. Oh, my Lord Mayor, a crew of good fellows that
for love to your Honor are come hither with a morris
dance.—Come in, my Mesopotamians, cheerily.   [70

Enter HODGE, LACY as HANS, RALPH, FIRK, and other
Shoemakers, in a morris; after a little dancing, the LORD
MAYOR speaks

L. MAYOR. Master Eyre, are all these shoemakers?
EYRE. All cordwainers, my good Lord Mayor.
ROSE (aside). How like my Lacy looks yond shoemaker!
HANS (aside). Oh, that I durst but speak unto my love!
L. MAYOR. Sybil, go fetch some wine to make these
drink.—You are all welcome.   76
ALL. We thank your Lordship.
                [ROSE takes a cup of wine and goes to HANS
ROSE. For his sake whose fair shape thou represent'st,
Good friend, I drink to thee.
HANS. Ic bedancke, good frister.[92]   80
MARG. I see, Mistress Rose, you do not want judgment;
you have drunk to the properest man I keep.
FIRK. Here be some have done their parts to be as proper
as he.
L. MAYOR. Well, urgent business calls me back to
    London.   85
Good fellows, first go in and taste our cheer;
And to make merry as you homeward go,
Spend these two angels in beer at Stratford-Bow.
EYRE. To these two, my mad lads, Sim Eyre adds   [89
another; then cheerily, Firk; tickle it, Hans, and all for the
honor of shoemakers.   [All the Shoemakers go dancing out
L. MAYOR. Come, Master Eyre, let's have your company.
                [Exeunt MAYOR, EYRE, and MARGERY
ROSE. Sybil, what shall I do?
SYBIL.   Why, what's the matter?
ROSE. That Hans the shoemaker is my love Lacy,
Disguised in that attire to find me out.   95
How should I find the means to speak with him?
SYBIL. What, mistress, never fear! I dare venture my
maidenhead to nothing, and that's great odds, that Hans
the Dutchman, when we come to London, shall not only
see and speak with you, but in spite of all your father's   [100
policies steal you away and marry you. Will not this please
you?
ROSE. Do this, and ever be assurèd of my love.
SYBIL. Away, then, and follow your father to   [104
London, lest your absence cause him to suspect something:
To-morrow, if my counsel be obeyed,
I'll bind you prentice to the gentle trade.   [Exeunt

---

87 Silly.
88 Handsome.   89 Fool.   90 Swill.   91 Small drum.   92 Miss.

ACT IV

SCENE I[1]

Enter JANE *in a seamster's shop, working; and* HAM-
MON, *muffled, at another door; he stands aloof*

HAM. Yonder 's the shop,[2] and there my fair love sits.
She's fair and lovely, but she is not mine.
Oh, would she were! Thrice have I courted her,
Thrice hath my hand been moist'ned with her hand,
Whilst my poor famished eyes do feed on that   5
Which made them famish. I am infortunate:
I still love one, yet nobody loves me.
I muse[3] in other men what women see
That I so want![4] Fine Mistress Rose was coy,
And this too curious![5] Oh, no, she is chaste;   10
And for[6] she thinks me wanton, she denies
To cheer my cold heart with her sunny eyes.
How prettily she works! O pretty hand!
O happy work! It doth me good to stand
Unseen to see her. Thus I oft have stood   15
In frosty evenings, a light burning by her,
Enduring biting cold, only to eye her.
One only look hath seemed as rich to me
As a king's crown; such is love's lunacy.
Muffled I'll pass along, and by that try   20
Whether she know me.

JANE.   Sir, what is't you buy?
What is't you lack, sir, calico, or lawn,
Fine cambric shirts, or bands,[7] what will you buy?

HAM. (*aside*). That which thou wilt not sell. Faith, yet
    I'll try.—
How do you sell this handkerchief?

JANE.   Good cheap.[8]   25

HAM. And how these ruffs?

JANE.   Cheap too.

HAM.   And how this band?

JANE. Cheap too.

HAM.   All cheap; how sell you then this hand?

JANE. My hands are not to be sold.

HAM.   To be given then!
Nay, faith, I come to buy.

JANE.   But none knows when.

HAM. Good sweet, leave work a little while; let's
    play.   30

JANE. I cannot live by keeping holiday.

HAM. I'll pay you for the time which shall be lost.

JANE. With me you shall not be at so much cost.

---

[1] A street in London.   [2] Within the inner stage.
[3] Wonder.   [4] Lack.   [5] Finicky.   [6] Because.
[7] Collars.   [8] At a reasonable price.

HAM. Look, how you wound this cloth, so you wound
    me.

JANE. It may be so.

HAM.   'T is so.

JANE.   What remedy?   35

HAM. Nay, faith, you are too coy.

JANE.   Let go my hand.

HAM. I will do any task at your command;
I would let go this beauty, were I not
In mind to disobey you by a power
That controls kings: I love you!

JANE.   So; now part.   40

HAM. With hands I may, but never with my heart.
In faith, I love you.

JANE.   I believe you do.

HAM. Shall a true love in me breed hate in you?

JANE. I hate you not.

HAM.   Then you must love?

JANE.   I do.
What, are you better now? I love not you.   45

HAM. All this, I hope, is but a woman's fray,
That means "Come to me" when she cries "Away!"
In earnest, mistress, I do not jest,
A true chaste love hath ent'red in my breast.
I love you dearly, as I love my life;   50
I love you as a husband loves a wife;
That, and no other love, my love requires.
Thy wealth, I know, is little; my desires
Thirst not for gold. Sweet, beauteous Jane, what's mine
Shall, if thou make myself thine, all be thine.   55
Say, judge, what is thy sentence, life or death?
Mercy or cruelty lies in thy breath.

JANE. Good sir, I do believe you love me well;
For 't is a silly conquest, silly pride,
For one like you—I mean a gentleman—   60
To boast that by his love-tricks he hath brought
Such and such women to his amorous lure.
I think you do not so; yet many do,
And make it even a very trade to woo.
I could be coy, as many women be,   65
Feed you with sunshine smiles and wanton looks,
But I detest witchcraft; say that I
Do constantly believe you, constant have—

HAM. Why dost thou not believe me?

JANE.   I believe you;
But yet, good sir, because I will not grieve you   70
With hopes to taste fruit which will never fall,
In simple truth this is the sum of all:
My husband lives, at least I hope he lives.
Pressed was he to these bitter wars in France;
Bitter they are to me by wanting him.   75

I have but one heart, and that heart's his due:
How can I then bestow the same on you?
Whilst he lives, his I live, be it ne'er so poor,
And rather be his wife than a king's whore.

HAM. Chaste and dear woman, I will not abuse thee, [80
Although it cost my life, if thou refuse me.
Thy husband, pressed for France, what was his name?

JANE. Ralph Damport.

HAM.   Damport?—Here's a letter sent
From France to me, from a dear friend of mine,
A gentleman of place; here he doth write   85
Their names that have been slain in every fight.

JANE. I hope death's scroll contains not my love's name.

HAM. Cannot you read?

JANE.   I can.

HAM.   Peruse the same.
To my remembrance such a name I read
Amongst the rest.—See here.

JANE.   Ay me, he's dead!   90
He's dead! If this be true, my dear heart's slain!

HAM. Have patience, dear love.

JANE.   Hence, hence!

HAM.   Nay, sweet Jane,
Make not poor sorrow proud with these rich tears.
I mourn thy husband's death, because thou mourn'st.

JANE. That bill is forged; 't is signed by forgery.   95

HAM. I'll bring thee letters sent besides to many,
Carrying the like report; Jane, 't is too true.
Come, weep not; mourning, though it rise from love,
Helps not the mournèd, yet hurts them that mourn.

JANE. For God's sake, leave me.

HAM.   Whither dost thou turn?   100
Forget the dead; love them that are alive.
His love is faded; try how mine will thrive.

JANE. 'T is now no time for me to think on love.

HAM. 'T is now best time for you to think on love,
Because your love lives not.

JANE.   Though he be dead,   105
My love to him shall not be buried;
For God's sake, leave me to myself alone.

HAM. 'T would kill my soul, to leave thee drowned in
moan.
Answer me to my suit, and I am gone;
Say to me yea or no.

JANE.   No.

HAM.   Then farewell!—   110
One farewell will not serve; I come again.
Come dry these wet cheeks; tell me, faith, sweet Jane,
Yea or no, once more.

JANE.   Once more I say no;
Once more begone, I pray; else will I go.

HAM. Nay, then I will grow rude, by this white
hand,   115

Until you change that cold "no"; here I'll stand
Till by your hard heart—

JANE.   Nay, for God's love, peace!
My sorrows by your presence more increase.
Not that you thus are present, but all grief
Desires to be alone; therefore in brief   120
Thus much I say, and saying bid adieu:
If ever I wed man, it shall be you.

HAM. O blessèd voice! Dear Jane, I'll urge no more;
Thy breath hath made me rich.

JANE.   Death makes me poor.

[Exeunt

SCENE II[9]

Enter HODGE, *at his shop-board,* RALPH, FIRK, LACY *as*
HANS, *and a* Boy, *at work*

ALL (*singing*). Hey, down a down, down derry.

HODGE. Well said,[10] my hearts; ply your work today;
we loit'red yesterday; to it pell-mell, that we may live to
be lord mayors, or aldermen at least!

FIRK. Hey, down a down, derry.   5

HODGE. Well said, i' faith! How say'st thou, Hans, doth
not Firk tickle it?

HANS. *Yaw, mester.*

FIRK. Not so neither; my organ-pipe squeaks this morning for want of liquoring. Hey, down a down, derry!   10

HANS. *Forware, Firk, tow best un jolly youngster. Hort*[11]
'ee, mester; ic bid yo cut me un pair vampres[12] *vor Mester*
Jeffre's boots.

HODGE. Thou shalt, Hans.

FIRK. Master!   15

HODGE. How now, boy?

FIRK. Pray, now you are in the cutting vein, cut me out
a pair of counterfeits,[13] or else my work will not pass
current. Hey, down a down!

HODGE. Tell me, sirs, are my cousin Mistress   [20
Priscilla's shoes done?

FIRK. Your cousin? No, master; one of your aunts,[14]
hang her; let them alone.

RALPH. I am in hand with them; she gave charge that
none but I should do them for her.   25

FIRK. Thou do for her? Then't will be a lame doing, and
that she loves not. Ralph, thou might'st have sent her to
me; in faith, I would have yarked and firked[15] your
Priscilla. Hey, down a down, derry. This gear will not
hold.   30

---

[9] Hodge's shop.   [10] Done.   [11] Hark.   [12] Vamps, uppers.
[13] I.e., patterns; *counterfeits* is for the sake of the pun.
[14] Mistresses.
[15] Synonyms, = drubbed. Here, of course, as elsewhere, with an
indecent meaning.

HODGE. How say'st thou, Firk, were we not merry at Old Ford?

FIRK. How, merry! Why, our buttocks went jiggy-joggy like a quagmire. Well, Sir Roger Oatmeal, if I thought all meal of that nature, I would eat noth-   [35 ing but bag-puddings.

RALPH. Of all good fortunes my fellow Hans had the best.

FIRK. 'T is true, because Mistress Rose drank to him.

HODGE. Well, well, work apace. They say seven   [40 of the aldermen be dead, or very sick.

FIRK. I care not; I'll be none.

RALPH. No, nor I; but then my Master Eyre will come quickly to be lord mayor.

Enter SYBIL

FIRK. Whoop, yonder comes Sybil.   45

HODGE. Sybil, welcome, i' faith; and how dost thou, mad wench?

FIRK. Syb, whore, welcome to London.

SYBIL. Godamercy, sweet Firk; good Lord, Hodge, what a delicious shop you have got! You tickle it, i' faith.   [50

RALPH. Godamercy, Sybil, for our good cheer at Old Ford.

SYBIL. That you shall have, Ralph.

FIRK. Nay, by the mass, we had tickling cheer, Sybil; and how the plague dost thou and Mistress Rose   [55 and my Lord Mayor?—I put the women in first.

SYBIL. Well, Godamercy. But God's me, I forget myself! Where's Hans the Fleming?

FIRK. Hark, butter-box, now you must yelp out some *spreken.*   60

HANS. *Wat begaie ou? Vat vod ou, Frister?*[16]

SYBIL. Marry, you must come to my young mistress, to pull on her shoes you made last.

HANS. *Vare ben your edle[17] fro, vare ben your mistris?*

SYBIL. Marry, here at our London house in Cornhill.[18]   [65

FIRK. Will nobody serve her turn but Hans?

SYBIL. No, sir.—Come, Hans, I stand upon needles.

HODGE. Why then, Sybil, take heed of pricking.

SYBIL. For that let me alone. I have a trick in my budget. Come, Hans.   70

HANS. *Yaw, yaw, ic sall meete yo gane.*[19]

[*Exeunt* HANS *and* SYBIL

HODGE. Go, Hans, make haste again.—Come, who lacks work?

FIRK. I, master, for I lack my breakfast; 't is munching-time, and past.   75

HODGE. Is't so?—Why, then leave work, Ralph.—To breakfast!—Boy, look to the tools.—Come, Ralph; come, Firk.   [*Exeunt*

SCENE III[20]

Enter a SERVING MAN

SERV. Let me see now, the sign of the Last in Tower Street. Mass,[21] yonder's the house. What, haw! Who's within?

Enter RALPH

RALPH. Who calls there? What want you, sir?

SERV. Marry, I would have a pair of shoes made   [5 for a gentlewoman against tomorrow morning. What, can you do them?

RALPH. Yes, sir, you shall have them. But what length's her foot?

SERV. Why, you must make them in all parts like   [10 this shoe; but, at any hand, fail not to do them, for the gentlewoman is to be married very early in the morning.

RALPH. How? by this shoe must it be made? By this? Are you sure, sir, by this?

SERV. How, by this? am I sure, by this? Art thou   [15 in thy wits? I tell thee, I must have a pair of shoes—dost thou mark me? A pair of shoes, two shoes, made by this very shoe, this same shoe, against tomorrow morning by four a'clock. Dost understand me? Canst thou do't?

RALPH. Yes, sir, yes—I—I—I can do't. By this   [20 shoe, you say? I should know this shoe. Yes, sir, yes, by this shoe, I can do't. Four a'clock. Well! Whither shall I bring them?

SERV. To the sign of the Golden Ball in Watling Street; inquire for one Master Hammon, a gentleman, my   [25 master.

RALPH. Yea, sir; by this shoe, you say?

SERV. I say, Master Hammon at the Golden Ball; he's the bridegroom, and those shoes are for his bride.

RALPH. They shall be done by this shoe. Well,   [30 well, Master Hammon at the Golden Shoe—I would say, the Golden Ball; very well, very well. But I pray you, sir, where must Master Hammon be married?

SERV. At St. Faith's Church, under Paul's.[22] But what's that to thee? Prithee, dispatch[23] those shoes, and   [35 so farewell.   [*Exit*

RALPH. By this shoe, said he. How am I amazed
At this strange accident! Upon my life,
This was the very shoe I gave my wife
When I was pressed for France; since when, alas,   40
I never could hear of her. It is the same,
And Hammon's bride no other but my Jane.

[16] What do you want? What would you, Miss?   [17] Noble.
[18] Corrected from *Cornewaile, Cornwall,* in the earliest editions.
[19] With you go.

[20] Before the shop.   [21] By the Mass.
[22] I.e., in the crypt of the cathedral.   [23] Hurry up with.

Enter FIRK

FIRK. 'Snails,[24] Ralph, thou hast lost thy part of three pots a countryman of mine gave me to breakfast.

RALPH. I care not; I have found a better thing.   45

FIRK. A thing? Away! Is it a man's thing, or a woman's thing?

RALPH. Firk, dost thou know this shoe?

FIRK. No, by my troth; neither doth that know me! I have no acquaintance with it; 't is a mere stranger   [50 to me.

RALPH. Why, then I do; this shoe, I durst be sworn, Once coverèd the instep of my Jane.
This is her size, her breadth, thus trod my love;
These true-love knots I pricked. I hold my life,   55
By this old shoe I shall find out my wife.

FIRK. Ha, ha! Old shoe, that wert new! How a murrain[25] came this ague-fit of foolishness upon thee?

RALPH. Thus, Firk: even now here came a servingman;
By this shoe would he have a new pair made   60
Against tomorrow morning for his mistress,
That's to be married to a gentleman.
And why may not this be my sweet Jane?

FIRK. And why mayst not thou be my sweet ass? Ha, ha!

RALPH. Well, laugh and spare not! But the truth is this: 65
Against tomorrow morning I'll provide
A lusty crew of honest shoemakers,
To watch the going of the bride to church.
If she prove Jane, I'll take her in despite
From Hammon and the Devil, were he by.   70
If it be not my Jane, what remedy?
Hereof am I sure, I shall live till I die
Although I never with a woman lie.   [*Exit*

FIRK. Thou lie with a woman to build nothing but Cripplegates! Well, God sends fools fortune, and   [75 it may be he may light upon his matrimony by such a device; for wedding and hanging goes by destiny.[26]   [*Exit*

SCENE IV[27]

Enter LACY *as* HANS *and* ROSE, *arm in arm*

HANS. How happy am I by embracing thee!
Oh, I did fear such cross mishaps did reign
That I should never see my Rose again.

ROSE. Sweet Lacy, since fair opportunity
Offers herself to furder our escape,   5
Let not too overfond esteem of me
Hinder that happy hour. Invent the means,
And Rose will follow thee through all the world.

HANS. Oh, how I surfeit with excess of joy,
Made happy by thy rich perfectiön!   10
But since thou pay'st sweet interest to my hopes,
Redoubling love on love, let me once more
Like to a bold-faced debtor crave of thee
This night to steal abroad, and at Eyre's house,
Who now by death of certain aldermen   15
Is mayor of London, and my master once,
Meet thou thy Lacy, where, in spite of change,
Your father's anger, and mine uncle's hate,
Our happy nuptials will we consummate.

Enter SYBIL

SYBIL. O God, what will you do, mistress? Shift   [20 for yourself, your father is at hand! He's coming, he's coming! Master Lacy, hide yourself in my mistress! For God's sake, shift for yourselves!

HANS. Your father come! Sweet Rose, what shall I do?
Where shall I hide me? How shall I escape?   25

ROSE. A man, and want wit in extremity?
Come, come, be Hans still; play the shoemaker;
Pull on my shoe.

Enter LORD MAYOR

HANS.   Mass, and that's well rememb'red.

SYBIL. Here comes your father.

HANS. *Forware,*[28] *mestresse,* 't *is un good skow; it*   [30 *sal vel dute,*[29] *or ye sal neit betallen.*[30]

ROSE. O God, it pincheth me; what will you do?

HANS (*aside*). Your father's presence pincheth, not the shoe.

L. MAYOR. Well done. Fit my daughter well, and she shall please thee well.   35

HANS. *Yaw, yaw, ick weit*[31] *dat well; forware,* 't *is un good skoo,* 't *is gimait van neits leither: se ever, mine here.*[32]

Enter a Prentice

L. MAYOR. I do believe it.—What's the news with you?

PRENTICE. Please you, the Earl of Lincoln at the gate
Is newly lighted,[33] and would speak with you.   40

L. MAYOR. The Earl of Lincoln come to speak with me?
Well, well, I know his errand.—Daughter Rose,
Send hence your shoemaker; dispatch, have done!
Syb, make things handsome! Sir boy, follow me.
[*Exit, with the* Prentice

HANS. Mine uncle come! Oh, what may this portend?
Sweet Rose, this of our love threatens an end.   46

ROSE. Be not dismayed at this; whate'er befall,
Rose is thine own. To witness I speak truth,

---

[24] By God's nails.   [25] How the plague.   [26] Proverbial.
[27] A room in the (former) Lord Mayor's house in London.

[28] Indeed.   [29] Do it, serve.   [30] Pay.   [31] Know.
[32] 'T is made of neat's leather; just look, sir.   [33] Dismounted.

Where thou appoints[34] the place, I'll meet with thee.—
I will not fix a day to follow thee,   50
But presently[35] steal hence. Do not reply;
Love, which gave strength to bear my father's hate,
Shall now add wings to further our escape.   [*Exeunt*

SCENE V[36]

Enter LORD MAYOR *and* EARL OF LINCOLN

L. MAYOR. Believe me, on my credit, I speak truth:
Since first your nephew Lacy went to France
I have not seen him. It seemed strange to me,
When Dodger told me that he stayed behind,
Neglecting the high charge the King imposed.   5
  LINCOLN. Trust me, Sir Roger Oateley, I did think
Your counsel had given head to this attempt,
Drawn to it by the love he bears your child.
Here I did hope to find him in your house;
But now I see mine error, and confess   10
My judgment wronged you by conceiving so.
  L. MAYOR. Lodge in my house, say you? Trust me, my
      Lord,
I love your nephew Lacy too too dearly,
So much to wrong his honor; and he hath done so,
That first gave him advice to stay from France.   15
To witness I speak truth, I let you know
How careful I have been to keep my daughter
Free from all conference or speech of him—
Not that I scorn your nephew, but in love
I bear your Honor, lest your noble blood   20
Should by my mean worth be dishonorèd.
  LINCOLN (*aside*). How far the churl's tongue wanders
      from his heart!—
Well, well, Sir Roger Oateley, I believe you,
With more than many thanks for the kind love
So much you seem to bear me. But, my Lord,   25
Let me request your help to seek my nephew,
Whom if I find, I'll straight embark for France.
So shall your Rose be free, my thoughts at rest,
And much care die which now lies in my breast.

Enter SYBIL

SYBIL. O Lord! Help, for God's sake! My mistress;   [30
oh, my young mistress!
  L. MAYOR. Where is thy mistress? What's become of
her?
  SYBIL. She's gone; she's fled!
  L. MAYOR. Gone! Whither is she fled?   35
  SYBIL. I know not, forsooth; she's fled out of doors with
Hans the shoemaker; I saw them scud, scud, scud, apace,
apace!

L. MAYOR. Which way?—What, John! Where be my
men?—Which way?   40
  SYBIL. I know not, an it please your Worship.
  L. MAYOR. Fled with a shoemaker? Can this be true?
  SYBIL. O Lord, sir, as true as God's in heaven.
  LINCOLN. Her love turned shoemaker?—(*aside*) I am glad
      of this.
  L. MAYOR. A Fleming butter-box, a shoemaker!   45
Will she forget her birth, requite my care
With such ingratitude? Scorned she young Hammon
To love a honniken,[37] a needy knave?
Well, let her fly; I'll not fly after her:
Let her starve, if she will—she's none of mine.   50
  LINCOLN. Be not so cruel, sir.

Enter FIRK *with shoes*

SYBIL (*aside*).   I am glad she's scaped.
  L. MAYOR. I'll not account of her as of my child.
Was there no better object for her eyes
But a foul drunken lubber, swill-belly,
A shoemaker? That's brave![38]   55
  FIRK. Yea, forsooth; 't is a very brave shoe, and as fit as
a pudding.
  L. MAYOR. How now, what knave is this? From whence
comest thou?
  FIRK. No knave, sir. I am Firk the shoemaker,   [60
lusty Roger's chief lusty journeyman, and I have come
hither to take up the pretty leg of sweet Mistress Rose;
and thus hoping your Worship is in as good health as I
was at the making hereof, I bid you farewell—yours, Firk.
  L. MAYOR. Stay, stay, sir knave!
  LINCOLN.   Come hither, shoemaker!   [65
  FIRK. 'T is happy the knave is put before the shoemaker,
or else I would not have vouchsafed to come back to you.
I am moved, for I stir.
  L. MAYOR. My Lord, this villain calls us knaves by craft.
  FIRK. Then 't is by the gentle craft, and to call one [70
knave gently, is no harm. Sit your Worship merry!—Syb,
your young mistress—(*aside*) I'll so bob[39] them, now my
master, Master Eyre, is Lord Mayor of London.
  L. MAYOR. Tell me, sirrah, whose man are you?
  FIRK. I am glad to see your Worship so merry. I   [75
have no maw to this gear,[40] no stomach as yet to a red
petticoat.   [*Pointing to* SYBIL
  LINCOLN. He means not, sir, to woo you to his maid,
But only doth demand whose man you are.
  FIRK. I sing now to the tune of Rogero.[41] Roger, [80
my fellow, is now my master.
  LINCOLN. Sirrah, know'st thou one Hans, a shoemaker?
  FIRK. Hans, shoemaker? Oh, yes, stay, yes, I have him.
I tell you what, I speak it in secret: Mistress Rose and he
are by this time—no, not so, but shortly are to come [85

---

[34] For the (for stage purposes) unpronounceable *appoint'st*.
[35] Immediately.   [36] The same.

[37] A low fellow.   [38] Fine, splendid.   [39] Cheat.
[40] Appetite for this affair.   [41] A well-known tune of the day.

over one another with[42] "Can you dance 'The Shaking of the Sheets'?"[43] It is that Hans—(*aside*) I'll so gull[44] these diggers![45]

L. MAYOR. Know'st thou, then, where he is?

FIRK. Yes, forsooth; yea, marry!   90

LINCOLN. Canst thou, in sadness[46]—

FIRK. No, forsooth, no, marry!

L. MAYOR. Tell me, good honest fellow, where he is, And thou shalt see what I'll bestow of thee.

FIRK. Honest fellow? No, sir; not so, sir; my pro- [95 fession is the gentle craft. I care not for seeing; I love feeling:[47] let me feel it here—*aurium tenus,* ten pieces of gold; *genuum tenus,* ten pieces of silver;[48] and then Firk is your man—(*aside*) in a new pair of stretchers.[49]

L. MAYOR. Here is an angel, part of thy reward   100 Which I will give thee; tell me where he is.

FIRK. No point. Shall I betray my brother? No! Shall I prove Judas to Hans? No! Shall I cry treason to my cor-poration? No, I shall be firked and yerked[50] then. But give me your angel; your angel shall tell you.   105

LINCOLN. Do so, good fellow; 't is no hurt to thee.

FIRK. Send simpering Syb away.

L. MAYOR.   Huswife,[51] get you in.

[*Exit* SYBIL

FIRK. Pitchers have ears, and maids have wide mouths; but for[52] Hans Prans, upon my word, tomorrow morning he and young Mistress Rose go to this gear: they   [110 shall be married together, by this rush,[53] or else turn Firk to a firkin of butter, to tan leather withal.

L. MAYOR. But art thou sure of this?

FIRK. Am I sure that Paul's steeple is a handful higher than London Stone,[54] or that the Pissing Conduit[55] [115 leaks nothing but pure Mother Bunch?[56] Am I sure I am lusty Firk? God's nails, do you think I am so base to[57] gull you?

LINCOLN. Where are they married? Dost thou know the church?

FIRK. I never go to church, but I know the name   [120

---

of it; it is a swearing church—stay awhile, 't is—ay, by the mass; no, no; 't is—ay, by my troth; no, nor that; 't is—ay, by my faith: that, that, 't is, ay, By My Faith's Church under Paul's Cross. There they shall be knit like a pair of stockings in matrimony; there they'll be inconie.[58]

LINCOLN. Upon my life, my nephew Lacy walks   126 In the disguise of this Dutch shoemaker.

FIRK. Yes, forsooth.

LINCOLN. Doth he not, honest fellow?

FIRK. No, forsooth; I think Hans is nobody but   [130 Hans, no spirit.

L. MAYOR. My mind misgives me now, 't is so, indeed.

LINCOLN. My cousin speaks the language, knows the trade.

L. MAYOR. Let me request your company, my Lord; Your honorable presence may, no doubt,   135 Refrain their headstrong rashness, when myself Going alone perchance may be o'erborne. Shall I request this favor?

LINCOLN.   This, or what else.

FIRK. Then you must rise betimes,[59] for they mean to fall to their hey-pass and repass,[60] pindy-pandy,[61] [140 which hand will you have, very early.

L. MAYOR. My care shall every way equal their haste. This night accept your lodging in my house; The earlier shall we stir, and at St. Faith's Prevent this giddy, harebrained nuptiäl.   145 This traffic of hot love shall yield cold gains: They ban[62] our loves, and we'll forbid their banns. [*Exit*

LINCOLN. At St. Faith's Church thou say'st?

FIRK.   Yes, by their troth.

LINCOLN. Be secret, on thy life.   [*Exit*

FIRK.   Yes, when I kiss your wife! [150 Ha, ha, here's no craft in the gentle craft! I came hither of purpose with shoes to Sir Roger's Worship, whilst Rose, his daughter, be cony-catched[63] by Hans. Soft now; these two gulls will be at St. Faith's Church tomorrow morning, to take Master Bridegroom and Mistress Bride [155 napping; and they, in the meantime, shall chop up the matter at the Savoy.[64] But the best sport is, Sir Roger Oateley will find my fellow lame Ralph's wife going to marry a gentleman, and then he'll stop her instead of his daughter. Oh, brave! there will be fine tickling   [160 sport. Soft now, what have I to do? Oh, I know; now a mess of shoemakers meet at the Woolsack[65] in Ivy Lane, to cozen[66] my gentleman of lame Ralph's wife, that's true.

　Alack, alack!
　Girl, hold out tack![67]   165
For now smocks for this jumbling
　Shall go to wrack.   [*Exit*

---

[42] Cf. III, i, 122.   [43] A popular tune and ballad.   [44] Dupe.
[45] Delvers (into secrets).   [46] Seriously.
[47] With reference to the supposed liberties taken by shoemakers with female customers.
[48] *Aurium tenus* = up to the ears; *genuum tenus* = up to the knees. Firk pretends (punningly) that *tenus* means *ten,* and that *aurium* means *pieces of gold.*
[49] Punning on the meanings (1) shoe-stretchers, (2) lies.
[50] Synonyms, = drubbed. Cf. IV, ii, 28, and note 15.
[51] Hussy, wench.   [52] As for.
[53] Elizabethan floors were often covered with rushes.
[54] It was supposed to mark the center from which the Romans' military roads radiated.
[55] A small but famous conduit, also mentioned in Shakespeare's *2 Henry VI,* IV, vi, 4.
[56] I.e., water. Mother Bunch's ale was famous, though Nashe (ed. McKerrow, I, 173–4) calls it "slimie." By the date of our play she was probably dead. Apparently her ale had lost its reputa-tion, and "Mother Bunch" had come to mean very thin drink, and hence (as here) water.   [57] As to.

[58] A pretty sight.   [59] Early.   [60] Jugglers' terms.
[61] Alluding to the children's game of handy-dandy, or which hand will you have?   [62] Curse.   [63] Beguiled.
[64] A hospital; its chapel served as a parish church.
[65] A well-known tavern.   [66] Cheat.   [67] Hold out, endure.

ACT V

SCENE I[1]

Enter EYRE, *his wife* MARGERY, LACY *as* HANS, *and* ROSE

EYRE. This is the morning, then; stay, my bully, my honest Hans, is it not?

HANS. This is the morning that must make us two
Happy or miserable; therefore, if you—

EYRE. Away with these ifs and ands, Hans, and   [5
these et ceteras! By mine honor, Rowland Lacy, none but the King shall wrong thee. Come, fear nothing; am not I Sim Eyre? Is not Sim Eyre Lord Mayor of London?—Fear nothing, Rose: let them all say what they can; dainty, come thou to me—laughest thou?   10

MARG. Good my Lord, stand her friend in what thing you may.

EYRE. Why, my sweet Lady Madgy, think you Simon Eyre can forget his fine Dutch journeyman? No, vah! Fie, I scorn it; it shall never be cast in my teeth that I was   [15 unthankful. Lady Madgy, thou hadst never covered thy Saracen's head[2] with this French flap, nor loaden thy bum with this farthingale ('t is trash, trumpery, vanity), Simon Eyre had never walked in a red petticoat, nor wore a chain of gold, but for my fine journeyman's Portu-   [20 guese.—And shall I leave him? No! Prince am I none, yet bear a princely mind.

HANS. My Lord, 't is time for us to part from hence.

EYRE. Lady Madgy, Lady Madgy, take two or three of my piecrust eaters, my buff-jerkin[3] varlets, that do   [25 walk in black gowns at Simon Eyre's heels; take them, good Lady Madgy; trip and go, my brown queen of periwigs,[4] with my delicate Rose and my jolly Rowland to the Savoy; see them linked, countenance the marriage; and when it is done, cling, cling together, you Ham-   [30 borow[5] turtledoves. I'll bear you out: come to Simon Eyre; come, dwell with me, Hans, thou shalt eat minced-pies and march-pane.[6]—Rose, away, cricket!—Trip and go, my Lady Madgy, to the Savoy.—Hans, wed, and to bed; kiss, and away! Go, vanish!   35

MARG. Farewell, my Lord.

ROSE. Make haste, sweet love.

MARG.   She'd fain the deed were done.

HANS. Come, my sweet Rose; faster than deer we'll run.

[*They go out*

EYRE. Go, vanish, vanish! Avaunt, I say! By the Lord of Ludgate, it's a mad life to be a lord mayor; it's a   [40 stirring life, a fine life, a velvet life, a careful[7] life. Well, Simon Eyre, yet set a good face on it, in the honor of St. Hugh. Soft,[8] the King this day comes to dine with me, to see my new buildings; his Majesty is welcome: he shall have good cheer, delicate cheer, princely cheer. This   [45 day, my fellow prentices of London come to dine with me too; they shall have fine cheer, gentlemanlike cheer. I promised the mad Cappadocians, when we all served at the conduit together,[9] that if ever I came to be mayor of London, I would feast them all; and I'll do 't, I'll   [50 do 't, by the life of Pharaoh: by this beard, Sim Eyre will be no flincher. Besides, I have procured that upon every Shrove Tuesday,[10] at the sound of the pancake[11] bell, my fine dapper Assyrian lads shall clap up their shop windows, and away. This is the day, and this day they shall do 't, they shall do 't.   56

Boys, that day are you free; let masters care;
And prentices shall pray for Simon Eyre.   [*Exit*

SCENE II[12]

Enter HODGE, FIRK, RALPH, *and five or six* Shoemakers, *all with cudgels or such weapons*

HODGE. Come, Ralph; stand to it, Firk. My masters,[13] as we are the brave bloods of the shoemakers, heirs apparent to St. Hugh, and perpetual benefactors to all good fellows, thou shalt have no wrong: were Hammon a king of spades, he should not delve in thy close[14] without   [5 thy sufferance. But tell me, Ralph, art thou sure 't is thy wife?

RALPH. Am I sure this is Firk? This morning, when I stroked on her shoes, I looked upon her, and she upon me, and she sighed, asked me if ever I knew one Ralph.   [10 Yes, said I. For his sake, said she—tears standing in her eyes—and for thou art somewhat like him, spend this piece of gold. I took it; my lame leg and my travel beyond sea made me unknown. All is one for that; I know she's mine.   15

FIRK. Did she give thee this gold? O glorious, glittering gold! She's thine own, 't is thy wife, and she loves thee; for I'll stand to 't, there's no woman will give gold to any man but she thinks better of him than she thinks of them

---

[1] A room in Eyre's house.
[2] Alluding to the numerous signs which bore a ferocious face so called.   [3] Leather jacket.
[4] Since she now has wigged flunkies to attend her.
[5] Hamburg.   [6] A sweatmeat of almond paste.

[7] Full of responsibilities.   [8] Hold on.
[9] The prentices had to serve as water-carriers for their masters.
[10] The day before Lent begins.
[11] The special dish for Shrove Tuesday.
[12] A street near St. Paul's.   [13] Gentlemen.
[14] Fenced (and so private) land.

378   THE RENAISSANCE

she gives silver to. And for Hammon, neither Ham-   [20
mon nor hangman shall wrong thee in London! Is not our
old master Eyre, lord mayor? Speak, my hearts!

ALL. Yes, and Hammon shall know it to his cost.

Enter HAMMON, *his* Man, JANE, *and* Others

HODGE. Peace, my bullies; yonder they come.

RALPH. Stand to 't, my hearts. Firk, let me speak   [25
first.

HODGE. No, Ralph, let me.—Hammon, whither away so
early?

HAM. Unmannerly, rude slave, what's that to thee?

FIRK. To him, sir? Yes, sir, and to me, and others.   [30
—Good morrow, Jane, how dost thou? Good Lord, how
the world is changed with you! God be thanked!

HAM. Villains, hands off! How dare you touch my love?

ALL. Villains? Down with them! Cry clubs[15] for prentices!

HODGE. Hold, my hearts!—Touch her, Hammon?   [35
Yea, and more than that: we'll carry her away with us.—
My masters and gentlemen, never draw your bird-spits;
shoemakers are steel to the back, men every inch of them,
all spirit.

ALL OF HAMMON'S SIDE. Well, and what of all this?   [40

HODGE. I'll show you.—Jane, dost thou know this man?
'T is Ralph, I can tell thee; nay, 't is he in faith, though he
be lamed by the wars. Yet look not strange, but run to
him, fold him about the neck and kiss him.

JANE. Lives then my husband? O God, let me go;   [45
Let me embrace my Ralph.

HAM.   What means my Jane?

JANE. Nay, what meant you, to tell me he was slain?

HAM. Pardon me, dear love, for being misled—
(*To* RALPH) 'T was rumored here in London thou wert
    dead.

FIRK. Thou seest he lives.—Lass, go, pack home with
    him.—   50
Now, Master Hammon, where's your mistress, your wife?

SERV. Swounds, master, fight for her!
Will you thus lose her?

ALL. Down with that creature! Clubs! Down with him!

HODGE. Hold, hold!   55

HAM. Hold, fool!—Sirs, he shall do no wrong.—
Will my Jane leave me thus, and break her faith?

FIRK. Yea, sir! She must, sir! She shall, sir! What then?
Mend it!

HODGE. Hark, fellow Ralph, follow my counsel: [60
set the wench in the midst, and let her choose her man,
and let her be his woman.

JANE. Whom shall I choose? Whom should my thoughts
    affect

But him whom heaven hath made to be my love?
Thou art my husband, and these humble weeds   65
Makes thee more beautiful than all his wealth.
Therefore, I will but put off his attire,
Returning it into the owner's hand,
And after ever be thy constant wife.

HODGE. Not a rag, Jane! The law's on our side: [70
he that sows in another man's ground forfeits his harvest.
Get thee home, Ralph; follow him, Jane; he shall not have
so much as a busk-point[16] from thee.

FIRK. Stand to that, Ralph; the appurtenances are thine
own.—Hammon, look not at her!   75

SERV. Oh, swounds,[17] no!

FIRK. Blue coat,[18] be quiet; we'll give you a new livery[19]
else; we'll make Shrove Tuesday St. George's Day[20] for
you.—Look not, Hammon, leer not! I'll firk you! For thy
head now, one glance, one sheep's eye, anything, at   [80
her! Touch not a rag, lest I and my brethren beat you to
clouts.

SERV. Come, Master Hammon, there's no striving here.

HAM. Good fellows, hear me speak; and, honest Ralph,
Whom I have injured most by loving Jane,   85
Mark what I offer thee: here in fair gold
Is twenty pound; I'll give it for thy Jane.
If this content thee not, thou shalt have more.

HODGE. Sell not thy wife, Ralph; make her not a whore.

HAM. Say, wilt thou freely cease thy claim in her,   90
And let her be my wife?

ALL.   No, do not, Ralph!

RALPH. Sirrah Hammon, Hammon, dost thou think a
shoemaker is so base to be a bawd to his own wife for
commodity? Take thy gold; choke with it! Were I not
lame, I would make thee eat thy words.   95

FIRK. A shoemaker sell his flesh and blood? O, indignity!

HODGE. Sirrah, take up your pelf, and be packing.

HAM. I will not touch one penny; but, in lieu
Of that great wrong I offerèd thy Jane,
To Jane and thee I give that twenty pound.   100
Since I have failed of her, during my life
I vow no woman else shall be my wife.
Farewell, good fellows of the gentle trade;
Your morning's mirth my mourning day hath made.

[*Exeunt* HAMMON *and his party*

FIRK (*to the* Serving Man). Touch the gold, crea-   [105
ture, if you dare! Y' are best be trudging.—Here, Jane,
take thou it.—Now let's home, my hearts.

HODGE. Stay! Who comes here? Jane, on again with thy
mask!

---

[16] The tagged lace that fastened the busk, the wooden strip which
    reënforced the front of the stays.
[17] By God's wounds (on the Cross).   [18] Servant.
[19] By beating you (black and blue).
[20] Blue was its appropriate color.

---
[15] The apprentices' call for help from their fellows and their rally-
    ing cry.

Enter EARL OF LINCOLN, LORD MAYOR, *and* Servants

LINCOLN. Yonder's the lying varlet mocked us so.   110

L. MAYOR. Come hither, sirrah![21]

FIRK. I, sir? I am sirrah? You mean me, do you not?

LINCOLN. Where is my nephew married?

FIRK. Is he married? God give him joy; I am glad of it.
They have a fair day, and the sign is in a good planet,   [115
Mars in Venus.

L. MAYOR. Villain, thou told'st me that my daughter Rose
This morning should be married at St. Faith's;
We have watched there these three hours at the least,
Yet see we no such thing.   120

FIRK. Truly, I am sorry for't; a bride's a pretty thing.

HODGE. Come to the purpose. Yonder's the bride and
bridegroom you look for, I hope. Though you be lords,
you are not to bar by your authority men from women,
are you?   125

L. MAYOR. See, see, my daughter's masked.

LINCOLN.   True, and my nephew,
To hide his guilt, counterfeits him lame.

FIRK. Yea, truly; God help the poor couple: they are
lame and blind.

L. MAYOR. I'll ease her blindness.

LINCOLN.   I'll his lameness cure.   [130

FIRK (*aside to the* Shoemakers). Lie down, sirs, and laugh!
My fellow Ralph is taken for Rowland Lacy, and Jane for
Mistress Damask Rose. This is all my knavery.

L. MAYOR. What, have I found you, minion?

LINCOLN.   O base wretch!
Nay, hide thy face: the horror of thy guilt   135
Can hardly be washed off. Where are thy powers?[22]
What battles have you made? Oh, yes, I see,
Thou fought'st with shame, and shame hath conquered
    thee.
This lameness will not serve.

L. MAYOR.   Unmask yourself.

LINCOLN. Lead home your daughter.

L. MAYOR.   Take your nephew hence.   [140

RALPH. Hence! Swounds, what mean you? Are you mad?
I hope you cannot enforce my wife from me. Where's
Hammon?

L. MAYOR. Your wife?

LINCOLN. What Hammon?   145

RALPH. Yea, my wife; and, therefore, the proudest of
you that lay hands on her first, I'll lay my crutch 'cross his
pate.

FIRK. To him, lame Ralph! Here's brave sport!

RALPH. Rose, call you her? Why, her name is   [150
Jane. Look here else; do you know her now?

[JANE *unmasks*

LINCOLN. Is this your daughter?

L. MAYOR.   No, nor this your nephew.
My Lord of Lincoln, we are both abused[23]
By this base, crafty varlet.

FIRK. Yea, forsooth, no varlet; forsooth, no base;   [155
forsooth, I am but mean; no crafty neither, but of the
gentle craft.

L. MAYOR. Where is my daughter Rose? Where is my
    child?

LINCOLN. Where is my nephew Lacy married?

FIRK. Why, here is good laced mutton,[24] as I   [160
promised you.

LINCOLN. Villain, I'll have thee punished for this wrong.

FIRK. Punish the journeyman villain, but not the journeyman shoemaker.

Enter DODGER

DODGER. My Lord, I come to bring unwelcome news.
Your nephew Lacy and your daughter Rose   166
Early this morning wedded at the Savoy,
None being present but the Lady Mayoress.
Besides, I learnt among the officers,
The Lord Mayor vows to stand in their defense   170
'Gainst any that shall seek to cross the match.

LINCOLN. Dares Eyre the shoemaker uphold the deed?

FIRK. Yes, sir, shoemakers dare stand in a woman's
quarrel, I warrant you, as deep as another, and deeper too.

DODGER. Besides, his Grace today dines with the Mayor;
Who on his knees humbly intends to fall   176
And beg a pardon for your nephew's fault.

LINCOLN. But I'll prevent[25] him! Come, Sir Roger
    Oateley;
The King will do us justice in this cause.
Howe'er their hands have made them man and wife,   180
I will disjoin the match or lose my life.

[*Exeunt* LINCOLN, MAYOR, DODGER, *and* Servants

FIRK. Adieu, Monsier Dodger! Farewell, fools!—Ha,
ha! Oh, if they had stayed, I would have so lambed[26]
them with flouts! O heart, my codpiece-point[27] is ready to
fly in pieces every time I think upon Mistress Rose.   [185
But let that pass, as my Lady Mayoress says.

HODGE. This matter is answered. Come, Ralph; home
with thy wife. Come, my fine shoemakers, let's to our
master's the new Lord Mayor, and there swagger this
Shrove Tuesday.[28] I'll promise you wine enough,   [190
for Madge keeps the cellar.

---

[23] Deceived.

[24] Slang for a strumpet; but the point is the pun with "Lacied,"
and no reflection on Jane's character is intended.

[25] Anticipate.   [26] Lammed, lambasted.

[27] The lacing of the bagged appendage worn at the front of tight
hose or breeches.

[28] The great holiday of the apprentices.

---

[21] A contemptuous vocative.   [22] Troops.

ALL. Oh, rare! Madge is a good wench.

FIRK. And I'll promise you meat enough, for simp'ring Susan keeps the larder. I'll lead you to victuals, my brave soldiers; follow your captain. Oh, brave! Hark, hark! [195

[Bell rings

ALL. The pancake bell[29] rings, the pancake bell! Trilill, my hearts!

FIRK. Oh, brave! O sweet bell! O delicate pancakes! Open the doors, my hearts, and shut up the windows! keep in the house, let out the pancakes! Oh, rare, [200 my hearts! Let's march together for the honor of St. Hugh to the great new hall[30] in Gracious Street corner, which our master, the new Lord Mayor, hath built.

RALPH. Oh, the crew of good fellows that will dine at my Lord Mayor's cost today! 205

HODGE. By the Lord, my Lord Mayor is a most brave man. How shall prentices be bound to pray for him and the honor of the gentlemen shoemakers! Let's feed and be fat with my Lord's bounty.

FIRK. O musical bell, still! O Hodge, O my [210 brethren! There's cheer for the heavens: venison pasties walk up and down piping hot, like serjeants; beef and brewis[31] comes marching in dry-vats;[32] fritters and pancakes comes trolling[33] in in wheelbarrows; hens and oranges hopping in porters' baskets, collops[34] and [215 eggs in scuttles;[35] and tarts and custards comes quavering in in malt-shovels.

Enter more Prentices

ALL. Whoop, look here, look here!

HODGE. How now, mad lads, whither away so fast?

1ST PRENTICE. Whither? Why, to the great new [220 hall; know you not why? The Lord Mayor hath bidden all the prentices in London to breakfast this morning.

ALL. O brave shoemaker, O brave lord of incomprehensible good-fellowship! Whoo! Hark you! The pancake bell rings. [*Cast up caps* [225

FIRK. Nay, more, my hearts! Every Shrove Tuesday is our year of jubilee; and when the pancake bell rings, we are as free as my Lord Mayor; we may shut up our shops, and make holiday; I'll have it called St. Hugh's Holiday.

ALL. Agreed, agreed! St. Hugh's Holiday. 230

HODGE. And this shall continue forever.

ALL. Oh, brave! Come, come, my hearts! Away, away!

FIRK. Oh, eternal credit to us of the gentle craft! March fair, my hearts! Oh, rare! [*Exeunt*

SCENE III[36]

Enter the KING *and his* Train *over the stage*

KING. Is our Lord Mayor of London such a gallant?

NOBLEMAN. One of the merriest madcaps in your land. Your Grace will think, when you behold the man, He's rather a wild ruffian than a mayor. Yet thus much I'll ensure your Majesty, 5 In all his actions that concern his state[37] He is as serious, provident, and wise, As full of gravity amongst the grave, As any mayor hath been these many years.

KING. I am with child[38] till I behold this huffcap.[39] 10 But all my doubt is, when we come in presence, His madness will be dashed clean out of countenance.

NOBLEMAN. It may be so, my liege.

KING. Which to prevent, Let someone give him notice 't is our pleasure That he put on his wonted merriment.— 15 Set forward!

ALL. On afore! [*Exeunt*

SCENE IV[40]

Enter EYRE, HODGE, FIRK, RALPH, *and other* Shoemakers, *all with napkins on their shoulders*

EYRE. Come, my fine Hodge, my jolly gentlemen shoemakers; soft, where be these cannibals, these varlets, my officers? Let them all walk and wait upon my brethren; for my meaning is that none but shoemakers, none but the livery of my company, shall in their satin hoods wait [5 upon the trencher of my sovereign.

FIRK. Oh, my Lord, it will be rare!

EYRE. No more, Firk; come, lively! Let your fellow prentices want no cheer; let wine be plentiful as beer, and beer as water. Hang these penny-pinching fathers, [10 that cram wealth in innocent lamb-skins.[41] Rip, knaves, avaunt! Look to my guests!

HODGE. My Lord, we are at our wits' end for room; those hundred tables will not feast the fourth part of them.

EYRE. Then cover me those hundred tables again, [15 and again, till all my jolly prentices be feasted. Avoid, Hodge! Run, Ralph! Frisk about, my nimble Firk! Carouse me fathom-healths to the honor of the shoemakers. Do they drink lively, Hodge? Do they tickle it, Firk?

FIRK. Tickle it? Some of them have taken their [20 liquor standing so long that they can stand no longer; but for meat, they would eat it an they had it.

---

29 In every parish the bell was rung early on Shrove Tuesday as a reminder of shriving. Pancakes being popular as a substitute for meat, it came to be called the pancake bell, and was the signal for the beginning of the holiday merriment.
30 Leadenhall. 31 Beef broth. 32 Casks. 33 Rolling.
34 Slices of meat. 35 Vegetable or fruit baskets.

36 A street. 37 Administration. 38 Impatiently expectant.
39 Swaggerer. 40 A great hall.
41 Probably alluding to their use as parchment for recording deeds, transfers, etc.

EYRE. Want they meat? Where's this swag-belly, this greasy kitchen-stuff cook? Call the varlet to me! Want meat? Firk, Hodge, lame Ralph, run, my tall men, [25 beleaguer the shambles,[42] beggar all Eastcheap, serve me whole oxen in chargers,[43] and let sheep whine upon the tables like pigs for want of good fellows to eat them. Want meat? Vanish, Firk! Avaunt, Hodge!

HODGE. Your Lordship mistakes my man Firk; [30 he means their bellies want meat, not the boards, for they have drunk so much they can eat nothing.

THE SECOND THREE-MAN'S SONG

(This is to be sung at the latter end)[44]

Cold's the wind, and wet's the rain;
  St. Hugh be our good speed;
Ill is the weather that bringeth no gain, 35
  Nor helps good hearts in need.

Troll[45] the bowl, the jolly nut-brown bowl,
  And here, kind mate, to thee;
Let's sing a dirge for St. Hugh's soul.
  And down it[46] merrily. 40

Down a down, hey down a down,
  Hey derry derry, down a down!
                (Close with the tenor boy)
Ho, well done; to me let come!
  Ring compass, gentle joy.[47]

Troll the bowl, the nut-brown bowl, 45
  And here, kind, etc. *[Repeat] as often as there be men to
                          drink; at last, when all have drunk,
                          this verse:*

Cold's the wind, and wet's the rain;
  St. Hugh be our good speed;
Ill is the weather that bringeth no gain,
  Nor helps good hearts in need. 50

Enter LACY *as* HANS, ROSE, *and wife* MARGERY

MARG. Where is my Lord?
EYRE. How now, Lady Madgy?
MARG. The King's most excellent Majesty is new come; he sends me for thy Honor; one of his most worshipful peers bade me tell thou must be merry, and so forth; [55 but let that pass.

EYRE. Is my sovereign come? Vanish, my tall shoemakers, my nimble brethren; look to my guests, the prentices. Yet stay a little! How now, Hans? How looks my little Rose?

HANS. Let me request you to remember me. 60
I know your Honor easily may obtain
Free pardon of the King for me and Rose,
And reconcile me to my uncle's grace.

EYRE. Have done, my good Hans, my honest journeyman; look cheerily! I'll fall upon both my knees, [65 till they be as hard as horn, but I'll get thy pardon.

MARG. Good my Lord, have a care what you speak to his Grace.

EYRE. Away, you Islington whitepot![48] hence, you hopper-arse![49] hence, you barley-pudding, full of [70 maggots! you broiled carbonado![50] avaunt, avaunt, avoid, Mephistophilus! Shall Sim Eyre learn to speak of you, Lady Madgy? Vanish, Mother Miniver-cap;[51] vanish, go, trip and go; meddle with your partlets[52] and your pishery-pashery, your flews[53] and your whirligigs; go, [75 rub,[54] out of mine alley! Sim Eyre knows how to speak to a pope, to Sultan Soliman,[55] to Tamburlaine, an he were here; and shall I melt, shall I droop before my sovereign? No, come, my Lady Madgy! Follow me, Hans! About your business, my frolic freebooters! Firk, [80 frisk about, and about, and about, for the honor of mad Simon Eyre, Lord Mayor of London.

FIRK. Hey, for the honor of the shoemakers! *[Exeunt*

SCENE V[56]

A long flourish or two. Enter KING, Nobles, EYRE, *his wife* MARGERY, LACY, *and* ROSE. LACY *and* ROSE *kneel*

KING. Well, Lacy, though the fact was very foul
Of your revolting from our kingly love
And your own duty, yet we pardon you.
Rise both, and, Mistress Lacy, thank my Lord Mayor
For your young bridegroom here. 5

EYRE. So, my dear liege, Sim Eyre and my brethren, the gentlemen shoemakers, shall set your sweet Majesty's image cheek by jowl by St. Hugh for this honor you have done poor Simon Eyre. I beseech your Grace, pardon my rude behavior; I am a handicraftsman, yet my heart [10 is without craft; I would be sorry at my soul that my boldness should offend my King.

---

42 The butchers' shops.
43 Great platters.   44 But precisely where is not stated.
45 Circulate.   46 Sing the burden, "down-a-down," etc.
47 Complete the circle, my dear love; i.e., let the drinks go round.

48 A dish made of milk, eggs, sugar, etc., boiled in a pot.
49 Presumably with reference to her shape in the farthingale. See III, iv, 38 f., above.   50 Steak.
51 I.e., trimmed or lined with that fur.   52 Neckerchiefs.
53 Probably the flaps of the French hood.
54 Obstacle (in bowling).
55 Evidently an allusion to the anonymous play, *Soliman and Perseda*, attributed by some to Kyd.   56 The same.

KING. Nay, I pray thee, good Lord Mayor, be even as merry
As if thou wert among thy shoemakers;
It does me good to see thee in this humor.   15

EYRE. Say'st thou me so, my sweet Dioclesian?[57] Then, hump![58] Prince am I none, yet am I princely born. By the Lord of Ludgate, my liege, I'll be as merry as a pie.[59]

KING. Tell me, in faith, mad Eyre, how old thou art.

EYRE. My liege, a very boy, a stripling, a younker;   [20
you see not a white hair on my head, not a gray in this beard. Every hair, I assure thy Majesty, that sticks in this beard, Sim Eyre values at the King of Babylon's ransom; Tamar Cham's[60] beard was a rubbing-brush to 't: yet I'll shave it off, and stuff tennis-balls with it, to please   [25
my bully King.

KING. But all this while I do not know your age.

EYRE. My liege, I am six-and-fifty year old, yet I can cry hump! with a sound heart for the honor of St. Hugh. Mark this old wench, my King: I danced the Shak-   [30
ing of the Sheets[61] with her six-and-thirty years ago, and yet I hope to get two or three young lord mayors, ere I die. I am lusty still, Sim Eyre still. Care and cold lodging brings white hairs. My sweet Majesty, let care vanish; cast it upon thy nobles; it will make thee look always   [35
young like Apollo, and cry hump! Prince am I none, yet am I princely born.

KING. Ha, ha! Say, Cornwall, didst thou ever see his like?

NOBLEMAN. Not I, my Lord.

Enter EARL OF LINCOLN *and the former* LORD MAYOR

KING.   Lincoln, what news with you?

LINCOLN. My gracious Lord, have care unto yourself,[40
For there are traitors here.

ALL.   Traitors? Where? Who?

EYRE. Traitors in my house? God forbid! Where be my officers? I'll spend my soul, ere my King feel harm.

KING. Where is the traitor, Lincoln?

LINCOLN.   Here he stands.

KING. Cornwall, lay hold on Lacy!—Lincoln, speak,   45
What canst thou lay unto thy nephew's charge?

LINCOLN. This, my dear liege: your Grace, to do me honor,
Heaped on the head of this degenerous[62] boy
Desertless[63] favors; you made choice of him
To be commander over powers in France.   50
But he—

57 Diocletian, i.e., emperor. St. Hugh's martyrdom occurred in his time. See II, iii, note 30.
58 Humph! An interjection of jollity.   59 Magpie.
60 I.e., the Khan Timur, Tamburlaine.
61 See IV, v, 86 f., and note.   62 Degenerate.
63 Undeserved.

KING.   Good Lincoln, prithee, pause awhile!
Even in thine eyes I read what thou wouldst speak.
I know how Lacy did neglect our love,
Ran himself deeply, in the highest degree,
Into vile treason.

LINCOLN.   Is he not a traitor?   55

KING. Lincoln, he was; now have we pard'ned him.
'T was not a base want of true valor's fire
That held him out of France, but love's desire.

LINCOLN. I will not bear his shame upon my back.

KING. Nor shalt thou, Lincoln; I forgive you both.   60

LINCOLN. Then, good my liege, forbid the boy to wed
One whose mean birth will much disgrace his bed.

KING. Are they not married?

LINCOLN.   No, my liege.

BOTH.   We are.

KING. Shall I divorce them then? Oh, be it far
That any hand on earth should dare untie   65
The sacred knot, knit by God's Majesty;
I would not for my crown disjoin their hands
That are conjoined in holy nuptial bands.
How say'st thou, Lacy, wouldst thou lose thy Rose?

LACY. Not for all India's wealth, my sovereign.   70

KING. But Rose, I am sure, her Lacy would forgo.

ROSE. If Rose were asked that question, she'd say no.

KING. You hear them, Lincoln.

LINCOLN.   Yea, my liege, I do.

KING. Yet canst thou find i' th' heart to part these two?
Who seeks, besides you, to divorce these lovers?   75

L. MAYOR. I do, my gracious Lord; I am her father.

KING. Sir Roger Oateley, our last mayor, I think?

NOBLEMAN. The same, my liege.

KING.   Would you offend Love's laws?
Well, you shall have your wills; you sue to me,
To prohibit the match. Soft, let me see—   80
You both are married, Lacy, art thou not?

LACY. I am, dread sovereign.

KING.   Then, upon thy life,
I charge thee not to call this woman wife.

L. MAYOR. I thank your Grace.

ROSE.   O my most gracious Lord! [Kneel

KING. Nay, Rose, never woo me; I tell you true,   85
Although as yet I am a bachelor,
Yet I believe I shall not marry you.

ROSE. Can you divide the body from the soul,
Yet make the body live?

KING.   Yea, so profound?
I cannot, Rose; but you I must divide.—   90
This fair maid, bridegroom, cannot be your bride.—
Are you pleased, Lincoln?—Oateley, are you pleased?

BOTH. Yes, my Lord.

KING.   Then must my heart be eased;
For, credit me, my conscience lives in pain,

Till these whom I divorced be joined again. 95
Lacy, give me thy hand; Rose, lend me thine!
Be what you would be! Kiss now! So, that's fine.
At night, lovers, to bed!—Now, let me see,
Which of you all mislikes this harmony.

L. MAYOR. Will you then take from me my child
    perforce? 100

KING. Why, tell me, Oateley: shines not Lacy's name
As bright in the world's eye as the gay beams
Of any citizen?

LINCOLN.   Yea; but, my gracious Lord,
I do mislike the match far more than he
Her blood is too, too base.

KING.   Lincoln, no more. 105
Dost thou not know that love respects no blood,
Cares not for difference of birth or state?
The maid is young, well born, fair, virtuous,
A worthy bride for any gentleman.
Besides, your nephew for her sake did stoop 110
To bare necessity, and, as I hear,
Forgetting honors and all courtly pleasures,
To gain her love became a shoemaker.
As for the honor which he lost in France,
Thus I redeem it: Lacy, kneel thee down!— 115
Arise, Sir Rowland Lacy! Tell me now,
Tell me in earnest, Oateley, canst thou chide,
Seeing thy Rose a lady and a bride?

L. MAYOR. I am content with what your Grace hath
    done.

LINCOLN. And I, my liege, since there's no remedy. [120

KING. Come on, then, all shake hands: I'll have you
    friends;
Where there is much love, all discord ends.
What says my mad Lord Mayor to all this love?

EYRE. O my liege, this honor you have done to my fine
journeyman here, Rowland Lacy, and all these   [125
favors which you have shown to me this day in my poor
house, will make Simon Eyre live longer by one dozen of
warm summers more than he should.

KING. Nay, my mad Lord Mayor—that shall be thy
    name—
If any grace of mine can length thy life, 130
One honor more I'll do thee: that new building,
Which at thy cost in Cornhill is erected,
Shall take a name from us; we'll have it called
The Leadenhall, because in digging it
You found the lead that covereth the same.[64] 135

EYRE. I thank your Majesty.

MARG.   God bless your Grace!

KING. Lincoln, a word with you!

Enter HODGE, FIRK, RALPH, _and more_ Shoemakers

EYRE. How now, my mad knaves? Peace, speak softly,
yonder is the King.

KING. With the old troop which there we keep in pay,
We will incorporate a new supply.
Before one summer more pass o'er my head,
France shall repent England was injurèd.—
What are all those?

LACY.   All shoemakers, my liege,
Sometimes[65] my fellows; in their companies 145
I lived as merry as an emperor.

KING. My mad Lord Mayor, are all these shoemakers?

EYRE. All shoemakers, my liege; all gentlemen of the
gentle craft, true Trojans, courageous cordwainers; they
all kneel to the shrine of holy St. Hugh. 150

ALL. God save your Majesty! all shoemakers!

KING. Mad Simon, would they anything with us?

EYRE. Mum, mad knaves! Not a word! I'll do't, I warrant
you.—They are all beggars, my liege; all for themselves,
and I for them all on both my knees, do entreat   [155
that for the honor of poor Simon Eyre and the good of
his brethren, these mad knaves, your Grace would vouchsafe some privilege to my new Leadenhall, that it may be
lawful for us to buy and sell leather[66] there two days a
week. 160

KING. Mad Sim, I grant your suit; you shall have patent
To hold two market days in Leadenhall,
Mondays and Fridays; those shall be the times.
Will this content you?

ALL.   Jesus bless your Grace!

EYRE. In the name of these my poor brethren   [165
shoemakers, I most humbly thank your Grace. But before
I rise, seeing you are in the giving vein and we in the begging, grant Sim Eyre one boon more.

KING. What is it, my Lord Mayor?

EYRE. Vouchsafe to taste of a poor banquet that   [170
stands sweetly waiting for your sweet presence.

KING. I shall undo[67] thee, Eyre, only with feasts;
Already have I been too troublesome;
Say, have I not?

EYRE. O my dear King, Sim Eyre was taken   [175
unawares upon a day of shroving,[68] which I promised
long ago to the prentices of London. For, an 't please your
Highness, in time past I bare the water-tankard, and my
coat sits not a whit the worse upon my back; and then,
upon a morning, some mad boys—it was Shrove   [180
Tuesday, even as 't is now—gave me my breakfast, and I
swore then by the stopple of my tankard if ever I came

---

[64] Actually the name long antedates the historical Eyre's erection
of a public granary in 1419.

[65] Formerly.
[66] Leadenhall as a leather market was an Elizabethan institution;
the historical Eyre seems to have been, not a shoemaker, but a
draper.   [67] Ruin.   [68] Carnival.

to be Lord Mayor of London, I would feast all the prentices.
This day, my liege, I did it, and the slaves had an hundred
tables five times covered; they are gone home and   [185
vanished.
Yet add more honor to the gentle trade:
Taste of Eyre's banquet, Simon's happy made.

KING. Eyre, I will taste of thy banquet, and will say

I have not met more pleasure on a day.—   190
Friends of the gentle craft, thanks to you all;
Thanks, my kind Lady May'ress, for our cheer.—
Come, lords, awhile let's revel it at home!
When all our sports and banquetings are done,
Wars must right wrongs which Frenchmen have
    begun.   [Exeunt   195

Thomas Campion
1567-1620

CAMPION was doubly endowed with the lyrical gift. He
was great as a lyric poet, great as a composer of songs, and
uncannily endowed with the knack of making the perfect
marriage between music and English words.

He was a Londoner by birth. Though orphaned at ten,
he was sent to Cambridge, where he may have begun his
medical studies. He was certainly well known as a "doctor
of physic," but where and when he obtained his degree is
unrevealed. For a while he had apparently aimed at the
law; he was entered at Gray's Inn in 1586. Thereafter we
know little of his life. He may have seen service under the
Earl of Essex in the civil wars of France.

In 1591 some of his poems appeared anonymously in the
unauthorized edition of Sidney's *Astrophel and Stella,* and
in 1595 he brought out a volume of Latin verses. His
Observations in the Art of English Poesy (1602), a condemnation of rime and a plea for the quantitative metrics of the
classical poets, provoked Samuel Daniel to *A Defense of
Rime,* a far abler performance. Fortunately for the treasury
of English poetry, Campion did not tie his practice to his
precepts. His verse, though it shows the chastening influence of Horace and Catullus, is rimed and thoroughly
English. Poem after poem, in its subtle metrical nuances,
is an unsurpassed example of the art of versification. Many
poets have sung with deeper passion, but none in English
has ever come closer to making actual melody out of words.

With Philip Rosseter he issued in 1601 a double *Book of
Airs,* each composer contributing half. There are two later
volumes of uncertain date by Campion alone, each consisting of two "books." His five "books" contain over a
hundred songs. In addition he wrote the words and music
of several masques, some of them for court performance.
As a poet he is a singer, not a trumpeter. There was no
thunder in his inkwell, nor did he as a composer essay the
elaborate musical structures which, especially in sacred
music, are among the most impressive of his contemporaries' compositions. Yet there is much variety in his lyricism, as our selections show. His is the apparent artlessness
of consummate art; and at his best, though in all simplicity
and quietness, he repeatedly achieves something that cannot be called by any lesser name than perfection.

The standard edition of Campion's literary works was
edited by P. Vivian (1909); it includes an account of his
life. There is a good article in *Grove's Dictionary of Music
and Musicians* (ed. H. C. Colles, 1938). The songs are available in E. H. Fellowes's *The English School of Lutenist Song
Writers* (16 vols., 1920-32; second series, 16 vols., 1925-27);
the volumes devoted to Campion are IV and XIII of the
first series, and I, II, X, and XI of the second series. See also
M. M. Kastendieck's *England's Musical Poet: Thomas Campion* (1938).

MY SWEETEST LESBIA

The first five of these poems are from a group of twenty-
one songs by Campion, "made at his vacant hours and
privately imparted to his friends," which he allowed Philip
Rosseter (d. 1623) to publish with an equal number of his
own in *A Book of Airs, Set Forth to Be Sung to the Lute,
Orpherian,*[1] *and Bass Viol* (1601). "My sweetest Lesbia" is
an imitation (in part actually a translation) of the fifth ode
of Catullus, "Vivamus, mea Lesbia, atque amemus."

My sweetest Lesbia, let us live and love;
And though the sager sort our deeds reprove,
Let us not weigh them: heaven's great lamps do dive
Into their west, and straight again revive;
But soon as once set is our little light,   5
Then must we sleep one ever-during night.

If all would lead their lives in love like me,
Then bloody swords and armor should not be;
No drum nor trumpet peaceful sleeps should move,
Unless alarm came from the camp of love.   10
But fools do live, and waste their little light,
And seek with pain their ever-during night.

When timely death my life and fortune ends,
Let not my hearse be vexed with mourning friends;
But let all lovers, rich in triumph, come   15
And with sweet pastimes grace my happy tomb;
And, Lesbia, close up thou my little light,
And crown with love my ever-during night.

---

[1] Orpharion or orpheoreon, an instrument much like the zither.

I CARE NOT FOR THESE LADIES

I care not for these ladies
That must be wooed and prayed;
Give me kind Amaryllis,
The wanton country maid.
Nature art disdaineth: 5
Her beauty is her own.
   Her when we court and kiss,
   She cries, "Forsooth,[2] let go!"
But when we come where comfort is,
She never will say no.   10

If I love Amaryllis,
She gives me fruit and flowers;
But if we love these ladies,
We must give golden showers.
Give them gold that sell love;   15
Give me the nut-brown lass,
   Who when we court and kiss,
   She cries, "Forsooth, let go!"
But when we come where comfort is,
She never will say no.   20

These ladies must have pillows
And beds by strangers wrought;[3]
Give me a bower of willows,
Of moss and leaves unbought,
And fresh Amaryllis,   25
With milk and honey fed,
   Who when we court and kiss,
   She cries, "Forsooth, let go!"
But when we come where comfort is,
She never will say no.

FOLLOW THY FAIR SUN

Follow thy fair sun, unhappy shadow,
Though thou be black as night,
And she made all of light,
Yet follow thy fair sun, unhappy shadow.

Follow her whose light thy light depriveth,   5
Though here thou liv'st disgracèd,
And she in heaven is placèd,
Yet follow her whose light the world reviveth.

Follow those pure beams whose beauty burneth,
That so have scorchèd thee,   10
As thou still[4] black must be,
Till her kind beams thy black to brightness turneth.

---

[2] In truth, really! By the end of the sixteenth century the use of
this expression was considered an indication of a lack of sophistication. [3] I.e., of foreign manufacture. [4] That thou ever.

Follow her while yet her glory shineth:
There comes a luckless night
That will dim all her light;   15
And this the black, unhappy shade divineth.

Follow still, since so thy fates ordainèd;
The sun must have his shade,
Till both at once do fade,
The sun still proud, the shadow still disdainèd.   20

WHEN TO HER LUTE

When to her lute Corinna sings,
Her voice revives the leaden strings,
And doth in highest notes appear,
As any challenged echo clear;
But when she doth of mourning speak,   5
Ev'n with her sighs the strings do break.

And as her lute doth live or die,
Led by her passion, so must I:
For when of pleasure she doth sing,
My thoughts enjoy a sudden spring;   10
But if she doth of sorrow speak,
Ev'n from my heart the strings do break.

THE MAN OF LIFE UPRIGHT

The man of life upright,
   Whose guiltless heart is free
From all dishonest deeds
   Or thought of vanity,

The man whose silent days   5
   In harmless joys are spent,
Whom hopes cannot delude
   Nor sorrow discontent,

That man needs neither towers
   Nor armor for defense   10
Nor secret vaults to fly
   From thunder's violence.

He only can behold
   With unaffrighted eyes
The horrors of the deep   15
   And terrors of the skies.

Thus, scorning all the cares
   That fate or fortune brings,
He makes the heav'n his book,
   His wisdom heav'nly things,   20

Good thoughts his only friends,
   His wealth a well-spent age,
The earth his sober inn
   And quiet pilgrimage.

ROSE-CHEEKED LAURA

This masterpiece of lyric smoothness is the best thing in Campion's *Observations in the Art of English Poesy* (1602), where it occurs to illustrate a "more compounded" (i.e., complex) type of versification.

Rose-cheeked Laura, come
Sing thou smoothly with thy beauty's
Silent music, either other
    Sweetly gracing.

Lovely forms do flow   5
From consent[5] divinely framèd;
Heav'n is music, and thy beauty's
    Birth is heavenly.

These dull notes we sing
Discords need for helps to grace them.   10
Only beauty purely loving
    Knows no discord,

But still moves delight,
Like clear springs renewed by flowing,
Ever perfect, ever in them-
    selves eternal.   15

NOW WINTER NIGHTS ENLARGE

The remainder of our selections are from Campion's *The Third and Fourth Book of Airs* (1617?). "Thrice toss these oaken ashes" is available in an arrangement for solo voice and piano in Frederick Keel's *Elizabethan Love-Songs, Second Set* (1913); "There is a garden in her face" is included in his *First Set* (1909).

Now winter nights enlarge
    The number of their hours,
And clouds their storms discharge
    Upon the airy towers.
Let now the chimneys blaze   5
    And cups o'erflow with wine;
Let well-tuned words amaze
    With harmony divine.
Now yellow waxen lights
    Shall wait on honey love,   10
While youthful revels, masques, and courtly sights
    Sleep's leaden spells remove.

This time doth well dispense
    With[6] lovers' long discourse;
Much speech hath some defense,   15
    Though beauty no remorse.
All do not all things well;
    Some measures[7] comely tread,
Some knotted riddles tell,
    Some poems smoothly read.   20

The summer hath his joys,
    And winter his delights;
Though love and all his[8] pleasures are but toys,
    They shorten tedious nights.

THRICE TOSS THESE OAKEN ASHES

Thrice toss these oaken ashes in the air,
Thrice sit thou mute in this enchanted chair,
And thrice three times tie up this true love's knot
And murmur soft, "She will, or she will not."

Go burn these pois'nous weeds in yon blue fire,   5
These screech-owl's feathers and this prickling brier,
This cypress gathered at a dead man's grave—
That all thy fears and cares an end may have.

Then come, you fairies, dance with me a round;
Melt her hard heart with your melodious sound!   10
In vain are all the charms I can devise:
She hath an art to break them with her eyes.

NEVER LOVE

Never love unless you can
Bear with all the faults of man:
Men sometimes will jealous be,
Though but little cause they see,
And hang the head, as discontent,   5
And speak what straight they will repent.

Men that but one saint adore
Make a show of love to more:
Beauty must be scorned in none,
Though but truly served in one;   10
For what is courtship but disguise?
True hearts may have dissembling eyes.

Men when their affairs require
Must a while themselves retire,
Sometimes hunt, and sometimes hawk,   15
And not ever sit and talk.
If these and such-like you can bear,
Then like, and love, and never fear.

THERE IS A GARDEN IN HER FACE

There is a garden in her face,
    Where roses and white lilies grow;
A heav'nly paradise is that place,
    Wherein all pleasant fruits do flow.
There cherries grow, which none may buy   5
Till "Cherry ripe!"[9] themselves do cry.

[5] Harmony.   [6] Give a dispensation to, warrant.
[7] Stately dances.

[8] Its.   [9] The street cry of the London huckster.

Those cherries fairly do enclose
  Of orient pearl a double row,
Which when her lovely laughter shows,
  They look like rose-buds filled with snow.   10
Yet them nor peer nor prince can buy,
Till "Cherry ripe!" themselves do cry.

Her eyes like angels watch them still;
  Her brows like bended bows do stand,
Threat'ning with piercing frowns to kill   15
  All that attempt with eye or hand
Those sacred cherries to come nigh,
Till "Cherry ripe!" themselves do cry.

The Seventeenth Century

THE SEVENTEENTH CENTURY

THE SEVENTEENTH century was probably the richest hundred years of English literature. If that is not enough to make it of absorbing interest to a twentieth-century American, it was Act I in the drama of the modern world, and the foundations of the United States were laid in and by it. There is no single key to it, nor for that matter to any century. In politics, revolution is the key; and there were revolutionary developments in many other departments of life. The seventeenth was a century of contrasts and change. The age-old struggle for liberty was intensified, and long strides were taken toward making the world considerably safer for the nonconformist in religion, the independent thinker, the individualist. The period begins with the attempted absolutism of James I and ends with the constitutional gains of the Glorious Revolution. As for literature, the century begins with the Renaissance still in full swing; much of our introduction to the Renaissance is no less applicable to the early seventeenth century. But the year 1700 finds us well into the age of cool rationalism: prose is more flourishing than poetry; common sense is more highly valued than imagination; the triumph of realism is complete.

COMMERCIAL EXPANSION AND SOCIAL PROGRESS

IN THIS same seventeenth century, English colonization took root, and the commercial expansion which had begun in the preceding age continued. In 1601 England was still the tight little island; in 1700 she was on her way to empire, and not alone because of Jamestown (1607), Plymouth (1620), and Boston (1630). Not till the next century was it certain that England and not France would found the most successful of modern empires; in 1623, moreover, the Dutch had driven the English from the rich archipelago of the Spice Islands or East Indies; but well before 1700 England had Jamaica and other West Indian possessions, while in India the East India Company was established in its trading posts, owned a fleet of big armed merchantmen, and was doing an importing business so profitable that in 1685 its stock stood at 500% of par. The old feeling against exacting interest for the use of money had gone by the board. Joint-stock companies, banks, and fire, maritime, and life insurance were important innovations in the business world. Another was the penny post, established for the City of London in the reign of Charles II.

With the growth of the foreign-trading companies, London's wealth and prosperity greatly increased. By 1700 the metropolitan area had over 600,000 inhabitants, of whom 200,000 lived in the city proper. (England and Wales together had 5,500,000.) There was no other large city; Bristol and Norwich came next with 30,000 apiece. Aside from some enlargement of the Elizabethan system of poor relief, any serious concern for social welfare was left to later centuries, though Locke championed the rights of children. There is nothing in the idea that the Great Fire of 1666 improved the housing of London's masses; the area which burned did not include the poorer districts.

For the upper and middle classes a greater refinement in living was possible, especially in Restoration times. More citrus fruit was used, and refined sugar became available. The importation of tea, coffee, and cocoa was responsible for a multiplicity of coffee and chocolate houses; some of these were meeting places for special groups—the world of fashion, party politicians, merchants, the literary coteries. In spite of these temptations to indolence, English life grew less easygoing, more precise and punctual. In this feature of its modernization, the manufacture and general use of clocks with minute hands was a factor. The introduction of forks revolutionized table manners. At the disposal of the well-to-do were Eastern silks and Chinese porcelain. Life in the Jacobean mansion no longer centered, as in medieval and Tudor times, in the hall. This central feature of the earlier house was replaced by smaller rooms which divided its functions, the drawing room and the dining room. Their floors were covered with carpets instead of rushes, which meant fewer fleas from the rats which carried the plague. All Americans who visit England are struck by the profusion of flowers, wild and cultivated. It was during the seventeenth century that the ornamental flower garden detached itself from the orchard and vegetable garden; and though it was nothing new for poets to express the Englishman's love of flowers, the garden received from Andrew Marvell (the poem will be found on pp. 529-30, below) perhaps the finest tribute it has had in verse.

In the intellectual world the Renaissance spirit of inquiry was stronger than ever. The telescope (1609) of the Italian Galileo (1564–1642) and the work of the German astronomer Kepler (1571–1630) insured the adoption of the Copernican theory (p. 216, above). In another direction, the microscope opened up boundless possibilities of exploration. Experimental research was aided and stimulated by a tremendous advance in mathematics: logarithms, the slide rule, analytic geometry, and calculus were products of seventeenth-century minds. To this progress Englishmen made vital contributions. Scientists honor the memory of William Harvey (1578–1657), for his epoch-making discovery of the circulation of the blood (1628); of Robert Boyle (1627–91), father of modern chemistry; of John Ray (1627–1705), for his studies in botany and zoology; and, above all, of Sir Isaac Newton (1647–1727), England's grandest name in science.

Modern philosophy begins with the great Frenchman Descartes (1596–1650), though (as we shall see) Sir Francis Bacon was an important forerunner. Descartes inaugurated the "Age of Reason." He begins, skeptically, by wiping the slate clean; he will have none of traditional knowledge as such. He also doubts the adequacy of what is presented to the mind by the senses alone. For him the great fact is the reason: *cogito, ergo sum* (I think, therefore I exist). From this proof of his own existence, he goes on to offer a proof of God's.[1]

Descartes's views were welcomed at Cambridge, where there had already been a healthy reaction against the medieval stranglehold of Aristotelian logic. It had also come under the fire of Bacon, who charged that Aristotle failed to "consult experience in order to make right propositions and axioms, but . . . twisted experience round and made her bend to his system." "Thus saith Aristotle" had long been an unanswerable argument. The immense improvement in methods of calculation afforded by the new mathematics, and the invention of more powerful and more accurate instruments (telescope, microscope, pendulum clock, thermometer, barometer, air pump), encouraged a bolder reliance on "experience," that is, on scientific observation and experiment. Bacon's principal weakness was his too exclusive devotion to the empirical method (the pursuit of knowledge by observation and experi-

---

[1] The insistence of Descartes on the mind's separability from matter, with which our senses are concerned, led to the seventeenth century's sharp distinction (a fundamental one in its literary theory) between reason and judgment on the one hand and imagination and fancy on the other.

ment); but others brought about a new and fruitful union—and to it scientific progress was largely due—between empiricism and rationalism (especially mathematical reasoning). In the sixties and seventies came Sir Isaac Newton's epoch-making contributions to mathematics, optics, and physics (for example, the binomial theorem, differential and integral calculus, the law of gravitation), culminating in 1687 in his *Principia*. The mechanistic and materialistic universe set forth in the *Principia*—it was an attempt to bring all phenomena under uniform law—shaped European thinking for the next two hundred years.

The scrutiny of received opinion and the tremendous accumulation of new information naturally led to considerable readjustment of traditional ideas, especially of religious ideas. The selections below reflect a good many shades of seventeenth-century religious views. Solutions to the problems posed by conflict of old and new ranged from stubborn rejection of scientific findings that conflicted with orthodox theology to out-and-out atheism. Here should be mentioned one group, called the Cambridge Platonists, who sought to reconcile Christian theology with modern philosophy and science, though they were resolute against the materialism of Hobbes.

But on his own century and the next, Thomas Hobbes (1588–1679) was immensely influential. His conception of the universe was mechanistic. The words "soul," "spirit," and "mind," he says, were invented to frighten people, as scarecrows frighten birds. The terms "good" and "evil" have neither divine sanction nor permanent meaning. Self-interest is the universal law governing human actions. Though his political philosophy of absolutism, expounded in his *Leviathan* (1651), was rejected by the English in favor of Locke's theory of government as a social contract to protect the rights of man, Hobbes's materialistic views seeped into much of the thought of the time. One effect of them is plainly visible in numerous writings of "the merry gang," the courtier-poets of Charles II. In their lives and in their verse they adopted the cynical, hardboiled attitude which at a certain age comes over many superior young men, but which most of them grow out of before it destroys their capacity to live a full life. Too many of the Restoration lads never grew out of it. We shall see what it did to one of the most promising, the Earl of Rochester.

GOVERNMENT AND RELIGION

Institutional religion must be considered along with government, for the religious quarrel was a vital element in the struggle which culminated in the two political revolutions. To be understood at all, some of the century's best literature must be read in the light of that struggle; hence, a rapid survey of historical events is necessary. The Great Rebellion did not arise from economic causes, although it is true that to manufacturers and tradesmen the Puritan way of life appealed with special force because it put a premium on the business virtues of thrift, sobriety, and application to the job in hand. The Protestant sectarians became a political party which steadily gained in numbers and influence until in the middle of the century it seized the government and set up a republic.

Hostile to art by temperament and also from their conviction that the world is but vanity, the supreme reality being the certainty of foreordained damnation for most and salvation for a few, "the saints" with their somber garb and grave, fanatic faces present a spectacle which neither charms nor cheers. Over the age that followed the English Renaissance they cast a dark, unlovely pall. Their mocking enemy the Cavalier, with his flowing locks, merry smile, and touch of swagger, is infinitely more appealing to the romantic instinct. But whether or not we like the Puritans, the fact is inescapable that on their Rebellion in 1642 and its aftermath, the Glorious Revolution of 1688, rests the modern framework of English liberty and to a considerable extent of ours. These political events established the supremacy of Parliament, put the king under the law, and confirmed the superiority of the Common Law to other kinds of law. Henceforth the legislative function was, for the English-speaking world, clearly vested in the legislative branch, not the executive. It is easy to condemn the Puritans for their narrowness and intolerance, but it must be remembered that few people in the seventeenth century believed in religious freedom; and it happened that the Puritans' fight for the right to hold their views, and later to impose them on others, furthered the historic cause of liberty.

JAMES I

ON THE death of Elizabeth in 1603, James VI of Scotland, a great-great-grandson of Henry VII, ascended the English throne as James I. His accession did not, however, unite the two countries; there were separate parliaments till 1707. James was remarkably learned for a king; but he was personally without dignity, and intellectually a pedant. He inherited a throne which under Elizabeth had been virtually absolute in fact, if not in name. But James was full of notions about the divine right of kings,

and his efforts and his son's to force acceptance of this doctrine on the English cost the house of Stuart both its thrones. Moreover, James lacked Elizabeth's genius for choosing able ministers. Nevertheless, his reign opened auspiciously. For one thing, the long war with Spain was wound up in 1604 by a satisfactory peace treaty. Soon, however, the monarch and his advisers were clashing with Parliament; and throughout the southeastern half of England, the Puritans gradually became a people's party and an opposition party. Eventually they obtained a majority of the seats in Commons.

Although a number of sectarians, the Independents, had left the Church of England, the bulk of the Puritans were not at first hostile to it; they merely wished to reform it. Their main object in the beginning was to simplify and still further Protestantize its ritual. Later, these aims being opposed by the bishops, they demanded abolition of the episcopal form of church government. In Scotland the king had already lost control of the national church; there the Presbyterian system was established, with control by the ministers and laity through synods or assemblies. James set himself against the spread of this form of religious organization to England, ordering the ejection of ministers who failed to conform to the Book of Common Prayer. Toward the oldest of the churches the reign began tolerantly enough; but the Gunpowder Plot of some desperate Catholics in 1605—they planned to blow up the Houses of Parliament along with the King and his advisers—made the vast majority of Englishmen deeply suspicious of Catholicism till long after the century's close.

James's un-English conviction that the king is above the law led him into a series of tyrannical actions which the House of Commons attempted to thwart by refusing to vote funds until grievances should be redressed. A long quarrel ensued. In the course of an attack on the King's administration, Parliament struck at him by impeaching the Lord Chancellor, Sir Francis Bacon.

CHARLES I

WHEN James died in 1625, his son succeeded as Charles I. This monarch, unlike his father a fine figure of a man and in his private life a decent sort, was politically obstinate and untrustworthy. He continued to press for recognition of the Stuarts' absolutist principles; finding Parliament intractable, he tried to rule without it. Under his program Puritan disaffection steadily increased. His chief advisers worked for royal supremacy and for High-Church Anglicanism. His foreign policy led him into futile wars with Spain and France. His marriage to a Catholic princess created alarm. Finally his attempt to seize control of the Scottish national church ended in failure. In 1640, after a gap of eleven years, he was obliged once more to summon Parliament. This was the Long Parliament, which put through the Puritan revolution. Under the leadership of John Pym (1584–1643), it passed act after act limiting the royal power.

In the summer of 1642 Charles decided on an appeal to arms. The royal party, or Cavaliers, were strongest in the north, west, and extreme southwest; on the whole the eastern and southern counties, commercially and culturally the more advanced, supported Parliament, from which the Cavalier members soon withdrew. Those members of the peerage who took the Parliamentary side were generally from families whose activities had brought them into some contact with the new commercial life of London. The royalists won early successes, but in the battles of Marston Moor (1644) and Naseby (1645) were routed by the Parliamentary army.

The military crisis brought to the front one of the greatest men in England's history. Oliver Cromwell (1599–1658) was a country squire, from near Huntingdon, with a genius for war and administration. He was a Puritan member of Parliament, but no fanatic. He perceived, however, that fanatics make superior fighting men. His disciplined cavalry, the Ironsides, played a decisive role in the battles. The Presbyterians in Parliament resisted his reorganization of the army, but he had his way and admitted the Puritan extremists or Independents; in the ranks of the "New Model" they came to predominate. The majority in Parliament, on the other hand, was composed of Presbyterians, who wanted to re-establish the national church along the lines of Scotland's; in order to secure Scottish aid for the Rebellion they had in fact agreed to do so. The Independents desired no such establishment, but toleration for all Protestant sects and complete self-government by the congregation of each local church.[2] Though a minority in Parliament, the Independents had the backing of Cromwell and of the army which he commanded; they were afraid the more conservative Presbyterians would compromise with Charles and throw away the political and religious fruits of the victory they had won in battle.[3]

Naseby ended the first Civil War. In the following year, 1646, Charles surrendered to the Scots, who turned him over to the English Parliament. The King was an incurable intriguer; and when the English Presbyterians began negotiations for his restoration, the resentful army seized him. In 1648 the second war broke out. A Scottish army marched southward, this time to fight for King Charles. Cromwell cut it to pieces at Preston, but the Presbyterians of Parliament continued dickering with the King. At this point, late in 1648, the army usurped the civil power by forcing the exclusion of the Presbyterian members from the House of Commons. The "Rump" Parliament which remained was the army's tool. Early in 1649 Charles was tried by an improvised court, found guilty of treason, and beheaded.

THE COMMONWEALTH AND PROTECTORATE

ENGLAND was declared a commonwealth, that is, a republic. But even the Rump was a vexation to the victorious commander-in-chief. Cromwell soon dismissed the last semblance of constitutional government, took the title of Lord Protector, and from 1653 till his death in 1658 ruled England as a military dictator.

In many ways his rule was highly successful. On the Irish, who had rebelled and massacred the English, Cromwell took a terrible vengeance; thousands of them perished in counter-massacres, as well as in battle. The Scots took up the cause of Charles's son; but the Protector shattered two more of their armies, at Dunbar in 1650 and at Worcester in 1651. His conduct of foreign affairs was brilliant. England's commercial rivals, the Dutch, were soundly beaten in 1652–54. In a Spanish war England seized the valuable island of Jamaica. English prestige and influence on the Continent rose to their greatest height since Elizabeth's triumphs over Spain.

But the regime was a dictatorship and rested on the support of a fanatical minority. Personal liberties were invaded under repressive acts designed to safeguard the nation's morals. The ban on plays which had been enacted in 1642 was continued in force till 1660. The Puritans' ban on Sunday sports and amusements still creates an issue in some American localities. Doubtless the people would have voted at any time for a return, with restrictions, to the old

[2] The adoption of local self-government by the churches of the Massachusetts Bay colony was the result of local conditions. Though congregational democracy finally won out, most of the early Boston leaders were Presbyterian in their views. But Plymouth, the "Old Colony," was settled by Independents or Separatists.

[3] Among the results of that victory was the abolition of the old system of royal monopolies, by which the exclusive right to manufacture and sell many commonly used articles had been granted, sometimes in sheer favoritism, sometimes as a means of raising money, to courtiers or to enterprising speculators.

form of government; and less than two years after Cromwell's death a new Parliament invited Charles Stuart to return from his exile in France and Holland.

CHARLES II

THE IMPORTANT thing about the Restoration was not the return of the King but the return of Parliament. The old struggle for supremacy was instantly renewed; yet Charles, who was a highly intelligent person, always gave in when he had to. He did not, he whimsically averred, wish to set out again on his travels. Temperamentally he was just the monarch for a post-Puritan era; and, despite its excesses, his court played a fostering role toward the national culture—the last English court to do so. The daily life of most plain men and women was probably little affected by the changeover from Puritanism; but the fashionable world, centered in the court, adopted new codes, cynical codes. Hobbes's view that selfishness underlies everything we do was widely held and acted on.

Symbol of the new life was the gay, witty King, a gentleman, a man of brains and taste, but lazy and unprincipled. The long-accepted view that he neglected public affairs has recently been disputed; but the fact is that, while his interest was keen enough, he displayed little energy for getting things done. A good deal of his energy was dissipated in the company of his mistresses, of whom he had a bevy, partly recruited from the playhouse, and including at least one French spy. Around him gathered a brilliant group of young courtiers, all of them wits, most of them poets. Their class, as Mr. Trevelyan says, had been put in cold storage; now they rejoiced in the warm sun, and begged rewards to help them thaw out. The older Cavaliers, who had cheerfully lost their estates for the King's father, and had fought and bled under the swords of the Ironsides, were not happy about the sovereign's habit of spending evening after evening with these youngsters, in talk for the sake of talk.

Unlike his father and grandfather, Charles, perhaps because he had a strong sense of humor, was not troubled with mystic sentiments about the divine right of kings. Nor was he prepared to risk his crown for religion's sake. It was partly his own preference, as a connoisseur, for the elegance of the French court, and his dislike of the Dutch republic's stolid burghers, that inclined him to follow France in his foreign policy. Catholic France was now the leading and most dreaded European power; while the Dutch, though they were Protestants, were England's business rivals at sea. One fine English gain from the war with Holland in 1664–67 was the island of Manhattan with its settlement of New Amsterdam, promptly renamed New York, and the territories northward and westward toward the Great Lakes;[4] but till the day of Neville Chamberlain and his appeasement of Hitler's Germany at Munich, English prestige touched its lowest point in 1667 when, on the heels of a terrible outbreak of the plague, followed by the Great Fire in which London lost 13,000 houses, a Dutch fleet sailed up the Thames and burned three English warships. In 1670 Charles actually signed a secret treaty with France and became a pensioner of King Louis, agreeing in return for an annual stipend to join the French in a second war with Holland, to become a Catholic openly when the time should be ripe, and to accept the aid of French troops in the event of an English rebellion. He did not, however, acknowledge his Catholic faith till he was on his deathbed; and as for the Dutch, he made a separate peace with them in 1674. Four years later Louis followed suit; already the implacable foe of his designs, the Protestant Prince William of Orange, was beginning to thwart them.

WHIG AND TORY

CHARLES's first Parliament lasted eighteen years, till 1679. "Loyalty" was now a catchword, and this Parliament was staunchly royalist in politics and Anglican in religion. The ministers whom the Puritans had ousted were reinstated; and two thousand others, who now refused to follow the prescribed service, were driven from their pulpits. This enforced exodus removed the last Puritan element from the clerical ranks of the Church of England. From then on it steadily declined as a spiritual force in English life, until in the middle of the eighteenth century it was revitalized by the Wesleyan or Methodist movement. Puritanism itself had lost most of its flaming idealism by the end of Charles's reign. No longer active in the councils of government, barred from the universities, ill at ease in the world of art, the Puritan rank and file directed its energy more and more into commercial channels. But the strength of mercantile England and the core of the Whig or liberal party (though not its leaders) came to be these same Dissenters, as the Protestant nonconformists were called.

Despite the uncompromising Anglicanism of Charles's Parliament, a reaction toward Catholicism soon developed, especially at court. Charles was sympathetic; and his brother James, Duke of York and heir to the throne, became a Catholic openly.

---

[4] The settlement of Pennsylvania and Delaware soon followed.

By 1678 there was such tension over religious questions that the so-called Popish Plot shook the nation to its depths. We shall return to this episode when we come to Dryden's satires. By this time, the party lines of Whig and Tory were well defined. The leader of the Whig or opposition party was the Earl of Shaftesbury, a great statesman and opponent of tyranny, but accustomed to fight fire with fire. He seized on the opportunity afforded by fears of a Catholic coup to agitate for the exclusion of James from the succession, in favor of Charles's illegitimate son the Duke of Monmouth, who was a Protestant. The excesses of the Whigs, which led to the execution of many innocent persons, kept the country in a turmoil for three years, and made a Tory reaction inevitable. Shaftesbury fled to Holland, where he died in 1683; for the remainder of the reign, the positions of both Charles and James were unchallenged.

JAMES II

WITH the accession of a Catholic king in 1685 there was an immediate challenge. James was an earnest soul, with neither the charm of Charles nor his easygoing temperament. In the interests of his fellow Catholics James issued a Declaration of Indulgence granting toleration to them and to the Dissenters, that is, the non-Anglican Protestant sects. A rebellion of the Duke of Monmouth was easily and bloodily suppressed; Charles's bastard paid with his own and many other lives for the ideas Shaftesbury had put into his head a decade earlier. But the Declaration of Indulgence had alienated the very party that would normally have supported James, the royalist and High-Church Tories. Their strength was in the country squires, that is, the landed gentry, and in the clergy of the Church of England. Both classes regarded toleration for non-Anglicans, including Catholics, as an attack on true religion and the safety of the country. There was now a social cleavage in the nation, more or less along the line which divided the Church of England from the Dissenters. It continued far into the nineteenth century. On the whole, the Anglican establishment was the church of the upper classes and their docile tenants in the country, while the Dissenters were mostly members of the middle or merchant class and workingmen. The division between Whigs and Tories did not, however, by any means follow the same line.

By his first wife James had two grown-up daughters, both Protestants. When his second wife gave birth to a son, who would be reared in the Catholic faith, the King's doom was sealed. Whig and Tory leaders joined in correspondence with the foremost of Europe's Protestant rulers, the archenemy of Louis XIV, William, Prince of Orange, head of the Dutch republic. He was the great-grandson of William the Silent (p. 223, above), a grandson on his mother's side of Charles I, and the husband of James's elder daughter, Mary Stuart. In November, 1688, he landed in England with a Dutch army. The whole country went over to him with enthusiasm. Among those who deserted James was the ablest soldier England has produced, John Churchill, destined to fame as the great Duke of Marlborough. James left for France in a hurry. He died in exile in 1701.

THE GLORIOUS REVOLUTION AND WILLIAM III

ON THE flight of James in 1688, Parliament declared the throne vacant and settled the succession; the very act implied for all subsequent sovereigns a denial of divine right and an acceptance of the legislature's authority. William and Mary were to rule jointly; should Mary's husband survive her (she died childless in 1694), he was to reign alone as William III; should issue be wanting, the crown was to pass to James's younger daughter, Mary's sister, Anne Stuart. A Bill of Rights, enacted in 1689, brought the monarch explicitly under the law of the land. A Toleration Act made no concessions to Catholics, but granted Dissenters the right to public worship.

With the Glorious Revolution, as it was called, England passed under parliamentary government. A further development, the cabinet system, by which the king's ministers as a body are held accountable to Parliament and can be dismissed at its pleasure, was the next step, an essential one. There were to be other important changes; but the form, though not yet the substance, of English democracy as we know it today had come into being. England was not yet, of course, a democracy. The Revolution simply meant that the country was not to go the way of France. There would be no absolute monarch in England, but rule by the propertied classes through a Parliament elected by them. Although the Tory leaders had joined in the Revolution, it was the Whigs' principles that triumphed in it, and it left their chiefs well entrenched.

Queen Mary carried little personal weight in politics. The new King was a moderate man, not brilliant, but distinguished by good sense and firmly opposed to religious persecution. From William's twenty-second year, when he was called to be stadholder, he had fought, on both religious and political grounds, against the tyranny of Louis XIV, despotic ruler of France and such other territories as he could lay hands on. Louis was not only a menace to the Dutch republic, the crushing of which was the main object of his foreign policy, but a general threat to European freedom who needed to be stopped as imperatively as a century later Napoleon needed to be stopped, and a century and more after that, Hitler. To resisting the aggressions of Louis, William dedicated his life. He looked on his new kingdom chiefly as an aid in carrying on that mission.

Already he had lined up Spain, Austria, and other German states in a Grand Alliance against France. The war dragged on. Peace was signed in 1697, but soon afterward it flared up again over the claim of a grandson of Louis to the Spanish throne. William formed a second Grand Alliance and then, worn out by a life of toil, failed to rally from the shock of a fall from his horse. He died on the eve of the final and victorious struggle, the War of the Spanish Succession (1702–13). His death, early in 1702, brings us to the new century and the age of Queen Anne. It is therefore time to turn back a hundred years and review the course of seventeenth-century literature.

PROSE WRITING

THREE extraordinary writers, whose careers began in the sixteenth century, led the way to the realism, disillusion, and cynicism which by and large distinguish seventeenth-century literature from Elizabethan or Renaissance writings: Francis Bacon, John Donne, and Ben Jonson. All three were masters of prose style, though only Bacon was exclusively or even mainly a writer of prose. Donne's major contribution was in poetry, Jonson's in drama.

There was much good prose in England before the general shift to a simpler style which historians have agreed to place in Dryden's time. Style is a very individual thing. As we have seen, from Tyndale on there was an excellent model in the English translations of the Bible; they culminated in 1611 in the noble prose of the King James Version. There was also much excellent prose writing in the drama, especially after 1600. But during the course of the seventeenth century a change occurred, at least in conceptions of what good prose is. It was a more self-conscious age, and those formulators of standards, the critics, were more heeded. They advocated a clean-cut, simple, sinewy, straightforward style. Toward the end of the century there was a premium on literal and precise rather than imaginative or suggestive expression. The fondness of some earlier writers for coining fantastic English derivatives from Latin words was frowned on, as were rhetorical tricks in general. The enormous activity of political and religious pamphleteers may have had something to do with this simplification. If you are really trying to change people's views, you will work for clearness

and persuasiveness, and resist the temptation to indulge in fancy writing for the sake of showing off.

The modernization of prose style was also related to the advance of science and philosophy. The Royal Society for Improving Natural Knowledge, founded in 1662 to encourage scientific experimentation, was interested in this problem, because it wanted English to become an effective medium for reporting findings. Dr. Thomas Sprat says in his *History of the Royal Society* (1667) that members were required to present their papers in "a close, naked, natural way of speaking," with "positive expressions, clear senses, a native easiness, bringing all things as near the mathematical plainness as they can and preferring the language of artisans, countrymen, and merchants before that of wits or scholars." It was a useful injunction. The application of critical and analytical methods to the study of society and of art likewise encouraged a more precise way of writing. The leading prose writer in the last third of the century was Dryden; as a critic of literature he had much to do with freeing prose style from the curlicues of ornament introduced for its own decorative sake. Yet a great deal of the century's best prose was not written with any special thought about what was happening in other fields. It was simply good, artistic prose. Shakespeare, Bacon, Jonson, and Webster wrote some of it in the early 1600's, and toward the end of the century the comic dramatists of the Restoration.

The prose of the century embraces many genres. The sermon was still immensely popular. *The seventeenth-century book* was the Bible, and many quite ordinary folk were deeply interested in interpretive comment on it. The inseparability of politics and religion increased public concern with theology, which occupied as a background for serious thought much the same undisputed position that science did in the first quarter of the twentieth century. Donne's sermons form a substantial body of remarkable prose. Jeremy Taylor (1613–67), "the Shakespeare of divines" as Emerson calls him, is still read for the poetic force of his sermons and for the eloquence of his plea for toleration in *A Discourse on the Liberty of Prophesying*. His devotional treatises on *Holy Living* and *Holy Dying* have often been reprinted.[5]

The "character," of which several examples will be found below, was not a new genre; but the popularity of this essaylike sketch of types of humanity exemplifies the age's self-consciousness and its urge toward the analysis of human nature and conduct. The essays of Bacon were another manifestation of

[5] See, for selections from Taylor, L. P. Smith, *The Golden Grove*, 1930.

the same urge, not to mention at the end of the century the diaries of Samuel Pepys (1633–1703) and John Evelyn (1620–76). So was the vogue for biography; that now popular art became established in English during the course of the seventeeth century. Antiquarians like Thomas Fuller (1608–61), John Aubrey (1626–97), and Anthony à Wood (1632–95) collected biographical data. Beginning in 1640, Izaak Walton wrote five short Lives, the first important biographical writings in English. Historical works form an important category. We have already glanced at Raleigh's history of the world. An important source book for its period was by Charles II's Lord Chancellor, Edward Hyde, Earl of Clarendon (1608–74), who began contemporaneously with the events it describes his *History of the Rebellion and Civil Wars in England*. He also wrote, among other works, an autobiography.

The selections below from Browne and Walton reflect the current spirit of inquiry, and the excerpt from Milton's *Areopagitica* shows you the highwater mark of the vast output of controversial prose. The writings of John Bunyan (1628–88) are not represented here, because his best work, *The Pilgrim's Progress*, is easy to come by and should be read entire rather than in extracts. Prose fiction is of small importance in the seventeenth century. Mrs. Aphra Behn (1640–89), England's first professional woman writer, produced plays and novels. Her *Oroonoko*, which appeared in both forms, is a forerunner of the next century's agitation against slavery.

THE REVOLUTION IN VERSE

IN POETRY, as in prose and the drama, there were immediate indications as the century opened that the spirit of the Renaissance was still at work, but less hopefully, more realistically. In every age and place there are enthusiasts, and also colder temperaments inclined to wet-blanket enthusiasm. The first class produces the artist, the second most of the critics. But though the major artist is usually a yea-sayer, in some men the two impulses are so unhappily mixed that the critical faculty (which like its opposite is usually present to some degree in any good man) thwarts rather than steadies an artist. That is the key to many a minor poet's predicament.

At first John Donne (1572–1631) was a nay-sayer. All he had to offer in the beginning was a jeer for the Elizabethan lovesong and even for love. Then, as we shall see, he was converted to a realism deeper than the superficial cynicism he had affected, and he became a yea-sayer, but still inquiring, still critical. Ben Jonson (1573–1637), though an even more revolutionary agent than Donne in the history of seven-

teenth-century poetry, is intellectually more conventional than Donne. It is the exuberant expression of Elizabethan verse against which Jonson turns. In love, not with the Elizabethans' favorite, Ovid, but with the classical lyrists—the Greek Anacreon, the Roman Horace and Catullus—Jonson writes as like them as he can. He is the first great neoclassical English poet, and possibly the best.

The triumph of neoclassicism was not, however, to come till the Restoration. Meanwhile, several poets, Herbert, Crashaw, and Vaughan in chief, had enriched English literature with its finest religious lyrics (they will be found under the heading "The Devotional Lyrists"); Robert Herrick, Jonson's principal successor on the poetic side, had made the largest contribution of first-rate lyricism anyone made in the seventeenth century; each of a swarm of lesser poets had written one or more things no reader can afford to miss—hence our "Miscellany of Stuart Verse"; and Milton, belonging to no school, had composed his finest verse, his so-called minor poems.

The last quarter of the century was not comparably productive on the lyric side. The tendency away from the creative and toward the critical, from poetry and imagination toward prose and common sense, bore a dry but firm and not unpleasing fruit, a kind of poetry that is as close to being prose as poetry can come. It is not prose, however; and a reader who, loving the great Elizabethan and Romantic singers, rejects the poetry of neoclassicism is sadly limiting his appreciations. This poetry was written mostly in rimed iambic pentameter couplets, and as time went on the poets tended more and more to make each couplet a self-contained unit of thought in the progression of a poem:

From point to point proceeds th' audacious minion,
And proves them all with "That is my opinion."

This tight and streamlined form lent itself admirably to the new fetish of clearness. "Though," wrote a learned bishop in 1666, "a huge, luscious style may relish sweet to childish and liquorish fancies, yet it rather loathes and nauseates a discreet understanding than forms and nourishes it." The restricted mold of the heroic couplet was a force for precision in thinking and writing, and it speedily became the normal vehicle of English poetry.

But not Milton's. The one great figure whose career as an active writer links the two halves of the century, Milton dwelt apart. He remained the last major writer of the English Renaissance, as Dryden was the advance agent of the eighteenth century. *Paradise Lost* is less admired now than formerly, but it towers above the little age in which its author, blind and defeated, serenely composed it.

JACOBEAN AND CAROLINE DRAMA

JONSON's is the great name in Jacobean comedy. How he laid the foundations of seventeenth-century realistic comedy will be described in the introductory sketch of his life and works. Other powerfully realistic pens were those of Thomas Middleton and John Marston. John Fletcher, who was Shakespeare's successor as principal playwright for the King's Men, "His Majesty's Servants" at the Blackfriars and the Globe, developed an unromantic kind of comedy which, at its best, is hardly realistic, though the general tone is one of disillusion. The mediocre Philip Massinger has the distinction of writing the only non-Shakespearean play of the seventeenth century that has continuously held a place in the professional repertory down to our own time, *A New Way to Pay Old Debts* (c. 1625), a comedy which ends in the villain's death. With the realistic comedies of James Shirley (e.g., *The Lady of Pleasure,* 1635), we are close to the tone though hardly to the wit of Restoration comedy. Shirley lived into the Restoration period; his plays were popular in the sixties, till the new men began coming forward with theirs.

In tragedy the story is of decline. We begin with a supreme peak of artistic achievement; for rivals to *Hamlet, Othello, King Lear, Macbeth,* and *Antony and Cleopatra* we have to go back, not forward—to the ancient Greeks. The tragedies of Beaumont and Fletcher are often theatrically effective and pleasingly phrased, but little more can be said for them. Jonson tried Roman tragedy and failed. The best of the century's non-Shakespearean tragedies are the two masterpieces of John Webster, *The White Devil* (c. 1611) and *The Duchess of Malfi* (c. 1613); the latter is reprinted below. Middleton, Marston, Massinger, and Shirley all wrote tragedies; but none is comparable to these. Long before the theaters were closed in 1642, the dramatists were manipulating well-worn situations, characters, and sentiments, invented in happier days. An exception is John Ford, who developed an original vein in such tragedies as *'Tis Pity She's a Whore* (c. 1631) and *The Broken Heart* (c. 1632).

RESTORATION TRAGEDY

THE MAIN effect of the enforced closing of the theaters from 1642 to 1660 was that, with the exceptions of Shirley and the minor playwright but important producer Sir William D'avenant, it was a new set of dramatists who took over in 1660. (A good many plays by Fletcher, Jonson, and Shakespeare, however, continued in the new repertory.) Oddly enough, the new tragedy started off with a romantic reaction, in the form of the Heroic drama, formulated by Dryden and others. "Heroic" means more than life-sized, as in "a heroic statue"; and the heroes of these plays evince both military prowess and emotion on a colossal scale. Composed in the most inflated style, though in rimed couplets, the Heroic play specializes in one of drama's best situations, the clash between love and honor. Between these two motives the hero vacillates; he is pushed in the direction of honor by the monumentally virtuous heroine, but pulled away from it by his passion for her. It is a grossly sentimental school of drama, and a hopelessly unrealistic one, perhaps because the age was itself so lacking in idealism that it had to go far afield for objects to admire. It was ridiculed in *The Rehearsal* (1671), a mock-heroic play by the second Duke of Buckingham, whose hero Drawcansir declaims in a fashion scarcely more extravagant than the speech of his original, Almanzor, in Dryden's *The Conquest of Granada*. Although the Heroic play regularly brings the distressed lovers out happily, it was and is often called Heroic tragedy, and for a while it was the closest approach to tragedy the playwrights made.

The vogue lasted only till 1677—that is, the vogue for *composing* heroic dramas; some of them long continued in the repertory, and for many decades traces of Almanzor-Drawcansir were likely to crop out anywhere. Dryden turned in 1677 from Heroic drama to a frankly confessed but none too happy attempt at imitating the style of Shakespeare's blank-verse tragedies while conforming more or less to the neoclassical Rules. His most successful play, *All for Love,* is based on *Antony and Cleopatra*. The best Restoration tragedies were not the work of Dryden, nor of Nathaniel Lee (1649?-92), who in the same year made the same turn from Heroic to blank-verse tragedy with *The Rival Queens, or The Death of Alexander the Great*. The best ones were written by Thomas Otway (1652-85): *The Orphan* (1680), a poignant domestic tragedy, and *Venice Preserved* (1682), the finest tragedy between Webster's *The Duchess of Malfi* and the turn of the twentieth century.

RESTORATION COMEDY

THE COMIC dramatists of the Restoration brilliantly exploited a narrow vein. Shakespeare and his fellows had staged a pageant of human life on every level of society. The best Restoration playwrights, except Shadwell, were not much interested in any level except high society. If the proletariat appears—servants, for instance—it is to be coldly ridiculed. The middle class exists in order that its wives may be seduced by the aristocratic rakes. Less and less was the drama a cross section of English life; more and more it was the affair of coteries. The nature of this comedy, its strength and its weakness, though not its obscenity, is well illustrated by its most scintillating example, Congreve's *The Way of the World;* see the headnote to that play, below.

Aside from Congreve, whose career began in the nineties, the most distinguished dramatists were Sir George Etherege (1635?–91?), with his graceful *The Man of Mode, or Sir Fopling Flutter*—it established the favorite Restoration characters of the rakish hero and the fop; William Wycherley (1641–1715), the most genuinely satirical and therefore least typical of them all, more typical in the funny but brutal comedy of *The Country Wife* than in the savage satire of *The Plain Dealer;* Thomas Shadwell (1642?–92), most Jonsonian but least polished of the group, with his sturdy *Bury Fair* and *The Squire of Alsatia;* and Sir John Vanbrugh (1664–1726), dramatist, soldier, and architect,—he built Blenheim Palace for the Duke of Marlborough,—and author of, for example, *The Relapse, or Virtue in Danger.* These titles are selected merely to indicate where to begin reading, if you find you like the flavor of Restoration comedy.

A limited course of reading in Restoration comedy is delightful; persisted in too long, it can turn sour, for the almost complete absence of honest emotion eventually becomes depressing. These people are clever and elegant and charming; but where are their hearts, not to say their morals? The age finally grew weary of its own wit, and shocked by its moral failures.

The Beaux' Stratagem (1707), the best play of George Farquhar (1678?–1707), is on the fence between Restoration comedy and the new, serious genre of the eighteenth century, called sentimental comedy. Near its close, a hero who has played the game of seduction with all the aplomb of the Restoration rake has a complete change of heart: "I find myself unequal to the task of villain; she has gained my soul, and made it honest like her own." That infusion of sentiment or feeling is pure eighteenth-century; the fine gentlemen of the Restoration do not talk in any such fashion. As we shall see, the eighteenth century was very much in earnest about trying to correct old abuses and improve society. Not to care about raising the tone of the town's manners and morals argued a man uncivilized. Too soft a head might be a misfortune, but a hard heart was worse. To laugh, as we are invited to do in pure comedy, at a cutting witticism or a fellow creature's plight was barbarous. In such a climate the comedy of manners could not flourish, and it gave way to sentimental comedy.

On both Restoration comedy and Heroic drama French influence was strong, but not so strong as the inheritance from earlier English drama. The seeds of the Heroic play are recognizable in Beaumont and Fletcher, but the actual plots were borrowed from the interminable Heroic romances of seventeenth-century France. In comedy the English playwrights drew on Molière (1622–73), sometimes for plots, often for inspiration.

THE RESTORATION STAGE

GREAT innovations revolutionized the English stage in the early sixties: actresses and scenery. The latter was even more important in opera, which, after the Restoration, at first in hybrid and then in quite separate forms from the drama, gave the latter stiff competition with its music, spectacle, and mechanical as well as scenic effects. Not, however, till the nineteenth century was there much realism in setting the dramatic stage. Scenery merely formed a more or less appropriate background. Furniture was mostly painted on the backdrop; sometimes even supernumeraries were. If chairs were brought out, they were put away again when no longer required; drawing-room scenes were regularly played standing—for cup-and-saucer drama we must wait till Victoria's reign. Though the stage was now framed by a proscenium arch, and artificially lighted, it was still essentially a platform for actors to speak from.

GENERAL REFERENCES

Among the books on the background of general European conditions and events G. N. Clark's *The Seventeenth Century* (1929) is particularly useful. G. M. Trevelyan's *England under the Stuarts* (1928) is a good history. *The Seventeenth Century Background* (1934) by Basil Willey contains "studies in the thought of the age in relation to poetry and religion." There are valuable chapters (VIII and IX) in G. M. Trevelyan's *English Social History* (1942). V. de S. Pinto's *The English Renaissance* (1938), already cited, covers the seventeenth century as well as the sixteenth.

E. K. Chambers's *The Elizabethan Stage* (1923), likewise already mentioned, runs into the Jacobean period. A continuation is now in progress, *The Jacobean and Caroline Stage,* by G. E. Bentley (2 vols. thus far, 1941). The best single-volume history of English plays is A. Nicoll's *British Drama* (1925). The standard history and bibliography of *Restoration Drama* is by A. Nicoll (revised ed., 1928).

References to the standard editions and treatises will be found in the headnotes to the various writers. Most of the pre-Wars dramas mentioned are in H. Spencer's *Elizabethan Plays* (1933). Good collections of later drama are G. H. Nettleton and A. E. Case's *British Dramatists from Dryden to Sheridan* (1939), and D. MacMillan and H. M. Jones's *Plays of the Restoration and Eighteenth Century* (revised ed., 1935).

Sir Francis Bacon

1561–1626

BACON is a logical choice to lead off this section, for he was much concerned with the search for truth which is one of the most characteristic features of the seventeenth century. He was hardly a creative genius; his was not what Emerson calls a "genial" (that is, a generating) mind. But it was a shrewd and inquiring mind, a mind of great critical power; and if he is no longer credited, as he once was, with a fundamental contribution to modern thought, he at least helped to prepare the ground for it.

He was born in London in 1561. As Lord Keeper of the Great Seal, his father was one of the Queen's ministers; and Francis was so precocious and so grave that he was only a dozen years old when she began calling him "the young Lord Keeper." Like many a promising youth before and since (as well as many a dull one), Bacon concluded that the education offered in his day was all wrong. He left Cambridge without taking a degree.

In 1579 his father's death called him home from a sojourn in France, and he began studying law at Gray's Inn. He intended to have a political as well as a legal career; but though he was called to the bar in 1582 and soon after was appointed Queen's Counsel and secured a seat in Parliament, his ambition for high office was thwarted by Lord Burghley (d. 1598), his mother's brother-in-law, apparently for fear lest Bacon's talents eclipse the chances of his own son, Robert, who did in fact succeed his father as Elizabeth's principal minister.

Only too well aware that the way to advancement lay through patronage, Bacon next made up to Elizabeth's favorite, Robert Devereux, Earl of Essex; but his applications for office were rejected despite the support of the Earl, who presented him with an estate worth at least $10,000. In 1597 appeared the first edition of the *Essays;* their disillusioned tone was natural enough in a brilliant man of thirty-six who was deeply in debt and without definite prospects, and it was in tune with the coming century. After Essex's fiasco in 1599 as commander in Ireland, the Earl sulked and brooded; in 1601 he attempted his ill-planned *coup d'état.* On its collapse he was tried for treason and executed. As special counsel for the prosecution, Bacon helped secure his friend's conviction. Politics was a rough game, and Essex was both guilty and foolish; but Bacon's behavior has seemed to many to show a lack of decent feeling.

Under James his fortunes were for a time better. He was knighted, given a small pension, and appointed King's Counsel. At forty-five he married the daughter of a rich London merchant. He continued to mount rapidly the ladder of office. Having held successively the posts of Solicitor General, Attorney General, and Lord Keeper, he was appointed in 1618 Lord Chancellor, and thus became head of the entire judicial system. In the same year he was raised to the peerage as Baron Verulam; three years later he became Viscount St. Albans. Since these were his titles, the use of "Lord Bacon" is quite incorrect.

By this time the struggle between Parliament and the King was intense. In 1621 Parliament met for the first time in seven years. Among its leaders' opening moves was a blow at James through Bacon, who had consistently supported the King's tyrannical proceedings. The Lord Chancellor presided over the high court known as Chancery. In common with most judges in those days, Bacon had accepted presents from litigants; charges of bribery were now pressed against him. He maintained, very likely with a good deal of truth, that his decisions had not been influenced; but he agreed that his practice had been wrong, and did not go to trial. The penalties included a prison sentence and a heavy fine; they were soon remitted by the King. Bacon's career, however, was over. He spent his five remaining years in retirement, chiefly in writing. The essay "Of Adversity" was written after his fall. He died in 1626 of a chill he caught when he stepped from his coach to get some snow with which to conduct an experiment in preserving meat from decay. He left debts of more than $100,000.

Bacon won his place in literature with his *Essays,* the first example of that genre in English. In his famous dictionary, Dr. Samuel Johnson defines an essay as "a loose sally of the mind"—which is well enough for many, but certainly not for Bacon's. His belong to the formal, precise, objective type; not, like Montaigne's (from which the term *essay* is derived), to the easy, conversational, and subjective. They lack the Frenchman's warm humanity. What they reflect is a remarkable experience of affairs, but an experience of life drastically restricted by the limitations of their author's temperament. In general, Bacon's weakness, both as a writer and as a man, was an excessive reliance on the purely rational powers of the mind and a minimizing of imagination, emotion, and intuition. With profitable wisdom he explains in "Of Great Place" how to be a successful executive; but to write "Of Love" he was simply not equipped, either by experience or by imagination.

Yet on the side of worldly wisdom the *Essays* have a great deal to offer, and in their style's superb rhythm they give pleasure. Until recently they were among the most popular of English books. There is irony in that, for Bacon elected to write what he considered his most important works in Latin, as likelier to endure. Yet his contemporaries were well aware of his mastery of English, both as writer and as orator. Ben Jonson declares of him:

There happened in my time one noble speaker. . . . No man ever spoke more neatly, more pressly,[1] more weightily, or suffered less emptiness, less idleness,[2] in what he spoke. . . . His hearers could not cough or look aside from him without loss. . . . The fear of every man that heard him was lest he should make an end.

Bacon's place in the history of thought he won by his insistence on the necessity for clearing the mind of obstructions to thinking and for fresh observation rather than authority as a basis for knowledge. His uncompleted *Instauratio Magna* (The Great Renewal [of Science]) was to be a comprehensive treatment of the state of knowledge in his own time and methods for its expansion and useful application to human affairs. About 1592 he wrote to Burghley: "I have taken all knowledge to be my province; and if I could purge it of two sorts of rovers, whereof the one with frivolous disputations, confutations, and verbosities, the other with blind experiments and auricular traditions and impostures, hath committed so many spoils, I hope I should bring in industrious observations, grounded conclusions, and profitable inventions and discoveries."
The Advancement of Learning, published in 1605, was a kind of preliminary sketch in English; the passages reprinted below reflect most of Bacon's key ideas. Two years later came *De Sapientia Veterum* (On the Wisdom of the Ancients). In 1620 was published the second section (though the first to appear) of the *Instauratio;* it contained part of the *Novum Organum* (The New Instrument), an argument for the use of the inductive method of reasoning (that is, of proceeding from the particular to the general) in place of the Aristotelian "instrument," the deductive method. There are several English translations of it. Other portions of the *Instauratio* came out in 1622–23. Also in 1622 appeared Bacon's *History of Henry VII. The New Atlantis* (1627), a fragment unpublished till after his death, is a scientific romance; its picture of a great research institute of science and philosophy rising on a Pacific isle, staffed by scholars who form the island's aristocracy, sets forth Bacon's conviction that science is the hope of mankind and reflects his steady emphasis on *useful* knowledge.

The following excerpt from the *Novum Organum* (sections 38–44) contains what has perhaps been Bacon's most influential single statement; hence it is given here, although the plan of this book regularly excludes works not written in English. You will find related ideas in Bacon's own prose in the excerpts from *The Advancement of Learning*

below. His attack on the "idols" (that is, the false conceptions and fallacies) which most men allow to obscure their thinking has helped many a reader clear his mind of rubbish.

The idols and false notions which have hitherto preoccupied the human intellect, and are deeply rooted in it, not only so blockade men's minds that an entrance for truth is difficult, but also, even when entrance has been granted, will again present themselves and prove troublesome in the instauration[3] of the sciences, unless men be forewarned and as far as possible guard themselves against them.

There are four kinds of idols that blockade the human mind. To them (for the sake of explanation) we have assigned names, and call the first kind *idols of the tribe,* the second *idols of the cave,* the third *idols of the market place,* the fourth *idols of the theater.*

The construction of conceptions and axioms through true induction is certainly the right remedy for warding off and clearing away the idols; yet it is a great advantage to indicate what they are. For this teaching concerning idols has the same relation to the interpretation of nature that the teaching concerning the confutation of sophisms[4] has to common logic.

The idols of the tribe are fundamental in human nature itself, and in the very tribe or race of man. For it is a false assertion that man's sense is the measure of things; on the contrary, all perceptions (of the senses as well as of the mind) are referable to man, not to the universe. And the human intellect resembles an uneven mirror, which receives the rays from things, but mingles its own nature with the nature of the things and distorts and obscures them.

The idols of the cave are the idols of the individual man. For, besides the errors common to human nature in general, every man has his individual cave or den, which weakens and perverts the light of nature: on account of either his own special nature, or his education and intercourse with others, or his reading of books and the authority of those he respects and admires, or the differences of impressions according to whether these occur in a mind preoccupied and predisposed or in a reasonable and tranquil mind, or the like. So that the human spirit, as it is placed in individual men, is a variable thing and utterly restless and, as it were, the result of chance. And so Heraclitus[5] says well that men seek for knowledge in lesser worlds and not in the greater or common world.

There are also idols arising from the intercourse and association of men with each other, which we call idols of the market place, from men's communication and society. For men are joined by their speech, but words are shaped by the capacity of the vulgar; and thus a bad and foolish imposition of words blockades the intellect in strange ways. Nor can the definitions and explanations with which learned men are accustomed to pave the way and liberate themselves make up for this fact in any respect. But words

---

[1] Concisely.   [2] Uselessness.

[3] Renewal.   [4] Refutation of fallacious arguments.
[5] A Greek philosopher who flourished *c.* 500 B.C.

evidently force the intellect and throw everything into confusion, and lead men into empty and innumerable controversies and fallacies.

Lastly, there are the idols which have made their way into men's minds from the various dogmas of philosophical systems, and also from perverted rules of demonstration. These we call idols of the theater, because we consider all the philosophies that have been accepted or invented as so many plays produced and acted, which create their own fictitious and scenic worlds. Nor do we speak merely of those we now have, or of the ancient philosophies and sects, since many other plays of the same sort could still be composed and produced, seeing that the causes of quite different errors may none the less be virtually the same. Nor, again, do we mean only the general systems of philosophy, but also many principles and axioms of the sciences, which have obtained strength from tradition, mere belief, and neglect.

The standard edition of the complete works (including Life and letters) is by J. Spedding, R. L. Ellis, and D. D. Heath (14 vols., 1857–74). P. E. and E. F. Matheson edited a volume of selections (1922). A good edition of the essays is that of S. H. Reynolds (1890); more usefully annotated is A. S. West's (1897, and often reprinted). The essays and *The Advancement of Learning* are also available in Everyman's Library and The World's Classics. The standard Life (too eulogistic) is by Spedding (see above). There is a good article by S. R. Gardiner in the *Dictionary of National Biography*. T. B. Macaulay wrote a sharp essay, part of which is reprinted in our second volume. More recent Lives are by R. W. Church (1884), I. Levine (1925), and C. Williams (1933). Estimates of Bacon by his various biographers differ perhaps more sharply than those of any other figure in this book.

Sir Francis Bacon

ESSAYS, OR COUNSELS CIVIL AND MORAL

Of the essays reprinted below, "Discourse," "Negotiating," and "Studies" appeared in the first edition, of 1597; it contained ten in all. A new edition in 1612 dropped one of the original essays and brought the number up to thirty-eight; among the twenty-nine additions were "Marriage and Single Life," "Parents and Children," "Great Place," "Love," "Wisdom for a Man's Self," "Riches," and "Custom and Education." In 1625 the collection took its final form, with nineteen new essays (fifty-eight in all), including "Truth" and "Adversity." Bacon revised, as well as added; his later style is somewhat less severe and plain than his earlier. Besides the usual modernizations, the text below has been paragraphed without reference to the original. Some of the essays have structure, and progress from point to point; others are merely a collection of observations on the chosen theme.

I

OF TRUTH

"What is truth?" said jesting[1] Pilate, and would not stay for an answer. Certainly there be that[2] delight in giddiness and count it a bondage to fix a belief, affecting[3] free will in thinking as well as in acting. And though the sects of philosophers of that kind[4] be gone, yet there remain certain discoursing wits[5]

which are of the same veins, though there be not so much blood in them as was in those of the ancients. But it is not only the difficulty and labor which men take in finding out of truth, nor again that when it is found it imposeth[6] upon men's thoughts, that doth bring lies in favor; but a natural, though corrupt, love of the lie itself. One of the later school of the Grecians[7] examineth the matter and is at a stand[8] to think what should be in it, that men should love lies, where neither they make for pleasure as with poets, nor for advantage as with the merchant, but for the lie's sake. But I cannot tell; this same truth is a naked and open daylight, that doth not show the masks and mummeries and triumphs[9] of the world, half so stately and daintily as candlelights. Truth may perhaps come to the price of a pearl, that showeth best by day; but it will not rise to the price of a diamond or carbuncle, that showeth best in varied lights.

A mixture of a lie doth ever add pleasure. Doth any man doubt that if there were taken out of men's minds vain opinions, flattering hopes, false valuations, imaginations as one would,[10] and the like, but it would leave the minds of a number of men poor shrunken things, full of melancholy and indisposition,

---

[1] Scoffing. See John 18: 37–38. Pilate was the Roman procurator of Judea before whom Jesus was tried.
[2] There are those who.   [3] Inclining to.
[4] Such as the skeptics of the fourth century B.C.
[5] Fluent intellects.

[6] Puts restraint.
[7] Lucian (d. 200? A.D.), the Greek satirist.
[8] Standstill.
[9] Spectacles. Bacon is thinking of entertainments at court.
[10] I.e., wishful thinking.

and unpleasing to themselves? One of the Fathers,[11] in great severity, called poesy *vinum daemonum,*[12] because it filleth the imagination and yet it is but with the shadow of a lie. But it is not the lie that passeth through the mind, but the lie that sinketh in and settleth in it, that doth the hurt, such as we spake of before.

But howsoever these things are thus in men's depraved judgments and affections,[13] yet truth, which only doth judge itself, teacheth that the inquiry of truth, which is the love-making or wooing of it, the knowledge of truth, which is the presence of it, and the belief of truth, which is the enjoying of it, is the sovereign good of human nature. The first creature[14] of God, in the works of the days, was the light of the sense; the last was the light of reason; and his sabbath work ever since is the illumination of his Spirit. First he breathed light upon the face of the matter or chaos; then he breathed light into the face of man; and still he breatheth and inspireth light into the face of his chosen. The poet[15] that beautified the sect[16] that was otherwise inferior to the rest, saith yet excellently well: "It is a pleasure to stand upon the shore and to see ships tossed upon the sea; a pleasure to stand in the window of a castle and to see a battle and the adventures thereof below; but no pleasure is comparable to the standing upon the vantage ground of truth [a hill not to be commanded, and where the air is always clear and serene], and to see the errors and wanderings and mists and tempests in the vale below": so[17] always that this prospect be with pity, and not with swelling or pride. Certainly, it is heaven upon earth to have a man's mind move in charity, rest in Providence, and turn upon the poles of truth.

To pass from theological and philosophical truth to the truth of civil business, it will be acknowledged even by those that practice it not that clear and round[18] dealing is the honor of man's nature, and that mixture of falsehood is like alloy in coin of gold and silver, which may make the metal work the better, but it embaseth it. For these winding and crooked courses are the goings of the serpent, which goeth basely upon the belly and not upon the feet. There is no vice that doth so cover a man with shame as to be found false and perfidious. And therefore

Montaigne[19] saith prettily, when he inquired the reason why the word of the lie should be such a disgrace and such an odious charge. Saith he, "If it be well weighed, to say that a man lieth is as much to say as that he is brave towards God and a coward towards men." For a lie faces God, and shrinks from man. Surely the wickedness of falsehood and breach of faith cannot possibly be so highly expressed as in that it shall be the last peal to call the judgments of God upon the generations of men: it being foretold that, when Christ cometh, "he shall not find faith upon the earth."[20]

5

OF ADVERSITY

It was an high speech of Seneca[21] (after the manner of the Stoics) that "the good things which belong to prosperity are to be wished, but the good things that belong to adversity are to be admired.[22] *Bona rerum secundarum optabilia; adversarum mirabilia.*" Certainly, if miracles be the command over nature, they appear most in adversity. It is yet a higher speech of his than the other (much too high for a heathen): "It is true greatness to have in one the frailty of a man, and the security[23] of a God. *Vere magnum habere fragilitatem hominis, securitatem Dei.*" This would have done better in poesy, where transcendences[24] are more allowed. And the poets indeed have been busy with it; for it is in effect the thing which is figured[25] in that strange fiction of the ancient poets, which seemeth not to be without mystery[26] (nay, and to have some approach to the state of a Christian): that Hercules, when he went to unbind Prometheus[27] (by whom human nature is represented), sailed the length of the great ocean in an earthen pot or pitcher—lively describing Christian resolution, that saileth in the frail bark of the flesh through the waves of the world.

But to speak in a mean.[28] The virtue of prosperity is temperance; the virtue of adversity is fortitude, which in morals is the more heroical virtue. Prosperity is the blessing of the Old Testament; ad-

[11] I.e., the early Church authorities, but Bacon's memory appears to be wrong.   [12] The wine of devils.
[13] Inclinations, feelings.   [14] Creation. See Genesis 1:3 ff.
[15] The Roman poet Lucretius (d.55 B.C.), in his *De Rerum Natura* (On the Nature of Things).   [16] The Epicureans.
[17] Provided.   [18] Plain, direct.

[19] The greatest of essayists (1533–92). The passage is from Book II, chap. 18; actually Montaigne is quoting Plutarch.
[20] Luke 18:8, but "faith" is used in another sense.
[21] The Roman philosopher and dramatist (d. 65 A.D.). These lines and the next are misquoted from his *Epistles,* lxvi, liii.
[22] Wondered at.   [23] Freedom from care.
[24] Exaggerations.   [25] Metaphorically expressed.
[26] Secret meaning.
[27] The Titan who was chained by Zeus on Mt. Caucasus as punishment for giving fire to man.
[28] With moderation.

versity is the blessing of the New, which carrieth the greater benediction and the clearer revelation of God's favor. Yet even in the Old Testament, if you listen to David's harp,[29] you shall hear as many hearse-like airs as carols; and the pencil of the Holy Ghost hath labored more in describing the afflictions of Job than the felicities of Solomon. Prosperity is not without many fears and distastes,[30] and adversity is not without comforts and hopes. We see in needle-works and embroideries it is more pleasing to have a lively work upon a sad and solemn[31] ground than to have a dark and melancholy work upon a lightsome ground; judge therefore of the pleasure of the heart by the pleasure of the eye. Certainly virtue is like precious odors, most fragrant when they are incensed[32] or crushed; for prosperity doth best discover[33] vice, but adversity doth best discover virtue.

7

OF PARENTS AND CHILDREN

The joys of parents are secret, and so are their griefs and fears; they cannot utter the one, nor they will not utter the other. Children sweeten labors, but they make misfortunes more bitter; they increase the cares of life, but they mitigate the remembrance of death. The perpetuity by generation[34] is common to beasts; but memory, merit, and noble works are proper to[35] men. And surely a man shall see the noblest works and foundations have proceeded from childless men, which have sought to express the images of their minds where those of their bodies have failed; so the care of posterity[36] is most in them that have no posterity. They that are the first raisers of their houses[37] are most indulgent towards their children, beholding them as the continuance, not only of their kind, but of their work, and so both children and creatures.[38]

The difference in affection[39] of parents towards their several children is many times unequal, and sometimes unworthy, especially in the mother; as Solomon saith, "A wise son rejoiceth the father, but an ungracious son shames the mother."[40] A man shall see, where there is a house full of children, one or two of the eldest respected[41] and the youngest made wantons,[42] but in the midst some that are as it were forgotten, who many times nevertheless prove the best.

The illiberality of parents in allowance towards their children is a harmful error, makes them base, acquaints them with shifts,[43] makes them sort[44] with mean company, and makes them surfeit[45] more when they come to plenty; and therefore the proof is[46] best when men keep their authority towards their children, but not their purse.

Men have a foolish manner (both parents, and schoolmasters and servants) in creating and breeding an emulation between brothers during childhood, which many times sorteth to[47] discord when they are men, and disturbeth families. The Italians make little difference between children and nephews or near kinsfolk; but so they be of the lump they care not, though they pass not through their own body. And, to say truth, in nature it is much a like matter; insomuch that we see a nephew sometimes resembleth an uncle or a kinsman more than his own parent, as the blood happens.

Let parents choose betimes[48] the vocations and courses they mean their children should take, for then they are most flexible; and let them not too much apply[49] themselves to the disposition of their children, as thinking they will take best to that which they have most mind to. It is true that, if the affection or aptness of the children be extraordinary, then it is good not to cross it; but generally the precept is good: *Optimum elige, suave et facile illud faciet consuetudo.*[50]

Younger brothers are commonly fortunate, but seldom or never where the elder are disinherited.

8

OF MARRIAGE AND SINGLE LIFE

He that hath wife and children hath given hostages to fortune; for they are impediments to great enterprises, either of virtue or mischief. Certainly the best works, and of greatest merit for the public, have proceeded from the unmarried or childless men, which both in affection and means have married and endowed the public. Yet it were great reason that those that have children should have greatest care of

---

29 Read David's Psalms.
30 Distasteful things.　　　31 Dull and sober.
32 Burned.　　33 Disclose.　　34 Propagation.
35 Natural to, distinctive of.　　36 Being remembered.
37 The first to make their families prosperous.
38 Creations, works.　　39 Inclination, feelings.
40 Proverbs 10:1.　　41 Given attention.

42 I.e., spoiled.　　43 Unworthy expedients.
44 Associate.　　　　45 Go to excess.
46 The test of experience turns out.　　47 Turns into.
48 Early.　　　　49 Conform.
50 Choose the best; habit will make it pleasant and easy. Plutarch (d.120? A.D.), in his *Morals*, ascribes this maxim to the followers of Pythagoras, the Greek philosopher of the sixth century B.C.

future times, unto which they know they must transmit their dearest pledges. Some there are who, though they lead a single life, yet their thoughts do end with themselves and account future times impertinences.[51] Nay, there are some other that account wife and children but as bills of charges. Nay more, there are some foolish rich covetous men that take a pride in having no children, because they may be thought so much the richer. For perhaps they have heard some talk, "Such an one is a great rich man," and another except to it, "Yea, but he hath a great charge of children," as if it were an abatement to his riches. But the most ordinary cause of a single life is liberty, especially in certain self-pleasing and humorous[52] minds, which are so sensible of every restraint as they will go near to think their girdles[53] and garters to be bonds and shackles.

Unmarried men are best friends, best masters, best servants; but not always best subjects: for they are light[54] to run away, and almost all fugitives are of that condition. A single life doth well with churchmen, for charity will hardly water the ground where it must first fill a pool. It is indifferent[55] for judges and magistrates; for if they be facile and corrupt, you shall have a servant five times worse than a wife. For soldiers, I find the generals commonly in their hortatives[56] put men in mind of their wives and children; and I think the despising of marriage amongst the Turks maketh the vulgar soldier more base. Certainly wife and children are a kind of discipline of humanity; and single men, though they be many times more charitable, because their means are less exhaust,[57] yet on the other side they are more cruel and hardhearted (good to make severe inquisitors), because their tenderness is not so oft called upon.

Grave natures, led by custom, and therefore constant, are commonly loving husbands, as was said of Ulysses: *Vetulam suam praetulit immortalitati.*[58] Chaste women are often proud and forward, as presuming upon the merit of their chastity. It is one of the best bonds, both of chastity and obedience, in the wife if she think her husband wise, which she will never do if she find him jealous. Wives are young men's mistresses, companions for middle age, and old men's nurses. So as a man may have a quarrel[59] to marry when he will. But yet he[60] was reputed one of the wise men, that made answer to the question when a man should marry, "A young man not yet, an elder man not at all."

It is often seen that bad husbands have very good wives, whether it be that it raiseth the price of their husbands' kindness when it comes or that the wives take a pride in their patience; but this never fails, if the bad husbands were of their own choosing, against their friends' consent, for then they will be sure to make good their own folly.

10

OF LOVE

The stage is more beholding[61] to love than the life of man: for as to the stage, love is ever matter of comedies, and now and then of tragedies; but in life it doth much mischief, sometimes like a Siren, sometimes like a Fury.[62] You may observe that amongst all the great and worthy persons whereof the memory remaineth, either ancient or recent, there is not one that hath been transported to the mad degree of love; which shows that great spirits and great business do keep out this weak passion. You must except, nevertheless, Marcus Antonius,[63] the half-partner of the empire of Rome, and Appius Claudius, the decemvir[64] and lawgiver; whereof the former was indeed a voluptuous man and inordinate, but the latter was an austere and wise man: and therefore it seems, though rarely, that love can find entrance, not only into an open heart, but also into a heart well fortified, if watch be not well kept. It is a poor saying of Epicurus,[65] *Satis magnum alter alteri theatrum sumus,*[66] as if man, made for the contemplation of heaven and all noble objects, should do nothing but kneel before a little idol, and make himself subject, though not of the mouth, as beasts are, yet of the eye, which was given him for higher purposes.

It is a strange thing to note the excess of this passion; and how it braves[67] the nature and value of

51 Things of no concern (to them).   52 Eccentric.
53 Belts.   54 Unencumbered.
55 An unimportant question.   56 Exhortations, speeches.
57 Exhausted.
58 He preferred his old wife to immortality. Ulysses, who had sojourned for seven years with the nymph Calypso and was offered immortality by her, was reproached by her on the eve of his departure. See the *Odyssey,* Book V.

59 Excuse.
60 Thales, the Greek philosopher (d. 546 B.C.).
61 Beholden, indebted.
62 In Greek mythology the Sirens were minor deities; the most famous were those who tried to lure Ulysses to destruction (*Odyssey,* Book XII). The Furies were terrible spirits of vengeance.   63 D. 30 B.C. He was Cleopatra's lover.
64 I.e., one of ten men appointed in 451 B.C. to codify the Roman law. His fraudulent claim that Virginia was his slave was foiled by her father's killing her.
65 The Greek philosopher (d. 270 B.C.).
66 We constitute a big enough theatrical show for each other.
67 Defies, sets at naught.

things by this, that the speaking in a perpetual hyperbole is comely in nothing but in love. Neither is it merely in the phrase; for whereas it hath been well said that the arch-flatterer, with whom all the petty flatterers have intelligence,[68] is a man's self, certainly the lover is more. For there was never proud man thought so absurdly well of himself as the lover doth of the person loved; and therefore it was well said, that "it is impossible to love and to be wise."[69] Neither doth this weakness appear to others only and not to the party loved, but to the loved most of all, except the love be reciproque.[70] For it is a true rule that love is ever rewarded either with the reciproque or with an inward and secret contempt. By how much the more men ought to beware of this passion, which loseth not only other things, but itself! As for the other losses, the poet's relation[71] doth well figure them: that he that preferred Helena quitted the gifts of Juno and Pallas; for whosoever esteemeth too much of amorous affection quitteth both riches and wisdom.

This passion hath his[72] floods in the very times of weakness, which are great prosperity and great adversity (though this latter hath been less observed), both which times kindle love and make it more fervent, and therefore show it to be the child of folly. They do best, who if they cannot but admit love, yet make it keep quarter,[73] and sever it wholly from their serious affairs and actions of life; for if it check once with[74] business, it troubleth men's fortunes, and maketh men that they can no ways be true to their own ends. I know not how, but martial men are given to love; I think it is but as they are given to wine, for perils commonly ask to be paid in pleasures.

There is in man's nature a secret inclination and motion towards love of others, which, if it be not spent upon some one or a few, doth naturally spread itself towards many and maketh men become humane and charitable, as it is seen sometimes in friars. Nuptial love maketh mankind; friendly love perfecteth it; but wanton love corrupteth and embaseth it.

Men in great place[1] are thrice servants: servants of the sovereign or state, servants of fame, and servants of business, so as[2] they have no freedom, neither in their persons nor in their actions nor in their times. It is a strange desire, to seek power and to lose liberty; or to seek power over others, and to lose power over a man's self. The rising unto place is laborious, and by pains men come to greater pains; and it is sometimes base, and by indignities men come to dignities.[3] The standing is slippery, and the regress[4] is either a downfall, or at least an eclipse, which is a melancholy thing: *Cum non sis qui fueris, non esse cur velis vivere.*[5] Nay, retire men cannot when they would, neither will they when it were reason; but are impatient of privateness, even in age and sickness, which require the shadow,[6] like old townsmen, that will be still[7] sitting at their street door, though thereby they offer age to scorn.

Certainly great persons had need to borrow other men's opinions, to think themselves happy; for if they judge by their own feeling, they cannot find it: but if they think with themselves what other men think of them, and that other men would fain be as they are, then they are happy as it were by report, when perhaps they find the contrary within. For they are the first that find their own griefs, though they be the last that find their own faults. Certainly men in great fortunes are strangers to themselves, and while they are in the puzzle of business they have no time to tend their health either of body or mind. *Illi mors gravis incubat, qui notus nimis omnibus, ignotus moritur sibi.*[8]

In place there is license to do good and evil; whereof the latter is a curse: for in evil the best condition is not to will; the second, not to can.[9] But power to do good is the true and lawful end of aspiring; for good thoughts (though God accept them) yet towards men are little better than good dreams except they be put in act, and that cannot be without power and place as the vantage and commanding ground. Merit and good works is the end of man's motion;[10] and conscience[11] of the same is the accomplishment of man's rest: for if a man can

---

68 Are allied.
69 By Plutarch—and others.   70 Reciprocal.
71 Narrative. The story of Paris and the golden apple has been told by many. Rejecting Juno and Pallas Athena (or Minerva), he awarded it to Venus, who gave him Helen, the wife of Menelaus; and that was the cause of the Trojan War.   72 Its.
73 Its proper place.   74 Once hinder.

1 Office.   2 That.   3 Offices.   4 Withdrawal.
5 When you are no longer what you were, there is no reason why you should desire to live (Cicero, *Epistles,* vii, 3).
6 Withdrawal from the heat of activity.   7 Ever.
8 Death lies heavy on him who, exceedingly well known to all, dies unknown to himself (Seneca, *Thyestes,* II, 401-3).
9 Be able.   10 Entire activity.   11 Consciousness.

be partaker of God's theater,[12] he shall likewise be partaker of God's rest. *Et conversus Deus, ut aspiceret opera quae fecerunt manus suae, vidit quod omnia essent bona nimis;*[13] and then the sabbath.

In the discharge of thy place set before thee the best examples, for imitation is a globe[14] of precepts. And after a time set before thee thine own example, and examine thyself strictly whether thou didst not best at first. Neglect not also the examples of those that have carried themselves ill in the same place; not to set off thyself by taxing[15] their memory, but to direct thyself what to avoid. Reform therefore, without bravery[16] or scandal of former times and persons; but yet set it down to thyself as well to create good precedents as to follow them. Reduce things to the first institution, and observe wherein and how they have degenerate;[17] but yet ask counsel of both times: of the ancient time, what is best; and of the latter time, what is fittest. Seek to make thy course regular, that men may know beforehand what they may expect; but be not too positive and peremptory, and express thyself well when thou digressest from thy rule. Preserve the right of thy place, but stir not questions of jurisdiction; and rather assume thy right in silence and *de facto,*[18] than voice it with claims and challenges. Preserve likewise the rights of inferior places; and think it more honor to direct in chief than to be busy in all. Embrace and invite helps and advices touching the execution of thy place; and do not drive away such as bring thee information, as meddlers, but accept of them in good part.

The vices of authority are chiefly four: delays, corruption, roughness, and facility.[19] For[20] delays: give easy access; keep times appointed; go through with that which is in hand, and interlace not business but of necessity. For corruption: do not only bind thine own hands or thy servants' hands from taking, but bind the hands of suitors also from offering; for integrity used doth the one, but integrity professed (and with a manifest detestation of bribery) doth the other; and avoid not only the fault, but the suspicion. Whosoever is found variable, and changeth manifestly without manifest cause, giveth suspicion of corruption. Therefore always, when thou changest thine opinion or course, profess it plainly, and de-

clare it, together with the reasons that move thee to change; and do not think to steal[21] it. A servant or a favorite, if he be inward,[22] and no other apparent cause of esteem, is commonly thought but a byway to close[23] corruption. For roughness: it is a needless cause of discontent; severity breedeth fear, but roughness breedeth hate. Even reproofs from authority ought to be grave, and not taunting. As for facility: it is worse than bribery; for bribes come but now and then, but if importunity or idle respects[24] lead a man, he shall never be without. As Solomon saith, "To respect persons is not good, for such a man will transgress for a piece of bread."[25]

It is most true that was anciently spoken: "A place showeth the man";[26] and it showeth some to the better, and some to the worse. *Omnium consensu capax imperii, nisi imperasset,*[27] saith Tacitus of Galba; but of Vespasian he saith, *Solus imperantium, Vespasianus mutatus in melius,*[28] though the one was meant of sufficiency,[29] the other of manners and affection. It is an assured sign of a worthy and generous spirit, whom honor amends. For honor is, or should be, the place of virtue; and as in nature things move violently to their place and calmly in their place, so virtue in ambition is violent, in authority settled and calm.

All rising to great place is by a winding stair; and if there be factions, it is good to side a man's self[30] whilst he is in the rising, and to balance himself when he is placed. Use the memory of thy predecessor fairly and tenderly; for if thou dost not, it is a debt will sure be paid when thou art gone. If thou have colleagues, respect[31] them; and rather call them when they look not for it, than exclude them when they have reason to look to be called. Be not too sensible or too remembering of thy place in conversation and private answers to suitors; but let it rather be said, "When he sits in place, he is another man."

---

[21] Effect stealthily.
[22] On confidential terms (with a holder of high office).
[23] Secret.   [24] I.e., special consideration for individuals.
[25] Cf. Proverbs 28:21.
[26] Quoted or mentioned by Aristotle and others, and variously ascribed.
[27] In everyone's opinion fit for empire—if he had not been emperor. Thus the Roman historian Tacitus (*History*, I, 49). Galba was emperor in 68–9.
[28] Alone of the emperors, Vespasian changed for the better (I, 50). He was emperor in 69–79.
[29] I.e., with reference to Galba, Tacitus meant his administrative capacity.   [30] Take a side.   [31] Be attentive to.

---

[12] I.e., if like God he can be a spectator of good works he has accomplished.
[13] And God, turning to look at the works his hands had made, saw that they were all exceedingly good. Cf. Genesis 1:31.
[14] Compact mass.   [15] Blaming.   [16] Bravado.
[17] Degenerated.   [18] As a fact; i.e., as a matter of course.
[19] Easygoingness.   [20] As for.

OF WISDOM FOR A MAN'S SELF

An ant is a wise creature for itself, but it is a shrewd[32] thing in an orchard or garden; and certainly men that are great lovers of themselves waste the public. Divide with reason between self-love and society; and be so true to thyself as[33] thou be not false to others, specially to thy king and country. It is a poor center of a man's actions, himself. It is right earth; for that only stands fast upon his own center,[34] whereas all things that have affinity with the heavens move upon the center of another, which they benefit. The referring of all to a man's self is more tolerable in a sovereign prince, because themselves are not only themselves, but their good and evil is at the peril of the public fortune; but it is a desperate evil in a servant to a prince, or a citizen in a republic. For whatsoever affairs pass such a man's hands, he crooketh them to his own ends, which must needs be often eccentric to[35] the ends of his master or state. Therefore let princes or states choose such servants as have not this mark, except they mean their service should be made but the accessory.[36] That which maketh the effect more pernicious is that all proportion is lost. It were disproportion enough for the servant's good to be preferred before the master's; but yet it is a greater extreme, when a little good of the servant shall carry things against a great good of the master's. And yet that is the case of bad officers, treasurers, ambassadors, generals, and other false and corrupt servants; which set a bias upon their bowl,[37] of their own petty ends and envies, to the overthrow of their master's great and important affairs. And for the most part, the good such servants receive is after the model[38] of their own fortune; but the hurt they sell for that good is after the model of their master's fortune. And certainly it is the nature of extreme self-lovers, as they will set an house on fire and[39] it were but to roast their eggs; and yet these men many times hold credit with their masters because their study is but to please them and profit themselves, and for either respect[40] they will abandon the good of their affairs.

Wisdom for a man's self is, in many branches thereof, a depraved thing: it is the wisdom of rats, that will be sure to leave a house somewhat before it fall; it is the wisdom of the fox, that thrusts out the badger who digged and made room for him; it is the wisdom of crocodiles, that shed tears when they would devour. But that which is specially to be noted is that those which (as Cicero says of Pompey) are *sui amantes sine rivali*[41] are many times unfortunate; and whereas they have all their time sacrificed to themselves, they become in the end themselves sacrifices to the inconstancy of fortune, whose wings they thought by their self-wisdom to have pinioned.[42]

32

OF DISCOURSE

Some in their discourse[43] desire rather commendation of wit,[44] in being able to hold all arguments,[45] than of judgment, in discerning what is true; as if it were a praise to know what might be said, and not what should be thought. Some have certain commonplaces and themes, wherein they are good, and want[46] variety; which kind of poverty is for the most part tedious, and, when it is once perceived, ridiculous. The honorablest part of talk is to give the occasion; and again to moderate,[47] and pass to somewhat else, for then a man leads the dance. It is good in discourse and speech of conversation to vary and intermingle speech of the present occasion with arguments, tales with reasons, asking of questions with telling of opinions, and jest with earnest; for it is a dull thing to tire, and as we say now, to jade[48] anything too far. As for jest, there be certain things which ought to be privileged from it: namely, religion, matters of state, great persons, any man's present business of importance, and any case that deserveth pity. Yet there be some that think their wits have been asleep, except they dart out somewhat that is piquant and to the quick; that is a vein which would be[49] bridled. *Parce, puer, stimulis, et fortius utere loris.*[50] And generally men ought to find the difference between saltness and bitterness. Certainly he that hath a satirical vein, as he maketh others afraid of his wit, so he had need be afraid of others' memory.

He that questioneth much shall learn much, and content much; but especially if he apply his questions

---

[32] Pernicious, "cussed."   [33] That.
[34] According to the Ptolemaic theory of astronomy (to which Bacon clung), the earth was the center of the universe.
[35] Differently centered from.   [36] I.e., secondary.
[37] Weight off center (with lead) the ball used in bowling, to deflect it.   [38] According to the scale.   [39] If.
[40] Consideration.

[41] Lovers of themselves, without a rival.
[42] Cut off.   [43] Conversation.   [44] Cleverness.
[45] I.e., maintain any proposition.   [46] Lack.
[47] Act as moderator; i.e., guide the discussion.
[48] Ride to exhaustion.   [49] Ought to be.
[50] Spare the goad, boy, and hold the reins more tightly (Ovid, *Metamorphoses*, II, 127).

to the skill of the persons whom he asketh, for he shall give them occasion to please themselves in speaking, and himself shall continually gather knowledge. But let his questions not be troublesome, for that is fit for a poser.[51] And let him be sure to leave other men their turns to speak; nay, if there be any that would reign, and take up all the time, let him find means to take them off and to bring others on, as musicians use to do with those that dance too long galliards.[52]

If you dissemble sometimes your knowledge of that you are thought to know, you shall be thought another time to know that you know not. Speech of a man's self ought to be seldom, and well chosen. I knew one was wont to say in scorn, "He must needs be a wise man, he speaks so much of himself." And there is but one case wherein a man may commend himself with good grace, and that is in commending virtue in another, especially if it be such a virtue whereunto himself pretendeth.[53] Speech of touch towards[54] others should be sparingly used, for discourse ought to be as a field, without coming home to any man. I knew two noblemen of the west part of England, whereof the one was given to scoff, but kept ever royal cheer in his house. The other would ask of those that had been at the other's table, "Tell truly, was there never a flout or dry[55] blow given?" To which the guest would answer, "Such and such a thing passed." The lord would say, "I thought he would mar a good dinner." Discretion of speech is more than eloquence, and to speak agreeably to him with whom we deal is more than to speak in good words or in good order.

A good continued speech, without a good speech of interlocution,[56] shows slowness; and a good reply, or second speech, without a good settled speech, showeth shallowness and weakness. As we see in beasts, that those that are weakest in the course[57] are yet nimblest in the turn, as it is betwixt the greyhound and the hare. To use too many circumstances[58] ere one come to the matter is wearisome; to use none at all is blunt.

OF RICHES

I cannot call riches better than the baggage of virtue. The Roman word is better, *impedimenta;* for as the baggage is to an army, so is riches to virtue: it cannot be spared nor left behind, but it hind'reth the march; yea, and the care of it sometimes loseth or disturbeth the victory. Of great riches there is no real use, except it be in the distribution; the rest is but conceit.[59] So saith Solomon: "Where much is, there are many to consume it; and what hath the owner but the sight of it with his eyes?"[60] The personal fruition in any man cannot reach to feel great riches; there is a custody of them, or a power of dole and donative of them, or a fame of them, but no solid use to the owner. Do you not see what feigned prices are set upon little stones and rarities? And what works of ostentation are undertaken, because[61] there might seem to be some use of great riches? But then you will say they may be of use to buy men out of dangers or troubles, as Solomon saith, "Riches are as a stronghold in the imagination of the rich man."[62] But this is excellently expressed, that it is in imagination, and not always in fact; for certainly great riches have sold more men than they have bought out.

Seek not proud riches, but such as thou mayest get justly, use soberly, distribute cheerfully, and leave contentedly. Yet have no abstract nor friarly contempt of them, but distinguish, as Cicero saith well of Rabirius Posthumus,[63] *In studio rei amplificandae, apparebat, non avaritiae praedam, sed instrumentum bonitati quaeri.*[64] Hearken also to Solomon, and beware of hasty gathering of riches: *Qui festinat ad divitias, non erit insons.*[65] The poets feign that when Plutus (which is riches) is sent from Jupiter, he limps and goes slowly; but when he is sent from Pluto,[66] he runs and is swift of foot. Meaning that riches gotten by good means and just labor pace slowly; but when they come by the death of others (as by the course of inheritance, testaments, and the like), they come tumbling upon a man. But it mought[67] be applied likewise to Pluto, taking him for the Devil; for when

---

[51] Examiner.   [52] A kind of lively dance.
[53] Lays claim.   [54] Which has a bearing on.
[55] Sharp but bloodless.
[56] I.e., ability to talk along continuously, without ability to respond well to what someone else says.
[57] Straightaway run.   [58] Circumstantial details.

[59] Imagination.   [60] Cf. Ecclesiastes 5:11.
[61] In order that.   [62] Cf. Proverbs 18:11.
[63] Actually of his father, in a speech in defense of Rabirius, who in his old age had been accused of responsibility for the death of a tribune many years before.
[64] It was evident that in desiring to increase his fortune his object was to obtain, not gratification of avarice, but means of benevolence.
[65] He that maketh haste to be rich shall not be innocent (Proverbs 28:20).   [66] The god of Hades.   [67] Might.

riches come from the Devil (as by fraud and oppression and unjust means), they come upon speed.

The ways to enrich are many, and most of them foul. Parsimony is one of the best, and yet is not innocent; for it withholdeth men from works of liberality and charity. The improvement of the ground is the most natural obtaining of riches, for it is our great mother's blessing, the earth's; but it is slow. And yet, where men of great wealth do stoop to husbandry,[68] it multiplieth riches exceedingly. I knew a nobleman in England that had the greatest audits of any man in my time: a great grazier, a great sheepmaster, a great timber man, a great collier, a great cornmaster, a great lead man, and so of iron, and a number of the like points of husbandry; so as the earth seemed a sea to him in respect of the perpetual importation. It was truly observed by one, that himself came very hardly to a little riches, and very easily to great riches. For when a man's stock is come to that, that he can expect[69] the prime[70] of markets, and overcome[71] those bargains which for their greatness are few men's money,[72] and be partner in the industries of younger men, he cannot but increase mainly.

The gains of ordinary trades and vocations are honest, and furthered by two things chiefly: by diligence, and by a good name for good and fair dealing. But the gains of bargains[73] are of a more doubtful nature: when men shall wait upon others' necessity, broke by[74] servants and instruments to draw them on, put off others cunningly that would be better chapmen,[75] and the like practices,[76] which are crafty and naught.[77] As for the chopping of bargains, when a man buys not to hold but to sell over again, that commonly grindeth double, both upon the seller and upon the buyer. Sharings[78] do greatly enrich, if the hands be well chosen that are trusted. Usury is the certainest means of gain, though one of the worst, as that whereby a man doth eat his bread *in sudori vultus alieni*[79] and besides, doth plow upon Sundays.[80] But yet certain though it be, it hath flaws; for that the scriveners and brokers do value unsound men[81] to serve their own turn. The fortune in being the first in an invention or in a privilege doth cause sometimes a wonderful overgrowth in riches, as it was with the first sugar man in the Canaries. Therefore, if a man can play the true logician, to have as well judgment as invention, he may do great matters, especially if the times be fit.

He that resteth upon gains certain, shall hardly grow to great riches; and he that puts all upon adventures,[82] doth oftentimes break[83] and come to poverty: it is good therefore to guard adventures with certainties, that may uphold[84] losses. Monopolies,[85] and coemption[86] of wares for resale, where they are not restrained,[87] are great means to enrich; especially if the party have intelligence what things are like to come into request, and so store himself beforehand. Riches gotten by service, though it be of the best rise, yet when they are gotten by flattery, feeding humors,[88] and other servile conditions, they may be placed amongst the worst. As for fishing for testaments and executorships (as Tacitus saith of Seneca, *Testamenta et orbos tanquam indagine capi*[89]), it is yet worse, by how much men submit themselves to meaner persons than in service.

Believe not much them that seem to despise riches; for they despise them that despair of them, and none worse[90] when they come to them. Be not pennywise; riches have wings, and sometimes they fly away of themselves, sometimes they must be set flying to bring in more. Men leave their riches either to their kindred or to the public, and moderate portions prosper best in both. A great estate[91] left to an heir is as a lure to all the birds of prey round about to seize on him, if he be not the better[92] stablished in years and judgment. Likewise glorious[93] gifts and foundations are like sacrifices without salt and but the painted sepulchers of alms, which soon will putrefy and corrupt inwardly. Therefore, measure not thine advancements[94] by quantity, but frame them by measure[95] and defer not charities till death; for certainly if a man weigh it rightly, he that doth so is rather liberal of another man's than of his own.

---

68 Working the land.
69 Wait for. I.e., when a man's capital is large enough to enable him to refrain from selling his produce until he can get the best price.   70 Best state.   71 Accomplish.
72 I.e., deals for which large capital is required.
73 Transactions.   74 Negotiate through.   75 Buyers.
76 Sharp practices.   77 Rascally.   78 Partnerships.
79 In the sweat of another's brow.
80 I.e., interest charges go right on seven days a week.
81 I.e., the intermediaries who arrange loans will put a false value on an applicant's resources.

82 Risks.
83 Go bankrupt.   84 I.e., compensate for.
85 Licenses by the crown granting the sole right to manufacture or to deal in various articles. They were rightly a great source of complaint under Elizabeth and James.
86 Buying up, often with a view to cornering the market.
87 By statute.   88 Catering to whims.
89 Wills and childless men were, so to speak, caught in a net (*Annals*, xiii, 42).   90 Behave worse.
91 Fortune.   92 Very well.
93 Ostentatious.   94 Gifts.
95 Proportionately to the object.

OF CUSTOM AND EDUCATION

Men's thoughts are much according to their inclination, their discourse and speeches according to their learning and infused[1] opinions; but their deeds are after as they have been accustomed. And therefore, as Machiavel[2] well noteth (though in an evil-favored[3] instance), there is no trusting to the force of nature nor to the bravery[4] of words, except it be corroborate by custom. His instance is, that for the achieving of a desperate conspiracy, a man should not rest upon the fierceness of any man's nature or his resolute undertakings,[5] but take such an one as hath had his hands formerly in blood. But Machiavel knew not of a Friar Clément,[6] nor a Ravaillac,[7] nor a Jaureguy,[8] nor a Baltazar Gerard; yet his rule holdeth still that nature nor the engagement of words are not so forcible as custom. Only superstition[9] is now so well advanced that men of the first blood[10] are as firm as butchers by occupation; and votary[11] resolution is made equipollent[12] to custom even in matter of blood. In other things the predominancy of custom is everywhere visible; insomuch as a man would wonder to hear men profess, protest, engage, give great words, and then do just as they have done before; as if they were dead images, and engines moved only by the wheels of custom.

We see also the reign or tyranny of custom, what it is. The Indians[13] (I mean the sect of their wise men) lay themselves quietly upon a stack of wood, and so sacrifice themselves by fire; nay the wives strive to be burned with the corpses of their husbands. The lads of Sparta, of ancient time, were wont to be scourged upon the altar of Diana, without so much as queching.[14] I remember, in the beginning of Queen Elizabeth's time of England, an Irish rebel condemned put up a petition to the deputy that he might be hanged in a withe[15] and not in an halter,[16] because it had been so used with former

rebels. There be monks in Russia, for penance, that will sit a whole night in a vessel of water, till they be engaged with hard ice. Many examples may be put of the force of custom, both upon mind and body.

Therefore, since custom is the principal magistrate of man's life, let men by all means endeavor to obtain good customs. Certainly, custom is most perfect when it beginneth in young years; this we call education, which is in effect but an early custom. So we see in languages the tongue is more pliant to all expressions and sounds, the joints are more supple to all feats of activity and motions, in youth than afterwards. For it is true that late learners cannot so well take the ply,[17] except it be in some minds that have not suffered themselves to fix, but have kept themselves open and prepared to receive continual amendment, which is exceeding rare. But if the force of custom simple and separate be great, the force of custom copulate and conjoined and collegiate[18] is far greater. For there example teacheth, company comforteth,[19] emulation quickeneth, glory raiseth; so as in such places the force of custom is in his exaltation.[20] Certainly the great multiplication of virtues upon human nature resteth upon societies well ordained and disciplined. For commonwealths and good governments do nourish virtue grown, but do not much mend the seeds. But the misery is that the most effectual means are now applied to the ends least to be desired.

47

OF NEGOTIATING

It is generally better to deal by speech than by letter, and by the mediation of a third than by a man's self. Letters are good when a man would draw an answer by letter back again, or when it may serve for a man's justification afterwards to produce his own letter, or where it[21] may be danger to be interrupted or heard by pieces. To deal in person is good when a man's face breedeth regard, as commonly with inferiors; or in tender cases, where a man's eye upon the countenance of him with whom he speaketh may give him a direction how far to go; and generally, where a man will reserve to himself liberty either to disavow or to expound.

In choice of instruments, it is better to choose men of a plainer sort, that are like to do that that is com-

---

[1] Acquired.
[2] Machiavelli, the Italian political theorist (d. 1527), author of *The Prince*.   [3] Ugly.   [4] Fine appearance.
[5] Promises to be resolute.
[6] Assassin of Henry III of France in 1589.
[7] Assassin of Henry IV of France in 1610.
[8] He wounded William the Silent in an attempted assassination in 1582; the great leader of the Dutch was killed two years later by Gerard.
[9] I.e., fanaticism. All the foregoing assassinations were in the interest of Catholic factions.   [10] I.e., novices in murder.
[11] Vowed.   [12] Equally effective.   [13] I.e., Hindus.
[14] Flinching.   [15] Flexible branch or twig.
[16] Rope.

[17] Are not so pliant.
[18] I.e., associated.   [19] Strengthens.
[20] At its strongest.   [21] There.

mitted to them and to report back again faithfully the success,[22] than those that are cunning to contrive out of other men's business somewhat to grace themselves, and will help the matter in report[23] for satisfaction sake. Use also such persons as affect[24] the business wherein they are employed, for that quickeneth much; and such as are fit for the matter, as bold men for expostulation, fair-spoken men for persuasion, crafty men for inquiry and observation, froward and absurd[25] men for business that doth not well bear out itself. Use also such as have been lucky and prevailed before in things wherein you have employed them; for that breeds confidence, and they will strive to maintain their prescription.[26]

It is better to sound a person with whom one deals afar off than to fall upon the point at first, except you mean to surprise him by some short question. It is better dealing with men in appetite[27] than with those that are where they would be. If a man deal with another upon conditions,[28] the start or first performance is all; which a man cannot reasonably demand,[29] except either the nature of the thing be such which must go before,[30] or else a man can persuade the other party that he shall still need him in some other thing,[31] or else that he be counted the honester man.[32] All practice[33] is to discover,[34] or to work.[35] Men discover[36] themselves in trust, in passion, at unawares, and of necessity when they would have somewhat done and cannot find an apt pretext. If you would work any man, you must either know his nature and fashions, and so lead him; or his ends, and so persuade him; or his weakness and disadvantages, and so awe him; or those that have interest in him, and so govern him. In dealing with cunning persons, we must ever consider their ends, to interpret their speeches; and it is good to say little to them, and that which they least look for.

In all negotiations of difficulty, a man may not look to sow and reap at once; but must prepare business, and so ripen it by degrees.

Studies serve for delight, for ornament, and for ability. Their chief use for delight is in privateness and retiring; for ornament, is in discourse;[37] and for ability, is in the judgment and disposition of business: for expert[38] men can execute and perhaps judge of particulars one by one; but the general counsels, and the plots and marshaling of affairs, come best from those that are learned. To spend too much time in studies is sloth; to use them too much for ornament is affectation; to make judgment wholly by their rules is the humor[39] of a scholar. They perfect nature, and are perfected by experience; for natural abilities are like natural plants, that need proyning[40] by study; and studies themselves do give forth directions too much at large, except they be bounded in by experience.

Crafty[41] men contemn studies, simple men admire[42] them, and wise men use them; for they teach not their own use, but that is a wisdom without[43] them and above them, won by observation. Read not to contradict and confute, nor to believe and take for granted, nor to find talk and discourse, but to weigh and consider. Some books are to be tasted, others to be swallowed, and some few to be chewed and digested; that is, some books are to be read only in parts, others to be read but not curiously,[44] and some few to be read wholly and with diligence and attention. Some books also may be read by deputy, and extracts made of them by others; but that would be only in the less important arguments[45] and the meaner sort of books; else, distilled books are like common distilled waters, flashy[46] things. Reading maketh a full man, conference[47] a ready man, and writing an exact man. And therefore, if a man write little, he had need have a great memory; if he confer little, he had need have a present wit; and if he read little, he had need have much cunning, to seem to know that[48] he doth not.

Histories make men wise, poets witty,[49] the mathematics subtile, natural philosophy[50] deep, moral[51] grave, logic and rhetoric able to contend. *Abeunt studia in mores.*[52] Nay, there is no stond[53] or impediment in the wit[54] but may be wrought out by fit

---

22 Outcome.
23 I.e., will report more favorably than the facts warrant.
24 Like.　　　　25 Obstinate and unreasonable.
26 Claim (on your confidence).
27 I.e., who want something.
28 I.e., if he does such and such, you will do so and so.
29 I.e., you can't insist on the other fellow's carrying out his part first.
30 I.e., what he is to do must precede what you are to do.
31 So that he will be confident you won't dare fail him now.
32 I.e., if you persuade the other fellow that you are a more reliable character than he, so that it is up to him to carry out his part of the bargain first.
33 I.e., the whole game or trick (of negotiating).
34 I.e., learn your man's character.
35 I.e., get your man to do what you want.　　　36 Reveal.

37 Conversation.　　38 Experienced.　　39 Eccentricity.
40 Pruning.　　41 "Practical."　　42 Marvel at.
43 Outside.　　44 Carefully.　　45 Subjects.
46 Flat, tasteless.　　47 Conversation.　　48 What.
49 Clever.　　50 Science.
51 Moral philosophy, i.e., ethics.
52 Studies develop into character (Ovid, *Heroides*, xv, 83).
53 Obstacle.　　54 Mind, intelligence.

studies, like as diseases of the body may have appropriate exercises: bowling is good for the stone and reins,[55] shooting[56] for the lungs and breast, gentle walking for the stomach, riding for the head, and the like. So if a man's wit be wandering, let him study the mathematics; for in demonstrations, if his wit be called away never so little, he must begin

again. If his wit be not apt to distinguish or find differences, let him study the Schoolmen,[57] for they are *cymini sectores*.[58] If he be not apt to beat over matters, and to call up one thing to prove and illustrate another, let him study the lawyers' cases. So every defect of the mind may have a special receipt.[59]

from THE ADVANCEMENT OF LEARNING

Bacon begins by refuting various general objections to learning and examining the "distempers" that afflict learning in his own day. In the excerpts reprinted from this section you will find, among other things, his answer to the charge that learning is hostile to religion (compare the theme of *Doctor Faustus*), his attitude toward the Ancients, and some valuable comments on prose style. From Book II, an analysis of the parts of learning and a sketch of their status in contemporary scholarship, come his account of natural history (note particularly his characteristic emphasis on the practical value of "history mechanical") and his description of "poesy," which offers interesting points of comparison with Sidney's.

from BOOK I

. . . To have the true testimonies concerning the dignity of learning to be better heard, without the interruption of tacit objections, I think good to deliver it from the discredits and disgraces which it hath received; all from ignorance, but ignorance severally disguised, appearing sometimes in the zeal and jealousy of divines, sometimes in the severity and arrogancy of politiques,[1] and sometimes in the errors and imperfections of learned men themselves.

I hear the former sort say that knowledge is of those things which are to be accepted of with great limitation and caution; that the aspiring to overmuch knowledge was the original temptation and sin whereupon ensued the fall of man; that knowledge hath in it somewhat of the serpent, and therefore where it entereth into a man it makes him swell—*scientia inflat;*[2] that Solomon gives a censure that "there is no end of making books, and that much reading is weariness of the flesh";[3] and again, in another place, that "in spacious knowledge there is much contristation, and that he that increaseth

knowledge increaseth anxiety";[4] that St. Paul gives a caveat that "we be not spoiled through vain philosophy";[5] that experience demonstrates how learned men have been arch-heretics, how learned times have been inclined to atheism, and how the contemplation of second causes derogates from our dependence upon God, who is the first cause.

To discover then the ignorance and error of this opinion and the misunderstanding in the grounds thereof, it may well appear these men do not observe or consider that it was not the pure knowledge of nature and universality, a knowledge by the light whereof man did give names unto other creatures in paradise, as they were brought before him,[6] according unto their proprieties, which gave the occasion to the fall; but it was the proud knowledge of good and evil, with an intent in man to give law unto himself and to depend no more upon God's commandments, which was the form of the temptation. Neither is it any quantity of knowledge, how great soever, that can make the mind of man to swell; for nothing can fill, much less extend, the soul of man but God and the contemplation of God; and therefore Solomon, speaking of the two principal senses of inquisition,[7] the eye and the ear, affirmeth that the eye is never satisfied with seeing, nor the ear with hearing;[8] and if there be no fulness, then is the continent[9] greater than the content: so of knowledge itself, and the mind of man, whereto the senses are but reporters, he defineth likewise in these words, placed after that calendar or ephemerides which he maketh of the diversities of times and seasons for all actions and purposes,[10] and concludeth thus: "God

---

55 Testicle(s) and kidneys.   56 Archery.
1 Politicians, those concerned with affairs of state.
2 "Knowledge puffeth up" (1 Corinthians 8:1).
3 Cf. Ecclesiastes 12:12.

57 The medieval theologians and philosophers.
58 Dividers of cumin seeds—by which Bacon means hairsplitters. The expression was originally Greek and meant skinflints.
59 Recipe.
4 Cf. Ecclesiastes 1:18.
5 Cf. Colossians 2:8.   6 See Genesis 2:19–20.
7 Inquiry, investigation.   8 See Ecclesiastes 1:8.
9 Container.   10 Ecclesiastes 3:1–8.

hath made all things beautiful, or decent, in the true return of their seasons; also he hath placed the world in man's heart, yet cannot man find out the work which God worketh from the beginning to the end":[11] declaring, not obscurely, that God hath framed the mind of man as a mirror or glass, capable of the image of the universal world, and joyful to receive the impression thereof, as the eye joyeth to receive light; and not only delighted in beholding the variety of things and vicissitude of times, but raised also to find out and discern the ordinances and decrees which throughout all those changes are infallibly observed. And although he doth insinuate that the supreme or summary law of nature, which he calleth "the work which God worketh from the beginning to the end," is not possible to be found out by man, yet that doth not derogate from the capacity of the mind, but may be referred to the impediments, as of shortness of life, ill conjunction of labors, ill tradition of knowledge over from hand to hand, and many other inconveniences, whereunto the condition of man is subject. For that nothing parcel[12] of the world is denied to man's inquiry and invention,[13] he doth in another place rule over,[14] when he saith, "The spirit of man is as the lamp of God, wherewith he searcheth the inwardness of all secrets."[15] If then such be the capacity and receipt[16] of the mind of man, it is manifest that there is no danger at all in the proportion or quantity of knowledge, how large soever, lest it should make it swell or outcompass itself; no, but it is merely the quality of knowledge, which, be it in quantity more or less, if it be taken without the true corrective thereof, hath in it some nature of venom or malignity, and some effects of that venom, which is ventosity[17] or swelling. This corrective spice, the mixture whereof maketh knowledge so sovereign, is charity, which the apostle immediately addeth to the former clause: for so he saith, "Knowledge bloweth up, but charity buildeth up";[18] not unlike unto that which he delivereth in another place: "If I spake," saith he, "with the tongues of men and angels, and had not charity, it were but as a tinkling cymbal";[19] not but that it is an excellent thing to speak with the tongues of men and angels, but because, if it be severed from charity and not referred to the good of men and mankind, it hath rather a sounding and unworthy glory than a

meriting and substantial virtue. And as for that censure of Solomon concerning the excess of writing and reading books and the anxiety of spirit which redoundeth from knowledge, and that admonition of St. Paul that "we be not seduced by vain philosophy," let those places be rightly understood and they do indeed excellently set forth the true bounds and limitations whereby human knowledge is confined and circumscribed, and yet without any such contracting or coarctation[20] but that it may comprehend all the universal nature of things. For these limits are three: the first, that we do not so place our felicity in knowledge, as we forget our mortality; the second, that we make application of our knowledge to give ourselves repose and contentment, and not distaste or repining; the third, that we do not presume by the contemplation of nature to attain to the mysteries of God. For as touching the first of these, Solomon doth excellently expound himself in another place of the same book, where he saith: "I saw well that knowledge recedeth as far from ignorance as light doth from darkness, and that the wise man's eyes keep watch in his head, whereas the fool roundeth about in darkness; but withal I learned that the same mortality involveth them both."[21] And for the second, certain it is, there is no vexation or anxiety of mind which resulteth from knowledge otherwise than merely by accident. For all knowledge and wonder (which is the seed of knowledge) is an impression of pleasure in itself; but when men fall to framing conclusions out of their knowledge, applying it to their particular,[22] and ministering to themselves thereby weak fears or vast desires, there groweth that carefulness[23] and trouble of mind which is spoken of. For then knowledge is no more *Lumen siccum*,[24] whereof Heraclitus the profound said, *Lumen siccum optima anima*;[25] but it becometh *Lumen madidum* or *maceratum*,[26] being steeped and infused in the humors of the affections. And as for the third point, it deserveth to be a little stood upon, and not to be lightly passed over. For if any man shall think by view and inquiry into these sensible and material things to attain that light whereby he may reveal unto himself the nature or will of God, then indeed is he spoiled by vain philosophy; for the contemplation of God's creatures and works produceth, having regard to the works and creatures themselves, knowl-

---

[11] Cf. Ecclesiastes 3:11.   [12] No part.
[13] Discovery.   [14] Pronounce judgment.
[15] Cf. Proverbs 20:27.   [16] Ability to receive.
[17] Windiness, flatulence.   [18] See note 2.
[19] Cf. 1 Corinthians 13:1.

[20] Constriction.
[21] Cf. Ecclesiastes 2:13–14.
[22] Individual case.   [23] Anxiety.   [24] A dry light.
[25] The best spirit is a dry light. Heraclitus appears to have said, "A dry spirit is best"; Bacon follows a textual corruption of long standing.   [26] Wet or soaked.

edge, but having regard to God, no perfect knowledge, but wonder, which is broken knowledge. And therefore it was most aptly said by one of Plato's school[27] that "the sense of man carrieth a resemblance with the sun, which, as we see, openeth and revealeth all the terrestrial globe, but then again it obscureth and concealeth the stars and celestial globe; so doth the sense discover natural things, but it darkeneth and shutteth up divine." And hence it is true that it hath proceeded that divers great learned men have been heretical whilst they have sought to fly up to the secrets of the Deity by the waxen wings[28] of the senses. And as for the conceit that too much knowledge should incline a man to atheism, and that the ignorance of second causes should make a more devout dependence upon God, which is the first cause, first it is good to ask the question which Job asked of his friends: "Will you lie for God, as one man will do for another, to gratify him?"[29] For certain it is that God worketh nothing in nature but by second causes: and if they would have it otherwise believed, it is mere imposture, as it were in favor towards God, and nothing else but to offer to the Author of truth the unclean sacrifice of a lie. But farther, it is an assured truth and a conclusion of experience that a little or superficial knowledge of philosophy may incline the mind of man to atheism, but a farther proceeding therein doth bring the mind back again to religion.[30] For in the entrance of philosophy, when the second causes, which are next unto the senses, do offer themselves to the mind of man, if it dwell and stay there it may induce some oblivion of the highest cause; but when a man passeth on farther and seeth the dependence of causes and the works of Providence, then, according to the allegory of the poets, he will easily believe that the highest link of nature's chain must needs be tied to the foot of Jupiter's chair.[31] To conclude, therefore, let no man upon a weak conceit of sobriety or an ill-applied moderation think or maintain that a man can search too far or be too well studied in the book of God's word or in the book of God's works, divinity or philosophy; but rather let men endeavor an endless progress or proficience in both. Only let men beware that they apply both to charity, and not to swelling; to use, and not to ostentation; and again, that they

do not unwisely mingle or confound these learnings together. . . .[32]

There be . . . chiefly three vanities in studies, whereby learning hath been most traduced. . . : the first, fantastical learning; the second, contentious learning; and the last, delicate learning; vain imaginations, vain altercations, and vain affectations; and with the last I will begin. Martin Luther, conducted no doubt by a higher providence, but in discourse of reason[33] finding what a province he had undertaken against the bishop of Rome and the degenerate traditions of the church, and finding his own solitude, being noways aided by the opinions of his own time, was enforced to awake all antiquity and to call former times to his succors to make a party against the present time. So that the ancient authors, both in divinity and in humanity, which had long time slept in libraries, began generally to be read and revolved. Thus by consequence did draw on a necessity of a more exquisite[34] travail in the languages original wherein those authors did write, for the better understanding of those authors and the better advantage of pressing and applying their words. And thereof grew again a delight in their manner of style and phrase and an admiration of that kind of writing, which was much furthered and precipitated by the enmity and opposition that the propounders of those primitive but seeming new opinions had against the schoolmen,[35] who were generally of the contrary part and whose writings were altogether in a different style and form; taking liberty to coin and frame new terms of art to express their own sense and to avoid circuit of speech,[36] without regard to the pureness, pleasantness, and, as I may call it, lawfulness of the phrase or word. And again, because the great labor that then was with the people (of whom the Pharisees were wont to say, *Execrabilis ista turba, quae non novit legem*[37]) for the winning and persuading of them, there grew of necessity in chief price[38] and request eloquence and variety of discourse, as the fittest and forciblest access into the capacity of the vulgar sort. So that these four causes concurring, the admiration of ancient authors, the hate of the schoolmen, the exact study of languages, and the efficacy of preaching, did bring in an affectionate[39] study of eloquence and copie[40] of speech, which then began to flourish. This grew speedily to an excess; for men

[27] Philo Judaeus (flourished 39 A.D.) in his treatise *Of Dreams*.
[28] Bacon alludes to the myth of Daedalus, who made waxen wings for himself and his son Icarus. Icarus flew too near the sun; his wings melted, and he fell into the sea and was drowned.
[29] Cf. Job 13:7, 9.
[30] Bacon argues similarly in his essay "Of Atheism."
[31] Homer, *Iliad*, VIII, 19.

[32] Bacon next considers the objections raised by "politiques" and then those arising from the imperfections and errors of learned men themselves.   [33] By discursive reasoning.
[34] Elaborate, minute.   [35] The scholastic philosophers.
[36] Circumlocution.
[37] "This people who knoweth not the law are cursed" (John 7:49).
[38] Esteem.   [39] Affected.   [40] Copiousness (Latin *copia*).

began to hunt more after words than matter—more after the choiceness of the phrase, and the round and clean composition of the sentence, and the sweet falling of the clauses, and the varying and illustration of their works with tropes and figures, than after the weight of matter, worth of subject, soundness of argument, life of invention, or depth of judgment. Then grew the flowing and watery vein of Osorius,[41] the Portugal bishop, to be in price. Then did Sturmius[42] spend such infinite and curious pains upon Cicero the orator and Hermogenes the rhetorician, besides his own books of periods and imitation, and the like. Then did Car of Cambridge[43] and Ascham with their lectures and writings almost deify Cicero and Demosthenes, and allure all young men that were studious unto that delicate and polished kind of learning. Then did Erasmus take occasion to make the scoffing Echo: "*Decem annos consumpsi in legendo Cicerone*";[44] and the Echo answered in Greek, "Ὄνε, *Asine*." Then grew the learning of the schoolmen to be utterly despised as barbarous. In sum, the whole inclination and bent of those times was rather towards copie than weight.

Here, therefore, is the first distemper of learning, when men study words and not matter. . . .[45]

Thus have I gone over these three diseases of learning; besides the which there are some other rather peccant humors[46] than formed diseases, which nevertheless are not so secret and intrinsic[47] but that they fall under a popular observation and traducement, and therefore are not to be passed over.

The first of these is the extreme affecting of two extremities: the one antiquity, the other novelty; wherein it seemeth the children of time do take after the nature and malice of the father.[48] For as he devoureth his children, so one of them seeketh to devour and suppress the other; while antiquity envieth there should be new additions, and novelty cannot be content to add but it must deface. Surely the advice of the prophet is the true direction in this matter: *State super vias antiquas, et videte quaenam sit via recta et bona, et ambulate in ea.*[49] Antiquity deserveth that

reverence, that men should make a stand thereupon and discover what is the best way; but when the discovery is well taken, then to make progression. And to speak truly, *Antiquitas saeculi juventus mundi.*[50] These times are the ancient times, when the world is ancient, and not those which we account ancient *ordine retrogrado,* by a computation backward from ourselves.

Another error induced by the former is a distrust that anything should be now to be found out, which the world should have missed and passed over so long time; as if the same objection were to be made to time that Lucian[51] maketh to Jupiter and order the heathen gods; of which he wondereth that they begot so many children in old time, and begot none in his time; and asketh whether they were become septuagenary, or whether the law *Papia,* made against old men's marriages, had restrained them. So it seemeth men doubt lest time is become past children and generation; wherein, contrariwise, we see commonly the levity[52] and unconstancy of men's judgments, which till a matter be done, wonder that it can be done; and as soon as it is done, wonder again that it was no sooner done: as we see in the expedition of Alexander into Asia, which at first was prejudged as a vast and impossible enterprise; and yet afterwards it pleaseth Livy[53] to make no more of it than this: *Nil aliud quam bene ausus vana contemnere;*[54] and the same happened to Columbus in the western navigation. But in intellectual matters it is much more common, as may be seen in most of the propositions of Euclid, which till they be demonstrate,[55] they seem strange to our assent; but being demonstrate, our mind accepteth of them by a kind of relation (as the lawyers speak), as if we had known them before.

Another error, that hath also some affinity with the former, is a conceit that of former opinions or sects, after variety and examination, the best hath still prevailed and suppressed the rest; so as if a man should begin the labor of a new search, he were but like to light upon somewhat formerly rejected, and by rejection brought into oblivion: as if the multitude, or the wisest for the multitude's sake, were not ready to give passage rather to that which is popular and superficial than to that which is substantial and profound; for the truth is that time seemeth to be of the nature of a river or stream, which carrieth

[41] A Portuguese theologian (d. 1580).
[42] A German humanist (1507–89).
[43] Nicholas Carr (1523–68), professor of Greek at Cambridge.— On Ascham and Erasmus see pp. 217, 219, 224, 226, above.
[44] "I have spent ten years studying Cicero." Echo replies, "Ass." The episode is from Erasmus's *Colloquies.*
[45] Bacon next considers "contentious learning" and "fantastical learning." [46] Morbid secretions.
[47] Internal and hence hidden.
[48] According to the myth, Cronos (Time) swallowed his children.
[49] Cf. Jeremiah 6:16: ". . . Stand ye in the ways, and see, and ask for the old paths, where is the good way, and walk therein. . . ."

[50] Ancient times were the world's youth.
[51] Actually, Seneca, the Roman philosopher and dramatist of the first century A.D. [52] Lightness.
[53] The famous Roman historian (59 B.C.–17 A.D.).
[54] His daring consisted only in scorning foolish objections.
[55] Demonstrated. Cf. *illustrate* in line 13 on the next page.

down to us that which is light and blown up, and sinketh and drowneth that which is weighty and solid.

Another error, of a diverse nature from all the former, is the over-early and peremptory reduction of knowledge into arts and methods; from which time commonly sciences receive small or no augmentation. But as young men, when they knit and shape perfectly, do seldom grow to a further stature; so knowledge, while it is in aphorisms and observations, it is in growth; but when it once is comprehended in exact methods, it may perchance be further polished and illustrate and accommodated for use and practice, but it increaseth no more in bulk and substance.

Another error, which doth succeed that which we last mentioned, is that after the distribution of particular arts and sciences, men have abandoned universality, or *philosophia prima;* which cannot but cease and stop all progression. For no perfect discovery can be made upon a flat or a level; neither is it possible to discover the more remote and deeper parts of any science if you stand but upon the level of the same science, and ascend not to a higher science.

Another error hath proceeded from too great a reverence, and a kind of adoration, of the mind and understanding of man; by means whereof men have withdrawn themselves too much from the contemplation of nature and the observations of experience, and have tumbled up and down in their own reason and conceits. Upon these intellectualists, which are notwithstanding commonly taken for the most sublime and divine philosophers, Heraclitus gave a just censure, saying, "Men sought truth in their own little worlds, and not in the great and common world"; for they disdain to spell, and so by degrees to read in the volume of God's works: and contrariwise by continual meditation and agitation of wit do urge and as it were invocate their own spirits to divine and give oracles unto them, whereby they are deservedly deluded.

Another error, that hath some connection with this latter, is that men have used to infect their meditations, opinions, and doctrines with some conceits which they have most admired, or some sciences which they have most applied, and given all things else a tincture according to them, utterly untrue and unproper. So hath Plato intermingled his philosophy with theology, and Aristotle with logic; and the second school of Plato,[56] Proclus and the rest, with

the mathematics. For these were the arts which had a kind of primogeniture with them severally. So have the alchemists made a philosophy out of a few experiments of the furnace; and Gilbertus,[57] our countryman, hath made a philosophy out of the observations of a loadstone. So Cicero, when, reciting the several opinions of the nature of the soul, he found a musician that held the soul was but a harmony, saith pleasantly, *Hic ab arte sua non recessit,*[58] etc. But of these conceits Aristotle speaketh seriously and wisely when he saith, *Qui respiciunt ad pauca de facili pronunciant.*[59]

Another error is an impatience of doubt, and haste to assertion without due and mature suspension of judgment. For the two ways of contemplation are not unlike the two ways of action commonly spoken of by the ancients: the one plain and smooth in the beginning, and in the end impassable; the other rough and troublesome in the entrance, but after a while fair and even. So it is in contemplation: if a man will begin with certainties, he shall end in doubts; but if he will be content to begin with doubts, he shall end in certainties.

Another error is in the manner of the tradition and delivery of knowledge, which is for the most part magistral and peremptory, and not ingenuous and faithful; in a sort as may be soonest believed, and not easiliest examined. It is true that in compendious treatises for practice that form is not to be disallowed; but in the true handling of knowledge, men ought not to fall either on the one side into the vein of Velleius the Epicurean: *Nil tam metuens, quam ne dubitare aliqua de re videretur;*[60] nor on the other side into Socrates his ironical doubting of all things; but to propound things sincerely with more or less asseveration as they stand in a man's own judgment proved more or less.

Other errors there are in the scope that men propound to themselves, whereunto they bend their endeavors; for whereas the more constant and devote[61] kind of professors of any science ought to propound to themselves to make some additions to their science, they convert their labors to aspire to certain second prizes: as to be a profound interpreter or commenter, to be a sharp champion or defender, to

<hr />

56 The Neoplatonic school. Proclus (411–85), its last important figure, also wrote a commentary on Euclid.

57 William Gilbert published in 1600 an important book on the magnet.
58 He did not depart from his own profession (*Tusculan Disputation,* Book I).
59 Those who take few things into consideration find it easy to pronounce judgment (*Of Generation and Corruption,* I, 2).
60 Fearing nothing so much as to seem to be in doubt about anything (Cicero, *Of the Nature of the Gods,* I, 8).
61 Devoted.

be a methodical compounder or abridger; and so the patrimony of knowledge cometh to be sometimes improved, but seldom augmented.

But the greatest error of all the rest is the mistaking or misplacing of the last or farthest end of knowledge. For men have entered into a desire of learning and knowledge, sometimes upon a natural curiosity and inquisitive appetite; sometimes to entertain their minds with variety and delight; sometimes for ornament and reputation; and sometimes to enable them to victory of wit and contradiction; and most times for lucre and profession; and seldom sincerely to give a true account of their gift of reason, to the benefit and use of men: as if there were sought in knowledge a couch, whereupon to rest a searching and restless spirit; or a terrace, for a wandering and variable mind to walk up and down with a fair prospect; or a tower of state, for a proud mind to raise itself upon; or a fort or commanding ground, for strife and contention; or a shop, for profit or sale; and not a rich storehouse for the glory of the Creator and the relief of man's estate. But this is that which will indeed dignify and exalt knowledge, if contemplation and action may be more nearly and straitly conjoined and united together than they have been; a conjunction like unto that of the two highest planets, Saturn, the planet of rest and contemplation, and Jupiter, the planet of civil society and action. Howbeit, I do not mean, when I speak of use and action, that end before mentioned of the applying of knowledge to lucre and profession; for I am not ignorant how much that diverteth and interrupteth the prosecution and advancement of knowledge, like unto the golden ball thrown before Atalanta, which while she goeth aside and stoopeth to take up, the race is hindered:

Declinat cursus, aurumque volubile tollit.[62]

Neither is my meaning, as was spoken of Socrates,[63] to call philosophy down from heaven to converse upon the earth; that is, to leave natural philosophy aside, and to apply knowledge only to manners and policy. But as both heaven and earth do conspire and contribute to the use and benefit of man; so the end ought to be, from both philosophies to separate and reject vain speculations, and whatsoever is empty and void, and to preserve and augment whatsoever is solid and fruitful: that knowledge may not be as a courtesan, for pleasure and vanity only, or as a bondwoman, to acquire and gain to her master's use; but as a spouse, for generation, fruit, and comfort.

Thus have I described and opened, as by a kind of dissection, those peccant humors (the principal of them) which have not only given impediment to the proficience of learning, but have given also occasion to the traducement thereof.

from BOOK II

THE PARTS of human learning have reference to the three parts of man's understanding, which is the seat of learning: history to his memory, poesy to his imagination, and philosophy to his reason. . . .

History is natural, civil, ecclesiastical, and literary; whereof the first three I allow as extant, the fourth I note as deficient.[1] For no man hath propounded to himself the general state of learning to be described and represented from age to age, as many have done the works of nature, and the state civil and ecclesiastical; without which the history of the world seemeth to me to be as the statua of Polyphemus[2] with his eye out, that part being wanting which doth most show the spirit and life of the person. And yet I am not ignorant that in divers particular sciences, as of the jurisconsults, the mathematicians, the rhetoricians, the philosophers, there are set down some small memorials of the schools, authors, and books; and so likewise some barren relations touching the invention of arts or usages. But a just story[3] of learning, containing the antiquities and originals of knowledges and their sects, their inventions, their traditions, their diverse administrations and managings, their flourishings, their oppositions, decays, depressions, oblivions, removes, with the causes and occasions of them, and all other events concerning learning, throughout the ages of the world, I may truly affirm to be wanting. The use and end of which work I do not so much design for curiosity or satisfaction of those that are the lovers of learning, but chiefly for a more serious and grave purpose, which is this in few words: that it will make learned men wise in the use and administration of learning. For it is not St. Augustine's nor St. Ambrose's works that will make so wise a divine as ecclesiastical history, thoroughly read and observed; and the same reason is of learning.

---

62 She turns aside from the course and picks up the golden ball (Ovid, *Metamorphoses*, X, 667). Atalanta agreed to marry Hippomenes if he could defeat her in a foot race; he won the victory by the device described here.
63 By Cicero in the *Tusculan Disputation*, Book V.

1 I.e., the extant accounts of the first three are adequate; the fourth has not been satisfactorily treated.
2 A one-eyed giant, one of the Cyclopes, whose eye was put out by Odysseus (*Odyssey*, Book IX).   3 Accurate history.

History of nature is of three sorts: of nature in course, of nature erring or varying, and of nature altered or wrought; that is, history of creatures, history of marvels, and history of arts. The first of these, no doubt, is extant, and that in good perfection; the two latter are handled so weakly and unprofitably as I am moved to note them as deficient. For I find no sufficient or competent collection of the works of nature which have a digression and deflection from the ordinary course of generations, productions, and motions; whether they be singularities of place and region, or the strange events of time and chance, or the effects of yet unknown properties, or the instances of exceptions to general kinds. It is true, I find a number of books of fabulous experiments and secrets, and frivolous impostures for pleasure and strangeness; but a substantial and severe collection of the heteroclites or irregulars of nature, well examined and described, I find not: especially not with due rejection of fables and popular errors; for as things now are, if an untruth in nature be once on foot, what by reason of the neglect of examination and countenance of antiquity, and what by reason of the use of the opinion in similitudes and ornaments of speech, it is never called down.[4]

The use of this work, honored with a precedent in Aristotle,[5] is nothing less than[6] to give contentment to the appetite of curious and vain wits, as the manner of mirabilaries[7] is to do; but for two reasons, both of great weight: the one to correct the partiality of axioms and opinions, which are commonly framed only upon common and familiar examples; the other because from the wonders of nature is the nearest intelligence and passage towards the wonders of art: for it is no more but by following and as it were hounding nature in her wanderings, to be able to lead her afterwards to the same place again. Neither am I of opinion, in this history of marvels, that superstitious narrations of sorceries, witchcrafts, dreams, divinations, and the like, where there is an assurance and clear evidence of the fact, be altogether excluded. For it is not yet known in what cases and how far effects attributed to superstition do participate of natural causes; and therefore howsoever the practice of such things is to be condemned, yet from the speculation and consideration of them light may be taken, not only for the discerning of the offences but for the further disclosing of nature.

Neither ought a man to make scruple of entering into these things for inquisition of truth, as your Majesty[8] hath showed in your own example; who with the two clear eyes of religion and natural philosophy have looked deeply and wisely into these shadows, and yet proved yourself to be of the nature of the sun, which passeth through pollutions and itself remains as pure as before. But this I hold fit, that these narrations which have mixture with superstition be sorted by themselves, and not be mingled with the narrations which are merely and sincerely[9] natural. But as for the narrations touching the prodigies and miracles of religions, they are either not true or not natural, and therefore impertinent for the story of nature.

For history of nature wrought or mechanical, I find some collections made of agriculture and likewise of manual arts, but commonly with a rejection of experiments familiar and vulgar. For it is esteemed a kind of dishonor unto learning to descend to inquiry or meditation upon matters mechanical, except they be such as may be thought secrets, rarities, and special subtilities; which humor of vain and supercilious arrogancy is justly derided in Plato,[10] where he brings in Hippias, a vaunting sophist, disputing with Socrates, a true and unfeigned inquisitor of truth; where the subject being touching beauty, Socrates, after his wandering manner of inductions, put first an example of a fair virgin, and then of a fair horse, and then of a fair pot well glazed, whereat Hippias was offended, and said, more than for courtesy's sake, he did think much to dispute with any that did allege such base and sordid instances; whereunto Socrates answered, "You have reason, and it becomes you well, being a man so trim in your vestments," etc., and so goeth on in an irony. But the truth is, they be not the highest instances that give the securest information; as may be well expressed in the tale so common of the philosopher,[11] that while he gazed upwards to the stars fell into the water; for if he had looked down he might have seen the stars in the water, but looking aloft he could not see the water in the stars. So it cometh often to pass that mean and small things discover great better than great can discover the small; and therefore Aristotle noteth well that "the nature of everything is best seen in its smallest portions."[12] And for that cause he inquireth the nature of a commonwealth,

---

[4] Cried down.
[5] The work referred to, *De Mirabilibus Auscultationibus*, is no longer ascribed to Aristotle.   [6] I.e., not at all.
[7] Collections of marvels.

[8] The book is addressed to James I, who was interested in "wonders" and wrote a treatise on demonology.
[9] Purely and simply.
[10] In his dialogue *Hippias Major*.
[11] This story was told of Thales (born 624 B.C.).   [12] *Politics*, I, 3.

first in a family, and the simple conjugations of man and wife, parent and child, master and servant, which are in every cottage. Even so likewise the nature of this great city of the world, and the policy thereof, must be first sought in mean concordances and small portions. So we see how that secret of nature, of the turning of iron touched with the loadstone towards the north, was found out in needles of iron, not in bars of iron.

But if my judgment be of any weight, the use of history mechanical is of all others the most radical[13] and fundamental towards natural philosophy—such natural philosophy as shall not vanish in the fume of subtile, sublime, or delectable speculation, but such as shall be operative to the endowment and benefit of man's life. For it will not only minister and suggest for the present many ingenious practices in all trades, by a connection and transferring of the observations of one art to the use of another, when the experiences of several mysteries shall fall under the consideration of one man's mind; but further, it will give a more true and real illumination concerning causes and axioms than is hitherto attained. For like as a man's disposition is never well known till he be crossed, nor Proteus[14] ever changed shapes till he was straitened and held fast, so the passages and variations of nature cannot appear so fully in the liberty of nature as in the trials and vexations of art. . . .[15]

Poesy is a part of learning in measure of words for the most part restrained, but in all other points extremely licensed, and doth truly refer to the imagination; which, being not tied to the laws of matter, may at pleasure join that which nature hath severed, and sever that which nature hath joined, and so make unlawful matches and divorces of things. *Pictoribus atque poetis,* etc.[16] It is taken in two senses in respect of words or matter: in the first sense it is but a character of style, and belongeth to arts of speech, and is not pertinent for the present; in the latter it is, as hath been said, one of the principal portions of learning, and is nothing else but feigned history, which may be styled as well in prose as in verse.

The use of this feigned history hath been to give some shadow of satisfaction to the mind of man in those points wherein the nature of things doth deny it, the world being in proportion inferior to the soul; by reason whereof there is, agreeable to the spirit of man, a more ample greatness, a more exact goodness, and a more absolute variety than can be found in the nature of things. Therefore, because the acts or events of true history have not that magnitude which satisfieth the mind of man, poesy feigneth acts and events greater and more heroical; because true history propoundeth the successes and issues of actions not so agreeable to the merits of virtue and vice, therefore poesy feigns them more just in retribution, and more according to revealed providence; because true history representeth actions and events more ordinary and less interchanged, therefore poesy endueth them with more rareness and more unexpected and alternative variations; so as it appeareth that poesy serveth and conferreth to magnanimity, morality, and to delectation. And therefore it was ever thought to have some participation of divineness, because it doth raise and erect the mind by submitting the shows of things to the desires of the mind, whereas reason doth buckle and bow the mind into the nature of things. And we see that by these insinuations and congruities with man's nature and pleasure, joined also with the agreement and comfort it hath with music, it hath had access and estimation in rude times and barbarous regions, where other learning stood excluded.

The division of poesy which is aptest in the propriety thereof[17] (besides those divisions which are common unto it with history, as feigned chronicles, feigned lives, and the appendices of history, as feigned epistles, feigned orations, and the rest) is into poesy narrative, representative, and allusive. The narrative is a mere imitation of history, with the excesses before remembered; choosing for subject commonly wars and love, rarely state, and sometimes pleasure or mirth. Representative is as a visible history, and is an image of actions as if they were present, as history is of actions in nature as they are, (that is) past. Allusive or parabolical is a narrative applied only to express some special purpose or conceit. Which latter kind of parabolical wisdom was much more in use in the ancient times, as by the fables of Aesop, and the brief sentences of the Seven,[18]

---

[13] I.e., basic.

[14] A sea god who when seized assumed various shapes to avoid being questioned.

[15] Bacon's analysis of the other kinds of history follows.

[16] The whole statement is *Pictoribus atque poetis quidlibet audendi semper fuit aequa potestas* (Horace, *Art of Poetry,* 9–10). Ben Jonson translated it:

"But equal power to painter and to poet
Of daring aught hath still been given, we know it."

[17] I.e., which is most appropriate to its peculiar nature.

[18] The Seven Sages (philosophers of the seventh and sixth centuries B.C.—the list of names varies), whose wisdom was handed down in aphorisms.

and the use of hieroglyphics[19] may appear. And the cause was, for that it was then of necessity to express any point of reason which was more sharp or subtile than the vulgar in that manner, because men in those times wanted[20] both variety of examples and subtility of conceit; and as hieroglyphics were before letters, so parables were before arguments; and nevertheless now, and at all times, they do retain much life and vigor, because reason cannot be so sensible,[21] nor examples so fit.

But there remaineth yet another use of poesy parabolical, opposite to that which we last mentioned; for that tendeth to demonstrate and illustrate that which is taught or delivered, and this other to retire and obscure it: that is, when the secrets and mysteries of religion, policy, or philosophy are involved in fables or parables. Of this in divine poesy we see the use is authorized. In heathen poesy we see the exposition of fables doth fall out sometimes with great felicity; as in the fable that the giants being overthrown in their war against the gods, the Earth their mother in revenge thereof brought forth Fame;[22] . . . expounded, that when princes and monarchs have suppressed actual and open rebels, then the malignity of the people, which is the mother of rebellion, doth bring libels and slanders, and taxations of the states, which is of the same kind with rebellion, but more feminine. So in the fable that the rest of the gods having conspired to bind Jupiter, Pallas[23] called Briareus with his hundred hands to his aid; expounded, that monarchs need not fear any curbing of their absoluteness by mighty subjects as long as by wisdom they keep the hearts of the people, who will be sure to come in on their side. So in the fable that Achilles was brought up under Chiron the centaur, who was part a man and part a beast; expounded ingeniously by Machiavel,[24] that it belongeth to the education and discipline of princes to know as well how to play the part of the lion in violence, and the fox in guile, as of the man in virtue and justice. Nevertheless, in many the like encounters I do rather think that the fable was first, and the exposition devised, than that the moral was first, and thereupon the fable framed. For I find it was an ancient vanity in Chrysippus,[25] that troubled himself with great contention to fasten the assertions of the Stoics upon the fictions of the ancient poets; but yet that all the fables and fictions of the poets were but pleasure and not figure, I interpose no opinion. Surely of those poets which are now extant, even Homer himself (notwithstanding he was made a kind of Scripture by the latter schools of the Grecians), yet I should without any difficulty pronounce that his fables had no such inwardness in his own meaning; but what they might have upon a more original tradition is not easy to affirm, for he was not the inventor of many of them.

In this third part of learning, which is poesy, I can report no deficience. For being as a plant that cometh of the lust of the earth, without a formal seed, it hath sprung up and spread abroad more than any other kind. But to ascribe unto it that which is due, for the expressing of affections, passions, corruptions, and customs, we are beholding to poets more than to the philosophers' works; and for wit and eloquence, not much less than to orator's harangue.

* * * * *

---

[19] Picture writing, which represented objects and ideas by means of pictorial symbols. [20] Lacked. [21] I.e., concrete.

[22] Rumor. Bacon quotes Vergil's account, *Aeneid*, IV, 178–80.

[23] According to Homer, not Pallas but Thetis, a sea goddess who became the mother of Achilles. Briareus was a huge hundred-handed monster.

[24] *The Prince*, chap. 18.

[25] A Stoic philosopher of the third century B.C.

John Donne

1572-1631

BEN JONSON, who admired him, proved a false prophet when he predicted that Donne "for not being understood would perish." His art is certainly a tough nut to crack; but there is no one quite like him, and his best poems richly reward the effort that is required to penetrate their meaning.

Donne began writing in conscious reaction against the Petrarchan solemnity and artificiality of the conventional tributes to love and beauty. We have seen how, even at Elizabeth's court, the poems of Raleigh sometimes strike a note of disillusion. In Donne's earliest verse it becomes the dominant note. He enjoyed, a bit sophomorically perhaps, giving his contemporaries a jolt of surprise. He repudiates the code of the right-thinking Elizabethan and willfully praises the wrong things, such as inconstancy in love. He flouts the standards by his meter's contemptuous roughness; Jonson roundly declared that "for not keeping of accent" he "deserved hanging." It was a profound personal experience which eventually led him to drop his youthful hardboiled pose and turn to writing a poetry of faith—faith in love, and in the end faith in God. After the smartly cynical verses of his youth came the wiser love poems which followed his marriage. To his third kind of poetry, the religious, he came late, after he entered the Anglican Church.

Whether Donne is a truly "metaphysical" poet (whether, that is, his poetic impulse arose from thought, which in the course of intellectual processing burst into emotional flame) is hard to say. Some think so; but it seems more likely that his better poems were more normally conceived, in emotional states, and that having *felt* he worked very hard to rationalize his emotion and to avoid conventionality in its expression. Certainly there is more *play* of the intellect in his than in most Elizabethan poetry, just as there is more in Congreve's *The Way of the World* (1700) than in Shakespeare's *Twelfth Night* (c. 1600). Which does not necessarily mean that the later work is in either case more profoundly *thoughtful* than the earlier.

It is true that love is a simpler emotion in Elizabethan verse than in Donne's poetry, behind which lie dualistic worries, almost medieval and not especially characteristic of the Renaissance, about the right relations of body and soul. Donne's conceits also differ from the characteristic Elizabethan type. He was impatient with the shopworn Petrarchan conceits and classical allusions. But in his anxiety to avoid them, he was frequently guilty of going too far afield to find his own; and so, while they are often brilliantly or poignantly effective, they are sometimes grotesque or cryptic. Dr. Johnson observed that Donne frequently brings them from "recesses of learning not very much frequented by common readers of poetry." The conceit is ordinarily more functional in Donne than in the Petrarchists; it is not superficially tacked on as an added beauty, but is intellectually worked out in the poem's meaning. In "A Valediction," for example, the comparison of the two lovers to a pair of compasses is certainly far-fetched, as Burns's "O my love's like a red, red rose" is not. But the compass conceit is built into Donne's thought. It elucidates the meaning, and despite its mechanistic realism contributes to the poem's great beauty. For his conceits Donne draws on his knowledge of the medieval theologians, the New Learning, contemporary science, and the Romance literatures, as well as on homely details of daily living.

His obsession with cleverness, and his grim pursuit (in the midst of his emotions) of an uncompromising intellectuality, spoiled a great deal of what he wrote, but in his finest work thought and feeling are completely interfused. There is a small section of his poetry that stands very close to the best that English literature can offer.

Someone like Donne was probably inevitable. Even in the seventeenth century there were Spenserian imitators, but Elizabethan poetry could not go on forever; and Donne's and Jonson's were the strongest influences in establishing new modes of expression. Under James I, Donne was a model for the younger secular poets; Thomas Carew (1594-1640) spoke for his generation when he wrote of him:

> Here lies a king that ruled as he saw fit
> The universal monarchy of wit.

His religious poetry greatly influenced the later group of devotional lyrists headed by Herbert and Vaughan. In satire he is the principal English forerunner of Dryden and Pope, though all three are, of course, followers of Horace, Juvenal, and the other Roman satirists. Donne's influence was not always for good; in the verse of some of his immediate disciples the eccentricity and cleverness are present without the passion and without the art which underlie his best poems. The same is true of some of his followers in the twentieth century, which has seen a remarkable revival of interest in his work.

Donne was born in the Catholic faith and in comfortable circumstances. Having studied at both Oxford and Cambridge, he began in London, at Lincoln's Inn, a not very serious study of the law, which was probably interrupted by travel on the Continent. He was known at this time as "a great visiter of ladies, a great frequenter of plays, a great writer of conceited verses." In 1596 he served as a volunteer under Essex in the raid on Cadiz, and the next year in Lord Thomas Howard's squadron on the "Island Voyage" to the Azores (see p. 277, above). By this time he appears to have run through his inheritance. On his return to England he secured a place as secretary to Sir Thomas Egerton, one of the Queen's ministers; but in 1601 he eloped with Anne More, a niece of Egerton's wife. His punishment was imprisonment and the loss of his job.

Donne's marriage seems to have altered his spiritual outlook even more than his material prospects. He had been living the life of courtier and man about town. Toward love his early poems had expressed an amusing but shallow cynicism. They are a wit's commentary on the sonnet vogue, on *Romeo and Juliet,* on Shakespeare's romantic comedies. Rallied by some reporters who caught up with him on his honeymoon, H. L. Mencken, who had done his share of railing at love and marriage, responded with admirable brevity and candor, "I am wiser now." Such was the experience of Donne; and while his poems cannot be dated with any certainty, it is clear that a number of them sprang from a new understanding which is not vouchsafed to all applicants.

For years this brilliant and learned man lived in poverty with his increasing family. He must have been desperate when, burdened with debt, he tried in vain to secure the secretaryship of the new colony of Virginia. Long before this his allegiance to the Catholic Church was broken; and, besides a galling dependence on patrons, he supported himself partly by writing propaganda pamphlets for a bishop of the Church of England. This prelate, as well as

King James himself, was eager that Donne's talents should be formally enlisted for that Church. After years of doubt and hesitation, he was ordained to the Anglican priesthood in 1615. Promotion came rapidly, and he was soon famous for the literary qualities of his sermons. But in 1617 his wife died; and in his grief he was, as Izaak Walton says, "crucified to the world." In 1621 the King made him dean of St. Paul's; by the time of his death ten years later he was in line for a bishopric.

From the pulpit of St. Paul's, Donne established himself as the leading preacher of his time. His religious verse, the bulk of which came after his wife's death, is correspondingly eloquent. Nevertheless he was far better known to his contemporaries as a divine than as a poet. He published practically nothing of his verse, which circulated in manuscript. The first edition appeared in 1633; there were six more in six years.

The standard edition of the poems is by H. J. C. Grierson (2 vols., 1912); it is inadequately annotated, but includes a valuable analytical essay. A carefully modernized text, unannotated, is R. E. Bennett's (1942). *Sermons, Selected Passages* was edited by L. P. Smith (1919). There is a one-volume edition of *The Complete Poetry and Selected Prose* (1929) by J. Hayward, and Everyman's Library includes a Donne volume. His Life by Izaak Walton, who was one of his parishioners at St. Dunstan's, Fleet Street, was first printed in 1640, in a volume of Donne's sermons; an enlarged revision appeared in 1658. There is a *Life and Letters* (1899) by E. Gosse. See also *The Metaphysical Poets,* by Helen C. White (1936). Whether the titles of the various poems are of Donne's choosing is uncertain. His name, by the way, rimes with *sun.*

John Donne

THE GOOD MORROW

This is, as Donne's verses go, a straightforward love poem, written in obedience to a lyric impulse rather than a desire to display cleverness or startle.

I wonder, by my troth, what thou and I
Did till we loved? Were we not weaned till then
But sucked on country pleasures childishly?
Or snorted[1] we in the Seven Sleepers' den?
'Twas so; but this,[2] all pleasures fancies be.   5
If ever any beauty I did see
Which I desired, and got, 'twas but a dream of thee.

And now good morrow to our waking souls,
Which watch not one another out of fear;
For love all love of other sights controls,   10
And makes one little room an everywhere.
Let sea discoverers to new worlds have gone;
Let maps to other,[3] worlds on worlds have shown;
Let us possess one world: each hath one, and is one.

My face in thine eye, thine in mine appears,   15
And true plain hearts do in the faces rest.
Where can we find two better hemispheres
Without sharp North, without declining West?
Whatever dies was not mixed equally;
If our two loves be one, or thou and I   20
Love so alike that none do slacken, none can die.[4]

---

[1] Snored.—According to one version of the legend, seven Christian youths sought refuge from persecution in a cave, where they slept for 230 years. When discovered and wakened, they lived for a few days and then died.
[2] I.e., except our love.

[3] Others.
[4] I.e., our united souls form, in philosophical parlance, a "simple" substance, and as such cannot perish.

GO AND CATCH A FALLING STAR

This poem and the next are two amusing morsels of cynicism, such as might today appear in the *New Yorker*— if as good a poet as Donne were writing for it. While they are certainly satirical, the tone is light, not bitter.

Go and catch a falling star,
   Get with child a mandrake[5] root,
Tell me where all past years are
   Or who cleft the devil's foot,
Teach me to hear mermaids singing   5
Or to keep off envy's stinging,
     And find
     What wind
Serves to advance an honest mind.

If thou be'st born to strange sights,[6]   10
   Things invisible to see,
Ride ten thousand days and nights
   Till age snow white hairs on thee.
Thou, when thou return'st, wilt tell me
All strange wonders that befell thee,   15
     And swear
     Nowhere
Lives a woman true, and fair.

If thou find'st one, let me know;
   Such a pilgrimage were sweet.   20
Yet do not; I would not go,
   Though at next door we might meet.
Though she were true when you met her,
And last till you write your letter,
     Yet she   25
     Will be
False ere I come, to two or three.

THE INDIFFERENT

I can love both fair and brown,[7]
Her whom abundance melts and her whom want betrays,
Her who loves loneness best and her who masks and plays,
Her whom the country formed and whom the town,
Her who believes and her who tries,[8]   5
Her who still[9] weeps with spongy eyes.
And her who is dry cork and never cries:
I can love her, and her, and you, and you;
I can love any, so[10] she be not true.

[5] A plant with a forked root. Its fancied resemblance to the human body gave rise to such superstitions as that it shrieked when pulled up.   [6] I.e., with second sight.
[7] Blonde and brunette.   [8] Tests.   [9] Constantly.
[10] Provided that.

Will no other vice content you?   10
Will it not serve your turn to do as did your mothers?
Or have you all old vices spent and now would find out
   others?
Or doth a fear that men are true torment you?
O, we are not: be not you so!
Let me—and do you—twenty know.   15
Rob me, but bind me not, and let me go.
Must I, who came to travel thorough[11] you,
Grow your fixed subject, because you are true?

Venus heard me sigh this song;
And by love's sweetest part, variety, she swore   20
She heard not this till now; and that it should be so no
   more.
She went, examined, and returned ere long,
And said, "Alas, some two or three
Poor heretics in love there be,
Which think to 'stablish dangerous constancy.   25
But I have told them, 'Since you will be true,
You shall be true to them who're false to you.' "

THE CANONIZATION

In style this love poem is poles apart from the Petrarchan modes of expression, but the theme is a familiar one of the Elizabethan sonneteers.

For God's sake hold your tongue, and let me love!
   Or[12] chide my palsy or my gout;
   My five gray hairs or ruined fortune flout;
With wealth your state, your mind with arts improve;
     Take you a course, get you a place,[13]   5
     Observe his Honor or his Grace;
Or the king's real or his stampèd face[14]
   Contemplate; what you will, approve:
   So you will let me love.

Alas, alas, who's injured by my love?   10
   What merchant's ships have my sighs drowned?
   Who says my tears have overflowed his ground?
When did my colds a forward spring remove?
     When did the heats which my veins fill
     Add one man to the plaguy bill?[15]   15
Soldiers find wars, and lawyers find out still
   Litigious men, which quarrels move:[16]
   Though she and I do love.

[11] Through; i.e., merely to visit.
[12] Either.   [13] Office.   [14] On coins.
[15] The notice of (the number of deaths from) the plague.
[16] Set in motion.

Call us what you will, we are made such by love:
Call her one, me another, fly; 20
We're tapers too, and at our own cost die,
And we in us find th' eagle and the dove.[17]
The phoenix[18] riddle hath more wit
By us;[19] we two, being one, are it;
So to one neutral thing both sexes fit. 25
We die and rise the same, and prove
Mysterious by this love.

We can die by it, if not live by love;
And if unfit for tombs and hearse
Our legend be, it will be fit for verse. 30
And if no piece of chronicle we prove,
We'll build in sonnets pretty rooms—
As well a well-wrought urn becomes
The greatest ashes as half-acre tombs—
And by these hymns all shall approve 35
Us canonized[20] for love,

And thus invoke us: "You, whom reverend love
Made one another's hermitage,
You, to whom love was peace, that now is rage,[21]
Who did the whole world's soul contract,[22] and drove 40
Into the glasses of your eyes
(So made such mirrors, and such spies,
That they did all to you epitomize)
Countries, towns, courts, beg from above
A pattern[23] of your love." 45

LOVERS' INFINITENESS

Some of Donne's editors are puzzled by this title, but the
poem explains how it is that lovers may possess "infinite-
ness." The explanation is a quibbling one, and it is strange
how the poem's beauty shines through the mere cleverness
of the verbal texture.

If yet I have not all thy love,
Dear, I shall never have it all:
I cannot breathe one other sigh to move,
Nor can intreat one other tear to fall;
And all my treasure which should purchase thee, 5
Sighs, tears, and oaths, and letters, I have spent.
Yet no more can be due to me
Than at the bargain made was meant.

---

[17] Symbols of strength and purity.
[18] This fabulous Arabian bird was supposed periodically (after a
life of centuries) to burn itself and its nest of spices, and then to
rise immortal from the ashes.
[19] Makes more sense because of our experience (of an immortal
love). [20] Made saints. [21] Stormy emotion.
[22] I.e., distill to its essence.
[23] Likeness, copy. I.e., you two, now saints, ask God to grant us
love like yours.

If then thy gift of love were partiäl,
That[24] some to me, some should to others fall, 10
Dear, I shall never have thee all.

Or if then thou gavest me all,
"All" was but all which thou hadst then;
But if in thy heart, since, there be or shall
New love created be by other men, 15
Which have their stocks entire, and can in tears,
In sighs, in oaths, and letters outbid me,
This new love may beget new fears,
For this love was not vowed by thee—
And yet it was: thy gift being general, 20
The ground, thy heart, is mine; whatever shall
Grow there, dear, I should have it all.

Yet I would not have all yet.
He that hath all can have no more;
And since my love doth every day admit 25
New growth, thou shouldst have new rewards in store.
Thou canst not every day give me thy heart;
If thou canst give it, then thou never gavest it.
Love's riddles are that though thy heart depart
It stays at home, and thou with losing savest it: 30
But we will have a way more liberal
Than changing hearts: to join them! So we shall
Be one, and one another's all.

SWEETEST LOVE, I DO NOT GO

Like "Go and catch a falling star," this is a song, though
its tenderness plucks a very different and lovely string. This
poem and the next may have been written for Donne's
wife when, in the company of one of his patrons, he left
England for a sojourn on the Continent in 1611–12. Such
at any rate was the occasion of "A Valediction Forbidding
Mourning," according to Izaak Walton in his Life of
Donne.

Sweetest love, I do not go
For weariness of thee,
Nor in hope the world can show
A fitter love for me;
But since that I 5
Must die at last, 'tis best
To use myself in jest[25]
Thus by feigned deaths to die.

Yesternight the sun went hence,
And yet is here today; 10
He hath no desire nor sense,
Nor half so short a way.

---

[24] So that. [25] To accustom myself by pretending.

Then fear not me,
But believe that I shall make
Speedier journeys, since I take   15
    More wings and spurs than he.

O how feeble is man's power,
    That, if good fortune fall,
Cannot add another hour
    Nor a lost hour recall!   20
        But come bad chance,
And we join it to our strength,
And we teach it art and length,
    Itself o'er us to advance.

When thou sigh'st thou sigh'st not wind,   25
    But sigh'st my soul away;
When thou weep'st, unkindly kind,
    My life's blood doth decay.
        It cannot be
That thou lov'st me as thou say'st,   30
If in thine my life thou waste:
    That art the best of me.

Let not thy divining heart
    Forethink me any ill;
Destiny may take thy part,   35
    And may thy fears fulfil.
        But think that we
Are but turned aside to sleep:
They who one another keep
    Alive, ne'er parted be.   40

A VALEDICTION
FORBIDDING MOURNING

As virtuous men pass mildly away,
And whisper to their souls to go,
Whilst some of their sad friends do say,
"The breath goes now," and some say, "No,"

So let us melt and make no noise,   5
No tear-floods, nor sigh-tempests move;
'Twere profanation of our joys,
To tell the laity our love.

Moving of th' earth brings harm and fears;
Men reckon what it did and meant.   10
But trepidation[26] of the spheres,
Though greater far, is innocent.

Dull sublunary lovers' love
(Whose soul is sense) cannot admit
Absence, because it doth remove   15
Those things which elemented[27] it.

But we by a love so much refined
That ourselves know not what it is,
Interassurèd of the mind,
Care less eyes, lips, and hands to miss.   20

Our two souls, therefore, which are one,
Though I must go, endure not yet
A breach, but an expansïon,
Like gold to airy thinness beat.

If they be two, they are two so   25
As stiff twin compasses are two;
Thy soul, the fixed foot, makes no show
To move, but doth if th' other do.

And though it in the center sit,
Yet when the other far doth roam,   30
It leans and hearkens after it,
And grows erect as that comes home.

Such wilt thou be to me, who must,
Like th' other foot, obliquely run;
Thy firmness makes my circle just,
And makes me end where I begun.   35

THE DREAM

Here again there appears, in unfamiliar guise, an old familiar theme, the precariousness of lovers' happiness. She
came, and stayed; but she must leave, and all is fear again
—save for the hope that lies in dreams. Donne's treatment
of the theme is more realistic than the sonneteers', for his
lover not only dreams his lady has come to him but is
awakened by her actual presence.

Dear love, for nothing less than thee
Would I have broke this happy dream.
        It was a theme
For reason, much too strong for fantasy;
Therefore thou wak'dst me wisely. Yet   5
My dream thou brok'st not, but continued'st it;
Thou art so Truth that thoughts of thee suffice
To make dreams truths, and fables histories.
Enter these arms, for since thou thought'st it best
Not to dream all my dream, let's act the rest.   10

---

[26] Quaking; i.e., great account is made of the earth's moving in
an earthquake, but not of the motion of the spheres, though that
is vaster and constant.

[27] Composed.

As lightning or a taper's light,
Thine eyes, and not thy noise, waked me.
        Yet I thought thee—
For thou lovest truth—an angel, at first sight;
But when I saw thou saw'st my heart,   15
And knew'st my thoughts, beyond an angel's art,
When thou knew'st what I dreamt, when thou knew'st
        when
Excess of joy would wake me, and cam'st then,
I must confess it could not choose but be
Profane to think thee anything but thee.   20

Coming and staying showed thee thee,[28]
But rising makes me doubt[29] that now
        Thou art not thou.[30]
That love is weak where fear's as strong as he;
'T is not all spirit, pure and brave,   25
If mixture it of fear, shame, honor, have.
Perchance as torches, which must ready be,
Men light and put out,[31] so thou deal'st with me.
Thou cam'st to kindle, go'st to come: then I
Will dream that hope again, but else would die.   30

THE ECSTASY

This poem is an attempt to put into words an experience
which artists repeatedly try to express but can only suggest. Donne's attempt is less subtle and more direct than
many. The word "love," as we use it, covers a wide
variety of experience. Donne's experience had touched
heights which not all lovers attain. He had learned that
there is a spiritual plane of inexpressible and almost disembodied exaltation which spiritually qualified lovers who
are perfectly in tune with each other can reach through the
physical expression of their love. That is what he means
by the neo-Platonic term *ecstasy*. The poem has been much
discussed, and much misunderstood by some because they
treat it as if it were the chronological narrative of a unique
experience. A recent writer thinks that it is not a love
poem—that Donne's real interest is in man's place in the
universe. But these concerns are not mutually exclusive:
the first often leads to the second.

Where, like a pillow on a bed,
    A pregnant bank swelled up to rest
The violet's reclining head,
        Sat we two, one another's best.

Our hands were firmly cémentèd   5
    With a fast balm, which thence did spring;[32]
Our eyebeams twisted, and did thread
        Our eyes upon one double string.

So t' intergraft our hands, as yet,
    Was all the means to make us one;   10
And pictures in our eyes to get
        Was all our propagatïon.

As 'twixt two equal armies fate
    Suspends uncertain victory,
Our souls (which to advance their state   15
        Were gone out) hung 'twixt her and me.

And whil'st our souls negotiate there,
    We like sepulchral statues lay;
All day the same our postures were,
        And we said nothing all the day.   20

If any, so by love refined
    That he soul's language understood
And by good love were grown all mind,
        Within convenient distance stood,

He (though he knew not which soul spake,   25
    Because both meant, both spake the same)
Might thence a new concoction[33] take,
        And part[34] far purer than he came.

This Ecstasy doth unperplex,
    We said, and tell us what we love.   30
We see by this it was not sex;
        We see we saw not what did move:[35]

But as all several souls contain
    Mixture of things, they know not what,
Love these mixed souls doth mix again,   35
        And makes both one, each this and that.

A single violet transplant,
    The strength, the color, and the size
(All which before was poor, and scant)
        Redoubles still, and multiplies.   40

When love with one another so
    Interinanimates two souls,
That abler soul, which thence doth flow,
        Defects of loneliness controls.[36]

We then, who are this new soul, know   45
    Of what we are composed and made,
For th' atomies of[37] which we grow
        Are souls, whom no change can invade.

---

[28] Showed that it was really you.   [29] Fear.
[30] I.e., my lover.
[31] Since a torch that had once been lighted would catch more
    quickly.   [32] I.e., the sweat from our hot hands.

[33] Ripening, perfection.   [34] Depart.
[35] I.e., now we know we did not understand what the cause of our
love was—that its origin was spiritual.
[36] I.e., the soul thus created of us and our love supplies what is
lacking in each of our individual souls.   [37] Atoms from.

But O, alas, so long, so far
   Our bodies why do we forbear?   50
They're ours, though they're not we; we are
   The intelligences, they the sphere.[38]

We owe them thanks, because they thus
   Did us to us at first convey,
Yielded their forces, sense, to us,   55
   Nor are dross to us, but allay.[39]

On man heaven's influence works not so
   But that it first imprints the air;[40]
So soul into the soul may flow,
   Though it to body first repair.[41]   60

As our blood labors to beget
   Spirits as like souls as it can,[42]
Because such fingers need to knit
   That subtle knot which makes us man:

So must pure lovers' souls descend   65
   T' affections[43] and to faculties
Which sense may reach and apprehend;
   Else a great prince in prison lies.

T' our bodies turn we then, that so
   Weak men on love revealed may look;   70
Love's mysteries in souls do grow,
   But yet the body is his book.

And if some lover, such as we,
   Have heard this dialogue of one,
Let him still mark us: he shall see   75
   Small change when we're to bodies gone.

THE FUNERAL

Once more Donne is wearing "with a difference" a flower often chosen by the sonneteers, the lover's complaint of his mistress's cruelty. The poem is probably more graceful than serious. It seems likely that, along with several others, it was addressed to the mother of George Herbert, one of seventeenth-century religious lyrists whose poetry we shall consider below.

---

[38] I.e., our bodies are the sphere which affords our real selves a ground on which to meet.
[39] Alloy; i.e., without them our real selves, remaining disembodied, could not function.
[40] Philosophers held that the air was the medium which transmitted planetary influences to man.   [41] Go, turn.
[42] The "vital spirits" were supposed to be formed in the heart and carried by the arteries to all parts of the body, which depended on them for its liveliness.
[43] Emotions.—The "prince" of line 68 is the soul.

Whoever comes to shroud me, do not harm
   Nor question much
That subtle wreath of hair[44] about mine arm:
The mystery, the sign, you must not touch,
   For 'tis my outward soul,   5
Viceroy to that[45] which, then to heav'n being gone,
   Will leave this to control
And keep these limbs, her[46] provinces, from dissolutiön.

For if the sinewy thread[47] my brain lets fall
   Through every part   10
Can tie those parts, and make me one of all,[48]
These hairs which upward grew, and strength and art
   Have from a better brain,[49]
Can better do't—except[50] she meant that I
   By this should know my pain,   15
As prisoners then are manacled when they're condemned
   to die.

Whate'er she meant by it, bury it with me;
   For since I am
Love's martyr, it might breed idolatry
If into others' hands these relics came.   20
   As 'twas humility
To afford to it all that a soul can do,
   So, 'tis some bravery[51]
That since you would have none of me,[52] I bury some
   of you.

ABSENCE

This poem first appeared in print anonymously, and attributions in the manuscripts vary. Scholars are divided as to whether it is Donne's. Very likely it is.

Absence, hear thou my protestation
   Against thy strength,
     Distance, and length:
Do what thou canst for alteration,
   For hearts of truest mettle   5
   Absence doth join and time doth settle.

Who loves a mistress of such quality,
     His mind hath found
     Affection's ground
Beyond time, place, and all mortality.   10
   To hearts that cannot vary,
   Absence is present, time doth tarry.

---

[44] Bracelet of the lady's hair.
[45] My actual soul.   [46] My soul's.
[47] I.e., the spinal cord and the branches of the nervous system.
[48] I.e., if my nervous system can unify my entire body.
[49] The lady's.   [50] Unless (by giving it to me).
[51] Bravado, defiance.
[52] I.e., would not prevent my martyrdom by loving me.

My senses want their outward motion,
    Which now within
      Reason doth win,   15
Redoubled by her secret notion,
    Like rich men that take pleasure
    In hiding more than handling treasure.

By absence this good means I gain:
    That I can catch her   20
      Where none can watch her,
In some close corner of my brain.
    There I embrace and kiss her,
    And so I both enjoy and miss her.

from HOLY SONNETS

5

I am a little world made cunningly
Of elements, and an angelic sprite;[53]
But black sin hath betrayed to endless night
My world's both parts, and, oh, both parts must die.
You which beyond that heaven which was most high   5
Have found new spheres, and of new lands can write,
Pour new seas in mine eyes, that so I might
Drown my world with my weeping earnestly,
Or wash it if it must be drowned no more:[54]
But oh, it must be burnt! alas, the fire   10
Of lust and envy have burnt it heretofore,
And made it fouler; let their flames retire,
And burn me, O Lord, with a fiery zeal
Of thee and thy house,[55] which doth in eating heal.

7

At the round earth's imagined corners, blow
Your trumpets, angels,[56] and arise, arise
From death, you numberless infinities
Of souls, and to your scattered bodies go;
All whom the flood did, and fire shall o'erthrow;   5
All whom war, dearth, age, agues, tyrannies,
Despair, law, chance, hath slain, and you whose eyes
Shall behold God, and never taste death's woe.
But let them sleep, Lord, and me mourn a space,
For if above all these my sins abound,   10

'Tis late to ask abundance of thy grace
When we are there; here on this lowly ground
Teach me how to repent; for that's as good
As if thou hadst sealed my pardon with thy blood.

10

Death, be not proud, though some have callèd thee
Mighty and dreadful, for thou art not so;
For those whom thou think'st thou dost overthrow
Die not, poor Death, nor yet canst thou kill me.
From rest and sleep, which but thy pictures be,   5
Much pleasure; then from thee much more must flow;
And soonest our best men with thee do go,
Rest of their bones and souls' delivery.
Thou'rt slave to fate, chance, kings, and desperate men,
And dost with poison, war, and sickness dwell;   10
And poppy or charms can make us sleep as well
And better than thy stroke. Why swell'st[57] thou then?
One short sleep past, we wake eternally,
And Death shall be no more: Death, thou shalt die.

A HYMN TO GOD THE FATHER

Wilt thou forgive that sin where I begun,
    Which was my sin, though it were done before?
Wilt thou forgive that sin through which I run,
    And do run still, though still I do deplore?
When thou hast done, thou hast not done;   5
      For I have more.

Wilt thou forgive that sin which I have won
    Others to sin, and made my sins their door?
Wilt thou forgive that sin which I did shun
    A year or two, but wallowed in a score?   10
When thou hast done, thou hast not done;
      For I have more.

I have a sin of fear, that when I've spun
    My last thread, I shall perish on the shore;
But swear by thyself that at my death thy Son   15
    Shall shine as he shines now and heretofore;
And having done that, thou hast done;
      I fear no more.

---

[53] Spirit.
[54] See Genesis 9:11: ". . . neither shall there any more be a flood to destroy the earth."
[55] See Psalms 69:9: "For the zeal of thine house hath eaten me up. . . ."
[56] See Revelation 7:1: "And after these things I saw four angels standing on the four corners of the earth. . . ."

[57] With pride.

The Character Writers

NOVELTY has an obvious appeal to everybody, and yet one of the great pleasures of reading is its exact opposite, the recognition of familiar things. No one with any powers of observation can read the seventeenth-century sketches called characters without being reminded of people he knows. True, these pieces are full of references to vanished manners and customs, and that enlarges their interest for us; but human nature has not changed appreciably, and since the character writers were often shrewd observers many of their descriptions remain remarkably applicable.

The genre is an old one. The character or analytical portrait of a type, independent of story or theme, was first written by Theophrastus (d. 284 B.C.). This Greek philosopher was a pupil of Aristotle and the greatest botanist of ancient times. His characters had long been forgotten when in 1592 Isaac Casaubon, a French critic, made them available in a Latin version.

Bishop Hall was the first English practitioner of the genre. Throughout the seventeenth century it was very popular, for one reason because it afforded ample scope for the display of wit; but the great increase in both the quantity and the quality of prose fiction killed it off in the eighteenth century as a separate genre. It was, in fact, absorbed by the novel.

Richard Aldington's *A Book of Characters* (1924) is an anthology, beginning with Theophrastus and including, besides the English writers, Jean de la Bruyère (1645-96), the leading French exponent.

Joseph Hall

1574–1656

HALL rose to be bishop, first of Exeter and then of Norwich; but his Puritan leanings got him into trouble, and shortly before the outbreak of the Civil Wars he was a prisoner in the Tower of London. The last decade of his life was spent in retirement on a small farm. Before he entered the Anglican priesthood he had won fame with his verse satires (1598), which Archbishop Whitgift ordered burnt. His *Characters of Virtues and Vices,* from which the sketch below is taken, appeared in 1608. Hall's tone is heavier and more didactic than his successors'.

THE HONEST MAN

He looks not to what he might do, but what he should. Justice is his first guide; the second law of his actions is expedience. He would rather complain than offend, and hates sin more for the indignity of it than the danger. His simple uprightness works in him that confidence which ofttimes wrongs him and gives advantage to the subtle, when he rather pities their faithlessness than repents of his credulity. He hath but one heart and that lies open to sight; and, were it not for discretion, he never thinks aught whereof he would avoid a witness. His word is his parchment and his yea his oath, which he will not violate for fear or for loss. The mishaps of following events may cause him to blame his providence, can never cause him to eat his promise; neither saith he, "This I saw not," but, "This I said." When he is made his friend's executor, he defrays debts, pays legacies, and scorneth to gain by orphans or to ransack graves: and therefore will be true to a dead friend, because he sees him not. All his dealings are square, and above the board; he bewrays[1] the fault of what he sells, and restores the overseen gain of a false reckoning. He esteems a bribe venomous, though it come gilded over with the color of gratuity. His cheeks are never stained with the blushes of recantation, neither doth his tongue falter to make good a lie with the secret glosses of double or reserved senses; and when his name is traduced, his innocency bears him out with courage: then, lo, he goes on in the plain way of truth, and will either triumph in his integrity or suffer with it. His conscience overrules his providence, so as in all things, good or ill, he respects[2] the nature of the actions, not the sequel. If he see what he must do, let God see what shall follow. He never loadeth himself with burdens above his strength, beyond his will; and, once bound, what he can he will do, neither doth he will but what he can do. His ear is the sanctuary of his absent friend's name, of his present friend's secret; neither of them can miscarry in his trust. He remembers the wrongs of his youth, and repays them with that usury which he himself would not take. He would rather want than borrow, and beg than not pay. His fair conditions are without dissembling, and he loves actions above words. Finally, he hates falsehood worse than death; he is a faithful client of truth, no man's enemy, and it is a question whether more another man's friend or his own. And if there were no heaven, yet he would be virtuous.

---

[1] Reveals.   [2] Considers.

Sir Thomas Overbury

1581–1613

THE career of this courtier poet and character writer was ended by one of the most famous crimes in England's annals. His patron was James I's favorite, Robert Carr, Earl of Rochester and Somerset. When Overbury opposed the Earl's marriage to the divorced Countess of Essex, she had him poisoned. That was in 1613. In the following year there was added to the second edition of Overbury's poem *A Wife* a series of twenty-two characters, not all from his pen. In subsequent editions the number was gradually increased to eighty-three. These later pieces were doubtless the work of professional writers; many of them, including "An Excellent Actor" (1615), are probably by John Webster, the great dramatist. "An Affectate Traveler" is very likely Overbury's. There is a good edition, *The Overburian Characters* (1936), by W. J. Paylor.

AN AFFECTATE TRAVELER

Is a speaking fashion; he hath taken pains to be ridiculous, and hath seen more than he hath perceived. His attire speaks French or Italian, and his gait cries, "Behold me." He censures[3] all things by countenances and shrugs, and speaks his own language with shame and lisping; he will choke rather than confess beer good drink, and his picktooth is a main part of his behavior. He chooseth rather to be counted a spy than not a politician, and maintains his reputation by naming great men familiarly. He chooseth rather to tell lies than not wonders, and talks with men singly; his discourse sounds big, but means nothing; and his boy is bound to admire him howsoever. He comes still from great personages, but goes with mean. He takes occasion to show jewels given him in regard of his virtue, that were bought in St. Martin's;[4] and not long after, having with a mountebank's method pronounced them worth thousands, impawneth them for a few shillings. Upon festival days he goes to court, and salutes without resaluting; at night in an ordinary[5] he confesseth the business in hand, and seems as conversant with all intents and plots as if he begot them. His extraordinary accompt[6] of men is first to tell them the ends of all matters of consequence and then to borrow money of them; he offers courtesies to show them, rather than himself, humble. He disdains all things above his reach, and preferreth all

---

[3] Judges.
[4] A district in London where cheap jewelry was made.
[5] Restaurant, tavern.   [6] Account, consideration.

countries before his own. He imputeth his wants and poverty to the ignorance of the time, not his own unworthiness; and concludes his discourse with a half period, or a word, and leaves the rest to imagination. In a word, his religion is fashion, and both body and soul are governed by fame; he loves most voices above truth.

AN EXCELLENT ACTOR

Whatsoever is commendable in the grave orator is most exquisitely perfect in him, for by a full and significant action of body he charms our attention: sit in a full theater, and you will think you see so many lines drawn from the circumference of so many ears, whiles the actor is the center. He doth not strive to make nature monstrous; she is often seen in the same scene with him, but neither on stilts nor crutches; and for his voice, 'tis not lower than the prompter, nor louder than the foil or target.[7] By his action he fortifies moral precepts with examples, for what we see him personate we think truly done before us: a man of a deep thought might apprehend the ghost of our ancient heroes walked again, and take him at several times for many of them. He is much affected[8] to painting, and 'tis a question whether that make him an excellent player, or his playing an exquisite painter.[9] He adds grace to the poet's labors; for what in the poet is but ditty,[10] in him is both ditty and music. He entertains us in the best leisure of our life, that is, between meals, the most unfit time either for study or bodily exercise. The flight of hawks and chase of wild beasts, either of them are delights noble; but some think this sport of men the worthier, despite all calumny. All men have been of his occupation; and indeed, what he doth feignedly, that do others essentially: this day one plays a monarch, the next a private person; here one acts a tyrant, on the morrow an exile; a parasite this man tonight, tomorrow a precisian;[11] and so of divers others. I observe, of all men living, a worthy actor in one kind[12] is the strongest motive of affection that can be; for, when he dies, we cannot be persuaded any man can do his parts like him. Therefore the imitating characterist[13] was extreme idle in

---

[7] I.e., the racket of sword on shield in a stage fight.
[8] Inclined.
[9] Almost certainly a reference to Richard Burbage (d. 1619), the principal actor of Shakespeare's company. He was also a painter.
[10] I.e., the words.   [11] Puritan.
[12] I.e., type of roles.
[13] John Stephens, who, in one of his *Satirical Essays, Characters, and Others* (1615), had attacked actors. The publisher of the Overburian characters considered him an interloper, hence "imitating."

calling them rogues. His Muse, it seems, with all his loud invocation, could not be waked to light him a snuff[14] to read the statute;[15] for I would let his malicious ignorance understand that rogues are not to be employed as main ornaments to his Majesty's Revels.[16] But the itch of bestriding the press, or getting up on this wooden Pacolet,[17] hath defiled more innocent paper than ever did laxative physic; yet is their invention such tired stuff that, like the Kentish posthorse, they cannot go beyond their ordinary stage,[18] should you flay them. But to conclude, I value a worthy actor, by[19] the corruption of some few of the quality,[20] as I would do gold in the ore: I should not mind the dross, but the purity of the metal.

John Earle

1601?–1665

EARLE spent twenty years at Oxford as student, fellow, and proctor; his *Microcosmography* reflects, among other things, his shrewd yet kindly observation of academic types. Though he took the royalist side, was chaplain to the future Charles II, and went into exile, he was esteemed by the Puritans; and when toward the end of his life he became a bishop, he did what he could to save them from persecution. "He was," declared the chancellor and historian Lord Clarendon (d.1674), "amongst the few excellent men who never had nor ever could have an enemy but such a one who was an enemy to all learning and virtue." Earle is the best of the character writers. His book appeared anonymously in 1628 with fifty-two sketches, including the three below. Like its Overburian predecessor it was very popular, and successive editions increased the number of characters to seventy-eight. All are reprinted, with an account of Earle, in A. S. West's edition (1897).

A YOUNG MAN

He is now out of Nature's protection, though not yet able to guide himself, but left loose to the world and fortune, from which the weakness of his childhood preserved him; and now his strength exposes him. He is indeed just of age to be miserable, yet in his own conceit[21] first begins to be happy; and he is happier in this imagination, and his misery not felt is less. He sees yet but the outside of the world and men, and conceives them according to their appearing glister, and out of this ignorance believes them. He pursues all vanities for happiness, and enjoys them best in this fancy. His reason serves, not to curb, but understand his appetite, and prosecute the motions[22] thereof with a more eager earnestness. Himself is his own temptation, and needs not Satan; and the world will come hereafter. He leaves repentance for gray hairs, and performs it in being covetous. He is mingled with the vices of the age as the fashion and custom with which he longs to be acquainted, and sins to better his understanding. He conceives his youth as the season of his lust, and the hour wherein he ought to be bad; and because he would not lose his time, spends it. He distastes religion as a sad thing, and is six years elder for a thought of heaven. He scorns and fears (and yet hopes for) old age, but dare not imagine it with wrinkles. He loves and hates with the same inflammation; and when the heat is over, is cool alike to friends and enemies. His friendship is seldom so steadfast but that lust, drink, or anger may overturn it. He offers you his blood today in kindness, and is ready to take yours tomorrow. He does seldom anything which he wishes not to do again,[23] and is only wise after a misfortune. He suffers much for his knowledge, and a great deal of folly it is makes him a wise man. He is free from many vices, by being not grown to the performance, and is only more virtuous out of weakness. Every action is his danger, and every man his ambush. He is a ship without pilot or tackling, and only good fortune may steer him. If he 'scape this age, he has 'scaped a tempest, and may live to be a man.

A VULGAR-SPIRITED MAN

Is one of the herd of the world. One that follows merely the common cry, and makes it louder by one. A man that loves none but who are publicly affected,[24] and he will not be wiser than the rest of the town. That never owns a friend after an ill name or some general imputation, though he knows it most unworthy. That opposes to reason "Thus men say" and "Thus most do" and "Thus the world goes," and thinks this enough to poise[25] the other. That worships men in place, and those only, and thinks all a great man speaks oracles. Much taken

---

14 Charred candlewick, candle end.
15 Regulating strolling actors.
16 Entertainments at court were under the jurisdiction of the Master of the Revels.
17 A dwarf in the romance of *Valentine and Orson*. He had a magic horse of wood.   18 Distance.   19 With respect to.
20 Profession of acting.   21 Opinion.

22 Promptings.
23 In the hope that if he had a second chance he would do better.
24 In public favor.   25 Counterbalance.

with my Lord's jest, and repeats you it all to a syllable. One that justifies nothing out of fashion, nor any opinion out of the applauded way. That thinks certainly all Spaniards and Jesuits very villains, and is still cursing the Pope and Spinola.[26] One that thinks the gravest cassock the best scholar, and the best clothes the finest man. That is taken only with broad and obscene wit, and hisses anything too deep for him. That cries, "Chaucer for his money," above all our English poets, because the voice[27] has gone so, and he had read none. That is much ravished with such a nobleman's courtesy, and would venture his life for him, because he put off his hat. One that is foremost still to kiss the King's hand, and cries "God bless his Majesty" loudest. That rails on all men condemned and out of favor, and the first that says, "Away with the traitors"; yet struck with much ruth at executions, and for pity to see a man die could kill the hangman. That comes to London to see it, and the pretty things in it, and the chief cause of his journey the bears.[28] That measures the happiness of the kingdom by the cheapness of corn,[29] and conceives no harm of state but ill trading. Within this compass, too, come those that are too much wedged into the world, and have no lifting thoughts above those things; that call to thrive[30] to do well, and preferment[31] only the grace of God. That aim all studies at this mark, and show you poor scholars as an example to take heed by. That think the prison and want a judgment for some sin, and never like well hereafter of a jailbird. That know no other content but wealth, bravery,[32] and the town-pleasures; that think all else but idle speculation, and the philosophers madmen. In short, men that are carried away with all outwardnesses, shows, appearances, the stream, the people; for there is no man of worth but has a piece of singularity, and scorns something.

A DOWNRIGHT SCHOLAR

Is one that has much learning in the ore, unwrought and untried, which time and experience fashions and refines. He is good metal in the inside, though rough and unscoured without, and therefore hated of the courtier, that is quite contrary. The time has got a vein of making him ridiculous, and men laugh at him by tradition; and no unlucky absurdity but is put upon his profession and done "like a scholar." But his fault is only this: that his mind is somewhat too much taken up with his mind, and his thoughts not loaden with any carriage besides. He has not put on the quaint garb of the age, which is now become a man's total. He has not humbled his meditations to the industry of compliment, nor afflicted his brain in an elaborate leg.[33] His body is not set upon nice pins, to be turning and flexible for every motion, but his scrape[34] is homely and his nod worse. He cannot kiss his hand and cry, "Madam," nor talk idly enough to bear her company. His smacking of a gentlewoman is somewhat too savory, and he mistakes her nose for her lip. A very woodcock[35] would puzzle him in carving, and he wants the logic of a capon.[36] He has not the glib faculty of sliding over a tale, but his words come squeamishly out of his mouth, and the laughter commonly before the jest. He names this word *college* too often, and his discourse beats too much on the university. The perplexity of mannerliness[37] will not let him feed, and he is sharp set at an argument when he should cut his meat. He is discarded for a gamester at all games but one-and-thirty,[38] and at tables[39] he reaches not beyond doublets. His fingers are not long and drawn out to handle a fiddle, but his fist is cluncht[40] with the habit of disputing. He ascends a horse somewhat sinisterly,[41] though not on the left side; and they both go jogging in grief together. He is exceedingly censured by the inns-a-court men[42] for that heinous vice, being out of fashion. He cannot speak to a dog in his own dialect, and understands Greek better than the language of a falconer. He has been used to a dark room and dark clothes, and his eyes dazzle at a satin doublet. The hermitage of his study has made him somewhat uncouth in the world, and men make him worse by staring on him. Thus is he silly and ridiculous, and it continues with him for some quarter of a year out of the university. But practice him a little in men, and brush him o'er with good company, and he shall outbalance those glisterers as much as a solid substance does a feather, or gold, gold-lace.

[26] The Marquis of Spinola (d. 1630), a famous Spanish commander-in-chief in the Low Countries.   [27] I.e., general opinion.
[28] Used in bear baiting.   [29] Grain, especially wheat.
[30] Prosperity.   [31] Getting ahead.   [32] Finery.

[33] Bow.
[34] Bow (from the scrape when the foot is drawn back).
[35] A proverbially simple (minded) bird.
[36] I.e., lacks knowledge of (how to carve) a chicken.
[37] The complications of etiquette—they embarrass him in public.
[38] A card game.   [39] Backgammon.   [40] Clenched.
[41] Awkwardly. A horse is mounted from the left.
[42] Inns-of-court men, law students. Many were rich young squires, without any serious purpose.

Thomas Fuller

1608–1661

THOUGH included here among the character writers, this famous divine and antiquary cut a much wider swath than the others. He was a versatile and popular writer in his own day, was vastly admired by Coleridge and Lamb, and still makes fascinating reading. Educated at Cambridge, he entered the Church but, having served the King as chaplain in the royal army, lost his appointments during the Commonwealth and had to turn for livelihood to his pen. He died soon after the Restoration reinstated him. *The History of the Holy War,* an account of the Crusades, was published in 1639; like most of his writings it went through numerous editions. In 1642 appeared two books in one, *The Holy and the Profane State;* this miscellany of characters, essays, and biographical sketches is not at all what the title leads one to expect. Among Fuller's other works are *The Church History of Britain* (1655) and *The History of the Worthies of England* (1662). The latter is a forerunner of the dictionaries of national biography. These are only a few of Fuller's writings, which include many sermons. For his life see *The Great Tom Fuller* (1935) by D. B. Lyman, and for a special study W. E. Houghton's *The Formation of Thomas Fuller's Holy and Profane States* (1938). There is a facsimile edition of this work, with notes, by M. G. Walten (2 vols., 1938). A selection from Fuller's writings was edited by E. K. Broadus (1928). The following essay is from *The Holy State,* Book II, Chapter 16.

THE GOOD SCHOOLMASTER

There is scarce any profession in the commonwealth more necessary, which is so slightly performed. The reasons whereof I conceive to be these. First, young scholars make this calling their refuge: yea, perchance before they have taken any degree in the university, commence schoolmasters in the country, as if nothing else were required to set up this profession, but only a rod and a ferula.[43] Secondly, others who are able use it only as a passage to better preferment, to patch the rents in their present fortune till they can provide a new one, and betake themselves to some more gainful calling. Thirdly, they are disheartened from doing their best with the miserable reward which in some places they receive, being masters to the children and slaves to their parents. Fourthly, being grown rich, they grow negligent, and scorn to touch the school but by the proxy of an usher.[44] But see how well our schoolmaster behaves himself.

His genius inclines him with delight to his profession.[45] Some men had as lief be schoolboys as schoolmasters, to be tied to the school as Cooper's Dictionary and Scapula's Lexicon[46] are chained to the desk therein; and though great scholars, and skillful in other arts, are bunglers in this. But God of his goodness hath fitted several men for several callings, that the necessity of Church and State in all conditions may be provided for. So that he who beholds the fabric thereof may say, "God hewed out this stone and appointed it to lie in this very place, for it would fit none other so well, and here it doth most excellent." And thus God moldeth some for a schoolmaster's life, undertaking it with desire and delight, and discharging it with dexterity and happy success.

He studieth his scholars' natures as carefully as they their books, and ranks their dispositions into several forms. And though it may seem difficult for him in a great school to descend to all particulars, yet experienced schoolmasters may quickly make a grammar of boys' natures, and reduce them all (saving some few exceptions) to these general rules.

1. Those that are ingenious[47] and industrious. The conjunction of two such planets in a youth presages much good unto him. To such a lad a frown may be a whipping, and a whipping a death; yea, where their master whips them once, shame whips them all the week after. Such natures he useth with all gentleness.

2. Those that are ingenious and idle. These think, with the hare in the fable, that running with snails (so they count the rest of their schoolfellows) they shall come soon enough to the post, though sleeping a good while before their starting. Oh, a good rod would finely take them napping.

3. Those that are dull and diligent. Wines, the stronger they be, the more lees they have when they are new. Many boys are muddy-headed till they be clarified with age, and such afterwards prove the best. Bristol diamonds[48] are both bright and squared and pointed by nature, and yet are soft and worthless; whereas orient[49] ones in India are rough and rugged naturally. Hard, rugged, and dull natures of youth acquit themselves afterwards the jewels of the country, and therefore their dullness at first is to be

---

[43] Switch.

[44] Assistant teacher.
[45] This and similar statements, eight in all, are italicized in the original and numbered marginally as maxims.
[46] Latin-English (1548) and Greek-Latin (1579) dictionaries.
[47] Clever.   [48] Transparent rock crystals found near that city.
[49] Lustrous.

borne with, if they be diligent. That schoolmaster deserves to be beaten himself who beats nature in a boy for a fault. And I question whether all the whipping in the world can make their parts, which are naturally sluggish, rise one minute before the hour nature hath appointed.

4. Those that are invincibly dull, and negligent also. Correction may reform the latter, not amend the former. All the whetting in the world can never set a razor's edge on that which hath no steel in it. Such boys he consigneth over to other professions. Shipwrights and boatmakers will choose those crooked pieces of timber which other carpenters refuse. Those may make excellent merchants and mechanics which will not serve for scholars.

He is able, diligent, and methodical in his teaching, not leading them rather in a circle than forwards. He minces his precepts for children to swallow, hanging clogs on the nimbleness of his own soul, that his scholars may go along with him.

He is, and will be known to be, an absolute monarch in his school. If cockering[50] mothers proffer him money to purchase their sons an exemption from his rod (to live as it were in a peculiar, out of their master's jurisdiction), with disdain he refuseth it, and scorns the late custom in some places of commuting whipping into money, and ransoming boys from the rod at a set price. If he hath a stubborn youth, correction-proof, he debaseth not his authority by contesting with him, but fairly, if he can, puts him away before his obstinacy hath infected others.

He is moderate in inflicting deserved correction. Many a schoolmaster better answereth the name παιδοτρίβης[51] than παιδαγωγός,[52] rather tearing his scholars' flesh with whipping than giving them good education. No wonder if his scholars hate the Muses, being presented unto them in the shapes of fiends and furies. Junius[53] complains *de insolenti carnificina*[54] of his schoolmaster, by whom *conscindebatur flagris septies aut octies in dies singulos.*[55] Yea, hear the lamentable verses of poor Tusser[56] in his own life:

> From Paul's I went, to Eton sent,
> To learn straightways the Latin phrase,
> Where fifty-three stripes given to me
> At once I had.

> For fault but small, or none at all,
> It came to pass thus beat I was;
> See, Udall,[57] see the mercy of thee
> To me, poor lad.

Such an Orbilius[58] mars more scholars than he makes: their tyranny hath caused many tongues to stammer which spake plain by nature, and whose stuttering at first was nothing else but fears quavering on their speech at their master's presence; and whose mauling them about their heads hath dulled those who, in quickness, exceeded their master.

He makes his school free to him who sues to him in forma pauperis.[59] And surely learning is the greatest alms that can be given. But he is a beast who, because the poor scholar cannot pay him his wages, pays the scholar in his whipping. Rather are diligent lads to be encouraged with all excitements to learning. This minds me of what I have heard concerning Mr. Bust, that worthy late schoolmaster of Eton, who would never suffer any wandering begging scholar (such as justly the statute hath ranked in the forefront of rogues) to come into his school, but would thrust him out with earnestness (however privately charitable unto him) lest his schoolboys should be disheartened from their books by seeing some scholars, after their studying in the university, preferred[60] to beggary.

He spoils not a good school to make thereof a bad college, therein to teach his scholars logic. For besides that logic may have an action of trespass against grammar for encroaching on her liberties, syllogisms are solecisms taught[61] in the school, and oftentimes they are forced afterwards in the university to unlearn the fumbling skill they had before.

Out of his school he is no whit pedantical in carriage or discourse, contenting himself to be rich in Latin, though he doth not jingle with it in every company wherein he comes.

To conclude, let this amongst other motives make schoolmasters careful in their place, that the eminencies of their scholars have commended the memories of their schoolmasters to posterity, who otherwise in obscurity had altogether been forgotten. Who had ever heard of R. Bond in Lancashire but for the breeding of learned Ascham,[62] his scholar? or

---

[50] Pampering.   [51] Paidotribes, wrestling teacher.
[52] Paidagogos, pedagogue.
[53] The Huguenot theologian Francis Junius (d. 1602).
[54] Of the excessive torture.
[55] By whom he was torn with scourges seven or eight times every day.
[56] Thomas Tusser (d. 1580), a writer of verse on agricultural subjects.

[57] Nicholas Udall (d. 1556), headmaster of Eton and author of the comedy *Ralph Roister Doister.*
[58] Horace (*Epistles,* II, i, 70, 71) says this Roman teacher was "full of floggings."   [59] As a poor person.   [60] Promoted.
[61] I.e., the forms of logic are blunders when taught.
[62] Roger Ascham (d. 1568), scholar, prose writer, and tutor to Queen Elizabeth.

of Hartgrave in Brundly school, in the same county, but because he was the first did teach worthy Doctor Whitaker?[63] Nor do I honor the memory of Mulcaster[64] for anything so much as for his scholar, that gulf of learning, Bishop Andrewes.[65] This made the Athenians, the day before the great feast of Theseus their founder, to sacrifice a ram to the memory of Conidas, his schoolmaster, that first instructed him.

Ben Jonson

1572–1637

ONE of the major personalities of literary history, Jonson was even more versatile than Shakespeare, who was his friend. As a playwright he stands, of all the age's authors, nearest to Shakespeare in excellence; and with the possible exception of Shakespeare, he was the greatest comic dramatist to appear between the death of Aristophanes (c. 480 B.C.) and Molière's first Parisian season (1658). Unlike Shakespeare, Jonson did not hesitate to introduce his own rugged personality into his plays. They are full of his opinions on a great variety of subjects, and more than once he actually brings himself on stage under some such transparent guise as the character Horace in *Poetaster*. He resembles Bernard Shaw in the cockiness and earnestness with which he lectures his audience—not in prefaces but in prologues and inductions. His contempt for his public was immense. "Come, leave the loathèd stage," he begins an "Ode to Himself," in 1631, after one of his plays had failed:

> Come, leave the loathèd stage,
>   And the more loathsome age,
> Where pride and impudence, in faction knit,
>   Usurp the chair of wit,
> Indicting and arraigning every day
>   Something they call a play.
> Let their fastidious, vain
> Commission of the brain
> Run on, and rage, sweat, censure, and condemn:
> They were not made for thee, less thou for them.

> Say that thou pour'st 'em wheat,
>   And they would acorns eat:
> 'Twere simple fury[1] still thyself to waste
>   On such as have no taste:
> To offer them a surfeit of pure bread
>   Whose appetites are dead.

> No, give them grains their fill,
>   Husks, draff to drink and swill.
> If they love lees, and leave the lusty wine,
>   Envy them not; their palate's with the swine. . . .

> Leave things so prostitute,
>   And take th' Alcaic[2] lute,
> Or thine own Horace' or Anacreon's lyre;
>   Warm thee by Pindar's fire.
> And though thy nerves[3] be shrunk and blood be cold,
>   Ere years have made thee old,
> Strike that[4] disdainful heat
> Throughout, to their defeat,
> As curious fools, and envious of thy strain,
> May blushing swear no palsy's in thy brain. . . .

Widely read in classical and modern literature, Jonson was the most scholarly of the playwrights. He is greatest as a dramatist; but that his powerful and critical mind might have found expression, as Bacon's did, in the formal essay is evident from his jottings in his commonplace-book, even though he never organized them for publication. They were collected after his death under the title *Timber, or Discoveries*.

Of his poems a handful seem likely to be immortal. In his own way, a different way from Donne's, he helps bring on the seventeenth century. His elegant, self-conscious, deliberate lyrics, more regular and more highly finished than those of the Elizabethan songsters, were models for Herrick and the other Cavalier poets. Jonson was a devoted admirer of the Latin lyrists, especially Horace. His own verse, though he is close to the Renaissance and not afraid of emotion and romantic ebullience, ordinarily shows the restraint of neoclassicism. This check, and a large fund of common sense, held back Jonson the

---

[63] William Whitaker (d. 1595), a Cambridge divine and professor. Fuller wrote a biographical sketch of him.

[64] Richard Mulcaster (d. 1611), the famous head of the Merchant Tailors School in London.

[1] Madness.

[65] Lancelot Andrewes (d. 1626), Bishop of Winchester, famous preacher, and a translator of the King James Version of the Bible.

[2] Like Anacreon (d. 478 B.C.), Alcaeus (d. 580) was one of the greatest of the Greek lyric poets. With Horace (d. 8 B.C.), the Roman lyrist, satirist, and critic, Jonson felt a special affinity. The Greek Pindar (d. 448? B.C.) was famous for his odes.

[3] Sinews.   [4] Such.

lyric poet from the passion and also from the crotchety extravagance of Donne. Both poets powerfully influenced the next generation, but it was Jonson who actually had a circle. Its members gloried in the name of "the sons of Ben." Much of his verse is in the smooth and social vein of "Inviting a Friend to Supper"; it is not meant to rise to any great height of feeling. How much emotion lies behind his best lyrics is an unanswerable question. Whatever the answer, Jonson has in his quiet way an extraordinary power to arouse deep feeling in his readers. Not that his personality, nor always his lines, were on the quiet side. Ben was two-fisted and tough-minded. With the Latin satirists for exemplars, he delighted to scourge his enemies in robust and sometimes foul-mouthed invective.

He was a Londoner born and bred. His father had died a month before his son's birth; his mother's second husband was a poor bricklayer. Ben was educated at Westminster School but not at the universities, though both eventually gave him honorary degrees. At Westminster he came under the teaching of the great antiquarian William Camden,

> to whom I owe
> All that I am in arts, all that I know.

For a time he unwillingly followed his stepfather's trade. Till he turns up as a playwright, in the middle nineties, not much is known about him. He says he served against the Spaniards in the Low Countries and killed one of the enemy in single combat. By 1594, when he married, he was back in London.

For a while Jonson was an actor. In 1598 his epoch-making comedy, *Every Man in His Humor,* produced by Shakespeare's company, was a hit. In the same year he killed a well-known fellow player, Gabriel Spencer, in a duel. He escaped the death penalty by pleading benefit of clergy, getting off with a brand on the ball of his thumb and the confiscation of his goods, if he had any. While in prison (he was not there for the first time) he became a Roman Catholic; in that faith he remained for a dozen years. He was also involved at the turn of the century in another quarrel, the War of the Theaters. A boy's company (Shakespeare mentions it in *Hamlet,* II, ii, 354 ff.) was all the rage; there was skirmishing between its writers and those of the adult troupes. In a series of satirical plays, Jonson on one side and Marston and Dekker on the other indulged in some sharp personalities. According to Ben, he also "beat Marston and took his pistol from him."

Jonson's career as dramatist is described in the headnote to his dramatic prologues. As in his poems, he led the turn away from Elizabethan romance; his plays inaugurated the realism and the disillusion of seventeenth-century comedy. He is far more the playwright of the London scene than Shakespeare ever was. Like Lamb and Dickens,

he writes with authority on metropolitan life; he puts it directly into his comedies. Not like Shakespeare, he is skeptical about the essential soundness of human nature, and in *Volpone* he gives a terrible picture of its potential baseness. Jonson seems to have had a larger capacity for moral indignation than the more tolerant and easygoing Shakespeare. Readers should not be misled by the picturesque vulgarity of parts of his plays; Jonson is always a moralist. He took the highest view of the writer's calling; for him the poet is charged with a sacred responsibility to society.

Under James he was long in favor at court, though in 1604 he was once more in jail, over some sarcastic references (he denied responsibility for them) to the new King's profuse creation of knights for a cash consideration, to the horde of Scots that had come to London on the make, and even to the King's northern accent. These gibes appeared in *Eastward Ho,* an amusing but serious social comedy, on which Jonson collaborated with George Chapman and his old antagonist Marston. As the reign went on, Ben's prestige increased. He was recognized as poet laureate and had a small pension. In 1616, to the vast amusement of rival coteries, which refused to accept modern plays as literature, he brought out a folio edition of his *Works,* a title which to many seemed pretentious. For nine years after this event he abandoned the theater for the amateur theatricals known as masques. James and his court lavished money on this semidramatic form, which combined poetry, music, dancing, and *décor.* In charge of the last of these elements was the leading architect of the day, Inigo Jones; not yet had stage design become a separate specialty from architecture. Eventually the collaborators quarreled, with lasting bitterness. Jones proved the more powerful at court, and the discarded poet went wearily back to writing for the stage. His last plays failed to recapture his public; and, there being no royalty system, the continued success of his masterpieces brought him nothing.

Meanwhile two journeys had taken him abroad. In 1612–13 he went to France as tutor to Raleigh's son, a wild youth destined, as we have seen, to perish in Venezuela. In 1618–19 Jonson walked to Edinburgh and back; there he was honored by the Scots, feted at a public dinner, and entertained at Christmas by the leading Scottish poet, William Drummond of Hawthornden. Drummond's record of their conversations is the source of much of what we know about Jonson.

Charles I had no interest in the ageing poet; painters, not writers, received his patronage. Jonson's last years were passed in sickness and poverty. But the young poets loved him; in the taverns where he presided, they hung on his every word. The Mermaid had been a famous rendezvous. For another, the Apollo room of the Devil, Ben drew up a set of *Leges Conviviales* or Convivial Regulations. He died in 1637 and was buried in Westminster Abbey. An unfinished pastoral play of rare beauty was found among his papers, *The Sad Shepherd, or A Tale of Robin Hood.*

The standard edition, a noble one, is *Ben Jonson*, also known as the Oxford *Jonson*, edited by C. H. Herford, P. Simpson, and Evelyn Simpson (in progress, 8 vols. thus far, 1925–). The first two volumes contain the best account of "The Man and His Work." There are two volumes of Jonson's plays in Everyman's Library. The best separate edition of the poems is by B. H. Newdigate (1936).

Ben Jonson

TO DOCTOR EMPIRIC[1]

The first four of the following poems appear in the Folio under "Epigrams," but this gibe at doctors is a better example of the genre than the other three. An epigram is properly a short and often satirical poem treating concisely and wittily a single idea or happening.

When men a dangerous disease did 'scape
  Of old, they gave a cock to Aesculape;[2]
Let me give two, that doubly am got free:
  From my disease's danger, and from thee.

ON MY FIRST SON

The boy was born in 1596 and died of the plague in 1603.

Farewell, thou child of my right hand, and joy;
  My sin was too much hope of thee, loved boy.
Seven years thou wert lent to me, and I thee pay,
  Exacted by thy fate, on the just[3] day.
O, could I lose all father now! For why   5
  Will man lament the state he should envý?
To have so soon 'scaped world's and flesh's rage,
  And, if no other misery, yet age?
Rest in soft peace, and, asked, say here doth lie
  Ben Jonson his best piece of poetry.   10
For whose sake, henceforth, all his vows be such
  As what he loves may never like[4] too much.

INVITING A FRIEND TO SUPPER

These rimed couplets, in their ease and social charm, mark the beginning of the seventeenth-century turn to the neo-classical. Jonson's models were Horace and Martial.

Tonight, grave sir, both my poor house and I
  Do equally desire your company;
Not that we think us worthy such a guest,
  But that your worth will dignify our feast

With those that come, whose grace may make that seem
  Something, which else could hope for no esteem.   6
It is the fair acceptance, sir, creates
  The entertainment perfect, not the cates.[5]
Yet shall you have, to rectify your palate,
  An olive, capers, or some better salad[6]   10
Ush'ring the mutton; with a short-legged hen,
  If we can get her, full of eggs, and then
Lemons and wine for sauce; to these, a coney[7]
  Is not to be despaired of, for our money;
And though fowl now be scarce, yet there are clarks,[8]   15
  The sky not falling, think we may have larks.
I'll tell you of more, and lie, so you will come:
  Of partrich, pheasant, woodcock, of which some
May yet be there; and godwit, if we can,
  Knat,[9] rail, and ruff too. Howsoe'er, my man[10]   20
Shall read a piece of Vergil, Tacitus,
  Livy, or of some better book to us,
Of which we'll speak our minds amidst our meat;
  And I'll profess no verses to repeat.
To this, if aught appear which I not know of,   25
  That will the pastry, not my paper, show of.
Digestive cheese and fruit there sure will be;
  But that which most doth take my Muse, and me,
Is a pure cup of rich Canary wine,
  Which is the Mermaid's now, but shall be mine;   30
Of which had Horace or Anacreon[11] tasted,
  Their lives, as do their lines, till now had lasted.
Tobacco, nectar, or the Thespian[12] spring
  Are all but Luther's beer to this I sing.
Of this we will sup free, but moderately,   35
  And we will have no polly or parrot by,
Nor shall our cups make any guilty men;
  But at our parting we will be as when
We innocently met. No simple word
  That shall be uttered at our mirthful board   40
Shall make us sad next morning, or affright
  The liberty that we'll enjoy tonight.

---

[1] Quack.   [2] I.e., sacrificed it to Aesculapius, god of medicine.
[3] Exactly on the.
[4] Thrive. The allusion here (and in line 2) is to the religious belief that God will punish a parent who gives too large a part of his love to a promising child, by ending the latter's life.

[5] Delicacies.   [6] Sometimes pronounced (and spelled) *sallet.—Rectify* = put right.   [7] Rabbit.   [8] Learned men.
[9] Knot. Like the others, a variety of game bird.
[10] Probably Richard Brome, afterwards a dramatist in his own right.   [11] The Greek lyric poet (d. 478 B.C.). He wrote of wine.
[12] Thespia, a town in central Greece, was associated with the Muses.

EPITAPH ON S. P., A CHILD OF QUEEN ELIZABETH'S CHAPEL

This charming tribute to little Solomon Pavy of the all-boy company known as the Children of the Chapel Royal is an important piece of evidence for the excellence of the child actors.

Weep with me, all you that read
　　This little story;
And know, for whom a tear you shed
　　Death's self is sorry.
'Twas a child, that so did thrive　　　　5
　　In grace and feature,
As heaven and nature seemed to strive
　　Which owned the creature.
Years he numb'red scarce thirteen
　　When fates turned cruel,　　　　10
Yet three filled zodiacs[13] had he been
　　The stage's jewel;
And did act, what now we moan,
　　Old men so duly
As, sooth, the Parcae[14] thought him one,　　15
　　He played so truly.
So, by error, to his fate
　　They all consented;
But viewing him since (alas, too late)
　　They have repented,　　　　20
And have sought, to give new birth,
　　In baths to steep him;
But being so much too good for earth,
　　Heaven vows to keep him.

SONG: TO CELIA (1)

This ardent but elegant song (its source is partly the fifth ode of another Roman poet, Catullus) is sung in *Volpone* (III, vii) by the brilliant hero-villain when, having shammed illness, he leaps from his couch to exert all his artfulness in an attempt to seduce the virtuous Celia.

Come, my Celia, let us prove,
While we may, the sports of love.
Time will not be ours for ever,
He, at length, our goods will sever.
Spend not then his gifts in vain:　　　　5
Suns that set may rise again;
But if once we lose this light,
'Tis with us perpetual night.
Why should we defer our joys?
Fame and rumor are but toys.　　　　10

---

[13] Full years.　　　　[14] The three Fates.

Cannot we delude the eyes
Of a few poor household spies?
Or his easier ears beguile,
Thus removèd by our wile?
'Tis no sin love's fruits to steal,　　　　15
But the sweet thefts to reveal;
To be taken, to be seen,
These have crimes accounted been.

SONG: TO CELIA (2)

This beautiful song, known to everyone in the eighteenth-century setting by Dr. Thomas Arne, is numbered IX in a group of Jonson's poems entitled "The Forest." "Come, my Celia" is number V.

Drink to me only with thine eyes,
　　And I will pledge with mine;
Or leave a kiss but in the cup,
　　And I'll not look for wine.
The thirst that from the soul doth rise　　5
　　Doth ask a drink divine;
But might I of Jove's nectar sup,
　　I would not change for thine.

I sent thee late a rosy wreath,
　　Not so much honoring thee　　　　10
As giving it a hope that there
　　It could not withered be.
But thou thereon didst only breathe,
　　And sent'st it back to me;
Since when it grows, and smells, I swear,　　15
　　Not of itself, but thee.

CHARIS: HER TRIUMPH

"Her Triumph" is as exquisite a thing as lyric verse affords. It is the fourth of a set of ten poems entitled "A Celebration of Charis." The lady's identity is unknown. In the opening lines she is compared to Venus in her chariot; "Love" is Cupid.

See the chariot at hand here of Love,
　　Wherein my lady rideth!
Each that draws is a swan or a dove,
　　And well the car Love guideth.
As she goes, all hearts do duty　　　　5
　　　　Unto her beauty,
And, enamored, do wish, so they might
　　　　But enjoy such a sight,
That they still were to run by her side
Through swords, through seas, whether[15] she
　　would ride.　　　　10

---

[15] Whither.—*Through* should here be pronounced *thorough.*

Do but look on her eyes, they do light
　All that Love's world compriseth!
Do but look on her hair, it is bright
　As Love's star when it riseth!
Do but mark her forehead's smoother　　　15
　　　Than words that soothe her!
And from her arched brows, such a grace
　　　Sheds itself through the face
As alone there triumphs to the life
All the gain, all the good, of the elements' strife.　20

Have you seen but a bright lily grow
　Before rude hands have touched it?
Ha' you marked but the fall o' the snow
　Before the soil hath smutched it?
Ha' you felt the wool of beaver?　　　25
　　　Or swan's down ever?
Or have smelt o' the bud o' the brier?
　　　Or the nard[16] in the fire?
Or have tasted the bag of the bee?
O so white! O so soft! O so sweet is she!　30

IT IS NOT GROWING LIKE A TREE

In a famous but unsuccessful poem "To the Immortal
Memory and Friendship of That Noble Pair, Sir Lucius
Cary and Sir H. Morison" Jonson attempted a Pindaric
ode, the third "turn" of which follows. Originated by the
Greek Pindar (fifth century B.C.), this verse form (with its
several sections each consisting of a "turn" or strophe, an
exactly parallel "counterturn" or antistrophe, and a "stand"
or epode) has never caught on in English; but these lines
are memorable. Cary and Morison were members of
Jonson's circle; Morison died young.

　　　It is not growing like a tree　　　65
　　　　In bulk, doth make man better be;
　　Or standing long an oak, three hundred year,
　　To fall a log at last, dry, bald, and sear:
　　　　　A lily of a day,
　　　　　Is fairer far, in May,　　　70
　　　Although it fall and die that night;
　　　It was the plant and flow'r of light.
　　In small proportions, we just beauties see;
　　And in short measures, life may perfect be.

---

[16] Spikenard, an odoriferous plant.

TO THE MEMORY OF MY BELOVED, THE AUTHOR, MR. WILLIAM SHAKESPEARE, AND WHAT HE HATH LEFT US

An occasional poem is one that is composed to be read
aloud at a special meeting or to be printed in connection
with some special event. Such an "occasion" was the posthumous publication in 1623 of Shakespeare's collected
plays, the First Folio. To that matchless volume a number
of poets contributed commendatory verses. Jonson's are a
warm but discriminating appreciation, perhaps the finest
Shakespeare has ever received, and probably the most
popular occasional poem in English. Incidentally, they
would be sufficient, if other evidence were lacking, to
expose the absurdity of the notion that Shakespeare did
not write his plays.

To draw no envy, Shakespeare, on thy name,
　Am I thus ample to thy book and fame;
While I confess thy writings to be such
　As neither man nor Muse can praise too much.
'Tis true, and all men's suffrage.[17] But these ways
　Were not the paths I meant unto thy praise:
For seeliest[18] ignorance on these may light,
　Which, when it sounds at best, but echoes right;
Or blind affection,[19] which doth ne'er advance
　The truth, but gropes, and urgeth all by chance;　　　10
Or crafty malice might pretend this praise,
　And think to ruin where it seemed to raise.
These are as some infamous bawd or whore
　Should praise a matron. What could hurt her more?
But thou are proof against them, and indeed　　　15
　Above th' ill fortune of them, or the need.
I therefore will begin. Soul of the age!
　The applause! delight! the wonder of our stage!
My Shakespeare, rise; I will not lodge thee by
　Chaucer or Spenser, or bid Beaumont lie　　　20
A little further, to make thee a room:[20]
　Thou art a monument, without a tomb;
And art alive still while thy book doth live,
　And we have wits to read and praise to give.
That I not mix thee so, my brain excuses;　　　25
　I mean with great, but disproportioned Muses:[21]
For, if I thought my judgment were of years,
　I should commit thee surely with thy peers,
And tell how far thou didst our Lyly outshine,
　Or sporting Kyd, or Marlowe's mighty line.　　　30
And though thou hadst small Latin, and less Greek,
　From thence to honor thee I would not seek

---

[17] Vote, judgment.　　[18] Feeblest.　　[19] Feeling.
[20] An elegy by an obscure writer named William Basse had enjoined these three poets to move over (they lie in Westminster Abbey) and make room for Shakespeare.
[21] I.e., inferior poets.

For names, but call forth thund'ring Aeschylus,
    Euripides, and Sophocles[22] to us,
Pacuvius, Accius,[23] him of Cordova dead,[24]   35
    To life again, to hear thy buskin[25] tread
And shake a stage; or, when thy socks were on,[26]
    Leave thee alone for the comparison
Of all that insolent Greece or haughty Rome
    Sent forth, or since did from their ashes come.[27]   40
Triumph, my Britain; thou hast one to show
    To whom all scenes of Europe homage owe.
He was not of an age, but for all time!
    And all the Muses still were in their prime
When like Apollo he came forth to warm   45
    Our ears, or like a Mercury to charm!
Nature herself was proud of his designs,
    And joyed to wear the dressing of his lines!
Which were so richly spun, and woven so fit,
    As, since, she will vouchsafe no other wit.   50
The merry Greek, tart Aristophanes,[28]
    Neat Terence, witty Plautus,[29] now not please,
But antiquated and deserted lie,
    As they were not of Nature's family.
Yet must I not give Nature all: thy art,   55
    My gentle Shakespeare, must enjoy a part.
For though the poet's matter Nature be,
    His art doth give the fashion; and that he[30]
Who casts[31] to write a living line must sweat
    (Such as thine are) and strike the second heat   60
Upon the Muses' anvil, turn the same,
    And himself with it, that he thinks to frame,
Or for[32] the laurel he may gain a scorn;
    For a good poet's made, as well as born.
And such wert thou. Look how the father's face   65
    Lives in his issue; even so the race
Of Shakespeare's mind and manners brightly shines
    In his well-turnèd and true-filèd lines,
In each of which he seems to shake a lance,
    As[33] brandished at the eyes of ignorance.   70
Sweet swan of Avon, what a sight it were
    To see thee in our waters yet appear,
And make those flights upon the banks of Thames
    That so did take Eliza and our James!

---

[22] The three greatest of the Greek tragic poets.
[23] Early Roman tragic poets.
[24] Seneca, chief of the Roman tragic poets.
[25] The tall shoe the Greek actors wore for height in tragedy. I.e., to hear your tragedies.
[26] I.e., in comedy—for which the Greek actors wore a low shoe (Latin *soccus*).
[27] I.e., Renaissance imitators of classical tragedy.
[28] One of the greatest of all comic dramatists.
[29] The two leading Roman comic dramatists.
[30] Man.   [31] Intends.   [32] Instead of.
[33] As if.—"Shake a lance" obviously alludes to Shakespeare's surname.

But stay, I see thee in the hemisphere   75
    Advanced, and made a constellation there!
Shine forth, thou star of poets, and with rage
    Or influence chide or cheer the drooping stage,
Which, since thy flight from hence, hath mourned like
    night
And despairs day, but for thy volume's light.   80

SLOW, SLOW, FRESH FOUNT

Sung in *Cynthia's Revels* (I, ii) by the nymph Echo, lamenting her unrequited love for the beautiful but indifferent youth Narcissus, who pined away with self-love and was changed into a flower.

Slow, slow, fresh fount, keep time with my salt tears;
    Yet slower, yet; oh, faintly, gentle springs:
List to the heavy part the music bears;
    Woe weeps out her division[34] when she sings.
        Droop herbs and flow'rs;   5
        Fall grief in show'rs;
        Our beauties are not ours.
        O, I could still,
Like melting snow upon some craggy hill,
    Drop, drop, drop, drop,   10
Since nature's pride is, now, a withered daffodil.

STILL TO BE NEAT

Composed by Clerimont and sung by his page early in *Epicoene, or The Silent Woman*.

    Still[35] to be neat, still to be drest,
    As you were going to a feast;
    Still to be powd'red, still perfumed:
    Lady, it is to be presumed,
    Though art's hid causes are not found,   5
    All is not sweet, all is not sound.

    Give me a look, give me a face,
    That makes simplicity a grace;
    Robes loosely flowing, hair as free:
    Such sweet neglect more taketh me   10
    Than all th' adulteries of art.
    They strike mine eyes, but not my heart.

TO A FRIEND: AN EPIGRAM OF INIGO JONES

Sir Inigo doth fear it, as I hear,
    (And labors to seem worthy of that fear)

---

[34] Added melody, counterpoint.   [35] Always. *Neat* = fastidious.

That I should write upon him some sharp verse,
  Able to eat into his bones and pierce[36]
The marrow!—Wretch! I quit[37] thee of thy pain;   5
  Thou art too ambitious, and dost fear in vain!
The Lybian lion hunts no butterflies!
  He makes the camel and dull ass his prize!

If thou be so desirous to be read,
  Seek out some hungry painter, that, for bread,   10
With rotten chalk or coal upon a wall
  Will well design thee, to be viewed of all
That sit upon the common draught or strand:[38]
  Thy forehead is too narrow for my brand.

from TIMBER, OR DISCOVERIES MADE UPON MEN AND MATTER

JONSON was accustomed to jot down ideas in a common-place-book. He never got around to organizing these jottings for publication; they did not see print till after his death, and are doubtless more fragmentary than he would have wished. All of them, however, bear the stamp of his powerful mind.

Consilia.[1]—No man is so foolish but may give another good counsel sometimes; and no man is so wise but may easily err, if he will take no others' counsel but his own. But very few men are wise by their own counsel, or learned by their own teaching. For he that was only taught by himself had a fool to his master.

Vita recta.[2]—Wisdom without honesty is mere craft and cozenage. And therefore the reputation of honesty must first be gotten, which cannot be but by living well. A good life is a main argument.

Natura non effoeta.[3]—I cannot think Nature is so spent and decayed that she can bring forth nothing worth her former years. She is always the same, like herself; and when she collects her strength is abler still. Men are decayed, and studies; she is not.

De Shakespeare nostrati.—Augustus in Hat.[4]—I remember the players have often mentioned it as an honor to Shakespeare that in his writing, whatsoever he penned, he never blotted out line. My answer hath been, would he had blotted a thousand. Which they thought a malevolent speech. I had not told posterity this but for their ignorance, who chose that circumstance to commend their friend by wherein he most faulted. And to justify mine own candor, for I loved the man, and do honor his

memory (on this side idolatry) as much as any. He was, indeed, honest, and of an open and free nature; had an excellent phantsie, brave[5] notions, and gentle expressions, wherein he flowed with that facility that sometime it was necessary he should be stopped. *Sufflaminandus erat,*[6] as Augustus said of Haterius. His wit was in his own power; would the rule of it had been so, too. Many times he fell into those things could not escape laughter; as when he said in the person of Caesar, one speaking to him: "Caesar, thou dost me wrong." He replied: "Caesar did never wrong but with just cause";[7] and such like, which were ridiculous. But he redeemed his vices with his virtues. There was ever more in him to be praised than to be pardoned.

De stilo, et optimo scribendi genere.[8]—For a man to write well, there are required three necessaries: to read the best authors, observe the best speakers, and much exercise of his own style. In style, to consider what ought to be written and after what manner, he must first think and excogitate his matter, then choose his words, and examine the weight of either. Then take care, in placing and ranking both matter and words, that the composition be comely; and to do this with diligence and often. No matter how slow the style be at first, so it be labored and accurate; seek the best, and be not glad of the forward conceits,[9] or first words, that offer themselves to us; but judge of what we invent, and order what we approve. Repeat often what we have formerly written; which, beside that it helps the consequence,[10] and makes the juncture[11] better, it quickens the heat

---

[36] Then pronounced as if spelled *purse*.   [37] Acquit, free.

[1] Counsel.   [2] An upright life.—*Cozenage* = fraud.

[3] Nature's creative powers not exhausted.

[4] On Shakespeare, our fellow countryman.—Augustus (the first Roman emperor) on Haterius (a senator and rhetorician of his time).

[38] Privy or drain.

[5] Fine.—*Phantsie* = imagination.   [6] He needed a brake.

[7] Cf. *Julius Caesar*, III, i, 47–8. Jonson is probably misquoting, without the text before him. Possibly, however, Shakespeare revised it in response to an objection by Ben.

[8] On style, and the best kind of writing.   [9] First notions.

[10] What follows.—I.e., frequently read over what you have already written, to gain momentum for the rest of the piece.

[11] Joint (between what you have already done and what is still to be written).

of imagination, that often cools in the time of setting down, and gives it new strength, as if it grew lustier by the going back. As we see in the contention of leaping, they jump farthest that fetch their race largest; or, as in throwing a dart or javelin, we force back our arms to make our loose the stronger. Yet, if we have a fair gale of wind, I forbid not the steering out of our sail, so[12] the favor of the gale deceive us not. For all that we invent doth please us in the conception of birth, else we would never set it down. But the safest is to return to our judgment, and handle over again those things the easiness of which might make them justly suspected. So did the best writers in their beginnings; they imposed upon themselves care and industry; they did nothing rashly: they obtained first to write well, and then custom made it easy and a habit. By little and little their matter showed itself to them more plentifully; their words answered, their composition followed; and all, as in a well-ordered family, presented itself in the place. So that the sum of all is, ready writing makes not good writing, but good writing brings on ready writing. Yet, when we think we have got the faculty, it is even then good to resist it, as to give a horse a check sometimes with a bit, which doth not so much stop his course as stir his mettle. Again, whither a man's genius is best able to reach, thither it should more and more contend, lift, and dilate itself; as men of low stature raise themselves on their toes, and so ofttimes get even, if not eminent. Besides, as it is fit for grown and able writers to stand of themselves, and work with their own strength, to trust and endeavor by their own faculties, so it is fit for the beginner and learner to study others and the best. For the mind and memory are more sharply exercised in comprehending another man's things than our own; and such as accustom themselves and are familiar with the best authors shall ever and anon find somewhat of them in themselves; and in the expression of their minds, even when they feel it not, be able to utter something like theirs, which hath an authority above their own. Nay, sometimes it is the reward of a man's study, the praise of quoting another man fitly; and though a man be more prone and able for one kind of writing than another, yet he must exercise all. For, as in an instrument, so in style: there must be a harmony and consent[13] of parts.

DRAMATIC PROLOGUES

Jonson's first play, *Every Man in His Humor,* was produced in 1598. Though it was acted by Shakespeare's company, just before he began writing his great romantic comedies, *Every Man in His Humor* blazed a trail in the opposite direction from *Much Ado about Nothing, As You Like It,* and *Twelfth Night*—the direction of realism.

Jonson wrote on a neoclassical theory much influenced by the Renaissance Italian critics who promulgated "the Rules" for dramatic composition. Thus Jonson observes the unities of time and place; the action of *Every Man in His Humor,* though not itself unified, all occurs on a single day and in or near London. Strict Separation is preserved; the play is a comedy, and nothing serious is allowed to intrude—in Shakespeare's comedies it always intrudes. Decorum, a neoclassical fetish, is exemplified in the complete and therefore narrow consistency of every character's thought and conduct. Above all, Jonson adopts the neoclassical precept that comedy should tend to the correction of manners and should therefore deal with the universal weaknesses of humankind.

He embodies these various weaknesses in characters created solely to illustrate them. The current physiology attributed both bodily and mental health to a proper pro-portion in the human system of four liquids called humors: blood, phlegm, bile (yellow bile or choler), and melancholy (black bile). If one of these was present in excess, your health and disposition were thrown out of balance; you were too sanguine, phlegmatic, choleric (bilious or irritable), or melancholy. Jonson extended this theory metaphorically by building a character around one dominant psychological trait. Preoccupied, as the comic dramatist usually is, with deviations from normal conduct, Jonson was ready to attribute any abnormality in a stage character to some ruling passion or fixed idea. Thus the jealous Kitely in *Every Man in His Humor* is not, like Othello, a normal man who becomes jealous when he thinks there is unimpeachable evidence against his wife's virtue; Kitely is jealous because he is naturally and irrationally jealous: jealousy is his ruling passion, the likelihood of his wife's infidelity is a fixed idea deeply rooted in the quality of his mind, and everything he does is dictated by that abnormal mental state. Often, however, Jonson himself—and the same is true of his imitators throughout the century—will draw a character whose "humor" is more superficial and less ingrained. Over his protest in *Every Man out of His Humor* (1599), but not without his example, mere eccen-

---

[12] Provided that.

[13] Agreement.

tricity in dress or manner, in some cases even the frequent repetition of a catch phrase, came to be called a humor.

Jonson followed up his first success with three other humors plays, of limited merit, and an unsuccessful attempt at tragedy, *Sejanus*. Then came his four best comedies—*Volpone, or The Fox* (1606), *Epicoene, or The Silent Woman* (c. 1609), *The Alchemist* (1610), and (after a second failure at tragedy, *Catiline*) *Bartholomew Fair* (1614). *Epicoene* is a farce, a brilliant trifle; but the other three are masterpieces of English comedy. Though they make some use of humors characterization, fortunately they do not rely on it—fortunately, because, however amusing humors may prove on the stage, a well-rounded and faithful likeness of human nature cannot be achieved by concentration on a single aspect of it. That method produces caricature, not characterization.

The prefaces printed below express the most important points of the neoclassical dramatic theory underlying Jonson's practice. Its influence on the development of drama was profound. With his masterpieces Jonson laid the foundations of English comedy for at least the next hundred years.

Prologue to
EVERY MAN IN HIS HUMOR

Though need make many poets, and some such
As art and nature have not bettered much,
Yet ours for want hath not so loved the stage
As he dare serve th'ill customs of the age,
Or purchase your delight at such a rate   5
As, for it, he himself must justly hate:
To make a child, now swaddled, to proceed
Man, and then shoot up, in one beard and weed,
Past threescore years; or, with three rusty swords,
And help of some few foot-and-half-foot words,   10
Fight over York and Lancaster's long jars,[1]
And in the tiring-house[2] bring wounds to scars.
He rather prays you will be pleased to see
One such today as other plays should be;
Where neither chorus wafts you o'er the seas,[3]   15
Nor creaking throne comes down the boys to please,
Nor nimble squib is seen to make afeard
The gentlewomen, nor rolled bullet[4] heard
To say it thunders, nor tempestuous drum
Rumbles to tell you when the storm doth come;   20
But deeds and language such as men do use,
And persons such as comedy would choose
When she would show an image of the times,
And sport with human follies, not with crimes;
Except we make 'em such, by loving still   25
Our popular errors, when we know th'are ill.
I mean such errors as you'll all confess,
By laughing at them, they deserve no less:
Which when you heartily do, there's hope left, then,
You, that have so graced monsters, may like men.   30

---

[1] A direct hit at Shakespeare's *Henry VI*.
[2] Dressing room.   [3] As in Shakespeare's *Henry V*.
[4] Cannon ball.

from the Induction to
EVERY MAN OUT OF HIS HUMOR

ASPER.[5] . . . Humor, as 'tis *ens*,[6] we thus define it,
To be a quality of air, or water,
And in itself holds these two properties,
Moisture and fluxure:[7] as, for demonstration,
Pour water on this floor, 'twill wet and run: 5
Likewise the air, forced through a horn or trumpet,
Flows instantly away, and leaves behind
A kind of dew; and hence we do conclude,
That whatsoe'er hath fluxure and humidity,
As wanting power to contain itself,   10
Is humor. So in every human body,
The choler, melancholy, phlegm, and blood,
By reason that they flow continually
In some one part, and are not continent,[8]
Receive the name of humors. Now thus far   15
It may, by metaphor, apply itself
Unto the general dispositiōn:
As when some one peculiar quality
Doth so possess a man, that it doth draw
All his affects,[9] his spirits, and his powers,   20
In their confluctions,[10] all to run one way,
This may be truly said to be a humor.
But that a rook,[11] by wearing a pied feather,
The cable hat-band, or the three-piled ruff,
A yard of shoe-tie, or the Switzer's knot   25
On his French garters, should affect a humor!
O, it is more than most ridiculous.

---

[5] Asper is Jonson himself, who here gives his definition of *humor* and complains of its current misuse to designate any superficial oddity.
[6] Being.   [7] State of being fluid.
[8] Contained in a fixed place.   [9] Affections.
[10] Flowing together.
[11] Fool. The following details refer to affectations of dress, frequently of foreign importation.

CORDATUS. He speaks pure truth; now if an idiot
Have but an apish or fantastic strain,
It is his humor.
    ASPER.   Well, I will scourge those apes,   30
And to these courteous eyes[12] oppose a mirror,
As large as is the stage whereon we act;
Where they shall see the time's deformity[13]
Anatomized[14] in every nerve and sinew
With constant courage and contempt of fear.   35

Prologue to VOLPONE, OR THE FOX

Now, luck yet send us, and a little wit
    Will serve to make our play hit;
According to the palates of the season,
    Here is rime, not empty of reason.
This we were bid to credit from our poet,   5
    Whose true scope, if you would know it,
In all his poems still hath been this measure,
    To mix profit with your pleasure;
And not as some, whose throats their envy failing,
    Cry hoarsely, "All he writes is railing,"   10
And when his plays come forth, think they can flout them
    With saying he was a year about them.[15]

To this there needs no lie[16] but this his creature,
    Which was two months since no feature;
And, though he dares give them five lives to mend it,   15
    'T is known, five weeks fully penned it,
From his own hand, without a coadjutor,
    Novice, journeyman, or tutor.
Yet thus much I can give you as a token
    Of his play's worth: no eggs are broken,   20
Nor quaking custards with fierce teeth affrighted,
    Wherewith your rout are so delighted;
Nor hales he in a gull, old ends reciting,
    To stop gaps in his loose writing;
With such a deal of monstrous and forced action,   25
    As might make Bet'lem a faction:[17]
Nor made he his play for jests stolen from each table,
    But makes jests to fit his fable;
And so presents quick comedy refined,
    As best critics have designed;   30
The laws of time, place, persons he observeth,
    From no needful rule he swerveth.
All gall and copperas[18] from his ink he draineth;
    Only, a little salt remaineth;
Wherewith he'll rub your cheeks, till, red with laughter,
    They shall look fresh a week after.   36

John Webster

1580?–1625?

WEBSTER wrote two plays which are still the best romantic tragedies since *Antony and Cleopatra,* yet almost nothing is known about his life. His father was a London tailor. His career as a playwright had begun by 1602; much of it was devoted to hack work in collaboration with Dekker and others. The earlier of his masterpieces, *The White Devil,* a tragedy of terrific intensity, was written about 1611; the second, *The Duchess of Malfi,* about 1613.

None of Webster's other plays approaches these two. Both are passionate tragedies of amorous and political intrigue in Renaissance Italy. Both are marked by Webster's crabbed but searing observations on the folly of human complacency, the vanity of human wishes, the emptiness of pride and pedantry, and the baseness to which the ambitious can descend in the service of great men by whom they hope to rise. Both are full of *double-entendres,* un-

dramatic and essaylike speeches, improbabilities and inconsistencies of plot, rather cheap physical violence, and grotesque horror effects. To some critics in the early-twentieth-century heyday of realism, things like the dead man's hand and the lunatics' dance in *The Duchess of Malfi* stamped Webster's plays as mere melodrama. A "Tussaud laureate," jeers Bernard Shaw, reminded of the Chamber of Horrors at the famous waxworks. There is certainly a minority that remains unmoved by Webster's great power to stir the heart and kindle the imagination. This power is manifested less in the play as a whole work of art than in the individual scene as a unit. In his best scenes Webster gives us poignant and breathtaking drama. Swinburne may be overenthusiastic, but he is nearer the truth than Shaw: "Except in Aeschylus, in Dante, and in Shakespeare, I at least do not know where to seek for passages which in

---

12 I.e., those of the audience.
13 Jonson reiterates here his constant emphasis on contemporary realism as the material of comedy, and on the corrective function of comedy.   14 Dissected.
15 Jonson was frequently charged with slow and laborious composition.

16 Denial.
17 I.e., as might provide Bedlam (the hospital for the insane) with a (still more) disorderly party.
18 Green vitriol, used, like gall, for making ink. Here they stand for bitterness and malignity, as salt stands for wit.

sheer force of tragic and noble horror . . . may be set against the subtlest, the deepest, the sublimest passages of Webster."

Webster carries on the tradition of *The Spanish Tragedy* and *Hamlet,* but his is the disillusion of the seventeenth century, even more than in Jonson's case. With a truly Elizabethan gusto Jonson denounces particular vices and iniquities and hopes to reform them. Webster is without hope, and his skepticism embraces nearly all life's aspects. His plays are the last flowering of Elizabethan drama, not so much a decadent flowering as a late one, nipped by the frosts of the new intellectual climate. But *The Duchess of Malfi* is a gentler play than *The White Devil,* slower in working out its plot, less tense, a good deal less bitter. There is an equal exhibition of depravity, but more tenderness, and, in the midst of all the cruelty and horror, an unforgettable portrait of ardent and noble womanhood.

Webster took his plot from Painter's *Palace of Pleasure* (p. 225, above), which adapts a story in the famous Italian collection of Bandello. Bandello's tale was based on actual events. Giovanna, Duchess of Amalfi, was the granddaughter of a Spanish king of Naples. Her brother Lodovico, after distinguishing himself by feats of arms, became while still a youth Cardinal of Aragon. He resigned his marquisate to his brother Carlo, the Duke Ferdinand of the play. Giovanna was about twenty when her first husband died; Antonio Bologna, a Sicilian of good family, became her major-domo about 1504. He and Giovanna fell in love and were secretly married. With two of their children and her waiting-woman, the Duchess was seized in 1512 by her brothers' agents. She was never seen again. She had persuaded Antonio to escape with their eldest son, arguing that her brothers would not harm her. Antonio was assassinated at Milan in 1513. The Cardinal died a natural death in 1519. The subplot of Julia and Castruchio was added by Webster. He is also responsible for the circumstances of the deaths and for the fascinating villain Bosola. For some of his ideas and phraseology he went to Montaigne's *Essays* and Sidney's *Arcadia,* as well as to Donne and other contemporaries.

The Duchess of Malfi was first printed in 1623: "As it was Presented priuatly, at the Black-Friers; and publiquely at the Globe, By the Kings Maiesties Seruants. The Perfect and exact Coppy, with diuerse things Printed, that the length of the Play would not beare in the Presentment." The following text is based on that edition. Stage directions have been slightly altered and amplified. Among Webster's other writings, the character of an actor (see pp. 432 f.) is probably his, as well as others in the Overburian collection. The standard edition of Webster's works is by F. L. Lucas (4 vols., 1928). *The White Devil* is reprinted in H. Spencer's *Elizabethan Plays* (1933).

CALL FOR THE ROBIN REDBREAST

Even Webster's most lyrical verse is preoccupied with decay and death, as the two following poems show. Both occur in plays, the first in *The White Devil,* V, iv, the second in *The Devil's Law Case,* V, iv.

Call for the robin redbreast and the wren,
  Since o'er shady groves they hover
  And with leaves and flow'rs do cover
The friendless bodies of unburied men.
  Call unto his funeral dole   5
  The ant, the fieldmouse, and the mole,
To rear him hillocks that shall keep him warm,
And (when gay tombs are robbed) sustain no harm;
But keep the wolf far thence, that's foe to men;
For with his nails he'll dig them up again.   10

ALL THE FLOWERS OF THE SPRING

All the flowers of the spring
Meet to perfume our burying.
These have but their growing prime,
And man does flourish but his time.
Survey our progress from our birth—   5
We are set, we grow, we turn to earth.
Courts adieu, and all delights,
All bewitching appetites.
Sweetest breath and clearest eye
Like perfúmes go out and die;   10
And consequently this is done
As shadows wait upon the sun.
Vain the ambitïon of kings,
Who seek by trophies and dead things
To leave a living name behind,   15
And weave but nets to catch the wind.

John Webster

THE DUCHESS OF MALFI

THE ACTORS' NAMES

BOSOLA, DANIEL DE, *Master of Horse to the* DUCHESS   J. LOWIN

FERDINAND, *Duke of Calabria*   1 R. BURBIDGE   2 J. TAYLOR

CARDINAL, *his brother*   1 H. CONDELL[1]   2 R. ROBINSON

ANTONIO BOLOGNA, *steward to the* DUCHESS   1 W. OSTLER   2 R. BENFIELD

DELIO, *his friend*   J. UNDERWOOD

FOROBOSCO, *an attendant*[2]   N. TOWLEY

MALATESTE, COUNT

CASTRUCHIO, *an old lord*

MARQUESS OF PESCARA   J. RICE

SILVIO, *a lord*   T. POLLARD

RODERIGO   ⎫
GRISOLAN   ⎬ *attendants of the* DUKE

The several MADMEN   N. TOWLEY, J. UNDERWOOD, &c.

The DUCHESS   R. SHARPE

The CARDINAL'S MISTRESS (JULIA, *wife of* CASTRUCHIO)   J. TOMSON

The DOCTOR   ⎫
CARIOLA, *the* DUCHESS'S *waiting-woman* ⎬   R. PALLANT

Court Officers

An OLD LADY

ECHO, *from the* DUCHESS'S *grave*

Three young Children, two Pilgrims, Ladies, Executioners, and Attendants

THE SCENE—*Amalfi, Rome, Loretto, Milan*

ACT I

SCENE I[3]

Enter ANTONIO *and* DELIO

DELIO. You are welcome to your country, dear Antonio.
You have been long in France, and you return
A very formal Frenchman in your habit.[4]
How do you like the French court?

---

[1] Of these players, Burbage was the leading actor of the King's
Men. (See the Overburian character, probably by Webster,
pp. 432 f.) On Burbage's death in 1619, Taylor entered the
company and took over many of his roles. Like Burbage,
Lowin was an associate of Shakespeare and one of the chief
players. Condell, with another old friend of the poet, assumed
the task of getting Shakespeare's collected plays published in
1623.

[2] But there is no such part in the surviving text.

[3] Amalfi. The palace of the Duchess.   [4] Clothes.

ANT.   I admire it.
In seeking to reduce both state and people   5
To a fixed order, their judicious king
Begins at home; quits[5] first his royal palace
Of flatt'ring sycophants, of dissolute
And infamous persons—which he sweetly terms
His Master's masterpiece, the work of heaven;   10
Consid'ring duly that a prince's court
Is like a common fountain, whence should flow
Pure silver drops in general;[6] but if't chance
Some cursed example poison't near the head,
Death and diseases through the whole land spread.   15
And what is't makes this blessèd government
But a most provident council, who dare freely
Inform him the corruption of the times?

[5] Rids.   [6] Invariably.

Though some o' th' court hold it presumptiön
To instruct princes what they ought to do,   20
It is a noble duty to inform them
What they ought to foresee.[7] Here comes Bosola,

Enter BOSOLA

The only court-gall;[8] yet I observe his railing
Is not for simple love of piety:
Indeed he rails at those things which he wants;   25
Would be as lecherous, covetous, or proud,
Bloody, or envious,[9] as any man,
If he had means to be so. Here's the Cardinal.

Enter CARDINAL

BOS. I do haunt you still.
CARD. So.   30
BOS. I have done you better service than to be slighted
thus. Miserable age, where only the[10] reward of doing
well is the doing of it!
CARD. You enforce your merit too much.
BOS. I fell into the galleys in your service,[11] where,   [35
for two years together, I wore two towels instead of a
shirt, with a knot on the shoulder, after the fashion of a
Roman mantle. Slighted thus! I will thrive some way.
Blackbirds fatten best in hard weather; why not I in these
dog days?   40
CARD. Would you could become honest—
BOS. With all your divinity[12] do but direct me the way
to it. I have known many travel far for it, and yet return
as arrant knaves as they went forth: because they carried
themselves always along with them. (*Exit* CARDINAL.)   [45
Are you gone? Some fellows, they say, are possessed with
the Devil, but this great fellow were able to possess the
greatest devil, and make him worse.
ANT. He hath denied thee some suit?
BOS. He and his brother are like plum trees that   [50
grow crooked over standing pools; they are rich, and
o'erladen with fruit, but none but crows, pies,[13] and
caterpillars feed on them. Could I be one of their flatt'ring
pandars, I would hang on their ears like a horseleech, till I
were full, and then drop off. I pray, leave me. Who   [55
would rely upon these miserable dependances, in expectation to be advanced tomorrow? What creature ever fed
worse than hoping Tantalus?[14] Nor ever died any man

more fearfully than he that hoped for a pardon. There
are rewards for hawks and dogs when they have   [60
done us service; but for a soldier, that hazards his limbs in
a battle, nothing but a kind of geometry is his last sup-
portation.[15]
DELIO. Geometry?
BOS. Ay, to hang in a fair pair of slings, take his   [65
latter swing in the world upon an honorable pair of
crutches, from hospital to hospital. Fare ye well, sir. And
yet do not you scorn us; for places in the court are but like
beds in the hospital, where this man's head lies at that man's
foot, and so lower, and lower.   [*Exit* 70
DELIO. I knew this fellow seven years in the galleys
For a notorious murther; and 't was thought
The Cardinal suborned[16] it. He was released
By the French general, Gaston de Foix,[17]
When he recovered Naples.
ANT.   'T is great pity   75
He should be thus neglected; I have heard
He's very valiant. This foul melancholy
Will poison all his goodness; for, I'll tell you,
If too immoderate sleep be truly said
To be an inward rust unto the soul,   80
It then doth follow, want of actiön
Breeds all black malcontents; and their close rearing,[18]
Like moths in cloth, do hurt for want of wearing.

SCENE II[19]

Enter ANTONIO, DELIO, SILVIO, CASTRUCHIO, ROD-
ERIGO, *and* GRISOLAN

DELIO. The presence 'gins to fill; you promised me
To make me the partaker of the natures
Of some of your great courtiers.
ANT.   The Lord Cardinal's
And other strangers' that are now in court?
I shall. Here comes the great Calabrian duke.   5

Enter FERDINAND *and* Attendants

FERD. Who took the ring[20] oft'nest?
SIL. Antonio Bologna, my Lord.
FERD. Our sister Duchess' great master of her household?
Give him the jewel.[21] When shall we leave this sportive
action, and fall to action indeed?   10

---

[7] And prevent.
[8] The utterly cynical courtier.   [9] Malicious.
[10] The only.
[11] I.e., I was sentenced to row as a convict in the galleys as a
result of executing your orders.
[12] Knowledge of theology.   [13] Magpies.
[14] Whose punishment in Hades was to be placed up to his chin
in water under a fruit-laden branch; water and fruit drew
away when he tried to eat and drink.

[15] Support.   [16] Induced him to commit.
[17] Killed in the moment of victory at Ravenna in 1512. The capture of Naples was earlier, and not by him.
[18] Breeding in secret.
[19] The presence chamber or ducal reception hall.
[20] In "riding at the ring." The ring was hung so that a skillful
contestant could hit it on the gallop and carry it off on the
point of his lance.   [21] I.e., the prize.

CAST. Methinks, my Lord, you should not desire to go to war in person.

FERD. Now for some gravity.—Why, my Lord?

CAST. It is fitting a soldier arise to be a prince, but not necessary a prince descend to be a captain.   15

FERD. No?

CAST. No, my Lord; he were far better do it by a deputy.

FERD. Why should he not as well sleep or eat by a deputy? This might take idle, offensive, and base office[22] from him, whereas the other deprives him of honor.   20

CAST. Believe my experience: that realm is never long in quiet where the ruler is a soldier.

FERD. Thou told'st me thy wife could not endure fighting.

CAST. True, my Lord.

FERD. And of a jest she broke[23] of a captain she   [25 met full of wounds—I have forgot it.

CAST. She told him, my Lord, he was a pitiful fellow, to lie, like the children of Israel, all in tents.[24]

FERD. Why, there's a wit were able to undo all the chirurgeons[25] o' the city; for although gallants should   [30 quarrel and had drawn their weapons and were ready to go to it, yet her persuasions would make them put up.

CAST. That she would, my Lord.—How do you like my Spanish jennet?[26]

ROD. He is all fire.   35

FERD. I am of Pliny's[27] opinion: I think he was begot by the wind. He runs as if he were ballassed[28] with quicksilver.

SIL. True, my Lord, he reels from the tilt often.

ROD., GRIS. Ha, ha, ha!

FERD. Why do you laugh? Methinks you that   [40 are courtiers should be my touchwood,[29] take fire when I give fire; that is, laugh when I laugh, were the subject never so witty.

CAST. True, my Lord; I myself have heard a very good jest, and have scorned to seem to have so silly a wit   [45 as to understand it.

FERD. But I can laugh at your fool, my Lord.

CAST. He cannot speak, you know, but he makes faces; my lady cannot abide him.

FERD. No?   50

CAST. Nor endure to be in merry company; for she says too much laughing, and too much company, fills her too full of the wrinkle.

FERD. I would, then, have a mathematical instrument made for her face, that she might not laugh out of   [55 compass.—I shall shortly visit you at Milan, Lord Silvio.

SIL. Your Grace shall arrive most welcome.

FERD. You are a good horseman, Antonio. You have[30] excellent riders in France. What do you think of good horsemanship?   60

ANT. Nobly, my Lord. As out of the Grecian horse[31] issued many famous princes, so out of brave horsemanship arise the first sparks of growing resolution,[32] that raise the mind to noble action.

FERD. You have bespoke it worthily.   65

SIL. Your brother, the Lord Cardinal, and sister Duchess.

Enter CARDINAL, DUCHESS, *and* CARIOLA

CARD. Are the galleys come about?

GRIS.   They are, my Lord.

FERD. Here's the Lord Silvio, is[33] come to take his leave.

DELIO. Now, sir, your promise. What's that Cardinal— I mean his temper? They say he's a brave[34] fellow,   70 Will[35] play his five thousand crowns at tennis, dance, Court ladies, and one that hath fought single combats.

ANT. Some such flashes superficially hang on him, for form; but observe his inward character: he is a melancholy churchman. The spring in his face is nothing but the   [75 engend'ring of toads;[36] where he is jealous of any man, he lays worse plots for them than ever was imposed on Hercules, for he strews in his way flatterers, pandars, intelligencers,[37] atheists, and a thousand such political monsters. He should have been Pope; but instead   [80 of coming to it by the primitive decency of the Church, he did bestow bribes so largely and so impudently as if he would have carried it away[38] without heaven's knowledge. Some good he hath done.

DELIO. You have given too much of him. What's his brother?   85

ANT. The Duke there? A most perverse and turbulent nature.

What appears in him mirth is merely outside;
If he laugh heartily, it is to laugh
All honesty out of fashion.

DELIO.   Twins?

ANT.   In quality.
He speaks with others' tongues, and hears men's suits   90
With others' ears; will seem to sleep o' th' bench
Only to entrap offenders in their answers;
Dooms men to death by informatïon;[39]
Rewards by hearsay.

---

[22] Duty, concerns.   [23] Cracked.
[24] See 2 Samuel 11:11. This passage is among the Biblical selections in our Renaissance section. *Tents* is a pun, for one meaning is absorbent rolls placed in wounds to keep them open and draining.   [25] Surgeons.
[26] A small Spanish horse.
[27] Pliny the Elder (d. 79 A.D.). This idea was widespread.
[28] Ballasted.   [29] Tinder.

[30] There are.
[31] The wooden horse in which the Greeks who captured Troy were concealed.   [32] Courage.   [33] Who has.
[34] Fine, showy.
[35] Who will. Webster often omits the relative pronoun.
[36] I.e., he looks fresh and open, but is really loathsome.
[37] Spies.   [38] Got away with it.   [39] Spies' reports.

DELIO.   Then the law to him
Is like a foul, black cobweb to a spider: 95
He makes it his dwelling, and a prison
To entangle those shall feed him.

ANT.   Most true.
He never pays debts unless they be shrewd turns,[40]
And those he will confess that he doth owe.
Last, for his brother there, the Cardinal,   100
They that do flatter him most say oracles
Hang at his lips; and verily I believe them,
For the Devil speaks in them.
But for their sister, the right noble Duchess,
You never fixed your eye on three fair medals   105
Cast in one figure,[41] of so different temper.
For[42] her discourse, it is so full of rapture
You only will begin then to be sorry
When she doth end her speech, and wish, in wonder,
She held it less vainglory to talk much   110
Than your penance to hear her.[43] Whilst she speaks,
She throws upon a man so sweet a look
That it were able raise one to a galliard[44]
That lay in a dead palsy, and to dote
On that sweet countenance. But in that look   115
There speaketh so divine a continence
As cuts off all lascivious and vain hope.
Her days are practiced in such noble virtue
That sure her nights, nay more, her very sleeps,
Are more in heaven than other ladies' shrifts.[45]   120
Let all sweet ladies break their flatt'ring glasses,
And dress themselves in[46] her.

DELIO.   Fie, Antonio,
You play the wire-drawer with her commendations.[47]

ANT. I'll case the picture up.[48] Only thus much:—
All her particular worth grows to this sum: 125
She stains[49] the time past, lights the time to come.

CARI. You must attend my Lady in the gallery,
Some half an hour hence.

ANT.   I shall.
                         [Exeunt ANTONIO and DELIO

FERD. Sister, I have a suit to you.

DUCH.   To me, sir?

FERD. A gentleman here, Daniel de Bosola,   130
One that was in the galleys—

DUCH.   Yes, I know him.

FERD. A worthy fellow h'is: pray let me entreat for
The provisorship[50] of your horse.[51]

DUCH.   Your knowledge of him
Commends him and prefers[52] him.

FERD.   Call him hither.
                         [Exit Attendant
We're now upon parting. Good Lord Silvio,   135
Do us commend to all our noble friends
At the leaguer.[53]

SIL.   Sir, I shall.

DUCH.   You are for Milan?

SIL. I am.

DUCH.   Bring the caroches:[54] we'll bring you down
To the haven.   [Exeunt all but CARDINAL and FERDINAND

CARD.   Be sure you entertain[55] that Bosola
For your intelligence.[56] I would not be seen in't;   140
And therefore many times I have slighted him,
When he did court our furtherance, as this morning.

FERD. Antonio, the great master of her household,
Had been far fitter.

CARD.   You are deceived in him;
His nature is too honest for such business.   145
He comes; I'll leave you.   [Exit

     Enter BOSOLA

BOS.   I was lured to you.

FERD. My brother here, the Cardinal, could never
Abide you.

BOS.   Never since he was in my debt.

FERD. May be some oblique character in your face
Made him suspect you?

BOS.   Doth he study physiognomy?   150
There's no more credit to be given to th' face
Than to a sick man's urine, which some call
The physician's whore, because she cozens[57] him.
He did suspect me wrongfully.

FERD.   For that
You must give great men leave to take their times: 155
Distrust doth cause us seldom be deceived.
You see the oft shaking of the cedar tree
Fastens it more at root.

BOS.   Yet, take heed.
For to suspect a friend unworthily
Instructs him the next[58] way to suspect you,   160
And prompts him to deceive you.

FERD.   There's gold.

BOS.   So.
What follows? Never rained such showers as these

---

40 Injuries.   41 Mold.   42 As for.
43 I.e., you regret that the Duchess is more convinced that to
  talk much is vanity than she is that people like to hear her.
44 A particularly lively dance.   45 Confessions.
46 I.e., model themselves on.
47 You spin out (exaggerate) your praises of her.
48 I.e., draw the curtain over it (pictures were protected by
  curtains); i.e., I'll stop.
49 Blots out (the merits of ladies in), i.e., surpasses.

50 Purveyorship, post of supply officer.   51 Horses, stables.
52 Gets him the post.   53 Camp.   54 Coaches.
55 Retain, take.   56 Spy service.   57 Cheats.
58 Nearest, quickest.

Without thunderbolts i' th' tail of them. Whose throat
    must I cut?

FERD. Your inclination to shed blood rides post[59]
Before my occasion to use you. I give you that   165
To live i' th' court here, and observe the Duchess;
To note all the particulars of her behavior:[60]
What suitors do solicit her for marriage,
And whom she best affects.[61] She's a young widow;
I would not have her marry again.

BOS.   No, sir?   170

FERD. Do not you ask the reason; but be satisfied
I say I would not.

BOS.   It seems you would create me
One of your familiars.

FERD.   Familiar? what's that?

BOS. Why, a very quaint invisible devil in flesh:
An intelligencer.

FERD.   Such a kind of thriving thing   175
I would wish thee; and, ere long, thou mayst arrive
At a higher place by't.

BOS.   Take your devils,
Which hell calls angels![62] These cursed gifts would make
You a corrupter, me an impudent traitor;
And should I take these, they'd take me to hell.   180

FERD. Sir, I'll take nothing from you that I have given.
There is a place that I procured for you
This morning, the provisorship o' the' horse.
Have you heard on't?

BOS.   No.

FERD.   'Tis yours. Is't not worth thanks?

BOS. I would have you curse yourself now, that your
    bounty   185
(Which makes men truly noble) e'er should make
Me a villain. Oh, that to avoid ingratitude
For the good deed you have done me, I must do
All the ill man can invent! Thus the Devil
Candies all sins o'er; and what heaven terms vild,[63]   190
That names he complimental.[64]

FERD.   Be yourself.
Keep your old garb of melancholy; 'twill express
You envy those that stand above your reach,
Yet strive not to come near 'em. This will gain
Access to private lodgings, where yourself   195
May, like a politic dormouse—

BOS.   As I have seen some
Feed in a lord's dish, half asleep, not seeming
To listen to any talk; and yet these rogues
Have cut his throat in a dream. What's my place?

The provisorship o' th' horse? Say, then, my corruption
Grew out of horse-dung. I am your creature.

FERD.   Away!   201

BOS. Let good men, for good deeds, covet good fame,
Since place and riches oft are bribes of shame—
Sometimes the Devil doth preach.   [Exeunt

SCENE III[65]

Enter FERDINAND, DUCHESS, CARDINAL, *and* CARIOLA

CARD. We are to part from you, and your own
    discretion
Must now be your director.

FERD.   You are a widow:
You know already what man is; and therefore
Let not youth, high promotion, eloquence—

CARD. No, nor anything without the addition, honor,   5
Sway your high blood.

FERD.   Marry! they are most luxurious,[66]
Will wed twice.

CARD.   O, fie!

FERD.   Their livers are more spotted
Than Laban's sheep.[67]

DUCH.   Diamonds are of most value,
They say, that have passed through most jewelers' hands.

FERD. Whores, by that rule, are precious—

DUCH.   Will you hear me?   10
I'll never marry.

CARD.   So most widows say;
But commonly that motion[68] lasts no longer
Than the turning of an hourglass: the funeral sermon
And it end both together.

FERD.   Now hear me.
You live in a rank pasture here, i' th' court.   15
There is a kind of honey-dew[69] that's deadly:
'Twill poison your fame; look to't. Be not cunning;
For they whose faces do belie their hearts
Are witches ere they arrive at twenty years,
Ay, and give the Devil suck.[70]

DUCH.   This is terrible good counsel.   20

FERD. Hypocrisy is woven of a fine small thread,
Subtler than Vulcan's engine;[71] yet, believe't,
Your darkest actions, nay, your privat'st thoughts,
Will come to light.

CARD.   You may flatter yourself
And take your own choice, privately be married   25
Under the eaves of night—

---

[59] Hastens.   [60] Behavior.
[61] Inclines to.   [62] A kind of gold coin.   [63] Vile.
[64] He calls courteous.

[65] A gallery in the palace.
[66] Lascivious.   [67] Genesis 30: 31–42.   [68] Resolution.
[69] Found on plants.
[70] With milk or blood. This was a common belief about witches.
[71] Device. Vulcan caught his wife Venus and her lover Mars in a
    net he had made.

FERD.   Think't the best voyage
That e'er you made; like the irregular crab,
Which, though 't goes backward, thinks that it goes right
Because it goes its own way. But, observe,
Such weddings may more properly be said   30
To be executed than celebrated.

CARD.   The marriage night
Is the entrance into some prison.

FERD.   And those joys,
Those lustful pleasures, are like heavy sleeps
Which do forerun man's mischief.

CARD.   Fare you well.
Wisdom begins at the end.[72] Remember it.   [Exit 35

DUCH. I think this speech between you both was
    studied,
It came so roundly off.

FERD.   You are my sister;
This was my father's poniard. Do you see?
I'd be loath to see 't look rusty, 'cause 't was his.
I would have you to give o'er these chargeable[73] revels;
A visor[74] and a mask are whispering-rooms   41
That were never built for goodness. Fare ye well.—
And women like that part which, like the lamprey,[75]
Hath never a bone in 't.

DUCH.   Fie, sir![76]

FERD.   Nay,
I mean the tongue: variety of courtship.   45
What cannot a neat knave with a smooth tale
Make a woman believe? Farewell, lusty widow.   [Exit

DUCH. Shall this move me? If all my royal kindred
Lay in my way unto this marriage,
I'd make them my low footsteps.[77] And even now,   50
Even in this hate, as men in some great battles
By apprehending danger have achieved
Almost impossible actions (I have heard soldiers say so),
So I, through frights and threat'nings, will assay
This dangerous venture. Let old wives[78] report   55
I winked[79] and chose a husband.—Cariola,
To thy known secrecy I have given up
More than my life—my fame.

CARI.   Both shall be safe;
For I'll conceal this secret from the world
As warily as those that trade in poison   60
Keep poison from their children.

DUCH.   Thy protestation
Is ingenious[80] and hearty; I believe it.
Is Antonio come?

CARI.   He attends you.

DUCH.   Good dear soul,
Leave me; but place thyself behind the arras,
Where thou mayst overhear us. Wish me good speed, 65
For I am going into a wilderness
Where I shall find nor path nor friendly clue
To be my guide.   [CARIOLA goes behind the arras

Enter ANTONIO

                    I sent for you; sit down;
Take pen and ink, and write. Are you ready?

ANT.   Yes.

DUCH. What did I say?   70

ANT. That I should write somewhat.[81]

DUCH.   Oh, I remember.
After these triumphs[82] and this large expense
It's fit, like thrifty husbands,[83] we inquire
What's laid up for tomorrow.

ANT. So please your beauteous Excellence.

DUCH.   Beauteous! 75
Indeed, I thank you. I look young for your sake;[84]
You have ta'en my cares upon you.

ANT.   I'll fetch your Grace
The particulars of your revenue and expense.

DUCH. Oh, you are an upright treasurer, but you
    mistook;
For when I said I meant to make inquiry   80
What's laid up for tomorrow, I did mean
What's laid up yonder for me.

ANT.   Where?

DUCH.   In heaven.
I am making my will (as 't is fit princes should,
In perfect memory), and, I pray, sir, tell me,
Were not one better make it smiling, thus,   85
Than in deep groans and terrible ghastly looks,
As if the gifts we parted with procured[85]
That violent distraction?

ANT.   Oh, much better.

DUCH. If I had a husband now, this care were quit;[86]
But I intend to make you overseer.   90
What good deed shall we first remember? Say.

ANT. Begin with that first good deed began[87] i' th'
    world,
After man's creation, the sacrament of marriage.
I'd have you first provide for a good husband:
Give him all.

DUCH.   All!

ANT.   Yes, your excellent self.   95

DUCH. In a winding sheet?

---

72 A wise man considers first the final end of an action.
73 Expensive.   74 Mask, worn at a masked ball.
75 An eel-like fish.   76 Since his real meaning is improper.
77 Stepping stones.   78 Women, crones.
79 Shut my eyes.   80 Ingenuous, free from guile.
81 Something.   82 Festivities.
83 Economical managers.   84 Because of you.
85 Caused.   86 Would be wiped out.
87 Which began.

ANT. In a couple.[88]

DUCH. Saint Winfrid,[89] that were a strange will!

ANT. 'T were strange if there were no will in you
To marry again.

DUCH. What do you think of marriage?

ANT. I take 't, as those that deny purgatory, 100
It locally[90] contains or heaven or hell;
There's no third place in 't.

DUCH. How do you affect[91] it?

ANT. My banishment, feeding my melancholy,
Would often reason thus—

DUCH. Pray, let's hear it.

ANT. Say a man never marry nor have children. 105
What takes that from him? Only the bare name
Of being a father, or the weak delight
To see the little wanton ride a-cock-horse
Upon a painted stick, or hear him chatter
Like a taught starling.

DUCH. Fie, fie, what's all this? 110
One of your eyes is bloodshot; use my ring to 't—
They say 't is very sovereign.[92] 'T was my wedding ring,
And I did vow never to part with it
But to my second husband.

ANT. You have parted with it now.

DUCH. Yes, to help your eyesight.

ANT. You have made me stark blind.

DUCH. How? 115

ANT. There is a saucy and ambitious devil
Is dancing in this circle.[93]

DUCH. Remove him.

ANT. How?

DUCH. There needs small conjuration, when your finger
May do it—thus. Is it fit?

[She puts the ring on his finger, and he kneels

ANT. What said you?

DUCH. Sir,
This goodly roof of yours is too low built; 120
I cannot stand upright in 't nor discourse,
Without I raise it higher. Raise yourself;
Or, if you please, my hand to help you. So. [He rises

ANT. Ambition, madam, is a great man's madness,
That is not kept in chains and close-pent rooms, 125
But in fair lightsome lodgings, and is girt
With the wild noise of prattling visitants,
Which makes it lunatic beyond all cure.
Conceive not I am so stupid but I aim

Whereto your favors tend; but he's a fool 130
That, being a-cold, would thrust his hands i' th' fire
To warm them.

DUCH. So, now the ground 's broke,
You may discover what a wealthy mine
I make you lord of.

ANT. Oh, my unworthiness!

DUCH. You were ill to sell yourself:[94] 135
This dark'ning of your worth is not like that
Which tradesmen use i' th' city: their false lights
Are to rid bad wares off;[95] and I must tell you,
If you will know where breathes a complete man
(I speak it without flattery), turn your eyes, 140
And progress[96] through yourself.

ANT. Were there nor heaven nor hell,
I should be honest. I have long served virtue,
And never ta'en wages of her.

DUCH. Now she pays it.
The misery of us that are born great! 145
We are forced to woo, because none dare woo us;
And as a tyrant doubles with his words
And fearfully equivocates, so we
Are forced to express our violent passiöns
In riddles and in dreams, and leave the path 150
Of simple virtue, which was never made
To seem the thing it is not. Go, go brag
You have left me heartless: mine is in your bosom;
I hope 't will multiply love there. You do tremble.
Make not your heart so dead a piece of flesh, 155
To fear more than to love me. Sir, be confident.
What is 't distracts you? This is flesh and blood, sir;
'T is not the figure cut in alablaster,[97]
Kneels[98] at my husband's tomb. Awake, awake, man!
I do here put off all vain ceremony, 160
And only do appear to you a young widow
That claims you for her husband; and, like a widow,
I use but half a blush in 't.

ANT. Truth speak for me,
I will remain the constant sanctuary
Of your good name.

DUCH. I thank you, gentle love; 165
And 'cause you shall not come to me in debt,
(Being now my steward) here upon your lips
I sign your *Quietus est*.[99] This you should have begged
now.

---

88 Of sheets; i.e., in the marriage bed.
89 St. Winifred (seventh century), patron saint of virgins. She
was beheaded by a rejected suitor.
90 In itself.   91 Incline to, like.   92 Effective.
93 I.e., the ring. With an allusion to a magician's drawing a
magic circle to protect himself when conjuring up spirits.

94 You would not be a good salesman of yourself.
95 A common complaint was that London shops were kept dark
to hide imperfections in the goods.
96 Make a royal journey.
97 Alabaster; it was used for the effigy (on the tomb) of the person
buried. Evidently the Duchess's effigy is already there, as well
as her first husband's.
98 Which kneels.
99 Acquittance, attesting that the accounts are in order.

I have seen children oft eat sweetmeats thus,
As fearful to devour them too soon.   170
    ANT. But for your brothers?
    DUCH.   Do not think of them.
All discord without this circumference[100]
Is only to be pitied, and not feared:
Yet should they know it, time will easily
Scatter the tempest.
    ANT.   These words should be mine,   175
And all the parts you have spoke, if some part of it
Would not have savored flattery.
    DUCH.   Kneel.
            [CARIOLA *comes from behind the arras*
    ANT.   Ha!
    DUCH. Be not amazed; this woman's of my counsel.
I have heard lawyers say a contract in a chamber
Per verba presenti[101] is absolute marriage.   180
Bless, heaven, this sacred gordian,[102] which let violence
Never untwine!
    ANT. And may our sweet affections, like the spheres,
Be still[103] in motiön.
    DUCH.   Quick'ning,[104] and make
The like soft music.[105]   185
    ANT. That we may imitate the loving palms,[106]

Best emblem of a peaceful marriage,
That never bore fruit divided.
    DUCH. What can the Church force more?
    ANT. That fortune may not know an accident,   190
Either of joy or sorrow, to divide
Our fixèd wishes!
    DUCH. How can the Church build faster?[107]
We now are man and wife, and 'tis the Church
That must but echo this.—Maid, stand apart;   195
I now am blind.
    ANT.   What's your conceit[108] in this?
    DUCH. I would have you lead your fortune by the hand
Unto your marriage bed
(You speak in me this, for we now are one).
We'll only lie and talk together, and plot   200
T' appease my humorous[109] kindred; and, if you please,
Like the old tale in *Alexander and Lodowick,*[110]
Lay a naked sword between us, keep us chaste—
Oh, let me shroud my blushes in your bosom,
Since 'tis the treasury of all my secrets!   205
            [*Exeunt* DUCHESS *and* ANTONIO
    CARI. Whether the spirit of greatness or of woman
Reign most in her, I know not; but it shows
A fearful madness. I owe her much of pity.   [*Exit*

ACT II

SCENE I[1]

Enter BOSOLA *and* CASTRUCHIO

    BOS. You say, you would fain be taken—for an eminent courtier?
    CAST. 'Tis the very main[2] of my ambition.
    BOS. Let me see. You have a reasonable good face for't already, and your nightcap[3] expresses your ears suf- [5
ficient largely. I would have you learn to twirl the strings of your band[4] with a good grace, and in a set speech, at th' end of every sentence, to hum three or four times or blow your nose till it smart again, to recover your memory. When you come to be a president in criminal causes, [10
if you smile upon a prisoner, hang him; but if you frown

upon him and threaten him, let him be sure to scape the gallows.
    CAST. I would be a very merry president.
    BOS. Do not sup o' nights; 'twill beget you an [15
admirable wit.
    CAST. Rather it would make me have a good stomach[5] to quarrel; for they say, your[6] roaring boys[7] eat meat seldom, and that makes them so valiant. But how shall I know whether the people take me for an eminent [20
fellow?
    BOS. I will teach a trick to know it: give out you lie a-dying, and if you hear the common people curse you, be sure you are taken for one of the prime nightcaps.[8]

Enter an OLD LADY

You come from painting now?   25
    OLD LADY. From what?
    BOS. Why, from your scurvy face-physic. To behold thee not painted inclines somewhat near a miracle; these,

---

[100] Outside the circle of our embracing arms.
[101] Properly, *per verba de presenti,* by words of the present. Such a marriage was valid in canon law, if the present tense was used: "I take you," not "I will take you."   [102] Knot.
[103] Ever.   [104] Living, growing.
[105] The planetary spheres were supposed to utter harmonies.
[106] Palm trees. They were supposed to entwine.

[1] The palace.   [2] Objective.
[3] Evidently he has on something like the white cap or coif worn by lawyers.   [4] Collar.

[107] Firmer.   [108] Idea.   [109] Capricious.
[110] A ballad version of an old romance.

[5] Appetite, inclination.   [6] The.   [7] Bullies.
[8] Lawyers. See note 3 of this series.

in thy face here, were deep ruts, and foul sloughs, the last progress.[9] There was a lady in France that, having [30 had the smallpox, flayed the skin off her face, to make it more level; and whereas before she looked like a nutmeg-grater, after she resembled an abortive hedgehog.

OLD LADY. Do you call this painting?

BOS. No, no, but I call it careening[10] of an old [35 morphewed[11] lady, to make her disembogue[12] again: there's roughcast phrase to your plastic.[13]

OLD LADY. It seems you are well acquainted with my closet.[14]

BOS. One would suspect it for a shop of witch- [40 craft, to find in it the fat of serpents, spawn of snakes, Jews' spittle, and their young children's ordures—and all these for the face. I would sooner eat a dead pigeon, taken from the soles of the feet of one sick of the plague, than kiss one of you fasting.[15] Here are two of you, [45 whose sin of your youth is the very patrimony of the physician—makes him renew his footcloth[16] with the spring, and change his high-prized[17] courtesan with the fall of the leaf. I do wonder you do not loathe yourselves.
Observe my meditation now: 50
What thing is in this outward form of man
To be beloved? We account it ominous
If nature do produce a colt, or lamb,
A fawn, or goat, in any limb resembling
A man, and fly from 't as a prodigy.   55
Man stands amazed to see his deformity
In any other creature but himself.
But in our own flesh, though we bear diseases
Which have their true names only ta'en from beasts—
As the most ulcerous wolf and swinish measle[18]—   60
Though we are eaten up of lice and worms,
And though continually we bear about us
A rotten and dead body, we delight
To hide it in rich tissue;[19] all our fear,
Nay, all our terror, is lest our physician   65
Should put us in the ground to be made sweet.—
Your wife 's gone to Rome. You two couple, and get
you to the wells at Lucca to recover[20] your aches. I have
other work on foot.   [Exeunt CASTRUCHIO and OLD LADY
I observe our Duchess   70
Is sick a-days, she pukes, her stomach seethes,

The fins of her eyelids look most teeming blue,[21]
She wanes i' th' cheek, and waxes fat i' th' flank,
And, contrary to our Italian fashion,
Wears a loose-bodied gown—there's somewhat in 't.   75
I have a trick may chance discover it,
A pretty one: I have bought some apricocks,
The first our spring yields.

Enter ANTONIO *and* DELIO

DELIO (*aside*).   And so long since married?
You amaze me.

ANT. (*aside*).   Let me seal your lips for ever;
For, did I think that anything but th' air   80
Could carry these words from you, I should wish
You had no breath at all.—Now, sir. In your
       contemplation?
You are studying to become a great wise fellow?

BOS. Oh, sir, the opinion of wisdom is a foul tetter[22]
that runs all over a man's body. If simplicity[23]   [85
direct us to have no evil, it directs us to a happy being;
for the subtlest folly proceeds from the subtlest wisdom.
Let me be simply honest.

ANT. I do understand your inside.

BOS.   Do you so?

ANT. Because you would not seem to appear to th'
       world   90
Puffed up with your preferment, you continue
This out-of-fashion melancholy. Leave it, leave it.

BOS. Give me leave to be honest in any phrase, in any compliment whatsoever. Shall I confess myself to you? I look no higher than I can reach. They are the gods [95 that must ride on winged horses; a lawyer's mule of a slow pace will both suit my disposition and business. For, mark me, when a man's mind rides faster than his horse can gallop, they quickly both tire.

ANT. You would look up to heaven, but I think 100
The Devil, that rules i' th' air, stands in your light.

BOS. O, sir, you are lord of the ascendant,[24] chief man with the Duchess; a duke was your cousin-german re-moved.[25] Say you were lineally descended from King Pepin,[26] or he himself, what of this? Search the [105 heads of the greatest rivers in the world, you shall find them but bubbles of water. Some would think the souls of princes were brought forth by some more weighty cause than those of meaner persons; they are deceived: there's the same hand to them; the like passions [110 sway them; the same reason that makes a vicar go to law

---

[9] See p. 454, note 96.
[10] Scraping, as when a ship is turned on its side.
[11] Scurfy.   [12] Put to sea, i.e., get her ready.
[13] There's a roughly plastered phrase to go with your face model-ing.   [14] Private room.
[15] When the breath is at its worst.—A freshly killed pigeon to draw out the infection was a common prescription.
[16] Caparison for horse or mule.   [17] High-priced.
[18] A disease of hogs; it has no connection with the more familiar measles.—*Lupus* (wolf)＝ulcer.   [19] Silk.   [20] Cure.

[21] Have the blue look of pregnancy.—Presumably *fins*＝edges.
[22] Skin disease.   [23] Foolishness.
[24] In astrology, the planet whose zodiacal sign is entering the first "mansion" or part of the sky just above the horizon; i.e., your fortune is rising.   [25] First cousin once removed.
[26] King of the Franks (d. 768).

for a tithe-pig, and undo[27] his neighbors, makes them spoil a whole province, and batter down goodly cities with the cannon.

Enter DUCHESS *and* Ladies

DUCH. Your arm, Antonio; do I not grow fat? 115
I am exceeding short-winded.—Bosola,
I would have you, sir, provide for me a litter,
Such a one as the Duchess of Florence rode in.
　BOS. The duchess used one when she was great with
　　child.
　DUCH. I think she did.—(*To a* Lady) Come hither,
　　mend[28] my ruff— 120
Here, when![29] Thou art such a tedious lady;
And thy breath smells of lemon-peels.[30] Would thou
　　hadst done!
Shall I sound[31] under thy fingers? I am so troubled
With the mother.[32]
　BOS. (*aside*). 　　　　I fear, too much.
　DUCH. 　　　　　　　I have heard you say
That the French courtiers wear their hats on 'fore 125
The king.
　ANT. 　I have seen it.
　DUCH. 　　　　In the presence?
　ANT. 　　　　　　　Yes.
　DUCH. Why should not we bring up that fashion?
'Tis ceremony more than duty that consists
In the removing of a piece of felt.
Be you the example to the rest o' th' court; 130
Put on your hat first.
　ANT. 　　　You must pardon me:
I have seen, in colder countries than in France,
Nobles stand bare to th' prince; and the distinction
Methought showed reverently.
　BOS. I have a present for your Grace.
　DUCH. 　　　　　　For me, sir? 135
　BOS. Apricocks, madam.
　DUCH. 　　　　O, sir, where are they?
I have heard of none to-year.[33]
　BOS. (*aside*). 　　　Good! her color rises.
　DUCH. Indeed, I thank you; they are wondrous fair ones.
What an unskillful fellow is our gardener!
We shall have none this month.
　BOS. 　　　Will not your Grace pare them? 140
　DUCH. No. They taste of musk, methinks; indeed they
　　do.
　BOS. I know not. Yet I wish your Grace had pared 'em.
　DUCH. Why?

BOS. 　　　I forgot to tell you, the knave gard'ner,
Only to raise his profit by them the sooner,
Did ripen them in horse-dung.
　DUCH. 　　　　O, you jest!— 145
(*To* ANTONIO) You shall judge; pray, taste one.
　ANT. 　　　　　　　Indeed, madam,
I do not love the fruit.
　DUCH. 　　　Sir, you are loath
To rob us of our dainties. 'Tis a delicate fruit;
They say they are restorative.
　BOS. 　　　　'Tis a pretty art,
This grafting.
　DUCH. 　'Tis so; a bett'ring of nature. 150
　BOS. To make a pippin grow upon a crab,[34]
A damson on a blackthorn.—(*Aside*) How greedily she
　　eats them!
A whirlwind strike off these bawd farthingales![35]
For, but for that and the loose-bodied gown,
I should have discovered apparently[36] 155
The young springal[37] cutting a caper in her belly.
　DUCH. I thank you, Bosola; they were right good ones,
If they do not make me sick.
　ANT. 　　　　How now, madam!
　DUCH. This green fruit and my stomach are not
　　friends. 159
How they swell me!
　BOS. (*aside*). 　Nay, you are too much swelled already.
　DUCH. Oh, I am in an extreme cold sweat.
　BOS. 　　　　I am very sorry. [*Exit*
　DUCH. Lights to my chamber!—(*Aside*) O good
　　Antonio,
I fear I am undone!
　DELIO. 　　　Lights there, lights!
　　　　　　　[*Exeunt* DUCHESS *and* Ladies
　ANT. O my most trusty Delio, we are lost.
I fear she's fall'n in labor; and there's left 165
No time for her remove.
　DELIO. 　　　Have you prepared
Those ladies to attend her, and procured
That politic safe conveyance for the midwife
Your Duchess plotted?
　ANT. 　I have.
　DELIO. Make use then of this forced occasïon. 170
Give out that Bosola hath poisoned her
With these apricocks; that will give some color[38]
For her keeping close.[39]
　ANT. 　　　Fie, fie, the physicians
Will then flock to her.

---

[27] Ruin. 　[28] Improve, i.e., arrange. 　[29] Hurry!
[30] A common remedy for bad breath. 　[31] Swoon.
[32] Hysteria. 　[33] This year.

[34] A crab-apple tree. 　[35] Hoop petticoats. 　[36] Plainly.
[37] Stripling, youngster. 　[38] Plausible excuse.
[39] In secret, in retirement.

DELIO.   For that you may pretend
She'll use some prepared antidote of her own,   175
Lest the physicians should re-poison her.

ANT. I am lost in amazement; I know not what to
        think on't.   [Exeunt

SCENE II[40]

Enter BOSOLA

BOS. So, so! there's no question but her techiness[41] and
most vulturous eating of the apricocks are apparent signs
of breeding.

Enter OLD LADY

Now?
    OLD LADY. I am in haste, sir.   5
    BOS. There was a young waiting-woman had a mon-
strous desire to see the glass-house—[42]
    OLD LADY. Nay, pray let me go.
    BOS. And it was only to know what strange instrument
it was, should swell up a glass to the fashion of a   [10
woman's belly.
    OLD LADY. I will hear no more of the glass-house. You
are still abusing women?
    BOS. Who, I? no, only, by the way now and then,
mention your frailties. The orange tree bears ripe   [15
and green fruit, and blossoms, all together; and some of
you give entertainment for pure love, but more for more
precious reward. The lusty spring smells well, but drooping
autumn tastes well. If we have the same golden show'rs
that rained in the time of Jupiter the Thunderer,   [20
you have the same Danaës still, to hold up their laps to
receive them. Didst thou never study the mathematics?
    OLD LADY. What's that, sir?
    BOS. Why, to know the trick how to make a-many
lines meet in one center. Go, go; give your foster-   [25
daughters good counsel: tell them that the Devil takes delight to hang at a woman's girdle, like a false rusty watch,
that she cannot discern how the time passes.
                                            [Exit OLD LADY

Enter ANTONIO, DELIO, RODERIGO, and GRISOLAN

ANT. Shut up the court gates.
    ROD.   Why, sir? what's the danger?
    ANT. Shut up the posterns presently,[43] and call   30
All the officers o' th' court.
    GRIS.   I shall instantly. [Exit

[40] The same or another room or courtyard.
[41] Irritability.   [42] Glass factory.   [43] At once.

ANT. Who keeps the key o' th' park gate?
    ROD.   Forobosco.
    ANT. Let him bring't presently.

Re-enter GRISOLAN and Servants

1 SERV. Oh, gentlemen o' th' court, the foulest treason!
    BOS. (aside). If that these apricocks should be poisoned,
        now,   35
Without my knowledge!
    1 SERV. There was taken even now a Switzer in the
Duchess' bedchamber.
    2 SERV. A Switzer!
    1 SERV. With a pistol in his great codpiece.[44]   40
    BOS. Ha, ha, ha!
    1 SERV. The codpiece was the case for't.
    2 SERV. There was a cunning traitor! Who would have
searched his codpiece?
    1 SERV. True, if he had kept out of the ladies' chambers.
And all the molds of his buttons were leaden bullets.   46
    2 SERV. O wicked cannibal! a firelock in's codpiece!
    1 SERV. 'Twas a French plot, upon my life!
    2 SERV. To see what the Devil can do!
    ANT. All the officers here?
    SERVANTS.   We are.
    ANT.   Gentlemen, we have lost
Much plate, you know; and but this evening   51
Jewels, to the value of four thousand ducats,
Are missing in the Duchess' cabinet.—
Are the gates shut?
    SERVANTS.   Yes.
    ANT.   'Tis the Duchess' pleasure
Each officer be locked into his chamber   55
Till the sun-rising, and to send the keys
Of all their chests, and of their outward doors,
Into her bedchamber. She is very sick.
    ROD. At her pleasure.
    ANT. She entreats you take't not ill; the innocent   60
Shall be the more approved[45] by it.
    BOS. Gentlemen o' th' wood-yard,[46] where's your
        Switzer now?
    1 SERV. By this hand, 'twas credibly reported by one o'
        th' black-guard.[47]   [Exeunt all but ANTONIO and DELIO
    DELIO. How fares it with the Duchess?
    ANT.   She's exposed
Unto the worst of torture: pain and fear.   65
    DELIO. Speak to her all happy comfort.
    ANT. How I do play the fool with mine own danger!
You are this night, dear friend, to post to Rome;
My life lies in your service.

[44] A baglike appendage worn at the opening of the tight trousers.
    It was the source of much ribald jesting.   [45] Vindicated.
[46] I.e., fuel carriers.   [47] The lowest class of kitchen helpers.

DELIO. Do not doubt me.

ANT. Oh, 'tis far from me; and yet fear presents me 70
Somewhat that looks like danger.

DELIO. Believe it,
'Tis but the shadow of your fear, no more.
How superstitiously we mind our evils!
The throwing down salt, or crossing of a hare,
Bleeding at nose, the stumbling of a horse, 75
Or singing of a cricket, are of power
To daunt whole man[48] in us. Sir, fare you well.
I wish you all the joys of a blessed father;
And, for my faith, lay this unto your breast:
Old friends, like old swords, still are trusted best. [Exit

Enter CARIOLA

CARI. Sir, you are the happy father of a son; 81
Your wife commends him to you.

ANT. Blessèd comfort!
For heaven-sake tend her well. I'll presently
Go set a figure[49] for's nativity. [Exeunt

SCENE III[50]

Enter BOSOLA, *with a dark lantern*

BOS. Sure I did hear a woman shriek. List, ha!
And the sound came, if I received it right,
From the Duchess' lodgings. There's some stratagem
In the confining all our courtiers
To their several wards; I must have part[51] of it— 5
My intelligence will freeze else. List, again!
It may be 't was the melancholy bird,
Best friend of silence and of solitariness,
The owl, that screamed so.—Ha! Antonio!

Enter ANTONIO *with a candle, his sword drawn*

ANT. I heard some noise.—Who's there? What art
thou? Speak. 10

BOS. Antonio? put not your face nor body
To such a forced expressïon of fear:
I am Bosola, your friend.

ANT. Bosola?—
(*Aside*) This mole does undermine me.—Heard you not
A noise even now?

BOS. From whence?

ANT. From the Duchess' lodging. 15

BOS. Not I; did you?

ANT. I did, or else I dreamed.

BOS. Let's walk towards it.

ANT. No. It may be 't was
But the rising of the wind.

BOS. Very likely.
Methinks 't is very cold, and yet you sweat.
You look wildly.

ANT. I have been setting a figure[52] 20
For the Duchess' jewels.

BOS. Ah, and how falls your question?
Do you find it radical?[53]

ANT. What 's that to you?
'T is rather to be questioned what design,
When all men were commanded to their lodgings,
Makes you a night-walker.

BOS. In sooth, I'll tell you. 25
Now all the court's asleep, I thought the Devil
Had least to do here. I came to say my prayers;
And if it do offend you I do so,
You are a fine courtier.

ANT. (*aside*). This fellow will undo me!—
You gave the Duchess apricocks today. 30
Pray heaven they were not poisoned!

BOS. Poisoned! a Spanish fig[54]
For the imputation.

ANT. Traitors are ever confident
Till they are discovered. There were jewels stol'n too.
In my conceit,[55] none are to be suspected
More than yourself.

BOS. You are a false steward. 35

ANT. Saucy slave, I'll pull thee up by the roots.

BOS. May be the ruin will crush you to pieces.

ANT. You are an impudent snake indeed, sir.
Are you scarce warm, and do you show your sting?[56]
You libel well, sir!

BOS. No, sir: copy it out, 40
And I will set my hand to 't.[57]

ANT. (*aside*). My nose bleeds.
One that were superstitïous would count
This ominous, when it merely comes by chance.
Two letters, that are wrought[58] here for my name,
Are drowned in blood! 45
Mere accident.—For you, sir, I'll take[59] order.

---

[48] All manhood. [49] Calculate a horoscope.
[50] The same or another room or courtyard.
[51] Learn something.

[52] Making an astrological calculation. Losers often tried to recover property through astrology.
[53] I.e., is the problem capable of solution by astrology?
[54] Here Bosola doubtless "makes the fig"; it was an obscene gesture.
[55] Opinion.
[56] Alluding to the fable of the countryman who warmed the frozen snake and was bitten.
[57] The meaning is not clear, and the text may be imperfect. Perhaps Antonio means, "You are apt at sharp statements (such as this false one that you can ruin me)"; to which Bosola replies, "It's not false; write it out, and I'll sign it (as true)."
[58] Worked, embroidered—on his initialed handkerchief.
[59] Give.

I' th' morn you shall be safe.[60]—(*Aside*) 'T is that must
color
Her lying-in.—Sir, this door you pass not.
I do not hold it fit that you come near
The Duchess' lodgings, till you have quit[61] yourself.—   50
(*Aside*) The great are like the base; nay, they are the same,
When they seek shameful ways to avoid shame.   [*Exit*

BOS. Antonio hereabout did drop a paper.—
Some of your help, false friend[62]—Oh, here it is.
What 's here? a child's nativity calculated!   55
*The Duchess was delivered of a son, 'tween the hours twelve
and one in the night, Anno Dom. 1504*—that 's this year—
decimo nono Decembris—that 's this night—*taken according to
the meridian of Malfi*—that 's our duchy. Happy discovery!
—*The lord of the first house being combust in the ascend-*   [60
ant[63] *signifies short life; and Mars being in a human sign,*[64]
joined to the tail of the Dragon,[65] *in the eight*[66] *house, doth
threaten a violent death. Caetera non scrutantur.*[67]
Why, now 't is most apparent. This precise[68] fellow
Is the Duchess' bawd. I have it to my wish.   65
This is a parcel of intelligency
Our courtiers were cased up for. It needs must follow
That I must be committed, on pretence
Of poisoning her; which I 'll endure, and laugh at.
If one could find the father now! but that   70
Time will discover. Old Castruchio
I' th' morning posts to Rome; by him I 'll send
A letter that shall make her brothers' galls
O'erflow their livers. This was a thrifty way.
Though Lust do mask in ne'er so strange disguise,   75
She 's oft found witty, but is never wise.   [*Exit*

SCENE IV[69]

Enter CARDINAL *and* JULIA

CARD. Sit; thou art my best of wishes. Prithee, tell me
What trick didst thou invent to come to Rome
Without thy husband?

JULIA.   Why, my Lord, I told him
I came to visit an old anchorite[70]
Here, for devotion.

CARD.   Thou art a witty false one—   5
I mean, to him.

JULIA.   You have prevailed with me
Beyond my strongest thoughts; I would not now
Find you inconstant.

CARD.   Do not put thyself
To such a voluntary torture, which proceeds
Out of your own guilt.

JULIA.   How, my Lord?

CARD.   You fear   10
My constancy, because you have approved[71]
Those giddy and wild turnings in yourself.

JULIA. Did you e'er find them?

CARD.   Sooth, generally for women,[72]
A man might strive to make glass malleable
Ere he should make them fixed.

JULIA.   So, my Lord!   15

CARD. We had need go borrow that fantastic glass[73]
Invented by Galileo, the Florentine,
To view another spacious world i' th' moon,
And look to find a constant woman there.

JULIA. This is very well, my Lord.

CARD.   Why do you weep?   20
Are tears your justification? The selfsame tears
Will fall into your husband's bosom, lady,
With a loud protestation that you love him
Above the world. Come, I 'll love you wisely,
That 's jealously; since I am very certain   25
You cannot make me cuckold.

JULIA.   I 'll go home
To my husband.

CARD.   You may thank me, lady.
I have taken you off your melancholy perch,
Bore you upon my fist,[74] and showed you game,
And let you fly at it. I pray thee, kiss me.   30
When thou wast with thy husband, thou wast watched
Like a tame elephant—still you are to thank me—
Thou hadst only kisses from him and high feeding,
But what delight was that? 'T was just like one
That hath[75] a little fing'ring on the lute,   35
Yet cannot tune it—still you are to thank me.

JULIA. You told me of a piteous wound i' th' heart
And a sick liver, when you wooed me first,
And spake like one in physic.[76]

CARD.   Who 's that?—

Enter Servant

Rest firm; for my affectïon to thee,   40
Lightning moves slow to 't.[77]

---

60 Under arrest.   61 Acquitted.   62 The dark lantern.
63 See p. 456, note 24. *Combust* (burned up) means in astrology
    that the planet is obscured by its nearness to the sun.
64 I.e., one of the signs of the zodiac called after human beings,
    not animals.
65 The Dragon was the two parts of the moon's path, lying south
    of the sun's path, the tail being the *descending* part of the moon's
    path after it crosses the sun's.   66 Eighth.
67 Other things are not examined.   68 Puritanical.
69 Rome. The Cardinal's palace.   70 Hermit.

71 Experienced.   72 As for women in general.
73 The telescope, invented early in the seventeenth century, a
    hundred years after the supposed events of the play.
74 Like a falcon.   75 I.e., has learned.
76 I.e., under medical treatment.   77 In comparison with it.

SERV.   Madam, a gentleman
That 's come post from Malfi desires to see you.
  CARD. Let him enter; I 'll withdraw.   [Exit
  SERV.   He says
Your husband, old Castruchio, is come to Rome,
Most pitifully tired with riding post.   [Exit 45

Enter DELIO

JULIA. Signior Delio!—(Aside) 'T is one of my old
    suitors.
  DELIO. I was bold to come and see you.
  JULIA.   Sir, you are welcome.
  DELIO. Do you lie[78] here?
  JULIA.   Sure, your own experience
Will satisfy you no. Our Roman prelates
Do not keep lodging for ladies.
  DELIO.   Very well.   50
I have brought you no commendations from your
    husband,
For I know none by him.
  JULIA.   I hear he 's come to Rome.
  DELIO. I never knew man and beast, of[79] a horse and a
    knight,
So weary of each other. If he had had a good back,
He would have undertook to have borne his horse,   55
His breech was so pitifully sore.
  JULIA.   Your laughter
Is my pity.
  DELIO.   Lady, I know not whether
You want money; but I have brought you some.
  JULIA. From my husband?
  DELIO.   No, from mine own allowance.[80]
  JULIA. I must hear the condition, ere I be bound to take
    it.   60
  DELIO. Look on't, 'tis gold; hath it not a fine color?
  JULIA. I have a bird more beautiful.
  DELIO.   Try the sound on't.
  JULIA. A lute-string far exceeds it.
It hath no smell, like cassia, or civet;
Nor is it physical,[81] though some fond[82] doctors   65
Persuade us seethe 't in cullises.[83] I'll tell you,
This is a creature bred by—

Enter Servant

  SERV.   Your husband's come;
Hath delivered a letter to the Duke of Calabria
That, to my thinking, hath put him out of his wits. [Exit

JULIA. Sir, you hear.   70
Pray let me know your business and your suit,
As briefly as can be.
  DELIO.   With good speed. I would wish you,
At such time as you are nonresident
With your husband, my mistress.[84]
  JULIA. Sir, I'll go ask my husband if I shall,   75
And straight return your answer.   [Exit
  DELIO.   Very fine!
Is this her wit, or honesty, that speaks thus?
I heard one say the Duke was highly moved
With a letter sent from Malfi. I do fear
Antonio is betrayed. How fearfully   80
Shows his ambition now! Unfortunate fortune!
They pass through whirlpools, and deep woes do shun,
Who the event weigh[85] ere the action's done.   [Exit

SCENE V[86]

Enter CARDINAL, and FERDINAND with a letter

FERD. I have this night digged up a mandrake.[87]
  CARD.   Say you?
  FERD. And I am grown mad with't.
  CARD.   What's the prodigy?
  FERD. Read there: a sister damned; she's loose i' th'
    hilts,[88]
Grown a notorious strumpet.
  CARD.   Speak lower.
  FERD.   Lower!
Rogues do not whisper't now, but seek to publish't   5
(As servants do the bounty of their lords)
Aloud; and, with a covetous searching eye,
To mark who note them. Oh, confusion seize her!
She hath had most cunning bawds to serve her turn,
And more secure conveyances for lust   10
Than towns of garrison for service.
  CARD.   Is't possible?
Can this be certain?
  FERD.   Rhubarb, oh, for rhubarb,
To purge this choler![89] here's the cursèd day[90]
To prompt my memory; and here't shall stick
Till of her bleeding heart I make a sponge   15
To wipe it out.
  CARD.   Why do you make yourself
So wild a tempest?

---

[84] To become my mistress. Presumably Delio hopes to persuade
her to spy out the Cardinal's plans.
[85] Consider the outcome.   [86] The same or another room.
[87] To dig up this sinister root was to run the risk of insanity.
[88] I.e., unchaste.
[89] Yellow bile, which predisposed to anger.
[90] The incriminating horoscope sent by Bosola.

---

[78] Lodge.   [79] In the form of.   [80] Grant.
[81] Medicinal.   [82] Foolish.   [83] Boil it in broths.

FERD.   Would I could be one,
That I might toss her palace 'bout her ears,
Root up her goodly forests, blast her meads,
And lay her general territory as waste   20
As she hath done her honors.

CARD.   Shall our blood,
The royal blood of Aragon and Castile,
Be thus attainted?

FERD.   Apply desperate physic;
We must not now use balsamum,[91] but fire,
The smarting cupping-glass,[92] for that's the mean   25
To purge infected blood, such blood as hers.
There is a kind of pity in mine eye:
I'll give it to my handkercher; and now 'tis here,
I'll bequeath this to her bastard.

CARD.   What to do?

FERD. Why, to make soft lint for his mother's
          wounds,   30
When I have hewed her to pieces.

CARD.   Cursed creature!
Unequal nature, to place women's hearts
So far upon the left[93] side!

FERD.   Foolish men,
That e'er will trust their honor in a bark
Made of so slight weak bulrush as is woman,   35
Apt every minute to sink it!

CARD. Thus ignorance, when it hath purchased honor,
It cannot wield it.

FERD.   Methinks I see her laughing,
Excellent hyena! Talk to me somewhat, quickly,
Or my imagination will carry me   40
To see her in the shameful act of sin.

CARD. With whom?

FERD.   Happily[94] with some strong-
          thighed bargeman;
Or one o' th' wood-yard, that can quoit the sledge[95]
Or toss the bar; or else some lovely squire[96]
That carries coals up to her privy[97] lodgings.   45

CARD. You fly beyond your reason.

FERD.   Go to, mistress!

'Tis not your whore's milk that shall quench my wildfire,
But your whore's blood.

CARD. How idly shows this rage, which carries you
As men conveyed by witches through the air,   50
On violent whirlwinds! This intemperate noise
Fitly resembles deaf men's shrill discourse,
Who talk aloud, thinking all other men
To have their imperfection.

FERD.   Have not you
My palsy?

CARD.   Yes, yet I can be angry   55
Without this rupture.[98] There is not in nature
A thing that makes man so deformed, so beastly,
As doth intemperate anger. Chide yourself.
You have divers men who never yet expressed
Their strong desire of rest, but by unrest,   60
By vexing of themselves. Come, put yourself
In tune.

FERD.   So. I will only study to seem
The thing I am not. I could kill her now,
In you, or in myself; for I do think
It is some sin in us heaven doth revenge   65
By her.

CARD.   Are you stark mad?

FERD.   I would have their bodies
Burnt in a coal-pit with the ventage stopped,
That their cursed smoke might not ascend to heaven;
Or dip the sheets they lie in, in pitch or sulphur,
Wrap them in't, and then light them like a match;   70
Or else to-boil[99] their bastard to a cullis,
And give't his lecherous father, to renew
The sin of his back.

CARD.   I'll leave you.

FERD.   Nay, I have done.
I am confident, had I been damned in hell
And should have heard of this, it would have put me   75
Into a cold sweat. In, in; I'll go sleep.
Till I know who leaps my sister, I'll not stir;
That known, I'll find scorpions to string my whips,
And fix her in a general eclipse.   [*Exeunt*

---

[91] Balm.
[92] Used in bleeding a patient.   [93] Or ill-omened.
[94] Haply, perhaps.   [95] Throw the hammer.   [96] Fellow.
[97] Private.

[98] Breaking out.   [99] Boil down.

ACT III

Enter ANTONIO *and* DELIO

ANT. Our noble friend, my most belovèd Delio!
Oh, you have been a stranger long at court.
Came you along with the Lord Ferdinand?

DELIO. I did, sir; and how fares your noble Duchess?

ANT. Right fortunately well; she's an excellent   5
Feeder of pedigrees: since you last saw her,
She hath had two children more, a son and daughter.

DELIO. Methinks 'twas yesterday; let me but wink,
And not behold your face—which to mine eye
Is somewhat leaner—verily I should dream   10
It were within this half hour.

ANT. You have not been in law, friend Delio,
Nor in prison, nor a suitor at the court,
Nor begged the reversion of some great man's place,
Nor troubled with an old wife, which doth make   15
Your time so insensibly hasten.

DELIO.   Pray, sir, tell me,
Hath not this news arrived yet to the ear
Of the Lord Cardinal?

ANT.   I fear it hath.
The Lord Ferdinand, that's newly come to court,
Doth bear himself right dangerously.

DELIO.   Pray, why?   20

ANT. He is so quiet that he seems to sleep
The tempest out, as dormice do in winter.
Those houses that are haunted are most still,
Till the Devil be up.

DELIO.   What say the common people?

ANT. The common rabble do directly say   25
She is a strumpet.

DELIO.   And your[2] graver heads,
Which would be politic, what censure they?[3]

ANT. They do observe I grow to infinite purchase[4]
The left-hand way; and all suppose the Duchess
Would amend it, if she could. For, say they,   30
Great princes, though they grudge their officers
Should have such large and unconfinèd means
To get wealth under them, will not complain,
Lest thereby they should make them odious
Unto the people. For other obligation,   35
Of love or marriage between her and me,
They never dream of.

DELIO.   The Lord Ferdinand
Is going to bed.

Enter DUCHESS, FERDINAND, *and* BOSOLA

FERD.   I 'll instantly to bed,
For I am weary.—I am to bespeak
A husband for you.

DUCH.   For me, sir! Pray, who is 't?   40

FERD. The great Count Malateste.

DUCH.   Fie upon him!
A count! He's a mere stick of sugar-candy;
You may look quite thorough[5] him. When I choose
A husband, I will marry for your honor.

FERD. You shall do well in 't.—How is 't, worthy
Antonio?   45

DUCH. But, sir, I am to have private conference with
you
About a scandalous report is spread
Touching mine honor.

FERD.   Let me be ever deaf to 't—
One of Pasquil's[6] paper-bullets, court-calumny,
A pestilent air, which princes' palaces   50
Are seldom purged of. Yet, say that it were true,
I pour it in your bosom my fixed love
Would strongly excuse, extenuate, nay, deny
Faults, were they apparent in you. Go, be safe
In your own innocency.

DUCH. (*aside*).   O blessed comfort!   55
This deadly air is purged.

          [*Exeunt all but* FERDINAND *and* BOSOLA

FERD. (*aside*).   Her guilt treads on
Hot-burning colters.[7]—Now, Bosola,
How thrives our intelligence?[8]

BOS.   Sir, uncertainly.
'T is rumored she hath had three bastards, but
By whom we may go read i' th' stars.

FERD.   Why, some   60
Hold opinion all things are written there.

BOS. Yes, if we could find spectacles to read them.
I do suspect there hath been some sorcery
Used on the Duchess.

FERD.   Sorcery! to what purpose?

BOS. To make her dote on some desertless fellow   65
She shames to acknowledge.

FERD.   Can your faith give way
To think there 's pow'r in potions or in charms,
To make us love whether we will or no?

BOS. Most certainly.

---

[5] Through.
[6] To a statue thus called the Romans of the Renaissance used to
attach satirical verses or pasquinades.
[7] The colter is the knife in front of the plowshare. The reference
is to the old trial by ordeal.   [8] Spying.

FERD. Away! these are mere gulleries,[9] horrid
    things,   70
Invented by some cheating mountebanks
To abuse us. Do you think that herbs or charms
Can force the will?[10] Some trials have been made
In this foolish practice, but the ingredients
Were lenitive[11] poisons, such as are of force   75
To make the patient mad; and straight the witch
Swears by equivocation[12] they are in love.
The witchcraft lies in her rank blood.[13] This night
I will force confession from her. You told me
You had got, within these two days, a false key   80
Into her bedchamber.

BOS.   I have.

FERD.   As I would wish.

BOS. What do you intend to do?

FERD.   Can you guess?

BOS.   No.

FERD.   Do not ask, then.
He that can compass[14] me, and know my drifts,[15]
May say he hath put a girdle 'bout the world,
And sounded all her quicksands.

BOS.   I do not   85
Think so.

FERD.   What do you think, then, pray?

BOS.   That you
Are your own chronicle too much, and grossly
Flatter yourself.

FERD.   Give me thy hand; I thank thee.
I never gave pension but to flatterers,
Till I entertainèd thee. Farewell.   90
That friend a great man's ruin strongly checks,
Who rails into his belief all his defects.

                               [*Exeunt*

SCENE II[16]

Enter DUCHESS, ANTONIO, *and* CARIOLA

DUCH. Bring me the casket hither, and the glass.—
You get no lodging here tonight, my Lord.

ANT. Indeed, I must persuade one.

DUCH.   Very good!
I hope in time 't will grow into a custom,
That noblemen shall come with cap and knee   5
To purchase a night's lodging of their wives.

ANT. I must lie here.

DUCH.   Must? You are a Lord of Misrule.[17]

ANT. Indeed, my rule is only in the night.

DUCH. To what use will you put me?

ANT.   We 'll sleep together.

DUCH. Alas, what pleasure can two lovers find in
    sleep?   10

CARI. My Lord, I lie with her often; and I know
She 'll much disquiet you—

ANT.   See, you are complained of.

CARI. For she 's the sprawling'st bedfellow.

ANT. I shall like her the better for that.

CARI. Sir, shall I ask you a question?   15

ANT. I pray thee, Cariola.

CARI. Wherefore still when[18] you lie with my lady
Do you rise so early?

ANT.   Laboring men
Count the clock oft'nest, Cariola,
Are glad when their task 's ended.

DUCH.   I 'll stop your mouth. [*Kisses him* 20

ANT. Nay, that 's but one; Venus had two soft doves
To draw her chariot: I must have another.—   [*Kisses her*
When wilt thou marry, Cariola?

CARI.   Never, my Lord.

ANT. O, fie upon this single life! forgo it.
We read how Daphne, for her peevish slight,[19]   25
Became a fruitless bay tree; Syrinx turned
To the pale empty reed;[20] Anaxarete
Was frozen into marble:[21] whereas those
Which married, or proved kind unto their friends,[22]
Were by a gracious influence[23] transshaped   30
Into the olive, pomegranate, mulberry,
Became flow'rs, precious stones, or eminent stars.

CARI. This is a vain poetry; but, I pray you, tell me,
If there were proposed me wisdom, riches, and beauty,
In three several young men, which should I choose?   35

ANT. 'T is a hard question. This was Paris' case,
And he was blind in 't, and there was great cause;
For how was 't possible he could judge right,
Having three amorous goddesses in view,
And they stark naked? 'T was a motiön[24]   40
Were able to benight the apprehension
Of the severest counsellor of Europe.
Now I look on both your faces so well formed,
It puts me in mind of a question I would ask.

CARI. What is 't?

ANT.   I do wonder why hard-favored[25] ladies,
For the most part, keep worse-favored waiting-women 46
To attend them, and cannot endure fair ones.

DUCH. Oh, that 's soon answered.
Did you ever in your life know an ill painter

---

[9] Cheats.   [10] Desire.   [11] Softening.
[12] A quibble—such as that lovers are all crazy.
[13] Wanton passions.   [14] Comprehend.   [15] Purposes.
[16] The Duchess's bedchamber.
[17] Who presided over Christmas revels.

[18] Whenever.   [19] When wooed by Apollo.
[20] From which Pan, her wooer, made his pipe.
[21] When her rejected lover hanged himself at her door.
[22] Lovers.   [23] The gods'.   [24] Puppet show, spectacle.
[25] Homely.

Desire to have his dwelling next door to the shop   50
Of an excellent picture-maker? 'T would disgrace
His face-making, and undo him. I prithee,
When were we so merry? My hair tangles.

    ANT. (*aside*). Pray thee, Cariola, let 's steal forth the
      room,
And let her talk to herself. I have divers times   55
Served her the like, when she hath chafed extremely—
I love to see her angry. Softly, Cariola.

                  [*Exeunt* ANTONIO *and* CARIOLA
    DUCH. Doth not the color of my hair 'gin to change?
When I wax gray, I shall have all the court
Powder their hair with arras,[26] to be like me.   60
You have cause to love me; I ent'red you into my heart

    Enter FERDINAND *unseen*

Before you would vouchsafe to call for the keys.
We shall one day have my brothers take you napping.
Methinks his presence, being now in court,
Should make you keep your own bed; but you 'll say   65
Love mixed with fear is sweetest. I 'll assure you,
You shall get no more children till my brothers
Consent to be your gossips.[27] Have you lost your
    tongue?—
'T is welcome.
For know, whether I am doomed to live or die,   70
I can do both like a prince.

    FERD.   Die, then, quickly.

               [FERDINAND *gives her a poniard*
Virtue, where art thou hid? What hideous thing
Is it that doth eclipse thee?

    DUCH.   Pray, sir, hear me.

    FERD. Or is it true thou art but a bare name,
And no essential thing?

    DUCH.   Sir!

    FERD.   Do not speak.   75
    DUCH. No, sir.
I will plant my soul in mine ears, to hear you.

    FERD. O most imperfect light of human reason,
That mak'st us so unhappy to[28] foresee
What we can least prevent! Pursue thy wishes,   80
And glory in them; there's in shame no comfort,
But to be past all bounds and sense of shame.

    DUCH. I pray, sir, hear me. I am married.

    FERD.   So!

    DUCH. Happily not to your liking; but for that,
Alas, your shears do come untimely now   85
To clip the bird's wings that's already flown.
Will you see my husband?

    FERD.   Yes, if I could change
Eyes with a basilisk.[29]

    DUCH.   Sure, you came hither
By his confederacy.

    FERD.   The howling of a wolf
Is music to[30] thee, screech owl; prithee, peace.—   90
Whate'er thou art that hast enjoyed my sister
(For I am sure thou hear'st me), for thine own sake
Let me not know thee. I came hither prepared
To work thy discovery; yet am now persuaded
It would beget such violent effects   95
As would damn us both. I would not for ten millions
I had beheld thee. Therefore use all means
I never may have knowledge of thy name.
Enjoy thy lust still, and a wretched life,
On that condition.—And for thee, vild woman,   100
If thou do wish thy lecher may grow old
In thy embracements, I would have thee build
Such a room for him as our anchorites
To holier use inhabit. Let not the sun
Shine on him, till he's dead. Let dogs and monkeys   105
Only converse with him, and such dumb things
To whom nature denies use to sound his name.
Do not keep a paraquito,[31] lest she learn it;
If thou do love him, cut out thine own tongue
Lest it bewray him.

    DUCH.   Why might not I marry?   110
I have not gone about in this to create
Any new world or custom.

    FERD.   Thou art undone;
And thou hast ta'en that massy sheet of lead
That hid thy husband's bones, and folded it
About my heart.

    DUCH.   Mine bleeds for't.

    FERD.   Thine! thy heart!   115
What should I name't, unless a hollow bullet
Filled with unquenchable wildfire?[32]

    DUCH.   You are in this
Too strict; and were you not my princely brother,
I would say too willful. My reputation
Is safe.

    FERD.   Dost thou know what reputation is?   120
I'll tell thee—to small purpose, since th' instruction
Comes now too late.
Upon a time Reputation, Love, and Death
Would travel o'er the world; and it was concluded
That they should part, and take three several ways.   125
Death told them they should find him in great battles,
Or cities plagued with plagues. Love gives them counsel
To inquire for him 'mongst unambitious shepherds,

[26] Or orris, a powder made from the root of a kind of iris.
[27] Sponsors at the christening of your children.   [28] As to.

[29] The fabulous serpent whose glance was fatal.
[30] In comparison with.   [31] Parakeet, a kind of parrot.
[32] A cannon shell.

Where dowries were not talked of, and sometimes
'Mongst quiet kindred, that had nothing left   130
By their dead parents. "Stay," quoth Reputation,
"Do not forsake me; for it is my nature
If once I part from any man I meet,
I am never found again." And so, for you.
You have shook hands with[33] Reputation,   135
And made him invisible. So fare you well;
I will never see you more.
    DUCH.   Why should only I,
Of all the other princes of the world,
Be cased up, like a holy relic? I have youth,
And a little beauty.
    FERD.   So you have some virgins   140
That are witches. I will never see thee more.   [Exit

Enter ANTONIO *with a pistol, and* CARIOLA

    DUCH. You saw this apparition?
    ANT.   Yes. We are
Betrayed. How came he hither?—(*To* CARIOLA) I should
    turn
This[34] to thee, for that.
    CARI.   Pray, sir, do; and when
That you have cleft my heart, you shall read there   145
Mine innocence.
    DUCH.   That gallery gave him entrance.
    ANT. I would this terrible thing would come again,
That, standing on my guard, I might relate
My warrantable love. Ha! what means this?
                       [*She shows the poniard*
    DUCH. He left this with me.
    ANT.   And it seems, did wish   150
You would use it on yourself.
    DUCH.   His action seemed
To intend so much.
    ANT.   This hath a handle to't,
As well as a point. Turn it towards him, and
So fasten the keen edge in his rank gall.   [*Knocking within*
How now! who knocks? more earthquakes?
    DUCH.   I stand   155
As if a mine beneath my feet were ready
To be blown up.
    CARI.   'Tis Bosola.
    DUCH.   Away!
Oh, misery! methinks unjust actions
Should wear these masks and curtains, and not we.
You must instantly part hence; I have fashioned it already.
                       [*Exit* ANTONIO

Enter BOSOLA

    BOS. The Duke your brother is ta'en up in a whirl-
    wind—   161
Hath took horse, and's rid post to Rome.
    DUCH.   So late?
    BOS. He told me, as he mounted into th' saddle,
You were undone.
    DUCH.   Indeed, I am very near it.
    BOS. What's the matter?
    DUCH.   Antonio, the master of our household,   165
Hath dealt so falsely with me in's accounts.
My brother stood engaged with me for money
Ta'en up of[35] certain Neapolitan Jews;
And Antonio lets the bonds be forfeit.[36]
    BOS.   Strange!—
    (*Aside*) This is cunning.
    DUCH.   And hereupon   170
My brother's bills[37] at Naples are protested
Against. Call up our officers.
    BOS.   I shall.   [*Exit*

Re-enter ANTONIO

    DUCH. The place that you must fly to is Ancona.
Hire a house there. I'll send after you
My treasure and my jewels. Our weak safety   175
Runs upon enginous[38] wheels; short syllables
Must stand for periods.[39] I must now accuse you
Of such a feignèd crime as Tasso[40] calls
Magnanima menzogna, a noble lie,
'Cause it must shield our honors.—Hark, they are
    coming.   180

Re-enter BOSOLA, *with* Officers

    ANT. Will your grace hear me?
    DUCH. I have got well by you; you have yielded me
A million of loss. I am like to inherit
The people's curses for your stewardship.
You had the trick in audit-time to be sick,   185
Till I had signed your quietus; and that cured you
Without help of a doctor.—Gentlemen,
I would have this man be an example to you all;
So shall you hold my favor. I pray, let him.[41]
For 'has done that, alas, you would not think of.   190
And, because I intend to be rid of him,
I mean not to publish.—Use your fortune elsewhere.

[35] Borrowed from—the Duke having endorsed the Duchess's
notes.
[36] I.e., by failing to make some payment.—*Bonds* = notes.
[37] Notes.
[38] I.e., swift and complicated.—*Runs on wheels* = moves fast.
[39] Sentences.   [40] In *Jerusalem Delivered,* II, 22.
[41] Let him go.

[33] Parted from.   [34] The pistol.

ANT. I am strongly armed to brook my overthrow,
As commonly men bear with a hard year.
I will not blame the cause on't, but do think   195
The necessity of my malevolent star
Procures this, not her humor.[42] Oh, the inconstant
And rotten ground of service, you may see.
'Tis ev'n like him that in a winter night
Takes a long slumber o'er a dying fire,   200
As loath to part from't, yet parts thence as cold
As when he first sat down.
    DUCH.   We do confiscate,
Towards the satisfying of your accounts,
All that you have.
    ANT.   I am all yours; and 'tis very fit
All mine should be so.
    DUCH.   So, sir, you have your pass.   205
    ANT. You may see, gentlemen, what 'tis to serve
A prince with body and soul.   [*Exit*
    BOS. Here's an example for extortion: what moisture
is drawn out of the sea, when foul weather comes pours
down and runs into the sea again.   210
    DUCH. I would know what are your opinions
Of this Antonio.
    2ND OFF. He could not abide to see a pig's head gaping;
I thought your Grace would find him a Jew.
    3RD OFF. I would you had been his officer, for your   [215
own sake.
    4TH OFF. You would have had more money.
    1ST OFF. He stopped his ears with black wool, and to
those came to him for money said he was thick of hearing.
    2ND OFF. Some said he was an hermaphrodite,   [220
for he could not abide a woman.
    4TH OFF. How scurvy proud he would look when the
treasury was full! Well, let him go.
    1ST OFF. Yes, and the chippings[43] of the buttery fly after
him, to scour his gold chain.[44]   225
    DUCH. Leave us.—   [*Exeunt* Officers
             What do you think of these?
    BOS. That these are rogues that in 's prosperity,
But to have waited on his fortune, could have wished
His dirty stirrup riveted through their noses,
And followed after 's mule, like a bear in a ring;   230
Would have prostituted their daughters to his lust,
Made their first-born intelligencers, thought none happy
But such as were born under his blest planet
And wore his livery. And do these lice drop off now?
Well, never look to have the like again.   235
He hath left a sort[45] of flatt'ring rogues behind him;
Their doom must follow. Princes pay flatterers

In their own money; flatterers dissemble their vices,
And they dissemble their lies: that 's justice.
Alas, poor gentleman!
    DUCH.   Poor! he hath amply filled his coffers.   240
    BOS. Sure he was too honest. Pluto,[46] the god of riches,
When he 's sent by Jupiter to any man,
He goes limping, to signify that wealth
That comes on God's name comes slowly; but when
    he 's sent
On the Devil's errand, he rides post and comes in by
    scuttles.[47]   245
Let me show you what a most unvalued[48] jewel
You have in a wanton humor thrown away,
To bless the man shall[49] find him. He was an excellent
Courtier and most faithful, a soldier that thought it
As beastly to know his own value too little   250
As devilish to acknowledge it too much.
Both his virtue and form deserved a far better fortune.
His discourse rather delighted to judge itself than show
    itself:
His breast was filled with all perfectiön,
And yet it seemed a private whisp'ring-room,   255
It made so little noise of 't.
    DUCH. But he was basely descended.
    BOS. Will you make yourself a mercenary herald,
Rather to examine men's pedigrees than virtues?
You shall want[50] him.   260
For know, an honest statesman to a prince
Is like a cedar planted by a spring;
The spring bathes the tree's root, the grateful tree
Rewards it with his shadow. You have not done so.
I would sooner swim to the Bermoothes[51] on   265
Two politicians' rotten bladders, tied
Together with an intelligencer's heartstring,
Than depend on so changeable a prince's favor.—
Fare thee well, Antonio! Since the malice of the world
Would needs down with thee, it cannot be said yet   270
That any ill happened unto thee, considering thy fall
Was accompanied with virtue.
    DUCH. Oh, you render me excellent music!
    BOS.   Say you?
    DUCH. This good one that you speak of is my husband.
    BOS. Do I not dream? Can this ambitious age   275
Have so much goodness in 't as to prefer[52]
A man merely for worth, without these shadows
Of wealth and painted honors? Possible?
    DUCH. I have had three children by him.
    BOS.   Fortunate lady!
For you have made your private nuptial bed   280

---

[42] Whim.   [43] Bread crumbs—used to clean gold.
[44] Worn officially by stewards.   [45] Set.

[46] *Plutus* is the correct name.   [47] I.e., running.
[48] Invaluable.   [49] Who shall.   [50] Feel the lack of.
[51] Bermudas.   [52] Promote, raise.

The humble and fair seminary[53] of peace—
No question but. Many an unbeneficed[54] scholar
Shall pray for you for this deed, and rejoice
That some preferment in the world can yet
Arise from merit. The virgins of your land   285
That have no dowries shall hope your example
Will raise them to rich husbands. Should you want
Soldiers, 't would make the very Turks and Moors
Turn Christians and serve you for this act.
Last, the neglected poets of your time,   290
In honor of this trophy[55] of a man,
Raised by that curious engine,[56] your white hand,
Shall thank you in your grave for 't, and make that
More reverend than all the cabinets[57]
Of living princes. For Antonio,   295
His fame shall likewise flow from many a pen,
When heralds shall want coats to sell to men.[58]
    DUCH. As I taste comfort in this friendly speech,
So would I find concealment.
    BOS.   Oh, the secret of my prince,
Which I will wear on th' inside of my heart!   300
    DUCH. You shall take charge of all my coin and
        jewels,
And follow him; for he retires himself
To Ancona.
    BOS.   So.
    DUCH.   Whither, within few days,
I mean to follow thee.
    BOS.   Let me think.
I would wish your Grace to feign a pilgrimage   305
To our Lady of Loretto,[59] scarce seven leagues
From fair Ancona; so may you depart
Your country with more honor, and your flight
Will seem a princely progress, retaining
Your usual train about you.
    DUCH.   Sir, your direction   310
Shall lead me by the hand.
    CARI.   In my opinion,
She were better progress to the baths at Lucca,
Or go visit the Spa
In Germany;[60] for, if you will believe me,
I do not like this jesting with religion,   315
This feignèd pilgrimage.
    DUCH.   Thou art a superstitious fool!
Prepare us instantly for our departure.
Past sorrows, let us moderately lament them;
For those to come, seek wisely to prevent them.
                [Exit DUCHESS with CARIOLA

----

53 Seed-plot.   54 Jobless.   55 Prize.
56 Remarkable instrument.   57 Council chambers.
58 A current scandal was the readiness of the college of heralds
    to grant coats of arms, for bribes, to unqualified persons.
59 A famous shrine.   60 Now Belgium.

    BOS. A politician is the Devil's quilted anvil: 320
He fashions all sins on him, and the blows
Are never heard; he may work in a lady's chamber
(As here, for proof). What rests[61] but I reveal
All to my Lord? Oh, this base quality[62]
Of intelligencer! Why, every quality i' th' world   325
Prefers but gain or commendatiön.
Now for this act I am certain to be raised,
And men that paint weeds, to the life, are praised.   [Exit

SCENE III[63]

Enter CARDINAL, FERDINAND, MALATESTE, PESCARA,
SILVIO, and DELIO

    CARD. Must we turn soldier, then?
    MAL.   The Emperor,[64]
Hearing your worth that way (ere you attained
This reverend garment), joins you in commission
With the right fortunate soldier, the Marquess of Pescara,[65]
And the famous Lannoy.[66]
    CARD.   He that had the honor   5
Of taking the French king[67] prisoner?
    MAL.   The same.
Here 's a plot[68] drawn for a new fortification
At Naples.
    FERD.   This great Count Malateste,[69] I perceive,
Hath got employment?
    DELIO.   No employment, my Lord;
A marginal note in the muster-book that he is   10
A voluntary lord.[70]
    FERD.   He 's no soldier?
    DELIO. He has worn gunpowder in 's hollow tooth for
        the toothache.
    SIL. He comes to the leaguer with a full intent
To eat fresh beef and garlic, means to stay
Till the scent be gone, and straight return to court.   15
    DELIO. He hath read all the late service
As the City Chronicle[71] relates it;
And keeps two pewterers going, only to express
Battles in model.[72]
    SIL.   Then he 'll fight by the book.[73]

----

61 Remains.   62 Profession.
63 Rome. The Cardinal's palace.   64 Charles V.
65 The historical Marquis (d. 1525) was Ferdinand's brother-in-
    law.
66 The historical Charles de Lannoy (d. 1527) was viceroy of
    Naples.   67 Francis I, at the battle of Pavia (1525).
68 Plan.
69 Not a historical character.—He goes on talking with the Car-
    dinal and does not hear this conversation.
70 I.e., a gentleman volunteer.
71 Written up by a city official.
72 I.e., by means of toy soldiers.
73 I.e., according to his reading, instead of experience.

DELIO. By the almanac, I think:
To choose good days and shun the critical.
That 's his mistress' scarf.

SIL.   Yes, he protests
He would do much for that taffeta.

DELIO. I think he would run away from a battle
To save it from taking[74] prisoner.

SIL.   He is horribly afraid 25
Gunpowder will spoil the perfume on 't.

DELIO. I saw a Dutchman break his pate once
For calling him a pot-gun;[75] he made his head
Have a bore in 't like a musket.

SIL. I would he had made a touchhole[76] to 't.   30
He is indeed a guarded[77] sumpter-cloth,[78]
Only for the remove of the court.

Enter BOSOLA[79]

PES. Bosola arrived! What should be the business?
Some falling-out amongst the cardinals.
These factions amongst great men, they are like   35
Foxes: when their heads are divided,
They carry fire in their tails;[80] and all the country
About them goes to wrack for 't.

SIL.   What 's that Bosola?

DELIO. I knew him in Padua—a fantastical scholar, like
such who study to know how many knots was in   [40
Hercules' club, of what color Achilles' beard was, or
whether Hector were not troubled with the toothache.
He hath studied himself half blear-eyed to know the true
symmetry of Caesar's nose by a shoeinghorn; and this he
did to gain the name of a speculative man.   45

PES. Mark Prince Ferdinand:
A very salamander lives in 's eye,
To mock the eager violence of fire.

SIL. That Cardinal hath made more bad faces with his
oppression[81] than ever Michael Angelo made good   [50
ones. He lifts up 's nose, like a foul porpoise before a storm.

PES. The Lord Ferdinand laughs.

DELIO.   Like a deadly cannon
That lightens ere it smokes.

PES. These are your true pangs of death,
The pangs of life that struggle with great statesmen.   55

DELIO. In such a deformed silence, witches whisper their
charms.

---

[74] Being taken.   [75] Popgun; i.e., full of wind, a braggart.
[76] The vent through which fire reached the charge of powder.
[77] Decorated, fancy.
[78] Ornamental cloth for horse or mule.
[79] He reports to the Cardinal and the Duke, while the courtiers
talk aside.
[80] Samson's method of burning the Philistines' standing grain
(Judges 15:4).   [81] From the stress of his emotion.

CARD. Doth she make religion her riding-hood
To keep her from the sun and tempest?

FERD. That, that damns her. Methinks her fault and
beauty,
Blended together, show like leprosy,   60
The whiter the fouler. I make it a question
Whether her beggarly brats were ever christ'ned.

CARD. I will instantly solicit the state of Ancona
To have them banished.

FERD.   You are for Loretto?
I shall not be at your ceremony; fare you well.—   65
Write to the Duke of Malfi, my young nephew
She had by her first husband, and acquaint him
With 's mother's honesty.[82]

BOS.   I will.

FERD.   Antonio!
A slave, that only smelled of ink and counters,[83]
And never in 's life looked like a gentleman   70
But in the audit-time.—Go, go presently,
Draw me out an hundreth and fifty of our horse,
And meet me at the fort-bridge.[84]   [*Exeunt*

SCENE IV[85]

Enter two PILGRIMS *to the shrine of Our Lady of
Loretto*

1 PIL. I have not seen a goodlier shrine than this;
Yet I have visited many.

2 PIL.   The Cardinal of Aragon
Is this day to resign his cardinal's hat.
His sister Duchess likewise is arrived
To pay her vow of pilgrimage. I expect   5
A noble ceremony.

1 PIL.   No question. They come.

Here the ceremony of the CARDINAL'S *instalment, in the
habit of a soldier, performed in delivering up his cross, hat,
robes, and ring, at the shrine, and investing him with sword,
helmet, shield, and spurs: then* ANTONIO, *the* DUCHESS, *and
their* Children, *having presented themselves at the shrine, are,
by a form of banishment in dumb show expressed towards them
by the* CARDINAL *and the state of Ancona, banished. During all
which ceremony, this ditty is sung, to very solemn music, by
divers churchmen, and then exeunt.*

Arms and honors deck thy story,[86]
To thy fame's eternal glory;
Adverse Fortune ever fly thee,
No disastrous fate come nigh thee.   10

---

[82] Chastity.   [83] Used in figuring up accounts.
[84] Drawbridge.   [85] Loretto. The shrine.
[86] "The author disclaims this ditty to be his" (marginal note in
the quarto of 1623).

I alone will sing thy praises,
Whom to honor virtue raises;
And thy study, that divine is,
Bent to martial discipline is.
Lay aside all those robes lie by thee;   15
Crown thy arts with arms: they'll beautify thee.

O worthy of worthiest name, adorned in this manner,
Lead bravely thy forces on, under war's warlike banner.
Oh, mayst thou prove fortunate in all martial courses;
Guide thou still by skill in arts and forces.   20
Victory attend thee nigh, whilst fame sings loud thy
    powers;
Triumphant conquest crown thy head, and blessings pour
    down showers!

I PIL. Here's a strange turn of state! who would have
    thought
So great a lady would have matched herself
Unto so mean a person? Yet the Cardinal   25
Bears himself much too cruel.
2 PIL.   They are banished.
I PIL. But I would ask what power hath this state
Of Ancona, to determine of a free prince?
2 PIL. They are a free state, sir, and her brother showed
How that the Pope, forehearing of her looseness,   30
Hath seized into the protection of the Church
The dukedom, which she held as dowager.
I PIL. But by what justice?
2 PIL.   Sure, I think by none,
Only her brother's instigatiön.
I PIL. What was it with such violence he took   35
Off from her finger?
2 PIL.   'Twas her wedding ring,
Which he vowed shortly he would sacrifice
To his revenge.
I PIL.   Alas, Antonio!
If that a man be thrust into a well,
No matter who sets hand to't, his own weight   40
Will bring him sooner to th' bottom. Come, let's hence.
Fortune makes this conclusion general:
All things do help th' unhappy[87] man to fall.   [Exeunt

SCENE V[88]

Enter DUCHESS, ANTONIO, Children, CARIOLA, and
Servants

DUCH. Banished Ancona!
ANT.   Yes, you see what pow'r
Lightens in great men's breath.

DUCH.   Is all our train
Shrunk to this poor remainder?
ANT.   These poor men,
Which have got little in your service, vow
To take[89] your fortune; but your wiser buntings,[90]   5
Now they are fledged, are gone.
DUCH.   They have done wisely.
This puts me in mind of death; physicians thus,
With their hands full of money, use to give o'er[91]
Their patients.
ANT.   Right[92] the fashion of the world:
From decayed fortunes every flatterer shrinks;   10
Men cease to build, where the foundation sinks.
DUCH. I had a very strange dream tonight.[93]
ANT.   What was't?
DUCH. Methought I wore my coronet of state,
And on a sudden all the diamonds
Were changed to pearls.
ANT.   My interpretation   15
Is you'll weep shortly, for to me the pearls
Do signify your tears.
DUCH.   The birds, that live i' th' field
On the wild benefit of nature, live
Happier than we; for they may choose their mates,
And carol their sweet pleasures to the spring.   20

Enter BOSOLA, with a letter

BOS. You are happily o'erta'en.
DUCH.   From my brother?
BOS. Yes, from the Lord Ferdinand, your brother,
All love and safety—
DUCH.   Thou dost blanch mischief,
Wouldst make it white. See, see; like to calm weather
At sea before a tempest, false hearts speak fair   25
To those they intend most mischief.   [Reads the letter
"Send Antonio to me; I want his head in a business."
A politic equivocatiön![94]
He doth not want your counsel, but your head;
That is, he cannot sleep till you be dead.   30
And here's another pitfall that's strewed o'er
With roses; mark it, 'tis a cunning one: [Reads
"I stand engaged for your husband, for several debts
at Naples. Let not that trouble him; I had rather have
his heart than his money."   [35
And I believe so, too.
BOS.   What do you believe?
DUCH. That he so much distrusts my husband's love
He will by no means believe his heart is with him,

87 Unfortunate.   88 A road, near Loretto.

89 Accept, share.   90 A kind of bird.
91 Are accustomed to give up.
92 Exactly.   93 Last night.
94 Ambiguous use of words.

Until he see it. The Devil is not cunning enough
To circumvent us in riddles.   40
  BOS. Will you reject that noble and free league
Of amity and love which I present you?
  DUCH. Their league is like that of some politic kings,
Only to make themselves of strength and pow'r
To be our after-ruin. Tell them so.   45
  BOS. And what from you?
  ANT.   Thus tell him; I will not come.
  BOS. And what of this?
  ANT.   My brothers have dispersed
Bloodhounds abroad; which till I hear are muzzled,
No truce, though hatched with ne'er such politic skill,
Is safe, that hangs upon our enemies' will.   50
I'll not come at them.
  BOS.   This proclaims your breeding.
Every small thing draws a base mind to fear,
As the adamant[95] draws iron. Fare you well, sir.
You shall shortly hear from 's.   [Exit
  DUCH.   I suspect some ambush.
Therefore, by all my love I do conjure you   55
To take your eldest son and fly towards Milan.
Let us not venture all this poor remainder
In one unlucky bottom.[96]
  ANT.   You counsel safely.
Best of my life, farewell. Since we must part,
Heaven hath a hand in 't; but no otherwise   60
Than as some curious artist[97] takes in sunder
A clock or watch, when it is out of frame,
To bring 't in better order.
  DUCH.   I know not which is best:
To see you dead, or part with you.—Farewell, boy.
Thou art happy that thou hast not understanding   65
To know thy misery. For all our wit
And reading brings us to a truer sense
Of sorrow.—In the eternal Church, sir,
I do hope we shall not part thus.
  ANT.   Oh, be of comfort.
Make patïence a noble fortitude,   70
And think not how unkindly we are used.
Man, like to cassia, is proved best, being bruised.
  DUCH. Must I, like to a slave-born Russiän,
Account it praise to suffer tyranny?
And yet, O heaven, thy heavy hand is in 't.   75
I have seen my little boy oft scourge his top,
And compared myself to 't: naught made me e'er
Go right but heaven's scourge-stick.[98]
  ANT.   Do not weep.
Heaven fashioned us of nothing; and we strive,
To bring ourselves to nothing.—Farewell, Cariola,   80

---

[95] Magnet.   [96] Ship.   [97] Painstaking craftsman.
[98] Whip for the top.

And thy sweet armful.—If I do never see thee more,
Be a good mother to your little ones,
And save them from the tiger. Fare you well.
  DUCH. Let me look upon you once more, for that
    speech
Came from a dying father. Your kiss is colder   85
Than that I have seen an holy anchorite
Give to a dead man's skull.
  ANT. My heart is turned to a heavy lump of lead,[99]
With which I sound my danger. Fare you well.
                              [Exit with his son
  DUCH. My laurel is all withered.   90
  CARI. Look, madam, what a troop of armèd men
Make toward us.

    Enter BOSOLA, masked, with a Guard

  DUCH.   Oh, they are very welcome:
When Fortune's wheel is overcharged[100] with princes,
The weight makes it move swift: I would have my
    ruin
Be sudden.—I am your adventure,[101] am I not?   95
  BOS. You are; you must see your husband no more.
  DUCH. What devil art thou that counterfeits heaven's
    thunder?
  BOS. Is that terrible? I would have you tell me whether
Is that note worse that frights the silly birds
Out of the corn, or that which doth allure them   100
To the nets? You have heark'ned to the last too much.
  DUCH. O misery! like to a rusty o'ercharged cannon,
Shall I never fly in pieces? Come, to what prison?
  BOS. To none.
  DUCH.   Whither, then?
  BOS.   To your palace.
  DUCH.   I have heard
That Charon's[102] boat serves to convey all o'er   105
The dismal lake, but brings none back again.
  BOS. Your brothers mean you safety and pity.
  DUCH.   Pity!
With such a pity, men preserve alive
Pheasants and quails, when they are not fat enough
To be eaten.
  BOS.   These are your children?
  DUCH.   Yes.
  BOS.   Can they prattle?
  DUCH. No.   111
But I intend, since they were born accursed,
Curses shall be their first language.

[99] Used by sailors in taking soundings.
[100] Overloaded.—Fortune was often depicted turning a great
    wheel; to its rim men and women were attached, all being on
    the way either up or down.
[101] (The object of) your enterprise.
[102] The ferryman who took souls across the river Styx to Hades.

BOS.   Fie, madam!
Forget this base, low fellow.
     DUCH.   Were I a man,
I'd beat that counterfeit face[103] into thy other.   115
     BOS. One of no birth.
     DUCH. Say[104] that he was born mean;
Man is most happy when 's own actiöns
Be arguments and examples of his virtue.
     BOS. A barren, beggarly virtue.
     DUCH. I prithee, who is greatest? Can you tell?   120
Sad tales befit my woe; I 'll tell you one.
A salmon, as she swam unto the sea,
Met with a dogfish, who encounters her
With this rough language: "Why art thou so bold
To mix thyself with our high state of floods,   125
Being no eminent courtier, but one
That for the calmest and fresh time o' th' year
Dost live in shallow rivers, rank'st thyself
With silly smelts and shrimps? And darest thou
Pass by our dogship without reverence?"   130
"Oh," quoth the salmon, "sister, be at peace.
Thank Jupiter we both have passed the net.
Our value never can be truly known
Till in the fisher's basket we be shown.
I' th' market then my price may be the higher,   135
Even when I am nearest to the cook and fire."
So to great men the moral may be stretchèd:
Men oft are valued high when th' are most wretched.
But come; whither you please. I am armed 'gainst
     misery,
Bent to all sways of the oppressor's will.   140
There's no deep valley but near some great hill.   [*Exeunt*

ACT IV

SCENE I[1]

Enter FERDINAND *and* BOSOLA

     FERD. How doth our sister Duchess bear herself
In her imprisonment?
     BOS.   Nobly. I 'll describe her.
She 's sad as one long used to 't, and she seems
Rather to welcome the end of misery
Than shun it; a behavior so noble   5
As gives a majesty to adversity.
You may discern the shape of loveliness
More perfect in her tears than in her smiles.
She will muse four hours together; and her silence,
Methinks, expresseth more than if she spake.   10
     FERD. Her melancholy seems to be fortified
With a strange disdain.
     BOS.   'T is so; and this restraint
(Like English mastiffs that grow fierce with tying)
Makes her too passionately apprehend
Those pleasures she 's kept from.
     FERD.   Curse upon her!   15
I will no longer study in the book
Of another's heart. Inform her what I told you.   [*Exit*

Enter DUCHESS *and* Attendants

     BOS. All comfort to your Grace!
     DUCH.   I will have none.
Pray thee, why dost thou wrap thy poisoned pills
In gold and sugar?   20

     BOS. Your elder brother, the Lord Ferdinand,
Is come to visit you, and sends you word,
'Cause once he rashly made a solemn vow
Never to see you more, he comes i' th' night;
And prays you gently neither torch nor taper   25
Shine in your chamber. He will kiss your hand,
And reconcile himself; but, for his vow,
He dares not see you.
     DUCH.   At his pleasure.—
Take hence the lights.—He 's come.
                    [*Exeunt* Attendants *with lights*

Re-enter FERDINAND

     FERD.   Where are you?
     DUCH.   Here, sir.
     FERD. This darkness suits you well.
     DUCH.   I would ask you pardon.   30
     FERD. You have it;
For I account it the honorablest revenge,
Where I may kill, to pardon.—Where are your cubs?
     DUCH. Whom?
     FERD.   Call them your children;
For though our national law distinguish bastards   35
From true legitimate issue, compassionate nature
Makes them all equal.
     DUCH.   Do you visit me for this?
You violate a sacrament o' th' Church[2]
Shall make you howl in hell for 't.
     FERD.   It had been well,
Could you have lived thus always; for, indeed,   40
You were too much i' th' light.[3] But no more;

---

103 Mask.   104 Suppose.
1 Unlocated; some castle, presumably.

2 By calling the offspring of a marriage bastards.
3 A pun. Your conduct was too light.

I come to seal my peace with you. Here 's a hand

[*Gives her a dead man's hand*

To which you have vowed much love; the ring upon 't
You gave.

DUCH.   I affectionately kiss it.

FERD. Pray, do, and bury the print of it in your
    heart.   45

I will leave this ring with you for a love token;
And the hand, as sure as the ring; and do not doubt
But you shall have the heart, too. When you need a
    friend,
Send it to him that owed[4] it; you shall see
Whether he can aid you.

DUCH.   You are very cold.   50
I fear you are not well after your travel.—

Re-enter Attendants *with lights*

Ha! lights! Oh, horrible!

FERD.   Let her have lights enough. [*Exit*

DUCH. What witchcraft doth he practice, that he hath
    left
A dead man's hand here?

*Here is discovered, behind a traverse,[5] the artificial
figures of* ANTONIO *and his* Children, *appearing as if
they were dead*

BOS. Look you. Here 's the piece from which 't was
    ta'en.   55
He doth present you this sad spectacle,
That, now you know directly they are dead,
Hereafter you may wisely cease to grieve
For that which cannot be recoverèd.

DUCH. There is not between heaven and earth one
    wish   60
I stay for, after this. It wastes me more
Than were 't my picture, fashioned out of wax,
Stuck with a magical needle, and then buried
In some foul dunghill;[6] and yond 's an excellent property
For a tyrant, which I would account mercy.

BOS.   What's that? 65

DUCH. If they would bind me to that lifeless trunk,
And let me freeze to death.

BOS.   Come, you must live.

DUCH. That's the greatest torture souls feel in hell,
In hell: that they must live, and cannot die.
Portia,[7] I'll new kindle thy coals again, 70

---

[4] Owned.

[5] The sliding curtain between the outer platform and the inner
stage.

[6] The warmth of which would slowly melt the image and thus,
by sympathetic magic, cause her death.

[7] Brutus's wife; she killed herself by swallowing hot coals.

And revive the rare and almost dead example
Of a loving wife.

BOS.   Oh, fie! Despair? remember
You are a Christian.

DUCH.   The Church enjoins fasting;
I'll starve myself to death.

BOS.   Leave this vain sorrow.
Things being at the worst, begin to mend; 75
The bee, when he hath shot his sting into your hand,
May then play with your eyelid.

DUCH.   Good comfortable[8] fellow,
Persuade a wretch that's broke upon the wheel
To have all his bones new set; entreat him live,
To be executed again. Who must dispatch me? 80
I account this world a tedious theater,
For I do play a part in't 'gainst my will.

BOS. Come, be of comfort; I will save your life.

DUCH. Indeed I have not leisure to tend so small a
    business.

BOS. Now, by my life, I pity you.

DUCH.   Thou art a fool then, 85
To waste thy pity on a thing so wretch'd
As cannot pity it.[9] I am full of daggers.
Puff, let me blow these vipers from me.—
(*To an* Attendant) What are you?

SERV.   One that wishes you long life.

DUCH. I would thou wert hanged for the horrible
    curse   90
Thou hast given me.—I shall shortly grow one
Of the miracles of pity. I'll go pray; no,
I'll go curse.

BOS.   Oh, fie!

DUCH.   I could curse the stars—

BOS.   Oh, fearful!

DUCH. And those three smiling seasons of the year,
Into a Russian winter; nay, the world 95
To its first chaos.

BOS.   Look you, the stars shine still.

DUCH. Oh, but you must remember, my curse hath a
    great way to go.
Plagues, that make lanes through largest families,
Consume them!

BOS.   Fie, lady!

DUCH.   Let them like tyrants
Never be remember'd, but for the ill they have done. 100
Let all the zealous prayers of mortified[10]
Churchmen forget them!

BOS.   Oh, uncharitable!

DUCH. Let heaven, a little while, cease crowning
    martyrs,
To punish them!

---

[8] Comforting.   [9] Itself.   [10] Humble, devout.

Go, howl them this, and say I long to bleed: 105
It is some mercy when men kill with speed.

[Exit with Attendants

Re-enter FERDINAND

FERD. Excellent! as I would wish! she's plagued in art:
These presentations are but framed in wax,
By the curious master in that quality,[11]
Vincentio Lauriola,[12] and she takes them   110
For true substantial bodies.
     BOS.   Why do you do this?
     FERD. To bring her to despair.[13]
     BOS.   'Faith, end here;
And go no farther in your cruelty;
Send her a penitential garment to put on
Next to her delicate skin, and furnish her   115
With beads and prayer books.
     FERD.   Damn her, that body of hers,
While that my blood ran pure in't, was more worth
Than that which thou wouldst comfort, called a soul.
I will send her masks of common courtesans,
Have her meat served up by bawds and ruffians;[14]   120
And, 'cause she'll needs be mad, I am resolved
To remove forth[15] the common hospital
All the mad folk, and place them near her lodging:
There let them practice together, sing and dance,
And act their gambols to the full o' th' moon.   125
If she can sleep the better for it, let her.
Your work is almost ended.
     BOS.   Must I see her again?
     FERD. Yes.
     BOS.   Never.
     FERD.   You must.
     BOS.   Never in mine own shape;[16]
That's forfeited by my intelligence,[17]
And this last cruel lie. When you send me next,   130
The business shall be comfort.
     FERD.   Very likely!
Thy pity is nothing of kin to thee. Antonio
Lurks about Milan; thou shalt shortly thither,
To feed a fire as great as my revenge,
Which never will slack till it have spent his[18] fuel: 135
Intemperate agues make physicians cruel.   *[Exeunt*

---

[11] Profession.   [12] Unidentified.
[13] Which was held a sin.
[14] Bullies, prostitutes' protectors.   [15] From.
[16] Undisguised.   [17] Spying.   [18] Its.

SCENE II[19]

Enter DUCHESS *and* CARIOLA

     DUCH. What hideous noise was that?
     CARI.   'Tis the wild consort
Of madmen, lady, which your tyrant brother
Hath placed about your lodging. This tyranny
I think, was never practiced till this hour.
     DUCH. Indeed, I thank him: nothing but noise and
          folly   5
Can keep me in my right wits; whereas reason
And silence make me stark mad. Sit down;
Discourse to me some dismal tragedy.
     CARI. Oh, 'twill increase your melancholy.
     DUCH.   Thou art deceived.
To hear of greater grief would lessen mine.   10
This is a prison?
     CARI.   Yes, but you shall live
To shake this durance off.
     DUCH.   Thou art a fool.
The robin redbreast and the nightingale
Never live long in cages.
     CARI.   Pray, dry your eyes:
What think you of, madam?
     DUCH.   Of nothing. When   15
I muse thus, I sleep.
     CARI.   Like a madman, with your eyes open?
     DUCH. Dost thou think we shall know one another
In th' other world?
     CARI.   Yes, out of questïon.
     DUCH. O that it were possible we might
But hold some two days' conference with the dead!   20
From them I should learn somewhat, I am sure,
I never shall know here. I'll tell thee a miracle:
I am not mad yet, to my cause of sorrow.
Th' heaven o'er my head seems made of molten brass,
The earth of flaming sulphur; yet I am not mad.   25
I am acquainted with sad misery
As the tanned galley-slave is with his oar.
Necessity makes me suffer constantly,
And custom makes it easy. Who do I look like now?
     CARI. Like to your picture in the gallery,   30
A deal of life in show, but none in practice;
Or, rather, like some reverend monument
Whose ruins are even pitied.
     DUCH.   Very proper;
And Fortune seems only to have her eyesight
To behold my tragedy.—How now!   35
What noise is that?

---

[19] The same.

Enter a Servant

SERV.   I am come to tell you
Your brother hath intended you some sport.
A great physician, when the Pope was sick
Of a deep melancholy, presented him
With several sorts[20] of madmen, which wild object,   40
Being full of change and sport, forced him to laugh,
And so th' imposthume[21] broke. The selfsame cure
The Duke intends on you.
    DUCH.   Let them come in.
    SERV. There's a mad lawyer; and a secular[22] priest;
A doctor that hath forfeited his wits   45
By jealousy; an astrologian,
That in his works said such a day o' th' month
Should be the day of doom, and, failing of't,
Ran mad; an English tailor crazed i' th' brain
With the study of new fashion; a gentleman-usher   50
Quite beside himself with care to keep in mind
The number of his lady's salutations
Or "How do you" she employed him in each morning;
A farmer, too, an excellent knave in grain,[23]
Mad 'cause he was hindered transportation;[24]   55
And, let one broker that's mad loose to these,
You'd think the Devil were among them.
    DUCH. Sit, Cariola.—Let them loose when you please,
For I am chained to endure all your tyranny.

Enter MADMEN. *Here by a* MADMAN *this song is sung,*
to a dismal kind of music

O let us howl some heavy note,   60
    Some deadly-doggèd howl,
Sounding as from the threat'ning throat
    Of beasts and fatal fowl!
As ravens, screech owls, bulls, and bears,
    We'll bell,[25] and bawl our parts,   65
Till yerksome[26] noise have cloyed your ears
    And corrosived[27] your hearts.
At last, whenas our choir wants breath,
    Our bodies being blest,
We'll sing, like swans, to welcome death,   70
    And die in love and rest.

IST MAD.[28] Doomsday not come yet! I'll draw it nearer
by a perspective,[29] or make a glass that shall set all the
world on fire upon an instant. I cannot sleep; my pillow
is stuffed with a litter of porcupines.   75

2ND MAD.[30] Hell is a mere glass-house, where the devils
are continually blowing up women's souls on hollow irons,
and the fire never goes out.

3RD MAD.[31] I will lie with every woman in my parish
the tenth night. I will tithe them over like haycocks.   [80

4TH MAD.[32] Shall my 'pothecary outgo me, because I
am a cuckold? I have found out his roguery: he makes
alum of his wife's urine, and sells it to Puritans that have
sore throats with overstraining.[33]

IST MAD. I have skill in heraldry.   85

2ND MAD. Hast?

IST MAD. You do give for your crest a woodcock's[34]
head with the brains picked out[35] on 't; you are a very
ancient[36] gentleman.

3RD MAD. Greek is turned Turk;[37] we are only   [90
to be saved by the Helvetian[38] translation.

IST MAD. Come on, sir, I will lay the law[39] to you.

2ND MAD. O, rather lay a corrosive; the law will eat to
the bone.

3RD MAD. He that drinks but to satisfy nature is   [95
damned.

4TH MAD. If I had my glass[40] here, I would show a sight
should make all the women here call me mad doctor.

IST MAD. What 's he? A ropemaker?[41]

2ND MAD. No, no, no; a snuffling[42] knave that,   [100
while he shows the tombs, will have his hand in a wench's
placket.[43]

3RD MAD. Woe to the caroche that brought home my
wife from the masque at three o'clock in the morning! It
had a large feather-bed in it.   105

4TH MAD. I have pared the Devil's nails forty times,
roasted them in raven's eggs, and cured agues with them.

3RD MAD. Get me three hundred milchbats, to make
possets[44] to procure sleep.

4TH MAD. All the college[45] may throw their caps   [110
at me:[46] I have made a soap-boiler[47] costive;[48] it was my
masterpiece.

[20] Sets.   [21] Ulcer.
[22] I.e., not a monk or friar. Actually, he turns out to be a caricature
of the Puritan ministers.
[23] A pun. *Grain* in the usual sense, and also =dye; he is a dyed-
in-the-wool knave.   [24] Forbidden to export his grain.
[25] Bellow.   [26] Irksome.   [27] Bitten into.
[28] The astrologer.   [29] Telescope.

[30] The lawyer.   [31] The priest.   [32] The physician.
[33] In preaching.   [34] A proverbially foolish bird.
[35] A pun on the meanings (1) removed and (2) depicted.
[36] I.e., of an old family. Webster is sneering at the upstart gentry
of his time.
[37] The Greek Testament has become unchristian.
[38] Swiss, i.e., Genevan, and thus Calvinistic.
[39] Explain it.
[40] Apparently one that showed something indecent.
[41] And thus an ally of the hangman.
[42] Alluding to the nasal whine of Puritan preachers.
[43] Petticoat.   [44] Drinks of milk and spiced wine.
[45] Of physicians.   [46] Give up trying to compete with me.
[47] Since soap was used as a suppository, his trade might be expected
to have the opposite tendency.   [48] Constipated.

Here the dance, consisting of EIGHT MADMEN, *with music answerable[49] thereunto; after which* BOSOLA (*like[50] an old man*) *enters*

DUCH. Is he mad, too?

SERV.   Pray question him. I 'll leave you.

                         [Exeunt Servant *and* MADMEN

BOS. I am come to make thy tomb.

DUCH.   Ha! my tomb?
Thou speak'st as if I lay upon my deathbed,   115
Gasping for breath. Dost thou perceive me sick?

BOS. Yes, and the more dangerously, since thy sickness is
insensible.

DUCH. Thou art not mad, sure. Dost know me?

BOS.   Yes.

DUCH.   Who am I?

BOS. Thou art a box of worm-seed, at best but a   [120
salvatory[51] of green[52] mummy. What 's this flesh? A little
crudded[53] milk, fantastical puff-paste.[54] Our bodies are
weaker than those paper prisons boys use to keep flies in;
more contemptible, since ours is to preserve earthworms.
Didst thou ever see a lark in a cage? Such is the soul   [125
in the body; this world is like her little turf of grass, and
the heaven o'er our heads, like her looking glass, only
gives us a miserable knowledge of the small compass of
our prison.

DUCH. Am not I thy duchess?   130

BOS. Thou art some great woman, sure; for riot[55] begins
to sit on thy forehead, clad in gray hairs, twenty years
sooner than on a merry milkmaid's. Thou sleep'st worse
than if a mouse should be forced to take up her lodging in
a cat's ear. A little infant, that breeds its teeth, should   [135
it lie with thee would cry out, as if thou wert the more
unquiet bedfellow.

DUCH. I am Duchess of Malfi still.

BOS. That makes thy sleeps so broken:
Glories, like glowworms, afar off shine bright,   140
But, looked to near, have neither heat nor light.

DUCH. Thou art very plain.

BOS. My trade is to flatter the dead, not the living; I am
a tombmaker.

DUCH. And thou com'st to make my tomb?   145

BOS. Yes.

DUCH. Let me be a little merry.—Of what stuff wilt
thou make it?

BOS. Nay, resolve[56] me first of what fashion?

DUCH. Why, do we grow fantastical in our deathbed?
Do we affect fashion in the grave?   151

BOS. Most ambitiously. Princes' images on their tombs
do not lie, as they were wont, seeming to pray up to
heaven; but with their hands under their cheeks, as if they
died of the toothache. They are not carved with   [155
their eyes fixed upon the stars; but, as their minds were
wholly bent upon the world, the selfsame way they seem
to turn their faces.

DUCH. Let me know fully therefore the effect
Of this thy dismal preparatiön,   160
This talk fit for a charnel.[57]

BOS.   Now I shall:—

Enter Executioners, *with a coffin, cords, and a bell*

Here is a present from your princely brothers;
And may it arrive welcome, for it brings
Last benefit, last sorrow.

DUCH.   Let me see it:
I have so much obedience in my blood,   165
I wish it in their veins to do them good.

BOS. This is your last presence-chamber.

CARI. O my sweet lady!

DUCH.   Peace; it affrights not me.

BOS. I am the common bellman
That usually is sent to condemned persons   170
The night before they suffer.[58]

DUCH.   Even now thou said'st
Thou wast a tombmaker.

BOS.   'T was to bring you
By degrees to mortification. Listen.   *[Rings the bell*

Hark, now everything is still,
The screech owl and the whistler[59] shrill   175
Call upon our dame aloud,
And bid her quickly don her shroud.
Much you had of land and rent;
Your length in clay 's now competent.[60]
A long war disturbed your mind;   180
Here your perfect peace is signed.
Of what is 't fools make such vain keeping?
Sin their conception, their birth weeping,
Their life a general mist of error,
Their death a hideous storm of terror.   185
Strew your hair with powders sweet,
Don clean linen, bathe your feet,
And (the foul fiend more to check)
A crucifix let bless your neck.
'T is now full tide 'tween night and day;   190
End your groan, and come away.

---

[49] Appropriate.   [50] Disguised as.   [51] Ointment box.
[52] Fresh. Mummy was used medicinally.   [53] Curdled.
[54] Flimsy pastry.   [55] Ruin.   [56] Inform.

[57] Burial place, or house in which were thrown bones dug up in
making new graves.
[58] A London tradesman established a foundation for this purpose
in 1605.   [59] Some kind of bird.   [60] Sufficient.

CARI. Hence, villains, tyrants, murderers! Alas!
What will you do with my lady?—Call for help!
  DUCH. To whom? To our next neighbors? They are
    mad folks.
  BOS. Remove that noise.
  DUCH.   Farewell, Cariola.   195
In my last will I have not much to give.
A many hungry guests have fed upon me;
Thine will be a poor reversion.⁶¹
  CARI.   I will die with her.
  DUCH. I pray thee, look thou giv'st my little boy
Some syrup for his cold, and let the girl   200
Say her prayers ere she sleep.—   [CARIOLA is forced off
                    Now what you please!
What death?
  BOS.   Strangling: here are your executioners.
  DUCH. I forgive them.
The apoplexy,⁶² catarrh, or cough o' th' lungs
Would do as much as they do.   205
  BOS. Doth not death fright you?
  DUCH.   Who would be afraid on 't,
Knowing to meet such excellent company
In th' other world?
  BOS.   Yet, methinks,
The manner of your death should much afflict you:
This cord should terrify you.
  DUCH.   Not a whit: 210
What would it pleasure me to have my throat cut
With diamonds? or to be smothered
With cassia?⁶³ or to be shot to death with pearls?
I know death hath ten thousand several doors
For men to take their exits; and 't is found   215
They go on such strange geometrical hinges,
You may open them both ways.⁶⁴—Any way, for
    heaven-sake,
So I were out of your whispering.—Tell my brothers
That I perceive death, now I am well awake,
Best gift is they can give or I can take.   220
I would fain put off my last woman's-fault:
I 'd not be tedious to you.
  EXECUT.   We are ready.
  DUCH. Dispose my breath how please you; but my body
Bestow upon my women, will you?
  EXECUT.   Yes.
  DUCH. Pull, and pull strongly, for your able strength
Must pull down heaven upon me—   226
Yet stay; heaven-gates are not so highly arched
As princes' palaces; they that enter there

Must go upon their knees.—(Kneeling) Come, violent
    death,
Serve for mandragora⁶⁵ to make me sleep!—   230
Go tell my brothers, when I am laid out,
They then may feed in quiet.   [They strangle her
  BOS.   Where 's the waiting-woman?
Fetch her. (Exeunt some of the Executioners.) Some other
    strangle the children.   [Exeunt others

  BOS. I think, not; her infelicity
Seemed to have years too many.—

And should I die this instant, I had lived

You have bloodily approved the ancient truth,
That kindred commonly do worse agree
Than remote strangers.

Again, Why did you
An excellent honest man didst thou desire

If thou dost love them, cast

  CARI.   Oh, you are damned
Perpetually for this. My turn is next—   235
Is 't not so ordered?
  BOS.   Yes, and I am glad
You are so well prepared for't.
  CARI.   You are deceived, sir.
I am not prepared for't; I will not die.
I will first come to my answer,⁶⁶ and know
How I have offended.
  BOS.   Come, dispatch her.—   240
You kept her counsel; now you shall keep ours.
  CARI. I will not die; I must not; I am contracted
To a young gentleman.
  EXECUT.   Here's your wedding ring.⁶⁷
  CARI. Let me but speak with the Duke. I'll discover⁶⁸
Treason to his person.
  BOS.   Delays! Throttle her.   245
  EXECUT. She bites and scratches.
  CARI.   If you kill me now,
I am damned; I have not been at confession
These two years.
  BOS. (to Executioners). When!
  CARI.   I am quick with child.
  BOS.   Why, then,
Your credit's⁶⁹ saved.   [They strangle her
                    Bear her into the next room;
Let this⁷⁰ lie still.
          [Exeunt Executioners with CARIOLA's body

    Enter FERDINAND

  FERD.   Is she dead?
  BOS.   She is what   250
You'd have her. But here begin your pity:
          [Shows⁷¹ the Children strangled
Alas, how have these offended?
  FERD.   The death
Of young wolves is never to be pitied.

---

⁶¹ Inheritance.   ⁶² Cerebral hemorrhage.
⁶³ I.e., spices.
⁶⁴ They can be opened from either side; i.e., either God or man can
    open them.

⁶⁵ A narcotic made from its root.
⁶⁶ Examination.   ⁶⁷ The noose.   ⁶⁸ Reveal.
⁶⁹ Reputation.   ⁷⁰ The Duchess's body.
⁷¹ By pulling aside the curtain before the inner stage.

BOS. Fix your eye here.[72]

FERD.   Constantly.

BOS.   Do you not weep?
Other sins only speak; murder shrieks out.   255
The element of water moistens the earth,
But blood flies upwards and bedews the heavens.

FERD. Cover her face; mine eyes dazzle. She died
    young.

BOS. I think not so; her infelicity
Seemed to have years too many.

FERD.   She and I were twins;   260
And should I die this instant, I had lived
Her time to a minute.

BOS.   It seems she was born first.
You have bloodily approved the ancient truth,
That kindred commonly do worse agree
Than remote strangers.

FERD.   Let me see her face   265
Again. Why didst not thou pity her? What
An excellent honest man mightst thou have been,
If thou hadst borne her to some sanctuary!
Or, bold in a good cause, opposed thyself,
With thy advancèd sword above thy head,   270
Between her innocence and my revenge!
I bade thee, when I was distracted of my wits,
Go kill my dearest friend; and thou hast done't.
For, let me but examine well the cause,
What was the meanness of her match to me?   275
Only I must confess I had a hope,
Had she continued widow, to have gained
An infinite mass of treasure by her death;
And that was the main cause, her marriage,
That drew a stream of gall quite through my heart.   280
For thee, as we observe in tragedies
That a good actor many times is cursed
For playing a villain's part, I hate thee for't,
And for my sake say thou hast done much ill, well.

BOS. Let me quicken your memory, for I perceive   285
You are falling into ingratitude; I challenge
The reward due to my service.

FERD.   I'll tell thee
What I'll give thee.

BOS.   Do.

FERD.   I'll give thee a pardon
For this murder.

BOS.   Ha!

FERD.   Yes, and 'tis
The largest bounty I can study to do thee.   290
By what authority didst thou execute
This bloody sentence?

BOS.   By yours.

FERD. Mine! was I her judge?
Did any ceremonial form of law
Doom her to not-being? Did a complete jury   295
Deliver her conviction up i' th' court?
Where shalt thou find this judgment registered,
Unless in hell? See, like a bloody fool,
Th' hast forfeited thy life, and thou shalt die for't.

BOS. The office of justice is perverted quite,   300
When one thief hangs another. Who shall dare
To reveal this?

FERD.   Oh, I'll tell thee;
The wolf shall find her grave, and scrape it up,
Not to devour the corpse, but to discover
The horrid murder.

BOS.   You, not I, shall quake for't.   305

FERD. Leave me.

BOS.   I will first receive my pension.

FERD. You are a villain.

BOS.   When your ingratitude
Is judge, I am so.

FERD.   O horror,
That not the fear of him which binds the devils
Can prescribe man obedience!   310
Never look upon me more.

BOS.   Why, fare thee well:
Your brother and yourself are worthy men.
You have a pair of hearts are hollow graves,
Rotten, and rotting others; and your vengeance,
Like two chained bullets, still goes arm in arm.   315
You may be brothers; for treason, like the plague,
Doth take much in a blood.[73] I stand like one
That long hath ta'en a sweet and golden dream.
I am angry with myself, now that I wake.

FERD. Get thee into some unknown part o' th' world,
That I may never see thee.

BOS.   Let me know   321
Wherefore I should be thus neglected. Sir,
I served your tyranny, and rather strove
To satisfy yourself than all the world;
And though I loathed the evil, yet I loved   325
You that did counsel it, and rather sought
To appear a true servant than an honest man.

FERD. I'll go hunt the badger by owl-light.
'Tis a deed of darkness.   [Exit

BOS. He's much distracted. Off, my painted[74] honor!
While with vain hopes our faculties we tire,   331
We seem to sweat in ice and freeze in fire.
What would I do, were this to do again?
I would not change my peace of consciënce
For all the wealth of Europe. She stirs; here's life!   335
Return, fair soul, from darkness, and lead mine

---

[72] On the Duchess.

[73] Runs in families.   [74] Unreal.

Out of this sensible hell. She's warm, she breathes!
Upon thy pale lips I will melt my heart,
To store them with fresh color.—Who's there?
Some cordial drink!—Alas! I dare not call;   340
So[75] pity would destroy pity.[76] Her eye opes,
And heaven in it seems to ope, that late was shut,
To take me up to mercy.
   DUCH. Antonio!
   BOS.   Yes, madam, he is living;
The dead bodies you saw were but feigned statues.   345
He's reconciled to your brothers; the Pope hath wrought
The atonement.
   DUCH.   Mercy!   [She dies
   BOS. Oh, she's gone again! there the cords of life broke.
O sacred innocence, that sweetly sleeps
On turtles'[77] feathers, whilst a guilty conscience   350
Is a black register, wherein is writ
All our good deeds and bad, a pérspective

That shows us hell. That we cannot be suffered
To do good when we have a mind to it!
This is manly sorrow;   355
These tears, I am very certain, never grew
In my mother's milk.[78] My estate is sunk
Below the degree of fear. Where were
These penitent fountains while she was living?
Oh, they were frozen up. Here is a sight   360
As direful to my soul as is the sword
Unto a wretch hath slain his father. Come,
I'll bear thee hence,
And execute thy last will; that's deliver
Thy body to the reverend dispose   365
Of some good women: that, the cruel tyrant
Shall not deny me. Then I'll post to Milan,
Where somewhat I will speedily enact
Worth[79] my dejection.
                                [Exit

ACT V

SCENE I[1]

Enter ANTONIO *and* DELIO

   ANT. What think you of my hope of reconcilement
To the Aragonian brethren?
   DELIO.   I misdoubt it;
For though they have sent their letters of safe conduct
For your repair to Milan, they appear
But nets to entrap you. The Marquess of Pescara,   5
Under whom you hold certain land in cheat,[2]
Much 'gainst his noble nature hath been moved
To seize those lands, and some of his dependents
Are at this instant making it their suit
To be invested in[3] your revenues.   10
I cannot think they mean well to your life
That do deprive you of your means of life,
Your living.
   ANT.   You are still an heretic[4]
To any safety I can shape myself.
   DELIO. Here comes the Marquess. I will make myself   [15
Petitioner for some part of your land,
To know whither it is flying.
   ANT.   I pray do.   [Withdraws

Enter PESCARA

   DELIO. Sir, I have a suit to you.
   PES.   To me?
   DELIO.   An easy one.
There is the Citadel of Saint Bennet,[5]
With some demesnes, of late in the possession   20
Of Antonio Bologna—please you bestow them on me?
   PES. You are my friend; but this is such a suit
Nor fit for me to give nor you to take.
   DELIO. No, sir?
   PES.   I will give you ample reason for 't
Soon in private. Here 's the Cardinal's mistress.   25

Enter JULIA

   JULIA. My Lord, I am grown your poor petitioner,
And should be an ill beggar, had I not
A great man's letter here (the Cardinal's)
To court you in my favor.   [Gives a letter
   PES.   He entreats for you
The Citadel of Saint Bennet, that belonged   30
To the banished Bologna.
   JULIA.   Yes.
   PES. I could not have thought of a friend I could rather
Pleasure with it; 't is yours.
   JULIA.   Sir, I thank you;
And he shall know how doubly I am engaged,

---

[75] I.e., if I did.
[76] I.e., to be so pitiful as to call for help would doom her to death.
[77] Doves'.

[1] Milan. Perhaps the palace of Pescara.
[2] Subject to forfeiture by the lord's resuming possession.
[3] To be granted.   [4] Skeptic.

[78] I.e., it is not natural for me to weep.   [79] Worthy of.
[5] Benedict.

Both in your gift and speediness of giving,   35
Which makes your grant the greater.   [Exit

ANT. (aside).   How they fortify
Themselves with my ruin!

DELIO.   Sir, I am
Little bound to you.

PES.   Why?

DELIO. Because you denied this suit, to me, and gave 't
To such a creature.

PES.   Do you know what it was?   40
It was Antonio's land, not forfeited
By course of law, but ravished from his throat
By the Cardinal's entreaty. It were not fit
I should bestow so main a piece of wrong
Upon my friend; 't is a gratification   45
Only due to a strumpet, for it is injustice.
Shall I sprinkle the pure blood of innocents
To make those followers I call my friends
Look ruddier upon me? I am glad
This land, ta'en from the owner by such wrong,   50
Returns again unto so foul an use
As salary for his lust. Learn, good Delio,
To ask noble things of me, and you shall find
I 'll be a noble giver.

DELIO.   You instruct me well.

ANT. (aside). Why, here 's a man now would fright
          impudence   55
From sauciest beggars.

PES.   Prince Ferdinand 's come to Milan,
Sick, as they give out, of an apoplexy;
But some say 't is a frenzy. I am going
To visit him.   [Exit

ANT.   'T is a noble old fellow.

DELIO. What course do you mean to take, Antonio?   60

ANT. This night I mean to venture all my fortune,
Which is no more than a poor ling'ring life,
To the Cardinal's worst of malice. I have got
Private access to his chamber, and intend
To visit him about the mid of night,   65
As once his brother did our noble Duchess.
It may be that the sudden apprehension
Of danger—for I 'll go in mine own shape—
When he shall see it fraight[6] with love and duty,
May draw the poison out of him, and work   70
A friendly reconcilement. If it fail,
Yet it shall rid me of this infamous calling;
For better fall once than be ever falling.

DELIO. I'll second you in all danger; and, howe'er,
My life keeps rank with yours.   75

ANT. You are still my loved and best friend.   [Exeunt

---

[6] Fraught.

Enter PESCARA, and a DOCTOR

PES. Now, doctor, may I visit your patient?

DOC. If 't please your Lordship; but he 's instantly
To take the air here in the gallery,
By my direction.

PES.   Pray thee, what 's his disease?

DOC. A very pestilent disease, my Lord;   5
They call lycanthropia.[8]

PES.   What 's that?
I need a dictionary to 't.

DOC.   I 'll tell you.
In those that are possessed with 't there o'erflows
Such melancholy humor[9] they imagine
Themselves to be transformèd into wolves,   10
Steal forth to churchyards in the dead of night,
And dig dead bodies up: as two nights since,
One met the Duke 'bout midnight in a lane
Behind Saint Mark's church, with the leg of a man
Upon his shoulder; and he howled fearfully;   15
Said he was a wolf, only the difference
Was, a wolf's skin was hairy on the outside,
His on the inside; bade them take their swords,
Rip up his flesh, and try. Straight I was sent for,
And, having ministered to him, found his Grace   20
Very well recovered.

PES. I am glad on 't.

DOC.   Yet not without some fear
Of a relapse. If he grow to his fit again,
I 'll go a nearer way to work with him
Than ever Paracelsus[10] dreamed of; if   25
They 'll give me leave, I 'll buffet[11] his madness out of
          him.
Stand aside; he comes.

Enter FERDINAND, CARDINAL, MALATESTE, and BOSOLA

FERD. Leave me.

MAL. Why doth your Lordship love this solitariness?

FERD. Eagles commonly fly alone; they are crows,   [30
daws, and starlings that flock together.
Look! what's that follows me?

MAL.   Nothing, my Lord.

FERD.   Yes.

MAL. 'T is your shadow.

FERD.   Stay it; let it not haunt me.

---

[7] The Cardinal's palace at Milan.
[8] Lycanthropy. It is a real mania.
[9] Bodily and mental condition.
[10] Swiss alchemist and physician (d. 1541).
[11] Whipping was a recognized treatment for lunacy.

MAL. Impossible, if you move, and the sun shine.

FERD. I will throttle it.   [*Throws himself on the ground*

MAL.   O, my Lord, you are angry with
    nothing.   35

FERD. You are a fool. How is 't possible I should catch
my shadow, unless I fall upon 't? When I go to hell, I
mean to carry a bribe; for, look you, good gifts evermore
make way for the worst persons.

PES. Rise, good my Lord.

FERD.   I am studying the art of patience.   40

PES. 'T is a noble virtue.

FERD. To drive six snails before me from this town to
Moscow; neither use goad nor whip to them, but let them
take their own time—the patient'st man i' th' world match
me for an experiment—and I 'll crawl after like a   [45
sheepbiter.[12]

CARD. Force him up.

FERD.   Use me well, you were best.
What I have done, I have done; I 'll confess nothing.

DOC. Now let me come to him.—Are you mad, my
    Lord?   49
Are you out of your princely wits?

FERD.   What 's he?

PES.   Your doctor.

FERD. Let me have his beard sawed off, and his eyebrows
filed more civil.

DOC. I must do mad tricks with him, for that 's the only
way on 't.—I have brought your Grace a salamander's[13]
skin to keep you from sunburning.   55

FERD. I have cruel sore eyes.

DOC. The white of a cockatrix's[14] egg is present remedy.

FERD. Let it be a new-laid one, you were best.
Hide me from him; physicians are like kings—   59
They brook no contradiction.

DOC.   Now he begins to fear me;
Now let me alone with him.   [*He takes off his gown*

CARD.   How now! put off your gown?

DOC. Let me have some forty urinals filled with rose-
water; he and I 'll go pelt one another with them.—Now
he begins to fear me.—Can you fetch a frisk,[15] sir?   [64
—Let him go, let him go, upon my peril. I find by his eye
he stands in awe of me. I 'll make him as tame as a dormouse.

FERD. Can you fetch your frisks, sir!—I will stamp him
into a cullis,[16] flay off his skin to cover one of the   [69
anatomies[17] this rogue hath set i' th' cold yonder in Barber-
Chirurgeon's Hall.—Hence, hence! you are all of you like
beasts for sacrifice. (*Throws the* DOCTOR *down and beats him.*)

[12] Dog.
[13] A mythical animal supposed to be able to live in fire.
[14] The cockatrice was a fabulous serpent hatched from a cock's egg.
[15] Cut a caper.   [16] Broth; i.e., I'll make soup of him.
[17] Skeleton's.

There's nothing left of you but tongue and belly: flattery
and lechery.   [*Exit*

PES. Doctor, he did not fear you throughly.   75

DOC. True; I was somewhat too forward.

BOS. Mercy upon me, what a fatal judgment
Hath fall'n upon this Ferdinand!

PES.   Knows your Grace
What accident hath brought unto the Prince
This strange distraction?   80

CARD. (*aside*). I must feign somewhat.—Thus they say
    it grew.
You have heard it rumored, for these many years,
None of our family dies but there is seen
The shape of an old woman, which is given
By tradition to us to have been murthered   85
By her nephews for her riches. Such a figure
One night, as the Prince sat up late at 's book,
Appeared to him; when, crying out for help,
The gentlemen of 's chamber found his Grace
All on a cold sweat, altered much in face   90
And language. Since which apparitiön,
He hath grown worse and worse; and I much fear
He cannot live.

BOS.   Sir, I would speak with you.

PES. We 'll leave your Grace,
Wishing to the sick prince, our noble lord,   95
All health of mind and body.

CARD.   You are most welcome.
                [*Exeunt all but the* CARDINAL *and* BOSOLA
Are you come? so.—(*Aside*) This fellow must not know
By any means I had intelligence
In our Duchess' death; for, though I counseled it,
The full of all th' engagement[18] seemed to grow   100
From Ferdinand.—Now, sir, how fares our sister?
I do not think but sorrow makes her look
Like to an oft-dyed garment. She shall now
Taste comfort from me. Why do you look so wildly?
Oh, the fortune of your master here, the Prince,   105
Dejects you; but be you of happy comfort:
If you'll do one thing for me I'll entreat,
Though he had a cold tombstone o'er his bones,
I'd make you what you would be.

BOS.   Anything!
Give it me in a breath, and let me fly to't.   110
They that think long, small expedition[19] win,
For musing much o' th' end cannot begin.

        Enter JULIA

JULIA. Sir, will you come in to supper?

CARD.   I am busy; leave me.

[18] Of Bosola.   [19] Speed.

JULIA (*aside*). What an excellent shape hath that
fellow! [*Exit*

CARD. 'Tis thus: Antonio lurks here in Milan. 115
Inquire him out, and kill him. While he lives,
Our sister cannot marry; and I have thought
Of an excellent match for her. Do this, and style me
Thy advancement.

BOS. But by what means shall I find him out?

CARD. There is a gentleman called Delio 120
Here in the camp, that hath been long approved
His loyal friend. Set eye upon that fellow;
Follow him to mass: may be Antonio,
Although he do account religiön
But a school-name, for fashion of the world 125
May accompany him; or else go inquire out
Delio's confessor, and see if you can bribe
Him to reveal it. There are a thousand ways
A man might find to trace him; as to know
What fellows haunt the Jews, for taking up 130
Great sums of money, for sure he's in want;
Or else to go to th' picture-makers, and learn
Who brought her[20] picture lately—some of these
Happily may take.

BOS. Well, I'll not freeze i' th' business.
I would see that wretched thing, Antonio, 135
Above all sights i' th' world.

CARD. Do, and be happy. [*Exit*

BOS. This fellow doth breed basilisks in's eyes;
He's nothing else but murder. Yet he seems
Not to have notice of the Duchess' death.
'Tis his cunning. I must follow his example; 140
There cannot be a surer way to trace[21]
Than that of an old fox.

Enter JULIA, *with a pistol*

JULIA. So, sir, you are well met.

BOS. How now?

JULIA. Nay, the doors are fast enough.
Now, sir, I will make you confess your treachery. 145

BOS. Treachery?

JULIA. Yes, confess to me
Which of my women 'twas you hired to put
Love-powder into my drink?

BOS. Love-powder!

JULIA. Yes, when I was at Malfi.
Why should I fall in love with such a face else? 150
I have already suffered for thee so much pain,
The only remedy to do me good
Is to kill my longing.

BOS. Sure your pistol holds
Nothing but perfumes or kissing-comfits.[22] Excellent
lady,
You have a pretty way on't to discover 155
Your longing. Come, come, I'll disarm you,
And arm[23] you thus—yet this is wondrous strange.

JULIA. Compare thy form and my eyes together,
You'll find my love no such great miracle. Now you'll
say
I am wanton. This nice modesty in ladies 160
Is but a troublesome familiar[24]
That haunts them.

BOS. Know you me, I am a blunt soldier.

JULIA. The better;
Sure, there wants fire where there are no lively sparks 164
Of roughness.

BOS. And I want compliment.[25]

JULIA. Why, ignorance
In courtship cannot make you do amiss,
If you have a heart to do well.

BOS. You are very fair.

JULIA. Nay, if you lay beauty to my charge,
I must plead unguilty.

BOS. Your bright eyes
Carry a quiver of darts in them, sharper 170
Than sunbeams.

JULIA. You will mar me with commendation,
Put yourself to the charge of courting me,
Whereas now I woo you.

BOS. (*aside*). I have it; I will work upon this creature.—
Let us grow most amorously familiar. [*They embrace*
If the great Cardinal now should see me thus, 176
Would he not count me a villain?

JULIA. No; he might count me a wanton,
Not lay a scruple of offense on you.
For if I see and steal a diamond, 180
The fault is not i' th' stone, but in me, the thief
That purloins it. I am sudden with you.
We that are great women of pleasure use to cut off
These uncertain wishes and unquiet longings,
And in an instant join the sweet delight 185
And the pretty excuse together. Had you been i' th'
street,
Under my chamber window, even there
I should have courted you.

BOS. Oh, you are an excellent lady!

JULIA. Bid me to do somewhat for you presently,
To express I love you.

BOS. I will; and if you love me, 190
Fail not to effect it.

---

[20] The Duchess's—in order to obtain cash. Not that Antonio has
done so. [21] Plan to follow.

[22] Candies to sweeten the breath. [23] Embrace.
[24] Spirit. [25] Courtliness.

The Cardinal is grown wondrous melancholy.
Demand the cause; let him not put you off
With feigned excuse; discover the main ground on't.

JULIA. Why would you know this?

BOS.   I have depended on him,
And I hear that he is fall'n in some disgrace   196
With the Emperor. If he be, like the mice
That forsake falling houses, I would shift
To other dependence.

JULIA.   You shall not need follow the wars;
I'll be your maintenance.

BOS.   And I your loyal servant;[26]   200
But I cannot leave my calling.

JULIA.   Not leave an
Ungrateful general, for the love of a sweet lady?
You are like some cannot sleep in featherbeds,
But must have blocks for their pillows.

BOS.   Will you do this?

JULIA. Cunningly.   205

BOS. Tomorrow, I'll expect th' intelligence.

JULIA. To-morrow! Get you into my cabinet;[27]
You shall have it with you. Do not delay me,
No more than I do you. I am like one
That is condemned; I have my pardon promised,   210
But I would see it sealed. Go, get you in.
You shall see me wind my tongue about his heart,
Like a skein of silk.   [*Exit* BOSOLA

Enter CARDINAL

CARD. Where are you?

Enter Servants

SERVANTS.   Here.

CARD.   Let none upon your lives
Have conference with the Prince Ferdinand,   215
Unless I know it.—(*Aside*) In this distractiön,
                     [*Exeunt* Servants
He may reveal the murther.
Yond's my lingering consumptiön;
I am weary of her, and by any means
Would be quit off.

JULIA.   How now, my Lord, what ails you?

CARD. Nothing.

JULIA.   Oh, you are much altered.   221
Come, I must be your secretary,[28] and remove
This lead from off your bosom. What's the matter?

CARD. I may not tell you.

JULIA.   Are you so far in love with sorrow,
You cannot part with part of it? Or think you   225

I cannot love your Grace when you are sad
As well as merry? Or do you suspect
I, that have been a secret to your heart
These many winters, cannot be the same
Unto your tongue?

CARD.   Satisfy thy longing.   230
The only way to make thee keep my counsel
Is not to tell thee.

JULIA.   Tell your echo this,
Or flatterers, that like echoes still report
What they hear, though most imperfect, and not me;
For, if that you be true unto yourself,   235
I'll know.

CARD.   Will you rack me?

JULIA.   No, judgment shall
Draw it from you; it is an equal fault
To tell one's secrets unto all or none.

CARD. The first argues folly.

JULIA.   But the last, tyranny.

CARD. Very well. Why, imagine I have committed   240
Some secret deed which I desire the world
May never hear of.

JULIA.   Therefore may not I know it?
You have concealed for me as great a sin
As adultery. Sir, never was occasion
For perfect trial of my constancy   245
Till now. Sir, I beseech you.

CARD.   You'll repent it.

JULIA. Never.

CARD. It hurries thee to ruin. I'll not tell thee.
Be well advised, and think what danger 'tis
To receive a prince's secrets. They that do   250
Had need have their breasts hooped with adamant
To contain them. I pray thee, yet be satisfied.
Examine thine own frailty; 'tis more easy
To tie knots than unloose them. 'Tis a secret
That, like a ling'ring poison, may chance lie   255
Spread in thy veins, and kill thee seven year hence.

JULIA. Now you dally with me.

CARD.   No more; thou shalt know it.
By my appointment, the great Duchess of Malfi
And two of her young children, four nights since,
Were strangled.

JULIA.   O heaven, sir! what have you done? 260

CARD. How now? How settles this? Think you your
     bosom
Will be a grave dark and obscure enough
For such a secret?

JULIA.   You have undone yourself, sir.

CARD. Why?

JULIA.   It lies not in me to conceal it.

CARD.   No?
Come, I will swear you to 't upon this book.   265

JULIA. Most religiously.

CARD.   Kiss it.
Now you shall never utter it; thy curiosity
Hath undone thee: thou 'rt poisoned with that book.
Because I knew thou couldst not keep my counsel,
I have bound thee to 't by death.   270

    Re-enter BOSOLA

BOS. For pity sake, hold!
CARD.   Ha, Bosola?
JULIA.   I forgive you
This equal piece of justice you have done,
For I betrayed your counsel to that fellow.
He overheard it; that was the cause I said
It lay not in me to conceal it.
BOS.   O foolish woman,   275
Couldst not thou have poisoned him?
JULIA.   'T is weakness
Too much to think what should have been done. I go,
I know not whither.   [*Dies*
CARD.   Wherefore com'st thou hither?
BOS. That I might find a great man, like yourself,
Not out of his wits as the Lord Ferdinand,   280
To remember my service.
CARD.   I'll have thee hewed in pieces.
BOS. Make not yourself such a promise of that life
Which is not yours to dispose of.
CARD.   Who placed thee here?
BOS. Her lust, as she intended.
CARD.   Very well.
Now you know me for your fellow-murderer.   285
BOS. And wherefore should you lay fair marble colors[29]
Upon your rotten purposes to me?
Unless you imitate some that do plot great treasons
And, when they have done, go hide themselves i' th'
    graves
Of those were actors in 't?
CARD.   No more; there is   290
A fortune attends thee.
BOS. Shall I go sue to Fortune any longer?
'T is the fool's pilgrimage.
CARD. I have honors in store for thee.   294
BOS. There are a-many ways that conduct to seeming
Honor, and some of them very dirty ones.
CARD. Throw to the Devil
Thy melancholy. The fire burns well;
What need we keep a-stirring of 't, and make
A greater smother?[30] Thou wilt kill Antonio?   300
BOS. Yes.
CARD.   Take up that body.

---

29 I.e., paint imitative of marble.   30 Smoke.

BOS.   I think I shall
Shortly grow the common bier for churchyards!
CARD. I will allow thee some dozen of attendants,
To aid thee in the murther.   304
BOS. Oh, by no means. Physicians that apply horse-
leeches to any rank swelling use to cut off their tails, that
the blood may run through them the faster. Let me have
no train when I go to shed blood, lest it make me have a
greater when I ride to the gallows.   309
CARD. Come to me after midnight, to help to remove
That body to her own lodging. I'll give out
She died o' th' plague; 't will breed the less inquiry
After her death.
BOS.   Where's Castruchio, her husband?
CARD. He's rode to Naples, to take possessiön
Of Antonio's citadel.   315
BOS. Believe me, you have done a very happy turn.
CARD. Fail not to come. There is the master-key
Of our lodgings; and by that you may conceive
What trust I plant in you.
BOS.   You shall find me ready.
                               [*Exit* CARDINAL
O poor Antonio, though nothing be so needful   320
To thy estate as pity, yet I find
Nothing so dangerous. I must look to my footing.
In such slippery ice-pavements, men had need
To be frost-nailed[31] well; they may break their necks
    else.
The precedent 's here afore me. How this man   325
Bears up in blood![32] seems fearless! Why, 't is well.
Security[33] some men call the suburbs of hell,
Only a dead wall between. Well, good Antonio,
I'll seek thee out; and all my care shall be
To put thee into safety from the reach   330
Of these most cruel biters, that have got
Some of thy blood already. It may be,
I'll join with thee in a most just revenge.
The weakest arm is strong enough, that strikes
With the sword of justice. Still methinks the Duchess 335
Haunts me. There, there!—'T is nothing but my
    melancholy.
O Penitence, let me truly taste thy cup,
That throws men down only to raise them up.   [*Exit*

---

31 Equipped with spiked boots.   32 Keeps up his courage.
33 Belief in one's own safety.

SCENE III[34]

Enter ANTONIO *and* DELIO. *A voice for* ECHO, *off stage, from the Duchess's grave*

DELIO. Yond's the Cardinal's window. This fortification
Grew from the ruins of an ancient abbey;
And to yond side o' th' river lies a wall,
Piece of a cloister, which in my opinion
Gives the best echo that you ever heard: 5
So hollow and so dismal, and withal
So plain in the distinction of our words,
That many have supposed it is a spirit
That answers.

ANT.   I do love these ancient ruins.
We never tread upon them but we set   10
Our foot upon some reverend history.
And, questionless, here in this open court,
Which now lies naked to the injuries
Of stormy weather, some men lie interred
Loved the church so well, and gave so largely to 't,   15
They thought it should have canopied their bones
Till doomsday. But all things have their end;
Churches and cities, which have diseases like to men,
Must have like death that we have.

ECHO.   Like death that we have.
DELIO. Now the echo hath caught you.
ANT.   It groaned, methought, and gave   20
A very deadly accent!
ECHO.   Deadly accent.
DELIO. I told you 't was a pretty one. You may make it
A huntsman, or a falconer, a musician,
Or a thing of sorrow.
ECHO.   A thing of sorrow.
ANT. Ay, sure, that suits it best.
ECHO.   That suits it best.   25
ANT. 'T is very like my wife's voice.
ECHO.   Ay, wife's voice.
DELIO. Come, let's us walk farther from 't. I would not
    have you
Go to th' Cardinal's tonight. Do not!
ECHO.   Do not.
DELIO. Wisdom doth not more moderate wasting
    sorrow
Than time. Take time for 't; be mindful of thy safety.   30
ECHO. Be mindful of thy safety.
ANT.   Necessity compels me.
Make scrutiny throughout the passages
Of your own life; you'll find it impossible
To fly your fate.

---

[34] Part of the fortifications of Milan.

ECHO.   O fly your fate.
DELIO. Hark! the dead stones seem to have pity on
    you,   35
And give you good counsel.
ANT.   Echo, I will not talk with thee,
For thou art a dead thing.
ECHO.   Thou art a dead thing.
ANT. My Duchess is asleep now,
And her little ones, I hope sweetly. O heaven,
Shall I never see her more?
ECHO.   Never see her more.   40
ANT. I marked not one repetition of the echo
But that; and on the sudden a clear light
Presented me a face folded in sorrow.
DELIO. Your fancy merely.
ANT.   Come, I'll be out of this ague.
For to live thus is not indeed to live;   45
It is a mockery and abuse of life.
I will not henceforth save myself by halves;
Lose all, or nothing.
DELIO.   Your own virtue save you!
I'll fetch your eldest son, and second you.
It may be that the sight of his[35] own blood,   50
Spread in so sweet a figure, may beget
The more compassion.
ANT.   However,[36] fare you well.
Though in our miseries Fortune have a part,
Yet in our noble suff'rings she hath none.
Contempt of pain, that we may call our own.   55
                                        [*Exeunt*

SCENE IV[37]

Enter CARDINAL, PESCARA, MALATESTE, RODERIGO, *and*
GRISOLAN

CARD. You shall not watch tonight by the sick prince;
His Grace is very well recovered.
MAL. Good my Lord, suffer us.
CARD.   Oh, by no means;
The noise, and change of object in his eye,
Doth more distract him. I pray, all to bed;   5
And though you hear him in his violent fit,
Do not rise, I entreat you.
PES. So, sir; we shall not.
CARD.   Nay, I must have you promise
Upon your honors, for I was enjoined to 't
By himself; and he seemed to urge it sensibly.   10
PES. Let our honors bind this trifle.
CARD. Nor any of your followers.
MAL. Neither.

---

[35] The Cardinal's. [36] Whatever happens.
[37] The Cardinal's palace.

CARD. It may be, to make trial of your promise,
When he's asleep, myself will rise and feign   15
Some of his mad tricks, and cry out for help,
And feign myself in danger.
    MAL. If your throat were cutting,
I'd not come at you, now I have protested against it.
    CARD. Why, I thank you.
    GRIS. (*aside*).   'Twas a foul storm tonight.[38] 20
    ROD. (*aside*). The Lord Ferdinand's chamber shook like
        an osier.
    MAL. (*aside*). 'Twas nothing but pure kindness in the
        Devil,
To rock his own child.   [*Exeunt all but the* CARDINAL
    CARD. The reason why I would not suffer these
About my brother is because at midnight   25
I may with better privacy convey
Julia's body to her own lodging. O my conscience!
I would pray now; but the Devil takes away my heart
For having any confidence in prayer.
About this hour I appointed Bosola   30
To fetch the body. When he hath served my turn,
He dies.   [*Exit*

            Enter BOSOLA

    BOS. Ha! 'twas the Cardinal's voice; I heard him name
Bosola and my death. Listen, I hear one's footing.

            Enter FERDINAND

    FERD. Strangling is a very quiet death.   35
    BOS. (*aside*). Nay then, I see, I must stand upon my
        guard.
    FERD. What say to that? whisper softly; do you agree
to't? So; it must be done i' th' dark; the Cardinal would
not for a thousand pounds the doctor should see   [39
it.   [*Exit*
    BOS. My death is plotted; here's the consequence of
        murther.
We value not desert nor Christian breath,
When we know black deeds must be cured with death.

            Enter ANTONIO *and a* Servant

    SERV. Here stay, sir, and be confident, I pray.   44
I'll fetch you a dark lantern.   [*Exit*
    ANT. Could I take him[39] at his prayers,
There were hope of pardon.
    BOS. Fall right my sword!—
I'll not give thee so much leisure as to pray.   [*He strikes*

    ANT. Oh, I am gone! Thou hast ended a long suit   50
In a minute.
    BOS.   What art thou?
    ANT.   A most wretched thing,
That only have thy benefit in death,
To appear myself.

        Re-enter Servant *with a light*

    SERV. Where are you, sir?
    ANT. Very near my home.—Bosola!   55
    SERV. Oh, misfortune!
    BOS. Smother thy pity; thou art dead else.—Antonio!
The man I would have saved 'bove mine own life!—
We are merely the stars' tennis balls, struck and banded[40]
Which way please them.—O good Antonio,   60
I'll whisper one thing in thy dying ear,
Shall make thy heart break quickly. Thy fair Duchess
And two sweet children—
    ANT.   Their very names
Kindle a little life in me.
    BOS.   Are murdered.
    ANT. Some men have wished to die   65
At the hearing of sad tidings. I am glad
That I shall do't, in sadness.[41] I would not now
Wish my wounds balmed nor healed, for I have no use
To put my life to. In all our quest of greatness,
Like wanton boys whose pastime is their care,   70
We follow after bubbles blown in th' air.
Pleasure of life, what is't? Only the good hours
Of an ague; merely a preparative to rest,
To endure vexation. I do not ask
The process[42] of my death; only commend me   75
To Delio.
    BOS. Break, heart!
    ANT. And let my son fly the courts of princes.   [*Dies*
    BOS. Thou seem'st to have loved Antonio?
    SERV. I brought him hither,   80
To have reconciled him to the Cardinal.
    BOS. I do not ask thee that:[43]
Take him up, if thou tender thine own life,
And bear him where the Lady Julia
Was wont to lodge.—Oh, my fate moves swift.   85
I have this Cardinal in the forge already,
Now I'll bring him to th' hammer. O direful misprision![44]
I will not imitate things glorious,
No more than base; I'll be mine own example.—
On, on, and look thou represent,[45] for silence,   90
The thing thou bear'st.   [*Exeunt*

---

[38] Last night.
[39] The Cardinal. But, in the darkness, Antonio is taken by Bosola
    for an assassin planning *his* death.

[40] Bandied.   [41] A pun. In sober truth.   [42] An account.
[43] Ask you to do that.   [44] Mistake.   [45] Imitate.

Enter CARDINAL, *with a book*

CARD. I am puzzled in a question about hell.
He says, in hell there's one material fire,
And yet it shall not burn all men alike.
Lay him by. How tedious is a guilty conscience!
When I look into the fishponds in my garden,   5
Methinks I see a thing armed with a rake,
That seems to strike at me.

Enter BOSOLA *and* Servant *bearing* ANTONIO's *body*

                    Now! art thou come?
Thou look'st ghastly;
There sits in thy face some great determination,
Mixed with some fear.
BOS.   Thus it lightens into action: 10
I am come to kill thee.
CARD.   Ha!—Help! our guard!
BOS. Thou art deceived; they are out of thy howling.
CARD. Hold; and I will faithfully divide
Revenues with thee.
BOS.   Thy prayers and proffers
Are both unseasonable.
CARD.   Raise the watch!   15
We are betrayed!
BOS.   I have confined your flight.
I'll suffer your retreat to Julia's chamber,
But no further.
CARD.   Help! we are betrayed!

Enter, above,[47] PESCARA, MALATESTE, RODERIGO, *and*
GRISOLAN

MAL. Listen.
CARD. My dukedom for rescue!   20
ROD. Fie upon his counterfeiting!
MAL. Why, 't is not the Cardinal.
ROD. Yes, yes, 't is he.
But I'll see him hanged ere I'll go down to him.
CARD. Here's a plot upon me; I am assaulted! I am
    lost,   25
Unless some rescue.
GRIS.   He doth this pretty well;
But it will not serve. To laugh me out of mine honor!
CARD. The sword 's at my throat!
ROD.   You would not bawl so loud then.
MAL. Come, come, let 's go to bed; he told us thus
    much aforehand.

PES. He wished you should not come at him; but,
    believe 't,   30
The accent of the voice sounds not in jest.
I'll down to him, howsoever, and with engines
Force ope the doors.   [*Exit above*
ROD.   Let's follow him aloof,
And note how the Cardinal will laugh at him.
                                        [*Exeunt above*
BOS. There's for you first,   35
'Cause you shall not unbarricade the door
To let in rescue.   [*He kills the* Servant
CARD. What cause hast thou to pursue my life?
BOS.   Look there.
CARD. Antonio?
BOS.   Slain by my hand unwittingly.
Pray, and be sudden. When thou killed'st thy sister,   40
Thou took'st from Justice her most equal balance,
And left her naught but her sword.
CARD.   Oh, mercy!
BOS. Now it seems thy greatness was only outward;
For thou fall'st faster of thyself than calamity
Can drive thee. I'll not waste longer time. There!   45
                                        [*Wounds him*
CARD. Thou hast hurt[48] me.
BOS.   Again!   [*Wounds him*
CARD.   Shall I die like a leveret,[49]
Without any resistance?—Help, help, help!
I am slain!

Enter FERDINAND

FERD.   Th' alarum! Give me a fresh horse!
Rally the vauntguard,[50] or the day is lost!
Yield, yield! I give you the honor of arms,[51]   50
Shake my sword over you; will you yield?
CARD. Help me; I am your brother!
FERD.   The devil!
My brother fight upon the adverse party!
    [*He wounds the* CARDINAL, *and (in the scuffle) gives*
    BOSOLA *his death-wound*
There flies your ransom.[52]
CARD. O justice!   55
I suffer now for what hath former been;
Sorrow is held the eldest child of sin.
FERD. Now you're brave fellows. Caesar's fortune was
harder than Pompey's. Caesar died in the arms of pros-
perity, Pompey at the feet of disgrace. You both   [60
died in the field. The pain 's nothing; pain many times is
taken away with the apprehension of greater, as the tooth-

---

48 Wounded.
49 Young hare.   50 Vanguard.
51 Fair terms of surrender.
52 I.e., I've lost it by killing you.

ache with the sight of a barber that comes to pull it out.
There's philosophy for you.

BOS. Now my revenge is perfect. Sink, thou main
 cause   [*He kills* FERDINAND 65
Of my undoing. The last part of my life
Hath done me best service.

FERD. Give me some wet hay, I am broken-winded.
I do account this world but a dog kennel.
I will vault credit[53] and affect high pleasures,   70
Beyond death.

BOS.   He seems to come to himself,
Now he's so near the bottom.

FERD. My sister, oh, my sister! there's the cause on't.
Whether we fall by ambition, blood, or lust,
Like diamonds we are cut with our own dust.   [*Dies* 75

CARD. Thou hast thy payment too.

BOS. Yes, I hold my weary soul in my teeth;
'Tis ready to part from me. I do glory
That thou, which stood'st like a huge pyramid
Begun upon a large and ample base,   80
Shalt end in a little point, a kind of nothing.

Enter PESCARA, MALATESTE, RODERIGO, *and* GRISOLAN

PES. How now, my Lord!

MAL.   O sad disaster!

ROD.   How comes this?

BOS. Revenge for the Duchess of Malfi, murdered
By the Aragonian brethren; for Antonio,
Slain by this hand; for lustful Julia,   85
Poisoned by this man; and lastly for myself,
That was an actor in the main of all,
Much 'gainst mine own good nature, yet i' th' end
Neglected.

PES.   How now, my Lord?

CARD.   Look to my brother.
He gave us these large wounds, as we were struggling 90
Here i' th' rushes.[54] And now, I pray, let me

Be laid by and never thought of.   [*Dies*

PES. How fatally, it seems, he did withstand
His own rescue!

MAL.   Thou wretched thing of blood,
How came Antonio by his death?   95

BOS. In a mist. I know not how—
Such a mistake as I have often seen
In a play. Oh, I am gone!
We are only like dead walls or vaulted graves,
That, ruined, yields no echo. Fare you well.   100
It may be pain, but no harm, to me to die
In so good a quarrel. O this gloomy world!
In what a shadow or deep pit of darkness
Doth (womanish, and fearful) mankind live!
Let worthy minds ne'er stagger in distrust   105
To suffer death or shame for what is just.
Mine is another voyage.   [*Dies*

PES. The noble Delio, as I came to th' palace,
Told me of Antonio's being here, and showed me
A pretty gentleman, his son and heir.   110

Enter DELIO *and* ANTONIO'S SON

MAL. O sir, you come too late!

DELIO.   I heard so, and
Was armed for't, ere I came. Let us make noble use
Of this great ruin, and join all our force
To establish this young hopeful[55] gentleman
In's mother's right. These wretched eminent things 115
Leave no more fame behind 'em than should one
Fall in a frost, and leave his print in snow:
As soon as the sun shines, it ever melts,
Both form and matter. I have ever thought
Nature doth nothing so great for great men   120
As when she's pleased to make them lords of truth.
Integrity of life is fame's best friend,
Which nobly, beyond death, shall crown the end.

     [*Exeunt*

---

[53] Aspire incredibly high.   [54] With which floors were strewn.   [55] Promising.

Robert Herrick

1591–1674

HERRICK is the most distinguished of the "sons of Ben." The garden he cultivated was a small one, but within its confines he comes nearer perfection than his master. Herrick has no such range as Jonson, no such intellectual force. He is a kind of miniaturist, painting perfectly, but on a small scale. His work is marked by a quiet mastery, rather than by energy or power. Even his love of nature is expressed on a small scale—in a portrait of a flower, not the sweep of a landscape. Yet this very intimacy endears him; he is among the best loved of the poets.

It was Jonson's Horatian side that appealed to Herrick, most of whose verse is really light verse, lacking deep feeling, with little in it of wildness or wonder. Nevertheless he has an excellent claim to first place among the century's lyrists: for the quantity as well as the quality of his poetry, for its engagingly personal flavor, and for its great charm. Sensuousness is another characteristic. Herrick's poems are fresh and close to life; his directness avoids both the Petrarchan and the metaphysical conceits. Much of his work is pagan in spirit; but except in his vituperative epigrams it is always sweet, even when his realism is frankly sensual, and there are many serious poems which show a genuine though not profound religious feeling. Another great merit is his master-craftsmanship; he is technically a virtuoso in the variety of his meters and in his verbal melody. Besides Jonson, his tutors were the great classical lyrists: Anacreon, Horace, and Catullus, and for his satirical epigrams—some are coarse, many are witty—Martial.

Herrick was born in London, the son of a prosperous goldsmith. His father's suicide, in Robert's second year, left the widow and her six children well provided for; she took them to Hampton, a few miles up the Thames, and there the poet was reared, in the country. Nothing is known of his schooling. In his seventeenth year he was apprenticed to his uncle, Sir William Herrick, a leading London goldsmith. The profusion of rich jewels in Herrick's verses may hark back to his apprenticeship. However that may be, at twenty-two the poet, who seems to have had little money of his own, changed his mind about his calling and entered Cambridge University. He was, of course, much older than most of the undergraduates. He took his B. A. in 1617, and his M. A. three years later. Residence was no longer required for the second degree, which did not involve much work.

What Herrick did with himself for the ten years after 1617 is uncertain. Probably, like Donne in his youth, he lived a pleasant and, except for his verse-writing, a rather aimless life in London. Evidently he was a member, till about 1625 an inconspicuous member, of Jonson's circle. To what extent his poems about his "mistresses" reflect actual experience is an unsolved question. Herrick never married. He may have had many a love affair; or, like some of the Elizabethan sonneteers, he may have been inspired

> Less by desire to kiss and tell
> Than by a lust for writing well.

The impossibility of drawing biographical conclusions from the unsupported evidence of his poetry is illustrated by the charming epitaph on his housekeeper, Prudence Baldwin. It was composed about thirty years before Herrick's death, and Prue outlived him four years. Nor does the arrangement of the poems in the original edition help us. Contrast, not order of composition, seems to be the principle; few of them can be dated.

When Herrick was ordained a minister of the Church of England is not known. In 1627 he was appointed chaplain to George Villiers, first Duke of Buckingham, and with that unprincipled favorite of King James and King Charles he embarked on a disastrous expedition intended to help the Huguenots besieged at La Rochelle. Presumably it was through Buckingham that Herrick won the favor of Charles, who in 1629 made him vicar at Dean Prior, a hamlet on the edge of Dartmoor, in the beautiful county of Devonshire. Herrick's life there—for eighteen years, till 1647—seems to have been one of mixed emotions. We should not, however, take too seriously his description of his parishioners as

> A people currish, churlish as the seas,
> And rude almost as rudest savages.

Dean Prior meant losing the fellowship of the wits in the capital; but Herrick's poems are full of zest for the simple pleasures of the neighborhood, the wakes, Maypoles, and harvest home. Such complaints as

> Search worlds of ice, and rather there
> Dwell than in loathèd Devonshire

were very likely inspired by his resentment when, at the triumph of the Puritan party, he was ejected from his parish by the new rulers of the Church. Herrick was a royalist, perhaps too stout a one for the taste of his flock. He went to London, where he had rich relatives. He lived to be restored by Charles II to his vicarage and twelve more years in Dean Prior. He knew well enough what he owed to his first sojourn there, even though tradition has him throwing the manuscript of his sermon at the heads of an unresponsive congregation:

DISCONTENTS IN DEVON

More discontents I never had
  Since I was born than here
Where I have been and still am sad,
  In this dull Devonshire.
Yet justly too I must confess
  I ne'er invented such
Ennobled numbers[1] for the press
  Than where I loathed so much.

The numbers, many of which had long circulated in manuscript, were not printed till 1648. Evidently their publication was Herrick's first concern when he reached London after the loss of his "living." He called the volume after the fabled garden of the golden apples: *Hesperides, or The Works Humane and Divine of Robert Herrick, Esq.* The "divine" poems, *Noble Numbers,* follow the lighter verse, with a title page of their own. The book came too late; taste had changed in favor of a drier, less lyric form of neoclassicism. The countryside was unfashionable, at any rate in literature. Set to music, however, especially by William and Henry Lawes, some of Herrick's poems became immensely popular as songs.

The standard edition is the *Poetical Works* (1915), edited by F. W. Moorman, author of *Robert Herrick, a Biographical and Critical Study* (1910). The poems are also reprinted in Everyman's Library and in The World's Classics.

from HESPERIDES
THE ARGUMENT[2] OF HIS BOOK

I sing of brooks, of blossoms, birds, and bowers:
Of April, May, of June, and July flowers.
I sing of Maypoles, hock-carts,[3] wassails, wakes,
Of bridegrooms, brides, and of their bridal cakes.
I write of youth, of love, and have access   5
By these to sing of cleanly wantonness.[4]
I sing of dews, of rains, and piece by piece
Of balm, of oil, of spice, and ambergris.[5]
I sing of Time's trans-shifting; and I write
How roses first came red, and lilies white.   10
I write of groves, of twilights, and I sing
The court of Mab,[6] and of the Fairy King.
I write of hell; I sing (and ever shall)
Of heaven, and hope to have it after all.

TO THE SOUR READER

If thou dislik'st the piece thou light'st on first,
Think that, of all that I have writ, the worst;
But if thou read'st my book unto the end,
And still dost this and that verse reprehend,—
O perverse man! If all disgustful be,   5
The extreme scab[7] take thee and thine, for me.

WHEN HE WOULD
HAVE HIS VERSES READ

In sober mornings, do not thou rehearse
The holy incantation of a verse;
But when that men have both well drunk and fed,
Let my enchantments then be sung, or read.
When laurel spirts[8] i' th' fire, and when the hearth   5
Smiles to itself and gilds the roof with mirth;
When up the thyrse[9] is raised, and when the sound
Of sacred orgies[10] flies—A round, a round![11]
When the rose reigns, and locks with ointments shine,
Let rigid Cato[12] read these lines of mine.   10

UPON THE LOSS OF HIS MISTRESSES

I have lost, and lately, these
Many dainty mistresses:
Stately Julia, prime of all;
Sappho next, a principal;
Smooth Anthea, for a skin   5
White and heavenlike crystalline;
Sweet Electra, and the choice
Myrrha, for the lute and voice.
Next, Corinna, for her wit,
And the graceful use of it;   10
With Perilla: all are gone;
Only Herrick's left alone,
For to number sorrow by
Their departures hence, and die.

---

[1] Verses.
[2] Theme, summary.
[3] The wagon that brought in the last load of the harvest was called a hock-cart. Its arrival was the signal for the merrymaking of harvest home.—*Wakes*=parish festivals.
[4] Wholesome gaiety.   [5] I.e., perfume.
[6] The fairy queen.   [7] A skin disease.

[8] Flares.   [9] Staff twined with ivy, a symbol of Bacchus.
[10] "Songs to Bacchus" (marginal note in original).
[11] The call for a song.   [12] I.e., critic or censor.

CHERRY-RIPE

"Cherry-ripe, ripe, ripe," I cry,
"Full and fair ones; come and buy!"
If so be you ask me where
They do grow, I answer, "There,
Where my Julia's lips do smile,   5
There's the land, or Cherry-Isle,
Whose plantations fully show,
All the year, where cherries grow."

DELIGHT IN DISORDER

A sweet disorder in the dress
Kindles in clothes a wantonness:
A lawn[13] about the shoulders thrown
Into a fine distractiön,
An erring lace which here and there   5
Enthralls the crimson stomacher,[14]
A cuff neglectful and thereby
Ribbands to flow confusedly,
A winning wave (deserving note)
In the tempestuous petticoat,   10
A careless shoestring in whose tie
I see a wild civility,[15]
Do more bewitch me than when art
Is too precise in every part.

TO DIANEME

Sweet, be not proud of those two eyes,
Which starlike sparkle in their skies;
Nor be you proud that you can see
All hearts your captives, yours, yet free;
Be you not proud of that rich hair,   5
Which wantons with the lovesick air:
Whenas that ruby which you wear,
Sunk from the tip of your soft ear,
Will last to be a precious stone,
When all your world of beauty's gone.   10

CORINNA'S GOING A-MAYING

Get up, get up, for shame; the blooming Morn[16]
Upon her wings presents the god unshorn.[17]
    See how Aurora throws her fair
    Fresh-quilted[18] colors through the air.
    Get up, sweet slug-a-bed, and see   5
    The dew bespangling herb and tree.

Each flower has wept, and bowed toward the East,
Above an hour since; yet you not dressed,
    Nay! not so much as out of bed?
    When all the birds have matins[19] said   10
    And sung their thankful hymns, 'tis sin,
    Nay, profanation to keep in,
Whenas[20] a thousand virgins on this day
Spring, sooner than the lark, to fetch in May.

Rise! and put on your foliage, and be seen   15
To come forth, like the springtime, fresh and green,
    And sweet as Flora.[21] Take no care
    For jewels for your gown, or hair;
    Fear not, the leaves will strew
    Gems in abundance upon you;   20
Besides, the childhood of the day has kept,
Against you come, some orient pearls unwept;[22]
    Come, and receive them while the light
    Hangs on the dewlocks of the night,
    And Titan[23] on the eastern hill   25
    Retires himself or else stands still
Till you come forth. Wash, dress, be brief in praying!
Few beads[24] are best, when once we go a-Maying.

Come, my Corinna, come; and, coming, mark
How each field turns a street, each street a park   30
    Made green and trimmed with trees. See how
    Devotion gives each house a bough
    Or branch; each porch, each door, ere this
    An ark, a tabernacle, is,
Made up of whitethorn, neatly interwove;   35
As if here were those cooler shades of love.
    Can such delights be in the street
    And open fields, and we not see 't?
    Come, we'll abroad; and let's obey
    The proclamation made for May,   40
And sin no more, as we have done, by staying;
But, my Corinna, come, let's go a-Maying.

There's not a budding boy or girl this day
But is got up, and gone to bring in May.
    A deal of youth, ere this, is come   45
    Back, and with whitethorn laden home.
    Some have dispatched their cakes and cream,
    Before that we have left to dream;
And some have wept and wooed and plighted troth,
And chose their priest, ere we can cast off sloth.   50
    Many a green-gown has been given,[25]
    Many a kiss, both odd and even;[26]

---

13 Sheer scarf.   14 Front of bodice.   15 Elegance.
16 Aurora, goddess of the dawn.
17 Apollo, the sun god, with his streaming hair (rays).
18 I.e., bright and variegated, as in a new patchwork quilt.

19 Service of Morning Prayer.   20 When.
21 Goddess of flowers.   22 I.e., dewdrops.   23 The sun.
24 Prayers.
25 I.e., there has been much lovemaking. *Green-gown* = one stained
    by the grass.   26 Perhaps = unreturned and returned.

Many a glance, too, has been sent
From out the eye, love's firmament;
Many a jest told of the keys' betraying   55
This night, and locks picked, yet w'are not a-Maying.

Come, let us go while we are in our prime,
And take the harmless folly of the time.
  We shall grow old apace, and die
  Before we know our liberty.   60
  Our life is short, and our days run
  As fast away as does the sun;
And, as a vapor or a drop of rain,
Once lost, can ne'er be found again,
  So, when or you or I are made   65
  A fable, song, or fleeting shade,
  All love, all liking, all delight,
  Lies drowned with us in endless night.
Then while time serves, and we are but decaying,
Come, my Corinna, come, let's go a-Maying.   70

TO THE VIRGINS, TO MAKE MUCH OF TIME[27]

  Gather ye rosebuds while ye may:
    Old Time is still a-flying;
  And this same flower that smiles today,
    Tomorrow will be dying.

  The glorious lamp of heaven, the sun,   5
    The higher he's a-getting,
  The sooner will his race be run,
    And nearer he's to setting.

  That age is best which is the first,
    When youth and blood are warmer;   10
  But being spent, the worse and worst
    Times, still succeed the former.

  Then be not coy, but use your time;
    And while ye may, go marry:
  For, having lost but once your prime,   15
    You may for ever tarry.

---

[27] This lyric was set by William Lawes (d. 1645). It seems to have been the most popular of all poems in the second half of the seventeenth century.

HIS POETRY HIS PILLAR

  Only a little more
    I have to write;
    Then I'll give o'er,
  And bid the world good night.

  'T is but a flying minute   5
    That I must stay,
    Or linger in it;
  And then I must away.

  O Time, that cut'st down all,
    And scarce leav'st here   10
    Memorial
  Of any men that were!

  How many lie forgot
    In vaults beneath,
    And piecemeal rot   15
  Without a fame in death?

  Behold this living stone
    I rear for me,
    Ne'er to be thrown
  Down, envious Time, by thee.   20

  Pillars let some set up,
    If so they please.
    Here is my hope,
  And my Pyrámidès.[28]

TO ANTHEA, WHO MAY COMMAND HIM ANYTHING

  Bid me to live, and I will live
    Thy protestant[29] to be;
  Or bid me love, and I will give
    A loving heart to thee.

  A heart as soft, a heart as kind,   5
    A heart as sound and free,
  As in the whole world thou canst find,
    That heart I'll give to thee.

  Bid that heart stay, and it will stay,
    To honor thy decree;   10
  Or bid it languish quite away,
    And 't shall do so for thee.

---

[28] Pyramids; i.e., monument.   [29] Devotee, suitor.

Bid me to weep, and I will weep,
  While I have eyes to see;
And having none, yet will I keep   15
  A heart to weep for thee.

Bid me despair, and I'll despair,
  Under that cypress tree;
Or bid me die, and I will dare
  E'en death, to die for thee.   20

Thou art my life, my love, my heart,
  The very eyes of me;
And hast command of every part,
  To live and die for thee.

UPON A CHILD THAT DIED

Here she lies, a pretty bud,
  Lately made of flesh and blood;
Who as soon fell fast asleep,
  As her little eyes did peep.
Give her strewings, but not stir   5
  The earth that lightly covers her.

TO DAFFODILS

Fair daffodils, we weep to see
  You haste away so soon.
As yet, the early-rising sun
  Has not attained his noon.
    Stay, stay,   5
    Until the hasting day
      Has run
    But to the evensong;[30]
And, having prayed together, we
    Will go with you along.   10

We have short time to stay, as you;
  We have as short a spring;
As quick a growth to meet decay,
  As you, or any thing.
    We die,   15
  As your hours do, and dry
      Away,
  Like to the summer's rain;
Or as the pearls of morning dew,
  Ne'er to be found again.   20

---

[30] Vesper service.

MEAT WITHOUT MIRTH

Eaten I have; and though I had good cheer,
I did not sup, because no friends were there.
Where mirth and friends are absent when we dine
Or sup, there wants the incense and the wine.

HIS PRAYER TO BEN JONSON

When I a verse shall make,
  Know I have prayed thee,
For old religion's sake,
  Saint Ben, to aid me.

Make the way smooth for me,   5
  When I, thy Herrick,
Honoring thee, on my knee
  Offer my lyric.

Candles I'll give to thee,
  And a new altar;   10
And thou, Saint Ben, shalt be
  Writ in my psalter.

THE NIGHT-PIECE, TO JULIA

Her eyes the glowworm lend thee;
The shooting stars attend thee;
  And the elves also,
  Whose little eyes glow
Like the sparks of fire, befriend thee.   5

No will-o'-th'-wisp mislight thee,
Nor snake nor slowworm bite thee;
  But on, on thy way
  Not making a stay,
Since ghost there's none to affright thee. 10

Let not the dark thee cumber;
What though the moon does slumber?
  The stars of the night
  Will lend thee their light,
Like tapers clear without number.   15

Then, Julia, let me woo thee,
Thus, thus, to come unto me;
  And when I shall meet
  Thy silv'ry feet,
My soul I'll pour into thee.   20

NOT EVERY DAY FIT FOR VERSE[31]

'Tis not ev'ry day that I
Fitted am to prophesy.
No, but when the spirit fills
The fantastic pannicles[32]
Full of fire, then I write   5
As the godhead doth indite.
Thus enraged,[33] my lines are hurled,
Like the Sibyl's,[34] through the world.
Look how next the holy fire
Either slakes,[35] or doth retire;   10
So the fancy[36] cools, till when
That brave[37] spirit comes again.

A TERNARY[38] OF LITTLES, UPON
A PIPKIN OF JELLY SENT TO A LADY

A little saint best fits a little shrine,
A little prop best fits a little vine,
As my small cruse[39] best fits my little wine.

A little seed best fits a little soil,
A little trade best fits a little toil,   5
As my small jar best fits my little oil.

A little bin best fits a little bread,
A little garland fits a little head,
As my small stuff best fits my little shed.

A little hearth best fits a little fire,   10
A little chapel fits a little quire,
As my small bell best fits my little spire.

A little stream best fits a little boat,
A little lead best fits a little float,[40]
As my small pipe best fits my little note.   15

A little meat best fits a little belly,
As sweetly, lady, give me leave to tell ye,
This little pipkin[41] fits this little jelly.

UPON JULIA'S CLOTHES

Whenas in silks my Julia goes,
Then, then, methinks, how sweetly flows
That liquefaction of her clothes.

Next, when I cast mine eyes and see
That brave vibration each way free,   5
O how that glittering taketh me!

UPON PRUE, HIS MAID

In this little urn is laid
Prudence Baldwin, once my maid,
From whose happy spark here let
Spring the purple violet.

AN ODE FOR HIM[42]

Ah, Ben!
Say how or when
Shall we, thy guests,
Meet at those lyric feasts
Made at the Sun,   5
The Dog, the Triple Tun?[43]
Where we such clusters[44] had
As made us nobly wild, not mad;
And yet each verse of thine
Outdid the meat, outdid the frolic wine.   10

My Ben,
Or come again,
Or send to us
Thy wit's great overplus;
But teach us yet   15
Wisely to husband it,
Lest we that talent spend,
And, having once brought to an end
That precious stock, the store   19
Of such a wit the world should have no more.

from NOBLE NUMBERS

HIS LITANY, TO THE HOLY SPIRIT

In the hour of my distress,
When temptations me oppress,
And when I my sins confess,
Sweet Spirit, comfort me!

---

[31] This poem is one of the best statements of the theory of poetic
inspiration.   [32] The imaginative membranes of the brain.
[33] I being in a frenzy of inspiration.
[34] Several prophetesses in classical mythology have this name.
[35] Slackens.   [36] Imagination.   [37] Fine.
[38] Something arranged by threes.   [39] Jar.
[40] On a fishing line.   [41] Small earthen pot.

[42] This poem immediately follows an epitaph "Upon Ben Jonson."
[43] Names of London taverns; the last was actually The Three Tuns.
[44] Of grapes; i.e., wine.

When I lie within my bed,   5
Sick in heart, and sick in head,
And with doubts discomforted,
　　Sweet Spirit, comfort me!

When the house doth sigh and weep,
And the world is drowned in sleep,   10
Yet mine eyes the watch do keep,
　　Sweet Spirit, comfort me!

When the artless doctor sees
No one hope, but of his fees,
And his skill runs on the lees,[45]   15
　　Sweet Spirit, comfort me!

When his potion and his pill
Has or none or little skill,
Meet for nothing but to kill,
　　Sweet Spirit, comfort me!   20

When the passing-bell doth toll,
And the Furies in a shoal
Come to fright a parting soul,
　　Sweet Spirit, comfort me!

When the tapers now burn blue,   25
And the comforters are few,
And that number more than true,
　　Sweet Spirit, comfort me!

When the priest his last hath prayed,
And I nod to what is said,   30
'Cause my speech is now decayed,
　　Sweet Spirit, comfort me!

When, God knows, I'm tossed about,
Either with despair or doubt,
Yet before the glass[46] be out,   35
　　Sweet Spirit, comfort me!

When the Tempter me pursu'th
With the sins of all my youth,
And half damns me with untruth,
　　Sweet Spirit, comfort me!   40

When the flames and hellish cries
Fright mine ears and fright mine eyes,
And all terrors me surprise,
　　Sweet Spirit, comfort me!

When the judgment is revealed,   45
And that opened which was sealed,
When to thee I have appealed,
　　Sweet Spirit, comfort me!

A THANKSGIVING TO GOD,
FOR HIS HOUSE

Lord, thou hast given me a cell
　　Wherein to dwell,
A little house, whose humble roof
　　Is weatherproof,
Under the spars of which I lie   5
　　Both soft and dry,
Where thou, my chamber for to ward,
　　Hast set a guard
Of harmless thoughts, to watch and keep
　　Me while I sleep.   10
Low is my porch, as is my fate,
　　Both void of state;
And yet the threshold of my door
　　Is worn by th' poor,
Who thither come and freely get   15
　　Good words or meat.
Like as my parlor, so my hall
　　And kitchen's small:
A little buttery, and therein
　　A little bin,   20
Which keeps my little loaf of bread
　　Unchipped, unflead.[47]
Some brittle sticks of thorn or briar
　　Make me a fire,
Close by whose living coal I sit,   25
　　And glow like it.
Lord, I confess too, when I dine,
　　The pulse[48] is thine,
And all those other bits that be
　　There placed by thee,   30
The worts,[49] the purslane,[50] and the mess
　　Of water cress,
Which of thy kindness thou hast sent;
　　And my content
Makes those, and my belovèd beet,   35
　　To be more sweet.
'Tis thou that crown'st my glittering hearth
　　With guiltless mirth,
And giv'st me wassail bowls to drink,
　　Spiced to the brink.   40

[47] Perhaps = unflayed, i.e., safe against nibbling mice. Possibly, a dialectal word meaning free from mold.
[48] Peas, beans, etc.　　　[49] Vegetables.
[50] A leafy herb used in soups and salads.

---

[45] I.e., runs low.　　　[46] Hourglass.

Lord, 'tis thy plenty-dropping hand
    That soils[51] my land,
And giv'st me, for my bushel sown,
    Twice ten for one.
Thou mak'st my teeming hen to lay   45
    Her egg each day,
Besides my healthful ewes to bear
    Me twins each year,
The while the conduits of my kine
    Run cream, for wine.   50
All these, and better, thou dost send
    Me, to this end,
That I should render, for my part,
    A thankful heart,
Which, fired with incense, I resign,   55
    As wholly thine;
But the acceptance, that must be,
    My Christ, by thee.

ANOTHER GRACE FOR A CHILD[52]

Here a little child I stand,
Heaving up my either hand;
Cold as paddocks[53] though they be,
Here I lift them up to thee,
For a benison to fall   5
On our meat, and on us all. Amen.

TO KEEP A TRUE LENT

Is this a fast, to keep
    The larder lean,
        And clean
From fat of veals and sheep?

Is it to quit the dish   5
    Of flesh, yet still
        To fill
The platter high with fish?

Is it to fast an hour,
    Or ragg'd to go,   10
        Or show
A downcast look and sour?

No; 'tis a fast, to dole
    Thy sheaf of wheat,
        And meat,   15
Unto the hungry soul.

It is to fast from strife,
    From old debate,
        And hate;
To circumcise[54] thy life;   20

To show a heart grief-rent;
    To starve thy sin,
        Not bin;
And that's to keep thy Lent.

The Devotional Lyrists

THE NUMBER of seventeenth-century sermons which found their way into print is staggering; the amount of religious verse is almost equally so. The men whose poems are reprinted below were not a coterie; but well along in the eighteenth century Dr. Johnson recognized that they had formed a chain of successive influence and that in their fondness for the "metaphysical" conceit or philosophically elaborated comparison they were all more or less influenced by Donne. Their combined efforts produced by far the finest body of religious poetry in English literature.

Dryden (and with him the neoclassical school which triumphed under the Restoration and held the field till its defeat by the Romantics at the end of the eighteenth century) disapproved of the frequent obscurity, extrava-

gance, and conceitfulness which mar many of the poems of these writers. In 1651 the philosopher Thomas Hobbes put the case against their style in an introduction he wrote for the *Gondibert* of Sir William D'avenant, the poet laureate. Hobbes objected to "the ambitious obscurity of expressing more than is perfectly conceived [i.e., thought out]" and charged that many lines are "no better than riddles." Hobbes exalts education, experience, and judgment in a poet above imagination. His was the winning side—till the Romantics blew it to the moon. Meanwhile, the immensely stimulating imaginative sallies of Donne and his followers were discarded for the clear but seldom exciting prose-in-verse of Dryden and Pope.

Dryden, in his "Discourse concerning Satire" (1692),

---

[51] Manures.   [52] Herrick wrote several.
[53] Frogs.

[54] Purify.

applied to Donne the somewhat misleading term which is still employed by some historians for him and for the devotional group: "He affects the *metaphysics* not only in his satires, but in his amorous verses, where nature only should reign, and perplexes the minds of the fair sex with nice speculations of philosophy, when he should engage their hearts." Nearly a century later (in his Life of Abraham Cowley, who along with Andrew Marvell is sometimes lumped in with Donne and the devotional poets) Dr. Johnson declared: "About the beginning of the seventeenth century appeared a race of writers that may be termed *the metaphysical poets*." It was their subtlety and complexity, and their going for their conceits to the abstractions of theology and philosophy instead of to the concrete objects perceived by the senses, which prompted Dr. Johnson's revival of Dryden's term.

A better classification is followed in the present volume. All the poets discussed in this subsection were influenced by Donne; but it is much more important to note that they made the religious lyric, which during the sixteenth century had lapsed from the high estate it reached in the later Middle Ages, an instrument of great beauty as well as of devotion.

For this group and the chain of poetry they forged, see Helen C. White's *The Metaphysical Poets: A Study in Religious Experience* (1936).

George Herbert

1593–1633

Less than a month after he entered Cambridge University, Herbert sent his mother two sonnets in which he dedicated himself to religious poetry. He was only sixteen, but as far as is known he kept that vow to the end of his life of forty years. Herbert had seemed marked by his birth for worldly success. He belonged to the great Herbert family whose heads were the earls of Pembroke. His brother Edward, also a poet, was Lord Herbert of Cherbury; he and several other brothers were soldiers or officials. That George's devotion to the religious life was sometimes troubled by thoughts of the worldly career he had rejected is evident in several poems, especially in "The Collar."

The boys' father died when George was three. They were brought up by their mother, a beautiful and strong-minded woman, a friend of John Donne; his "The Autumnal," with its beautiful opening,

> No spring nor summer beauty hath such grace
> As I have seen in one autumnal face,

may have been written for her. Herbert was educated at Westminster, then England's best school, and at Cambridge. Soon after he took his M. A. he was appointed Reader in Rhetoric. The conspicuous post of Public Orator of the University followed when he was only twenty-seven; his predecessor had stepped directly from it to the secretaryship of state. For several years Herbert seems to have hoped that he might obtain high office; eventually he entered holy orders as a deacon. Family influence brought him ecclesiastical sinecures, but he was plagued with ill health. In 1629 he married, and not long after was ordained to the Anglican priesthood. He was doubtful of his worthiness, and had to be persuaded to accept the rectory of a little church in Wiltshire, at Bemerton, near Salisbury. Once a minister, he proceeded to justify, by his humility, serenity, and devotion to his pastoral duties, the phrase which Izaak Walton was to use in his Life of "holy Mr. Herbert." He was the friend and adviser of the humblest of his flock.

The best of his poems are more fervently lyric than most of the amatory verse of the day; even his fondness for conceits fails to dampen their fire. Donne was the great influence on his style. Herbert was not Donne's intellectual equal, nor has he the older man's power of evoking the mood of wonder; but of their religious poems Herbert's best are far more powerfully winged as lyrics. Like most excellent poets, he wrote a good deal of bad poetry. In some of it his share of the seventeenth-century weakness for "wit" betrays him into such extravagances as acrostic verses, and poems with lines arranged to form the shape of an altar or a pair of wings. He knew such tricks were absurd; his object was to consecrate "wit" to the service of God. In his fervor he sometimes addresses God in the terms of a lover to his mistress. But poets are entitled to be judged at their best; and the best of Herbert stands high, not only among English religious poems but among lyrics in general. His interest in the lyric was aesthetic as well as devotional; he liked to experiment, as the extraordinary variety of his meters testifies.

Herbert wrote Latin as well as English verses. The latter were not printed in his lifetime, but their circulation in manuscript made him famous. They were brought out as a book, *The Temple*, immediately after his death in 1633. A prose work, *A Priest to the Temple, or The Country Parson*, was published in 1652. The standard edition of his works, with commentary and biographical sketch, is by F. E. Hutchinson (1941). There is also an Everyman's Library edition.

VIRTUE

Sweet day, so cool, so calm, so bright,
    The bridal of the earth and sky,
The dew shall weep thy fall tonight,
    For thou must die.

Sweet rose, whose hue, angry[1] and brave,   5
    Bids the rash gazer wipe his eye,
Thy root is ever in its grave,
    And thou must die.

Sweet spring, full of sweet days and roses,
    A box where sweets compacted lie,   10
My music shows ye have your closes,[2]
    And all must die.

Only a sweet and virtuous soul,
    Like seasoned timber, never gives;
But though the whole world turn to coal,[3]   15
    Then chiefly lives.

DULLNESS

In its curious mingling of the witty and the intensely devotional, this poem is characteristic of much seventeenth-century religious verse. To Herbert it seemed perfectly natural to address a love lyric to Christ.

Why do I languish thus, drooping and dull,
    As if I were all earth?
O give me quickness,[4] that I may with mirth
    Praise thee brimful!

The wanton lover in a curious strain   5
    Can praise his fairest fair,
And with quaint metaphors her curlèd hair
    Curl o'er again.

Thou art my loveliness, my life, my light,
    Beauty alone to me;   10
Thy bloody death and undeserved makes thee
    Pure red and white.

When all perfections as but one appear,
    That those[5] thy form doth show,
The very dust where thou dost tread and go[6]   15
    Makes beauties here.

Where are my lines then, my approaches, views?
    Where are my window songs?[7]
Lovers are still pretending,[8] and even wrongs
    Sharpen their Muse.   20

But I am lost in flesh, whose sug'red lies
    Still mock me, and grow bold.
Sure thou didst put a mind there, if I could
    Find where it lies.

Lord, clear thy gift, that with a constant wit   25
    I may but look towards thee—
Look only; for to *love* thee who can be,
    What angel, fit?

THE COLLAR

It is not essential that a reader should be religious to respond to the emotion of this beautiful poem. The collar, once a sign of slavery, is here a symbol of religious submission.

I struck the board and cried, "No more!
    I will abroad!"[9]
What, shall I ever sigh and pine?
My lines and life are free: free as the road,
    Loose as the wind, as large as store.[10]   5
        Shall I be still in suit?[11]
Have I no harvest but a thorn,
    To let me blood and not restore
What I have lost with cordial[12] fruit?
        Sure there was wine,   10
Before my sighs did dry it; there was corn,
    Before my tears did drown it.
    Is the year only lost to me?
    Have I no bays[13] to crown it,
No flowers, no garlands gay? all blasted?   15
        All wasted?
Not so, my heart; but there is fruit,
    And thou hast hands.

[5] So that those perfections.   [6] Walk.
[7] Serenades.   [8] Proffering, wooing.
[9] I.e., I will go out into the world.
[10] Abundance itself.
[11] Always petitioning (instead of striking out **on my own**).
[12] Restorative.   [13] Laureate wreath.

---

[1] I.e., red.   [2] Concluding strains.
[3] Alone survive the final conflagration which is to burn the world to cinders.   [4] Animation.

Recover all thy sigh-blown age
On double pleasures. Leave thy cold dispute   20
Of what is fit and not. Forsake thy cage,
     Thy rope of sands,[14]
Which petty thoughts have made (and made
     to thee
Good cable, to enforce and draw,
     And be thy law,   25
While thou didst wink[15] and wouldst not see).
     Away! take heed!
     I will abroad!
Call in thy death's-head there! Tie up thy fears!
     He that forbears   30
     To suit and serve his need
     Deserves his load."
But as I raved, and grew more fierce and wild
     At every word,
Methought I heard one calling, "Child!"   35
     And I replied, "My Lord."

THE PULLEY

The meaning of *pulley* is explained by the final stanza. It is the means God has devised for ensuring that man will be drawn to him.

When God at first made man,
Having a glass of blessings standing by,
     "Let us," said he, "pour on him all we can:
Let the world's riches, which dispersèd lie,
     Contract into a span."   5

So Strength first made a way;
Then Beauty flowed; then Wisdom, Honor, Pleasure.
     When almost all was out, God made a stay,
Perceiving that alone of all his treasure
     Rest in the bottom lay.   10

"For if I should," said he,
"Bestow this jewel also on my creature,
     He would adore my gifts instead of me,
And rest in Nature, not the God of Nature;
     So both should losers be.   15

"Yet let him keep the rest,
But keep them with repining restlessness:
     Let him be rich and weary, that at least,
If goodness lead him not, yet weariness
     May toss him to my breast."   20

THE ELIXIR

This noble poem is built on a "conceit." "For thy sake" is compared to the elixir or "philosophers' stone," the substance sought by the alchemists, who believed that it would turn baser metals to gold.

Teach me, my God and King,
     In all things thee to see,
And what I do in any thing,
     To do it as for thee:

Not rudely, as a beast,   5
     To run into an actiön;
But still to make thee prepossessed,[16]
     And give it his[17] perfectiön.

A man that looks on glass
     On it may stay his eye,   10
Or, if he pleaseth, through it pass,
     And then the heav'n espy.

All may of thee partake;
     Nothing can be so mean
Which with his tincture[18] "for thy sake"   15
     Will not grow bright and clean.

A servant with this clause[19]
     Makes drudgery divine.
Who sweeps a room as for thy laws
     Makes that and th' action fine.   20

This is the famous stone
     That turneth all to gold;
For that which God doth touch[20] and own
     Cannot for less be told.[21]

LOVE

This is the third and, despite the pun in line 12, the most exquisite of Herbert's poems with this title.

Love bade me welcome; yet my soul drew back,
     Guilty of dust and sin.
But quick-eyed Love, observing me grow slack
     From my first entrance in,
Drew nearer to me, sweetly questioning   5
     If I lacked anything.

[16] To give thee a prior claim (on what I do).   [17] Its.
[18] An alchemical term: a purifying infusion. *His* means *its*. I.e., nothing can be so mean that, if it be infused with the principle "I do it for thy sake," it will not become beautiful.
[19] Phrase; i.e., for thy sake.
[20] Apply a touchstone to, testing its purity as gold.
[21] I.e., cannot be reckoned less than gold.

---

[14] For, at the moment, religion seems equally futile.
[15] Shut your eyes.—these words are a parenthetical observation on the mood of rebellion, not an expression of that mood.

"A guest," I answered, "worthy to be here."
Love said, "You shall be he."
"I, the unkind, ungrateful? Ah, my dear,
    I cannot look on thee."   10
Love took my hand, and smiling did reply,
    "Who made the eyes but I?"

"Truth, Lord, but I have marred them; let my shame
    Go where it doth deserve."
"And know you not," says Love, "who bore the blame?"[22]
    "My dear, then I will serve."   16
"You must sit down," says Love, "and taste my meat."
    So I did sit and eat.

Richard Crashaw

1612?–1649

CRASHAW was about fourteen when, his mother and his stepmother already being dead, he lost his father, an Anglican clergyman bitterly hostile to Catholicism. The boy was educated at the Charterhouse, a famous London school, where he obtained a scholarship to Cambridge. He took his B.A. in 1634, and soon after was elected a fellow of Peterhouse, one of the Cambridge colleges. It was a high-church center, strongly anti-Puritan. Its chapel was adorned and its ritual elaborated with an elegance which aroused the horror of the reforming or low-church party. Crashaw found its Anglo-Catholic atmosphere congenial to his devotion and his tastes; he soon entered the Anglican ministry.

His choice of the royalist side, on the outbreak of the first of the Civil Wars, was inevitable; it cost him his fel-

lowship, for the Parliamentarians speedily made themselves masters of Cambridge. Crashaw fled to the Continent; whether he ever saw England again is uncertain. Several years before his death he became a Roman Catholic, and for the last few weeks of his life he held a minor appointment at the famous shrine of Loretto in Italy, where he died. His religious ecstasy is particularly well illustrated in the poems inspired by St. Teresa.

Crashaw's *Steps to the Temple, Sacred Poems with Other Delights of the Muses* (1646) contains both religious and secular verse. The standard edition is by L. C. Martin (1927). Valuable studies are A. Warren's *Richard Crashaw: A Study in Baroque Sensibility* (1939) and Ruth C. Wallerstein's *Richard Crashaw: A Study in Style and Poetic Development* (1935).

ON MR. G. HERBERT'S BOOK, ENTITLED THE TEMPLE OF SACRED POEMS, SENT TO A GENTLEWOMAN

Know you, fair, on what you look:
Divinest love lies in this book,
Expecting[1] fire from your eyes
To kindle this his sacrifice.
When your hands untie these strings,[2]   5
Think you have an angel by the wings,
One that gladly will be nigh
To wait upon each morning sigh,
To flutter in the balmy air
Of your well-perfumèd prayer.   10
These white plumes of his he'll lend you,
Which every day to heaven will send you
To take acquaintance of the sphere
And all the smooth-faced kindred there.
And though Herbert's name do owe[3]   15
These devotions, fairest, know
That while I lay them on the shrine
Of your white hand, they are mine.

---

[1] Waiting for.   [2] Which held a book shut.   [3] Own.

A HYMN IN THE NAME AND HONOR OF THE ADMIRABLE ST. TERESA[4]

Foundress of the Reformation of the Discalced[5] Carmelites, both men and women; a woman for angelical height of speculation, for masculine courage of performance, more than a woman, who yet a child outran maturity, and durst plot a martyrdom[6]

Love, thou art absolute sole lord
Of life and death. To prove the word,
We'll now appeal to none of all
Those thy old soldiers, great and tall,
Ripe men of martyrdom, that could reach down   5
With strong arms their triumphant crown,

[22] By Christ's atonement.

[4] A Spanish nun and mystic (1515–82), the author of several works which have become classics of mysticism and which inspired Crashaw even before his conversion to Roman Catholicism. She was canonized in 1622.

[5] Barefoot. Teresa, disturbed by the relaxation of monastic discipline in her day, secured permission to found religious houses, both nunneries and monasteries, in which all the original rules of the Carmelite order were to be strictly practiced.

[6] While she was still a child she and her brother planned to go among the Moors in search of martyrdom.

Such as could with lusty breath
Speak loud into the face of death
Their great Lord's glorious name, to none
Of those whose spacious bosoms spread a throne   10
For Love at large to fill; spare blood and sweat,
And see him take a private seat,
Making his mansion in the mild
And milky soul of a soft child.

    Scarce has she learned to lisp the name   15
Of martyr; yet she thinks it shame
Life should so long play with that breath
Which, spent, can buy so brave a death.
She never undertook to know
What death with Love should have to do;   20
Nor has she e'er yet understood
Why, to show love, she should shed blood;
Yet, though she cannot tell you why,
She can love, and she can die.

    Scarce has she blood enough to make   25
A guilty sword blush for her sake;
Yet has she a heart dares hope to prove
How much less strong is death than Love.

    Be Love but there, let poor six years
Be posed with the maturest fears   30
Man trembles at, you straight shall find
Love knows no nonage,[7] nor the mind;
'Tis Love, not years or limbs, that can
Make the martyr or the man.

    Love touched her heart, and, lo, it beats   35
High, and burns with such brave heats,
Such thirsts to die, as dares drink up
A thousand cold deaths in one cup.
Good reason; for she breathes all fire;
Her white breast heaves with strong desire   40
Of what she may, with fruitless wishes,
Seek for amongst her mother's kisses.

    Since 'tis not to be had at home,
She'll travel to a martyrdom.
No home for hers confesses she   45
But where she may a martyr be.

    She'll to the Moors, and trade with them
For this unvalued[8] diadem.
She'll offer them her dearest breath,
With Christ's name in it, in change for death.   50
She'll bargain with them, and will give
Them God; teach them how to live
In him; or, if they this deny,
For him she'll teach them how to die.
So shall she leave amongst them sown   55
Her Lord's blood, or at least her own.

Farewell, then, all the world! adieu!
Teresa is no more for you.
Farewell, all pleasures, sports, and joys
(Never till now esteemèd toys);   60
Farewell, whatever dear may be,
Mother's arms, or father's knee;
Farewell, house, and farewell, home!
She's for the Moors and martyrdom.

    Sweet, not so fast! lo, thy fair Spouse,   65
Whom thou seek'st with so swift vows,
Calls thee back, and bids thee come
To embrace a milder martyrdom.

    Blest powers forbid thy tender life
Should bleed upon a barbarous knife,   70
Or some base hand have power to rase
Thy breast's chaste cabinet, and uncase
A soul kept there so sweet; O no,
Wise heaven will not have it so.
Thou art Love's victim, and must die   75
A death more mystical and high.
Into Love's arms thou shalt let fall
A still-surviving funeral.
His is the dart must make the death
Whose stroke shall taste thy hallowed breath;   80
A dart thrice dipped in that rich flame[9]
Which writes thy Spouse's radiant name
Upon the roof of heaven, where ay
It shines, and with a sovereign ray
Beats bright upon the burning faces   85
Of souls which in that name's sweet graces
Find everlasting smiles. So rare,
So spiritual, pure, and fair
Must be the immortal instrument
Upon whose choice point shall be sent   90
A life so loved; and that there be
Fit executioners for thee,
The fairest and first-born sons of fire,
Bright seraphim, shall leave their choir,
And turn Love's soldiers, upon thee   95
To exercise their archery.

    O how oft shalt thou complain
Of a sweet and subtle pain;
Of intolerable joys;
Of a death in which who dies   100
Loves his death, and dies again,
And would forever so be slain,
And lives, and dies, and knows not why
To live, but that he thus may never leave[10] to die.

    How kindly will thy gentle heart   105
Kiss the sweetly killing dart,

---

[7] Immaturity.   [8] Invaluable, priceless.

[9] In mystical visions St. Teresa was visited by an angel who pierced her heart with a flame-tipped spear and thus increased the ardor of her love for God.   [10] Cease.

And close in his embraces keep
Those delicious wounds, that weep
Balsam to heal themselves with. Thus
When these thy deaths, so numerous,   110
Shall all at last die into one,
And melt thy soul's sweet mansion,
Like a soft lump of incense, hasted
By too hot a fire, and wasted
Into perfuming clouds, so fast   115
Shalt thou exhale to heaven at last
In a resolving sigh, and then—
O what? Ask not the tongues of men.
Angels cannot tell; suffice
Thyself shall feel thine own full joys   120
And hold them fast forever there.
So soon as thou shalt first appear,
The moon of maiden stars,[11] thy white
Mistress, attended by such bright
Souls as thy shining self, shall come,   125
And in her first ranks make thee room;
Where 'mongst her snowy family
Immortal welcomes wait for thee.
　　O what delight, when revealed Life shall stand
And teach thy lips heaven with his hand;   130
On which thou now may'st to thy wishes
Heap up thy consecrated kisses.
What joys shall seize thy soul when she,
Bending her blessed eyes on thee
(Those second smiles of heaven), shall dart   135
Her mild rays through thy melting heart!
　　Angels, thy old friends, there shall greet thee,
Glad at their own home now to meet thee.
　　All thy good works which went before
And waited for thee at the door   140
Shall own thee there; and all in one
Weave a constellatïon
Of crowns, with which the King, thy Spouse,
Shall build up thy triumphant brows.
　　All thy old woes shall now smile on thee,   145
And thy pains sit bright upon thee;
All thy sorrows here shall shine,
All thy sufferings be divine.
Tears shall take comfort and turn gems,
And wrongs repent to diadems.   150
Even thy deaths shall live, and new
Dress the soul that erst they slew.
Thy wounds shall blush to such bright scars
As keep account of the Lamb's wars.
　　Those rare works where thou shalt leave writ   155
Love's noble history, with wit

Taught thee by none but him, while here
They feed our souls, shall clothe thine there.
Each heavenly word by whose hid flame
Our hard hearts shall strike fire, the same   160
Shall flourish on thy brows, and be
Both fire to us and flame to thee,
Whose light shall live bright in thy face
By glory, in our hearts by grace.
　　Thou shalt look round about and see   165
Thousands of crowned souls throng to be
Themselves thy crown, sons of thy vows,
The virgin-births with which thy sovereign Spouse
Made fruitful thy fair soul. Go now,
And with them all about thee, bow   170
To him. "Put on," he'll say, "put on,
My rosy love, that thy rich zone[12]
Sparkling with the sacred flames
Of thousand souls, whose happy names
Heaven keep upon thy score": thy bright   175
Life brought them first to kiss the light
That kindled them to stars. And so
Thou with the Lamb, thy Lord, shalt go;
And wheresoe'er he sets his white
Steps, walk with him those ways of light,   180
Which who in death would live to see
Must learn in life to die like thee.

from THE FLAMING HEART

*Upon the book and picture of the seraphical St. Teresa (as
she is usually expressed with a seraphim beside her)*

The title is that of an English translation of St. Teresa's
autobiography. This selection gives the last 34 of the poem's
108 lines.

. . . O heart, the equal poise of love's both parts,[13]
Big alike with wounds and darts,
Live in these conquering leaves; live all the same,
And walk through all tongues one triumphant flame!
Live here, great heart, and love and die and kill,   5
And bleed and wound, and yield and conquer still!
Let this immortal life, where'er it comes,
Walk in a crowd of loves and martyrdoms.
Let mystic deaths wait on 't, and wise souls be
The love-slain witnesses of this life of thee.   10
O sweet incendiary! show here thy art,
Upon this carcass of a hard, cold heart.
Let all thy scattered shafts of light, that play
Among the leaves of thy large books of day,
Combined against this breast at once break in   15
And take away from me my self and sin.

---

[11] The Blessed Virgin.

[12] Girdle.　　[13] Active and passive.

This gracious robbery shall thy bounty be,
And my best fortunes such fair spoils of me.[14]
O thou undaunted daughter of desires!
By all thy dow'r of lights and fires,   20
By all the eagle in thee, all the dove,[15]
By all thy lives and deaths of love,
By thy large draughts of intellectual day,
And by thy thirsts of love more large than they,
By all thy brim-filled bowls of fierce desire,   25
By thy last morning's draught of liquid fire,
By the full kingdom of that final kiss
That seized thy parting soul and sealed thee his,
By all the heav'ns thou hast in him,
Fair sister of the seraphim,   30
By all of him we have in thee,
Leave nothing of myself in me!
Let me so read thy life that I
Unto all life of mine may die.

IN THE HOLY NATIVITY
OF OUR LORD GOD
A HYMN SUNG AS BY THE SHEPHERDS

CHORUS

Come, we shepherds, whose blest sight
Hath met love's noon in nature's night;
Come, lift we up our loftier song
And wake the sun that lies too long.

To all our world of well-stolen joy   5
He slept, and dreamt of no such thing,
  While we found out heaven's fairer eye
And kissed the cradle of our King.
  Tell him he rises now too late
To show us aught worth looking at.   10

Tell him we now can show him more
Than he e'er showed to mortal sight,
  Than he himself e'er saw before,
Which to be seen needs not his light.
  Tell him, Tityrus, where th'hast been   15
Tell him, Thyrsis, what th'hast seen.

TITYRUS. Gloomy night embraced the place
Where the noble Infant lay.
  The Babe looked up and showed his face;
In spite of darkness, it was day.   20
  It was thy day, Sweet! and did rise
Not from the east, but from thine eyes.

CHORUS. It was thy day, Sweet, etc.

THYRSIS. Winter chid aloud, and sent
The angry North[16] to wage his wars;   25
  The North forgot his fierce intent,
And left perfumes instead of scars.
  By those sweet eyes' persuasive powers
Where he meant frost he scattered flowers.

CHO. By those sweet eyes, etc.   30

BOTH. We saw thee in thy balmy nest,
Young dawn of our eternal day;
  We saw thine eyes break from their east
And chase the trembling shades away.
  We saw thee, and we blest the sight,   35
We saw thee by thine own sweet light.

CHO. We saw thee, etc.

TIT. Poor world, said I, what wilt thou do
To entertain this starry stranger?
  Is this the best thou canst bestow—   40
A cold and not too cleanly manger?
  Contend, the powers of heaven and earth,
To fit a bed for this huge birth!

CHO. Contend, the powers, etc.

THYR. Proud world, said I, cease your contest,   45
And let the mighty Babe alone;
  The phoenix builds the phoenix' nest,
Love's architecture is his own;
  The Babe whose birth embraves this morn,
Made his own bed e'er he was born.   50

CHO. The Babe whose, etc.

TIT. I saw the curled drops, soft and slow,
Come hovering o'er the place's head,
  Offering their whitest sheets of snow
To furnish the fair Infant's bed.   55
  Forbear, said I; be not too bold;
Your fleece is white, but 'tis too cold.

CHO. Forbear, said I, etc.

THYR. I saw the obsequious seraphim
Their rosy fleece of fire bestow,   60
  For well they now can spare their wing
Since heaven itself lies here below.
  Well done, said I; but are you sure
Your down so warm will pass for pure?

---

[14] I.e., the best thing that could happen to me would be such a
"robbery."   [15] Symbols of strength and purity.

[16] North wind.

TIT. No, no, your King's not yet to seek
Where to repose his royal head;
   See, see how soon his new-bloomed cheek
'Twixt mother's breasts is gone to bed!
   Sweet choice, said we; no way but so   70
Not to lie cold, yet sleep in snow.

CHO. Sweet choice, said we, etc.

BOTH. We saw thee in thy balmy nest,
Bright dawn of our eternal day;
   We saw thine eyes break from their east   75
And chase the trembling shades away.
   We saw thee, and we blest the sight,
We saw thee by thine own sweet light.

CHO. We saw thee, etc.

FULL CHORUS

Welcome, all wonders in one sight!   80
Eternity shut in a span!
   Summer in winter! day in night!
Heaven in earth! and God in man!
   Great little one, whose all-embracing birth
Lifts earth to heaven, stoops heaven to earth!   85

Welcome, though nor to gold nor silk,
To more than Caesar's birthright is;
   Two sister-seas of virgin-milk,

With many a rarely-tempered kiss,
   That breathes at once both maid and mother,   90
Warms in the one, cools in the other.

   She sings thy tears asleep, and dips
Her kisses in thy weeping eye;
   She spreads the red leaves of thy lips
That in their buds yet blushing lie;   95
   She 'gainst those mother-diamonds tries
The points of her young eagle's eyes.

   Welcome, though not to those gay flies
Gilded i'th' beams of earthly kings,
   Slippery souls in smiling eyes—   100
But to poor shepherds, homespun things,
   Whose wealth's their flock, whose wit, to be
Well read in their simplicity.

   Yet, when young April's husband showers
Shall bless the fruitful Maia's bed,   105
   We'll bring the first-born of her flowers
To kiss thy feet and crown thy head.
   To thee, dread Lamb! whose love must keep
The shepherds, more than they the sheep.

   To thee, meek Majesty, soft King   110
Of simple graces and sweet loves,
   Each of us his lamb will bring,
Each his pair of silver doves;
   Till burnt at last in fire of thy fair eyes,
Ourselves become our own best sacrifice!

Henry Vaughan

1622?–1695

FOR sheer beauty Vaughan is probably the greatest of Britain's religious writers. He loves nature with a tender delight in her loveliness but also with a constant and mystical awareness of God's presence in her and in man, her stepchild. Vaughan's poetry is full of allusions to the immanence of God, as this doctrine of the divine indwelling is termed. And so, with all the desire and need of the artist to communicate his own experience, in the hope that others may enter the same kingdoms of beauty and joy, Vaughan sorrows over the poor estate of those who cannot or will not perceive what seems so plain to him. Man, he thinks, has abdicated his rightful place and privileges as the child of God. He fails to embrace his spiritual opportunities, and Vaughan eloquently laments his failure.

Vaughan was the first Welshman to win a place among the English poets. He was born and brought up in Breck-nockshire, and was nearly in his teens before he began learning English. Not a great deal is known of his life. With his twin brother he went to Oxford, but he left without a degree in order to study law at the inns of court in London. His plans, he says, were upset by the Civil Wars. He probably served awhile in the royal army. When and where he studied medicine is unrecorded, but before the Wars were over he had settled down in South Wales as a country doctor. The ancient Britons of that region were known to the Romans as the Silures; and with all a Welshman's pride in his origin, Vaughan called himself "the Silurist." He married twice and had eight children.

He had already written two volumes of verse when his *Silex Scintillans* (i.e., sparks from the flint) appeared in 1650; by "flint" he probably meant, in his humility, his heart. The book was reissued in 1655, enlarged; on it

Vaughan's reputation chiefly rests. Though in earlier poems he had penned the conventional tributes to "Amoret" and even an occasional bit of ribaldry, *Silex Scintillans* is exclusively religious. So is a volume of prose, *The Mount of Olives, or Solitary Devotions* (1652). The standard text is L. C. Martin's edition of the *Works* (2 vols., 1914). For an estimate of Vaughan see Helen C. White's *The Metaphysical Poets*.

THE RETREAT

Regret for lost childhood is a common emotion; in Vaughan it takes the form of regret for lost innocence and for paradise lost or at least jeopardized. In his conception of the special divinity of childhood, Vaughan anticipates Wordsworth's great ode on "Intimations of Immortality."

Happy those early days! when I
Shined in my angel-infancy;
Before I understood this place
Appointed for my second race,[1]
Or taught my soul to fancy aught   5
But a white, celestial thought;
When yet I had not walked above
A mile, or two, from my first love,
And looking back at that short space
Could see a glimpse of His bright face;   10
When on some gilded cloud or flow'r
My gazing soul would dwell an hour,
And in those weaker glories spy
Some shadows of eternity;
Before I taught my tongue to wound   15
My conscience with a sinful sound,
Or had the black art to dispense
A sev'ral[2] sin to ev'ry sense;
But felt through all this fleshly dress[3]
Bright shoots of everlastingness.   20
   O, how I long to travel back,
And tread again that ancient track!
That I might once more reach that plain,
Where first I left my glorious train;
From whence th' enlightened spirit sees   25
That shady city of palm trees[4]—
But ah! my soul with too much stay
Is drunk, and staggers in the way!
Some men a forward motion love,
But I by backward steps would move,   30
And when this dust falls to the urn,
In that state I came, return.

---

[1] Earthly existence.   [2] Different.   [3] Garb of flesh.
[4] Probably = paradise; possibly with an allusion also to Jericho (2 Chronicles 28:15).

PEACE

My soul, there is a country
   Far beyond the stars,
Where stands a wingèd sentry,
   All skillful in the wars.
There, above noise and danger,   5
   Sweet peace sits crowned with smiles;
And one born in a manger
   Commands the beauteous files.
He is thy gracious friend,
   And (O my soul, awake!)   10
Did in pure love descend
   To die here for thy sake.
If thou canst get but thither,
   There grows the flow'r of peace,
The rose that cannot wither,   15
   Thy fortress, and thy ease.
Leave then thy foolish ranges;
   For none can thee secure,
But one who never changes,
   Thy God, thy life, thy cure.   20

CORRUPTION

Sure, it was so. Man in those early days
   Was not all stone and earth;
He shined a little, and by those weak rays
   Had some glimpse of his birth.
He saw heaven o'er his head, and knew from whence   5
   He came, condemnèd, hither;
And, as first love draws strongest, so from hence
   His mind sure prógressed thither.
Things here were strange unto him, sweat and till:[5]
   All was a thorn or weed;   10
Nor did those last, but like himself died still
   As soon as they did seed.
They seemed to quarrel with him, for that act
   That fell[6] him foiled them all;
He drew the curse upon the world, and cracked   15
   The whole frame with his fall.
This made him long for home, as loath to stay
   With murmurers and foes;
He sighed for Eden and would often say,
   "Ah, what bright days were those!"   20
Nor was heav'n cold unto him; for each day
   The valley or the mountain
Afforded visits, and still Paradise lay
   In some green shade or fountain.[7]
Angels lay lieger[8] here: each bush and cell,[9]   25
   Each oak and highway, knew them;

---

[5] Tilling the soil.   [6] Befell. I.e., Adam's fall.
[7] Spring.   [8] Were in residence as ambassadors.   [9] Nook.

Walk but the fields or sit down at some well,
    And he was sure to view them.
Almighty Love! where art thou now? Mad man
    Sits down, and freezeth on;   30
He raves, and swears to stir nor fire nor fan,
    But bids the thread be spun.[10]
I see thy curtains are close drawn; thy bow[11]
    Looks dim, too, in the cloud.
Sin triumphs still; and man is sunk below   35
    The center,[12] and his shroud.
All's in deep sleep and night; thick darkness lies
    And hatcheth[13] o'er thy people.
But hark! what trumpet's that? what angel cries,
    "Arise! Thrust in thy sickle!"   40

THE WORLD

To this poem Vaughan appended the following passage
from the First Epistle of John (2:16,17): "For all that is
in the world, the lust of the flesh, and the lust of the eyes,
and the pride of life, is not of the Father, but is of the world.
And the world passeth away, and the lust thereof: but he
that doeth the will of God abideth for ever."

I saw eternity the other night
Like a great ring of pure and endless light,
    All calm, as it was bright;
And round beneath it, time, in hours, days, years,
    Driv'n by the spheres,[14]   5
Like a vast shadow moved, in which the world
    And all her train were hurled.
The doting lover in his quaintest strain
    Did there complain;
Near him, his lute, his fancy, and his flights,[15]   10
    Wit's sour delights,
With gloves and knots,[16] the silly snares of pleasure.
    Yet his dear treasure,
All scattered lay, while he his eyes did pour
    Upon a flow'r.   15

The darksome statesman, hung with weights and woe
Like a thick midnight fog, moved there so slow
    He did not stay, nor go.
Condemning thoughts, like sad eclipses, scowl
    Upon his soul;   20
And clouds of crying witnesses without
    Pursued him with one shout.

---

10 I.e., inactively resigns himself to fate.
11 Rainbow, God's promise.   12 Of the earth.
13 Broods.
14 Of the Ptolemaic system of astronomy.
15 Of love verses.
16 Bows or bunches of ribbon; like the gloves, presents.

Yet digged the mole and, lest his ways be found,
    Worked underground,
Where he did clutch his prey; but One did see   25
    That policy.[17]
Churches and altars fed him;[18] perjuries
    Were[19] gnats and flies;
It rained about him blood and tears, but he
    Drank them as free.[20]   30

The fearful miser on a heap of rust
Sat pining all his life there, did scarce trust
    His own hands with the dust,
Yet would not place one piece above,[21] but lives
    In fear of thieves.   35
Thousands there were as frantic as himself,
    And hugged each one his pelf;
The downright epicure placed heav'n in sense,
    And scorned pretence;
While others, slipped into a wide excess,   40
    Said little less.
The weaker sort slight, trivial wares enslave,
    Who think them brave;[22]
And poor, despisèd Truth sat counting by[23]
    Their victory.   45

Yet some, who all this while did weep and sing,
And sing and weep, soared up into the ring;[24]
    But most would use no wing.
"O fools," said I, "thus to prefer dark night
    Before true light!   50
To live in grots and caves, and hate the day
    Because it shows the way,
The way which from this dead and dark abode
    Leads up to God,
A way where you might tread the sun, and be   55
    More bright than he!"
But, as I did their madness so discuss,
    One whispered thus:
"This ring the Bridegroom[25] did for none provide
    But for his bride."[26]   60

MAN

    Weighing the steadfastness and state
Of some mean things which here below reside,
Where birds like watchful clocks the noiseless date
    And intercourse of times divide,

---

17 Maneuver.
18 Perhaps a reference to the Puritans' attacks on the bishops.
19 Were of no more importance than.
20 As freely as they rained down.
21 Would not lay up one piece of treasure in heaven (see Matthew
    6:19,20).   22 Fine, splendid.   23 Observing.
24 See line 2.   25 Christ.   26 The Church.

Where bees at night get home and hive, and flow'rs   5
    Early, as well as late,
Rise with the sun, and set in the same bow'rs,

  I would (said I) my God would give
The staidness of these things to man! for these
To his divine appointments ever cleave,   10
  And no new business breaks their peace.
The birds nor sow nor reap, yet sup and dine;
    The flow'rs without clothes live,
Yet Solomon was never dressed so fine.

  Man hath still either toys[27] or care;   15
He hath no root, nor to one place is tied,
But ever restless and irregular
  About this earth doth run and ride.
He knows he hath a home, but scarce knows where;
    He says it is so far   20
That he hath quite forgot how to go there.

  He knocks at all doors, strays and roams,
Nay, hath not so much wit as some stones[28] have
Which in the darkest nights point to their homes,
  By some hid sense their Maker gave.   25
Man is the shuttle, to whose winding quest
    And passage through these looms
God ordered motion, but ordained no rest.

THEY ARE ALL GONE

They are all gone into the world of light!
  And I alone sit ling'ring here;
Their very memory is fair and bright,
  And my sad thoughts doth clear.

It glows and glitters in my cloudy breast   5
  Like stars upon some gloomy grove,
Or those faint beams in which this hill is dressed,
  After the sun's remove.

I see them walking in an air of glory,
  Whose light doth trample on[29] my days: 10
My days, which are at best but dull and hoary,
  Mere glimmering and decays.

O holy hope! and high humility,
  High as the heavens above!
These are your walks, and you have showed them me   15
  To kindle my cold love.

---

27 Trifles.
28 Loadstones; here, the magnetized needles in compasses.
29 Follows closely after.

Dear, beauteous death! the jewel of the just,
  Shining nowhere but in the dark;
What mysteries do lie beyond thy dust,
  Could man outlook that mark![30]   20

He that hath found some fledged bird's nest may know
  At first sight if the bird be flown;
But what fair well or grove he sings in now,
  That is to him unknown.

And yet, as angels in some brighter dreams   25
  Call to the soul when man doth sleep,
So some strange thoughts transcend our wonted themes,
  And into glory peep.

If a star were confined into a tomb,
  Her captive flames must needs burn there;   30
But when the hand that locked her up gives room,
  She'll shine through all the sphere.

O Father of eternal life, and all
  Created glories under thee!
Resume thy spirit[31] from this world of thrall   35
  Into true liberty.

Either disperse these mists, which blot and fill
  My pérspective[32] still as they pass,
Or else remove me hence unto that hill
  Where I shall need no glass.   40

THE REVIVAL

The foregoing poems are all from *Silex Scintillans: Sacred Poems and Private Ejaculations*. This beautiful lyric is from Vaughan's final volume of verse, *Thalia Rediviva: The Pastimes and Diversions of a Country Muse, in Choice Poems on Several Occasions*. It should be observed that sixteenth- and seventeenth-century title pages were often composed by the publisher, not the author.

Unfold, unfold! Take in his light
Who makes thy cares more short than night.
The joys which with his daystar rise
He deals to all, but drowsy eyes,
And what the men of this world miss,   5
Some drops and dews of future bliss.
  Hark! how his winds have changed their note,
And with warm whispers call thee out.
The frosts are past, the storms are gone,
And backward life at last comes on.   10
The lofty groves in express joys
Reply unto the turtle's[33] voice;
And here in dust and dirt, oh, here,
The lilies of his love appear!

---

30 Boundary.   31 I.e., take back my soul, which belongs to thee.
32 Telescope.   33 Dove's.

HENRY VAUGHAN   507

A Miscellany of Stuart Verse

Good anthologies are N. Ault's SEVENTEENTH CENTURY LYRICS *(revised ed., 1950), R. Florence Brinkley's* ENGLISH POETRY OF THE SEVENTEENTH CENTURY *(revised ed., 1942), M. W. Black's* ELIZABETHAN AND SEVENTEENTH-CENTURY LYRICS *(1938), H. J. C. Grierson and G. Bullough's* THE OXFORD BOOK OF SEVENTEENTH CENTURY VERSE *(1934), J. W. Hebel and H. H. Hudson's* POETRY OF THE ENGLISH RENAISSANCE, 1509–1660 *(1929), and the first two hundred pages of R. S. Crane's* A COLLECTION OF ENGLISH POEMS, 1660–1800 *(1932).*

Sir Henry Wotton

1568–1639

WOTTON began, after his Oxford B. A., as a courtier poet in the 1590's. He was a friend of Bacon, Donne, and Walton. Much of his life was passed on the Continent, at first in the service of the Earl of Essex (d. 1601). For sixteen years he was British ambassador to Venice, but he fell out with King James and ended his career as provost of Eton. "How happy is he born or taught" became famous; even better known is the pun in his definition of an ambassador: "an honest man sent to lie abroad for the good of his country." Wotton was the earliest important English collector of Italian painting. His works were published in 1651 as *Reliquiae Wottonianae.* There is a modern edition, in the Aldine Poets series, by J. Hannah (*The Poems of Sir Walter Raleigh . . . with Those of Sir Henry Wotton and Other Court Poets* (1892), and a *Life and Letters* (2 vols., 1907) by L. P. Smith.

THE CHARACTER OF A HAPPY LIFE

Ben Jonson knew this poem by heart. The title appears in the volume of 1651 but not in an earlier manuscript.

How happy is he born or taught
  That serveth not another's will;
Whose armor is his honest thought,
  And simple truth his highest skill;

Whose passions not his masters are;   5
  Whose soul is still prepared for death,
Untied unto the world with care
  Of princes' grace or vulgar breath;

Who envies none whom chance doth raise,
  Or vice; who never understood   10
The deepest wounds are given by praise,
  By rule of state but not of good;

Who hath his life from rumors freed,
  Whose conscience is his strong retreat,
Whose state can neither flatterers feed   15
  Nor ruins make accusers great;

Who God doth late and early pray
  More of his grace than goods to send,
And entertains the harmless day
  With a well-chosen book or friend.   20

This man is free from servile bands[1]
  Of hope to rise or fear to fall,
Lord of himself, though not of lands,
  And having nothing, yet hath all.

ON HIS MISTRESS, THE QUEEN OF BOHEMIA

King James's beautiful daughter Elizabeth (1596–1662) married the Elector Palatine in 1613. Six years later he became King of Bohemia, but soon lost his throne. Their grandson, the Elector of Hanover, succeeded to the English crown as George I in 1714.

You meaner beauties of the night,
  That poorly satisfy our eyes
More by your number than your light,
  You common people of the skies,
    What are you when the sun shall rise?   5

You curious chanters of the wood,
  That warble forth Dame Nature's lays,
Thinking your voices understood
  By your weak accents, what 's your praise
    When Philomel[2] her voice shall raise?   10

You violets that first appear,
  By your pure purple mantles known,
Like the proud virgins of the year,
  As if the spring were all your own,
    What are you when the rose is blown?[3]   15

So, when my mistress shall be seen
  In form and beauty of her mind,
By virtue first, then choice, a queen,
  Tell me if she were not designed
    The eclipse and glory of her kind?   20

---

[1] Bonds.   [2] The nightingale.   [3] Has bloomed.

ON THE DEATH OF
SIR ALBERT MORTON'S WIFE

Morton was Wotton's nephew and secretary. He died in 1625, about a year after his marriage. His widow died in 1627.

> He first deceasèd; she for a little tried
> To live without him, liked it not, and died.

John Marston
1576–1634

MARSTON'S erotic and satirical verses brought him into prominence, not to say notoriety, in the closing years of the sixteenth century. He soon fell foul of Ben Jonson, who according to his own account "beat him and took his pistol from him." Jonson also pilloried him in a play, *Poetaster* (1601). Marston had already begun his own short but brilliant career as a dramatist; his best piece is *The Malcontent* (1604?). He soon left the theater for the Church. In 1609 he was ordained to the Anglican priesthood, and in 1616 received the living of Christchurch in Hampshire, which he held for fifteen years. Marston was by no means a perfect writer; for one thing, he loved to toy with high-flown new words coined from Latin. But he was an uncommonly pungent writer, and as a playwright ranks with Jonson, Chapman, Heywood, and Dekker in the foremost group of Shakespeare's immediate contemporaries. There is a poor edition of his plays by H. H. Wood (3 vols., 1934–39). A. H. Bullen edited the *Works* (3 vols., 1887).

from ANTONIO'S REVENGE

Probably in 1601, and probably after *Hamlet* was first acted, Marston wrote this revenge tragedy as a sequel to his *Antonio and Mellida*. The best thing in it is the opening speech.

THE PROLOGUE

The rawish dank of clumsy winter ramps[4]
The fluent summer's vein; and drizzling sleet
Chilleth the wan bleak cheek of the numbed earth,
Whilst snarling gusts nibble the juiceless leaves
From the nak't[5] shudd'ring branch, and pills[6] the skin   5
From off the soft and delicate aspécts.
O now, methinks, a sullen tragic scene
Would suit the time, with pleasing congruence.
May we be happy in our weak devoir,[7]
And all part pleasèd, in most wished content!   10
But sweat of Hercules can ne'er beget
So blest an issue. Therefore, we proclaim,

---

[4] Storms on.   [5] Naked.   [6] Peels, strips.
[7] Duty (of pleasing you); so that you will leave ("part") satisfied.
  —*Happy* = fortunate.

If any spirit breathes within this round[8]
Uncapable of weighty passïon
(As from his birth being huggèd in the arms,   15
And nuzzled 'twixt the breasts, of happiness);
Who winks,[9] and shuts his apprehension up
From common sense of what men were, and are;
Who would not know what men must be: let such
Hurry amain from our black-visaged shows!   20
We shall affright their eyes. But if a breast
Nailed to the earth with grief, if any heart
Pierced through with anguish, pant within this ring;
If there be any blood whose heat is choked
And stifled with true sense of misery;   25
If aught of these strains fill this consort[10] up:
Th' arrive most welcome. O that our power
Could lackey or keep wing with our desires,
That with unusèd paize[11] of style and sense
We might weigh massy in judicious scale.—   30
Yet here's the prop that doth support our hopes:
> When our scenes falter or invention halts,[12]
> Your favor will give crutches to our faults.

Francis Beaumont
1584–1616

NEXT to the collaboration of Gilbert and Sullivan, the most memorable in the history of the English theater is that of Beaumont and Fletcher. A student at Oxford, one of the sons of Ben, and like Fletcher both wellborn and well educated, Beaumont was about twenty-three when he wrote his charming mock-heroic play *The Knight of the Burning Pestle*. He was still in his middle twenties when, about 1610, he and Fletcher composed their masterpieces, *Philaster* and *The Maid's Tragedy*. In 1613 Beaumont married and abandoned his career; he died three years later. Collected editions of Beaumont and Fletcher were edited by A. Dyce (11 vols., 1843–46), A. Glover and A. R. Waller (10 vols., 1905–12), and A. H. Bullen (4 vols. only, 1904–12).

MR. FRANCIS BEAUMONT'S
LETTER TO BEN JONSON

Written before he and Mr. Fletcher came to London with two . . . comedies then not finished, which deferred their merry meetings at the Mermaid[13]

The sun, which doth the greatest comfort bring
To absent friends, because the selfsame thing
They know they see, however absent, is
Here our best haymaker—forgive me this;

---

[8] Circle, the theater.   [9] Shuts his eyes.
[10] Assemblage, with a pun on the meaning *harmony*.
[11] Unusual weight.   [12] Goes lame.
[13] A well-known tavern in the City.

It is our country's style. In this warm shine,   5
I lie and dream of your full Mermaid wine.
Oh, we have water mixed with claret lees,
Drink apt to bring in drier heresies
Than beer—good only for the sonnet's strain,
With fustian[14] metaphors to stuff the brain;   10
So mixed, that, given to the thirstiest one,
'Twill not prove alms, unless he have the stone:[15]
I think that with one draught man's invention[16] fades;
Two cups had[17] quite spoiled Homer's Iliads;
'Tis liquor that will find out Sutcliffe's[18] wit,   15
Lie where he will, and make him write worse yet.
Filled with such moisture, in most grievous qualms,
Did Robert Wisdom[19] write his singing psalms;
And so must I do this: and yet I think
It is a potion sent us down to drink,   20
By special Providence, keeps us from fights,
Makes us not laugh when we make legs[20] to knights.
'Tis this that keeps our minds fit for our states,
A medicine to obey our magistrates.
For we do live more free than you: no hate,   25
No envy at one another's happy state,
Moves us; we are all equal, every whit;
Of land,[21] that God gives men here, is their wit,
If we consider fully; for our best
And gravest man will with his main house-jest[22]   30
Scarce please you; we want subtlety to do
The city tricks, lie, hate, and flatter too.
Here are none that can bear a painted show,
Strike when you wince[23] and then lament the blow,
Who (like mills set the right way for to grind)   35
Can make their gains alike with every wind—
Only some fellows, with the subtl'st pate
Amongst us, may perchance equivocate
At selling of a horse, and that's the most.[24]
Methinks the little wit I had is lost   40
Since I saw you. For wit is like a rest
Held up[25] at tennis, which men do the best
With the best gamesters.[26] What things have we seen
Done at the Mermaid! heard words that have been
So nimble and so full of subtle flame,   45
As if that everyone from whence they came

Had meant to put his whole wit in a jest
And had resolved to live a fool the rest
Of his dull life! Then, when there hath been thrown
Wit able enough to justify the town   50
For three days past—wit, that might warrant be
For the whole city to talk foolishly
Till that were canceled—and, when that was gone,
We left an air behind us, which alone
Was able to make the two next companies   55
Right witty—though but downright fools, more wise.
When I remember this, and see that now
The country gentlemen begin to allow
My wit for dry bobs,[27] then I needs must cry,
"I see my days of ballating[28] grow nigh."   60
I can already riddle, and can sing
Catches, sell bargains, and I fear shall bring
Myself to speak the hardest words I find
Over as oft as any, with one wind,
That takes no medicines.[29] But one thought of thee   65
Makes me remember all these things to be
The wit of our young men, fellows that show
No part of good, yet utter all they know;
Who, like trees of the gard,[30] have growing[31] souls.
Only, strong Destiny, which all controls,   70
I hope hath left a better fate in store
For me, thy friend, than to live ever poor,
Banished unto this home. Fate, once again,
Bring me to thee, who canst make smooth and plain
The way of knowledge for me! and then I,   75
Who have no good but in thy company,
Protest it will my greatest comfort be
To acknowledge all I have to flow from thee.
Ben, when these scenes are perfect,[32] we'll taste wine:
I'll drink thy Muse's health, thou shalt quaff mine.   80

John Fletcher

1579–1625

FLETCHER's father was a bishop and courtier. The poet was educated at Cambridge. The date of the first work with Beaumont (see p. 509) is uncertain. In 1613, the year of Beaumont's retirement, Fletcher seems to have collaborated with Shakespeare on *Henry VIII* and *The Two Noble Kinsmen*. The evidence is chiefly internal: Fletcher wrote a distinctive kind of blank verse, often ending in an unstressed syllable and containing more than the usual number of syllables, thus:

---

14 Claptrap.
15 Kidney stone. Heavy wine was supposed to be a cause; watered claret would therefore be in order.
16 Ability to compose.   17 Would have.
18 Dr. William Sutcliffe, a contemporary who wrote controversial pamphlets on theology.
19 Supposed to have contributed to a popular psalter.
20 Bow. King James knighted so many and such unworthy persons that knighthood became a laughingstock.
21 I.e., dull earth.   22 Stock family joke.
23 Wink, have your eyes closed.
24 I.e., the extent of their deceitfulness.
25 A rally kept up.   26 Players.

27 Esteem my wit as mere harmless jesting.
28 Making ballads; i.e., I fear I'll have to earn my living as a hack ballad writer, trying to please simple-minded folk.
29 Cathartics. I.e., I can expel a hard word without taking a purge.
30 Garden.   31 I.e., vegetable.
32 When I have finished writing the plays.

If either of these two women were offered to me now,
I would think otherwise and do accordingly;
Yes, and recant my heresies; I would, sir.

Fletcher is a competent lyric poet, but the best things he wrote independently are his comedies. He succeeded Shakespeare as the principal dramatist of the King's Men; his plays were extremely popular. Of all the Elizabethans, Shakespeare, Jonson, and Fletcher were the great names in the Restoration theater, where Fletcher was considered the best for pathos. (See under Beaumont, p. 509, for bibliography.)

ORPHEUS WITH HIS LUTE

This song is from *Henry VIII,* and therefore is not certainly Fletcher's. It is sung by a waiting woman to the discarded Queen Katherine.

> Orpheus with his lute made trees
> And the mountain-tops that freeze
>   Bow themselves when he did sing.
> To his music plants and flowers
> Ever sprung, as[33] sun and showers   5
>   There had made a lasting spring.
>
> Every thing that heard him play,
> Even the billows of the sea,[34]
>   Hung their heads, and then lay by.
> In sweet music is such art,   10
> Killing care and grief of heart
>   Fall asleep or, hearing, die.

CARE-CHARMING SLEEP

From one of Fletcher's strongest tragedies, *Valentinian.* This song is sung for the dying Emperor, who has been poisoned.

> Care-charming Sleep, thou easer of all woes,
> Brother to Death, sweetly thyself dispose
> On this afflicted prince; fall like a cloud,
> In gentle showers; give nothing that is loud
> Or painful to his slumbers; easy, sweet,   5
> And as a purling stream, thou son of Night,
> Pass by his troubled senses; sing his pain
> Like hollow murmuring wind or silver rain;
> Into this prince gently, oh, gently slide,
> And kiss him into slumbers like a bride.   10

---

[33] As if.   [34] A good rime as then pronounced.

DRINK TODAY

From *The Bloody Brother.* Since on this play Fletcher collaborated with other writers, his authorship of the lyric is not certain. The singers are a quartet of servants, headed by a jovial cook.

> Drink today, and drown all sorrow;
> You shall perhaps not do it tomorrow.
> Best, while you have it, use your breath;
> There is no drinking after death.
>
> Wine works the heart up, wakes the wit,   5
> There is no cure 'gainst age but it;
> It helps the headache, cough, and tisic,[35]
> And is for all diseases physic.
>
> Then let us swill, boys, for our health;
> Who drinks well, loves the commonwealth.   10
> And he that will to bed go sober
> Falls with the leaf still in October.

O FAIR SWEET FACE

This fine song of Petrarchan sentiment is from *Women Pleased.* It is sung by a jealous husband to his sleeping wife.

> O fair sweet face! O eyes celestial bright,
> Twin stars in heaven, that now adorn the night!
> O fruitful lips, where cherries ever grow;
> And damask[36] cheeks, where all sweet beauties blow!
> O thou from head to foot divinely fair,   5
> Cupid's most cunning net's made of that hair;
> And as he weaves himself for curious eyes,
> "Oh, me! oh, me! I am caught myself!" he cries.
> Sweet rest about thee, sweet and golden sleep!
> Soft peaceful thoughts your hourly watches keep!   10
> Whilst I in wonder sing this sacrifice,
> To beauty sacred, and those angel eyes.

Thomas Heywood

1575?–1641

THE DATE and place of Heywood's birth, his parentage, and whether he was educated (as seems likely) at Cambridge, are not certainly known. He was writing for the stage before the turn of the century; in all, he says, he had "either an entire hand or at least a main finger" in 220 plays. As a poet he reaches a higher level in his best lyrics than in his

---

[35] Phthisic, consumption.
[36] Red and white, like damask roses.

dramas; but the latter are infused by a warmth of sympathy with human nature which ranges him with Shakespeare and Dekker rather than with Jonson, Webster, and Marston. *A Woman Killed with Kindness* is the time's best tragedy of domestic life. It is reprinted in H. Spencer's *Elizabethan Plays* (1933) and, with *The Fair Maid of the West,* in a Belles Lettres volume edited by Katharine L. Bates. There is no good collected edition of Heywood (see, however, the Pearson reprint of his plays, 6 vols., 1874); nor is there a reliable book on him (see, however, A. M. Clark's *Thomas Heywood, Playwright and Miscellanist,* 1931).

PACK, CLOUDS, AWAY

Probably composed for a wedding, this ecstatic *aubade* or morning serenade was afterwards used in one of Heywood's poorest plays, *The Rape of Lucrece.*

> Pack, clouds, away! and welcome, day!
> With night we banish sorrow.
> Sweet air, blow soft; mount, lark, aloft,
> To give my love good morrow!
> Wings from the wind, to please her mind, 5
> Notes from the lark, I'll borrow:
> Bird, prune thy wing; nightingale, sing,
> To give my love good morrow!
>   To give my love good morrow
>   Notes from them all I'll borrow. 10
>
> Wake from thy nest, robin redbreast;
> Sing, birds, in every furrow;
> And from each bill, let music shrill
> Give my fair love good morrow!
> Blackbird and thrush in every bush, 15
> Stare,[37] linnet, and cock sparrow,
> You pretty elves, amongst yourselves
> Sing my fair love good morrow!
>   To give my love good morrow
>   Sing, birds, in every furrow! 20

YE LITTLE BIRDS

The charm of this lyric, as of the preceding one, lies in its straightforward simplicity and tenderness, qualities that also mark Heywood's plays. "Ye little birds" is from *The Fair Maid of the Exchange;* it is sung by Frank Golding, in love with Phyllis.

> Ye little birds that sit and sing
> Amidst the shady valleys,
> And see how Phyllis sweetly walks
> Within her garden alleys,

---

37 Starling.

> Go, pretty birds, about her bower; 5
> Sing, pretty birds, she may not lour!
> Ah, me! methinks I see her frown.
>   Ye pretty wantons, warble!
>
> Go, tell her through your chirping bills,
> As you by me are bidden, 10
> To her is only known my love,
> Which from the world is hidden.
> Go, pretty birds, and tell her so;
> See that your notes strain not too low!
> For still, methinks, I see her frown. 15
>   Ye pretty wantons, warble!
>
> Go, tune your voices' harmony,
> And sing I am her lover;
> Strain loud and sweet, that every note
> With sweet content may move her; 20
> And she that hath the sweetest voice,
> Tell her I will not change my choice!
> Yet still, methinks, I see her frown.
>   Ye pretty wantons, warble!
>
> Oh, fly! make haste! see, see, she falls 25
> Into a pretty slumber.
> Sing round about her rosy bed
> That, waking, she may wonder;
> Say to her, 'tis her lover true
> That sendeth love to you, to you! 30
> And when you hear her kind reply,
> Return with pleasant warblings!

THE AUTHOR TO HIS BOOK

Heywood's life spanned the whole course of Elizabethan drama. The first theater was built about the time of his birth, and he died the year before the playhouses were closed by the Puritans. Their attacks had persisted throughout the entire period. In 1612 Heywood answered them with *An Apology for Actors,* a temperate defense in prose, which he prefaced with the following lines.

> The world's a theater, the earth a stage,
> Which God and nature doth with actors fill;
> Kings have their entrance in due equipage,
> And some their parts play well and others ill.
> The best no better are, in this theater, 5
> Where every humor's fitted in his[38] kind:
> This a true subject acts and that a traitor,
> The first applauded and the last confined,
> This plays an honest man and that a knave,

---

38 Its.

A gentle person this and he a clown; 10
One man is ragged and another brave;[39]
All men have parts, and each man acts his own.
She a chaste lady acteth all her life;
A wanton courtesan another plays.
This covets marriage love, that nuptial strife; 15
Both in continual action spend their days.
Some citizens, some soldiers born to adventer,
Shepherds, and seamen. Then our play's begun
When we are born, and to the world first enter,
And all find exits when their parts are done. 20
If then the world a theater present,
As by the roundness it appears most fit,
Built with star-galleries of high ascent
In which Jehove doth as spectator sit,
And chief determiner, to applaud the best 25
And their endeavors crown with more than merit,
But by their evil actions dooms the rest
To end disgraced, whilst others praise inherit:
  He that denies, then, theaters should be,
  He may as well deny a world to me. 30

Anonymous

A MEMENTO FOR MORTALITY

Taken from the view of sepulchers of so many kings and nobles as lie interred in the Abbey of Westminster

In a shortened form, unwarrantably ascribed to Francis Beaumont, this poem is among the most famous of the period. It originally appeared in a miscellany published in 1619 (W. B. and E. P.'s *A Help to Discourse*).

Mortality, behold and fear!
What a change of flesh is here!
Think how many royal bones
Sleep within this heap of stones,
Hence removed from beds of ease, 5
Dainty fare, and what might please,
Fretted[40] roofs, and costly shows,
To a roof that flats the nose:
Which proclaims all flesh is grass,
How the world's fair glories pass; 10
That there is no trust in health,
In youth, in age, in greatness, wealth;
For if such could have reprieved,
Those had been immortal lived.
Know from this the world a snare, 15
How that greatness is but care,

How all pleasures are but pain,
And how short they do remain;
For here they lie had realms and lands,
That now want strength to stir their hands; 20
Where from their pulpits ceiled[41] with dust
They preach, "In greatness is no trust."
Here's an acre sown indeed
With the richest royal'st seed
That the earth did e'er suck in 25
Since the first man died for sin.
Here the bones of birth have cried,
"Though gods they were, as men they died."
Here are sands, ignoble things,
Dropped from the ruined sides of kings, 30
With whom the poor man's earth being shown,
The difference is not easily known.
Here's a world of pomp and state
Forgotten, dead, disconsolate.
Think then this scythe, that mows down kings, 35
Exempts no meaner mortal things.
Then bid the wanton[42] lady tread
Amid these mazes of the dead,
And these, truly understood,
More shall cool and quench the blood 40
Than her many sports a-day
And her nightly wanton play.
Bid her paint till day of doom,
To this favor[43] she must come.
Bid the merchant gather wealth, 45
The usurer exact by stealth,
The proud man beat it from his thought,
Yet to this shape all must be brought.

YET IF HIS MAJESTY

The date of this beautiful poem is unknown. It must have been written before 1648, for in that year Thomas Ford, who set it to music, died.

Yet if his Majesty, our sovereign lord,
    Should of his own accord
    Friendly himself invite
And say, "I'll be your guest tomorrow night,"
How should we stir ourselves, call and command 5
All hands to work! "Let no man idle stand!

"Set me fine Spanish tables in the hall—
    See they be fitted all;
    Let there be room to eat,
And order taken that there want no meat. 10
See every sconce[44] and candlestick made bright,
That without tapers they may give a light.

---

[39] Finely dressed.   [40] Ornamented.

[41] Canopied.   [42] Gay.
[43] These looks.   [44] Wall bracket for candles.

"Look to the presence:[45] are the carpets spread,
    The dazie[46] o'er the head,
        The cushions in the chairs,   15
And all the candles lighted on the stairs?
Perfume the chambers, and in any case
Let each man give attendance in his place!"

Thus if the king were coming would we do,
    And 'twere good reason, too;   20
        For 'tis a duteous thing
To show all honor to an earthly king,
And, after all our travail and our cost,
So he be pleased, to think no labor lost.

But at the coming of the King of Heaven   25
    All's set at six and seven;
        We wallow in our sin;
Christ cannot find a chamber in the inn.
We entertain him always like a stranger,
And, as at first, still lodge him in the manger.   30

George Wither

1588–1667

A VOLUMINOUS and varied writer, with about a hundred
works of prose and poetry to his credit, Wither is at his
poorest in his most typical verse, written in the Spenserian
tradition and frequently blemished by excessive facility.
He is at his best in the light verse which follows; it was
written in his youth. By the outbreak of the Civil War,
Wither had become a zealous Puritan. He was a captain
in the Parliamentary army, and when he was captured by
the royalists came within an ace of hanging for his writings
against the King. His poems were edited by F. Sidgwick
(2 vols., 1902) for the Muses' Library.

SHALL I, WASTING?

Shall I, wasting in despair,
Die because a woman's fair?
Or make pale my cheeks with care,
'Cause another's rosy are?
Be she fairer than the day   5
Or the flowery meads in May:
    If she be not so to me,
    What care I how fair she be?

Should my heart be grieved or pined,
'Cause I see a woman kind?   10

Or a well disposèd nature
Joinèd with a lovely feature?[47]
Be she meeker, kinder, than
Turtledove or pelican:[48]
    If she be not so to me,   15
    What care I how kind she be?

Shall a woman's virtues move
Me to perish for her love?
Or, her well-deserving known,
Make me quite forget mine own?   20
Be she with that goodness blest
Which may gain her name of best:
    If she be not such to me,
    What care I how good she be?

'Cause her fortune seems too high,   25
Shall I play the fool, and die?
Those that bear a noble mind,
Where they want of riches find,
Think what, with them, they would do
That, without them, dare to woo.   30
    And, unless that mind I see,
    What care I though great she be?

Great, or good, or kind, or fair,
I will ne'er the more despair.
If she love me (this believe)   35
I will die ere she shall grieve!
If she slight me when I woo,
I can scorn, and let her go.
    For if she be not for me,
    What care I for whom she be?   40

A LOVE SONNET

I loved a lass, a fair one,
    As fair as e'er was seen;
She was indeed a rare one,
    Another Sheba Queen:
But, fool as then I was,   5
    I thought she loved me too;
But now, alas, sh'as left me—
    Falero, lero, loo!

Her hair like gold did glister,
    Each eye was like a star;   10
She did surpass her sister,
    Which passed all others far.

[45] Reception hall.   [46] Dais, canopy.

[47] *Ea* was pronounced as in *great*.
[48] Reputed to feed her young with her own flesh.

She would me honey call,
  She 'd, oh, she 'd kiss me too;
But now, alas, sh'as left me—   15
  Falero, lero, loo!

In summer time to Medley[49]
  My love and I would go;
The boatmen there stood ready
  My love and I to row.   20
For cream there would we call,
  For cakes and for prunes, too;
But now, alas! sh'as left me—
  Falero, lero, loo!

Many a merry meeting   25
  My love and I have had;
She was my only sweeting;
  She made my heart full glad;
The tears stood in her eyes,
  Like to the morning dew;   30
But now, alas, sh'as left me—
  Falero, lero, loo!

And as abroad we walkèd,
  As lovers' fashion is,
Oft as we sweetly talkèd   35
  The sun would steal a kiss;
The wind upon her lips
  Likewise most sweetly blew;
But now, alas, sh'as left me—
  Falero, lero, loo!   40

Her cheeks were like the cherry,
  Her skin was white as snow;
When she was blithe and merry,
  She angel-like did show;
Her waist exceeding small;   45
  The fives did fit her shoe;
But now, alas, she's left me—
  Falero, lero, loo!

In summer time or winter
  She had her heart's desire;   50
I still did scorn to stint her
  From sugar, sack,[50] or fire;[51]
The world went round about,
  No cares we ever knew;
But now, alas, she's left me—   55
  Falero, lero, loo!

As we walked home together
  At midnight through the town,
To keep away the weather
  O'er her I'd cast my gown;[52]   60
No cold my love should feel,
  Whate'er the heavens could do;
But now, alas, sh'as left me—
  Falero, lero, loo!

Like doves we would be billing,   65
  And clip[53] and kiss so fast,
Yet she would be unwilling
  That I should kiss the last.
They're Judas kisses now,
  Since that they proved untrue;   70
For now, alas, sh'as left me—
  Falero, lero, loo!

To maidens' vows and swearing
  Henceforth no credit give;
You may give them the hearing,   75
  But never them believe;
They are as false as fair,
  Unconstant, frail, untrue;
For mine, alas, has left me—
  Falero, lero, loo!   80

'Twas I that paid for all things,
  'Twas others drank the wine;
I cannot now recall things,
  Live but a fool to pine.
'Twas I that beat the bush;   85
  The bird to others flew.
For she, alas, hath left me—
  Falero, lero, loo!

If ever that Dame Nature,
  For this false lover's sake,   90
Another pleasing creature
  Like unto her would make,
Let her remember this:
  To make the other true.
For this, alas, hath left me—   95
  Falero, lero, loo!

No riches now can raise me,
  No want make me despair,
No misery amaze me,
  Nor yet for want I care.   100
I have lost a world itself;
  My earthly heaven, adieu!
Since she, alas, hath left me—
  Falero, lero, loo!

---

[49] A short way up the Thames from Oxford.   [50] Sherry.
[51] One still pays extra in most English inns for a fire in one's room. Central heating is infrequent.

[52] This poem was probably written when Wither was an undergraduate at Oxford, or soon after.   [53] Embrace.

Thomas Carew

1598?–1639?

This "son of Ben" was one of the master lyrists of the Caroline period, as the times of Charles I are called. With Waller, Suckling, and Lovelace, he ranks at the head of a new group of literary courtiers, the Cavalier poets. Educated at Oxford and the Inns of Court, Carew held minor diplomatic appointments but failed to find his place in life, except as a writer of extremely graceful verse. Charles I finally gave him a post in his personal entourage as sewer, that is, taster and server at the royal table. The merits of the following poems are obvious; of its kind, "Ask me no more" comes pretty close to perfection. The titles were probably supplied by the publisher of the earliest edition (1640). The best modern edition is by A. Vincent (an undated volume in The Muses' Library). In R. G. Howarth's *Minor Poets of the 17th Century* (Everyman's Library), pp. 65–181 reprint poems by Carew. Pronounce this poet's surname as if it were spelled Carey.

PERSUASIONS TO ENJOY

If the quick spirits in your eye
Now languish and anon must die,
If every sweet and every grace
Must fly from that forsaken face,
    Then, Celia, let us reap our joys   5
    Ere Time such goodly fruit destroys.

Or, if that golden fleece must grow
For ever free from agèd snow,
If those bright suns must know no shade,
Nor your fresh beauties ever fade,   10
    Then fear not, Celia, to bestow
    What, still being gathered, still must grow.

Thus either Time his sickle brings
In vain, or else in vain his wings.

INGRATEFUL BEAUTY THREATENED

Know, Celia, since thou art so proud,
    'Twas I that gave thee thy renown;
Thou hadst in the forgotten crowd
    Of common beauties lived unknown,
Had not my verse exhaled thy name,   5
And with it imped[54] the wings of Fame.

That killing power is none of thine:
    I gave it to thy voice and eyes;
Thy sweets, thy graces, all are mine;
    Thou art my star, shin'st in my skies.   10
Then dart not from thy borrowed sphere[55]
Lightning on him that fixed thee there.

Tempt me with such affrights no more,
    Lest what I made I uncreate;
Let fools thy mystic form adore,   15
    I'll know thee in thy mortal state.
Wise poets, that wrapped Truth in tales,
Knew her themselves through all her veils.

DISDAIN RETURNED

He that loves a rosy cheek,
    Or a coral lip admires,
Or from starlike eyes doth seek
    Fuel to maintain his fires,
As old Time makes these decay   5
So his flames must waste away.

But a smooth and steadfast mind,
    Gentle thoughts, and calm desires,
Hearts with equal love combined,
    Kindle never-dying fires.   10
Where these are not, I despise
Lovely cheeks or lips or eyes.

No tears, Celia, now shall win
    My resolved heart to return;
I have searched thy soul within,   15
    And find nought but pride and scorn.
I have learned thy arts, and now
Can disdain as much as thou.

Some power, in my revenge, convey
That love to her I cast away.   20

UPON A RIBBON

This silken wreath, which circles in mine arm,
Is but an emblem of that mystic charm
Wherewith the magic of your beauties binds
My captive soul, and round about it winds
Fetters of lasting love. This hath entwined   5
My flesh alone; that hath empaled[56] my mind.
Time may wear out these soft weak bands, but those
Strong chains of brass Fate shall not discompose.

---

[54] Mended (as a falconer fastened additional feathers on a hawk's wing).

[55] The outer sphere of fixed stars in the Ptolemaic astronomy.
[56] That (your "mystic charm") has enclosed.

This holy relic may preserve my wrist,
But my whole frame doth by that power subsist: 10
To that, my prayers and sacrifice; to this,
I only pay a superstitious kiss.
This but the idol, that's the deity;
Religion there is due, here ceremony;
That I receive by faith, this but in trust;   15
Here I may tender duty, there I must;
This order as a layman I may bear,
But I become Love's priest when that I wear;
This moves like air, that as the center[57] stands;
That knot your virtue tied, this but your hands;   20
That nature framed, but this was made by art;
This makes my arm your prisoner, that my heart.

A SONG

Ask me no more where Jove bestows,
When June is past, the fading rose;
For in your beauty's orient deep[58]
These flowers, as in their causes,[59] sleep.

Ask me no more whither do stray   5
The golden atoms of the day;[60]
For in pure love heaven did prepare
Those powders to enrich your hair.

Ask me no more whither doth haste
The nightingale, when May is past;   10
For in your sweet dividing[61] throat
She winters, and keeps warm her note.

Ask me no more where those stars light
That downwards fall in dead of night;
For in your eyes they sit, and there   15
Fixèd become, as in their sphere.

Ask me no more if east or west
The phoenix[62] builds her spicy nest;
For unto you at last she flies,
And in your fragrant bosom dies.   20

---

[57] The earth, in the Ptolemaic system the center of the universe.
It *stands* immovable.
[58] In the oriental depths of your beauty. The East was considered
the source of being.
[59] I.e., as the rose remains unseen in the stalk (till the next impulse
from the East).   [60] The motes seen in sunbeams.
[61] Melodious.
[62] The fabulous Arabian bird. Periodically it gathered a nest of
spices which the sun set on fire. Both nest and bird were consumed, but the phoenix rose renewed from the ashes.

Sir William D'avenant

1606–1668

THE SON of an Oxford tavern-keeper, D'avenant (as he
preferred to have his name spelled) became a Cavalier poet
by dint of industry, not talent. He succeeded Jonson as poet
laureate, though not till Dryden, who followed D'avenant,
was that title used officially. His knighthood was for his
services in the royal army at the siege of Gloucester. Like
most of his writings, the heroic poem *Gondibert* is a dreadful
bore; but D'avenant achieved one fine lyric, the following
aubade. In the history of the English stage he is of considerable importance, since he links the pre-Wars with the
Restoration theater. As a playwright, and still more as one
of the two courtiers to whom Charles II granted a monopoly of acting in London, D'avenant was prominent
in the revival of the drama. He led the way in putting
scenery on the public stage, and in rewriting Shakespeare
to suit contemporary taste. There is a good book by A. H.
Nethercot, *Sir William D'avenant, Poet Laureate and Play-
wright-Manager* (1938).

THE LARK NOW LEAVES HIS WAT'RY NEST

The lark now leaves his wat'ry nest,
  And climbing shakes his dewy wings;
He takes this window for the east,
  And to implore your light he sings:
Awake, awake! the morn will never rise   5
Till she can dress her beauty at your eyes.

The merchant bows unto the seaman's star;
  The plowman from the sun his season takes.
But still the lover wonders what they are
  Who look for day before his mistress wakes.   10
Awake, awake! break through your veils of lawn!
Then draw your curtains, and begin the dawn.

Edmund Waller

1606–1687

THE EARLY life of this accomplished Cavalier poet, "smooth
Waller" as he was called for his verses' polish, was smoothed
by circumstances; but wealthy parents, an inherited fortune,
Eton, Cambridge, a brilliant success in the House of
Commons, and a rich marriage failed to produce a character
of integrity. After beginning on the Parliamentary side,
he was heavily fined and banished in 1643 for participation
in a royalist plot; and his reputation was tarnished by his
abjectness and the alacrity with which he betrayed his
associates to their deaths. Later on he made his peace with

the Puritans, returned to England, and composed a poetic eulogy of Cromwell. At the Restoration he did the same for Charles II, who took him into favor but pointed out that the earlier panegyric was the better poem. "Sir," replied Waller, "we poets never succeed so well in writing truth as in fiction." His poems were first published in 1645; by the neoclassicists of the Restoration and eighteenth century they were praised to the skies. Dryden credited Waller with perfecting the rimed couplet, by using it as a unit of expression instead of letting the sense run on past the second line (see the last of our selections). This claim of priority is hardly warranted, but several of Waller's poems are unsurpassed for elegance. There is an edition by G. T. Drury (1893) in The Muses' Library.

TO MR. HENRY LAWES[63]

Who Had Then Newly Set a Song of Mine
in the Year 1635

Verse makes heroic virtue live,
But you can life to verses give.
As, when in open air we blow,
The breath, though strained, sounds flat and low,
But if a trumpet take the blast,   5
It lifts it high and makes it last:
So in your airs our numbers[64] dressed
Make a shrill sally from the breast
Of nymphs, who, singing what we penned,
Our passions to themselves commend;   10
While love, victorious with thy art,
Governs at once their voice and heart.
You, by the help of tune and time,
Can make that song that was but rime.
Noy pleading, no man doubts the cause,[65]   15
Or questions verses set by Lawes.
As a church window, thick with paint,
Lets in a light but dim and faint,
So others with division[66] hide
The light of sense, the poet's pride;   20
But you alone may truly boast
That not a syllable is lost:
The writer's and the setter's skill
At once the ravished ears do fill.
Let those which only warble long,   25
And gargle in their throats a song,
Content themselves with ut,[67] re, mi:
Let words, and sense, be set by thee.

ON A GIRDLE

That which her slender waist confined
Shall now my joyful temples bind;
No monarch but would give his crown,
His arms might do what this has done.

It was my heaven's extremest sphere,[68]   5
The pale[69] which held that lovely deer.
My joy, my grief, my hope, my love,
Did all within this circle move.

A narrow compass! and yet there
Dwelt all that's good and all that's fair.   10
Give me but what this riband bound,
Take all the rest the sun goes round!

GO, LOVELY ROSE!

Go, lovely rose!
Tell her that wastes her time and me
That now she knows,
When I resemble her to thee,
How sweet and fair she seems to be.   5

Tell her that's young,
And shuns to have her graces spied,
That hadst thou sprung
In deserts, where no men abide,
Thou must have uncommended died.   10

Small is the worth
Of beauty from the light retired;
Bid her come forth,
Suffer herself to be desired,
And not blush so to be admired.   15

Then die! that she
The common fate of all things rare
May read in thee:
How small a part of time they share
That are so wondrous sweet and fair.   20

OF THE LAST VERSES IN THE BOOK[70]

When we for age could neither read nor write,
The subject made us able to indite;
The soul, with nobler resolutions decked,
The body stooping, does herself erect.

---

63 The leading Caroline composer.   64 Verses.
65 When Noy pleads, no one doubts the merits of the case. William
   Noy (1577–1634) was a leading lawyer.
66 Florid melodies.   67 Do.

68 The outermost sphere of the Ptolemaic system.
69 Fence.
70 According to a manuscript note by Waller's son, "the last
   verses my dear father made." He had written poetry for upwards of sixty years.

No mortal parts are requisite to raise 5
Her that, unbodied, can her Maker praise.

    The seas are quiet when the winds give o'er;
So, calm are we when passions are no more.
For then we know how vain it was to boast
Of fleeting things, so certain to be lost. 10
Clouds of affection from our younger eyes
Conceal that emptiness which age descries.

    The soul's dark cottage, battered and decayed,
Lets in new light through chinks that time has made;
Stronger by weakness, wiser men become 15
As they draw near to their eternal home.
Leaving the old, both worlds at once they view
That stand upon the threshold of the new.

Sir John Suckling

1609–1642

"Natural, easy Suckling!" cries Mistress Millamant in Congreve's *The Way of the World*. He was possibly the most brilliant of the Cavalier poets, renowned at the court of Charles I for his reckless gambling and general extravagance, for the gracefulness of his verses, and for the sparkling charm of his talk. Dryden thought Suckling's the closest approximation to the ideal conversation of a gentleman. He has been credited with inventing the excellent game of cribbage; it was not played for fun in his day.

Educated at Cambridge and the Inns of Court, Suckling was only eighteen when he came into a large inheritance. He traveled in France and Italy, and saw military service under the great Swedish king and general Gustavus Adolphus (d. 1632). Suckling was a member of the Long Parliament. On the discovery of his part in the conspiracy to rescue from the Tower Charles's hated minister, the Earl of Strafford, he fled to France; and there he died in the following year, by suicide. Besides his light verse he wrote some inferior plays. His work was published in 1646 under the title of *Fragmenta Aurea*. Both verse and prose were edited by A. H. Thompson (1910). For the poems see also R. G. Howarth's *Minor Poets of the 17th Century* (Everyman's Library), pp. 183–244.

WHY SO PALE AND WAN?

Why so pale and wan, fond lover?
    Prithee, why so pale?
Will, when looking well can't move her,
    Looking ill prevail?
    Prithee, why so pale? 5

Why so dull and mute, young sinner?
    Prithee, why so mute?
Will, when speaking well can't win her,
    Saying nothing do't?
    Prithee, why so mute? 10

Quit, quit for shame! This will not move,
    This cannot take her.
If of herself she will not love,
    Nothing can make her:
    The devil take her! 15

THE CONSTANT LOVER

Out upon it! I have loved
    Three whole days together,
And am like to love three more—
    If it prove fair weather.

Time shall moult away his wings 5
    Ere he shall discover
In the whole wide world again
    Such a constant lover.

But the spite on't is, no praise
    Is due at all to me: 10
Love with me had made no stays,
    Had it any been but she.

Had it any been but she,
    And that very face,
There had been at least ere this 15
    A dozen dozen in her place.

Samuel Butler

1612–1680

Two Samuel Butlers, in two centuries born,
The Seventeenth and Nineteenth did adorn—
Adorn with Satire's pleasing virulence,
Much as small boys adorn the vacant fence.

This judgment, if such it can be termed, is not wholly unjust but it is too severe. Both Butlers were, and meant to be, smart—no man can set up for satirist without a certain confidence in his own wit—yet the writings of both are high-powered by intellectual force and artistic mastery.

Samuel the First was earliest in the field of the major neoclassical satirists; Part I of his masterly burlesque of the Puritans appeared in 1663, Part II the year after, Part III in 1678. The indebtedness to *Don Quixote* is obvious, yet

Butler is less humane than Cervantes. He handles his octosyllabic couplet with a wit and precision which have made "Hudibrastic" verse almost a genre. On Swift his influence was considerable; and though in his roughness and horseplay he is not a typical neoclassical satirist, he had many followers among the eighteenth-century poets.

As secretary or steward Butler, who was not a university man, served several landed gentlemen of the Puritan persuasion; evidently he took copious notes. Though inspired by royalist partisanship, many of his gibes in *Hudibras,* which is his best work, are doubly effective because they fit fanaticism, pedantry, and hypocrisy in general. Butler's was not an ingratiating temperament; and despite the immense popularity of his satire, in which Charles II took extraordinary pleasure, he was inadequately rewarded and died in poverty. The standard edition is by A. R. Waller and R. Lamar (*Complete Works,* 3 vols., 1905–28). The following are the opening lines of Butler's masterpiece; the text is from the edition of 1674, which incorporates the author's revisions.

HUDIBRAS

WRITTEN IN THE TIME OF THE LATE WARS

Corrected and emended
with several additions and annotations

FIRST PART, CANTO I

THE ARGUMENT OF THE FIRST CANTO

Sir Hudibras his passing worth,
The manner how he sallied forth,
His arms and equipage, are shown,
His horse's virtues and his own.
Th' adventure of the bear and fiddle
Is sung, but breaks off in the middle.

When civil fury[1] first grew high,
And men fell out they knew not why;
When hard words, jealousies, and fears
Set folks together by the ears
And made them fight, like mad or drunk,   5
For Dame Religion as for punk,[2]
Whose honesty they all durst swear for,
Though not a man of them knew wherefore;
When gospel-trumpeter,[3] surrounded
With long-eared[4] rout,[5] to battle sounded,   10
And pulpit, drum ecclesiastic,
Was beat with fist instead of a stick:
Then did Sir Knight abandon dwelling,
And out he rode a-colonelling.[6]

A wight he was whose very sight would   15
Entitle him Mirror of Knighthood:
That never bowed his stubborn knee
To anything but chivalry,
Nor put up[7] blow, but that which laid
Right Worshipful on shoulder blade;[8]   20
Chief of domestic knights and errant,
Either for chartel[9] or for warrant;[10]
Great on the bench,[11] great in the saddle,
That could as well bind o'er[12] as swaddle.[13]
Mighty he was at both of these,   25
And styled[14] of war as well as peace
(So some rats, of amphibious nature,
Are either for the land or water).
But here our authors make a doubt
Whether he were more wise or stout.[15]   30
Some hold the one, and some the other;
But, howso'er they make a pother,
The diff'rence was so small, his brain
Outweighed his rage but half a grain;
Which made some take him for a tool   35
That knaves do work with, called a fool,
And offer to lay wagers that,
As Montaigne,[16] playing with his cat,
Complains she thought him but an ass,
Much more she would Sir Hudibras   40
(For that's the name our valiant knight
To all his challenges did write).
But they're mistaken very much;
'Tis plain enough he was no such.
We grant, although he had much wit,   45
H' was very shy of using it,
As being loth to wear it out,
And therefore bore it not about—
Unless on holidays or so,
As men their best apparel do.   50
Beside, 'tis known he could speak Greek
As naturally as pigs squeak,
That Latin was no more difficile,
Than to a blackbird 'tis to whistle.
Being rich in both, he never scanted   55
His bounty unto such as wanted;
But much of either would afford
To many that had not one word.
For Hebrew roots, although th' are found
To flourish most in barren ground,   60

---

[7] Submitted to.
[8] I.e., when he was tapped with a sword and knighted.
[9] Challenge to a duel.   [10] Officer's commission.
[11] As a country justice of the peace.
[12] Put (an offender or suspect) under bond.
[13] A pun: (1) bind an infant with a swaddling band, (2) beat.
[14] Called, known as.   [15] Valiant.
[16] The great French essayist (1533–92). See *Essays,* Book II, chap. 12 (trans. E. J. Trechmann, I, 444).

---

[1] I.e., the Civil Wars between the Puritans and royalists.
[2] Prostitute.   [3] I.e., the Puritan ministers.
[4] Since the Puritans cut their hair short, their ears were prominent —like a donkey's.   [5] Mob.
[6] *Colonel* was a trisyllable.

He had such plenty as sufficed
To make some think him circumcised.
And truly so, perhaps, he was;
'Tis many a pious Christian's case.

He was in logic a great critic, 65
Profoundly skilled in analytic.
He could distinguish, and divide
A hair 'twixt south and southwest side;
On either which he would dispute,
Confute, change hands, and still confute. 70
He'd undertake to prove, by force
Of argument, a man's no horse;
He'd prove a buzzard is no fowl,
And that a lord may be an owl,
A calf an alderman, a goose a justice, 75
And rooks committeemen[17] and trustees.
He'd run in debt by disputation,
And pay with ratiocination.[18]
All this by syllogism, true
In mood and figure, he would do. 80

For[19] rhetoric, he could not ope
His mouth but out there flew a trope;[20]
And when he happ'ned to break off
I' th' middle of his speech, or cough,
H' had hard words ready to show why, 85
And tell what rules he did it by;
Else, when with greatest art he spoke,
You'd think he talked like other folk:
For all a rhetorician's rules
Teach nothing but to name his tools. 90
His ordinary rate of speech
In loftiness of sound was rich—
A Babylonish dialect,
Which learnèd pedants much affect;
It was a parti-colored dress 95
Of patched and piebald languages:
'T was English cut on Greek and Latin,
Like fustian[21] heretofore on satin.
It had an odd promiscuous tone,
As if h' had talked three parts in one; 100
Which made some think, when he did gabble,
Th' had heard three laborers of Babel,[22]
Or Cerberus[23] himself pronounce
A leash[24] of languages at once.

This he as volubly would vent, 105
As if his stock would ne'er be spent.
And truly, to support that charge,
He had supplies as vast and large;
For he could coin or counterfeit
New words with little or no wit, 110
Words so debased and hard, no stone
Was hard enough to touch them on.[25]
And when with hasty noise he spoke 'em,
The ignorant for current took 'em;
That,[26] had the orator who once 115
Did fill his mouth with pebble stones
When he harangued[27] but known his phrase,
He would have used no other ways.

In mathematics he was greater
Than Tycho Brahe[28] or Erra Pater:[29] 120
For he by geometric scale
Could take the size of pots of ale,
Resolve by sines and tangents straight[30]
If bread or butter wanted weight,
And wisely tell what hour o' th' day 125
The clock does strike by algebra.

Besides, he was a shrewd philosopher,
And had read every text and gloss over.
Whate'er the crabbed'st author hath,
He understood b' implicit faith; 130
Whatever skeptic could inquire for,
For every why he had a wherefore;
Knew more than forty of them do,
As far as words and terms could go:
All which he understood by rote, 135
And, as occasion served, would quote,
No matter whether right or wrong;
They might be either said or sung.
His notions fitted things so well
That which was which he could not tell, 140
But oftentimes mistook the one
For th' other, as great clerks[31] have done.
He could reduce all things to acts,
And knew their natures by abstracts:
Where entity and quiddity,[32] 145
The ghosts of defunct bodies, fly;

[17] I.e., officious members of Parliamentary committees. They often served as trustees of confiscated royalist estates. The rook, i.e. crow, is of course a thief.   [18] Formal reasoning.
[19] As for.   [20] Figure of speech.
[21] A kind of coarse cloth. Suits made of it were sometimes slit to show the silk lining.   [22] See Genesis 11:1-9.
[23] The triple-headed dog who, in classical mythology, guarded the gate of Hades.   [24] A set of three.

[25] To serve (like the goldsmith's touchstone) to test their value.
[26] So that.
[27] Thus the great Greek orator Demosthenes (d. 322 B.C.) trained himself to speak clearly.
[28] Famous Danish astronomer (d. 1601).
[29] A satirist had termed the Puritan members of Parliament sons of Erra Pater (said to be an old astrologer) on account of the credulity with which they accepted the predictions of the astrologer William Lilly (d. 1681).   [30] Immediately.
[31] Savants.
[32] Scholastic terms professing to distinguish between "essential identity" and "characteristic identity."

Where truth in person does appear,
Like words congealed in northern air;[33]
He knew what's what, and that's as high
As metaphysic wit can fly;   150
In school divinity[34] as able
As he that hight[35] Irrefragable;
Profound in all the nominal[36]
And real ways beyond them all;
And with as delicate a hand   155
Could twist as tough a rope of sand,
And weave fine cobwebs, fit for skull
That's empty when the moon is full,
Such as take lodgings in a head
That's to be let unfurnishèd.   160
He could raise scruples dark and nice,[37]
And after solve 'em in a trice;
As if divinity had catched
The itch, of purpose to be scratched,
Or like a mountebank did wound   165
And stab herself with doubts profound,
Only to show with how small pain
The sores of faith are cured again,
Although by woeful proof we find
They always leave a scar behind.   170
He knew the seat[38] of Paradise,
Could tell in what degree it lies,
And, as he was disposed, could prove it
Below the moon, or else above it;
What Adam dreamt of when his bride   175
Came from her closet in his side;
Whether the Devil tempted her
By a High-Dutch[39] interpreter;
If either of them had a navel;[40]
Who first made music malleable;[41]   180
Whether the serpent, at the fall,
Had cloven feet or none at all.
All this without a gloss or comment
He could unriddle in a moment,
In proper terms, such as men smatter   185
When they throw out and miss the matter.

For his religion, it was fit
To match his learning and his wit:—

'Twas Presbyterian true blue,
For he was of that stubborn crew   190
Of errant[42] saints whom all men grant
To be the true Church Militant:
Such as do build their faith upon
The holy text of pike and gun;
Decide all controversies by   195
Infallible artillery,
And prove their doctrine orthodox
By apostolic blows and knocks;
Call fire and sword and desolation
A godly, thorough reformation,   200
Which always must be carried on
And still be doing, never done—
As if religion were intended
For nothing else but to be mended—
A sect whose chief devotion lies   205
In odd, perverse antipathies;[43]
In falling out with that or this,
And finding somewhat still amiss;
More peevish, cross, and splénetic[44]
Than dog distract or monkey sick;   210
That with more care keep holiday[45]
The wrong, than others the right, way;
Compound[46] for sins they are inclined to
By damning those they have no mind to;
Still so perverse and opposite   215
(As if they worshipped God for spite),
The selfsame thing they will abhor
One way, and long another for.
Free will they one way disavow,[47]
Another, nothing else allow.   220
All piety consists therein
In them, in other men all sin.
Rather than fail, they will defy
That which they love most tenderly:
Quarrel with minced pies, and disparage   225
Their best and dearest friend, plum porridge;
Fat pig and goose itself oppose,
And blaspheme custard through the nose.[48]
Th' apostles of this fierce religion,
Like Máhomet's, were ass and widgeon;[49]   230

[33] This phenomenon is reported by Rabelais (Book IV, chap. 56).
[34] Scholastic theology.
[35] Is called.—*Irrefragable* = the unbreakable, the irrefutable; Alexander Hales (d. 1245).
[36] An allusion to the great controversy of medieval scholasticism over realism and nominalism.   [37] Subtle.   [38] Site.
[39] German. Claims were actually made for its being God's language at the Creation.
[40] A point of theological interest, in view of their origin.
[41] Percussive music. The Greek philosopher Pythagoras (sixth century B.C.) was alleged to have invented music after hearing a blacksmith at his anvil.

[42] Rascally.
[43] Alluding to the Puritans' disapproval of many of the pleasures of life.   [44] Fretful.   [45] Religious feast days.
[46] Settle, pay.—This is one of the most famous couplets in English.
[47] Calvinism taught that man has no freedom of choice but acts according to a divinely imposed necessity. But it insisted on freedom of the individual conscience as against ecclesiastical authority.
[48] I.e., in the nasal singsong of the Puritan fanatic.
[49] A kind of wild duck, but = simpleton. The allusions are to the dove that was supposed to bring the prophet divine messages, and to the ass which he dreamed would bear him into God's presence.

To whom our knight, by fast instinct
Of wit and temper, was so linked
As if hypocrisy and nonsense
Had got th' advowson[50] of his conscience. . . .

Richard Lovelace

1618–1657?

LOVELACE was an uncommonly handsome fellow. He was
still in his teens when, through the influence of "a great
lady" he had favorably impressed, he received his M.A.—
at the end of his second year at Oxford! He was soon leading the life of a Cavalier poet at court. In 1642, on the eve
of the fighting, he spent seven weeks in jail for presenting
a royalist petition to the Long Parliament; this was the
occasion of "To Althea from Prison." He had already seen
service against the Scots, but almost nothing is known about
his share in the Civil Wars. He was much in the Low Countries, part of the time in the French army fighting the
Spaniards. "To Lucasta, Going beyond the Seas" was
evidently written on his departure, but whether there
actually was such a lady has never been determined. He is
said to have been wounded at the seige of Dunkirk in
1646. Not long afterwards he was back in England, and in
1648, in connection with the Kentish rebellion, was again
imprisoned. On his release he published his poems in a
volume entitled *Lucasta* (1649). He must have dedicated
his fortune to his King's service; apparently he died in
poverty. Lovelace wrote little of merit, but the exceptions
are shining ones. His poems were edited by C. H. Wilkin-
son (2 vols., 1925). Another edition is by R. G. Howarth,
Minor Poets of the 17th Century (Everyman's Library), pp.
245–375. There is a Life by C. H. Hartmann (*The Cavalier
Spirit*, 1925).

TO ALTHEA, FROM PRISON

When Love with unconfinèd wings
  Hovers within my gates,
And my divine Althea brings
  To whisper at the grates;
When I lie tangled in her hair   5
  And fettered to her eye:
The gods[1] that wanton in the air
  Know no such liberty.

When flowing cups run swiftly round,
  With no allaying Thames,[2]   10
Our careless heads with roses bound,
  Our hearts with loyal flames;

When thirsty grief in wine we steep,
  When healths and draughts go free:
Fishes that tipple in the deep   15
  Know no such liberty.

When, like committed[3] linnets, I
  With shriller throat shall sing
The sweetness, mercy, majesty,
  And glories of my King;   20
When I shall voice aloud how good
  He is, how great should be:
Enlargèd winds that curl the flood
  Know no such liberty.

Stone walls do not a prison make,   25
  Nor iron bars a cage;
Minds innocent and quiet take
  That for an hermitage.

If I have freedom in my love,
  And in my soul am free,   30
Angels alone, that soar above,
  Enjoy such liberty.

TO LUCASTA, GOING TO THE WARS

Tell me not, sweet, I am unkind,
  That from the nunnery
Of thy chaste breast and quiet mind
  To war and arms I fly.

True, a new mistress now I chase,   5
  The first foe in the field;
And with a stronger faith embrace
  A sword, a horse, a shield.

Yet this inconstancy is such
  As you too shall adore;   10
I could not love thee, dear, so much,
  Loved I not honor more.

TO LUCASTA, GOING BEYOND THE SEAS

If to be absent were to be
  Away from thee,
  Or that when I am gone
  You or I were alone,
Then, my Lucasta, might I crave   5
Pity from blust'ring wind or swallowing wave.

---

[50] Ecclesiastical patronage, right to occupancy.

[1] *Gods* is Lovelace's final choice instead of the *birds* of earlier texts.
[2] Unweakened with water.

[3] Imprisoned.

But I'll not sigh one blast or gale
　　To swell my sail,
　　Or pay a tear to 'suage
　　The foaming blue god's[4] rage;　　　10
For whether he will let me pass
Or no, I'm still as happy as I was.

Though seas and land betwixt us both,
　　Our faith and troth,
　　Like separated souls,　　　15
　　All time and space controls:
Above the highest sphere we meet,
Unseen, unknown, and greet as angels greet.

So then we do anticipate
　　Our after-fate,　　　20
　　And are alive i' th' skies,
　　If thus our lips and eyes
Can speak like spirits unconfined,
In heav'n, their earthy bodies left behind.

Abraham Cowley

1618–1667

COWLEY'S first volume of poetry was published when he was about fourteen; it went through three editions in four years. His contemporaries thought him a great poet, a judgment which was soon reversed. His faults do not appear in the selections below; the chief one was over-fondness for the metaphysical conceit. "He could never," said Dryden at the end of the century, "forgive any conceit that came in his way, but swept like a dragnet great and small." From Westminster School Cowley went to Cambridge, where Crashaw was among his friends and he won praise as an amateur playwright. (On the Restoration stage he was to have a minor success with a comedy, *Cutter of Coleman Street.*) During the Civil Wars he was a confidential secretary to the exiled Queen, and then a secret agent. On a trip to England in the latter capacity he was caught, but was released on bail in view of his decision to accept the new order. In 1657 he took the M.D. degree at Oxford. His subsequent writings show the seriousness of his interest in science; he was an early member of the Royal Society, to which he addressed an ode. His rewards, when the King was restored, were small; eventually he retired to country life.

Aside from a very few good poems and some of the earliest familiar essays in our language, Cowley's main impress on English literature came from his repeated use of a verse form which, though called the Pindaric Ode, lacks the

balanced structure of the original. (See p. 441, above.) The lines and stanzas of the Cowleian species are irregular in length; the idea was to achieve a lofty effect without adhering to a set pattern. Cowley's own odes are frequently poor, but better poets afterwards adopted the form. His *English Writings* were edited by A. R. Waller (2 vols., 1905–6). Dr. Johnson leads off his *Lives of the Poets* with a study of Cowley which is of general importance. There is an excellent biography by A. H. Nethercot (*Abraham Cowley, The Muse's Hannibal,* 1931). In his own time his name was pronounced (and sometimes spelled) Cooley.

THE WISH

This poem, with most of Cowley's best pieces, appeared in *The Mistress* (1647).

Well then, I now do plainly see
This busy world and I shall ne'er agree.
The very honey of all earthly joy
Does of all meats the soonest cloy;
　　And they, methinks, deserve my pity　　　5
Who for it can endure the stings,
The crowd, and buzz, and murmurings,
　　Of this great hive, the city,

Ah, yet, ere I descend to th' grave,
May I a small house and large garden have　　　10
And a few friends, and many books, both true,
Both wise, and both delightful, too!
　　And since love ne'er will from me flee,
A mistress moderately fair,
And good as guardian angels are,　　　15
　　Only beloved, and loving me!

O fountains, when in you shall I
Myself, eased of unpeaceful thoughts, espy?
O fields! O woods! when, when shall I be made
The happy tenant of your shade?　　　20
　　Here's the spring-head of pleasure's flood;[5]
Here's wealthy nature's treasury,
Where all the riches lie that she
　　Has coined and stamped for good.

Pride and ambition here　　　25
Only in far-fetched metaphors appear;
Here nought but winds can hurtful murmurs scatter,
And nought but Echo flatter.
　　The gods, when they descended, hither
From heaven did always choose their way;　　　30
And therefore we may boldly say
　　That 'tis the way, too, thither.

---

[4] Neptune's.

[5] River.

How happy here should I
And one dear she live, and embracing die!
She who is all the world, and can exclude,   35
In deserts, solitude.
　　I should have then this only fear:
Lest men, when they my pleasures see,
Should hither throng to live like me,
　　And so make a city here.   40

ON THE DEATH OF MR. CRASHAW

This elegy for his friend and fellow poet (see pp. 500 ff.,
above) is one of Cowley's best poems.

Poet and saint! to thee alone are given
The two most sacred names of earth and heaven,
The hard and rarest[6] union which can be
Next that of godhead with humanity.
Long did the Muses banished slaves abide   5
And built vain pyramids to mortal pride;[7]
Like Moses thou—though spells and charms withstand—
Hast brought them nobly home, back to their Holy Land.
　　Ah wretched we, poets of earth! but thou
Wert, living, the same poet which thou art now[8]   10
Whilst angels sing to thee their airs divine
And joy in an applause so great as thine.
Equal society with them to hold,
Thou need'st not make new songs, but say the old.
And they, kind spirits! shall all rejoice to see   15
How little less than they exalted man may be.
Still the old heathen gods in numbers dwell;
The heavenliest thing on earth still keeps up hell.
Nor have we yet quite purged the Christian land;
Still idols here, like calves at Bethel,[9] stand.   20
And though Pan's death long since all oracles broke,
Yet still in rime the fiend Apollo spoke.[10]
Nay, with the worst of heathen dotage we,
Vain men, the monster woman deify,
Find stars and tie our fates there in a face,   25
And paradise in them, by whom we lost it, place.
What different faults corrupt our Muses thus?
Wanton as girls, as old wives fabulous!
　　Thy spotless Muse, like Mary, did contain
The boundless godhead; she[11] did well disdain   30

That her eternal verse employed should be
On a less subject than eternity,
And for a sacred mistress scorned to take
But her whom God himself scorned not his spouse to
　　make.
It, in a kind, her miracle did do: 35
A fruitful mother was, and virgin too.
　　How well, blest swan, did fate contrive thy death;
And made thee render up thy tuneful breath
In thy great mistress' arms, thou most divine
And richest offering of Loretto's shrine![12]   40
Where, like some holy sacrifice to expire,
A fever burns thee, and love lights the fire.
Angels—they say—brought the famed chapel there,
And bore the sacred load in triumph through the air.
'Tis surer much they brought thee there; and they   45
And thou, their charge, went singing all the way.
　　Pardon, my mother church,[13] if I consent
That angels led him when from thee he went,
For even in error sure no danger is
When joined with so much piety as his.   50
Ah, mighty God, with shame I speak 't and grief,
Ah, that our greatest faults were in belief!
And our weak reason were even weaker yet,
Rather than thus our wills too strong for it.
His faith perhaps in some nice tenets might   55
Be wrong; his life, I'm sure, was in the right.
And I myself a Catholic will be
So far at least, great saint, to pray to thee.
　　Hail, bard triumphant! and some care bestow
On us, the poets militant below![14]   60
Opposed by our old enemy, adverse chance,
Attacked by envy and by ignorance,
Enchained by beauty, tortured by desires,
Exposed by tyrant love to savage beasts and fires.
Thou from low earth in nobler flames didst rise,   65
And like Elijah[15] mount alive the skies.
Elisha-like (but with a wish much less,
More fit thy greatness and my littleness),
Lo, here I beg (I whom thou once didst prove
So humble to esteem, so good to love)   70

---

[6] I.e., hardest and rarest.
[7] Cowley refers here and in lines 17 ff. below to what he considers
the debasement of poetry by its addiction to secular themes,
especially love. Crashaw has shown poets the way to the highest
theme, religion, as Moses led the Jews out of bondage in Egypt
to the Promised Land.
[8] I.e., you sang God's praise on earth just as you now do in heaven.
[9] See 1 Kings 12:26–33.
[10] I.e., although Christianity has long since superseded paganism,
poetry continues to celebrate pagan themes.
[11] The antecedent is Muse.

[12] On Crashaw's death at Loretto, see p. 500, above. According
to Catholic tradition, the house in which Mary lived during
much of her life and in which Jesus lived as a child was carried
away from Nazareth by angels at the end of the thirteenth
century, when it was threatened with destruction by the Turks,
and was finally deposited at Loretto, where it became a celebrated
shrine.　　　　[13] Cowley was an Anglican.
[14] These lines utilize the distinction between the church triumphant
(the church in heaven) and the church militant (the church on
earth, waging war against the powers of evil). The participles
in the following lines continue the parallel between the trials
of the church militant and the temptations of the poet on earth.
[15] See 2 Kings 2:8–15.

Not that thy spirit might on me doubled be,
I ask but half thy mighty spirit for me;
And when my Muse soars with so strong a wing,
'Twill learn of things divine, and first of thee to sing.

from ANACREONTICS

In 1656 Cowley published several poems paraphrasing or
imitating the light verse attributed to the Greek poet
Anacreon (d. 478 B.C.).

II. DRINKING

The thirsty earth soaks up the rain,
And drinks, and gapes for drink again.
The plants suck in the earth, and are
With constant drinking fresh and fair.
The sea itself, which one would think   5
Should have but little need of drink,
Drinks twice ten thousand rivers up,
So filled that they o'erflow the cup.
The busy sun (and one would guess
By's drunken fiery face no less)   10
Drinks up the sea, and when h'as done,
The moon and stars drink up the sun.
They drink and dance by their own light;
They drink and revel all the night.
Nothing in nature's sober found,   15
But an eternal health goes round.
Fill up the bowl, then, fill it high,
Fill all the glasses there, for why
Should every creature drink but I?
Why, man of morals, tell me why?   20

Andrew Marvell

1621–1678

IN HIS use of the metaphysical conceit Marvell stands in the
Donne tradition, somewhat closer to the devotional lyrists
than to the Cavaliers; but, unlike Cowley, he writes with
a lyric freshness that is quite his own. He was better known
in his day for his prose writings on political and ecclesiastical
questions than for his poetry. Under the Restoration he
used his literary gifts in satire; it is his earlier verse that has
won him the high reputation he enjoys today: next to
Milton he is the best of the Puritan (or semi-Puritan) poets.

Like Milton he was educated at Cambridge; but soon
after he took his B.A. the death of his father, an Anglican
minister at Winestead in Yorkshire, ended what might
have been an academic career. At first he earned a living
as clerk and tutor, standing aside from the controversies
of the forties, part of which he spent abroad; but in 1657
he was appointed assistant to Milton, who was Latin secretary to the Commonwealth government. Two years later
Marvell was elected to the House of Commons. He sat
there for Hull throughout the remainder of his life, and
his lyric impulse was submerged in public affairs. His was
a character of incorruptibility and (except in his satires and
controversial pamphlets) of moderation, for which he was
respected by both parties.

To sum up, Marvell is one of the most remarkable
personalities in English literature: a wise and practical
statesman; a devoted representative of his constituents; a
proficient student of many languages, ancient and modern;
a great lover of nature's beauty; a savage satirist; and, above
all, one of the masters of the English lyric, fusing in his
best poems the metaphysical boldness and intellectuality,
the Cavalier directness, and the neoclassical polish. Practically all his verse was posthumously published. The standard
edition is by H. M. Margoliouth (*Poems and Letters,* 2 vols.,
1927). Marvell seems to have been a bachelor, but the ladies
have done best by him in books; see Muriel C. Bradbrook
and M. Gwyneth Lloyd Thomas's *Andrew Marvell* (1940)
and Victoria Sackville-West's appreciative booklet, *Andrew
Marvell* (1929).

AN HORATION ODE UPON CROMWELL'S RETURN FROM IRELAND[16]

The forward youth that would appear
Must now forsake his muses dear,
    Nor in the shadows sing
    His numbers languishing:

'Tis time to leave the books in dust,   5
And oil the unused armor's rust,
    Removing from the wall
    The corselet of the hall.

So restless Cromwell would not cease
In the inglorious arts of peace,   10
    But through adventurous war
    Urgèd his active star;

And, like the three-forked lightning, first
Breaking the clouds where it was nursed,
    Did thorough his own side   15
    His fiery way divide;[17]

For 'tis all one to courage high,
The emulous, or enemy,
    And with such to inclose,
    Is more than to oppose.   20

16 In 1650, after a bloody subjugation of the Irish rebels against the
Commonwealth.
17 On the split in the Puritan party between Presbyterians and
Independents see p. 394, above.

Then burning through the air he went,
And palaces and temples rent;
  And Caesar's[18] head at last
  Did through his laurels blast.

'Tis madness to resist or blame   25
The face of angry heaven's flame;
  And if we would speak true,
  Much to the man is due,

Who from his private gardens, where
He lived reservèd and austere,   30
  As if his highest plot
  To plant the bergamot,[19]

Could by industrious valor climb
To ruin the great work of time,
  And cast the kingdoms old   35
  Into another mold,

Though Justice against Fate complain,
And plead the ancient rights in vain;
  But those do hold or break,
  As men are strong or weak.   40

Nature, that hateth emptiness,[20]
Allows of penetration[21] less,
  And therefore must make room
  Where greater spirits come.

What field of all the civil war,   45
Where his were not the deepest scar?
  And Hampton[22] shows what part
  He had of wiser art;

Where, twining subtle fears with hope,
He wove a net of such a scope   50
  That Charles himself might chase
  To Carisbrooke's narrow case,

That thence the royal actor borne
The tragic scaffold might adorn,
  While round the armèd bands   55
  Did clap their bloody hands.

He nothing common did, or mean,
Upon that memorable scene,
  But with his keener eye
  The ax's edge did try;   60

Nor called the gods with vulgar spite
To vindicate his helpless right,
  But bowed his comely head
  Down, as upon a bed.

This was that memorable hour   65
Which first assured the forcèd power;[23]
  So, when they did design
  The Capitol's first line,[24]

A bleeding head, where they begun,
Did fright the architects to run;   70
  And yet in that the state
  Foresaw its happy fate.[25]

And now the Irish are ashamed
To see themselves in one year tamed;
  So much one man can do,   75
  That does both act and know.

They can affirm his praises best,
And have, though overcome, confessed
  How good he is, how just,
  And fit for highest trust;   80

Nor yet grown stiffer with command,
But still in the republic's hand,
  How fit he is to sway,
  That can so well obey!

He to the Commons' feet presents   85
A kingdom[26] for his first year's rents;
  And, what he may, forbears[27]
  His fame, to make it theirs;

And has his sword and spoils ungirt,
To lay them at the public's skirt: 90
  So when the falcon high
  Falls heavy[28] from the sky,

She, having killed, no more doth search
But on the next green bough to perch;
  Where, when he first does lure,   95
  The falconer has her sure.

---

[18] Charles I's. *Laurels* in the next line = royal crown.
[19] A variety of pear.—Cromwell had been a country squire before his entry into politics.   [20] A vacuum.
[21] Occupation of the same space by two bodies simultaneously.
[22] In 1647 Charles I fled from Hampton Court to Carisbrooke Castle on the Isle of Wight. Marvell's statement that Cromwell instigated Charles's flight to serve his own ends is no longer accepted.

[23] I.e., the Commonwealth.   [24] In Rome.
[25] The event was interpreted by the soothsayers as a favorable omen.   [26] Ireland.   [27] As far as he is able, minimizes.
[28] With its prey.

What may not then our isle presume,
While victory his crest does plume?
    What may not others fear,
    If thus he crowns each year?   100

A Caesar, he, ere long, to Gaul,
To Italy a Hannibal,
    And to all states not free
    Shall climacteric[29] be.

The Pict[30] no shelter now shall find   105
Within his parti-colored[31] mind,
    But, from this valor sad,[32]
    Shrink underneath the plaid;

Happy if in the tufted brake
The English hunter him mistake,[33]   110
    Nor lay[34] his hounds in near
    The Caledonian deer.

But thou, the war's and Fortune's son,
March undefatigably on;
    And for the least effect,   115
    Still keep the sword erect;

Besides the force it has to fright
The spirits of the shady night,
    The same arts that did gain
    A power, must it maintain.   120

BERMUDAS

Marvell went to Eton in 1653 as tutor of a ward of Cromwell. They lodged in the house of the Rev. John Oxen-
bridge, who had been a leader of a group of nonconformist
settlers in the islands.

Where the remote Bermudas ride
In th' ocean's bosom unespied,
From a small boat that rowed along
The listening winds received this song.

"What should we do but sing his praise   5
That led us through the wat'ry maze,
Unto an isle so long unknown,
And yet far kinder than our own?
Where he the huge sea-monsters wracks,[35]

That lift the deep upon their backs,   10
He lands us on a grassy stage,
Safe from the storms' and prelates' rage.
He gave us this eternal spring,
Which here enamels everything,
And sends the fowls to us in care,   15
On daily visits through the air;
He hangs in shades the orange bright,
Like golden lamps in a green night;
And does in the pomegranates close
Jewels more rich than Ormus[36] shows.   20
He makes the figs our mouths to meet,
And throws the melons at our feet;
But apples[37] plants of such a price
No tree could ever bear them twice.
With cedars chosen by his hand   25
From Lebanon he stores the land,
And makes the hollow seas, that roar,
Proclaim the ambergris[38] on shore.
He cast (of which we rather boast)
The Gospel's pearl upon our coast,   30
And in these rocks for us did frame
A temple, where to sound his name.
Oh, let our voice his praise exalt,
Till it arrive at heaven's vault,
Which, thence perhaps rebounding, may   35
Echo beyond the Mexique Bay."

Thus sung they, in the English boat,
An holy and a cheerful note;
And all the way, to guide their chime,
With falling oars they kept the time.   40

TO HIS COY MISTRESS

Had we but world[39] enough, and time,
This coyness, lady, were no crime.
We would sit down, and think which way
To walk, and pass our long love's day.
Thou by the Indian Ganges' side   5
Shouldst rubies find; I by the tide
Of Humber[40] would complain.[41] I would
Love you ten years before the Flood,
And you should, if you please, refuse
Till the conversion of the Jews.   10
My vegetable love should grow
Vaster than empires, and more slow;

---

29 A decisive force at a critical time.
30 Scot. Cromwell had returned from Ireland in order to deal with
opposition in Scotland.
31 Variegated, like his tartan—hence, fickle.
32 Determined, resolute.   33 Fail to observe.   34 Send.
35 I.e., strands whales.

36 Hormuz, an island in the Persian gulf; it was a commercial
center for trade with India.   37 Pineapples.
38 A secretion of sperm whales, used in perfumery. It figures in
the early history of the colony.   39 I.e., space.
40 Hull, Marvell's home town, is on the estuary of this river.
41 Write love poems.

BEN JONSON

An engraving by Houbraken. (Boston Public Library)

JOHN DONNE

The portrait facing the title page of Donne's *Poems*, 1635, shows him at the age of 18. He had died at the age of 58 in 1631. The first collected edition of his poems came out in 1633; the one shown here was the second. The engraving, by William Marshall, has great charm. (Harvard College Library)

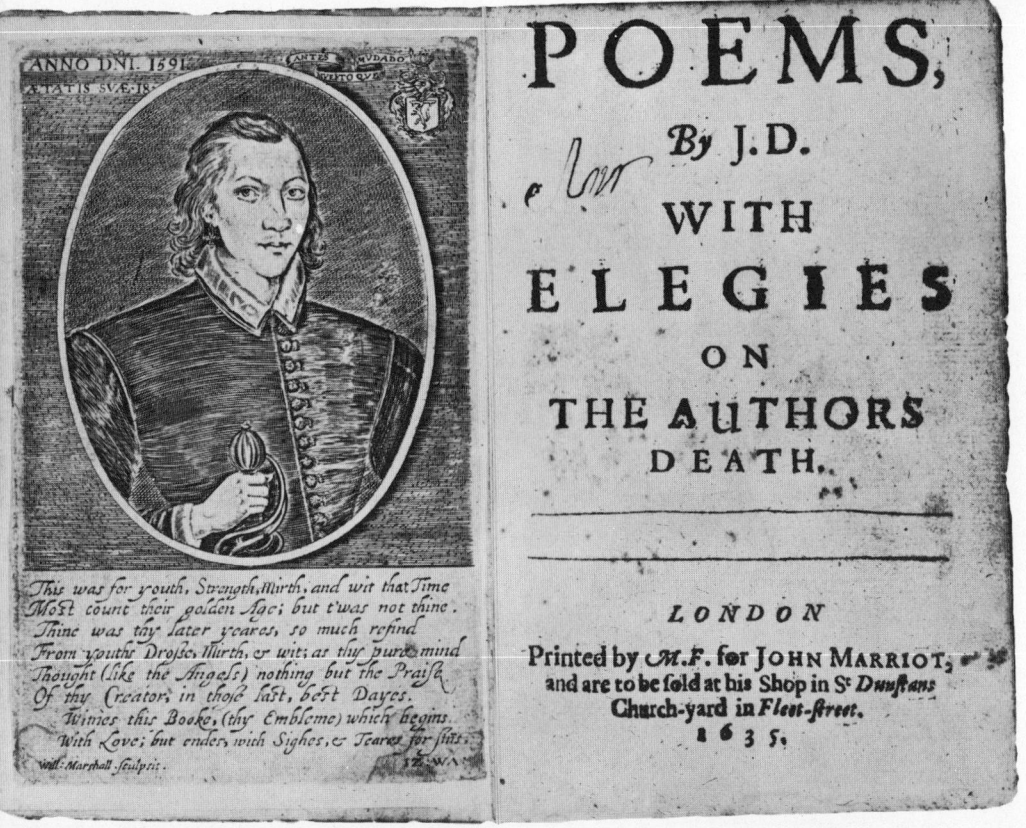

ANNO DNI. 1591
ÆTATIS SVÆ 18

ANTES MVDADO
QVITO QVE

POEMS,

By J.D.

WITH

ELEGIES

ON

THE AUTHORS

DEATH.

This was for youth, Strength, Mirth, and wit that Time
Most count their golden Age; but t'was not thine.
Thine was thy later yeares, so much refin'd
From youths Drosse, Mirth, & wit; as thy pure mind
Thought (like the Angels) nothing but the Praise
Of thy Creator, in those last, best Dayes.
Witnes this Booke, (thy Emblem) which begins
With Love; but endes, with Sighes, & Teares for sins.

Will: Marshall sculpsit.

LONDON

Printed by *M.F.* for JOHN MARRIOT,
and are to be sold at his Shop in St *Dunstans*
Church-yard in *Fleet-street.*
1635.

LUTE PLAYER

This picture is not English, possibly French, but England cou[ld]
easily have provided models. The lute was long the gener[al]
instrument for accompaniment, although forms of the viol[in]
began to gain popularity during the seventeenth century. T[he]
lute had a large number of strings, which were plucked. [A]
great deal of the player's time went into tuning it. (Museu[m]
of Fine Arts, Boston)

Author and publisher, John Playford had almost a monopo[ly]
of music publishing in London from the middle of the seve[n]
teenth century into the 80's. The large number of editions [of]
his *Brief Introduction to the Skill of Music* is good evidence [of]
the nearly universal devotion of his contemporaries to singi[ng]
and playing—an enthusiasm which had been equally characte[r]
istic of the preceding century. On November 22, 1662, Samu[el]
Pepys wrote in his diary: "This day . . . , meeting Mr. Pla[y]
ford, he did give me his Latin songs of Mr. Deering's [*Canti[ca]
Sacra ad duas et tres voces composita*] which he lately printed[."]
(Boston Public Library)

PLAYFORD'S
SKILL OF MUSIC

88   An Introduction to

the Skill of Musick.   89

A BRIEF
INTRODUCTION
To the Playing on the
Bafs-Viol.

The Second BOOK.

THe *Viol* (ufually called) *de Gambo*, or
Confort Viol, becaufe the Mufick thereon
is play'd from the Rules of the *Gam-vt*, and
not as the *Lyra-Viol*, which is by Letters or
Tablature. Of this *Viol de Gambo* there are
three feveral fizes, one larger than the other,
according to the three Parts of Mufick fet
forth in the *Gam-vt*, *viz.* *Treble-Viol*, *Tenor-
Viol*, and *Bafs-Viol*. The *Treble-Viol* plays the
higheft Part, and its Leffons are prick'd by
the *G fol re vt* Cliff 𝄞; the *Tenor-Viol*, or
middle Part, its Leffons are by the *C fol fa vt*
Cliff 𝄡; and the *Bafs-Viol*, which is the lar-
geft;

An hundred years should go to praise
Thine eyes and on thy forehead gaze,
Two hundred to adore each breast,   15
But thirty thousand to the rest:
An age at least to every part,
And the last age should show your heart.
For, lady, you deserve this state,[42]
Nor would I love at lower rate.   20
   But at my back I always hear
Time's wingèd chariot hurrying near;
And yonder all before us lie
Deserts of vast eternity.
Thy beauty shall no more be found,   25
Nor in thy marble vault shall sound
My echoing song; then worms shall try
That long preserved virginity,
And your quaint[43] honor turn to dust,
And into ashes all my lust.   30
The grave's a fine and private place,
But none, I think, do there embrace.
   Now, therefore, while the youthful hue
Sits on thy skin like morning dew,[44]
And while thy willing soul transpires   35
At every pore with instant fires,
Now let us sport us while we may,
And now, like am'rous birds of prey,
Rather at once our time devour
Than languish in his slow-chapped[45] power.   40
Let us roll all our strength and all
Our sweetness up into one ball,
And tear our pleasures with rough strife
Thorough[46] the iron gates of life.
Thus, though we cannot make our sun   45
Stand still, yet we will make him run.[47]

THE DEFINITION OF LOVE

My love is of a birth as rare
As 'tis for object strange and high:
It was begotten by Despair
Upon Impossibility.

Magnanimous Despair alone   5
Could show me so divine a thing,
Where feeble Hope could ne'er have flown
But vainly flapped its tinsel wing.

And yet I quickly might arrive
Where my extended soul is fixed,   10
But Fate does iron wedges drive
And always crowds itself betwixt.

For Fate with jealous eye does see
Two perfect loves, nor lets them close;[48]
Their union would her ruin be,   15
And her tyrannic power depose.

And therefore her decrees of steel
Us as the distant poles have placed,
(Though love's whole world on us doth wheel)
Not by themselves to be embraced,   20

Unless the giddy heaven fall
And earth some new convulsion tear
And, us to join, the world should all
Be cramped into a planisphere.[49]

As lines so loves oblique may well   25
Themselves in every angle greet;
But ours, so truly parallel,
Though infinite can never meet.

Therefore the love which us doth bind,
But Fate so enviously[50] debars,   30
Is the conjunction of the mind,
And opposition of the stars.

THE GARDEN

It seems likely that this remarkable poem was written
during or soon after Marvell's sojourn of two years at
Nunappleton House in Yorkshire, where he was tutor to
the daughter of Lord Fairfax, the general of the Parliamentary army.

How vainly men themselves amaze[51]
To win the palm, the oak, or bays,
And their uncessant labors see
Crowned from some single herb or tree,
Whose short and narrow-vergèd shade   5
Does prudently[52] their toils upbraid,
While all flow'rs and all trees do close
To weave the garlands of repose!

Fair Quiet, have I found thee here,
And Innocence, thy sister dear?   10

[42] Stately procedure.   [43] Overfastidious.
[44] The original reads *glew*, and various emendations have been
proposed. There can be little doubt that Marvell wrote *dew*.
[45] Slow-jawed, i.e., slowly devouring.   [46] Through.
[47] To catch up with us.

[48] Join.   [49] Circular map of the earth.
[50] Maliciously.—*Conjunction* and *opposition* (in the next two lines)
are astrological terms; the former means the apparent proximity
of two planets or stars, the latter their appearance opposite each
other as seen from the earth.   [51] Perplex, trouble.
[52] Wisely.

Mistaken long, I sought you then
In busy companies of men.
Your sacred plants, if here below,
Only among the plants will grow.
Society is all but rude,   15
To[53] this delicious solitude.

No white nor red[54] was ever seen
So am'rous[55] as this lovely green.
Fond lovers, cruel as their flame,
Cut in these trees their mistress' name: 20
Little, alas, they know or heed
How far these beauties hers exceed!
Fair trees, wheres'e'er your barks I wound,
No name shall but your own be found.

When we have run our passion's heat,   25
Love hither makes his best retreat.
The gods, that mortal beauty chase,
Still in a tree did end their race.
Apollo hunted Daphne so,
Only that she might laurel grow;[56]   30
And Pan did after Syrinx speed,
Not as a nymph, but for a reed.

What wondrous life is this I lead!
Ripe apples drop about my head;
The luscious clusters of the vine   35
Upon my mouth do crush their wine;
The nectarine and curious[57] peach
Into my hands themselves do reach;
Stumbling on melons, as I pass,
Insnared with flow'rs, I fall on grass.   40

Meanwhile the mind, from pleasure less,[58]
Withdraws into its happiness;
The mind, that ocean where each kind
Does straight its own resemblance find;[59]
Yet it creates, transcending these,   45
Far other worlds and other seas,
Annihilating all that's made
To a green thought in a green shade.[60]

Here at the fountain's sliding foot,
Or at some fruit tree's mossy root,   50
Casting the body's vest[61] aside,
My soul into the boughs does glide:
There, like a bird, it sits and sings,
Then whets[62] and combs its silver wings,
And, till prepared for longer flight,   55
Waves in its plumes the various light.

Such was that happy garden state,
While man there walked without a mate.
After a place so pure and sweet,
What other help could yet be meet?   60
But 'twas beyond a mortal's share
To wander solitary there:
Two paradises 'twere in one
To live in paradise alone.

How well the skillful gard'ner drew,   65
Of flowers and herbs, this dial new![63]
Where, from above, the milder sun
Does through a fragrant zodiac run,
And, as it works, the industrious bee
Computes its time as well as we.   70
How could such sweet and wholesome hours
Be reckoned but with herbs and flow'rs?

Charles Sackville, Earl of Dorset

1643–1706

"GAY, vigorous, and airy," said Dr. Johnson of Dorset's poems; they are "what they pretend to be, the effusion of a man of wit." As Lord Buckhurst, Charles Sackville was one of the wildest of the new coterie of young poet-aristocrats who adorned, and sometimes disgraced, the court of Charles II. They were the final group of England's courtier poets, as Wyatt and Surrey were conspicuous among the first. In 1677 Buckhurst succeeded his father as Earl of Dorset, and by the time James II came to the throne had begun sobering off. He had a minor part in the Glorious Revolution, and under William III held the high office of lord chamberlain. In this capacity he aided numerous writers, among them Dryden, a friend of long standing. Dorset's lyrics and satires have never been collected and properly edited. The best attempt is still in *The Works of the Most Celebrated Minor Poets* (2 vols., 1749). There is a biography by B. Harris (*Charles Sackville, Sixth Earl of Dorset: Patron and Poet of the Restoration*, 1940).

[53] Compared with.   [54] In a woman's face.   [55] Lovely.
[56] I.e., be metamorphosed to a laurel tree (in order to escape him).
[57] Exquisite.
[58] I.e., rendered for the moment less intellectual by pleasure in the garden.
[59] There was, some believed, a counterpart in the sea of every land animal.
[60] I.e., reducing material things to nothingness and replacing them with "other worlds and other seas" by means of the garden-inspired imagination. (Or, possibly: reducing everything to one overwhelming impression of green; the mind here in the green, shady garden is completely occupied by the thought of greenness.)

[61] The body, the soul's vestment.   [62] Preens.
[63] The gardener has planted a flower bed in the shape of a sundial. He has done it well, and it is well that he has chosen this form.

SONG

Written at Sea, in the First Dutch War, 1665,
the Night before an Engagement

This spirited song was not, as stated in the subtitle supplied by an early version, composed on the eve of the naval battle of June 3, 1665 ("seldom," observes Dr. Johnson, "any splendid story is wholly true"). On January 2 of that year, Samuel Pepys boasts that he "occasioned much mirth with a ballet . . . made from the seamen at sea to their ladies in town"; it had been published on or about December 30, 1664. Sackville had cruised with the fleet a few weeks earlier. With the exception of the refrain, the text below follows that of N. Ault (*Seventeenth Century Lyrics*, revised ed., 1950), who prints from an early manuscript.

To all you ladies now at land
    We men at sea do write,
But first I hope you'll understand
    How hard 'tis to indite;
The Muses now, and Neptune too,   5
We must implore, to write to you.
    With a fa, la, la, la, la.

For though the Muses should be kind
    And fill our empty brain,
Yet when rough Neptune calls the wind   10
    To rouse the azure main,
Our paper, ink, and pen, and we
Roll up and down our ship at sea.
    With a fa, la, la, la, la.

Then if we write not by each post,   15
    Think not we are unkind,
Nor yet conclude that we are lost
    By Dutch or else by wind.
Our tears we'll send a speedier way:
The tide shall bring them twice a day.   20
    With a fa, la, la, la, la.

With wonder and amaze the King
    Will vow his seas grow bold,
Because the tides more water bring
    Than they were wont of old;   25
But you must tell him that our cares
Send floods of grief to Whitehall Stairs.[64]
    With a fa, la, la, la, la.

To pass the tedious hours away
    We throw the merry main,[65]   30
Or else at serious ombre[66] play.
    But why should we in vain
Each other's ruin thus pursue?

We were undone when we left you!
    With a fa, la, la, la, la.   35

If foggy Opdam[67] did but know
    Our sad and dismal story,
The Dutch would scorn so weak a foe
    And leave the port of Goree.[68]
For what resistance can they find   40
From men that left their hearts behind?
    With a fa, la, la, la, la.

Let wind and weather do their worst,
    Be you to us but kind;
Let Frenchmen vapor,[69] Dutchmen curse,   45
    No sorrow shall we find:
'Tis then no matter how things go,
Nor who's our friend nor who's our foe.
    With a fa, la, la, la, la.

In justice, you cannot refuse   50
    To think of our distress,
Since we in hope of honor lose
    Our certain happiness.
All our designs are but to prove
Ourselves more worthy of your love.   55
    With a fa, la, la, la, la.

Alas, out tears tempestuous grow
    And cast our hopes away,
While you, unmindful of our woe,
    Sit careless at a play,   60
And now permit some happier man
To kiss your busk[70] and wag your fan.
    With a fa, la, la, la, la.

When any mournful tune you hear,
    That dies in every note   65
As if it sighed for each man's care
    For being so remote,
Think then how oft our love we made
To you while all those tunes were played.
    With a fa, la, la, la, la.   70

And now we have told all our love
    And also all our tears,
We hope our declarations move
    Some pity for our cares.
Let's hear of no unconstancy—   75
We have too much of that at sea!
    With a fa, la, la, la, la.

---

[64] The landing place for the palace on the Thames.
[65] Shoot craps; the game was then known as *hazard*.
[66] A card game.

[67] The Dutch admiral. In the battle of June 3 he was killed when his flagship blew up.
[68] Goeree, an island in South Holland. The Dutch fleet lay there while the English cruised in search of an engagement.
[69] Bluster.
[70] The wooden strip reinforcing the front of the stomacher.

Sir Charles Sedley

1639?–1701

SEDLEY inherited the wealth and the baronetcy of a landed family long established in Kent. A few months at Oxford satisfied his taste for formal learning, and he was soon a leader of the rakehelly wits at the court of Charles II, who was particularly fond of his company. The King spent a great deal of time with this group of his younger courtiers, to the neglect of many an "old Cavalier" whose services during "the troubles" could not make up for his lack of conversational brilliance. Some of Sedley's escapades were pretty wild, but he managed to survive to years of discretion. His dissolute daughter Katherine became a mistress of James II, who conferred on her the title of Countess of Dorchester. In 1688 Sedley was a warm supporter of King William, whose wife, Queen Mary, was James's daughter. Sedley airily observed that he was only returning James's kindness: "for, as he made my daughter a countess, so I have helped to make his daughter a queen." It is easy to see why the gay baronet was reputed one of the best talkers of the age. After the Glorious Revolution he saw that the House of Commons was to be the place where talk would count. He had been a member for twenty years; now he became one of its ablest and most sensible speakers. Sedley wrote several plays as well as some prose, dramatic and nondramatic; but his literary fame rests chiefly on a handful of extremely graceful songs. The standard edition is V. de Sola Pinto's (*The Poetical and Dramatic Works*, 2 vols., 1928). Professor Pinto's *Sir Charles Sedley . . . A Study in the Life and Literature of the Restoration* (1927) is an interesting though overspeculative biography.

NOT, CELIA

Not, Celia, that I juster am
  Or better than the rest,
For I would change each hour like them,
  Were not my heart at rest.

But I am tied to very thee,   5
  By every thought I have;
Thy face I only care to see,
  Thy heart I only crave.

All that in woman is adored,
  In thy dear self I find,   10
For the whole sex can but afford
  The handsome and the kind.

Why then should I seek farther store,
  And still make love anew?
When change itself can give no more,   15
  'Tis easy to be true.

LOVE STILL HAS SOMETHING OF THE SEA

Love still has something of the sea,
  From whence his mother rose;[71]
No time his slaves from doubt can free,
  Nor give their thoughts repose:

They are becalmed in clearest days,   5
  And in rough weather tossed;
They wither under cold delays,
  Or are in tempests lost.

One while they seem to touch the port,
  Then straight into the main   10
Some angry wind in cruel sport
  The vessel drives again.

At first disdain and pride they fear,
  Which if they chance to 'scape,
Rivals and falsehood soon appear   15
  In a more dreadful shape.

By such degrees to joy they come,
  And are so long withstood,
So slowly they receive the sum,
  It hardly does them good.   20

'Tis cruel to prolong a pain;
  And to defer a joy,
Believe me, gentle Célimène,
  Offends the wingèd boy.

An hundred thousand oaths your fears   25
  Perhaps would not remove;
And if I gazed a thousand years,
  I could no deeper love.

John Wilmot, Earl of Rochester

1647–1680

JOHN WILMOT succeeded his exiled father in the earldom of Rochester when he was eleven. Six years later, after Oxford and foreign travel, he joined the "merry gang" at the court of Charles II. Sedley, Buckhurst (afterwards Earl of Dorset), and George Villiers, second Duke of Buckingham,

---

[71] According to one of the classical myths, Venus was born of the sea.

were other conspicuous members. Rochester equaled them in dissipation; in force of intellect he surpassed them all. He was the best of the Restoration courtier poets (Marvell was not a courtier), but his portrait shows a haunted face. Driven by some demon within, he sought experience at all points and at all costs—in the naval battles of the Dutch War, in marriage, in strenuous writing (some of it beautiful, some obscene), and in debauchery. His rank, the wealth he acquired by his marriage, the standards of his circle, and his intense lust for life inevitably made the pursuit of pleasure a primary object at first; but he also had a mind, and it gave him no rest. He was an utterly disillusioned realist, about himself as well as the world. Unfortunately for him, he had surrendered while still a youth to the writings of the philosopher Thomas Hobbes (1588-1679), whose system was a thoroughgoing materialism which denied the existence of moral or social feeling. Like most men, Rochester stood in need of some ideal or faith, but he could believe in nothing. Syphilis scourged him throughout his adult life; it is not impossible that he contracted it while still a young boy. He tried to escape from himself by getting drunk, and staying drunk. At thirty-three he was burned out.

The winter before he died he had a series of conversations with Gilbert Burnet (1643-1715), a distinguished theologian and historian. Burnet, afterwards Bishop of Salisbury, became his friend and biographer. A few weeks before the end, Rochester summoned his family and servants, and solemnly announced his conversion to Christianity. He told Burnet that "all the pleasures he had ever known in sin were not worth that torture he had felt in his mind." His *Collected Works* were edited by J. Hayward (1926), and *The Poetical Works* by Q. Johns (1933). V. de Sola Pinto, who terms him the Marlowe of the Restoration, is the author of the best Life, *Rochester: Portrait of a Restoration Poet* (1935).

ABSENT FROM THEE

It seems likely that this poem was addressed to Lady Rochester. While the poet spent most of his time in London, she lived on their country estates and bore him four children.

Absent from thee, I languish still;[1]
    Then ask me not when I return:
The straying fool 'twill plainly kill
    To wish all day, all night to mourn.

Dear, from thine arms then let me fly,   5
    That my fantastic mind may prove[2]
The torments it deserves to try,
    That tears my fixed heart from my love.

_____
[1] Always.   [2] Experience.

When, wearied with a world of woe,
    To thy safe bosom I retire,   10
Where love and peace and truth does flow,
    May I contented there expire!

Lest, once more wand'ring from that heaven,
    I fall on some base heart unblest,
Faithless to thee, false, unforgiven,   15
    And lose my everlasting rest.

LOVE AND LIFE

A Song

This is not merely another suave love lyric. Thought is behind it, and a deep despair is in it.

All my past life is mine no more,
    The flying hours are gone:
Like transitory dreams giv'n o'er,
Whose images are kept in store,
    By memory alone.   5

The time that is to come is not;
    How can it then be mine?
The present moment's all my lot;
And that, as fast as it is got,
    Phyllis, is only thine.   10

Then talk not of inconstancy,
    False hearts, and broken vows;
If I, by miracle, can be
This livelong minute true to thee,
    'Tis all that heav'n allows.   15

THE KING'S "EPITAPH"

These famous lines have survived in several versions. This one may be authentic. According to the antiquary Thomas Hearne (1678-1735), the occasion was "His Majesty's saying he would leave everyone to his own liberty in talking, and would not take what was said at all amiss."

We have a pretty, witty king,
    Whose word no man relies on.
He never said a foolish thing,
    And never did a wise one.

A SATIRE AGAINST MANKIND

This bitter poem, a culmination of seventeenth-century disillusion, and in its satirical couplets an advance guard for Dryden, Pope, and the eighteenth century, was probably composed five or six years before Rochester's death. It owes something to the eighth satire of the influential French poet and critic Boileau (1636–1711); but Rochester's poem is shorter, more forceful, and more personal. In a way it was a prelude to his conversion, for it was evidently inspired by his despairing recognition of the ethical nihilism to which his adoption of Hobbes's philosophy as a pattern of thought and conduct had finally brought him.

Were I, who to my cost already am
One of those strange prodigious creatures *Man*,
A spirit, free to choose for my own share
What sort of flesh and blood I pleased to wear,
I'd be a dog, a monkey, or a bear,   5
Or anything, but that vain animal
Who is so proud of being rational.
The senses are too gross; and he'll contrive
A sixth,[3] to contradict the other five:
And, before certain instinct, will prefer   10
Reason, which fifty times for one does err—
Reason, an *ignis fatuus*[4] of the mind,
Which leaves the light of nature, sense,[5] behind.
Pathless and dangerous wand'ring ways it takes,
Through error's fenny bogs and thorny brakes;[6]   15
Whilst the misguided follower climbs with pain
Mountains of whimsies heaped in his own brain—
Stumbling from thought to thought, falls headlong down
Into doubt's boundless sea, where, like to drown,
Books bear him up a while and make him try   20
To swim with bladders of philosophy,
In hopes still to o'ertake the skipping light.
The vapor dances in his dazzled sight,
Till, spent, it leaves him to eternal night.
Then old age and experience, hand in hand,   25
Lead him to death, and make him understand,
After a search so painful and so long,
That all his life he has been in the wrong.
Huddled in dirt, reas'ning Engine[7] lies,
Who was so proud, so witty,[8] and so wise.   30
Pride drew him in, as cheats their bubbles[9] catch,
And made him venture to be made a wretch.
His wisdom did his happiness destroy,
Aiming to *know* the world he should *enjoy*.
And wit was his vain, frivolous pretense   35
Of pleasing others at his own expense.
For wits are treated just like common whores:
First they're enjoyed, and then kicked out of doors.

The pleasure past, a threat'ning doubt remains,
That frights th' enjoyer with succeeding pains.   40
Women, and men of wit, are dang'rous tools,
And ever fatal to admiring fools.
Pleasure allures; and when the fops escape,
'Tis not that they're beloved, but fortunate;
And therefore what they fear, at heart they hate.   45

But now, methinks, some formal band and beard[10]
Takes me to task. Come on, sir, I'm prepared!
"Then, by your favor,[11] anything that's writ
Against this gibing, jingling knack called wit
Likes[12] me abundantly; but you'll take care   50
Upon this point not to be too severe.
Perhaps *my* Muse were fitter for this part;
For I profess I can be very smart
On wit, which I abhor with all my heart.
I long to lash it in some sharp essáy;   55
But your grand indiscretion bids me stay,
And turns my tide of ink another way.
What rage ferments in your degen'rate mind,
To make you rail at reason and mankind?
Blest, glorious Man! to whom alone kind heav'n   60
An everlasting soul hath freely giv'n;
Whom his great Maker took such care to make
That from himself he did the image take,
And this fair frame in shining reason dressed,
To dignify his nature above beast—   65
Reason! by whose aspiring influence
We take a flight beyond material sense,
Dive into mysteries, then soaring pierce
The flaming limits of the universe,
Search heav'n and hell, find out what's acted there,   70
And give the world true grounds of hope and fear!"

"Hold, mighty man!" I cry; "all this we know
From the pathetic pen of Ingelo,[13]
From Patrick's *Pilgrim*,[14] Sibb's *Soliloquies;*[15]
And 'tis this very 'reason' I despise,   75
This supernat'ral gift, that makes a mite
Think he's the image of the Infinite,
Comparing his short life, void of all rest,
To the eternal and the ever blest—
This busy, puzzling stirrer up of doubt,   80
That frames deep mysteries, then finds 'em out,
Filling, with frantic crowds of thinking fools,

---

[3] I.e., a superior one (as he thinks), which discriminates among and synthesizes the reports of the others.
[4] Will-o'-the-wisp, misleading influence.
[5] The senses (which report the facts of nature to the mind).
[6] Thickets.—*Fenny* = marshy.
[7] A proper noun; i.e., man as a machine that reasons.
[8] Ingenious.   [9] Dupes.

[10] I.e., dignified old gentleman. Bands were collars on the gowns of professors, lawyers, and the clergy.
[11] I.e., if I may speak.   [12] Is pleasing to.
[13] Nathaniel Ingelo, a contemporary theologian.
[14] By Simon Patrick (d. 1707), Bishop of Ely.
[15] Presumably the *Divine Meditations* of Richard Sibbes (d. 1635), a Puritan.

The reverend bedlams: colleges and schools—
Borne on whose wings, each heavy sot[16] can pierce
The limits of the boundless universe: 85
So charming[17] ointments make on old witch fly
And bear a crippled carcass through the sky.
'Tis this exalted pow'r whose business lies
In nonsense and impossibilities.
This made a whimsical philosopher[18] 90
Before the spacious world his tub prefer;
And we have many modern coxcombs[19] who
Retire to think, 'cause they have nought to do.
But thoughts were giv'n for action's government;
Where action ceases, thought's impertinent. 95
Our sphere of action is life's happiness;
And he that thinks beyond thinks like an ass.
Thus, whilst against false reas'ning I inveigh,
I own right reason,[20] which I would obey:
That reason which distinguishes by sense, 100
That gives us rules of good and ill from thence;
That bounds desires with a reforming will,
To keep them more in vigor, not to kill.
Your reason hinders; mine helps to enjoy,
Renewing appetites yours would destroy. 105
My reason is my friend; yours is a cheat:
Hunger calls out, my reason bids me eat;
Perversely, yours your appetite doth mock.
This asks for food; that answers, 'What's o'clock?'

"This plain distinction, sir, your doubt secures; 110
'Tis not true reason I despise, but yours.
Thus, I think reason righted. But for[21] Man,
I'll ne'er recant. Defend him if you can.
For all his pride and his philosophy,
'Tis evident beasts are, in their degree, } 115
As wise, at least, and better far than he.
Those creatures are the wisest who attain
By surest means the ends at which they aim.
If, therefore, Jowler finds and kills his hare
Better than Meres[22] supplies committee chair, 120
Though one's a statesman, th'other but a hound,
Jowler in justice will be wiser found.
You see how far Man's wisdom here extends;

Look next if human nature makes amends:
Whose principles are more generous and just, 125
And to whose morals you would sooner trust.
Be judge yourself; I'll bring it to the test:
Which is the basest creature, man or beast?
Birds feed on birds, beasts on each other prey;
But savage man alone does man betray. 130
Pressed by necessity, *they* kill for food;
Man undoes man, to do himself no good.
With teeth and claws by nature armed, *they* hunt
Nature's allowance, to supply their want;
But Man, with smiles, embraces, friendships, praise, 135
Inhumanly his fellow's life betrays,
With voluntary pains works his distress,
Not through necessity but wantonness.
For hunger or for love *they* bite or tear,
Whilst wretched Man is still in arms for fear: 140
For fear he arms, and is of arms afraid;
From fear to fear successively betrayed—
Base fear! the source whence his best passions came,
His boasted honor, and his dear-bought fame,
The lust of pow'r, to which he's such a slave 145
And for the which alone he dares be brave—
To which his various projects are designed,
Which makes him gen'rous, affable, and kind,
For which he takes such pains to be thought wise,
And screws his actions in a forced disguise, 150
Leads a most tedious life in misery
Under laborious, mean hypocrisy.
Look to the bottom of his vast design,
Wherein Man's wisdom, pow'r, and glory join:
The good he acts, the ill he does endure, 155
'Tis all from fear, to make himself secure.
Merely for safety, after fame they thirst;
For all men would be cowards, if they durst.
And honesty's against all common sense:
Men must be knaves; 'tis in their own defense 160
Mankind's dishonest: if they think it fair
Amongst known cheats to play upon the square,
You'll be undone—
Nor can weak truth your reputation save:
The knaves will all agree to call you knave." 165

---

[16] Dull fool.   [17] Magical.
[18] Diogenes (d. 323 B.C.).   [19] Fools.
[20] Acknowledge true reason, i.e., common sense.—*Sense,* in the
    next line, =the senses.
[21] As for.
[22] Sir Thomas Meres, a prominent member of the anticourt party
    in the House of Commons.

Izaak Walton

1593–1683

WALTON expressed the modest hope that a second edition of *The Complete Angler* might be required. As a matter of fact there have been nearly three hundred, and it looks as though the procession would stretch out to the crack of doom, or at any rate till the human race has done with rod and line. Walton was born in Stafford; of his education no record has survived. He went into business in London, and in 1626 he married. Between that date and 1641 came a dreadful series of bereavements, the loss of his wife and all of their children. He married again in 1646. One child by his second wife died in infancy; a son and a daughter survived. Walton was a royalist; but his only adventure during the Wars was when, after the Battle of Worcester, he brought one of the fleeing King's jeweled trinkets from Stafford to London for safekeeping.

His friendships were many and included some of the most distinguished men of his times, especially among the clergy. He had been a parishioner and an intimate of John Donne; a Life of Donne (1640) was his first important publication. Walton was sixty when, in 1653, the appearance of *The Complete Angler* established him in what appears to be a permanent niche in English literature. Most readers subscribe to the estimate of Charles Lamb: "It breathes the very spirit of innocence, purity, and simplicity of heart . . . it would sweeten a man's temper at any time to read it." The book's merit resides mainly in its tone and style. Walton is much more the enthusiast than the inquiring observer or precise recorder; many state-

ments in *The Complete Angler* have no basis in fact. Its conversational ease, as is often the case, was achieved only after much labor; Walton kept reworking its texture, improving the flow of its cadences. By 1676 the original thirteen chapters had grown to twenty-one, and a second part (by his friend Charles Cotton, poet, translator, and miscellaneous writer) was added.

Andrew Lang, one of Walton's editors, says he "had a natural taste for a bishop." At the Restoration his episcopal friends were re-established in their sees; and when his second wife died, in 1662, he went to live with one of these prelates, Dr. George Morley, Bishop of Winchester, as his steward. He died aged ninety and was buried in the great cathedral there.

Besides his masterpiece, he wrote five short Lives: of Donne, Wotton, Hooker (p. 226, above), George Herbert, and Robert Sanderson, Bishop of Lincoln. These are among the best of the earlier biographies of any length in English, and their charm is such that they have often been reprinted. Two years after *The Complete Angler, or The Contemplative Man's Recreation* was first published, there was an enlarged second edition. The text below is based on the fifth (1676), the last Walton prepared himself. Lang's edition is now available in Everyman's Library. Walton's writings have been collected by G. Keynes (1929). The World's Classics devotes two volumes to *The Complete Angler* and the *Lives*. S. Martin's *Izaak Walton and His Friends* (second ed., 1904) is a pleasant, harmless book.

---

from THE COMPLETE ANGLER

from CHAPTER I

A conference betwixt an angler, a falconer, and a hunter, each commending his recreation

PISCATOR, VENATOR, AUCEPS[1]

PISCATOR. You are well overtaken, gentlemen! A good morning to you both! I have stretched my legs up Tottenham Hill to overtake you, hoping your [10]

business may occasion you towards Ware,[2] whither I am going this fine, fresh May morning.

VENATOR. Sir, I, for my part, shall almost answer your hopes, for my purpose is to drink my morning's [5] draught at the Thatched House in Hodsden; and I think not to rest till I come thither, where I have appointed a friend or two to meet me. But for[3] this gentleman that you see with me, I know not how far he intends his journey; he came so lately into my

---

[1] Fisherman, hunter, falconer.

[2] About 20 miles north of London. Tottenham was a northern suburb of London. Hoddesdon was near Ware; Theobald's, about 12 miles from London.

[3] As for.

company that I have scarce had time to ask him the question.

AUCEPS. Sir, I shall by your favor bear you company as far as Theobald's, and there leave you; for then I turn up to a friend's house, who mews[4] a hawk for me, which I now long to see.

VENATOR. Sir, we are all so happy as to have a fine, fresh, cool morning; and I hope we shall each be the happier in the others' company. And, gentlemen, that I may not lose yours, I shall either abate or amend my pace to enjoy it, knowing that, as the Italians say, "Good company in a journey makes the way to seem the shorter."

AUCEPS. It may do so, sir, with the help of good discourse, which methinks we may promise from you, that both look and speak so cheerfully; and for my part, I promise you, as an invitation to it, that I will be as free and open-hearted as discretion will allow me to be with strangers.

VENATOR. And, sir, I promise the like.

PISCATOR. I am right glad to hear your answers; and, in confidence you speak the truth, I shall put on a boldness to ask you, sir, whether business or pleasure caused you to be so early up, and walk so fast? For this other gentleman hath declared he is going to see a hawk, that a friend mews for him.

VENATOR. Sir, mine is a mixture of both, a little business and more pleasure; for I intend this day to do all my business, and then bestow another day or two in hunting the otter, which a friend, that I go to meet, tells me is much pleasanter than any other chase whatsoever. Howsoever, I mean to try it; for tomorrow morning we shall meet a pack of otter-dogs of noble Mr. Sadler's,[5] upon Amwell Hill, who will be there so early that they intend to prevent[6] the sunrising.

PISCATOR. Sir, my fortune has answered my desires, and my purpose is to bestow a day or two in helping to destroy some of those villainous vermin; for I hate them perfectly, because they love fish so well, or rather, because they destroy so much: indeed so much that, in my judgment, all men that keep otter-dogs ought to have pensions from the king, to encourage them to destroy the very breed of those base otters, they do so much mischief.

VENATOR. But what say you to the foxes of the nation? would not you as willingly have them destroyed? for doubtless they do as much mischief as otters do.

PISCATOR. Oh, sir, if they do, it is not so much to me and my fraternity, as those base vermin the otters do.

AUCEPS. Why, sir, I pray, of what fraternity are you, that you are so angry with the poor otters?

PISCATOR. I am, sir, a brother of the angle, and therefore an enemy to the otter; for you are to note that we anglers all love one another, and therefore do I hate the otter both for my own and their sakes who are of my brotherhood.

VENATOR. And I am a lover of hounds; I have followed many a pack of dogs many a mile, and heard many merry huntsmen make sport and scoff at anglers.

AUCEPS. And I profess myself a falconer, and have heard many grave, serious men pity them, 'tis such a heavy, contemptible, dull recreation.

PISCATOR. You know, gentlemen, 'tis an easy thing to scoff at any art or recreation; a little wit mixed with ill nature, confidence, and malice will do it; but though they often venture boldly, yet they are often caught, even in their own trap, according to that of Lucian,[7] the father of the family of scoffers.

Lucian, well skilled in scoffing, this hath writ:
Friend, that's your folly, which you think your wit.
This you vent oft, void both of wit and fear,
Meaning another, when yourself you jeer.

If to this you add what Solomon says of scoffers, that they are abomination to mankind,[8] let him that thinks fit scoff on and be a scoffer still; but I account them enemies to me and to all that love virtue and angling.

And for you that have heard many grave, serious men pity anglers, let me tell you, sir, there be many men that are by others taken to be serious and grave men, whom we contemn and pity. Men that are taken to be grave, because nature hath made them of a sour complexion; money-getting men, men that spend all their time, first in getting, and next in anxious care to keep it; men that are condemned to be rich, and then always busy or discontented: for these poor rich-men, we anglers pity them perfectly, and stand in no need to borrow their thoughts to think ourselves so happy. No, no, sir, we enjoy a contentedness above the reach of such dispositions, and as the learned and ingenuous[9] Montaigne says, like himself, freely, "When my cat and I entertain each other with mutual apish tricks, as playing with a garter, who knows but that I make my cat more

---

[4] Cages (i.e., keeps) in moulting time.
[5] A well-known sportsman.   [6] Precede.

[7] The second-century Greek satirist.   [8] Proverbs 24:9.
[9] Ingenious, full of genius.

sport than she makes me? Shall I conclude her to be simple, that has her time to begin or refuse to play as freely as I myself have? Nay, who knows but that it is a defect of my not understanding her language (for doubtless cats talk and reason with one another) that we agree no better; and who knows but that she pities me for being no wiser, and laughs and censures my folly for making sport for her, when we two play together?"[10]

Thus freely speaks Montaigne concerning cats, and I hope I may take as great a liberty to blame any man, and laugh at him too, let him be never so grave, that hath not heard what anglers can say in the justification of their art and recreation; which I may again tell you is so full of pleasure that we need not borrow their thoughts to think ourselves happy.

VENATOR. Sir, you have almost amazed me, for though I am no scoffer, yet I have (I pray let me speak it without offense) always looked upon anglers as more patient and more simple men than I fear I shall find you to be.

PISCATOR. Sir, I hope you will not judge my earnestness to be impatience. And for my simplicity, if by that you mean a harmlessness, or that simplicity which was usually found in the primitive Christians, who were, as most anglers are, quiet men and followers of peace, men that were so simply wise as not to sell their consciences to buy riches and with them vexation and a fear to die, if you mean such simple men as lived in those times when there were fewer lawyers—when men might have had a lordship safely conveyed to them in a piece of parchment no bigger than your hand (though several sheets will not do it safely in this wiser age)—I say, sir, if you take us anglers to be such simple men as I have spoken of, then myself and those of my profession will be glad to be so understood. But if by simplicity you meant to express a general defect in those that profess and practice the excellent art of angling, I hope in time to disabuse you, and make the contrary appear so evidently that, if you will but have patience to hear me, I shall remove all the anticipations that discourse or time or prejudice have possessed you with against that laudable and ancient art; for I know it is worthy the knowledge and practice of a wise man. . . .

Observations of the nature and breeding of the trout, and how to fish for him. And the milkmaid's song.

PISCATOR. The trout is a fish highly valued both in this and foreign nations: he may be justly said, as we English say of venison, to be a generous[12] fish; a fish that is so like the buck that he also has his seasons, for it is observed that he comes in and goes out of season with the stag and buck. Gesner[13] says his name is of a German offspring,[14] and says he is a fish that feeds clean and purely, in the swiftest streams and on the hardest gravel, and that he may justly contend with all freshwater fish, as the mullet may with all sea fish, for precedency and daintiness of taste, and that, being in right season, the most dainty palates have allowed precedency to him.

And before I go further in my discourse, let me tell you that you are to observe that, as there be some barren does that are good in summer, so there be some barren trouts that are good in winter; but there are not many that are so; for usually they be in their perfection in the month of May, and decline with the buck. Now you are to take notice that in several countries, as in Germany and in other parts, compared to ours, fish do differ much in their bigness and shape and other ways; and so do trouts. It is well known that in the Lake Leman, the Lake of Geneva, there are trouts taken of three cubits long, as is affirmed by Gesner, a writer of good credit; and Mercator[15] says the trouts that are taken in the Lake of Geneva are a great part of the merchandise of that famous city. And you are further to know that there be certain waters that breed trouts remarkable both for their number and smallness. I know a little brook in Kent that breeds them to a number incredible, and you may take them twenty or forty in an hour, but none greater than about the size of a gudgeon. There are also, in divers rivers, especially that relate to, or be near to the sea, as Winchester, or the Thames about Windsor, a little trout called a samlet, or skegger trout—in both which places I have caught twenty or forty at a standing—that will bite as fast and as freely as minnows. These be by some taken to be young salmons, but in those waters they never grow to be bigger than a herring.

---

[10] *Essays,* Book II, chap. 12 (trans. E. J. Trechmann, I, 444).

[11] The discussion has continued in Chapters II and III; there is an otter hunt at Amwell Hill, and then a fishing trip for chub. By this time Venator, who is ambitious for a trout, is humbly addressing Piscator as Master.   [12] Noble.

[13] Conrad von Gesner (d. 1565), a German-Swiss naturalist.

[14] Origin.   [15] The famous Flemish geographer.

There is also in Kent, near to Canterbury, a trout called there a Fordidge[16] trout, a trout that bears the name of the town where it is usually caught, that is accounted the rarest of fish, many of them near the bigness of a salmon but known by their different color; and in their best season they cut very white; and none of these have been known to be caught with an angle, unless it were one that was caught by Sir George Hastings, an excellent angler and now with God; and he hath told me he thought that trout bit not for hunger but wantonness; and it is the rather to be believed, because both he then, and many others before him, have been curious to search into their bellies, what the food was by which they lived, and have found out nothing by which they might satisfy their curiosity.

Concerning which you are to take notice that it is reported by good authors that grasshoppers and some fish have no mouths, but are nourished and take breath by the porousness of their gills, man knows not how; and this may be believed, if we consider that when the raven hath hatched her eggs she takes no further care, but leaves her young ones to the care of the God of nature, who is said, in the Psalms (Psal. 147:9) "to feed the young ravens that call upon him." And they be kept alive and fed by a dew, or worms that breed in their nests, or some other ways that we mortals know not. And this may be believed of the Fordidge trout, which, as it is said of the stork (Jerem. 8:7) that he knows his season, so he knows his times, I think almost his day of coming into that river out of the sea; where he lives and, it is like, feeds nine months of the year, and fasts three in the river of Fordidge. And you are to note, that those townsmen are very punctual in observing the time of beginning to fish for them, and boast much that their river affords a trout that exceeds all others. And just so does Sussex boast of several fish; as, namely, a Shelsey cockle, a Chichester lobster, an Arundel mullet, and an Amerly trout.

And, now, for some confirmation of the Fordidge trout: you are to know that this trout is thought to eat nothing in the fresh water; and it may be the better believed, because it is well known that swallows and bats and wagtails, which are called half-year birds, and not seen to fly in England for six months in the year, but about Michaelmas[17] leave us for a better climate, yet some of them that have been left behind their fellows have been found, many thousands at a time, in hollow trees or clay caves, where they have been observed to live and sleep out the whole winter without meat. And so Albertus[18] observes that there is one kind of frog that hath her mouth naturally shut up about the end of August, and that she lives so all the winter; and though it be strange to some, yet it is known to too many among us to be doubted.

And so much for these Fordidge trouts, which never afford an angler sport, but either live their time of being in the fresh water, by their meat formerly gotten in the sea, not unlike the swallow or frog, or by the virtue of the fresh water only, or, as the birds of paradise and the chameleon are said to live, by the sun and the air.

There is also in Northumberland a trout called a bull-trout, of a much greater length and bigness than any in these southern parts; and there are, in many rivers that relate to[19] the sea, salmon-trouts, as much different from others, both in shape and in their spots, as we see sheep in some countries differ one from another in their shape and bigness, and in the fineness of the wool. And certainly, as some pastures breed larger sheep, so do some rivers, by reason of the ground over which they run, breed larger trouts.

Now the next thing that I will commend to your consideration is that the trout is of a more sudden growth than other fish; concerning which you are also to take notice that he lives not so long as the perch and divers other fishes do, as Sir Francis Bacon hath observed in his *History of Life and Death*.

And next you are to take notice that he is not like the crocodile, which, if he lives never so long, yet always thrives till his death; but 'tis not so with the trout: for after he is come to his full growth, he declines in his body, and keeps his bigness, or thrives only in his head till his death. And you are to know that he will, about (especially before) the time of his spawning, get almost miraculously through weirs and floodgates against the streams, even through such high and swift places as is almost incredible. Next, that the trout usually spawns about October or November, but in some rivers a little sooner or later; which is the more observable because most other fish spawn in the spring or summer, when the sun hath warmed both the earth and water, and made it fit for generation. And you are to note that he continues many months out of season; for it may be observed of the trout that he is like the buck or the ox, that will not be fat in many months, though he go in the very same pasture that horses do, which

[16] Fordwich, near Canterbury.   [17] September 29.

[18] Albertus Magnus, a thirteenth-century Bavarian monk, famous as a philosopher.   [19] Are connected with.

will be fat in one month; and so you may observe that most other fishes recover strength, and grow sooner fat and in season, than the trout doth.

And next you are to note that, till the sun gets to such a height as to warm the earth and the water, the trout is sick and lean and lousy and unwholesome, for you shall in winter find him to have a big head and then to be lank and thin and lean; at which time many of them have sticking on them sugs, or trout-lice, which is a kind of a worm in shape like a clove or pin with a big head, and sticks close to him and sucks his moisture. Those, I think, the trout breeds himself, and never thrives till he free himself from them, which is when warm weather comes; and then, as he grows stronger, he gets from the dead, still water into the sharp streams and the gravel, and there rubs off these worms or lice, and then, as he grows stronger, so he gets himself into swifter and swifter streams, and there lies at the watch for any fly or minnow that comes near to him. And he especially loves the May fly, which is bred of the cod-worm or caddis; and these make the trout bold and lusty, and he is usually fatter and better meat at the end of that month than at any time of the year.

Now you are to know that it is observed that usually the best trouts are either red or yellow, though some, as the Fordidge trout, be white and yet good; but that is not usual. And it is a note observable that the female trout hath usually a less head and a deeper body than the male trout, and is usually the better meat. And note that a hog back and a little head, to either trout, salmon, or any other fish, is a sign that that fish is in season.

But yet you are to note that, as you see some willows or palm trees bud and blossom sooner than others do, so some trouts be in rivers sooner in season; and as some hollies or oaks are longer before they cast their leaves, so are some trouts in rivers longer before they go out of season.

And you are to note that there are several kinds of trouts. But these several kinds are not considered but by very few men; for they go under the general name of trouts, just as pigeons do in most places, though it is certain there are tame and wild pigeons; and of the tame there be helmits and runts and carriers and cropers, and indeed too many to name. Nay, the Royal Society have found and published lately that there be thirty and three kinds of spiders; and yet all, for aught I know, go under that one general name of spider. And it is so with many kinds of fish, and of trouts especially, which differ in their bigness and shape and spots and color. The great

Kentish hens may be an instance, compared to other hens; and doubtless there is a kind of small trout which will never thrive to be big, that breeds very many more than others do that be of a larger size. Which you may rather believe, if you consider that the little wren and titmouse will have twenty young ones at a time, when usually the noble hawk, or the musical thrassel[20] or blackbird, exceed not four or five.

And now you shall see me try my skill to catch a trout; and at my next walking, either this evening or tomorrow morning, I will give you direction how you yourself shall fish for him.

VENATOR. Trust me, master, I see now it is a harder matter to catch a trout than a chub; for I have put on patience, and followed you these two hours, and not seen a fish stir, neither at your minnow nor your worm.

PISCATOR. Well, scholar, you must endure worse luck sometime, or you will never make a good angler. But what say you now? There is a trout now, and a good one too, if I can but hold him; and two or three turns more will tire him. Now you see where he lies still, and the sleight is to land him. Reach me that landing net. So, sir, now he is mine own. What say you now? is not this worth all my labor and your patience?

VENATOR. On my word, master, this is a gallant trout. What shall we do with him?

PISCATOR. Marry, e'en eat him to supper. We'll go to my hostess,[21] from whence we came; she told me, as I was going out of door, that my brother Peter, a good angler and a cheerful companion, had sent word he would lodge there tonight and bring a friend with him. My hostess has two beds, and I know you and I may have the best. We'll rejoice with my brother Peter and his friend, tell tales, or sing ballads, or make a catch,[22] or find some harmless sport to content us, and pass away a little time without offense to God or man.

VENATOR. A match, good master! let's go to that house, for the linen looks white and smells of lavender, and I long to lie in a pair of sheets that smell so. Let's be going, good master, for I am hungry again with fishing.

PISCATOR. Nay, stay a little, good scholar. I caught my last trout with a worm; now I will put on a minnow and try a quarter of an hour about yonder trees for another, and so walk towards our lodging. Look you, scholar, thereabout we shall have a bite

20 Throstle, thrush. 21 At their inn.
22 Sing a round.

presently, or not at all. Have with you,[23] sir! O' my word, I have hold of him. Oh, it is a great logger-headed[24] chub! Come, hang him upon that willow twig, and let's be going. But turn out of the way a little, good scholar, towards yonder high honey-suckle hedge. There we'll sit and sing whilst this shower falls so gently upon the teeming earth and gives yet a sweeter smell to the lovely flowers that adorn these verdant meadows.

Look! under that broad beech tree I sat down when I was last this way a-fishing; and the birds in the adjoining grove seemed to have a friendly con-tention with an echo, whose dead voice seemed to live in a hollow tree near to the brow of that prim-rose hill. There I sat viewing the silver streams glide silently towards their center, the tempestuous sea, yet sometimes opposed by rugged roots and pebble-stones, which broke their waves and turned them into foam. And sometimes I beguiled time by view-ing the harmless lambs, some leaping securely in the cool shade, whilst others sported themselves in the cheerful sun; and saw others craving comfort from the swollen udders of their bleating dams. As I thus sat, these and other sights had so fully possessed my soul with content that I thought, as the poet has happily expressed it,

> I was for that time lifted above earth,
> And possessed joys not promised in my birth.

As I left this place, and entered into the next field, a second pleasure entertained me; 'twas a handsome milkmaid that had not yet attained so much age and wisdom as to load her mind with any fears of many things that will never be, as too many men often do; but she cast away all care, and sung like a night-ingale. Her voice was good, and the ditty fitted for it; 'twas that smooth song which was made by Kit Marlowe, now at least fifty years ago: and the milk-maid's mother sung an answer to it, which was made by Sir Walter Raleigh in his younger days.

They were old-fashioned poetry, but choicely good, I think much better than the strong lines that are now in fashion in this critical age. Look yonder! on my word, yonder they both be a-milking again. I will give her the chub, and persuade them to sing those two songs to us.

God speed you, good woman! I have been a-fish-ing, and am going to Bleak Hall to my bed, and having caught more fish than will sup myself and

my friend, I will bestow this upon you and your daughter, for I use to sell none.

MILKWOMAN. Marry, God requite you, sir! and we'll eat it cheerfully. And if you come this way a-fishing two months hence, a' grace of God I'll give you a sillabub[25] of new verjuice,[26] in a new-made haycock,[27] for it. And my Maudlin shall sing you one of her best ballads, for she and I both love all anglers, they be such honest, civil, quiet men. In the meantime, will you drink a draught of red cow's milk? You shall have it freely.

PISCATOR. No, I thank you; but I pray do us a courtesy that shall stand you and your daughter in nothing,[28] and yet we will think ourselves still some-thing in your debt. It is but to sing us a song that was sung by your daughter when I last passed over this meadow, about eight or nine days since.

MILKWOMAN. What song was it, I pray? Was it "Come, shepherds, deck your herds," or "As at noon Dulcina rested," or "Phillida flouts me," or "Chevy Chase," or "Johnny Armstrong," or "Troy Town"?

PISCATOR. No, it is none of those; it is a song that your daughter sung the first part, and you sung the answer to it.

MILKWOMAN. Oh, I know it now. I learned the first part in my golden age, when I was about the age of my poor daughter, and the latter part, which indeed fits me best now, but two or three years ago, when the cares of the world began to take hold of me; but you shall, God willing, hear them both; and sung as well as we can, for we both love anglers. Come, Maudlin, sing the first part to the gentlemen, with a merry heart; and I'll sing the second when you have done.

THE MILKMAID'S SONG[29]

> Come live with me, and be my love,
> And we will all the pleasures prove
> That hills and valleys, dales and fields,
> And all the craggy mountains yields.

---

[25] A frothy drink of cider or wine mixed with milk or cream.
[26] Sour juice of apples or grapes.
[27] Where the jug has been set to keep cool.
[28] Cost you nothing.
[29] This is Marlowe's "The Passionate Shepherd to His Love." There are several early versions, besides this. The present text, which varies considerably from Walton's, follows the standard edition of Marlowe's *Poems* (ed. L. C. Martin, 1931). The next to the last stanza was first printed in the second edition of *The Complete Angler*, but there is a garbled version of it in an Eliza-bethan commonplace-book; so it is probably genuine.

---

[23] I'm going to get you (said to the trout).
[24] Big headed.

And we will sit upon the rocks,
Seeing the shepherds feed their flocks,
By shallow rivers, to whose falls
Melodious birds sings madrigals.

And I will make thee beds of roses
And a thousand fragrant posies,
A cap of flowers, and a kirtle
Embroidered all with leaves of myrtle,

A gown made of the finest wool,
Which from our pretty lambs we pull,
Fair linèd slippers, for the cold,
With buckles of the purest gold,

A belt of straw and ivy-buds
With coral clasps and amber studs.
And if these pleasures may thee move,
Come live with me, and be my love.

Thy silver dishes for thy meat,
As precious as the gods do eat,
Shall on an ivory table be
Prepared each day for thee and me.

The shepherd swains shall dance and sing
For thy delight each May morning.
If these delights thy mind may move,
Then live with me, and be my love.

VENATOR. Trust me, master, it is a choice song, and sweetly sung by honest Maudlin. I now see it was not without cause that our good Queen Elizabeth did so often wish herself a milkmaid all the month of May, because they are not troubled with fears and cares, but sing sweetly all the day and sleep securely all the night; and without doubt honest, innocent, pretty Maudlin does so. I'll bestow Sir Thomas Overbury's milkmaid's wish[30] upon her: "that she may die in the spring, and being dead may have good store of flowers stuck round about her winding sheet."

THE MILKMAID'S MOTHER'S ANSWER[31]

If all the world and love were young,
And truth in every shepherd's tongue,

---

[30] In one of the Overburian characters (see p. 432, above).
[31] This is "The Nymph's Reply to the Shepherd," and Walton's ascription of it to Raleigh (just before the appearance of the Milkwoman) is generally accepted. The present text follows the standard edition of The Poems of Raleigh (ed. Agnes M. C. Latham, 1929). In the second edition of The Complete Angler the following stanza appears before the final one:
"What should we talk of dainties, then,
    Of better meat than's fit for men?
These are but vain; that's only good
    Which God hath blessed, and sent for food."

These pretty pleasures might me move
To live with thee, and be thy love.

Time drives the flocks from field to fold,
When rivers rage, and rocks grow cold,
And Philomel becometh dumb;
The rest complains of cares to come.

The flowers do fade, and wanton fields
To wayward winter reckoning yields;
A honey tongue, a heart of gall,
Is fancy's spring but sorrow's fall.

Thy gowns, thy shoes, thy beds of roses,
Thy cap, thy kirtle, and thy posies,
Soon break, soon wither, soon forgotten:
In folly ripe, in reason rotten.

Thy belt of straw and ivy buds,
Thy coral clasps and amber studs,
All these in me no means can move
To come to thee, and be thy love.

But could youth last and love still breed,[32]
Had joys no date nor age no need,
Then those delights my mind might move
To live with thee, and be thy love.

MOTHER. Well, I have done my song. But stay, honest anglers, for I will make Maudlin sing you one short song more. Maudlin, sing that song that you sung last night, when young Corydon the shepherd played so purely on his oaten pipe to you and your cousin Betty.

MAUDLIN. I will, Mother.

I married a wife of late,
The more's my unhappy fate:
    I married her for love,
    As my fancy did me move,
And not for a worldly estate.
    But oh, the green sickness[33]
    Soon changed her likeness,
And all her beauty did fail;
        But 'tis not so
        With those that go
        Through frost and snow,
        As all men know,
And carry the milking-pail.

---

[32] Increase.
[33] Chlorosis, an anemic disease of young women.

PISCATOR. Well sung, good woman; I thank you; I'll give you another dish of fish one of these days, and then beg another song of you. Come, scholar, let Maudlin alone; do not you offer[34] to spoil her voice. Look! yonder comes mine hostess, to call us to supper. How now! is my brother Peter come?

HOSTESS. Yes, and a friend with him. They are both glad to hear that you are in these parts, and long to see you, and long to be at supper, for they be very hungry.

Sir Thomas Browne

1605–1682

BROWNE was a physician who won a permanent place in English literature largely because of his style. It is not a style that anyone would wish to adopt today, for it is usually involved and sometimes obscure, in fact the kind of writing the Royal Society wanted to abolish. But even though literary expression in England veered in a different direction, Browne's style remains a magnificent thing: lofty, rich, imaginative, rhythmical, imbued with a sense of largeness. The very sound of it is glorious, in a calm, dignified way; and if the meaning is occasionally hard to follow by reason of inordinately long sentences and too many strange words and idioms never naturalized in English, at least (and this is no minor merit) the mind is constantly stimulated.

The wielder of this stately measure (for in *Hydriotaphia* Browne's prose is actually a species of poetry) was the son of a London merchant. His education was prolonged into his thirties. After Winchester, one of England's most famous schools, came Oxford and then studies abroad, chiefly medical, at the universities of Montpellier, Padua, and Leyden. In recognition of these, Oxford added in 1637 the degree of M.D. to the B.A. and M.A. he had already taken there. Then he settled in Norwich, where he practiced medicine for the remainder of his life. In 1641 he made a happy marriage; a large family of successful sons and well-married daughters increased his happiness. He was a royalist, but absorption in his profession and his scientific and metaphysical pursuits seems to have kept him from any great concern over the Civil Wars. He was less interested in politics than in the possible existence of sidehill badgers conveniently equipped with longer legs to port or starboard, in the vocal habits of dying swans, or in the effect on himself of an experimental meal consisting of spiders.

Browne's writings show that he was a great reader. He collected one of the largest scientific libraries in England, and one reason why his works are still so readable is that their allusions range so widely. The bent of his mind was reversible, and he turns his back on scientific principles about as frequently as he sticks to them. He warns against incredulity as solemnly as against superstition. His was a mind in love with the mysterious. Anything odd, any reminder of what a queer place our world is, anything suggestive of the invisible atmosphere of wonder which enfolds our world and makes it strange—such things always aroused Browne's curiosity and fired his imagination. And in his extraordinary style he had an instrument capable of communicating to others his mood as well as his facts or alleged facts.

In 1643 he published his *Religio Medici,* a doctor's religion. He was impelled to write it mainly by the fascination for him of "those involved enigmas and riddles of the Trinity, with Incarnation, and Resurrection." He had written it about eight years earlier, for his own satisfaction. not for publication. Copies had been available to his friends in manuscript, and one had got into print without his authorization. In spite of its breathing a spirit of tolerance alien to the times, the book became popular at once; there were eight editions by 1685. In it his contemporaries found greatly to their taste Browne's unique blend of devout religious feeling with a skeptical and inquiring attitude which, while it reflected the age's scientific trend, did not lead like Rochester's speculations[1] to an intellectual nihilism. Browne was aware of the limitations of the reason; its weakness made faith imperative. In 1646 came his largest work: *Pseudodoxia Epidemica, or Enquiries into Very Many Received Tenets and Commonly Presumed Truths;* it is also known, from its running title, as *Vulgar Errors.* In 1658 appeared the most imaginative and beautiful of his compositions: *Hydriotaphia: Urn-Burial, or A Discourse of the Sepulchral Urns Lately Found in Norfolk.* Of its kind this essay is unmatched in English prose for the organlike effect of its rhythms and its stately diction.

Browne received his knighthood under unusual circumstances. On a visit to Norwich in 1671 Charles II offered

---

[34] Try.

[1] See pp. 532 ff., above.

to knight the mayor, who gracefully declined in favor of the Norfolk capital's most distinguished citizen. The standard edition is *The Works,* edited by G. Keynes (6 vols., 1928–31). There is a Browne volume in Everyman's Library. His relation to the thought of his time is discussed by B. Willey in *The Seventeenth Century Background* (1934), pp. 41–69. On Browne's style, see W. M. Croll, "The Baroque Style in Prose," *Studies in . . . Honor of Frederick Klaeber* (1929), pp. 427–56. You are advised to begin your acquaintance with Browne by reading aloud the extract from *Hydriotaphia,* ignoring the notes and even the ideas, and yielding yourself to the spell of the sound and rhythm and to the images or pictures that they call up in your mind.

from RELIGIO MEDICI

from THE SECOND PART

Now for that other virtue of charity, without which faith is a mere notion, and of no existence, I have ever endeavored to nourish the merciful disposition and humane inclination I borrowed from my parents, and regulate it to the written and prescribed laws of charity. And if I hold the true anatomy of myself,[2] I am delineated and naturally framed to such a piece of virtue; for I am of a constitution so general that it consorts and sympathizeth with all things. I have no antipathy, or rather idiosyncrasy, in diet, humor, air, anything. I wonder not at the French for their dishes of frogs, snails, and toadstools, nor at the Jews for locusts and grasshoppers, but, being amongst them, make them my common viands; and I find they agree with my stomach as well as theirs. I could digest a salad gathered in a churchyard, as well as in a garden. I cannot start at the presence of a serpent, scorpion, lizard, or salamander; at the sight of a toad[3] or viper I find in me no desire to take up a stone to destroy them. I feel not in myself those common antipathies that I can discover in others; those national repugnances do not touch me, nor do I behold with prejudice the French, Italian, Spaniard, or Dutch; but where I find their actions in balance with my countrymen's, I honor, love, and embrace them in the same degree. I was born in the eighth climate,[4] but seem for to be framed and constellated[5] unto all. I am no plant that will not prosper out of a garden. All places, all airs, make unto me one country; I am in England everywhere, and under any meridian. I have been shipwrackt, yet am not enemy with the sea or winds; I can study, play, or sleep in a tempest. In brief, I am averse from nothing; my conscience would give me the lie if I should say I absolutely detest or hate any essence but the Devil, or so at least abhor anything but that we might come to composition.[6] If there be any among those common objects of hatred I do contemn and laugh at, it is that great enemy of reason, virtue, and religion, the multitude: that numerous piece of monstrosity which, taken asunder, seem men and the reasonable creatures of God, but, confused together, make but one great beast and a monstrosity more prodigious than Hydra.[7] It is no breach of charity to call these fools; it is the style all holy writers have afforded them, set down by Solomon in canonical Scripture,[8] and a point of our faith to believe so. Neither in the name of Multitude do I only include the base and minor sort of people; there is a rabble even amongst the gentry, a sort of plebeian heads, whose fancy moves with the same wheel as these—men in the same level with mechanics, though their fortunes do somewhat gild their infirmities, and their purses compound[9] for their follies. But as, in casting account, three or four men together come short in account of one man placed by himself below them; so neither are a troop of these ignorant Doradoes[10] of that[11] true esteem and value as many a forlorn person whose condition doth place him below their feet. Let us speak like politicians: there is a nobility without heraldry, a natural dignity, whereby one man is ranked with another, another filed before him, according to the quality of his desert, and pre-eminence of his good parts. Though the corruption of these times and the bias of present practice wheel another way, thus it was in the first and primitive commonwealths, and is yet in the integrity and cradle of well-ordered polities, till corruption getteth ground, ruder desires laboring after that which wiser generations contemn, everyone having a liberty to amass and heap up riches, and they a license or faculty to do or purchase anything. . . .

But to return from philosophy to charity. I hold not so narrow a conceit[12] of this virtue as to con-

[2] If I correctly analyze myself.
[3] Then supposed to be venomous.   [4] Zone.
[5] Astrologically adjusted.

[6] Agreement.   [7] The nine-headed monster slain by Hercules.
[8] Proverbs.   [9] Settle, square up.
[10] I.e., rich men.   [11] Such.   [12] Conception.

ceive that to give alms is only to be[13] charitable, or think a piece of liberality can comprehend the total of charity. Divinity[14] hath wisely divided the act thereof into many branches, and hath taught us in this narrow way many paths unto goodness; as many ways as we may do good, so many ways we may be charitable. There are infirmities, not only of body but of soul and fortunes, which do require the merciful hand of our abilities. I cannot contemn a man for ignorance, but behold him with as much pity as I do Lazarus.[15] It is no greater charity to clothe his body than apparel the nakedness of his soul. It is an honorable object to see the reasons of other men wear our liveries, and their borrowed understandings do homage to the bounty of ours; it is the cheapest way of beneficence, and, like the natural charity of the sun, illuminates another without obscuring itself. To be reserved and caitiff[16] in this part of goodness is the sordidest piece of covetousness, and more contemptible than pecuniary avarice. To this (as calling myself a scholar) I am obliged by the duty of my condition: I make not therefore my head a grave, but a treasure, of knowledge; I intend no monopoly, but a community, in learning; I study not for my own sake only, but for theirs that study not for themselves. I envy no man that knows more than myself, but pity them that know less. I instruct no man as an exercise of my knowledge, or with an intent rather to nourish and keep it alive in mine own head then beget and propagate it in his. And in the midst of all my endeavors there is but one thought that dejects me, that my acquired parts must perish with myself, nor can be legacied among my honored friends. I cannot fall out or contemn a man for an error, or conceive why a difference in opinion should divide an affection; for controversies, disputes, and argumentations, both in philosophy and in divinity, if they meet with discreet and peaceable natures, do not infringe the laws of charity. In all disputes, so much as there is of passion, so much there is of nothing to the purpose; for then reason, like a bad hound, spends upon a false scent, and forsakes the question first started. And this is one reason why controversies are never determined; for, though they be amply proposed, they are scarce at all handled, they do so swell with unnecessary digressions, and the parenthesis on the party[17] is often as large as the main discourse upon the subject. The foundations of religion are already established, and the principles of salvation subscribed unto by all; there remain not many controversies worth a passion, and yet never any disputed without, not only in divinity, but in inferior arts. What a βατραχο-μυομαχία[18] and hot skirmish is betwixt S and T in Lucian![19] How do grammarians hack and slash for the genitive case in Jupiter![20] How do they break their own pates to salve that of Priscian![21]

Si foret in terris, rideret Democritus.[22]

Yea, even amongst wiser militants, how many wounds have been given, and credits slain, for the poor victory of an opinion or beggarly conquest of a distinction! Scholars are men of peace; they bear no arms, but their tongues are sharper than Actius[23] his razor; their pens carry farther, and give a louder report than thunder: I had rather stand the shock of a basilisco,[24] than the fury of a merciless pen. It is not mere zeal to learning, or devotion to the muses, that wiser princes patron the arts and carry an indulgent aspect unto scholars, but a desire to have their names eternized by the memory of their writings, and a fear of the revengeful pen of succeeding ages; for these are the men, that, when they have played their parts and had their exits, must step out and give the moral of their scenes and deliver unto posterity an inventory of their virtues and vices. And surely there goes a great deal of conscience to the compiling of an history: there is no reproach to the scandal of a story; it is such an authentic kind of falsehood that with authority belies our good names to all nations and posterity.

There is another offence unto charity, which no author hath ever written of, and few take notice of; and that's the reproach, not of whole professions, mysteries,[25] and conditions,[26] but of whole nations, wherein by opprobrious epithets we miscall each

---

13 Is the only way of being.   14 Theology.
15 The beggar full of sores in the parable (Luke 16: 19–31).
16 Mean.   17 Part, i.e., side issue.

18 Batrachomyomachía, battle of the frogs and mice. A poem of this title burlesquing the Iliad was once ascribed to Homer.
19 The second-century Greek satirist. In his dialogue, "Trial in the Court of Vowels," the letter sigma complains that tau has stolen many words that ought to begin with sigma.
20 Whether it should be Jovis or Jupitris.
21 A Roman grammarian who flourished about 500 A.D.
22 If he were back on earth, Democritus would laugh. This Greek (d. 362? B.C.) was known as the Laughing Philosopher. The line is from Horace, Epistles, II, i, 194.
23 Attus Navius, a soothsayer. According to the Roman historian Livy, he was trapped into predicting that the idea in the king's mind could be executed. The idea turned out to be cutting a whetstone in two, and at Navius's bidding the king performed the feat.   24 A kind of cannon.   25 Trades.
26 Ranks.

other, and, by an uncharitable logic, from a disposition in a few conclude a habit in all.

> Le mutin Anglois, et le bravache Escossois,
> Le bougre Italian, et le fol François,
> Le poultron Romain, le larron de Gascongne,
> L'Espagnol superbe, et l'Aleman yvrongne.[27]

St. Paul, that calls the Cretians[28] liars, doth it but indirectly, and upon quotation of their own poet. It is as bloody a thought in one way as Nero's was in another; for by a word we wound a thousand, and at one blow assassine the honor of a nation. It is as complete a piece of madness to miscall and rave against the times, or think to recall men to reason by a fit of passion. Democritus, that thought to laugh the times into goodness, seems to me as deeply hypochondriac as Heraclitus,[29] that bewailed them. It moves not my spleen[30] to behold the multitude in their proper[31] humors, that is, in their fits of folly and madness; as well understanding that wisdom is not profaned unto the world, and 'tis the privilege of a few to be virtuous. They that endeavour to abolish vice destroy also virtue; for contraries, though they destroy one another, are yet the life of one another. Thus virtue (abolish vice) is an idea. Again, the community of sin doth not disparage goodness; for when vice gains upon the major part, virtue, in whom it remains, becomes more excellent, and, being lost in some, multiplies its goodness in others which remain untouched and persist entire in the general inundation. I can therefore behold vice without a satire, content only with an admonition or instructive reprehension: for noble natures, and such as are capable of goodness, are railed into vice, that might as easily be admonished into virtue; and we should all be so far the orators of goodness as to protect her from the power of vice, and maintain the cause of injured truth. No man can justly censure or condemn another, because indeed no man truly knows another. This I perceive in myself; for I am in the dark to all the world, and my nearest friends behold me but in a cloud. Those that know me but superficially think less of me than I do of myself; those of my near acquaintance think more; God, who truly knows me, knows that I am nothing: for

he only[32] beholds me and all the world, who looks not on us through a derived ray, or a trajection of a sensible species,[33] but beholds the substance without the helps of accidents,[34] and the forms of things as we their operations. Further, no man can judge another, because no man knows himself: for we censure others but as they disagree from that humor which we fancy laudable in ourselves, and commend others but for that wherein they seem to quadrate[35] and consent with us. So that, in conclusion, all is but that we all condemn, self-love. 'Tis the general complaint of these times, and perhaps of those past, that charity grows cold; which I perceive most verified in those which most do manifest the fires and flames of zeal, for it is a virtue that best agrees with coldest natures, and such as are complexioned for[36] humility. But how shall we expect charity towards others, when we are uncharitable to ourselves? *Charity begins at home* is the voice of the world; yet is every man his greatest enemy, and, as it were, his own executioner. *Non occides*[37] is the commandment of God, yet scarce observed by any man; for I perceive every man is his own Atropos,[38] and lends a hand to cut the thread of his own days. Cain was not therefore the first murtherer, but Adam, who brought in death; whereof he beheld the practice and example in his own son Abel,[39] and saw that verified, in the experience of another, which faith could not persuade him in the theory of himself.

There is, I think, no man that apprehends his own miseries less than myself, and no man that so nearly apprehends another's. I could lose an arm without a tear, and with few groans, methinks, be quartered into pieces; yet can I weep most seriously at a play, and receive with true passion the counterfeit grief of those known and professed impostures. It is a barbarous part of inhumanity to add unto any afflicted party's misery, or endeavor to multiply in any man a passion whose single nature is already above his patience. This was the greatest affliction of Job,[40] and those oblique expostulations of his friends a deeper injury than the downright blows of the Devil. It is not the tears of our own eyes only, but of our friends also, that do exhaust the current of our sor-

---

[27] The rebellious Englishman, and the Scottish braggart, the Italian debauchee, and the French fool, the Roman coward, the thief from Gascony, the haughty Spaniard, and the drunken German.

[28] Cretans. See Titus 1:12. St. Paul quotes the poet Epimenides (seventh century B.C.).

[29] The Greek known as the Weeping Philosopher. He flourished about 500 B.C. [30] Anger. [31] Own.

[32] Alone.

[33] I.e., God does not see us as we see each other by means of rays reflected from our bodies, that is, by dimensions, color, etc.

[34] Mere phenomena, the objects perceived by the senses (in contrast with *substance*, the real).

[35] Square, agree.—*Consent* is a synonym.

[36] Temperamentally inclined to.

[37] Thou shalt not kill. (Exodus 20:13.)

[38] That one of the three Fates who cut the thread of man's life.

[39] Genesis 4. [40] See pp. 233-40, above.

rows; which, falling into many streams, runs more peaceably and is contented with a narrower channel. It is an act within the power of charity, to translate a passion out of one breast into another, and to divide a sorrow almost out of itself; for an affliction, like a dimension, may be so divided, as, if not indivisible,[41] at least to become insensible. Now with my friend I desire not to share or participate, but to engross, his sorrows: that, by making them mine own, I may more easily discuss them; for in mine own reason, and within myself, I can command that which I cannot entreat without myself, and within the circle of another. I have often thought those noble pairs and examples of friendship not so truly histories of what had been, as fictions of what should be; but I now perceive nothing in them but possibilities, nor any thing in the heroic examples of Damon and Pythias,[42] Achilles and Patroclus,[43] which methinks upon some grounds I could not perform within the narrow compass of myself. That a man should lay down his life for his friend seems strange to vulgar affections and such as confine themselves within that worldly principle, *Charity begins at home.* For mine own part I could never remember the relations that I held unto myself, nor the respect that I owe unto my own nature, in the cause of God, my country, and my friends. Next to these three, I do embrace myself. I confess I do not observe that order that the schools[44] ordain our affections, to love our parents, wives, children, and then our friends; for, excepting the injunctions of religion, I do not find in myself such a necessary and indissoluble sympathy to all those of my blood.[45] I hope I do not break the fifth Commandment, if I conceive I may love my friend before the nearest of my blood, even those to whom I owe the principles of life. I never yet cast a true affection on a woman; but I have loved my friend as I do virtue, my soul, my God. From hence methinks I do conceive how God loves man, what happiness there is in the love of God. Omitting all other, there are three most mystical unions: two natures in one person,[46] three persons in one nature,[47] one soul in two bodies:[48] for though indeed they be really divided, yet are they so united as they seem but one, and make rather a duality than two distinct souls.

There are wonders in true affection: it is a body of enigmas, mysteries, and riddles; wherein two so become one, as they both become two. I love my friend before myself, and yet methinks I do not love him enough; some few months hence my multiplied affection will make me believe I have not loved him at all. When I am from him, I am dead till I be with him; when I am with him, I am not satisfied, but would still be nearer him. United souls are not satisfied with embraces, but desire to be truly each other; which being impossible, their desires are infinite, and must proceed without a possibility of satisfaction. Another misery there is in affection, that whom we truly love like our own selves, we forget their looks, nor can our memory retain the idea of their faces; and it is no wonder, for they are ourselves, and our affection makes their looks our own. This noble affection falls not on vulgar and common constitutions, but on such as are marked for virtue; he that can love his friend with this noble ardor, will in a competent degree affect all. Now, if we can bring our affections to look beyond the body, and cast an eye upon the soul, we have found out the true object, not only of friendship, but charity; and the greatest happiness that we can bequeath the soul, is that wherein we all do place our last felicity, salvation: which, though it be not in our power to bestow, it is in our charity and pious invocations to desire, if not procure and further. I cannot contentedly frame a prayer for myself in particular without a catalogue for my friends, nor request a happiness wherein my sociable disposition doth not desire the fellowship of my neighbor. I never hear the toll of a passing bell, though in my mirth, without my prayers and best wishes for the departing spirit; I cannot go to cure the body of my patient but I forget my profession, and call unto God for his soul; I cannot see one say his prayers but, instead of imitating him, I fall into a supplication for him, who perhaps is no more to me than a common nature; and if God hath vouchsafed an ear to my supplications, there are surely many happy that never saw me, and enjoy the blessing of mine unknown devotions. To pray for enemies, that is, for their salvation, is no harsh precept, but the practice of our daily and ordinary devotions. I cannot believe the story of the Italian:[49] our bad wishes and uncharitable

---

41 When it has been divided into fractions so small as to be incapable of further division.

42 Pythias, under sentence of death, was allowed a leave of absence by the tyrant Dionysus of Syracuse (d. 367 B.C.), when Damon pledged his life for his friend's return.

43 The bosom friend of Achilles in the *Iliad.*

44 I.e., the philosophers.

45 Browne was still a bachelor when he wrote this.

46 Christ as both God and man. 47 The Trinity.

48 Friendship, especially between men.

49 "Who, after he had inveigled his enemy to disclaim his faith for the redemption of his life, did presently [i.e., immediately] poniard him, to prevent repentance and assure his eternal death." (Browne, *Pseudodoxia Epidemica,* Book VII, chap. 19.)

desires proceed no further than this life; it is the Devil, and the uncharitable votes of hell, that desire our misery in the world to come. . . .

I thank God, amongst those millions of vices I do inherit and hold from Adam, I have escaped one, and that a mortal enemy to charity, the first and father-sin, not only of man, but of the Devil, Pride: a vice whose name is comprehended in a monosyllable, but in its nature not circumscribed with a world. I have escaped it in a condition[50] that can hardly avoid it. Those petty acquisitions and reputed perfections that advance and elevate the conceits of other men, add no feathers unto mine. I have seen a grammarian tow'r and plume himself over a single line in Horace, and show more pride in the construction[51] of one ode than the author in the composure of the whole book. For my own part, besides the jargon and patois of several provinces, I understand no less than six languages; yet I protest I have no higher conceit of myself than had our fathers before the confusion of Babel, when there was but one language in the world and none to boast himself either linguist or critic. I have not only seen several countries, beheld the nature of their climes, the chorography[52] of their provinces, topography of their cities, but understood their several laws, customs, and policies; yet cannot all this persuade the dulness of my spirit unto such an opinion of myself, as I behold in nimbler and conceited heads, that never looked a degree beyond their nests. I know the names, and somewhat more, of all the constellations in my horizon; yet I have seen a prating mariner, that could only name the pointers[53] and the North Star, outtalk me, and conceit himself a whole sphere above me. I know most of the plants of my country, and of those about me; yet methinks I do not know so many as when I did but know a hundred, and had scarcely ever simpled[54] further than Cheapside.[55] For, indeed, heads of capacity, and such as are not full with a handful or easy measure of knowledge, think they know nothing till they know all; which being impossible, they fall upon the opinion of Socrates,[56] and only know they know not anything. I cannot think that Homer pined away upon the riddle of the fishermen;[57] or that Aristotle,

who understood the uncertainty of knowledge and confessed so often the reason of man too weak for the works of nature, did ever drown himself upon the flux and reflux of Euripus.[58] We do but learn today what our better advanced judgments will unteach tomorrow; and Aristotle doth but instruct us, as Plato did him, that is, to confute himself. I have run through all sorts, yet find no rest in any: though our first studies and junior endeavors may style us Peripatetics, Stoics, or Academics;[59] yet I perceive the wisest heads prove, at last, almost all Skeptics, and stand like Janus[60] in the field of knowledge. I have therefore one common and authentic philosophy I learned in the schools, whereby I discourse and satisfy the reason of other men; another more reserved, and drawn from experience, whereby I content mine own. Solomon, that complained of ignorance in the height of knowledge, hath not only humbled my conceits but discouraged my endeavors. There is yet another conceit that hath sometimes made me shut my books, which tells me it is a vanity to waste our days in the blind pursuit of knowledge; it is but attending a little longer, and we shall enjoy that by instinct and infusion which we endeavor at here by labor and inquisition. It is better to sit down in a modest ignorance, and rest contented with the natural blessing of our own reasons, than buy the uncertain knowledge of this life with sweat and vexation, which Death gives every fool gratis and is an accessory of our glorification. . . .

For my conversation, it is like the sun's, with all men, and with a friendly aspect to good and bad. Methinks there is no man bad, and the worst, best, that is, while they are kept within the circle of those qualities wherein they are good: there is no man's mind of such discordant and jarring a temper to which a tunable disposition may not strike a harmony. *Magnae virtutes, nec minora vitia:*[61] it is the posy[62] of the best natures, and may be inverted on the worst; there are in the most depraved and venomous dispositions certain pieces that remain untouched, which by an *antiperistasis*[63] become more excellent, or by the excellency of their antipathies

<hr/>

50 Position in life.   51 Interpretation.
52 Geographical features.
53 The stars in Ursa Major (the Great Bear or Big Dipper) which point to the North Star.   54 Gone botanizing.
55 The famous street in the heart of London.
56 Athenian philosopher (d. 399 B.C.).
57 According to Plutarch's Life of Homer, he grieved to death because he could not answer it.

58 A euripus is a narrow body of water through which the tides or currents rush violently; here, the strait between the Greek island of Euboea and the mainland, at Chalcis. There, according to this absurd legend, he committed suicide because he could not figure out why the tide flowed more frequently than is normal.
59 Like *Skeptics,* schools of ancient philosophy.
60 The Roman god of beginnings, depicted with two faces, looking both ways.
61 His virtues were great and his faults no less (author unidentified).
62 Motto.   63 Opposition through which strength is acquired.

are able to preserve themselves from the contagion of their enemy vices, and persist entire beyond the general corruption. For it is also thus in nature: the greatest balsams do lie enveloped in the bodies of most powerful corrosives. I say, moreover, and I ground upon experience, that poisons contain within themselves their own antidote and that which preserves them from the venom of themselves, without which they were not deleterious to others only, but to themselves also. But it is the corruption that I fear within me, not the contagion of commerce[64] without me. 'Tis that unruly regiment within me that will destroy me; 'tis I that do infect myself; the man without a navel[65] yet lives in me; I feel that original canker corrode and devour me; and therefore *Defenda me Dios de me,* "Lord, deliver me from myself," is a part of my litany, and the first voice of my retired imaginations. There is no man alone, because every man is a microcosm and carries the whole world about him.[66] *Nunquam minus solus quam cum solus,*[67] though it be the apothegm of a wise man, is yet true in the mouth of a fool. Indeed, though in a wilderness, a man is never alone, not only because he is with himself and his own thoughts, but because he is with the Devil, who ever consorts with our solitude, and is that unruly rebel that musters up those disordered motions[68] which accompany our sequest'red imaginations. And to speak more narrowly, there is no such thing as solitude, nor anything that can be said to be alone and by itself, but God, who is his own circle and can subsist by himself; all others, besides their dissimilar and heterogeneous parts, which in a manner multiply their natures, cannot subsist without the concourse[69] of God, and the society of that hand which doth uphold their natures. In brief, there can be nothing truly alone and by itself which is not truly one; and such is only God: all others do transcend an unity, and so by consequence are many.

Now for my life, it is a miracle of thirty years, which to relate were not a history but a piece of poetry, and would sound to common ears like a fable. For the world, I count it not an inn, but an hospital; and a place not to live, but to die in. The world that I regard is myself; it is the microcosm[70]

of my own frame that I cast mine eye on; for the other, I use it but like my globe, and turn it round sometimes for my recreation. Men that look upon my outside, perusing only my condition and fortunes, do err in my altitude; for I am above Atlas[71] his shoulders. The earth is a point, not only in respect of the heavens above us, but of that heavenly and celestial part within us: that mass of flesh that circumscribes me, limits not my mind; that surface that tells the heavens it hath an end, cannot persuade me I have any; I take my circle to be above three hundred and sixty; though the number of the Ark[72] do measure my body, it comprehendeth not my mind; whilst I study to find how I am a microcosm, or little world, I find myself something more than the great. There is surely a piece of divinity in us, something that was before the elements, and owes no homage unto the sun. Nature tells me I am the image of God, as well as Scripture; he that understands not thus much hath not his introduction or first lesson, and is yet to begin the alphabet of man. Let me not injure the felicity of others, if I say I am as happy as any: *Ruat coelum, fiat voluntas tua*[73] salveth all; so that whatsoever happens, it is but what our daily prayers desire. In brief, I am content; and what should Providence add more? Surely this is it we call happiness, and this do I enjoy; with this I am happy in a dream, and as content to enjoy a happiness in a fancy as others in a more apparent truth and reality. There is surely a nearer apprehension of anything that delights us in our dreams than in our waked senses: without this I were unhappy; for my awaked judgment discontents me, ever whispering unto me that I am from my friend; but my friendly dreams in the night requite me, and make me think I am within his arms. I thank God for my happy dreams, as I do for my good rest; for there is a satisfaction in them unto reasonable desires, and such as can be content with a fit of happiness: and surely it is not a melancholy conceit[74] to think we are all asleep in this world, and that the conceits of this life are as mere dreams to those of the next, as the phantasms of the night to the conceits of the day. There is an equal delusion in both, and the one doth but seem to be the emblem or picture of the other; we are somewhat more than ourselves in our sleeps, and the slumber of the body seems to be but the waking of the soul. It is the ligation[75] of sense, but

---

[64] Intercourse with others in the affairs of life.
[65] Adam. Browne's note: "whom I conceive to want a navel because he was not born of a woman."
[66] I.e., in him. *Microcosm* = little world, i.e., man, as an epitome of the macrocosm, or great world (the universe).
[67] Never less alone than when alone. (Ascribed to Scipio Africanus by Cicero, *De Officiis,* III, sec. 1.)
[68] Impulses.   [69] Concurrence.   [70] See note 66, above.

[71] In Greek mythology a Titan represented as supporting on his shoulders the heavens or the world.
[72] Measurement. According to the Church Fathers, the Ark was built on the proportions of the human body.   [73] Though the heavens fall, thy will be done.   [74] Idea.   [75] Bondage

the liberty of reason; and our waking conceptions do not match the fancies of our sleeps. At my nativity my ascendant[76] was the watery sign of Scorpius; I was born in the planetary hour of Saturn, and I think I have a piece of that leaden planet in me. I am no way facetious, nor disposed for the mirth and galliardize[77] of company; yet in one dream I can compose a whole comedy, behold the action, apprehend the jests, and laugh myself awake at the conceits thereof. Were my memory as faithful as my reason is then fruitful, I would never study but in my dreams; and this time also would I choose for my devotions. But our grosser memories have then so little hold of our abstracted understandings that they forget the story, and can only relate to our awaked souls a confused and broken tale of that that hath passed. Aristotle, who hath written a singular

tract *Of Sleep,* hath not, methinks, throughly defined it, nor yet Galen,[78] though he seem to have corrected it; for those *noctambuloes* and nightwalkers, though in their sleep, do yet enjoy the action of their senses. We must therefore say that there is something in us that is not in the jurisdiction of Morpheus;[79] and that those abstracted and ecstatic souls do walk about in their own corpse,[80] as[81] spirits with the bodies they assume, wherein they seem to hear, see, and feel, though indeed the organs are destitute of sense, and their natures of those faculties that should inform[82] them. Thus it is observed that men sometimes, upon the hour of their departure, do speak and reason above themselves; for then the soul, beginning to be freed from the ligaments[83] of the body, begins to reason like herself, and to discourse in a strain above mortality. . . .

from HYDRIOTAPHIA: URN-BURIAL

CHAPTER V

Now since these dead bones[1] have already outlasted the living ones of Methuselah,[2] and in a yard under ground, and thin walls of clay, outworn all the strong and specious buildings above it, and quietly rested under the drums and tramplings of three conquests,[3] what prince can promise such diuturnity[4] unto his relics, or might not gladly say,

Sic ego componi versus in ossa velim?[5]

Time, which antiquates antiquities, and hath an art to make dust of all things, hath yet spared these minor monuments. In vain we hope to be known by open and visible conservatories,[6] when to be unknown was the means of their continuation, and obscurity their protection. If they died by violent hands, and were thrust into their urns, these bones become considerable, and some old philosophers would honor them, whose souls they conceived most pure which were thus snatched from their

bodies, and to retain a stronger propension[7] unto them; whereas they weariedly left a languishing corpse, and with faint desires of reunion. If they fell by long and aged decay, yet wrapped up in the bundle of time, they fall into indistinction, and make but one blot with infants. If we begin to die when we live, and long life be but a prolongation of death, our life is a sad composition; we live with death, and die not in a moment. How many pulses made up the life of Methuselah, were work for Archimedes;[8] common counters sum up the life of Moses his man.[9] Our days become considerable, like petty sums, by minute accumulations, where numerous fractions make up but small round numbers; and our days of a span long, make not one little finger.[10]

If the nearness of our last necessity brought a nearer conformity into it, there were a happiness in hoary hairs, and no calamity in half-senses. But the long habit of living indisposeth us for dying; when avarice makes us the sport of death, when even David grew politicly cruel, and Solomon could hardly be said to be the wisest of men. But many

---

[76] The newly risen sign of the zodiac.   [77] Gaiety.

[1] The occasion (but obviously not the exclusive subject) of *Hydriotaphia* was the discovery near Walsingham, Norfolk, of several urns filled with human bones now believed Saxon but then supposed to be earlier. This is the last chapter of the essay.
[2] The patriarch who, according to Genesis 5:27, lived 969 years.
[3] Roman, English, and Norman.   [4] Lastingness.
[5] Thus, when turned to bones, would I be laid away (Tibullus, III, ii, 26).   [6] Repositories, tombs.

[78] The great Greek medical authority of the second century.
[79] The god of dreams.   [80] Bodies.   [81] Like.
[82] Animate.   [83] Bonds, fetters.

[7] Propensity, inclination.
[8] Greek mathematician (d. 212 B.C.).
[9] Moses's man. Psalm 90 (attributed to Moses) contains the famous pronouncement (verse 10) on "the days of our years."
[10] Browne's marginal note: "According to the ancient arithmetic of the hand, wherein the little finger of the right hand, contracted, signifieth an hundred."

are too early old, and before the date of age. Adversity stretcheth our days, misery makes Alcmena's nights,[11] and time hath no wings unto it. But the most tedious being is that which can unwish itself, content to be nothing, or never to have been, which was beyond the malcontent of Job, who cursed not the day of his life, but his nativity, content to have so far been, as to have a title to future being, although he had lived here but in an hidden state of life, and as it were an abortion.

What song the Sirens[12] sang, or what name Achilles assumed when he hid himself among women,[13] though puzzling questions,[14] are not beyond all conjecture. What time the persons of these ossuaries[15] entered the famous nations of the dead, and slept with princes and counselors, might admit a wide solution. But who were the proprietaries of these bones, or what bodies these ashes made up, were a question above antiquarism, not to be resolved by man nor easily perhaps by spirits, except we consult the provincial guardians, or tutelary observators.[16] Had they made as good provision for their names as they have done for their relics, they had not so grossly erred in the art of perpetuation. But to subsist in bones, and be but pyramidally[17] extant, is a fallacy in duration. Vain ashes, which in the oblivion of names, persons, times, and sexes, have found unto themselves a fruitless continuation, and only arise unto late posterity, as emblems of mortal vanities, antidotes against pride, vainglory, and madding vices! Pagan vainglories, which thought the world might last for ever, had encouragement for ambition; and, finding no Atropos[18] unto the immortality of their names, were never damped with the necessity[19] of oblivion. Even old ambitions had the advantage of ours, in the attempts of their vainglories, who acting early and before the probable meridian of time,[20] have by this time found great accomplishment of their designs, whereby the ancient heroes have already outlasted their monu-ments and mechanical preservations. But in this latter scene of time, we cannot expect such mummies unto our memories, when ambition may fear the prophecy of Elias;[21] and Charles the Fifth[22] can never hope to live within two Methuselahs of Hector.[23]

And therefore restless unquiet for the diuturnity of our memories unto present considerations seems a vanity almost out of date, and superannuated piece of folly. We cannot hope to live so long in our names as some have done in their persons. One face of Janus[24] holds no proportion unto the other. 'Tis too late to be ambitious. The great mutations of the world are acted, or time may be too short for our designs. To extend our memories by monuments, whose death we daily pray for, and whose duration we cannot hope without injury to our expectations in the advent of the last day, were a contradiction to our beliefs. We whose generations are ordained in this setting part of time, are providentially taken off from such imaginations and, being necessitated to eye the remaining particle of futurity, are naturally constituted unto thoughts of the next world, and cannot excusably decline the consideration of that duration which maketh pyramids pillars of snow, and all that's past a moment.

Circles and right[25] lines limit and close[26] all bodies; and the mortal right-lined circle[27] must conclude and shut up all. There is no antidote against the opium of time, which temporally considereth all things. Our fathers find their graves in our short memories, and sadly tell us how we may be buried in our survivors. Gravestones tell truth scarce forty years.[28] Generations pass while some trees stand, and old families last not three oaks. To be read by bare inscriptions like many in Gruter,[29] to hope for eternity by enigmatical epithets or first letters of our names, to be studied by antiquaries who we were, and have new names given us like many of the mummies,[30] are cold consolations unto the students of perpetuity, even by everlasting languages.

---

11 According to the classical myth, the conception of Hercules took longer than that of mortals. He was the son of Alcmena; in the absence of her husband Amphitruo, she was visited by Zeus, who had assumed his form. Browne's marginal note: "One night as long as three."

12 When these minor divinities of classical mythology tried to lure sailors to destruction.

13 To avoid joining the expedition against Troy, where he became the chief Greek hero.

14 Browne's note: ". . . of Tiberius unto grammarians."

15 Depositories for bones.   16 Guardian spirits.

17 By means of a monument or tomb.

18 One of the Fates of classical mythology; she cut the thread of life.

19 Discouraged by the inevitability.

20 Noon of the world's duration.

21 Elijah. Browne's note: "That the world may last but six thousand years."   22 German Emperor and King of Spain (d. 1558).

23 In the *Iliad* the chief hero of the Trojans.

24 The two-faced Roman god of gates and beginnings.

25 Straight.   26 Enclose.

27 The Greek letter θ (theta), standing for θάνατος (thanatos), death.

28 Browne's note: "Old ones being taken up, and other bodies laid under them."

29 Jan Gruter (d. 1627), a Dutch scholar who wrote on Latin inscriptions.

30 Browne's note: "Which men show in several countries, giving them what names they please, and unto some the names of the old Egyptian kings out of Herodotus."

To be content that times to come should only know there was such a man, not caring whether they knew more of him, was a frigid ambition in Cardan,[31] disparaging his horoscopical inclination and judgment of himself. Who cares to subsist, like Hippocrates'[32] patients or Achilles' horses in Homer, under naked nominations,[33] without deserts and noble acts, which are the balsam[34] of our memories, the *entelechia*[35] and soul of our subsistences? To be nameless in worthy deeds exceeds an infamous history. The Canaanitish woman[36] lives more happily without a name than Herodias[37] with one. And who had not rather have been the good thief[38] than Pilate?[39]

But the iniquity of oblivion blindly scattereth her poppy,[40] and deals with the memory of men without distinction to merit of perpetuity. Who can but pity the founder of the pyramids? Herostratus lives that burnt the temple of Diana;[41] he is almost lost that built it; time hath spared the epitaph of Adrian's[42] horse, confounded that of himself. In vain we compute our felicities by the advantage of our good names, since bad have equal durations; and Thersites[43] is like to live as long as Agamemnon. Who knows whether the best of men be known? or whether there be not more remarkable persons forgot than any that stand rememb'red in the known account of time? Without the favor of the everlasting register, the first man had been as unknown as the last, and Methuselah's long life had been his only chronicle.

Oblivion is not to be hired: the greater part must be content to be as though they had not been: to be found in the register of God, not in the record of man. Twenty-seven names make up the first story,[44] and the recorded names ever since contain not one living century.[45] The number of the dead long ex-

ceedeth all that shall live. The night of time far surpasseth the day, and who knows when was the equinox?[46] Every hour adds unto that current arithmetic[47] which scarce stands[48] one moment. And since death must be the Lucina[49] of life, and even pagans[50] could doubt whether thus to live were to die; since our longest sun sets at right descensions, and makes but winter arches, and therefore it cannot be long before we lie down in darkness and have our light in ashes;[51] since the brother of death[52] daily haunts us with dying mementos,[53] and time (that grows old itself) bids us hope no long duration: diuturnity is a dream and folly of expectation.

Darkness and light divide the course of time, and oblivion shares with memory a great part even of our living beings; we slightly remember our felicities, and the smartest strokes of affliction leave but short smart upon us. Sense endureth no extremities, and sorrows destroy us or themselves. To weep into stones are fables.[54] Afflictions induce callosities;[55] miseries are slippery, or fall like snow upon us; which notwithstanding is no unhappy stupidity. To be ignorant of evils to come, and forgetful of evils past, is a merciful provision in nature, whereby we digest the mixture of our few and evil days, and, our delivered senses not relapsing into cutting remembrances, our sorrows are not kept raw by the edge of repetitions. A great part of antiquity contented their hopes of subsistency with a transmigration of their souls, a good way to continue their memories: while having the advantage of plural successions, they could not but act something remarkable in such variety of beings, and enjoying the fame of their passed selves, make accumulation of glory unto their last durations. Others, rather than be lost in the uncomfortable night of nothing, were content to recede into the common being, and make one particle of the public soul of all things, which was no more than to return into their unknown and divine original again. Egyptian ingenuity was more unsatisfied, contriving their bodies in sweet consisten-

[31] Girolamo Cardano (d. 1576), an Italian physician, mathematician, and astrologer.

[32] The great Greek physician of the fourth and fifth centuries B.C.

[33] Bare names.   [34] Preservative.   [35] Being.

[36] Matthew 15:22–28. Because of her faith, her daughter was cured by Jesus.

[37] Herod's wife; through her daughter Salome, she procured the murder of John the Baptist (Mark 6:17–28).

[38] Luke 23:39–43.   [39] The Roman procurator of Judea. He surrendered Jesus for crucifixion.

[40] A source of opium.

[41] At Ephesus (fourth century B.C.). It was one of the Seven Wonders of the ancient world. His object was merely to perpetuate his name.

[42] Hadrian, Roman emperor (d. 138).

[43] In Homer (and in Shakespeare's *Troilus and Cressida*), a scurrilous Greek in the army commanded by King Agamemnon at the siege of Troy.

[44] Browne's note: "Before the Flood." (Genesis 5.)

[45] Hundred (living at the same time).

[46] I.e., when the world's age reached the halfway mark.

[47] I.e., steadily mounting sum of time.   [48] Halts.

[49] The Roman goddess of childbirth.

[50] In a marginal note Browne refers to the Greek dramatist Euripides (d. 406 B.C.).

[51] Browne's note: "According to the custom of the Jews, who place a lighted wax candle in a pot of ashes by the corpse."

[52] Sleep, like Death the child of Night.

[53] Reminders of death.

[54] Weeping (according to the myth) for the slaughter of her twelve children, Niobe was changed to stone, and continued to weep streams.   [55] Make us callous.

cies,[56] to attend the return of their souls. But all was vanity, feeding the wind, and folly. The Egyptian mummies, which Cambyses[57] or time hath spared, avarice now consumeth. Mummy is become merchandise,[58] Mizraim[59] cures wounds, and Pharaoh[60] is sold for balsams.

In vain do individuals hope for immortality, or any patent from oblivion, in preservations below the moon; men have been deceived even in their flatteries above the sun, and studied conceits to perpetuate their names in heaven. The various cosmography of that part hath already varied the names of contrived constellations; Nimrod[61] is lost in Orion,[62] and Osiris[63] in the Dog Star.[64] While we look for incorruption in the heavens, we find they are but like the earth: durable in their main bodies, alterable in their parts; whereof, beside comets and new stars, perspectives[65] begin to tell tales. And the spots that wander about the sun, with Phaëton's[66] favor, would make clear conviction.

There is nothing strictly immortal, but immortality; whatever hath no beginning may be confident of no end (all others have a dependent being, and within the reach of destruction); which is the peculiar[67] of that necessary essence that cannot destroy itself, and the highest strain of omnipotency: to be so powerfully constituted as not to suffer even from the power of itself. But the sufficiency of Christian immortality frustrates all earthly glory, and the quality of either state after death makes a folly of posthumous memory. God who can only[68] destroy our souls, and hath assured our resurrection, either of our bodies or names hath directly promised no duration. Wherein there is so much of chance that the boldest expectants have found unhappy frustration; and to hold long subsistence seems but a scape in[69] oblivion. But man is a noble animal, splendid in ashes and pompous in the grave, solemnizing nativities and deaths with equal luster, nor omitting ceremonies of bravery[70] in the infamy of his nature.

Life is a pure flame, and we live by an invisible sun within us. A small fire sufficeth for life; great flames seemed too little after death, while men vainly affected precious pyres, and to burn like Sardanapalus:[71] but the wisdom of funeral laws found the folly of prodigal blazes, and reduced undoing[72] fires unto the rule of sober obsequies, wherein few could be so mean as not to provide wood, pitch, a mourner, and an urn.

Five languages secured not the epitaph of Gordianus.[73] The man of God lives longer without a tomb than any by one, invisibly interred by angels, and adjudged to obscurity, though not without some marks directing human discovery. Enoch and Elias,[74] without either tomb or burial, in an anomalous state of being, are the great examples of perpetuity, in their long and living memory, in strict account being still on this side death, and having a late part yet to act upon this stage of earth. If in the decretory term[75] of the world we shall not all die but be changed,[76] according to received translation, the last day will make but few graves; at least quick resurrections will anticipate lasting sepultures, some graves will be opened before they be quite closed, and Lazarus[77] be no wonder. When many that feared to die shall groan that they can die but once, the dismal state is the second and living death, when life puts despair on the damned, when men shall wish the coverings of mountains,[78] not of monuments, and annihilation shall be courted.

While some have studied[79] monuments, others have studiously declined them; and some have been so vainly boisterous that they durst not acknowledge their graves, wherein Alaricus[80] seems most subtle, who had a river turned to hide his bones at the bottom. Even Sylla,[81] that thought himself safe in his urn, could not prevent revenging tongues, and stones thrown at his monument. Happy are they whom privacy makes innocent, who deal so with men in this world that they are not afraid to meet them in

---

56 I.e., embalming them in spices.
57 King of the Medes and Persians (d. 522 B.C.).
58 You could buy it in any drugstore.
59 Mentioned in Genesis 10:6,13. His descendants were supposed to have peopled Egypt.
60 The title of the Egyptian king.
61 The mighty hunter (Genesis 10:8–10).
62 A constellation sometimes represented as the figure of a hunter.
63 One of the great gods of the Egyptians, presiding over the underworld.   64 Sirius, the brightest star.
65 Telescopes (invented early in the seventeenth century).
66 The sungod's son.   67 Special characteristic.
68 Alone.   69 I.e., a poor way of avoiding.
70 Gaudy ceremonies.

71 An ancient king of Assyria, said to have burned himself up to avoid capture by besiegers.
72 Destroying.
73 The third Roman emperor so named (d. 244). Browne's note: ". . . in Greek, Latin, Hebrew, Egyptian, Arabic, defaced by Licinius [d. 324] the emperor."
74 The prophet Elijah. Like the patriarch Enoch (Genesis 5:24), he did not (according to 2 Kings 2:1–11) die but was "taken" by God.   75 Decreed end.
76 Cf. 1 Corinthians 15:51 ff.
77 Whom (according to John 11:1–46) Jesus raised from the dead.
78 Cf. Luke 23:29–30 and Revelation 6:15–16.
79 Have been studious for, have gone in for.
80 Alaric the Visigoth, the conqueror of Rome (410 A.D.). He was afraid his enemies would desecrate a tomb.
81 Sulla (d. 78 B.C.), the Roman dictator.

the next, who when they die make no commotion among the dead and are not touched with that poetical taunt of Isaiah.[82]

Pyramids, arches, obelisks, were but the irregularities of vainglory, and wild enormities of ancient magnanimity. But the most magnanimous resolution rests in the Christian religion, which trampleth upon pride, and sets[83] on the neck of ambition, humbly pursuing that infallible perpetuity unto which all others must diminish their diameters and be poorly seen in angles of contingency.[84]

Pious spirits, who passed their days in raptures of futurity, made little more of this world than the world that was before it, while they lay obscure in the chaos of preordination and night of their fore-beings. And if any have been so happy as truly to understand Christian annihilation, extasis, exolution, liquefaction, transformation, the kiss of the Spouse,

gustation of God, and ingression into the divine shadow,[85] they have already had an handsome anticipation of heaven: the glory of the world is surely over, and the earth in ashes unto them.

To subsist in lasting monuments, to live in their productions, to exist in their names and predicament of chimeras,[86] was large satisfaction unto old expectations, and made one part of their Elysiums.[87] But all this is nothing in the metaphysics of true belief. To live indeed, is to be again ourselves, which being not only an hope but an evidence in noble believers, 'tis all one[88] to lie in St. Innocent's[89] churchyard, as in the sands of Egypt. Ready to be anything, in the ecstasy of being ever, and as content with six foot as the moles of Adrianus.[90]

Tabesne cadavera solvat
An rogus haud refert.[91]

John Milton

1608-1674

MILTON was born in 1608 in London, where his father was a well-to-do scrivener. The functions of this calling included some of those now performed by lawyers and bankers as well as by notaries public. The poet was brought up in a home of wealth, piety, and refinement. As a boy he learned from his father to love music; to the end of his life he played the organ, and he was an accomplished singer. Special gifts for languages and for writing appeared early.

Milton prepared at St. Paul's School and at sixteen entered Cambridge. At the university he was soon in conflict with authority in the person of his tutor. He was suspended, and apparently whipped. On his return another tutor took charge of him, and he proceeded to show what he could do, particularly in Latin composition. Nevertheless he thought his university a hopeless nest of intellectual reaction. A Platonic idealist, he despised the traditional emphasis on Aristotelian logic; and he deplored the inadequacy of the curriculum on the scientific side. He took his B.A. in 1629 and his M.A. in 1632.

The next five years were spent at Horton, a hamlet across the Thames from Windsor; his father had retired to a country estate there. During his student days Milton had composed Latin and Italian verse, and in English had written a number of his best things, including his ode "On the Morning of Christ's Nativity" and probably "L'Al-

legro" and "Il Penseroso." On the whole these early poems reflect normal attitudes and feelings. Their author shows a healthy interest in social pleasures as well as in reading and music, in nature, and even in girls. Milton was no hermit; every now and then he took time out and went up to London to "keep a gaudy day."

He had come to know an influential family, the Egertons; its head, the Earl of Bridgewater, was son of the Sir Thomas Egerton whom John Donne had served as secretary. For these royalist and High-Church friends Milton wrote Comus, an elaborate masque. Their children acted it at Ludlow Castle in 1634, with music by Henry Lawes, the leading composer of the time. On this undramatic but melodiously lyrical work, the theme of which is the superlative merit of chastity, the influence of Spenser was paramount. The next of Milton's important poems was also occasional, for "Lycidas" was composed in response to a request for a contribution to a volume in memory of a young Cambridge man, Edward King, who was drowned in 1637. In the opinion of many, these early pieces consti-

[82] Browne's note: "Isaiah 14."   [83] I.e., sits.
[84] Browne's note: ". . . the least of angles."

[85] Phrases of Christian mysticism expressing the idea of union with the divine.
[86] I.e., in the same state as mere creatures of the imagination.
[87] Blessed abodes, paradises.   [88] The same.
[89] In Paris, where bodies soon consume.
[90] Browne's note: "A stately mausoleum or sepulchral pile built by Adrianus [Hadrian] in Rome where now standeth the Castle of St. Angelo."
[91] It matters not whether decomposition or the funeral pyre consume our corpses (Lucan, Pharsalia, VII, 809-10).

tute Milton's finest work as a poet; but he himself, studying hard at mathematics, music, and the classics, looked on this period of his life as a phase of postgraduate preparation for some great achievement. It ended in 1637 with his mother's death. The following year he left England for fifteen months on the Continent. The Grand Tour, which included France, Switzerland, and above all Italy, was for him another phase of his educational program. He found a warm welcome in cultivated circles at Florence and Rome; he was, he says, "a constant attendant at their literary parties." During his absence political and religious conflicts were rapidly approaching a crisis in England. He felt the tension, and in 1639 it brought him home.

He took lodgings in London and began a decade of schoolteaching; his pupils were two nephews and some "sons of gentlemen that were his intimate friends." Meanwhile the pamphlet warfare between the Puritans and royalists was raging hotly. Milton felt that in general the Reformation in England had lagged behind its counterparts on the Continent; in 1641 he leaped into the fray with a series of attacks on the episcopal form of church government. He himself insisted that he wrote these and subsequent tracts with his left hand, but they won him a European reputation. Eventually he became the chief literary spokesman for the Puritan party and state. Literary controversy was then a ferocious business; a slanderous hit below the belt was no less applauded than a clean logical uppercut. Milton learned both to give and to receive.

In 1642, the year that saw the commencement of the military struggle, Milton, now nearly thirty-four, positively asked for trouble by marrying a girl who was half his age and a royalist in her upbringing. She left him in a month. This episode lies behind his four pamphlets on divorce, which mark his break with the Presbyterian majority and his alignment with the Independents. Like the pamphlets against the High-Church wing of the Anglicans, the divorce tracts are an argument for freedom, in this case the liberalization of the divorce law. Milton's point of view, for which he was roundly denounced by the Presbyterians, is a modern one. The essence of true marriage, he holds, is a spiritual union, to which the physical relationship is secondary; spiritual incompatibility should therefore be added to the grounds for divorce.

Other important works of the 1640's were the great plea for freedom of the press (*Areopagitica*), the tract *Of Education*, and a few sonnets. Milton's occasional use of the sonnet form, not as a lover's lute but as a trumpet call to action on public questions, marks an important turn in its English history. In 1645 appeared a collected edition of his poems, both English and Latin. In the same year his wife came back to him; unfortunately she brought her royalist relatives with her, and they camped on the poet. The result of the reconciliation was more concrete than spiritual:

three daughters and a son were born, but Shakespeare's "marriage of true minds" seems never to have been realized.

Till after the beheading of Charles I in 1649, Milton's pen had been concerned more with general aspects of the problems of freedom than with partisan issues; in that year he was drawn into the actual machinery of the Puritan government. This may have been due to the publication, soon after the King's death, of *The Tenure of Kings and Magistrates,* an argument for the legal liability of monarchs to deposition and execution; it was written, Milton said, "to reconcile the minds of the people to the event." At any rate, he was soon appointed Latin secretary to the Council of State, and he continued in that office under the dictatorship of Cromwell. His main duties were to draft the correspondence with foreign governments and to defend the administration of the Commonwealth by controversial pamphlets in both Latin and English. All this was exhilarating; but it took its toll, especially in eyestrain. Milton overworked, his health suffered, his eyes failed, and by 1652 he was totally blind. In the same year his wife and infant son died.

Milton continued to serve the government with his pen. In 1656 he made a happy second marriage, but little more than a year later his wife died. Perhaps he turned to the most famous of his works in order to dull the edge of grief. He had long meditated the composition of an epic poem, and in his early thirties had drawn up a list of possible subjects from English history and the Bible. By the restoration of Charles II in 1660, Milton's career as a public servant was ended; fourteen years remained, with leisure for poetry, though they were not free from trouble. As a prominent member of the Puritan administration, he was sentenced to death and went into hiding; contemporary accounts variously ascribe to Andrew Marvell and Sir William D'avenant the honor of interceding for him. The sentence was not carried out, and his was not among the names excepted from the general Act of Oblivion issued when the easygoing Charles reached London. Milton lost his salary, of course, and that portion of his capital invested in government securities. He had to live on a reduced scale, without money enough to buy the books he wanted or to hire competent secretaries. He tried to train his daughters, but they were not eager to assist in the production of *Paradise Lost.*

In a way, Milton had himself lost paradise. The wife he loved was dead; the Commonwealth was shattered;

the sons
Of Belial, flown with insolence and wine,

roamed London streets and had the King's ear. This was Milton's finest hour. The blind old man sits amid the wreckage of his hopes, and the sounds that reach his ears from the new order of things are dreadful to him. But the unconquerable will is there, and courage indomitable. Satan is certainly not the hero of *Paradise Lost,* as some have urged, but Milton has put something of himself into the portrait of him in the first two Books.

Milton's third marriage, in 1663, to a bride of twenty-four, seems to have turned out sufficiently well. He had regained his health, music remained a consolation, and he was launched on the great enterprise of his boyhood dreams. *Paradise Lost* was finished in 1665 and published two years later. *Paradise Regained* (on the temptation of Christ) and *Samson Agonistes* (Samson the Champion) appeared in a single volume in 1671. For his account of the Biblical hero (see Judges 14–16) Milton adopted the forms of Greek tragedy, including the chorus. He died in 1674.

The standard edition is the Columbia Milton (18 vols. in 21, 1931–8). The New Cambridge edition of *The Complete Poetical Works* in one volume, by H. H. Fletcher, affords a modernized but carefully constructed text. More ambitious in their annotations are M. Y. Hughes's three volumes: *Paradise Lost* (1935), *Paradise Regained, the Minor Poems, and Samson Agonistes* (1937), and selected prose (1947). F. A. Patterson's *The Student's Milton* (revised ed., 1933) gives all the poetry and most of the prose. J. H. Hanford's *A Milton Handbook* (3rd ed., 1939) is invaluable. *Milton,* by E. M. W. Tillyard (1930), though occasionally wanting in common sense, is an able and readable study. The latest study is J. H. Hanford's *John Milton, Englishman* (1949).

John Milton

L'ALLEGRO

"L'Allegro" (The Lively Man) and its companion piece, "Il Penseroso" (The Contemplative Man), were probably written in the summer of one of Milton's last years at Cambridge. In them you see a young man pulled, not unpleasantly, two ways: by the genial aspects of the Renaissance and by its more somber side, Puritanism even. And the young *poet* is likewise pulled two ways: by the Renaissance, its encouragement of free expression, its love of color and rhetorical ornament; and also by neoclassicism, with its devotion to purity of form as a major excellence. It may be this tension which, aside from the main factor of Milton's genius, is responsible for the chaste but far from pallid beauty of this pair of poems.

It is through the ear that they are mainly to be enjoyed, even though they are full of excellent suggestions about how either kind of temperament, social or solitary—which is only to say, any man in either of man's moods—may advantageously expend life's leisure hours. For many they reach the ear like a little orchestra of strings and woodwinds discoursing the most melodious of simple airs. You are advised to read them aloud, in as sonorous a voice as you can muster. After that no objection will be made if you turn to the explanatory footnotes, to learn what certain lines mean. If the string of mythological allusions with which each begins seems pedantic, remember that to the lips of the educated of the seventeenth century the names of the classical gods and demigods came very naturally.

Hence, loathèd Melancholy,
    Of Cerberus[1] and blackest Midnight born
In Stygian cave forlorn,
'Mongst horrid shapes, and shrieks, and sights unholy!

Find out some uncouth[2] cell,   5
    Where brooding Darkness spreads his jealous wings,
And the night-raven sings;
    There, under ebon shades, and low-browed rocks
As ragged as thy locks,
    In dark Cimmerian[3] desert ever dwell.   10
But come, thou goddess fair and free,
In heaven ycleped[4] Euphrosyne,
And by men heart-easing Mirth,
Whom lovely Venus, at a[5] birth,
With two sister Graces more,   15
To ivy-crownèd Bacchus bore;
Or whether (as some sager sing)
The frolic wind that breathes the spring,
Zephyr, with Aurora[6] playing,
As he met her once a-Maying,   20
There on beds of violets blue,
And fresh-blown roses washed in dew,
Filled her with thee, a daughter fair,
So buxom,[7] blithe, and debonair.
Haste thee, nymph, and bring with thee   25
Jest and youthful Jollity,
Quips and cranks[8] and wanton wiles,
Nods and becks[9] and wreathèd smiles,
Such as hang on Hebe's[10] cheek,
And love to live in dimple sleek;   30
Sport that wrinkled Care derides,
And Laughter holding both his sides.
Come, and trip it as you go
On the light fantastic toe,

[2] Dismal.
[3] Gloomy (from a fabled land of perpetual mist and darkness).
[4] Called.   [5] One.
[6] Goddess of the dawn.—Zephyr was god of the west wind.
[7] Gay.   [8] Humorous turns of speech.—*Wanton* = playful.
[9] Gestures of salutation.   [10] Goddess of youth.

---

[1] The three-headed dog which guarded the gate to Hades, on the Styx, its principal river (whence *Stygian*). The genealogies in these poems are often from Milton's fancy, not classical mythology.

And in thy right hand lead with thee 35
The mountain nymph, sweet Liberty;
And, if I give thee honor due,
Mirth, admit me of thy crew,
To live with her and live with thee,
In unreprovèd[11] pleasures free: 40
To hear the lark begin his flight
And singing startle the dull night
From his watchtower in the skies,
Till the dappled dawn doth rise;
Then to come, in spite[12] of sorrow, 45
And at my window bid good morrow,
Through the sweetbrier or the vine
Or the twisted eglantine;
While the cock, with lively din,
Scatters the rear of darkness thin, 50
And to the stack or the barn door
Stoutly struts his dames before—
Oft listening how the hounds and horn
Cheerly rouse the slumbering morn,
From the side of some hoar[13] hill, 55
Through the high wood echoing shrill;
Sometime walking, not unseen,[14]
By hedgerow elms, on hillocks green,
Right against the eastern gate
Where the great sun begins his state,[15] 60
Robed in flames and amber light,
The clouds in thousand liveries dight;[16]
While the plowman near at hand
Whistles o'er the furrowed land,
And the milkmaid singeth blithe, 65
And the mower whets his scythe,
And every shepherd tells his tale[17]
Under the hawthorn in the dale.
Straight mine eye hath caught new pleasures,
Whilst the lantskip[18] round it measures: 70
Russet lawns and fallows grey,
Where the nibbling flocks do stray;
Mountains, on whose barren breast
The laboring clouds do often rest;
Meadows trim with daisies pied, 75
Shallow brooks, and rivers wide.
Towers and battlements it sees
Bosomed high in tufted trees,
Where perhaps some beauty lies,
The cynosure[19] of neighboring eyes. 80

Hard by, a cottage chimney smokes
From betwixt two agèd oaks,
Where Corydon and Thyrsis[20] met
Are at their savory dinner set
Of herbs and other country messes, 85
Which the neat-handed Phyllis dresses;
And then in haste her bower[21] she leaves,
With Thestylis to bind the sheaves,
Or, if the earlier season lead,
To the tanned haycock in the mead. 90
Sometimes with secure[22] delight
The upland hamlets will invite,
When the merry bells ring round,
And the jocund rebecks[23] sound
To many a youth and many a maid 95
Dancing in the chequered shade,
And young and old come forth to play
On a sunshine holiday,
Till the livelong daylight fail;
Then to the spicy nut-brown ale, 100
With stories told of many a feat,
How Fairy Mab[24] the junkets eat.[25]
She was pinched and pulled, she said;
And he, by friar's lanthorn[26] led,
Tells how the drudging goblin[27] sweat 105
To earn his cream bowl duly set,
When in one night, ere glimpse of morn,
His shadowy flail hath threshed the corn[28]
That ten day-laborers could not end;
Then lies him down, the lubber fiend, 110
And, stretched out all the chimney's[29] length,
Basks at the fire his hairy strength;
And cropfull out of doors he flings,
Ere the first cock his matin rings.
Thus done the tales, to bed they creep, 115
By whispering winds soon lulled asleep.
Towered cities please us then,
And the busy hum of men,
Where throngs of knights and barons bold,
In weeds[30] of peace, high triumphs[31] hold, 120
With store of ladies, whose bright eyes
Rain influence,[32] and judge the prize
Of wit or arms, while both contend
To win her grace whom all commend.
There let Hymen[33] oft appear 125
In saffron robe, with taper clear,

[20] Favorite names in pastoral poetry, like those in lines 86, 88.
[21] Cottage.   [22] Free from care.
[23] A primitive kind of viol.   [24] The fairy queen.
[25] Ate, *feat* being pronounced *fate*.   [26] Will-o'-the-wisp.
[27] Hobgoblin, or Robin Goodfellow, the Puck of Shakespeare's *A Midsummer Night's Dream*.   [28] Grain.
[29] Fireplace's.   [30] Garments.   [31] Festivals.
[32] Since their eyes are like the stars, which astrologers believed controlled men's fortunes.   [33] God of marriage.

[11] Unreprovable, harmless.
[12] Despite, scorn. It is the poet who looks *from* his window.
[13] Gray in the morning mist or dew.
[14] I.e., not trying to avoid people.   [15] Royal progress.
[16] Arrayed—like attendants in livery of a thousand colors.
[17] Counts up the tally (of his sheep).   [18] Landscape.
[19] Center of attention.

And pomp and feast and revelry,
With masque and ántique pageantry—
Such sights as youthful poets dream
On summer eves by haunted stream.   130
Then to the well-trod stage anon,
If Jonson's learnèd sock[34] be on,
Or sweetest Shakespeare, fancy's[35] child,
Warble his native wood-notes wild.
And ever, against eating cares,   135
Lap me in soft Lydian[36] airs,
Married to immortal verse,
Such as the meeting soul may pierce,[37]
In notes with many a winding bout[38]
Of linkèd sweetness long drawn out,   140
With wanton heed and giddy cunning,
The melting voice through mazes running,
Untwisting all the chains that tie
The hidden soul of harmony:
That[39] Orpheus'[40] self may heave his head   145
From golden slumber on a bed
Of heaped Elysian[41] flowers, and hear
Such strains as would have won the ear
Of Pluto to have quite set free
His half-regained Eurydice.   150

These delights if thou canst give,
Mirth, with thee I mean to live.

IL PENSEROSO

Hence, vain deluding joys,
    The brood of Folly without father bred!
How little you bestead,[1]
    Or fill the fixèd mind with all your toys!
Dwell in some idle brain,   5
    And fancies fond[2] with gaudy shapes possess,
As thick and numberless
    As the gay motes that people the sunbeams,
Or likest hovering dreams,

The fickle pensioners[3] of Morpheus' train.   10
    But hail, thou goddess sage and holy,
Hail, divinest Melancholy![4]
Whose saintly visage is too bright
To hit the sense of human sight,
And therefore to our weaker view   15
O'erlaid with black, staid Wisdom's hue.
Black, but such as in esteem[5]
Prince Memnon's[6] sister might beseem,[7]
Or that starred Ethiop queen[8] that strove
To set her beauty's praise above   20
The sea nymphs, and their powers offended;
Yet thou art higher far descended:
Thee bright-haired Vesta long of yore
To solitary Saturn[9] bore;
His daughter she (in Saturn's reign   25
Such mixture was not held a stain).
Oft in glimmering bowers and glades
He met her, and in secret shades
Of woody Ida's inmost grove,
While yet there was no fear of Jove.   30
Come, pensive nun, devout and pure,
Sober, steadfast, and demure,
All in a robe of darkest grain,[10]
Flowing with majestic train,
And sable stole[11] of cypress lawn[12]   35
Over thy decent[13] shoulders drawn.
Come, but keep thy wonted state,[14]
With even step and musing gait
And looks commercing[15] with the skies,
Thy rapt soul sitting in thine eyes;   40
There held in holy passion still,
Forget thyself to marble,[16] till
With a sad[17] leaden downward cast
Thou fix them on the earth as fast.
And join with thee calm Peace and Quiet,   45
Spare Fast, that oft with gods doth diet
And hears the Muses in a ring
Aye round about Jove's altar sing.
And add to these retirèd Leisure,
That in trim gardens takes his pleasure;   50

[34] Symbol of comedy (from Latin *soccus*, light shoe, in contrast with the cothurnus or buskin, the raised shoe worn by the Greek actors in tragedy, to add to their height).

[35] Imagination's. Shakespeare had come to be regarded as a natural genius in contrast with Jonson, whose writings were supposed to be the fruit of his classical reading.

[36] I.e., soft and sweet. The Lydian was one of the three "modes" of Greek music.   [37] Then pronounced *purse*.

[38] Circuit, turn; perhaps with reference to counterpoint: cf. "linked."   [39] So that.

[40] The fabled musician who by his playing persuaded Pluto, ruler of the underworld, to release his dead wife, Eurydice. The condition was that as she followed him to the upper regions he should not look back; but he proved unable to fulfill it, and lost her.   [41] In Elysium, the abode of the happy dead.

[1] Help, are of service.   [2] Foolish.

[3] Attendants.—Morpheus was the god of dreams.
[4] Pensive meditation.   [5] Worth.
[6] A mythical Ethiopian, according to Homer of great beauty.
[7] Befit.
[8] Cassiopeia, who was changed into a constellation for boasting not of her own but her daughter's beauty.
[9] King of the gods in the golden age, before Zeus or Jove. Saturn reigned on Mt. Ida in Crete. Vesta was goddess of the hearth.
[10] Dye, color.   [11] A garment for neck and shoulders.
[12] A fine gauzy fabric.
[13] Seemly (because decorously covered).
[14] Customary dignity.   [15] Communing.
[16] Be motionless as a statue.   [17] Serious.

But first, and chiefest, with thee bring
Him that yon soars on golden wing,
Guiding the fiery-wheelèd throne,[18]
The cherub[19] Contemplatiön;
And the mute Silence hist[20] along,   55
'Less Philomel[21] will deign a song,
In her sweetest, saddest plight,
Smoothing the rugged brow of Night,
While Cynthia[22] checks her dragon yoke
Gently o'er the accustomed oak: 60
Sweet bird, that shunn'st the noise of folly,
Most musical, most melancholy!
Thee, chauntress, oft the woods among
I woo to hear thy evensong;
And missing thee, I walk unseen   65
On the dry, smooth-shaven green,
To behold the wandering moon,
Riding near her highest noon,
Like one that had beén led astray
Through the heaven's wide pathless way,   70
And oft, as if her head she bowed,
Stooping through a fleecy cloud.
Oft, on a plat of rising ground,
I hear the far-off curfew sound,
Over some wide-watered shore,   75
Swinging slow with sullen roar;
Or if the air will not permit,
Some still removèd place will fit,
Where glowing embers through the room
Teach light to counterfeit a gloom,   80
Far from all resort of mirth,
Save the cricket on the hearth,
Or the bellman's drowsy charm
To bless the doors from nightly harm.
Or let my lamp, at midnight hour,   85
Be seen in some high lonely tower,
Where I may oft outwatch the Bear,[23]
With thrice great Hermes,[24] or unsphere[25]
The spirit of Plato, to unfold
What worlds or what vast regions hold   90
The immortal mind that hath forsook
Her mansion in this fleshly nook;
And of those demons that are found
In fire, air, flood, or under ground,

Whose power hath a true consent[26]   95
With planet or with element.
Sometime let gorgeous Tragedy
In sceptered pall[27] come sweeping by,
Presenting Thebes, or Pelops' line,
Or the tale of Troy divine,[28]   100
Or what (though rare) of later age
Ennobled hath the buskined[29] stage.
But, O sad virgin, that thy power
Might raise Musaeus[30] from his bower;
Or bid the soul of Orpheus sing   105
Such notes as, warbled to the string,
Drew iron tears down Pluto's cheek,
And made hell grant what love did seek;[31]
Or call up him[32] that left half told
The story of Cambuscan bold,   110
Of Camball, and of Algarsife,
And who had Canacee to wife,
That owned the virtuous[33] ring and glass,
And of the wondrous horse of brass
On which the Tartar king did ride;   115
And if aught else great bards beside
In sage and solemn tunes have sung,
Of tourneys, and of trophies hung,
Of forests, and inchantments drear,
Where more is meant than meets the ear.   120
Thus, Night, oft see me in thy pale career,
Till civil-suited Morn[34] appear,
Not tricked[35] and frounced,[36] as she was wont
With the Attic boy to hunt,
But kerchiefed in a comely cloud,   125
While rocking winds are piping loud,
Or ushered with a shower still,
When the gust hath blown his fill,
Ending on the rustling leaves,
With minute-drops from off the eaves.   130
And when the sun begins to fling
His flaring beams, me, goddess, bring

---

[26] Agreement, correspondence. Each of these demons was supposed
to have special sympathy with, and powers corresponding to,
some element or planet.
[27] Robe.—*Sceptered* = royal, i.e., splendid.
[28] Themes of Greek tragedies. Oedipus, central figure of one of
the greatest plays ever written (*Oedipus the King,* by Sophocles),
was ruler of Thebes, and his children's fate is the subject of other
tragedies. Agamemnon (in Aeschylus's play so entitled) and his
children (heroes and heroines of many tragedies) were descendants of Pelops. Numerous plays were written about the figures
of the Trojan War, e.g., *The Trojan Women* of Euripides.
[29] See "L'Allegro," note 34.
[30] A semilegendary Greek poet.
[31] See "L'Allegro," note 40.
[32] Chaucer, who left "The Squire's Tale" unfinished.
[33] (Magically) powerful.
[34] Aurora dressed soberly, not in bright array as when she hunted
with Cephalus of Attica.   [35] Dressed in bright colors.
[36] With hair curled.

---

[18] Ezekiel 10.   [19] Not a child angel. The cherubim were the
second highest of the nine orders of angels.
[20] Summon quietly.   [21] The nightingale.
[22] Diana, the moon goddess, sometimes described as driving a team
of dragons.
[23] Stay up longer than the Great Bear or Big Dipper, i.e., till
dawn, since in the north that constellation never sets.
[24] Hermes Trismegistus, a legendary philosopher supposed to be
the author of a number of writings of the third and fourth
centuries.   [25] I.e., recall from its abode on high.

To archèd walks of twilight groves,
And shadows brown, that Sylvan[37] loves,
Of pine or monumental oak,   135
Where the rude ax with heavèd stroke
Was never heard the nymphs[38] to daunt,
Or fright them from their hallowed haunt.
There, in close covert, by some brook,
Where no profaner eye may look,   140
Hide me from day's garish eye,
While the bee with honeyed thigh,
That at her flowery work doth sing,
And the waters murmuring,
With such consort[39] as they keep,   145
Entice the dewy-feathered Sleep.
And let some strange, mysterious dream
Wave at[40] his wings, in airy stream
Of lively portraiture[41] displayed,
Softly on my eyelids laid.   150
And, as I wake, sweet music breathe
Above, about, or underneath,
Sent by some spirit to mortals good,
Or the unseen genius[42] of the wood.
But let my due feet never fail   155
To walk the studious cloister's pale,[43]
And love the high embowèd[44] roof,
With ántique pillars massy-proof,[45]
And storied windows richly dight,[46]
Casting a dim religious light.   160
There let the pealing organ blow,
To the full-voiced quire below,
In service high and anthems clear,
As may with sweetness, through mine ear,
Dissolve me into ecstasies,   165
And bring all heaven before mine eyes.
And may at last my weary age
Find out the peaceful hermitage,
The hairy gown[47] and mossy cell,
Where I may sit and rightly spell[48]   170
Of every star that heaven doth shew,
And every herb that sips the dew,
Till old experience do attain
To something like prophetic strain.

These pleasures, Melancholy, give,   175
And I with thee will choose to live.

---

37 Sylvanus, god of the woods.
38 Minor deities of nature.   39 Harmony.
40 I.e., flutter on.   41 I.e., with a series of vivid images.
42 Guardian spirit.
43 I.e., the enclosure of the cloister of some college or school which
    had a chapel attached to it.   44 Vaulted.
45 I.e., secure because so massive.
46 I.e., richly furnished with (stained glass) pictures of Biblical
    episodes.   47 I.e., coarsely woven, rough, shaggy.   48 Study.

LYCIDAS

THIS great elegy, the most perfect thing of its kind we
have, is not great because it is an inspired poem, but because consummate craftsmanship went into the making of
it. Artists often take delight in fashioning intricate beauties
within the form of what seems to the layman an overelaborate and artificial convention. In music the fugue is
an example; in poetry, the pastoral elegy, which has a
tradition reaching back at least as far as the third century
B.C. Like other poems in the memorial volume for Edward
King, "Lycidas" follows this long tradition, even in its
more warmly phrased digressions (the poet's own ambitions, lines 64–84; St. Peter's lament for the dead "shepherd," with its rebuke to the corrupt clergy, lines 108–131).
"Lycidas" was never intended to be a passionate outpouring
of personal emotion. King (1612–37) was Milton's fellow
student at Cambridge, but he may have been only an
acquaintance. Milton felt his loss as one feels the death of
any promising young man entering a profession where he
is needed.

The significant thing is not the conformity to a now
outmoded tradition but what Milton accomplished inside
its framework. To appreciate the degree of the achievement one need but compare Milton's poem with the companion pieces from other pens. Almost every line of
"Lycidas" is exquisitely molded. To the ear its music is
perfection; for full appreciation it must be read aloud.

*In this monody the author bewails a learned friend, unfortunately
drowned in his passage from Chester on the Irish seas, 1637.
And by occasion foretells the ruin of our corrupted clergy, then
in their height.*[1]

Yet once more, O ye laurels, and once more,
Ye myrtles brown, with ivy never sere,[2]
I come to pluck your berries harsh and crude,
And with forced fingers rude
Shatter your leaves before the mellowing year.   5
Bitter constraint and sad occasion dear
Compels me to disturb your season due;[3]
For Lycidas[4] is dead, dead ere his prime,
Young Lycidas, and hath not left his peer.
Who would not sing for Lycidas? he knew   10
Himself to sing, and build the lofty rime.
He must not float upon his watery bier
Unwept, and welter to the parching wind
Without the meed[5] of some melodious tear.

---

1 This note was first printed in 1645 during the first Civil War.
2 And ever-green ivy. Like laurel and myrtle, a symbol of poetic
  distinction.
3 I.e., my friend's death compels me to compose this poem in
  advance of the ripening of my poetic powers.
4 Milton borrows this name from the seventh idyl of Theocritus.
5 Tribute.

JOHN MILTON

This portrait by an unknown English painter of the
seventeenth century once belonged to Charles Lamb.
(New York Public Library)

CHRIST'S COLLEGE,

CAMBRIDGE

Here Milton was a student from 1625 to 1632. (Boston Public Library)

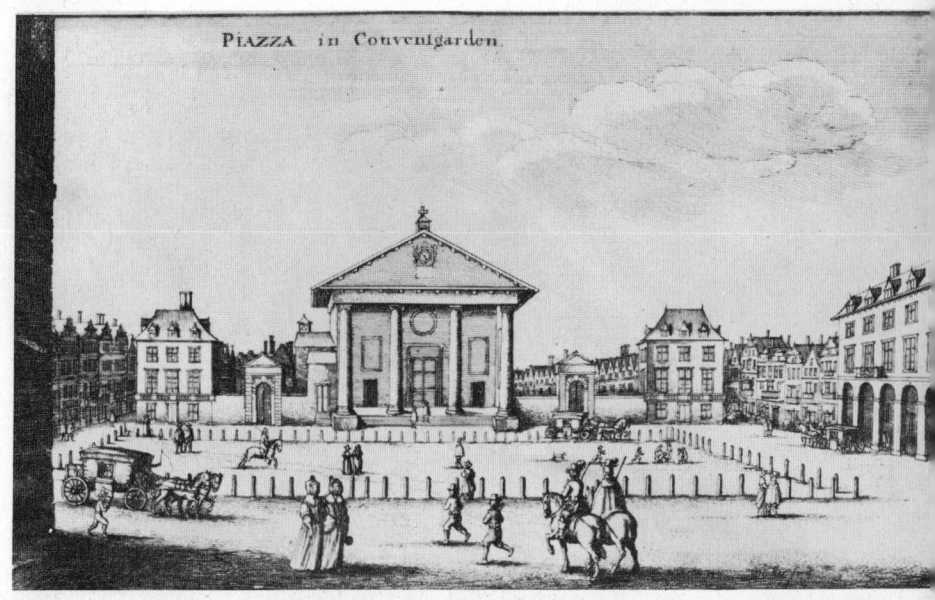

The GREAT FIRE of LONDON in the Year 1666.

From the Original Picture in the Possession of
Robert Golden Esq. Painted by Old Griffier at the time of the Fire. The Scene is the Original Ludgate taken at the instant of time when the Walls of the Goal
adjoining it fell, and exhibited to the View Old St. Pauls Church just taking fire, and Old Bow Church in the back ground.

Unlike most fire pictures, this one has an air of authenticity. The engraving is from a painting by a Dutch artist know
as Old Griffier who settled in England just about the time of the fire. St. Paul's in the background is the Gothic cathed⟨ral⟩
which had stood since the twelfth century. It was replaced by Sir Christopher Wren's classic cathedral (see sketch ⟨on⟩
back end paper). (Boston Public Library)

COVENT GARDEN

This early view is by the
German engraver Wences-
laus Hollar (1607-77).
(New York Public Li-
brary)

Covent Garden, constantly mentioned in the literature of London, is a square on th⟨e⟩
edge of the old part of the city. It was designed by Inigo Jones in 1630-31 and bui⟨lt⟩
in what was then open ground. The houses surrounding two sides were arcaded on th⟨e⟩
ground floor. In neighboring streets stood the house of Dryden, Will's coffee hous⟨e⟩
which he frequented, and Davies's bookshop, where Boswell first met Dr. Johnso⟨n⟩

Begin, then, sisters of the sacred well   15
That from beneath the seat of Jove[6] doth spring,
Begin, and somewhat loudly sweep the string.
Hence with denial vain, and coy excuse!
So may some gentle Muse[7]
With lucky[8] words favor my destined urn,   20
And as he passes turn,
And bid fair peace be to my sable shroud.
For we were nursed upon the selfsame hill,
Fed the same flock, by fountain,[9] shade, and rill.

    Together both, ere the high lawns[10] appeared   25
Under the opening eyelids of the Morn,
We drove afield, and both together heard
What time the gray-fly winds[11] her sultry horn,
Battening[12] our flocks with the fresh dews of night,
Oft till the star that rose, at evening, bright,   30
Toward heaven's descent had sloped his westering wheel.
Meanwhile the rural ditties were not mute:
Tempered[13] to the oaten flute,
Rough satyrs danced, and fauns[14] with cloven heel
From the glad sound would not be absent long,   35
And old Damoetas[15] loved to hear our song.

    But, oh, the heavy change, now thou art gone,
Now thou art gone, and never must return!
Thee, shepherd, thee the woods and desert caves,
With wild thyme and the gadding vine o'ergrown,   40
And all their echoes mourn.
The willows, and the hazel copses[16] green,
Shall now no more be seen
Fanning their joyous leaves to thy soft lays.
As killing as the canker[17] to the rose,   45
Or taint-worm to the weanling[18] herds that graze,
Or frost to flowers, that their gay wardrop[19] wear
When first the white-thorn blows:
Such, Lycidas, thy loss to shepherd's ear.

    Where were ye, nymphs, when the remorseless deep   50
Closed o'er the head of your loved Lycidas?
For neither were ye playing on the steep[20]
Where your old bards, the famous Druids, lie,

Nor on the shaggy top of Mona[21] high,
Nor yet where Deva[22] spreads her wizard stream.   55
Ay me, I fondly[23] dream!
Had ye been there—for what could that have done?
What could the Muse herself that Orpheus bore,[24]
The Muse herself, for her enchanting son,
Whom universal nature did lament,   60
When, by the rout that made the hideous roar,
His gory visage down the stream was sent,
Down the swift Hebrus to the Lesbian shore?[25]

    Alas! what boots[26] it with uncessant care
To tend the homely, slighted shepherd's trade,[27]   65
And strictly meditate the thankless Muse?
Were it not better done, as others use,[28]
To sport with Amaryllis[29] in the shade,
Or with the tangles of Neaera's hair?
Fame is the spur that the clear[30] spirit doth raise   70
(That last infirmity of noble mind[31])
To scorn delights, and live laborious days;
But the fair guerdon when we hope to find,
And think to burst out into sudden blaze,
Comes the blind Fury with the abhorrèd shears,[32]   75
And slits the thin-spun life. "But not the praise,"
Phoebus replied, and touched my trembling ears;[33]
"Fame is no plant that grows on mortal soil,
Nor in the glistering foil[34]
Set off to the world, nor in broad rumor[35] lies,   80
But lives and spreads aloft by those pure eyes
And perfect witness of all-judging Jove;[36]
As he pronounces lastly on each deed,
Of so much fame in heaven expect thy meed."

    O fountain Arethuse[37] and thou honored flood,   85
Smooth-sliding Mincius, crowned with vocal reeds,

---

6 Mt. Olympus. At its foot was the Pierian spring, associated with the Muses.   7 I.e., a Muse-inspired poet.
8 Happy, felicitous.   9 Spring.   10 Grassy uplands.
11 Blows; i.e., hums in the sultry heat of midday.
12 Fattening. These phrases in the idiom of pastoralism refer, of course, to undergraduate studies at Cambridge, and the experiments of the young poets.
13 Conforming.—The traditional instrument of the shepherds of pastoral poetry was the pipe made of oat straw or reeds.
14 Minor rural divinities: satyrs were part man, part horse; fauns part man, part goat.
15 Very likely some Cambridge tutor.
16 Coppices, thickets.   17 Cankerworm.
18 Just weaned, young.—The taint-worm was supposed to infect cattle.   19 Wardrobe.
20 Cliff.—The Druids were the priests of the ancient Britons.

21 The island of Anglesey, off the north coast of Wales.
22 The river Dee; its estuary separates Cheshire from North Wales. Its shifting fords were supposed to foretell future events.
23 Foolishly.   24 Calliope, the Muse of epic poetry.
25 According to the myth, Orpheus was torn to pieces by Thracian women because he would not join their Bacchic orgies. His head floated across the Aegean Sea to the island of Lesbos.
26 Profits.   27 I.e., to lead the life of the serious poet.
28 I.e., as other poets are accustomed to.
29 Like Neaera, a conventional name in pastoral poetry. I.e., to write love poetry.   30 Pure.
31 I.e., the last weakness a high-minded man is able to free himself from is the desire for fame.
32 Atropos, that one of the Fates who cut the thread of life. She was not a Fury.
33 Vergil (Eclogues, VI, 3–4) says that Phoebus Apollo, god of poetry, warned him against ambition by pulling his ear.
34 Glittering gold or silver leaf placed under a jewel to enhance its brilliance; hence, showy deceptiveness.
35 Worldly reputation.   36 I.e., God.
37 Near Syracuse in Sicily, home of Theocritus and Greek pastoral poetry.—Vergil (famous for pastoral as well as epic poetry) was born near Mantua in northern Italy, not far from where the river Mincius joins the Po. The reeds were vocal because they were used for shepherds' pipes.

That strain I heard was of a higher mood.
But now my oat[38] proceeds,
And listens to the Herald of the Sea[39]
That came in Neptune's plea.[40]   90
He asked the waves, and asked the felon winds,
"What hard mishap hath doomed this gentle swain?"
And questioned every guest of rugged wings
That blows from off each beakèd promontory.
They knew not of his story;   95
And sage Hippotades[41] their answer brings
That not a blast was from his dungeon strayed;
The air was calm, and on the level brine
Sleek Panope[42] with all her sisters played.
It was that fatal and perfidious bark,   100
Built in the eclipse, and rigged with curses dark,
That sunk so low that sacred head of thine.
    Next, Camus,[43] reverend sire, went footing slow,
His mantle hairy, and his bonnet sedge,
Inwrought with figures dim, and on the edge   105
Like to that sanguine flower inscribed with woe.[44]
"Ah! who hath reft," quoth he, "my dearest pledge?"[45]
Last came, and last did go,
The Pilot of the Galilean Lake;[46]
Two massy keys he bore of metals twain   110
(The golden opes, the iron shuts amain[47]).
He shook his mitered[48] locks, and stern bespake:
"How well could I have spared for thee, young swain,
Enow[49] of such as, for their bellies' sake,
Creep, and intrude, and climb into the fold![50]   115
Of other care they little reckoning make
Than how to scramble at the shearers' feast,
And shove away the worthy bidden guest.
Blind mouths![51] that scarce themselves know how to hold
A sheep-hook,[52] or have learned aught else the least   120
That to the faithful herdman's art belongs!
What recks it them? What need they? They are sped;[53]
And when they list, their lean and flashy songs[54]

Grate on their scrannel[55] pipes of wretched straw.
The hungry sheep look up, and are not fed,   125
But, swol'n with wind and the rank mist they draw,
Rot inwardly, and foul contagion spread;
Besides what the grim wolf[56] with privy[57] paw
Daily devours apace, and nothing said.
But that two-handed engine[58] at the door   130
Stands ready to smite once, and smite no more."
    Return, Alphéus![59] the dread voice is past
That shrunk thy streams. Return, Sicilian Muse![60]
And call the vales, and bid them hither cast
Their bells and flow'rets of a thousand hues.   135
Ye valleys low, where the mild whispers use[61]
Of shades and wanton winds and gushing brooks,
On whose fresh lap the swart star[62] sparely looks,
Throw hither all your quaint enameled eyes,
That on the green turf suck the honeyed showers,   140
And purple all the ground with vernal flowers.
Bring the rathe[63] primrose that forsaken dies,[64]
The tufted crow-toe,[65] and pale jessamine,
The white pink, and the pansy freaked[66] with jet,
The glowing violet,   145
The musk rose, and the well-attired woodbine,
With cowslips wan that hang the pensive head,
And every flower that sad embroidery wears.
Bid amarantus[67] all his beauty shed,
And daffadillies fill their cups with tears,   150
To strew the laureate hearse[68] where Lycid lies.
For, so to interpose a little ease,
Let our frail thoughts dally with false surmise.[69]
Ay me! Whilst thee the shores and sounding seas
Wash far away, where'er thy bones are hurled,   155
Whether beyond the stormy Hebrides,[70]
Where thou perhaps under the whelming tide
Visit'st the bottom of the monstrous world,[71]
Or whether thou, to our moist vows[72] denied,

---

38 See note 13, above.
39 A sea demigod, with a conch-shell trumpet.
40 To defend the god of the sea against the charge of responsibility for King's death.   41 Aeolus, god of the winds.
42 One of the sea nymphs.
43 The god of the Cam, the river of Cambridge.
44 When the youth Hyacinthus was accidentally killed at discus throwing, Apollo caused a flower to spring from his blood. Its petals were inscribed with the Greek exclamation of grief, *ai, ai.*
45 Child, i.e., of the university.
46 St. Peter, who keeps the gate of heaven.
47 I.e., firmly.
48 As the original Bishop of Rome, he wears the high head-covering known as the miter.   49 Enough; i.e., plenty.
50 I.e., the corrupt non-Puritan ministers of the Church of England.
51 I.e., ignorant and corrupt ones.
52 Shepherd's crook; i.e., their pastoral duties.
53 They are prosperous; i.e., they have their "livings."
54 I.e., meager and insipid sermons.

55 Scrawny; i.e., harsh.   56 The Roman Catholic Church.
57 Secret. I.e., the negligence of the Anglican clergy is responsible for numerous secret conversions to Catholicism.
58 I.e., a great sword. Probably with reference to the capture of the government by the Puritans, who can now employ the civil power (the sword of justice) against reactionaries in the Church. *Two-handed* = big.
59 A Greek river-god whose pursuit of the nymph Arethusa resulted in her metamorphosis into a fountain (see note 37, above). He was associated with pastoral poetry.
60 I.e., the Muse that inspired the Sicilian Greek, Theocritus.
61 Are usual.
62 Sirius, the Dog Star, supposed to burn vegetation dark in the late summer's heat.   63 Early.
64 I.e., droops in the sun's absence.
65 The wild hyacinth, not our crowfoot or buttercup.
66 Spotted.   67 Amaranth.   68 Coffin.
69 I.e., I have been playing with the false notion that the body might be here, for burial.
70 Or Western Isles, off Scotland.   71 World of monsters.
72 Tearful rites.

Sleep'st by the fable of Bellerus old,[73]   160
Where the great vision of the guarded mount[74]
Looks toward Namancos,[75] and Bayona's hold.
Look homeward, angel,[76] now, and melt with ruth.
And, O ye dolphins,[77] waft the hapless youth.

Weep no more, woeful shepherds, weep no more,   165
For Lycidas, your sorrow, is not dead,
Sunk though he be beneath the watery floor.
So sinks the daystar[78] in the ocean bed,
And yet anon repairs his drooping head,
And tricks[79] his beams, and with new-spangled ore[80]   170
Flames in the forehead of the morning sky:
So Lycidas sunk low, but mounted high,
Through the dear might of Him that walked the waves;[81]
Where, other groves and other streams along,
With nectar pure his oozy locks he laves,   175
And hears the unexpressive[82] nuptial song,[83]
In the blest kingdoms meek of joy and love.
There entertain[84] him all the saints above,
In solemn troops, and sweet societies
That sing, and singing in their glory move,   180
And wipe the tears for ever from his eyes.
Now, Lycidas, the shepherds weep no more;
Henceforth thou art the genius[85] of the shore,
In thy large recompense, and shalt be good
To all that wander in that perilous flood.   185

Thus sang the uncouth swain[86] to the oaks and rills,
While the still morn went out with sandals gray;
He touched the tender stops of various quills,[87]
With eager thought warbling his Doric lay.[88]
And now the sun had stretched out all the hills,   190
And now was dropped into the western bay;
At last he rose, and twitched[89] his mantle blue:
Tomorrow to fresh woods, and pastures new.

---

[73] I.e., the fabulous Bellerus, for whom Bellerium, as the Romans
called Land's End (the southwestern tip of England), was supposed to be named.
[74] Mount St. Michael, a 200-foot island rock in Mount's Bay, near
Land's End. The archangel was supposed to be visible sometimes
on its summit.
[75] Nemancos is in the Spanish province of Galicia east of Cape
Finisterre; Bayona is south of the Cape. A naval expedition
against England would leave the coast of Spain in this vicinity.
—*Hold* = stronghold.
[76] St. Michael.
[77] Who, according to legend, bore the Greek poet and musician
Arion to safety.   [78] The sun.   [79] Makes splendid.
[80] Gold fresh and glittering from its bath in the sea.
[81] Matthew 14: 25–33.   [82] Inexpressibly beautiful.
[83] At the "marriage of the Lamb" (Revelation 19: 6,7).
[84] Receive.   [85] Local divinity.
[86] Unpolished countryman, i.e., Milton.   [87] Reed pipes.
[88] Pastoral song (since Theocritus and the other Sicilian pastoralists
wrote in the Doric dialect of Greek).   [89] Pulled closer.

HOW SOON HATH TIME

"In his hand," says Wordsworth of Milton's use of the
sonnet form, "the thing became a trumpet." In the elevation of its style, adoption of the Italian instead of the English
or Shakespearean form (see p. 247, above), and abandon-
ment of romantic love as the subject matter, the Miltonic
sonnet has had a profound influence on nineteenth- and
twentieth-century poetry.

How soon hath Time, the subtle thief of youth,
Stolen on his wing my three-and-twentieth year!
My hasting days fly on with full career,[1]
But my late spring no bud or blossom shew'th.
Perhaps my semblance[2] might deceive the truth   5
That I to manhood am arrived so near;
And inward ripeness doth much less appear,
That some more timely-happy[3] spirits endu'th.[4]
Yet be it less or more, or soon or slow,
It shall be still in strictest measure even   10
To[5] that same lot, however mean or high,
Toward which Time leads me, and the will of Heaven;
All is, if I have grace to use it so,
As ever in my great Taskmaster's eye.[6]

TO THE LORD GENERAL CROMWELL,
MAY, 1652 (Presbyterians tried to establish a church state)

*On the proposals of certain ministers at the committee for prop-
agation of the gospel*[7]

Cromwell, our chief of men, who through a cloud
Not of war only, but detractions rude,
Guided by faith and matchless fortitude,
To peace and truth thy glorious way hast plowed,
And on the neck of crownèd Fortune proud   5
Hast reared God's trophies, and his work pursued,

---

[1] *Fast.*—Since early in the eighteenth century, this sonnet has usually been entitled "On His Having Arrived at the Age of Twenty-
three." There is much dispute over the meaning of the final lines,
the obscurity of which is due to Milton's imperfect mastery of
the sonnet form at this early stage of his career.
[2] I.e., boyish appearance.   [3] Early fortunate.
[4] Endows. Milton has in mind those of his contemporaries to
whom life has (thus far) given a greater chance for distinction
than he has had.
[5] Exactly corresponding to. *It* (lines 9 f.) means "what is coming
to me," "my chance to show what I can do."
[6] I.e., everything exists in the mind of God, and therefore my
great chance is already in existence there. Accordingly, my task
is (with the help of God's grace) to make use of the opportunity
when it comes.
[7] The entire title appears, crossed out, in a manuscript at Trinity
College, Cambridge, in the hand of one of Milton's amanuenses.
The poem was not printed till 1694. When the sonnet was
written, Cromwell was not yet Lord Protector. The clergymen
mentioned had proposed the establishment of a new state
Church, a threat to freedom which Milton here opposes.

While Darwen[8] stream, with blood of Scots imbrued,
And Dunbar[9] field, resounds thy praises loud,
And Worcester's[10] laureate wreath. Yet much remains
To conquer still; peace hath her victories   10
No less renowned than war: new foes arise,
Threatening to bind our souls with secular chains.
Help us to save free conscience from the paw
Of hireling wolves whose gospel is their maw.

ON HIS BLINDNESS[11]

When I consider how my light is spent,
Ere half my days, in this dark world and wide,
And that one talent which is death to hide[12]
Lodged with me useless, though my soul more bent
To serve therewith my Maker, and present   5
My true account, lest he returning chide,
"Doth God exact day labor, light denied?"
I fondly[13] ask; but Patience, to prevent
That murmur, soon replies: "God doth not need
Either man's work or his own gifts; who best   10
Bear his mild yoke, they serve him best. His state
Is kingly: thousands[14] at his bidding speed
And post o'er land and ocean without rest.
They also serve who only stand and wait."

TO CYRIACK SKINNER[15]

Cyriack, this three years' day these eyes, though clear,
To outward view, of blemish or of spot,
Bereft of light their seeing have forgot.
Nor to their idle orbs doth sight appear
Of sun, or moon, or star, throughout the year,   5
Of man, or woman. Yet I argue not
Against heaven's hand or will, nor bate a jot
Of heart or hope; but still bear up and steer
Right onward. What supports me, dost thou ask?
The conscience,[16] friend, to have lost them overplied   10

In liberty's defense, my noble task,
Of which all Europe talks from side to side.
This thought might lead me through the world's vain
     mask,
Content, though blind, had I no better guide.

ON THE LATE MASSACRE IN PIEMONT[17]

Avenge, O Lord, thy slaughtered saints, whose bones
Lie scattered on the Alpine mountains cold;
Even them who kept thy truth so pure of old
When all our fathers worshipped stocks and stones,
Forget not: in thy book record their groans   5
Who were thy sheep and in their ancient fold
Slain by the bloody Piemontese, that rolled
Mother with infant down the rocks. Their moans
The vales redoubled to the hills, and they
To heaven. Their martyred blood and ashes sow[18]   10
O'er all the Italian fields where still doth sway
The triple tyrant;[19] that from these may grow
A hundredfold, who, having learnt thy way,
Early may fly the Babylonian woe.[20]

ON HIS DECEASED WIFE

Methought I saw my late espousèd saint[21]
Brought to me like Alcestis[22] from the grave,
Whom Jove's great son to her glad husband gave,
Rescued from death by force though pale and faint.
Mine, as whom washed from spot of childbed taint   5
Purification in the old law[23] did save,
And such as yet once more I trust to have
Full sight of her in heaven without restraint,
Came vested all in white, pure as her mind.
Her face was veiled,[24] yet to my fancied sight   10
Love, sweetness, goodness in her person shined
So clear as in no face with more delight.
But oh, as to embrace me she inclined,
I waked, she fled, and day brought back my night.

---

8 In Yorkshire, where, in the second Civil War, Cromwell
   defeated an army of Scottish royalists at Preston on August 18,
   1648.
9 In southeastern Scotland. Cromwell cut an army to pieces there
   on Sept. 3, 1650.
10 Where, on Sept. 3, 1651, Cromwell won the final victory of the
   Civil Wars, against an invading army of Scots under the future
   Charles II.
11 This sonnet, possibly Milton's best poem, was first printed in
   1673. The title is not Milton's, but its brevity and its use since
   the middle of the eighteenth century dictate its retention. It is
   likely that he wrote the poem in 1652, when he became totally
   blind.
12 See the parable of the talents, Matthew 25:14-30.
13 Foolishly.   14 The angels.
15 A former pupil and close friend of Milton's.
16 Consciousness.

17 Piedmont. April 25, 1655, saw a massacre of the Waldenses, a
   sect of western Alpine Franco-Italian mountaineers which had
   broken away from the Roman Catholic Church in the twelfth
   century. As Latin secretary, Milton handled Cromwell's protest
   to the Duke of Savoy, who in the following summer granted the
   survivors freedom of worship.
18 The metaphor, from the parable of the sower (Matthew 13:23),
   is completed in lines 12 f.
19 The Pope, because of his triple tiara.
20 To the Roman Catholic Church the Puritans, like Petrarch,
   applied the depiction of Babylon in Revelation 17-18.
21 His second wife, Katherine Woodcock.
22 Alcestis offered her life to save that of her husband, Admetus,
   king of Thessaly, but was rescued from death by Hercules, the
   son of Jupiter, and restored to her husband.
23 See Leviticus 12.
24 Milton was already blind when he married her.

AREOPAGITICA

[see also sonnet to Cromwell p563, Cromwell (p563,

THIS is one of the great historic blasts for freedom. Though entitled a speech, it was written to be read. Milton called it *Areopagitica* by analogy with the *Areopagitic Speech* (likewise composed for reading) of the Greek rhetorician Isocrates (fourth century B.C.), a call for a revival of the power and prestige of the high court of Athens, the Areopagus. All Milton's prose is concerned with liberty—intellectual, political, religious, or domestic—and his disappointment was great when he realized that the Puritans were no more disposed to bring freedom to pass than the King and the Anglican Church had been.

In June, 1643, the Puritans had put through a Parliamentary statute requiring the licensing of books by a government censor in advance of publication. For about three years the press had been free, and discussion of public questions in controversial pamphlets had been lively. This Milton considered a healthy state of affairs, but the reversion to the old censorship showed that the Presbyterians intended to force their views on Church and state by suppressing the free press. In *Areopagitica,* which appeared in November, 1644, without having been submitted to the censor, Milton sought to persuade Parliament to repeal its action of the previous year. The tract embraces an historical review of censorship as the servant of tyranny, a defense of freedom in the use of books, an argument against trying to make men virtuous by legislation, and a plea for complete liberty in the pursuit of truth, of whose final victory over error Milton was confident. He failed in his immediate object, and England had to wait for unlicensed printing till 1696; but to this powerful document in the history of freedom its advocates in many lands and generations have repeatedly returned for ammunition.

from AREOPAGITICA

A Speech of MR. JOHN MILTON *for the* LIBERTY OF UNLICENSED PRINTING, *to the Parliament of England*

. . . I deny not but that it is of greatest concernment, in the Church and Commonwealth, to have a vigilant eye how books demean themselves, as well as men; and thereafter to confine, imprison, and do sharpest justice on them as malefactors. For books are not absolutely dead things, but do contain a potency of life in them to be as active as that soul was whose progeny they are; nay, they do preserve as in a vial the purest efficacy and extraction of that living intellect that bred them. I know they are as lively and as vigorously productive as those fabulous dragon's teeth, and being sown up and down may chance to spring up armed men.[1] And yet on the other hand, unless wariness be used, as good almost kill a man as kill a good book; who kills a man kills a reasonable creature, God's image; but he who destroys a good book kills reason itself, kills the image of God, as it were in the eye. Many a man lives a burden to the earth; but a good book is the precious lifeblood of a master spirit, imbalmed and treasured up on purpose to a life beyond life. 'Tis true, no age can restore a life, whereof perhaps there is no great loss; and revolutions of ages do not oft recover the loss of a rejected truth, for the want of which whole nations fare the worse. We should be wary therefore what persecution we raise against the living labors of public men, how we spill that seasoned life of man preserved and stored up in books; since we see a kind of homicide may be thus committed, sometimes a martyrdom, and if it extend to the whole impression,[2] a kind of massacre, whereof the execution ends not in the slaying of an elemental life, but strikes at that ethereal and fifth essence,[3] the breath of reason itself—slays an immortality rather than a life. . . .

Dionysius Alexandrinus was about the year 240 a person of great name in the Church for piety and learning, who had wont to avail himself much against heretics by being conversant in their books, until a certain presbyter[4] laid it scrupulously to his

---

[1] Cadmus, the mythical founder of Thebes (in Greece), sowed dragon's teeth from which warriors sprang up. A similar myth was told of Jason, who won the Golden Fleece.

[2] The entire number of copies printed at the same time.

[3] Life being also dependent on the four "elements": earth, air, fire, water.

[4] Elder of the early Christian Church.—Milton found this account in Eusebius, the fourth-century historian of the Church. Dionysius was Bishop of Alexandria.

conscience how he durst venture himself among those defiling volumes. The worthy man, loath to give offense,[5] fell into a new debate with himself what was to be thought; when suddenly a vision sent from God (it is his own epistle that so avers it) confirmed him in these words: "Read any books whatever come to thy hands, for thou art sufficient both to judge aright and to examine each matter." To this revelation he assented the sooner, as he confesses, because it was answerable to that of the Apostle to the Thessalonians: "Prove all things; hold fast that which is good."[6] And he might have added another remarkable saying of the same author: "To the pure all things are pure,"[7] not only meats and drinks, but all kind of knowledge whether of good or evil; the knowledge cannot defile, nor consequently the books, if the will and conscience be not defiled.

For books are as meats and viands are, some of good, some of evil, substance; and yet God in that unapocryphal[8] vision said without exception, "Rise, Peter; kill and eat," leaving the choice to each man's discretion. Wholesome meats to a vitiated stomach differ little or nothing from unwholesome; and best books to a naughty[9] mind are not unappliable to occasions of evil. Bad meats will scarce breed good nourishment in the healthiest concoction;[10] but herein the difference is of bad books: that they to a discreet and judicious reader serve in many respects to discover, to confute, to forewarn, and to illustrate. Whereof what better witness can ye expect I should produce than one of your own now sitting in Parliament, the chief of learned men reputed in this land, Mr. Selden,[11] whose volume of natural and national laws proves, not only by great authorities brought together, but by exquisite reasons and theorems almost mathematically demonstrative, that all opinions, yea, errors, known, read, and collated, are of main service and assistance toward the speedy attainment of what is truest? I conceive, therefore, that when God did enlarge the universal diet of man's body, saving ever[12] the rules of temperance, he then also, as before, left arbitrary the dieting and repasting of our minds, as wherein every mature man might have to exercise his own leading capacity.[13] How

great a virtue is temperance, how much of moment through the whole life of man! Yet God commits the managing so great a trust, without particular law or prescription, wholly to the demeanor[14] of every grown man. And therefore, when he himself tabled the Jews from heaven, that omer[15] which was every man's daily portion of manna is computed to have been more than might have well sufficed the heartiest feeder thrice as many meals. For those actions which enter into a man rather than issue out of him, and therefore defile not,[16] God uses not[17] to captivate under a perpetual childhood of prescription, but trusts him with the gift of reason to be his own chooser; there were but little work left for preaching if law and compulsion should grow so fast upon those things which heretofore were governed only by exhortation.

Solomon informs us that much reading is a weariness to the flesh;[18] but neither he nor other inspired author tells us that such or such reading is unlawful: yet certainly had God thought good to limit us herein, it had been much more expedient to have told us what was unlawful than what was wearisome. As for the burning of those Ephesian books by St. Paul's converts,[19] 'tis replied the books were magic; the Syriac[20] so renders them. It was a private act, a voluntary act, and leaves us to a voluntary imitation; the men in remorse burnt those books which were their own; the magistrate by this example is not appointed: these men practiced the books; another might perhaps have read them in some sort usefully. Good and evil we know in the field of this world grow up together almost inseparably; and the knowledge of good is so involved and interwoven with the knowledge of evil, and in so many cunning resemblances hardly to be discerned, that those confused seeds which were imposed on Psyche[21] as an incessant labor to cull out, and sort asunder, were not more intermixed. It was from out the rind of one apple tasted, that the knowledge of good and evil as two twins cleaving together leaped forth into the world. And perhaps this is that doom which

---

[5] Cause (by a bad example) others to sin.
[6] Paul, 1 Thessalonians 5:21.   [7] Titus 1:15.
[8] Canonically part of the Bible. See Acts 10:9–16.
[9] Wicked.   [10] Digestion.
[11] John Selden (1584–1654), the great scholar and legal authority. The author of many learned works (Milton refers to his *De Jure Naturali et Gentium*), he is now best known for his *Table Talk*.
[12] Always excepting.
[13] Principal faculty, i.e., judgment.

[14] Management.   [15] See Exodus 16:11–36.
[16] "Whatsoever entereth in at the mouth goeth into the belly, and is cast out. . . . But those things which proceed out of the mouth come forth from the heart; and they defile the man. For out of the heart proceed evil thoughts," etc. (Matthew 15:17–19.)
[17] Is not accustomed.   [18] Ecclesiastes 12:12.
[19] Acts 19:19.   [20] The dialect of a version.
[21] With whom Cupid fell in love. His mother, the jealous Venus, imposed the task. According to *The Golden Ass* of Apuleius, Books IV–VI, the ants came to Psyche's aid.

Adam fell into of knowing good and evil, that is to say of knowing good by evil.

As therefore the state of man now is, what wisdom can there be to choose, what continence to forbear, without the knowledge of evil? He that can apprehend and consider vice with all her baits and seeming pleasures, and yet abstain, and yet distinguish, and yet prefer that which is truly better, he is the true warfaring Christian. I cannot praise a fugitive and cloistered virtue, unexercised and unbreathed, that never sallies out and sees her adversary, but slinks out of the race where that immortal garland is to be run for, not without dust and heat. Assuredly we bring not innocence into the world, we bring impurity much rather: that which purifies us is trial, and trial is by what is contrary. That virtue therefore which is but a youngling in the contemplation of evil, and knows not the utmost that vice promises to her followers and rejects it, is but a blank virtue, not a pure; her whiteness is but an excremental[22] whiteness. Which was the reason why our sage and serious poet Spenser, whom I dare be known to think a better teacher than Scotus or Aquinas,[23] describing true temperance under the person of Guyon, brings him in with his palmer through the cave of Mammon, and the bower of earthly bliss, that he might see and know, and yet abstain.[24]

Since, therefore, the knowledge and survey of vice is in this world so necessary to the constituting of human virtue, and the scanning of error to the confirmation of truth, how can we more safely, and with less danger, scout into the regions of sin and falsity than by reading all manner of tractates and hearing all manner of reason? And this is the benefit which may be had of books promiscuously read. . . .

Seeing, therefore, that those books, and those in great abundance which are likeliest to taint both life and doctrine, cannot be suppressed without the fall of learning and of all ability in disputation, and that these books of either sort are most and soonest catching to the learned, from whom to the common people whatever is heretical or dissolute may quickly be conveyed; and that evil manners are as perfectly learned without books a thousand other ways which cannot be stopped, and evil doctrine not with books can propagate, except a teacher guide, which he might also do without writing, and so beyond pro-

hibiting: I am not able to unfold how this cautelous[25] enterprise of licensing can be exempted from the number of vain and impossible attempts. And he who were pleasantly disposed[26] could not well avoid to liken it to the exploit of that gallant man who thought to pound up the crows by shutting his park gate. . . .

If we think to regulate printing, thereby to rectify manners, we must regulate all recreations and pastimes, all that is delightful to man. No music must be heard, no song be set or sung, but what is grave and Doric.[27] There must be licensing dancers, that no gesture, motion, or deportment be taught our youth but what by their allowance shall be thought honest;[28] for such Plato was provided of.[29] It will ask more than the work of twenty licensers to examine all the lutes, the violins, and the guitars in every house; they must not be suffered to prattle as they do, but must be licensed what they may say. And who shall silence all the airs and madrigals, that whisper softness in chambers? The windows also and the balconies must be thought on. There are shrewd[30] books with dangerous frontispieces set to sale; who shall prohibit them? shall twenty licensers? The villages also must have their visitors[31] to inquire what lectures the bagpipe and the rebec[32] reads, even to the ballatry[33] and the gamut[34] of every municipal fiddler, for these are the countryman's *Arcadias,* and his Montemayors.[35] Next, what more national corruption, for which England hears ill[36] abroad, than household gluttony? Who shall be the rectors of our daily rioting? And what shall be done to inhibit the multitudes that frequent those houses where drunkenness is sold and harbored? Our garments also should be referred to the licensing of some more sober workmasters to see them cut into a less wanton garb. Who shall regulate all the mixed conversation of our youth, male and female together, as is the fashion of this country? who shall still appoint what shall be discoursed, what presumed, and no furder? Lastly, who shall forbid and separate all idle resort, all evil company? These things will be, and must be; but how they shall be least hurtful, how least enticing, herein consists the grave and governing wisdom of a state.

---

22 Superficial.
23 Duns Scotus (d. 1308), a Scot who taught at Oxford and Paris, and St. Thomas Aquinas (d. 1274?), an Italian who lectured at Paris, Rome, and Bologna, were famous scholastic theologians.
24 *Faery Queen,* Book II, Cantos 7, 12.

25 Deceitful.
26 Inclined to joke.   27 Austere.   28 Chaste.
29 I.e., prescribed.   30 Mischievous.
31 Visiting inquisitors.   32 See "L'Allegro," note 23, above.
33 Ballads.   34 Full range.
35 I.e., rustic substitutes for romances like Sidney's *Arcadia* or the Spanish *Diana* of the Portuguese Jorge de Montemayor (d. 1561), which started the vogue of pastoral romance.
36 Is ill reputed.

To sequester out of the world into Atlantic and Utopian polities,[37] which never can be drawn into use, will not mend our condition, but to ordain wisely as in this world of evil, in the midst whereof God hath placed us unavoidably. Nor is it Plato's licensing of books will do this, which necessarily pulls along with it so many other kinds of licensing as will make us all both ridiculous and weary, and yet frustrate, but those unwritten, or at least unconstraining laws of virtuous education, religious and civil nurture, which Plato there[38] mentions as the bonds and ligaments of the commonwealth, the pillars and the sustainers of every written statute; these they be which will bear chief sway in such matters as these, when all licensing will be easily eluded. Impunity and remissness for certain are the bane of a commonwealth; but here the great art lies to discern in what the law is to bid restraint and punishment, and in what things persuasion only is to work. If every action which is good or evil in man at ripe years were to be under pittance[39] and prescription and compulsion, what were virtue but a name? what praise could be then due to well-doing? what gramercy[40] to be sober, just, or continent? Many there be that complain of divine Providence for suffering Adam to transgress: foolish tongues! When God gave him reason, he gave him freedom to choose, for reason is but choosing; he had been else a mere artificial Adam, such an Adam as he is in the motions.[41] We ourselves esteem not of that obedience, or love, or gift, which is of force; God therefore left him free, set before him a provoking object, ever almost in his eyes; herein consisted his merit, herein the right of his reward, the praise of his abstinence. Wherefore did he create passions within us, pleasures round about us, but that these rightly tempered are the very ingredients of virtue? They are not skillful considerers of human things who imagine to remove sin by removing the matter of sin; for, besides that it is a huge heap increasing under the very act of diminishing, though some part of it may for a time be withdrawn from some persons, it cannot from all in such a universal thing as books are; and when this is done, yet the sin remains entire. Though ye take from a covetous man all his treasure, he has yet one jewel left: ye cannot bereave him of his covetousness. Banish all objects of lust, shut up all youth into the severest discipline that can be exercised in any

hermitage; ye cannot make them chaste that came not thither so: such great care and wisdom is required to the right managing of this point. Suppose we could expel sin by this means; look how much we thus expel of sin, so much we expel of virtue, for the matter of them both is the same; remove that, and ye remove them both alike.

This justifies the high providence of God, who though he commands us temperance, justice, continence, yet pours out before us even to a profuseness all desirable things, and gives us minds that can wander beyond all limit and satiety. Why should we then affect a rigor contrary to the manner of God and of nature, by abridging or scanting those means, which books freely permitted are, both to the trial of virtue and the exercise of truth? It would be better done to learn that the law must needs be frivolous which goes to restrain things uncertainly and yet equally working to good and to evil. And were I the chooser, a dram of welldoing should be preferred before many times as much the forcible hindrance of evildoing. For God sure esteems the growth and completing of one virtuous person more than the restraint of ten vicious. And albeit whatever thing we hear or see, sitting, walking, traveling, or conversing, may be fitly called our book, and is of the same effect that writings are, yet, grant the thing to be prohibited were only books, it appears that this order hitherto is far insufficient to the end which it intends. . . .

I lastly proceed from the no good it can do, to the manifest hurt it causes in being, first, the greatest discouragement and affront that can be offered to learning and to learned men. It was the complaint and lamentation of prelates, upon every least breath of a motion to remove pluralities[42] and distribute more equally Church revenues, that then all learning would be forever dashed and discouraged. But as for that opinion, I never found cause to think that the tenth part of learning stood or fell with the clergy; nor could I ever but hold it for a sordid and unworthy speech of any churchman who had a competency left him. If, therefore, ye be loath to dishearten utterly and discontent, not the mercenary crew of false pretenders to learning, but the free and ingenuous sort of such as evidently were born to study, and love learning for itself, not for lucre or any other end but the service of God and of truth and perhaps that lasting fame and perpetuity of praise which God and good men have consented shall be

---

[37] Governmental systems, like Bacon's New Atlantis or More's Utopia.
[38] There are statements more or less to this effect in Plato's Republic and Laws.   [39] Rationing.   [40] Merit.
[41] Puppet shows.

[42] The practice of one minister's holding more than one appointment in the Church.

the reward of those whose published labors advance the good of mankind, then know that so far to distrust the judgment and the honesty of one who hath but a common repute in learning, and never yet offended, as not to count him fit to print his mind without a tutor and examiner, lest he should drop a schism or something of corruption, is the greatest displeasure and indignity to a free and knowing spirit that can be put upon him.

What advantage is it to be a man over it is to be a boy at school, if we have only scaped the ferular,[43] to come under the fescu[44] of an imprimatur,[45] if serious and elaborate writings, as if they were no more than the theme of a grammar lad under his pedagogue, must not be uttered[46] without the cursory eyes of a temporizing and extemporizing licenser? He who is not trusted with his own actions, his drift not being known to be evil, and standing to the hazard of law and penalty, has no great argument to think himself reputed in the commonwealth wherein he was born for other than a fool or a foreigner. When a man writes to the world, he summons up all his reason and deliberation to assist him; he searches, meditates, is industrious, and likely consults and confers with his judicious friends; after all which done, he takes himself to be informed in what he writes, as well as any that writ before him; if in this the most consummate act of his fidelity and ripeness, no years, no industry, no former proof of his abilities can bring him to that state of maturity as not to be still mistrusted and suspected, unless he carry all his considerate diligence, all his midnight watchings and expense of Palladian[47] oil, to the hasty view of an unleisured licenser, perhaps much his younger, perhaps far his inferior in judgment, perhaps one who never knew the labor of book-writing, and, if he be not repulsed or slighted, must appear in print like a puny[48] with his guardian, and his censor's hand[49] on the back of his title to be his bail and surety that he is no idiot or seducer, it cannot be but a dishonor and derogation to the author, to the book, to the privilege and dignity of learning.

And what if the author shall be one so copious of fancy as to have many things well worth the adding come into his mind after licensing, while the book is yet under the press, which not seldom happens to the best and diligentest writers, and that perhaps a dozen times in one book? The printer dares not go beyond his licensed copy; so often then must the author trudge to his leave-giver, that those his new insertions may be viewed; and many a jaunt will be made ere that licenser, for it must be the same man, can either be found or found at leisure; meanwhile either the press must stand still, which is no small damage, or the author lose his accuratest thoughts and send the book forth worse than he had made it, which to a diligent writer is the greatest melancholy and vexation that can befall.

And how can a man teach with authority, which is the life of teaching, how can he be a doctor in his book, as he ought to be or else had better be silent, whenas all he teaches, all he delivers, is but under the tuition, under the correction, of his patriarchal licenser to blot or alter what precisely accords not with the hidebound humor[50] which he calls his judgment? When every acute reader, upon the first sight of a pedantic license, will be ready with these like words to ding the book a coit's[51] distance from him: "I hate a pupil teacher, I endure not an instructor that comes to me under the wardship of an overseeing fist.[52] I know nothing of the licenser, but that I have his own hand here for his arrogance; who shall warrant me his judgment?" "The state, sir," replies the stationer,[53] but has a quick return: "The state shall be my governors, but not my critics; they may be mistaken in the choice of a licenser as easily as this licenser may be mistaken in an author: this is some common stuff"; and he might add from Sir Francis Bacon, that "such authorized books are but the language of the times." For though a licenser should happen to be judicious more than ordinary, which will be a great jeopardy of the next succession,[54] yet his very office and his commission enjoins him to let pass nothing but what is vulgarly[55] received already. . . .

And as it is a particular disesteem of every knowing person alive, and most injurious to the written labors and monuments of the dead, so to me it seems an undervaluing and vilifying of the whole nation. I cannot set so light by all the invention, the art, the wit, the grave and solid judgment, which is in England, as that it can be comprehended in any twenty capacities how good soever, much less that it should not pass except their superintendence be over it, except it be sifted and strained with their strainers, that it should be uncurrent without their manual stamp. Truth and understanding are not such wares

---

[43] Rod. [44] Teacher's pointer. [45] License to publish.
[46] Circulated.
[47] Pertaining to Pallas or Minerva, the goddess of wisdom. The olive (whence the scholar's midnight oil) was sacred to her.
[48] Minor. [49] Signature.

[50] Whim.
[51] Quoit's. [52] Handwriting. [53] Publisher-bookseller.
[54] His successor, who will probably be inferior.
[55] Generally.

as to be monopolized and traded in by tickets and statutes and standards. We must not think to make a staple commodity of all the knowledge in the land, to mark and license it like our broadcloth and our woolpacks. What is it but a servitude like that imposed by the Philistines, not to be allowed the sharpening of our own axes and colters,[56] but we must repair from all quarters to twenty licensing forges? Had anyone written and divulged erroneous things and scandalous to honest life, misusing and forfeiting the esteem had of his reason among men, if after conviction this only censure were adjudged him, that he should never henceforth write but what were first examined by an appointed officer whose hand should be annexed to pass his credit for him that now he might be safely read, it could not be apprehended less than a disgraceful punishment. Whence, to include the whole nation, and those that never yet thus offended, under such a diffident and suspectful prohibition, may plainly be understood what a disparagement it is. So much the more, whenas debtors and delinquents may walk abroad without a keeper, but unoffensive books must not stir forth without a visible jailer in their title. Nor is it to the common people less than a reproach; for if we be so jealous[57] over them as that we dare not trust them with an English pamphlet, what do we but censure them for a giddy, vicious, and ungrounded people, in such a sick and weak estate of faith and discretion as to be able to take nothing down but through the pipe[58] of a licenser? . . .

And in conclusion, it reflects to the disrepute of our ministers also, of whose labors we should hope better, and of the proficiency which their flock reaps by them, than that after all this light of the gospel which is, and is to be, and all this continual preaching, they should be still frequented with such an unprincipled, unedified, and laic rabble as that the whiff of every new pamphlet should stagger them out of their catechism and Christian walking. . . .

And lest some should persuade ye, Lords and Commons, that these arguments of learned men's discouragement at this your order are mere flourishes and not real, I could recount what I have seen and heard in other countries, where this kind of inquisition tyrannizes; when I have sat among their learned men, for that honor I had, and been counted happy to be born in such a place of philosophic freedom as they supposed England was, while themselves did nothing but bemoan the servile condition into which learning amongst them was brought: that this was it which had damped the glory of Italian wits; that nothing had been there written now these many years but flattery and fustian. There it was that I found and visited the famous Galileo grown old, a prisoner to the Inquisition,[59] for thinking in astronomy otherwise than the Franciscan and Dominican licensers thought. And though I knew that England then was groaning loudest under the prelatical yoke,[60] nevertheless I took it as a pledge of future happiness that other nations were so persuaded of her liberty. Yet was it beyond my hope that those worthies were then breathing in her air who should be her leaders to such a deliverance as shall never be forgotten by any revolution of time that this world hath to finish. . . .

Methinks I see in my mind a noble and puissant nation rousing herself like a strong man after sleep, and shaking her invincible locks; methinks I see her as an eagle renewing[61] her mighty youth and kindling her undazzled eyes at the full midday beam, purging and unscaling her long abused sight at the fountain itself of heavenly radiance; while the whole noise[62] of timorous and flocking birds, with those also that love the twilight, flutter about, amazed at what she means, and in their envious gabble would prognosticate a year of sects and schisms.

What should ye do then, should ye suppress all this flowery crop of knowledge and new light sprung up and yet springing daily in this city, should ye set an oligarchy of twenty ingrossers[63] over it, to bring a famine upon our minds again, when we shall know nothing but what is measured to us by their bushel? Believe it, Lords and Commons, they who counsel ye to such a suppressing do as good as bid ye suppress yourselves; and I will soon shew how. If it be desired to know the immediate cause of all this free writing and free speaking, there cannot be assigned a truer than your own mild and free and humane government; it is the liberty, Lords and Commons, which your own valorous and happy counsels have purchased us: liberty, which is the nurse of all great wits; this is that which hath rarefied and enlight'ned our spirits like the influence of heaven[64]; this is that which hath enfranchised, enlarged, and lifted up our apprehensions degrees above

---

[56] Cutting edges of plows. See 1 Samuel 13: 19–22.
[57] Suspicious.   [58] Feeding tube.

[59] Milton saw the great astronomer (1564–1642) in 1638. He had been obliged to recant his adoption of the Copernican system.
[60] Of Archbishop Laud.
[61] The original text reads *muing;* but cf. Psalms 103:5.
[62] Band.   [63] Monopolists.
[64] The astrological "influence" of the stars.

themselves. Ye cannot make us now less capable, less knowing, less eagerly pursuing of the truth, unless ye first make yourselves, that made us so, less the lovers, less the founders, of our true liberty. We can grow ignorant again, brutish, formal, and slavish as ye found us; but you then must first become that which ye cannot be: oppressive, arbitrary, and tyrannous, as they were from whom ye have freed us. That our hearts are now more capacious, our thoughts more erected to the search and expectation of greatest and exactest things, is the issue[65] of your own virtue propagated in us; ye cannot suppress that unless ye reinforce an abrogated and merciless law, that fathers may dispatch[66] at will their own children. And who shall then stick closest to ye, and excite others? . . . Give me the liberty to know, to utter, and to argue freely according to conscience, above all liberties. . . .

from PARADISE LOST

EDMUND WALLER thought *Paradise Lost* remarkable only for its length, and Poe denied that it is a poem. On the other hand its admirers have not only ranked it as the chief epic in English but have insisted that in grandeur of plan and high artistry of execution it surpasses the classical epics. Certainly no major poem has been the subject of livelier controversy. In recent years its popularity has undeniably receded; to many who love Shakespeare and Chaucer, *Paradise Lost* seems tedious and below the best of Milton's so-called minor poems. You will have to make up your mind for yourself. What exalts me may not exalt you; what leaves me cold may lift you to the heights. "The great poets," says Emerson, "are to be judged by the frame of mind which they induce"; and it is the business of every man who takes himself at all seriously to examine those works of art that are or have been called great, and to ascertain which of them have something to say *to him*. If from your reading of the selections below you find *Paradise Lost* the kind of poetry you like, the remainder is easily accessible.

The poem was first printed in 1667 and appeared in a second edition in 1674. The best annotated edition is by A. W. Verity (2 vols., 1929). C. S. Lewis's *A Preface to Paradise Lost* (1942) is a lively little book; it includes a survey of epic poetry in general. See also D. Bush's *Paradise Lost in Our Time* (1945).

THE VERSE

THE MEASURE is English heroic verse without rime, as that of Homer in Greek and of Vergil in Latin, rime being no necessary adjunct or true ornament of poem or good verse, in longer works especially, but the invention of a barbarous age, to set off wretched matter and lame meter, graced indeed since by the use of some famous modern poets, carried away by custom, but much to their own vexation, hindrance, and constraint to express many things otherwise and for the most part worse than else they would have expressed them. Not without cause, therefore, some both Italian and Spanish poets of prime note have rejected rime both in longer and shorter works, as have also long since our best English tragedies, as a thing of itself, to all judicious ears, trivial and of no true musical delight: which consists only in apt numbers, fit quantity of syllables, and the sense variously drawn out from one verse into another, not in the jingling sound of like endings, a fault avoided by the learned ancients both in poetry and all good oratory. This neglect then of rime so little is to be taken for a defect, though it may seem so perhaps to vulgar readers, that it rather is to be esteemed an example set, the first in English, of ancient liberty recovered to heroic poem from the troublesome and modern bondage of riming.

BOOK I

THE ARGUMENT[1]

THIS FIRST BOOK proposes, first in brief, the whole subject, man's disobedience, and the loss thereupon of Paradise, wherein he was placed; then touches the prime cause of his fall, the Serpent, or rather Satan in the Serpent, who revolting from God, and drawing to his side many legions of angels, was by the command of God driven out of heaven with all his crew into the great deep. Which action passed over, the poem hastes into the midst of things, presenting Satan with his angels now fallen into hell, described here not in the center (for heaven and earth may be supposed as yet not made, certainly not yet accursed) but in a place of utter darkness, fitliest called Chaos. Here Satan

---

[1] Theme.   [65] Offspring.   [66] Kill.

with his angels lying on the burning lake, thunderstruck and astonished, after a certain space recovers, as from confusion, calls up him who next in order and dignity lay by him; they confer of their miserable fall. Satan awakens all his legions, who lay till then in the same manner confounded; they rise, their numbers, array of battle, their chief leaders named, according to the idols known afterwards in Canaan and the countries adjoining. To these Satan directs his speech, comforts them with hope yet of regaining heaven, but tells them lastly of a new world and new kind of creature to be created, according to an ancient prophecy or report in heaven; for that angels were long before this visible creation was the opinion of many ancient Fathers. To find out the truth of this prophecy, and what to determine thereon, he refers to a full council. What his associates thence attempt. Pandemonium, the palace of Satan, rises, suddenly built out of the deep; the infernal peers there sit in council.

Of man's first disobedience, and the fruit
Of that forbidden tree whose mortal taste
Brought death into the world and all our woe,
With loss of Eden, till one greater Man[2]
Restore us, and regain the blissful seat,   5
Sing, Heavenly Muse,[3] that on the secret top
Of Oreb, or of Sinai, didst inspire
That shepherd[4] who first taught the chosen seed
In the beginning how the heavens and earth
Rose out of Chaos: or, if Sion hill   10
Delight thee more, and Siloa's brook, that flowed
Fast by the oracle of God,[5] I thence
Invoke thy aid to my adventurous song,
That with no middle flight intends to soar
Above the Aonian mount,[6] while it pursues   15
Things unattempted yet in prose or rime.
And chiefly thou, O Spirit,[7] that dost prefer
Before all temples the upright heart and pure,
Instruct me, for thou know'st; thou from the first
Wast present, and with mighty wings outspread   20
Dovelike sat'st brooding on the vast abyss,
And mad'st it pregnant: what in me is dark
Illumine, what is low raise and support;
That, to the highth of this great argument,

---

[2] Christ.
[3] Urania, the Muse of astronomy and hence of heavenly wisdom.
[4] Moses, leader of the chosen people, the Jews. See Exodus 19 for his reception of the Law on Mt. Sinai, a spur of Mt. Horeb.
[5] On the hill of Zion in Jerusalem, near the spring of Siloam, stood the Temple, where the Jewish prophets received inspiration.
[6] Mt. Helicon, sacred to the Muses. I.e., Milton has chosen a more exalted theme than the writers of the classical epics. Like them he announces his subject, invokes the Muse, and begins the narrative *in medias res*.   [7] The Holy Ghost.

I may assert Eternal Providence,   25
And justify the ways of God to men.
   Say first, for heaven hides nothing from thy view
Nor the deep tract of hell, say first what cause
Moved our grand parents, in that happy state,
Favored of heaven so highly, to fall off   30
From their Creator, and transgress his will
For one restraint, lords of the world besides.
Who first seduced them to that foul revolt?
The infernal Serpent; he it was whose guile,
Stirred up with envy and revenge, deceived   35
The mother of mankind, what time[8] his pride
Had cast him out from heaven, with all his host
Of rebel angels, by whose aid aspiring
To set himself in glory above his peers,
He trusted to have equaled the Most High,   40
If he opposed, and with ambitious aim
Against the throne and monarchy of God,
Raised impious war in heaven and battle proud,
With vain attempt. Him the Almighty Power
Hurled headlong flaming from the ethereal sky,   45
With hideous ruin and combustion, down
To bottomless perdition, there to dwell
In adamantine chains and penal fire,
Who durst defy the Omnipotent to arms.
   Nine times the space that measures day and night   50
To mortal men, he with his horrid crew
Lay vanquished, rolling in the fiery gulf,
Confounded,[9] though immortal. But his doom
Reserved him to more wrath; for now the thought
Both of lost happiness and lasting pain   55
Torments him: round he throws his baleful eyes,
That witnessed[10] huge affliction and dismay,
Mixed with obdurate pride and steadfast hate.
At once, as far as angel's ken,[11] he views
The dismal situation waste and wild.   60
A dungeon horrible, on all sides round,
As one great furnace flamed; yet from those flames
No light; but rather darkness visible
Served only to discover sights of woe,
Regions of sorrow, doleful shades, where peace   65
And rest can never dwell, hope never comes
That comes to all, but torture without end
Still urges,[12] and a fiery deluge, fed
With ever-burning sulphur unconsumed.
Such place eternal justice had prepared   70
For those rebellious; here their prison ordained
In utter darkness, and their portion set
As far removed from God and light of heaven

---

[8] When.   [9] Defeated and ruined.   [10] Showed.
[11] Sight.   [12] Presses, plies.

As from the center thrice to the utmost pole.[13]
Oh, how unlike the place from whence they fell!   75
There the companions of his fall, o'erwhelmed
With floods and whirlwinds of tempestuous fire,
He soon discerns, and weltering by his side
One next himself in power, and next in crime,
Long after known in Palestine, and named   80
Beëlzebub. To whom the arch-enemy,
And thence in heaven called Satan,[14] with bold words
Breaking the horrid silence, thus began:
   "If thou beest he—but oh, how fallen! how changed
From him who in the happy realms of light,   85
Clothed with transcendent brightness, didst outshine
Myriads, though bright!—if he whom mutual league,
United thoughts and counsels, equal hope
And hazard in the glorious enterprise
Joined with me once, now misery hath joined   90
In equal ruin; into what pit thou seest
From what highth fallen: so much the stronger proved
He with his thunder: and till then who knew
The force of those dire arms? Yet not for those,
Nor what the potent Victor in his rage   95
Can else inflict, do I repent or change,
Though changed in outward luster, that fixed mind
And high disdain, from sense of injured merit,
That with the Mightiest raised me to contend,
And to the fierce contention brought along   100
Innumerable force of spirits armed
That durst dislike his reign, and, me preferring,
His utmost power with adverse power opposed
In dubious[15] battle on the plains of heaven,
And shook his throne. What though the field be lost?   105
All is not lost; the unconquerable will,
And study[16] of revenge, immortal hate,
And courage never to submit or yield:
And what is else not to be overcome?[17]
That glory never shall his wrath or might   110
Extort from me. To bow and sue for grace
With suppliant knee, and deify his power
Who, from the terror of this arm, so late
Doubted his empire[18]—that were low indeed;
That were an ignominy and shame beneath   115
This downfall; since by fate the strength of gods
And this empyreal[19] substance cannot fail;[20]
Since, through experience of this great event,
In arms not worse, in foresight much advanced,

We may with more successful hope[21] resolve   120
To wage by force or guile eternal war,
Irreconcilable to our grand Foe,
Who now triúmphs, and in the excess of joy
Sole reigning holds the tyranny of heaven."
   So spake the apostate angel, though in pain,   125
Vaunting aloud, but racked with deep despair;
And him thus answered soon his bold compeer:
   "O prince, O chief of many thronèd powers[22]
That led the embattled seraphim to war
Under thy conduct, and, in dreadful deeds   130
Fearless, endangered heaven's perpetual King,
And put to proof his high supremacy,
Whether upheld by strength, or chance, or fate!
Too well I see and rue the dire event
That with sad overthrow and foul defeat   135
Hath lost us heaven, and all this mighty host
In horrible destruction laid thus low,
As far as gods and heavenly essences
Can perish: for the mind and spirit remains
Invincible, and vigor soon returns,   140
Though all our glory extinct, and happy state
Here swallowed up in endless misery.
But what if he our Conqueror (whom I now
Of force[23] believe almighty, since no less
Than such could have o'erpowered such force as ours)   145
Have left us this our spirit and strength entire
Strongly to suffer and support our pains,
That we may so suffice[24] his vengeful ire,
Or do him mightier service as his thralls
By right of war, whate'er his business be   150
Here in the heart of hell to work in fire,
Or do his errands in the gloomy deep?[25]
What can it then avail though yet we feel
Strength undiminished, or eternal being
To undergo eternal punishment?"   155
   Whereto with speedy words the archfiend replied:
"Fallen cherub, to be weak is miserable,
Doing or suffering; but of this be sure:
To do aught good never will be our task,
But ever to do ill our sole delight,   160
As being the contrary to his high will
Whom we resist. If then his providence
Out of our evil seek to bring forth good,
Our labor must be to pervert that end,
And out of good still to find means of evil;   165

[13] I.e., three times the distance from the center of the earth to the
   outermost sphere of the universe (in the Ptolemaic astronomy).
[14] I.e., the adversary.   [15] Of uncertain outcome.
[16] Pursuit, attempt.
[17] What other test of not being overcome is there?
[18] Was afraid for his sovereignty.   [19] Nonmaterial.
[20] I.e., perish.

[21] Hope of success.
[22] Throughout there are frequent references to the medieval
   classification of angels in three hierarchies, each of which was
   subdivided into three orders, as follows (in descending order):
   (1) seraphim, cherubim, thrones; (2) dominations (or dominions), virtues, powers; (3) principalities, archangels, angels.
[23] Perforce, of necessity.   [24] Satisfy.   [25] In Chaos.

Which ofttimes may succeed so as perhaps
Shall grieve him, if I fail[26] not, and disturb
His inmost counsels from their destined aim.
But see! the angry Victor hath recalled
His ministers of vengeance and pursuit   170
Back to the gates of heaven: the sulphurous hail,
Shot after us in storm, o'erblown hath laid
The fiery surge that from the precipice
Of heaven received us falling; and the thunder,
Winged with red lightning and impetuous rage,   175
Perhaps hath spent his shafts, and ceases now
To bellow through the vast and boundless deep.
Let us not slip[27] the occasion, whether scorn
Or satiate fury yield it from our foe.
Seest thou yon dreary plain, forlorn and wild,   180
The seat of desolation, void of light,
Save what the glimmering of these livid flames
Casts pale and dreadful? Thither let us tend
From off the tossing of these fiery waves;
There rest, if any rest can harbor there;   185
And, reassembling our afflicted powers,[28]
Consult how we may henceforth most offend
Our enemy, our own loss how repair,
How overcome this dire calamity,
What reinforcement we may gain from hope,   190
If not, what resolution from despair."

    Thus Satan, talking to his nearest mate,
With head uplift above the wave, and eyes
That sparkling blazed; his other parts besides,
Prone on the flood, extended long and large,   195
Lay floating many a rood,[29] in bulk as huge
As whom the fables name of monstrous size,
Titanian or Earth-born, that warred on Jove,
Briareos or Typhon,[30] whom the den
By ancient Tarsus[31] held, or that sea-beast   200
Leviathan,[32] which God of all his works
Created hugest that swim the ocean stream:
Him, haply slumbering on the Norway foam,
The pilot of some small night-foundered[33] skiff,
Deeming some island, oft, as seamen tell,   205
With fixèd anchor in his scaly rind,
Moors by his side under the lee, while night

---

[26] Mistake.   [27] Let slip.
[28] Stricken forces.
[29] A square measure of about a quarter of an acre.
[30] Two huge monsters of Greek mythology, the first having a hundred hands, the second a hundred serpents' heads with fiery eyes. Both were sons of Ge (Earth).
[31] The capital of Cilicia, the province in which ancient writers localize Typhon's abode.
[32] An aquatic monster mentioned several times in the Bible and variously interpreted: apparently a crocodile in Job 41:1, for example (see above, p. 238, note 32), and a whale in Psalms 104:26.   [33] I.e., brought to a halt by the coming of night.

Invests the sea, and wishèd morn delays.
So stretched out huge in length the archfiend lay
Chained on the burning lake; nor ever thence   210
Had risen, or heaved his head, but that the will
And high permission of all-ruling heaven
Left him at large to his own dark designs,
That with reiterated crimes he might
Heap on himself damnation, while he sought   215
Evil to others, and enraged might see
How all his malice served but to bring forth
Infinite goodness, grace, and mercy, shown
On man by him seduced, but on himself
Treble confusion, wrath, and vengeance poured.   220
    Forthwith upright he rears from off the pool
His mighty stature; on each hand the flames
Driven backward slope their pointing spires, and, rolled
In billows, leave i' the midst a horrid vale.
Then with expanded wings he steers his flight   225
Aloft, incumbent[34] on the dusky air,
That felt unusual weight, till on dry land
He lights—if it were land, that ever burned
With solid, as the lake with liquid, fire,
And such appeared in hue as when the force   230
Of subterranean wind transports a hill
Torn from Pelorus,[35] or the shattered side
Of thundering Etna, whose combustible
And fueled entrails, thence conceiving fire,
Sublimed with[36] mineral fury, aid the winds,   235
And leave a singèd bottom all involved
With stench and smoke: such resting found the sole
Of unblest feet. Him followed his next mate,
Both glorying to have scaped the Stygian[37] flood
As gods, and by their own recovered strength,   240
Not by the sufferance of supernal power.
    "Is this the region, this the soil, the clime,"
Said then the lost archangel, "this the seat
That we must change for heaven, this mournful gloom
For that celestial light? Be it so, since he   245
Who now is sovran can dispose and bid
What shall be right: fardest from him[38] is best,
Whom reason hath equaled, force hath made supreme
Above his equals.[39] Farewell, happy fields,
Where joy for ever dwells! Hail, horrors! hail,   250
Infernal world! and thou, profoundest hell,
Receive thy new possessor: one who brings
A mind not to be changed by place or time.
The mind is its own place, and in itself
Can make a heaven of hell, a hell of heaven.   255

---

[34] Lying.   [35] Cape Faro, in Sicily, near Mt. Etna.
[36] Vaporized by.
[37] I.e., hellish, since the Styx was the principal river of Hades.
[38] Farthest distant from God.
[39] I.e., we are his equals in reason but not in power.

What matter where, if I be still the same
And what I should be, all but less than he[40]
Whom thunder hath made greater? Here at least
We shall be free; the Almighty hath not built
Here for his envy, will not drive us hence: 260
Here we may reign secure; and, in my choice,
To reign is worth ambition, though in hell:
Better to reign in hell than serve in heaven.
But wherefore let we then our faithful friends,
The associates and copartners of our loss,   265
Lie thus astonished[41] on the oblivious[42] pool,
And call them not to share with us their part
In this unhappy mansion,[43] or once more
With rallied arms to try what may be yet
Regained in heaven, or what more lost in hell?"   270
    So Satan spake, and him Beëlzebub
Thus answered: "Leader of those armies bright
Which, but the Omnipotent, none could have foiled!
If once they hear that voice, their liveliest pledge
Of hope in fears and dangers—heard so oft   275
In worst extremes, and on the perilous edge
Of battle, when it raged, in all assaults
Their surest signal—they will soon resume
New courage and revive, though now they lie
Groveling[44] and prostrate on yon lake of fire,   280
As we erewhile, astounded and amazed;
No wonder, fallen such a pernicious highth!"
    He scarce had ceased when the superior fiend
Was moving toward the shore; his ponderous shield,
Ethereal[45] temper, massy, large, and round,   285
Behind him cast; the broad circumference
Hung on his shoulders like the moon, whose orb
Through optic glass[46] the Tuscan artist[47] views
At evening, from the top of Fesolè,[48]
Or in Valdarno,[49] to descry new lands,   290
Rivers, or mountains, in her spotty globe.
His spear, to equal which the tallest pine
Hewn on Norwegian hills, to be the mast
Of some great ammiral,[50] were but a wand,
He walked with, to support uneasy steps   295
Over the burning marle,[51] not like those steps
On heaven's azure; and the torrid clime
Smote on him sore besides, vaulted with fire.
Nathless[52] he so endured, till on the beach
Of that inflamèd sea he stood, and called   300

His legions—angel forms, who lay entranced
Thick as autumnal leaves that strow the brooks
In Vallombrosa,[53] where the Etrurian shades
High over-arched embower; or scattered sedge
Afloat, when with fierce winds Orion[54] armed   305
Hath vexed the Red Sea coast, whose waves o'erthrew
Busiris and his Memphian chivalry,[55]
While with perfidious hatred they pursued
The sojourners of Goshen,[56] who beheld
From the safe shore their floating carcasses   310
And broken chariot wheels; so thick bestrown,
Abject and lost, lay these, covering the flood,
Under amazement of[57] their hideous change.
He called so loud that all the hollow deep
Of hell resounded:—"Princes, potentates,   315
Warriors, the flower of heaven, once yours, now lost,
If such astonishment as this can seize
Eternal spirits! Or have ye chosen this place
After the toil of battle to repose
Your wearied virtue,[58] for the ease you find   320
To slumber here, as in the vales of heaven?
Or in this abject posture have ye sworn
To adore the Conqueror? who now beholds
Cherub and seraph rolling in the flood
With scattered arms and ensigns, till anon   325
His swift pursuers from heaven gates discern
The advantage, and, descending, tread us down
Thus drooping, or with linkèd thunderbolts
Transfix us to the bottom of this gulf.
Awake, arise! or be for ever fallen!"   330
    They heard, and were abashed, and up they sprung
Upon the wing, as when men wont to watch,
On duty sleeping found by whom they dread,
Rouse and bestir themselves ere well awake.
Nor did they not perceive the evil plight   335
In which they were, or the fierce pains not feel;
Yet to their general's voice they soon obeyed
Innumerable. As when the potent rod
Of Amram's son,[59] in Egypt's evil day,
Waved round the coast, up called a pitchy cloud   340
Of locusts, warping[60] on the eastern wind,
That o'er the realm of impious Pharaoh hung
Like night, and darkened all the land of Nile:

---

[40] Nearly equal to him.
[41] Astounded, stunned (see also line 317).
[42] Causing forgetfulness.   [43] Abode.   [44] Lying prone.
[45] Celestial, heavenly.   [46] Telescope.
[47] Galileo, whom Milton had met in Florence.
[48] Fiesole, a hill outside Florence.
[49] Valley of the river Arno, in which Florence is situated.
[50] Flagship.   [51] Soil, earth.   [52] Nevertheless.

[53] A valley not far from Florence. Tuscany, in which it is situated, was part of ancient Etruria.
[54] A constellation named for a mighty hunter of Greek myth ("armed" with a sword in pictorial charts of the stars); its setting early in November was often accompanied by stormy weather.
[55] I.e., Pharaoh and his Egyptian horsemen and charioteers. Busiris was not in fact the Pharaoh of the account in Exodus 14, but an earlier, mythical Egyptian king.
[56] A district in Egypt where the Jews had lived (see Genesis 47:27).
[57] Utterly confounded by.   [58] Valor.
[59] Moses. See Exodus 10:12–15.   [60] Making their way.

So numberless were those bad angels seen
Hovering on wing under the cope[61] of hell,   345
'Twixt upper, nether, and surrounding fires;
Till, as a signal given, the uplifted spear
Of their great sultan waving to direct
Their course, in even balance down they light
On the firm brimstone, and fill all the plain—   350
A multitude like which the populous North
Poured never from her frozen loins to pass
Rhene or the Danaw,[62] when her barbarous sons
Came like a deluge on the South, and spread
Beneath[63] Gibraltar to the Libyan sands.   355
Forthwith, from every squadron and each band,
The heads and leaders thither haste where stood
Their great commander: godlike shapes, and forms
Excelling human, princely dignities,
And powers that erst[64] in heaven sat on thrones,   360
Though of their names in heavenly records now
Be no memorial, blotted out and rased
By their rebellion from the books of life.
Nor had they yet among the sons of Eve
Got them new names, till, wandering o'er the earth,   365
Through God's high sufferance for the trial of man,
By falsities and lies the greatest part
Of mankind they corrupted to forsake
God their Creator and the invisible
Glory of him that made them, to transform   370
Oft to the image of a brute, adorned
With gay religions full of pomp and gold,
And devils to adore for deities:
Then were they known to men by various names,
And various idols through the heathen world.   375
    Say, Muse, their names then known, who first, who
      last,
Roused from the slumber on that fiery couch,
At their great emperor's call, as next in worth
Came singly where he stood on the bare strand,
While the promiscuous crowd stood yet aloof.[65]   380
    The chief were those who, from the pit of hell
Roaming to seek their prey on earth, durst fix
Their seats, long after, next the seat of God,[66]

Their altars by his altar, gods adored
Among the nations round, and durst abide   385
Jehovah thundering out of Sion, throned
Between the cherubim; yea, often placed
Within his sanctuary itself their shrines,
Abominations; and with cursèd things[67]
His holy rites and solemn feasts profaned,   390
And with their darkness durst affront his light.
First, Moloch,[68] horrid king, besmeared with blood
Of human sacrifice and parents' tears;
Though, for the noise of drums and timbrels loud,
Their children's cries unheard that passed through fire   395
To his grim idol. Him the Ammonite
Worshiped in Rabba and her watery plain,
In Argob and in Basan, to the stream
Of utmost Arnon.[69] Nor content with such
Audacious neighborhood,[70] the wisest heart   400
Of Solomon he led by fraud to build
His temple right against the temple of God
On that opprobrious hill, and made his grove
The pleasant valley of Hinnom,[71] Tophet thence
And black Gehenna called, the type of hell.   405
Next Chemos,[72] the obscene dread of Moab's sons,
From Aroar to Nebo and the wild
Of southmost Abarim; in Hesebon
And Horonaim, Seon's[73] realm, beyond
The flowery dale of Sibma clad with vines,   410
And Elealè to the Asphaltic Pool:[74]
Peor his other name, when he enticed
Israel in Sittim, on their march from Nile,
To do him wanton rites, which cost them woe.[75]
Yet thence his lustful orgies he enlarged   415
Even to that hill of scandal,[76] by the grove
Of Moloch homicide, lust hard by hate,[77]
Till good Josiah drove them thence to hell.[78]
With these came they who, from the bordering flood
Of old Euphrates to the brook that parts   420

---

[61] Vault, roof.

[62] Latin *Rhenus*, German *Donau:* Rhine, Danube. The reference is to the invasions of the Goths, Vandals, and Huns.

[63] South of.   [64] Formerly.

[65] I.e., the mingled throng of lesser angels remain at a distance until their leaders have approached Satan singly.

[66] A reference to various occasions in Hebrew history when altars to heathen gods were set up in or near the Temple of Jehovah. In the following passage Milton names the chief angels, as he says in the Argument to Book I, "according to the idols known afterward in Canaan and the countries adjoining." The whole section shows his fondness for catalogs of sonorous and exotic names.

[67] Religious observances.

[68] God of the Ammonites, worshiped by the sacrifice of children, who were burned to death in his heated image. Solomon reared a shrine for him near the Temple (see 1 Kings 11:5–7).

[69] Places in the Ammonite kingdom.

[70] Bold nearness (to God's chosen people).

[71] A valley near Jerusalem, called Gehenna in Greek. Tophet was probably the site of the sacrifices to Moloch, not (as Milton makes it) an alternative name for the whole valley. Gehenna was later made a receptacle for refuse, with perpetual fires burning in it (hence it is called "the type of hell").

[72] God of the Moabites, in whose realm were the places named in the following lines.   [73] An Ammonite king.

[74] The Dead Sea, so called because of the asphalt or bitumen in it.

[75] See Numbers 25.

[76] Like Moloch, he had a shrine erected by Solomon near the Temple (see the reference in note 68).

[77] I.e., the god of lust (Chemos) close beside the god of hate (Moloch).   [78] See 2 Kings 23.

Egypt from Syrian ground, had general names
Of Baalim and Ashtaroth,[79] those male,
These feminine. For spirits when they please
Can either sex assume, or both; so soft
And uncompounded is their essence pure,   425
Not tied or manacled with joint or limb,
Nor founded on the brittle strength of bones,
Like cumbrous flesh; but in what shape they choose,
Dilated or condensed, bright or obscure,
Can execute their aery purposes,   430
And works of love or enmity fulfill.
For those the race of Israel oft forsook
Their Living Strength, and unfrequented left
His righteous altar, bowing lowly down
To bestial gods; for which their heads, as low   435
Bowed down in battle, sunk before the spear
Of despicable foes. With these in troop
Came Astoreth, whom the Phoenicians called
Astarte, queen of heaven, with crescent horns;
To whose bright image nightly by the moon   440
Sidonian[80] virgins paid their vows and songs;
In Sion also not unsung, where stood
Her temple on the offensive mountain, built
By that uxorious king[81] whose heart, though large,
Beguiled by fair idolatresses, fell   445
To idols foul. Thammuz[82] came next behind,
Whose annual wound in Lebanon allured
The Syrian damsels to lament his fate
In amorous ditties all a summer's day,
While smooth Adonis from his native rock   450
Ran purple to the sea, supposed with blood
Of Thammuz yearly wounded: the love-tale
Infected Sion's daughters[83] with like heat,
Whose wanton passions in the sacred porch
Ezekiel saw, when by the vision led   455
His eye surveyed the dark idolatries
Of alienated Judah. Next came one
Who mourned in earnest, when the captive ark
Maimed his brute image, head and hands lopped off,
In his own temple, on the grunsel[84] edge.   460
Where he fell flat and shamed his worshipers:
Dagon his name, sea monster, upward man
And downward fish; yet had his temple high

Reared in Azotus, dreaded through the coast
Of Palestine, in Gath and Ascalon   465
And Accaron and Gaza's[85] frontier bounds.
Him followed Rimmon, whose delightful seat
Was fair Damascus, on the fertile banks
Of Abbana and Pharphar, lucid streams.
He also against the house of God was bold.   470
A leper once he lost and gained a king,[86]
Ahaz, his sottish conqueror, whom he drew
God's altar to disparage and displace
For one of Syrian mode, whereon to burn
His odious offerings, and adore the gods   475
Whom he had vanquished. After these appeared
A crew who, under names of old renown,
Osiris, Isis, Orus, and their train,
With monstrous shapes and sorceries abused
Fanatic Egypt and her priests to seek   480
Their wandering gods disguised in brutish forms[87]
Rather than human. Nor did Israel scape
The infection, when their borrowed gold composed
The calf in Oreb;[88] and the rebel king[89]
Doubled that sin in Bethel and in Dan,   485
Likening his Maker to the grazèd ox—
Jehovah, who, in one night, when he passed
From Egypt marching, equaled[90] with one stroke
Both her first-born and all her bleating gods.
Belial came last; than whom a spirit more lewd   490
Fell not from heaven, or more gross to love
Vice for itself. To him no temple stood
Or altar smoked; yet who more oft than he
In temples and at altars, when the priest
Turns atheist, as did Eli's sons,[91] who filled   495
With lust and violence the house of God?
In courts and palaces he also reigns,
And in luxurious[92] cities, where the noise
Of riot ascends above their loftiest towers,
And injury and outrage; and, when night   500
Darkens the streets, then wander forth the sons
Of Belial, flown[93] with insolence and wine.
Witness the streets of Sodom,[94] and that night
In Gibeah, where the hospitable door
Exposed a matron, to avoid worse rape.[95]   505

---

79 Collective names for Phoenician sun and moon deities.
80 From Sidon, a city of Phoenicia.
81 Solomon; see the reference in note 68. *Uxorious* =dotingly wife-loving.
82 Originally a vegetation deity, slain by a boar but fabled to revive every spring. When the river Adonis was reddened by mud washed from Lebanon by the spring rains, it was thought to be discolored by the wound of Thammuz bleeding afresh. His Greek equivalent was Adonis.
83 The women of Jerusalem; see Ezekiel 8:14.
84 Groundsill, threshold. See 1 Samuel 5:1–5.

85 Cities of the Philistines, who worshiped Dagon.
86 See 2 Kings 5 and 12.
87 Osiris as a bull, Isis as a cow, Orus as a hawk.
88 See Exodus 32.
89 Jeroboam, who rebelled with ten tribes against Rehoboam, Solomon's son and successor, and set up the northern kingdom of Israel. On the next line see 1 Kings 12:28–33.
90 Made equal in destruction. The allusion is to the tenth plague, in which "the Lord smote all the first-born in the land of Egypt . . . and all the first-born of cattle" (Exodus 12:29).
91 See 1 Samuel 2:12–17.   92 Lustful.   93 Flushed.
94 See Genesis 19.   95 See Judges 19.

These were the prime in order and in might:
The rest were long to tell; though far renowned
The Ionian[96] gods—of Javan's issue[97] held
Gods, yet confessed later than Heaven and Earth,[98]
Their boasted parents;—Titan, Heaven's first-born,   510
With his enormous brood, and birthright seized
By younger Saturn: he from mightier Jove,
His own and Rhea's son, like measure found;
So Jove usurping reigned. These, first in Crete
And Ida[99] known, thence on the snowy top   515
Of cold Olympus[1] ruled the middle air,
Their highest heaven; or on the Delphian cliff,[2]
Or in Dodona,[3] and through all the bounds
Of Doric[4] land; or who with Saturn old
Fled over Adria to the Hesperian fields,   520
And o'er the Celtic roamed the utmost isles.[5]

  All these and more came flocking, but with looks
Downcast and damp,[6] yet such wherein appeared
Obscure some glimpse of joy, to have found their chief
Not in despair, to have found themselves not lost   525
In loss itself, which on his countenance cast
Like doubtful hue; but he, his wonted pride
Soon recollecting, with high words, that bore
Semblance of worth, not substance, gently raised
Their fainting courage, and dispelled their fears.   530
Then straight commands that, at the warlike sound
Of trumpets loud and clarions, be upreared
His mighty standard. That proud honor claimed
Azazel as his right, a cherub tall:
Who forthwith from the glittering staff unfurled   535
The imperial ensign, which, full high advanced,[7]
Shone like a meteor streaming to the wind,
With gems and golden luster rich emblazed,
Seraphic arms and trophies; all the while
Sonorous metal blowing martial sounds: 540
At which the universal host upsent
A shout that tore hell's concave,[8] and beyond
Frighted the reign of Chaos and old Night.
All in a moment through the gloom were seen
Ten thousand banners rise into the air,   545

With orient[9] colors waving; with them rose
A forest huge of spears; and thronging helms
Appeared, and serried[10] shields in thick array
Of depth immeasurable. Anon they move
In perfect phalanx[11] to the Dorian[12] mood   550
Of flutes and soft recorders;[13] such as raised
To highth of noblest temper heroes old
Arming to battle, and instead of rage
Deliberate valor breathed, firm and unmoved
With dread of death to flight or foul retreat,   555
Nor wanting power to mitigate and swage[14]
With solemn touches troubled thoughts, and chase
Anguish and doubt and fear and sorrow and pain
From mortal or immortal minds. Thus they,
Breathing united force with fixèd thought,   560
Moved on in silence to soft pipes that charmed
Their painful steps o'er the burnt soil. And now
Advanced in view, they stand, a horrid front
Of dreadful length and dazzling arms, in guise
Of warriors old, with ordered spear and shield,   565
Awaiting what command their mighty chief
Had to impose. He through the armèd files
Darts his experienced eye, and soon traverse[15]
The whole battalion views, their order due,
Their visages and stature as of gods;   570
Their number last he sums. And now his heart
Distends with pride, and hardening in his strength
Glories: for never, since created man,
Met such embodied force as, named[16] with these,
Could merit more than that small infantry   575
Warred on by cranes, though all the giant brood
Of Phlegra[17] with the heroic race were joined
That fought at Thebes and Ilium,[18] on each side
Mixed with auxiliar gods; and what resounds
In fable or romance of Uther's son,[19]   580
Begirt with British and Armoric[20] knights;
And all who since, baptized or infidel,[21]
Jousted in Aspramont, or Montalban,
Damasco, or Marocco, or Trebisond,[22]
Or whom Biserta[23] sent from Afric shore   585

---

[96] Greek.

[97] By the descendants of Javan, grandson of Noah.

[98] Uranus (Heaven) and Ge (Earth) were parents of the Titans. Uranus was dethroned by his son Cronos (Saturn), who was in turn dethroned by Zeus (Jove), his son by Rhea.

[99] The birthplace of Zeus.

[1] The abode of the Greek gods.

[2] The seat of a famous oracle of Apollo, on Mt. Parnassus.

[3] The seat of an oracle of Zeus, on Mt. Tomarus in Epirus.

[4] Greek.

[5] I.e., the worship of the older dynasty of gods was transferred across the Adriatic to Italy and through the western provinces as far as the British Isles.   [6] Depressed.

[7] Lifted.   [8] Vault.

[9] Splendid.   [10] Massed.   [11] Close order.

[12] One of the "modes" of Greek music; it was grave and often martial.   [13] An ancestor of the flute.

[14] Assuage.   [15] Across.

[16] I.e., compared with this force any other in history was as negligible as the army of the pygmies, on which according to Homer the cranes made war.

[17] The peninsula in Macedonia where the gods warred on the giants.

[18] Troy; like Thebes it was the scene of battles famous in Greek legend.   [19] King Arthur.   [20] Of Brittany.

[21] I.e., Saracen.

[22] These place names all figure in French and Italian romances.

[23] According to romance, an army which invaded Spain and attacked the emperor Charlemagne (d. 814) embarked at Bizerte in Tunis.

When Charlemagne with all his peerage fell
By Fontarabbia.[24] Thus far these beyond
Compare of mortal prowess, yet observed
Their dread commander. He, above the rest
In shape and gesture proudly eminent,   590
Stood like a tower. His form had yet not lost
All her original brightness, nor appeared
Less than archangel ruined, and the excess
Of glory obscured: as when the sun new risen
Looks through the horizontal misty air   595
Shorn of his beams, or from behind the moon
In dim eclipse, disastrous[25] twilight sheds
On half the nations, and with fear of change
Perplexes monarchs. Darkened so, yet shone
Above them all the archangel; but his face   600
Deep scars of thunder had intrenched, and care
Sat on his faded cheek, but under brows
Of dauntless courage, and considerate[26] pride
Waiting revenge; cruel his eye, but cast
Signs of remorse and passion,[27] to behold   605
The fellows of his crime, the followers rather
(Far other once beheld in bliss), condemned
For ever now to have their lot in pain,
Millions of spirits for his fault amerced[28]
Of heaven, and from eternal splendors flung   610
For his revolt, yet faithful how they stood,
Their glory withered; as, when heaven's fire
Hath scathed the forest oaks or mountain pines,
With singèd top their stately growth, though bare,
Stands on the blasted heath. He now prepared   615
To speak; whereat their doubled ranks they bend
From wing to wing, and half enclose him round
With all his peers: attention held them mute.
Thrice he assayed, and thrice, in spite of scorn,
Tears such as angels weep burst forth; at last   620
Words interwove with sighs found out their way:
    "O myriads of immortal spirits! O powers
Matchless, but with the Almighty!—and that strife
Was not inglorious, though the event[29] was dire,
As this place testifies and this dire change,   625
Hateful to utter. But what power of mind,
Foreseeing or presaging, from the depth
Of knowledge past or present, could have feared
How such united force of gods, how such
As stood like these, could ever know repulse?   630

For who can yet believe, though after loss,
That all these puissant legions, whose exile
Hath emptied heaven, shall fail to reascend,
Self-raised, and repossess their native seat?
For me be witness all the host of heaven,   635
If counsels different, or danger shunned
By me, have lost our hopes. But he who reigns
Monarch in heaven till then as one secure
Sat on his throne, upheld by old repute,
Consent, or custom, and his regal state   640
Put forth at full, but still his strength concealed,
Which tempted our attempt, and wrought our fall.
Henceforth his might we know, and know our own,
So as not either to provoke, or dread
New war provoked: our better part remains,   645
To work in close[30] design, by fraud or guile,
What force effected not, that he no less
At length from us may find, who overcomes
By force hath overcome but half his foe.
Space may produce new worlds; whereof so rife[31]   650
There went a fame[32] in heaven that he ere long
Intended to create, and therein plant
A generation whom his choice regard
Should favor equal to the sons of heaven.
Thither, if but to pry, shall be perhaps   655
Our first eruption, thither or elsewhere;
For this infernal pit shall never hold
Celestial spirits in bondage, nor the abyss
Long under darkness cover. But these thoughts
Full counsel must mature. Peace is despaired,   660
For who can think submission? War, then, war
Open or understood, must be resolved."
    He spake; and, to confirm his words, outflew
Millions of flaming swords, drawn from the thighs
Of mighty cherubim; the sudden blaze   665
Far round illumined hell; highly they raged
Against the Highest, and fierce with graspèd arms
Clashed on their sounding shields the din of war,
Hurling defiance toward the vault of heaven.
    There stood a hill not far, whose grisly top   670
Belched fire and rolling smoke; the rest entire
Shone with a glossy scurf, undoubted sign
That in his[33] womb was hid metallic ore,
The work of sulphur.[34] Thither, winged with speed,
A numerous brígade hastened: as when bands   675
Of pioners,[35] with spade and pickax armed,
Forerun the royal camp, to trench a field
Or cast a rampart. Mammon led them on,
Mammon, the least erected spirit that fell
From heaven; for even in heaven his looks and thoughts

---

[24] Roncesvalles, in the Pyrenees, where Charlemagne's rearguard
was cut to pieces, is actually some distance from the coastal town
of Fuenterrabia. According to romance all but one of the twelve
"peers" or knightly companions, including the Emperor's
nephew Roland or Orlando, died there (778), but not Charlemagne.   [25] Threatening disaster.
[26] Thoughtful, deliberate.   [27] Pity and deep feeling.
[28] Punished by fine, i.e., deprived.   [29] Outcome.

[30] Secret.   [31] Prevalent.   [32] Rumor.   [33] Its.
[34] The alchemists held that sulphur and mercury were the "parents"
of metals.   [35] Pioneers, army engineers.

Were always downward bent, admiring more 681
The riches of heaven's pavement, trodden gold,
Than aught divine or holy else enjoyed
In vision beatific; by him first
Men also, and by his suggestion taught, 685
Ransacked the center, and with impious hands
Rifled the bowels of their mother earth
For treasures better hid. Soon had his crew
Opened into the hill a spacious wound,
And digged out ribs of gold. Let none admire³⁶ 690
That riches grow in hell; that soil may best
Deserve the precious bane.³⁷ And here let those
Who boast in mortal things, and wondering tell
Of Babel,³⁸ and the works of Memphian kings,³⁹
Learn how their greatest monuments of fame 695
And strength and art are easily outdone
By spirits reprobate, and in an hour
What in an age they with incessant toil
And hands innumerable scarce perform.
Nigh on the plain, in many cells prepared, 700
That underneath had veins of liquid fire
Sluiced from the lake, a second multitude
With wondrous art found out⁴⁰ the massy ore,
Severing each kind, and scummed the bullion dross.
A third as soon had formed within the ground 705
A various mold, and from the boiling cells
By strange conveyance filled each hollow nook,
As in an organ, from one blast of wind,
To many a row of pipes the soundboard breathes.
Anon out of the earth a fabric huge 710
Rose like an exhalation, with the sound
Of dulcet symphonies and voices sweet,
Built like a temple, where pilasters round
Were set, and Doric pillars overlaid
With golden architrave; nor did there want 715
Cornice or frieze, with bossy⁴¹ sculptures graven;
The roof was fretted gold. Not Babylon
Nor great Alcairo⁴² such magnificence
Equaled in all their glories, to enshrine
Belus or Serapis⁴³ their gods, or seat 720
Their kings, when Egypt with Assyria strove
In wealth and luxury. The ascending pile
Stood fixed her stately highth, and straight the doors,
Opening their brazen folds, discover, wide
Within, her ample spaces o'er the smooth 725
And level pavement; from the archèd roof,

Pendent by subtle magic, many a row
Of starry lamps and blazing cressets,⁴⁴ fed
With naphtha and asphaltus, yielded light
As from a sky. The hasty multitude 730
Admiring entered, and the work some praise,
And some the architect; his hand was known
In heaven by many a towered structure high,
Where sceptered angels held their residence,
And sat as princes, whom the supreme King 735
Exalted to such power, and gave to rule,
Each in his hierarchy, the orders bright.
Nor was his name unheard or unadored
In ancient Greece; and in Ausonian land⁴⁵
Men called him Mulciber; and how he fell 740
From heaven they fabled, thrown by angry Jove
Sheer o'er the crystal battlements; from morn
To noon he fell, from noon to dewy eve,
A summer's day, and with the setting sun
Dropped from the zenith, like a falling star, 745
On Lemnos, the Aegean isle: thus they relate,
Erring; for he with this rebellious rout
Fell long before; nor aught availed him now
To have built in heaven high towers; nor did he scape
By all his engines,⁴⁶ but was headlong sent, 750
With his industrious crew, to build in hell.
    Meanwhile the wingèd haralds,⁴⁷ by command
Of sovran power, with awful ceremony
And trumpet's sound, throughout the host proclaim
A solemn council forthwith to be held 755
At Pandemonium,⁴⁸ the high capital
Of Satan and his peers: their summons called
From every band and squarèd regiment
By place or choice the worthiest; they anon
With hundreds and with thousands trooping came 760
Attended: all access was thronged; the gates
And porches wide, but chief the spacious hall
(Though like a covered field, where champions bold
Wont⁴⁹ ride in armed, and at the soldan's⁵⁰ chair
Defied the best of paynim chivalry⁵¹ 765
To mortal combat, or career⁵² with lance)
Thick swarmed, both on the ground and in the air,
Brushed with the hiss of rustling wings. As bees
In springtime, when the sun with Taurus⁵³ rides,
Pour fourth their populous youth about the hive 770
In clusters; they among fresh dews and flowers

---

³⁶ Wonder.   ³⁷ Evil.
³⁸ For the Tower of Babel see Genesis 11:1–9.
³⁹ The Pyramids.   ⁴⁰ I.e., separated, refined.
⁴¹ In relief. Milton is thinking of baroque architecture.
⁴² The ancient Memphis, near modern Cairo.
⁴³ The Babylonian god Bel, and an Egyptian god of the underworld.

⁴⁴ Pots used for fixed torches.
⁴⁵ Italy.—*Mulciber* = Vulcan (Greek Hephaistos).
⁴⁶ Contrivances.   ⁴⁷ Heralds.
⁴⁸ The place of all demons (Milton coined the word).
⁴⁹ Were accustomed to.   ⁵⁰ Sultan's.
⁵¹ Pagan knights.   ⁵² Gallop, joust.
⁵³ The Bull, one of the signs of the zodiac. The sun is in Taurus between April 19 and May 20.

Fly to and fro, or on the smoothèd plank,
The suburb of their straw-built citadel,
New rubbed with balm, expatiate, and confer[54]
Their state affairs. So thick the aery crowd   775
Swarmed and were straitened;[55] till, the signal given,
Behold a wonder! they but now who seemed
In bigness to surpass Earth's giant sons,
Now less than smallest dwarfs, in narrow room
Throng numberless, like that pygmean race   780
Beyond the Indian mount,[56] or faery elves,
Whose midnight revels by a forest side
Of fountain some belated peasant sees,
Or dreams he sees, while overhead the moon
Sits arbitress,[57] and nearer to the earth   785

Wheels her pale course: they, on their mirth and dance
Intent, with jocund music charm his ear;
At once with joy and fear his heart rebounds.
Thus incorporeal spirits to smallest forms
Reduced their shapes immense, and were at large,   790
Though without number still, amidst the hall
Of that infernal court. But far within,
And in their own dimensions like themselves,
The great seraphic lords and cherubim
In close recess and secret conclave sat,   795
A thousand demigods on golden seats,
Frequent[58] and full. After short silence then,
And summons read, the great consult[59] began.

THE END OF THE FIRST BOOK

BOOK II

THE ARGUMENT

THE CONSULTATION begun, Satan debates whether another
battle be to be hazarded for the recovery of heaven: some
advise it, others dissuade. A third proposal is preferred,
mentioned before by Satan, to search the truth of that
prophecy or tradition in heaven concerning another world
and another kind of creature, equal or not much inferior
to themselves, about this time to be created. Their doubt
who shall be sent on this difficult search: Satan, their chief,
undertakes alone the voyage, is honored and applauded.
The council thus ended, the rest betake them several ways
and to several employments, as their inclinations lead
them, to entertain the time till Satan return. He passes on
his journey to hell gates, finds them shut, and who sat
there to guard them, by whom at length they are opened,
and discover to him the great gulf between hell and
heaven; with what difficulty he passes through, directed by
Chaos, the power of that place, to the sight of this new
world which he sought.

High on a throne of royal state, which far
Outshone the wealth of Ormus[1] and of Ind,
Or where the gorgeous East with richest hand
Showers on her kings barbaric pearl and gold,
Satan exalted sat, by merit raised   5
To that bad eminence, and, from despair
Thus high uplifted beyond hope, aspires
Beyond thus high, insatiate to pursue
Vain war with heaven, and, by success[2] untaught,
His proud imaginations thus displayed: 10

"Powers and dominions,[3] deities of heaven,
For since no deep within her gulf can hold
Immortal vigor, though oppressed and fallen,
I give not heaven for lost. From this descent
Celestial virtues rising will appear   15
More glorious and more dread than from no fall,
And trust themselves to fear no second fate.
Me, though just right and the fixed laws of heaven
Did first create your leader, next free choice,
With what besides, in council or in fight,   20
Hath been achieved of merit, yet this loss,
Thus far at least recovered, hath much more
Established in a safe, unenvied throne,
Yielded with full consent. The happier state
In heaven, which follows dignity,[4] might draw   25
Envy from each inferior; but who here
Will envy whom the highest place exposes
Foremost to stand against the Thunderer's aim
Your bulwark, and condemns to greatest share
Of endless pain? Where there is, then, no good   30
For which to strive, no strife can grow up there
From faction; for none sure will claim in hell
Precedence, none, whose portion is so small
Of present pain, that with ambitious mind
Will covet more. With this advantage, then,   35
To union and firm faith and firm accord,
More than can be in heaven, we now return
To claim our just inheritance of old,
Surer to prosper than prosperity
Could have assured us; and by what best way,   40
Whether of open war or covert guile,
We now debate; who can advise, may speak."

---

[54] Walk out and discuss.   [55] Crowded.
[56] The ancient belief that the pygmies lived in the mountains of
India had not yet been discarded.   [57] Spectator.

[1] Hormuz, an island in the Persian gulf, famous as a jewel mart.
[2] The outcome (of his first attempt).

[53] Crowded.   [59] Consultation.
[3] See note on Book I, line 128.   [4] Rank.

He ceased; and next him Moloch,[5] sceptered king,
Stood up, the strongest and the fiercest spirit
That fought in heaven, now fiercer by despair;   45
His trust was with the Eternal to be deemed
Equal in strength, and rather than be less
Cared not to be at all; with that care lost
Went all his fear: of God, or hell, or worse,
He recked not, and these words thereafter[6] spake: 50
   "My sentence[7] is for open war: of wiles,
More unexpert,[8] I boast not; them let those
Contrive who need, or when they need, not now.
For, while they sit contriving, shall the rest—
Millions that stand in arms, and longing wait   55
The signal to ascend—sit lingering here,
Heaven's fugitives, and for their dwelling place
Accept this dark opprobrious den of shame,
The prison of his tyranny who reigns
By our delay? No, let us rather choose,   60
Armed with hell-flames and fury, all at once
O'er heaven's high towers to force resistless way,
Turning our tortures[9] into horrid arms
Against the Torturer; when, to meet the noise
Of his almighty engine,[10] he shall hear   65
Infernal thunder, and, for lightning, see
Black fire and horror shot with equal rage
Among his angels, and his throne itself
Mixed with Tartarean[11] sulphur and strange fire,
His own invented torments. But perhaps   70
The way seems difficult and steep to scale
With upright wing against a higher foe.
Let such bethink them, if the sleepy drench
Of that forgetful lake[12] benumb not still,
That in our proper[13] motion we ascend   75
Up to our native seat; descent and fall
To us is adverse. Who but felt of late,
When the fierce foe hung on our broken rear
Insulting,[14] and pursued us through the deep,
With what compulsion and laborious flight   80
We sunk thus low? The ascent is easy, then;
The event[15] is feared: should we again provoke
Our stronger, some worse way his wrath may find
To our destruction, if there be in hell
Fear to be worse destroyed. What can be worse   85
Than to dwell here, driven out from bliss, condemned
In this abhorrèd deep to utter woe;

Where pain of unextinguishable fire
Must exercise[16] us without hope of end,
The vassals of his anger, when the scourge   90
Inexorably, and the torturing hour,
Calls us to penance? More destroyed than thus,
We should be quite abolished, and expire.
What fear we, then? what doubt we[17] to incense
His utmost ire? which, to the highth enraged,   95
Will either quite consume us, and reduce
To nothing this essential[18]—happier far
Than miserable to have eternal being!—
Or, if our substance be indeed divine,
And cannot cease to be, we are at worst   100
On this side nothing; and by proof we feel
Our power sufficient to disturb his heaven,
And with perpetual inroads to alarm,
Though inaccessible, his fatal[19] throne:
Which, if not victory, is yet revenge."   105
   He ended frowning, and his look denounced[20]
Desperate revenge, and battle dangerous
To less than gods. On the other side up rose
Belial,[21] in act more graceful and humane;
A fairer person lost not heaven; he seemed   110
For dignity composed, and high exploit.
But all was false and hollow, though his tongue
Dropped manna, and could make the worse appear
The better reason, to perplex and dash
Maturest counsels; for his thoughts were low;   115
To vice industrious, but to nobler deeds
Timorous and slothful; yet he pleased the ear,
And with persuasive accent thus began:
   "I should be much for open war, O peers,
As not behind in hate, if what was urged   120
Main reason to persuade immediate war
Did not dissuade me most, and seem to cast
Ominous conjecture on the whole success;[22]
When he who most excels in fact[23] of arms,
In what he counsels and in what excels   125
Mistrustful, grounds his courage on despair
And utter dissolution, as the scope
Of all his aim, after some dire revenge.
First, what revenge? The towers of heaven are filled
With armèd watch, that render all access   130
Impregnable; oft on the bordering deep
Encamp their legions, or with óbscure wing
Scout far and wide into the realm of Night,
Scorning surprise. Or could we break our way

---

[5] See Book I, lines 392 ff.   [6] Accordingly.
[7] Opinion, vote.   [8] I being less experienced in them.
[9] I.e., the flames.   [10] I.e., the thunderbolt.
[11] Infernal; *Tartarus* = hell.
[12] If the sleep-inducing drenching in the fiery lake, which made us forget for a time our true nature. Cf. Book I, line 266.
[13] Own natural; i.e., ascent is the motion natural to us.
[14] Assaulting.   [15] Outcome.

[16] Torment.   [17] Why are we afraid?   [18] Essence, being.
[19] Established by fate.   [20] Proclaimed.
[21] See Book I, lines 490 ff.
[22] I.e., seem to forecast a disastrous issue. *Success* (as in line 9 and elsewhere) = outcome (what succeeds or follows), whether favorable or unfavorable.   [23] Deed, feat.

By force, and at our heels all hell should rise 135
With blackest insurrection, to confound
Heaven's purest light, yet our great Enemy
All incorruptible would on his thron
Sit unpolluted, and the ethereal mold,[24]
Incapable of stain, would soon expel 140
Her mischief,[25] and purge off the baser fire,
Victorious. Thus repulsed, our final hope
Is flat despair: we must exasperate
The almighty Victor to spend all his rage;
And that must end us; that must be our cure; 145
To be no more; sad cure! for who would lose,
Though full of pain, this intellectual being,
Those thoughts that wander through eternity,
To perish rather, swallowed up and lost
In the wide womb of uncreated night, 150
Devoid of sense and motion? and who knows,
Let this be good,[26] whether our angry Foe
Can give it, or will ever? How he can
Is doubtful; that he never will is sure.
Will he, so wise, let loose at once his ire, 155
Belike[27] through impotence[28] or unaware,
To give his enemies their wish, and end
Them in his anger whom his anger saves
To punish endless? 'Wherefore cease we, then?'
Say they who counsel war; 'we are decreed, 160
Reserved, and destined to eternal woe;
Whatever doing, what can we suffer more,
What can we suffer worse?' Is this then worst,
Thus sitting, thus consulting, thus in arms?
What[29] when we fled amain,[30] pursued and struck 165
With heaven's afflicting thunder, and besought
The deep to shelter us? this hell then seemed
A refuge from those wounds: or when we lay
Chained on the burning lake? that sure was worse.
What if the breath that kindled those grim fires, 170
Awaked should blow them into sevenfold rage,
And plunge us in the flames? or from above
Should intermitted vengeance arm again
His red right hand to plague us? What if all
Her stores were opened, and this firmament 175
Of hell should spout her cataracts of fire,
Impendent[31] horrors, threatening hideous fall
One day upon our heads; while we perhaps,
Designing or exhorting glorious war,
Caught in a fiery tempest shall be hurled, 180
Each on his rock transfixed, the sport and prey
Of racking whirlwinds, or for ever sunk

Under yon boiling ocean, wrapped in chains,
There to converse with everlasting groans,
Unrespited, unpitied, unreprieved, 185
Ages of hopeless end?[32] This would be worse.
War, therefore, open or concealed, alike
My voice[33] dissuades; for what can force or guile
With him, or who deceive his mind, whose eye
Views all things at one view? He from heaven's height
All these our motions[34] vain sees and derides, 191
Not more almighty to resist our might
Than wise to frustrate all our plots and wiles.
Shall we, then, live thus vile, the race of heaven
Thus trampled, thus expelled, to suffer here 195
Chains and these torments? Better these than worse,
By my advice; since fate inevitable
Subdues us, and omnipotent decree,
The victor's will. To suffer, as to do,
Our strength is equal, nor the law unjust 200
That so ordains; this was at first resolved,
If we were wise,[35] against so great a foe
Contending, and so doubtful what might fall.[36]
I laugh, when those who at the spear are bold
And venturous, if that fail them, shrink and fear 205
What yet they know must follow, to endure
Exile or ignominy or bonds or pain,
The sentence of their conqueror: this is now
Our doom; which if we can sustain and bear,
Our súpreme Foe in time may much remit 210
His anger, and perhaps, thus far removed,
Not mind us not offending, satisfied
With what is punished;[37] whence these raging fires
Will slacken, if his breath stir not their flames.
Our purer essence then will overcome 215
Their noxious vapor, or inured not feel;
Or, changed at length and to the place conformed
In temper[38] and in nature, will receive
Familiar the fierce heat, and void of pain;
This horror will grow mild, this darkness light, 220
Besides what hope the never-ending flight
Of future days may bring, what chance, what change
Worth waiting, since our present lot appears
For happy[39] though but ill, for ill not worst,
If we procure not to ourselves more woe." 225
    Thus Belial with words clothed in reason's garb
Counseled ignoble ease and peaceful sloth,
Not peace; and after him thus Mammon[40] spake:

---

[24] Substance.   [25] The damage done to it ("her").
[26] Supposing we grant that annihilation might be desirable.
[27] Perhaps, no doubt (said ironically).
[28] Lack of self-control.   [29] What about? How was it?
[30] At top speed.   [31] Overhanging.

[32] Without hope of an end.   [33] Vote, opinion.
[34] Proposals.
[35] I.e., it was the part of wisdom to come to this resolution in
    advance of the action.   [36] Befall, happen.
[37] With the extent of the punishment.   [38] Temperament.
[39] With respect to happiness.   [40] See Book I, lines 679 ff.

"Either to disenthrone the King of heaven
We war, if war be best, or to regain   230
Our own right lost; him to unthrone we then
May hope, when everlasting Fate shall yield
To fickle Chance, and Chaos judge the strife.
The former, vain to hope, argues[41] as vain
The latter; for what place can be for us   235
Within heaven's bound, unless heaven's Lord supreme
We overpower? Suppose he should relent,
And publish grace to all, on promise made
Of new subjection; with what eyes could we
Stand in his presence humble, and receive   240
Strict laws imposed, to celebrate his throne
With warbled hymns, and to his Godhead sing
Forced halleluiahs, while he lordly sits
Our envied sovran, and his altar breathes
Ambrosial odors and ambrosial flowers,   245
Our servile offerings? This must be our task
In heaven, this our delight; how wearisome
Eternity so spent in worship paid
To whom we hate! Let us not then pursue,[42]
By force impossible, by leave obtained   250
Unacceptable, though in heaven, our state
Of splendid vassalage, but rather seek
Our own good from ourselves, and from our own
Live to ourselves, though in this vast recess,
Free, and to none accountable, preferring   255
Hard liberty before the easy yoke
Of servile pomp. Our greatness will appear
Then most conspicuous when great things of small,
Useful of hurtful, prosperous of adverse,
We can create, and in what place soe'er   260
Thrive under evil, and work ease out of pain
Through labor and endurance. This deep world
Of darkness do we dread? How oft amidst
Thick clouds and dark doth heaven's all-ruling Sire
Choose to reside, his glory unobscured,   265
And with the majesty of darkness round
Covers his throne, from whence deep thunders roar,
Mustering their rage, and heaven resembles hell!
As he our darkness, cannot we his light
Imitate when we please? This desert soil   270
Wants not her hidden luster, gems and gold;
Nor want we skill or art from whence to raise
Magnificence; and what can heaven show more?
Our torments also may in length of time
Become our elements, these piercing fires   275
As soft as now severe, our temper changed
Into their temper; which must needs remove
The sensible[43] of pain. All things invite
To peaceful counsels, and the settled state

Of order, how in safety best we may   280
Compose[44] our present evils, with regard
Of what we are and where, dismissing quite
All thoughts of war: ye have what I advise."
    He scarce had finished when such murmur filled
The assembly as when hollow rocks retain   285
The sound of blustering winds, which all night long
Had roused the sea, now with hoarse cadence lull
Seafaring men o'erwatched,[45] whose bark by chance,
Or pinnace, anchors in a craggy bay
After the tempest: such applause was heard   290
As Mammon ended, and his sentence pleased,
Advising peace; for such another field[46]
They dreaded worse than hell: so much the fear
Of thunder and the sword of Michaël[47]
Wrought still within them; and no less desire   295
To found this nether empire, which might rise,
By policy and long process of time,
In emulation opposite to heaven.
Which when Beëlzebub[48] perceived—than whom,
Satan except, none higher sat—with grave   300
Aspéct he rose, and in his rising seemed
A pillar of state; deep on his front[49] engraven
Deliberation sat, and public care;
And princely counsel in his face yet shone,
Majestic, though in ruin: sage he stood,   305
With Atlantean[50] shoulders, fit to bear
The weight of mightiest monarchies; his look
Drew audience and attention still as night
Or summer's noontide air, while thus he spake:
    "Thrones and imperial powers, offspring of heaven,   310
Ethereal virtues![51] or these titles now
Must we renounce, and, changing style,[52] be called
Princes of hell? for so the popular vote
Inclines, here to continue, and build up here
A growing empire; doubtless![53] while we dream,   315
And know not that the King of heaven hath doomed
This place our dungeon, not our safe retreat
Beyond his potent arm, to live exempt
From heaven's high jurisdiction, in new league
Banded against his throne, but to remain   320
In strictest bondage, though thus far removed,
Under the inevitable curb, reserved
His captive multitude: for he, be sure,
In highth or depth, still first and last[54] will reign

---

41 Proves.   42 I.e., try to regain.   43 Feeling.

44 Adjust, allay.   45 Worn out with standing watch.
46 Battle.   47 The archangel commanding the army of God.
48 See Book I, lines 78–81.   49 Face.
50 Like those of Atlas, the Titan credited in classical mythology
with holding up the sky or the earth.
51 See note on Book I, line 128.   52 Title.
53 Spoken sarcastically.
54 "I am Alpha and Omega, the first and the last" (Revelation
1:11).

Sole king, and of his kingdom lose no part 325
By our revolt, but over hell extend
His empire, and with iron scepter rule
Us here, as with his golden those in heaven.
What[55] sit we then projecting peace and war?
War hath determined[56] us and foiled with loss 330
Irreparable; terms of peace yet none
Voutsafed[57] or sought; for what peace will be given
To us enslaved, but custody severe,
And stripes,[58] and arbitrary punishment
Inflicted? and what peace can we return 335
But, to[59] our power, hostility and hate,
Untamed reluctance,[60] and revenge though slow,
Yet ever plotting how the Conqueror least
May reap his conquest, and may least rejoice
In doing what we most in suffering feel? 340
Nor will occasion want, nor shall we need
With dangerous expedition to invade
Heaven, whose high walls fear no assault or siege,
Or ambush from the deep. What if we find
Some easier enterprise? There is a place 345
(If ancient and prophetic fame[61] in heaven
Err not), another world, the happy seat
Of some new race called man, about this time
To be created like to us, though less
In power and excellence, but favored more 350
Of him who rules above; so was his will
Pronounced among the gods, and by an oath
That shook heaven's whole circumference confirmed.
Thither let us bend all our thoughts, to learn
What creatures there inhabit, of what mold 355
Or substance, how endued,[62] and what their power,
And where their weakness, how attempted best,
By force or subtlety. Though heaven be shut,
And heaven's high Arbitrator sit secure
In his own strength, this place may lie exposed, 360
The utmost border of his kingdom, left
To their defense who hold it; here, perhaps,
Some advantageous act may be achieved
By sudden onset—either with hell-fire
To waste his whole creation, or possess 365
All as our own, and drive, as we were driven,
The puny habitants; or, if not drive,
Seduce them to our party, that their God
May prove their foe, and with repenting hand
Abolish his own works. This would surpass 370
Common revenge, and interrupt his joy
In our confusion,[63] and our joy upraise

In his disturbance, when his darling sons,
Hurled headlong to partake with us, shall curse
Their frail original,[64] and faded bliss— 375
Faded so soon. Advise[65] if this be worth
Attempting, or to sit in darkness here
Hatching vain empires." Thus Beëlzebub
Pleaded his devilish counsel, first devised
By Satan, and in part proposed; for whence 380
But from the author of all ill could spring
So deep a malice, to confound the race
Of mankind in one root, and earth with hell
To mingle and involve, done all to spite
The great Creator? But their spite still serves 385
His glory to augment. The bold design
Pleased highly those infernal states,[66] and joy
Sparkled in all their eyes; with full assent
They vote; whereat his speech he thus renews:
"Well have ye judged, well ended long debate, 390
Synod[67] of gods, and, like to what ye are,
Great things resolved, which from the lowest deep
Will once more lift us up, in spite of fate,
Nearer our ancient seat, perhaps in view
Of those bright confines whence, with neighboring arms
And opportune excursion, we may chance 396
Re-enter heaven, or else in some mild zone
Dwell, not unvisited of heaven's fair light,
Secure, and at the brightening orient beam
Purge off this gloom; the soft delicious air, 400
To heal the scar of these corrosive fires,
Shall breathe her balm. But first whom shall we send
In search of this new world, whom shall we find
Sufficient? who shall tempt[68] with wandering feet
The dark, unbottomed, infinite abyss, 405
And through the palpable obscure[69] find out
His uncouth[70] way, or spread his aery flight,
Upborne with indefatigable wings
Over the vast abrupt,[71] ere he arrive
The happy isle?[72] What strength, what art, can then 410
Suffice, or what evasion bear him safe
Through the strict senteries and stations[73] thick
Of angels watching round? Here he had need
All circumspection, and we now no less
Choice in our suffrage;[74] for on whom we send 415
The weight of all, and our last hope, relies."
    This said, he sat; and expectation held
His look suspense,[75] awaiting who appeared
To second, or oppose, or undertake

---

55 Why.   56 Ended, done for.
57 Vouchsafed, granted.   58 Lashes.
59 To the extent of.   60 Untamable resistance.
61 Rumor.   62 Endowed, invested, gifted.   63 Ruin.

64 Adam.   65 Consider.
66 Members of the assembly.   67 Assembly.
68 Attempt.   69 Tangible darkness.   70 Unknown.
71 Gulf.   72 The world, suspended in chaos.
73 Sentries and guards.   74 Care in our selection.
75 In suspense.

The perilous attempt: but all sat mute,   420
Pondering the danger with deep thoughts; and each
In other's countenance read his own dismay,
Astonished.[76] None among the choice and prime
Of those heaven-warring champions could be found
So hardy as to proffer or accept   425
Alone the dreadful voyage; till at last
Satan, whom now transcendent glory raised
Above his fellows, with monarchal pride
Conscious of highest worth, unmoved thus spake:
  "O progeny of heaven, empyreal thrones,   430
With reason hath deep silence and demur
Seized us, though undismayed: long is the way
And hard, that out of hell leads up to light;
Our prison strong, this huge convex of fire,
Outrageous to devour, immures us round   435
Ninefold; and gates of burning adamant,
Barred over us, prohibit all egress.
These passed, if any pass, the void profound
Of unessential[77] night receives him next,
Wide-gaping, and with utter loss of being   440
Threatens him, plunged in that abortive[78] gulf.
If thence he scape, into whatever world
Or unknown region, what remains him less
Than unknown dangers and as hard escape?
But I should ill become this throne, O peers,   445
And this imperial sovranty, adorned
With splendor, armed with power, if aught, proposed
And judged of public moment,[79] in the shape
Of difficulty or danger could deter
Me from attempting. Wherefore do I assume   450
These royalties, and not refuse to reign,
Refusing[80] to accept as great a share
Of hazard as of honor, due alike
To him who reigns, and so much to him due
Of hazard more, as he above the rest   455
High honored sits? Go, therefore, mighty powers,
Terror of heaven, though fallen; intend[81] at home,
While here shall be our home, what best may ease
The present misery, and render hell
More tolerable, if there be cure or charm   460
To respite or deceive or slack the pain
Of this ill mansion; intermit no watch
Against a wakeful foe, while I abroad
Through all the coasts of dark destruction seek
Deliverance for us all: this enterprise   465
None shall partake with me." Thus saying, rose
The monarch, and prevented all reply;
Prudent, lest, from his resolution raised,[82]

Others among the chief might offer now
(Certain to be refused) what erst they feared,   470
And, so refused, might in opinion stand
His rivals, winning cheap the high repute
Which he through hazard huge must earn. But they
Dreaded not more the adventure than his voice
Forbidding; and at once with him they rose;   475
Their rising all at once was as the sound
Of thunder heard remote. Towards him they bend
With awful reverence prone, and as a god
Extol him equal to the Highest in heaven:
Nor failed they to express how much they praised   480
That for the general safety he despised
His own; for neither do the spirits damned
Lose all their virtue, lest bad men should boast
Their specious deeds on earth, which glory excites,
Or close[83] ambition varnished o'er with zeal.[84]   485
  Thus they their doubtful consultations dark
Ended, rejoicing in their matchless chief:
As when from mountain tops the dusky clouds
Ascending, while the north wind sleeps, o'erspread
Heaven's cheerful face, the louring element[85]   490
Scowls o'er the darkened lantskip[86] snow, or shower,
If chance the radiant sun, with farewell sweet,
Extend his evening beam, the fields revive,
The birds their notes renew, and bleating herds
Attest their joy, that hill and valley rings.   495
O shame to men! Devil with devil damned
Firm concord holds; men only disagree
Of creatures rational, though under hope
Of heavenly grace, and, God proclaiming peace,
Yet live in hatred, enmity, and strife   500
Among themselves, and levy cruel wars,
Wasting the earth, each other to destroy:
As if (which might induce us to accord)
Man had not hellish foes anow[87] besides,
That day and night for his destruction wait.   505
  The Stygian council thus dissolved; and forth
In order came the grand infernal peers:
Midst came their mighty paramount,[88] and seemed
Alone the antagonist of heaven, nor less
Than hell's dread emperor, with pomp supreme,   510
And godlike imitated state; him round
A globe[89] of fiery seraphim inclosed
With bright imblazonry,[90] and horrent[91] arms.
Then of their session ended they bid cry
With trumpets' regal sound the great result: 515
Toward the four winds four speedy cherubim
Put to their mouths the sounding alchemy,[92]

---

[76] Stunned.
[77] Without substance, vacant.   [78] Formless.
[79] Importance.   [80] If I should refuse.   [81] Consider.
[82] Encouraged by his boldness.

[83] Secret.   [84] Religious devotion.   [85] Frowning sky.
[86] Landscape.   [87] Enow, enough.   [88] Chief.
[89] Circle.   [90] Coats of arms.   [91] Bristling.
[92] I.e., trumpets of (goldlike) brass.

By harald's voice explained; the hollow abyss
Heard far and wide, and all the host of hell
With deafening shout returned them loud acclaim. 520
Thence more at ease their minds, and somewhat raised
By false presumptuous hope, the rangèd powers[93]
Disband, and, wandering, each his several way
Pursues, as inclination or sad choice
Leads him perplexed, where he may likeliest find 525
Truce to his restless thoughts, and entertain
The irksome hours, till his great chief return.
Part on the plain, or in the air sublime,[94]
Upon the wing or in swift race contend,
As at the Olympian games or Pythian fields;[95] 530
Part curb their fiery steeds,[96] or shun the goal
With rapid wheels,[97] or fronted brígades[98] form.
As when, to warn proud cities, war appears
Waged in the troubled sky, and armies rush
To battle in the clouds;[99] before each van[1] 535
Prick[2] forth the aery knights, and couch their spears
Till thickest legions close; with feats of arms
From either end of heaven the welkin[3] burns.
Others, with vast Typhoean[4] rage more fell,
Rend up both rocks and hills, and ride the air 540
In whirlwind; hell scarce holds the wild uproar.
As when Alcides,[5] from Oechalia[6] crowned
With conquest, felt the envenomed robe, and tore
Through pain up by the roots Thessalian pines,
And Lichas from the top of Oeta[7] threw 545
Into the Euboic[8] sea. Others, more mild,
Retreated in a silent valley, sing
With notes angelical to many a harp
Their own heroic deeds, and hapless fall
By doom of battle, and complain that fate 550
Free virtue[9] should enthrall to force or chance.
Their song was partial; but the harmony
(What could it less when spirits immortal sing?)

Suspended[10] hell, and took[11] with ravishment
The thronging audience. In discourse more sweet 555
(For eloquence the soul, song charms the sense)
Others apart sat on a hill retired,
In thoughts more elevate, and reasoned high
Of providence, foreknowledge, will, and fate—
Fixed fate, free will, foreknowledge absolute— 560
And found no end, in wandering mazes lost.
Of good and evil much they argued then,
Of happiness and final misery,
Passion and apathy,[12] and glory and shame:
Vain wisdom all, and false philosophy! 565
Yet with a pleasing sorcery could charm
Pain for a while or anguish, and excite
Fallacious hope, or arm the obdurèd[13] breast
With stubborn patience as with triple steel.
Another part, in squadrons and gross[14] bands, 570
On bold adventure to discover[15] wide
That dismal world, if any clime[16] perhaps
Might yield them easier habitation, bend
Four ways their flying march, along the banks
Of four infernal rivers that disgorge 575
Into the burning lake their baleful streams:
Abhorrèd Styx, the flood of deadly hate;
Sad Acheron, of sorrow, black and deep;
Cocytus, named of lamentation loud
Heard on the rueful stream; fierce Phlegeton,[17] 580
Whose waves of torrent fire inflame with rage.
Far off from these, a slow and silent stream,
Lethe, the river of oblivion, rolls
Her watery labyrinth, whereof who drinks
Forthwith his former state and being forgets, 585
Forgets both joy and grief, pleasure and pain.
Beyond this flood a frozen continent
Lies dark and wild, beat with perpetual storms
Of whirlwind and dire hail, which on firm land
Thaws not, but gathers heap, and ruin seems 590
Of ancient pile;[18] all else deep snow and ice,
A gulf profound as that Serbonian bog[19]
Betwixt Damiata and Mount Casius old,
Where armies whole have sunk: the parching air
Burns frore,[20] and cold performs the effect of fire. 595
Thither, by harpy-footed[21] Furies haled,

---

93 Troops.   94 Lofty.
95 As the Olympics (held at Olympia in southern Greece every
four years) honored Zeus, games were held in honor of the
Pythian god (Apollo, who slew a huge python) at Delphi in
central Greece, the seat of his oracle.
96 I.e., race their horses.
97 I.e., in making the turns around the posts in chariot races.
98 In mock battles or tournaments.
99 What this means no one knows; guesses have ranged from the
aurora borealis down.
1 Vanguard.   2 Spur.   3 Air.
4 Typhoeus, a hundred-headed monster confined by Zeus under
Mt. Etna—the Typhon of Book I, line 199.
5 Hercules. His servant Lichas brought him the robe, unaware that
it had been poisoned.
6 In Thessaly, where he won a victory.
7 A mountain in Thessaly.
8 Between the island of Euboea and the mainland.
9 Power, i.e., rugged individualism.

10 Held enrapt.   11 Charmed.
12 The Stoic ideal of freedom from feeling.
13 Hardened.   14 Compact.   15 Explore.   16 Region.
17 Phlegethon. Like the other rivers, this one is transferred by
Milton from classical mythology to his Christian hell.
18 Building.
19 Lake Serbonis (now dried up), near Damietta, at the mouth of
the Nile.
20 Frosty. The idea of hellish cold as well as heat is an old one.
21 Claw-footed. The Harpies of Greek mythology were soul-
snatchers, part bird, part woman. The Furies were divinities
who avenged crime.

At certain revolutions[22] all the damned
Are brought and feel by turns the bitter change
Of fierce extremes, extremes by change more fierce,
From beds of raging fire to starve[23] in ice   600
Their soft ethereal warmth, and there to pine
Immovable, infixed, and frozen round,
Periods of time, thence hurried back to fire.
They ferry over this Lethean sound
Both to and fro, their sorrow to augment,   605
And wish and struggle, as they pass, to reach
The tempting stream, with one small drop to lose
In sweet forgetfulness all pain and woe,
All in one moment, and so near the brink;
But fate withstands, and, to oppose the attempt,   610
Medusa[24] with Gorgonian terror guards
The ford, and of itself the water flies
All taste of living wight, as once it fled
The lip of Tantalus.[25] Thus roving on
In cónfused march forlorn, the adventurous bands,   615
With shuddering horror pale and eyes aghast,
Viewed first their lamentable lot, and found
No rest: through many a dark and dreary vale
They passed, and many a region dolorous,
O'er many a frozen, many a fiery alp,[26]   620
Rocks, caves, lakes, fens, bogs, dens, and shades of death,
A universe of death, which God by curse
Created evil, for evil only good,
Where all life dies, death lives, and nature breeds,
Perverse, all monstrous, all prodigious[27] things,   625
Abominable, inutterable, and worse
Than fables yet have feigned or fear conceived,
Gorgons, and hydras, and chimeras[28] dire.

Meanwhile the adversary of God and man,
Satan, with thoughts inflamed of highest design,   630
Puts on swift wings, and toward the gates of hell
Explores[29] his solitary flight; sometimes
He scours the right-hand coast, sometimes the left,
Now shaves with level wing the deep, then soars
Up to the fiery concave towering high.   635
As when far off at sea a fleet descried
Hangs in the clouds, by equinoctial winds
Close sailing from Bengala,[30] or the isles
Of Ternate and Tidore,[31] whence merchants bring

Their spicy drugs; they on the trading flood,   640
Through the wide Ethiopian[32] to the Cape,[33]
Ply stemming nightly toward the pole: so seemed
Far off the flying fiend. At last appear
Hell bounds, high reaching to the horrid roof,
And thrice threefold the gates: three folds were brass,   645
Three iron, three of adamantine rock,
Impenetrable, impaled with circling fire,
Yet unconsumed. Before the gates there sat
On either side a formidable shape.
The one seemed woman to the waist, and fair,   650
But ended foul in many a scaly fold,
Voluminous and vast, a serpent armed
With mortal sting. About her middle round
A cry of hellhounds never ceasing barked
With wide Cerberean[34] mouths full loud, and rung   655
A hideous peal; yet, when they list, would creep,
If aught disturbed their noise, into her womb,
And kennel there; yet there still barked and howled
Within unseen. Far less abhorred than these
Vexed Scylla,[35] bathing in the sea that parts   660
Calabria from the hoarse Trinacrian shore;
Nor uglier follow the night hag, when, called
In secret, riding through the air she comes,
Lured with the smell of infant blood, to dance
With Lapland[36] witches, while the laboring moon   665
Eclipses at their charms. The other shape—
If shape it might be called that shape had none
Distinguishable in member, joint, or limb;
Or substance might be called that shadow seemed,
For each seemed either—black it stood as night,   670
Fierce as ten Furies, terrible as hell,
And shook a dreadful dart; what seemed his head
The likeness of a kingly crown had on.
Satan was now at hand, and from his seat
The monster moving onward came as fast   675
With horrid strides; hell trembled as he strode.
The undaunted fiend what this might be admired—[37]
Admired, not feared (God and his Son except,
Created thing naught valued he nor shunned),
And with disdainful look thus first began: 680
"Whence and what art thou, execrable shape,
That dar'st, though grim and terrible, advance
Thy miscreated front athwart my way
To yonder gates? Through them I mean to pass,
That be assured, without leave asked of thee.   685

---

[22] Periodically.   [23] Destroy.
[24] The most famous of the Gorgons, the three snake-haired sister
monsters of classical mythology, whose gaze turned the spectator
to stone.
[25] According to the classical myth, his punishment was to be placed
between water and fruit, which receded when he tried to touch
them.   [26] High mountain.   [27] Unnatural.
[28] The Hydra was the nine-headed serpent killed by Hercules. The
Chimera was a fiery monster, part goat, lion, and dragon.
[29] Pursues in a tentative or uncertain fashion.
[30] A province of India.   [31] Islands in the Dutch Indies.

[32] Indian Ocean.   [33] Cape of Good Hope, South Africa.
[34] Cerberus was the three-headed hound that guarded the gates of
Hades in classical myth.
[35] A female sea-monster who was thought to inhabit a rock in the
Strait of Messina, between Italy and Sicily. Opposite her, near
the Sicilian ("Trinacrian") shore, was the whirlpool Charybdis.
[36] Thought to be a favorite meeting place and abode of witches.
[37] Wondered.

Retire; or taste thy folly, and learn by proof,
Hellborn, not to contend with spirits of heaven."
    To whom the goblin, full of wrath, replied:
"Art thou that traitor angel, art thou he,
Who first broke peace in heaven, and faith, till then   690
Unbroken, and in proud rebellious arms
Drew after him the third part of heaven's sons,
Conjured[38] against the Highest, for which both thou
And they, outcast from God, are here condemned
To waste eternal days in woe and pain?   695
And reckon'st thou thyself with spirits of heaven,
Hell-doomed, and breath'st defiance here and scorn,
Where I reign king, and, to enrage thee more,
Thy king and lord? Back to thy punishment,
False fugitive; and to thy speed add wings,   700
Lest with a whip of scorpions I pursue
Thy lingering, or with one stroke of this dart
Strange horror seize thee, and pangs unfelt before."
    So spake the grisly terror, and in shape,
So speaking and so threatening, grew tenfold   705
More dreadful and deform. On the other side,
Incensed with indignation, Satan stood
Unterrified, and like a comet burned,
That fires the length of Ophiuchus[39] huge
In the arctic sky, and from his horrid[40] hair   710
Shakes pestilence and war. Each at the head
Leveled his deadly aim; their fatal hands
No second stroke intend; and such a frown
Each cast at the other as when two black clouds,
With heaven's artillery fraught, come rattling on   715
Over the Caspian, then stand front to front
Hovering a space, till winds the signal blow
To join their dark encounter in mid-air.
So frowned the mighty combatants that hell
Grew darker at their frown; so matched they stood;   720
For never but once more was either like
To meet so great a foe. And now great deeds
Had been achieved, whereof all hell had rung,
Had not the snaky sorceress, that sat
Fast by hell gate and kept the fatal key,   725
Risen, and with hideous outcry rushed between.
    "O father, what intends thy hand," she cried,
"Against thy only son? What fury, O son,
Possesses thee to bend that mortal dart
Against thy father's head? And know'st for whom?   730
For him who sits above, and laughs the while
At thee, ordained his drudge to execute
Whate'er his wrath, which he calls justice, bids,
His wrath which one day will destroy ye both!"

[38] United by an oath.
[39] A constellation. Comets were regarded as portents, usually of
    disaster.   [40] Bristling.

She spake, and at her words the hellish pest[41]   735
Forbore: then these to her Satan returned:
    "So strange thy outcry, and thy words so strange
Thou interposest, that my sudden hand,
Prevented, spares to tell thee yet by deeds
What it intends, till first I know of thee   740
What thing thou art, thus double-formed, and why,
In this infernal vale first met, thou call'st
Me father, and that phantasm call'st my son.
I know thee not, nor ever saw till now
Sight more detestable than him and thee."   745
    To whom thus the portress of hell gate replied:
"Hast thou forgot me, then, and do I seem
Now in thine eyes so foul?—once deemed so fair
In heaven, when at the assembly, and in sight
Of all the seraphim with thee combined   750
In bold conspiracy against heaven's King,
All on a sudden miserable pain
Surprised thee, dim thine eyes, and dizzy swum
In darkness, while thy head flames thick and fast
Threw forth, till on the left side opening wide,   755
Likest to thee in shape and countenance bright,
Then shining heavenly fair, a goddess armed,
Out of thy head I sprung.[42] Amazement seized
All the host of heaven; back they recoiled afraid
At first, and called me Sin, and for a sign   760
Portentous held me; but, familiar grown,
I pleased, and with attractive graces won
The most averse, thee chiefly, who, full oft
Thyself in me thy perfect image viewing,
Becam'st enamored; and such joy thou took'st   765
With me in secret that my womb conceived
A growing burden. Meanwhile war arose,
And fields were fought in heaven: wherein remained
(For what could else?) to our almighty Foe
Clear victory; to our part loss and rout   770
Through all the empyrean. Down they fell,
Driven headlong from the pitch of heaven, down
Into this deep, and in the general fall
I also; at which time this powerful key
Into my hands was given, with charge to keep   775
These gates for ever shut, which none can pass
Without my opening. Pensive here I sat
Alone, but long I sat not till my womb,
Pregnant by thee, and now excessive grown,
Prodigious motion felt and rueful throes.   780
At last this odious offspring whom thou seest,
Thine own begotten, breaking violent way,
Tore through my entrails, that, with fear and pain
Distorted, all my nether shape thus grew

[41] Pestilential creature.
[42] Compare the myth of the emergence of Pallas Athena fully
    armed from the head of Zeus.

Transformed: but he my inbred enemy   785
Forth issued, brandishing his fatal dart
Made to destroy. I fled, and cried out 'Death!'
Hell trembled at the hideous name, and sighed
From all her caves, and back resounded 'Death!'
I fled; but he pursued (though more, it seems,   790
Inflamed with lust than rage), and, swifter far,
Me overtook, his mother, all dismayed,
And, in embraces forcible and foul
Engendering with me, of that rape begot
These yelling monsters, that with ceaseless cry   795
Surround me, as thou saw'st, hourly conceived
And hourly born, with sorrow infinite
To me, for, when they list, into the womb
That bred them they return, and howl, and gnaw
My bowels, their repast; then, bursting forth   800
Afresh, with conscious terrors vex me round,
That rest or intermission none I find.
Before mine eyes in opposition sits
Grim Death, my son and foe, who sets them on,
And me, his parent, would full soon devour   805
For want of other prey, but that he knows
His end with mine involved, and knows that I
Should prove a bitter morsel, and his bane,
Whenever that shall be: so Fate pronounced.
But thou, O father, I forewarn thee, shun   810
His deadly arrow; neither vainly hope
To be invulnerable in those bright arms,
Though tempered heavenly; for that mortal dint,[43]
Save he who reigns above, none can resist."
She finished; and the subtle fiend his lore   815
Soon learned, now milder, and thus answered smooth:
"Dear daughter—since thou claim'st me for thy sire,
And my fair son here show'st me, the dear pledge
Of dalliance had with thee in heaven, and joys
Then sweet, now sad to mention, through dire change
Befallen us unforeseen, unthought-of—know   821
I come no enemy, but to set free
From out this dark and dismal house of pain
Both him and thee, and all the heavenly host
Of spirits that, in our just pretenses[44] armed,   825
Fell with us from on high; from them I go
This uncouth[45] errand sole, and one for all
Myself expose, with lonely steps to tread
The unfounded deep, and through the void immense
To search with wandering quest a place foretold   830
Should be, and, by concurring signs,[46] ere now
Created vast and round, a place of bliss
In the purlieus of heaven; and therein placed

A race of upstart creatures, to supply
Perhaps our vacant room,[47] though more removed,[48] 835
Lest heaven, surcharged with potent multitude,
Might hap to move new broils. Be this, or aught
Than this more secret, now designed, I haste
To know; and, this once known, shall soon return,
And bring ye to the place where thou and Death   840
Shall dwell at ease, and up and down unseen
Wing silently the buxom[49] air, embalmed
With odors; there ye shall be fed and filled
Immeasurably; all things shall be your prey."
He ceased; for both seemed highly pleased,
     and Death   845
Grinned horrible a ghastly smile, to hear
His famine should be filled, and blessed his maw
Destined to that good hour. No less rejoiced
His mother bad, and thus bespake her sire:
"The key of this infernal pit, by due   850
And by command of heaven's all-powerful King,
I keep, by him forbidden to unlock
These adamantine gates; against all force
Death ready stands to interpose his dart,
Fearless to be o'ermatched by living might.   855
But what owe I to his commands above,
Who hates me, and hath hither thrust me down
Into this gloom of Tartarus profound,
To sit in hateful office here confined,
Inhabitant of heaven and heavenly-born,   860
Here in perpetual agony and pain,
With terrors and with clamors compassed round
Of mine own brood, that on my bowels feed?
Thou art my father, thou my author, thou
My being gav'st me; whom should I obey   865
But thee? whom follow? Thou wilt bring me soon
To that new world of light and bliss, among
The gods who live at ease, where I shall reign
At thy right hand voluptuous, as beseems
Thy daughter and thy darling, without end."   870
Thus saying, from her side the fatal key,
Sad instrument of all our woe, she took;
And, toward the gate rolling her bestial train,
Forthwith the huge portcullis high updrew,
Which, but herself, not all the Stygian powers   875
Could once have moved; then in the keyhole turns
The intricate wards, and every bolt and bar
Of massy iron or solid rock with ease
Unfastens; on a sudden open fly
With impetuous recoil and jarring sound   880
The infernal doors, and on their hinges grate
Harsh thunder, that the lowest bottom shook

---

[43] Blow.   [44] Claims.
[45] Unknown, unfamiliar.
[46] To judge by confirming indications.

[47] To fill perhaps the space left vacant by our removal.
[48] Farther distant; i.e., not in heaven itself.   [49] Yielding.

Of Erebus.[50] She opened, but to shut
Excelled her power: the gates wide open stood,
That with extended wings a bannered host   885
Under spread ensigns marching might pass through
With horse and chariots ranked in loose array;
So wide they stood, and like a furnace mouth
Cast forth redounding[51] smoke and ruddy flame.
Before their eyes in sudden view appear   890
The secrets of the hoary deep, a dark
Illimitable ocean without bound,
Without dimension, where length, breadth, and highth,
And time, and place, are lost; where eldest Night
And Chaos, ancestors of Nature, hold   895
Eternal anarchy, amidst the noise
Of endless wars, and by confusion stand.
For hot, cold, moist, and dry,[52] four champions fierce,
Strive here for mastery, and to battle bring
Their embryon atoms; they around the flag   900
Of each his faction, in their several clans,
Light-armed or heavy, sharp, smooth, swift, or slow,
Swarm populous, unnumbered as the sands
Of Barca or Cyrene's[53] torrid soil,
Levied to side with warring winds, and poise   905
Their lighter wings. To whom these most adhere,
He rules a moment; Chaos umpire sits,
And by decision more embroils the fray
By which he reigns; next him, high arbiter,
Chance governs all. Into this wild abyss,   910
The womb of Nature, and perhaps her grave,
Of neither sea, nor shore, nor air, nor fire,
But all these in their pregnant causes mixed
Confusedly, and which thus might ever fight,
Unless the almighty Maker them ordain   915
His dark materials to create more worlds—
Into this wild abyss the wary fiend
Stood on the brink of hell and looked a while,
Pondering his voyage; for no narrow frith[54]
He had to cross. Nor was his ear less pealed   920
With noises loud and ruinous (to compare
Great things with small) than when Bellona[55] storms
With all her battering engines, bent to rase
Some capital city; or less than if this frame
Of heaven were falling, and these elements   925
In mutiny had from her axle torn
The steadfast earth. At last his sail-broad vans[56]

He spreads for flight, and, in the surging smoke
Uplifted, spurns the ground; thence many a league
As in a cloudy chair ascending rides   930
Audacious, but, that seat soon failing, meets
A vast vacuity; all unawares,
Fluttering his pennons vain, plumb down he drops
Ten thousand fadom[57] deep, and to this hour
Down had been falling, had not by ill chance   935
The strong rebuff of some tumultuous cloud,
Instinct[58] with fire and niter, hurried him
As many miles aloft. That fury stayed,
Quenched in a boggy Syrtis,[59] neither sea
Nor good dry land, nigh foundered on he fares,   940
Treading the crude consistence, half on foot,
Half flying; behoves him now both oar and sail.
As when a gryphon[60] through the wilderness
With wingèd course, o'er hill or moory dale,
Pursues the Arimaspian,[61] who by stealth   945
Had from his wakeful custody purloined
The guarded gold; so eagerly the fiend
O'er bog or steep, through strait, rough, dense, or rare,[62]
With head, hands, wings, or feet, pursues his way,
And swims, or sinks, or wades, or creeps, or flies.   950
At length a universal hubbub wild
Of stunning sounds, and voices all confused,
Borne through the hollow dark, assaults his ear
With loudest vehemence; thither he plies
Undaunted, to meet there whatever power   955
Or spirit of the nethermost abyss
Might in that noise reside, of whom to ask
Which way the nearest coast of darkness lies
Bordering on light; when straight behold the throne
Of Chaos, and his dark pavilion spread   960
Wide on the wasteful deep; with him enthroned
Sat sable-vested Night, eldest of things,
The consort of his reign; and by them stood
Orcus and Ades, and the dreaded name
Of Demogorgon;[63] Rumor next, and Chance,   965
And Tumult, and Confusion, all embroiled,
And Discord with a thousand various mouths.
    To whom Satan, turning boldly, thus: "Ye powers
And spirits of this nethermost abyss,
Chaos and ancient Night, I come no spy   970
With purpose to explore or to disturb
The secrets of your realm; but, by constraint[64]
Wandering this darksome desert, as my way

---

[50] I.e., hell.   [51] Surging, billowing in clouds.
[52] In Chaos these four elemental qualities are in conflict; Nature
    succeeds Chaos when by God's command (see lines 915 f.) they
    combine harmoniously to produce material objects. Hence
    Milton calls Chaos the ancestor of Nature and "the womb of
    Nature" (lines 895, 911).   [53] Cities in northern Africa.
[54] Firth, arm of the sea.   [55] The Roman goddess of war.
[56] Wings.

[57] Fathoms. A fathom is six feet.   [58] Filled, charged.
[59] Quicksands off the northern coast of Africa.
[60] Usually spelled *griffin* or *griffon;* a mythical monster with a lion's
    body and an eagle's wings.
[61] The Arimaspians, one-eyed people of Scythia, were fabled to be
    in constant war with the griffins to obtain the gold they guarded.
[62] Thin.   [63] Names of infernal deities in classical myth.
[64] Necessity.

Lies through your spacious empire up to light,
Alone and without guide, half lost, I seek   975
What readiest path leads where your gloomy bounds
Confine with[65] heaven; or, if some other place,
From your dominion won, the Ethereal King
Possesses lately, thither to arrive
I travel this profound. Direct my course;   980
Directed, no mean recompense it brings
To your behoof, if I that region lost,
All usurpation thence expelled, reduce
To her original darkness and your sway
(Which is my present journey[66]), and once more   985
Erect the standard there of ancient Night.
Yours be the advantage all, mine the revenge!"

      Thus Satan; and him thus the anarch old,
With faltering speech and visage incomposed,
Answered: "I know thee, stranger, who thou art,   990
That mighty leading angel, who of late
Made head against heaven's King, though overthrown.
I saw and heard, for such a numerous host
Fled not in silence through the frighted deep
With ruin upon ruin, rout on rout,   995
Confusion worse confounded; and heaven gates
Poured out by millions her victorious bands
Pursuing. I upon my frontiers here
Keep residence; if all I can will serve
That little which is left so to defend,   1000
Encroached on still through our intestine broils
Weakening the scepter of old Night: first hell,
Your dungeon, stretching far and wide beneath;
Now lately heaven and earth, another world
Hung o'er my realm, linked in a golden chain   1005
To that side heaven from whence your legions fell.
If that way be your walk, you have not far;
So much the nearer danger. Go, and speed;
Havoc and spoil and ruin are my gain."

      He ceased; and Satan stayed not to reply,   1010
But, glad that now his sea should find a shore,
With fresh alacrity and force renewed
Springs upward, like a pyramid of fire,
Into the wild expanse, and through the shock
Of fighting elements, on all sides round   1015

Environed, wins his way; harder beset
And more endangered than when Argo[67] passed
Through Bosporus betwixt the justling rocks,[68]
Or when Ulysses on the larboard shunned
Charybdis, and by the other whirlpool steered.[69]   1020
So he with difficulty and labor hard
Moved on, with difficulty and labor he;
But, he once passed, soon after, when man fell,
Strange alteration! Sin and Death, amain
Following his track (such was the will of heaven),   1025
Paved after him a broad and beaten way
Over the dark abyss, whose boiling gulf
Tamely endured a bridge of wondrous length,
From hell continued, reaching the utmost orb[70]
Of this frail world; by which the spirits perverse   1030
With easy intercourse pass to and fro
To tempt or punish mortals, except whom
God and good angels guard by special grace.

      But now at last the sacred influence
Of light appears, and from the walls of heaven   1035
Shoots far into the bosom of dim night
A glimmering dawn. Here Nature first begins
Her fardest verge, and Chaos to retire,
As from her outmost works, a broken foe,
With tumult less and with less hostile din;   1040
That[71] Satan with less toil, and now with ease,
Wafts on the calmer wave by dubious light,
And, like a weather-beaten vessel, holds[72]
Gladly the port, though shrouds and tackle torn;
Or in the emptier waste, resembling air,   1045
Weighs[73] his spread wings, at leisure to behold
Far off the empyreal[74] heaven, extended wide
In circuit, undetermined[75] square or round,
With opal towers and battlements adorned
Of living sapphire, once his native seat;   1050
And, fast by, hanging in a golden chain,
This pendent world, in bigness as a star
Of smallest magnitude close by the moon.
Thither, full fraught with mischievous revenge,
Accurst, and in a cursèd hour, he hies.   1055

THE END OF THE SECOND BOOK[76]

---

[67] The vessel in which Jason sailed in search of the Golden Fleece.
[68] The Symplegades, two rocks at the entrance of the Black Sea, which dashed against each other at intervals to destroy boats sailing between.   [69] See the note on line 60, above.
[70] The outermost sphere of the Ptolemaic universe. *World* in the next line (as in line 1052 and elsewhere) = the universe.
[71] So that.   [72] Makes for.   [73] Poises.   [74] Celestial.
[75] I.e., its vastness prevents the eye from making out its shape.
[76] At the end of the first four Books, Satan has reached Paradise and is ready for the temptation. The next four, through Book VIII, go back and narrate Satan's rebellion, his fall, and the creation of the world.

---

[65] Border on.
[66] I.e., the purpose of my present journey.

from BOOK IX

THE ARGUMENT

SATAN, having compassed the earth, with meditated guile returns as a mist by night into Paradise; enters into the serpent sleeping. Adam and Eve in the morning go forth to their labors, which Eve proposes to divide in several places, each laboring apart: Adam consents not, alleging the danger lest that enemy of whom they were forewarned should attempt her found alone. Eve, loath to be thought not circumspect or firm enough, urges her going apart, the rather desirous to make trial of her strength; Adam at last yields. The serpent finds her alone; his subtle approach, first gazing, then speaking, with much flattery extolling Eve above all other creatures. Eve, wondering to hear the serpent speak, asks how he attained to human speech and such understanding not till now; the serpent answers that by tasting of a certain tree in the garden he attained both to speech and reason, till then void of both; Eve requires him to bring her to that tree, and finds it to be the tree of knowledge forbidden. The serpent, now grown bolder, with many wiles and arguments induces her at length to eat; she, pleased with the taste, deliberates a while whether to impart thereof to Adam or not; at last brings him of the fruit, relates what persuaded her to eat thereof. Adam, at first amazed, but perceiving her lost, resolves, through vehemence of love, to perish with her, and, extenuating the trespass, eats also of the fruit. The effects thereof in them both; they seek to cover their nakedness; then fall to variance and accusation of one another.

... For now, and since first break of dawn, the fiend,
Mere[1] serpent in appearance, forth was come,
And on his quest where likeliest he might find
The only two of mankind, but in them   415
The whole included race, his purposed prey.
In bower and field he sought, where any tuft
Of grove or garden-plot more pleasant[2] lay,
Their tendance or plantation[3] for delight;
By fountain or by shady rivulet   420
He sought them both, but wished his hap might find
Eve separate; he wished, but not with hope
Of what so seldom chanced, when to his wish,
Beyond his hope, Eve separate he spies,
Veiled in a cloud of fragrance, where she stood,   425
Half spied, so thick the roses bushing round
About her glowed, oft stooping to support
Each flower of slender stalk, whose head, though gay
Carnation,[4] purple, azure, or specked with gold,

Hung drooping unsustained. Them she upstays   430
Gently with myrtle band, mindless[5] the while
Herself, though fairest unsupported flower,
From her best prop so far, and storm so nigh.
Nearer he drew, and many a walk traversed
Of stateliest covert, cedar, pine, or palm;   435
Then voluble[6] and bold, now hid, now seen
Among thick-woven arborets[7] and flowers
Imbordered on each bank, the hand[8] of Eve:
Spot more delicious than those gardens feigned
Or[9] of revived Adonis,[10] or renowned   440
Alcinous, host of old Laertes' son,[11]
Or that, not mystic,[12] where the sapient king[13]
Held dalliance with his fair Egyptian spouse.
Much he the place admired, the person more.
As one who, long in populous city pent,   445
Where houses thick and sewers annoy[14] the air,
Forth issuing on a summer's morn to breathe
Among the pleasant villages and farms
Adjoined, from each thing met conceives delight,
The smell of grain, or tedded[15] grass, or kine,   450
Or dairy, each rural sight, each rural sound;
If chance with nymphlike step fair virgin pass,
What pleasing seemed, for her[16] now pleases more,
She most, and in her look sums all delight.
Such pleasure took the serpent to behold   455
This flowery plat,[17] the sweet recess of Eve
Thus early, thus alone; her heavenly form
Angelic, but more soft, and feminine,
Her graceful innocence, her every air
Of gesture or least action, overawed   460
His malice, and with rapine sweet bereaved
His fierceness of the fierce intent it brought.
That space the evil one abstracted stood
From his own evil, and for the time remained
Stupidly[18] good, of enmity disarmed,   465
Of guile, of hate, of envy, of revenge.
But the hot hell that always in him burns,
Though in mid heaven, soon ended his delight,
And tortures him now more, the more he sees
Of pleasure not for him ordained. Then soon   470
Fierce hate he recollects, and all his thoughts
Of mischief, gratulating, thus excites:

---

[1] I.e., entirely.
[2] More pleasant than the rest; i.e., most pleasant.
[3] Either what they, finding it growing, had tended or what they themselves had planted.   [4] Flesh-colored, pink.

[5] Unmindful of.   [6] Advancing easily.
[7] Small trees, shrubs.   [8] Handiwork.   [9] Either.
[10] On Adonis, the god of reviving vegetation, see the note on I, 446.
[11] Ulysses, whose entertainment by Alcinous, king of the Phaeacians, is described by Homer in the *Odyssey*, Book VII.
[12] Not fabulous, like those just mentioned.
[13] Solomon, who married Pharaoh's daughter (1 Kings 3:1).
[14] Pollute.   [15] Cut and spread to dry.
[16] Because of her presence.   [17] Plot.
[18] I.e., with his evil faculties stupefied.

"Thoughts, whither have ye led me? with what sweet
Compulsion thus transported to forget
What hither brought us? hate, not love, nor hope   475
Of Paradise for hell, hope here to taste
Of pleasure, but all pleasure to destroy,
Save what is in destroying; other joy
To me is lost. Then let me not let pass
Occasion which now smiles: behold alone   480
The woman, opportune to all attempts;
Her husband, for I view far round, not nigh,
Whose higher intellectual[19] more I shun,
And strength, of courage haughty,[20] and of limb
Heroic built, though of terrestrial mold;   485
Foe not informidable, exempt from wound,
I not; so much hath hell debased, and pain
Enfeebled me, to what I was in heaven.
She fair, divinely fair, fit love for gods,
Not terrible, though terror be in love,   490
And beauty, not[21] approached by stronger hate,
Hate stronger under show of love well feigned,
The way which to her ruin now I tend."
     So spake the enemy of mankind, enclosed
In serpent, inmate bad, and toward Eve   495
Addressed his way, not with indented wave,
Prone on the ground, as since, but on his rear,
Circular base of rising folds, that towered
Fold above fold, a surging maze; his head
Crested aloft, and carbuncle[22] his eyes;   500
With burnished neck of verdant gold, erect
Amidst his circling spires,[23] that on the grass
Floated redundant.[24] Pleasing was his shape
And lovely; never since of serpent kind
Lovelier—not those that in Illyria changed   505
Hermione and Cadmus,[25] or the god
In Epidaurus;[26] nor to which transformed
Ammonian Jove, or Capitoline,[27] was seen,
He with Olympias, this with her who bore
Scipio, the highth of Rome. With tract[28] oblique   510
At first, as one who sought access but feared
To interrupt, sidelong he works his way.

As when a ship by skillful steersman wrought
Nigh river's mouth or foreland, where the wind
Veers oft, as oft so steers, and shifts her sail: 515
So varied he, and of his tortuous train
Curled many a wanton wreath in sight of Eve,
To lure her eye; she, busied, heard the sound
Of rustling leaves, but minded not, as used
To such disport before her through the field   520
From every beast, more duteous at her call
Than at Circean call the herd disguised.[29]
He, bolder now, uncalled before her stood,
But as in gaze admiring. Oft he bowed
His turret[30] crest and sleek enameled neck,   525
Fawning, and licked the ground whereon she trod.
His gentle dumb expression turned at length
The eye of Eve to mark his play; he, glad
Of her attention gained, with serpent tongue
Organic, or impulse of vocal air,   530
His fraudulent temptation thus began:
     "Wonder not, sovran mistress, if perhaps
Thou canst who art sole wonder, much less arm
Thy looks, the heaven of mildness, with disdain,
Displeased that I approach thee thus, and gaze   535
Insatiate, I thus single, nor have feared
Thy awful brow, more awful thus retired.
Fairest resemblance of thy Maker fair,
Thee all things living gaze on, all things thine
By gift, and thy celestial beauty adore,   540
With ravishment beheld, there best beheld
Where universally admired. But here,
In this enclosure wild, these beasts among,
Beholders rude, and shallow to discern
Half what in thee is fair, one man except,   545
Who sees thee? (and what is one?) who shouldst be seen
A goddess among gods, adored and served
By angels numberless, thy daily train."
     So glozed[31] the tempter, and his proem[32] tuned;
Into the heart of Eve his words made way,   550
Though at the voice much marveling; at length
Not unamazed she thus in answer spake:
     "What may this mean? Language of man pronounced
By tongue of brute, and human sense expressed!
The first at least of these I thought denied   555
To beasts, whom God on their creation-day
Created mute to all articulate sound;
The latter I demur,[33] for in their looks
Much reason, and in their actions, oft appears.
Thee, serpent, subtlest beast of all the field   560
I knew, but not with human voice endued;

---

[19] Intellect.   [20] Lofty.   [21] I.e., when it is not.
[22] Deep red.   [23] Coils.   [24] Luxuriant.
[25] Cadmus, founder of Thebes, and his wife Harmonia were turned
     into serpents. *Changed* = took the place of.
[26] Asclepius (Latin Aesculapius), the god of healing, whose chief
     shrine was at Epidaurus in Greece, was fabled to assume at times
     the shape of one of the serpents held sacred to him by his devo-
     tees.
[27] Jupiter Ammon (the Greeks identified the Egyptian god Ammon
     with Zeus) was said to have visited Olympias, the mother of
     Alexander the Great, in the form of a serpent; Jupiter Capitolinus
     (so called from his temple on the Capitol in Rome) similarly
     appeared to the mother of Scipio Africanus.
[28] Track, course.

[29] The enchantress Circe turned men into animals and made them
     obedient to her (*Odyssey*, Book X).   [30] Towerlike.
[31] Flattered.   [32] Preface, prelude.
[33] I.e., I doubt that reason is denied to beasts.

Redouble, then, this miracle, and say,
How cam'st thou speakable of mute,[34] and how
To me so friendly grown above the rest
Of brutal kind that daily are in sight?   565
Say, for such wonder claims attention due."
    To whom the guileful tempter thus replied:
"Empress of this fair world, resplendent Eve!
Easy to me it is to tell thee all
What thou command'st, and right thou shouldst be
        obeyed.   570
I was at first as other beasts that graze
The trodden herb, of abject thoughts and low,
As was my food, nor aught but food discerned
Or sex, and apprehended nothing high:
Till on a day, roving the field, I chanced   575
A goodly tree far distant to behold,
Loaden with fruit of fairest colors mixed,
Ruddy and gold: I nearer drew to gaze;
When from the boughs a savory odor blown,
Grateful to appetite, more pleased my sense   580
Than smell of sweetest fennel, or the teats
Of ewe or goat dropping with milk at even,
Unsucked of lamb or kid, that tend their play.
To satisfy the sharp desire I had
Of tasting those fair apples, I resolved   585
Not to defer; hunger and thirst at once,
Powerful persuaders, quickened at the scent
Of that alluring fruit, urged me so keen.
About the mossy trunk I wound me soon;
For, high from ground, the branches would require 590
Thy utmost reach, or Adam's: round the tree
All other beasts that saw, with like desire
Longing and envying stood, but could not reach.
Amid the tree now got, where plenty hung
Tempting so nigh, to pluck and eat my fill   595
I spared not; for such pleasure till that hour
At feed or fountain never had I found.
Sated at length, ere long I might perceive
Strange alteration in me, to degree
Of reason[35] in my inward powers, and speech   600
Wanted not long, though to this shape retained.
Thenceforth to speculations high or deep
I turned my thoughts, and with capacious mind
Considered all things visible in heaven,
Or earth, or middle, all things fair and good;   605
But all that fair and good in thy divine
Semblance and in thy beauty's heavenly ray
United I beheld; no fair[36] to thine
Equivalent or second; which compelled

Me thus, though importune[37] perhaps, to come   610
And gaze, and worship thee of right declared
Sovran of creatures, universal dame!"[38]
    So talked the spirited[39] sly snake; and Eve,
Yet more amazed, unwary thus replied:
"Serpent, thy overpraising leaves in doubt   615
The virtue[40] of that fruit, in thee first proved.
But say, where grows the tree? from hence how far?
For many are the trees of God that grow
In Paradise, and various, yet unknown
To us; in such abundance lies our choice   620
As leaves a greater store of fruit untouched,
Still hanging incorruptible, till men
Grow up to their provision, and more hands
Help to disburden nature of her bearth."[41]
    To whom the wily adder, blithe and glad: 625
"Empress, the way is ready, and not long—
Beyond a row of myrtles, on a flat,
Fast by a fountain, one small thicket past
Of blowing[42] myrrh and balm. If thou accept
My conduct,[43] I can bring thee thither soon."   630
    "Lead, then," said Eve. He, leading, swiftly rolled
In tangles, and made intricate seem straight,
To mischief swift. Hope elevates and joy
Brightens his crest. As when a wandering fire,[44]
Compact of unctuous[45] vapor, which the night   635
Condenses, and the cold environs round,
Kindled through agitation to a flame,
Which oft, they say, some evil spirit attends,
Hovering and blazing with delusive light,
Misleads the amazed night-wanderer from his way   640
To bogs and mires, and oft through pond or pool,
There swallowed up and lost, from succor far:
So glistered the dire snake, and into fraud[46]
Led Eve, our credulous mother, to the tree
Of prohibition,[47] root of all our woe;   645
Which when she saw, thus to her guide she spake:
    "Serpent, we might have spared our coming hither,
Fruitless to me, though fruit be here to excess,
The credit of whose virtue rest with thee,[48]
Wondrous indeed, if cause of such effects!   650
But of this tree we may not taste nor touch;
God so commanded, and left that command
Sole daughter of his voice: the rest,[49] we live
Law to ourselves; our reason is our law."

[37] Importunate.
[38] Mistress of the universe. Cf. line 684.
[39] I.e., inhabited by the spirit of Satan.
[40] Power, efficacy.   [41] What she bears.   [42] Blooming.
[43] Guidance.   [44] Will-o'-the-wisp.   [45] Oily.
[46] Evil.   [47] The prohibited or forbidden tree.
[48] *Rest* is hortatory: let the claims for its powers rest on your
    authority (since I cannot eat of it).
[49] With respect to everything else.

[34] How did you, from being mute, become able to speak?
[35] Going so far as to produce reason.   [36] Beauty.

To whom the tempter guilefully replied: 655
"Indeed! Hath God then said that of the fruit
Of all these garden trees ye shall not eat,
Yet lords declared of all in earth or air?"

To whom thus Eve, yet sinless: "Of the fruit
Of each tree in the garden we may eat, 660
But of the fruit of this fair tree, amidst
The garden, God hath said, 'Ye shall not eat
Thereof, nor shall ye touch it, lest ye die.'"

She scarce had said, though brief, when now more bold
The tempter, but with show of zeal and love 665
To man, and indignation at his wrong,
New part puts on, and, as to passion moved,
Fluctuates[50] disturbed, yet comely and in act
Raised, as of some great matter to begin.
As when of old some orator renowned 670
In Athens or free Rome, where eloquence
Flourished, since mute, to some great cause addressed,
Stood in himself collected, while each part,
Motion, each act, won audience ere the tongue
Sometimes in highth[51] began, as no delay 675
Of preface brooking through his zeal of right:
So standing, moving, or to highth upgrown,
The tempter all impassioned thus began:

"O sacred, wise, and wisdom-giving plant,
Mother of science,[52] now I feel thy power 680
Within me clear, not only to discern
Things in their causes, but to trace the ways
Of highest agents, deemed however wise.[53]
Queen of this universe, do not believe
Those rigid threats of death; ye shall not die. 685
How should ye? by the fruit? it gives you life
To knowledge. By the threatener? look on me,
Me who have touched and tasted, yet both live,
And life more perfect have attained than fate
Meant me, by venturing higher than my lot. 690
Shall that be shut to man which to the beast
Is open? or will God incense his ire
For such a petty trespass, and not praise
Rather your dauntless virtue, whom the pain
Of death denounced,[54] whatever thing death be, 695
Deterred not from achieving what might lead
To happier life, knowledge of good and evil?
Of good, how just? of evil, if what is evil
Be real, why not known, since easier shunned?
God therefore cannot hurt ye, and be just; 700
Not just, not God; not feared then, nor obeyed;
Your fear itself of death removes the fear.
Why, then, was this forbid? Why but to awe,

Why but to keep ye low and ignorant,
His worshippers? He knows that in the day 705
Ye eat thereof, your eyes, that seem so clear,
Yet are but dim, shall perfectly be then
Opened and cleared, and ye shall be as gods,
Knowing both good and evil, as they know.
That ye should be as gods, since I as man, 710
Internal man,[55] is but proportion meet,
I, of brute, human; ye, of human, gods.
So ye shall die perhaps, by putting off
Human, to put on gods—death to be wished,
Though threatened, which no worse than this can bring!
And what are gods, that man may not become 716
As they, participating godlike food?
The gods are first, and that advantage use
On our belief, that all from them proceeds.
I question it, for this fair earth I see, 720
Warmed by the sun, producing every kind;
Them nothing. If they all things, who enclosed
Knowledge of good and evil in this tree,
That whoso eats thereof forthwith attains
Wisdom without their leave? and wherein lies 725
The offence, that man should thus attain to know?
What can your knowledge hurt him, or this tree
Impart against his will, if all be his?
Or is it envy? and can envy dwell
In heavenly breasts? These, these and many more 730
Causes import your need of this fair fruit.
Goddess humane, reach then, and freely taste!"

He ended, and his words replete with guile
Into her heart too easy entrance won:
Fixed on the fruit she gazed, which to behold 735
Might tempt alone; and in her ears the sound
Yet rung of his persuasive words, impregned[56]
With reason, to her seeming, and with truth.
Meanwhile the hour of noon drew on, and waked
An eager appetite, raised by the smell 740
So savory of that fruit, which with desire,
Inclinable now grown to touch or taste,
Solicited her longing eye; yet first
Pausing a while, thus to herself she mused:

"Great are thy virtues, doubtless, best of fruits, 745
Though kept from man, and worthy to be admired,
Whose taste, too long forborne, at first assay
Gave elocution to the mute, and taught
The tongue not made for speech to speak thy praise.
Thy praise he also who forbids thy use 750
Conceals not from us, naming thee the tree
Of knowledge, knowledge both of good and evil;
Forbids us then to taste; but his forbidding

---

[50] Waves his body to and fro.
[51] I.e., without introductory remarks.   [52] Knowledge.
[53] However wise they be deemed.   [54] Threatened.

[55] A man in my inner faculties, though still having a serpent's body.
[56] Impregnated.

Commends thee more, while it infers the good
By thee communicated, and our want;   755
For good unknown sure is not had, or, had
And yet unknown, is as not had at all.
In plain, then, what forbids he but to know,
Forbids us good, forbids us to be wise?
Such prohibitions bind not. But if death   760
Bind us with after-bands, what profits then
Our inward freedom? In the day we eat
Of this fair fruit, our doom is we shall die.
How dies the serpent? He hath eaten and lives,
And knows, and speaks, and reasons, and discerns,   765
Irrational till then. For us alone
Was death invented? or to us denied
This intellectual food, for beasts reserved?
For beasts it seems; yet that one beast which first
Hath tasted envies not, but brings with joy   770
The good befallen him, author unsuspect,[57]
Friendly to man, far from deceit or guile.
What fear I then? rather, what know to fear
Under this ignorance of good and evil,
Of God or Death, of law or penalty?   775
Here grows the cure of all, this fruit divine,
Fair to the eye, inviting to the taste,
Of virtue[58] to make wise. What hinders then
To reach, and feed at once both body and mind?"

    So saying, her rash hand in evil hour   780
Forth reaching to the fruit, she plucked, she eat.[59]
Earth felt the wound, and Nature from her seat
Sighing through all her works gave signs of woe
That all was lost. Back to the thicket slunk
The guilty serpent, and well might, for Eve,   785
Intent now only on her taste, naught else
Regarded; such delight till then, as seemed,
In fruit she never tasted, whether true,
Or fancied so through expectation high
Of knowledge; nor was godhead from her thought.   790
Greedily she ingorged without restraint,
And knew not eating death. Satiate at length,
And heightened as with wine, jocund and boon,[60]
Thus to herself she pleasingly began:

    "O sovran, virtuous, precious of all trees   795
In Paradise! of operation blest
To sapience,[61] hitherto obscured, infamed,[62]
And thy fair fruit let hang, as to no end
Created! but henceforth my early care,
Not without song, each morning, and due praise,   800

Shall tend thee, and the fertile burden ease
Of thy full branches, offered free to all;
Till dieted by thee I grow mature
In knowledge, as the gods who all things know;
Though others envy what they cannot give;   805
For, had the gift been theirs, it had not here
Thus grown! Experience, next to thee I owe,
Best guide: not following thee, I had remained
In ignorance; thou open'st wisdom's way,
And giv'st access, though secret she retire.   810
And I perhaps am secret: heaven is high,
High and remote to see from thence distinct
Each thing on earth; and other care perhaps
May have diverted from continual watch
Our great Forbidder, safe[63] with all his spies   815
About him. But to Adam in what sort
Shall I appear? Shall I to him make known
As yet my change, and give him to partake
Full happiness with me, or rather not,
But keep the odds of knowledge in my power   820
Without copartner? so to add what wants
In female sex, the more to draw his love,
And render me more equal, and perhaps,
A thing not undesirable, sometime
Superior; for, inferior, who is free?   825
This may be well; but what if God have seen,
And death ensue? Then I shall be no more;
And Adam wedded to another Eve
Shall live with her enjoying, I extinct!
A death to think! Confirmed then I resolve,   830
Adam shall share with me in bliss or woe.
So dear I love him that with him all deaths
I could endure, without him live no life."

    So saying, from the tree her step she turned,
But first low reverence done, as to the power   835
That dwelt within, whose presence had infused
Into the plant sciential[64] sap, derived
From nectar, drink of gods. Adam the while,
Waiting desirous her return, had wove
Of choicest flowers a garland, to adorn   840
Her tresses, and her rural labors crown,
As reapers oft are wont their harvest queen.
Great joy he promised to his thoughts, and new
Solace in her return, so long delayed;
Yet oft his heart, divine[65] of something ill,   845
Misgave him; he the faltering measure[66] felt,
And forth to meet her went, the way she took
That morn when first they parted; by the tree
Of knowledge he must pass; there he her met,
Scarce from the tree returning; in her hand   850

---

[57] Authority not to be distrusted.
[58] Power.   [59] Ate (pronounced ĕt).   [60] Gay, merry.
[61] Blessed with the power of producing wisdom.
[62] Perhaps=defamed, slandered (as deadly), but the context favors "not known."

[63] As regards any danger of punishment from him.
[64] Producing knowledge.   [65] Feeling a premonition.
[66] Irregular beating of his heart.

JOHN MILTON   597

A bough of fairest fruit, that downy smiled,
New gathered, and ambrosial smell diffused.
To him she hasted; in her face excuse
Came prologue, and apology to prompt,
Which, with bland words at will, she thus addressed: 855
    "Hast thou not wondered, Adam, at my stay?
Thee I have missed, and thought it long, deprived
Thy presence, agony of love till now
Not felt, nor shall be twice; for never more
Mean I to try, what rash untried I sought,   860
The pain of absence from thy sight. But strange
Hath been the cause, and wonderful to hear.
This tree is not, as we are told, a tree
Of danger tasted,[67] nor to evil unknown
Opening the way, but of divine effect   865
To open eyes, and make them gods who taste;
And hath been tasted such.[68] The serpent wise,
Or not restrained as we, or not obeying,
Hath eaten of the fruit, and is become
Not dead, as we are threatened, but thenceforth   870
Endued with human voice and human sense,
Reasoning to admiration,[69] and with me
Persuasively hath so prevailed that I
Have also tasted, and have also found
The effects to correspond, opener mine eyes,   875
Dim erst, dilated spirits, ampler heart,
And growing up to godhead; which for thee
Chiefly I sought, without thee can despise.
For bliss, as thou hast part, to me is bliss;
Tedious, unshared with thee, and odious soon.   880
Thou therefore also taste, that equal lot
May join us, equal joy, as equal love;
Lest, thou not tasting, different degree
Disjoin us, and I then too late renounce
Deity for thee, when fate will not permit."   885
    Thus Eve with countenance blithe her story told;
But in her cheek distemper flushing glowed.
On the other side, Adam, soon as he heard
The fatal trespass done by Eve, amazed,
Astonied stood and blank, while horror chill   890
Ran through his veins, and all his joints relaxed.
From his slack hand the garland wreathed for Eve
Down dropped, and all the faded roses shed.
Speechless he stood and pale, till thus at length
First to himself he inward silence broke: 895
    "O fairest of creation, last and best
Of all God's works, creature in whom excelled
Whatever can to sight or thought be formed,
Holy, divine, good, amiable, or sweet!
How art thou lost! how on a sudden lost,   900

Defaced, deflowered, and now to death devote![70]
Rather, how hast thou yielded to transgress
The strict forbiddance, how to violate
The sacred fruit forbidden? Some cursed fraud
Of enemy hath beguiled thee, yet unknown,   905
And me with thee hath ruined; for with thee
Certain my resolution is to die.
How can I live without thee? how forgo
Thy sweet converse and love so dearly joined,
To live again in these wild woods forlorn?   910
Should God create another Eve, and I
Another rib afford, yet loss of thee
Would never from my heart. No, no, I feel
The link of nature draw me: flesh of flesh,
Bone of my bone thou art, and from thy state   915
Mine never shall be parted, bliss or woe."
    So having said, as one from sad dismay
Recomforted, and, after thoughts disturbed,
Submitting to what seemed remediless,
Thus in calm mood his words to Eve he turned: 920
    "Bold deed thou hast presumed, adventurous Eve,
And peril great provoked, who thus hast dared,
Had it been only coveting to eye
That sacred fruit, sacred to abstinence,
Much more to taste it, under ban to touch.   925
But past who can recall, or done undo?
Not God omnipotent, nor fate! Yet so
Perhaps thou shalt not die; perhaps the fact[71]
Is not so heinous now—foretasted fruit,
Profaned first by the serpent, by him first   930
Made common and unhallowed ere our taste,
Nor yet on him found deadly; he yet lives,
Lives, as thou saidst, and gains to live as man
Higher degree of life, inducement strong
To us, as likely, tasting, to attain   935
Proportional ascent; which cannot be
But to be gods, or angels, demigods.
Nor can I think that God, creator wise,
Though threatening, will in earnest so destroy
Us his prime creatures, dignified so high,   940
Set over all his works, which in our fall,
For us created, needs with us must fail,
Dependent made; so God shall uncreate,
Be frustrate, do, undo, and labor lose—
Not well conceived[72] of God; who, though his power
Creation could repeat, yet would be loath   946
Us to abolish, lest the adversary
Triumph and say: 'Fickle their state whom God
Most favors; who can please him long? Me first
He ruined, now mankind; whom will he next?'   950
Matter of scorn not to be given the foe.

---

[67] If tasted.   [68] Proved such by being tasted.
[69] In such a way as to produce wonder.

[70] Doomed.   [71] Act.   [72] Easily conceivable.

However, I with thee have fixed my lot,
Certain[73] to undergo like doom. If death
Consort with thee, death is to me as life;
So forcible within my heart I feel   955
The bond of nature draw me to my own,
My own in thee, for what thou art is mine.
Our state cannot be severed; we are one,
One flesh; to lose thee were to lose myself."
    So Adam; and thus Eve to him replied: 960
"O glorious trial of exceeding love,
Illustrious evidence, example high!
Engaging me to emulate; but, short
Of thy perfection, how shall I attain,
Adam? from whose dear side I boast me sprung,   965
And gladly of our union hear thee speak,
One heart, one soul in both; whereof good proof
This day affords, declaring thee resolved,
Rather than death, or aught than death more dread,
Shall separate us, linked in love so dear,   970
To undergo with me one guilt, one crime,
If any be, of tasting this fair fruit;
Whose virtue (for of good still good proceeds,
Direct, or by occasion) hath presented
This happy trial of thy love, which else   975
So eminently never had been known.
Were it I thought death menaced[74] would ensue
This my attempt, I would sustain alone
The worst, and not persuade thee, rather die
Deserted than oblige[75] thee with a fact[76]   980
Pernicious to thy peace, chiefly assured
Remarkably so late of thy so true,
So faithful, love unequaled. But I feel
Far otherwise the event,[77] not death, but life
Augmented, opened eyes, new hopes, new joys,   985
Taste so divine that what of sweet before
Hath touched my sense, flat seems to this, and harsh.
On my experience, Adam, freely taste,
And fear of death deliver to the winds."
    So saying, she embraced him, and for joy   990
Tenderly wept, much won that he his love
Had so ennobled as of choice to incur
Divine displeasure for her sake, or death.
In recompense (for such compliance bad
Such recompense best merits) from the bough   995
She gave him of that fair enticing fruit
With liberal hand; he scrupled not to eat,
Against his better knowledge, not deceived,
But fondly overcome with female charm.
Earth trembled from her entrails, as again   1000
In pangs, and Nature gave a second groan;

Sky loured, and, muttering thunder, some sad drops
Wept at completing of the mortal sin
Original; while Adam took no thought,
Eating his fill, nor Eve to iterate   1005
Her former trespass feared, the more to soothe
Him with her loved society; that now,
As with new wine intoxicated both,
They swim in mirth, and fancy that they feel
Divinity within them breeding wings   1010
Wherewith to scorn the earth: but that false fruit
Far other operation first displayed,
Carnal desire inflaming; he on Eve
Began to cast lascivious eyes; she him
As wantonly repaid; in lust they burn,   1015
Till Adam thus 'gan Eve to dalliance move:
    "Eve, now I see thou art exact of taste
And elegant, of sapience no small part,
Since to each meaning savor we apply,
And palate call judicious;[78] I the praise   1020
Yield thee, so well this day thou hast purveyed.
Much pleasure we have lost while we abstained
From this delightful fruit, nor known till now
True relish, tasting; if such pleasure be
In things to us forbidden, it might be wished   1025
For[79] this one tree had been forbidden ten.
But come; so well refreshed, now let us play,
As meet is, after such delicious fare;
For never did thy beauty, since the day
I saw thee first and wedded thee, adorned   1030
With all perfections, so enflame my sense
With ardor to enjoy thee, fairer now
Than ever—bounty of this virtuous tree!"
    So said he, and forbore not glance or toy
Of amorous intent, well understand   1035
Of Eve, whose eye darted contagious fire.
Her hand he seized, and to a shady bank,
Thick overhead with verdant roof embowered,
He led her, nothing loath; flowers were the couch,
Pansies, and violets, and asphodel,   1040
And hyacinth, earth's freshest, softest lap.
There they their fill of love and love's disport
Took largely, of their mutual guilt the seal,
The solace of their sin, till dewy sleep
Oppressed them, wearied with their amorous play.   1045
    Soon as the force of that fallacious fruit,
That with exhilarating vapor bland
About their spirits had played, and inmost powers

---

[78] A discriminating sense of taste, says Adam, is a part of wisdom—
and our idiomatic use of language testifies to this connection,
for we apply the word *taste* to certain intellectual matters, and
in turn we apply an intellectual word to the sense of taste when
we speak of a "judicious" palate. Latin *sapere*, to which both
savor and *sapience* are related, means both "to taste" and "to
know."   [79] In place of.

---

[73] Resolved.   [74] Threatened.   [75] Obligate, involve.
[76] Action.   [77] Effect, result.

Made err, was now exhaled, and grosser sleep,
Bred of unkindly[80] fumes, with conscious dreams   1050
Encumbered, now had left them, up they rose
As from unrest, and each the other viewing,
Soon found their eyes how opened, and their minds
How darkened; innocence, that as a veil
Had shadowed them from knowing ill, was gone;   1055
Just confidence, and native righteousness,
And honor, from about them, naked left
To guilty shame: he covered, but his robe
Uncovered more. So rose the Danite strong,[81]
Herculean Samson, from the harlot-lap   1060
Of Philistean Dálilah, and waked
Shorn of his strength; they destitute and bare
Of all their virtue. Silent, and in face
Confounded, long they sat, as stricken mute;
Till Adam, though not less than Eve abashed,   1065
At length gave utterance to these words constrained:
"O Eve, in evil hour thou didst give ear
To that false worm,[82] of whomsoever taught
To counterfeit man's voice—true in our fall,
False in our promised rising; since our eyes   1070
Opened we find indeed, and find we know
Both good and evil, good lost and evil got:
Bad fruit of knowledge, if this be to know,
Which leaves us naked thus, of honor void,
Of innocence, of faith, of purity,   1075
Our wonted ornaments now soiled and stained,
And in our faces evident the signs
Of foul concupiscence; whence evil store,[83]
Even shame, the last[84] of evils; of the first
Be sure then. How shall I behold the face   1080
Henceforth of God or angel, erst with joy
And rapture so oft beheld? Those heavenly shapes
Will dazzle now this earthly with their blaze
Insufferably bright. Oh, might I here
In solitude live savage, in some glade   1085
Obscured, where highest woods, impenetrable
To star or sunlight, spread their umbrage[85] broad,
And brown[86] as evening! Cover me, ye pines!
Ye cedars, with innumerable boughs
Hide me, where I may never see them more!   1090
But let us now, as in bad plight, devise
What best may, for the present, serve to hide
The parts of each from other that seem most
To shame obnoxious,[87] and unseemliest seen—
Some tree, whose broad smooth leaves, together sewed,
And girded on our loins, may cover round   1096

Those middle parts, that this new comer, shame,
There sit not, and reproach us as unclean."
So counseled he, and both together went
Into the thickest wood; there soon they chose   1100
The fig tree, not that kind for fruit renowned,
But such as at this day to Indians known[88]
In Malabar or Deccan[89] spreads her arms
Branching so broad and long that in the ground
The bended twigs take root, and daughters grow   1105
About the mother tree, a pillared shade
High overarched, and echoing walks between;
There oft the Indian herdsman, shunning heat,
Shelters in cool, and tends his pasturing herds
At loopholes cut through thickest shade. Those leaves
They gathered, broad as Amazonian targe,[90]   1111
And with what skill they had together sewed,
To gird their waist—vain covering, if to hide
Their guilt and dreaded shame! O how unlike
To that first naked glory! Such of late   1115
Columbus found the American, so girt
With feathered cincture,[91] naked else and wild
Among the trees on isles and woody shores.
Thus fenced, and, as they thought, their shame in part
Covered, but not at rest or ease of mind,   1120
They sat them down to weep. Nor only tears
Rained at their eyes, but high winds worse within
Began to rise, high passions, anger, hate,
Mistrust, suspicion, discord, and shook sore
Their inward state of mind, calm region once   1125
And full of peace, now tossed and turbulent:
For understanding ruled not, and the will
Heard not her lore, both in subjection now
To sensual appetite, who, from beneath
Usurping over sovran reason, claimed   1130
Superior sway. From thus distempered breast
Adam, estranged in look and altered style,[92]
Speech intermitted thus to Eve renewed:
"Would thou hadst hearkened to my words, and stayed
With me, as I besought thee, when that strange   1135
Desire of wandering, this unhappy morn,
I know not whence possessed thee! We had then
Remained still happy, not, as now, despoiled
Of all our good, shamed, naked, miserable!
Let none henceforth seek needless cause to approve[93]   1140
The faith they owe;[94] when earnestly they seek
Such proof, conclude they then begin to fail."
To whom soon moved with touch of blame, thus Eve:
"What words have passed thy lips, Adam severe?
Imput'st thou that to my default, or will   1145
Of wandering, as thou call'st it, which who knows

---

[80] Unnatural.   [81] See Judges 16:4–20.   [82] Serpent.
[83] Abundance of evil.
[84] Greatest; *first*=all the lesser evils.   [85] Shade.
[86] Dark.   [87] Liable, subject.

[88] The banyan tree.   [89] Districts of India.
[90] Shield. The Amazons were a legendary race of female warriors.
[91] Belt.   [92] Manner.   [93] Test.   [94] Own.

But might as ill have happened thou being by,
Or to thyself perhaps? Hadst thou been there,
Or here the attempt, thou couldst not have discerned
Fraud in the serpent, speaking as he spake;   1150
No ground of enmity between us known,
Why he should mean me ill or seek to harm.
Was I to have never parted from thy side?
As good have grown there still a lifeless rib.
Being as I am, why didst not thou, the head,   1155
Command me absolutely not to go,
Going into such danger, as thou saidst?
Too facile then, thou didst not much gainsay,
Nay, didst permit, approve, and fair dismiss.
Hadst thou been firm and fixed in thy dissent,   1160
Neither had I transgressed, nor thou with me."

    To whom, then first incensed, Adam replied:
"Is this the love, is this the recompense
Of mine to thee, ingrateful Eve, expressed
Immutable when thou wert lost, not I,   1165
Who might have lived, and joyed immortal bliss,
Yet willingly chose rather death with thee?
And am I now upbraided as the cause

Of thy transgressing? not enough severe,
It seems, in thy restraint! What could I more?   1170
I warned thee, I admonished thee, foretold
The danger, and the lurking enemy
That lay in wait; beyond this had been force,
And force upon free will hath here no place.
But confidence then bore thee on, secure   1175
Either to meet no danger, or to find
Matter of glorious trial; and perhaps
I also erred in overmuch admiring
What seemed in thee so perfect that I thought
No evil durst attempt thee; but I rue   1180
That error now, which is become my crime,
And thou the accuser. Thus it shall befall
Him who, to worth in women overtrusting,
Lets her will rule; restraint she will not brook;
And, left to herself, if evil thence ensue,   1185
She first his weak indulgence will accuse."

    Thus they in mutual accusation spent
The fruitless hours, but neither self-condemning;
And of their vain contèst appeared no end.

THE END OF THE NINTH BOOK[95]

from BOOK XII

THE ARGUMENT

THE ANGEL MICHAEL continues, from the Flood, to relate
what shall succeed; then, in the mention of Abraham, comes
by degrees to explain who that seed of the woman shall
be which was promised Adam and Eve in the Fall: his
incarnation, death, resurrection, and ascension; the state of
the Church till his second coming. Adam, greatly satisfied
and recomforted by these relations and promises, descends
the hill with Michael; wakens Eve, who all this while had
slept, but with gentle dreams composed to quietness of
mind and submission. Michael in either hand leads them
out of Paradise, the fiery sword waving behind them, and
the cherubim taking their stations to guard the place.

. . . He[1] ended; and thus Adam last replied:
"How soon hath thy prediction, seer blest,
Measured this transient world, the race of time,
Till time stand fixed! Beyond is all abyss,   555
Eternity, whose end no eye can reach.
Greatly instructed I shall hence depart,
Greatly in peace of thought, and have my fill
Of knowledge, what this vessel[2] can contain,
Beyond which was my folly to aspire.   560

Henceforth I learn that to obey is best,
And love with fear the only God, to walk
As in his presence, ever to observe
His providence, and on him sole depend,
Merciful over all his works, with good   565
Still overcoming evil, and by small
Accomplishing great things, by things deemed weak
Subverting worldly strong, and worldly wise
By simply meek; that suffering for truth's sake
Is fortitude to highest victory,   570
And to the faithful death the gate of life,
Taught this by his example whom I now
Acknowledge my Redeemer ever blest."

    To whom thus also the angel last replied:
"This having learned, thou hast attained the sum   575
Of wisdom; hope no higher, though all the stars
Thou knew'st by name, and all the ethereal powers,
All secrets of the deep, all nature's works,
Or works of God in heaven, air, earth, or sea,
And all the riches of this world enjoy'dst,   580
And all the rule, one empire. Only add
Deeds to thy knowledge answerable; add faith;

---

1 Michael.   2 I.e., mind.

95 In Books X and XI Adam and Eve are sentenced, and the archangel Michael is sent "to dispossess them, but first to reveal to
Adam future things." Michael sets before Adam "in vision
what shall happen till the Flood."

Add virtue, patience, temperance; add love,
By name to come called charity,[3] the soul
Of all the rest: then wilt thou not be loath   585
To leave this Paradise, but shalt possess
A paradise within thee, happier far.
Let us descend now, therefore, from this top
Of speculation[4]; for the hour precise
Exacts our parting hence; and, see, the guards,   590
By me encamped on yonder hill, expect
Their motion, at whose front a flaming sword
In signal of remove waves fiercely round.
We may no longer stay. Go, waken Eve;
Her also I with gentle dreams have calmed,   595
Portending good, and all her spirits composed
To meek submission: thou at season fit
Let her with thee partake what thou hast heard,
Chiefly what may concern her faith to know,
The great deliverance by her seed to come   600
(For by the woman's seed) on all mankind,
That ye may live, which will be many days,[5]
Both in one faith unanimous; though sad
With cause for evils past, yet much more cheered
With meditation on the happy end."   605
   He ended, and they both descend the hill;
Descended, Adam to the bower where Eve
Lay sleeping ran before, but found her waked;
And thus with words not sad she him received:
   "Whence thou return'st and whither went'st I know;
For God is also in sleep, and dreams advise,   611
Which he hath sent propitious, some great good
Presaging, since, with sorrow and heart's distress
Wearied, I fell asleep: but now lead on;
In me is no delay; with thee to go   615
Is to stay here; without thee here to stay

Is to go hence unwilling; thou to me
Art all things under heaven, all places thou,
Who for my willful crime art banished hence.
This further consolation yet secure   620
I carry hence: though all by me is lost,
Such favor I unworthy am vouchsafed,
By me the promised seed shall all restore."
   So spake our mother Eve, and Adam heard
Well pleased, but answered not; for now too nigh   625
The archangel stood, and from the other hill
To their fixed station, all in bright array,
The cherubim descended, on the ground
Gliding meteorous, as evening mist
Risen from a river o'er the marish[6] glides   630
And gathers ground fast at the laborer's heel
Homeward returning. High in front advanced,
The brandished sword of God before them blazed
Fierce as a comet, which with torrid heat,
And vapor as the Libyan air adust,[7]   635
Began to parch that temperate clime; whereat
In either hand the hastening angel caught
Our lingering parents, and to the eastern gate
Led them direct, and down the cliff as fast
To the subjected[8] plain; then disappeared.   640
They, looking back, all the eastern side beheld
Of Paradise, so late their happy seat,
Waved over by that flaming brand, the gate
With dreadful faces thronged and fiery arms.
Some natural tears they dropped, but wiped them soon;
The world was all before them, where to choose   646
Their place of rest, and Providence their guide:
They hand in hand, with wandering steps and slow,
Through Eden took their solitary way.

THE END

Samuel Pepys

1633–1703

DIARIES are interesting or boring according to the quality of the author, not the importance of the events recorded. Pepys was a connoisseur and an amateur in several arts; he was also an extraordinarily able administrator, and as such is termed the father of the British Navy; but in the art of composing a diary he was really an artist. He wrote in shorthand, for he resolved to be frank about himself as well as others and had no intention of letting his contemporaries see him with his mask off. Yet he knew well enough he would be read some day; and to insure that he would be, he bound the three thousand pages in six leather volumes and placed them with the fine library he had collected. It was in accordance with his wishes that the books went, after his death and his nephew's, to Magdalene, his own college at Cambridge. There the Diary was ignored till early in the nineteenth century, when it was deciphered, transcribed, and published in part. Since then

---

[3] See 1 Corinthians 13.
[4] "Top of speculation" refers both to the lofty subject of their discourse and to the high hill on which they have been talking (speculation=observation).
[5] Adam lived 930 years (Genesis 5:5).

[6] Marsh.   [7] Scorched by the sun.   [8] Situated below.

it has all been printed, save for a few passages of unusual frankness.

"Nothing so honest," says a biographer, "has ever been written by a man of his own self." What is the portrait the *Diary* paints? There was formerly a notion that Pepys is fascinating because he is the perfect example of the average Restoration man; but average men do not sire navies or write books of 1,300,000 words which three centuries later make readers think them too short. Pepys was obviously a most unusual man; yet because he had his full share of human frailty, and put it on record, he does not seem remote. The sexual irregularities described in the *Diary* have alienated some readers. It is clear that his ideas and too often his practices were brutal; he failed, as many men do, to understand the spiritual in love and to fuse it with its physical expression. But this was his only failure. In all other aspects of life he was a success—in practical affairs (he served his country and simultaneously made a fortune) and in the enrichment of his experience through art. He was a man of *capacity*, for both.

Pepys's start came through family influence. Though he was the son of an obscure London tailor, he was a cousin of the statesman and admiral Edward Montagu, Earl of Sandwich, at the Restoration one of the most influential of the men around King Charles. Montagu got Pepys a key post at the Admiralty. The start was all he needed; his rise was on sheer merit. As Clerk of the Acts, Pepys systematically proceeded to acquire an unrivaled knowledge of the Navy's affairs. Eventually he revolutionized them, and the present establishment rests on the foundations he laid, first as Clerk of the Acts and afterwards as Secretary of the Admiralty and a great officer of state.

This was his principal achievement, though his other activities were many and various. He sat in Parliament, served on numerous committees and boards, was an enthusiastic member of the Royal Society and for a term its president, became a notable book collector, and was always a devotee of music and the drama. In an age when no one else thought ballads worth saving, he formed a collection which is now of first-rate importance. His attention was easily caught by anything, old or new, that seemed out of the ordinary run of things; but his manifold interests, while they tickled his mind, did not distract it. The *Diary* would be fascinating if only because it passes the Restoration in review for us; it is the honesty, curiosity, alertness, versatility, and (in most affairs) sagacity of Pepys that make it the best of diaries.

To his career as ruler of the Navy the Glorious Revolution put an end, and he spent the rest of his life quietly but not unhappily. He was insured against a dull old age by his genius for friendship and by his love, acquired early, for literature and music. Weakened eyesight had long before put an end to the keeping of the *Diary;* it covers only the years 1660–69.

The best edition is by H. B. Wheatley (9 vols., 1893–96; reissued in 3 vols., 1923). With the generous permission of Messrs. Harcourt, Brace and Company, the text of the following extracts is from that edition. Besides the *Diary,* Pepys wrote *Memoirs of the Royal Navy* (1690). There are several Lives; the best is by A. Bryant (3 vols. thus far, 1933–39).

In a satirical poem by a contemporary, Pepys's name rimes with *lips.* It seems to have been pronounced in various ways, but the usual form now is *peeps.*

from the DIARY

AUGUST 18, 1660. This morning I took my wife towards Westminster by water, and landed her at Whitefriars,[1] with £5 to buy her a petticoat, and I to the Privy Seal.[2] By and by comes my wife to tell me that my father has persuaded her to buy a most fine cloth of 26s. a yard, and a rich lace, that[3] the petticoat will come to £5, at which I was somewhat troubled; but she doing it very innocently, I could not be angry. I did give her more money, and sent her away; and I and Creed[4] and Captain Hayward[5] 10 (who is now unkindly put out of the *Plymouth* to make way for Captain Allen[6] to go to Constantinople, and put into his ship the *Dover,* which I know will trouble my Lord[7]) went and dined at the Leg in King Street,[8] where Captain Ferrers, my Lord's cornet,[9] comes to us, who after dinner took me and Creed to the Cockpit[10] play, the first that I have had time to see since my coming from sea, *The Loyal Subject,*[11] where one Kynaston,[12] a boy, acted the

---

1 A district between Fleet Street and the Thames. The Pepyses lived at the Navy Office, a little to the west of the Tower of London, in a house on Seething Lane.

2 An office of the Crown, where the royal seal was affixed to certain documents.   3 So that.

4 John Creed, an early associate of Pepys in the affairs of the Navy.

5 John Hayward; the *Plymouth* was one of the Navy's big ships.

6 Afterwards Sir Thomas Allen and a prominent admiral.

7 Sir Edward Montagu, Earl of Sandwich, one of the leading courtiers, and a kinsman of Pepys, who owed him his place. Montagu commanded the fleet which brought Charles II back to England.   8 In Westminster.

9 The fifth grade of commissioned officer in a cavalry troop. He was on Sandwich's staff.   10 In Drury Lane.

11 By John Fletcher.

12 Edward Kynaston, afterwards a leading actor of male roles.

Duke's sister, but made the loveliest lady that ever I saw in my life, only her voice not very good. After the play done, we three went to drink; and by Captain Ferrers' means, Kynaston and another that acted Archas, the general, came and drank with us. Hence home by coach; and after being trimmed, leaving my wife to look after her little bitch, which was just now a-whelping, I to bed.

OCTOBER 13, 1660. To my Lord's in the morning, where I met with Captain Cuttance;[13] but my Lord not being up I went out to Charing Cross, to see Major-General Harrison[14] hanged, drawn, and quartered; which was done there, he looking as cheerful as any man could do in that condition. He was presently cut down, and his head and heart shown to the people, at which there was great shouts of joy. It is said that he said that he was sure to come shortly at the right hand of Christ to judge them that now had judged him, and that his wife do expect his coming again. Thus it was my chance to see the King beheaded at Whitehall,[15] and to see the first blood shed in revenge for the blood of the King at Charing Cross. From thence to my Lord's, and took Captain Cuttance and Mr. Shepley[16] to the Sun Tavern,[17] and did give them some oysters. After that I went by water home, where I was angry with my wife for her things lying about, and in my passion kicked the little fine basket which I bought her in Holland, and broke it, which troubled me after I had done it. Within all the afternoon setting up shelves in my study. At night to bed.

JANUARY 28, 1661. At the office all the morning; dine at home, and after dinner to Fleet Street, with my sword to Mr. Brigden (lately made Captain of the Auxiliaries) to be refreshed, and with him to an ale house, where I met Mr. Davenport, and after some talk of Cromwell, Ireton,[18] and Bradshaw's[19] bodies being taken out of their graves today, I went to Mr. Crewe's[20] and thence to the Theater, where I saw again *The Lost Lady*,[21] which do now please

me better than before; and here I sitting behind in a dark place, a lady spit backward upon me by a mistake, not seeing me, but after seeing her to be a very pretty lady, I was not troubled at it at all. Thence to Mr. Crewe's, and there met Mr. Moore,[22] who came lately to me, and went with me to my father's, and with him to Standing's,[23] whither came to us Dr. Fairbrother,[24] who I took and my father to the Bear[25] and gave a pint of sack and a pint of claret. He do still continue his expressions of respect and love to me, and tells me my brother John will make a good scholar. Thence to see the Doctor at his lodging at Mr. Holden's, where I bought a hat, cost me 35s. So home by moonshine, and by the way was overtaken by the Comptroller's[26] coach, and so home to his house with him. So home and to bed. This noon I had my press set up in my chamber for papers to be put in.

MAY 30, 1663. Up betimes,[27] and Creed and I by water to Fleet Street, and my brother not being ready, he and I walked to the New Exchange,[28] and there drank our morning draft of whey, the first I have done this year; but I perceive the lawyers come all in as they go to the Hall,[29] and I believe it is very good. So to my brother's, and there I found my aunt James,[30] a poor, religious, well-meaning, good soul, talking of nothing but God Almighty, and that with so much innocence that mightily pleased me. Here was a fellow that said grace so long like a prayer; I believe the fellow is a cunning fellow, and yet I by my brother's desire did give him a crown, he being in great want, and, it seems, a parson among the fanatics, and a cousin of my poor aunt's, whose prayers she told me did do me good among the many good souls that did by my father's desires pray for me when I was cut of the stone,[31] and which God did hear, which I also in complaisance did own; but, God forgive me, my mind was otherwise. I had a couple of lobsters and some wine for her; and so, she going out of town today, and being not willing to come home with me to dinner, I parted and home, where we sat at the office all the morning, and after dinner all the afternoon till night, there at

---

13 Afterwards Sir Roger Cuttance.
14 Thomas Harrison, one of the signers of the death warrant of Charles I. 15 The royal palace at Westminster.
16 Steward at Sandwich's country seat, Hinchingbrooke, near Huntingdon.
17 There were several taverns with this name.
18 Henry Ireton, Cromwell's son-in-law, second in command of the Parliamentary army.
19 John Bradshaw, president of the special court which tried Charles I. The bodies were exhumed and hanged.
20 John (afterwards Lord) Crew, a member of the House of Commons.
21 A pre-Wars tragicomedy by Sir William Berkeley.

22 A relative of Lord Sandwich.
23 A tavern in Fleet Street.
24 William Fairbrother, a fellow of King's College, Cambridge.
25 A tavern at the south end of London Bridge.—*Sack*=sherry.
26 Colonel Robert Slingsby, Comptroller of the Navy.
27 Early.
28 A bazaar in the Strand.—The "morning draft," often at a tavern, took the place of our breakfast.
29 Westminster Hall, where the courts sat.   30 Mrs. James.
31 Pepys was operated on for kidney stones in 1658.

my office getting up the time that I have of late lost by not following my business, but I hope now to settle my mind again very well to my business. So home, and after supper did wash my feet, and so to bed.

JUNE 13, 1663. Up and betimes to Thames Street among the tar men, to look the price of tar, and so by water to Whitehall, thinking to speak with Sir G. Carteret;[32] but he lying in the city all night, and meeting with Mr. Cutler the merchant, I with him in his coach into the city to Sir G. Carteret; but missing him there, he and I walked to find him at Sir Tho. Allen's[33] in Bread Street, where not finding him he and I walked towards our office, he discoursing well of the business of the Navy, and particularly of the victualing, in which he was once I perceive concerned; and he and I parted, and I to the office and there had a difference with Sir W. Batten[34] about Mr. Bowyer's tar, which I am resolved to cross, though he sent me last night, as a bribe, a barrel of sturgeon, which, it may be, I shall send back, for I will not have the King abused[35] so abominably in the price of what we buy, by Sir W. Batten's corruption and underhand dealing. So from the office, Mr. Wayth[36] with me, to the Parliament House, and there I spoke and told Sir G. Carteret all, with which he is well pleased, and do recall his willingness yesterday, it seems, to Sir W. Batten, that we should buy a great quantity of tar, being abused by him. Thence with Mr. Wayth after drinking a cup of ale at the Swan,[37] talking of the corruption of the Navy, by water. I landed him at Whitefriars, and I to the Exchange, and so home to dinner, where I found my wife's brother, and thence after dinner by water to the Royal Theater,[38] where I resolve to bid farewell, as shall appear by my oaths tomorrow against all plays either at public houses or court till Christmas be over. Here we saw *The Faithful Shepherdess,*[39] a most simple thing, and yet much thronged after and often shown, but it is only for the scene's sake, which is very fine indeed and worth seeing; but I am quite out of opinion with any of their actings, but Lacy's,[40] compared with the other house. Thence to see Mrs. Hunt,[41] which

we did and were much made of; and in our way saw my Lady Castlemaine,[42] who, I fear, is not so handsome as I have taken her for, and now she begins to decay something.[43] This is my wife's opinion also, for which I am sorry. Thence by coach, with a mad coachman, that drove like mad, and down byways, through Bucklersbury[44] home, everybody through the street cursing him, being ready to run over them. So home, and after writing letters by the post, home to supper and bed. Yesterday, upon conference with the King in the Banqueting House,[45] the Parliament did agree with much ado, it being carried out by forty-two voices, that they would supply him with a sum of money; but what and how is not yet known, but expected to be done with great disputes the next week. But if done at all, it is well.

NOVEMBER 29, 1663 (*Lord's day*). This morning I put on my best black cloth suit, trimmed with scarlet ribbon, very neat, with my cloak lined with velvet, and a new beaver,[46] which altogether is very noble, with my black silk knit canons[47] I bought a month ago. I to church alone, my wife not going, and there I found my Lady Batten[48] in a velvet gown, which vexed me that she should be in it before my wife, or that I am able to put her into one; but what cannot be, cannot be. However, when I came home I told my wife of it, and (to see my weakness!) I could on the sudden have found my heart to have offered her one, but second thoughts put it by; and indeed it would undo me to think of doing as Sir W. Batten and his Lady do, who has a good estate besides his office. A good dinner we had of *bœuf à la mode,* but not roasted so well as my wife used to do it. So after dinner I to the French Church,[49] but that being too far begun I came back to St. Dunstan's[50] by six and heard a good sermon, and so home and to my office all the evening making up my accounts of this month; and blessed be God I have got up my crumb again to £770, the most that ever I had yet, and good clothes a great many besides, which is a great mercy of God to me. So home to supper and to bed.

32 Sir George was Treasurer of the Navy.
33 See note 6, above.
34 Sir William was one of the Commissioners of the Navy.
35 Deceived.   36 Robert Wayth, Navy Paymaster.
37 A tavern in the Palace Yard, at Westminster.
38 In Drury Lane.   39 A pastoral play by John Fletcher.
40 A favorite comedian.
41 The Hunts were friends of the Pepyses.

42 Barbara Villiers, afterwards Mrs. Palmer, Countess of Castlemaine, and Duchess of Cleveland. She was one of the King's mistresses and had six children by him.   43 Somewhat.
44 A district east of Cheapside, the central mercantile street northeast of St. Paul's.   45 In the palace of Whitehall.
46 Hat.
47 Or canions; ornamental, sausagelike rolls around the ends of the breeches legs.   48 See note 34, above.
49 A Huguenot church in Threadneedle Street.
50 St. Dunstan's in the East; it was near the Tower of London.

SEPTEMBER 20, 1665. . . . So I up, and after being trimmed, the first time I have been touched by a barber these twelvemonths, I think, and more, went to Sir J. Mennes's,[51] where I find all out of order still, they having not seen one another till by and by Sir J. Mennes and Sir W. Batten met, to go into my Lord Brouncker's[52] coach, and so we four to Lambeth,[53] and thence to the Duke of Albemarle,[54] to inform him what we have done as to the fleet, which is very little, and to receive his direction. But, Lord! what a sad time it is to see no boats upon the river; and grass grows all up and down Whitehall court, and nobody but poor wretches in the streets! And, which is worst of all, the Duke showed us the number of the plague this week, brought in the last night from the Lord Mayor; that it is increased about 600 more than the last, which is quite contrary to all our hopes and expectations from the coldness of the late season. For the whole general number is 8,297, and of them the plague 7,165 which is more in the whole by above 50, than the biggest bill yet; which is very grievous to us all. . . .

MAY 5, 1666. At the office all the morning. After dinner, upon a letter from the fleet from Sir W. Coventry,[55] I did do a great deal of work for the sending away of the victualers that are in the river, &c., too much to remember. Till 10 at night busy about letters and other necessary matter of the office. About 11 I home, it being a fine moonshine; and so my wife and Mercer[56] come into the garden, and, my business being done, we sang till about twelve at night, with mighty pleasure to ourselves and neighbors, by their casements opening, and so home to supper and to bed.

SEPTEMBER 2, 1666 (*Lord's day*). Some of our maids sitting up late last night to get things ready against our feast today, Jane[57] called us up about three in the morning, to tell us of a great fire they saw in the City. So I rose and slipped on my nightgown and went to her window, and thought it to be on the back side of Mark Lane[58] at the farthest; but,

being unused to such fires as followed, I thought it far enough off, and so went to bed again and to sleep. About seven rose again to dress myself, and there looked out at the window, and saw the fire not so much as it was and further off. So to my closet to set things to rights after yesterday's cleaning. By and by Jane comes and tells me that she hears that above 300 houses have been burned down tonight by the fire we saw, and that it is now burning down all Fish Street, by London Bridge. So I made myself ready presently and walked to the Tower and there got up upon one of the high places, Sir J. Robinson's[59] little son going up with me; and there I did see the houses at that end of the bridge all on fire, and an infinite great fire on this and the other side the end of the bridge; which, among other people, did trouble me for poor little Michell[60] and our Sarah on the bridge. So down, with my heart full of trouble, to the Lieutenant of the Tower, who tells me that it begun this morning in the King's baker's house in Pudding Lane,[61] and that it hath burned St. Magnus's Church and most part of Fish Street already. So I down to the waterside, and there got a boat and through bridge, and there saw a lamentable fire. Poor Michell's house, as far as the Old Swan,[62] already burned that way, and the fire running further, that in a very little time it got as far as the Steelyard,[63] while I was there. Everybody endeavoring to remove their goods, and flinging into the river or bringing them into lighters that lay off; poor people staying in their houses as long as till the very fire touched them, and then running into boats or clambering from one pair of stairs by the waterside to another. And among other things, the poor pigeons, I perceive, were loath to leave their houses, but hovered about the windows and balconies till they were, some of them, burned, their wings, and fell down. Having stayed, and in an hour's time seen the fire rage every way, and nobody, to my sight, endeavoring to quench it, but to remove their goods and leave all to the fire, and having seen it get as far as the Steelyard, and the wind mighty high and driving it into the City; and everything, after so long a drought, proving combustible, even the very stones of churches, and among other

---

[51] Vice-Admiral Sir John Mennes, Comptroller of the Navy after Slingsby's death.
[52] William, Viscount Brouncker, one of the Commissioners of the Navy. He was president of the Royal Society.
[53] A district above Westminster, on the other side of the Thames.
[54] General George Monk, Duke of Albemarle, Acting Lord Admiral.
[55] Sir William Coventry, one of the Commissioners of the Navy.
[56] Mary Mercer, Mrs. Pepys's maid.
[57] Jane Birch, the Pepyses' cook.
[58] On the other side of the Navy Office.

[59] Sir John Robinson, Lieutenant of the Tower.
[60] Betty Howlet, a shopkeeper's daughter, and from childhood a pet of Pepys. She had recently married "young Michell," a tradesman.—Sarah was the name of a former maid of Mrs. Pepys.
[61] Between Eastcheap and Lower Thames Street.—St. Magnus's was near London Bridge, from which Fish Street ran north.
[62] A landing-place a little above the bridge.
[63] A little way up the river from the Old Swan.

things the poor steeple by which pretty Mrs. ———— lives, and whereof my old schoolfellow Elborough[64] is parson, taken fire in the very top, and there burned till it fell down: I to Whitehall (with a gentleman with me who desired to go off from the Tower, to see the fire, in my boat); to Whitehall, and there up to the King's closet in the Chapel, where people come about me, and I did give them an account dismayed them all, and word was carried in to the King. So I was called for, and did tell the King and Duke of York what I saw, and that unless his Majesty did command houses to be pulled down nothing could stop the fire. They seemed much troubled, and the King commanded me to go to my Lord Mayor from him, and command him to spare no houses, but to pull down before the fire every way. The Duke of York bid me tell him that if he would have any more soldiers he shall; and so did my Lord Arlington[65] afterwards, as a great secret. Here meeting with Captain Cocke,[66] I in his coach, which he lent me, and Creed with me to Paul's, and there walked along Watling Street, as well as I could, every creature coming away loaden with goods to save, and here and there sick people carried away in beds. Extraordinary good goods carried in carts and on backs. At last met my Lord Mayor in Canning Street,[67] like a man spent, with a handkercher about his neck. To the King's message he cried, like a fainting woman, "Lord! what can I do? I am spent; people will not obey me. I have been pulling down houses, but the fire overtakes us faster than we can do it." That he needed no more soldiers; and that, for himself, he must go and refresh himself, having been up all night. So he left me, and I him, and walked home, seeing people all almost distracted, and no manner of means used to quench the fire. The houses, too, so very thick thereabouts, and full of matter for burning, as pitch and tar, in Thames Street, and warehouses of oil and wines and brandy and other things. Here I saw Mr. Isaac Houblon, the handsome man, prettily dressed and dirty, at his door at Dowgate,[68] receiving some of his brother's things, whose houses were on fire, and, as he says, have been removed twice already; and he doubts (as it soon proved) that they must be in a little time removed from his house also, which was a sad consideration.

And to see the churches all filling with goods by people who themselves should have been quietly there at this time! By this time it was about twelve o'clock; and so home, and there find my guests, which was Mr. Wood[69] and his wife Barbary Sheldon, and also Mr. Moone:[70] she mighty fine, and her husband, for aught I see, a likely man. But Mr. Moone's design and mine, which was to look over my closet and please him with the sight thereof, which he hath long desired, was wholly disappointed; for we were in great trouble and disturbance at this fire, not knowing what to think of it. However, we had an extraordinary good dinner, and as merry as at this time we could be. While at dinner Mrs. Batelier[71] come to enquire after Mr. Wolfe and Stanes (who, it seems, are related to them), whose houses in Fish Street are all burned, and they in a sad condition. She would not stay in the fright. Soon as dined, I and Moone away, and walked through the City, the streets full of nothing but people and horses and carts loaden with goods, ready to run over one another, and removing goods from one burned house to another. They now removing out of Canning Street (which received goods in the morning) into Lombard Street, and further; and among others I now saw my little goldsmith, Stokes, receiving some friend's goods, whose house itself was burned the day after. We parted at Paul's; he home, and I to Paul's Wharf, where I had appointed a boat to attend me, and took in Mr. Carcasse[72] and his brother, whom I met in the street, and carried them below and above bridge to and again to see the fire, which was now got further, both below and above, and no likelihood of stopping it. Met with the King and Duke of York in their barge, and with them to Queenhithe,[73] and there called Sir Richard Browne[74] to them. Their order was only to pull down houses apace, and so below bridge at the waterside; but little was or could be done, the fire coming upon them so fast. Good hopes there was of stopping it at the Three Cranes[75] above, and at Buttolph's Wharf below bridge, if care be used; but the wind carries it into the City, so as we know not by the waterside what it do there. River full of lighters and boats taking in goods, and good goods swimming in the water, and only I observed that

64 Thomas Elborough, curate of St. Lawrence Poultney, between Cannon and Thames Streets.
65 The Earl of Arlington, Secretary of State.
66 Captain George Cocke, wealthy merchant.
67 Or Cannon Street.
68 A district between Cannon and Thames streets.

69 A mast-maker.   70 Secretary to Lord Bellasyse.
71 Mary Batelier, a linendraper; she and her family were friends of the Pepyses.
72 James Carcasse, a clerk in the Navy Office.
73 A quay to the east of Paul's Wharf, which was south of the cathedral.   74 The Lord Mayor.
75 A wharf a little to the east of Queenhithe.

hardly one lighter or boat in three, that had the goods of a house in, but there was a pair of virginals[76] in it. Having seen as much as I could now, I away to Whitehall by appointment, and there walked to St. James's Park, and there met my wife and Creed and Wood and his wife, and walked to my boat; and there upon the water again, and to the fire up and down, it still increasing, and the wind great. So near the fire as we could for smoke; and all over the Thames, with one's face in the wind, you were almost burned with a shower of fire-drops. This is very true; so as houses were burned by these drops and flakes of fire, three or four, nay, five or six houses, one from another. When we could endure no more upon the water, we to a little alehouse on the Bankside, over against[77] the Three Cranes, and there stayed till it was dark almost, and saw the fire grow; and, as it grew darker, appeared more and more, and in corners and upon steeples, and between churches and houses, as far as we could see up the hill of the City, in a most horrid, malicious, bloody flame, not like the fine flame of an ordinary fire. Barbary and her husband away before us. We stayed till, it being darkish, we saw the fire as only one entire arch of fire from this to the other side of the bridge, and in a bow up the hill for an arch of above a mile long: it made me weep to see it. The churches, houses, and all on fire and flaming at once; and a horrid noise the flames made, and the cracking of houses at their ruin. So home with a sad heart, and there find everybody discoursing and lamenting the fire; and poor Tom Hater[78] come with some few of his goods saved out of his house, which is burned upon Fish Street Hill. I invited him to lie at my house, and did receive his goods, but was deceived in his lying there, the news coming every moment of the growth of the fire, so as we were forced to begin to pack up our own goods and prepare for their removal, and did by moonshine (it being brave[79] dry, and moonshine, and warm weather) carry much of my goods into the garden, and Mr. Hater and I did remove my money and iron chests into my cellar, as thinking that the safest place. And got my bags of gold into my office, ready to carry away, and my chief papers of accounts also there, and my tallies into a box by themselves. So great was our fear as Sir W. Batten hath carts come out of the country to fetch away his goods this night. We did put Mr. Hater, poor man, to bed a little;

but he got but very little rest, so much noise being in my house, taking down of goods.

3rd. About four o'clock in the morning, my Lady Batten sent me a cart to carry away all my money and plate and best things, to Sir W. Rider's at Bednal Green.[80] Which I did, riding myself in my nightgown[81] in the cart; and, Lord! to see how the streets and the highways are crowded with people running and riding, and getting of carts at any rate to fetch away things. I find Sir W. Rider tired with being called up all night, and receiving things from several friends. His house full of goods, and much of Sir W. Batten's and Sir W. Penn's.[82] I am eased at my heart to have my treasure so well secured. Then home, with much ado to find a way, nor any sleep all this night to me nor my poor wife. But then and all this day, she and I and all my people laboring to get away the rest of our things, and did get Mr. Tooker[83] to get me a lighter to take them in, and we did carry them (myself some) over Tower Hill, which was by this time full of people's goods, bringing their goods thither; and down to the lighter, which lay at the next quay, above the Tower Dock. And here was my neighbor's wife, Mrs. ———, with her pretty child, and some few of her things, which I did willingly give way to be saved with mine; but there was no passing with anything through the postern, the crowd was so great. The Duke of York come this day by the office, and spoke to us, and did ride with his guard up and down the City to keep all quiet (he being now General, and having the care of all). This day, Mercer being not at home, but against her mistress's order gone to her mother's, and my wife going thither to speak with W. Hewer,[84] met her there, and was angry; and her mother saying that she was not a prentice girl, to ask leave every time she goes abroad, my wife with good reason was angry, and when she came home bid her be gone again. And so she went away, which troubled me, but yet less than it would, because of the condition we are in, fear of coming into in a little time of being less able to keep one in[85] her quality. At night lay down a little upon a quilt of

---

76 A small rectangular spinet.
77 Opposite, i.e., across the river from.
78 One of Pepys's clerks. 79 Fine.

80 Bethnal Green, a suburb northeast of London.—Sir William Rider and Pepys were fellow-members of the Commission for Tangier. 81 Dressing gown.
82 Vice-Admiral Penn, father of the founder of Pennsylvania, was one of the Commissioners of the Navy. He had been second in command to the Duke of York when the Dutch fleet was beaten on June 3, 1665.
83 John Tooker, messenger to the Commissioners of the Navy.
84 William Hewer, Pepys's chief clerk. 85 Of.

W. Hewer's in the office, all my own things being packed up or gone; and after me my poor wife did the like, we having fed upon the remains of yesterday's dinner, having no fire nor dishes, nor any opportunity of dressing anything.

4th. Up by break of day to get away the remainder of my things; which I did by a lighter at the Iron Gate,[86] and my hands so few that it was the afternoon before we could get them all away. Sir W. Penn and I to Tower Street, and there met the fire burning three or four doors beyond Mr. Howell's,[87] whose goods, poor man, his trays and dishes, shovels, &c., were flung all along Tower Street in the kennels,[88] and people working therewith from one end to the other, the fire coming on in that narrow street, on both sides, with infinite fury. Sir W. Batten not knowing how to remove his wine, did dig a pit in the garden, and laid it in there; and I took the opportunity of laying all the papers of my office that I could not otherwise dispose of. And in the evening Sir W. Penn and I did dig another, and put our wine in it; and I my Parmesan cheese, as well as my wine and some other things. The Duke of York was at the office this day, at Sir W. Penn's; but I happened not to be within. This afternoon, sitting melancholy with Sir W. Penn in our garden, and thinking of the certain burning of this office, without extraordinary means, I did propose for the sending up of all our workmen from Woolwich and Deptford yards[89] (none whereof yet appeared), and to write to Sir W. Coventry to have the Duke of York's permission to pull down houses rather than lose this office, which would much hinder the King's business. So Sir W. Penn he went down this night, in order to the sending them up tomorrow morning; and I wrote to Sir W. Coventry about the business, but received no answer. This night Mrs. Turner (who, poor woman, was removing her goods all this day, good goods into the garden, and knows not how to dispose of them), and her husband[90] supped with my wife and I at night, in the office, upon a shoulder of mutton from the cook's, without any napkin or anything, in a sad manner, but were merry. Only now and then walking into the garden, and saw how horridly the sky looks, all on a fire in the night, was enough to put us out of our wits; and, indeed, it was extremely dreadful, for it looks just as if it was at us, and the whole heaven on fire.

I after supper walked in the dark down to Tower Street, and there saw it all on fire, at the Trinity House on that[91] side, and the Dolphin Tavern on this side, which was very near us; and the fire with extraordinary vehemence. Now begins the practice of blowing up of houses in Tower Street, those next the Tower, which at first did frighten people more than anything; but it stopped the fire where it was done, it bringing down the houses to the ground in the same places they stood, and then it was easy to quench what little fire was in it, though it kindled nothing almost. W. Hewer this day went to see how his mother did, and comes late home, telling us how he hath been forced to remove her to Islington,[92] her house in Pie Corner[93] being burned; so that the fire is got so far that way, and all the Old Bailey,[94] and was running down to Fleet Street; and Paul's is burned, and all Cheapside. I wrote to my father this night, but the posthouse being burned, the letter could not go.

5th. I lay down in the office again upon W. Hewer's quilt, being mighty weary, and sore in my feet with going till I was hardly able to stand. About two in the morning my wife calls me up and tells me of new cries of fire, it being come to Barking Church, which is the bottom of our lane. I up, and finding it so, resolved presently to take her away, and did, and took my gold, which was about £2,350, W. Hewer, and Jane, down by Poundy's[95] boat to Woolwich; but, Lord! what a sad sight it was by moonlight to see the whole City almost on fire, that you might see it plain at Woolwich, as if you were by it. There, when I come, I find the gates shut, but no guard kept at all, which troubled me, because of discourse now begun that there is plot in it and that the French had done it. I got the gates open, and to Mr. Sheldon's,[96] where I locked up my gold, and charged my wife and W. Hewer never to leave the room without one of them in it, night or day. So back again, by the way seeing my goods well in the lighters at Deptford, and watched well by people. Home, and whereas I expected to have seen our house on fire, it being now about seven o'clock, it was not. But to the fire, and there find greater hopes than I expected; for my confidence of finding our office on fire was such that I durst not ask anybody how it was with us, till I come and saw it not burned. But going to

---

86 Of the Tower.   87 He was a turner.   88 Gutters.
89 Down the Thames.
90 Thomas Turner was General Clerk at the Navy Office.

91 I.e., toward the river.   92 A northern suburb.
93 The Great Fire, which began at Pudding Lane, ended at Pie Corner, in West Smithfield, to the northwest of the City.
94 North of Ludgate Hill.   95 A waterman.
96 A clerk in the Navy Yard.

the fire, I find by the blowing up of houses, and the great help given by the workmen out of the King's yards, sent up by Sir W. Penn, there is a good stop given to it, as well as at Mark Lane end as ours; it having only burned the dial of Barking Church[97] and part of the porch, and was there quenched. I up to the top of Barking steeple, and there saw the saddest sight of desolation that I ever saw; everywhere great fires, oilcellars, and brimstone, and other things burning. I became afeard to stay there long, and therefore down again as fast as I could, the fire being spread as far as I could see it; and to Sir W. Penn's, and there eat a piece of cold meat, having eaten nothing since Sunday but the remains of Sunday's dinner. Here I met with Mr. Young and Whistler;[98] and having removed all my things, and received good hopes that the fire at our end is stopped, they and I walked into the town, and find Fanchurch Street, Gracious Street, and Lombard Street all in dust. The Exchange a sad sight, nothing standing there of all the statues or pillars but Sir Thomas Gresham's[99] picture in the corner. Walked into Moorfields[1] (our feet ready to burn, walking through the town among the hot coals), and find that full of people, and poor wretches carrying their goods there, and everybody keeping his goods together by themselves (and a great blessing it is to them that it is fair weather for them to keep abroad night and day); drank there, and paid twopence for a plain penny loaf. Thence homeward, having passed through Cheapside and Newgate Market,[2] all burned, and seen Anthony Joyce's[3] house in fire. And took up (which I keep by me) a piece of glass of Mercers' Chapel in the street,[4] where much more was, so melted and buckled with the heat of the fire like parchment. I also did see a poor cat taken out of a hole in the chimney, joining to the wall of the Exchange, with the hair all burned off the body, and yet alive. So home at night, and find there good hopes of saving our office; but great endeavors of watching all night, and having men ready; and so we lodged them in the office, and had drink and bread and cheese for them. And I lay down and slept a good night about midnight, though when I rose I heard that there had been a great alarm of

French and Dutch being risen, which proved nothing. But it is a strange thing to see how long this time did look since Sunday, having been always full of variety of actions and little sleep, that it looked like a week or more, and I had forgot almost the day of the week.

JULY 8, 1667. Up, and to my chamber, and by and by comes Greeting,[5] and to my flageolet with him with a pretty deal of pleasure, and then to the office, where W. Batten, W. Penn and I met about putting men to work for the weighing of the ships in the river sunk.[6] Then home again, and there heard Mr. Caesar[7] play some very good things on the lute together with myself on the viol[8] and Greeting on the violin. Then with my wife abroad by coach, she to her tailor's, I to Westminster to Burgess[9] about my Tangier business, and thence to Whitehall, where I spoke with Sir John Nicholas,[10] who tells me that Mr. Coventry is come from Breda as was expected, but contrary to expectation brings with him two or three articles[11] which do not please the King: as, to retrench the Act of Navigation, and then to ascertain what are contraband goods; and then that those exiled persons, who are or shall take refuge in their country, may be secure from any further prosecution. Whether these will be enough to break the peace upon, or no, he cannot tell; but I perceive the certainty of peace is blown over. So called on my wife and met Creed by the way, and they two and I to Charing Cross,[12] there to see the great boy and girl that are lately come out of Ireland, the latter eight, the former but four years old, of most prodigious bigness for their age. I tried to weigh them in my arms, and find them twice as heavy as people almost twice their age; and yet I am apt to believe they are very young. Their father a little sorry fellow, and their mother an old Irish woman. They have had four children of this bigness, and four of ordinary growth, whereof two of each are dead. If, as my Lord Ormond[13] certifies, it be true that they are no older, it is very monstrous. So home and to dinner with my wife and to pipe,[14] and then

---

[97] Allhallows Barking, in Great Tower Street, near the end of Seething Lane.   [98] Flagmakers.
[99] The founder of the Royal Exchange, a bazaar in Cornhill. It was opened in 1571.

[1] A large park north of the City.
[2] To the west of Cheapside.   [3] Pepys's cousin.
[4] Cheapside.

[5] A music teacher.
[6] The month before. The object was to keep the Dutch fleet from coming up the river.
[7] William Caesar, composer and lute player.
[8] A stringed instrument played with a bow but distinct from the violin.   [9] An official of the Exchequer.
[10] Son of the Secretary of State, Sir Edward Nicholas.
[11] Of the peace treaty under negotiation at the Dutch town of Breda.   [12] North of Whitehall.
[13] The Duke of Ormond, Lord Deputy of Ireland.
[14] On the flageolet.

I to the office, where busy all the afternoon till the evening; and then with my wife by coach abroad to Bow and Stratford,[15] it being so dusty weather that there was little pleasure in it, and so home and to walk in the garden, and thither comes Pelling[16] to us to talk, and so in and to supper, and then to bed. All the world being as I hear very much damped that their hopes of peace is become uncertain again.

FEBRUARY 27, 1668. All the morning at the office, and at noon home to dinner, and thence with my wife and Deb[17] to the King's House,[18] to see *The Virgin Martyr,*[19] the first time it hath been acted a great while, and it is mighty pleasant; not that the play is worth much, but it is finely acted by Beck Marshall. But that which did please me beyond anything in the whole world was the wind music when the angel comes down, which is so sweet that it ravished me, and indeed, in a word, did wrap up my soul so that it made me really sick, just as I have formerly been when in love with my wife: that neither then, nor all the evening going home, and at home, I was able to think of anything, but remained all night transported, so as I could not believe that ever any music hath that real command over the soul of a man as this did upon me; and makes me resolve to practice wind music, and to make my wife do the like.

APRIL 2, 1668. . . . With Lord Brouncker[20] to the Royal Society, where they were just done; but there I was forced to subscribe to the building of a college, and did give £40; and several others did subscribe, some greater and some less sums, but several I saw hang off; and I doubt it will spoil the Society, for it breeds faction and ill will, and becomes burdensome to some that cannot, or would not, do it. Here, to my great content, I did try the use of the autocousticon,[21] which was only a great glass bottle broke at the bottom, putting the neck to my ear, and there I did plainly hear the dashing of the oars of the boats in the Thames to Arundel[22] gallery window, which, without it, I could not in the least do, and may, I believe, be improved to a great height, which I am mighty glad of. Thence with Lord Brouncker and several of them to the King's

Head Tavern by Chancery Lane, and there did drink and eat and talk, and above the rest I did hear of Mr. Hooke[23] and my Lord an account of the reason of concords and discords in music, which they say is from the equality of vibrations; but I am not satisfied in it, but will at my leisure think of it more, and see how far that do go to explain it. . . .

SEPTEMBER 4, 1668. Up, and met at the office all the morning; and at noon my wife and Deb and Mercer and W. Hewer and I to the Fair, and there, at the old house, did eat a pig and was pretty merry, but saw no sights, my wife having a mind to see the play *Bartholomew Fair,*[24] with puppets. Which we did, and it is an excellent play; the more I see it, the more I love the wit of it; only the business of abusing the Puritans begins to grow stale and of no use, they being the people that at last will be found the wisest. . . .

MAY 31, 1669. Up very betimes, and so continued all the morning with W. Hewer, upon examining and stating my accounts, in order to the fitting myself to go abroad beyond sea,[25] which the ill condition of my eyes and my neglect for a year or two hath kept me behindhand in, and so as to render it very difficult now, and troublesome to my mind to do it; but I this day made a satisfactory entrance therein. . . .

And thus ends all that I doubt I shall ever be able to do with my own eyes in the keeping of my journal, I being not able to do it any longer, having done now so long as to undo my eyes almost every time that I take a pen in my hand; and, therefore, whatever comes of it, I must forbear: and therefore resolve, from this time forward, to have it kept by my people in longhand, and must therefore be contented to set down no more than is fit for them and all the world to know; or if there be anything, which cannot be much (now my amours to Deb are past and my eyes hindering me in almost all other pleasures), I must endeavor to keep a margin in my book open, to add here and there a note in shorthand with my own hand.

And so I betake myself to that course which is almost as much as to see myself go into my grave; for which, and all the discomforts that will accompany my being blind, the good God prepare me!

---

[15] Stratford Le Bow, an eastern suburb, to which Londoners resorted for cakes and cream.　　[16] An apothecary.
[17] Deb Willet, Mrs. Pepys's maid.
[18] The Theater Royal, Drury Lane.
[19] A tragedy by Philip Massinger and Thomas Dekker.
[20] See note 52, above.　　[21] Ear trumpet.
[22] The Royal Society met at Arundel House, in the Strand.

[23] Dr. Robert Hook, a professor of geometry, and the Royal Society's "Curator of the Experiments."
[24] One of Ben Jonson's masterpieces. The puppets appear in its final act, to ridicule the Puritans.
[25] He had obtained a leave of absence. With his wife he made a tour of France and Holland.

John Dryden

1631–1700

No OTHER Englishman was ever so generally acknowledged in his own time the foremost writer of an age as was Dryden—in drama, poetry, and prose criticism. Nowadays his pre-eminence is not accepted without reservations. There were certainly better dramatists and perhaps better poets—except in satire. In the whole range of English literature only Pope and Byron are his rivals as verse satirists, though if Rochester had lived he might have equaled them. As a critic Dryden stands very high, and not only for intellectual acumen. A robust and thoroughly masculine personality animates his direct and forceful style; as a stylist he has been called, with pardonable exaggeration, the father of modern English prose. His prose is like his best satirical verse: clean-cut, "nervous" (that is, sinewy), and unaffected. Dryden's was a strong intellect; it invests most of what he wrote with a strength that of itself is still exhilarating. The more you read his criticism and satire the better you will think of him.

A Northamptonshire man, he was educated at Westminster School, where he became a sound Latinist, and at Cambridge, where he took his B.A. in 1654. In due course he married and had three sons, the youngest of whom eventually succeeded the poet's cousins in the family baronetcy; he saw England change from Puritan domination to a licentious and somewhat arbitrary monarchy, and then to a constitutional one; he was a member of the Royal Society and a reader of Descartes and Hobbes; he was interested though not active in politics; and he changed his religion—at the wrong moment, as far as worldly advantage went. Yet his was a life essentially of letters; its most significant mileposts are the dates of his writings.

In 1658 Dryden composed his first notable poem, "Heroic Stanzas on the Death of Oliver Cromwell." Two years later he welcomed the return of Charles II with the rimed couplets of Astraea Redux (Justice Restored). Those who condemn this sudden shift forget that a large section of English opinion felt the same way on both occasions. His principal poems, besides those printed in part or in whole below, are Annus Mirabilis (The Wonderful Year, 1666), on the Dutch War and the Great Fire; The Medal (1682), a satire against the Whigs; Religio Laici (A Layman's Religion, 1683), a defense of the Church of England; The Hind and the Panther (1687), a defense of Catholicism, to which he had become, at a time when the current was running strongly against Rome, a sincere convert; a translation of Vergil (1697); and a miscellany entitled

Fables (1700). Dryden had turned to the last of these and to other translations, as formerly to the theater, for a livelihood.

His career as a playwright was long but disappointing. He lacked a natural talent for drama, and wrote for the stage only because that was still the readiest way for a poet to make a living. He helped establish the brief vogue of the Heroic play, and in such pieces as The Conquest of Granada (in two parts, first acted 1670–71) became its leading exponent. In Aurengzebe (1675) he is less remote from the common sense which, so characteristic of him in other genres, he abandoned in this. In All for Love (1677), an attempt at treating the subject of Shakespeare's Antony and Cleopatra within the confines of the neoclassical Rules, he turns from the rimed couplet to blank verse. Another example of his zeal for "improving" Shakespeare is his adaptation of Troilus and Cressida. But in tragedy Dryden was surpassed by Thomas Otway's The Orphan (1680) and Venice Preserved (1682), while in comedy Etherege, Wycherley, Shadwell, Vanbrugh, and Congreve were all his betters. As a writer of prologues distinguished by ease and charm he had, however, few equals.

As a critic Dryden is both brilliant and solid. His essays, many of them prefaces to his plays, form the earliest considerable body of literary criticism in English. In the first place, he has taste; it is remarkably catholic, and he goes straight for the good things. His general position is neoclassical, and he is strongly impressed by the French critics; but he is not hidebound. He respects the Rules, but retains his own liberty of opinion and practice. In the second place, then, he is a vigorous and independent thinker. In the third, he writes with a combination of strength, clearness, and winning charm. His shortcomings, in both prose and verse, arise from his haste—he seldom perfected his work— and from his failure to cultivate his own imagination and a consequent tendency to depreciate its value.

At the revolution of 1688 Dryden refused to alter his politics. In 1670 he had succeeded D'avenant as poet laureate; now he was ousted, and the place was filled by a stout Whig, Thomas Shadwell. No one thought Shadwell the better poet, however; and at Will's coffee house Dryden laid down the law for the world of letters, as in a former day Jonson had taken the lead at the Mermaid and the Devil. If anyone has ever deserved the name of literary dictator it was Dryden. He established the rimed couplet as the principal English meter; it was to remain such for a century. He was the most conspicuous figure of the revolution in English prose style. His example helped form Addison and Pope, and with them the eighteenth century.

The standard edition of the *Works* is by Sir Walter Scott, re-edited by G. Saintsbury (18 vols., 1882-93). There is an excellent one-volume edition of *The Poetical Works* (1909) by G. R. Noyes, who also edited *Selected Dramas* (1910). For the essays, see W. P. Ker's edition (2 vols., 1900). L. I. Bredvold's *The Best of Dryden* (1933) is a good selection. There is an Everyman volume of essays and another of poems; two volumes of plays are given in the Mermaid edition. Scott's is still the best biography (1808); the latest, by C. Hollis (1933), is unreliable; a new one is needed. The best critical study of the poems is Mark Van Doren's *The Poetry of John Dryden* (revised ed., 1946). L. I. Bredvold's *The Intellectual Milieu of John Dryden* (1934) is an important book. T. S. Eliot's criticism has done much to increase interest in Dryden in our day.

from ABSALOM AND ACHITOPHEL

THIS masterly political satire of 1031 lines was published anonymously in 1681. Three years earlier the nation had been rocked by disclosure of the so-called Popish Plot. A conspiracy was on foot to restore the Catholic religion, but it was of small proportions compared to the story told the authorities by an infamous and fantastic liar named Titus Oates. According to Oates the plotters intended to burn London, massacre the Protestants, assassinate Charles II, and establish a Catholic state. Before the excitement subsided, many innocent persons had been falsely accused and executed.

The leader of the Whig party, the Earl of Shaftesbury, tried to make political capital out of this unhappy affair. A bill was brought into Parliament to exclude from the succession Charles's Catholic brother, James, Duke of York. The Whigs hoped to supplant him with the popular and Protestant Duke of Monmouth, an illegitimate son of King Charles. In 1680 the Exclusion Bill passed the House of Commons, but it was voted down in the House of Lords. By the summer of 1681 the scare was over, and Charles's Tory government felt strong enough to arrest Shaftesbury on a charge of treason. In November, however, the grand jury rightly refused to indict him, and he was freed. Dryden's poem had appeared the week before; it was meant to encourage a verdict against Shaftesbury.

In 2 Samuel 13-18 will be found the Biblical account which, with modifications, Dryden used as a parallel to the political situation in England. He writes as a conservative, alarmed by the specter of mob rule. In his Life of Dryden, Dr. Johnson praises the poem's "acrimony of censure, elegance of praise, artful delineation of characters, variety and vigor of sentiment, happy turns of language, and pleasing harmony of numbers." The portrait of Zimri is universally regarded as one of the most brilliant satirical efforts in English. Dryden's own estimate, in his essay on "The Original and Progress of Satire" (1693), embodies a definition of his method:

How easy is it to call rogue and villain . . . ! But how hard to make a man appear a fool, a blockhead, or a knave, without using any of those opprobrious terms! . . . Neither is it true that this fineness of raillery is offensive. A witty man is tickled while he is hurt in this manner, and a fool feels it not. . . . There is still a vast difference betwixt the slovenly butchering of a man and the fineness of a stroke that separates the head from the body, and leaves it standing in its place. . . . The character of Zimri[1] in my *Absalom* is, in my opinion, worth the whole poem: it is not bloody, but it is ridiculous enough; and he for whom it was intended was too witty to resent it as an injury. If I had railed, I might have suffered for it justly; but I managed my own work more happily, perhaps more dexterously. I avoided the mention of great crimes, and applied myself to the representing of blindsides and little extravagances; to which, the wittier a man is, he is generally the more obnoxious.[2] It succeeded as I wished; the jest went round, and he was laughed at in his turn who began the frolic.

The last words refer to Buckingham's hilarious mock-heroic play, *The Rehearsal* (1671), in which Dryden is caricatured as the ridiculous poet laureate Bayes.

Absalom and Achitophel appeals to the intellect rather than the heart. One does not turn to satire for inspiration, but for essentially the same kinds of pleasure that witty prose affords. These are chiefly two: first, the exhilaration which comes from contact with a penetrating and energetic mind, and second, the delight which any man of taste is bound to take in recognizing expert workmanship. Dryden's poetic tools are precision tools, though their manipulation was to be further refined by Pope in the next century. The use of the heroic couplet is always dogged by the danger of monotony, and all the neoclassicists employed certain tricks to thwart it—for example, the occasional use of a triplet instead of a couplet, and of an Alexandrine or six-stress iambic line instead of the normal pentameter. But an artist like Dryden has less mechanical ways of achieving variety and flexibility within the couplet form, which you will discover as you read.

---

[1] The Duke of Buckingham. See lines 543-68 and note 74, below.
[2] Liable, subject.

In pious times, ere priestcraft did begin,
Before polygamy was made a sin,
When man on many multiplied his kind,
Ere one to one was cursedly confined,
When nature prompted and no law denied   5
Promiscuous use of concubine and bride,
Then Israel's monarch[2] after heaven's own heart
His vigorous warmth did variously impart
To wives and slaves, and, wide as his command,
Scattered his Maker's image through the land.   10
Michal,[3] of royal blood, the crown did wear,
A soil ungrateful to the tiller's care:
Not so the rest; for several mothers[4] bore
To godlike David several sons before.
But since like slaves his bed they did ascend,   15
No true succession could their seed attend.
Of all this numerous progeny was none
So beautiful, so brave, as Absalon,[5]
Whether, inspired by some diviner lust,
His father got him with a greater gust,[6]   20
Or that his conscious destiny made way
By manly beauty to imperial sway.
Early in foreign fields he won renown,
With kings and states allied to Israel's crown;
In peace the thoughts of war he could remove,   25
And seemed as he were only born for love.
Whate'er he did was done with so much ease,
In him alone 'twas natural to please;
His motions all accompanied with grace,
And paradise was opened in his face.   30
With secret joy, indulgent David viewed
His youthful image in his son renewed;
To all his wishes nothing he denied,
And made the charming Annabel[7] his bride.
What faults he had (for who from faults is free?)   35
His father could not or he would not see.
Some warm excesses, which the law forbore,
Were construed youth that purged by boiling o'er;
And Amnon's murder,[8] by a specious name,
Was called a just revenge for injured fame.   40

Thus praised and loved the noble youth remained,
While David, undisturbed, in Sion[9] reigned.
But life can never be sincerely blest:
Heav'n punishes the bad, and proves[10] the best.
The Jews,[11] a headstrong, moody, murm'ring race   45
As ever tried th' extent and stretch of grace,
God's pampered people, whom, debauched with ease,
No king could govern nor no God could please
(Gods they had tried of every shape and size,
That god-smiths could produce, or priests devise),   50
These Adam-wits,[12] too fortunately free,
Began to dream they wanted[13] liberty;
And when no rule, no precedent, was found
Of men by laws less circumscribed and bound,
They led their wild desires to woods and caves,   55
And thought that all but savages were slaves.
They who, when Saul[14] was dead, without a blow
Made foolish Ishbosheth[15] the crown forgo,
Who banished David did from Hebron[16] bring,
And with a general shout proclaimed him king,   60
Those very Jews who, at their very best,
Their humor[17] more than loyalty expressed,
Now wondered why so long they had obeyed
An idol monarch, which their hands had made,
Thought they might ruin him they could create,   65
Or melt him to that golden calf, a state.[18]
But these were random bolts:[19] no formed design
Nor interest made the factious crowd to join;[20]
The sober part of Israel, free from stain,
Well knew the value of a peaceful reign   70
And, looking backward with a wise affright,
Saw seams of wounds, dishonest to the sight;
In contemplation of whose ugly scars,
They cursed the memory of civil wars.
The moderate sort of men, thus qualified,[21]   75
Inclined the balance to the better side;
And David's mildness managed it so well
The bad found no occasion to rebel.
But when to sin our biased nature leans,
The careful Devil is still[22] at hand with means,   80

---

[1] I.e., the closer you get, the more you'll see in it (Horace, *Art of Poetry*). [2] David; i.e., Charles II.
[3] David's queen; i.e., Charles's Portuguese wife, the childless Catharine of Braganza. [4] I.e., Charles's mistresses.
[5] Absalom, David's favorite son; i.e., the Duke of Monmouth, illegitimate son of Charles II. [6] Gusto.—*Got*=begot.
[7] I.e., Anne Scott, Countess of Buccleugh.
[8] Absalom procured the murder of Amnon, another of David's sons, in revenge for his rape of their sister Tamar. The allusion is probably to a brutal attack instigated by Monmouth on Sir John Coventry, who had publicly criticized King Charles's morals.

[9] London. [10] Tests. [11] English.
[12] I.e., fools who, like Adam in the Garden of Eden, failed to know when they were well off. [13] Lacked.
[14] David's predecessor as king of Israel; i.e., Oliver Cromwell.
[15] A son of Saul; on his father's death he was crowned king by one faction, and reigned for two years as a rival to David. He stands for the great Cromwell's ineffective son Richard, who ruled for a few months as Lord Protector.
[16] Where David was anointed king; i.e., Scotland, where Charles had been crowned in 1651. He was actually living in Holland at the time of his restoration to the English throne in 1660.
[17] Caprice, whim.
[18] I.e., might reduce the king to a mere figurehead. The "golden calf" is a symbol of rebellion; see Exodus 32.
[19] Shots. [20] Pronounced *jine*. [21] Made moderate.
[22] Always.

And providently pimps for ill desires;
The Good Old Cause,[23] revived, a plot requires:
Plots, true or false, are necessary things
To raise up commonwealths and ruin kings.

The inhabitants of old Jerusalem[24]   85
Were Jebusites;[25] the town so called from them;
And theirs the native right—
But when the chosen people[26] grew more strong,
The rightful cause at length became the wrong;
And every loss the men of Jebus bore,   90
They still were thought God's enemies the more.
Thus, worn and weakened, well or ill content,
Submit they must to David's government:
Impoverished and deprived of all command,
Their taxes doubled as they lost their land,   95
And, what was harder yet to flesh and blood,
Their gods disgraced, and burnt like common wood.
This set the heathen priesthood in a flame,
For priests of all religions are the same;
Of whatsoe'er descent their godhead be,   100
Stock, stone, or other homely pedigree,
In his defense his servants are as bold
As if he had been born of beaten gold.
The Jewish rabbins,[27] though their enemies,
In this conclude them honest men and wise: 105
For 'twas their duty, all the learnèd think,
To espouse his cause by whom they eat and drink.
From hence began that plot,[28] the nation's curse,
Bad in itself, but represented worse,
Raised in extremes and in extremes decried,   110
With oaths affirmed, with dying vows denied,
Not weighed or winnowed by the multitude
But swallowed in the mass, unchewed and crude.
Some truth there was, but dashed and brewed with lies,
To please the fools and puzzle all the wise.   115
Succeeding times did equal folly call
Believing nothing or believing all.
The Egyptian[29] rites the Jebusites embraced,
Where gods were recommended by their taste.
Such sav'ry deities must needs be good,   120
As served at once for worship and for food.
By force they could not introduce these gods,

For ten to one in former days was odds;[30]
So fraud was used (the sacrificer's trade):
Fools are more hard to conquer than persuade.   125
Their busy teachers[31] mingled with the Jews
And raked for converts even the court and stews,[32]
Which Hebrew priests[33] the more unkindly took
Because the fleece accompanies the flock.
Some thought they God's anointed[34] meant to slay   130
By guns, invented since full many a day;
Our author swears it not, but who can know
How far the Devil and Jebusites may go?
This plot, which failed for want of common sense,
Had yet a deep and dangerous consequence;   135
For, as when raging fevers boil the blood,
The standing lake soon floats into a flood,
And ev'ry hostile humor,[35] which before
Slept quiet in its channels, bubbles o'er;
So several factions from this first fermént   140
Work up to foam, and threat the government.
Some by their friends, more by themselves, thought wise,
Opposed the pow'r to which they could not rise.
Some had in courts been great and, thrown from thence,
Like fiends were hardened in impenitence.   145
Some by their monarch's fatal mercy grown,
From pardoned rebels, kinsmen to the throne
Were raised in pow'r and public office high;
Strong bands, if bands ungrateful men could tie.
Of these the false Achitophel[36] was first,   150
A name to all succeeding ages curst:
For close[37] designs and crooked counsels fit,
Sagacious, bold, and turbulent of wit,
Restless, unfixed in principles and place,
In pow'r unpleased, impatient of disgrace;   155
A fiery soul, which, working out its way,
Fretted the pigmy body[38] to decay,
And o'er-informed[39] the tenement of clay.
A daring pilot in extremity,[40]
Pleased with the danger when the waves went high,   160
He sought the storms; but, for a calm unfit,
Would steer too nigh the sands, to boast his wit.
Great wits are sure to madness near allied,
And thin partitions do their bounds divide;

_____

[23] The Puritan revolution.   [24] London.
[25] I.e., Roman Catholics.   [26] The Jews; i.e., the Protestants.
[27] Rabbis; i.e., the clergy of the Church of England.
[28] The alleged Popish Plot of 1678.
[29] French; i.e., Catholic. The following lines are a sneer at transubstantiation, the doctrine that the elements of the Eucharist change to the body and blood of Christ. Dryden was later to defend it in _The Hind and the Panther_. The agitation over the Popish Plot was increased by the disclosure that Charles was receiving a subsidy from France. Invasion by a French army was feared.

[30] I.e., the chances of war had always favored the English army if there were no more than ten times as many Frenchmen against it.
[31] The Jesuits.
[32] Brothels. Some of Charles's mistresses were Catholics; so was, openly, the Duke of York, his brother; and the King was rightly suspected of secret Catholic leanings.
[33] The Anglican ministers. The _fleece_ is the tithes paid by their parishioners.   [34] The King.
[35] Dangerous secretion.
[36] Or Ahithophel; i.e., Anthony Ashley Cooper (1621-83), first Earl of Shaftesbury, once a principal minister of the King.
[37] Secret.   [38] He was a small man.
[39] Too intensely animated.   [40] Danger.

Else why should he, with wealth and honor blest,   165
Refuse his age the needful hours of rest?
Punish a body which he could not please;
Bankrupt of life, yet prodigal of ease?
And all to leave what with his toil he won
To that unfeathered two-legged thing, a son,   170
Got while his soul did huddled notions try,[41]
And born a shapeless lump, like anarchy.
In friendship false, implacable in hate,
Resolved to ruin or to rule the state.
To compass this the triple bond[42] he broke,   175
The pillars of the public safety shook,
And fitted Israel for a foreign yoke;
Then, seized with fear, yet still affecting fame,[43]
Usurped a patriot's all-atoning name.
So easy still it proves in factious times   180
With public zeal to cancel private crimes.
How safe is treason, and how sacred ill,
Where none can sin against the people's will![44]
Where crowds can wink,[45] and no offense be known,
Since in another's guilt they find their own!   185
Yet fame deserved, no enemy can grudge;
The statesman we abhor, but praise the judge,[46]
In Israel's courts ne'er sat an Abbethdin[47]
With more discerning eyes or hands more clean,
Unbribed, unsought, the wretched to redress,   190
Swift of dispatch, and easy of access.
Oh, had he been content to serve the crown
With virtues only proper to the gown,[48]
Or had the rankness of the soil been freed
From cockle,[49] that oppressed the noble seed,   195
David for him his tuneful harp had strung,
And heav'n had wanted one immortal song.[50]
But wild ambition loves to slide, not stand,
And fortune's ice prefers to virtue's land.
Achitophel, grown weary to possess   200
A lawful fame and lazy happiness,
Disdained the golden fruit to gather free

And lent the crowd his arm to shake the tree.
Now, manifest of[51] crimes contrived long since,
He stood at bold defiance with his prince,   205
Held up the buckler of the people's cause
Against the crown, and skulked behind the laws.
The wished occasion of the plot he takes,
Some circumstances finds, but more he makes;
By buzzing emissaries fills the ears   210
Of listening crowds with jealousies and fears
Of arbitrary counsels brought to light,
And proves the King himself a Jebusite.
Weak arguments! which yet he knew full well
Were strong with people easy to rebel.   215
For, governed by the moon, the giddy Jews
Tread the same track when she the prime renews;[52]
And once in twenty years, their scribes record,
By natural instinct they change their lord.
Achitophel still wants a chief, and none   220
Was found so fit as warlike Absalon:
Not that he wished his greatness to create
(For politicians neither love nor hate),
But, for he knew his title not allowed,[53]
Would keep him still depending on the crowd;   225
That kingly power, thus ebbing out, might be
Drawn to the dregs of a democracy.
Him he attempts with studied arts to please,
And sheds his venom in such words as these:
  "Auspicious prince! at whose nativity   230
Some royal planet ruled the southern sky;
Thy longing country's darling and desire,
Their cloudy pillar and their guardian fire,[54]
Their second Moses, whose extended wand
Divides the seas and shows the promised land,   235
Whose dawning day in every distant age
Has exercised the sacred prophets' rage,[55]
The people's pray'r, the glad diviners' theme,
The young men's vision, and the old men's dream!
Thee, savior, thee, the nation's vows confess,   240
And, never satisfied with seeing, bless:
Swift, unbespoken pomps thy steps proclaim,
And stammering babes are taught to lisp thy name.
How long wilt thou the general joy detain,
Starve and defraud the people of thy reign?   245
Content ingloriously to pass thy days
Like one of virtue's fools that feeds on praise,
Till thy fresh glories, which now shine so bright,
Grow stale and tarnish with our daily sight.
Believe me, royal youth, thy fruit must be   250
Or gathered ripe or rot upon the tree.

---

[41] Conceived while he was thinking of various other things.
[42] The alliance against France (broken in 1670) between England, Sweden, and the Dutch Republic. Dryden's statement is unfair; Shaftesbury and other ministers were deceived by Charles, who negotiated a secret treaty with France against the Dutch.
[43] Desiring a good reputation.
[44] I.e., as long as the mob holds them innocent. Lines 180–91 were not printed in the first edition, but added in the second, also of 1681, after Shaftesbury's acquittal.   [45] Shut their eyes.
[46] Shaftesbury had formerly, as lord chancellor, presided justly over the highest court.
[47] Head of the Jewish judiciary.
[48] Only characteristic of the judge.
[49] A weed that grows in grainfields.
[50] David (there is here no reference to Charles) would have composed a poem in honor of Achitophel instead of writing one of the Psalms.

[51] Open in.   [52] Is once more the new moon.
[53] Monmouth was an illegitimate son of Charles.
[54] See Exodus 13:21.   [55] Fervor, ecstasy.

Heav'n has to all allotted, soon or late,
Some lucky revolution of their fate:
Whose motions if we watch and guide with skill
(For human good depends on human will),   255
Our Fortune rolls as from a smooth descent,
And from the first impression takes the bent;
But if unseized she glides away like wind,
And leaves repenting Folly far behind.
Now, now she meets you with a glorious prize,   260
And spreads her locks before her as she flies.[56]
Had thus old David, from whose loins you spring,
Not dared, when Fortune called him, to be king,
At Gath[57] an exile he might still remain,
And heaven's anointing oil had been in vain.   265
Let his successful youth your hopes engage,
But shun th' example of declining age.
Behold him setting in his western skies,
The shadows lengthening as the vapors rise.
He is not now as when on Jordan's sand[58]   270
The joyful people thronged to see him land,
Cov'ring the beach, and black'ning all the strand;
But, like the prince of angels,[59] from his height
Comes tumbling downward with diminished light,
Betrayed by one poor plot to public scorn   275
(Our only blessing since his curst return),
Those heaps of people, which one sheaf did bind,
Blown off and scattered by a puff of wind.
What strength can he to your designs oppose,
Naked of friends, and round beset with foes?   280
If Pharaoh's[60] doubtful succor he should use,
A foreign aid would more incense the Jews;
Proud Egypt would dissembled friendship bring:
Foment the war, but not support the King.
Nor would the royal party e'er unite   285
With Pharaoh's arms t' assist the Jebusite;
Or if they should, their interest soon would break,
And with such odious aid make David weak.
All sorts of men by my successful arts,
Abhorring kings, estrange their altered hearts   290
From David's rule; and 'tis the general cry,
'Religion, commonwealth, and liberty.'
If you, as champion of the public good,
Add to their arms a chief of royal blood,
What may not Israel hope, and what applause   295
Might such a general gain by such a cause?
Not barren praise alone, that gaudy flow'r,

Fair only to the sight, but solid pow'r;
And nobler is a limited command,
Giv'n by the love of all your native land,   300
Than a successive title, long and dark,
Drawn from the moldy rolls of Noah's ark."
    What cannot praise effect in mighty minds,
When flattery soothes and when ambition blinds!
Desire of pow'r, on earth a vicious weed,   305
Yet, sprung from high, is of celestial seed;
In God 'tis glory, and when men aspire
'Tis but a spark too much of heavenly fire.
Th' ambitious youth, too covetous of fame,
Too full of angels' metal[61] in his frame,   310
Unwarily was led from virtue's ways,
Made drunk with honor, and debauched with praise.
Half loath, and half consenting to the ill
(For loyal blood within him struggled still),
He thus replied: "And what pretense have I   315
To take up arms for public liberty?
My father governs with unquestioned right,
The Faith's defender and mankind's delight,
Good, gracious, just, observant of the laws;
And heav'n by wonders has espoused his cause.   320
Whom has he wronged in all his peaceful reign?
Who sues for justice to his throne in vain?
What millions has he pardoned of his foes,
Whom just revenge did to his wrath expose?
Mild, easy, humble, studious of our good,   325
Inclined to mercy, and averse from blood.
If mildness ill with stubborn Israel suit,
His crime is God's belovèd attribute.
What could he gain, his people to betray,
Or change his right for arbitrary sway?   330
Let haughty Pharaoh curse with such a reign
His fruitful Nile, and yoke a servile train.
If David's rule Jerusalem displease,
The Dog Star heats their brains to this disease.
Why then should I, encouraging the bad,   335
Turn rebel and run popularly mad?
Were he a tyrant, who by lawless might
Oppressed the Jews, and raised the Jebusite,
Well might I mourn; but nature's holy bands
Would curb my spirits and restrain my hands;   340
The people might assert their liberty,
But what was right in them were crime in me.
His favor leaves me nothing to require,
Prevents[62] my wishes and outruns desire.
What more can I expect while David lives?   345
All but his kingly diadem he gives;
And that"—but there he paused; then, sighing, said—
"Is justly destined for a worthier head.

---

[56] I.e., you should seize her by the forelock.
[57] Where, before he was king, David sought refuge, among the
Philistines; i.e., the Low Countries, where Charles had lived in
exile, especially Brussels.
[58] I.e., the beach of the English Channel, at Dover.
[59] Lucifer or Satan.   [60] King Louis XIV of France.

[61] Mettle.   [62] Anticipates.

For, when my father from his toils shall rest,
And late augment the number of the blest, 350
His lawful issue shall the throne ascend,
Or the collat'ral line, where that shall end.
His brother,[63] though oppressed with vulgar spite,
Yet dauntless, and secure of native right,
Of every royal virtue stands possessed, 355
Still dear to all the bravest and the best.
His courage foes, his friends his truth, proclaim;
His loyalty the King, the world his fame.
His mercy ev'n the offending crowd will find,
For sure he comes of a forgiving kind. 360
Why should I then repine at heaven's decree,
Which gives me no pretense to royalty?
Yet oh, that Fate, propitiously inclined,
Had raised my birth or had debased my mind;
To my large soul not all her treasure lent, 365
And then betrayed it to a mean descent!
I find, I find my mounting spirits bold,
And David's part disdains my mother's[64] mold.
Why am I scanted by a niggard birth?
My soul disclaims the kindred of her earth; 370
And, made for empire, whispers me within, _shaftesbury_
'Desire of greatness is a godlike sin.' "
charles —Him staggering so when hell's dire agent found,
While fainting Virtue scarce maintained her ground,
He pours fresh forces in and thus replies: 375
  "Th' eternal God, supremely good and wise,
Imparts not these prodigious gifts in vain:
What wonders are reserved to bless your reign!
Against your will, your arguments have shown
Such virtue's only giv'n to guide a throne. 380
Not that your father's mildness I contemn,
But manly force becomes the diadem.
'Tis true he grants the people all they crave,
And more perhaps than subjects ought to have;
For lavish grants suppose a monarch tame, 385
And more his goodness than his wit proclaim.
But when should people strive their bonds to break,
If not when kings are negligent or weak?
Let him give on till he can give no more,
The thrifty Sanhedrin[65] shall keep him poor; 390
And every shekel which he can receive
Shall cost a limb of his prerogative.[66]
To ply him with new plots shall be my care,
Or plunge him deep in some expensive war;

Which, when his treasure can no more supply, 395
He must with the remains of kingship buy.[67]
His faithful friends our jealousies and fears
Call Jebusites and Pharaoh's pensioners;
Whom when our fury from his aid has torn,
He shall be naked left to public scorn. 400
The next[68] successor, whom I fear and hate,
My arts have made obnoxious to the state,
Turned all his virtues to his overthrow,
And gained our elders to pronounce a foe.
His right, for sums of necessary gold, 405
Shall first be pawned and afterwards be sold;
Till time shall ever-wanting David draw
To pass your doubtful title into law.
If not, the people have a right supreme
To make their kings; for kings are made for them.[69] 410
All empire is no more than pow'r in trust,
Which, when resumed, can be no longer just.
Succession, for the general good designed,
In its own wrong a nation cannot bind;
If, altering that, the people can relieve, 415
Better one suffer than a nation grieve.
The Jews well know their pow'r: ere Saul they chose,
God was their king,[70] and God they durst depose.
Urge now your piety, your filial name,
A father's right, and fear of future fame; 420
The public good, that universal call
To which even heav'n submitted, answers all.
Nor let his love enchant your generous mind;
'Tis Nature's trick to propagate her kind.
Our fond begetters, who would never die, 425
Love but themselves in their posterity.
Or let his kindness by th' effects be tried
Or let him lay his vain pretense aside.
God said he loved your father; could he bring
A better proof than to anoint him king? 430
It surely showed he loved the shepherd well,
Who gave so fair a flock as Israel.
Would David have you thought his darling son?
What means he then, to alienate the crown?
The name of godly he may blush to bear: 435
'Tis after God's own heart to cheat his heir.
He to his brother gives supreme command,
To you a legacy of barren land;
Perhaps th' old harp, on which he thrums his lays,
Or some dull Hebrew ballad in your praise. 440

---

[67] I.e., secure a Parliamentary appropriation by making concessions.   [68] Nearest, presumptive; the Duke of York.
[69] These sentiments were, prior to the American Revolution,
  horrifying to most people.
[70] Before Saul became king the Jewish state was a theocracy, under
  the priestly Judges. Similarly, after the overthrow of Charles I,
  England had until the dictatorship of Cromwell been governed
  by a religious group, the Presbyterians.

---

[63] The Duke of York, later James II. Charles II had no legitimate
  children.
[64] Monmouth's mother was Lucy Waters, a girl of good family
  who was one of Charles's mistresses during his exile.
[65] The supreme council of the Jews; i.e., Parliament.
[66] The rights of the Crown.

Then the next heir, a prince severe and wise,
Already looks on you with jealous eyes;
Sees through the thin disguises of your arts,
And marks your progress in the people's hearts.
Though now his mighty soul its grief contains,   445
He meditates revenge who least complains;
And, like a lion, slumb'ring in the way,
Or sleep dissembling, while he waits his prey,
His fearless foes within his distance draws,
Constrains his roaring, and contracts his paws;   450
Till at the last, his time for fury found,
He shoots with sudden vengeance from the ground,
The prostrate vulgar passes o'er and spares,
But with a lordly rage his hunters tears.
Your case no tame expedients will afford: 455
Resolve on death, or conquest by the sword,
Which for no less a stake than life you draw;
And self-defense is nature's eldest law.
Leave the warm people no considering time,
For then rebellion may be thought a crime.   460
Prevail[71] yourself of what occasion gives:
But try your title while your father lives;
And, that your arms may have a fair pretense,
Proclaim you take them in the King's defense,
Whose sacred life each minute would expose   465
To plots from seeming friends and secret foes.
And who can sound the depth of David's soul?
Perhaps his fear his kindness may control.
He fears his brother, though he loves his son,
For plighted vows[72] too late to be undone.   470
If so, by force he wishes to be gained,
Like women's lechery, to seem constrained.
Doubt not; but, when he most affects the frown,
Commit a pleasing rape upon the crown.
Secure his person to secure your cause: 475
They who possess the prince, possess the laws."
    He said, and this advice above the rest,
With Absalom's mild nature suited best;
Unblamed of life (ambition set aside),
Not stained with cruelty, nor puffed with pride.   480

How happy had he been, if destiny
Had higher placed his birth, or not so high!
His kingly virtues might have claimed a throne,
And blessed all other countries but his own;
But charming greatness since so few refuse,   485
'Tis juster to lament him than accuse.
Strong were his hopes a rival to remove,
With blandishments to gain the public love,
To head the faction while their zeal was hot,
And popularly prosecute the plot.   490
To further this, Achitophel unites
The malcontents of all the Israelites;
Whose differing parties he could wisely join,
For several ends, to serve the same design. . . .[73]

Some of their chiefs were princes of the land;
In the first rank of these did Zimri[74] stand:
A man so various that he seemed to be   545
Not one, but all mankind's, epitome.
Stiff in opinions, always in the wrong;
Was everything by starts, and nothing long;
But, in the course of one revolving moon,
Was chymist, fiddler, statesman, and buffoon;   550
Then all for women, painting, riming, drinking,
Besides ten thousand freaks that died in thinking.
Blest madman, who could every hour employ
With something new to wish, or to enjoy!
Railing and praising were his usual themes;   555
And both (to show his judgment) in extremes:
So over violent, or over civil,
That every man, with him, was God or Devil.
In squand'ring wealth was his peculiar art:
Nothing went unrewarded but desert.[75]   560
Beggared by fools, whom still he found too late;
He had his jest, and they had his estate.
He laughed himself from court; then sought relief
By forming parties, but could ne'er be chief:
For, spite of him, the weight of business fell   565
On Absalom and wise Achitophel.
Thus, wicked but in will, of means bereft,
He left not faction, but of [76] that was left. . . .

---

[71] Avail.   [72] Promises to the Duke of York.

[73] In the intervening lines these factions are enumerated, after which Dryden turns to their leaders.
[74] The brilliant and profligate George Villiers, second Duke of Buckingham, once an intimate friend of the King and one of his ministers.   [75] Pronounced *desart*.   [76] By.

MACFLECKNOE

or A SATIRE UPON THE TRUE-BLUE PROTESTANT POET, T. S.

This satire is literary and personal, not political. To be sure, the victim, Thomas Shadwell (1642?-92), was a Whig; after the Glorious Revolution of 1688 he was to replace Dryden as poet laureate. But *MacFlecknoe* (Son of Flecknoe), though published in 1682 (probably without the author's permission), was very likely written three years earlier. Dryden had been on friendly terms with Shadwell; some private quarrel may have occasioned the attack. Satirical thrusts at Dryden and the Heroic drama in Shadwell's *The Virtuoso* (1676), a comedy ridiculing the Royal Society, hardly seem cause enough for treatment like this, nor does a long argument, carried on some years earlier in the prefaces to both men's plays, concerning the nature of comedy. As a matter of fact, Shadwell was a much better writer than Dryden allows, and the poem is a startling example of how the reputation of a good man can be blasted for posterity by the enmity of a great man. It is true that Shadwell was not highly gifted as a poet, and that as a playwright he lacked the grace and wit of an Etherege or a Congreve. But of all the Restoration dramatists, he probably gives the most comprehensive picture of his times; and such plays as *Bury Fair* and *The Squire of Alsatia* are more enjoyable reading than any of Dryden's comedies. If Dryden's motive in pillorying him is far from clear, neither is the choice of Richard Flecknoe (d. 1678?) as Shadwell's predecessor and the great symbol of stupidity. There were worse writers than Flecknoe. Perhaps his recent death suggested the name of this very minor author to Dryden.

A reader's pleasure in a satire like *MacFlecknoe* is much the same as one takes in the more devastating of the "Profiles" that appear in the *New Yorker*. With this great difference: that besides relishing the exposure of human fallibility and admiring the dexterity with which the unhappy subject is dissected, we are conscious of a special delight in recognizing a genius's contribution of those elements of concentration and intellectual force which, along with a virtuoso handling of the rimed couplet, raise a tirade of personal abuse to the plane of art. *MacFlecknoe* is like a savage newspaper cartoon, but a cartoon on which a Daumier has lavished all the skill and power of a master. The result is one of the best of satires. Pope acknowledged it as his inspiration for *The Dunciad,* which for the most part is nothing like so good. Both poems are in the mock-heroic vein; the designed pretentiousness of the opening lines of *MacFlecknoe* strikes the keynote, the investment of trivial things and persons with a solemnity appropriate only to great ones.

All human things are subject to decay,
And, when fate summons, monarchs must obey.
This Flecknoe found, who, like Augustus,[1] young
Was called to empire and had governed long:
In prose and verse was owned, without dispute, 5
Through all the realms of Nonsense, absolute.
This agèd prince, now flourishing in peace,
And blest with issue of a large increase,
Worn out with business, did at length debate
To settle the succession of the state; 10
And, pond'ring which of all his sons was fit
To reign, and wage immortal war with wit,[2]
Cried, " 'Tis resolved; for nature pleads that he
Should only rule who most resembles me:
Sh——[3] alone my perfect image bears, 15
Mature in dullness from his tender years;
Sh—— alone of all my sons is he
Who stands confirmed in full stupidity.
The rest to some faint meaning make pretense,
But Sh—— never deviates into sense. 20
Some beams of wit on other souls may fall,
Strike through, and make a lucid interval;
But Sh——'s genuine night admits no ray,
His rising fogs prevail upon the day:
Besides, his goodly fabric fills the eye,[4] 25
And seems designed for thoughtless majesty:
Thoughtless as monarch oaks that shade the plain
And, spread in solemn state, supinely reign.
Heywood and Shirley[5] were but types of thee,
Thou last great prophet of tautology: 30
Even I, a dunce of more renown than they,
Was sent before but to prepare thy way,
And, coarsely clad in Norwich drugget,[6] came
To teach the nations in thy greater name.
My warbling lute, the lute I whilom[7] strung, 35
When to King John of Portugal I sung,[8]
Was but the prelude to that glorious day
When thou on silver Thames didst cut thy way,
With well-timed oars before the royal barge,

---

[1] The first of the Roman emperors.   [2] Intelligence, sense.
[3] This was a common trick of the neoclassical satirists, not to conceal the victim's name but to add piquancy.
[4] Shadwell was a fat man.
[5] For Heywood, see pp. 511-13, above. By the date of this poem his reputation and that of James Shirley (1596-1666), the last of the major "Elizabethan" dramatists, were at a low ebb.
[6] A coarse woolen fabric. Dryden is comparing Flecknoe to John the Baptist.   [7] Formerly.
[8] Flecknoe had visited the court of John IV.

Swelled with the pride of thy celestial charge; 40
And big with hymn, commander of an host,
The like was ne'er in Epsom[9] blankets tossed.
Methinks I see the new Arion[10] sail,
The lute still trembling underneath thy nail.
At thy well-sharpened thumb from shore to shore 45
The treble squeaks for fear, the basses roar;
Echoes from Pissing Alley[11] Sh—— call,
And Sh—— they resound from Aston Hall.
About thy boat the little fishes throng,
As at the morning toast[12] that floats along. 50
Sometimes, as prince of thy harmonious band,
Thou wield'st thy papers in thy threshing hand.
St. André's[13] feet ne'er kept more equal time,
Not ev'n the feet of thy own *Psyche's*[14] rime;
Though they in number as in sense excel, 55
So just, so like tautology, they fell
That, pale with envy, Singleton[15] forswore
The lute and sword which he in triumph bore,
And vowed he ne'er would act Villerius[16] more."
Here stopped the good old sire, and wept for joy, 60
In silent raptures of the hopeful boy.
All arguments, but most his plays, persuade
That for anointed dullness he was made.

Close to the walls which fair Augusta[17] bind
(The fair Augusta much to fears inclined), 65
An ancient fabric raised t' inform the sight
There stood of yore, and Barbican it hight:[18]
A watchtower once; but now, so fate ordains,
Of all the pile an empty name remains.
From its old ruins brothel houses rise, 70
Scenes of lewd loves and of polluted joys,
Where their vast courts the mother-strumpets keep,
And, undisturbed by watch, in silence sleep.
Near these a Nursery[19] erects its head,
Where queens are formed and future heroes bred, 75

Where unfledged actors learn to laugh and cry,
Where infant punks[20] their tender voices try,
And little Maximins[21] the gods defy.
Great Fletcher[22] never treads in buskins[23] here,
Nor greater Jonson dares in socks appear; 80
But gentle Simkin[24] just reception finds
Amidst this monument of vanished minds:
Pure clinches[25] the suburbian Muse affords,
And Panton[26] waging harmless war with words.
Here Flecknoe, as a place to fame well known, 85
Ambitiously designed his Sh——'s throne.
For ancient Dekker[27] prophesied long since
That in this pile should reign a mighty prince,
Born for a scourge of wit and flail of sense,
To whom true dullness should some *Psyches* owe, 90
But worlds of *Misers*[28] from his pen should flow;
Humorists and hypocrites it should produce,
Whole Raymond families, and tribes of Bruce.[29]

Now Empress Fame had published the renown
Of Sh——'s coronation through the town. 95
Roused by report of Fame, the nations meet,
From near Bunhill, and distant Watling Street.[30]
No Persian carpets spread th' imperial way,
But scattered limbs of mangled poets lay;
From dusty shops neglected authors come, 100
Martyrs of pies and relics of the bum.[31]
Much Heywood, Shirley, Ogleby[32] there lay,
But loads of Sh—— almost choked the way.
Bilked stationers for yeomen stood prepared,[33]
And H——[34] was captain of the guard. 105
The hoary prince in majesty appeared,
High on a throne of his own labors reared.
At his right hand our young Ascanius[35] sate,
Rome's other hope, and pillar of the state.

---

[9] *Epsom Wells* is one of Shadwell's comedies; in *The Virtuoso* there is a blanket-tossing episode.

[10] The Greek musician (c.700 B.C.) who, according to legend, saved himself from drowning by charming some dolphins and getting ashore on their backs. Shadwell plumed himself on his talent for music. In 1674 he had made a very successful operatic version of Dryden's adaptation of *The Tempest*. The allusion here is apparently to Shadwell's direction of some pageant on the Thames.

[11] Off the Strand. Aston Hall has not been identified.

[12] I.e., excrement collected in the morning and dumped into the river. It is compared to a piece of toast floating in a cup of wine or ale.   [13] A popular French dancing-master.

[14] An opera for which Shadwell wrote the libretto.

[15] An eminent opera-singer.

[16] In D'avenant's *The Siege of Rhodes*.

[17] London. For its "fears" (over the Popish Plot) see the headnote to *Absalom and Achitophel*.

[18] Was called. The use of archaic words is part of the mock-heroic style.—The Barbican was near Smithfield, the site of Bartholomew Fair.

[19] A training school and theater for young actors.

[20] Prostitutes. A number of the Restoration actresses were mistresses of Charles II and his courtiers.

[21] The Roman emperor Maximinus, a ranting character in Dryden's *Tyrannic Love*.   [22] John Fletcher. See pp. 510 f., above.

[23] The high shoes worn by the Greek actors in tragedy and therefore its symbol, as the sock (low shoe) was of comedy.

[24] A clown in a contemporary farce, *The Humors of Simpkin*.

[25] Puns.

[26] Perhaps Thomas Panton (d. 1685), a well-known gambler and gallant, said to have been a punster.

[27] Thomas Dekker; see pp. 354 f.,, above.

[28] *The Miser* (from Molière's *L'Avare*) and *The Humorists* are plays by Shadwell.

[29] Characters in, respectively, *The Humorists* and *The Virtuoso*.

[30] A mock-heroic touch, since these localities are not far apart.

[31] I.e., leaves from their unsold books had been used in pastry making and as toilet paper.

[32] John Ogilby (d. 1676), a poetaster.

[33] Publishers defrauded (by the unsalability of the books) were ready as guardsmen or household troops.

[34] Henry Herringman, for years London's leading publisher. Both Dryden and Shadwell were among his authors.

[35] I.e., prince, heir; Shadwell. Ascanius is the son of Aeneas in Vergil's poem.

His brows thick fogs, instead of glories, grace,   110
And lambent dullness played around his face.
As Hannibal did to the altars come,
Sworn by his sire a mortal foe to Rome,
So Sh—— swore, nor should his vow be vain,
That he till death true dullness would maintain,   115
And, in his father's right, and realm's defense,
Ne'er to have peace with wit nor truce with sense.
The King himself the sacred unction made,
As king by office and as priest by trade.
In his siníster hand, instead of ball,[36]   120
He placed a mighty mug of potent ale;
Love's Kingdom[37] to his right he did convey,
At once his scepter and his rule of sway;
Whose righteous lore the prince had practiced young,
And from whose loins recorded[38] *Psyche* sprung.   125
His temples, last, with poppies were o'erspread,
That nodding seemed to consecrate his head.
Just at that point of time, if fame not lie,
On his left hand twelve reverend owls did fly.
So Romulus,[39] 'tis sung, by Tiber's brook,   130
Presage of sway from twice six vultures took.
Th' admiring throng loud acclamations make,
And omens of his future empire take.
The sire then shook the honors of his head,
And from his brows damps of oblivion shed   135
Full on the filial dullness: long he stood,
Repelling from his breast the raging god;[40]
At length burst out in this prophetic mood:
    "Heavens bless my son; from Ireland let him reign
To far Barbadoes on the western main;   140
Of his dominion may no end be known,
And greater than his father's be his throne;
Beyond *Love's Kingdom* let him stretch his pen!"
He paused, and all the people cried, "Amen."
Then thus continued he: "My son, advance   145
Still in new impudence, new ignorance.
Success let others teach; learn thou from me
Pangs without birth, and fruitless industry.
Let *Virtuosos* in five years be writ,
Yet not one thought accuse thy toil of wit.   150
Let gentle George[41] in triumph tread the stage,
Make Dorimant betray and Loveit rage;
Let Cully, Cockwood, Fopling, charm the pit,

And in their folly show the writer's wit.
Yet still thy fools shall stand in thy defense,   155
And justify their author's want of sense.
Let 'em be all by thy own model made
Of dullness, and desire no foreign aid;
That they to future ages may be known,
Not copies drawn, but issue of thy own.   160
Nay, let thy men of wit too be the same,
All full of thee, and differing but in name.
But let no alien S—dl—y[42] interpose,
To lard with wit thy hungry *Epsom* prose.
And when false flowers of rhetoric thou wouldst cull,   165
Trust nature, do not labor to be dull;
But write thy best, and top; and, in each line,
Sir Formal's[43] oratory will be thine.
Sir Formal, though unsought, attends thy quill,
And does thy northern dedications[44] fill.   170
Nor let false friends seduce thy mind to fame
By arrogating Jonson's[45] hostile name.
Let father Flecknoe fire thy mind with praise,
And uncle Ogleby thy envy raise.
Thou art my blood, where Jonson has no part: 175
What share have we in nature or in art?
Where did his wit on learning fix a brand,
And rail at arts he did not understand?
Where made he love in Prince Nicander's[46] vein,
Or swept the dust in *Psyche's* humble strain?   180
Where sold he bargains,[47] 'Whip-stitch,[48] kiss my arse,'
Promised a play and dwindled to a farce?
When did his Muse from Fletcher scenes purloin,
As thou whole Eth'rege dost transfuse to thine?
But so transfused as oils on water flow: 185
His always floats above, thine sinks below.
This is thy province, this thy wondrous way,
New humors to invent for each new play:[49]
This is that boasted bias of thy mind,
By which one way, to dullness, 'tis inclined;   190
Which makes thy writings lean on one side still,
And in all changes that way bends thy will.[50]
Nor let thy mountain belly make pretense

---

[36] Symbol of sovereign power.
[37] A play by Flecknoe.
[38] Remembered. The opera was pretentious, but not so successful as its predecessor, an operatic version by Shadwell of Dryden's adaptation of *The Tempest*.
[39] One of the legendary founders of Rome.
[40] I.e., divine inspiration.
[41] Sir George Etherege (d. 1691), author of *The Man of Mode, or Sir Fopling Flutter* and other witty comedies. The characters mentioned are from his plays.
[42] See p. 532, above. Dryden hints that Sedley, who wrote a prologue for *Epsom Wells*, helped Shadwell with the play.
[43] Sir Formal Trifle, a foolish character in *The Virtuoso*.
[44] Shadwell had dedicated a number of his plays to the Duke of Newcastle and members of his family.
[45] Shadwell rightly considered himself the leading Restoration exponent of Jonsonian comedy.
[46] In Shadwell's *Psyche*.
[47] Made fools of people. I.e., what he did was a "sell."
[48] Quick, presto.
[49] Shadwell had bragged, in his dedication of *The Virtuoso*, of his skill in inventing new humors.
[50] A parody of *The Humorists*:
    "A humor is the bias of the mind
        By which with violence 'tis one way inclined;
    It makes our actions lean on one side still,
    And in all changes that way bends the will."

Of likeness; thine's a tympany[51] of sense.
A tun of man in thy large bulk is writ,   195
But sure thou 'rt but a kilderkin[52] of wit.
Like mine, thy gentle numbers feebly creep;
Thy tragic Muse gives smiles, thy comic sleep.
With whate'er gall thou sett'st thyself to write,
Thy inoffensive satires never bite.   200
In thy felonious heart though venom lies,
It does but touch thy Irish pen, and dies.[53]
Thy genius calls thee not to purchase fame
In keen iambics[54] but mild anagram.
Leave writing plays, and choose for thy command   205
Some peaceful province in acrostic land.
There thou may'st wings display and altars raise,[55]
And torture one poor word ten thousand ways;
Or, if thou wouldst thy diff'rent talents suit,
Set thy own songs, and sing them to thy lute."   210
    He said; but his last words were scarcely heard,
For Bruce and Longvil[56] had a trap prepared,
And down they sent the yet declaiming bard.
Sinking he left his drugget robe behind,
Borne upwards by a subterranean wind.   215
The mantle fell to the young prophet's part,
With double portion of his father's art.[57]

A SONG FOR ST. CECILIA'S DAY

This poem and another called *Alexander's Feast* were
written, in 1687 and 1697, for a London musical society
which annually on her day, November 22, performed an
original ode in honor of the martyred Roman lady who
became the patron saint of music and was traditionally
credited with inventing the organ. Dryden thought
Alexander's Feast not only his best poem but the equal of
any ode ever produced. Today it seems overstrained and
melodramatic; the poet and critic Mark Van Doren aptly
calls it "only immortal ragtime." The less rhetorical and
more truly lyric *A Song for St. Cecilia's Day*, while it too
is a tour de force, is not only a superb tribute to music;
it is itself musical, and musically varied. Both odes offered
unusual opportunities to the composers who set them to
music.

---

[51] Inflation.
[52] Cask or small barrel; a tun is a big one.
[53] There being no snakes in Ireland. Flecknoe was an Irishman;
Shadwell spent a few months there in his early twenties.
[54] The traditional meter of satire.
[55] I.e., show your wit (as even George Herbert had done) by
writing poems which when printed formed such shapes.
[56] Characters in *The Virtuoso*. Two ladies in that play spring a trap-
door under Sir Formal Trifle.
[57] As the young Elisha received the mantle and a double portion
of the spirit of the prophet Elijah (2 Kings 2:9-15).

I

From harmony, from heav'nly harmony,
    This universal frame began;
    When Nature underneath a heap
        Of jarring atoms lay,
    And could not heave her head,   5
The tuneful voice was heard from high,
    "Arise, ye more than dead."
Then cold and hot and moist and dry[1]
    In order to their stations leap,
        And Music's pow'r obey.   10
From harmony, from heav'nly harmony,
    This universal frame began;
        From harmony to harmony
Through all the compass of the notes it ran,
The diapason[2] closing full in man.   15

2

What passion cannot Music raise and quell!
    When Jubal[3] struck the corded shell,
    His list'ning brethren stood around,
        And, wond'ring, on their faces fell
    To worship that celestial sound.   20
Less than a god they thought there could not dwell
        Within the hollow of that shell
        That spoke so sweetly and so well.
What passion cannot Music raise and quell!

3

    The trumpet's loud clangor   25
        Excites us to arms,
    With shrill notes of anger
        And mortal alarms.
    The double double double beat
        Of the thund'ring drum   30
        Cries, "Hark! the foes come;
Charge, charge, 'tis too late to retreat!"

4

    The soft complaining flute
    In dying notes discovers
    The woes of hopeless lovers,   35
Whose dirge is whispered by the warbling lute.

---

[1] I.e., the four so-called elements of which all matter is composed,
since these were their qualities.
[2] When this stop is pulled out, the organ sounds all the variously
toned pitches in octaves with the keys played.
[3] "The father of all such as handle the harp and organ" (Genesis
4:21).

5

Sharp violins proclaim
Their jealous pangs, and desperation,
Fury, frantic indignation,
Depth of pains, and height of passion   40
   For the fair, disdainful dame.

6

But oh! what art can teach,
What human voice can reach
   The sacred organ's praise?
Notes inspiring holy love,   45
Notes that wing their heav'nly ways
   To mend the choirs above.

7

Orpheus[4] could lead the savage race;
And trees unrooted left their place,
   Sequacious of[5] the lyre;   50
But bright Cecilia raised the wonder high'r:
When to her organ vocal breath was giv'n,
An angel heard and straight appeared,
   Mistaking earth for heav'n.

GRAND CHORUS

As from the pow'r of sacred lays
   The spheres began to move,   55
And sung the great Creator's praise
   To all the blessed above,
So, when the last and dreadful hour
This crumbling pageant shall devour,   60
The trumpet shall be heard on high,
The dead shall live, the living die,
And Music shall untune the sky.[6]

TO THE MEMORY OF MR. OLDHAM[7]

Farewell, too little and too lately known,
Whom I began to think and call my own:
For sure our souls were near allied, and thine
Cast in the same poetic mold with mine.
One common note on either lyre did strike,   5
And knaves and fools we both abhorred alike.
To the same goal did both our studies drive;

The last set out the soonest did arrive.
Thus Nisus fell upon the slippery place,
While his young friend performed and won the race.[8]   10
O early ripe! to thy abundant store
What could advancing age have added more?
It might (what nature never gives the young)
Have taught the numbers of thy native tongue.[9]
But satire needs not those, and wit will shine   15
Through the harsh cadence of a rugged line.
A noble error, and but seldom made,
When poets are by too much force betrayed.
Thy gen'rous fruits, though gathered ere their prime,
Still showed a quickness; and maturing time   20
But mellows what we write to the dull sweets of rime.
Once more, hail, and farewell! farewell, thou young,
But ah! too short, Marcellus[10] of our tongue!
Thy brows with ivy and with laurels bound;
But fate and gloomy night encompass thee around.   25

THE SECULAR[11] MASQUE

Enter JANUS[12]

JANUS. Chronos,[13] Chronos, mend thy pace:
   An hundred times the rolling sun
   Around the radiant belt[14] has run
     In his revolving race.
   Behold, behold, the goal in sight;   5
   Spread thy fans, and wing thy flight.

Enter CHRONOS, *with a scythe in his hand and a great
globe on his back, which he sets down at his entrance*

CHRONOS. Weary, weary of my weight,
   Let me, let me drop my freight,
   And leave the world behind.
     I could not bear   10
     Another year
   The load of humankind.

---

[8] The race which Nisus lost to his close friend Euryalus is described by Vergil in the *Aeneid,* Book V.
[9] I.e., it might have taught Oldham greater smoothness in versification.
[10] Marcellus (43–23 B.C.) was the nephew and adopted son of the emperor Augustus, whom it was supposed he would succeed. His death was lamented as a national loss—for example, by Vergil (*Aeneid,* VI, 861 ff.).
[11] Coming once in a long period—here, a century: the masque was written as an addition to Fletcher's comedy *The Pilgrim* for its revival in 1700, and so celebrates the end of one century and the beginning of another.
[12] The god of beginnings and hence of the first month, which derives its name from him.   [13] Father Time.
[14] The zodiac, which the sun traverses once a year.

---

[4] The Greek musician mythically credited with the power of pleasing even beasts and trees.
[5] Following.
[6] At doomsday, announced by the last trumpet, the world and therefore the music of the spheres will end.
[7] John Oldham (1653–83), a vigorous, often savage, political satirist.

Enter MOMUS,[15] *laughing*

MOMUS. Ha! ha! ha! Ha! ha! ha! well hast thou done
  To lay down thy pack,
  And lighten thy back.
 The world was a fool e'er since it begun,   15
 And since neither Janus, nor Chronos, nor I
  Can hinder the crimes
  Or mend the bad times,
 'Tis better to laugh than to cry.   20

CHORUS OF ALL 3. 'Tis better to laugh than to cry.

JANUS. Since Momus comes to laugh below,
 Old Time, begin the show,
 That he may see, in every scene,
 What changes in this age have been.   25

CHRONOS. Then goddess of the silver bow begin.

    Horns or hunting music within

  Enter DIANA

DIANA. With horns and with hounds I waken the day,
 And hie to my woodland walks away;
 I tuck up my robe, and am buskined soon,
 And tie to my forehead a waxing moon.   30
 I course the fleet stag, unkennel the fox,
 And chase the wild goats o'er summits of rocks.
 With shouting and hooting we pierce through the sky,
 And echo turns hunter and doubles the cry.

CHORUS OF ALL. With shouting and hooting we pierce
  through the sky,   35
 And echo turns hunter and doubles the cry.

JANUS. Then our age was in its prime.
CHRONOS. Free from rage.
DIANA.   And free from crime.
MOMUS. A very merry, dancing, drinking,
 Laughing, quaffing, and unthinking time. 40

CHORUS OF ALL. Then our age was in its prime,
 Free from rage, and free from crime,
 A very merry, dancing, drinking,
 Laughing, quaffing, and unthinking time.

    Dance of DIANA'S *attendants*

  Enter MARS

MARS. Inspire the vocal brass, inspire;   45
 The world is past its infant age.
  Arms and honor,
  Arms and honor,

---

[15] The personification of scoffing humor and ridicule.

 Set the martial mind on fire
 And kindle manly rage.   50
  Mars has looked the sky to red,
  And peace, the lazy good, is fled.
 Plenty, peace, and pleasure fly;
  The sprightly green
 In woodland walks no more is seen; 55
 The sprightly green has drunk the Tyrian dye.[16]

CHORUS OF ALL. Plenty, peace, &c.

MARS. Sound the trumpet, beat the drum;
 Through all the world around,
 Sound a reveille, sound, sound;   60
 The warrior god is come.

CHORUS OF ALL. Sound the trumpet, &c.

MOMUS. Thy sword within the scabbard keep,
 And let mankind agree;
 Better the world were fast asleep   65
 Than kept awake by thee.
 The fools are only thinner,
  With all our cost and care;
 But neither side a winner,
  For things are as they were.   70

CHORUS OF ALL. The fools are only, &c.

  Enter VENUS

VENUS. Calms appear when storms are past;
 Love will have his hour at last.
 Nature is my kindly care;
 Mars destroys and I repair.   75
 Take me, take me, while you may;
 Venus comes not ev'ry day.

CHORUS OF ALL. Take her, take her, &c.

CHRONOS. The world was then so light,
 I scarcely felt the weight;   80
 Joy ruled the day, and love the night.
 But since the queen of pleasure left the ground,
  I faint, I lag,
  And feebly drag
 The pond'rous orb around.   85

MOMUS. All, all of a piece throughout:
         (*Pointing to* DIANA)
 Thy chase had a beast in view;
         (*Pointing to* MARS)
 Thy wars brought nothing about;
        (*Pointing to* VENUS)
 Thy lovers were all untrue.

---

[16] Purple or crimson; i.e., the woodland is bloodstained.

Thy wars brought nothing about;
   Thy lovers were all untrue.   95
'Tis well an old age is out,
   And time to begin a new.

Dance of huntsmen, nymphs, warriors, and lovers

from AN ESSAY OF DRAMATIC POESY

"IT WAS," the essay begins,

that memorable day, in the first summer of the late war, when our navy engaged the Dutch; a day wherein the two most mighty and best appointed fleets which any age had ever seen disputed the command of the greater half of the globe, the commerce of nations, and the riches of the universe. While these vast floating bodies, on either side, moved against each other in parallel lines, and our countrymen, under the happy conduct of his Royal Highness, went breaking by little and little into the line of the enemies, the noise of the cannon from both navies reached our ears about the City; so that, all men being alarmed with it, and in a dreadful suspense of the event which we knew was then deciding, everyone went following the sound as his fancy led him, and, leaving the town almost empty, some took towards the Park, some cross the river, others down it, all seeking the noise in the depth of silence.

Among the rest, it was the fortune of Eugenius, Crites, Lisideius, and Neander to be in company together: three of them persons whom their wit and quality have made known to all the town, and whom I have chose to hide under these borrowed names, that they may not suffer by so ill a relation as I am going to make of their discourse.

Neander is Dryden himself; Crites, his brother-in-law, the minor dramatist Sir Robert Howard; Eugenius, the future Earl of Dorset (see p. 530, above); and Lisideius, Sir Charles Sedley (p. 532). Eventually their talk turns to the subject of literature. The essay is in dialogue form, and the opinions of the participants are those they actually held.

Dryden's purpose was "to vindicate the honor of our English writers from the censure of those who unjustly prefer the French before them," and the worth of the moderns as compared with the ancients. He includes a defense of rime in tragedy; the essay appeared in 1668, eight years before he was to confess in his prologue to *Aurengzebe* that he had grown "weary of his long-loved mistress, rime." Of special interest today are his estimates of the great writers of the earlier part of his century. Dryden knew that the Restoration smoothness had been gained at the expense of more important qualities. In his generous epistle "To My Dear Friend Mr. Congreve" (1694) he acknowledges that

Our age was cultivated thus at length,
But what we gained in skill we lost in strength.
Our builders were with want of genius cursed;
The second temple was not like the first.

Dryden's understanding of Shakespeare was always somewhat limited, but his appreciation overrode his neoclassical reservations. The following excerpt comes about two-thirds of the way through the essay, which is a long one.

It has been said of this essay that modern English prose begins here. Dryden's purpose was poles apart from Sir Thomas Browne's (p. 543, above). Browne lays on the rhetoric, trying for beauty by a lavish use of ornament and stately cadences far removed from the rhythms of speech. Even Milton tries to destroy an adversary not as a rule with the cutting edge of direct simplicity but by an avalanche that overwhelms with figures of speech, invective, and the sheer crushing weight of massive verbiage. Dryden writes like a man talking—a very gifted man, talking uncommonly well. It would be a shallow woman who would love a man for easy and graceful manners, and only a shallow reader falls in love with a writer mainly for his style. Yet there is an exquisite and only partly sensuous pleasure to be had from a well-turned sentence when it serves to speed, like an arrow from the bow, a thought worth our hearing. Dryden's mind is in his style. English prose became a crisper, tauter thing for the example he set; and these qualities were achieved by him with no loss of charm. His great merits as a prose stylist are illustrated by the extract which follows; in the Preface to the *Fables*, also represented below, they appear at their best.

Unless your mind has a natural bent like Dryden's, you are not likely to find so much delight in critical as in creative literature. The pleasures of reading criticism are, none the less, considerable. Good critical writing sharpens a reader's wits. There is, moreover, the special pleasure of recognition; it is gratifying to find an acute intelligence liking the same things one does oneself, and to see one's own response put better than one could oneself. When, on the other hand, you disagree with a critic, there is a pleasing stimulus in that. It is a good sign if you get stirred up by a literary opinion you do not share. Some men are irritated to the extent of coming forward with criticism of their own, and it is the hope of your editor that you for one will not rest content with all the observations and judgments set before you in this book.

"BUT to return whence I[1] have digressed. I dare boldly affirm these two things of the English drama: first, that we have many plays of ours as regular as any of theirs,[2] and which, besides, have more variety of plot and characters; and secondly, that in most of the irregular plays of Shakespeare or Fletcher (for Ben Jonson's are for the most part regular), there is a more masculine fancy and greater spirit in the writing than there is in any of the French. I could produce, even in Shakespeare's and Fletcher's works, some plays which are almost exactly formed, as *The Merry Wives of Windsor* and *The Scornful Lady;* but because (generally speaking) Shakespeare, who writ first, did not perfectly observe the laws of comedy, and Fletcher, who came nearer to perfection, yet through carelessness made many faults, I will take the pattern of a perfect play from Ben Jonson, who was a careful and learned observer of the dramatic laws, and from all his comedies I shall select *The Silent Woman;* of which I will make a short examen, according to those rules which the French observe."

As Neander was beginning to examine *The Silent Woman,* Eugenius, earnestly regarding him, "I beseech you, Neander," said he, "gratify the company, and me in particular, so far as, before you speak of the play, to give us a character of the author; and tell us frankly your opinion, whether you do not think all writers, both French and English, ought to give place to him."

"I fear," replied Neander, "that in obeying your commands I shall draw some envy[3] on myself. Besides, in performing them, it will be first necessary to speak somewhat of Shakespeare and Fletcher, his rivals in poesy; and one of them, in my opinion, at least his equal, perhaps his superior.

"To begin, then, with Shakespeare. He was the man who, of all modern and perhaps ancient poets, had the largest and most comprehensive soul. All the images of nature were still[4] present to him, and he drew them, not laboriously, but luckily; when he describes anything, you more than see it, you feel it too. Those who accuse him to have wanted learning give him the greater commendation: he was

naturally learned; he needed not the spectacles of books to read nature; he looked inwards, and found her there. I cannot say he is everywhere alike; were he so, I should do him injury to compare him with the greatest of mankind. He is many times flat, insipid; his comic wit degenerating into clenches,[5] his serious swelling into bombast. But he is always great when some great occasion is presented to him; no man can say he ever had a fit subject for his wit[6] and did not then raise himself as high above the rest of poets,

Quantum lenta solent inter viburna cupressi[7]

The consideration of this made Mr. Hales[8] of Eton say that there was no subject of which any poet ever writ but he would produce it much better done in Shakespeare; and however others are now generally preferred before him,[9] yet the age wherein he lived, which had contemporaries with him Fletcher and Jonson, never equaled them to him in their esteem; and in the last king's[10] court, when Ben's reputation was at highest, Sir John Suckling,[11] and with him the greater part of the courtiers, set our Shakespeare far above him.

"Beaumont and Fletcher,[12] of whom I am next to speak, had, with the advantage of Shakespeare's wit, which was their precedent, great natural gifts, improved by study: Beaumont especially being so accurate a judge of plays that Ben Jonson, while he lived, submitted all his writings to his censure, and, 'tis thought, used his judgment in correcting, if not contriving, all his plots. What value he had for him,[13] appears by the verses he writ to him; and therefore I need speak no farther of it. The first play that brought Fletcher and him in esteem was their *Philaster;* for before that, they had written two or three very unsuccessfully, as the like is reported of Ben Jonson, before he writ *Every Man in His Humor.* Their plots were generally more regular than Shakespeare's, especially those which were made before Beaumont's death; and they understood and imitated the conversation of gentlemen much better, whose wild debaucheries and quickness of wit in

---

1 Neander is speaking.
2 Conforming as strictly to the Rules as any of the French.
3 Spite.   4 Constantly.

5 Puns.   6 Intellectual powers.
7 As cypresses are accustomed (to rise) over yielding shrubs (Vergil, *Eclogues,* I, 25).
8 John Hales (1584–1656), a fellow of Eton.
9 Shakespeare's reputation touched its lowest point in the 1660's.
10 Charles I.   11 See p. 519, above.
12 See pp. 509–11, above.
13 What esteem Jonson had for Beaumont. The verses referred to are probably those beginning, "How I do love thee, Beaumont, and thy Muse."

repartees no poet before them could paint as they have done. Humor, which Ben Jonson derived from particular persons, they made it not their business to describe; they represented all the passions very lively, but above all, love. I am apt to believe the English language in them arrived to its highest perfection; what words have since been taken in are rather superfluous than ornamental. Their plays are now the most pleasant and frequent entertainments of the stage, two of theirs being acted through the year for one of Shakespeare's or Jonson's. The reason is because there is a certain gaiety in their comedies and pathos in their more serious plays which suits generally with all men's humors. Shakespeare's language is likewise a little obsolete, and Ben Jonson's wit comes short of theirs.

"As for Jonson, to whose character I am now arrived, if we look upon him while he was himself (for his last plays were but his dotages), I think him the most learned and judicious writer which any theater ever had. He was a most severe judge of himself, as well as others. One cannot say he wanted wit, but rather that he was frugal of it. In his works you find little to retrench or alter. Wit and language and humor also in some measure we had before him, but something of art was wanting to the drama till he came. He managed his strength to more advantage than any who preceded him. You seldom find him making love in any of his scenes, or endeavoring to move the passions; his genius was too sullen and saturnine to do it gracefully, especially when he knew he came after those who had performed both

to such a height. Humor was his proper sphere; and in that he delighted most to represent mechanic people.[14] He was deeply conversant in the ancients, both Greek and Latin, and he borrowed boldly from them; there is scarce a poet or historian among the Roman authors of those times whom he has not translated in *Sejanus* and *Catiline*. But he has done his robberies so openly that one may see he fears not to be taxed by any law. He invades authors like a monarch; and what would be theft in other poets is only victory in him. With the spoils of these writers he so represents old Rome to us, in its rites, ceremonies, and customs, that if one of their poets had written either of his tragedies, we had seen less of it than in him. If there was any fault in his language, 'twas that he weaved it too closely and laboriously, in his comedies especially. Perhaps, too, he did a little too much Romanize our tongue, leaving the words which he translated almost as much Latin as he found them; wherein, though he learnedly followed their language, he did not enough comply with the idiom of ours. If I would compare him with Shakespeare, I must acknowledge him the more correct poet, but Shakespeare the greater wit. Shakespeare was the Homer, or father, of our dramatic poets; Jonson was the Vergil, the pattern of elaborate writing. I admire him, but I love Shakespeare. To conclude of him: as he has given us the most correct plays, so, in the precepts which he has laid down in his *Discoveries,* we have as many and profitable rules for perfecting the stage, as any wherewith the French can furnish us. . . ."

from the PREFACE TO THE *FABLES*

This essay is probably Dryden's finest piece of prose. It was published in March, 1700, with *Fables, Ancient and Modern, Translated into Verse from Homer, Ovid, Boccace, and Chaucer, with Original Poems.* Dryden died on May 1.

It is with a poet as with a man who designs to build and is very exact, as he supposes, in casting up the cost beforehand; but, generally speaking, he is mistaken in his account, and reckons short of the expense he first intended. He alters his mind as the work proceeds, and will have this or that convenience more, of which he had not thought when he began. So has it happened to me: I have built a house, where I intended but a lodge; yet with better

success than a certain nobleman[1] who, beginning with a dog kennel, never lived to finish the palace he had contrived.

From translating the first of Homer's *Iliads* (which I intended as an essay[2] to the whole work), I proceeded to the translation of the twelfth book of Ovid's *Metamorphoses,* because it contains, among other things, the causes, the beginning, and ending,

---

[14] Tradesfolk.

[1] The Duke of Buckingham, author of *The Rehearsal,* in which Dryden was ridiculed, and the subject of the portrait of Zimri in *Absalom and Achitophel.* The palace was Cliveden, recently the home of Viscountess Astor.   [2] First attempt.

of the Trojan war. Here I ought in reason to have stopped; but the speeches of Ajax and Ulysses lying next in my way, I could not balk 'em.[3] When I had compassed them, I was so taken with the former part of the fifteenth book (which is the masterpiece of the whole *Metamorphoses*), that I enjoined myself the pleasing task of rendering it into English. And now I found, by the number of my verses, that they began to swell into a little volume; which gave me an occasion of looking backward on some beauties of my author in his former books. . . .

This is what I thought needful in this place to say of Homer. I proceed to Ovid and Chaucer, considering the former only in relation to the latter. With Ovid ended the golden age of the Roman tongue; from Chaucer the purity of the English tongue began. The manners of the poets were not unlike. Both of them were well-bred, well-natured, amorous, and libertine, at least in their writings; it may be, also in their lives. . . .

Both of them built on the inventions of other men; yet since Chaucer had something of his own, as "The Wife of Bath's Tale," "The Cock and the Fox,"[4] which I have translated, and some others, I may justly give our countryman the precedence in that part, since I can remember nothing of Ovid which was wholly his. Both of them understood the manners; under which name I comprehend the passions, and, in a larger sense, the descriptions of persons, and their very habits.[5] For an example, I see Baucis and Philemon[6] as perfectly before me as if some ancient painter had drawn them; and all the pilgrims in *The Canterbury Tales,* their humors, their features, and the very dress, as distinctly as if I had supped with them at the Tabard in Southwark. Yet even there, too, the figures of Chaucer are much more lively,[7] and set in a better light; which though I have not time to prove, yet I appeal to the reader, and am sure he will clear me from partiality. The thoughts and words remain to be considered, in the comparison of the two poets, and I have saved myself one-half of the labor, by owning that Ovid lived when the Roman tongue was in its meridian;[8] Chaucer, in the dawning of our language: therefore that part of the comparison stands not on an equal foot, any more than the diction of Ennius[9] and Ovid,

or of Chaucer and our present English. The words are given up, as a post not to be defended in our poet, because he wanted the modern art of fortifying. The thoughts remain to be considered; and they are to be measured only by their propriety, that is, as they flow more or less naturally from the persons described, on such and such occasions. The vulgar judges, which are nine parts in ten of all nations, who call conceits and jingles wit, who see Ovid full of them, and Chaucer altogether without them, will think me little less than mad for preferring the Englishman to the Roman. Yet, with their leave, I must presume to say that the things they admire are only glittering trifles, and so far from being witty that in a serious poem they are nauseous, because they are unnatural. Would any man, who is ready to die for love, describe his passion like Narcissus? Would he think of *inopem me copia fecit,*[10] and a dozen more of such expressions, poured on the neck of one another, and signifying all the same thing? If this were wit, was this a time to be witty, when the poor wretch was in the agony of death? This is just John Littlewit, in *Bartholomew Fair,* who had a conceit (as he tells you) left him in his misery; a miserable conceit. On these occasions the poet should endeavor to raise pity; but, instead of this, Ovid is tickling you to laugh. Vergil never made use of such machines when he was moving you to commiserate the death of Dido;[11] he would not destroy what he was building. Chaucer makes Arcite[12] violent in his love and unjust in the pursuit of it; yet, when he came to die, he made him think more reasonably: he repents not of his love, for that had[13] altered his character, but acknowledges the injustice of his proceedings and resigns Emilia to Palamon. What would Ovid have done on this occasion? He would certainly have made Arcite witty on his deathbed; he had complained he was further off from possession, by being so near, and a thousand such boyisms, which Chaucer rejected as below the dignity of the subject. They who think otherwise, would, by the same reason, prefer Lucan[14] and Ovid to Homer and Vergil, and Martial[15] to all four of them. As for the turn of words,[16] in which Ovid particularly excels all poets, they are sometimes a fault and sometimes a beauty, as they are used properly or improperly, but in strong passions always to be shunned, because passions are serious and will admit no playing. The

---

[3] Pass them by.
[4] "The Nun's Priest's Tale"; see pp. 155 ff., above.
[5] And even their clothes.
[6] *Metamorphoses,* VIII, 611–724.   [7] Lifelike.
[8] Midday.
[9] Quintus Ennius (d. 170 B.C.), an early Roman tragic dramatist and poet.

[10] Plenty has made me poor. Thus speaks Narcissus, *Metamorphoses,* III, 466.   [11] *Aeneid,* Book IV.
[12] In "The Knight's Tale."   [13] Would have.
[14] Roman epic poet (d. 65).   [15] Roman satirist (d. 102?).
[16] I.e., unexpected turns of thought and expression.

French have a high value for them; and, I confess, they are often what they call delicate, when they are introduced with judgment; but Chaucer writ with more simplicity, and followed nature more closely than to use them. I have thus far, to the best of my knowledge, been an upright judge betwixt the parties in competition, not meddling with the design nor the disposition of it; because the design was not their own, and in the disposing of it they were equal. It remains that I say somewhat of Chaucer in particular.

In the first place, as he is the father of English poetry, so I hold him in the same degree of veneration as the Grecians held Homer, or the Romans Vergil. He is a perpetual fountain of good sense; learned in all sciences; and, therefore, speaks properly on all subjects. As he knew what to say, so he knows also when to leave off, a continence which is practiced by few writers, and scarcely by any of the ancients, excepting Vergil and Horace. One of our late great poets[17] is sunk in his reputation because he could never forgive any conceit which came in his way, but swept like a dragnet, great and small. There was plenty enough, but the dishes were ill sorted; whole pyramids of sweetmeats for boys and women, but little of solid meat for men. All this proceeded not from any want of knowledge, but of judgment. Neither did he want that in discerning the beauties and faults of other poets, but only indulged himself in the luxury of writing; and perhaps knew it was a fault, but hoped the reader would not find it. For this reason, though he must always be thought a great poet, he is no longer esteemed a good writer; and for ten impressions which his works have had in so many successive years, yet at present a hundred books are scarcely purchased once a twelvemonth; for, as my last Lord Rochester[18] said, though somewhat profanely, "Not being of God, he could not stand."

Chaucer followed nature everywhere, but was never so bold to go beyond her; and there is a great difference of being *poeta* and *nimis poeta*,[19] if we may believe Catullus, as much as betwixt a modest behavior and affectation. The verse of Chaucer, I confess, is not harmonious to us; but 'tis like the eloquence of one whom Tacitus commends, it was *auribus istius temporis accommodata*.[20] They who lived with him, and some time after him, thought it musical; and it continues so, even in our judgment, if compared with the numbers of Lydgate[21] and Gower,[22] his contemporaries: there is the rude sweetness of a Scotch tune in it, which is natural and pleasing, though not perfect. It is true, I cannot go so far as he who published the last edition of him,[23] for he would make us believe the fault is in our ears, and that there were really ten syllables in a verse where we find but nine; but this opinion is not worth confuting; 'tis so gross and obvious an error that common sense (which is a rule in everything but matters of faith and revelation) must convince the reader that equality of numbers, in every verse which we call Heroic, was either not known, or not always practiced, in Chaucer's age. It were an easy matter to produce some thousands of his verses which are lame for want of half a foot, and sometimes a whole one, and which no pronunciation can make otherwise. We can only say that he lived in the infancy of our poetry, and that nothing is brought to perfection at the first. We must be children before we grow men. . . . As for the religion of our poet, he seems to have some little bias towards the opinions of Wyclif,[24] after John of Gaunt his patron; somewhat of which appears in the tale of "Piers Plowman."[25] Yet I cannot blame him for inveighing so sharply against the vices of the clergy in his age; their pride, their ambition, their pomp, their avarice, their worldly interest, deserved the lashes which he gave them, both in that, and in most of his *Canterbury Tales*. Neither has his contemporary Boccace[26] spared them; yet both those poets lived in much esteem with good and holy men in orders, for the scandal which is given by particular priests reflects not on the sacred function. Chaucer's Monk, his Canon, and his Friar, took not from the character of his Good Parson. A satirical poet is the check of the laymen on bad priests. We are only to take care that we involve not the innocent with the guilty in the same condemnation. The good cannot be too much honored, nor the bad too coarsely used; for the corruption of the best becomes the worst. . . .

---

[17] Cowley; see p. 524, above.   [18] See pp. 532 ff., above.

[19] A poet and too much of a poet. The source is actually Martial, III, 44.

[20] Suited to the ears of that time. Cf. Tacitus (the Roman historian —d. 120? A.D.), Dialogue XXI. By Dryden's time, as we have seen, the pronunciation of Chaucer's English had been lost.

[21] John Lydgate (d. 1450?), English poet and follower of Chaucer.
[22] The poet John Gower (d. 1408), contemporary and friend of Chaucer.
[23] Thomas Speght's edition appeared in 1598 and 1602; it was reprinted in 1687. Speght has, of course, been proved right by modern scholarship.
[24] The fourteenth-century reformer; see pp. 60, 67, above.
[25] A reference not to the famous *Piers Plowman* but to "The Plowman's Tale," not by Chaucer, but formerly ascribed to him and included in all the editions till 1775.
[26] Boccaccio, the Italian storyteller (d. 1375).

He must have been a man of a most wonderful comprehensive nature, because, as it has been truly observed of him, he has taken into the compass of his *Canterbury Tales* the various manners and humors (as we now call them) of the whole English nation, in his age. Not a single character has escaped him. All his pilgrims are severally distinguished from each other; and not only in their inclinations, but in their very physiognomies and persons. Baptista Porta[27] could not have described their natures better than by the marks which the poet gives them. The matter and manner of their tales, and of their telling, are so suited to their different educations, humors, and callings that each of them would be improper in any other mouth. Even the grave and serious characters are distinguished by their several sorts of gravity: their discourses are such as belong to their age, their calling, and their breeding; such as are becoming of them, and of them only. Some of his persons are vicious, and some virtuous; some are unlearned, or (as Chaucer calls them) lewd, and some are learned. Even the ribaldry of the low characters is different: the Reeve, the Miller, and the Cook are several men, and distinguished from each other as much as the mincing Lady-Prioress and the broad-speaking, gap-toothed Wife of Bath. But enough of this; there is such a variety of game springing up before me that I am distracted in my choice, and know not which to follow. 'Tis sufficient to say, according to the proverb, that "Here is God's plenty." We have our forefathers and great-grand-dames all before us, as they were in Chaucer's days; their general characters are still remaining in mankind, and even in England, though they are called by other names than those of Monks and Friars and Canons, and Lady Abbesses and Nuns, for mankind is ever the same, and nothing lost out of Nature, though everything is altered. . . .

27 Giambattista della Porta (d. 1615), a Neapolitan physician and writer on physiognomy.

William Congreve

1670–1729

CONGREVE was born in Yorkshire but brought up in Ireland, where his father, an army officer, was stationed. Lieutenant Congreve was a younger son of a landed English family that had fought for Charles I. Kilkenny was a little capital; its school was known as Ireland's Eton. There and at Trinity College, Dublin, young Congreve was educated. Swift, a lifelong friend, was a fellow student at both places. There were plenty of opportunities for the future dramatist to see plays, since Dublin had the best theater outside London; the English stars often acted there. When the political troubles of 1688–89 forced the closing of Trinity, Congreve had already left for London; in 1691 he was half-heartedly studying law at the Middle Temple, but he was more attracted by the theater and the literary talk at Will's coffee house. Dryden became his firm friend and encourager. Congreve was soon writing verse, bringing out a novel, and composing his first play, *The Old Bachelor*, which Dryden helped him prepare for the stage. At the Theater Royal, Drury Lane, early in 1693, it had a run of fourteen days, an extraordinary success for those times. The repertory system was still in vogue, as in Shakespeare's day; but a successful play was allowed to continue, if patronage warranted, for a few days after the opening performance.

To a leading actress, the beautiful Anne Bracegirdle, seven years older than Congreve, he lost his heart. She was the toast of the town; it was said that when she acted, half the audience was in love with her. Her reputation was then as spotless as her beauty—a rare thing for an actress in those days. Congreve pursued her, presumably (but not certainly) without success:

> Pious Selinda goes to prayers
> If I but ask the favor;
> And yet the tender fool's in tears
> When she believes I'll leave her.
>
> Would I were free from this restraint,
> Or else had hopes to win her;
> Would she could make of me a saint,
> Or I of her a sinner.

Apparently he never offered marriage, but a long friendship ensued; and the dramatist's passion bore fruit in the brilliant roles he wrote for the charming Bracey, especially Millamant in *The Way of the World*, the best coquette in English drama. Congreve's next piece, however, *The Double Dealer*, acted late in 1693, was not liked. Dryden said the women resented it because it "exposed their bitchery too much."

Next to *The Way of the World*, Congreve's finest play—as an acting drama it is his best—is another comedy, *Love for Love;* it was a great hit in 1695, with a famous low-comedian, Thomas Doggett, in the character part of Ben the Sailor. *Love for Love* opened a new theater in Lincoln's Inn Fields, to which the principal actors had seceded from a tyrannical regime at Drury Lane. Among them were Thomas Betterton, a really great actor, perhaps the greatest the English stage has had, and the two leading actresses, Elizabeth Barry and Anne Bracegirdle. Congreve agreed to write a play for them once a year. Another friend of theirs was the elderly Earl of Dorset (p. 530, above), poet and patron of poets. To him Congreve dedicated *Love for Love.* Both men were Whigs, and Dorset was King William's lord chamberlain. It was the policy of both parties to enlist the services of able writers by granting them sinecures. Congreve, for instance, was a commissioner for the licensing of hackney coaches; but not till much later did a really good plum fall his way. In 1697 was acted his sole tragedy, *The Mourning Bride;* though it is very inferior to his comedies, it proved the most popular of all his plays. Everyone has heard its opening line, "Music has charms to soothe a savage breast."

The next year Congreve found himself one of Jeremy Collier's main targets in *A Short View of the Immorality and Profaneness of the English Stage.* Most unwisely he chose to defend himself; his reply merely gave another opening to the ferocious parson, who was able to cite chapter and verse (that is, act and scene) for all his charges. Collier's attack was intemperate, but he had all the best of the debate. It was, in fact, time for a new deal in comedy. *The Way of the World,* Congreve's last and greatest play, came just too late. It was acted in the final year of the seventeenth century, and public taste was wavering on the threshold of the eighteenth. Comedy of manners now seemed brittle and heartless, its witty heroines and hero-rakes corrupt. Already the best of the new men were putting sentiment into their plays, and a dash of morality. Young Colley Cibber had pointed the way with the fifth-act repentance of *Love's Last Shift* (1696), and George Farquhar was soon to follow with a similar denouement in *The Beaux' Stratagem* (1707). By 1722 the sentimental comedy would be in full swing with Steele's earnest comedy, *The Conscious Lovers. The Way of the World* is a great comedy almost exclusively because its style is almost inhumanly brilliant. Congreve had polished and repolished it. When the public failed to appreciate it, he left the theater, never to return.

If London audiences were done with high comedy, so much the worse for them. He had set the highwater mark of pure comedy in English; he would let the record stand. It was London's loss, and ours; perhaps it was also Congreve's.

From then on he was only the man about town. He had aimed at a social success, had brilliantly achieved it, and was proud of it. At the exclusive assembly of Whig politicians and wits, the Kit-Cat Club, he shone; and when George I was crowned in 1714 and the Tory ministry fell, Congreve was well rewarded by the secretaryship of Jamaica, with permission to perform its duties by deputy. His finances were now secure; he had Swift, Pope, Gay, and Steele for friends; and, except for a temporary blindness from cataracts and the common penalty of gout, he led a pleasant, unproductive existence. When Voltaire called on him in 1726, he pooh-poohed his real accomplishment, asking to be taken "upon no other foot than that of a gentleman" leading a plain and quiet life. Voltaire, bubbling with enthusiasm for Congreve's writings because they were like a Frenchman's, was disgusted.

The central interest of Congreve's later years was his love for Henrietta, Duchess of Marlborough, which she returned with equal devotion. She was the daughter of the great Duke, whose title had passed to her by a special act of Parliament. Eleven years younger than her lover, she was the wife of the Earl of Godolphin, by whom she had two surviving children. They were no longer children when, in 1723, a daughter was born to her and Congreve. This explains the terms of his will, much criticized by literary historians. Dying in 1729, he left practically all his money to the wealthy Duchess and remembered Anne Bracegirdle to the extent of only £200. The actress had retired, however, in comfortable circumstances; and the will of her lover, the Earl of Scarsdale, had made a substantial addition to her capital. Congreve's bequest to the Duchess was unquestionably in behalf of their daughter, to whom she afterwards willed it.

There is no satisfactory edition of Congreve's works. The comedies have been edited by B. Dobrée for The World's Classics and by J. W. Krutch for The Modern Readers' Series. The *Works* (actually a selection) appear in a single volume by F. W. Bateson (1930), and the five plays in a Mermaid volume. The best Life is J. C. Hodges's *William Congreve, the Man* (1941).

William Congreve

THE WAY OF THE WORLD

ON MARCH 12, 1700, a lady of fashion wrote in a letter from London: "*The Way of the World,* Congreve's new play, doth not answer expectation, there being no plot in it, but many witty things to ridicule the chocolate house and the fantastical part of the world." The commercial stage has accepted that verdict, but not readers. This is perhaps the best example of pure comedy in our language, the closest any English-speaking writer has come to Molière. The complaint about the absence of plot touches the play's weakness. Plot, as a reader quickly discovers, is usually a minor consideration in the comedy of manners. Character, ideas, the social code—these are its preoccupations; and they are likely to be handled skeptically, not sympathetically. From Jonson, however, Congreve differs profoundly; Congreve's comedy is not really corrective. He admires Mirabell and Millamant; he does not wish to change their manners, nor to convert his audience from the fashionable ideal they stand for. We shall admire them, too, but as figures no less remote from reality than Orlando and Rosalind in *As You Like It*—indeed, more remote. For although the adventures in the Forest of Arden are unrealistic, the concerns of those lovers are humanity's concerns. Mirabell and Millamant are not drawn wholly without truth, but it is a very limited truth. Their brilliance is matchless; there is not much behind it. They are citizens, as Charles Lamb said, of Cloud-Cuckoo Land, not London. Rosalind and Orlando are solid humanity; beside them Millamant and Mirabell seem a little thin. They live only in their speech, and *The Way of the World* is mostly speech. On that side there is nothing to give it but praise; even Sheridan is not quite so witty, though he is more humane. Not till Bernard Shaw left Ireland was England to own a comic dramatist who could combine a Congreve's stylistic brilliance with the social values of corrective comedy.

The following text is based on the earliest quarto (1700), for this play the most authoritative edition despite the claim of the *Works* of 1710 to be "the least faulty impression." A few stage directions have been added. It should be remembered that by this time the London stages had front curtains, backdrops or flats, and side-wings. There was, however, little furniture on the stage.

PERSONAE DRAMATIS

FAINALL, *in love with* MRS.[1] MARWOOD   MR. BETTERTON[2]

EDWARD MIRABELL, *in love with* MRS. MILLAMANT   MR. VERBRUGGEN[3]

ANTHONY WITWOUD ⎱
PETULANT ⎰ *followers of* MRS. MILLAMANT   MR. BOWEN / MR. BOWMAN

SIR WILFULL WITWOUD, *half brother to* WITWOUD, *and nephew to* LADY WISHFORT   MR. UNDERHILL[4]

WAITWELL, *servant to* MIRABELL   MR. BRIGHT

LADY WISHFORT, *enemy to* MIRABELL, *for having falsely pretended love to her*   MRS. LEIGH

MRS. MILLAMANT, *a fine lady, niece to* LADY WISHFORT, *and loves* MIRABELL   MRS. BRACEGIRDLE[5]

MRS. MARWOOD, *friend to*[6] MR. FAINALL, *and likes* MIRABELL   MRS. BARRY[7]

MRS. FAINALL, *daughter to* LADY WISHFORT, *and wife to* FAINALL, *formerly friend to* MIRABELL   MRS. BOWMAN

FOIBLE, *woman to* LADY WISHFORT   MRS. WILLIS

MINCING, *woman to* MRS. MILLAMANT   MRS. PRINCE

BETTY, *waiting woman at a chocolate house*

PEG, *maid to* LADY WISHFORT

Dancers, footmen, and attendants

---

[1] *Mrs.* (Mistress) was the usual title for unmarried women; *Miss* was reserved for very young girls and kept mistresses.—Fainall= he who wants everything.

[2] Thomas Betterton (c. 1635–1710), the leading actor of the age and possibly the greatest tragedian the English theater has known.

[3] John Verbruggen became a leading actor in the 1690's.

[4] Cave Underhill; he had been a leading low-comedian for forty years, being endowed, says a contemporary, with a "face very like the *homo sylvestris* or champanza."

[5] See introduction to Congreve.—*Millamant*=she who has a thousand lovers.   [6] I.e., mistress of.

[7] A great actress, the Restoration's best in tragedy.

PROLOGUE

Spoken by MR. BETTERTON

Of those few fools who with ill stars are curst,
Sure scribbling fools, called poets, fare the worst;
For they're a sort of fools which Fortune makes,
And, after she has made 'em fools, forsakes.
With Nature's oafs 'tis quite a diff'rent case,   5
For Fortune favors all her idiot race;
In her own nest the cuckoo eggs we find,
O'er which she broods to hatch the changeling kind.[9]
No portion for her own she has to spare,
So much she dotes on her adopted care.   10
    Poets are bubbles,[10] by the town drawn in,
Suffered at first some trifling stakes to win;
But what unequal hazards do they run!
Each time they write they venture all they've won: ⎫
The squire[11] that's buttered still[12] is sure to be undone. ⎭
This author, heretofore, has found your favor,   16
But pleads no merit from his past behavior.
To build on that might prove a vain presumption,
Should grants to poets made admit resumption;

And in Parnassus[13] he must lose his seat,   20
If that be found a forfeited estate.
    He owns, with toil he wrought the following scenes,
But, if they're naught, ne'er spare him for his pains.
Damn him the more; have no commiseration
For dullness on mature deliberation.   25
He swears he'll not resent one hissed-off scene, ⎫
Nor, like those peevish wits, his play maintain, ⎬
Who, to assert their sense, your taste arraign. ⎭
Some plot we think he has, and some new thought,
Some humor too, no farce; but that's a fault.[14]   30
Satire, he thinks, you ought not to expect,
For so reformed a town who dares correct?[15]
To please, this time, has been his sole pretense;
He'll not instruct, lest it should give offense.
Should he by chance a knave or fool expose,   35
That hurts none here; sure here are none of those.
In short, our play shall (with your leave to show it)
Give you one instance of a passive poet,
Who to your judgments yields all resignation;
So save or damn, after your own discretion.   40

ACT I

A chocolate house. MIRABELL *and* FAINALL,[16] *rising from cards.* BETTY *waiting.*

MIRA. You are a fortunate man, Mr. Fainall.
FAIN. Have we done?   5
MIRA. What you please. I'll play on to entertain you.
FAIN. No, I'll give you your revenge another time, when you are not so indifferent; you are thinking of something else now, and play too negligently; the   10
coldness of a losing gamester lessens the pleasure of

the winner. I'd no more play with a man that slighted his ill fortune than I'd make love to a woman who undervalued the loss of her reputation.
MIRA. You have a taste extremely delicate, and are for refining on your pleasures.
FAIN. Prithee, why so reserved? Something has put you out of humor.
MIRA. Not at all. I happen to be grave today, and you are gay; that's all.
FAIN. Confess, Millamant and you quarreled last night, after I left you; my fair cousin has some humors[17] that would tempt the patience of a Stoic. What! some coxcomb[18] came in, and was well received by her, while you were by.
MIRA. Witwoud and Petulant; and what was   15
worse, her aunt, your wife's mother, my evil genius, or to sum up all in her own name, my old Lady Wishfort came in—

---

[8] I.e., time, the present.

[9] I.e., not her own. A changeling was properly an ugly child left by the fairies in place of one stolen by them.

[10] Dupes.   [11] Fellow.

[12] Continually flattered, i.e., into risking his reputation by further writing, like a "buttered" gambler who pyramids his bets, till, having staked all his winnings on the last throw, he loses and is ruined ("undone").

[16] They are discovered by raising the front curtain. Acting in the Restoration theater was still chiefly downstage, close to the audience; there was little furniture on stage, but painted scenery and actresses had been introduced soon after the theaters reopened in 1660.

[13] A mountain in central Greece sacred to Apollo and the Muses. I.e., in the poets' hall of fame. *Seat* rimes with *estate.*

[14] The *l* was not pronounced.

[15] An allusion to the activities of the professional reformers.

[17] Whims, moods.   [18] Foolish gallant.

FAIN. Oh, there it is then! she has a lasting passion for you, and with reason.—What, then my wife was there?

MIRA. Yes, and Mrs. Marwood and three or four more whom I never saw before; seeing me, they all put on their grave faces, whispered one another, then complained aloud of the vapors,[19] and after fell into a profound silence.

FAIN. They had a mind to be rid of you.

MIRA. For which reason I resolved not to stir. At last the good old lady broke through her painful taciturnity, with an invective against long visits. I would not have understood[20] her; but Millamant joining in the argument, I rose and with a constrained smile told her I thought nothing was so easy as to know when a visit began to be troublesome; she reddened and I withdrew, without expecting[21] her reply.

FAIN. You were to blame to resent what she spoke only in compliance with her aunt.

MIRA. She is more mistress of herself than to be under the necessity of such a resignation.

FAIN. What? though half her fortune depends upon her marrying with my Lady's approbation?

MIRA. I was then in such a humor that I should have been better pleased if she had been less discreet.

FAIN. Now I remember, I wonder not they were weary of you; last night was one of their cabal nights; they have 'em three times a week, and meet by turns at one another's apartments, where they come together like the coroner's inquest, to sit upon the murdered reputations of the week. You and I are excluded; and it was once proposed that all the male sex should be excepted; but somebody moved that to avoid scandal there might be one man of the community; upon which motion Witwoud and Petulant were enrolled members.

MIRA. And who may have been the foundress of this sect? My Lady Wishfort, I warrant, who publishes her detestation of mankind and, full of the vigor of fifty-five, declares for a friend and ratafia,[22] and let posterity shift for itself: she'll breed no more.

FAIN. The discovery of your sham addresses to her, to conceal your love to her niece, has provoked this separation; had you dissembled better, things might have continued in the state of nature.

MIRA. I did as much as man could with any reasonable conscience; I proceeded to the very last act of flattery with her, and was guilty of a song in her commendation. Nay, I got a friend to put her into a lampoon and compliment her with the imputation of an affair with a young fellow, which I carried so far that I told her the malicious town took notice that she was grown fat of a sudden; and when she lay in of a dropsy, persuaded her she was reported to be in labor. The Devil's in't if an old woman is to be flattered further, unless a man should endeavor downright personally to debauch her; and that my virtue forbade me. But, for the discovery of that amour, I am indebted to your friend, or your wife's friend, Mrs. Marwood.

FAIN. What should provoke her to be your enemy, without she has made you advances which you have slighted? Women do not easily forgive omissions of that nature.

MIRA. She was always civil to me till of late; I confess I am not one of those coxcombs who are apt to interpret a woman's good manners to her prejudice, and think that she who does not refuse 'em everything can refuse 'em nothing.

FAIN. You are a gallant man, Mirabell; and though you may have cruelty enough not to satisfy a lady's longing, you have too much generosity not to be tender of her honor. Yet you speak with an indifference which seems to be affected, and confesses you are conscious of a negligence.

MIRA. You pursue the argument with a distrust that seems to be unaffected, and confesses you are conscious of a concern for which the lady is more indebted to you than your wife.

FAIN. Fie, fie, friend; if you grow censorious I must leave you. I'll look upon the gamesters in the next room.

MIRA. Who are they?

FAIN. Petulant and Witwoud.—(*To* BETTY) Bring me some chocolate.   [*Exit*

MIRA. Betty, what says your clock?

BET. Turned of the last canonical hour,[23] sir.

                                                          [*Exit*

MIRA. How pertinently[24] the jade answers me! Ha! almost one o'clock! (*Looking on his watch*) Oh, y'are come—

Enter a Servant

Well, is the grand affair over? You have been something tedious.

---

19 The blues.   20 I.e., I pretended not to understand.
21 Awaiting.
22 A liqueur flavored with fruit pits.—*Friend* is here intentionally ambiguous; it often meant *lover*. Lady Wishfort declares she is through with marriage and childbearing.

23 Past twelve o'clock.
24 Because of Mirabell's plot, which he soon discloses. Marriages could be peformed only during certain canonical hours, which ended at noon.

SERV. Sir, there's such coupling at Pancras[25] that they stand behind one another, as 'twere in a country dance. Ours was the last couple to lead up; and no hopes appearing of dispatch, besides, the parson growing hoarse, we were afraid his lungs would have failed before it came to our turn; so we drove round to Duke's Place; and there they were riveted in a trice.

MIRA. So, so, you are sure they are married.

SERV. Married and bedded, sir; I am witness.

MIRA. Have you the certificate?

SERV. Here it is, sir.

MIRA. Has the tailor brought Waitwell's clothes home, and the new liveries?

SERV. Yes, sir.

MIRA. That's well. Do you go home again, d'ee hear, and adjourn the consummation till farther order; bid Waitwell shake his ears, and Dame Partlet[26] rustle up her feathers, and meet me at one o'clock by Rosamond's Pond,[27] that I may see her before she returns to her lady; and as you tender your ears, be secret. [*Exit* Servant

Re-enter FAINALL *and* BETTY

FAIN. Joy of your success, Mirabell; you look pleased.

MIRA. Ay; I have been engaged in a matter of some sort of mirth, which is not yet ripe for discovery. I am glad this is not a cabal night. I wonder, Fainall, that you who are married, and of consequence should be discreet, will suffer your wife to be of such a party.

FAIN. Faith, I am not jealous. Besides, most who are engaged are women and relations; and for the men, they are of a kind too contemptible to give scandal.

MIRA. I am of another opinion. The greater the coxcomb, always the more the scandal; for a woman who is not a fool can have but one reason for associating with a man that is.

FAIN. Are you jealous as often as you see Witwoud entertained by Millamant?

MIRA. Of her understanding I am, if not of her person.

FAIN. You do her wrong; for to give her her due, she has wit.

MIRA. She has beauty enough to make any man think so, and complaisance enough not to contradict him who shall tell her so.

FAIN. For a passionate lover, methinks you are a man somewhat too discerning in the failings of your mistress.

MIRA. And for a discerning man, somewhat too passionate a lover; for I like her with all her faults—nay, like her for her faults. Her follies are so natural, or so artful, that they become her; and those affectations which in another woman would be odious, serve but to make her more agreeable. I'll tell thee, Fainall, she once used me with that[28] insolence that in revenge I took her to pieces: sifted her, and separated her failings; I studied 'em, and got 'em by rote. The catalogue was so large that I was not without hopes, one day or other, to hate her heartily: to which end I so used myself to think of 'em, that at length, contrary to my design and expectation, they gave me every hour less and less disturbance; till in a few days it became habitual to me to remember 'em without being displeased. They are now grown as familiar to me as my own frailties; and in all probability in a little time longer I shall like 'em as well.

FAIN. Marry her, marry her; be half as well acquainted with her charms as you are with her defects, and, my life on't, you are your own man again.

MIRA. Say you so?

FAIN. Ay, ay, I have experience; I have a wife, and so forth.

Enter Messenger

MESS. Is one Squire Witwoud here?

BET. Yes; what's your business?

MESS. I have a letter for him from his brother, Sir Wilfull, which I am charged to deliver into his own hands.

BET. He's in the next room, friend—that way.

[*Exit* Messenger

MIRA. What, is the chief of that noble family in town, Sir Wilfull Witwoud?

FAIN. He is expected today. Do you know him?

MIRA. I have seen him; he promises to be an extraordinary person; I think you have the honor to be related to him.

FAIN. Yes; he is half-brother to this Witwoud by a former wife, who was sister to my Lady Wishfort, my wife's mother. If you marry Millamant, you must call cousins too.

---

[25] At St. Pancras's Church, in a northwestern suburb, and at St. James's in Duke's Place, Aldgate, marriages were celebrated without banns or license.

[26] I.e., the hen. See Chaucer's "Nun's Priest's Tale," above.

[27] In St. James's Park.

[28] Such.

MIRA. I had rather be his relation than his acquaintance.

FAIN. He comes to town in order to equip himself for travel.

MIRA. For travel! Why, the man that I mean is above forty.[29]

FAIN. No matter for that; 'tis for the honor of England that all Europe should know we have blockheads of all ages.

MIRA. I wonder there is not an act of Parliament to save the credit[30] of the nation, and prohibit the exportation of fools.

FAIN. By no means; 'tis better as 'tis: 'tis better to trade with a little loss than to be quite eaten up with being overstocked.

MIRA. Pray, are the follies of this knight-errant, and those of the squire his brother, anything related?

FAIN. Not at all; Witwoud grows by the knight, like a medlar[31] grafted on a crab. One will melt in your mouth, and t'other set your teeth on edge; one is all pulp, and the other all core.

MIRA. So one[32] will be rotten before he be ripe, and the other will be rotten without ever being ripe at all.

FAIN. Sir Wilfull is an odd mixture of bashfulness and obstinacy. But when he's drunk, he's as loving as the monster in *The Tempest*,[33] and much after the same manner. To give the t'other his due, he has something of good nature, and does not always want wit.

MIRA. Not always; but as often as his memory fails him, and his commonplace[34] of comparisons. He is a fool with a good memory, and some few scraps of other folks' wit. He is one whose conversation can never be approved, yet it is now and then to be endured. He has indeed one good quality, he is not exceptious;[35] for he so passionately affects the reputation of understanding raillery that he will construe an affront into a jest, and call downright rudeness and ill language, satire and fire.

FAIN. If you have a mind to finish his picture, you have an opportunity to do it at full length. Behold the original.

Enter WITWOUD

WIT. Afford me your compassion, my dears; pity me, Fainall; Mirabell, pity me.

MIRA. I do from my soul.

FAIN. Why, what's the matter?

WIT. No letters for me, Betty?

BET. Did not the messenger bring you one but now, sir?

WIT. Ay, but no other?

BET. No, sir.

WIT. That's hard, that's very hard. A messenger, a mule, a beast of burden, he has brought me a letter from the fool my brother, as heavy as a panegyric in a funeral sermon, or a copy of commendatory verses from one poet to another. And what's worse, 'tis as sure a forerunner of the author as an epistle dedicatory.

MIRA. A fool, and your brother, Witwoud!

WIT. Ay, ay, my half brother. My half brother he is, no nearer, upon honor.

MIRA. Then 'tis possible he may be but half a fool.

WIT. Good, good, Mirabell, *le drôle!*[36] Good, good! Hang him, don't let's talk of him.—Fainall, how does your lady? Gad, I say anything in the world to get this fellow out of my head. I beg pardon that I should ask a man of pleasure, and the town, a question at once so foreign and domestic. But I talk like an old maid at a marriage: I don't know what I say; but she's the best woman in the world.

FAIN. 'Tis well you don't know what you say, or else your commendation would go near to make me either vain or jealous.

WIT. No man in town lives well with a wife but Fainall.—Your judgment, Mirabell?

MIRA. You had better step and ask his wife, if you would be credibly informed.

WIT. Mirabell?

MIRA. Ay.

WIT. My dear, I ask ten thousand pardons.—Gad, I have forgot what I was going to say to you.

MIRA. I thank you heartily, heartily.

WIT. No, but prithee excuse me—my memory is such a memory.

MIRA. Have a care of such apologies, Witwoud; for I never knew a fool but he affected to complain, either of the spleen[37] or his memory.

FAIN. What have you done with Petulant?

WIT. He's reckoning his money—my money it was—I have no luck today.

---

29 While the Grand Tour, to round off a man's education, was usually taken immediately after he left the university.
30 Reputation.   31 A soft fruit somewhat like a crab apple.
32 The medlar—and Sir Wilfull.
33 Caliban's sister, the foul and amorous Sycorax in the D'avenant-Dryden-Shadwell operatic adaptation of Shakespeare's *The Tempest*.   34 The private collection he has compiled.
35 Quarrelsome.

36 The witty fellow!   37 Melancholy.

FAIN. You may allow him to win of you at play, for you are sure to be too hard for him at repartee. Since you monopolize the wit that is between you, the fortune must be his of course.

MIRA. I don't find that Petulant confesses the superiority of wit to be your talent, Witwoud.

WIT. Come, come, you are malicious now, and would breed debates. Petulant's my friend, and a very honest fellow, and a very pretty fellow, and has a smattering—faith and troth, a pretty deal of an odd sort of a small wit; nay, I'll do him justice. I'm his friend; I won't wrong him neither. And if he had but any judgment in the world, he would not be altogether contemptible. Come, come, don't detract from the merits of my friend.

FAIN. You don't take your friend to be overnicely bred.

WIT. No, no, hang him, the rogue has no manners at all, that I must own—no more breeding than a bumbailey,[38] that I grant you. 'Tis pity, faith; the fellow has fire and life.

MIRA. What, courage?

WIT. Hum; faith, I don't know as to that—I can't say as to that. Yes, faith, in a controversy he'll contradict anybody.

MIRA. Though 'twere a man whom he feared, or a woman whom he loved.

WIT. Well, well, he does not always think before he speaks. We have all our failings; you're too hard upon him, you are, faith. Let me excuse him—I can defend most of his faults, except one or two; one he has, that's the truth on't, if he were my brother, I could not acquit him. That indeed I could wish were otherwise.

MIRA. Ay, marry, what's that, Witwoud?

WIT. Oh, pardon me. Expose the infirmities of my friend? No, my dear, excuse me there.

FAIN. What, I warrant he's unsincere, or 'tis some such trifle.

WIT. No, no, what if he be? 'Tis no matter for that; his wit will excuse that. A wit should no more be sincere than a woman constant; one argues a decay of parts, as t'other of beauty.

MIRA. May be you think him too positive?

WIT. No, no, his being positive is an incentive to argument, and keeps up conversation.

FAIN. Too illiterate.

WIT. That! that's his happiness. His want of learning gives him the more opportunities to shew his natural parts.

MIRA. He wants words.

WIT. Ay; but I like him for that now: for his want of words gives me the pleasure very often to explain his meaning.

FAIN. He's impudent.

WIT. No, that's not it.

MIRA. Vain.

WIT. No.

MIRA. What, he speaks unseasonable truths sometimes, because he has not wit enough to invent an evasion.

WIT. Truths! Ha, ha, ha! No, no, since you will have it—I mean, he never speaks truth at all—that's all. He will lie like a chambermaid, or a woman of quality's porter. Now that is a fault.

Enter Coachman

COACH. Is Master Petulant here, mistress?

BET. Yes.

COACH. Three gentlewomen in the coach would speak with him.

FAIN. O brave Petulant, three!

BET. I'll tell him.

COACH. You must bring two dishes of chocolate and a glass of cinnamon-water.[39]

[*Exeunt* BETTY *and* Coachman

WIT. That should be for two fasting strumpets, and a bawd troubled with wind. Now you may know what the three are.

MIRA. You are very free with your friend's acquaintance.

WIT. Ay, ay, friendship without freedom is as dull as love without enjoyment, or wine without toasting; but to tell you a secret, these are trulls that he allows coach-hire, and something more by the week, to call on him once a day at public places.

MIRA. How!

WIT. You shall see he won't go to 'em because there's no more company here to take notice of him. Why, this is nothing to what he used to do; before he found out this way, I have known him call for himself—

FAIN. Call for himself? What dost thou mean?

WIT. Mean? why, he would slip you out of this chocolate house, just when you had been talking to him. As soon as your back was turned—whip he was gone; then trip to his lodging, clap on a hood and scarf and mask, slap into a hackney-coach, and drive hither to the door again in a trice; where he would send in for himself—that I mean—call for

---

[38] A contemptuous name for a bailiff, suggestive of his arresting his man by sneaking up on him from the rear.

[39] A cordial.

himself, wait for himself, nay and what's more, not finding himself, sometimes leave a letter for himself.

MIRA. I confess this is something extraordinary—I believe he waits for himself now, he is so long a-coming. Oh, I ask his pardon.

Enter PETULANT *and* BETTY

BET. Sir, the coach stays. [*Exit*

PET. Well, well; I come.—'Sbud,[40] a man had as good be a professed midwife as a professed whore-master, at this rate; to be knocked up and raised at all hours, and in all places! Pox on 'em, I won't come.—D'ee hear, tell 'em I won't come. Let 'em snivel and cry their hearts out.

FAIN. You are very cruel, Petulant.

PET. All's one,[41] let it pass—I have a humor to be cruel.

MIRA. I hope they are not persons of condition[42] that you use at this rate.

PET. Condition! condition's a dried fig, if I am not in humor. By this hand, if they were your[43]—a—a—your what-d'ee-call-'ems themselves, they must wait or rub off,[44] if I want appetite.

MIRA. What-d'ee-call-'ems! What are they, Wit-woud?

WIT. Empresses, my dear—by your what-d'ee-call-'ems he means sultana queens.[45]

PET. Ay, Roxolanas.[46]

MIRA. Cry you mercy.

FAIN. Witwoud says they are—

PET. What does he say th' are?

WIT. I—fine ladies, I say.

PET. Pass on, Witwoud.—Hark 'ee, by this light, his relations—two co-heiresses his cousins, and an old aunt, that loves caterwauling[47] better than a conventicle.[48]

WIT. Ha, ha, ha! I had a mind to see how the rogue would come off. Ha, ha, ha! Gad, I can't be angry with him, if he said they were my mother and my sisters.

MIRA. No?

WIT. No; the rogue's wit and readiness of invention charm me: dear Petulant!

Re-enter BETTY

BET. They are gone, sir, in great anger.

PET. Enough, let 'em trundle. Anger helps complexion, saves paint.

FAIN. This continence is all dissembled; this is in order to have something to brag of the next time he makes court to Millamant, and swears he has abandoned the whole sex for her sake.

MIRA. Have you not left off your impudent pretensions there yet? I shall cut your throat, sometime or other, Petulant, about that business.

PET. Ay, ay, let that pass—there are other throats to be cut—

MIRA. Meaning mine, sir?

PET. Not I—I mean nobody—I know nothing. But there are uncles and nephews in the world—and they may be rivals. What then? All's one for that—

MIRA. How! Harkee, Petulant, come hither. Explain, or I shall call your interpreter.

PET. Explain! I know nothing. Why, you have an uncle, have you not, lately come to town, and lodges by my Lady Wishfort's?

MIRA. True.

PET. Why, that's enough. You and he are not friends; and if he should marry and have a child, you may be disinherited, ha?

MIRA. Where hast thou stumbled upon all this truth?

PET. All's one for that; why, then say I know something.

MIRA. Come, thou art an honest fellow, Petulant, and shalt make love to my mistress, thou sha't, faith. What hast thou heard of my uncle?

PET. I? nothing I. If throats are to be cut, let swords clash; snug's the word, I shrug and am silent.

MIRA. O raillery, raillery. Come, I know thou art in the women's secrets. What, you're a cabalist; I know you stayed at Millamant's last night, after I went. Was there any mention made of my uncle, or me? Tell me; if thou hadst but good nature equal to thy wit, Petulant, Tony Witwoud, who is now thy competitor in fame, would show as dim by thee as a dead whiting's eye by a pearl of orient;[49] he would no more be seen by[50] thee than Mercury is by the sun. Come, I'm sure thou wo't[51] tell me.

PET. If I do, will you grant me common sense then, for the future?

MIRA. Faith, I'll do what I can for thee, and I'll pray that heaven may grant it thee in the meantime.

PET. Well, hark 'ee. [*They step aside*

---

40 I.e., by God's body.
41 It makes no difference, never mind. 42 Standing.
43 *Your* does not refer to Mirabell or Witwoud; it is used as in "If you know your kings of England." 44 Clear out.
45 Queans, prostitutes.
46 Wife of the Turkish sultan Soliman the Magnificent (1494–1566). She figured in Heroic romance and drama.
47 Miaowing like an amorous cat. 48 A religious meeting.

49 A lustrous pearl. 50 Beside. 51 Wilt.

FAIN. Petulant and you both will find Mirabell as warm a rival as a lover.

WIT. Pshaw, pshaw, that she laughs at Petulant is plain. And for my part—but that it is almost a fashion to admire her, I should—hark'ee—to tell you a secret, but let it go no further—between friends, I shall never break my heart for her.

FAIN. How!

WIT. She's handsome; but she's a sort of an uncertain woman.

FAIN. I thought you had died for her.

WIT. Umh—no—

FAIN. She has wit.

WIT. 'Tis what she will hardly allow anybody else. Now, demme,[52] I should hate that, if she were as handsome as Cleopatra. Mirabell is not so sure of her as he thinks for.

FAIN. Why do you think so?

WIT. We stayed pretty late there last night, and heard something of an uncle to Mirabell, who is lately come to town—and is between him and the best part of his estate. Mirabell and he are at some distance,[53] as my Lady Wishfort has been told; and you know she hates Mirabell, worse than a Quaker hates a parrot,[54] or than a fishmonger hates a hard frost. Whether this uncle has seen Mrs. Millamant or not, I cannot say; but there were items of such a treaty being in embryo; and if it should come to life, poor Mirabell would be in some sort unfortunately fobbed,[55] i'faith.

FAIN. 'Tis impossible Millamant should hearken to it.

WIT. Faith, my dear, I can't tell; she's a woman and a kind of a humorist.[56]

MIRA. (to PETULANT). And this is the sum of what you could collect last night.

PET. The quintessence. Maybe Witwoud knows more; he stayed longer. Besides, they never mind him; they say anything before him.

MIRA. I thought you had been the greatest favorite.

PET. Ay, tête-à-tête; but not in public, because I make remarks.

MIRA. Do you?

PET. Ay, ay; pox, I'm malicious, man. Now, he's soft, you know; they are not in awe of him—the fellow's well-bred; he's what you call a—what-d'ee-call-'em. A fine gentleman, but he's silly withal.[57]

MIRA. I thank you; I know as much as my curiosity requires.—Fainall, are you for the Mall?[58]

FAIN. Ay, I'll take a turn before dinner.

WIT. Ay, we'll all walk in the Park; the ladies talked of being there.

MIRA. I thought you were obliged to watch for your brother Sir Wilfull's arrival.

WIT. No, no, he comes to his aunt's, my Lady Wishfort; pox on him, I shall be troubled with him too; what shall I do with the fool?

PET. Beg him for his estate, that I may beg you afterwards, and so have but one trouble with you both.

WIT. O rare Petulant! thou art as quick as a fire in a frosty morning; thou shalt to the Mall with us, and we'll be very severe.

PET. Enough! I'm in a humor to be severe.

MIRA. Are you? Pray then walk by yourselves—let not us be accessory to your putting the ladies out of countenance, with your senseless ribaldry, which you roar out aloud as often as they pass by you; and when you have made a handsome woman blush, then you think you have been severe.

PET. What, what? Then let 'em either show their innocence by not understanding what they hear, or else show their discretion by not hearing what they would not be thought to understand.

MIRA. But hast not thou then sense enough to know that thou ought'st to be most ashamed of thyself when thou hast put another out of countenance?

PET. Not I, by this hand—I always take blushing either for a sign of guilt or ill breeding.

MIRA. I confess you ought to think so. You are in the right, that you may plead the error of your judgment in defence of your practice.

Where modesty's ill manners, 'tis but fit
That impudence and malice pass for wit.

[Exeunt

---

[52] Damn me.
[53] Not on good terms. There is, of course, no such person; the report is a part of Mirabell's scheme, soon to be disclosed.
[54] Perhaps because some parrots swear.   [55] Tricked.
[56] Whimsical person.

[57] Besides.
[58] Pall Mall (pronounced *pell mell*), the fashionable walk in St. James's Park.

St. James's Park. MRS. FAINALL *and* MRS. MARWOOD

MRS. FAIN. Ay, ay, dear Marwood, if we will be happy, we must find the means in ourselves, and among ourselves. Men are ever in extremes, either doting or averse. While they are lovers, if they have fire and sense, their jealousies are insupportable; and when they cease to love (we ought to think at least) they loathe; they look upon us with horror and distaste; they meet us like the ghosts of what we were, and as such, fly from us.

MRS. MAR. True, 'tis an unhappy circumstance of life that love should ever die before us, and that the man so often should outlive the lover. But say what you will, 'tis better to be left than never to have been loved. To pass your youth in dull indifference, to refuse the sweets of life because they once must leave us, is as preposterous as to wish to have been born old because we one day must be old. For my part, my youth may wear and waste, but it shall never rust in my possession.

MRS. FAIN. Then it seems you dissemble an aversion to mankind, only in compliance with my mother's humor.

MRS. MAR. Certainly. To be free, I have no taste of those insipid dry discourses with which our sex of force must entertain themselves, apart from men. We may affect endearments to each other, profess eternal friendships, and seem to dote like lovers; but 'tis not in our natures long to persevere. Love will resume his empire in our breasts, and every heart, or soon or late, receive and readmit him as its lawful tyrant.

MRS. FAIN. Bless me, how have I been deceived! Why, you profess a libertine.

MRS. MAR. You see my friendship by my freedom. Come, be as sincere, acknowledge that your sentiments agree with mine.

MRS. FAIN. Never.

MRS. MAR. You hate mankind?

MRS. FAIN. Heartily, inveterately.

MRS. MAR. Your husband?

MRS. FAIN. Most transcendently; ay, though I say it, meritoriously.

MRS. MAR. Give me your hand upon it.

MRS. FAIN. There.

MRS. MAR. I join with you; what I have said has been to try you.

MRS. FAIN. Is it possible? Dost thou hate those vipers, men?

MRS. MAR. I have done hating 'em, and am now come to despise 'em; the next thing I have to do, is eternally to forget 'em.

MRS. FAIN. There spoke the spirit of an Amazon, a Penthesilea.[1]

MRS. MAR. And yet I am thinking sometimes to carry my aversion further.

MRS. FAIN. How?

MRS. MAR. Faith, by marrying; if I could but find one that loved me very well, and would be thoroughly sensible of ill usage, I think I should do myself the violence of undergoing the ceremony.

MRS. FAIN. You would not make him a cuckold?

MRS. MAR. No; but I'd make him believe I did, and that's as bad.

MRS. FAIN. Why had not you as good do it?

MRS. MAR. Oh, if he should ever discover it, he would then know the worst, and be out of his pain; but I would have him ever to continue upon the rack of fear and jealousy.

MRS. FAIN. Ingenious mischief! Would thou wert married to Mirabell.

MRS. MAR. Would I were.

MRS. FAIN. You change color.

MRS. MAR. Because I hate him.

MRS. FAIN. So do I; but I can hear him named. But what reason have you to hate him in particular?

MRS. MAR. I never loved him; he is, and always was, insufferably proud.

MRS. FAIN. By the reason you give for your aversion, one would think it dissembled; for you have laid a fault to his charge of which his enemies must acquit him.

MRS. MAR. Oh, then it seems you are one of his favorable enemies. Methinks you look a little pale, and now you flush again.

MRS. FAIN. Do I? I think I am a little sick o' the sudden.

MRS. MAR. What ails you?

MRS. FAIN. My husband. Don't you see him? He turned short upon me unawares, and has almost overcome me.

Enter FAINALL *and* MIRABELL

MRS. MAR. Ha, ha, ha; he comes opportunely for you.

---

[1] Queen of the Amazons, in the Trojan War.

MRS. FAIN. For you, for he has brought Mirabell with him.

FAIN. My dear.

MRS. FAIN. My soul.

FAIN. You don't look well today, child.

MRS. FAIN. D'ee think so?

MIRA. He is the only man that does, madam.

MRS. FAIN. The only man that would tell me so, at least; and the only man from whom I could hear it without mortification.

FAIN. Oh, my dear, I am satisfied of your tenderness; I know you cannot resent anything from me, especially what is an effect of my concern.

MRS. FAIN. Mr. Mirabell, my mother interrupted you in a pleasant relation last night; I would fain hear it out.

MIRA. The persons concerned in that affair have yet a tolerable reputation. I am afraid Mr. Fainall will be censorious.

MRS. FAIN. He has a humor more prevailing than his curiosity, and will willingly dispense with the hearing of one scandalous story, to avoid giving an occasion to make another by being seen to walk with his wife. This way, Mr. Mirabell; and I dare promise you will oblige us both.

[*Exeunt* MRS. FAINALL *and* MIRABELL

FAIN. Excellent creature! Well, sure if I should live to be rid of my wife, I should be a miserable man.

MRS. MAR. Ay!

FAIN. For having only that one hope, the accomplishment of it, of consequence, must put an end to all my hopes; and what a wretch is he who must survive his hopes! Nothing remains when that day comes but to sit down and weep like Alexander, when he wanted other worlds to conquer.

MRS. MAR. Will you not follow 'em?

FAIN. Faith, I think not.

MRS. MAR. Pray let us; I have a reason.

FAIN. You are not jealous?

MRS. MAR. Of whom?

FAIN. Of Mirabell.

MRS. MAR. If I am, is it inconsistent with my love to you that I am tender of your honor?

FAIN. You would intimate, then, as if there were a fellow-feeling between my wife and him.

MRS. MAR. I think she does not hate him to that degree she would be thought.

FAIN. But he, I fear, is too insensible.

MRS. MAR. It may be you are deceived.

FAIN. It may be so. I do now begin to apprehend it.

MRS. MAR. What?

FAIN. That I have been deceived, madam, and you are false.

MRS. MAR. That I am false! What mean you?

FAIN. To let you know I see through all your little arts. Come, you both love him; and both have equally dissembled your aversion. Your mutual jealousies of one another have made you clash till you have both struck fire. I have seen the warm confession redd'ning on your cheeks, and sparkling from your eyes.

MRS. MAR. You do me wrong.

FAIN. I do not. 'Twas for my ease to oversee[2] and willfully neglect the gross advances made him by my wife; that, by permitting her to be engaged, I might continue unsuspected in my pleasures, and take you oft'ner to my arms in full security. But could you think, because the nodding husband would not wake, that e'er the watchful lover slept?

MRS. MAR. And wherewithal can you reproach me?

FAIN. With infidelity, with loving of another, with love of Mirabell.

MRS. MAR. 'Tis false. I challenge you to show an instance that can confirm your groundless accusation. I hate him.

FAIN. And wherefore do you hate him? He is insensible, and your resentment follows his neglect. An instance! The injuries you have done him are a proof: your interposing in his love. What cause had you to make discoveries of his pretended passion?[3] to undeceive the credulous aunt, and be the officious obstacle of his match with Millamant?

MRS. MAR. My obligations to my Lady urged me; I had professed a friendship to her, and could not see her easy nature so abused by that dissembler.

FAIN. What, was it conscience then? Professed a friendship! Oh, the pious friendships of the female sex!

MRS. MAR. More tender, more sincere, and more enduring than all the vain and empty vows of men, whether professing love to us or mutual faith to one another.

FAIN. Ha, ha, ha; you are my wife's friend too.

MRS. MAR. Shame and ingratitude! Do you reproach me? Have I been false to her, through strict fidelity to you, and sacrificed my friendship to keep my love inviolate? And have you the baseness to charge me with the guilt, unmindful of the merit! To you it should be meritorious that I have been

---

[2] Overlook.

[3] For Lady Wishfort. Mrs. Marwood's disclosure of the truth is a main reason for Lady Wishfort's opposition to Mirabell's suit to Millamant, her niece.

vicious; and do you reflect that guilt upon me which should lie buried in your bosom?

FAIN. You misinterpret my reproof. I meant but to remind you of the slight account you once could make of strictest ties when set in competition with your love to me.

MRS. MAR. 'Tis false; you urged it with deliberate malice—'twas spoke in scorn, and I never will forgive it.

FAIN. Your guilt, not your resentment, begets your rage. If yet you loved, you could forgive a jealousy; but you are stung to find you are discovered.

MRS. MAR. It shall be all discovered. You too shall be discovered; be sure you shall. I can but be exposed—if I do it myself I shall prevent[4] your baseness.

FAIN. Why, what will you do?

MRS. MAR. Disclose it to your wife; own what has passed between us.

FAIN. Frenzy!

MRS. MAR. By all my wrongs I'll do't—I'll publish to the world the injuries you have done me, both in my fame and fortune. With both I trusted you, you bankrupt in honor, as indigent of wealth.

FAIN. Your fame I have preserved. Your fortune has been bestowed as the prodigality of your love would have it, in pleasures which we both have shared. Yet, had not you been false, I had ere this repaid it. 'Tis true: had you permitted Mirabell with Millamant to have stolen their marriage, my Lady had been incensed beyond all means of reconcilement; Millamant had forfeited the moiety[5] of her fortune, which then would have descended to my wife. And wherefore did I marry, but to make lawful prize of a rich widow's wealth, and squander it on love and you?

MRS. MAR. Deceit and frivolous pretense!

FAIN. Death, am I not married? What's pretense? Am I not imprisoned, fettered? Have I not a wife? Nay, a wife that was a widow, a young widow, a handsome widow; and would be again a widow, but that I have a heart of proof,[6] and something of a constitution to bustle through the ways of wedlock and this world. Will you yet be reconciled to truth and me?

MRS. MAR. Impossible. Truth and you are inconsistent—I hate you, and shall for ever.

FAIN. For loving you?

MRS. MAR. I loathe the name of love after such usage; and next to the guilt with which you would asperse me, I scorn you most. Farewell.

FAIN. Nay, we must not part thus.

MRS. MAR. Let me go.

FAIN. Come, I'm sorry.

MRS. MAR. I care not—let me go—break my hands, do—I'd leave 'em to get loose.

FAIN. I would not hurt you for the world. Have I no other hold to keep you here?

MRS. MAR. Well, I have deserved it all.

FAIN. You know I love you.

MRS. MAR. Poor dissembling!—Oh, that—well, it is not yet—

FAIN. What? What is it not? What is it not yet? It is not yet too late—

MRS. MAR. No, it is not yet too late—I have that comfort.

FAIN. It is, to love another.

MRS. MAR. But not to loathe, detest, abhor mankind, myself, and the whole treacherous world.

FAIN. Nay, this is extravagance. Come, I ask your pardon—no tears—I was to blame; I could not love you and be easy in my doubts. Pray forbear—I believe you; I'm convinced I've done you wrong; and any way, every way, will make amends—I'll hate my wife yet more, damn her; I'll part with her, rob her of all she's worth, and we'll retire somewhere, anywhere, to another world. I'll marry thee—be pacified.—'Sdeath, they come; hide your face, your tears. You have a mask;[7] wear it a moment. This way, this way; be persuaded. [Exeunt

Enter MIRABELL *and* MRS. FAINALL

MRS. FAIN. They are here yet.

MIRA. They are turning into the other walk.

MRS. FAIN. While I only hated my husband, I could bear to see him; but since I have despised him, he's too offensive.

MIRA. Oh, you should hate with prudence.

MRS. FAIN. Yes, for I have loved with indiscretion.

MIRA. You should have just so much disgust for your husband as may be sufficient to make you relish your lover.

MRS. FAIN. You have been the cause that I have loved without bounds, and would you set limits to that aversion of which you have been the occasion? Why did you make me marry this man?

MIRA. Why do we daily commit disagreeable and dangerous actions? To save that idol, reputation. If

---

[4] Anticipate.   [5] Half.   [6] Strength.

[7] Formerly worn by ladies, as a veil was in later times; but by 1700 respectable women did not ordinarily wear masks.

the familiarities of our loves had produced that consequence of which you were apprehensive, where could you have fixed a father's name with credit, but on a husband? I knew Fainall to be a man lavish of his morals, an interested and professing friend, a false and a designing lover; yet one whose wit and outward fair behavior have gained a reputation with the town, enough to make that woman stand excused who has suffered herself to be won by his addresses. A better man ought not to have been sacrificed to the occasion; a worse had not answered to the purpose. When you are weary of him, you know your remedy.

MRS. FAIN. I ought to stand in some degree of credit with you, Mirabell.

MIRA. In justice to you, I have made you privy to my whole design, and put it in your power to ruin or advance my fortune.

MRS. FAIN. Whom have you instructed to represent your pretended uncle?

MIRA. Waitwell, my servant.

MRS. FAIN. He is an humble servant[8] to Foible, my mother's woman, and may win her to your interest.

MIRA. Care is taken for that; she is won and worn by this time. They were married this morning.

MRS. FAIN. Who?

MIRA. Waitwell and Foible. I would not tempt my servant to betray me by trusting him too far. If your mother, in hopes to ruin me, should consent to marry my pretended uncle, he might, like Mosca in *The Fox*,[9] stand upon terms; so I made him sure beforehand.

MRS. FAIN. So, if my poor mother is caught in a contract, you will discover the imposture betimes,[10] and release her by producing a certificate of her gallant's former marriage.

MIRA. Yes, upon condition she consent to my marriage with her niece, and surrender the moiety of her fortune in her possession.

MRS. FAIN. She talked last night of endeavoring at a match between Millamant and your uncle.

MIRA. That was by Foible's direction and my instruction, that she might seem to carry it more privately.

MRS. FAIN. Well, I have an opinion of your success, for I believe my Lady will do anything to get a husband; and when she has this, which you have provided for her, I suppose she will submit to anything to get rid of him.

MIRA. Yes, I think the good lady would marry anything that resembled a man, though 'twere no more than what a butler could pinch out of a napkin.[11]

MRS. FAIN. Female frailty! We must all come to it, if we live to be old, and feel the craving of a false appetite when the true is decayed.

MIRA. An old woman's appetite is depraved like that of a girl—'tis the greensickness[12] of a second childhood; and, like the faint offer[13] of a latter spring, serves but to usher in the fall, and withers in an affected bloom.

MRS. FAIN. Here's your mistress.

Enter MRS. MILLAMANT, WITWOUD, *and* MINCING

MIRA. Here she comes, i'faith, full sail, with her fan spread and her streamers out, and a shoal[14] of fools for tenders.—Ha, no, I cry her mercy!

MRS. FAIN. I see but one poor empty sculler; and he tows her woman after him.

MIRA. You seem to be unattended, madam. You used to have the beau monde[15] throng after you, and a flock of gay fine perukes[16] hovering around you.

WIT. Like moths about a candle.—I had like to have lost my comparison for want of breath.

MILLA. Oh, I have denied myself airs today. I have walked as fast through the crowd—

WIT. As a favorite in disgrace, and with as few followers.

MILLA. Dear Mr. Witwoud, truce with your similitudes; for I am as sick of 'em—

WIT. As a physician of a good air.—I cannot help it, madam, though 'tis against myself.

MILLA. Yet again! Mincing, stand between me and his wit.

WIT. Do, Mrs. Mincing, like a screen before a great fire. I confess I do blaze today, I am too bright.

MRS. FAIN. But, dear Millamant, why were you so long?

MILLA. Long! Lord, have I not made violent haste? I have asked every living thing I met for you; I have enquired after you, as after a new fashion.

WIT. Madam, truce with your similitudes.—No, you met her husband, and did not ask him for her.

MIRA. By your leave, Witwoud, that were like enquiring after an old fashion, to ask a husband for his wife.

---

[8] Suitor, lover.
[9] Jonson's *Volpone*. Mosca, Volpone's agent in crime, blackmails his master.   [10] Early, in time.
[11] I.e., in folding a napkin decoratively for the table.
[12] Chlorosis, an anemic disease of young women.
[13] Attempt, effort.   [14] Throng.
[15] World of fashion.   [16] Wigs, worn by men of fashion.

WIT. Hum, a hit, a hit, a palpable hit, I confess it.

MRS. FAIN. You were dressed before I came abroad.

MILLA. Ay, that's true—oh, but then I had—Mincing, what had I? Why was I so long?

MINC. Oh, mem, your La'ship stayed to peruse a pecquet[17] of letters.

MILLA. Oh, ay, letters—I had letters—I am persecuted with letters—I hate letters—nobody knows how to write letters; and yet one has 'em, one does not know why—they serve one to pin up one's hair.

WIT. Is that the way? Pray, madam, do you pin up your hair with all your letters? I find I must keep copies.

MILLA. Only with those in verse, Mr. Witwoud. I never pin up my hair with prose. I fancy one's hair would not curl if it were pinned up with prose. I think I tried once, Mincing.

MINC. Oh, mem, I shall never forget it.

MILLA. Ay, poor Mincing tifft[18] and tifft all the morning.

MINC. Till I had the cremp in my fingers, I'll vow, mem. And all to no purpose. But when your La'ship pins it up with poetry, it sits so pleasant the next day as anything, and is so pure and so crips.[19]

WIT. Indeed, so "crips"?

MINC. You're such a critic, Mr. Witwoud.

MILLA. Mirabell, did not you take exceptions last night? Oh, ay, and went away. Now I think on't, I'm angry—no, now I think on't, I'm pleased—for I believe I gave you some pain.

MIRA. Does that please you?

MILLA. Infinitely; I love to give pain.

MIRA. You would affect a cruelty which is not in your nature; your true vanity is in the power of pleasing.

MILLA. Oh, I ask your pardon for that. One's cruelty is one's power, and when one parts with one's cruelty, one parts with one's power; and when one has parted with that, I fancy one's old and ugly.

MIRA. Ay, ay, suffer your cruelty to ruin the object of your power, to destroy your lover—and then how vain, how lost a thing you'll be! Nay, 'tis true: you are no longer handsome when you've lost your lover; your beauty dies upon the instant. For beauty is the lover's gift; 'tis he bestows your charms—your glass is all a cheat. The ugly and the old, whom the looking glass mortifies, yet after commendation can be flattered by it, and discover beauties in it; for that reflects our praises, rather than your face.

MILLA. Oh, the vanity of these men! Fainall,[20] d'ee hear him? If they did not commend us, we were not handsome! Now you must know they could not commend one, if one was not handsome. Beauty the lover's gift—Lord, what is a lover, that it can give? Why, one makes lovers as fast as one pleases, and they live as long as one pleases, and they die as soon as one pleases; and then, if one pleases, one makes more.

WIT. Very pretty. Why, you make no more of making of lovers, madam, than of making so many card-matches.[21]

MILLA. One no more owes one's beauty to a lover than one's wit to an echo; they can but reflect what we look and say: vain empty things if we are silent or unseen, and want a being.

MIRA. Yet, to those two vain empty things, you owe two the greatest pleasures of your life.

MILLA. How so?

MIRA. To your lover you owe the pleasure of hearing yourselves praised, and to an echo the pleasure of hearing yourselves talk.

WIT. But I know a lady that loves talking so incessantly she won't give an echo fair play; she has that everlasting rotation of tongue that an echo must wait till she dies before it can catch her last words.

MILLA. Oh, fiction; Fainall, let us leave these men.

MIRA. (aside to MRS. FAINALL). Draw off Witwoud.

MRS. FAIN. (aside). Immediately.—I have a word or two for Mr. Witwoud.

[Exeunt MRS. FAINALL and WITWOUD

MIRA. I would beg a little private audience, too. You had the tyranny to deny me last night; though you knew I came to impart a secret to you that concerned my love.

MILLA. You saw I was engaged.

MIRA. Unkind. You had the leisure to entertain[22] a herd of fools, things who visit you from their excessive idleness, bestowing on your easiness that time which is the incumbrance of their lives. How can you find delight in such society? It is impossible they should admire you; they are not capable; or, if they were, it should be to you as a mortification: for, sure, to please a fool is some degree of folly.

MILLA. I please myself—besides, sometimes to converse with fools is for my health.

MIRA. Your health! Is there a worse disease than the conversation of fools?

MILLA. Yes, the vapors; fools are physic for it, next to asafetida.[23]

---

[17] Packet. Mincing's speech is often provincial.
[18] Arranged, tricked out.   [19] Dialect for *crisp*, i.e., curly.

[20] Mrs. Fainall.   [21] Matches in a card dipped in sulphur.
[22] Receive.   [23] Used as a sedative.

MIRA. You are not in a course[24] of fools?

MILLA. Mirabell, if you persist in this offensive freedom, you'll displease me. I think I must resolve after all, not to have you—we shan't agree.

MIRA. Not in our physic, it may be.

MILLA. And yet our distemper in all likelihood will be the same; for we shall be sick of one another. I shan't endure to be reprimanded, nor instructed; 'tis so dull to act always by advice, and so tedious to be told of one's faults—I can't bear it. Well, I won't have you, Mirabell—I'm resolved—I think—you may go—ha, ha, ha. What would you give, that you could help loving me?

MIRA. I would give something that you did not know I could not help it.

MILLA. Come, don't look grave, then. Well, what do you say to me?

MIRA. I say that a man may as soon make a friend by his wit, or a fortune by his honesty, as win a woman with plain dealing and sincerity.

MILLA. Sententious Mirabell! Prithee, don't look with that violent and inflexible wise face, like Solomon at the dividing of the child[25] in an old tapestry hanging.

MIRA. You are merry, madam, but I would persuade you for one moment to be serious.

MILLA. What, with that face? No, if you keep your countenance, 'tis impossible I should hold mine. Well, after all, there is something very moving in a lovesick face. Ha, ha, ha—well, I won't laugh; don't be peevish—heigho! Now I'll be melancholy, as melancholy as a watch light.[26] Well, Mirabell, if ever you will win me, woo me now— nay, if you are so tedious, fare you well—I see they are walking away.

MIRA. Can you not find in the variety of your disposition one moment—

MILLA. To hear you tell me that Foible's married and your plot like to speed?[27] No.

MIRA. But how you came to know it—

MILLA. Unless by the help of the Devil, you can't imagine, unless she should tell me herself. Which of the two it may have been, I will leave you to consider; and when you have done thinking of that, think of me.   [Exit

MIRA. I have something more—gone—think of you! To think of a whirlwind, though 'twere in a whirlwind, were a case of more steady contempla- tion, a very tranquillity of mind and mansion. A fellow that lives in a windmill has not a more whimsical dwelling than the heart of a man that is lodged in a woman. There is no point of the compass to which they cannot turn, and by which they are not turned, and by one as well as another; for motion, not method, is their occupation. To know this, and yet continue to be in love, is to be made wise from the dictates of reason and yet persevere to play the fool by the force of instinct. Oh, here come my pair of turtles.[28]—What, billing so sweetly! Is not Valentine's Day over with you yet?

Enter WAITWELL *and* FOIBLE

Sirrah, Waitwell, why sure you think you were married for your own recreation, and not for my conveniency.

WAIT. Your pardon, sir. With submission, we have indeed been solacing in lawful delights; but still with an eye to business, sir. I have instructed her as well as I could. If she can take your directions as readily as my instructions, sir, your affairs are in a prosperous way.

MIRA. Give you joy, Mrs. Foible.

FOIB. Oh, 'las, sir, I'm so ashamed—I'm afraid my Lady has been in a thousand inquietudes for me. But I protest, sir, I made as much haste as I could.

WAIT. That she did indeed, sir. It was my fault that she did not make more.

MIRA. That I believe.

FOIB. But I told my Lady as you instructed me, sir. That I had a prospect of seeing Sir Rowland, your uncle, and that I would put her Ladyship's picture in my pocket to show him; which I'll be sure to say has made him so enamored of her beauty that he burns with impatience to lie at her Ladyship's feet and worship the original.

MIRA. Excellent Foible! Matrimony has made you eloquent in love.

WAIT. I think she has profited, sir. I think so.

FOIB. You have seen madam Millamant, sir?

MIRA. Yes.

FOIB. I told her, sir, because I did not know that you might find an opportunity; she had so much company last night.

MIRA. Your diligence will merit more.—In the mean time—   [Gives money

FOIB. Oh, dear sir, your humble servant.

WAIT. Spouse.

---

24 Series of remedies.
25 See 1 Kings 3:16–28. Solomon proposed dividing the child in order to determine which of two claimants was the mother.
26 Night light, in a bedroom.   27 Succeed.

28 Turtledoves.

MIRA. Stand off, sir; not a penny.—Go on and prosper, Foible. The lease shall be made good and the farm stocked, if we succeed.

FOIB. I don't question your generosity, sir; and you need not doubt of success. If you have no more commands, sir, I'll be gone; I'm sure my Lady is at her toilet, and can't dress till I come.—Oh, dear, I'm sure that (*looking out*) was Mrs. Marwood that went by in a mask; if she has seen me with you I'm sure she'll tell my Lady. I'll make haste home and prevent[29] her. Your servant sir. B'w'y,[30] Waitwell.

[*Exit*

WAIT. Sir Rowland, if you please.—The jade's so pert upon her preferment[31] she forgets herself.

MIRA. Come, sir, will you endeavor to forget yourself—and transform into Sir Rowland?

WAIT. Why, sir, it will be impossible I should remember myself—married, knighted, and attended all in one day! 'Tis enough to make any man forget himself. The difficulty will be how to recover my acquaintance and familiarity with my former self, and fall from my transformation to a reformation into Waitwell. Nay, I shan't be quite the same Waitwell neither—for now I remember me, I am married, and can't be my own man again.

Ay, there's the grief; that's the sad change of life:
To lose my title, and yet keep my wife. [*Exeunt*

ACT III

A room in LADY WISHFORT'S *house.* LADY WISHFORT *at her toilet,* PEG *waiting*

LADY W. Merciful,[1] no news of Foible yet?

PEG. No, madam.

LADY W. I have no more patience. If I have not fretted myself till I am pale again, there's no veracity in me. Fetch me the red—the red, do you hear, sweetheart? An errant[2] ash color, as I'm a person. Look you how this wench stirs! Didst thou not hear me, mopus?[3]

PEG. The red ratafia, does your Ladyship mean, or the cherry brandy?

LADY W. Ratafia, fool! No, fool. Not the ratafia, fool—grant me patience! I mean the Spanish paper,[4] idiot—complexion, darling. Paint, paint, paint; dost thou understand that, changeling, dangling thy hands like bobbins before thee? Why dost thou not stir, puppet?—thou wooden thing upon wires!

PEG. Lord, madam, your Ladyship is so impatient. I cannot come at the paint, madam; Mrs. Foible has locked it up, and carried the key with her.

LADY W. A pox take you both! Fetch me the cherry brandy, then. (*Exit* PEG.) I'm as pale and as faint, I look like Mrs. Qualmsick, the curate's wife, that's always breeding.—Wench, come, come, wench, what art thou doing, sipping? tasting? Save thee, dost thou not know the bottle?

Re-enter PEG *with a bottle and china cup*

PEG. Madam, I was looking for a cup.

LADY W. A cup, save thee, and what a cup hast thou brought! Dost thou take me for a fairy, to drink out of an acorn? Why didst thou not bring thy thimble? Hast thou ne'er a brass thimble clinking in thy pocket with a bit of nutmeg? I warrant thee. Come, fill, fill.—So—again. (*One knocks.*) See who that is.—Set down the bottle first. Here, here, under the table. What, wouldst thou go with the bottle in thy hand like a tapster? (*Exit* PEG.) As I'm a person, this wench has lived in an inn upon the road, before she came to me, like Maritornes the Asturian in *Don Quixote*.[5] (*Re-enter* PEG.) No Foible yet?

PEG. No, madam—Mrs. Marwood.

LADY W. Oh, Marwood! let her come in. Come in, good Marwood.

Enter MRS. MARWOOD

MRS. MAR. I'm surprised to find your Ladyship in dishabille at this time of day.

LADY W. Foible's a lost thing; has been abroad since morning, and never heard of since.

MRS. MAR. I saw her but now, as I came masked through the Park, in conference with Mirabell.

LADY W. With Mirabell! You call my blood into my face, with mentioning that traitor. She durst not have the confidence. I sent her to negotiate an affair, in which if I'm detected I'm undone. If that whee-

---

[29] Get ahead of.
[30] 'Bye, (God) be with you.   [31] Advancement.

[1] *Heavens* understood.   [2] Arrant.   [3] Mope, dull one.
[4] I. e., rouge.

[5] An ugly inn servant from the Asturias in *Don Quixote,* Part I, chap. 16.

dling villain has wrought upon Foible to detect me, I'm ruined. Oh, my dear friend, I'm a wretch of wretches if I'm detected.

MRS. MAR. Oh, madam, you cannot suspect Mrs. Foible's integrity.

LADY W. Oh, he carries poison in his tongue, that would corrupt integrity itself. If she has given him an opportunity, she has as good as put her integrity into his hands. Ah, dear Marwood, what's integrity to an opportunity?—Hark! I hear her. (*To* PEG) Go, you thing, and send her in. (*Exit* PEG.)—Dear friend, retire into my closet, that I may examine her with more freedom.—You'll pardon me, dear friend, I can make bold with you.—There are books over the chimney—Quarles[6] and Prynne,[7] and the *Short View of the Stage,*[8] with Bunyan's works[9] to entertain you. [*Exit* MARWOOD

Enter FOIBLE

LADY W. Oh, Foible, where hast thou been? What hast thou been doing?

FOIB. Madam, I have seen the party.

LADY W. But what hast thou done?

FOIB. Nay, 'tis your Ladyship has done, and are to do; I have only promised. But a man so enamored —so transported! Well, here it is, all that is left; all that is not kissed away. Well, if worshipping of pictures be a sin[10]—poor Sir Rowland, I say.

LADY W. The miniature has been counted like— but hast thou not betrayed me, Foible? Hast thou not detected me to that faithless Mirabell?—What hadst thou to do with him in the Park? Answer me, has he got nothing out of thee?

FOIB. (*aside*). So, the devil has been beforehand with me; what shall I say?—Alas, madam, could I help it, if I met that confident thing? Was I in fault? If you had heard how he used me, and all upon your Ladyship's account, I'm sure you would not suspect my fidelity. Nay, if that had been the worst, I could have borne; but he had a fling at your Ladyship too; and then I could not hold, but, i'faith, I gave him his own.

LADY W. Me? What did the filthy fellow say?

FOIB. Oh, madam, 'tis a shame to say what he said —with his taunts and his fleers,[11] tossing up his nose. "Humh," says he, "what, you are a-hatching some plot," says he, "you are so early abroad, or catering," says he, "ferreting[12] for some disbanded officer, I warrant—half pay is but thin subsistence," says he. "Well, what pension does your lady propose? Let me see," says he, "what, she must come down pretty deep now, she's superannuated," says he, "and ——"

LADY W. Ods my life, I'll have him—I'll have him murdered. I'll have him poisoned. Where does he eat? I'll marry a drawer[13] to have him poisoned in his wine. I'll send for Robin from Locket's[14]— immediately.

FOIB. Poison him? Poisoning's too good for him. Starve him, madam, starve him; marry Sir Rowland, and get him disinherited. Oh, you would bless yourself, to hear what he said.

LADY W. A villain! "Superannuated!"

FOIB. "Humh," says he, "I hear you are laying designs against me, too," says he, "and Mrs. Millamant is to marry my uncle" (he does not suspect a word of your Ladyship); "but," says he, "I'll fit you for that, I warrant you," says he, "I'll hamper you for that," says he, "you and your old frippery[15] too," says he, "I'll handle you—"

LADY W. Audacious villain! handle me, would he durst—"Frippery! old frippery!" Was there ever such a foul-mouthed fellow? I'll be married tomorrow, I'll be contracted tonight.

FOIB. The sooner the better, madam.

LADY W. Will Sir Rowland be here, say'st thou? when, Foible?

FOIB. Incontinently,[16] madam. No new sheriff's wife expects the return of her husband after knighthood with that impatience in which Sir Rowland burns for the dear hour of kissing your Ladyship's hands after dinner.

LADY W. "Frippery! superannuated frippery!" I'll frippery the villain; I'll reduce him to frippery and rags. A tatterdemalion—I hope to see him hung with tatters, like a Long Lane penthouse,[17] or a gibbet-thief.[18] A slander-mouthed railer; I warrant the spendthrift prodigal's in debt as much as the

---

[6] Francis Quarles (1592–1644), whose *Divine Emblems* was one of the most popular religious books of the century.

[7] William Prynne (1600–69), a Puritan lawyer and voluminous author, was heavily fined, imprisoned, pilloried, and branded, and had his ears cut off, a decade before the Civil Wars, for his fanatical writings, among them *Histriomastix, or a Scourge for Stage Players.*

[8] *A Short View of the Immorality and Profaneness of the English Stage* (1698), by Jeremy Collier, the most famous of recent attacks.

[9] Such as *The Pilgrim's Progress* (1678–84). Lady Wishfort's library is not an exhilarating one.

[10] A reference to a Puritan charge.

[11] Gibes.   [12] I.e., in Lady Wishfort's behalf.

[13] Tapster. *Robin* was a standard name for a tavern servant.

[14] A fashionable tavern at Charing Cross.

[15] Cast-off clothes, i.e., old-clothes bag.   [16] Speedily.

[17] Stall, in front of a tradesman's house; it would have a sloping roof. Long Lane, in West Smithfield, was an old-clothes street.

[18] A hanged thief.

million lottery, or the whole court upon a birthday.[19] I'll spoil his credit with his tailor. Yes, he shall have my niece with her fortune, he shall.

FOIB. He! I hope to see him lodge in Ludgate[20] first, and angle into Blackfriars for brass farthings, with an old mitten.

LADY W. Ay, dear Foible; thank thee for that, dear Foible. He has put me out of all patience. I shall never recompose my features to receive Sir Rowland with any economy of face. This wretch has fretted me that I am absolutely decayed. Look, Foible.

FOIB. Your Ladyship has frowned a little too rashly, indeed, madam. There are some cracks discernible in the white varnish.

LADY W. Let me see the glass. Cracks, say'st thou? Why, I am arrantly flayed. I look like an old peeled wall. Thou must repair me, Foible, before Sir Rowland comes, or I shall never keep up to my picture.

FOIB. I warrant you, madam; a little art once made your picture like you; and now a little of the same art must make you like your picture. Your picture must sit for you, madam.

LADY W. But art thou sure Sir Rowland will not fail to come? Or will 'a not fail when he does come? Will he be importunate, Foible, and push? For if he should not be importunate—I shall never break decorums—I shall die with confusion, if I am forced to advance—oh, no, I can never advance—I shall swoon if he should expect advances. No, I hope Sir Rowland is better bred than to put a lady to the necessity of breaking her forms.—I won't be too coy neither. I won't give him despair—but a little disdain is not amiss; a little scorn is alluring.

FOIB. A little scorn becomes your Ladyship.

LADY W. Yes, but tenderness becomes me best—a sort of dyingness. You see that picture has a sort of a—ha, Foible? A swimminess in the eyes—yes, I'll look so—my niece affects it; but she wants features. Is Sir Rowland handsome? Let my toilet be removed —I'll dress above. I'll receive Sir Rowland here. Is he handsome? Don't answer me. I won't know; I'll be surprised. I'll be taken by surprise.

FOIB. By storm, madam. Sir Rowland's a brisk man.

LADY W. Is he! Oh, then he'll importune, if he's a brisk man. I shall save decorums if Sir Rowland

importunes. I have a mortal terror at the apprehension of offending against decorums. Nothing but importunity can surmount decorums. Oh, I'm glad he's a brisk man. Let my things be removed, good Foible.   [Exit

Enter MRS. FAINALL

MRS. FAIN. Oh, Foible, I have been in a fright, lest I should come too late. That devil Marwood saw you in the Park with Mirabell, and I'm afraid will discover it to my Lady.

FOIB. Discover what, madam?

MRS. FAIN. Nay, nay, put not on that strange face. I am privy to the whole design, and know that Waitwell, to whom thou wert this morning married, is to personate Mirabell's uncle, and as such, winning my Lady, to involve her in those difficulties from which Mirabell only must release her, by his making his conditions to have my cousin and her fortune left to her own disposal.

FOIB. Oh, dear madam, I beg your pardon. It was not my confidence in your Ladyship that was deficient; but I thought the former good correspondence between your Ladyship and Mr. Mirabell[21] might have hindered his communicating this secret.

MRS. FAIN. Dear Foible, forget that.

FOIB. Oh, dear madam, Mr. Mirabell is such a sweet, winning gentleman—but your Ladyship is the pattern of generosity. Sweet lady, to be so good! Mr. Mirabell cannot choose but be grateful. I find your Ladyship has his heart still. Now, madam, I can safely tell your Ladyship our success; Mrs. Marwood had told my Lady, but I warrant I managed myself. I turned it all for the better. I told my Lady that Mr. Mirabell railed at her. I laid horrid things to his charge, I'll vow; and my Lady is so incensed that she'll be contracted to Sir Rowland tonight, she says; I warrant I worked her up, that he may have her for asking for, as they say of a Welsh maidenhead.

MRS. FAIN. Oh, rare Foible!

FOIB. Madam, I beg your Ladyship to acquaint Mr. Mirabell of his success. I would be seen as little as possible to speak to him; besides, I believe Madam Marwood watches me. She has a month's mind;[22] but I know Mr. Mirabell can't abide her.—(*Calls.*) John! (*Enter* Footman.) Remove my Lady's toilet. (*Exit* Footman.)—Madam, your servant. My Lady is so impatient, I fear she'll come for me, if I stay.

MRS. FAIN. I'll go with you up the back stairs, lest I should meet her.   [*Exeunt*

[19] The government had raised money by selling chances in a lottery. Apparently it had defaulted payments of the prizes, which were long-term annuities.—On the king's birthday, courtiers were expected to appear in new clothes.

[20] A debtor's prison, in the Blackfriars district. Such appeals for charity were common.

[21] For Mrs. Fainall had been his mistress.

[22] Longing (for Mirabell).

Enter MRS. MARWOOD

MRS. MAR. Indeed, Mrs. Engine,[23] is it thus with you? Are you become a go-between of this importance? Yes, I shall watch you. Why, this wench is the *passe-partout,* a very master-key to everybody's strongbox. My friend Fainall, have you carried it so swimmingly? I thought there was something in it; but it seems it's over with you. Your loathing is not from a want of appetite, then, but from a surfeit. Else you could never be so cool to fall from a principal to be an assistant, to procure for him! A pattern of generosity, that I confess. Well, Mr. Fainall, you have met with your match.—O man, man! Woman, woman! The Devil's an ass: if I were a painter, I would draw him like an idiot, a driveler with a bib and bells. Man should have his head and horns,[24] and woman the rest of him. Poor simple fiend! "Madam Marwood has a month's mind, but he can't abide her."—'Twere better for him you had not been his confessor in that affair, without you could have kept his counsel closer. I shall not prove another pattern of generosity and stalk for him, till he takes his stand to aim at a fortune; he has not obliged me to that with those excesses of himself; and now I'll have none of him. Here comes the good lady, panting ripe; with a heart full of hope, and a head full of care, like any chemist upon the day of projection.[25]

Enter LADY WISHFORT

LADY W. Oh, dear Marwood, what shall I say for this rude forgetfulness—but my dear friend is all goodness.

MRS. MAR. No apologies, dear madam. I have been very well entertained.

LADY W. As I'm a person, I am in a very chaos to think I should so forget myself—but I have such an olio[26] of affairs really I know not what to do.— (*Calls.*) Foible!—I expect my nephew Sir Wilfull every moment too.—Why, Foible!—He means to travel for improvement.

MRS. MAR. Methinks Sir Wilfull should rather think of marrying than traveling at his years. I hear he is turned of forty.

LADY W. Oh, he's in less danger of being spoiled by his travels—I am against my nephew's marrying too young. It will be time enough when he comes back, and has acquired discretion to choose for himself.

MRS. MAR. Methinks Mrs. Millamant and he would make a very fit match. He may travel afterwards. 'Tis a thing very usual with young gentlemen.

LADY W. I promise you I have thought on't—and since 'tis your judgment, I'll think on't again. I assure you I will; I value your judgment extremely. On my word, I'll propose it.

Enter FOIBLE

LADY W. Come, come, Foible—I had forgot my nephew will be here before dinner—I must make haste.

FOIB. Mr. Witwoud and Mr. Petulant are come to dine with your Ladyship.

LADY W. Oh, dear, I can't appear till I'm dressed. Dear Marwood, shall I be free with you again, and beg you to entertain 'em? I'll make all imaginable haste. Dear friend, excuse me.

[*Exeunt* LADY WISHFORT *and* FOIBLE

Enter MRS. MILLAMANT *and* MINCING

MILLA. Sure never anything was so unbred as that odious man.—Marwood, your servant.

MRS. MAR. You have a color; what's the matter?

MILLA. That horrid fellow Petulant has provoked me into a flame—I have broke my fan—Mincing, lend me yours.—Is not all the powder out of my hair?

MRS. MAR. No. What has he done?

MILLA. Nay, he has done nothing; he has only talked. Nay, he has said nothing neither; but he has contradicted everything that has been said. For my part, I thought Witwoud and he would have quarreled.

MINC. I vow, mem, I thought once they would have fit.

MILLA. Well, 'tis a lamentable thing, I'll swear, that one has not the liberty of choosing one's acquaintance as one does one's clothes.

MRS. MAR. If we had the liberty, we should be as weary of one set of acquaintance, though never so good, as we are of one suit, though never so fine. A fool and a doily stuff[27] would now and then find days of grace, and be worn for variety.

MILLA. I could consent to wear 'em, if they would wear alike; but fools never wear out—they are such *drap-de-berry*[28] things!—without one could give 'em to one's chambermaid after a day or two.

---

[23] Contrivance. Mrs. Marwood has heard everything.
[24] Symbol of the cuckold. "The Devil is an ass" was a proverb; Jonson used it as the title of one of his plays.
[25] The final alchemical process.   [26] Hodgepodge.

[27] A cheap woolen fabric.
[28] A woolen textile from Berry in France.

MRS. MAR. 'Twere better so, indeed. Or what think you of the playhouse? A fine gay glossy fool should be given there, like a new masking habit, after the masquerade is over, and we have done with the disguise. For a fool's visit is always a disguise, and never admitted by a woman of wit but to blind her affair with a lover of sense. If you would but appear barefaced now, and own Mirabell, you might as easily put off Petulant and Witwoud as your hood and scarf. And indeed 'tis time, for the town has found it: the secret is grown too big for the pretense: 'tis like Mrs. Primly's great belly; she may lace it down before, but it burnishes[29] on her hips. Indeed, Millamant, you can no more conceal it than my Lady Strammel[30] can her face, that goodly face, which, in defiance of her Rhenish-wine tea,[31] will not be comprehended[32] in a mask.

MILLA. I'll take my death, Marwood, you are more censorious than a decayed beauty, or a discarded toast.[33]—Mincing, tell the men they may come up. My aunt is not dressing. Their folly is less provoking than your malice. (*Exit* MINCING.) The town has found it! What has it found? That Mirabell loves me is no more a secret than it is a secret that you discovered it to my aunt, or than the reason why you discovered it is a secret.

MRS. MAR. You are nettled.

MILLA. You're mistaken. Ridiculous!

MRS. MAR. Indeed, my dear, you'll tear another fan if you don't mitigate those violent airs.

MILLA. Oh, silly! Ha, ha, ha. I could laugh immoderately. Poor Mirabell! His constancy to me has quite destroyed his complaisance for all the world beside. I swear, I never enjoined it him to be so coy. If I had the vanity to think he would obey me, I would command him to show more gallantry. 'Tis hardly well-bred to be so particular on one hand, and so insensible on the other. But I despair to prevail; and so let him follow his own way. Ha, ha, ha. Pardon me, dear creature, I must laugh, ha, ha, ha; though I grant you 'tis a little barbarous, ha, ha, ha.

MRS. MAR. What pity 'tis, so much fine raillery, and delivered with so significant gesture, should be so unhappily directed to miscarry.

MILLA. Heh? Dear creature I ask your pardon—I swear I did not mind you.[34]

MRS. MAR. Mr. Mirabell and you both may think it a thing impossible, when I shall tell him by telling you—

MILLA. Oh, dear, what? for it is the same thing, if I hear it—ha, ha, ha.

MRS. MAR. That I detest him, hate him, madam.

MILLA. Oh, madam, why, so do I—and yet the creature loves me, ha, ha, ha. How can one forbear laughing to think of it—I am a sibyl[35] if I am not amazed to think what he can see in me. I'll take my death, I think you are handsomer—and within a year or two as young. If you could but stay for me, I should overtake you—but that cannot be. Well, that thought makes me melancholy. Now I'll be sad.

MRS. MAR. Your merry note may be changed sooner than you think.

MILLA. D'ee say so? Then I'm resolved I'll have a song to keep up my spirits.

Enter MINCING

MINC. The gentlemen stay but to comb,[36] madam, and will wait on you.

MILLA. Desire Mrs. ——, that is in the next room, to sing the song I would have learnt yesterday.— You shall hear it, madam. Not that there's any great matter in it—but 'tis agreeable to my humor.

SONG

Set by MR. JOHN ECCLES,[37] *and sung by* MRS. HODGSON

1

Love's but the frailty of the mind,
    When 'tis not with ambition joined;
A sickly flame, which if not fed expires,
And, feeding, wastes in self-consuming fires.

2

'Tis not to wound a wanton boy
    Or amorous youth that gives the joy;
But 'tis the glory to have pierced a swain
For whom inferior beauties sighed in vain.

3

Then I alone the conquest prize,
    When I insult a rival's eyes;
If there's delight in love, 'tis when I see
That heart which others bleed for, bleed for me.

Enter PETULANT *and* WITWOUD

MILLA. Is your animosity composed, gentlemen?

---

29 Spreads out.   30 Gaunt; perhaps=horse-face.
31 Taken for reducing.   32 Enclosed.
33 A former beauty, no longer the toast of the town.
34 Pay attention.

35 I.e., an old crone.   36 Their wigs.
37 Eccles (d. 1735) wrote incidental music for many plays. Mrs. Hodgson was a well-known singer.

WIT. Raillery, raillery, madam; we have no animosity—we hit off a little wit now and then, but no animosity. The falling out of wits is like the falling out of lovers. We agree in the main, like treble and bass. Ha, Petulant?

PET. Ay, in the main. But when I have a humor to contradict—

WIT. Ay, when he has a humor to contradict, then I contradict too. What, I know my cue. Then we contradict one another like two battledores, for contradictions beget one another like Jews.

PET. If he says black's black—if I have a humor to say 'tis blue—let that pass—all's one for that. If I have a humor to prove it, it must be granted.

WIT. Not positively must—but it may—it may.

PET. Yes, it positively must, upon proof positive.

WIT. Ay, upon proof positive it must; but upon proof presumptive it only may. That's a logical distinction now, madam.

MRS. MAR. I perceive your debates are of importance, and very learnedly handled.

PET. Importance is one thing, and learning's another; but a debate's a debate, that I assert.

WIT. Petulant's an enemy to learning; he relies altogether on his parts.[38]

PET. No, I'm no enemy to learning; it hurts not me.

MRS. MAR. That's a sign indeed it's no enemy to you.

PET. No, no, it's no enemy to anybody, but them that have it.

MILLA. Well, an illiterate man's my aversion. I wonder at the impudence of any illiterate man, to offer to make love.

WIT. That I confess I wonder at too.

MILLA. Ah! to marry an ignorant! that can hardly read or write.

PET. Why should a man be ever the further from being married though he can't read, any more than he is from being hanged? The ordinary's[39] paid for setting the psalm, and the parish priest for reading the ceremony. And for the rest which is to follow in both cases, a man may do it[40] without book—so all's one for that.

MILLA. D'ee hear the creature? Lord, here's company; I'll be gone. [Exeunt MILLAMANT and MINCING

WIT. In the name of Bartlemew and his fair,[41] what have we here?

MRS. MAR. 'Tis your brother, I fancy. Don't you know him?

WIT. Not I—yes, I think it is he—I've almost forgot him; I have not seen him since the Revolution.[42]

Enter SIR WILFULL WITWOUD in a country riding-habit, and a Servant to LADY WISHFORT

SERV. Sir, my Lady's dressing. Here's company, if you please to walk in, in the meantime.

SIR WIL. Dressing! What, it's but morning here, I warrant, with you in London; we should count it towards afternoon in our parts, down in Shropshire. Why, then belike my aunt han't dined yet—ha, friend?

SERV. Your aunt, sir?

SIR WIL. My aunt, sir, yes, my aunt, sir, and your lady, sir; your lady is my aunt, sir. Why, what, dost thou not know me, friend? Why, then send somebody here that does. How long hast thou lived with thy lady, fellow, ha?

SERV. A week, sir; longer than anybody in the house, except my Lady's woman.

SIR WIL. Why, then belike thou dost not know thy lady if thou see'st her, ha, friend?

SERV. Why, truly, sir, I cannot safely swear to her face in a morning, before she is dressed. 'Tis like I may give a shrewd guess at her by this time.

SIR WIL. Well, prithee try what thou canst do; if thou canst not guess, enquire her out, dost hear, fellow? And tell her, her nephew, Sir Wilfull Witwoud, is in the house.

SERV. I shall, sir.

SIR WIL. Hold ye, hear me, friend; a word with you in your ear; prithee who are these gallants?

SERV. Really, sir, I can't tell; here come so many here, 'tis hard to know 'em all. [Exit

SIR WIL. Oons,[43] this fellow knows less than a starling; I don't think a knows his own name.

MRS. MAR. Mr. Witwoud, your brother is not behindhand in forgetfulness—I fancy he has forgot you too.

WIT. I hope so—the Devil take him that remembers first, I say.

SIR WIL. Save you, gentlemen and lady.

MRS. MAR. For shame, Mr. Witwoud; why won't you speak to him? And you, sir.

WIT. Petulant, speak.

PET. And you, sir.

SIR WIL. No offense, I hope. [Salutes[44] MARWOOD

MRS. MAR. No, sure, sir.

---

[38] Talents. [39] Prison chaplain. [40] Be hanged or married.
[41] He implies that the approaching Sir Wilfull looks like one of the freaks exhibited at Bartholomew Fair.

[42] Which dethroned James II in 1688. [43] For God's wounds.
[44] Kisses. An old English custom, once as common as shaking hands.

WIT. This is a vile dog, I see that already. No offense! Ha, ha, ha. To him; to him, Petulant; smoke[45] him.

PET. It seems as if you had come a journey, sir; hem, hem. [Surveying him round

SIR WIL. Very likely, sir, that it may seem so.

PET. No offense, I hope, sir.

WIT. Smoke the boots, the boots; Petulant, the boots; ha, ha, ha!

SIR WIL. Maybe not, sir; thereafter as 'tis meant, sir.

PET. Sir, I presume upon the information of your boots.

SIR WIL. Why, 'tis like you may, sir. If you are not satisfied with the information of my boots, sir, if you will step to the stable, you may enquire further of my horse, sir.

PET. Your horse, sir! Your horse is an ass, sir!

SIR WIL. Do you speak by way of offense, sir?

MRS. MAR. The gentleman's merry, that's all, sir.— (Aside) 'Slife, we shall have a quarrel betwixt an horse and an ass, before they find one another out.— You must not take anything amiss from your friends, sir. You are among your friends here, though it may be you don't know it. If I am not mistaken, you are Sir Wilfull Witwoud.

SIR WIL. Right, lady; I am Sir Wilfull Witwoud, so I write myself, no offense to anybody, I hope, and nephew to the Lady Wishfort of this mansion.

MRS. MAR. Don't you know this gentleman, sir?

SIR WIL. Hum! What, sure 'tis not—yea, by'r Lady, but 'tis—'sheart, I know not whether 'tis or no.— Yea, but 'tis, by the Wrekin.[46] Brother Antony! What, Tony, i' faith! What, dost thou not know me? By'r Lady, nor I thee, thou art so becravated and so beperiwigged.—'Sheart, why dost not speak? Art thou o'erjoyed?

WIT. Odso,[47] brother, is it you? Your servant, brother.

SIR WIL. Your servant! Why, yours, sir. Your servant again.—'Sheart, and your friend and servant to that—and a—(puff) and a flapdragon[48] for your service, sir; and a hare's foot and a hare's scut[49] for your service, sir, an[50] you be so cold and so courtly!

WIT. No offense, I hope, brother.

SIR WIL. 'Sheart, sir, but there is, and much offense. —A pox, is this your Inns o' Court[51] breeding, not to know your friends and your relations, your elders, and your betters?

WIT. Why, brother Wilfull of Salop,[52] you may be as short as a Shrewsbury cake, if you please. But I tell you 'tis not modish to know relations in town. You think you're in the country, where great lubberly brothers slabber and kiss one another when they meet, like a call of sergeants.[53] 'Tis not the fashion here; 'tis not indeed, dear brother.

SIR WIL. The fashion's a fool, and you're a fop, dear brother. 'Sheart, I've suspected this. By'r Lady, I conjectured you were a fop since you began to change the style of your letters and write in a scrap of paper gilt round the edges, no broader than a subpoena. I might expect this when you left off "Honored Brother" and "Hoping you are in good health," and so forth—to begin with a "Rat[54] me, knight, I'm so sick of a last night's debauch"—Od's-heart, and then tell a familiar tale of a cock and a bull,[55] and a whore and a bottle, and so conclude. You could write news before you were out of your time,[56] when you lived with honest Pumple-Nose, the attorney of Furnival's Inn.[57] You could entreat to be remembered then to your friends round the Wrekin. We could have gazettes then, and Dawks's Letter,[58] and the weekly bill,[59] till of late days.

PET. 'Slife, Witwoud, were you ever an attorney's clerk? Of the family of the Furnivals. Ha, ha, ha!

WIT. Ay, ay, but that was for a while. Not long, not long; pshaw, I was not in my own power then. An orphan, and this fellow was my guardian; ay, ay, I was glad to consent to that, man, to come to London. He had the disposal of me then. If I had not agreed to that, I might have been bound prentice to a feltmaker in Shrewsbury; this fellow would have bound me to a maker of felts.

SIR WIL. 'Sheart, and better than to be bound to a maker of fops; where, I suppose, you have served your time; and now you may set up for yourself.

MRS. MAR. You intend to travel, sir, as I'm informed.

SIR WIL. Belike I may, madam. I may chance to sail upon the salt seas, if my mind hold.

---

45 Banter, chaff.
46 A high hill in the middle of Shropshire.
47 For the exclamation Godso.
48 A raisin, in burning brandy, from which the game was to snatch and eat it.   49 Tail.   50 If.

51 The four inns of court, where the law students lived, had charge of admission to the bar.
52 Shropshire. Shrewsbury is the county town. Cake=cookie.
53 A group of sergeants at law (a superior rank of lawyers) called to that rank at the same time.   54 For God rot.
55 I.e., an incredible one.
56 Had finished your apprenticeship.—Pumple=pimple.
57 An adjunct of Lincoln's, one of the four inns of court.
58 A news sheet, printed in type imitative of handwriting, with space left for private correspondence.
59 List of deaths.

PET. And the wind serve.

SIR WIL. Serve or not serve, I shan't ask license of you, sir; nor the weathercock, your companion. I direct my discourse to the lady, sir.—'Tis like my aunt may have told you, madam—yes, I have settled my concerns, I may say now, and am minded to see foreign parts. If an how that the peace holds, whereby, that is, taxes abate.[60]

MRS. MAR. I thought you had designed for France at all adventures.[61]

SIR WIL. I can't tell that; 'tis like I may, and 'tis like I may not. I am somewhat dainty in making a resolution—because when I make it I keep it. I don't stand shill I, shall I, then; if I say't, I'll do't. But I have thoughts to tarry a small matter in town, to learn somewhat of your[62] lingo first, before I cross the seas. I'd gladly have a spice of your French, as they say, whereby to hold discourse in foreign countries.

MRS. MAR. Here is an academy in town for that use.

SIR WIL. There is? 'Tis like there may.

MRS. MAR. No doubt you will return very much improved.

WIT. Yes, refined, like a Dutch skipper from a whale-fishing.[63]

Enter LADY WISHFORT *and* FAINALL

LADY W. Nephew, you are welcome.

SIR WIL. Aunt, your servant.

FAIN. Sir Wilfull, your most faithful servant.

SIR WIL. Cousin Fainall, give me your hand.

LADY W. Cousin Witwoud, your servant; Mr. Petulant, your servant.—Nephew, you are welcome again. Will you drink anything after your journey, nephew, before you eat? Dinner's almost ready.

SIR WIL. I'm very well, I thank you, aunt—however, I thank you for your courteous offer. 'Sheart, I was afraid you would have been in the fashion too, and have remembered to have forgot your relations. Here's your cousin Tony; belike I mayn't call him brother for fear of offense.

LADY W. Oh, he's a rallier, nephew—my cousin's a wit; and your great wits always rally their best friends to choose.[64] When you have been abroad, nephew, you'll understand raillery better.

[FAINALL *and* MRS. MARWOOD *talk apart*

SIR WIL. Why, then let him hold his tongue in the meantime, and rail when that day comes.

Enter MINCING

MINC. Mem, I come to acquaint your La'ship that dinner is impatient.

SIR WIL. Impatient? Why, then belike it won't stay till I pull off my boots. Sweetheart, can you help me to a pair of slippers? My man's with his horses, I warrant.

LADY W. Fie, fie, nephew, you would not pull off your boots here. Go down into the hall—dinner shall stay for you.—My nephew's a little unbred; you'll pardon him, madam.—Gentlemen, will you walk?—Marwood?

MRS. MAR. I'll follow you, madam, before Sir Wilfull is ready.

[*Exeunt all except* MRS. MARWOOD *and* FAINALL

FAIN. Why, then Foible's a bawd, an errant, rank matchmaking bawd. And I, it seems, am a husband, a rank husband; and my wife a very errant, rank wife—all in the way of the world. 'Sdeath, to be an anticipated cuckold, a cuckold in embryo! Sure I was born with budding antlers like a young satyr, or a citizen's child.[65] 'Sdeath, to be outwitted, to be out-jilted—out-matrimonied! If I had kept my speed like a stag, 'twere somewhat; but to crawl after, with my horns, like a snail, and be outstripped by my wife—'tis scurvy wedlock.

MRS. MAR. Then shake it off; you have often wished for an opportunity to part, and now you have it. But first prevent their plot—the half of Millamant's fortune is too considerable to be parted with, to a foe, to Mirabell.

FAIN. Damn him, that had been mine, had you not made that fond[66] discovery—that had been forfeited, had they been married. My wife had added luster to my horns, by that increase of fortune. I could have worn 'em tipt with gold, though my forehead had been furnished like a deputy-lieutenant's hall.[67]

MRS. MAR. They may prove a cap of maintenance[68] to you still, if you can away with your wife. And she's no worse than when you had her—I dare swear she had given up her game before she was married.

---

[60] Taxes had been less since the war with France was suspended by the Peace of Ryswick (1697). [61] Anyway.
[62] I.e., the.
[63] The smelly process of refining was carried out on board.
[64] By choice.

[65] Daughter—destined to be seduced by a gallant. *Citizen*=tradesman, bourgeois. [66] Foolish.
[67] I.e., though I had been cuckolded as many times as there are horns of deer hung in the hall of the deputy lord-lieutenant of a county.
[68] A cap worn or carried before certain high officials; a pun on the meaning *support*.

FAIN. Hum! That may be. She might throw up her cards, but I'll be hanged if she did not put Pam[69] in her pocket.

MRS. MAR. You married her to keep you; and if you can contrive to have her keep you better than you expected, why should you not keep her longer than you intended?

FAIN. The means, the means!

MRS. MAR. Discover to my Lady your wife's conduct; threaten to part with her. My Lady loves her, and will come to any composition[70] to save her reputation. Take the opportunity of breaking it,[71] just upon the discovery of this imposture. My Lady will be enraged beyond bounds, and sacrifice niece and fortune and all at that conjuncture. And let me alone[72] to keep her warm; if she should flag in her part, I will not fail to prompt her.

FAIN. Faith, this has an appearance.

MRS. MAR. I'm sorry I hinted to my Lady to endeavor a match between Millamant and Sir Wilfull; that may be an obstacle.

FAIN. Oh, for that matter leave me to manage him. I'll disable him for that; he will drink like a Dane—after dinner, I'll set his hand in.[73]

MRS. MAR. Well, how do you stand affected towards your lady?

FAIN. Why, faith, I'm thinking of it.—Let me see—I am married already; so that's over.—My wife has played the jade with me—well, that's over, too.—I never loved her, or if I had, why, that would have been over too by this time.—Jealous[74] of her I cannot be, for I am certain; so there's an end of jealousy. Weary of her, I am and shall be.—No, there's no end of that; no, no, that were too much to hope. Thus far concerning my repose. Now for my reputation. As to my own, I married not for it; so that's out of the question. And as to my part in my wife's—why, she had parted with hers before; so, bringing none to me, she can take none from me; 'tis against all rule of play, that I should lose to one who has not wherewithal to stake.

MRS. MAR. Besides, you forget, marriage is honorable.

FAIN. Hum! Faith, and that's well thought on; marriage is honorable, as you say; and if so, wherefore should cuckoldom be a discredit, being derived from so honorable a root?

MRS. MAR. Nay, I know not; if the root be honorable, why not the branches?[75]

FAIN. So, so; why, this point's clear.—Well, how do we proceed?

MRS. MAR. I will contrive a letter which shall be delivered to my Lady at the time when that rascal who is to act Sir Rowland is with her. It shall come as from an unknown hand—for the less I appear to know of the truth, the better I can play the incendiary. Besides, I would not have Foible provoked if I could help it, because you know she knows some passages. Nay, I expect all will come out—but let the mine be sprung first, and then I care not if I'm discovered.

FAIN. If the worst come to the worst, I'll turn my wife out to grass. I have already a deed of settlement of the best part of her estate, which I wheedled out of her; and that you shall partake at least.

MRS. MAR. I hope you are convinced that I hate Mirabell; now you'll be no more jealous.

FAIN. Jealous, no—by this kiss; let husbands be jealous, but let the lover still believe; or if he doubt, let it be only to endear his pleasure, and prepare the joy that follows, when he proves his mistress true. But let husbands' doubts convert to endless jealousy; or if they have belief, let it corrupt to superstition and blind credulity. I am single, and will herd no more with 'em. True, I wear the badge;[76] but I'll disown the order. And since I take my leave of 'em, I care not if I leave 'em a common motto to their common crest:

All husbands must or pain or shame endure;
The wise too jealous are, fools too secure.

[*Exeunt*

---

[69] The jack of clubs, highest trump in the fashionable game of 100.
[70] Terms.   [71] The news.   [72] Leave it to me.
[73] Start him.   [74] Suspicious.

[75] With another allusion to the cuckold's horns.
[76] I.e., my horns.

Scene continues. Enter LADY WISHFORT *and* FOIBLE

LADY W. Is Sir Rowland coming, say'st thou, Foible? and are things in order?

FOIB. Yes, madam. I have put waxlights in the sconces, and placed the footmen in a row in the hall, in their best liveries, with the coachman and postilion to fill up the equipage.[1]

LADY W. Have you pulvilled[2] the coachman and postilion, that they may not stink of the stable when Sir Rowland comes by?

FOIB. Yes, madam.

LADY W. And are the dancers and the music ready, that he may be entertained in all points with correspondence to his passion?

FOIB. All is ready, madam.

LADY W. And—well—and how do I look, Foible?

FOIB. Most killing well, madam.

LADY W. Well, and how shall I receive him? In what figure shall I give his heart the first impression? There is a great deal in the first impression. Shall I sit?—No, I won't sit—I'll walk—ay, I'll walk from the door upon his entrance; and then turn full upon him—no, that will be too sudden. I'll lie—ay, I'll lie down—I'll receive him in my little dressing-room; there's a couch—yes, yes, I'll give the first impression on a couch.—I won't lie neither, but loll and lean upon one elbow, with one foot a little dangling off, jogging in a thoughtful way—yes—and then, as soon as he appears, start, ay, start and be surprised, and rise to meet him in a pretty disorder—yes—oh, nothing is more alluring than a levee[3] from a couch in some confusion—it shows the foot to advantage, and furnishes with blushes and recomposing airs beyond comparison. Hark! There's a coach.

FOIB. 'Tis he, madam.

LADY W. Oh, dear, has my nephew made his addresses to Millamant? I ordered him.

FOIB. Sir Wilfull is set in[4] to drinking, madam, in the parlor.

LADY W. Ods my life, I'll send him to her. Call her down, Foible; bring her hither. I'll send him as I go. When they are together, then come to me, Foible, that I may not be too long alone with Sir Rowland. [*Exit*

Enter MRS. MILLAMANT *and* MRS. FAINALL

FOIB. Madam, I stayed here, to tell your Ladyship that Mr. Mirabell has waited this half hour for an opportunity to talk with you, though my Lady's orders were to leave you and Sir Wilfull together. Shall I tell Mr. Mirabell that you are at leisure?

MILLA. No—what would the dear man have? I am thoughtful, and would amuse myself—bid him come another time. (*Repeating and walking about*)

> There never yet was woman made,
> Nor shall, but to be cursed—

That's hard!

MRS. FAIN. You are very fond of Sir John Suckling[5] today, Millamant, and the poets.

MILLA. He? Ay, and filthy verses—so I am.

FOIB. Sir Wilfull is coming, madam. Shall I send Mr. Mirabell away?

MILLA. Ay, if you please, Foible, send him away—or send him hither—just as you will, dear Foible.—I think I'll see him—shall I? Ay, let the wretch come. (*Exit* FOIB.) (*Repeating*)

> Thyrsis, a youth of the inspirèd train—[6]

Dear Fainall, entertain Sir Wilfull—thou hast philosophy to undergo a fool; thou art married, and hast patience—I would confer with my own thoughts.

MRS. FAIN. I am obliged to you, that you would make me your proxy in this affair; but I have business of my own.

Enter SIR WILFULL

Oh, Sir Wilfull, you are come at the critical instant. There's your mistress up to the ears in love and contemplation; pursue your point, now or never.

SIR WIL. Yes; my aunt would have it so—I would gladly have been encouraged with a bottle or two, because I'm somewhat wary at first, before I am acquainted. (*This while* MILLAMANT *walks about repeating to herself.*) But I hope, after a time, I shall break

---

[1] Retinue.   [2] Perfumed with powder.   [3] Rising.
[4] Cf. Act III, note 73.

[5] See p. 519, above. These are the opening lines of an untitled poem by Suckling.
[6] From "The Story of Phoebus and Daphne, Applied," by Edmund Waller (pp. 517 ff., above). The same poem is the source of the line quoted by Millamant as Mirabell enters, below, and the line with which he caps her quotation.

my mind—that is, upon further acquaintance.—So for the present, cousin, I'll take my leave—if so be you'll be so kind to make my excuse, I'll return to my company—

MRS. FAIN. Oh, fie, Sir Wilfull! What, you must not be daunted.

SIR WIL. Daunted! no, that's not it, it is not so much for that—for if so be that I set on't, I'll do't. But only for the present, 'tis sufficient till further acquaintance, that's all—your servant.

MRS. FAIN. Nay, I'll swear you shall never lose so favorable an opportunity, if I can help it. I'll leave you together, and lock the door.   [*Exit*

SIR WIL. Nay, nay, cousin—I have forgot my gloves. What d'ee do?—'Sheart, a has locked the door indeed, I think.—Nay, cousin Fainall, open the door.—Pshaw, what a vixen trick is this!—Nay, now a has seen me, too.—Cousin, I made bold to pass through, as it were—I think this door's enchanted—

MILLA. (*repeating*).

> I prithee spare me, gentle boy;
> Press me no more for that slight toy—[7]

SIR WIL. Anan?[8] Cousin, your servant.

MILLA. (*repeating*).

> That foolish trifle of a heart—

Sir Wilfull!

SIR WIL. Yes—your servant. No offense, I hope, cousin.

MILLA. (*repeating*).

> I swear it will not do its part,
> Though thou dost thine, employ'st thy power and art.

Natural, easy Suckling!

SIR WIL. Anan? Suckling? No such suckling neither, cousin, nor stripling. I thank heaven, I'm no minor.

MILLA. Ah, rustic, ruder than Gothic.[9]

SIR WIL. Well, well, I shall understand your lingo one of these days, cousin; in the meanwhile I must answer in plain English.

MILLA. Have you any business with me, Sir Wilfull?

SIR WIL. Not at present, cousin.—Yes, I made bold to see, to come and know if that how you were disposed to fetch a walk this evening; if so be that I might not be troublesome, I would have fought[10] a walk with you.

MILLA. A walk? What then?

SIR WIL. Nay, nothing—only for the walk's sake, that's all—

MILLA. I nauseate walking; 'tis a country diversion; I loathe the country and everything that relates to it.

SIR WIL. Indeed! Hah! Look ye, look ye, you do? Nay, 'tis like you may.—Here are choice of pastimes here in town, as plays and the like; that must be confessed indeed—

MILLA. Ah, *l'étourdie*![11] I hate the town too.

SIR WIL. Dear heart, that's much. Hah! that you should hate 'em both! Hah! 'tis like you may; there are some can't relish the town, and others can't away with the country—'tis like you may be one of those, cousin.

MILLA. Ha, ha, ha! Yes, 'tis like I may.—You have nothing further to say to me?

SIR WIL. Not at present, cousin.—'Tis like when I have an opportunity to be more private, I may break my mind in some measure—I conjecture you partly guess.—However, that's as time shall try—but spare to speak and spare to speed, as they say.

MILLA. If it is of no great importance, Sir Wilfull, you will oblige me to leave me. I have just now a little business—

SIR WIL. Enough, enough, cousin; yes, yes, all a case[12]—when you're disposed, when you're disposed. Now's as well as another time; and another time as well as now. All's one for that—yes, yes, if your concerns call you, there's no haste; it will keep cold, as they say.—Cousin, your servant.—I think this door's locked.

MILLA. You may go this way, sir.

SIR WIL. Your servant! then with your leave I'll return to my company.   [*Exit*

MILLA. Ay, ay; ha, ha, ha!

> Like Phoebus sung the no less am'rous boy.

Enter MIRABELL

MIRA.

> Like Daphne she, as lovely and as coy.

Do you lock yourself up from me to make my search more curious?[13] Or is this pretty artifice contrived to signify that here the chase must end, and my pursuit be crowned; for you can fly no further?

MILLA. Vanity! No—I'll fly and be followed to the last moment. Though I am upon the very verge of matrimony, I expect you should solicit me as much

---

[7] *Trifle.*—The five lines are the first stanza of another untitled poem by Suckling.   [8] *How's that?*

[9] I.e., a barbarian.

[10] Fetched; cf. Sir Wilfull's provincialism with our own *fotched.*

[11] The giddy (town).   [12] All the same.   [13] Intricate.

as if I were wavering at the grate of a monastery,[14] with one foot over the threshold. I'll be solicited to the very last, nay, and afterwards.

MIRA. What, after the last?

MILLA. Oh, I should think I was poor and had nothing to bestow, if I were reduced to an inglorious ease, and freed from the agreeable fatigues of solicitation.

MIRA. But do not you know that, when favors are conferred upon instant[15] and tedious solicitation, that they diminish in their value, and that both the giver loses the grace and the receiver lessens his pleasure?

MILLA. It may be in things of common application, but never sure in love. Oh, I hate a lover that can dare to think he draws a moment's air, independent on[16] the bounty of his mistress. There is not so impudent a thing in nature as the saucy look of an assured man, confident of success. The pedantic arrogance of a very husband has not so pragmatical[17] an air. Ah! I'll never marry, unless I am first made sure of my will and pleasure.

MIRA. Would you have 'em both before marriage? Or will you be contented with the first now, and stay for the other till after grace?[18]

MILLA. Ah, don't be impertinent.—My dear liberty, shall I leave thee? My faithful solitude, my darling contemplation, must I bid you then adieu? Ay-h, adieu—my morning thoughts, agreeable wakings, indolent slumbers, all ye *douceurs,* ye *sommeils du matin,*[19] adieu—I can't do 't, 'tis more than impossible. Positively, Mirabell, I'll lie abed in a morning as long as I please.

MIRA. Then I'll get up in a morning as early as I please.

MILLA. Ah! Idle creature, get up when you will.—And d'ee hear, I won't be called names after I'm married; positively I won't be called names.

MIRA. Names!

MILLA. Ay, as wife, spouse, my dear, joy, jewel, love, sweetheart, and the rest of that nauseous cant, in which men and their wives are so fulsomely familiar—I shall never bear that. Good Mirabell, don't let us be familiar or fond, nor kiss before folks, like my Lady Fadler[20] and Sir Francis; nor go to Hyde Park together the first Sunday in a new chariot, to provoke eyes and whispers, and then never to be seen there together again, as if we were proud of one another the first week, and ashamed of one another for ever after. Let us never visit together, nor go to a play together; but let us be very strange[21] and well-bred: let us be as strange as if we had been married a great while, and as well-bred as if we were not married at all.

MIRA. Have you any more conditions to offer? Hitherto your demands are pretty reasonable.

MILLA. Trifles—as liberty to pay and receive visits to and from whom I please; to write and receive letters, without interrogatories or wry faces on your part; to wear what I please, and choose conversation with regard only to my own taste; to have no obligation upon me to converse with wits that I don't like, because they are your acquaintance, or to be intimate with fools because they may be your relations. Come to dinner when I please, dine in my dressing-room when I'm out of humor, without giving a reason. To have my closet[22] inviolate; to be sole empress of my tea-table, which you must never presume to approach without first asking leave. And lastly, wherever I am, you shall always knock at the door before you come in. These articles subscribed, if I continue to endure you a little longer, I may by degrees dwindle into a wife.

MIRA. Your bill of fare is something advanced[23] in this latter account. Well, have I liberty to offer conditions—that, when you are dwindled into a wife, I may not be beyond measure enlarged into a husband?

MILLA. You have free leave; propose your utmost: speak and spare not.

MIRA. I thank you. *Imprimis*[24] then, I covenant that your acquaintance be general; that you admit no sworn confidant or intimate of your own sex, no she-friend to screen her affairs under your countenance,[25] and tempt you to make trial of a mutual secrecy. No decoy-duck to wheedle you a-fop-scrambling to the play[26] in a mask—then bring you home in a pretended fright, when you think you shall be found out—and rail at me for missing the play, and disappointing the frolic which you had, to pick me up and prove my constancy.

MILLA. Detestable *imprimis*! I go to the play in a mask!

MIRA. *Item*, I article,[27] that you continue to like your own face as long as I shall; and while it passes current with me, that you endeavor not to new coin it. To which end, together with all vizards for the

[14] Barred window of a convent.   [15] Urgent.   [16] Of.
[17] Officious.   [18] I.e., the ceremony.
[19] Ye sweetnesses, ye morning slumbers.   [20] Fondler.

[21] Distant, reserved.   [22] Private room, boudoir.
[23] Increased.   [24] In the first place.   [25] Approval, aid.
[26] Wheedle you into going to the play in order to scramble for (the attentions of) a fop.   [27] Stipulate.

day, I prohibit all masks[28] for the night, made of oiled skins and I know not what—hog's bones, hare's gall, pig water,[29] and the marrow of a roasted cat. In short, I forbid all commerce with the gentlewoman in What-d'ye-call-it Court.[30] *Item,* I shut my doors against all bawds with baskets, and pennyworths of muslin, china, fans, atlases,[31] etc.—*Item,* when you shall be breeding—

MILLA. Ah, name it not.

MIRA. Which may be presumed, with a blessing on our endeavors—

MILLA. Odious endeavors!

MIRA. I denounce against all strait[32] lacing, squeezing for a shape, till you mold my boy's head like a sugar-loaf; and instead of a man-child, make me the father to a crooked billet. Lastly, to the dominion of the tea-table I submit—but with proviso that you exceed not in your province, but restrain yourself to native and simple tea-table drinks, as tea, chocolate, and coffee; as likewise to genuine and authorized tea-table talk—such as mending of fashions, spoiling reputations, railing at absent friends, and so forth—but that on no account you encroach upon the men's prerogative, and presume to drink healths or toast fellows; for prevention of which I banish all foreign forces, all auxiliaries to the tea-table, as orange brandy, all aniseed, cinnamon, citron, and Barbadoes[33] waters, together with ratafia and the most noble spirit of clary.[34] But for[35] cowslip wine, poppy water, and all dormitives,[36] those I allow.—These provisos admitted, in other things I may prove a tractable and complying husband.

MILLA. Oh, horrid provisos! filthy strong waters! I toast fellows, odious men! I hate your odious provisos.

MIRA. Then we're agreed. Shall I kiss your hand upon the contract? and here comes one to be a witness to the sealing of the deed.

Enter MRS. FAINALL

MILLA. Fainall, what shall I do? Shall I have him? I think I must have him.

MRS. FAIN. Ay, ay, take him, take him; what should you do?

MILLA. Well, then—I'll take my death, I'm in a horrid fright—Fainall, I shall never say it—well—I think—I'll endure you.

MRS. FAIN. Fie, fie! have him, have him, and tell him so in plain terms; for I am sure you have a mind to him.

MILLA. Are you? I think I have—and the horrid man looks as if he thought so too.—Well, you ridiculous thing, you, I'll have you—I won't be kissed, nor I won't be thanked—here, kiss my hand, though—so, hold your tongue now, and don't say a word.

MRS. FAIN. Mirabell, there's a necessity for your obedience—you have neither time to talk nor stay. My mother is coming, and in my conscience, if she should see you, would fall into fits, and maybe not recover time enough to return to Sir Rowland; who, as Foible tells me, is in a fair way to succeed. Therefore, spare your ecstasies for another occasion, and slip down the back stairs, where Foible waits to consult you.

MILLA. Ay, go, go. In the meantime, I suppose you have said something to please me.

MIRA. I am all obedience.   [*Exit*

MRS. FAIN. Yonder Sir Wilfull's drunk, and so noisy that my mother has been forced to leave Sir Rowland to appease him; but he answers her only with singing and drinking. What they have done by this time I know not, but Petulant and he were upon quarreling as I came by.

MILLA. Well, if Mirabell should not make a good husband, I am a lost thing; for I find I love him violently.

MRS. FAIN. So it seems, when you mind not what's said to you. If you doubt him, you had best take up with Sir Wilfull.

MILLA. How can you name that superannuated lubber? foh!

Enter WITWOUD *from drinking*

MRS. FAIN. So, is the fray made up, that you have left 'em?

WIT. Left 'em? I could stay no longer—I have laughed like ten christ'nings—I am tipsy with laughing—if I had stayed any longer I should have burst—I must have been let out and pieced in the sides like an unsized[37] camlet.[38]—Yes, yes, the fray is

---

28 Of facial creams.—*Vizards*=masks.
29 Urine. The urine of certain small animals was a valued ingredient in some cosmetics.
30 I.e., the proprietress of a beauty shop.   31 Satins.
32 Tight.   33 All these were brandies or liqueurs.
34 Or clary water, made of brandy, sugar, cinnamon, a kind of mint (clary), etc.   35 As for.
36 Sleep-inducing drinks, like the two just mentioned.

37 I.e., undersized.
38 A garment made of this fabric, the composition of which varied. It was originally of camel or Angora hair.

composed; my lady came in like a *nolle prosequi*,[39] and stopped their proceedings.

MILLA. What was the dispute?

WIT. That's the jest; there was no dispute. They could neither of 'em speak for rage, and so fell a-sputt'ring at one another like two roasting apples.

Enter PETULANT *drunk*

Now Petulant, all's over, all's well. Gad, my head begins to whim it about.—Why dost thou not speak? Thou art both as drunk and as mute as a fish.

PET. Look you, Mrs. Millamant—if you can love me, dear nymph—say it—and that's the conclusion—pass on, or pass off—that's all.

WIT. Thou hast uttered volumes, folios, in less than *decimo sexto*,[40] my dear Lacedaemonian.[41] Sirrah, Petulant, thou art an epitomizer of words.

PET. Witwoud—you are an annihilator of sense.

WIT. Thou art a retailer of phrases, and dost deal in remnants of remnants, like a maker of pincushions—thou art in truth (metaphorically speaking) a speaker of shorthand.

PET. Thou art (without a figure) just one half of an ass, and Baldwin[42] yonder, thy half brother, is the rest. A gemini[43] of asses, split, would make just four of you.

WIT. Thou dost bite, my dear mustard seed;[44] kiss me for that.

PET. Stand off—I'll kiss no more males—I have kissed your twin yonder in a humor of reconciliation, till he (*hiccup*) rises upon my stomach like a radish.

MILLA. Eh! filthy creature—what was the quarrel?

PET. There was no quarrel—there might have been a quarrel.

WIT. If there had been words enow between 'em to have expressed provocation, they had gone together by the ears like a pair of castanets.

PET. You were the quarrel.

MILLA. Me!

PET. If I have a humor to quarrel, I can make less matters conclude premises.[45]—If you are not handsome, what then, if I have a humor to prove it?—If I shall have my reward, say so; if not, fight for your face the next time yourself.—I'll go sleep.

WIT. Do; wrap thyself up like a woodlouse, and dream revenge—and, hear me, if thou canst learn to write by tomorrow morning, pen me a challenge—I'll carry it for thee.

PET. Carry your mistress's monkey a spider—go flea dogs,[46] and read romances—I'll go to bed to my maid. [*Exit*

MRS. FAIN. He's horridly drunk.—How came you all in this pickle?

WIT. A plot, a plot, to get rid of the knight—your husband's advice; but he sneaked off.

Enter LADY WISHFORT, *and* SIR WILFULL *drunk*

LADY W. Out upon't, out upon't; at years of discretion, and comport yourself at this rantipole[47] rate.

SIR WIL. No offense, aunt.

LADY W. Offense? As I'm a person, I'm ashamed of you—fogh! how you stink of wine! D'ee think my niece will ever endure such a *borachio*?[48] You're an absolute *borachio*.

SIR WIL. *Borachio!*

LADY W. At a time when you should commence an amour, and put your best foot foremost—

SIR WIL. 'Sheart, an you grutch me your liquor, make a bill. Give me more drink, and take my purse. [*Sings*

Prithee fill me the glass
Till it laugh in my face,
With ale that is potent and mellow;
He that whines for a lass
Is an ignorant ass,
For a bumper has not its fellow.

But if you would have me marry my cousin, say the word, and I'll do't—Wilfull will do't, that's the word—Wilfull will do't, that's my crest[49]—my motto I have forgot.

LADY W. My nephew's a little overtaken, cousin—but 'tis with drinking your health. O' my word, you are obliged to him—

SIR WIL. *In vino veritas*,[50] aunt.—If I drunk your health today, Cousin, I am a *borachio*. But if you have a mind to be married, say the word, and send for the piper; Wilfull will do't. If not, dust it away,[51] and let's have t'other round.—Tony, 'odsheart, where's Tony?—Tony's an honest fellow, but he spits after a bumper; and that's a fault. [*Sings*

---

[39] A motion by the plaintiff to withdraw a legal action.

[40] Or 16mo, a very small book size, as *folio* is a large one.

[41] I.e., Spartan; the Spartans were famous for sparing speech.

[42] The name of the ass.   [43] Pair.

[44] Evidently Petulant is short, for mustard seed is very small, though it bites.   [45] Bring things to a head.

[46] I.e., her lapdogs.   [47] Wild.   [48] Drunkard.

[49] An heraldic bearing, often used ornamentally.

[50] In wine, truth; i.e., you hear the truth when a man's drunk.

[51] I.e., down the drink.

We'll drink and we'll never ha' done, boys,
Put the glass then around with the sun, boys,
Let Apollo's example invite us;
For he's drunk every night,
And that makes him so bright
That he's able next morning to light us.

The sun's a good pimple,[52] an honest soaker; he has a cellar at your[53] Antipodes. If I travel, aunt, I touch at your Antipodes—your Antipodes are a good rascally sort of topsy-turvy fellows. If I had a bumper, I'd stand upon my head and drink a health to 'em. —A match or no match, cousin with the hard name? —Aunt, Wilfull will do't. If she has her maidenhead, let her look to't; if she has not, let her keep her own counsel in the meantime, and cry out at the nine months' end.

MILLA. Your pardon, madam, I can stay no longer —Sir Wilfull grows very powerful. Egh! how he smells! I shall be overcome if I stay. Come, cousin.

[*Exeunt* MRS. MILLAMANT *and* MRS. FAINALL

LADY W. Smells! he would poison a tallow-chandler and his family.—Beastly creature, I know not what to do with him.—Travel, quoth a; ay, travel, travel, get thee gone, get thee but far enough, to the Saracens, or the Tartars, or the Turks—for thou art not fit to live in a Christian commonwealth, thou beastly pagan.

SIR WIL. Turks, no; no Turks, aunt: your Turks are infidels, and believe not in the grape. Your Mahometan, your Mussulman, is a dry stinkard[54]— no offense, aunt. My map says that your Turk is not so honest a man as your Christian—I cannot find by the map that your mufti[55] is orthodox—whereby it is a plain case that orthodox is a hard word, aunt, and (*hiccup*) Greek for claret.   [*Sings*

Let Mahometan fools
Live by heathenish rules,
And be damned over teacups and coffee;
But let British lads sing,
Crown a health to the King,
And a fig for your sultan and sophy.[56]

Ah, Tony!

Enter FOIBLE *and whispers* LADY WISHFORT

LADY W. Sir Rowland impatient? Good lack! what shall I do with this beastly tumbril?[57]—Go lie down

and sleep, you sot—or as I'm a person, I'll have you bastinadoed with broomsticks. Call up the wenches.

SIR WIL. Ahey? Wenches, where are the wenches?

LADY W. Dear Cousin Witwoud, get him away, and you will bind me to you inviolably. I have an affair of moment that invades me with some precipitation.—You will oblige me to all futurity.

WIT. Come, knight.—Pox on him, I don't know what to say to him.—Will you go to a cock match?

SIR WIL. With a wench, Tony? Is she a shakebag,[58] sirrah? Let me bite your cheek for that.

WIT. Horrible! He has a breath like a bagpipe.— Ay, ay; come, will you march, my Salopian?[59]

SIR WIL. Lead on, little Tony—I'll follow thee, my Antony, my Tantony. Sirrah, thou sha't be my Tantony, and I'll be thy pig.[60]

And a fig for your sultan and sophy.

[*Exit singing, with* WITWOUD

LADY W. This will never do. It will never make a match—at least before he has been abroad.

Enter WAITWELL *disguised as for Sir Rowland*

Dear Sir Rowland, I am confounded with confusion at the retrospection of my own rudeness—I have more pardons to ask than the Pope distributes in the year of jubilee.[61] But I hope where there is likely to be so near an alliance, we may unbend the severity of decorum, and dispense with a little ceremony.

WAIT. My impatience, madam, is the effect of my transport; and till I have the possession of your adorable person, I am tantalized on a rack, and do but hang, madam, on the tenter[62] of expectation.

LADY W. You have excess of gallantry, Sir Rowland, and press things to a conclusion with a most prevailing vehemence.—But a day or two for decency of marriage—

WAIT. For decency of funeral, madam. The delay will break my heart—or if that should fail, I shall be poisoned. My nephew will get an inkling of my designs, and poison me—and I would willingly starve him before I die—I would gladly go out of the world with that satisfaction. That would be some comfort to me, if I could but live so long as to be revenged on that unnatural viper.

---

[52] Boon companion.   [53] The.
[54] Stinker; as today, in a general derogatory sense.
[55] Moslem official.   [56] Shah of Persia.
[57] Farmer's tipcart.

[58] I.e., plump and lively. *Shakebag* was the name of the larger kind of gamecock.   [59] Native of Shropshire.
[60] St. Anthony ("Tantony"), as patron of swineherds, was painted with a pig.
[61] 1700 was a jubilee year. The Catholic Church celebrates one every twenty-five years.   [62] Tenterhook.

LADY W. Is he so unnatural, say you? Truly, I would contribute much both to the saving of your life and the accomplishment of your revenge—not that I respect[63] myself; though he has been a perfidious wretch to me.

WAIT. Perfidious to you!

LADY W. Oh, Sir Rowland, the hours that he has died away at my feet, the tears that he has shed, the oaths that he has sworn, the palpitations that he has felt, the trances and the tremblings, the ardors and the ecstasies, the kneelings and the risings, the heart-heavings and the hand-gripings, the pangs and the pathetic regards of his protesting eyes! oh, no memory can register.

WAIT. What, my rival! Is the rebel my rival? a dies.

LADY W. No, don't kill him at once, Sir Rowland; starve him gradually inch by inch.

WAIT. I'll do't. In three weeks he shall be barefoot, in a month out at knees with begging an alms—he shall starve upward and upward, till he has nothing living but his head, and then go out in a stink, like a candle's end upon a save-all.[64]

LADY W. Well, Sir Rowland, you have the way—you are no novice in the labyrinth of love—you have the clue.—But as I am a person, Sir Rowland, you must not attribute my yielding to any sinister appetite or indigestion of widowhood, nor impute my complacency to any lethargy of continence. I hope you do not think me prone to any iteration of nuptials.

WAIT. Far be it from me—

LADY W. If you do, I protest I must recede—or think that I have made a prostitution of decorums, but[65] in the vehemence of compassion, and to save the life of a person of so much importance—

WAIT. I esteem it so—

LADY W. Or else you wrong my condescension—

WAIT. I do not, I do not—

LADY W. Indeed you do.

WAIT. I do not, fair shrine of virtue.

LADY W. If you think the least scruple of carnality was an ingredient—

WAIT. Dear madam, no. You are all camphire[66] and frankincense, all chastity and odor.

LADY W. Or that—

---

[63] Am considering.
[64] A device (fitted to a socket of a candlestick) for letting a candle burn completely up. You stuck the candle on a pin in the middle of a small pan that caught the grease. [65] Except.
[66] Camphor. It was taken as an antaphrodisiac.

Enter FOIBLE

FOIB. Madam, the dancers are ready; and there's one with a letter, who must deliver it into your own hands.

LADY W. Sir Rowland, will you give me leave? Think favorably, judge candidly, and conclude you have found a person who would suffer racks in honor's cause, dear Sir Rowland, and will wait on you incessantly.[67]   [*Exit*

WAIT. Fie, fie!—What a slavery have I undergone! Spouse, hast thou any cordial—I want spirits.

FOIB. What a washy rogue art thou, to pant thus for a quarter of an hour's lying and swearing to a fine lady!

WAIT. Oh, she is the antidote to desire. Spouse, thou wilt fare the worse for't—I shall have no "appetite to iteration of nuptials" this eight-and-forty hours. By this hand, I'd rather be a chairman[68] in the dog days than act Sir Rowland till this time tomorrow.

Enter LADY WISHFORT *with a letter*

LADY W. Call in the dancers.—Sir Rowland, we'll sit, if you please, and see the entertainment. [*Dance* Now with your permission, Sir Rowland, I will peruse my letter—I would open it in your presence, because I would not make you uneasy. If it should make you uneasy, I would burn it—speak, if it does—but you may see by the superscription it is like a woman's hand.

FOIB. (*aside*). By heaven! Mrs. Marwood's, I know it—my heart aches.—(*To him*) Get it from her—

WAIT. A woman's hand? No, madam, that's no woman's hand, I see that already. That's somebody whose throat must be cut.

LADY W. Nay, Sir Rowland, since you give me a proof of your passion by your jealousy, I promise you I'll make you a return by a frank communication. You shall see it—we'll open it together—look you here. (*Reads.*) "Madam, though unknown to you"—look you there; 'tis from nobody that I know—"I have that honor for your character that I think myself obliged to let you know you are abused.[69] He who pretends to be Sir Rowland is a cheat and a rascal—" Oh, heavens! what's this?

FOIB. (*aside*). Unfortunate, all's ruined.

WAIT. How, how, let me see, let me see! (*Reading*) "A rascal, and disguised and suborned for that im-

---

[67] Without delay.   [68] Sedan chair bearer.
[69] Deceived.

posture"—Oh, villainy! Oh, villainy!—"by the contrivance of—"

LADY W. I shall faint, I shall die, I shall die, oh!

FOIB. (to him). Say 'tis your nephew's hand. Quickly, his plot, swear, swear it.

WAIT. Here's a villain! Madam, don't you perceive it, don't you see it?

LADY W. Too well, too well. I have seen too much.

WAIT. I told you at first I knew the hand. A woman's hand? The rascal writes a sort of a large hand, your Roman hand. I saw there was a throat to be cut presently. If he were my son, as he is my nephew, I'd pistol him—

FOIB. Oh, treachery! But are you sure, Sir Rowland, it is his writing?

WAIT. Sure? Am I here? do I live? do I love this pearl of India? I have twenty letters in my pocket from him, in the same character.

LADY W. How!

FOIB. Oh, what luck it is, Sir Rowland, that you were present at this juncture! This was the business that brought Mr. Mirabell disguised to Madam Millamant this afternoon. I thought something was contriving, when he stole by me and would have hid his face.

LADY W. How, how!—I heard the villain was in the house indeed; and now I remember, my niece went away abruptly, when Sir Wilfull was to have made his addresses.

FOIB. Then, then, madam, Mr. Mirabell waited for her in her chamber; but I would not tell your Lady-

ship to discompose you when you were to receive Sir Rowland.

WAIT. Enough, his date is short.

FOIB. No, good Sir Rowland, don't incur the law.

WAIT. Law! I care not for law. I can but die, and 'tis in a good cause—my Lady shall be satisfied of my truth and innocence, though it cost me my life.

LADY W. No, dear Sir Rowland, don't fight; if you should be killed I must never show my face; or hanged—oh, consider my reputation, Sir Rowland! No, you shan't fight.—I'll go in and examine my niece; I'll make her confess. I conjure you, Sir Rowland, by all your love, not to fight.

WAIT. I am charmed, madam, I obey. But some proof you must let me give you; I'll go for a black box, which contains the writings of my whole estate, and deliver that into your hands.

LADY W. Ay, dear Sir Rowland, that will be some comfort; bring the black box.

WAIT. And may I presume to bring a contract to be signed this night? May I hope so far?

LADY W. Bring what you will; but come alive, pray come alive. Oh, this is a happy discovery.

WAIT. Dead or alive I'll come—and married we will be in spite of treachery; ay, and get an heir that shall defeat the last remaining glimpse of hope in my abandoned nephew. Come, my buxom widow:

E'er long you shall substantial proof receive
That I'm an arrant[70] knight—

FOIB. (aside).   Or arrant knave.

[Exeunt

ACT V

Scene continues.[1] LADY WISHFORT and FOIBLE

LADY W. Out of my house, out of my house, thou viper, thou serpent, that I have fostered! thou bosom traitress, that I raised from nothing!—begone, begone, begone, go, go!—that I took from washing of old gauze and weaving of dead hair,[2] with a bleak blue nose, over a chafing dish of starved embers, and dining behind a traverse rag,[3] in a shop no bigger than a bird cage—go, go, starve again, do, do!

FOIB. Dear madam, I'll beg pardon on my knees.

LADY W. Away, out, out, go set up for yourself again!—do, drive a trade, do, with your three-

pennyworth of small ware, flaunting upon a packthread, under a brandy seller's bulk,[4] or against a dead wall by a balladmonger. Go, hang out an old Frisoneer gorget,[5] with a yard of yellow colberteen[6] again! do! an old gnawed mask, two rows of pins, and a child's fiddle, a glass necklace with the beads broken, and a quilted nightcap with one ear. Go, go, drive a trade!—These were your commodities, you treacherous trull, this was your merchandise you dealt in, when I took you into my house, placed you next myself, and made you governante of my whole family.[7] You have forgot this, have you, now you have feathered your nest?

[70] Errant (and chivalrous).

[4] Stall.   [5] A coarse woolen scarf or wimple.
[6] A cheap French lace.
[7] Housekeeper of my entire household.

---

[1] I.e., the scenery is the same as for Act IV. There is an interval of time.   [2] Making wigs.
[3] A rag hung up to curtain off part of the room.

FOIB. No, no, dear madam. Do but hear me, have but a moment's patience—I'll confess all. Mr. Mirabell seduced[8] me; I am not the first that he has wheedled with his dissembling tongue; your Ladyship's own wisdom has been deluded by him; then how should I, a poor ignorant, defend myself? Oh, madam, if you knew but what he promised me, and how he assured me your Ladyship should come to no damage—or else the wealth of the Indies should not have bribed me to conspire against so good, so sweet, so kind a lady as you have been to me.

LADY W. No damage? What, to betray me, to marry me to a cast[9] servingman, to make me a receptacle, an hospital for a decayed pimp? No damage? Oh, thou frontless[10] impudence, more than a big-bellied actress.

FOIB. Pray do but hear me, madam; he could not marry your Ladyship, madam, no indeed, his marriage was to have been void in law; for he was married to me first, to secure your Ladyship. He could not have bedded your Ladyship; for if he had consummated with your Ladyship, he must have run the risk of the law and been put upon his clergy.[11] Yes indeed, I enquired of the law in that case before I would meddle or make.

LADY W. What, then I have been your property, have I? I have been convenient to you, it seems, while you were catering for Mirabell; I have been broker for you? What, have you made a passive bawd of me?—This exceeds all precedent; I am brought to fine uses, to become a botcher[12] of second-hand marriages between Abigails and Andrews![13] I'll couple you. Yes, I'll baste you together, you and your Philander. I'll Duke's Place you, as I'm a person. Your turtle[14] is in custody already; you shall coo in the same cage, if there be constable or warrant in the parish.   [Exit

FOIB. Oh, that ever I was born! Oh, that I was ever married!—A bride, ay, I shall be a Bridewell[15] bride. Oh!

[8] From my loyalty to you.   [9] Discharged.
[10] Shameless.
[11] Had to plead benefit of clergy; i.e., got off, as a first offender, by demonstrating that he could read.
[12] A second-rate tailor, only making repairs.
[13] Lady's maids and valets. From characters in the Beaumont-Fletcher plays: Abigail from *The Scornful Lady*, Andrew from *The Elder Brother*. Cf. *Philander* (erroneously taken to mean *loving man*) from *The Laws of Candy*.—On *Duke's Place* see Act I, note 25, above.   [14] Dove, lover.
[15] The famous house of correction.

Enter MRS. FAINALL

MRS. FAIN. Poor Foible, what's the matter?

FOIB. Oh, madam, my Lady's gone for a constable; I shall be had to a justice, and put to Bridewell to beat hemp; poor Waitwell's gone to prison already.

MRS. FAIN. Have a good heart, Foible; Mirabell's gone to give security for him. This is all Marwood's and my husband's doing.

FOIB. Yes, yes, I know it, madam; she was in my Lady's closet, and overheard all that you said to me before dinner. She sent the letter to my Lady; and, that missing effect,[16] Mr. Fainall laid this plot to arrest Waitwell, when he pretended to go for the papers; and in the meantime Mrs. Marwood declared all to my Lady.

MRS. FAIN. Was there no mention made of me in the letter? My mother does not suspect my being in the confederacy? I fancy Marwood has not told her, though she has told my husband.

FOIB. Yes, madam, but my Lady did not see that part; we stifled the letter before she read so far. Has that mischievous devil told Mr. Fainall of your Ladyship, then?

MRS. FAIN. Ay, all's out, my affair with Mirabell, everything discovered. This is the last day of our living together, that's my comfort.

FOIB. Indeed, madam, and so 'tis a comfort if you knew all: he has been even with your Ladyship, which I could have told you long enough since, but I love to keep peace and quietness by my good will. I had rather bring friends together than set 'em at distance. But Mrs. Marwood and he are nearer related than ever their parents thought for.

MRS. FAIN. Say'st thou so, Foible? Canst thou prove this?

FOIB. I can take my oath of it, madam; so can Mrs. Mincing. We have had many a fair word from Madam Marwood, to conceal something that passed in our chamber one evening when you were at Hyde Park, and we were thought to have gone a-walking; but we went up unawares—though we were sworn to secrecy, too. Madam Marwood took a book and swore us upon it; but it was but a book of verses and poems—so as long as it was not a Bible oath, we may break it with a safe conscience.

MRS. FAIN. This discovery is the most opportune thing I could wish. Now, Mincing?

[16] I.e., the letter failing to accomplish its purpose.

Enter MINCING

MINC. My Lady[17] would speak with Mrs. Foible, mem. Mr. Mirabell is with her; he has set your spouse at liberty, Mrs. Foible, and would have you hide yourself in my Lady's closet, till my old Lady's anger is abated. Oh, my old Lady is in a perilous[18] passion at something Mr. Fainall has said; he swears, and my old Lady cries. There's a fearful hurricane, I vow. He says, mem, how that he'll have my Lady's fortune made over to him, or he'll be divorced.

MRS. FAIN. Does your lady and Mirabell know that?

MINC. Yes, mem, they have sent me to see if Sir Wilfull be sober, and to bring him to them. My Lady is resolved to have him, I think, rather than lose such a vast sum as six thousand pound. Oh, come, Mrs. Foible, I hear my old Lady.

MRS. FAIN. Foible, you must tell Mincing that she must prepare to vouch when I call her.

FOIB. Yes, yes, madam.

MINC. Oh, yes, mem, I'll vouch anything for your Ladyship's service, be what it will.

[*Exeunt* MINCING *and* FOIBLE

Enter LADY WISHFORT *and* MRS. MARWOOD

LADY W. Oh, my dear friend, how can I enumerate the benefits that I have received from your goodness? To you I owe the timely discovery of the false vows of Mirabell, to you the detection of the impostor Sir Rowland. And now you are become an intercessor with my son-in-law, to save the honor of my house and compound for the frailties of my daughter. Well, friend, you are enough to reconcile me to the bad world, or else I would retire to deserts and solitudes, and feed harmless sheep by groves and purling streams. Dear Marwood, let us leave the world, and retire by ourselves and be shepherdesses.

MRS. MAR. Let us first dispatch the affair in hand, madam. We shall have leisure to think of retirement afterwards. Here is one who is concerned in the treaty.

LADY W. Oh, daughter, daughter, is it possible thou shouldst be my child, bone of my bone, and flesh of my flesh, and, as I may say, another me, and yet transgress the most minute particle of severe virtue? Is it possible you should lean aside to iniquity, who have been cast in the direct mold of virtue? I have not only been a mold but a pattern for you, and a model for you, after you were brought into the world.

MRS. FAIN. I don't understand your Ladyship.

LADY W. Not understand? Why, have you not been naught?[19] Have you not been sophisticated?[20] Not understand? Here I am ruined to compound[21] for your caprices and your cuckoldoms. I must pawn my plate and my jewels, and ruin my niece, and all little enough—

MRS. FAIN. I am wronged and abused, and so are you. 'Tis a false accusation, as false as hell, as false as your friend there, ay, or your friend's friend,[22] my false husband.

MRS. MAR. My friend, Mrs. Fainall? Your husband my friend! what do you mean?

MRS. FAIN. I know what I mean, madam, and so do you; and so shall the world, at a time convenient.

MRS. MAR. I am sorry to see you so passionate, madam. More temper[23] would look more like innocence. But I have done. I am sorry my zeal to serve your Ladyship and family should admit of misconstruction, or make me liable to affronts. You will pardon me, madam, if I meddle no more with an affair in which I am not personally concerned.

LADY W. Oh, dear friend, I am so ashamed that you should meet with such returns.—You ought to ask pardon on your knees, ungrateful creature; she deserves more from you than all your life can accomplish.—Oh, don't leave me destitute in this perplexity; no, stick to me, my good genius.

MRS. FAIN. I tell you, madam, you're abused. Stick to you? ay, like a leech, to suck your best blood—she'll drop off when she's full. Madam, you sha' not pawn a bodkin, nor part with a brass counter,[24] in composition[25] for me. I defy 'em all. Let 'em prove their aspersions; I know my own innocence, and dare stand by[26] a trial. [*Exit*

LADY W. Why, if she should be innocent, if she should be wronged after all, ha? I don't know what to think—and, I promise you, her education has been unexceptionable—I may say it; for I chiefly made it my own care to initiate her very infancy in the rudiments of virtue, and to impress upon her tender years a young odium and aversion to the very sight of men; ay, friend, she would ha' shrieked if she had but seen a man, till she was in her teens. As I'm a person, 'tis true. She was never suffered to play with a male-child, though but in coats;[27] nay, her

---

[17] Millamant.   [18] Parlous, extreme.

[19] Wicked.   [20] Corrupted.   [21] Pay (to get you off).
[22] Lover.   [23] Composure.   [24] Token.
[25] Compounding. See note 21.   [26] On, according to.
[27] Skirt, dress.

very babies[28] were of the feminine gender. Oh, she never looked a man in the face but her own father, or the chaplain, and him we made a shift to put upon her for a woman, by the help of his long garments and his sleek face, till she was going in her fifteen.

MRS. MAR. 'Twas much she should be deceived so long.

LADY W. I warrant you, or she would never have borne to have been catechised by him, and have heard his long lectures against singing and dancing, and such debaucheries, and going to filthy plays, and profane music-meetings where the lewd trebles squeak nothing but bawdy, and the basses roar blasphemy. Oh, she would have swooned at the sight or name of an obscene playbook—and can I think, after all this, that my daughter can be naught? What, a whore? And thought it excommunication to set her foot within the door of a playhouse. Oh, my dear friend, I can't believe it, no, no; as she says, let him prove it, let him prove it.

MRS. MAR. Prove it, madam? What, and have your name prostituted in a public court; yours and your daughter's reputation worried at the bar by a pack of bawling lawyers? To be ushered in with an oyez[29] of scandal; and have your case opened by an old fumbling lecher in a quoif[30] like a man midwife, to bring your daughter's infamy to light; to be a theme for legal punsters, and quibblers by the statute; and become a jest, against a rule of court, where there is no precedent for a jest in any record, not even in Doomsday Book;[31] to discompose the gravity of the bench, and provoke naughty interrogatories in more naughty law Latin, while the good judge, tickled with the proceeding, simpers under a gray beard, and fidges[32] off and on his cushion as if he had swallowed cantharides[33] or sat upon cow-itch.[34]

LADY W. Oh, 'tis very hard!

MRS. MAR. And then to have my[35] young revelers of the Temple[36] take notes, like prentices at a conventicle;[37] and, after, talk it all over again in commons,[38] or before drawers in an eating-house.

LADY W. Worse and worse.

MRS. MAR. Nay, this is nothing; if it would end here 'twere well. But it must after this be consigned by the shorthand writers to the public press; and from thence be transferred to the hands, nay, into the throats and lungs, of hawkers, with voices more licentious than the loud flounder-man's[39] or the woman that cries grey-pease; this you must hear till you are stunned; nay, you must hear nothing else for some days.

LADY W. Oh, 'tis insupportable. No, no, dear friend, make it up, make it up; ay, ay, I'll compound. I'll give up all, myself and my all, my niece and her all—anything, everything, for composition.

MRS. MAR. Nay, madam, I advise nothing, I only lay before you, as a friend, the inconveniencies which perhaps you have overseen.[40] Here comes Mr. Fainall. If he will be satisfied to huddle up all in silence, I shall be glad. You must think I would rather congratulate than condole with you.

Enter FAINALL

LADY W. Ay, ay, I do not doubt it, dear Marwood; no, no, I do not doubt it.

FAIN. Well, madam; I have suffered myself to be overcome by the importunity of this lady, your friend, and am content you shall enjoy your own proper[41] estate during life; on condition you oblige yourself never to marry, under such penalty as I think convenient.

LADY W. Never to marry?

FAIN. No more Sir Rowlands—the next imposture may not be so timely detected.

MRS. MAR. That condition, I dare answer, my Lady will consent to, without difficulty; she has already but too much experienced the perfidiousness of men. Besides, madam, when we retire to our pastoral solitude we shall bid adieu to all other thoughts.

LADY W. Ay, that's true; but in case of necessity, as of health, or some such emergency—

FAIN. Oh, if you are prescribed marriage, you shall be considered; I will only reserve to myself the power to choose for you. If your physic be wholesome, it matters not who is your apothecary. Next, my wife shall settle on me the remainder of her fortune not made over already, and for her maintenance depend entirely on my discretion.

LADY W. This is most inhumanly savage, exceeding the barbarity of a Muscovite[42] husband.

---

[28] Dolls.
[29] Hear ye; the crier's call at the opening of a court.
[30] Coif, a white cap once worn by lawyers, especially the sergeants.
[31] The record of William the Conqueror's great survey of English landholdings.   [32] Fidgets.   [33] An aphrodisiac.
[34] Cowhage, a tropical vine with hairy pods which cause itching.
[35] The.   [36] The law students.
[37] They were sometimes quizzed on the sermon by their masters.
[38] The dining hall.

[39] A well-known character of the London streets.
[40] Overlooked.   [41] Belonging to you.   [42] Russian.

FAIN. I learned it from his Czarish majesty's retinue,[43] in a winter evening's conference over brandy and pepper, amongst other secrets of matrimony and policy as they are at present practiced in the northern hemisphere. But this must be agreed unto, and that positively. Lastly, I will be endowed, in right of my wife, with that six thousand pound which is the moiety of Mrs. Millamant's fortune in your possession, and which she has forfeited (as will appear by the last will and testament of your deceased husband, Sir Jonathan Wishfort) by her disobedience in contracting herself against your consent or knowledge, and by refusing the offered match with Sir Wilfull Witwoud, which you, like a careful aunt, had provided for her.

LADY W. My nephew was *non compos*,[44] and could not make his addresses.

FAIN. I come to make demands—I'll hear no objections.

LADY W. You will grant me time to consider?

FAIN. Yes, while the instrument is drawing,[45] to which you must set your hand till more sufficient deeds can be perfected, which I will take care shall be done with all possible speed. In the meanwhile, I will go for the said instrument; and till my return you may balance this matter in your own discretion.
[*Exit*

LADY W. This insolence is beyond all precedent, all parallel; must I be subject to this merciless villain?

MRS. MAR. 'Tis severe indeed, madam, that you should smart for your daughter's wantonness.

LADY W. 'Twas against my consent that she married this barbarian; but she would have him, though her year[46] was not out.—Ah! her first husband, my son Languish, would not have carried it thus. Well, that was my choice, this is hers; she is matched now, with a witness.[47] I shall be mad, dear friend; is there no comfort for me? Must I live to be confiscated at this rebel-rate?[48]—Here come two more of my Egyptian plagues,[49] too.

Enter MILLAMANT *and* SIR WILFULL

SIR WIL. Aunt, your servant.

LADY W. Out, caterpillar, call not me aunt; I know thee not.

SIR WIL. I confess I have been a little in disguise,[50] as they say—'sheart! and I'm sorry for't. What would you have? I hope I committed no offense, aunt—and if I did I am willing to make satisfaction; and what can a man say fairer? If I have broke anything I'll pay for't, an it cost a pound. And so let that content for what's past, and make no more words. For what's to come, to pleasure you I'm willing to marry my cousin. So pray let's all be friends; she and I are agreed upon the matter before a witness.

LADY W. How's this, dear niece? Have I any comfort? Can this be true?

MILLA. I am content to be a sacrifice to your repose, madam; and to convince you that I had no hand in the plot, as you were misinformed, I have laid my commands on Mirabell to come in person, and be a witness that I give my hand to this flower of knighthood; and for[51] the contract that passed between Mirabell and me, I have obliged him to make a resignation of it in your Ladyship's presence. He is without, and waits your leave for admittance.

LADY W. Well, I'll swear I am something revived at this testimony of your obedience; but I cannot admit that traitor—I fear I cannot fortify myself to support his appearance. He is as terrible to me as a Gorgon; if I see him I fear I shall turn to stone, petrify incessantly.[52]

MILLA. If you disoblige him, he may resent your refusal, and insist upon the contract still. Then, 'tis the last time he will be offensive to you.

LADY W. Are you sure it will be the last time?—If I were sure of that—shall I never see him again?

MILLA. Sir Wilfull, you and he are to travel together, are you not?

SIR WIL. 'Sheart, the gentleman's a civil gentleman, aunt; let him come in; why, we are sworn brothers and fellow-travelers.—We are to be Pylades and Orestes,[53] he and I—he is to be my interpreter in foreign parts. He has been overseas once already; and with proviso that I marry my cousin, will cross 'em once again, only to bear me company.—'Sheart, I'll call him in—an I set on't once, he shall come in; and see who'll hinder him.
[*Exit*

MRS. MAR. (*aside*). This is precious fooling, if it would pass; but I'll know the bottom of it.

LADY W. Oh, dear Marwood, you are not going?

MAR. Not far, madam; I'll return immediately.
[*Exit*

---

[43] Peter the Great had spent three months in England in 1697.
[44] *Non compos mentis*, not of sound mind.
[45] While the document is being drawn up.
[46] Of widowhood.   [47] And no mistake!
[48] As rebels' property is subject to confiscation—100%.
[49] A reference to the ten plagues of Egypt (Exodus 7-12).

[50] Not myself, drunk.   [51] As for.   [52] Immediately.
[53] Proverbially faithful friends. The avenger of his father's murder, Orestes is the Hamlet of Greek tragedy. He and Pylades wandered in many lands.

SIR WIL. Look up, man; I'll stand by you, 'sbud; and she do frown, she can't kill you.—Besides—hark'ee, she dare not frown desperately, because her face is none of her own; 'sheart, an she should, her forehead would wrinkle like the coat of a cream cheese; but mum for that, fellow-traveler.

MIRA. If a deep sense of the many injuries I have offered to so good a lady, with a sincere remorse and a hearty contrition, can but obtain the least glance of compassion, I am too happy. Ah, madam, there was a time—but let it be forgotten—I confess I have deservedly forfeited the high place I once held, of sighing at your feet; nay, kill me not, by turning from me in disdain—I come not to plead for favor—nay, not for pardon; I am a suppliant only for your pity—I am going where I never shall behold you more—

SIR WIL. How, fellow-traveler! You shall go by yourself then.

MIRA. Let me be pitied first, and afterwards forgotten—I ask no more.

SIR WIL. By'r Lady, a very reasonable request, and will cost you nothing, aunt. Come, come, forgive and forget, aunt; why, you must, an you are a Christian.

MIRA. Consider, madam, in reality you could not receive much prejudice; it was an innocent device; though I confess it had a face of guiltiness, it was at most an artifice which love contrived—and errors which love produces have ever been accounted venial. At least, think it is punishment enough that I have lost what in my heart I hold most dear, that to your cruel indignation I have offered up this beauty, and with her my peace and quiet, nay, all my hopes of future comfort.

SIR WIL. An he does not move me, would I might never be o' the quorum![54] An it were not as good a deed as to drink, to give her to him again, I would I might never take shipping!—Aunt, if you don't forgive quickly, I shall melt, I can tell you that. My contract went no further than a little mouth glue,[55] and that's hardly dry—one doleful sigh more from my fellow-traveler and 'tis dissolved.

LADY W. Well, nephew, upon your account.—Ah, he has a false insinuating tongue!—Well, sir, I will stifle my just resentment, at my nephew's request.—I will endeavor what I can to forget—but on pro-viso that you resign the contract with my niece immediately.

MIRA. It is in writing and with papers of concern; but I have sent my servant for it, and will deliver it to you, with all acknowledgments for your transcendent goodness.

LADY W. (*apart*). Oh, he has witchcraft in his eyes and tongue! When I did not see him, I could have bribed a villain to his assassination; but his appearance rakes the embers which have so long lain smothered in my breast.

Enter FAINALL *and* MRS. MARWOOD

FAIN. Your date of deliberation, madam, is expired. Here is the instrument; are you prepared to sign?

LADY W. If I were prepared, I am not empowered. My niece exerts a lawful claim, having matched herself by my direction to Sir Wilfull.

FAIN. That sham is too gross to pass on me, though 'tis imposed on you, madam.

MILLA. Sir, I have given my consent.

MIRA. And, sir, I have resigned my pretensions.

SIR WIL. And, sir, I assert my right, and will maintain it in defiance of you, sir, and of your instrument. 'Sheart, an you talk of an instrument, sir, I have an old fox[56] by my thigh shall hack your instrument of ram vellum[57] to shreds, sir. It shall not be sufficient for a mittimus[58] or a tailor's measure; therefore withdraw your instrument, sir, or by'r Lady I shall draw mine.

LADY W. Hold, nephew, hold.

MILLA. Good Sir Wilfull, respite your valor.

FAIN. Indeed? Are you provided of a guard, with your single beefeater[59] there? But I'm prepared for you, and insist upon my first proposal. You shall submit your own estate to my management, and absolutely make over my wife's to my sole use, as pursuant to the purport and tenor of this other covenant.—(*To* MILLAMANT) I suppose, madam, your consent is not requisite in this case—nor, Mr. Mirabell, your resignation—nor, Sir Wilfull, your right. You may draw your fox if you please, sir, and make a bear-garden flourish somewhere else, for here it will not avail. This, my Lady Wishfort, must be subscribed, or your darling daughter's turned adrift, like a leaky hulk, to sink or swim as she and the current of this lewd town can agree.

---

[54] Be one of the select justices of the peace, whose presence was required for court sessions.   [55] I.e., an oral agreement.

[56] Sword.   [57] Parchment.   [58] Warrant for arrest.
[59] Yeoman of the royal guard, the old household troops.

LADY W. Is there no means, no remedy, to stop my ruin? Ungrateful wretch! dost thou not owe thy being, thy subsistence, to my daughter's fortune?

FAIN. I'll answer you when I have the rest of it in my possession.

MIRA. But that you would not accept of a remedy from my hands—I own I have not deserved you should owe any obligation to me, or else perhaps I could advise—

LADY W. Oh, what? what? to save me and my child from ruin, from want, I'll forgive all that's past; nay, I'll consent to anything to come, to be delivered from this tyranny.

MIRA. Ay, madam; but that is too late, my reward is intercepted. You have disposed of her who only could have made me a compensation for all my services—but be it as it may, I am resolved I'll serve you; you shall not be wronged in this savage manner.

LADY W. How! Dear Mr. Mirabell, can you be so generous at last? But it is not possible. Hark'ee, I'll break my nephew's match; you shall have my niece yet, and all her fortune, if you can but save me from this imminent danger.

MIRA. Will you? I take you at your word. I ask no more. I must have leave for two criminals to appear.

LADY W. Ay, ay, anybody, anybody!

MIRA. Foible is one, and a penitent.

Enter MRS. FAINALL, FOIBLE, *and* MINCING

MRS. MAR. (*to* FAINALL). Oh, my shame! these corrupt things are bought, and brought hither to expose me.

[MIRABELL *and* LADY WISHFORT *go to* MRS. FAINALL *and* FOIBLE

FAIN. If it must all come out, why, let 'em know it; 'tis but *the way of the world*. That shall not urge me to relinquish or abate one tittle of my terms; no, I will insist the more.

FOIB. Yes indeed, madam, I'll take my Bible oath of it.

MINC. And so will I, mem.

LADY W. Oh, Marwood, Marwood, art thou false? my friend deceive me? Hast thou been a wicked accomplice with that profligate man?

MRS. MAR. Have you so much ingratitude and injustice, to give credit, against your friend, to the aspersions of two such mercenary trulls?

MINC. Mercenary, mem? I scorn your words. 'Tis true we found you and Mr. Fainall in the blue garret; by the same token, you swore us to secrecy upon Messalinas's[60] poems. Mercenary? No, if we would have been mercenary, we should have held our tongues; you would have bribed us sufficiently.

FAIN. Go, you are an insignificant thing!—Well, what are you the better for this? Is this Mr. Mirabell's expedient? I'll be put off no longer.—You thing, that was a wife, shall smart for this. I will not leave thee wherewithal to hide thy shame; your body shall be naked as your reputation.

MRS. FAIN. I despise you, and defy your malice. You have aspersed me wrongfully—I have proved your falsehood. Go, you and your treacherous—I will not name it; but starve together—perish!

FAIN. Not while you are worth a groat, indeed, my dear. Madam, I'll be fooled no longer.

LADY W. Ah, Mr. Mirabell, this is small comfort, the detection of this affair.

MIRA. Oh, in good time. Your leave for the other offender and penitent to appear, madam.

Enter WAITWELL *with a box of writings*

LADY W. Oh, Sir Rowland!—Well, rascal!

WAIT. What your Ladyship pleases.—I have brought the black box at last, madam.

MIRA. Give it me.—Madam, you remember your promise.

LADY W. Ay, dear sir.

MIRA. Where are the gentlemen?

WAIT. At hand, sir, rubbing their eyes—just risen from sleep.

FAIN. S'death, what's this to me? I'll not wait your private concerns.

Enter PETULANT *and* WITWOUD

PET. How now? and what's the matter? whose hand's out?

WIT. Hey day! what, are you all got together, like players at the end of the last act?

MIRA. You may remember, gentlemen, I once requested your hands as witnesses to a certain parchment.

WIT. Ay, I do; my hand I remember—Petulant set his mark.

MIRA. You wrong him; his name is fairly written, as shall appear. You do not remember, gentlemen, anything of what that parchment contained?

[*Undoing the box*

---

[60] The ignorant Mincing makes an unintentional joke. Messalina was the dissolute wife of the Roman emperor Claudius. Probably Mincing saw the title *Miscellaneous Poems.*

WILLIAM CONGREVE   669

WIT. No.

PET. Not I. I writ; I read nothing.

MIRA. Very well, now you shall know.—Madam, your promise.

LADY W. Ay, ay, sir, upon my honor.

MIRA. Mr. Fainall, it is now time that you should know that your lady, while she was at her own disposal, and before you had by your insinuations wheedled her out of a pretended settlement of the greatest part of her fortune—

FAIN. Sir! pretended!

MIRA. Yes, sir. I say that this lady, while a widow, having it seems received some cautions respecting your inconstancy and tyranny of temper—which from her own partial opinion and fondness of you she could never have suspected—she did, I say, by the wholesome advice of friends and of sages learned in the laws of this land, deliver this same as her act and deed to me in trust, and to the uses within mentioned. You may read if you please (*holding out the parchment*)—though perhaps what is inscribed on the back may serve your occasions.

FAIN. Very likely, sir. What's here? Damnation! (*Reads.*) "A deed of conveyance of the whole estate real of Arabella Languish, widow, in trust to Edward Mirabell."—Confusion!

MIRA. Even so, sir; 'tis *the way of the world*, sir—of the widows of the world. I suppose this deed may bear an elder date than what you have obtained from your lady.

FAIN. Perfidious fiend! then thus I'll be revenged.

[*Offers*[61] *to run at* MRS. FAINALL

SIR WIL. Hold, sir, now you may make your beargarden flourish somewhere else, sir.

FAIN. Mirabell, you shall hear of this, sir; be sure you shall.—Let me pass, oaf. [*Exit*

MRS. FAIN. (*to* MRS. MARWOOD). Madam, you seem to stifle your resentment. You had better give it vent.

MRS. MAR. Yes, it shall have vent—and to your confusion, or I'll perish in the attempt. [*Exit*

LADY W. O daughter, daughter! 'tis plain thou hast inherited thy mother's prudence.

MRS. FAIN. Thank Mr. Mirabell, a cautious friend, to whose advice all is owing.

LADY W. Well, Mr. Mirabell, you have kept your promise—and I must perform mine.—First, I pardon for your sake Sir Rowland there and Foible. The next thing is to break the matter to my nephew—and how to do that—

MIRA. For that, madam, give yourself no trouble; let me have your consent. Sir Wilfull is my friend;

he has had compassion upon lovers, and generously engaged a volunteer in this action, for our service, and now designs to prosecute his travels.

SIR WIL. 'Sheart, aunt, I have no mind to marry. My cousin's a fine lady, and the gentleman loves her, and she loves him, and they deserve one another; my resolution is to see foreign parts—I have set on't—and when I'm set on't, I must do 't. And if these two gentlemen would travel too, I think they may be spared.

PET. For my part, I say little—I think things are best off or on.[62]

WIT. I'gad, I understand nothing of the matter; I'm in a maze yet, like a dog in a dancing-school.

LADY W. Well, sir, take her, and with her all the joy I can give you.

MILLA. Why does not the man take me? Would you have me give myself to you over again?

MIRA. Ay, and over and over again; for (*kisses her hand*) I would have you as often as possibly I can. Well, heaven grant I love you not too well, that's all my fear.

SIR WIL. 'Sheart, you'll have him time enough to toy, after you're married; or, if you will toy now, let us have a dance in the meantime, that we who are not lovers may have some other employment besides looking on.

MIRA. With all my heart, dear Sir Wilfull. What shall we do for music?

FOIB. Oh, sir, some that were provided for Sir Rowland's entertainment are yet within call. [*A dance*

LADY W. As I am a person, I can hold out no longer; I have wasted my spirits so today, already, that I am ready to sink under the fatigue; and I cannot but have some fears upon me yet that my son Fainall will pursue some desperate course.

MIRA. Madam, disquiet not yourself on that account; to my knowledge his circumstances are such he must of force comply. For my part, I will contribute all that in me lies to a reunion; in the mean time, madam (*to* MRS. FAINALL), let me before these witnesses restore to you this deed of trust. It may be a means, well managed, to make you live easily together.

From hence let those be warned who mean to wed,
Lest mutual falsehood stain the bridal bed;
For each deceiver to his cost may find
That marriage frauds too oft are paid in kind.

[*Exeunt omnes*

---

[61] Tries.

[62] Either way.

EPILOGUE

Spoken by MRS. BRACEGIRDLE

After our epilogue this crowd dismisses,
I'm thinking how this play'll be pulled to pieces.
But pray consider, ere you doom its fall,
How hard a thing 'twould be to please you all.
There are some critics so with spleen[1] diseased   5
They scarcely come inclining to be pleased;
And sure he must have more than mortal skill
Who pleases anyone against his will.
Then, all bad poets we are sure are foes,
And how their number's swelled the town well knows; 10
In shoals, I've marked 'em judging in the pit,
Though they're on no pretense for judgment fit,
But that they have been damned for want of wit.
Since when they, by their own offenses taught,
Set up for spies on plays, and finding fault.   15
Others there are, whose malice we'd prevent:
Such who watch plays with scurrilous intent
To mark out who by characters are meant;

And though no perfect likeness they can trace,
Yet each pretends to know the copied face.   20
These with false glosses feed their own ill nature,
And turn to libel what was meant a satire.
May such malicious fops this fortune find,
To think themselves alone the fools designed,
If any are so arrogantly vain   25
To think they singly can support a scene,
And furnish fool enough to entertain.
For well the learn'd and the judicious know
That satire scorns to stoop so meanly low
As any one abstracted[2] fop to show.   30
For, as when painters form a matchless face,
They from each fair one catch some diff'rent grace,
And shining features in one portrait blend,
To which no single beauty must pretend:
So poets oft do in one piece expose   35
Whole belles assemblées[3] of coquettes and beaux.

---

[1] Supposed to be the seat of spite.   [2] Separate.   [3] Fashionable gatherings.

WILLIAM CONGREVE   671

The Eighteenth Century

THE EIGHTEENTH CENTURY

EIGHTEENTH-CENTURY literature lacks the imaginative power of the seventeenth-century masterpieces which preceded it and of the great Romantic poetry which followed it. Yet the eighteenth-century writers make to the twentieth century a curiously intimate appeal. For all their knee breeches and long stockings, their ruffles, wigs, and snuffboxes, they seem more like ourselves. This is largely due to the fact that eighteenth-century literature keeps pretty consistently to life's familiar objects and so gives us a knowledge of the life of the time that allows us to move at ease within it. The major writers were men of the world who centered their thoughts on society and made it the theme of their writing. Many of their best performances are executed, not at all in the grand manner, but over the teacups, practically on the level of gossip—of a wonderfully brilliant and cutting sort. So we know a great deal concerning the men of the period. We should doubtless feel considerably more at home over a cup of coffee or "tay" with Pope or even Swift than over a bottle of sack with Bacon or Jonson; and though we may feel no great confidence that we could have sustained an acceptable part in the Club of Dr. Johnson and his friends, we know we should not find the talk of Goldsmith and Burke couched in an unfamiliar idiom.

ARTS AND CRAFTS

THE MEN of the age were civilized and urbane. Their century set a high value on a gracious way of living, on elegance in manners, and on a gay, serene attitude toward life. To be sure, the attainment of that attitude by thoughtful people has been none too common in our troubled era; but we understand it, wish we had it, and savor the taste of it whenever we can through the medium of the arts and crafts which exemplify it. There is a refreshing element of playfulness in it. From, for example, the music of Mozart we whose times have been grim with horrors, whose art has often been strident, overstrained, or hysterical, derive a peculiar satisfaction; it springs from a perfect balance of beauty, elegance, and playfulness, which we have not been able to achieve either in our lives or in our art.

Mozart, never more adored than today, is but one of many eighteenth-century Europeans to whom nearly all cultivated people feel a personal indebtedness. As for music in England, Handel came from Germany to London for his career as oratorio and opera composer, and there were visitors of genius like Haydn; there were also a few native song-composers of talent, but after the death of Purcell in 1695 no British musician held a leading position. The highest artistic accomplishments of eighteenth-century Englishmen were in more worldly fields than music. We admire their architecture of the style called Georgian, so simple, so well proportioned, and so thoroughly assimilated in America that, in sharp contrast with our imitation-Gothic cathedrals and colleges, it seems to "belong"—and indeed it was transplanted here and flourished while we were still English colonies. We copy their light and graceful furniture by Adam and Chippendale. The distinction of their "china" or earthenware (its use was general by the end of the century) and of the work of their silversmiths enchants us.

Whether or not we have seen their pictures in the galleries, we all know some of them through prints. To be sure, William Hogarth (1697-1764), whom many now esteem the best English artist of the century, was hardly typical of his time. Like Swift, and like the novelists Fielding and Smollett, he lacked the complacency of his period. He had a vivid sense of the reality of evil, along with a powerful social conscience, and the scope of his brush and pencil embraced the poor, the weak, the vicious. But most of the leading painters were content to glorify, if not the best of all possible worlds, at any rate the most enlightened age of the most nearly perfect of nations; more especially, they loved to paint the pillars of its aristocratic society: the gentlemen; the ladies; the clustered offspring with their clean and shining faces, who in later decades would succeed automatically to this title and those acres, step into that "place" in state or church, or marry by parental arrangement such and such a fortune and position. We think of patrician ladies with large hats painted by Thomas Gainsborough (1727-88) and of the simpler and nobler portraits by George Romney (1734-1802). The recognized chief of the painters was Sir Joshua Reynolds (1723-92), the close friend of Dr. Johnson and other authors, and himself a writer. Like them he had a strong historical sense, venerating the masters of the past as they did its great writers. Some of his portraits are intimate, almost conversational; some, a little self-consciously, are executed in the grand manner. Nearly all have a touch of suavity; and on that account his reputation sank almost immediately after his death to a more modest level, where it has remained to the present day.

NEOCLASSICISM AND ITS PERSONALITIES

To COME to English letters, no age can be characterized by a single adjective; nevertheless the literature of the eighteenth century was mainly neoclassical. That is to say, the principal writers thought that the great virtues of art lay in regularity of form, not novelty or variety; in taking for subjects the normal or universal rather than the unusual or eccentric; and in following, instead of impulse, the guidance of the reason, especially as it had been applied in the formulation of the Rules, which were thought to embody all that the age-old experience of man had found most reasonable. To none of these prescripts have the best writers of recent times been willing to subscribe without extensive reservations, any more than they were unreservedly subscribed to by the great Elizabethans or the great Romantics; but our divergence in literary theory and practice has not alienated us from the eighteenth-century personalities. The restraints of neoclassicism did not inhibit a number of them from being very great personalities indeed.

The reader of English literature will find in the eighteenth century few sublime peaks of emotional or spiritual experience; but at a lower altitude an interesting degree of intellectual companionship is available with two groups of uncommonly able men: the Queen Anne or Augustan group, and the circle of Dr. Johnson. The literary history of this century breaks into two forty-year portions; no major writer overlapped them with a long career, and when we arrive at the last decade or two we are in the Romantic period. Pope died not long before the middle of the century, the first forty-odd years of which are sometimes called the Age of Pope. Echoing the name given to the golden era of Roman literature, this period liked to call itself the Augustan age of English letters—evidence both of its complacency and of the sympathy it felt with the Latin authors and with the doctrines of order and refinement preached by Horace. The second period, like the first, is often designated by the name of one of its major literary figures—the Age of Johnson.

Perhaps one would give all that was printed between 1700 and 1798 for the plays of Shakespeare or the poems of Wordsworth. Happily, no such choice confronts us; we have no expectation of retiring to a desert island with a single volume; and the young man or woman who should neglect Swift's critical view of human nature, Dr. Johnson's universal sagacity, or the political good sense of Burke, would be setting out on the journey through life, perhaps no worse off in the matter of personal ideals, but certainly in a deplorable state of innocence regarding the ways of human society. For common sense, urbanity, and knowledge of the world this eighteenth is the one to turn to.

PHILOSOPHY AND RELIGION

SUCH seemed its philosophy, which began by exalting the reason, assigned an increasingly important place to experience and common sense, and wound up with a firm conviction that the eighteenth century was the great age of Enlightenment. While in France the absolute monarchy of Louis XIV remained outwardly intact through the long reign (1715–74) of Louis XV, till under Louis XVI it fell to pieces toward the end of the century, England had decided against absolutism before the century began. We have seen that the theory of political absolutism propounded by the archmaterialist Hobbes (d. 1679) proved obnoxious to the temper of the English. They rejected it in favor of the political philosophy of John Locke (1632–1704), which was a product of the Revolution of 1688. According to Locke, men possess "natural rights"—to life, liberty, and property—and establish governments in order to secure these rights. When the state fails to maintain them, the people are justified in revolution, the implied contract having been broken. This view of the state as a kind of corporation organized by property owners for their defense and profit was a view thoroughly acceptable to the great Whig families who emerged from the Civil Wars and the Glorious Revolution as England's rulers, and it was tremendously influential throughout the eighteenth century. Revolutionary societies in England were dedicated, not to undermining the constitution, but to maintaining the principles of 1688. To the Englishman, Whig or Tory, an absolute sovereign seemed abhorrent to reason.

So did the arbitrary deity of the Old Testament. Deism became the philosophy of the English intellectuals (and of the American intellectuals, too); it was also a substitute, and as such roundly denounced, for orthodox religion. The Deist could call himself a Christian, while rejecting as incompatible with reason and science such articles of belief as, for example, miracles and supernatural revelation. To the Deist, God was no longer the despotic monarch, suspending natural law on special occasions and directly intervening in the details of human affairs; he was a benevolent creator who, having set the universe in motion, allowed it to keep on running in accordance with immutable principles, and revealed himself in its order and beauty.

This conception, a product of the late seventeenth-century Age of Reason, rested on a confidence in abstract logic which the twentieth century has been unable to share. The argument ran thus: if God is obliged to intervene in a world he made, his creation was an imperfect act to begin with; such a conclusion being inconsistent with the idea of an omniscient and omnipotent deity, we must reject the notion that he interferes with the operation of natural laws. According to this view, which the German philosopher Leibnitz (d. 1716) had worked up into a formal system, the "spacious firmament on high" is a perfectly functioning mechanism; and, as Pope insists, "Whatever is, is right": that is, given our conflicting aims and interests, the world is as right as it is possible for a world to be. To be sure, the rightness may not be in every respect immediately perceptible to the naked eye; and in *Candide* (1759) the great French skeptic Voltaire derides the whole conception, asking what part such calamities as the earthquake at Lisbon were supposed to play in the perfect scheme of things. To this objection the answer would be that, as Newton had shown, the task of science is to ascertain the laws of nature; when fully understood they would presumably demonstrate the perfection of God's plan. That conception and that expectation were optimistic to a degree which has proved unacceptable to later generations and, for that matter, was rejected by many in its own time; Swift was obviously out of sympathy with it. But Deism flourished, though never among the rank and file, to the comfort and satisfaction of that portion of the community which is always in search of a formula to reconcile supernaturalism with the rational. Deism sought to work out a *reasonable* religion. Its adherents in England were eager to bring it into line with the lowest common denominator of all the Christian faiths, even Catholicism; but in France the Deists vigorously attacked the Church.

In natural law lay the explanation of things; and since it was the human reason that was engaged in the discovery of natural law, in reason lay the hope of progress. Locke had expounded, however, the limitations of the tool. Since, he held, the mind receives nothing but impressions conveyed to it by the senses, its conclusions are dependent on obviously imperfect reports of the world outside itself. Nevertheless the tool functioned; at any rate, man's experience seemed to indicate that it did. The Earl of Chesterfield advises his son to "consult your reason. . . . I do not say it will always prove an unerring guide . . . but it will prove the least erring guide that you can follow." Reason was not only to be applied to scientific investigation; it was to be used for improving man's lot, as an instrument of social progress. Thus the betterment of society, or humanitarianism, was one of the goals of the Enlightenment. In France, particularly, all the established institutions, legal, political, economic, religious, were subjected by the philosophers to a new, rational, and skeptical scrutiny which paved the way for the French Revolution. North of the Channel, a good deal of the best writing, in both prose and verse, was concerned (like Pope's *Essay on Man*) with expounding the logic of Deism, or (as in the periodical essays of Addison and Johnson) with improving manners and morals, or (as in Swift's Irish pamphlets and the orations of Burke) with exposing injustice.

METHODISM

MEANWHILE the Established Church suffered from dry rot. The exclusion of the Dissenters, with their emphasis on a personal religion, had removed from influence in both Church and state the most vital of the religious constituencies. The main lay support of the Church of England, the country squires, many of them incapable of either ideas or spirituality,[1] dozed in their pews under the sermons of worldly divines, who aimed to please by flattering their patrons' prejudices or even vices. Some of the clergy lived far from their flocks, subsisting on the income from the "living" while a curate hired at starvation wages performed the parish duties. Gibbon alludes in his autobiography to "the fat slumbers of the Church." As for its bishops, their elevation to their lordly rank almost never resulted from anything they had done in a priestly capacity; bishoprics were important items in the vast system of party patronage.

From this moribund spiritual state the Church of England was finally roused by the religious revival of which Methodism was the spearhead. Though its

---

[1] Some, however, were men of education and taste; and the great landowning magnates lived like princes in country houses full of books and paintings.

leader, John Wesley (1703–91), never renounced his Anglican priesthood, the congregations he organized eventually constituted a new sect. Barred from the pulpits of the state Church, the Methodist preachers carried a message of hope and salvation directly to the masses, whom the Church of England had largely ignored. Great open-air meetings were held; and instead of sitting back quiescently while indifferent priest and execrable choir rattled perfunctorily through a glorious but stereotyped ritual, vast throngs of workingmen were stirred emotionally by singing hymns as well as by hearing the sermons of the exhorters. To the Methodist, religion was less a matter of subscribing to doctrine than of undergoing a vital religious experience. In its earnestness, its insistence on soul-searching, and the strictness of its code of moral prohibitions, the movement was a revival of Puritanism. One wing of it, led by the eloquent evangelist George Whitefield (1714–70), was in fact Calvinistic; the itinerants or roving preachers of this persuasion laid lurid stress on the inescapability of hellfire for the unconverted soul. Wesley himself was more interested in the beauty and sweetness of the religious life, and to many the Methodist preaching opened new vistas of spiritual comfort.

This revival, which began about 1740, not only founded the Wesleyan and Methodist churches; it galvanized into an activity which still persists the evangelical, Low-Church branch of the Church of England. The Methodists did not expect to be carried to the skies on flowery beds of ease; they emphasized the importance of good works. They were not ashamed of enthusiasm,[2] and they stood in the forefront of social reform. In their recognition of the values of feeling and in their respect for the common people they were romantic; the Methodist Revival was the manifestation in England's religious life of much the same tendencies which were soon to inspire the Romantic Movement in European literature and the fine arts, as well as the revolutionary uprisings in European politics.

HUMANITARIANISM

NOTHING is more characteristic of the eighteenth century than its zeal for making improvements (in this respect, incidentally, no Englishman or Frenchman is more typical of the age than Benjamin Franklin and Thomas Jefferson, with their multifarious interests, schemes, and inventions). Horrible

things could happen in that century, though not more horrible than we have witnessed in the twentieth; but while it was a less spectacular age than its predecessor, and produced fewer great men, it made great social and political progress. *Refinement* is a finicky-sounding word, though anyone who has lived in a foxhole will not object to it. The eighteenth century in England was marked by a great advance in refinement; on the whole men behaved more like reasoning beings and less like savages. It is true that drunkenness, gambling, and the duel were prevalent on an appalling scale; little progress was made against them by the reformers. Yet, by and large, people were more decent to one another. Though the penal code multiplied the number of capital offenses, there was more mercy, and a purer justice. The sick, the poor, the insane, and to some extent the imprisoned, got better treatment. Burke regarded his championship of India as his chief public service. Medicine and surgery saw immense gains, not only in knowledge but also in the number of their practitioners and a consequently wider application to the mass of the population. Education made enormous strides, especially through the establishment of the "charity schools," which provided elementary training for the poor; and literacy was vastly increased because girls as well as boys received more schooling. With the expansion of the reading public arrived the day of the newspaper, the magazine, and the novel. At the top of the educational system, however, the two English universities had gone to seed. The dons, appointed for life, relaxed in shameless ease; some of them drank themselves to death in a more or less genteel sort of way. Others increased their own learning, but not many paid any attention to the students. Except in Scotland, a professor who troubled to give lectures was a rarity. The Scottish universities were in a healthier state in this and most respects, and the latter half of the century saw a remarkable burst of intellectual activity at the city of Edinburgh.

But if an academic sense of responsibility to society was virtually nonexistent, and if the religious zeal of the early seventeenth century had no counterpart till the appearance of the Methodists and even then chiefly affected the working and not the governing classes, eighteenth-century England saw the awakening of a social conscience. On the political side, Burke had more to do with this than anyone else; but the change went far deeper than politics. With all the talk about rationalism, the new conviction of responsibility for others' welfare was from the first charged with feeling, as well as with a

---

[2] During the course of the eighteenth century this word had become a term of reproach, signifying an irrational emotionalism.

rationale. In the second half of the century feeling is more and more in evidence; and although, almost to the end, eighteenth-century literature remains dominated by neoclassicism, honest middle-class sentiment is catered to at the very outset by Defoe, there is moral feeling behind the pamphlets of Swift and the essays of Addison and Steele, Dr. Johnson is always concerned for the community and subject to a strong emotional drive, Burke is passionate in his advocacy of the measures he conceives necessary for the benefit of mankind, and in the novel and the drama a flood of feeling, "sensibility," or "sentiment" too often submerges everything else. As the century proceeds we shall see, not a general disregard of the cautionary signals of rationalism and neoclassicism—the signals remained set almost to the end of the run—but an increased disposition to admit feeling and imagination more and more freely into all the forms of literary expression.

POLITICS

IF LITERATURE is the most intimate record of human life, a look at general history is an essential preliminary to any literary survey; and before we tackle eighteenth-century literature such a glance must include the ever-shifting political scene. It is not merely that nearly all the major authors were convinced Tories or Whigs, but that some of the greatest were actually in the employ of one or the other of the two parties. Partisan politics was a dirty game in eighteenth-century England; even national politics was quite as corrupt as municipal politics in some American cities today. But the Glorious Revolution, and after William's death a succession of royal mediocrities, reduced the powers of the throne. No Englishman had to submit to the foul tyrannies the peasants and working class of France were subject to. The British workman or farm laborer had, however, no part in government, being disfranchised by property qualifications; for example, Robert Burns (d. 1796) was only a tenant farmer and therefore had no vote. The new manufacturing cities rising in the midlands and the north were unrepresented in Parliament; and though the country squires were Tories, election to the House of Commons was largely controlled by great Whig landowners allied with the great merchants. Even so, Commons was not likely to be entirely unresponsive when a strong current of public opinion was unmistakably setting one way. Once a member of the House, whether by actual election or by the gift or purchase of a seat in some magnate's pocket, a politician could, if he wanted to, fight as Burke

did for what he thought was right; yet the existence, at the disposal of the ministry in power, of an enormous number of well-paid legitimate jobs, as well as numerous sinecures (posts involving either no work at all, or work done by a deputy hired by the incumbent at a fraction of the salary), often enabled the chief of the administration, the first or prime minister, to buy the votes of a majority of Commons. A truly democratic franchise and a reformed Parliament were the work of the next century.

MARLBOROUGH

WE HAVE seen (p. 397) how the War of the Spanish Succession had broken out against France, and how William III, before his death in 1702, had arranged the coalition which was to wage it. Queen Anne, William's sister-in-law and successor, continued his policy, which was based upon reluctance to allow any power to become master of the Continent and upon a commercial nation's need of keeping open the trade routes and the foreign markets for her exports. To John Churchill (1650-1722), Duke of Marlborough and the greatest military genius England has produced, Anne committed not only the war but also the constant diplomatic maneuvering required to maintain the Grand Alliance against Louis XIV. Marlborough spent his summers fighting and his winters keeping England's allies in line. For a time he was the real ruler of England. His campaigns and victories put an end, till the time of Napoleon a century later, to the menace of a French tyranny over Europe.

The prosecution of the war became a political issue in England, where taxes soared in consequence of it. Marlborough advised making peace after the battle of Oudenarde, in 1708, but the Whig ministry and the Continental allies demanded impossible terms. The war became identified with the Whig party; and Marlborough, originally a Tory, had to go along with the Whigs. In 1710 the Queen, persuaded that the one great interest of her life, the Church of England, would be safer under a Tory government, succumbed to the wiles of Tory intriguers and began dismissing Marlborough's supporters, the Whig ministers. We shall see how this political overturn changed the luck of nearly all the leading writers. Public opinion was against a further sacrifice of money and lives. By 1712 it was all over. Led by two brilliant but unprincipled politicians, Robert Harley (afterwards Earl of Oxford) and Henry St. John (afterwards Viscount Bolingbroke), the Tories drove Marlborough into exile and betrayed England's allies by opening negotiations with

Louis which led to the Peace of Utrecht in 1713. This was the brief day of Swift's political glory, for his trenchant pen was the mainstay of the triumphant party.

A constitutional development of first-rate significance marked this episode. Marlborough had been opposed by a Tory House of Commons, but he was able to maintain himself as long as there was a Whig majority in the House of Lords. His fall was engineered by reversing that majority, through the Queen's creation of a dozen new Tory lords. This she did on the advice of her Tory ministers, whose party had triumphed in the election of a new House of Commons. Thus a precedent was established for the supremacy of the lower house, of which the leading British statesmen have as a rule been members ever since. To the House of Commons the ministers are all responsible, rather than to the monarch, who is unable even to pay "his" army without an annual appropriation. When backed by public opinion as well as by their majority in Commons, the ministry has usually been able to override a recalcitrant upper chamber by the mere threat of inducing or obliging the sovereign to create enough new peers of their own party to give them a working majority in the House of Lords.

WALPOLE AND THE ELDER PITT

THE short-lived Tory triumph ended with Anne's death in 1714. A conspiracy had been forming to void the Protestant succession and bestow the crown at the Queen's death on James II's exiled son James Stuart, the "Old Pretender"; but Anne died before the Jacobite conspirators' plans were matured, and without opposition the Whigs were able to proclaim the accession of the Elector of Hanover, a great-grandson of James I. From him the present royal family derives its tenure.

George I (reigned 1714-27) and his son George II (reigned 1727-60) were both personally insignificant. The throne sank to relative unimportance; England was governed by a Whig majority in the House of Commons, which did the bidding of the real rulers, the great Whig landowning families. George I never even learned to speak English. Naturally, he had to choose his ministers from the party that had put him on the throne and that controlled the House of Commons. Thus the principle was established that *all* the ministers must come from the dominant party; this was a decisive step in the development of the British constitution toward party rule and the joint responsibility of the cabinet to the majority in the lower house.

By enacting statutes favorable to commerce, the landed Whig magnates enlisted the support of the mercantilists and financiers. Between these two ruling classes, on the one hand the agricultural and mining aristocracy and on the other the new grandees of trade, there was as yet no great cleavage. Unlike the scions of the French gentry, the younger sons of the country gentlemen of England often went into business; many others sought their fortunes overseas. These men formed a strong link between the landed caste or squirearchy and the world of commerce. Another was forged by those of the city merchants who spent some of their accumulations in the purchase of land, either because they liked country life or in order to raise their families to the status of landowning gentry.

The foreign policy of the Whigs was now peace—trade flourished best in peacetime. Their domestic policy was to preserve the fruits of the Glorious Revolution and maintain their political supremacy, without introducing further reforms in government. England prospered under their rule. Its principal instrument from 1721 to 1742 was Sir Robert Walpole (1676-1745). On the whole, his do-nothing policy worked well in an age of expanding commerce. As we shall see when we come to Swift, Walpole was hated by the Tories; but he kept a majority in the House of Commons, by a system of almost open bribery. George II, who succeeded his father in 1727, detested the prime minister; but Queen Caroline, a better politician than her husband, was steadfast in his support. After her death in 1737 "Booty Bob" kept afloat with growing difficulty. In 1739 England's commercial rivalry with France and Spain created a popular demand for war, to which against his own judgment Walpole was obliged to yield. In 1740 the War of the Austrian Succession broke out, and two years later the ill success of England's part in it brought about Walpole's fall.

The struggle with France was suspended in 1748 but renewed in 1756 on a world-wide scale as the Seven Years' War. A string of defeats at the start called to the head of affairs the "Great Commoner," William Pitt (1708-78). Under his vigorous leadership England rose to heights she had not known since Marlborough. The eloquence of the prime minister tamed the House of Commons; though he led the Whigs, his personal austerity, incorruptibility, and patriotism raised him above party. The end of the war left the British Empire immensely strengthened. In India the victories of Robert Clive wrested from France control of what came to be regarded as the most valuable of England's possessions; while across the Atlantic the expulsion of the French from Canada insured the future of a great British dominion and opened the Ohio and Mississippi basins and also the western prairies to American settlement.

GEORGE III

WITH the accession in 1760 of George III (1738–1820), grandson of George II, we come to the last English monarch who played a major role in politics. It proved a disastrous one, for the attempt at personal government made by this narrow-minded and badly educated king was responsible for the mishandling of relations with the American colonies. Under his immediate predecessors the innumerable appointments to lucrative office in state and Church, nominally disposed of by the monarch, had actually been made by the prime minister. George III seized this patronage into his own hands, kept it from the Whigs, and with it built up a court party. Pitt fell in 1761, and soon withdrew from Commons with the title of Earl of Chatham. In 1763 the conclusion of a favorable peace treaty with France left the King free to consolidate his hold on the government of Great Britain. The direct purchase of seats in Commons and the systematic bribery of its members deprived that house for a time of its character as a responsive agency of the national will. The Whigs split into factions; a subservient Tory ministry executed the King's wishes; from 1768 to 1784 George III was England's ruler.

It was largely the King's failure either to conciliate or to suppress the American rebellion that terminated his personal government. With our cause the Whig leaders were in full sympathy, and its triumph proved a victory of lasting importance for British liberalism. When France and Spain finally ventured to come in on our side, the old struggle for primacy flared up again all round the globe. Though England lost the North American colonies, except Canada, her conquest of India was extended; and soon her greatness was more powerfully displayed than ever when again she led Europe in resistance to a French despot. Sympathetic at first with the French Revolution, she was horrified (as we shall see when we read Burke) by its excesses. Their effect was more than merely to send cold chills along the spines of British property owners; French violence and French political theorizing outraged the deep English feeling for order, continuity, and common sense. With the rise of Napoleon Bonaparte and the subjection of Europe to yet another series of blood baths, England was faced once more with the prospect of a

Continent organized for world conquest by a tyrant who would stop at nothing to gain his ends. It was in the midst of a cataclysmic political upheaval, war on a larger Continental scale than ever, and a revolution in the economic system that the Romantic Movement in English literature was born.

ECONOMIC CHANGES

FUNDAMENTAL economic changes occurred during this century. To a large extent their cause was the necessity of feeding, clothing, and giving employment to a rapidly increasing population, which grew during the century from five and a half millions in England and Wales to nine millions. There were various reasons for this growth; the chief was the reduction of the death rate accomplished by the advances already noted in the art of medicine and by the multiplication of hospitals and dispensaries. Another factor was an improved diet. Food was easier to get. Scientific methods in agriculture made the operation of large farms more productive than ever. Two million acres of previously untilled land were brought under cultivation. Root crops and artificial grasses were introduced for winter feed. No longer was it necessary to slaughter a large part of the herd and salt down the meat for winter consumption; the cattle could be kept alive till spring grazing was again available. Crops were rotated. The quality of cattle and sheep was improved under the new system of enclosures, that is, of privately fenced fields and pastures; improvement through breeding had been impossible when the village herds and flocks grazed together under the old conditions of pasturage in common. The average weight of marketed English sheep and cattle doubled during the course of the century, and by the end of it England had the best horses in the world.

The dispossession of many small tenant-farmers, who had been scrabbling along on a marginal existence, aroused the indignation of Goldsmith in *The Deserted Village;* but, though theirs was an unhappy destiny, getting rid of them was probably an economic blessing. They were inefficient farmers, and they were soon to swell the ranks of the new laboring class that manned the machines of the Industrial Revolution. Many small freeholders, yeomen who owned small farms, saw the writing on the wall and sold out. So did some of the lesser squires, in spite of the persistence of the connection between gentility and the ownership of land. Particularly among tenant farmers dispossessed because under the new competitive conditions they were unable to pay their rents, there was much hardship;

but the production of food increased, and before the century was over even the common people were demanding the luxury of white bread. The distressing feature of the change was that in rural areas the poor man who had at least made an independent living from his little strip of land was likely to become a pauper or a landless, unskilled laborer; the farmers who survived had to be capitalists.

In the sixties and seventies a series of inventions made possible the application of steam power to spinning and weaving; the result was the enormous textile industry of Lancashire. Coal and pottery also became major exports. Roads and canals were improved and extended, and the great manufacturing cities of the midlands and the north took first-rate economic, though not as yet political, place. British commerce was furthered by the free-trade policy of the younger Pitt (1759-1806), whose inspiration was the first important treatise on economics, Adam Smith's *The Wealth of Nations* (1776).

THE QUALITY OF EIGHTEENTH-CENTURY POETRY

THE HISTORY of the century's literature is traced in the introductions to the major writers, from whose works our selections have been drawn. Except for genres unrepresented by them, only the main trends need be noted here.

Both the Age of Pope and the Age of Johnson were in their temper more critical than creative, and with one exception their greatest figures were writers principally of prose. The exception is Pope. His own idea as to the relation of poetry to prose is indicated in a comment on "the Design" of *An Essay on Man*. Having summarized the content of the poem, he continues: "This I might have done in prose, but I chose verse, and even rime, for two reasons. The one will appear obvious: that principles, maxims, or precepts so written both strike the reader more strongly at first, and are more easily retained by him afterwards. The other may seem odd but is true: I found I could express them more *shortly* this way than in prose itself; and nothing is more certain than that much of the *force* as well as *grace* of arguments or instructions depends on their *conciseness*. I was unable to treat this part of my subject . . . more *poetically* without sacrificing perspicuity to ornament, without wandering from the precision, or breaking the chain of reasoning." Poetry, like prose, was explicitly didactic; its material was rational truth; the function of imagination was to provide pleasing embellishment in the form of imagery drawn from the store conveyed to it by the senses; imagination was to be rigorously subjected

to judgment lest it break the design. The conception of imagination as an instrument for discovering truth of a kind that transcends reason was to be the revolutionary contribution of the Romantic period; to the rationalism of the eighteenth century it was wholly repugnant.

Pope's gifts of language and versification allowed him to bring his kind of poetry to the highest development it has ever reached. Too many of those who followed him wrote with a mechanical regularity or with a pompous dullness of which he was never guilty. In particular, the attempt to find in style as distinct from matter the difference between poetry and prose led to the development of an artificial poetic diction that blemishes the work of even the better writers. Gray wrote one of the minor masterpieces of English poetry; but one of his inferior poems, an ode on "The Progress of Poesy," will serve to illustrate some of the vices which eventually brought eighteenth-century poetry into disesteem. Here we have the "poetic" circumlocution: "feathered king" for eagle, "Ceres' golden reign" for wheatfields; the pallid personification: "antic Sports and blue-eyed Pleasures"; the conventional epithet: "nodding groves" and "verdant vales"; the inflated and insufficiently particularized imagery:

> O'er her warm cheek, and rising bosom, move
> The bloom of young Desire, and purple light of Love.

The man who writes like that is comparable to an artist painting indoors, with all the shades down, from his recollection of pictures he has seen in the galleries. A part of the trouble comes from the age's emphasis on the general, the typical, the universal, which has its most famous statement in Johnson's *Rasselas,* chapter 10, reprinted below. "The business of a poet," he declares, "is to examine, not the individual but the species; to remark general properties and large appearances; he does not number the streaks of the tulip, or describe the different shades in the verdure of the forest." In this perversion of Aristotle's illuminating remark that poetry is more significantly true than history because it deals with universals, Johnson confused the object of poetry with the means by which it is attained. His knowledge of Shakespeare, whose regular method is to create by the selection of vivid detail an impression of universality, should have kept him from this error. But he was stating orthodox contemporary theory.

Yet the merits of eighteenth-century poetry at its best are far from negligible. There is much pleasure to be got from the shapely work of the gifted craftsman. The Romantic genius of the next era was sometimes divorced from humor, and the artist who enthralls us when we are in the right mood may bore us or wear us down when we are not. Great poetry rarely soothes, but everyone is the better for occasional relaxation. Often the eighteenth-century poet is a pleasant person who charms us into a good humor by his ease and intimate manner as of one social being to another, or a man of great good sense and worldly experience who can tell us a good deal about human nature, or a sharp fellow who amuses us and, inviting us to join him on a high intellectual plane, flatters our self-esteem by showing us what fools and rascals less admirable folk can be. These pleasing methods, whether applied to polite small-talk or to moral discourse or to bitter satire, he presents in a vocabulary and syntax easy to understand and a verse form which delights by the simplicity and regularity of its pattern and the artfulness with which every second line clicks into its appointed place in the couplet. He composes, our eighteenth-century poet, like a well-informed gentleman whose conversation is so calculatedly urbane and witty that it reaches the level of art.

It is often drawing-room talk, principally concerned with men's and women's manners—giving to that word its older and wider sense, which included character. An ecstatic response to nature, to the beauty of the countryside, of forest, hill, or ocean, would be as out of place in this poetry as an eighteenth-century man of fashion would feel if he found himself in public without his wig. The nature of *humanity* was the great subject. If a poet went out of doors, it was preferably into a garden of studied arrangements—no longer, to be sure, the ruler-straight walks and clipped hedges of King William's time (we shall see what Addison and Pope had to say of such gardens), but a kind of pretended and miniature wilderness. At a real hill the early eighteenth century was apt to shudder; English travelers en route to Italy considered the Alps at best a nuisance, at worst a horrible menace. Even in the lovely English northland where Wordsworth was soon to find inspiration and glory, the lakes and mountains, which to an American who knows his country seem far from stupendous, were not much visited till late in the century; nature was too disorderly there for the neoclassicist. Only faintly appears in the most typical writers any trace of that ardent feeling for natural beauty which would have its way at the century's end; and almost never, even where there is some response to the outward charms

of Nature, is there any indication that a poet's ear is listening for her message.

After 1750 the turn of the tide against the exclusively rational and the narrowly neoclassical is plain to see. One milestone, it is now apparent, was the appearance in 1765 of Thomas Percy's *Reliques of Ancient English Poetry*. The neoclassicists in general underestimated earlier English literature. Despite frequent admonitions against unreasoning worship of the classics, and despite the vigor with which the Modernists defended their side in the old controversy between the Ancients and the Moderns, it was the ancient world that chiefly offered literary models and inspiration to the eighteenth century. Secondary and college education was still mainly classical; the period abounds in translations of ancient authors and imitation of the classical genres, to say nothing of the countless allusions that make necessary a large proportion of the footnotes attached to the selections in this section. Bishop Percy's collection of the old ballads, new studies by philologists in Chaucer and Old English literature, and a revaluation upward of the Elizabethan writers were all signs pointing toward a shift in taste that was to culminate in the next epoch.

Despite such symptoms of change, the century remained dominantly rational and neoclassical until very near its end. Collins, Gray, and Cowper, sometimes cited as the advance guard of Romanticism, are all fundamentally neoclassical. Not till the advent of Blake, Burns, Wordsworth, and Coleridge, with their new conception of the imagination, can any important writer of the eighteenth century properly be called a Romantic.

THE NOVEL

THE MAJOR types of prose writing in the eighteenth century are dealt with below—with one exception. Unfortunately the novel cannot be illustrated in this book. In the age of Johnson it burst into a bloom which has been perennial ever since. As a rule, sixteenth- and seventeenth-century storytelling seems bald and artless compared with the fiction of the eighteenth-century masters. Defoe began his tales of adventure in 1719 with *Robinson Crusoe;* but the modern novel of character, devoted mainly to showing how people behave, flowers with Samuel Richardson (1689–1761) and his *Pamela* (1740; sequel in 1741). Richardson was a printer who, like Defoe, turned late to fiction. His three novels are cast in the form of letters; for us their interest and strength lie in analysis of emotion and the untangling of motives. As a rule, the eighteenth-century novel is leisurely;

Richardson's are often tedious, and occasionally absurd. His masterpiece, the tragic *Clarissa* (1747-8), and the inferior *Sir Charles Grandison* (1753-4) originally appeared in seven volumes each. Their author's tone is heavily moral and rankly sentimental. Pamela is a maidservant who resists the repeated attempts of her wealthy young master to seduce her, falls in love with him, reforms him, and marries him. Clarissa is a virtuous girl seduced by the unscrupulous Lovelace. Yet the books are not romances but novels—the first really modern novels—because, instead of telling wild tales of extraordinary adventure, they treat contemporary characters with psychological realism.

A more robust atmosphere prevails in the works of Henry Fielding (1707-54), who was not, like Defoe and Richardson, a tradesman. Some think his *Tom Jones* the greatest English novel. Educated for the law, Fielding began his literary career with mediocre comedies, farces, and burlesques. After a satirical piece on Sir Robert Walpole, he ended his connection with the theater when the Licensing Act of 1737 was passed, requiring (as is still the case in England) the Lord Chamberlain's permission in advance of any play's production. Fielding resumed his legal studies, went into journalism, and continued to attack Walpole. He was called to the bar in 1740; in 1748 he became a magistrate in London, and began introducing epoch-making reforms in the police system and his court at Bow Street. His first novel, *Joseph Andrews* (1742), was conceived as a parody of Richardson (Joseph is Pamela's brother and a virtuous servant who resists the wicked wiles of his mistress, Lady Booby); but it developed into a serious work on its own account. In *Tom Jones* (1749), along with a wealth of realistic detail, there is an almost Shakespearean sweep of events and breadth of understanding of human nature. This is one of those few of the world's novels that will bear repeated rereadings; it is much better than Fielding's others.

Tobias George Smollett (1721-71), a Scottish doctor, was surgeon's mate on a naval expedition, tried with little success to practice medicine in London, and soon found his real métier in fiction. His novels are rambling, adventurous tales, coarser and less acute than Fielding's and Richardson's, but vigorous, comic, and racy. *Roderick Random* (1748) and *Humphrey Clinker* (1771) are the best; in the former he exploits his experience at sea, while the latter gives a full and vivid picture of how daily life was lived in contemporary England.

The Reverend Laurence Sterne (1713-68) did not become a novelist till his last years. *Tristram Shandy* (1760-67), in its humor, impropriety, and wild whimsicality, is unlike any other novel; and its Uncle Toby and Corporal Trim are among the unforgettable creations of prose fiction. *A Sentimental Journey* (1768) is slighter, but in its fragile essays the prevailing sensibility of the time is exquisitely distilled.

Goldsmith's one novel, *The Vicar of Wakefield* (1766), long continued to win the affection of readers, but is not of much importance in the development of the genre. The so-called Gothic romance, beginning with *The Castle of Otranto* (1765) by Horace Walpole (who was possibly the greatest of English letter writers), is hopelessly inferior to the work of the century's four major novelists. As a return to the medieval and an attempt, a misguided one, at infusing fiction with a renewal of imagination, it properly belongs to the Romantic Movement.

COMEDY

WE HAVE seen how the final phase of seventeenth-century drama was a superbly polished comedy of manners, which culminated in 1700 with Congreve's *The Way of the World,* and ended in 1707 with *The Beaux' Stratagem* of Farquhar. The reaction of the new century against this type of play has also been described (p. 400). Humanitarian feeling and the Enlightenment's earnestness about improving society condemned a genre which provoked laughter at the follies and the predicaments, however deserved, of our fellow creatures. Restoration comedy was replaced by a type called sentimental comedy, displaying characters of the most exalted virtue who for four acts are embroiled in complications that seriously threaten their happiness but who emerge in the fifth triumphant. The aim was to draw from the audience not laughter at human folly but tearful sympathy for virtue in distress and satisfaction at virtue rewarded.

Early in the century Steele flatly advocated banishing laughter from the comic stage, and he was proud that over certain scenes in his comedy of *The Conscious Lovers* (1722) audiences wept. Later on, Richard Cumberland (1732-1811), whom Sheridan satirized in *The Critic,* pleased the public with the deadly seriousness of humanitarian propaganda disguised as comedy. Cumberland was the arch-sentimentalist; a close second was another stage moralist, Hugh Kelly (1739-77), whose comedies were replete with genteel distresses irresistible to tender sensibilities.

In vain in the late sixties and the seventies two better writers of comedy, Goldsmith and Sheridan, protested against the hybrid genre and attempted to restore laughter to the stage (see below, pp. 893, 938). There were farces galore; but true comedy on a rational and literary level attracted few good writers—an unhappy contrast with conditions in earlier epochs. The best comedy between Congreve's exit from the stage (1700) and Goldsmith's entrance (1768) was not a legitimate drama but a ballad opera, John Gay's merry, satirical, and tuneful masterpiece, *The Beggar's Opera* (1728). With a few exceptions, the tendency of comedy was toward either the maudlin or the farcical; and such on the whole it remained till past the middle of the nineteenth century.

TRAGEDY

As FOR English tragedy, neoclassicism had a soporific effect on it. The drama thrives on passion, not on restraining it; and the stately or would-be stately speeches of the eighteenth-century heroes dug up out of Roman history have a hollow sound, as if composed for slightly animated statues robed in marble (or wooden) togas. Another tragic genre, no better written than the neoclassical type, had at least the merit of bearing some relation to contemporary life. This was the bourgeois or domestic tragedy. With the rise of the middle class to political consequence and to better educational and cultural advantages, the merchant or tradesman becomes for the dramatist a serious subject, even a hero, instead of a figure of fun to be laughed at when his wife or daughter makes a fool of him with the assistance of a rakehelly young aristocrat. As early as 1722, Steele had halted the action of *The Conscious Lovers* to voice a panegyric of the merchant's "service" to the community. In the tragedy of *The London Merchant* (1731) by George Lillo, a whole play is dedicated to showing the apprentices that honesty pays the best dividends. In its ethical code this is a middle-class play, and Lillo writes it in prose instead of in the customary blank verse. Unfortunately, his powers were unequal to his aims.

Tragedy became even more sentimental than comedy; and when the Romantic movement reached the theater, it did no good to either genre: both were encouraged to go in more recklessly than ever for feeling for the sake of feeling. Tears were regarded as infallible signs of a heart in the right place; and the tragic dramatist conceived that his business was not so much to reconstruct life, or to illuminate its mystery, as to invent pressure situations for moody heroes and distraught heroines over whom an audience could have a delicious cry. After the death of Thomas Otway in 1685 London saw no more good new English tragedies until the first decade of our own century.

What it did see, besides a very mixed grill of contemporary plays, was a long line of revivals of Shakespeare. Beginning with David Garrick in the early years of the Age of Johnson, on down through the productions of Sir Henry Irving (d. 1905), a series of brilliant actor-managers kept Shakespeare's best plays continuously before the public, chiefly in repertory companies. Actors and public alike learned about drama from him. There is something to be said for a theater which is faithful to the greatest works of its past; but that is the most which can be said for the English theater of the eighteenth and nineteenth centuries. Drama shirked its duty, as defined by Shakespeare, of holding the mirror up to nature; for the facts and for the criticism of contemporary life during both centuries we must turn, not to the drama, but to poetry, the essay, and the novel.

GENERAL REFERENCES

Good books for the general background are: P. Smith's *A History of Modern Culture,* vol. II, *The Enlightenment, 1687–1776* (1934); and two books edited by A. S. Turberville: the lavishly illustrated *English Men and Manners in the Eighteenth Century* (2nd ed., 1929), and *Johnson's England* (2 vols, 1933). Chapters X–XIV in G. M. Trevelyan's *English Social History* (1942) deal with this period. H. V. D. Dyson and J. Butt's *Augustans and Romantics, 1689–1830* (1940) is equally divided between a sketch of literary history with its background, and a well-organized bibliography.

Among the useful anthologies are C. A. Moore's *English Poetry of the Eighteenth Century* (1935), R. S. Crane's *A Collection of English Poems, 1660–1800* (1932), D. N. Smith's *The Oxford Book of Eighteenth Century Verse* (1926), and L. I. Bredvold, R. K. Root, and G. Sherburn's *Eighteenth Century Prose* (1932).

References to the standard editions and biographies of the leading writers will be found in the special introductions below. The best guides to the plays of the period are A. Nicoll's *A History of Early Eighteenth Century Drama, 1700–1750* (1925) and *A History of Late Eighteenth Century Drama, 1750–1800* (1927). Good anthologies are G. H. Nettleton and A. E. Case's *British Dramatists from Dryden to Sheridan* (1939) and D. MacMillan and H. M. Jones's *Plays of the Restoration and Eighteenth Century* (revised ed., 1935).

Daniel Defoe

1660-1731

NOTHING else that Defoe wrote is comparable, as literature, to his novels; and for obvious reasons that genre is beyond the scope of this book. A novel may be read piecemeal; but if it is worth the reading, it must be thought about whole, since in any serious work of art the whole is greater than the sum of its parts. The next best way of taking Defoe's measure is through *A Journal of the Plague Year.* In a way this account of the epidemic of 1665 is more an historical novel than anything else, for it purports to be the recollections of an elderly tradesman, a saddler, who is just as fictitious as any character in the novels proper, and its material is drawn not only from earlier accounts of the plague and the weekly "bills of mortality" but also from Defoe's imagination. Just as a piece of prose, it has even been called his masterpiece.

Though intellectually Defoe was at least the equal of Addison and Pope, he was no Swift. Yet an extract from *The Plague Year* will serve well enough for our initiation into the eighteenth century. The first four of its writers to be considered here are all prose writers; the fact is significant. Defoe's is a far from faultless prose; the *New York Times* would not tolerate such writing by its staff today. But if its sentences ramble, and sometimes creak at the joints, his style has the admirable simplicity and straightforwardness which mark good reporting and were noted in our introduction to the seventeenth century among the major aims of its later critics. Defoe was forty when the eighteenth century began. In that same introduction we observed that well before 1700 the trend was away from the hardboiled Restoration attitude, toward a candid expression of feeling. In this respect, too, *A Journal of the Plague Year* is appropriate for an opening selection. There is no cynicism in it, but tears for suffering. When it appeared, in 1722, not to weep for another's woe argued a man unfeeling; and not to bestir oneself in the relief of misery exposed one's unworthiness of living in the Age of Enlightenment. Sympathy bedews every page of the *Journal,* a more personal sympathy than that expressed by Samuel Pepys over the identical calamity. The narrator's streaming eye is not unmanly; no properly brought up citizen of the full-blown eighteenth century could think it unmanly. By compassion for distress and suffering you showed yourself a man, distinguished from the beasts by sensibility as well as reason.

Defoe was a London businessman who turned in middle life to writing on politics and economics, and in later life turned again, to fiction. He was Daniel Foe till he was in his forties, when, like Sir William D'avenant (see p. 517), who inserted his own apostrophe, he added the *De.* The son of a Puritan butcher in London, he was intended for the Presbyterian ministry, but his preaching was fated to be done in books, pamphlets, and newspapers. At an academy maintained by Dissenters he received a reasonably good education; from the universities his religion barred him. Many details about his life, such as the extent to which he traveled, are still obscure. He married in 1684, and had eight children. According to his own account, he was "in arms" as a rebel when the Duke of Monmouth made his bid for King James's throne. By the date of his marriage he was evidently well established as a commission merchant. It was an expansive moment in the commercial history of London. Defoe dealt in various commodities, for instance in hosiery, wine, and tobacco. In 1692 he went bankrupt, to the tune of £17,000. He was pretty clearly an adventurous speculator, and some of the litigation he was constantly involved in suggests that his business methods were far from scrupulous. An agreement was arranged with his creditors, and he escaped the horrors of debtor's prison; but apparently he never got free from debt nor from the possibility of being jailed for it. He did his best to pay it off; by 1705 he had reduced it to £5000.

Defoe was writing verse at least as early as 1691, but his first important work was the prose *An Essay upon Projects,* published in the spring of 1698. This 300-page book shows the eighteenth-century zeal for improving things, the same urge which on a higher level of accomplishment pushed Benjamin Franklin into his diversified activities. Defoe brings forward projects, or proposals, in fields as varied as education, road making, banking, taxation, insurance, and the care of idiot children. Most of his early writing, however, was political pamphleteering for the Whigs. He was a warm supporter of William III, and in several trenchant pamphlets he took up the cudgels for the King's policy of war against France. In 1701 Defoe argued in a verse satire, *The True-born Englishman,* that William's foreign birth should not be held against him; in view of the variety of peoples that composed the island's stock, England was "Europe's sink" anyway. Defoe's rough verses hit the public fancy and seem to have influenced opinion. The poem had an immense sale, and Defoe says (the statement is far from conclusive evidence) that he became an intimate of the King.

The Shortest Way with Dissenters (1702) is a piece of ironical prose, purporting to maintain, in the interest of the Church of England, that the nonconforming Protestant sects "ought to be destroyed, hanged, banished, and the devil and all." This pamphlet appeared anonymously in the first year of the reign of Queen Anne, whose main interest in life was the Established Church. Parliament was debating a bill to deny the right of holding office to those Dissenters who got round their exclusion from it by occasionally taking communion at an Anglican altar. Defoe's authorship of the pamphlet was soon discovered. Unfortunately, both the Dissenters and the High Churchmen at first took the irony seriously. When the hoax was somewhat tardily recognized and the complacent Anglicans realized that the attack was actually against them, the pamphlet was pronounced seditious and its author became a fugitive from justice. He was caught several months later and harshly punished by fine, imprisonment, and exposure in the pillory. This last mode of punishment was no joke. Its victims were often favored by the rabble with showers of dirt, decayed fruit and vegetables, and eggs that were past serving other purposes; it was a dreadful ordeal, and death from it was not unknown. On this occasion, however, the mob decided that the victim was a hero and astonished him with flowers in token of their sympathy.

His imprisonment was terminated by the good offices of the future Tory prime minister, Robert Harley. Defoe's latest business now being ruined (he had gone into brick and tile making), he became a secret agent for Harley. One of his duties was to spy on the Jacobites in Scotland, as well as in England; and he spent long periods riding the roads to pick up "intelligence." Another task was to support his employer's policy of moderation by anonymous pamphlets attacking both Whig and Tory extremists. From 1704 to 1713 Defoe edited a newspaper, the *Review,* which appeared three times a week. The *Review,* the bulk of which Defoe wrote himself, was the most important English periodical before the *Tatler;* it originated two standard features of journalism, the leading article and the "column," for it was even more a journal of opinion than a newspaper. Despite his employment by Harley, Defoe's pen was always for sale; he secretly composed an immense amount of political prose and verse, for both sides. Harley was out of office from 1707 to 1710, and Defoe went to work for the Whigs till his master regained power. In 1714, when the accession of George I brought the Whigs their decisive triumph, Defoe went on their secret payroll. Some of his activities were well enough known to give him an unsavory name. Swift, who called him a rogue, and Addison, who found him "a false, shuffling, prevaricating rascal," would have raised their eyebrows if anyone had told them that Defoe would be more widely read by posterity than they. Till the appearance of *Robinson Crusoe,* when he was nearly sixty, his reputation as a writer was principally for his contributions, often highly statistical, to economics.

Now, of course, it is for his novels. *The Life and Strange Surprising Adventures of Robinson Crusoe of York, Mariner,* was published in 1719; it had a tremendous sale. In 1720 appeared *Memoirs of a Cavalier* and *The Life, Adventures, and Piracies of the Famous Captain Singleton;* in 1722, besides *A Journal of the Plague Year,* came *Colonel Jack* and the second-best of the novels, *The Fortunes and Misfortunes of the Famous Moll Flanders;* in 1724 there was *Roxana, or The Fortunate Mistress.* Defoe had a widely ranging curiosity and an extraordinary sense of concrete fact. A wealth of detail gives his novels an air of actuality, whether as in *Crusoe* we are wafted to the remotest isles or, as in the picaresque or rogue novel of *Moll Flanders,* we are conducted through London's underworld. In these works, and in the *Journal,* the sheer narrative power sweeps us along; few men have equaled Defoe in ability to absorb a reader's attention.

He says in his *Complete English Tradesman* (1726) that "easy, plain, and familiar language is the beauty of speech in general, and is the excellency of all writing," and that "the end of speech is that men might understand one another's meaning." He achieves these goals so admirably that it is easy to excuse the inaccuracy of his grammar and the looseness of his sentences. His output was enormous, and he turned it out at a journalist's pace. He writes as his alleged narrators would talk if they had Defoe's flair for talk. We who come to his pages fresh from Congreve's sparkling prose can easily assess the changes that had occurred since 1700. Congreve had written with a wit's elegance and verve, for aristocrats—of taste as well as birth. Defoe was a middle-class Londoner. He writes about people of the middle, lower, and lowest classes, for the middle and lower classes.

> Down in the kitchen, honest Dick and Doll
> Are studying Colonel Jack and Flanders Moll.

So reports the *Flying Post* of March 1, 1729, quoted in Professor Sutherland's biography. Two marks of the superior reader are his pleasure in recognizing the rapier-flash of wit and, when a master's thrust is too quick for the naked eye, a willingness to spend a few moments searching for the wound. Defoe's characteristic merits are of a different order. He pleases because he is so easy to follow. He also pleased the readers of his day because he combined racy realism with plenty of right thinking, right feeling, and pious exhortation. But with all this success, he was born to trouble, as the sparks fly upward. He was in hiding again—this time in flight from a creditor—when his stormy life ended in 1731.

In all, Defoe wrote some four hundred works. There is no edition that is anything like complete. A selection of his writings is given in the Shakespeare Head edition (14 vols., 1927–28). The *Romances and Narratives* were edited by G. A. Aitken (16 vols., 1895–96), whose edition of *A Journal of the Plague Year,* as well as several of the novels,

is included in Everyman's Library. For an authoritative study of the epidemic, see W. G. Bell's *The Great Plague in London in 1665* (1924). A good Life is J. R. Sutherland's *Defoe* (1938).

Daniel Defoe

from A JOURNAL OF THE PLAGUE YEAR

Written by a Citizen Who Continued All the While in London

THE occasion of *A Journal of the Plague Year,* which came out early in 1722, was an epidemic at Marseilles in 1720–21. Defoe exploited the current fear that the Great Plague of 1665 might not prove England's last. His picture is hardly overdrawn; of the half million inhabitants of the metropolitan area it seems likely that the plague of 1665 killed a hundred thousand. The following selections are from various parts of the book.

As I went along Houndsditch[1] one morning about eight o'clock, there was a great noise. It is true, indeed, there was not much crowd, because people were not very free to gather together, or to stay long together when they were there; nor did I stay long there. But the outcry was loud enough to prompt my curiosity, and I called to one that looked out of a window, and asked what was the matter.

A watchman, it seems, had been employed to keep his post at the door of a house which was infected, or said to be infected, and was shut up. He had been there all night for two nights together, as he told his story, and the day watchman had been there one day, and was now come to relieve him. All this while no noise had been heard in the house, no light had been seen; they called for nothing, sent him of no errands, which used to be the chief business of the watchmen; neither had they given him any disturbance, as he said, from the Monday afternoon, when he heard great crying and screaming in the house, which, as he supposed, was occasioned by some of the family dying just at that time. It seems the night before the dead-cart, as it was called, had been stopped there, and a servant-maid had been brought down to the door dead, and the buriers or bearers, as they were called, put her into the cart, wrapt only in a green rug, and carried her away.

The watchman had knocked at the door, it seems, when he heard that noise and crying, as above, and nobody answered a great while; but at last one looked out and said with an angry, quick tone, and yet a kind of crying voice, or a voice of one that was crying, "What d'ye want, that ye make such a knocking?" He answered, "I am the watchman! How do you do? What is the matter?" The person answered, "What is that to you? Stop the dead-cart." This, it seems, was about one o'clock. Soon after, as the fellow said, he stopped the dead-cart, and then knocked again, but nobody answered. He continued knocking, and the bellman called out several times, "Bring out your dead!" but nobody answered, till the man that drove the cart, being called to other houses, would stay no longer, and drove away.

The watchman knew not what to make of all this; so he let them alone till the morning man or day watchman, as they called him, came to relieve him. Giving him an account of the particulars, they knocked at the door a great while, but nobody answered; and they observed that the window or casement at which the person had looked out who had answered before continued open, being up two pair of stairs.

Upon this, the two men to satisfy their curiosity got a long ladder, and one of them went up to the window and looked into the room, where he saw a woman lying dead upon the floor in a dismal manner, having no clothes on her but her shift. But though he called aloud and, putting in his long staff, knocked hard on the floor, yet nobody stirred or answered; neither could he hear any noise in the house.

He came down again upon this, and acquainted his fellow, who went up also; and finding it just so, they resolved to acquaint either the Lord Mayor or some other magistrate of it, but did not offer[2] to go

[1] A street on the site of the old moat running northwest along the city wall from Aldgate to Bishopsgate. The supposed narrator lived in the vicinity, which was one of the hardest hit.

[2] Attempt.

in at the window. The magistrate, it seems, upon the information of the two men, ordered the house to be broke open, a constable and other persons being appointed to be present, that nothing might be plundered; and accordingly it was so done, when nobody was found in the house but that young woman, who, having been infected and past recovery, the rest had left her to die by herself, and were every one gone, having found some way to delude the watchman, and to get open the door, or get out at some back door, or over the tops of the houses, so that he knew nothing of it; and as to those cries and shrieks which he heard, it was supposed they were the passionate cries of the family at the bitter parting, which, to be sure, it was to them all, this being the sister to the mistress of the family. The man of the house, his wife, several children, and servants, being all gone and fled, whether sick or sound, that I could never learn; nor, indeed, did I make much inquiry after it. . . .

I remember, and while I am writing this story I think I hear the very sound of it, a certain lady had an only daughter, a young maiden about nineteen years old, and who was possessed of a very considerable fortune. They were only lodgers in the house where they were. The young woman, her mother, and the maid had been abroad[3] on some occasion, I do not remember what, for the house was not shut up; but about two hours after they came home the young lady complained she was not well; in a quarter of an hour more she vomited and had a violent pain in her head. "Pray God," says her mother, in a terrible fright, "my child has not the distemper!" The pain in her head increasing, her mother ordered the bed to be warmed, and resolved to put her to bed, and prepared to give her things to sweat, which was the ordinary remedy to be taken when the first apprehensions of the distemper began.

While the bed was airing, the mother undressed the young woman, and just as she was laid down in the bed, she, looking upon her body with a candle, immediately discovered the fatal tokens on the inside of her thighs. Her mother, not being able to contain herself, threw down her candle and screeched out in such a frightful manner that it was enough to place horror upon the stoutest heart in the world; nor was it one scream or one cry, but, the fright having seized her spirits, she fainted first, then recovered, then ran all over the house, up the stairs and down the stairs, like one distracted, and indeed really was distracted, and continued screeching and

crying out for several hours void of all sense, or, at least, government of her senses, and, as I was told, never came thoroughly to herself again. As to the young maiden, she was a dead corpse from that moment, for the gangrene which occasions the spots had spread over her whole body, and she died in less than two hours. But still the mother continued crying out, not knowing anything more of her child, several hours after she was dead. It is so long ago that I am not certain; but I think the mother never recovered, but died in two or three weeks after.

This was an extraordinary case, and I am therefore the more particular in it, because I came so much to the knowledge of it; but there were innumerable suchlike cases, and it was seldom that the weekly bill[4] came in but there were two or three put in frighted, that is, that may well be called frighted to death. . . .

I went all the first part of the time freely about the streets, though not so freely as to run myself into apparent danger, except when they dug the great pit in the churchyard of our parish of Aldgate. A terrible pit it was, and I could not resist my curiosity to go and see it. As near as I may judge, it was about forty feet in length, and about fifteen or sixteen feet broad, and, at the time I first looked at it, about nine feet deep; but it was said they dug it near twenty feet deep afterwards in one part of it, till they could go no deeper for[5] the water; for they had, it seems, dug several large pits before this. For though the plague was long a-coming to our parish, yet, when it did come, there was no parish in or about London where it raged with such violence as in the two parishes of Aldgate and Whitechapel.[6]

I say they had dug several pits in another ground, when the distemper began to spread in our parish, and especially when the dead-carts began to go about, which was not, in our parish, till the beginning of August. Into these pits they had put perhaps fifty or sixty bodies each; then they made larger holes, wherein they buried all that the cart brought in a week, which, by the middle to the end of August, came to from 200 to 400 a week; and they could not well dig them larger, because of the order of the magistrates confining them to leave no bodies within six feet of the surface; and the water coming on at about seventeen or eighteen feet, they could not well, I say, put more in one pit. But now, at the beginning of September, the plague raging in a dreadful manner, and the number of burials in our

---

3 Out.

4 List of deaths, with causes.   5 On account of.
6 East of Aldgate; it is still a crowded area.

parish increasing to more than was ever buried in any parish about London of no larger extent, they ordered this dreadful gulf to be dug, for such it was rather than a pit.

They had supposed this pit would have supplied them for a month or more, when they dug it, and some blamed the churchwardens for suffering such a frightful thing, telling them they were making preparations to bury the whole parish, and the like; but time made it appear the churchwardens knew the condition of the parish better than they did, for, the pit being finished the 4th of September, I think, they began to bury in it the 6th, and by the 20th, which was just two weeks, they had thrown into it 1114 bodies, when they were obliged to fill it up, the bodies being then come to lie within six feet of the surface. I doubt not but there may be some ancient persons alive in the parish who can justify the fact of this, and are able to show even in what place of the churchyard the pit lay better than I can. The mark of it also was many years to be seen in the churchyard on the surface, lying in length parallel with the passage which goes by the west wall of the churchyard out of Houndsditch, and turns east again into Whitechapel, coming out near the Three Nuns' Inn.

It was about the 10th of September that my curiosity led, or rather drove, me to go and see this pit again, when there had been near 400 people buried in it; and I was not content to see it in the daytime, as I had done before, for then there would have been nothing to have been seen but the loose earth; for all the bodies that were thrown in were immediately covered with earth by those they called the buriers, which at other times were called bearers; but I resolved to go in the night and see some of them thrown in.

There was a strict order to prevent people coming to those pits, and that was only to prevent infection. But after some time that order was more necessary, for people that were infected and near their end, and delirious also, would run to those pits, wrapt in blankets or rugs, and throw themselves in, and, as they said, bury themselves. I cannot say that the officers suffered any willingly to lie there; but I have heard that in a great pit in Finsbury, in the parish of Cripplegate, it lying open then to the fields, for it was not then walled about, some came and threw themselves in, and expired there before they threw any earth upon them; and that when they came to bury others, and found them there, they were quite dead, though not cold.

This may serve a little to describe the dreadful condition of that day, though it is impossible to say anything that is able to give a true idea of it to those who did not see it, other than this: that it was indeed very, very, very dreadful, and such as no tongue can express.

I got admittance into the churchyard by being acquainted with the sexton who attended, who, though he did not refuse me at all, yet earnestly persuaded me not to go, telling me very seriously, for he was a good, religious, and sensible man, that it was indeed their business and duty to venture, and to run all hazards, and that in it they might hope to be preserved; but that I had no apparent call to it but my own curiosity, which, he said, he believed I would not pretend was sufficient to justify my running that hazard. I told him I had been pressed in my mind to go, and that perhaps it might be an instructing sight, that might not be without its uses. "Nay," says the good man, "if you will venture upon that score, name of God go in; for, depend upon it, 'twill be a sermon to you—it may be, the best that ever you heard in your life. 'Tis a speaking sight," says he, "and has a voice with it, and a loud one, to call us all to repentance." And with that he opened the door and said, "Go, if you will."

His discourse had shocked my resolution a little, and I stood wavering for a good while; but just at that interval I saw two links[7] come over from the end of the Minories,[8] and heard the bellman, and then appeared a dead-cart, as they called it, coming over the streets; so I could no longer resist my desire of seeing it, and went in. There was nobody, as[9] I could perceive at first, in the churchyard, or going into it, but the buriers and the fellow that drove the cart, or rather led the horse and cart; but when they came up to the pit they saw a man go to and again,[10] muffled up in a brown cloak, and making motions with his hands under his cloak, as if he was in a great agony, and the buriers immediately gathered about him, supposing he was one of those poor delirious or desperate creatures that used to pretend, as I have said, to bury themselves. He said nothing as he walked about, but two or three times groaned very deeply and loud, and sighed as he would break his heart.

When the buriers came up to him, they soon found he was neither a person infected and desperate, as I have observed above, or a person distempered in mind, but one oppressed with a dreadful weight of

---

7 Torches.   8 A street between Aldgate and the Tower.
9 As far as, that.   10 To and fro.

grief indeed, having his wife and several of his children all in the cart that was just come in with him, and he followed in an agony and excess of sorrow. He mourned heartily, as it was easy to see, but with a kind of masculine grief that could not give itself vent by tears; and, calmly defying the buriers to let him alone, said he would only see the bodies thrown in and go away; so they left importuning him. But no sooner was the cart turned round and the bodies shot into the pit promiscuously, which was a surprise to him, for he at least expected they would have been decently laid in, though indeed he was afterwards convinced that was impracticable—I say, no sooner did he see the sight but he cried out aloud, unable to contain himself. I could not hear what he said, but he went backward two or three steps and fell down in a swoon. The buriers ran to him and took him up, and in a little while he came to himself, and they led him away to the Pie Tavern over against the end of Houndsditch, where, it seems, the man was known, and where they took care of him. He looked into the pit again as he went away, but the buriers had covered the bodies so immediately, with throwing in earth, that though there was light enough, for there were lanterns, and candles in them, placed all night round the sides of the pit, upon heaps of earth, seven or eight or perhaps more, yet nothing could be seen.

This was a mournful scene indeed, and affected me almost as much as the rest; but the other was awful and full of terror: the cart had in it sixteen or seventeen bodies; some were wrapt up in linen sheets, some in rags, some little other than naked, or so loose that what covering they had fell from them in the shooting out of the cart, and they fell quite naked among the rest; but the matter was not much to them, or the indecency much to anyone else, seeing they were all dead and were to be huddled together into the common grave of mankind, as we may call it, for here was no difference made, but poor and rich went together; there was no other way of burials, neither was it possible there should, for coffins were not to be had for the prodigious numbers that fell in such a calamity as this. . . .

I had in family only an ancient woman that managed the house, a maid-servant, two apprentices, and myself; and the plague beginning to increase about us, I had many sad thoughts about what course I should take, and how I should act. The many dismal objects, which happened everywhere as I went about the streets, had filled my mind with a great deal of horror, for fear of the distemper, which was, indeed, very horrible in itself, and in some more than in others. The swellings, which were generally in the neck or groin, when they grew hard and would not break grew so painful that it was equal to the most exquisite torture; and some, not able to bear the torment, threw themselves out at windows or shot themselves or otherwise made themselves away; and I saw several dismal objects of that kind. Others, unable to contain themselves, vented their pain by incessant roarings, and such loud and lamentable cries were to be heard as we walked along the streets that would pierce the very heart to think of, especially when it was to be considered that the same dreadful scourge might be expected every moment to seize upon ourselves.

I cannot say but that now I began to faint in my resolutions; my heart failed me very much, and sorely I repented of my rashness. When I had been out, and met with such terrible things as these I have talked of, I say I repented my rashness in venturing to abide in town. I wished often that I had not taken upon me to stay, but had gone away with my brother and his family.

Terrified by those frightful objects, I would retire home sometimes and resolve to go out no more; and perhaps I would keep those resolutions for three or four days, which time I spent in the most serious thankfulness for my preservation and the preservation of my family, and the constant confession of my sins, giving myself up to God every day, and applying to him with fasting, humiliation, and meditation. Such intervals as I had I employed in reading books and in writing down my memorandums of what occurred to me every day, and out of which, afterwards, I took most of this work, as it relates to my observations without doors. What I wrote of my private meditations I reserve for private use, and desire it may not be made public on any account whatever.

I also wrote other meditations upon divine subjects, such as occurred to me at that time and were profitable to myself, but not fit for any other view, and therefore I say no more of that.

I had a very good friend, a physician, whose name was Heath, whom I frequently visited during this dismal time, and to whose advice I was very much obliged for many things which he directed me to take, by way of preventing the infection when I went out, as he found I frequently did, and to hold in my mouth when I was in the streets. He also came very often to see me, and as he was a good Christian as well as a good physician, his agreeable conversation was a very great support to me in the worst of this terrible time.

It was now the beginning of August, and the plague grew very violent and terrible in the place where I lived, and Dr. Heath coming to visit me, and finding that I ventured so often out in the streets, earnestly persuaded me to lock myself up and my family, and not to suffer any of us to go out of doors; to keep all our windows fast, shutters and curtains close, and never to open them; but first, to make a very strong smoke in the room where the window or door was to be opened, with rosin and pitch, brimstone or gunpowder, and the like; and we did this for some time; but as I had not laid in a store of provision for such a retreat, it was impossible that we could keep within doors entirely. However, I attempted, though it was so very late, to do something towards it; and first, as I had convenience both for brewing and baking, I went and bought two sacks of meal, and for several weeks, having an oven, we baked all our own bread; also I bought malt, and brewed as much beer as all the casks I had would hold, and which seemed enough to serve my house for five or six weeks; also I laid in a quantity of salt butter and Cheshire cheese; but I had no flesh-meat, and the plague raged so violently among the butchers and slaughterhouses on the other side of our street, where they are known to dwell in great numbers, that it was not advisable so much as to go over the street among them. . . .

But though I confined my family, I could not prevail upon my unsatisfied curiosity to stay within entirely myself; and though I generally came frighted and terrified home, yet I could not restrain; only that indeed I did not do it so frequently as at first.

I had some little obligations, indeed, upon me to go to my brother's house, which was in Coleman Street parish,[11] and which he had left to my care; and I went at first every day, but afterwards only once or twice a week.

In these walks I had many dismal scenes before my eyes, as particularly of persons falling dead in the streets, terrible shrieks and screechings of women, who, in their agonies, would throw open their chamber windows and cry out in a dismal, surprising manner. It is impossible to describe the variety of postures in which the passions of the poor people would express themselves.

Passing through Tokenhouse Yard, in Lothbury,[12] of a sudden a casement violently opened just over my head, and a woman gave three frightful screeches, and then cried, "Oh! death, death, death!" in a most inimitable tone, and which struck me with horror and a chillness in my very blood. There was nobody to be seen in the whole street, neither did any other window open, for people had no curiosity now in any case, nor could anybody help one another; so I went on to pass into Bell Alley.

Just in Bell Alley, on the right hand of the passage, there was a more terrible cry than that, though it was not so directed out at the window; but the whole family was in a terrible fright, and I could hear women and children run screaming about the rooms like distracted, when a garret window opened, and somebody from a window on the other side the alley called and asked, "What is the matter?" upon which, from the first window it was answered, "O Lord, my old master has hanged himself!" The other asked again, "Is he quite dead?" and the first answered, "Ay, ay, quite dead; quite dead and cold!" This person was a merchant and a deputy alderman, and very rich. I care not to mention the name, though I knew his name too, but that would be an hardship to the family, which is now flourishing again.

But this is but one; it is scarce credible what dreadful cases happened in particular families every day. People in the rage of the distemper, or in the torment of their swellings, which was indeed intolerable, running out of their own government, raving and distracted, and oftentimes laying violent hands upon themselves, throwing themselves out at their windows, shooting themselves, &c.; mothers murdering their own children in their lunacy, some dying of mere grief as a passion, some of mere fright and surprise without any infection at all, others frighted into idiotism and foolish distractions, some into despair and lunacy, others into melancholy madness.

The pain of the swelling was in particular very violent, and to some intolerable; the physicians and surgeons may be said to have tortured many poor creatures even to death. The swellings in some grew hard, and they applied violent drawing-plaisters or poultices to break them; and if these did not do, they cut and scarified them in a terrible manner. In some those swellings were made hard partly by the force of the distemper and partly by their being too violently drawn, and were so hard that no instrument could cut them; and then they burnt them with caustics, so that many died raving mad with the torment, and some in the very operation. In these distresses, some, for want of help to hold them down

11 About half a mile westward from the narrator's district, and nearer the center of the city.
12 A street running westward to the south end of Coleman Street; Bell Alley is on the east side of Coleman Street.

in their beds, or to look to them, laid hands upon themselves, as above. Some broke out into the streets, perhaps naked, and would run directly down to the river, if they were not stopped by the watchmen or other officers, and plunge themselves into the water wherever they found it.

It often pierced my very soul to hear the groans and cries of those who were thus tormented, but of the two this was counted the most promising particular in the whole infection; for, if these swellings could be brought to a head, and to break and run, or, as the surgeons call it, to digest, the patient generally recovered; whereas those who, like the gentlewoman's daughter, were struck with death at the beginning, and had the tokens come out upon them, often went about indifferent easy[13] till a little before they died, and some till the moment they dropped down, as in apoplexies and epilepsies is often the case. Such would be taken suddenly very sick, and would run to a bench or bulk,[14] or any convenient place that offered itself, or to their own houses if possible, as I mentioned before, and there sit down, grow faint, and die. This kind of dying was much the same as it was with those who die of common mortifications,[15] who die swooning, and, as it were, go away in a dream. Such as died thus had very little notice of their being infected at all till the gangrene was spread through their whole body; nor could physicians themselves know certainly how it was with them, till they opened their breasts or other parts of their body, and saw the tokens. . . .

It must be confessed that though the plague was chiefly among the poor, yet were the poor the most venturous and fearless of it, and went about their employment with a sort of brutal courage; I must call it so, for it was founded neither on religion nor prudence; scarce did they use any caution, but ran into any business which they could get employment in, though it was the most hazardous. Such was that of tending the sick, watching houses shut up, carrying infected persons to the pesthouse, and, which was still worse, carrying the dead away to their graves.

It was under this John Hayward's[16] care, and

within his bounds, that the story of the piper, with which people have made themselves so merry, happened; and he assured me that it was true. It is said that it was a blind piper; but, as John told me, the fellow was not blind, but an ignorant, weak, poor man, and usually walked his rounds about ten o'clock at night and went piping along from door to door; and the people usually took him in at public houses[17] where they knew him, and would give him drink and victuals, and sometimes farthings; and he in return would pipe and sing and talk simply,[18] which diverted the people; and thus he lived. It was but a very bad time for this diversion while things were as I have told, yet the poor fellow went about as usual, but was almost starved; and when anybody asked how he did he would answer, the dead-cart had not taken him yet, but that they had promised to call for him next week.

It happened one night that this poor fellow, whether somebody had given him too much drink or no—John Hayward said he had not drink in his house, but that they had given him a little more victuals than ordinary at a public house in Coleman Street—and the poor fellow, having not usually had a bellyful for perhaps not a good while, was laid all along upon the top of a bulk or stall, and fast asleep, at a door in the street near London Wall, towards Cripplegate, and that upon the same bulk or stall the people of some house, in the alley of which the house was a corner, hearing a bell, which they always rang before the cart came, had laid a body really dead of the plague just by him, thinking, too, that this poor fellow had been a dead body, as the other was, and laid there by some of the neighbors.

Accordingly, when John Hayward with his bell and the cart came along, finding two dead bodies lie upon the stall, they took them up with the instrument they used and threw them into the cart; and all this while the piper slept soundly.

From hence they passed along and took in other dead bodies, till, as honest John Hayward told me, they almost buried him alive in the cart; yet all this while he slept soundly. At length the cart came to the place where the bodies were to be thrown into the ground, which, as I do remember, was at Mount Mill;[19] and as the cart usually stopped some time before they were ready to shoot out the melancholy load they had in it, as soon as the cart stopped the fellow awaked and struggled a little to get his head out from among the dead bodies, when, raising him-

[13] Fairly comfortable.
[14] The stall in front of a London shop.
[15] Gangrene or death of tissue.
[16] Mentioned in a passage here omitted. As undersexton and grave-digger of St. Stephen's, Coleman Street, according to the narrator, Hayward went about the parish with the dead-cart and bell, without taking any precautions "other than holding garlic and rue in his mouth, and smoking tobacco." Actually, the plague was carried by fleas from infected rats.

[17] Taverns, saloons.   [18] Foolishly.
[19] Near Seward Street, Clerkenwell, north of the City.

self up in the cart, he called out, "Hey! where am I?" This frighted the fellow that attended about the work; but after some pause John Hayward, recovering himself, said, "Lord, bless us! There's somebody in the cart not quite dead!" So another called to him and said, "Who are you?" The fellow answered, "I am the poor piper. Where am I?" "Where are you?" says Hayward. "Why, you are in the dead-cart, and we are going to bury you." "But I an't dead, though, am I?" says the piper, which made them laugh a little, though, as John said, they were heartily frighted at first; so they helped the poor fellow down, and he went about his business.

I know the story goes he set up his pipes in the cart and frighted the bearers and others so that they ran away; but John Hayward did not tell the story so, nor say anything of his piping at all; but that he was a poor piper, and that he was carried away as above, I am fully satisfied of the truth of. . . .

One of the worst days we had in the whole time, as I thought, was in the beginning of September, when, indeed, good people began to think that God was resolved to make a full end of the people in this miserable city. This was at that time when the plague was fully come into the eastern parishes. The parish of Aldgate, if I may give my opinion, buried above a thousand a week for two weeks, though the bills did not say so many; but it surrounded me at so dismal a rate that there was not a house in twenty uninfected in the Minories, in Houndsditch, and in those parts of Aldgate Parish about the Butcher Row and the alleys over against me.[20] I say, in those places death reigned in every corner. Whitechapel parish was in the same condition, and though much less[21] than the parish I lived in, yet buried near 600 a week by the bills, and in my opinion near twice as many. Whole families, and indeed whole streets of families, were swept away together; insomuch that it was frequent for neighbors to call to the bellman to go to such and such houses and fetch out the people, for that they were all dead.

And, indeed, the work of removing the dead bodies by carts was now grown so very odious and dangerous that it was complained of that the bearers did not take care to clear such houses where all the inhabitants were dead, but that sometimes the bodies lay several days unburied, till the neighboring families were offended with the stench, and consequently infected; and this neglect of the officers was such that the churchwardens and constables were summoned to look after it, and even the justices of the hamlets were obliged to venture their lives among them to quicken and encourage them, for innumerable of the bearers died of the distemper, infected by the bodies they were obliged to come so near. And had it not been that the number of poor people who wanted employment and wanted bread (as I have said before) was so great that necessity drove them to undertake anything and venture anything, they would never have found people to be employed. And then the bodies of the dead would have lain above ground, and have perished and rotted in a dreadful manner. . . .

Much about the same time I walked out into the fields towards Bow,[22] for I had a great mind to see how things were managed in the river and among the ships; and as I had some concern in shipping, I had a notion that it had[23] been one of the best ways of securing oneself from the infection to have retired into a ship; and musing how to satisfy my curiosity in that point, I turned away over the fields, from Bow to Bromley[24] and down to Blackwall, to the stairs which are there for landing or taking water.[25]

Here I saw a poor man walking on the bank or sea wall, as they call it, by himself. I walked a while also about, seeing the houses all shut up; at last I fell into some talk, at a distance, with this poor man. First I asked him how people did thereabouts. "Alas, sir!" says he, "almost desolate, all dead or sick. Here are very few families in this part, or in that village," pointing at Poplar,[26] "where half of them are dead already, and the rest sick." Then he pointing to one house, "There they are all dead," said he, "and the house stands open; nobody dares go into it. A poor thief," says he, "ventured in to steal something; but he paid dear for his theft, for he was carried to the churchyard too last night." Then he pointed to several other houses. "There," says he, "they are all dead, the man and his wife and five children. There," says he, "they are shut up; you see a watchman at the door"; and so of other houses. "Why," says I, "what do you here all alone?" "Why," says he, "I am a poor, desolate man; it hath pleased God I am not yet visited, though my family is, and one of my children dead." "How do you mean, then," said I, "that you are not visited?" "Why," says he, "that is my house," pointing to a very little low, boarded

[20] Opposite my residence.   [21] Smaller.

[22] Stratford le Bow, about two miles east of the city.
[23] Would have.
[24] Between Bow and the Thames. Blackwall is a docks area on the north bank.   [25] Going onto the river.
[26] Between Bromley and Blackwell.

house; "and there my poor wife and two children live," said he, "if they may be said to live, for my wife and one of the children are visited; but I do not come at them." And with that word I saw the tears run very plentifully down his face; and so they did down mine, too, I assure you.

"But," said I, "why do you not come at them? How can you abandon your own flesh and blood?" "Oh, sir," says he, "the Lord forbid! I do not abandon them; I work for them as much as I am able; and, blessed be the Lord, I keep them from want." And with that I observed he lifted up his eyes to heaven with a countenance that presently told me I had happened on a man that was no hypocrite, but a serious, religious, good man; and his ejaculation was an expression of thankfulness that, in such a condition as he was in, he should be able to say his family did not want. "Well," says I, "honest man, that is a great mercy, as things go now with the poor. But how do you live, then, and how are you kept from the dreadful calamity that is now upon us all?" "Why, sir," says he, "I am a waterman, and there 's my boat," says he, "and the boat serves me for a house; I work in it in the day, and I sleep in it in the night; and what I get I lay down upon that stone," says he, showing me a broad stone on the other side of the street, a good way from the house; "and then," says he, "I halloo, and call to them till I make them hear, and they come and fetch it."

"Well, friend," says I, "but how can you get any money as a waterman? Does anybody go by water these times?" "Yes, sir," says he, "in the way I am employed there does. Do you see there," says he, "five ships lie at anchor," pointing down the river a good way below the town; "and do you see," says he, "eight or ten ships lie at the chain there, and at anchor yonder?" pointing above the town. "All those ships have families on board, of their merchants and owners and such like, who have locked themselves up and live on board, close shut in for fear of the infection; and I tend on them to fetch things for them, carry letters, and do what is absolutely necessary, that they may not be obliged to come on shore; and every night I fasten my boat on board one of the ship's boats, and there I sleep by myself, and, blessed be God, I am preserved hitherto."

"Well," said I, "friend, but will they let you come on board after you have been on shore here, when this is such a terrible place, and so infected as it is?"

"Why, as to that," said he, "I very seldom go up the ship side, but deliver what I bring to their boat, or lie by the side and they hoist it on board. If I did,

I think they are in no danger from me, for I never go into any house on shore, or touch anybody, no, not of my own family; but I fetch provisions for them."

"Nay," says I, "but that may be worse, for you must have those provisions of somebody or other; and since all this part of the town is so infected, it is dangerous so much as to speak with anybody; for the village," said I, "is, as it were, the beginning of London, though it be at some distance from it."

"That is true," added he, "but you do not understand me right. I do not buy provisions for them here; I row up to Greenwich[27] and buy fresh meat there, and sometimes I row down the river to Woolwich[28] and buy there; then I go to single farmhouses on the Kentish side,[29] where I am known, and buy fowls and eggs and butter, and bring to the ships as they direct me, sometimes one, sometimes the other. I seldom come on shore here; and I came now only to call my wife and hear how my little family do, and give them a little money which I received last night."

"Poor man!" said I, "and how much hast thou gotten for them?"

"I have gotten four shillings," said he, "which is a great sum as things go now with poor men; but they have given me a bag of bread, too, and a salt fish and some flesh; so all helps out."

"Well," said I, "and have you given it them yet?"

"No," said he, "but I have called, and my wife has answered that she cannot come out yet, but in half an hour she hopes to come; and I am waiting for her. Poor woman!" says he, "she is brought sadly down. She has a swelling, and it is broke, and I hope she will recover; but I fear the child will die; but it is the Lord—" Here he stopped and wept very much.

"Well, honest friend," said I, "thou hast a sure comforter if thou hast brought thyself to be resigned to the will of God; he is dealing with us all in judgment."

"Oh, sir," says he, "it is infinite mercy if any of us are spared; and who am I to repine?"

"Sayest thou so?" said I, "and how much less is my faith than thine!" And here my heart smote me, suggesting how much better this poor man's foundation was, on which he stayed in the danger, than mine; that he had nowhere to fly; that he had a family to bind him to attendance, which I had not;

---

27 A short way up the river, on the south bank.
28 Two miles down the river, on the south bank, and nine miles from London.   29 The southern side.

and mine was mere presumption, his a true dependence and a courage resting on God; and yet that he used all possible caution for his safety.

I turned a little away from the man while these thoughts engaged me; for, indeed, I could no more refrain from tears than he.

At length, after some further talk, the poor woman opened the door and called, "Robert, Robert!" He answered, and bid her stay a few moments, and he would come; so he ran down the common stairs to his boat and fetched up a sack, in which were the provisions he had brought from the ships; and when he returned he hallooed again. Then he went to the great stone which he showed me and emptied the sack, and laid all out, everything by themselves, and then retired; and his wife came with a little boy to fetch them away, and he called and said such a captain had sent such a thing, and such a captain such a thing, and at the end adds, "God has sent it all; give thanks to him." When the poor woman had taken up all, she was so weak she could not carry it at once in, though the weight was not much neither; so she left the biscuit,[30] which was in a little bag, and left a little boy to watch it till she came again.

"Well, but," says I to him, "did you leave her the four shillings too, which you said was your week's pay?"

"Yes, yes," says he; "you shall hear her own it." So he calls again, "Rachel, Rachel," which, it seems, was her name, "did you take up the money?" "Yes," said she. "How much was it?" said he. "Four shillings and a groat," said she. "Well, well," says he, "the Lord keep you all"; and so he turned to go away.

As I could not refrain contributing tears to this man's story, so neither could I refrain my charity for his assistance. So I called him; "Hark thee, friend," said I, "come hither, for I believe thou art in health, that I may venture thee"; so I pulled out my hand, which was in my pocket before, "Here," says I, "go and call thy Rachel once more, and give her a little more comfort from me. God will never forsake a family that trusts in him as thou dost." So I gave him four other shillings, and bid him go lay them on the stone and call his wife.

I have not words to express the poor man's thankfulness, neither could he express it himself but by tears running down his face. He called his wife, and told her God had moved the heart of a stranger,

upon hearing their condition, to give them all that money; and a great deal more such as that, he said to her. The woman, too, made signs of the like thankfulness, as well to heaven as to me, and joyfully picked it up; and I parted with no money all that year that I thought better bestowed. . . .

It is here, however, to be observed that after the funerals became so many that people could not toll the bell, mourn, or weep, or wear black for one another, as they did before, no, nor so much as make coffins for those that died, so after a while the fury of the infection appeared to be so increased that, in short, they shut up no houses at all. It seemed enough that all the remedies of that kind had been used till they were found fruitless, and that the plague spread itself with an irresistible fury; so that as the fire the succeeding year spread itself, and burned with such violence that the citizens, in despair, gave over their endeavors to extinguish it, so in the plague it came at last to such violence that the people sat still looking at one another, and seemed quite abandoned to despair; whole streets seemed to be desolated, and not to be shut up only, but to be emptied of their inhabitants; doors were left open, windows stood shattering with the wind in empty houses for want of people to shut them. In a word, people began to give up themselves to their fears, and to think that all regulations and methods were in vain, and that there was nothing to be hoped for but an universal desolation; and it was even in the height of this general despair that it pleased God to stay his hand, and to slacken the fury of the contagion in such a manner as was even surprising, like its beginning, and demonstrated it to be his own particular hand, and that above, if not without the agency of means[31] as I shall take notice of in its proper place.

But I must still speak of the plague as in its height, raging even to desolation, and the people under the most dreadful consternation, even, as I have said, to despair. It is hardly credible to what excesses the passions of men carried them in this extremity of the distemper; and this part, I think, was as moving as the rest. What could affect a man in his full power of reflection, and what could make deeper impressions on the soul, than to see a man almost naked and got out of his house, or perhaps out of his bed, into the street, come out of Harrow Alley, a populous conjunction or collection of alleys, courts, and passages

---

[30] Crackers, hardtack.

[31] I.e., even though natural causes were the agency of his intervention. As a matter of fact, the plague did not end so suddenly as Defoe asserts.

in the Butcher Row in Whitechapel—I say, what could be more affecting than to see this poor man come out into the open street, run dancing and singing, and making a thousand antic gestures, with five or six women and children running after him, crying and calling upon him for the Lord's sake to come back, and entreating the help of others to bring him back; but all in vain, nobody daring to lay a hand upon him or to come near him?

This was a most grievous and afflicting thing to me, who saw it all from my own windows; for all this while the poor afflicted man was, as I observed it, even then in the utmost agony of pain, having, as they said, two swellings upon him, which could not be brought to break or to suppurate; but by laying strong caustics on them, the surgeons had, it seems, hopes to break them, which caustics were then upon him, burning his flesh as with a hot iron. I cannot say what became of this poor man, but I think he continued roving about in that manner till he fell down and died. . . .

I would be glad if I could close the account of this melancholy year with some particular examples historically; I mean of the thankfulness to God, our preserver, for our being delivered from this dreadful calamity. Certainly the circumstance of the deliverance, as well as the terrible enemy we were delivered from, called upon the whole nation for it. The circumstances of the deliverance were indeed very remarkable, as I have in part mentioned already, and particularly the dreadful condition which we were all in, when we were, to the surprise of the whole town, made joyful with the hope of a stop of the infection.

Nothing but the immediate finger of God, nothing but omnipotent power, could have done it. The contagion despised all medicine; death raged in every corner; and had it gone on as it did then, a few weeks more would have cleared the town of all, and everything that had a soul. Men everywhere began to despair; every heart failed them for fear; people were made desperate through the anguish of their souls, and the terrors of death sat in the very faces and countenances of the people.

In that very moment, when we might very well say, "Vain was the help of man"—I say, in that very moment it pleased God, with a most agreeable surprise, to cause the fury of it to abate, even of itself; and the malignity declining, as I have said, though infinite numbers were sick, yet fewer died, and the very first week's bill decreased 1843, a vast number indeed!

It is impossible to express the change that appeared in the very countenances of the people that Thursday morning when the weekly bill came out. It might have been perceived in their countenances that a secret surprise and smile of joy sat on everybody's face. They shook one another by the hands in the streets, who would hardly go on the same side of the way with one another before. Where the streets were not too broad, they would open their windows and call from one house to another, and ask how they did, and if they had heard the good news that the plague was abated. Some would return, when they said good news, and ask, "What good news?" and when they answered that the plague was abated and the bills decreased almost 2000, they would cry out, "God be praised," and would weep aloud for joy, telling them they had heard nothing of it; and such was the joy of the people that it was, as it were, life to them from the grave. I could almost set down as many extravagant things done in the excess of their joy as of their grief; but that would be to lessen the value of it. . . .

Addison and Steele

1672–1719   1672–1729

DURING a period of four years, in the *Tatler* and the *Spectator*, Addison and Steele turned out a series of essays which, especially Addison's, were regarded for two centuries as the best models on which to form a prose style. When Benjamin Franklin, who was born three years before the *Tatler*, decided in his ambitious youth to improve his way of writing, one of his methods was to turn a *Spectator* essay into verse and, after a lengthy interval, back into prose; then he would compare the result with the

original. Dr. Johnson called Addison's prose "the model of the middle style; on grave subjects not formal, on light occasions not groveling; pure without scrupulosity, and exact without apparent elaboration; always equable, and always easy, without glowing words or pointed sentences." Beside it, Steele's sometimes seems hasty and careless, but it has greater warmth. The difference between their styles reflects the divergence of temperaments. Though Addison's are on the whole the better essays,

Steele's is the more winning personality; and it is worth noting that Addison produced by far his best work during the period of his collaboration with Steele.

JOSEPH ADDISON came from Wiltshire; Steele, born in the same year and orphaned in early childhood, was a Dubliner. Addison's father was a well-known Anglican priest, dean of the cathedral at Lichfield. Steele's was an English lawyer, married to an Irish wife. The future essayists were educated together at the Charterhouse, one of London's famous schools, and at Oxford.

After graduation Addison stayed on at Oxford, first a demy or scholar, and then a fellow, of Magdalen College. He was about twenty-seven when his talent for smooth Latin verse was noticed by influential Whig politicians. Here was a man worth enlisting as a party writer. They got him a pension, which during the next four years he used for travel and study on the Continent. Back in London, he wrote to order *The Campaign,* a somewhat stilted poem celebrating Marlborough's spectacular victory at Blenheim in 1704. Blenheim was a Whig victory, since the Whigs were the war party; Marlborough was fighting Jacobitism, among other things, in far-off Bavaria. His success had inspired such bad verses that the Whig chiefs feared it might be made to look absurd, and they were pleased with Addison's response to their demand for something better.

His path in life was now plainly marked, and it proved on the whole a smooth one. Both he and Steele were office-holding Whigs and members of the exclusive Whig club, the Kit-Cats; but though as a member of Parliament Addison always followed the party line, which Steele did not, he never made a speech there, and was in fact the most moderate of partisans. No man of real force was ever more chary of exposing himself to the slings and arrows of controversy; none of the Queen Anne wits, except Pope, was more afraid of ridicule. Good manners in public debate and imperturbability in private relationships seemed to him more important than winning a cause or trouncing an adversary. Addison had a congenital aversion to extremes and risks.

When in 1710 the Whigs were put out of office, he turned to literary activity. It was Steele who began the *Tatler;* Addison recognized his own opportunity, and offered contributions which were enthusiastically accepted and paid for. Of the *Spectator* papers he wrote more than Steele did. At Button's coffee house he presided over his "little senate," as Pope venomously styled it, of minor literary lights, who showered adulation upon him. In 1713 his *Cato* was acted, with great popular acclaim. It is a wooden neo-classical tragedy with few merits, but it was the eighteenth-century British theater's greatest success till Gay laid the world in his debt with *The Beggar's Opera* fifteen years

later. The Whigs applauded the liberal sentiments in Cato's speeches, and the Tories did the same to show that they, too, approved of liberty.

In 1714, when the Tories fell, Addison went back into office. His was not a distinguished talent for government; but in 1716 he became one of the secretaries of state, though illness soon forced his resignation. In the same year, at forty-four, he made a rich and fashionable marriage, to the widowed Countess of Warwick, mistress of the famous mansion, Holland House. He died three years later.

SIR RICHARD STEELE rose by other means. He left Oxford without a degree, was thereupon disinherited by his uncle, and at thirty had won promotion to a captaincy in the army, although he never saw action. Steele's temperament was ardent; unlike Addison's, his talent for the stage was genuine. His literary career began while he was still an ensign in the Coldstream Guards, with an amateurish treatise, *The Christian Hero* (1701). His motive in writing it was partly to brace up his own morals, his satisfaction with which had been considerably shaken by his recent paternity of an illegitimate baby girl. The child's mother was a daughter of the publisher Jacob Tonson, a fellow Kit-Cat. Another ethical question also gave Steele pause about the same time, for he quarreled with a fellow officer and wounded him severely in a duel. From then on Steele took a strong stand against the current code of honor, as may be seen in the first of the following essays. Throughout the *Tatler* and *Spectator* he preaches more openly than his partner.

His next works were comedies: *The Funeral, or Grief a la Mode* (1701), *The Lying Lover* (1703), and *The Tender Husband* (1705). These plays, though no more than forerunners of *The Conscious Lovers* (1722), break in some respects with Restoration comedy and point the way toward the sentimental school which was to prevail in the eighteenth century. The purpose of *The Lying Lover* is frankly announced in the preface: to show that a comedy may "be no improper entertainment in a Christian community." The idea behind the *Tatler* (1709-11) and the *Spectator* (1711-12) was Steele's. He was already experienced in journalism; in 1707 Addison had got him the job of gazetteer, with the duty of writing the government newspaper, the *Gazette.* He lost the post, of course, when the Tories ousted the Whigs in 1710.

Less orderly and less reserved than Addison, Steele lived a more emotional and consequently more turbulent life. He drank too much, and he was wildly extravagant. Of his first wife little is known, save that she brought him money, a commodity he was never able to keep very long. His second marriage was happy, and far from humdrum. A hundred of his letters have survived to his "dear Prue";

they are too charming to leave entirely unquoted. The first was written before his marriage in September, 1707.

SEPBR. 1ST, 1707
S^nt James's Coffee House

Madam,

It is the hardest thing in the world to be in love, and yet attend business. As for me, all that speak to me find me out; and I must lock myself up, or other people will do it for me.

A gentleman asked me this morning what news from Lisbon; and I answered, "She's exquisitely handsome. . . ."

Methinks I could write a volume to you, but all the language on earth would fail in saying how much, and with what disinterested passion, I am ever y^rs,

RICH^D STEELE

The rest were written after the marriage. "I wish," wrote Lady Mary Wortley Montagu (1690–1762) to her husband —her own letters are famous—"I wish you would learn of Mr. Steele to write to your wife."

Lord Sunderland's Office
MAY 19, 1708, 11 O'CLOCK

Dear Prue,

I desire of you to get the coach and yourself ready, as soon as you can conveniently, and call for me here, from whence we will go and spend some time together in the fresh air in free conference. Let my best periwig be put in the coach box, and my new shoes, for it is a comfort to be well-dressed in agreeable company. You are vital to your obliged, affectionate husband and humble servant,

RICH. STEELE

SEPT. 20, 1708

Dear Prue,

If a servant I sent last night got to Hampton Court, you received 29 walnuts and a letter from me. I enclose the *Gazette;* and am, with all my soul,

Your passionate lover and faithful husband,

RICH. STEELE

Since I writ the above, I have found half an hundred more of walnuts, which I send herewith. . . .

Monday, 7 at night
SEPT. 27, 1708

Dear Prue,

You see that you are obeyed in everything, and that I write overnight for the day following. I shall now in earnest, by Mr. Clay's good conduct, manage my business

with that method as shall make me easy. . . . I shall send by tomorrow's coach.

I am, dear Prue, a little in drink, but at all times your faithful husband,

RICH. STEELE

Half-hour after ten
SEPT. 28, 1708

Dear Prue,

It being three hours since I writ to you, I send this to assure you I am now going very soberly to bed, and that you shall be the last thing in my thoughts tonight, as well as the first tomorrow morning. I am, with the utmost fondness,

Your faithful husband,
RICH. STEELE

In politics Steele was a hot fighter, and took chances which Addison balked at. Having expressed his views with considerable freedom and been elected to a Tory-dominated House of Commons, he was promptly expelled on a trumped-up charge of sedition. But when the Whigs returned to power, Steele's services were well rewarded. He was re-elected to Parliament and was knighted. Among his lucrative offices was the nominal control of Drury Lane Theater. His last and best play, *The Conscious Lovers* (1722), is a milestone in eighteenth-century drama. His last years were still, however, stormy. He quarreled with Addison, who died before they were fully reconciled. He lost his wife and two of their four children. His financial worries never ended, and he spent his final years in sickness and retirement, far from London. He died in 1729.

THE *Tatler* was begun by Steele in 1709, without the knowledge of Addison. The form, a journal with various news items and essays, was already established; but the *Tatler* was the first of substantial literary importance, and with Addison's help Steele soon developed it into the single-essay periodical. His purpose was serious. Too sensible to believe in such enterprises as the Society for the Reformation of Manners, he aimed at raising the moral tone of the community by sugar-coating the pill of instruction. Thus the essay on dueling (*Tatler,* no. 25) is dead in earnest, but couched in an agreeably ironical vein. The *Tatler* appeared three times a week; of its 271 issues Steele produced by far the larger number. The *Spectator,* which succeeded the *Tatler* in 1711 and appeared six times weekly, ran to the end of 1712; here the larger share was Addison's, and it was Addison who revived it for some months in 1714. In 1713 Steele inaugurated another periodical, the *Guardian,* which ran for several months, again with some assistance from Addison.

As we have seen, Defoe had invented the leading article as a journalistic feature. Montaigne (1533–92) had created the modern essay. John Dunton's *Athenian Mercury* (1691–97) had regaled its readers with questions and answers on many topics, reserving one number every month for the special satisfaction of feminine interests. Steele's contribution was the *serial* essay, with its running commentary on the follies of the day. Johnson and Goldsmith, later on, followed his lead; and the form was also adopted on the Continent. Nowadays, the *Tatler, Spectator,* and *Guardian* are too sedate to be as interesting as they unquestionably were at the Queen Anne breakfast table. But if their authors—there were others besides the two foremost—never rolled up their sleeves and took on all comers in the style of Defoe or Swift, or deftly nailed a contemporary hide to the barn door in the manner of a *New Yorker* Profile, they exercised a gentle yet steady pressure toward the humanitarian improvements made during the second half of the century. Wit had been employed by Restora-

tion writers to flatter wrong. To have brought it over to serve the other side was an honorable and lasting achievement.

For the genre, see W. Graham's *English Literary Periodicals* (1930). The best edition of the *Tatler* is by G. A. Aitken (4 vols., 1898–9). The *Spectator* was also edited by Aitken (8 vols., 1898), and there is a good edition by G. G. Smith (8 vols., 1897–8), reprinted in Everyman's Library (4 vols.). There are numerous cheap editions of selected essays by Addison and Steele. Aitken wrote the most authoritative Life of Steele (2 vols., 1889); a less formidable Life is by W. Connely (1934), and there is a delightful biographical sketch in Austin Dobson's volume of selections from Steele (revised ed., 1896). Rae Blanchard has edited Steele's *Correspondence* (1941) and a volume of his *Tracts and Pamphlets* (1944). W. J. Courthope wrote a Life of Addison (1884) for the English Men of Letters series. For a tart handling of Addison in the debunking style, see B. Dobrée's *Essays in Biography, 1680–1726* (1925).

Periodical Essays

STEELE: ON DUELING

THE TATLER, NO. 25   *Tuesday,* JUNE 7, 1709

Quicquid agunt homines . . .
. . . nostri est farrago libelli.[1]
        JUVENAL, *Satires,* I, 85–6

White's Chocolate House,[2] JUNE 6

A LETTER from a young lady, written in the most passionate terms, wherein she laments the misfortune of a gentleman, her lover, who was lately wounded in a duel, has turned my thoughts to that subject and inclined me to examine into the causes which precipitate men into so fatal a folly. And as it has been proposed to treat of subjects of gallantry in the article from hence, and no one point in nature is more proper to be considered by the company who frequent this place than that of duels,[3] it is worth our consideration to examine into this chimerical,

groundless humor[4] and to lay every other thought aside, until we have stripped it of all its false pretenses to credit and reputation amongst men.

But I must confess, when I consider what I am going about, and run over in my imagination all the endless crowd of men of honor who will be offended at such a discourse, I am undertaking, methinks, a work worthy an invulnerable hero in romance, rather than a private gentleman with a single rapier; but as I am pretty well acquainted, by great opportunities, with the nature of man, and know of a truth that all men fight against their will, the danger vanishes and resolution rises upon this subject. For this reason, I shall talk very freely on a custom which all men wish exploded, though no man has courage enough to resist it.

But there is one unintelligible word, which I fear will extremely perplex my dissertation, and I confess to you I find very hard to explain, which is the term "satisfaction." An honest country gentleman had the misfortune to fall into company with two or three modern men of honor, where he happened to be very ill-treated; and one of the company, being conscious of his offense, sends a note to him in the morning and tells him he was ready to give him *satisfaction.* "This is fine doing," says the plain fel-

---

[1] Everything human goes into our hodgepodge of a book, i.e., is grist for our mill. This is the motto of the first forty numbers. The essay on dueling is the first part of no. 25.

[2] In St. James's Street, Piccadilly. *Tatler* no. 1 had announced that "all accounts of gallantry, pleasure, and entertainment shall be under the article of White's Chocolate House."

[3] Quarrels often arose from gambling, for which White's was notorious.

[4] Whim, notion.

low; "last night he sent me away cursedly out of humor, and this morning he fancies it would be a *satisfaction* to be run through the body."

As the matter at present stands, it is not to do handsome actions denominates a man of honor; it is enough if he dares to defend ill ones. Thus you often see a common sharper in competition with a gentleman of the first rank, though all mankind is convinced that a fighting gamester is only a pickpocket with the courage of a highwayman. One cannot with any patience reflect on the unaccountable jumble of persons and things in this town and nation; which occasions very frequently that a brave man falls by a hand below that of a common hangman, and yet his executioner escapes the clutches of the hangman for doing it. I shall therefore hereafter consider how the bravest men in other ages and nations have behaved themselves upon such incidents as we decide by combat; and show, from their practice, that this resentment neither has its foundation from true reason or solid fame; but is an imposture, made of cowardice, falsehood, and want of understanding. For this work, a good history of quarrels would be very edifying to the public; and I apply myself to the town for particulars and circumstances within their knowledge, which may serve to embellish the dissertation with proper cuts.[5] Most of the quarrels I have ever known have proceeded from some valiant coxcomb's persisting in the wrong, to defend some prevailing folly, and preserve himself from the ingenuity[6] of owning a mistake.

By this means it is called "giving a man satisfaction" to urge your offense against him with your sword; which puts me in mind of Peter's order to the keeper in *The Tale of a Tub:*[7] "If you neglect to do all this, damn you and your generation for ever; and so we bid you heartily farewell." If the contradiction in the very terms of one of our challenges were as well explained, and turned into downright English, would it not run after this manner?

"*Sir,*
"Your extraordinary behavior last night, and the liberty you were pleased to take with me, makes me this morning give you this, to tell you, because you are an ill-bred puppy, I will meet you in Hyde Park an hour hence; and because you want both breeding and humanity, I desire you would come with a pistol in your hand, on horseback, and endeavor to shoot me through the head, to teach you more manners. If you fail of doing me this pleasure, I shall say you are a rascal on every post in town; and so, sir, if you will not injure me more, I shall never forgive what you have done already. Pray, sir, do not fail of getting everything ready, and you will infinitely oblige, sir, Your most obedient humble servant, etc."

STEELE: ON THE PASSION OF LOVE

THE TATLER, NO. 40   *Tuesday,* JULY 12, 1709

... From my own apartment, JULY 11

THIS evening some ladies came to visit my sister Jenny; and the discourse, after very many frivolous and public matters, turned upon the main point among the women, the passion of love. Sappho, who always leads on this occasion, began to show her reading, and told us that Sir John Suckling and Milton had, upon a parallel occasion, said the tenderest things she ever read. "The circumstance," said she, "is such as gives us a notion of that protecting part which is the duty of men in their honorable designs upon or possession of women. In Suckling's tragedy of *Brennoralt*[1] he makes the lover steal into his mistress's bedchamber, and draw the curtains;[2] then, when his heart is full of her charms as she lies sleeping, instead of being carried away by the violence of his desires into thoughts of a warmer nature, Sleep, which is the image of death, gives this generous lover reflections of a different kind, which regard rather her safety than his own passion. For, beholding her as she lies sleeping, he utters these words:

So Misers look upon their gold,
Which, while they joy to see, they fear to lose;
The pleasure of the sight scarce equaling
The jealousy of being dispossessed by others.
Her face is like the Milky Way i' th' sky,
A meeting of gentle lights without name!
Heav'ns! Shall this fresh ornament of the world,
This precious loveliness, pass with other common things
Amongst the wastes of time? What pity 'twere!

"When Milton makes Adam leaning on his arm beholding Eve, and lying in the contemplation of

---

[5] Illustrations.   [6] Ingenuousness, frankness.
[7] By Swift (see p. 723, below). Peter (the Catholic Church) orders criminals released from jail (i.e., grants absolution). Steele has toned down Swift's language.

[1] Published in 1646. For Suckling, see p. 519, above.
[2] Open the curtains of the bed. In Act III, Scene i.

her beauty, he describes the utmost tenderness and guardian affection in one word:

> Adam, with *looks of* cordial love,
> Hung over her enamored.[3]

"This is that sort of passion which truly deserves the name of love, and has something more generous than friendship itself; for it has a constant care of the object beloved, abstracted from its own interests in the possession of it." Sappho was proceeding on this subject, when my sister produced a letter sent to her in the time of my absence, in celebration of the marriage state, which is the condition wherein only this sort of passion reigns in full authority. The epistle is as follows:

Dear Madam,

Your Brother being absent, I dare take the liberty of writing to you my thoughts of that state which our whole sex either is or desires to be in. You'll easily guess I mean matrimony, which I hear so much decried that it was with no small labor I maintained my ground against two opponents; but, as your brother observed of Socrates, I drew them into my conclusion from their own concessions, thus:

> In marriage are two happy things allowed,
> A wife in wedding sheets, and in a shroud.
> How can a marriage state be then accursed,
> Since the last day's as happy as the first?

If you think they were too easily confuted, you may conclude them not of the first sense, by their talking against Marriage. *Yours,*

MARIANA

I observed Sappho began to redden at this epistle; and turning to a lady who was playing with a dog she was so fond of as to carry him abroad with her, "Nay," says she, "I cannot blame the men if they have mean ideas of our souls and affections, and wonder so many are brought to take us for companions for life, when they see our endearments so triflingly placed; for, to my knowledge, Mr. Truman would give half his estate for half the affection you have shewn to that shock.[4] Nor do I believe you would be ashamed to confess that I saw you cry when he had the colic last week with lapping sour milk. What more could you do for your lover himself?" "What more!" replied the lady: "There is not a man in England for whom I could lament half so much." Then she stifled the animal with kisses, and

---

[3] Cf. *Paradise Lost*, V, 12–13.   [4] Long-haired dog.

called him beau, life, dear, monsieur, pretty fellow, and what not, in the hurry of her impertinence. Sappho rose up, as she always does at anything she observes done which discovers in her own sex a levity of mind that renders them inconsiderable in the opinion of ours.

ADDISON: ON MR. SPECTATOR

THE SPECTATOR, NO. 1 *Thursday,* MARCH 1, 1711

> *Non fumum ex fulgore, sed ex fumo dare lucem*
> *Cogitat, ut speciosa dehinc miracula promat.*[1]
> HORACE, *Ars Poetica*, 143–4

I HAVE observed that a reader seldom peruses a book with pleasure till he knows whether the writer of it be a black[2] or a fair man, of a mild or choleric disposition, married or a bachelor, with other particulars of the like nature, that conduce very much to the right understanding of an author. To gratify this curiosity, which is so natural to a reader, I design this paper and my next as prefatory discourses to my following writings, and shall give some account in them of the several persons that are engaged in this work. As the chief trouble of compiling, digesting, and correcting will fall to my share, I must do myself the justice to open the work with my own history.

I was born to a small hereditary estate, which, according to the tradition of the village where it lies, was bounded by the same hedges and ditches in William the Conqueror's time that it is at present, and has been delivered down from father to son whole and entire, without the loss or acquisition of a single field or meadow, during the space of six hundred years. There runs a story in the family, that when my mother was gone with child of me about three months, she dreamt that she was brought to bed of a judge. Whether this might proceed from a lawsuit which was then depending in the family, or my father's being a justice of the peace, I cannot determine; for I am not so vain as to think it presaged any dignity that I should arrive at in my future life, though that was the interpretation which the neighborhood put upon it. The gravity of my behavior at my very first appearance in the world, and all the time that I sucked, seemed to favor my mother's dream; for, as she has often told me, I threw away

---

[1] He intends to bring, not smoke from flame, but light from smoke, in order to disclose his fine wonders.
[2] Dark complexioned.

my rattle before I was two months old, and would not make use of my coral[3] till they had taken away the bells from it.

As for the rest of my infancy, there being nothing in it remarkable, I shall pass it over in silence. I find that during my nonage I had the reputation of a very sullen youth, but was always a favorite of my schoolmaster, who used to say that my parts[4] were solid and would wear well. I had not been long at the university before I distinguished myself by a most profound silence; for during the space of eight years, excepting in the public exercises of the college, I scarce uttered the quantity of an hundred words; and indeed do not remember that I ever spoke three sentences together in my whole life. Whilst I was in this learned body, I applied myself with so much diligence to my studies that there are very few celebrated books, either in the learned or the modern tongues, which I am not acquainted with.

Upon the death of my father I was resolved to travel into foreign countries and therefore left the university, with the character of an odd, unaccountable fellow that had a great deal of learning if I would but show it. An insatiable thirst after knowledge carried me into all the countries of Europe in which there was anything new or strange to be seen; nay, to such a degree was my curiosity raised, that, having read the controversies of some great men concerning the antiquities of Egypt, I made a voyage to Grand Cairo, on purpose to take the measure of a pyramid, and, as soon as I had set myself right in that particular, returned to my native country with great satisfaction.

I have passed my latter years in this city, where I am frequently seen in most public places, though there are not above half a dozen of my select friends that know me; of whom my next paper shall give a more particular account. There is no place of general resort wherein I do not often make my appearance; sometimes I am seen thrusting my head into a round of politicians at Will's,[5] and listening with great attention to the narratives that are made in those little circular audiences. Sometimes I smoke a pipe at Child's,[6] and, whilst I seem attentive to nothing but the *Postman,*[7] overhear the conversation of every table in the room. I appear on Sunday nights at St. James's Coffee House,[8] and sometimes join the little committee of politics in the inner room, as one who comes there to hear and improve. My face is likewise very well known at the Grecian,[9] the Cocoa Tree,[10] and in the theaters both of Drury Lane and the Haymarket. I have been taken for a merchant upon the Exchange for above these ten years, and sometimes pass for a Jew in the assembly of stockjobbers[11] at Jonathan's.[12] In short, wherever I see a cluster of people I always mix with them, though I never open my lips but in my own club.

Thus I live in the world rather as a spectator of mankind than as one of the species; by which means I have made myself a speculative[13] statesman, soldier, merchant, and artisan, without ever meddling with any practical part in life. I am very well versed in the theory of an husband or a father, and can discern the errors in the economy, business, and diversion of others better than those who are engaged in them; as standers-by discover blots which are apt to escape those who are in the game. I never espoused any party with violence, and am resolved to observe an exact neutrality between the Whigs and Tories, unless I shall be forced to declare myself by the hostilities of either side. In short, I have acted in all the parts of my life as a looker-on, which is the character I intend to preserve in this paper.

I have given the reader just so much of my history and character as to let him see I am not altogether unqualified for the business I have undertaken. As for other particulars in my life and adventures, I shall insert them in following papers, as I shall see occasion. In the meantime, when I consider how much I have seen, read, and heard, I begin to blame my own taciturnity; and since I have neither time nor inclination to communicate the fullness of my heart in speech, I am resolved to do it in writing, and to print myself out, if possible, before I die. I have been often told by my friends that it is pity so many useful discoveries which I have made should be in the possession of a silent man. For this reason, therefore, I shall publish a sheetful of thoughts every morning for the benefit of my contemporaries; and if I can any way contribute to the diversion or improvement of the country in which I live, I shall leave it, when

---

[3] Teething ring.   [4] Talents.
[5] This coffee house in Covent Garden had acquired in Dryden's time its reputation as a resort of the poets and wits.
[6] In St. Paul's Churchyard. It was frequented by physicians, the clergy, and other professional men, especially those of the Tory persuasion.   [7] A Whig newspaper.

[8] A Whig rendezvous in St. James's Street.
[9] Off the Strand. In *Tatler* no. 1 Steele assigns learning to the Grecian. It was a favorite resort of lawyers and scholars.
[10] In St. James's Street. It attracted a Tory clientele.
[11] Brokers.
[12] A coffee house in Change Alley off Cornhill; it served as a stock exchange.   [13] Theoretical.

I am summoned out of it, with the secret satisfaction of thinking that I have not lived in vain.

There are three very material points which I have not spoken to in this paper, and which, for several important reasons, I must keep to myself, at least for some time: I mean, an account of my name, my age, and my lodgings. I must confess I would gratify my reader in anything that is reasonable; but, as for these three particulars, though I am sensible they might tend very much to the embellishment of my paper, I cannot yet come to a resolution of communicating them to the public. They would indeed draw me out of that obscurity which I have enjoyed for many years, and expose me in public places to several salutes and civilities, which have been always very disagreeable to me; for the greatest pain I can suffer is the being talked to and being stared at. It is for this reason, likewise, that I keep my complexion and dress as very great secrets, though it is not impossible but I may make discoveries of both in the progress of the work I have undertaken.

After having been thus particular upon myself, I shall in tomorrow's paper give an account of those gentlemen who are concerned with me in this work; for, as I have before intimated, a plan of it is laid and concerted (as all other matters of importance are) in a club. However, as my friends have engaged me to stand in the front, those who have a mind to correspond with me may direct their letters "To the Spectator, at Mr. Buckley's in Little Britain."[14] For I must further acquaint the reader that, though our club meets only on Tuesdays and Thursdays, we have appointed a committee to sit every night for the inspection of all such papers as may contribute to the advancement of the public weal.

Steele: ON THE SPECTATOR CLUB

THE SPECTATOR, NO. 2 *Friday*, MARCH 2, 1711

*Haec alii sex
Et plures uno conclamant ore.*[1]
JUVENAL, *Satires*, VII, 166–7

THE first of our society is a gentleman of Worcestershire, of ancient descent, a baronet, his name Sir Roger de Coverley. His great-grandfather was inventor of that famous country-dance which is called after him. All who know that shire are very well acquainted with the parts and merits of Sir Roger. He is a gentleman that is very singular in his behavior; but his singularities proceed from his good sense, and are contradictions to the manners of the world only as he thinks the world is in the wrong. However, this humor creates him no enemies, for he does nothing with sourness or obstinacy; and his being unconfined to modes and forms makes him but the readier and more capable to please and oblige all who know him. When he is in town, he lives in Soho Square.[2] It is said he keeps himself a bachelor by reason he was crossed in love by a perverse, beautiful widow of the next county to him. Before this disappointment, Sir Roger was what you call a fine gentleman, had often supped with my Lord Rochester and Sir George Etherege,[3] fought a duel upon his first coming to town, and kicked Bully Dawson[4] in a public coffee house for calling him "youngster." But being ill used by the above-mentioned widow, he was very serious for a year and a half; and though, his temper being naturally jovial, he at last got over it, he grew careless of himself and never dressed afterwards; he continues to wear a coat and doublet of the same cut that were in fashion at the time of his repulse, which, in his merry humors, he tells us has been in and out twelve times since he first wore it. 'Tis said Sir Roger grew humble in his desires after he had forgot this cruel beauty, insomuch that it is reported he has frequently offended in point of chastity with beggars and gypsies; but this is looked upon by his friends rather as matter of raillery than truth. He is now in his fifty-sixth year, cheerful, gay, and hearty; keeps a good house both in town and country; a great lover of mankind; but there is such a mirthful cast in his behavior that he is rather beloved than esteemed. His tenants grow rich, his servants look satisfied, all the young women profess love to him, and the young men are glad of his company. When he comes into a house he calls the servants by their names, and talks all the way upstairs to a visit. I must not omit that Sir Roger is a justice of the quorum;[5] that he fills the chair at a quarter session[6] with great abilities; and, three months ago, gained

---

[2] Then a fashionable suburban neighborhood west of the City.
[3] The famous Restoration courtiers and writers. See pp. 400, 532–5, above.
[4] A notorious character of Restoration times.
[5] I.e., one of the select group of justices of the peace some of whom had to be present before a court could proceed.
[6] A court of limited jurisdiction held quarterly by country justices of the peace.

---

[14] A street of printers and booksellers near Aldersgate. Samuel Buckley printed the *Spectator*. This invitation was accepted by many.

[1] Six others and more cry out with one voice.

universal applause by explaining a passage in the Game Act.

The gentleman next in esteem and authority among us is another bachelor, who is a member of the Inner Temple;[7] a man of great probity, wit, and understanding; but he has chosen his place of residence rather to obey the direction of an old humorsome father than in pursuit of his own inclinations. He was placed there to study the laws of the land, and is the most learned of any of the house in those of the stage. Aristotle[8] and Longinus[9] are much better understood by him than Littleton or Coke.[10] The father sends up, every post, questions relating to marriage articles, leases, and tenures, in the neighborhood; all which questions he agrees with an attorney to answer and take care of in the lump. He is studying the passions themselves, when he should be inquiring into the debates among men which arise from them. He knows the argument of each of the orations of Demosthenes[11] and Tully,[12] but not one case in the reports of our own courts. No one ever took him for a fool; but none, except his intimate friends, know he has a great deal of wit. This turn makes him at once both disinterested and agreeable; as few of his thoughts are drawn from business, they are most of them fit for conversation. His taste of books is a little too just for the age he lives in; he has read all, but approves of very few. His familiarity with the customs, manners, actions, and writings of the ancients makes him a very delicate observer of what occurs to him in the present world. He is an excellent critic, and the time of the play is his hour of business; exactly at five he passes through New Inn, crosses through Russell Court, and takes a turn at Will's till the play begins; he has his shoes rubbed and his periwig powdered at the barber's as you go into the Rose.[13] It is for the good of the audience when he is at a play, for the actors have an ambition to please him.

The person of next consideration is Sir Andrew Freeport, a merchant of great eminence in the City[14] of London, a person of indefatigable industry, strong reason, and great experience. His notions of trade are noble and generous, and (as every rich man has usually some sly way of jesting which would make no great figure were he not a rich man) he calls the sea the British Common. He is acquainted with commerce in all its parts, and will tell you that it is a stupid and barbarous way to extend dominion by arms; for true power is to be got by arts and industry. He will often argue that if this part of our trade were well cultivated, we should gain from one nation; and if another, from another. I have heard him prove that diligence makes more lasting acquisitions than valor, and that sloth has ruined more nations than the sword. He abounds in several frugal maxims, among which the greatest favorite is "A penny saved is a penny got." A general trader of good sense is pleasanter company than a general scholar; and Sir Andrew having a natural unaffected eloquence, the perspicuity of his discourse gives the same pleasure that wit would in another man. He has made his fortunes himself, and says that England may be richer than other kingdoms by as plain methods as he himself is richer than other men; though at the same time I can say this of him, that there is not a point in the compass but blows home a ship in which he is an owner.

Next to Sir Andrew in the club-room sits Captain Sentry, a gentleman of great courage, good understanding, but invincible modesty. He is one of those that deserve very well, but are very awkward at putting their talents within the observation of such as should take notice of them. He was some years a captain, and behaved himself with great gallantry in several engagements and at several sieges; but having a small estate of his own, and being next heir to Sir Roger, he has quitted a way of life in which no man can rise suitably to his merit who is not something of a courtier as well as a soldier. I have heard him often lament that in a profession where merit is placed in so conspicuous a view, impudence should get the better of modesty. When he has talked to this purpose I never heard him make a sour expression, but frankly confess that he left the world because he was not fit for it. A strict honesty and an even, regular behavior are in themselves obstacles to him that must press through crowds who endeavor at the same end with himself, the favor of a commander. He will, however, in his way of talk, excuse generals for not disposing according to men's desert, or inquiring into it; "for," says he, "that great man who has a mind to help me has as many to break through to come at me as I have to come at him." Therefore he will conclude that the man who would make a figure, especially in a military way, must

---

[7] One of the inns of court.

[8] The first and greatest of dramatic critics.

[9] The Greek author of a valuable critical treatise *On the Sublime* (probably of the first or second century).

[10] The great legal authorities Sir Thomas Littleton (1402–81) and Sir Edward Coke (1552–1634).

[11] Most famous of the Greek orators (d. 322 B.C.).

[12] Marcus Tullius Cicero (d. 43 B.C.), the Roman orator, statesman, and prose stylist.

[13] A tavern near the Theater Royal, Drury Lane.

[14] I.e., the central portion, the business district.

get over all false modesty, and assist his patron against the importunity of other pretenders by a proper assurance in his own vindication. He says it is a civil cowardice to be backward in asserting what you ought to expect, as it is a military fear to be slow in attacking when it is your duty. With this candor does the gentleman speak of himself and others. The same frankness runs through all his conversation. The military part of his life has furnished him with many adventures, in the relation of which he is very agreeable to the company; for he is never overbearing, though accustomed to command men in the utmost degree below him, nor ever too obsequious from an habit of obeying men highly above him.

But that our society may not appear a set of humorists[15] unacquainted with the gallantries and pleasures of the age, we have among us the gallant Will Honeycomb, a gentleman who according to his years should be in the decline of his life, but, having ever been very careful of his person and always had a very easy fortune, time has made but very little impression, either by wrinkles on his forehead or traces in his brain. His person is well turned and of a good height. He is very ready at that sort of discourse with which men usually entertain women. He has all his life dressed very well, and remembers habits as others do men. He can smile when one speaks to him, and laughs easily. He knows the history of every mode, and can inform you from which of the French king's wenches our wives and daughters had this manner of curling their hair, that way of placing their hoods; whose frailty was covered by such a sort of petticoat,[16] and whose vanity to show her foot made that part of the dress so short in such a year. In a word, all his conversation and knowledge has been in the female world: as other men of his age will take notice to you what such a minister said upon such and such an occasion, he will tell you when the Duke of Monmouth[17] danced at court such a woman was then smitten, another was taken with him at the head of his troop in the park. In all these important relations, he has ever about the same time received a kind glance or a blow of a fan from some celebrated beauty, mother of the present Lord Such-a-one. If you speak of a young commoner that said a lively thing in the House, he starts up: "He has good blood in his veins; Tom Mirabell begot him; the rogue cheated me in that affair; that young fellow's mother used me more

like a dog than any woman I ever made advances to." This way of talking of his very much enlivens the conversation among us of a more sedate turn; and I find there is not one of the company but myself, who rarely speak at all, but speaks of him as of that sort of man who is usually called a well-bred fine gentleman. To conclude his character, where women are not concerned, he is an honest, worthy man.

I cannot tell whether I am to account him whom I am next to speak of as one of our company, for he visits us but seldom; but when he does, it adds to every man else a new enjoyment of himself. He is a clergyman, a very philosophic man, of general learning, great sanctity of life, and the most exact good breeding. He has the misfortune to be of a very weak constitution, and consequently cannot accept of such cares and business as preferments in his function[18] would oblige him to; he is therefore among divines what a chamber-counselor[19] is among lawyers. The probity of his mind and the integrity of his life create him followers, as being eloquent or loud advances others. He seldom introduces the subject he speaks upon; but we are so far gone in years that he observes, when he is among us, an earnestness to have him fall on some divine topic, which he always treats with much authority, as one who has no interests in this world, as one who is hastening to the object of all his wishes, and conceives hope from his decays and infirmities. These are my ordinary companions.

Addison: ON THE SPECTATOR'S USES

THE SPECTATOR, NO. 10 *Monday*, MARCH 12, 1711

Non aliter quam qui adverso vix flumine lembum
Remigiis subigit; si brachia forte remisit,
Atque illum in praeceps prono rapit alveus amni.[1]
VERGIL, *Georgics*, I, 201-3

IT IS with much satisfaction that I hear this great city inquiring day by day after these my papers, and receiving my morning lectures with a becoming seriousness and attention. My publisher tells me that

---

[15] Eccentrics.   [16] Designed to conceal pregnancy.
[17] Bastard son of Charles II.

[18] Advancement in his profession.
[19] A lawyer who gives advice but does not appear in court.

[1] So the boat's brawny crew the current stem,
And, slow advancing, struggle with the stream;
But if they slack their hands, or cease to strive,
Then down the flood with headlong haste they drive.
(Dryden's translation.)

there are already three thousand[2] of them distributed every day; so that if I allow twenty readers to every paper, which I look upon as a modest computation, I may reckon about threescore thousand disciples in London and Westminster, who I hope will take care to distinguish themselves from the thoughtless herd of their ignorant and unattentive brethren. Since I have raised to myself so great an audience, I shall spare no pains to make their instruction agreeable, and their diversion useful. For which reasons I shall endeavor to enliven morality with wit, and to temper wit with morality, that my readers may, if possible, both ways find their account in the speculation of the day. And to the end that their virtue and discretion may not be short, transient, intermittent starts of thought, I have resolved to refresh their memories from day to day, till I have recovered them out of that desperate state of vice and folly into which the age is fallen. The mind that lies fallow but a single day sprouts up in follies that are only to be killed by a constant and assiduous culture. It was said of Socrates that he brought philosophy down from heaven, to inhabit among men; and I shall be ambitious to have it said of me that I have brought philosophy out of closets[3] and libraries, schools and colleges, to dwell in clubs and assemblies, at tea tables and in coffee houses.

I would therefore in a very particular manner recommend these my speculations to all well-regulated families, that set apart an hour in every morning for tea and bread and butter; and would earnestly advise them for their good to order this paper to be served up, and to be looked upon as a part of the tea equipage.

Sir Francis Bacon[4] observes that a well-written book, compared with its rivals and antagonists, is like Moses's serpent, that immediately swallowed up and devoured those of the Egyptians. I shall not be so vain as to think, that where the SPECTATOR appears, the other public prints will vanish; but shall leave it to my reader's consideration whether it is not much better to be let into the knowledge of oneself than to hear what passes in Muscovy or Poland, and to amuse ourselves with such writings as tend to the wearing out of ignorance, passion, and prejudice than such as naturally conduce to inflame hatreds and make enmities irreconcilable.

In the next place, I would recommend this paper to the daily perusal of those gentlemen whom I cannot but consider as my good brothers and allies; I mean the fraternity of spectators who live in the world without having anything to do in it, and either by the affluence of their fortunes or laziness of their dispositions have no other business with the rest of mankind but to look upon them. Under this class of men are comprehended all contemplative tradesmen, titular physicians, fellows of the Royal Society, Templars[5] that are not given to be contentious, and statesmen that are out of business; in short, everyone that considers the world as a theater, and desires to form a right judgment of those who are the actors on it.

There is another set of men that I must likewise lay a claim to, whom I have lately called the blanks of society, as being altogether unfurnished with ideas till the business and conversation of the day has supplied them. I have often considered these poor souls with an eye of great commiseration, when I have heard them asking the first man they have met with whether there was any news stirring, and by that means gathering together materials for thinking. These needy persons do not know what to talk of till about twelve o'clock in the morning; for by that time they are pretty good judges of the weather, know which way the wind sits, and whether the Dutch mail be come in. As they lie at the mercy of the first man they meet, and are grave or impertinent all the day long, according to the notions which they have imbibed in the morning, I would earnestly entreat them not to stir out of their chambers till they have read this paper, and do promise them that I will daily instil into them such sound and wholesome sentiments, as shall have a good effect on their conversation for the ensuing twelve hours.

But there are none to whom this paper will be more useful, than to the female world. I have often thought there has not been sufficient pains taken in finding out proper employments and diversions for the fair ones. Their amusements seem contrived for them rather as they are women than as they are reasonable creatures, and are more adapted to the sex than to the species. The toilet is their great scene of business, and the right adjusting of their hair the principal employment of their lives. The sorting of a suit of ribbons is reckoned a very good morning's work; and if they make an excursion to a mercer's[6] or a toy shop, so great a fatigue makes them unfit for anything else all the day after. Their more serious occupations are sewing and embroidery, and their greatest drudgery the preparation of jellies and

---

2 Eventually the sale rose to about 25,000 copies an issue.
3 Private rooms.
4 *The Advancement of Learning*, II, introduction.

5 Lawyers or law students.   6 Dry-goods shop.

sweetmeats. This, I say, is the state of ordinary women, though I know there are multitudes of those of a more elevated life and conversation, that move in an exalted sphere of knowledge and virtue, that join all the beauties of the mind to the ornaments of dress, and inspire a kind of awe and respect, as well as love, into their male beholders. I hope to increase the number of these by publishing this daily paper, which I shall always endeavor to make an innocent if not an improving entertainment, and by that means at least divert the minds of my female readers from greater trifles. At the same time, as I would fain give some finishing touches to those which are already the most beautiful pieces in human nature, I shall endeavor to point out all those imperfections that are the blemishes, as well as those virtues which are the embellishments, of the sex. In the meanwhile I hope these my gentle readers, who have so much time on their hands, will not grudge throwing away a quarter of an hour in a day on this paper, since they may do it without any hindrance to business.

I know several of my friends and well-wishers are in great pain for me, lest I should not be able to keep up the spirit of a paper which I oblige myself to furnish every day; but to make them easy in this particular, I will promise them faithfully to give it over as soon as I grow dull. This I know will be matter of great raillery to the small wits, who will frequently put me in mind of my promise, desire me to keep my word, assure me that it is high time to give over, with many other little pleasantries of the like nature, which men of a little smart genius cannot forbear throwing out against their best friends, when they have such a handle given them of being witty. But let them remember that I do hereby enter my caveat against this piece of raillery.

ADDISON: ON NICOLINI AND THE LIONS

THE SPECTATOR, NO. 13 *Thursday*, MARCH 15, 1711

Dic mihi, si fias tu leo, qualis eris?[1]
MARTIAL, XII, 93

THERE is nothing that of late years has afforded matter of greater amusement to the town than Signior Nicolini's[2] combat with a lion in the Haymarket, which has been very often exhibited to the general satisfaction of most of the nobility and gentry in the kingdom of Great Britain. Upon the first rumor of this intended combat, it was confidently affirmed, and is still believed by many in both galleries, that there would be a tame lion sent from the Tower every opera night, in order to be killed by Hydaspes; this report, though altogether groundless, so universally prevailed in the upper regions of the playhouse, that some of the most refined politicians in those parts of the audience gave it out in whisper that the lion was a cousin-german of the tiger who made his appearance in King William's days, and that the stage would be supplied with lions at the public expense during the whole session. Many, likewise, were the conjectures of the treatment which this lion was to meet with from the hands of Signior Nicolini; some supposed that he was to subdue him in *recitativo*, as Orpheus used to serve the wild beasts in his time, and afterwards to knock him on the head; some fancied that the lion would not pretend to lay his paws upon the hero, by reason of the received opinion that a lion will not hurt a virgin. Several, who pretended to have seen the opera in Italy, had informed their friends that the lion was to act a part in High Dutch, and roar twice or thrice to a thorough bass[3] before he fell at the feet of Hydaspes. To clear up a matter that was so variously reported, I have made it my business to examine whether this pretended lion is really the savage he appears to be, or only a counterfeit.

But before I communicate my discoveries, I must acquaint the reader that upon my walking behind the scenes last winter, as I was thinking on something else I accidentally justled against a monstrous animal that extremely startled me, and upon my nearer survey of it appeared to be a lion rampant. The lion, seeing me very much surprised, told me in a gentle voice that I might come by him if I pleased. "For," says he, "I do not intend to hurt anybody." I thanked him very kindly, and passed by him. And in a little time after saw him leap upon the stage, and act his part with very great applause. It has been observed by several that the lion has changed his manner of acting twice or thrice since his first appearance,

---

[1] Were you a lion, say to me
What kind of lion you would be.

[2] The *castrato* Nicolino Grimaldi, known as the Cavaliere Nicolini, was a famous Neapolitan contralto. Born about 1673, he was now the leading singer of the newly established opera at the Haymarket. He was said to be a better actor than the actors. The opera with a lion was *Hydaspes*, libretto by Nicolini, music by Francesco Mancini.

[3] To the accompaniment of a very low chord.

which will not seem strange when I acquaint my reader that the lion has been changed upon the audience three several times. The first lion was a candle snuffer,[4] who, being a fellow of a testy, choleric temper, overdid his part and would not suffer himself to be killed so easily as he ought to have done; besides, it was observed of him that he grew more surly every time he came out of the lion; and having dropped some words in ordinary conversation, as if he had not fought his best and that he suffered himself to be thrown upon his back in the scuffle and that he would wrestle with Mr. Nicolini for what he pleased, out of his lion's skin, it was thought proper to discard him. And it is verily believed to this day that had he been brought upon the stage another time, he would certainly have done mischief. Besides, it was objected against the first lion that he reared himself so high upon his hinder paws and walked in so erect a posture that he looked more like an old man than a lion.

The second lion was a tailor by trade, who belonged to the playhouse and had the character of a mild and peaceable man in his profession. If the former was too furious, this was too sheepish, for his part; insomuch that, after a short modest walk upon the stage, he would fall at the first touch of Hydaspas, without grappling with him and giving him an opportunity of showing his variety of Italian trips. It is said indeed, that he once gave him a rip in his flesh-color doublet, but this was only to make work for himself, in his private character of a tailor. I must not omit that it was this second lion who treated me with so much humanity behind the scenes.

The acting lion at present is, as I am informed, a country gentleman, who does it for his diversion but desires his name may be concealed. He says very handsomely, in his own excuse, that he does not act for gain, that he indulges an innocent pleasure in it, and that it is better to pass away an evening in this manner than in gaming and drinking; but at the same time says, with a very agreeable raillery upon himself, that if his name should be known, the ill-natured world might call him "the ass in the lion's skin." This gentleman's temper is made out of such a happy mixture of the mild and the choleric, that he outdoes both his predecessors, and has drawn together greater audiences than have been known in the memory of man.

I must not conclude my narrative without taking notice of a groundless report that has been raised to a gentleman's disadvantage, of whom I must declare myself an admirer; namely, that Signior Nicolini and the lion have been seen sitting peaceably by one another and smoking a pipe together, behind the scenes; by which their common enemies would insinuate that it is but a sham combat which they represent upon the stage; but upon inquiry I find that, if any such correspondence has passed between them, it was not till the combat was over, when the lion was to be looked upon as dead, according to the received rules of the drama. Besides, this is what is practiced every day in Westminster Hall, where nothing is more usual than to see a couple of lawyers, who have been tearing each other to pieces in the court, embracing one another as soon as they are out of it.

I would not be thought, in any part of this relation, to reflect upon Signor Nicolini, who in acting this part only complies with the wretched taste of his audience. He knows very well that the lion has many more admirers than himself; as they say of the famous equestrian statue on the Pont Neuf at Paris, that more people go to see the horse than the king[5] who sits upon it. On the contrary, it gives me a just indignation to see a person whose action gives new majesty to kings, resolution to heroes, and softness to lovers, thus sinking from the greatness of his behavior and degraded into the character of the London Prentice.[6] I have often wished that our tragedians would copy after this great master in action. Could they make the same use of their arms and legs, and inform their faces with as significant looks and passions, how glorious would an English tragedy appear with that action, which is capable of giving a dignity to the forced thoughts, cold conceits, and unnatural expressions of an Italian opera! In the meantime, I have related this combat of the lion to show what are at present the reigning entertainments of the politer part of Great Britain.

Audiences have often been reproached by writers for the coarseness of their taste; but our present grievance does not seem to be the want of a good taste, but of common sense.

---

[4] To lower the light, the candle snuffer had to come on stage.   [5] Henri IV.   [6] Hero of absurd melodramas.

THE SPECTATOR, NO. 112 *Monday,* JULY 9, 1711

Ἀθανάτους μὲν πρῶτα θεοὺς, νόμῳ ὡς διάκειται,
Τίμα.[1]

PYTHAGORAS, *Carmina Aurea,* 1–2

I AM always very well pleased with a country Sunday, and think, if keeping holy the seventh day were only a human institution, it would be the best method that could have been thought of for the polishing and civilizing of mankind. It is certain the country people would soon degenerate into a kind of savages and barbarians were there not such frequent returns of a stated time in which the whole village meet together with their best faces, and in their cleanliest habits, to converse with one another upon indifferent[2] subjects, hear their duties explained to them, and join together in adoration of the Supreme Being. Sunday clears away the rust of the whole week, not only as it refreshes in their minds the notions of religion, but as it puts both the sexes upon appearing in their most agreeable forms and exerting all such qualities as are apt to give them a figure in the eye of the village. A country fellow distinguishes himself as much in the churchyard as a citizen does upon the 'Change,[3] the whole parish politics being generally discussed in that place either after sermon or before the bell rings.

My friend Sir Roger, being a good churchman, has beautified the inside of his church with several texts of his own choosing; he has likewise given a handsome pulpit cloth, and railed in the communion table at his own expense. He has often told me that, at his coming to his estate, he found his parishioners very irregular; and that, in order to make them kneel and join in the responses, he gave every one of them a hassock and a common-prayer-book, and at the same time employed an itinerant singing-master, who goes about the country for that purpose, to instruct them rightly in the tunes of the Psalms, upon which they now very much value themselves, and indeed outdo most of the country churches that I have ever heard.

As Sir Roger is landlord to the whole congregation, he keeps them in very good order, and will suffer nobody to sleep in it besides himself; for if by chance he has been surprised into a short nap at sermon, upon recovering out of it he stands up and looks about him, and if he sees anybody else nodding either wakes them himself or sends his servants to them. Several other of the old knight's particularities break out upon these occasions. Sometimes he will be lengthening out a verse in the Singing Psalms half a minute after the rest of the congregation have done with it; sometimes, when he is pleased with the matter of his devotion, he pronounces "Amen" three or four times to the same prayer; and sometimes stands up when everybody else is upon their knees, to count the congregation, or see if any of his tenants are missing.

I was yesterday very much surprised to hear my old friend, in the midst of the service, calling out to one John Matthews to mind what he was about and not disturb the congregation. This John Matthews, it seems, is remarkable for being an idle fellow, and at that time was kicking his heels for his diversion. This authority of the knight, though exerted in that odd manner which accompanies him in all circumstances of life, has a very good effect upon the parish, who are not polite[4] enough to see anything ridiculous in his behavior; besides that, the general good sense and worthiness of his character makes his friends observe these little singularities as foils that rather set off than blemish his good qualities.

As soon as the sermon is finished, nobody presumes to stir till Sir Roger is gone out of the church. The knight walks down from his seat in the chancel between a double row of his tenants, that stand bowing to him on each side, and every now and then inquires how such an one's wife or mother or son or father do, whom he does not see at church; which is understood as a secret reprimand to the person that is absent.

The chaplain has often told me that, upon a catechizing day, when Sir Roger has been pleased with a boy that answers well, he has ordered a Bible to be given him next day for his encouragement, and sometimes accompanies it with a flitch of bacon to his mother. Sir Roger has likewise added five pounds a year to the clerk's place and, that he may encourage the young fellows to make themselves perfect in the church service, has promised upon the death of the present incumbent, who is very old, to bestow it according to merit.

The fair understanding between Sir Roger and his chaplain, and their mutual concurrence in doing good, is the more remarkable because the very next

---

[1] First worship the immortal gods, as custom doth decree.
[2] Different.
[3] The Royal Exchange, a bazaar and mercantile center, between Threadneedle Street and Cornhill.

[4] Polished.

village is famous for the differences and contentions that rise between the parson and the squire, who live in a perpetual state of war. The parson is always preaching at the squire, and the squire to be revenged on the parson never comes to church. The squire has made all his tenants atheists, and tithe stealers;[5] while the parson instructs them every Sunday in the dignity of his order, and insinuates to them in almost every sermon that he is a better man than his patron. In short, matters have come to such an extremity that the squire has not said his prayers either in public or private this half year, and that the parson threatens him, if he does not mend his manners, to pray for him in the face of the whole congregation.

Feuds of this nature, though too frequent in the country, are very fatal to the ordinary people, who are so used to be dazzled with riches that they pay as much deference to the understanding of a man of an estate as of a man of learning, and are very hardly brought to regard any truth, how important soever it may be, that is preached to them, when they know there are several men of five hundred a year who do not believe it.

ADDISON: ON GENIUS

THE SPECTATOR, NO. 291   *Monday*, SEPT. 3, 1711

> . . . *Cui mens divinior, atque os*
> *Magna sonaturum, des nominis hujus honorem.*[1]
>   HORACE, *Satires*, I, 4, 43–4

THERE is no character more frequently given to a writer than that of being a "genius." I have heard many a little sonneteer called a *fine genius*. There is not an heroic scribbler[2] in the nation that has not his admirers who think him a *great genius;* and as for your smatterers in tragedy, there is scarce a man among them who is not cried up by one or other for a *prodigious genius*.

My design in this paper is to consider what is properly a great genius, and throw some thoughts together on so uncommon a subject.

Among great geniuses those few draw the admiration of all the world upon them, and stand up as the prodigies of mankind, who by the mere strength of natural parts,[3] and without the assistance of arts or learning, have produced works that were the delight of their own times and the wonder of posterity. There appears something nobly wild and extravagant in these great natural geniuses that is infinitely more beautiful than all the turn and polishing of what the French call a *bel esprit,* by which they would express a genius refined by conversation, reflection, and the reading of the most polite authors. The greatest genius which runs through the arts and sciences takes a kind of tincture from them, and falls unavoidably into imitation.

Many of these great natural geniuses that were never disciplined and broken by rules of art are to be found among the ancients, and in particular among those of the more eastern parts of the world. Homer has innumerable flights that Vergil was not able to reach, and in the Old Testament we find several passages more elevated and sublime than any in Homer. At the same time that we allow a greater and more daring genius to the ancients, we must own that the greatest of them very much failed in, or if you will that they were much above, the nicety and correctness of the moderns. In their similitudes and allusions, provided there was a likeness, they did not much trouble themselves about the decency[4] of the comparison. Thus Solomon resembles the nose of his beloved to the tower of Lebanon which looketh toward Damascus;[5] as the coming of a thief in the night is a similitude of the same kind in the New Testament.[6] It would be endless to make collections of this nature. Homer illustrates one of his heroes encompassed by the enemy by an ass in a field of corn that has his sides belabored by all the boys of the village without stirring a foot for it;[7] and another of them tossing to and fro in his bed and burning with resentment, to a piece of flesh broiled on the coals.[8] This particular failure in the ancients opens a large field of raillery to the little wits, who can laugh at an indecency but not relish the sublime in these sorts of writings. The present emperor of Persia, conformable to this eastern way of thinking, amidst a great many pompous titles, denominates himself the sun of glory and the nutmeg of delight. In short, to cut off all caviling against the ancients and particularly those of the warmer climates who had most heat and life in their imaginations, we are to consider that the rule of observing what the

---

[5] I.e., withholders of the tithes legally due the Church.

[1] On him confer the Poet's sacred name
  Whose lofty voice proclaims the heavenly flame.
                  (Pope's translation.)

[2] Scribbler of epics.

[3] Talents.   [4] Appropriateness.
[5] Song of Solomon 7:4.
[6] See 1 Thessalonians 5:2, 2 Peter 3:10.
[7] Ajax (*Iliad*, II, 558).   [8] Ulysses (*Odyssey*, XX, 25).

French call the *bienséance*[9] in an allusion has been found out of latter years, and in the colder regions of the world; where we could make some amends for our want of force and spirit, by a scrupulous nicety and exactness in our compositions. Our countryman Shakespeare was a remarkable instance of this first kind of great geniuses.

I cannot quit this head without observing that Pindar[10] was a great genius of the first class, who was hurried on by a natural fire and impetuosity to vast conceptions of things and noble sallies of imagination. At the same time, can anything be more ridiculous than for men of a sober and moderate fancy to imitate this poet's way of writing in those monstrous compositions which go among us under the name of Pindarics? When I see people copying works which, as Horace has represented them, are singular in their kind, and inimitable; when I see men following irregularities by rule, and by the little tricks of art straining after the most unbounded flights of nature, I cannot but apply to them that passage in Terence:

> . . . Incerta haec si tu postules
> Ratione certa facere, nihilo plus agas,
> Quam si des operam, ut cum ratione insanias.[11]

In short, a modern Pindaric writer, compared with Pindar, is like a sister among the Camisars[12] compared with Vergil's Sibyl.[13] There is the distortion, grimace, and outward figure, but nothing of that divine impulse which raises the mind above itself, and makes the sounds more than human.

There is another kind of great geniuses which I shall place in a second class, not as I think them inferior to the first, but only for distinction's sake, as they are of a different kind. This second class of great geniuses are those that have formed themselves by rules, and submitted the greatness of their natural talents to the corrections and restraints of art. Such among the Greeks were Plato and Aristotle; among the Romans, Vergil and Tully; among the English, Milton and Sir Francis Bacon.

The genius in both these classes of authors may be equally great, but shows itself after a different manner. In the first it is like a rich soil in a happy climate, that produces a whole wilderness of noble plants rising in a thousand beautiful landskips without any certain order or regularity. In the other it is the same rich soil under the same happy climate, that has been laid out in walks and parterres and cut into shape and beauty by the skill of the gardener.

The great danger in the latter kind of geniuses is lest they cramp their own abilities too much by imitation, and form themselves altogether upon models, without giving the full play to their own natural parts. An imitation of the best authors is not to compare with a good original; and I believe we may observe that very few writers make an extraordinary figure in the world who have not something in their way of thinking or expressing themselves that is peculiar to them and entirely their own.

It is odd to consider what great geniuses are sometimes thrown away upon trifles.

I once saw a shepherd, says a famous Italian author, who used to divert himself in his solitudes with tossing up eggs and catching them again without breaking them; in which he had arrived to so great a degree of perfection that he would keep up four at a time for several minutes together playing in the air and falling into his hand by turns. I think, says the author, I never saw a greater severity than in this man's face; for by his wonderful perseverance and application he had contracted the seriousness and gravity of a privy-councillor; and I could not but reflect with myself that the same assiduity and attention, had they been rightly applied, might have made him a greater mathematician than Archimedes.[14]

ADDISON: ON DYING FOR LOVE

THE SPECTATOR, NO. 377   *Tuesday*, MAY 13, 1712

> *Quid quisque vitet, nunquam homini satis*
> *Cautum est in horas.*[1]
> HORACE, *Odes*, II, xiii, 13–14

LOVE was the mother of poetry, and still produces, among the most ignorant and barbarous, a thousand imaginary distresses and poetical complaints. It makes a footman talk like Oroondates,[2] and converts a

---

[9] Propriety, decorum.

[10] On Pindar and the Pindaric ode, see p. 441, above.

[11] *Eunuch,* I, i, 16–18. W. Ritchie translates:
> "So if you thought to make secure
> By reason things so insecure, you'd fail as much
> As if you strove by reason's rules to be insane."

[12] French Protestants who revolted against the persecutions that followed the revocation of the Edict of Nantes.

[13] The Cumaean Sibyl, a prophetess consulted by Aeneas before his descent into Hades (*Aeneid,* Book VI).

[14] The great Greek mathematician and physicist of the third century B.C.

[1] While dangers hourly round us rise,
No caution guards us from surprise.
(Butler's translation.)

[2] A character in the long-winded romance of *Artamène ou Le Grand Cyrus* (1648–53) by Madeleine de Scudéry.

brutal rustic into a gentle swain. The most ordinary plebeian or mechanic in love bleeds and pines away with a certain elegance and tenderness of sentiments which this passion naturally inspires.

These inward languishings of a mind infected with this softness have given birth to a phrase which is made use of by all the melting tribe, from the highest to the lowest, I mean that of *dying for love*.

Romances, which owe their very being to this passion, are full of these metaphorical deaths. Heroes and heroines, knights, squires, and damsels, are all of them in a dying condition. There is the same kind of mortality in our modern tragedies, where every one gasps, faints, bleeds, and dies. Many of the poets, to describe the execution which is done by this passion, represent the fair sex as basilisks, that destroy with their eyes; but I think Mr. Cowley has with great justness of thought compared a beautiful woman to a porcupine, that sends an arrow from every part.[3]

I have often thought that there is no way so effectual for the cure of this general infirmity as a man's reflecting upon the motives that produce it. When the passion proceeds from the sense of any virtue or perfection in the person beloved, I would by no means discourage it; but if a man considers that all his heavy complaints of wounds and deaths rise from some little affectations of coquetry, which are improved into charms by his own fond imagination, the very laying before himself the cause of his distemper may be sufficient to effect the cure of it.

It is in this view that I have looked over the several bundles of letters which I have received from dying people, and composed out of them the following bill of mortality,[4] which I shall lay before my reader without any further preface, as hoping that it may be useful to him in discovering those several places where there is most danger, and those fatal arts which are made use of to destroy the heedless and unwary.

Lysander, slain at a puppet show on the 3rd of September.

Thyrsis, shot from a casement in Piccadilly.

T. S., wounded by Zelinda's scarlet stocking, as she was stepping out of a coach.

Will Simple, smitten at the opera by the glance of an eye that was aimed at one who stood by him.

Tho. Vainlove, lost his life at a ball.

Tim Tattle, killed by the tap of a fan on his left shoulder by Coquetilla, as he was talking carelessly with her in a bow window.

Sir Simon Softly, murdered at the playhouse in Drury Lane by a frown.

Philander, mortally wounded by Cleora, as she was adjusting her tucker.[5]

Ralph Gapely, Esq., hit by a random shot at the ring.[6]

F. R., caught his death upon the water, April the 31st.

W. W., killed by an unknown hand, that was playing, with the glove off, upon the side of the front box in Drury Lane.

Sir Christopher Crazy, Bar.,[7] hurt by the brush of a whalebone petticoat.

Sylvius, shot through the sticks of a fan at St. James's Church.

Damon, struck through the heart by a diamond necklace.

Thomas Trusty, Francis Goosequill, William Meanwell, Edward Callow, Esqrs., standing in a row, fell all four at the same time by an ogle of the Widow Trapland.

Tom Rattle, chancing to tread upon a lady's tail[8] as he came out of the playhouse, she turned full upon him, and laid him dead upon the spot.

Dick Tastewell, slain by a blush from the Queen's box in the third act of the *Trip to the Jubilee*.[9]

Samuel Felt, Haberdasher, wounded in his walk to Islington by Mrs. Susannah Cross-stitch, as she was clamb'ring over a stile.

R. F., T. W., S. I., M. P., &c., put to death in the last Birthday[10] massacre.

Roger Blinko, cut off in the twenty-first year of his age by a whitewash.

Musidorus, slain by an arrow that flew out of a dimple in Belinda's left cheek.

Ned Courtly, presenting Flavia with her glove (which she had dropped on purpose), she received it, and took away his life with a curtsy.

John Gosselin, having received a slight hurt[11] from a pair of blue eyes, as he was making his escape was dispatched by a smile.

---

[3] The second of Cowley's *Anacreontics* is given on p. 526, above. The absurd conceit appears in the third.
[4] They were issued weekly in London, and listed the deaths from various causes.

[5] Neckerchief.
[6] A fashionable promenade and riding circle in Hyde Park.
[7] Baronet.　　　　　　[8] Train.
[9] George Farquhar's *The Constant Couple, or A Trip to the Jubilee*.
[10] Celebration of the Queen's birthday.　　[11] Wound.

Strephon, killed by Clarinda as she looked down into the pit.[12]

Charles Careless, shot flying by a girl of fifteen, who unexpectedly popped her head upon him out of a coach.

Josiah Wither, aged threescore and three, sent to his long home by Elizabeth Jettwell, spinster.

Jack Freelove, murdered by Melissa in her hair.

William Wiseaker, Gent., drowned in a flood of tears by Moll Common.

John Pleadwell, Esq., of the Middle Temple, barrister-at-law, assassinated in his chambers the sixth instant by Kitty Sly, who pretended to come to him for his advice.

ADDISON: ON THE PLEASURES OF THE IMAGINATION

THE SPECTATOR, NO. 411   *Saturday*, JUNE 21, 1712

Avia Pieridum peragro loca, nullius ante
Trita solo; juvat integros accedere fonteis,
Atque haurire.[1]

LUCRETIUS, I, 925–7

OUR sight is the most perfect and most delightful of all our senses. It fills the mind with the largest variety of ideas, converses with its objects at the greatest distance, and continues the longest in action without being tired or satiated with its proper enjoyments. The sense of feeling can indeed give us a notion of extension, shape, and all other ideas that enter at the eye, except colors; but at the same time it is very much straitened and confined in its operations to the number, bulk, and distance of its particular objects. Our sight seems designed to supply all these defects, and may be considered as a more delicate and diffusive kind of touch, that spreads itself over an infinite multitude of bodies, comprehends the largest figures, and brings into our reach some of the most remote parts of the universe.

It is this sense which furnishes the imagination with its ideas; so that by the pleasures of the imagination or fancy (which I shall use promiscuously) I here mean such as arise from visible objects, either when we have them actually in our view or when we call up their ideas into our minds by paintings, statues, descriptions, or any the like occasion. We cannot indeed have a single image in the fancy that did not make its first entrance through the sight; but we have the power of retaining, altering, and compounding those images which we have once received, into all the varieties of picture and vision that are most agreeable to the imagination; for by this faculty a man in a dungeon is capable of entertaining himself with scenes and landskips more beautiful than any that can be found in the whole compass of nature.

There are few words in the English language which are employed in a more loose and uncircumscribed sense than those of the fancy and the imagination. I therefore thought it necessary to fix and determine the notion of these two words, as I intend to make use of them in the thread of my following speculations, that the reader may conceive rightly what is the subject which I proceed upon. I must therefore desire him to remember that by the pleasures of the imagination I mean only such pleasures as arise originally from sight, and that I divide these pleasures into two kinds: my design being first of all to discourse of those primary pleasures of the imagination, which entirely proceed from such objects as are before our eyes; and in the next place to speak of those secondary pleasures of the imagination which flow from the ideas of visible objects, when the objects are not actually before the eye but are called up into our memories, or formed into agreeable visions of things that are either absent or fictitious.

The pleasures of the imagination, taken in the full extent, are not so gross as those of sense, nor so refined as those of the understanding. The last are, indeed, more preferable, because they are founded on some new knowledge or improvement in the mind of man; yet it must be confessed that those of the imagination are as great and as transporting as the other. A beautiful prospect delights the soul, as much as a demonstration; and a description in Homer has charmed more readers than a chapter in Aristotle. Besides, the pleasures of the imagination have this advantage, above those of the understanding: that they are more obvious, and more easy to be acquired. It is but opening the eye, and the scene enters. The colors paint themselves on the fancy, with very little attention of thought or application of mind in the beholder. We are struck, we know not how, with the symmetry of anything we see, and immediately assent to the beauty of an object,

---

[12] From a box, at the theater.

[1] I wander afield, thriving in sturdy thought,
Through unpathed haunts of the Pierides [or Muses],
Trodden of step by none before. I joy
To come on undefilèd fountains there,
To drain them deep. (W. E. Leonard's translation.)

without inquiring into the particular causes and occasions of it.

A man of a polite[2] imagination is let into a great many pleasures that the vulgar are not capable of receiving. He can converse with a picture, and find an agreeable companion in a statue. He meets with a secret refreshment in a description, and often feels a greater satisfaction in the prospect of fields and meadows than another does in the possession. It gives him, indeed, a kind of property in everything he sees, and makes the most rude, uncultivated parts of nature administer to his pleasures; so that he looks upon the world, as it were, in another light, and discovers in it a multitude of charms that conceal themselves from the generality of mankind.

There are, indeed, but very few who know how to be idle and innocent, or have a relish of any pleasures that are not criminal; every diversion they take is at the expense of some one virtue or another, and their very first step out of business is into vice or folly. A man should endeavor, therefore, to make the sphere of his innocent pleasures as wide as possible, that he may retire into them with safety, and find in them such a satisfaction as a wise man would not blush to take. Of this nature are those of the imagination, which do not require such a bent of thought as is necessary to our more serious employments, nor, at the same time, suffer the mind to sink into that negligence and remissness which are apt to accompany our more sensual delights, but, like a gentle exercise to the faculties, awaken them from sloth and idleness, without putting them upon any labor or difficulty.

We might here add that the pleasures of the fancy are more conducive to health than those of the understanding, which are worked out by dint of thinking and attended with too violent a labor of the brain. Delightful scenes, whether in nature, painting, or poetry, have a kindly influence on the body, as well as the mind, and not only serve to clear and brighten the imagination, but are able to disperse grief and melancholy, and to set the animal spirits in pleasing and agreeable motions. For this reason Sir Francis Bacon, in his essay upon health, has not thought it improper to prescribe to his reader a poem or a prospect, where[3] he particularly dissuades him from knotty and subtile disquisitions, and advises him to pursue studies that fill the mind with splendid and illustrious objects, as histories, fables, and contemplations of nature.

I have in this paper, by way of introduction, settled the notion of those pleasures of the imagination which are the subject of my present undertaking, and endeavored by several considerations to recommend to my reader the pursuit of those pleasures. I shall, in my next paper, examine the several sources from whence these pleasures are derived.

Addison: ON THE PLEASURES OF THE IMAGINATION

THE SPECTATOR, NO. 412 *Monday,* JUNE 23, 1712

. . . Divisum sic breve fiet opus.[1]
MARTIAL, *Epigrams,* IV, 83

I SHALL first consider those pleasures of the imagination which arise from the actual view and survey of outward objects. And these, I think, all proceed from the sight of what is great, uncommon, or beautiful. There may, indeed, be something so terrible or offensive that the horror or loathsomeness of an object may overbear the pleasure which results from its greatness, novelty, or beauty; but still there will be such a mixture of delight in the very disgust it gives us, as any of these three qualifications are most conspicuous and prevailing.

By greatness, I do not only mean the bulk of any single object, but the largeness of a whole view, considered as one entire piece. Such are the prospects of an open champian[2] country, a vast uncultivated desert, of huge heaps of mountains, high rocks and precipices, or a wide expanse of waters, where we are not struck with the novelty or beauty of the sight, but with that rude kind of magnificence which appears in many of these stupendous works of nature. Our imagination loves to be filled with an object, or to grasp at anything that is too big for its capacity. We are flung into a pleasing astonishment at such unbounded views, and feel a delightful stillness and amazement in the soul at the apprehension of them. The mind of man naturally hates everything that looks like a restraint upon it, and is apt to fancy itself under a sort of confinement when the sight is pent up in a narrow compass and shortened on every side by the neighborhood of walls or mountains. On the contrary, a spacious horizon is an image of liberty, where the eye has room to range abroad, to expatiate[3] at large on the immensity of its

---

2 Cultivated, refined.   3 Whereas.

1 Divided thus, the work will be made brief.
2 Champaign; flat and open.   3 Range freely.

views, and to lose itself amidst the variety of objects that offer themselves to its observation. Such wide and undetermined prospects are as pleasing to the fancy as the speculations of eternity or infinitude are to the understanding. But if there be a beauty or uncommonness joined with this grandeur, as in a troubled ocean, a heaven adorned with stars and meteors, or a spacious landscape cut out into rivers, woods, rocks, and meadows, the pleasure still grows upon us, as it arises from more than a single principle.

Everything that is new or uncommon raises a pleasure in the imagination, because it fills the soul with an agreeable surprise, gratifies its curiosity, and gives it an idea of which it was not before possessed. We are, indeed, so often conversant with one set of objects, and tired out with so many repeated shows of the same things, that whatever is new or uncommon contributes a little to vary human life and to divert our minds, for a while, with the strangeness of its appearance: it serves us for a kind of refreshment, and takes off from that satiety we are apt to complain of in our usual and ordinary entertainments. It is this that bestows charms on a monster, and makes even the imperfections of nature please us. It is this that recommends variety, where the mind is every instant called off to something new, and the attention not suffered to dwell too long, and waste itself on any particular object. It is this, likewise, that improves what is great or beautiful, and makes it afford the mind a double entertainment. Groves, fields, and meadows are at any season of the year pleasant to look upon, but never so much as in the opening of the spring, when they are all new and fresh with their first gloss upon them, and not yet too much accustomed and familiar to the eye. For this reason there is nothing that more enlivens a prospect than rivers, jetteaus,[4] or falls of water, where the scene is perpetually shifting and entertaining the sight every moment with something that is new. We are quickly tired with looking upon hills and valleys, where everything continues fixed and settled in the same place and posture, but find our thoughts a little agitated and relieved at the sight of such objects as are ever in motion, and sliding away from beneath the eye of the beholder.

But there is nothing that makes its way more directly to the soul than beauty, which immediately diffuses a secret satisfaction and complacency through the imagination, and gives a finishing to anything that is great or uncommon. The very first discovery of it strikes the mind with an inward joy, and spreads a cheerfulness and delight through all its faculties. There is not, perhaps, any real beauty or deformity more in one piece of matter than another, because we might have been so made that whatsoever now appears loathsome to us might have shown itself agreeable; but we find by experience that there are several modifications of matter which the mind, without any previous consideration, pronounces at first sight beautiful or deformed. Thus we see that every different species of sensible creatures has its different notions of beauty, and that each of them is most affected with the beauties of its own kind. This is nowhere more remarkable than in birds of the same shape and proportion, where we often see the male determined in his courtship by the single grain[5] or tincture of a feather, and never discovering any charms but in the color of its species. . . .[6]

There is a second kind of beauty that we find in the several products of art and nature which does not work in the imagination with that warmth and violence as the beauty that appears in our proper species, but is apt, however, to raise in us a secret delight and a kind of fondness for the places or objects in which we discover it. This consists either in the gaiety or variety of colors, in the symmetry and proportion of parts, in the arrangement and disposition of bodies, or in a just mixture and concurrence of all together. Among these several kinds of beauty the eye takes most delight in colors. We nowhere meet with a more glorious or pleasing show in nature than what appears in the heavens at the rising and setting of the sun, which is wholly made up of those different stains of light that show themselves in clouds of a different situation. For this reason we find the poets, who are always addressing themselves to the imagination, borrowing more of their epithets from colors than from any other topic.

As the fancy delights in everything that is great, strange, or beautiful, and is still more pleased the more it finds of these perfections in the same object, so it is capable of receiving a new satisfaction by the assistance of another sense. Thus any continued sound, as the music of birds, or a fall of water, awakens every moment the mind of the beholder, and makes him more attentive to the several beauties of the place that lie before him. Thus if there arises a fragrancy of smells or perfumes, they heighten the

---

[4] Jets, fountains.

[5] Hue.
[6] Here are omitted some Latin verses probably of Addison's own composition.

pleasures of the imagination, and make even the colors and verdure of the landscape appear more agreeable; for the ideas of both senses recommend each other, and are pleasanter together than when they enter the mind separately; as the different colors of a picture, when they are well disposed, set off one another, and receive an additional beauty from the advantage of their situation.

ADDISON: ON GARDENS

THE SPECTATOR, NO. 414 *Wednesday*, JUNE 25, 1712

> . . . *Alterius sic*
> *Altera poscit opem res, et conjurat amice.*[1]
> HORACE, *Ars Poetica,* 410-11

IF WE consider the works of nature and art, as they are qualified to entertain the imagination, we shall find the last very defective in comparison of the former; for though they may sometimes appear as beautiful or strange, they can have nothing in them of the vastness and immensity which afford so great an entertainment to the mind of the beholder. The one may be as polite and delicate as the other, but can never show herself so august and magnificent in the design. There is something more bold and masterly in the rough, careless strokes of nature than in the nice touches and embellishments of art. The beauties of the most stately garden or palace lie in a narrow compass, the imagination immediately runs them over and requires something else to gratify her; but in the wide fields of nature the sight wanders up and down without confinement, and is fed with an infinite variety of images, without any certain stint or number. For this reason we always find the poet in love with a country life, where nature appears in the greatest perfection and furnishes out all those scenes that are most apt to delight the imagination.

> Scriptorum chorus omnis amat nemus et fugit urbes.
> HORACE, *Epodes,* II, ii, 77.[2]

> Hic secura quies, et nescia fallere vita,
> Dives opum variarum; hic latis otia fundis,
> Speluncae, vivique lacus, hic frigida Tempe,
> Mugitusque boum, mollesque sub arbore somni.
> VERGIL, *Georgics,* II, 476-9.[3]

But though there are several of these wild scenes that are more delightful than any artificial shows, yet we find the works of nature still more pleasant the more they resemble those of art. For in this case our pleasure rises from a double principle—from the agreeableness of the objects to the eye, and from their similitude to other objects; we are pleased as well with comparing their beauties as with surveying them, and can represent them to our minds either as copies or originals. Hence it is that we take delight in a prospect which is well laid out and diversified with fields and meadows, woods and rivers; in those accidental landscapes of trees, clouds, and cities that are sometimes found in the veins of marble; in the curious fretwork of rocks and grottoes; and, in a word, in anything that hath such a variety or regularity as may seem the effect of design, in what we call the works of chance.

If the products of nature rise in value according as they more or less resemble those of art, we may be sure that artificial works receive a greater advantage from their resemblance of such as are natural; because here the similitude is not only pleasant, but the pattern more perfect. The prettiest landscape I ever saw was one drawn on the walls of a dark room,[4] which stood opposite on one side to a navigable river and on the other to a park. The experiment is very common in optics. Here you might discover the waves and fluctuations of the water in strong and proper colors, with the picture of a ship entering at one end and failing by degrees through the whole piece. On another there appeared the green shadows of trees waving to and fro with the wind, and herds of deer among them in miniature, leaping about upon the wall. I must confess, the novelty of such a sight may be one occasion of its pleasantness to the imagination; but certainly the chief reason is its near resemblance to nature, as it does not only, like other pictures, give the color and figure, but the motion of the things it represents.

___
[1] So doth the one the other's help require,
  And friendly should unto their end conspire.
        (Ben Jonson's translation.)
[2] The whole chorus of poets loves a grove and flees the city.
[3] But calm security and a life that will not cheat you,
  Rich in its own rewards are here; the broad ease of
    the farmlands,
  Caves, living lakes, and combes that are cool even
    at midsummer,
  Mooing of herds, and slumbers mild in the trees' shade.
        (C. Day Lewis's translation.)
[4] The Camera Obscura at Greenwich.

We have before observed that there is generally in nature something more grand and august than what we meet with in the curiosities of art. When, therefore, we see this imitated in any measure, it gives us a nobler and more exalted kind of pleasure than what we receive from the nicer and more accurate productions of art. On this account our English gardens are not so entertaining to the fancy as those in France and Italy, where we see a large extent of ground covered over with an agreeable mixture of garden and forest, which represent everywhere an artificial rudeness, much more charming than that neatness and elegancy which we meet with in those of our own country. It might, indeed, be of ill consequence to the public, as well as unprofitable to private persons, to alienate so much ground from pasturage and the plow in many parts of a country that is so well peopled, and cultivated to a far greater advantage. But why may not a whole estate be thrown into a kind of garden by frequent plantations, that may turn as much to the profit as the pleasure of the owner? A marsh overgrown with willows, or a mountain shaded with oaks, are not only more beautiful but more beneficial than when they lie bare and unadorned. Fields of corn make a pleasant prospect, and if the walks were a little taken care of that lie between them, if the natural embroidery of the meadows were helped and improved by some small additions of art, and the several rows of hedges set off by trees and flowers that the soil was capable of receiving, a man might make a pretty landscape of his own possessions.

Writers who have given us an account of China tell us, the inhabitants of that country laugh at the plantations of our Europeans, which are laid by the rule and line; because, they say, anyone may place trees in equal rows and uniform figures. They choose rather to show a genius in works of this nature, and therefore always conceal the art by which they direct themselves. They have a word, it seems, in their language by which they express the particular beauty of a plantation that thus strikes the imagination at first sight without discovering what it is that has so agreeable an effect. Our British gardeners, on the contrary, instead of humoring nature, love to deviate from it as much as possible. Our trees rise in cones, globes, and pyramids. We see the marks of the scissors upon every plant and bush. I do not know whether I am singular in my opinion, but for my own part I would rather look upon a tree in all its luxuriancy and diffusion of boughs and branches than when it is thus cut and trimmed into a mathematical figure; and cannot but fancy that an orchard

in flower looks infinitely more delightful than all the little labyrinths of the most finished parterre. But as our great modelers of gardens have their magazines of plants to dispose of, it is very natural for them to tear up all the beautiful plantations of fruit trees and contrive a plan that may most turn to their own profit, in taking off their evergreens and the like movable plants with which their shops are plentifully stocked.

ADDISON: ON THE MEANS OF FAITH

THE SPECTATOR, NO. 465 *Saturday*, AUG. 23, 1712

Qua ratione queas traducere leniter aevum;
Ne te semper inops agitet vexetque cupido,
Ne pavor et rerum mediocriter utilium spes.[1]
HORACE, *Epistles,* I, xviii, 97-9

HAVING endeavored in my last Saturday's paper to show the great excellency of faith, I shall here consider what are proper means of strengthening and confirming it in the mind of man. . . .

The last method which I shall mention for the giving life to a man's faith is frequent retirement from the world, accompanied with religious meditation. When a man thinks of anything in the darkness of the night, whatever deep impressions it may make in his mind, they are apt to vanish as soon as the day breaks about him. The light and noise of the day, which are perpetually soliciting his senses and calling off his attention, wear out of his mind the thoughts that imprinted themselves in it with so much strength during the silence and darkness of the night. A man finds the same difference as to himself in a crowd and in a solitude; the mind is stunned and dazzled amidst that variety of objects which press upon her in a great city. She cannot apply herself to the consideration of those things which are of the utmost concern to her. The cares or pleasures of the world strike in with every thought, and a multitude of vicious examples give a kind of justification to our folly. In our retirements, everything disposes us to be serious. In courts and cities we are entertained with the works of men, in the country with those of God. One is the province of art, the other of nature. Faith and devotion naturally grow in the mind of every reasonable man who sees

[1] What things in life go happily and well;
How cure desire, the soul's perpetual dearth,
How moderate care for things of trifling worth?
(Conington's translation.)
Only a part of this essay is given here.

the impressions of divine power and wisdom in every object on which he casts his eye. The Supreme Being has made the best arguments for his own existence, in the formation of the heavens and the earth; and these are arguments which a man of sense cannot forbear attending to, who is out of the noise and hurry of human affairs. . . .[2]

I

The spacious firmament on high,
With all the blue ethereal sky,
And spangled heav'ns, a shining frame,
Their great Original proclaim;
Th' unwearied sun, from day to day,
Does his Creator's power display,
And publishes to every land
The work of an almighty hand.

II

Soon as the evening shades prevail,
The moon takes up the wondrous tale,
And nightly to the list'ning earth
Repeats the story of her birth;
Whilst all the stars that round her burn,
And all the planets in their turn,
Confirm the tidings as they roll,
And spread the truth from pole to pole.

III

What though in solemn silence all
Move round the dark terrestrial ball?
What though nor real voice nor sound
Amid their radiant orbs be found?
In reason's ear, they all rejoice
And utter forth a glorious voice,
For ever singing, as they shine,
"The hand that made us is divine."

ADDISON: ON NATURAL RELIGION

THE SPECTATOR, NO. 543 *Saturday*, NOV. 22, 1712

. . . facies non omnibus una
Nec diversa tamen.[1]
                    OVID, *Metamorphoses*, II, 13

THOSE who were skillful in anatomy among the ancients concluded from the outward and inward

---

[2] This is the "argument from design": the perfect mechanism of the heavens and the earth proves the existence of God. In the next essay (No. 543) the same argument is based upon the design of animal bodies.—In an omitted passage Addison refers to Psalm 19, "The heavens declare the glory of God." Haydn's setting of the following ode is in many hymnals.

[1] People all look different and yet alike.

make of an human body that it was the work of a Being transcendently wise and powerful. As the world grew more enlightened in this art, their discoveries gave them fresh opportunities of admiring the conduct of Providence in the formation of an human body. Galen[2] was converted by his dissections, and could not but own a Supreme Being upon a survey of this his handiwork. There were, indeed, many parts of which the old anatomists did not know the certain use, but as they saw that most of those which they examined were adapted with admirable art to their several functions, they did not question but those whose uses they could not determine were contrived with the same wisdom for respective ends and purposes. Since the circulation of the blood has been found out and many other great discoveries have been made by our modern anatomists, we see new wonders in the human frame and discern several important uses for those parts, which uses the ancients knew nothing of. In short, the body of man is such a subject as stands the utmost test of examination. Though it appears formed with the nicest wisdom upon the most superficial survey of it, it still mends upon the search, and produces our surprise and amazement in proportion as we pry into it. What I have here said of an human body may be applied to the body of every animal which has been the subject of anatomical observations.

The body of an animal is an object adequate to our senses. It is a particular system of Providence, that lies in a narrow compass. The eye is able to command it, and by successive inquiries can search into all its parts. Could the body of the whole earth, or indeed the whole universe, be thus submitted to the examination of our senses, were it not too big and disproportioned for our inquiries, too unwieldy for the management of the eye and hand, there is no question but it would appear to us as curious and well-contrived a frame as that of an human body. We should see the same concatenation and subserviency, the same necessity and usefulness, the same beauty and harmony, in all and every of its parts as what we discover in the body of every single animal.

The more extended our reason is, and the more able to grapple with immense objects, the greater still are those discoveries which it makes of wisdom and providence in the work of the creation. A Sir Isaac Newton, who stands up as the miracle of the present age, can look through a whole planetary system, consider it in its weight, number, and measure, and draw from it as many demonstrations

---

[2] The great classical authority on medicine (second century A.D.).

of infinite power and wisdom as a more confined understanding is able to deduce from the system of an human body.

But to return to our speculations on anatomy, I shall here consider the fabric and texture of the bodies of animals in one particular view, which, in my opinion, shows the hand of a thinking and all-wise Being in their formation, with the evidence of a thousand demonstrations. I think we may lay this down as an incontested principle, that chance never acts in a perpetual uniformity and consistence with itself. If one should always fling the same number with ten thousand dice, or see every throw just five times less, or five times more, in number than the throw which immediately preceded it, who would not imagine there is some invisible power which directs the cast? This is the proceeding which we find in the operations of nature. Every kind of animal is diversified by different magnitudes, each of which gives rise to a different species. Let a man trace the dog or lion kind, and he will observe how many of the works of nature are published, if I may use the expression, in a variety of editions. If we look into the reptile world, or into those different kind of animals that fill the element of water, we meet with the same repetitions among several species, that differ very little from one another but in size and bulk. You find the same creature that is drawn at large, copied out in several proportions, and ending in miniature. It would be tedious to produce instances of this regular conduct in Providence, as it would be superfluous to those who are versed in the natural history of animals. The magnificent harmony of the universe is such that we may observe innumerable divisions running upon the same ground. I might also extend this speculation to the dead parts of nature, in which we may find matter disposed into many similar systems, as well in our survey of stars and planets as of stones, vegetables, and other sublunary[3] parts of the creation. In a word, Providence has shown the richness of its goodness and wisdom not only in the production of many original species but in the multiplicity of descants[4] which it has made on every original species in particular.

But to pursue this thought still farther. Every living creature, considered in itself, has many very complicated parts that are exact copies of some other parts which it possesses and which are complicated in the same manner. One eye would have been sufficient for the subsistence and preservation of an animal; but, in order to better his condition, we see another placed with a mathematical exactness in the same most advantageous situation, and in every particular of the same size and texture. Is it possible for chance to be thus delicate and uniform in her operations? Should a million of dice turn up twice together the same number, the wonder would be nothing in comparison with this. But when we see this similitude and resemblance in the arm, the hand, and fingers; when we see one half of the body entirely correspond with the other in all those minute strokes without which a man might have very well subsisted; nay, when we often see a single part repeated an hundred times in the same body, notwithstanding it consists of the most intricate weaving of numberless fibers, and these parts differing still in magnitude as the convenience of their particular situation requires, sure a man must have a strange cast of understanding who does not discover the finger of God in so wonderful a work. These duplicates in those parts of the body, without which a man might have very well subsisted, though not so well as with them, are a plain demonstration of an all-wise Contriver; as those more numerous copyings which are found among the vessels of the same body are evident demonstrations that they could not be the work of chance. This argument receives additional strength if we apply it to every animal and insect within our knowledge, as well as to those numberless living creatures that are objects too minute for an human eye, and if we consider how the several species in this whole world of life resemble one another in very many particulars, so far as is convenient for their respective states of existence. It is much more probable that an hundred million of dice should be casually thrown an hundred million of times in the same number than that the body of any single animal should be produced by the fortuitous concourse of matter. And that the like chance should arise in innumerable instances, requires a degree of credulity that is not under the direction of common sense. We may carry this consideration yet further if we reflect on the two sexes in every living species, with their resemblances to each other and those particular distinctions that were necessary for the keeping up of this great world of life.

There are many more demonstrations of a Supreme Being and of his transcendent wisdom, power, and goodness in the formation of the body of a living creature, for which I refer my reader to other writings, particularly to the sixth book of the poem entitled *Creation*,[5] where the anatomy of the human

---

[3] Pertaining to this world, earthly.   [4] Variations.

[5] A poem by Sir Richard Blackmore, published in 1712.

body is described with great perspicuity and elegance. I have been particular on the thought which runs through this speculation because I have not seen it enlarged upon by others.

STEELE: ON STORY TELLING

THE GUARDIAN, NO. 42 *Wednesday*, APRIL 29, 1713

Non missura cutem, nisi plena cruoris hirudo.[1]
HORACE, *Ars Poetica*, last verse

TOM LIZARD[2] told us a story the other day of some persons which our family know very well, with so much humor and life that it caused a great deal of mirth at the tea table. His brother Will, the templar,[3] was highly delighted with it, and the next day, being with some of his inns-of-court acquaintance, resolved (whether out of the benevolence or the pride of his heart I will not determine) to entertain them with what he called "a pleasant humor enough." I was in great pain for him when I heard him begin, and was not at all surprised to find the company very little moved by it. Will blushed, looked round the room, and with a forced laugh, "Faith, gentlemen," said he, "I do not know what makes you look so grave; it was an admirable story when I heard it."

When I came home I fell into a profound contemplation upon story telling; and as I have nothing so much at heart as the good of my country, I resolved to lay down some precautions upon this subject.

I have often thought that a story teller is born, as well as a poet. It is, I think, certain that some men have such a peculiar cast of mind that they see things in another light than men of grave dispositions. Men of a lively imagination and a mirthful temper will represent things to their hearers in the same manner as they themselves were affected with them; and whereas serious spirits might perhaps have been disgusted at the sight of some odd occurrences in life, yet the very same occurrences shall please them in a well-told story, where the disagreeable parts of the images are concealed, and those only which are pleasing exhibited to the fancy. Story telling is therefore not an art, but what we call a *knack;* it doth not so much subsist upon wit as upon humor; and I will add that it is not perfect without proper gesticula-

---

[1] As leeches stick till they have sucked their fills.
(Conington's translation.)

[2] Introduced in no. 13 as an agreeable young society man.

[3] Law student. Will has already been introduced in no. 13 as more serious and socially less at ease than Tom.

tions of the body, which naturally attend such merry emotions of the mind. I know very well that a certain gravity of countenance sets some stories off to advantage, where the hearer is to be surprised in the end; but this is by no means a general rule, for it is frequently convenient to aid and assist by cheerful looks and whimsical agitations. I will go yet further and affirm that the success of a story very often depends upon the make of the body and formation of the features of him who relates it. I have been of this opinion ever since I criticized upon the chin of Dick Dewlap. I very often had the weakness to repine at the prosperity of his conceits, which made him pass for a wit with the widow at the coffee house, and the ordinary mechanics that frequent it; nor could I myself forbear laughing at them most heartily, though upon examination I thought most of them very flat and insipid. I found after some time that the merit of his wit was founded upon the shaking of a fat paunch and the tossing up of a pair of rosy jowls. Poor Dick had a fit of sickness, which robbed him of his fat and his fame at once; and it was full three months before he regained his reputation, which rose in proportion to his floridity. He is now very jolly and ingenious, and hath a good constitution for wit.

Those who are thus adorned with the gifts of nature are apt to shew their parts with too much ostentation. I would therefore advise all the professors of this art never to tell stories but as they seem to grow out of the subject matter of the conversation, or as they serve to illustrate or enliven it. Stories that are very common are generally irksome, but may be aptly introduced provided they be only hinted at and mentioned by way of allusion. Those that are altogether new should never be ushered in without a short and pertinent character of the chief persons concerned, because by that means you make the company acquainted with them; and it is a certain rule that slight and trivial accounts of those who are familiar to us administer more mirth than the brightest points of wit in unknown characters. A little circumstance in the complexion or dress of the man you are talking of sets his image before the hearer, if it be chosen aptly for the story. Thus I remember Tom Lizard, after having made his sisters merry with an account of a formal old man's way of complimenting, owned very frankly that his story would not have been worth one farthing if he had made the hat of him whom he represented one inch narrower. Besides the marking distinct characters and selecting pertinent circumstances, it is likewise necessary to leave off in time and end smartly. So that there is a kind of drama in the forming of a story, and the manner of conducting and pointing it is the same as in an epigram. It is a miserable thing, after one hath raised the expectation of the company by humorous characters and a pretty conceit, to pursue the matter too far. There is no retreating; and how poor is it for a story teller to end his relation by saying, "That's all!"

As the choosing of pertinent circumstances is the life of a story and that wherein humor principally consists, so the collectors of impertinent particulars are the very bane and opiates of conversation. Old men are great transgressors this way. Poor Ned Poppy—he's gone—was a very honest man, but was so excessively tedious over his pipe that he was not to be endured. He knew so exactly what they had for dinner, when such a thing happened, in what ditch his bay stone-horse[4] had his sprain at that time, and how his man John,—no! it was William—started a hare in the common field, that he never got to the end of his tale. Then he was extremely particular in marriages and intermarriages, and cousins twice or thrice removed, and whether such a thing happened at the latter end of July or the beginning of August. He had a marvelous tendency likewise to digressions, insomuch that if a considerable person was mentioned in his story he would straightway launch out into an episode on him; and again, if in that person's story he had occasion to remember a third man, he broke off and gave us his history, and so on. He always put me in mind of what Sir William Temple[5] informs us of the tale tellers in the north of Ireland, who are hired to tell stories of giants and enchanters to lull people asleep. These historians are obliged, by their bargain, to go on without stopping; so that after the patient hath by this benefit enjoyed a long nap, he is sure to find the operator proceeding in his work. Ned procured the like effect in me, the last time I was with him. As he was in the third hour of his story, and very thankful that his memory did not fail him, I fairly nodded in the elbow chair. He was much affronted at this, till I told him, "Old friend, you have your infirmity, and I have mine."

But of all evils in story telling, the humor of telling tales one after another, in great numbers, is the least supportable. Sir Harry Pandolf and his son gave my Lady Lizard great offence in this particular. Sir Harry hath what they call a string of stories, which he tells over every Christmas. When our family visits there, we are constantly, after supper, entertained with the Glastonbury thorn.[6] When we have wondered at that a little, "Ay, but, Father," saith the son, "let us have the spirit in the wood." After that hath been laughed at, "Ay, but, Father," cries the booby again, "tell us how you served the robber." "Alack-a-day," saith Sir Harry with a smile and rubbing his forehead, "I have almost forgot that; but 't is a pleasant conceit, to be sure." Accordingly he tells that and twenty more in the same independent order and without the least variation at this day, as he hath done, to my knowledge ever since the revolution.[7] I must not forget a very odd compliment that Sir Harry always makes my Lady when he dines here. After dinner he strokes his belly and says, with a feigned concern in his countenance, "Madam, I have lost by you today." "How so, Sir Harry?" replies my Lady. "Madam," says he, "I have lost an excellent stomach."[8] At this, his son and heir laughs immoderately, and winks upon Mrs. Arabella. This is the thirty-third time that Sir Harry hath been thus arch, and I can bear it no longer.

As the telling of stories is a great help and life to conversation, I always encourage them, if they are pertinent and innocent; in opposition to those gloomy mortals who disdain everything but matter of fact. Those grave fellows are my aversion, who sift everything with the utmost nicety, and find the malignity of a lie in a piece of humor pushed a little beyond the exact truth. I likewise have a poor opinion of those who have got a trick of keeping a steady countenance, that cock their hats and look glum when a pleasant thing is said, and ask, "Well! and what then?" Men of wit and parts should treat one another with benevolence; and I will lay it down as a maxim that if you seem to have a good opinion of another man's wit he will allow you to have judgment.

---

[4] Stallion.
[5] The Whig statesman and writer (1628–99), in his essay "Of Poetry."

[6] According to legend, Joseph of Arimathea stuck his staff of thorn in the ground at Glastonbury, the ancient abbey town in Somersetshire, his and King Arthur's reputed burial place; the thorn was said to bloom every Christmas Day.
[7] Of 1688.   [8] Appetite.

Jonathan Swift

1667-1745

SWIFT is one of the great masters of English prose. He is also the foremost English writer of satire. He had no wish to be anything in letters but a satirist and a reformer; writing to Pope he confesses as much: "The chief end I propose to myself in all my labors is to vex the world rather than divert it." There is much in his writings, both prose and verse, which no one not in love with dirt can really enjoy; and of the rest a good deal would be unpalatably bitter if it were not that the precision with which the jaws of his traps snap shut on their victims compels a kind of awed admiration. Swift was a charming social companion but not a happy man, and his pages are not buoyant reading. What any man gets out of life is his own business; yet the conclusion can hardly be avoided that Swift, who was for a few years in the thick of great events and the close friend of some of the most eminent and interesting men of his time, missed a good many of the best things in life.

He was born in Ireland (much to his chagrin later on), though of English parentage. To a career mainly in Ireland he seemed doomed by a fate he considered malignant. He resented his destiny and never ceased struggling against it. He was a posthumous child, dependent on his uncles' generosity. Like Congreve and at the same time, he was educated at a celebrated school in Kilkenny and at the famous Protestant college of Trinity, Dublin. At Trinity he remained for three years after taking his B.A. When he fled, early in 1689, from "the troubles" which followed the Revolution, he had nearly completed his work for the M.A.; through influence and without much if any further study, he obtained it at Oxford some years later. Soon after his arrival in England, he was engaged as secretary by the distinguished Whig statesman and writer Sir William Temple (1628-99), himself an excellent modern stylist. Temple's father had been a friend of the Swifts in Ireland. Retired from politics, Sir William lived at his country seat of Moor Park, near Farnham in Surrey. In that household was a little girl of eight, Hester Johnson, the "Stella" of Swift's later life. She was the housekeeper's daughter; Swift was her tutor. Their friendship was to last for nearly forty years. In time it ripened into something like love, but it is still a puzzle to biographers.

Swift lived mostly at Moor Park till Temple's death in 1699; but during an interlude he became a priest of the Church of England and was given a "living" in Ireland. The last thing in his mind, however, was to base his career on attention to the cares of a parish. He was consumed with ambition, yet handicapped by ill health. For the rest of his life he had trouble with his stomach; and he often suffered from spells of dizziness, deafness, and depression, as well as sharp pain. After the death of Temple, Swift returned to Ireland and various ecclesiastical pursuits there. Visits to England had by 1708 brought him in touch with Addison, Steele, Congreve, and other Whig notables; but for a dozen years the career he frankly sought eluded him. Appointment after appointment went to others, in the face of his direct applications.

Not till Swift was thirty-seven did he attract favorable notice as a writer; his early verse is worthless. Dryden, a distant relative, told him bluntly he would never make a poet. It was the anonymous appearance of *A Tale of a Tub*, practically finished by 1697 but not published till 1704, that showed where his real genius lay, in prose satire. The title means a playful yarn or hoax. This one is an allegorical account of Christianity and its warring sects, typified by three brothers: Peter (the Catholics), Martin (the Anglicans), and Jack (the Dissenters). Sandwiched along in the story are the "digressions," essays on a variety of topics. *A Tale of a Tub* is replete with brilliant and biting satire. "Good God!" Swift exclaimed long afterwards, "what a genius I had when I wrote that book!" Included in the same volume was *A Full and True Account of the Battle Fought Last Friday between the Ancient and the Modern Books in St. James's Library*. With this sprightly essay Swift entered a controversy which Europe had debated since the Renaissance began, the "Quarrel between the Ancients and the Moderns." Temple had recently taken a prominent part, on the side of the superiority of classical literature. Swift adopted the same side; later, when he was a famous author himself, he changed his mind. His main point, however, in *The Battle of the Books* was the futility of literary controversy. Another satirical masterpiece came in 1708: *An Argument to Prove that the Abolishing of Christianity in England May, as Things Now Stand, Be Attended with Some Inconveniences and Perhaps Not Produce Those Many Good Effects Proposed Thereby*. His defense, he says, is not of "real Christianity, such as used . . . to have an influence upon men's belief and actions." Instead, he pours out his irony in a pretended argument for what currently passes as Christianity. The essay is an indictment of the hypocrisy of nominal Christians, and a protest against attempts to substitute Deism for the Christian religion.

Meanwhile, he had written in 1701 the first of a long line of political pamphlets. He began as a Whig; but when the Tories came to power in 1710 Swift accepted the invitation of their leaders, Harley and Bolingbroke, to enlist his pen with them. It was a logical shift; he was an Anglican priest, and it was the Tories who upheld the Established Church. For four exciting years, till the death of Queen Anne collapsed the Tory house of cards, Swift was close to the fountain of power. He lost his old Whig literary friends, but gained Arbuthnot, Prior, Gay, and Pope. He belonged to the exclusive clubs, the Brothers and Scriblerus; and he sat down to the political breakfasts of Bolingbroke, where the Tory strategy was mapped for the ensuing week. These were Swift's happiest years. He held no "place," but his hopes soared. He fought the party's battles in pamphlet after pamphlet and in the *Examiner*, the Tories' journal, which he edited and wrote. He exulted in his prominence, and knew the satisfaction of being run after. To a considerable extent it was his pen that kept the ministry in office; for a brief period he was the most influential man in England. In 1711 his political tract, *The Conduct of the Allies*, was instrumental in molding popular sentiment to accept the ending of the war with France. Soon after the close of that year Marlborough was dismissed from his command and all his offices, and the ground was prepared for the betrayal of England's allies by the Peace of Utrecht (1713). Swift's high spirits are evident in his *Journal to Stella* (the title is not his), a record of his doings periodically dispatched to Hester Johnson in Dublin, where she lived under Swift's protection, without scandal, on a legacy Temple had left her. Swift never got over this experience with great affairs. His life was soured by his party's fall in 1714 and by the failure of Queen Anne to award him an ecclesiastical plum. Along with others who should have known better, she had been scandalized by *A Tale of a Tub*, in which she thought he had ridiculed religion. Swift wanted a bishopric. What he got was the deanery of St. Patrick's, Dublin's Anglican cathedral.

With the Tory chieftains' Jacobite intrigues Swift had nothing to do. He thought the worst Whig ministry preferable to the return of the Pretender. When the crash came, he withdrew to Dublin; and in Ireland, save for occasional English visits, he remained. He was to do his greatest work there. After an interval of six years largely concerned with his duties as dean, he went on the warpath again in 1720. The real rulers of Ireland were Walpole and his Whigs, and they ruled with an eye to England's and their own advantage. In pleading Ireland's cause Swift was therefore striking at his old enemies. But this was not his sole motive. Jaundiced as his writings often are, he had a heart of deep compassion for human suffering. Abominably misgoverned, as we shall see when we come to *A Modest Proposal*, Ireland was in a dreadful state of ruin and starvation. In a series of pamphlets, especially the *Drapier's Letters*, purporting to be the work of a Dublin dry-goods merchant, Swift fought a long and spectacular fight against English exploitation. On the whole it was a losing cam-

paign; but there were victories, such as his successful attack in 1724 on a proposed copper currency ("Wood's halfpence"), which appears to have been an attempt, not as he thought at debasing the Irish coinage, but at joint racketeering by a profiteer and one of George I's mistresses. In this and other battles Swift brought all his resources to bear: his gifts for logic and clear exposition, his armory of savage invective, and above all the genius for irony which appears at its terrible best in *A Modest Proposal* (1729). His services were warmly appreciated in Ireland, where he became a national hero. When he returned from a sojourn in England with Pope, Dublin's bells rang in jubilation, the Corporation rowed out to greet his ship, and there were bonfires in every street.

That did not, however, bring him any measure of content. Swift thought wisdom incompatible with happiness, and he deliberately chose wisdom and reason—as far as he had any choice. For sheer intellectual force he is the superior of all his friends, including Pope. But the cost was profound disillusion and mental anguish. It was from this abyss that he drew his masterpiece. He was working on *Gulliver's Travels* all through the campaign for Irish rights which began in 1720. The book was finished in 1725; early in the following year he took it to London for publication.

From the views which put *Gulliver's Travels* among the most appalling condemnations of human nature, many a man might have been saved by marriage to the right woman. However masculine Swift's mind, he was evidently not strongly masculine in his physical make-up. That he never married Stella is probable but not certain. In any case, the physical bond was absent. Yet theirs was a romance of great tenderness, and Stella's death in 1728 left Swift miserable. Five years earlier Hester Vanhomrigh had died. She was his "Vanessa," to whom long years before he had been a kind of tutor. When she fell in love with him and pursued him to Ireland, he was made a little ridiculous and Stella not a little unhappy.

As the years ground inexorably on, there was in Swift, though his secret charities to individuals were many, less of the old zeal for righting the world's wrongs. Satire became, not a weapon to crusade with, but a defensive mechanism behind which he could withdraw for the comfort that lay in laughing sardonically at the baseness of men. In short, Swift turned the complete misanthrope. The final phase of his genius was verse satire. Two poems in this genre, one given below in full and the other briefly sampled, are among his chefs-d'oeuvre. Toward the end his mind gave way, and for his three remaining years he was in a keeper's charge. He had predicted that he would die like a tree, at the top first. Death came in 1745. He left his estate to charity.

There is no satisfactory edition of Swift's works. T. Scott edited the prose (12 vols., 1897–1908), and this is still the most useful edition. Another, by H. Davis (14 vols.), is in progress; the texts and introductions are good, but there is no annotation. The poems have been edited by H. Williams (3 vols., 1937). The principal prose writings have often been separately reprinted. Swift's letters are fascinating; the standard edition is by F. E. Ball (6 vols., 1910–14). Everyman's Library has three volumes of Swift: the *Journal to Stella, A Tale of a Tub* and *The Battle of the Books,* and *Gulliver's Travels.* The standard Life is by H. Craik (2nd ed., 2 vols., 1894). C. Van Doren's *Swift* is a readable popular biography. The best critical study is R. Quintana's *The Mind and Art of Jonathan Swift* (1936); it includes an adequate biography, as well as interesting material on the eighteenth-century milieu.

Jonathan Swift

from THOUGHTS ON VARIOUS SUBJECTS

THE following aphorisms have been chosen from an early group jotted down during the decade 1696–1706. To it Swift afterwards added others. They are a good introduction to the realistic grasp of his mind, and to the limitations imposed on it by a preoccupation with disillusion.

WE HAVE just religion enough to make us hate, but not enough to make us love, one another.

Reflect on things past, as wars, negotiations, factions, and the like: we enter so little into those interests that we wonder how men could possibly be so busy and concerned for things so transitory. Look on the present times, we find the same humor;[1] yet wonder not at all.

How is it possible to expect that mankind will take *advice,* when they will not so much as take *warning?*

No preacher is listened to but Time, which gives us the same train and turn of thought that elder people have tried in vain to put into our heads before.

The latter part of a wise man's life is taken up in curing the follies, prejudices, and false opinions he had contracted in the former.

When a true genius appears in the world, you may know him by this infallible sign: that the dunces are all in confederacy against him.

One argument to prove that the common relations[2] of ghosts and specters are generally false may be drawn from the opinion held that spirits are never seen by more than one person at a time; that is to say, it seldom happens that above one person in a company is possessed with any high degree of spleen or melancholy.

It is grown a word of course for writers to say "this *critical age,*" as divines say "this *sinful age.*"

In all well-instituted commonwealths, care hath been taken to limit men's possessions; which is done for many reasons, and among the rest for one that perhaps is not often considered: because, when bounds are set to men's desires, after they have acquired as much as the laws will permit them their private interest is at an end, and they have nothing to do but to take care of[3] the public.

There are but three ways for a man to revenge himself of a censorious world: to despise it, to return the like, or to endeavor to live so as to avoid it. The first of these is usually pretended; the last is almost impossible; the universal practice is for the second.

I have known some men possessed of good qualities which were very serviceable to others but useless to themselves; like a sundial on the front of a house, to inform the neighbors and passengers, but not the owner within.

The Stoical[4] scheme of supplying our wants by lopping off our desires is like cutting off our feet when we want shoes.

The reason why so few marriages are happy is because young ladies spend their time in making nets, and not in making cages.

If a man will observe as he walks the streets, I believe he will find the merriest countenances in mourning coaches.

The power of Fortune is confessed only by the miserable, for the happy impute all their success to prudence or merit.

Ambition often puts men upon doing the meanest offices; so climbing is performed in the same posture with creeping.

Ill company is like a dog, who fouls those most whom he loves best.

Censure is the tax a man pays to the public for being eminent.

---

[1] Trait.   [2] Tales.

[3] For.
[4] The Stoics were followers of a Greek philosophical sect which held that a passive attitude toward joy and sorrow is best.

THIS famous book was published in 1726; Swift had been working at it for about five years. It was an immediate success; the first printing sold out in a week. There have been innumerable reprints of it since, and it is one of the oddities of literary history that it should have become, in expurgated form, a children's classic, for it is possibly the most uncompromising indictment of the human race ever penned. Its genre is the imaginary voyage, a vehicle for satire ever since the *True History* of Lucian (d. 200 A. D.); and at first it appears no more than a burlesque of current travel-literature. But soon the pettiness of human beings and affairs is exposed by being exhibited on the reduced scale of one to twelve, and after that the baseness of mankind comes directly under Swift's lash. The reader should not allow himself to be misled by the easy and blandly ironic style.

Captain Gulliver makes four voyages. The first, here reprinted in full, has always been the most popular. Swift had begun it, with different intentions, in England many years before; and since his plans were originally more innocent, Part I is invested with a charm which is lacking in the later voyages. To them the reader must turn if he desires to experience the full blast of Swift's satire. In Part II the Captain is in Brobdingnag, a land of amiable giants, whose monarch, after hearing from Gulliver a detailed account of European civilization, concludes that "the bulk of your natives" must be "the most pernicious race of little odious vermin that nature ever suffered to crawl upon the surface of the earth." The least successful part, the third, is a miscellany. Its best-known satire is on the new experimental science; the researchers of Laputa are engaged in such fantastic enterprises as the extraction of sunbeams from cucumbers. In the light of more recent scientific achievements, Swift's fancies in this part now seem less extravagant. Part IV, a substantial portion of which is reprinted below, contains the sharpest satire of all. The contrast between the loathsome and degraded Yahoos and the noble and enlightened Houyhnhnms is a powerful and terrible picture, not without objective truth, but very far from telling the whole truth. Swift's rationalistic philosophy and his disappointed ambition joined to draw it, and the grief and pain life brought him colored it.

TRAVELS INTO SEVERAL REMOTE NATIONS OF THE WORLD

BY LEMUEL GULLIVER

First a surgeon, and then a captain of several ships

PART I

A VOYAGE TO LILLIPUT

CHAPTER I

The Author giveth some account of himself and family; his first inducements to travel. He is shipwrecked, and swims for his life; gets safe on shore in the country of Lilliput; is made a prisoner, and carried up the country.

MY FATHER had a small estate in Nottinghamshire; I was the third of five sons. He sent me to Emanuel College in Cambridge, at fourteen years old, where I resided three years, and applied myself close to my studies; but the charge of maintaining me (although I had a very scanty allowance) being too great for a narrow fortune, I was bound apprentice to Mr. James Bates, an eminent surgeon in London, with whom I continued four years; and my father now and then sending me small sums of money, I laid 20 them out in learning navigation and other parts of the mathematics useful to those who intend to travel, as I always believed it would be some time or other my fortune to do. When I left Mr. Bates, I went down to my father; where, by the assistance of him 5 and my uncle John and some other relations, I got forty pounds, and a promise of thirty pounds a year to maintain me at Leyden: there I studied physic[1] two years and seven months, knowing it would be useful in long voyages.

10 Soon after my return from Leyden, I was recommended by my good master, Mr. Bates, to be surgeon to the *Swallow,* Captain Abraham Pannell, commander; with whom I continued three years and a half, making a voyage or two into the Levant and 15 some other parts. When I came back I resolved to settle in London, to which Mr. Bates, my master, encouraged me; and by him I was recommended to

---

[1] Medicine. The leading medical school was then at Leyden, in South Holland.

several patients. I took part of a small house in the Old Jewry;[2] and, being advised to alter my condition, I married Mrs.[3] Mary Burton, second daughter to Mr. Edmond Burton, hosier, in Newgate Street,[4] with whom I received four hundred pounds for a portion.

But, my good master Bates dying in two years after, and I having few friends, my business began to fail; for my conscience would not suffer me to imitate the bad practice of too many among my brethren. Having therefore consulted with my wife and some of my acquaintance, I determined to go again to sea. I was surgeon successively in two ships, and made several voyages, for six years, to the East and West Indies, by which I got some addition to my fortune. My hours of leisure I spent in reading the best authors, ancient and modern, being always provided with a good number of books; and when I was ashore, in observing the manners and dispositions of the people, as well as learning their language, wherein I had a great facility by the strength of my memory.

The last of these voyages not proving very fortunate, I grew weary of the sea, and intended to stay at home with my wife and family. I removed from the Old Jewry to Fetter Lane,[5] and from thence to Wapping,[6] hoping to get business among the sailors; but it would not turn to account. After three years' expectation that things would[7] mend, I accepted an advantageous offer from Captain William Prichard, master of the *Antelope,* who was making a voyage to the South Sea.[8] We set sail from Bristol May 4th, 1699, and our voyage at first was very prosperous.

It would not be proper, for some reasons, to trouble the reader with the particulars of our adventures in those seas; let it suffice to inform him that, in our passage from thence to the East Indies, we were driven by a violent storm to the northwest of Van Diemen's Land.[9] By an observation, we found ourselves in the latitude of 30 degrees 2 minutes south. Twelve of our crew were dead by immoderate labor and ill food; the rest were in a very weak condition. On the fifth of November, which was the beginning of summer in those parts, the weather being very hazy, the seamen spied a rock,

within half a cable's length of the ship; but the wind was so strong that we were driven directly upon it, and immediately split. Six of the crew, of whom I was one, having let down the boat into the sea, made a shift to get clear of the ship and the rock. We rowed, by my computation, about three leagues, till we were able to work no longer, being already spent with labor while we were in the ship. We therefore trusted ourselves to the mercy of the waves, and in about half an hour the boat was overset by a sudden flurry from the north. What became of my companions in the boat, as well as of those who escaped on the rock or were left in the vessel, I cannot tell, but conclude they were all lost. For my own part, I swam as fortune directed me, and was pushed forward by wind and tide. I often let my legs drop, and could feel no bottom; but when I was almost gone, and able to struggle no longer, I found myself within my depth; and by this time the storm was much abated. The declivity was so small that I walked near a mile before I got to the shore, which I conjectured was about eight o'clock in the evening. I then advanced forward near half a mile, but could not discover any sign of houses or inhabitants; at least I was in so weak a condition that I did not observe them. I was extremely tired, and with that, and the heat of the weather, and about half a pint of brandy that I drank as I left the ship, I found myself much inclined to sleep. I lay down on the grass, which was very short and soft, where I slept sounder than ever I remember to have done in my life, and, as I reckoned, above nine hours; for when I awaked, it was just daylight. I attempted to rise, but was not able to stir; for, as I happened to lie on my back, I found my arms and legs were strongly fastened on each side to the ground, and my hair, which was long and thick, tied down in the same manner. I likewise felt several slender ligatures across my body, from my armpits to my thighs. I could only look upwards; the sun began to grow hot, and the light offended my eyes. I heard a confused noise about me, but, in the posture I lay, could see nothing except the sky. In a little time I felt something alive moving on my left leg, which, advancing gently forward over my breast, came almost up to my chin; when, bending my eyes downwards as much as I could, I perceived it to be a human creature not six inches high,[10] with a bow and arrow in his hands, and a quiver at his back. In

2 A street near the center of the city, running north into Coleman Street from near the east end of Cheapside.

3 Mistress; here = Miss.

4 It runs westward from the west end of Cheapside.

5 It runs north from Fleet Street to Holborn.

6 A docks area east of the Tower.

7 Waiting for things to.   8 The South Pacific.

9 Probably Tasmania, though the longitude indicates Australia, about which, however, geographers were then pretty hazy.

10 *Lilliput* probably means *little fellow. Lilli* meant *little* in Swift's private playful language; *put=person,* elsewhere in his writings. In all the Lilliputian measurements, the scale is one inch to our foot. In Part II, "A Voyage to Brobdingnag," the scale is reversed: one Brobdingnagian foot to our inch.

the mean time, I felt at least forty more of the same kind (as I conjectured) following the first. I was in the utmost astonishment, and roared so loud that they all ran back in a fright; and some of them, as I was afterwards told, were hurt with the falls they got by leaping from my sides upon the ground. However, they soon returned; and one of them, who ventured so far as to get a full sight of my face, lifting up his hands and eyes by way of admiration,[11] cried out in a shrill but distinct voice, "Hekinah degul." The others repeated the same words several times, but I then knew not what they meant. I lay all this while, as the reader may believe, in great uneasiness. At length, struggling to get loose, I had the fortune to break the strings and wrench out the pegs that fastened my left arm to the ground; for, by lifting it up to my face, I discovered the methods they had taken to bind me, and at the same time with a violent pull, which gave me excessive pain, I a little loosened the strings that tied down my hair on the left side; so that I was just able to turn my head about two inches. But the creatures ran off a second time, before I could seize them; whereupon there was a great shout in a very shrill accent; and after it ceased, I heard one of them cry aloud, "Tolgo phonac"; when in an instant I felt above an hundred arrows discharged on my left hand, which pricked me like so many needles; and besides, they shot another flight into the air, as we do bombs in Europe, whereof many, I suppose, fell on my body (though I felt them not) and some on my face, which I immediately covered with my left hand. When this shower of arrows was over, I fell a-groaning with grief and pain; and then striving again to get loose, they discharged another volley larger than the first, and some of them attempted with spears to stick me in the sides; but, by good luck, I had on me a buff jerkin, which they could not pierce. I thought it the most prudent method to lie still; and my design was to continue so till night, when, my left hand being already loose, I could easily free myself. And as for the inhabitants, I had reason to believe I might be a match for the greatest armies they could bring against me, if they were all of the same size with him that I saw. But fortune disposed otherwise of me. When the people observed I was quiet, they discharged no more arrows. But by the noise increasing I knew their numbers were greater; and about four yards from me, over against my right ear, I heard a knocking for above an hour, like people at work; when, turning my head that way, as well as the pegs and

strings would permit me, I saw a stage erected, about a foot and a half from the ground, capable of holding four of the inhabitants, with two or three ladders to mount it: from whence one of them, who seemed to be a person of quality,[12] made me a long speech, whereof I understood not one syllable. But I should have mentioned that before the principal person began his oration, he cried out three times, "Langro dehul san" (these words and the former were afterwards repeated and explained to me). Whereupon immediately about fifty of the inhabitants came and cut the strings that fastened the left side of my head, which gave me the liberty of turning it to the right, and of observing the person and gesture of him who was to speak. He appeared to be of a middle age, and taller than any of the other three who attended him, whereof one was a page who held up his train, and seemed to be somewhat longer than my middle finger; the other two stood one on each side to support him. He acted every part of an orator; and I could observe many periods of threatenings, and others of promises, pity, and kindness. I answered in a few words, but in the most submissive manner, lifting up my left hand and both my eyes to the sun, as calling him for a witness; and being almost famished with hunger, having not eaten a morsel for some hours before I left the ship, I found the demands of nature so strong upon me that I could not forbear showing my impatience (perhaps against the strict rules of decency) by putting my finger frequently on my mouth, to signify that I wanted food. The *hurgo* (for so they call a great lord, as I afterwards learnt) understood me very well. He descended from the stage, and commanded that several ladders should be applied to my sides, on which above an hundred of the inhabitants mounted and walked towards my mouth, laden with baskets full of meat,[13] which had been provided and sent thither by the King's orders, upon the first intelligence he received of me. I observed there was the flesh of several animals, but could not distinguish them by the taste. There were shoulders, legs, and loins, shaped like those of mutton, and very well dressed, but smaller than the wings of a lark. I eat[14] them by two or three at a mouthful, and took three loaves at a time, about the bigness of musket bullets. They supplied me as fast as they could, showing a thousand marks of wonder and astonishment at my bulk and appetite. I then made another sign that I wanted drink. They found by my eating that a small quantity would not suffice me; and, being a most ingenious people, they

---

[11] Wonder.

[12] Rank.   [13] Food.   [14] Ate; pronounced *ĕt*.

slung up with great dexterity one of their largest hogsheads, then rolled it towards my hand, and beat out the top; I drank it off at a draught, which I might well do, for it hardly held half a pint, and tasted like a small[15] wine of Burgundy, but much more delicious. They brought me a second hogshead, which I drank in the same manner, and made signs for more; but they had none to give me. When I had performed these wonders, they shouted for joy and danced upon my breast, repeating several times as they did at first, "Hekinah degul." They made me a sign that I should throw down the two hogsheads, but first warned the people below to stand out of the way, crying aloud, "Borach mivola"; and when they saw the vessels in the air, there was an universal shout of "Hekinah degul." I confess I was often tempted, while they were passing backwards and forwards on my body, to seize forty or fifty of the first that came in my reach, and dash them against the ground. But the remembrance of what I had felt, which probably might not be the worst they could do, and the promise of honor I made them, for so I interpreted my submissive behavior, soon drove out those imaginations. Besides, I now considered myself as bound by the laws of hospitality to a people who had treated me with so much expense and magnificence. However, in my thoughts I could not sufficiently wonder at the intrepidity of these diminutive mortals, who durst venture to mount and walk on my body, while one of my hands was at liberty, without trembling at the very sight of so prodigious a creature as I must appear to them. After some time, when they observed that I made no more demands for meat, there appeared before me a person of high rank from his Imperial Majesty. His Excellency, having mounted on the small of my right leg, advanced forwards up to my face with about a dozen of his retinue, and, producing his credentials under the signet royal, which he applied close to mine eyes, spoke about ten minutes, without any signs of anger, but with a kind of determinate resolution, often pointing forwards, which, as I afterwards found, was towards the capital city, about half a mile distant, whither it was agreed by his Majesty in council that I must be conveyed. I answered in few words, but to no purpose, and made a sign with my hand that was loose, putting it to the other (but over his Excellency's head, for fear of hurting him or his train) and then to my own head and body, to signify that I desired my liberty. It appeared that he understood me well enough, for he

shook his head by way of disapprobation, and held his hand in a posture to show that I must be carried as a prisoner. However, he made other signs to let me understand that I should have meat and drink enough, and very good treatment. Whereupon I once more thought of attempting to break my bonds; but again, when I felt the smart of their arrows upon my face and hands, which were all in blisters, and many of the darts still sticking in them, and observing likewise that the number of my enemies increased, I gave tokens to let them know that they might do with me what they pleased. Upon this, the *hurgo* and his train withdrew, with much civility and cheerful countenances. Soon after I heard a general shout, with frequent repetitions of the words "peplom selan," and I felt great numbers of people on my left side relaxing the cords to such a degree that I was able to turn upon my right and to ease myself with making water; which I very plentifully did, to the great astonishment of the people, who, conjecturing by my motions what I was going to do, immediately opened to the right and left on that side to avoid the torrent which fell with such noise and violence from me. But before this, they had daubed my face and both my hands with a sort of ointment very pleasant to the smell, which in a few minutes removed all the smart of their arrows. These circumstances, added to the refreshment I had received by their victuals and drink, which were very nourishing, disposed me to sleep. I slept about eight hours, as I was afterwards assured; and it was no wonder, for the physicians, by the Emperor's order, had mingled a sleeping potion in the hogsheads of wine.

It seems that upon the first moment I was discovered sleeping on the ground after my landing, the Emperor had early notice of it by an express,[16] and determined in council that I should be tied in the manner I have related (which was done in the night while I slept), that plenty of meat and drink should be sent me, and a machine prepared to carry me to the capital city.

This resolution perhaps may appear very bold and dangerous, and I am confident would not be imitated by any prince in Europe on the like occasion; however, in my opinion it was extremely prudent as well as generous. For supposing these people had endeavored to kill me with their spears and arrows while I was asleep, I should certainly have awaked with the first sense of smart, which might so far have roused my rage and strength as to have enabled me

---

15 Weak.

16 Special messenger.

to break the strings wherewith I was tied; after which, as they were not able to make resistance, so they could expect no mercy.

These people are most excellent mathematicians, and arrived to a great perfection in mechanics, by the countenance and encouragement of the Emperor, who is a renowned patron of learning. This prince hath several machines fixed on wheels, for the carriage of trees and other great weights. He often buildeth his largest men-of-war, whereof some are nine foot long, in the woods where the timber grows, and has them carried on these engines three or four hundred yards to the sea. Five hundred carpenters and engineers were immediately set at work to prepare the greatest engine they had. It was a frame of wood raised three inches from the ground, about seven foot long and four wide, moving upon twenty-two wheels. The shout I heard was upon the arrival of this engine, which it seems set out in four hours after my landing. It was brought parallel to me as I lay. But the principal difficulty was to raise and place me in this vehicle. Eighty poles, each of one foot high, were erected for this purpose; and very strong cords of the bigness of packthread were fastened by hooks to many bandages which the workmen had girt round my neck, my hands, my body, and my legs. Nine hundred of the strongest men were employed to draw up these cords by many pulleys fastened on the poles; and thus, in less than three hours, I was raised and slung into the engine, and there tied fast. All this I was told, for, while the whole operation was performing, I lay in a profound sleep by the force of that soporiferous medicine infused into my liquor. Fifteen hundred of the emperor's largest horses, each about four inches and a half high, were employed to draw me towards the metropolis, which, as I said, was half a mile distant.

About four hours after we began our journey, I awaked by a very ridiculous accident; for the carriage being stopped awhile to adjust something that was out of order, two or three of the young natives had the curiosity to see how I looked when I was asleep; they climbed up into the engine and, advancing very softly to my face, one of them, an officer in the guards, put the sharp end of his half-pike[17] a good way up into my left nostril, which tickled my nose like a straw, and made me sneeze violently; whereupon they stole off unperceived, and it was three weeks before I knew the cause of my awaking so suddenly. We made a long march the remaining part of that day, and rested at night with five hundred guards on each side of me, half with torches and half with bows and arrows, ready to shoot me if I should offer to stir. The next morning at sunrise we continued our march, and arrived within two hundred yards of the city gates about noon. The Emperor and all his court came out to meet us, but his great officers would by no means suffer his Majesty to endanger his person by mounting on my body.

At the place where the carriage stopped, there stood an ancient temple, esteemed to be the largest in the whole kingdom; which, having been polluted some years before by an unnatural murder, was, according to the zeal[18] of those people, looked upon as profane, and therefore had been applied to common use, and all the ornaments and furniture carried away. In this edifice it was determined I should lodge. The great gate fronting to the north was about four foot high and almost two foot wide, through which I could easily creep. On each side of the gate was a small window not above six inches from the ground. Into that on the left side, the King's smiths conveyed fourscore and eleven chains, like those that hang to a lady's watch in Europe, and almost as large, which were locked to my left leg with six-and-thirty padlocks. Over against this temple, on the other side of the great highway, at twenty foot distance, there was a turret at least five foot high. Here the Emperor ascended, with many principal lords of his court, to have an opportunity of viewing me, as I was told, for I could not see them. It was reckoned that above an hundred thousand inhabitants came out of the town upon the same errand; and, in spite of my guards, I believe there could not be fewer than ten thousand, at several[19] times, who mounted upon my body by the help of ladders. But a proclamation was soon issued to forbid it upon pain of death. When the workmen found it was impossible for me to break loose, they cut all the strings that bound me; whereupon I rose up, with as melancholy a disposition as ever I had in my life. But the noise and astonishment of the people at seeing me rise and walk are not to be expressed. The chains that held my left leg were about two yards long, and gave me not only the liberty of walking backwards and forwards in a semicircle, but, being fixed within four inches of the gate, allowed me to creep in, and lie at my full length in the temple.

---

[17] Or spontoon; it was carried by infantry officers. Like the pike, it was (though not yet attached to the musket) a precursor of the bayonet.

[18] Piety.—This is probably an allusion to Westminster Hall, where Charles I was tried.   [19] Different.

The Emperor of Lilliput, attended by several of the nobility, comes to see the Author in his confinement. The Emperor's person and habit described. Learned men appointed to teach the Author their language. He gains favor by his mild disposition. His pockets are searched, and his sword and pistols taken from him.

When I found myself on my feet, I looked about me, and must confess I never beheld a more entertaining prospect.[20] The country round appeared like a continued garden; and the enclosed fields, which were generally forty foot square, resembled so many beds of flowers. These fields were intermingled with woods of half a stang,[21] and the tallest trees, as I could judge, appeared to be seven foot high. I viewed the town on my left hand, which looked like the painted scene of a city in a theater.

I had been for some hours extremely pressed by the necessities of nature; which was no wonder, it being almost two days since I had last disburthened myself. I was under great difficulties between urgency and shame. The best expedient I could think on was to creep into my house, which I accordingly did; and shutting the gate after me, I went as far as the length of my chain would suffer, and discharged my body of that uneasy load. But this was the only time I was ever guilty of so uncleanly an action; for which I cannot but hope the candid reader will give some allowance, after he hath maturely and impartially considered my case and the distress I was in. From this time my constant practice was, as soon as I rose, to perform that business in open air, at the full extent of my chain; and due care was taken every morning before company came that the offensive matter should be carried off in wheelbarrows by two servants appointed for that purpose. I would not have dwelt so long upon a circumstance that perhaps at first sight may appear not very momentous, if I had not thought it necessary to justify my character in point of cleanliness to the world, which I am told some of my maligners have been pleased, upon this and other occasions, to call in question.

When this adventure was at an end, I came back out of my house, having occasion for fresh air. The Emperor was already descended from the tower and advancing on horseback towards me, which had like to have cost him dear; for the beast, though very well trained, yet wholly unused to such a sight, which appeared as if a mountain moved before him,

reared up on his hinder feet; but that prince, who is an excellent horseman, kept his seat till his attendants ran in and held the bridle while his Majesty had time to dismount. When he alighted, he surveyed me round with great admiration, but kept beyond the length of my chains. He ordered his cooks and butlers, who were already prepared, to give me victuals and drink, which pushed forward in a sort of vehicles upon wheels until I could reach them. I took these vehicles and soon emptied them all; twenty of them were filled with meat and ten with liquor; each of the former afforded me two or three good mouthfuls, and I emptied the liquor of ten vessels, which was contained in earthen vials, into one vehicle, drinking it off at a draught; and so I did with the rest. The Empress, and young princes of the blood of both sexes, attended by many ladies, sat at some distance in their chairs;[22] but upon the accident that happened to the Emperor's horse, they alighted and came near his person, which I am now going to describe.[23] He is taller by almost the breadth of my nail than any of his court, which alone is enough to strike an awe into the beholders. His features are strong and masculine, with an Austrian lip[24] and arched nose, his complexion olive, his countenance erect, his body and limbs well proportioned, all his motions graceful, and his deportment majestic. He was then past his prime, being twenty-eight years and three-quarters old, of which he had reigned about seven, in great felicity and generally victorious. For the better convenience of beholding him, I lay on my side, so that my face was parallel to his, and he stood but three yards off. However, I have had him since many times in my hand, and therefore cannot be deceived in the description. His dress was very plain and simple, and the fashion of it between the Asiatic and the European; but he had on his head a light helmet of gold, adorned with jewels, and a plume on the crest. He held his sword drawn in his hand, to defend himself, if I should happen to break loose; it was almost three inches long; the hilt and scabbard were gold enriched with diamonds. His voice was shrill, but very clear and articulate; and I could distinctly hear it when I stood up. The ladies and courtiers were all most magnificently clad, so that the spot they stood upon seemed to resemble a petticoat spread on the ground,

---

20 View. 21 Rod, 16½ feet.

22 Sedan chairs.
23 This is not a description of George I, who was the Lilliputian monarch's inferior in person and manners. As the narrative proceeds, however, the latter's policy alludes to that of George and his ministry.
24 The protruding lower lip of the Hapsburgs.

embroidered with figures of gold and silver. His Imperial Majesty spoke often to me, and I returned answers; but neither of us could understand a syllable. There were several of his priests and lawyers present (as I conjectured by their habits[25]), who were commanded to address themselves to me; and I spoke to them in as many languages as I had the least smattering of, which were High and Low Dutch,[26] Latin, French, Spanish, Italian, and Lingua Franca,[27] but all to no purpose. After about two hours the court retired, and I was left with a strong guard, to prevent the impertinence and probably the malice of the rabble, who were very impatient to crowd about me as near as they durst; and some of them had the impudence to shoot their arrows at me as I sat on the ground by the door of my house, whereof one very narrowly missed my left eye. But the colonel ordered six of the ringleaders to be seized, and thought no punishment so proper as to deliver them bound into my hands, which some of his soldiers accordingly did, pushing them forwards with the butt-ends of their pikes into my reach. I took them all in my right hand, put five of them into my coat pocket, and as to the sixth I made a countenance as if I would eat him alive. The poor man squalled terribly, and the colonel and his officers were in much pain, especially when they saw me take out my penknife; but I soon put them out of fear, for, looking mildly, and immediately cutting the strings he was bound with, I set him gently on the ground, and away he ran. I treated the rest in the same manner, taking them one by one out of my pocket; and I observed both the soldiers and people were highly obliged at this mark of my clemency, which was represented very much to my advantage at court.

Towards night I got with some difficulty into my house, where I lay on the ground and continued to do so about a fortnight, during which time the Emperor gave orders to have a bed prepared for me. Six hundred beds of the common measure were brought in carriages and worked up in my house; an hundred and fifty of their beds sewn together made up the breadth and length, and these were four double, which however kept me but very indifferently from the hardness of the floor, that was of smooth stone. By the same computation they provided me with sheets, blankets, and coverlets, tolerable enough for one who had been so long enured to hardships as I.

As the news of my arrival spread through the kingdom, it brought prodigious numbers of rich, idle, and curious people to see me; so that the villages were almost emptied, and great neglect of tillage and household affairs must have ensued, if his Imperial Majesty had not provided, by several proclamations and orders of state, against this inconveniency. He directed that those who had already beheld me should return home, and not presume to come within fifty yards of my house without license from court; whereby the secretaries of state got considerable fees.

In the meantime, the Emperor held frequent councils to debate what course should be taken with me; and I was afterwards assured by a particular friend, a person of great quality who was as much in the secret as any, that the court was under many difficulties concerning me. They apprehended my breaking loose, that my diet would be very expensive and might cause a famine. Sometimes they determined to starve me, or at least to shoot me in the face and hands with poisoned arrows, which would soon dispatch me; but again they considered that the stench of so large a carcass might produce a plague in the metropolis, and probably spread through the whole kingdom. In the midst of these consultations, several officers of the army went to the door of the great council-chamber; and two of them, being admitted, gave an account of my behavior to the six criminals above-mentioned; which made so favorable an impression in the breast of his Majesty and the whole board, in my behalf, that an imperial commission was issued out, obliging all the villages nine hundred yards round the city to deliver in every morning six beeves, forty sheep, and other victuals for my sustenance, together with a proportionable quantity of bread and wine and other liquors, for the due payment of which his Majesty gave assignments upon his treasury. For this prince lives chiefly upon his own demesnes,[28] seldom, except upon great occasions, raising any subsidies upon his subjects, who are bound to attend him in his wars at their own expense. An establishment was also made of six hundred persons to be my domestics, who had board-wages[29] allowed for their maintenance, and tents built for them very conveniently on each side of my door. It was likewise ordered that three hundred tailors should make me a suit of

---

25 Clothes.   26 German and Dutch.
27 A mixed language used by traders and sailors in Mediterranean ports.

28 Crown lands.   29 An allowance in lieu of board.

clothes after the fashion of the country; that six of his Majesty's greatest scholars should be employed to instruct me in their language; and, lastly, that the Emperor's horses, and those of the nobility and troops of guards, should be exercised in my sight to accustom themselves to me. All these orders were duly put in execution; and in about three weeks I made a great progress in learning their language, during which time the Emperor frequently honored me with his visits and was pleased to assist my masters in teaching me. We began already to converse together in some sort; and the first words I learnt were to express my desire that he would please to give me my liberty, which I every day repeated on my knees. His answer, as I could comprehend it, was that this must be a work of time, not to be thought on without the advice of his council, and that first I must "Lumos kelmin pesso desmar lon emposo," that is, swear a peace with him and his kingdom. However, that I should be used with all kindness; and he advised me to acquire, by my patience and discreet behavior, the good opinion of himself and his subjects. He desired I would not take it ill if he gave orders to certain proper officers to search me; for probably I might carry about me several weapons, which must needs be dangerous things if they answered the bulk of so prodigious a person. I said his Majesty should be satisfied, for I was ready to strip myself and turn up my pockets before him. This I delivered part in words and part in signs. He replied that by the laws of the kingdom I must be searched by two of his officers, that he knew this could not be done without my consent and assistance, that he had so good an opinion of my generosity and justice as to trust their persons in my hands, that whatever they took from me should be returned when I left the country or paid for at the rate which I would set upon them. I took up the two officers in my hands, put them first into my coat pockets, and then into every other pocket about me, except my two fobs[30] and another secret pocket which I had no mind should be searched, wherein I had some little necessaries of no consequence to any but myself. In one of my fobs there was a silver watch, and in the other a small quantity of gold in a purse. These gentlemen, having pen, ink, and paper about them, made an exact inventory of everything they saw, and when they had done desired I would set them down that they might deliver it to the Emperor.

This inventory I afterwards translated into English, and is word for word as follows:[31]

Imprimis, In the right coat-pocket of the Great Man Mountain (for so I interpret the words *quinbus flestrin*) after the strictest search, we found only one great piece of coarse cloth, large enough to be a footcloth for your Majesty's chief room of state. In the left pocket we saw a huge silver chest, with a cover of the same metal, which we, the searchers, were not able to lift. We desired it should be opened, and one of us stepping into it, found himself up to the mid-leg in a sort of dust, some part whereof, flying up to our faces, set us both a-sneezing for several times together. In his right waistcoat-pocket we found a prodigious bundle of white thin substances, folded one over another, about the bigness of three men, tied with a strong cable and marked with black figures, which we humbly conceive to be writings, every letter almost half as large as the palm of our hands. In the left there was a sort of engine, from the back of which were extended twenty long poles resembling the palisadoes before your Majesty's court, wherewith we conjecture the Man Mountain combs his head; for we did not always trouble him with questions, because we found it a great difficulty to make him understand us. In the large pocket on the right side of his middle cover (so I translate the word *ranfu-lo,* by which they meant my breeches) we saw a hollow pillar of iron, about the length of a man, fastened to a strong piece of timber larger than the pillar; and upon one side of the pillar were huge pieces of iron sticking out, cut into strange figures, which we know not what to make of. In the left pocket, another engine of the same kind. In the smaller pocket on the right side, were several round flat pieces of white and red metal of different bulk; some of the white, which seemed to be silver, were so large and heavy that my comrade and I could hardly lift them. In the left pocket were two black pillars irregularly shaped; we could not, without difficulty, reach the top of them as we stood at the bottom of his pocket. One of them was covered, and seemed all of a piece; but at the upper end of the other, there appeared a white round substance, about twice the bigness of our heads. Within each of these was enclosed a prodigious plate of steel, which by our orders we obliged him to show us, because we apprehended they might be dangerous engines. He

---

30 Small pockets, especially for watches.

31 The search seems intended to ridicule the results of a secret committee of the Whigs appointed by Walpole to investigate Tory connections with the Jacobite movement.

took them out of their cases, and told us that in his own country his practice was to shave his beard with one of these, and to cut his meat with the other. There were two pockets which we could not enter. These he called his fobs; they were two large slits cut into the top of his middle cover, but squeezed close by the pressure of his belly. Out of the right fob hung a great silver chain, with a wonderful kind of engine at the bottom. We directed him to draw out whatever was at the end of that chain; which appeared to be a globe, half silver, and half of some transparent metal; for, on the transparent side, we saw certain strange figures circularly drawn, and thought we could touch them, till we found our fingers stopped with that lucid substance. He put this engine to our ears, which made an incessant noise like that of a watermill. And we conjecture it is either some unknown animal or the god that he worships; but we are more inclined to the latter opinion, because he assured us (if we understood him right, for he expressed himself very imperfectly) that he seldom did anything without consulting it. He called it his oracle, and said it pointed out the time for every action of his life. From the left fob he took out a net almost large enough for a fisherman, but contrived to open and shut like a purse, and served him for the same use; we found therein several massy pieces of yellow metal, which, if they be real gold, must be of immense value.

Having thus, in obedience to your Majesty's commands, diligently searched all his pockets, we observed a girdle about his waist made of the hide of some prodigious animal; from which, on the left side, hung a sword of the length of five men; and on the right, a bag or pouch divided into two cells, each cell capable of holding three of your Majesty's subjects. In one of these cells were several globes or balls of a most ponderous metal, about the bigness of our heads, and required a strong hand to lift them; the other cell contained a heap of certain black grains, but of no great bulk or weight, for we could hold above fifty of them in the palms of our hands.

This is an exact inventory of what we found about the body of the Man Mountain, who used us with great civility and due respect to your Majesty's commission. Signed and sealed on the fourth day of the eighty-ninth moon of your Majesty's auspicious reign.

CLEFRIN FRELOCK, MARSI FRELOCK.

When this inventory was read over to the Emperor, he directed me to deliver up the several particulars. He first called for my scimitar, which I took out, scabbard and all. In the meantime he ordered three thousand of his choicest troops (who then attended him) to surround me at a distance, with their bows and arrows just ready to discharge; but I did not observe it, for my eyes were wholly fixed upon his Majesty. He then desired me to draw my scimitar, which, although it had got some rust by the sea-water, was in most parts exceeding bright. I did so, and immediately all the troops gave a shout between terror and surprise; for the sun shone clear, and the reflection dazzled their eyes as I waved the scimitar to and fro in my hand. His Majesty, who is a most magnanimous prince, was less daunted than I could expect; he ordered me to return it into the scabbard and cast it on the ground as gently as I could, about six foot from the end of my chain. The next thing he demanded was one of the hollow iron pillars, by which he meant my pocket pistols. I drew it out, and at his desire, as well as I could, expressed to him the use of it; and charging it only with powder, which by the closeness of my pouch happened to escape wetting in the sea (an inconvenience that all prudent mariners take special care to provide against), I first cautioned the Emperor not to be afraid and then I let it off in the air. The astonishment here was much greater than at the sight of my scimitar. Hundreds fell down as if they had been struck dead; and even the Emperor, although he stood his ground, could not recover himself in some time. I delivered up both my pistols in the same manner as I had done my scimitar, and then my pouch of powder and bullets, begging him that the former might be kept from fire, for it would kindle with the smallest spark and blow up his imperial palace into the air. I likewise delivered up my watch, which the Emperor was very curious to see, and commanded two of his tallest yeomen of the guards to bear it on a pole upon their shoulders as draymen in England do a barrel of ale. He was amazed at the continual noise it made, and the motion of the minute hand, which he could easily discern, for their sight is much more acute than ours, and asked the opinions of his learned men about him, which were various and remote,[32] as the reader may well imagine without my repeating, although indeed I could not very perfectly understand them. I then gave up my silver and copper money, my purse, with nine large pieces of gold and some smaller ones, my knife and razor, my comb and silver snuffbox, my handkerchief and journal-book. My scimitar, pistols, and pouch

---

[32] Far-fetched.

were conveyed in carriages to his Majesty's stores; but the rest of my goods were returned to me.

I had, as I before observed, one private pocket which escaped their search, wherein there was a pair of spectacles (which I sometimes use for the weakness of mine eyes), a pocket perspective,[33] and several other little conveniences; which, being of no consequence to the Emperor, I did not think myself bound in honor to discover, and I apprehended they might be lost or spoiled if I ventured them out of my possession.

CHAPTER 3

The Author diverts the Emperor and his nobility of both sexes in a very uncommon manner. The diversions of the court of Lilliput described. The Author hath his liberty granted him upon certain conditions.

My gentleness and good behavior had gained so far on the Emperor and his court, and indeed upon the army and people in general, that I began to conceive hopes of getting my liberty in a short time. I took all possible methods to cultivate this favorable disposition. The natives came by degrees to be less apprehensive of any danger from me. I would sometimes lie down and let five or six of them dance on my hand. And at last the boys and girls would venture to come and play at hide and seek in my hair. I had now made a good progress in understanding and speaking their language. The Emperor had a mind one day to entertain me with several of the country[34] shows, wherein they exceed all nations I have known, both for dexterity and magnificence. I was diverted with none so much as that of the rope dancers, performed upon a slender white thread extended about two foot and twelve inches from the ground. Upon which I shall desire liberty, with the reader's patience, to enlarge a little.

This diversion is only practiced by those persons who are candidates for great employments and high favor at court. They are trained in this art from their youth, and are not always of noble birth or liberal education. When a great office is vacant, either by death or disgrace (which often happens), five or six of those candidates petition the Emperor to entertain his Majesty and the court with a dance on the rope; and whoever jumps the highest without falling succeeds in the office. Very often the chief ministers themselves are commanded to show their skill and to convince the Emperor that they have not lost

their faculty. Flimnap, the treasurer,[35] is allowed[36] to cut a caper on the straight rope at least an inch higher than any other lord in the whole empire. I have seen him do the somerset several times together upon a trencher[37] fixed on the rope, which is no thicker than a common packthread in England. My friend Reldresal, principal secretary for private affairs,[38] is, in my opinion, if I am not partial, the second after the Treasurer; the rest of the great officers are much upon a par.

These diversions are often attended with fatal accidents, whereof great numbers are on record. I myself have seen two or three candidates break a limb. But the danger is much greater when the ministers themselves are commanded to show their dexterity; for, by contending to excel themselves and their fellows, they strain so far that there is hardly one of them who hath not received a fall, and some of them two or three. I was assured that, a year or two before my arrival, Flimnap would have infallibly broke his neck, if one of the King's cushions,[39] that accidentally lay on the ground, had not weakened the force of his fall.

There is likewise another diversion, which is only shown before the Emperor and Empress and First Minister upon particular occasions. The Emperor lays on the table three fine silken threads of six inches long. One is blue, the other red, and the third green.[40] These threads are proposed as prizes for those persons whom the Emperor hath a mind to distinguish by a peculiar mark of his favor. The ceremony is performed in his Majesty's great chamber of state, where the candidates are to undergo a trial of dexterity very different from the former, and such as I have not observed the least resemblance of in any other country of the Old or the New World. The Emperor holds a stick in his hands, both ends parallel to the horizon, while the candidates advancing one by one sometimes leap over the stick, sometimes creep under it backwards and forwards several times, according as the stick is advanced or depressed. Sometimes the Emperor holds one end of the stick and his First Minister the other; sometimes the minister has it entirely to himself. Who-

---

[33] Spyglass.   [34] Country's.

[35] I.e., Sir Robert Walpole, Whig statesman, who as First Lord of the Treasury ruled England from 1721 to 1742.
[36] Conceded.   [37] Wooden plate.
[38] Perhaps Lord Carteret, who had been a Secretary of State and was a friend of Swift, but was obliged as Lord Lieutenant of Ireland to offer a reward for discovery of the authorship of a pamphlet everyone knew Swift had written.
[39] One of the mistresses of George I. She seems to have had a part in restoring Walpole to power in 1721.
[40] I.e., the ribbons of the Garter, Bath, and Thistle. Walpole was instrumental in having the second of these orders revived.

ever performs his part with most agility, and holds out the longest in leaping and creeping, is rewarded with the blue-colored silk; the red is given to the next, and the green to the third, which they all wear girt twice round about the middle; and you see few great persons about this court who are not adorned with one of these girdles.

The horses of the army, and those of the royal stables, having been daily led before me, were no longer shy but would come up to my very feet without starting. The riders would leap them over my hand as I held it on the ground, and one of the Emperor's huntsmen upon a large courser took my foot, shoe and all, which was indeed a prodigious leap. I had the good fortune to divert the Emperor one day after a very extraordinary manner. I desired he would order several sticks of two foot high and the thickness of an ordinary cane to be brought me; whereupon his Majesty commanded the master of his woods to give directions accordingly; and the next morning six woodmen arrived with as many carriages, drawn by eight horses to each. I took nine of these sticks, fixing them firmly in the ground in a quadrangular figure, two foot and a half square. I took four other sticks, and tied them parallel at each corner, about two foot from the ground; then I fastened my handkerchief to the nine sticks that stood erect, and extended it on all sides till it was tight as the top of a drum; and the four parallel sticks, rising about five inches higher than the handkerchief, served as ledges on each side. When I had finished my work, I desired the Emperor to let a troop of his best horse, twenty-four in number, come and exercise upon this plain. His Majesty approved of the proposal, and I took them up, one by one, in my hands, ready mounted and armed, with the proper officers to exercise them. As soon as they got into order, they divided into two parties, performed mock skirmishes, discharged blunt arrows, drew their swords, fled and pursued, attacked and retired, and in short discovered the best military discipline I ever beheld. The parallel sticks secured them and their horses from falling over the stage; and the Emperor was so much delighted that he ordered this entertainment to be repeated several days, and once was pleased to be lifted up and give the word of command; and, with great difficulty, persuaded even the Empress herself to let me hold her in her close chair within two yards of the stage, from whence she was able to take a full view of the whole performance. It was my good fortune that no ill accident happened in these entertainments, only once a fiery horse that belonged to one of the captains, paw-

ing with his hoof, struck a hole in my handkerchief, and, his foot slipping, he overthrew his rider and himself; but I immediately relieved them both: for, covering the hole with one hand, I set down the troop with the other, in the same manner as I took them up. The horse that fell was strained in the left shoulder, but the rider got no hurt, and I repaired my handkerchief as well as I could. However, I would not trust to the strength of it any more in such dangerous enterprises.

About two or three days before I was set at liberty, as I was entertaining the court with these kinds of feats, there arrived an express to inform his Majesty that some of his subjects, riding near the place where I was first taken up, had seen a great black substance lying on the ground, very oddly shaped, extending its edges round as wide as his Majesty's bedchamber, and rising up in the middle as high as a man; that it was no living creature, as they at first apprehended, for it lay on the grass without motion and some of them had walked round it several times; that by mounting upon each other's shoulders they had got to the top, which was flat and even, and stamping upon it they found it was hollow within; that they humbly conceived it might be something belonging to the Man Mountain; and if his Majesty pleased, they would undertake to bring it with only five horses. I presently[41] knew what they meant, and was glad at heart to receive this intelligence. It seems, upon my first reaching the shore after our shipwreck, I was in such confusion that before I came to the place where I went to sleep my hat, which I had fastened with a string to my head while I was rowing, and had stuck on all the time I was swimming, fell off after I came to land, the string, as I conjecture, breaking by some accident which I never observed but thought my hat had been lost at sea. I entreated his Imperial Majesty to give orders it might be brought to me as soon as possible, describing to him the use and the nature of it; and the next day the wagoners arrived with it, but not in a very good condition: they had bored two holes in the brim, within an inch and half of the edge, and fastened two hooks in the holes; these hooks were tied by a long cord to the harness, and thus my hat was dragged along for above half an English mile; but the ground in that country being extremely smooth and level, it received less damage than I expected.

Two days after this adventure the Emperor, having ordered that part of his army which quarters in

----

41 Immediately.

and about his metropolis to be in a readiness, took a fancy of diverting himself in a very singular manner. He desired I would stand like a colossus, with my legs as far asunder as I conveniently could. He then commanded his general (who was an old experienced leader, and a great patron of mine) to draw up the troops in close order and march them under me, the foot by twenty-four in a breast, and the horse by sixteen, with drums beating, colors flying, and pikes advanced. This body consisted of three thousand foot and a thousand horse. His Majesty gave orders, upon pain of death, that every soldier in his march should observe the strictest decency with regard to my person, which, however, could not prevent some of the younger officers from turning up their eyes as they passed under me. And, to confess the truth, my breeches were at that time in so ill a condition that they afforded some opportunities for laughter and admiration.

I had sent so many memorials and petitions for my liberty that his Majesty at length mentioned the matter, first in the cabinet and then in a full council, where it was opposed by none except Skyresh Bolgolam,[42] who was pleased, without any provocation, to be my mortal enemy. But it was carried against him by the whole board, and confirmed by the Emperor. That minister was *galbet,* or admiral of the realm, very much in his master's confidence, and a person well versed in affairs, but of a morose and sour complexion. However, he was at length persuaded to comply, but prevailed that the articles and conditions upon which I should be set free, and to which I must swear, should be drawn up by himself. These articles were brought to me by Skyresh Bolgolam in person, attended by two under-secretaries and several persons of distinction. After they were read, I was demanded to swear to the performance of them, first in the manner of my own country and afterwards in the method prescribed by their laws, which was to hold my right foot in my left hand, to place the middle finger of my right hand on the crown of my head, and my thumb on the tip of my right ear. But because the reader may be curious to have some idea of the style and manner of expression peculiar to that people, as well as to know the articles upon which I recovered my liberty, I have made a translation of the whole instrument word for word, as near as I was able, which I here offer to the public.

"GOLBASTO MOMAREM EVLAME GURDILO SHEFIN MULLY ULLY GUE, most mighty Emperor of Lilliput, delight and terror of the universe, whose dominions extend five thousand *blustrugs* [about twelve miles in circumference] to the extremities of the globe; monarch of all monarchs, taller than the sons of men; whose feet press down to the center, and whose head strikes against the sun; at whose nod the princes of the earth shake their knees; pleasant as the spring, comfortable as the summer, fruitful as autumn, dreadful as winter. His most sublime Majesty proposeth to the Man Mountain, lately arrived to our celestial dominions, the following articles, which by a solemn oath he shall be obliged to perform.

"First, the Man Mountain shall not depart from our dominions without our license under our great seal.

"Secondly, he shall not presume to come into our metropolis without our express order, at which time the inhabitants shall have two hours' warning to keep within their doors.

"Thirdly, the said Man Mountain shall confine his walks to our principal highroads, and not offer to walk or lie down in a meadow or field of corn.[43]

"Fourthly, as he walks the said roads, he shall take the utmost care not to trample upon the bodies of any of our loving subjects, their horses or carriages, nor take any of our subjects into his hands without their own consent.

"Fifthly, if an express require extraordinary dispatch, the Man Mountain shall be obliged to carry in his pocket the messenger and horse a six days' journey once in every moon, and return the said messenger back (if so required) safe to our imperial presence.

"Sixthly, he shall be our ally against our enemies in the island of Blefuscu,[44] and do his utmost to destroy their fleet, which is now preparing to invade us.

"Seventhly, that the said Man Mountain shall, at his times of leisure, be aiding and assisting to our workmen in helping to raise certain great stones towards covering the wall of the principal park and other our royal buildings.

"Eighthly, that the said Man Mountain shall, in two moons' time, deliver in an exact survey of the circumference of our dominions, by a computation of his own paces round the coast.

---

[42] Probably the Earl of Nottingham, an enemy of Defoe as well as of Swift. He was a High Churchman and Tory extremist. His nickname was "Dismal." Having been First Lord of the Admiralty many years before, he sometimes meddled with naval affairs, in which the experts considered him incompetent.

[43] Grain.   [44] I.e., France.

"Lastly, that, upon his solemn oath to observe all the above articles, the said Man Mountain shall have a daily allowance of meat and drink sufficient for the support of 1728 of our subjects, with free access to our royal person and other marks of our favor. Given at our palace at Belfaborac, the twelfth day of the ninety-first moon of our reign."

I swore and subscribed to these articles with great cheerfulness and content, although some of them were not so honorable as I could have wished, which proceeded wholly from the malice of Skyresh Bolgolam, the high admiral; whereupon my chains were immediately unlocked, and I was at full liberty. The Emperor himself in person did me the honor to be by at the whole ceremony. I made my acknowledgments by prostrating myself at his Majesty's feet; but he commanded me to rise, and, after many gracious expressions, which, to avoid the censure of vanity, I shall not repeat, he added that he hoped I should prove a useful servant and well deserve all the favors he had already conferred upon me or might do for the future.

The reader may please to observe that, in the last article for the recovery of my liberty, the Emperor stipulates to allow me a quantity of meat and drink sufficient for the support of 1728 Lilliputians. Some time after, asking a friend at court how they came to fix on that determinate number, he told me that his Majesty's mathematicians, having taken the height of my body by the help of a quadrant, and finding it to exceed theirs in the proportion of twelve to one, they concluded from the similarity of their bodies that mine must contain at least 1728 of theirs, and consequently would require as much food as was necessary to support that number of Lilliputians. By which the reader may conceive an idea of the ingenuity of that people, as well as the prudent and exact economy of so great a prince.

CHAPTER 4

Mildendo, the metropolis of Lilliput, described, together with the Emperor's palace. A conversation between the Author and a principal secretary, concerning the affairs of that empire. The Author's offers to serve the Emperor in his wars.

The first request I made after I had obtained my liberty was that I might have license to see Mildendo, the metropolis, which the Emperor easily granted me, but with a special charge to do no hurt either to the inhabitants or their houses. The people had notice by proclamation of my design to visit the town. The wall which encompassed it is two foot and an half high and at least eleven inches broad, so that a coach and horses may be driven very safely round it; and it is flanked with strong towers at ten foot distance. I stepped over the great western gate, and passed very gently, and sideling through the two principal streets, only in my short waistcoat, for fear of damaging the roofs and eaves of the houses with the skirts of my coat. I walked with the utmost circumspection to avoid treading on any stragglers who might remain in the streets, although the orders were very strict that all people should keep in their houses, at their own peril. The garret windows and tops of houses were so crowded with spectators that I thought in all my travels I had not seen a more populous place. The city is an exact square, each side of the wall being five hundred foot long. The two great streets, which run across and divide it into four quarters, are five foot wide. The lanes and alleys, which I could not enter but only viewed them as I passed, are from twelve to eighteen inches. The town is capable of holding five hundred thousand souls. The houses are from three to five stories. The shops and markets well provided.

The Emperor's palace is in the center of the city, where the two great streets meet. It is enclosed by a wall of two foot high, and twenty foot distant from the buildings. I had his Majesty's permission to step over this wall; and the space being so wide between that and the palace, I could easily view it on every side. The outward court is a square of forty foot, and includes two other courts; in the inmost are the royal apartments, which I was very desirous to see, but found it extremely difficult, for the great gates, from one square into another, were but eighteen inches high and seven inches wide. Now the buildings of the outer court were at least five foot high, and it was impossible for me to stride over them without infinite damage to the pile, though the walls were strongly built of hewn stone, and four inches thick. At the same time the Emperor had a great desire that I should see the magnificence of his palace; but this I was not able to do till three days after, which I spent in cutting down with my knife some of the largest trees in the royal park, about an hundred yards distant from the city. Of these trees I made two stools, each about three foot high and strong enough to bear my weight. The people having received notice a second time, I went again through the city to the palace, with my two stools in my hands. When I came to the side of the outer court, I stood upon one stool and took the other in my hand; this I lifted over the roof, and gently set it down on the space between the first and second court, which was eight foot wide. I then stepped over the buildings very conveniently from one stool to the other, and drew up the first after me with a hooked stick. By this contrivance I got into the inmost court; and lying down upon my side, I applied my face to the windows of the middle stories, which were left open on purpose, and discovered the most splendid apartments that can be imagined. There I saw the Empress and the young princes, in their several lodgings, with their chief attendants about them. Her Imperial Majesty was pleased to smile very graciously upon me, and gave me out of the window her hand to kiss.

But I shall not anticipate the reader with farther descriptions of this kind, because I reserve them for a greater work, which is now almost ready for the press, containing a general description of this empire, from its first erection, through a long series of princes, with a particular account of their wars and politics, laws, learning, and religion; their plants and animals, their peculiar manners and customs, with other matters very curious and useful, my chief design at present being only to relate such events and transactions as happened to the public or to myself during a residence of about nine months in that empire.

One morning, about a fortnight after I had obtained my liberty, Reldresal, principal secretary (as they style him) of private affairs, came to my house attended only by one servant. He ordered his coach to wait at a distance, and desired I would give him an hour's audience; which I readily consented to, on account of his quality and personal merits, as well as the many good offices he had done me during my solicitations at court. I offered to lie down that he might the more conveniently reach my ear; but he chose rather to let me hold him in my hand during our conversation. He began with compliments on my liberty; said he might pretend to some merit in it; but, however, added that if it had not been for the present situation of things at court, perhaps I might not have obtained it so soon. "For," said he, "as flourishing a condition as we appear to be in to foreigners, we labor under two mighty evils: a violent faction at home, and the danger of an invasion by a most potent enemy from abroad. As to the first, you are to understand that for about seventy moons past there have been two struggling parties in this empire, under the names of *Tramecksan* and *Slamecksan*, from the high and low heels on their shoes, by which they distinguish themselves.[45] It is

alleged, indeed, that the high heels are most agreeable to our ancient constitution; but however this be, his Majesty hath determined to make use of only low heels in the administration of the government, and all offices in the gift of the Crown, as you cannot but observe; and particularly, that his Majesty's imperial heels are lower at least by a *drurr* than any of his court [*drurr* is a measure about the fourteenth part of an inch].[46] The animosities between these two parties run so high that they will neither eat nor drink nor talk with each other. We compute the *Tramecksan*, or High Heels, to exceed us in number; but the power is wholly on our side. We apprehend his imperial Highness, the heir to the crown, to have some tendency towards the High Heels; at least we can plainly discover one of his heels higher than the other, which gives him a hobble in his gait.[47] Now, in the midst of these intestine disquiets, we are threatened with an invasion from the island of Blefuscu, which is the other great empire of the universe, almost as large and powerful as this of his Majesty. For as to what we have heard you affirm, that there are other kingdoms and states in the world inhabited by human creatures as large as yourself, our philosophers are in much doubt, and would rather conjecture that you dropped from the moon, or one of the stars; because it is certain that an hundred mortals of your bulk would, in a short time, destroy all the fruits and cattle of his Majesty's dominions. Besides, our histories of six thousand moons make no mention of any other regions than the two great empires of Lilliput and Blefuscu. Which two mighty powers have, as I was going to tell you, been engaged in a most obstinate war for six-and-thirty moons past.[48] It began upon the following occasion. It is allowed on all hands that the primitive way of breaking eggs before we eat them was upon the larger end; but his present Majesty's grandfather, while he was a boy, going to eat an egg, and breaking it according to the ancient practice, happened to cut one of his fingers. Whereupon the emperor his father published an edict commanding all his subjects, upon great penalties, to break the smaller end of their eggs.[49] The people so highly resented this law that our histories tell us there have

45 Tories and Whigs. The former were High Churchmen, the latter Low.

46 George I had turned the Tories out of office on his accession in 1714.
47 When the Prince of Wales, who opposed his father's policies, came to the throne as George II in 1727, the Whigs remained in office. In 1726, when *Gulliver* was published, his intentions were not clear.
48 The War of the Spanish Succession, 1702–13 (p. 397, above).
49 The Big-Endians are the Catholics, the Little-Endians Protestants.

been six rebellions raised on that account; wherein one emperor lost his life, and another his crown.[50] These civil commotions were constantly fomented by the monarchs of Blefuscu; and when they were quelled, the exiles always fled for refuge to that empire. It is computed that eleven thousand persons have, at several times, suffered death rather than submit to break their eggs at the smaller end. Many hundred large volumes have been published upon this controversy. But the books of the Big-Endians have been long forbidden, and the whole party rendered incapable by law of holding employments.[51] During the course of these troubles the emperors of Blefuscu did frequently expostulate by their ambassadors, accusing us of making a schism in religion by offending against a fundamental doctrine of our great prophet Lustrog, in the fifty-fourth chapter of the Blundecral [which is their Alcoran]. This, however, is thought to be a mere strain upon the text, for the words are these: 'That all true believers break their eggs at the convenient end'; and which is the convenient end seems, in my humble opinion, to be left to every man's conscience, or at least in the power of the chief magistrate to determine. Now the Big-Endian exiles have found so much credit in the Emperor of Blefuscu's court, and so much private assistance and encouragement from their party here at home, that a bloody war hath been carried on between the two empires for six-and-thirty moons, with various success; during which time we have lost forty capital ships and a much greater number of smaller vessels, together with thirty thousand of our best seamen and soldiers; and the damage received by the enemy is reckoned to be somewhat greater than ours. However, they have now equipped a numerous fleet and are just preparing to make a descent upon us; and his Imperial Majesty, placing great confidence in your valor and strength, hath commanded me to lay this account of his affairs before you."

I desired the Secretary to present my humble duty to the Emperor, and to let him know that I thought it would not become me, who was a foreigner, to interfere with parties; but I was ready, with the hazard of my life, to defend his person and state against all invaders.

The Author, by an extraordinary stratagem, prevents an invasion. A high title of honor is conferred upon him. Ambassadors arrive from the Emperor of Blefuscu, and sue for peace. The Empress's apartment on fire by an accident; the Author instrumental in saving the rest of the palace.

The Empire of Blefuscu is an island situated to the north-northeast side of Lilliput, from whence it is parted only by a channel of eight hundred yards wide. I had not yet seen it; and upon this notice of an intended invasion, I avoided appearing on that side of the coast, for fear of being discovered by some of the enemy's ships, who had received no intelligence of me, all intercourse between the two empires having been strictly forbidden during the war, upon pain of death, and an embargo laid by our Emperor upon all vessels whatsoever. I communicated to his Majesty a project I had formed of seizing the enemy's whole fleet, which, as our scouts assured us, lay at anchor in the harbor ready to sail with the first fair wind. I consulted the most experienced seamen upon the depth of the channel, which they had often plumbed, who told me that in the middle at high water it was seventy *glumgluffs* deep, which is about six foot of European measure, and the rest of it fifty *glumgluffs* at most. I walked to the northeast coast over against Blefuscu, where, lying down behind a hillock, I took out my small pocket perspective-glass and viewed the enemy's fleet at anchor, consisting of about fifty men-of-war and a great number of transports. I then came back to my house and gave order (for which I had a warrant) for a great quantity of the strongest cable and bars of iron. The cable was about as thick as packthread, and the bars of the length and size of a knitting needle. I trebled the cable to make it stronger, and for the same reason I twisted three of the iron bars together, bending the extremities into a hook. Having thus fixed fifty hooks to as many cables, I went back to the northeast coast, and, putting off my coat, shoes, and stockings, walked into the sea in my leathern jerkin, about half an hour before high water. I waded with what haste I could, and swam in the middle about thirty yards till I felt ground; I arrived to the fleet in less than half an hour. The enemy was so frighted when they saw me that they leaped out of their ships and swam to shore, where there could not be fewer than thirty thousand souls. I then took my tackling, and fastening a hook to the hole at the prow of each, I tied all the cords together at the end. While I was thus employed, the enemy discharged several thousand arrows, many of which

---

[50] Charles I and James II.   [51] Political office.

stuck in my hands and face, and besides the excessive smart gave me much disturbance in my work. My greatest apprehension was for mine eyes, which I should have infallibly lost if I had not suddenly thought of an expedient. I kept among other little necessaries a pair of spectacles in a private pocket, which, as I observed before, had escaped the Emperor's searchers. These I took out and fastened as strongly as I could upon my nose, and thus armed went on boldly with my work in spite of the enemy's arrows, many of which struck against the glasses of my spectacles, but without any other effect further than a little to discompose them. I had now fastened all the hooks, and taking the knot in my hand began to pull; but not a ship would stir, for they were all too fast held by their anchors; so that the boldest part of my enterprise remained. I therefore let go the cord, and, leaving the hooks fixed to the ships, I resolutely cut with my knife the cables that fastened the anchors, receiving above two hundred shots in my face and hands; then I took up the knotted end of the cables to which my hooks were tied, and with great ease drew fifty of the enemy's largest men-of-war after me.

The Blefuscudians, who had not the least imagination of what I intended, were at first confounded with astonishment. They had seen me cut the cables, and thought my design was only to let the ships run adrift or fall foul on each other; but when they perceived the whole fleet moving in order, and saw me pulling at the end, they set up such a scream of grief and despair that it is almost impossible to describe or conceive. When I had got out of danger, I stopped awhile to pick out the arrows that stuck in my hands and face, and rubbed on some of the same ointment that was given me at my first arrival, as I have formerly mentioned. I then took off my spectacles, and waiting about an hour, till the tide was a little fallen, I waded through the middle with my cargo and arrived safe at the royal port of Lilliput.

The Emperor and his whole court stood on the shore, expecting the issue[52] of this great adventure. They saw the ships move forward in a large half-moon, but could not discern me, who was up to my breast in water. When I advanced to the middle of the channel, they were yet in more pain, because I was under water to my neck. The Emperor concluded me to be drowned, and that the enemy's fleet was approaching in a hostile manner; but he was soon eased of his fears, for, the channel growing shallower every step I made, I came in a short time within hearing; and holding up the end of the cable by which the fleet was fastened, I cried in a loud voice, "Long live the most puissant Emperor of Lilliput!" This great prince received me at my landing with all possible encomiums, and created me a *nardac* upon the spot, which is the highest title of honor among them.

His Majesty desired I would take some other opportunity of bringing all the rest of his enemy's ships into his ports. And so unmeasurable is the ambition of princes that he seemed to think of nothing less than reducing the whole empire of Blefuscu into a province and governing it by a viceroy, of destroying the Big-Endian exiles,[53] and compelling that people to break the smaller end of their eggs, by which he would remain the sole monarch of the whole world. But I endeavored to divert him from this design by many arguments drawn from the topics of policy as well as justice; and I plainly protested that I would never be an instrument of bringing a free and brave people into slavery. And when the matter was debated in council, the wisest part of the ministry were of my opinion.

This open bold declaration of mine was so opposite to the schemes and politics of his Imperial Majesty that he could never forgive me. He mentioned it in a very artful manner at council, where I was told that some of the wisest appeared, at least by their silence, to be of my opinion; but others, who were my secret enemies, could not forbear some expressions which by a side wind reflected on me. And from this time began an intrigue between his Majesty and a junta of ministers maliciously bent against me, which broke out in less than two months, and had like to have ended in my utter destruction. Of so little weight are the greatest services to princes, when put into the balance with a refusal to gratify their passions.

About three weeks after this exploit, there arrived a solemn embassy from Blefuscu with humble offers of a peace, which was soon concluded upon conditions very advantageous to our emperor,[54] wherewith I shall not trouble the reader. There were six ambassadors, with a train of about five hundred persons; and their entry was very magnificent, suitable to the grandeur of their master and the importance of their business. When their treaty was finished, wherein I did them several good offices by

---

[52] Awaiting the outcome.

[53] The Jacobite exiles in France. It was the Whigs who had supported Marlborough's prosecution of the War of the Spanish Succession, which the Tories brought to an end.

[54] The Peace of Utrecht (1713).

the credit I now had or at least appeared to have at court, their Excellencies, who were privately told how much I had been their friend, made me a visit in form. They began with many compliments upon my valor and generosity, invited me to that kingdom in the Emperor their master's name, and desired me to show them some proofs of my prodigious strength, of which they had heard so many wonders; wherein I readily obliged them, but shall not interrupt the reader with the particulars.

When I had for some time entertained their Excellencies, to their infinite satisfaction and surprise, I desired they would do me the honor to present my most humble respects to the Emperor their master, the renown of whose virtues had so justly filled the whole world with admiration, and whose royal person I resolved to attend before I returned to my own country. Accordingly, the next time I had the honor to see our Emperor, I desired his general license to wait on the Blefuscudian monarch, which he was pleased to grant me, as I could perceive, in a very cold manner, but could not guess the reason till I had a whisper from a certain person that Flimnap and Bolgolam had represented my intercourse with those ambassadors as a mark of disaffection, from which I am sure my heart was wholly free. And this was the first time I began to conceive some imperfect idea of courts and ministers.

It is to be observed that these ambassadors spoke to me by an interpreter, the languages of both empires differing as much from each other as any two in Europe, and each nation priding itself upon the antiquity, beauty, and energy of their own tongues, with an avowed contempt for that of their neighbor. Yet our emperor, standing upon the advantage he had got by the seizure of their fleet, obliged them to deliver their credentials and make their speech in the Lilliputian tongue. And it must be confessed that from the great intercourse of trade and commerce between both realms, from the continual reception of exiles, which is mutual among them, and from the custom in each empire to send their young nobility and richer gentry to the other, in order to polish themselves by seeing the world and understanding men and manners, there are few persons of distinction, or merchants or seamen who dwell in the maritime parts, but what can hold conversation in both tongues, as I found some weeks after, when I went to pay my respects to the Emperor of Blefuscu, which in the midst of great misfortunes, through the malice of my enemies, proved a very happy adventure to me, as I shall relate in its proper place.

The reader may remember that, when I signed those articles upon which I recovered my liberty, there were some which I disliked upon account of their being too servile; neither could anything but an extreme necessity have forced me to submit. But being now a *nardac,* of the highest rank in that empire, such offices were looked upon as below my dignity; and the Emperor (to do him justice) never once mentioned them to me. However, it was not long before I had an opportunity of doing his Majesty, at least as I then thought, a most signal service. I was alarmed at midnight with the cries of many hundred people at my door; by which being suddenly awaked, I was in some kind of terror. I heard the word *burglum* repeated incessantly; several of the Emperor's court, making their way through the crowd, entreated me to come immediately to the palace, where her Imperial Majesty's apartment was on fire, by the carelessness of a maid of honor, who fell asleep while she was reading a romance. I got up in an instant; and orders being given to clear the way before me, and it being likewise a moonshine night, I made a shift to get to the palace without trampling on any of the people. I found they had already applied ladders to the walls of the apartment, and were well provided with buckets; but the water was at some distance. These buckets were about the size of a large thimble, and the poor people supplied me with them as fast as they could; but the flame was so violent that they did little good. I might easily have stifled it with my coat, which I unfortunately left behind me for haste, and came away only in my leathern jerkin. The case seemed wholly desperate and deplorable; and this magnificent palace would have infallibly been burnt down to the ground, if, by a presence of mind unusual to me, I had not suddenly thought of an expedient. I had the evening before drank plentifully of a most delicious wine called *glimigrim* (the Blefuscudians call it *flunec,* but ours is esteemed the better sort), which is very diuretic. By the luckiest chance in the world, I had not discharged myself of any part of it. The heat I had contracted by coming very near the flames and by laboring to quench them, made the wine begin to operate by urine, which I voided in such a quantity, and applied so well to the proper places, that in three minutes the fire was wholly extinguished, and the rest of that noble pile, which had cost so many ages in erecting, preserved from destruction.

It was now daylight, and I returned to my house without waiting to congratulate with the Emperor; because, although I had done a very eminent piece of service, yet I could not tell how his Majesty might resent the manner by which I had performed it. For, by the fundamental laws of the realm, it is capital[55] in any person, of what quality soever, to make water within the precincts of the palace. But I was a little comforted by a message from his Majesty that he would give orders to the grand justiciary for passing my pardon in form; which, however, I could not obtain. And I was privately assured that the Empress, conceiving the greatest abhorrence of what I had done, removed to the most distant side of the court, firmly resolved that those buildings should never be repaired for her use, and in the presence of her chief confidants could not forbear vowing revenge.[56]

CHAPTER 6

Of the inhabitants of Lilliput; their learning, laws, and customs. The manner of educating their children. The Author's way of living in that country. His vindication of a great lady.

Although I intend to leave the description of this empire to a particular treatise, yet in the meantime I am content to gratify the curious reader with some general ideas. As the common size of the natives is somewhat under six inches high, so there is an exact proportion in all other animals, as well as plants and trees. For instance, the tallest horses and oxen are between four and five inches in height; the sheep an inch and a half, more or less; their geese about the bigness of a sparrow; and so the several gradations downwards till you come to the smallest, which, to my sight, were almost invisible; but nature hath adapted the eyes of the Lilliputians to all objects proper for their view: they see with great exactness, but at no great distance. And to show the sharpness of their sight towards objects that are near, I have been much pleased with observing a cook pulling a lark, which was not so large as a common fly, and a young girl threading an invisible needle with invisible silk. Their tallest trees are about seven foot high: I mean some of those in the great royal park, the tops whereof I could but just reach with my fist clinched. The other vegetables are in the same proportion; but this I leave to the reader's imagination.

I shall say but little at present of their learning, which for many ages hath flourished in all its branches among them; but their manner of writing is very peculiar, being neither from the left to the right like the Europeans, nor from the right to the left like the Arabians, nor from up to down like the Chinese, nor from down to up like the Cascagians,[57] but aslant from one corner of the paper to the other, like ladies in England.

They bury their dead with their heads directly downwards, because they hold an opinion that in eleven thousand moons they are all to rise again; in which period the earth (which they conceive to be flat) will turn upside down, and by this means they shall, at their resurrection, be found ready standing on their feet. The learned among them confess the absurdity of this doctrine; but the practice still continues, in compliance to the vulgar.

There are some laws and customs in this empire very peculiar; and if they were not so directly contrary to those of my own dear country, I should be tempted to say a little in their justification. It is only to be wished that they were as well executed. The first I shall mention relateth to informers. All crimes against the state are punished here with the utmost severity; but if the person accused make his innocence plainly to appear upon his trial, the accuser is immediately put to an ignominious death; and out of his goods or lands the innocent person is quadruply recompensed for the loss of his time, for the danger he underwent, for the hardship of his imprisonment, and for all the charges he hath been at in making his defense. Or, if that fund be deficient, it is largely supplied by the Crown. The emperor doth also confer on him some public mark of his favor, and proclamation is made of his innocence through the whole city.

They look upon fraud as a greater crime than theft, and therefore seldom fail to punish it with death; for they allege that care and vigilance, with a very common understanding, may preserve a man's goods from thieves, but honesty hath no fence against superior cunning. And since it is necessary that there should be a perpetual intercourse of buying and selling, and dealing upon credit, where fraud is permitted and connived at, or hath no law to punish it, the honest dealer is always undone and the knave gets the advantage. I remember when I was once interceding with the Emperor for a criminal who had wronged his master of a great sum of money, which he had received by order and ran away with; and happening to tell his Majesty, by way of extenuation, that it was only a breach of trust, the Emperor thought it monstrous in me to offer as a defense the greatest aggravation of the

---

[55] A capital crime.
[56] Probably an allusion to Queen Anne's refusal to give Swift a bishopric because of her disgust with *A Tale of a Tub*.

[57] Presumably invented by Swift, to round out the pattern.

crime. And truly I had little to say in return, farther than the common answer, that different nations had different customs; for, I confess, I was heartily ashamed.

Although we usually call reward and punishment the two hinges upon which all government turns, yet I could never observe this maxim to be put in practice by any nation except that of Lilliput. Whoever can there bring sufficient proof that he hath strictly observed the laws of his country for seventy-three moons hath a claim to certain privileges, according to his quality and condition of life, with a proportionable sum of money out of a fund appropriated for that use. He likewise acquires the title of *snilpall*, or legal, which is added to his name, but doth not descend to his posterity. And these people thought it a prodigious defect of policy among us, when I told them that our laws were enforced only by penalties, without any mention of reward. It is upon this account that the image of Justice, in their courts of judicature, is formed with six eyes, two before, as many behind, and on each side one, to signify circumspection; with a bag of gold open in her right hand, and a sword sheathed in her left, to show she is more disposed to reward than to punish.

In choosing persons for all employments, they have more regard to good morals than to great abilities; for, since government is necessary to mankind, they believe that the common size of human understandings is fitted to some station or other, and that Providence never intended to make the management of public affairs a mystery, to be comprehended only by a few persons of sublime genius, of which there seldom are three born in an age. But they suppose truth, justice, temperance, and the like, to be in every man's power; the practice of which virtues, assisted by experience and a good intention, would qualify any man for the service of his country, except where a course of study is required. But they thought the want of moral virtues was so far from being supplied by superior endowments of the mind that employments could never be put into such dangerous hands as those of persons so qualified, and at least that the mistakes committed by ignorance in a virtuous disposition would never be of such fatal consequence to the public weal as the practices of a man whose inclinations led him to be corrupt, and had great abilities to manage, to multiply, and defend his corruptions.

In like manner, the disbelief of a Divine Providence renders a man uncapable of holding any public station; for, since kings avow themselves to be the deputies of Providence, the Lilliputians think nothing

can be more absurd than for a prince to employ such men as disown the authority under which he acteth.

In relating these and the following laws, I would only be understood to mean the original institutions, and not the most scandalous corruptions into which these people are fallen by the degenerate nature of man. For as to that infamous practice of acquiring great employments by dancing on the ropes, or badges of favor and distinction by leaping over sticks and creeping under them, the reader is to observe that they were first introduced by the grandfather of the emperor now reigning, and grew to the present height by the gradual increase of party and faction.

Ingratitude is among them a capital crime, as we read it to have been in some other countries. For they reason thus: that whoever makes ill returns to his benefactor must needs be a common enemy to the rest of mankind, from whom he hath received no obligation, and therefore such a man is not fit to live.

Their notions relating to the duties of parents and children differ extremely from ours. For, since the conjunction of male and female is founded upon the great law of nature, in order to propagate and continue the species, the Lilliputians will needs have it that men and women are joined together like other animals, by the motives of concupiscence, and that their tenderness towards their young proceedeth from the like natural principle. For which reason they will never allow that a child is under any obligation to his father for begetting him, or to his mother for bringing him into the world, which, considering the miseries of human life, was neither a benefit in itself nor intended so by his parents, whose thoughts in their love encounters were otherwise employed. Upon these and the like reasonings, their opinion is that parents are the last of all others to be trusted with the education of their own children. And therefore they have in every town public nurseries, where all parents, except cottagers[58] and laborers, are obliged to send their infants of both sexes to be reared and educated when they come to the age of twenty moons, at which time they are supposed to have some rudiments of docility. These schools are of several kinds, suited to different qualities and to both sexes. They have certain professors well skilled in preparing children for such a condition of life as befits the rank of their parents and their own capacities as well as inclinations. I shall first say something of the male nurseries, and then of the female.

---

58 Small tenant-farmers.

The nurseries for males of noble or eminent birth are provided with grave and learned professors and their several deputies. The clothes and food of the children are plain and simple. They are bred up in the principles of honor, justice, courage, modesty, clemency, religion, and love of their country. They are always employed in some business, except in the times of eating and sleeping, which are very short, and two hours for diversions, consisting of bodily exercises. They are dressed by men till four years of age, and then are obliged to dress themselves, although their quality be ever so great; and the women attendants, who are aged proportionably to ours at fifty, perform only the most menial offices. They are never suffered to converse with servants, but go together in small or greater numbers to take their diversions, and always in the presence of a professor or one of his deputies; whereby they avoid those early bad impressions of folly and vice to which our children are subject. Their parents are suffered to see them only twice a year; the visit is to last but an hour; they are allowed to kiss the child at meeting and parting; but a professor, who always standeth by on those occasions, will not suffer them to whisper, or use any fondling expressions, or bring any presents of toys, sweetmeats, and the like.

The pension from each family for the education and entertainment[59] of a child, upon failure of due payment, is levied by the emperor's officers.

The nurseries for children of ordinary gentlemen, merchants, traders, and handicrafts are managed proportionably after the same manner; only those designed for trades are put out apprentices at seven years old, whereas those of persons of quality continue in their exercises till fifteen, which answers to one-and-twenty with us. But the confinement is gradually lessened for the last three years.

In the female nurseries, the young girls of quality are educated much like the males, only they are dressed by orderly servants of their own sex, but always in the presence of a professor or deputy, until they come to dress themselves, which is at five years old. And if it be found that these nurses ever presume to entertain the girls with frightful or foolish stories, or the common follies practiced by chambermaids among us, they are publicly whipped thrice about the city, imprisoned for a year, and banished for life to the most desolate parts of the country. Thus the young ladies there are as much ashamed of being cowards and fools as the men, and despise all personal ornaments beyond decency and cleanliness; neither did I perceive any difference in their education made by their difference of sex, only that the exercises of the females were not altogether so robust, and that some rules were given them relating to domestic life, and a smaller compass of learning was enjoined them. For their maxim is that among people of quality a wife should be always a reasonable and agreeable companion, because she cannot always be young. When the girls are twelve years old, which among them is the marriageable age, their parents or guardians take them home, with great expressions of gratitude to the professors, and seldom without tears of the young lady and her companions.

In the nurseries of females of the meaner sort, the children are instructed in all kinds of works proper for their sex and their several degrees. Those intended for apprentices are dismissed at seven years old; the rest are kept to eleven.

The meaner families who have children at these nurseries are obliged, besides their annual pension, which is as low as possible, to return to the steward of the nursery a small monthly share of their gettings, to be a portion for the child; and therefore all parents are limited in their expenses by the law. For the Lilliputians think nothing can be more unjust than that people, in subservience to their own appetites, should bring children into the world and leave the burthen of supporting them on the public. As to persons of quality, they give security to appropriate a certain sum for each child, suitable to their condition; and these funds are always managed with good husbandry and the most exact justice.

The cottagers and laborers keep their children at home, their business being only to till and cultivate the earth, and therefore their education is of little consequence to the public; but the old and diseased among them are supported by hospitals, for begging is a trade unknown in this empire.

And here it may perhaps divert the curious reader, to give some account of my domestic,[60] and my manner of living in this country, during a residence of nine months and thirteen days. Having a head mechanically turned, and being likewise forced by necessity, I had made for myself a table and chair convenient enough, out of the largest trees in the royal park. Two hundred sempstresses were employed to make me shirts, and linen for my bed and table, all of the strongest and coarsest kind they could get; which, however, they were forced to quilt together in several folds, for the thickest was

---

59 Maintenance.

60 Housekeeping.

some degrees finer than lawn. Their linen is usually three inches wide, and three foot make a piece. The sempstresses took my measure as I lay on the ground, one standing at my neck and another at my mid-leg, with a strong cord extended that each held by the end, while the third measured the length of the cord with a rule of an inch long. Then they measured my right thumb, and desired no more; for by a mathematical computation that twice round the thumb is once round the wrist, and so on to the neck and the waist, and by the help of my old shirt, which I displayed on the ground before them for a pattern, they fitted me exactly. Three hundred tailors were employed in the same manner to make me clothes; but they had another contrivance for taking my measure. I kneeled down, and they raised a ladder from the ground to my neck; upon this ladder one of them mounted, and let fall a plumb line from my collar to the floor, which just answered the length of my coat; but my waist and arms I measured myself. When my clothes were finished, which was done in my house (for the largest of theirs would not have been able to hold them), they looked like the patchwork made by the ladies in England, only that mine were all of a color.

I had three hundred cooks to dress my victuals, in little convenient huts built about my house, where they and their families lived, and prepared me two dishes apiece. I took up twenty waiters in my hand and placed them on the table; an hundred more attended below on the ground, some with dishes of meat and some with barrels of wine and other liquors slung on their shoulders, all which the waiters above drew up as I wanted, in a very ingenious manner, by certain cords, as we draw the bucket up a well in Europe. A dish of their meat was a good mouthful, and a barrel of their liquor a reasonable draught. Their mutton yields to ours, but their beef is excellent. I have had a sirloin so large that I have been forced to make three bits of it; but this is rare. My servants were astonished to see me eat it bones and all, as in our country we do the leg of a lark. Their geese and turkeys I usually eat at a mouthful, and I must confess they far exceed ours. Of their smaller fowl I could take up twenty or thirty at the end of my knife.

One day his Imperial Majesty, being informed of my way of living, desired that himself and his royal consort, with the young princes of the blood of both sexes, might have the happiness (as he was pleased to call it) of dining with me. They came accordingly, and I placed them upon chairs of state on my table, just over against me, with their guards about them. Flimnap, the lord high treasurer, attended there likewise with his white staff;[61] and I observed he often looked on me with a sour countenance, which I would not seem to regard, but eat more than usual, in honor to my dear country as well as to fill the court with admiration. I have some private reasons to believe that this visit from his Majesty gave Flimnap an opportunity of doing me ill offices to his master. That minister had always been my secret enemy, although he outwardly caressed me more than was usual to the moroseness of his nature. He represented to the Emperor the low condition of his treasury, that he was forced to take up money at great discount, that exchequer bills would not circulate under nine per cent below par, that I had cost his Majesty above a million and a half of *sprugs* (their greatest gold coin, about the bigness of a spangle), and upon the whole that it would be advisable in the Emperor to take the first fair occasion of dismissing me.

I am here obliged to vindicate the reputation of an excellent lady who was an innocent sufferer upon my account. The Treasurer took a fancy to be jealous of his wife, from the malice of some evil tongues, who informed him that her Grace had taken a violent affection for my person; and the court scandal ran for some time that she once came privately to my lodging. This I solemnly declare to be a most infamous falsehood, without any grounds farther than that her Grace was pleased to treat me with all innocent marks of freedom and friendship. I own she came often to my house, but always publicly, nor ever without three more in the coach, who were usually her sister and young daughter and some particular acquaintance; but this was common to many other ladies of the court. And I still appeal to my servants round, whether they at any time saw a coach at my door without knowing what persons were in it. On those occasions, when a servant had given me notice, my custom was to go immediately to the door; and, after paying my respects, to take up the coach and two horses very carefully in my hands (for, if there were six horses, the postillion always unharnessed four) and place them on a table, where I had fixed a movable rim quite round, of five inches high, to prevent accidents. And I have often had four coaches and horses at once on my table full of company, while I sat in my chair leaning my face towards them; and when I was engaged with one set, the coachmen would gently drive the others

---

61 The symbol of that office in England.

round my table. I have passed many an afternoon very agreeably in these conversations. But I defy the Treasurer or his two informers (I will name them, and let them make their best of it) Clustril and Drunlo to prove that any person ever came to me incognito, except the secretary Reldresal, who was sent by express command of his Imperial Majesty, as I have before related. I should not have dwelt so long upon this particular, if it had not been a point wherein the reputation of a great lady is so nearly concerned, to say nothing of my own; although I had the honor to be a *nardac,* which the Treasurer himself is not;[62] for all the world knows he is only a *glumglum,* a title inferior by one degree, as that of a marquess is to a duke in England; yet I allow he preceded me in right of his post.[63] These false informations, which I afterwards came to the knowledge of by an accident not proper to mention, made the Treasurer show his lady for some time an ill countenance, and me a worse. For although he were at last undeceived and reconciled to her, yet I lost all credit with him, and found my interest decline very fast with the Emperor himself, who was indeed too much governed by that favorite.

CHAPTER 7

The Author, being informed of a design to accuse him of high treason, makes his escape to Blefuscu. His reception there.

Before I proceed to give an account of my leaving this kingdom, it may be proper to inform the reader of a private intrigue which had been for two months forming against me.

I had been hitherto all my life a stranger to courts, for which I was unqualified by the meanness of my condition. I had indeed heard and read enough of the dispositions of great princes and ministers, but never expected to have found such terrible effects of them in so remote a country, governed, as I thought, by very different maxims from those in Europe.

When I was just preparing to pay my attendance on the Emperor of Blefuscu, a considerable person at court (to whom I had been very serviceable at a time when he lay under the highest displeasure of his Imperial Majesty) came to my house very privately at night in a close chair, and without sending his name desired admittance. The chairmen were dismissed; I put the chair, with his Lordship in it, into my coat pocket; and giving orders to a trusty servant to say I was indisposed and gone to sleep, I fastened the door of my house, placed the chair on the table, according to my usual custom, and sat down by it. After the common salutations were over, observing his Lordship's countenance full of concern and enquiring into the reason, he desired I would hear him with patience in a matter that highly concerned my honor and my life. His speech was to the following effect, for I took notes of it as soon as he left me.

"You are to know," said he, "that several committees of council have been lately called in the most private manner on your account; and it is but two days since his Majesty came to a full resolution.

"You are very sensible that Skyresh Bolgolam [*galbet,* or high admiral] hath been your mortal enemy almost ever since your arrival. His original reasons I know not; but his hatred is much increased since your great success against Blefuscu, by which his glory as admiral is obscured. This lord, in conjunction with Flimnap the high treasurer, whose enmity against you is notorious on account of his lady, Limtoc the general, Lalcon the chamberlain, and Balmuff the grand justiciary, have prepared articles of impeachment against you, for treason and other capital crimes."[64]

This preface made me so impatient, being conscious of my own merits and innocence, that I was going to interrupt, when he entreated me to be silent, and thus proceeded.

"Out of gratitude for the favors you have done me, I procured information of the whole proceedings and a copy of the articles, wherein I venture my head for your service.

"'*Articles of Impeachment against Quinbus Flestrin (the Man Mountain)*

"'ARTICLE I

"'Whereas, by a statute made in the reign of his Imperial Majesty Calin Deffar Plune, it is enacted that whoever shall make water within the precincts of the royal palace shall be liable to the pains and

---

62 Walpole was not at this time a peer. Till 1742, when he was made Earl of Orford, he preferred to remain in the House of Commons. There was much talk when he received the Garter, a rare honor for a commoner.

63 Outranked me by virtue of his office.

64 The charges which follow are intended to burlesque those brought against the Tory leaders who were impeached after the Whig triumph of 1714–15. Harley (Earl of Oxford) was sent to the Tower. Bolingbroke and the Duke of Ormond fled overseas. (On Ormond see "On the Death of Dr. Swift," note 41, below.) Gulliver stands for Bolingbroke to some extent, though not consistently. Bolingbroke had, like Gulliver, brought an end to a great war, against the wishes of an opposition party.

penalties of high treason; notwithstanding, the said Quinbus Flestrin in open breach of the said law, under color of extinguishing the fire kindled in the apartment of his Majesty's most dear imperial consort, did maliciously, traitorously, and devilishly, by discharge of his urine, put out the said fire kindled in the said apartment, lying and being within the precincts of the said royal palace, against the statute in that case provided, &c., against the duty, &c.

" 'ARTICLE II

" 'That, the said Quinbus Flestrin having brought the imperial fleet of Blefuscu into the royal port, and being afterwards commanded by his Imperial Majesty to seize all the other ships of the said empire of Blefuscu, and reduce that empire to a province, to be governed by a viceroy from hence, and to destroy and put to death not only all the Big-Endian exiles, but likewise all the people of that empire who would not immediately forsake the Big-Endian heresy, he, the said Flestrin, like a false traitor against his most Auspicious, Serene, Imperial Majesty, did petition to be excused from the said service, upon pretense of unwillingness to force the consciences or destroy the liberties and lives of an innocent people.

" 'ARTICLE III

" 'That, whereas certain ambassadors arrived from the court of Blefuscu to sue for peace in his Majesty's court, he, the said Flestrin, did, like a false traitor, aid, abet, comfort, and divert the said ambassadors, although he knew them to be servants to a prince who was lately an open enemy to his Imperial Majesty, and in open war against his said Majesty.

" 'ARTICLE IV

" 'That the said Quinbus Flestrin, contrary to the duty of a faithful subject, is now preparing to make a voyage to the court and empire of Blefuscu, for which he hath received only verbal license from his Imperial Majesty, and under color of the said license doth falsely and traitorously intend to take the said voyage, and thereby to aid, comfort, and abet the Emperor of Blefuscu, so late an enemy and in open war with his Imperial Majesty aforesaid.'

"There are some other articles, but these are the most important, of which I have read you an abstract.

"In the several debates upon this impeachment, it must be confessed that his Majesty gave many marks of his great lenity, often urging the services you had done him and endeavoring to extenuate your crimes. The Treasurer and Admiral insisted that you

should be put to the most painful and ignominious death, by setting fire on your house at night; and the General was to attend with twenty thousand men armed with poisoned arrows to shoot you on the face and hands. Some of your servants were to have private orders to strew a poisonous juice on your shirts and sheets, which would soon make you tear your own flesh and die in the utmost torture. The General came into the same opinion; so that for a long time there was a majority against you. But his Majesty resolving, if possible, to spare your life, at last brought off[65] the Chamberlain.

"Upon this incident, Reldresal, principal secretary for private affairs, who always approved[66] himself your true friend, was commanded by the Emperor to deliver his opinion, which he accordingly did, and therein justified the good thoughts you have of him. He allowed your crimes to be great, but that still there was room for mercy, the most commendable virtue in a prince, and for which his Majesty was so justly celebrated. He said the friendship between you and him was so well known to the world that perhaps the most honorable board might think him partial; however, in obedience to the command he had received he would freely offer his sentiments. That if his Majesty, in consideration of your services and pursuant to his own merciful disposition, would please to spare your life and only give order to put out both your eyes, he humbly conceived that by this expedient justice might in some measure be satisfied, and all the world would applaud the lenity of the Emperor, as well as the fair and generous proceedings of those who have the honor to be his counselors. That the loss of your eyes would be no impediment to your bodily strength, by which you might still be useful to his Majesty. That blindness is an addition to courage, by concealing dangers from us; that the fear you had for your eyes was the greatest difficulty in bringing over the enemy's fleet; and it would be sufficient for you to see by the eyes of the ministers, since the greatest princes do no more.

"This proposal was received with the utmost disapprobation by the whole board. Bolgolam, the admiral, could not preserve his temper, but rising up in fury said he wondered how the Secretary durst presume to give his opinion for preserving the life of a traitor; that the services you had performed were, by all true reasons of state, the great aggravation of your crimes; that you, who were able to extinguish the fire by discharge of urine in her Majesty's apartment (which he mentioned with

---

[65] Dissuaded.   [66] Proved.

horror), might at another time raise an inundation by the same means, to drown the whole palace; and the same strength which enabled you to bring over the enemy's fleet might serve upon the first discontent to carry it back; that he had good reasons to think you were a Big-Endian in your heart; and as treason begins in the heart before it appears in overt acts, so he accused you as a traitor on that account, and therefore insisted you should be put to death.

"The Treasurer was of the same opinion; he showed to what straits his Majesty's revenue was reduced by the charge of maintaining you, which would soon grow insupportable; that the Secretary's expedient of putting out your eyes was so far from being a remedy against this evil that it would probably increase it, as it is manifest from the common practice of blinding some kind of fowl, after which they fed the faster and grew sooner fat; that his sacred Majesty and the council, who are your judges, were in their own consciences fully convinced of your guilt, which was a sufficient argument to condemn you to death, without the *formal proofs required by the strict letter of the law*.

"But his Imperial Majesty, fully determined against capital punishment, was graciously pleased to say that since the council thought the loss of your eyes too easy a censure, some other may be inflicted hereafter. And your friend the Secretary humbly desiring to be heard again, in answer to what the Treasurer had objected concerning the great charge his Majesty was at in maintaining you, said that his Excellency, who had the sole disposal of the Emperor's revenue, might easily provide against that evil by gradually lessening your establishment; by which, for want of sufficient food, you would grow weak and faint, and lose your appetite, and consequently decay and consume[67] in a few months; neither would the stench of your carcass be then so dangerous, when it should become more than half diminished; and immediately upon your death, five or six thousand of his Majesty's subjects might, in two or three days, cut your flesh from your bones, take it away by cartloads, and bury it in distant parts to prevent infection, leaving the skeleton as a monument of admiration to posterity.

"Thus by the great friendship of the Secretary, the whole affair was compromised. It was strictly enjoined that the project of starving you by degrees should be kept a secret; but the sentence of putting out your eyes was entered on the books, none dissenting except Bolgolam the admiral, who, being a creature of the Empress, was perpetually instigated by her Majesty to insist upon your death, she having borne perpetual malice against you on account of that infamous and illegal method you took to extinguish the fire in her apartment.

"In three days your friend the Secretary will be directed to come to your house and read before you the articles of impeachment, and then to signify the great lenity and favor of his Majesty and council, whereby you are only condemned to the loss of your eyes, which his Majesty doth not question you will gratefully and humbly submit to; and twenty of his Majesty's surgeons will attend, in order to see the operation well performed, by discharging very sharp-pointed arrows into the balls of your eyes, as you lie on the ground.

"I leave to your prudence what measures you will take; and to avoid suspicion, I must immediately return in as private a manner as I came."

His Lordship did so, and I remained alone, under many doubts and perplexities of mind.

It was a custom introduced by this prince and his ministry (very different, as I have been assured, from the practices of former times) that after the court had decreed any cruel execution, either to gratify the monarch's resentment or the malice of a favorite, the Emperor always made a speech to his whole council, expressing *his great lenity and tenderness, as qualities known and confessed by all the world.*[68] This speech was immediately published through the kingdom; nor did anything terrify the people so much as those encomiums on his Majesty's mercy, because it was observed that the more these praises were enlarged and insisted on, the more inhuman was the punishment, and the *sufferer more innocent.* Yet, as to myself, I must confess, having never been designed for a courtier either by my birth or education, I was so ill a judge of things that I could not discover the lenity and favor of this sentence, but conceived it (perhaps erroneously) rather to be rigorous than gentle. I sometimes thought of standing my trial; for although I could not deny the facts alleged in the several articles, yet I hoped they would admit of some extenuations. But having in my life perused many state trials, which I ever observed to terminate as the judges thought fit to direct, I durst not rely on so dangerous a decision in so critical a juncture and against such powerful enemies. Once I was strongly bent upon resistance; for while I had liberty, the whole strength of that empire could hardly subdue me, and I might easily with stones pelt the metropolis

---

[67] Waste away.

[68] Perhaps an ironical reference to the savage punishment of the rebels of 1715.

to pieces. But I soon rejected that project with horror, by remembering the oath I had made to the Emperor, the favors I received from him, and the high title of *nardac* he conferred upon me. Neither had I so soon learned the gratitude of courtiers, to persuade myself that his Majesty's *present severities acquitted me of all past obligations.*

At last I fixed upon a resolution for which it is probable I may incur some censure, and not unjustly; for I confess I owe the preserving of my eyes, and consequently my liberty, to my own great rashness and want of experience. Because if I had then known the nature of princes and ministers, which I have since observed in many other courts, and their methods of treating criminals less obnoxious than myself, I should with great alacrity and readiness have submitted to so *easy* a punishment.[69] But hurried on by the precipitancy of youth, and, having his Imperial Majesty's license to pay my attendance upon the Emperor of Blefuscu, I took this opportunity, before the three days were elapsed, to send a letter to my friend the Secretary, signifying my resolution of setting out that morning for Blefuscu pursuant to the leave I had got; and without waiting for an answer, I went to that side of the island where our fleet lay. I seized a large man-of-war, tied a cable to the prow, and, lifting up the anchors, I stripped myself, put my clothes (together with my coverlet, which I brought under my arm) into the vessel, and, drawing it after me, between wading and swimming arrived at the royal port of Blefuscu, where the people had long expected me. They lent me two guides to direct me to the capital city, which is of the same name. I held them in my hands until I came within two hundred yards of the gate, and desired them to signify my arrival to one of the secretaries, and let him know I there waited his Majesty's commands. I had an answer in about an hour that his Majesty, attended by the royal family and great officers of the court, was coming out to receive me. I advanced a hundred yards. The Emperor and his train alighted from their horses, the Empress and ladies from their coaches; and I did not perceive they were in any fright or concern. I lay on the ground to kiss his Majesty's and the Empress's hands. I told his Majesty that I was come according to my promise and with the license of the Emperor my master, to have the honor of seeing so mighty a monarch and to offer him any service in my power consistent with my duty to my own prince, not mentioning a word of my disgrace, because I had hitherto no regular information of it, and might suppose myself wholly ignorant of any such design; neither could I reasonably conceive that the Emperor would discover the secret while I was out of his power; wherein, however, it soon appeared I was deceived.

I shall not trouble the reader with the particular account of my reception at this court, which was suitable to the generosity of so great a prince, nor of the difficulties I was in for want of a house and bed, being forced to lie on the ground, wrapped up in my coverlet.[70]

CHAPTER 8

The Author by a lucky accident finds means to leave Blefuscu, and after some difficulties returns safe to his native country.

Three days after my arrival, walking out of curiosity to the northeast coast of the island, I observed, about half a league off in the sea, somewhat that looked like a boat overturned. I pulled off my shoes and stockings and, wading two or three hundred yards, I found the object to approach nearer by force of the tide, and then plainly saw it to be a real boat, which I supposed might by some tempest have been driven from a ship. Whereupon I returned immediately towards the city and desired his Imperial Majesty to lend me twenty of the tallest vessels he had left after the loss of his fleet, and three thousand seamen under the command of his vice-admiral. This fleet sailed round, while I went back the shortest way to the coast where I first discovered the boat; I found the tide had driven it still nearer; the seamen were all provided with cordage, which I had beforehand twisted to a sufficient strength. When the ships came up, I stripped myself and waded till I came within an hundred yards of the boat, after which I was forced to swim till I got up to it. The seamen threw me the end of the cord, which I fastened to a hole in the forepart of the boat, and the other end to a man-of-war. But I found all my labor to little purpose; for, being out of my depth, I was not able to work. In this necessity, I was forced to swim behind and push the boat forwards as often as I could with one of my hands; and the tide favoring me, I advanced so far that I could just hold up my chin and feel the ground. I rested two or three minutes and then gave

---

[69] This passage seems intended as a defense of Bolingbroke's flight from the impeachment proceedings. He was granted a limited pardon and returned to England in 1723.

[70] A reference to the hardships of the Jacobite exiles at the court of France.

the boat another shove, and so on till the sea was no higher than my armpits. And now the most laborious part being over, I took out my other cables, which were stowed in one of the ships, and fastening them first to the boat and then to nine of the vessels which attended me, the wind being favorable, the seamen towed and I shoved till we arrived within forty yards of the shore; and waiting till the tide was out, I got dry to the boat, and by the assistance of two thousand men with ropes and engines I made a shift to turn it on its bottom and found it was but little damaged.

I shall not trouble the reader with the difficulties I was under by the help of certain paddles, which cost me ten days making, to get my boat to the royal port of Blefuscu, where a mighty concourse of people appeared upon my arrival, full of wonder at the sight of so prodigious a vessel. I told the Emperor that my good fortune had thrown this boat in my way to carry me to some place from whence I might return into my native country, and begged his Majesty's orders for getting materials to fit it up, together with his license to depart; which, after some kind expostulations, he was pleased to grant.

I did very much wonder, in all this time, not to have heard of any express relating to me from our Emperor to the court of Blefuscu. But I was afterwards given privately to understand that his Imperial Majesty, never imagining I had the least notice of his designs, believed I was only gone to Blefuscu in performance of my promise, according to the license he had given me, which was well known at our court, and would return in a few days when that ceremony was ended. But he was at last in pain at my long absence; and after consulting with the Treasurer and the rest of that cabal, a person of quality was dispatched with the copy of the articles against me. This envoy had instructions to represent to the monarch of Blefuscu the great lenity of his master, who was content to punish me no further than with the loss of my eyes; that I had fled from justice and, if I did not return in two hours, I should be deprived of my title of *nardac* and declared a traitor. The envoy further added that in order to maintain the peace and amity between both empires his master expected that his brother of Blefuscu would give orders to have me sent back to Lilliput, bound hand and foot, to be punished as a traitor.

The Emperor of Blefuscu having taken three days to consult, returned an answer consisting of many civilities and excuses. He said that, as for sending me bound, his brother knew it was impossible; that although I had deprived him of his fleet, yet he owed great obligations to me for many good offices I had done him in making the peace. That, however, both their Majesties would soon be made easy, for I had found a prodigious vessel on the shore, able to carry me on the sea, which he had given order to fit up with my own assistance and direction; and he hoped in a few weeks both empires would be freed from so insupportable an incumbrance.

With this answer the envoy returned to Lilliput, and the monarch of Blefuscu related to me all that had passed, offering me at the same time (but under the strictest confidence) his gracious protection if I would continue in his service, wherein, although I believed him sincere, yet I resolved never more to put any confidence in princes or ministers where I could possibly avoid it; and therefore, with all due acknowledgments for his favorable intentions, I humbly begged to be excused. I told him, that since fortune, whether good or evil, had thrown a vessel in my way, I was resolved to venture myself in the ocean rather than be an occasion of difference between two such mighty monarchs. Neither did I find the Emperor at all displeased; and I discovered by a certain accident that he was very glad of my resolution, and so were most of his ministers.

These considerations moved me to hasten my departure somewhat sooner than I intended; to which the court, impatient to have me gone, very readily contributed. Five hundred workmen were employed to make two sails to my boat, according to my directions, by quilting thirteen fold of their strongest linen together. I was at the pains of making ropes and cables, by twisting ten, twenty, or thirty of the thickest and strongest of theirs. A great stone that I happened to find, after a long search by the seashore, served me for an anchor. I had the tallow of three hundred cows for greasing my boat and other uses. I was at incredible pains in cutting down some of the largest timber trees for oars and masts; wherein I was, however, much assisted by his Majesty's ship carpenters, who helped me in smoothing them, after I had done the rough work.

In about a month, when all was prepared, I sent to receive his Majesty's commands and to take my leave. The Emperor and royal family came out of the palace; I lay down on my face to kiss his hand, which he very graciously gave me; so did the Empress and young princes of the blood. His Majesty presented me with fifty purses of two hundred *sprugs* apiece, together with his picture at full length, which I put immediately into one of my gloves, to keep it from being hurt. The ceremonies at my departure were too many to trouble the reader with at this time.

I stored the boat with the carcasses of an hundred oxen and three hundred sheep, with bread and drink proportionable, and as much meat ready dressed as four hundred cooks could provide. I took with me six cows and two bulls alive, with as many ewes and rams, intending to carry them into my own country and propagate the breed. And to feed them on board, I had a good bundle of hay and a bag of corn. I would gladly have taken a dozen of the natives, but this was a thing the Emperor would by no means permit; and besides a diligent search into my pockets, his Majesty engaged my honor not to carry away any of his subjects, although with their own consent and desire.

Having thus prepared all things as well as I was able, I set sail on the twenty-fourth day of September, 1701, at six in the morning; and when I had gone about four leagues to the northward, the wind being at southeast, at six in the evening I descried a small island about half a league to the northwest. I advanced forward and cast anchor on the lee side of the island, which seemed to be uninhabited. I then took some refreshment and went to my rest. I slept well, and as I conjecture at least six hours, for I found the day broke in two hours after I awaked. It was a clear night; I eat my breakfast before the sun was up; and heaving anchor, the wind being favorable, I steered the same course that I had done the day before, wherein I was directed by my pocket compass. My intention was to reach, if possible, one of those islands which I had reason to believe lay to the northeast of Van Diemen's Land. I discovered nothing all that day; but upon the next, about three in the afternoon, when I had by my computation made twenty-four leagues from Blefuscu, I descried a sail steering to the southeast; my course was due east. I hailed her, but could get no answer; yet I found I gained upon her, for the wind slackened. I made all the sail I could, and in half an hour she spied me, then hung out her ancient[71] and discharged a gun. It is not easy to express the joy I was in upon the unexpected hope of once more seeing my beloved country and the dear pledges I had left in it. The ship slackened her sails, and I came up with her between five and six in the evening, September 26; but my heart leaped within me to see her English colors. I put my cows and sheep into my coat pockets, and got on board with all my little cargo of provisions. The vessel was an English merchantman, returning from Japan by the North and South Seas; the captain,

Mr. John Biddel of Deptford, a very civil man and an excellent sailor. We were now in the latitude of 30 degrees south; there were about fifty men in the ship; and here I met an old comrade of mine, one Peter Williams, who gave me a good character to the Captain. This gentleman treated me with kindness, and desired I would let him know what place I came from last and whither I was bound; which I did in a few words, but he thought I was raving, and that the dangers I underwent had disturbed my head; whereupon I took my black cattle[72] and sheep out of my pocket, which, after great astonishment, clearly convinced him of my veracity. I then showed him the gold given me by the Emperor of Blefuscu, together with his Majesty's picture at full length, and some other rarities of that country. I gave him two purses of two hundred *sprugs* each, and promised, when we arrived in England, to make him a present of a cow and a sheep big with young.

I shall not trouble the reader with a particular account of this voyage, which was very prosperous for the most part. We arrived in the Downs[73] on the 13th of April, 1702. I had only one misfortune, that the rats on board carried away one of my sheep; I found her bones in a hole, picked clean from the flesh. The rest of my cattle I got safe on shore, and set them a-grazing in a bowling green at Greenwich, where the fineness of the grass made them feed very heartily, although I had always feared the contrary. Neither could I possibly have preserved them in so long a voyage if the Captain had not allowed me some of his best biscuit, which, rubbed to powder and mingled with water, was their constant food. The short time I continued in England I made a considerable profit by showing my cattle to many persons of quality and others; and before I began my second voyage, I sold them for six hundred pounds. Since my last return I find the breed is considerably increased, especially the sheep; which I hope will prove much to the advantage of the woolen manufacture, by the fineness of the fleeces.

I stayed but two months with my wife and family, for my insatiable desire of seeing foreign countries would suffer me to continue no longer. I left fifteen hundred pounds with my wife, and fixed her in a good house at Redriff.[74] My remaining stock I carried with me, part in money and part in goods, in hopes to improve my fortunes. My eldest uncle,

---

71 Ensign.

72 "Black cattle" had come to mean cattle in general.
73 The famous roadstead off Deal and Sandwich on the coast of Kent.
74 Rotherhithe, on the south bank of the Thames, about a mile below London Bridge.

John, had left me an estate in land near Epping,[75] of about thirty pounds a year; and I had a long lease of the Black Bull[76] in Fetter Lane, which yielded me as much more; so that I was not in any danger of leaving my family upon the parish. My son Johnny, named so after his uncle, was at the grammar school, and a towardly child. My daughter Betty (who is now well married, and has children) was then at her needlework. I took leave of my wife and boy and girl with tears on both sides, and went on board the *Adventure,* a merchant-ship of three hundred tons, bound for Surat,[77] Captain John Nicholas of Liverpool, commander. But my account of this voyage must be referred to the second part of my travels.

The End of the First Part

from PART IV

A VOYAGE TO THE HOUYHNHNMS[1]

CHAPTER I

. . . The land was divided by long rows of trees, not regularly planted, but naturally growing; there was great plenty of grass, and several fields of oats. I walked very circumspectly for fear of being surprised, or suddenly shot with an arrow from behind or on either side. I fell into a beaten road, where I saw many tracks of human feet, and some of cows, but most of horses. At last I beheld several animals in a field, and one or two of the same kind sitting in trees. Their shape was very singular and deformed, which a little discomposed me, so that I lay down behind a thicket to observe them better. Some of them coming forward near the place where I lay, gave me an opportunity of distinctly marking their form. Their heads and breasts were covered with a thick hair, some frizzled and others lank; they had beards like goats, and a long ridge of hair down their backs and the fore-parts of their legs and feet, but the rest of their bodies were bare, so that I might see their skins, which were of a brown buff color. They had no tails, nor any hair at all on their buttocks, except about the anus; which, I presume, nature had placed there to defend them as they sat on the

ground; for this posture they used, as well as lying down, and often stood on their hind feet. They climbed high trees as nimbly as a squirrel, for they had strong extended claws before and behind, terminating in sharp points, and hooked. They would often spring and bound and leap with prodigious agility. The females were not so large as the males; they had long lank hair on their heads, but none on their faces, nor anything more than a sort of down on the rest of their bodies, except about the anus and pudenda. Their dugs hung between their forefeet and often reached almost to the ground as they walked. The hair of both sexes was of several colors, brown, red, black, and yellow. Upon the whole, I never beheld in all my travels so disagreeable an animal, nor one against which I naturally conceived so strong an antipathy. So that thinking I had seen enough, full of contempt and aversion, I got up and pursued the beaten road, hoping it might direct me to the cabin of some Indian. I had not got far when I met one of these creatures full in my way, and coming up directly to me. The ugly monster, when he saw me, distorted several ways every feature of his visage, and stared as at an object he had never seen before; then approaching nearer, lifted up his forepaw, whether out of curiosity or mischief I could not tell. But I drew my hanger[2] and gave him a good blow with the flat side of it, for I durst not strike him with the edge, fearing the inhabitants might be provoked against me if they should come to know that I had killed or maimed any of their cattle. When the beast felt the smart, he drew back and roared so loud that a herd of at least forty came flocking about me from the next field, howling and making odious faces; but I ran to the body of a tree, and leaning my back against it, kept them off by waving my hanger. Several of this cursed brood, getting hold of the branches behind, leapt up into the tree, from whence they began to discharge their excrements on my head; however, I escaped pretty well by sticking close to the stem of the tree, but was almost stifled with the filth, which fell about me on every side.

In the midst of this distress I observed them all to run away on a sudden as fast as they could, at which I ventured to leave the tree and pursue the road, wondering what it was that could put them into this fright. But looking on my left hand, I saw a horse walking softly in the field; which my persecutors having sooner discovered, was the cause of their flight. The horse started a little when he came near

---

[75] In Essex, about fifteen miles north of London.
[76] An imaginary tavern.
[77] In India, north of Bombay.
   [1] Pronounced *Whinnums.*—Gulliver's account of his fourth voyage and his arrival in the country of the Houyhnhnms precedes our excerpt.

[2] Short sword.

me, but soon recovering himself, looked full in my face with manifest tokens of wonder; he viewed my hands and feet, walking round me several times. I would have pursued my journey, but he placed himself directly in the way, yet looking with a very mild aspect, never offering the least violence. We stood gazing at each other for some time; at last I took the boldness to reach my hand towards his neck, with a design to stroke it, using the common style and whistle of jockeys when they are going to handle a strange horse. But this animal, seeming to receive my civilities with disdain, shook his head and bent his brows, softly raising up his right forefoot to remove my hand. Then he neighed three or four times, but in so different a cadence that I almost began to think he was speaking to himself in some language of his own.

While he and I were thus employed, another horse came up; who applying himself to the first in a very formal manner, they gently struck each other's right hoof before, neighing several times by turns, and varying the sound, which seemed to be almost articulate. They went some paces off, as if it were to confer together, walking side by side, backward and forward, like persons deliberating upon some affair of weight, but often turning their eyes towards me, as it were to watch that I might not escape. I was amazed to see such actions and behavior in brute beasts, and concluded with myself that if the inhabitants of this country were endued with a proportionable degree of reason, they must needs be the wisest people upon earth. This thought gave me so much comfort that I resolved to go forward until I could discover some house or village, or meet with any of the natives, leaving the two horses to discourse together as they pleased. But the first, who was a dapple gray, observing me to steal off, neighed after me in so expressive a tone that I fancied myself to understand what he meant; whereupon I turned back and came near him, to expect his farther commands, but concealing my fear as much as I could, for I began to be in some pain[3] how this adventure might terminate; and the reader will easily believe I did not much like my present situation.

The two horses came up close to me, looking with great earnestness upon my face and hands. The gray steed rubbed my hat all round with his right forehoof, and discomposed it so much that I was forced to adjust it better by taking it off and settling it again; whereat both he and his companion (who

was a brown bay) appeared to be much surprised; the latter felt the lappet of my coat, and finding it to hang loose about me, they both looked with new signs of wonder. He stroked my right hand, seeming to admire the softness and color; but he squeezed it so hard between his hoof and his pastern that I was forced to roar; after which they both touched me with all possible tenderness. They were under great perplexity about my shoes and stockings, which they felt very often, neighing to each other and using various gestures, not unlike those of a philosopher when he would attempt to solve some new and difficult phenomenon.

Upon the whole, the behavior of these animals was so orderly and rational, so acute and judicious, that I at last concluded they must needs be magicians who had thus metamorphosed themselves upon some design, and seeing a stranger in the way, were resolved to divert themselves with him; or perhaps were really amazed at the sight of a man so very different in habit, feature, and complexion from those who might probably live in so remote a climate. Upon the strength of this reasoning, I ventured to address them in the following manner: "Gentlemen, if you be conjurers, as I have good cause to believe, you can understand any language; therefore I make bold to let your worships know that I am a poor distressed Englishman, driven by his misfortunes upon your coast, and I entreat one of you to let me ride upon his back, as if he were a real horse, to some house or village where I can be relieved. In return of which favor I will make you a present of this knife and bracelet" (taking them out of my pocket). The two creatures stood silent while I spoke, seeming to listen with great attention; and when I had ended, they neighed frequently towards each other, as if they were engaged in serious conversation. I plainly observed that their language expressed the passions very well, and the words might with little pains be resolved into an alphabet more easily than the Chinese.

I could frequently distinguish the word *Yahoo*, which was repeated by each of them several times; and although it was impossible for me to conjecture what it meant, yet while the two horses were busy in conversation I endeavored to practice this word upon my tongue; and as soon as they were silent I boldly pronounced *Yahoo* in a loud voice, imitating, at the same time, as near as I could, the neighing of a horse; at which they were both visibly surprised, and the gray repeated the same word twice, as if he meant to teach me the right accent, wherein I spoke after him as well as I could, and found myself

---

[3] Anxiety.

perceivably to improve every time, though very far from any degree of perfection. Then the bay tried me with a second word, much harder to be pronounced; but reducing it to the English orthography, may be spelt thus, *Houyhnhnm.* I did not succeed in this so well as the former, but after two or three farther trials, I had better fortune; and they both appeared amazed at my capacity.

After some further discourse, which I then conjectured might relate to me, the two friends took their leaves, with the same compliment of striking each other's hoof; and the gray made me signs that I should walk before him, wherein I thought it prudent to comply, till I could find a better director. When I offered to slacken my pace, he would cry "Hhuun Hhuun"; I guessed his meaning, and gave him to understand as well as I could that I was weary and not able to walk faster; upon which he would stand a while to let me rest. . . .[4]

CHAPTER 5

The Author, at his master's command, informs him of the state of England. The causes of war among the princes of Europe. The Author begins to explain the English constitution.

The reader may please to observe that the following extract of many conversations I had with my master contains a summary of the most material points which were discoursed at several times for above two years; his Honor often desiring fuller satisfaction as I farther improved in the Houyhnhnm tongue. I laid before him, as well as I could, the whole state of Europe; I discoursed of trade and manufactures, of arts and sciences; and the answers I gave to all the questions he made, as they arose upon several subjects, were a fund of conversation not to be exhausted. But I shall here only set down the substance of what passed between us concerning my own country, reducing it into order as well as I can, without any regard to time or other circumstances, while I strictly adhere to truth. My only concern is that I shall hardly be able to do justice to my master's arguments and expressions, which must needs suffer by my want of capacity, as well as by a translation into our barbarous English.

In obedience therefore to his Honor's commands, I related to him the Revolution under the Prince of Orange; the long war with France entered into by the said prince, and renewed by his successor the present Queen, wherein the greatest powers of Christendom were engaged, and which still continued: I computed at his request that about a million of Yahoos might have been killed in the whole progress of it, and perhaps a hundred or more cities taken, and thrice as many ships burnt or sunk.

He asked me what were the usual causes or motives that made one country go to war with another. I answered they were innumerable, but I should only mention a few of the chief. Sometimes the ambition of princes, who never think they have land or people enough to govern; sometimes the corruption of ministers, who engage their master in a war in order to stifle or divert the clamor of the subjects against their evil administration. Difference in opinions hath cost many millions of lives: for instance, whether flesh be bread, or bread be flesh; whether the juice of a certain berry be blood or wine; whether whistling be a vice or a virtue; whether it be better to kiss a post, or throw it into the fire; what is the best color for a coat, whether black, white, red, or gray; and whether it should be long or short, narrow or wide, dirty or clean; with many more. Neither are any wars so furious and bloody, or of so long continuance, as those occasioned by difference in opinion, especially if it be in things indifferent.

Sometimes the quarrel between two princes is to decide which of them shall dispossess a third of his dominions, where neither of them pretend to any right. Sometimes one prince quarreleth with another, for fear the other should quarrel with him. Sometimes a war is entered upon because the enemy is too strong, and sometimes because he is too weak. Sometimes our neighbors want the things which we have, or have the things which we want; and we both fight, till they take ours or give us theirs. It is a very justifiable cause of a war to invade a country after the people have been wasted by famine, destroyed by pestilence, or embroiled by factions among themselves. It is justifiable to enter into war against our nearest ally, when one of his towns lies convenient for us, or a territory of land, that would render our dominions round and complete. If a prince sends forces into a nation where the people are poor and ignorant, he may lawfully put half of them to death, and make slaves of the rest, in order to civilize and reduce them from their barbarous way of living. It is a very kingly, honorable, and

---

4 Gulliver soon learns that the horses are the rulers of the country. He becomes a member of the household of the Houyhnhnm who has found him; there his admiration for the noble horses and his detestation of the subject Yahoos (only too closely resembling his fellow Europeans, whom he comes to think of as Yahoos) steadily increase.

frequent practice, when one prince desires the assistance of another to secure him against an invasion, that the assistant, when he hath driven out the invader, should seize on the dominions himself, and kill, imprison, or banish the prince he came to relieve. Alliance by blood or marriage is a frequent cause of war between princes; and the nearer the kindred is, the greater is their disposition to quarrel. Poor nations are hungry, and rich nations are proud; and pride and hunger will ever be at variance. For these reasons, the trade of a soldier is held the most honorable of all others; because a soldier is a Yahoo hired to kill in cold blood as many of his own species, who have never offended him, as possibly he can.

There is likewise a kind of beggarly princes in Europe, not able to make war by themselves, who hire out their troops to richer nations, for so much a day to each man; of which they keep three fourths to themselves, and it is the best part of their maintenance; such are those in Germany and other northern parts of Europe.

"What you have told me," said my master, "upon the subject of war, does indeed discover most admirably the effects of that reason you pretend to: however, it is happy that the shame is greater than the danger; and that nature hath left you utterly uncapable of doing much mischief.

"For your mouths lying flat with your faces, you can hardly bite each other to any purpose, unless by consent. Then as to the claws upon your feet before and behind, they are so short and tender that one of our Yahoos would drive a dozen of yours before him. And therefore in recounting the numbers of those who have been killed in battle, I cannot but think that you have *said the thing which is not*."[5]

I could not forbear shaking my head and smiling a little at his ignorance. And being no stranger to the art of war, I gave him a description of cannons, culverins, muskets, carabines, pistols, bullets, powder, swords, bayonets, battles, sieges, retreats, attacks, undermines, countermines, bombardments, sea fights; ships sunk with a thousand men, twenty thousand killed on each side; dying groans, limbs flying in the air, smoke, noise, confusion, trampling to death under horses' feet; flight, pursuit, victory; fields strewed with carcasses left for food to dogs and wolves and birds of prey; plundering, stripping, ravishing, burning, and destroying. And to set

forth the valor of my own dear countrymen, I assured him that I had seen them blow up a hundred enemies at once in a siege, and as many in a ship, and beheld the dead bodies come down in pieces from the clouds, to the great diversion of the spectators.

I was going on to more particulars, when my master commanded me silence. He said whoever understood the nature of Yahoos might easily believe it possible for so vile an animal to be capable of every action I had named, if their strength and cunning equaled their malice. But as my discourse had increased his abhorrence of the whole species, so he found it gave him a disturbance in his mind, to which he was wholly a stranger before. He thought his ears being used to such abominable words, might by degrees admit them with less detestation. That although he hated the Yahoos of this country, yet he no more blamed them for their odious qualities than he did a *gnnayh* (a bird of prey) for its cruelty, or a sharp stone for cutting his hoof. But when a creature pretending to reason could be capable of such enormities, he dreaded lest the corruption of that faculty might be worse than brutality itself. He seemed therefore confident that instead of reason we were only possessed of some quality fitted to increase our natural vices; as the reflection from a troubled stream returns the image of an ill-shapen body not only larger but more distorted.

He added that he had heard too much upon the subject of war, both in this and some former discourses. There was another point which a little perplexed him at present. I had informed him, that some of our crew left their country on account of being ruined by *Law;* that I had already explained the meaning of the word; but he was at a loss how it should come to pass that the law, which was intended for every man's preservation, should be any man's ruin. Therefore he desired to be farther satisfied what I meant by law, and the dispensers thereof, according to the present practice in my own country; because he thought nature and reason were sufficient guides for a reasonable animal, as we pretended to be, in showing us what we ought to do and what to avoid.

I assured his Honor that law was a science wherein I had not much conversed, further than by employing advocates, in vain, upon some injustices that had been done me: however, I would give him all the satisfaction I was able.

I said there was a society of men among us, bred up from their youth in the art of proving by words multiplied for the purpose that white is black, and

---

[5] The Houyhnhnms' language has no verb meaning "to tell a lie," since lying is unknown among them. Hence Gulliver's master resorts to this periphrasis.

black is white, according as they are paid. To this society all the rest of the people are slaves. For example, if my neighbor hath a mind to my cow, he hires a lawyer to prove that he ought to have my cow from me. I must then hire another to defend my right, it being against all rules of law that any man should be allowed to speak for himself. Now in this case I who am the right owner lie under two great disadvantages. First, my lawyer, being practiced almost from his cradle in defending falsehood, is quite out of his element when he would be an advocate for justice, which as an office unnatural, he always attempts with ill will. The second disadvantage is that my lawyer must proceed with great caution, or else he will be reprimanded by the judges, and abhorred by his brethren, as one that would lessen the practice of the law. And therefore I have but two methods to preserve my cow. The first is to gain over my adversary's lawyer with a double fee, who will then betray his client by insinuating that he hath justice on his side. The second way is for my lawyer to make my cause appear as unjust as he can, by allowing the cow to belong to my adversary: and this, if it be skillfully done, will certainly bespeak the favor of the bench.

Now, your Honor is to know that these judges are persons appointed to decide all controversies of property, as well as for the trial of criminals, and picked out from the most dexterous lawyers, who are grown old or lazy, and having been biased all their lives against truth and equity, are under such a fatal necessity of favoring fraud, perjury, and oppression that I have known several of them refuse a large bribe from the side where justice lay, rather than injure the faculty by doing anything unbecoming their nature or their office.

It is a maxim among these lawyers, that whatever hath been done before may legally be done again: and therefore they take special care to record all the decisions formerly made against common justice and the general reason of mankind. These, under the name of *precedents,* they produce as authorities, to justify the most iniquitous opinions; and the judges never fail of directing accordingly.

In pleading they studiously avoid entering into the merits of the cause, but are loud, violent, and tedious in dwelling upon all circumstances which are not to the purpose. For instance, in the case already mentioned, they never desire to know what claim or title my adversary hath to my cow; but whether the said cow were red or black, her horns long or short, whether the field I graze her in be round or square, whether she was milked at home

or abroad, what diseases she is subject to, and the like; after which they consult precedents, adjourn the cause from time to time, and in ten, twenty, or thirty years come to an issue.

It is likewise to be observed, that this society hath a peculiar cant and jargon of their own that no other mortal can understand, and wherein all their laws are written, which they take special care to multiply; whereby they have wholly confounded the very essence of truth and falsehood, of right and wrong; so that it will take thirty years to decide whether the field left me by my ancestors for six generations belongs to me or to a stranger three hundred miles off.

In the trial of persons accused for crimes against the state the method is much more short and commendable: the judge first sends to sound the disposition of those in power, after which he can easily hang or save the criminal, strictly preserving all due forms of law.

Here my master, interposing, said it was a pity that creatures endowed with such prodigious abilities of mind as these lawyers, by the description I gave of them, must certainly be, were not rather encouraged to be instructors of others in wisdom and knowledge. In answer to which I assured his Honor that in all points out of their own trade they were the most ignorant and stupid generation among us, the most despicable in common conversation, avowed enemies to all knowledge and learning, and equally disposed to pervert the general reason of mankind in every other subject of discourse as in that of their own profession.

CHAPTER 6

A continuation of the state of England under Queen Anne. The character of a first minister in the courts of Europe.

My master was yet wholly at a loss to understand what motives could incite this race of lawyers to perplex, disquiet, and weary themselves, and engage in a confederacy of injustice, merely for the sake of injuring their fellow animals; neither could he comprehend what I meant in saying they did it for hire. Whereupon I was at much pains to describe to him the use of money, the materials it was made of, and the value of the metals; that when a Yahoo had got a great store of this precious substance, he was able to purchase whatever he had a mind to— the finest clothing, the noblest houses, great tracts of land, the most costly meats and drinks—and have his choice of the most beautiful females. Therefore since money alone was able to perform all these feats, our Yahoos thought they could never have enough of it to spend or save, as they found themselves inclined from their natural bent either to profusion or avarice. That the rich man enjoyed the fruit of the poor man's labor, and the latter were a thousand to one in proportion to the former. That the bulk of our people were forced to live miserably by laboring every day for small wages to make a few live plentifully. I enlarged myself much on these and many other particulars to the same purpose; but his Honor was still to seek;[6] for he went upon a supposition that all animals had a title to their share in the productions of the earth, and especially those who presided over the rest. Therefore he desired I would let him know what these costly meats were, and how any of us happened to want them. Whereupon I enumerated as many sorts as came into my head, with the various methods of dressing them, which could not be done without sending vessels by sea to every part of the world, as well for liquors to drink as for sauces and innumerable other conveniences. I assured him that this whole globe of earth must be at least three times gone round before one of our better female Yahoos could get her breakfast or a cup to put it in. He said that must needs be a miserable country which cannot furnish food for its own inhabitants. But what he chiefly wondered at, was how such vast tracts of ground as I described should be wholly without fresh water, and the people put to the necessity of sending over the sea for drink. I replied that England (the dear place of my nativity) was computed to produce three times the quantity of food, more than its inhabitants are able to consume, as well as liquors extracted from grain, or pressed out of the fruit of certain trees, which made excellent drink, and the same proportion in every other convenience of life. But in order to feed the luxury and intemperance of the males and the vanity of the females, we sent away the greatest part of our necessary things to other countries, from whence in return we brought the materials of diseases, folly, and vice, to spend among ourselves. Hence it follows of necessity that vast numbers of our people are compelled to seek their livelihood by begging, robbing, stealing, cheating, pimping, forswearing, flattering, suborning, forging, gaming, lying, fawning, hectoring, voting, scribbling, stargazing, poisoning, whoring, canting, libeling, freethinking, and the like occupations: every one of which terms I was at much pains to make him understand.

That wine was not imported among us from foreign countries to supply the want of water or other drinks, but because it was a sort of liquid which made us merry by putting us out of our senses, diverted all melancholy thoughts, begat wild extravagant imaginations in the brain, raised our hopes and banished our fears, suspended every office of reason for a time, and deprived us of the use of our limbs, till we fell into a profound sleep; although it must be confessed that we always awaked sick and dispirited and that the use of this liquor filled us with diseases, which made our lives uncomfortable and short.

But beside all this, the bulk of our people supported themselves by furnishing the necessities or conveniences of life to the rich, and to each other. For instance, when I am at home and dressed as I ought to be, I carry on my body the workmanship of an hundred tradesmen; the building and furniture of my house employ as many more, and five times the number to adorn my wife. . . .[7]

I had formerly upon occasion discoursed with my master upon the nature of government in general, and particularly of our own excellent constitution, deservedly the wonder and envy of the whole world. But having here accidentally mentioned a minister of state, he commanded me some time after to inform him what species of Yahoo I particularly meant by that appellation.

I told him that a first or chief minister of state, who was the person I intended to describe, was a creature wholly exempt from joy and grief, love and hatred, pity and anger; at least made use of no other passions but a violent desire of wealth, power, and titles; that he applies his words to all uses, except to the indication of his mind; that he never tells a truth but with an intent that you should take it for a lie; nor a lie but with a design that you should take it for a truth; that those he speaks worst of behind their backs are in the surest way of preferment; and whenever he begins to praise you to others or to yourself, you are from that day forlorn. The worst mark you can receive is a promise, especially when it is confirmed with an oath; after which every wise man retires, and gives over all hopes.

There are three methods by which a man may rise to be chief minister: the first is by knowing how with prudence to dispose of a wife, a daughter, or a sister; the second, by betraying or undermining his predecessor; and the third is by a furious zeal in public assemblies against the corruptions of the

---

[6] I.e., wanted still more information.

[7] Gulliver next describes the diseases to which the Europeans are subject and pays his respects to the medical profession.

court. But a wise prince would rather choose to employ those who practice the last of these methods, because such zealots prove always the most obsequious and subservient to the will and passions of their master. That these ministers, having all employments at their disposal, preserve themselves in power by bribing the majority of a senate or great council; and at last, by an expedient called an act of indemnity (whereof I described the nature to him), they secure themselves from after-reckonings, and retire from the public, laden with the spoils of the nation.

The palace of a chief minister is a seminary to breed up others in his own trade: the pages, lackeys, and porter, by imitating their master, become ministers of state in their several districts, and learn to excel in the three principal ingredients, of insolence, lying, and bribery. Accordingly they have a subaltern court paid to them by persons of the best rank, and sometimes by the force of dexterity and impudence arrive through several gradations to be successors to their lord.

He is usually governed by a decayed wench or favorite footman, who are the tunnels through which all graces are conveyed, and may properly be called, in the last resort, the governors of the kingdom. . . .

CHAPTER 7

The Author's great love of his native country. His master's observations upon the constitution and administration of England, as described by the Author, with parallel cases and comparisons. His master's observations upon human nature.

The reader may be disposed to wonder how I could prevail on myself to give so free a representation of my own species, among a race of mortals who were already too apt to conceive the vilest opinion of humankind, from that entire congruity betwixt me and their Yahoos. But I must freely confess that the many virtues of those excellent quadrupeds, placed in opposite view to human corruptions, had so far opened my eyes and enlarged my understanding that I began to view the actions and passions of man in a very different light, and to think the honor of my own kind not worth managing; which, besides, it was impossible for me to do before a person of so acute a judgment as my master, who daily convinced me of a thousand faults in myself, whereof I had not the least perception before, and which among us would never be numbered even among human infirmities. I had likewise learned from his example

an utter detestation of all falsehood or disguise, and truth appeared so amiable to me that I determined upon sacrificing everything to it.

Let me deal so candidly with the reader as to confess that there was yet a much stronger motive for the freedom I took in my representation of things. I had not been a year in this country before I contracted such a love and veneration for the inhabitants that I entered on a firm resolution never to return to humankind, but to pass the rest of my life among these admirable Houyhnhnms in the contemplation and practice of every virtue; where I could have no example or incitement to vice. But it was decreed by fortune, my perpetual enemy, that so great a felicity should not fall to my share. However, it is now some comfort to reflect that in what I said of my countrymen I extenuated their faults as much as I durst before so strict an examiner, and upon every article gave as favorable a turn as the matter would bear. For indeed who is there alive that will not be swayed by his bias and partiality to the place of his birth?

I have related the substance of several conversations I had with my master, during the greatest part of the time I had the honor to be in his service, but have indeed for brevity's sake omitted much more than is here set down.

When I had answered all his questions, and his curiosity seemed to be fully satisfied, he sent for me one morning early, and commanding me to sit down at some distance (an honor which he had never before conferred upon me), he said he had been very seriously considering my whole story, as far as it related both to myself and my country; that he looked upon us as a sort of animals to whose share, by what accident he could not conjecture, some small pittance of reason had fallen, whereof we made no other use than by its assistance to aggravate our natural corruptions and to acquire new ones which nature had not given us. That we disarmed ourselves of the few abilities she had bestowed, had been very successful in multiplying our original wants, and seemed to spend our whole lives in vain endeavors to supply them by our own inventions. That as to myself, it was manifest I had neither the strength nor agility of a common Yahoo, that I walked infirmly on my hinder feet, had found out a contrivance to make my claws of no use or defence, and to remove the hair from my chin, which was intended as a shelter from the sun and the weather. Lastly, that I could neither run with speed, nor climb trees like my brethren (as he called them) the Yahoos in this country.

That our institutions of government and law were plainly owing to our gross defects in reason and, by consequence, in virtue; because reason alone is sufficient to govern a rational creature; which was therefore a character we had no pretence to challenge, even from the account I had given of my own people; although he manifestly perceived that in order to favor them I had concealed many particulars and often *said the thing which was not.*

He was the more confirmed in this opinion because he observed that as I agreed in every feature of my body with other Yahoos, except where it was to my real disadvantage in point of strength, speed, and activity, the shortness of my claws, and some other particulars where nature had no part; so from the representation I had given him of our lives, our manners, and our actions, he found as near a resemblance in the disposition of our minds. He said the Yahoos were known to hate one another more than they did any different species of animals; and the reason usually assigned was the odiousness of their own shapes, which all could see in the rest, but not in themselves. He had therefore begun to think it not unwise in us to cover our bodies, and by that invention conceal many of our own deformities from each other, which would else be hardly supportable. But he now found he had been mistaken, and that the dissensions of those brutes in his country were owing to the same cause with ours, as I had described them. For if (said he) you throw among five Yahoos as much food as would be sufficient for fifty, they will, instead of eating peaceably, fall together by the ears, each single one impatient to have all to itself; and therefore a servant was usually employed to stand by while they were feeding abroad, and those kept at home were tied at a distance from each other: that if a cow died of age or accident, before a Houyhnhnm could secure it for his own Yahoos, those in the neighborhood would come in herds to seize it, and then would ensue such a battle as I had described, with terrible wounds made by their claws on both sides, although they seldom were able to kill one another, for want of such convenient instruments of death as we had invented. At other times the like battles have been fought between the Yahoos of several neighborhoods without any visible cause; those of one district watching all opportunities to surprise the next before they are prepared. But if they find their project hath miscarried, they return home, and, for want of enemies, engage in what I call a civil war among themselves.

That in some fields of his country there are certain shining stones of several colors, whereof the Yahoos are violently fond, and when part of these stones is fixed in the earth, as it sometimes happeneth, they will dig with their claws for whole days to get them out, then carry them away, and hide them by heaps in their kennels; but still looking round with great caution, for fear their comrades should find out their treasure. My master said he could never discover the reason of this unnatural appetite, or how these stones could be of any use to a Yahoo; but now he believed it might proceed from the same principle of avarice which I had ascribed to mankind: that he had once, by way of experiment, privately removed a heap of these stones from the place where one of his Yahoos had buried it: whereupon the sordid animal missing his treasure, by his loud lamenting brought the whole herd to the place, there miserably howled, then fell to biting and tearing the rest, began to pine away, would neither eat nor sleep nor work, till he ordered a servant privately to convey the stones into the same hole and hide them as before; which when his Yahoo had found, he presently recovered his spirits and good humor, but took good care to remove them to a better hiding-place, and hath ever since been a very serviceable brute.

My master farther assured me, which I also observed myself, that in the fields where these shining stones abound, the fiercest and most frequent battles are fought, occasioned by perpetual inroads of the neighboring Yahoos.

He said it was common when two Yahoos discovered such a stone in a field, and were contending which of them should be the proprietor, a third would take the advantage, and carry it away from them both; which my master would needs contend to have some kind of resemblance with our suits at law; wherein I thought it for our credit not to undeceive him; since the decision he mentioned was much more equitable than many decrees among us; because the plaintiff and defendant there lost nothing beside the stone they contended for, whereas our courts of equity would never have dismissed the cause while either of them had anything left.

My master, continuing his discourse, said there was nothing that rendered the Yahoos more odious than their undistinguishing appetite to devour everything that came in their way, whether herbs, roots, berries, the corrupted flesh of animals, or all mingled together; and it was peculiar in their temper that they were fonder of what they could get by rapine or stealth at a greater distance than much better food provided for them at home. If their prey held out, they would eat till they were ready to burst, after which nature had pointed out to them a certain root that gave them a general evacuation.

There was also another kind of root very juicy, but somewhat rare and difficult to be found, which the Yahoos sought for with much eagerness, and would suck it with great delight; and it produced in them the same effects that wine hath upon us. It would make them sometimes hug and sometimes tear one another; they would howl and grin, and chatter, and reel, and tumble, and then fall asleep in the dirt.

I did indeed observe that the Yahoos were the only animals in this country subject to any diseases; which, however, were much fewer than horses have among us, and contracted not by any ill treatment they meet with but by the nastiness and greediness of that sordid brute. Neither has their language any more than a general appellation for those maladies, which is borrowed from the name of the beast, and called *Hnea-Yahoo,* or the *Yahoo's evil,* and the cure prescribed is a mixture of their own dung and urine forcibly put down the Yahoo's throat. This I have since often known to have been taken with success, and do freely recommend it to my countrymen, for the public good, as an admirable specific against all diseases produced by repletion.

As to learning, government, arts, manufactures, and the like, my master confessed he could find little or no resemblance between the Yahoos of that country and those in ours. For he only meant to observe what parity there was in our natures. He had heard indeed some curious Houyhnhnms observe that in most herds there was a sort of ruling Yahoo (as among us there is generally some leading or principal stag in a park), who was always more deformed in body and mischievous in disposition than any of the rest. That this leader had usually a favorite as like himself as he could get, whose employment was to lick his master's feet and posteriors, and drive the female Yahoos to his kennel; for which he was now and then rewarded with a piece of ass's flesh. This favorite is hated by the whole herd, and therefore to protect himself keeps always near the person of his leader. He usually continues in office till a worse can be found; but the very moment he is discarded, his successor, at the head of all the Yahoos in that district, young and old, male and female, come in a body, and discharge their excrements upon him from head to foot. But how far this might be applicable to our courts and favorites and ministers of state, my master said I could best determine.

I durst make no return to this malicious insinuation, which debased human understanding below the sagacity of a common hound, who has judgment enough to distinguish and follow the cry of the ablest dog in the pack, without being ever mistaken. . . .

CHAPTER 8

. . . Having lived three years in this country, the reader I suppose will expect that I should, like other travelers, give him some account of the manners and customs of its inhabitants, which it was indeed my principal study to learn.

As these noble Houyhnhnms are endowed by nature with a general disposition to all virtues, and have no conceptions or ideas of what is evil in a rational creature, so their grand maxim is to cultivate reason and to be wholly governed by it. Neither is reason among them a point problematical as with us, where men can argue with plausibility on both sides of the question; but strikes you with immediate conviction; as it must needs do where it is not mingled, obscured, or discolored by passion and interest. I remember it was with extreme difficulty that I could bring my master to understand the meaning of the word *opinion,* or how a point could be disputable; because reason taught us to affirm or deny only where we are certain, and beyond our knowledge we cannot do either. So that controversies, wranglings, disputes, and positiveness in false or dubious propositions are evils unknown among the Houyhnhnms. In the like manner when I used to explain to him our several systems of natural philosophy, he would laugh that a creature pretending to reason should value itself upon the knowledge of other people's conjectures, and in things where that knowledge, if it were certain, could be of no use. Wherein he agreed entirely with the sentiments of Socrates, as Plato delivers them; which I mention as the highest honor I can do that prince of philosophers. I have often since reflected what destruction such a doctrine would make in the libraries of Europe, and how many paths to fame would be then shut up in the learned world.

Friendship and benevolence are the two principal virtues among the Houyhnhnms, and these not confined to particular objects, but universal to the whole race. For a stranger from the remotest part is equally treated with the nearest neighbor, and wherever he goes looks upon himself as at home. They preserve decency and civility in the highest degrees, but are altogether ignorant of ceremony. They have no fondness for their colts or foals, but the care they take in educating them proceeds entirely from the dictates of reason. And I observed my master to show the same affection to his neighbor's issue that he had for his own. They will have it that nature teaches them to love the whole species, and it is reason only that maketh a distinction of persons where there is a superior degree of virtue.

When the matron Houyhnhnms have produced one of each sex, they no longer accompany with their consorts, except they lose one of their issue by some casualty, which very seldom happens; but in such a case they meet again; or when the like accident befalls a person whose wife is past bearing, some other couple bestow him one of their own colts, and then go together again till the mother is pregnant. This caution is necessary to prevent the country from being over-burthened with numbers. But the race of inferior Houyhnhnms bred up to be servants is not so strictly limited upon this article; these are allowed to produce three of each sex, to be domestics in the noble families.

In their marriages they are exactly careful to choose such colors as will not make any disagreeable mixture in the breed. Strength is chiefly valued in the male, and comeliness in the female; not upon the account of love, but to preserve the race from degenerating; for where a female happens to excel in strength, a consort is chosen with regard to comeliness. Courtship, love, presents, jointures, settlements, have no place in their thoughts, or terms whereby to express them in their language. The young couple meet and are joined, merely because it is the determination of their parents and friends; it is what they see done every day, and they look upon it as one of the necessary actions of a rational being. But the violation of marriage, or any other unchastity, was never heard of; and the married pair pass their lives with the same friendship and mutual benevolence that they bear to all others of the same species who come in their way; without jealousy, fondness, quarreling, or discontent.

In educating the youth of both sexes, their method is admirable, and highly deserves our imitation. These are not suffered to taste a grain of oats, except upon certain days, till eighteen years old; nor milk, but very rarely; and in summer they graze two hours in the morning, and as long in the evening, which their parents likewise observe; but the servants are not allowed above half that time, and a great part of their grass is brought home, which they eat at the most convenient hours, when they can be best spared from work.

Temperance, industry, exercise, and cleanliness are the lessons equally enjoined to the young ones of both sexes; and my master thought it monstrous in us to give the females a different kind of education from the males, except in some articles of domestic management; whereby, as he truly observed, one half of our natives were good for nothing but bringing children into the world; and to trust the care of our children to such useless animals, he said, was yet a greater instance of brutality.

But the Houyhnhnms train up their youth to strength, speed, and hardiness, by exercising them in running races up and down steep hills, and over hard stony grounds; and when they are all in a sweat, they are ordered to leap over head and ears into a pond or river. Four times a year the youth of a certain district meet to show their proficiency in running and leaping, and other feats of strength and agility; where the victor is rewarded with a song made in his or her praise. On this festival the servants drive a herd of Yahoos into the field, laden with hay and oats and milk, for a repast to the Houyhnhnms; after which these brutes are immediately driven back again, for fear of being noisome to the assembly.

Every fourth year, at the vernal equinox, there is a representative council of the whole nation, which meets in a plain about twenty miles from our house, and continues about five or six days. Here they enquire into the state and condition of the several districts; whether they abound or be deficient in hay or oats, or cows or Yahoos. And wherever there is any want (which is but seldom) it is immediately supplied by unanimous consent and contribution. Here likewise the regulation of children is settled: as for instance, if a Houyhnhnm hath two males, he changeth one of them with another that hath two females; and when a child hath been lost by any casualty, where the mother is past breeding, it is determined what family in the district shall breed another to supply the loss.

CHAPTER 9

. . . The Houyhnhnms have no letters, and consequently their knowledge is all traditional. But there happening few events of any moment among a people so well united, naturally disposed to every virtue, wholly governed by reason, and cut off from all commerce with other nations, the historical part is easily preserved without burthening their memories. I have already observed that they are subject to no diseases, and therefore can have no need of physicians. However, they have excellent medicines composed of herbs, to cure accidental bruises and cuts in the pastern or frog of the foot by sharp stones, as well as other maims and hurts in the several parts of the body.

They calculate the year by the revolution of the sun and the moon, but use no subdivisions into weeks. They are well enough acquainted with the motions of those two luminaries, and understand the nature of eclipses; and this is the utmost progress of their astronomy.

In poetry they must be allowed to excel all other mortals; wherein the justness of their similes and the minuteness, as well as exactness, of their descriptions are indeed inimitable. Their verses abound very much in both of these, and usually contain either some exalted notions of friendship and benevolence, or the praises of those who were victors in races and other bodily exercises. Their buildings, although very rude and simple, are not inconvenient, but well contrived to defend them from all injuries of cold and heat. They have a kind of tree which at forty years old loosens in the root and falls with the first storm; they grow very straight, and being pointed like stakes with a sharp stone (for the Houyhnhnms know not the use of iron), they stick them erect in the ground about ten inches asunder, and then weave in oat straw, or sometimes wattles, betwixt them. The roof is made after the same manner, and so are the doors.

The Houyhnhnms use the hollow part between the pastern and the hoof of their forefeet as we do our hands, and this with greater dexterity than I could at first imagine. I have seen a white mare of our family thread a needle (which I lent her on purpose) with that joint. They milk their cows, reap their oats, and do all the work which requires hands, in the same manner. They have a kind of hard flints, which by grinding against other stones they form into instruments that serve instead of wedges, axes, and hammers. With tools made of these flints they likewise cut their hay and reap their oats, which there groweth naturally in several fields; the Yahoos draw home the sheaves in carriages, and the servants tread them in certain covered huts, to get out the grain, which is kept in stores. They make a rude kind of earthen and wooden vessels, and bake the former in the sun.

If they can avoid casualties, they die only of old age, and are buried in the obscurest places that can be found, their friends and relations expressing neither joy nor grief at their departure; nor does the dying person discover the least regret that he is leaving the world, any more than if he were upon returning home from a visit to one of his neighbors. I remember my master having once made an appointment with a friend and his family to come to his house upon some affair of importance, on the day fixed the mistress and her two children came very late; she made two excuses, first for her husband, who, as she said, happened that very morning to *shnuwnh*. The word is strongly expressive in their language, but not easily rendered into English; it signifies, *to retire to his first mother*. Her excuse for not coming sooner was that her husband dying late in the morning, she was a good while consulting her servants about a convenient place where his body should be laid; and I observed she behaved herself at our house as cheerfully as the rest, and died about three months after.

They live generally to seventy or seventy-five years, very seldom to fourscore: some weeks before their death they feel a gradual decay, but without pain. During this time they are much visited by their friends, because they cannot go abroad with their usual ease and satisfaction. However, about ten days before their death, which they seldom fail in computing, they return the visits that have been made them by those who are nearest in the neighborhood, being carried in a convenient sledge drawn by Yahoos; which vehicle they use, not only upon this occasion, but when they grow old, upon long journeys, or when they are lamed by any accident. And therefore when the dying Houyhnhnms return those visits, they take a solemn leave of their friends, as if they were going to some remote part of the country, where they designed to pass the rest of their lives.

I know not whether it may be worth observing that the Houyhnhnms have no word in their language to express anything that is evil, except what they borrow from the deformities or ill qualities of the Yahoos. Thus they denote the folly of a servant, an omission of a child, a stone that cuts their feet, a continuance of foul or unseasonable weather, and the like, by adding to each the epithet of *Yahoo*. For instance, *Hhnm Yahoo, Whnaholm Yahoo, Ynlhmndwihlma Yahoo*, and an ill-contrived house *Ynholmhnmrohlnw Yahoo*.

I could with great pleasure enlarge further upon the manners and virtues of this excellent people; but intending in a short time to publish a volume by itself expressly upon that subject, I refer the reader thither, and in the meantime proceed to relate my own sad catastrophe.

The Author's economy, and happy life among the Houyhnhnms. His great improvement in virtue, by conversing with them. Their conversations. The Author has notice given him by his master that he must depart from the country. He falls into a swoon for grief, but submits. He contrives and finishes a canoe, by the help of a fellow-servant, and puts to sea at a venture.

I had settled my little economy to my own heart's content. My master had ordered a room to be made for me after their manner, about six yards from the house, the sides and floors of which I plastered with clay and covered with rush-mats of my own contriving. I had beaten hemp, which there grows wild, and made of it a sort of ticking; this I filled with the feathers of several birds I had taken with springes made of Yahoos' hairs, and were excellent food. I had worked two chairs with my knife, the sorrel nag helping me in the grosser and more laborious part. When my clothes were worn to rags, I made myself others with the skins of rabbits and of a certain beautiful animal about the same size, called *nnuhnoh,* the skin of which is covered with a fine down. Of these I likewise made very tolerable stockings. I soled my shoes with wood which I cut from a tree and fitted to the upper leather, and when this was worn out I supplied it with the skins of Yahoos dried in the sun. I often got honey out of hollow trees, which I mingled with water, or ate with my bread. No man could more verify the truth of these two maxims, that "nature is very easily satisfied," and that "necessity is the mother of invention." I enjoyed perfect health of body and tranquillity of mind; I did not feel the treachery or inconstancy of a friend, nor the injuries of a secret or open enemy. I had no occasion of bribing, flattering, or pimping to procure the favor of any great man or of his minion. I wanted no fence against fraud or oppression; here was neither physician to destroy my body, nor lawyer to ruin my fortune; no informer to watch my words and actions, or forge accusations against me for hire; here were no gibers, censurers, backbiters, pickpockets, highwaymen, housebreakers, attorneys, bawds, buffoons, gamesters, politicians, wits, splenetics, tedious talkers, controvertists, ravishers, murderers, robbers, virtuosos; no leaders or followers of party and faction; no encouragers to vice, by seducement or examples; no dungeon, axes, gibbets, whipping posts, or pillories; no cheating shopkeepers or mechanics; no pride, vanity, or affectation; no fops, bullies, drunkards, strolling whores, or poxes; no ranting, lewd, expensive wives; no stupid, proud pedants; no importunate, overbearing, quarrelsome,

noisy, roaring, empty, conceited, swearing companions; no scoundrels, raised from the dust for the sake of their vices, or nobility thrown into it on account of their virtues; no lords, fiddlers, judges, or dancing masters.

I had the favor of being admitted to several Houyhnhnms, who came to visit or dine with my master; where his Honor graciously suffered me to wait in the room and listen to their discourse. Both he and his company would often descend to ask me questions, and receive my answers. I had also sometimes the honor of attending my master in his visits to others. I never presumed to speak, except in answer to a question; and then I did it with inward regret, because it was a loss of so much time for improving myself; but I was infinitely delighted with the station of an humble auditor in such conversations, where nothing passed but what was useful, expressed in the fewest and most significant words; where the greatest decency was observed, without the least degree of ceremony; where no person spoke without being pleased himself, and pleasing his companions; where there was no interruption, tediousness, heat, or difference of sentiments. They have a notion that when people are met together, a short silence doth much improve conversation: this I found to be true; for during those little intermissions of talk, new ideas would arise in their thoughts, which very much enlivened the discourse. Their subjects are generally on friendship and benevolence, or order and economy; sometimes upon the visible operations of nature, or ancient traditions; upon the bounds and limits of virtue; upon the unerring rules of reason, or upon some determinations to be taken at the next great assembly; and often upon the various excellencies of poetry. I may add without vanity that my presence often gave them sufficient matter for discourse, because it afforded my master an occasion of letting his friends into the history of me and my country, upon which they were all pleased to descant in a manner not very advantageous to humankind; and for that reason I shall not repeat what they said: only I may be allowed to observe that his Honor, to my great admiration, appeared to understand the nature of Yahoos in all countries much better than myself. He went through all our vices and follies, and discovered many which I had never mentioned to him, by only supposing what qualities a Yahoo of their country, with a small proportion of reason, might be capable of exerting; and concluded, with too much probability, how vile as well as miserable such a creature must be.

I freely confess that all the little knowledge I have

of any value was acquired by the lectures I received from my master, and from hearing the discourses of him and his friends; to which I should be prouder to listen than to dictate to the greatest and wisest assembly in Europe. I admired the strength, comeliness, and speed of the inhabitants; and such a constellation of virtues in such amiable persons produced in me the highest veneration. At first, indeed, I did not feel that natural awe which the Yahoos and all other animals bear towards them; but it grew upon me by degrees, much sooner than I imagined, and was mingled with a respectful love and gratitude, that they would condescend to distinguish me from the rest of my species.

When I thought of my family, my friends, my countrymen, or human race in general, I considered them as they really were, Yahoos in shape and disposition, perhaps a little more civilized, and qualified with the gift of speech, but making no other use of reason than to improve and multiply those vices whereof their brethren in this country had only the share that nature allotted them. When I happened to behold the reflection of my own form in a lake or fountain, I turned away my face in horror and detestation of myself, and could better endure the sight of a common Yahoo than of my own person. By conversing with the Houyhnhnms, and looking upon them with delight, I fell to imitate their gait and gesture, which is now grown into an habit, and my friends often tell me in a blunt way that I trot like a horse; which, however, I take for a great compliment. Neither shall I disown that in speaking I am apt to fall into the voice and manner of the Houyhnhnms, and hear myself ridiculed on that account without the least mortification. . . .[8]

CHAPTER II

. . . As soon as I entered the house, my wife took me in her arms and kissed me, at which, having not been used to the touch of that odious animal for so many years, I fell in a swoon for almost an hour. At the time I am writing it is five years since my last return to England. During the first year I could not endure my wife or children in my presence; the very smell of them was intolerable, much less could I suffer them to eat in the same room. To this hour they dare not presume to touch my bread, or drink out of the same cup, neither was I ever able to let one of them take me by the hand. The first money I laid out was to buy two young stone-horses,[9] which I keep in a good stable, and next to them the groom is my greatest favorite; for I feel my spirits revived by the smell he contracts in the stable. My horses understand me tolerably well; I converse with them at least four hours every day. They are strangers to bridle or saddle; they live in great amity with me and friendship to each other.

A MODEST PROPOSAL

EVER since the reconquest of Ireland by William III, conditions there had been going from bad to worse. The country was ruled, as far as it was not ruled from England, by the Irish membership of the Established Church, comprising about one-twelfth of the island's population. Behind this group and its Irish Parliament was the Whig ministry in England, which cared nothing for Ireland's welfare. It appointed the officials of the Irish government and the prelates of the Established Church in Ireland. Not all these men became Walpole's agents in exploitation, but many did. In northern Ireland most of the English settlers were Presbyterians; as Dissenters they were excluded from any part in government. The worst injustice was the exclusion of the bulk of the Irish people, the Catholics, who were treated like foreigners in their own country. The economic plight of the island was dreadful. English legislation forbade Irish trade with England's colonies and barred the importation of Irish goods into England. The consequence was the ruin of Irish manufacturing. Absentee landlords, some of whom were spending their incomes on high living in England, sucked the country's blood. In Ireland the ruling caste, to which Swift belonged and for which he felt the sternest contempt, resisted most proposals of reform. The masses lived on the edge of starvation.

Statistics on questions of economic and social welfare can seem horribly unfeeling to the layman. It was in a mood of revulsion from such treatises that Swift came forward with A Modest Proposal. At first glance the tone seems callously light; actually Swift writes out of a profound despair over man's inhumanity to man, and his satire is a bitter protest for a people under the harrow. He has no illusions about the merits of the victims, and he would never have advocated admitting either Catholics or Dissenters to a share in the government; but he blazes with indignation against their oppressors. The tract was published, in Dublin and London, in 1729.

---

[8] Gulliver is finally required to leave the country because of his resemblance to the detested Yahoos. He departs in a boat he has constructed and is picked up by a Portuguese vessel that takes him back to Europe. [9] Stallions.

A MODEST PROPOSAL

FOR PREVENTING THE CHILDREN OF POOR PEOPLE FROM BEING A BURTHEN TO
THEIR PARENTS OR COUNTRY, AND FOR MAKING THEM BENEFICIAL TO THE PUBLIC

IT IS a melancholy object to those who walk through this great town[1] or travel in the country, when they see the streets, the roads, and cabin doors crowded with beggars of the female sex, followed by three, four, or six children, all in rags, and importuning every passenger for an alms. These mothers, instead of being able to work for their honest livelihood, are forced to employ all their time in strolling, to beg sustenance for their helpless infants, who, as they grow up, either turn thieves for want of work or leave their dear native country to fight for the Pretender in Spain,[2] or sell themselves[3] to the Barbados.

I think it is agreed by all parties that this prodigious number of children in the arms or on the backs or at the heels of their mothers, and frequently of their fathers, is in the present deplorable state of the kingdom a very great additional grievance; and therefore whoever could find out a fair, cheap, and easy method of making these children sound, useful members of the commonwealth would deserve so well of the public as to have his statue set up for a preserver of the nation.

But my intention is very far from being confined to provide only for the children of professed beggars; it is of a much greater extent, and shall take in the whole number of infants at a certain age who are born of parents in effect as little able to support them as those who demand our charity in the streets.

As to my own part, having turned my thoughts for many years upon this important subject and maturely weighed the several schemes of other projectors, I have always found them grossly mistaken in their computation. It is true a child just dropped from its dam may be supported by her milk for a solar year with little other nourishment, at most not above the value of two shillings, which the mother may certainly get, or the value in scraps, by her lawful occupation of begging; and it is exactly at one year old that I propose to provide for them in such a manner as, instead of being a charge upon their parents or the parish, or wanting food and raiment for the rest of their lives, they shall, on the contrary, contribute to the feeding and partly to the clothing of many thousands.

There is likewise another great advantage in my scheme, that it will prevent those voluntary abortions and that horrid practice of women murdering their bastard children, alas, too frequent among us, sacrificing the poor innocent babes, I doubt,[4] more to avoid the expense than the shame, which would move tears and pity in the most savage and inhuman breast.

The number of souls in this kingdom being usually reckoned one million and a half, of these I calculate there may be about two hundred thousand couple whose wives are breeders; from which number I subtract thirty thousand couple who are able to maintain their own children, although I apprehend there cannot be so many under the present distresses of the kingdom; but this being granted, there will remain an hundred and seventy thousand breeders. I again subtract fifty thousand for those women who miscarry, or whose children die by accident or disease within the year. There only remain an hundred and twenty thousand children of poor parents annually born: the question therefore is how this number shall be reared and provided for, which, as I have already said, under the present situation of affairs, is utterly impossible by all the methods hitherto proposed; for we can neither employ them in handicraft or agriculture: we neither build houses (I mean in the country) nor cultivate land; they can very seldom pick up a livelihood by stealing till they arrive at six years old, except where they are of towardly parts;[5] although I confess they learn the rudiments much earlier, during which time they can however be properly looked upon only as probationers, as I have been informed by a principal gentleman in the county of Cavan, who protested to me that he never knew above one or two instances under the age of six, even in a part of the kingdom so renowned for the quickest proficiency in that art.

I am assured by our merchants that a boy or a girl before twelve years old is no salable commodity,

---

[1] Dublin.

[2] Many Irish Catholics had emigrated in despair to France and Spain, where some became mercenary soldiers. There may be an allusion to a small expedition sent in 1718 to aid the Scottish Jacobites by Cardinal Alberoni (1664–1752), prime minister of Spain. It was wrecked en route.—The *Pretender* was James III, as the Jacobites styled him, the son of James II.

[3] As indentured servants. To secure transportation to the New World, a man would agree that his services for a term of years might be sold on arrival.

[4] Suspect.   [5] Precocious talents.

and even when they come to this age they will not yield above three pounds, or three pounds and half a crown at most, on the Exchange, which cannot turn to account either to the parents or kingdom, the charge of nutriment and rags having been at least four times that value.

I shall now therefore humbly propose my own thoughts, which I hope will not be liable to the least objection.

I have been assured by a very knowing American[6] of my acquaintance in London, that a young healthy child well nursed is at a year old a most delicious, nourishing, and wholesome food, whether stewed, roasted, baked, or boiled; and I make no doubt that it will equally serve in a fricassee or a ragout.

I do therefore humbly offer it to public consideration that, of the hundred and twenty thousand children already computed, twenty thousand may be reserved for breed, whereof only one fourth part to be males, which is more than we allow to sheep, black cattle,[7] or swine; and my reason is that these children are seldom the fruits of marriage, a circumstance not much regarded by our savages; therefore one male will be sufficient to serve four females. That the remaining hundred thousand may at a year old be offered in sale to the persons of quality and fortune through the kingdom, always advising the mother to let them suck plentifully in the last month, so as to render them plump and fat for a good table. A child will make two dishes at an entertainment for friends; and when the family dines alone, the fore or hind quarter will make a reasonable dish, and seasoned with a little pepper or salt will be very good boiled on the fourth day, especially in winter.

I have reckoned, upon a medium,[8] that a child just born will weigh twelve pounds, and in a solar year if tolerably nursed increaseth to twenty-eight pounds.

I grant this food will be somewhat dear, and therefore very proper for landlords, who, as they have already devoured most of the parents, seem to have the best title to the children.

Infants' flesh will be in season throughout the year, but more plentiful in March and a little before and after; for we are told by a grave author, an eminent French physician,[9] that, fish being a prolific diet, there are more children born in Roman Catholic countries about nine months after Lent than at any other season; therefore reckoning a year after Lent, the markets will be more glutted than usual, because the number of Popish infants is at least three to one in this kingdom, and therefore it will have one other collateral advantage by lessening the number of Papists among us.

I have already computed the charge of nursing a beggar's child (in which list I reckon all cottagers,[10] laborers, and four-fifths of the farmers) to be about two shillings per annum, rags included; and I believe no gentleman would repine to give ten shillings for the carcass of a good fat child, which, as I have said, will make four dishes of excellent nutritive meat when he hath only some particular friend or his own family to dine with him. Thus the squire will learn to be a good landlord, and grow popular among his tenants; the mother will have eight shillings net profit, and be fit for work till she produces another child.

Those who are more thrifty (as I must confess the times require) may flay the carcass, the skin of which, artificially dressed, will make admirable gloves for ladies and summer boots for fine gentlemen.

As to our city of Dublin, shambles may be appointed for this purpose in the most convenient parts of it, and butchers we may be assured will not be wanting, although I rather recommend buying the children alive and dressing them hot from the knife, as we do roasting pigs.

A very worthy person, a true lover of his country, and whose virtues I highly esteem, was lately pleased in discoursing on this matter to offer a refinement upon my scheme. He said that many gentlemen of this kingdom having of late destroyed their deer, he conceived that the want of venison might be well supplied by the bodies of young lads and maidens, not exceeding fourteen years of age nor under twelve, so great a number of both sexes in every country being now ready to starve for want of work and service; and these to be disposed of by their parents if alive, or otherwise by their nearest relations. But with due deference to so excellent a friend and so deserving a patriot, I cannot be altogether in his sentiments; for as to the males, my American acquaintance assured me from frequent experience that their flesh was generally tough and lean, like that of our schoolboys, by continual exercise, and their taste disagreeable, and to fatten them would not answer the charge. Then as to the females, it would, I think with humble submission, be a loss to the public, because they soon would become breeders themselves.

---

[6] Englishmen long held equally strange ideas about America.
[7] Cattle in general.   [8] An average.
[9] Rabelais.

[10] Small tenant-farmers.

And besides, it is not improbable that some scrupulous people might be apt to censure such a practice (although indeed very unjustly) as a little bordering upon cruelty, which, I confess, hath always been with me the strongest objection against any project, however so well.

But in order to justify my friend, he confessed that this expedient was put into his head by the famous Psalmanazar,[11] a native of the island Formosa, who came from thence to London above twenty years ago, and in conversation told my friend that in his country, when any young person happened to be put to death, the executioner sold the carcass to persons of quality, as a prime dainty, and that in his time the body of a plump girl of fifteen, who was crucified for an attempt to poison the emperor, was sold to his Imperial Majesty's prime minister of state and other great mandarins of the court, in joints from the gibbet, at four hundred crowns. Neither indeed can I deny that if the same use were made of several plump young girls in this town, who, without one single groat[12] to their fortunes, cannot stir abroad without a chair,[13] and appear at the playhouse and assemblies in foreign fineries, which they never will pay for, the kingdom would not be the worse.

Some persons of a desponding spirit are in great concern about that vast number of poor people who are aged, diseased, or maimed; and I have been desired to employ my thoughts what course may be taken to ease the nation of so grievous an encumbrance. But I am not in the least pain upon that matter, because it is very well known that they are every day dying and rotting by cold and famine and filth and vermin, as fast as can be reasonably expected. And as to the younger laborers, they are now in almost as hopeful a condition. They cannot get work, and consequently pine away for want of nourishment, to a degree that, if at any time they are accidentally hired to common labor, they have not strength to perform it; and thus the country and themselves are happily delivered from the evils to come.

I have too long digressed, and therefore shall return to my subject. I think the advantages by the proposal which I have made are obvious and many, as well as of the highest importance.

For first, as I have already observed, it would greatly lessen the number of Papists, with whom we are yearly overrun, being the principal breeders of the nation as well as our most dangerous enemies, and who stay at home on purpose with a design to deliver the kingdom to the Pretender, hoping to take their advantage by the absence of so many good Protestants[14] who have chosen rather to leave their country than stay at home and pay tithes against their conscience to an episcopal curate.

Secondly, the poorer tenants will have something valuable of their own, which by law may be made liable to distress,[15] and help to pay their landlord's rent, their corn and cattle being already seized, and money a thing unknown.

Thirdly, whereas the maintenance of an hundred thousand children, from two years old and upwards, cannot be computed at less than ten shillings apiece per annum, the nation's stock will be thereby increased fifty thousand pounds per annum, besides the profit of a new dish introduced to the tables of all gentlemen of fortune in the kingdom who have any refinement in taste; and the money will circulate among ourselves, the goods being entirely of our own growth and manufacture.

Fourthly, the constant breeders, besides the gain of eight shillings sterling per annum by the sale of their children, will be rid of the charge of maintaining them after the first year.

Fifthly, this food would likewise bring great custom to taverns, where the vintners will certainly be so prudent as to procure the best receipts for dressing it to perfection, and consequently have their houses frequented by all the fine gentlemen who justly value themselves upon their knowledge in good eating; and a skillful cook who understands how to oblige his guests will contrive to make it as expensive as they please.

Sixthly, this would be a great inducement to marriage, which all wise nations have either encouraged by rewards or enforced by laws and penalties. It would increase the care and tenderness of mothers toward their children, when they were sure of a settlement for life to the poor babes, provided in some sort by the public to their annual profit instead of expense. We should soon see an honest emulation among the married women, which of them could bring the fattest child to the market. Men would become as fond of their wives, during the time of their pregnancy, as they are now of their mares in foal, their cows in calf, or sows when they are ready to farrow, nor offer to beat or kick them (as is too frequent a practice) for fear of a miscarriage.

---

11 "George Psalmanazar" (1679?–1763)—his real name is unknown—was a French impostor who wrote a *Description of Formosa* (1704); he pretended he was a native.

12 Silver fourpence.   13 Sedan chair.

14 In this case, the Dissenters.   15 Seizure for taxes, rent, etc.

Many other advantages might be enumerated: for instance, the addition of some thousand carcasses in our exportation of barreled beef; the propagation of swine's flesh, and improvement in the art of making good bacon, so much wanted among us by the great destruction of pigs, too frequent at our tables, which are no way comparable in taste or magnificence to a well-grown, fat yearling child, which roasted whole will make a considerable figure at a lord mayor's feast or any other public entertainment. But this and many others I omit, being studious of brevity.

Supposing that one thousand families in this city would be constant customers for infants' flesh, besides others who might have it at merry meetings, particularly weddings and christenings, I compute that Dublin would take off annually about twenty thousand carcasses, and the rest of the kingdom (where probably they will be sold somewhat cheaper) the remaining eighty thousand.

I can think of no one objection that will possibly be raised against this proposal, unless it should be urged that the number of people will be thereby much lessened in the kingdom. This I freely own, and was indeed one principal design in offering it to the world. I desire the reader will observe that I calculate my remedy *for this one individual kingdom of Ireland, and for no other that ever was, is, or, I think, ever can be upon earth.* Therefore let no man talk to me of other expedients:[16] *of taxing our absentees[17] at five shillings a pound; of using neither clothes nor household furniture, except what is of our own growth and manufacture; of utterly rejecting the materials and instruments that promote foreign luxury; of curing the expensiveness of pride, vanity, idleness, and gaming in our women; of introducing a vein of parsimony, prudence, and temperance; of learning to love our country, wherein we differ even from Laplanders, and the inhabitants of Topinamboo;[18] of quitting our animosities and factions, nor act any longer like the Jews who were murdering one another at the very moment their city was taken;[19] of being a little cautious not to sell our country and consciences for nothing; of teaching landlords to have at least one degree of mercy toward their tenants. Lastly, of putting a spirit of honesty, industry, and skill into our shopkeepers, who, if a resolution could now be taken to buy* only our native goods, *would immediately unite to cheat and exact upon us in the price, the measure, and the goodness, nor could ever yet be brought to make one fair proposal of just dealing, though often and earnestly invited to it.*

Therefore, I repeat, let no man talk to me of these and the like expedients till he hath at least some glimpse of hope that there will ever be some hearty and sincere attempt to put them in practice.

But as to myself, having been wearied out for many years with offering vain, idle, visionary thoughts, and at length utterly despairing of success, I fortunately fell upon this proposal; which, as it is wholly new, so it hath something solid and real, of no expense and little trouble, full in our own power, and whereby we can incur no danger in *disobliging England.* For this kind of commodity will not bear exportation, the flesh being of too tender a consistence to admit a long continuance in salt, *although perhaps I could name a country which would be glad to eat up our whole nation without it.*

After all, I am not so violently bent upon my own opinion as to reject any offer proposed by wise men which shall be found equally innocent, cheap, easy, and effectual. But before something of that kind shall be advanced in contradiction to my scheme and offering a better, I desire the author or authors will be pleased maturely to consider two points. First, as things now stand, how they will be able to find food and raiment for an hundred thousand useless mouths and backs. And secondly, there being a round million of creatures in human figure throughout this kingdom, whose whole subsistence put into a common stock would leave them in debt two millions of pounds sterling, adding those who are beggars by profession to the bulk of farmers, cottagers, and laborers, with their wives and children, who are beggars in effect; I desire those politicians who dislike my overture, and may perhaps be so bold to attempt an answer, that they will first ask the parents of these mortals whether they would not at this day think it a great happiness to have been sold for food at a year old in the manner I prescribe, and thereby have avoided such a perpetual scene of misfortunes as they have since gone through by the oppression of landlords, the impossibility of paying rent without money or trade, the want of common sustenance, with neither house nor clothes to cover them from the inclemencies of the weather, and the most inevitable prospect of entailing the like or greater miseries upon their breed for ever.

I profess in the sincerity of my heart that I have not the least personal interest in endeavoring to promote

---

16 Those listed Swift had advocated in earlier writings.
17 Absentee landlords.
18 A district in Brazil, supposedly inhabited by savages.
19 An allusion to the capture of Jerusalem in 70 A.D. by the Romans under Titus.

this necessary work, having no other motive than the *public good of my country, by advancing our trade, providing for infants, relieving the poor, and giving some pleasure to the rich*. I have no children by which I can propose to get a single penny; the youngest being nine years old, and my wife past childbearing.

VERSES ON THE DEATH OF DR. SWIFT

"I have been several months," says Swift in a letter to John Gay on December 1, 1731, "writing near five hundred lines on a pleasant subject, only to tell what my friends and enemies will say on me after I am dead. I shall finish it soon, for I add two lines every week, and blot out four and alter eight." The poem was not published on completion. The first edition, in 1739, was printed in London without Swift's permission; about a third of the text and all of his notes were left out, on the "advice and opinion" of friends in England who feared offense might be taken. In the same year an imperfect but more faithful edition was published in Dublin; but Swift's final intentions remain uncertain at many points, and the poem has to be pieced out from later editions. The most careful attempt at reconstruction is by H. Williams (*Swift's Poems,* vol. II).

This is Swift's highest achievement in verse, one of those rare compositions which succeed in being extremely amusing, and yet in touching also a subtle chord of pathos.

VERSES ON THE DEATH OF DR. SWIFT, D.S.P.D.[1]

Occasioned by Reading a Maxim in Rochefoucault[2]

Dans l'adversité de nos meilleurs amis nous trouvons quelque chose qui ne nous deplaist pas.

In the adversity of our best friends, we find something that doth not displease us.

As Rochefoucault his maxims drew
From nature, I believe 'em true:
They argue no corrupted mind
In him; the fault is in mankind.

This maxim more than all the rest   5
Is thought too base for human breast:
"In all distresses of our friends
We first consult our private ends,
While nature, kindly bent to ease us,
Points out some circumstance to please us."   10

If this perhaps your patience move,
Let reason and experience prove.

We all behold with envious eyes
Our equal raised above our size.
Who would not, at a crowded show,   15
Stand high himself, keep others low?
I love my friend as well as you,
But would not have him stop my view.
Then let me have the higher post;
I ask but for an inch at most.   20

If in a battle you should find
One, whom you love of all mankind,
Had some heroic action done,
A champion killed, or trophy won,
Rather than thus be overtopped   25
Would you not wish his laurels cropped?

Dear honest Ned is in the gout,
Lies racked with pain, and you without.
How patiently you hear him groan!
How glad the case is not your own!   30

What poet would not grieve to see
His brethren write as well as he?
But rather than they should excel,
He'd wish his rivals all in hell.

Her end when Emulation misses,   35
She turns to envy, stings, and hisses;
The strongest friendship yields to pride,
Unless the odds be on our side.

Vain humankind! fantastic race!
Thy various follies who can trace?   40
Self-love, ambition, envy, pride,
Their empire in our hearts divide;
Give others riches, power, and station,
'Tis all on me an usurpation.
I have no title to aspire,   45
Yet when you sink I seem the higher.

---

[1] Dean of St. Patrick's, Dublin.
[2] François de la Rochefoucauld (1613–80), author of a famous book of maxims.

In Pope[3] I cannot read a line
But with a sigh I wish it mine;
When he can in one couplet fix
More sense than I can do in six,   50
It gives me such a jealous fit
I cry, "Pox take him, and his wit!"

Why must I be outdone by Gay,[4]
In my own hum'rous biting way?

Arbuthnot[5] is no more my friend,   55
Who dares to irony pretend,
Which I was born to introduce,
Refined it first, and showed its use.

St. John,[6] as well as Pultney,[7] knows
That I had some repute for prose   60
And, till they drove me out of date,
Could maul a minister of state.
If they have mortified my pride
And made me throw my pen aside,
If with such talents heav'n hath blest 'em,   65
Have I not reason to detest 'em?

To all my foes, dear Fortune, send
Thy gifts, but never to my friend;
I tamely can endure the first,
But this with envy makes me burst.   70

Thus much may serve by way of proem;[8]
Proceed we therefore to our poem.

The time is not remote when I
Must by the course of nature die,
When I foresee my special friends   75
Will try to find their private ends;
Though it is hardly understood
Which way my death can do them good,
Yet thus, methinks, I hear 'em speak:[9]
"See how the Dean begins to break.   80
Poor gentleman, he droops apace,
You plainly find it in his face.
That old vertigo in his head
Will never leave him till he's dead.

Besides, his memory decays: 85
He recollects not what he says;
He cannot call his friends to mind,
Forgets the place where last he dined,
Plies you with stories o'er and o'er—
He told them fifty times before.   90
How does he fancy we can sit
To hear his out-of-fashioned wit?
But he takes up with younger folks,
Who for his wine will bear his jokes;
Faith, he must make his stories shorter,   95
Or change his comrades once a quarter:
In half the time, he talks them round;
There must another set be found.

"For poetry, he's past his prime;
He takes an hour to find a rime.   100
His fire is out, his wit decayed,
His fancy sunk, his muse a jade.
I'd have him throw away his pen;
But there's no talking to some men."

And then their tenderness appears   105
By adding largely to my years:
"He's older than he would be reckoned,
And well remembers Charles the Second.

"He hardly drinks a pint of wine;
And that, I doubt,[10] is no good sign.   110
His stomach, too, begins to fail:
Last year we thought him strong and hale,
But now he's quite another thing;
I wish he may hold out till spring."

Then hug themselves, and reason thus: 115
"It is not yet so bad with us."

In such a case they talk in tropes,[11]
And by their fears express their hopes:
Some great misfortune to portend,
No enemy can match a friend;   120
With all the kindness they profess,
The merit of a lucky guess
(When daily howd'y's come of course,
And servants answer, "Worse and worse")
Would please 'em better than to tell   125
That, God be praised, the Dean is well.
Then he who prophesied the best
Approves his foresight to the rest:
"You know, I always feared the worst,
And often told you so at first."   130

---

[3] See below, pp. 777 ff.   [4] See below, pp. 811 ff.
[5] Queen Anne's physician, and a friend of Swift and Pope.
[6] Henry St. John, Viscount Bolingbroke, the Tory statesman.
Swift calls him "the most universal genius in Europe." "St.
John" was probably pronounced *Sínjon* (see also lines 373, 434).
[7] The statesman and journalist William Pultney, afterwards Earl
of Bath. As Swift says in a note, he had once been "Mr. Walpole's intimate friend"; but in 1726 he had left the Whigs and
made an alliance with Bolingbroke in opposition to Walpole.
[8] Preface.   [9] *Ea* was then pronounced as in *break*.

[10] Fear.   [11] Figures of speech.

He'd rather choose that I should die
Than his prediction prove a lie.
Not one foretells I shall recover;
But all agree to give me over.

Yet should some neighbor feel a pain,   135
Just in the parts where I complain,
How many a message would he send!
What hearty prayers that I should mend!
Enquire what regimen I kept,
What gave me ease, and how I slept!   140
And more lament, when I was dead,
Than all the sniv'lers round my bed.

My good companions, never fear;
For though you may mistake a year,
Though your prognostics run too fast,   145
They must be verified at last.

Behold the fatal day arrive!
"How is the Dean?" "He's just alive."
"Now the departing prayer is read."
"He hardly breathes." "The Dean is dead."   150
Before the passing bell begun,
The news through half the town has run.
"Oh, may we all for death prepare!
What has he left? And who's his heir?"
"I know no more than what the news is: 155
'Tis all bequeathed to public uses."
"To public use! A perfect whim!
What had the public done for him?
Mere envy, avarice, and pride!
He gave it all"—but first he died.   160
"And had the Dean, in all the nation,
No worthy friend, no poor relation?
So ready to do strangers good,
Forgetting his own flesh and blood?"

Now Grub Street[12] wits are all employed;   165
With elegies the town is cloyed;
Some paragraph in ev'ry paper,
To curse the Dean, or bless the Drapier.[13]

The doctors, tender of their fame,
Wisely on me lay all the blame: 170
"We must confess his case was nice;[14]
But he would never take advice.
Had he been ruled, for aught appears,
He might have lived these twenty years;
For when we opened him, we found   175
That all his vital parts were sound."

From Dublin soon to London spread,
'Tis told at court, the Dean is dead.

Kind Lady Suffolk,[15] in the spleen,[16]
Runs laughing up to tell the Queen.   180
The Queen, so gracious, mild, and good,
Cries, "Is he gone? 'Tis time he should.
He's dead, you say; why, let him rot;
I'm glad the medals were forgot.
I promised them, 'tis true; but when?   185
I only was the Princess then;
But now, as consort of the King,
You know 'tis quite a different thing."

Now Chartres,[17] at Sir Robert's[18] levee,
Tells, with a sneer, the tidings heavy: 190
"Why, is he dead without his shoes?"
Cries Bob; "I'm sorry for the news;
Oh, were the wretch but living still,
And in his place my good friend Will,[19]
Or had a miter[20] on his head   195
Provided Bolingbroke were dead."

Now Curll[21] his shop from rubbish drains:
Three genuine tomes of Swift's remains.

---

14 Called for delicate treatment.
15 In two notes Swift explains that the "Countess of Suffolk, then of the bedchamber to the Queen [Caroline, wife of George II— Lady Suffolk had also been the King's official mistress] professed much friendship for the Dean. The Queen, then Princess, sent a dozen times to the Dean (then in London) with her command to attend her." He says the Princess asked him to get her some Irish plaid. He made her a present of some, worth £35; but certain medals she had promised him were never received, nor was a promised "settlement in England."
16 Fit of excitement.
17 Colonel Francis Chartres (1675–1732), characterized by Lord Chesterfield (see below) as "the most notorious blasted rascal in the world." He was cashiered from the army for cheating. Swift tells in a note how Chartres had made "a prodigious fortune," and how "he was tried at seventy for a rape"; actually he was then about fifty-five.   18 Walpole's.
19 William Pultney; see note 7, above.
20 The headdress of a bishop. I.e., I wish Swift had been promoted from dean to bishop—"provided Bolingbroke were dead."
21 Swift's note: "[Edmund] Curll [1675–1747] hath been the most infamous bookseller of any age or country. . . . He published three volumes all charged on the Dean, who never writ three pages of them. . . ."

---

12 "The name of a street in London [near Cripplegate] much inhabited by writers of small histories, dictionaries, and temporary [i.e., occasional] poems" (Dr. Johnson's Dictionary). This former abode of hack writers and pamphleteers now rejoices in the name of Milton Street.
13 Note by Swift: "The Author imagines that the scribblers of the prevailing party, which he always opposed, will libel him after his death; but that others will remember him with gratitude who consider the service he had done to Ireland, under the name of M. B., drapier, by utterly defeating the destructive project of Wood's halfpence, in five letters to the people of Ireland, at that time read universally and convincing every reader."

And then, to make them pass the glibber,
Revised by Tibbalds, Moore, and Cibber.[22]   200
He'll treat me as he does my betters:
Publish my will, my Life, my letters,
Revive the libels born to die,
Which Pope must bear, as well as I.

Here shift the scene, to represent   205
How those I love my death lament.
Poor Pope will grieve a month, and Gay
A week, and Arbuthnot a day.

St. John himself will scarce forbear
To bite his pen and drop a tear.   210
The rest will give a shrug and cry,
"I'm sorry; but we all must die."
Indifference, clad in wisdom's guise,
All fortitude of mind supplies;
For how can stony bowels melt   215
In those who never pity felt?
When *we* are lashed *they* kiss the rod,
Resigning to the will of God.

The fools, my juniors by a year,
Are tortured with suspense and fear—   220
Who wisely thought my age a screen,
When death approached, to stand between.
The screen removed, their hearts are trembling;
They mourn for me without dissembling.

My female friends, whose tender hearts   225
Have better learned to act their parts,
Receive the news in doleful dumps:
"The Dean is dead (and what is trumps?)."
"Then Lord have mercy on his soul!
(Ladies, I'll venture for the vole.[23])"   230
"Six deans, they say, must bear the pall.
(I wish I knew what king to call.)"
"Madam, your husband will attend
The funeral of so good a friend."
"No, madam, 'tis a shocking sight,   235
And he's engaged tomorrow night!

My Lady Club would take it ill
If he should fail her at quadrille.[24]
He loved the Dean. (I lead a heart.)
But dearest friends, they say, must part.   240
His time was come, he ran his race;
We hope he's in a better place."

Why do we grieve that friends should die?
No loss more easy to supply.
One year is past; a different scene: 245
No further mention of the Dean,
Who now, alas, no more is missed
Than if he never did exist.
Where's now this fav'rite of Apollo?
Departed; and his works must follow: 250
Must undergo the common fate;
His kind of wit is out of date.
Some country squire to Lintot[25] goes,
Inquires for Swift in verse and prose.
Says Lintot, "I have heard the name;   255
He died a year ago." "The same."
He searcheth all his shop in vain;
"Sir, you may find them in Duck Lane;[26]
I sent them with a load of books,
Last Monday, to the pastry cooks.[27]   260
To fancy they could live a year!
I find you're but a stranger here.
The Dean was famous in his time,
And had a kind of knack at rime.
His way of writing now is past;   265
The Town hath got a better taste.
I keep no antiquated stuff;
But spick and span I have enough.
Pray, do but give me leave to show 'em;
Here's Colley Cibber's[28] birthday poem.   270
This ode you never yet have seen,
By Stephen Duck,[29] upon the Queen.
Then, here's a letter finely penned
Against the *Craftsman*[30] and his friend;
It clearly shows that all reflection   275
On ministers is disaffection.

---

22 I.e., Curll asserts that the three alleged volumes of Swift's un-published "remains" have been revised by the three writers mentioned. "Tibbalds" is the great editor of Shakespeare, Lewis Theobald (1688–1744). His criticism of the edition by Pope, a better writer but an inferior editor, earned Pope's hatred (see below, Pope's "Epistle to Dr. Arbuthnot," p. 807, note 52). James Moore Smythe was a minor writer who incurred Pope's enmity. Colley Cibber (1671–1757) was a bad poet, a good actor, a fair dramatist, and a charming autobiographer.
23 The taking of all the tricks, in quadrille and other card games.
24 The fashionable card game of the day.
25 Barnaby Bernard Lintot (1675–1736), a famous "bookseller." Not yet was the retail book trade a separate business from pub-lishing.
26 In West Smithfield. Swift's note: "A place in London where old books are sold."
27 Who needed paper for use in baking.
28 See note 22, above. As poet laureate Cibber had annually to write an ode on the King's birthday.
29 Duck (1705–56) was a farmhand who became a poet and clergy-man. He was taken up by Society, and Queen Caroline was his patroness.
30 A political journal founded in 1726 by Bolingbroke and Pultney to attack Walpole.

Next, here's Sir Robert's vindication,
And Mr. Henley's[31] last oration.
The hawkers have not got 'em yet;
Your Honor please to buy a set?   280

"Here's Wolston's tracts, the twelfth edition;[32]
'Tis read by ev'ry politician:
The country Members,[33] when in town,
To all their boroughs send them down.
You never met a thing so smart;   285
The courtiers have them all by heart.
Those maids of honor (who can read)
Are taught to use them for their creed.
The rev'rend author's good intention
Hath been rewarded with a pension.   290
He doth an honor to his gown
By bravely running priestcraft down;
He shows, as sure as God's in Gloucester,[34]
That Jesus was a grand impostor:
That all his miracles were cheats,   295
Performed as jugglers do their feats.
The Church had never such a writer;
A shame he hath not got a miter!"

Suppose me dead; and then suppose
A club assembled at the Rose,[35]   300
Where, from discourse of this and that,
I grow the subject of their chat;
And, while they toss my name about,
With favor some, and some without,
One quite indiff'rent in the cause   305
My character impartial draws:
"The Dean, if we believe report,
Was never ill received at court.
As for his works in verse and prose,
I own myself no judge of those;   310
Nor can I tell what critics thought 'em,
But this I know: all people bought 'em,
As[36] with a moral view designed
To cure the vices of mankind.
His vein, ironically grave,   315
Exposed the fool and lashed the knave;
To steal a hint was never known,
But what he writ was all his own.

"He never thought an honor done him
Because a duke was proud to own[37] him;   320
Would rather slip aside and choose
To talk with wits in dirty shoes;
Despised the fools with Stars and Garters,
So often seen caressing Chartres.
He never courted men in station,   325
Nor persons had in admiration;
Of no man's greatness was afraid,
Because he sought for no man's aid.
Though trusted long in great affairs,
He gave himself no haughty airs;   330
Without regarding private ends,
Spent all his credit for his friends,
And only chose the wise and good,
No flatt'rers, no allies in blood;
But succored virtue in distress,   335
And seldom failed of good success,
As numbers in their hearts must own,
Who, but for him, had been unknown.

"With princes kept a due decorum,
But never stood in awe before 'em;   340
He followed David's lesson just:
'In princes never put thy trust.'
And, would you make him truly sour,
Provoke him with *a slave in power.*
The Irish Senate, if you named,   345
With what impatience he declaimed!
Fair LIBERTY was all his cry;
For her he stood prepared to die;
For her he boldly stood alone;
For her he oft exposed his own.   350
Two kingdoms,[38] just as faction led,
Had set a price upon his head;
But not a traitor could be found
To sell him for six hundred pound.

"Had he but spared his tongue and pen,   355
He might have rose like other men;
But power was never in his thought,
And wealth he valued not a groat.
Ingratitude he often found,
And pitied those who meant the wound;   360
But kept the tenor of his mind,
To merit well of humankind,
Nor made a sacrifice of those
Who still were true, to please his foes.

---

[31] The eccentric Rev. George Henley (1692–1756) left the Established Church and set up an independent pulpit. He was a retainer of Walpole. Swift's note calls him "an absolute dunce, but generally reputed crazy."
[32] The Rev. Thomas Woolston (1670–1733) professed deism, was convicted of blasphemy, and died in prison.
[33] Of Parliament.   [34] Pronounced *Gloster.*
[35] Adjoining Drury Lane Theater.
[36] As if; i.e., apparently.

[37] Acknowledge.
[38] England and Ireland; Swift explains that rewards had been offered twice for identifying the author of two of his anonymous pamphlets.

He labored many a fruitless hour 365
To reconcile his friends in power;[39]
Saw mischief by a faction brewing,
While they pursued each other's ruin.
But finding vain was all his care,
He left the court in mere[40] despair. 370

"And, oh! how short are human schemes!
Here ended all our golden dreams.
What St. John's skill in state affairs,
What Ormond's[41] valor, Oxford's[42] cares,
To save their sinking country lent, 375
Was all destroyed by one event:
Too soon that precious life was ended
On which, alone, our weal depended.[43]
When up a dangerous faction starts,
With wrath and vengeance in their hearts: 380
By solemn league and cov'nant bound
To ruin, slaughter, and confound;
To turn religion to a fable,
And make the government a Babel;
Pervert the law, disgrace the gown, 385
Corrupt the senate, rob the Crown;
To sacrifice old England's glory,
And make her infamous in story.
When such a tempest shook the land,
How could unguarded Virtue stand? 390

"With horror, grief, despair, the Dean
Beheld the dire destructive scene:
His friends in exile, or the Tower;
Himself within the frown of power,[44]
Pursued by base envenomed pens 395
Far to the land of slaves and fens,[45]
A servile race, in folly nursed,
Who truckle most when treated worst.

"By innocence and resolution
He bore continual persecution, 400
While numbers to preferment rose
Whose merits were—to be his foes.
When *ev'n his own familiar friends,*
Intent upon their private ends,
Like renegadoes now he feels 405
Against him lifting up their heels.

"The Dean did by his pen defeat
An infamous destructive cheat:[46]
Taught fools their int'rest how to know,
And gave them arms to ward the blow. 410
Envy hath owned it was his doing,
To save that helpless land from ruin;
While they who at the steerage stood,
And reaped the profit, sought his blood.

"To save them from their evil fate, 415
In him was held a crime of state.
A wicked monster on the bench,[47]
Whose fury blood could never quench,
As vile and profligate a villain
As modern Scroggs[48] or old Tresilian,[49] 420
Who long all justice had discarded,
Nor feared he God, nor man regarded,
Vowed on the Dean his rage to vent
And make him of his zeal repent;
But heav'n his innocence defends, 425
The grateful people stand his friends:
Not strains of law, nor judge's frown,
Nor topics brought to please the Crown,
Nor witness hired, nor jury picked,
Prevail to bring him in convict. 430

"In exile,[50] with a steady heart,
He spent his life's declining part,
Where folly, pride, and faction sway,
Remote from St. John, Pope, and Gay.

---

[39] In a note Swift refers to his past efforts to compose quarrels within the Tory ministry. Before it fell there had been a bitter struggle between Harley and Bolingbroke.   [40] Utter.

[41] James Butler, second Duke of Ormond (1665–1745), was appointed commander-in-chief on the fall of Marlborough in 1710. When the Tories lost power he was impeached as a Jacobite and fled the country.

[42] Robert Harley (1661–1724), Defoe's employer, left the Whigs and became one of the Tory leaders. He was afterwards made Earl of Oxford.

[43] When Queen Anne died, in 1714, the Tories fell and the Whigs triumphed with the accession of George I.

[44] Swift's note: "Upon the Queen's death, the Dean returned to live in Dublin. . . . Numberless libels were writ against him in England as a Jacobite; he was insulted in the street, and at nights was forced to be attended by his servants armed."

[45] Swift's note: "The land of slaves and fens is Ireland."

[46] The project for the Irish copper coinage. See p. 724, above.

[47] William Whitshed, who presided when printers were tried for publishing some of Swift's pamphlets. He was appointed chief justice in Ireland at the accession of George I.

[48] Sir William Scroggs (1623?–83), a lord chief justice of England under Charles II. He was impeached by the House of Commons in 1680. He was an unjust judge to some of the victims of Titus Oates at the time of the Popish Plot.

[49] Sir Robert Tresilian, the severe chief justice who punished some of the rebels of the Peasants' Revolt in the fourteenth century.

[50] Swift's note: "In Ireland, which he had reason to call a place of exile; to which country nothing could have driven him but the Queen's death, who had determined to fix him in England. . . ."

"His friendships there, to few confined,   435
Were always of the middling kind:[51]
No fools of rank, a mongrel breed,
Who fain would pass for lords indeed.
Where titles give no right or power,
And peerage is a withered flower,   440
He would have held it a disgrace
If such a wretch had known his face.
On rural squires, that kingdom's bane,
He vented oft his wrath in vain:
Biennial squires, to market brought,[52]   445
Who sell their souls and votes for naught;
The nation stripped, go joyful back,
To rob the Church, their tenants rack,
Go snacks with rogues and rapparees,[53]
And keep the peace, to pick up fees—   450
In every job to have a share,
A jail or barrack to repair,[54]
And turn the tax for public roads
Commodious[55] to their own abodes.

"Perhaps, I may allow, the Dean   455
Had too much satire in his vein,
And seemed determined not to starve it,
Because no age could more deserve[56] it.
Yet malice never was his aim;
He lashed the vice, but spared the name.   460
No individual could resent,
Where thousands equally were meant.
His satire points at no defect
But what all mortals may correct;
For he abhorred that senseless tribe   465
Who call it humor when they jibe:
He spared a hump or crooked nose
Whose owners set not up for beaux.
True genuine dullness moved his pity,
Unless it offered[57] to be witty.   470
Those who their ignorance confessed
He ne'er offended with a jest,
But laughed to hear an idiot quote
A verse from Horace, learned by rote.

"He knew an hundred pleasant stories,   475
With all the turns of Whigs and Tories;
Was cheerful to his dying day,
And friends would let him have his way.

"He gave the little wealth he had
To build a house for fools and mad,   480
And showed by one satiric touch[58]
No nation wanted[59] it so much.
That kingdom[60] he hath left his debtor,
I wish it soon may have a better."

from ON POETRY: A RHAPSODY

This piece of disillusioned advice to aspirant poets is a
494-line geyser of unflagging wit and cynicism. It appeared
soon after Swift finished it, in 1733. The following extract
is a pleasing indictment of a familiar pest: the minor artist
who, unable to scale the peak himself, turns critic and tries
to prove that the major artist, who did get there, arrived
by the wrong route.

Hobbes[1] clearly proves that ev'ry creature
Lives in a state of war, by nature.   320
The greater for the smallest watch,
But meddle seldom with their match.
A whale of moderate size will draw
A shoal of herrings down his maw.
A fox with geese his belly crams;   325
A wolf destroys a thousand lambs.
But search among the riming race,
The brave are worried by the base.
If on Parnassus'[2] top you sit,
You rarely bite, are always bit: 330
Each poet of an inferior size
On you shall rail and criticize;
And strive to tear you limb from limb,
While others do as much for him.

The vermin only tease and pinch   335
Their foes superior by an inch.
So nat'ralists observe a flea
Hath smaller fleas that on him prey;
And these have smaller fleas to bite 'em,
And so proceed ad infinitum.   340
Thus ev'ry poet in his kind
Is bit by him that comes behind;

[51] Swift's note: "In Ireland the Dean was not acquainted with one
single lord spiritual [i.e., bishop] or temporal [i.e., of the
peerage]. He only conversed with private gentlemen of the
clergy or laity, and but a small number of either."
[52] I.e., the landowners elected to membership in the Irish Parliament, which met once in two years.
[53] Plunderers, robbers.
[54] Swift's note: "The army in Ireland is lodged in barracks, the
building and repairing whereof . . . have cost a prodigious sum
to that unhappy kingdom." [55] Serviceable.
[56] Then pronounced to rime with starve.
[57] Tried, professed.

[58] I.e., the gift.   [59] Needed.
[60] That kingdom which. Swift's note: "Meaning Ireland, where he
now lives, and probably may die."
[1] See p. 392, above.
[2] The Greek mountain sacred to Apollo and the Muses.

Who, though too little to be seen,
Can tease and gall and give the spleen;[3]
Call dunces, fools, and sons of whores,   345
Lay Grub Street[4] at each other's doors;
Extol the Greek and Roman masters,
And curse our modern poetasters.
Complain, as many an ancient bard did,

How genius is no more rewarded,   350
How wrong a taste prevails among us,
How much our ancestors outsung us;
Can personate an awkward scorn
For those who are not poets born;
And all their brother dunces lash,   355
Who crowd the press with hourly trash. . . .

Alexander Pope

1688–1744

POPE was not a great spirit, but he was an uncommonly interesting man and a consummate craftsman. Neither by nature nor by accomplishment was he a poet in the fullest sense of the word. Nevertheless, while his verse seldom moves the heart, it constantly stirs up the mind. It is first-rate fun to read; few Englishmen have written more wittily. To a considerable extent the merits of his poems are those of sparkling prose: clearness, cleverness, charm, sting—all achieved to the nth degree of precision. In addition, he has a complete mastery over his favorite meter. Thousands of rimesters have ticked off heroic couplets, but no one else has been able to get such a polish on them, or to endow them with such variety of sound and movement. Pope's are usually "closed" couplets: there is a stop at the end, and the sense unit rarely runs over from one couplet into the next. Pope brought to their writing a genius for selecting the *mot juste,* the one right word, and a knack of compression so extraordinary that again and again he distills a whole doctrine into a single couplet. Because of these qualities the best of his couplets stick in the memory. Pope is probably more quoted than any other English poet except Shakespeare—not because he is still widely read, but because his nuggets passed into the general currency two hundred years ago and have been in circulation ever since, independently of the poems in which they originally glittered.

Pope was the son of a well-to-do wholesale linen-dealer of London, where he was born in 1688. The restrictions imposed on Catholics after the Revolution of that year included a law forbidding them to reside within ten miles of the capital. Pope's father gave up his business and moved to an estate in Windsor Forest. When the poet was twelve he was crippled by an infection of the spine which left him a hunchback. In maturity his height was only four feet six; at table he had to have a higher seat, like a child's. That

he overcame this handicap and made himself one of the most eminent and sought-after men of his century remains an inspiring achievement. He spent his boyhood reading. On his body, he knew, he could not rely for aid when the time should come to face the world; his excuse for existing, his only means of leading a more than animal existence, must be his mind. It was therefore vital to equip that mind, and to perfect the means by which he could bring it into play. Accordingly, with the help of the priests who were his tutors (even had his health permitted, his Catholic faith would have barred him from the great schools and the universities), he cultivated his intellect. Critical as he was, his was not an original mind; its strength was in deftness and discrimination, joined with powers of steady application. By their aid he sharpened his pen to a stiletto's point. It could make the neatest of punctures, and he gloried in the knowledge that men and women were afraid of it. He himself had one of the most sensitive skins that ever stood thinly between a human spirit and a lacerating world. When he scratched or stabbed another's, he knew exactly how it felt.

Pope started out with unimportant translations and imitations of classical writers. He was so eager for praise that he later insisted he had written some of his best things before he was in his teens; veracity was not among his most salient traits. Whenever he began them, he was twenty-one when his *Pastorals* were published in 1709. They gave him some valuable practice in handling the couplet, but are nearly lifeless. Two years later, in 1711, appeared *An Essay on Criticism,* with which our selections begin. Horace in his *Ars Poetica* had formulated aesthetic theory for the Augustan age of Rome; Boileau had done it for French neoclassicism in *L'Art Poétique* (1674). The merit of Pope's essay lies not in what he has to say but in his saying a number of things more brilliantly and concisely than any of his predecessors, a remarkable feat for a young man of twenty-three. Before long everyone realized that a new talent of great distinction had arrived. Years

---

[3] Make the victim angry.
[4] See "On the Death of Dr. Swift," note 12.

before this, the older wits who had hobnobbed with Dryden at Will's had taken notice of the gifted boy. Now he had won his spurs. He came out of his seclusion and began frequenting newer circles, Addison's at first. For a while he sat in the little senate at Button's coffee house, and to him fell the honor of providing the prologue when *Cato* was acted. But Addison's friends thought, or professed to think, that the pastorals of Ambrose Philips were better than Pope's; and Pope thought that Addison was jealous and had egged them on. Even before Addison, who may not have known who wrote it, had deplored the tone of his attack on the critic John Dennis, Pope began gravitating away from the Whigs toward the more brilliant and congenial coterie of Swift, Arbuthnot, Gay, and Bolingbroke. These men became his lifelong friends; with them he shared the fun of the Scriblerus Club.

This pleasant interlude was ended in 1714 by the fall of the Tories. Swift retreated to Ireland, Bolingbroke fled to France, Arbuthnot lost the post of crown physician, and Pope abandoned the gaiety of London. In 1716 he moved to a suburb. In 1719 he went a little farther up the river, leasing an estate at Twickenham, beyond Kew and Richmond, just below Hampton Court; he was to be known as "the wasp of Twickenham." His five acres he turned into a remarkable garden; and on this estate he lived for the rest of his life, but not in seclusion. For making enemies Pope possessed one of the most notable talents in the history of the human race; he also had a deep capacity for friendship. His friends came to Twickenham, and for Swift the highlight of English visits was always the stay with Pope.

Meanwhile, one of his most admired works had been published, the charming mock-epic, *The Rape of the Lock* (1712, revised 1714). It is given in full below. In 1713 came *Windsor Forest,* none too happy in its description of nature; Pope would have liked to be her lover, but how to unbend in the presence of her charms he did not know. By this time, when he was only twenty-five, he was generally recognized as the foremost living English poet. In 1717 he brought out his collected poems. In two of them, the "Elegy to the Memory of an Unfortunate Lady" and "Eloisa to Abelard," he comes closer to the romantic than is usual with him.

One reason for his withdrawal to the country in 1716 was his need of leisure for the famous translations of the *Iliad* and *Odyssey* (1715–26). They were published by subscription; and though to us they seem to substitute an inappropriate artificiality for the naturalness of their glorious originals, they made Pope a fortune. His mediocre edition of Shakespeare appeared in 1725.

In his next important work, *The Dunciad* (1728), another mock-heroic poem, he turned to satire, not political but personal. He had quarreled with scores of people; now he decided to pay off scores. He struck with all the venom which in some sensitive natures is secreted by unhappiness. By the time Pope reached middle life he was physically so nearly helpless that he required aid to put on his clothes. Until it was laced into a heavy canvas corset, he could not hold his little figure erect. He was always cold; under his shirt he wore a fur jacket, and three pairs of stockings swathed his pipe-stem legs. His bodily misery bit deep into his mind; his spirit was corroded by something very like a persecution complex. As the reigning dunce in his new poem he crowned the Shakespeare scholar Lewis Theobald, who had dared expose the defects of Pope's edition. In subsequent versions of *The Dunciad* numerous changes were made; in the last (1743), Theobald was replaced as hero by the laureate, Colley Cibber. *The Dunciad* is the most elaborate personal satire in our language, and some of it makes pretty dull reading now. But much of it rises above personal satire to cast deserved ridicule upon dullness in general—upon pedantic critics and scholars and upon pretentious poetasters; and some critics find Pope at his best in certain passages in this poem. The method of such satires as *The Dunciad* is defended in Pope's brilliant *Epistle to Dr. Arbuthnot* (1735), which will be found below. Of the other works the most notable are the four *Moral Essays* (1731–35) and *An Essay on Man* (1732–34), also represented in the selections.

Pope died in 1744 at the age of fifty-six, of dropsy and asthma. His place in English poetry was unshaken till the Romantic triumph in the nineteenth century revised it sharply downward. In the twentieth his reputation has undergone, like Donne's, a substantial and perhaps even exaggerated rehabilitation.

The standard edition is still that of W. Elwin and W. J. Courthope (10 vols., 1871–89), but it is being superseded. A better edition of the original poetry is in progress under the general editorship of J. Butt (3 vols. thus far, 1939–). A handy one-volume edition is H. W. Boynton's (1902), and there is a good volume of selections by G. Sherburn (1931). Everyman's Library has a volume of the poems, and two volumes of The World's Classics give the translations from Homer. Parts of Dr. Johnson's biography are reprinted a little later in this section. G. Sherburn's *The Early Career of Alexander Pope* (1934) is an authoritative piece of scholarship, addressed to the specialist. Edith Sitwell's *Alexander Pope* (1930) is interesting but wildly uncritical. Among the more valuable studies are R. K. Root's *The Poetical Career of Alexander Pope* (1938) and G. Tillotson's *On the Poetry of Pope* (1938).

Alexander Pope

from AN ESSAY ON CRITICISM

THIS scintillating restatement of current principles was published in 1711, when Pope was twenty-three. Except for a favorable mention by Addison in the *Spectator* (no. 253), it met with little praise at first. The vindictive critic John Dennis (1657–1734), who is satirized in Part III, denounced it and called its author a hunchbacked toad. But the poem won its way. It was no accident that Pope's first important writing was an effort more critical than creative. Its precepts are not original; Pope is much indebted to the pronouncements of Horace, Dryden, and many others. The merit of the poem lies in its expression; it exemplifies its own famous definition (II, 297–8):

> True wit is nature to advantage dressed,
> What oft was thought, but ne'er so well expressed.

PART I

INTRODUCTION. *That 'tis as great a fault to judge ill as to write ill, and a more dangerous one to the public, verse 1. That a true taste is as rare to be found as a true genius, verses 9 to 18. That most men are born with some taste, but spoiled by false education, verses 19 to 25. The multitude of critics, and causes of them, verses 26 to 45. That we are to study our own taste, and know the limits of it, verses 46 to 67. Nature the best guide of judgment, verses 68 to 87. Improved by art and rules, which are but methodized nature, verse 88. Rules derived from the practice of the ancient poets, verses 88 to 110. That therefore the ancients are necessary to be studied by a critic, particularly Homer and Vergil, verses 120 to 138. Of licenses, and the use of them by the ancients, verses 142 to 180. Reverence due to the ancients, and praise of them, verses 181, &c.*

'Tis hard to say if greater want of skill
Appear in writing or in judging ill;
But, of the two, less dang'rous is the offense
To tire our patience than mislead our sense.
Some few in that, but numbers err in this;   5
Ten censure wrong for one who writes amiss;
A fool might once himself alone expose;
Now one in verse makes many more in prose.
'Tis with our judgments as our watches: none
Go just alike, yet each believes his own.   10
In poets as true genius is but rare,
True taste as seldom is the critic's share;
Both must alike from heav'n derive their light,
These born to judge, as well as those to write.
Let such teach others who themselves excel,   15
And censure freely, who have written well.

Many of its couplets have become common property among cultivated people. There is much sound advice in them; and there are few writers who are not the better for a course of discipline while they are learning how to write. The danger in such general instructions is that the small fry among the critics accept them as if they were the law and the gospel, and use them as a club with which to tame the boldness of the man who dares come forward with something new. Not that Pope demands an absolute worship of the Rules; his is a later phase of neoclassicism than that of its uncompromising heyday in Italy and France: let nature be your guide, though as a matter of common sense you had better abide by those laws of nature which the critics have discovered and which the greatest of the ancient writers have long since exemplified.

Authors are partial to their wit, 'tis true;
But are not critics to their judgment, too?
    Yet, if we look more closely, we shall find
Most have the seeds of judgment in their mind;   20
Nature affords at least a glimm'ring light;
The lines, though touched but faintly, are drawn right;
But as the slightest sketch, if justly traced,
Is by ill-coloring but the more disgraced,
So by false learning is good sense defaced: 25
Some are bewildered in the maze of schools,
And some made coxcombs[1] nature meant but fools.
In search of wit these lose their common sense,
And then turn critics in their own defense;
Each burns alike, who can or cannot write,   30
Or with a rival's or an eunuch's spite.
All fools have still an itching to deride,
And fain would be upon the laughing side.
If Maevius[2] scribble in Apollo's spite,
There are who judge still worse than he can write.   35
    Some have at first for wits, then poets passed,
Turned critics next, and proved plain fools at last.
Some neither can for wits nor critics pass,
As heavy mules are neither horse nor ass.
Those half-learned witlings, num'rous in our isle   40
As half-formed insects on the banks of Nile,[3]

---

[1] Conceited asses.
[2] A Roman writer who attacked Vergil; his name had become a byword.
[3] It was supposed that the mud of the Nile bred living creatures.

Unfinished things, one knows not what to call,
Their generation's[4] so equivocal,
To tell 'em would a hundred tongues require,
Or one vain wit's, that might a hundred tire.

But you who seek to give and merit fame,   45
And justly bear a critic's noble name,
Be sure yourself and your own reach to know,
How far your genius, taste, and learning go;
Launch not beyond your depth, but be discreet,   50
And mark that point where sense and dullness meet.

Nature to all things fixed the limits fit,
And wisely curbed proud man's pretending wit.
As on the land, while here the ocean gains,
In other parts it leaves wide sandy plains,   55
Thus in the soul, while memory prevails,
The solid pow'r of understanding fails;
Where beams of warm imagination play,
The memory's soft figures melt away.
One science only will one genius fit;   60
So vast is art, so narrow human wit,
Not only bounded to peculiar arts,
But oft in those confined to single parts.
Like kings, we lose the conquests gained before,
By vain ambition still to make them more;   65
Each might his sev'ral province well command,
Would all but stoop to what they understand.

First follow nature,[5] and your judgment frame
By her just standard, which is still the same:
Unerring nature, still divinely bright,   70
One clear, unchanged, and universal light,
Life, force, and beauty, must to all impart,
At once the source and end and test of art.
Art from that fund each just supply provides,
Works without show, and without pomp presides;   75
In some fair body thus th' informing soul
With spirits feeds, with vigor fills the whole,
Each motion guides, and ev'ry nerve sustains;
Itself unseen, but in the effects remains.
Some, to whom heav'n in wit[6] has been profuse,   80
Want as much more, to turn it to its use;
For wit and judgment often are at strife,
Though meant each other's aid, like man and wife.
'Tis more to guide than spur the Muse's steed,
Restrain his fury than provoke his speed;   85

The wingèd courser,[7] like a gen'rous[8] horse,
Shows most true mettle when you check his course.
Those rules of old discovered, not devised,
Are nature still, but nature methodized;
Nature, like liberty, is but restrained   90
By the same laws which first herself ordained.

Hear how learn'd Greece her useful rules indites,
When to repress and when indulge our flights:
High on Parnassus'[9] top her sons she showed,
And pointed out those arduous paths they trod;   95
Held from afar, aloft, the immortal prize,
And urged the rest by equal steps to rise.
Just precepts thus from great examples giv'n,
She drew from them what they derived from heav'n.
The gen'rous critic fanned the poet's fire,   100
And taught the world with reason to admire.
Then Criticism the Muse's handmaid proved,
To dress her charms, and make her more beloved;
But following wits from that intention strayed:
Who could not win the mistress, wooed the maid;   105
Against the poets their own arms they turned,
Sure to hate most the men from whom they learned.
So modern 'pothecaries, taught the art
By doctors' bills[10] to play the doctor's part,
Bold in the practice of mistaken rules,   110
Prescribe, apply, and call their masters fools.
Some on the leaves of ancient authors prey;
Nor time nor moths e'er spoiled so much as they.
Some drily plain, without invention's aid,
Write dull receipts how poems may be made.   115
These leave the sense, their learning to display;
And those explain the meaning quite away.

You, then, whose judgment the right course would
      steer,
Know well each ancient's proper character;
His fable, subject, scope in ev'ry page,   120
Religion, country, genius of his age;
Without all these at once before your eyes,
Cavil you may, but never criticize.
Be Homer's works your study and delight;
Read them by day, and meditate by night;   125
Thence form your judgment, thence your maxims bring,
And trace the Muses upward to their spring.[11]
Still with itself compared, his text peruse;
And let your comment be the Mantuan Muse.[12]

---

4 The way they are given life.
5 Here, not simply the outside world of physical phenomena,
but also the sum total of what mankind has experienced. Pope
uses the word *nature* (like the word *wit*) in a variety of meanings. By *nature* he usually means the reasonable, the sensible,
the regular, the orderly, the universal.
6 Here, inventive power, fancy. Cf. lines 53, 61, where *wit* =na-
tive intelligence.

7 Pegasus, the Muses' winged horse.
8 Noble.
9 A mountain range in central Greece, the haunt of the Muses.
10 Prescriptions.
11 On Mt. Helicon, sacred to the Muses, in central Greece.
12 Publius Vergilius Maro (d. 19 B.C.), author of the *Aeneid*, etc.
He was born near Mantua.

When first young Maro in his boundless mind   130
A work t' outlast immortal Rome designed,
Perhaps he seemed above the critic's law,
And but from nature's fountains scorned to draw;
But when t' examine ev'ry part he came,
Nature and Homer were, he found, the same.   135
Convinced, amazed, he checks the bold design;
And rules as strict his labored work confine
As if the Stagirite[13] o'erlooked each line.
Learn hence for ancient rules a just esteem;
To copy nature is to copy them.   140
    Some beauties yet no precepts can declare,
For there's a happiness[14] as well as care.
Music resembles poetry; in each
Are nameless graces which no methods teach,
And which a master hand alone can reach.   145
If, where the rules not far enough extend
(Since rules were made but to promote their end),
Some lucky license answer to the full
Th' intent proposed, that license is a rule.
Thus Pegasus, a nearer way to take,   150
May boldly deviate from the common track.
From vulgar bounds with brave disorder part,
And snatch a grace beyond the reach of art,
Which, without passing through the judgment, gains
The heart, and all its end at once attains.   155
In prospects, thus some objects please our eyes,
Which out of nature's common order rise:
The shapeless rock, or hanging precipice.
Great wits sometimes may gloriously offend,
And rise to faults true critics dare not mend.   160
But though the ancients thus their rules invade
(As kings dispense which laws themselves have made),
Moderns, beware! or if you must offend
Against the precept, ne'er transgress its end;
Let it be seldom, and compelled by need,   165
And have at least their precedent to plead.
The critic else proceeds without remorse,
Seizes your fame, and puts his laws in force.
    I know there are[15] to whose presumptuous thoughts
Those freer beauties, ev'n in them, seem faults.[16]   170
Some figures monstrous and misshaped appear,
Considered singly, or beheld too near,
Which, but proportioned to their light or place,
Due distance reconciles to form and grace.
A prudent chief not always must display   175
His pow'rs[17] in equal ranks and fair array,

But with th' occasion and the place comply,
Conceal his force, nay, seem sometimes to fly.
Those oft are stratagems which errors seem;
Nor is it Homer nods, but we that dream.   180
    Still green with bays each ancient altar stands,
Above the reach of sacrilegious hands,
Secure from flames, from envy's fiercer rage,
Destructive war, and all-involving age.
See from each clime the learn'd their incense bring!   185
Hear in all tongues consenting paeans ring!
In praise so just let ev'ry voice be joined,
And fill the gen'ral chorus of mankind.
Hail, bards triumphant! born in happier days,
Immortal heirs of universal praise!   190
Whose honors with increase of ages grow,
As streams roll down, enlarging as they flow;
Nations unborn your mighty names shall sound,
And worlds applaud that must not yet be found!
O may some spark of your celestial fire   195
The last, the meanest, of your sons inspire
(That on weak wings, from far, pursues your flights,
Glows while he reads, but trembles as he writes)
To teach vain wits a science little known,
T' admire superior sense, and doubt their own!   200

PART II

CAUSES *hindering a true judgment:* 1. *Pride, verse* 208. 2. *Imperfect learning, verse* 215. 3. *Judging by parts and not by the whole, verses* 233 *to* 288; *critics in wit, language, versification, only, verses* 288, 305, 339, &c. 4. *Being too hard to please, or too apt to admire, verse* 384. 5. *Partiality, too much love to a sect, to the ancients or moderns, verse* 394. 6. *Prejudice or prevention,*[18] *verse* 408. 7. *Singularity, verse* 424. 8. *Inconstancy, verse* 430. 9. *Party spirit, verses* 452, &c. 10. *Envy, verse* 466; *against envy and in praise of good nature, verses* 508, &c.; *when severity is chiefly to be used by critics, verses* 526, &c.

Of all the causes which conspire to blind
Man's erring judgment and misguide the mind,
What the weak head with strongest bias rules
Is pride, the never-failing vice of fools.
Whatever nature has in worth denied   205
She gives in large recruits[19] of needful pride;
For, as in bodies, thus in souls we find
What wants in blood and spirits swelled with wind:
Pride, where wit fails, steps in to our defense,
And fills up all the mighty void of sense.   210
If once right reason drives that cloud away,
Truth breaks upon us with resistless day.
Trust not yourself; but, your defects to know,
Make use of ev'ry friend—and ev'ry foe.

---

[13] The first great critic, Aristotle (d. 322 B.C.); he was born at Stagira in Macedonia.
[14] I.e., there are lucky or inspired strokes in writing. Lines 141–58 are remarkably liberal.   [15] There are those.
[16] The *l* was not pronounced.   [17] Troops.

[18] Prepossession, bias.   [19] Supplies.

A little learning is a dang'rous thing;   215
Drink deep, or taste not the Pierian spring:[20]
There shallow draughts intoxicate the brain,
And drinking largely sobers us again.
Fired at first sight with what the Muse imparts,
In fearless youth we tempt the heights of arts,   220
While from the bounded level of our mind
Short views we take, nor see the lengths behind;
But more advanced, behold with strange surprise
New distant scenes of endless science rise!
So pleased at first the tow'ring Alps we try,   225
Mount o'er the vales, and seem to tread the sky;
Th' eternal snows appear already past,
And the first clouds and mountains seem the last.
But those attained, we tremble to survey
The growing labors of the lengthened way;   230
Th' increasing prospect tires our wand'ring eyes,
Hills peep o'er hills, and Alps on Alps arise!
     A perfect judge will read each work of wit
With the same spirit that its author writ:
Survey the whole, nor seek slight faults to find   235
Where nature moves, and rapture warms the mind;
Nor lose, for that malignant dull delight,
The gen'rous pleasure to be charmed with wit.
But in such lays as neither ebb nor flow,
Correctly cold, and regularly low,   240
That, shunning faults, one quiet tenor keep,
We cannot blame indeed—but we may sleep.
In wit, as nature, what affects our hearts
Is not th' exactness of peculiar parts;
'Tis not a lip or eye we beauty call,   245
But the joint force and full result of all.
Thus when we view some well proportioned dome[21]
(The world's just wonder, and ev'n thine, O Rome!)
No single parts unequally surprise;
All comes united to th' admiring eyes;   250
No monstrous height or breadth or length appear;
The whole at once is bold, and regular.
     Whoever thinks a faultless piece to see,
Thinks what ne'er was, nor is, nor e'er shall be.
In ev'ry work regard the writer's end,   255
Since none can compass more than they intend;
And if the means be just, the conduct true,
Applause, in spite of trivial faults, is due.
As men of breeding, sometimes men of wit,
T' avoid great errors must the less commit,   260
Neglect the rules each verbal critic lays,
For not to know some trifles is a praise.
Most critics, fond of some subservient art,
Still make the whole depend upon a part;

They talk of principles, but notions prize,   265
And all to one loved folly sacrifice.
     Once on a time La Mancha's knight,[22] they say,
A certain bard encount'ring on the way,
Discoursed in terms as just, with looks as sage,
As e'er could Dennis,[23] of the Grecian stage;   270
Concluding all were desp'rate sots and fools
Who durst depart from Aristotle's rules.
Our author, happy in a judge so nice,
Produced his play, and begged the knight's advice;
Made him observe the subject and the plot,   275
The manners, passions, unities—what not?
All which exact to rule were brought about,
Were but a combat in the lists left out.
"What! leave the combat out?" exclaims the knight.
"Yes, or we must renounce the Stagirite."   280
"Not so, by heav'n!" he answers in a rage;
"Knights, squires, and steeds must enter on the stage."
"So vast a throng the stage can ne'er contain."
"Then build a new, or act it in a plain."
     Thus critics of less judgment than caprice,   285
Curious, not knowing, not exact but nice,
Form short ideas, and offend in arts
(As most in manners) by a love to parts.
     Some to conceit[24] alone their taste confine,
And glitt'ring thoughts struck out at ev'ry line;   290
Pleased with a work where nothing's just or fit,
One glaring chaos and wild heap of wit.
Poets, like painters, thus unskilled to trace
The naked nature and the living grace,
With gold and jewels cover ev'ry part,   295
And hide with ornaments their want of art.
True wit is nature to advantage dressed,
What oft was thought, but ne'er so well expressed;[25]
Something whose truth convinced at sight we find,
That gives us back the image of our mind.   300
As shades more sweetly recommend the light,
So modest plainness sets off sprightly wit;
For works may have more wit than does 'em good,
As bodies perish through excess of blood.
     Others for language all their care express,   305
And value books, as women men, for dress.
Their praise is still, "The style is excellent."—
The sense they humbly take upon content.[26]
Words are like leaves; and where they most abound,
Much fruit of sense beneath is rarely found.   310

[22] Don Quixote, but this incident is from a spurious continuation, not by Cervantes.
[23] John Dennis (1657–1734), a well-known critic.
[24] Striking (sometimes far-fetched) metaphors or comparisons.
[25] This couplet sums up neoclassical conservatism.
[26] On trust.

[20] Pieria in Macedonia was an early seat of the worship of the Muses.   [21] The Pantheon, or possibly St. Peter's.

False eloquence, like the prismatic glass,
Its gaudy colors spreads on ev'ry place;
The face of nature we no more survey:
All glares alike, without distinction gay.
But true expression, like th' unchanging sun,⎫
Clears and improves whate'er it shines upon;⎬ 315
It gilds all objects, but it alters none.⎭
Expression is the dress of thought, and still
Appears more decent as more suitable;
A vile conceit in pompous words expressed   320
Is like a clown in regal purple dressed;
For diff'rent styles with diff'rent subjects sort,[27]
As sev'ral garbs with country, town, and court.
Some by old words to fame have made pretense,
Ancients in phrase, mere moderns in their sense;   325
Such labored nothings, in so strange a style,
Amaze th' unlearn'd, and make the learned smile.
Unlucky as Fungoso in the play,[28]⎫
These sparks with awkward vanity display⎬
What the fine gentleman wore yesterday;⎭   330
And but so mimic ancient wits, at best,
As apes our grandsires, in their doublets dressed.
In words as fashions the same rule will hold,
Alike fantastic if too new or old:
Be not the first by whom the new are tried,   335
Nor yet the last to lay the old aside.
    But most by numbers[29] judge a poet's song,
And smooth or rough with them is right or wrong:
In the bright Muse though thousand charms conspire,
Her voice is all these tuneful fools admire;   340
Who haunt Parnassus but to please their ear,⎫
Not mend their minds; as some to church repair,⎬
Not for the doctrine, but the music there.⎭
These equal syllables alone require,
Though oft the ear the open vowels tire;[30]   345
While expletives their feeble aid do join,
And ten low words oft creep in one dull line;
While they ring round the same unvaried chimes,
With sure returns of still-expected rimes:
Where'er you find "the cooling western breeze,"   350
In the next line it "whispers through the trees";
If crystal streams "with pleasing murmurs creep,"
The reader's threatened (not in vain) with "sleep";

Then, at the last and only couplet fraught
With some unmeaning thing they call a thought,   355
A needless Alexandrine[31] ends the song,
That, like a wounded snake, drags its slow length along.
Leave such to tune their own dull rimes, and know
What's roundly smooth or languishingly slow;
And praise the easy vigor of a line   360
Where Denham's[32] strength and Waller's sweetness join.
True ease in writing comes from art, not chance,
As those move easiest who have learned to dance.
'Tis not enough no harshness gives offense;
The sound must seem an echo to the sense.   365
Soft is the strain when zephyr gently blows,
And the smooth stream in smoother numbers flows;
But when loud surges lash the sounding shore,
The hoarse, rough verse should like the torrent roar.
When Ajax[33] strives some rock's vast weight to throw,
The line too labors, and the words move slow;   371
Not so when swift Camilla[34] scours the plain,
Flies o'er the unbending corn,[35] and skims along the main.
Hear how Timotheus'[36] varied lays surprise,
And bid alternate passions fall and rise!   375
While, at each change, the son of Libyan Jove[37]
Now burns with glory and then melts with love;
Now his fierce eyes with sparkling fury glow,
Now sighs steal out and tears begin to flow:
Persians and Greeks like turns of nature found,   380
And the world's victor stood subdued by sound!
The pow'r of music all our hearts allow,
And what Timotheus was, is Dryden now.
    Avoid extremes, and shun the fault of such
Who still are pleased too little or too much.   385
At ev'ry trifle scorn to take offense;
That always shows great pride or little sense.
Those heads, as stomachs, are not sure the best
Which nauseate all,[38] and nothing can digest.
Yet let not each gay turn thy rapture move,   390
For fools admire,[39] but men of sense approve;[40]

---

27 Consort, harmonize.
28 A would-be fop in Jonson's *Every Man out of His Humor.*
29 Versification.
30 I.e., such critics ask only that the syllables total up to the proper
   number, irrespective of the tiresome effect of "open" vowels.
   By the last Pope means the effect that results from following a
   word ending in a vowel by a word beginning with one. He has
   three examples in line 345. This is the reason why elisions of
   vowels are so frequent in neoclassical verse; the correct form
   was *th' open*, not *the open*. Lines 344-73 illustrate Pope's various
   points.

31 A line of six iambic feet, normally with twelve syllables; the
   next line is an example.
32 Sir John Denham (1615-69) and Edmund Waller (pp. 517-19,
   above), though minor poets, were credited with developing the
   heroic couplet.
33 Pictured in the *Iliad* as surpassing the other Greek chieftains in
   bodily strength.
34 A woman warrior who fought against the Trojans in Italy
   (*Aeneid*, VII, 808 ff.).   35 Grain.
36 Musician of Alexander the Great. Doubtless Pope is thinking of
   Dryden's "Alexander's Feast."
37 Alexander. On the eastern border of Libya there was a temple
   to Jupiter Ammon, who Alexander liked to believe was his
   father.   38 Are nauseated by everything.   39 Wonder.
40 I.e., are quiet in their approval, without indulging in that
   reprehensible thing "enthusiasm."

As things seem large which we through mists descry,
Dullness is ever apt to magnify.

Some foreign writers, some our own despise;
The ancients only, or the moderns prize.   395
Thus wit, like faith, by each man is applied
To one small sect, and all are damned beside.
Meanly they seek the blessing to confine,
And force that sun but on a part to shine,
Which not alone the southern wit sublimes,   400
But ripens spirits in cold northern climes;
Which from the first has shone on ages past,
Enlights the present, and shall warm the last;
Though each may feel increases and decays,
And see now clearer and now darker days: 405
Regard not, then, if wit be old or new,
But blame the false and value still the true.

Some ne'er advance a judgment of their own,
But catch the spreading notion of the town;
They reason and conclude by precedent,   410
And own stale nonsense which they ne'er invent.
Some judge of authors' names, not works, and then
Nor praise nor blame the writings, but the men.
Of all this servile herd, the worst is he
That in proud dullness joins with quality,[41]   415
A constant critic at the great man's board,
To fetch and carry nonsense for my Lord.
What woeful stuff this madrigal would be
In some starved hackney[42] sonneteer, or me!
But let a lord once own the happy lines,   420
How the wit brightens! how the style refines!
Before his sacred name flies ev'ry fault,
And each exalted stanza teems with thought!

The vulgar thus through imitation err,
As oft the learn'd by being singular;   425
So much they scorn the crowd, that if the throng
By chance go right, they purposely go wrong;
So schísmatics[43] the plain believers quit,
And are but damned for having too much wit.
Some praise at morning what they blame at night,   430
But always think the last opinion right.
A Muse by these is like a mistress used:
This hour she's idolized, the next abused;
While their weak heads, like towns unfortified,
'Twixt sense and nonsense daily change their side.   435
Ask them the cause; they're wiser still, they say;
And still tomorrow's wiser than today.
We think our fathers fools, so wise we grow;
Our wiser sons no doubt will think us so.
Once school divines[44] this zealous isle o'erspread;   440

Who knew most sentences[45] was deepest read.
Faith, gospel, all, seemed made to be disputed;
And none had sense enough to be confuted.
Scotists and Thomists[46] now in peace remain
Amidst their kindred cobwebs in Duck Lane.[47]   445
If faith itself has diff'rent dresses worn,
What wonder modes in wit should take their turn?
Oft, leaving what is natural and fit,
The current folly proves the ready wit;[48]
And authors think their reputation safe,   450
Which lives as long as fools are pleased to laugh.

Some, valuing those of their own side or mind,
Still[49] make themselves the measure of mankind;
Fondly we think we honor merit then,
When we but praise ourselves in other men.   455
Parties in wit attend on those of state,
And public faction doubles private hate.
Pride, malice, folly, against Dryden rose,
In various shapes of parsons,[50] critics, beaus;[51]
But sense survived when merry jests were past,   460
For rising merit will buoy up at last.
Might he return and bless once more our eyes,
New Blackmores and new Milbournes[52] must arise:
Nay, should great Homer lift his awful head,
Zoilus[53] again would start up from the dead.   465
Envy will merit as its shade pursue,
But, like a shadow, proves the substance true;
For envied wit, like Sol eclipsed, makes known
The opposing body's grossness, not its own.
When first that sun too pow'rful beams displays,   470
It draws up vapors which obscure its rays;
But ev'n those clouds at last adorn its way,
Reflect new glories, and augment the day.

Be thou the first true merit to befriend;
His praise is lost who stays till all commend.   475
Short is the date, alas, of modern rimes,
And 'tis but just to let them live betimes.[54]
No longer now that golden age appears,
When patriarch wits[55] survived a thousand years;
Now length of fame (our second life) is lost,   480
And bare threescore is all ev'n that can boast:
Our sons their fathers' failing language see,
And such as Chaucer is shall Dryden be.

[45] Sayings (especially from the Church Fathers).
[46] Followers of the scholastic controversialists Duns Scotus (d. 1308) and St. Thomas Aquinas (d. 1274?).
[47] A street of second-hand booksellers, near Smithfield.
[48] Approves of facile cleverness.   [49] Always.
[50] E.g., Jeremy Collier (see p. 632, above).
[51] Probably the second Duke of Buckingham (see p. 619, note 74).
[52] Dryden was belittled in Sir Richard Blackmore's *Satire against Wit* (1700) and attacked in Luke Milbourne's *Notes on Dryden's Vergil* (1898).
[53] Greek grammarian of the fourth century B.C. who attacked the *Iliad* and *Odyssey*.   [54] In good season.   [55] Authors.

[41] People of rank.
[42] Hack.   [43] Followers of eccentric religious sects.
[44] Scholastic theologians.

Compositium jus, fasque animi, sanctosque recessus
Mentis, & incoctum generoso pectus honesto.

TRAVELS

INTO SEVERAL

Remote Nations

OF THE

WORLD.

In Four PARTS.

By *LEMUEL GULLIVER*,
First a SURGEON, and then a CAP-
TAIN of several SHIPS.

VOL. I.

LONDON:

Printed for BENJ. MOTTE, *at the*
Middle Temple-Gate *in* Fleet-ſtreet.
MDCCXXVI.

GULLIVER'S TRAVELS
The frontiſpiece and title page of the firſt edition. (Harvard College Library)

The SPECTATOR.

Non fumum ex fulgore, ſed ex fumo dare lucem
Cogitat, ut ſpecioſa dehinc miracula promat. Hor.

To be Continued every Day.

THE SPECTATOR, NO. 1

Printed on a folio half-ſheet, the
paper ſold for a penny, until the
price was doubled in August, 1712.
(Harvard College Library)

Thurſday, March 1. 1711.

I Have obſerved, that a Reader ſeldom peruſes
a Book with Pleaſure 'till he knows whether
the Writer of it be a black or a fair Man, of
a mild or cholerick Diſpoſition, Married or a
Batchelor, with other Particulars of the like
nature, that conduce very much to the right Un-
derſtanding of an Author. To gratify this Curio-
ſity, which is ſo natural to a Reader, I deſign this
ſtinguiſhed my ſelf by a moſt profound Silence: For
during the Space of eight Years, excepting in
the publick Exerciſes of the College, I ſcarce uttered the Quantity of an hundred Words; and indeed do not remember that I ever ſpoke three Sentences together in my whole Life. Whilſt I was
in this Learned Body I applied my ſelf with ſo
much Diligence to my Studies, that there are very

ALEXANDER POPE
An engraving by Houbraken.

ALEXANDER POPE Esq.

Twickenham is on the Thames not far west of
London. The villa shown here (the wings are
later) was bought by Pope in 1719. The
grounds were his special delight; they contained
a shell temple, a vineyard, an obelisk in memory
of Pope's mother, a bowling green, a grove, an
orangery, a kitchen garden, and a grotto. Dr
Johnson wrote: "Being under the necessity of
making a subterranean passage to a garden on
the other side of the road, he adorned it with
fossil bodies, and dignified it with the title of
a grotto; a place of silence and retreat, from
which he endeavored to persuade his friends
that cares and passions could be excluded."

POPE'S VILLA AT
TWICKENHAM

Engraving by William
Watts. (Harvard Col-
lege Library)

So when the faithful pencil has designed
Some bright idea of the master's mind,   485
Where a new world leaps out at his command,
And ready nature waits upon his hand;
When the ripe colors soften and unite,
And sweetly melt into just shade and light;
When mellowing years their full perfection give,   490
And each bold figure just begins to live:
The treach'rous colors the fair art betray,
And all the bright creation fades away!

   Unhappy wit, like most mistaken things,
Atones not for that envy which it brings.   495
In youth alone its empty praise we boast,
But soon the short-lived vanity is lost;
Like some fair flower the early spring supplies,
That gaily blooms, but ev'n in blooming dies.
What is this wit, which must our cares employ?   500
The owner's wife that other men enjoy;
Then most our trouble still when most admired,
And still the more we give, the more required;
Whose fame with pains we guard, but lose with ease,
Sure some to vex, but never all to please;   505
'Tis what the vicious fear, the virtuous shun;
By fools 'tis hated, and by knaves undone!

   If wit so much from ign'rance undergo,
Ah, let not learning too commence its foe!
Of old those met rewards who could excel,   510
And such were praised who but endeavored well;
Though triumphs were to gen'rals only due,
Crowns were reserved to grace the soldiers too.
Now, they who reach Parnassus' lofty crown
Employ their pains to spurn[56] some others down;   515
And while self-love each jealous writer rules,
Contending wits become the sport of fools:
But still the worst with most regret commend,
For each ill author is as bad a friend.
To what base ends, and by what abject ways,   520
Are mortals urged through sacred lust of praise!

Ah, ne'er so dire a thirst of glory boast,
Nor in the critic let the man be lost.
Good nature and good sense must ever join;
To err is human: to forgive, divine.   525
   But if in noble minds some dregs remain,
Not yet purged off, of spleen and sour disdain,
Discharge that rage on more provoking crimes,
Nor fear a dearth in these flagitious[57] times.
No pardon vile obscenity should find,   530
Though wit and art conspire to move your mind;
But dullness with obscenity must prove
As shameful sure as impotence in love.
In the fat age of pleasure, wealth, and ease,
Sprung the rank weed, and thrived with large increase:
When love was all an easy monarch's[58] care,   536
Seldom at council, never in a war;
Jilts ruled the state, and statesmen farces writ;
Nay wits had pensions, and young lords had wit;
The fair sat panting at a courtier's play,   540
And not a mask[59] went unimproved away;
The modest fan was lifted up no more,
And virgins smiled at what they blushed before.
The following license of a foreign reign[60]
Did all the dregs of bold Socinus[61] drain;   545
Then unbelieving priests reformed the nation,
And taught more pleasant methods of salvation;
Where heav'n's free subjects might their rights dispute,
Lest God himself should seem too absolute;
Pulpits their sacred satire learned to spare,   550
And vice admired[62] to find a flatt'rer there!
Encouraged thus, wit's titans braved the skies,
And the press groaned with licensed blasphemies.
These monsters, critics, with your darts engage!
Here point your thunder, and exhaust your rage!   555
Yet shun their fault, who, scandalously nice,
Will needs mistake an author into vice:
All seems infected that th' infected spy,
As all looks yellow to the jaundiced eye.

THE RAPE OF THE LOCK

AN HEROI-COMICAL POEM

POPE was friendly with a group of Catholic families who
owned estates in the "home counties," some near Windsor.
Two of them were involved in the incident which occasioned this clever, airy trifle of a masterpiece. The birth
date of Arabella Fermor, the poem's Belinda, is unknown;
she was married, presumably young, but not to the bold
Baron, about two years after Pope wrote the first version.

From her pretty head, Robert, seventh Lord Petre, had
snipped the lock in question; and the theft was so seriously
resented that a friend of the families, John Caryll, who
was also a friend of Pope, suggested an attempt to smooth

57 Wicked.   58 Charles II.
59 Lady. It was fashionable to wear a mask at the theater.
60 Of William III.
61 Faustus Socinus (d. 1604) was an Italian theologian who denied
   the divinity of Christ and adopted a Unitarian position.
62 Was amazed.

56 Kick.

things over with some light verse. How accurate Pope's details are has never been ascertained. He was not acquainted with Lord Petre; Miss Fermor he may have met. The original version, in two cantos, was composed in 1711 and published the following spring. In manuscript the families had liked it; but a number of Pope's lines have double meanings, and when it was offered to the town in print the Fermors changed their minds. Pope knew he had written a masterpiece and decided to expand it. He added the "machinery" of the sylphs, and in 1714 brought it out again, in five cantos.

The form is the mock-epic, a branch of the mock-heroic. It is the opposite of burlesque, in which great affairs and persons are handled ridiculously. The mock-heroic treats trivial matters and private persons with pretended gravity, in an inflated style, as in Chaucer's "The Nun's Priest's Tale" of the cock and hen. For *The Rape of the Lock* Pope uses the stock devices of the epic: the formal harangue, the extended simile, the battle, the supernatural machinery, the lofty tone, the moral elevation. The satire, always playful, is aimed at the foibles of fashionable society. Much of it is sufficiently general to remain applicable; and to that and to its intimate glimpses into the customs of our ancestors, still more our ancestresses, is due a large part of the pleasure the poem affords. But it is primarily the sparkling play of Pope's fancy and wit that delights the reader.

Nolueram, Belinda,[1] tuos violare capillos,
Sed juvat hoc precibus me tribuisse tuis.
MARTIAL, *Epigrams*, XII, 84

CANTO I

What dire offense from am'rous causes springs,
What mighty contests rise from trivial things,
I sing—this verse to Caryll,[2] Muse! is due;
This, ev'n Belinda may vouchsafe to view:
Slight is the subject, but not so the praise,   5
If she inspire, and he approve my lays.
    Say what strange motive, goddess! could compel
A well-bred lord t' assault a gentle belle!
Oh, say what stranger cause, yet unexplored,
Could make a gentle belle reject a lord!   10
In tasks so bold can little men engage,
And in soft bosoms dwells such mighty rage?
    Sol through white curtains shot a tim'rous ray,
And oped those eyes that must eclipse the day;
Now lap dogs give themselves the rousing shake,   15
And sleepless lovers, just at twelve, awake:
Thrice rung the bell, the slipper knocked the ground,
And the pressed watch[3] returned a silver sound.
Belinda still her downy pillow pressed;
Her guardian sylph[4] prolonged the balmy rest: 20

'Twas he had summoned to her silent bed
The morning dream that hovered o'er her head.
A youth more glitt'ring than a birthnight[5] beau
(That ev'n in slumber caused her cheek to glow)
Seemed to her ear his winning lips to lay,   25
And thus in whispers said, or seemed to say:
    "Fairest of mortals, thou distinguished care
Of thousand bright inhabitants of air!
If e'er one vision touched thy infant thought,
Of all the nurse and all the priest have taught—   30
Of airy elves by moonlight shadows seen,
The silver token,[6] and the circled green,[7]
Or virgins visited by angel pow'rs,
With golden crowns and wreaths of heav'nly flow'rs—
Hear and believe! thy own importance know,   35
Nor bound thy narrow views to things below.
Some secret truths, from learned pride concealed,
To maids alone and children are revealed:
What though no credit doubting wits may give?
The fair and innocent shall still believe.   40
Know, then, unnumbered spirits round thee fly,
The light militia of the lower sky;
These, though unseen, are ever on the wing,
Hang o'er the box,[8] and hover round the ring.[9]
Think what an equipage thou hast in air,   45
And view with scorn two pages and a chair.
As now your own, our beings were of old,
And once inclosed in woman's beauteous mold;
Thence, by a soft transition, we repair
From earthly vehicles to these of air.   50
Think not, when woman's transient breath is fled,

---

[1] Pope substitutes this name for the one in the original. Translation: I did not wish, Belinda, to do violence to your locks, but I am glad to grant this much to your request. (The implication, rightly or not, is that Miss Fermor had asked Pope to write the poem.)
[2] John Caryll (1666?–1736), a nephew of the minor poet and playwright (1625–1711) of the same name. See headnote.
[3] A "repeater"; when a pin was pressed, it struck the latest hour.
[4] In the dedicatory epistle to Arabella Fermor ("Belinda"), Pope playfully explains that the four "elements" (air, earth, water, fire) are said to be "inhabited by spirits, which they call sylphs, gnomes, nymphs, and salamanders." The gnomes, the earth spirits, "delight in mischief; but the sylphs, whose habitation is the air," are benevolent, and such mortals as preserve their chastity may become intimate with them. In this mock-epic, these spirits replace the deities of the classical epic.

[5] I.e., at the ball on the royal birthday.
[6] The silver penny which the fairies dropped at night into the shoe of a maid who did her work tidily.
[7] Rings of darker grass were supposed to show where the fairies danced.   [8] At the theater.
[9] The fashionable drive and promenade in Hyde Park.

That all her vanities at once are dead;
Succeeding vanities she still regards,
And, though she plays no more, o'erlooks the cards.
Her joy in gilded chariots, when alive,   55
And love of ombre,[10] after death survive.
For when the fair in all their pride expire,
To their first elements their souls retire:
The sprites of fiery termagants in flame
Mount up, and take a salamander's name.   60
Soft, yielding minds to water glide away,
And sip, with nymphs, their elemental tea.[11]
The graver prude sinks downward to a gnome,
In search of mischief still on earth to roam.
The light coquettes in sylphs aloft repair,   65
And sport and flutter in the fields of air.
    "Know farther yet: whoever fair and chaste
Rejects mankind, is by some sylph embraced;
For spirits, freed from mortal laws, with ease
Assume what sexes and what shapes they please.   70
What guards the purity of melting maids,
In courtly balls, and midnight masquerades,
Safe from the treach'rous friend, the daring spark,
The glance by day, the whisper in the dark,
When kind occasion prompts their warm desires,   75
When music softens, and when dancing fires?
'Tis but their sylph, the wise celestials know,
Though *honor* is the word with men below.
    "Some nymphs there are, too conscious of their face,
For life predestined to the gnomes' embrace.   80
These swell their prospects and exalt their pride,
When offers are disdained, and love denied.
Then gay ideas crowd the vacant brain,
While peers and dukes and all their sweeping train,
And garters, stars, and coronets, appear,   85
And in soft sounds 'Your Grace' salutes their ear.
'Tis these that early taint the female soul,
Instruct the eyes of young coquettes to roll,
Teach infant cheeks a bidden blush to know,
And little hearts to flutter at a beau.   90
    "Oft, when the world imagine women stray,
The sylphs through mystic mazes guide their way;
Through all the giddy circle they pursue,
And old impertinence[12] expel by new.
What tender maid but must a victim fall   95
To one man's treat, but for another's ball?
When Florio speaks, what virgin could withstand,
If gentle Damon[13] did not squeeze her hand?
With varying vanities, from ev'ry part,

They shift the moving toyshop of their heart: 100
Where wigs with wigs, with sword knots[14] sword knots
    strive,
Beaus banish beaus, and coaches coaches drive.
This erring mortals levity may call;
Oh, blind to truth! the sylphs contrive it all.
    "Of these am I, who thy protection claim,   105
A watchful sprite, and Ariel is my name.
Late, as I ranged the crystal wilds of air,
In the clear mirror of thy ruling star
I saw, alas! some dread event impend,
Ere to the main this morning sun descend;   110
But heav'n reveals not what or how or where:
Warned by the sylph, oh, pious maid, beware!
This to disclose is all thy guardian can:
Beware of all, but most beware of man!"
    He said; when Shock,[15] who thought she slept too long,
Leaped up and waked his mistress with his tongue.   116
'Twas then, Belinda, if report say true,
Thy eyes first opened on a billet-doux;
Wounds, charms, and ardors were no sooner read
But all the vision vanished from thy head.   120
    And now, unveiled, the toilet stands displayed,
Each silver vase in mystic order laid.
First, robed in white, the nymph intent adores,
With head uncovered, the cosmetic pow'rs.
A heav'nly image in the glass appears;   125
To that she bends, to that her eyes she rears;
The inferior priestess,[16] at her altar's side,
Trembling begins the sacred rites of pride.
Unnumbered treasures ope at once, and here
The various off'rings of the world appear;   130
From each she nicely culls with curious toil,
And decks the goddess with the glitt'ring spoil.
This casket India's glowing gems unlocks,
And all Arabia[17] breathes from yonder box.
The tortoise here and elephant unite,   135
Transformed to combs, the speckled and the white.
Here files of pins extend their shining rows,
Puffs, powders, patches, bibles, billets-doux.
Now awful beauty puts on all its arms;
The fair each moment rises in her charms,   140
Repairs her smiles, awakens ev'ry grace,
And calls forth all the wonders of her face;
Sees by degrees a purer blush arise,
And keener lightnings quicken in her eyes.
The busy sylphs surround their darling care,   145
These set the head, and those divide the hair,
Some fold the sleeve, whilst other plait the gown;
And Betty's praised for labors not her own.

---

10 The fashionable card game of the day; pronounced ŏmber (from
    Spanish *hombre,* man).
11 *Ea* was then pronounced as in *great.*   12 Trifles.
13 Like *Florio,* a conventional name for a lover.

14 Ribbons or tassels on hilts.
15 The shock was a long-haired dog, popular as a lap dog.
16 Betty, her maid.   17 Famous for perfumes.

CANTO II

Not with more glories, in th' ethereal plain,
The sun first rises o'er the purpled main,
Than, issuing forth, the rival of his beams
Launched on the bosom of the silver Thames.
Fair nymphs and well-dressed youths around her shone, 5
But ev'ry eye was fixed on her alone.
On her white breast a sparkling cross she wore,
Which Jews might kiss, and infidels adore.
Her lively looks a sprightly mind disclose,
Quick as her eyes, and as unfixed as those: 10
Favors to none, to all she smiles extends;
Oft she rejects, but never once offends.
Bright as the sun, her eyes the gazers strike,
And, like the sun, they shine on all alike.
Yet graceful ease, and sweetness void of pride,   15
Might hide her faults, if belles had faults to hide;
If to her share some female errors fall,
Look on her face, and you'll forget 'em all.

   This nymph, to the destruction of mankind,
Nourished two locks, which graceful hung behind   20
In equal curls, and well conspired to deck
With shining ringlets her smooth iv'ry neck.
Love in these labyrinths his slaves detains,
And mighty hearts are held in slender chains.
With hairy springes[18] we the birds betray;   25
Slight lines of hair surprise[19] the finny prey;
Fair tresses man's imperial race insnare,
And beauty draws us with a single hair.

   Th' advent'rous Baron the bright locks admired;
He saw, he wished, and to the prize aspired.   30
Resolved to win, he meditates the way,
By force to ravish or by fraud betray;
For when success a lover's toil attends,
Few ask if fraud or force attained his ends.

   For this, ere Phoebus rose, he had implored   35
Propitious heav'n, and ev'ry pow'r adored,
But chiefly Love—to Love an altar built
Of twelve vast French romances, neatly gilt.
There lay three garters,[20] half a pair of gloves,
And all the trophies of his former loves;   40
With tender billet-doux he lights the pyre,
And breathes three am'rous sighs to raise the fire.
Then prostrate falls, and begs with ardent eyes
Soon to obtain, and long possess the prize.
The pow'rs gave ear, and granted half his prayer; 45
The rest the winds dispersed in empty air.

   But now secure the painted vessel glides,
The sunbeams trembling on the floating tides,

While melting music steals upon the sky,
And softened sounds along the waters die.   50
Smooth flow the waves, the zephyrs gently play,
Belinda smiled, and all the world was gay.
All but the sylph—with careful thoughts oppressed,
Th' impending woe sat heavy on his breast.
He summons straight his denizens of air;   55
The lucid squadrons round the sails repair:
Soft o'er the shrouds aerial whispers breathe,
That seemed but zephyrs to the train beneath.
Some to the sun their insect wings unfold,
Waft on the breeze, or sink in clouds of gold;   60
Transparent forms, too fine for mortal sight,
Their fluid bodies half dissolved in light.
Loose to the wind their airy garments flew,
Thin glitt'ring textures of the filmy dew,
Dipt in the richest tincture of the skies,   65
Where light disports in ever-mingling dyes,
While ev'ry beam new transient colors flings,
Colors that change whene'er they wave their wings.
Amid the circle, on the gilded mast,
Superior by the head was Ariel placed;   70
His purple pinions op'ning to the sun,
He raised his azure wand, and thus begun:
  "Ye sylphs and sylphids,[21] to your chief give ear;
Fays, fairies, genii, elves, and daemons, hear!
Ye know the spheres and various tasks assigned   75
By laws eternal to th' aerial kind.
Some in the fields of purest ether play,
And bask and whiten in the blaze of day.
Some guide the course of wand'ring orbs on high,
Or roll the planets through the boundless sky.   80
Some, less refined, beneath the moon's pale light
Pursue the stars that shoot athwart the night,
Or suck the mists in grosser air below,
Or dip their pinions in the painted bow,
Or brew fierce tempests on the wintry main,   85
Or o'er the glebe distil the kindly rain.
Others, on earth, o'er human race preside,
Watch all their ways, and all their actions guide:
Of these the chief the care of nations own,
And guard with arms divine the British throne.   90

  "Our humbler province is to tend the fair,
Not a less pleasing, though less glorious care;
To save the powder from too rude a gale,
Nor let the imprisoned essences exhale;
To draw fresh colors from the vernal flow'rs,   95
To steal from rainbows ere they drop in show'rs
A brighter wash; to curl their waving hairs,
Assist their blushes, and inspire their airs;
Nay oft, in dreams, invention we bestow,
To change a flounce or add a furbelow.   100

---

18 Snares made of hair.   19 Capture.
20 Quite another thing from the garter of the famous Order, in
   Canto I, line 85.

21 Female sylphs.

"This day, black omens threat the brightest fair
That e'er deserved a watchful spirit's care;
Some dire disaster, or by force or sleight;
But what, or where, the Fates have wrapt in night:
Whether the nymph shall break Diana's law,[22]   105
Or some frail china jar receive a flaw;
Or stain her honor, or her new brocade,
Forget her pray'rs, or miss a masquerade;
Or lose her heart, or necklace, at a ball;
Or whether heav'n has doomed that Shock must fall. 110
Haste, then, ye spirits! to your charge repair:
The flutt'ring fan be Zephyretta's care;
The drops to thee, Brillante, we consign;
And, Momentilla, let the watch be thine;
Do thou, Crispissa, tend her fav'rite lock;   115
Ariel himself shall be the guard of Shock.
    "To fifty chosen sylphs, of special note,
We trust the important charge, the petticoat;
Oft have we known that sev'n-fold fence to fail,
Though stiff with hoops, and armed with ribs of whale.
Form a strong line about the silver bound,   121
And guard the wide circumference around.
    "Whatever spirit, careless of his charge,
His post neglects, or leaves the fair at large,
Shall feel sharp vengeance soon o'ertake his sins,   125
Be stopped in vials, or transfixed with pins;
Or plunged in lakes of bitter washes lie,
Or wedged whole ages in a bodkin's eye;
Gums and pomatums[23] shall his flight restrain,
While clogged he beats his silken wings in vain;   130
Or alum styptics with contracting power
Shrink his thin essence like a riveled[24] flower;
Or, as Ixion fixed,[25] the wretch shall feel
The giddy motion of the whirling mill,[26]
In fumes of burning chocolate shall glow,   135
And tremble at the sea that froths below!"
    He spoke; the spirits from the sails descend:
Some, orb in orb, around the nymph extend;
Some thrid[27] the mazy ringlets of her hair;
Some hang upon the pendants of her ear;   140
With beating hearts the dire event they wait,
Anxious, and trembling for the birth of fate.

Close by those meads, for ever crowned with flow'rs,
Where Thames with pride surveys his rising tow'rs,
There stands a structure[28] of majestic frame,
Which from the neighb'ring Hampton takes its name.
Here Britain's statesmen oft the fall foredoom   5
Of foreign tyrants, and of nymphs at home;
Here thou, great Anna! whom three realms obey,
Dost sometimes counsel take—and sometimes tea.
    Hither the heroes and the nymphs resort,
To taste awhile the pleasures of a court;   10
In various talk th' instructive hours they passed:
Who gave the ball, or paid the visit last;
One speaks the glory of the British queen,
And one describes a charming Indian screen;
A third interprets motions, looks, and eyes;   15
At ev'ry word a reputation dies.
Snuff or the fan supply each pause of chat,
With singing, laughing, ogling, and all that.
    Meanwhile, declining from the noon of day,
The sun obliquely shoots his burning ray;   20
The hungry judges soon the sentence sign,
And wretches hang that jurymen may dine;
The merchant from th' Exchange returns in peace,
And the long labors of the toilet cease.
Belinda now, whom thirst of fame invites,   25
Burns to encounter two advent'rous knights,
At ombre singly to decide their doom,
And swells her breast with conquests yet to come.
Straight the three bands prepare in arms to join,
Each band the number of the sacred Nine.[29]   30
Soon as she spreads her hand, the aerial guard
Descend, and sit on each important card:
First Ariel perched upon a matadore,[30]
Then each according to the rank they bore;
For sylphs, yet mindful of their ancient race,   35
Are, as when women, wondrous fond of place.
    Behold four kings in majesty revered,
With hoary whiskers and a forky beard;
And four fair queens, whose hands sustain a flow'r,
The expressive emblem of their softer pow'r;   40
Four knaves, in garbs succinct,[31] a trusty band,
Caps on their heads, and halberds in their hand;
And parti-colored troops, a shining train,
Draw forth to combat on the velvet plain.

22 Of chastity.
23 Pomades, scented ointments.   24 Withered.
25 In classical mythology his punishment in hell was to be bound
on a ceaselessly revolving wheel.
26 In which the chocolate was ground.
27 Threaded their way through.

28 Hampton Court, one of the royal palaces, twenty miles up the
Thames from Westminster.
29 The Muses. Nine cards were dealt to each player in a three-
handed game of ombre.
30 The three highest cards were called matadores (Spanish *matador*,
killer).   31 Belted.

The skillful nymph reviews her force with care: 45
"Let spades be trumps!"[32] she said, and trumps they were.
　　Now move to war her sable matadores,
In show like leaders of the swarthy Moors.
Spadillio[33] first, unconquerable lord!
Led off two captive trumps, and swept the board.   50
As many more Manillio forced to yield,
And marched a victor from the verdant field.
Him Basto followed, but his fate more hard
Gained but one trump and one plebeian card.
With his broad saber next, a chief in years,   55
The hoary Majesty of spades appears,
Puts forth one manly leg, to sight revealed;
The rest his many-colored robe concealed.
The rebel knave, who dares his prince engage,
Proves the just victim of his royal rage.   60
Ev'n mighty Pam,[34] that kings and queens o'erthrew,
And mowed down armies, in the fights of loo,
Sad chance of war! now, destitute of aid,
Falls undistinguished by the victor spade!
　　Thus far both armies to Belinda yield;   65
Now to the Baron fate inclines the field.
His warlike amazon her host invades,
Th' imperial consort of the crown of spades.
The club's black tyrant first her victim died,
Spite of his haughty mien and barb'rous pride.[35]   70
What boots the regal circle on his head,
His giant limbs, in state unwieldy spread;
That long behind he trails his pompous robe,
And of all monarchs only grasps the globe?
　　The Baron now his diamonds pours apace;   75
Th' embroidered king who shows but half his face,
And his refulgent queen, with pow'rs combined,

Of broken troops an easy conquest find.[36]
Clubs, diamonds, hearts, in wild disorder seen,
With throngs promiscuous strow the level green.   80
Thus, when dispersed, a routed army runs,
Of Asia's troops, and Afric's sable sons;
With like confusion different nations fly,
Of various habit, and of various dye;
The pierced battalions disunited fall   85
In heaps on heaps: one fate o'erwhelms them all.
　　The knave of diamonds tries his wily arts,
And wins (oh, shameful chance!) the queen of hearts.
At this, the blood the virgin's cheek forsook,
A livid paleness spreads o'er all her look;   90
She sees, and trembles at th' approaching ill,
Just in the jaws of ruin, and codille.[37]
And now (as oft in some distempered state)
On one nice[38] trick depends the gen'ral fate.
An ace of hearts steps forth: the king unseen   95
Lurked in her hand, and mourned his captive queen.
He springs to vengeance with an eager pace,
And falls like thunder on the prostrate ace.
The nymph, exulting, fills with shouts the sky;
The walls, the woods, and long canals reply.   100
　　Oh, thoughtless mortals! ever blind to fate,
Too soon dejected, and too soon elate.
Sudden these honors shall be snatched away,
And cursed for ever this victorious day.
　　For lo! the board with cups and spoons is crowned, 105
The berries crackle, and the mill[39] turns round;
On shining altars of Japan[40] they raise
The silver lamp; the fiery spirits blaze.
From silver spouts the grateful liquors glide,
While China's earth receives the smoking tide.   110
At once they gratify their scent and taste,
And frequent cups prolong the rich repast.
Straight hover round the fair her airy band;
Some, as she sipped, the fuming liquor fanned;
Some o'er her lap their careful plumes displayed,[41]   115
Trembling, and conscious of the rich brocade.
Coffee (which makes the politician[42] wise,
And see through all things with his half-shut eyes)
Sent up in vapors to the Baron's brain
New stratagems, the radiant lock to gain.   120

---

[32] Since, in the preliminaries (not described by Pope), she has secured the privilege of being the *ombre*, which involves her playing against the other two, with the obligation of taking more tricks than either, she names trumps.

[33] The ace of spades, the top matadore. Belinda begins by taking out her opponents' trumps. Her next leads are her second and third highest matadores, the deuce of spades (Manillio) and the ace of clubs (Basto). Her fourth lead is the king of spades. She takes the first four tricks. The king of spades has a "broad saber" because, in cards, *spade* (Spanish *espada*) means *sword*. The design of the face cards was much as it is today, except that they showed the figure full length instead of cut off and reversed.

[34] The jack or knave of clubs, the highest card in the game of loo. It is discarded by the third player. The Baron has followed suit (lines 59–60) with the jack of spades. Belinda now has four tricks; she must win a fifth, in case one of her opponents should take the other four. She knows the Baron has one trump left; she is out of trumps, but she holds the kings of hearts and clubs, and her hope is to make one of them good. In ombre the black aces were always trumps, but the red aces (when not trumps) were outranked by the face cards of their respective suits.

[35] Belinda leads the king of clubs; the Baron is unable to follow suit, and trumps with the queen of spades.

[36] The Baron leads the three highest diamonds, the king, queen, and jack, all of which take tricks.

[37] If either opponent won, he gave "codille" to the ombre, i.e., set him. Belinda and the Baron now have four tricks each, and everything depends on the ninth and last. Each has one card left; the Baron leads the ace of hearts, which is topped by Belinda's king, and she wins the game.   [38] Ticklish.

[39] Coffee mill. The beans crackle as they are ground.

[40] Lacquered tables.   [41] Acted as napkins.

[42] I.e., the amateur politician who haunted the coffee house.

Ah, cease, rash youth! desist ere 'tis too late;
Fear the just gods, and think of Scylla's fate!
Changed to a bird, and sent to flit in air,
She dearly pays for Nisus' injured hair![43]

But when to mischief mortals bend their will,   125
How soon they find fit instruments of ill!
Just then, Clarissa drew with tempting grace
A two-edged weapon from her shining case;
So ladies in romance assist their knight,
Present the spear, and arm him for the fight.   130
He takes the gift with rev'rence, and extends
The little engine on his fingers' ends;
This just behind Belinda's neck he spread,
As o'er the fragrant steams she bends her head.
Swift to the lock a thousand sprites repair;   135
A thousand wings, by turns, blow back the hair;
And thrice they twitched the diamond in her ear;
Thrice she looked back, and thrice the foe drew near.
Just in that instant, anxious Ariel sought
The close recesses of the virgin's thought: 140
As on the nosegay in her breast reclined,
He watched th' ideas rising in her mind,
Sudden he viewed, in spite of all her art,
An earthly lover lurking at her heart.
Amazed, confused, he found his pow'r expired,   145
Resigned to fate, and with a sigh retired.

The peer now spreads the glitt'ring forfex[44] wide,
T' inclose the lock; now joins it, to divide.
Ev'n then, before the fatal engine closed,
A wretched sylph too fondly[45] interposed;   150
Fate urged the shears, and cut the sylph in twain
(But airy substance soon unites again).
The meeting points the sacred hair dissever
From the fair head, for ever, and for ever!

Then flashed the living lightning from her eyes,   155
And screams of horror rend th' affrighted skies.
Not louder shrieks to pitying heav'n are cast
When husbands or when lap dogs breathe their last,
Or when rich china vessels, fall'n from high,
In glitt'ring dust and painted fragments lie!   160

"Let wreaths of triumph now my temples twine,"
The victor cried; "the glorious prize is mine!
While fish in streams, or birds delight in air,
Or in a coach and six the British fair,
As long as *Atalantis*[46] shall be read,   165

Or the small pillow[47] grace a lady's bed,
While visits shall be paid on solemn days
When num'rous wax-lights in bright order blaze,[48]
While nymphs take treats, or assignations give,
So long my honor, name, and praise shall live!   170
    "What time would spare, from steel receives its date,
And monuments, like men, submit to fate!
Steel could the labor of the gods destroy,
And strike to dust th' imperial tow'rs of Troy;
Steel could the works of mortal pride confound,   175
And hew triumphal arches to the ground.
What wonder, then, fair nymph! thy hairs should feel
The conqu'ring force of unresisted steel?"

CANTO IV

But anxious cares the pensive nymph oppressed,
And secret passions labored in her breast.
Not youthful kings in battle seized alive,
Not scornful virgins who their charms survive,
Not ardent lovers robbed of all their bliss,   5
Not ancient ladies when refused a kiss,
Not tyrants fierce that unrepenting die,
Not Cynthia when her manteau's pinned awry,
E'er felt such rage, resentment, and despair,
As thou, sad virgin! for thy ravished hair.   10
    For, that sad moment, when the sylphs withdrew,
And Ariel weeping from Belinda flew,
Umbriel, a dusky, melancholy sprite
As ever sullied the fair face of light,
Down to the central earth, his proper scene,   15
Repaired to search the gloomy cave of Spleen.[49]
    Swift on his sooty pinions flits the gnome,
And in a vapor reached the dismal dome.
No cheerful breeze this sullen region knows;
The dreaded east[50] is all the wind that blows.   20
Here in a grotto shelt'red close from air,
And screened in shades from day's detested glare,
She sighs for ever on her pensive bed,
Pain at her side, and Megrim[51] at her head.
    Two handmaids wait the throne, alike in place,   25
But diff'ring far in figure and in face.
Here stood Ill Nature, like an ancient maid,
Her wrinkled form in black and white arrayed;
With store of pray'rs for mornings, nights, and noons,
Her hand is filled; her bosom with lampoons.

---

[43] In Greek myth, Nisus, king of Megara, had a daughter, Scylla (not connected with the monster of the Strait of Messina). She stole from his head a hair on which his safety depended and gave it to his enemy. For this undaughterly action she was changed by the gods into a bird.   [44] Scissors.   [45] Foolishly.
[46] *Secret Memoirs and Manners of Several Persons of Quality, of Both Sexes. From the New Atalantis, an Island in the Mediterranean* (1709–10) was a notorious book of gossip by Mrs. Mary Manley (1663–1724).

[47] A fashionable ornament.
[48] The fashionable lady's formal visits, after dark, attended by servants, with blazing lights, were often satirized.
[49] Hypochondria, morbid depression. Mr. Tillotson observes in his note that this disease was confined to the idle rich.
[50] Credited with causing spleen.   [51] Migraine, headache.

There Affectation, with a sickly mien,
Shows in her cheek the roses of eighteen,
Practiced to lisp, and hang the head aside,
Faints into airs, and languishes with pride;
On the rich quilt sinks with becoming woe,   35
Wrapped in a gown, for sickness, and for show.
The fair ones feel such maladies as these,
When each new nightdress gives a new disease.

     A constant vapor o'er the palace flies;
Strange phantoms rising as the mists arise;   40
Dreadful as hermits' dreams in haunted shades,
Or bright as visions of expiring maids.
Now glaring fiends, and snakes on rolling spires,
Pale specters, gaping tombs, and purple fires;
Now lakes of liquid gold, Elysian scenes,   45
And crystal domes, and angels in machines.[52]

     Unnumbered throngs on ev'ry side are seen,
Of bodies changed to various forms by Spleen.
Here living teapots stand, one arm held out,
One bent; the handle this, and that the spout;   50
A pipkin[53] there, like Homer's tripod walks;
Here sighs a jar, and there a goose pie[54] talks;
Men prove with child, as pow'rful fancy works;
And maids turned bottles call aloud for corks.

     Safe passed the gnome through this fantastic band,   55
A branch of healing spleenwort[55] in his hand.
Then thus addressed the pow'r: "Hail, wayward queen!
Who rule the sex to fifty from fifteen:
Parent of vapors[56] and of female wit,
Who give the hysteric or poetic fit,   60
On various tempers act by various ways,
Make some take physic, others scribble plays;
Who cause the proud their visits to delay,
And send the godly in a pet to pray.
A nymph there is that all thy pow'r disdains,   65
And thousands more in equal mirth maintains.
But oh! if e'er thy gnome could spoil a grace,
Or raise a pimple on a beauteous face,
Like citron waters[57] matrons' cheeks inflame,
Or change complexions at a losing game;   70
If e'er with airy horns[58] I planted heads,
Or rumpled petticoats, or tumbled beds,
Or caused suspicion when no soul was rude,
Or discomposed the headdress of a prude,

Or e'er to costive lap dog gave disease   75
Which not the tears of brightest eyes could ease,
Hear me, and touch Belinda with chagrin;
That single act gives half the world the spleen."
     The goddess, with a discontented air,
Seems to reject him though she grants his pray'r.   80
A wondrous bag with both her hands she binds,
Like that where once Ulysses held the winds;[59]
There she collects the force of female lungs,
Sighs, sobs, and passions, and the war of tongues.
A vial next she fills with fainting fears,   85
Soft sorrows, melting griefs, and flowing tears.
The gnome rejoicing bears her gifts away,
Spreads his black wings, and slowly mounts to day.

     Sunk in Thalestris'[60] arms the nymph he found,
Her eyes dejected, and her hair unbound.   90
Full o'er their heads the swelling bag he rent,
And all the Furies issued at the vent.
Belinda burns with more than mortal ire,
And fierce Thalestris fans the rising fire.
"O wretched maid!" she spread her hands and cried   95
(While Hampton's echoes "Wretched maid!" replied),
"Was it for this you took such constant care
The bodkin, comb, and essence to prepare?
For this your locks in paper durance bound?
For this with tort'ring irons wreathed around?   100
For this with fillets strained your tender head,
And bravely bore the double loads of lead?[61]
Gods! shall the ravisher display your hair,
While the fops envy, and the ladies stare?
Honor forbid! at whose unrivaled shrine   105
Ease, pleasure, virtue, all, our sex resign.
Methinks already I your tears survey,
Already hear the horrid things they say,
Already see you a degraded toast,[62]
And all your honor in a whisper lost!   110
How shall I, then, your helpless fame defend?
'Twill then be infamy to seem your friend!
And shall this prize, th' inestimable prize,
Exposed through crystal to the gazing eyes,
And heightened by the diamond's circling rays,   115
On that rapacious hand for ever blaze?
Sooner shall grass in Hyde Park Circus[63] grow,
And wits take lodgings in the sound of Bow;[64]

[52] I.e., as they appear suspended by mechanical contrivances on the operatic stage.
[53] Small earthen pot. For Vulcan's walking tripods, see the *Iliad*, XVIII, 372 ff.
[54] Pope's comment: "Alludes to a real fact; a lady of distinction imagined herself in this condition."
[55] A kind of fern, credited with curing the disease.
[56] The blues.   [57] Citron-flavored brandy.
[58] Of the cuckold.

[59] Aeolus, god of the winds, made him this present (*Odyssey*, X, 19 ff.).
[60] Miss Fermor's friend Gertrude, wife of Sir George Browne, nee Morley.
[61] Flexible bits of leads were used to fasten curl papers.
[62] Toasted in an unpleasant way.   [63] See Canto I, note 9.
[64] The church of St. Mary-le-Bow was off Cheapside, in the heart of the City; the fashionable residential districts were far away, in the West End. To be born within the sound of Bow Bells was to be a true citizen or cockney.

Sooner let earth, air, sea, to chaos fall,
Men, monkeys, lap dogs, parrots, perish all!"   120

    She said; then raging to Sir Plume[65] repairs,
And bids her beau demand the precious hairs
(Sir Plume of amber snuffbox justly vain,
And the nice conduct of a clouded[66] cane):
With earnest eyes, and round, unthinking face,   125
He first the snuffbox opened, then the case,
And thus broke out, "My Lord, why, what the devil!
Z—ds![67] damn the lock! 'fore Gad, you must be civil!
Plague on 't! 'tis past a jest—nay, prithee, pox![68]
Give her the hair."—He spoke, and rapped his box.   130

    "It grieves me much," replied the Peer again,
"Who speaks so well should ever speak in vain.
But by this lock, this sacred lock, I swear
(Which nevermore shall join its parted hair;
Which nevermore its honors shall renew,   135
Clipped from the lovely head where late it grew)
That, while my nostrils draw the vital air,
This hand, which won it, shall for ever wear."
He spoke, and speaking, in proud triumph spread
The long-contended honors of her head.   140

    But Umbriel, hateful gnome! forbears not so;
He breaks the vial whence the sorrows flow.
Then see! the nymph in beauteous grief appears,
Her eyes half languishing, half drowned in tears;
On her heaved bosom hung her drooping head,   145
Which with a sigh she raised, and thus she said:

    "For ever cursed be this detested day,
Which snatched my best, my fav'rite curl away!
Happy! ah, ten times happy had I been,
If Hampton Court these eyes had never seen!   150
Yet am not I the first mistaken maid,
By love of courts to num'rous ills betrayed.
Oh, had I rather unadmired remained
In some lone isle, or distant northern land;
Where the gilt chariot never marks the way,   155
Where none learn ombre, none e'er taste bohea![69]
There kept my charms concealed from mortal eye,
Like roses, that in deserts bloom and die.
What moved my mind with youthful lords to roam?
Oh, had I stayed, and said my pray'rs at home!   160
'T was this the morning omens seemed to tell:
Thrice from my trembling hand the patchbox[70] fell;

The tott'ring china shook without a wind;
Nay, Poll sat mute, and Shock was most unkind!
A sylph, too, warned me of the threats of fate,   165
In mystic visions, now believed too late!
See the poor remnants of these slighted hairs!
My hands shall rend what ev'n thy rapine spares.
These, in two sable ringlets taught to break,
Once gave new beauties to the snowy neck;   170
The sister lock now sits uncouth alone,
And in its fellow's fate foresees its own;
Uncurled it hangs, the fatal shears demands,
And tempts once more thy sacrilegious hands.
Oh, hadst thou, cruel! been content to seize   175
Hairs less in sight, or any hairs but these!"

CANTO V

She said: the pitying audience melt in tears;
But fate and Jove had stopped the Baron's ears.
In vain Thalestris with reproach assails,
For who can move when fair Belinda fails?
Not half so fixed the Trojan could remain,   5
While Anna begged and Dido raged in vain.[71]
Then grave Clarissa[72] graceful waved her fan;
Silence ensued, and thus the nymph began:

    "Say, why are beauties praised and honored most,
The wise man's passion, and the vain man's toast?   10
Why decked with all that land and sea afford,
Why angels called, and angel-like adored?
Why round our coaches crowd the white-gloved beaus?
Why bows the side-box from its inmost rows?
How vain are all these glories, all our pains,   15
Unless good sense preserve what beauty gains;
That men may say when we the front-box grace,
'Behold the first in virtue as in face!'
Oh! if to dance all night, and dress all day,
Charmed the smallpox or chased old age away,   20
Who would not scorn what huswife's cares produce,
Or who would learn one earthly thing of use?
To patch, nay, ogle, might become a saint,
Nor could it, sure, be such a sin to paint.
But since, alas! frail beauty must decay,   25
Curled or uncurled, since locks will turn to gray,
Since painted, or not painted, all shall fade,
And she who scorns a man must die a maid,
What then remains but well our power to use,
And keep good humor still whate'er we lose?   30

---

65 Actually, her husband, Sir George Browne. He was a cousin of
    Miss Fermor's mother. Not unnaturally, he resented the foolish
    figure Pope makes him cut.
66 Both light and dark, on account of the grain.
67 Zounds. Literally, by God's wounds.
68 Cf. plague. Literally, pox=syphilis, but the word was used
    lightly.   69 A superior variety of Chinese tea.
70 Ladies enhanced their beauty by sticking a small black patch of
    silk or courtplaster on the cheek.

71 The Trojan hero Aeneas (see Aeneid, opening of Book IV)
    broke off his amour with Dido and left Carthage despite the
    entreaties of the Queen and her sister, Anna.
72 Mentioned in Canto III, line 127. Pope explains that she is
    introduced "to open more clearly the moral of the poem."

And trust me, dear! good humor can prevail,
When airs and flights and screams and scolding fail.
Beauties in vain their pretty eyes may roll;
Charms strike the sight, but merit wins the soul."

So spoke the dame, but no applause ensued;   35
Belinda frowned, Thalestris called her prude.
"To arms, to arms!" the fierce virago cries,
And swift as lightning to the combat flies.
All side in parties, and begin th' attack;
Fans clap, silks rustle, and tough whalebones crack; 40
Heroes' and heroines' shouts confus'dly rise,
And bass and treble voices strike the skies.
No common weapons in their hands are found;
Like gods they fight, nor dread a mortal wound.

So when bold Homer makes the gods engage,   45
And heav'nly breasts with human passions rage;
'Gainst Pallas Mars, Latona Hermes arms;[73]
And all Olympus rings with loud alarms;
Jove's thunder roars, heav'n trembles all around,
Blue Neptune storms, the bellowing deeps resound: 50
Earth shakes her nodding tow'rs, the ground gives way,
And the pale ghosts start at the flash of day!

Triumphant Umbriel, on a sconce's[74] height,
Clapped his glad wings, and sat to view the fight;
Propped on their bodkin-spears, the sprites survey   55
The growing combat, or assist the fray.

While through the press enraged Thalestris flies,
And scatters death around from both her eyes,
A beau and witling perished in the throng,
One died in metaphor, and one in song.   60
"O cruel nymph! a living death I bear,"
Cried Dapperwit,[75] and sunk beside his chair.
A mournful glance Sir Fopling upwards cast,
"Those eyes are made so killing" was his last.
Thus on Maeander's[76] flow'ry margin lies   65
Th' expiring swan, and as he sings he dies.

When bold Sir Plume had drawn Clarissa down,
Chloe stepped in, and killed him with a frown;
She smiled to see the doughty hero slain,
But, at her smile, the beau revived again.   70

Now Jove suspends his golden scales in air,
Weighs the men's wits against the lady's hair;
The doubtful beam long nods from side to side;
At length the wits mount up, the hairs subside.

See fierce Belinda on the Baron flies,   75
With more than usual lightning in her eyes;
Nor feared the chief th' unequal fight to try,
Who sought no more than on his foe to die.
But this bold lord, with manly strength indued,
She with one finger and a thumb subdued: 80
Just where the breath of life his nostrils drew,
A charge of snuff the wily virgin threw;
The gnomes direct, to ev'ry atom just,
The pungent grains of titillating dust.
Sudden, with starting tears each eye o'erflows,   85
And the high dome re-echoes to his nose.

"Now meet thy fate," incensed Belinda cried,
And drew a deadly bodkin from her side.
(The same, his ancient personage to deck,
Her great-great-grandsire wore about his neck,   90
In three seal-rings; which after, melted down,
Formed a vast buckle for his widow's gown.
Her infant grandame's whistle next it grew,
The bells she jingled, and the whistle blew;
Then in a bodkin graced her mother's hairs,   95
Which long she wore and now Belinda wears.)

"Boast not my fall," he cried, "insulting[77] foe!
Thou by some other shalt be laid as low.
Nor think to die dejects my lofty mind;
All that I dread is leaving you behind!   100
Rather than so, ah, let me still survive,
And burn in Cupid's flames—but burn alive."

"Restore the lock!" she cries; and all around
"Restore the lock!" the vaulted roofs rebound.
Not fierce Othello in so loud a strain   105
Roared for the handkerchief that caused his pain.[78]
But see how oft ambitious aims are crossed,
And chiefs contend till all the prize is lost!
The lock, obtained with guilt, and kept with pain,
In ev'ry place is sought, but sought in vain: 110
With such a prize no mortal must be blest;
So heav'n decrees! with heav'n who can contest?

Some thought it mounted to the lunar sphere,
Since all things lost on earth are treasured there.
There heroes' wits are kept in pond'rous vases,   115
And beaus' in snuffboxes and tweezer-cases.
There broken vows, and deathbed alms are found,
And lovers' hearts with ends of riband bound,
The courtier's promises, and sick man's prayers,
The smiles of harlots, and the tears of heirs,   120
Cages for gnats, and chains to yoke a flea,
Dried butterflies, and tomes of casuistry.[79]

---

[73] Pallas Athena or Minerva (goddess of wisdom) is attacked by
Mars (god of war); Latona (mother of Apollo and Diana), by
Mercury (messenger of the gods). Olympus is the mountain in
Thessaly where the Greek gods lived. Neptune was god of the
sea.   [74] Hanging candlestick.
[75] Pope takes these names from Restoration comedies: Dapperwit
is in William Wycherley's *Love in a Wood,* and Sir Fopling
Flutter in George Etherege's *The Man of Mode.*
[76] The ancient name of the Menderes River in Asia Minor. It flows
through the Trojan plain.

[77] Insolently exulting.
[78] In Shakespeare's tragedy. Cassio's possession of the handkerchief
is wrongly supposed by Othello to be evidence of his wife's
adultery.
[79] Volumes of specious reasoning about questions of conduct.

But trust the Muse—she saw it upward rise,
Though marked by none but quick poetic eyes
(So Rome's great founder[80] to the heav'ns withdrew,   125
To Proculus alone confessed in view):
A sudden star, it shot through liquid air,
And drew behind a radiant trail of hair.
Not Berenice's locks first rose so bright,[81]
The heav'ns bespangling with disheveled light.   130
The sylphs behold it kindling as it flies,
And pleased pursue its progress through the skies.
   This the beau monde shall from the Mall[82] survey,
And hail with music its propitious ray;
This the blest lover shall for Venus take,   135
And send up vows from Rosamonda's lake;[83]

This Partridge[84] soon shall view in cloudless skies,
When next he looks through Galileo's eyes;[85]
And hence th' egregious wizard shall foredoom
The fate of Louis, and the fall of Rome.[86]   140
   Then cease, bright nymph! to mourn thy ravished hair,
Which adds new glory to the shining sphere!
Not all the tresses that fair head can boast
Shall draw such envy as the lock you lost.
For after all the murders of your eye,   145
When, after millions slain, yourself shall die,
When those fair suns shall set, as set they must,
And all those tresses shall be laid in dust,
This lock the Muse shall consecrate to fame,
And 'midst the stars inscribe Belinda's name!   150

from AN ESSAY ON MAN

If Swift called Bolingbroke "the most universal genius in Europe," Pope may be excused for taking the retired politician seriously as a philosopher. Bolingbroke's gifts were more flashy than solid. They showed at their height in oratory—a dangerous sign in any man. With Harley, Bolingbroke had governed England from 1710 to 1714; just before the death of Anne, he had edged his colleague off the seat of government and ruled alone. He had betrayed Marlborough and England's allies, intrigued with the Jacobites, and escaped to France from the vengeance of the Whigs. While in exile he became interested in deism. In 1732 he came home under a pardon, but was excluded from the House of Lords. For ten years he lived near Twickenham, a constant stimulus to Pope. Some have alleged that Pope merely versified what Bolingbroke told him; but Dr. Johnson is doubtless nearer the mark: "The *Essay* plainly appears the fabric of a poet: what Bolingbroke supplied could be only the first principles; the order, illustration, and embellishments must all be Pope's."

And these are what make the poem. Expert workmanship and wit, not inspiration nor hard thinking, distinguish it. Pope was a devotee of polish; it is the brilliant finish of these couplets that has made many of them into familiar quotations. "Whatever is, is right" reflects (through more than one intervening medium) the optimistic philosophy of Leibnitz (1646–1716), which the Enlightenment hugged to its bosom. To the twentieth-century reader it may well

seem cheerful nonsense. But Pope is saying what was fast coming to be his century's accepted solution of the Problem of Evil. For a total rejection of it, see Voltaire's *Candide* (1759). To Pope, whatever is, is right because the universe God created is rational through and through, even though we cannot see to the ends of it. His verses are no glorification of the human mind; on the contrary, they repeatedly deny the unlimited scope of *human* reason. But the universe, he is confident, is built on order and rational necessity. In so far as the mind can comprehend any portion of it, the rationality of its laws is, Pope thinks, apparent. It would, however, be a mistake to lay much stress on the thought of this poem, which is not a systematic exposition but a collection of remarks brilliantly put. The four epistles were published separately 1732–34.

EPISTLE I

OF THE NATURE AND STATE OF MAN
WITH RESPECT TO THE UNIVERSE

ARGUMENT

Of man in the abstract. I. That we can judge only with regard to our own system, being ignorant of the relations of systems and things, verses 17, &c. II. That man is not to

---

80 Romulus. According to the Roman historian Livy, he told Proculus Julius that Mars had taken him to heaven.

81 Berenice was an Egyptian queen (d. 216 B.C.). She dedicated her hair to the gods for her husband's safe return; when she hung it up in the temple it was stolen, and according to the legend it eventually appeared as part of a constellation.

82 Pall Mall (pronounced *pell mell*), the fashionable promenade on the north side of St. James's Park.

83 Rosamond's Pond, in St. James's Park, "long consecrated to disastrous love and elegiac poetry."

84 In 1707–9, over the signature "Isaac Bickerstaff," Swift had played a huge practical joke on "John Partridge" (his real name was Hewson), an astrologer and almanac maker, one of the most eminent quacks of the day. Swift wrote a pamphlet of predictions, among them that Partridge would die on March 29. On March 30 an elegy on his death appeared. In vain he protested in his almanac for 1709 that he was still alive; Bickerstaff insisted he had died.

85 The telescope. It was greatly improved by the Italian astronomer Galileo Galilei (1564–1642).

86 Louis XIV, and the Papacy. Partridge had frequently predicted their downfall.

be deemed imperfect, but a being suited to his place and rank in the creation, agreeable to the general order of things, and comfortable to ends and relations to him unknown, verses 35, &c. III. That it is partly upon his ignorance of future events, and partly upon the hope of a future state, that all his happiness in the present depends, verses 77, &c. IV. The pride of aiming at more knowledge, and pretending to more perfection, the cause of man's error and misery. The impiety of putting himself in the place of God, and judging of the fitness or unfitness, perfection or imperfection, justice or injustice, of his dispensations, verses 113, &c. V. The absurdity of conceiving himself the final cause of the creation, or expecting that perfection in the moral world which is not in the natural, verses 131, &c. VI. The unreasonableness of his complaints against Providence, while, on the one hand, he demands the perfections of the angels, and, on the other, the bodily qualifications of the brutes; though to possess any of the sensitive faculties in a higher degree would render him miserable, verses 173, &c. VII. That throughout the whole visible world an universal order and gradation in the sensual and mental faculties is observed, which causes a subordination of creature to creature, and of all creatures to man. The gradations of sense, instinct, thought, reflection, reason; that reason alone countervails all the other faculties, verse 207. VIII. How much further this order and subordination of living creatures may extend above and below us; were any part of which broken, not that part only, but the whole connected creation must be destroyed, verse 233. IX. The extravagance, madness, and pride of such a desire, verse 259. X. The consequence of all, the absolute submission due to Providence, both as to our present and future state, verses 281, &c., to the end.

Awake, my St. John![1] leave all meaner things
To low ambition and the pride of kings.
Let us (since life can little more supply
Than just to look about us and to die)
Expatiate[2] free o'er all this scene of man;   5
A mighty maze! but not without a plan;
A wild where weeds and flow'rs promiscuous shoot,
Or garden tempting with forbidden fruit.
Together let us beat[3] this ample field,
Try what the open, what the covert yield;   10
The latent tracts, the giddy heights, explore
Of all who blindly creep or sightless soar;
Eye nature's walks, shoot folly as it flies,
And catch the manners living as they rise;
Laugh where we must, be candid[4] where we can,   15
But vindicate the ways of God to man.[5]

I. Say first, of God above or man below,
What can we reason but from what we know?
Of man what see we but his station here
From which to reason, or to which refer?   20
Through worlds unnumbered though the God be known,
'Tis ours to trace him only in our own.
He who through vast immensity can pierce,[6]
See worlds on worlds compose one universe,
Observe how system into system runs,   25
What other planets circle other suns,
What varied being peoples ev'ry star,
May tell why heav'n has made us as we are.
But of this frame the bearings and the ties,
The strong connections, nice[7] dependencies,   30
Gradations just, has thy pervading soul
Looked through? or can a part contain the whole?
   Is the great chain that draws all to agree,
And drawn supports, upheld by God or thee?

II. Presumptuous man! the reason wouldst thou find, 35
Why formed so weak, so little, and so blind?
First, if thou canst, the harder reason guess
Why formed no weaker, blinder, and no less?
Ask of thy mother earth why oaks are made
Taller or stronger than the weeds they shade!   40
Or ask of yonder argent[8] fields above
Why Jove's satellites[9] are less than Jove!
   Of systems possible, if 'tis confessed
That wisdom infinite must form the best,
Where all must full or not coherent be,   45
And all that rises rise in due degree;
Then in the scale of reas'ning life, 'tis plain,
There must be, somewhere, such a rank as man:
And all the question (wrangle e'er so long)
Is only this: if God has placed him wrong.   50
   Respecting man, whatever wrong we call,
May, must be, right, as relative to all.
In human works though labored on with pain,
A thousand movements scarce one purpose gain;
In God's, one single can its end produce,   55
Yet serves to second too some other use.
So man, who here seems principal alone,
Perhaps acts second to some sphere unknown,
Touches some wheel, or verges to some goal;
'Tis but a part we see, and not a whole.   60
   When the proud steed shall know why man restrains
His fiery course, or drives him o'er the plains;
When the dull ox, why now he breaks the clod,
Is now a victim, and now Egypt's god;

---

[1] Henry St. John, Viscount Bolingbroke (1678–1751).
[2] Range.   [3] As sportsmen do, to start up the birds.
[4] Kindly.   [5] Cf. Milton, *Paradise Lost*, I, 26.

[6] Then pronounced *purse*.   [7] Subtle.   [8] Silvery.
[9] Pronounced in four syllables, with the second accented.

Then shall man's pride and dullness comprehend   65
His actions', passions', being's, use and end;
Why doing, suff'ring, checked, impelled; and why
This hour a slave, the next a deity.

Then say not man's imperfect, heav'n in fault;
Say rather man's as perfect as he ought: 70
His knowledge measured to his state and place,
His time a moment, and a point his space.
If to be perfect in a certain sphere,
What matter soon or late, or here or there?
The blest today is as completely so   75
As who began a thousand years ago.

III. Heav'n from all creatures hides the book of fate,
All but the page prescribed, their present state;
From brutes what men, from men what spirits know;
Or who could suffer being here below?
The lamb thy riot[10] dooms to bleed today,
Had he thy reason, would he skip and play?
Pleased to the last, he crops the flow'ry food,
And licks the hand just raised to shed his blood.
Oh, blindness to the future! kindly giv'n,   85
That each may fill the circle marked by heav'n;
Who sees with equal eye, as God of all,
A hero perish or a sparrow fall,
Atoms or systems into ruin hurled,
And now a bubble burst, and now a world.   90

Hope humbly, then; with trembling pinions soar;
Wait the great teacher, death; and God adore.
What future bliss he gives not thee to know,
But gives that hope to be thy blessing now.
Hope springs eternal in the human breast;   95
Man never is, but always to be, blessed.
The soul, uneasy and confined from home,
Rests and expatiates in a life to come.

Lo, the poor Indian! whose untutored mind
Sees God in clouds, or hears him in the wind;   100
His soul proud science never taught to stray
Far as the solar walk[11] or Milky Way;
Yet simple nature to his hope has giv'n,
Behind the cloud-topped hill, an humbler heav'n,
Some safer world in depth of woods embraced,   105
Some happier island in the wat'ry waste,
Where slaves once more their native land behold,
No fiends torment, no Christians thirst for gold.
To be, contents his natural desire;
He asks no angel's wing, no seraph's fire;   110
But thinks, admitted to that equal sky,
His faithful dog shall bear him company.

IV. Go, wiser thou! and in thy scale of sense
Weigh thy opinion against Providence;
Call imperfection what thou fanci'st such;   115
Say, "Here he gives too little, there too much";
Destroy all creatures for thy sport or gust,[12]
Yet cry, "If man's unhappy, God's unjust";
If man alone ingross not heav'n's high care,
Alone made perfect here, immortal there,   120
Snatch from his hand the balance and the rod,
Rejudge his justice, be the god of God.
In pride, in reas'ning pride, our error lies;
All quit their sphere and rush into the skies.
Pride still is aiming at the blessed abodes;   125
Men would be angels, angels would be gods.
Aspiring to be gods if angels fell,
Aspiring to be angels men rebel;
And who but wishes to invert the laws
Of order sins against th' Eternal Cause.   130

V. Ask for what end the heav'nly bodies shine,
Earth for whose use, Pride answers, " 'Tis for mine!
For me kind nature wakes her genial[13] pow'r,
Suckles each herb, and spreads out ev'ry flow'r;
Annual for me the grape, the rose, renew   135
The juice nectareous and the balmy dew;
For me the mine a thousand treasures brings;
For me health gushes from a thousand springs;
Seas roll to waft me, suns to light me rise;
My footstool earth, my canopy the skies."   140

But errs not nature from this gracious end,
From burning suns when livid deaths descend,
When earthquakes swallow, or when tempests sweep
Towns to one grave, whole nations to the deep?
"No," 'tis replied, "the first Almighty Cause   145
Acts not by partial but by gen'ral laws:
Th' exceptions few; some change since all began;
And what created perfect?"—Why then man?
If the great end be human happiness,
Then nature deviates; and can man do less?   150
As much that end a constant course requires
Of show'rs and sunshine, as of man's desires;
As much eternal springs and cloudless skies,
As men for ever temp'rate, calm, and wise.
If plagues or earthquakes break not heav'n's design,   155
Why then a Borgia or a Catiline?[14]
Who knows but He, whose hand the lightning forms,
Who heaves old ocean, and who wings the storms,
Pours fierce ambition in a Caesar's mind,

[12] Pleasure.   [13] Generative.

[14] Caesar Borgia (1476–1507), brother of Lucrezia Borgia, and an even more notorious member of that murderous Italian family. Catiline (d. 62 B.C.) was the conspirator against the Roman republic whom Cicero exposed in his most famous orations.

[10] Luxury.   [11] The sun's path or orbit.

Or turns young Ammon[15] loose to scourge mankind? 160
From pride, from pride, our very reas'ning springs;
Account for moral as for nat'ral things:
Why charge we heav'n in those, in these acquit?
In both, to reason right is to submit.

    Better for us, perhaps, it might appear, 165
Were there all harmony, all virtue here;
That never air or ocean felt the wind;
That never passion discomposed the mind.
But all subsists by elemental strife,
And passions are the elements of life. 170
The gen'ral order, since the whole began,
Is kept in nature, and is kept in man.

    VI. What would this Man? Now upward will he soar,
And, little less than angel, would be more;
Now, looking downwards, just as grieved appears 175
To want[16] the strength of bulls, the fur of bears.
Made for his use all creatures if he call,
Say what their use, had he the powers of all?
Nature to these without profusion kind,
The proper organs, proper pow'rs assigned; 180
Each seeming want compensated of course,
Here with degrees of swiftness, there of force;
All in exact proportion to the state;
Nothing to add, and nothing to abate.
Each beast, each insect, happy in its own: 185
Is heav'n unkind to man, and man alone?
Shall he alone, whom rational we call,
Be pleased with nothing if not blessed with all?
    The bliss of man (could pride that blessing find)
Is not to act or think beyond mankind; 190
No pow'rs of body or of soul to share,
But what his nature and his state can bear.
Why has not man a microscopic eye?[17]
For this plain reason, man is not a fly.
Say what the use, were finer optics giv'n, 195
T' inspect a mite, not comprehend the heav'n?
Or touch, if tremblingly alive all o'er,
To smart and agonize at ev'ry pore?
Or, quick effluvia[18] darting through the brain,
Die of a rose in aromatic pain? 200
If nature thundered in his op'ning ears,
And stunned him with the music of the spheres,[19]

How would he wish that heav'n had left him still
The whisp'ring zephyr and the purling rill!
Who finds not Providence all good and wise, 205
Alike in what it gives and what denies?

    VII. Far as creation's ample range extends,
The scale of sensual, mental pow'rs ascends:
Mark how it mounts to man's imperial race
From the green myriads in the peopled grass; 210
What modes of sight betwixt each wide extreme,
The mole's dim curtain and the lynx's beam:
Of smell, the headlong lioness between,
And hound sagacious on the tainted green:
Of hearing, from the life that fills the flood 215
To that which warbles through the vernal wood:
The spider's touch, how exquisitely fine!
Feels at each thread, and lives along the line:
In the nice[20] bee what sense, so subtly true,
From pois'nous herbs extracts the healing dew? 220
How instinct varies in the grov'ling swine,
Compared, half-reas'ning elephant, with thine!
'Twixt that and reason what a nice[21] barrier!
For ever sep'rate, yet for ever near!
Remembrance and reflection how allied; 225
What thin partitions sense from thought divide:
And middle natures how they long to join,
Yet never pass th' insuperable line!
Without this just gradation could they be
Subjected, these to those, or all to thee? 230
The pow'rs of all subdued by thee alone,
Is not thy reason all these pow'rs in one?

    VIII. See, through this air, this ocean, and this earth,
All matter quick,[22] and bursting into birth.
Above, how high progressive life may go! 235
Around, how wide! how deep extend below!
Vast chain of being![23] which from God began,
Natures ethereal, human, angel, man,
Beast, bird, fish, insect, what no eye can see,
No glass can reach; from infinite to thee, 240
From thee to nothing. On superior pow'rs
Were we to press, inferior might on ours:
Or in the full creation leave a void,
Where, one step broken, the great scale's destroyed:
From nature's chain whatever link you strike, 245
Tenth, or ten thousandth, breaks the chain alike.

---

[15] Alexander the Great. See, above, Pope's *Essay on Criticism*, line 376, note 37.   [16] Lack.

[17] This line of reasoning Pope takes from Locke's *Essay on the Human Understanding* (Book II, chap. iii, sec. 12).

[18] Exhalations.

[19] An allusion to the ancient belief that a music beyond man's capacity to hear was made by the spheres which, according to the Ptolemaic astronomy, revolved around the earth and contained all the stars.

[20] Discriminating.   [21] Fine.

[22] Alive.

[23] According to the view Pope presents, God has created the universe complete (with all possible forms and ideas) and continuous (without gaps)—see lines 43 ff. Each form shades off into the next both above and below; gradation necessarily follows from order and continuity. The Great Chain (or ladder) of Being runs up from next-to-nothing to next-to-God.

And if each system in gradation roll,
Alike essential to th' amazing whole,
The least confusion but in one, not all
That system only, but the whole, must fall.   250
Let earth unbalanced from her orbit fly,
Planets and suns run lawless through the sky;
Let ruling angels from their spheres be hurled,
Being on being wrecked, and world on world;
Heav'n's whole foundations to their center nod,   255
And nature tremble to the throne of God!
All this dread order break—for whom? for thee?
Vile worm!—oh, madness! pride! impiety!

   IX. What if the foot, ordained the dust to tread,
Or hand, to toil, aspired to be the head?   260
What if the head, the eye, or ear repined
To serve mere engines to the ruling mind?
Just as absurd for any part to claim
To be another in this gen'ral frame;
Just as absurd to mourn the tasks or pains   265
The great directing Mind of All ordains.
   All are but parts of one stupendous whole,
Whose body nature is, and God the soul;
That changed through all, and yet in all the same,
Great in the earth as in th' ethereal frame,   270
Warms in the sun, refreshes in the breeze,
Glows in the stars, and blossoms in the trees;
Lives through all life, extends through all extent,
Spreads undivided, operates unspent;
Breathes in our soul, informs our mortal part,   275
As full, as perfect, in a hair as heart;
As full, as perfect, in vile man that mourns,
As the rapt seraph that adores and burns:[24]
To him no high, no low, no great, no small;
He fills, he bounds, connects, and equals all.   280

   X. Cease, then, nor order imperfection name;
Our proper bliss depends on what we blame.
Know thy own point: this kind, this due degree
Of blindness, weakness, heav'n bestows on thee.
Submit: in this or any other sphere,   285
Secure to be as blessed as thou canst bear;
Safe in the hand of one disposing Pow'r,
Or in the natal or the mortal hour.
All nature is but art, unknown to thee;
All chance, direction which thou canst not see;   290
All discord, harmony not understood;
All partial evil, universal good;
And, spite of pride, in erring reason's spite,
One truth is clear, WHATEVER IS, IS RIGHT.

---

[24] Cf. Spenser, "Hymn of Heavenly Beauty," lines 94–5:
    "And those eternal burning seraphins,
      Which from their faces dart out fiery light."

from EPISTLE II

OF THE NATURE AND STATE OF MAN
WITH RESPECT TO HIMSELF AS AN INDIVIDUAL

ARGUMENT

I. The business of man not to pry into God, but to study himself. His middle nature; his powers and frailties, verses 1 to 19. The limits of his capacity, verses 19, &c. II. The two principles of man, self-love and reason, both necessary, verses 53, &c. Self-love the stronger, and why, verses 67, &c. Their end the same, verses 81, &c. III. The passions, and their use, verses 93 to 130. The predominant passion, and its force, verses 132 to 160. Its necessity, in directing men to different purposes, verses 165, &c. Its providential use, in fixing our principle, and ascertaining our virtue, verse 177. IV. Virtue and vice joined in our mixed nature; the limits near, yet the things separate and evident: what is the office of reason, verses 202 to 216. V. How odious vice in itself, and how we deceive ourselves into it, verse 217. VI. That, however, the ends of Providence and general good are answered in our passions and imperfections, verses 238, &c. How usefully these are distributed to all orders of men, verse 241. How useful they are to society, verse 251. And to individuals, verse 263. In every state, and every age of life, verses 273, &c.

I. Know then thyself; presume not God to scan:
The proper study of mankind is man.
Placed on this isthmus of a middle state,
A being darkly wise and rudely great:
With too much knowledge for the skeptic side,   5
With too much weakness for the Stoic's pride,
He hangs between, in doubt to act or rest;
In doubt to deem himself a god or beast;
In doubt his mind or body to prefer;
Born but to die, and reas'ning but to err;   10
Alike in ignorance, his reason such,
Whether he thinks too little or too much;
Chaos of thought and passion, all confused;
Still by himself abused[25] or disabused;
Created half to rise, and half to fall;   15
Great lord of all things, yet a prey to all;
Sole judge of truth, in endless error hurled;
The glory, jest, and riddle of the world!
   Go, wondrous creature! mount where science guides;
Go, measure earth, weigh air, and state the tides;   20
Instruct the planets in what orbs to run,
Correct old time, and regulate the sun;[26]

---

[25] Deceived.

[26] An allusion to Europe's gradual replacement of the Julian calendar (Old Style) by the Gregorian (New Style). The former had fallen ten days behind by 1582, when Pope Gregory XIII adopted the present system. England did not change over till 1751; by that time Old Style was eleven days behind.

Go, soar with Plato to th' empyreal sphere,[27]
To the first good, first perfect, and first fair;
Or tread the mazy round his follow'rs trod,   25
And quitting sense call imitating God;[28]
As eastern priests in giddy circles run,
And turn their heads to imitate the sun.
Go, teach Eternal Wisdom how to rule—
Then drop into thyself, and be a fool!   30
    Superior beings, when of late they saw
A mortal man unfold all nature's law,
Admired such wisdom in an earthly shape,
And showed a Newton[29] as we show an ape.
    Could he, whose rules the rapid comet bind,   35
Describe or fix one movement of his mind?
Who saw its fires here rise, and there descend,
Explain his own beginning or his end?
Alas! what wonder! man's superior part
Unchecked may rise, and climb from art to art;   40
But when his own great work is but begun,
What reason weaves, by passion is undone.
    Trace science then, with modesty thy guide;
First strip off all her equipage of pride;
Deduct what is but vanity or dress,   45
Or learning's luxury, or idleness,
Or tricks to show the stretch of human brain,
Mere curious pleasure, or ingenious pain;
Expunge the whole, or lop th' excrescent parts
Of all[30] our vices have created arts;   50
Then see how little the remaining sum,
Which served the past, and must the times to come!

    II. Two principles in human nature reign,
Self-love to urge, and reason to restrain;
Nor this a good, nor that a bad we call;   55
Each works its end, to move or govern all:
And to their proper operation still[31]
Ascribe all good; to their improper, ill. . . .
    As fruits ungrateful to the planter's care,   181
On savage stocks inserted, learn to bear,
The surest virtues thus from passions shoot,
Wild nature's vigor working at the root.
What crops of wit and honesty appear   185
From spleen, from obstinacy, hate, or fear!
See anger, zeal and fortitude supply;
Ev'n av'rice, prudence; sloth, philosophy;

Lust, through some certain strainers well refined,
Is gentle love, and charms all womankind;   190
Envy, to which th' ignoble mind's a slave,
Is emulation in the learn'd or brave;
Nor virtue male or female can we name,
But what will grow on pride or grow on shame.
    Thus nature gives us (let it check our pride)   195
The virtue nearest to our vice allied:
Reason the bias turns to good from ill,
And Nero reigns a Titus[32] if he will.
The fiery soul abhorred in Catiline,
In Decius charms, in Curtius[33] is divine: 200
The same ambition can destroy or save,
And makes a patriot as it makes a knave. . . .

from EPISTLE III

OF THE NATURE AND STATE OF MAN
WITH RESPECT TO SOCIETY

ARGUMENT

I. The whole universe one system of society, verses 7, &c.
Nothing made wholly for itself, nor yet wholly for
another, verse 27. The happiness of animals mutual, verse
49. II. Reason or instinct operate alike to the good of each
individual, verse 79. Reason or instinct operate also to
society, in all animals, verse 109. III. How far society carried by instinct, verse 115. How much farther by reason,
verse 131. IV. Of that which is called the state of nature,
verse 144. Reason instructed by instinct in the invention of
arts, verse 169, and in the forms of society, verse 179. V.
Origin of political societies, verse 199. Origin of monarchy,
verse 207. Patriarchal government, verse 215. VI. Origin
of true religion and government, from the same principle,
of love, 231, &c. Origin of superstition and tyranny, from
the same principle, of fear, verses 241, &c. The influence of
self-love operating to the social and public good, verse 269.
Restoration of true religion and government on their first
principle, verse 283. Mixed government, verse 288. Various
forms of each, and the true end of all, verses 303, &c.

IV. Nor think, in nature's state they blindly trod;
The state of nature was the reign of God:
Self-love and social at her birth began,
Union the bond of all things, and of man.   150

---

[27] The outermost of the concentric spheres of the old astronomy.
Pope follows Bolingbroke in rejecting Plato's idealism and
denying the validity of intuition.
[28] "I dare not . . . talk of imitating God" (Bolingbroke). *Sense*=
common sense, i.e., here, sound judgment based on experience
(the factual reports of the senses, plus reason).
[29] Sir Isaac Newton (1642–1727). See p. 392, above.
[30] Everything which.   [31] Ever.

[32] Roman emperors who reigned wickedly (Nero, 54–68) and
benevolently (Titus, 79–81).
[33] On Catiline, see Epistle I, note 14, above. Decius and Curtius
were legendary Roman heroes of the fourth century B.C.
Decius, warned in a vision that the general who died would
win the battle, rushed ahead where he would be sure to be
killed. Curtius rode in full armor into a chasm which had appeared in the Forum and thus satisfied the requirement for
closing it, the sacrifice of Rome's greatest treasure, i.e., the brave
citizen and his arms.

Pride then was not; nor arts, that pride to aid;
Man walked with beast, joint tenant of the shade;
The same his table, and the same his bed;
No murder clothed him, and no murder fed.
In the same temple, the resounding wood,   155
All vocal beings hymned their equal God;
The shrine with gore unstained, with gold undressed;
Unbribed, unbloody, stood the blameless priest:
Heaven's attribute was universal care,
And man's prerogative to rule, but spare.   160
Ah! how unlike the man of times to come!
Of half that live the butcher and the tomb;
Who, foe to nature, hears the gen'ral groan,
Murders their species, and betrays his own.
But just disease to luxury succeeds,   165
And every death its own avenger breeds;
The Fury-passions[34] from that blood began,
And turned on man a fiercer savage, man. . . .

    'Twas then the studious head or gen'rous mind,
Follower of God or friend of humankind,
Poet or patriot, rose but to restore   285
The faith and moral nature gave before;
Relumed her ancient light, not kindled new;
If not God's image, yet his shadow drew:
Taught power's due use to people and to kings;
Taught nor to slack nor strain its tender strings,   290
The less or greater set so justly true,
That touching one must strike the other too;
Till jarring int'rests, of themselves create
Th' according music of a well-mixed state.
Such is the world's great harmony, that springs   295
From order, union, full consent of things:
Where small and great, where weak and mighty, made
To serve, not suffer, strengthen, not invade;
More powerful each as needful to the rest,
And, in proportion as it blesses, blessed;   300
Draw to one point, and to one center bring
Beast, man, or angel, servant, lord, or king.

    For forms of government let fools contest;
Whate'er is best administered is best:
For modes of faith let graceless zealots fight;   305
His can't be wrong whose life is in the right:
In faith and hope the world will disagree,
But all mankind's concern is charity:
All must be false that thwart this one great end;
And all of God, that bless mankind or mend.   310

    Man, like the gen'rous vine, supported lives;
The strength he gains is from th' embrace he gives.
On their own axis as the planets run,
Yet make at once their circle round the sun;

So two consistent motions act the soul;   315
And one regards itself, and one the whole.
    Thus God and nature linked the gen'ral frame,
And bade self-love and social be the same.

from EPISTLE IV

OF THE NATURE AND STATE OF MAN
WITH RESPECT TO HAPPINESS

ARGUMENT

I. False notions of happiness, philosophical and popular,
answered, from verse 19 to 26. II. It is the end of all men,
and attainable by all, verse 29. God intends happiness to be
equal; and to be so, it must be social, since all particular
happiness depends on general, and since he governs by
general, not particular, laws, verse 35. As it is necessary
for order, and the peace and welfare of society, that external goods should be unequal, happiness is not made to
consist in these, verse 49. But, notwithstanding that in-
equality, the balance of happiness among mankind is kept
even by Providence, by the two passions of hope and fear,
verse 67. III. What the happiness of individuals is, as far as
is consistent with the constitution of this world; and that
the good man has here the advantage, verse 77. The error
of imputing to virtue what are only the calamities of
nature or of fortune, verse 93. IV. The folly of expecting
that God should alter his general laws in favor of particulars, verse 121. V. That we are not judges who are good;
but that, whoever they are, they must be happiest, verses
131, &c. VI. That external goods are not the proper rewards, but often inconsistent with, or destructive of,
virtue, verse 167. That even these can make no man happy
without virtue: instanced in riches, verse 185; honors,
verse 193; nobility, verse 205; greatness, verse 217; fame,
verse 237; superior talents, verses 259, &c. With pictures
of human infelicity in men possessed of them all, verses
269, &c. VII. That virtue only constitutes a happiness
whose object is universal and whose prospect eternal,
verse 309. That the perfection of virtue and happiness
consists in a conformity to the order of Providence here,
and a resignation to it here and hereafter, verses 327, &c.

VI. . . . Honor and shame from no condition[35] rise;
Act well your part, there all the honor lies.
Fortune in men has some small diff'rence made: 195
One flaunts in rags, one flutters in brocade;
The cobbler aproned, and the parson gowned,
The friar hooded, and the monarch crowned.
"What differ more," you cry, "than crown and cowl?"
I'll tell you, friend! a wise man and a fool. . . .   200

---

[34] The Furies of Greek myth were avenging deities.

[35] Rank, status in life.

VII. Know then this truth (enough for man to know),
Virtue alone is happiness below: 310
The only point where human bliss stands still,
And tastes the good without the fall to ill;
Where only merit constant pay receives,
Is blest in what it takes, and what it gives;
The joy unequaled, if its end it gain,   315
And if it lose, attended with no pain:
Without satiety, though e'er so blessed,
And but more relished as the more distressed:
The broadest mirth unfeeling folly wears,
Less pleasing far than virtue's very tears: 320
Good, from each object, from each place acquired,
For ever exercised, yet never tired;
Never elated, while one man's oppressed;
Never dejected, while another's blessed;

And where no wants, no wishes can remain,   325
Since but to wish more virtue, is to gain.
   See the sole bliss heaven could on all bestow!
Which who but feels can taste, but thinks can know:
Yet poor with fortune, and with learning blind,
The bad must miss; the good, untaught will find;   330
Slave to no sect, who takes no private road,
But looks through nature up to nature's God;
Pursues that chain which links the immense design,
Joins heaven and earth, and mortal and divine;
Sees that no being any bliss can know,   335
But touches some above, and some below;
Learns, from this union of the rising whole,
The first, last purpose of the human soul;
And knows, where faith, law, morals, all began,
All end: in LOVE OF GOD, and LOVE OF MAN. . . .   340

from MORAL ESSAYS

Of the four *Moral Essays,* the one now numbered IV was the first to appear; it was published in 1731. Here Pope extends the application of his canons of good sense and "nature" to architecture and landscape gardening. Compare his remarks on gardens with those of Addison (pp. 717-18, above).

EPISTLE IV

To Richard Boyle, Earl of Burlington[1]

OF THE USE OF RICHES

ARGUMENT

THE VANITY of expense in people of wealth and quality. The abuse of the word *taste.* That the first principle and foundation in this, as in everything else, is good sense. The chief proof of it is to follow nature, even in works of mere luxury and elegance. Instanced in architecture and gardening, where all must be adapted to the genius and use of the place, and the beauties not forced into it, but resulting from it. How men are disappointed in their most expensive undertakings for want of this true foundation, without which nothing can please long, if at all; and the best examples and rules will but be perverted into something burdensome and ridiculous. A description of the false taste of magnificence; the first grand error of which is to imagine that greatness consists in the size and dimension, instead of the proportion and harmony, of the whole; and the second, either in joining together parts incoherent, or too minutely resembling, or in the repetition of the same too frequently. A word or two of false taste in books, in music, in painting, even in preaching and prayer, and lastly in entertainments.

Yet Providence is justified in giving wealth to be squandered in this manner, since it is dispersed to the poor and laborious part of mankind. What are the proper objects of magnificence, and a proper field for the expense of great men, and finally, the great and public works which become a prince.

'Tis strange the miser should his cares employ
To gain those riches he can ne'er enjoy:
Is it less strange the prodigal should waste
His wealth to purchase what he ne'er can taste?
Not for himself he sees, or hears, or eats;   5
Artists must choose his pictures, music, meats:
He buys for Topham[2] drawings and designs;
For Pembroke statues, dirty gods, and coins;
Rare monkish manuscripts for Hearne alone,
And books for Mead, and butterflies for Sloane.   10
Think we all these are for himself? no more
Than his fine wife, alas! or finer whore.
   For what has Virro painted, built, and planted?
Only to show how many tastes he wanted.[3]
What brought Sir Visto's ill-got wealth to waste?   15
Some demon whispered, "Visto! have a taste."
Heaven visits with a taste the wealthy fool,
And needs no rod but Ripley[4] with a rule.
See! sportive fate, to punish awkward pride,
Bids Bubo build, and sends him such a guide: 20
A standing sermon, at each year's expense,
That never coxcomb reached magnificence!

---

[1] An old friend of Pope's and a distinguished patron of the arts.

[2] A collector of drawings. The individuals named in the next lines were collectors of the objects mentioned in connection with them.   [3] Lacked.   [4] An incompetent architect.

You show us Rome was glorious, not profuse,[5]
And pompous buildings once were things of use;
Yet shall, my Lord, your just, your noble rules   25
Fill half the land with imitating fools;
Who random drawings from your sheets shall take,
And of one beauty many blunders make;
Load some vain church with old theatric state,
Turn arcs of triumph to a garden gate;   30
Reverse your ornaments, and hang them all
On some patched dog-hole eked with ends of wall,
Then clap four slices of pilaster on 't,
That laced with bits of rustic[6] makes a front;
Shall call the winds through long arcades to roar,   35
Proud to catch cold at a Venetian door:
Conscious they act a true Palladian part,
And if they starve, they starve by rules of art.
    Oft have you hinted to your brother peer
A certain truth, which many buy too dear: 40
Something there is more needful than expense,
And something previous even to taste—'tis sense;
Good sense, which only is the gift of heaven,
And though no science, fairly worth the seven;
A light which in yourself you must perceive;   45
Jones and Le Nôtre[7] have it not to give.
    To build, to plant, whatever you intend,
To rear the column, or the arch to bend,
To swell the terrace, or to sink the grot,
In all, let Nature never be forgot.   50
But treat the goddess like a modest fair,[8]
Nor overdress, nor leave her wholly bare;
Let not each beauty everywhere be spied,
Where half the skill is decently to hide.
He gains all points who pleasingly confounds,   55
Surprises, varies, and conceals the bounds.
    Consult the genius of the place in all;
That tells the waters or to rise or fall;
Or helps th' ambitious hill the heavens to scale,
Or scoops in circling theaters the vale;   60
Calls in the country, catches op'ning glades,
Joins willing woods, and varies shades from shades;
Now breaks, or now directs, th' intending lines;
Paints as you plant, and as you work designs.
    Still follow sense, of every art the soul;   65
Parts answ'ring parts shall slide into a whole,
Spontaneous beauties all around advance,
Start even from difficulty, strike from chance:

Nature shall join you; time shall make it grow
A work to wonder at—perhaps a Stowe.[9]   70
    Without it, proud Versailles! thy glory falls,
And Nero's terraces desert their walls:
The vast parterres a thousand hands shall make,
Lo! Cobham comes, and floats them with a lake;
Or cut wide views through mountains to the plain,   75
You'll wish your hill or sheltered seat again.
Even in an ornament its place remark,
Nor in a hermitage set Dr. Clarke.[10]
    Behold Villario's ten years' toil complete:
His quincunx[11] darkens, his espaliers meet,   80
The wood supports the plain, the parts unite,
And strength of shade contends with strength of light;
A waving glow the bloomy beds display,
Blushing in bright diversities of day,
With silver-quiv'ring rills meandered o'er—   85
Enjoy them, you! Villario can no more:
Tired of the scene parterres and fountains yield,
He finds at last he better likes a field.
    Through his young woods how pleased Sabinus strayed,
Or sat delighted in the thick'ning shade,   90
With annual joy the redd'ning shoots to greet,
Or see the stretching branches long to meet.
His son's fine taste an op'ner vista loves,
Foe to the dryads of his father's groves;
One boundless green or flourished carpet views,[12]   95
With all the mournful family of yews;
The thriving plants, ignoble broomsticks made,
Now sweep those alleys they were born to shade.
    At Timon's villa[13] let us pass a day,
Where all cry out, "What sums are thrown away!"   100
So proud, so grand; of that stupendous air,
Soft and agreeable come never there;
Greatness with Timon dwells in such a draught
As brings all Brobdingnag[14] before your thought.
To compass this, his building is a town,   105
His pond an ocean, his parterre a down:[15]
Who but must laugh, the master when he sees,
A puny insect shivering at a breeze!

---

[5] The year before Pope's poem appeared, Lord Burlington had
published a volume of designs of ancient Roman structures by
Palladio, a neoclassical Italian architect of the sixteenth century.
[6] Rough-surfaced material.
[7] Inigo Jones (see p. 438, above) and André Le Nôtre, French
architect and designer of gardens.   [8] Lady.

[9] An estate in Buckinghamshire rebuilt by the Lord Viscount
Cobham, a friend of Pope's, to whom he addressed the first of
the Moral Essays. See line 74.
[10] Pope's note: "Dr. L. Clarke's busto placed by the Queen in the
Hermitage, while the doctor duly frequented the court."
[11] Arrangement of five trees with one at each corner and one at
the center of a square. Espaliers are trees trained to grow flat
against a support.
[12] I.e., an uninterrupted stretch of lawn or a lawn cut up into small
units.
[13] Pope's enemies identified Timon's villa with Canons, the estate
of the Duke of Chandos, who had befriended Pope; thus they
used the following passage as evidence of Pope's ingratitude and
hypocrisy. See An Epistle to Dr. Arbuthnot, lines 299–300.
[14] The land of the giants in Swift's Gulliver's Travels, Book II.
[15] I.e., a great open tract.

Lo, what huge heaps of littleness around!
The whole a labored quarry above ground. 110
Two Cupids squirt before; a lake behind
Improves the keenness of the northern wind.
His gardens next your admiration call;
On every side you look, behold the wall!
No pleasing intricacies intervene; 115
No artful wildness to perplex the scene;
Grove nods at grove, each alley has a brother,
And half the platform just reflects the other.
The suff'ring eye inverted nature sees,
Trees cut to statues, statues thick as trees; 120
With here a fountain never to be played,
And there a summerhouse that knows no shade;
Here Amphitrite[16] sails through myrtle bowers;
There gladiators fight or die in flowers;
Unwatered see the drooping seahorse mourn, 125
And swallows roost in Nilus' dusty urn.
    My Lord advances with majestic mien,
Smit with the mighty pleasure to be seen:
But soft! by regular approach—not yet—
First through the length of yon hot terrace sweat; 130
And when up ten steep slopes you've dragged your
        thighs,
Just at his study door he'll bless your eyes.
    His study! with what authors is it stored?
In books, not authors, curious is my Lord.
To all their dated backs he turns you round; 135
These Aldus printed, those Du Sueil[17] has bound;
Lo, some are vellum, and the rest as good,
For all his Lordship knows,—but they are wood.
For Locke or Milton 'tis in vain to look;
These shelves admit not any modern book. 140
    And now the chapel's silver bell you hear,
That summons you to all the pride of prayer.
Light quirks of music, broken and uneven,
Make the soul dance upon a jig to heaven.
On painted ceilings you devoutly stare, 145
Where sprawl the saints of Verrio or Laguerre,[18]
On gilded clouds in fair expansion lie,
And bring all paradise before your eye.
To rest, the cushion and soft dean invite,
Who never mentions hell to ears polite. 150
    But hark! the chiming clocks to dinner call:
A hundred footsteps scrape the marble hall;
The rich buffet well-colored serpents grace,
And gaping Tritons spew to wash your face.

Is this a dinner? this a genial room? 155
No, 'tis a temple, and a hecatomb;
A solemn sacrifice performed in state;
You drink by measure, and to minutes eat.
So quick retires each flying course, you'd swear
Sancho's dread doctor and his wand were there.[19] 160
Between each act the trembling salvers ring,
From soup to sweet wine and God bless the King.[20]
In plenty starving, tantalized in state,
And complaisantly helped to all I hate,
Treated, caressed, and tired, I take my leave, 165
Sick of his civil pride from morn to eve;
I curse such lavish cost and little skill,
And swear no day was ever passed so ill.
    Yet hence the poor are clothed, the hungry fed;
Health to himself, and to his infants bread 170
The lab'rer bears: what his hard heart denies,
His charitable vanity supplies.
    Another age shall see the golden ear[21]
Imbrown the slope, and nod on the parterre,
Deep harvests bury all his pride has planned, 175
And laughing Ceres[22] reassume the land.
    Who then shall grace or who improve the soil?
Who[23] plants like Bathurst,[24] or who builds like Boyle.
'Tis use alone that sanctifies expense,
And splendor borrows all her rays from sense. 180
    His father's acres who enjoys in peace,
Or makes his neighbors glad if he increase;
Whose cheerful tenants bless their yearly toil,
Yet to their lord owe more than to the soil;
Whose ample lawns are not ashamed to feed 185
The milky heifer and deserving steed;
Whose rising forests, not for pride or show,
But future buildings, future navies, grow:
Let his plantations stretch from down to down,
First shade a country, and then raise a town. 190
    You, too, proceed! make falling arts your care;
Erect new wonders, and the old repair;
Jones and Palladio to themselves restore,
And be whate'er Vitruvius[25] was before,
Till kings call forth th' ideas of your mind 195
(Proud to accomplish what such hands designed),
Bid harbors open, public ways extend,
Bid temples, worthier of the God, ascend,

---

16 A sea goddess, wife of Poseidon (Neptune).
17 Aldus Manutius (1450–1515), a famous Italian printer, and
    Augustin Du Sueil or Du Seuil (1673–1746), a French book-
    binder.
18 Two decorative painters whose work was to be seen in various
    great houses in England.

19 In Cervantes's *Don Quixote,* Pt. II, chap. 47, the squire Sancho
    is present at a feast where the dishes disappear before he has
    time to taste them.   20 I.e., the toast to the king at the end.
21 Of grain—i.e., the lawns and gardens will be sown with wheat.
22 Goddess of the harvest.   23 He who.
24 Allen, Lord Bathurst, to whom Pope addressed the third of the
    Moral Essays, was deeply interested in gardening.
25 The Roman author (first century B.C.) of a treatise on archi-
    tecture.

Bid the broad arch the dang'rous flood contain,
The mole[26] projected break the roaring main,   200
Back to his bounds their subject sea command,

And roll obedient rivers through the land.
These honors peace to happy Britain brings;
These are imperial works, and worthy kings.

AN EPISTLE TO DR. ARBUTHNOT

JOHN ARBUTHNOT (1667–1735) was a doctor, a wit, a delightful companion, and an influential Tory. He had been Queen Anne's physician; more than that, he had belonged to Scriblerus. Both Swift and Pope were devoted to him. About a year before he died, knowing that the end was not distant, he wrote to Pope advising him to continue with his satires but to avoid rousing animosity by indulgence in personalities. Pope, who had ample reason to be interested in the question of how far personal satire can ethically be carried, replied that he proposed to offer Arbuthnot a poetic discussion of the subject. "It pleases me much," he wrote, "to take this occasion of testifying (to the public at least, if not to posterity) my obligation and friendship for and from you, for so many years; that is all that's in it; for compliments are fulsome, and go for nothing." The poem appeared early in 1735. It contains some of the ablest personal satire in English, most notably the cool but scathing lines on Addison. In a letter to John Caryll (see the headnote to *The Rape of the Lock*) Pope described the *Epistle* as a "just vindication from slanders of all sorts, and slanderers of what rank or quality soever." In other words, this is a literary platform, an *apologia pro vita sua*. Your editor deplores the amount of underpinning visible on the following pages; but this poem is worth enjoying, and its enjoyment depends on understanding its allusions as well as on recognizing its wit and gracefulness.

"Shut, shut the door, good John!"[1] fatigued I said;
"Tie up the knocker; say I'm sick, I'm dead."
The Dog Star rages![2] nay, 'tis past a doubt
All Bedlam, or Parnassus,[3] is let out:
Fire in each eye, and papers in each hand,   5
They rave, recite, and madden round the land.
    What walls can guard me, or what shades can hide?
They pierce my thickets, through my grot[4] they glide;
By land, by water, they renew the charge;
They stop the chariot, and they board the barge.[5]   10
No place is sacred; not the church is free;
Ev'n Sunday shines no Sabbath day to me:

Then from the Mint[6] walks forth the man of rime,
Happy to catch me just at dinner time.
    Is there a parson much bemused in beer,   15
A maudlin poetess, a riming peer,
A clerk, foredoomed his father's soul to cross,
Who pens a stanza when he should engross?
Is there who, locked from ink and paper, scrawls
With desp'rate charcoal round his darkened walls?   20
All fly to Twit'nam, and in humble strain
Apply to me to keep them mad or vain.
Arthur,[7] whose giddy son neglects the laws,
Imputes to me and my damned works the cause:
Poor Cornus[8] sees his frantic wife elope,   25
And curses wit, and poetry, and Pope.
    Friend to my life (which did not you prolong,
The world had wanted many an idle song),
What drop or nostrum can this plague remove?
Or which must end me, a fool's wrath or love?   30
A dire dilemma! either way I'm sped:[9]
If foes, they write; if friends, they read me dead.
Seized and tied down to judge, how wretched I!
Who can't be silent, and who will not lie.
To laugh were want of goodness and of grace,   35
And to be grave exceeds all pow'r of face.
I sit with sad civility; I read
With honest anguish and an aching head;
And drop at last, but in unwilling ears,
This saving counsel, "Keep your piece nine years."[10]   40
    "Nine years!" cries he, who, high in Drury Lane,[11]
Lulled by soft zephyrs through the broken pane,
Rimes ere he wakes, and prints before term[12] ends,
Obliged by hunger, and request of friends:[13]

---

26 Breakwater.

1 John Serle, Pope's gardener.
2 The brilliance of Sirius, in August, was supposed to be connected with the heat and with madness.—*Bedlam* (for *Bethlehem*) was London's insane hospital.   3 I.e., the poets.
4 Grotto. Pope took pleasure in ornamenting an underpass on his Twickenham estate.
5 Pope went to and from London by the Thames.

6 A district in Southwark, near the south end of London Bridge. It was long a refuge for crooks, whores, and poor debtors. Mat of the Mint is one of the rogues in *The Beggar's Opera*.—Cf. *Sabbath,* in the preceding line; debtors were exempt from arrest on Sunday.
7 Arthur Moore (1666?–1730), a member of Parliament. His son, the minor poet and eccentric, James Moore Smythe, a prominent Freemason, had incurred Pope's enmity, and had retaliated by collaborating with Welsted (note 14) in an attack.
8 I.e., cuckold (Latin *cornu*=horn).   9 Done for.
10 The advice of Horace (*Art of Poetry,* lines 386–9).
11 I.e., a hack writer living in a garret in that disreputable quarter.
12 The *terms,* when the London law courts were sitting, were the "seasons"; publishing dates were geared to them.
13 The former being, of course, the real reason.

"The piece, you think, is incorrect? why, take it;   45
I'm all submission; what you'd have it, make it."
    Three things another's modest wishes bound:
My friendship, and a prologue, and ten pound.
    Pitholeon[14] sends to me: "You know his Grace;
I want a patron: ask him for a place."   50
Pitholeon libeled me—"But here's a letter
Informs you, sir, 'twas when he knew no better.
Dare you refuse him? Curll[15] invites to dine;
He'll write a *Journal*, or he'll turn divine."
    Bless me! a packet. " 'Tis a stranger sues: 55
A virgin tragedy, an orphan Muse."
If I dislike it, "Furies, death, and rage!"
If I approve, "Commend it to the stage."
There (thank my stars) my whole commission ends;
The play'rs and I are, luckily, no friends.   60
Fired that the house reject him, " 'Sdeath, I'll print it,
And shame the fools—your int'rest, sir, with Lintot."[16]
"Lintot, dull rogue! will think your price too much."
"Not, sir, if you revise it, and retouch."
All my demurs but double his attacks;   65
At last he whispers, "Do, and we go snacks."
Glad of a quarrel, straight I clap the door:
"Sir, let me see your works and you no more."
    'Tis sung, when Midas' ears began to spring
(Midas, a sacred person and a king),   70
His very minister who spied them first
(Some say his queen) was forced to speak, or burst.[17]
And is not mine, my friend, a sorer case,
When ev'ry coxcomb perks them in my face?
"Good friend, forbear![18] you deal in dang'rous things;
I'd never name queens, ministers, or kings;   76
Keep close to ears, and those let asses prick,
'Tis nothing—" Nothing? if they bite and kick?

Out with it, *Dunciad!*[19] let the secret pass,
That secret to each fool, that he's an ass:[20]   80
The truth once told (and wherefore should we lie?),
The queen of Midas slept, and so may I.
    You think this cruel? take it for a rule,
No creature smarts so little as a fool.
Let peals of laughter, Codrus![21] round thee break,   85
Thou unconcerned canst hear the mighty crack:
Pit, box, and gall'ry in convulsions hurled,
Thou stand'st unshook amidst a bursting world.
Who shames a scribbler? break one cobweb[22] through,
He spins the slight, self-pleasing thread anew;   90
Destroy his fib, or sophistry—in vain!
The creature's at his dirty work again,
Throned in the center of his thin designs,
Proud of a vast extent of flimsy lines!
Whom have I hurt? has poet yet, or peer,   95
Lost the arched eyebrow or Parnassian sneer?
And has not Colley[23] still his lord and whore?
His butchers, Henley?[24] his Freemasons, Moore?[25]
Does not one table Bavius[26] still admit?
Still to one bishop, Philips[27] seem a wit?   100
Still Sappho[28]—"Hold! for God's sake!—you'll offend:
No names—be calm—learn prudence of a friend:
I too could write, and I am twice as tall;
But foes like these—" One flatt'rer's worse than all.
Of all mad creatures, if the learn'd are right,   105
It is the slaver kills, and not the bite.
A fool quite angry is quite innocent:
Alas! 'tis ten times worse when they repent.
    One dedicates in high heroic prose,
And ridicules beyond a hundred foes: 110
One from all Grub Street[29] will my fame defend,
And, more abusive, calls himself my friend.
This prints my letters,[30] that expects a bribe,

---

[14] Pope's note: "The name taken from a foolish poet at Rhodes, who pretended much to Greek." Apparently he means the minor poet Leonard Welsted (1688–1747), a friend of Addison's. Cf. line 375. The London *Journal* (line 54) was a Whig paper; "turn divine" seems to allude to Welsted's being at work on a theological treatise which came out in 1736. "His Grace" is the Duke of Argyle (1678–1743), head of the Campbell clan.

[15] Edmund Curll (1675–1747), a notoriously unscrupulous publisher, and Pope's enemy.—The "virgin tragedy" may be a reference to *The Virgin Queen* (1729) by Richard Barford, who had angered Pope by using in a poem of his own the machinery of the sylphs in *The Rape of the Lock*.

[16] Bernard Lintot (1675–1736), Pope's publisher.

[17] In Greek myth King Midas was punished by Apollo with ass's ears for judging him second to Pan in a musical contest. In some versions it was the barber who discovered what had happened; he dug a hole, whispered the secret into it, and then filled it up. The satire, not very pointed, glances at George II and the political understanding between Queen Caroline and Walpole.

[18] This and similar interjections seem to be intended for the responses Pope assumes Arbuthnot might make. The actual assignment of speeches to Pope and Arbuthnot in late editions may not, however, represent Pope's intentions.

[19] One of the satires in which Pope had pilloried his enemies.

[20] That his folly (like the ears of Midas) is visible.

[21] A fictitious poet, ridiculed by Vergil and Juvenal; the name was applied to any poet who bores by reading his works to others.

[22] Spider web.

[23] The poet laureate, comedian, and theater manager Colley Cibber (1671–1757).

[24] John Henley (1692–1756), an eccentric preacher and elocution teacher. On Easter Day, 1729, he addressed the butchers of London, with extravagant praises of their calling.

[25] See note 7, above.

[26] A dull poet ridiculed by Vergil, and hence a name for a poetaster.

[27] Ambrose Philips (1675?–1749), known as Namby Pamby, a member of Addison's circle, excited Pope's jealousy by writing pastoral poetry. He had served as secretary to a bishop.

[28] The great Greek lyric poetess (seventh century B.C.). The allusion is to Lady Mary Wortley Montagu (1689–1762), famous for her charming letters. She had been Pope's friend; but they were estranged and he had put her into the *Dunciad*, perhaps because her response when he offered his love was a hearty laugh.

[29] Near Cripplegate. Many hack writers lived there.

[30] Curll (note 15, above) had done so.

And others roar aloud, "Subscribe, subscribe!"[31]
There are who to my person pay their court: 115
I cough like Horace; and though lean, am short;
Ammon's great son one shoulder had too high,[32]
Such Ovid's[33] nose, and, "Sir! you have an eye."
Go on, obliging creatures; make me see
All that disgraced my betters met in me.   120
Say, for my comfort, languishing in bed,
"Just so immortal Maro[34] held his head";
And when I die, be sure you let me know
Great Homer died three thousand years ago.

    Why did I write? what sin to me unknown   125
Dipped me in ink, my parents', or my own?
As yet a child, nor yet a fool to fame,
I lisped in numbers,[35] for the numbers came.
I left no calling for this idle trade,
No duty broke, no father disobeyed.   130
The Muse but served to ease some friend, not wife,
To help me through this long disease, my life;
To second, Arbuthnot! thy art and care,
And teach the being you preserved, to bear.

    "But why then publish?"[36] Granville the polite,[37]   135
And knowing Walsh,[38] would tell me I could write;
Well-natured Garth[39] inflamed with early praise,
And Congreve loved, and Swift endured my lays;
The courtly Talbot,[40] Somers,[41] Sheffield,[42] read;
Ev'n mitered Rochester[43] would nod the head,   140
And St. John's[44] self (great Dryden's friends before)
With open arms received one poet more.
Happy my studies, when by these approved!
Happier their author, when by these beloved!
From these the world will judge of men and books,   145
Not from the Burnets,[45] Oldmixons,[46] and Cookes.[47]

Soft were my numbers; who could take offense
While pure description held the place of sense?[48]
Like gentle Fanny's[49] was my flowery theme,
A painted mistress or a purling stream.   150
Yet then did Gildon draw his venal quill;[50]
I wished the man a dinner, and sat still.
Yet then did Dennis rave in furious fret;
I never answered—I was not in debt.
If want provoked, or madness made them print,   155
I waged no war with Bedlam or the Mint.

    Did some more sober critic come abroad;
If wrong, I smiled; if right, I kissed the rod.
Pains, reading, study, are their just pretense;
And all they want[51] is spirit, taste, and sense.   160
Commas and points they set exactly right,
And 'twere a sin to rob them of their mite.
Yet ne'er one sprig of laurel graced these ribalds,
From slashing Bentley down to piddling Tibbalds:[52]
Each wight who reads not, and but scans and spells,   165
Each word catcher that lives on syllables,
Ev'n such small critics some regard may claim,
Preserved in Milton's or in Shakespeare's name.
Pretty! in amber to observe the forms
Of hairs or straws or dirt or grubs or worms;   170
The things, we know, are neither rich nor rare,
But wonder how the devil they got there!

    Were others angry? I excused them too;
Well might they rage: I gave them but their due.
A man's true merit 'tis not hard to find;   175
But each man's secret standard in his mind,

31 For a projected edition.
32 Alexander. See Pope's *Essay on Criticism,* line 376, note 20. According to one historian, his shoulders were not symmetrical.
33 The Roman poet Publius Ovidius Naso (43 B.C.–17 A.D.).
34 Publius Vergilius Maro (70–19 B.C.).
35 Verse.
36 Says Arbuthnot.
37 Polished. George Granville (1667–1735), first Baron Lansdowne, poet, playwright, and Tory statesman. He and the others encouraged Pope when he was in his teens.
38 William Walsh (1663–1708), poet, critic, and Whig M.P.
39 Dr. Samuel Garth, poet, and physician to George I.
40 Charles Talbot (1660–1718), Duke of Shrewsbury, and minister of William III, Anne, and George I.
41 John, Baron Somers (1651–1716), leader of the Whigs and minister of William III.
42 John Sheffield, first Duke of Buckinghamshire (1648–1721), statesman, and minor poet and playwright.
43 Francis Atterbury, Bishop of Rochester (1662–1732), banished in 1732 for Jacobite plotting. The *miter* is the headdress of a bishop.
44 See headnote to *An Essay on Man.*

45 Thomas Burnet (1694–1743), son of Bishop Gilbert Burnet (see p. 533, above), and afterwards a judge. A friend of Addison, he had attacked Pope.
46 John Oldmixon (1673–1742), a Whig writer; among his sins was the stealing of three of Pope's poems for a miscellany.
47 Thomas Cooke (1703–56), a translator, pamphleteer, and minor poet; he first aroused Pope's ire by ranking him below Ambrose Philips.   48 Pope's judgment on his early works.
49 *Lord Fanny* was Pope's name for his former friend, the Whig statesman John, Baron Hervey (1696–1743), who had sided with Lady Montagu in her quarrel with Pope. He is the Sporus of lines 305 ff.—Line 150 refers to *The Rape of the Lock* and *Windsor Forest.*
50 Pope thought Addison had inspired some of the numerous attacks of the well-known critics Charles Gildon (1665–1724) and John Dennis (1657–1734).   51 Lack.
52 I.e., they are not creative artists. The great classical scholar Richard Bentley (1662–1742), of Cambridge, had tried to dodge Pope's demand for an opinion on his translation of Homer. Pope pressed him, and deserved what he is said to have got: "It is a pretty poem, Mr. Pope, but you must not call it Homer." Bentley had published a bad edition of Milton (see line 168). Lewis Theobald (1688–1744—pronounced *Tibbald*) was a hack writer, but a great Shakespearean scholar. In 1726 he had issued his *Shakespeare Restored, or A Specimen of the Many Errors . . . by Mr. Pope in His Late Edition;* in 1733 his own edition was published, a much better one than Pope's. He was the original hero of the *Dunciad.*

That casting weight[53] pride adds to emptiness,
This, who can gratify? for who can guess?
The bard whom pilfered pastorals renown,
Who turns a Persian tale for half a crown,[54]   180
Just writes to make his barrenness appear,
And strains from hard-bound brains eight lines a year;
He who, still wanting, though he lives on theft,
Steals much, spends little, yet has nothing left;
And he who now to sense, now nonsense, leaning,   185
Means not, but blunders round about a meaning;
And he whose fustian's[55] so sublimely bad
It is not poetry, but prose run mad:
All these my modest satire[56] bade translate,
And owned that nine such poets made a Tate.[57]   190
How did they fume and stamp and roar and chafe!
And swear not Addison himself was safe.

　　Peace to all such! but were there one whose fires
True genius kindles and fair fame inspires,
Blest with each talent and each art to please,   195
And born to write, converse, and live with ease:
Should such a man, too fond to rule[58] alone,
Bear like the Turk no brother near the throne;[59]
View him with scornful yet with jealous eyes,
And hate for arts that caused himself to rise;   200
Damn with faint praise, assent with civil leer,
And, without sneering, teach the rest to sneer;
Willing to wound, and yet afraid to strike,
Just hint a fault, and hesitate dislike;
Alike reserved to blame or to commend,   205
A tim'rous foe, and a suspicious friend;
Dreading ev'n fools, by flatterers besieged,
And so obliging that he ne'er obliged;[60]
Like Cato, give his little senate[61] laws,
And sit attentive to his own applause,   210
While wits and templars[62] ev'ry sentence raise,[63]
And wonder with a foolish face of praise—
Who but must laugh if such a man there be?

Who would not weep, if Atticus[64] were he?
　　What though my name stood rubric[65] on the walls, 215
Or plastered posts,[66] with claps, in capitals?
Or smoking forth, a hundred hawkers' load,
On wings of winds came flying all abroad?
I sought no homage from the race that write;
I kept, like Asian monarchs, from their sight.   220
Poems I heeded (now berimed so long)
No more than thou, great George! a birthday song.[67]
I ne'er with wits or witlings passed my days,
To spread about the itch of verse and praise;
Nor like a puppy daggled[68] through the town,   225
To fetch and carry singsong[69] up and down;
Nor at rehearsals[70] sweat and mouthed and cried,
With handkerchief and orange[71] at my side;
But sick of fops and poetry and prate,
To Bufo[72] left the whole Castalian state.[73]   230
　　Proud as Apollo on his forkèd hill[74]
Sat full-blown Bufo, puffed[75] by ev'ry quill;
Fed with soft dedication all day long,
Horace and he went hand in hand in song.
His library (where busts of poets dead,   235
And a true Pindar[76] stood without a head)
Received of wits an undistinguished race,
Who first his judgment asked, and then a place.[77]
Much they extolled his pictures, much his seat,[78]
And flattered ev'ry day, and some days ate;   240
Till, grown more frugal in his riper days,
He paid some bards with port, and some with praise;

[64] A Roman scholar of the first century B.C.; but everyone knew
Addison was meant. Part of this devastating portrait was composed not later than 1716; Pope had sent it to Addison, as a
kind of warning. The main cause of Pope's resentment seems
to have been that Addison had shown more interest in another
new translation of Homer than in his. The early version had
been printed anonymously, very likely without Pope's consent,
in 1722, three years after Addison's death.
[65] Printed in red on Lintot's advertisements of new books.
[66] Where booksellers advertised with "claps," which were bills
(small posters) to be clapped (i.e., pasted) on.
[67] A jeer at the poet laureate, Colley Cibber, who had to write an
annual birthday ode (see note 23).
[68] Trailed through the mud.　　　　[69] Doggerel.
[70] I.e., of some play by me.
[71] Half a rind, filled with scented rags, as a recourse against playhouse odors.
[72] I.e., some patron. Probably no one in particular is meant. Pope
proceeds with a "character," doubtless composed from the
traits of several persons, among them Charles Montagu (1661–
1751), first Earl of Halifax, a statesman, minor poet, and patron
of poets.
[73] I.e., all the poems. Castalia was the spring on Mt. Parnassus,
sacred to Apollo and the Muses.
[74] Parnassus has two main peaks.　　　[75] Extravagantly praised.
[76] A major Greek lyric poet (d. 448? B.C.). Pope's note: "Ridicules
the affectation of antiquaries, who frequently exhibit the headless trunks of statues, for Plato, Homer, Pindar, &c."
[77] Political job.　　　　[78] Country place.

[53] The adjustment of which turns the scale.
[54] Philips (see note 27, above). He had translated a book of Persian
tales.
[55] Bombast is.
[56] In the Dunciad.
[57] Shadwell's ridiculous successor (1692) as poet laureate was
Nahum Tate (1652–1715), playwright and versifier of the
Psalms.
[58] Desirous of ruling.
[59] It was an old Turkish custom for a new sultan to murder his
half brothers by his father's other wives.
[60] Then pronounced obleeged.
[61] Addison's circle of admirers at Button's (see headnote to Addison, p. 698, above).
[62] Law students, or at any rate residents of the inns of court. They
often paid more attention to literature than to the law.
[63] Overestimate.

To some a dry rehearsal was assigned,[79]
And others (harder still) he paid in kind.[80]
Dryden alone (what wonder?) came not nigh;   245
Dryden alone escaped this judging eye:
But still the great have kindness in reserve;
He helped to bury whom he helped to starve.[81]
   May some choice patron bless each gray goose quill!
May every Bavius have his Bufo still!   250
So, when a statesman wants a day's defense,
Or envy holds a whole week's war with sense,
Or simple pride for flatt'ry makes demands,
May dunce by dunce be whistled off my hands!
Blest be the great! for those they take away,   255
And those they left me—for they left me Gay,[82]
Left me to see neglected genius bloom,
Neglected die, and tell it on his tomb;
Of all thy blameless life the sole return
My verse, and Queensb'ry[83] weeping o'er thy urn!   260
Oh, let me live my own! and die so too!
("To live and die is all I have to do"):[84]
Maintain a poet's dignity and ease,
And see what friends and read what books I please.
Above a patron, though I condescend   265
Sometimes to call a minister my friend,
I was not born for courts or great affairs;
I pay my debts, believe, and say my pray'rs,
Can sleep without a poem in my head,
Nor know if Dennis be alive or dead.   270
   Why am I asked what next shall see the light?
Heav'ns! was I born for nothing but to write?
Has life no joys for me? or (to be grave)
Have I no friend to serve, no soul to save?
"I found him close with Swift."—"Indeed? no doubt," 275
Cries prating Balbus,[85] "something will come out."
'Tis all in vain, deny it as I will.
"No, such a genius never can lie still";
And then for mine obligingly mistakes
The first lampoon Sir Will or Bubo[86] makes.   280
Poor guiltless I! and can I choose but smile,
When ev'ry coxcomb knows me by my style?

---

[79] I.e., he gave them neither wine nor praise while they read him their poems.   [80] I.e., by reading his poems to them.
[81] Not true of Halifax. Pope's note: "Mr. Dryden, after having lived in exigencies, had a magnificent funeral bestowed upon him by the contribution of several persons of quality."
[82] See introduction to John Gay, pp. 811 f., below.
[83] The Duchess of Queensberry, Gay's friend and patroness.
[84] Quoted from "Of Prudence," by Sir John Denham (1615–69).
[85] Viscount Dupplin, eldest son of the eighth Earl of Kinnoul; he was known as an incessant talker.
[86] Sir William Yonge (d. 1755), a Whig politician; and George Bubb Dodington, Baron Melcombe (1691–1762), an ostentatious rich man who wielded political influence and posed as a patron of letters.

Cursed be the verse, how well soe'er it flow,
That tends to make one worthy man my foe,
Give virtue scandal, innocence a fear,   285
Or from the soft-eyed virgin steal a tear!
But he who hurts a harmless neighbor's peace,
Insults fall'n worth, or beauty in distress,
Who loves a lie, lame slander helps about,
Who writes a libel, or who copies out;   290
That fop whose pride affects a patron's name,
Yet, absent, wounds an author's honest fame;
Who can your merit selfishly approve,
And show the sense of it without the love;
Who has the vanity to call you friend,   295
Yet wants the honor, injured, to defend;
Who tells whate'er you think, whate'er you say,
And, if he lie not, must at least betray;
Who to the *dean* and *silver bell* can swear,
And sees at Canons what was never there;[87]   300
Who reads but with a lust to misapply,
Make satire a lampoon, and fiction lie:
A lash like mine no honest man shall dread,
But all such babbling blockheads in his stead.
   Let Sporus[88] tremble—"What? that thing of silk,   305
Sporus, that mere white curd of ass's milk?[89]
Satire or sense, alas! can Sporus feel?
Who breaks a butterfly upon a wheel?"
Yet let me flap this bug with gilded wings,
This painted child of dirt, that stinks and stings,   310
Whose buzz the witty and the fair annoys,
Yet wit ne'er tastes, and beauty ne'er enjoys:
So well-bred spaniels civilly delight
In mumbling of the game they dare not bite.
Eternal smiles his emptiness betray,   315
As shallow streams run dimpling all the way.
Whether in florid impotence he speaks,
And, as the prompter breathes, the puppet squeaks;
Or at the ear of Eve, familiar toad,[90]
Half froth, half venom, spits himself abroad,   320
In puns or politics or tales or lies
Or spite or smut or rimes or blasphemies.
His wit all seesaw between that and this, ⎫
Now high, now low, now master up, now miss, ⎬
And he himself one vile antithesis.   ⎭   325
Amphibious thing! that acting either part,
The trifling head, or the corrupted heart!
Fop at the toilet, flatt'rer at the board,
Now trips a lady, and now struts a lord.

[87] See *Moral Essays,* IV, note on line 99.
[88] The name of this eunuch, a favorite of the Emperor Nero, stands for Lord Hervey (see note 49).
[89] Both Hervey and Pope drank it for their health.
[90] Like Satan in the form of a serpent. Here, Eve=Queen Caroline.

Eve's tempter thus the rabbins[91] have expressed,   330
A cherub's face, a reptile all the rest;
Beauty that shocks you, parts[92] that none will trust,
Wit that can creep, and pride that licks the dust.

    Not fortune's worshipper, nor fashion's fool,
Not lucre's madman, nor ambition's tool,   335
Not proud nor servile: be one poet's praise,
That if he pleased, he pleased by manly ways;
That flatt'ry, ev'n to kings, he held a shame,
And thought a lie in verse or prose the same;
That not in fancy's maze he wandered long,   340
But stooped to[93] truth, and moralized his song;
That not for fame, but virtue's better end,
He stood the furious foe, the timid friend,
The damning critic, half-approving wit,
The coxcomb hit, or fearing to be hit;   345
Laughed at the loss of friends he never had,
The dull, the proud, the wicked, and the mad;
The distant threats of vengeance on his head,
The blow unfelt, the tear he never shed;
The tale revived, the lie so oft o'erthrown,   350
Th' imputed trash, and dullness not his own;
The morals blackened when the writings 'scape,
The libeled person, and the pictured shape;
Abuse on all he loved, or loved him, spread,
A friend in exile, or a father dead;   355
The whisper[94] that, to greatness still too near,
Perhaps yet vibrates on his sov'reign's ear—
Welcome for thee, fair virtue! all the past;
For thee, fair virtue! welcome ev'n the last!

    "But why insult the poor? affront the great?"   360
A knave's a knave to me, in ev'ry state;
Alike my scorn if he succeed or fail,
Sporus at court, or Japhet in a jail,[95]
A hireling scribbler, or a hireling peer,
Knight of the post corrupt,[96] or of the shire;[97]   365
If on a pillory, or near a throne,
He gain his prince's ear, or lose his own.

    Yet soft by nature, more a dupe than wit,
Sappho can tell you how this man was bit;[98]
This dreaded sat'rist Dennis will confess   370
Foe to his pride, but friend to his distress:[99]

So humble, he has knocked at Tibbald's door,
Has drunk with Cibber, nay, has rimed for Moore.
Full ten years slandered, did he once reply?
Three thousand suns went down on Welsted's lie.[1]   375
To please a mistress one aspersed his life;[2]
He lashed him not, but let her be his wife.
Let Budgell charge low Grub Street on his quill,
And write whate'er he pleased, except his will;[3]
Let the two Curlls of town and court[4] abuse   380
His father, mother, body, soul, and Muse.
Yet why? that father held it for a rule,
It was a sin to call our neighbor fool;
That harmless mother thought no wife a whore—
Hear this, and spare his family, James Moore![5]   385
Unspotted names! and memorable long,
If there be force in virtue, or in song.

    Of gentle blood (part shed in honor's cause,
While yet in Britain honor had applause)
Each parent sprung—"What fortune, pray?"—Their own,
And better got than Bestia's from the throne.[6]   391
Born to no pride, inheriting no strife,
Nor marrying discord in a noble wife,[7]
Stranger to civil and religious rage,
The good man walked innoxious through his age.   395
No courts he saw, no suits would ever try,
Nor dared an oath,[8] nor hazarded a lie.
Unlearn'd, he knew no schoolman's subtle art,
No language but the language of the heart.
By nature honest, by experience wise,   400
Healthy by temp'rance and by exercise;
His life, though long, to sickness passed unknown;
His death was instant, and without a groan.
Oh, grant me thus to live, and thus to die!
Who sprung from kings shall know less joy than I.   405

    O friend! may each domestic bliss be thine!
Be no unpleasing melancholy mine:
Me, let the tender office long engage
To rock the cradle of reposing age,
With lenient arts extend a mother's breath,   410
Make languor smile, and smooth the bed of death;

---

91 Rabbis, Jewish scholars.   92 Accomplishments.
93 Swooped on (as a falcon "stoops" to her prey).
94 I.e., Hervey's.
95 Japhet Crook (1662–1734), rightly named, for he was a notorious forger.   96 A professional perjurer.
97 Representative of a county in the House of Commons.
98 Stung, victimized.
99 In 1733 Pope provided a prologue for a benefit performance in aid of his old enemy. Despite line 270, Dennis had died shortly before.

1 See note 14, above.
2 This reference remains unexplained.
3 Eustace Budgell (1686–1737), a cousin of Addison. He seems to have acquired a fortune by forging a will. He had attacked Pope.
4 I.e., the publisher (note 15) and Lord Hervey (note 49).
5 There were scandalous stories about his mother.
6 L. Calpurnius Bestia was a venal Roman consul of the second century B.C. (mentioned by Sallust). Pope probably means the Duke of Marlborough.
7 Perhaps an allusion to the marriage of Addison and Lady Warwick.
8 As a Catholic he had refused to take the oath of allegiance to William and Mary.

Explore the thought, explain the asking eye,
And keep awhile one parent from the sky![9]
On cares like these if length of days attend,
May heav'n, to bless those days, preserve my friend,   415

Preserve him social, cheerful, and serene,
And just as rich as when he served a queen.
Whether that blessing be denied or giv'n,
Thus far was right; the rest belongs to heav'n.

John Gay

1685–1732

It is not customary to begin a biographical sketch with an epitaph, but the two bits of verse which appear on his tomb in Westminster Abbey make a good introduction to Gay. Pope contributed the first:

> Of manners gentle, of affections mild;
> In wit, a man; simplicity, a child:
> With native humor temp'ring virtuous rage,
> Formed to delight at once and lash the age:
> Above temptation in a low estate,
> And uncorrupted, ev'n among the great:
> A safe companion, and an easy friend,
> Unblamed through life, lamented in thy end.
> These are thy honors! not that here thy bust
> Is mixed with heroes, or with kings thy dust;
> But that the worthy and the good shall say,
> Striking their pensive bosoms, "Here lies Gay."

It was a daring but sound judgment which decided to comply with Gay's request that his own lines should also be inscribed:

> Life is a jest, and all things show it;
> I thought so once, and now I know it.

This couplet is the report of a man who found fun and friendship in life, refused to be a sedate citizen, and gave the world better than he received.

He was born in 1685 at the port of Barnstaple in Devonshire. His parents left him an orphan at ten, and his only education was at the excellent grammar school of his native town. When he was seventeen he went up to London and entered the silk trade as an apprentice; apparently he came into an inheritance, and for a while went back to Devonshire. When he returned, it was to be secretary to Aaron Hill (1685–1750), a wealthy young man and a boyhood friend, whose poems and plays won him a minor reputation. Gay helped him with his new journal, the British Apollo (1708–11), and through him was brought in touch with a number of second-rate literary figures. In

1711 he moved into higher circles. Steele praised his account of The Present State of Wit, in which Gay had heaped encomiums on Steele and Addison. Pope became a close friend, and introduced him to Swift and Arbuthnot. Gay was never a strong party man. It was the Whigs who had first taken notice of him; but he went along with Pope and Swift, and became more or less identified with the Tories. For a while (1712–14) he held the not very exacting post of secretary-steward to the Duchess of Monmouth. When the Tory wits started the Scriblerus Club, the inclusion of Gay was a matter of course. Just before the fall of the party in 1714, Swift got him the secretaryship of a special mission to the Elector of Hanover, who was soon to wear the English crown as George I; but Gay's hopes of a career in political sinecures were almost immediately dashed by the Tories' catastrophe. Nothing else came his way till 1724, when Walpole's generosity (ill rewarded four years later by the satire of The Beggar's Opera) assigned Gay a lottery commissionership. The stipend, though it carried official lodgings, was a small one.

Gay was not, in fact, the sort of man to carve out a place for himself; till quite recently he has been regarded as an amiable weakling. As Pope's verses show, that was not the view of those who knew him best. The Dean of St. Patrick's, moreover, was not one who suffered fools gladly. When the letter came announcing Gay's death, Swift suspected the contents and let it lie unopened for five days before he could bring himself to read it. To be sure, there is no denying that like many artists Gay was irresponsible about things that bored him, and lacked judgment in handling money. He made a thousand pounds from his collected poems in 1720, and proceeded to lose it all in the South Sea Bubble.

But this does not alter the gratitude of the host of theatergoers who, in the twentieth as in the eighteenth century, have taken (to borrow a phrase from one of its lyrics) a joy beyond expression in The Beggar's Opera (1728). It was his one grand, imperishable success. Walpole was stung by the satire, though he pretended otherwise on the opening night; and the performance of Polly, an inferior sequel, was banned by the censor. Gay at once had

---

[9] Pope's mother died in 1733, a year and a half before the poem was published. A version of lines 406–19 was written before her death.

Polly printed and acted as his own publisher; he made a very good thing out of it, but he could never keep the money he got. Fortunately he had a genius for friendship with the great of the three worlds, then intimately related, of fashion, politics, and letters. His presence enlivened any dinner table; and there was always someone ready to be his host for a long visit, or to take him to Bath or over to France for a pleasant sojourn. From 1727 till his death in 1732, he lived with the Duke and Duchess of Queensberry; the Duke looked after his money, and the Duchess after his clothes. Gay's health was delicate; he was only forty-seven when he died.

Meanwhile he had written some mediocre plays and a long string of poems, some of them delightful pieces. Their popularity continued throughout the eighteenth century; and though his reputation declined during the nineteenth century, of late it has been rising, especially since the revival of *The Beggar's Opera* in England and the United States in 1920, which swept everything before it. As a rule Gay's verse, though some of it is trash, is easy, unpretentious, and charming. *The Shepherd's Week* (1714), composed at Pope's suggestion, consists of six pastorals, not in the traditional vein but peopled with real English rustics. His realism is continued in *Trivia* (1716), probably the best picture of London in verse. His *Fables* (2 vols., 1727-28) are nothing like so good as *Trivia,* but they have pleased many readers.

The standard edition is *The Poetical Works* by G. C. Faber (1926); it includes the text of *The Beggar's Opera* and selections from Gay's other dramatic writings. The best Life is W. H. Irving's delightful *John Gay, Favorite of the Wits* (1940).

John Gay

from TRIVIA, OR THE ART OF WALKING

Trivia is not exactly poetry; it is a descriptive essay in verse. Its appeal is to man's interest in man. For everyone who is fascinated by the sights of a great city, and loves to watch the panorama of its streets at all hours and in all weathers, Gay's verses cast an unfailing spell. They are good, honest realism, with now and then a flick of satire for the inflated epic mannerisms of that neoclassical day. For Gay there is not, at least in *Trivia,* any mystery or wonder in the gigantic spectacle, though he was capable of a higher flight in "A Contemplation on Night" and has therefore been most exaggeratedly likened to Wordsworth. But if he misses a good deal, and cannot see the wood for the trees, the trees are the subject here. He has the priceless gifts of responsiveness and enthusiasm; he is no less delighted than the most devoted Cockney to be a part of London, and he communicates his delight.

A good book to read along with *Trivia* is W. H. Irving's *John Gay's London* (1928). *Trivia* (from Latin *trivium,* fork in the road, meeting of three streets) was an epithet of the goddess Diana, who had a threefold function, in heaven, earth, and hell. Gay therefore selects her as an appropriate deity to invoke, in mock-epic style, on behalf of walkers.

BOOK II

OF WALKING THE STREETS BY DAY

Thus far the Muse has traced, in useful lays,
The proper implements for wintry ways;
Has taught the walker, with judicious eyes,
To read the various warnings of the skies.
Now venture, Muse, from home, to range the town,   5
And for the public safety risk thy own. . . .
  Let due civilities be strictly paid.   45
The wall surrender to the hooded maid;
Nor let thy sturdy elbow's hasty rage
Jostle the feeble steps of trembling age;
And when the porter bends beneath his load
And pants for breath, clear thou the crowded road.   50
But, above all, the groping blind direct,
And from the pressing throng the lame protect.

You'll sometimes meet a fop, of nicest tread,
Whose mantling peruke veils his empty head;
At ev'ry step he dreads the wall to lose,   55
And risks, to save a coach, his red-heeled shoes;
Him, like the miller, pass with caution by,
Lest from his shoulder clouds of powder fly.
But when the bully, with assuming pace,
Cocks his broad hat, edged round with tarnished lace,   60
Yield not the way; defy his strutting pride,
And thrust him to the muddy kennel's[1] side;
He never turns again, nor dares oppose,
But mutters coward curses as he goes. . . .
  Where, elevated o'er the gaping crowd,   221
Clasped in the board the perjured head is bowed,[2]
Betimes[3] retreat; here thick as hailstones pour
Turnips, and half-hatched eggs (a mingled show'r)

---

[1] Gutter's.   [2] In the pillory.   [3] Promptly.

Among the rabble rain. Some random throw   225
May with the trickling yolk thy cheek o'erflow. . . .

    Where Covent Garden's famous temple[4] stands,
That boasts the work of Jones' immortal hands,
Columns with plain magnificence appear,   345
And graceful porches lead along the square.
Here oft my course I bend, when lo! from far
I spy the furies of the football war:
The prentice quits his shop, to join the crew,
Encreasing crowds the flying game pursue.   350
Thus, as you roll the ball o'er snowy ground,
The gath'ring globe augments with ev'ry round.
But whither shall I run? The throng draws nigh,
The ball now skims the street, now soars on high;
The dext'rous glazier strong returns the bound,   355
And jingling sashes on the penthouse[5] sound. . . .

    Experienced men, inured to city ways,   405
Need not the calendar to count their days.
When through the town with slow and solemn air,
Led by the nostril walks the muzzled bear—
Behind him moves, majestically dull,
The pride of Hockley Hole,[6] the surly bull—   410
Learn hence the periods of the week to name:
Mondays and Thursdays are the days of game.

    When fishy stalls with double store are laid,
The golden-bellied carp, the broad-finned maid,[7]
Red-speckled trouts, the salmon's silver jowl,   415
The jointed lobster, and unscaly sole,
And luscious scallops, to allure the tastes
Of rigid zealots to delicious fasts—
Wednesdays and Fridays you'll observe from hence,
Days when our sires were doomed to abstinence.   420

    When dirty waters from balcónies drop,
And dext'rous damsels twirl the sprinkling mop,
And cleanse the spattered sash, and scrub the stairs,
Know Saturday's conclusive morn appears. . . .

    Proud coaches pass, regardless of the moan   451
Of infant orphans, and the widow's groan;
While charity still[8] moves the walker's mind:
His lib'ral purse relieves the lame and blind.
Judiciously thy halfpence are bestowed   455
Where the laborious beggar sweeps the road.
Whate'er you give, give ever at demand,
Nor let old age long stretch his palsied hand.
Those who give late are importuned each day,
And still are teased because they still delay.   460

---

[4] St. Paul's, Covent Garden, north of the Strand and west of
  Drury Lane. The famous square of Covent Garden, its arcades,
  and perhaps the church were designed by Inigo Jones (p. 438,
  above).
[5] Sloping roof of a shed or a stall attached to a building.
[6] Hockley in the Hole, now Ray Street, in the northern suburb
  of Clerkenwell. Bulls and bears were baited there.
[7] A kind of skate.   [8] Always.

If e'er the miser durst his farthings spare,
He thinly spreads them through the public square,
Where all beside the rail ranged beggars lie
And from each other catch the doleful cry,
With heav'n for twopence cheaply wipes his score,   465
Lifts up his eyes, and hastes to beggar more. . . .

BOOK III

OF WALKING THE STREETS BY NIGHT

O Trivia, goddess, leave these low abodes,
And traverse o'er the wide ethereal roads;
Celestial queen, put on thy robes of light,
Now Cynthia[9] named, fair regent of the night.
At sight of thee the villain sheathes his sword,   5
Nor scales the wall, to steal the wealthy hoard.
O may thy silver lamp from heav'n's high bow'r
Direct my footsteps in the midnight hour! . . .

    Forth issuing from steep lanes, the collier's steeds   25
Drag the black load; another cart succeeds,
Team follows team, crowds heaped on crowds appear,
And wait impatient till the road grow clear.
Now all the pavement sounds with trampling feet,
And the mixed hurry barricades the street.   30
Entangled here, the wagon's lengthened team
Cracks the tough harness; here a pond'rous beam
Lies overturned athwart; for slaughter fed,
Here lowing bullocks raise their hornèd head.
Now oaths grow loud, with coaches coaches jar,   35
And the smart blow provokes the sturdy war;
From the high box they whirl the thong around,
And with the twining lash their shins resound.
Their rage ferments, more dang'rous wounds they try,
And the blood gushes down their painful eye.   40
And now on foot the frowning warriors light,
And with their pond'rous fists renew the fight;
Blow answers blow, their cheeks are smeared with blood,
Till down they fall, and grappling roll in mud.
So when two boars, in wild Ytene[10] bred,   45
Or on Westphalia's fatt'ning chestnuts fed,
Gnash their sharp tusks and, roused with equal fire,
Dispute the reign of some luxurious mire;
In the black flood they wallow o'er and o'er,
Till their armed jaws distill with foam and gore.   50
    Where the mob gathers, swiftly shoot along,
Nor idly mingle in the noisy throng.
Lured by the silver hilt, amid the swarm
The subtle artist will thy side disarm.

---

[9] In heaven Diana (see headnote) is Cynthia, the moon.
[10] Gay's footnote: "New Forest in Hampshire, anciently so called."
  —The formal comparison, introduced by *so*, lightly burlesques
  the Homeric simile.

JOHN GAY   813

Nor is thy flaxen wig with safety worn; 55
High on the shoulder, in a basket borne,
Lurks the sly boy, whose hand, to rapine bred,
Plucks off the curling honors of thy head.
Here dives the skulking thief with practiced sleight,
And unfelt fingers make thy pocket light. 60
Where's now thy watch, with all its trinkets, flown?
And thy late snuffbox is no more thy own.
But lo! his bolder theft some tradesman spies,
Swift from his prey the scudding lurcher[11] flies;
Dext'rous he 'scapes the coach with nimble bounds, 65
Whilst ev'ry honest tongue *Stop thief!* resounds.
So speeds the wily fox, alarmed by fear,
Who lately filched the turkey's callow care;
Hounds following hounds grow louder as he flies,
And injured tenants join the hunter's cries. 70
Breathless he stumbling falls. Ill-fated boy!
Why did not honest work thy youth employ?
Seized by rough hands, he's dragged amid the rout,
And stretched beneath the pump's incessant spout;
Or plunged in miry ponds, he gasping lies: 75
Mud chokes his mouth, and plasters o'er his eyes.

Let not the ballad singer's shrilling strain
Amid the swarm thy list'ning ear detain;
Guard well thy pocket, for these sirens stand
To aid the labors of the diving hand; 80
Confed'rate in the cheat, they draw the throng,
And cambric handkerchiefs reward the song.
But soon as coach or cart drives rattling on,
The rabble part; in shoals they backward run.
So Jove's loud bolts the mingled war divide, 85
And Greece and Troy retreat on either side. . . .

Let constant vigilance thy footsteps guide,
And wary circumspection guard thy side;
Then shalt thou walk unharmed the dang'rous night,
Nor need th' officious linkboy's[12] smoky light.
Thou never wilt attempt to cross the road 115
Where alehouse benches rest the porter's load,
Grievous to heedless shins; no barrow's wheel,
That bruises oft the truant schoolboy's heel,
Behind thee rolling, with insidious pace,
Shall mark thy stocking with a miry trace. 120
Let not thy vent'rous steps approach too nigh
Where, gaping wide, low steepy cellars lie:
Should thy shoe wrench aside, down, down you fall,
And overturn the scolding huckster's stall;
The scolding huckster shall not o'er thee moan, 125
But pence exact for nuts and pears o'erthrown.

Though you through cleanlier alleys wind by day,
To shun the hurries of the public way,

Yet ne'er to those dark paths by night retire;
Mind only safety, and contemn[13] the mire. 130
Then no impervious courts thy haste detain,
Nor sneering alewives bid thee turn again.

Where Lincoln's Inn,[14] wide space, is railed around,
Cross not with vent'rous step; there oft is found
The lurking thief, who, while the daylight shone, 135
Made the walls echo with his begging tone.
That crutch, which late compassion moved, shall wound
Thy bleeding head, and fell thee to the ground.
Though thou art tempted by the linkman's call,
Yet trust him not along the lonely wall; 140
In the mid-way he'll quench the flaming brand,
And share the booty with the pilf'ring band.
Still keep the public streets, where oily rays,
Shot from the crystal lamp, o'erspread the ways. . . .

If wheels bar up the road where streets are crossed 165
With gentle words the coachman's ear accost;
He ne'er the threat or harsh command obeys,
But with contempt the spattered shoe surveys.
Now man with utmost fortitude thy soul,
To cross the way where carts and coaches roll; 170
Yet do not in thy hardy skill confide,
Nor rashly risk the kennel's spacious stride.
Stay, till afar the distant wheel you hear,
Like dying thunder in the breaking air;
Thy foot will slide upon the miry stone, 175
And passing coaches crush thy tortured bone,
Or wheels enclose the road: on either hand
Pent round with perils, in the midst you stand,
And call for aid in vain; the coachman swears,
And car-men drive, unmindful of thy prayers. 180
Where wilt thou turn? ah! whither wilt thou fly?
On ev'ry side the pressing spokes are nigh.
So sailors, while Charybdis' gulf[15] they shun,
Amazed, on Scylla's craggy dangers run.

Be sure observe where brown Ostrea[16] stands, 185
Who boasts her shelly ware from Wallfleet[17] sands;
There mayst thou pass, with safe unmiry feet,
Where the raised pavement leads athwart the street.
If where Fleet Ditch[18] with muddy current flows
You chance to roam, where oyster tubs in rows 190
Are ranged beside the posts, there stay thy haste,
And with the sav'ry fish indulge thy taste;

---

[11] Sneak thief.   [12] Torchbearer.

[13] Scorn, don't mind.
[14] A fine square between the Strand and High Holborn.
[15] The famous whirlpool off Sicily, in the Straits of Messina. On the Italian shore opposite it was the rock Scylla (see line 184).
[16] I.e., an oyster woman; Latin *ostrea* = oyster.
[17] Another name for the peninsula of Wallasey, in Essex, on the estuary of the Crouch, famous for its oyster beds.
[18] The Fleet, in Gay's time still an open sewer, flowed into the Thames at Blackfriars.

The damsel's knife the gaping shell commands,
While the salt liquor streams between her hands.

 The man had sure a palate covered o'er   195
With brass or steel, that on the rocky shore
First broke the oozy oyster's pearly coat,
And risked the living morsel down his throat.
What will not lux'ry taste? Earth, sea, and air
Are daily ransacked for the bill of fare.   200
Blood stuffed in skins is British Christians' food,
And France robs marshes of the croaking brood;
Spongy morels[19] in strong ragousts[20] are found,
And in the soup the slimy snail is drowned. . . .

 Oh, may thy virtue guard thee through the roads
Of Drury's mazy courts and dark abodes,   260
The harlots' guileful paths, who nightly stand
Where Catherine Street[21] descends into the Strand.
Say, vagrant Muse, their wiles and subtle arts,
To lure the strangers' unsuspecting hearts;
So shall our youth on healthful sinews tread,   265
And city cheeks grow warm with rural red.

 'Tis she who nightly strolls with saunt'ring pace;[22]
No stubborn stays her yielding shape embrace;
Beneath the lamp her tawdry ribbons glare,
The new-scoured manteau,[23] and the slattern air;   270
High-draggled petticoats her travels show,
And hollow cheeks with artful blushes glow;
With flatt'ring sounds she soothes the cred'lous ear,
"My noble captain! charmer! love! my dear!"
In riding hood near tavern doors she plies,   275
Or muffled pinners[24] hide her livid eyes.
With empty bandbox she delights to range,
And feigns a distant errand from the Change;[25]
Nay, she will oft the Quaker's hood profane,
And trudge demure the rounds of Drury Lane.   280
She darts from sarcenet[26] ambush wily leers,
Twitches thy sleeve, or with familiar airs
Her fan will pat thy cheek; these snares disdain,
Nor gaze behind thee when she turns again. . . .

Now is the time that rakes their revels keep,   321
Kindlers of riot, enemies of sleep.
His scattered pence the flying Nicker[27] flings,
And with the copper show'r the casement rings.
Who has not heard the Scourer's midnight fame?   325
Who has not trembled at the Mohock's[28] name?
Was there a watchman took his hourly rounds
Safe from their blows or new-invented wounds?
I pass their desp'rate deeds, and mischiefs done
Where from Snow Hill[29] black steepy torrents run: 330
How matrons, hooped within the hoghead's womb,
Were tumbled furious thence; the rolling tomb
O'er the stones thunders, bounds from side to side.
So Regulus[30] to save his country died. . . .

 Consider, reader, what fatigues I've known,
The toils, the perils of the wintry town;
What riots seen, what bustling crowds I bored,   395
How oft I crossed where carts and coaches roared;
Yet shall I bless my labors, if mankind
Their future safety from my dangers find.
Thus the bold traveler, inured to toil,
Whose steps have printed Asia's desert soil,   400
The barb'rous Arabs' haunt, or shiv'ring crossed
Dark Greenland's mountains of eternal frost,
Whom providence in length of years restores
To the wished harbor of his native shores,
Sets forth his journals to the public view   405
To caution, by his woes, the wand'ring crew.

 And now complete my gen'rous labors lie,
Finished, and ripe for immortality.
Death shall entomb in dust this mold'ring frame,
But never reach th' eternal part, my fame.   410
When W* and G**,[31] mighty names, are dead,
Or but at Chelsea under custards read;[32]
When critics crazy bandboxes repair,[33]
And tragedies, turned rockets,[34] bounce in air,
High-raised on Fleet Street posts,[35] consigned to fame,   415
This work shall shine, and walkers bless my name.

[27] Gay's footnote: "Gentlemen who delighted to break windows with halfpence."
[28] The Scourers, especially in Restoration times, and their successors the Mohocks were gangs of rowdies, sometimes fashionable young men, who ranged the streets at night.
[29] The highway between Holborn Bridge and Newgate.
[30] This Roman general was captured by the Carthaginians. He was tortured to death by being rolled in a nail-studded barrel.
[31] Probably Edward Ward (1667–1731), a tavern keeper who also wrote, badly; and Charles Gildon (1665–1724), a bad critic and worse playwright, who had attacked both Pope and Gay.
[32] Chelsea, on the north bank of the Thames above Westminster, was famous for buns and pastries. Cooks used leaves from unsalable books to line baking dishes.
[33] I.e., leaves from their works are used to line and strengthen rickety bandboxes.
[34] Their leaves used for the paper part of rockets.
[35] Where booksellers advertised their wares, in front of their shops.

---

[19] Edible fungi.
[20] Ragouts, stews.   [21] By Drury Lane Theater.
[22] The topics of *Trivia* are set forth in marginal notes; here, "How to know a whore."   [23] Loose-bodied robe.
[24] A caplike headdress, with a long hanging flap on each side.
[25] The Royal Exchange, the great bazaar in Cornhill.
[26] I.e., silken.

SONGS *from* THE BEGGAR'S OPERA

Swift's suggestion, which he made in 1716 in a letter to Pope, that Gay should write "a Newgate pastoral, among the whores and thieves" in that celebrated jail, probably had little to do with *The Beggar's Opera,* which came eight years later and is not a pastoral. It is merely the best musical comedy in English; the only possible exceptions are the cream of Gilbert and Sullivan. The hero is a highwayman, surrounded principally by rogues and women of the town. Unlike most musical dramas, *The Beggar's Opera* is a good play. It is also full of excellent songs. Gay stole a little from Purcell, and also from Handel, who was his friend and never resented the theft; but for almost all of his lyrics he selected either traditionally or currently popular tunes, and graceful ones they mostly are. The scoring by Dr. John C. Pepusch (a minor German composer who had come to England in 1688) of an overture and basses to the airs was only decided on, at the insistence of the Duchess of Queensberry, after rehearsals were under way.

This jewel of ballad operas proved one of the English theater's greatest successes. The latest major revival was in London in 1920; it ran for three years, and a second company toured this country several times. It can be, and by most of its more recent audiences has been, enjoyed without reference to its satire. Contemporaries had additional pleasure from the jeering allusions to Italian opera, then all the rage at the Haymarket, and wicked thrusts at Booty Bob Walpole and his Whig ministry.

The text has often been reprinted, in anthologies of eighteenth-century drama as well as separately. W. E. Schultz's *Gay's Beggar's Opera* (1923) is an elaborate study. An arrangement, for piano and voices, of the score prepared by Frederic Austin for the opera's revival in 1920 in an adapted version by Arnold Bennett, was published in the same year.

THROUGH ALL THE EMPLOYMENTS OF LIFE

AIR I

AN OLD WOMAN CLOTHED IN GRAY[36]

Through all the employments of life
　Each neighbor abuses his brother;
Whore and rogue they call husband and wife:
　All professions berogue one another.
The priest calls the lawyer a cheat; 5
　The lawyer beknaves the divine;
And the statesman, because he's so great,
　Thinks his trade as honest as mine.

---

[36] The name of the tune. It is sung by Peachum when the curtain rises on the first act. He is the head of a gang of thieves, and in part is intended for Walpole.

WERE I LAID ON GREENLAND'S COAST

AIR XVI

OVER THE HILLS AND FAR AWAY[37]

MACHEATH.　Were I laid on Greenland's coast,
　　　　　And in my arms embraced my lass,
　　　　　Warm amidst eternal frost,
　　　　　Too soon the half-year's night would pass.
POLLY.　　Were I sold on Indian soil, 5
　　　　　Soon as the burning day was closed
　　　　　I could mock the sultry toil,
　　　　　When on my charmer's breast reposed.
MACHEATH.　And I would love you all the day,
POLLY.　　Every night would kiss and play, 10
MACHEATH.　If with me you'd fondly stray
POLLY.　　Over the hills and far away.

YOUTH'S THE SEASON

A dance à la ronde in the French manner; near the end of it this song and chorus:

AIR XXII

COTILLON[38]

Youth's the season made for joys,
　Love is then our duty;
She alone who that employs,
　Well deserves her beauty.
　　Let's be gay, 5
　　While we may,
Beauty's a flower despised in decay.
CHORUS.　Youth's the season made for joys,
　　　　　Love is then our duty.

Let us drink and sport today, 10
　Ours is not tomorrow.
Love with youth flies swift away,
　Age is nought but sorrow.
　　Dance and sing,
　　Time's on the wing, 15
Life never knows the return of spring.
CHORUS.　Let us drink and sport today,
　　　　　Ours is not tomorrow.

---

[37] Sung in Act I, Scene xiii, by Peachum's daughter Polly and her husband, the highwayman Macheath.
[38] In Act II, Scene iv; Macheath and chorus of women of the town.

SONGS in the BEGGAR's OPERA.

The cries of London street peddlers were recorded with a great variety of appropriate illustrations. Here, the cry "Fresh gathered peas" has summoned a purchaser.

The first page of the score of *The Beggar's Opera*, third edition, 1729. (Boston Public Library)

Robert Baddeley, who had been a footman, distinguished himself in low comedy parts, particularly those of footmen. He is shown here in the role of Moses in the original production of *The School for Scandal*, which opened at the Theater Royal, Drury Lane, on May 8, 1777. The painting is by Johann Zoffany, who did many paintings of Garrick and of the comedian Samuel Foote in parts for which they were famous.

David Garrick and his wife entertain Dr. Johnson. The painting is by Zoffany.

Ranelagh Gardens, favorite resort of Londoners in the eighteenth century, were laid out in 1742. Eating, drinking, singing, fireworks, concerts, enjoyed in an atmosphere in which fashion and mild rowdiness mingled, drew throngs to the place. Dr. Johnson, however, found himself depressed after visits to it.

James Thomson

1700–1748

"Hail, mildly pleasing Solitude!"
Thus was the Muse by Thomson wooed.
She yielded to his am'rous teasing,
And bore him verses—mildly pleasing.

But if the satirist meant to disparage *The Seasons,* he was quite wrong. It is true that only art which is intensely what it is can be called great; the major artist captures us by assault, not by sitting down to an uneventful siege. Yet there have been victories in war, and in art, by the latter method. There is a place in painting for the quiet landscape, the peaceful face; and in poetry there are mild delights as well as exciting ones. Such is the pleasure Thomson affords his readers.

Though Pope encouraged him, Thomson's appearance in the age of Pope is a somewhat surprising phenomenon. He was the first writer in the history of English literature to base his poetry on the beauty of the countryside. At the Hampton Court tea table, while the smoking tides fill China's earth, the ladies and gentlemen of fashion are considering such topics as "Who gave the ball, or paid the visit last." Thomson's mind is occupied with less fragile, more solidly satisfying thoughts. No doubt his preference for the country over the city, for natural scenery over metropolitan society, is atypical of his age. Yet he is fundamentally a neoclassicist. It is true that nature moves him as a revelation of God; but the revelation does not come through intuition and imagination, as for the Romantic poet, but through reason, as for the Deist. Basically, Thomson's approach to nature is no more romantic than Addison's in "The spacious firmament." Man, the favorite subject of the neoclassicist, has a large place in Thomson's nature poem; and Thomson thinks of his response to nature not as an individual and personal feeling but as one that any thoughtful rational man will share. Dr. Johnson's comment is significant: "The reader of *The Seasons* wonders that he never saw before what Thomson shows him, and that he never yet has felt what Thomson impresses." If Thomson was also atypical in his choice of blank verse (and later the Spenserian stanza) in preference to the reigning heroic couplet, he nevertheless follows current poetic fashion in the generalized description and the "elevated" diction of *The Seasons.*

Thomson was the son of a Presbyterian minister in Scotland. He was born in 1700, the fourth of nine children, and was brought up in the romantic border country among the Cheviot Hills. It is largely the scenes of his boyhood that he describes in *The Seasons.* His father died shortly after the poet entered Edinburgh University; but by dint of a hard struggle his remarkable mother managed to support the family and keep the talented James in college. After finishing his undergraduate course, he was a divinity student for about four years; in 1724 he decided to try for a career in London, and left the university. Friends got him a place as a private tutor; and though he was desperately poor, he had time for a serious poetic effort. *Winter* was published in 1726, with immediate success; it ran through five editions in less than three years and won Thomson influential friends. He gave up his tutoring and went to work on *Summer* (1727) and *Spring* (1728). In 1730, on the completion of *Autumn,* he brought out the whole poem as *The Seasons.* It was probably the most popular poem throughout the remainder of the eighteenth century.

Thomson also attempted the stage; but though four of his five tragedies were produced with some success, they are pretty tame. For two years he was enabled by another tutorship to travel in France and Italy. On his return he wrote a long, dull epic on *Liberty* (1734–36). For several years he held, through a patron's favor, a secretaryship in the Court of Chancery. When he lost it, he was again in financial straits; he was even arrested for debt. But a pension of £100 a year was soon granted by the Prince of Wales, and it was enough to live on. In 1740 Thomson was co-author of *Alfred, a Masque;* one of its lyrics is his best-known poem, the patriotic song "Rule Britannia." It has no poetic worth, but it shows where Thomson stood politically. He was an enthusiastic Whig; yet since he gloried in England's expanding commerce, he despised the pacific policy of Walpole, who in the opinion of many partisans failed to give England's merchant fleet adequate protection against French and Spanish agression.

Thomson was far from unresponsive to women, but he never married. He was in his forties when the rejection of a proposal plunged him into a permanent mood of depression and of indifference to his future. Nevertheless, during the five years that remained to him he wrote another play, which Garrick staged, and revised a final edition of *The Seasons.* For three years he held a government sinecure as surveyor-general of the Leeward Islands, hiring a deputy to do the work and pocketing £300 a year himself. Shortly before his death in 1748 appeared the second in importance of his poems, the eighty-one Spenserian stanzas of *The Castle of Indolence.*

The most useful edition of *The Seasons* is by J. L. Robertson (1891); *The Castle of Indolence* is included with it. Another volume by the same editor gives the *Complete*

Poetical Works (1908). Dr. Johnson wrote a Life; another is G. C. Macaulay's (1908). A. D. McKillop's *The Background of Thomson's Seasons* (1942), while not denying that Thomson's direct observation is what made the poem, shows (as in note 14, below) that he also drew on a wide range of philosophical and scientific reading.

James Thomson

from THE SEASONS

from SPRING

Come, gentle Spring, ethereal mildness, come;[1]
And from the bosom of yon dropping cloud,
While music wakes around, veiled in a shower
Of shadowing roses, on our plains descend.

    O Hartford,[2] fitted or to shine in courts   5
With unaffected grace or walk the plain
With innocence and meditation joined
In soft assemblage, listen to my song,
Which thy own season paints, when nature all
Is blooming and benevolent, like thee.   10

    And see where surly Winter passes off
Far to the north, and calls his ruffian blasts:
His blasts obey, and quit the howling hill,
The shattered forest, and the ravished vale;
While softer gales succeed, at whose kind touch,   15
Dissolving snows in livid torrents lost,
The mountains lift their green heads to the sky.

    As yet the trembling year is unconfirmed;
And Winter oft at eve resumes the breeze,
Chills the pale morn, and bids his driving sleets   20
Deform the day delightless; so that scarce
The bittern knows his time[3] with bill ingulfed
To shake the sounding marsh, or from the shore
The plovers when to scatter o'er the heath
And sing their wild notes to the listening waste.   25

    At last from Aries[4] rolls the bounteous sun,
And the bright Bull receives him. Then no more
Th' expansive atmosphere is cramped with cold,

But, full of life and vivifying soul,
Lifts the light clouds sublime, and spreads them thin,   30
Fleecy, and white o'er all-surrounding heaven.

    Forth fly the tepid airs; and unconfined,
Unbinding earth, the moving softness strays.
Joyous th' impatient husbandman perceives
Relenting nature, and his lusty steers   35
Drives from their stalls to where the well-used plow
Lies in the furrow loosened from the frost.
There, unrefusing, to the harnessed yoke
They lend their shoulder, and begin their toil,
Cheered by the simple song and soaring lark.   40
Meanwhile incumbent o'er the shining share
The master leans, removes th' obstructing clay,
Winds[5] the whole work, and sidelong lays the glebe.[6]

    White through the neighboring fields the sower stalks
With measured step, and liberal throws the grain   45
Into the faithful bosom of the ground;
The harrow follows harsh, and shuts the scene.

    Be gracious, heaven, for now laborious man
Has done his part. Ye fostering breezes, blow;
Ye softening dews, ye tender showers, descend;   50
And temper all, thou world-reviving sun,
Into the perfect year. Nor, ye who live
In luxury and ease, in pomp and pride,
Think these lost themes unworthy of your ear:
Such themes as these the rural Maro[7] sung   55
To wide-imperial Rome, in the full height
Of elegance and taste, by Greece refined.
In ancient times the sacred plow employed
The kings and awful fathers of mankind;
And some, with whom compared your insect-tribes   60
Are but the beings of a summer's day,
Have held the scale of empire, ruled the storm
Of mighty war, then with victorious hand,
Disdaining little delicacies, seized
The plow, and greatly independent scorned   65
All the vile stores corruption can bestow.

---

[1] *Spring* was first published in 1728. Thomson revised and added to *The Seasons* for the edition of 1744. The present text is based on the last of the many editions published in his lifetime (1746).
[2] Frances Thynne Seymour (d. 1754), Countess of Hertford and afterwards Duchess of Somerset. According to Dr. Johnson, she invited a poet every summer to visit her in Wiltshire "to hear her verses and assist her studies." Thomson wrote *Spring* there in 1727; but Johnson says he spent more time drinking with the Earl "than assisting her Ladyship's poetical operations, and therefore never received another summons."
[3] Mating season, when he sounds his booming cry. It was (erroneously) supposed that he made it by thrusting his bill into a reed.
[4] The Ram, a sign of the zodiac. Taurus or the Bull is another. It is toward the end of April.

[5] I.e., plows back and forth, furrow by furrow, as yarn is wound on hand and elbow.   [6] Soil.
[7] Vergil (Publius Vergilius Maro), in his *Georgics*.

Ye generous Britons, venerate the plow;
And o'er your hills and long withdrawing vales
Let Autumn spread his treasures to the sun,
Luxuriant and unbounded. As the sea   70
Far through his azure turbulent domain
Your empire owns,[8] and from a thousand shores
Wafts all the pomp of life into your ports;
So with superior boon may your rich soil,
Exuberant, nature's better blessings pour   75
O'er every land, the naked nations clothe,
And be th' exhaustless granary of a world!
    Nor only through the lenient air this change
Delicious breathes: the penetrative sun,
His force deep-darting to the dark retreat   80
Of vegetation,[9] sets the steaming power[10]
At large, to wander o'er the vernant[11] earth
In various hues—but chiefly thee, gay green!
Thou smiling nature's universal robe!
United light and shade! where the sight dwells 85
With growing strength and ever-new delight.
    From the moist meadow to the withered hill,
Led by the breeze, the vivid verdure runs,
And swells, and deepens to the cherished eye.
The hawthorn whitens; and the juicy groves   90
Put forth their buds, unfolding by degrees,
Till the whole leafy forest stands displayed
In full luxuriance to the sighing gales,
Where the deer rustle through the twining brake,[12]
And the birds sing concealed. At once arrayed 95
In all the colors of the flushing year
By nature's swift and secret-working hand,
The garden glows, and fills the liberal air
With lavish fragrance; while the promised fruit
Lies yet a little embryo, unperceived,   100
Within its crimson folds. Now from the town,
Buried in smoke and sleep and noisome damps,
Oft let me wander o'er the dewy fields
Where freshness breathes, and dash the trembling drops
From the bent bush, as through the verdant maze 105
Of sweetbrier hedges I pursue my walk;
Or taste the smell of dairy; or ascend
Some eminence, Augusta,[13] in thy plains,
And see the country, far-diffused around,
One boundless blush, one white-empurpled shower 110
Of mingled blossoms, where the raptured eye
Hurries from joy to joy, and, hid beneath
The fair profusion, yellow Autumn spies. . . .
    Hail, Source of Being! Universal Soul   556
Of heaven and earth! Essential Presence, hail!

To thee I bend the knee; to thee my thoughts
Continual climb, who with a master-hand
Hast the great whole into perfection touched.   560
By thee the various vegetative tribes,
Wrapt in a filmy net and clad with leaves,
Draw the live ether, and imbibe the dew.
By thee disposed into congenial soils
Stands each attractive plant, and sucks and swells 565
The juicy tide, a twining mass of tubes.
At thy command the vernal sun awakes
The torpid sap, detruded[14] to the root
By wintry winds, that now, in fluent dance
And lively fermentation mounting, spreads   570
All this innumerous-coloured scene of things.
    As rising from the vegetable world
My theme ascends, with equal wing ascend,
My panting Muse; and hark, how loud the woods
Invite you forth in all your gayest trim.   575
Lend me your song, ye nightingales! oh, pour
The mazy-running soul of melody
Into my varied verse! while I deduce,
From the first note the hollow cuckoo sings,
The symphony of Spring, and touch a theme   580
Unknown to fame—the passion of the groves.
    When first the soul of love is sent abroad
Warm through the vital air, and on the heart
Harmonious seizes, the gay troops begin
In gallant thought to plume the painted wing,   585
And try again the long-forgotten strain,
At first faint-warbled. But no sooner grows
The soft infusion prevalent and wide
Than all alive at once their joy o'erflows
In music unconfined. Up springs the lark,   590
Shrill-voiced and loud, the messenger of morn:
Ere yet the shadows fly, he mounted sings
Amid the dawning clouds, and from their haunts
Calls up the tuneful nations. Every copse[15]
Deep-tangled, tree irregular, and bush   595
Bending with dewy moisture, o'er the heads
Of the coy quiristers[16] that lodge within,
Are prodigal of harmony. The thrush
And woodlark, o'er the kind-contending throng
Superior heard, run through the sweetest length 600
Of notes; when listening Philomela[17] deigns
To let them joy, and purposes, in thought
Elate, to make her night excel their day.
The blackbird whistles from the thorny brake;

---

[14] Forced down.—"This passage seems to be a phrasing in brief of
Stephen Hales's findings in his *Vegetable Statics* (1727) . . . the
first full scientific account of the flow of sap in plants and the
function of the leaves in plant respiration and nutrition" (A. D.
McKillop).   [15] Coppice, thicket.   [16] Choristers.
[17] The nightingale.

---

[8] Acknowledges.   [9] Roots.   [10] Sap.
[11] Vernal, flourishing.   [12] Underbrush.
[13] An old Roman name for London.

The mellow bullfinch answers from the grove; 605
Nor are the linnets, o'er the flowering furze
Poured out profusely, silent. Joined to these,
Innumerous songsters, in the freshening shade
Of new-sprung leaves, their modulations mix
Mellifluous. The jay, the rook, the daw, 610
And each harsh pipe, discordant heard alone,
Aid the full concert; while the stockdove breathes
A melancholy murmur through the whole.

'Tis love creates their melody, and all
This waste of music is the voice of love, 615
That even to birds and beasts the tender arts
Of pleasing teaches. Hence the glossy kind
Try every winning way inventive love
Can dictate, and in courtship to their mates
Pour forth their little souls. First, wide around, 620
With distant awe, in airy rings they rove,
Endeavoring by a thousand tricks to catch
The cunning, conscious, half-averted glance
Of their regardless charmer. Should she seem,
Softening, the least approvance to bestow, 625
Their colors burnish, and, by hope inspired,
They brisk advance; then, on a sudden struck,
Retire disordered; then again approach;
In fond rotation spread the spotted wing,
And shiver every feather with desire. . . . 630

Be not the Muse ashamed, here to bemoan
Her brothers of the grove, by tyrant man
Inhuman caught, and in the narrow cage
From liberty confined and boundless air. 705
Dull are the pretty slaves, their plumage dull,
Ragged, and all its brightening luster lost;
Nor is that sprightly wildness in their notes,
Which, clear and vigorous, warbles from the beech.
Oh then, ye friends of love and love-taught song, 710
Spare the soft tribes, this barbarous art forbear!
If on your bosom innocence can win,
Music engage, or piety persuade.

But let not chief the nightingale lament
Her ruined care, too delicately framed 715
To brook the harsh confinement of the cage.
Oft when, returning with her loaded bill,
Th' astonished mother finds a vacant nest,
By the hard hand of unrelenting clowns[18]
Robbed, to the ground the vain provision falls; 720

Her pinions ruffle, and, low-drooping, scarce
Can bear the mourner to the poplar shade;
Where, all abandoned to derpair, she sings
Her sorrows through the night, and, on the bough
Sole-sitting, still at every dying fall 725
Takes up again her lamentable strain
Of winding woe, till wide around the woods
Sigh to her song and with her wail resound. . . .

Still let my song a nobler note assume,
And sing th' infusive force of Spring on man;
When heaven and earth, as if contending, vie
To raise his being, and serene[19] his soul. 870
Can he forbear to join the general smile
Of nature? Can fierce passions vex his breast
While every gale is peace, and every grove
Is melody? Hence! from the bounteous walks
Of flowing Spring, ye sordid sons of earth, 875
Hard, and unfeeling of another's woe,
Or only lavish to yourselves—away!
But come, ye generous minds, in whose wide thought,
Of all his works, Creative Bounty burns
With warmest beam, and on your open front[20] 880
And liberal eye sits, from his dark retreat
Inviting modest want. Nor till invoked
Can restless goodness wait; your active search
Leaves no cold wintry corner unexplored;
Like silent-working heaven, surprising oft 885
The lonely heart with unexpected good.
For you the roving spirit of the wind
Blows Spring abroad; for you the teeming clouds
Descend in gladsome plenty o'er the world;
And the sun sheds his kindest rays for you, 890
Ye flower of human race! In these green days
Reviving sickness lifts her languid head;
Life flows afresh; and young-eyed health exalts
The whole creation round. Contentment walks
The sunny glade, and feels an inward bliss 895
Spring o'er his mind, beyond the power of kings
To purchase. Pure serenity apace
Induces thought and contemplation still.
By swift degrees the love of nature works,
And warms the bosom; till at last, sublimed 900
To rapture and enthusiastic heat,
We feel the present Deity, and taste
The joy of God to see a happy world! . . .

---

[18] Country folk.

[19] Make serene.   [20] Forehead.

THE THEME of this poem was only too characteristic of the author: he was not in youth especially inclined to laziness, but it grew upon him in middle life, and the composition of his last poem dragged on for years. It has been warmly praised, and indeed Thomson does handle the intricate stanza skillfully; but it is hard to escape the final judgment that he only tries to do what Spenser has done better. The narrative interest of Thomson's poem is nil; what virtue it has lies in the remarkable smoothness of such lines as the following from the first of the two cantos.

1

O mortal man! who livest here by toil,
Do not complain of this thy hard estate;
That like an emmet[1] thou must ever moil
Is a sad sentence of an ancient date;
And, certes, there is for it reason great;   5
For, though sometimes it makes thee weep and wail,
And curse thy star,[2] and early drudge and late,
Withouten that would come an heavier bale,
Loose life, unruly passions, and diseases pale.

2

In lowly dale, fast by a river's side,   10
With woody hill o'er hill encompassed round,
A most enchanting[3] wizard did abide,
Than whom a fiend more fell is nowhere found.
It was, I ween, a lovely spot of ground;
And there a season atween June and May,   15
Half prankt[4] with spring, with summer half embrowned,
A listless climate made, where, sooth to say,
No living wight could work, ne carèd ev'n for play.

3

Was nought around but images of rest:
Sleep-soothing groves, and quiet lawns between;   20
And flowery beds that slumbrous influence kest[5]
From poppies breathed; and beds of pleasant green,
Where never yet was creeping creature seen.
Meantime unnumbered glittering streamlets played,
And hurlèd everywhere their waters sheen;[6]   25
That, as they bickered through the sunny glade,
Though restless still themselves, a lulling murmur made.

4

Joined to the prattle of the purling rills,
Were heard the lowing herds along the vale,
And flocks loud-bleating from the distant hills,   30
And vacant[7] shepherds piping in the dale:
And now and then sweet Philomel[8] would wail,
Or stockdoves plain[9] amid the forest deep,
That drowsy rustled to the sighing gale;
And still a coil[10] the grasshopper did keep: 35
Yet all these sounds yblent[11] inclinèd all to sleep.

5

Full in the passage of the vale, above,
A sable, silent, solemn forest stood,
Where nought but shadowy forms were seen to move,
As Idless[12] fancied in her dreaming mood;   40
And up the hills, on either side, a wood
Of blackening pines, ay waving to and fro,
Sent forth a sleepy horror through the blood;
And where this valley winded out, below,
The murmuring main was heard, and scarcely heard, to
flow.   45

6

A pleasing land of drowsyhed[13] it was:
Of dreams that wave before the half-shut eye;
And of gay castles in the clouds that pass,
For ever flushing round a summer sky;
There eke[14] the soft delights, that witchingly   50
Instil a wanton sweetness through the breast,
And the calm pleasures, always hovered nigh;
But whate'er smacked of noyance, or unrest,
Was far far off expelled from this delicious nest. . . .

---

[1] Ant.
[2] I.e., destiny.
[3] Skilled in magic arts.
[4] Decked.
[5] Cast.
[6] Bright.

[7] With nothing on their minds.
[8] The nightingale.
[9] Complain, make plaintive sounds.
[10] Noise.
[11] Blended.
[12] Idleness.
[13] Drowsiness.
[14] Also.

A Sheaf of Lesser Augustans

Matthew Prior

1664–1721

THE LITERARY Earl of Dorset (p. 530, above) stepped into the Rhenish, a popular tavern in Westminster run by Prior's uncle, and saw a prentice bartender so deep in a volume of Horace that he failed to look up. Dorset put the boy back into Westminster School, from which his father's death had forced him to drop out. Then Prior won a scholarship at Cambridge, where he took his B.A. in 1687. After the Revolution he became a trusted diplomat in King William's foreign service, first as secretary at the Hague. In 1699 he was for a brief period under-secretary of state; other "places" followed. In Queen Anne's time he lost his offices, gradually went over to the Tories, became an intimate of Swift and the rest, and was taken into the Tories' exclusive politico-literary club, the Brothers. When the Tories triumphed in 1710, Prior's fortunes also rose. Already experienced at the court of Louis XIV, he played a leading role in negotiating the Peace of Utrecht, and for a gilded interval was acting ambassador to Paris. When the Tories fell, Prior was subjected by the vengeful Whigs to thirteen months of imprisonment. His friends rallied round and pushed a subscription volume of his collected poems (1719), by which he got 4000 guineas. A patron gave him a country estate in Essex, where he ended his days. A man of easy morals, he never married.

Poetry was a side line with Prior. Except in his youth, he refrained from satire; it was not to his pen that he owed his public career. He is at his best in *vers de société;* some of his extremely elegant trifles are among the best light verse we have. They illustrate an important side of neoclassicism, one which is too often overlooked. The standard edition is by A. R. Waller (2 vols., 1905–7). There is an excellent essay on Prior in A. Dobson's volume of selections (1889). The latest Life is by C. K. Eves (1939).

TO A CHILD OF QUALITY FIVE YEARS OLD, THE AUTHOR FORTY

Lords, knights, and squires, the num'rous band
  That wear the fair Miss Mary's fetters,
Were summoned by her high command
  To show their passions by their letters.

My pen among the rest I took,   5
  Lest those bright eyes that cannot read
Should dart their kindling fires, and look
  The power they have to be obeyed.

Nor quality[1] nor reputation
  Forbid me yet my flame to tell: 10
Dear five years old befriends my passion,
  And I may write till she can spell.

For, while she makes her silk-worms' beds
  With all the tender things I swear,
Whilst all the house my passion reads   15
  In papers round her baby's[2] hair,

She may receive and own my flame;
  For though the strictest prudes should know it,
She'll pass for a most virtuous dame,
  And I for an unhappy poet.   20

Then, too, alas! when she shall tear
  The lines some younger rival sends,
She'll give me leave to write, I fear,
  And we shall still continue friends.

For, as our diff'rent ages move,   25
  'Tis so ordained—would Fate but mend it!—
That I shall be past making love
  When she begins to comprehend it.

WRITTEN IN THE BEGINNING OF MEZERAY'S *HISTORY OF FRANCE*

Whate'er thy countrymen have done,
By law and wit, by sword and gun,
  In thee is faithfully recited;
And all the living world, that view
Thy work, give thee the praises due,   5
  At once instructed and delighted.

Yet for the fame of all these deeds,
What beggar in the *Invalides,*[3]
  With lameness broke, with blindness smitten,
Wished ever decently to die,   10
To have been either Mezeray[4]
  Or any monarch he has written?

---

[1] Rank. "Miss Mary" was the daughter of Prior's close friend, the Earl of Jersey. The title of the poem first appears in the edition of 1740, with the note "written in 1704." The correct date is more likely 1700, when the child was ten and Prior thirty-six. He wrote other charming poems to or about children.   [2] Doll's.   [3] The famous establishment in Paris for aged and wounded veterans.   [4] François de Mézeray (1610–83), author of a history of France.

It strange, dear author, yet it true is,
That down from Pharamond[5] to Louis[6]
    All covet life, yet call it pain;   15
All feel the ill, yet shun the cure.
    Can sense this paradox endure?
    Resolve me, Cambray or Fontaine.[7]

The man in graver tragic known,
Though his best part long since was done,   20
    Still on the stage desires to tarry;
And he who played the harlequin,[8]
After the jest still loads the scene,
    Unwilling to retire, though weary.

THE FEMALE PHAETON[9]

Thus Kitty,[10] beautiful and young,
    And wild as colt untamed,
Bespoke the fair from whom she sprung,
    With little rage inflamed,

Inflamed with rage at sad restraint   5
    Which wise Mamma ordained,
And sorely vexed to play the saint
    Whilst wit and beauty reigned:

"Shall I thumb holy books, confined
    With Abigails[11] forsaken?   10
Kitty's for other things designed,
    Or I am much mistaken.

"Must Lady Jenny[12] frisk about,
    And visit with her cousins?
At balls must *she* make all the rout,   15
    And bring home hearts by dozens?

"What has she better, pray, than I?
    What hidden charms to boast,
That all mankind for her should die,
    Whilst I am scarce a toast?   20

---

[5] The legendary first king of France.   [6] Louis XIV.
[7] Fénelon (1651–1715), Archbishop of Cambrai, writer and educator; and Jean de la Fontaine (1621–95), poet and author of the *Fables*.   [8] Buffoon.
[9] Phaethon, a son of the sun-god, borrowed his chariot for a day and drove so low in the sky that only Jove's striking him with a thunderbolt saved the earth from burning up.
[10] Lady Catharine Hyde (d. 1777), daughter of the Earl of Clarendon, afterwards Duchess of Queensberry and Gay's patroness. This delightful poem was originally printed in 1718, with a title naming as its occasion the young lady's "first appearing at the playhouse in Drury Lane."   [11] Lady's maids.
[12] Her sister, Lady Jane Hyde; she married the Earl of Essex.

"Dearest Mamma, for once let me,
    Unchained, my fortune try;
I'll have my earl as well as she,
    Or know the reason why.

"I'll soon with Jenny's pride quit score,   25
    Make all her lovers fall;
They'll grieve I was not loosed before,
    She, I was loosed at all."

Fondness prevailed; Mamma gave way:
    Kitty, at heart's desire,   30
Obtained the chariot for a day,
    And set the world on fire.

Isaac Watts

1674–1748

SINCE not many hymns reach the level of poetry, exceptions are doubly welcome. Several of the best hymn-writers were eighteenth-century men. The earliest and most influential was Isaac Watts, a Dissenting minister, who wrote in addition to his other poems about six hundred hymns, marked in general by dignity, feeling, and unpretentiousness. Many of his contemporaries composed on stilts. Watts, who loved music and childhood, followed nature and actually achieved the simplicity which too many of his fellow neoclassicists praised without exemplifying. Among his best hymns are, besides the one below, "When I survey the wondrous cross" and "Jesus shall reign where'er the sun." During the century's first two decades Watts brought out four volumes; until quite recently everyone knew the little homilies from *Divine Songs for Children,* "Let dogs delight to bark and bite," "How doth the little busy bee," and " 'Tis the voice of the sluggard," as well as the tender lullaby, "Hush, my dear, lie still and slumber," which has been compared to Blake's *Songs of Innocence* and was praised by A. E. Housman as "beyond Pope." Watts rebelled against the prevalent low conceptions which would have limited poetry to purveying social entertainment, and against the formal restrictions of the neoclassical critics. Religion, he insisted, was a proper theme for verse; and he experimented with a wide variety of forms, from blank verse and ballad meters to the intricate stanza of Sappho. In terms most un-Augustan he calls for boldness and imagination:

Give me the chariot whose diviner wheels
    Mark their own route and, unconfined,
    Bound o'er the everlasting hills
And lose the clouds below, and leave the stars behind.

His verse may be found in A. Chalmers's *English Poets* (1810), XIII, 1–96. There is an appreciative sketch by

V. de S. Pinto (*Essays and Studies by Members of the English Association*, XX, 86–107), as well as a Life, *Isaac Watts and Contemporary Hymn Writers* (1914), by T. Wright. G. Sampson gives a concise account of eighteenth-century hymnology in *The Century of Divine Songs* (separately reprinted, 1943, from *Proceedings of the British Academy*, XXIX).

OUR GOD, OUR HELP

Our God, our help in ages past,[13]
   Our hope for years to come,
Our shelter from the stormy blast,
   And our eternal home:

Under the shadow of thy throne   5
   Thy saints have dwelt secure;
Sufficient is thine arm alone,
   And our defense is sure.

Before the hills in order stood
   Or earth received her frame,   10
From everlasting thou art God,
   To endless years the same.

Thy word commands our flesh to dust,
   "Return, ye sons of men";
All nations rose from earth at first,   15
   And turn to earth again.

A thousand ages in thy sight
   Are like an evening gone;
Short as the watch that ends the night
   Before the rising sun.   20

The busy tribes of flesh and blood,
   With all their lives and cares,
Are carried downwards by thy flood,
   And lost in following years.

Time, like an ever-rolling stream,   25
   Bears all its sons away;
They fly forgotten, as a dream
   Dies at the opening day.

Like flow'ry fields the nations stand,
   Pleased with the morning light;   30
The flowers beneath the mower's hand
   Lie withering e'er 'tis night.

Our God, our help in ages past,
   Our hope for years to come,
Be thou our guard while troubles last,   35
   And our eternal home.

---

[13] The theme is from Psalm 90.

Allan Ramsay
1685?–1758

THIS forerunner and influencer of Robert Burns was apprenticed to an Edinburgh wigmaker, and in due course rose to be a master of his craft. In 1718 he added a bookselling department to his shop and published his first volume of poetry. Some of this he wrote in English, but he is best in his own "braid Scots." He was a patriot, and heartily disliked the union with England in 1707. Besides his own works, he brought out at intervals four volumes of *The Tea-Table Miscellany*, in which, though he tampered with their texts, he included old Scottish songs. Many of these Sir Walter Scott came to love, and memorized in his childhood. *The Ever Green* is another collection of older Scottish poetry. Ramsay's own poetry is largely neoclassical, but the new currency he gave the old songs influenced public taste and helped prepare the way for the appreciation of folk literature that marked the Romantic Movement. Ramsay also wrote a pastoral play, *The Gentle Shepherd* (1725), which, revised by the author as a ballad opera, had a popular success on both sides of the Atlantic. The following song is from Act I. Ramsay's poems were collected by G. Chalmers (2 vols., 1800). B. Martin is the author of *Allan Ramsay: A Study of His Life and Works* (1931).

MY PEGGY IS A YOUNG THING

My Peggy is a young thing,
   Just entered in her teens,
Fair as the day, and sweet as May,
Fair as the day, and always gay;
   My Peggy is a young thing,   5
   And I'm not very auld,
Yet well I like to meet her at
   The wauking[14] of the fauld.

My Peggy speaks sae sweetly,
   Whene'er we meet alane,   10
I wish nae mair to lay my care,
I wish nae mair of a'[15] that's rare.
   My Peggy speaks sae sweetly,
   To a' the lave I'm cauld;[16]
But she gars[17] a' my spirits glow,   15
   At wauking of the fauld.

---

[14] Scottish for *waking*, keeping vigil—over the sheepfold.
[15] No more of all.   [16] To all the rest I'm cold.
[17] Makes.

My Peggy smiles sae kindly,
  Whene'er I whisper love,
That I look down on a' the town,
That I look down upon a crown.   20
  My Peggy smiles sae kindly,
    It makes me blithe and bauld;
And naething gi'es me sic delight
As wauking of the fauld.

My Peggy sings sae saftly,   25
  When on my pipe I play,
By a' the rest it is confest,
By a' the rest, that she sings best.
  My Peggy sings sae saftly,
    And in her sangs are tald,   30
With innocence, the wale[18] of sense,
At wauking of the fauld.

Henry Carey

1687?–1743

CAREY may have been an illegitimate son or grandson of
George Savile, Marquis of Halifax. He was versed in music
as well as literature and worked in both fields for the
theater. In 1713 he published his *Poems on Several Occasions;*
the third edition (1729) contained "Sally in Our Alley,"
and "Namby Pamby." The latter, a poem in ridicule of
Ambrose Philips, gave Addison's friend and Pope's enemy
his nickname, and enriched our language with a striking
synonym of *insipid.* Carey wrote many farces and burlesques; the best known is *Chrononhotonthologos* (1734),
which pokes fun at current trends in the drama. Carey
married and had four children. None of his writings
brought financial security, and in destitution and despair
he died, probably by his own hand, in 1743.

SALLY IN OUR ALLEY

Of all the girls that are so smart
  There's none like pretty Sally;
She is the darling of my heart,
  And she lives in our alley.
There is no lady in the land   5
  Is half so sweet as Sally;
She is the darling of my heart,
  And she lives in our alley.

Her father he makes cabbage nets,[19]
  And through the streets does cry 'em;   10

Her mother she sells laces long
  To such as please to buy 'em:
But sure such folks could ne'er beget
  So sweet a girl as Sally!
She is the darling of my heart,   15
  And she lives in our alley.

When she is by, I leave my work,
  I love her so sincerely;
My master comes like any Turk,
  And bangs me most severely;   20
But let him bang his bellyful,
  I'll bear it all for Sally;
She is the darling of my heart,
  And she lives in our alley.

Of all the days that's in the week   25
  I dearly love but one day,
And that's the day that comes betwixt
  A Saturday and Monday;
For then I'm dressed all in my best
  To walk abroad with Sally;   30
She is the darling of my heart,
  And she lives in our alley.

My master carries me to church,
  And often am I blamèd
Because I leave him in the lurch   35
  As soon as text is namèd;
I leave the church in sermon time
  And slink away to Sally;
She is the darling of my heart,
  And she lives in our alley.   40

When Christmas comes about again,
  O, then I shall have money;
I'll hoard it up, and box and all,
  I'll give it to my honey;
I would it were ten thousand pounds—   45
  I'd give it all to Sally;
She is the darling of my heart,
  And she lives in our alley.

My master and the neighbors all
  Make game of me and Sally,   50
And, but for her, I'd better be
  A slave and row a galley;
But when my seven long years are out,
  Oh, then I'll marry Sally;
Oh, then we'll wed, and then we'll bed,   55
  But not in our alley.

---

[18] Best, choicest.   [19] Small nets, for boiling cabbage.

George Berkeley

1685–1753

BERKELEY was an Anglo-Irishman, educated at Kilkenny School and Trinity College, Dublin, where he remained as a teacher till 1713. In England he became the friend of Steele, Addison, Swift, and Pope. He entered the priesthood of the Established Church, married, and in 1728 went to America; he remained for three years. His main object was to found a university where the settlers could educate their sons, but promised support did not materialize. On his return he was made Bishop of Cloyne in Ireland. His importance as a writer lies in his fight against the materialism of Hobbes and Locke; his is one of the great names in eighteenth-century philosophy. He also made an important contribution to the theory of optics. The standard edition is by A. C. Fraser (4 vols., 1871).

VERSES ON THE PROSPECT OF PLANTING ARTS AND LEARNING IN AMERICA

The Muse, disgusted at an age and clime
  Barren of every glorious theme,
In distant lands now waits a better time,
  Producing subjects worthy fame:

In happy climes, where from the genial[20] sun   5
  And virgin earth such scenes ensue,
The force of art by nature seems outdone,
  And fancied beauties by the true:

In happy climes, the seat of innocence,
  Where nature guides and virtue rules,   10
Where men shall not impose for truth and sense
  The pedantry of courts and schools:

There shall be sung another golden age,
  The rise of empire and of arts,
The good and great inspiring epic rage,[21]   15
  The wisest heads and noblest hearts.

Not such as Europe breeds in her decay;
  Such as she bred when fresh and young,
When heav'nly flame did animate her clay,
  By future poets shall be sung.   20

Westward the course of empire takes its way;
  The four first acts already past,
A fifth shall close the drama with the day;
  Time's noblest offspring is the last.

---

[20] Creative, generative.   [21] Fervor.

Anonymous

THE VICAR OF BRAY

In good King Charles's golden days,
  When Loyalty no harm meant,
A furious High-Church man I was,
  And so I gained preferment.
Unto my flock I daily preached   5
  Kings are by God appointed,
And damned are those who dare resist
  Or touch the Lord's anointed.
    And this is law, I will maintain
      Unto my dying day, sir,   10
    That, whatsoever king shall reign,
    I will be vicar of Bray,[22] sir!

When royal James possessed the crown
  And popery grew in fashion,
The Penal Law I hooted down   15
  And read the Declaration;[23]
The Church of Rome I found would fit
  Full well my constitution,
And I had been a Jesuit
  But for the Revolution.   20
    And this is law, &c.

When William our deliverer came
  To heal the nation's grievance,
I turned the cat in pan[24] again
  And swore to him allegiance.   25
Old principles I did revoke,
  Set conscience at a distance;
Passive Obedience is a joke,
  A jest is Nonresistance.
    And this is law, &c.   30

When glorious Anne became our queen,
  The Church of England's glory,
Another face of things was seen,
  And I became a Tory.
Occasional Conformists[25] base   35
  I damned, and Moderation,
And thought the Church in danger was
  From such prevarication.
    And this is law, &c.

---

[22] A village five miles up the Thames from Windsor.
[23] In 1687 James issued a Declaration of Indulgence revoking the penal laws against Dissenters and Catholics.
[24] Changed sides.
[25] Some Dissenters got around the law against their participating in politics by occasionally taking Communion at an Anglican altar.

When George in pudding[26] time came o'er, 40
   And Moderate men looked big, sir,
My principles I changed once more,
   And so became a Whig, sir;
And thus preferment I procured
   From our faith's great Defender, 45
And almost every day abjured
   The Pope and the Pretender.
     And this is law, &c.

The illustrious house of Hanover
   And Protestant succession, 50
To these I lustily will swear,
   Whilst they can keep possession.
For in my faith and loyalty
   I never once will falter,
But George my lawful king shall be, 55
   Except the times should alter.
     And this is law, &c.

Charles Wesley

1707–1788

JOHN and Charles Wesley, the founders of Methodism, were born at Epworth in Lincolnshire, where their father (Charles was his eighteenth child) was a rector of the Established Church. Both were educated at Oxford. John (1703–91) took an M.A. and then became an Anglican priest. He was the organizer; he also wrote hymns, but the real poet was Charles. They followed Watts in emphasizing congregational singing. Their first hymn book appeared in 1737, during their three-year missionary enterprise in the colony of Georgia. It was followed by many others. In all, Charles wrote about 6500 hymns. In 1739 Charles became an itinerant preacher, but his great contribution to the Methodist revival was his hymns. Besides "Love divine," his "Hark, the herald angels sing" and "Jesu, lover of my soul" are among the best known. There is a Life by J. Telford (1886).

LOVE DIVINE

Love divine, all loves excelling,
   Joy of heaven, to earth come down,
Fix in us thy humble dwelling,
   All thy faithful mercies crown.
Jesus, thou art all compassion, 5
   Pure unbounded love thou art;
Visit us with thy salvation,
   Enter every trembling heart.

---

[26] Sausage. This is a jeer at George's German birth.

Breathe, oh, breathe thy loving spirit
   Into every troubled breast! 10
Let us all in thee inherit,
   Let us find that second rest;
Take away our bent to sinning;
   Alpha and Omega be;
End of faith, as its beginning, 15
   Set our hearts at liberty.

Come, almighty to deliver,
   Let us all thy grace receive;
Suddenly return, and never,
   Never more thy temples leave. 20
Thee we would be always blessing,
   Serve thee as thy hosts above,
Pray and praise thee without ceasing,
   Glory in thy perfect love.

Finish then thy new creation: 25
   Pure and spotless let us be;
Let us see thy great salvation,
   Perfectly restored in thee:
Changed from glory into glory,
   Till in heaven we take our place, 30
Till we cast our crowns before thee,
   Lost in wonder, love, and praise.

William Collins

1721–1759

COLLINS came from Chichester in Sussex; his father, a tradesman, was twice its mayor. He was educated at Winchester, one of England's leading schools, and at Oxford. Then he went to London, vaguely hoping to make his way as a poet. Unfortunately his health was bad, he was constitutionally lazy, and he was oppressed by debts. He wrote very little. A slender volume of *Odes* in 1746 made no impression on the public; James Thomson, however, praised it and gave him his friendship. A few years later Collins came into a small legacy. But his mind was now clouded. For a while he was in an asylum; and he spent the rest of his life in his sister's care, with only occasional intervals of sanity. The second of the following poems shows his gifts of quiet beauty, discriminating feeling, and a verse music which requires neither rime nor obvious rhythms. Collins is neoclassical, but his ear was attuned to the lyricism of the Greeks and the Elizabethans, and in his "Ode on the Popular Superstitions of the Highlands" he foreshadows the Romantic Movement. A good edition is W. C. Bronson's (1898); E. Blunden edited another (1929). The poems are also reprinted in a volume with Gray's, edited by A. L. Poole and C. Stone (3rd ed., 1937). Useful studies are E. G. Ainsworth's *Poor Collins: His Life, His Art, and His Influence* (1937), H. W. Garrod's *Collins* (1928), and A. S. P. Woodhouse's "Collins and the Creative Imagination" (*Studies in English by Members of University College, Toronto*, 1931, pp. 59–130).

ODE

WRITTEN IN THE BEGINNING OF THE YEAR 1746[27]

How sleep the brave, who sink to rest
By all their country's wishes blest!
When Spring, with dewy fingers cold,
Returns to deck their hallowed mold,
She there shall dress a sweeter sod   5
Than Fancy's feet have ever trod.

By fairy hands their knell is rung,
By forms unseen their dirge is sung;
There Honor comes, a pilgrim grey,
To bless the turf that wraps their clay;   10
And Freedom shall a while repair,
To dwell a weeping hermit there!

ODE TO EVENING

If aught of oaten stop,[28] or pastoral song,
May hope, chaste Eve, to soothe thy modest ear,
Like thy own solemn springs,
Thy springs, and dying gales,
O nymph reserved, while now the bright-haired sun   5
Sits in yon western tent, whose cloudy skirts,
With brede[29] ethereal wove,
O'erhang his wavy bed:
Now[30] air is hushed, save where the weak-eyed bat
With short shrill shriek flits by on leathern wing,   10
Or where the beetle winds
His small but sullen horn,
As oft he rises midst the twilight path,
Against the pilgrim born in heedless hum:

Now teach me, maid composed,   15
To breathe some softened strain,
Whose numbers, stealing through thy dark'ning vale,
May not unseemly with its stillness suit,
As, musing slow, I hail
Thy genial loved return!   20
For when thy folding star[31] arising shows
His paly circlet, at his warning lamp
The fragrant Hours, and elves
Who slept in flow'rs the day,
And many a nymph who wreathes her brows with
       sedge,   25
And sheds the fresh'ning dew, and, lovelier still,
The pensive Pleasures sweet
Prepare thy shadowy car.
Then lead, calm vot'ress, where some sheety lake
Cheers the lone heath, or some time-hallowed pile,   30
Or upland fallows gray
Reflect its last cool gleam.
But when chill blust'ring winds, or driving rain,
Forbid my willing feet, be mine the hut,
That from the mountain's side   35
Views wilds, and swelling floods,
And hamlets brown, and dim-discovered spires,
And hears their simple bell, and marks o'er all
Thy dewy fingers draw
The gradual dusky veil.   40
While Spring shall pour his show'rs, as oft he wont,[32]
And bathe thy breathing tresses, meekest Eve;
While Summer loves to sport
Beneath thy ling'ring light;
While sallow Autumn fills thy lap with leaves;   45
Or Winter, yelling through the troublous air,
Affrights thy shrinking train,
And rudely rends thy robes;
So long, sure-found beneath the sylvan shed,
Shall Fancy, Friendship, Science, rose-lipped Health,   50
Thy gentlest influence own,
And hymn thy fav'rite name!

---

[27] The Battle of Fontenoy, on May 11, 1745, was a bloody defeat for the English, who were allied with the Dutch and Hanoverians against the French in the War of the Austrian Succession. The British infantry, advancing in column with great gallantry, was shot to pieces by a concentration of the French artillery. Two months later the Young Pretender, James II's grandson, landed in Scotland. In two battles, at Preston Pans in September and at Falkirk in January, wild charges by the Highland clans beat the English. Collins may have had any or all of these defeats in mind. The rebellion was soon quelled, at Culloden Moor, on April 16.
[28] If anything from the straw pipe, i.e., of a pastoral sort.
[29] Embroidery.   [30] Now while.

[31] I.e., the evening star, at whose rising the shepherds lead their sheep to the fold.   [32] As is often his custom.

828   THE EIGHTEENTH CENTURY

Philip Dormer Stanhope, Earl of Chesterfield

1694–1773

PHILIP DORMER STANHOPE was born and brought up in London. Since his father disliked him and his mother died in his early childhood, he was reared, not by his parents, but in the brilliant household of his maternal grandmother, the widow of the great Whig statesman, George Savile, Marquis of Halifax, who had presided over the Revolution of 1688. Lady Halifax saw carefully to his education by private tutors, after which he studied for a year at Cambridge. He left the university to travel in the Low Countries and in France; polish was his object in settling down for a while in Paris. From 1715 to 1722 he sat in the House of Commons, and in 1726 he succeeded to the title and estates of his father as fourth Earl of Chesterfield. His eminence in the reign of George II was not as a writer; he was an able diplomat and a model of fashionable urbanity. Ambassador to Holland, a notably successful viceroy of Ireland, and for a short time one of the two secretaries of state, he was long a leading orator in the House of Lords, whether in or out of office. He lived to a ripe old age. Deafness afflicted his last years and his health failed early, but he never lost his reputation for distinguished manners.

That he gave our language the adjective "Chesterfieldian" is now a more impressive claim to remembrance than his public services. Weightier still is his authorship of the famous letters, especially those to Philip Stanhope (1732–68), his illegitimate son by a lady who became his mistress during his residence at The Hague. They were meant for the boy's eye alone. Though Chesterfield married a wife the year after Philip's birth, it was for money, not love, and there were no children; the earldom passed to an adopted godchild, the son of a distant cousin. Apparently Philip Stanhope was the only being for whom his father ever cared deeply. He turned out as disappointingly as if he had never been the recipient of so much advice on how to turn out well. He remained shy and awkward, he failed in the House of Commons, his brief career as a diplomat was undistinguished, he made a secret marriage much below his father's expectations, and he died at thirty-six.

The letters were published by Philip's widow the year after Lord Chesterfield's death. Though moralists have denounced them, a great deal of the advice is sound. No one is born with good manners or habits of self-improvement, and what Chesterfield has to say about acquiring them is admirably practical. But the upshot of his instruction in the artful use of the prescribed accomplishments amounts to advising a man to play a role instead of being himself. Self-interest, he concludes, dictates deception. His program, completely wanting in idealism, is too likely to lead on the one hand to the stuffed shirt and on the other to the go-getter.

Chesterfield wrote with a polish equal to that of his deportment. We shall shortly come to Dr. Johnson and the Earl's clash with that less suave, more direct personality; it inspired a letter to Chesterfield which, though unjust, is no less famous than those of his own writing. The standard edition of the latter, including those to his son, is by B. Dobrée (6 vols., 1932); the first volume includes a laudatory Life. There is a volume of selected letters in Everyman's Library, and another in The World's Classics. S. Shellbarger has written a more critical biography (1935), which gives a spirited picture of the times.

LETTERS TO HIS SON

Spa,[1] 25 JULY, N. S.,[2] 1741

Dear Boy,

I have often told you in my former letters (and it is most certainly true) that the strictest and most scrupulous honor and virtue can alone make you 5 esteemed and valued by mankind; that parts and learning can alone make you admired and celebrated by them; but that the possession of lesser talents was most absolutely necessary towards making you 10

liked, beloved, and sought after in private life. Of these lesser talents, good breeding is the principal and most necessary one, not only as it is very important in itself, but as it adds great luster to the more solid advantages both of the heart and the mind.

I have often touched upon good breeding to you before; so that this letter shall be upon the next necessary qualification to it, which is a genteel, easy manner and carriage, wholly free from those odd tricks, ill habits, and awkwardnesses, which even very many worthy and sensible people have in their behavior. However trifling a genteel manner may

---

[1] The Belgian watering place.
[2] For Old and New Style see above, p. 799, note 26.

sound, it is of very great consequence towards pleasing in private life, especially the women; which, one time or other, you will think worth pleasing; and I have known many a man, from his awkwardness, give people such a dislike of him at first, that all his merit could not get the better of it afterwards. Whereas a genteel manner prepossesses people in your favor, bends them towards you, and makes them wish to like you.

Awkwardness can proceed but from two causes: either from not having kept good company, or from not having attended to it. As for your keeping good company, I will take care of that; do you take care to observe their ways and manners, and to form your own upon them. Attention is absolutely necessary for this, as indeed it is for everything else; and a man without attention is not fit to live in the world. When an awkward fellow first comes into a room, it is highly probable that his sword gets between his legs, and throws him down, or makes him stumble at least; when he has recovered this accident, he goes and places himself in the very place of the whole room where he should not; there he soon lets his hat fall down; and, taking it up again, throws down his cane; in recovering his cane, his hat falls a second time; so that he is a quarter of an hour before he is in order again. If he drinks tea or coffee, he certainly scalds his mouth, and lets either the cup or the saucer fall, and spills the tea or coffee in his breeches. At dinner, his awkwardness distinguishes itself particularly, as he has more to do; there he holds his knife, fork, and spoon differently from other people, eats with his knife to the great danger of his mouth, picks his teeth with his fork, and puts his spoon, which has been in his throat twenty times, into the dishes again. If he is to carve, he can never hit the joint; but, in his vain efforts to cut through the bone, scatters the sauce in everybody's face. He generally daubs himself with soup and grease, though his napkin is commonly stuck through a buttonhole, and tickles his chin. When he drinks, he infallibly coughs in his glass, and besprinkles the company. Besides all this, he has strange tricks and gestures; such as snuffing up his nose, making faces, putting his fingers in his nose, or blowing it and looking afterwards in his handkerchief, so as to make the company sick. His hands are troublesome to him when he has not something in them, and he does not know where to put them; but they are in perpetual motion between his bosom and his breeches; he does not wear his clothes, and in short does nothing, like other people. All this, I own, is not in any degree criminal; but it is highly disagreeable and ridiculous in company, and ought most carefully to be avoided by whoever desires to please.

From this account of what you should not do, you may easily judge what you should do; and a due attention to the manners of people of fashion, and who have seen the world, will make it habitual and familiar to you.

There is, likewise, an awkwardness of expression and words, most carefully to be avoided; such as false English, bad pronunciation, old sayings, and common proverbs; which are so many proofs of having kept bad and low company. For example: if, instead of saying that tastes are different, and that every man has his own peculiar one, you should let off a proverb, and say that what is one man's meat is another man's poison, or else, "Everyone as they like, as the good man said when he kissed his cow," everybody would be persuaded that you had never kept company with anybody above footmen and housemaids.

Attention will do all this; and without attention nothing is to be done: want of attention, which is really want of thought, is either folly or madness. You should not only have attention to everything, but a quickness of attention, so as to observe, at once, all the people in the room; their motions, their looks, and their words; and yet without staring at them, and seeming to be an observer. This quick and unobserved observation is of infinite advantage in life, and is to be acquired with care; and, on the contrary, what is called absence, which is a thoughtlessness, and want of attention about what is doing, makes a man so like either a fool or a madman, that, for my part, I see no real difference. A fool never has thought; a madman has lost it; and an absent man is, for the time, without it.

Adieu! Direct your next to me, *chez Monsieur Chabert, Banquier, à Paris;* and take care that I find the improvements I expect at my return.

London, 9 OCTOBER, O.S., 1747

Dear Boy,

People of your age have, commonly, an unguarded frankness about them, which makes them the easy prey and bubbles of the artful and experienced; they look upon every knave or fool who tells them that he is their friend to be really so, and pay that profession of simulated friendship with an indiscreet and unbounded confidence, always to their loss, often to their ruin. Beware, therefore, now that you are coming into the world, of these proffered friendships. Receive them with great civility, but with great incredulity too; and pay them with compliments, but not with confidence. Do not let your vanity, and self-love, make you suppose that people become your friends at first sight, or even upon a short acquaintance. Real friendship is a slow grower, and never thrives unless ingrafted upon a stock of known and reciprocal merit. There is another kind of nominal friendship, among young people, which is warm for the time, but, by good luck, of short duration. This friendship is hastily produced by their being accidentally thrown together, and pursuing the same course of riot and debauchery. A fine friendship, truly; and well cemented by drunkenness and lewdness. It should rather be called a conspiracy against morals and good manners, and be punished as such by the civil magistrate. However, they have the impudence, and the folly, to call this confederacy a friendship. They lend one another money, for bad purposes; they engage in quarrels, offensive and defensive, for their accomplices; they tell one another all they know, and often more too; when, of a sudden, some accident disperses them, and they think no more of each other, unless it be to betray and laugh at their imprudent confidence. Remember to make a great difference between companions and friends; for a very complaisant and agreeable companion may, and often does, prove a very improper and a very dangerous friend. People will, in a great degree, and not without reason, form their opinion of you upon that which they have of your friends; and there is a Spanish proverb which says very justly, "Tell me whom you live with, and I will tell you who you are." One may fairly suppose that a man who makes a knave or a fool his friend has something very bad to do or to conceal. But, at the same time that you carefully decline the friendship of knaves and fools, if it can be called friendship, there is no occasion to make either of them your enemies, wantonly, and unprovoked; for they are numerous bodies, and I would rather choose a secure neutrality than alliance, or war, with either of them. You may be a declared enemy to their vices and follies, without being marked out by them as a personal one. Their enmity is the next dangerous thing to their friendship. Have a real reserve with almost everybody, and have a seeming reserve with almost nobody; for it is very disagreeable to seem reserved, and very dangerous not to be so. Few people find the true medium; many are ridiculously mysterious and reserved upon trifles, and many imprudently communicative of all they know.

The next thing to the choice of your friends is the choice of your company. Endeavor, as much as you can, to keep company with people above you. There you rise, as much as you sink with people below you; for (as I have mentioned before) you are whatever the company you keep is. Do not mistake, when I say company above you, and think that I mean with regard to their birth; that is the least consideration: but I mean with regard to their merit, and the light in which the world considers them.

There are two sorts of good company: one, which is called the beau monde, and consists of those people who have the lead in courts and in the gay part of life; the other consists of those who are distinguished by some peculiar merit, or who excel in some particular and valuable art or science. For my own part, I used to think myself in company as much above me, when I was with Mr. Addison and Mr. Pope, as if I had been with all the princes in Europe. What I mean by low company which should by all means be avoided, is the company of those who, absolutely insignificant and contemptible in themselves, think they are honored by being in your company, and who flatter every vice and folly you have, in order to engage you to converse with them. The pride of being the first of the company is but too common; but it is very silly, and very prejudicial. Nothing in the world lets down a character more than that wrong turn.

You may possibly ask me whether a man has it always in his power to get into the best company, and how. I say, yes, he has, by deserving it; provided he is but in circumstances which enable him to appear upon the footing of a gentleman. Merit and good breeding will make their way everywhere. Knowledge will introduce him, and good breeding will endear him, to the best companies; for, as I have often told you, politeness and good breeding are absolutely necessary to adorn any or all other good qualities or talents. Without them, no knowledge, no perfection whatsoever, is seen in its best light. The scholar, without good breeding, is a pedant; the philosopher, a cynic; the soldier, a brute; and every man disagreeable.

I long to hear, from my several correspondents at Leipzig, of your arrival there, and what impression you make on them at first; for I have Arguses, with a hundred eyes each, who will watch you narrowly, and relate to me faithfully. My accounts will certainly be true; it depends upon you, entirely, of what kind they shall be. Adieu!

London, 16 OCTOBER, O.S., 1747

Dear Boy,

The art of pleasing is a very necessary one to possess, but a very difficult one to acquire. It can hardly be reduced to rules; and your own good sense and observation will teach you more of it than I can. "Do as you would be done by" is the surest method that I know of pleasing. Observe carefully what pleases you in others, and probably the same things in you will please others. If you are pleased with the complaisance and attention of others to your humors, your tastes, or your weaknesses, depend upon it the same complaisance and attention on your part to theirs will equally please them. Take the tone of the company that you are in, and do not pretend to give it; be serious, gay, or even trifling, as you find the present humor of the company: this is an attention due from every individual to the majority. Do not tell stories in company; there is nothing more tedious and disagreeable. If by chance you know a very short story, and exceedingly applicable to the present subject of conversation, tell it in as few words as possible; and even then throw out that you do not love to tell stories, but that the shortness of it tempted you.

Of all things, banish the egotism out of your conversation, and never think of entertaining people with your own personal concerns or private affairs; though they are interesting to you, they are tedious and impertinent to everybody else; besides that, one cannot keep one's own private affairs too secret. Whatever you think your own excellencies may be, do not affectedly display them in company, nor labor, as many people do, to give that turn to the conversation which may supply you with an opportunity of exhibiting them. If they are real, they will infallibly be discovered without your pointing them out yourself, and with much more advantage. Never maintain an argument with heat and clamor, though you think or know yourself to be in the right; but give your opinion modestly and coolly, which is the only way to convince; and, if that does not do, try to change the conversation, by saying, with good humor, "We shall hardly convince one another, nor is it necessary that we should; so let us talk of something else." Remember that there is a local propriety to be observed in all companies, and that what is extremely proper in one company may be, and often is, highly improper in another. The jokes, the bon mots, the little adventures, which may do very well in one company, will seem flat and tedious when related in another. The particular characters, the habits, the cant of one company may give merit to a word or a gesture which would have none at all if divested of those accidental circumstances. Here people very commonly err; and, fond of something that has entertained them in one company and in certain circumstances, repeat it with emphasis in another, where it is either insipid or, it may be, offensive, by being ill-timed or misplaced. Nay, they often do it with this silly preamble, "I will tell you an excellent thing," or, "I will tell you the best thing in the world." This raises expectations, which, when absolutely disappointed, make the relater of this excellent thing look, very deservedly, like a fool.

If you would particularly gain the affection and friendship of particular people, whether men or women, endeavor to find out their predominant excellency, if they have one, and their prevailing weakness, which everybody has; and do justice to the one, and something more than justice to the other. Men have various objects in which they may excel, or at least would be thought to excel; and, though they love to hear justice done to them where they know that they excel, yet they are most and best flattered upon those points where they wish to excel and yet are doubtful whether they do or not. As, for example: Cardinal Richelieu,[3] who was undoubtedly the ablest statesman of his time, or perhaps of any other, had the idle vanity of being thought the best poet too: he envied the great Corneille[4] his reputation, and ordered a criticism to be written upon the *Cid.* Those, therefore, who flattered skillfully said little to him of his abilities in state affairs, or at least but *en passant,*[5] and as it might naturally occur. But the incense which they gave him, the smoke of which they knew would turn his head in their favor, was as a *bel-esprit*[6] and a poet. Why? Because he was sure of one excellency, and distrustful as to the other. You will easily discover every man's prevailing vanity by observing his favorite topic of conversation; for every man talks most of what he has most a mind to be thought to excel in. Touch him but there, and you touch him to the quick. The late Sir Robert Walpole[7] (who was certainly an able man) was little open to flattery upon that head, for he was in no doubt himself about it; but his prevailing weakness was to

---

[3] The great minister (d. 1642) of Louis XIII.
[4] Pierre Corneille (1606–84), the great French dramatist. *The Cid* is his most famous play.   [5] In passing, by the way.
[6] A highly cultivated person, a "wit."
[7] As Whig prime minister, the ruler of England from 1721 to 1742.

be thought to have a polite and happy turn to gallantry—of which he had undoubtedly less than any man living. It was his favorite and frequent subject of conversation; which proved, to those who had any penetration, that it was his prevailing weakness, and they applied to it with success.

Women have, in general, but one object, which is their beauty, upon which scarce any flattery is too gross for them to swallow. Nature has hardly formed a woman ugly enough to be insensible to flattery upon her person; if her face is so shocking that she must in some degree be conscious of it, her figure and air, she trusts, make ample amends for it. If her figure is deformed, her face, she thinks, counterbalances it. If they are both bad, she comforts herself that she has graces, a certain manner, a *je ne sais quoi*,[8] still more engaging than beauty. This truth is evident from the studied and elaborate dress of the ugliest woman in the world. An undoubted, uncontested, conscious beauty is, of all women, the least sensible of flattery upon that head; she knows that it is her due, and is therefore obliged to nobody for giving it her. She must be flattered upon her understanding, which though she may possibly not doubt of herself, yet she suspects that men may distrust.

Do not mistake me, and think that I mean to recommend to you abject and criminal flattery: no, flatter nobody's vices or crimes; on the contrary, abhor and discourage them. But there is no living in the world without a complaisant indulgence for people's weaknesses and innocent, though ridiculous, vanities. If a man has a mind to be thought wiser, and a woman handsomer, than they really are, their error is a comfortable one to themselves, and an innocent one with regard to other people; and I would rather make them my friends by indulging them in it than my enemies by endeavoring (and that to no purpose) to undeceive them.

There are little attentions, likewise, which are infinitely engaging, and which sensibly affect that degree of pride and self-love which is inseparable from human nature, as they are unquestionable proofs of the regard and consideration which we have for the persons to whom we pay them. As, for example: to observe the little habits, the likings, the antipathies, and the tastes of those whom we would gain; and then take care to provide them with the one, and to secure them from the other, giving them genteelly to understand that you had observed they liked such a dish or such a room, for which reason you had prepared it; or, on the contrary, that having observed they had an aversion to such a dish, a dislike to such a person, etc., you had taken care to avoid presenting them. Such attention to such trifles flatters self-love much more than greater things, as it makes people think themselves almost the only objects of your thoughts and care.

These are some of the arcana[9] necessary for your initiation in the great society of the world. I wish I had known them better at your age; I have paid the price of three-and-fifty years for them, and shall not grudge it if you reap the advantage. Adieu.

London, 5 SEPTEMBER, O.S., 1748

Dear Boy,

I have received yours, with the inclosed German letter to Mr. Grevenkop,[10] which he assures me is extremely well written, considering the little time that you have applied yourself to that language. As you have now got over the most difficult part, pray go on diligently, and make yourself absolutely master of the rest. Whoever does not entirely possess a language will never appear to advantage, or even equal to himself, either in speaking or writing it; his ideas are fettered, and seem imperfect or confused, if he is not master of all the words and phrases necessary to express them. I therefore desire that you will not fail writing a German letter once every fortnight to Mr. Grevenkop, which will make the writing of that language familiar to you; and moreover, when you shall have left Germany and be arrived at Turin, I shall require you to write even to me in German, that you may not forget with ease what you have with difficulty learned. I likewise desire that while you are in Germany you will take all opportunities of conversing in German, which is the only way of knowing that or any language accurately. You will also desire your German master to teach you the proper titles and superscriptions to be used to people of all ranks, which is a point so material in Germany that I have known many a letter returned unopened because one title in twenty has been omitted in the direction. . . .

As women are a considerable or at least a pretty numerous part of company, and as their suffrages go a great way towards establishing a man's character in the fashionable part of the world (which is of great importance to the fortune and figure he proposes to make in it), it is necessary to please them. I will therefore, upon this subject, let you into

---

[8] An I-know-not-what, an inexpressible something.

[9] Secrets.
[10] Gaspar Grevenkop, a Dane, one of Chesterfield's secretaries.

certain arcana, that will be very useful for you to know, but which you must, with the utmost care, conceal and never seem to know.

Women, then, are only children of a larger growth;[11] they have an entertaining tattle, and sometimes wit; but for solid, reasoning good sense, I never knew in my life one that had it, or who reasoned or acted consequentially for four-and-twenty hours together. Some little passion or humor always breaks in upon their best resolutions. Their beauty neglected or controverted, their age increased or their supposed understandings depreciated, instantly kindles their little passions, and overturns any system of consequential conduct that in their most reasonable moments they might have been capable of forming. A man of sense only trifles with them, plays with them, humors and flatters them, as he does with a sprightly, forward child; but he neither consults them about, nor trusts them with, serious matters, though he often makes them believe that he does both, which is the thing in the world that they are proud of; for they love mightily to be dabbling in business (which, by the way, they always spoil); and being justly distrustful, that men in general look upon them in a trifling light, they almost adore that man who talks more seriously to them, and who seems to consult and trust them; I say, who seems, for weak men really do, but wise ones only seem to do it. No flattery is either too high or too low for them. They will greedily swallow the highest, and gratefully accept of the lowest; and you may safely flatter any woman, from her understanding down to the exquisite taste of her fan.

Women who are either indisputably beautiful or indisputably ugly are best flattered upon the score of their understandings; but those who are in a state of mediocrity are best flattered upon their beauty, or at least their graces; for every woman who is not absolutely ugly thinks herself handsome, but, not hearing often that she is so, is the more grateful and the more obliged to the few who tell her so; whereas a decided and conscious beauty looks upon every tribute paid to her beauty only as her due, but wants to shine and to be considered on the side of her understanding; and a woman who is ugly enough to know that she is so knows that she has nothing left for her but her understanding, which is consequently (and probably in more senses than one) her weak side. But these are secrets, which you must keep inviolably, if you would not, like Orpheus,[12] be torn to pieces by the whole sex; on the contrary, a man who thinks of living in the great world must be gallant, polite, and attentive to please the women. They have, from the weakness of men, more or less influence in all courts; they absolutely stamp every man's character in the beau monde, and make it either current or cry it down and stop it in payments. It is, therefore, absolutely necessary to manage, please, and flatter them, and never to discover[13] the least marks of contempt, which is what they never forgive; but in this they are not singular, for it is the same with men, who will much sooner forgive an injustice than an insult. Every man is not ambitious, or covetous, or passionate; but every man has pride enough in his composition to feel and resent the least slight and contempt. Remember, therefore, most carefully to conceal your contempt, however just, wherever you would not make an implacable enemy. Men are much more unwilling to have their weaknesses and their imperfections known than their crimes; and if you hint to a man that you think him silly, ignorant, or even ill-bred or awkward, he will hate you more and longer than if you tell him plainly that you think him a rogue. Never yield to that temptation, which to most young men is very strong, of exposing other people's weaknesses and infirmities, for the sake either of diverting the company or showing your own superiority. You may get the laugh on your side by it, for the present; but you will make enemies by it forever; and even those who laugh with you then, will, upon reflection, fear and consequently hate you; besides that, it is ill-natured, and a good heart desires rather to conceal than expose other people's weaknesses or misfortunes. If you have wit, use it to please, and not to hurt; you may shine, like the sun in the temperate zones, without scorching. Here it is wished for; under the line[14] it is dreaded.

These are some of the hints which my long experience in the great world enables me to give you, and which, if you attend to them, may prove useful to you in your journey through it. I wish it may be a prosperous one; at least I am sure that it must be your own fault if it is not.

Make my compliments to Mr. Harte,[15] who, I am very sorry to hear, is not well. I hope by this time he is recovered. Adieu!

---

[11] Cf. Dryden, *All for Love* (IV, i, 43): "Men are but children of a larger growth."

[12] The mythical Thracian poet and musician. He was torn to pieces because he refused to join the women in their Bacchic orgies. [13] Reveal. [14] Equator.
[15] The Rev. Walter Harte (1709–74), the boy's tutor.

Thomas Gray

1716-1771

GRAY was primarily a scholar, though he made no important contribution to scholarship. He died in his fifty-fifth year, having published thirteen short English poems. Twenty-six others, some of them fragments, survived in manuscript. He had nothing else to show for his life, except some Latin verse and his letters. Yet he is one of England's most famous poets, for he wrote one poem which the English-speaking world immediately took to its heart and has kept there. Was he fastidious, donnish, affected, reticent, or morbid? His real personality remains his secret; what is clear is that the great "Elegy" is a weightier achievement than most men's.

Gray was born in 1716, the fifth of twelve children and the only one that lived past infancy. His father, a London businessman, was a brutal wretch. Thomas was supported at Eton and Cambridge by his mother, who kept a millinery shop. At Eton, where her brother was one of the masters, Gray formed several close friendships, especially with Horace Walpole (1717–97), third son of the great statesman. Walpole was to be the foremost of English letter writers; in *The Castle of Otranto* he was to lead the way in the Gothic romance; but a main interest came to be his imitation Gothic castle called Strawberry Hill, at Twickenham, and the curios and objects of art with which he crammed it.

Gray disliked the university and left without a degree in 1738. The year after, he accepted Walpole's invitation to make the Grand Tour. After crossing the Alps to Italy (an incident of that journey is described in one of the following letters) they quarreled and separated; they were fast friends again, however, later on. In 1741 Gray came home alone. His father died in that year, and for a while he lived with his mother and aunt at the village of Stoke Poges, near Eton and Windsor. Then he returned to Cambridge and took rooms in one of the colleges. At Cambridge he spent the rest of his life, except for vacations and a short period in London, where he went, after the British Museum opened in 1759, to be near its library. Gray took a law degree at Cambridge, and he began writing poetry there in 1742; but his main energies went into the study of language and literature, architecture, and zoology and botany. In all these fields he became a learned man. He never married. He had a few friends, but for the most part lived completely to himself. His poems brought him fame; he was tendered the poet laureateship, but declined it. In 1768 he was appointed professor of modern history and languages; he was not required to teach, and did not. A recluse to the last, he went on adding to his private store of knowledge.

Gray's poems were edited by W. L. Phelps (1902), D. C. Tovey (revised ed., 1904), and A. L. Poole and L. Whibley (3rd ed., 1937). Dr. Johnson included a sketch in his *Lives of the Poets,* but for obvious reasons Gray has not attracted biographers. Phelps's edition (which includes most of the poems and some selections from the letters) gives a good general account. The biographical facts are carefully set forth in a thesis by R. Martin, *Chronologie de la Vie et de l'Oeuvre de Thomas Gray* (1931). There is an edition of the letters by P. Toynbee and L. Whibley (3 vols., 1935). An Everyman's Library volume includes selected letters as well as the poems, and two World's Classics volumes are devoted to both.

ODE ON A DISTANT PROSPECT OF ETON COLLEGE

Eton is one of England's great "public" schools or, as we would call them, preparatory schools. On its playing fields, said the Duke of Wellington, the victory of Waterloo was won. He meant that the discipline of the sports at such schools, exclusively for the upper classes, formed the type of man on whom the country depended for public service, including the officering of his regiments. This poem was the first Gray published. It appeared separately, as a pamphlet, in 1747, five years after it was written. In its generalized description, its numerous personifications, its frank didacticism, and its smooth versification it is typically neoclassical.

Ye distant spires, ye antique towers,
   That crown the wat'ry glade,
Where grateful Science[1] still adores
   Her Henry's holy shade;[2]
And ye, that from the stately brow   5
Of Windsor's[3] heights th' expanse below
   Of grove, of lawn, of mead survey,
Whose turf, whose shade, whose flowers among
Wanders the hoary[4] Thames along
   His silver-winding way;   10

---

[1] Knowledge.   [2] The spirit of Henry VI, who founded Eton. He was an unsuccessful ruler, but pious.
[3] Windsor Castle is built on a height across the river.
[4] I.e., ancient.

Ah, happy hills! ah, pleasing shade!
　Ah, fields beloved in vain,
Where once my careless childhood strayed
　A stranger yet to pain!
I feel the gales that from ye blow　　　　15
A momentary bliss bestow,
　As waving fresh their gladsome wing,
My weary soul they seem to sooth,[5]
And, redolent of joy and youth,
　To breathe a second spring.　　　　　20

Say, Father Thames, for thou hast seen
　Full many a sprightly race
Disporting on thy margent green
　The paths of pleasure trace,
Who foremost now delight to cleave　　25
With pliant arm thy glassy wave?
　The captive linnet which enthrall?
What idle progeny succeed
To chase the rolling circle's[6] speed,
　Or urge the flying ball?　　　　　　30

While some on earnest business bent
　Their murm'ring labors ply[7]
'Gainst graver hours, that bring constraint
　To sweeten liberty:
Some bold adventurers disdain　　　　35
The limits of their little reign,
　And unknown regions dare descry;
Still as they run they look behind,
They hear a voice in every wind,
　And snatch a fearful joy.　　　　　40

Gay hope is theirs by fancy fed,
　Less pleasing when possest;
The tear forgot as soon as shed,
　The sunshine of the breast:
Theirs buxom health of rosy hue,　　　45
Wild wit, invention ever-new,
　And lively cheer of vigor born;
The thoughtless day, the easy night,
The spirits pure, the slumbers light,
　That fly th' approach of morn.　　　50

Alas, regardless of their doom,
　The little victims play!
No sense have they of ills to come,
　Nor care beyond today:
Yet see how all around 'em wait　　　55

The ministers of human fate,
　And black Misfortune's baleful train!
Ah, show them where in ambush stand
To seize their prey the murth'rous band!
　Ah, tell them they are men!　　　　60

These shall the fury Passions tear,
　The vultures of the mind,
Disdainful Anger, pallid Fear,
　And Shame that skulks behind;
Or pining Love shall waste their youth,　65
Or Jealousy with rankling tooth,
　That inly gnaws the secret heart,
And Envy wan, and faded Care,
Grim-visaged comfortless Despair,
　And Sorrow's piercing dart.　　　　70

Ambition this shall tempt to rise,
　Then whirl the wretch from high,
To bitter Scorn a sacrifice,
　And grinning Infamy.
The stings of Falsehood those shall try,　75
And hard Unkindness' altered eye,
　That mocks the tear it forced to flow;
And keen Remorse with blood defiled,
And moody Madness laughing wild
　Amid severest woe.　　　　　　80

Lo, in the vale of years beneath
　A grisly troop are seen,
The painful family of Death,
　More hideous than their Queen:
This racks the joints, this fires the veins,　85
That every laboring sinew strains,
　Those in the deeper vitals rage:
Lo, Poverty, to fill the band,
That numbs the soul with icy hand,
　And slow-consuming Age.　　　　90

To each his suff'rings: all are men,
　Condemned alike to groan,
The tender for another's pain,
　Th' unfeeling for his own.
Yet, ah! why should they know their fate?　95
Since sorrow never comes too late,
　And happiness too swiftly flies.
Thought would destroy their paradise.
No more; where ignorance is bliss,
　'Tis folly to be wise.　　　　　100

---

[5] Soothe.　　　[6] Hoop's.
[7] Study aloud.

HYMN TO ADVERSITY

Daughter of Jove, relentless power,
Thou tamer of the human breast,
Whose iron scourge and tort'ring hour
The bad affright, afflict the best!
Bound in thy adamantine chain   5
The proud are taught to taste of pain,
And purple[8] tyrants vainly groan
With pangs unfelt before, unpitied and alone.

When first thy sire to send on earth
Virtue, his darling child, designed,   10
To thee he gave the heav'nly birth,
And bade to form her infant mind.
Stern, rugged nurse! thy rigid lore
With patience many a year she bore:
What sorrow was, thou bad'st her know,   15
And from her own she learned to melt at others' woe.

Scared at thy frown terrific, fly
Self-pleasing Folly's idle brood,
Wild Laughter, Noise, and thoughtless Joy,
And leave us leisure to be good.   20
Light[9] they disperse, and with them go
The summer Friend, the flatt'ring Foe;
By vain Prosperity received,
To her they vow their truth, and are again believed.

Wisdom in sable garb arrayed,   25
Immersed in rapt'rous thought profound,
And Melancholy, silent maid
With leaden eye, that loves the ground,
Still on thy solemn steps attend:
Warm Charity, the gen'ral friend,   30
With Justice, to herself severe,
And Pity, dropping soft the sadly-pleasing tear.

Oh, gently on thy suppliant's head,
Dread goddess, lay thy chast'ning hand!
Not in thy Gorgon[10] terrors clad,   35
Nor circled with the vengeful band[11]
(As by the impious thou art seen)
With thund'ring voice, and threat'ning mien,
With screaming Horror's funeral cry,
Despair, and fell Disease, and ghastly Poverty.   40

---

[8] Robed in royal crimson.—This poem was also written in 1742.
[9] Swiftly.
[10] To look upon the Gorgons, three snake-haired sisters of Greek
  myth, was to turn to stone.
[11] The Furies, the avenging deities of Greek mythology.

Thy form benign, Oh goddess, wear;
Thy milder influence impart;
Thy philosophic train be there
To soften, not to wound, my heart.
The gen'rous spark extinct revive,   45
Teach me to love and to forgive,
Exact my own defects to scan,
What others are to feel, and know myself a Man.

ON THE DEATH OF A FAVORITE CAT
DROWNED IN A TUB OF GOLD-FISHES

Gray wrote this *jeu d'esprit* in 1747. It is one of the most
elegant bits of light verse in English.

'Twas on a lofty vase's side,
Where China's gayest art had dyed
  The azure flowers that blow;
Demurest of the tabby kind,[12]
The pensive Selima reclined,   5
  Gazed on the lake below.

Her conscious tail her joy declared;
The fair round face, the snowy beard,
  The velvet of her paws,
Her coat, that with the tortoise vies,   10
Her ears of jet, and emerald eyes,
  She saw; and purred applause.

Still had she gazed; but midst the tide
Two angel forms were seen to glide,
  The Genii[13] of the stream: 15
Their scaly armor's Tyrian[14] hue
Through richest purple to the view
  Betrayed a golden gleam.

The hapless nymph with wonder saw:
A whisker first, and then a claw,   20
  With many an ardent wish,
She stretched in vain to reach the prize.
What female heart can gold despise?
  What cat's averse to fish?

Presumptuous maid! with looks intent   25
Again she stretched, again she bent,
  Nor knew the gulf between.
(Malignant Fate sat by, and smiled.)
The slipp'ry verge her feet beguiled;
  She tumbled headlong in.   30

---

[12] The cat belonged to Horace Walpole.
[13] Attendant deities.
[14] "Purple," i.e., crimson. From *Tyre,* where the mollusk was
  found from which the dye was made in ancient times.

Eight times emerging from the flood
She mewed to ev'ry wat'ry god,
    Some speedy aid to send.
No dolphin[15] came, no Nereid[16] stirred:
Nor cruel Tom nor Susan[17] heard.   35
    A fav'rite has no friend!

From hence, ye beauties, undeceived,
Know, one false step is ne'er retrieved,
    And be with caution bold.
Not all that tempts your wand'ring eyes   40
And heedless hearts is lawful prize;
    Nor all that glisters, gold.

ELEGY WRITTEN IN A COUNTRY CHURCHYARD

If it can be said of any English poem that it is universally known, this is the one. There are thousands of poems about death; it is the sheer artistry of this one that makes it supreme. Perhaps another reason for its unchanging popularity is its tinge of romantic melancholy: the wonderful evocation of twilight at the beginning; the perfection with which atmosphere is maintained throughout; the pervading sense of life's mystery; the touch of romantic self-pity in the epitaph and the stanzas just before it, in which Gray seems to identify himself with the youthful solitary and his untimely end.

Yet the poem is thoroughly neoclassical. What makes it so is perhaps best indicated by Dr. Johnson's well-known comment at the end of his Life of Gray: "In the character of his *Elegy* I rejoice to concur with the common reader; for by the common sense of readers uncorrupted with literary prejudices, after all the refinements of subtilty and the dogmatism of learning, must be finally decided all claim to poetical honors. The *Churchyard* abounds with images which find a mirror in every mind, and with sentiments to which every bosom returns an echo. The four stanzas beginning 'Yet ev'n these bones' are to me original: I have never seen the notions in any other place; yet he that reads them here persuades himself that he has always felt them. Had Gray written often thus, it had been vain to blame and useless to praise him."

Gray began the poem in 1742, soon after the death of his best friend and fellow Etonian, Richard West, of whom he was thinking when he wrote the closing epitaph. He finished it at Stoke Poges some years later. In the churchyard there he lies, as he wished, without a word of in-

scription to identify his grave. The natives will point out the yew under which he wrote; whether or not the tradition is reliable, the scene fits the mood of the verses. They were completed by 1750 and published anonymously in 1751. Gray continued to polish them; the present text is from the edition of 1768.

The curfew tolls the knell of parting day;
The lowing herd wind slowly o'er the lea;
The plowman homeward plods his weary way,
And leaves the world to darkness and to me.

Now fades the glimmering landscape on the sight,   5
And all the air a solemn stillness holds,
Save where the beetle wheels his droning flight,
And drowsy tinklings lull the distant folds;

Save that from yonder ivy-mantled tow'r,
The moping owl does to the moon complain   10
Of such as, wand'ring near her secret bow'r,
Molest her ancient solitary reign.

Beneath those rugged elms, that yew tree's shade,
Where heaves the turf in many a mold'ring heap,
Each in his narrow cell for ever laid,   15
The rude forefathers of the hamlet sleep.

The breezy call of incense-breathing Morn,
The swallow twitt'ring from the straw-built shed,
The cock's shrill clarion, or the echoing horn,[18]
No more shall rouse them from their lowly bed.   20

For them no more the blazing hearth shall burn,
Or busy housewife ply her evening care;
No children run to lisp their sire's return,
Or climb his knees the envied kiss to share.

Oft did the harvest to their sickle yield;   25
Their furrow oft the stubborn glebe has broke;
How jocund did they drive their team afield!
How bowed the woods beneath their sturdy stroke!

Let not Ambition mock their useful toil,
Their homely joys, and destiny obscure;   30
Nor Grandeur hear with a disdainful smile,
The short and simple annals of the poor.

The boast of heraldry, the pomp of pow'r,
And all that beauty, all that wealth, e'er gave
Awaits[19] alike th' inevitable hour.   35
The paths of glory lead but to the grave.

[15] According to fable, the Greek musician Arion was rescued from a watery grave by a dolphin.   [16] Sea nymph.
[17] I.e., neither footman nor parlormaid.

[18] Of the hunt, early in the morning.
[19] The subject of *awaits* is *hour*.

Nor you, ye proud, impute to these the fault
If Mem'ry o'er their tomb no trophies raise,
Where, through the long-drawn aisle and fretted vault,[20]
The pealing anthem swells the note of praise.   40

Can storied urn[21] or animated[22] bust
Back to its mansion call the fleeting breath?
Can Honor's voice provoke[23] the silent dust,
Or Flattery soothe the dull cold ear of Death?

Perhaps in this neglected spot is laid   45
Some heart once pregnant with celestial fire;
Hands that the rod of empire might have swayed,
Or waked to ecstasy the living lyre.

But Knowledge to their eyes her ample page,
Rich with the spoils of time, did ne'er unroll;   50
Chill Penury repressed their noble rage,[24]
And froze the genial[25] current of the soul.

Full many a gem of purest ray serene
The dark unfathomed caves of ocean bear;
Full many a flower is born to blush unseen,   55
And waste its sweetness on the desert air.

Some village Hampden,[26] that with dauntless breast
The little tyrant of his fields withstood;
Some mute inglorious Milton here may rest,
Some Cromwell guiltless of his country's blood.   60

Th' applause of list'ning senates to command,
The threats of pain and ruin to despise,
To scatter plenty o'er a smiling land,
And read their hist'ry in a nation's eyes,

Their lot forbade: nor circumscribed alone   65
Their growing virtues, but their crimes confined;
Forbade to wade through slaughter to a throne
And shut the gates of mercy on mankind,

The struggling pangs of conscious truth to hide,
To quench the blushes of ingenuous shame,   70
Or heap the shrine of Luxury and Pride
With incense kindled at the Muse's flame.

Far from the madding crowd's ignoble strife,
Their sober wishes never learned to stray;
Along the cool sequestered vale of life   75
They kept the noiseless tenor of their way.

Yet ev'n these bones from insult to protect,
Some frail memorial still erected nigh,
With uncouth rimes and shapeless sculpture decked,
Implores the passing tribute of a sigh.   80

Their name, their years, spelt by th' unlettered Muse,
The place of fame and elegy supply;
And many a holy text around she strews,
That teach the rustic moralist to die.

For who, to dumb Forgetfulness a prey,   85
This pleasing anxious being e'er resigned,
Left the warm precincts of the cheerful day,
Nor cast one longing ling'ring look behind?

On some fond breast the parting soul relies,
Some pious drops the closing eye requires;   90
Ev'n from the tomb the voice of Nature cries,
Ev'n in our ashes live their wonted fires.

For[27] thee who, mindful of th' unhonored dead,
Dost in these lines their artless tale relate,
If chance,[28] by lonely contemplation led,   95
Some kindred spirit shall inquire thy fate,

Haply some hoary-headed swain may say,
"Oft have we seen him at the peep of dawn
Brushing with hasty steps the dews away
To meet the sun upon the upland lawn.   100

"There at the foot of yonder nodding beech
That wreathes its old fantastic roots so high,
His listless length at noontide would he stretch,
And pore upon the brook that babbles by.

"Hard by yon wood, now smiling as in scorn,   105
Mutt'ring his wayward fancies he would rove,
Now drooping, woeful wan, like one forlorn,
Or crazed with care, or crossed in hopeless love.

"One morn I missed him on the customed hill,
Along the heath and near his fav'rite tree;   110
Another came; nor yet beside the rill,
Nor up the lawn, nor at the wood was he;

---

[20] The arched ceilings, with stone tracery, of the aisles of a Gothic
church.
[21] Such as Keats describes in his "Ode on a Grecian Urn"; i.e., one
with paintings suggesting a story.   [22] Lifelike.
[23] Evoke, call forth.   [24] Inspired mood.   [25] Creative.
[26] John Hampden (1594–1643), a high-minded leader of Parliament's resistance to the tyranny of Charles I.

[27] As for.   [28] If it should chance.

"The next, with dirges due in sad array
Slow through the church-way path we saw him borne.
Approach and read (for thou canst read) the lay,   115
Graved on the stone beneath yon agèd thorn."

The Epitaph

Here rests his head upon the lap of Earth
A youth to fortune and to fame unknown.
Fair Science frowned not on his humble birth,
And Melancholy marked him for her own.   120

Large was his bounty, and his soul sincere,
Heav'n did a recompense as largely send:
He gave to Misery all he had, a tear;
He gained from heav'n ('twas all he wished) a friend.

No farther seek his merits to disclose,   125
Or draw his frailties from their dread abode
(There they alike in trembling hope repose),
The bosom of his Father and his God.

THE BARD

A PINDARIC ODE

Attempts to domesticate the Pindaric ode in England have
not proved successful, though one good strophe has already
been quoted from Ben Jonson's memorial to Cary and
Morison. Gray does better than anyone else with it; but
all such imitations of the structure and manner of the
Greek lyric poet Pindar (fifth century B.C.) are hopelessly
stilted. The Pindaric ode consists of several divisions or
ternaries, each of which is made up of three parts, a strophe
(or as Jonson terms it, a "turn"), an antistrophe (or "counterturn"), and an epode (or "stand"). The strophe and
antistrophe have the same metrical and rime scheme; the
epode has a different one. The parts in each division run
precisely parallel with the corresponding parts in the other
divisions of the poem. The idea is to achieve at once symmetry and variety.

Neither "The Bard" nor another Pindaric ode by Gray,
"The Progress of Poesy," can be called an exception to our
opening generalization. But in "The Bard" his imagination
is at least kindled as he thinks of the medieval past (that interest is in itself a sign of the changing tastes which were
eventually to bring in the Romantic Movement)—of the
picturesque scenery of the Welsh mountains, of battles long
ago and the bards who sang the chieftains into battle, of
the dramatic pageant of the successive English kings, of
the more glorious succession of the great English poets.
And so he writes with more of the romantic intensity of
feeling than is usual for him. He began the poem in 1754,
dropped it, and then, reminded of its theme by hearing a

Welsh harper, picked it up and finished it in 1757. With
"The Progress of Poesy" it was printed in the first volume
to come off Horace Walpole's private press at Strawberry
Hill. Gray explains in a note that the poem "is founded
on a tradition current in Wales"—actually it is a false one
—"that Edward the First, when he completed the conquest
of that country, ordered all the bards that fell into his
hands to be put to death."

Gray's odes were not liked in their own time. His historical notes to this poem (for the most part not reproduced here) were a late addition; the public thought the
poems obscure. In a conversation with Boswell, Dr.
Johnson gave them a tremendous raking, fore and aft, and
in his Life of Gray he returned to the attack: "These odes
are marked by glittering accumulations of ungraceful
ornaments; they strike, rather than please; the images are
magnified by affectation; the language is labored into
harshness. The mind of the writer seems to work with
unnatural violence. 'Double, double, toil and trouble.' He
has a kind of strutting dignity, and is tall by walking on
tiptoe. His art and his struggle are too visible, and there is
too little appearance of ease and nature."

There, perhaps, is the best clue to Gray's weakness. His
one great serious poem was neoclassical, and in harmony
with his temperament. He felt, sooner than most, the first
faint wandering airs of the coming gale of romanticism.
But he lacked emotional depths which could be stirred
by them into creative energy.

I, 1

"Ruin seize thee, ruthless King!
Confusion[1] on thy banners wait!
Though fanned by Conquest's crimson wing,
They mock the air with idle state.
Helm, nor hauberk's[2] twisted mail,   5
Nor e'en thy virtues, tyrant, shall avail
To save thy secret soul from nightly fears,
From Cambria's[3] curse, from Cambria's tears!"
Such were the sounds that o'er the crested pride
Of the first Edward scattered wild dismay,   10
As down the steep of Snowdon's[4] shaggy side
He wound with toilsome march his long array.
Stout Gloster[5] stood aghast in speechless trance:
"To arms!" cried Mortimer,[6] and couched his quiv'ring
    lance.

---

[1] Destruction.   [2] Coat of ringed mail.
[3] Wales's. The conquest of Wales was completed by Edward I in
1282.
[4] The highest of the Welsh mountains, in Carnarvonshire.
[5] Gilbert de Clare (1243–95), Earl of Gloucester, the King's son-
in-law and the most powerful of the English barons.
[6] Edmond de Mortimer, Lord of Wigmore, one of the English
barons.

On a rock, whose haughty brow   15
Frowns o'er old Conway's[7] foaming flood,
Robed in the sable garb of woe,
With haggard eyes the poet stood
(Loose his beard and hoary hair
Streamed, like a meteor, to the troubled air)   20
And with a master's hand, and prophet's fire,
Struck the deep sorrows of his lyre.
"Hark, how each giant oak and desert cave
Sighs to the torrent's awful voice beneath!
O'er thee, O King! their hundred arms they wave,   25
Revenge on thee in hoarser murmurs breathe;
Vocal no more, since Cambria's fatal day,
To high-born Hoel's[8] harp, or soft Llewellyn's[9] lay.

"Cold is Cadwallo's tongue,
That hushed the stormy main;   30
Brave Urien[10] sleeps upon his craggy bed;
Mountains, ye mourn in vain
Modred, whose magic song
Made huge Plinlimmon[11] bow his cloud-topped head.
On dreary Arvon's[12] shore they lie,   35
Smeared with gore and ghastly pale:
Far, far aloof th' affrighted ravens sail;
The famished eagle screams, and passes by.
Dear lost companions of my tuneful art,
Dear as the light that visits these sad eyes,   40
Dear as the ruddy drops that warm my heart,
Ye died amidst your dying country's cries—
No more I weep. They do not sleep.
On yonder cliffs, a grisly band,
I see them sit; they linger yet,   45
Avengers of their native land.
With me in dreadful harmony they join,
And weave with bloody hands the tissue of thy line:

"Weave the warp, and weave the woof,
The winding sheet of Edward's race.   50
Give ample room and verge enough
The characters of hell to trace.
Mark the year, and mark the night,

When Severn shall re-echo with affright
The shrieks of death, through Berkeley's roof that ring,
Shrieks of an agonizing king![13]   56
She-wolf of France, with unrelenting fangs,
That tear'st the bowels of thy mangled mate,
From thee be born, who[14] o'er thy country hangs,
The scourge of heav'n. What terrors round him wait!   60
Amazement[15] in his van, with Flight combined,
And Sorrow's faded form, and Solitude behind.

"Mighty victor, mighty lord,
Low on his funeral couch he lies!
No pitying heart, no eye, afford   65
A tear to grace his obsequies.
Is the sable warrior fled?[16]
Thy son is gone. He rests among the dead.
The swarm that in thy noontide beam were born?
Gone to salute the rising morn.[17]   70
Fair laughs the morn, and soft the zephyr blows,
While proudly riding o'er the azure realm
In gallant trim the gilded vessel goes,
Youth on the prow and Pleasure at the helm,
Regardless of the sweeping whirlwind's sway,   75
That, hushed in grim repose, expects[18] his evening prey.

"Fill high the sparkling bowl,
The rich repast prepare;
Reft of a crown, he yet may share the feast.[19]
Close by the regal chair   80
Fell Thirst and Famine scowl
A baleful smile upon their baffled guest.
Heard ye the din of battle bray,
Lance to lance, and horse to horse?
Long years of havoc urge their destined course,   85
And through the kindred squadrons[20] mow their way.

---

7 A river in North Wales.
8 Or Howel. A Welsh warrior and poet.
9 The leader of the Welsh against Edward was Llewellyn ab Gruffyd, but "soft" is not the word for him. There are many Llewellyns in Welsh history.
10 Like Cadwallo, a Welsh bard. No bard named Modred is known.
11 A Welsh mountain.   12 Carnarvonshire's.

13 At Berkeley Castle, in the valley of the Severn, Edward II, son of Edward I, was murdered in 1327 by a particularly cruel means. His shrieks were heard all over the town. His adulterous queen, Isabel of France, consented to the murder.
14 He who. Edward III; his conquests in France ruined that country.   15 Consternation.
16 Edward the Black Prince, eldest son of Edward III; he died before his father.
17 I.e., the courtiers, created by the sunshine of your favor, have deserted you in order to curry favor with your successor. This was the son of the Black Prince, Richard II, whose reign began auspiciously (lines 71 ff.).   18 Awaits.
19 Richard II was deposed and imprisoned in 1399 by his Lancastrian cousin, Henry IV. According to one tradition, he was starved to death.
20 Of the adherents of the related houses of York and Lancaster, in their long struggle for the crown, the Wars of the Roses, which began in the reign of Henry IV's grandson, Henry VI.

Ye towers of Julius,[21] London's lasting shame,
With many a foul and midnight murther fed,
Revere his consort's faith,[22] his father's fame,
And spare the meek usurper's[23] holy head.   90
Above, below, the rose of snow,
Twined with her blushing foe,[24] we spread:
The bristled boar in infant gore[25]
Wallows beneath the thorny shade.
Now, brothers, bending o'er th' accursèd loom,   95
Stamp we our vengeance deep, and ratify his doom.

III, 1

"Edward, lo! to sudden fate
(Weave we the woof. The thread is spun.)
Half of thy heart[26] we consecrate.
(The web is wove. The work is done.)[27]—   100
Stay, oh, stay! nor thus forlorn
Leave me unblessed, unpitied, here to mourn!
In yon bright track, that fires the western skies,
They melt, they vanish from my eyes.
But oh! what solemn scenes on Snowdon's height   105
Descending slow their glitt'ring skirts unroll?
Visions of glory, spare my aching sight;
Ye unborn ages, crowd not on my soul!
No more our long-lost Arthur[28] we bewail.
All-hail, ye genuine kings,[29] Britannia's issue, hail!   110

III, 2.

"Girt with many a baron bold,
Sublime their starry fronts[30] they rear;
And gorgeous dames, and statesmen old
In bearded majesty, appear.
In the midst a form divine![31]   115
Her eye proclaims her of the Briton line;
Her lion port, her awe-commanding face,
Attempered sweet to virgin grace.
What strings symphonious tremble in the air,
What strains of vocal transport round her play!   120
Hear from the grave, great Taliesin,[32] hear;
They breathe a soul to animate thy clay.
Bright Rapture calls, and soaring, as she sings,
Waves in the eye of heav'n her many-colored wings.

III, 3

"The verse adorn again   125
Fierce War, and faithful Love,
And Truth severe, by fairy Fiction drest.[33]
In buskined measures[34] move
Pale Grief, and pleasing Pain,
With Horror, tyrant of the throbbing breast.   130
A voice,[35] as of the cherub choir,
Gales from blooming Eden bear;
And distant warblings[36] lessen on my ear,
That lost in long futurity expire.
Fond[37] impious man,[38] think'st thou yon sanguine cloud,
Raised by thy breath, has quenched the orb of day?   136
Tomorrow he repairs the golden flood,
And warms the nations with redoubled ray.
Enough for me: with joy I see
The different doom our fates assign.   140
Be thine despair, and scept'red care;
To triumph, and to die, are mine."
He spoke, and headlong from the mountain's height
Deep in the roaring tide he plunged to endless night.

---

21 The Tower of London. Henry VI was murdered there, soon
after the triumph of his Yorkist rival, Edward IV. Other
murders mentioned in Gray's note were those of Edward IV's
brother Clarence and of Edward's two sons, "the little princes
in the Tower." Richard III may have been the children's
murderer.

22 Henry VI's queen, Margaret of Anjou. Gray's note calls her
"heroic," but she was an unscrupulous and vindictive politician.
The father of Henry VI was the hero king Henry V, victor of
Agincourt.

23 So called because the house of Lancaster reached the throne by
the usurpation of Henry VI's grandfather, Henry IV (see note
19).

24 The badges of York and Lancaster were the white and the red
rose.

25 The badge of Richard III was a boar. He seized the throne in
1683 on the death of his brother Edward IV.

26 A reference to Eleanor of Castile (d. 1290), wife of Edward I.
There was a legend that she died from the effect of sucking the
poison from the King's wound.

27 At this point the spirits of his dead colleagues, who have joined
with him in the predictions of lines 49–100, leave the bard.

28 The Welsh believed that King Arthur would return and rule.

29 The accession of the Welshman Henry Tudor as Henry VII in
1485 was considered a fulfillment of the prophecy that Welsh
kings should rule Britain.

30 Foreheads.
31 Queen Elizabeth, granddaughter of Henry VII.
32 A famous sixth-century bard.
33 A reference to the allegory of Spenser's *The Faery Queen*.
34 Tragic meters, Shakespeare's tragedies.   35 Milton.
36 Poetry after Milton.   37 Foolish.   38 Edward I.

I. TO HORACE WALPOLE

I was hindered in my last, and so could not give you all the trouble I would have done; the description of a road which your coach wheels have so often honored it would be needless to give you; suffice it that I arrived at Birnam Wood[1] without the loss of any of my fine jewels, and that no little cacaturient[2] gentlewoman made me any reverences by the way; I live with my uncle, a great hunter in imagination; his dogs take up every chair in the house, so I'm forced to stand at this present writing, and though the gout forbids him galloping after 'em in the field, yet he continues still to regale his ears and nose with their comfortable noise and stink; he holds me mighty cheap, I perceive, for walking when I should ride, and reading when I should hunt; my comfort amidst all this is that I have at the distance of half a mile, through a green lane, a forest (the vulgar call it a common) all my own; at least as good as so, for I spy no human thing in it but myself; it is a little chaos of mountains and precipices; mountains, it is true, that don't ascend much above the clouds, nor are the declivities quite so amazing as Dover Cliff; but just such hills as people who love their necks as well as I do may venture to climb, and crags that give the eye as much pleasure as if they were more dangerous: both vale and hill is covered over with most venerable beeches, and other very reverend vegetables, that, like most other ancient people, are always dreaming out their old stories to the winds

And, as they bow their hoary tops, relate
In murmuring sounds the dark decrees of fate;
While visions, as poetic eyes avow,
Cling to each leaf, and swarm on ev'ry bough.[3]

At the foot of one of these squats me I, *il penseroso,* and there grow to the trunk for a whole morning

—the tim'rous hare and sportive squirrel
Gambol around me—

like Adam in Paradise, but commonly without an Eve, and besides I think he did not use to read

Vergil, as I usually do there: in this situation I often converse with my Horace aloud too, that is, talk to you; but I don't remember that I ever heard you answer me; I beg pardon for taking all the conversation to myself, but it is your own fault indeed. We have old Mr. Southerne[4] at a gentleman's house a little way off, who often comes to see us; he is now 77 year old, and has almost wholly lost his memory, but is as agreeable as an old man can be; at least I persuade myself so when I look upon him, and think of Isabella and Oroonoko. I shall be in town in about 3 weeks, I believe; if you direct your letters to London, they will take care to send 'em safe; but I must desire you would fold 'em with a little more art, for your last had been opened without breaking the seal. Adieu.

Yours ever,

T. Gray

II. TO HIS MOTHER

Rheims, 21 JUNE, N.S., 1739

We have now been settled almost three weeks in this city, which is more considerable upon account of its size and antiquity than from the number of its inhabitants or any advantages of commerce. There is little in it worth a stranger's curiosity besides the cathedral church, which is a vast Gothic building of a surprising beauty and lightness, all covered over with a profusion of little statues and other ornaments. It is here the kings of France are crowned by the archbishop of Rheims, who is the first peer and the primate of the kingdom. The holy vessel made use of on that occasion, which contains the oil, is kept in the church of St. Nicasius hard by, and is believed to have been brought by an angel from heaven at the coronation of Clovis, the first Christian king. The streets in general have but a melancholy aspect, the houses all old; the public walks run along the side of a great moat under the ramparts, where one hears a continual croaking of frogs; the country round about is one great plain covered with vines, which at this time of the year afford no very pleasing prospect, as being not above a foot high. What pleasures the place denies to the sight it makes up to the palate, since you have nothing to drink but the best champagne in the world, and all sorts of

---

[1] A jocular allusion to *Macbeth.* Gray was in Burnham, in Buckinghamshire, not far from Stoke Poges; Burnham Beeches is a forest. He was staying with his aunt and her husband, Jonathan Rogers, a lawyer. The letter was written in August, 1736.

[2] Desirous of evacuating the bowels.

[3] Presumably these lines are by Gray.

[4] Thomas Southerne (1660–1746), the dramatist. His most famous plays are *The Fatal Marriage* (Isabella is the heroine) and *Oroonoko,* the latter based on the novel by Aphra Behn (p. 398, above).

provisions equally good. As to other pleasures, there is not that freedom of conversation among the people of fashion here that one sees in other parts of France; for, though they are not very numerous in this place, and consequently must live a good deal together, yet they never come to any great familiarity with one another. As my Lord Conway had spent a good part of his time among them, his brother[5] and we with him were soon introduced into all their assemblies. As soon as you enter, the lady of the house presents each of you a card, and offers you a party at quadrille; you sit down and play forty deals without intermission, excepting one quarter of an hour when everybody rises to eat of what they call the *gouter,* which supplies the place of our tea, and is a service of wine, fruits, cream, sweetmeats, crawfish, and cheese. People take what they like, and sit down again to play; after that, they make little parties to go to the walks together, and then all the company retire to their separate habitations. Very seldom any suppers or dinners are given; and this is the manner they live among one another, not so much out of any aversion they have to pleasure as out of a sort of formality they have contracted by not being much frequented by people who have lived at Paris. It is sure they do not hate gaiety any more than the rest of their countrypeople, and can enter into diversions that are once proposed, with a good grace enough; for instance, the other evening we happened to be got together in a company of eighteen people, men and women of the best fashion here, at a garden in the town to walk; when one of the ladies bethought herself of asking, "Why should not we sup here?" Immediately the cloth was laid by the side of a fountain under the trees, and a very elegant supper served up; after which another said, "Come, let us sing"; and directly began herself: from singing we insensibly fell to dancing, and singing in a round, when somebody mentioned the violins, and immediately a company of them was ordered. Minuets were begun in the open air, and then came country-dances, which held till four o'clock next morning; at which hour the gayest lady there proposed that such as were weary should get into their coaches, and the rest of them should dance before them with the music in the van[6]; and in this manner we paraded through all the principal streets of the city, and waked everybody in it. Mr. Walpole had a mind to make a custom of the

thing, and would have given a ball in the same manner next week, but the women did not come into it; so I believe it will drop, and they will return to their dull cards and usual formalities. We are not to stay above a month longer here, and shall then go to Dijon, the chief city of Burgundy, a very splendid and very gay town; at least such is the present design.

III. TO HIS MOTHER

Turin, Nov. 7, N.S., 1739

I am this night arrived here, and have just set down to rest me after eight days' tiresome journey.[7] For the first three we had the same road we before passed through to go to Geneva; the fourth we turned out of it, and for that day and the next traveled rather among than upon the Alps, the way commonly running through a deep valley by the side of the river Arc, which works itself a passage, with great difficulty and a mighty noise, among vast quantities of rocks, that have rolled down from the mountain tops. The winter was so far advanced as in great measure to spoil the beauty of the prospect; however, there was still somewhat fine remaining amidst the savageness and horror of the place. The sixth we began to go up several of these mountains; and as we were passing one, met with an odd accident enough. Mr. Walpole had a little fat black spaniel, that he was very fond of, which he sometimes used to set down, and let it run by the chaise side. We were at that time in a very rough road, not two yards broad at most; on one side was a great wood of pines, and on the other a vast precipice; it was noonday, and the sun shone bright, when all of a sudden, from the woodside (which was as steep upwards as the other part was downwards), out rushed a great wolf, came close to the head of the horses, seized the dog by the throat, and rushed up the hill again with him in his mouth. This was done in less than a quarter of a minute; we all saw it, and yet the servants had not time to draw their pistols, or do anything to save the dog. If he had not been there, and the creature had thought fit to lay hold of one of the horses, chaise and we and all must inevitably have tumbled above fifty fathoms perpendicular down the precipice. The seventh we came to Lanslebourg, the last town in Savoy; it lies at the foot of the famous Mount Cenis, which is so situated as to allow no room for any way

---

[5] Gray's companions were Horace Walpole and the latter's cousin, Henry Seymour Conway.　　[6] Lead.

[7] This letter is interesting in itself, but is also significant as an early example of the Romantic delight in wild nature.

but over the very top of it. Here the chaise was forced to be pulled to pieces, and the baggage and that to be carried by mules. We ourselves were wrapped up in our furs, and seated upon a sort of matted chair without legs, which is carried upon poles in the manner of a bier, and so begun to ascend by the help of eight men. It was six miles to the top, where a plain opens itself about as many more in breadth, covered perpetually with very deep snow, and in the midst of that a great lake of unfathomable depth, from whence a river takes its rise, and tumbles over monstrous rocks quite down the other side of the mountain. The descent is six miles more, but infinitely more steep than the going up; and here the men perfectly fly down with you, stepping from stone to stone with incredible swiftness in places where none but they could go three paces without falling. The immensity of the precipices, the roaring of the river and torrents that run into it, the huge crags covered with ice and snow, and the clouds below you and about you, are objects it is impossible to conceive without seeing them; and though we had heard many strange descriptions of the scene, none of them at all came up to it. . . .

IV. TO WILLIAM MASON[8]

DEC. 19, 1757

Dear Mason,

Though I very well know the bland, emollient, saponaceous qualities both of sack[9] and silver, yet if any great man would say to me, "I make you rat catcher to his Majesty, with a salary of £300 a year and two butts of the best Malaga; and though it has been usual to catch a mouse or two (for form's sake) in public once a year, yet to you, sir, we shall not stand upon these things"—I can not say I should jump at it. Nay, if they would drop the very name of the office, and call me Sinecure to the King's Majesty, I should still feel a little awkward, and think everybody I saw smelt a rat about me; but I do not pretend to blame anyone else that has not the same sensations. For my part, I would rather be Sergeant-Trumpeter, or Pin-Maker to the Palace. Nevertheless I interest myself a little in the history of it, and rather wish somebody may accept it that will retrieve the credit of the thing, if it be retrievable, or ever had any credit.[10] Rowe[11] was, I think, the last man of character that had it. As to Settle, whom you mention, he belonged to my Lord Mayor, not to the king.[12] Eusden[13] was a person of great hopes in his youth, though at last he turned out a drunken parson. Dryden was as disgraceful to the office from his character as the poorest scribbler could have been from his verses.[14] In short, the office itself has always humbled the possessor hitherto (even in an age when kings were somebody): if he were a poor writer, by making him more conspicuous; and if he were a good one, by setting him at war with the little fry of his own profession, for there are poets little enough to envy even a poet laureate. . . .

Christopher Smart

1722–1771

A FEW pages further on we shall have a glimpse of Smart as Dr. Johnson saw him:

Madness frequently discovers itself merely by unnecessary deviation from the usual modes of the world. My poor friend Smart showed the disturbance of his mind by falling upon his knees and saying his prayers in the street. . . . I did not think he ought to be shut up. His infirmities were not noxious to society. He insisted on people praying with him; and I'd as lief pray with Kit Smart as anyone else.

Johnson might have added that genius also has been known to deviate from the usual modes. In nearly everything he wrote Smart remained strictly within the contemporary pattern, a third-rate neoclassicist; but in two poems, the

8 This clergyman and minor poet (1724–97) wrote a Life of Gray.
9 Sherry, in particular; but the term was applied in general to strong wines from southern Europe. Gray had just refused an offer of the poet laureateship; the stipend included besides money a hogshead of Canary wine.

10 William Whitehead (1715–85), an inferior poet, succeeded Colley Cibber, the well-known actor and dramatist, on the day Gray wrote this letter.
11 Nicholas Rowe (1674–1718) succeeded Nahum Tate in 1715. Rowe was a fair dramatist, a poor poet, and the earliest editor of Shakespeare.
12 Elkanah Settle (1628–74), minor poet and dramatist. I.e., he was official poet of London, not poet laureate of England.
13 The appointment of Laurence Eusden (1688–1730) was one of the worst of many bad ones. He succeeded Rowe in 1718; Cibber followed him.
14 A biased judgment. Actually, Dryden's was the only first-rate appointment between Jonson's and Wordsworth's.

only two of interest today, he broke the mold of convention, and it was the touch of insanity that freed him. *A Song to David* is one of the great English lyrics. As Browning says in *Parleyings with Certain People of Importance in Their Day,* Smart "reached the zenith from his madhouse cell." His masterpiece, declares the critic Churton Collins, is "the one rapt strain in the poetry of the eighteenth century." Actually, of course, there are others, among them Smart's own *Rejoice in the Lamb;* but the reader whose taste has not been dulled by an exclusive diet of realism will not quarrel with anyone who applies superlatives to Smart's great poem.

This phenomenon among the mid-century poets, this stranger from another than the eighteenth-century world, was born in 1722 in Kent, where his father was steward of an estate. After the latter's death he went to school in Durham; in that county the family which his father had served owned a country seat. Aided by a relative of this family, Smart entered Cambridge; by 1745 he was a fellow of Pembroke College. His prospects seemed excellent, but they were thrown away in the tavern. Smart ran up debts he could not pay; he became a drunkard; and about 1749 he left the university for a Bohemian existence in London, subsisting on what he could pick up as a hack writer and a tavern entertainer. Yet five times in the next six years his entries won the Seatonian prize at Cambridge for religious poetry. His most popular poem, however, was a georgic (that is, a piece on agriculture), *The Hop Garden* (1752).

Smart married the stepdaughter of a London publisher and had two children. How early his eccentricities passed the verge of lunacy is not known. His literal obedience to the precept "pray without ceasing" was certainly irrational; and when he was drunk he prayed all the harder. This excess of Christian zeal ran shockingly counter to the eighteenth century's distrust of "enthusiasm"; to call a man enthusiastic was then the reverse of complimentary. In the opinion of his contemporaries, Smart's best poem lay wide open to that charge. Attacks of worse than "enthusiasm" apparently led to private confinement as early as 1756. He remained in duress about seven years, part of the time in a public asylum. Johnson befriended him, and Garrick gave a benefit performance for him. Soon after his release Smart published *A Song to David;* some took it for conclusive proof that his madness was incurable. Even in 1791, when his poems were edited by his nephew, this masterpiece was omitted as unworthy of him. Smart never completely regained his balance. He lived alone, showing little or no interest in his family. Among his later works were verse translations of the Psalms (1765) and of Horace (1767). The government gave him a small pension, but he was in debtor's prison when he died in 1771.

Selections from the poems were edited by Edmund Blunden (1924). More recent editions are by Norman Callan (2 vols., 1949) and Robert Brittain (1950). *The Case of Christopher Smart* (1934) is an appreciative essay by L. Binyon.

from A SONG TO DAVID

The central idea of this ecstatic poem is that all living things, because each is in its separate way so marvelous, unite to praise the Lord. Praise was the object of David's art in the Psalms; and Smart points out in an analytical table of contents that "the best poet which ever lived was thought worthy of the highest honor which possibly can be conceived, as the Saviour of the world was ascribed to his house and called his son in the body." Smart's allusions were drawn from much reading, especially in the Bible, but also in both occult and scientific works. For the twentieth century the poem's appeal lies mainly in the intensity of its author's response to the world's beauty and wonder and his enraptured perception of deity. Smart lets himself go, and the agency which burned away the barriers was presumably his madness.

Yet he managed to retain control of his pen. If the boldness of the repetitions seems in wild disregard of restraint, actually they shape the poem's form. The structure, as Professor Havens has shown, is carefully wrought. The stanzas are organized in groups, especially of three and seven—mystic numbers. The following excerpt (it includes the last thirty-eight stanzas) begins with no. 49, addressed to David, whose merits and poetic mission have already been described. No. 50, "Praise above all," introduces the theme of the next three groups, of seven stanzas each; every stanza contains the phrase "for adoration." Finally (nos. 72–86), we have five groups of three stanzas each. Within each of these groups the first two stanzas begin with the same adjective, which reappears at the opening of the third stanza in the comparative degree (e.g., "precious," "more precious"). Accordingly, although the poet's rush of feeling imbues his lines with romantic warmth, we must conclude that he composed "with unusual attention to parallelism, formal design, and pattern—to the ordered beauty of classic and neo-classic art." The poem is not only among the most remarkable examples of English song; it is among the most successful.

It appeared in 1763, on Smart's emergence from the asylum. A reprint was published by the Oxford University Press in 1926. R. D. Havens has explained "The Structure of Smart's *Song to David*" (*Review of English Studies,* XIV [1938], 178–82).

O DAVID, highest in the list
Of worthies, on God's ways insist, 290
      The genuine word repeat:
Vain are the documents of men,
And vain the flourish of the pen
      That keeps the fool's conceit.

PRAISE above all—for praise prevails; 295
Heap up the measure, load the scales,
      And good to goodness add:
The gen'rous soul her Saviour aids,
But peevish obloquy degrades;
      The Lord is great and glad. 300

For ADORATION all the ranks
Of angels yield eternal thanks,
      And DAVID in the midst;
With God's good poor, which, last and least
In man's esteem, thou to thy feast, 305
      O blessèd bridegroom, bidst.

For ADORATION seasons change,
And order, truth, and beauty range,
      Adjust, attract, and fill:
The grass the polyanthus checks;[1] 310
And polished porphyry reflects,
      By the descending rill.

Rich almonds color to the prime[2]
For ADORATION; tendrils climb,
      And fruit trees pledge their gems; 315
And Ivis[3] with her gorgeous vest
Builds for her eggs her cunning nest,
      And bellflowers[4] bow their stems.

With vinous syrup cedars spout;
From rocks pure honey gushing out 320
      For ADORATION springs:
All scenes of painting crowd the map
Of nature; to the mermaid's pap
      The scalèd infant clings.

The spotted ounce[5] and playsome cubs 325
Run rustling 'mongst the flow'ring shrubs,
      And lizards feed[6] the moss;
For ADORATION beasts embark,[7]
While waves upholding halycon's[8] ark
      No longer roar and toss. 330

While Israel sits beneath his fig,[9]
With coral root and amber sprig
      The weaned advent'rer sports;[10]
Where to the palm the jasmine cleaves,
For ADORATION 'mongst the leaves 335
      The gale his peace reports.

Increasing days their reign exalt,
Nor in the pink and mottled vault
      Th' opposing spirits tilt;[11]
And, by the coasting reader[12] spied, 340
The silverlings[13] and crusians[14] glide
      For ADORATION gilt.

For ADORATION rip'ning canes
And cocoa's[15] purest milk detains
      The western pilgrim's staff, 345
Where rain in clasping boughs inclosed,
And vines with oranges disposed,
      Embow'r the social laugh.

Now labor his reward receives,
For ADORATION counts his sheaves 350
      To peace, her bounteous prince;
The nectarine his strong tint imbibes,
And apples of ten thousand tribes,
      And quick peculiar quince.

The wealthy crops of whit'ning rice 355
'Mongst thyine[16] woods and groves of spice,
      For ADORATION grow;
And, marshaled in the fencèd land,
The peaches and pomegranates stand,
      Where wild carnations blow. 360

The laurels with the winter strive;
The crocus burnishes alive
      Upon the snow-clad earth.
For ADORATION myrtles stay
To keep the garden from dismay, 365
      And bless the sight from dearth.

The pheasant shows his pompous neck;
And ermine, jealous[17] of a speck,
      With fear eludes offense:[18]
The sable, with his glossy pride, 370
For ADORATION is descried,
      Where frosts the wave condense.

---

[1] Checkers.   [2] I.e., ripen to the height of excellence.
[3] The hummingbird.   [4] Canterbury bells, etc.
[5] A variety of large, pantherlike cat.   [6] Feed on.
[7] I.e., it is a tribute to God's wondrous power that certain beasts can swim out from shore.
[8] The kingfisher's. It was supposed to build its nest on the water, which it charmed to smoothness.

[9] Micah 4:4: "But they shall sit every man under his vine and under his fig tree; and none shall make them afraid. . . ."
[10] I.e., the adventurous child plays.
[11] I.e., in the tropical paradise all is peace; the skies are calm and still—storms are not in control.
[12] The observer moving along the shore in a boat.
[13] Silver-colored fish.   [14] Carp.   [15] The cocoanuts.
[16] An epithet of uncertain meaning applied to wood in Revelation 18:12.   [17] Suspicious.   [18] Injury.

The cheerful holly, pensive yew,
And holy thorn[19] their trim renew;
     The squirrel hoards his nuts: 375
All creatures batten[20] o'er their stores,
And careful nature all her doors
     For ADORATION shuts.

For ADORATION, DAVID's Psalms
Lift up the heart to deeds of alms;   380
     And he who kneels and chants
Prevails his passions to control,
Finds meat and med'cine to the soul,
     Which for translation[21] pants.

For ADORATION, beyond match,   385
The scholar bullfinch[22] aims to catch
     The soft flute's iv'ry touch;
And, careless on the hazel spray,
The daring redbreast keeps at bay
     The damsel's greedy clutch.   390

For ADORATION, in the skies,
The Lord's philosopher[23] espies
     The Dog, the Ram, and Rose,
The planet's[24] ring, Orion's sword;
Nor is his greatness less adored   395
     In the vile worm that glows.

For ADORATION on the strings[25]
The western breezes work their wings,
     The captive ear to soothe.—
Hark! 'tis a voice—how still, and small—   400
That makes the cataracts to fall,
     Or bids the sea be smooth.

For ADORATION, incense comes
From bezoar,[26] and Arabian gums,
     And on the civet's fur: 405
But as for prayer, or e'er it faints,
Far better is the breath of saints
     Than galbanum[27] and myrrh.

For ADORATION, from the down
Of damsons to th' anana's[28] crown,   410
     God sends to tempt the taste;
And while the luscious zest invites
The sense, that in the scene delights,
     Commands desire be chaste.

For ADORATION, all the paths   415
Of grace are open, all the baths
     Of purity refresh;
And all the rays of glory beam
To deck the man of God's esteem,
     Who triumphs o'er the flesh.   420

For ADORATION, in the dome
Of Christ the sparrows find an home,
     And on his olives perch:
The swallow also dwells with thee,
O man of God's humility,   425
     Within his Saviour's CHURCH.

Sweet is the dew that falls betimes,[29]
And drops upon the leafy limes;
     Sweet, Hermon's[30] fragrant air:
Sweet is the lily's silver bell,   430
And sweet the wakeful tapers smell
     That watch for early prayer.

Sweet the young nurse with love intense,
Which smiles o'er sleeping innocence;
     Sweet when the lost arrive: 435
Sweet the musician's ardor beats,
While his vague mind's in quest of sweets,
     The choicest flow'rs to hive.

Sweeter in all the strains of love
The language of thy turtledove,   440
     Paired to thy swelling chord;
Sweeter with ev'ry grace endued
The glory of thy gratitude,
     Respired unto the Lord.

Strong is the horse upon his speed;   445
Strong in pursuit the rapid glede,[31]
     Which makes at once his game;
Strong the tall ostrich on the ground;
Strong through the turbulent profound[32]
     Shoots xiphias[33] to his aim.   450

---

19 "Holy" because of the famous thorn at Glastonbury supposed
   to have sprung from the staff of Joseph of Arimathea, who
   brought the Holy Grail to Britain.   20 Cover.
21 Removal to heaven.
22 The European bird, which can learn to whistle a short tune.
23 Scientist. He seeks to understand God by studying his works.
24 Saturn's.   25 Of the aeolian harp.
26 A resinous stone found in the intestines of certain animals. It
   was not, however, used as perfume.
27 A Persian gum.

28 Pineapple's.   29 Early.
30 A mountain in the Anti-Lebanon range in Syria.
31 Hawk.   32 Deep, ocean.   33 The swordfish.

Strong is the lion—like a coal
His eyeball—like a bastion's mole
    His chest against the foes:
Strong the gier-eagle[34] on his sail;
Strong against tide, th' enormous whale   455
    Emerges as he goes.

But stronger still, in earth and air
And in the sea, the man of prayer;
    And far beneath the tide;[35]
And in the seat to faith assigned,   460
Where ask is have, where seek is find,
    Where knock is open wide.[36]

Beauteous the fleet before the gale;
Beauteous the multitudes in mail,
    Ranked arms and crested heads: 465
Beauteous the garden's umbrage mild,
Walk, water, meditated wild,[37]
    And all the bloomy beds.

Beauteous the moon full on the lawn;
And beauteous, when the veil's withdrawn,   470
    The virgin to her spouse:
Beauteous the temple decked and filled,
When to the heav'n of heav'ns they build
    Their heart-directed vows.

Beauteous, yea, beauteous more than these,   475
The shepherd king[38] upon his knees,
    For his momentous trust,
With wish of infinite conceit[39]
For man, beast, mute, the small and great,
    And prostrate dust to dust.   480

Precious the bounteous widow's mite;[40]
And precious, for extreme delight,
    The largess from the churl:[41]
Precious the ruby's blushing blaze,
And alba's[42] blest imperial rays,   485
    And pure cerulean pearl.

Precious the penitential tear;
And precious is the sigh sincere,
    Acceptable to God:
And precious are the winning flow'rs,   490
In gladsome Israel's feast of bow'rs,
    Bound on the hallowed sod.

---

[34] Vulture.   [35] As in the case of Jonah.   [36] Matthew 7:7.
[37] I.e., a part intentionally left uncultivated.   [38] David.
[39] Conception, comprehension.   [40] Mark 12:41–44.
[41] 1 Samuel 25:2–42.   [42] The white stone of Revelation 2:17.

More precious that diviner part
Of David, ev'n the Lord's own heart,
    Great, beautiful, and new: 495
In all things where it was intent,
In all extremes, in each event,
    Proof[43]—answ'ring true to true.

Glorious the sun in mid career;
Glorious th' assembled fires appear;   500
    Glorious the comet's train:
Glorious the trumpet and alarm;
Glorious th' almighty stretched-out arm;
    Glorious th' enraptured main:

Glorious the northern lights astream;   505
Glorious the song, when God's the theme;
    Glorious the thunder's roar:
Glorious hosanna from the den;
Glorious the catholic amen;
    Glorious the martyr's gore.   510

Glorious—more glorious is the crown
Of him who brought salvation down
    By meekness, called thy Son;
Thou that stupendous truth believed;
And now the matchless deed's achieved,   515
    DETERMINED, DARED, and DONE.

from REJOICE IN THE LAMB

Like *A Song to David*, this poem is a remarkable illustration of Emerson's doctrine of compensation, for it too
owes its character to the release conferred on Smart by
his affliction. This time, however, he is unable to maintain
steady control; parts of *Rejoice in the Lamb* (or *Jubilate
Agno*) are quite mad. Yet from the welter of these free-verse
lines in Biblical style—about half of them begin with
"For" and the rest with "Let"—rises the same radiant
theme. David sang of how the heavens declare the glory
of God; to Smart, every created thing makes the same
announcement, not least his cat Jeoffry, sole companion of
his confinement, whose life is an act of constant worship
by virtue of the simple fact that he exists—because he is
cat, with the great and numerous talents of cat.

    Rejoice in the Lamb was written during Smart's madness,
sometime between 1756 and 1763. Only recently was the
manuscript discovered and edited by W. F. Stead (1939);
the following lines are reprinted by permission of the
publisher, Jonathan Cape Ltd. (London)—the American
publisher is Henry Holt and Company. The passage on

[43] Firm.

Jeoffry (which is decidedly *not* mad) begins with section XIX, line 50, and runs through section XX, in Mr. Stead's arrangement of the disordered manuscript. A new edition, by W. H. Bond, is in preparation (see *Harvard Library Bulletin*, IV, 39–52).

For I will consider my Cat Jeoffry.

For he is the servant of the Living God, duly and daily serving him.

For at the first glance of the glory of God in the East he worships in his way.

For is this done by wreathing his body seven times round with elegant quickness.

For then he leaps up to catch the musk,[1] which is the blessing of God upon his prayer.   5

For he rolls upon prank to work it in.

For having done duty and received blessing he begins to consider himself.

For this he performs in ten degrees.

For first he looks upon his forepaws to see if they are clean.

For secondly he kicks up behind to clear away there.   10

For thirdly he works it upon stretch[2] with the forepaws extended.

For fourthly he sharpens his paws by wood.

For fifthly he washes himself.

For sixthly he rolls upon wash.

For seventhly he fleas himself, that he may not be interrupted upon the beat.[3]   15

For eighthly he rubs himself against a post.

For ninthly he looks up for his instructions.

For tenthly he goes in quest of food.

For having considered God and himself he will consider his neighbor.

For if he meets another cat he will kiss her in kindness.   20

For when he takes his prey he plays with it to give it chance.

For one mouse in seven escapes by his dallying.

For when his day's work is done his business more properly begins.

For he keeps the Lord's watch in the night against the adversary.

For he counteracts the powers of darkness by his electrical skin and glaring eyes.   25

For he counteracts the Devil, who is death, by brisking about the life.[4]

For in his morning orisons he loves the sun and the sun loves him.

For he is of the tribe of Tiger.

For the Cherub Cat is a term of the Angel Tiger.[5]

For he has the subtlety and hissing of a serpent, which in goodness he suppresses.   30

For he will not do destruction, if he is well-fed, neither will he spit without provocation.

For he purrs in thankfulness, when God tells him he's a good Cat.

For he is an instrument for the children to learn benevolence upon.

For every house is incomplete without him and a blessing is lacking in the spirit.

For the Lord commanded Moses concerning the cats at the departure of the Children of Israel from Egypt.[6]

For every family had one cat at least in the bag.   36

For the English Cats are the best in Europe.

For he is the cleanest in the use of his forepaws of any quadruped.

For the dexterity of his defense is an instance of the love of God to him exceedingly.

For he is the quickest to his mark of any creature.   40

For he is tenacious of his point.

For he is a mixture of gravity and waggery.

For he knows that God is his Saviour.

For there is nothing sweeter than his peace when at rest.

For there is nothing brisker than his life when in motion.

For he is of the Lord's poor and so indeed is he called by benevolence perpetually—Poor Jeoffry! poor Jeoffry! the rat has bit thy throat.   46

For I bless the name of the Lord Jesus that Jeoffry is better.

For the divine spirit comes about his body to sustain it in complete cat.

For his tongue is exceeding pure so that it has in purity what it wants in music.

For he is docile and can learn certain things.   50

For he can set up with gravity, which is patience upon approbation.

For he can fetch and carry, which is patience in employment.

For he can jump over a stick, which is patience upon proof positive.

For he can spraggle upon waggle[7] at the word of command.

For he can jump from an eminence into his master's bosom.   55

---

[1] Evidently Smart would swing or toss a musk-ball; having caught it, Jeoffry would roll on it.
[2] I.e., gives himself a workout by stretching.
[3] I.e., when on his rounds.
[4] I.e., because he is so full of life.

[5] I.e., a cherub is a little angel, and a cat a little tiger.
[6] They were commanded to take along some loot, and Smart fancies that among other things they stole cats.
[7] Can sprawl when his master shakes the stick or makes a sign with his hand.

For he can catch the cork and toss it again.

For he is hated by the hypocrite and miser.

For the former is afraid of detection.

For the latter refuses the charge.[8]

For he camels his back to bear the first notion of business.

For he is good to think on, if a man would express
    himself neatly.   61

For he made a great figure in Egypt for his signal
    services.

For he killed the ichneumon-rat[9] very pernicious by land.

For his ears are so acute that they sting[10] again.

For from this proceeds the passing quickness of his
    attention.   65

For by stroking him I have found out electricity.

For I perceived God's light about him both wax and
    fire.[11]

For the electrical fire is the spiritual substance, which
    God sends from heaven to sustain the bodies both of
    man and beast.

For God has blessed him in the variety of his movements.

For, though he cannot fly, he is an excellent clamberer. 70

For his motions upon the face of the earth are more than
    any other quadruped.

For he can tread to all the measures upon the music.

For he can swim for life.

For he can creep.

Samuel Johnson

1709–1784

THE FULL flavor of Johnson must be sought in Boswell's record of his talk; Johnson is also to be found in his own writings, though not so pungently. All that he wrote, like all that he said, is colored with the richness of his own experience in the world of men. Unlike Addison, he did not shun intimate exchanges with the strongest minds of his time. Many of the ablest men of the age flocked about him, and every one of them fell under the spell of his personality. His is, indeed, probably the greatest personality in English literature.

His pre-eminence does not arise solely from his intellectual force, his vast fund of common sense, or the pointedness of his wit. More than most writers he had the knack of drawing not merely on his own but on the sum total of human experience in order to formulate a generalization about how men behave. Dr. Dodd is under sentence of death, and to someone who rightly suspects Johnson's authorship of an address purporting to be the work of the doomed man, "Why," Johnson rejoins, "should you think so? Depend upon it, sir, when a man knows he is to be hanged in a fortnight, it concentrates his mind wonderfully." "All theory is against freedom of the will; all experience for it." "All censure of a man's self is oblique praise. It is in order to show how much he can spare." But men are not so in love with instruction that we can suppose Johnson's company was valued entirely for that reason. He was the exact opposite of Lord Chesterfield, allowing his emotions plenty of rein in conversation, so

that sometimes he roared with laughter and sometimes stormed with contempt or indignation. And he gave his wit free play. He says he never calculated how he should talk. It was that spontaneous emotional warmth which endeared him to his friends. He was incredibly dictatorial in his talk, and his frequent brusqueness made enemies; but he was plainly a lovable man. Some called him Ursa Major, the Great Bear; but Goldsmith said that no man alive had a more tender heart: "he has nothing of the bear but his skin."

His father was a bookseller at the cathedral town of Lichfield in Staffordshire, where Johnson was born in 1709. His boyhood reading in his father's shop was an important element in his education. Not for him were the famous "public" schools; but, poor as he was, he spent three years at Oxford, though he had to leave before taking a degree. Thirty years later Trinity College, Dublin, gave him an honorary D.C.L., and in 1775 Oxford conferred an honorary LL.D. Till he was in his forties, Johnson was obscure, and miserably oppressed by poverty. He was twenty-four when he married a widow twenty years his senior. To others she appeared endowed with neither beauty nor charm, yet he was devoted to her. With his wife's money, not a large sum, Johnson tried to establish a school near Lichfield. He secured only three pupils; but one of them was David Garrick, destined to become the most famous actor in the history of the English stage. Johnson next determined to try his luck in London, and Garrick went with him. The following year (1738) saw the publication of Johnson's first substantial composition, the poem *London*. It was well received; Pope praised it gen-

---

[8] Is unwilling to bear the expense of feeding a cat.

[9] Mongoose. It was not, however, pernicious; on the contrary, it was valued as a destroyer of crocodile eggs, snakes, and rats.

[10] That at any sound they pierce his consciousness and put him on the alert.

[11] Candle and flame.

erously, and it went into a second edition. For the next few years, however, Johnson's mainstay was the job of writing reports of speeches in Parliament for the *Gentleman's Magazine*. Debates were supposed to be secret; but their substance could be worked up from notes, under the transparent guise of recording the proceedings of the senate of Lilliput.

Through these and other prose writings, such as a Life of the unfortunate young poet Richard Savage, Johnson became known; but it was very gradually, and for years he was wretchedly poor. In 1747 he published the *Plan* of his dictionary. A pool of London booksellers agreed to give him £1575 on its completion. With the aid of six assistants he expected to finish it in three years, but it was not ready till 1755. By that time he had spent the stipulated sum, and even owed money to his publishers. It long remained the best English dictionary, even though some of the definitions were distorted by Johnson's prejudices. Here, for example, is his definition of *pension:* "an allowance made to anyone without an equivalent. In England it is generally understood to mean pay given to a state hireling for treason to his country." Among the *Dictionary's* great merits is Johnson's practice of illustrating meanings by quotations from good writers. His wife did not live to see the end of this heavy task; she died in 1752. Meanwhile, in 1749, *The Vanity of Human Wishes,* a poem of much strength, had been published. In the same year his tragedy *Irene* was produced by Garrick. Johnson had no talent for the theater, and the play failed. In 1750 appeared the first number of the *Rambler,* a literary periodical of the *Spectator* type. As a periodical it never had many subscribers, but ten editions in book form were printed in Johnson's lifetime. For ten years, off and on, he continued to write periodical essays under the titles of the *Rambler,* the *Adventurer,* and the *Idler.*

No sooner was the *Dictionary* finished than Johnson issued a prospectus for a new edition of Shakespeare. He found this task so wearisome that he kept putting it off; but when in 1765, goaded by the taunts of his enemies, he finally completed it, he had produced one of the most valuable of the innumerable editions; it is still regularly consulted by scholars. His most important work in the interval was *The History of Rasselas, Prince of Abyssinia,* which is represented below. Hard-pressed for money, he wrote it in a week in 1759. His financial situation was stabilized in 1762 by his acceptance of a pension of three hundred pounds a year from George III. Johnson, who had formed the estimate of pensions quoted above as a Tory living under Whig administrations, was naturally hesitant about becoming a pensioner; but on being assured that his stipend was intended not as a political retaining-fee but as a recognition of past services to the nation's culture, he consented. Considering the greater purchasing power of

money at that time, the annuity was enough for him to live on comfortably; but his own pensioners were a heavy drain on his purse. He took into his house—these charities began even before his wife's death in 1752—a motley crew of unfortunates, most of them wholly dependent on him for food and shelter. There were the blind poetess Anna Williams; a down-at-heels physician, Dr. Levet; the destitute Mrs. Desmoulins and her daughter; Frank Barber, an unneeded Negro servant, for whose education he provided; and Miss "Poll" Carmichael.

Johnson loved social intercourse and had a host of friends. Humanity enthralled him; moreover, he was subject to morbid fits of depression, and he sought relief from his melancholy in conversation. He liked to dine out; he told Boswell he felt under an obligation to any man who called on him; above all, he liked to play the leading role in a lively and intellectual discussion. In 1764 he and the foremost living painter, Sir Joshua Reynolds, founded the Club, later called the Literary Club. Goldsmith and Edmund Burke were among the original members; by the time Boswell's *Life of Johnson* was published (1791) its roster had included Garrick, Boswell, the economist Adam Smith, the ballad collector Bishop Thomas Percy, the great historian Edward Gibbon, the Whig statesman Charles James Fox, the dramatist and Whig statesman Richard Brinsley Sheridan, the Shakespearean scholar Edmond Malone, and the historian of music Charles Burney, besides others less well known. The members dined together, at first weekly and afterwards fortnightly.

About the time the Club was established, Johnson met the Thrales. Henry Thrale, a rich brewer, was merely an amiable Babbitt who ate himself to death. His vivacious wife became one of Johnson's closest friends, and at the Thrales' suburban house in Streatham he visited them for long periods. The friendship with Mrs. Thrale ended shortly before Johnson's death in 1784 when, three years after her husband's death, she married an Italian music teacher named Gabriel Piozzi. Johnson disapproved of the marriage and broke with her. In 1774 he had traveled in France with the Thrales, and in the preceding year made in Boswell's company his famous journey through Scotland to some of the primitive islands of the Hebrides. Two books were the fruit of this northern excursion: Johnson's *Journey to the Western Islands of Scotland* (1775) and Boswell's *Journal of a Tour to the Hebrides* (1785). The last of Johnson's important works was *The Lives of the Most Eminent English Poets, with Critical Observations on Their Works* (1779–81); it is discussed below, in the headnote to extracts from the Life of Pope.

It is in Boswell that Johnson is alive for the twentieth-century reading public, and to Boswell we shall come in a few pages. But even Boswell does not give us all of Johnson. Great as his portrait is, it is a portrait, not a photograph. Boswell's conception is *his* conception. It would be a mistake not to sample the writings that Johnson himself has left us.

Johnson's collected works were first published in 1787, and like the *Dictionary* were often reprinted till about the middle of the nineteenth century. The *Preface* to his edition of Shakespeare is given, along with a selection of his notes, in W. Raleigh's *Johnson on Shakespeare* (1916). The standard edition of the poems is by D. N. Smith and E. L. McAdam (1941), and of *The Lives of the Poets* by G. B. Hill (3rd ed. of Hill's ed., 3 vols., 1905). Hill also edited the letters (2 vols., 1892). R. W. Chapman edited *Rasselas* (1927) and the *Journey to the Western Islands* (1930). Two

handy volumes of general selections are C. H. Conley's *The Reader's Johnson* (1940) and C. G. Osgood's *Selections from the Works of Samuel Johnson* (1909); each includes some of the periodical essays. The World's Classics reprints selected letters and *The Lives of the Poets* (2 vols.), and the latter also appears in Everyman's Library (2 vols.). The standard edition of James Boswell's *Life of Johnson* is by G. B. Hill (revised ed. by L. F. Powell, 6 vols., in progress, 1934—; 4 vols. thus far, completing the text of the *Life*). There is a recent Life by J. W. Krutch (1944). Useful studies are J. Bailey's *Dr. Johnson and His Circle* (Home University Library, no. 59) and W. Raleigh's *Six Essays on Johnson* (1910).

Samuel Johnson

PROLOGUE

SPOKEN BY MR. GARRICK AT THE OPENING OF THE THEATER IN DRURY LANE, 1747

ON September 15, 1747, David Garrick began his long reign as manager of the Theater Royal with a revival of *The Merchant of Venice*. Prologues had long before become a verse genre of some importance; Dryden, for instance, had written a good many. Two lines of Johnson's poem (53 f.) have become proverbial.

When Learning's triumph o'er her barb'rous foes
First reared the stage, immortal Shakespeare rose;
Each change of many-colored life he drew,
Exhausted worlds, and then imagined new:
Existence saw him spurn her bounded reign,   5
And panting Time toiled after him in vain;
His pow'rful strokes presiding truth impressed,
And unresisted passion stormed the breast.
    Then Jonson came, instructed from the school,
To please in method and invent by rule;   10
His studious patience and laborious art
By regular approach essayed the heart;
Cold approbation gave the ling'ring bays,[1]
For those who durst not censure scarce could praise.
A mortal born, he met the gen'ral doom,   15
But left, like Egypt's kings, a lasting tomb.
    The wits of Charles[2] found easier ways to fame,
Nor wished for Jonson's art or Shakespeare's flame;
Themselves they studied; as they felt, they writ;
Intrigue was plot, obscenity was wit.   20

Vice always found a sympathetic friend;
They pleased their age, and did not aim to mend.
Yet bards like these aspired to lasting praise,
And proudly hoped to pimp in future days.
Their cause was gen'ral, their supports were strong;   25
Their slaves were willing, and their reign was long:
Till shame regained the post that sense betrayed,
And virtue called oblivion to her aid.
    Then, crushed by rules, and weakened as refined,
For years the pow'r of tragedy declined;   30
From bard to bard the frigid caution crept,
Till declamation roared, while passion slept.
Yet still did virtue deign the stage to tread;
Philosophy remained though nature fled.
But forced at length her ancient reign to quit,   35
She saw great Faustus[3] lay the ghost of wit:
Exulting folly hailed the joyous day,
And pantomime and song confirmed her sway.
    But who the coming changes can presage,
And mark the future periods of the stage?   40
Perhaps if skill could distant times explore,
New Behns,[4] new Durfeys,[5] yet remain in store.

[3] Marlowe's *Doctor Faustus* was degraded in successive adaptations. Pope had complained against the practice of playing a *Faustus* farce as an after-piece.
[4] Mrs. Aphra Behn (1640–89), the first Englishwoman to become a professional writer; she was the author of indecent plays.
[5] Thomas D'Urfey (1653–1723), a minor dramatist and songwriter, also notorious for the obscenity of his works.

---

[1] I.e., hesitantly granted the poet's crown.
[2] In the time of Charles II.

Perhaps where Lear has raved and Hamlet died,
On flying cars[6] new sorcerers may ride.
Perhaps (for who can guess th' effects of chance?)   45
Here Hunt[7] may box, or Mahomet[8] may dance.

   Hard is his lot that, here by fortune placed,
Must watch the wild vicissitudes of taste:
With ev'ry meteor of caprice must play,
And chase the new-blown bubbles of the day.   50
Ah! let not censure term our fate our choice;
The stage but echoes back the public voice.

The drama's laws the drama's patrons give,
For we that live to please must please to live.
   Then prompt no more the follies you decry,   55
As tyrants doom their tools of guilt to die;
'Tis yours this night to bid the reign commence
Of rescued nature and reviving sense;
To chase the charms of sound, the pomp of show,
For useful mirth and salutary woe;   60
Bid scenic virtue form the rising age,
And truth diffuse her radiance from the stage.

THE VANITY OF HUMAN WISHES

THE subtitle is "The Tenth Satire of Juvenal Imitated";
Johnson's indebtedness to the Roman poet is not, however,
very serious. This is not a great poem; but it is finely eloquent, and a good example of rimed couplets handled with
strength and feeling instead of mere smoothness. Here we
are at the opposite pole from Pope's cheery assurances in
An Essay on Man; Johnson's attitude toward life is more
rugged and (many will feel) more realistic. The subject,
treated again in *Rasselas,* was never far from Johnson's
thought; it weighed also on his heart. On one occasion
when he was reading the poem aloud to some friends, he
burst into tears when he came to the passage (lines 135 ff.)
on the scholar's lot. The situation was saved by one of his
hearers, who "clapped him on the back and said, 'What's
all this, my dear sir? Why, you and I and Hercules, you
know, were all troubled with melancholy.'" The poem
appeared in 1749. Johnson revised it for the *Collection of
Poems* made by the publisher Dodsley (1755), and the
present text is based on the later edition.

Let observation, with extensive view,
Survey mankind, from China to Peru;
Remark each anxious toil, each eager strife,
And watch the busy scenes of crowded life;
Then say how hope and fear, desire and hate,   5
O'erspread with snares the clouded maze of fate,
Where wav'ring man, betrayed by vent'rous pride
To tread the dreary paths without a guide,
As treach'rous phantoms in the mist delude,
Shuns fancied ills, or chases airy[1] good.   10
How rarely reason guides the stubborn choice,
Rules the bold hand, or prompts the suppliant voice;
How nations sink, by darling schemes oppressed,
When vengeance listens to the fool's request.

Fate wings with ev'ry wish th'afflictive dart,   15
Each gift of nature, and each grace of art;
With fatal heat impetuous courage glows,
With fatal sweetness elocution flows;
Impeachment stops the speaker's pow'rful breath,
And restless fire precipitates on death.   20
   But scarce observed, the knowing and the bold
Fall in the gen'ral massacre of gold;
Wide-wasting pest! that rages unconfined,
And crowds with crimes the records of mankind;
For gold his sword the hireling ruffian draws,   25
For gold the hireling judge distorts the laws;
Wealth heaped on wealth nor truth nor safety buys:
The dangers gather as the treasures rise.
   Let hist'ry tell, where rival kings command,
And dubious title shakes the maddened land,   30
When statutes glean the refuse of the sword,[2]
How much more safe the vassal than the lord;
Low skulks the hind[3] beneath the rage of pow'r,
And leaves the wealthy traitor in the Tow'r,
Untouched his cottage, and his slumbers sound,   35
Though confiscation's[4] vultures hover round.
   The needy traveler, serene and gay,
Walks the wild heath, and sings his toil away.
Does envy seize thee? crush th'upbraiding joy,
Increase his riches, and his peace destroy;   40
Now fears in dire vicissitude invade,
The rustling brake alarms, and quiv'ring shade;
Nor light nor darkness bring his pain relief:
One shows the plunder, and one hides the thief.
   Yet still one gen'ral cry the skies assails,   45
And gain and grandeur load the tainted gales;[5]

---

[6] Stage chariots suspended in the air.
[7] Edward Hunt, a well-known lightweight.
[8] A ropedancer who had performed at Covent Garden Theater
the season before.

[1] I.e., unreal.

[2] I.e., special acts (bills of attainder) are passed for the execution
of surviving leaders of the opposition. Johnson has in mind the
punishments which followed the Jacobite rising of 1745.
[3] Peasant.   [4] The estates of a traitor were forfeit.
[5] I.e., the wind bears the scent.

Few know the toiling statesman's fear or care,
Th'insidious rival and the gaping heir.[6]

Once more, Democritus,[7] arise on earth,
With cheerful wisdom and instructive mirth;   50
See motley life in modern trappings dressed,
And feed with varied fools th'eternal jest:
Thou who couldst laugh where want enchained caprice,
Toil crushed conceit,[8] and man was of a piece;
Where wealth unloved without a mourner died,   55
And scarce a sycophant was fed by pride;
Where ne'er was known the form of mock debate,[9]
Or seen a new-made mayor's unwieldy state;[10]
Where change of fav'rites made no change of laws,
And senates heard before they judged a cause;   60
How wouldst thou shake at Britain's modish tribe,
Dart the quick taunt, and edge the piercing gibe?
Attentive truth and nature to descry,
And pierce each scene with philosophic eye,
To thee were solemn toys, or empty show,   65
The robes of pleasure and the veils of woe:
All aid the farce, and all thy mirth maintain,
Whose joys are causeless or whose griefs are vain.

Such was the scorn that filled the sage's mind,
Renewed at ev'ry glance on humankind;   70
How just that scorn ere yet thy voice declare,
Search ev'ry state, and canvass ev'ry pray'r.

Unnumbered suppliants crowd Preferment's gate,
Athirst for wealth, and burning to be great;
Delusive Fortune hears th'incessant call;   75
They mount, they shine, evaporate, and fall.
On ev'ry stage the foes of peace attend;
Hate dogs their flight, and insult mocks their end.
Love ends with hope: the sinking statesman's door
Pours in the morning worshiper no more;   80
For growing names the weekly scribbler lies,
To growing wealth the dedicator flies;
From ev'ry room descends the painted face
That hung the bright palladium[11] of the place,
And, smoked in kitchens, or in auctions sold,   85
To better features yields the frame of gold;
For now no more we trace in ev'ry line
Heroic worth, benevolence divine:

The form distorted justifies the fall,
And detestation rids th'indignant wall.   90
But will not Britain hear the last appeal,
Sign her foes' doom, or guard her fav'rites' zeal?
Through Freedom's sons no more remonstrance[12] rings,
Degrading nobles and controlling kings;
Our supple tribes repress their patriot throats,   95
And ask no questions but the price of votes;
With weekly libels[13] and septennial ale,[14]
Their wish is full to riot and to rail.

In full-blown dignity see Wolsey[15] stand,
Law in his voice and fortune in his hand;   100
To him the church, the realm, their pow'rs consign;
Through him the rays of regal bounty shine;
Turned by his nod the stream of honor flows;
His smile alone security bestows:
Still to new heights his restless wishes tow'r,   105
Claim leads to claim, and pow'r advances pow'r;
Till conquest unresisted ceased to please,
And rights submitted left him none to seize.
At length his sov'reign frowns—the train of state
Mark the keen glance, and watch the sign of hate.   110
Where'er he turns he meets a stranger's eye,
His suppliants scorn him, and his followers fly;
At once is lost the pride of awful state,
The golden canopy, the glitt'ring plate,
The regal palace,[16] the luxurious board,   115
The liv'ried army, and the menial lord.
With age, with cares, with maladies oppressed,
He seeks the refuge of monastic rest.
Grief aids disease, remembered folly stings,
And his last sighs reproach the faith of kings.   120

Speak thou, whose thoughts at humble peace repine,
Shall Wolsey's wealth, with Wolsey's end, be thine?
Or liv'st thou now, with safer pride content,
The wisest justice on the banks of Trent?[17]
For why did Wolsey, near the steeps of fate,   125
On weak foundations raise th'enormous weight?
Why but to sink, beneath misfortune's blow,
With louder ruin to the gulfs below?

6 Frederick, Prince of Wales, was in opposition to his father, George II, but died before him. He had "gaped" for nine years; but the next king was Frederick's son, George III.
7 The Greek (fifth century B.C.) known as the laughing philosopher.   8 Mere opinion.
9 I.e., debate in Parliament was merely a matter of form, since the administration was in control and had already made its decision.
10 The "lord mayor's show," a festive procession, is still one of London's annual events.
11 Safeguard, symbol of protection. I.e., the patron's portrait is taken off the wall.

12 Against tyranny. Such as the Grand Remonstrance adopted by the House of Commons and presented to Charles I in 1641.
13 In the political journals.
14 Dispensed by candidates at elections every seven years, the term of the House of Commons.
15 Thomas, Cardinal Wolsey (d. 1530), was Henry VIII's chief minister of state till he was dismissed in disgrace for failing to push the King's divorce.
16 Wolsey built Hampton Court, a finer palace than any belonging to the King, to whom he was eventually obliged to present it.
17 Lichfield is near the Trent. Johnson is contrasting conspicuous wealth and power with the obscure, useful work of a provincial justice of the peace.

What gave great Villiers[18] to th'assassin's knife,
And fixed disease on Harley's[19] closing life? 130
What murdered Wentworth,[20] and what exiled Hyde,[21]
By kings protected, and to kings allied?
What but their wish indulged in courts to shine,
And pow'r too great to keep, or to resign?

When first the college rolls receive his name, 135
The young enthusiast quits his ease for fame;
Through all his veins the fever of renown
Burns from the strong contagion of the gown;
O'er Bodley's dome[22] his future labors spread,
And Bacon's mansion[23] trembles o'er his head. 140
Are these thy views? Proceed, illustrious youth,
And Virtue guard thee to the throne of Truth!
Yet, should thy soul indulge the gen'rous heat
Till captive Science yields her last retreat;
Should Reason guide thee with her brightest ray, 145
And pour on misty doubt resistless day;
Should no false kindness lure to loose delight,
Nor praise relax, nor difficulty fright;
Should tempting Novelty thy cell refrain,
And Sloth effuse her opiate fumes in vain; 150
Should Beauty blunt on fops her fatal dart,
Nor claim the triumph of a lettered heart;
Should no disease thy torpid veins invade,
Nor melancholy's phantoms haunt thy shade;
Yet hope not life from grief or danger free, 155
Nor think the doom of man reversed for thee:
Deign on the passing world to turn thine eyes,
And pause awhile from letters, to be wise;
There mark what ills the scholar's life assail,
Toil, envy, want, the patron, and the jail. 160
See nations, slowly wise and meanly just,
To buried merit raise the tardy bust.
If dreams yet flatter, once again attend;
Here Lydiat's[24] life, and Galileo's end.[25]

Nor deem, when Learning her vast prize bestows, 165
The glitt'ring eminence exempt from foes;
See, when the vulgar 'scape, despised or awed,
Rebellion's vengeful talons seize on Laud:[26]
From meaner minds, though smaller fines content,
The plundered palace or sequestered rent,[27] 170
Marked out by dang'rous parts[28] he meets the shock,
And fatal Learning leads him to the block:
Around his tomb let Art and Genius weep,
But hear his death, ye blockheads, hear and sleep.

The festal blazes, the triumphal show, 175
The ravished standard, and the captive foe,
The senate's thanks, the gázette's[29] pompous tale,
With force resistless o'er the brave prevail
Such bribes the rapid Greek[30] o'er Asia whirled;
For such the steady Romans shook the world; 180
For such in distant lands the Britons shine,
And stain with blood the Danube or the Rhine;[31]
This pow'r has praise, that virtue scarce can warm,
Till fame supplies the universal charm.
Yet Reason frowns on war's unequal game, 185
Where wasted nations raise a single name,
And mortgaged states their grandsires' wreaths regret,
From age to age in everlasting debt;
Wreaths which at last the dear-bought right convey
To rust on medals, or on stones decay. 190

On what foundation stands the warrior's pride,
How just his hopes, let Swedish Charles[32] decide;
A frame of adamant, a soul of fire,
No dangers fright him, and no labors tire;
O'er love, o'er fear, extends his wide domain, 195
Unconquered lord of pleasure and of pain;
No joys to him pacific scepters yield:
War sounds the trump, he rushes to the field;
Behold surrounding kings their pow'r combine,
And one capitulate, and one resign;[33] 200
Peace courts his hand, but spreads her charms in vain;
"Think nothing gained," he cries, "till nought remain,
On Moscow's walls till Gothic[34] standards fly,

---

18 George Villiers (1592–1628), first Duke of Buckingham, favorite of James I and Charles I.
19 Robert Harley (1661–1724), Earl of Oxford, the Tory leader. His bad health was not, however, due to his party's fall in 1714.
20 Thomas Wentworth (1593–1641), Earl of Strafford, principal minister of Charles I, who tried to protect him but was forced to allow Parliament to execute him.
21 The historian and statesman Edward Hyde (1609–74), first Earl of Clarendon, lord chancellor of Charles II, but exiled in 1667. The Duke of York, afterwards James II, was his son-in-law. Queens Mary and Anne were his granddaughters.
22 The Bodleian, the university library at Oxford.
23 Friar Roger Bacon, the great thirteenth-century scientist, was said to have lived in a certain gatehouse on a bridge at Oxford. There was a tradition that he had arranged by his magic that it should fall when a greater man than he should pass under it.
24 Thomas Lydiat (1572–1646), an Oxford mathematician and Biblical scholar; his reputation and his poverty were great.
25 Galileo (1564–1642), the eminent Italian scientist, was imprisoned by the Inquisition during his last years.

26 William Laud (1573–1645), Archbishop of Canterbury. For his persecution of the Puritan clergy he was executed by Parliament. Johnson's High-Church views are obvious here.
27 Confiscated income.   28 Accomplishments.
29 The Gazette was the government newspaper. In his Dictionary Johnson puts the accent on the first syllable.
30 Alexander the Great.
31 A reference to the campaigns of Marlborough (1702–4) early in the War of the Spanish Succession. No doubt his is the "single name" of line 186. The War of the Austrian Succession may also be meant; the British had campaigned along the Rhine.
32 Charles XII (1682–1718). This warrior king beat the Danes, Poles, and Saxons, but was defeated at Pultowa in 1709 by the Russians under Peter the Great.
33 Frederick IV of Denmark capitulated; Augustus II, Elector of Saxony, was deposed from his Polish throne.
34 I.e., Swedish.

And all be mine beneath the polar sky."
The march begins in military state,   205
And nations on his eye suspended wait;
Stern Famine guards the solitary coast,
And Winter barricades the realms of Frost;
He comes, nor want nor cold his course delay—
Hide, blushing Glory, hide Pultowa's day: 210
The vanquished hero leaves his broken bands,
And shows his miseries in distant lands;[35]
Condemned a needy supplicant to wait,
While ladies interpose, and slaves debate.[36]
But did not Chance at length her error mend?   215
Did no subverted empire mark his end?
Did rival monarchs give the fatal wound?
Or hostile millions press him to the ground?
His fall was destined to a barren strand,
A petty fortress, and a dubious hand;[37]   220
He left the name at which the world grew pale
To point a moral, or adorn a tale.

All times their scenes of pompous woes afford,
From Persia's tyrant[38] to Bavaria's lord.[39]
In gay hostility and barb'rous pride,   225
With half mankind embattled at his side,
Great Xerxes comes to seize the certain prey,
And starves exhausted regions in his way;
Attendant Flatt'ry counts his myriads o'er,
Till counted myriads soothe his pride no more;   230
Fresh praise is tried till madness fires his mind,
The waves he lashes,[40] and enchains the wind.
New pow'rs are claimed, new pow'rs are still bestowed,
Till rude resistance lops the spreading god;
The daring Greeks deride the martial show,   235
And heap their valleys with the gaudy foe;[41]
Th' insulted sea with humbler thoughts he gains:
A single skiff to speed his flight remains;
Th' encumbered oar scarce leaves the dreaded coast
Through purple[42] billows and a floating host.   240

The bold Bavarian, in a luckless hour,
Tries the dread summits of Caesarean pow'r,
With unexpected legions bursts away,
And sees defenseless realms receive his sway.
Short sway! fair Austria[43] spreads her mournful charms,
The queen, the beauty, sets the world in arms;   246
From hill to hill the beacon's rousing blaze
Spreads wide the hope of plunder and of praise;
The fierce Croatian and the wild hussar,[44]
With all the sons of ravage, crowd the war;   250
The baffled prince, in honor's flatt'ring bloom
Of hasty greatness, finds the fatal doom,
His foes' derision, and his subjects' blame,
And steals to death from anguish and from shame.

"Enlarge my life with multitude of days!"   255
In health, in sickness, thus the suppliant prays;
Hides from himself his state, and shuns to know
That life protracted is protracted woe.
Time hovers o'er, impatient to destroy,
And shuts up all the passages of joy: 260
In vain their gifts the bounteous seasons pour,
The fruit autumnal, and the vernal flow'r;
With listless eyes the dotard views the store,
He views, and wonders that they please no more.
Now pall the tasteless meats and joyless wines,   265
And Luxury with sighs her slave resigns.
Approach, ye minstrels, try the soothing strain;
Diffuse the tuneful lenitives[45] of pain:
No sounds, alas, would teach th'impervious ear,
Though dancing mountains witnessed Orpheus near;[46]
Nor lute nor lyre his feeble pow'rs attend,[47]   271
Nor sweeter music of a virtuous friend;
But everlasting dictates crowd his tongue,
Perversely grave, or positively wrong.
The still-returning tale and ling'ring jest   275
Perplex the fawning niece and pampered guest,
While growing hopes scarce awe the gath'ring sneer,
And scarce a legacy can bribe to hear;
The watchful guests still hint the last offense;
The daughter's petulance, the son's expense,   280
Improve[48] his heady rage with treach'rous skill,
And mold his passions till they make his will.

Unnumbered maladies his joints invade,
Lay siege to life, and press the dire blockade;
But unextinguished Avarice still remains,   285
And dreaded losses aggravate his pains;

---

[35] Charles spent five years in exile in Turkey.
[36] I.e., in the midst of the political intrigues of court.
[37] Charles died on a minor campaign in Norway.
[38] Xerxes, king of Persia. The naval battle was the great Greek victory at Salamis in 480 B.C.
[39] Charles Albert, Elector of Bavaria, died in 1745. His attempt to wrest the crown of the Empire from the rightful heiress, Queen Maria Theresa of Austria (1717–80), led to the War of the Austrian Succession, which ended in 1748, a few months before Johnson's poem appeared. The Elector was backed by France, Spain, Prussia, Saxony, and Poland (all shamelessly on the make), and opposed by England and Holland. This was the struggle known in American colonial history as "King George's War" against the French and Indians.
[40] He is said to have ordered the sea scourged when a bridge of boats at the Dardanelles was smashed by the currents.
[41] When Leonidas with 300 Spartans held back the army of Xerxes for three days at Thermopylae.
[42] Red with the blood of the Persians killed at Salamis.

[43] Maria Theresa. She appealed successfully to the loyalty of her Hungarian and Croatian subjects.
[44] Originally a Hungarian light cavalryman.
[45] Palliatives, remedies.
[46] According to fable, Orpheus could move inanimate objects with his music.   [47] Regard.   [48] Increase.

He turns, with anxious heart and crippled hands,
His bonds of debt and mortgages of lands,
Or views his coffers with suspicious eyes,
Unlocks his gold, and counts it till he dies.   290

But grant the virtues of a temp'rate prime
Bless with an age exempt from scorn and crime,
An age that melts with unperceived decay,
And glides in modest innocence away;
Whose peaceful day benevolence endears,   295
Whose night congratulating conscience cheers,
The gen'ral fav'rite as the gen'ral friend:
Such age there is, and who shall wish its end?

Yet ev'n on this her load Misfortune flings,
To press the weary minutes' flagging wings;   300
New sorrow rises as the day returns,
A sister sickens, or a daughter mourns.
Now kindred merit fills the sable bier;
Now lacerated friendship claims a tear.
Year chases year, decay pursues decay: 305
Still drops some joy from with'ring life away;
New forms arise, and diff'rent views engage,
Superfluous lags the vet'ran on the stage,
Till pitying Nature signs the last release,
And bids afflicted worth retire to peace.   310

But few there are whom hours like these await,
Who set unclouded in the gulfs of fate.
From Lydia's monarch[49] should the search descend,
By Solon cautioned to regard his end,
In life's last scene what prodigies surprise,   315
Fears of the brave, and follies of the wise!
From Marlb'rough's eyes the streams of dotage flow,
And Swift expires a driv'ler and a show.[50]

The teeming mother anxious for her race
Begs for each birth the fortune of a face;   320
Yet Vane[51] could tell what ills from beauty spring;
And Sedley[52] cursed the form that pleased a king.
Ye nymphs of rosy lips and radiant eyes,
Whom pleasure keeps too busy to be wise,
Whom joys with soft varieties invite,   325
By day the frolic, and the dance by night,
Who frown with vanity, who smile with art,

And ask the latest fashion of the heart:
What care, what rules, your heedless charms shall save,
Each nymph your rival, and each youth your slave?   330
Against your fame with fondness hate combines,
The rival batters, and the lover mines.[53]
With distant voice neglected Virtue calls;
Less heard and less, the faint remonstrance falls;
Tired with contempt, she quits the slipp'ry reign,   335
And Pride and Prudence take her seat in vain.
In crowd at once, where none the pass defend,
The harmless Freedom, and the private Friend.
The guardians yield, by force superior plied;
By Int'rest, Prudence; and by Flatt'ry, Pride.   340
Now Beauty falls betrayed, despised, distressed;
And hissing Infamy proclaims the rest.

Where then shall Hope and Fear their objects find?
Must dull Suspense corrupt the stagnant mind?
Must helpless man, in ignorance sedate,   345
Roll darkling down the torrent of his fate?
Must no dislike alarm, no wishes rise,
No cries attempt the mercies of the skies?
Enquirer, cease; petitions yet remain,
Which heav'n may hear; nor deem religion vain.   350
Still raise for good the supplicating voice,
But leave to heav'n the measure and the choice,
Safe in his pow'r whose eyes discern afar
The secret ambush of a specious pray'r.
Implore his aid, in his decisions rest;   355
Secure[54] whate'er he gives, he gives the best.
Yet when the sense of sacred presence fires,
And strong devotion to the skies aspires,
Pour forth thy fervors for a healthful mind,
Obedient passions, and a will resigned;   360
For love, which scarce collective man can fill;
For patience, sov'reign o'er transmuted ill;
For faith, that, panting for a happier seat,
Counts death kind Nature's signal of retreat:
These goods for man the laws of heav'n ordain;   365
These goods he grants who grants the pow'r to gain;
With these celestial wisdom calms the mind,
And makes the happiness she does not find.

---

[49] Croesus. Solon (d. 559 B.C.), the Athenian sage, refused to call this king of Lydia happy since his end was still unknown.

[50] Swift lost his mind toward the end of his life. According to an unauthenticated story his servants used to exhibit him for a fee.

[51] Anne Vane, the deserted mistress of Frederick, Prince of Wales (note 6, above).

[52] Catherine Sedley, Countess of Dorchester, daughter of the Restoration poet, and mistress of James II but discarded before his accession.

[53] Another figure from siege warfare.
[54] Certain that.

THERE were 208 numbers of the *Rambler,* nearly all by Johnson. It ran, as a separate periodical, from March, 1750, to March, 1752. Johnson's contributions to the *Adventurer* were few; but the *Idler* also ran two years, from April, 1758, to April, 1760. These later papers appeared weekly in the *Universal Chronicle and Weekly Register.* Johnson's periodical essays are obviously modeled on the *Tatler* and *Spectator;* the main difference is that the emphasis of Addison and Steele is on manners, Johnson's on morals. Most of his essays are heavy-handed, but he is worth listening to because his idealism is not cloistered. Here, as in everything he wrote, Johnson draws on his extraordinary knowledge of the world.

THE NOVEL

THE RAMBLER, NO. 4 *Saturday,* MARCH 31, 1750

Simul et jucunda et idonea dicere vitae.[1]
HORACE, *Art of Poetry,* line 334

THE works of fiction with which the present generation seems more particularly delighted are such as exhibit life in its true state, diversified only by accidents that daily happen in the world, and influenced by passions and qualities which are really to be found in conversing with mankind.[2]

This kind of writing may be termed not improperly the comedy of romance, and is to be conducted nearly by the rules of comic poetry. Its province is to bring about natural events by easy means, and to keep up curiosity without the help of wonder: it is therefore precluded from the machines and expedients of the heroic romance, and can neither employ giants to snatch away a lady from the nuptial rites, nor knights to bring her back from captivity; it can neither bewilder its personages in deserts, nor lodge them in imaginary castles.

I remember a remark made by Scaliger upon Pontanus,[3] that all his writings are filled with the same images; and that if you take from him his lilies and his roses, his satyrs and his dryads,[4] he will have nothing left that can be called poetry. In like manner almost all the fictions of the last age will vanish if you deprive them of a hermit and a wood, a battle and a shipwreck.

Why this wild strain of imagination found reception so long in polite and learned ages, it is not easy to conceive; but we cannot wonder that while readers could be procured the authors were willing to continue it; for when a man had by practice gained some fluency of language, he had no further care than to retire to his closet, let loose his invention, and heat his mind with incredibilities; a book was thus produced without fear of criticism, without the toil of study, without knowledge of nature, or acquaintance with life.

The task of our present writers is very different; it requires, together with that learning which is to be gained from books, that experience which can never be attained by solitary diligence, but must arise from general converse and accurate observation of the living world. Their performances have, as Horace expresses it, *plus oneris quantum veniae minus,* little indulgence, and therefore more difficulty.[5] They are engaged in portraits of which everyone knows the original, and can detect any deviation from exactness of resemblance. Other writings are safe except from the malice of learning, but these are in danger from every common reader; as the slipper ill executed was censured by a shoemaker, who happened to stop in his way at the Venus of Apelles.[6]

But the fear of not being approved as just copiers of human manners is not the most important concern that an author of this sort ought to have before him. These books are written chiefly to the young, the ignorant, and the idle, to whom they serve as lectures of conduct and introductions into life. They are the entertainment of minds unfurnished with ideas, and therefore easily susceptible of impressions; not fixed by principles, and therefore easily following the current of fancy; not informed by experience, and consequently open to every false suggestion and partial account.

That the highest degree of reverence should be paid to youth, and that nothing indecent should be

[1] And join both profit and delight in one (Creech's translation).
[2] Johnson was probably thinking of the recent success of two racy and relatively realistic novels, Tobias Smollett's *Roderick Random* (1748) and Henry Fielding's *Tom Jones* (1749). Johnson preferred the milder and more psychological novels of Samuel Richardson, whose *Pamela* and *Clarissa* had appeared in 1740–41 and 1747–48.
[3] Julius Caesar Scaliger (1484–1558), an eminent Italian scholar, comments in his *Poetics* on the style of the Italian poet Jovianus Pontanus (1426–1503).
[4] Sylvan deities and wood nymphs, in classical mythology.
[5] *Sed habet comoedia tanto plus oneris quanto veniae minus* (*Epistles,* II, i, 170). Horace makes the point that comedy, supposedly easy because it rests on observation of daily life, is really difficult and judged the more severely by the critics.
[6] The most famous of the ancient Greek painters (fourth century B.C.).

suffered to approach their eyes or ears, are precepts extorted by sense and virtue from an ancient writer,[7] by no means eminent for chastity of thought. The same kind, though not the same degree, of caution, is required in everything which is laid before them, to secure them from unjust prejudices, perverse opinions, and incongruous combinations of images.

In the romances formerly written, every transaction and sentiment was so remote from all that passes among men that the reader was in very little danger of making any applications to himself; the virtues and crimes were equally beyond his sphere of activity; and he amused himself with heroes and with traitors, deliverers and persecutors, as with beings of another species, whose actions were regulated upon motives of their own, and who had neither faults nor excellencies in common with himself.

But when an adventurer is leveled with the rest of the world, and acts in such scenes of the universal drama as may be the lot of any other man, young spectators fix their eyes upon him with closer attention, and hope, by observing his behavior and success, to regulate their own practices, when they shall be engaged in the like part.

For this reason these familiar histories may perhaps be made of greater use than the solemnities of professed morality, and convey the knowledge of vice and virtue with more efficacy than axioms and definitions. But if the power of example is so great as to take possession of the memory by a kind of violence, and produce effects almost without the intervention of the will, care ought to be taken that, when the choice is unrestrained, the best examples only should be exhibited; and that which is likely to operate so strongly should not be mischievous or uncertain in its effects.

The chief advantage which these fictions have over real life is that their authors are at liberty, though not to invent, yet to select objects, and to cull from the mass of mankind those individuals upon which the attention ought most to be employed; as a diamond, though it cannot be made, may be polished by art, and placed in such a situation as to display that luster which before was buried among common stones.

It is justly considered as the greatest excellency of art, to imitate nature; but it is necessary to distinguish those parts of nature which are most proper for imitation: greater care is still required in representing life, which is so often discolored by passion or deformed by wickedness. If the world be promiscuously described, I cannot see of what use it can be to read the account; or why it may not be as safe to turn the eye immediately upon mankind as upon a mirror which shows all that presents itself without discrimination.

It is therefore not a sufficient vindication of a character, that it is drawn as it appears, for many characters ought never to be drawn; nor of a narrative, that the train of events is agreeable to observation and experience, for that observation which is called knowledge of the world, will be found much more frequently to make men cunning than good. The purpose of these writings is surely not only to show mankind, but to provide that they may be seen hereafter with less hazard; to teach the means of avoiding the snares which are laid by TREACHERY for INNOCENCE, without infusing any wish for that superiority with which the betrayer flatters his vanity; to give the power of counteracting fraud, without the temptation to practice it; to initiate youth by mock encounters in the art of necessary defense, and to increase prudence without impairing virtue.

Many writers, for the sake of following nature, so mingle good and bad qualities in their principal personages that they are both equally conspicuous; and as we accompany them through their adventures with delight, and are led by degrees to interest ourselves in their favor, we lose the abhorrence of their faults, because they do not hinder our pleasure, or, perhaps, regard them with some kindness for being united with so much merit.[8]

There have been men indeed splendidly wicked, whose endowments threw a brightness on their crimes, and whom scarce any villainy made perfectly detestable, because they never could be wholly divested of their excellencies; but such have been in all ages the great corrupters of the world, and their resemblance ought no more to be preserved than the art of murdering without pain.

Some have advanced, without due attention to the consequence of this notion, that certain virtues have their correspondent faults, and therefore that to exhibit either apart is to deviate from probability. Thus men are observed by Swift to be "grateful in the same degree as they are resentful." This principle, with others of the same kind, supposes man to act from a brute impulse, and pursue a certain degree of inclination, without any choice of the object; for,

---

[7] Juvenal (d. 140? A.D.), *Satires*, XIV.

[8] Tom Jones is a good example.

otherwise, though it should be allowed that gratitude and resentment arise from the same constitution of the passions, it follows not that they will be equally indulged when reason is consulted; yet unless that consequence be admitted, this sagacious maxim becomes an empty sound, without any relation to practice or to life.

Nor is it evident that even the first motions to these effects are always in the same proportion. For pride, which produces quickness of resentment, will obstruct gratitude by unwillingness to admit that inferiority which obligation implies; and it is very unlikely that he who cannot think he receives a favor will acknowledge or repay it.

It is of the utmost importance to mankind that positions of this tendency should be laid open and confuted; for while men consider good and evil as springing from the same root, they will spare the one for the sake of the other, and in judging, if not of others, at least of themselves, will be apt to estimate their virtues by their vices. To this fatal error all those will contribute who confound the colors of right and wrong, and, instead of helping to settle their boundaries, mix them with so much art that no common mind is able to disunite them.

In narratives where historical veracity has no place, I cannot discover why there should not be exhibited the most perfect idea of virtue: of virtue not angelical, nor above probability, for what we cannot credit we shall never imitate, but the highest and purest that humanity can reach; which, exercised in such trials as the various revolutions of things shall bring upon it, may, by conquering some calamities and enduring others, teach us what we may hope and what we can perform. Vice, for vice is necessary to be shown, should always disgust; nor should the graces of gaiety, or the dignity of courage, be so united with it as to reconcile it to the mind. Wherever it appears, it should raise hatred by the malignity of its practices, and contempt by the meanness of its stratagems: for while it is supported by either parts or spirit, it will be seldom heartily abhorred. The Roman tyrant[9] was content to be hated, if he was but feared; and there are thousands of the readers of romances willing to be thought wicked, if they may be allowed to be wits. It is therefore to be steadily inculcated that virtue is the highest proof of understanding, and the only solid basis of greatness; and that vice is the natural consequence of narrow thoughts; that it begins in mistake, and ends in ignominy.

---

[9] The Emperor Caligula (d. 41 A.D.).

SPRING

THE RAMBLER, NO. 5   *Tuesday*, APRIL 3, 1750

Et nunc omnis ager, nunc omnis parturit arbos,
Nunc frondent silvae, nunc formosissimus annus.[10]
VERGIL, *Eclogues*, III, 56–7

EVERY man is sufficiently discontented with some circumstances of his present state to suffer his imagination to range more or less in quest of future happiness, and to fix upon some point of time in which, by the removal of the inconvenience which now perplexes him, or acquisition of the advantage which he at present wants, he shall find the condition of his life very much improved.

When this time, which is too often expected with great impatience, at last arrives, it generally comes without the blessing for which it was desired; but we solace ourselves with some new prospect, and press forward again with equal eagerness.

It is lucky for a man in whom this temper prevails, when he turns his hopes upon things wholly out of his own power; since he forbears then to precipitate his affairs for the sake of the great event that is to complete his felicity, and waits for the blissful hour with less neglect of the measures necessary to be taken in the meantime.

I have long known a person of this temper, who indulged his dream of happiness with less hurt to himself than such chimerical wishes commonly produce and adjusted his scheme with such address that his hopes were in full bloom three parts of the year, and in the other part never wholly blasted. Many, perhaps, would be desirous of learning by what means he procured to himself such a cheap and lasting satisfaction. It was gained by a constant practice of referring the removal of all his uneasiness to the coming of the next spring; if his health was impaired, the spring would restore it; if what he wanted was at a high price, it would fall its value in the spring.

The spring indeed did often come without any of these effects, but he was always certain that the next would be more propitious; nor was ever convinced that the present spring would fail him before the middle of summer; for he always talked of the spring as coming till it was past, and when it was once past everyone agreed with him that it was coming.

By long converse with this man, I am, perhaps,

---

[10] Now ev'ry field, now ev'ry tree, is green;
Now genial Nature's fairest face is seen.
(Elphinston's translation.)

brought to feel immoderate pleasure in the contemplation of this delightful season; but I have the satisfaction of finding many, whom it can be no shame to resemble, infected with the same enthusiasm; for there is, I believe, scarce any poet of eminence who has not left some testimony of his fondness for the flowers, the zephyrs, and the warblers of the spring. Nor has the most luxuriant imagination been able to describe the serenity and happiness of the Golden Age otherwise than by giving a perpetual spring, as the highest reward of uncorrupted innocence.

There is, indeed, something inexpressibly pleasing in the annual renovation of the world, and the new display of the treasures of nature. The cold and darkness of winter, with the naked deformity of every object on which we turn our eyes, make us rejoice at the succeeding season, as well for what we have escaped, as for what we may enjoy; and every budding flower which a warm situation brings early to our view is considered by us as a messenger to notify the approach of more joyous days.

The spring affords to a mind, so free from the disturbance of cares or passions as to be vacant to calm amusements, almost everything that our present state makes us capable of enjoying. The variegated verdure of the fields and woods, the succession of grateful odors, the voice of pleasure pouring out its notes on every side, with the gladness apparently conceived by every animal from the growth of his food and the clemency of the weather, throw over the whole earth an air of gaiety, significantly expressed by the smile of nature.

Yet there are men to whom these scenes are able to give no delight, and who hurry away from all the varieties of rural beauty, to lose their hours and divert their thoughts by cards or assemblies,[11] a tavern dinner, or the prattle of the day.

It may be laid down as a position which will seldom deceive, that when a man cannot bear his own company there is something wrong. He must fly from himself, either because he feels a tediousness in life from the equipoise of an empty mind, which, having no tendency to one motion more than another but as it is impelled by some external power, must always have recourse to foreign objects; or he must be afraid of the intrusion of some unpleasing ideas, and perhaps is struggling to escape from the remembrance of a loss, the fear of a calamity, or some other thought of greater horror.

Those whom sorrow incapacitates to enjoy the pleasures of contemplation may properly apply to such diversions, provided they are innocent, as lay strong hold on the attention; and those whom fear of any future affliction chains down to misery must endeavor to obviate the danger.

My considerations shall, on this occasion, be turned on such as are burdensome to themselves merely because they want subjects for reflection, and to whom the volume of nature is thrown open without affording them pleasure or instruction, because they never learned to read the characters.

A French author has advanced this seeming paradox, that *very few men know how to take a walk;* and, indeed, it is true that few know how to take a walk with a prospect of any other pleasure than the same company would have afforded them at home.

There are animals that borrow their color from the neighboring body, and consequently vary their hue as they happen to change their place. In like manner it ought to be the endeavor of every man to derive his reflections from the objects about him; for it is to no purpose that he alters his position, if his attention continues fixed to the same point. The mind should be kept open to the access of every new idea, and so far disengaged from the predominance of particular thoughts as easily to accommodate itself to occasional entertainment.

A man that has formed this habit of turning every new object to his entertainment, finds in the productions of nature an inexhaustible stock of materials upon which he can employ himself, without any temptations to envy or malevolence; faults, perhaps, seldom totally avoided by those, whose judgment is much exercised upon the works of art. He has always a certain prospect of discovering new reasons for adoring the sovereign Author of the universe, and probable hopes of making some discovery of benefit to others, or of profit to himself. There is no doubt but many vegetables and animals have qualities that might be of great use, to the knowledge of which there is not required much force of penetration or fatigue of study, but only frequent experiments and close attention. What is said by the chemists of their darling mercury, is, perhaps, true of every body through the whole creation, that, if a thousand lives should be spent upon it, all its properties would not be found out.

Mankind must necessarily be diversified by various tastes, since life affords and requires such multiplicity of employments, and a nation of naturalists is neither

---

[11] Social gatherings, for conversation, cards, etc.

to be hoped nor desired; but it is surely not improper to point out a fresh amusement to those who languish in health, and repine in plenty, for want of some source of diversion that may be less easily exhausted, and to inform the multitudes of both sexes, who are burthened with every new day, that there are many shows which they have not seen.

He that enlarges his curiosity after the works of nature demonstrably multiplies the inlets to happiness; and therefore the younger part of my readers, to whom I dedicate this vernal speculation, must excuse me for calling upon them to make use at once of the spring of the year, and the spring of life; to acquire, while their minds may be yet impressed with new images, a love of innocent pleasures and an ardor for useful knowledge; and to remember that a blighted spring makes a barren year, and that the vernal flowers, however beautiful and gay, are only intended by nature as preparatives to autumnal fruits.

LETTER TO CHESTERFIELD

THIS is one of the most famous letters ever penned, but the wrath it conveys is hardly of the righteous variety. In 1747 Johnson was unknown, except for the poem *London* and the Life of the minor poet Richard Savage. A rough draft of the prospectus of his *Dictionary* came into the hands of the Earl of Chesterfield (pp. 829 ff., above), one of the most eminent men of the day. He granted Johnson an interview, which seems to have gone well. The *Plan* was then published, with a dedication to the Earl, who gave Johnson ten pounds. Why further aid was expected does not appear, though it would have been a noble action if Chesterfield had thought of it; Johnson certainly needed it. Toward the end of 1754 Chesterfield heard from Dodsley the publisher that the *Dictionary* was about ready, and warmly endorsed it in two of the anonymous articles he was writing for the *World*. Perhaps Johnson was offended by the touch of humor with which Chesterfield had disclaimed collusion: "I most solemnly protest that neither Mr. Johnson, nor any person employed by him, nor any bookseller or booksellers concerned in the success of it, have ever offered me the usual compliment of a pair of gloves or a bottle of wine." Johnson afterwards regretted sending the letter, and indeed it is unjust; for instance, it seems clear that he was never actually repulsed from Chesterfield's door. But that the letter is a masterpiece Johnson well knew. He was proud of its style, and in admiring it was joined by his victim. Lord Chesterfield could hardly have been pleased to receive it; but with his usual imperturbability he left it where it could be seen on his table, and at least once called a visitor's attention to the stylistic merits of the more cutting portions.

TO THE RIGHT HONORABLE THE EARL OF CHESTERFIELD

FEBRUARY 7, 1755

My Lord,

I have been lately informed by the proprietor of the *World,* that two papers in which my *Dictionary* is recommended to the public were written by your Lordship. To be so distinguished is an honor which, being very little accustomed to favors from the great, I know not well how to receive, or in what terms to acknowledge.

When, upon some slight encouragement, I first visited your Lordship, I was overpowered, like the rest of mankind, by the enchantment of your address; and I could not forbear to wish that I might boast myself *le vainqueur du vainqueur de la terre,*[1] that I might obtain that regard for which I saw the world contending; but I found my attendance so little encouraged that neither pride nor modesty would suffer me to continue it. When I had once addressed your Lordship in public, I had exhausted all the art of pleasing which a retired and uncourtly scholar can possess. I had done all that I could; and no man is well pleased to have his all neglected, be it ever so little.

Seven years, my Lord, have now passed since I waited in your outward rooms or was repulsed from your door; during which time I have been pushing on my work through difficulties of which it is useless to complain, and have brought it at last to the verge of publication, without one act of assistance, one word of encouragement, or one smile of favor. Such treatment I did not expect, for I never had a patron before.

The shepherd in Vergil[2] grew at last acquainted with Love, and found him a native of the rocks.

Is not a patron, my Lord, one who looks with unconcern on a man struggling for life in the water and, when he has reached ground, encumbers him with help? The notice which you have been pleased to take of my labors, had it been early, had been kind; but it has been delayed till I am indifferent,

---

[1] The conqueror of the conqueror of the earth. This is part of a line from the epic *Alaric* of Georges de Scudéry (1601–67).
[2] *Eclogues*, VIII, 43 ff.

and cannot enjoy it; till I am solitary,[3] and cannot impart it; till I am known, and do not want it. I hope it is no very cynical asperity not to confess obligations where no benefit has been received, or to be unwilling that the public should consider me as owing that to a patron which Providence has enabled me to do for myself.

Having carried on my work thus far with so little obligation to any favorer of learning, I shall not be disappointed though I should conclude it, if less be possible, with less; for I have been long wakened from that dream of hope in which I once boasted myself with so much exultation, my Lord,

Your Lordship's most humble,
most obedient servant,

SAM. JOHNSON

from THE HISTORY OF RASSELAS, PRINCE OF ABYSSINIA

THOUGH it is cast in the currently popular form of Oriental narrative, *Rasselas* is mainly a series of essays. The hero, his sister, and the wise Imlac leave the Happy Valley in search of a happy state of society. Their travels fail to discover one, and they return whence they came. It is another discourse on "the vanity of human wishes." The following chapter, an excerpt from Imlac's account of his life, embodies some important current critical beliefs. See p. 682, above.

CHAPTER 10

IMLAC'S HISTORY CONTINUED. A DISSERTATION
UPON POETRY

"WHEREVER I went, I found that poetry was considered as the highest learning, and regarded with a veneration somewhat approaching to that which man would pay to the Angelic Nature. And yet it fills me with wonder that in almost all countries the most ancient poets are considered as the best: whether it be that every other kind of knowledge is an acquisition gradually attained, and poetry is a gift conferred at once; or that the first poetry of every nation surprised them as a novelty, and retained the credit by consent which it received by accident at first; or whether, as the province of poetry is to describe nature and passion, which are always the same, the first writers took possession of the most striking objects for description and the most probable occurrences for fiction, and left nothing to those that followed them but transcription of the same events and new combinations of the same images. Whatever be the reason, it is commonly observed that the early writers are in possession of nature, and their followers of art: that the first excel in strength and invention, and the latter in elegance and refinement.

"I was desirous to add my name to this illustrious fraternity. I read all the poets of Persia and Arabia, and was able to repeat by memory the volumes that are suspended in the mosque of Mecca. But I soon found that no man was ever great by imitation. My desire of excellence impelled me to transfer my attention to nature and to life. Nature was to be my subject, and men to be my auditors. I could never describe what I had not seen. I could not hope to move those with delight or terror whose interests and opinions I did not understand.

"Being now resolved to be a poet, I saw everything with a new purpose; my sphere of attention was suddenly magnified: no kind of knowledge was to be overlooked. I ranged mountains and deserts for images and resemblances, and pictured upon my mind every tree of the forest and flower of the valley. I observed with equal care the crags of the rock and the pinnacles of the palace. Sometimes I wandered along the mazes of the rivulet, and sometimes watched the changes of the summer clouds. To a poet nothing can be useless. Whatever is beautiful and whatever is dreadful must be familiar to his imagination: he must be conversant with all that is awfully vast or elegantly little. The plants of the garden, the animals of the wood, the minerals of the earth, and meteors of the sky, must all concur to store his mind with inexhaustible variety: for every idea[1] is useful for the enforcement or decoration of moral or religious truth; and he who knows most will have most power of diversifying his scenes and of gratifying his reader with remote allusions and unexpected instruction.

"All the appearances of nature I was therefore

[3] Johnson's wife had died three years before.

[1] Image.

careful to study, and every country which I have surveyed has contributed something to my poetical powers."

"In so wide a survey," said the prince, "you must surely have left much unobserved. I have lived, till now, within the circuit of these mountains, and yet cannot walk abroad without the sight of something which I had never beheld before, or never heeded."

"The business of a poet," said Imlac, "is to examine not the individual but the species; to remark general properties and large appearances. He does not number the streaks of the tulip, or describe the different shades in the verdure of the forest. He is to exhibit in his portraits of nature such prominent and striking features as recall the original to every mind; and must neglect the minuter discriminations, which one may have remarked and another have neglected, for those characteristics which are alike obvious to vigilance and carelessness.

"But the knowledge of nature is only half the task of a poet; he must be acquainted likewise with all the modes of life. His character requires that he estimate the happiness and misery of every condition; observe the power of all the passions in all their combinations; and trace the changes of the human mind, as they are modified by various institutions and accidental influences of climate or custom, from the sprightliness of infancy to the despondence of decrepitude. He must divest himself of the prejudices of his age or country; he must consider right and wrong in their abstracted and invariable state; he must disregard present laws and opinions, and rise to general and transcendental truths, which will always be the same. He must therefore content himself with the slow progress of his name, contemn the applause of his own time, and commit his claims to the justice of posterity. He must write as the interpreter of nature and the legislator of mankind, and consider himself as presiding over the thoughts and manners of future generations, as a being superior to time and place.

"His labor is not yet at an end; he must know many languages and many sciences; and, that his style may be worthy of his thoughts, must by incessant practice familiarize to himself every delicacy of speech and grace of harmony."

from the PREFACE TO SHAKESPEARE

JOHNSON's edition was published in 1765. Its merit, which is very great, lies chiefly in his illuminating notes, where he brings to bear both his learning and his fund of experience in observing and dealing with human nature. His criticism is not infallible, but on the whole he is the best of the long line of commentators. The Preface embodies a revision of prevailing critical opinions, which had not kept pace with the enthusiasm of audiences. Johnson was a neoclassicist; he objects as well as praises; but when the Rules get in the way of common sense, he discards them. "There is always," he writes, "an appeal open from criticism to nature." In particular, he condemns the use of the Three Unities as a touchstone of excellence in drama. Recognizing that unity of time (limiting the action to a single day), unity of place (barring transfers of the action from place to place), and unity of action (restricting it to a single plot) may all contribute to a desirable compactness of structure, he exposes the absurdity of maintaining that they insure a play's plausibility and insists that some plays can profitably dispense with them.

The introductory paragraphs are reprinted here, not only for their estimate of Shakespeare but for what Johnson has to say about the claim of older writings to our attention.

If the reader of this anthology has ever wondered why an acquaintance with noncontemporary literature is considered indispensable to the educated man or woman, Johnson's explanation of its importance can hardly be bettered.

THAT praises are without reason lavished on the dead, and that the honors due only to excellence are paid to antiquity, is a complaint likely to be always continued by those, who, being able to add nothing to truth, hope for eminence from the heresies of paradox; or those who, being forced by disappointment upon consolatory expedients, are willing to hope from posterity what the present age refuses, and flatter themselves that the regard which is yet denied by envy will be at last bestowed by time.

Antiquity, like every other quality that attracts the notice of mankind, has undoubtedly votaries that reverence it not from reason but from prejudice. Some seem to admire indiscriminately whatever has been long preserved, without considering that time has sometimes cooperated with chance; all perhaps are more willing to honor past than present excellence; and the mind contemplates genius through the shades of age, as the eye surveys the sun through artificial opacity. The great contention of criticism is to find the faults of the moderns and the beauties of the ancients. While an author is yet living, we estimate his powers by his worst performance; and when he is dead, we rate them by his best.

To works, however, of which the excellence is not absolute and definite but gradual and comparative; to works not raised upon principles demonstrative and scientific but appealing wholly to observation and experience, no other test can be applied than length of duration and continuance of esteem. What mankind have long possessed, they have often examined and compared; and if they persist to value the possession, it is because frequent comparisons have confirmed opinion in its favor. As among the works of nature no man can properly call a river deep or a mountain high without the knowledge of many mountains and many rivers, so in the productions of genius nothing can be styled excellent till it has been compared with other works of the same kind. Demonstration immediately displays its power, and has nothing to hope or fear from the flux of years; but works tentative and experimental must be estimated by their proportion to the general and collective ability of man as it is discovered in a long succession of endeavors. Of the first building that was raised, it might be with certainty determined that it was round or square; but whether it was spacious or lofty must have been referred to time. The Pythagorean scale of numbers[1] was at once discovered to be perfect; but the poems of Homer we yet know not to transcend the common limits of human intelligence but by remarking that nation after nation, and century after century, has been able to do little more than transpose his incidents, new name his characters, and paraphrase his sentiments.

The reverence due to writings that have long subsisted arises, therefore, not from any credulous confidence in the superior wisdom of past ages or gloomy persuasion of the degeneracy of mankind, but is the consequence of acknowledged and indubitable positions: that what has been longest known has been most considered, and what is most considered is best understood.

The poet of whose works I have undertaken the revision may now begin to assume the dignity of an ancient, and claim the privilege of established fame and prescriptive veneration. He has long outlived his century, the term commonly fixed as the test of literary merit. Whatever advantages he might once derive from personal allusions, local customs, or temporary opinions have for many years been lost; and every topic of merriment or motive of sorrow which the modes of artificial life afforded him, now only obscure the scenes which they once illuminated. The effects of favor and competition are at an end; the tradition of his friendships and his enmities has perished; his works support no opinion with arguments, nor supply any faction with invectives; they can neither indulge vanity nor gratify malignity, but are read without any other reason than the desire of pleasure, and are therefore praised only as pleasure is obtained; yet, thus unassisted by interest or passion, they have passed through variations of taste and changes of manners, and, as they devolved from one generation to another, have received new honors at every transmission.

But because human judgment, though it be gradually gaining upon certainty, never becomes infallible, and approbation, though long continued, may yet be only the approbation of prejudice or fashion, it is proper to inquire by what peculiarities of excellence Shakespeare has gained and kept the favor of his countrymen.

Nothing can please many and please long but just representations of general nature. Particular manners can be known to few, and therefore few only can judge how nearly they are copied. The irregular combinations of fanciful invention may delight awhile by that novelty of which the common satiety of life sends us all in quest; but the pleasures of sudden wonder are soon exhausted, and the mind can only repose on the stability of truth.

Shakespeare is above all writers, at least above all modern writers, the poet of nature; the poet that holds up to his readers a faithful mirror of manners and of life. His characters are not modified by the customs of particular places, unpracticed by the rest of the world, by the peculiarities of studies or professions which can operate but upon small numbers or by the accidents of transient fashions or temporary opinions; they are the genuine progeny of common humanity, such as the world will always supply and observation will always find. His persons act and speak by the influence of those general passions and principles by which all minds are agitated, and the whole system of life is continued in motion. In the writings of other poets a character is too often an

---

[1] To the Greek philosopher Pythagoras (sixth century B.C.) numerous mathematical discoveries were ascribed.

individual; in those of Shakespeare it is commonly a species.

It is from this wide extension of design that so much instruction is derived. It is this which fills the plays of Shakespeare with practical axioms and domestic wisdom. It was said of Euripides that every verse was a precept; and it may be said of Shakespeare that from his works may be collected a system of civil and economical prudence. Yet his real power is not shown in the splendor of particular passages, but by the progress of his fable[2] and the tenor of his dialogue; and he that tries to recommend him by select quotations will succeed like the pedant in Hierocles,[3] who, when he offered his house to sale, carried a brick in his pocket as a specimen.

It will not easily be imagined how much Shakespeare excels in accommodating his sentiments to real life but by comparing him with other authors. It was observed[4] of the ancient schools of declamation that the more diligently they were frequented, the more was the student disqualified for the world, because he found nothing there which he should ever meet in any other place. The same remark may be applied to every stage but that of Shakespeare. The theater, when it is under any other direction, is peopled by such characters as were never seen, conversing in a language which was never heard, upon topics which will never arise in the commerce of mankind. But the dialogue of this author is often so evidently determined by the incident which produces it, and is pursued with so much ease and simplicity, that it seems scarcely to claim the merit of fiction, but to have been gleaned by diligent selection out of common conversation and common occurrences.

Upon every other stage the universal agent is love, by whose power all good and evil is distributed, and every action quickened or retarded. To bring a lover, a lady, and a rival into the fable; to entangle them in contradictory obligations, perplex them with oppositions of interest, and harass them with violence of desires inconsistent with each other; to make them meet in rapture, and part in agony; to fill their mouths with hyperbolical joy and outrageous sorrow; to distress them as nothing human ever was distressed; to deliver them as nothing human ever was delivered, is the business of a modern dramatist. For this, probability is violated, life is misrepresented, and language is depraved. But love is only one of many passions; and as it has no great influence upon the sum of life, it has little operation in the dramas of a poet who caught his ideas from the living world and exhibited only what he saw before him. He knew that any other passion, as it was regular or exorbitant, was a cause of happiness or calamity.

Characters thus ample and general were not easily discriminated and preserved, yet perhaps no poet ever kept his personages more distinct from each other. I will not say, with Pope,[5] that every speech may be assigned to the proper speaker, because many speeches there are which have nothing characteristical; but perhaps, though some may be equally adapted to every person, it will be difficult to find that any can be properly transferred from the present possessor to another claimant. The choice is right when there is reason for choice.

Other dramatists can only gain attention by hyperbolical or aggravated characters, by fabulous and unexampled excellence or depravity, as the writers of barbarous romances invigorated the reader by a giant and a dwarf; and he that should form his expectations of human affairs from the play, or from the tale, would be equally deceived. Shakespeare has no heroes; his scenes are occupied only by men who act and speak as the reader thinks that he should himself have spoken or acted on the same occasion: even where the agency is supernatural, the dialogue is level with life. Other writers disguise the most natural passions and most frequent incidents, so that he who contemplates them in the book will not know them in the world. Shakespeare approximates the remote and familiarizes the wonderful; the event which he represents will not happen, but, if it were possible, its effects would probably be such as he has assigned; and it may be said that he has not only shown human nature as it acts in real exigencies, but as it would be found in trials to which it cannot be exposed.

This, therefore, is the praise of Shakespeare, that his drama is the mirror of life.

* * * * *

---

[2] Plot.

[3] A fifth-century Alexandrian philosopher. A book of humorous anecdotes has survived under his name.

[4] By the satirist Petronius (d. 66? A.D.) in his *Satyricon*.

[5] In the preface to his edition of Shakespeare.

from THE LIVES OF THE MOST EMINENT ENGLISH POETS

PROFESSOR SHERBURN, our leading authority on the life of Pope, has pronounced Johnson's biography still the best. It was the last of his *Lives* to be written, and his masterpiece in this genre. As was usual, it falls into three portions. Johnson begins with the biographical facts and a running account of the works. The second part (with which our selections open) is devoted to personal description and analysis. The third gives the critical estimate.

A pool of London publishers having decided to issue an edition of all the important English poets since Chaucer, Johnson was retained in 1777 to supply brief introductions. The project was soon restricted to writers not earlier than Cowley (1618-67), but Johnson found he had more to say than was originally planned. His fifty-two Lives vary in length. About half are mere sketches; seven are substantial biographies. They appeared in ten volumes in 1779-81. Naturally, their merits also vary; Johnson is at his best with the best poets of the neoclassical school. In Pope he had a particularly congenial subject.

Besides Hill's edition of the *Lives,* there are cheap reprints in Everyman's Library and the World's Classics.

POPE

. . . The person of Pope is well known not to have been formed by the nicest model. He has, in his account of the "Little Club,"[1] compared himself to a spider, and by another is described as protuberant behind and before. He is said to have been beautiful in his infancy; but he was of a constitution originally feeble and weak; and as bodies of a tender frame are easily distorted, his deformity was probably in part the effect of his application.[2] His stature was so low that to bring him to a level with common tables it was necessary to raise his seat. But his face was not displeasing, and his eyes were animated and vivid.

By natural deformity or accidental distortion his vital functions were so much disordered that his life was a "long disease."[3] His most frequent assailant was the headache, which he used to relieve by inhaling the steam of coffee, which he very frequently required.

Most of what can be told concerning his petty peculiarities was communicated by a female domestic of the Earl of Oxford,[4] who knew him perhaps after the middle of life. He was then so weak as to stand in perpetual need of female attendance; extremely sensible of cold, so that he wore a kind of fur doublet under a shirt of very coarse warm linen with fine sleeves. When he rose, he was invested in bodice[5] made of stiff canvas, being scarce able to hold himself erect till they were laced, and he then put on a flannel waistcoat. One side was contracted. His legs were so slender that he enlarged their bulk with three pair of stockings, which were drawn on and off by the maid; for he was not able to dress or undress himself, and neither went to bed nor rose without help. His weakness made it very difficult for him to be clean.

His hair had fallen almost all away, and he used to dine sometimes with Lord Oxford, privately, in a velvet cap. His dress of ceremony was black, with a tie-wig and a little sword.

The indulgence and accommodation which his sickness required had taught him all the unpleasing and unsocial qualities of a valetudinary[6] man. He expected that everything should give way to his ease or humor, as a child whose parents will not hear her cry has an unresisted dominion in the nursery.

C'est que l'enfant toujours est homme;
C'est que l'homme est toujours enfant.[7]

When he wanted to sleep, he "nodded in company," and once slumbered at his own table while the Prince of Wales was talking of poetry.

The reputation which his friendship gave procured him many invitations; but he was a very troublesome inmate. He brought no servant, and had so many wants that a numerous attendance was scarcely able to supply them. Wherever he was he left no room for another, because he exacted the attention and employed the activity of the whole family. His errands were so frequent and frivolous that the footmen in time avoided and neglected him, and the Earl of Oxford discharged some of the servants for their resolute refusal of his messages. The maids, when they had neglected their business, alleged that they had been employed by Mr. Pope. One of his constant demands was of coffee in the night, and to the woman that waited on him in his chamber he was very burthensome; but he was careful to re-

---

[1] For Steele's *Guardian* Pope wrote two humorous papers (nos. 91, 92) about a club of small men.   [2] To study.
[3] See, above, Pope's *Epistle to Dr. Arbuthnot,* line 132.
[4] Robert Harley, the Tory statesman.

[5] This word was considered a plural; cf. "a pair of bodices" or stays.   [6] Sickly.
[7] Ever the child's the man; ever the man's the child.

compense her want of sleep, and Lord Oxford's servant declared that in a house where her business was to answer his call she would not ask for wages.

He had another fault, easily incident to those who, suffering much pain, think themselves entitled to whatever pleasures they can snatch. He was too indulgent to his appetite: he loved meat highly seasoned and of strong taste, and, at the intervals of the table, amused himself with biscuits and dry conserves. If he sat down to a variety of dishes, he would oppress his stomach with repletion, and though he seemed angry when a dram was offered him, did not forbear to drink it. His friends, who knew the avenues to his heart, pampered him with presents of luxury, which he did not suffer to stand neglected. The death of great men is not always proportioned to the luster of their lives. Hannibal, says Juvenal,[8] did not perish by a javelin or a sword; the slaughters of Cannae were revenged by a ring. The death of Pope was imputed by some of his friends to a silver saucepan, in which it was his delight to heat potted lampreys.

That he loved too well to eat is certain; but that his sensuality shortened his life will not be hastily concluded when it is remembered that a conformation so irregular lasted six and fifty years, notwithstanding such pertinacious diligence of study and meditation.

In all his intercourse with mankind he had great delight in artifice, and endeavored to attain all his purposes by indirect and unsuspected methods. "He hardly drank tea without a stratagem."[9] If at the house of his friends he wanted any accommodation, he was not willing to ask for it in plain terms, but would mention it remotely as something convenient; though, when it was procured, he soon made it appear for whose sake it had been recommended. Thus he teased Lord Orrery[10] till he obtained a screen. He practiced his arts on such small occasions that Lady Bolingbroke[11] used to say, in a French phrase, that "he played the politician about cabbages and turnips." His unjustifiable impression[12]

of *The Patriot King*, as it can be imputed to no particular motive, must have proceeded from his general habit of secrecy and cunning: he caught an opportunity of a sly trick, and pleased himself with the thought of outwitting Bolingbroke.

In familiar or convivial conversation it does not appear that he excelled. He may be said to have resembled Dryden, as being not one that was distinguished by vivacity in company. It is remarkable that, so near his time, so much should be known of what he has written, and so little of what he has said: traditional memory retains no sallies of raillery nor sentences[13] of observation; nothing either pointed or solid, either wise or merry. One apophthegm[14] only stands upon record. When an objection raised against his inscription for Shakespeare was defended by the authority of Patrick,[15] he replied—*horresco referens*[16]—that he would allow the publisher of a dictionary to know the meaning of a single word, but not of two words put together.

He was fretful and easily displeased, and allowed himself to be capriciously resentful. He would sometimes leave Lord Oxford silently, no one could tell why, and was to be courted back by more letters and messages than the footmen were willing to carry. The table was indeed infested by Lady Mary Wortley,[17] who was the friend of Lady Oxford, and who, knowing his peevishness, could by no intreaties be restrained from contradicting him, till their disputes were sharpened to such asperity that one or the other quitted the house.

He sometimes condescended to be jocular with servants or inferiors; but by no merriment, either of others or his own, was he ever seen excited to laughter.

Of his domestic character frugality was a part eminently remarkable. Having determined not to be dependent, he determined not to be in want, and therefore wisely and magnanimously rejected all temptations to expense unsuitable to his fortune. This general care must be universally approved; but it sometimes appeared in petty artifices of parsimony, such as the practice of writing his compositions on the back of letters, as may be seen in the remaining copy of the *Iliad*, by which perhaps in five years five shillings were saved; or in a niggardly reception of his friends and scantiness of entertainment, as

---

8 *Satires*, X, 163–6. Hannibal (d. 183 B.C.), the Carthaginian general, victor over the Romans at Cannae in 216 B.C., was said to have taken poison which he kept in a ring.

9 Adapted from a line in the satires (VI, 188) of Edward Young (d. 1765).

10 John Boyle, fifth Earl of Orrery and Cork (1707–62).

11 Wife of Henry St. John, Viscount Bolingbroke, the Tory statesman.

12 Printing. Earlier in this Life, Johnson mentions Pope's having this pamphlet by Bolingbroke printed without the latter's knowledge.

13 Sayings.   14 Apothegm, witty saying.

15 Samuel Patrick edited a Latin dictionary (1746).

16 I shudder to think of it (Vergil, *Aeneid*, II, 204). That is, Johnson, as a dictionary-maker himself, shudders at the aspersion.

17 Lady Mary Wortley Montagu, famous letter-writer, once Pope's friend but afterwards his enemy (see above, on Pope's *Epistle to Dr. Arbuthnot*, note 28).

when he had two guests in his house he would set at supper a single pint upon the table and having himself taken two small glasses would retire and say, "Gentlemen, I leave you to your wine." Yet he tells his friends that he has a heart for all, a house for all, and, whatever they may think, a fortune for all.[18]

He sometimes, however, made a splendid dinner, and is said to have wanted no part of the skill or elegance which such performances require. That this magnificence should be often displayed, that obstinate prudence with which he conducted his affairs would not permit; for his revenue, certain and casual, amounted only to about eight hundred pounds[19] a year, of which, however, he declares himself able to assign one hundred to charity.

Of this fortune, which, as it arose from public approbation, was very honorably obtained, his imagination seems to have been too full: it would be hard to find a man so well entitled to notice by his wit that ever delighted so much in talking of his money. In his letters and in his poems his garden and his grotto, his quincunx[20] and his vines, or some hints of his opulence, are always to be found. The great topic of his ridicule is poverty: the crimes with which he reproaches his antagonists are their debts, their habitation in the Mint,[21] and their want of a dinner. He seems to be of an opinion, not very uncommon in the world, that to want[22] money is to want everything.

Next to the pleasure of contemplating his possessions seems to be that of enumerating the men of high rank with whom he was acquainted, and whose notice he loudly proclaims not to have been obtained by any practices of meanness or servility; a boast which was never denied to be true, and to which very few poets have ever aspired. Pope never set genius to sale: he never flattered those whom he did not love, or praised those whom he did not esteem. Savage, however, remarked that he began a little to relax his dignity when he wrote a distich for "his Highness's[23] dog."

---

[18] In a letter of invitation to Swift.
[19] Worth much more in purchasing power then than now.
[20] An arrangement of five things in a square, with one at each corner and the fifth in the center; here probably trees.
[21] A notorious district in Southwark, across the Thames, where (among other fugitives) poor debtors hid.   [22] Lack.
[23] Frederick, Prince of Wales. See on *The Vanity of Human Wishes*, note 6. Richard Savage (d. 1743) was an unfortunate minor poet; Johnson wrote his Life. The distich was engraved on the dog's collar:
    "I am his Highness' dog at Kew;
      Pray tell me, sir, whose dog are you?"
The "sir" is not addressed to visiting dogs, but to men.

His admiration of the great seems to have increased in the advance of life. He passed over peers and statesmen to inscribe his *Iliad* to Congreve, with a magnanimity of which the praise had been complete had his friend's virtue been equal to his wit. Why he was chosen for so great an honor it is not now possible to know; there is no trace in literary history of any particular intimacy between them. The name of Congreve appears in the letters among those of his other friends, but without any observable distinction or consequence.

To his latter works, however, he took care to annex names dignified with titles, but was not very happy in his choice. . . .

Of his social qualities, if an estimate be made from his letters, an opinion too favorable cannot easily be formed; they exhibit a perpetual and unclouded effulgence of general benevolence and particular fondness. There is nothing but liberality, gratitude, constancy, and tenderness. It has been so long said as to be commonly believed that the true characters of men may be found in their letters, and that he who writes to his friend lays his heart open before him. But the truth is that such were the simple friendships of the Golden Age, and are now the friendships only of children. Very few can boast of hearts which they dare lay open to themselves, and of which, by whatever accident exposed, they do not shun a distinct and continued view; and, certainly, what we hide from ourselves we do not show to our friends. There is, indeed, no transaction which offers stronger temptations to fallacy and sophistication than epistolary intercourse. In the eagerness of conversation the first emotions of the mind often burst out before they are considered; in the tumult of business, interest and passion have their genuine effect; but a friendly letter is a calm and deliberate performance in the cool of leisure, in the stillness of solitude; and surely no man sits down to depreciate by design his own character.

Friendship has no tendency to secure veracity, for by whom can a man so much wish to be thought better than he is as by him whose kindness he desires to gain or keep? Even in writing to the world there is less constraint: the author is not confronted with his reader, and takes his chance of approbation among the different dispositions of mankind; but a letter is addressed to a single mind of which the prejudices and partialities are known, and must therefore please, if not by favoring them, by forbearing to oppose them. . . .

One of his favorite topics is contempt of his own poetry. For this, if it had been real, he would deserve no commendation, and in this he certainly was not sincere; for his high value of himself was sufficiently observed, and of what could he be proud but of his poetry? He writes, he says, when he has just nothing else to do; yet Swift complains that he was never at leisure for conversation because he "had always some poetical scheme in his head." It was punctually required that his writing box should be set upon his bed before he rose; and Lord Oxford's domestic related that in the dreadful winter of Forty[24] she was called from her bed by him four times in one night to supply him with paper, lest he should lose a thought.

He pretends insensibility to censure and criticism, though it was observed by all who knew him that every pamphlet disturbed his quiet, and that his extreme irritability laid him open to perpetual vexation; but he wished to despise his critics, and therefore hoped that he did despise them. . . .

In the letters both of Swift and Pope there appears such narrowness of mind as makes them insensible of any excellence that has not some affinity with their own, and confines their esteem and approbation to so small a number that whoever should form his opinion of the age from their representation would suppose them to have lived amidst ignorance and barbarity, unable to find among their contemporaries either virtue or intelligence, and persecuted by those that could not understand them. . . .

The virtues which seem to have had most of his affection were liberality, and fidelity of friendship, in which it does not appear that he was other than he describes himself. His fortune did not suffer his charity to be splendid and conspicuous, but he assisted Dodsley[25] with a hundred pounds that he might open a shop; and of the subscription of forty pounds a year that he raised for Savage twenty were paid by himself. He was accused of loving money; but his love was eagerness to gain, not solicitude to keep it.

In the duties of friendship he was zealous and constant: his early maturity of mind commonly united him with men older than himself, and therefore, without attaining any considerable length of life, he saw many companions of his youth sink into the grave; but it does not appear that he lost a single friend by coldness or by injury: those who loved him once continued their kindness. . . .

Of his intellectual character the constituent and fundamental principle was good sense, a prompt and intuitive perception of consonance and propriety. He saw immediately, of his own conceptions, what was to be chosen and what to be rejected; and, in the works of others, what was to be shunned and what was to be copied.

But good sense alone is a sedate and quiescent quality, which manages its possessions well, but does not increase them; it collects few materials for its own operations, and preserves safety, but never gains supremacy. Pope had likewise genius; a mind active, ambitious, and adventurous, always investigating, always aspiring; in its widest searches still longing to go forward, in its highest flights still wishing to be higher; always imagining something greater than it knows, always endeavoring more than it can do.

To assist these powers he is said to have had great strength and exactness of memory. That which he had heard or read was not easily lost; and he had before him not only what his own meditation suggested, but what he had found in other writers that might be accommodated to his present purpose.

These benefits of nature he improved by incessant and unwearied diligence; he had recourse to every source of intelligence, and lost no opportunity of information; he consulted the living as well as the dead; he read his compositions to his friends, and was never content with mediocrity when excellence could be attained. He considered poetry as the business of his life; and, however he might seem to lament his occupation, he followed it with constancy: to make verses was his first labor, and to mend them was his last. . . .

He professed to have learned his poetry from Dryden, whom, whenever an opportunity was presented, he praised through his whole life with unvaried liberality; and perhaps his character may receive some illustration if he be compared with his master.

Integrity of understanding and nicety of discernment were not allotted in a less proportion to Dryden than to Pope. The rectitude of Dryden's mind was sufficiently shown by the dismission of his poetical prejudices, and the rejection of unnatural thoughts and rugged numbers. But Dryden never desired to apply all the judgment that he had. He wrote, and professed to write, merely for the people; and when he pleased others, he contented himself. He spent no time in struggles to rouse latent powers; he never attempted to make that better which was already good, nor often to mend what

---

[24] An especially cold one.
[25] Robert Dodsley (1703–64), publisher and minor poet and dramatist. He had been a footman.

he must have known to be faulty. He wrote, as he tells us, with very little consideration; when occasion or necessity called upon him, he poured out what the present moment happened to supply, and, when once it had passed the press, ejected it from his mind; for when he had no pecuniary interest, he had no further solicitude.

Pope was not content to satisfy; he desired to excel, and therefore always endeavored to do his best: he did not court the candor, but dared the judgment, of his reader, and, expecting no indulgence from others, he showed none to himself. He examined lines and words with minute and punctilious observation, and retouched every part with indefatigable diligence, till he had left nothing to be forgiven. . . .

In acquired knowledge the superiority must be allowed to Dryden, whose education was more scholastic, and who before he became an author had been allowed more time for study, with better means of information. His mind has a larger range, and he collects his images and illustrations from a more extensive circumference of science. Dryden knew more of man in his general nature, and Pope in his local manners. The notions of Dryden were formed by comprehensive speculation, and those of Pope by minute attention. There is more dignity in the knowledge of Dryden, and more certainty in that of Pope.

Poetry was not the sole praise of either, for both excelled likewise in prose; but Pope did not borrow his prose from his predecessor. The style of Dryden is capricious and varied; that of Pope is cautious and uniform. Dryden obeys the motions of his own mind; Pope constrains his mind to his own rules of composition. Dryden is sometimes vehement and rapid; Pope is always smooth, uniform, and gentle.

Dryden's page is a natural field, rising into inequalities, and diversified by the varied exuberance of abundant vegetation; Pope's is a velvet lawn, shaven by the scythe and leveled by the roller. 5

Of genius, that power which constitutes a poet, that quality without which judgment is cold and knowledge is inert, that energy which collects, combines, amplifies, and animates—the superiority must, with some hesitation, be allowed to Dryden. It is 10 not to be inferred that of this poetical vigor Pope had only a little because Dryden had more, for every other writer since Milton must give place to Pope; and even of Dryden it must be said that, if he has brighter paragraphs, he has not better poems. Dryden's performances were always hasty, either excited by some external occasion, or extorted by domestic necessity; he composed without consideration and published without correction. What his mind could supply at call, or gather in one excursion, was all that he sought and all that he 20 gave. The dilatory caution of Pope enabled him to condense his sentiments, to multiply his images, and to accumulate all that study might produce or chance might supply. If the flights of Dryden therefore are higher, Pope continues longer on the wing. 25 If of Dryden's fire the blaze is brighter, of Pope's the heat is more regular and constant. Dryden often surpasses expectation, and Pope never falls below it. Dryden is read with frequent astonishment, and Pope with perpetual delight. 30

This parallel will, I hope, when it is well considered, be found just; and if the reader should suspect me, as I suspect myself, of some partial fondness for the memory of Dryden, let him not too hastily condemn me; for meditation and enquiry may, 35 perhaps, show him the reasonableness of my determination. . . .

James Boswell

1740–1795

JOHNSON's conversation, faithfully recorded through the agency of unusual powers of concentration and an extraordinary memory for dialogue, is what gives Boswell's great book its fascination; but that does not mean, as used to be alleged against its author, that his was a passive role. The greatest of biographies could not possibly have been written by anyone except a great biographer. Nor was it Boswell's only first-rate book. To say that Boswell was a great biographer is not to say that he was a great man; but

he was a remarkable man, and a writer with an unusual faculty of observation and a knack, not only for selecting the telling detail, but for asking the questions and even arranging the situations which would produce the materials he wanted. His veneration for Johnson has perversely been cited in belittlement of his own personality. Of course it was highly creditable to his taste and judgment. Boswell the eager youngster and Boswell the sot who died at fifty-four are parts of a tragic story which began happily. "Good-humored" was what everyone said of the youth Boswell. In those hopeful days it is likely enough that of all Johnson's friends he loved Boswell best.

Boswell's father was a distinguished Scottish judge and a laird, that is, one of the landed gentry; at his death in 1782 James Boswell, as the eldest son, became Master of Auchinleck, the family estate in Ayrshire. It was on his father's insistence that he became a lawyer, after studies at Edinburgh, Glasgow, and Utrecht; he was admitted to the Scottish bar in 1766, three years after his first meeting with Johnson. He seems to have been a competent advocate, till drink got the better of him; but his heart was never in his profession. On his visits to London he made the acquaintance of a number of the leading men of his time; and their society, above all Johnson's, made his life in Edinburgh and on circuit seem intolerable.

He was still in his teens when it became evident that he had the biographer's primary trait, an irrational delight in personality, especially the personalities of the eminent. Moreover, like almost all artists, he was sometimes engrossed, often to a comic degree, with his own personality. Scotland's leading man of letters was the philosopher and historian David Hume (1711–76). He was forty-seven; but the eighteen-year-old Boswell secured an introduction. Then he wrote to his lifelong college friend, William Johnson Temple:

Few such people are to be met with nowadays. . . . Mr. Hume, I think, is a very proper person for a young man to cultivate an acquaintance with; though he has not, perhaps, the most delicate taste, yet he has applied himself with great attention to the study of the ancients, and is likeways a great historian, so that you are not only entertained in his company, but may reap a good deal of useful information.

There you have it! One may quarrel with Boswell or with anyone for running after great men, or for wanting to be a biographer at all; but that was the way he was naturally inclined, and his literary achievements were not accidents. He was only twenty-two when he met Johnson, who was fifty-three. Boswell's charm conquered the great man immediately.

A few weeks later Bozzy was off for the Continent, to continue his legal studies at the University of Utrecht, with the promise of a European tour to follow. What he studied mostly, besides women and drinking, was men of genius. It is only fair to add that it was melancholia which drove him to the bottle, and that the most repellent episodes in which women were concerned occurred when he was drunk. He paid a dreadful price for both varieties of intemperance. As for his researches in greatness, *crust* is the only word for the manner in which he scraped acquaintance with Jean Jacques Rousseau and Voltaire. Another who yielded to his winning ways was the Corsican

patriot, Pasquale Paoli. Armed with a letter from Rousseau, Boswell pursued General Paoli to his mountain lair and spent several days in the stimulating company of the sons of freedom. He came home with a Corsican guerrilla's outfit, a colorful costume, worn with pistol on belt and a slung musket; he did not hesitate to appear thus in public on what he regarded as suitable occasions. There was obvious exhibitionism in this, but he was sincerely interested in Corsican liberty. When the French crushed it and Paoli became a refugee in London, he and Boswell renewed a friendship which was to last throughout Boswell's life. Meanwhile the latter had turned their first meeting to good purpose with his *Account of Corsica* (1768).

After various courtships and, besides the fathering of two illegitimate children, numerous even less creditable adventures, all reported in his letters to Temple, who though now a clergyman continued to be the recipient of extremely frank confidences, Boswell married a cousin. It proved a bad bargain for her. Unquestionably he meant well by her, and his numerous repentances of infidelity were painful to him, at the moment. He loved his children. But the lure of London was constant; it was on his excursions there that he felt he really lived. In 1773, ten years after he first saw Johnson and nearly ten after its foundation, he was somewhat grudgingly admitted, on Johnson's insistence, to the Literary Club. The reluctance of some of its members is understandable; till the appearance of his magnum opus, as he loved to call it, few suspected his caliber. It was also in 1773 that he guided Johnson, now sixty-four, on a three-months tour of Scotland and its Western Islands. They penetrated, by land and by sea, into some rough regions. Of the intimate opportunities this journey afforded for observation of his companion, Boswell took full advantage. His *Journal of a Tour to the Hebrides,* with its close and revealing study of Johnson, is one of the eighteenth century's most entertaining books. It was not printed till 1785, the year after Johnson's death. Edmond Malone, the Shakespearean scholar, helped prepare it for the press, for by that time Boswell was deteriorating.

After the famous tour Johnson went back to London, and Boswell did not see him again for well over a year.[1] He resumed his life as an Edinburgh advocate, with increased distaste for that city and for the law. During the course of the next few years he became a confirmed drunkard. After Johnson's death he may have realized that his one sure claim to distinction would be the biography. At any rate he transferred his activities and his family to London, and secured admission to the English bar. He never worked up a practice there, but he cherished ill-

---

[1] It has been estimated that during their twenty-year friendship Boswell saw Johnson on no more than 870 days.

founded hopes of political preferment. In 1769 his wife died, to his genuine distress.

With the help once more of Malone, Boswell got his notes on Johnson into final form. He worked hard and painstakingly, fully aware that the *Life* would be a departure from the accepted pattern. On February 24, 1788, he had written to Temple: "I am absolutely certain that *my* mode of biography, which gives not only a *history* of Johnson's *visible* progress through the world and of his publications, but a *view* of his mind in his letters and conversations, is the most perfect that can be conceived, and will be *more* of a *Life* than any work that has ever yet appeared." The book came out in 1791, and there is now no serious dissent from that prediction. With its publication Boswell's work was done. He died in 1795.

The selections below are reprinted without the topical headings inserted by some anthologists, a helpful practice in many cases but not when introducing Boswell's *Johnson.* It is better that a new reader should see for himself how the book's varied store of wisdom and wit lies undisplayed along its pages. This is not one of the books which must be read at systematically; it can be opened anywhere, for five minutes or a day. If you have an intelligent reader's normal curiosity about personalities and ideas, you are not likely to read far anywhere in it without renewing the pleasure it is hoped you will find in the following extracts.

The standard edition is Boswell's *Life of Johnson . . . with Boswell's Journal of a Tour to the Hebrides and Johnson's Diary of a Journey into North Wales,* edited by G. B. Hill (revised ed. by L. F. Powell, 6 vols., in progress, 4 vols. thus far, constituting the *Life,* 1934—). This is a massive work of reference, but there are several simpler and cheaper reprints of the *Life,* for example in Everyman's Library (2 vols.) The *Tour* has been edited by F. A. Pottle and C. H. Bennett (1936), and it is also reprinted in Everyman's Library. Boswell's letters were edited by C. B. Tinker (2 vols., 1924); since then many more have been discovered. It was long supposed that Boswell's private papers had been lost; but in 1926 and 1930 large quantities were found (*Private Papers of James Boswell,* ed. G. Scott and F. A. Pottle, 18 vols., 1928–34), and since then still more have turned up. These finds, which are now in the library of Yale University, have rendered earlier biographies unsatisfactory, though C. B. Tinker's *Young Boswell* (1922) is still valuable. Publication of the new material has been inaugurated with an edition of Boswell's private journal of his London sojourn in 1762–63 (ed. F. A. Pottle, 1950).

James Boswell

from THE LIFE OF SAMUEL JOHNSON, LL.D.

FROM THE YEAR 1763

. . . This is to me a memorable year; for in it I had the happiness to obtain the acquaintance of that extraordinary man whose memoirs I am now writing, an acquaintance which I shall ever esteem as one of the most fortunate circumstances in my life. Though then but two-and-twenty, I had for several years read his works with delight and instruction, and had the highest reverence for their author, which had grown up in my fancy into a kind of mysterious veneration, by figuring to myself a state of solemn elevated abstraction, in which I supposed him to live in the immense metropolis of London. Mr. Gentleman,[1] a native of Ireland, who passed some years in Scotland as a player, and as an instructor in the English language, a man whose talents and worth were depressed by misfortunes, had given me a representation of the figure and manner of DICTIONARY JOHNSON! as he was then generally called; and during my first visit to London, which was for three months in 1760, Mr. Derrick the poet,[2] who was Gentleman's friend and countryman, flattered me with hopes that he would introduce me to Johnson, an honor of which I was very ambitious. But he never found an opportunity; which made me doubt[3] that he had promised to do what was not in his power; till Johnson some years afterwards told me, "Derrick, sir, might very well have introduced you. I had a kindness for Derrick, and am sorry he is dead."

In the summer of 1761 Mr. Thomas Sheridan[4] was at Edinburgh, and delivered lectures upon the English

---

[1] Francis Gentleman (1728–84), actor and playwright.

[2] Samuel Derrick (1724–69). Johnson had been kind to him, but had no illusions about his talents. Asked on another occasion whether this poet or Smart was the better, Johnson replied, "Sir, there is no settling the point of precedency between a louse and a flea."   [3] Suspect.

[4] Father of the dramatist.

language and public speaking to large and respectable audiences. I was often in his company, and heard him frequently expatiate upon Johnson's extraordinary knowledge, talents, and virtues, repeat his pointed sayings, describe his particularities, and boast of his being his guest sometimes till two or three in the morning. At his house I hoped to have many opportunities of seeing the sage, as Mr. Sheridan obligingly assured me I should not be disappointed.

When I returned to London in the end of 1762, to my surprise and regret I found an irreconcilable difference had taken place between Johnson and Sheridan. A pension of two hundred pounds a year had been given to Sheridan. Johnson, who, as has been already mentioned, thought slightingly of Sheridan's art, upon hearing that he was also pensioned, exclaimed, "What! have they given *him* a pension? Then it is time for me to give up mine." Whether this proceeded from a momentary indignation, as if it were an affront to his exalted merit that a player should be rewarded in the same manner with him, or was the sudden effect of a fit of peevishness, it was unluckily said and, indeed, cannot be justified. Mr. Sheridan's pension was granted to him, not as a player, but as a sufferer in the cause of government when he was manager of the Theater Royal in Ireland, when parties ran high in 1753.[5] And it must also be allowed that he was a man of literature, and had considerably improved the arts of reading and speaking with distinctness and propriety. . . .

Johnson complained that a man who disliked him repeated his sarcasm to Mr. Sheridan, without telling him what followed, which was that after a pause he added, "However, I am glad that Mr. Sheridan has a pension, for he is a very good man." Sheridan could never forgive this hasty contemptuous expression. It rankled in his mind; and though I informed him of all that Johnson said, and that he would be very glad to meet him amicably, he positively declined repeated offers which I made, and once went off abruptly from a house where he and I were engaged to dine, because he was told that Dr. Johnson was to be there. . . .

This rupture with Sheridan deprived Johnson of one of his most agreeable resources for amusement in his lonely evenings; for Sheridan's well-informed, animated, and bustling mind never suffered conversation to stagnate; and Mrs. Sheridan was a most agreeable companion to an intellectual man. She was sensible, ingenious, unassuming, yet communicative. I recollect, with satisfaction, many pleasing hours which I passed with her under the hospitable roof of her husband, who was to me a very kind friend. Her novel, entitled *Memoirs of Miss Sydney Biddulph,* contains an excellent moral, while it inculcates a future state of retribution; and what it teaches is impressed upon the mind by a series of as deep distress as can affect humanity, in the amiable and pious heroine who goes to her grave unrelieved, but resigned, and full of hope of "heaven's mercy." Johnson paid her this high compliment upon it: "I know not, madam, that you have a right, upon moral principles, to make your readers suffer so much."

Mr. Thomas Davies the actor, who then kept a bookseller's shop in Russell Street, Covent Garden, told me that Johnson was very much his friend, and came frequently to his house, where he more than once invited me to meet him; but by some unlucky accident or other he was prevented from coming to us.

Mr. Thomas Davies was a man of good understanding and talents, with the advantage of a liberal education. Though somewhat pompous, he was an entertaining companion; and his literary performances[6] have no inconsiderable share of merit. He was a friendly and very hospitable man. Both he and his wife (who has been celebrated for her beauty), though upon the stage for many years, maintained an uniform decency of character; and Johnson esteemed them, and lived in as easy an intimacy with them as with any family which he used to visit. Mr. Davies recollected several of Johnson's remarkable sayings, and was one of the best of the many imitators of his voice and manner, while relating them. He increased my impatience more and more to see the extraordinary man whose works I highly valued, and whose conversation was reported to be so peculiarly excellent.

At last, on Monday the 16th of May, when I was sitting in Mr. Davies's back parlor, after having drunk tea with him and Mrs. Davies, Johnson unexpectedly came into the shop; and Mr. Davies having perceived him through the glass door in the room in which we were sitting, advancing towards us, he announced his awful approach to me, somewhat in the manner of an actor in the part of Horatio, when he addresses Hamlet on the appearance of his

---

[5] Actually in 1754. Interpreting some lines as applicable against the government, the audience demanded their repetition and, when Sheridan ordered the actor to refuse, wrecked the theater.

[6] A Life of Garrick (1780) and *Dramatic Miscellanies* (1785).

father's ghost, "Look, my Lord, it comes." I found that I had a very perfect idea of Johnson's figure, from the portrait of him painted by Sir Joshua Reynolds[7] soon after he had published his *Dictionary*, in the attitude of sitting in his easy chair in deep meditation, which was the first picture his friend did for him, which Sir Joshua very kindly presented to me, and from which an engraving has been made for this work. Mr. Davies mentioned my name, and respectfully introduced me to him. I was much agitated; and recollecting his prejudice against the Scotch, of which I had heard much, I said to Davies, "Don't tell where I come from."—"From Scotland," cried Davies, roguishly. "Mr. Johnson," said I, "I do indeed come from Scotland, but I cannot help it." I am willing to flatter myself that I meant this as light pleasantry to soothe and conciliate him, and not as an humiliating abasement at the expense of my country. But however that might be, this speech was somewhat unlucky; for with that quickness of wit for which he was so remarkable, he seized the expression "come from Scotland," which I used in the sense of being of that country; and, as if I had said that I had come away from it, or left it, retorted, "That, sir, I find is what a very great many of your countrymen cannot help." This stroke stunned me a good deal; and when we had sat down, I felt myself not a little embarrassed, and apprehensive of what might come next. He then addressed himself to Davies: "What do you think of Garrick? He has refused me an order for the play for Miss Williams,[8] because he knows the house will be full, and that an order would be worth three shillings." Eager to take any opening to get into conversation with him, I ventured to say, "Oh, sir, I cannot think Mr. Garrick would grudge such a trifle to you." "Sir," said he, with a stern look, "I have known David Garrick longer than you have done; and I know no right you have to talk to me on the subject." Perhaps I deserved this check; for it was rather presumptuous in me, an entire stranger, to express any doubt of the justice of his animadversion upon his old acquaintance and pupil. I now felt myself much mortified, and began to think that the hope which I had long indulged of obtaining his acquaintance was blasted. And, in truth, had not my ardor been uncommonly strong, and my resolution uncommonly persevering, so rough a reception might have deterred me for ever from making any further

attempts. Fortunately, however, I remained upon the field not wholly discomfited, and was soon rewarded by hearing some of his conversation . . . .

I was highly pleased with the extraordinary vigor of his conversation, and regretted that I was drawn away from it by an engagement at another place. I had, for a part of the evening, been left alone with him, and had ventured to make an observation now and then, which he received very civilly; so that I was satisfied that, though there was a roughness in his manner, there was no ill nature in his disposition. Davies followed me to the door, and when I complained to him a little of the hard blows which the great man had given me, he kindly took upon him to console me by saying, "Don't be uneasy. I can see he likes you very well."

A few days afterwards I called on Davies, and asked him if he thought I might take the liberty of waiting on Mr. Johnson at his chambers in the Temple. He said I certainly might, and that Mr. Johnson would take it as a compliment. So upon Tuesday the 24th of May . . . I boldly repaired to Johnson. His chambers were on the first floor of No. 1, Inner Temple Lane, and I entered them with an impression given me by the Reverend Dr. Blair,[9] of Edinburgh, who had been introduced to him not long before, and described his having "found the giant in his den"; an expression which, when I came to be pretty well acquainted with Johnson, I repeated to him, and he was diverted at this picturesque account of himself. Dr. Blair had been presented to him by Dr. James Fordyce.[10] At this time the controversy concerning the pieces published by Mr. James Macpherson, as translations of Ossian, was at its height.[11] Johnson had all along denied their authenticity; and, what was still more provoking to their admirers, maintained that they had no merit. The subject having been introduced by Dr. Fordyce, Dr. Blair, relying on the internal evidence of their antiquity, asked Dr. Johnson whether he thought any man of a modern age could have written such poems? Johnson replied, "Yes, sir, many men, many women, and many children." Johnson, at this time, did not know that Dr. Blair

---

[7] The famous portrait painter (1723–92), and a friend of Johnson's.
[8] Anna Williams (1706–83), the blind poetess, one of Johnson's "inmates."

[9] The Rev. Hugh Blair (1718–1800), Professor of Rhetoric and Belles Lettres at Edinburgh, and author of four volumes of extremely popular sermons.
[10] The Rev. James Fordyce (1720–96), a popular preacher and minor poet.
[11] Macpherson (d. 1796) had a great success with *Fingal* and other poems, which he alleged to be his translations of ancient Gaelic writings by Ossian, a warrior bard. Johnson was right in denying both their authenticity and any great merit in them.

had just published a *Dissertation,* not only defending their authenticity, but seriously ranking them with the poems of Homer and Vergil; and when he was afterwards informed of this circumstance, he expressed some displeasure at Dr. Fordyce's having suggested the topic, and said, "I am not sorry that they got thus much for their pains. Sir, it was like leading one to talk of a book when the author is concealed behind the door."

He received me very courteously, but it must be confessed that his apartment and furniture and morning dress were sufficiently uncouth. His brown suit of clothes looked very rusty; he had on a little old shriveled unpowdered wig, which was too small for his head; his shirt-neck and knees of his breeches were loose; his black worsted stockings ill drawn up; and he had a pair of unbuckled shoes by way of slippers. But all these slovenly particularities were forgotten the moment that he began to talk. Some gentlemen, whom I do not recollect, were sitting with him; and when they went away, I also rose; but he said to me, "Nay, don't go."—"Sir," said I, "I am afraid that I intrude upon you. It is benevolent to allow me to sit and hear you." He seemed pleased with this compliment, which I sincerely paid him, and answered, "Sir, I am obliged to any man who visits me." I have preserved the following short minute of what passed this day.

"Madness frequently discovers itself merely by unnecessary deviation from the usual modes of the world. My poor friend Smart showed the disturbance of his mind by falling upon his knees and saying his prayers in the street or in any other unusual place. Now although, rationally speaking, it is greater madness not to pray at all than to pray as Smart did, I am afraid there are so many who do not pray that their understanding is not called in question."

Concerning this unfortunate poet, Christopher Smart, who was confined in a madhouse, he had, at another time, the following conversation with Dr. Burney.[12]—BURNEY. "How does poor Smart do, sir; is he likely to recover?" JOHNSON. "It seems as if his mind had ceased to struggle with the disease; for he grows fat upon it." BURNEY. "Perhaps, sir, that may be from want of exercise." JOHNSON. "No, sir; he has partly as much exercise as he used to have, for he digs in the garden. Indeed, before his confinement, he used for exercise to walk to the alehouse; but he was *carried* back again. I did not think he ought

to be shut up. His infirmities were not noxious to society. He insisted on people praying with him; and I'd as lief pray with Kit Smart as anyone else. Another charge was that he did not love clean linen; and I have no passion for it."

Johnson continued: "Mankind have a great aversion to intellectual labor; but even supposing knowledge to be easily attainable, more people would be content to be ignorant than would take even a little trouble to acquire it." . . .

Talking of Garrick, he said, "He is the first man in the world for sprightly conversation."

When I rose a second time he again pressed me to stay, which I did.

He told me that he generally went abroad at four in the afternoon, and seldom came home till two in the morning. I took the liberty to ask if he did not think it wrong to live thus, and not make more use of his great talents. He owned it was a bad habit. On reviewing, at the distance of many years, my journal of this period, I wonder how, at my first visit, I ventured to talk to him so freely, and that he bore it with so much indulgence.

Before we parted, he was so good as to promise to favor me with his company one evening at my lodgings; and, as I took my leave, shook me cordially by the hand. It is almost needless to add that I felt no little elation at having now so happily established an acquaintance of which I had been so long ambitious. . . .

I did not visit him again till Monday, June 13, at which time I recollect no part of his conversation, except that when I told him I had been to see Johnson ride upon three horses, he said, "Such a man, sir, should be encouraged; for his performances show the extent of the human powers in one instance, and thus tend to raise our opinion of the faculties of man. He shows what may be attained by persevering application; so that every man may hope that by giving as much application, although perhaps he may never ride three horses at a time or dance upon a wire, yet he may be equally expert in whatever profession he has chosen to pursue."

He again shook me by the hand at parting, and asked me why I did not come oftener to him. Trusting that I was now in his good graces, I answered that he had not given me much encouragement, and reminded him of the check I had received from him at our first interview. "Poh, poh!" said he, with a complacent smile, "never mind these things. Come to me as often as you can. I shall be glad to see you."

I had learnt that his place of frequent resort was the Mitre tavern in Fleet Street, where he loved to

<hr />

12 Charles Burney (1726–1814), a musician and a noted historian of music. For Smart, see pp. 845 ff., above.

sit up late; and I begged I might be allowed to pass an evening with him there soon, which he promised I should. A few days afterwards I met him near Temple Bar,[13] about one o'clock in the morning, and asked if he would then go to the Mitre. "Sir," said he, "it is too late; they won't let us in. But I'll go with you another night with all my heart."

A revolution of some importance in my plan of life had just taken place; for instead of procuring a commission in the Foot Guards, which was my own inclination, I had, in compliance with my father's wishes, agreed to study the law, and was soon to set out for Utrecht, to hear the lectures of an excellent Civilian[14] in that university, and then to proceed on my travels. Though very desirous of obtaining Dr. Johnson's advice and instructions on the mode of pursuing my studies, I was at this time so occupied, shall I call it? or so dissipated, by the amusements of London, that our next meeting was not till Saturday, June 25, when happening to dine at Clifton's eating-house, in Butcher Row,[15] I was surprised to perceive Johnson come in and take his seat at another table. The mode of dining, or rather being fed, at such houses in London is well known to many to be particularly unsocial, as there is no ordinary,[16] or united company, but each person has his own mess, and is under no obligation to hold any intercourse with anyone. A liberal and full-minded man, however, who loves to talk will break through this churlish and unsocial restraint. Johnson and an Irish gentleman got into a dispute concerning the cause of some part of mankind being black. "Why, sir," said Johnson, "it has been accounted for in three ways: either by supposing that they are the posterity of Ham, who was cursed; or that God at first created two kinds of men, one black and another white; or that by the heat of the sun the skin is scorched, and so acquires a sooty hue. This matter has been much canvassed among naturalists, but has never been brought to any certain issue." What the Irishman said is totally obliterated from my mind; but I remember that he became very warm and intemperate in his expressions; upon which Johnson rose, and quietly walked away. When he had retired, his antagonist took his revenge, as he thought, by saying, "He has a most ungainly figure, and an affectation of pomposity, unworthy of a man of genius."

Johnson had not observed that I was in the room. I followed him, however, and he agreed to meet me in the evening at the Mitre. I called on him, and we went thither at nine. We had a good supper, and port wine, of which he then sometimes drank a bottle. The orthodox High-Church sound of the Mitre[17]—the figure and manner of the celebrated SAMUEL JOHNSON—the extraordinary power and precision of his conversation, and the pride arising from finding myself admitted as his companion, produced a variety of sensations, and a pleasing elevation of mind beyond what I had ever before experienced. I find in my journal the following minute of our conversation, which, though it will give but a very faint notion of what passed, is in some degree a valuable record; and it will be curious in this view, as showing how habitual to his mind were some opinions which appear in his works. . . .

"Colley Cibber[18] sir, was by no means a blockhead; but by arrogating to himself too much, he was in danger of losing that degree of estimation to which he was entitled. His friends gave out that he *intended* his birthday odes should be bad: but that was not the case, sir; for he kept them many months by him, and a few years before he died he showed me one of them, with great solicitude to render it as perfect as might be, and I made some corrections, to which he was not very willing to submit. I remember the following couplet in allusion to the King and himself:

> Perched on the eagle's soaring wing,
> The lowly linnet loves to sing.

Sir, he had heard something of the fabulous tale of the wren sitting upon the eagle's wing, and he had applied it to a linnet. Cibber's familiar style, however, was better than that which Whitehead[19] has assumed. *Grand* nonsense is insupportable. Whitehead is but a little man to inscribe verses to players.[20] . . .

"Sir, I do not think Gray a first-rate poet. He has not a bold imagination, nor much command of words. The obscurity in which he has involved him-

---

[13] A gateway between the Strand and Fleet Street.
[14] Professor of civil law.   [15] Off the Strand.
[16] Table d'hôte, common table.

[17] A miter is a bishop's headdress.
[18] Pope made Cibber (1671–1757) the hero of the final version of his *Dunciad*. Cibber's poet laureateship was a joke; but he was an excellent comedian and a fairly good comic dramatist, as well as a delightful autobiographer. As the laureate he had to write an annual birthday ode to the King.
[19] The poetaster William Whitehead (1715–85) followed Cibber as poet laureate.
[20] Whitehead had written verses to Garrick, whom he served for a time as playreader.

self will not persuade us that he is sublime. His 'Elegy in a Churchyard' has a happy selection of images, but I don't like what are called his great things. His ode[21] which begins

> Ruin seize thee, ruthless King!
> Confusion on thy banners wait!

has been celebrated for its abruptness, and plunging into the subject all at once. But such arts as these have no merit, unless when they are original. We admire them only once; and this abruptness has nothing new in it. We have had it often before. Nay, we have it in the old song of Johnny Armstrong:

> Is there ever a man in all Scotland
> From the highest estate to the lowest degree, &c.

And then, sir,

> Yes, there is a man in Westmoreland,
> And Johnny Armstrong they do him call.

There, now, you plunge at once into the subject. You have no previous narration to lead you to it.— The two next lines in that ode are, I think, very good:

> Though fanned by Conquest's crimson wing,
> They mock the air with idle state."

Here let it be observed that although his opinion of Gray's poetry was widely different from mine, and I believe from that of most men of taste, by whom it is with justice highly admired, there is certainly much absurdity in the clamor which has been raised, as if he had been culpably injurious to the merit of that bard, and had been actuated by envy. Alas! ye little short-sighted critics, could Johnson be envious of the talents of any of his contemporaries? That his opinion on this subject was what in private and in public he uniformly expressed, regardless of what others might think, we may wonder, and perhaps regret; but it is shallow and unjust to charge him with expressing what he did not think.

Finding him in a placid humor, and wishing to avail myself of the opportunity which I fortunately had of consulting a sage, to hear whose wisdom, I conceived, in the ardor of youthful imagination, that men filled with a noble enthusiasm for intellectual improvement would gladly have resorted from distant lands,—I opened my mind to him ingenuously, and gave him a little sketch of my life, to which he was pleased to listen with great attention....

I complained to him that I had not yet acquired much knowledge, and asked his advice as to my studies. He said, "Don't talk of study now. I will give you a plan; but it will require some time to consider of it."—"It is very good in you," I replied, "to allow me to be with you thus. Had it been foretold to me some years ago that I should pass an evening with the author of the *Rambler,* how should I have exulted!" What I then expressed was sincerely from the heart. He was satisfied that it was, and cordially answered, "Sir, I am glad we have met. I hope we shall pass many evenings, and mornings too, together." We finished a couple of bottles of port, and sat till between one and two in the morning....

As Dr. Oliver Goldsmith will frequently appear in this narrative, I shall endeavor to make my readers in some degree acquainted with his singular character. He was a native of Ireland, and a contemporary with Mr. Burke[22] at Trinity College, Dublin, but did not then give much promise of future celebrity. He, however, observed to Mr. Malone[23] that though he "made no great figure in mathematics," which was a study in much repute there, he "could turn an ode of Horace into English better than any of them." He afterwards studied physic at Edinburgh, and upon the Continent, and, I have been informed, was enabled to pursue his travels on foot, partly by demanding at universities to enter the lists as a disputant, by which, according to the custom of many of them, he was entitled to the premium of a crown, when luckily for him his challenge was not accepted; so that, as I once observed to Dr. Johnson, he *disputed* his passage through Europe. He then came to England, and was employed successively in the capacities of an usher[24] to an academy, a corrector of the press,[25] a reviewer, and a writer for a newspaper. He had sagacity enough to cultivate assiduously the acquaintance of Johnson, and his faculties were gradually enlarged by the contemplation of such a model. To me and many others it appeared that he studiously copied the manner of Johnson, though, indeed, upon a smaller scale.

At this time I think he had published nothing with his name, though it was pretty generally known that "one Dr. Goldsmith" was the author of *An*

---

21 "The Bard" (pp. 840–42, above).

22 On Edmund Burke, the great statesman, political thinker, and orator, see pp. 907 ff., below.
23 Edmond Malone (1741–1812), the Shakespearean scholar.
24 Teacher.   25 Proofreader.

Enquiry into the Present State of Polite Learning in Europe, and of *The Citizen of the World,* a series of letters supposed to be written from London by a Chinese. No man had the art of displaying with more advantage as a writer whatever literary acquisitions he made. *Nihil quod tetigit non ornavit.*[26] His mind resembled a fertile but thin soil. There was a quick but not a strong vegetation, of whatever chanced to be thrown upon it. No deep root could be struck. The oak of the forest did not grow there; but the elegant shrubbery and the fragrant parterre[27] appeared in gay succession. It has been generally circulated and believed that he was a mere fool in conversation; but, in truth, this has been greatly exaggerated. He had, no doubt, a more than common share of that hurry of ideas which we often find in his countrymen, and which sometimes produces a laughable confusion in expressing them. He was very much what the French call *un étourdi,*[28] and from vanity and an eager desire of being conspicuous wherever he was, he frequently talked carelessly without knowledge of the subject, or even without thought. His person was short, his countenance coarse and vulgar, his deportment that of a scholar awkwardly affecting the easy gentleman. Those who were in any way distinguished excited envy in him to so ridiculous an excess that the instances of it are hardly credible. When accompanying two beautiful young ladies with their mother on a tour in France, he was seriously angry that more attention was paid to them than to him;[29] and once at the exhibition of the *fantoccini*[30] in London, when those who sat next to him observed with what dexterity a puppet was made to toss[31] a pike, he could not bear that it should have such praise, and exclaimed, with some warmth, "Pshaw! I can do it better myself."[32]

He, I am afraid, had no settled system of any sort, so that his conduct must not be strictly scrutinized; but his affections were social and generous, and when he had money he gave it away very liberally. His desire of imaginary consequence predominated over his attention to truth. When he began to rise into notice, he said he had a brother who was Dean of Durham,[33] a fiction so easily detected that it is wonderful how he should have been so inconsiderate as to hazard it. He boasted to me at this time of the power of his pen in commanding money, which I believe was true in a certain degree, though in the instance he gave he was by no means correct. He told me that he had sold a novel for four hundred pounds. This was his *Vicar of Wakefield.* But Johnson informed me that he had made the bargain for Goldsmith, and the price was sixty pounds. "And, sir," said he, "a sufficient price, too, when it was sold; for then the fame of Goldsmith had not been elevated, as it afterwards was, by his *Traveler;* and the bookseller had such faint hopes of profit by his bargain that he kept the manuscript by him a long time, and did not publish it till after the *Traveler* had appeared. Then, to be sure, it was accidentally worth more money."

Mrs. Piozzi[34] and Sir John Hawkins[35] have

---

[26] There was nothing he touched that he did not adorn (Dr. Johnson's inscription on the monument to Goldsmith erected in Westminster Abbey by the Literary Club).

[27] Ornamental arrangement of flower plots.

[28] A rattlebrain.—Later on Boswell notes a comment on this subject made by Johnson on April 27, 1773:

"He said, 'Goldsmith should not be for ever attempting to shine in conversation: he has not temper for it; he is so much mortified when he fails. Sir, a game of jokes is composed partly of skill, partly of chance. A man may be beat at times by one who has not the tenth part of his wit. Now Goldsmith's putting himself against another is like a man laying a hundred to one who cannot spare the hundred. It is not worth a man's while. A man should not lay a hundred to one unless he can easily spare it, though he has a hundred chances for him; he can get but a guinea, and he may lose a hundred. Goldsmith is in this state. When he contends, if he gets the better it is a very little addition to a man of his literary reputation; if he does not get the better, he is miserably vexed.'

"Johnson's own superlative powers of wit set him above any risk of such uneasiness. Garrick had remarked to me of him, a few days before, 'Rabelais and all other wits are nothing compared with him. You may be diverted by them; but Johnson gives you a forcible hug, and shakes laughter out of you, whether you will or no.'

"Goldsmith, however, was often very fortunate in his witty contests, even when he entered the lists with Johnson himself. Sir Joshua Reynolds was in company with them one day when Goldsmith said that he thought he could write a good fable, mentioned the simplicity which that kind of composition requires, and observed that in most fables the animals introduced seldom talk in character. 'For instance, said he, 'the fable of the little fishes who saw birds fly over their heads and, envying them, petitioned Jupiter to be changed into birds. The skill,' continued he, 'consists in making them talk like little fishes.' While he indulged himself in this fanciful reverie, he observed Johnson shaking his sides and laughing. Upon which he smartly proceeded, 'Why, Dr. Johnson, this is not so easy as you seem to think; for if you were to make little fishes talk, they would talk like WHALES.'"

[29] The young ladies were the Misses Horneck; but one of them afterwards explained that the incident Boswell refers to was in reality a bit of playfulness on Goldsmith's part. [30] Puppets.

[31] Probably=perform the manual of arms with.

[32] According to Boswell, "he went home with Mr. Burke to supper, and broke his shin by attempting to exhibit to the company how much better he could jump over a stick than the puppets."

[33] I.e., head of the canons of the cathedral there.

[34] The former Mrs. Thrale, Johnson's friend and benefactress. Her *Anecdotes of the Late Samuel Johnson* was published in 1786.

[35] A London lawyer and friend of Johnson, whose Life he wrote (1787).

strangely misstated the history of Goldsmith's situation and Johnson's friendly interference, when this novel was sold. I shall give it authentically from Johnson's own exact narration: "I received one morning a message from poor Goldsmith that he was in great distress, and, as it was not in his power to come to me, begging that I would come to him as soon as possible. I sent him a guinea, and promised to come to him directly. I accordingly went as soon as I was dressed, and found that his landlady had arrested him for his rent, at which he was in a violent passion. I perceived that he had already changed my guinea, and had got a bottle of Madeira and a glass before him. I put the cork into the bottle, desired he would be calm, and began to talk to him of the means by which he might be extricated. He then told me that he had a novel ready for the press, which he produced to me. I looked into it and saw its merit, told the landlady I should soon return, and having gone to a bookseller, sold it for sixty pounds. I brought Goldsmith the money, and he discharged his rent, not without rating his landlady in a high tone for having used him so ill."

My next meeting with Johnson was on Friday the 1st of July, when he and I and Dr. Goldsmith supped together at the Mitre. I was before this time pretty well acquainted with Goldsmith, who was one of the brightest ornaments of the Johnsonian school. Goldsmith's respectful attachment to Johnson was then at its height, for his own literary reputation had not yet distinguished him so much as to excite a vain desire of competition with his great master. He had increased my admiration of the goodness of Johnson's heart by incidental remarks in the course of conversation, such as, when I mentioned Mr. Levet,[36] whom he entertained under his roof, "He is poor and honest, which is recommendation enough to Johnson"; and when I wondered that he was very kind to a man of whom I had heard a very bad character, "He is now become miserable, and that insures the protection of Johnson."

Goldsmith attempted this evening to maintain, I suppose from an affectation of paradox, "that knowledge was not desirable on its own account, for it often was a source of unhappiness." JOHNSON.

"Why, sir, that knowledge may in some cases produce unhappiness, I allow. But, upon the whole, knowledge, per se,[37] is certainly an object which every man would wish to attain, although, perhaps, he may not take the trouble necessary for attaining it.". . .

On Tuesday the 5th of July, I again visited Johnson. . . .

Talking of London, he observed, "Sir, if you wish to have a just notion of the magnitude of this city, you must not be satisfied with seeing its great streets and squares, but must survey the innumerable little lanes and courts. It is not in the showy evolutions of buildings but in the multiplicity of human habitations which are crowded together that the wonderful immensity of London consists.". . .

On Wednesday, July 6, he was engaged to sup with me at my lodgings in Downing Street, Westminster. But on the preceding night my landlord having behaved very rudely to me and some company who were with me, I had resolved not to remain another night in his house. I was exceedingly uneasy at the awkward appearance I supposed I should make to Johnson and the other gentlemen whom I had invited, not being able to receive them at home, and being obliged to order supper at the Mitre. I went to Johnson in the morning, and talked of it as a serious distress. He laughed, and said, "Consider, sir, how insignificant this will appear a twelvemonth hence." Were this consideration to be applied to most of the little vexatious incidents of life by which our quiet is too often disturbed, it would prevent many painful sensations. I have tried it frequently, with good effect. "There is nothing," continued he, "in this mighty misfortune; nay, we shall be better at the Mitre." I told him that I had been at Sir John Fielding's[38] office, complaining of my landlord, and had been informed that though I had taken my lodgings for a year, I might, upon proof of his bad behavior, quit them when I pleased without being under an obligation to pay rent for any longer time than while I possessed them. The fertility of Johnson's mind could show itself even upon so small a matter as this. "Why, sir," said he, "I suppose this must be the law, since you have been told so in Bow Street. But if your landlord could hold you to your bargain, and the lodgings should

36 Dr. Robert Levet died in 1782 aged seventy-six. This poverty-stricken physician was one of Johnson's "inmates." His death was the occasion of one of Johnson's better poems; it includes the fine stanza

"His virtues walked their narrow round,
Nor made a pause, nor left a void;
And sure th' Eternal Master found
The single talent well employed."

37 As such, of itself.
38 A well-known judge, the blind half-brother of the great novelist, Henry Fielding (1707-54). Sir John (d. 1780) followed his brother as magistrate. In Bow Street, near Drury Lane, both the Fieldings lived. London's principal magistrate's-court is still in Bow Street.

be yours for a year, you may certainly use them as you think fit. So, sir, you may quarter two Life Guardmen upon him; or you may send the greatest scoundrel you can find into your apartments; or you may say that you want to make some experiments in natural philosophy,[39] and may burn a large quantity of asafetida in his house."

I had as my guests this evening at the Mitre tavern, Dr. Johnson, Dr. Goldsmith, Mr. Thomas Davies, Mr. Eccles, an Irish gentleman for whose agreeable company I was obliged to Mr. Davies, and the Rev. Mr. John Ogilvie,[40] who was desirous of being in company with my illustrious friend, while I, in my turn, was proud to have the honor of showing one of my countrymen upon what easy terms Johnson permitted me to live with him.

Goldsmith, as usual, endeavored with too much eagerness to *shine,* and disputed very warmly with Johnson against the well-known maxim of the British constitution, "the king can do no wrong"; affirming that "what was morally false could not be politically true; and as the king might, in the exercise of his regal power, command and cause the doing of what was wrong, it certainly might be said, in sense and in reason, that he could do wrong." JOHNSON. "Sir, you are to consider that in our constitution, according to its true principles, the king is the head, he is supreme; he is above everything, and there is no power by which he can be tried. Therefore it is, sir, that we hold the king can do no wrong, that whatever may happen to be wrong in government may not be above our reach by being ascribed to majesty. Redress is always to be had against oppression, by punishing the immediate agents. The king, though he should command, cannot force a judge to condemn a man unjustly; therefore it is the judge whom we prosecute and punish. Political institutions are formed upon the consideration of what will most frequently tend to the good of the whole, although now and then exceptions may occur. Thus it is better in general that a nation should have a supreme legislative power, although it may at times be abused. And then, sir, there is this consideration, that *if the abuse be enormous, nature will rise up, and, claiming her original rights, overturn a corrupt political system.*" I mark this animated sentence with peculiar pleasure, as a noble instance of that truly dignified spirit of freedom which ever glowed in his heart, though he was charged with slavish tenets by superficial observers; because he was at all times indignant against that false patriotism, that pretended love of freedom, that unruly restlessness, which is inconsistent with the stable authority of any good government.

This generous sentiment, which he uttered with great fervor, struck me exceedingly, and stirred my blood to that pitch of fancied resistance, the possibility of which I am glad to keep in mind, but to which I trust I never shall be forced.

"Great abilities," said he, "are not requisite for an historian; for in historical composition, all the greatest powers of the human mind are quiescent. He has facts ready to his hand; so there is no exercise of invention. Imagination is not required in any high degree, only about as much as is used in the lower kinds of poetry. Some penetration, accuracy, and coloring will fit a man for the task, if he can give the application which is necessary.". . .

Talking of the eminent writers in Queen Anne's reign, he observed, "I think Dr. Arbuthnot[41] the first man among them. He was the most universal genius, being an excellent physician, a man of deep learning, and a man of much humor. Mr. Addison was, to be sure, a great man: his learning was not profound; but his morality, his humor, and his elegance of writing set him very high."

Mr. Ogilvie was unlucky enough to choose for the topic of his conversation the praises of his native country. He began with saying that there was very rich land round Edinburgh. Goldsmith, who had studied physic there, contradicted this, very untruly, with a sneering laugh. Disconcerted a little by this, Mr. Ogilvie then took new ground, where, I suppose, he thought himself perfectly safe; for he observed that Scotland had a great many noble wild prospects. JOHNSON. "I believe, sir, you have a great many. Norway, too, has noble wild prospects; and Lapland is remarkable for prodigious noble wild prospects. But, sir, let me tell you, the noblest prospect which a Scotchman ever sees is the high road that leads him to England!" This unexpected and pointed sally produced a roar of applause. After all, however, those who admire the rude grandeur of nature cannot deny it to Caledonia.

On Saturday, July 9, I found Johnson surrounded with a numerous levee, but have not preserved any part of his conversation. On the 14th we had another evening by ourselves at the Mitre. . . .

Feeling myself now quite at ease as his companion, though I had all possible reverence for him, I

---

39 Science.

40 Ogilvie (1733–1813), a Presbyterian minister, was the author of *Poems on Several Subjects* and other volumes.

41 See p. 805, above.

expressed a regret that I could not be so easy with my father, though he was not much older than Johnson, and certainly however respectable had not more learning and greater abilities to depress me. I asked him the reason of this. JOHNSON. "Why, sir, I am a man of the world. I live in the world, and I take, in some degree, the color of the world as it moves along. Your father is a judge in a remote part of the island, and all his notions are taken from the old world. Besides, sir, there must always be a struggle between a father and son while one aims at power and the other at independence.". . .

He enlarged very convincingly upon the excellence of rime over blank verse in English poetry. I mentioned to him that Dr. Adam Smith,[42] in his lectures upon composition, when I studied under him in the College of Glasgow, had maintained the same opinion strenuously, and I repeated some of his arguments. JOHNSON. "Sir, I was once in company with Smith, and we did not take to each other; but had I known that he loved rime as much as you tell me he does, I should have HUGGED him.". . .

One day when dining at old Mr. Langton's[43] where Miss Roberts, his niece, was one of the company, Johnson, with his usual complacent attention to the fair sex, took her by the hand and said, "My dear, I hope you are a Jacobite."[44] Old Mr. Langton, who, though a high and steady Tory, was attached to the present royal family, seemed offended, and asked Johnson, with great warmth, what he could mean by putting such a question to his niece. "Why, sir," said Johnson, "I meant no offense to your niece; I meant her a great compliment. A Jacobite, sir, believes in the divine right of kings. He that believes in the divine right of kings believes in a Divinity. A Jacobite believes in the divine right of bishops. He that believes in the divine right of bishops believes in the divine authority of the Christian religion. Therefore, sir, a Jacobite is neither an atheist nor a Deist. That cannot be said of a Whig; for *Whiggism is a negation of all principle.*"

He advised me, when abroad, to be as much as I could with the professors in the universities, and with the clergy; for from their conversation I might expect the best accounts of everything in whatever country I should be, with the additional advantage of keeping my learning alive.

It will be observed that when giving me advice as to my travels, Dr. Johnson did not dwell upon cities and palaces and pictures and shows and Arcadian[45] scenes. He was of Lord Essex's[46] opinion, who advises his kinsman Roger, Earl of Rutland, "rather to go an hundred miles to speak with one wise man than five miles to see a fair town."

I described to him an impudent fellow from Scotland,[47] who affected to be a savage, and railed at all established systems. JOHNSON. "There is nothing surprising in this, sir. He wants to make himself conspicuous. He would tumble in a hogsty, as long as you looked at him and called to him to come out. But let him alone, never mind him, and he'll soon give it over."

I added that the same person maintained that there was no distinction between virtue and vice. JOHNSON. "Why, sir, if the fellow does not think as he speaks, he is lying; and I see not what honor he can propose to himself from having the character of a liar. But if he does really think that there is no distinction between virtue and vice, why, sir, when he leaves our houses let us count our spoons.". . .

He recommended to me to keep a journal of my life, full and unreserved. He said it would be a very good exercise, and would yield me great satisfaction when the particulars were faded from my remembrance. I was uncommonly fortunate in having had a previous coincidence of opinion with him upon this subject, for I had kept such a journal for some time; and it was no small pleasure to me to have this to tell him, and to receive his approbation. He counseled me to keep it private, and said I might surely have a friend who would burn it in case of my death. From this habit I have been enabled to give the world so many anecdotes, which would otherwise have been lost to posterity. I mentioned that I was afraid I put into my journal too many little incidents. JOHNSON. "There is nothing, sir, too little for so little a creature as man. It is by studying little things that we attain the great art of having as little misery and as much happiness as possible.". . .

At night, Mr. Johnson and I supped in a private room at the Turk's Head coffee house, in the Strand. "I encourage this house," said he, "for the mistress of it is a good civil woman, and has not much business.

---

[42] The great economist (1723–90). Years before his *Wealth of Nations* (1776) he had held chairs of logic and moral philosophy at Glasgow.

[43] The father of Bennet Langton (1737–1801), who was an original member of the Literary Club and one of Johnson's closest friends.

[44] From *Jacobus,* the Latin word for *James;* i.e., an upholder of the Stuart claim to the throne.

[45] I.e., merely pleasant (from the traditional idealization of pastoral scenes, supposed to abound in Arcadia, Greece).

[46] Robert Devereux, second Earl of Essex (d. 1601). The letter (1596) may have been written by Bacon.

[47] Elsewhere identified by Boswell as the poet Macpherson (see note 11, above).

"Sir, I love the acquaintance of young people; because, in the first place, I don't like to think myself growing old. In the next place, young acquaintances must last longest, if they do last; and then, sir, young men have more virtue than old men; they have more generous sentiments in every respect. I love the young dogs of this age: they have more wit and humor and knowledge of life than we had; but then, the dogs are not so good scholars. Sir, in my early years I read very hard. It is a sad reflection but a true one, that I knew almost as much at eighteen as I do now. My judgment, to be sure, was not so good; but I had all the facts. I remember very well, when I was at Oxford, an old gentleman said to me, 'Young man, ply your book diligently now, and acquire a stock of knowledge; for when years come upon you, you will find that poring upon books will be but an irksome task.' "...

He mentioned to me now, for the first time, that he had been distressed by melancholy, and for that reason had been obliged to fly from study and meditation, to the dissipating variety of life. Against melancholy he recommended constant occupation of mind, a great deal of exercise, moderation in eating and drinking, and especially to shun drinking at night. He said melancholy people were apt to fly to intemperance for relief, but that it sunk them much deeper in misery. He observed, that laboring men who work hard, and live sparingly, are seldom or never troubled with low spirits.

He again insisted on the duty of maintaining subordination of rank. "Sir, I would no more deprive a nobleman of his respect than of his money. I consider myself as acting a part in the great system of society, and I do to others as I would have them to do to me. I would behave to a nobleman as I should expect he would behave to me, were I a nobleman and he Sam Johnson. Sir, there is one Mrs. Macaulay[48] in this town, a great republican. One day when I was at her house, I put on a very grave countenance, and said to her, 'Madam, I am now become a convert to your way of thinking. I am convinced that all mankind are upon an equal footing; and to give you an unquestionable proof, madam, that I am in earnest, here is a very sensible, civil, well-behaved fellow-citizen, your footman; I desire that he may be allowed to sit down and dine with us.' I thus, sir, showed her the absurdity of the leveling doctrine. She has never liked me since.

Sir, your levelers wish to level down as far as themselves; but they cannot bear leveling up to themselves. They would all have some people under them; why not then have some people above them?" I mentioned a certain author who disgusted me by his forwardness, and by showing no deference to noblemen into whose company he was admitted. JOHNSON. "Suppose a shoemaker should claim an equality with him, as he does with a lord; how he would stare. 'Why, sir, do you stare?' says the shoemaker; 'I do great service to society. 'Tis true, I am paid for doing it; but so are you, sir: and I am sorry to say it, paid better than I am, for doing something not so necessary. For mankind could do better without your books, than without my shoes.' Thus, sir, there would be a perpetual struggle for precedence, were there no fixed invariable rules for the distinction of rank, which creates no jealousy, as it is allowed to be accidental."...

He said he would go to the Hebrides with me, when I returned from my travels, unless some very good companion should offer when I was absent, which he did not think probable; adding, "There are few people to whom I take so much to as you." And when I talked of my leaving England, he said with a very affectionate air, "My dear Boswell, I should be very unhappy at parting, did I think we were not to meet again." I cannot too often remind my readers that, although such instances of his kindness are doubtless very flattering to me, yet I hope my recording them will be ascribed to a better motive than to vanity; for they afford unquestionable evidence of his tenderness and complacency,[49] which some, while they were forced to acknowledge his great powers, have been so strenuous to deny.

He maintained that a boy at school was the happiest of human beings. I supported a different opinion, from which I have never yet varied, that a man is happier; and I enlarged upon the anxiety and sufferings which are endured at school. JOHNSON. "Ah! sir, a boy's being flogged is not so severe as a man's having the hiss of the world against him. Men have a solicitude about fame; and the greater share they have of it, the more afraid they are of losing it." I silently asked myself, "Is it possible that the great SAMUEL JOHNSON really entertains any such apprehension, and is not confident that his exalted fame is established upon a foundation never to be shaken?"...

I again begged his advice as to my method of study at Utrecht. "Come," said he, "let us make a

---

[48] Catherine Macaulay (1731-91), author of a popular history of England.

[49] Good nature.

day of it. Let us go down to Greenwich and dine, and talk of it there." The following Saturday was fixed for this excursion.

As we walked along the Strand tonight, arm in arm, a woman of the town accosted us, in the usual enticing manner. "No, no, my girl," said Johnson, "it won't do." He, however, did not treat her with harshness; and we talked of the wretched life of such women, and agreed that much more misery than happiness, upon the whole, is produced by illicit commerce between the sexes.

On Saturday, July 30, Dr. Johnson and I took a sculler[50] at the Temple Stairs, and set out for Greenwich. I asked him if he really thought a knowledge of the Greek and Latin languages an essential requisite to a good education. JOHNSON. "Most certainly, sir, for those who know them have a very great advantage over those who do not. Nay, sir, it is wonderful what a difference learning makes upon people even in the common intercourse of life, which does not appear to be much connected with it."—"And yet," said I, "people go through the world very well, and carry on the business of life to good advantage, without learning." JOHNSON. "Why, sir, that may be true in cases where learning cannot possibly be of any use; for instance, this boy rows us as well without learning, as if he could sing the song of Orpheus to the Argonauts,[51] who were the first sailors." He then called to the boy, "What would you give, my lad, to know about the Argonauts?" —"Sir," said the boy, "I would give what I have." Johnson was much pleased with his answer, and we gave him a double fare. Dr. Johnson then turning to me, "Sir," said he, "a desire of knowledge is the natural feeling of mankind; and every human being whose mind is not debauched will be willing to give all that he has, to get knowledge."

We landed at the Old Swan,[52] and walked to Billingsgate, where we took oars and moved smoothly along the silver Thames. It was a very fine day. We were entertained with the immense number and variety of ships that were lying at anchor, and with the beautiful country on each side of the river.

I talked of preaching, and of the great success which those called Methodists have. JOHNSON. "Sir, it is owing to their expressing themselves in a plain and familiar manner, which is the only way to do good to the common people, and which clergymen of genius and learning ought to do from a principle of duty, when it is suited to their congregations, a practice for which they will be praised by men of sense. To insist against drunkenness as a crime because it debases reason, the noblest faculty of man, would be of no service to the common people; but to tell them that they may die in a fit of drunkenness, and show them how dreadful that would be, cannot fail to make a deep impression. Sir, when your Scotch clergy give up their homely manner, religion will soon decay in that country." Let this observation, as Johnson meant it, be ever remembered.

I was much pleased to find myself with Johnson at Greenwich, which he celebrates in his *London* as a favorite scene. I had the poem in my pocket, and read the lines aloud with enthusiasm:

On Thames's banks in silent thought we stood,
Where Greenwich smiles upon the silver flood:
Pleased with the seat which gave ELIZA[53] birth,
We kneel, and kiss the consecrated earth.

. . . Afterwards he entered upon the business of the day, which was to give me his advice as to a course of study. And here I am to mention with much regret that my record of what he said is miserably scanty. I recollect with admiration an animating blaze of eloquence, which roused every intellectual power in me to the highest pitch, but must have dazzled me so much that my memory could not preserve the substance of his discourse; for the note which I find of it is no more than this:—"He ran over the grand scale of human knowledge; advised me to select some particular branch to excel in, but to acquire a little of every kind." The defect of my minutes will be fully supplied by a long letter upon the subject, which he favored me with after I had been some time at Utrecht, and which my readers will have the pleasure to peruse in its proper place.

We walked in the evening in Greenwich Park. He asked me, I suppose by way of trying my disposition, "Is not this very fine?" Having no exquisite relish of the beauties of nature, and being more delighted with "the busy hum of men,"[54] I answered, "Yes, sir; but not equal to Fleet Street." JOHNSON. "You are right, sir.". . .

We stayed so long at Greenwich that our sail up the river, in our return to London, was by no means

---

50 A small rowboat.
51 Jason's companions on his search for the Golden Fleece.
52 Landing stairs above London Bridge. Since the tide ran so strongly that there was an element of danger in shooting the narrow arches of the Bridge, passengers often landed above it, walked to the district of Billingsgate below it, and took another boat there.

53 Queen Elizabeth was born in the palace there.
54 Milton, "L'Allegro," line 118.

so pleasant as in the morning; for the night air was so cold that it made me shiver. I was the more sensible of it from having sat up all the night before recollecting and writing in my journal what I thought worthy of preservation, an exertion which, during the first part of my acquaintance with Johnson, I frequently made. I remember having sat up four nights in one week, without being much incommoded in the daytime.

Johnson, whose robust frame was not in the least affected by the cold, scolded me, as if my shivering had been a paltry effeminacy, saying, "Why do you shiver?". . . It is not easy to make allowance for sensations in others, which we ourselves have not at the time. . . .

We concluded the day at the Turk's Head coffee house very socially. He was pleased to listen to a particular account which I gave him of my family, and of its hereditary estate, as to the extent and population of which he asked questions, and made calculations, recommending at the same time a liberal kindness to the tenantry, as people over whom the proprietor was placed by Providence. He took delight in hearing my description of the romantic seat of my ancestors. "I must be there, sir," said he, "and we will live in the old castle; and if there is not a room in it remaining, we will build one." I was highly flattered, but could scarcely indulge a hope that Auchinleck would indeed be honored by his presence, and celebrated by a description, as it afterwards was, in his *Journey to the Western Islands.*

After we had again talked of my setting out for Holland, he said, "I must see thee out of England; I will accompany you to Harwich." I could not find words to express what I felt upon this unexpected and very great mark of his affectionate regard.

Next day, Sunday, July 31, I told him I had been that morning at a meeting of the people called Quakers, where I had heard a woman preach. JOHNSON. "Sir, a woman's preaching is like a dog's walking on his hinder legs. It is not done well; but you are surprised to find it done at all."

On Tuesday, August 2 (the day of my departure from London having been fixed for the 5th), Dr. Johnson did me the honor to pass a part of the morning with me at my chambers. He said that he "always felt an inclination to do nothing." I observed that it was strange to think that the most indolent man in Britain had written the most laborious work, *The English Dictionary.* . . .

On Friday, August 5, we set out early in the morning in the Harwich stagecoach. A fat elderly gentlewoman and a young Dutchman seemed the most inclined among us to conversation. At the inn where we dined, the gentlewoman said that she had done her best to educate her children, and particularly that she had never suffered them to be a moment idle. JOHNSON. "I wish, madam, you would educate me too; for I have been an idle fellow all my life." "I am sure, sir," said she, "you have not been idle." JOHNSON. "Nay, madam, it is very true; and that gentleman there," pointing to me, "has been idle. He was idle at Edinburgh. His father sent him to Glasgow, where he continued to be idle. He then came to London, where he has been very idle; and now he is going to Utrecht, where he will be as idle as ever." I asked him privately how he could expose me so. JOHNSON. "Poh, poh!" said he; "they knew nothing about you, and will think of it no more." In the afternoon the gentlewoman talked violently against the Roman Catholics, and of the horrors of the Inquisition. To the utter astonishment of all the passengers but myself, who knew that he could talk upon any side of a question, he defended the Inquisition, and maintained that "false doctrine should be checked on its first appearance; that the civil power should unite with the church in punishing those who dared to attack the established religion, and that such only were punished by the Inquisition.". . . Though by no means niggardly, his attention to what was generally right was so minute that, having observed at one of the stages that I ostentatiously gave a shilling to the coachman, when the custom was for each passenger to give only sixpence, he took me aside and scolded me, saying that what I had done would make the coachman dissatisfied with all the rest of the passengers, who gave him no more than his due. This was a just reprimand; for in whatever way a man may indulge his generosity or his vanity in spending his money, for the sake of others he ought not to raise the price of any article for which there is a constant demand. . . .

At supper this night he talked of good eating with uncommon satisfaction. "Some people," said he, "have a foolish way of not minding, or pretending not to mind, what they eat. For my part, I mind my belly very studiously, and very carefully; for I look upon it that he who does not mind his belly will hardly mind anything else." He now appeared to me *Jean Bull philosophe;*[55] and he was, for the moment, not only serious but vehement. Yet I have heard him, upon other occasions, talk with great contempt of people who were anxious to gratify their palates;

---

[55] John Bull as philosopher.

and the 206th number of his *Rambler* is a masterly essay against gulosity. His practice, indeed, I must acknowledge, may be considered as casting the balance of his different opinions upon this subject; for I never knew any man who relished good eating more than he did. When at table, he was totally absorbed in the business of the moment; his looks seemed riveted to his plate; nor would he, unless when in very high company, say one word, or even pay the least attention to what was said by others, till he had satisfied his appetite, which was so fierce, and indulged with such intenseness, that while in the act of eating the veins of his forehead swelled, and generally a strong perspiration was visible. To those whose sensations were delicate, this could not but be disgusting; and it was doubtless not very suitable to the character of a philosopher, who should be distinguished by self-command. But it must be owned that Johnson, though he could be rigidly *abstemious,* was not a *temperate* man either in eating or drinking. He could refrain, but he could not use moderately. He told me that he had fasted two days without inconvenience, and that he had never been hungry but once. They who beheld with wonder how much he ate upon all occasions, when his dinner was to his taste, could not easily conceive what he must have meant by hunger; and not only was he remarkable for the extraordinary quantity which he ate, but he was, or affected to be, a man of very nice discernment in the science of cookery. He used to descant critically on the dishes which had been at table where he had dined or supped, and to recollect very minutely what he had liked. I remember, when he was in Scotland, his praising "Gordon's palates" (a dish of palates[56] at the Honorable Alexander Gordon's) with a warmth of expression which might have done honor to more important subjects. "As for Maclaurin's[57] imitation of a made dish, it was a wretched attempt." He about the same time was so much displeased with the performances of a nobleman's French cook that he exclaimed with vehemence, "I'd throw such a rascal into the river"; and he then proceeded to alarm a lady at whose house he was to sup, by the following manifesto of his skill: "I, madam, who live at a variety of good tables, am a much better judge of cookery than any person who has a very tolerable cook but lives much at home; for his palate is gradually adapted to the taste of his cook; whereas, madam, in trying by a wider range,

I can more exquisitely judge." When invited to dine, even with an intimate friend, he was not pleased if something better than a plain dinner was not prepared for him. I have heard him say on such an occasion, "This was a good dinner enough, to be sure: but it was not a dinner to *ask* a man to." On the other hand, he was wont to express, with great glee, his satisfaction when he had been entertained quite to his mind. One day when he had dined with his neighbor and landlord, in Bolt Court,[58] Mr. Allen, the printer, whose old housekeeper had studied his taste in everything, he pronounced this eulogy: "Sir, we could not have had a better dinner, had there been a *synod of cooks.*"

While we were left by ourselves, after the Dutchman had gone to bed, Dr. Johnson talked of that studied behavior which many have recommended and practiced. He disapproved of it and said, "I never considered whether I should be a grave man or a merry man, but just let inclination, for the time, have its course.". . .

Next day we got to Harwich, to dinner; and my passage in the packet-boat to Helvoetsluys being secured, and my baggage put on board, we dined at our inn by ourselves. I happened to say it would be terrible if he should not find a speedy opportunity of returning to London, and be confined in so dull a place. JOHNSON. "Don't, sir, accustom yourself to use big words for little matters. It would *not* be *terrible,* though I *were* to be detained some time here.". . .

My revered friend walked down with me to the beach, where we embraced and parted with tenderness, and engaged to correspond by letters. I said, "I hope, sir, you will not forget me in my absence." JOHNSON. "Nay, sir, it is more likely you should forget me than that I should forget you." As the vessel put out to sea, I kept my eyes upon him for a considerable time, while he remained rolling his majestic frame in his usual manner; and at last I perceived him walk back into the town, and he disappeared.

FROM THE YEAR 1764

About this time he was afflicted with a very severe return of the hypochondriac disorder which was ever lurking about him. He was so ill as, notwithstanding his remarkable love of company, to be

56 I.e., soft palates, presumably of beef cattle.
57 Another gentleman visited by Johnson during his tour of Scotland and the Hebrides.

58 It leads off the north side of Fleet Street. Johnson lived at no. 8 from 1776 till his death. It was there that the great actress Mrs. Siddons called on him. When she left, his servant had some difficulty in finding a sedan chair for her; and Johnson gallantly remarked that wherever she came there were no seats to be had.

entirely averse to society, the most fatal symptom of that malady. Dr. Adams[1] told me that as an old friend he was admitted to visit him, and that he found him in a deplorable state, sighing, groaning, talking to himself, and restlessly walking from room to room. He then used this emphatical expression of the misery which he felt: "I would consent to have a limb amputated to recover my spirits."

Talking to himself was, indeed, one of his singularities ever since I knew him. I was certain that he was frequently uttering pious ejaculations; for fragments of the Lord's Prayer have been distinctly overheard. His friend Mr. Thomas Davies, of whom Churchill says, "That Davies hath a very pretty wife,"[2] when Dr. Johnson muttered, "Lead us not into temptation," used with waggish and gallant humor to whisper Mrs. Davies, "You, my dear, are the cause of this."

He had another particularity, of which none of his friends ever ventured to ask an explanation. It appeared to me some superstitious habit which he had contracted early, and from which he had never called upon his reason to disentangle him. This was his anxious care to go out or in at a door or passage by a certain number of steps from a certain point, or at least so as that either his right or his left foot (I am not certain which) should constantly make the first actual movement when he came close to the door or passage. Thus I conjecture: for I have upon innumerable occasions observed him suddenly stop, and then seem to count his steps with a deep earnestness; and when he had neglected or gone wrong in this sort of magical movement, I have seen him go back again, put himself in a proper posture to begin the ceremony, and, having gone through it, break from his abstraction, walk briskly on, and join his companion. A strange instance of something of this nature, even when on horseback, happened when he was in the Isle of Skye.[3] Sir Joshua Reynolds has observed him to go a good way about rather than cross a particular alley in Leicester Fields;[4] but this Sir Joshua imputed to his having had some disagreeable recollection associated with it.

That the most minute singularities which belonged to him, and made very observable parts of his appearance and manner, may not be omitted, it is requisite to mention that while talking or even musing as he sat in his chair, he commonly held his head to one side towards his right shoulder, and shook it in a tremulous manner, moving his body backwards and forwards, and rubbing his left knee in the same direction with the palm of his hand. In the intervals of articulating he made various sounds with his mouth, sometimes as if ruminating or what is called chewing the cud, sometimes giving a half whistle, sometimes making his tongue play backwards from the roof of his mouth as if clucking like a hen, and sometimes protruding it against his upper gums in front, as if pronouncing quickly under his breath *too, too, too:* all this accompanied sometimes with a thoughtful look, but more frequently with a smile. Generally when he had concluded a period in the course of a dispute, by which time he was a good deal exhausted by violence and vociferation, he used to blow out his breath like a whale. This I supposed was a relief to his lungs, and seemed in him to be a contemptuous mode of expression, as if he had made the arguments of his opponent fly like chaff before the wind.

I am fully aware how very obvious an occasion I here give for the sneering jocularity of such as have no relish of an exact likeness; which to render complete, he who draws it must not disdain the slightest strokes. But if witlings should be inclined to attack this account, let them have the candor to quote what I have offered in my defense.

FROM THE YEAR 1776

I am now to record a very curious incident in Dr. Johnson's life, which fell under my own observation; of which *pars magna fui,*[1] and which I am persuaded will, with the liberal minded, be much to his credit.

My desire of being acquainted with celebrated men of every description had made me, much about the same time, obtain an introduction to Dr. Samuel Johnson and to John Wilkes, Esq.[2] Two men more different could perhaps not be selected out of all mankind. They had even attacked one

---

[1] The Rev. William Adams (1706–89), a fellow student at Pembroke College, Oxford, and afterwards its Master.
[2] Charles Churchill (1731–64), author of the *Rosciad,* a satire on actors and theater managers. The quotation is line 320.
[3] In the Hebrides.
[4] Now Leicester Square, near Piccadilly Circus.

[1] I was a large part.
[2] Wilkes (1727–97) was a brilliant but unprincipled and dissolute politician; through his expulsion from the House of Commons (to which he had eventually to be readmitted), he became a champion of free representation. His liberal opinions were, of course, highly obnoxious to the Toryism of Johnson. In *The False Alarm* (1770) Johnson had called him "a retailer of sedition and obscenity," while in no. 12 of his paper the *North Briton* Wilkes had suggested that Johnson was "a slave of the state, hired by a stipend to obey his master."

another with some asperity in their writings; yet I lived in habits of friendship with both. I could fully relish the excellence of each; for I have ever delighted in that intellectual chemistry which can separate good qualities from evil in the same person. . . . But I conceived an irresistible wish, if possible, to bring Dr. Johnson and Mr. Wilkes together. How to manage it was a nice and difficult matter.

My worthy booksellers and friends, Messieurs Dilly in the Poultry,[3] at whose hospitable and well-covered table I have seen a greater number of literary men than at any other except that of Sir Joshua Reynolds, had invited me to meet Mr. Wilkes and some more gentlemen on Wednesday, May 15. "Pray," said I, "let us have Dr. Johnson."—"What, with Mr. Wilkes? not for the world," said Mr. Edward Dilly; "Dr. Johnson would never forgive me."—"Come," said I, "if you'll let me negotiate for you, I will be answerable that all shall go well." DILLY. "Nay, if you will take it upon you, I am sure I shall be very happy to see them both here."

Notwithstanding the high veneration which I entertained for Dr. Johnson, I was sensible that he was sometimes a little actuated by the spirit of contradiction, and by means of that I hoped I should gain my point. I was persuaded that if I had come upon him with a direct proposal, "Sir, will you dine in company with Jack Wilkes?" he would have flown into a passion, and would probably have answered, "Dine with Jack Wilkes, sir! I'd as soon dine with Jack Ketch."[4] I therefore, while we were sitting quietly by ourselves at his house in an evening, took occasion to open my plan thus:—"Mr. Dilly, sir, sends his respectful compliments to you, and would be happy if you would do him the honor to dine with him on Wednesday next along with me, as I must soon go to Scotland." JOHNSON. "Sir, I am obliged to Mr. Dilly. I will wait upon him—" BOSWELL. "Provided, sir, I suppose, that the company which he is to have is agreeable to you." JOHNSON. "What do you mean, sir? What do you take me for? Do you think I am so ignorant of the world as to imagine that I am to prescribe to a gentleman what company he is to have at his table?" BOSWELL. "I beg your pardon, sir, for wishing to prevent you from meeting people whom you might not like. Perhaps he may have some of what he calls his patriotic friends with him." JOHNSON.

"Well, sir, and what then? What care *I* for his *patriotic friends*? Poh!" BOSWELL. "I should not be surprised to find Jack Wilkes there." JOHNSON. "And if Jack Wilkes *should* be there, what is that to *me, sir*? My dear friend, let us have no more of this. I am sorry to be angry with you; but really it is treating me strangely to talk to me as if I could not meet any company whatever, occasionally." BOSWELL. "Pray forgive me, sir: I meant well. But you shall meet whoever comes, for me." Thus I secured him, and told Dilly that he would find him very well pleased to be one of his guests on the day appointed. . . .

When we entered Mr. Dilly's drawing room, he found himself in the midst of a company he did not know. I kept myself snug and silent, watching how he would conduct himself. I observed him whispering to Mr. Dilly, "Who is that gentleman, sir?"—"Mr. Arthur Lee."—JOHNSON. "Too, too, too" (under his breath), which was one of his habitual mutterings. Mr. Arthur Lee could not but be very obnoxious to Johnson, for he was not only a *patriot* but an *American*.[5] He was afterwards minister from the United States at the court of Madrid. "And who is the gentleman in lace?"—"Mr. Wilkes, sir." This information confounded him still more; he had some difficulty to restrain himself, and, taking up a book, sat down upon a window seat and read, or at least kept his eye upon it intently for some time, till he composed himself. His feelings, I dare say, were awkward enough. But he no doubt recollected his having rated me for supposing that he could be at all disconcerted by any company, and he therefore resolutely set himself to behave quite as an easy man

[5] Lee (1740–92) was an agent of the Continental Congress. One of the Virginia Lees, he had been educated at Eton, Edinburgh, and the Inns of Court. He was a great friend of Wilkes. On the colonial question Johnson was, of course, a hot Tory. In the midst of a discussion of some religious books on April 15, 1778, says Boswell, "he, I know not how or why, made a sudden transition to one upon which he was a violent aggressor; for he said, 'I am willing to love all mankind, *except an American';* and his inflammable corruption bursting into horrid fire, he 'breathed out threatenings and slaughter,' calling them 'rascals—robbers—pirates,' and exclaiming he'd 'burn and destroy them.' Miss Seward, looking to him with mild but steady astonishment, said, 'Sir, this is an instance that we are always most violent against those whom we have injured.' He was irritated still more by this delicate and keen reproach, and roared out another tremendous volley, which one might fancy could be heard across the Atlantic. During this tempest I sat in great uneasiness, lamenting his heat of temper, till by degrees I diverted his attention to other topics."

Of the other guests, Miller and Slater are not identified in the index to Hill's edition, nor in the *Dictionary of National Biography*. Dr. John C. Lettsom (1744–1815) was a distinguished Quaker physician and also a writer.

[3] A street connecting Cheapside and Cornhill.
[4] The public executioner; from the name of a notorious one (d. 1686) in Restoration times.

of the world, who could adapt himself at once to the disposition and manners of those whom he might chance to meet.

The cheering sound of "Dinner is upon the table" dissolved his reverie, and we *all* sat down without any symptom of ill humor. There were present, besides Mr. Wilkes, and Mr. Arthur Lee, who was an old companion of mine when he studied physic at Edinburgh, Mr. (now Sir John) Miller, Dr. Lettsom, and Mr. Slater the druggist. Mr. Wilkes placed himself next to Dr. Johnson, and behaved to him with so much attention and politeness that he gained upon him insensibly. No man ate more heartily than Johnson, or loved better what was nice and delicate. Mr. Wilkes was very assiduous in helping him to some fine veal. "Pray give me leave, sir:—It is better here—A little of the brown—Some fat, sir—A little of the stuffing—Some gravy—Let me have the pleasure of giving you some butter—Allow me to recommend a squeeze of this orange;—or the lemon, perhaps, may have more zest."—"Sir, sir, I am obliged to you, sir," cried Johnson, bowing, and turning his head to him with a look for some time of "surly virtue,"[6] but, in a short while, of complacency.

Foote[7] being mentioned, Johnson said, "He is not a good mimic." One of the company added, "A merry Andrew, a buffoon." JOHNSON. "But he has wit too, and is not deficient in ideas, or in fertility and variety of imagery, and not empty of reading; he has knowledge enough to fill up his part. One species of wit he has in an eminent degree, that of escape. You drive him into a corner with both hands; but he's gone, sir, when you think you have got him—like an animal that jumps over your head. Then he has a great range for his wit; he never lets truth stand between him and a jest, and he is sometimes mighty coarse. Garrick is under many restraints from which Foote is free." WILKES. "Garrick's wit is more like Lord Chesterfield's." JOHNSON. "The first time I was in company with Foote was at Fitzherbert's. Having no good opinion of the fellow, I was resolved not to be pleased; and it is very difficult to please a man against his will. I went on eating my dinner pretty sullenly, affecting not to mind him. But the dog was so very comical, that I was obliged to lay down my knife and fork, throw

myself back upon my chair, and fairly laugh it out. No, sir, he was irresistible. He upon one occasion experienced, in an extraordinary degree, the efficacy of his powers of entertaining. Amongst the many and various modes which he tried of getting money, he became a partner with a small-beer[8] brewer, and he was to have a share of the profits for procuring customers amongst his numerous acquaintance. Fitzherbert was one who took his small beer, but it was so bad that the servants resolved not to drink it. They were at some loss how to notify their resolution, being afraid of offending their master, who they knew liked Foote much as a companion. At last they fixed upon a little black boy, who was rather a favorite, to be their deputy, and deliver their remonstrance; and having invested him with the whole authority of the kitchen, he was to inform Mr. Fitzherbert, in all their names, upon a certain day, that they would drink Foote's small beer no longer. On that day Foote happened to dine at Fitzherbert's, and this boy served at table; he was so delighted with Foote's stories and merriment and grimace that, when he went downstairs, he told them, 'This is the finest man I have ever seen. I will not deliver your message. I will drink his small beer.' "

Somebody observed that Garrick could not have done this. WILKES. "Garrick would have made the small beer still smaller. He is now leaving the stage; but he will play Scrub[9] all his life." I knew that Johnson would let nobody attack Garrick but himself, as Garrick once said to me, and I had heard him praise his liberality; so to bring out his commendation of his celebrated pupil, I said, loudly, "I have heard Garrick is liberal." JOHNSON. "Yes, sir, I know that Garrick has given away more money than any man in England that I am acquainted with, and that not from ostentatious views. Garrick was very poor when he began life; so when he came to have money, he probably was very unskillful in giving away, and saved when he should not. But Garrick began to be liberal as soon as he could; and I am of opinion the reputation of avarice which he has had has been very lucky for him, and prevented his having many enemies. You despise a man for avarice, but do not hate him. Garrick might have been much better attacked for living with more splendor than is suitable to a player: if they had had

---

[6] Johnson's *London,* line 145: "Can surly virtue hope to fix a friend?"

[7] Samuel Foote (1720–77) was a sprightly comedian and playwright, and also a celebrated conversationalist.

[8] A weak kind of beer.—William Fitzherbert was a member of Parliament.

[9] A money-loving servant in George Farquhar's *The Beaux' Stratagem* (1707).

the wit to have assaulted him in that quarter, they might have galled him more. But they have kept clamoring about his avarice, which has rescued him from much obloquy and envy."

Talking of the great difficulty of obtaining authentic information for biography, Johnson told us, "When I was a young fellow I wanted to write the *Life of Dryden,* and in order to get materials I applied to the only two persons then alive who had seen him; these were old Swinney[10] and old Cibber.[11] Swinney's information was no more than this, 'That at Will's coffee house Dryden had a particular chair for himself, which was set by the fire in winter, and was then called his winter chair; and that it was carried out for him to the balcony in summer, and was then called his summer chair.' Cibber could tell no more but 'That he remembered him a decent old man, arbiter of critical disputes at Wills's.' You are to consider that Cibber was then at a great distance from Dryden, had perhaps one leg only in the room, and durst not draw in the other." BOSWELL. "Yet Cibber was a man of observation?" JOHNSON. "I think not." BOSWELL. "You will allow his *Apology*[12] to be well done." JOHNSON. "Very well done, to be sure, sir. That book is a striking proof of the justice of Pope's remark:

> Each might his several province well command,
> Would all but stoop to what they understand."[13]

BOSWELL. "And his plays are good." JOHNSON. "Yes; but that was his trade; *l'esprit du corps:*[14] he had been all his life among players and play writers. I wondered that he had so little to say in conversation, for he had kept the best company, and learnt all that can be got by the ear. He abused Pindar[15] to me, and then showed me an ode of his own, with an absurd couplet, making a linnet soar on an eagle's wing. I told him that when the ancients made a simile, they always made it like something real."

Mr. Wilkes remarked that "among all the bold flights of Shakespeare's imagination, the boldest was making Birnam Wood march to Dunsinane;[16] creating a wood where there never was a shrub; a

wood in Scotland! ha! ha! ha!" And he also observed that "the clannish slavery of the Highlands of Scotland was the single exception to Milton's remark of 'The mountain nymph, sweet Liberty,' being worshipped in all hilly countries.[17] When I was at Inverary," said he, "on a visit to my old friend, Archibald, Duke of Argyle, his dependents congratulated me on being such a favorite of his Grace. I said, 'It is then, gentlemen, truly lucky for me; for if I had displeased the Duke, and he had wished it, there is not a Campbell among you but would have been ready to bring John Wilkes's head to him in a charger.'[18] It would have been only

> Off with his head! So much for Aylesbury.[19]

I was then member[20] for Aylesbury.". . .

Mr. Arthur Lee mentioned some Scotch who had taken possession of a barren part of America, and wondered why they should choose it. JOHNSON. "Why, sir, all barrenness is comparative. The *Scotch* would not know it to be barren." BOSWELL. "Come, come, he is flattering the English. You have now been in Scotland, sir, and say if you did not see meat and drink enough there." JOHNSON. "Why, yes, sir; meat and drink enough to give the inhabitants sufficient strength to run away from home." All these quick and lively sallies were said sportively, quite in jest, and with a smile, which showed that he meant only wit. Upon this topic he and Mr. Wilkes could perfectly assimilate; here was a bond of union between them, and I was conscious that, as both of them had visited Caledonia, both were fully satisfied of the strange narrow ignorance of those who imagine that it is a land of famine. But they amused themselves with persevering in the old jokes. When I claimed a superiority for Scotland over England in one respect, that no man can be arrested there for a debt merely because another swears it against him, but there must first be the judgment of a court of law ascertaining its justice, and that a seizure of the person before judgment is obtained can take place only if his creditor should swear that he is about to fly from the country, or as it is technically expressed is *in meditatione fugae:*[21] WILKES. "That, I should think, may be safely sworn of all the Scotch nation." JOHNSON (to Mr. Wilkes). "You must know, sir, I lately took my friend Boswell and showed him

---

[10] Owen Mac Swinney (d. 1754) was a theater manager and minor playwright.
[11] See p. 878, note 18, above.
[12] Cibber's autobiography.
[13] See above, *Essay on Criticism,* I, 66–7.
[14] The spirit pervading the group.
[15] A Greek poet of the fifth century B.C.   [16] In *Macbeth.*

[17] Milton, "L'Allegro," line 36.   [18] Platter.
[19] A parody of the famous line inserted by Colley Cibber in his adaptation (1700) of Shakespeare's *Richard III, Aylesbury* being substituted for *Buckingham.*   [20] Of the House of Commons.
[21] Considering flight.

genuine civilized life in an English provincial town. I turned him loose at Lichfield, my native city, that he might see for once real civility: for you know he lives among savages in Scotland, and among rakes in London." WILKES. "Except when he is with grave, sober, decent people like you and me." JOHNSON (smiling). "And we ashamed of him."

They were quite frank and easy. Johnson told the story of his asking Mrs. Macaulay to allow her footman to sit down with them, to prove the ridiculousness of the argument for the equality of mankind; and he said to me afterwards, with a nod of satisfaction, "You saw Mr. Wilkes acquiesced." Wilkes talked with all imaginable freedom of the ludicrous title given to the Attorney-General, *Diabolus Regis*;[22] adding, "I have reason to know something about that officer; for I was prosecuted for a libel." Johnson, who many people would have supposed must have been furiously angry at hearing this talked of so lightly, said not a word. He was now, *indeed,* "a good-humored fellow."[23]

After dinner we had an accession of Mrs. Knowles, the Quaker lady, well known for her various talents, and of Mr. Alderman Lee. Amidst some patriotic groans, somebody (I think the Alderman) said, "Poor old England is lost." JOHNSON. "Sir, it is not so much to be lamented that old England is lost, as that the Scotch have found it.". . .

Mr. Wilkes held a candle to show a fine print of a beautiful female figure which hung in the room, and pointed out the elegant contour of the bosom with the finger of an arch connoisseur. He afterwards, in a conversation with me, waggishly insisted that all the time Johnson showed visible signs of a fervent admiration of the corresponding charms of the fair Quaker.

This record, though by no means so perfect as I could wish, will serve to give a notion of a very curious interview, which was not only pleasing at the time, but had the agreeable and benignant effect of reconciling any animosity, and sweetening any acidity, which, in the various bustle of political contest, had been produced in the minds of two men, who, though widely different, had so many things in common—classical learning, modern literature, wit, and humor, and ready repartee—that it would have been much to be regretted if they had been for ever at a distance from each other.

Mr. Burke gave me much credit for this successful *negotiation;* and pleasantly said that "there was nothing to equal it in the whole history of the *Corps Diplomatique.*"

I attended Dr. Johnson home, and had the satisfaction to hear him tell Mrs. Williams how much he had been pleased with Mr. Wilkes's company, and what an agreeable day he had passed.

Oliver Goldsmith

1730?–1774

WE HAVE already seen Goldsmith (pp. 879–81) through the eyes of Boswell, who did not like him; doubtless Bozzy was a little jealous of Johnson's affection for the happy-go-lucky Irishman, and was willing he should cut a somewhat clownish figure in the great Life. Certainly he was no match, at any rate in conversation, for wits like Johnson and Garrick; there was even some opposition to including him when the Club was founded in 1764, on the ground

22 King's devil.
23 Boswell had noted that on April 18, 1775, Johnson observed, "It is wonderful, sir, how rare a quality good humor is in life. We meet with very few good-humored men." Boswell proposed four of their acquaintances, to all of whom Johnson found objections. "Then, shaking his head and stretching himself at his ease in the coach, and smiling with much complacency [i.e., good humor], he turned to me and said, 'I look upon *myself* as a good-humored fellow.'"

that he was only a hack writer. That was after his periodical essays, the *Bee* (1759) and *The Citizen of the World* (1762), were written, but before he made his mark in poetry, prose fiction, and the drama. In each of these four fields he was soon established among the leading authors of his time; he was one of the most versatile men in literary history. His permanent success is due principally to his style, which accurately mirrors his droll and lovable personality. To Oliver Goldsmith belonged that indefinable asset we call charm; it distinguishes everything he wrote. He was a neoclassicist, but an Irish neoclassicist—and therefore a living paradox. Not many first-rate writers are always readable, even when not at their best. Goldsmith is. He seems to compose in a flood of affection for his readers, as if his chief pleasure in life was to give them pleasure, and he seldom fails of his object.

Goldsmith, a clergyman's son, was born in County Longford, Ireland, and educated at Trinity College, Dublin. An attack of smallpox in early childhood left his face deeply scarred. He was a small, homely, ungainly creature; but neither personal defects nor the slings and arrows of outrageous fortune could defeat his temperament. He took life as it came; eventually he learned how to work hard. He never married, though he was no woman hater; apparently he was not a man who appealed to women. Between his graduation from Trinity and his London success, his career reads like a comedy. For a while he thought of the Church. The story goes that he turned up to be examined for holy orders in a pair of scarlet breeches, which the bishop considered prima-facie evidence of unfitness; more probably a propensity for sitting around in taverns had too drastically reduced the time Goldsmith had devoted to theological studies. Upon his rejection, a long-suffering uncle gave him fifty pounds to study law in London; but a gambler fleeced him of it before he could tear himself away from Dublin. Goldsmith then decided for medicine. This time, again with his uncle's aid, he succeeded in leaving Ireland's shore; apparently he never saw it again. First he went to Edinburgh and next to Leyden; but in 1755 he set out from Holland on an original version of the Grand Tour—walking. He made his way through Flanders, France, Germany, Switzerland, and Italy, financing his journey by playing his flute and by engaging, for the sake of the nominal fee, in the formal disputations at the universities he visited. Where he picked up his dubious degree of Bachelor of Medicine is uncertain. In 1756 he returned to England and tried his hand at a variety of jobs in London. He was an apothecary's assistant, practiced after a fashion among the poor, tried proofreading and schoolteaching, applied unsuccessfully for a medical post in India, and finally drifted into journalism and hack writing.

In 1759-62 he began to attract serious attention with his *Enquiry into the Present State of Polite Learning in Europe* and also with his periodical essays, the best since the *Spectator*. He soon won the invaluable friendship of Johnson. In 1764 his reputation was raised by his first long poem, *The Traveler*. Two years later his only novel, *The Vicar of Wakefield,* won him the devotion of a wide circle of readers; Primrose the vicar was long one of the favorite characters in English fiction. In 1770 came *The Deserted Village,* Goldsmith's best poem. Throughout his entire career he continued turning out miscellaneous works,

especially histories and biographies, on order from the publishers; he was always in need of money. His major contribution to literature was a play, the perennially popular *She Stoops to Conquer,* first acted in 1773. In an earlier comedy, *The Good-Natured Man* (1768), and in "An Essay on the Theater, or A Comparison between Laughing and Sentimental Comedy," he had already protested against the

new species of dramatic composition . . . under the name of *sentimental* comedy, in which the virtues of private life are exhibited, rather than the vices exposed, and the distresses rather than the faults of mankind make our interest in the piece. . . . Almost all the characters are good, and exceedingly generous; they are lavish enough of their *tin* money on the stage; and, though they want humor, have abundance of sentiment and feeling. If they happen to have faults or foibles, the spectator is taught not only to pardon but to applaud them, in consideration of the goodness of their hearts; so that folly, instead of being ridiculed, is commended.

"Bastard tragedy" he calls this, the prevailing, kind of comedy; and in *She Stoops to Conquer,* while feeling is by no means excluded, Goldsmith tries to recapture the wit and gaiety of Restoration comedy without its immorality and inhumanity. Of the other eighteenth-century dramatists only Sheridan equals him. Horace Walpole thought parts of *She Stoops to Conquer* disgustingly "low," but Dr. Johnson led the laughter and applause on the opening night. By including the farcical character of Tony Lumpkin and the "low" scene of conviviality at the Three Pigeons tavern, Goldsmith protested against the over-refinement of the fashionable "genteel" comedy.

Goldsmith had his faults—of vanity, financial irresponsibility, a loud taste in dress, and general instability; but these seem trivial when compared with what his genius gave the world and with his unfailing generosity to all who asked for help. When in 1774 his friends heard the news that he was dead, Burke burst into tears. Reynolds threw down his brush, and could not take it up again that day.

The standard edition, unfortunately an inadequate one, is by J. W. M. Gibbs (5 vols., 1884-6). There are numerous editions of the most important of the separate works, including several volumes in Everyman's Library and The World's Classics. Katharine C. Balderston has edited the letters (1928). A good Life is A. Dobson's (1888). S. Gwynn's (1935) is a readable popular biography.

Oliver Goldsmith

from THE CITIZEN OF THE WORLD

NEARLY all the 123 essays of this series, thinly disguised in the form of the pseudo-letter, appeared in 1760–61 in the *Public Ledger* of John Newbery, Christopher Smart's father-in-law, and in the following year came out in book form as *The Citizen of the World*. They were Goldsmith's first real success. A French translation went through seven editions in four years; but although the good sense and charm of the letters had appealed to newspaper readers, the book was largely ignored in England. "Light, agreeable summer reading, partly original, partly borrowed," said the reviewer in the *Public Ledger* itself. As a matter of fact Goldsmith knew nothing of the East. He helped himself liberally to the books in which he read up for his undertaking; it was essentially hack work, raised to a superior level by a unique light touch. "Is there a man, sir, now," Johnson asked, "who can pen an essay with such ease and elegance as Goldsmith?"

The Citizen of the World exemplifies the foreign-visitor genre, an effective device for enlivening comment upon the contemporary scene. In adopting a pretended Asiatic's point of view Goldsmith follows the Frenchmen Montesquieu and Voltaire, as well as Horace Walpole. Beginning in Queen Anne's time with the first English translation of the *Arabian Nights,* the eighteenth century succumbed to a wave of enthusiasm for the entire Orient, from Turkey to China. Tales with Oriental settings were devoured. Chinese gardening and decoration were all the rage. Walpole collected Chinese bric-a-brac. Goldsmith was moving with the tide when he ascribed his mildly critical observations to the nonexistent philosopher Lien Chi Altangi from Honan Province. In the following letters the sage addresses Fum Hoam, "First President of the Ceremonial Academy at Pekin." A volume in Everyman's Library reprints *The Citizen of the World* along with the eight essays of the *Bee.*

LETTER 4

ENGLISH PRIDE—LIBERTY—
AN INSTANCE OF BOTH—
NEWSPAPERS—POLITENESS

THE English seem as silent as the Japanese, yet vainer than the inhabitants of Siam. Upon my arrival I attributed that reserve to modesty which, I now find, has its origin in pride. Condescend to address them first, and you are sure of their acquaintance; stoop to flattery, and you conciliate their friendship and esteem. They bear hunger, cold, fatigue, and all the miseries of life without shrinking; danger only calls forth their fortitude; they even exult in calamity; but contempt is what they cannot bear. An Englishman fears contempt more than death; he often flies to death as a refuge from its pressure, and dies when he fancies the world has ceased to esteem him.

Pride seems the source, not only of their national vices, but of their national virtues also. An Englishman is taught to love his king as his friend, but to acknowledge no other master than the laws which himself has contributed to enact. He despises those nations who, that one may be free, are all content to be slaves; who first lift a tyrant into terror, and then shrink under his power as if delegated from heaven. Liberty is echoed in all their assemblies; and thousands might be found ready to offer up their lives for the sound, though perhaps not one of all the number understands the meaning. The lowest mechanic, however, looks upon it as his duty to be a watchful guardian of his country's freedom, and often uses a language that might seem haughty even in the mouth of the Great Emperor, who traces his ancestry to the Moon.

A few days ago, passing by one of their prisons, I could not avoid stopping, in order to listen to a dialogue which I thought might afford me some entertainment. The conversation was carried on between a debtor through the grate of his prison, a porter who had stopped to rest his burthen, and a soldier at the window. The subject was upon a threatened invasion from France, and each seemed extremely anxious to rescue his country from the impending danger. "For my part," cries the prisoner, "the greatest of my apprehensions is for our freedom; if the French should conquer, what would become of English liberty? My dear friends, liberty is the Englishman's prerogative; we must preserve that at the expense of our lives; of that the French shall never deprive us. It is not to be expected that men who are slaves themselves would preserve our freedom should they happen to conquer."—"Ay, slaves," cries the porter, "they are all slaves, fit only to carry burthens, every one of them. Before I would stoop to slavery, may this be my poison," and he held the goblet in his hand, "may this be my poison—but I would sooner 'list for a soldier."

The soldier, taking the goblet from his friend, with much awe fervently cried out, "It is not so much our liberties as our religion that would suffer by such a change; ay, our religion, my lads. May the Devil sink me into flames," such was the solemnity of his adjuration, "if the French should come over but our religion would be utterly undone!" So saying, instead of a libation, he applied the goblet to his lips, and confirmed his sentiments with a ceremony of the most persevering devotion.

In short, every man here pretends to be a politician; even the fair sex are sometimes found to mix the severity of national altercation with the blandishments of love, and often become conquerors by more weapons of destruction than their eyes.

This universal passion for politics is gratified by daily gazettes, as with us in China. But, as in ours the Emperor endeavors to instruct his people, in theirs the people endeavor to instruct the administration. You must not, however, imagine that they who compile these papers have any actual knowledge of the politics or the government of a state; they only collect their materials from the oracle of some coffee house, which oracle has himself gathered them the night before from a beau at a gaming table, who has pillaged his knowledge from a great man's porter, who has had his information from the great man's gentleman,[1] who has invented the whole story for his own amusement the night preceding.

The English, in general, seem fonder of gaining the esteem than the love of those they converse with. This gives a formality to their amusements: their gayest conversations have something too wise for innocent relaxation; though in company you are seldom disgusted with the absurdity of a fool, you are seldom lifted into rapture by those strokes of vivacity which give instant though not permanent pleasure.

What they want, however, in gaiety they make up in politeness. You smile at hearing me praise the English for their politeness, you who have heard very different accounts from the missionaries at Pekin,[2] who have seen such a different behavior in their merchants and seamen at home. But I must still repeat it: the English seem more polite than any of their neighbors; their great art in this respect lies in endeavoring, while they oblige, to lessen the force of the favor. Other countries are fond of obliging a stranger, but seem desirous that he should be sensible of the obligation. The English confer their kindness with an appearance of indifference, and give away benefits with an air as if they despised them.

Walking a few days ago, between an Englishman and a Frenchman, in the suburbs of the city, we were overtaken by a heavy shower of rain. I was unprepared; but they had each large coats, which defended them from what seemed to me a perfect inundation. The Englishman, seeing me shrink from the weather, accosted me thus: "Pshaw, man, what dost shrink at? Here, take this coat; I don't want it; I find it no way useful to me; I had as lief be without it." The Frenchman began to show his politeness in turn. "My dear friend," cries he, "why won't you oblige me by making use of my coat? You see how well it defends me from the rain; I should not choose to part with it to others, but to such a friend as you I could even part with my skin to do him service."

From such minute instances as these, most reverend Fum Hoam, I am sensible your sagacity will collect instruction. The volume of nature is the book of knowledge; and he becomes most wise who makes the most judicious selection. Farewell.

LETTER 54

THE CHARACTER OF AN IMPORTANT TRIFLER[3]

THOUGH naturally pensive, yet I am fond of gay company, and take every opportunity of thus dismissing the mind from duty. From this motive, I am often found in the center of a crowd, and wherever pleasure is to be sold am always a purchaser. In those places, without being remarked by any, I join in whatever goes forward, work my passions into a similitude of frivolous earnestness, shout as they shout, and condemn as they happen to disapprove. A mind thus sunk for a while below its natural standard is qualified for stronger flights, as those first retire who would spring forward with greater vigor.

Attracted by the serenity of the evening, my friend and I lately went to gaze upon the company in one of the public walks near the city. Here we sauntered together for some time, either praising the beauty of such as were handsome, or the dresses of such as had nothing else to recommend them. We had gone thus deliberately forward for some time,

---

[1] Valet.   [2] Peking, Peiping.

[3] "Beau Tibbs." Some recent editions insert this name in the title.

when, stopping on a sudden, my friend caught me by the elbow, and led me out of the public walk. I could perceive, by the quickness of his pace and by his frequently looking behind, that he was attempting to avoid somebody who followed: we now turned to the right, then to the left; as we went forward he still went faster, but in vain; the person whom he attempted to escape hunted us through every doubling and gained upon us each moment, so that at last we fairly stood still, resolving to face what we could not avoid.

Our pursuer soon came up, and joined us with all the familiarity of an old acquaintance. "My dear Drybone," cries he, shaking my friend's hand, "where have you been hiding this half a century? Positively I had fancied you were gone to cultivate matrimony and your estate in the country." During the reply, I had an opportunity of surveying the appearance of our new companion: his hat was pinched up with peculiar smartness; his looks were pale, thin, and sharp; round his neck he wore a broad black riband, and in his bosom a buckle studded with glass; his coat was trimmed with tarnished twist;[4] he wore by his side a sword with a black hilt; and his stockings of silk, though newly washed, were grown yellow by long service. I was so much engaged with the peculiarity of his dress that I attended only to the latter part of my friend's reply, in which he complimented Mr. Tibbs on the taste of his clothes and the bloom in his countenance. "Pshaw, pshaw, Will!" cried the figure, "no more of that, if you love me; you know I hate flattery, on my soul I do; and yet, to be sure, an intimacy with the great will improve one's appearance, and a course of venison will fatten; and yet, faith, I despise the great as much as you do; but there are a great many damned honest fellows among them, and we must not quarrel with one half because the other wants breeding. If they were all such as my Lord Mudler, one of the most good-natured creatures that ever squeezed a lemon, I should myself be among the number of their admirers. I was yesterday to dine at the Duchess of Piccadilly's. My Lord was there. 'Ned,' says he to me, 'Ned,' says he, 'I'll hold gold to silver I can tell where you were poaching last night.'—'Poaching, my Lord?' says I; 'faith, you have missed already; for I stayed at home, and let the girls poach for me. That's my way; I take a fine woman as some animals do their prey—stand still, and swoop; they fall into my mouth.'"

"Ah, Tibbs, thou art a happy fellow," cried my companion, with looks of infinite pity; "I hope your fortune is as much improved as your understanding in such company?"—"Improved," replied the other; "you shall know—but let it go no further—a great secret—five hundred a year to begin with. My Lord's word of honor for it—his Lordship took me down in his own chariot yesterday, and we had a tête-à-tête dinner in the country, where we talked of nothing else."—"I fancy you forget, sir," cried I, "you told us but this moment of your dining yesterday in town."—"Did I say so?" replied he coolly; "to be sure, if I said so, it was so—dined in town; egad, now I do remember, I did dine in town, but I dined in the country too; for you must know, my boys, I ate two dinners. By the by, I am grown as nice as the Devil in my eating. I'll tell you a pleasant affair about that.—We were a select party of us to dine at Lady Grogram's—an affected piece, but let it go no farther—a secret—well, there happened to be no asafetida in the sauce to a turkey, upon which, says I, 'I'll hold a thousand guineas, and say done first, that—' but, dear Drybone, you are an honest creature; lend me half a crown for a minute or two, or so, just till—but harkee, ask me for it the next time we meet, or it may be twenty to one but I forget to pay you."

When he left us, our conversation naturally turned upon so extraordinary a character. "His very dress," cries my friend, "is not less extraordinary than his conduct. If you meet him this day you find him in rags; if the next, in embroidery. With those persons of distinction of whom he talks so familiarly, he has scarce a coffee-house acquaintance. However, both for the interests of society, and perhaps for his own, heaven has made him poor; and while all the world perceive his wants, he fancies them concealed from every eye. An agreeable companion, because he understands flattery; and all must be pleased with the first part of his conversation, though all are sure of its ending with a demand on their purse. While his youth countenances the levity of his conduct, he may thus earn a precarious subsistence; but when age comes on, the gravity of which is incompatible with buffoonery, then will he find himself forsaken by all, condemned in the decline of life to hang upon some rich family whom he once despised, there to undergo all the ingenuity of studied contempt, to be employed only as a spy upon the servants, or a bugbear to fright the children into obedience." Adieu.

---

[4] Cord.

LETTER 55

THE CHARACTER OF THE TRIFLER CONTINUED;
WITH THAT OF HIS WIFE, HIS HOUSE,
HIS FURNITURE

I AM apt to fancy I have contracted a new acquaintance whom it will be no easy matter to shake
off. My little beau yesterday overtook me again in
one of the public walks and, slapping me on the
shoulder, saluted me with an air of the most perfect
familiarity. His dress was the same as usual, except
that he had more powder in his hair, wore a dirtier
shirt, a pair of temple[5] spectacles, and his hat under
his arm.

As I knew him to be a harmless, amusing little
thing, I could not return his smiles with any degree
of severity; so we walked forward on terms of the
utmost intimacy, and in a few minutes discussed all
the usual topics preliminary to particular conversation. The oddities that marked his character, however, soon began to appear; he bowed to several
well-dressed persons, who, by their manner of returning the compliment, appeared perfect strangers.
At intervals he drew out a pocketbook, seeming to
take memorandums before all the company, with
much importance and assiduity. In this manner he
led me through the length of the whole walk, fretting
at his absurdities, and fancying myself laughed at
not less than him by every spectator.

When we were got to the end of our procession,
"Blast me," cries he, with an air of vivacity, "I
never saw the Park so thin in my life before! There's
no company at all today; not a single face to be seen."
—"No company!" interrupted I peevishly; "no
company where there is such a crowd? why, man,
there's too much. What are the thousands that have
been laughing at us but company?"—"Lord, my
dear," returned he, with the utmost good humor,
"you seem immensely chagrined; but blast me, when
the world laughs at me, I laugh at the world, and so
we are even. My Lord Trip, Bill Squash the Cre-
olian,[6] and I sometimes make a party at being
ridiculous; and so we say and do a thousand things
for the joke's sake. But I see you are grave; and if
you are for a fine grave sentimental companion, you
shall dine with me and my wife today; I must insist
on't. I'll introduce you to Mrs. Tibbs, a lady of as
elegant qualifications as any in nature; she was bred
(but that's between ourselves) under the inspection

of the Countess of Allnight. A charming body of
voice; but no more of that—she will give us a song.
You shall see my little girl too, Carolina Wilhelmina
Amelia Tibbs, a sweet pretty creature. I design her
for my Lord Drumstick's eldest son; but that's in
friendship—let it go no further; she's but six years
old, and yet she walks a minuet, and plays on the
guitar immensely already. I intend she shall be as
perfect as possible in every accomplishment. In the
first place, I'll make her a scholar: I'll teach her
Greek myself, and learn that language purposely to
instruct her; but let that be a secret."

Thus saying, without waiting for a reply, he took
me by the arm and hauled me along. We passed
through many dark alleys and winding ways; for,
from some motives to me unknown, he seemed to
have a particular aversion to every frequented street;
at last, however, we got to the door of a dismal-
looking house in the outlets[7] of the town, where
he informed me he chose to reside for the benefit
of the air.

We entered the lower door, which ever seemed
to lie most hospitably open; and I began to ascend
an old and creaking staircase, when, as he mounted
to show me the way, he demanded whether I delighted in prospects; to which answering in the
affirmative, "Then," says he, "I shall show you one
of the most charming in the world, out of my
window; we shall see the ships sailing, and the whole
country for twenty miles round, tiptop, quite high.
My Lord Swamp would give ten thousand guineas
for such a one; but, as I sometimes pleasantly tell
him, I always love to keep my prospects at home,
that my friends may visit me the oftener."

By this time we were arrived as high as the stairs
would permit us to ascend, till we came to what he
was facetiously pleased to call the first floor down
the chimney; and, knocking at the door, a voice
from within demanded, "Who's there?" My con-
ductor answered that it was him. But this not satisfying the querist, the voice again repeated the demand, to which he answered louder than before; and
now the door was opened by an old woman with
cautious reluctance.

When we were got in, he welcomed me to his
house with great ceremony and, turning to the old
woman, asked where was her lady? "Good troth,"
replied she in a peculiar dialect, "she's washing your
twa shirts at the next door, because they have taken
an oath against lending out the tub any longer."—
"My twa shirts," cried he in a tone that faltered with

---

[5] I.e., with side-pieces.   [6] Creole.   [7] Outskirts.

confusion, "what does the idiot mean?"—"I ken what I mean weel enough," replied the other; "she's washing your twa shirts at the next door, because—" —"Fire and fury! no more of thy stupid explanations," cried he; "go and inform her we have got company.—Were that Scotch hag," continued he, "to be for ever in my family, she would never learn politeness, nor forget that absurd poisonous accent of hers, or testify the smallest specimen of breeding or high life; and yet it is very surprising too, as I had her from a Parliament man, a friend of mine from the Highlands, one of the politest men in the world; but that's a secret."

We waited some time for Mrs. Tibbs's arrival, during which interval I had a full opportunity of surveying the chamber and all its furniture, which consisted of four chairs with old wrought bottoms that he assured me were his wife's embroidery; a square table that had been once japanned, a cradle in one corner, a lumbering cabinet in the other; a broken shepherdess and a mandarin without a head were stuck over the chimney; and round the walls several paltry unframed pictures, which, he observed, were all his own drawing. "What do you think, sir, of that head in the corner, done in the manner of Grisoni?[8] there's the true keeping in it; it is my own face, and though there happens to be no likeness, a countess offered me a hundred for its fellow. I refused her, for, hang it, that would be mechanical,[9] you know."

The wife at last made her appearance, at once a slattern and a coquette; much emaciated, but still carrying the remains of beauty. She made twenty apologies for being seen in such odious dishabille, but hoped to be excused, as she had stayed all night at the Gardens[10] with the Countess, who was excessively fond of the horns.[11] "And, indeed, my dear," added she, turning to her husband, "his Lordship drank your health in a bumper."—"Poor Jack!" cries he, "a dear good-natured creature, I know he loves me. But I hope, my dear, you have given orders for dinner; you need make no great preparations neither; there are but three of us; something elegant, and little will do; a turbot, an ortolan, a—"[12]—"Or what do you think, my dear," interrupts the wife, "of a nice pretty bit of ox-cheek, piping hot, and dressed with a little of my own

sauce?"—"The very thing!" replies he; "it will eat best with some smart bottled beer; but be sure to let us have the sauce his Grace was so fond of. I hate your immense loads of meat; that is country all over, extremely disgusting to those who are in the least acquainted with high life."

By this time my curiosity began to abate, and my appetite to increase; the company of fools may at first make us smile, but at last never fails of rendering us melancholy. I therefore pretended to recollect a prior engagement, and, after having shown my respect to the house, according to the fashion of the English, by giving the old servant a piece of money at the door, I took my leave; Mr. Tibbs assuring me that dinner, if I stayed, would be ready at least in less than two hours.

LETTER 86

THE RACES OF NEWMARKET RIDICULED—
DESCRIPTION OF A CART RACE

OF ALL the places of amusement where gentlemen and ladies are entertained, I have not been yet to visit Newmarket.[13] This, I am told, is a large field where, upon certain occasions, three or four horses are brought together, then set a-running, and that horse which runs fastest wins the wager.

This is reckoned a very polite and fashionable amusement here, much more followed by the nobility than partridge fighting at Java, or paper kites in Madagascar. Several of the great here, I am told, understand as much of farriery as their grooms; and a horse with any share of merit can never want a patron among the nobility.

We have a description of this entertainment almost every day in some of the gazettes, as for instance: "On such a day the Give and Take Plate was run for between his Grace's Crab, his Lordship's Periwinkle, and Squire Smackem's Slamerkin. All rode their own horses. There was the greatest concourse of nobility that has been known here for several seasons. The odds were in favor of Crab in the beginning; but Slamerkin, after the first heat, seemed to have the match hollow: however, it was soon seen that Periwinkle improved in wind, which at last turned out accordingly; Crab was run to a standstill, Slamerkin was knocked up, and Periwinkle was brought in with universal applause." Thus, you see,

---

[8] Giuseppe Grisoni (1692-1769), an Italian painter who lived in England from 1715 to 1728. [9] Tradesmanlike, commercial.
[10] Spring Gardens, a pleasure garden at Vauxhall, across the Thames from Westminster. [11] Of the band.
[12] Both the fish and the bird are choice dishes.

[13] The headquarters of English racing, fourteen miles from Cambridge.

Periwinkle received universal applause, and, no doubt, his Lordship came in for some share of that praise which was so liberally bestowed upon Periwinkle. Sun of China! how glorious must the senator[14] appear in his cap and leather breeches, his whip crossed in his mouth, and thus coming to the goal, amongst the shouts of grooms, jockeys, pimps, stable-bred dukes, and degraded generals!

From the description of this princely amusement now transcribed, and from the great veneration I have for the characters of its principal promoters, I make no doubt but I shall look upon a horse race with becoming reverence, predisposed as I am by a similar amusement, of which I have lately been a spectator; for just now I happened to have an opportunity of being present at a cart race.

Whether this contention between three carts of different parishes was promoted by a subscription among the nobility, or whether the grand jury, in council assembled, had gloriously combined to encourage plaustral[15] merit, I cannot take upon me to determine; but certain it is, the whole was conducted with the utmost regularity and decorum, and the company, which made a brilliant appearance, were universally of opinion that the sport was high, the running fine, and the riders influenced by no bribe.

It was run on the road from London to a village called Brentford, between a turnip cart, a dust[16] cart and a dung cart, each of the owners condescending to mount, and be his own driver. The odds, at starting, were Dust against Dung, five to four; but, after half a mile's going, the knowing ones found themselves all on the wrong side, and it was Turnip against the field, brass to silver.

Soon, however, the contest became more doubtful; Turnip indeed kept the way, but it was perceived that Dung had better bottom.[17] The road re-echoed with the shouts of the spectators—"Dung against Turnip! Turnip against Dung!" was now the universal cry; neck and neck; one rode lighter, but the other had more judgment. I could not but particularly observe the ardor with which the fair sex espoused the cause of the different riders on this occasion; one was charmed with the unwashed beauties of Dung; another was captivated with the patibulary[18] aspect of Turnip; while, in the meantime, unfortunate gloomy Dust, who came whipping behind, was cheered by the encouragement of some and pity of all.

The contention now continued for some time, without a possibility of determining to whom victory designed the prize. The winning post appeared in view, and he who drove the turnip cart assured himself of success; and successful he might have been, had his horse been as ambitious as he; but, upon approaching a turn from the road, which led homewards, the horse fairly stood still and refused to move a foot farther. The dung cart had scarce time to enjoy this temporary triumph, when it was pitched headlong into a ditch by the wayside, and the rider left to wallow in congenial mud. Dust, in the meantime, soon came up, and, not being far from the post, came in, amidst the shouts and acclamations of all the spectators, and greatly caressed by all the quality[19] of Brentford. Fortune was kind only to one, who ought to have been favorable to all; each had peculiar merit, each labored hard to earn the prize, and each richly deserved the cart he drove.

I do not know whether this description may not have anticipated that which I intended giving of Newmarket. I am told there is little else to be seen even there. There may be some minute differences in the dress of the spectators, but none at all in their understandings: the quality of Brentford are as remarkable for politeness and delicacy as the breeders of Newmarket. The quality of Brentford drive their own carts, and the honorable fraternity of Newmarket ride their own horses. In short, the matches in one place are as rational as those in the other; and it is more than probable that turnips, dust, and dung are all that can be found to furnish out description in either.

Forgive me, my friend; but a person like me, bred up in a philosophic seclusion, is apt to regard perhaps with too much asperity those occurrences which sink man below his station in nature, and diminish the intrinsic value of humanity. Adieu.

AN ELEGY
ON THE DEATH OF A MAD DOG

Good people all, of every sort,
  Give ear unto my song;
And if you find it wondrous short,
  It cannot hold you long.

---

[14] I.e., member of the House of Lords.
[15] Like "patibulary" (note 18), a jocose coinage by Goldsmith. Latin *plaustrum*=cart.
[16] Refuse, trash.—A letter in the *Public Ledger,* complaining of cart races near Brentford (seven miles up the Thames), may have given Goldsmith the idea. It appeared eight days before the essay.   [17] Staying power.

[18] Gallowslike.   [19] Upper class.

In Isling town[1] there was a man   5
  Of whom the world might say
That still a godly race he ran,
  Whene'er he went to pray.

A kind and gentle heart he had,
  To comfort friends and foes;   10
The naked every day he clad,
  When he put on his clothes.

And in that town a dog was found,
  As many dogs there be,
Both mongrel, puppy, whelp, and hound,   15
  And curs of low degree.

This dog and man at first were friends;
  But when a pique began,
The dog, to gain some private ends,
  Went mad and bit the man.   20

Around from all the neighboring streets
  The wond'ring neighbors ran,
And swore the dog had lost his wits,
  To bite so good a man.

The wound it seemed both sore and sad   25
  To every Christian eye;
And while they swore the dog was mad,
  They swore the man would die.

But soon a wonder came to light,
  That showed the rogues they lied;   30
The man recovered of the bite,
  The dog it was that died.

THE DESERTED VILLAGE

This poem has endeared itself to the English-speaking
world because its nostalgic picture of the good days, now
gone for ever, is touched with both sentiment and humor.
The best and best-liked passages come in the first half—
village scenes and characters when all was well with the
countryside. But the title is "The *Deserted* Village"; and
whether or not Goldsmith's economic views were sound,
the poem is serious, didactic, and humanitarian.

In *Lloyd's Evening Post* for June 14–16, 1762, Goldsmith
had described the eviction of some cottagers. He adds: "In
almost every part of the kingdom the laborious husband-

man has been reduced, and the lands are now either occupied by some general undertaker or turned into enclosures destined for purposes of amusement or luxury."
About the middle of the eighteenth century a series of
Enclosure Acts wiped out many small tenant-farmers who
were still operating under the medieval system of open-
field agriculture and pasturage in common. Under that
system, the tenant-farmer cultivated his share of the
narrow strips into which the fields had anciently been
divided for the sake of insuring an equitable distribution
of good land and bad. The eighteenth-century landowner
who wanted to get rid of his tenants would induce Parliament to pass an act requiring the separate enclosure of
every share, including his own. This involved a redistribu-
tion of the allotments, in order to throw each man's share
into one piece; as a rule the little man got the poorest land.
The size of the portion cultivated by the owner enabled
him, now that it was no longer scattered about in strips,
to improve it by drainage and to farm it more effectively
in accordance with the new scientific methods. The
diminutive plot of the small tenant could not compete.
The cost of the required fencing was often prohibitive,
and it was harder than ever to pay the rent exacted by
the landowner. The result was to squeeze the small tenant
out. He was evicted for failure to meet his payments, or,
seeing no future, he sold out in despair. His little field was
added by the squire to his own holdings; the larger the
farm, whether operated directly by the squire or leased to
a new and more efficient tenant, the larger the revenue
per acre. It is this kind of magnate—he might own hundreds
of thousands of acres—that Goldsmith refers to as an
"undertaker" in his newspaper article. The other class of
"tyrant" was the landowner who secured an Enclosure
Act in order to increase the size of his "park" or game
preserve. The heyday of these magnates, whether or not
they kept all their arable land in production, lasted from
the middle of the eighteenth century till about 1880. After
that, cheap wheat from America brought down the price
of native grains. The taxation and land reforms of David
Lloyd George early in the twentieth century administered
the final blow to the magnates' ability to retain their vast
holdings. As for the dispossessed tenant for whom Goldsmith pleads, he could become a hired farmhand, drift to
the city and find work as a laborer, or emigrate. The
millhands required by the Industrial Revolution were to a
large extent recruited from this unhappy class.

While for some details of his fictitious village of Auburn
Goldsmith may have drawn on memories of his childhood,
he is thinking principally of England, not Ireland. The
poem, which appeared in 1770, became popular immediately.

---

[1] Islington, then a suburban village north of London.—This
famous piece of light verse is a burlesque elegy; it first appeared
in *The Vicar of Wakefield* (1766). The present text follows the
last edition published in Goldsmith's lifetime (1773).

TO SIR JOSHUA REYNOLDS[1]

DEAR SIR,—*I can have no expectations in an address of this kind, either to add to your reputation, or to establish my own. You can gain nothing from my admiration, as I am ignorant of that art in which you are said to excel; and I may lose much by the severity of your judgment, as few have a juster taste in poetry than you. Setting interest therefore aside, to which I never paid much attention, I must be indulged at present in following my affections. The only dedication I ever made was to my brother,[2] because I loved him better than most other men. He is since dead. Permit me to inscribe this poem to you.*

How far you may be pleased with the versification and mere mechanical parts of this attempt, I don't pretend to enquire; but I know you will object (and indeed several of our best and wisest friends concur in the opinion) that the depopulation it deplores is nowhere to be seen, and the disorders it laments are only to be found in the poet's own imagination. To this I can scarce make any other answer than that I sincerely believe what I have written; that I have taken all possible pains, in my country excursions, for these four or five years past, to be certain of what I allege; and that all my views and enquiries have led me to believe those miseries real which I here attempt to display. But this is not the place to enter into an enquiry whether the country be depopulating, or not; the discussion would take up much room, and I should prove myself, at best, an indifferent politician, to tire the reader with a long preface, when I want his unfatigued attention to a long poem.

In regretting the depopulation of the country, I inveigh against the increase of our luxuries; and here also I expect the shout of modern politicians against me. For twenty or thirty years past, it has been the fashion to consider luxury as one of the greatest national advantages, and all the wisdom of antiquity in that particular as erroneous. Still, however, I must remain a professed ancient on that head, and continue to think those luxuries prejudicial to states by which so many vices are introduced and so many kingdoms have been undone. Indeed so much has been poured out of late on the other side of the question, that, merely for the sake of novelty and variety, one would sometimes wish to be in the right.

> *I am, dear sir,*
> *Your sincere friend and ardent admirer,*
> OLIVER GOLDSMITH

Sweet AUBURN, loveliest village of the plain,
Where health and plenty cheered the laboring swain,[3]
Where smiling spring its earliest visit paid,
And parting summer's lingering blooms delayed,
Dear lovely bowers of innocence and ease,   5
Seats of my youth, when every sport could please,

---

[1] The foremost English portrait-painter (1723–92). He was also a writer on art, and an intimate friend of Goldsmith, Burke, and Johnson; with the latter he founded the Literary Club.
[2] The Rev. Henry Goldsmith, to whom *The Traveler* was dedicated.   [3] Rustic.

How often have I loitered o'er thy green,
Where humble happiness endeared each scene;
How often have I paused on every charm,
The sheltered cot, the cultivated farm,   10
The never-failing brook, the busy mill,
The decent church that topped the neighboring hill,
The hawthorn bush, with seats beneath the shade,
For talking age and whispering lovers made;
How often have I blessed the coming day,   15
When toil remitting lent its turn to play,
And all the village train, from labor free,
Led up their sports beneath the spreading tree;
While many a pastime circled in the shade,
The young contending as the old surveyed;   20
And many a gambol frolicked o'er the ground,
And sleights of art and feats of strength went round;
And still, as each repeated pleasure tired,
Succeeding sports the mirthful band inspired;
The dancing pair that simply sought renown   25
By holding out to tire each other down,
The swain mistrustless of his smutted face
While secret laughter tittered round the place,
The bashful virgin's sidelong looks of love,
The matron's glance that would those looks reprove: 30
These were thy charms, sweet village; sports like these,
With sweet succession, taught even toil to please;
These round thy bowers their cheerful influence shed,
These were thy charms—but all these charms are fled.

Sweet smiling village, loveliest of the lawn,   35
Thy sports are fled, and all thy charms withdrawn;
Amidst thy bowers the tyrant's hand is seen,
And desolation saddens all thy green:
One only master grasps the whole domain,
And half a tillage stints thy smiling plain;   40
No more thy glassy brook reflects the day,
But, choked with sedges, works its weedy way.
Along thy glades, a solitary guest,
The hollow-sounding bittern guards its nest;
Amidst thy desert walks the lapwing flies,   45
And tires their echoes with unvaried cries.
Sunk are thy bowers, in shapeless ruin all,
And the long grass o'ertops the moldering wall;
And, trembling, shrinking from the spoiler's hand,
Far, far away, thy children leave the land.   50

Ill fares the land, to hastening ills a prey,
Where wealth accumulates, and men decay;
Princes and lords may flourish, or may fade;
A breath can make them, as a breath has made;
But a bold peasantry, their country's pride,   55
When once destroyed, can never be supplied.

A time there was, ere England's griefs began,
When every rood[4] of ground maintained its man;
For him light labor spread her wholesome store,
Just gave what life required, but gave no more: 60
His best companions, innocence and health;
And his best riches, ignorance of wealth.

But times are altered; trade's unfeeling train[5]
Usurp the land, and dispossess the swain;
Along the lawn, where scattered hamlets rose,   65
Unwieldy wealth and cumbrous pomp repose;
And every want to opulence allied,[6]
And every pang that folly pays to pride.
Those gentle hours that plenty bade to bloom,
Those calm desires that asked but little room,   70
Those healthful sports that graced the peaceful scene,
Lived in each look, and brightened all the green—
These far departing seek a kinder shore,
And rural mirth and manners are no more.

Sweet AUBURN! parent of the blissful hour,   75
Thy glades forlorn confess the tyrant's power.
Here, as I take my solitary rounds,
Amidst thy tangling walks and ruined grounds,
And, many a year elapsed, return to view
Where once the cottage stood, the hawthorn grew,   80
Remembrance wakes with all her busy train,
Swells at my breast, and turns the past to pain.

In all my wanderings round this world of care,
In all my griefs—and God has given my share—
I still had hopes, my latest hours to crown,   85
Amidst these humble bowers to lay me down;
To husband out life's taper at the close,
And keep the flame from wasting by repose.
I still had hopes, for pride attends us still,
Amidst the swains to show my book-learned skill,   90
Around my fire an evening group to draw,
And tell of all I felt, and all I saw;
And, as a hare whom hounds and horns pursue
Pants to the place from whence at first she flew,
I still had hopes, my long vexations past,   95
Here to return—and die at home at last.

O blest retirement, friend to life's decline,
Retreats from care, that never must be mine,
How happy he who crowns, in shades like these,
A youth of labor with an age of ease;   100

Who quits a world where strong temptations try,
And, since 'tis hard to combat, learns to fly.
For him no wretches, born to work and weep,
Explore the mine or tempt the dangerous deep;
No surly porter stands, in guilty state,   105
To spurn imploring famine from the gate;
But on he moves to meet his latter end,
Angels around befriending virtue's friend;
Bends to the grave with unperceived decay,
While resignation gently slopes the way;   110
And, all his prospects brightening to the last,
His heaven commences ere the world be past!

Sweet was the sound when oft, at evening's close,
Up yonder hill the village murmur rose.
There, as I passed with careless[7] steps and slow,   115
The mingled notes came softened from below;
The swain responsive as the milkmaid sung,
The sober herd that lowed to meet their young,
The noisy geese that gabbled o'er the pool,
The playful children just let loose from school,   120
The watchdog's voice that bayed the whispering wind,
And the loud laugh that spoke the vacant[8] mind—
These all in sweet confusion sought the shade,
And filled each pause the nightingale had made.
But now the sounds of population fail,   125
No cheerful murmurs fluctuate in the gale,
No busy steps the grass-grown footway tread,
For all the bloomy flush of life is fled.
All but yon widowed, solitary thing,
That feebly bends beside the plashy spring;   130
She, wretched matron—forced, in age, for bread,
To strip the brook with mantling cresses spread,
To pick her wintry faggot from the thorn,
To seek her nightly shed, and weep till morn—
She only left of all the harmless train,   135
The sad historian of the pensive plain.

Near yonder copse, where once the garden smiled,
And still where many a garden flower grows wild,
There, where a few torn shrubs the place disclose,
The village preacher's modest mansion rose.   140
A man he was to all the country dear,
And passing rich with forty pounds a year;
Remote from towns he ran his godly race,
Nor e'er had changed, nor wished to change, his place;
Unpracticed he to fawn, or seek for power,   145
By doctrines fashioned to the varying hour;
Far other aims his heart had learned to prize,
More skilled to raise the wretched than to rise.

---

[4] Quarter-acre.   [5] Attendants, company.
[6] I.e., every lack which is inevitable when wealth is in the hands
of the few.

[7] Carefree.   [8] I.e., untroubled.

His house was known to all the vagrant train;
He chid their wanderings, but relieved their pain; 150
The long-remembered beggar was his guest,
Whose beard descending swept his agèd breast;
The ruined spendthrift, now no longer proud,
Claimed kindred there, and had his claims allowed;
The broken soldier, kindly bade to stay, 155
Sat by his fire, and talked the night away,
Wept o'er his wounds, or, tales of sorrow done,
Shouldered his crutch and showed how fields were won.
Pleased with his guests, the good man learned to glow,
And quite forgot their vices in their woe; 160
Careless their merits or their faults to scan,
His pity gave ere charity began.

Thus to relieve the wretched was his pride,
And e'en his failings leaned to virtue's side;
But in his duty prompt at every call, 165
He watched and wept, he prayed and felt, for all;
And, as a bird each fond endearment tries
To tempt its new-fledged offspring to the skies,
He tried each art, reproved each dull delay,
Allured to brighter worlds, and led the way. 170

Beside the bed where parting life was laid,
And sorrow, guilt, and pain by turns dismayed,
The reverend champion stood. At his control,
Despair and anguish fled the struggling soul;
Comfort came down the trembling wretch to raise, 175
And his last faltering accents whispered praise.

At church, with meek and unaffected grace,
His looks adorned the venerable place;
Truth from his lips prevailed with double sway,
And fools who came to scoff remained to pray. 180
The service past, around the pious man
With steady zeal each honest rustic ran;
E'en children followed with endearing wile,
And plucked his gown, to share the good man's smile;
His ready smile a parent's warmth expressed: 185
Their welfare pleased him, and their cares distressed;
To them his heart, his love, his griefs were given,
But all his serious thoughts had rest in heaven.
As some tall cliff that lifts its awful form,
Swells from the vale, and midway leaves the storm, 190
Though round its breast the rolling clouds are spread,
Eternal sunshine settles on its head.

Beside yon straggling fence that skirts the way,
With blossomed furze unprofitably gay,
There, in his noisy mansion, skilled to rule, 195
The village master taught his little school;

A man severe he was, and stern to view;
I knew him well, and every truant knew;
Well had the boding tremblers learned to trace
The day's disasters in his morning face; 200
Full well they laughed with counterfeited glee
At all his jokes, for many a joke had he;
Full well the busy whisper, circling round,
Conveyed the dismal tidings when he frowned;
Yet he was kind, or if severe in aught, 205
The love he bore to learning was in fault;
The village all declared how much he knew:
'Twas certain he could write, and cipher too;
Lands he could measure, terms and tides presage,
And even the story ran that he could gauge:[9] 210
In arguing, too, the parson owned his skill,
For, even though vanquished, he could argue still;
While words of learned length and thundering sound
Amazed the gazing rustics ranged around;
And still they gazed, and still the wonder grew 215
That one small head could carry all he knew.

But past is all his fame. The very spot
Where many a time he triumphed is forgot.
Near yonder thorn, that lifts its head on high,
Where once the signpost caught the passing eye, 220
Low lies that house where nut-brown draughts[10] inspired,
Where gray-beard mirth and smiling toil retired,
Where village statesmen talked with looks profound,
And news much older than their ale went round.
Imagination fondly stoops to trace 225
The parlor splendors of that festive place:
The whitewashed wall, the nicely sanded floor,
The varnished clock that clicked behind the door;
The chest, contrived a double debt to pay,
A bed by night, a chest of drawers by day; 230
The pictures placed for ornament and use,[11]
The twelve good rules,[12] the royal game of goose;[13]
The hearth, except when winter chilled the day,
With aspen boughs and flowers and fennel gay;
While broken teacups, wisely kept for show, 235
Ranged o'er the chimney, glistened in a row.

Vain transitory splendors! Could not all
Reprieve the tottering mansion from its fall?
Obscure it sinks, nor shall it more impart
An hour's importance to the poor man's heart; 240

---

9 Calculate the capacity of circular containers.   10 Of ale.
11 Instruction.
12 Hung on the wall. They were rules of conduct, supposed to
have been composed by Charles I.
13 A dice game somewhat like parcheesi. If a piece landed on one
of the squares where a goose was pictured, it moved forward
double the value of the throw.

Thither no more the peasant shall repair
To sweet oblivion of his daily care;
No more the farmer's news, the barber's tale,
No more the woodman's ballad shall prevail;
No more the smith his dusky brow shall clear,   245
Relax his ponderous strength, and lean to hear;
The host himself no longer shall be found
Careful to see the mantling[14] bliss go round;
Nor the coy maid, half willing to be pressed,
Shall kiss the cup to pass it to the rest.   250

Yes! let the rich deride, the proud disdain,
These simple blessings of the lowly train;
To me more dear, congenial to my heart,
One native charm than all the gloss of art;
Spontaneous joys, where nature has its play,   255
The soul adopts, and owns their first-born sway;
Lightly they frolic o'er the vacant mind,
Unenvied, unmolested, unconfined.
But the long pomp, the midnight masquerade,
With all the freaks of wanton wealth arrayed,   260
In these, ere triflers half their wish obtain,
The toiling pleasure sickens into pain;
And, even while fashion's brightest arts decoy,
The heart distrusting asks if this be joy.

Ye friends to truth, ye statesmen, who survey   265
The rich man's joys increase, the poor's decay,
'Tis yours to judge how wide the limits stand
Between a splendid and a happy land.
Proud swells the tide with loads of freighted ore,
And shouting Folly hails them from her shore;   270
Hoards even beyond the miser's wish abound,
And rich men flock from all the world around.
Yet count our gains. This wealth is but a name,
That leaves our useful products still the same.
Not so the loss. The man of wealth and pride   275
Takes up a space that many poor supplied;
Space for his lake, his park's extended bounds,
Space for his horses, equipage, and hounds;
The robe that wraps his limbs in silken sloth
Has robbed the neighboring fields of half their growth;
His seat, where solitary sports are seen,   281
Indignant spurns the cottage from the green;
Around the world each needful product flies,
For all the luxuries the world supplies;
While thus the land, adorned for pleasure, all   285
In barren splendor feebly waits the fall.

As some fair female, unadorned and plain,
Secure to please while youth confirms her reign,
Slights every borrowed charm that dress supplies,
Nor shares with art the triumph of her eyes;   290
But when those charms are past, for charms are frail,
When time advances, and when lovers fail,
She then shines forth, solicitous to bless,
In all the glaring impotence of dress:
Thus fares the land, by luxury betrayed;   295
In nature's simplest charms at first arrayed;
But, verging to decline, its splendors rise,
Its vistas strike, its palaces surprise;
While, scourged by famine from the smiling land,
The mournful peasant leads his humble band;   300
And while he sinks without one arm to save,
The country blooms—a garden, and a grave.

Where then, ah, where, shall poverty reside,
To 'scape the pressure of contiguous pride?[15]
If, to some common's fenceless limits strayed,   305
He drives his flock to pick the scanty blade,
Those fenceless fields the sons of wealth divide,
And even the bare-worn common is denied.

If to the city sped—what waits him there?
To see profusion that he must not share;   310
To see ten thousand baneful arts combined
To pamper luxury, and thin mankind;
To see those joys the sons of pleasure know
Extorted from his fellow creature's woe.
Here while the courtier glitters in brocade,   315
There the pale artist[16] plies the sickly trade;
Here while the proud their long-drawn pomps display,
There the black gibbet glooms beside the way;
The dome where Pleasure holds her midnight reign,
Here, richly decked, admits the gorgeous train;   320
Tumultuous grandeur crowds the blazing square,
The rattling chariots clash, the torches glare.

Sure, scenes like these no troubles e'er annoy!
Sure, these denote one universal joy!
Are these thy serious thoughts?—Ah, turn thine eyes   325
Where the poor houseless shivering female lies.
She once, perhaps, in village plenty blessed,
Has wept at tales of innocence distressed;
Her modest looks the cottage might adorn,
Sweet as the primrose peeps beneath the thorn;   330
Now lost to all; her friends, her virtue, fled,
Near her betrayer's door she lays her head,

---

[14] Foaming.

[15] I.e., the encroachments of a rich neighbor.
[16] Artisan, workman.

And, pinched with cold, and shrinking from the shower,
With heavy heart deplores that luckless hour,
When idly first, ambitious of the town,   335
She left her wheel and robes of country brown.

Do thine, sweet AUBURN, thine, the loveliest train,
Do thy fair tribes participate her pain?
Even now, perhaps, by cold and hunger led,
At proud men's doors they ask a little bread!   340

Ah, no. To distant climes, a dreary scene,
Where half the convex world intrudes between,
Through torrid tracts with fainting steps they go,
Where wild Altama[17] murmurs to their woe.
Far different there from all that charmed before,   345
The various terrors of that horrid shore;
Those blazing suns that dart a downward ray,
And fiercely shed intolerable day;
Those matted woods where birds forget to sing,
But silent bats in drowsy clusters cling;   350
Those poisonous fields with rank luxuriance crowned,
Where the dark scorpion gathers death around;
Where at each step the stranger fears to wake
The rattling terrors of the vengeful snake;
Where crouching tigers wait their hapless prey,   355
And savage men more murderous still than they;
While oft in whirls the mad tornado flies,
Mingling the ravaged landscape with the skies.
Far different these from every former scene,
The cooling brook, the grassy-vested green,   360
The breezy covert of the warbling grove,
That only sheltered thefts of harmless love.

Good heaven! what sorrows gloomed that parting day
That called them from their native walks away;
When the poor exiles, every pleasure past,   365
Hung round their bowers, and fondly looked their last,
And took a long farewell, and wished in vain
For seats like these beyond the western main;
And shuddering still to face the distant deep,
Returned and wept, and still returned to weep.   370
The good old sire the first prepared to go
To new-found worlds, and wept for others' woe;
But for himself, in conscious virtue brave,
He only wished for worlds beyond the grave.
His lovely daughter, lovelier in her tears,   375
The fond companion of his helpless years,
Silent went next, neglectful of her charms,
And left a lover's for a father's arms.

With louder plaints the mother spoke her woes,
And blessed the cot where every pleasure rose,   380
And kissed her thoughtless babes with many a tear,
And clasped them close, in sorrow doubly dear;
Whilst her fond husband strove to lend relief
In all the silent manliness of grief.

O luxury! thou cursed by heaven's decree,   385
How ill exchanged are things like these for thee!
How do thy potions, with insidious joy,
Diffuse their pleasures only to destroy!
Kingdoms, by thee to sickly greatness grown,
Boast of a florid vigor not their own;   390
At every draught more large and large they grow,
A bloated mass of rank, unwieldy woe;
Till sapped their strength, and every part unsound,
Down, down they sink, and spread a ruin round.

Even now the devastation is begun,   395
And half the business of destruction done;
Even now, methinks, as pondering here I stand,
I see the rural virtues leave the land:
Down where yon anchoring vessel spreads the sail,
That idly waiting flaps with every gale,   400
Downward they move, a melancholy band,
Pass from the shore, and darken all the strand.
Contented toil and hospitable care
And kind connubial tenderness are there;
And piety, with wishes placed above,   405
And steady loyalty, and faithful love.
And thou, sweet Poetry, thou loveliest maid,
Still first to fly where sensual joys invade,
Unfit, in these degenerate times of shame,
To catch the heart or strike for honest fame,   410
Dear charming nymph, neglected and decried,
My shame in crowds, my solitary pride,
Thou source of all my bliss and all my woe,
That found'st me poor at first, and keep'st me so,
Thou guide by which the nobler arts excel,   415
Thou nurse of every virtue, fare thee well!
Farewell! and oh, where'er thy voice be tried,
On Torno's cliffs or Pambamarca's[18] side,
Whether where equinoctial[19] fervors glow,
Or winter wraps the polar world in snow,   420
Still let thy voice, prevailing over time,
Redress the rigors of the inclement clime;
Aid slighted truth; with thy persuasive strain
Teach erring man to spurn the rage of gain;

---

17 The Altamaha River in Georgia. Goldsmith knew General
Oglethorpe, who had founded that colony in 1732.

18 These names occurred to Goldsmith because Newton's contention that the earth's curvature flattens slightly at the poles had
been confirmed by recent scientific expeditions which made
studies at the Tornea River, between Sweden and Finland, and
Mount Pambamarca in Ecuador.   19 Equatorial.

Teach him that states of native strength possessed,   425
Though very poor, may still be very blest;
That trade's proud empire hastes to swift decay,
As ocean sweeps the labored mole away;
While self-dependent power can time defy,
As rocks resist the billows and the sky.[20]   430

from RETALIATION

According to David Garrick these amusing verses were the aftermath of a "meeting of a company of gentlemen who were well known to each other," at which he was challenged by Goldsmith to a trial of their "epigrammatic powers." Each was to write the other's epitaph. Garrick immediately declared he had finished, and offered the following couplet extempore:

Here lies Nolly Goldsmith, for shortness called Noll,
Who wrote like an angel, but talked like poor Poll.

"Goldsmith, upon the company's laughing very heartily, grew very thoughtful, and either would not or could not write anything at that time; however, he went to work and, some weeks after, he produced the . . . poem called 'Retaliation.'" As a matter of fact, it was still unfinished when he died, in 1774; it was published shortly afterward, with notes identifying the persons mentioned.

. . . Here, waiter, more wine, let me sit while I'm able,
Till all my companions sink under the table;   20
Then, with chaos and blunders encircling my head,
Let me ponder, and tell what I think of the dead. . . .

Here lies our good Edmund, whose genius was such
We scarcely can praise it, or blame it, too much;   30
Who, born for the universe, narrowed his mind,
And to party gave up what was meant for mankind.[1]
Though fraught with all learning, yet straining his throat
To persuade Tommy Townshend[2] to lend him a vote;
Who, too deep for his hearers, still went on refining,   35
And thought of convincing while they thought of dining;
Though equal to all things, for all things unfit,
Too nice for a statesman, too proud for a wit;
For a patriot, too cool; for a drudge, disobedient;
And too fond of the *right* to pursue the *expedient*.   40
In short, 'twas his fate, unemployed or in place, sir,
To eat mutton cold, and cut blocks with a razor. . . .

Here lies David Garrick, describe me who can,[3]
An abridgment[4] of all that was pleasant in man;
As an actor, confessed without rival to shine;   95
As a wit, if not first, in the very first line;
Yet, with talents like these, and an excellent heart,
The man had his failings, a dupe to his art:
Like an ill-judging beauty, his colors he spread,
And beplastered with rouge his own natural red.   100
On the stage he was natural, simple, affecting;
'Twas only that when he was off he was acting.
With no reason on earth to go out of his way,
He turned and he varied full ten times a day.
Though secure of our hearts, yet confoundedly sick   105
If they were not his own by finessing and trick,
He cast off his friends, as a huntsman his pack,
For he knew when he pleased he could whistle them back.
Of praise a mere glutton, he swallowed what came,
And the puff of a dunce, he mistook it for fame;   110
Till, his relish grown callous, almost to disease,
Who peppered the highest was surest to please.
But let us be candid, and speak out our mind;
If dunces applauded, he paid them in kind.
Ye Kenricks,[5] ye Kellys,[6] and Woodfalls[7] so grave,   115
What a commerce was yours, while you got and you gave!
How did Grub Street[8] re-echo the shouts that you raised,
While he was be-Rosciused,[9] and you were bepraised!
But peace to his spirit, wherever it flies,
To act as an angel, and mix with the skies.   120
Those poets who owe their best fame to his skill
Shall still be his flatterers, go where he will.
Old Shakespeare, receive him, with praise and with love,
And Beaumonts and Bens[10] be his Kellys[11] above. . . .

Here Reynolds[12] is laid, and to tell you my mind,
He has not left a better or wiser behind;
His pencil was striking, resistless, and grand;

[20] According to Boswell the last four lines were written by Dr. Johnson.

[1] Not a sage observation. See headnote to selections from the works of Edmund Burke, below. Burke was an exponent of the political party as an instrument of good government and a better lot for mankind.   [2] A Whig leader.

[3] Let him who can adequately do so describe him for me.
[4] He was a small man.
[5] William Kenrick (1725?–79), a libelous hack writer, hostile to Goldsmith and Johnson.
[6] Hugh Kelly (1739–77), author of a famous comedy, *False Delicacy*. Many preferred his comedies to Goldsmith's.
[7] William Woodfall (1746–1803), a London editor and dramatic critic.   [8] Where the hack writers labored.
[9] Roscius (d. 62 B.C.) was the greatest of the Roman actors. Garrick was called the English Roscius. Charles Churchill (1731–64), author of the *Rosciad*, a satire on the actors, was an enemy of Dr. Johnson and his circle.
[10] Francis Beaumont and Ben Jonson, the Jacobean dramatists.
[11] I.e., playwrights (see note 6).
[12] Sir Joshua Reynolds, president of the Royal Academy; see above, on *The Deserted Village*, note 1.

His manners were gentle, complying, and bland;   140
Still born to improve us in every part,
His pencil our faces, his manners our heart;
To coxcombs averse, yet most civilly steering,

When they judged without skill he was still hard of
        hearing;   144
When they talked of their Raphaels, Correggios,[13] and stuff,
He shifted his trumpet,[14] and only took snuff.

Edmund Burke

1729–1797

TO THOSE, says Sir Philip Magnus, who may wish to acquire the art of politics, "a knowledge of Burke is the beginning of wisdom." Certainly he is more often quoted than any other British statesman. From the floor of the House of Commons, and also with his pen, he fought a series of losing battles; on all three of the major issues he championed, the course of events was against him—on the retention of the American colonies as free partners in the imperial system, on the punishment of India's despoilers, on the preservation in Britain and Europe of a way of life that was already doomed by the opening phase of the Industrial Revolution. Yet, in the midst of the chaos and corruption into which politics had fallen during the long rule of the Whigs and the subsequent attempt of George III to be in effect his own prime minister, Burke's tracts and speeches restored to English life a political philosophy which towered above the selfish aims of unprincipled men; it was a conception of a state guided by principle and dedicated to human welfare. In a way, therefore, hated as he was in the latter part of his career, Burke emerged victor in the long run. The imperial system was eventually liberalized, the aroused conscience of the British people called a halt to the looting of India, and the French Revolution was not duplicated in England.

Burke's great reputation rests, however, less on his having been right on these issues than on his faculty of formulating political generalizations, not, as the French philosophers did, in the vacuum of abstract reasoning, but in the vital atmosphere of fact and experience. "I never govern myself," he says, "no rational man ever did govern himself, by abstractions and universals." And "He who does not take circumstances into consideration is not erroneous, but stark mad." And again, "Nothing universal can be rationally affirmed on any moral or political subject." Quite aside from his formulations of principle, it was above all the great service of revitalizing politics that ranks his among the major eighteenth-century contributions to civilization. He has been called the John Wesley of politics. Wesley and Burke alike injected new life into moribund institutions; and scarcely less than Wesley's, the pattern of Burke's ideas was worked out within a framework of religious faith.

Burke's wisdom is apparent even in the fragment given below from his famous oration *On Conciliation with the Colonies*—"with *America*," it is often styled. That masterpiece of organization, the bane of many a high-school senior, is not, however, the best introduction to Burke. To be sure, in his insistence on the superior strength of intangible bonds over immediate materialistic considerations, he was not only idealistic: he was correct, as the great idealists usually are, and as the history of the British Empire was to demonstrate. Yet, for all its statesmanship, the *Conciliation* speech, though it earned its author a permanent place in American esteem, is not among his richest and most eloquent writings. We are here concerned, naturally, with Burke as a literary figure—*artist* is not too strong a word. On that score, and probably politically too, first place must go to the *Reflections on the Revolution in France,* from which an extract will be found below. In this passage Burke writes with more color, under the stimulus of a spectacular occasion, the thought of which worked powerfully on his highly emotional nature. He looked at France, and was alarmed for England. Burke was no democrat; as an abstract principle, the Rights of Man made no appeal to him. The modern reader will respond less warmly to the notion that the plight of Louis XVI and his family was more pathetic because they were royal. On that point our feelings might have been different in 1790; but no one can now regard as cast in the heroic mold either the bewildered King or his shallow wife, nor can we accept Burke's romantic lament over the whited sepulchre of chivalry. Yet the surge of the mob into Versailles on October 5–6, 1789, contains the essence of wild drama. Burke, to whom order was a paramount consideration, makes the most of that episode as a horrifying symbol of disorder; and the reproaches he hurls at English supporters of the Revolution are charged with mordant irony and appalling prophecies—most of which were borne out by subsequent events. He foresaw, for example, the military dictatorship in which the Revolution

---

[13] Raphael (1483–1520) and Correggio (1494–1534) were among the greatest Italian Renaissance painters.
[14] Ear trumpet. Reynolds was deaf.

ended. If we cannot follow him in basing liberty on every man's knowing his place, his warnings against the naive theorist and the unscrupulous extremist must be accepted by every intelligent and well-meaning citizen who has acquired any experience in the world, against which to weigh either the conclusions of the abstract or doctrinaire thinker, or the proposals of the opportunist who sees in abrupt change a likelier prospect of personal advantage.

Burke was born in Dublin in 1729. His father, a leading lawyer there, was a Protestant; and though his mother was a Roman Catholic, Burke was reared in the Established Church. In 1750, two years after he took his degree at Trinity College, he went to London to study law. He was never admitted to the bar; literature and politics claimed him, and his disgusted father withdrew his allowance. In 1756 he revealed something of his mind's quality in a little book called *A Vindication of Natural Society,* an ironical handling of the deistic philosophy of Bolingbroke (p. 795, above), whose works had been posthumously published. For Burke both religious and political truth must be rooted in faith. In 1757 he made a marriage that brought him lifelong happiness. In the same year appeared a second essay, *The Origin of Our Ideas of the Sublime and Beautiful,* which won him a Continental reputation; the much better and better-known *Laokoön* (1766) of the German critic Lessing is indebted to it. Literary success led to important friendships, to a reconciliation with his father, and to several years of editorial and secretarial employment.

Burke's connection with politics began with a secretaryship to a member of Parliament, and in 1766 he entered the House of Commons himself. By this time the Whigs had split into factions dominated by one or another of the families whose ancestors had managed the Glorious Revolution. For about a year the Marquis of Rockingham headed a Whig ministry. Burke served him as private secretary and party manager; hence his own election to Parliament, from a pocket borough, and his long association with the Rockingham Whigs, a group of great landowners who professed to be imbued with the principles of 1688. Once in the House, Burke leaped into prominence. Though for brief periods he was in office as Paymaster-General, he never held a ministerial portfolio or entered the cabinet, for which his inability to conduct his private affairs on a sound financial basis indicates a temperamental unfitness. He was fully aware of it. Practically his whole career was spent as a member of the Opposition. Though the tangible rewards of his services were not remarkable—under the younger Pitt he was granted a pension in 1794—and though when he died three years later he was heavily in debt, partly because of the great house and estate he had purchased at Beaconsfield in Buckinghamshire, nevertheless Burke did not lack

ample recognition of what he was. His friends, both within and outside the Literary Club, numbered many of the age's most eminent men. To Johnson, Reynolds, Goldsmith, and Garrick he was particularly close; with Johnson there was, not rivalry, but the keenest mutual admiration. "Yes, sir," declared Johnson, "if a man were to go by chance at the same time with Burke under a shed to shun a shower, he would say, 'This is an extraordinary man.' If Burke should go into a stable to see his horse dressed, the ostler would say, 'We have had an extraordinary man here.'"

As for his position on public questions, in the pamphlet *Thoughts on the Cause of the Present Discontents* (1770) Burke attacked encroachments on English liberty by King George's "personal government," offering what has become the classic exposition of the necessity for political parties. This was the year when, through the subserviency of the Tory prime minister, Lord North, the King began his twelve-year attempt to rule in fact as well as name. Public feeling was at a high pitch. There had been rioting and bloodshed over the refusal of the House of Commons to seat the duly elected John Wilkes.[1] The freedom of the press was also a burning issue, and it was largely through Burke's efforts that the order of the House against reporting its debates was nullified. In the *Speech on American Taxation* (1774), the *Conciliation* speech (1775), and the *Letter to the Sheriffs of Bristol* (1777)—Bristol was now his constituency—Burke condemned the Tory policy on America. This series of pronouncements is described by John Morley (1838–1923), himself both statesman and man of letters, as "the most perfect manual in our literature, or in any literature, for one who approaches the study of public affairs, whether for knowledge or for practice. They are an example without fault of all the qualities which the critic, whether a theorist or an actor, of great political situations should strive by night and by day to possess." This series is vastly more than an argument on the immediate American issue; it is a great contribution to constitutional theory. Burke's accomplishment rests on a rare combination of learning, practical experience, and the imagination of a poet. Other causes he espoused were the abolition of the slave trade, Catholic emancipation and other reforms for Ireland, and the reform of England's government of India.[2]

---

[1] See above, p. 888, note 2.

[2] Still others were free trade, the rights of Dissenters, milder bankruptcy laws, abolition of army enlistments for life, and a plan of economic reform in the royal household and government departments. The last of these causes was of more than economic importance, since by greatly reducing the number of jobs in the gift of a ministry, its eventual adoption put an end to control of the House of Commons by bribery.

Burke had long since been informing himself on eastern affairs when in 1785 his speech on *The Nabob of Arcot's Debts* began the campaign to impeach Warren Hastings (1732–1818), the governor-general of British India. Burke pursued Hastings for ten years. Some of his hearers actually fainted as, in the four-day speech with which he opened the trial in 1788, he poured out, with a phraseology enriched by the Oriental background of the case, details of the extortions and cruelties which marked the operations of the empire builders. The proceedings, on charges brought by the House of Commons and heard by the House of Lords, with Burke as principal manager for Commons, ended in 1795 in acquittal. There were 142 sessions in all. Burke, many of whose speeches were wildly intemperate, had never expected to secure a conviction; he was probably mistaken in holding Hastings personally corrupt or directly responsible for needless severity, but during the long course of the trial he gave passionate utterance to sentiments which were beginning to stir a social conscience in England. He considered his service to the peoples of India the major achievement of his life. Thereafter the sahibs who ruled the great dependency were obliged to recognize the existence of limits beyond which English public opinion would not tolerate their going. For us today the most significant feature of the whole affair is Burke's insistence that nations are not a law unto themselves. The Fascist conception of a non-moral state accountable to no power outside itself Burke would have repudiated as contrary to the laws of God and the experience of mankind.

Until the day in 1792 when, during the Paris Terror, he formally crossed the floor of the House to sit with Pitt and the Tories, Burke was a moderate Whig, of what we would call liberal but not radical views. Now that he began laying greater emphasis on radicalism than on Tory conservatism as a menace to liberty, his old associates called him a renegade. Actually, as Lord Morley observes, he had changed his front but never his ground. Burke was not opposed to change; most of his career was spent

fighting for it. But he thought continuity an indispensable feature of national life; he set a high value on our legacy from the past, and he was not favorably impressed by the French philosophers who urged a complete break with it. It was the ideological excesses of the French, as well as their violence, that turned him into an enemy of their revolution and inspired his *Reflections* (1790). How influential he was on the subsequent course of events is difficult to say; but it is probable that his rejection of the French Revolution helped form the English decision to intervene against it.

Charles James Fox and Richard Brinsley Sheridan, whose friendship he now lost, both outshone him on the floor of Commons. Burke often spoke too long; his delivery was marred by awkwardness and a heavy brogue, and lacked the advantages of a good voice and an engaging manner. These defects, above which, to the rapt attention of the House, he sometimes rose triumphant, did not include lack of animation. He was extremely excitable, and when carried away by an occasion would say anything. Sometimes his friends, alarmed by the possibility of an outburst beyond even his usual vitriolic indulgence in personalities, would seize his coat-tails and pull him down into his seat. In his last years the younger members yawned through his magnificently cadenced periods, and even called him the dinner bell because they stole away when he rose to speak; but in printed form his orations were widely read. Whether or not we should willingly hear Burke from the platform today, that he is one of the masters of English prose is beyond dispute.

The works are available in various editions; particularly useful is E. J. Payne's *Burke: Select Works* (new ed., 3 vols., 1904). Everyman's Library includes the *Reflections* and a volume of the American speeches; The World's Classics has the *Works* in six volumes, and a volume of letters; and there is a volume of selections in The Modern Student's Library. J. Morley's *Life* (1867) is still important and there is a new one by P. Magnus (1939). See also J. MacCunn's *The Political Philosophy of Edmund Burke* (1913).

Edmund Burke

from the SPEECH ON CONCILIATION WITH THE COLONIES

MARCH 22, 1775

MY HOLD of the colonies[1] is in the close affection which grows from common names, from kindred blood, from similar privileges, and equal protection.

These are ties which, though light as air, are as strong as links of iron. Let the colonies always keep the idea of their civil rights associated with your government; they will cling and grapple to you, and no force under heaven will be of power to tear them from their allegiance. But let it be once under-

---

[1] I.e., my plan for holding them.—These are the final paragraphs of the speech.

stood that your government may be one thing and their privileges another, that these two things may exist without any mutual relation—the cement is gone, the cohesion is loosened, and everything hastens to decay and dissolution. As long as you have the wisdom to keep the sovereign authority of this country as the sanctuary of liberty, the sacred temple consecrated to our common faith, wherever the chosen race and sons of England worship Freedom they will turn their faces towards you. The more they multiply, the more friends you will have; the more ardently they love liberty, the more perfect will be their obedience. Slavery they can have anywhere. It is a weed that grows in every soil. They may have it from Spain; they may have it from Prussia. But, until you become lost to all feeling of your true interest and your natural dignity, freedom they can have from none but you. This is the commodity of price, of which you have the monopoly. This is the true Act of Navigation, which binds to you the commerce of the colonies, and through them secures to you the wealth of the world. Deny them this participation of freedom, and you break that sole bond which originally made, and must still[2] preserve, the unity of the Empire. Do not entertain so weak an imagination[3] as that your registers and your bonds, your affidavits and your sufferances,[4] your cockets[5] and your clearances are what form the great securities of your commerce. Do not dream that your letters of office, and your instructions, and your suspending clauses are the things that hold together the great contexture of the mysterious whole. Dead instruments, passive tools as they are, it is the spirit of the English communion that gives all their life and efficacy to them. It is the spirit of the English Constitution, which, infused through the mighty mass, pervades, feeds, unites, invigorates, vivifies every part of the Empire, even down to the minutest member.

Is it not the same virtue[6] which does everything for us here in England? Do you imagine, then, that it is the Land Tax[7] Act which raises your revenue? that it is the annual vote in the Committee of Supply which gives you your army? or that it is the Mutiny Bill[8] which inspires it with bravery and discipline? No! surely no! It is the love of the people; it is their attachment to their government, from the sense of the deep stake they have in such a glorious institution, which gives you your army and your navy, and infuses into both that liberal obedience without which your army would be a base rabble and your navy nothing but rotten timber.

All this, I know well enough, will sound wild and chimerical to the profane herd of those vulgar and mechanical politicians who have no place[9] among us, a sort of people who think that nothing exists but what is gross and material, and who, therefore, far from being qualified to be directors of the great movement of empire, are not fit to turn a wheel in the machine. But to men truly initiated and rightly taught, these ruling and master principles, which, in the opinion of such men as I have mentioned, have no substantial existence, are in truth everything, and all in all. Magnanimity in politics is not seldom the truest wisdom; and a great empire and little minds go ill together. If we are conscious of our station and glow with zeal to fill our place as becomes our situation and ourselves, we aught to auspicate[10] all our public proceedings on America with the old warning of the Church, *Sursum corda!*[11] We ought to elevate our minds to the greatness of that trust to which the order of Providence has called us. By adverting to the dignity of this high calling, our ancestors have turned a savage wilderness into a glorious empire, and have made the most extensive and the only honorable conquests, not by destroying but by promoting the wealth, the number, the happiness of the human race. Let us get an American revenue as we have got an American empire. English privileges have made it all that it is; English privileges alone will make it all it can be.

In full confidence of this unalterable truth, I now (*quod felix faustumque sit*)[12] lay the first stone of the temple of peace; and I move you

"That the colonies and plantations of Great Britain in North America, consisting of fourteen separate governments, and containing two millions and upwards of free inhabitants, have not had the liberty and privilege of electing and sending any knights and burgesses or others to represent them in the high court of Parliament."[13]

---

[2] Ever.   [3] Thought, idea.   [4] Permits.
[5] Certificates that the customs have been paid on imported goods.
[6] Power, efficacy.
[7] It then brought in a major portion of the government's revenue.
[8] The annual bill by which Parliament concedes, for a term, the right of the army to try soldiers by military law.

[9] I.e., no right.   [10] Begin.
[11] Lift up your hearts. These words begin the Preface to the Mass.
[12] May it be fruitful and fortunate.
[13] The resolution was lost by a vote of 270 to 78.

from REFLECTIONS ON THE REVOLUTION IN FRANCE

THE FULL title of the essay is *Reflections on the Revolution in France, and on the Proceedings in Certain Societies in London Relative to That Event, in a Letter Intended to Have Been Sent to a Gentleman in Paris*. It originally appeared in 1790; the text of the following selections, which begin about one-fourth of the way through the essay, is from the most authoritative edition, the eleventh. Burke is denying the alleged similarity between the French Revolution and the Glorious Revolution of 1688, and emphasizing the difference between the French and English conceptions of liberty.

IN FRANCE you are now in the crisis of a revolution, and in the transit from one form of government to another—you cannot see that character of men[1] exactly in the same situation in which we see it in this country. With us it is militant; with you it is triumphant; and you know how it can act when its power is commensurate to its will. I would not be supposed to confine those observations to any description of men, or to comprehend all men of any description within them—no! far from it. I am as incapable of that injustice as I am of keeping terms with those who profess principles of extremes; and who, under the name of religion, teach little else than wild and dangerous politics. The worst of these politics of revolution is this: they temper and harden the breast, in order to prepare it for the desperate strokes which are sometimes used in extreme occasions. But as these occasions may never arrive, the mind receives a gratuitous taint; and the moral sentiments suffer not a little, when no political purpose is served by the depravation.[2] This sort of people are so taken up with their theories about the rights of man that they have totally forgot his nature. Without opening one new avenue to the understanding, they have succeeded in stopping up those that lead to the heart. They have perverted in themselves, and in those that attend to them, all the well-placed sympathies of the human breast.

This famous sermon[3] of the Old Jewry breathes nothing but this spirit through all the political part.

Plots, massacres, assassinations, seem to some people a trivial price for obtaining a revolution. A cheap, bloodless reformation, a guiltless liberty, appear flat and vapid in their taste. There must be a great change of scene; there must be a magnificent stage effect; there must be a grand spectacle to rouse the imagination, grown torpid with the lazy enjoyment of sixty years' security, and the still unanimating repose of public prosperity. The preacher found them all in the French Revolution. This inspires a juvenile warmth through his whole frame. His enthusiasm kindles as he advances; and when he arrives at his peroration, it is in a full blaze. Then viewing, from the Pisgah[4] of his pulpit, the free, moral, happy, flourishing, and glorious state of France, as in a bird-eye landscape of a promised land, he breaks out into the following rapture:

"What an eventful period is this! I am *thankful* that I have lived to it; I could almost say, *Lord, now lettest thou thy servant depart in peace, for mine eyes have seen thy salvation.*[5]—I have lived to see a *diffusion* of knowledge, which has undermined superstition and error.—I have lived to see *the rights of men* better understood than ever; and nations panting for liberty which seemed to have lost the idea of it.—I have lived to see *thirty millions of people,* indignant and resolute, spurning at slavery, and demanding liberty with an irresistible voice. *Their king led in triumph, and an arbitrary monarch surrendering himself to his subjects.*"[6]

I find a preacher of the gospel profaning the beautiful and prophetic ejaculation, commonly called *nunc dimittis,*[7] made on the first presentation of our Saviour in the Temple, and applying it, with an inhuman and unnatural rapture, to the most horrid, atrocious, and afflicting spectacle that perhaps ever was exhibited to the pity and indignation of mankind. This "leading in triumph," a thing in its best form unmanly and irreligious, which fills our preacher with such unhallowed transports, must

[1] Extreme radicals, who "see no merit in the good, and no fault in the vicious management of public affairs; they rather rejoice in the latter, as more propitious to revolution."

[2] Depravity.

[3] The immediate occasion of Burke's pamphlet was a sermon which he has described in an earlier passage. It was delivered on Nov. 4, 1789, before a group of revolutionary sympathizers by Dr. Richard Price (1723–91), a well-known Dissenting minister. The meetinghouse stood in the Old Jewry, a street in the heart of London.

[4] The mountain from which the Lord showed Moses the Promised Land (Deuteronomy 34:1).   [5] Luke 2:29, 30.

[6] Burke's note: "Another of these reverend gentlemen, who was witness to some of the spectacles which Paris has lately exhibited, expresses himself thus: '*A king dragged in submissive triumph by his conquering subjects,* is one of those appearances of grandeur which seldom rise in the prospect of human affairs, and which, during the remainder of my life, I shall think of with wonder and gratification.' These gentlemen agree marvelously in their feelings."

[7] From the opening words, in the Vulgate, of the text quoted by Price (note 5).

shock, I believe, the moral taste of every well-born[8] mind. Several English were the stupefied and indignant spectators of that triumph. It was (unless we have been strangely deceived) a spectacle more resembling a procession of American savages, entering into Onondaga,[9] after some of their murders called victories, and leading into hovels hung round with scalps, their captives, overpowered with the scoffs and buffets of women as ferocious as themselves, much more than it resembled the triumphal pomp of a civilized, martial nation—if a civilized nation, or any men who had a sense of generosity, were capable of a personal triumph over the fallen and afflicted.[10]

This, my dear sir, was not the triumph of France. I must believe that, as a nation, it overwhelmed you with shame and horror. I must believe that the National Assembly[11] find themselves in a state of the greatest humiliation in not being able to punish the authors of this triumph, or the actors in it; and that they are in a situation in which any enquiry they may make upon the subject must be destitute even of the appearance of liberty or impartiality. The apology of that Assembly is found in their situation; but when we approve what they *must* bear, it is in us the degenerate choice of a vitiated mind.

With a compelled appearance of deliberation, they vote under the dominion of a stern necessity. They sit in the heart, as it were, of a foreign republic:[12] they have their residence in a city whose constitution has emanated neither from the charter of their king nor from their legislative power. There they are surrounded by an army[13] not raised either by the authority of their crown or by their command; and which, if they should order to dissolve itself, would instantly dissolve them. There they sit, after a gang of assassins had driven away some hundreds of the members; whilst those who held the same moderate principles, with more patience or better hope, continued every day exposed to outrageous insults and murderous threats. There a majority, sometimes real, sometimes pretended, captive itself, compels a captive king to issue as royal edicts, at third hand,

the polluted nonsense of their most licentious and giddy coffee houses. It is notorious that all their measures are decided before they are debated.[14] It is beyond doubt that, under the terror of the bayonet and the lamp post and the torch to their houses, they are obliged to adopt all the crude and desperate measures suggested by clubs composed of a monstrous medley of all conditions,[15] tongues, and nations. Among these are found persons, in comparison of whom Catiline[16] would be thought scrupulous, and Cethegus a man of sobriety and moderation. Nor is it in these clubs alone that the public measures are deformed into monsters. They undergo a previous distortion in academies, intended as so many seminaries for these clubs, which are set up in all the places of public resort.[17] In these meetings of all sorts, every counsel, in proportion as it is daring and violent and perfidious, is taken for the mark of superior genius. Humanity and compassion are ridiculed as the fruits of superstition and ignorance. Tenderness to individuals is considered as treason to the public. Liberty is always to be estimated perfect as property is rendered insecure. Amidst assassination, massacre, and confiscation, perpetrated or meditated, they are forming plans for the good order of future society. Embracing in their arms the carcasses of base criminals, and promoting their relations on the title of their offenses,[18] they drive hundreds of virtuous persons to the same end, by forcing them to subsist by beggary or by crime.

The Assembly, their organ, acts before them the farce of deliberation, with as little decency as liberty. They act like the comedians of a fair before a riotous audience; they act amidst the tumultuous cries of a mixed mob of ferocious men, and of women lost to shame, who, according to their insolent fancies, direct, control, applaud, explode them, and sometimes mix and take their seats amongst them, domineering over them with a strange mixture of servile petulance and proud, presumptuous authority.

---

[8] Generous, liberal.

[9] An Indian village in western New York.

[10] On Oct. 6, 1789, a mob had brought Louis XVI, Queen Marie Antoinette, and their son back to Paris from Versailles. The National Assembly followed them.

[11] It was charged with the duty of framing a new constitution, but found itself obliged to assume the task of governing France.

[12] I.e., Paris, where a new municipal government had been set up.

[13] The newly created National Guard, commanded by Lafayette.

[14] Since, through the municipal government of Paris, the radical clubs controlled the National Assembly. The most important were the Cordeliers, led by Danton, and the Jacobins, whose more moderate leaders had to give way to Robespierre.

[15] Ranks.

[16] The conspirator (d. 62 B.C.) against the Roman republic; Cicero denounced him in the famous orations. Cethegus was a fellow plotter.

[17] Attempts were made to form discussion groups in the cafés.

[18] A reference to the promotion to lieutenancies in the National Guard of two relatives of a pair of forgers who had been sentenced to death. The promotion was to mark the passage of a law freeing the relatives of a condemned man from the old feudal taint of felony.

As they have inverted order in all things, the gallery is in the place of the house. This Assembly, which overthrows kings and kingdoms, has not even the physiognomy and aspect of a grave legislative body —*nec color imperii, nec frons ulla senatus.*[19] They have a power given to them, like that of the evil principle, to subvert and destroy; but none to construct, except such machines as may be fitted for further subversion and further destruction.

Who is it that admires, and from the heart is attached to national representative assemblies, but must turn with horror and disgust from such a profane burlesque and abominable perversion of that sacred institute? Lovers of monarchy, lovers of republics, must alike abhor it. The members of your Assembly must themselves groan under the tyranny of which they have all the shame, none of the direction, and little of the profit. I am sure many of the members who compose even the majority of that body must feel as I do, notwithstanding the applauses of the Revolution Society.[20]—Miserable King! miserable Assembly! How must that Assembly be silently scandalized with those of their members who could call a day[21] which seemed to blot the sun out of heaven "un beau jour"! How must they be inwardly indignant at hearing others, who thought fit to declare to them that "the vessel of the state would fly forward in her course towards regeneration with more speed than ever," from the stiff gale of treason and murder which preceded our preacher's triumph! What must they have felt, whilst with outward patience and inward indignation they heard of the slaughter of innocent gentlemen in their houses, that "the blood spilled was not the most pure"![22] What must they have felt, when they were besieged by complaints of disorders which shook their country to its foundations, at being compelled coolly to tell the complainants that they were under the protection of the law, and that they would address the King (the captive King) to cause the laws to be enforced for their protection; when the enslaved ministers of that captive King had formally notified to them that there were neither law nor authority nor power left to protect! What must they have felt at being obliged, as a felicitation on the present New Year, to request their captive King to forget the stormy period of the last, on account of the great good which *he* was likely to produce to his people; to the complete attainment of which good they adjourned the practical demonstrations of their loyalty, assuring him of their obedience, when he should no longer possess any authority to command!

This address was made with much good nature and affection, to be sure. But among the revolutions in France must be reckoned a considerable revolution in their ideas of politeness. In England we are said to learn manners at second-hand from your side of the water, and that we dress our behavior in the frippery[23] of France. If so, we are still in the old cut; and have not so far conformed to the new Parisian mode of good breeding as to think it quite in the most refined strain of delicate compliment, whether in condolence or congratulation, to say, to the most humiliated creature that crawls upon the earth, that great public benefits are derived from the murder of his servants, the attempted assassination of himself and of his wife, and the mortification, disgrace, and degradation that he has personally suffered. It is a topic of consolation which our ordinary[24] of Newgate would be too humane to use to a criminal at the foot of the gallows. I should have thought that the hangman of Paris, now that he is liberalized by the vote of the National Assembly, and is allowed his rank and arms in the heralds' college[25] of the rights of men, would be too generous, too gallant a man, too full of the sense of his new dignity, to employ that cutting consolation to any of the persons whom the *leze nation*[26] might bring under the administration of his *executive powers.*

A man is fallen indeed, when he is thus flattered. The anodyne draught of oblivion, thus drugged, is well calculated to preserve a galling wakefulness, and to feed the living ulcer of a corroding memory. Thus to administer the opiate potion of amnesty, powdered with all the ingredients of scorn and contempt, is to hold to his lips, instead of "the balm of hurt minds,"[27] the cup of human misery full to the brim, and to force him to drink it to the dregs.

Yielding to reasons at least as forcible as those which were so delicately urged in the compliment

---

[19] They have neither the aspect of sovereignty nor the appearance of a senate (cf. Lucan, *Pharsalia,* IX, 207).

[20] An English association, formed to commemorate the Glorious Revolution of 1688. It had recently sent a congratulatory address to the National Assembly.

[21] Oct. 6, 1789; see note 10, above.

[22] A remark by the moderate Jacobin leader A.P.J.M. Barnave (1671–93).

[23] Second-hand clothes.

[24] Chaplain (of the famous London prison).

[25] The Heralds' College in England has jurisdiction over coats of arms, genealogies, etc.

[26] Treason to the nation. The National Assembly had set up this category of crime, on the analogy of *lèse-majesté.*

[27] *Macbeth,* II, ii, 39.

on the New Year, the King of France will probably endeavor to forget these events and that compliment. But History, who keeps a durable record of all our acts, and exercises her awful censure over the proceedings of all sorts of sovereigns, will not forget either those events or the era of this liberal refinement in the intercourse of mankind. History will record that on the morning of the 6th of October, 1789, the King and Queen of France, after a day of confusion, alarm, dismay, and slaughter, lay down, under the pledged security of public faith, to indulge nature in a few hours of respite, and troubled, melancholy repose. From this sleep the Queen was first startled by the voice of the sentinel at her door, who cried out to her to save herself by flight—that this was the last proof of fidelity he could give— that they were upon him, and he was dead. Instantly he was cut down.[28] A band of cruel ruffians and assassins, reeking with his blood, rushed into the chamber of the Queen, and pierced with an hundred strokes of bayonets and poniards the bed, from whence this persecuted woman had but just had time to fly almost naked, and, through ways unknown to the murderers, had escaped to seek refuge at the feet of a king and husband not secure of his own life for a moment.

This King, to say no more of him, and this Queen, and their infant children (who once would have been the pride and hope of a great and generous people), were then forced to abandon the sanctuary of the most splendid palace[29] in the world, which they left swimming in blood, polluted by massacre, and strewed with scattered limbs and mutilated carcasses. Thence they were conducted into the capital of their kingdom. Two had been selected from the unprovoked, unresisted, promiscuous slaughter which was made of the gentlemen of birth and family who composed the King's bodyguard. These two gentlemen, with all the parade of an execution of justice, were cruelly and publicly dragged to the block, and beheaded in the great court of the palace. Their heads were stuck upon spears, and led the procession; whilst the royal captives who followed in the train were slowly moved along, amidst the horrid yells and shrilling screams and frantic dances and infamous contumelies; and all the unutterable abominations of the furies of hell, in the abused shape of the vilest of women.[30]

After they had been made to taste, drop by drop, more than the bitterness of death, in the slow torture of a journey of twelve miles, protracted to six hours, they were, under a guard, composed of those very soldiers[31] who had thus conducted them through this famous triumph, lodged in one of the old palaces[32] of Paris now converted into a bastille for kings.

Is this a triumph to be consecrated at altars? to be commemorated with grateful thanksgiving? to be offered to the divine humanity with fervent prayer and enthusiastic ejaculation?—These Theban and Thracian orgies,[33] acted in France, and applauded only in the Old Jewry, I assure you, kindle prophetic enthusiasm in the minds but of very few people in this kingdom: although a saint and apostle, who may have revelations of his own, and who has so completely vanquished all the mean superstitions of the heart, may incline to think it pious and decorous to compare it with the entrance into the world of the Prince of Peace, proclaimed in an holy temple by a venerable sage, and not long before not worse announced by the voice of angels to the quiet innocence of shepherds.

At first I was at a loss to account for this fit of unguarded transport. I knew, indeed, that the sufferings of monarchs make a delicious repast to some sort of palates. There were reflections which might serve to keep this appetite within some bounds of temperance. But when I took one circumstance into my consideration, I was obliged to confess that much allowance ought to be made for the Society,[34] and that the temptation was too strong for common discretion; I mean, the circumstance of the *Io Paean*[35] of the triumph, the animating cry which called "for all the BISHOPS to be hanged on the lamp posts,"[36] might well have brought forth a burst of enthusiasm on the foreseen consequences of this happy day. I allow to so much enthusiasm some little deviation from prudence. I allow this prophet to break forth into hymns of joy and thanksgiving on an event which appears like the precursor of the millennium and the projected fifth

---

[31] Troops of the National Guard, under Lafayette; they arrived at Versailles after the mob and saved the King's life.
[32] The Tuileries. The King was still held there when Burke wrote this tract.
[33] I.e., frenzied rites. At Thebes (in central Greece) and in Thrace the worship of Dionysus flourished.
[34] See note 20, above.
[35] Paean, though an attribute of Apollo, was sometimes used by the Romans with *Io* (=hurrah) simply as an exclamation.
[36] Burke's note: "Tous les évêques à la lanterne."

---

[28] He recovered, however, from his wounds.   [29] Versailles.
[30] Ten thousand women formed the nucleus of the mob that seized the royal family.

monarchy,[37] in the destruction of all church establishments. There was, however (as in all human affairs there is), in the midst of this joy something to exercise the patience of these worthy gentlemen, and to try the long-suffering of their faith. The actual murder of the King and Queen, and their child, was wanting to the other auspicious circumstances of this "beautiful day." The actual murder of the bishops, though called for by so many holy ejaculations, was also wanting. A group of regicide and sacrilegious slaughter was indeed boldly sketched, but it was only sketched. It unhappily was left unfinished, in this great history-piece of the massacre of innocents. What hardy pencil of a great master from the school of the rights of men will finish it, is to be seen hereafter. The age has not yet the complete benefit of that diffusion of knowledge that has undermined superstition and error; and the King of France wants another object or two to consign to oblivion, in consideration of all the good which is to arise from his own sufferings, and the patriotic crimes of an enlightened age.[38]

Although this work of our new light and knowledge did not go to the length that in all probability it was intended it should be carried, yet I must think that such treatment of any human creatures must be shocking to any but those who are made for accomplishing revolutions. But I cannot stop here. Influenced by the inborn feelings of my nature, and not being illuminated by a single ray of this new-sprung modern light, I confess to you, sir, that the exalted rank of the persons suffering, and particularly the sex, the beauty, and the amiable qualities of the descendant of so many kings and emperors, with the tender age of royal infants, insensible only through infancy and innocence of the cruel outrages to which their parents were exposed, instead of being a subject of exultation, adds not a little to my sensibility on that most melancholy occasion.

I hear that the august person who was the principal object of our preacher's triumph, though he supported himself, felt much on that shameful occasion. As a man, it became him to feel for his wife and his children, and the faithful guards of his person that were massacred in cold blood about him. As a prince, it became him to feel for the strange and frightful transformation of his civilized subjects, and to be more grieved for them than solicitous for himself. It derogates little from his fortitude, while it adds infinitely to the honor of his humanity. I am very sorry to say it, very sorry indeed, that such personages are in a situation in which it is not unbecoming in us to praise the virtues of the great.

I hear, and I rejoice to hear, that the great lady, the other object of the triumph, has borne that day (one is interested that beings made for suffering should suffer well) and that she bears all the succeeding days, that she bears the imprisonment of her husband and her captivity and the exile of her friends and the insulting adulation of addresses and the whole weight of her accumulated wrongs, with a serene patience, in a manner suited to her rank and race, and becoming the offspring of a sovereign[39] distinguished for her piety and her courage; that, like her, she has lofty sentiments; that she feels with the dignity of a Roman matron; that in the last extremity she will save herself from the last disgrace; and that, if she must fall, she will fall by no ignoble hand.[40]

It is now sixteen or seventeen years since I saw the Queen of France, then the Dauphiness,[41] at Versailles; and surely never lighted on this orb, which she hardly seemed to touch, a more delightful vision. I saw her just above the horizon, decorating and cheering the elevated sphere she just began to move in, glittering like the morning star, full of life and splendor and joy. Oh! what a revolution! and what an heart must I have, to contemplate without emotion that elevation and that fall! Little did I dream, when she added titles of veneration to those of enthusiastic, distant, respectful love, that she should ever be obliged to carry the sharp antidote[42] against disgrace concealed in that bosom; little did I dream that I should have lived to see such disasters fallen upon her in a nation of gallant men, in a nation of men of honor and of cavaliers. I thought ten thousand swords must have leaped from their scabbards to avenge even a look that threatened her with insult.—But the age of chivalry is gone. That of sophisters, economists, and calculators has succeeded; and the glory of Europe is extinguished for ever. Never, never more shall we behold that generous loyalty to rank and sex, that proud submission,

---

[37] The Fifth Monarchy Men were a sect in Puritan times who thought that the millennium, during which Christ would reign over a world-wide kingdom, was near at hand. The four preceding monarchies were the Assyrian, Persian, Greek, and Roman.

[38] In a note Burke quotes at length from the letter of a French eyewitness.

[39] Marie Antoinette was the daughter of the great Austrian empress, Maria Theresa.

[40] I.e., that she will take her own life, as (for example) the ravished Lucrece did.

[41] Wife of the Dauphin, i.e., the heir to the throne.   [42] Poison.

that dignified obedience, that subordination of the heart, which kept alive, even in servitude itself, the spirit of an exalted freedom. The unbought grace of life, the cheap defense of nations, the nurse of manly sentiment and heroic enterprise, is gone! It is gone, that sensibility of principle, that chastity of honor, which felt a stain like a wound, which inspired courage whilst it mitigated ferocity, which ennobled whatever it touched, and under which vice itself lost half its evil, by losing all its grossness.

This mixed system of opinion and sentiment had its origin in the ancient chivalry; and the principle, though varied in its appearance by the varying state of human affairs, subsisted and influenced through a long succession of generations, even to the time we live in. If it should ever be totally extinguished, the loss, I fear, will be great. It is this which has given its character to modern Europe. It is this which has distinguished it under all its forms of government, and distinguished it to its advantage, from the states of Asia, and possibly from those states which flourished in the most brilliant periods of the antique world. It was this which, without confounding ranks, had produced a noble equality, and handed it down through all the gradations of social life. It was this opinion which mitigated kings into companions, and raised private men to be fellows with kings. Without force or opposition, it subdued the fierceness of pride and power; it obliged sovereigns to submit to the soft collar of social esteem, compelled stern authority to submit to elegance, and gave a dominating vanquisher of laws to be subdued by manners.

But now all is to be changed. All the pleasing illusions which made power gentle and obedience liberal, which harmonized the different shades of life, and which by a bland assimilation incorporated into politics the sentiments which beautify and soften private society, are to be dissolved by this new conquering empire of light and reason. All the decent drapery of life is to be rudely torn off. All the superadded ideas, furnished from the wardrobe of a moral imagination, which the heart owns and the understanding ratifies, as necessary to cover the defects of our naked, shivering nature and to raise it to dignity in our own estimation, are to be exploded as a ridiculous, absurd, and antiquated fashion.

On this scheme of things, a king is but a man, a queen is but a woman; a woman is but an animal, and an animal not of the highest order. All homage paid to the sex in general as such, and without distinct views, is to be regarded as romance and folly. Regicide and parricide and sacrilege are but fictions of superstition, corrupting jurisprudence by destroying its simplicity. The murder of a king or a queen or a bishop or a father are only common homicide; and if the people are by any chance or in any way gainers by it, a sort of homicide much the most pardonable, and into which we ought not to make too severe a scrutiny.

On the scheme of this barbarous philosophy, which is the offspring of cold hearts and muddy understandings, and which is as void of solid wisdom as it is destitute of all taste and elegance, laws are to be supported only by their own terrors, and by the concern which each individual may find in them from his own private speculations, or can spare to them from his own private interests. In the groves of *their* academy, at the end of every visto,[43] you see nothing but the gallows. Nothing is left which engages the affections on the part of the commonwealth. On the principles of this mechanic philosophy, our institutions can never be embodied, if I may use the expression, in persons, so as to create in us love, veneration, admiration, or attachment. But that sort of reason which banishes the affections is incapable of filling their place. These public affections, combined with manners, are required sometimes as supplements, sometimes as correctives, always as aids to law. The precept given by a wise man, as well as a great critic, for the construction of poems, is equally true as to states: *Non satis est pulchra esse poemata; dulcia sunto.*[44] There ought to be a system of manners, in every nation, which a well-formed mind would be disposed to relish. To make us love our country, our country ought to be lovely.

But power, of some kind or other, will survive the shock in which manners and opinions perish; and it will find other and worse means for its support. The usurpation which, in order to subvert ancient institutions, has destroyed ancient principles, will hold power by arts similar to those by which it has acquired it. When the old feudal and chivalrous spirit of *fealty,* which, by freeing kings from fear, freed both kings and subjects from the precautions of tyranny, shall be extinct in the minds of men, plots and assassinations will be anticipated by preventive murder and preventive confiscation, and that long roll of grim and bloody maxims which

---

43 Vista.
44 It is not enough that poems should be beautiful; they must also be charming.

form the political code of all power not standing on its own honor and the honor of those who are to obey it. Kings will be tyrants from policy, when subjects are rebels from principle.

When ancient opinions and rules of life are taken away, the loss cannot possibly be estimated. From that moment we have no compass to govern us; nor can we know distinctly to what port we steer. Europe, undoubtedly, taken in a mass, was in a flourishing condition the day on which your Revolution was completed. How much of that prosperous state was owing to the spirit of our old manners and opinions is not easy to say; but as such causes cannot be indifferent in their operation, we must presume that, on the whole, their operation was beneficial.

We are but too apt to consider things in the state in which we find them, without sufficiently adverting to the causes by which they have been produced, and possibly may be upheld. Nothing is more certain than that our manners, our civilization, and all the good things which are connected with manners and with civilization, have, in this European world of ours, depended for ages upon two principles, and were indeed the result of both combined; I mean the spirit of a gentleman, and the spirit of religion. The nobility and the clergy, the one by profession, the other by patronage, kept learning in existence, even in the midst of arms and confusions, and whilst governments were rather in their causes, than formed. Learning paid back what it received to nobility and to priesthood; and paid it with usury, by enlarging their ideas and by furnishing their minds. Happy if they had all continued to know their indissoluble union, and their proper place!

Happy if learning, not debauched by ambition, had been satisfied to continue the instructor, and not aspired to be the master! Along with its natural protectors and guardians, learning will be cast into the mire, and trodden down under the hoofs of a swinish multitude.[45]

If, as I suspect, modern letters owe more than they are always willing to own to ancient manners, so do other interests which we value full as much as they are worth. Even commerce and trade and manufacture, the gods of our economical politicians, are themselves perhaps but creatures; are themselves but effects, which, as first causes, we choose to worship. They certainly grew under the same shade in which learning flourished. They too may decay with their natural protecting principles. With you, for the present at least, they all threaten to disappear together. Where trade and manufactures are wanting to a people, and the spirit of nobility and religion remains, sentiment supplies, and not always ill supplies, their place; but if commerce and the arts should be lost in an experiment to try how well a state may stand without these old fundamental principles, what sort of a thing must be a nation of gross, stupid, ferocious, and, at the same time, poor and sordid barbarians, destitute of religion, honor, or manly pride, possessing nothing at present, and hoping for nothing hereafter?

I wish you may not be going fast, and by the shortest cut, to that horrible and disgustful situation. Already there appears a poverty of conception, a coarseness and vulgarity, in all the proceedings of the Assembly and of all their instructors. Their liberty is not liberal. Their science is presumptuous ignorance. Their humanity is savage and brutal. . . .

William Cowper

1731–1800

"I WAS a stricken deer, that left the herd." Neither the gentleness of his lovable temperament nor the affection of a host of friends could save Cowper from the tragedy of a clouded mind. Melancholy, as Gray says of his imagined poet in the "Elegy," had marked him for her own; five times he crossed the mysterious borderland between depression and insanity. Out of that life of fears and sorrows came noble poems, some of our best humorous verse, and a large body of private letters so delightful that the world has been unwilling to respect their privacy.

Cowper's father, a member of a distinguished and influential family, was rector at the village of Berkhampstead in Hertfordshire. The poet's mother died when he was six; her death was the earliest of the blows fate had in store for him. The second seems to have been the bullying he suffered at the school to which, according to British

---

45 This phrase was bitterly resented. English radicals began drinking toasts to "the swinish multitude." Throughout the *Reflections,* Burke is animated chiefly by his fear of *English* radicalism.

custom, he was sent away when he was little more than a baby. Later on he was happy enough at a better school, Westminster, except for attacks of melancholia. He did not attend either university; his father wanted him to be a lawyer, and so he was "articled" to a London solicitor, in whose office he studied for three years. Cowper found the law completely distasteful, and was therefore all the more attracted by the charms of two of his London cousins, with whom he began spending all the time he could. Harriet, afterwards Lady Hesketh, was a brilliant, lively girl; they became fast friends. With her younger sister Theodora he fell in love.

When his three years expired, Cowper engaged chambers in the Middle Temple and went on with his legal studies. In 1754 he was admitted to the bar; after that, he sat about in his cheerless quarters waiting for clients who never came. Meanwhile, in 1752, he had his first mental illness: "day and night I was upon the rack, lying down in horror, and rising up in despair." He turned to religion, but instead of comfort found terror. He was an evangelical or Low-Church Anglican; with the Methodists, though he never joined their sect, he was strongly in sympathy. For him religion was not a mere matter of belief and membership; it was intensely personal. If he had come directly under John Wesley's influence, he might have found joy and consolation. Unfortunately, his contact with the evangelical movement was with the Calvinist side, and by its doctrines he was literally scared out of his wits. Eventually he thought he had committed that mysterious offense, the Unpardonable Sin (Matthew 12: 31-32); belief that he was certain of damnation became an obsession. There were times when he paced the floor in agony, waiting for the Devil to appear and drag him off to hell. From this first attack he soon recovered; but twice in 1756, two years after his admission to the bar, he felt the heavy hand of destiny again. His father died; and he parted for ever from his cousin Theodora, with whom his uncle, doubtless wisely, forbade marriage. In time Cowper forgot her, but Theodora lived on the memory of their shattered hopes. She never married. The poems he had written to her remained her greatest treasure, and in the days of his direst poverty she sent him aid anonymously.

The years dragged on, nine years—of utter failure since his admission to the bar. In 1763 family influence obtained him the clerkship of the journals of the House of Lords, but when he found he would have to go through the formality of an examination before the peers, his fear of a disgraceful failure was so morbid that he made three attempts to commit suicide, and for a time he was shut up in a madhouse. On his recovery from this second attack, he took lodgings in Huntingdon, near Cambridge, where his younger brother held a fellowship. At Hunting-

don he made the acquaintance of the Reverend and Mrs. Morley Unwin and their two children. Of this family Cowper was soon practically a member, as a paying guest; Mary Unwin, seven years older than the poet, was to become the mainstay of his life. When in 1767 her elderly husband was killed by a fall from his horse, Cowper went with her and her children to live in the village of Olney in northern Buckinghamshire. The reason for this move was to be near the curate of that place, the Reverend John Newton, formerly the captain of a slaveship. As it turned out, Newton's evangelical fervor was the worst thing in the world for Cowper; it kept his nerves in a constant state of tension. Newton saw the danger and induced his friend to join him in writing a volume of hymns, hoping the work would have a soothing effect; but in 1773 Cowper succumbed for the third time. He fled to Newton's house; the devoted Mrs. Unwin followed him there and nursed him throughout his illness, which lasted over a year. They had intended to marry; but the new seizure, during which he again attempted suicide, put an end to that hope. Mary remained his closest friend; probably her love for him had always been chiefly maternal.

The five years which followed his recovery were the happiest he was ever to know. Newton was called to a parish in London, and the poet was better off without him. Cowper found relaxation by turning to things outside himself. He did a little carpentry and gardening, and like many high-strung people found association with animals soothing—he loved his pet hares and his dog and cat. Verse was another outlet; in 1782, when he was over fifty, he published his first volume of poems. The best of these verses is "The Shrubbery," which will be found below; the bulk of the volume consists of dull moral essays in heroic couplets, more or less imitative of Pope. Meanwhile Cowper had made a new friend, Lady Austen, a vivacious widow. She could rouse him from his broodings, and under the stimulus of her high spirits he did his best work. She told him the story of John Gilpin, and to her we also owe the whimsical proposal of a blank-verse poem on the parlor sofa (see headnote to *The Task*, below). Lady Austen saw that Cowper, a recluse, had been trying to write about a world he had withdrawn from. She turned him to the near and familiar. His approach to nature in *The Task* is not in the least romantic—not for him the unity of God and nature soon to be proclaimed by Wordsworth; but it is an appealing series he gives us of little pictures, lovingly painted, of the quiet round of country life and domestic life. In this poem, and in his letters, he is perhaps of all English writers the foremost devotee of home and fireside. From his peaceful hearth he looks out on a stormy world. He has no wish to re-enter it, but now and again he launches a vigorous comment on it. Humanitarian convictions were strong in him, and so was his patriotism; on both these subjects he could blaze with eloquence and conviction.

In the end Lady Austen turned out rather too much of a good thing. It was well enough to be stirred up to the making of poetry; but when it came to being roused to romantic love, Cowper shied off. Loyalty to Mary Unwin stood in the way of that; and in a letter he put an end to a friendship which, at least on Lady Austen's part, was ripening into something more intense. She left Olney, never to return; eventually she remarried. Cowper continued to follow another of her suggestions, and 1791 saw the appearance of his blank-verse translations of the *Iliad* and the *Odyssey*. Meanwhile, in 1786, he had moved with Mrs. Unwin to the near-by village of Weston. His relatives, who, although they contributed to his support, had thought of him only as a remote, mad kinsman, took more interest in him when they heard the world talking about *The Task* and calling its author a great poet. His cousin Harriet, Lady Hesketh, now a widow, left London and for several months in 1786 devoted herself to his welfare; but in 1787 he was once again—for the fourth time—a raving lunatic. He recovered, but Mrs. Unwin's years of unremitting care had left her worn out, in mind as well as body. In 1792 she had a second paralytic stroke; and two years later Cowper suffered his fifth attack of madness, from which he never fully recovered. For over a year Lady Hesketh took charge of them, and then another of Cowper's cousins gave them shelter at his home in Norfolk. There the poet passed the rest of his life, in what despair the closing lines of "The Castaway" attest. He died in 1800, four years after his faithful Mary.

R. Southey edited Cowper's works (15 vols., 1835-37). The best edition of the poems is by H. S. Milford (revised ed., 1934). Everyman's Library contains a volume of the poems and another of the letters; selected letters are also available in The World's Classics. The pathos of this life has attracted many biographers. T. Wright's study (2nd ed., 1921) is fully documented; it first appeared in 1892, and later Lives are all indebted to it. More readable is D. Cecil's *The Stricken Deer* (1929), a thoughtful popular biography. H. Fausset's *William Cowper* (1928) is also excellent. On the whole, G. Thomas's *Cowper and the Eighteenth Century* (1935) is the soundest of recent attempts to pluck out the heart of what must always remain something of a mystery.

William Cowper

ON OPENING A PLACE
FOR SOCIAL PRAYER

This is one of the *Olney Hymns*. Other famous ones are "Oh! for a closer walk with God," "There is a fountain filled with blood," "God moves in a mysterious way," and "Sometimes a light surprises." In all Cowper wrote sixty-seven, chiefly in 1771-72; the remainder of the volume, which was published in 1779, was the work of his friend the Rev. John Newton, then curate at Olney. "Jesus, where'er thy people meet" was written for the first of a series of prayer meetings at a large vacant house in Olney which Newton engaged for that purpose.

Jesus, where'er thy people meet,
There they behold thy mercy-seat;
Where'er they seek thee thou art found,
And ev'ry place is hallowed ground.

For thou, within no walls confined,   5
Inhabitest the human mind;
Such ever bring thee where they come,
And, going, take thee to their home.

Dear Shepherd of thy chosen few!
Thy former mercies here renew;   10

Here, to our waiting hearts, proclaim
The sweetness of thy saving name.

Here may we prove the pow'r of pray'r
To strengthen faith and sweeten care,
To teach our faint desires to rise,   15
And bring all heav'n before our eyes.

Behold! at thy commanding word
We stretch the curtain and the cord;[1]
Come thou, and fill this wider space,
And help us with a large encrease.   20

Lord, we are few, but thou art near;
Nor short thine arm nor deaf thine ear;
Oh, rend the heav'ns, come quickly down,
And make a thousand hearts thine own!

---

[1] Isaiah 54:2-3: "Enlarge the place of thy tent, and let them stretch forth the curtains of thine habitations: spare not, lengthen thy cords, and strengthen thy stakes; for thou shalt break forth on the right hand and on the left; and thy seed shall . . . make the desolate cities to be inhabited."

THE SHRUBBERY

WRITTEN IN A TIME OF AFFLICTION

This sad little poem was composed in the year of 1773, during the course of which Cowper suffered his third attack of insanity, his engagement was broken, and he attempted suicide. This is a cry from the heart, if there ever was one; yet not for an instant does the surge of emotion break the smooth regularity of the neoclassical form.

Oh, happy shades—to me unblest!
    Friendly to peace, but not to me!
How ill the scene that offers rest
    And heart that cannot rest, agree!

This glassy stream, that spreading pine, 5
    Those alders quiv'ring to the breeze,
Might soothe a soul less hurt than mine,
    And please, if anything could please.

But fixed, unalterable care
    Forgoes not what she feels within, 10
Shows the same sadness ev'rywhere,
    And slights the season and the scene.

For all that pleased in wood or lawn
    While peace possessed these silent bow'rs,
Her animating smile withdrawn, 15
    Has lost its beauties and its pow'rs.

The saint or moralist should tread
    This moss-grown alley, musing, slow;
They seek, like me, the secret shade,
    But not, like me, to nourish woe! 20

Me fruitful scenes and prospects waste
    Alike admonish not to roam;
These tell me of enjoyments past,
    And those of sorrows yet to come.

THE DIVERTING HISTORY OF JOHN GILPIN

SHOWING HOW HE WENT FARTHER THAN HE INTENDED AND CAME SAFE HOME AGAIN

Aside from some of his hymns, this is Cowper's best-known work; it was composed in 1782, and is still one of the great favorites in English light verse. It has not kept that place merely because the story is "diverting," but also because the carefully finished texture of the verse is full of sly characterizing strokes, applicable to members of more families than the Gilpins, and above all because the spirit of the whole thing is so infectiously gay. The ballad style and meter, comically handled, also contribute to the fun. Cowper's name is more likely to live on for this poem than for anything else; and by most readers he will continue to be taken for a merry soul, bubbling over with natural gifts for playing the jester's role. Such are life's ironies; here is his own view of the case: "If I trifle, and merely trifle, it is because I am reduced to it by necessity—a melancholy, that nothing else so effectually disperses, engages me sometimes in the arduous task of being merry by force. And, strange as it may seem, the most ludicrous lines I ever wrote have been written in the saddest mood, and, but for that saddest mood, perhaps had never been written at all."[1]

John Gilpin was a citizen
    Of credit and renown;
A trainband[2] captain eke was he
    Of famous London town.

John Gilpin's spouse said to her dear, 5
    "Though wedded we have been
These twice ten tedious years, yet we
    No holiday have seen.

"Tomorrow is our wedding day,
    And we will then repair 10
Unto the Bell[3] at Edmonton
    All in a chaise and pair.

"My sister, and my sister's child,
    Myself, and children three,
Will fill the chaise; so you must ride 15
    On horseback after we."

He soon replied, "I do admire
    Of womankind but one;
And you are she, my dearest dear;
    Therefore it shall be done. 20

"I am a linen-draper bold,
    As all the world doth know;
And my good friend the calender[4]
    Will lend his horse to go."

Quoth Mrs. Gilpin, "That's well said; 25
    And, for that[5] wine is dear,
We will be furnished with our own,
    Which is both bright and clear."

---

[1] Letter to William Unwin, Nov. 18, 1782.
[2] Militia.—*Eke*=also.
[3] An inn. Edmonton is a suburb about ten miles north of the City.
[4] Calendering is a finishing process in clothmaking; the cloth is pressed between rollers. [5] Because.

John Gilpin kissed his loving wife;
O'erjoyed was he to find   30
That, though on pleasure she was bent,
She had a frugal mind.

The morning came, the chaise was brought,
But yet was not allowed
To drive up to the door, lest all   35
Should say that she was proud.

So three doors off the chaise was stayed,
Where they did all get in;
Six precious souls, and all agog
To dash through thick and thin!   40

Smack went the whip, round went the wheels,
Were never folk so glad;
The stones did rattle underneath,
As if Cheapside⁶ were mad.

John Gilpin at his horse's side   45
Seized fast the flowing mane,
And up he got, in haste to ride,
But soon came down again;

For saddletree scarce reached had he,
His journey to begin,   50
When, turning round his head, he saw
Three customers come in.

So down he came; for loss of time,
Although it grieved him sore,
Yet loss of pence, full well he knew,   55
Would trouble him much more.

'Twas long before the customers
Were suited to their mind,
When Betty screaming came downstairs—
"The wine is left behind!"   60

"Good lack!" quoth he, "yet bring it me,
My leathern belt likewise,
In which I bear my trusty sword
When I do exercise."

Now Mistress Gilpin (careful soul!)   65
Had two stone bottles found,
To hold the liquor that she loved,
And keep it safe and sound.

Each bottle had a curling ear,
Through which the belt he drew,   70
And hung a bottle on each side,
To make his balance true.

Then, over all, that he might be
Equipped from top to toe,
His long red cloak, well brushed and neat,   75
He manfully did throw.

Now see him mounted once again
Upon his nimble steed,
Full slowly pacing o'er the stones,
With caution and good heed!   80

But, finding soon a smoother road
Beneath his well-shod feet,
The snorting beast began to trot,
Which galled him in his seat.

So, "Fair and softly," John he cried,   85
But John he cried in vain;
That trot became a gallop soon,
In spite of curb and rein.

So, stooping down, as needs he must
Who cannot sit upright,   90
He grasped the mane with both his hands,
And eke with all his might.

His horse, who never in that sort
Had handled been before,
What thing upon his back had got   95
Did wonder more and more.

Away went Gilpin, neck or nought;⁷
Away went hat and wig!—
He little dreamt, when he set out,
Of running such a rig!⁸   100

The wind did blow, the cloak did fly,
Like streamer long and gay,
Till, loop and button failing both,
At last it flew away.

Then might all people well discern   105
The bottles he had slung;
A bottle swinging at each side,
As hath been said or sung.

---

⁶ Then the principal business street of London.

⁷ Neck or nothing, running all risks.
⁸ Playing such a prank.

The dogs did bark, the children screamed,
    Up flew the windows all;
And ev'ry soul cried out, "Well done!"   110
    As loud as he could bawl.

Away went Gilpin—who but he?
    His fame soon spread around;
"He carries weight!" "He rides a race!"   115
    " 'T is for a thousand pound!"

And still, as fast as he drew near,
    'T was wonderful to view,
How in a trice the turnpike men
    Their gates wide open threw.   120

And now, as he went bowing down
    His reeking head full low,
The bottles twain behind his back
    Were shattered at a blow.

Down ran the wine into the road,   125
    Most piteous to be seen,
Which made his horse's flanks to smoke
    As they had basted been.

But still he seemed to carry weight,
    With leathern girdle braced;   130
For all might see the bottlenecks
    Still dangling at his waist.

Thus all through merry Islington
    These gambols he did play,
And till he came unto the Wash[9]   135
    Of Edmonton so gay;

And there he threw the wash about,
    On both sides of the way,
Just like unto a trundling mop,
    Or a wild goose at play.   140

At Edmonton, his loving wife
    From the balcóny spied
Her tender husband, wond'ring much
    To see how he did ride.

"Stop, stop, John Gilpin!—here's the house!"   145
    They all at once did cry;
"The dinner waits, and we are tired."
    Said Gilpin, "So am I!"

But yet his horse was not a whit
    Inclined to tarry there;   150
For why?—his owner had a house
    Full ten miles off, at Ware.

So like an arrow swift he flew,
    Shot by an archer strong;
So did he fly—which brings me to   155
    The middle of my song.

Away went Gilpin, out of breath,
    And sore against his will,
Till at his friend the calender's
    His horse at last stood still.   160

The calender, amazed to see
    His neighbor in such trim,
Laid down his pipe, flew to the gate
    And thus accosted him:

"What news? what news? your tidings tell;   165
    Tell me you must and shall—
Say why bareheaded you are come,
    Or why you come at all?"

Now Gilpin had a pleasant wit,
    And loved a timely joke;   170
And thus unto the calender
    In merry guise he spoke:

"I came because your horse would come;
    And, if I well forebode,
My hat and wig will soon be here—   175
    They are upon the road."

The calender, right glad to find
    His friend in merry pin,[10]
Returned him not a single word,
    But to the house went in;   180

Whence straight he came with hat and wig;
    A wig that flowed behind,
A hat not much the worse for wear,
    Each comely in its kind.

He held them up, and, in his turn,   185
    Thus showed his ready wit:
"My head is twice as big as yours;
    They therefore needs must fit.

---

[9] A shallow body of water. Here a ford.

[10] Humor, mood.

"But let me scrape the dirt away
  That hangs upon your face;
And stop and eat, for well you may
  Be in a hungry case."   190

Said John, "It is my wedding day,
  And all the world would stare
If wife should dine at Edmonton   195
  And I should dine at Ware!"

So turning to his horse, he said,
  "I am in haste to dine;
'T was for your pleasure you came here—
  You shall go back for mine."   200

Ah, luckless speech, and bootless boast!
  For which he paid full dear;
For while he spake, a braying ass
  Did sing most loud and clear;

Whereat his horse did snort, as he   205
  Had heard a lion roar,
And galloped off with all his might,
  As he had done before.

Away went Gilpin, and away
  Went Gilpin's hat and wig!   210
He lost them sooner than at first—
  For why?—they were too big!

Now Mistress Gilpin, when she saw
  Her husband posting down
Into the country far away,   215
  She pulled out half-a-crown;[11]

And thus unto the youth she said
  That drove them to the Bell,
"This shall be yours when you bring back
  My husband safe and well."   220

The youth did ride, and soon did meet
  John coming back amain;
Whom in a trice he tried to stop,
  By catching at his rein;

But, not performing what he meant   225
  And gladly would have done,
The frighted steed he frighted more,
  And made him faster run.

Away went Gilpin, and away
  Went postboy at his heels!—   230
The postboy's horse right glad to miss
  The lumb'ring of the wheels.

Six gentlemen upon the road,
  Thus seeing Gilpin fly,
With postboy scamp'ring in the rear,   235
  They raised the hue and cry:

"Stop thief! stop thief!—a highwayman!"
  Not one of them was mute;
And all and each that passed that way
  Did join in the pursuit.   240

And now the turnpike gates again
  Flew open in short space,
The toll-men thinking, as before,
  That Gilpin rode a race.

And so he did—and won it too!—   245
  For he got first to town;
Nor stopped till where he had got up
  He did again get down.

Now let us sing—Long live the King,
  And Gilpin, long live he;   250
And when he next doth ride abroad,
  May I be there to see!

from THE TASK

When Cowper's friend, Lady Austen, suggested something in lighter vein, a blank-verse poem on the parlor sofa, he obeyed, as he says in a foreword (hence the title *The Task*), "and, having much leisure, connected another subject with it, and, pursuing the train of thought to which his situation and turn of mind led him, brought forth at length, instead of the trifle which he at first intended, a serious affair—a Volume!" The result is a rambling but rewarding pastoral-domestic symphony, remarkable for the skill with which it sustains a conversational tone. The poem was composed in 1783–84 and published with "John Gilpin" in 1785.

from BOOK I

THE SOFA

I sing the SOFA. I, who lately sang
Truth, Hope, and Charity,[1] and touched with awe
The solemn chords, and, with a trembling hand,

---

[11] Approximately the equivalent of a fifty-cent piece.

[1] Titles of earlier poems.

Escaped with pain from that advent'rous flight,
Now seek repose upon an humbler theme;   5
The theme though humble, yet august and proud
Th' occasion—for the Fair commands the song.

Time was, when clothing sumptuous or for use,
Save their own painted skins, our sires had none.
As yet black breeches were not; satin smooth,   10
Or velvet soft, or plush with shaggy pile:
The hardy chief upon the rugged rock
Washed by the sea, or on the grav'lly bank
Thrown up by wintry torrents roaring loud,
Fearless of wrong, reposed his weary strength.   15
Those barb'rous ages past, succeeded next
The birthday of invention; weak at first,
Dull in design, and clumsy to perform.
Joint-stools were then created; on three legs
Upborne they stood. Three legs upholding firm   20
A massy slab, in fashion square or round.
On such a stool immortal Alfred sat,
And swayed the scepter of his infant realms:
And such in ancient halls and mansions drear
May still be seen; but perforated sore,   25
And drilled in holes, the solid oak is found,
By worms voracious eating through and through.

At length a generation more refined
Improved the simple plan; made three legs four,
Gave them a twisted form vermicular,   30
And o'er the seat, with plenteous wadding stuffed,
Induced a splendid cover, green and blue,
Yellow and red, of tap'stry richly wrought
And woven close, or needlework sublime.
There might ye see the peony spread wide,   35
The full-blown rose, the shepherd and his lass,
Lap dog and lambkin with black staring eyes,
And parrots with twin cherries in their beak.
Now came the cane from India, smooth and bright
With nature's varnish; severed into stripes   40
That interlaced each other, these supplied
Of texture firm a latticework, that braced
The new machine, and it became a chair.
But restless was the chair; the back erect
Distressed the weary loins, that felt no ease;   45
The slipp'ry seat betrayed the sliding part
That pressed it, and the feet hung dangling down,
Anxious in vain to find the distant floor.
These for the rich: the rest, whom fate had placed
In modest mediocrity, content   50
With base materials, sat on well-tanned hides,
Obdurate and unyielding, glassy smooth,
With here and there a tuft of crimson yarn
Or scarlet crewel[2] in the cushion fixed;

If cushion might be called, what harder seemed   55
Than the firm oak of which the frame was formed.
No want of timber then was felt or feared
In Albion's happy isle. The lumber stood
Pond'rous and fixed by its own massy weight.
But elbows still were wanting; these, some say,   60
An alderman of Cripplegate contrived:
And some ascribe th' invention to a priest,
Burly and big, and studious of his ease.
But, rude at first, and not with easy slope
Receding wide, they pressed against the ribs   65
And bruised the side, and, elevated high,
Taught the raised shoulders to invade the ears.
Long time elapsed or e'er our rugged sires
Complained, though incommodiously pent in,
And ill at ease behind. The ladies first   70
'Gan murmur, as became the softer sex.
Ingenious fancy, never better pleased
Than when employed t' accommodate the fair,
Heard the sweet moan with pity, and devised
The soft settee; one elbow at each end,   75
And in the midst an elbow it received,
United yet divided, twain at once.
So sit two kings of Brentford[3] on one throne;
And so two citizens who take the air,
Close packed and smiling, in a chaise and one.   80
But relaxation of the languid frame,
By soft recumbency of outstretched limbs,
Was bliss reserved for happier days. So slow
The growth of what is excellent; so hard
T' attain perfection in this nether world.   85
Thus first necessity invented stools,
Convenience next suggested elbow-chairs,
And luxury th' accomplished SOFA last. . . .

Oh, may I live exempted (while I live
Guiltless of pampered appetite obscene)
From pangs arthritic that infest the toe   105
Of libertine excess. The SOFA suits
The gouty limb, 'tis true; but gouty limb,
Though on a SOFA, may I never feel:
For I have loved the rural walk through lanes
Of grassy swarth, close cropped by nibbling sheep,   110
And skirted thick with intertexture firm
Of thorny boughs; have loved the rural walk
O'er hills, through valleys, and by rivers' brink,
E'er since, a truant boy, I passed my bounds
T' enjoy a ramble on the banks of Thames;   115
And still remember, nor without regret
Of hours that sorrow since has much endeared,

---

[2] Twisted yarn.

[3] Then a village and popular resort near London. The two kings,
who share a single throne, are absurd characters in Buckingham's mock-heroic play *The Rehearsal* (1671).

How oft, my slice of pocket store consumed,
Still hung'ring, penniless and far from home,
I fed on scarlet hips and stony haws,   120
Or blushing crabs,[4] or berries that emboss
The bramble black as jet, or sloes austere.
Hard fare! but such as boyish appetite
Disdains not, nor the palate undepraved
By culinary arts unsav'ry deems.   125
No SOFA then awaited my return;
Nor SOFA then I needed. Youth repairs
His wasted spirits quickly, by long toil
Incurring short fatigue; and, though our years
As life declines speed rapidly away,   130
And not a year but pilfers as he goes
Some youthful grace that age would gladly keep—
A tooth or auburn lock, and by degrees
Their length and color from the locks they spare—
Th' elastic spring of an unwearied foot   135
That mounts the stile with ease or leaps the fence,
That play of lungs inhaling and again
Respiring freely the fresh air that makes
Swift pace or steep ascent no toil to me,
Mine have not pilfered yet; nor yet impaired   140
My relish of fair prospect; scenes that soothed
Or charmed me young, no longer young I find
Still soothing and of pow'r to charm me still. . . .
    God made the country, and man made the town.
What wonder then that health and virtue, gifts   750
That can alone make sweet the bitter draught
That life holds out to all, should most abound
And least be threatened in the fields and groves?
Possess ye, therefore, ye who, borne about
In chariots and sedans,[5] know no fatigue   755
But that of idleness, and taste no scenes
But such as art contrives, possess ye still
Your element; there only can ye shine,
There only minds like yours can do no harm.
Our groves were planted to console at noon   760
The pensive wand'rer in their shades. At eve
The moonbeam, sliding softly in between
The sleeping leaves, is all the light they wish;
Birds warbling, all the music. We can spare
The splendor of your lamps; they but eclipse   765
Our softer satellite. Your songs confound
Our more harmonious notes: the thrush departs
Scared, and th' offended nightingale is mute.
There is a public mischief in your mirth;
It plagues your country. Folly such as yours,   770

---

[4] Crab apples. *Hips* are the fruit of the rosebush, *haws* of the hawthorn, and *sloes* of the blackthorn. *Austere*=sour.
[5] Carriages and sedan chairs.

Graced with a sword, and worthier of a fan,
Has made, which enemies could ne'er have done,
Our arch of empire, steadfast but for you,
A mutilated structure, soon to fall.

from BOOK II

THE TIMEPIECE

Oh, for a lodge in some vast wilderness,
Some boundless contiguity of shade,
Where rumor of oppression and deceit,
Of unsuccessful or successful war,
Might never reach me more! My ear is pained,   5
My soul is sick, with every day's report
Of wrong and outrage with which earth is filled.
There is no flesh in man's obdurate heart;
It does not feel for man; the nat'ral bond
Of brotherhood is severed as the flax   10
That falls asunder at the touch of fire.
He finds his fellow guilty of a skin
Not colored like his own, and, having power
T' enforce the wrong, for such a worthy cause
Dooms and devotes[6] him as his lawful prey.   15
Lands intersected by a narrow frith[7]
Abhor each other. Mountains interposed
Make enemies of nations who had else,
Like kindred drops, been mingled into one.
Thus man devotes his brother, and destroys;   20
And worse than all, and most to be deplored,
As human nature's broadest, foulest blot,
Chains him, and tasks him, and exacts his sweat
With stripes that Mercy, with a bleeding heart,
Weeps when she sees inflicted on a beast.   25
Then what is man? And what man, seeing this,
And having human feelings, does not blush
And hang his head, to think himself a man?
I would not have a slave to till my ground,
To carry me, to fan me while I sleep,   30
And tremble when I wake, for all the wealth
That sinews bought and sold have ever earned.
No: dear as freedom is, and in my heart's
Just estimation prized above all price,
I had much rather be myself the slave   35
And wear the bonds, than fasten them on him.
We have no slaves at home.—Then why abroad?
And they themselves, once ferried o'er the wave
That parts us, are emancipate and loosed.
Slaves cannot breathe in England; if their lungs   40
Receive our air, that moment they are free;
They touch our country, and their shackles fall.

---

[6] Consigns to destruction.   [7] Firth, arm of the sea.

That's noble, and bespeaks a nation proud
And jealous of the blessing. Spread it, then,
And let it circulate through ev'ry vein   45
Of all your empire; that, where Britain's pow'r
Is felt, mankind may feel her mercy too. . . .

from BOOK III

THE GARDEN

I was a stricken deer, that left the herd
Long since; with many an arrow deep infixed
My panting side was charged, when I withdrew   110
To seek a tranquil death in distant shades.
There was I found by One who had himself
Been hurt by th' archers. In his side he bore,
And in his hands and feet, the cruel scars.
With gentle force soliciting the darts,   115
He drew them forth, and healed, and bade me live.
Since then, with few associates, in remote
And silent woods I wander, far from those
My former partners of the peopled scene;
With few associates, and not wishing more.   120
Here much I ruminate, as much I may,
With other views of men and manners now
Than once, and others of a life to come.
I see that all are wand'rers, gone astray
Each in his own delusions; they are lost   125
In chase of fancied happiness, still wooed
And never won. Dream after dream ensues;
And still they dream that they shall still succeed,
And still are disappointed. Rings the world
With the vain stir. I sum up half mankind,   130
And add two-thirds of the remaining half,
And find the total of their hopes and fears
Dreams, empty dreams. . . .

from BOOK IV

THE WINTER EVENING

Hark! 'tis the twanging horn! O'er yonder bridge,
That with its wearisome but needful length
Bestrides the wintry flood, in which the moon
Sees her unwrinkled face reflected bright,
He comes, the herald of a noisy world,   5
With spattered boots, strapped waist, and frozen locks,
News from all nations lumb'ring at his back.
True to his charge, the close-packed load behind,
Yet careless what he brings, his one concern
Is to conduct it to the destined inn: 10
And, having dropped th' expected bag, pass on.
He whistles as he goes, light-hearted wretch,

Cold and yet cheerful: messenger of grief
Perhaps to thousands, and of joy to some;
To him indiff'rent whether grief or joy.   15
Houses in ashes, and the fall of stocks,
Births, deaths, and marriages, epistles wet
With tears, that trickled down the writer's cheeks
Fast as the periods[8] from his fluent quill,
Or charged with am'rous sighs of absent swains   20
Or nymphs responsive, equally affect
His horse and him, unconscious of them all.
But oh, th' important budget! ushered in
With such heart-shaking music, who can say
What are its tidings? have our troops awaked?   25
Or do they still, as if with opium drugged,
Snore to the murmurs of th' Atlantic wave?[9]
Is India free? and does she wear her plumed
And jeweled turban with a smile of peace,
Or do we grind her still? The grand debate,   30
The popular harangue, the tart reply,
The logic, and the wisdom, and the wit,
And the loud laugh—I long to know them all;
I burn to set th' imprisoned wranglers free,
And give them voice and utt'rance once again.   35
   Now stir the fire, and close the shutters fast,
Let fall the curtains, wheel the sofa round,
And, while the bubbling and loud-hissing urn
Throws up a steamy column, and the cups
That cheer but not inebriate, wait on each,   40
So let us welcome peaceful ev'ning in.
Not such his ev'ning, who with shining face
Sweats in the crowded theater, and, squeezed
And bored with elbow-points through both his sides,
Outscolds the ranting actor on the stage: 45
Nor his who patient stands, till his feet throb
And his head thumps, to feed upon the breath
Of patriots, bursting with heroic rage,
Or placemen,[10] all tranquillity and smiles.
This folio of four pages,[11] happy work!   50
Which not ev'n critics criticize; that holds
Inquisitive attention, while I read,
Fast bound in chains of silence, which the fair,
Though eloquent themselves, yet fear to break;
What is it, but a map of busy life,   55
Its fluctuations and its vast concerns?
Here runs the mountainous and craggy ridge
That tempts ambition. On the summit see
The seals of office glitter in his eyes;
He climbs, he pants, he grasps them! At his heels, 60
Close at his heels, a demagogue ascends,

---

[8] Sentences.
[9] Evidently written during the closing stage of the American
Revolution.   [10] Officeholders.   [11] I.e., newspaper.

And with a dext'rous jerk soon twists him down,
And wins them, but to lose them in his turn.
Here rills of oily eloquence in soft
Meanders lubricate the course they take;   65
The modest speaker is ashamed and grieved
T' engross a moment's notice, and yet begs,
Begs a propitious ear for his poor thoughts,
However trivial all that he conceives.
Sweet bashfulness! it claims at least this praise,   70
The dearth of information and good sense
That it foretells us always comes to pass.
Cat'racts of declamation thunder here;
There forests of no meaning spread the page,
In which all comprehension wanders, lost;   75
While fields of pleasantry amuse us there
With merry descants on a nation's woes.
The rest appears a wilderness of strange
But gay confusion: roses for the cheeks,
And lilies for the brows, of faded age;   80
Teeth for the toothless, ringlets for the bald,
Heav'n, earth, and ocean, plundered of their sweets,
Nectareous essences, Olympian dews,
Sermons, and city feasts, and fav'rite airs,
Aethereal journeys,[12] submarine exploits,   85
And Katterfelto,[13] with his hair on end
At his own wonders, wond'ring for his bread.
    'Tis pleasant through the loopholes of retreat
To peep at such a world; to see the stir
Of the great Babel, and not feel the crowd;   90
To hear the roar she sends through all her gates
At a safe distance, where the dying sound
Falls a soft murmur on th' uninjured ear.
Thus sitting, and surveying thus at ease
The globe and its concerns, I seem advanced   95
To some secure and more than mortal height,
That lib'rates and exempts me from them all.
It turns submitted to my view, turns round
With all its generations; I behold
The tumult, and am still. The sound of war   100
Has lost its terrors ere it reaches me;
Grieves, but alarms me not. I mourn the pride
And av'rice that make man a wolf to man,
Hear the faint echo of those brazen throats
By which he speaks the language of his heart,   105
And sigh but never tremble at the sound.
He travels and expatiates,[14] as the bee
From flow'r to flow'r, so he from land to land;

The manners, customs, policy of all
Pay contribution to the store he gleans;   110
He sucks intelligence in ev'ry clime,
And spreads the honey of his deep research
At his return—a rich repast for me.
He travels, and I too. I tread his deck,
Ascend his topmast, through his peering eyes   115
Discover countries, with a kindred heart
Suffer his woes, and share in his escapes;
While fancy, like the finger of a clock,[15]
Runs the great circuit, and is still at home.
    O Winter, ruler of th' inverted year,   120
Thy scattered hair with sleet like ashes filled,
Thy breath congealed upon thy lips, thy cheeks
Fringed with a beard made white with other snows
Than those of age, thy forehead wrapped in clouds,
A leafless branch thy scepter, and thy throne   125
A sliding car, indebted to no wheels,
But urged by storms along its slipp'ry way,
I love thee, all unlovely as thou seem'st,
And dreaded as thou art! Thou hold'st the sun
A pris'ner in the yet undawning east,   130
Short'ning his journey between morn and noon,
And hurrying him, impatient of his stay,
Down to the rosy west; but kindly still
Compensating his loss with added hours
Of social converse and instructive ease,   135
And gath'ring, at short notice, in one group
The family dispersed, and fixing thought,
Not less dispersed by daylight and its cares.
I crown thee king of intimate delights,
Fireside enjoyments, home-born happiness,   140
And all the comforts that the lowly roof
Of undisturbed retirement, and the hours
Of long uninterrupted ev'ning, know.
No rattling wheels stop short before these gates;
No powdered pert, proficient in the art   145
Of sounding an alarm, assaults these doors
Till the street rings; no stationary steeds
Cough their own knell, while, heedless of the sound,
The silent circle fan themselves, and quake:
But here the needle plies its busy task,   150
The pattern grows, the well-depicted flow'r,
Wrought patiently into the snowy lawn,
Unfolds its bosom; buds and leaves and sprigs
And curling tendrils, gracefully disposed,
Follow the nimble finger of the fair,   155
A wreath that cannot fade, of flow'rs that blow
With most success when all besides decay.
The poet's or historian's page by one
Made vocal for th' amusement of the rest,   159

---

12 Balloon ascents.
13 Gustavus Katterfelto (d. 1799), a Prussian by birth, had a
   notable success in England as a conjuror and quack. His advertisements were headed "Wonders, wonders, wonders!"
14 Ranges.

15 See the title of Book II.

The sprightly lyre whose treasure of sweet sounds
The touch from many a trembling chord shakes out,
And the clear voice symphonious yet distinct
And in the charming strife triumphant still,
Beguile the night, and set a keener edge   165
On female industry: the threaded steel
Flies swiftly, and unfelt the task proceeds.
The volume closed, the customary rites
Of the last meal commence. A Roman meal,
Such as the mistress of the world once found
Delicious, when her patriots of high note,   170
Perhaps by moonlight, at their humble doors,
And under an old oak's domestic shade,
Enjoyed—spare feast!—a radish and an egg!
Discourse ensues, not trivial, yet not dull,
Nor such as with a frown forbids the play   175
Of fancy or proscribes the sound of mirth:
Nor do we madly, like an impious world,
Who deem religion frenzy, and the God
That made them an intruder on their joys,
Start at his awful name, or deem his praise   180
A jarring note—themes of a graver tone
Exciting oft our gratitude and love,
While we retrace with mem'ry's pointing wand,
That calls the past to our exact review,
The dangers we have 'scaped, the broken snare,   185
The disappointed foe, deliv'rance found
Unlooked for, life preserved and peace restored—
Fruits of omnipotent eternal love.
"Oh, ev'nings worthy of the gods!" exclaimed
The Sabine bard.[16] "Oh, ev'nings," I reply,   190
"More to be prized and coveted than yours,
As more illumined and with nobler truths,
That I and mine and those we love enjoy."
    Is winter hideous in a garb like this?
Needs he the tragic[17] fur, the smoke of lamps   195
The pent-up breath of an unsav'ry throng,
To thaw him into feeling; or the smart
And snappish dialogue that flippant wits
Call comedy, to prompt him with a smile?
The self-complacent actor, when he views   200
(Stealing a sidelong glance at a full house)
The slope of faces, from the floor to th' roof
(As if one master spring controlled them all),
Relaxed into an universal grin,
Sees not a countenance there that speaks of joy   205
Half so refined or so sincere as ours. . . .[18]

---

[16] Cf. Horace, *Satires*, II, vi, 65.
[17] Because of the animals killed to obtain it.
[18] Book V is entitled "The Winter Morning Walk," Book VI
"The Winter Walk at Noon."

ON THE RECEIPT OF MY MOTHER'S PICTURE OUT OF NORFOLK

THE GIFT OF MY COUSIN ANN BODHAM

Cowper's mother died when he was six. This poem of
love and devotion was written in 1790.

Oh, that those lips had language! Life has passed
With me but roughly since I heard thee last.
Those lips are thine—thy own sweet smiles I see,
The same that oft in childhood solaced me;
Voice only fails, else, how distinct they say,   5
"Grieve not, my child; chase all thy fears away!"
The meek intelligence of those dear eyes
(Blest be the art that can immortalize,
The art that baffles time's tyrannic claim
To quench it) here shines on me still the same.   10
    Faithful remembrancer of one so dear,
O welcome guest, though unexpected, here!
Who bidd'st me honor with an artless song,
Affectionate, a mother lost so long,
I will obey, not willingly alone,   15
But gladly, as[1] the precept were her own;
And, while that face renews my filial grief,
Fancy shall weave a charm for my relief—
Shall steep me in Elysian[2] reverie,
A momentary dream, that thou art she.   20
    My mother! when I learned that thou wast dead,
Say, wast thou conscious of the tears I shed?
Hovered thy spirit o'er thy sorrowing son,
Wretch even then, life's journey just begun?
Perhaps thou gav'st me, though unseen, a kiss;   25
Perhaps a tear, if souls can weep in bliss—
Ah, that maternal smile! it answers—Yes.
I heard the bell tolled on thy burial day,
I saw the hearse that bore thee slow away,
And, turning from my nurs'ry window, drew   30
A long, long sigh, and wept a last adieu!
But was it such?—It was.—Where thou art gone,
Adieus and farewells are a sound unknown.
May I but meet thee on that peaceful shore,
The parting word shall pass my lips no more!   35
Thy maidens grieved themselves at my concern,
Oft gave me promise of thy quick return.
What ardently I wished I long believed,
And, disappointed still, was still deceived;
By expectation every day beguiled,   40
Dupe of *tomorrow* even from a child.
Thus many a sad tomorrow came and went,
Till, all my stock of infant sorrow spent,

---

[1] As if.   [2] Blissful.

I learned at last submission to my lot;
But, though I less deplored thee, ne'er forgot.   45
    Where once we dwelt our name is heard no more,
Children not thine have trod my nurs'ry floor;
And where the gard'ner Robin, day by day,
Drew me to school along the public way,
Delighted with my bauble coach, and wrapped   50
In scarlet mantle warm, and velvet capped,
'Tis now become a history little known,
That once we called the past'ral house[3] our own.
Short-lived possession! but the record fair
That mem'ry keeps of all thy kindness there   55
Still outlives many a storm that has effaced
A thousand other themes less deeply traced.
Thy nightly visits to my chamber made,
That thou mightst know me safe and warmly laid;
Thy morning bounties ere I left my home,   60
The biscuit, or confectionary plum;
The fragrant waters on my cheeks bestowed
By thy own hand, till fresh they shone and glowed;
All this, and more endearing still than all,
Thy constant flow of love, that knew no fall,   65
Ne'er roughened by those cataracts and brakes[4]
That humor[5] interposed too often makes;
All this still legible in mem'ry's page,
And still to be so, to my latest age,
Adds joy to duty, makes me glad to pay   70
Such honors to thee as my numbers[6] may;
Perhaps a frail memorial, but sincere,
Not scorned in heav'n, though little noticed here.
    Could time, his flight reversed, restore the hours
When, playing with thy vesture's tissued flow'rs,   75
The violet, the pink, and jessamine,
I pricked them into paper with a pin
(And thou wast happier than myself the while,
Wouldst softly speak, and stroke my head and smile),
Could those few pleasant hours again appear,   80
Might one wish bring them, would I wish them here?
I would not trust my heart—the dear delight
Seems so to be desired, perhaps I might.—
But no—what here we call our life is such,
So little to be loved, and thou so much,   85
That I should ill requite thee to constrain
Thy unbound spirit into bonds again.
    Thou, as a gallant bark from Albion's[7] coast
(The storms all weathered and the ocean crossed)
Shoots into port at some well-havened isle,   90
Where spices breathe and brighter seasons smile,
There sits quiescent on the floods[8] that show
Her beauteous form reflected clear below,

While airs impregnated with incense play
Around her, fanning light her streamers gay;   95
So thou, with sails how swift! hast reached the shore
"Where tempests never beat nor billows roar,"[9]
And thy loved consort on the dang'rous tide
Of life, long since, has anchored at thy side.[10]
But me, scarce hoping to attain that rest,   100
Always from port withheld, always distressed—
Me howling winds drive devious, tempest-tossed,
Sails ripped, seams op'ning wide, and compass lost,
And day by day some current's thwarting force
Sets me more distant from a prosp'rous course.   105
But oh, the thought that thou art safe, and he!
That thought is joy, arrive what may to me.
My boast is not that I deduce my birth
From loins enthroned, and rulers of the earth;
But higher far my proud pretensions rise—   110
The son of parents passed into the skies.
And now, farewell—time, unrevoked, has run
His wonted course, yet what I wished is done.
By contemplation's help, not sought in vain,
I seem t' have lived my childhood o'er again;   115
To have renewed the joys that once were mine,
Without the sin of violating thine:
And, while the wings of fancy still are free,
And I can view this mimic show of thee,
Time has but half succeeded in his theft—   120
Thyself removed, thy power to soothe me left.

TO MARY

Cowper's engagement to Mrs. Unwin was broken in 1773,
when he had his third attack of insanity. The poem was
written in 1793. A few months before, Mrs. Unwin had
suffered a second paralytic stroke.

    The twentieth year is well-nigh past,
    Since first our sky was overcast;
    Ah, would that this might be the last!
            My Mary!

    Thy spirits have a fainter flow,   5
    I see thee daily weaker grow—
    'Twas my distress that brought thee low,
            My Mary!

    Thy needles, once a shining store,
    For my sake restless heretofore,   10
    Now rust disused, and shine no more,
            My Mary!

[3] The rectory at Great Berkhampstead, Hertfordshire, where
Cowper was born.   [4] Or bracks, spurts of water.
[5] Caprice.   [6] Verses.   [7] England's.   [8] Waters.

[9] Misquoted from The Dispensary (III, 242), a satire by the
physician and poet Sir Samuel Garth (1661–1719).
[10] Cowper's father died in 1756.

For though thou gladly wouldst fulfil
The same kind office for me still,
Thy sight now seconds not thy will,   15
    My Mary!

But well thou played'st the housewife's part,
And all thy threads with magic art
Have wound themselves about this heart,
    My Mary!   20

Thy indistinct expressions seem
Like language uttered in a dream;
Yet me they charm, whate'er the theme
    My Mary!

Thy silver locks, once auburn bright,   25
Are still more lovely in my sight
Than golden beams of orient light,
    My Mary!

For could I view nor them nor thee,
What sight worth seeing could I see?   30
The sun would rise in vain for me,
    My Mary!

Partakers of thy sad decline,
Thy hands their little force resign;
Yet, gently pressed, press gently mine,   35
    My Mary!

And then I feel that still I hold
A richer store ten thousandfold
Than misers fancy in their gold,
    My Mary!   40

Such feebleness of limbs thou prov'st,
That now at every step thou mov'st
Upheld by two; yet still thou lov'st,
    My Mary!

And still to love, though pressed with ill,   45
In wintry age to feel no chill,
With me is to be lovely still,
    My Mary!

But ah! by constant heed I know
How oft the sadness that I show   50
Transforms thy smiles to looks of woe,
    My Mary!

And should my future lot be cast
With much resemblance of the past,
Thy worn-out heart will break at last,   55
    My Mary!

THE CASTAWAY

This anguished poem was written in 1799, the year before
Cowper's death. He found the incident he describes in *A
Voyage round the World* (1748) by the great British admiral
George Anson.

Obscurest night involved the sky,
    Th' Atlantic billows roared,
When such a destined wretch as I,
    Washed headlong from on board,
Of friends, of hope, of all bereft,   5
His floating home for ever left.

No braver chief could Albion boast
    Than he with whom he went,
Nor ever ship left Albion's coast
    With warmer wishes sent.   10
He loved them both, but both in vain,
Nor him beheld, nor her again.

Not long beneath the whelming brine,
    Expert to swim, he lay;
Nor soon he felt his strength decline,   15
    Or courage die away;
But waged with death a lasting strife,
Supported by despair of life.

He shouted: nor his friends had failed
    To check the vessel's course,   20
But so the furious blast prevailed
    That, pitiless perforce,
They left their outcast mate behind,
And scudded still before the wind.

Some succor yet they could afford;   25
    And, such as storms allow,
The cask, the coop, the floated cord,
    Delayed not to bestow.
But he (they knew) nor ship nor shore,
Whate'er they gave, should visit more.   30

Nor, cruel as it seemed, could he
    Their haste himself condemn,
Aware that flight, in such a sea,
    Alone could rescue them;
Yet bitter felt it still to die   35
Deserted, and his friends so nigh.

He long survives, who lives an hour
    In ocean, self-upheld;
And so long he, with unspent pow'r,
    His destiny repelled;   40
And ever, as the minutes flew,
Entreated help, or cried, "Adieu!"

At length, his transient respite past,
　His comrades, who before
Had heard his voice in ev'ry blast,　　　45
　Could catch the sound no more.
For then, by toil subdued, he drank
The stifling wave, and then he sank.

No poet wept him: but the page
　Of narrative sincere,　　　　　　50
That tells his name, his worth, his age,
　Is wet with Anson's tear.
And tears by bards or heroes shed
Alike immortalize the dead.

I therefore purpose not, or dream,　　　55
　Descanting on his fate,
To give the melancholy theme
　A more enduring date:
But misery still delights to trace
Its semblance in another's case.　　　　60

No voice divine the storm allayed,
　No light propitious shone,
When, snatched from all effectual aid,
　We perished, each alone:
But I beneath a rougher sea,　　　　　65
And whelmed in deeper gulfs than he.

LETTERS

COWPER is among the best of the English letter-writers; by some he has been called the greatest. His touch is light, whimsical, and charming. As his editor observes, he "seems like a next-door neighbor," but an uncommonly gifted one. His *Correspondence* has often been edited, best by T. Wright (4 vols., 1904; additional vol., 1925). There is a good volume of selections by E. V. Lucas and M. L. Milford (1911); Everyman's Library also contains a volume.

I. TO MRS. NEWTON

5TH JUNE, 1780

Dear Madam,—When I write to Mr. Newton,[1] he answers me by letter; when I write to you, you answer me in fish. I return you many thanks for the 15 mackerel and lobster. They assured me in terms as intelligible as pen and ink could have spoken that you still remember Orchardside;[2] and though they never spoke in their lives, and it was still less to be expected from them that they should speak, being 20 dead, they gave us an assurance of your affection that corresponds exactly with that which Mr. Newton expresses towards us in all his letters. For my own part, I never in my life began a letter more at a venture than the present. It is possible that I may 25 finish it, but perhaps more than probable that I shall not. I have had several indifferent nights, and the wind is easterly: two circumstances so unfavorable to me in all my occupations, but especially that of writing, that it was with the greatest difficulty I 30 could even bring myself to attempt it.

You have never yet perhaps been made acquainted with the unfortunate Tom Freeman's misadventure. He and his wife, returning from Hanslope fair, were coming down Weston Lane: to wit, themselves, 5 their horse, and their great wooden panniers, at ten o'clock at night. The horse, having a lively imagination and very weak nerves, fancied he either saw or heard something, but has never been able to say what. A sudden fright will impart activity and a 10 momentary vigor, even to lameness itself. Accordingly, he started, and sprung from the middle of the road to the side of it, with such surprising alacrity that he dismounted the gingerbread baker and his gingerbread wife in a moment. Not contented with this effort, nor thinking himself yet out of danger, he proceeded as fast as he could to a full gallop, rushed against the gate at the bottom of the lane, and opened it for himself, without perceiving that there was any gate there. Still he galloped, and with 20 a velocity and momentum continually increasing, till he arrived in Olney. I had been in bed about ten minutes when I heard the most uncommon and unaccountable noise that can be imagined. It was, in fact, occasioned by the clattering of tin pattypans[3] and a Dutch oven against the sides of the panniers. Much gingerbread was picked up in the street, and Mr. Lucy's windows were broken all to pieces. Had this been all, it would have been a comedy; but we learned the next morning that the poor woman's 30 collarbone was broken, and she has hardly been able to resume her occupation since. . . .

　　　　　　Yours, dear Madam,
　　　　　　　　　WM. COWPER

[1] Newton had recently been called to the rectorship of St. Mary Woolnoth, in London.
[2] The house where Cowper was then living, at Olney, with Mrs. Unwin.
[3] For small pies.

II. TO THE REV. WILLIAM UNWIN[4]

AUGUST 6, 1780

My dear Friend,—You like to hear from me—this is a very good reason why I should write; but I have nothing to say—this seems equally a good reason why I should not. Yet if you had alighted from your horse at our door this morning, and at this present writing, being five o'clock in the afternoon, had found occasion to say to me, "Mr. Cowper, you have not spoke since I came in; have you resolved never to speak again?" it would be but a poor reply if, in answer to the summons, I should plead inability as my best and only excuse. And this, by the way, suggests to me a seasonable piece of instruction, and reminds me of what I am very apt to forget when I have any epistolary business in hand: that a letter may be written upon anything or nothing, just as that anything or nothing happens to occur. A man that has a journey before him twenty miles in length, which he is to perform on foot, will not hesitate and doubt whether he shall set out or not, because he does not readily conceive how he shall ever reach the end of it; for he knows that, by the simple operation of moving one foot forward first and then the other, he shall be sure to accomplish it. So it is in the present case, and so it is in every similar case. A letter is written as a conversation is maintained or a journey performed, not by preconcerted or premeditated means, a new contrivance, or an invention never heard of before, but merely by maintaining a progress, and resolving, as a postilion does, having once set out, never to stop till we reach the appointed end. If a man may talk without thinking, why may he not write upon the same terms? A grave gentleman of the last century, a tiewig, square-toe, Steinkirk[5] figure, would say, "My good sir, a man has no right to do either." But it is to be hoped that the present century has nothing to do with the moldy opinions of the last; and so, good Sir Launcelot, or St. Paul, or whatever be your name, step into your picture frame again, and look as if you thought for another century, and leave us moderns in the meantime to think when we can, and to write whether we can or not, else we might as well be dead as you are.

When we look back upon our forefathers, we seem to look back upon the people of another nation, almost upon creatures of another species. Their vast rambling mansions, spacious halls, and painted casements, the gothic porch smothered with honeysuckles, their little gardens and high walls, their box-edgings, balls of holly, and yew-tree statues,[6] are become so entirely unfashionable now that we can hardly believe it possible that a people who resembled us so little in their taste should resemble us in anything else. But in everything else, I suppose, they were our counterparts exactly; and time, that has sewed up the slashed sleeve, and reduced the large trunk hose to a neat pair of silk stockings, has left human nature just where it found it. The inside of the man at least has undergone no change. His passions, appetites, and aims are just what they ever were. They wear perhaps a handsomer disguise than they did in the days of yore, for philosophy and literature will have their effect upon the exterior; but in every other respect a modern is only an ancient in a different dress.

W. C.

III. TO JOHN NEWTON

NOVEMBER 17, 1783

My dear Friend,—A parcel arrived last night, the contents of which shall be disposed of according to order. We thank Mrs. Newton (not from the teeth outwards) for the toothbrushes.

The country around us is much alarmed with apprehensions of fire. Two have happened since that of Olney. One at Hitchin, where the damage is said to amount to eleven thousand pounds, and another at a place not far from Hitchin, of which I have not learnt the name. Letters have been dropped at Bedford, threatening to burn the town; and the inhabitants have been so intimidated as to have placed a guard in many parts of it several nights past. Some madman or some devil has broke loose, who it is to be hoped will pay dear for these effusions of his malignity. Since our conflagration here, we have sent two women and a boy to the justice, for depredation; Sue Riviss, for stealing a piece of beef, which, in her excuse, she said she intended to take care of. This lady, whom you well remember, escaped for want of evidence; not that evidence was indeed wanting, but our men of Gotham[7] judged it unnecessary to send it. With her went the woman

---

[4] Mrs. Unwin's son; he was rector of Stock, in Essex.
[5] Or Steenkirk; a kind of loose neckcloth.—A *tiewig* was a small wig, with the lower part tied, unlike the large, full-bottomed kind.

[6] All three were features of the formal garden.
[7] I.e., fools.

I mentioned before, who, it seems, has made some sort of profession,[8] but upon this occasion allowed herself a latitude of conduct rather inconsistent with it, having filled her apron with wearing apparel, which she likewise intended to take care of. She would have gone to the county gaol had Billy Raban, the baker's son, who prosecuted, insisted upon it; but he good-naturedly, though I think weakly, interposed in her favor, and begged her off. The young gentleman who accompanied these fair ones is the junior son of Molly Boswell. He had stolen some ironwork, the property of Griggs, the butcher. Being convicted, he was ordered to be whipped, which operation he underwent at the cart's tail, from the stone house to the high arch,[9] and back again. He seemed to show great fortitude, but it was all an imposition upon the public. The beadle who performed it had filled his left hand with red ochre, through which, after every stroke, he drew the lash of his whip, leaving the appearance of a wound upon the skin, but in reality not hurting him at all. This being perceived by Mr. Constable Handscomb, who followed the beadle, he applied his cane, without any such management or precaution, to the shoulders of the too merciful executioner. The scene immediately became more interesting. The beadle could by no means be prevailed upon to strike hard, which provoked the constable to strike harder; and this double flogging continued, till a lass of Silver End,[10] pitying the pitiful beadle thus suffering under the hands of the pitiless constable, joined the procession, and, placing herself immediately behind the latter, seized him by his capillary[11] club, and pulling him backwards by the same, slapped his face with a most Amazonian fury. This concatenation of events has taken up more of my paper than I intended it should; but I could not forbear to inform you how the beadle threshed the thief, the constable the beadle, and the lady the constable, and how the thief was the only person concerned who suffered nothing. Mr. Teedon[12] has been here, and is gone again. He came to thank me for an old pair of breeches. In answer to our inquiries after his health, he replied that he had a slow fever which made him take all possible care not to inflame his blood. I admitted his prudence, but in his particular instance could not very clearly discern the need of it. Pump water will not heat him much;

and, to speak a little in his own style, more inebriating fluids are to him, I fancy, not very attainable. He brought us news, the truth of which, however, I do not vouch for, that the town of Bedford was actually on fire yesterday, and the flames not extinguished when the bearer of the tidings left it.

Swift observes, when he is giving his reasons why the preacher is elevated always above his hearers, that let the crowd be as great as it will below, there is always room enough overhead. If the French philosophers can carry their art of flying to the perfection they desire, the observation may be reversed; the crowd will be overhead, and they will have most room who stay below. I can assure you, however, upon my own experience, that this way of traveling is very delightful. I dreamt, a night or two since, that I drove myself through the upper regions in a balloon and pair, with the greatest ease and security. Having finished the tour I intended, I made a short turn, and, with one flourish of my whip, descended, my horses prancing and curveting with an infinite share of spirit, but without the least danger either to me or my vehicle. The time, we may suppose, is at hand, and seems to be prognosticated by my dream, when these airy excursions will be universal, when judges will fly the circuit, and bishops their visitations; and when the tour of Europe will be performed with much greater speed, and with equal advantage, by all who travel merely for the sake of having it to say that they have made it.

I beg you will accept for yourself and yours our unfeigned love; and remember me affectionately to Mr. Bacon,[13] when you see him.

Yours, my dear friend,
WM. COWPER

IV. TO LADY HESKETH[14]

JUNE 12, 1786

I am neither young nor superannuated, yet am I a child. When I had read your letter I grumbled: not at you, my dearest cousin, for you are in no fault, but at the whole generation of coachmakers, as you may suppose, and at yours in particular. I foresaw and foreknew that he would fail in his promise, and yet was disappointed; was, in truth, no more prepared for what I expected with so much reason, than if I had not at all expected it. I grumbled till we went to dinner, and at intervals till we had dined;

---

[8] I.e., announced her religious conversion.
[9] Two landmarks in Olney.   [10] A street in Olney.
[11] Pigtail, done up in a clublike knot.
[12] Samuel Teedon, the schoolmaster at Olney.

[13] The sculptor John Bacon (1740–99).
[14] "Dearest Cuzzy-Wuzzy," Cowper's cousin Harriet, widow of Sir Thomas Hesketh. Cowper had not seen her for twenty years.

and when dinner was over, with very little encouragement, I could actually have cried. And if I had, I should in truth have thought them tears as well bestowed as most that I have shed for many years. At first I numbered months, then weeks, then days, and was just beginning to number hours; and now I am thrown back to days again. My first speech was, after folding up your letter (for I will honestly tell you all), "I am crazed with Mondays, Tuesdays, and Wednesdays and St. Albans,[15] and Totteridge, and Hadley. When is she to set out?—When is she to be here? Do tell me, for perhaps you understand it better than I."—"Why," says Mrs. Unwin (with much more composure in her air than properly belonged to her, for she also had her feelings on the occasion), "she sets out tomorrow se'nnight, and will be here on the Wednesday after."—"And who knows that?" replied I; "will the coachmaker be at all more punctual in repairing the old carriage than in making the new one? For my part, I have no hope of seeing her this month; and if it be possible, I will not think of it, lest I should be again disappointed." And to say the truth, my dear, though hours have passed since thus I said, and I have had time for cooler consideration, the suspicion still sticks close to me that more delays may happen. A philosopher would prepare himself for such an event; but I am no philosopher, at least when the comfort of seeing you is in question. I believe in my heart that there have been just as many true philosophers upon earth as there have been men that have had little or no feeling, and not one more. Swift truly says,

> Indifference, clad in reason's guise,
> All want of fortitude supplies.[16]

When I wake in the night, I feel my spirits the lighter because you are coming. When I am not at Troy,[17] I am either occupied in the recollection of a thousand passages of my past life in which you were a partaker with me, or conversing about you with Mrs. Unwin. Thus my days and nights have been spent principally, ever since you determined upon this journey, and especially, and almost without interruption from any other subject, since the time of your journey has seemed near at hand. While I despaired, as I did for many years, that I should ever

see you more, I thought of you, indeed, and often, but with less solicitude. I used to say to myself, "Providence has so ordered it, and it is my duty to submit. He has cast me at a distance from her, and from all whom I once knew. He did it, and not I; it is he who has chosen my situation for me. Have I not reason to be thankful that, since he designed me to pass a part of my life, and no inconsiderable one neither, in a state of the deepest melancholy, he appointed me a friend in Mrs. Unwin, who should share all my sorrows with me, and watch over me in my helpless condition, night and day? What, and where, had I been without her?" Such considerations were sufficient to reconcile me at that time to perpetual separation even from you, because perpetual I supposed it must be, and without remedy. But now every hour of your absence seems long, for this very natural reason: because the same Providence has given me a hope that you will be present with me soon. A good that seems at an immeasurable distance, and that we cannot hope to reach, has therefore the less influence on our affections.[18] But the same good brought nearer, made to appear practicable, promised to our hopes, and almost in possession, engages all our faculties and desires. All this is according to the natural and necessary course of things in the human heart; and the philosophy that would interfere with it is folly at least, if not frenzy. A throne has at present but little sensible attraction for me. And why? Perhaps only because I know that should I break my heart with wishes for a throne, I should never reach one. But did I know assuredly that I should put on a crown tomorrow, perhaps I too should feel ambition, and account the interposing night tedious. The sum of the whole matter, my dear, is this: that this villainous coachmaker has mortified me monstrously, and that I tremble lest he should do so again. From you I have no fears. I see in your letter, and all the way through it, what pains you take to assure me and give me comfort. I am and will be comforted for that very reason; and will wait still other ten days with all the patience that I can muster. You, I know, will be punctual if you can, and that at least is matter of real consolation.

I approve altogether, my cousin beloved, of your sending your goods to the wagon on Saturday, and cookee by the coach on Tuesday. She will be here perhaps by four in the afternoon, at the latest by five, and will have quite time enough to find out all the cupboards and shelves in her department before

---

[15] Through which Lady Hesketh would pass on her way from London to Olney.

[16] Misquoted from "The Death of Swift," lines 213–14 (p. 773, above).

[17] I.e., working on his translation of Homer's *Iliad*.

[18] Feelings.

you arrive. But I declare and protest that cookee shall sleep that night at our house, and get her breakfast here next morning. You will break her heart, child, if you send her into a strange house where she will find nothing that has life but the curate, who has not much neither. Servant he keeps none. A woman makes his bed, and after a fashion, as they say, dresses his dinner, and then leaves him to his lucubrations. I do therefore insist on it, and so does Mrs. Unwin, that cookee shall be our guest for that time; and from this we will not depart. I tell thee besides, that I shall be more glad to see her than ever I was in my life to see one whom I never saw before. Guess why, if you can.

You must number your miles fifty-six instead of fifty-four. The fifty-sixth mile ends but a few yards beyond the vicarage. Soon after you shall have entered Olney, you will find an opening on your right hand. It is a lane that leads to your dwelling. There your coach may stop and set down Mrs. Eaton;[19] when she has walked about forty yards she will spy a green gate and rails on her left hand; and when she has opened the gate and reached the house door, she will find herself at home. But we have another maneuver to play off upon you, and in which we positively will not be opposed, or, if we are, it shall be to no purpose. I have an honest fellow that works in my garden; his name is Kitchener, and we call him Kitch for brevity. He is sober, and as trusty as the day. He has a smart blue coat, that, when I had worn it some years, I gave him, and he has now worn it some years himself. I shall set him on horseback, and order him to the Swan at Newport, there to wait your arrival, and, if you should not stop at that place, as perhaps you may not, immediately to throw himself into your suite, and to officiate as your guide. For though the way from Newport hither is short, there are turnings that might puzzle your coachman; and he will be of use, too, in conducting you to our house, which otherwise you might not easily find, partly through the stupidity of those of whom you might inquire, and partly from its out-of-the-way situation. My brother drove up and down Olney in quest of us, almost as often as you up and down Chancery Lane in quest of the Madans,[20] with fifty boys and girls at his tail, before he could find us. The first man, therefore, you shall see in a blue coat with white buttons, in the famous town of Newport, cry "Kitch!" He will immediately answer, "My Lady!" and from that moment you are sure not to be lost.

Your house shall be as clean as scrubbing and dry-rubbing can make it, and in all respects fit to receive you. My friend the Quaker, in all that I have seen of his doings, has acquitted himself much to my satisfaction. Some little things, he says, will perhaps be missing at first, in such a multiplicity, but they shall be produced as soon as called for. Mrs. U. has bought you six ducks, and is fatting them for you. She has also rummaged up a coop that will hold six chickens, and designs to people it for you by the first opportunity; for these things are not to be got fit for the table at Olney. Thus, my dear, are all things in the best train possible, and nothing remains but that you come and show yourself. Oh, that moment! Shall we not both enjoy it?—That we shall.

I have received an anonymous complimentary Pindaric Ode from a little poet who calls himself a schoolboy. I send you the first stanza by way of specimen. You shall see it all soon.

TO WM. COWPER, OF THE INNER TEMPLE, ESQ.

On His Poems in the Second Volume

In what high strains, my Muse, wilt thou
Attempt great Cowper's worth to show?
    Pindaric strains shall tune the lyre,
        And 'twould require
        A Pindar's fire
    To sing great Cowper's worth,
The lofty bard, delightful sage,
Ever the wonder of the age,
    And *blessing to the earth.*

Adieu, my precious cousin; your lofty bard and delightful sage expects you with all possible affection.

Ever yours,
WM. COWPER. . . .

V. TO LADY HESKETH

The Lodge,[21] MARCH 3, 1788

One day last week Mrs. Unwin and I, having taken our morning walk and returning homeward through the wilderness, met the Throckmortons.[22] A minute

---

[19] Lady Hesketh had rented the vicarage. Mrs. Eaton was one of the three servants she brought.

[20] Judith Cowper, Mrs. Madan, was a sister of Cowper's father.

[21] Cowper was now living at Weston Underwood, two miles from Olney.

[22] John (afterwards Sir John) Throckmorton occupied an estate in the vicinity; he and his wife had become great friends with Cowper.

after we had met them, we heard the cry of hounds at no great distance; and, mounting the broad stump of an elm which had been felled, and by the aid of which we were enabled to look over the wall, we saw them. They were all at that time in our orchard; presently we heard a terrier, belonging to Mrs. Throckmorton, which you may remember by the name of Fury, yelping with much vehemence, and saw her running through the thickets within a few yards of us at her utmost speed, as if in pursuit of something which we doubted not was the fox. Before we could reach the other end of the wilderness, the hounds entered also; and when we arrived at the gate which opens into the grove, there we found the whole weary cavalcade assembled. The huntsman, dismounting, begged leave to follow his hounds on foot, for he was sure, he said, that they had killed him: a conclusion which I suppose he drew from their profound silence. He was accordingly admitted, and with a sagacity that would not have dishonored the best hound in the world, pursuing precisely the same track which the fox and the dogs had taken, though he had never had a glimpse of either after their first entrance through the rails, arrived where he found the slaughtered prey. He soon produced dead reynard, and rejoined us in the grove with all his dogs about him. Having an opportunity to see a ceremony which I was pretty sure would never fall in my way again, I determined to stay, and to notice all that passed with the most minute attention. The huntsman, having by the aid of a pitchfork lodged reynard on the arm of an elm, at the height of about nine feet from the ground, there left him for a considerable time. The gentlemen sat on their horses, contemplating the fox, for which they had toiled so hard; and the hounds assembled at the foot of the tree, with faces not less expressive of the most rational delight, contemplated the same object. The huntsman remounted, cut off a foot, and threw it to the hounds; one of them swallowed it whole, like a bolus.[23] He then once more alighted, and, drawing down the fox by the hinder legs, desired the people, who were by this time rather numerous, to open a lane for him to the right and left. He was instantly obeyed; when, throwing the fox to the distance of some yards, and screaming like a fiend, "Tear him to pieces!"—at least six times repeatedly—he consigned him over absolutely to the pack, who in a few minutes devoured him completely. Thus, my dear, as Vergil says,[24] what none of the gods could have ventured to promise me, time itself, pursuing its accustomed course, has of its own accord presented me with. I have been in at the death of a fox; and you now know as much of the matter as I, who am as well informed as any sportsman in England.

Yours,

W. C.

Richard Brinsley Sheridan

1751–1816

In *The School for Scandal* Sheridan provided the English stage with the best comedy of manners between Congreve and Shaw. Not content with that contribution, he also wrote the best ballad opera and the best burlesque of his time. After Gay's *Beggar's Opera* (1728) there is nothing so good as *The Duenna* until the operettas of Gilbert and Sullivan, while *The Critic* remains to this day the wittiest take-off of silly tendencies in the drama since the Duke of Buckingham wrote *The Rehearsal* (1671) to guy John Dryden and the Heroic drama of the Restoration. All this, Sheridan accomplished between the ages of twenty-four and twenty-nine. After such a beginning, one might expect a young author to remain for life grappled to the stage with hoops of steel; but Sheridan's ambition was boundless. Having conquered the theater in his twenties, he proceeded in his thirties to duplicate that success on the stage of politics. No less than boxes, pit, and galleries, the House of Commons was hypnotized by the inexhaustible flow of his brilliance.

On brilliance, indeed, more than on principle, Sheridan's success as a statesman was based, and more on his extraordinary gifts as an orator than on solid qualities of intellect and character. In these respects he is the opposite of his fellow countryman and fellow Whig, Edmund Burke. In the drama, his wit was displayed in a setting more substantial than the disputations of party. He condemned the sentimental comedy which flourished in his day, but he did not revert to the Restoration coldness and cynicism. Sheridan was a man of feeling as well as wit, and his comic pen was enlisted for morality as well as common sense. That is evident when you compare *The School for Scandal* with *The Way of the World,* and it is a fact that the greatest

---

[23] Large pill, especially for a horse.   [24] *Aeneid,* IX, 6–7.

comedies all have a sound conception of the seriousness, the dignity even, of human life.

Sheridan was born in Dublin. His father, Thomas Sheridan, was a well-known actor and theater manager, who soon moved to London and opened a school of oratory. Richard was sent to the famous "public" school of Harrow, Eton's great rival; subjected to snubbing as an actor's son and therefore hardly a gentleman, he seems to have been miserable there. Instead of proceeding from Harrow to one of the universities, he was next enrolled in his father's "academy." This enterprise was transferred in 1770 to Bath, the famous watering place and second capital of the beau monde. The school soon failed, and the elder Sheridan resumed acting in Dublin. Meanwhile the family had made the acquaintance of the Linleys. Thomas Linley was one of the leading musicians of the time; and his beautiful daughter Elizabeth, aged seventeen, was already a distinguished singer as well as a beauty. She was beset with suitors, whose importunities she determined to escape by withdrawing for a few years to a convent, and Sheridan chivalrously offered to escort her to France for that purpose. He was in love with her, of course; and this escapade, romantic enough for a hero in a cloak-and-sword melodrama, led through two duels to their marriage in 1773.

The happy pair settled in London—with no visible means of support, since Sheridan, to the very end of his career keenly apprehensive of sneers from the snobs, was unwilling to have his wife go on with her professional work. He himself turned to the stage only because he was desperately in need of money. The opening performance of The Rivals early in 1775 came so close to being a flat failure that Sheridan withdrew the play and slaved over it anew for eleven days before it was put on again, this time with a success which has continued ever since. Mrs. Malaprop has become a household word; and the very names of Bob Acres, Sir Lucius O'Trigger, Lydia Languish, and Sir Anthony and Captain Jack Absolute evoke the most delightful of memories. Every few years an all-star cast is assembled for a revival of this sparkling play, and numberless amateurs look back complacently on having acted one or another of these roles in a high school or college production.

The year after he captivated the town with The Rivals, Sheridan and several associates, among them his father-in-law, acquired a controlling interest in the Theater Royal, Drury Lane; for Garrick's reign was over. At first Sheridan himself was manager, but his political interests became paramount and he delegated the actual direction to others. After The Rivals his next play of any importance was The Duenna; it was a great hit in the fall of 1775. In 1777, The School for Scandal, also a popular triumph, put him per-manently in the front rank of Europe's comic dramatists; it also won him admission to Johnson's Literary Club. His only other important play is The Critic, or A Tragedy Rehearsed (1779), an uproarious attack on the sentimental drama. Since the sentimentalists were only carrying to an extreme tendencies more or less latent in all drama from which emotion is not excluded, The Critic is still both funny and pointedly satirical, even for an audience unread in the particular playwrights Sheridan was ridiculing. Of the first act he declared that he thought more of it than of anything else he had written.

Our concern is with the dramatist, and Sheridan's subsequent career can only be outlined here. In 1780 he entered the House of Commons. There, within the arena of parliamentary debate, he and Burke and Fox were the three horsemen of the Whigs. Sheridan opposed the war with America, was a leading advocate of Catholic Emancipation and other reforms, and stood in the forefront of the prosecution of Warren Hastings (p. 909, above). His speech in 1787 on the wrongs of the Begums or Princesses of Oude was one of the major oratorical efforts of the entire Indian affair. On the issue of the French Revolution he broke with Burke and stuck with Fox on the radical side. For short periods, when the Whigs were in office, he was undersecretary for foreign affairs, secretary to the treasury, and treasurer of the navy.

His private life was one of wild extravagance. Like many of the brilliant men of those times, he was a devotee of the bottle. His debts were mountainous, and Drury Lane increased them. From the wife of his youth his notorious infidelities estranged him, but they were reconciled shortly before her death in 1792. His sorrow was effusive and genuine, but within two months he was proposing to a famous beauty still in her teens. In 1795 he made a second marriage, to a woman half his age. His last years were unhappy. In 1809 Drury Lane burned to the ground, and the insurance was negligible. Money was raised for a new theater on the same site; it opened in 1812, but Sheridan was kept out of the actual management. In the same year he lost his seat in Commons, for want of money to contest it. Once out of Parliament he was no longer immune from arrest for debt, and the following year saw him in prison. After his release he subsisted chiefly on presents which wealthy friends offered in the guise of loans. His finances were in irremediable chaos, and only threats of his physician saved him from being dragged to jail from his death-bed. He was buried in Westminster Abbey.

The standard edition of The Plays and Poems (3 vols., 1928) is by R. C. Rhodes, who also wrote the most reliable of the biographies, Harlequin Sheridan: The Man and the Legends (1933). Sheridan's speeches were collected in five volumes in 1816.

Richard Brinsley Sheridan

THE SCHOOL FOR SCANDAL

SHERIDAN's aim, like Goldsmith's, was to restore to the stage the wit and laughter of Restoration comedy without its lack of morality and normal human sentiment. He is no Goldsmith for tenderness; but he rises to heights of his own in the great screen scene (IV, iii), in which, at Lady Teazle's "Not one word of it," after the screen is thrown down, comes an astounding elevation, with character replacing situation as the center of interest. "Few plays," said the New York *Times* reviewer of a recent revival, "ever turn so sharp a corner at such amazing speed." After all

the jokes and nudgings about the smart little French milliner, the cleansing tide of decent human feeling surges in. *The School for Scandal* is a better comedy because it does, and Lady Teazle's is a greater part because it shows a real growth in stature.

Sheridan was justly proud of this play, and repeatedly repolished it. He never authorized an edition, but he once corrected a manuscript copy for a friend. The text which follows is probably close to the version performed at Drury Lane, but there is no perfect text in existence.

DRAMATIS PERSONAE

SIR PETER TEAZLE	Mr. King[1]
SIR OLIVER SURFACE	Mr. Yates
JOSEPH SURFACE	Mr. Palmer
CHARLES SURFACE	Mr. Smith
CRABTREE	Mr. Parsons
SIR BENJAMIN BACKBITE	Mr. Dodd
ROWLEY	Mr. Aickin
TRIP	Mr. Lamash
MOSES	Mr. Baddeley
SNAKE	Mr. Packer
CARELESS	Mr. Farren

and other companions to CHARLES, servants, etc.

LADY TEAZLE	Mrs. Abington
MARIA	Miss P. Hopkins
LADY SNEERWELL	Miss Sherry
MRS. CANDOUR	Miss Pope

THE SCENE—*London*

PROLOGUE

Written by D. GARRICK, ESQ.

Spoken by MR. KING

A School for Scandal! Tell me, I beseech you,
Needs there a school this modish art to teach you?
No need of lessons now, the knowing think;
We might as well be taught to eat and drink.
Caused by a dearth of scandal, should the vapors[2]   5
Distress our fair ones, let 'em read the papers;

Their pow'rful mixtures such disorders hit,
Crave what you will, there's *quantum sufficit*.[3]
"Lord!" cries my Lady Wormwood (who loves tattle,
And puts much salt and pepper in her prattle),   10
Just ris'n at noon, all night at cards when threshing
Strong tea and scandal, "Bless me, how refreshing!
Give me the papers, Lisp—how bold and free! [*Sips*
'Last night Lord L. [*sips*] was caught with Lady D.'
For aching heads what charming *sal volatile!*[4] [*Sips* 15

---

[1] The cast is that of the original production.   [2] Blues.   [3] Sufficient amount.   [4] Smelling salts.

'If Mrs. B. will still continue flirting,
We hope she'll *draw*, or we'll *undraw* the curtain.'
Fine satire, poz![5] In public all abuse it,
But by ourselves [*sips*] our praise we can't refuse it.
Now, Lisp, read you—there, at that dash and star."[6]— 20
"Yes, ma'am. 'A certain lord had best beware,
Who lives not twenty miles from Grosv'nor Square;[7]
For, should he Lady W. find willing,
Wormwood is bitter—' " "Oh! that's me! the villain!
Throw it behind the fire and never more 25
Let that vile paper come within my door."
Thus at our friends we laugh, who feel the dart;
To reach our feelings, we ourselves must smart.

Is our young bard so young, to think that he
Can stop the full spring tide of calumny? 30
Knows he the world so little, and its trade?
Alas! the Devil's sooner raised than laid.
So strong, so swift, the monster there's no gagging;
Cut Scandal's head off, still the tongue is wagging.
Proud of your smiles once lavishly bestowed,[8] 35
Again our young Don Quixote takes the road;
To show his gratitude he draws his pen
And seeks this hydra, Scandal, in his den.
For your applause all perils he would through—
He'll fight (that's *write*) a cavalliero true, 40
Till every drop of blood (that's *ink*) is spilt for you.

ACT I

SCENE I. LADY SNEERWELL'S *house*

LADY SNEERWELL *at the dressing table;* SNAKE *drinking chocolate*

LADY SNEER. The paragraphs, you say, Mr. Snake, were all inserted?

SNAKE. They were, madam; and as I copied them myself in a feigned hand, there can be no suspicion whence they came.

LADY SNEER. Did you circulate the report of Lady Brittle's intrigue with Captain Boastall?

SNAKE. That's in as fine a train as your Ladyship could wish. In the common course of things, I think it must reach Mrs. Clackitt's ears within four-and-twenty hours; and then, you know, the business is as good as done.

LADY SNEER. Why, truly, Mrs. Clackitt has a very pretty talent and a great deal of industry.

SNAKE. True, madam, and has been tolerably successful in her day. To my knowledge, she has been the cause of six matches being broken off and three sons being disinherited, of four forced elopements, as many close confinements, nine separate maintenances, and two divorces. Nay, I have more than once traced her causing a tête-à-tête in the *Town and Country Magazine*[9] when the parties, perhaps, had never seen each other's faces before in the course of their lives.

LADY SNEER. She certainly has talents, but her manner is gross.

SNAKE. 'Tis very true. She generally designs well, has a free tongue and a bold invention; but her coloring is too dark and her outline often extravagant.

She wants that *delicacy of hint* and *mellowness* of *sneer* which distinguish your Ladyship's scandal.

LADY SNEER. Ah! you are partial, Snake.

SNAKE. Not in the least; everybody allows that Lady Sneerwell can do more with a *word* or a *look* than many can with the most labored detail, even when they happen to have a little truth on their side to support it.

LADY SNEER. Yes, my dear Snake; and I am no hypocrite to deny the satisfaction I reap from the success of my efforts. Wounded myself, in the early part of my life, by the envenomed tongue of slander, I confess I have since known no pleasure equal to the reducing others to the level of my own injured reputation.

SNAKE. Nothing can be more natural. But, Lady Sneerwell, there is one affair in which you have lately employed me, wherein, I confess, I am at a loss to guess your motives.

LADY SNEER. I conceive you mean with respect to my neighbor, Sir Peter Teazle, and his family?

SNAKE. I do. Here are two young men to whom Sir Peter has acted as a kind of guardian since their father's death: the eldest possessing the most amiable character, and universally well spoken of; the youngest, the most dissipated and extravagant young fellow in the kingdom, without friends or character; the former an avowed admirer of your Ladyship, and apparently your favorite; the latter attached to Maria, Sir Peter's ward, and confessedly beloved by her. Now, on the face of these circumstances, it is utterly unaccountable to me why you, the widow of a city knight,[10] with a good jointure,[11] should not close[12] with the passion of a man of such character

---

[5] Positively.   [6] Substituted for the victim's name.
[7] One of the most fashionable residential squares in the West End.
[9] A gossip sheet of the time.

[8] On *The Rivals*, two years before.
[10] I.e., not a courtier, but a merchant who had been knighted.
[11] An estate settled on a wife.   [12] Come to terms.

RICHARD BRINSLEY SHERIDAN   939

and expectations as Mr. Surface; and more so, why you should be so uncommonly earnest to destroy the mutual attachment subsisting between his brother Charles and Maria.

LADY SNEER. Then at once to unravel this mystery, I must inform you that love has no share whatever in the intercourse between Mr. Surface and me.

SNAKE. No!

LADY SNEER. His real attachment is to Maria, or her fortune; but, finding in his brother a favored rival, he has been obliged to mask his pretensions, and profit by my assistance.

SNAKE. Yet still I am more puzzled why you should interest yourself in his success.

LADY SNEER. Heavens! how dull you are! Cannot you surmise the weakness which I hitherto, through shame, have concealed even from *you*? Must I confess that Charles, that libertine, that extravagant, that bankrupt in fortune and reputation—that he it is for whom I am thus anxious and malicious, and to gain whom I would sacrifice everything?

SNAKE. Now, indeed, your conduct appears consistent; but how came you and Mr. Surface so confidential?

LADY SNEER. For our mutual interest. I have found him out a long time since. I know him to be artful, selfish, and malicious—in short, a sentimental knave.

SNAKE. Yet Sir Peter vows he has not his equal in England—and, above all, he praises him as a man of sentiment.

LADY SNEER. True—and, with the assistance of his sentiment and hypocrisy, he has brought Sir Peter entirely into his interest with regard to Maria; while poor Charles has no friend in the house, though I fear he has a powerful one in Maria's heart, against whom we must direct our schemes.

Enter Servant

SERV. Mr. Surface.

LADY SNEER. Show him up. (*Exit* Servant.) He generally calls about this time. I don't wonder at people giving him to me for a lover.

Enter JOSEPH SURFACE

JOSEPH. My dear Lady Sneerwell, how do you do today?—Mr. Snake, your most obedient.

LADY SNEER. Snake has just been arraigning me on our mutual attachment, but I have informed him of our real views. You know how useful he has been to us, and, believe me, the confidence is not ill placed.

JOSEPH. Madam, it is impossible for me to suspect a man of Mr. Snake's sensibility and discernment.

LADY SNEER. Well, well, no compliments now; but tell me when you saw your mistress, Maria—or, what is more material to me, your brother.

JOSEPH. I have not seen either since I left you; but I can inform you that they never meet. Some of your stories have taken a good effect on Maria.

LADY SNEER. Ah! my dear Snake! the merit of this belongs to you.—But do your brother's distresses increase?

JOSEPH. Every hour. I am told he has had another execution[13] in the house yesterday. In short, his dissipation and extravagance exceed anything I ever heard of.

LADY SNEER. Poor Charles!

JOSEPH. True, madam; notwithstanding his vices, one cannot help feeling for him. Ay, poor Charles! I'm sure I wish it was in *my* power to be of any essential service to him. For the man who does not share in the distresses of a brother, even though merited by his own misconduct, deserves—

LADY SNEER. Oh, Lud![14] you are going to be moral, and forget that you are among friends.

JOSEPH. Egad, that's true!—I'll keep that sentiment till I see Sir Peter. However, it is certainly a charity to rescue Maria from such a libertine, who, if he is to be reclaimed, can be so only by a person of your Ladyship's superior accomplishments and understanding.

SNAKE. I believe, Lady Sneerwell, here's company coming; I'll go and copy the letter I mentioned to you.—Mr. Surface, your most obedient. [*Exit*

JOSEPH. Sir, your very devoted.—Lady Sneerwell, I am very sorry you have put any further confidence in that fellow.

LADY SNEER. Why so?

JOSEPH. I have lately detected him in frequent conference with old Rowley, who was formerly my father's steward, and has never, you know, been a friend of mine.

LADY SNEER. And do you think he would betray us?

JOSEPH. Nothing more likely; take my word for't, Lady Sneerwell, that fellow hasn't virtue enough to be faithful even to his own villainy.—Hah! Maria!

---

13 Seizure of goods by legal action.   14 Lord.

Enter MARIA

LADY SNEER. Maria, my dear, how do you do? What's the matter?

MARIA. Oh! there is that disagreeable lover of mine, Sir Benjamin Backbite, has just called at my guardian's, with his odious uncle, Crabtree; so I slipped out, and run hither to avoid them.

LADY SNEER. Is that all?

JOSEPH. If my brother Charles had been of the party, madam, perhaps you would not have been so much alarmed.

LADY SNEER. Nay, now you are severe; for I dare swear the truth of the matter is, Maria heard *you* were here.—But, my dear, what has Sir Benjamin done, that you should avoid him so?

MARIA. Oh, he has done nothing; but 'tis for what he has said: his conversation is a perpetual libel on all his acquaintance.

JOSEPH. Ay, and the worst of it is, there is no advantage in not knowing him; for he'll abuse a stranger just as soon as his best friend; and his uncle's as bad.

LADY SNEER. Nay, but we should make allowance; Sir Benjamin is a wit and a poet.

MARIA. For my part, I confess, madam, wit loses its respect with me when I see it in company with malice.—What do you think, Mr. Surface?

JOSEPH. Certainly, madam; to smile at the jest which plants a thorn in another's breast is to become a principal in the mischief.

LADY SNEER. Pshaw! there's no possibility of being witty without a little ill nature: the malice of a good thing is the barb that makes it stick.—What's your opinion, Mr. Surface?

JOSEPH. To be sure, madam, that conversation where the spirit of raillery is suppressed will ever appear tedious and insipid.

MARIA. Well, I'll not debate how far scandal may be allowable; but in a man, I am sure, it is always contemptible. We have pride, envy, rivalship, and a thousand motives to depreciate each other; but the male slanderer must have the cowardice of a woman before he can traduce one.

Enter Servant

SERV. Madam, Mrs. Candour is below, and, if your Ladyship's at leisure, will leave her carriage.

LADY SNEER. Beg her to walk in. (*Exit* Servant.) Now, Maria, here is a character to your taste; for though Mrs. Candour is a little talkative, everybody allows her to be the best-natured and best sort of woman.

MARIA. Yes, with a very gross affectation of good nature and benevolence, she does more mischief than the direct malice of old Crabtree.

JOSEPH. I' faith, that's true, Lady Sneerwell; whenever I hear the current running against the characters of my friends, I never think them in such danger as when Candour undertakes their defense.

LADY SNEER. Hush! here she is!

Enter MRS. CANDOUR

MRS. CAN. My dear Lady Sneerwell, how have you been this century?—Mr. Surface, what news do you hear? though indeed it is no matter, for I think one hears nothing else but scandal.

JOSEPH. Just so, indeed, madam.

MRS. CAN. Ah, Maria! child, what, is the whole affair off between you and Charles? His extravagance, I presume; the town talks of nothing else.

MARIA. Indeed! I am very sorry, ma'am, the town has so little to do.

MRS. CAN. True, true, child; but there is no stopping people's tongues. I own I was hurt to hear it, as I indeed was to learn, from the same quarter, that your guardian, Sir Peter, and Lady Teazle have not agreed lately so well as could be wished.

MARIA. 'Tis strangely impertinent for people to busy themselves so.

MRS. CAN. Very true, child; but what's to be done? People will talk; there's no preventing it. Why, it was but yesterday I was told that Miss Gadabout had eloped with Sir Filigree Flirt. But, Lord! there's no minding what one hears; though, to be sure, I had this from very good authority.

MARIA. Such reports are highly scandalous.

MRS. CAN. So they are, child; shameful, shameful! But the world is so censorious, no character escapes. —Lord, now who would have suspected your friend, Miss Prim, of an indiscretion? Yet such is the ill nature of people that they say her uncle stopped her last week, just as she was stepping into the York diligence[15] with her dancing master.

MARIA. I'll answer for't there are no grounds for the report.

MRS. CAN. Oh, no foundation in the world, I dare swear; no more, probably, than for the story circulated last month, of Mrs. Festino's affair with Colonel Cassino—though, to be sure, that matter was never rightly cleared up.

---

15 Stagecoach.

JOSEPH. The license of invention some people take is monstrous indeed.

MARIA. 'Tis so—but, in my opinion, those who report such things are equally culpable.

MRS. CAN. To be sure they are; talebearers are as bad as the talemakers—'tis an old observation, and a very true one; but what's to be done, as I said before? how will you prevent people from talking? Today, Mrs. Clackitt assured me Mr. and Mrs. Honeymoon were at last become mere man and wife, like the rest of their acquaintance. She likewise hinted that a certain widow, in the next street, had got rid of her dropsy and recovered her shape in a most surprising manner. And at the same time, Miss Tattle, who was by, affirmed that Lord Buffalo had discovered his lady at a house of no extraordinary fame; and that Sir Harry Bouquet and Tom Saunter were to measure swords on a similar provocation.— But, Lord, do you think I would report these things? No, no! talebearers, as I said before, are just as bad as the talemakers.

JOSEPH. Ah! Mrs. Candour, if everybody had your forbearance and good nature!

MRS. CAN. I confess, Mr. Surface, I cannot bear to hear people attacked behind their backs; and when ugly circumstances come out against one's acquaintance, I own I always love to think the best.— By-the-bye, I hope it is not true that your brother is absolutely ruined.

JOSEPH. I am afraid his circumstances are very bad indeed, ma'am.

MRS. CAN. Ah! I heard so—but you must tell him to keep up his spirits; everybody almost is in the same way—Lord Spindle, Sir Thomas Splint, Captain Quinze, and Mr. Nickit—all up, I hear, within this week; so if Charles is undone, he'll find half his acquaintance ruined too, and that, you know, is a consolation.

JOSEPH. Doubtless, ma'am—a very great one.

Enter Servant

SERV. Mr. Crabtree and Sir Benjamin Backbite.   [*Exit*

LADY SNEER. So, Maria, you see your lover pursues you; positively you shan't escape.

Enter CRABTREE *and* SIR BENJAMIN BACKBITE

CRAB. Lady Sneerwell, I kiss your hands.—Mrs. Candour, I don't believe you are acquainted with my nephew, Sir Benjamin Backbite? Egad! ma'am, he has a pretty wit, and is a pretty poet too; isn't he, Lady Sneerwell?

SIR BEN. Oh, fie, uncle!

CRAB. Nay, egad, it's true; I back him at a rebus or a charade against the best rimer in the kingdom. —Has your Ladyship heard the epigram he wrote last week on Lady Frizzle's feather catching fire?— Do, Benjamin, repeat it, or the charade you made last night extempore at Mrs. Drowzie's *conversazione*.[16] Come now;—your *first* is the name of a fish, your *second* a great naval commander, and—

SIR BEN. Uncle, now—prithee—

CRAB. I'faith, ma'am, 'twould surprise you to hear how ready he is at these things.

LADY SNEER. I wonder, Sir Benjamin, you never publish anything.

SIR BEN. To say truth, ma'am, 'tis very vulgar to print; and as my little productions are mostly satires and lampoons on particular people, I find they circulate more by giving copies in confidence to the friends of the parties. However, I have some love elegies, which, when favored with this lady's smiles, I mean to give to the public.

CRAB. 'Fore heaven, ma'am, they'll immortalize you!—you'll be handed down to posterity, like Petrarch's Laura,[17] or Waller's Sacharissa.

SIR BEN. Yes, madam, I think you will like them, when you shall see them on a beautiful quarto page, where a neat rivulet of text shall murmur through a meadow of margin.[18] 'Fore Gad, they will be the most elegant things of their kind!

CRAB. But, ladies, that's true. Have you heard the news?

MRS. CAN. What, sir, do you mean the report of—

CRAB. No, ma'am, that's not it.—Miss Nicely is going to be married to her own footman.

MRS. CAN. Impossible!

CRAB. Ask Sir Benjamin.

SIR BEN. 'Tis very true, ma'am; everything is fixed, and the wedding liveries bespoke.

CRAB. Yes; and they *do* say there were pressing reasons for it.

LADY SNEER. Why, I *have* heard something of this before.

MRS. CAN. It can't be; and I wonder anyone should believe such a story of so prudent a lady as Miss Nicely.

---

16 Social gathering for conversation on literature, art, etc.
17 To whom the sonnets of Petrarch were addressed, as some of Waller's poems (pp. 517–19, above) were to "Sacharissa" (Lady Dorothy Sidney).   18 Marginal notes.

SIR BEN. Oh, Lud! ma'am, that's the very reason 'twas believed at once. She has always been so *cautious* and so *reserved,* that everybody was sure there was some reason for it at bottom.

MRS. CAN. Why, to be sure, a tale of scandal is as fatal to the credit of a prudent lady of her stamp as a fever is generally to those of the strongest constitutions; but there is a sort of puny, sickly reputation, that is always ailing, yet will outlive the robuster characters of a hundred prudes.

SIR BEN. True, madam; there are valetudinarians in reputation as well as constitution; who, being conscious of their weak part, avoid the least breath of air, and supply their want of stamina by care and circumspection.

MRS. CAN. Well, but this may be all a mistake. You know, Sir Benjamin, very trifling circumstances often give rise to the most injurious tales.

CRAB. That they do, I'll be sworn, ma'am. Did you ever hear how Miss Piper came to lose her lover and her character last summer at Tunbridge?[19]—Sir Benjamin, you remember it?

SIR BEN. Oh, to be sure!—the most whimsical circumstance.

LADY SNEER. How was it, pray?

CRAB. Why, one evening, at Mrs. Ponto's assembly, the conversation happened to turn on the difficulty of breeding Nova Scotia sheep in this country. Says a young lady in company, "I have known instances of it; for Miss Letitia Piper, a first cousin of mine, had a Nova Scotia sheep that produced her twins."—"What!" cries the dowager Lady Dundizzy (who you know is as deaf as a post), "has Miss Piper had twins?" This mistake, as you may imagine, threw the whole company into a fit of laughing. However, 'twas the next morning everywhere reported, and in a few days believed by the whole town, that Miss Letitia Piper had actually been brought to bed of a fine boy and a girl; and in less than a week there were some people who could name the father, and the farmhouse where the babies were put out to nurse.

LADY SNEER. Strange, indeed!

CRAB. Matter of fact, I assure you.—Oh, Lud! Mr. Surface, pray is it true that your uncle, Sir Oliver, is coming home?

JOSEPH. Not that I know of, indeed, sir.

CRAB. He has been in the East Indies a long time. You can scarcely remember him, I believe. Sad comfort whenever he returns, to hear how your brother has gone on!

JOSEPH. Charles has been imprudent, sir, to be sure; but I hope no busy people have already prejudiced Sir Oliver against him—he may reform.

SIR BEN. To be sure he may; for my part, I never believed him to be so utterly void of principle as people say; and though he has lost all his friends, I am told nobody is better spoken of by the Jews.

CRAB. That's true, egad, nephew. If the Old Jewry[20] was a ward, I believe Charles would be an alderman; no man more popular there, 'fore Gad! I hear he pays as many annuities as the Irish tontine;[21] and that, whenever he is sick, they have prayers for the recovery of his health in the synagogues.

SIR BEN. Yet no man lives in greater splendor. They tell me when he entertains his friends he can sit down to dinner with a dozen of his own securities, have a score of tradesmen waiting in the antechamber, and an officer behind every guest's chair.

JOSEPH. This may be entertainment to you, gentlemen, but you pay very little regard to the feelings of a brother.

MARIA (*aside*). Their malice is intolerable!—Lady Sneerwell, I must wish you a good morning; I'm not very well. [*Exit*

MRS. CAN. Oh, dear! she changes color very much!

LADY SNEER. Do, Mrs. Candour, follow her: she may want assistance.

MRS. CAN. That I will, with all my soul, ma'am.—Poor dear girl, who knows what her situation may be! [*Exit*

LADY SNEER. 'Twas nothing but that she could not bear to hear Charles reflected on, notwithstanding their difference.

SIR BEN. The young lady's penchant is obvious.

CRAB. But, Benjamin, you mustn't give up the pursuit for that—follow her, and put her into good humor. Repeat her some of your own verses. Come, I'll assist you.

SIR BEN. Mr. Surface, I did not mean to hurt you; but depend upon't your brother is utterly undone. [*Going*

CRAB. Oh, Lud, ay! undone as ever man was—can't raise a guinea! [*Going*

SIR BEN. Everything sold, I am told, that was movable. [*Going*

CRAB. I have seen one that was at his house—not a thing left but some empty bottles that were over-

---

[19] Tunbridge Wells, a resort in Kent.

[20] A London street where moneylenders lived.

[21] An insurance scheme by which the government raised money. Subscribers received life annuities, the amount of which increased as the number of subscribers was reduced by death. The scheme got its name from its inventor, Tonti, a seventeenth-century Neapolitan banker.

looked, and the family pictures, which I believe are framed in the wainscot. [*Going*

SIR BEN. And I am very sorry to hear also some bad stories against him. [*Going*

CRAB. Oh, he has done many mean things, that's certain.

SIR BEN. But, however, as he's your brother— [*Going*

CRAB. We'll tell you all another opportunity.

[*Exeunt* CRABTREE *and* SIR BENJAMIN

LADY SNEER. Ha! ha! ha! 'tis very hard for them to leave a subject they have not quite run down.

JOSEPH. And I believe the abuse was not more acceptable to your Ladyship than to Maria.

LADY SNEER. I doubt[22] her affections are farther engaged than we imagined. But the family are to be here this evening; so you may as well dine where you are, and we shall have an opportunity of observing farther—in the meantime, I'll go and plot mischief, and you shall study sentiments. [*Exeunt*

SCENE II. SIR PETER TEAZLE'S *house*

Enter SIR PETER

SIR PETER. When an old bachelor takes a young wife, what is he to expect? 'Tis now six months since Lady Teazle made me the happiest of men—and I have been the miserablest dog ever since that ever committed wedlock! We tiffed a little going to church, and came to a quarrel before the bells were done ringing. I was more than once nearly choked with gall during the honeymoon, and had lost all comfort in life before my friends had done wishing me joy! Yet I chose with caution—a girl bred wholly in the country, who never knew luxury beyond one silk gown, nor dissipation beyond the annual gala of a race ball. Yet now she plays her part in all the extravagant fopperies of the fashion and the town, with as ready a grace as if she had never seen a bush or a grass-plot out of Grosvenor Square! I am sneered at by my old acquaintance—paragraphed in the newspapers. She dissipates my fortune, and contradicts all my humors; yet the worst of it is, I doubt I love her, or I should never bear all this. However, I'll never be weak enough to own it.

Enter ROWLEY

ROW. Oh, Sir Peter, your servant; how is it with you, sir?

SIR PETER. Very bad, Master Rowley, very bad. I meet with nothing but crosses and vexations.

ROW. What can have happened to trouble you since yesterday?

SIR PETER. A good question to a married man!

ROW. Nay, I'm sure your lady, Sir Peter, can't be the cause of your uneasiness.

SIR PETER. Why, has anyone told you she was dead?

ROW. Come, come, Sir Peter, you love her, notwithstanding your tempers don't exactly agree.

SIR PETER. But the fault is entirely hers, Master Rowley. I am, myself, the sweetest-tempered man alive, and hate a teasing temper; and so I tell her a hundred times a day.

ROW. Indeed!

SIR PETER. Ay; and what is very extraordinary, in all our disputes she is always in the wrong! But Lady Sneerwell, and the set she meets at her house, encourage the perverseness of her disposition. Then, to complete my vexation, Maria, my ward, whom I ought to have the power of a father over, is determined to turn rebel too, and absolutely refuses the man whom I have long resolved on for her husband; meaning, I suppose, to bestow herself on his profligate brother.

ROW. You know, Sir Peter, I have always taken the liberty to differ with you on the subject of these two young gentlemen. I only wish you may not be deceived in your opinion of the elder. For Charles, my life on 't, he will retrieve his errors yet. Their worthy father, once my honored master, was at his years nearly as wild a spark; yet when he died, he did not leave a more benevolent heart to lament his loss.

SIR PETER. You are wrong, Master Rowley. On their father's death, you know, I acted as a kind of guardian to them both till their uncle Sir Oliver's liberality gave them an early independence. Of course, no person could have more opportunities of judging of their hearts, and I was never mistaken in my life. Joseph is indeed a model for the young men of the age. He is a man of sentiment, and acts up to the sentiments he professes; but for the other, take my word for 't, if he had any grains of virtue by descent, he has dissipated them with the rest of his inheritance. Ah! my old friend Sir Oliver will be deeply mortified when he finds how part of his bounty has been misapplied.

ROW. I am sorry to find you so violent against the

---

[22] Suspect.

young man, because this may be the most critical period of his fortune. I came hither with news that will surprise you.

SIR PETER. What! Let me hear!

ROW. Sir Oliver *is* arrived and at this moment in town.

SIR PETER. How! You astonish me! I thought you did not expect him this month.

ROW. I did not; but his passage has been remarkably quick.

SIR PETER. Egad, I shall rejoice to see my old friend. 'Tis sixteen years since we met. We have had many a day together. But does he still enjoin us not to inform his nephews of his arrival?

ROW. Most strictly. He means, before it is known, to make some trial of their dispositions.

SIR PETER. Ah! There needs no art to discover their merits. He shall have his way; but, pray, does he know I am married?

ACT II

SCENE I. SIR PETER's *house*

Enter SIR PETER *and* LADY TEAZLE

SIR PETER. Lady Teazle, Lady Teazle, I'll not bear it!

LADY T. Sir Peter, Sir Peter, you may bear it or not as you please; but I ought to have my own way in everything, and, what's more, I *will*, too. What! though I was educated in the country, I know very well that women of fashion in London are accountable to nobody after they are married.

SIR PETER. Very well, ma'am, very well; so a husband is to have no influence, no authority?

LADY T. Authority! No, to be sure! If you wanted authority over me, you should have adopted me, and not married me; I am sure you were old enough.

SIR PETER. Old enough! ay, there it is. Well, well, Lady Teazle, though my life may be made unhappy by your temper, I'll not be ruined by your extravagance.

LADY T. My extravagance! I'm sure I'm not more extravagant than a woman of fashion ought to be.

SIR PETER. No, no, madam, you shall throw away no more sums on such unmeaning luxury. 'Slife![1] to spend as much to furnish your dressing-room with flowers in winter as would suffice to turn the Pan-

ROW. Yes, and will soon wish you joy.

SIR PETER. What, as we drink health to a friend in a consumption? Ah! Oliver will laugh at me. We used to rail at matrimony together, but he has been steady to his text. Well, he must be at my house, though—I'll instantly give orders for his reception. But, Master Rowley, don't drop a word that Lady Teazle and I ever disagree.

ROW. By no means.

SIR PETER. For I should never be able to stand Noll's jokes; so I'd have him think, Lord forgive me! that we are a very happy couple.

ROW. I understand you; but then you must be very careful not to differ while he is in the house with you.

SIR PETER. Egad, and so we must—and that's impossible. Ah! Master Rowley, when an old bachelor marries a young wife, he deserves—no, the crime carries its punishment along with it.

[*Exeunt*

theon[2] into a greenhouse, and give a *fête champêtre*[3] at Christmas.

LADY T. Lord, Sir Peter, am I to blame because flowers are dear in cold weather? You should find fault with the climate, and not with me. For my part, I'm sure I wish it was spring all the year round, and that roses grew under one's feet.

SIR PETER. Oons![4] madam; if you had been born to this, I shouldn't wonder at your talking thus; but you forget what your situation was when I married you.

LADY T. No, no, I don't; 'twas a very disagreeable one, or I should never have married *you*.

SIR PETER. Yes, yes, madam; you were then in somewhat an humbler style: the daughter of a plain country squire. Recollect, Lady Teazle, when I saw you first sitting at your tambour,[5] in a pretty figured linen gown, with a bunch of keys by your side, your hair combed smooth over a roll, and your apartment hung round with fruits in worsted, of your own working.

LADY T. Oh, yes! I remember it very well, and a curious life I led—my daily occupation to inspect the dairy, superintend the poultry, make extracts

---

[1] Literally, by God's life.

[2] A new and fashionable hall in Oxford Street, with rooms for balls, concerts, refreshments, etc.   [3] Outdoor party.
[4] Literally, by God's wounds.
[5] Embroidery frame (of two hoops, one fitting tightly inside the other).

from the family receipt book, and comb my aunt Deborah's lap dog.

SIR PETER. Yes, yes, ma'am, 'twas so indeed.

LADY T. And then, you know, my evening amusements! To draw patterns for ruffles, which I had not the materials to make up; to play Pope Joan[6] with the curate; to read a sermon to my aunt; or to be stuck down to an old spinet to strum my father to sleep after a fox-chase.

SIR PETER. I am glad you have so good a memory. Yes, madam, these were the recreations I took you from; but now you must have your coach—vis-à-vis[7]—and three powdered footmen before your chair;[8] and in the summer, a pair of white cats[9] to draw you to Kensington Gardens.[10] No recollection, I suppose, when you were content to ride double, behind the butler, on a docked coach horse?

LADY T. No; I swear I never did that. I deny the butler and the coach horse.

SIR PETER. This, madam, was your situation; and what have I done for you? I have made you a woman of fashion, of fortune, of rank; in short, I have made you my wife.

LADY T. Well, then, and there is but one thing more you can make me to add to the obligation, and that is—

SIR PETER. My widow, I suppose?

LADY T. Hem! hem!

SIR PETER. I thank you, madam; but don't flatter yourself; for though your ill conduct may disturb my peace, it shall never break my heart, I promise you; however, I am equally obliged to you for the hint.

LADY T. Then why will you endeavor to make yourself so disagreeable to me, and thwart me in every little elegant expense?

SIR PETER. 'Slife, madam, I say, had you any of these little elegant expenses when you married me?

LADY T. Lud, Sir Peter! would you have me be out of the fashion?

SIR PETER. The fashion, indeed! what had you to do with the fashion before you married me?

LADY T. For my part, I should think you would like to have your wife thought a woman of taste.

SIR PETER. Ay—there again—taste! Zounds! madam, you had no taste when you married me!

LADY T. That's very true indeed, Sir Peter! and after having married you, I should never pretend to taste again! But now, Sir Peter, if we have finished our daily jangle, I presume I may go to my engagement at Lady Sneerwell's?

SIR PETER. Ay, there's another precious circumstance; a charming set of acquaintance you have made there!

LADY T. Nay, Sir Peter, they are all people of rank and fortune, and remarkably tenacious of reputation.

SIR PETER. Yes, egad, they are tenacious of reputation with a vengeance; for they don't choose anybody should have a character but themselves! Such a crew! Ah! many a wretch has rid on a hurdle[11] who has done less mischief than these utterers of forged tales, coiners of scandal, and clippers of reputation.

LADY T. What! would you restrain the freedom of speech?

SIR PETER. Oh! they have made you just as bad as any one of the society.

LADY T. Why, I believe I do bear a part with a tolerable grace. But I vow I have no malice against the people I abuse. When I say an ill-natured thing, 'tis out of pure good humor; and I take it for granted they deal exactly in the same manner with me. But, Sir Peter, you know you promised to come to Lady Sneerwell's too.

SIR PETER. Well, well, I'll call in just to look after my own character.

LADY T. Then indeed you must make haste after me, or you'll be too late. So, good-by to ye. [Exit

SIR PETER. So, I have gained much by my intended expostulation! Yet, with what a charming air she contradicts everything I say, and how pleasingly she shows her contempt for my authority! Well, though I can't make her love me, there is great satisfaction in quarreling with her; and I think she never appears to such advantage as when she is doing everything in her power to plague me. [Exit

SCENE II. *At* LADY SNEERWELL'S

LADY SNEERWELL, MRS. CANDOUR, CRABTREE, SIR BENJAMIN BACKBITE, *and* JOSEPH SURFACE.

LADY SNEER. Nay, positively, we will hear it.

JOSEPH. Yes, yes, the epigram, by all means.

SIR BEN. Oh, plague on't, uncle! 'tis mere nonsense.

CRAB. No, no; 'fore Gad, very clever for an extempore!

---

6 A card game.
7 I.e., of a type with seats facing each other.   8 Sedan chair.
9 Ponies.   10 Still a much frequented West End park.

11 The sled or drag on which criminals were hauled to the place of execution.

SIR BEN. But, ladies, you should be acquainted with the circumstance. You must know that one day last week, as Lady Betty Curricle was taking the dust in Hyde Park, in a sort of duodecimo[12] phaeton, she desired me to write some verses on her ponies; upon which, I took out my pocketbook, and in one moment produced the following:

> Sure never were seen two such beautiful ponies!
> Other horses are clowns, but these macaronies:[13]
> To give 'em this title I'm sure isn't wrong,
> Their legs are so slim, and their tails are so long.

CRAB. There, ladies, done in the smack of a whip, and on horseback too!

JOSEPH. A very Phoebus,[14] mounted—indeed, Sir Benjamin.

SIR BEN. Oh, dear sir—trifles—trifles.

Enter LADY TEAZLE *and* MARIA

MRS. CAN. I must have a copy.

LADY SNEER. Lady Teazle, I hope we shall see Sir Peter?

LADY T. I believe he'll wait on your Ladyship presently.

LADY SNEER. Maria, my love, you look grave. Come, you shall sit down to cards with Mr. Surface.

MARIA. I take very little pleasure in cards—however, I'll do as your Ladyship pleases.

LADY T. (*aside*). I am surprised Mr. Surface should sit down with *her;* I thought he would have embraced this opportunity of speaking to me before Sir Peter came.

MRS. CAN. Now, I'll die but you are so scandalous, I'll forswear your society.

LADY T. What's the matter, Mrs. Candour?

MRS. CAN. They'll not allow our friend Miss Vermilion to be handsome.

LADY SNEER. Oh, surely she's a pretty woman.

CRAB. I am very glad you think so, madam.

MRS. CAN. She has a charming fresh color.

LADY T. Yes, when it is fresh put on.

MRS. CAN. Oh, fie! I'll swear her color is natural: I have seen it come and go.

LADY T. I dare swear you have, ma'am; it goes of a night, and comes again in the morning.

MRS. CAN. Ha! ha! ha! how I hate to hear you talk so! But surely now, her sister *is,* or *was,* very handsome.

CRAB. Who? Mrs. Evergreen? Oh, Lord! She's six-and-fifty if she's an hour!

MRS. CAN. Now positively you wrong her; fifty-two or fifty-three is the utmost—and I don't think she looks more.

SIR BEN. Ah! there's no judging by her looks, unless one could see her face.

LADY SNEER. Well, well, if Mrs. Evergreen *does* take some pains to repair the ravages of time, you must allow she effects it with great ingenuity; and surely that's better than the careless manner in which the widow Ochre caulks her wrinkles.

SIR BEN. Nay, now, Lady Sneerwell, you are severe upon the widow. Come, come, 'tis not that she paints so ill—but when she has finished her face, she joins it so badly to her neck that she looks like a mended statue in which the connoisseur sees at once that the head's modern, though the trunk's antique.

CRAB. Ha! ha! ha! Well said, nephew!

MRS. CAN. Ha! ha! ha! Well, you make me laugh; but I vow I hate you for it.—What do you think of Miss Simper?

SIR BEN. Why, she has very pretty teeth.

LADY T. Yes; and on that account, when she is neither speaking nor laughing (which very seldom happens), she never absolutely shuts her mouth, but leaves it always on a jar, as it were.

MRS. CAN. How can you be so ill-natured?

LADY T. Nay, I'll allow even that's better than the pains Mrs. Prim takes to conceal her losses in front. She draws her mouth till it positively resembles the aperture of a poor's box,[15] and all her words appear to slide out edgeways.

LADY SNEER. Very well, Lady Teazle; I see you can be a little severe.

LADY T. In defense of a friend it is but justice.— But here comes Sir Peter to spoil our pleasantry.

Enter SIR PETER TEAZLE

SIR PETER. Ladies, your most obedient.—(*Aside*) Mercy on me! here is the whole set! a character dead at every word, I suppose.

MRS. CAN. I am rejoiced you are come, Sir Peter. They have been *so* censorious—they will allow good qualities to nobody; not even good nature to our friend Mrs. Pursy.

LADY T. What, the fat dowager who was at Mrs. Codille's last night?

---

[12] I.e., diminutive (duodecimo being one of the smallest book sizes).   [13] Dandies.   [14] Apollo, god of poetry.

[15] Contribution box in a church for the poor of the parish.

MRS. CAN. Nay, her bulk is her misfortune; and when she takes such pains to get rid of it, you ought not to reflect on her.

LADY SNEER. That's very true, indeed.

LADY T. Yes, I know she almost lives on acids and small[16] whey; laces herself by pulleys; and often, in the hottest noon in summer, you may see her on a little squat pony, with her hair plaited up behind like a drummer's, and puffing round the Ring[17] on a full trot.

MRS. CAN. I thank you, Lady Teazle, for defending her.

SIR PETER. Yes, a good defense, truly!

MRS. CAN. But Sir Benjamin is as censorious as Miss Shallow.

CRAB. Yes, and she is a curious being to pretend to be censorious—an awkward gawky, without any one good point under heaven.

MRS. CAN. Positively you shall not be so very severe. Miss Sallow is a relation of mine by marriage, and, as for her person, great allowance is to be made; for, let me tell you, a woman labors under many disadvantages who tries to pass for a girl at six-and-thirty.

LADY SNEER. Though, surely, she is handsome still—and for the weakness in her eyes, considering how much she reads by candlelight, it is not to be wondered at.

MRS. CAN. True; and then, as to her manner, upon my word I think it is particularly graceful, considering she never had the least education: for you know her mother was a Welsh milliner, and her father a sugar-baker at Bristol.

SIR BEN. Ah! you are both of you too good-natured!

SIR PETER (aside). Yes, damned good-natured! This their own relation! mercy on me!

SIR BEN. And Mrs. Candour is of so moral a turn, she can sit for an hour and hear Lady Stucco talk sentiments.

LADY T. Nay, I vow Lady Stucco is very well with the dessert after dinner; for she's just like the French fruit one cracks for mottoes—made up of paint and proverb.

MRS. CAN. Well, I never will join in ridiculing a friend; and so I constantly tell my cousin Ogle, and you all know what pretensions she has to be critical on beauty.

CRAB. Oh, to be sure! she has herself the oddest countenance that ever was seen; 'tis a collection of features from all the different countries of the globe.

SIR BEN. So she has, indeed—an Irish front[18]—

CRAB. Caledonian locks—

SIR BEN. Dutch nose—

CRAB. Austrian lip—

SIR BEN. Complexion of a Spaniard—

CRAB. And teeth à la Chinoise![19]

SIR BEN. In short, her face resembles a table d'hôte at Spa[20]—where no two guests are of a nation—

CRAB. Or a congress at the close of a general war—wherein all the members, even to her eyes, appear to have a different interest, and her nose and chin are the only parties likely to join issue.

MRS. CAN. Ha! ha! ha!

SIR PETER (aside). Mercy on my life!—a person they dine with twice a week.

LADY SNEER. Go, go; you are a couple of provoking toads.

MRS. CAN. Nay, but I vow you shall not carry the laugh off so—for give me leave to say that Mrs. Ogle—

SIR PETER. Madam, madam, I beg your pardon—there's no stopping these good gentlemen's tongues.—But when I tell you, Mrs. Candour, that the lady they are abusing is a particular friend of mine, I hope you'll not take her part.

LADY SNEER. Well said, Sir Peter! but you are a cruel creature—too phlegmatic yourself for a jest, and too peevish to allow wit in others.

SIR PETER. Ah, madam, true wit is more nearly allied to good nature than your Ladyship is aware of.

LADY T. True, Sir Peter. I believe they are so near akin that they can never be united.[21]

SIR BEN. Or rather, madam, suppose them to be man and wife, because one seldom sees them together.

LADY T. But Sir Peter is such an enemy to scandal, I believe he would have it put down by Parliament.

SIR PETER. 'Fore heaven, madam, if they were to consider the sporting with reputation of as much importance as poaching on manors, and pass an Act for the preservation of fame, I believe there are many would thank them for the bill.

LADY SNEER. Oh, Lud! Sir Peter; would you deprive us of our privileges?

SIR PETER. Ay, madam; and then no person should be permitted to kill characters and run down reputa-

---

16 Weak; cf. "small beer."
17 The fashionable drive in Hyde Park.

18 Forehead.
19 In Chinese style.   20 The famous Belgian watering place.
21 An allusion to the prohibition of marriage between close relatives.

tions, but qualified old maids and disappointed widows.

LADY SNEER. Go, you monster!

MRS. CAN. But, sure, you would not be quite so severe on those who only report what they hear?

SIR PETER. Yes, madam, I would have law merchant[22] for them too; and in all cases of slander currency, whenever the drawer of the lie was not to be found, the injured parties should have a right to come on any of the endorsers.

CRAB. Well, for my part, I believe there never was a scandalous tale without some foundation.

LADY SNEER. Come, ladies, shall we sit down to cards in the next room?

Enter a Servant, *who whispers* SIR PETER

SIR PETER. I'll be with them directly. (*Exit* Servant.) —(*Aside*) I'll get away unperceived.

LADY SNEER. Sir Peter, you are not going to leave us?

SIR PETER. Your Ladyship must excuse me; I'm called away by particular business. But I leave my character behind me. [*Exit*

SIR BEN. Well, certainly, Lady Teazle, that lord of yours is a strange being; I could tell you some stories of him would make you laugh heartily, if he were not your husband.

LADY T. Oh, pray don't mind that; come, do let's hear them.

[*They join the rest of the company going into the next room*

JOSEPH (*rising with* MARIA). Maria, I see you have no satisfaction in this society.

MARIA. How is it possible I should? If to raise malicious smiles at the infirmities and misfortunes of those who have never injured us be the province of wit or humor, heaven grant me a double portion of dullness!

JOSEPH. Yet they appear more ill-natured than they are; they have no malice at heart.

MARIA. Then is their conduct still more contemptible; for, in my opinion, nothing could excuse the intemperance of their tongues but a natural and ungovernable bitterness of mind.

JOSEPH. But can you, Maria, feel thus for others, and be unkind to me alone? Is hope to be denied the tenderest passion?

MARIA. Why will you distress me by renewing this subject?

JOSEPH. Ah, Maria! you would not treat me thus, and oppose your guardian Sir Peter's will, but that I see that profligate Charles is still a favored rival.

MARIA. Ungenerously urged! But whatever my sentiments are for that unfortunate young man, be assured I shall not feel more bound to give him up because his distresses have lost him the regard even of a brother.

LADY TEAZLE *returns*

JOSEPH. Nay, but Maria, do not leave me with a frown; by all that's honest, I swear (*kneels*)—(*aside*) Gad's life, here's Lady Teazle!—You must not; no, you shall not; for, though I have the greatest regard for Lady Teazle—

MARIA. Lady Teazle!

JOSEPH. Yet were Sir Peter to suspect—

LADY T. (*coming forward*). What is this, pray? Do you take her for me?—Child, you are wanted in the next room. (*Exit* MARIA.)—What is all this, pray?

JOSEPH. Oh, the most unlucky circumstance in nature! Maria has somehow suspected the tender concern I have for your happiness, and threatened to acquaint Sir Peter with her suspicions; and I was just endeavoring to reason with her when you came in.

LADY T. Indeed! but you seemed to adopt a very tender mode of reasoning; do you *usually* argue on your knees?

JOSEPH. Oh, she's a child, and I thought a little bombast—But, Lady Teazle, when are you to give me your judgment on my library, as you promised?

LADY T. No, no; I begin to think it would be imprudent, and you know I admit you as a lover no farther than *fashion* sanctions.

JOSEPH. True, a mere platonic cicisbeo[23]—what every London wife is *entitled* to.

LADY T. Certainly, one must not be out of the fashion. However, I have so many of my country prejudices left, that, though Sir Peter's ill humor may vex me ever so, it never shall provoke me to—

JOSEPH. The only revenge in your power. Well, I applaud your moderation.

LADY T. Go; you are an insinuating wretch! But we shall be missed; let us join the company.

JOSEPH. But we had best not return together.

LADY T. Well, don't stay; for Maria shan't come to hear any more of your *reasoning*, I promise you.

[*Exit*

JOSEPH. A curious dilemma, truly, my politics have run me into! I wanted, at first, only to in-

---

[22] Commercial law.

[23] Gallant of a married woman.

gratiate myself with Lady Teazle, that she might not be my enemy with Maria; and I have, I don't know how, become her serious lover. Sincerely I begin to wish I had never made such a point of gaining so *very good* a character, for it has led me into so many cursed rogueries that I doubt I shall be exposed at last. [*Exit*

SCENE III. SIR PETER TEAZLE'S

Enter ROWLEY *and* SIR OLIVER SURFACE

SIR OLIVER. Ha! ha! ha! So my old friend is married, hey?—a young wife out of the country. Ha! ha! ha! that he should have stood bluff[24] to old bachelor so long, and sink into a husband at last!

ROW. But you must not rally him on the subject, Sir Oliver; 'tis a tender point, I assure you, though he has been married only seven months.

SIR OLIVER. Then he has been just half a year on the stool of repentance! Poor Peter! But you say he has entirely given up Charles; never sees him, hey?

ROW. His prejudice against him is astonishing, and I am sure greatly increased by a jealousy of him with Lady Teazle, which he has been industriously led into by a scandalous society in the neighborhood, who have contributed not a little to Charles's ill name. Whereas the truth is, I believe, if the lady is partial to either of them, his brother is the favorite.

SIR OLIVER. Ay, I know there are a set of malicious, prating, prudent gossips, both male and female, who murder characters to kill time, and will rob a young fellow of his good name before he has years to know the value of it. But I am not to be prejudiced against my nephew by such, I promise you. No, no; if Charles has done nothing false or mean, I shall compound[25] for his extravagance.

ROW. Then, my life on't, you will reclaim him. Ah, sir! it gives me new life to find that *your* heart is not turned against him, and that the son of my good old master has one friend, however, left.

SIR OLIVER. What! shall I forget, Master Rowley, when I was at his years myself? Egad, my brother and I were neither of us very *prudent* youths; and yet, I believe, you have not seen many better men than your old master was.

ROW. Sir, 'tis this reflection gives me assurance that Charles may yet be a credit to his family.—But here comes Sir Peter.

SIR OLIVER. Egad, so he does. Mercy on me! he's greatly altered, and seems to have a settled married look! One may read *husband* in his face at this distance!

Enter SIR PETER TEAZLE

SIR PETER. Ha! Sir Oliver, my old friend! Welcome to England a thousand times!

SIR OLIVER. Thank you, thank you, Sir Peter! And i' faith I am glad to find you well, believe me!

SIR PETER. Oh, 'tis a long time since we met—sixteen years, I doubt, Sir Oliver, and many a cross accident in the time.

SIR OLIVER. Ay, I have had my share. But, what! I find you are married, hey, my old boy! Well, well, it can't be helped; and so—I wish you joy with all my heart!

SIR PETER. Thank you, thank you, Sir Oliver. Yes, I have entered into—the happy state; but we'll not talk of that now.

SIR OLIVER. True, true, Sir Peter. Old friends should not begin on grievances at first meeting. No, no, no.

ROW. (*aside to* SIR OLIVER). Take care, pray, sir.

SIR OLIVER. Well, so one of my nephews is a wild rogue, hey?

SIR PETER. Wild! Ah, my old friend, I grieve for your disappointment there. He's a lost young man, indeed. However, his brother will make you amends; *Joseph* is, indeed, what a youth should be—everybody in the world speaks well of him.

SIR OLIVER. I am sorry to hear it; he has too good a character to be an honest fellow. Everybody speaks well of him! Pshaw! then he has bowed as low to knaves and fools as to the honest dignity of genius and virtue.

SIR PETER. What, Sir Oliver! do you blame him for not making enemies?

SIR OLIVER. Yes, if he has merit enough to deserve them.

SIR PETER. Well, well—you'll be convinced when you know him. 'Tis edification to hear him converse; he professes the noblest sentiments.

SIR OLIVER. Oh! plague of his sentiments! If he salutes me with a scrap of morality in his mouth, I shall be sick directly.—But, however, don't mistake me, Sir Peter; I don't mean to defend Charles's errors: but before I form my judgment of either of them, I intend to make a trial of their hearts, and my friend Rowley and I have planned something for the purpose.

ROW. And Sir Peter shall own he has been for once mistaken.

---

24 Stiff, staunch.   25 Settle, square accounts.

SIR PETER. Oh! my life on Joseph's honor.

SIR OLIVER. Well, come, give us a bottle of good wine, and we'll drink your lady's health, and tell you our scheme.

SIR PETER. *Allons,*[26] then!

SIR OLIVER. And don't, Sir Peter, be so severe against your old friend's son. Odds my life! I am not sorry that he has run out of the course a little: for my part, I hate to see prudence clinging to the green suckers of youth; 'tis like ivy round a sapling, and spoils the growth of the tree.

[*Exeunt*

ACT III

SCENE I. SIR PETER TEAZLE'S *house*

SIR PETER TEAZLE, SIR OLIVER SURFACE, *and* ROWLEY

SIR PETER. Well, then, we will see this fellow first, and have our wine afterwards. But how is this, Master Rowley? I don't see the jet[1] of your scheme.

ROW. Why, sir, this Mr. Stanley, whom I was speaking of, is nearly related to them, by their mother. He was a merchant in Dublin, but has been ruined by a series of undeserved misfortunes. He has applied, by letter, since his confinement, both to Mr. Surface and Charles: from the former he has received nothing but evasive promises of future service, while Charles has done all that his extravagance has left him power to do; and he is, at this time, endeavoring to raise a sum of money, part of which, in the midst of his own distresses, I know he intends for the service of poor Stanley.

SIR OLIVER. Ah!—he is my brother's son.

SIR PETER. Well, but how is Sir Oliver personally to—

ROW. Why, sir, I will inform Charles and his brother that Stanley has obtained permission to apply in person to his friends, and, as they have neither of them ever seen him, let Sir Oliver assume his character, and he will have a fair opportunity of judging, at least, of the benevolence of their dispositions; and believe me, sir, you will find in the youngest brother one who, in the midst of folly and dissipation, has still, as our immortal bard[2] expresses it,

a tear, for pity, and a hand,
Open as day for melting charity.

SIR PETER. Pshaw! What signifies his having an open hand or purse either, when he has nothing left to give? Well, well, make the trial, if you please.

But where is the fellow whom you brought for Sir Oliver to examine, relative to Charles's affairs?

ROW. Below, waiting his commands, and no one can give him better intelligence. This, Sir Oliver, is a friendly Jew, who, to do him justice, has done everything in his power to bring your nephew to a proper sense of his extravagance.

SIR PETER. Pray let us have him in.

ROW. (*calls to* SERVANT). Desire Mr. Moses to walk upstairs.

SIR PETER. But, pray, why should you suppose he will speak the truth?

ROW. Oh, I have convinced him that he has no chance of recovering certain sums advanced to Charles but through the bounty of Sir Oliver, who he knows is arrived; so that you may depend on his fidelity to his own interest. I have also another evidence in my power, one Snake, whom I have detected in a matter little short of forgery, and shall shortly produce him to remove some of *your* prejudices, Sir Peter, relative to Charles and Lady Teazle.

SIR PETER. I have heard too much on that subject.

ROW. Here comes the honest Israelite.

Enter MOSES

This is Sir Oliver.

SIR OLIVER. Sir, I understand you have lately had great dealing with my nephew Charles.

MOSES. Yes, Sir Oliver, I have done all I could for him; but he was ruined before he came to me for assistance.

SIR OLIVER. That was unlucky, truly—you have had no opportunity of showing your talents.

MOSES. None at all; I hadn't the pleasure of knowing his distresses till he was some thousands worse than nothing.

SIR OLIVER. Unfortunate, indeed! But I suppose you have done all in your power for him, honest Moses?

MOSES. Yes, he knows that. This very evening I was to have brought him a gentleman from the

---

[26] Let's go.

[1] Point, pith.

[2] Shakespeare (*2 Henry IV*, IV, iv, 31-2).

city, who does not know him, and will, I believe, advance him some money.

SIR PETER. What, one Charles has never had money from before?

MOSES. Yes; Mr. Premium, of Crutched Friars,[3] formerly a broker.

SIR PETER. Egad, Sir Oliver, a thought strikes me!—Charles, you say, does not know Mr. Premium?

MOSES. Not at all.

SIR PETER. Now then, Sir Oliver, you may have a better opportunity of satisfying yourself than by an old romancing tale of a poor relation: go with my friend Moses, and represent Premium, and then, I'll answer for it, you'll see your nephew in all his glory.

SIR OLIVER. Egad, I like this idea better than the other, and I may visit Joseph afterwards as old Stanley.

SIR PETER. True—so you may.

ROW. Well, this is taking Charles rather at a disadvantage, to be sure.—However, Moses, you understand Sir Peter, and will be faithful?

MOSES. You may depend upon me; this is near the time I was to have gone.

SIR OLIVER. I'll accompany you as soon as you please, Moses.—But hold! I forgot one thing—how the plague shall I be able to pass for a Jew?

MOSES. There is no need—the principal is Christian.

SIR OLIVER. Is he? I am very sorry to hear it. But then again, a'n't I rather too smartly dressed to look like a moneylender?

SIR PETER. Not at all; 'twould not be out of character if you went in your own carriage—would it, Moses?

MOSES. Not in the least.

SIR OLIVER. Well, but how must I talk? There's certainly some cant of usury, and mode of treating, that I ought to know.

SIR PETER. Oh, there's not much to learn. The great point, as I take it, is to be exorbitant enough in your demands—hey, Moses?

MOSES. Yes, that's a very great point.

SIR OLIVER. I'll answer for't I'll not be wanting in that. I'll ask him eight or ten per cent on the loan, at least.

MOSES. If you ask him no more than that, you'll be discovered immediately.

SIR OLIVER. Hey! what the plague! how much then?

MOSES. That depends upon the circumstances. If he appears not very anxious for the supply, you should require only forty or fifty per cent; but if you find him in great distress, and want the moneys very bad, you must ask double.

SIR PETER. A good honest trade you're learning, Sir Oliver!

SIR OLIVER. Truly, I think so—and not unprofitable.

MOSES. Then, you know, you haven't the moneys yourself, but are forced to borrow them for him of an old friend.

SIR OLIVER. Oh! I borrow it of a friend, do I?

MOSES. And your friend is an unconscionable dog; but you can't help it!

SIR OLIVER. My friend is an unconscionable dog, is he?

MOSES. Yes, and he himself has not the moneys by him, but is forced to sell stock at a great loss.

SIR OLIVER. He is forced to sell stock at a great loss, is he? Well, that's very kind of him.

SIR PETER. I'faith, Sir Oliver—Mr. Premium, I mean, you'll soon be master of the trade. But, Moses! wouldn't you have him run out a little against the Annuity Bill?[4] That would be in character, I should think.

MOSES. Very much.

ROW. And lament that a young man now must be at years of discretion before he is suffered to ruin himself?

MOSES. Ay, great pity!

SIR PETER. And abuse the public for allowing merit to an Act whose only object is to snatch misfortune and imprudence from the rapacious relief of usury, and give the minor a chance of inheriting his estate without being undone by coming into possession.

SIR OLIVER. So, so; Moses shall give me further instructions as we go together.

SIR PETER. You will not have much time, for your nephew lives hard by.

SIR OLIVER. Oh, never fear; my tutor appears so able that, though Charles lived in the next street, it must be my own fault if I am not a complete rogue before I turn the corner.

[Exeunt SIR OLIVER SURFACE and MOSES

SIR PETER. So now I think Sir Oliver will be convinced. You are partial, Rowley, and would have prepared Charles for the other plot.

ROW. No, upon my word, Sir Peter.

SIR PETER. Well, go bring me this Snake, and I'll hear what he has to say presently. I see Maria, and want to speak with her. (Exit ROWLEY.) I should be glad to be convinced my suspicions of Lady Teazle and Charles were unjust. I have never yet opened

---

[3] A street in the east end of the City proper.

[4] This bill, under discussion when *The School for Scandal* was produced and passed shortly afterward, was intended to protect the fortunes of minors.

my mind on this subject to my friend Joseph. I'm determined I will do it; *he* will give me his opinion sincerely.

Enter MARIA

So, child, has Mr. Surface returned with you?

MARIA. No, sir; he was engaged.

SIR PETER. Well, Maria, do you not reflect, the more you converse with that amiable young man, what return his partiality for you deserves?

MARIA. Indeed, Sir Peter, your frequent importunity on this subject distresses me extremely; you compel me to declare that I know no man who has ever paid me a particular attention whom I would not prefer to Mr. Surface.

SIR PETER. So, here's perverseness! No, no, Maria, 'tis Charles only whom you would prefer. 'Tis evident his vices and follies have won your heart.

MARIA. This is unkind, sir. You know I have obeyed you in neither seeing nor corresponding with him. I have heard enough to convince me that he is unworthy my regard. Yet I cannot think it culpable if, while my understanding severely condemns his vices, my heart suggests some pity for his distresses.

SIR PETER. Well, well, pity him as much as you please; but give your heart and hand to a worthier object.

MARIA. Never to his brother!

SIR PETER. Go, perverse and obstinate! But take care, madam; you have never yet known what the authority of a guardian is. Don't compel me to inform you of it.

MARIA. I can only say, you shall not have *just* reason. 'Tis true, by my father's will I am for a short period bound to regard you as his substitute, but must cease to think you so when you would compel me to be miserable. [*Exit*

SIR PETER. Was ever man so crossed as I am? everything conspiring to fret me! I had not been involved in matrimony a fortnight, before her father, a hale and hearty man, died—on purpose, I believe, for the pleasure of plaguing me with the care of his daughter. But here comes my helpmate! She appears in great good humor. How happy I should be if I could tease her into loving me, though but a little!

Enter LADY TEAZLE

LADY T. Lud! Sir Peter, I hope you haven't been quarreling with Maria? It is not using me well to be ill-humored when I am not by.

SIR PETER. Ah, Lady Teazle, you might have the power to make me good-humored at all times.

LADY T. I am sure I wish I had; for I want you to be in a charming sweet temper at this moment. Do be good-humored now, and let me have two hundred pounds, will you?

SIR PETER. Two hundred pounds! What, a'n't I to be in a good humor without paying for it? But speak to me thus, and i' faith there's nothing I could refuse you. You shall have it; but seal me a bond for the repayment.

LADY T. Oh, no—there: my note of hand will do as well.

SIR PETER (*kissing her hand*). And you shall no longer reproach me with not giving you an independent settlement. I mean shortly to surprise you. But shall we always live thus, hey?

LADY T. If you please. I'm sure I don't care how soon we leave off quarreling, provided you'll own *you* were tired first.

SIR PETER. Well, then let our future contest be who shall be most obliging.

LADY T. I assure you, Sir Peter, good nature becomes you. You look now as you did before we were married, when you used to walk with me under the elms, and tell me stories of what a gallant you were in your youth, and chuck me under the chin, you would, and ask me if I thought I could love an old fellow who would deny me nothing—didn't you?

SIR PETER. Yes, yes; and you were as kind and attentive—

LADY T. Ay, so I was, and would always take your part when my acquaintance used to abuse you and turn you into ridicule.

SIR PETER. Indeed!

LADY T. Ay, and when my cousin Sophy has called you a stiff, peevish old bachelor, and laughed at me for thinking of marrying one who might be my father, I have always defended you, and said I didn't think you so ugly by any means, and I dared say you'd make a very good sort of a husband.

SIR PETER. And you prophesied right; and we shall certainly now be the happiest couple—

LADY T. And never differ again?

SIR PETER. No, never!—though at the same time, indeed, my dear Lady Teazle, you must watch your temper very narrowly; for in all our little quarrels, my dear, if you recollect, my love, you always began first.

LADY T. I beg your pardon, my dear Sir Peter; indeed, you always gave the provocation.

SIR PETER. Now see, my angel! take care—contradicting isn't the way to keep friends.

LADY T. Then don't *you* begin it, my love!

SIR PETER. There, now! you—you are going on. You don't perceive, my life, that you are just doing the very thing which you know always makes me angry.

LADY T. Nay, you know if you will be angry without any reason, my dear—

SIR PETER. There! now you want to quarrel again.

LADY T. No, I am sure I don't; but if you will be so peevish—

SIR PETER. There now! who begins first?

LADY T. Why, you, to be sure. I said nothing—but there's no bearing your temper.

SIR PETER. No, no, madam; the fault's in your own temper.

LADY T. Ay, you are just what my cousin Sophy said you would be.

SIR PETER. Your cousin Sophy is a forward, impertinent gypsy.

LADY T. You are a great bear, I'm sure, to abuse my relations.

SIR PETER. Now may all the plagues of marriage be doubled on me if ever I try to be friends with you any more!

LADY T. So much the better.

SIR PETER. No, no, madam. 'Tis evident you never cared a pin for me, and I was a madman to marry you—a pert, rural coquette that had refused half the honest squires in the neighborhood.

LADY T. And I am sure I was a fool to marry you—an old dangling bachelor, who was single at fifty only because he never could meet with anyone who would have him.

SIR PETER. Ay, ay, madam; but you were pleased enough to listen to me—*you* never had such an offer before.

LADY T. No? Didn't I refuse Sir Tivy Terrier, who everybody said would have been a better match, for his estate is just as good as yours and he has broke his neck since we have been married?

SIR PETER. I have done with you, madam! You are an unfeeling, ungrateful—but there's an end of everything. I believe you capable of anything that is bad. Yes, madam, I now believe the reports relative to you and Charles, madam. Yes, madam, you and Charles are, not without grounds—

LADY T. Take care, Sir Peter! You had better not insinuate any such thing! I'll not be suspected without cause, I promise you.

SIR PETER. Very well, madam, very well! A separate maintenance as soon as you please. Yes, madam,

or a divorce! I'll make an example of myself for the benefit of all old bachelors. Let us separate, madam.

LADY T. Agreed, agreed! And now, my dear Sir Peter, we are of a mind once more, we may be the happiest couple and never differ again, you know. Ha, ha, ha! Well, you are going to be in a passion, I see, and I shall only interrupt you; so bye, bye! [*Exit*

SIR PETER. Plagues and tortures! Can't I make her angry neither? Oh, I am the miserablest fellow! But I'll not bear her presuming to keep her temper. No! she may break my heart, but she shan't keep her temper. [*Exit*

SCENE II. CHARLES SURFACE'S *house*

Enter TRIP, MOSES, *and* SIR OLIVER SURFACE

TRIP. Here, Master Moses! If you'll stay a moment, I'll try whether—what's the gentleman's name?

SIR OLIVER (*aside to* MOSES). Mr. Moses, what *is* my name?

MOSES. Mr. Premium.

TRIP. Premium. Very well. [*Exit, taking snuff*

SIR OLIVER. To judge by the servants, one wouldn't believe the master was ruined. But what!—sure, this was my brother's house?

MOSES. Yes, sir; Mr. Charles bought it of Mr. Joseph, with the furniture, pictures, &c., just as the old gentleman left it. Sir Peter thought it a piece of extravagance in him.

SIR OLIVER. In my mind, the other's economy in *selling* it to him was more reprehensible by half.

Re-enter TRIP

TRIP. My master says you must wait, gentlemen; he has company, and can't speak with you yet.

SIR OLIVER. If he knew *who* it was wanted to see him, perhaps he would not have sent such a message?

TRIP. Yes, yes, sir; he knows *you* are here—I did not forget little Premium; no, no, no.

SIR OLIVER. Very well; and I pray, sir, what may be your name?

TRIP. Trip, sir; my name is Trip, at your service.

SIR OLIVER. Well, then, Mr. Trip, you have a pleasant sort of place here, I guess?

TRIP. Why, yes—here are three or four of us pass our time agreeably enough; but then our wages are sometimes a little in arrear—and not very great either—but fifty pounds a year, and find our own bags[5] and bouquets.

---

[5] The back hair of a bagwig was enclosed in a silk bag.

SIR OLIVER (*aside*). Bags and bouquets! halters and bastinadoes!

TRIP. But, apropos,[6] Moses—have you been able to get me that little bill discounted?

SIR OLIVER (*aside*). Wants to raise money too!— mercy on me! Has his distresses, I warrant, like a lord, and affects creditors and duns.

MOSES. 'Twas not to be done, indeed, Mr. Trip.

TRIP. Good lack, you surprise me! My friend Brush has endorsed it, and I thought when he put his name at the back of a bill 'twas as good as cash.

MOSES. No, 'twouldn't do.

TRIP. A small sum—but twenty pounds. Hark'ee, Moses, do you think you couldn't get it me by way of annuity?

SIR OLIVER (*aside*). An annuity! ha! ha! ha! a footman raise money by way of annuity! Well done, luxury, egad!

MOSES. But you must insure your place.

TRIP. Oh, with all my heart! I'll insure my place, and my life too, if you please.

SIR OLIVER (*aside*). It's more than I would your neck.

TRIP. But then, Moses, it must be done before this d——d Register[7] takes place; one wouldn't like to have one's name made public, you know.

MOSES. No, certainly. But is there nothing you could deposit?

TRIP. Why, nothing capital of my master's wardrobe has dropped lately; but I could give you a mortgage on some of his winter clothes, with equity of redemption before November—or you shall have the reversion of the French velvet, or a post-obit[8] on the blue and silver—these, I should think, Moses, with a few pair of point ruffles, as a collateral security—hey, my little fellow?

MOSES. Well, well.   [*Bell rings*

TRIP. Egad, I heard the bell! I believe, gentlemen, I can now introduce you.—Don't forget the annuity, little Moses!—This way, gentlemen; insure my place, you know.

SIR OLIVER (*aside*). If the man be a shadow of his master, this is the temple of dissipation indeed!

---

6 By the way.
7 The Annuity Bill (note 4, above) provided for the registration of grants of life annuities.
8 A bond payable after someone's death.

CHARLES SURFACE, CARELESS, SIR TOBY BUMPER, *&c., discovered at a table, drinking wine*

CHARLES. 'Fore heaven, 'tis true!—there's the great degeneracy of the age. Many of our acquaintance have taste, spirit, and politeness; but, plague on't, they won't drink.

CARE. It is so indeed, Charles! they give in to all the substantial luxuries of the table, and abstain from nothing but wine and wit.

CHARLES. Oh, certainly society suffers by it intolerably; for now, instead of the social spirit of raillery that used to mantle over a glass of bright Burgundy, their conversation is become just like the Spa water they drink, which has all the pertness and flatulence of champagne, without its spirit or flavor.

1ST GENT. But what are they to do who love play better than wine?

CARE. True! there's Harry diets himself for gaming,[9] and is now under a hazard regimen.

CHARLES. Then he'll have the worst of it. What! you wouldn't train a horse for the course by keeping him from corn! For my part, egad, I am never so successful as when I am a little merry: let me throw on a bottle of champagne, and I never lose—at least, I never feel my losses, which is exactly the same thing.

2ND GENT. Ay, that I believe.

CHARLES. And then, what man can pretend to be a believer in love who is an abjurer of wine? 'Tis the test by which the lover knows his own heart. Fill a dozen bumpers to a dozen beauties, and she that floats atop is the maid that has bewitched you.

CARE. Now then, Charles, be honest, and give us your real favorite.

CHARLES. Why, I have withheld her only in compassion to you. If I toast her, you must give a round of her peers, which is impossible—on earth.

CARE. Oh, then we'll find some canonized vestals or heathen goddesses that will do, I warrant!

CHARLES. Here then, bumpers, you rogues! bumpers! Maria! Maria—

1ST GENT. Maria who?

CHARLES. Oh, damn the surname—'tis too formal to be registered in Love's calendar; but now, Sir Toby Bumper, beware—we must have beauty superlative.

CARE. Nay, never study, Sir Toby; we'll stand to the toast, though your mistress should want an eye —and you know you have a song will excuse you.

---

9 I.e., keeps in training for gambling.

SIR TOBY. Egad, so I have! and I'll give him the song instead of the lady.

SONG

Here's to the maiden of bashful fifteen;
Here's to the widow of fifty;
Here's to the flaunting extravagant quean,[10]
And here's to the housewife that's thrifty.

Chorus

Let the toast pass—
Drink to the lass—
I'll warrant she'll prove an excuse for the glass.

Here's to the charmer whose dimples we prize;
Now to the maid who has none, sir;
Here's to the girl with a pair of blue eyes,
And here's to the nymph with but one, sir.
Chorus. Let the toast pass, &c.

Here's to the maid with a bosom of snow;
Now to her that's as brown as a berry;
Here's to the wife with her face full of woe,
And now to the damsel that's merry.
Chorus. Let the toast pass, &c.

For let 'em be clumsy, or let 'em be slim,
Young or ancient, I care not a feather;
So fill a pint bumper quite up to the brim,
And let us e'en toast them together.
Chorus. Let the toast pass, &c.

ALL. Bravo! bravo!

Enter TRIP, *and whispers* CHARLES

CHARLES. Gentlemen you must excuse me a little. —Careless, take the chair, will you?

CARE. Nay, prithee, Charles, what now? This is one of your peerless beauties, I suppose, has dropped in by chance?

CHARLES. No, faith! To tell you the truth, 'tis a Jew and a broker, who are come by appointment.

CARE. Oh, damn it! let's have the Jew in.

1ST GENT. Ay, and the broker too, by all means.

2ND GENT. Yes, yes, the Jew and the broker.

CHARLES. Egad, with all my heart!—Trip, bid the gentlemen walk in (*Exit* TRIP.)—though there's one of them a stranger; I can tell you.

---

10 Jade, wench.

CARE. Charles, let us give them some generous Burgundy, and perhaps they'll grow conscientious.

CHARLES. Oh, hang 'em, no! wine does but draw forth a man's *natural* qualities; and to make *them* drink would only be to whet their knavery.

Enter TRIP, SIR OLIVER SURFACE, *and* MOSES

CHARLES. So, honest Moses; walk in; walk in, pray, Mr. Premium—that's the gentleman's name, isn't it, Moses?

MOSES. Yes, sir.

CHARLES. Set chairs, Trip—sit down, Mr. Premium —glasses, Trip—sit down, Moses. Come, Mr. Premium, I'll give you a sentiment; here's *Success to usury*—Moses, fill the gentleman a bumper.

MOSES. Success to usury!

CARE. Right, Moses—usury is prudence and industry, and deserves to succeed.

SIR OLIVER. Then here's *All the success it deserves!*

CARE. No, no, that won't do. Mr. Premium, you have demurred at the toast, and must drink it in a pint bumper.

1ST GENT. A pint bumper, at least.

MOSES. Oh, pray, sir, consider; Mr. Premium's a gentleman.

CARE. And therefore loves good wine.

2ND GENT. Give Moses a quart glass; this is mutiny, and a high contempt of the chair.

CARE. Here, now for't! I'll see justice done, to the last drop of my bottle.

SIR OLIVER. Nay, pray, gentlemen; I did not expect this usage.

CHARLES. No, hang it, Careless, you sha'n't! Mr. Premium's a stranger.

SIR OLIVER (*aside*). Odd! I wish I was well out of this company.

CARE. Plague on 'em, then! if they won't drink, we'll not sit down with them —Come, Harry, the dice are in the next room.—Charles, you'll join us, when you have finished your business with the gentlemen?

CHARLES. I will! I will! (*Exeunt.*) Careless!

CARE. (*returning*). Well!

CHARLES. Perhaps I may want *you.*

CARE. Oh, you know I am always ready: word, note, or bond, 'tis all the same to me. [*Exit*

MOSES. Sir, this is Mr. Premium, a gentleman of the strictest honor and secrecy, and always performs what he undertakes. Mr. Premium, this is—

CHARLES. Pshaw! have done.—Sir, my friend Moses is a very honest fellow, but a little slow at expression; he'll be an hour giving us our titles. Mr.

Premium, the plain state of the matter is this: I am an extravagant young fellow who wants to borrow money; you I take to be a prudent old fellow, who have got money to lend. I am blockhead enough to give fifty per cent sooner than not have it; and you, I presume, are rogue enough to take a hundred if you can get it. Now, sir, you see we are acquainted at once, and may proceed to business without farther ceremony.

SIR OLIVER. Exceeding frank, upon my word. I see, sir, you are not a man of many compliments.

CHARLES. Oh, no, sir! plain dealing in business I always think best.

SIR OLIVER. Sir, I like you the better for it. However, you are mistaken in one thing; I have no money to lend, but I believe I could procure some of a friend; but then he's an unconscionable dog— isn't he, Moses? And must sell stock to accommodate you—mustn't he, Moses?

MOSES. Yes, indeed! You know I always speak the truth, and scorn to tell a lie!

CHARLES. Right! People that speak truth generally do. But these are trifles, Mr. Premium. What! I know money isn't to be bought without paying for't!

SIR OLIVER. Well, but what security could you give? You have no land, I suppose?

CHARLES. Not a molehill, nor a twig, but what's in the beau-pots[11] out at the window!

SIR OLIVER. Nor any stock, I presume?

CHARLES. Nothing but live stock, and that's only a few pointers and ponies. But pray, Mr. Premium, are you acquainted at all with any of my connections?

SIR OLIVER. Why, to say truth, I am.

CHARLES. Then you must know that I have a dev'lish rich uncle in the East Indies, Sir Oliver Surface, from whom I have the greatest expectations.

SIR OLIVER. That you have a wealthy uncle I have heard; but how your expectations will turn out is more, I believe, than you can tell.

CHARLES. Oh, no! there can be no doubt. They tell me I'm a prodigious favorite, and that he talks of leaving me everything.

SIR OLIVER. Indeed! this is the first I've heard of it.

CHARLES. Yes, yes, 'tis just so. Moses knows 'tis true; don't you, Moses?

MOSES. Oh, yes! I'll swear to't.

SIR OLIVER (aside). Egad, they'll persuade me presently I'm at Bengal.

CHARLES. Now, I propose, Mr. Premium, if it's agreeable to you, a post-obit on Sir Oliver's life; though at the same time the old fellow has been so

liberal to me that I give you my word I should be very sorry to hear that anything had happened to him.

SIR OLIVER. Not more than I should, I assure you. But the bond you mention happens to be just the worst security you could offer me, for I might live to a hundred, and never recover the principal.

CHARLES. Oh, yes, you would; the moment Sir Oliver dies, you know, you would come on me for the money.

SIR OLIVER. Then I believe I should be the most unwelcome dun you ever had in your life.

CHARLES. What! I suppose you're afraid now that Sir Oliver is too good a life?

SIR OLIVER. No, indeed, I am not—though I have heard he is as hale and healthy as any man of his years in Christendom.

CHARLES. There again now you are misinformed. No, no, the climate has hurt him considerably, poor uncle Oliver! Yes, he breaks apace, I'm told, and is so much altered lately that his nearest relations don't know him.

SIR OLIVER. No! ha! ha! ha! so much altered lately that his nearest relations don't know him! Ha! ha! ha! egad—ha! ha! ha!

CHARLES. Ha! ha! you're glad to hear that, little Premium?

SIR OLIVER. No, no, I'm not.

CHARLES. Yes, yes, you are— ha! ha! ha! You know that mends your chance.

SIR OLIVER. But I'm told Sir Oliver is coming over —nay, some say he is actually arrived.

CHARLES. Pshaw! Sure I must know better than you whether he's come or not. No, no, rely on't, he's at this moment at Calcutta, isn't he, Moses?

MOSES. Oh, yes, certainly.

SIR OLIVER. Very true, as you say, you must know better than I, though I have it from pretty good authority—haven't I, Moses?

MOSES. Yes, most undoubted!

SIR OLIVER. But, sir, as I understand you want a few hundreds immediately, is there nothing you would dispose of?

CHARLES. How do you mean?

SIR OLIVER. For instance, now, I have heard that your father left behind him a great quantity of massy old plate.

CHARLES. Oh, Lud! that's gone long ago. Moses can tell you how, better than I can.

SIR OLIVER (aside). Good lack, all the family race-cups and corporation bowls![12]—Then it was also

[11] Vases or ornamental flowerpots.

[12] Presented as testimonials by the city government.

supposed that his library was one of the most valuable and complete.

CHARLES. Yes, yes, so it was—vastly too much so for a private gentleman. For my part, I was always of a communicative disposition; so I thought it a shame to keep so much knowledge to myself.

SIR OLIVER (*aside*). Mercy upon me! learning that had run in the family like an heirloom!—Pray what are become of the books?

CHARLES. You must inquire of the auctioneer, Master Premium, for I don't believe even Moses can direct you there.

MOSES. I know nothing of books.

SIR OLIVER. So, so, nothing of the family property left, I suppose?

CHARLES. Not much, indeed, unless you have a mind to the family pictures. I have got a room full of ancestors above; and if you have a taste for paintings, egad, you shall have 'em a bargain.

SIR OLIVER. Hey, and the Devil! Sure, you wouldn't sell your forefathers, would you?

CHARLES. Every man of 'em to the best bidder.

SIR OLIVER. What! Your great-uncles and aunts?

CHARLES. Ay, and my great-grandfathers and grandmothers too.

SIR OLIVER (*aside*). Now I give him up!— What the plague, have you no bowels for your own kindred? Odd's life, do you take me for Shylock in the play that you would raise money of me on your own flesh and blood?

CHARLES. Nay, my little broker, don't be angry. What need *you* care, if you have your money's worth?

SIR OLIVER. Well, I'll be the purchaser. I think I can dispose of the family canvas.—(*Aside*) Oh, I'll never forgive him this! never!

Enter CARELESS

CARE. Come, Charles, what keeps you?

CHARLES. I can't come yet. I' faith, we are going to have a sale above stairs. Here's little Premium will buy all my ancestors!

CARE. Oh, burn your ancestors!

CHARLES. No, he may do that afterwards, if he pleases. Stay, Careless, we want you; egad, you shall be auctioneer—so come along with us.

CARE. Oh, have with you, if that's the case. I can handle a hammer as well as a dice box!

SIR OLIVER (*aside*). Oh, the profligates!

CHARLES. Come, Moses, you shall be appraiser, if we want one.—Gad's life, little Premium, you don't seem to like the business.

SIR OLIVER. Oh, yes, I do, vastly! Ha, ha, ha! Yes, yes, I think it a rare joke to sell one's family by auction. Ha, ha!—(*Aside*) Oh, the prodigal!

CHARLES. To be sure! When a man wants money, where the plague should he get assistance if he can't make free with his own relations?

[*Exeunt*

ACT IV

SCENE I. *Picture room at* CHARLES's *house*

Enter CHARLES SURFACE, SIR OLIVER SURFACE, MOSES, *and* CARELESS

CHARLES. Walk in, gentlemen, pray walk in! Here they are, the family of the Surfaces, up to the Conquest.

SIR OLIVER. And, in my opinion, a goodly collection.

CHARLES. Ay, ay, these are done in the true spirit of portrait painting; no volunteer[1] grace and expression: not like the works of your modern Raphael,[2] who gives you the strongest resemblance, yet contrives to make your own portrait independent of you; so that you may sink the original and not hurt

the picture. No, no; the merit of these is the inveterate likeness—all stiff and awkward as the originals, and like nothing in human nature besides.

SIR OLIVER. Ah! we shall never see such figures of men again.

CHARLES. I hope not.—Well, you see, Master Premium, what a domestic character I am; here I sit of an evening surrounded by my family.—But come, get to your pulpit, Mr. Auctioneer; here's an old gouty chair of my grandfather's will answer the purpose.

CARE. Ay, ay, this will do.—But, Charles, I have ne'er a hammer; and what's an auctioneer without his hammer?

CHARLES. Egad, that's true. What parchment have we here? (*Takes down a roll.*) "Richard heir to Thomas."—Oh, our genealogy in full.—Here, Careless, you shall have no common bit of mahogany; here's the family tree for you, you rogue—this

---

[1] I.e., added by the artist.   [2] I.e., portrait painter.

shall be your hammer, and now you may knock down my ancestors with their own pedigree.

SIR OLIVER (*aside*). What an unnatural rogue!—an ex post facto[3] parricide!

CARE. Yes, yes, here's a list of your generation indeed; faith, Charles, this is the most convenient thing you could have found for the business, for 'twill serve not only as a hammer, but a catalogue into the bargain.—But come, begin—a-going, a-going, a-going!

CHARLES. Bravo, Careless!—Well, here's my great-uncle, Sir Richard Ravelin,[4] a marvelous good general in his day, I assure you. He served in all the Duke of Marlborough's wars, and got that cut over his eye at the battle of Malplaquet.[5]—What say you, Mr. Premium?—look at him—there's a hero for you, not cut out of his feathers, as your modern clipped captains are, but enveloped in wig and regimentals, as a general should be. What do you bid?

SIR OLIVER (*aside to* MOSES). Bid him speak.

MOSES. Mr. Premium would have *you* speak.

CHARLES. Why, then, he shall have him for ten pounds, and I'm sure that's not dear for a staff officer.

SIR OLIVER (*aside*). Heaven deliver me! his famous uncle Richard for ten pounds!—Very well, sir, I take him at that.

CHARLES. Careless, knock him down my uncle Richard.—Here, now, is a maiden sister of his, my great-aunt Deborah, done by Kneller,[6] thought to be in his best manner, and esteemed a very formidable likeness.—There she is, you see, a shepherdess feeding her flock.—You shall have her for five pounds ten—the sheep are worth the money.

SIR OLIVER (*aside*). Ah! poor Deborah! a woman who set such a value on herself!—Five pounds ten—she's mine.

CHARLES. Knock down my aunt Deborah!—Here, now, are two that were a sort of cousins of theirs.—You see, Moses, these pictures were done some time ago, when beaux wore wigs, and the ladies their own hair.

SIR OLIVER. Yes, truly, headdresses appear to have been a little lower in those days.

CHARLES. Well, take that couple for the same.

MOSES. 'Tis good bargain.

CHARLES. This, now, is a grandfather of my mother's, a learned judge, well known on the western circuit.—What do you rate him at, Moses?

MOSES. Four guineas.

CHARLES. Four guineas!—Gad's life, you don't bid me the price of his wig.—Mr. Premium, you have more respect for the woolsack;[7] do let us knock his Lordship down at fifteen.

SIR OLIVER. By all means.

CARE. Gone!

CHARLES. And there are two brothers of his, William and Walter Blunt, Esquires, both members of Parliament, and noted speakers, and what's very extraordinary, I believe this is the first time they were ever bought and sold.

SIR OLIVER. That is very extraordinary, indeed! I'll take them at your own price, for the honor of Parliament.

CARE. Well said, little Premium!—I'll knock them down at forty.

CHARLES. Here's a jolly fellow—I don't know what relation, but he was mayor of Norwich; take him at eight pounds.

SIR OLIVER. No, no; six will do for the mayor.

CHARLES. Come, make it guineas,[8] and I'll throw you the two aldermen there into the bargain.

SIR OLIVER. They're mine.

CHARLES. Careless, knock down the mayor and aldermen.—But plague on't, we shall be all day, retailing in this manner; do let us deal wholesale: what say you, little Premium? Give me three hundred pounds for the rest of the family in the lump.

CARE. Ay, ay, that will be the best way.

SIR OLIVER. Well, well, anything to accommodate you; they are mine. But there is one portrait which you have always passed over.

CARE. What, that ill-looking little fellow over the settee?

SIR OLIVER. Yes, sir, I mean that, though I don't think him so ill-looking a little fellow, by any means.

CHARLES. What, that? Oh, that's my uncle Oliver; 'twas done before he went to India.

CARE. Your uncle Oliver! Gad, then you'll never be friends, Charles. That, now, to me, is as stern a looking rogue as ever I saw—an unforgiving eye, and a damned disinheriting countenance! an inveterate knave, depend on't.—Don't you think so, little Premium?

SIR OLIVER. Upon my soul, sir, I do not; I think it is as honest a looking face as any in the room, dead

---

[3] Retroactive.

[4] A ravelin is a detached angle in a fortification.

[5] ... of Marlborough's famous victories over the French, in ... nglish casualties were heavy.

[6] ... nt portrait painter Sir Godfrey Kneller (1648–1723).

[7] I.e., judiciary. The woolsack is the seat of the head of the judicial system, the lord chancellor, in the House of Lords.

[8] A pound is 20 shillings, a guinea 21.

or alive.—But I suppose uncle Oliver goes with the rest of the lumber?

CHARLES. No, hang it! I'll not part with poor Noll. The old fellow has been very good to me, and, egad, I'll keep his picture while I've a room to put it in.

SIR OLIVER (aside). The rogue's my nephew after all!—But, sir, I have somehow taken a fancy to that picture.

CHARLES. I'm sorry for't, for you certainly will not have it. Oons, haven't you got enough of 'em?

SIR OLIVER (aside). I forgive him everything!—But, sir, when I take a whim in my head, I don't value money. I'll give you as much for that as for all the rest.

CHARLES. Don't tease me, master broker; I tell you I'll not part with it, and there's an end of it.

SIR OLIVER (aside). How like his father the dog is! —Well, well, I have done.—(Aside) I did not perceive it before, but I think I never saw such a striking resemblance.—Here is a draught for your sum.

CHARLES. Why, 'tis for eight hundred pounds.

SIR OLIVER. You will not let Sir Oliver go?

CHARLES. Zounds! no!—I tell you once more.

SIR OLIVER. Then never mind the difference; we'll balance that another time. But give me your hand on the bargain; you are an honest fellow, Charles— I beg pardon, sir, for being so free.—Come, Moses.

CHARLES. Egad, this is a whimsical old fellow!— But hark'ee, Premium, you'll prepare lodgings for these gentlemen.

SIR OLIVER. Yes, yes, I'll send for them in a day or two.

CHARLES. But hold; do now—send a genteel conveyance for them, for, I assure you, they were most of them used to ride in their own carriages.

SIR OLIVER. I will, I will—for all but Oliver.

CHARLES. Ay, all but the little honest nabob.

SIR OLIVER. You're fixed on that?

CHARLES. Peremptorily.

SIR OLIVER (aside). A dear extravagant rogue!— Good day!—Come, Moses.—(Aside) Let me hear now who dares call him profligate!

[Exeunt SIR OLIVER SURFACE and MOSES

CARE. Why, this is the oddest genius of the sort I ever saw!

CHARLES. Egad, he's the prince of brokers, I think. I wonder how the devil Moses got acquainted with so honest a fellow.—Ha! here's Rowley.—Do, Careless, say I'll join the company in a moment.

CARE. I will—but don't let that old blockhead persuade you to squander any of that money on old musty debts, or any such nonsense; for tradesmen, Charles, are the most exorbitant fellows.

CHARLES. Very true, and paying them is only encouraging them.

CARE. Nothing else.

CHARLES. Ay, ay, never fear. (Exit CARELESS.)—So! this was an odd old fellow, indeed!—Let me see— two-thirds of this is mine by right—five hundred and thirty odd pounds. 'Fore heaven! I find one's ancestors are more valuable relations than I took them for!—Ladies and gentlemen, your most obedient and very grateful humble servant.—

Enter ROWLEY

Ha! old Rowley! Egad, you are just come in time to take leave of your old acquaintance.

ROW. Yes, I heard they were a-going. But I wonder you can have such spirits under so many distresses.

CHARLES. Why, there's the point: my distresses are so many that I can't afford to part with my spirits; but I shall be rich and splenetic, all in good time. However, I suppose you are surprised that I am not more sorrowful at parting with so many near relations. To be sure, 'tis very affecting; but, rot 'em, you see they never move a muscle, so why should I?

ROW. There's no making you serious a moment.

CHARLES. Yes, faith; I am so now. Here, my honest Rowley, here, get me this changed directly and take a hundred pounds of it immediately to old Stanley.

ROW. A hundred pounds! Consider only—

CHARLES. Gad's life, don't talk about it! Poor Stanley's wants are pressing; and, if you don't make haste, we shall have someone call that has a better right to the money.

ROW. Ah, there's the point! I never will cease dunning you with the old proverb—

CHARLES. "Be *just* before you're *generous*."—Why, so I would if I could; but Justice is an old, lame, hobbling beldame, and I can't get her to keep pace with Generosity, for the soul of me.

ROW. Yet, Charles, believe me, one hour's reflection—

CHARLES. Ay, ay, it's all very true; but hark'ee, Rowley, while I have, by heaven I'll give; so damn your economy. And now for hazard! [*Exeunt*

SCENE II. *The parlor*[9]

Enter SIR OLIVER SURFACE *and* MOSES

MOSES. Well, sir, I think, as Sir Peter said, you have seen Mr. Charles in high glory; 'tis great pity he's so extravagant.

SIR OLIVER. True, but he would not sell my picture.

MOSES. And loves wine and women so much.

SIR OLIVER. But he would not sell my picture.

MOSES. And games so deep.

SIR OLIVER. But he would not sell my picture. Oh, here's Rowley!

Enter ROWLEY

ROW. So, Sir Oliver, I find you have made a purchase—

SIR OLIVER. Yes, yes, our young rake has parted with his ancestors like old tapestry.

ROW. And here has he commissioned me to re-deliver you part of the purchase money—I mean, though, in your necessitous character of old Stanley.

MOSES. Ah, there's the pity of all; he is so damned charitable.

ROW. And I left a hosier and two tailors in the hall, who, I'm sure, won't be paid; and this hundred would satisfy them.

SIR OLIVER. Well, well, I'll pay his debts— and his benevolence, too. But now I am no more a broker, and you shall introduce me to the elder brother as old Stanley.

ROW. Not yet awhile. Sir Peter, I know, means to call there about this time.

Enter TRIP

TRIP. Oh, gentlemen, I beg pardon for not show-ing you out. This way.—Moses, a word.

[*Exeunt* TRIP *and* MOSES

SIR OLIVER. There's a fellow for you! Would you believe it, that puppy intercepted the Jew on our coming, and wanted to raise money before he got to his master!

ROW. Indeed!

SIR OLIVER. Yes, they are now planning an annuity business. Ah, Master Rowley, in my days servants were content with the follies of their masters, when they were worn a little threadbare; but now they have their vices, like their birthday clothes,[10] with the gloss on. [*Exeunt*

---

[9] In Charles Surface's house.

[10] I.e., they get their masters' best clothes, discarded while still new. Courtiers appeared in new clothes on the king's birthday.

SCENE III. *A library*[11]

JOSEPH SURFACE *and a* Servant

JOSEPH. No letter from Lady Teazle?

SERV. No, sir.

JOSEPH (*aside*). I am surprised she has not sent, if she is prevented from coming. Sir Peter certainly does not suspect me. Yet I wish I may not lose the heiress, through the scrape I have drawn myself in with the wife; however, Charles's imprudence and bad character are great points in my favor.

[*Knocking*

SERV. Sir, I believe that must be Lady Teazle.

JOSEPH. Hold! See whether it is or not, before you go to the door; I have a particular message for you, if it should be my brother.

SERV. 'Tis her Ladyship, sir; she always leaves her chair at the milliner's in the next street.

JOSEPH. Stay, stay; draw that screen before the window—that will do; my opposite neighbor is a maiden lady of so curious a temper. (Servant *draws the screen, and exit.*)—I have a difficult hand to play in this affair. Lady Teazle has lately suspected my views on Maria; but she must by no means be let into that secret—at least, not till I have her more in my power.

Enter LADY TEAZLE

LADY T. What, sentiment in soliloquy? Have you been very impatient now? Oh, Lud! don't pretend to look grave. I vow I couldn't come before.

JOSEPH. Oh, madam, punctuality is a species of constancy, a very unfashionable quality in a lady.

LADY T. Upon my word you ought to pity me. Do you know, Sir Peter is grown so ill-natured to me of late, and so jealous of Charles too—that's the best of the story, isn't it?

JOSEPH (*aside*). I am glad my scandalous friends keep that up.

LADY T. I am sure I wish he would let Maria marry him, and then perhaps he would be convinced. Don't you, Mr. Surface?

JOSEPH (*aside*). Indeed I do not.—Oh, certainly I do! for then my dear Lady Teazle would also be convinced how wrong her suspicions were of my having any design on the silly girl.

LADY T. Well, well, I'm inclined to believe you. But isn't it provoking, to have the most ill-natured things said of one? And there's my friend, Lady

---

[11] At Joseph Surface's.

Sneerwell, has circulated I don't know how many scandalous tales of me, and all without any foundation too; that's what vexes me.

JOSEPH. Ay, madam, to be sure, that *is* the provoking circumstance—without foundation. Yes, yes, there's the mortification, indeed; for when a scandalous story is believed against one, there certainly is no comfort like the consciousness of having deserved it.

LADY T. No, to be sure—then I'd forgive their malice; but to attack me, who am really so innocent, and who never say an ill-natured thing of anybody —that is, of any friend; and then Sir Peter too, to have him so peevish, and so suspicious, when I know the integrity of my own heart! indeed 'tis monstrous!

JOSEPH. But, my dear Lady Teazle, 'tis your own fault if you suffer it. When a husband entertains a groundless suspicion of his wife, and withdraws his confidence from her, the original compact is broke, and she owes it to the honor of her sex to endeavor to outwit him.

LADY T. Indeed! so that if he suspects me without cause, it follows that the best way of curing his jealousy is to give him reason for't?

JOSEPH. Undoubtedly; for your husband should never be deceived in you; and in that case it becomes *you* to be frail, in compliment to *his* discernment.

LADY T. To be sure, what you say is very reasonable, and when the consciousness of my innocence—

JOSEPH. Ah, my dear madam, there is the great mistake: 'tis this very conscious innocence that is of the greatest prejudice to you. What is it makes you negligent of forms, and careless of the world's opinion? Why, the *consciousness* of your own innocence. What makes you thoughtless in your conduct, and apt to run into a thousand little imprudences? Why, the *consciousness* of your own innocence. What makes you impatient of Sir Peter's temper, and outrageous at his suspicions? Why, the *consciousness* of your innocence.

LADY T. 'Tis very true!

JOSEPH. Now, my dear Lady Teazle, if you would but once make a trifling *faux pas,* you can't conceive how cautious you would grow, and how ready to humor and agree with your husband.

LADY T. Do you think so?

JOSEPH. Oh, I'm sure on't; and then you would find all scandal would cease at once; for, in short, your character at present is like a person in a plethora,[12] absolutely dying from too much health.

LADY T. So, so; then I perceive your prescription is that I must sin in my own defense, and part with my virtue to preserve my reputation?

JOSEPH. Exactly so, upon my credit, ma'am.

LADY T. Well, certainly this is the oddest doctrine, and the newest receipt for avoiding calumny!

JOSEPH. An infallible one, believe me. *Prudence,* like *experience,* must be paid for.

LADY T. Why, if my understanding were once convinced—

JOSEPH. Oh, certainly, madam, your understanding *should* be convinced. Yes, yes; heaven forbid I should persuade you to do anything you *thought* wrong. No, no, I have too much honor to desire it.

LADY T. Don't you think we may as well leave honor out of the argument?

JOSEPH. Ah! the ill effects of your country education, I see, still remain with you.

LADY T. I doubt they do indeed; and I will fairly own to you that if I could be persuaded to do wrong, it would be by Sir Peter's ill usage sooner than your honorable logic, after all.

JOSEPH (*taking her hand*). Then, by this hand, which he is unworthy of—

Re-enter Servant

'Sdeath, you blockhead! What do you want?

SERV. I beg pardon, sir, but I thought you would not choose Sir Peter to come up without announcing him.

JOSEPH. Sir Peter! Oons—the devil!

LADY T. Sir Peter! Oh, Lud, I'm ruined! I'm ruined!

SERV. Sir, 'twasn't I let him in.

LADY T. Oh, I'm quite undone![13] What will become of me now, Mr. Logic? Oh! mercy, he's on the stairs. I'll get behind here; and if ever I'm so imprudent again—   [*Goes behind the screen*

JOSEPH. Give me that book.

[*Sits down. Servant pretends to adjust his hair*

Enter SIR PETER TEAZLE

SIR PETER. Ay, ever improving himself!—Mr. Surface, Mr. Surface!

JOSEPH. Oh, my dear Sir Peter, I beg your pardon. (*Gaping, and throws away the book.*) I have been dozing over a stupid book. Well, I am much obliged to you for this call. You haven't been here, I believe, since I fitted up this room. Books, you know, are the only things I am a coxcomb in.

---

[12] A state of having too much blood.

[13] Ruined.

SIR PETER. 'Tis very neat indeed. Well, well, that's proper; and you can make even your screen a source of knowledge; hung, I perceive, with maps.

JOSEPH. Oh, yes, I find great use in that screen.

SIR PETER. I dare say you must, certainly, when you want to find anything in a hurry.

JOSEPH (aside). Ay, or to hide anything in a hurry, either.

SIR PETER. Well, I have a little private business—

JOSEPH (to the Servant). You need not stay.

SERV. No, sir. [Exit

JOSEPH. Here's a chair, Sir Peter. I beg—

SIR PETER. Well, now we are alone, there is a subject, my dear friend, on which I wish to unburden my mind to you—a point of the greatest moment to my peace; in short, my dear friend, Lady Teazle's conduct of late has made me extremely unhappy.

JOSEPH. Indeed! I am very sorry to hear it.

SIR PETER. Ay, 'tis but too plain she has not the least regard for me; but, what's worse, I have a pretty good authority to suspect she has formed an attachment to another.

JOSEPH. You astonish me!

SIR PETER. Yes; and, between ourselves, I think I've discovered the person.

JOSEPH. How! you alarm me exceedingly.

SIR PETER. Ah, my dear friend, I knew you would sympathize with me!

JOSEPH. Yes—believe me, Sir Peter, such a discovery would hurt me just as much as it would you.

SIR PETER. I am convinced of it.—Ah! it is a happiness to have a friend whom one can trust even with one's family secrets. But have you no guess who I mean?

JOSEPH. I haven't the most distant idea. It can't be Sir Benjamin Backbite!

SIR PETER. Oh, no! What say you to Charles?

JOSEPH. My brother! impossible! Oh, no, Sir Peter, you must not credit the scandalous insinuations you may hear. No, no, Charles to be sure has been charged with many things of this kind, but I can never think he would meditate so gross an injury.

SIR PETER. Ah, my dear friend, the goodness of your own heart misleads you; you judge of others by yourself.

JOSEPH. Certainly, Sir Peter, the heart that is conscious of its own integrity is ever slow to credit another's treachery.

SIR PETER. True; but your brother has no sentiment—you never hear him talk so.

JOSEPH. Yet, I can't but think Lady Teazle herself has too much principle.

SIR PETER. Ay; but what is principle against the flattery of a handsome, lively young fellow?

JOSEPH. That's very true.

SIR PETER. And then, you know, the difference of our ages makes it very improbable that she should have a great affection for me; and if she were to be frail, and I were to make it public, why the town would only laugh at me, the foolish old bachelor, who had married a girl.

JOSEPH. That's true, to be sure—they would laugh.

SIR PETER. Laugh—ay, and make ballads, and paragraphs, and the devil knows what of me.

JOSEPH. No, you must never make it public.

SIR PETER. But then again—that the nephew of my old friend, Sir Oliver, should be the person to attempt such a wrong, hurts me more nearly.

JOSEPH. Ay, there's the point. When ingratitude barbs the dart of injury, the wound has double danger in it.

SIR PETER. Ay—I, that was, in a manner, left his guardian; in whose house he had been so often entertained; who never in my life denied him—my advice.

JOSEPH. Oh, 'tis not to be credited. There may be a man capable of such baseness, to be sure; but, for my part, till you can give me positive proofs, I cannot but doubt it. However, if this should be proved on him, he is no longer a brother of mine! I disclaim kindred with him: for the man who can break through the laws of hospitality, and attempt the wife of his friend, deserves to be branded as the pest of society.

SIR PETER. What a difference there is between you! What noble sentiments!

JOSEPH. Yet, I cannot suspect Lady Teazle's honor.

SIR PETER. I am sure I wish to think well of her, and to remove all ground of quarrel between us. She has lately reproached me more than once with having made no settlement on her; and, in our last quarrel, she almost hinted that she should not break her heart if I was dead. Now, as we seem to differ in our ideas of expense, I have resolved she shall be her own mistress in that respect for the future; and if I were to die, she shall find that I have not been inattentive to her interests while living. Here, my friend, are the drafts of two deeds, which I wish to have your opinion on. By one she will enjoy eight hundred a year independent while I live, and by the other the bulk of my fortune after my death.

JOSEPH. This conduct, Sir Peter, is indeed truly generous.—(Aside) I wish it may not corrupt my pupil.

SIR PETER. Yes, I am determined she shall have no

cause to complain, though I would not have her acquainted with the latter instance of my affection yet awhile.

JOSEPH (*aside*). Nor I, if I could help it.

SIR PETER. And now, my dear friend, if you please, we will talk over the situation of your hopes with Maria.

JOSEPH (*softly*). No, no, Sir Peter; another time, if you please.

SIR PETER. I am sensibly chagrined at the little progress you seem to make in her affections.

JOSEPH (*softly*). I beg you will not mention it. What are my disappointments, when your happiness is in debate!—(*Aside*) 'Sdeath, I shall be ruined every way.

SIR PETER. And though you are so averse to my acquainting Lady Teazle with your passion, I am sure she's not your enemy in the affair.

JOSEPH. Pray, Sir Peter, now, oblige me. I am really too much affected by the subject we have been speaking of, to bestow a thought on my own concerns. The man who is entrusted with his friend's distresses can never—

Re-enter Servant

Well, sir?

SERV. Your brother, sir, is speaking to a gentleman in the street, and says he knows you are within.

JOSEPH. 'Sdeath, blockhead, I'm not within—I'm out for the day.

SIR PETER. Stay—hold—a thought has struck me: you shall be at home.

JOSEPH. Well, well, let him up. (*Exit* Servant.)— (*Aside*) He'll interrupt Sir Peter, however.

SIR PETER. Now, my good friend, oblige me, I entreat you. Before Charles comes, let me conceal myself somewhere; then do you tax him on the point we have been talking on, and his answers may satisfy me at once.

JOSEPH. Oh, fie, Sir Peter! would you have me join in so mean a trick?—to trepan[14] my brother too?

SIR PETER. Nay, you tell me you are *sure* he is innocent; if so, you do him the greatest service by giving him an opportunity to clear himself, and you will set my heart at rest. Come, you shall not refuse me; here, behind this screen will be—Hey! what the devil! there seems to be *one* listener there already—I'll swear I saw a petticoat!

JOSEPH. Ha! ha! ha! Well, this is ridiculous

enough. I'll tell you, Sir Peter, though I hold a man of intrigue to be a most despicable character, yet, you know, it does not follow that one is to be an absolute Joseph[15] either! Hark'ee, 'tis a little French milliner—a silly rogue that plagues me—and having some character to lose, on your coming, sir, she ran behind the screen.

SIR PETER. Ah, you rogue!—But, egad, she has overheard all I have been saying of my wife.

JOSEPH. Oh, 'twill never go any farther, you may depend upon it!

SIR PETER. No? Then, faith, let her hear it out.— Here's a closet will do as well.

JOSEPH. Well, go in there.

SIR PETER. Sly rogue! Sly rogue!

[*Goes into the closet*

JOSEPH (*aside*). A narrow escape, indeed! and a curious situation I'm in, to part man and wife in this manner.

LADY T. (*peeping*). Couldn't I steal off?

JOSEPH. Keep close, my angel!

SIR PETER (*peeping*). Joseph, tax him home!

JOSEPH. Back, my dear friend!

LADY T. (*peeping*). Couldn't you lock Sir Peter in?

JOSEPH. Be still, my life!

SIR PETER (*peeping*). You're sure the little milliner won't blab?

JOSEPH. In, in, my dear Sir Peter!—'Fore gad, I wish I had a key to the door!

Enter CHARLES SURFACE

CHARLES. Holla, brother, what has been the matter? Your fellow would not let me up at first. What, have you had a Jew or a wench with you?

JOSEPH. Neither, brother, I assure you.

CHARLES. But what has made Sir Peter steal off? I thought he had been with you.

JOSEPH. He was, brother; but, hearing *you* were coming, he did not choose to stay.

CHARLES. What, was the old gentleman afraid I wanted to borrow money of him?

JOSEPH. No, sir; but I am sorry to find, Charles, you have lately given that worthy man grounds for great uneasiness.

CHARLES. Yes, they tell me I do that to a great many worthy men. But how so, pray?

JOSEPH. To be plain with you, brother, he thinks you are endeavoring to gain Lady Teazle's affections from him.

---

[14] Trap.

[15] See Genesis 39, where Joseph resists the advances of Potiphar's wife.

CHARLES. Who, I? Oh, Lud! not I, upon my word. Ha! ha! ha! so the old fellow has found out that he has got a young wife, has he? Or, what's worse, has her Ladyship discovered that she has an old husband?

JOSEPH. This is no subject to jest on, brother. He who can laugh—

CHARLES. True, true, as you were going to say— then, seriously, I never had the least idea of what you charge me with, upon my honor.

JOSEPH (aloud). Well, it will give Sir Peter great satisfaction to hear this.

CHARLES. To be sure, I once thought the lady seemed to have taken a fancy to me; but, upon my soul, I never gave her the least encouragement. Besides, you know my attachment to Maria.

JOSEPH. But sure, brother, even if Lady Teazle had betrayed the fondest partiality for you—

CHARLES. Why, look'ee, Joseph, I hope I shall never deliberately do a dishonorable action; but if a pretty woman was purposely to throw herself in my way, and that pretty woman married to a man old enough to be her father—

JOSEPH. Well—

CHARLES. Why, I believe I should be obliged to borrow a little of your morality, that's all. But, brother, do you know now that you surprise me exceedingly, by naming me with Lady Teazle? for, 'faith, I always understood you were her favorite.

JOSEPH. Oh, for shame, Charles! This retort is foolish.

CHARLES. Nay, I swear I have seen you exchange such significant glances—

JOSEPH. Nay, nay, sir, this is no jest.

CHARLES. Egad, I'm serious. Don't you remember, one day when I called here—

JOSEPH. Nay, prithee, Charles—

CHARLES. And found you together—

JOSEPH. Zounds, sir! I insist—

CHARLES. And another time, when your servant—

JOSEPH. Brother, brother, a word with you!— (Aside) Gad, I must stop him.

CHARLES. Informed, I say, that—

JOSEPH. Hush! I beg your pardon, but Sir Peter has overheard all we have been saying. I knew you would clear yourself, or I should not have consented.

CHARLES. How, Sir Peter! Where is he?

JOSEPH. Softly, there! [Points to the closet

CHARLES. Oh, 'fore heaven, I'll have him out.— Sir Peter, come forth!

JOSEPH. No, no—

CHARLES. I say, Sir Peter, come into court. (Pulls in SIR PETER.) What! my old guardian! What! turn inquisitor, and take evidence incog?

SIR PETER. Give me your hand, Charles. I believe I have suspected you wrongfully; but you mustn't be angry with Joseph— 'twas my plan!

CHARLES. Indeed!

SIR PETER. But I acquit you. I promise you I don't think near so ill of you as I did. What I have heard has given me great satisfaction.

CHARLES. Egad, then, 'twas lucky you didn't hear any more—(half aside) wasn't it, Joseph?

SIR PETER. Ah! you would have retorted on him.

CHARLES. Ay, ay, that was a joke.

SIR PETER. Yes, yes, I know his honor too well.

CHARLES. But you might as well have suspected him as me in this matter, for all that—(half aside) mightn't he, Joseph?

SIR PETER. Well, well, I believe you.

JOSEPH (aside). Would they were both well out of the room!

SIR PETER. And in future perhaps we may not be such strangers.

Enter Servant, *and whispers* JOSEPH SURFACE

JOSEPH. Lady Sneerwell! Stop her, by all means. (*Exit* Servant.)—Gentlemen, I beg pardon; I must wait on you downstairs; here is a person come on particular business.

CHARLES. Well, you can see him in another room. Sir Peter and I have not met a long time, and I have something to say to him.

JOSEPH (aside). They must not be left together. I'll send Lady Sneerwell away, and return directly. (*Apart to* SIR PETER) Sir Peter, not a word of the French milliner.

SIR PETER (apart to JOSEPH). Oh, not for the world. (*Exit* JOSEPH.)—Ah! Charles, if you associated more with your brother, one might indeed hope for your reformation. He is a man of sentiment. Well, there is nothing in the world so noble as a man of sentiment.

CHARLES. Pshaw! he is too moral by half, and so apprehensive of his good name, as he calls it, that I suppose he would as soon let a priest into his house as a girl.

SIR PETER. No, no; come, come; you wrong him. No, no! Joseph is no rake, but he is no such saint in that respect either.—(*Aside*) I have a great mind to tell him—we should have a laugh at Joseph.

CHARLES. Oh, hang him! he's a very anchorite, a young hermit.

SIR PETER. Hark'ee, you must not abuse him; he may chance to hear of it again, I promise you.

CHARLES. Why, you won't tell him?

SIR PETER. No—but—this way.—(*Aside*) Egad, I'll tell him.—Hark'ee, have you a mind to have a good laugh at Joseph?

CHARLES. I should like it of all things.

SIR PETER. Then, i'faith, we will.—(*Aside*) I'll be quit with him for discovering me.—He had a girl with him when I called.

CHARLES. What! Joseph? you jest.

SIR PETER. Hush!—a little—French milliner—and the best of the jest is—she's in the room now.

CHARLES. The devil she is!

SIR PETER. Hush! I tell you! [*Points*

CHARLES. Behind the screen! 'Slife, let's unveil her!

SIR PETER. No, no—he's coming—you shan't, indeed!

CHARLES. Oh, egad, we'll have a peep at the little milliner!

SIR PETER. Not for the world; Joseph will never forgive me—

CHARLES. I'll stand by you—

SIR PETER (*struggling with* CHARLES). Odds, here he is!

JOSEPH SURFACE *enters just as* CHARLES *throws down the screen*

CHARLES. Lady Teazle, by all that's wonderful!

SIR PETER. Lady Teazle, by all that's damnable!

CHARLES. Sir Peter, this is one of the smartest French milliners I ever saw.—Egad, you seem all to have been diverting yourselves here at hide and seek, and I don't see who is out of the secret.—Shall I beg your Ladyship to inform me?—Not a word!—Brother, will you be pleased to explain this matter?—What! Morality dumb too!—Sir Peter, though I *found* you in the dark, perhaps you are not so now!—All mute!—Well, though *I* can make nothing of the affair, I suppose you perfectly understand one another; so I'll leave you to yourselves.—(*Going*) Brother, I'm sorry to find you *have given that worthy man cause for so much uneasiness.*—Sir Peter! there's nothing *in the world* so *noble as a man of sentiment!*

[*Exit. They stand for some time looking at each other*

JOSEPH. Sir Peter—notwithstanding I confess that appearances are against me—if you will afford me your patience—I make no doubt but I shall explain everything to your satisfaction.

SIR PETER. If you please—

JOSEPH. The fact is, sir, that Lady Teazle, knowing my pretensions to your ward Maria—I say, sir, Lady Teazle, being apprehensive of the jealousy of your temper—and knowing my friendship to the family—she, sir, I say—called here—in order that—

I might explain those pretensions—but on your coming—being apprehensive—as I said—of your jealousy—she withdrew—and this, you may depend on it, is the whole truth of the matter.

SIR PETER. A very clear account, upon my word; and I dare swear the lady will vouch for every article of it.

LADY T. (*coming forward*). For not one word of it, Sir Peter!

SIR PETER. How! don't you think it worth while to agree in the lie?

LADY T. There is not one syllable of truth in what that gentleman has told you.

SIR PETER. I believe you, upon my soul, ma'am!

JOSEPH (*aside*). 'Sdeath, madam, will you betray me?

LADY T. Good Mr. Hypocrite, by your leave, I will speak for myself.

SIR PETER. Ay, let her alone, sir; you'll find she'll make out a better story than *you*, without prompting.

LADY T. Hear me, Sir Peter!—I came hither on no matter relating to your ward, and even ignorant of this gentleman's pretensions to her; but I came, seduced by his insidious arguments, at least to listen to his pretended passion, if not to sacrifice *your* honor to his baseness.

SIR PETER. Now, I believe, the truth *is* coming out, indeed!

JOSEPH. The woman's mad!

LADY T. No, sir; she has recovered her senses, and your own arts have furnished her with the means.—Sir Peter, I do not expect you to credit me—but the tenderness you expressed for me, when I am sure you could not think I was a witness to it, has penetrated so to my heart that had I left the place without the shame of this discovery, my future life should have spoken the sincerity of my gratitude. As for that smooth-tongued hypocrite, who would have seduced the wife of his too credulous friend, while he affected honorable addresses to his ward—I behold him now in a light so truly despicable that I shall never again respect myself for having listened to him. [*Exit*

JOSEPH. Notwithstanding all this, Sir Peter, heaven knows—

SIR PETER. That you are a villain!—and so I leave you to your conscience.

JOSEPH. You are too rash, Sir Peter; you *shall* hear me. The man who shuts out conviction by refusing to—

SIR PETER. Oh, damn your sentiments.

[*Exeunt,* JOSEPH *following and speaking*

SCENE I. *The library*[1]

Enter JOSEPH SURFACE *and* Servant

JOSEPH. Mr. Stanley!—and why should you think I would see him? you *must* know he comes to ask something.

SERV. Sir, I should not have let him in, but that Mr. Rowley came to the door with him.

JOSEPH. Pshaw! blockhead! to suppose that I should *now* be in a temper to receive visits from poor relations!—Well, why don't you show the fellow up?

SERV. I will, sir.—Why, sir, it was not my fault that Sir Peter discovered my Lady—

JOSEPH. Go, fool! (*Exit* Servant.)—Sure Fortune never played a man of my policy such a trick before. My character with Sir Peter, my hopes with Maria, destroyed in a moment! I'm in a rare humor to listen to other people's distresses! I shan't be able to bestow even a benevolent sentiment on Stanley.— So! here he comes, and Rowley with him. I must try to recover myself, and put a little charity into my face, however. [*Exit*

Enter SIR OLIVER SURFACE *and* ROWLEY

SIR OLIVER. What! does he avoid us?—That was he, was it not?

ROW. It was, sir. But I doubt you are come a little too abruptly. His nerves are so weak that the sight of a poor relation may be too much for him. I should have gone first to break you to him.

SIR OLIVER. Oh, plague of his nerves! Yet this is he whom Sir Peter extols as a man of the most benevolent way of thinking!

ROW. As to his way of thinking, I cannot pretend to decide, for, to do him justice, he appears to have as much speculative benevolence as any private gentleman in the kingdom, though he is seldom so sensual as to indulge himself in the exercise of it.

SIR OLIVER. Yet has a string of charitable sentiments, I suppose, at his fingers' ends!

ROW. Or rather, at his tongue's end, Sir Oliver; for I believe there is no sentiment he has more faith in than that "Charity begins at home."

SIR OLIVER. And his, I presume, is of that domestic sort; it never stirs abroad at all.

ROW. I doubt[2] you'll find it so;—but he's coming. I mustn't seem to interrupt you; and you know,

immediately as you leave him, I come in to announce your arrival in your real character.

SIR OLIVER. True; and afterwards you'll meet me at Sir Peter's.

ROW. Without losing a moment. [*Exit*

SIR OLIVER. So! I don't like the complaisance of his features.

Re-enter JOSEPH SURFACE

JOSEPH. Sir, I beg you ten thousand pardons for keeping you a moment waiting.—Mr. Stanley, I presume.

SIR OLIVER. At your service.

JOSEPH. Sir, I beg you will do me the honor to sit down—I entreat you, sir!

SIR OLIVER. Dear sir, there's no occasion.—(*Aside*) Too civil by half!

JOSEPH. I have not the pleasure of knowing you, Mr. Stanley; but I am extremely happy to see you look so well. You were nearly related to my mother, I think, Mr. Stanley?

SIR OLIVER. I was, sir—so nearly that my present poverty, I fear, may do discredit to her wealthy children; else I should not have presumed to trouble you.

JOSEPH. Dear sir, there needs no apology: he that is in distress, though a stranger, has a right to claim kindred with the wealthy. I am sure I wish *I* was of that class, and had it in my power to offer you even a small relief.

SIR OLIVER. If your uncle, Sir Oliver, were here, I should have a friend.

JOSEPH. I wish he was, sir, with all my heart; you should not want an advocate with him, believe me, sir.

SIR OLIVER. I should not *need* one—my distresses would recommend me. But I imagined his bounty had enabled *you* to become the agent of his charity.

JOSEPH. My dear sir, you were strangely misinformed. Sir Oliver is a worthy man, a very worthy sort of man; but—avarice, Mr. Stanley, is the vice of age. I will tell you, my good sir, in confidence, what he has done for me has been a mere nothing; though people, I know, have thought otherwise, and, for my part, I never chose to contradict the report.

SIR OLIVER. What! has he never transmitted you bullion—rupees—pagodas?[3]

---

[1] In Joseph Surface's house.   [2] Suspect.

[3] A gold coin worth about two dollars; the rupee is silver, and was then worth about fifty cents.

JOSEPH. Oh, dear sir, nothing of the kind! No, no; a few presents now and then—china, shawls, congou tea, avadavats,[4] and Indian crackers[5]—little more, believe me.

SIR OLIVER (aside). Here's gratitude for twelve thousand pounds!—Avadavats and Indian crackers!

JOSEPH. Then, my dear sir, you have heard, I doubt not, of the extravagance of my brother; there are very few would credit what I have done for that unfortunate young man.

SIR OLIVER (aside). Not I, for one!

JOSEPH. The sums I have lent him!—Indeed, I have been exceedingly to blame; it was an amiable weakness—however, I don't pretend to defend it—and now I feel it doubly culpable, since it has deprived me of the power of serving *you,* Mr. Stanley, as my heart dictates.

SIR OLIVER (aside). Dissembler!—Then, sir, you can't assist me?

JOSEPH. At present, it grieves me to say, I cannot; but, whenever I have the ability, you may depend upon hearing from me.

SIR OLIVER. I am extremely sorry—

JOSEPH. Not more than I, believe me; to pity without the power to relieve is still more painful than to ask and be denied.

SIR OLIVER. Kind sir, your most obedient humble servant.

JOSEPH. You leave me deeply affected, Mr. Stanley.—William, be ready to open the door.

SIR OLIVER. Oh, dear sir, no ceremony.

JOSEPH. Your very obedient.

SIR OLIVER. Sir, your most obsequious.

JOSEPH. You may depend upon hearing from me, whenever I can be of service.

SIR OLIVER. Sweet sir, you are too good!

JOSEPH. In the meantime, I wish you health and spirits.

SIR OLIVER. Your ever grateful and perpetual humble servant.

JOSEPH. Sir, yours as sincerely.

SIR OLIVER (aside). Now, I am satisfied.   [Exit

JOSEPH. This is one bad effect of a good character: it invites applications from the unfortunate; and there needs no small degree of address to gain the reputation of benevolence without incurring the expense. The silver ore of pure charity is an expensive article in the catalogue of a man's good qualities; whereas the sentimental French plate I use instead of it makes just as good a show, and pays no tax.

---

[4] A kind of Indian songbird.   [5] Firecrackers.

Enter ROWLEY

ROW. Mr. Surface, your servant. I was apprehensive of interrupting you, though my business demands immediate attention, as this note will inform you.

JOSEPH. Always happy to see Mr. Rowley.—(*Reads.*)—How! "Oliver—Surface!" My uncle arrived!

ROW. He is, indeed; we have just parted—quite well, after a speedy voyage, and impatient to embrace his worthy nephew.

JOSEPH. I am astonished!—William! stop Mr. Stanley, if he's not gone.

ROW. Oh! he's out of reach, I believe.

JOSEPH. Why did not you let me know this when you came in together?

ROW. I thought you had particular business. But I must be gone to inform your brother, and appoint him here to meet your uncle. He will be with you in a quarter of an hour.

JOSEPH. So he says. Well, I am strangely overjoyed at his coming.—(*Aside*) Never, to be sure, was anything so damned unlucky!

ROW. You will be delighted to see how well he looks.

JOSEPH. Oh! I'm rejoiced to hear it.—(*Aside*) Just at this time!

ROW. I'll tell him how impatiently you expect him.

JOSEPH. Do, do; pray give my best duty and affection. Indeed, I cannot express the sensations I feel at the thought of seeing him. (*Exit* ROWLEY.)—Certainly his coming just at this time is the cruelest piece of ill fortune!   [*Exit*

SCENE II. SIR PETER TEAZLE'S

Enter MRS. CANDOUR *and* Maid

MAID. Indeed, ma'am, my Lady will see nobody at present.

MRS. CAN. Did you tell her it was her friend Mrs. Candour?

MAID. Yes, ma'am; but she begs you will excuse her.

MRS. CAN. Do go again; I shall be glad to see her, if it be only for a moment, for I am sure she must be in great distress. (*Exit* Maid.)—Dear heart, how provoking! I'm not mistress of half the circumstances! We shall have the whole affair in the newspapers, with the names of the parties at length, before I have dropped the story at a dozen houses.

Enter SIR BENJAMIN BACKBITE

Oh, dear Sir Benjamin, you have heard, I suppose—

SIR BEN. Of Lady Teazle and Mr. Surface—

MRS. CAN. And Sir Peter's discovery—

SIR BEN. Oh! the strangest piece of business, to be sure!

MRS. CAN. Well, I never was so surprised in my life. I am so sorry for all parties, indeed I am.

SIR BEN. Now, I don't pity Sir Peter at all; he was so extravagantly partial to Mr. Surface.

MRS. CAN. Mr. Surface! Why, 'twas with Charles Lady Teazle was detected.

SIR BEN. No such thing—Mr. Surface is the gallant.

MRS. CAN. No, no! Charles is the man. 'Twas Mr. Surface brought Sir Peter on purpose to discover them.

SIR BEN. I tell you I had it from one—

MRS. CAN. And I have it from one—

SIR BEN. Who had it from one, who had it—

MRS. CAN. From one immediately—but here comes Lady Sneerwell; perhaps she knows the whole affair.

Enter LADY SNEERWELL

LADY SNEER. So, my dear Mrs. Candour, here's a sad affair of our friend, Lady Teazle!

MRS. CAN. Ay, my dear friend; who could have thought it?

LADY SNEER. Well, there is no trusting appearances; though, indeed, she was always too lively for me.

MRS. CAN. To be sure, her manners were a little too free; but then she was very young!

LADY SNEER. And had, indeed, some good qualities.

MRS. CAN. So she had, indeed. But have you heard the particulars?

LADY SNEER. No; but everybody says that Mr. Surface—

SIR BEN. Ay, there, I told you Mr. Surface was the man.

MRS. CAN. No, no, indeed; the assignation was with Charles.

LADY SNEER. With Charles! You alarm me, Mrs. Candour!

MRS. CAN. Yes, yes, he was the lover. Mr. Surface —do him justice—was only the informer.

SIR BEN. Well, I'll not dispute with you, Mrs. Candour; but, be it which it may, I hope that Sir Peter's wound will not—

MRS. CAN. Sir Peter's wound! Oh, mercy! I didn't hear a word of their fighting.

LADY SNEER. Nor I, a syllable.

SIR BEN. No! what, no mention of the duel?

MRS. CAN. Not a word.

SIR BEN. Oh, Lord, yes, yes—they fought before they left the room.

LADY SNEER. Pray let us hear.

MRS. CAN. Ay, do oblige us with the duel.

SIR BEN. "Sir," says Sir Peter, immediately after the discovery, "you are a most ungrateful fellow."

MRS. CAN. Ay, to Charles.

SIR BEN. No, no, to Mr. Surface—"a most ungrateful fellow; and, old as I am, sir," says he, "I insist on immediate satisfaction."

MRS. CAN. Ay, that must have been to Charles; for 'tis very unlikely Mr. Surface should go fight in his own house.

SIR BEN. Gad's life, ma'am, not at all—"giving me satisfaction." On this, ma'am, Lady Teazle, seeing Sir Peter in such danger, ran out of the room in strong hysterics, and Charles after her, calling out for hartshorn[6] and water. Then, madam, they began to fight with swords—

Enter CRABTREE

CRAB. With pistols, nephew—pistols. I have it from undoubted authority.

MRS. CAN. Oh, Mr. Crabtree, then it is all true!

CRAB. Too true, indeed, ma'am, and Sir Peter dangerously wounded—

SIR BEN. By a thrust in *segoon*[7] quite through his left side—

CRAB. By a bullet lodged in the thorax.

MRS. CAN. Mercy on me! Poor Sir Peter!

CRAB. Yes, madam; though Charles would have avoided the matter, if he could.

MRS. CAN. I knew Charles was the person.

SIR BEN. My uncle, I see, knows nothing of the matter.

CRAB. But Sir Peter taxed him with the basest ingratitude—

SIR BEN. That I told you, you know.

CRAB. Do, nephew, let me speak! and insisted on immediate—

SIR BEN. Just as I said—

CRAB. Odds life, nephew, allow others to know something too! A pair of pistols lay on the bureau (for Mr. Surface, it seems, had come home the night before late from Salthill, where he had been to see the Montem[8] with a friend who has a son at Eton); so, unluckily, the pistols were left charged.

---

[6] Smelling salts.   [7] *Seconde,* a position in fencing.

[8] It was a triennial custom at Eton for the boys to go to the hill (*montem*) and beg money from passers-by and from the crowd that gathered to watch. This "salt money" was for the expenses of the senior scholars.

SIR BEN. I heard nothing of this.

CRAB. Sir Peter forced Charles to take one, and they fired, it seems, pretty nearly together. Charles's shot took place, as I told you, and Sir Peter's missed; but what is very extraordinary, the ball struck against a little bronze Shakespeare that stood over the chimney-place, grazed out of the window at a right angle, and wounded the postman, who was just coming to the door with a double[9] letter from Northamptonshire.

SIR BEN. My uncle's account is more circumstantial, I confess; but I believe mine is the true one, for all that.

LADY SNEER. (aside). I am more interested in this affair than they imagine, and must have better information. [Exit

SIR BEN. Ah! Lady Sneerwell's alarm is very easily accounted for.

CRAB. Yes, yes, they certainly do say—but that's neither here nor there.

MRS. CAN. But, pray, where is Sir Peter at present?

CRAB. Oh! they brought him home, and he is now in the house, though the servants are ordered to deny it.

MRS. CAN. I believe so; and Lady Teazle, I suppose, attending him.

CRAB. Yes, yes; and I saw one of the faculty[10] enter just before me.

SIR BEN. Hey! Who comes here?

CRAB. Oh, this is he, the physician, depend on't.

MRS. CAN. Oh, certainly, it must be the physician; and now we shall know.

Enter SIR OLIVER SURFACE

CRAB. Well, doctor, what hopes?

MRS. CAN. Ay, doctor, how's your patient?

SIR BEN. Now, doctor, isn't it a wound with a smallsword?

CRAB. A bullet lodged in the thorax, for a hundred!

SIR OLIVER. Doctor! a wound with a smallsword! and a bullet in the thorax! What! are you mad, good people?

SIR BEN. Perhaps, sir, you are not a doctor?

SIR OLIVER. Truly, I am to thank you for my degree if I am.

CRAB. Only a friend of Sir Peter's, then, I presume. But, sir, you must have heard of his accident?

SIR OLIVER. Not a word!

CRAB. Not of his being dangerously wounded?

---

[9] Written on two sheets, and therefore charged double postage.
[10] Medical profession.

SIR OLIVER. The devil he is!

SIR BEN. Run through the body—

CRAB. Shot in the breast—

SIR BEN. By one Mr. Surface—

CRAB. Ay, the younger.

SIR OLIVER. Hey! what the plague! you seem to differ strangely in your accounts; however, you agree that Sir Peter is dangerously wounded.

SIR BEN. Oh, yes, we agree there.

CRAB. Yes, yes, I believe there can be no doubt of that.

SIR OLIVER. Then, upon my word, for a person in that situation, he is the most imprudent man alive; for here he comes, walking as if nothing at all was the matter.

Enter SIR PETER TEAZLE

Odds heart, Sir Peter, you are come in good time, I promise you, for we had just given you over.

SIR BEN. Egad, uncle, this is the most sudden recovery!

SIR OLIVER. Why, man, what do you out of bed with a smallsword through your body, and a bullet lodged in your thorax?

SIR PETER. A smallsword, and a bullet!

SIR OLIVER. Ay, these gentlemen would have killed you without law or physic, and wanted to dub me a doctor, to make me an accomplice.

SIR PETER. Why, what is all this?

SIR BEN. We rejoice, Sir Peter, that the story of the duel is not true, and are sincerely sorry for your other misfortunes.

SIR PETER (aside). So, so; all over the town already.

CRAB. Though, Sir Peter, you were certainly vastly to blame to marry at all, at your years.

SIR PETER. Sir, what business is that of yours?

MRS. CAN. Though, indeed, as Sir Peter made so good a husband, he's very much to be pitied.

SIR PETER. Plague on your pity, ma'am! I desire none of it.

SIR BEN. However, Sir Peter, you must not mind the laughing and jests you will meet with on the occasion.

SIR PETER. Sir, sir, I desire to be master in my own house.

CRAB. 'Tis no uncommon case, that's one comfort.

SIR PETER. I insist on being left to myself: without ceremony, I insist on your leaving my house directly.

MRS. CAN. Well, well, we are going; and depend on't, we'll make the best report of you we can. [Exit

SIR PETER. Leave my house!

CRAB. And tell how hardly you've been treated.

[Exit

SIR PETER. Leave my house!

SIR BEN. And how patiently you bear it. [*Exit*

SIR PETER. Fiends! vipers! furies! Oh! that their own venom would choke them!

SIR OLIVER. They are very provoking, indeed, Sir Peter.

Enter ROWLEY

ROW. I heard high words. What has ruffled you, Sir Peter?

SIR PETER. Pshaw! what signifies asking? Do I ever pass a day without my vexations?

SIR OLIVER. Well, I'm not inquisitive. I come only to tell you that I have seen both my nephews in the manner we proposed.

SIR PETER. A precious couple they are!

ROW. Yes, and Sir Oliver is convinced that your judgment was right, Sir Peter.

SIR OLIVER. Yes, I find Joseph is indeed the man, after all.

ROW. Ay, as Sir Peter says, he is a man of sentiment.

SIR OLIVER. And acts up to the sentiments he professes.

ROW. It certainly is edification to hear him talk.

SIR OLIVER. Oh, he's a model for the young men of the age!—But how's this, Sir Peter? you don't join us in your friend Joseph's praise, as I expected.

SIR PETER. Sir Oliver, we live in a damned wicked world, and the fewer we praise the better.

ROW. What! do *you* say so, Sir Peter, who were never mistaken in your life?

SIR PETER. Pshaw! Plague on you both! I see by your sneering you have heard the whole affair. I shall go mad among you!

ROW. Then, to fret you no longer, Sir Peter, we are indeed acquainted with it all. I met Lady Teazle coming from Mr. Surface's, so humbled that she deigned to request me to be her advocate with you.

SIR PETER. And does Sir Oliver know all, too?

SIR OLIVER. Every circumstance.

SIR PETER. What, of the closet—and the screen, hey?

SIR OLIVER. Yes, yes, and the little French milliner. Oh, I have been vastly diverted with the story! Ha! ha! ha!

SIR PETER. 'Twas very pleasant.

SIR OLIVER. I never laughed more in my life, I assure you; ha! ha! ha!

SIR PETER. Oh, vastly diverting! ha! ha! ha!

ROW. To be sure, Joseph with his sentiments! ha! ha! ha!

SIR PETER. Yes, yes, his sentiments! ha! ha! ha! A hypocritical villain!

SIR OLIVER. Ay, and that rogue Charles to pull Sir Peter out of the closet! ha! ha! ha!

SIR PETER. Ha! ha! 'twas devilish entertaining, to be sure!

SIR OLIVER. Ha! ha! ha! Egad, Sir Peter, I should like to have seen your face when the screen was thrown down! ha! ha!

SIR PETER. Yes, yes, my face when the screen was thrown down; ha! ha! ha! Oh, I must never show my head again!

SIR OLIVER. But come, come, it isn't fair to laugh at you neither, my old friend; though, upon my soul, I can't help it.

SIR PETER. Oh, pray don't restrain your mirth on my account; it does not hurt me at all! I laugh at the whole affair myself. Yes, yes, I think being a standing jest for all one's acquaintance a very happy situation. Oh, yes, and then of a morning to read the paragraphs about Mr. S——, Lady T——, and Sir P—— will be so diverting!

ROW. Without affectation, Sir Peter, you may despise the ridicule of fools. But I see Lady Teazle going towards the next room; I am sure you must desire a reconciliation as earnestly as she does.

SIR OLIVER. Perhaps my being here prevents her coming to you. Well, I'll leave honest Rowley to mediate between you; but he must bring you all presently to Mr. Surface's, where I am now returning, if not to reclaim a libertine, at least to expose hypocrisy.

SIR PETER. Ah, I'll be present at your discovering yourself there with all my heart—though 'tis a vile unlucky place for discoveries!

ROW. We'll follow. [*Exit* SIR OLIVER

SIR PETER. She is not coming here, you see, Rowley.

ROW. No, but she has left the door of that room open, you perceive. See, she's in tears.

SIR PETER. Certainly a little mortification appears very becoming in a wife. Don't you think it will do her good to let her pine a little?

ROW. Oh, this is ungenerous in you!

SIR PETER. Well, I know not what to think. You remember the letter I found of hers, evidently intended for Charles?

ROW. A mere forgery, Sir Peter! laid in your way on purpose. This is one of the points which I intend Snake shall give you conviction on.

SIR PETER. I wish I were once satisfied of that. She looks this way. What a remarkably elegant turn of the head she has! Rowley, I'll go to her.

ROW. Certainly.

SIR PETER. Though when it is known that we are reconciled, people will laugh at me ten times more.

ROW. Let them laugh, and retort their malice only by showing them you are happy in spite of it.

SIR PETER. I'faith, so I will! and if I'm not mistaken, we may yet be the happiest couple in the country.

ROW. Nay, Sir Peter, he who once lays aside suspicion—

SIR PETER. Hold, my dear Rowley! if you have any regard for me, never let me hear you utter anything like a sentiment—I have had enough of them to serve me the rest of my life. [*Exeunt*

SCENE III. *The library in* JOSEPH SURFACE'S *house*

Enter JOSEPH SURFACE *and* LADY SNEERWELL

LADY SNEER. Impossible! Will not Sir Peter immediately be reconciled to Charles, and of consequence no longer oppose his union with Maria? The thought is distraction to me.

JOSEPH. Can passion furnish a remedy?

LADY SNEER. No, nor cunning either. Oh, I was a fool, an idiot, to league with such a blunderer!

JOSEPH. Sure, Lady Sneerwell, *I* am the greatest sufferer; yet you see I bear the accident with calmness.

LADY SNEER. Because the disappointment doesn't reach your *heart;* your *interest* only attached you to Maria. Had you felt for *her* what *I* have for that ungrateful libertine, neither your temper nor hypocrisy could prevent your showing the sharpness of your vexation.

JOSEPH. But why should your reproaches fall on *me* for this disappointment?

LADY SNEER. Are you not the cause of it? Had you not a sufficient field for your roguery in blinding Sir Peter, and supplanting your brother, but you must endeavor to seduce his wife? I hate such an avarice of crimes; 'tis an unfair monopoly, and never prospers.

JOSEPH. Well, I admit I have been to blame. I confess I deviated from the direct road of wrong, but I don't think we're so totally defeated neither.

LADY SNEER. No!

JOSEPH. You tell me you have made a trial of Snake since we met, and that you still believe him faithful to us—

LADY SNEER. I do believe so.

JOSEPH. And that he has undertaken, should it be necessary, to swear and prove that Charles is at this time contracted by vows and honor to your Lady-

ship—which some of his former letters to you will serve to support?

LADY SNEER. This, indeed, might have assisted.

JOSEPH. Come, come; it is not too late yet. (*Knocking at the door.*) But hark! this is probably my uncle, Sir Oliver; retire to that room—we'll consult farther when he is gone.

LADY SNEER. Well, but if *he* should find you out too?

JOSEPH. Oh, I have no fear of that. Sir Peter will hold his tongue for his own credit's sake; and you may depend on it I shall soon discover Sir Oliver's weak side!

LADY SNEER. I have no diffidence of your abilities—only be constant to one roguery at a time! [*Exit*

JOSEPH. I will, I will.—So! 'tis confounded hard, after such bad fortune, to be baited by one's confederate in evil. Well, at all events my character is so much better than Charles's that I certainly—hey!—what!—this is not Sir Oliver, but old Stanley again. Plague on't that he should return to tease me just now. I shall have Sir Oliver come and find him here—and—

Enter SIR OLIVER SURFACE

Gad's life, Mr. Stanley, why have you come back to plague me just at this time? You must not stay now, upon my word.

SIR OLIVER. Sir, I hear your uncle Oliver is expected here; and though he has been so penurious to *you,* I'll try what he'll do for *me.*

JOSEPH. Sir, 'tis impossible for you to stay now, so I must beg—come any other time, and I promise you, you shall be assisted.

SIR OLIVER. No; Sir Oliver and I must be acquainted.

JOSEPH. Zounds, sir! then I insist on your quitting the room directly.

SIR OLIVER. Nay, sir.

JOSEPH. Sir, I insist on't. Here, William! show this gentleman out.—Since you compel me, sir—not one moment—this is such insolence!

[*Going to push him out*

Enter CHARLES SURFACE

CHARLES. Heyday! what's the matter now? What the devil, have you got hold of my little broker here? Zounds, brother! don't hurt little Premium.—What's the matter, my little fellow?

JOSEPH. So! he has been with you too, has he?

CHARLES. To be sure he has. Why, he's as honest a

little—But sure, Joseph, you have not been borrowing money too, have you?

JOSEPH. Borrowing! no! But, brother, you know we expect Sir Oliver here every—

CHARLES. Oh, Gad, that's true! Noll mustn't find the little broker here, to be sure.

JOSEPH. Yet Mr. Stanley insists—

CHARLES. Stanley! why, his name's Premium.

JOSEPH. No, sir, Stanley.

CHARLES. No, no, Premium.

JOSEPH. Well, no matter which—but—

CHARLES. Ay, ay, Stanley or Premium, 'tis the same thing, as you say; for I suppose he goes by half a hundred names, besides A. B. at the coffee houses.[11]

[*Knocking*

JOSEPH. 'Sdeath, here's Sir Oliver at the door!—Now I beg, Mr. Stanley—

CHARLES. Ay, ay, and I beg, Mr. Premium—

SIR OLIVER. Gentlemen—

JOSEPH. Sir, by heaven you shall go!

CHARLES. Ay, out with him, certainly!

SIR OLIVER. This violence—

JOSEPH. 'Tis your own fault.

CHARLES. Out with him, to be sure.

[*Both forcing* SIR OLIVER *out*

Enter SIR PETER *and* LADY TEAZLE, MARIA, *and* ROWLEY

SIR PETER. My old friend, Sir Oliver; hey! What in the name of wonder! here are dutiful nephews! assault their uncle at a first visit!

LADY T. Indeed, Sir Oliver, 'twas well we came in to rescue you.

ROW. Truly, it was; for I perceive, Sir Oliver, the character of old Stanley was no protection to you.

SIR OLIVER. Nor of Premium either: the necessities of the *former* could not extort a shilling from *that* benevolent gentleman; and now, egad, I stood a chance of faring worse than my ancestors, and being knocked down without being bid for.

JOSEPH. Charles!

CHARLES. Joseph!

JOSEPH. 'Tis now complete!

CHARLES. Very!

SIR OLIVER. Sir Peter, my friend, and Rowley too—look on that elder nephew of mine. You know what he has already received from my bounty, and you also know how gladly I would have regarded half

my fortune as held in trust for him; judge then my disappointment in discovering him to be destitute of faith, charity, and gratitude!

SIR PETER. Sir Oliver, I should be more surprised at this declaration if I had not myself found him to be selfish, treacherous, and hypocritical.

LADY T. And if the gentleman pleads not guilty to these, pray let him call *me* to his character.

SIR PETER. Then, I believe, we need add no more. If he knows himself, he will consider it as the most perfect punishment that he is known to the world.

CHARLES (*aside*). If they talk this way to *Honesty*, what will they say to *me*, by and by?

SIR OLIVER. As for that prodigal, his brother, there—

CHARLES (*aside*). Ay, now comes my turn; the damned family pictures will ruin me.

JOSEPH. Sir Oliver!—Uncle!—will you honor me with a hearing?

CHARLES (*aside*). Now if Joseph would make one of his long speeches I might recollect myself a little.

SIR PETER (*to* JOSEPH). I suppose you would undertake to justify yourself entirely?

JOSEPH. I trust I could.

SIR OLIVER. Pshaw! Nay, if you desert your roguery in this distress and try to be justified, you have even less principle than I thought you had. (*Turns from him in contempt.*)——Well, sir (*to* CHARLES), and *you* could justify yourself too, I suppose?

CHARLES. Not that I know of, Sir Oliver.

SIR OLIVER. What! Little Premium has been let too much into the secret, I presume?

CHARLES. True, sir; but they were *family* secrets, and should never be mentioned again, you know.

ROW. Come, Sir Oliver, I know you cannot speak of Charles's follies with anger.

SIR OLIVER. Odds heart, no more I can—nor with gravity either.—Sir Peter, do you know, the rogue bargained with me for all his ancestors—sold me judges and generals by the foot, and maiden aunts as cheap as broken china.

CHARLES. To be sure, Sir Oliver, I did make a little free with the family canvas, that's the truth on't. My ancestors may certainly rise in evidence against me, there's no denying it; but believe me sincere when I tell you—and upon my soul I would not say so if I was not—that if I do not appear mortified at the exposure of my follies, it is because I feel at this moment the warmest satisfaction in seeing you, my liberal benefactor.

SIR OLIVER. Charles, I believe you; give me your hand again: the ill-looking little fellow over the settee has made your peace.

[11] Where appointments were often made under assumed names or initials.

CHARLES. Then, sir, my gratitude to the original is still increased.

LADY T. (*pointing to* MARIA). Yet, I believe, Sir Oliver, here is one whom Charles is still more anxious to be reconciled to.

SIR OLIVER. Oh, I have heard of his attachment there; and with the young lady's pardon, if I construe right—that blush—

SIR PETER. Well, child, speak your sentiments.

MARIA. Sir, I have little to say, but that I shall rejoice to hear that he is happy; for me, whatever claim I had to his affection I willingly resign to one who has a better title.

CHARLES. How, Maria!

SIR PETER. Heyday! what's the mystery now?—While he appeared an incorrigible rake, you would give your hand to no one else; and now that he is likely to reform, I'll warrant you won't have him.

MARIA. His own heart, and Lady Sneerwell, know the cause.

CHARLES. Lady Sneerwell!

JOSEPH. Brother, it is with great concern I am obliged to speak on this point; but my regard for justice compels me, and Lady Sneerwell's injuries can no longer be concealed. [*Goes to the door*

Enter LADY SNEERWELL

SIR PETER. So! Another French milliner! Egad, he has one in every room in the house, I suppose!

LADY SNEER. Ungrateful Charles! Well may you be surprised, and feel for the indelicate situation your perfidy has forced me into.

CHARLES. Pray, uncle, is this another plot of yours? For, as I have life, I don't understand it.

JOSEPH. I believe, sir, there is but the evidence of one person more necessary to make it extremely clear.

SIR PETER. And that person, I imagine, is Mr. Snake.—Rowley, you were perfectly right to bring him with us, and pray let him appear.

ROW. Walk in, Mr. Snake.

Enter SNAKE

I thought his testimony might be wanted; however, it happens unluckily that he comes to confront Lady Sneerwell, not to support her.

LADY SNEER. (*aside*). A villain! Treacherous to me at last!—Speak, fellow, have *you*, too, conspired against me?

SNAKE. I beg your Ladyship ten thousand pardons. You paid me extremely liberally for the lie in

question, but I have unfortunately been offered double to speak the truth.

SIR PETER. Plot and counterplot, egad!—I wish your Ladyship joy of the success of your negotiation.

LADY SNEER. The torments of shame and disappointment on you all!

LADY T. Hold, Lady Sneerwell! Before you go, let me thank you for the trouble you and that gentleman have taken in writing letters from me to Charles, and answering them yourself; and let me also request you to make my respects to the scandalous college, of which you are president, and inform them that Lady Teazle, licentiate,[12] begs leave to return the diploma they gave her, as she leaves off practice and kills characters no longer.

LADY SNEER. You too, madam!—provoking!—insolent! May your husband live these fifty years!
[*Exit*

SIR PETER. Oons! what a fury!

LADY T. A malicious creature, indeed!

SIR PETER. Hey! Not for her last wish?

LADY T. Oh, no!

SIR OLIVER. Well, sir, and what have you to say now?

JOSEPH. Sir, I am so confounded, to find that Lady Sneerwell could be guilty of suborning Mr. Snake in this manner, to impose on us all, that I know not what to say; however, lest her revengeful spirit should prompt her to injure my brother, I had certainly better follow her directly. [*Exit*

SIR PETER. Moral to the last drop!

SIR OLIVER. Ay, and marry her, Joseph, if you can. Oil and vinegar, egad! you'll do very well together.

ROW. I believe we have no more occasion for Mr. Snake at present.

SNAKE. Before I go, I beg pardon once for all, for whatever uneasiness I have been the humble instrument of causing to the parties present.

SIR PETER. Well, well, you have made atonement by a good deed at last.

SNAKE. But I must request of the company that it shall never be known.

SIR PETER. Hey! What the plague! Are you ashamed of having done a right thing once in your life?

SNAKE. Ah, sir! consider I live by the badness of my character. I have nothing but my infamy to depend on! and, if it were once known that I had been betrayed into an honest action, I should lose every friend I have in the world.

---

12 Degree holder.

SIR OLIVER. Well, well; we'll not traduce you by saying anything in your praise, never fear.

[*Exit* SNAKE

SIR PETER. There's a precious rogue!

[CHARLES *and* MARIA *apart*

LADY T. See, Sir Oliver, there needs no persuasion now to reconcile your nephew and Maria.

SIR OLIVER. Ay, ay, that's as it should be; and egad, we'll have the wedding tomorrow morning.

CHARLES. Thank you, my dear uncle!

SIR PETER. What, you rogue! don't you ask the girl's consent first?

CHARLES. Oh, I have done that a long time—above a minute ago—and she has looked yes.

MARIA. For shame, Charles!—I protest, Sir Peter, there has not been a word—

SIR OLIVER. Well, then, the fewer the better. May your love for each other never know abatement!

SIR PETER. And may you live as happily together as Lady Teazle and I—intend to do!

CHARLES. Rowley, my old friend, I am sure you congratulate me; and I suspect that I owe you much.

SIR OLIVER. You do, indeed, Charles.

ROW. If my efforts to serve you had not succeeded, you would have been in my debt for the attempt: but deserve to be happy, and you overpay me.

SIR PETER. Ay, honest Rowley always said you would reform.

CHARLES. Why, as to reforming, Sir Peter, I'll make no promises, and that I take to be a proof that I intend to set about it; but here shall be my monitor —my gentle guide. Ah! can I leave the virtuous path those eyes illumine?
Though thou, dear maid, shouldst waive thy
    beauty's sway,
Thou still must rule, because I will obey:
An humble fugitive from Folly view,
No sanctuary near but Love and you.

[*To the audience*

You can, indeed, each anxious fear remove,
For even Scandal dies if *you* approve.[13]

[*Exeunt*

---

[13] The epilogue, by George Colman the Elder (1732–94), dramatist and theatrical manager, is of little merit and is here omitted.

An ABC of Prosody

by KARL SHAPIRO

AN ABC OF PROSODY

by Karl Shapiro

PROSODY, or versification, is the science of poetical forms, of the way in which syllables and words are combined so that they become verse as distinguished from prose. There is no need to approach this technical side of poetry with fear if we keep in mind a few general truths about it. One of these is that prosody appears after the poetry has been written. It is not a set of rules which a poet follows; it is a partial account of how a poet writes, a description of verse as we find it. Another point to keep in mind is that prosody can be called a "science" only in the broadest sense of the term: no one has ever set down a complete body of rules for the right analysis of verse. Indeed, poets themselves often disagree about the scansion, or measuring, of a line of verse, as we find exemplified by those poets who have written directly about prosody—Coleridge, Poe, Hopkins, Lanier, Bridges, Patmore, to name only a few. And finally we should remember that one may know little about prosody and yet may develop a mature and sensitive knowledge of poetry. A knowledge of prosody will be helpful in our analysis of the patterns of sounds which we find in poetry, but at the best it is an imperfect implement, and we may develop our awareness of the melody of poetry quite apart from it.

Beyond question, the most valuable approach to prosody is the memorizing of good poems in one's own language. In committing to memory a fine passage of English verse, one becomes aware of prosody in several ways at once. He fixes in his mind a specific metrical pattern—for every poem has its own metrical character—which will be helpful in learning to judge other poems with discrimination. Second, he fixes in his mind a definite sound-structure, which will apply to no other poem, but which will be retained as a model of the music of English. Thirdly, when he recites the poem he will grasp and understand the union of meter, sound, and sense which makes poetry. If he but knows the pronunciation of English words, the meter will speak itself to his ear. And if he but knows the sense of the words, the larger rhythms of phrase and stanza will speak to his mind and his feelings.

A complete prosody would include all the elements of sound that enter into the making of poetry. It would embrace not only the basic rhythmical pattern, or meter, of the line, but also rime schemes, the melody of vowel and consonant sounds, rhythmic phrasing, even tempo, volume, and pitch, and the relation of all these elements to meaning. Prosody has too often been considered in the narrow sense of meter; it is much more. Yet the study of meter alone is a good approach to the wider range of effects if we bear in mind that it is only one characteristic of verse. For meter is probably the most significant as well as the most obvious formal characteristic, and the harmony of poetry can be traced largely to it.

We have said that meter is the basic rhythmical pattern of verse—what might be called the ground rhythm, as distinguished from larger and vaguer rhythms of phrase and period. Rhythm, of course, is found also in prose. It is found wherever sounds are broken into more or less regular intervals of time. It is in the familiar words of the Lord's Prayer: "Thy kingdom come, Thy will be done, on earth, as it is in heaven." But the rhythm of prose is not regular; it is occasional. The metrical pattern of verse is continuous and highly regular. What is the nature of this rhythm of verse and what different kinds of rhythm do the English poets use? The answers to these questions, which follow, form a brief introduction to the study of meters.

THE METRICAL SYSTEM OF ENGLISH

The rhythm of English verse is governed by two main factors. One of these is stress, or accent. The other is time, or what was called *quantity* in classical Greek and Latin versification. Some writers have claimed that English verse is based on time durations alone—that its basis is temporal variations—and they have attempted to scan our poetry by using a system of time measurement similar to musical notation. Others have disregarded the time element completely and have merely marked the accents of the line. Take what is the commonest type of verse in English poetry, the ten-syllable line:

Ti-tum ti-tum ti-tum ti-tum ti-tum.

The accentualist, reading the line with alternating light and heavy accents, would represent it thus:

Ti-tum ti-tum ti-tum ti-tum ti-tum.

The quantitivist, reading it with alternating short and long syllables, would represent it thus:

Ti-tumm ti-tumm ti-tumm ti-tumm ti-tumm.

Neither system is truly satisfactory. By reading aloud any actual line of poetry, one can see that the melody of the line is in fact based on both accentual and temporal variations. Some syllables are more heavily accented than others. And it may be further observed that heavy accent and prolongation of sound usually occur in the same syllable. A syllable or word on which an accent falls is likely to be more prolonged in pronunciation than the same syllable or word if it does not receive an accent. Either system of notation is an approximation, not a full description of the facts. We use below the notation of the accentualist (x ′) in order to avoid unnecessary complication in the marking of lines.

In the preceding paragraph we represented a typical line of poetry by alternate unstressed and stressed syllables. The reading of a real line of poetry will show us that there is almost never a completely regular alternation of this sort. Such an alternation (ti-tum ti-tum ti-tum ti-tum ti-tum) is, as it were, an imaginary pattern against which the line plays, but which is seldom reproduced exactly. For example, in a typical line from *Hamlet* the imaginary pattern or "ideal" meter would be

Oh, that this too, too solid flesh would melt.

But actually no one would wrench the words thus. We make the ideal metrical pattern yield to normal speech habits, distributing the accents approximately as follows:

Oh, that this too, too solid flesh would melt.

The stress we give to produce this variation from the ideal comes from the accent given to a word in normal speech. It is obvious that no two readers will render a given line identically. Verse, like music, must be "interpreted." Anyone who can read English prose should be able to give a reasonably satisfactory rendering of an English poem. To analyze one's rendering, to identify the meter of the poem, is what is meant by *scanning* a poem.

We have seen that meter is a rhythm, more or less regular but not completely so, produced by combinations of accented and unaccented syllables. Considering again the line from *Hamlet,* we notice the following combinations:

(1) Oh, that
(2) this too
(3) too sol-
(4) id flesh
(5) would melt

Or, as commonly written:

Oh, that| this too| too sol|id flesh| would melt.|

The units into which we thus divide a line in scanning it are technically known as *feet.* Names have been given to the kinds of feet shown here (and to others), and the kinds of line are identified by the nature and number of the feet they contain. A one-foot line is called monometer; lines of two, three, four, five, six, seven, and eight feet are called respectively dimeter, trimeter, tetrameter, pentameter, hexameter, heptameter, and octameter.

THE IAMBIC FOOT. By far the commonest English foot is the one we have represented by x ′ above— the one occurring in the second, fourth, and fifth feet of the line from *Hamlet.* It has two syllables, the first lightly stressed, the second heavily stressed. On the analogy of the Greek iambus, which was composed of two syllables, the first half as long in time as the second, we call this English foot the iambus or the iambic foot.

English iambic is most successful in lines of five and four feet. Below four it has a certain lyrical value but cannot be used for sustained passages. The six-foot iambic, called the alexandrine, is used sparingly because of its tendency to break in two; it occurs most frequently in combination with lines of other length, as in the Spenserian stanza, where it follows eight five-foot lines. It is the five-foot iambic line that has proved the real backbone of English poetry. Its pre-eminence is due to its immense adaptability and internal fluidity. There is no kind of poetry, from the lightest to the most heroic, that cannot find expression in this meter. Dramatic, narrative, elegiac, epic, and didactic poets have all used it with great success. It is the meter of the sonnet as well.

The English developed this line from one of the very old French meters. It existed in English long before Chaucer, but Chaucer was the first great English poet to recognize its power and flexibility. From his time to ours the essential nature of this line has remained unaltered and has proved adaptable to the linguistic and ideational changes of five and a half centuries.

THE TROCHAIC FOOT. If we examine a collection of Shakespeare's lyrics, we will notice a remarkable fact, namely, that many of them are written not in the iambic foot of the plays themselves but in a foot that is the reverse of the iambus—a foot in which the accented syllable precedes the unaccented one (´ x). This foot is called a trochee or a trochaic foot. Trochaic meter, or *falling meter,* as it is sometimes called in contrast to the *rising meter* of the iambus, is hardly ever successful in the five-foot line, and it has never competed with the iambic as a vehicle for the larger verse forms. On the other hand, it is the meter chosen for such poems as "Who is Sylvia?"; "Where the bee sucks, there suck I"; "Tell me where is fancy bred"; "Take, O take those lips away." It is, in short, the meter of songs. We know that many nursery rimes are in falling meters:

> Jáck and| Jíll wènt| úp the| híll|

or

> Bóbby| Sháftoe's| góne to| séa.|

(The last unaccented syllable of a trochaic line is frequently omitted.) In music, measures begin with the accent in the initial place, and a great deal of English lyric verse, especially that intended for singing, is therefore quite naturally trochaic. Blake's *Songs of Innocence* are frequently in falling meters, and the "sprung rhythm" of Gerard Manley Hopkins is an elaboration of this "musical" structure for the purposes of spoken poetry.

THE SPONDAIC FOOT. The spondaic foot or spondee consists of two accented syllables (´ ´). This foot is not used in English verse as a basic meter; it occurs, as we see it in the third foot of our line from *Hamlet,* as an occasional substitute for some other type of foot.

THE ANAPESTIC FOOT AND THE DACTYLIC FOOT. The anapest (x x ´) and the dactyl (´ x x) are relatively infrequent in English poetry as basic meters. There are illustrious examples throughout the literature of poems in these trisyllabic meters, and we note an increase in them in the Victorian period and the twentieth century, but on the whole such poems are exhibition pieces and feats of metrical skill. The chief importance of trisyllabic feet is as substitute feet in iambic or trochaic verse.

SUBSTITUTION. We have already seen that the usual verse line does not reproduce exactly the regular structure of the "ideal" line. An iambic line, for example, is only predominantly iambic; one or more of its feet may be trochaic or anapestic or spondaic. Consider

> Wé two| alóne| will síng| like bírds| in the cáge,|

or

> Cóme thèn| and táke| the lást| warmth óf| my líps,|

or

> Lády,| by yón|der bléss|èd móon| I swéar,
> That típs| with síl|ver áll| these frúit-|tree tóps.|

Substitutions such as these play one of the largest parts in producing variety and metrical beauty in verse. In scanning a poem, recognition of the basic foot is necessary for the identification of the meter. Recognition of substitutions for this foot lead the beginner to an understanding of much of the subtlety of English verse. The following examples of typical English meters are fairly regular in movement, but the student will profit by analyzing the variations and considering their effect.

IAMBIC HEXAMETER

So dark are earthly things compared to things divine.
SPENSER, *Faery Queen*

Like pageantry of mist on an autumnal stream.
SHELLEY, *Adonais*

IAMBIC PENTAMETER

Alas, 'tis true I have gone here and there
And made myself a motley to the view,
Gored mine own thoughts, sold cheap what is most dear,
Made old offences of affections new.
SHAKESPEARE, *Sonnet 110*

IAMBIC TETRAMETER

I sometimes hold it half a sin
To put in words the grief I feel;
For words, like Nature, half reveal
And half conceal the Soul within.
TENNYSON, *In Memoriam*

IAMBIC TRIMETER

Grow old along with me;
The best is yet to be.
BROWNING, *Rabbi Ben Ezra*

TROCHAIC OCTAMETER

Hope the best, but hold the Present fatal daughter of the Past,
Shape your heart to front the hour, but dream not that the hour will last.
TENNYSON, *Locksley Hall Sixty Years After*

TROCHAIC PENTAMETER

Weary of myself and sick of asking
What I am and what I ought to be,
At this vessel's prow I stand, which bears me
Forwards, forwards, o'er the starlit sea.

ARNOLD, *Self-Dependence*

TROCHAIC TETRAMETER

Queen and huntress, chaste and fair,
Now the sun is laid to sleep,
Seated in thy silver chair,
State in wonted manner keep.
Hesperus entreats thy light,
Goddess excellently bright.

JONSON, *Hymn to Diana*

ANAPESTIC HEXAMETER

In the darkness of time, in the deeps of the years, in the
    changes of things,
Ye shall sleep as a slain man sleeps, and the world shall
    forget you for kings.

SWINBURNE, *Hymn to Proserpine*

ANAPESTIC PENTAMETER

"I have gone the whole round of creation: I saw and I
    spoke:
I, a work of God's hand for that purpose, received in my
    brain
And pronounced on the rest of his handwork—returned
    him again
His creation's approval or censure: I spoke as I saw."

BROWNING, *Saul*

ANAPESTIC TETRAMETER

Not a word to each other; we kept the great pace
Neck by neck, stride by stride, never changing our pace.

BROWNING, *How They Brought the Good News*

DACTYLIC HEXAMETER

Hope evermore and believe, O man, for e'en as thy
    thought
So are the things that thou seest; e'en as thy hope and
    belief.

CLOUGH, *Hope Evermore and Believe*

DACTYLIC PENTAMETER

What will it please you, my darling, hereafter to be?
Fame upon land will you look for, or glory by sea?
Gallant your life will be always, and all of it free.

SWINBURNE, *A Child's Future*

DACTYLIC TRIMETER

Yes! I believe that there lived
Others like thee in the past,

Not like the men of the crowd
Who all round me today
Blunder or cringe, and make life
Hideous, and arid, and vile.

ARNOLD, *Rugby Chapel*

RIME, BLANK VERSE, AND THE MUSIC OF ENGLISH

Two words are said to rime when they are alike in their stressed vowel and all that follows it and unlike in the sound or sounds preceding the stressed vowel. *Day-May* and *ride-hide* are monosyllabic or so-called masculine rimes. When an entire unstressed syllable follows the stressed syllable, the rime is called double or feminine, as in *riding-hiding*. When two unstressed syllables follow the stressed syllable, the rime is called triple, as in *tenderly-slenderly*.

Particularly in recent poetry, two types of partial rime have been utilized by poets as occasional or regular substitutes for complete rime in a poem. In *assonance* two words have the same accented vowel but different consonants before and after the vowel, as in *gold-rode*. Assonance was characteristic of much early Romance poetry—it occurs, for example, in the early French *Song of Roland*—but it has not achieved much prominence in English. *Dissonance* (also called half-rime, para-rime, and off-rime) is the reverse of assonance in that the accented vowel in the pair is changed while the surrounding consonants remain the same, as in *leaves-lives, scooped-escaped*. The masters of this radical device are Yeats and Wilfred Owen, the World War poet. Yeats used it tentatively, and in reality developed the use of *imperfect rime,* that is, pairs of words which are spelled for riming but which are pronounced differently (for example, *love-move*). Owen was the first to employ dissonance systematically and in place of the conventional complete rime. The introduction of this half-riming scale has enriched English riming a thousandfold.

At its best, rime is not simply a poetic ornament, enriching the musical texture, but a structural factor. It is a time-beater for the poem and it gives to the stanza an inner pattern of temporal design. Because of its conspicuousness among the sound effects of verse, its importance may be overestimated by some readers. It must be remembered that much of the greatest English verse has dispensed with rime. True, unrimed lyrics are rare in English, though notable exceptions may be mentioned, such as Campion's "Rose-cheeked Laura," Collins's "Ode to Evening," and some of Tennyson's lyrics. But *blank verse*—that is, unrimed iambic pentameter—has been one of the mainstays of longer English poems, especially of our

982   AN ABC OF PROSODY

verse drama and our epics. Blank verse, however, implies much more than the mere absence of rime. It is a form that implies size, together with the great variety of internal rhythmical and musical device and the great range of dramatic feeling that are appropriate to size.

We have been speaking of rime used at the ends of lines. End-rime, however, is only one (though the most conspicuous) type of sound-echo in poetry. Assonance and dissonance occur within lines as well as at their end. Another device involving repetition of sound is *alliteration* (sometimes described as initial rime), once a structural element of English poetry, as we have seen in *Beowulf, Piers Plowman,* and *Sir Gawain and the Green Knight,* but now employed sporadically, not only to provide a second pattern of prosody but also to emphasize phrasing.

How *p*oor are they that have not *p*atience!

Thou know'st *w*e *w*ork by *w*it and not by *w*itchcraft.

Shadwell alone of all my sons is he
Who *s*tands confirmed in *f*ull *s*tupidity.

Beyond such definable devices, patterns of similar or related vowel and consonant sounds appear in infinite variety to help create the music of English verse. The ear picks up, for example, the repetitions of *l* and of *m* and *n,* as well as the pattern of related vowels, in the following passage:

The long day wanes; the slow moon climbs; the deep
Moans round with many voices,

and finds the music of the lines exquisitely adapted to their sense. It is impossible here to do more than suggest the variety of means by which such marriage of sound and meaning has been achieved; the student will find his ear becoming more delicately attuned to them the more he reads of English poetry.

FORM IN THE SHORT POEM

It has been overwhelmingly the practice of the poet who works in the "short poem" to devise or borrow a pattern which results in a group of stanzas. What is a stanza? It is essentially a kind of larger rhythm, larger than foot and larger than line or verse, which forms a suitable period. It becomes a stanza by virtue of its repetition within a single poem. It corresponds in some ways to a paragraph in prose; but it has more internal regularity and, as between stanzas, more external similarity. The word *stanza* originally meant a room; thus the stanza is a spatial conception, the area where a significant section of a poem takes place.

Ordinarily a poem in stanzas employs the same stanza throughout, though there are poems in which the stanzas are not all alike, and even poems in which all the stanzas are different. A stanza may have as its recurrent feature only a set number of unrimed lines of equal length. Most unrimed stanzaic poems, however, use a pattern of lines of varying length; for example, the stanza of Collins's "Ode to Evening" has two iambic pentameter lines followed by two iambic trimeter lines. By far the majority of English stanzas employ a pattern of end-rime, either with or without a pattern of different line-lengths.

The simplest type of rimed stanza is the couplet, which appears in a variety of meters, most notably in iambic pentameter. Occasionally used is a three-line stanza with all lines riming; so is another three-line stanza, the Italian *terza rima,* with interlinking rime (*aba bcb cdc ded,* etc.). Four-line stanzas, or quatrains, appear in a great variety of forms. One of these is the "ballad stanza," which rimes *abcb,* the first and third lines iambic tetrameter, the second and fourth iambic trimeter. Quatrains riming *abab* occur in a variety of meters. Mention should also be made of the *In Memoriam* stanza, an iambic tetrameter quatrain riming *abba.*

Of longer stanzas there is room here to name only three particularly important ones: *rime royal,* which is composed of seven iambic pentameter lines riming *ababbcc;* the *Spenserian stanza,* which has eight iambic pentameter lines and an alexandrine, riming *ababbcc;* and *ottava rima,* used notably by Byron in *Don Juan* and other poems, which consists of eight iambic pentameter lines riming *abababcc.*

In the Romance languages there are many elaborate poetic structures which are carried intact from poem to poem. For example, the *triolet* consists of eight lines riming *abaaabab,* with the first line repeated entire as the fourth and seventh lines and the second repeated as the eighth. Versifying of this kind is relatively foreign to English poetry except in its early stages, and our prosodists usually refer to such forms as "artificial." One "set" form, however, has been of the utmost importance in English poetry since its importation from Italy in the sixteenth century. This is the *sonnet,* a fourteen-line iambic pentameter poem with rime in one or another of several established schemes (see I, 247, 302). The sonnet has proved peculiarly adaptable to many serious poetic occasions.

MODERN VERSE

The English prosody we have described up to this point is characterized, in comparison with much recent verse, by its regularity of metrical pattern. It is, as we have seen, by no means rigid in its regularity; it is an extraordinarily subtle medium in which repetition and variation of feet give almost unlimited opportunity of wedding ever-varying thought to form. In the twentieth century, however, has appeared a development of prosody, only suggested in earlier poetry, which has remarkably extended the boundaries of English verse forms. Modern verse, with little regularity of rhythm—or, at least, with a regularity hard to describe—offers the obstacle of newness to the reader whose ear is not yet accustomed to it, and to anyone who expects that all poetry must be measurable entirely by the counting of syllables.

The new movement in versification was largely of American origin, although it occurred simultaneously in England. It began, of course, in practice and not in theory; the new poetry appeared before it began to be explained. And the new poetry was never purely and simply a question of verse and meters; at the root of the change lay a new conception of imagery in poetry, a new conception of poetic diction, and a whole re-examination of earlier notions of what poetry is. The metrical change, while certainly not a minor innovation, was not the fundamental cause of the reaction.

What the new poets—Free Versers and Imagists—advocated was a line based on the natural flow of the contemporary language, not on syllable counting. The rhythmic phrasing therefore was not measured by the foot but, more broadly, by cadence, or the *fall of the voice*. Cadences usually include more syllables than traditional feet, and, in fact, there is usually no point in attempting to scan them in the ordinary sense. They are marked for the most part by the grammatical or rhetorical pauses of normal speech. Take three lines from T. S. Eliot's *The Waste Land*:

> He who was living is now dead
> We who were living are now dying
> With a little patience.[1]

These lines do not conform to any traditional pattern of metrics; they are the cadences of ordinary everyday modern speech. The first two lines can be divided into phrasal groups by observing a pause after the word "living" and another at the end of the line. The third line is a phrase in itself.

If we know, as Ezra Pound put it, that free verse proceeds by the sequence of the musical phrase, we know that the foot scansion does not apply to poetry composed in this style. And if we know, as T. S. Eliot suggested, that free verse does not imply complete metrical license, we are aware that limitations exist in this form too. The following illustration will show the problem of finding a "typical" meter for a free verse poem.

SALUTATION[2]

O| generation| of the thoroughly| smug|
    and thoroughly| uncomfortable,|
I have seen| fishermen| picnicking| in the sun,|
I have seen them| with untidy| families,|
I have seen| their smiles| full of teeth|
    and heard| ungainly| laughter.|
And I| am happier| than you are,|
And they| were happier| than I am;|
And the fish| swim| in the lake|
    and do not| even| own clothing.|

The cadences are read as they are marked off above—at least by the present reader. It is obvious that the feet named earlier have little utility in describing the rhythmical movement here. A reader beginning the poem might identify the first line as iambic pentameter, but he need not go much farther before discovering that that is not the metrical principle of the poem. He will discover recognizable feet, but he will find them combined with other rhythms to which he can give no name. He must give up any attempt at exact syllabic reading and try to savor the rhythms of the cadences. He may be puzzled and at first repelled by the unorthodoxy of the lines, but wider reading will train his ear and eventually enable him to distinguish good free verse from bad.

Following the liberation of English verse in the early twentieth century, poets began in earnest to experiment with meters, some reviving forms as old as the Anglo-Saxon, and others drawing more and more freely on prose rhythms for their verse effects. The result has been to produce two parallel tendencies in present-day poetry. One is the free verse line, which offers infinite metrical possibilities; the other is a new formalism, the revival of stanzaic and metrical forms for the sake of those forms. It appears that the two tendencies are not at variance, for poets today recognize that old meters may be used in new ways, and that new meters do not always signify new poetry.

[1] From *Collected Poems 1909–1935* by T. S. Eliot, copyright 1936 by Harcourt, Brace and Company, Inc. Reprinted by permission of the publisher.

[2] From *Personae: The Collected Poems of Ezra Pound*, copyright 1926 by New Directions. Reprinted by permission of the publisher.

Index of Authors
Titles
and First Lines of Poems

INDEX OF AUTHORS, TITLES, AND FIRST LINES OF POEMS

Authors' names are in small capitals, titles in italic, first lines of poems in roman. When the first line of a poem, in whole or in part, supplies the title, only a first-line entry is given. Except for authors, only the initial page reference is given. Suspension points before a first-line entry indicate that the first line of the excerpt in this volume is not the first line of the complete poem.

Royal Palace, GREENWICH

St.

VIEW of THE City of London, ENGLAND
LONDON
During the Eighteenth
Century: WHEREON are indicated
Many Historic & Literary LANDMARKS

From Old Prints: Drawings, Engravings from the PERIOD.

DRAWN by Aldren A. Watson; Putney, Vt.

British Museum

Bloomsbury Square

Red Lion Square

HIGH HOL

Lincoln's Inn Fields

Soho Square

Drury Lane

GEORGE ST.

St. George's Church

St. Anne's Church

Covent Garden Theater

BOW ST.

RUSSELL ST.

Drury Lane Theater

Shakespeare Tavern

Covent Garden Market

Will's Coffee House

St.

Berkeley Square

LEICESTER ST.

Leicester Fields

HENRIETTA ST.

Turk's Head Coffee House

THE STRAND

Savoy

Somerset House

Burlington House

St. Martin's Lane

SAVOY STAIRS

SOMERSET WATER GATE

PICCADILLY

St. James's Church

The Haymarket

St. Martin's in-the-Fields

Chesterfield House

QUEEN ST.

Devonshire House

St. James's Square

Royal Opera House

Charing Cross

Northumberland House

SHEPHERD'S MARKET

St. James's St.

PALL MALL

Spring Gardens

WHITEHALL

Scotland Yard

WHITEHALL STAIRS

HYDE PARK CORNER

Marlborough House

Privy Garden

THE GREEN PARK

St. James's Palace

Downing St.

PARLIAMENT ST.

PRIVY GARDEN STAIRS

St. James's Park

Buckingham House

WESTMINSTER

Pimlico

Gt. George St.

Westminster Br.

W—

WESTMINSTER BRIDGE STAIRS

the King's Road

Westminster Abbey

Houses of Parliament

Westminster Hall

Navy Office

London